# Pratt & Kulsrud

AF676237

Dear Student,

Thank you for purchasing this textbook. We hope you find it a useful tool as you examine the topic of taxation.

A *Study Guide to Accompany Federal Taxation* is available through your bookstore. With its chapter review, study exercises, and true-false / multiple-choice questions, the Study Guide is designed to help you study and review the text material, while providing you a means of self-testing.

If the Study Guide is not in stock at your bookstore, ask the bookstore manager to order a copy for you. In addition, the supplement may be purchased online; simply go to **www.cengagebrain.com** and enter ISBN 1111824215 to be directed to the Study Guide site.

At **www.cengagebrain.com** you will also find all book-specific legislative updates and inflation adjustments posted on a regular basis.

Best wishes for a great year!

Cordially,
James W. Pratt and William N. Kulsrud

TAXATION SERIES

# Federal Taxation

## 2012 EDITION

James W. Pratt
William N. Kulsrud

Contributing Authors

Gregory A. Carnes, Ph.D., C.P.A. | The University of North Alabama
Marguerite R. Hutton, Ph.D., C.P.A. | Western Washington University
Robert W. Jamison, Ph.D., C.P.A. | Indiana University
William N. Kulsrud, Ph.D., C.P.A. | Indiana University
Nathan Oestreich, Ph.D., C.P.A. | San Diego State University
James W. Pratt, D.B.A., C.P.A. | University of Houston
Edward J. Schnee, Ph.D., C.P.A. | University of Alabama
Steven C. Thompson, Ph.D., C.P.A. | Texas State University
John C. Tripp, Ph.D., C.P.A. | University of Denver
Michael J. Tucker, J.D., Ph.D., C.P.A
James L. Wittenbach, D.B.A., C.P.A. | University of Notre Dame

SOUTH-WESTERN
CENGAGE Learning™

Australia • Brazil • Japan • Korea • Mexico • Singapore • Spain • United Kingdom • United States

CENGAGE Learning™

**Federal Taxation**
**2012 Edition**

James W. Pratt
William N. Kulsrud

Executive Editor:
Maureen Staudt

Senior Acquisitions Editor:
Mike Schenk

Senior Marketing Communications Manager:
Libby Shipp

Marketing Manager:
Natalie Livingston

Product Development Manager:
Greg Albert

Production Editorial Manager:
Kim Fry

Content Project Editor:
Jennifer Flinchpaugh

Senior Rights Acquisition Account Manager:
Todd Osborne

Production Manager:
Robin Richie

Project Coordinator:
Kathryn Nussbaum

Cover and Preface Designer:
Candice Swanson

Compositor:
MPS Limited

Cover and Chapter Opener Images:
© 2011 Jupiterimages Corporation



Library of Congress Control Number: 2011926811

ISBN-13: 978-1-1118-2421-1 | PKG ISBN-13: 978-1-1118-2411-2
ISBN-10: 1-1118-2421-5 | PKG ISBN-10: 1-1118-2411-8

**Cengage Learning**
5191 Natorp Blvd.
Mason, OH 45040
USA

Cengage Learning is a leading provider of customized learning solutions with office locations around the globe, including Singapore, the United Kingdom, Australia, Mexico, Brazil, and Japan. Locate your local office at: www.**international.cengage.com/region**

Cengage Learning products are represented in Canada by Nelson Education, Ltd.

For your lifelong learning solutions, visit www.**cengage.com/custom**

Visit our corporate website at www.**cengage.com**

Printed in the United States of America

# PREFACE

## WELCOME TO THE PRATT & KULSRUD TAXATION SERIES

For more than 25 years, the Pratt & Kulsrud Taxation Series has provided educators, students, and professionals an engaging and clear presentation of tax law. In 1984, the series began with *Federal Taxation*, a unique textbook exploring issues relating to the taxation of individuals and businesses. The success of that text and the demand for additional topics led to the creation of two separate titles: *Corporate, Partnership, Estate and Gift Taxation* and *Individual Taxation*.

In every edition, the series' unique pedagogy has emphasized that the key to learning taxation is to understand the underlying principle behind every rule. For this reason, conceptual background and historical foundation are clearly explained as concepts are explored. This approach is bolstered by more than 1,000 examples and review questions that address the most important aspects of the law.

The 2012 series continues the tradition of excellence with timely updates reflecting the latest tax law changes, the inclusion of CPAexcel, the integration of H&R Block At Home™ Premium & Business Software, and rich online instructor resources.

## THE 2012 EDITION

This textbook has been revised to reflect tax law changes and significant judicial and administrative developments during the past year. As we go to press, Congress is considering various proposals that may lead to significant and immediate changes in the tax law. Should any of these proposals be enacted, we will continue our long-standing policy of posting these changes to the Pratt & Kulsrud instructor companion web site, which can be accessed by signing on to **login.cengage.com** and clicking on the appropriate title, and to the South-Western tax community website, **www.cengage.com/community/tax**.

## FEATURES FOR LEARNERS

- **Learning Objectives.** A summary of key learning outcomes can be found at the beginning of each chapter. Each summary outlines what students should understand after reading that chapter. Furthermore, each Learning Objective is referenced within the text as related content is introduced to the reader.

- **Problem Materials.** Available at the end of each chapter, a variety of assessment tools are offered to gauge comprehension. These include discussion questions and computational problems, as well as tax-return problems that highlight important topics.

- **You Make the Call.** Students are challenged by hypothetical situations that require reasoning and judgment to resolve practical tax problems.

- **Check Your Knowledge.** Many chapters include objective and short-answer review questions that check comprehension of key concepts. These review questions ensure that students grasp the critical aspects of each topic.

- **CPAexcel CPA Exam Review.** Every new copy of this text is packaged with an access code for CPAexcel, at no additional cost. This online resource gives students access to the same tax content from the CPA Review course that thousands of candidates take annually to prepare for the CPA Exam. CPAexcel includes hundreds of past exam questions and simulations that use formats identical to those found on the CPA exam. Students can follow along with video lectures on individual tax topics, view practice exam results, and track their progress.

- **H&R Block at Home™ Premium and Business Software.** Providing students an additional tax-preparation tool, H&R Block At Home™ features basic and complex problems that allow students to prepare returns for individuals, C and S corporations, partnerships, estates, and trusts. Furthermore, the software's website, **www.hrblock.com**, offers useful tips, calculators, and other up-to-the-minute, relevant, tax information. We do not anticipate any problems loading the software; however, Cengage Learning Technical Support (1-800-423-0563) is available for help, if necessary.

In addition , a *Study Guide to Accompany Federal Taxation* (1-1119-6856-X) is available. The Study Guide provides chapter reviews, study exercises, and true-false / multiple-choice questions. These materials may be used in students' initial study of the chapter content, and also in their review. The Study Guide may be purchased through collegiate bookstores. In addition, the supplement may be purchased online; students need only visit **www.cengagebrain.com** and enter ISBN 111196856X to be directed to the Study Guide site.

## **ENHANCED SUPPORT** FOR INSTRUCTORS

**Companion Web Site — login.cengage.com**
This Pratt & Kulsrud instructor companion site is your one-stop-shop for the following resources:

- **Solutions Manual.** Solutions to end-of-chapter discussion questions and computational problems are included in this manual. Specific pages and examples from the text are referenced, as are supporting statutory and administrative authorities, when appropriate.

- **Instructor's Resource Guide and Test Bank.** This guide includes solutions to comprehensive and tax research problems and tax-return problems, along with a test bank of more than 750 objective questions (true-false and multiple choice), whose answers reference specific pages and examples in the text.

- **PowerPoint Slides.** Designed for classroom use, there are slides for each chapter's principle topics, as well as slides containing solutions for many problems.

- **Lecture Outlines.** These outlines help instructors organize class discussions for greatest efficacy.

- **Legislative Updates.** Book-specific updates, tax law changes, and inflation adjustments are posted on a regular basis to the Pratt & Kulsrud instructor companion site, which can be accessed by signing on to **login.cengage.com** and clicking on the appropriate title, and to the South-Western tax community website, **www.cengage.com/community/tax**.

## **INSTRUCTOR'S RESOURCE CD** WITH EXAMVIEW®

Instructor ancillaries — including the Solutions Manual, Instructor's Resource Guide and Test Bank, PowerPoint Slides, and Lecture Outlines — are provided on a CD-ROM (ISBN 1-1118-2581-5). This gives instructors the ultimate tool for preparing and customizing lectures, presentations, and exams.

The test bank files on the CD are provided in two formats: Microsoft® Word and ExamView®. ExamView® is an easy-to-use test-creation software compatible with Microsoft® Windows.

## CENGAGE LEARNING CUSTOM SOLUTIONS

Cengage Learning Custom Solutions can work with you to develop a specialized publication that will make the educational experience unique and personal for all learners. Through our Custom publishing service, authors can publish original learning materials as a standalone book or as a supplement to another text; your materials can then be bundled with other Cengage Learning products. Our Custom services give you nearly limitless options for developing materials tailored to suit individual needs.

- **Derivative Solutions.** Derivative solutions let you build a book or a collection of course material using content from previously published Cengage textbooks. Include your own content to customize your materials even more.

- **TextChoice.** With TextChoice, our online database publishing program, you can access Cengage Learning's database of content to develop custom learning materials for your course. Explore **www.textchoice.com** to select readings, chapters, and excerpts from more than 40 subject areas.

- **Cover Gallery.** Our recently expanded cover gallery allows you to select a professional cover design to complement your customized book, or create a unique, course-specific design. Visit our online gallery at **www.custom.cengage.com/covers**.

- **Original Learning Materials.** Custom Solutions can publish your original learning materials with the help of our Custom publishing editors and our original works program. Textbooks, supplements, study guides…the possibilities are endless!

- **Custom Technology.** Technology Services can provide you with tailored learning materials in a variety of delivery methods.

Please visit **www.custom.cengage.com** for more information on Cengage Learning Custom Solutions' services.

## ADDITIONAL OFFERINGS FROM THE PRATT & KULSRUD TAXATION SERIES

The series includes new editions of:

***Corporate, Partnership, Estate and Gift Taxation***
**2012 Edition**
ISBN 1-1118-2579-3
Areas of taxation essential to the education of individuals pursuing careers in taxation or tax-related fields are emphasized. The first eight chapters are devoted to the tax problems of regular corporations and their shareholders. Two chapters consider the taxation of partnerships and partners, while one chapter examines S corporations. These chapters are followed by a separate chapter examining the special problems of international taxation, an area of growing importance. Another chapter discusses Federal estate and gift taxation. And two additional chapters contain related topics for the income taxation of estates, trusts and beneficiaries, and the major aspects of family tax planning. The text also includes a chapter on state and local taxation. The scope of this text is intentionally broad to accommodate a variety of uses and to provide flexibility for instructors designing advanced tax courses. Includes CPAexcel and H&R Block At Home™.

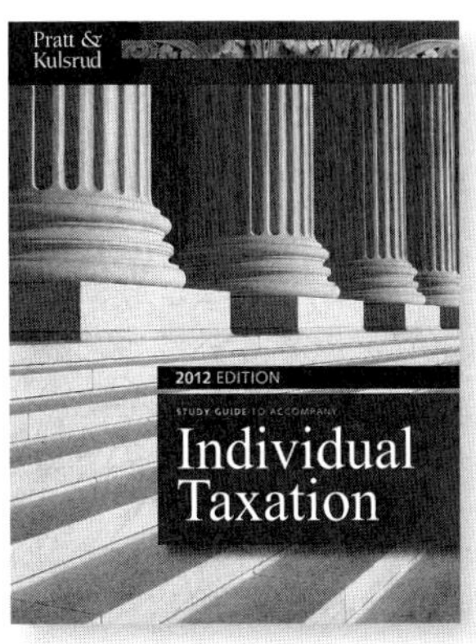


***Individual Taxation***
**2012 Edition**
ISBN 1-1118-2559-9
Numerous examples and computational illustrations explain the more complex rules concerning the Federal income taxation of individuals, making this text ideal for a first course in Federal taxation, undergraduate or graduate accounting, business or law students. Includes CPAexcel and H&R Block At Home™.

## ACKNOWLEDGMENTS

The editor and author team would like to thank particularly Linda Curry of Indiana University and Leonard Goodman of Rutgers University for their comments and suggestions. In addition, the editors and authors would like to acknowledge the tireless efforts of Cengage Learning's Managing Development Editor Greg Albert and Content Project Editor Jennifer Flinchpaugh. Their work on this edition has led to a strong revision that will benefit both students and instructors. Thanks also to our Senior Acquisitions Editor Mike Schenk, Marketing Manager Natalie Livingston, Senior Marketing Communications Manager Libby Shipp, and Executive Editor Maureen Staudt. Finally, we appreciate the efforts of the South-Western editors and sales representatives who put this book into your hands for adoption consideration.

## ABOUT **THE EDITORS**

**James W. Pratt**

James W. (Jim) Pratt is the PriceWaterhouse Coopers Professor of Accountancy & Taxation at the University of Houston's C.T. Bauer College of Business. Jim joined the faculty in 1972 after receiving his doctorate degree from the University of Southern California. He has published articles in leading professional journals, such as the *Journal of Accountancy*, *Journal of Taxation*, *Journal of Corporate Taxation*, *Journal of Partnership Taxation*, and *The Tax Adviser*. In addition to his contributions as an author and editor, Jim has received several awards for outstanding teaching. He has also taught in continuing professional education programs for more than 30 years, and has served as a tax training consultant for several national and local accounting firms.

**William N. Kulsrud**

William N. (Bill) Kulsrud is an Associate Professor of Accounting at the Kelley School of Business of Indiana University, Indianapolis/Bloomington, and serves as Chair of the Master of Science in Accounting and Master of Science in Taxation programs. Bill joined the faculty in 1979 after receiving his Ph.D. from the University of Texas. He has published numerous articles, which have appeared in leading professional journals such as the *Journal of Taxation*, *Journal of Corporate Taxation*, *The Tax Adviser*, *Taxation for Accountants*, and *Taxes — The Tax Magazine*. In addition to his contributions as an author and editor, Bill has received many awards for outstanding teaching. In 1990, he was named Accounting Educator of the Year by the Indiana C.P.A. Society. He has also taught hundreds of professional education programs for national and local accounting firms, and has developed materials used in their continuing education programs. Bill is currently the co-coordinator of the National Tax Education Program sponsored by the AICPA.

# Brief Contents


Preface iii

## Part 1 Introduction to the Federal Tax System

Chapter 1 An Overview of Federal Taxation 1-1

Chapter 2 Tax Practice and Research 2-1

Chapter 3 Taxable Entities; Tax Formula; Introduction to Property Transactions 3-1

Chapter 4 Personal and Dependency Exemptions; Filing Status; Determination of Tax for an Individual; Filing Requirements 4-1

## Part 2 Gross Income

Chapter 5 Gross Income 5-1

Chapter 6 Gross Income: Inclusions and Exclusions 6-1

## Part 3 Deductions and Losses

Chapter 7 Overview of Deductions and Losses 7-1

Chapter 8 Employee Business Expenses 8-1

Chapter 9 Capital Recovery: Depreciation, Amortization, and Depletion 9-1

Chapter 10 Certain Business Deductions and Losses 10-1

Chapter 11 Itemized Deductions 11-1

Chapter 12 Deductions for Certain Investment Expenses and Losses 12-1

## Part 4 Alternative Minimum Tax and Tax Credits

Chapter 13 The Alternative Minimum Tax and Tax Credits 13-1

## Part 5 Property Transactions

Chapter 14 Property Transactions: Basis Determination and Recognition of Gain or Loss 14-1

Chapter 15 Nontaxable Exchanges 15-1

Chapter 16 Property Transactions: Capital Gains and Losses 16-1

Chapter 17 Property Transactions: Dispositions of Trade or Business Property 17-1

## Part 6 Employee Compensation and Retirement Plans

Chapter 18 Employee Compensation and Retirement Plans 18-1

## Part 7 Corporate Taxation

Chapter 19 Corporations: Formation and Operation 19-1

Chapter 20 Corporate Distributions, Redemptions and Liquidations 20-1

Chapter 21 Taxation of Corporate Accumulations 21-1

## Part 8 Flow-Through Entities

Chapter 22 Taxation of Partnerships and Partners 22-1

Chapter 23 S Corporations 23-1

## Part 9 Family Tax Planning

Chapter 24 The Federal Transfer Taxes 24-1

Chapter 25 Income Taxation of Estates and Trusts 25-1

Chapter 26 Family Tax Planning 26-1

## Appendices and Index

**Appendix A:** Tax Rate Schedules and Tables A-1

**Appendix B:** Tax Forms B-1

**Appendix C:** Modified ACRS Tables C-1

**Appendix D:** Continuous Individual Tax Return Problems and Two Comprehensive Individual Tax Return Problems for 2010 D-1

**Appendix E:** Glossary of Tax Terms E-1

**Index** IN-1

# Contents


Preface iii

**Part 1** Introduction to the Federal Tax System

**Chapter 1** **An Overview of Federal Taxation 1-1**

**Introduction 1-2** | The Nature of a Tax 1-2 | **Development of U.S. Taxation 1-3** | Excise and Customs Duties 1-3 | Federal Income Tax 1-3 | Federal Wealth Transfer Taxes 1-4 | Federal Taxes as a Source of Revenue 1-4 | Key Tax Terms 1-4 | **Major Types of Taxes 1-10** | Income Taxes 1-10 | Wealth Transfer Taxes 1-12 | Employment Taxes 1-18 | Excise Taxes 1-24 | Additional Types of Taxes 1-24 | **Goals of Taxation 1-25** | Economic Objectives 1-26 | Social Objectives 1-27 | Other Objectives 1-28 | **A Prelude to Tax Planning 1-29** | **Problem Materials 1-31**

**Chapter 2** **Tax Practice and Research 2-1**

**Introduction 2-2** | **Tax Practice in General 2-2** | **Taxation as a Professional Career 2-4** | **Sources and Applications of Tax Law 2-5** | **Primary vs. Secondary Authority 2-5** | **Authoritative Sources of Tax Law 2-6** | **Statutory Law 2-6** | The Making of a Tax Law 2-6 | Committee Reports 2-7 | Organization of the Internal Revenue Code 2-9 | Tax Treaties 2-12 | **Administrative Interpretations 2-12** | Regulations 2-12 | Revenue Rulings 2-14 | Revenue Procedures 2-15 | Letter Rulings 2-15 | **Judicial Interpretations 2-16** | Trial Courts 2-17 | Appellate Courts 2-19 | Case Citation 2-21 | **Secondary Sources 2-25** | Tax Services 2-25 | Tax Periodicals 2-26 | **Tax Research 2-26** | Obtaining the Facts 2-27 | Diagnosing the Issue 2-27 | Locating the Authorities 2-28 | Evaluating the Authority 2-28 | Deriving the Solution 2-31 | Communicating the Findings 2-31 | **Rules of Tax Practice: Responsibilities and Ethics 2-31** | Taxpayer Penalties 2-32 | Accuracy-Related Penalties 2-33 | Economic Substance Doctrine 2-35 | Fraud 2-38 | Tax Preparer Penalties 2-39 | **Problem Materials 2-45**

**Chapter 3** **Taxable Entities; Tax Formula; Introduction to Property Transactions 3-1**

**Introduction 3-2** | The Taxable Entity 3-2 | **Taxable Entities 3-3** | Individual Taxpayers 3-3 | Corporate Taxpayers 3-5 | Fiduciary Taxpayers 3-7 | **Flow–Through Entities 3-8** | Sole Proprietorships 3-8 | Partnerships 3-9 | Electing Small Business Corporations: "S" Corporations 3-11 | Limited Liability Companies 3-11 | Tax–Exempt Organizations 3-12 | **Tax Formula 3-15** | Analyzing the Tax Formula 3-15 | **Introduction to Property Transactions 3-28** | Gain or Loss Realized 3-28 | Gain or Loss Recognized 3-30 | Character of the Gain or Loss 3-31 | Trade or Business Property 3-34 | **Tax Planning Considerations 3-36** | Choice of Business Form 3-36 | Itemized Deductions versus Standard Deduction 3-37 | Employee Business Expenses 3-37 | **Problem Materials 3-38**

**Chapter 4** **Personal and Dependency Exemptions; Filing Status; Determination of Tax for an Individual; Filing Requirements 4-1**

**Introduction 4-2 | Personal and Dependency Exemptions 4-2 |** Personal Exemptions 4-2 | Exemptions for Dependents 4-3 | Exemption for Qualifying Child 4-3 | Exemption for Qualifying Relative 4-4 | Provisions Common to all Dependency Exemptions 4-9 | Children of Divorced or Separated Parents 4-11 | Phase–Out of Personal and Dependency Exemptions 4-12 | Child Tax Credit 4-12 | **Filing Status 4-14 |** Evolution of Filing Status 4-14 | Married Individuals 4-16 | Head of Household 4-17 | **Computation of Tax for Individual Taxpayers 4-22 |** Tax Tables 4-22 | Tax Rate Schedules 4-25 | Special Tax Computation Rules 4-26 | Determination of Net Tax Due or Refund 4-31 | **Filing Requirements 4-32 |** Due Dates for Filing Returns 4-35 | Penalties 4-36 | Claim for Refund 4-40 | Statute of Limitations 4-41 | Indexation and the Federal Income Tax 4-43 | **Appendix 4-45 |** Tax Return Illustrations 4-45 | **Problem Materials 4-54**

**Part 2** Gross Income

**Chapter 5** **Gross Income 5-1**

**Introduction 5-2 | Gross Income Defined 5-2 |** Economic Concept of Income 5-3 | Accounting Concept of Income 5-5 | Income for Tax Purposes: The Judicial Concept 5-5 | **Refinements of the Gross Income Definition 5-6 |** Form-of-Benefit Principle 5-7 | Return of Capital Doctrine 5-8 | Indirect Economic Benefits 5-10 | **Reporting Income: Tax Accounting 5-12 |** Accounting Periods 5-12 | Accounting Methods 5-14 | Cash Method of Accounting 5-15 | Accrual Method of Accounting 5-20 | Changes in Accounting Methods 5-21 | **Accounting for Income: Special Rules 5-24 |** Claim of Right Doctrine 5-24 | Prepaid Income 5-26 | Interest Income 5-29 | **Identification of the Taxpayer 5-33 |** Income from Personal Services 5-34 | Income from Property 5-34 | Unearned Income of Children 5-34 | Interest-Free and Below-Market Loans 5-34 | Income from Community Property 5-38 | **Tax Planning 5-40 |** Timing Income Recognition 5-40 | Income-Splitting Techniques 5-40 | Excluded Economic Income 5-41 | **Problem Materials 5-42**

**Chapter 6** **Gross Income: Inclusions and Exclusions 6-1**

**Introduction 6-2 | Investment Income 6-2 |** Dividends 6-3 | Interest 6-6 | Annuities 6-10 | 529 Plans: Qualified Tuition Programs 6-14 | **Employee Compensation and Other Benefits 6-17 |** Reimbursement of Employee Expenses 6-19 | Employer Gifts 6-19 | Employer Awards 6-19 | Social Security Benefits 6-20 | Unemployment Benefits 6-22 | Employee Insurance 6-22 | Employer-Provided Meals and Lodging 6-26 | Child and Dependent Care Assistance 6-28 | Adoption Assistance Programs 6-28 | Educational Assistance Plans 6-28 | Section 132 Fringe Benefits 6-29 | Military Personnel 6-34 | Reparations to Holocaust Victims 6-34 | **Personal Transfers between Individuals 6-34 |** Gifts and Inheritances 6-35 | Alimony and Separate Maintenance 6-35 | **Transfers by Unrelated Parties 6-40 |** Life Insurance Proceeds and Other Death Benefits 6-40 | Employee Death Benefits 6-42 | Prizes and Awards 6-42 | Scholarships and Fellowships 6-43 | Cancellation of Indebtedness 6-44 | Government Transfer Payments 6-47 | **Business Gross Income 6-48 |** Agreement not to Compete and Goodwill 6-48 | Business Interruption Insurance Proceeds 6-48 | Damages Awarded 6-49 | Lease Cancellation Payments 6-49 | Leasehold Improvements 6-50 | Contributions to Capital 6-51 | **Miscellaneous Items 6-51 |** Fees Received 6-51 | Asset Discovery 6-51 | Car Pool Receipts 6-51 |

Income Tax Refunds 6-51 | Temporary Living Costs 6-52 | Damages Awarded to Individuals 6-52 | **Tax Planning 6-53** | Investments 6-53 | Employee Benefits 6-54 | Employee Versus Self-Employed 6-55 | Divorce 6-56 | **Problem Materials 6-57**

## Part 3 Deductions and Losses

### Chapter 7 Overview of Deductions and Losses 7-1

**Introduction 7-2** | Deduction Defined 7-2 | **Deductions for Expenses: General Requirements 7-3** | General Rules: Code §§ 162 and 212 7-3 | Related to Carrying on a Business or an Income-Producing Activity 7-4 | Ordinary and Necessary Expenses 7-7 | Reasonable Expenses 7-8 | Paid or Incurred During the Taxable Year 7-8 | Employee Business Expenses 7-9 | **Accounting for Deductions 7-9** | Cash Method of Accounting 7-9 | Accrual Method of Accounting 7-13 | Relationship to Financial Accounting 7-17 | **Deductions for Losses 7-18** | **Classification of Expenses 7-19** | Importance of Classification 7-19 | Deductions for A.G.I 7-20 | Itemized Deductions 7-20 | Self-Employed Versus Employee 7-21 | **Limitations on Deductions 7-24** | Hobby Expenses and Losses 7-24 | Personal Living Expenses 7-26 | Capital Expenditures 7-28 | Business Investigation Expenses and Start-up Costs 7-31 | Public Policy Restrictions 7-34 | Lobbying and Political Contributions 7-36 | Expenses and Interest Relating to Tax-Exempt Income 7-37 | Related Taxpayer Transactions 7-38 | Payment of Another Taxpayer's Obligation 7-41 | Substantiation 7-42 | **Tax Planning Considerations 7-42** | Maximizing Deductions 7-42 | Timing of Deductions 7-43 | Expenses Relating to Tax-Exempt Income 7-43 | "Points" on Mortgages 7-43 | Hobbies 7-44 | **Problem Materials 7-44**

### Chapter 8 Employee Business Expenses 8-1

**Introduction 8-2** | **Education Expenses 8-2** | Requirements for Deduction 8-3 | Travel as a form of Education 8-4 | Types and Classification of Education Deductions 8-4 | Deduction for Qualified Tuition and Related Expenses 8-5 | Relationship to Education Credits and Qualified Prepaid Tuition 8-6 | Deduction for Expenses of Primary and Secondary School Teachers 8-8 | **Moving Expenses 8-9** | Distance Requirement 8-9 | Time Test 8-10 | Deductible Moving Expenses 8-10 | Classifying and Reporting the Moving Expense Deduction 8-12 | **Home Office Expenses 8-13** | Requirements for Deductibility 8-13 | Amount Deductible 8-16 | Daycare and Storage Use 8-17 | Residential Phone Service 8-18 | **Transportation Expenses 8-19** | Deductible Transportation Versus Nondeductible Commuting 8-19 | Computing Car Expenses 8-24 | Classification of Transportation and Travel Expenses 8-26 | **Travel Expenses 8-26** | Away-from-Home Test 8-27 | Combined Business and Pleasure Travel 8-28 | Foreign Conventions 8-32 | Cruise Ships 8-32 | **Entertainment Expenses 8-33** | Deduction Requirements 8-33 | Entertainment Facilities 8-37 | Exceptions to Directly-Related-to and Associated-with Tests 8-37 | Fifty Percent Limitation on Entertainment and Meal Expenses 8-38 | Limitations on Deductions for Tickets 8-39 | Business Gifts 8-40 | **Travel and Entertainment Record Keeping Requirements 8-41** | **Reporting Business Expenses and Losses 8-44** | Sole Proprietors and Self–Employed Persons 8-44 | Statutory Employees 8-44 | Employees 8-46 | **Tax Planning Considerations 8-50** | Moving Expenses 8-50 | Travel and Entertainment Expenses 8-50 | **Problem Materials 8-53**

**Chapter 9** **Capital Recovery: Depreciation, Amortization, and Depletion 9-1**

**Introduction 9-2** | **Depreciation and Amortization for Tax Purposes 9-2** | General Rules for Depreciation Deductions 9-2 | Historical Perspective 9-4 | **Modified Accelerated Cost Recovery System 9-5** | An Overview of MACRS 9-5 | Property Subject to MACRS 9-5 | Classes of Property 9-6 | Calculating Depreciation 9-9 | Other Methods 9-16 | Changes in Depreciation 9-19 | **Limited Expensing Election: Code § 179 9-21** | Additional First-Year (Bonus) Depreciation 9-23 | Limitations for Automobiles 9-25 | Limitations for Personal Use 9-30 | Other Considerations 9-36 | **Amortization 9-37** | Goodwill and Covenants not to Compete 9-38 | Five-Year Elective Amortization 9-39 | Leasehold Improvements 9-39 | **Depletion 9-39** | Computing the Depletion Deduction 9-39 | **Research and Experimental Expenditures 9-42** | Research and Experimental Expenditures Defined 9-42 | Alternative Tax Treatments 9-42 | Other Related Provisions 9-44 | **Expenses of Farmers and Ranchers 9-44** | Expenses Related to Livestock 9-44 | Soil and Water Conservation, Fertilizer, Land Clearing 9-44 | Development Expenses 9-45 | **Tax Planning Considerations 9-45** | Depreciation and After-Tax Cash Flow 9-45 | Accelerating Depreciation with Cost Segregation 9-46 | Goodwill Amortization Rule Benefits Buyers and Sellers 9-47 | **Problem Materials 9-48**

**Chapter 10** **Certain Business Deductions and Losses 10-1**

**Introduction 10-2** | **Bad Debts 10-2** | Treatment of Business Versus Nonbusiness Bad Debts 10-2 | General Requirements 10-4 | Deduction Methods 10-5 | **Casualty and Theft Losses 10-7** | General Rules 10-7 | Casualty and Theft Defined 10-8 | Loss Computation 10-8 | Casualty Gains and Losses 10-10 | Year Deductible 10-11 | **Net Operating Losses 10-13** | Carryback and Carryforward Years 10-14 | Net Operating Loss Computation 10-15 | Recomputing Taxable Income for Year to Which Net Operating Loss is Carried 10-18 | **Inventories 10-19** | Exceptions to the Inventory Requirement 10-20 | Inventory Accounting in General 10-22 | Costs to be Inventoried 10-22 | Allocating Inventoriable Costs 10-25 | Dollar Value LIFO 10-26 | The LIFO Election 10-29 | Lower of Cost or Market 10-29 | Qualified Production Activities Deduction 10-30 | **Tax Planning Considerations 10-36** | Casualty and Theft Losses 10-36 | Bad Debts 10-37 | Net Operating Losses 10-37 | **Problem Materials 10-37**

**Chapter 11** **Itemized Deductions 11-1**

**Introduction 11-2** | **Medical Expenses 11-2** | In General 11-2 | When Deductible 11-3 | Deduction Limitations 11-4 | Special Items and Equipment 11-5 | Special Care Facilities 11-6 | Long-Term Care Costs 11-7 | Medical Travel and Transportation 11-7 | Medical Insurance Costs and Reimbursements 11-8 | Health Savings Accounts and Medical Savings Accounts 11-9 | Health Insurance Costs of Self-Employed Taxpayers 11-12 | **Personal Casualty and Theft Losses 11-13** | Year Deductible 11-13 | Reporting Casualty Losses 11-13 | **Taxes 11-13** | General Requirements for Deductibility 11-14 | Income Taxes 11-15 | Deduction for State and Local General Sales Tax 11-16 | Property Taxes 11-17 | Reporting Deductions for Taxes 11-19 | **Interest Expense 11-20** | Limitations on Deductions of Interest Expense 11-20 | Classification of Interest Expense 11-29 | When Deductible 11-33 | Where Reported 11-34 | **Charitable Contributions 11-35** | Deduction Requirements 11-35 | Limitations on Deductions 11-37 | Contribution Carryovers 11-45 | **Miscellaneous Itemized Deductions 11-46** | Other Itemized Deductions 11-47 | **Tax Planning Considerations 11-48** | Maximizing Personal Deductions 11-48 | Medical Expenses 11-48 | Charitable Contributions 11-49 | Miscellaneous Deductions 11-49 | **Problem Materials 11-50**

Chapter 12 **Deductions for Certain Investment Expenses and Losses 12-1**

**Introduction 12-2 | Introduction to Tax Shelters 12-2 |** Structure of a Tax Shelter 12-3 | Elements of a Tax Shelter 12-3 | **At–Risk Rules 12-6 |** At-Risk Computation 12-7 | **Passive Activity Loss Limitations 12-9 |** General Rule 12-9 | Taxpayers Subject to Limitations 12-13 | Passive Activities 12-14 | Definition of an Activity 12-14 | Rental Versus Nonrental Activities 12-18 | Material Participation 12-20 | Recharacterized Passive Income 12-24 | **Passive–Activity Interest Expense 12-25 | Rental of Residence (Vacation Home Rentals) 12-28 |** Basic Rules 12-28 | Allocation of Expenses 12-31 | **Problem Materials 12-34**

Part 4 Alternative Minimum Tax and Tax Credits

Chapter 13 **The Alternative Minimum Tax and Tax Credits 13-1**

**Introduction 13-2 | Alternative Minimum Tax 13-3 |** Policy Objectives 13-3 | Overview of AMT 13-3 | AMT Rates and Exemptions 13-5 | Adjustments and Tax Preference Items in General 13-7 | AMT Adjustments 13-7 | AMT Adjustments Applicable to All Taxpayers 13-7 | AMT Adjustments Applicable Only to Individuals 13-10 | Adjustment Applicable Only to Corporations 13-13 | Special Tax Shelter Loss Adjustments 13-14 | Tax Preference Items 13-15 | Alternative Minimum Tax Computations 13-17 | Minimum Tax Credit 13-19 | AMT Refundable Tax Credit 13-23 | **Income Tax Credits 13-25 |** Overview of Tax Credits 13-26 | General Business Credit 13-28 | Investment Credit 13-29 | Work Opportunity Credit 13-33 | Alcohol Fuel Credit 13-34 | Research and Experimental (R&E) Credit 13-34 | Low-Income Housing Credit 13-38 | Disabled Access Credit 13-38 | Empowerment Zone Employment Credit 13-39 | Credit for Employer-Provided Child-Care 13-39 | Other Components of the General Business Credit 13-40 | General Business Credit Carryover Rules 13-41 | Foreign Tax Credit 13-42 | **Nonbusiness Credits 13-43 |** Child Tax Credit 13-43 | Child and Dependent Care Credit 13-44 | Education Credits 13-49 | Credit for Adoption Expenses 13-52 | Credit for the Elderly and Permanently Disabled 13-53 | Credit for Interest on Certain Home Mortgages 13-54 | Refundable Credits 13-55 Tax Withheld at the Source 13-55 | Earned Income Credit 13-55 | Refundable Child Tax Credits 13-59 | Other Refundable Credits 13-61 | **Problem Materials 13-61**

Part 5 Property Transactions

Chapter 14 **Property Transactions: Basis Determination and Recognition of Gain or Loss 14-1**

**Introduction 14-2 | Determination of Gain or Loss 14-2 |** Introduction 14-2 | General Rule of Recognition 14-3 | Computing Amount Realized 14-4 | **Basis Determination Rules 14-6 |** Property Acquired by Purchase 14-6 | Property Acquired by Gift 14-7 | Property Acquired from a Decedent 14-9 | Property Acquired in a Nontaxable Exchange 14-10 | Property Converted from Personal Use to Business Use 14-11 | Property Converted from Business Use to Personal Use 14-11 | Adjustments to Basis 14-12 | **Effect of Liabilities on Amount Realized and Adjusted Basis 14-13 | Concepts Related to Realization and Recognition 14-13 |** Sale or Other Disposition 14-13 | Allocations of Purchase Price and Basis 14-18 | **Installment Sale Method 14-19 |** General Rules 14-19 | Election out of Installment Reporting 14-20 | Gain Reported Under the Installment Method 14-21 | Limitations on Certain Installment Sales 14-23 | Reporting Gain on Installment Sales 14-26 | **Disallowed Losses 14-27 |**

Wash Sales 14-27 | Sales Between Related Parties 14-28 | **Tax Planning Considerations 14-29** | Gift Versus Bequest 14-29 | Charitable Transfers Involving Property Other than Cash 14-29 | Changes in the Use of Property 14-29 | Sales to Related Parties 14-30 | Use of Installment Sales 14-30 | **Problem Materials 14-30**

Chapter 15 **Nontaxable Exchanges 15-1**

**Introduction 15-2** | **Types of Nontaxable Exchanges 15-3** | **Sale of a Personal Residence 15-3** | Computation of Basis of Residence and Gain or Loss Realized 15-3 | Section 121 Exclusion of Gain 15-4 | Frequency Limitation: One Sale Every Two Years 15-7 | Exceptions to Ownership, Use, and Frequency Tests 15-7 | **Involuntary Conversions 15-15** | Involuntary Conversion Defined 15-16 | Replacement Property 15-18 | Replacement Period 15-19 | Election Required 15-20 | Amount of Gain Recognized 15-21 | **Like–Kind Exchanges 15-24** | Qualified Property 15-24 | Like-Kind Property 15-25 | Receipt of Property Not of a Like–Kind (Boot) 15-28 | Basis in Property Received 15-30 | Exchange Requirement 15-33 | Treatment Mandatory 15-35 | Holding Period 15-36 | **Other Nontaxable Transactions 15-38** | Changes in form of Doing Business 15-38 | Certain Exchanges of Stock in Same Corporation 15-38 | Certain Exchanges of U.S. Obligations 15-38 | Repossession of Real Property 15-38 | Certain Exchanges of Insurance Policies 15-38 | **Tax Planning Considerations 15-39** | Current Recognition Versus Deferral 15-39 | Current Gain Resulting in Future Reductions 15-39 | Importance of Capital Budgeting in Decision Making 15-39 | **Problem Materials 15-39**

Chapter 16 **Property Transactions: Capital Gains and Losses 16-1**

**Introduction 16-2** | **General Requirements for Capital Gain 16-3** | **Capital Assets 16-4** | Definition of a Capital Asset 16-4 | Inventory 16-5 | Copyrights, Artistic Works, Letters and Similar Items 16-5 | Federal Publications 16-6 | Disposition of a Business 16-6 | **Sale or Exchange Requirement 16-7** | Worthless and Abandoned Property 16-7 | Certain Casualties and Thefts 16-9 | Other Transactions 16-10 | **Holding Period 16-10** | Stock Exchange Transactions 16-11 | Special Rules and Exceptions 16-11 | **Treatment of Capital Gains and Losses 16-13** | The Process in General 16-13 | Netting Process 16-14 | Dividends Taxed at Capital Gain Rates 16-18 | Corporate Taxpayers 16-19 | Calculating the Tax 16-20 | Reporting Capital Gains and Losses 16-24 | **Capital Gain Treatment Extended to Certain Transactions 16-25** | Patents 16-25 | Lease Cancellation Payments 16-26 | **Incentives for Investments in Small Businesses 16-26** | Losses on Small Business Stock: § 1244 16-26 | Qualified Small Business Stock (§ 1202 Stock) 16-27 | Rollover of Gain on Certain Publicly Traded Securities 16-30 | **Dealers and Developers 16-30** | Dealers, Investors and Traders of Securities 16-31 | Subdivided Real Estate 16-32 | **Other Related Provisions 16-33** | Nonbusiness Bad Debts 16-33 | Franchise Agreements, Trademarks, and Trade Names 16-33 | Short Sales 16-34 | Options 16-35 | **Corporate Bonds and Other Indebtedness 16-37** | Original Issue Discount 16-38 | Market Discount 16-41 | Conversion Transactions 16-41 | Bond Premium 16-42 | **Tax Planning Considerations 16-42** | Timing of Capital Asset Transactions 16-42 | Section 1244 Stock 16-43 | **Problem Materials 16-44**

Chapter 17 **Property Transactions: Dispositions of Trade or Business Property 17-1**

**Introduction 17-2** | **Section 1231 17-2** | Historical Perspective 17-2 | Section 1231 Property 17-3 | Other § 1231 Property 17-4 | Section 1231 Netting Process 17-6 | Look-Back Rule 17-10 | Applicability of Lower Rates 17-11 | **Depreciation**

**Recapture 17-13 |** Historical Perspective 17-13 | When Applicable 17-14 | Types of Depreciation Recapture 17-14 | Full Recapture—§ 1245 17-15 | Partial Recapture—§ 1250 17-17 | Additional Recapture—Corporations 17-27 | Other Recapture Provisions 17-33 | **Related Business Issues 17-35 |** Installment Sales of Trade or Business Property 17-35 | Intangible Business Assets 17-35 | Dispositions of Business Assets and the Self-Employment Tax 17-36 | **Tax Planning Considerations 17-36 |** Timing of Sales and Other Dispositions 17-36 | Selecting Depreciation Methods 17-36 | Installment Sales 17-37 | Sales of Businesses 17-37 | Dispositions of Business Assets and the Self-Employment Tax 17-37 | **Problem Materials 17-38**

## Part 6 Employee Compensation and Retirement Plans

### Chapter 18 Employee Compensation and Retirement Plans 18-1

**Introduction 18-2 | Taxation of Current Compensation 18-2 |** Statutory Fringe Benefits 18-2 | **Deferred Compensation 18-3 | Receipt of Property for Services 18-4 |** General Rule of § 83 18-4 | The § 83(B) Election 18-5 | **Qualified Retirement Plans for Corporations 18-6 |** Tax Benefits of Qualified Plans 18-6 | Taxability of Qualified Plan Lump-Sum Distributions 18-7 | Additional Taxes on Premature or Excess Distributions 18-8 | Rollover Contribution 18-8 | Plan Loans 18-9 | Types of Qualified Plans 18-10 | **Qualification Requirements 18-13 |** Existence of a Qualified Trust 18-13 | Anti-Discrimination Rules 18-13 | Scope of Plan Participation and Coverage 18-14 | Vesting Requirements and Forfeitures 18-15 | Funding and Contribution Limitations 18-15 | Top Heavy Plans 18-17 | Deductibility of Contributions by Employer 18-17 | Determination Letters 18-17 | **Qualified Plans for Self–Employed Individuals 18-17 |** Contribution Limitations 18-18 | **Qualified Plans for Employees 18-19 |** Cash or Deferred Arrangements [§ 401(k) Plans] 18-19 | Individual Retirement Accounts 18-22 | Traditional IRA 18-22 | Roth IRAs 18-27 | Credit for Contributions to Plans by Low-Income Individuals 18-28 | Education IRAs (Coverdell Education Savings Accounts) 18-29 | Simplified Employee Pensions 18-31 | **Retirement Planning Using Nonqualified Deferred Compensation 18-31 |** Constructive Receipt 18-31 | Treatment of Nonqualified Deferred Compensation Plans 18-32 | Unfunded Deferred Compensation Plans 18-33 | Funded Deferred Compensation Plans 18-34 | **Stock Options 18-34 |** Option Exercise 18-35 | **Incentive Stock Options 18-35 |** Holding Period Requirements 18-36 | Qualification Requirements 18-37 | Nonqualified Stock Options 18-38 | Stock Appreciation Rights 18-38 | **Tax Planning Considerations 18-39 |** Planning for Retirement Income 18-39 | Advantages of IRAs 18-40 | Spousal IRAs 18-40 | What Is an Active Participant? 18-40 | Making a Nondeductible Contribution to an IRA 18-40 | **Problem Materials 18-42**

## Part 7 Corporate Taxation

### Chapter 19 Corporations: Formation and Operation 19-1

**Introduction 19-2 | What is a Corporation? 19-2 |** Associations 19-2 | Limited Liability Companies 19-3 | Sham Corporations 19-3 | **Comparison of Corporate and Individual Income Taxation 19-4 |** Gross Income 19-5 | Deductions 19-5 | Dividends-Received Deduction 19-6 | Organizational Expenditures 19-10 | Net Operating Loss 19-11 | Charitable Contributions 19-12 | Capital Gains and Losses 19-15 | Sales of Depreciable Property 19-16 | Transactions between Corporations and

Their Shareholders 19-17 | Deduction Attributable to Domestic Production 19-18 | **Computation of Corporate Income Tax 19-18** | Corporate Surtax 19-18 | Personal Service Corporations 19-20 | Alternative Minimum Tax 19-20 | Tax Credits 19-20 | Accounting Periods and Methods 19-20 | **Corporate Tax Forms and Filing Requirements 19-21** | Filing Requirements 19-22 | Estimated Tax Payments 19-22 | Example of Corporate Tax Return 19-22 | **Corporate Formation 19-29** | Transfer of Property 19-29 | By One or More Persons 19-29 | Solely for Stock 19-30 | Control 19-30 | Receipt of Boot 19-30 | Assumption of Liabilities 19-31 | Effect of § 351 on the Transferee Corporation 19-33 | Basis to Shareholders 19-33 | Basis to Transferee Corporation 19-34 | Depreciation Recapture 19-34 | **Capital Contributions 19-36** | Made by Shareholders 19-36 | Made by Nonshareholders 19-37 | **Problem Materials 19-37**

**Chapter 20** **Corporate Distributions, Redemptions and Liquidations 20-1**

**Introduction 20-2** | **Dividends 20-2** | Earnings and Profits 20-2 | Distributions from Earnings and Profits 20-5 | Cash Dividends 20-8 | Property Dividends 20-8 | Constructive Dividends 20-9 | Stock Dividends and Stock Rights 20-9 | Nondeductibility of Dividends To Corporation 20-13 | **Stock Redemptions 20-13** | In General 20-14 | Redemptions Not Equivalent to Dividends 20-14 | Substantially Disproportionate Redemptions 20-15 | Termination of a Shareholder's Interest 20-17 | Redemption from Noncorporate Shareholder in Partial Liquidation 20-17 | Redemptions of Stock to Pay Death Taxes 20-17 | Constructive Ownership of Stock 20-18 | Redemptions through Related Corporations 20-20 | Effect of Redemptions on Redeeming Corporation 20-21 | **Complete Liquidations 20-22** | Introduction 20-22 | Complete Liquidations: The General Rules 20-22 | Liquidation of a Subsidiary 20-25 | **Problem Materials 20-30**

**Chapter 21** **Taxation of Corporate Accumulations 21-1**

**Introduction 21-2** | **Accumulated Earnings Tax 21-3** | An Overview 21-3 | Intent 21-4 | Reasonable Needs of the Business 21-5 | Computation of the Accumulated Earnings Tax 21-10 | Accumulated Earnings Credit 21-12 | Dividends-Paid Deduction 21-14 | **Personal Holding Company Tax 21-15** | Personal Holding Company Defined 21-16 | PHC Ownership Test 21-17 | Income Test 21-17 | Adjusted Ordinary Gross Income 21-18 | Personal Holding Company Income (PHCI) 21-20 | Computation of the PHC Tax 21-25 | **Tax Planning 21-28** | Accumulated Earnings Tax 21-28 | Personal Holding Company Tax 21-29 | **Problem Materials 21-34**

## Part 8 Flow-Through Entities

**Chapter 22** **Taxation of Partnerships and Partners 22-1**

**Introduction 22-2** | **Definitions 22-2** | What Is a Partnership? 22-2 | Electing out of Subchapter K Partnerships 22-3 | General and Limited Partnerships 22-3 | Entity and Aggregate Theories 22-4 | **Forming a Partnership 22-4** | Contributions of Property 22-5 | Effect of Partnership Liabilities on Basis 22-6 | Contribution of Services 22-11 | Proposed Regulations Change Rules for Services 22-12 | **Operating the Partnership 22-12** | The Partnership's Taxable Year 22-13 | Organization Costs and Syndication Fees 22-14 | Computation of Partnership Taxable Income 22-15 | Reporting of Partnership Items by Partners 22-16 | Adjustments to Partner's Basis 22-16 | **Partner's Distributive Shares 22-17** | Substantial Economic Effect 22-18 | Allocations with Respect to Contributed Property 22-19 | Retroactive Allocations 22-20 |

Basis Limitation on Loss Deductibility 22-21 | **Transactions between Partners and Partnerships 22-22 |** Sales between Partners and Controlled Partnerships 22-23 | **Partnership Distributions 22-24 |** Current Distributions 22-24 | Liquidating Distributions 22-27 | Section 736 Payments 22-32 | Dispositions of Distributed Property 22-34 | Basis Adjustments to Partnership Property 22-35 | **Dispositions of Partnership Interests 22-38 |** Sales of Partnership Interests 22-38 | Gifts of Partnership Interests and Family Partnerships 22-45 | Death of a Partner 22-46 | **Partnership Termination 22-47 |** Technical Terminations 22-47 | Effect of Termination 22-48 | **Problem Materials 22-48**

Chapter 23 **S Corporations 23-1**

**Introduction 23-2 | S Corporation Eligibility Requirements 23-3 |** Eligible Corporations 23-3 | Shareholder Requirements 23-4 | One Class of Stock 23-7 | **Election of S Corporation Status 23-8 |** Making the Election: Manner and Period of Effect 23-8 | Termination of the Election 23-11 | Election after Termination 23-16 | **Operating the S Corporation 23-16 |** Determining S Corporation Net Income 23-16 | Reporting S Corporation Income 23-21 | Allocations to Shareholders 23-28 | Losses of the S Corporation 23-30 | **Determining Shareholder Basis 23-31 |** Basis in S Corporate Stock 23-31 | Basis in S Corporation Debt 23-33 | **Relationship between an S Corporation and Its Shareholders 23-36 |** Transactions between S Corporations and Their Shareholders 23-36 | Selecting a Taxable Year 23-37 | **Family Ownership 23-39 | Current Distributions of Corporate Assets 23-40 |** The E&P Question 23-40 | S Corporations with no AE&P 23-40 | S Corporations With AE&P 23-42 | Distributions of Property 23-47 | Special Rules Relating to Source of Distributions 23-47 | Post-Termination Transactions 23-48 | **Taxes Imposed on the S Corporation 23-49 |** Tax on Excessive Passive Income 23-49 | Tax on Built-in Gains 23-51 | LIFO Recapture 23-54 | Estimated Taxes 23-55 | **Disposition of Ownership Interest 23-55 |** Worthless Securities 23-56 | Corporate Liquidation 23-56 | **Tax Planning 23-56 |** Choice of Entity: Comparing S Corporations, C Corporations, Partnerships, and LLCS 23-56 | **Problem Materials 23-61**

Part 9 Family Tax Planning

Chapter 24 **The Federal Transfer Taxes 24-1**

**Introduction 24-2 |** History and Overview 24-2 | **Property Interests 24-3 |** Forms of Co-Ownership 24-4 | Life Estates, Reversions, and Remainders 24-4 | **The Gift Tax 24-5 |** Transfers Subject to Tax 24-6 | Valuation 24-7 | Basis 24-9 | The Gift Tax Exclusion 24-9 | Gift Splitting 24-10 | Gifts to Political and Charitable Organizations 24-10 | The Gift Tax Marital Deduction 24-10 | Computation and Filing 24-11 | The Overlap between the Gift and Estate Taxes 24-13 | **Transfers of Property at Death 24-14 |** Role of a Will 24-14 | Intestacy 24-14 | Probate 24-14 | **The Taxable Estate 24-15 | The Gross Estate Concept 24-16 |** Valuation of Gross Estate and Basis 24-16 | Basis 24-18 | Special Use Valuation: § 2032A 24-18 | **Gross Estate Inclusions 24-19 |** Insurance on the Life of the Decedent 24-19 | Survivor Benefits 24-19 | Joint Interests 24-20 | General Powers of Appointment 24-20 | Transfers Taking Effect at Death 24-22 | Gifts in Contemplation of Death 24-24 | Transfers for Insufficient Consideration 24-24 | **Deductions from the Gross Estate 14-25 |** Expenses, Indebtedness, and Taxes 24-25 | Losses 24-26 | State Death Taxes 24-27 | Charitable Contributions 24-27 | The Marital Deduction 24-28 | **Computation of the Estate Tax 24-29 |** Estate Tax Credits 24-30 | A Comprehensive

Example 24-31 | Payment of the Estate Tax 24-32 | **The Generation-Skipping Transfer Tax 24-34 | Tax Planning Considerations 24-34 | Problem Materials 24-35**

Chapter 25 **Income Taxation of Estates and Trusts 25-1**

**Introduction 25-2 | The Function of Estates and Trusts 25-2 |** Estates 25-2 | Trusts 25-2 | Trust Beneficiaries 25-3 | Fiduciary Accounting Income 25-3 | **Income Taxation of Fiduciaries 25-5 | Fiduciary Taxable Income 25-6 |** Fiduciary Tax Rates 25-6 | Standard Deduction and Personal Exemption 25-6 | Limitations on Deductibility of Fiduciary Expenses 25-6 | Charitable Contributions 25-9 | Depreciation, Depletion, and Amortization 25-9 | Fiduciary Losses 25-10 | **Income and Deductions in Respect of a Decedent 25-11 |** Estate Tax Treatment and the § 691(c) Deduction 25-11 | **The Distribution Deduction and the Taxation of Beneficiaries 25-13 |** Computation of Distribution Deduction and DNI 25-14 | The Computation of DNI 25-15 | Simple Trusts 25-16 | Complex Trusts and Estates 25-16 | Character of Beneficiary's Income 25-19 | Reporting Requirements for Beneficiaries 25-21 | The Separate Share Rule 25-21 | A Comprehensive Example 25-22 | The Sixty-Five Day Rule 25-24 | **Tax Planning Considerations 25-30 | Problem Materials 25-30**

Chapter 26 **Family Tax Planning 26-1**

**Introduction 26-2 | Family Income Shifting 26-2 |** Judicial Constraints on Income Shifting 26-3 | Joint Filing and the Singles Penalty 26-4 | The Marriage Penalty 26-4 | Income Shifting to Children and Other Family Members 26-5 | **Income-Shifting Techniques 26-6 |** Family Members as Employees 26-6 | Family Employees of Partnerships and Corporations 26-6 | Family Members as Owners of the Family Business 26-7 | Family Partnerships 26-8 | Regular Corporations 26-9 | S Corporations 26-10 | Negative Aspects of Ownership Transfers 26-11 | Preservation of Control of the Business 26-11 | Shifts of Investment Income 26-12 | Taxation of Unearned Income of Minor Children 26-12 | **The Trust as a Tax Planning Vehicle 26-13 |** Advantages of the Trust Form 26-13 | Tax Consequences of Transfers into Trust 26-14 | Gift-Leasebacks 26-14 | Gift Tax Considerations 26-14 | Section 2503(c) and Crummey Trusts 26-15 | **Grantor Trusts 26-15 |** Reversionary Trusts 26-16 | Interest-Free Loans 26-16 | Power to Control Beneficial Enjoyment 26-17 | Other Grantor Trusts 26-18 | Grantor Trusts and the Transfer Tax Rules 26-19 | **Transfer Tax Planning 26-19 |** Tax Planning with Intrafamily Gifts 26-20 | "Freezing" the Value of Assets in the Gross Estate 26-21 | Charitable Giving 26-30 | **Liquidity Planning 26-31 |** Source of Funds 26-32 | Flower Bonds 26-32 | Planning for Deferred Payment of the Estate Tax 26-32 | **Conclusion 26-33 | Problem Materials 26-33**

## Appendices and Index

**Appendix A:** Tax Rate Schedules and Tables A-1

**Appendix B:** Tax Forms B-1

**Appendix C:** Modified ACRS Tables C-1

**Appendix D:** Continuous Individual Tax Return Problems and Two Comprehensive Individual Tax Return Problems for 2010 D-1

**Appendix E:** Glossary of Tax Terms E-1

**Index** IN-1

# Introduction to the Federal Tax System

# PART 1

**CHAPTER 1** An Overview of Federal Taxation

**CHAPTER 2** Tax Practice and Research

**CHAPTER 3** Taxable Entities; Tax Formula; Introduction to Property Transactions

**CHAPTER 4** Personal and Dependency Exemptions; Filing Status; Determination of Tax for an Individual; Filing Requirements

# 1

# An Overview of Federal Taxation

## Learning Objectives

Upon completion of this chapter you will be able to:

- LO.1 Explain what a tax is and distinguish it from other types of government charges.
- LO.2 Trace the historical development of our Federal income tax system.
- LO.3 Explain the key terms used to describe most taxes.
- LO.4 Identify the different types of Federal taxes found in the United States.
- LO.5 Describe the estate tax and the gift tax and their relationship.
- LO.6 Explain the differences in the employment taxes levied on employees versus those levied on self-employed individuals.
- LO.7 Identify some of the more common social and economic goals of our Federal tax system.

## Chapter Outline


Introduction 1-2
  The Nature of a Tax 1-2
Development of U.S. Taxation 1-3
  Excise and Customs Duties 1-3
  Federal Income Tax 1-3
  Federal Wealth Transfer Taxes 1-4
  Federal Taxes as a Source of Revenue 1-4
  Key Tax Terms 1-4
Major Types of Taxes 1-10
  Income Taxes 1-10
  Wealth Transfer Taxes 1-12
  Employment Taxes 1-18
  Excise Taxes 1-24
  Additional Types of Taxes 1-24
Goals of Taxation 1-25
  Economic Objectives 1-26
  Social Objectives 1-27
  Other Objectives 1-28
A Prelude to Tax Planning 1-29
Problem Materials 1-31

# Introduction

The United States has developed what is perhaps the most sophisticated and complex national tax programs in the world today. This system of taxation has an impact on almost every business and investment decision as well as many personal decisions. Decisions a business enterprise must make, such as the form it will take (i.e., sole proprietorship, partnership, limited liability company, or corporation), the length and nature of its operations, and the manner in which it will be terminated cannot be made without consideration of the tax consequences. An individual's decisions regarding employment contracts and alternative forms of compensation, as well as place and duration of employment, will be affected by the Federal tax structure. Even such personal choices as housing, family size, marital relationships, and termination of these relationships by divorce or death involve some of the most complex rules of the Federal tax law. This complexity places a *premium* on knowledge of the various types of Federal taxes imposed on those who by chance or choice must operate within the system's boundaries.

The purpose of this book is to introduce the reader to the major elements of Federal taxation. A corollary objective of the authors is to aid the reader in the development of his or her *tax awareness* (i.e., ability to recognize tax problems, pitfalls, and planning opportunities). Such an awareness is not only an important attribute of accountants and lawyers—it is *essential* for everyone who chooses a career in business.

## The Nature of a Tax

**LO.1**
Explain what a tax is and distinguish it from other types of government charges.

The Supreme Court of the United States has defined a *tax* as "an exaction for the support of the Government."[1] Thus, what a tax does is to provide a means through which the government derives a majority of the revenues necessary to keep it in operation. A tax is not merely a source of revenue, however. As discussed in a later section of this chapter, taxes have become a powerful instrument that policymakers use to attain social as well as economic goals.

A tax normally has one or more of the following characteristics:

1. There is no *direct relationship* between the exaction of revenue and any benefit to be received by the taxpayer. Thus, a taxpayer cannot trace his or her tax payment to an Army jeep, an unemployment payment, a weather satellite, or any of the myriad expenditures that the Federal government authorizes.
2. Taxes are levied on the basis of *predetermined criteria*. In other words, taxes can be objectively determined, calculated, and even planned around.
3. Taxes are levied on a *recurring* or *predictable* basis. Most taxes are levied on an annual basis, although some, like the estate tax, are levied only once.
4. Taxes *may be distinguished* from regulations or penalties. A regulation or penalty is a measure specifically designed to control or stop a particular activity. For instance, at one time Congress imposed a charge on the products of child labor. This charge was specifically aimed at stopping the use of children in manufacturing and thus was a regulation rather than a tax, even though it was called a "tax." Also, taxes can be distinguished from licenses and fees, which are payments made for some special privilege granted or services rendered (e.g., marriage license or automobile registration fee).

The major types of taxes imposed by taxing authorities within the United States (e.g., income, employment, and wealth transfer taxes) are discussed later in this chapter. As will be noted, one or more of the above characteristics can be found in each of these various taxes.

---

[1] *U.S. v. Butler*, 36-1 USTC ¶9039, 16 AFTR 1289, 297 U.S. 1, 70 (USSC, 1936). An explanation of case citations such as this is presented in Chapter 2.

## Development of U.S. Taxation

**LO.2**
Trace the historical development of our Federal income tax system.

The entire history of the United States, from its beginnings as a colony of England to the present day, is entwined with the development of Federal taxation. From its infancy until well into the current century, the United States Federal tax system closely paralleled the tax laws of its mother country, England.[2]

### Excise and Customs Duties

Shortly after the colonies won independence and became the United States of America, tariffs became the Federal government's principal revenue-raising source.[3] At the time of its adoption in 1789, the U.S. Constitution gave Congress the power to levy and collect taxes. Promptly exercising this authority, Congress passed as its first act the Tariff Act of 1789, which imposed a system of duties (called excise taxes) on imports.

### Federal Income Tax

As time passed and the Federal government enlarged the scope of its activities, it became more and more apparent to political leaders that they would need to identify additional sources of revenue to supplement the tariff system. Congress enacted the first Federal income tax in 1861 to finance the vastly increased expenditures brought on by the Civil War. The income tax was reasonably successful. However, when the Civil War came to an end so did the need for additional revenues as well as need for an income tax. The tax was repealed officially in 1872. With the repeal of the income tax, the burden of financing government once again was placed on a system of tariffs and duties.

But the tariff system had its opponents. Many believed that a tax system that relied on tariffs protected capitalists by protecting their products from competition from imports. They also argued that tariffs increased the prices of goods, and consequently, the burden of taxation was disproportionately imposed on the poor and middle class. As a result, the allure of an income tax—reducing tariffs and increasing the tax burden on the affluent—did not die, particularly among populist politicians. From 1872 to 1894, Congress introduced more than sixty bills to restore the income tax. This effort culminated in the reenactment of the income tax in 1894. However, less than a year later, the Supreme Court ultimately held that it was unconstitutional.[4]

Shortly thereafter, in 1909, Congress was able to enact an income tax on corporations. Interestingly, this tax was found to be constitutional on other grounds.[5] More importantly, with the passage of the corporate income tax, Congress proposed an amendment to the Constitution that would allow it to levy a tax on *all* incomes. This effort resulted in the passage of the Sixteenth Amendment on February 25, 1913, which provided that:

> The Congress shall have the power to lay and collect taxes on incomes from whatever source derived, without apportionment among the several States, and without regard to any census or enumeration.

Without hesitation, Congress enacted the Revenue Act of 1913 on October 3, 1913 and made it retroactive to March 1, 1913.

Because of special exemptions and the progressive tax rates of the 1913 income tax law, it too was challenged as a denial of due process of law as guaranteed by the Fifth Amendment to the Constitution. In 1916 the Supreme Court upheld the validity of the new income tax law in *Brushaber v. Union Pacific Railroad Co.*[6] Although many changes have taken place, the United States has not been without a Federal income tax since 1913.

---

[2] The states in turn have developed their own systems of taxation which often parallel—but sometimes diverge from—the Federal tax system.

[3] A tariff is a duty imposed on an importer. Since it is a cost of the product being imported, it usually is passed on to the consumer as part of the product's price. Thus, the higher the tariff imposed on a product, the higher must be its price if importation is to be profitable.

[4] *Pollock v. Farmers' Loan and Trust Co.*, 3 AFTR 2602, 157 U.S. 429 (USSC, 1895).

[5] *Flint v. Stone Tracy Co.*, 3 AFTR 2834, 220 U.S. 107 (USSC, 1911).

[6] 240 U.S. 1 (USSC, 1916).

As historical conditions changed and the Federal government's need for additional revenues increased, Congress exercised its income taxing authority by the passage of many separate pieces of legislation that resulted in greater complexity in the Federal income tax law. Each new revenue act was a reenactment of a previous revenue act with added amendments. This process created great confusion for those working with the law, since it could be necessary to research more than 100 separate sources to determine exactly what law was currently in effect. In addition, the reenactment of a statute sometimes suggested that any intervening interpretation of that statute (law) by the courts or the Treasury was approved by Congress, although no such Congressional approval was expressly stated. Congress resolved the confusion in 1939 with its systematic arrangement of all tax laws into the Internal Revenue Code of 1939, a permanent codification that required no reenactment.

The 1939 Code was revised in 1954 and again in 1986. Thus, today's governing Federal tax law is the *Internal Revenue Code of 1986*. The 1986 Code has been amended by significant tax changes made since 1986, and it will continue to be amended to incorporate changes in the tax law as those changes are enacted.

## Federal Wealth Transfer Taxes

In 1916, the very same year the Supreme Court upheld the constitutionality of the Federal income tax, Congress enacted the first Federal law to impose a tax on the transfer of property triggered by the death of an individual. The value of the transfer was measured by the fair market value of the various assets included in the decedent's estate, and consequently the tax imposed on the transfer is referred to as the estate tax. The Federal estate tax imposed a progressive tax on the value on the decedent's taxable estate.

Because an individual could avoid the imposition of the Federal estate tax simply by giving away his or her property before death, Congress enacted the first Federal gift tax in 1924[7] to prevent full scale avoidance of the estate tax.

Like the Federal income tax, these Federal wealth transfer taxes have undergone significant changes since first enacted, adding to their complexity. These taxes are discussed later in this chapter.

## Federal Taxes as a Source of Revenue

Among sources of revenue, only the Federal income tax can claim a dominant role in providing the funds with which the U.S. government operates. The chart in Exhibit 1-1 illustrates the role of the Federal income tax in providing funding for President Obama's proposed 2011 budget. Note the limited role of excise taxes. Federal transfer taxes are even less significant and are included in the "other" category as a revenue source. It is also worth noting that the proposed budget shows an operating deficit of over a $1 trillion ($3.728 trillion of expenditures − $2.583 trillion of revenues = $1.145 trillion deficit).

## Key Tax Terms

**LO.3**
Explain the key terms used to describe most taxes.

Before examining the various types of Federal taxes in more detail, the reader must first become familiar with basic tax terminology. Some of the more common terms are briefly presented below.

### Tax Base

A tax base is that amount upon which a tax is levied. For instance, in the case of Federal income taxation, the tax base is *taxable income*. Taxable income is the taxpayer's total income less exclusions, deductions, and exemptions that might be available to a particular taxpayer. In the case of the Federal wealth transfer taxes, the tax base is the fair market value of the property transferred by gift or at death *reduced* by certain exclusions, exemptions, or deductions allowed by Congress.

[7] Although repealed in 1926, the Federal gift tax was reinstated in 1932.

**EXHIBIT 1.1** 2011 Proposed Budget

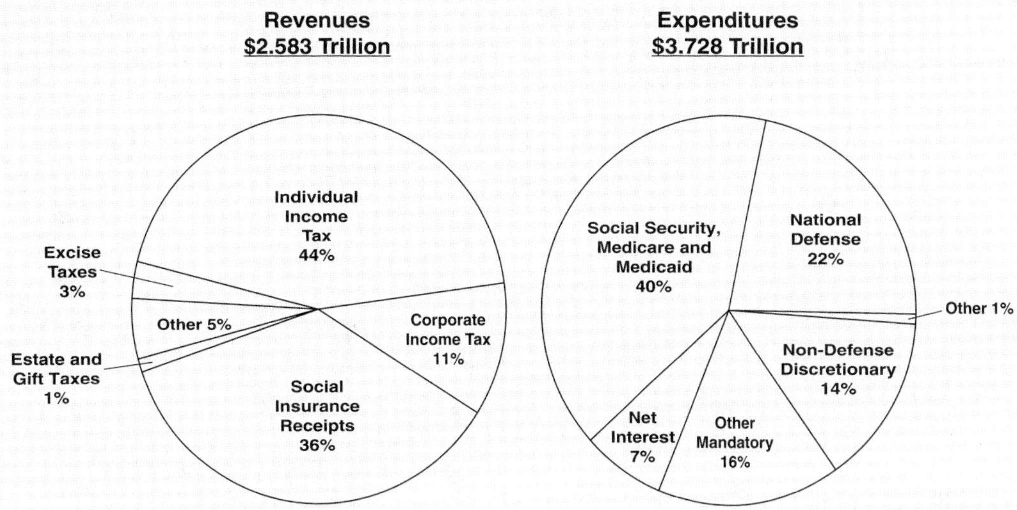


Source: Office of Management & Budget.

## Income

Any *permanent* increment to wealth generally is defined as income. Temporary increments such as loans are not considered to be income. Sometimes income is subject to Federal taxation and other times it is not. The taxability of these increments to wealth generally depends upon whether Congress has *exempted* a particular form of income from taxation. Increments to wealth take many forms. Such increments may take the form of cash, property other than cash, or even services that are rendered to the taxpayer. As a general rule, Congress—and the various Federal courts assigned to interpret its laws—consider *any* increment to wealth to be taxable income *unless* it is *excluded* by definition (e.g., loans that must be repaid), by specific statutory authority in the Internal Revenue Code of 1986, or by the Constitution. Each of these possibilities is examined in detail in Chapters 5 and 6, which deal with gross income.

## Exclusion

Certain increments to wealth that are *not included* in a particular Federal tax base are referred to as exclusions. Since the Constitution grants Congress the authority to tax income *from whatever source derived*, exclusions are the creations of Congress. For various social, political, or economic reasons, Congress has chosen to exclude many sources of income and wealth transfers from their usual Federal tax base. The more common Congressional objectives of exclusions are discussed in a later section of this chapter.

### Example 1

N receives a $13,000 graduation gift from her aunt. N does not have to include this amount in determining taxable income because Congress has specifically excluded gifts from income. If N had received the $13,000 in exchange for rendering services to her aunt, or if N had received the $13,000 for appearing on a television game show, then in both cases she would have to include (report) the amount in income subject to taxation.

> **Example 2**
>
> Refer to *Example 3* above. If N's aunt transfers $13,000 to N in the current year as a graduation gift, and this is the only gift made by the aunt to N in the current year, this transfer will not be subjected to the Federal gift tax. Congress has provided an annual exclusion from gift taxation of $13,000 per donee in 2011.

### Deduction

A deduction is a reduction in the gross (total) amount that must be included in the taxable base. For instance, when an individual taxpayer incurs expenses such as medical expenses, interest on a home mortgage, or property taxes, he or she generally will be allowed to deduct these expenses to arrive at taxable income for Federal tax purposes. Similarly, corporations are allowed to deduct most of their costs of doing business to determine corporate taxable income. It is *extremely important* to note, however, that deductions are a matter of legislative grace—unless Congress has specifically authorized a particular deduction, the expense will not be deductible.

> **Example 3**
>
> Individual T purchased his family residence in 2004 for $90,000. T sells his home in 2011 for $80,000. T may not take a deduction for the $10,000 loss (a permanent reduction in wealth) in determining his taxable income *because* Congress has not authorized a deduction for this particular type of loss.

Most deductions available to individual taxpayers and to other taxable entities (i.e., corporations, estates, and trusts) are discussed in detail in Chapters 7 through 12 of this text.

### Tax Rates

A tax rate is some percentage applied to the tax base to determine a taxpayer's liability. Tax rate structures usually are either proportional or progressive. A *proportional* tax rate is one that remains at a constant percentage regardless of the size of the tax base. A *progressive* tax rate structure is one in which an increasing percentage rate is applied to increasing increments of the tax base. A *regressive* tax rate structure is one in which a decreasing percentage rate is applied to increasing increments of the tax base.

> **Example 4**
>
> B has a tax base of $5,000 and pays a tax of $500, or 10% of the tax base. C's tax base is $10,000 and the tax on this amount is $1,000, or 10%. If the same constant rate of 10% is applied to any amount of tax base, the tax is proportional.

> **Example 5**
>
> R has a tax base of $10,000 and pays a tax of $500 on the first $5,000, and a tax of $1,000 on the next $5,000. The total tax of $1,500 was calculated by applying a 10% rate to the first $5,000 increment of the tax base and then applying a 20% rate to the excess tax base over $5,000. Since a higher percentage rate is applied as the tax base increases, this is a progressive rate structure.

Most excise taxes (e.g., sales taxes) employ a proportional tax rate. However, both the Federal income and transfer tax rates, as well as most state income tax rates, are progressive. The 2011 Federal income tax rate schedules for individual taxpayers appear on the inside front cover of this text for ready reference. The income tax rates for corporations, estates, and trusts are presented on the inside back cover of the text. The Federal gift and estate tax rates are reproduced in Appendix A-3 at the back of the text. A glance at either of these sources will indicate the progressive nature of the Federal tax system.

## Marginal, Average, and Effective Tax Rates

It is not surprising that tax rates receive a great deal of attention. Since taxes have such a significant impact on taxpayer's lives, everyone has an interest in—as well as an opinion about—tax rates. Are tax rates too high or too low? Are they too progressive or too flat? In any dialogue regarding tax rates, it is important to understand the terminology and distinguish between three different tax rate concepts: the marginal rate, the average rate and the effective tax rate.

**Marginal Tax Rates** The marginal tax rate of any tax rate structure is that percentage at which the next unit of the tax base will be taxed. For example, in the case of the income tax, if a taxpayer earns an additional dollar of income, the marginal rate would be the rate that applied to that dollar. The marginal tax rates of the Federal income tax rate structure for single and married taxpayers for 2011 and the amounts of income to which they apply are shown below:

| Tax Rate | Single Taxpayers Taxable Income | Married Taxpayers Taxable Income |
|---|---|---|
| 10% | $ 0 – $ 8,500 | $ 0 – $ 17,000 |
| 15 | 8,500 – 34,500 | 17,000 – 69,000 |
| 25 | 34,500 – 83,600 | 69,000 – 139,350 |
| 28 | 83,600 – 174,400 | 139,350 – 212,300 |
| 33 | 174,400 – 379,150 | 212,300 – 379,150 |
| 35 | Over 379,150 | Over 379,150 |

Note the progressive nature of the rate structure. There are currently six marginal tax rates for individuals, starting at 10% and climbing to a high of 35%. Each of these rates applies to a range of income known as a tax bracket. It is not uncommon to hear people say they are in a particular tax bracket. If a single person says he is in the "25% bracket," it simply means that his taxable income is at a level ($34,500 – $83,600 in 2011) such that the next dollar of income is taxed at 25%. While the tax rates for married taxpayers are the same as those for singles, they generally apply to different brackets of income. For the 10% and 15% rates, the married brackets are exactly twice the size of those for single taxpayers but vary thereafter until the top rate is reached. The potential for implicit tax "penalties" for being married or single, depending on a couple's income, who earns it and other factors, is discussed in Chapter 4.

Over the years, the tax rates and ranges of income to which they apply have varied dramatically. The first income tax that applied in 1913 had seven rates, ranging from 1% to 7%. In contrast, in 1962 there were 23 brackets, beginning at a rate of 22% and ending at 91%! No doubt rates and brackets will continue to change as Congress deems it necessary to balance the budget, raise revenues or to provide a tax cut. A typical tax computation using the current tax rate schedule is illustrated below.

### Example 6

H, an unmarried taxpayer, has taxable income of $65,500 for 2011. Referring to tax rate Schedule X on the inside front cover of this text, an unmarried taxpayer with taxable income of $65,500 has a tax of $12,500.00 as computed below. H's marginal tax rate is 25%.

| | |
|---|---|
| 2011 tax on $34,500 | $ 4,750.00 |
| Plus: Tax on income above $34,500 [($65,500 – $34,500 = $31,000) × 25%] | 7,750.00 |
| Tax liability | $12,500.00 |

A taxpayer's knowledge of his or her marginal tax rate is essential in any tax-planning effort to minimize taxes. Without such knowledge, the tax impact of an additional dollar of the tax base or an additional dollar deduction cannot be determined.

### Example 7

Refer to *Example 8*. If unmarried taxpayer H, age 40, is considering depositing $5,000 in an Individual Retirement Account (the maximum amount allowed in 2011 as a deduction for Federal income tax purposes for persons under 50 years old), he could determine his immediate tax savings to be $1,250 (the 25% marginal tax rate × the $5,000 income not taxed). Similarly, if H had a 33% marginal tax rate and wanted to know the after-tax amount of a proposed $10,000 increase in salary, he would simply multiply $10,000 by 67% (100% – 33%). In such case, the after-tax value of the $10,000 salary increase would be $6,700.

Many individuals, including those who are highly educated, do not understand the marginal tax rate concept. All too often one hears the expression, "I can't afford to earn more because it will throw me into a higher tax bracket and I will keep less than I do now after taxes." This theoretically cannot occur unless the marginal tax rate exceeds 100 percent.

While the rates above normally are used to compute an individual's tax liability, a lower rate can apply. An individual's gains from the sale of so-called capital assets (e.g., corporate stocks) held for more than a year receive preferential treatment. Such gains, referred to as long-term capital gains, usually are taxed at 15 percent but could be taxed as high as 28 percent. However, for 2011 or 2012 any long-term capital gains of taxpayers in either the 10 or 15 percent income tax bracket are tax-free (a 0% rate). Gains from sales of capital assets that are held for a year or less, short-term capital gains, are tax at an individual's ordinary rates.

Corporate tax rates, like individual rates, are progressive (see inside back cover). The rates run from 15% to 35%. Corporations with taxable incomes less than $75,000 may take advantage of the lower rates. When taxable income exceeds the $75,000 threshold, corporations generally face marginal rates of 34% up to $10,000,000 of taxable income and 35% for taxable incomes exceeding the $10,000,000 mark. The long-term capital gains of a corporation receive no preferential treatment and are taxed at regular rates.

**Average Tax Rates** The average rate is computed by dividing the taxpayer's tax liability by the tax base. For the income tax, the average tax rate is simply the tax divided by taxable income (tax ÷ taxable income).

### Example 8

K, an unmarried taxpayer, has 2011 taxable income of $82,400 and pays a tax of $16,725. Although her marginal tax rate is 25%, K's average tax rate is only 20.30% ($16,725 ÷ $82,400).

Average tax rates are a bit misleading in that they seem to suggest that all units of the tax base (e.g., all dollars of income) are treated equally. But as seen above, in a progressive tax rate system where marginal rates increase as income increases, some dollars of income are taxed higher than others. The average tax rate is just that, an average. While providing some insight about the overall rate structure, average rates say little about the true impact of a tax on the taxpayer. For this information, effective tax rates are the preferred statistic.

**Effective Tax Rates** The effective tax rate is computed by dividing the tax by some broader measure other than the tax base, often some quantity reflecting taxpayer's ability to pay. For example, for the income tax, the effective tax rate is normally determined by dividing the tax by total economic income (tax ÷ total economic income).

### Example 9

Assume the same facts as in *Example 10* except that K's total economic income is $100,000 the $17,600 difference between total income and taxable income being attributable to exclusions and deductions (e.g., interest on tax-exempt bonds and the personal exemption). In such case, K would pay taxes at an effective rate of 16.73% [$16,725 ÷ $100,000].

Marginal rates are often confused with average rates and effective rates. For example, in decrying the harshness of the income tax, people often point to their marginal rate and declare that they are paying that percent (e.g., 25%) of their income to the government. A comparison of Examples 10 and 11 above reveals that this clearly is not the case. Although the taxpayer has a marginal tax rate of 25%, the average rate is 20.30% and the effective rate is only 16.73%.

While effective tax rates provide meaningful information about a taxpayer's tax burden, it is not without problems, the most difficult of which is that there is no uniform definition of total economic income or the amount that will serve as the denominator in the formula. Any use of effective tax rates must recognize this potential weakness. In practice, however, the denominator for any particular purpose such as financial reporting or economic studies is usually well-defined from the outset. As a result, effective tax rates (ETRs) usually provide a relatively straightforward measure of the percentage of income siphoned away by taxes. For this reason, ETRs are of great interest not only to individual taxpayers but also businesses, governments (U.S. and foreign), investors, analysts, academics, public interest groups and others.

One of the most common uses of the ETR concept can be found in financial reporting. Since taxes have a significant impact on a company's earnings, management, investors, creditors and other users of financial statements are particularly interested in the company's ETR. Due to the importance of taxes on a company's net income, generally accepted accounting principles—specifically FAS 109 and its interpretations—require public companies to provide additional disclosures, a detailed footnote, regarding the impact of income taxes on financial statement income (book income).[8] This information includes the company's ETR. In this context, ETR generally is the percentage of taxes paid on pre-tax book income (tax ÷ pre-tax book income). Although a corporation's statutory U.S. tax rate is normally a flat 35 percent, the ETR usually differs. For example, the footnotes to the financial statements of Microsoft reported an ETR of 31% in 2006 and 26.3% in 2005. Such differences occur because book income may be higher or lower than taxable income. For example, interest income from municipal bonds is included in book income but is excluded from taxable income. Similarly dividend income is fully included in book income but corporations normally pay taxes on only 30 percent of their dividends. On the expense side, book income includes fines and penalties and life insurance premiums on key executives but taxable income does not allow deductions for such costs. In addition, book income includes income from foreign subsidiaries but is not included in a corporation's consolidated taxable income (until is repatriated or paid back to the U.S. usually through dividend payments).

The ETR is a useful tool since it provides a snapshot of whether a business is or is not paying taxes and if so, how much. In addition, the ETR provides a criterion for determining how well a business is managing its tax liability relative to other firms in the same industry or businesses as a whole.

## Tax Credits

A tax credit is a dollar-for-dollar offset against a tax liability. A credit is quite different from a deduction, since it directly reduces the tax liability itself, whereas a deduction simply reduces the base amount subject to the tax.

[8] See *Accounting for Income Taxes*, Statement of Financial Accounting Standards No. 109, Financial Accounting Standards Board, 1992. For financial statement purposes, FAS 109 requires income tax expense to be based on financial statement income rather than actual taxable income. Thus actual taxes paid may differ significantly from the reported amount. The ETR provides a picture of the taxes actually paid relative to book income rather than taxable income.

**Example 10**

T is a single taxpayer with a 28% marginal tax rate. An additional $100 tax deduction would reduce T's tax by $28 (28% × $100). If the $100 qualified as a tax credit, however, T would have a $100 tax reduction—the equivalent of a $357 tax deduction at a marginal tax rate of 28% ($357 × 28% = $100).

Tax credits are discussed in detail in Chapter 13 of this text.

## Major Types of Taxes

**LO.4**
Identify the different types of Federal taxes found in the United States.

Taxing authorities within the United States have a wide array of taxes with which they raise revenues or attempt to effect social, political, or economic change. The average individual will feel the impact of quite a number of taxes during his or her lifetime. Any attempt to accumulate wealth requires diligent tax planning, and to ignore the impact of Federal, state, and local taxes will serve no useful purpose toward this end. Although the principal thrust of this text is aimed at the Federal income and wealth transfer taxes, some of the other types of taxes merit a brief introduction.

### Income Taxes

An income tax is an extraction of some of the taxpayer's economic gain, usually on a periodic basis. In addition to the Federal government, many states and some local governments impose a tax on income. For example, New York City residents could pay not only a federal income tax of 35 percent but also a state income tax of 7.7 percent and a city income tax of 4.45 percent. As noted earlier in Exhibit 1-1, the individual income tax was expected to provide 44 percent of the Federal government's fiscal 2011 revenues. Of all the sources providing revenues to the Federal government, the individual income tax is the largest. In contrast, the corporate income tax was expected to provide only 11 percent of the Federal government's projected revenues in fiscal 2011.[9]

The Federal government imposes an income tax on individuals, corporations, estates, and trusts. Usually, a final tax reckoning (reporting and paying taxes due) is made at the end of each year. In order to ensure tax collections, however, Congress has created a pay-as-you-go requirement. Basically, this process requires employers to withhold and remit to the Federal government income taxes on wages paid to employees. Individuals with income from sources other than wages, and most other taxable entities, are required to make estimated tax prepayments during the year.[10]

Application of the Federal income tax to individuals is discussed in Chapters 3 and 4. Computation of a corporation's Federal income tax is explained in Chapter 19. The Federal income taxation of partnerships, estates, and trusts is examined in Chapters 22 and 25. For now, the procedures for determining the Federal income tax liability of corporate and individual taxpayers are reduced to computational formulas presented in Exhibits 1-2 and 1-3

[9] Such heavy reliance on the income tax as a source of government revenues is peculiar to the United States. Most Western European nations have turned to a Value-Added Tax (VAT). A VAT is a system of taxing the increment in value of goods as they move through the production and manufacturing process to the market place. The VAT operates very much like a national sales tax and has occasionally been proposed, though unsuccessfully, for the United States.

[10] This procedure was developed by Congress during World War II to accelerate annual tax payments needed to finance the war effort. The process served so well to increase compliance with, and facilitate administration of, the Federal income tax law that Congress chose not to abandon it at the close of the war.

**EXHIBIT 1.2** Tax Formula for Corporate Taxpayers

| | |
|---|---|
| ***Income (from whatever source)*** | $xxx,xxx |
| Less: Exclusions from gross income | −xx,xxx |
| ***Gross income*** | $xxx,xxx |
| Less: Deductions | −xx,xxx |
| ***Taxable income*** | $xxx,xxx |
| Applicable tax rates | xx% |
| ***Gross tax*** | $ xx,xxx |
| Less: Tax credits and prepayments | −x,xxx |
| ***Tax due (or refund)*** | $ xx,xxx |

**EXHIBIT 1.3** Tax Formula for Individual Taxpayers

| | | |
|---|---|---|
| ***Income (from whatever source)*** | | $xxx,xxx |
| Less: Exclusions from gross income | | −xx,xxx |
| ***Gross income*** | | $xxx,xxx |
| Less: Deductions for adjusted gross income | | −xx,xxx |
| ***Adjusted gross income*** | | $xxx,xxx |
| Less: 1. The larger of: | | |
| a. Standard deduction | $x,xxx | |
| *or* | *or* | −x,xxx |
| b. Total itemized deductions | $x,xxx | |
| 2. Personal and dependency exemptions × exemption amount | | −x,xxx |
| ***Taxable income*** | | $xxx,xxx |
| Applicable tax rates (from Tables or Schedules X, Y, or Z) | | xx% |
| ***Gross tax*** | | $ xx,xxx |
| Less: Tax credits and prepayments | | −x,xxx |
| ***Tax due (or refund)*** | | $ xx,xxx |

as follows. The components of these formulas are introduced and discussed in greater detail in Chapter 3.

Most states in the United States impose an income tax of some sort.[11] Generally, state income taxes are designed to operate much like the Federal income tax. Almost all the states

[11] States *not* currently imposing an income tax on individuals are Alaska, Florida, Nevada, South Dakota, Texas, Washington, and Wyoming. Tennessee and New Hampshire impose an income tax on an individual's dividend and interest income. Every state imposes either a corporate income tax or a tax on the privilege of conducting business within the state's boundaries. See subsequent discussion of franchise taxes.

have a tax-withholding procedure and most use the income determination for Federal income tax purposes as the tax base. Some states allow a deduction for Federal income taxes, while others exclude income that is subject to Federal income taxation. Interest income from Federal government obligations is not subject to state income taxation, and interest income from state and local government obligations generally is not subject to either Federal or state income taxation. Most states have developed their own set of rates, exemptions, and credits; however, the filing date for the state income tax return generally coincides with the due date of the taxpayer's Federal income tax return.[12]

One particular problem that has developed in the area of state taxation is the so-called unitary tax. Several states[13] tax businesses on the basis of their global activities, not just their local operations. This asserted right to tax income that has not been earned within the state's boundaries has been subjected to many challenges in the courts; but, as of this date, the unitary tax has not been struck down as unconstitutional.[14] Foreign corporations object to this worldwide combined reporting for many reasons, the most obvious being that it may result in the imposition of state taxation even when no taxable income has been generated by intrastate operations.

## Wealth Transfer Taxes

Unlike Federal and state income taxes, wealth transfer taxes are not significant revenue producers. For example, Federal transfer tax revenues for fiscal year 2011 represent less than 1 percent of Federal government revenues.[15] Historically, the primary function of wealth transfer taxes has been to *hinder* the accumulation of wealth by family units. Thus, the goal of wealth redistribution generally underlies the design of estate and gift tax systems.

The estate tax and its partner, the gift tax, are both excise taxes on the transfers of property. The estate tax, enacted in 1916, is imposed on the amount of a decedent's *net* wealth (fair market value of total assets less debts and expenses) that passes to his or her heirs at death. Absent any other rule, the estate tax easily could be avoided by giving away property before death. For this reason, Congress enacted a tax on gifts in 1932. The gift tax is imposed on the value of property transferred during an individual's life. As explained below, only a relatively small percentage of taxpayers are affected by the gift or estate tax since they apply only when the transfer of wealth is substantial. As a result of changes in 2010, the taxes generally are triggered only when transfers exceed $5,000,000 ($10,000,000 for married couples). Despite their limited application, for those to whom the taxes do apply, the cost can be significant. For this reason and the fact that there are a number of income tax issues related to the gift and estate tax, it is important to have a basic understanding of how they work.

Prior to 1977, the gift tax and estate tax were two separate taxes. Taxable gifts made during life generally did not impact the estate tax calculation. However, in 1976, the gift tax and estate tax were combined into what is conceptually a unified transfer tax. The taxes are unified in the way that the taxes are calculated. As an individual makes taxable gifts during life, the gift tax is computed on a cumulative basis. To calculate the tax on current year gifts, the donor must add all taxable gifts made in prior years (since 1976) to the current gifts, calculate the gross tax on the sum of the lifetime transfers, and then subtract gift taxes assessed on the prior years' gifts. The remainder is the current year gift tax. When the individual dies, the estate tax is computed in a similar manner by adding all prior taxable gifts to the taxable estate, applying the appropriate rate and subtracting any prior gift taxes assessed. It is sometimes useful to think of the transfer at death as the final gift. Note that in both cases, the addition of prior taxable gifts does not result in the gifts being taxed twice but only raises the marginal rate at which the current transfers are taxed. Like the Federal income tax rate structure, the gift tax and the estate tax rates are progressive.

As a practical matter, the estate and gift tax do not apply to most taxpayers. For starters, to eliminate the vast administrative problems that would result if the gift tax were imposed on

---

[12] For individuals and partnerships, the due date of the Federal income tax return is the fifteenth day of the fourth month following the close of the tax year. For corporate taxpayers, the due date of the Federal return is the fifteenth day of the *third* month following the close of the tax year.

[13] Among those states that tax businesses on the basis of worldwide income are Alaska, California, Colorado, Florida, Idaho, Illinois, Indiana, Massachusetts, Montana, New Hampshire, New York (oil companies only), North Dakota, Oregon, and Utah.

[14] The U.S. Supreme Court upheld California's system of taxing global profits of U.S.-based multinational businesses in *Container Corporation of America v. Franchise Tax Board*, 103 S.Ct. 2933 (USSC, 1983).

[15] Office of Management and Budget, 2011 *Fiscal Year Budget*.

all gifts (e.g., birthday presents), the tax is imposed only on those transfers that exceed a certain threshold. In 2011, this amount is $13,000. Technically, individuals are entitled to an exclusion of $13,000 per donee per year. The exclusion enables an individual to make an unlimited number of gifts as long as they do not exceed $13,000 per donee in one year. For married couples, these rules permit a husband and wife to give $26,000 a year to a particular donee (e.g., a child) tax free. In addition, to the annual exclusion, gifts to a spouse, charity or transfers for educational or medical purposes normally are not taxable.

Provisions also exist to ensure that only transfers of substantial wealth are subject to tax. For gift tax purposes, gifts in excess of amounts excluded are not subject to tax until the cumulative amount of all gifts exceeds $5,000,000. Similarly, at death, in 2011, there is no estate tax unless total transfers during life and at death exceed $5,000,000. It should be noted that once transfers exceed these levels, the tax is 35 percent.

## The Federal Estate Tax

**LO.5**
Describe the estate tax and the gift tax and their relationship.

A decedent's estate tax liability is based on his or her net wealth and whether he or she leaves it to a surviving spouse or charity. As discussed in detail in Chapter 24, the procedure for computing the Federal estate tax liability is illustrated in Exhibit 1-4 and is explained below.

The first step in computing the estate tax is to identify the decedent's gross estate. A decedent's gross estate includes the value of *all* property owned at date of death, wherever located. This includes the proceeds of an insurance policy on the life of the decedent if the decedent's estate is the beneficiary, or if the decedent had any ownership rights[16] in the policy at time of death. Property is generally included in the gross estate at its *fair market value* as of the date of death.[17]

The taxable estate is the gross estate reduced by deductions allowed for funeral and administrative expenses, debts of the decedent, certain taxes and losses, state dealth taxes and charitable gifts made from the decedent's estate. It is important to note that there is no limit imposed on the charitable deduction. If an individual is willing to leave his or her entire estate

**EXHIBIT 1.4** Computation of Federal Estate Tax Liability

| | | |
|---|---|---|
| ***Gross estate*** | | $x,xxx,xxx |
| Less the sum of: | | |
| Expenses, indebtedness, and taxes | $ xx,xxx | |
| State death taxes | x,xxx | |
| Losses | x,xxx | |
| Charitable bequests | xx,xxx | |
| Marital deduction | xxx,xxx | −xxx,xxx |
| ***Taxable estate*** | | $ xxx,xxx |
| Plus: Taxable gifts made after December 31, 1976 | | +xx,xxx |
| ***Total taxable transfers*** | | $ xxx,xxx |
| ***Tentative tax on total transfer*** | | $ xxx,xxx |
| Less the sum of: | | |
| Gift taxes paid on post-1976 taxable gifts | $ x,xxx | |
| Estate tax credit | xx,xxx | |
| Other tax credits | x,xxx | −xx,xxx |
| ***Estate tax liability*** | | $ xx,xxx |

[16] Ownership rights in a life insurance policy include the power to change the policy's beneficiary, the right to cancel or assign the policy, and the right to borrow against the policy.

[17] An executor of a taxable estate may elect an alternative valuation date of six months after death. See Chapter 24 for more details.

for public, charitable, or religious use, there will be no taxable estate. Finally, an *unlimited* marital deduction is allowed for the value of property passing to a surviving spouse. Thus, if a married taxpayer leaves all of his or her property to the surviving spouse, no Federal estate tax will be imposed on the estate. On the death of the surviving spouse, the couple's wealth may be subject to taxation.[18]

Under current Federal estate tax laws, taxable gifts made after 1976 are added to the taxable estate to arrive at total taxable transfers. A tentative estate tax is then computed on the base amount. All gift taxes paid on post-1976 gifts, as well as certain tax credits, are subtracted from this tentative tax in arriving at the Federal estate tax due, if any. Most estate tax credits have a single underlying purpose—to reduce or eliminate the effect of multiple taxation of a single estate. Estate taxes paid to the various states or foreign countries on property owned by the decedent and located within their boundaries are examples of estate tax credits. However, the major credit available to reduce the Federal estate tax has been the *unified credit*. The unified credit protects all but the wealthiest of taxpayers from the estate and gift tax. For 2011 the credit is $1,730,800 and has the effect of eliminating the tax on taxable transfers of $5,000,000 or less. The credit is unified in the sense that it can be used to offset gift taxes during the taxpayer's life. However, any credit used for gift tax purposes is not available at death.

### Example 11

In 2011, D died owning Google stock worth $5,000,000. D had never made a taxable gift. D was not married and had no deductions. In such case, the taxable estate and total taxable transfers would be $5,000,000, and there would be no estate tax computed as follows:

| | |
|---|---|
| Taxable estate and total taxable transfers . . . . . . . . . . | $5,000,000 |
| | |
| Gross estate tax (see Appendix A-3). . . . . . . . . . . . . . | $1,730,800 |
| Estate tax credit . . . . . . . . . . . . . . . . . . . . . . . . . . . . | (1,730,800) |
| Tax due. . . . . . . . . . . . . . . . . . . . . . . . . . . . . . . . . . . | $ 0 |

Note how the estate tax credit operates to exempt $5,000,000 of total taxable transfers from tax. For this reason, it is commonly said that taxpayers have an estate tax exemption equal to $5,000,000.

## Portability of the Unused Unified Credit

Beginning in 2011, taxpayers can take advantage of the so-called portability rule.[19] This rule provides that any credit that remains unused as of the death of a spouse who dies after 2010 is portable; that is, the unused amount is generally available for use by the surviving spouse as an addition to the surviving spouse's exemption. This effectively allows a married couple to exempt up to $10 million from the estate tax.

### Example 12

H and W are husband and wife. H dies in 2011 and uses $3,000,000 of his $5,000,000 exemption to eliminate his estate. As a result, $2,000,000 of his exemption is unused. In 2012, W dies. W's exemption amount is $7,000,000 (her $5,000,000 + the unused amount of her last deceased husband of $2,000,000). In effect, the couple is able to exempt up to $10 million from estate taxes ($3,000,000 when H died and $7,000,000 when W died).

[18] Planning for maximizing the benefit of the marital deduction is discussed in Chapter 26.

[19] § 2010(c).

If a surviving spouse is predeceased by more than one spouse, the amount of unused exclusion that is available for use by such surviving spouse is limited to the lesser of $5 million or the unused exclusion of the last such deceased spouse.

### Example 13

H and W are married. H dies and his unused exclusion is $5,000,000. W remarried NH, a new husband. NH died and his unused exclusion is $2,000,000. By what amount can W increase her exemption? She can use only the unused amount of her last spouse, $2,000,000 (and not the $5,000,000 of her first spouse). The rule may discourage W from remarrying in this case.

The unused exclusion amount is available to a surviving spouse only if the executor of the estate of the deceased spouse files an estate tax return on which such amount is computed and makes an election on such return that such amount may be used. The election is irrevocable. The election cannot be made unless that estate tax return is filed on a timely basis as extended. Thus, even if a decedent normally is not required to file an estate tax return, it appears that a return is now necessary simply to preserve the unused exclusion amount.

## The Federal Gift Tax

The purpose of the federal gift tax is to prevent a taxpayer's avoidance of the federal estate tax simply by giving away his or her property prior to death. The procedure for computing the federal gift tax liability is presented as a formula in Exhibit 1-5. To arrive at taxable gifts for the year, the taxpayer's total gifts may be reduced by the annual exclusion and by the deductions allowed for property transferred to a spouse or charity. The annual exclusion $13,000 per donee in 2011. The annual exclusion is allowed *each year* even if the donor has made gifts in the prior years to the same donee.

**EXHIBIT 1.5 Computation of Federal Gift Tax Liability**

| | | |
|---|---|---|
| Fair market value of all gifts made in the current year | | $xxx,xxx |
| Less the sum of: | | |
| Annual exclusions ($13,000 per donee in 2011) | $xx,xxx | |
| Marital deduction | xx,xxx | |
| Charitable deduction | x,xxx | −xx,xxx |
| Taxable gifts for current year | | $xxx,xxx |
| Plus: Taxable gifts made in prior years | | +xx,xxx |
| Taxable transfers to date | | $xxx,xxx |
| Tentative tax on total transfers to date | | $ xx,xxx |
| Less the sum of: | | |
| Gift taxes computed at current rates on prior years' taxable gifts | $ x,xxx | |
| Gift tax credit | x,xxx | −x,xxx |
| Gift tax due on current gifts | | $ xx,xxx |

### Example 14

T, a widower, wanted his son, daughter-in-law, and their five children to share his wealth. On December 25, 2011 he gave $13,000 to each family member. He repeats these gifts in 2010. Although T has transferred $182,000 [$13,000 × 7 (number of donees) × 2], he has not made taxable gifts in either 2009 or 2010.

Another unique feature of the Federal gift tax involves the *gift-splitting* election available to a married donor. If a donor makes the election on his or her current gift tax return, one half of all gifts made during the year will be considered to have been made by the donor's spouse. The election is valid *only if* both spouses *consent* to gift-splitting.

### Example 15

H and W are married. In 2011 H makes two gifts of $100,000 each to his son and daughter. W makes a gift of $5,000 to the daughter only. H and W elect gift-splitting on their 2011 gift tax returns. As a result, H will report a gift to the son of $50,000 and a gift to the daughter of $52,500 [½ of ($100,000 + $5,000)], and will claim two $13,000 gift tax exclusions. W will report exactly the same gifts and claim two annual exclusions. Without gift-splitting, H would still be entitled to $26,000 of exclusions, but W could only claim an exclusion of $5,000 for her gift to the daughter. Thus, by electing to split gifts, a married donor can, in effect, make use of any annual exclusions not needed by his or her spouse. More importantly, if taxable gifts are made under a gift-splitting arrangement, H can use his unified credit and W can use her lifetime credit to reduce the tax liability.

The marital and charitable deductions for Federal gift tax purposes are the same as for the Federal estate tax—*unlimited.* Thus, if a taxpayer gives his or her spouse a $2,000,000 anniversary present or transfers $100,000 to his or her church, a taxable gift has not been made.

If taxable gifts have been made for the current year, the cumulative computational procedure of the gift transfer tax must be applied.

### Example 16

In 2000, X made his first taxable gift of $100,000 (after the exclusion). The tax (before credits) on this amount was $23,800. X made a second taxable gift of $85,000 in 2011. The tax (before credits) on the second gift is $26,200, computed as follows:

| | |
|---|---|
| 2000 taxable gift | $100,000 |
| 2011 taxable gift | +85,000 |
| Cumulative gifts | $185,000 |
| Tax on cumulative taxable gifts of $185,000 | $ 50,000 |
| 2000 taxable gift | −23,800* |
| Tax on 2011 gift | $ 26,200 |

*See the estate and gift transfer tax rate schedules in Appendix A. Note that the current year's tax rate is used to compute the tax reduction for the 2000 gift.

Note that the cumulative system of wealth transfer taxation *and* the progressive rate schedule cause a higher tax on the 2011 gift, even though the 2010 gift was $15,000 *less* than the 2000 gift.

The tentative tax liability in the above example is reduced by the unified credit available for the gift tax, $1,730,800. The gift tax credit is the only credit available to offset the federal gift tax liability.

The unified credit for the gift tax is the same as that for the estate tax, $1,730,800 and is equivalent to an exemption of $5,000,000. In applying the credit, it is important to understand that whatever amount is used in one year reduces the amount of the credit available in future years or at death. In other words, if a taxpayer makes no taxable gifts during his or her lifetime, the entire unified credit of $1,730,800 in 2011 is available to reduce any estate taxes that otherwise may be due at the taxpayer's death (see Example above). In contrast, if the taxpayer uses all $1,730,800 of the unified credit to reduce gift taxes, such amount is not available at death.

As a practical matter, the $5,000,000 exemption (effectively $10,000,000 for married couples), protects most individual from the estate and gift tax.[20] However, for high wealth individuals, gifts can produce substantial savings. For example, a gift of income producing property (e.g., dividend paying stock or rental real estate) to children who may be in lower tax brackets not only reduces the income tax that might be paid but also removes all of the accumulated income from the donor's estate. In addition, a gift of property that is appreciating or will increase in value (e.g., land, stock, art, life insurance), removes all of the appreciation from the estate by transferring ownership of the property. Lastly, making gifts of up to $5,000,000 now may prove to be particularly wise if the unified credit is reduced when Congress revisits this area in 2013.

## State and Local Transfer Taxes

Many states and some local jurisdictions impose an inheritance tax on the *right to receive* property at death. Unlike an estate tax, which is imposed on the estate according to value of property transferred by the decedent at death, an inheritance tax is imposed on the recipient of property from an estate.[21] The amount of an inheritance tax payable usually is directly affected by the degree of kinship between the recipient and the decedent. The inheritance tax typically provides an exemption from the tax, which increases as the relationship between the recipient (e.g., surviving spouse, children, grandchildren, parents, etc.) and the decedent becomes closer. In addition, as the relationship becomes closer, the transfer tax rates decrease. Thus, the more closely related one is, the smaller the inheritance tax will be. Generally, little if any inheritance tax exemption is available for transfers to unrelated recipients, and the highest rate is imposed.

### Example 17

The Indiana inheritance tax is similar to most inheritance taxes. For example, transfers to a surviving spouse and charities are totally exempt. In contrast, the exemption for transfers to children and grandchildren is $100,000 for each child or grandchild, and the rates on the excess run from 1 to 10 percent. As the relationship between the decedent and the beneficiary grows more distant, the exemption shrinks and the rates grow. The exemption for transfers to brothers and sisters and their descendants (e.g., nieces and nephews) is only $500, and the rates range from 7 to 15 percent. Finally, transfers to nonrelatives (e.g., friends) are subject to an even lower exemption, $100, and the rates extend from 10 to 20 percent.

In addition to state and local inheritance taxes on beneficiaries, many states also impose estate taxes on the decedent's estate. The rates imposed on the taxable estate are considerably lower than those of the federal estate tax rates.[22] Beginning in 2005, any inheritance or estate

[20] According to a survey by the SpectremGroup, the number of persons in the U.S. that had a net worth of $1 million or more (excluding the value of their primary residence) rose 16 percent in 2009 to 7.8 million. The increase in those with $5 million in net worth was 17 percent to 980,000. See www.spectrem.com press release March 9, 2010.

[21] It is not uncommon for the decedent's will to provide that his or her estate pay any inheritance tax imposed on the recipient of property from the estate.

[22] States that impose both an estate and inheritance tax generally allow a credit against the state estate tax for any inheritance tax imposed on the heirs.

taxes imposed by a state are deductible in computing the Federal taxable estate. While most states impose some type of death tax, only a few states have a gift tax. In those states where there is no gift tax, wholesale avoidance of any state death tax is prohibited by certain special rules. For example, a state law may require that transfers made within one year of death to be included in the death tax base.

## EMPLOYMENT TAXES

**LO.6**
Explain the differences in the employment taxes levied on employees versus those levied on self-employed individuals.

The Federal government and most states impose some form of employment tax on either self-employed individuals, employees,[23] or employers. The most common form of state employment tax is levied on wages, with the proceeds used to finance the state's unemployment benefits program. State unemployment taxes are imposed on employers who have employees working within the state's boundaries, but only if the employees would be eligible for unemployment benefits from the state. Most states' unemployment taxes are based on the same taxable wage base as that used for the Federal unemployment tax (see discussion below), and employers are allowed to take state unemployment taxes paid as a credit against the Federal unemployment tax liability.

The Federal government imposes two types of taxes on employment—a social security tax and an unemployment tax. The Federal Insurance Contribution Act (FICA) imposes a tax on self-employed individuals, employees, and employers. The FICA tax is paid by both an employee and his or her employer if the employee is eligible for social security and Medicare health insurance benefits. Although subject to a different tax rate, self-employed individuals are required to pay FICA taxes on net earnings from self-employment. The Federal Unemployment Tax Act (FUTA) imposes a tax *only* on the employer. Self-employed individuals are not eligible for unemployment benefits and thus are not subject to the FUTA tax. The tax base and rate structure of both these Federal employment taxes are presented below.

### FICA Taxes

FICA taxes, often referred to as Social Security and Medicare taxes, have a long history. Both taxes help pay for a variety of federal programs that together assist individuals in times of need such as old-age, disability, death and illness. Social Security was enacted in 1935 to pay a guaranteed source of income to retired workers normally when they reach age 65. Since 1935 the Act has been modified many, many times, providing more and more benefits. For example, major additions occurred in 1956 and 1960 when the Act was amended to extend benefits for most disabled workers and their families. The programs established by these amendments are now collectively known as the Old Age, Survivors and Disability Insurance (OASDI) programs. In addition to these programs, Congress addressed problems of health care for the aged with the creation of Medicare Health Insurance (MHI) in 1965. Medicare helps pay hospital and medical expenses for persons who have reached age 65. In 2006, Medicare was amended to help pay for prescription drugs.

The Social Security and Medicare programs are paid for primarily through taxes on wages and self-employment income. Taxes to pay for Social Security benefits were first collected in January 1937 at a rate of 1 percent on the first $3,000 of wages or a maximum of only $30! In 1966, tax collections began for Medicare at a rate of .35 percent on the same wage base as for Social Security. At that point, 1966, the total tax for the two components of FICA, Social Security and Medicare, was 4.2 percent (3.85 + .35) on wages of $6,600 or a maximum of $2,772. Since those early days both the tax rates as well as the base have swelled. The rates stopped climbing—at least temporarily—in 1990 when they reached what they are currently: 6.2 percent for Social Security and 1.45 percent for Medicare. However, to provide some tax relief, Congress reduced the employee's social security tax for 2011 by 2 percentage points to 4.2 percent. The reduction is only for one year and will return to 6.2 percent in 2012. The wage base for Social Security is adjusted for inflation every year and in 2011 is $106,800. Until 1992, the wage base for Medicare was the same as for Social Security but starting in

[23] The term "employee" is used to identify persons whose work effort, tools, place of work, and work time periods are subject to the supervision and control of another (the employer). A person who provides his or her own tools and who has the *right* to exercise control over when, where, and for whom services are rendered (i.e., an independent contractor) generally is classified as self-employed rather than as an employee. See Chapter 8 for a discussion of the importance this classification has in the deductions allowed to individuals for Federal income tax purposes.

1993 the base for Medicare became unlimited and remains unlimited today. Many believe that it is only a matter of time before the Social Security base also will become unlimited.

It is important to note that Congress has already agreed to increase the Medicare tax in 2013. In early 2010, Congress enacted and the President Obama signed into law the *Patient Protection and Affordable Care Act,* as amended by the *Health Care and Reconciliation Act of 2010* (the Health Care Act). To help pay for the cost of the Health Care Act, the law provides for an increase in the Medicare tax in 2013 on *employees* (i.e., but *not* on employers). Although there is talk of repeal, without action the rate will increase .9 percentage points on wages in excess of $200,000 for individuals and $250,000 for joint filers (i.e., the rate increases from 1.45% to 2.34%). The additional MHI tax means that the portion of wages received in connection with "employment" in excess of $200,000 ($250,000 for joint filers) will, after the effective date, be subject to a total Medicare tax rate (combined employer and employee portions) of 3.8 percent (i.e., 1.45% by the employer, and (1.45% + .9%) by the employee). A similar increase would apply to self-employed persons.

In addition, in a dramatic extension of the Medicare tax, an additional 3.8% tax would be imposed on *investment income* (i.e., not just wages) but only to the extent it exceeded $200,000 ($250,000 for joint filers). For this purpose, the additional Medicare tax would be imposed on the *lesser* of: (1) net investment income from interest, dividends, annuities, royalties, rents and certain other income and gains *not* generated in the ordinary course of an active trade or business, or (2) modified AGI. This change is estimated to generate $210 billion to help fund the health care plan.

### Employees and Employers

(Note: the following discussion ignores the temporary 2 percentage point reduction in the employee's share of Social Security taxes that applies only for 2011.) FICA taxes are imposed at the combined rate of 7.65 percent (6.2% social security + 1.45% MHI) on each dollar of an employee's wages up to $106,800 plus 1.45 percent on each additional dollar of wages in 2010. As explained above, there is no maximum amount on the MHI component of the FICA tax because the 1.45 percent MHI tax is applicable to *all* compensation. The employer is required to pay a matching amount of FICA taxes for each employee (i.e., the same tax rates on each employee's wage base up to the same limits).[24]

#### Example 18

During 2010 employee E earns wages of $70,000. As a result, E will pay $5,355 (7.65% × $70,000) FICA taxes, and her employer must pay the same amount as an employment tax.

#### Example 19

During 2010 employee F earns wages of $240,000. As a result F will pay $10,102 FICA taxes, and her employer must pay the same amount as an employment tax. It is important to note that the 1.45% MHI tax has no ceiling amount. The calculation is as follows:

| | |
|---|---|
| Social security portion = 6.2% × $106,800 limit | $ 6,622 |
| Plus: MHI portion = 1.45% × $240,000 | +3,480 |
| Total FICA taxes | $10,102 |

[24] Employers are allowed a tax deduction for all payroll taxes. See Chapter 7 for a discussion of business deductions.

An employer is required to withhold both Federal income taxes and FICA taxes from each employee's wages paid during the year. The employer is then required to remit these withheld amounts plus the employer's matching FICA taxes for each employee to the IRS on a regular basis, usually weekly or monthly.[25] Employers also are required to file Form 941, Employer's Quarterly Federal Tax Return, by the end of the first month following each quarter of the calendar year (e.g., by April 30, 2010 for the quarter ended March 31, 2010) and pay any remaining amount of employment taxes due for the previous quarter.[26]

In some instances, an employee who has had more than one employer during the year may have paid *excess* FICA taxes for the year and will be entitled to a Federal income tax credit or refund for the excess.

### Example 20

During 2010 E earned \$100,000 from his regular job and \$50,000 from a part-time job. E's full time employer withheld \$7,650 (\$100,000 × 7.65%) and E's part time employer withheld \$3,825 (\$50,000 × 7.65%). Each employer made matching contributions and paid the withheld amount and the employer's match to the IRS. Since E has paid a total of \$11,475 (\$7,650 + \$3,825) FICA taxes and the maximum amount due for 2010 is \$8,797 [(\$106,800 × 6.2% = \$6,622) + (\$150,000 × 1.45% = \$2,175)], E will be entitled to a tax credit or refund of the \$2,678, the difference between the \$11,475 he paid and the \$8,797 that is due. Note that this simply represents the FICA taxes withheld on E's wages in excess of the \$102,000 maximum amount subject to the 6.2% Social Security rate in 2010 (\$150,000 − \$106,800 = \$43,200 × 6.2% = \$2,678).

## Self-Employed Taxpayers

(Note: the following discussion ignores the temporary 2 percentage point reduction in Social Security taxes that applies only for 2011.) Like employees, self-employed individuals are normally required to pay FICA taxes on their self-employment income (commonly known as self-employment tax or the SE tax). The social security portion of self-employment tax rate is 12.4 percent and the MHI portion is 2.9 percent. These rates are *twice* the FICA tax rates imposed on an employee's wages. In 2010, the ceiling amount for the social security portion of the SE tax is \$106,800, the same as for employees. As a result, taxpayers with self-employment income not exceeding this amount will pay an SE tax of 15.3 percent on their self-employment income. This tax is computed as part of Form 1040 on Schedule SE. (See Appendix B for this form.) Note that a taxpayer is not required to pay self-employment taxes unless he or she has self-employment income of \$400 or more.[27]

## Self-Employment Income

Self-employed persons do not receive wages. Employees receive wages. The equivalent of wages for a self-employed person is self-employment income. Self-employment income is generally the trade or business income earned by an individual as an independent contractor, a sole proprietor or a general partner in a partnership. Self-employment income does not include income passive in nature or investment income such as interest, dividends or rents. Nor does it include gains from the sale of property (other than sales of inventory or property customarily held for sale to customers). Note that self-employment income is a "net" concept so expenses related to producing the income may be subtracted in reaching the base.

---

[25] The frequency of these payments depends on the total amount of Federal income taxes withheld and the FICA taxes due on the employer's periodic payroll. The amount of Federal income and FICA taxes to be withheld from each employee's wages, and the reporting and payment requirements are specified in Circular E, *Employer's Tax Guide*, a free publication of the Internal Revenue Service.

[26] Because of significant penalties for underpayment of these Federal employment taxes, most employers exercise great care to make payments on a timely basis. See Circular E for a discussion of these penalties and due dates.

[27] Technically, self-employment income is defined as "net earnings from self-employment." Because the amount of net earnings from self-employment is 92.35% of self-employment income, there is no self-employment tax unless the taxpayer's self-employment income is \$433 (\$400/92.35%) or more. See §§ 1401 and 1402(b).

The most common type of self-employment income is that received by for providing services *other than in an employee capacity*. For example, it includes income earned by accountants, tax preparers, doctors, dentists, veterinarians, engineers, lawyers and consultants as long as they are independent contractors, sole proprietors or general partners. But self-employment income is not limited to income earned by professionals. It also includes income earned by such persons as farmers, fisherman, contractors, subcontractors, massage therapists, graphic designers, hair stylists, salesmen and freelance writers. Income from odd jobs also counts as self-employment income such as income from babysitting and child care, mowing lawns, driving a taxi, painting, tutoring, selling handicrafts, operating a bed and breakfast or serving on a board of directors. In all cases, the services must have been performed as an independent contractor, sole proprietor or partner to be considered self-employment income.

Whether an individual is an independent contractor or an employee depends on the facts in each case. An individual is normally considered an independent contractor if the payer has the right to control or direct only the result of the work and not how it will be done. Unfortunately, this is a dreadfully controversial area. As might be expected, payers, wanting to avoid payment of a 7.65 percent employment tax, are inclined to call a worker an independent contractor. Conversely, the government, hoping to ensure the collection of employment and income taxes, wants to classify the worker as an employee. To dissuade employers from misclassification, the government imposes severe penalties if the employer intentionally classifies a worker as an independent contractor when it is clear he or she is an employee.

In most cases, an independent contractor's self-employment income is reported to the taxpayer on Form 1099. Just like an employer that must provide an employee with a Form W-2 reporting wages earned, businesses must give a Form 1099 to any "independent contractor" who provides $600 or more of services to the business during the year. Generally a payer is not required to provide a Form 1099 to a corporation but there are a number of exceptions. For example, businesses must always give attorneys a Form 1099 regardless of the form of business in which the attorneys perform their services. Note that while the reporting threshold for a payer is $600, an individual is not required to pay self-employment tax unless his or her total self-employment income is $400 or more.

## Calculation of Self-Employment Tax

As a general rule, the self-employment tax is 15.3 percent of self-employment income. However, in computing the amount of a taxpayer's self-employment income subject to tax, a special adjustment is required as explained in the following example.

### Example 21

S is a sole proprietor who prepares tax returns. This year his income from operations net of all expenses *except* the self-employment tax related to such income is $10,000. To arrive at the correct measure of *net* income for the sole proprietorship, the taxpayer must reduce the $10,000 by the portion of the self-employment tax that represents a cost of doing business. This is analogous to an employer whose labor expenses include the 7.65 percent FICA tax on an employee's wages (i.e., the employer's matching share of FICA). A self-employed person incurs a similar cost and that cost is one-half of the individual's self-employment tax. Consequently, to determine the self-employment tax base, the tax preparer's income of $10,000 is reduced by one-half of the hypothetical self-employment tax on the $10,000 or $765 [$10,000 × 7.65% (15.3% × $^1/_2$)]. This results in self-employment income subject to tax of $9,235 ($10,000 − $765). The actual self-employment tax is $1,412.96 (15.3% × $9,235).

Following the approach above, in computing the amount subject to tax for each of the self-employment tax bases (both the 12.4 percent and the 2.9 percent), the taxpayer always reduces net earnings from self-employment by an amount equal to one-half the combined 15.3 percent tax rate times net earnings from self-employment (i.e., 7.65% × net earnings from self-employment).[28] Note that this adjustment applies only in the computation of the

[28] § 1402(a)(12).

amount of the self-employment tax bases. However, consistent with the theory above, a self-employed individual is entitled to an actual deduction for one-half of the self-employment tax as a business expense in computing adjusted gross income. Using the facts of the example, the actual deduction would be $706.48 (1/2 × actual self-employment tax of $1,412.96). Observe that the actual deduction in computing adjusted gross income is $706.48 and not the $765 used to compute the self-employment tax bases. Examples of these calculations are given below.

Each component of the self-employment tax required to be paid is computed as follows:

1. Multiply net earnings from self-employment by one-half of the self-employment tax rate, 7.65% (1/2 × 15.3%) and subtract that amount to reach a tentative tax base of 92.35% of the original amount.[29]
2. Compare the result in step 1 with the maximum base amount for the social security portion of the self-employment tax ($106,800 for 2010) and select the smaller amount.
3. Multiply the amount in step 1 by the Medicare rate of 2.9% and the amount in step 2 by the Social Security rate of 12.4%.
4. Add the amounts of the separate components from step 3. This is the amount of self-employment tax required to be paid.

## Example 22

Individuals C and D have net earnings from self-employment for 2010 of $50,000 and $150,000, respectively. Self-employment taxes for C and D are determined as follows:

| Self-employment tax computation | C | | D | |
|---|---|---|---|---|
| Social Security (12.4% portion) | | | | |
| Net earnings from self-employment . . | $50,000 | | $150,000 | |
| – (1/2 × 15.3% = 7.65%) of net earnings | (3,825) | | (11,475) | |
| SE tax base (92.35% net earnings)* | $46,175 | | $138,525 | |
| Smaller of SE tax base above or maximum wage base ($106,800 for 2010). . . . . . . . . . . . . . . . . . . . . | $46,175 | | $106,800 | |
| × 12.4%. . . . . . . | ×12.4% | | ×12.4% | |
| Social Security tax . . . . . . . . . . . . . . . | | $5,726 | | $13,243 |
| MHI (2.9% portion) | | | | |
| Net earnings from self-employment . . | $50,000 | | $150,000 | |
| – (1/2 × 15.3% = 7.65%) of net earnings | (3,825) | | (11,475) | |
| SE tax base (92.35% net earnings)** | $46,175 | | $138,525 | |
| × 2.9% . . . . . . . . | × 2.9% | | ×2.9% | |
| MHI tax | | 1,339 | | 4,017 |
| Total self-employment tax. . . . . . . . . . . | | $7,065 | | $17,260 |
| Deduct 1/2 SE tax for A.G.I. . . . . . . . . . | | $3,533 | | $ 8,630 |

*Not to exceed wage base–wages received
**No reduction for wages

[29] Note that the steps can be combined simply by multiplying the individual's net earnings from self-employment by 100% – one-half the current combined self-employment tax rate (i.e., 100% – 7.65% = 92.35%).

C will be allowed to deduct $3,533 (one-half of $7,065 self-employment tax paid) for income tax purposes, and D will be allowed to deduct $8,630 (one-half of $17,260). Although both will receive a benefit from the income tax deduction, note that only C has received any benefit from the so-called second deduction in arriving at his self-employment tax base for the social security component. Because D's reduced net earnings for self-employment are still greater than the maximum tax base for the social security component, she is required to pay the maximum amount of this component of the self-employment tax for 2010 (i.e., $106,800 × 12.4% = $13,243).

In some instances, a self-employed individual may also earn wages subject to FICA withholding while working as a full or part-time employee. In such a case, the maximum earnings base subject to the social security component of the self-employment tax is reduced by the wages earned as an employee.

## Example 23

During 2010 T received wages of $88,000 and had self-employment income of $50,000. In computing T's self-employment tax, the maximum taxable base for the social security tax is reduced by the wages paid because T's employer has already withheld the appropriate FICA amount on these wages.

| | *Social Security* |
|---|---|
| Maximum tax base | $106,800 |
| Less: Wages subject to FICA tax | (88,000) |
| Reduced maximum tax base | $ 18,800 |
| Net earnings from self-employment | $ 50,000 |
| Subtract: 7.65% of net earnings from self-employment | (3,825) |
| | $ 46,175 |
| Smaller of reduced maximum tax base or amount determined above | $ 18,800 |
| Times: Social security tax rate | ×12.4% |
| Tax on social security component | $ 2,331 |
| Social security tax | $ 2,331 |
| Plus: MHI tax ($46,175 × 2.9%) | 1,339 |
| Equals: T's self-employment tax | $ 3,670 |

T will also have an income tax deduction of $1,835 (one-half of the $3,670 self-employment taxes paid).

## FUTA Taxes

A Federal unemployment tax is imposed on employers who pay wages of $1,500 or more during any calendar quarter in the calendar year, or who employ at least one individual on each of some 20 days during the calendar year or previous year.[30] Certain exceptions are made for persons employing agricultural or domestic workers.

FUTA tax revenues are used by the Federal government to augment unemployment benefit programs of the various states. The current FUTA tax rate is 6.2 percent of the first $7,000 of wages paid during the year to each covered employee. This translates into a *maximum*

---

[30] § 3306(a)(1).

FUTA tax of $434 (6.2% × $7,000) *per employee* per year. Since most states also impose an unemployment tax on employers, a credit is allowed against an employer's FUTA tax liability for any similar tax paid to a state. Currently, the maximum FUTA tax credit allowed for this purpose is 5.4 percent of the covered wages (i.e., maximum of $378 per employee). Thus, the maximum FUTA tax paid is normally $56 ($434 – $378, or 0.8% × $7,000) per employee.

All employers subject to FUTA taxes must file Form 940, Employer's Annual Federal Unemployment Tax Return, on or before January 31 of the following year. If the employer's tax liability exceeds certain limits, estimated tax payments must be made during the year.[31] Most states require an employer to file unemployment tax returns and make tax payments quarterly.

## EXCISE TAXES

The purpose of an excise tax is to tax certain privileges as well as the manufacture, sale, or consumption of specified commodities. Federal excise taxes are imposed on the sale of specified articles, various transactions, occupations, and the use of certain items. This type of tax is not imposed on the profits of a business or profession, however. The major types of excise taxes are as follows:

1. Occupational taxes;
2. Facilities and services taxes;
3. Manufacturers' taxes; and
4. Retail sales of products and commodities taxes.

### Occupational Taxes

Some businesses must pay a fee before engaging in their business. These types of businesses include, but are not limited to, liquor dealers, dealers in medicines and dealers in firearms.

### Facilities and Services Taxes

The person who pays for services and facilities must pay the tax on these items. The institution or person who furnishes the facilities or services must collect the tax, file returns, and turn over the taxes to the taxing authorities. A few of the common services subject to the facilities and services excise tax include air travel, hotel or motel lodging, and telephone service.

### Manufacturers' Taxes

As a rule, certain manufactured goods are taxed at the manufacturing level to make collection easier. Most of these items are of a semi-luxurious or specialized nature, such as sporting goods or firearms. This excise tax applies to the sale or use by the manufacturer, producer, or importer of specified articles. The taxes may be determined by quantity of production (e.g., pounds or gallons) or by a percentage of the sales price. When sales price is used as an index, the tax is based on the sales price of the manufacturer, producer, or importer.

### Retail Sales of Products and Commodities Taxes

This excise tax applies to the retail sale or use of diesel fuel, special motor fuels, and fuel used in noncommercial aviation. The tax is collected from the person buying the product by the seller, and the seller must file and pay the tax unless the buyer purchased it tax-free.

### State Excise Taxes

Many states and local governments also have excise taxes. They vary in range of coverage and impact, but most parallel the Federal excise taxes. For instance, most states have an excise tax on gasoline, liquor, and cigarettes, as does the Federal government.

## ADDITIONAL TYPES OF TAXES

Many other types of taxes are used to augment state, local, and Federal income, employment, excise, and wealth transfer taxes. The three levels of government have never been reluctant to exercise their imagination in creating and developing new ways of supplementing

---

[31] See instructions in Circular E, *Supra*, Footnote 27.

governmental revenues. A few of the other more common types of taxes are briefly explained below.

### Franchise Tax

A franchise tax is a tax on the privilege of doing business in a state or local jurisdiction. The measure of the tax generally is the net income of the business or the value of the capital used within the taxing authority's jurisdiction.

### Sales Tax

A sales tax is imposed on the gross receipts from the retail sale of tangible personal property (e.g., clothing, automobiles, and equipment) and certain services. Each state or local government determines the tax rate and the services and articles to be taxed. The seller will collect the tax from the consumer at the time of the sale, and then periodically remit the taxes to the appropriate taxing authority. Often a state or local government allows the seller to retain a nominal percentage of the collected taxes to compensate for the additional costs incurred by the seller in complying with the tax requirements.

### Use Tax

A use tax is a tax imposed on the use within a state or local jurisdiction of tangible property on which a sales tax was not paid. The tax rate normally equals that of the taxing authority's sales tax.

### Doing-Business Penalty

This penalty tax is imposed on a business that has not obtained authorization from the state or local government to operate within its border. Usually, a business must pay a fee for a state charter or some other kind of license as permission to enter business within the state.

### Real Property Tax

A real property tax is a tax on the value of realty (land, buildings, homes, etc.) owned by nonexempt individuals or organizations within a jurisdiction. Rates vary with location. This type of tax normally supports local services, such as the public school system or the fire department, and is levied on a recurring annual basis.

### Tangible Personal Property Tax

This tax is levied on the value of tangible personalty located within a jurisdiction. Tangible personalty is property not classified as realtyand includes such items as office furniture, machinery and equipment, inventories, and supplies. The tax normally must be paid annually, with each local jurisdiction determining its own tax rate and the items to tax.

### Intangible Personal Property Tax

This tax is imposed on the value of intangible personalty (i.e., stocks, bonds, and accounts and notes receivable) located within a jurisdiction. The tax generally is paid annually, with each local jurisdiction setting its own tax rate and items to be taxed.

## Goals of Taxation

**LO.7**
Identify some of the more common social and economic goals of our Federal tax system.

In subsequent chapters, the specific provisions that must be followed to compute the Federal income tax will be discussed in detail. Some may view this discussion as a hopeless attempt to explain what seems like an endless barrage of boring rules—rules that, despite their apparent lack of "rhyme or reason," must be considered if the final tax liability is to be determined. The frustration that students of taxation often feel when studying the rules of Federal tax law is not completely unfounded. Indeed, a famous tax scholar, Boris Bittker, once commented on the increasing intricacy of the tax law, saying, "Can one hope to find a way through a statutory thicket so bristling with detail?"[32] As this statement suggests, many provisions of

[32] Boris I. Bittker and Lawrence M. Stone, *Federal Income Taxation*, 5th Ed. (Boston: Little, Brown & Co., 1980) liii.

the law are, in fact, obscure and often appear to be without purpose. However, each provision of the tax law originated with some goal, even if no more than to grant a benefit to some Congressperson's constituency. A knowledge of the goals underlying a particular provision is an important first step toward a comprehension of the provision. An understanding of the purpose of the law is an invaluable tool in attacking the "statutory thicket." In studying taxation, it becomes apparent that many provisions have been enacted with similar objectives. The following discussion reviews some of the goals of taxation that often serve as the reasons behind the rule.

## Economic Objectives

At first glance, it seems clear that the primary goal of taxation is to provide the resources necessary to fund governmental expenditures. At the Federal level, however, this is not entirely true. As many economists have pointed out, any taxing authority that has the power to control the money supply—as does our Federal government—can satisfy its revenue needs by merely creating money. Nevertheless, complete reliance on the Treasury's printing press to provide the needed resources is not a viable alternative. If the government's expenditures were financed predominantly with funds that it created rather than those obtained through taxation, excess demand would result, which in turn would cause prices to rise, or inflation. Thus, taxation in serving a revenue function also operates along with other instruments of policy to attain a stable price level.

Although Congress can create its own resources, revenue objectives often can explain a particular feature of the law. Consider the personal and dependency exemption deductions, the purpose of which is to free from tax the income needed to maintain a minimum standard of living. Although the cost of living has risen substantially over the years, Congress has been reluctant to increase the amount of these exemptions. The exemption deduction was set at $600 from 1948 to 1969. It slowly crept to $1,000 in 1979 where it essentially stayed until Congress started requiring inflation adjustments in 1985. In effect, the deduction has changed very little over the years, despite significant increases in the price level during this time. The reluctance to alter the exemption amount derives primarily from the potential impact on revenues. A slight increase in the exemption without a corresponding increase in revenues from other sources would result in a tremendous revenue loss because of the number of exemptions taxpayers claim—approximately 269 million in 2005. For similar reasons, Congress has refrained, until recently, from adjusting the tax rate schedules to compensate for inflation, since to do so would significantly reduce its inflow of resources. In 1985, however, both the personal and dependency exemption amount, the standard deduction *and* the individual tax rate schedules were adjusted (indexed) for the increase in the Consumer Price Index that occurred during the previous year.

Revenue considerations also can explain why tax accounting methods sometimes differ from those used for financial accounting. Prior to 1954, an accrual basis taxpayer could neither defer taxation of prepaid income nor deduct estimates of certain expenses, such as the expected costs of servicing warranty contracts. In 1954, the treatment of such items was changed to conform with financial accounting principles that permit deferral of income and accrual of expenses in most situations. The expected revenue loss attributed to this change was $50 million. Within a year after the change, however, the Treasury requested that Congress repeal the new provisions retroactively because estimates of the revenue loss were in excess of several billion dollars. In short, Congress responded and, as a result, the treatment of prepaid income and certain accruals for tax and financial accounting purposes differs—a difference attributable to revenue considerations.

The role of Federal taxation in carrying out economic policy extends beyond the realm of revenue raising and price stability. Taxation is a major tool used by the government to attain satisfactory economic growth with full employment. The title of the 1981 tax bill is illustrative: *The Economic Recovery Tax Act of 1981* (ERTA). As the title suggests, a major purpose of this legislation was directed toward revitalizing the health of the economy. ERTA significantly lowered tax rates to spur the economy out of a recession. Its objective was to place more *after-tax* income in the hands of taxpayers for their disposal. By so doing, it was hoped that taxpayers would consume more and thus increase aggregate demand, resulting in economic growth.

Congress also has used the tax structure to directly attack the problem of unemployment. In 1977, employers were encouraged to increase employment by the introduction of a general jobs tax credit, which effectively reduced the cost of labor. In 1978, Congress eliminated the general jobs credit and substituted a targeted jobs credit. This credit could be obtained only if employers hired certain targeted groups of individuals who were considered disadvantaged or handicapped. This credit was expanded in 1983 to stimulate the hiring of economically disadvantaged youth during the summer. The credit was further refined and is now referred to as the work opportunity credit. As the credit for jobs suggests, Congress believes that major economic problems can be solved using the tax system.

A subject closely related to economic growth and full employment is investment. To stimulate investment spending, Congress has enacted numerous provisions. For example, accelerated depreciation methods—the modified accelerated cost recovery system (MACRS)—may be used to compute the deduction for depreciation, thus enabling rapid recovery of the taxpayer's investment.

Congress encourages certain industries by granting them favorable tax treatment. For example, the credit for research and experimental expenditures cited above clearly benefits those engaged in technology businesses. Other tax provisions are particularly advantageous for other groups such as builders, farmers, and producers of natural resources. Special incentives also are available for manufacturers. As will become clear in later chapters, the income tax law is replete with rules designed to encourage, stimulate, and assist various enterprises as Congress has deemed necessary over the years.

## Social Objectives

The tax system is used to achieve not only economic goals but social objectives as well. Some examples are listed below:

1. The deduction for charitable contributions helps to finance the cost of important activities that otherwise would be funded by the government.
2. The deduction for interest on home mortgages subsidizes the cost of a home and thus encourages home ownership.
3. The work opportunity credit noted above exists to fight unemployment problems of certain disadvantaged groups of citizens.
4. Larger standard deductions are granted to taxpayers who are 65 or over, or who are blind, to relieve their tax burden.
5. Deductions for contributions to retirement savings accounts encourage individuals to provide for their future needs.

These examples are representative of the many provisions where social considerations provide the underlying rationale.

The above discussion is but a brief glimpse of how social and economic considerations have shaped our tax law. Interestingly, most of the provisions mentioned have been enacted in the past 25 years. During this time, Congress has relied increasingly on the tax system as a means to strike at the nation's ills. Whether the tax law can be used successfully in this manner is unclear. Many believe that attacking such problems should be done directly through government expenditure programs—not through so-called *tax expenditures*. A *tax expenditure* is the estimated amount of revenue lost for failing to tax a particular item (e.g., scholarships), for granting a certain deduction (e.g., charitable contributions), or for allowing a credit (e.g., work opportunity credit). The concept of tax expenditures was developed by noted tax authority Stanley S. Surrey. While Assistant Secretary of the Treasury for Tax Policy during 1961–1969, Surrey and his supporters urged that certain activities should not be encouraged by subsidizing them through reduced tax liabilities. They argued that paying for government-financed activities in such a roundabout fashion makes their costs difficult if not impossible to determine. In addition, they asserted that such expenditures are concealed from the public eye as well as from the standard budgetary review process.[33] Others, however, argued that the tax system could be used effectively for this purpose. Whether either view is correct, Congress currently shows no apparent signs of discontinuing use of the tax system to influence taxpayers' behavior.

[33] The annual U.S. budget now contains a projection of annual tax expenditures.

## Other Objectives

Although social and economic goals provide the rationale for much of our tax law, many provisions can be explained in terms of certain well-established principles of taxation. These principles are simply the characteristics that "good" taxes exhibit. Most tax experts agree that a tax is good if it satisfies the following conditions:[34]

1. The tax is *equitable* or fair;
2. The tax is *economically efficient* (i.e., it advances a goal where appropriate and otherwise is as neutral as possible);
3. The tax is *certain* and not arbitrary;
4. The tax can be administered by the government and complied with by the taxpayer at a *low cost* (i.e., it is *economical* to operate); and
5. The tax is *convenient* (i.e., administration and compliance can be carried out with the utmost simplicity).

These five qualities represent important principles of taxation that must be conformed with in pursuing social and economic goals. As discussed below, these criteria have greatly influenced our tax law.

### Equity

A tax system is considered equitable if it treats all persons who are in the same economic situation in the same fashion. This aspect of equity is referred to as *horizontal equity*. In contrast, *vertical equity* implies that taxpayers who are not in the same situation will be treated differently—the difference in treatment being fair and just. There are two major obstacles in implementing the equity concept as explained. First, there must be some method to determine when taxpayers are in the same economic situation. Second, there must be agreement on reasonable distinctions between those who are in different situations. The manner in which these obstacles are addressed explains two significant features of our tax system.

As indicated above, the first major difficulty in implementing the equity concept is identification of some technique to determine when taxpayers are similarly situated. For tax purposes, it is well settled that similarity is measured in terms of a taxpayer's *ability to pay*. Hence, taxpayers with equal abilities to pay should pay equal taxes. To the dismay of some tax policymakers, however, there is no simple, unambiguous index of an individual's ability. A taxpayer's ability to pay is the composite of numerous factors including his or her wealth, income, family situation, health, and attitude. Clearly, no one measure captures all of these factors. This being so, tax specialists generally have agreed that the best objective measure of ability to pay is income. This agreement, that income is a reasonable surrogate for ability to pay and thus serves the equity principle, explains in part why the primary tax used by the Federal government is an *income* tax.

The second obstacle in implementing the equity concept concerns the treatment of taxpayers who are differently situated. In terms of income, the problem may best be explained by reference to two taxpayers, A and B. If A's income (e.g., $100,000) exceeds B's (e.g., $20,000), it is assumed that A has more ability to pay and thus should pay more tax. The dilemma posed is not whether A and B should pay differing amounts of tax, but rather, what additional amount may be fairly charged to A. If a proportional tax of five percent is levied against A and B, A pays $5,000 (5% of $100,000) and B pays $1,000 (5% of $20,000). While application of this tax rate structure results in A paying $4,000 more than B absolutely, A pays the same amount in relative terms; that is, they both pay the *same* 5 percent. Those charged with the responsibility of developing Federal tax policy have concluded that paying more tax in absolute terms does not adequately serve the equity goal. For this reason, a progressive tax rate structure is used, requiring relatively more tax to be paid by those having more income. With respect to A and B above, this structure would require that A pay a greater percentage of his income than B.

---

[34] These qualities were first identified by Adam Smith. See The *Wealth of Nations*, Book V, Chapter II, Part II (New York: Dutton, 1910).

The equity principle explains (at least partially) not only the basic structure of our predominant tax device—an income tax and its progressive tax rate structure—but also explains many other provisions in our law. In fact, some of the factors mentioned earlier that affect a taxpayer's ability to pay are recognized explicitly by separate provisions in the Code. For example, a taxpayer may deduct medical expenses and casualty losses—items over which the taxpayer has little or no power—if such items exceed a certain level. Similarly, a taxpayer's family situation is considered by allowing exemption deductions for dependents whose support is the taxpayer's responsibility.

There are many other specific situations where the equity principle controls the tax consequences. For example, fairness dictates that taxes should not be paid when the taxpayer does not have the *wherewithal to pay* (i.e., the money to pay the tax). This is true even though the transaction results in income to the taxpayer.

### Example 24

Upon the theft of valuable machinery, LJM Corporation received a $20,000 insurance reimbursement. Assuming the machinery had a cost (adjusted for depreciation) of $5,000, LJM has realized a $15,000 gain ($20,000 – $5,000). Although the corporation has realized a gain, it also has lost the productive capacity of the machinery. If LJM reinvests the entire $20,000 proceeds in similar assets within two years of the theft, the gain is not taxed but rather deferred. This rule derives from Congressional belief that equity would not be served if taxes were levied when the taxpayer did not have the wherewithal to pay. In addition, the taxpayer's total economic situation has not been so materially altered as to require recognition of the gain.

### Administrative Concerns

The final three qualities of a good tax—certainty, economy, and simplicity—might be aptly characterized as administrative in nature. Numerous provisions exist to meet administrative goals. Some of these are so obvious as to be easily overlooked. For example, the certainty requirement underlies the provision that a tax return generally is due each April 15, while economy of collection is the purpose, at least in part, for withholding. Similarly, provisions requiring the taxpayer to compute the tax using tables provided by the IRS are motivated by concerns for simplicity.

Perhaps the most important aspect of the administrative principles is that they often conflict with other principles of taxation. Consequently, one principle must often be adhered to at the expense of another. For example, our tax system could no doubt be more equitable if each individual's ability to pay was personally assessed, much like welfare agents assess the needs of their clients. However, this improvement could be obtained only at a substantial administrative cost. The administrative principle is first in importance in this case, as well as in many others.

## A Prelude to Tax Planning

Although taxes affect numerous aspects of our lives, their impact is not uncontrollable. Given an understanding of the rules, taxes can be managed with considerable success. Successful management, however, is predicated on good tax planning.

Tax planning is simply the process of arranging one's actions in light of their potential tax consequences. It should be emphasized that the tax consequences sometimes turn on how a particular transaction is structured—that is, *form* often controls taxation.

### Example 25

Z is obligated to make monthly payments of interest and principal on a note secured by his home. During the year, he was short of cash so his mother, B, who lives with Z, made the payments for him. Even though B made the payments directly, she may not deduct the interest expense because interest is deductible only if it relates to a debt for which the taxpayer is personally liable. Moreover, her son cannot deduct the expense since he did not make payment. Note that the deduction could have been obtained had the payment been structured properly. If Z had received a gift of cash from his mother and then made payment, he could have claimed the interest deduction. Alternatively, if B had been jointly liable on the note, she could have deducted the interest payments she made.

In the example above, note that regardless of how the transaction is structured, the result is the same *except for* the tax ramifications. By merely planning and changing the form of the transaction, tax benefits are obtained. Before jumping to the conclusion that form always governs taxation, a caveat is warranted. Courts often are obliged to disregard form and let substance prevail. Notwithstanding the form versus substance difficulty, the point to be gained is that the pattern of a transaction often determines the tax outcome.

The obvious goal of most tax planning is the minimization of the amount that a person or other entity must transfer to the government. The legal minimization of taxes is usually referred to as *tax avoidance*. Although the phrase "tax avoidance" may have a criminal connotation, there is no injustice in legally reducing one's taxes. The most profound statement regarding the propriety of tax avoidance is found in a dissenting opinion authored by Judge Learned Hand in the case of *Commissioner v. Newman*. Judge Hand wrote:[35]

> Over and over again courts have said that there is nothing sinister in so arranging one's affairs so as to keep taxes as low as possible. Everybody does so, rich or poor, and all do right, for nobody owes any public duty to pay more than the law demands: taxes are enforced exactions, not voluntary contributions. To demand more in the name of morals is pure cant.

This statement is routinely cited as authority for taking those steps necessary to reduce one's taxes. It should be emphasized that tax planning and tax avoidance involve only those actions that are legal. *Tax evasion* is the label given to illegal activities that are designed to reduce the tax liability.

The planning effort for Federal income taxation (the principal area covered in this text) requires an understanding of the answer to *four* basic questions regarding the flow of cash and cash equivalents into and out of various tax entities. These questions regard the amount, character, and timing of income, deductions and credits, and recognition (reporting) of these items. The answers depend upon the tax entity that receives or transfers the cash or cash equivalents, its tax accounting period and methods, and whether the entity is considered a taxpayer separate from its owners or simply a conduit through which items of income, gain, loss, deduction, or credit flow to its owners. The tax entities recognized for Federal tax purposes, and the tax planning questions, are presented in Exhibit 1-6.

Tax planning efforts often involve deferring the recognition of income or shifting the incidence of its tax to a lower tax bracket entity (e.g., from parents to children), or accelerating, deferring, or shifting deductions and credits to tax periods or among tax entities with higher or lower tax rates. Keeping this overall scheme of tax minimization in mind, many of the subsequent chapters of this text conclude with a discussion of tax planning considerations.

---

[35] 159 F.2d 848 (CA-2. 1947).

**EXHIBIT 1.6** **Tax Planning Perspective**

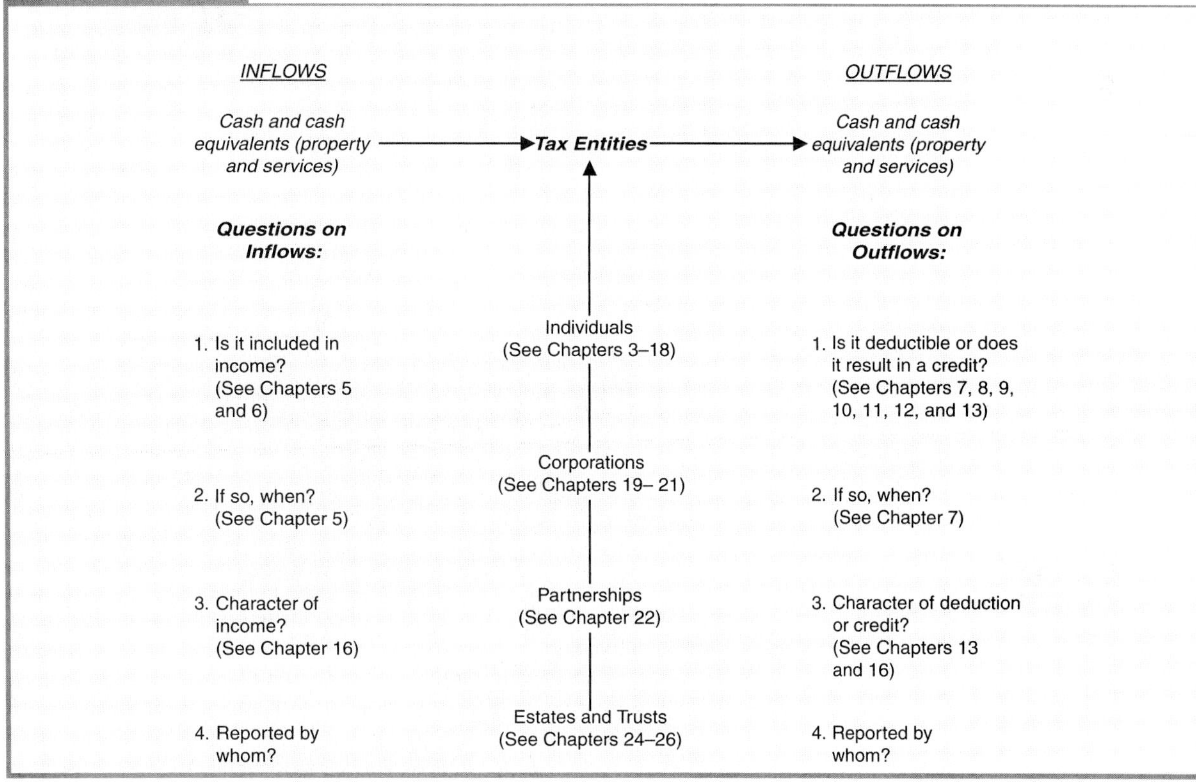


## Problem Materials

### DISCUSSION QUESTIONS

**1-1** *Tax Bases.* Describe the tax bases for the Federal income tax and for each of the Federal wealth transfer taxes.

**1-2** *Tax Rates.* Distinguish between a proportional tax rate structure and a progressive tax rate structure. What is the significance of the marginal tax rate under either a proportional or a progressive rate structure?

**1-3** *Progressive, Proportional, and Regressive Taxes.* The media often refer to sales taxes as regressive. Similar comments are made when discussing social security taxes (FICA). Are the media correct? Include in your comments an explanation of the different types of tax rate structures.

**1-4** *Deduction versus Credit.* Distinguish between a deduction and a credit. If a credit is allowed for 20 percent of an expenditure in lieu of a deduction for the total expenditure, under what circumstances should you prefer the credit? The deduction?

**1-5** *Individual versus Corporate Taxable Income.* Based on the tax formulas contained in Exhibits 1-2 and 1-3, what are the significant differences in computing a corporation's taxable income as opposed to computing an individual's taxable income?

**1-6** *Withholding Taxes at Source.* What do you believe is the principal reason that Congress continues the pay-as-you-go requirements of employers withholding Federal income taxes from the wages paid their employees?

**1-7** *Marital Deduction.* Describe the marital deduction allowed for Federal estate and gift taxes. How might an individual use this deduction to avoid all Federal wealth transfer taxes?

**1-8** *Estate Tax Credit.* How is the estate transfer tax credit applied in determining taxable wealth transfers?

**1-9** *Annual Gift Tax Exclusion.* What is the amount of the annual Federal gift tax exclusion? If a widow were interested in making gifts to her daughter and seven grandchildren, how much could she transfer to them in any given year before incurring a taxable gift?

**1-10** *Gift-Splitting Election.* What is the gift-splitting election allowed for Federal gift tax purposes? How might the marital deduction be used to explain why Congress allows this election?

**1-11** *Estate versus Inheritance Taxes.* Distinguish between an estate and an inheritance transfer tax.

**1-12** *Federal Employment Taxes.* Distinguish between FICA and FUTA taxes. Between an employee and his or her employer, who bears the greater burden of these taxes?

**1-13** *Unemployment Taxes.* For 2011 what is the maximum FUTA tax an employer can expect to pay if he or she has three employees during the year and the minimum salary paid is $10,000? If the employer also is subject to state unemployment taxes, what is the maximum amount of credit he or she will be allowed against the FUTA tax liability?

**1-14** *Sales versus Use Tax.* Distinguish between a sales and a use tax. Assume you live in state A but near the border of state B and that state A imposes a much higher sales tax than does state B. If you were planning to purchase a new automobile, what might you be tempted to do? How might state A discourage your plan?

**1-15** *Tax Expenditures.* It is often suggested that many of our social problems can be cured through use of tax incentives.

**a.** Discuss the concept of tax expenditures.

**b.** Expand on the text's discussion of the pros and cons of tax expenditures vis-a-vis direct governmental expenditures.

**1-16** *Goals of Taxation.* In a recent discussion concerning what a fair tax is, the following comments were made: (1) the fairest tax is one that someone else has to pay; (2) people should be taxed in accordance with the benefits they obtain (i.e., taxes are the price paid for the benefit); (3) a head tax would be the fairest; and (4) why tax at all?—just use the printing press. Discuss the first three of these comments in terms of equity and explain whether the fourth represents a viable alternative.

## PROBLEMS

**1-17** *Marginal Tax Rates.* T, a single taxpayer, has taxable income of $40,000 for 2011. If T anticipates a marginal tax rate of 15 percent for 2012, what income tax savings could she expect by accelerating $1,000 of deductible expenditures planned for 2011 into the 2011 tax year?

**1-18** *Tax Rate Schedules and Rate Concepts.* An examination of the tax rate schedules for single taxpayers for 2011 (see the inside cover of the text) indicates that the tax is a "given dollar amount" plus a percentage of taxable income exceeding a particular level.

**a.** Explain how the "given dollar amounts" are determined.

**b.** Assuming the taxpayer has a taxable income of $50,000 and is single, what is his tax liability for 2011?

**c.** Same facts as (b). What is the taxpayer's marginal tax rate?

**d.** Same facts as (b). What is the taxpayer's average tax rate?

**e.** Assuming the taxpayer has tax-exempt interest income from municipal bonds of $30,000, what is the taxpayer's effective tax rate?

**1-19** *Tax Equity.* Taxpayer R has income of $20,000. Similarly, S has income of $20,000. Each taxpayer pays a tax of $1,000 on his income.

**a.** Discuss whether the tax imposed is equitable. Include in your discussion comments concerning horizontal and vertical equity.

**b.** Assume S has a taxable income of $40,000 and pays a tax of $2,000 on his income. Discuss whether the tax imposed is equitable in light of this new information.

**1-20** *Tax Fairness.* R and S both own homes in Houston. Both have an appraised value of $200,000 and, consequently, both R and S pay $5,000 in real property taxes. Explain why such a tax may be considered fair by some and unfair by others.

**1-21** *Understanding Tax Rate Concepts.* Indicate whether the following statements are true or false and, if false, explain why.

**a.** Tax-exempt income would cause the taxpayer's average tax rate to increase.
**b.** Tax-exempt income would cause the taxpayer's marginal tax rate to decrease.
**c.** Tax-exempt income would cause the taxpayer's effective tax rate to decrease.

**1-22** *Understanding Tax Rate Concepts.* Indicate whether the following statements are true or false and, if false, explain why.

**a.** From a technical point of view, sales taxes are progressive.
**b.** From a popular point of view, sales taxes are regressive.
**c.** From a popular point of view, sales taxes are proportional.
**d.** From a technical point of view, there are no regressive taxes in the United States.

**1-23** *Think Tax.* From a tax perspective, a transaction that may make sense for one taxpayer may be complete nonsense for another. Consider two married taxpayers, H and W who have taxable income of $500,000 per year and L and M who have taxable income of $20,000 per year. Both plan on buying interest-paying bonds with a face value of $1,000, either State of Indiana bonds paying 6% tax-exempt interest or AT&T bonds paying eight percent taxable interest. Assume the bonds are in all other respects equivalent (e.g., price, risk, etc.). Show (with calculations) why it would make perfect sense for H and W to buy the Indiana bonds but it would be foolish for L and M to buy the Indiana bonds.

**1-24** *Identifying Tax Expenditures.* Indicate whether the following would be considered a tax expenditure.

**a.** Tax deduction allowed for payment of gasoline purchased by a taxicab driver who owns and operates his own taxicab business.
**b.** Deduction for charitable contributions made by individual taxpayers.
**c.** Postponement of taxation of income earned on an individual's savings in an Individual Retirement Account until such income is distributed (ignore the time value of money).
**d.** Straight-line depreciation of an office building used in a trade or business.
**e.** Tax credit for purchase of electric automobile.
**f.** Deduction for interest paid on a home mortgage.

**1-25** *Advantages and Disadvantages of Tax Expenditures.* Indicate whether the following would be considered an advantage or disadvantage of a tax expenditure.

**a.** Administrative costs less than other forms of government financial assistance
**b.** Beneficiaries easily identified
**c.** Only those entitled to financial assistance receive it
**d.** Costs and budgetary effects readily assessed
**e.** Benefits (e.g., from deductions) rise and fall without direct approval from the government
**f.** Less palatable to beneficiaries
**g.** Effect on tax system

**1-26** *Taxable Gifts.* M made the following cash gifts during 2011:

| | |
|---|---|
| To her son . . . . . . . . . . . . . . . . . . . . . | $50,000 |
| To her daughter . . . . . . . . . . . . . . . . . | 50,000 |
| To her niece . . . . . . . . . . . . . . . . . . . . | 10,000 |

**a.** If M is unmarried, what is the amount of taxable gifts she has made in 2011?
**b.** If M is married and her husband agrees to split gifts with her, what is the total amount of taxable gifts made by M and her husband for 2011?

**1-27** *Taxable Estate.* R dies in 2011. R made taxable gifts during his lifetime in 1990, 1991, 1993, 1997, and 1999 but paid no Federal transfer taxes due to the unified transfer tax credit in effect in those years. What effect will these taxable gifts have on determining the following:

**a.** R's Federal taxable estate?
**b.** The rates imposed on the Federal taxable estate?

**1-28** *Estate Tax Computation.* T died on January 4, 2011. He owned the following property on his date of death:

| | |
|---|---|
| Cash | $10,000,000 |
| Stocks and bonds | 700,000 |
| Residence | 800,000 |
| Interest in partnership | 350,000 |
| Miscellaneous personal property | 25,000 |

Upon T's death, he owed $80,000 on the mortgage on his residence. T also owned a life insurance policy. The policy was term life insurance which paid $200,000 to his mother upon his death. Its value immediately before his death was $0. T had all of the incidents of ownership with regard to the policy.

During his life, T had made only one gift. He gave a diamond ring worth $30,000 (it was an old family heirloom) to his daughter in 1995. No gift taxes were paid on the gift due to the annual exclusion (gift-splitting was elected and the annual exclusion was $10,000) and the unified transfer tax credit in effect for that year. The ring was worth $50 000 on his date of death.

T's will contained the following provisions:

**a.** To my wife I leave all of the stocks and bonds.

**b.** To my alma mater, State University, I leave $50,000 to establish a chair for a tax professor in the Department of Accounting in the School of Business.

**c.** The residue of my estate is to go to my daughter.

Compute T's estate tax before any credits other than the Federal estate tax credit.

**1-29** *Inheritance Taxes.* This year Bob died, leaving $500,000 to his heirs. His state of residence imposes an inheritance tax. Indicate whether the following statements are true or false and, if false, explain why. Consider using the Internet to find information on how the inheritance tax laws of your state operate.

**a.** The amount of the inheritance tax is $0 since Bob's estate does not exceed the 2010 taxable threshold of $2 million.

**b.** Assume Bob is single. The amount of inheritance tax due from Bob's estate, like the Federal estate tax, is the same regardless of whom he names as the beneficiaries.

**c.** Assume Bob is married. The amount of inheritance tax due from Bob's estate—like the Federal estate tax—is zero if he leaves the entire amount to his surviving spouse or children.

**d.** Any inheritance tax paid by Bob's estate may be used to reduce any Federal estate tax his estate owes.

**1-30** *Excess FICA Taxes.* During 2011 E earned $70,000 of wages from employer X and $50,000 of wages from employer Y. Both employers withheld and paid the appropriate amount of FICA taxes on E's wages. Ignore the temporary reduction in the FICA tax for 2011.

**a.** What is the amount of excess taxes paid by E for 2011?

**b.** Would it make any difference in the amount of E's refund or credit of the excess of FICA taxes if he was a full-time employee of each employer for different periods of the year, as opposed to a full-time employee of X and a part-time employee of Y for the entire year?

**1-31** *Self-Employment Tax.* During 2011 H had earnings from self-employment of $50,000 and wages of $78,000 from employer X. Employer X withheld and paid the appropriate amount of FICA taxes on H's wages. Compute H's self-employment tax liability for 2011. What is the amount of H's income tax deduction for the self-employment taxes paid? Ignore the temporary reduction in the FICA tax for 2011.

**1-32** *Tax Awareness.* Assume that you are currently employed by Corporation X in state A. Without your solicitation, Corporation Y offers you a 20 percent higher salary if you will relocate to state B and become its employee. What tax factors should you consider in making a decision as to the offer?

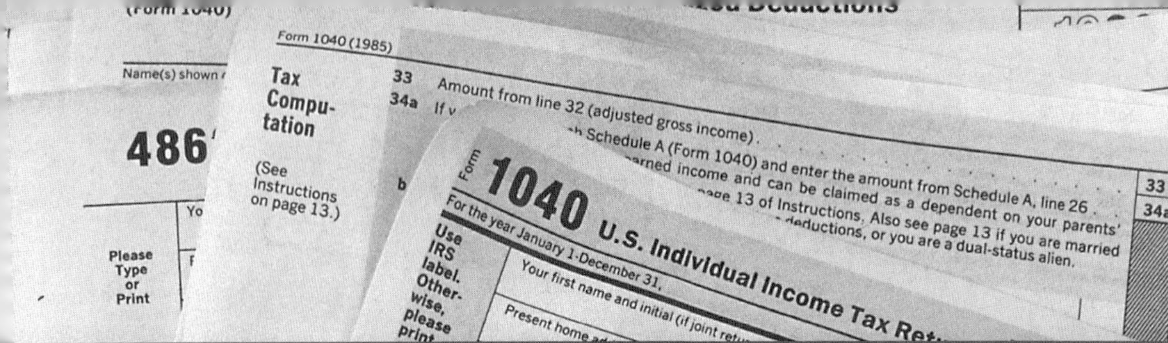


# 2

# Tax Practice and Research

## Learning Objectives

Upon completion of this chapter you will be able to:

- LO.1 Describe the basic features of tax practice: compliance, planning, litigation, and research.
- LO.2 Identify typical career paths in taxation.
- LO.3 Understand the difference between primary and secondary authority.
- LO.4 Understand the composition of statutory authority.
- LO.5 Describe the process in which Federal tax law is enacted and subsequently modified or evaluated by the judiciary.
- LO.6 Understand the significance of the Internal Revenue Code.
- LO.7 Identify the various types of administrative authority.
- LO.8 Understand the judicial system as it relates to tax matters.
- LO.9 Explain secondary authority.
- LO.10 Evaluate the relative strength of various tax authorities.
- LO.11 Understand the importance of communicating the results of tax research.
- LO.12 Explain the key penalties that influence positions taken on tax returns.
- LO.13 Understand the rules of conduct that must be followed by those who perform tax services.
- LO.14 Appreciate the role of ethics in tax practice and the responsibilities of tax practitioners.

## Chapter Outline


| | |
|---|---|
| Introduction | 2-2 |
| Tax Practice in General | 2-2 |
| Taxation as a Professional Career | 2-4 |
| Sources and Applications of Tax Law | 2-5 |
| Primary vs. Secondary Authority | 2-5 |
| Authoritative Sources of Tax Law | 2-6 |
| Statutory Law | 2-6 |
| The Making of a Tax Law | 2-6 |
| Committee Reports | 2-7 |
| Organization of the Internal Revenue Code | 2-9 |
| Tax Treaties | 2-12 |
| Administrative Interpretations | 2-12 |
| Regulations | 2-12 |
| Revenue Rulings | 2-14 |
| Revenue Procedures | 2-15 |
| Letter Rulings | 2-15 |
| Judicial Interpretations | 2-16 |
| Trial Courts | 2-17 |
| Appellate Courts | 2-19 |
| Case Citation | 2-21 |
| Secondary Sources | 2-25 |
| Tax Services | 2-25 |
| Tax Periodicals | 2-26 |

Tax Research 2-26
Obtaining the Facts 2-27
Diagnosing the Issue 2-27
Locating the Authorities 2-28
Evaluating the Authority 2-28
Deriving the Solution 2-31
Communicating the Findings 2-31
Rules of Tax Practice: Responsibilities and Ethics 2-31
Taxpayer Penalties 2-32
Accuracy-Related Penalties 2-33
Economic Substance Doctrine 2-35
Fraud 2-38
Tax Preparer Penalties 2-39
Problem Materials 2-45

## Introduction

Before discussing the rules and regulations that must be applied to determine the taxpayer's tax liability, one should have an appreciation of the nature of tax practice and how to go about finding answers to tax questions. This chapter lays the necessary foundation by first exploring exactly what it is that tax professionals do and the rules of conduct that they must observe while doing it. The chapter concludes by identifying the various sources of tax law and how they may be accessed and used to solve tax questions.

## Tax Practice in General

There are four aspects of tax practice: compliance, planning, litigation, and research. Although these may be thought of as discrete areas, as a practical matter, tax professionals are normally involved in all four.

**LO.1**
Describe the basic features of tax practice: compliance, planning, litigation, and research.

### Tax Compliance

Tax compliance encompasses all of the activities necessary to meet the statutory requirements of the tax law. This largely involves the preparation of the millions of tax returns that must be filed by individuals and other organizations each year. Interestingly, the reliance of individuals on professional return preparation is rather a recent phenomenon. There was a time when most individuals prepared their own returns and H&R Block was unheard of. However, the ever-increasing complexity of the tax law has made professional assistance almost a necessity and in fact created a tax preparation industry. In 2008, 57.7 percent of all the individual tax returns filed were completed by a paid preparer.[1] Tax preparation services are typically performed by Certified Public Accountants (CPAs), attorneys, enrolled agents (individuals who have passed a two-day examination given by the IRS), and commercial tax return preparation services. Until recently, there were no special requirements to be met to become a tax return preparer. Consequently, anyone willing to try his or her hand at mastering the tax law—as well as any shysters who thought there is a buck to be made—could hang out a shingle. However, this all changed in 2010 when the IRS instituted sweeping changes in the rules governing tax return preparers. Before looking at these rules, it should be emphasized that only CPAs, attorneys, and enrolled agents are authorized to practice before the IRS and are therefore able to represent taxpayers beyond the initial audit.

### Tax Return Preparers

After an extensive review that included significant public input, the IRS made fundamental changes in how it regulates the tax return preparation industry. In 2010, the IRS began implementing new regulations and procedures that it believes better serves taxpayers, tax administration and the tax professional industry.[2] The new requirements became effective on January 1, 2011, and include: *mandatory* preparer tax identification numbers (PTINs), continuing education, competency testing, ethical standards and electronic filing. Those who meet all of the requirements are designated as "Registered Tax Return Preparers." These individuals will be limited to preparing individual income tax returns. The IRS plans to issue additional guidance for those preparing other tax returns.

---

[1] See "Tax Statistics at a Glance," IRS Statistics of Income (preliminary data, revised August, 2010) http://www.irs.gov/taxstats

[2] See § 6019 and Reg. § 1.6019-2

*PTIN Requirements.* All tax return preparers who are compensated for preparing, or assisting in the preparation of, all or substantially all of a federal tax return after December 31, 2010 must be registered and have a PTIN. The preparer's PTIN must be disclosed on the return. Prior to the new rules, preparers could use either their social security number or their PTIN but this option no longer exists. Only the PTIN can be use.

The PTIN requirement applies to virtually anyone who prepares or assists in the preparation of a return. The rule extends to attorneys, certified public accountants, and enrolled agents who are compensated for preparing returns. Note that the IRS has indicated that students who have internships with accounting firms and who prepare returns, regardless of their simplicity, must have a PTIN. In contrast, individuals who volunteer and prepare returns as part of the IRS' VITA program (voluntary income tax assistance program) need not have PTINs.

Preparers can obtain a PTIN, using an online sign-up system available through the following website: www.IRS.gov/taxpros. An annual fee of $64.25 is charged. All applicants must be at least 18 years old.

*Competency Testing.* Beginning in 2011, tax return preparers normally must pass a competency test to become a registered tax return preparer. For now there are two tests. The tests generally cover the Form 1040 series returns, Schedules, C, E and F and other 1040 related forms. The IRS plans to add an additional test that covers business returns at a future date.

Tax return preparers, who have PTINs before testing becomes available, have until December 31, 2013 to pass the compctency test. After testing becomes available, new tax return preparers will be required to pass the competency test before they can obtain a PTIN. Attorneys, certified public accountants, and enrolled agents are exempt from the competency test requirement. Enrolled actuaries and enrolled retirement plan agents are exempt from the competency test requirement if they only prepare returns within the limited practice areas of these groups.

*Continuing Education.* In addition to passing a competency test, preparers are subject to a continuing education requirement of 15 hours per year. As of this writing, the start date for the education requirement has not been determined. Courses must include 3 hours of federal tax law updates, 2 hours of ethics, and 10 hours of other federal tax law. The education requirement does not apply to attorneys, certified public accountants, enrolled agents, enrolled actuaries, or enrolled retirement plan agents since all of these are already subject to education requirements to maintain their credentials.

As might be imagined, the day-to-day tasks of those working in the tax compliance area typically surround preparation of a tax return. They collect the appropriate information from the taxpayer and then analyze and evaluate such data for use in preparing the required tax return or other tax filing. But tax compliance goes far beyond merely placing numbers in boxes. In many cases, completion of the return requires tax research to determine the appropriate treatment of a particular item. Preparation of a return may also uncover tax planning opportunities that can be shared with the client to obtain future savings. In addition, tax compliance involves representation of the taxpayer before the IRS during audits and appeals.

## Tax Planning

Perhaps the most rewarding part of tax practice is tax planning and the sense of satisfaction one gets from helping clients minimize their tax liability. As explained in the previous chapter, tax planning is simply the process of arranging one's financial affairs in light of their potential tax consequences. Unlike the weather, taxpayers often have some degree of control over their tax liability, and it is the job of the tax adviser to help the taxpayer whenever possible. A great deal of tax planning is simply an outgrowth of the tax compliance process. Well-trained tax professionals often recognize a situation where a little planning could have brought a more favorable result. In these so-called *closed fact* situations, it is typically too late to do anything until the opportunity once again presents itself, typically the next year. On the other hand, taxpayers about to embark on a transaction—an *open fact* situation—may engage a tax adviser to determine the tax consequences and how to structure the transaction to obtain the most beneficial outcome.

## Tax Litigation

As might be expected, taxpayers and the IRS do not always agree on the tax treatment of a particular item. Many disputes and controversies are settled during an appeals process within the IRS itself. Others, however, are ultimately resolved in a court of law. Tax litigation is a very specialized but often lucrative area of tax practice. In most cases, tax litigation is conducted only by licensed attorneys. However, accountants and others, including the taxpayer himself, can represent the taxpayer in certain situations. In addition, accountants often assist legal counsel and provide litigation support.

### Tax Research

Most practitioners believe that tax research is the most interesting part of tax practice. Tax research is simply the process of obtaining information and synthesizing it to answer a particular tax question. Regardless of the area of tax practice—compliance, planning, or litigation—tax research plays an important part.

Tax research generally involves identifying tax issues, finding relevant information on the issues, and assessing the pertinent authority to arrive at a conclusion. Unfortunately, the law is not so straightforward that the answer to any tax question is readily available. Consequently, being able to do the research is an important skill for anyone involved in tax. For example, a decorator that works out of her home may want to know whether the cost of maintaining a home office can be deducted in computing taxable income. It may seem that a common problem like this could be easily resolved, but it is often much more difficult than might be imagined. To answer this question, the tax adviser may be required to sift through mounds of information—rules, regulations, IRS pronouncements, and court cases—in order to determine the proper treatment. Even if an answer seems apparent, the dynamic nature of the tax law often requires the practitioner to constantly update his or her research to ensure that it is current and has not been changed by some recent development.

## Taxation as a Professional Career

**LO.2**
Identify typical career paths in taxation.

The need for tax advisory services has grown almost exponentially in recent years. The growth is not surprising given the growth in the tax law. In recent years, there have been tax law changes virtually every year. During this time Congress has turned to the tax system again and again to attack not only the country's economic ills but its social problems as well. The end result is a tax law, both Federal and state, that is forever changing and quite complex. Consequently, individuals and organizations have increasingly needed to call upon tax specialists to help them cope with the law. These demands on the tax profession have created tremendous opportunities for those interested in careers in taxation.

The tax specialists of today wear a number of hats. They act as tax consultants as well as business advisers. They help individuals and business owners with tax compliance, keep them informed of changes in the tax law, and assist them in personal financial planning. Tax advisers not only consult on Federal and state income tax matters; they also prepare sales, payroll, and franchise tax returns. Industry and government also employ tax specialists who are involved in planning and compliance. Here are some examples of activities in which the tax specialist might be involved:

- A husband and wife want to transfer their business to their children. Should they sell the business to the kids or would they be better off just giving it to them? A tax specialist can compare the income tax consequences of a sale to that of a gift or bequest and help design the best plan in light of the couple's wishes.
- A taxpayer wants to sell her corporation. Should she sell the stock or cause the corporation to sell its assets? A tax specialist can explain the tax and nontax factors affecting the decision.
- An individual and his son are forming a new business. Should it be operated as a corporation, an S corporation, a partnership, or a limited liability company? A tax specialist can help with the analysis.
- A corporation is planning on opening operations in a foreign country. A tax specialist can help reorganize the company to help minimize U.S. and foreign taxes.
- A corporation is considering the establishment of a retirement plan. A tax adviser who specializes in employee benefits can provide information regarding the tax considerations.
- A taxpayer is seeking a divorce. A tax specialist can explain the tax consequences.

- A corporation and its subsidiaries are thinking about filing a consolidated tax return. The tax specialist can assist the taxpayer in filing such a return, preparing estimated tax payments, or reviewing a corporation's tax returns.
- The IRS wants to deny the taxpayer a deduction for meals and entertainment. The tax specialist might represent an individual during the IRS examination or present oral and written arguments before an IRS appeals conference and (if qualified) before the U.S. Tax Court.

In these and similar matters, the tax specialist is often an important member of the client's professional advisory team and works with other high-caliber individuals to minimize client costs. For example, if a business owner is seeking estate planning advice, the team typically includes the individual's attorney, accountant, life insurance agent, and tax adviser.

Thousands of men and women enjoy successful careers in taxation. They are highly respected as professionals and are well compensated for their work. Those in tax rarely find their jobs boring or dull. Tax work, particularly once one has paid one's dues and built a firm foundation, is interesting and challenging. Moreover, working in a tax department along with other professionals with like interests can be a vastly rewarding personal experience. Tax professionals also serve the public good by raising the standard of tax practice and administration and by working with other groups to improve the tax system.

## Sources and Applications of Tax Law

As stated at the outset of this chapter, before delving into the rules and regulations of taxation, it is important at a minimum to have an appreciation of not only the nature of tax practice but also the sources of the tax law and how they can be used for solving questions. The second half of this chapter identifies the various components of the tax law, explains how they can be accessed, and reviews the basic methods of tax research.

## Primary vs. Secondary Authority

**LO.3**
Understand the difference between primary and secondary authority.

Without doubt, the most important task of a tax professional is answering tax questions. Indeed, tax professionals spend much of their careers—much of their daily lives—determining the tax treatment of some transaction. Unfortunately, the tax law does not provide clear-cut definitive answers to all questions. There is no certainty in these matters. Consequently, in these *gray* areas, the job of the tax professional is not to find the perfect solution but rather to reach an answer that is defensibly or authoritatively correct. In this regard, the type of authority is critical.

In legal matters, like taxation, all "authority" is classified as either primary authority or secondary authority. The distinction is important because in tax controversies, as in any legal dispute, courts normally are obligated to follow primary authority and not secondary authority.

Primary authority generally refers to the written laws passed by the legislative branch of government (e.g., Congress). Primary authority also includes "official" interpretations of these laws. These interpretations include those issued by either the executive branch (e.g., the Treasury Department including the I.R.S) or the judicial branch (the courts). In short, primary authority generally has some official source that courts normally are obligated to follow.

Secondary authority is generally anything other than primary authority. Secondary authority essentially consists of any information that is not issued by the executive, legislative or judicial branches of government. It could be a scholarly article written by a professor or practicing attorney or a book or a treatise. Courts are not required to follow secondary authority. However, courts as well as lawyers and tax professionals often use secondary authority to support their arguments that are rooted in primary authority.

Primary authority and secondary authority are broad classifications of the various types of authority. As might be expected, there are different types of authority within each group. These different types of authority are discussed in detail below.

## Authoritative Sources of Tax Law

Primary authority can be classified into two broad categories: (1) the law, and (2) official interpretations of the law. The law consists primarily of the Constitution, the laws enacted by Congress (the Acts of Congress), and tax treaties. In general, these sources are referred to as the *statutory* law. Most statutory law is written in general terms for a typical situation. Since general rules, no matter how carefully drafted, cannot be written to cover variations on the normal scheme, interpretation is usually required. The task of interpreting the statute is one of the principal duties of the Internal Revenue Service (IRS) as representative of the Secretary of the Treasury. The IRS annually produces thousands of documents that explain and clarify the law. To no one's surprise, however, taxpayers and the government do not always agree on how a particular law should be interpreted. In situations where the taxpayer or the government decides to litigate the question, the courts, as final arbiters, are given the opportunity to interpret the law. These judicial interpretations, administrative interpretations, and the statutory law are considered in detail below.

## Statutory Law

**LO.4**
Understand the composition of statutory authority.

The Constitution of the United States provides the Federal government with the power to tax. Disputes concerning the constitutionality of an income tax levied on taxpayers without apportionment among the states were resolved in 1913 with passage of the Sixteenth Amendment. Between 1913 and 1939, Congress enacted revenue acts that amounted to a complete rewrite of all tax law to date, including the desired changes. In 1939, due primarily to the increasing complexity of the earlier process, Congress codified all Federal tax laws into Title 26 of the *United States Code*, which was then called the *Internal Revenue Code of 1939*. Significant changes in the Federal tax laws were made during World War II and the postwar period of the late 1940s. Each change resulted in amendments to the 1939 Code. By 1954, the codification process had to be repeated in order to organize all additions to the law and to eliminate obsolete provisions. The product of this effort was the *Internal Revenue Code of 1954*. After 1954, Congress took great care to ensure that each new amendment to the 1954 Code was incorporated within its organizational structure with appropriate cross-references to any prior provisions affected by a new law. In 1986, Congress again made substantial revision in the tax law. Consistent with this massive redesign of the 1954 Code, Congress changed the title to the *Internal Revenue Code of 1986*. Like the 1954 Code, the 1986 Code is subject to revisions introduced by a new law. Recent changes incorporated into the 1986 Code include the American Recovery and Reinvestment Tax Act of 2009 and the Worker, Homeownership and Business Assistance Act of 2009.

The legislative provisions contained in the Code are by far the most important component of tax law. Although procedure necessary to enact a law is generally well known, it is necessary to review this process with a special emphasis on taxation. From a tax perspective, the *intention* of Congress in producing the legislation is extremely important since the primary purpose of tax research is to interpret the legislative intent of Congress.

### The Making of a Tax Law

**LO.5**
Describe the process in which Federal tax law is enacted and subsequently modified or evaluated by the judiciary.

Article I, Section 7, Clause 1 of the Constitution provides that the House of Representatives of the U.S. Congress has the basic responsibility for initiating revenue bills.[3] The Ways and Means Committee of the House of Representatives must consider any tax bill before it is presented for vote by the full House of Representatives. On bills of major public interest, the Ways and Means Committee holds public hearings where interested organizations may send representatives to express their views about the bill. The first witness at such hearings is usually the Secretary of the Treasury, representing the President of the United States. In many cases, proposals for new tax legislation or changes in existing legislation come from the President as a part of his political or economic programs.

[3] Tax bills do not originate in the Senate, except when they are attached to other bills.

After the public hearings have been held, the Ways and Means Committee usually goes into closed session, where the Committee prepares the tax bill for consideration by the entire House. The members of the Committee receive invaluable assistance from their highly skilled staff, which includes economists, accountants, and lawyers. The product of this session is a proposed bill that is submitted to the entire House for debate and vote.

After a bill has been approved by the entire House, it is sent to the Senate and assigned to the Senate Finance Committee. The Senate Finance Committee may also hold hearings on the bill before its consideration by the full Senate. The Senate's bill generally differs from the House's bill. In these situations, both versions are sent to the Joint Conference Committee on Taxation, which is composed of members selected from the House Ways and Means Committee and from the Senate Finance Committee. The objective of this Joint Committee is to produce a compromise bill acceptable to both sides. On occasion, when compromise cannot be achieved by the Joint Committee or the compromise bill is unacceptable to the House or the Senate, the bill "dies." If, however, compromise is reached and the Senate and House approve the compromise bill, it is then referred to the President for his or her approval or veto. If the President vetoes the bill, the legislation is "killed" unless two-thirds of both the House and the Senate vote to override the veto. If the veto is overridden, the legislation becomes law.

When a bill is signed into law by the President it is sent to the Office of the Federal Register to be assigned a "public law number." For example, the Tax Reform Act of 1986 is designated P.L. 99-514 and is explained in the following diagram.

Citation P.L. 99- 514

Public Law → P.L.

"99" is the session of Congress that passed the Act → 99-

"514" is the 514th public bill adopted by Congress of that two year session → 514

References to the various laws are often made using their public law numbers. Unfortunately, the public law number does not indicate the year in which the bill was enacted. However, the legislative session in which a public law was enacted can be determined using the following formula:

$$(\text{Session number} \times 2) - 112 = \text{Second year of session}$$

Using this formula, P.L. 99-514 was enacted during the 1985–1986 legislative session ($99 \times 2 = 198 - 112 = 86$). The Tax Relief and Health Care Act of 2006 was P.L. 109-432. Using the formula reveals that this Act was enacted during the 2005–2006 legislative session ($109 \times 2 = 218 - 112 = 106$).

## Committee Reports

At each stage of the legislative process, information is produced that may be useful in assessing the intent of Congress. One of the better sources of Congressional intent is a report issued by the House Ways and Means Committee. This report contains the bill as well as a general explanation. This explanation usually provides the historical background of the proposed legislation along with the reasons for enactment. The Senate Finance Committee also issues a report similar to that of the House. Because the Senate often makes changes in the House version of the bill, the Senate's report is also an important source. Additionally, the Joint Conference Committee on Taxation issues its own report, which is sometimes helpful. Two other sources of intent are the records of the debates on the bill and publications of the initial hearings.

Committee reports and debates appear in several publications. Committee reports are officially published in pamphlet form by the U.S. Government Printing Office as the bill proceeds through Congress. The enacted bill is published in the *Internal Revenue Bulletin* and the *Internal Revenue Cumulative Bulletin*. The debates are published in the *Congressional Record*. In addition to these official government publications, several commercial publishers make this information available to subscribers.

The diagram below illustrates the normal flow of a bill through the legislative process and the documents that are generated in this process.

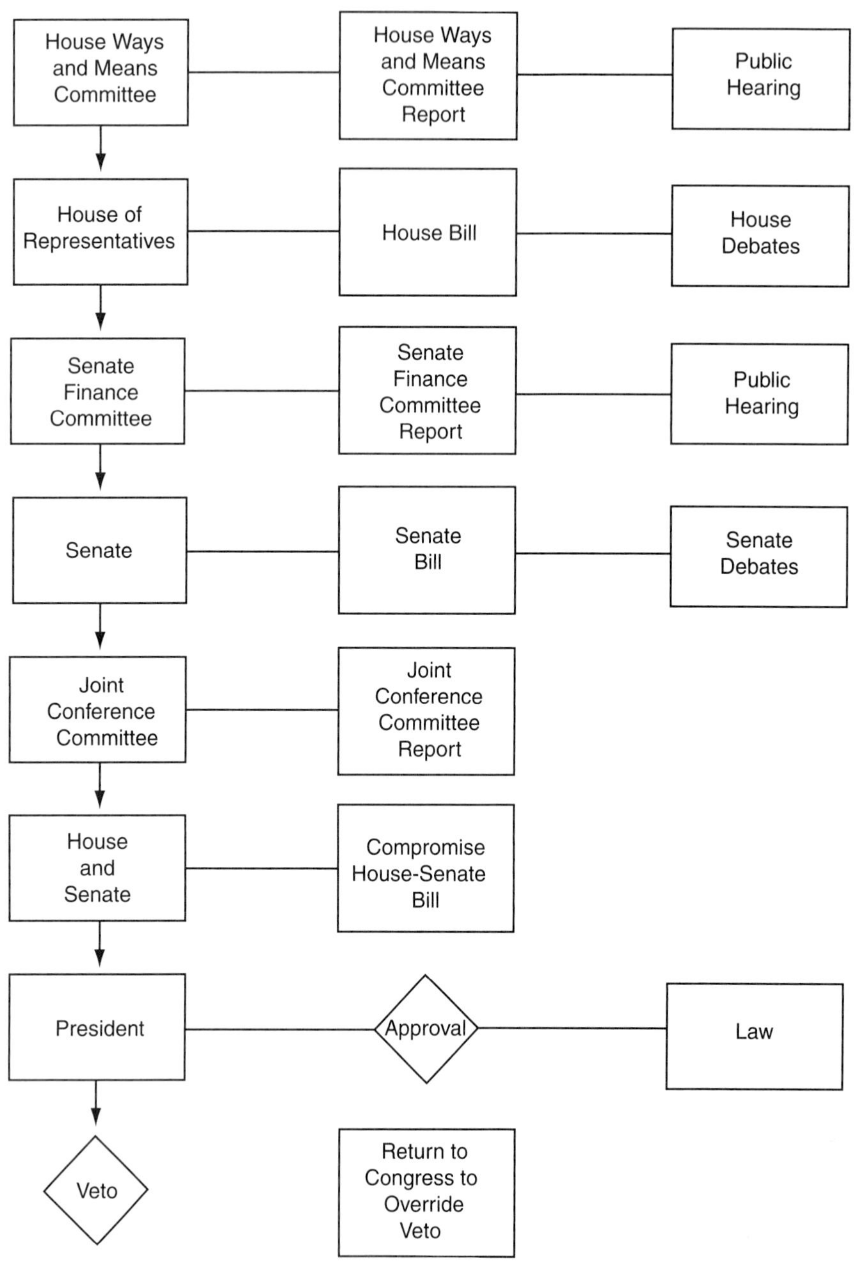

## ORGANIZATION OF THE INTERNAL REVENUE CODE

**LO.6**
Understand the significance of the Internal Revenue Code.

Once a tax bill becomes tax law, it is incorporated into the existing structure of the U.S. federal laws known as the *United States Code*. As mentioned above, the *U.S. Code* is the collection of all laws enacted by Congress. Laws concerning the same subject matter (e.g., taxation) are consolidated in a single "title." As shown in Exhibit 2-1, there are 50 titles. Tax laws are incorporated directly into Title 26 entitled *Internal Revenue Code.*[4]

**EXHIBIT 2.1 United States Code**

| TITLE NUMBER | TITLE NAME | TITLE NUMBER | TITLE NAME |
|---|---|---|---|
| Title 1 | General Provisions | **Title 26** | **Internal Revenue Code** |
| Title 2 | The Congress | Title 27 | Intoxicating Liquors |
| Title 3 | The President | Title 28 | Judiciary and Judicial Procedure |
| Title 4 | Flag and Seal, Seat Of Government, ... | Title 29 | Labor |
| Title 5 | Government Organization and Employees | Title 30 | Mineral Lands and Mining |
| Title 6 | Domestic Security | Title 31 | Money and Finance |
| Title 7 | Agriculture | Title 32 | National Guard |
| Title 8 | Aliens and Nationality | Title 33 | Navigation and Navigable Waters |
| Title 9 | Arbitration | Title 34 | Navy (repealed) |
| Title 10 | Armed Forces | Title 35 | Patents |
| Title 11 | Bankruptcy | Title 36 | Patriotic Societies and Observances |
| Title 12 | Banks and Banking | Title 37 | Pay and Allowances Of the Uniformed Services |
| Title 13 | Census | Title 38 | Veterans' Benefits |
| Title 14 | Coast Guard | Title 39 | Postal Service |
| Title 15 | Commerce and Trade | Title 40 | Public Buildings, Property, and Works |
| Title 16 | Conservation | Title 41 | Public Contracts |
| Title 17 | Copyrights | Title 42 | The Public Health and Welfare |
| Title 18 | Crimes and Criminal Procedure | Title 43 | Public Lands |
| Title 19 | Customs Duties | Title 44 | Public Printing and Documents |
| Title 20 | Education | Title 45 | Railroads |
| Title 21 | Food and Drugs | Title 46 | Shipping |
| Title 22 | Foreign Relations and Intercourse | Title 47 | Telegraphs, Telephones, and Radiotelegraphs |
| Title 23 | Highways | Title 48 | Territories and Insular Possessions |
| Title 24 | Hospitals and Asylums | Title 49 | Transportation |
| Title 25 | Indians | Title 50 | War and National Defense |

Title 26 (the Internal Revenue Code) is further divided as follows:

**Title 26** of the United States Code (referred to as the Internal Revenue Code)
**Subtitle A**—Income Taxes
**Chapter 1**—Normal Taxes and Surtaxes
**Subchapter A**—Determination of Tax Liability
**Part I**—Tax on Individuals
**Sections**—1 through 5

Exhibit 2-2 reveals the contents of the various subdivisions. As a practical matter, virtually all of a tax practitioner's work is done in Subtitle A, Chapter 1, which deals with

[4] All future use of the term Code or Internal Revenue Code refers to the *Internal Revenue Code of 1986*, as amended.

**EXHIBIT 2.2** **Internal Revenue Code: Subtitles, Chapters and Subchapters**

| Subtitle | Subject | First Code Section |
|---|---|---|
| Subtitle A | Income Taxes | § 1 |
| Subtitle B | Estate and Gift Taxes | § 2001 |
| Subtitle C | Employment Taxes | § 3101 |
| Subtitle D | Miscellaneous Excise Taxes | § 4001 |
| Subtitle E | Alcohol, Tobacco, and Certain Other Excise Taxes | § 5001 |
| Subtitle F | Procedure and Administration | § 6001 |
| Subtitle G | The Joint Committee on Taxation | § 8001 |
| Subtitle H | Financing of Presidential Election Campaigns | § 9001 |
| Subtitle I | Trust Fund Code | § 9501 |

| Chapters in Subtitle A | Name | First Code Section |
|---|---|---|
| 1 | Income Taxes | § 1 |
| 2 | Tax on Self-Employment Income | § 1401 |
| 3 | Withholding of Tax on Nonresident Aliens and Foreign Corporations | § 1441 |
| 4 | [Repealed] | |
| 5 | [Repealed] | § 1491 |
| 6 | Consolidated Returns | § 1501 |

| Selected Subchapters of Chapter 1 | Name | Code Sections |
|---|---|---|
| A | Determination of Tax Liability | §§ 1-59B |
| B | Computation of Taxable Income | §§ 61-291 |
| C | Corporate Distributions and Adjustments | §§ 301-385 |
| D | Deferred Compensation, etc. | §§ 401-436 |
| E | Accounting Periods and Methods of Accounting | §§ 441-483 |
| F | Exempt Organizations | §§ 501-530 |
| G | Corporations Used to Avoid Income Tax on Shareholders | §§ 531-565 |
| H | Banking Institutions | §§ 581-597 |
| I | Natural Resources | §§ 611-638 |
| J | Estates, Trusts, Beneficiaries, and Decedents | §§ 641-692 |
| K | Partners and Partnerships | §§ 701-777 |
| L | Insurance Companies | §§ 801-848 |
| M | Regulated Investment Companies and Real Estate Investment Trusts | §§ 851-860L |
| N | Tax Based on Income From Sources Within or Without the United States | §§ 861-999 |
| O | Gain or Loss on Disposition of Property | §§ 1001-1111 |
| P | Capital Gains and Losses | §§ 1201-1298 |
| S | Tax Treatment of S Corporations and Their Shareholders | §§ 1361-1379 |

income taxes. Note that subtitles are further divided into chapters, subchapters, parts, subparts and finally the most important element: sections.

The most critical portions of the Internal Revenue Code are its "sections." The sections contain the laws—often referred to as provisions or rules—that a taxpayer must follow to determine taxable income and ultimately the final tax liability. For example, the starting point in determining taxable income is gross income and Code Section 61 provides the definition of gross income as follows: income. Section 61 appears below.

*Section 61: Gross Income Defined*

**(a)** *General definition. Except as otherwise provided in this subtitle (A), gross income means all income from whatever source derived, including (but not limited to) the following items:*

**(1)** *Compensation for services, including fees, commissions, fringe benefits, and similar items;*
**(2)** *Gross income derived from business;*
**(3)** *Gains derived from dealings in property*
**(4)** *Interest*
**(5)** *Rents*

.
.
.

**(14)** *Income in respect of a decedent and*
**(15)** *Income from an interest in an estate or trust.*

The ability to use the Internal Revenue Code is essential for all individuals who have any involvement with the tax laws.

When working with the tax law, it is often necessary to make reference to, or *cite*, a particular source with respect to the Code. The *section* of the Code is the source normally cited. A complete citation for a section of the Code would be too cumbersome. For instance, a formal citation for Section 1 of the Code would be "Subtitle A, Chapter 1, Subchapter A, Part I, Section 1." In most cases, citation of the section alone is sufficient. Sections are numbered consecutively throughout the Code so that each section number is used only once. Currently the numbers run from Section 1 through Section 9833. Not all section numbers are used, so that additional ones may be added by Congress in the future without the need for renumbering.[5]

Citation of a particular Code section in tax literature ordinarily does not require the prefix "Internal Revenue Code" because it is generally understood that, unless otherwise stated, references to section numbers concern the Internal Revenue Code of 1986 as amended. However, since most Code sections are divided into subparts, reference to a specific subpart requires more than just its section number. Section 170(a)(2)(B) serves as an example.

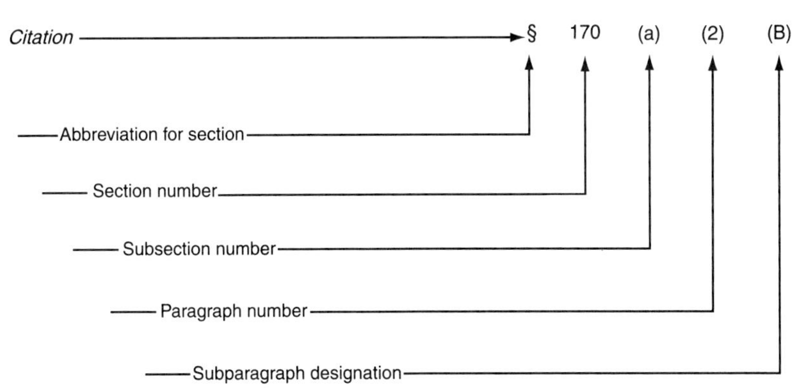


All footnote references used throughout this text are made in the form given above. In most cases, the "§" or "§§" symbols are used in place of the terms "section" or "sections," respectively.

Single-volume or double-volume editions of the Internal Revenue Code are published after every major change in the law. Private publishing companies such as

[5] It is interesting to note that when it adopted the 1954 Code, Congress deliberately left section numbers unassigned to provide room for future additions. Recently, however, Congress has been forced to identify new sections by alphabetical letters following a particular section number. See, for example, Sections 280, 280A, 280B, and 280C of the 1986 Code.

Commerce Clearing House, Inc. (CCH) and the Research Institute of America (RIA) publish these editions as well as a wealth of other tax information. All of this tax information is included in so-called tax services—massive tax libraries—compiled and published by these companies and others. The major tax services, all available electronically, are discussed in a later section of this chapter.

### TAX TREATIES

The laws contained in tax treaties represent the third and final component of the statutory law. Tax treaties (also referred to as tax conventions) are agreements between the United States and other countries that provide rules governing the taxation of residents of one country by another. For example, the tax treaty between the United States and France indicates how the French government taxes U.S. citizens residing in France and vice versa. Tax treaties, as law, have the same authority as those laws contained in the Code.[6] Treaty provisions may override provisions of the Internal Revenue Code if the treaty was signed after August 16, 1954.[7] For this reason, persons involved with an international tax question must be aware of tax treaties and recognize that the Code may be superseded by a tax treaty.

## Administrative Interpretations

**LO.7**
Identify the various types of administrative authority.

After Congress has enacted a tax law, the Executive branch of the Federal government has the responsibility for enforcing it. In the process of enforcing the law, the Treasury interprets, clarifies, defines, and analyzes the Code in order to apply Congressional intention of the law to the specific facts of a taxpayer's situation. This process results in numerous administrative releases, such as regulations, rulings, procedures and other pronouncements discussed below.

### REGULATIONS

Regulations are the Treasury's official interpretation of the Internal Revenue Code. To illustrate, consider the problem of a couple who discovered $4,467 of old currency in a piano seven years after they purchased it at an auction for $15.[8] Is this taxable income? Note that the definition of gross income contained in § 61 above provides little guidance, indicating only that "income is income from whatever source derived." However, one of the regulations explaining what constitutes gross income, Reg. § 1.61-14, indicates that buried treasure is to be included in income. Other regulations concerning gross income discuss in detail the treatment of such items as dividends, interest and rents. The major purpose of the regulations is to interpret, explain, clarify and elaborate on the various provisions of the Internal Revenue Code.

Code § 7805(a) authorizes the Secretary of the Treasury to "prescribe all needful rules and regulations for the enforcement of this title, including all rules and regulations as may be necessary of any alteration of law in relation to internal revenue." Section 7805(b) provides authority to the Secretary to prescribe the extent, if any, to which any ruling or regulation relating to the internal revenue laws will be applied without retroactive effect. In most cases the Secretary delegates the power to write the regulations to the Commissioner of the Internal Revenue Service. In practice, this means that the regulations are written by the technical staff of the IRS or by the office of the Chief Counsel of the IRS, an official who is also an assistant General Counsel of the Treasury Department.

#### Final and Proposed Regulations

Regulations are issued in the form of *Treasury Decisions* (often referred to as TDs), which are published in the *Federal Register* and sometimes later in the *Internal Revenue Bulletin*. The *Federal Register* is the official publication for regulations and legal notices issued by the

---

[6] See Code § 7852(d)(1).

[7] § 7852(d)(2).

[8] *Ermenegildo Cesarini v. U.S.*, 69-1 USTC ¶9270, 23 AFTR 2d 69-997, 296 F Supp 3 (DC-OH, 1969).

executive branch of the Federal government. The *Federal Register* is published every business day. Before a TD is published in final form, it must be issued in proposed form, a *proposed regulation*, for a period of at least 30 days before it is scheduled to become final.

Upon publication, interested parties have at least 30 days to comment on proposed regulations. In addition, public hearings are often scheduled. In theory, at the end of this comment period, the Treasury responds in any one of three ways; it may withdraw the proposed regulation, amend it, or leave it unchanged. In the latter two cases, the Treasury normally issues the regulation in its final form as a TD, published in the *Federal Register*. The final version of any given regulation is quite frequently significantly different from the proposed version.

Afterwards, the new regulation is included in Title 26 of the *Code of Federal Regulations*. In fact, however, proposed regulations sometimes remain in proposed form for many years. Proposed regulations do not have the force of law and are not the Treasury's official position on a particular issue.

## Temporary Regulations

The National Office of the Treasury issues temporary regulations as the need arises. Often such regulations are issued in response to substantive changes in the tax law when tax practitioners, in particular, need immediate guidance in applying a new or revised statute. Such regulations usually deal with immediate filing requirements or details regarding a mandated accounting method change. Temporary regulations are effective immediately without the comment period. This is true even though temporary regulations normally are also issued as proposed regulations which are subject to the comment period. Temporary regulations expire three years after issuance and are given the same respect and precedential value as final regulations.

The primary purpose of the regulations is to explain and interpret particular Code sections. Although regulations have not been issued for all Code sections, they have been issued for the great majority. In those cases where regulations exist, they are an important authoritative source on which one can usually rely. Regulations can be classified into three groups: (1) legislative; (2) interpretive; and (3) procedural.

## Legislative Regulations

Occasionally, Congress will give specific authorization to the Secretary of the Treasury to issue regulations on a particular Code section. For example, under § 1502, the Secretary is charged with prescribing the regulations for the filing of a consolidated return by an affiliated group of corporations. There are virtually no Code sections governing consolidated returns, and the regulations in effect serve in lieu of the Code. In this case and others where it occurs, the regulation has the force and effect of a law, with the result that a court reviewing the regulation usually will not substitute its judgment for that of the Treasury Department unless the Treasury has clearly abused its discretion.[9]

## Interpretative Regulations

Interpretative regulations explain the meaning of a Code section and commit the Treasury and the Internal Revenue Service to a particular position relative to the Code section in question. This type of regulation is binding on the IRS but not on the courts, although it is "a body of experience and informed judgment to which courts and litigants may properly resort for guidance."[10] Interpretive regulations have considerable authority and normally are invalidated only if they are inconsistent with the Code or are unreasonable.

## Procedural Regulations

Procedural regulations cover such areas as the information a taxpayer must supply to the IRS and the internal management and conduct of the IRS in certain matters. Those regulations affecting vital interests of the taxpayers are generally binding on the IRS, and those regulations stating the taxpayer's obligation to file particular forms or other types of information are given the effect of law.

---

[9] *Anderson, Clayton & Co. v. U.S.*, 77-2 USTC ¶9727, 40 AFTR2d 77-6102, 562 F.2d 972 (CA-5, 1977), Cert. den. at 436 U.S. 944 (USSC, 1978).

[10] *Skidmore v. Swift and Co.*, 323 U.S. 134 (USSC, 1944).

### Citation for Regulations

Regulations are arranged in the same sequence as the Code sections they interpret. Thus, a regulation begins with a number that designates the type of tax or administrative, definitional, or procedural matter and is followed by the applicable Code section number. For example, Treasury Regulation Section 1.614-3(f)(5) below is as an illustration of how regulations are cited throughout this text.

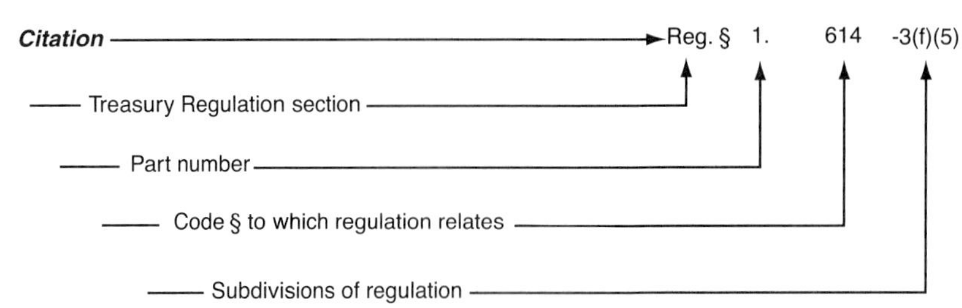


If a regulation is proposed, the word "Prop." is added prior to the word "Treas." or more simply, Prop. Reg. An example is Prop. Reg. § 1.280A-1. Similarly, for a temporary regulation the word "Temp." is usually added and the letter "T" follows the number of the regulation such as Temp. Reg. § 1.67-4T.

The part number of a Treasury regulation is used to identify the general area covered by the regulation as follows:

| *Part Number* | *Law Subject* |
|---|---|
| 1 | Income Tax |
| 20 | Estate Tax |
| 25 | Gift Tax |
| 31 | Employment Tax |
| 48–49 | Excise Tax |
| 301 | Procedural Matters |

The various subdivisions of a regulation are not necessarily related to a specific subdivision of the Code.

Treasury often issues temporary regulations when it is necessary to meet a compelling need such as shortly after enactment of a major change in the tax law. These temporary regulations have the same binding effect as final regulations until they are withdrawn or replaced.

Temporary regulations should not be confused with proposed regulations. The latter have no force or effect.[11] Nevertheless, proposed regulations provide insight into how the IRS currently interprets a particular Code section. For this reason, they should not be ignored.

## Revenue Rulings

Revenue rulings also are official interpretations of the Federal tax laws and are issued by the National Office of the IRS. Revenue rulings do not have quite the authority of regulations, however. Regulations are a direct extension of the law-making powers of Congress, whereas revenue rulings are an application of the administrative powers of the Internal Revenue Service. In contrast to rulings, regulations are usually issued only after public hearings and must be approved by the Secretary of the Treasury.

Unlike regulations, revenue rulings are limited to a given set of facts. For example, in Rev. Rul. 97-9, the IRS addressed whether the provision that concerns medical expenses, § 213, allowed a deduction for the costs of controlled substances such as marijuana when used for medical care. The ruling evaluated § 213 as it applied to this specific set of facts and held that because such purchases were in violation of Federal law they were not deductible.

---

[11] Federal law (i.e., the Administrative Procedure Act) requires any federal agency, including the Internal Revenue Service, that wishes to adopt a substantive rule to publish the rule in proposed form in order to give interested persons an opportunity to comment. Proposed regulations are issued in compliance with this directive.

Taxpayers may rely on revenue rulings in determining the tax consequences of their transactions; however, taxpayers must determine for themselves if the facts of their cases are substantially the same as those set forth in the revenue ruling.

Revenue rulings are published in the weekly issues of the *Internal Revenue Bulletin*. The information contained in the *Internal Revenue Bulletins* (including, among other things, revenue rulings) is accumulated and usually published semiannually in the *Cumulative Bulletin*. The *Cumulative Bulletin* reorganizes the material according to Code section. Citations for the *Internal Revenue Bulletin* and the *Cumulative Bulletin* are illustrated below.

## Revenue Procedures

Revenue procedures are statements reflecting the internal management practices of the IRS that affect the rights and duties of taxpayers. Occasionally they are also used to announce procedures to guide individuals in dealing with the IRS or to make public something the IRS believes should be brought to the attention of taxpayers. For example, each year the IRS announces the rate at which business mileage can be deducted (e.g., Rev. Proc. 2009-54 provides that the rate for 2010 is 50 cents per mile).

Revenue procedures are published in the weekly *Internal Revenue Bulletins* and bound in the *Cumulative Bulletin* along with revenue rulings issued in the same year. The citation system for revenue procedures is the same as for revenue rulings except that the prefix "Rev. Proc." is substituted for "Rev. Rul."

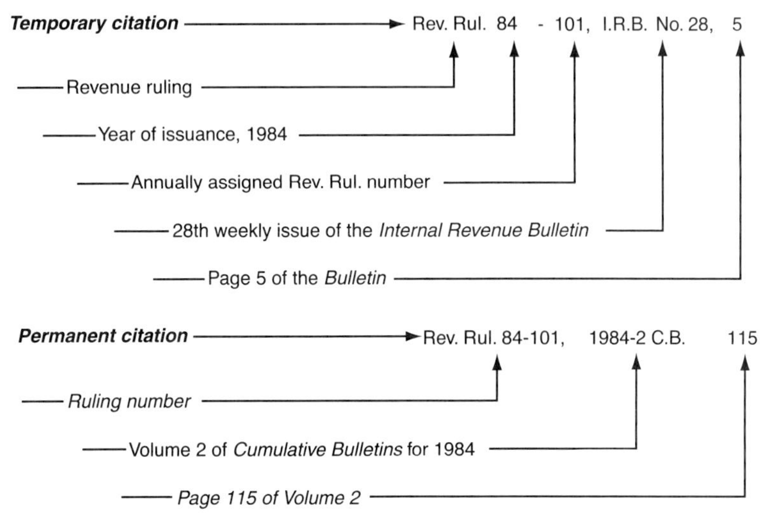


## Letter Rulings

The term *letter ruling* actually encompasses three different types of rulings: private letter rulings, determination letters, and technical advice memoranda. These items are not published in an official government publication but are available from commercial sources.

### Private Letter Ruling

Taxpayers who are in doubt about the tax consequences of a contemplated transaction can ask the National Office of the IRS for a ruling. Generally, the IRS has discretion about whether to rule or not, and it has issued guidelines describing the circumstances under which it will rule.[12]

Unlike revenue rulings, private letter rulings apply only to the particular taxpayer asking for the ruling and are thus not applicable to taxpayers in general. Section 6110(j)(3) specifically states that "unless the Secretary otherwise establishes by regulations, a written determination may not be used or cited as a precedent." Recently, however, the IRS has

[12] See Rev. Proc. 2009-3, 2009-1 I.R.B. 107 for a description of the areas in which the IRS has refused to issue advanced rulings. Note, also, that the IRS is required to charge taxpayers a fee for letter rulings, opinion letters, determination letters, and similar requests. A sense of the various fees charged can be found in Rev. Proc. 2009-1, 2009-1 IRB 1 248, (Appendix A). See § 6591.

expanded the list of authorities constituting "substantial" authority for Section 6662 purposes to include private letter rulings. As discussed in the previous section, § 6662 imposes an accuracy-related penalty equal to 20 percent of the underpayment unless the taxpayer can cite "substantial authority" for his or her position.

For those requesting a ruling, the IRS's response might provide insurance against surprises. As a practical matter, a favorable ruling should preclude any controversies with the IRS on an audit of that transaction, at least with respect to the matters addressed in the private letter ruling. During the process of obtaining a private letter ruling, the IRS often recommends changes in a proposed transaction to assist the taxpayer in achieving the tax result he or she wishes. Since 1976, the IRS has made individual private letter rulings publicly available after deleting names and other information that would tend to identify the taxpayer. Private letter rulings are published by both CCH and RIA.

### Determination Letter

A determination letter is similar to a private letter ruling, except that it is issued by the office of the local IRS district director, rather than by the National Office. Unlike private letter rulings, determination letters usually relate to completed transactions. Like private letter rulings, they are not published in any official government publication but are available commercially. In most instances, determination letters deal with issues and transactions that are not overtly controversial. Obtaining a determination letter in order to ensure that a pension plan is qualified is a typical use of a determination letter.

### Technical Advice Memorandum

A technical advice memorandum ("tech advice") is typically requested by an IRS agent during an audit. The request is normally made to the National Office when the agent has a question that cannot be answered by sources in his or her local office. The technical advice memorandum only applies to the taxpayer for whose audit the technical advice was requested and cannot be relied upon by other taxpayers. Technical advice memoranda are available from private publishers but are not published by the government.

Citations for letter rulings and technical advice follow a multi-digit file number system. IRS Letter Ruling 200434039 serves as an example.

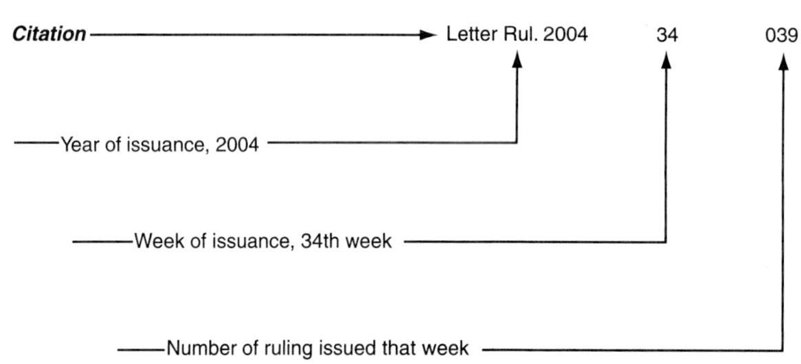


## Judicial Interpretations

**LO.8**
Understand the judicial system as it relates to tax matters.

Although Congress passes the tax law and the Executive branch of the Federal government enforces and interprets it, under the American system of checks and balances, it is the Judiciary branch that ultimately determines whether the Executive branch's interpretation is correct. This provides yet another source of tax law—court decisions. It is therefore absolutely essential for the student of tax as well as the tax practitioner to have a grasp of the judicial system of the United States and how tax cases move through this system.

Before litigating a case in court, the taxpayer must have exhausted the administrative remedies available to him or her within the Internal Revenue Service. If the taxpayer has not exhausted his or her administrative remedies, a court will deny a hearing because the claim filed in the court is premature.

All litigation begins in what are referred to as *courts of original jurisdiction*, or *trial courts*, which "try" the case. There are three trial courts: (1) the Tax Court; (2) the U.S. District Court; and (3) the U.S. Court of Federal Claims. Note that the taxpayer may select any one (and only one) of these three courts to hear the case. If the taxpayer or government disagrees with the decision by the trial court, it has the right to appeal to either the U.S. Court of Appeals or the U.S. Court of Appeals for the Federal Circuit, whichever is appropriate in the particular case. If a litigating party is dissatisfied with the decision by the appellate court, it may ask for review by the Supreme Court, but this is rarely granted. The judicial system is illustrated and discussed on the following page.

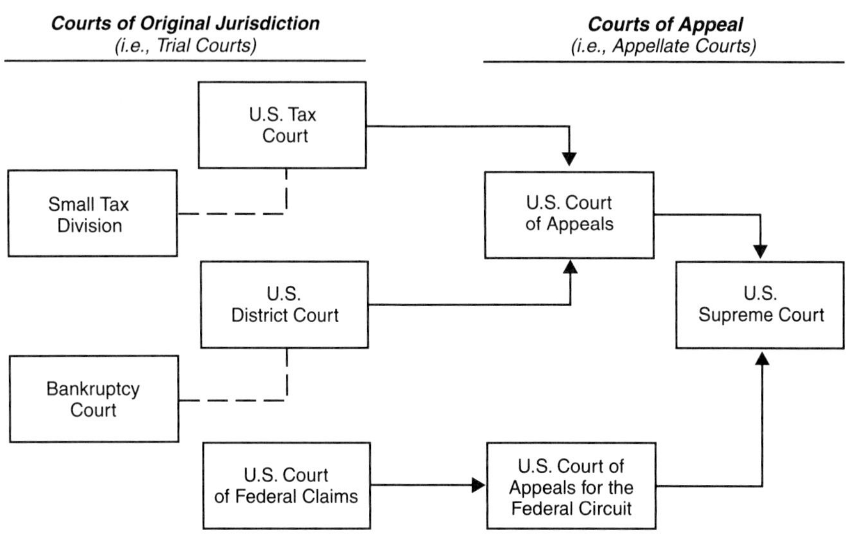


## TRIAL COURTS

### U.S. Tax Court

The Tax Court, as its name suggests, specializes in tax matters and hears no other types of cases. The judges on the court are especially skilled in taxation. Usually, prior to being selected as a judge by the President, the individual was a practitioner or IRS official who was noted for his or her expertise. This Court is composed of 19 judges who "ride circuit" throughout the United States (i.e., they travel and hear cases in various parts of the country as can be seen in the map contained in Exhibit 2-3). Occasionally, the full Tax Court hears a case, but most cases are heard by a single judge who submits his or her opinion to the chief judge, who then decides whether the full court should review the decision.

Besides its expertise in tax matters, two other characteristics of the Tax Court should be noted. Perhaps the most important feature of the Tax Court is that the taxpayer does not pay the alleged tax deficiency before bringing his or her action before the court. The second facet of the Tax Court that bears mentioning is that a trial by jury is not available.

### U.S. District Courts

For purposes of the Federal judicial system, the United States is divided into 11 geographic areas called circuits, which are subdivided into districts. For example, the second circuit, which is composed of Vermont, Connecticut, and New York, contains the District Court for the Southern District of New York, which covers parts of New York City. Other districts may include very large areas, such as the District Court for the State of Arizona, which covers the entire state. A taxpayer may take a case into the District Court for the district in which he or she resides, but only after the disputed tax deficiency has been paid. The taxpayer then sues the IRS for a refund of the disputed amount. The District Court is a court of general jurisdiction and hears many types of cases in addition to tax cases. This is the only court in which the taxpayer may obtain a jury trial. The jury decides matters of fact but not matters of law. However, even in issues of fact, the judge may, and occasionally does, disregard the jury's decision.

## U.S. Court of Federal Claims

The United States Court of Federal Claims hears cases involving certain claims against the Federal government, including tax refunds. The Court is made up of 16 judges and usually meets in Washington, D.C. A taxpayer must pay the disputed tax deficiency before bringing an action in this court, and may not obtain a jury trial. Appeals from the U.S. Court of Federal Claims are taken to the U.S. Court of Appeals for the Federal Circuit.

The chart below illustrates the position of the taxpayer in bringing an action in these courts.

## Small Claims Cases

When the amount of tax and penalties or a claim for refund are $50,000 per year or less, the taxpayer may elect to submit the case to the division of the Tax Court hearing small claims cases, called the Small Tax Division of the Tax Court. This procedure allows a taxpayer to obtain a decision with a minimum of formality, delay, and expense. However, the taxpayer loses the right to appeal the decision. The Small Tax Division is administered by the chief judge of the Tax Court, who is authorized to assign small claims cases to special trial judges. These cases receive priority on the trial calendars, and relatively informal rules are followed whenever possible. The special trial judges' opinions are published on these cases, but the decisions are not reviewed by any other court or treated as precedents in any other case.

## Bankruptcy Court

Under limited circumstances, it is possible for the bankruptcy court to have jurisdiction over tax matters. The filing of a bankruptcy petition prevents creditors, including the IRS, from taking action against a taxpayer, including the filing of a proceeding before the Tax Court if a notice of deficiency is sent after the filing of a petition in bankruptcy. In such cases, a tax claim may be determined by the bankruptcy court.

| | *U.S. Tax Court* | *U.S. District Court* | *U.S. Court of Federal Claims* |
|---|---|---|---|
| *Jurisdiction* | Nationwide | Specific district in which court is sitting | Nationwide |
| *Subject Matter* | Tax cases only | Many different types of cases, both criminal and civil | Claims against the Federal government, including tax refunds |
| *Payment of Contested Amount* | Taxpayer does not pay deficiency, but files suit against IRS Commissioner to stop collection of tax | Taxpayer pays alleged deficiency and then files suit against the U.S. government for refund | Taxpayer pays alleged deficiency and then files suit against the U.S. government for refund |
| *Availability of Jury Trial* | No | Yes | No |
| *Appeal Taken to* | U.S. Court of Appeals | U.S. Court of Appeals | U.S. Court of Appeals for the Federal Circuit |
| *Number of Courts* | 1 | 95 | 1 |
| *Number of Judges per Court* | 19 | 1 | 16 |

## Appellate Courts

### U.S. Courts of Appeals

Which appellate court is appropriate depends on which trial court hears the case. Taxpayer or government appeals from the District Courts and the Tax Court are taken to the U.S. Court of Appeals that has jurisdiction over the court in which the taxpayer lives. Appeals from the U.S. Court of Federal Claims are taken to the U.S. Court of Appeals for the Federal Circuit, which has the same powers and jurisdictions as any of the other Courts of Appeals except that it only hears specialized appeals. Courts of Appeals are national courts of appellate jurisdiction. With the exceptions of the Court of Appeals for the Federal Circuit and the Court of Appeals for the District of Columbia, these appellate courts are assigned various geographic areas of jurisdiction as shown in the map in Exhibit 2-3 and in the table below.

| *Court of Appeals for the Federal Circuit (CA-FC)* | *District of Columbia Circuit (CA-DC)* | *First Circuit (CA-1)* |
|---|---|---|
| U.S. Court of Federal Claims | District of Columbia | Maine |
| | | Massachusetts |
| | | New Hampshire |
| | | Puerto Rico |
| | | Rhode Island |

| *Second Circuit (CA-2)* | *Third Circuit (CA-3)* | *Fourth Circuit (CA-4)* | *Fifth Circuit (CA-5)* | *Sixth Circuit (CA-6)* |
|---|---|---|---|---|
| Connecticut | Delaware | Maryland | Louisiana | Kentucky |
| New York | New Jersey | N. Carolina | Mississippi | Michigan |
| Vermont | Pennsylvania | S. Carolina | Texas | Ohio |
| | Virgin Islands | Virginia | | Tennessee |
| | | W. Virginia | | |

| *Seventh Circuit (CA-7)* | *Eighth Circuit (CA-8)* | *Ninth Circuit (CA-9)* | *Tenth Circuit (CA-10)* | *Eleventh Circuit (CA-11)* |
|---|---|---|---|---|
| Illinois | Arkansas | Alaska | Colorado | Alabama |
| Indiana | Iowa | Arizona | New Mexico | Florida |
| Wisconsin | Minnesota | California | Kansas | Georgia |
| | Missouri | Guam | Oklahoma | |
| | Nebraska | Hawaii | Utah | |
| | N. Dakota | Idaho | Wyoming | |
| | S. Dakota | Montana | | |
| | | Nevada | | |
| | | Oregon | | |
| | | Washington | | |

Taxpayers may appeal to the Courts of Appeal as a matter of right, and the Courts must hear their cases. Very often, however, the expense of such an appeal deters many from proceeding with an appeal. Appellate courts review the record of the trial court to determine whether the lower court completed its responsibility of fact finding and applied the proper law in arriving at its decision.

District Courts must follow the decision of the Appeals Court for the circuit in which they are located. For instance, the District Court in the Eastern District of Missouri must follow the decision of the Eighth Circuit Court of Appeals because Missouri is in the Eighth Circuit. If the Eighth Circuit has not rendered a decision on the particular issue involved, then the District Court may make its own decision or follow the decision in another Circuit.

The Tax Court is a national court with jurisdiction throughout the entire country. Prior to 1970, the Tax Court considered itself independent and indicated that it would not be bound by the decisions of the Circuit Court to which its decision would be appealed. In *Golsen*,[13] however, the Tax Court reversed its position. Under the *Golsen rule*, the Tax Court now follows the decisions of the Circuit Court to which a particular case would be appealed. Even if the Tax Court disagrees with a Circuit Court's view, it will decide based upon the Circuit

---

[13] *Jack E. Golsen*. 54 T.C. 742 (1970).

**EXHIBIT 2.3** **United State Tax Court: Places of Trial and U.S. Courts of Appeals**

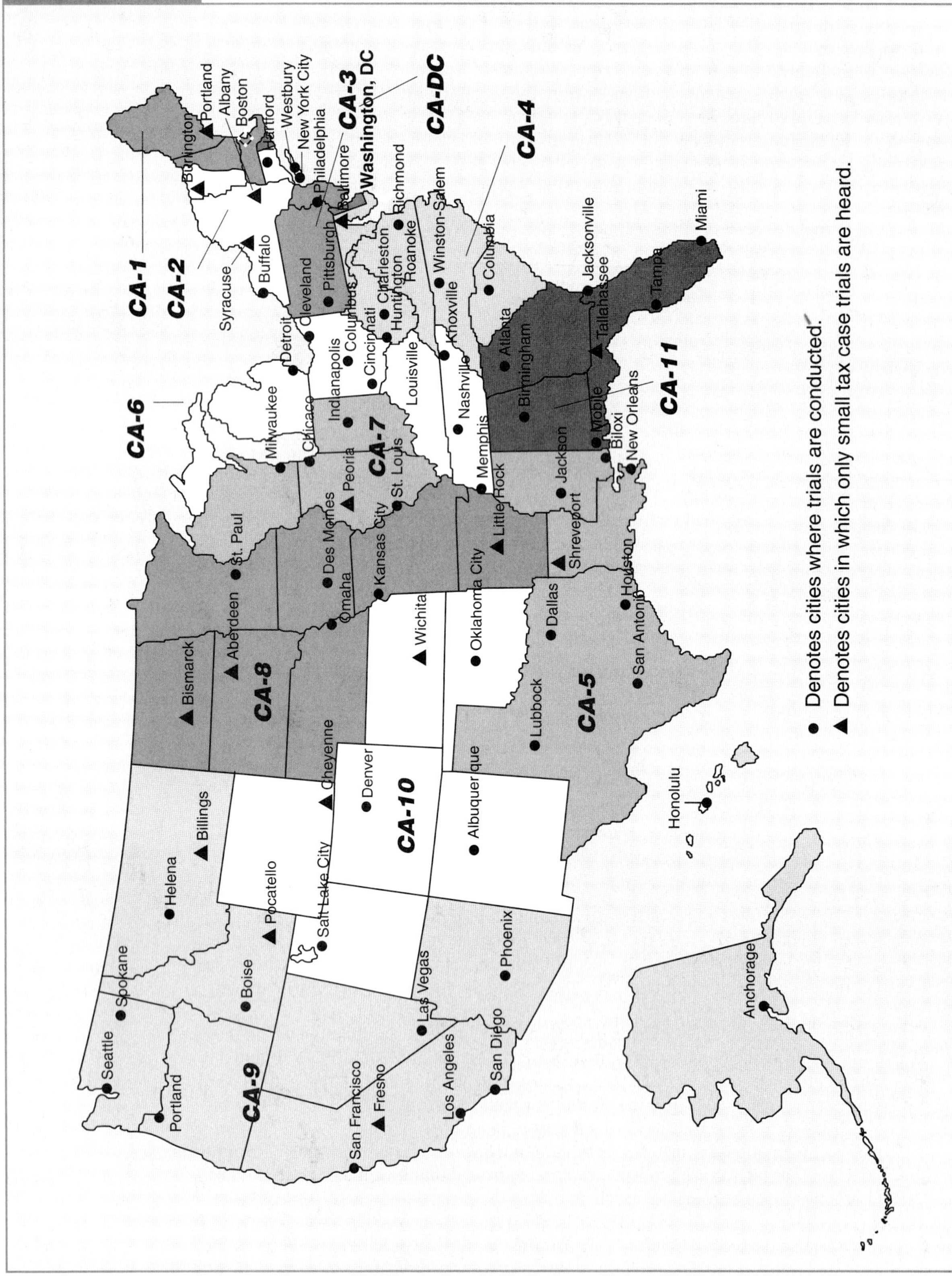

Court's view. On the other hand, if a similar case arises in the jurisdiction of another Circuit Court that has not yet ruled on the same issue, the Tax Court will follow its own view, despite its earlier decision following a contrary Circuit Court decision.

The U.S. Courts of Appeals generally sit in panels of three judges, although the entire court may sit in particularly important cases. They may reach a decision that affirms the lower court or that reverses the lower court. Additionally, the Appellate Court could send the case back to the lower court (remand the case) for another trial or for rehearing on another point not previously covered. It is possible for the Appellate Court to affirm the decision of the lower court on one particular issue and reverse it on another.

Generally, only one judge writes a decision for the Appeals Court, although in some cases no decision is written and an order is simply made. Such an order might hold that the lower court is sustained, or that the lower court's decision is reversed as being inconsistent with one of the Appellate Court's decisions. Sometimes other judges (besides the one assigned to write the opinion) will write additional opinions agreeing with (concurring opinion) or disagreeing with (dissenting opinion) the majority opinion. These opinions often contain valuable insights into the law controlling the case, and often set the ground for a change in the court's opinion at a later date.

### U.S. Supreme Court

The U.S. Supreme Court is the highest court in the U.S. judicial system. No one has a *right* to be heard by this Court. It only accepts cases it wishes to hear, and generally those involve issues that the Court feels are of national importance. The Supreme Court generally hears very few tax cases. Consequently, taxpayers desiring a review of their trial court decision find it solely at the Court of Appeals. Cases that are appealed to the Supreme Court are submitted through a request process known as the "Writ of Certiorari." Certiorari is a Latin word meaning "to be informed of." Thus the Writ of Certiorari informs the Supreme Court of the losing party's desire to have the case reviewed. If the Supreme Court decides to hear the case, it grants the Writ of Certiorari; if not, it denies the Writ of Certiorari. In a citation, the Court's refusal to review the case is indicated by "cert. den." If certiorari is granted, it would be reflected in the fact that the court issued a decision. It is important to note that there is another path to review by the U.S. Supreme Court—*by appeal*—as opposed to by Writ of Certiorari. This "review by appeal" may be available when a U.S. Court of Appeals has held that a state statute is in conflict with the laws or treaties of the United States. The "review by appeal" may also be available when the highest court in a state has decided a case on grounds that a Federal statute or treaty is invalid, or when the state court has held a state statute valid despite the claim of the losing party that the statute is in conflict with the U.S. Constitution or a Federal law. Review by the U.S. Supreme Court is still discretionary, but a Writ of Certiorari is not involved.

The Supreme Court, like the Courts of Appeals, does not conduct another trial. Its responsibility is to review the record and determine whether or not the trial court correctly applied the law in deciding the case. The Supreme Court also reviews the decision of the Court of Appeals to determine if the court used the correct reasoning.

In general, the Supreme Court hears cases only when one or more of the following conditions apply:

1. When the Court of Appeals has not used accepted or usual methods of judicial procedure or has sanctioned an unusual method by the trial court;
2. When a Court of Appeals has settled an important question of Federal law and the Supreme Court feels such an important question should have one more review by the most prestigious court of the nation;
3. When a decision of a Court of Appeals is in apparent conflict with a decision of the Supreme Court;
4. When two or more Courts of Appeals are in conflict on an issue; or
5. When the Supreme Court has already decided an issue but feels that the issue should be looked at again, possibly to reverse its previous decision.

## Case Citation

### Tax Court Decisions

Prior to 1943, the Tax Court was called the Board of Tax Appeals. The decisions of the Board of Tax Appeals were published as the *United States Board of Tax Appeals Reports* (BTA). Board of Tax Appeals cases are cited as follows:

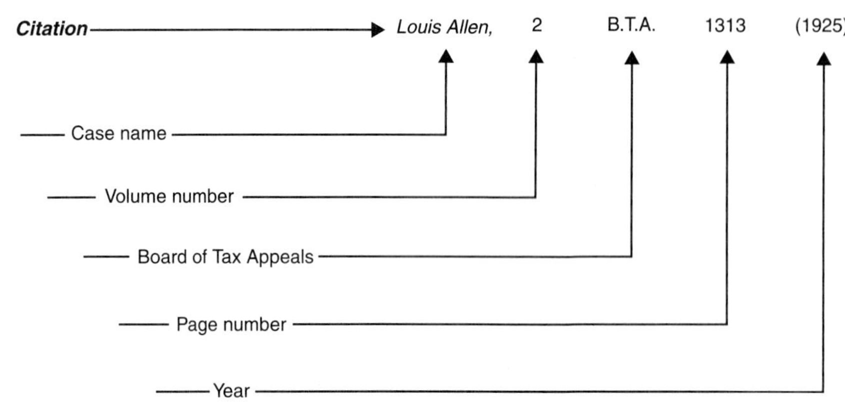


The Tax Court renders two different types of decisions with two different citation systems: Regular decisions and Memorandum decisions.

Tax Court *Regular* decisions deal with new issues that the court has not yet resolved. In contrast, decisions that deal only with the application of already established principles of law are called *Memorandum* decisions. The United States government publishes Regular decisions in *United States Tax Court Reports* (T.C.). Tax Court Regular decisions are cited as follows:

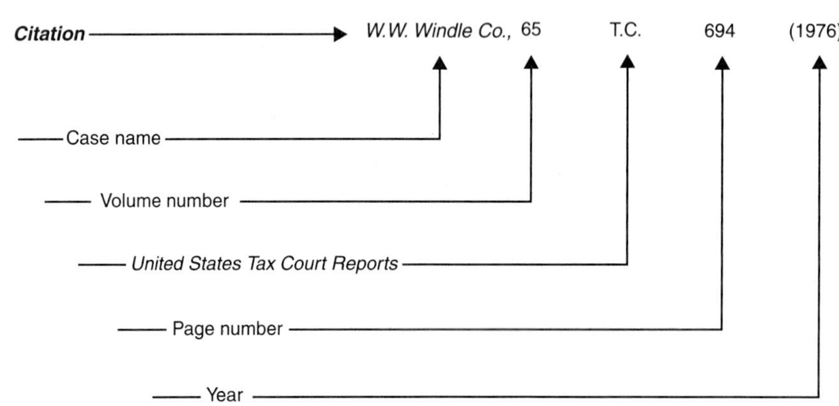


Like revenue rulings and the *Cumulative Bulletins*, there is a time lag between the date a Tax Court Regular decision is issued and the date it is bound in a *U.S. Tax Court Report* volume. In this case, the citation appears as follows:

***Temporary Citation:***

*W.W. Windle Co.*, 65 T.C. ______, No. 79(1976).

Here the page is left out, but the citation tells the reader that this is the 79th Regular decision issued by the Tax Court since Volume 64 ended. When the new volume (65th) of the Tax Court Report is issued, then the permanent citation may be substituted for the old one. Both CCH and RIA have tax services that allow the researcher to find these temporary citations.

The IRS has adopted the practice of announcing whether it agrees or disagrees with a decision issued by a court by announcing its acquiescence or nonacquiescence. Until 1991, this practice was limited to certain Regular decisions of the Tax Court. At that time, however, the IRS began to acquiesce or nonacquiesce to other cases where it thought it would be useful.[14] The IRS may withdraw its acquiescence or nonacquiescence at any time and may do

[14] The IRS's acquiescence is symbolized by "A" or "Acq." and its nonacquiescence by "NA" or "Nonacq."

so even retroactively. Acquiescences and nonacquiescences are published in the weekly *Internal Revenue Bulletins* and the *Cumulative Bulletins*.

The U.S. government publishes the Tax Court's Regular decisions, and also posts the decisions to its website (http://www.ustaxcourt.gov). The website currently has both Regular and Memorandum decisions since September 25, 1995. The Tax Court does not publish memorandum decisions. However, both CCH and RIA publish them. CCH publishes the memorandum decisions under the title *Tax Court Memorandum Decisions* (TCM), while RIA publishes these decisions as *Tax Court Reporter and Memorandum Decisions* (T.C. Memo). In citing Tax Court memorandum decisions, some authors prefer to use both the RIA and the CCH citations for their cases.

Decisions of the Small Claims division of the Tax Court were first published on the U.S. Tax Court Web site as U.S. Tax Court Summary Opinions in 2001. All of these decisions appear with the caveat that such cases may not be treated as precedent for any other case.

In an effort to provide the reader the greatest latitude of research sources, this dual citation policy has been adopted for this text. The case of *Alan K. Minor* serves as an example of the dual citation of Tax Court memorandum decisions.

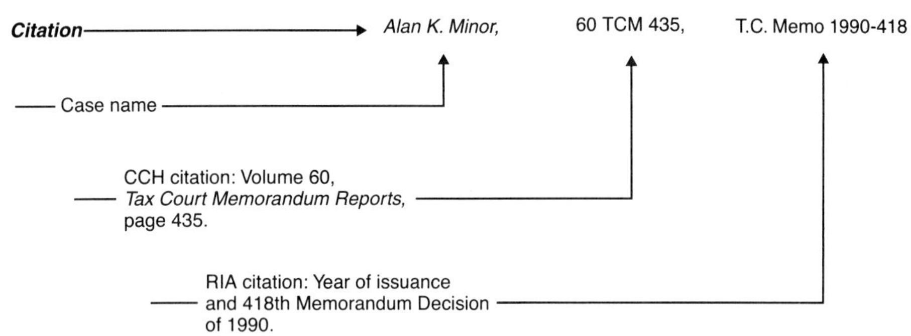


As noted above, Tax Court Summary Opinions can be found at the website of the Tax Court or through RIA and CCH. All use the same form of citation. For example, the decision in Richard Bradley on January 21, 2006 would be cited as follows:

*Richard Bradley*, T.C. Summary Opinion, 2006–61

## Citations for U.S. District Court, Court of Appeals, and Claims Court

Commerce Clearing House, Research Institute of America, and West Publishing Company all publish decisions of the District Courts, Courts of Appeals, and the Court of Federal Claims. When available, all three citations of a case are provided in this text.[15] CCH publishes the decisions of these courts in its *U.S. Tax Cases* (USTC—not to be confused with the *U.S. Tax Court Reports*) volumes, and RIA offers these decisions in its *American Federal Tax Reports* (AFTR) series.[16] West Publishing Company reports these decisions in either its *Federal Supplement Series* (F. Supp.—District Court decisions), or its *Federal Second Series or Federal Third Series* (F.2d or F.3d—Court of Federal Claims and Courts of Appeals decisions).

The citation of the U.S. District Court decision of *Cam F. Dowell, Jr. v. U.S.* is illustrated for each of the three publishing companies as follows:

*CCH Citation:*

*Cam F. Dowell, Jr. v. U.S.*, 74-1 USTC ¶9243, (D.Ct. Tx., 1974).

Interpretation: This case is reported in the first volume of the *U.S. Tax Cases*, published by CCH for calendar year 1974 (74-1), located at paragraph (¶) 9243, and is a decision rendered in 1974 by a U.S. District Court located in Texas (Tx.).

---

[15] When all three publishers have not printed the case, only the citations to the cases published are provided.

[16] Until the acquisition of Prentice Hall by RIA, Prentice Hall published cases under its own name. Accordingly, researchers needing cases from before 1993 will often encounter Prentice Hall as publisher of these reporters now carried under RIA's name.

***RIA Citation:***

*Cam F. Dowell, Jr. v. U.S.*, 33 AFTR2d 74-739, (D.Ct. Tx., 1974).

Interpretation: Reported in the 33rd volume of the second series of the *American Federal Tax Reports* (AFTR2d), published by RIA for 1974, and located at page 739.

***West Citation:***

*Cam F. Dowell, Jr. v. U.S.*, 370 F.Supp. 69 (D.Ct. Tx., 1974).

Interpretation: Located in the 370th volume of the *Federal Supplement Series* (F.Supp), published by West Publishing Company, and located at page 69.

The multiple citation of the U.S. District Court case illustrated above appears as follows:

*Cam F. Dowell, Jr. v. U.S.*, 74-1 USTC ¶9243, 33 AFTR2d 74-739, 370 F.Supp. 69 (D.Ct. Tx., 1974).

Decisions of the Court of Federal Claims (Ct. Cls.), the Courts of Appeals (e.g., CA-1, CA-2, etc.), and the Supreme Court (USSC) are published by CCH and RIA in the same reporting source as District Court decisions (i.e., USTCs and AFTRs). Court of Federal Claims and Court of Appeals decisions are reported by West Publishing Company in its *Federal Second Series* (F.2d) or *Federal Third Series* (F.3d). West also publishes the *Federal Appendix* (Fed. Appx.) which includes opinions not selected by the Courts of Appeals for publication in the Federal reporters. Supreme Court decisions are published by West Publishing Company in its *Supreme Court Reports* (S.Ct.), and the U.S. Government Printing Office publishes Supreme Court decisions in its *Supreme Court Reports* (U.S.).

An example of the multiple citation of a Court of Appeals decision follows:

***Citation:***

*Millar v. Comm.*, 78-2 USTC ¶9514, 42 AFTR2d 78-5246, 577 F.2d 212 (CA-3, 1978).

A multiple citation of a Supreme Court decision would appear as follows:

***Citation:***

*Fausner v. Comm.*, 73-2 USTC ¶9515, 32 AFTR2d 73-5202, 413 U.S. 838 (USSC, 1973).

Note that in each of the citations above, the designation "Commissioner of the Internal Revenue Service" is simply abbreviated to "Comm." In some instances, the IRS or U.S. is substituted for Comm., and older cases used the Commissioner's name. For example, in *Gregory v. Helvering*, 293 U.S. 465 (USSC, 1935), Mr. Helvering was the Commissioner of the Internal Revenue Service at the time the case was brought to the Court. Also note that the citation contains a reference to the Appellate Court rendering the decision (i.e., CA-3, or USSC) and the year of issuance.

Exhibits 2-4 and 2-5 summarize the sources of case citations from various reporter services.

**EXHIBIT 2.4 Reporters of Tax Court Decisions**

| *Reporter* | *Abbr.* | *Type* | *Publisher* |
|---|---|---|---|
| Tax Court Reports | TC | Regular | Government Printing Office |
| Tax Court Memorandum Decisions | TCM | Memorandum | Commerce Clearing House |
| Tax Court Memorandum Decisions | TC Memo | Memorandum | Research Institute of America |

**EXHIBIT 2.5** **Reporters of Decisions Other Than Tax Court**

| *Reporter* | *Abbr.* | *Courts Reported* | *Publisher* |
|---|---|---|---|
| Supreme Court Reports | U.S. | Supreme Court | Government Printing Office |
| Supreme Court Reporter | S.Ct | Supreme Court | West Publishing |
| Federal Supplement | F.Supp | District Courts | West Publishing |
| Federal Reporter | F.<br>F.2d<br>F.3d | Cts. of Appeals and Ct. of Fed. Cls. | West Publishing |
| Federal Appendix | Fed. Appx. | Cts. of Appeals Unreported cases | West Publishing |
| American Federal Tax Reports | AFTR2d | Ct. of Fed. Cls. Cts. of Appeals, and Supreme Ct. | Research Institute of America |
| United States Tax Cases | USTC | Same as AFTR and AFTR2d | Commerce Clearing House |

## Secondary Sources

**LO.9**
Explain secondary authority.

The importance of understanding the sources discussed thus far stems from their role in the taxation process. As mentioned earlier, the statutory law and its official interpretations constitute the legal authorities that set forth the tax consequences for a particular set of facts. These legal authorities, sometimes referred to as *primary authorities*, must be distinguished from so-called *secondary sources* or *secondary authorities*. The secondary sources of tax information consist mainly of books, periodicals, articles, newsletters, and editorial judgments in tax services. When working with the tax law, it must be recognized that secondary sources are unofficial interpretations—mere opinions—that have no legal authority.

Although secondary sources should not be used as the supporting authority for a particular tax treatment (except as a supplement to primary authority or in cases where primary authority is absent), they are an indispensable aid when seeking an understanding of the tax law. Several of these secondary materials are discussed briefly below.

### Tax Services

"Tax service" is the name given to a set of organized materials that contains a vast quantity of tax-related information organized so as to make it useful and accessible to tax practitioners. In general, a tax service is a paper or electronic compilation of some or all of the following: the Code, regulations, court decisions, IRS releases, and explanations of these primary authorities by the editors. As the listing of contents suggests, a tax service is invaluable since it contains, all in one place, a wealth of tax information, including both primary and secondary sources. Most tax services are available on CD-ROM or the Internet, or both. Moreover, these materials are updated constantly to reflect current developments—an extremely important feature given the dynamic nature of tax law. The major tax services are:

| *Publisher* | *Name of Publication* |
|---|---|
| Commerce Clearing House | *Standard Federal Tax Reporter—Income Taxes* |
| Research Institute of America | *United States Tax Reporter and Federal Tax Coordinator—2nd Series* |
| The Bureau of National Affairs, Inc. | *Tax Management Portfolios—U.S. Income* |

The widespread use of computers has found applications in tax research. For example, *LEXIS* is a computerized data base that a user can access through his or her personal computer. The *LEXIS* data base contains almost all information available in an extensive tax library. Suppliers of tax services currently make computer-based tax liabraries available to their customers. Undoubtedly computers are basic to tax research.

Commerce Clearing House, Research Institute of America, and other publishers issue weekly summaries of important cases and other tax developments that many practitioners and scholars find helpful in keeping current with developments in the tax field. The Bureau of National Affairs publishes the *Daily Tax Bulletin*, a comprehensive daily journal of late-breaking tax news that often reprints entire cases or regulations of particular importance. *Tax Notes*, published by Tax Analysts, is a weekly publication addressing legislative and judicial developments in the tax field. *Tax Notes* is particularly helpful in following the progress of tax legislation through the legislative process.

### Tax Periodicals

In addition to these services, there are a number of quality publications (usually published monthly) that contain articles on a variety of important tax topics. These publications are very helpful when new tax acts are passed, because they often contain clear, concise summaries of the new law in a readable format. In addition, they serve to convey new planning opportunities and relay the latest IRS and judicial developments in many important subspecialities of the tax profession. Some of the leading periodicals include the following:

- *ATA Journal of Legal Tax Research*
- *Estate Planning*
- *Journal of Corporate Taxation*
- *Journal of Partnership Taxation*
- *Journal of Real Estate Taxation*
- *Journal of Taxation*
- *Tax Law Journal*
- *Tax Law Review*
- *Taxes—The Tax Magazine*
- *The International Tax Journal*
- *The Review of Taxation of Individuals*
- *The Tax Advisor*
- *The Tax Executive*
- *The Tax Lawyer*
- *Trusts and Estates*

In addition to these publications, many law journals contain excellent articles on tax subjects.

Several indexes exist that may be used to locate a journal article. Through the use of a subject index, author index, and in some instances a Code section index, articles dealing with a particular topic may be found. Three of these indexes are:

| *Title* | *Publisher* |
|---|---|
| *Index to Federal Tax Articles* | Warren, Gorham and Lamont |
| *Federal Tax Articles* | Commerce Clearing House |
| *The Accountant's Index* | American Institute of Certified Public Accountants |

In addition, the *United States Tax Reporter*, published by RIA, contains a section entitled "Index to Tax Articles."

## Tax Research

Having introduced the sources of tax law, the remainder of this chapter is devoted to working with the law—or more specifically, the art of tax research. Tax research may be defined as the process used to ascertain the optimal answer to a question with tax implications. Although there is no perfect technique for researching a question, the following approach normally is used:

1. Obtain all of the facts
2. Diagnose the problem from the facts
3. Locate the authorities
4. Evaluate the authorities
5. Derive the solution and possible alternative solutions
6. Communicate the answer

Each of these steps is discussed below.

## Obtaining the Facts

Before discussing the importance of obtaining all the facts, the distinction between closed fact research and open- or controlled-fact research should be noted. If the research relates to a problem with transactions that are complete, it is referred to as closed-fact research and normally falls within the realm of tax practice known as tax compliance. On the other hand, if the research relates to contemplated transactions, it is called controlled- or open-fact research and is an integral part of tax planning.

In researching a closed-fact problem, the first step is gathering all of the facts. Unfortunately, it is difficult to obtain all relevant facts upon first inquiry. This is true because it is essentially impossible to understand the law so thoroughly that all of the proper questions can be asked before the research task begins. After the general area of the problem is identified and research has begun, it usually becomes apparent that more facts must be obtained before an answer can be derived. Consequently, additional inquiries must be made until all facts necessary for a solution are acquired.

## Diagnosing the Issue

Once the initial set of facts is gathered, the tax issue or question must be identified. Most tax problems involve very basic questions such as these:

1. Does the taxpayer have gross income that must be recognized?
2. Is the taxpayer entitled to a deduction?
3. Is the taxpayer entitled to a credit?
4. In what period is the gross income, deduction, or credit reported?
5. What amount of gross income, deduction, or credit must be reported?

As research progresses, however, such fundamental questions can be answered only after more specific issues have been resolved.

### Example 1

R's employer owns a home in which R lives. The basic question that must be asked is whether use of the home constitutes income to R. After consulting the various tax sources, it can be determined that § 61 requires virtually all benefits to be included in income unless another provision specifically grants an exclusion. In this case, § 119 allows a taxpayer to exclude the value employer-provided of housing if the housing is on the employer's premises, the lodging is furnished for the convenience of the employer, and the employee is required by the employer to accept the housing. Due to the additional research, three more specific questions must be asked:

1. Is the home on the employer's premises?
2. Is the home provided for the employer's convenience?
3. Is R required to live in the home?

As the above example suggests, diagnosing the problem requires a continuing refinement of the questions until the critical issue is identified. The refinement that occurs results from the awareness that is gained through reading and rereading the primary and secondary authorities.

### Example 2

Assume the same facts as in *Example 1*. After determining that one of the issues concerns whether R's home is on the business premises, a second inquiry is made of R concerning the location of his residence. (Note that as the research progresses, additional facts must be gathered.) According to R, the house is located in a suburb, 25 miles from his employer's downtown office. However, the house is owned by the employer, and hence R suggests that he lives on the employer's premises. He also explains that he often brings work home and frequently entertains clients in his home. Having uncovered this information, the primary authorities are reexamined. Upon review, it is determined that in *Charles N. Anderson*,[17] the court indicated that an employee would be considered on the business premises if the employee performed a significant portion of his duties at the place of lodging. Again the question must be refined to ask: Do R's work and entertainment activities in the home constitute a significant portion of his duties?

## Locating the Authorities

Identification of the critical issue presented by any tax question begins by first locating, then reading and studying the appropriate authority. Locating the authority is ordinarily done using a tax service. With the issue stated in general terms, the subject is found in the index volume and the location is determined. At this point, the appropriate Code sections, regulations, and editorial commentary may be perused to determine their applicability to the question.

### Example 3

In the case of R above, the problem stated in general terms concerns income. Using an index, the key word, *income*, could be located and a reference to information concerning the income aspects of lodging would be given.

Once information relating to the issue is identified, the authoritative materials must be read. That is, the appropriate Code sections, regulations, rulings, and cases must be examined and studied to determine how they relate to the question. As suggested above, this process normally results in refinement of the question, which in turn may require acquisition of additional facts.

## Evaluating the Authority

**LO.10**
Evaluate the relative strength of various tax authorities.

After the various authorities have been identified and it has been *verified* that they are applicable, their value must be appraised. This evaluation process, as will become clear below, primarily involves appraisal of court decisions and revenue rulings.

### The Code

The Internal Revenue Code is the final authority on most tax issues since it is the Federal tax law as passed by Congress. Only the courts can offset this authority by declaring part of the law unconstitutional, and this happens rarely. Most of the time, however, the Code itself is

[17] 67-1 USTC ¶9136, 19 AFTR2d 318, 371 F.2d 59 (CA-6, 1966).

only of partial help. It is written in a style that is not always easy to understand, and it contains no examples of its application. Accordingly, to the extent the Code can be understood as clearly applicable, no stronger authority exists, except possibly a treaty. But in most cases, the Code cannot be used without further support.

### Treasury Regulations

As previously discussed, the regulations are used to expand and explain the Code. Because Congress has given its authority to make laws to the Executive branch's administrative agency—the Treasury—the regulations that are produced are a very strong source of authority, second only to the Code itself. Normally, the major issue when a regulation is under scrutiny by a Court is whether the regulation is consistent with the Code. If the regulations are inconsistent, the Court will not hesitate to invalidate them.

### Judicial Authority

The value of a court decision depends on numerous factors. On appraising a decision, the most crucial determination concerns whether the outcome is consistent with other decisions on the same issue. In other words, consideration must be given to how other decisions have evaluated the one in question. An invaluable tool in determining the validity of a case is a *citator*. A tax citator provides an alphabetical listing by last name of virtually all tax cases and other administrative pronouncements (e.g. rulings). After the name of each case, there is a record of other decisions that have cited (in the text of their facts and opinions) the first case. The list of cases is organized by type of court and then by year. Exhibit 2-4 provides sample entries from the citators published by RIA and CCH for the Supreme Court's decision in *Indianapolis Power and Light Co.*

#### Example 4

Refer to Exhibit 2-6 and the sample entries from the RIA and CCH citators. Observe that the Supreme Court's decision in *Indianapolis Power and Light Co. (IPL)* was cited (mentioned) in a number of cases at various levels as well in several rulings. For instance, the *IPL* decision was cited by the Supreme Court in *Banks II*, by the Ninth Circuit in *Westpac-Pacific Foods* and by the Tax Court in *Tampa Bay Devil Rays, Ltd.* Similarly, *IPL* was cited in Rev. Proc. 91-31 and Rev. Rul. 2003-39.

It is important to note that tax citators often use abbreviations for subsequent case history. For example, the abbreviations *aff'g* and *aff'd* mean "affirming" and "affirmed" and indicate that an appeals court has upheld the decision in question. Similarly, *rev'g* and *rev'd* mean "reversing" and "reversed" and indicate that a trial court's decision was overturned. Finally, *rem'g* and *rem'd* mean "remanding" and "remanded" and indicate that the case has been sent back to a lower court for reconsideration.

The validity of a particular decision may be assessed by examining how the subsequent cases viewed the cited decision. For example, subsequent cases may have agreed or disagreed with the decision in question, or distinguished the facts of the cited case from those examined in a later case. In this regard, note how the RIA citator provides a notation, indicating the relationship between the cited and citing cases. For example, the Banks II decision is shown as having "cited favorably" the IPL decision. The CCH citator does not provide this information.

Another important factor that must be considered in evaluating a court decision is the level of the court that issued it. Decisions issued by trial courts have less value than those issued by appellate courts. And, of course, decisions of the Supreme Court are the ultimate authority.

A court decision's value rises appreciably if the IRS agrees with its result. As discussed earlier, the IRS usually indicates whether it acquiesces or does not acquiesce to Regular Tax Court decisions. The position of the Service may also be published in a revenue ruling.

**EXHIBIT 2.6** **Tax Citators: RIA and CCH**

**RIA Citator**
**(Online; Partial List of Entries)**

*Name of cited case*

**INDIANAPOLIS POWER & LIGHT CO.; COMM v,** 65 AFTR 2d 90-394 , 493 US 203 , 110 S Ct 589 , 107 L Ed 2d 591 , 90-1 USTC ¶50,007 (US, 1/9/1990)

*Alternative citations for cited case, includes citations from RIA, West and CCH*

**Judicial History**

**Affirming earlier case:** Indianapolis Power & Light Co. v Comm., 62 AFTR 2d 88-5708 , 857 F2d 1162 (CA7, 9/20/1988)
**Affirming earlier case:** Indianapolis Power & Light Co., 88 TC 964 , ¶88.52 PH TC (4/20/1987)

*Supreme Court decision agreed with decisions made earlier by 7th Circuit and the Tax Court*

**Cited In**

*Indicates how citing case (Banks) treated the cited case (IPL)*

**Cited favorably :** Banks, John W., II; Com. v., 95 AFTR 2d 2005-664,125 S Ct 831 (US, 1/24/2005) [See 65 AFTR 2d 90-397, 493 US 209]
**Reasoning followed:** Ware, R. Timmis v Comm., 66 AFTR 2d 90-5198, 906 F2d 64 (CA2, 6/21/1990) [See 65 AFTR 2d 90-397, 110 S Ct 593-594]
**Cited generally:** Webb, Frederick L. v I.R.S., 73 AFTR 2d 94-1021, 15 F3d 205 (CA1, 2/3/1994)
**Cases distinguished :** George, Randolph; U.S. v., 96 AFTR 2d 2005-5821, 420 F3d 996 (CA9, 8/23/2005) [See 65 AFTR 2d 90-397, 493 US 209-210]
**Cited favorably :** Westpac Pacific Food v. Com., 97 AFTR 2d 2006-3018, 451 F3d 975 (CA9, 6/21/2006) [See 65 AFTR 2d 90-396, 493 US 207]
**Cases reconciled :** Tampa Bay Devil Rays, Ltd., 2002 RIA TC Memo 2002-1539 [See 65 AFTR 2d 90-495, 90-499, 493 US 204-205, 214]
**Reasoning followed 1** : Rev Proc 91-31 , 1991-1 CB 567
**Cited generally 1** : Rev Rul 2003-39 , 2003-1 CB 811

*Cases and rulings that have cited the Supreme Court's decision in Indianapolis Power and Light Co.*

---

**CCH Citator**
**(Online; Partial List of Entries)**

*Name of cited case*

**Indianapolis Power and Light Co.**

*Locations in CCH where case and issues are discussed*

ANNOTATED AT ... 2007FED ¶5504.6992; ¶21,005.027; ¶21,005.035; ¶21,005.7039; ¶21,005.7080; ¶21,017.18

- **SCt**--(aff'g CA), 90-1 USTC ¶50,007; 493 US 203; 110 SCt 589

*Alternative citations for cited case (IPL)*

Banks II, SCt, 2005-1 USTC ¶50,155, 543 US 426, 125 SCt 826
Westpac Pacific Foods, CA-9, 2006-2 USTC ¶50,369, 451 F3d 970
George, CA-9, 2005-2 USTC ¶50,546, 420 F3d 991
Webb, CA-1, 94-1 USTC ¶50,071, 15 F3d 203
Ware, CA-2, 90-2 USTC ¶50,342, 906 F2d 62
Tampa Bay Devil Rays, Ltd., TC, Dec. 54,893(M), 84 TCM 394, TC Memo. 2002-248
Let. Rul. 200110002, October 4, 2000
Let. Rul. 200347014, August 4, 2003
Rev. Proc. 91-31
Rev. Rul. 2003-39, IRB 2003-17, 811; 2003-1 CB 811

*Cases and rulings that have cited the Supreme Court's decision in Indianapolis Power and Light Co.*

## Rulings

The significance of revenue rulings lies in the fact that they reflect current IRS policy. Since agents of the IRS are usually reluctant to vary from that policy, revenue rulings carry considerable weight.

Revenue rulings are often evaluated in court decisions. Thus, a tax service should be used to determine whether relevant rulings have been considered in any decisions. By examining the Court's view of the ruling, possible flaws may be discovered.

The IRS must adhere to private letter rulings issued to the taxpayer as long as the transaction is carried out in the manner initially approved. Variation from the facts on which the ruling was based permits the Service to revise its position. As mentioned earlier, a private letter ruling applies only to the particular taxpayer to whom it was issued. It does not apply to other taxpayers. However, such a ruling should prove helpful to any other taxpayer faced with a substantially identical fact pattern.

## Deriving the Solution

Once all the relevant authorities have been evaluated, a conclusion must be drawn. Before deriving the final answer or answers, however, an important caveat is warranted: the researcher must ensure that the research reflects all current developments. The new matters section of a tax service can aid in this regard. The new matters section updates the textual discussion with any late-breaking developments. For instance, the section will contain any new cases, regulations, or pronouncements of the Internal Revenue Service that may bear on the discussion of the topic covered in the main text.

## Communicating the Findings

**LO.11**
Understand the importance of communicating the results of tax research.

The final product of the research effort is a memorandum recording the research and a letter to the interested parties. Although many formats are suitable for the memorandum, one technique typically used is structured as follows:

1. Description of the facts
2. Statement of the issues or questions researched
3. Report of the conclusions (brief answers to the research questions)
4. Discussion of the rationale and authorities that support the conclusions
5. Summary of the authorities consulted in the research

A good tax memorandum is essential. If the research findings are not communicated intelligently and effectively, the entire research effort is wasted.

# Rules of Tax Practice: Responsibilities and Ethics

Over the past several years there has been a great deal of attention focused on ethics in business. The world of taxation has not escaped this attention. Unethical behavior of taxpayers and tax preparers has always been a serious concern of the tax system, primarily because of its reliance on voluntary compliance.

Anyone who has ever filed an income tax return recognizes the potential for bilking the system. It is as easy as underreporting income or overstating deductions. What is perhaps more important is that it can be done with so little risk. The current audit rate is so low—approximately 1 percent—that many dishonest taxpayers think they can exploit the system with little chance that they will ever get caught. That the tax system is such an easy mark was underscored recently in testimony given before the House Ways and Means Oversight Subcommittee by two practitioners convicted of tax fraud for illegal refund schemes. In his testimony, Barry Becht, a 36-year-old former tax return preparer, explained that, before he was convicted and sent to Federal prison, he had "helped" his clients reduce their tax liabilities by over $750,000 simply by overstating their deductions. Surprisingly, Becht did not share in his client's windfalls. Allegedly his only purpose was to build up his practice! The other convicted felon, Frazier Todd, reported that he had gained more than $500,000 in only two years using electronic filing schemes. Shortly after college and with the help of a few courses on computers, accounting, and business, Todd had set up a tax-preparation service near public housing in Atlanta. There he was able to strike deals with low-income taxpayers who allowed him to use their names and social security numbers to falsify wage statements (W-2 forms). He then proceeded to file returns electronically, which enabled him to obtain a refund before the IRS discovered that the returns were phony. Unfortunately, the stories of Becht and Todd are just two illustrations of how easy it is to abuse the system. Near the close of 1993, the IRS estimated that the "tax gap," the amount of unpaid taxes (income, payroll, and excise) due to cheating and fraud, was over $150 billion annually. By 2001, the gap had increased to as much as $353 billion.[18]

The problems of tax fraud do not go unnoticed, however. To safeguard the system, encourage compliance, and promote ethical behavior, the government has adopted a number of mechanisms. Among these is an intricate set of penalties that can be applied to both taxpayers and tax return preparers. These penalties cover a variety of violations, such as failure to file and pay taxes on a timely basis, negligence in preparing the tax return, and outright fraud. While the penalties are usually monetary in nature, criminal penalties—such as the jail sentences given to Mr. Becht and Mr. Todd—may result if the taxpayer goes beyond these civil offenses and purposefully attempts to evade tax. The failure-to-file and failure-to-pay penalties—penalties that typically result not because taxpayers are trying to deceive the government but simply because they are late in filing and paying their taxes—are discussed in Chapter 4. The focus in this chapter is on the responsibilities of taxpayers and tax return preparers in filing returns and the major penalties that may be imposed with respect to positions taken on returns.

## TAXPAYER PENALTIES

**LO.12**
Explain the key penalties that influence positions taken on tax returns.

In a 1985 IRS survey, one out of every five people reported that they cheated on their tax return. In the same survey, 41 percent said they believed that their fellow taxpayers also cheated. Similarly, Professor Peggy Hite found in a 1993 survey of Indiana residents that 40 percent of the individuals asked indicated that they definitely would not voluntarily report prize income, such as money won in a lottery or similar contests and sweepstakes.[19] Another 30 percent were somewhat wishy-washy in their answers, suggesting that, depending on the circumstances, they also would not report the income. But anyone thinking about cheating should recognize that it can be quite expensive. The IRS has over 140 penalties in its arsenal that it could apply. In their simplest form, these penalties provide that as long as taxpayers do not cheat and make a good faith effort to determine their tax liability, they have no reason to worry. But in reality the ethical problems created by the tax system for taxpayers and tax preparers can be difficult to resolve. Unfortunately, the law rarely provides clear-cut answers, leaving taxpayers wondering what they should do.

As an illustration, consider two taxpayers, both with bad backs, who bought $5,000 hot tubs on the hope that they might have some therapeutic value. Can the taxpayers deduct their costs as a medical expense? Even if they researched the question every day of the week for a month, the answer may not be clear. Should the fact that the answer is not clear preclude them from deducting their expenses? Some taxpayers might be inclined to simply abandon the issue, pay the tax and never worry about it again. But others might believe that there is some support for their position and want to take the deduction. So assume in this case taxpayer A deducts the expense and taxpayer B deducts not only the cost of the tub but, banking on the audit lottery, also deducts the entire cost of the house on the grounds that it serves as a rehabilitation facility. What happens if both returns are audited and the agent rejects the deductions of both taxpayers? Obviously the system of punishment should fit the crime. And this is what Congress has attempted to do by creating a penalty system that fairly treats taxpayers who in good faith believe that their position has validity but at the same time discourages taxpayers from taking frivolous positions, hoping that the audit lottery will never pick their number.

As the penalty discussion below will reveal, the tax law has its own way of dealing with taxpayers who stray too far from the correct position. While the system is complex, it is somewhat analogous to the way a mother treats her teenage son who is apt to stay out beyond his 12 o'clock curfew. If the son is a few minutes late, there will probably be no penalty if he has a reasonable explanation. On the other hand, if he gets home two hours late, the penalty will probably be severe unless he called to say he would be late. But if he never called, punishment is a virtual certainty unless his story is truly believable and backed by witnesses. And, of course, if her son lies, he will be grounded forever. Although the rules for breaking curfew are not completely analogous to those for taxpayers that take erroneous positions on returns, the comparison may be useful. If a taxpayer takes an incorrect position with respect to a *small* amount, there will be no penalty as long as there is a *reasonable basis* for the position. On the other hand, if the tax dollars involved are *substantial*, a penalty is normally imposed unless the

[18] IR News Release 2005-38 (Mar. 29, 2005).

[19] "Nearly 1 in 3 Would Cheat on Taxes," *The Indianapolis Star*, April 7, 1994, B1.

taxpayer has *substantial authority* for the position or, alternatively, has disclosed the position and has a reasonable basis for it. Of course, if the taxpayer commits blatant fraud, the penalties could be quite harsh. These ethical standards for taxpayers are embedded in two types of penalties: accuracy-related penalties and penalties for fraud.

## ACCURACY-RELATED PENALTIES

What happens if a waiter simply fails to report all of his tips? What if a 70-year-old grandmother fails to file her return believing that senior citizens do not have to pay tax? And what if the taxpayer deducts the cost of his daughter's wedding as business entertainment? As might be expected, the IRS does not treat such transgressions lightly. If the taxpayer's behavior can be characterized as negligent, a penalty in addition to the regular tax may be imposed. In 1989, Congress consolidated several existing penalties relating to negligence into a so-called accuracy-related penalty. The accuracy-related penalty is generally 20 percent of the portion of the tax underpayment. The principal accuracy-related penalties include:[20]

- Negligence or disregard of rules and regulations
- Substantial understatement of income tax
- Substantial valuation misstatement.

Note that these penalties do not stack on top of each other. The IRS must pick which one it wants to assess.

### Negligence Penalty (Insubstantial)

The negligence penalty, as an accuracy-related penalty, is 20 percent of the portion of the tax underpayment that is attributable to negligence or disregard of the rules and regulations.[21] For example, assume a taxpayer forgets to report $1,000 that he received for consulting during the year. If the taxpayer is in the 28 percent tax bracket, the underpayment is $280 and the penalty would be $56 (20% × $280). Note that when the day of reckoning comes, the taxpayer will be required to pay the underpayment, interest on the underpayment from the original due date, and the penalty, if any. The taxpayer may also owe interest on the penalty. Interest on the penalty generally starts to run when the taxpayer has been notified of the penalty, usually sometime after the audit. Under § 6601(e)(2)(B) interest must be paid on the failure-to-file penalty, accuracy-related penalties, and the fraud penalty.

Negligence is generally defined as any failure to do what a reasonable and ordinarily prudent person would do under the circumstances. To avoid the negligence penalty, the taxpayer must make a reasonable attempt to comply with the law. The negligence penalty is usually imposed when the taxpayer fails to report income or claims large amounts of unsubstantiated expenses. For example, a waitress who fails to report her cash tips would probably get hit with the penalty, as would the businessperson who claims thousands of dollars of business entertainment expenses with little or no substantiation—a specific requirement for travel and entertainment expenses. A taxpayer is automatically considered negligent and liable for the 20 percent penalty if he or she fails to report any type of income for which there is an information return filed by the party paying the income (e.g., Form 1099). In other situations, determination of whether the penalty should be imposed is in the hands of the auditor. It is important to note, however, that taxpayers who intentionally attempt to deceive the government are normally not subject to the negligence penalty but rather the more severe fraud penalty discussed below.

For most taxpayers, the most important aspect of the negligence penalty concerns its relationship to positions taken on returns.

#### Example 5

This year D graduated with a marketing degree from the University of Arkansas and immediately took a job with a publishing company as a sales representative. The company did not provide her with an office, so she worked out of her home. After

[20] § 6662.

[21] § 6662(c).

talking with her boss at work, she found out that he deducted his home office expenses as business expenses on his return. Knowing little about tax, she followed her boss's lead and deducted $3,000 of expenses related to her home office. Two years later D's return was audited and the agent informed her that he planned to deny her deduction for the home office expenses. Assuming the agent is correct, another issue is raised: should the negligence penalty apply since D has taken an incorrect position on the return?

Prior to 1994, the taxpayer could avoid the negligence penalty as long as the position was not frivolous and it was disclosed on the return. But that approach inspired taxpayers to play the audit lottery. For example, aggressive taxpayers might take a questionable deduction, disclose it, then hope that they would never be audited. Even if they got caught, there was little risk of punishment since disclosure protected them against a negligence penalty in every situation except where the position was frivolous or patently improper. In other words, as long as the position was nonfrivolous—that is, the taxpayer had some basis on which to argue the disclosed position (e.g., a merely arguable or merely colorable claim)—the negligence penalty could be avoided.[22] Believing that the ethical standard set by this rule was far too low, the Revenue Reconciliation Act of 1993 changed the rules. Under the current approach, taxpayers are forced to be more cautious about the positions they take on their returns.

A negligence penalty can be assessed unless the taxpayer has a *reasonable basis* for the position taken on the return regardless of whether it is disclosed on the return. What the current approach means to taxpayers is that in situations where the potential tax understatement is insubstantial they can ethically take a position that is contrary to the rules and regulations without fear of the negligence penalty as long as there is a reasonable basis for believing that if the matter were litigated, the taxpayer would prevail against the IRS. Of course, the critical issue here is what constitutes a reasonable basis.

Although any definition of a "reasonable basis" would be subject to debate, the regulations do provide some guidance. According to the regulations, the reasonable basis standard is met if the return position is "arguable, but fairly unlikely to prevail in court."[23] Practitioners generally interpret this to mean that a position has a reasonable basis if it has at least a 20 percent chance of succeeding (without regard to the possibility that it might not be discovered at all). Apparently, this represents a slight increase in the level of support required by the nonfrivolous standard for disclosed positions under prior law. In the final analysis, however, the standard leaves a great deal to be desired. The regulations do provide one additional insight that may be useful: the "too good to be true" rule. This rule indicates that the reasonable basis standard is not met if the taxpayer fails to make a reasonable attempt to determine the correctness of a position that seems too good to be true.

## Substantial Understatement Penalty

The substantial understatement penalty, like its sibling, the negligence penalty, is an accuracy-related penalty that is 20 percent of the portion of the underpayment of tax due to any substantial understatement of income tax.[24] The understatement is considered substantial if it exceeds the larger of (1) 10 percent of the correct tax or (2) $5,000.

The major difference between the substantial understatement penalty and the negligence penalty concerns the level of authority required to avoid penalty for an erroneous *undisclosed* position. In effect, Congress is telling taxpayers that if the risky position they are taking involves a substantial amount of tax and they are *unwilling to disclose* the position, the degree of support they must have is greater than simply a reasonable basis. The substantial understatement penalty applies to undisclosed positions unless the taxpayer has *substantial authority* for the position. It is unclear what the substantial authority requirement calls for, but it seems clear that it is somewhat more stringent than the 1 in 3 test of the realistic possibility of success standard discussed below but less demanding than the more-likely-than-not requirement, a more than 50 percent chance, related to certain positions taken with

[22] Reg. §§ 1.6662-3(b)(3) and 1.6694-2(c)(2).

[23] § 6662(d).

[24] § 6662(d)(2)(B). A corporate taxpayer has a substantial understatement if the amount of the understatement exceeds the lesser of (1) 10% of the tax required to be shown on the return for the tax year (or, if greater, $10,000), or (2) $10 million.

respect to certain tax shelter investments. For purposes of the substantial authority analysis, only materials published by Congress, the IRS, and the courts are relevant. Conclusions suggested by tax professionals in treatises, legal periodicals (which provide the basis of many arguments), or the like are not to be considered.[25]

The degree of support necessary to avoid the substantial understatement penalty drops down a notch if the taxpayer is willing to disclose the position. The substantial understatement penalty can be avoided if the taxpayer makes *adequate disclosure* and has a *reasonable* basis for his position. What constitutes adequate disclosure is clearer than what constitutes a reasonable basis. Disclosure is considered adequate if the position is explained on a special form intended just for this purpose. Form 8275 or 8275-R, or on the return in accordance with rules issued by the IRS each year.[26] In effect, when the tax dollars involved are material, taxpayers must meet a much higher standard—substantial authority—than is normally applied unless they are willing to disclose the position.

### Substantial Valuation Misstatement

The tax law often requires taxpayers and tax return preparers to provide valuations for certain items. For example, taxpayers are generally entitled to a deduction for the fair market value of property given to qualified charitable organizations. What happens if a taxpayer in the 30 percent bracket gives a work of art that he says is worth $6,000 when its value is really closer to $2,000? The answer is that he has saved $1,200 ($4,000 × 30%) if he wins the audit lottery. But if the IRS does catch him, the taxpayer may face an accuracy-related penalty for substantial valuation misstatement. A 20 percent penalty is imposed on the underpayment of tax attributable to the misstatement.[27] The taxpayer avoids the penalty, however, if the misstatement does not exceed 150 percent of the correct value or if the amount of tax underpayment attributable to the misstatement is less than $5,000 ($10,000 for corporations). Thus the taxpayer above, who overstated the correct value by 300 percent, would still escape the valuation penalty since the amount of tax attributable to the misstatement, $1,200, is less than the $5,000 threshold. However, the taxpayer could still be subject to the negligence or the substantial understatement penalties.

### Summary of Penalties for Inaccurate Returns

There is a great deal of confusion over penalties concerning erroneous positions on tax returns and what one can do to avoid them. Nevertheless, Exhibit 2-7 summarizes the three accuracy-related penalties discussed above and what defenses are available to the taxpayer. After a great deal of studying, it may become clear that the likelihood of a penalty depends on three factors: the amount of the potential understatement, whether the taxpayer has disclosed the position adequately, and the level of support that there is for the position. As a rule, if the tax dollars are not significant, a reasonable basis protects the taxpayer from penalty. On the other hand, if the tax dollars are substantial, the taxpayer is protected only if there is substantial authority or if there is disclosure with reasonable basis. Exhibit 2-8 summarizes the various standards of compliance and ranks them according to their level of certainty. Note that in all cases the taxpayer can avoid the penalties by showing that there was *reasonable cause* for the position taken or that he or she acted in *good faith*. Obviously, these are both purely subjective determinations based on the individual facts and circumstances.

## Economic Substance Doctrine

It is not surprising that some taxpayers—both individuals and businesses—go to great lengths, often concocting intricate transactions, to avoid paying taxes. Some schemes are the ingenious creation of a company's legal or accounting department, sometimes with the aid of tax professionals at big name accounting or law firms. Some are the outrageous products of charlatan promoters. Others fall somewhere in between. Interestingly, many of these plans actually adhere to the letter of the law, meeting all of the statutory and administrative requirements. Nevertheless, courts often deny taxpayers the tax benefits of these otherwise "legal" transactions if they lack so-called *economic substance*. A transaction is said to lack economic substance if it did not result in a meaningful change to the taxpayer's economic

---

[25] Reg. § 1.6692-4(d)(3)(iii).

[26] Reg. § 1.6694-2(c)(3).

[27] § 6662(e). The penalty is 40 percent if the claimed value is 200 percent or more of the correct value.

**EXHIBIT 2.7** **The 20 Percent Penalty for Inaccurate Returns and Defenses: § 6662**

1. Negligence (insubstantial)
   - Defined: Reasonable attempt to comply with the tax laws
   - Defenses:
     - Reasonable basis (disclosure is unnecessary)
     - Exercise of reasonable care in preparing tax return
     - Reasonable cause and good faith
2. Substantial understatement
   - Defined: Understatement greater than 10% of tax or $5,000, whichever is larger
   - Defenses:
     - Understatement does not exceed threshold
     - Disclosure with reasonable basis
     - No disclosure with substantial authority
     - Reasonable cause and good faith
3. Substantial valuation misstatement
   - Defined: Misstatement more than 150% of correct valuation
   - Defenses:
     - Misstatement does not exceed threshold
     - Amount of underpayment of tax is less than $5,000
     - Reasonable cause and good faith

**EXHIBIT 2.8** **Standards of Compliance Required to Avoid Penalties**

1. Frivolous position
   - Defined: Patently improper
     - No protection for frivolous positions
2. Not frivolous position
   - Defined: Not patently improper, merely arguable
     - Pre-1994: Protection against negligence with disclosure
     - Post-1993: Apparently no protection
3. Reasonable basis
   - Defined: Arguable but fairly unlikely to prevail in court
     - Protects against insubstantial negligence
     - Protects against substantial understatement if position disclosed
4. Realistic possibility of success
   - Defined: More than one in three chances for success
     - Protects against insubstantial negligence without disclosure
     - Protects against substantial negligence with disclosure
5. Substantial authority
   - Defined: Supporting authorities are substantial (Congress, IRS, or court cases)
     - Protects against insubstantial and substantial negligence without disclosure (except tax shelter items)
6. More-likely-than-not
   - Defined: Greater than 50 percent chance of prevailing against the IRS if the matter were litigated
     - Protects against insubstantial and substantial negligence without disclosure related to certain positions taken with respect to certain tax shelter investments
7. Reasonable cause and good faith
   - Defined: Facts and circumstances determination
     - Protects normally against all penalties

position other than reducing federal income taxes. In short, if the transaction was solely for tax purposes, it will be disregarded. This principle is referred to as the "economic substance doctrine."

The economic substance doctrine is just one of several judicial theories that have been used to attack tax avoidance schemes. Another theory is the "business purpose doctrine."

This principle says that the transaction must be motivated by business considerations and reducing taxes is *not* a business purpose. In other situations, where the alleged activity never took place or what took place was merely a facade, the court often asserts that the events were a "sham transaction" and disregards the outcome. Similarly, the court may disallow the tax benefits by invoking the "substance over form" principle. This well-known doctrine stands for the proposition that the tax results of an arrangement should be based on the underlying substance rather than a simple evaluation of the formal steps by which the arrangement was undertaken. Yet another weapon in the court's arsenal is the "step transaction" doctrine. This doctrine treats what are purportedly separate steps as a single transaction if the steps are integrated, interdependent, and focused toward a particular result. The purpose of each of these doctrines is to test the transactions and sort out those that are primarily or solely motivated by tax savings from those that have a substantial business purpose or economic motive.

In 2010, Congress created § 7701(o)(1) that effectively enacts into law the economic substance doctrine and its variations, and importantly, imposes a significant penalty for transactions that fail its tests. It is important to note, however, that the legislative history indicates that the codification was not intended to replace or supplant existing judicial principles.

Under § 7701(o), a transaction has economic substance only if it (1) changes in a meaningful way (apart from federal taxes) the taxpayer's economic position and (2) the taxpayer has a substantial purpose for entering the transaction (other than federal income taxes purposes). This is a two prong test where the taxpayer must meet both tests for the transaction to be honored. The law does allow an exception for personal transactions of individuals. Individuals will be subject to the economic substance doctrine only for transactions entered in connection with a trade or business or an activity entered into for the production of income.

For transactions not meeting the two-part test, there is a penalty based on the underpayment of taxes resulting from the transaction. If the transaction is disclosed, the penalty is 20 percent of the underpayment. For undisclosed transactions, the penalty is doubled to 40 percent.

The impact of § 7701(o) is yet to be determined. Most commentators believe that many tax professionals will now lose a great deal of sleep wondering whether even the most common transactions have economic substance. Indeed, the provision is quite broad, and many legitimate business transactions, if tested for economic substance, could fail the statutory tests. Because of the uncertainty and because of the strict liability penalty, it does seem that taxpayers will face increased tax risk with respect to some transactions and, in some cases, will be deterred from engaging in transactions that otherwise would have been undertaken.

## Uncertain Tax Positions: Financial Accounting Reporting

Part of the difficulty encountered in tax practice is uncertainty. For many transactions, the tax treatment may not be clear. In such case, companies, as might be expected, usually take positions that reduce their tax liability. For example, a company may exclude income that it may believe is tax-exempt or take a tax credit that it believes is appropriate. Similarly, a company may not file a tax return in a particular state because it believes it is not required. These positions normally have a sound legal basis and are taken in good faith. However, given the complexities and varying interpretations of the tax law, these positions may not ultimately prevail. Consequently, uncertainty exists regarding the actual benefit a company will derive from a position taken on its tax return. This has an impact not only on a company's tax return but also its financial statements.

Over time, the Financial Accounting Standards Board (FASB) became concerned about the accounting for uncertainty in income taxes and how it was reported for financial accounting purposes. In June 2006, the FASB issued FASB Interpretation (FIN) No. 48, *Accounting for Uncertainty in Income Taxes* (now contained in Accounting Standards Codification Topic 740). FIN 48 or ASC 740 was created primarily as a mechanism to provide greater transparency for uncertain tax positions and greater uniformity in the financial reporting of tax issues.

FIN 48 requires companies to identify their uncertain tax positions and determine the likelihood that they will or will not survive audit, appeals and litigation. Once that is determined, FIN 48 forces companies to disclose and create a reserve for uncertain tax positions that are more likely than not to occur. Basically, FIN 48 contains a two step-process that must be applied to all tax positions: recognition and measurement. First, a tax position is recognized for financial accounting purposes only if it is "more likely than not" (i.e., greater than 50 percent) that the position will be sustained upon examination by a taxing authority. Second, if the tax position is recognized, the effect is measured. Using probability techniques, measurement determines what amount of a tax position will be sustainable upon a potential examination or settlement. Finally, FIN 48 requires certain disclosures to be footnoted in the financial statements. In short, it has completely changed the way companies account for uncertainty with respect to tax positions.

### Uncertain Tax Positions: Tax Reporting

It was not long after the issuance of FIN 48 that the government decided it deserved similar treatment. In 2010, the IRS released Announcement 2010-9 that explained it was creating a new schedule, requiring certain companies to report *on their tax returns* their uncertain tax positions beginning with the 2010 tax year. The schedule is appropriately titled Schedule UTP. Generally, a corporation that is required to file a corporate income tax return, Form 1120 (and certain others) must attach Schedule UTP if it meets the following requirements:

1. The corporation has assets that equal or exceed $100 million;
2. The corporation or a related party issued *audited* financial statements; and
3. The corporation has one or more tax positions that must be reported on Schedule UTP.

Schedule UTP requires the reporting of an income tax position taken by the corporation on its tax return if it recorded a reserve for that tax position in audited financial statements or did not record a reserve because the corporation expects to litigate the position.

## Fraud

When the taxpayer attempts to defraud the government, the tax law imposes a minimum penalty equal to 75 percent of the amount of underpayment attributable to the fraud.[28] *In addition*, the taxpayer may also be subject to the criminal penalties for fraud. Criminal penalties can be as high as $100,000 ($500,000 for corporate taxpayers) and imprisonment for up to five years. Despite these penalties, it appears that some taxpayers continue to play the audit lottery, including some rich and famous tax felons:[29]

- Leona Helmsley, New York hotel magnate, who will forever be remembered for her offhand comment to her housekeeper, "we don't pay taxes; only the little people pay taxes." Helmsley, convicted in 1992 for deducting millions of dollars of personal expenses, including renovations to her personal residence, was fined more than $7 million and sentenced to four years in prison (served 18 months).
- Pete Rose, baseball player and all-time leader in hits (4,256). Rose failed to report income from memorabilia shows and gambling and served five months in prison.
- Spiro Agnew, vice-president during the Nixon era. Agnew, who failed to report income from bribes, was fined $10,000 and had a three-year suspended sentence.
- Chuck Berry, famous rock and roll star of Johnny B. Goode fame. Berry underreported his income by $110,000 in 1979 and served four months in prison.
- Aldo Gucci, famous designer. Gucci pleaded guilty to $7 million of tax fraud in 1989 and was sentenced to one year in jail and fined $30,000.
- Al Capone, racketeer and mobster. Capone, convicted of tax evasion in 1931, was fined $50,000 and served eight years of a ten-year sentence, then retired to his Miami estate.
- Willie Nelson, country and western singing star. Nelson ran up his tax bill to over $32 million. He served no time in prison, but part of the bill was paid from part of his ranch, which was seized by the IRS.

---

[28] § 6663.

[29] See in part "Famous Faces from IRS Hall of Shame," *Sacramento Bee*, March 29, 1994. Metro Final Scene, D3.

- Richard Hatch, winner in the debut season of reality show "Survivor." Hatch failed to report $1,000,000 and pay taxes on the winnings. He reportedly asked an accountant to prepare two tax returns, one with the winnings and the other without, and chose to file the latter. Hatch was found guilty of tax evasion and was sentenced in 2006 to serve 51 months in prison.

Civil fraud has not been clearly defined, but it requires more than simply negligent acts or omissions by the taxpayer. There is a fine line between fraud and negligence (to which a lesser penalty applies, as explained above). Fraud does not occur by accident. It is a willful and deliberate attempt to evade tax. For example, consider a taxpayer who is entitled to a deduction of $19,000. What penalty applies if he transposed the digits and claimed a deduction of $91,000? Fraud occurs only if it can be shown that the taxpayer knew that the amounts reported on the return were false. In this regard, the IRS must prove this to be true by a "preponderance of evidence." Thus for the transposition error above, the fraud penalty can be upheld if the IRS can carry its burden of proof and show that the taxpayer intentionally transposed the numbers. Lacking this, the negligence or substantial understatement penalty would probably be assessed. Note that before the *criminal* fraud penalty can be imposed, the IRS must show that the taxpayer intentionally tried to evade tax "beyond a shadow of any reasonable doubt." All of those in the "hall of shame" above found that this is not an impossible task. As a practical matter, the penalty imposed—negligence, civil, or criminal fraud—depends on the severity of the offense and the ability of the IRS to carry the burden of proof.

### Example 6

Dr. Bradford Calloway paid his children, all of whom were under 12 years of age, $11,000 for performing various tasks relating to his business. The kids did such chores as mail sorting, trash collecting, and answering the telephone. Although expenses incurred in carrying on a business such as these are normally deductible, the IRS did not believe that children that age could perform work worth that much money for any business. The Tax Court agreed with the IRS, and the judge added a fraud penalty, explaining that "We find it inherently incredible that Calloway, an intelligent and educated professional man, would pay a total of $11,138.56 for such services, performed by small children on a part-time basis, or that he could seriously believe that such payments represented reasonable and deductible compensation for services rendered in his medical practice . . . particularly in the face of his accountant's contrary advice."[30]

## Tax Preparer Penalties

**LO.13**
Understand the rules of conduct that must be followed by those who perform tax services.

Understanding the penalty structure becomes doubly hard when a tax preparer is involved. What are the responsibilities of tax preparers when the client is unscrupulous or simply wants to take an aggressive position? As a practical matter, it is not the totally dishonest taxpayer that presents difficulties for tax return preparers. Most practitioners can easily walk away from such engagements. The more perplexing and more common problems concern situations where the client wants the preparer to take an aggressive position on issues for which the answer is unclear. Similarly, taxpayers may want to pursue a particular position because they view the law as arbitrary or capricious or they are not receptive to the preparer's response. These situations often present an ethical dilemma for the preparer. What side should the practitioner take? Should the preparer sign the return if he or she disagrees with the taxpayer? First, it needs to be emphasized that the tax practitioner is being paid to be an advocate for the client, not an independent third party hired to provide an unbiased or neutral opinion. It is the job of the tax expert to explain the relevant considerations and possible consequences, including positions that may be contrary to the law but which may be defensible. That done, it is not the right of the practitioner to impose his or her own set of moral values on the client. The final decision is to be made by the client after reviewing the

---

[30] A. J. Cook, *A. J.'s Tax Court* (St. Luke's Press, 1987), p. 96.

alternatives provided. If the practitioner believes that the client's actions violate his or her personal code of ethics, the practitioner should withdraw from the engagement.

Beyond the basic preparer-client relationship, there are a number of other forces at work that affect whether the preparer signs the return containing a risky position. First, even if an answer to a particular question does exist, the costs of uncovering it probably cannot be recovered from the client. Second, given the small percentage of tax returns that are audited, there is only a slight chance that either the taxpayer or preparer will ever come face to face with the IRS. Third, preparers, like most people, want to please their customers and find it hard to just say no. When these dynamics are present, they make it relatively easy for practitioners to resolve an issue in favor of the client, notwithstanding the lack of reasonable support for the position. This is particularly true when the practitioner knows that the unprincipled competitor down the street will do whatever the client wants and at a cheaper price. On the other hand, the practitioner's sense of public duty, concern about his or her personal and professional reputation, and possible legal liability may cause him or her to be something less than an advocate for the client. As might be expected, the practitioner's proper role in these situations is not clearly defined. There are, however, in addition to the preparer's own personal code of ethics, some guidelines that a preparer generally must follow in carrying on a tax practice.

Individuals who prepare tax returns are subject to a variety of rules regulating their professional conduct. The rules governing tax practice are contained in Treasury Circular 230 and various provisions of the Internal Revenue Code. In addition, CPAs and attorneys engaged in tax practice must also follow the rules of conduct imposed by their professional organizations: the American Institute of Certified Public Accountants (AICPA) and the American Bar Association (ABA). The general rules of conduct prescribed by the AICPA for all CPAs concern a variety of matters such as independence, integrity, objectivity, advertising, contingent fees, and responsibilities of the accountant when undertaking an engagement—but none of these are directly related to tax practice. Acknowledging that individuals engaged in tax practice have ethical concerns beyond those covered in the general rules of conduct, the AICPA has developed Statements on Standards for Tax Services (SSTSs). These statements, currently seven in number, provide additional guidelines for professional conduct of CPAs in tax practice. Similarly, the ABA Standing Committee on Ethics and Professional Responsibility has also issued certain opinions regarding an attorney's conduct when practicing before the IRS.

## Tax Return Positions

As might be imagined, the rules and applicable penalties concerning practitioner conduct as set forth by Circular 230, the Internal Revenue Code, the AICPA, and the ABA deserve a chapter devoted solely to these topics. In essence, however, the most important penalty for those preparing returns is that contained in § 6694(a). Section 6694(a) provides that a penalty of $1,000 (or if greater, 50% of the income from preparing the return) is imposed on the preparer of a tax return if any part of an understatement of the liability on a return is due to an unreasonable position taken on the tax return and the return preparer knew (or reasonably should have known) of the position.[31] If the position is properly disclosed on the return, the penalty does not apply if there was a reasonable basis for the position.[32] If the position is not disclosed, the penalty applies unless there is substantial authority for the position. As noted earlier, substantial authority includes the Internal Revenue Code, Regulations (final, temporary and proposed), court cases, tax treaties, and administrative pronouncements (Revenue Rulings, Revenue Procedures, Private Letter Rulings, Technical Advice Memoranda, Notices and similar documents). If the position is with respect to a tax shelter investment, the threshold for authority is raised, and the penalty is imposed unless it was reasonable to believe that the position would "more likely than not" be sustained on its merits if the position were litigated. The preparer penalty is not imposed in any case if it is shown that there is reasonable cause for the understatement and the preparer acted in good faith. Note that the penalty applies to any

---

[31] The penalty increases to the greater of $5,000 or 50% of the income derived from preparation of the return if it is attributable to willful or reckless conduct. See § 6694(b).

[32] Disclosure must be made on Form 8275 or, when the position is contrary to a Regulation, Form 8275-R. See Reg. § 1.6694-2(c)(3)(i).

paid preparer regardless of whether the person is a CPA, enrolled agent, friend, or relative. If the preparer is compensated, the penalty could apply.[33]

### Example 7

T purchased a computer this year that he uses in his job as a financial planner. His friends at the office say that he can deduct it. His accountant, P, explained that it might be deductible but only if T can demonstrate that the computer's use is for his employer's convenience and not his own. If the position is disclosed, neither P nor T will be subject to penalty if there is a reasonable basis for the position. If the position is not disclosed, then normally substantial authority must exist to avoid penalty.

At first glance, it would appear that the size of penalty imposed by the IRS, $1,000, is so small that it would do little to dissuade preparers from taking whatever position a client wishes. What may not be apparent, however, is the significance of this standard *and* its violation should a disgruntled client end up suing the preparer for malpractice. In a civil action against a preparer, the courts, both judges and juries, typically rely on expert testimony to assess whether the preparer should be held liable. In such case, it is not too hard to imagine a judge or jury believing that the preparer was negligent once an expert has explained that the preparer has already been penalized under § 6694(a). Even if the preparer is ultimately exonerated, the costs to defend such action could be substantial. Moreover, failing to observe such a standard could ultimately cost the practitioner the loss of his or her professional license to practice as a CPA or attorney. In short, it is not the size of the penalty that the practitioner fears but the other consequences that the penalty may trigger.

### Example 8

T, a CPA, has prepared the tax return for D&G Home Products for the past 15 years. It is normally a week-long job and worth well over $10,000 to T's practice. He also does the monthly preparation of financial statements worth another $20,000 per year. This year G spent more than $100,000 on a Super Bowl excursion for its customers. In preparing the return, D&G insists that it should be able to deduct all of the expenses, but T has some reservations. T understands there have been some recent changes in the law in this area but does not have time to adequately research the issue, and, even if he did, he doubts whether he could charge for the time spent. He also knows that this is a lucrative engagement and he wants to continue the relationship with the client. Finally, T recognizes that it is highly unlikely that the return will ever be audited. Consequently, T decides to sign the return and worry about it only if a problem arises. But what happens if the return is audited, the position is overturned, and a preparer penalty is assessed on the grounds that the return contained an undisclosed position that did not have substantial authority supporting it. While the penalty would be monetarily small, the real concern is the effect of the reversal on the client. D&G may have a short memory once it is forced to pay the tax, interest, and perhaps a substantial understatement penalty and interest on the penalty. It may not remember conversations with T and his admonitions. In the end, the corporation may feel that it was misled and sue T for malpractice and thousands of dollars. In such a proceeding, D&G may have the upper hand since it has been determined by a court of law that the position was unrealistic under that standards of § 6694(a) and T has therefore failed to meet his ethical responsibilities.

[33] See § 7701(a)(36) for a definition of preparer.

The decision that all practitioners ultimately face with every return they prepare is whether they can in good faith sign the tax return as preparer. Under the current rules, preparers normally will be reluctant to sign if the return contains an undisclosed position that does not have substantial authority.[34]

In addition to the $1,000 penalty, the tax law provides a number of other penalties to encourage ethical conduct by preparers. For example, a penalty of $1,000 per return is imposed where the preparer willfully attempts to understate the liability of the taxpayer or where the preparer understates the taxpayer's liability by reckless or intentional disregard of the rules or regulations.[35] The law also contains a number of criminal penalties for preparers with fines of up to $10,000 and imprisonment for up to three years.[36]

## Other Guidelines for CPAs

**LO.14**
Appreciate the role of ethics in tax practice and the responsibilities of tax practitioners.

As suggested above, the Statements on Standards for Tax Services provide a number of other guidelines for members of the AICPA who are tax practitioners. There are currently seven statements. *SSTS No. 1*, regarding tax positions, was mentioned above. The remaining statements generally fall into one of two categories: (1) return preparation issues (SSTS Numbers 2, 3, and 4) and (2) issues that arise after a return is filed (SSTS Numbers 5 and 6). Statement Number 7 addresses the form and content of advice given to taxpayers. Some of these statements are summarized below.

- *SSTS No. 2: Answers to Questions on the Return.* When there are questions on a return that have not been answered, the CPA should make a reasonable effort to obtain appropriate answers from the taxpayer and provide the answers to the questions on the return. The significance of the question in terms of the information's effect on taxable income or loss and tax liability may be considered in determining whether the answer to a question may be omitted. However, omission of an answer is not justified simply because the answer may prove to be disadvantageous to the taxpayer.
- *SSTS No. 3: Certain Procedural Aspects of Preparing Returns.* In preparing or signing a return, a CPA may, without verification, rely in good faith on information furnished by the taxpayer or a third party. However, the CPA cannot ignore the implications of information furnished, and should make reasonable inquiries if the information appears to be incorrect, incomplete, or inconsistent either by itself or on the basis of other facts known to the CPA. When preparing the current return, the CPA should make use of returns from prior years wherever feasible. If the tax law or regulations impose conditions with respect to the tax treatment of an item (e.g., substantiating documentation), the CPA should make appropriate inquiries to determine if the conditions are met. In addition, when preparing a return, the CPA should consider relevant information known to the CPA from the tax return of another taxpayer, but should also consider any legal limitations relating to confidentiality.
- *SSTS No. 4: Use of Estimates.* Unless it is prohibited by the Internal Revenue Code or other tax rule, a CPA may prepare returns involving the use of the taxpayer's estimates, if under the circumstances, exact data cannot be obtained in a practical manner. When estimates are used, they should be presented in such a manner as to avoid the implication of greater accuracy than that which exists. The CPA should be satisfied that estimated amounts are reasonable under the circumstances.
- *SSTS No. 6: Knowledge of Error (Return Preparation and Administrative Proceeding).* A CPA should advise the taxpayer promptly upon learning of an error in a previously filed return, or upon learning of a taxpayer's failure to file a required return. The advice of the CPA may be oral, and should include a recommendation of the measures to be taken. The CPA is not obliged to inform the IRS and may not do so without the permission of the taxpayer, except where required by law. If the CPA is requested to prepare the current year's return and the taxpayer has not taken appropriate steps to correct an error on a prior year's return, the CPA should consider whether to withdraw from preparing the return and whether to continue a professional or employment relationship with the taxpayer.

  When the CPA represents a taxpayer in an administrative proceeding regarding a return with an error known to the CPA that has resulted or may result in more than an insignificant effect on the taxpayer's tax liability, the CPA should notify the taxpayer and

---

[34] Prop. Reg. § 10.34.

[35] § 6694(b).

[36] See §§ 7206, 7207, and 7216.

recommend corrective measures to be taken. The recommendations may be given orally. The CPA is not obligated to inform the IRS or other taxing authority, and may not do so without the taxpayer's permission, except where required by law. However, the CPA should request permission from the taxpayer to disclose the error to the IRS. Absent such permission, the CPA should consider withdrawing from the engagement.

## Circular 230 Changes

In 2005, Circular 230 was changed to require those who practice before the IRS to disclose to their clients when the advice they give to them cannot be relied on for purposes of mitigating penalties that might be imposed on them. In practice, this means that lawyers, CPAs and other tax practitioners affix a disclaimer somewhat like that which follows to all written communications with clients that do not constitute a full legal option. The disclaimer must be placed on faxes, e-mails, blackberries and regular written correspondence.

> DISCLAIMER: Any federal tax advice contained in this communication (including attachments) was not intended or written to be used, and it cannot be used, by you for the purpose of (1) avoiding any penalty that may be imposed by the Internal Revenue Service or (2) promoting, marketing or recommending to another party any transaction or matter addressed herein.

The above discussion is just a brief introduction to the penalties and rules of practice that serve to define the proper conduct for taxpayers and preparers. In reality, there are a number of other penalties and rules that may apply in certain situations.[37] Nevertheless, this introduction may provide a sense of what are the most common ethical problems facing tax practitioners. Moreover, it underscores the importance of being able to find authoritative answers for questions, the subject of the next section.

## CHECK YOUR KNOWLEDGE

### Review Question 1

The system of penalties provides an escape for taxpayers if the positions taken on their returns meet certain standards. In effect, meeting a certain standard enables the taxpayer to avoid a penalty. Practitioners generally associate a probability of success rate for each standard. What probabilities would you assign?

| | |
|---|---|
| Frivolous | ________ |
| Substantial authority | ________ |
| Nonfrivolous | ________ |
| More-likely-than-not | ________ |
| Reasonable basis | ________ |
| Realistic possibility of success | ________ |

None of these probabilities other than *realistic possibility of success* have been quantified by the law. However, practitioners would typically rank the standards in the following order with the associated probabilities of success. Although the probabilities might vary from firm to firm and practitioner to practitioner, the order would remain the same.

| | | |
|---|---|---|
| 1. | More-likely-than-not | > 50% |
| 2. | Substantial authority | ≥ 40 |
| 3. | Realistic possibility of success | ≥ 33 |
| 4. | Reasonable basis | ≥ 20 |
| 5. | Nonfrivolous | ≥ 5 |
| 6. | Frivolous | < 5 |

[37] For a more complete discussion, see the related text, *Corporate Partnership, Estate and Gift Taxation, 2011 Edition*, Chapter 18.

## Review Question 2

Pete Hartman operates an accounting practice in northern Virginia just outside of Washington. One of his long-time clients is Jim Anderson. Last year the IRS audited Jim's 2008 tax return, and he ultimately had to pay additional taxes as well as interest on that amount. Jim now wants to deduct a portion of this interest as a business expense. He reasons that because business expenses are deductible and the interest was directly attributable to back taxes on business income, the deduction should be allowed. There has also been another development this year. Jim's daughter has been diagnosed to have dyslexia. The problem is not severe but it was enough to cause Jim to enroll his daughter in a private school that is better equipped to provide the additional help she needs. The tuition for the school is $20,000, and Jim wants to deduct the cost as a medical expense. After some research, Pete believes that both positions are somewhat risky. Jim has asked Pete about the downside risk of taking this position on his return. Pete estimates that taking the deduction for the interest will reduce Jim's tax liability of $30,000 about $1,000. If he were to claim only the medical expense deduction by itself, it would reduce his tax liability by about $6,000. Try to answer the following questions.

**a.** What is the maximum penalty that Jim might pay if he deducts only the interest and it is considered erroneous but not fraudulent?

Jim would be subject to an accuracy-related penalty (negligence), which is 20 percent of the amount of the underpayment due to the overstatement of deductions. In this case, the penalty would be $200 (20% × $ 1,000). In addition, Jim would owe the additional $1,000 in tax plus interest on the underpayment *and* interest on the penalty.

**b.** True-False. Jim will not be subject to penalty with respect to the interest deduction as long as his position has a reasonable basis even if he does not specifically disclose the position on the return since the amount of tax at stake is not substantial.

*True.* The negligence penalty will not be assessed as long as the taxpayer has a reasonable basis for the position regardless of whether the position is disclosed on the tax return.

**c.** True-False. Jim will not be subject to penalty with respect to the tuition deduction as long as his position has a reasonable basis even if he does not specifically disclose the position on the return.

*False.* In this situation, Jim's $6,000 understatement would be considered substantial since it exceeds the larger of $5,000 or 10 percent of the correct tax, $3,000 (10% × $30,000). When the understatement in question is substantial, the substantial understatement penalty applies. This penalty can be avoided only if the taxpayer has substantial authority for his position *or* he discloses the position and such position has reasonable basis. Here Jim will not have disclosed the position, so a reasonable basis for the position will not suffice.

**d.** Jim has indicated that he does not want to flag either position. Pete would not be subject to a preparer penalty with respect to the tuition deduction if the position is *not* disclosed as long as the position:

(1) has a reasonable basis
(2) is nonfrivolous
(3) has a realistic possibility of success
(4) has a more-likely-than-not chance of prevailing
(5) all of the above

*(4).* To avoid the $1,000 preparer penalty of § 6694(a), an undisclosed position must be supported with substantial authority. However, if the position is disclosed, the preparer penalty will not apply as long as it there is a reasonable basis for the position.

**e.** Pete understands that the SSTS indicate that he is not supposed to sign the return where there is an undisclosed position unless the position has a realistic possibility of success. However, he has no real idea whether the chances are 20 percent, 30 percent, 40 percent, or whatever based on what he has found. Can Pete sign a return containing a position for which there is no reasonable basis without violating the AICPA statements if he discloses the position?

*Yes.* The SSTS provide that a practitioner can sign any return as long as the position is disclosed and it is not frivolous.

## Problem Materials

### DISCUSSION QUESTIONS

**2-1** *Taxpayer Penalties.* In reviewing his last year's return, T noticed that he had inadvertently deducted the entire cost of a new air-conditioning system. Such cost should have been capitalized and depreciated.

**a.** T wants to know what penalties, if any, might be assessed if his return is audited and the IRS uncovers his mistake.

**b.** What should T do?

**2-2** *Tax Positions.* R operates a small accounting practice in Columbus, Ohio. While preparing the return for his long-time client C, he found out that C wants to deduct the cost of lawn care for her home. C is a landscape architect who recently started using a room at her home as an office. She feels that this is clearly a business expense. During the interview she seemed to have a point. "What if my clients came to my house and the yard was less than picture perfect? It would kill my business," she explained. R has reviewed the proposed regulations on the home office deduction, and they specifically state that lawn care is not deductible. Nevertheless, he understands C's point. R just cannot say no, and he is thinking about preparing the return and deducting a portion of lawn care allocable to C's home office.

**a.** Assume the position is erroneous and is not disclosed. Will C be subject to any penalty? Explain.

**b.** Assume the position is erroneous and is disclosed. Will C be subject to any penalty? Explain.

**2-3** *Avoiding Preparer Penalties.* H recently quit a national public accounting firm and purchased the practice of a local accountant. Her first busy season with this new set of clients has been eye-opening. Some of the taxpayers have been taking very questionable positions on certain recurring items. Somewhat paranoid, H is now quite concerned about incurring penalties. What can she do to guard against possible preparer penalties?

**2-4** *Knowledge of Error.* Last March, P put the finishing touches on the tax return of one of his most prized clients, Great Buy Corporation. When preparing the monthly financial statement for June, P noticed that $30,000 of sales somehow got left off of the return. What should P do?

**2-5** *Knowledge of Error.* This year P got a new client from the firm down the street, Dewey, Cheatham and Howe. After reviewing the client's prior year return, he found, as he had expected, an error in the way Dewey had computed depreciation. What should P do?

**2-6** *Making a New Tax Law.* Describe the Congressional process of making a tax bill into final law.

**2-7** *Legislative versus Interpretative Regulations.* Explain the difference between a legislative Treasury Regulation and an interpretative Regulation.

**2-8** *Proposed versus Final Regulations.* Distinguish between proposed and final Regulations. How would either type of Regulation involving Code § 704 be cited?

**2-9** *Revenue Rulings and Revenue Procedures.* Distinguish between a Revenue Ruling and a Revenue Procedure. Where can either be found in printed form?

**2-10** *Private versus Published Rulings.* Distinguish between a private letter ruling and a Revenue Ruling. Under what circumstances would a taxpayer prefer to rely on either of these sources?

**2-11** *Technical Advice Memoranda.* What are Technical Advice Memoranda? Under what circumstances are they issued?

**2-12** *Trial Courts.* Describe the trial courts that hear tax cases. What are the advantages or disadvantages of litigating a tax issue in each of these courts?

**2-13** *The Appeals Process.* A taxpayer living in Indiana has exhausted her appeals within the IRS. If she chooses to litigate her case, trace the appeals process assuming she begins her effort in each of the following trial courts:

**a.** The U.S. Court of Federal Claims
**b.** The U.S. District Court
**c.** The U.S. Tax Court
**d.** The Small Tax Division of the U.S. Tax Court

**2-14** *Tax Court Decisions.* Distinguish between a Regular Tax Court decision and a Memorandum decision.

**2-15** *Authority of Tax Law Sources.* Assume that you have discovered favorable support for your position taken in a controversy with an IRS agent in each of the sources listed below. Which of these has the greater weight of authority? Rank them from strongest to weakest.

**a.** A decision of the U.S. District Court having jurisdiction over your case if litigated
**b.** Treasury Regulation
**c.** The Internal Revenue Code
**d.** A decision of the Supreme Court
**e.** A decision of the Court of Appeals
**f.** A decision of the Small Claims Court
**g.** A decision of the U.S. Tax Court
**h.** A private letter ruling issued to another taxpayer
**i.** A Revenue Ruling
**j.** A tax article in a leading periodical

**2-16** *Tax Services.* What materials are generally found in leading tax services? Which does your library have?

## YOU MAKE THE CALL

**2-17** T is the owner of a small CPA firm that has developed a very good auditing and tax practice over the years. Recently, while visiting the home of S, his best client (revenues of about $50,000 annually for audit and tax services), T learned some very disturbing information about S's business practices. During a tour of her home, S accidentally revealed that some very expensive personal entertainment equipment acquired this year had been charged to her corporation (cost of approximately $100,000). S stated that everyone she knew charged personal assets to their business accounts and that it appeared to be generally accepted practice. She said she hoped T would not mind.

When T returned to his office, he immediately checked S's 2010 corporate income tax return and found that depreciation had been taken on the $100,000 cost of assets listed simply as "Equipment." Of course, T never suspected the assets were for personal use in S's home.

What should T do? This client is too good to lose, but T is worried about the consequences of allowing this type of behavior to continue.

## PROBLEMS

**2-18** *Interpreting Citations.* Interpret each of the following citations:

**a.** Reg. § 1.721-1(a).
**b.** Rev. Rul. 60-314, 1960-2 C.B. 48.
**c.** Rev. Proc. 86-46, 1986-2 C.B. 739.
**d.** Rev. Rul. 98-36, I.R.B. No. 31, 6.
**e.** § 351.

**2-19** *Citation Abbreviations.* Explain each of the abbreviations below.

**a.** B.T.A.
**b.** Acq.
**c.** D. Ct.
**d.** CA-9
**e.** F.Supp.
**f.** NA.
**g.** Ct. Cls.
**h.** USTC
**i.** AFTR
**j.** *Cert. Den.*
**k.** *aff'g* and *aff'd*
**l.** *rev'g* and *rev'd*
**m.** *rem'g* and *rem'd*

**2-20** *Interpreting Citations.* Identify the publisher and interpret each of the following citations:

**a.** 41 TCM 289.
**b.** 71-1 USTC ¶9241 (CA-2, 1971).
**c.** 236 F.Supp. 761 (D. Ct. Va., 1974).
**d.** T.C. Memo 1977-20.
**e.** 48 T.C. 430 (1967).
**f.** 6 AFTR2d 5095 (CA-2, 1960).
**g.** 589 F.2d 446 (CA-9, 1979).
**h.** 277 U.S. 508 (USSC, 1928).

**2-21** *Citation Form.* Record the following information in its proper citation form.

**a.** Part 7, subdivision (a)(2) of the income tax Regulation under Code § 165
**b.** The 34th Revenue Ruling issued March 2, 1987, and printed on page 168 of the Cumulative Bulletin
**c.** The 113th letter ruling issued the last week of 1986

**2-22** *Citation Form.* Record the following information in its proper citation form.

**a.** A 1982 U.S. Tax Court case in which Roger A. Schubel sued the IRS Commissioner for a refund, published in volume 77 on pages 701 through 715 as a Regular decision
**b.** A 1974 U.S. Tax Court case in which H. N. Schilling, Jr. sued the IRS Commissioner for a refund, published by (1) Commerce Clearing House in volume 33 on pages 1097 through 1110 and (2) Research Institute of America (Prentice Hall) as its 246th decision that year
**c.** A 1966 Court of Appeals case in which Boris Nodiak sued the IRS Commissioner in the second Circuit for a refund, published by (1) Commerce Clearing House in volume 1 of that year at paragraph 9262, (2) Prentice Hall in volume 17 on pages 396 through 402, and (3) West Publishing Company in volume 356 on pages 911 through 919.

## TAX RESEARCH PROBLEMS

**2-23** *Using a Citator.* Use either the Commerce Clearing House or Research Institute of America Citator in your library and locate *Richard L. Kroll, Exec. v. U.S.*

**a.** Which Court of Appeals Circuit heard this case?
**b.** Was this case heard by the Supreme Court?
**c.** James B. and Doris E. Wallach are included in the listing below the citation for Kroll. In what court was the Wallach case heard?

**2-24** *Using a Citator.* Using any available citator, locate the case of *Corn Products v. Comm.*, 350 U.S. 46. What effect did the decision in *Arkansas Best v. Comm.* (58 AFTR2d 86-5748, 800 F.2d 219) have on the precedential value of the *Corn Products* case?

**2-25** *Locating Court Cases.* Locate the case of *Robert Autrey, Jr. v. United States*, 89-2 USTC ¶9659, and answer the following questions.

**a.** What court decided the case on appeal?
**b.** What court originally tried the case?
**c.** Was the trial court's decision upheld or reversed?

**2-26** *Locating Court Cases.* Locate the case of *Fabry v. Commissioner*, 111 T.C. 305, and answer the following questions.

**a.** What court tried the case?

**b.** Identify the various types of precedential authority the judge used in framing his opinion.

**2-27** *Locating Court Cases.* Locate the cited court cases and answer the questions below.

**a.** *Stanley A. and Lorriee M. Golanty*, 72 T.C. 411 (1979). Did the taxpayers win their case?

**b.** *Hamilton D. Hill*, 41 TCM 700, T.C. Memo ¶71,127 (1971). Who was the presiding judge?

**c.** *Patterson (Jefferson) v. Comm.*, 72-1 USTC ¶9420, 29 AFTR2d 1181 (Ct. Cls., 1972). What was the issue being questioned in this case?

**2-28** *Completing Citations.* To the extent the materials are available to you, complete the following citations:

**a.** Rev. Rul. 98-60, ______C.B. ______.

**b.** *Lawrence W. McCoy*, ______T.C. ______1962.

**c.** *Reginald Turner*______TCM ______T.C. Memo 1954-38.

**d.** *RCA Corp. v. U.S.*,______USTC ______ (CA-2, 1981).

**e.** *RCA Corp. v. U.S.*,______AFTR2d ______ (CA-2, 1981).

**f.** *RCA Corp. v. U.S.*,______F.2.d ______ (CA-2, 1981).

**g.** *Comm. v. Wilcox*,______S. Ct. ______(USSC, 1946).

**h.** ______, 79-1 USTC ¶9139 (USSC, 1979).

**i.** ______, 34 T.C. 842 (1960).

**j.** *Brian E. Knutson*, 60 TCM 540, T.C. Memo ______

**k.** *Samuel B. Levin v. Comm.*, 43 AFTR2d 79-1057 ( ______).

**2-29** *Examination of Tax Sources.* For each of the tax sources listed below, identify at least one of the tax issues involved. In addition, if the source has a temporary citation, provide its permanent citation (if available).

**a.** *Battelstein Investment Co. v. U.S.*, 71-1 USTC ¶9227, 27 AFTR2d 71-713, 442 F.2d 87 (CA-5, 1971).

**b.** *Joel Kerns*, 47 TCM, __________T.C. Memo 1984-22.

**c.** *Patterson v. U.S.*, 84-1 USTC ¶9315 (CA-6, 1984).

**d.** *Webster Lair*, 95 T.C. 484 (1990).

**e.** *Thompson Engineering Co., Inc.*, 80 T.C. 672 (1983).

**f.** *Towne Square, Inc.*, 45 TCM 478, T.C. Memo 1983-10.

**g.** Rev. Rul. 85-13, I.R.B. No. 7, 28.

**h.** Rev. Proc. 85-49, I.R.B. No. 40, 26.

**i.** *William E Sutton, et al. v. Comm.*, 84 T.C.__________No. 17.

**j.** Rev. Rul. 86-103, I.R.B. No. 36, 13.

**k.** *Hughes Properties, Inc.*, 86-1 USTC ¶9440, 58 AFTR2d 86-5062, __________ U.S. __________(USSC, 1986).

**l.** Rev. Rul. 98-27, I.R.B. No. 22, 4.

**2-30** *Office in the Home.* T comes to you for advice regarding the deductibility of expenses for maintaining an office in his home. T is currently employed as an executive vice president for Zandy Corporation. He has found it impossible to complete his job responsibilities during the normal forty-hour weekly period. Although the office building in which he works is open nights and weekends, the heating and air-conditioning systems are shut down at night (from 6 p.m.) and during the entire weekend. As a result, T has begun taking work home with him on a regular basis. The work is generally done in the den of T's home. Although T's employer does not require him to work at home, T is convinced that he would be fired if his work assignments were not completed on a timely basis. Given these facts, what would you advise T about taking a home-office deduction?

***Partial list of research aids:***

§ 280A
Proposed Reg. § 1.280A
*M.G. Hill*, 43 TCM 832, T.C. Memo 1982-143

**2-31** *Journal Articles.* Refer to *Problem 2-30*. Consult an index to periodicals (e.g., AICPA's *Accountants Index*; Warren, Gorham, and Lamont's *Index to Federal Tax Articles*; or CCH's *Federal Tax Articles*) and locate a journal article on the topic of tax deductions for an office in the home. Copy the article. Record the citation for the article (i.e., author's name, article title, journal name, publication date, and first and last pages of the article) at the top of your paper. Prepare a two-page summary of the article, including all relevant issues, research sources, and conclusions. Staple your two-page summary to the article. The grade for this exercise will be based on the relevance of your article to the topic, the accuracy and quality of your summary, and the quality of your written communication skills.

**2-32** *Deductible Medical Expenses.* B suffers from a severe form of degenerative arthritis. Her doctor strongly recommended that she swim for at least one hour per day in order to stretch and exercise her leg and arm muscles. There are no swimming pools nearby, so B spent $15,000 to have a swimming pool installed in her back yard. This expenditure increased the fair market value of her house by $5,000. B consults you about whether she can deduct the cost of the swimming pool on her individual tax return. What do you recommend?

***Hint:*** You should approach this problem by using the tax service volumes of either Commerce Clearing House or Research Institute of America. Both tax services are organized according to Code Sections, so you should start with Code § 213. You will find the Code Sections on the back binding of the volumes. Research Institute of America has a very extensive index, so look under the term "medical expenses."

**2-33** *Deductible Educational Expenses.* T is a CPA with a large accounting firm in Houston, Texas. He has been assigned to the international taxation group of his firm's tax department. As a result of this assignment, T enrolls in an international tax law course at the University of Houston Law School. The authorities of the University require T to enroll as a regular law student; and, theoretically, if he continues to attend courses, T will graduate with a law degree. Will T be able to deduct his tuition for the international tax law course as a business expense?

***Hint:*** Go to either the RIA or CCH tax service and use it to find the analysis of Code § 162. When you have found the discussion of § 162, find that part of the subsection dealing with educational deductions. Read the appropriate Regulations and then note the authorities listed after the Regulations. Read over the summaries provided and then choose those you think have the most relevance to the question asked above. Read these cases and other listed authorities, and formulate a written response to the question asked in light of these cases and other authorities Finally, for the authorities you choose, go to the RIA or CCH Citator and use it to ensure that your authorities are current.

3

# Taxable Entities; Tax Formula; Introduction to Property Transactions

## Learning Objectives

Upon completion of this chapter you will be able to:

LO.1 Identify the entities that are subject to the Federal income tax.

LO.2 Explain the basic tax treatment of individuals, corporations, partnerships, S corporations, and fiduciary taxpayers (trusts and estates).

LO.3 Understand the basic tax formulas to be followed in computing the tax liability for individuals and corporations.

LO.4 Define many of the basic terms used in the tax formula such as gross income, adjusted gross income, taxable income, exclusion, deduction, and credit.

LO.5 Calculate the gain or loss on the disposition of property and explain the tax consequences, including the special treatment of capital gains and losses.

## Chapter Outline

Introduction 3-2
The Taxable Entity 3-2
Taxable Entities 3-3
Individual Taxpayers 3-3
Corporate Taxpayers 3-5
Fiduciary Taxpayers 3-7
Flow-Through Entities 3-8
Sole Proprietorships 3-8
Partnerships 3-9
Electing Small Business Corporations: "S"Corporations 3-11
Limited Liability Companies 3-11
Tax-Exempt Organizations 3-12
Tax Formula 3-15
Analyzing the Tax Formula 3-15
Introduction to Property Transactions 3-28
Gain or Loss Realized 3-28
Gain or Loss Recognized 3-30
Character of the Gain or Loss 3-31
Trade or Business Property 3-34
Tax Planning Considerations 3-36
Choice of Business Form 3-36
Itemized Deductions versus Standard Deduction 3-37
Employee Business Expenses 3-37
Problem Materials 3-38

## Introduction

The amount of income tax ultimately paid by any taxpayer is determined by applying the many rules comprising our income tax system. This chapter examines some of the fundamental features of this system. They are

- *Taxable Entities*—those entities that are subject to taxation and those that are merely conduits
- *Tax Formulas*—the mathematical relationships used to compute the tax for the various taxable entities
- *Property Transactions*—the tax treatment of sales, exchanges, and other dispositions of property

This chapter, in covering the essentials, provides a bird's-eye view of the entire income tax system. For many, this may be sufficient. This one chapter may contain enough tax law and have more than enough detail for some. Nevertheless, it is just part of the picture. Many of the details as well as the conceptual basis for some of these provisions are left to later chapters. This can be frustrating to those who want more or know that more exists, but the major purpose of this chapter is to establish the basic framework in which the implications of any particular transaction on taxable income can be assessed. To this end, the chapter gives not only a brief description of what is taxable and what is deductible but also a glimpse of such complex topics as the passive loss rules and the alternative minimum tax. Remember, the goal is not necessarily to provide a detailed discussion of all the rules but to provide a foundation so that problems, pitfalls, and opportunities can be recognized.

## The Taxable Entity

**LO.1**
Identify the entities that are subject to the Federal income tax.

The income tax is imposed on the income of some type of entity. Unfortunately, there is no uniform agreement on what is the theoretically correct unit of taxation. There are a variety of legal, economic, social, and natural entities that Congress could select: individuals (natural persons), family units, households (those living together), sole proprietorships, partnerships, corporations, trusts, estates, governments, religious groups, nonprofit organizations, and other voluntary or cooperative associations. Despite the disagreement over which of these or other entities are the proper choices, Congress has provided that only certain entities are responsible for actually paying the tax. According to the Code, individuals, most corporations, and fiduciaries (estates and trusts) are taxable entities. Other entities, such as sole proprietorships, partnerships, and so-called "S" corporations, are not required to pay tax on any taxable income they might have. Instead, the taxable income of these entities is passed through or allocated to their owners, who bear the responsibility for paying any tax that may be due. For this reason, these entities are often referred to as flow-through entities or conduits. Exhibit 3-1 summarizes the various types of entities.

**EXHIBIT 3.1 Types of Entities**

| Taxpaying Entities | Flow-Through Entities or Conduits |
|---|---|
| Individuals | Sole proprietorships |
| C Corporations (regular corporations) | Partnerships and limited liability companies |
| Trusts | S corporations |
| Estates | |

> **Example 1**
>
> R and S are equal partners in a partnership that had taxable income of $50,000 in the current year. The partnership does not pay tax on the $50,000. Rather, the income is allocated equally between R and S. Thus, both R and S will report $25,000 of partnership income on their individual returns and pay the required tax regardless of whether they received distributions from the partnership.

In the following sections, the general tax treatment of the taxable entities—individuals, corporations, and fiduciaries—is explained along with the treatment of flow-through entities, sole proprietorships, partnerships and "S" corporations. The specific tax treatment of entities other than individuals is discussed separately in later chapters. However, it should be emphasized that many of the tax rules applying to one entity also apply to other entities. These similarities are pointed out as the various rules are discussed.

# Taxable Entities

## Individual Taxpayers

**LO.2**
Explain the basic tax treatment of individuals, corporations, partnerships, S corporations, and fiduciary taxpayers (trusts and estates).

The primary target for the income tax is the *individual* taxpayer. For 2007, 138.4 million individual returns were filed (Forms 1040, 1040A and 1040 EZ), and these were responsible for 51 percent of the total tax revenue collected by the federal government. This amount easily exceeded the second and third place finishers, employment taxes (31.6 percent) and corporate income taxes (14.7 percent). These statistics leave little doubt about the importance of the individual income tax in the United States.

### Citizens and Residents of the United States

Section 1 of the Internal Revenue Code provides that a tax is imposed on the taxable income of all individuals. As might be expected, the term *individual* generally applies to U.S. citizens. However, it also includes persons who are *not* U.S. citizens but who are considered residents, so-called *resident aliens.* Thus, if Prince Harry decides to move to New York to escape the tabloids of London, he could be subject to U.S. taxes even though he is not a U.S. citizen. The same could be said for a Japanese citizen working for Honda in Marysville, Ohio or a Canadian citizen who lives and works in Detroit. Whether these people are residents requires application of a complicated test.[1] The key point to remember is that foreign citizens who are not merely visiting but stay for an extended period must worry about the need for filing.[2] As discussed below, the tax would be levied on both their U.S. income and any foreign income.

### Foreign Taxpayers

Individuals who are not U.S. citizens and who do not qualify as residents may be subject to U.S. tax. These persons, referred to as *nonresident aliens*, are taxed on certain types of income that are received from U.S. sources.[3] If the income is derived from a trade or business carried on in the United States, that income is taxed in the same way as it is for a citizen or resident. Most other income earned in the United States is taxed at a flat rate of 30 percent. However, there are a number of special rules that must be observed.

### Age

It should be noted that the age of an individual is not a factor in determining if he or she is a taxpaying entity. Whether the individual is eight years old or eighty years old, he or she is still

[1] See § 7701(b) for a definition of the "substantial presence test" that is used to determine if an individual is a resident alien and subject to U.S. tax.

[2] Reg. § 1.871-2(b).

[3] § 871.

subject to tax on any taxable income received. Contrary to the belief of some people, a child's income is taxed to the child and not the parent. As explained later, age may have an impact on *both* the method of computing the tax and the amount of tax owed; it does not, however, impact the individual's status as a taxpayer.

### Worldwide Income

The Federal income tax on individuals applies not only to domestic (U.S.) source income, but also to income from foreign sources. In other words, a U.S. citizen is subject to U.S. taxation on his or her worldwide income regardless of where he or she lives (e.g., Rhode Island or Rome) or the source of the income (e.g., Connecticut or Copenhagen). It is therefore possible to have foreign source income taxed by more than one country (e.g., the foreign country and the United States). Several provisions exist to prevent or minimize double taxation, however. For example, U.S. citizens and residents living abroad may claim either the foreign tax credit (a direct reduction in the tax)[4] or deduct such taxes.[5]

In lieu of claiming a credit or deduction for foreign taxes, a U.S. citizen who works and lives in a foreign country may exclude from his or her U.S. income certain amounts of income earned abroad.[6] The foreign earned income exclusion is adjusted annually for inflation and for 2011 is $92,900. An individual qualifies for the exclusion if he or she maintains his tax home in a foreign country (i.e., his principal place of business is in the foreign country) and he or she is either a bona fide resident of a foreign country or is physically present in a foreign country for 330 days in any 12 consecutive months.

#### Example 2

Z, a U.S. citizen, is an aircraft mechanic who was temporarily assigned to a lucrative job in Seoul, South Korea. Z lived in Seoul all of 2011 except for two weeks when he came back to the United States to visit relatives. From his Korean job, he earned $101,500 in 2011. Because Z's tax home is in a foreign country and he was present in the foreign country for at least 330 days during 12 consecutive months, he meets the physical presence test and may exclude $92,900 of his $101,500 salary. The remaining $10,000 plus any other income, such as dividends and interest, are subject to tax.

In addition to the relief measures mentioned above, taxpayers may exclude, subject to certain limitations, allowances (in-kind or cash) for foreign housing. Also, tax treaties often exist that deal with the problem of double taxation by the United States and foreign countries.

### State Income Taxes

While virtually the entire focus of this text is on the federal income tax, state income taxes cannot be ignored. All but seven states have a state income tax imposed on individuals. The seven that do not have an income tax are: Alaska, Florida, Nevada, South Dakota, Texas, Washington and Wyoming. However, the income taxes of New Hampshire and Tennessee extend only to interest and dividends. Thus the vast majority of all individuals must pay not only federal income taxes but also state and local income taxes.

As might be expected, states that impose an income tax do not necessarily follow the federal rules. Each has its own unique method to compute taxable income. Of the 41 states with an income tax, 25 begin their calculation with federal adjusted gross income, 8 use federal taxable income as the starting point and 3 use the federal income tax liability as the basis for their tax. To make matters more challenging, some states conform with the methods allowed for federal tax purposes (e.g., depreciation) while others do not. As might be imagined, the world of state and local taxes can become quite complex.

The important concept to grasp here is not how the various state laws work but whether they apply to the taxpayer at all. Those working in tax must not overlook the possibility that a taxpayer may be responsible not only for federal taxes but for state or local taxes as well.

---

[4] § 901.

[5] § 164(a).

[6] § 911(a).

For example, consider a professional football player, say Peyton Manning of the Indianapolis Colts who lives in Indianapolis and files an Indiana income tax return. If he plays a game in Philadelphia, must he file a state income tax return for Pennsylvania and perhaps another return for the city of Philadelphia? Similarly, if a staff accountant working for a national accounting firm in Chicago is assigned temporarily to an audit in Denver, must he pay income taxes in Colorado? If a son is a professor at Michigan State but is a shareholder in his father's S corporation that operates a farm in Iowa, must the son pay Iowa taxes? At this juncture, the answer is not as important as asking the question!

## Corporate Taxpayers

Section 11 of the Internal Revenue Code imposes a tax on all corporations. The corporate income tax applies to both domestic corporations and foreign corporations that operate a trade or business in the United States.[7] However, the federal tax treatment of a corporation differs depending on whether it is a "C" corporation (a regular corporation) or an "S" corporation. For tax purposes, a corporation is treated as a C corporations unless it is eligible and elects to be treated as an S corporation. C corporations, like individuals, are treated as separate taxable entities. On the other hand, S corporations normally are not separate taxable entities but are treated as conduits, passing their income and losses through to their shareholders (as discussed below). It should be emphasized that this difference—C or S—is made only for tax purposes. For all other purposes (e.g., liability), the applicable state laws make no distincition.

The overall income tax treatment of corporations is quite similar to that of individuals. In fact, all of the basic rules governing income, exclusions, deductions, and credits apply to individuals as well as C corporations and, for that matter, fiduciaries. For example, the general rule concerning what is deductible, found in § 162, allows *all* taxpayers a deduction for trade or business expenses. Similarly, § 103 provides that *all* taxpayers are allowed to exclude interest income from state and local bonds. Although many of the general rules are the same for both individuals and corporations, there are several key differences.

The most obvious difference can be seen by comparing the corporate and individual formulas for determining taxable income as found in Exhibits 3-2 and 3-3. The concepts of adjusted gross income and itemized deductions found in the individual tax formula are conspicuously absent from the corporate formula. Other major differences in determining taxable income involve the treatment of particular items, such as dividend income and

**LO.3**
Understand the basic tax formulas to be followed in computing the tax liability for individuals and corporations.

**EXHIBIT 3.2 Tax Formula for Corporate Taxpayers**

| | |
|---|---|
| ***Total Income (from whatever source)*** | $xxx,xxx |
| Less: Exclusions from gross income | −xx,xxx |
| ***Gross income*** | $xxx,xxx |
| Less: Deductions | −xx,xxx |
| ***Taxable income*** | $xxx,xxx |
| Applicable tax rates | xx% |
| ***Gross tax*** | $ xx,xxx |
| Less: Tax credits and prepayments | −x,xxx |
| ***Tax due (or refund)*** | $ xx,xxx |

[7] § 882(a). See Chapter 19 for more details.

**EXHIBIT 3.3** **Tax Formula for Individual Taxpayers**

| | | | |
|---|---|---|---|
| ***Total income (from whatever source)*** | | | $xxx,xxx |
| Less: | Exclusions from gross income | | −xx,xxx |
| ***Gross income*** | | | $xxx,xxx |
| Less: | Deductions **for** adjusted gross income | | −xx,xxx |
| ***Adjusted gross income*** | | | $xxx,xxx |
| Less: | 1. The larger of: | | |
| | a. Standard deduction | $x,xxx | |
| | *or* | or | −x,xxx |
| | b. Total itemized deductions | $x,xxx | |
| | 2. Number of personal and dependency exemptions × exemption amount | | −x,xxx |
| ***Taxable income*** | | | $xxx,xxx |
| Applicable tax rates (from Tables or Schedules X, Y, or Z) | | | xx% |
| ***Gross income tax*** | | | $ xx,xxx |
| Plus: | Additional taxes (e.g., self-employment tax, alternative minimum tax, recapture of tax credits) | | +x,xxx |
| Less: | Tax credits and prepayments | | −x,xxx |
| ***Tax due (or refund)*** | | | $ xx,xxx |

charitable contributions. These and other differences are discussed in detail in Chapter 19. It should be emphasized once again, however, that most of the basic rules apply whether the taxpayer is a corporation or an individual.

One difference in the taxation of individuals and corporations that is not apparent from the basic formula, but which should be noted, concerns the tax rates that each uses in computing the tax liability (see the inside back cover of the text). A comparison of the individual and corporate tax rates shows a somewhat similar progression: 10 to 35 percent for individuals and 15 to 39 percent for corporations. But note that the rates apply at quite different levels of income.

Perhaps the most critical aspect of corporate taxation that is generally not shared with any other taxable entity concerns the potential for double taxation. When a corporation receives income and subsequently distributes that income as a dividend to its shareholders, the effect is to tax the income twice: once at the corporate level and again at the shareholder level. Double taxation can occur because the corporation is not allowed to deduct any dividend payments to its shareholders. As one might suspect, many have questioned the equity of this treatment, arguing that it penalizes those who elect to do business in the corporate form. Note, however, that this treatment is consistent with the fact that the corporation is considered a separate legal entity. Moreover, it is often argued that the corporation and its owners in reality do not bear the burden of the corporate tax. According to the argument, corporations are able to shift the tax burden either to consumers by charging higher prices or to employees by paying lower wages. In addition, those who reject the double tax theory often note that closely held corporations, whose owners may also be employees of the business, are able to avoid double taxation to the extent they can characterize any corporate distributions as deductible salary payments rather than nondeductible dividends. Whether in fact double taxation does or does not occur, it appears that this feature, which has been part of the U.S. tax system since its inception, is unlikely to change in the immediate future.

### Example 3

J owns all of the stock of ZZ Inc., a C corporation. This year ZZ reported taxable income of $1,000,000 before considering any distributions to J. Assume that ZZ is in the 34 percent marginal tax bracket while J is in 35 percent bracket. J plans on withdrawing $600,000 from the corporation. Ignoring payroll taxes, is J better off if he causes the corporation to distribute $600,000 as a qualifying dividend or $600,000 as a salary?

| Distribution Treated as a Dividend | ZZ Inc. | J | Total |
|---|---|---|---|
| Taxable income before distributions to J | $1,000,000 | | |
| Distributions to J | | | |
| Nondeductible dividend | — | $600,000 | |
| Taxable income | $1,000,000 | $600,000 | |
| Tax rate | x 34% | x 15% | |
| Total tax | $ 340,000 | 90,000 | $430,000 |
| **Distribution Treated as a Salary** | | | |
| Taxable income before distributions to J | $1,000,000 | | |
| Distributions to J | | | |
| Deductible salary | (600,000) | $600,000 | |
| Taxable income | $ 400,000 | $600,000 | |
| Tax rate | x 34% | x 35% | |
| Total tax | $ 136,000 | $210,000 | $346,000 |
| Savings | | | $ 84,000 |

As calculated above, J saves $84,000 by withdrawing the $600,000 as a salary rather than as a dividend. The savings result because $600,000 of the total income is taxed twice when it is distributed as a dividend (once at the corporate level and again at the individual level) but only once when the distribution is treated as a salary because the corporation is allowed to deduct the salary payment as a business expense. Note that currently the qualifying dividend is taxed at a maximum rate of 15 percent (2011 and 2012). In 2013 dividends are scheduled to be treated as ordinary income potentially taxed at the highest marginal rate as they were prior to 2003.

Special rules apply to the formation of a corporation, corporate dividend distributions, and distributions made to shareholders in exchange for their stock. Penalty taxes also may be assessed against corporations that try to shelter income from high personal tax rates by accumulating it in the corporation, rather than making dividend distributions. These topics and others related to the income taxation of corporations and their owners are discussed in Chapters 19, 20, and 21.

## Fiduciary Taxpayers

A *fiduciary* is a person who is entrusted with property for the benefit of another, the *beneficiary*. The individual or entity that acts as a fiduciary is responsible for managing and administering the entrusted property, at all times faithfully performing the required duties with the utmost care and prudence.

Two types of fiduciary relationships are the trust and the estate. The trust is a legal entity created when the title of property is transferred by a person (the *grantor*) to the fiduciary (the *trustee*). The trustee is required to implement the instructions of the grantor as specified in the trust agreement. Typically, the property is held in trust for a minor or some other person until he or she reaches a certain age or until some specified event occurs.

An estate is also recognized as a legal entity, established by law when a person dies. Upon the person's death, his or her property generally passes to the estate, where it is administered by the fiduciary until it is distributed to the beneficiaries. Both trusts and estates are treated as taxpaying entities.

The Code specifically provides for a tax on the taxable income of estates and trusts.[8] Determining the tax for such entities is very similar to determining the tax for individuals, with one major exception.[9] When distributions are made to beneficiaries, the distributed income is generally taxed to the beneficiary rather than to the estate or trust.[10] In essence, the trust or estate is permitted to reduce its taxable income by the amount of the distribution—acting as a *conduit*, since the distributed income flows through to the beneficiaries.

### Example 4

T is the trustee of a trust established for the benefit of A and B. The trust generated $4,000 of income subject to tax for the current year and no distributions were made to either A or B during the year. The trustee files an annual fiduciary tax return for the year and pays the tax based on the $4,000 taxable amount.

### Example 5

Assume that for the next year the trust in *Example 4* had $10,000 of income subject to tax and that distributions of $2,000 each were made to A and B. The trustee files an annual trust return for the year and pays a tax based on $6,000 ($10,000 taxable income − $4,000 distributions). A and B each include $2,000 in their income tax returns for the year.

Distributions made by a trust or estate from its corpus (also called the trust property or principal), including undistributed profits from prior years, generally are not taxable to the beneficiary.[11] This is because these distributions are part of a gift or inheritance or have been taxed previously. Similarly, the trust or estate is not entitled to deductions for these nontaxable distributions.[12]

## Flow-Through Entities

### Sole Proprietorships

**LO.2**
Explain the basic tax treatment of individuals, corporations, partnerships, S corporations, and fiduciary taxpayers (trusts and estates).

The first of the nontaxpaying, flow-through entities is the sole proprietorship. A sole proprietorship is commonly defined as an unincorporated business owned by one individual. The definition includes essentially all individuals who are in business for themselves. Indeed, while they may not think of themselves as proprietors, individuals who are self-employed (e.g., doctors, lawyers, accountants, consultants, plumbers, carpenters) as well as independent contractors are taxed as sole proprietorships. In addition, for tax purposes, a single member limited liability company (SMLLC) that does not elect to be treated as a corporation is disregarded as an entity separate from its owner and is treated as a sole proprietorship.

The tax treatment of sole proprietorships differs somewhat from that of financial accounting. For financial accounting purposes, the business activities of the proprietor are treated as distinct from other activities of the owner. The sole proprietorship is considered a totally independent accounting entity for which separate records and reports are maintained. For tax purposes, a similar approach applies except the sole proprietorship is not a separate

[8] §§ 1(e) and 641(a).

[9] § 641(b).

[10] §§ 651 and 661.

[11] § 662.

[12] § 661. These and other provisions related to the Federal income taxation of estates, trusts, and beneficiaries are discussed in Chapter 25.

taxable entity. For this reason, it does not file its own tax return. Instead, the income and deductions from operating a proprietorship are summarized and reported on Schedule C of the owner's personal income tax return along with other tax items (See Appendix B for Form 1040 and Schedule C).

Although some might not consider a sole proprietorship as a "flow-through" entity in the same sense that partnerships and S corporations are, they clearly function in much the same way. In essence, a sole proprietorship serves as a conduit through which its net income or loss flows through to the individual. Any item of income or deduction of the proprietorship that might receive some type of special treatment had the owner received or paid it directly—rather than running it through the business—is not included on the Schedule C but is reported separately on the owner's personal return (e.g., interest income, capital gains, charitable contributions). Distributions or withdrawals that an owner receives from a proprietorship are not considered salary or other income since all of the proprietorship income is included on the individual's return regardless of whether it is distributed. Therefore, a proprietor's "draw" is ignored.

### Example 6

K is employed as a law professor at State University, where she earns a salary of $102,000. K also operates a part-time consulting practice as a sole proprietorship. She maintains a separate checking account for the business. The business earned net income of $30,000 this year before considering $50 of interest earned on the money in the business' checking account, a $100 charitable contribution drawn on the business account to the United Way and a withdrawal of $18,000. How are the activities reported?

The sole proprietorship does not file a separate return and pay tax. Instead, K reports the sole proprietorship's income of $30,000 on her Schedule C. This amount is subsequently combined with her salary of $102,000 and other income and deductions on her return to compute her taxable income. She then pays both the income and self-employment taxes required. The $50 of interest income is not considered part of the proprietorship income but is aggregated with other interest income that K might have and is reported separately (Schedule B). The same approach is used for the charitable contribution. The contribution is treated as if K had made it personally and would be deducted as an itemized deduction on Schedule A if K itemizes. The $18,000 withdrawal is ignored since it represents either part of her original investment in the business or income that is currently or previously reported on Schedule C.

It is easy to dismiss sole proprietorships in a world dominated by multinational corporations. Indeed IRS statistics bare this out, indicating that in 2005, proprietorships accounted for only 9.7 percent of the net income reported by businesses. Nevertheless, based on returns filed for that year, proprietorships cannot be ignored. The number of proprietorships far exceeded the number of corporations and partnerships: 21.4 million proprietorships (71.8%) versus 5.7 million corporations (19%) and 2.7 million partnerships (9.2%).[13]

## PARTNERSHIPS

**LO.2**
Explain the basic tax treatment of individuals, corporations, partnerships, S corporations, and fiduciary taxpayers (trusts and estates).

A partnership is a conduit for Federal income tax purposes. This means that the partnership itself is not subject to Federal income tax and that all items of partnership income, expense, gain, loss, or credit pass through to the partners and are given their tax effect at the partner level.[14] The partnership is required to file an information return (Form 1065) reporting the results of the partnership's transactions and how those results are divided among the partners.

[13] *The 2009 Statistical Abstract (Table 722. Number of Tax Returns, Receipts, and Net Income by Type of Business: 1990 to 2005)*, U.S. Census Bureau.

[14] § 701.

Each partner's share of the various items are reported to the partner on Schedule K-1. Using this information, the partners each report their respective shares of the items on their own tax returns.[15] Because partners pay taxes on their shares of the partnership income regardless of whether it is distributed, distributions made by the partnership generally are not taxable to the partners.[16]

### Example 7

For its current calendar year, EG Partnership had taxable income of $18,000. During the year, each of its two equal partners received cash distributions of $4,000. The partnership is not subject to tax, and each partner must include $9,000 in his annual income tax return, despite the fact that each partner actually received less than this amount in cash. The distributions normally are not taxable since they represent previously taxed income. The partnership must file an annual information return reporting the results of its operations and the effect of these operations on each partner.

A characteristic of a partnership (as well as an S corporation or sole proprietorship) that deserves special emphasis is the treatment of losses. If a business is typical, it will take several years of operation before it can be declared a profitable venture. Until that time, expenses normally exceed revenues and the result is a net loss. In the case of a conduit entity such as a partnership, that net loss flows through to the owners, who are generally allowed to offset it against any other income they may have. In contrast, if a regular C corporation sustains a loss, referred to as a net operating loss, or NOL, the shareholders do not benefit from that loss directly. A C corporation is allowed, like individuals, to use the loss to offset taxable income of prior or subsequent years. Generally, losses are carried back two years and forward 20 years. For example, the taxpayer would first carry back the loss to the second prior year and offset it against any taxable income. In such case, the taxpayer would file a claim for a tax refund. Any remaining loss is carried to the first prior year. Any remaining loss is carried forward for 20 years. The key point to remember is that the losses of a partnership flow through and thus may provide immediate benefit, whereas those of a C corporation do not flow through and can be used only if the corporation has income in other tax years.

In some respects, the partnership is treated as a separate entity for tax purposes. For example, many tax elections are made by the partnership,[17] and a partnership interest generally is treated as a single asset when sold.[18] On the other hand, transactions between the partners and partnership are sometimes treated as if the partner was an independent third party and sometimes special rules apply.[19] For example, an individual partner who performs services for the partnership in his or her role as a partner is generally not considered an employee for tax purposes. Such payments are not considered salaries or wages. Consequently, the payments are not subject to withholding or employment taxes and are not reported to the partner at the end of the year on form W-2. Instead, these so-called "guaranteed payments" are reported to the partner on a Schedule K-1 and are subject to self-employment taxes. Consistent with this approach, a partner does not qualify for the favorable tax treatment of certain employee fringe benefits (see Chapter 6). In addition, a partner's share of any trade or business income of the partnership is generally subject to self-employment taxes. These and other controlling provisions related to the Federal income tax treatment of partnerships are covered in detail in Chapter 22.

---

[15] § 702(a).

[16] § 731(a).

[17] § 703(b).

[18] § 741 states that the sale or exchange of an interest in a partnership shall generally be treated as the sale of a capital asset.

[19] § 707(a).

## ELECTING SMALL BUSINESS CORPORATIONS: "S" CORPORATIONS

The Internal Revenue Code allows certain closely held corporations to elect to be treated as conduits (like partnerships) for Federal income tax purposes. The election is made pursuant to the rules contained in Subchapter S of the Code.[20] For this reason, such corporations are referred to as *S corporations*. Not all corporations are eligible to elect S status. The only corporations that qualify are those that have 100 or fewer shareholders and meet certain other tests.

If a corporation elects S corporation status, it is taxed in virtually the same fashion as a partnership. Like a partnership, the S corporation's items of income, expense, gain, or loss pass through to the shareholders to be given their tax effect at the shareholder level. Salaries and wages of shareholders who work for the corporation and other employees are reported on a Form W-2 and are subject to withholding of income taxes and FICA (that is matched by the employer corporation). Although employees generally qualify for favorable treatment of fringe benefits, shareholder-employees owning 2 percent or more of the corporation's stock do not. As a result, the value of any fringe benefits, such as medical insurance coverage, is taxable as compensation to the employee-shareholder (who is allowed to deduct it). Distributions from an S corporation, like those from partnerships, normally are nontaxable since they usually represent previously taxed income.

The S corporation files an information return (Form 1120S) similar to that of a partnership, reporting the results of the corporation's transactions and how those results are allocated among the shareholders. The individual shareholders report their respective shares of the various items on their own tax returns. Chapter 23 contains a detailed discussion of the taxation of S corporations and their shareholders.

## LIMITED LIABILITY COMPANIES

All 50 states and the District of Columbia have passed legislation creating a relatively new form of business entity: the limited liability company (LLC). What is this new creature and how is it taxed? Perhaps the best characterization of an LLC is that it is a cross between a partnership and a corporation. LLCs are created under state law by filing articles of organization. The owners of an LLC are called members and can be individuals, partnerships, regular corporations, S corporations, trusts, or other LLCs. Although some states allow single-member LLCs, two or more members usually form the entity. Like a corporation, an LLC can act on its own behalf and sue and be sued. Also like a corporation, members generally possess limited liability except that they may be liable for their own acts of malpractice in those states that allow professionals to form LLCs.

The tax law does not specifically address the tax treatment of an LLC. Initially, this omission caused some uncertainty as to whether an LLC should be taxed as a corpora tion or a partnership. To eliminate this confusion, the Treasury issued the so-called check-the-box regulations.[21] Under these rules, an LLC with two or more owners is treated as a partnership for tax purposes unless it elects to be treated as a corporation (i.e., the LLC is a partnership unless it checks the box on Form 8832 to be treated as a regular C corporation). An LLC with only one member is disregarded and treated as a sole proprietorship, unless it elects to be treated as a corporation.

The treatment of LLCs for self-employment tax purposes has also produced some confusion. As noted above, in the case of a partnership, a partner's share of partnership income is generally self-employment income subject to self-employment taxes. However, this rule is true only for general partners. Historically, limited partners have been treated differently on the theory that their role is similar to that of an investor rather than someone who is actively involved in the business. Consequently, a limited partner's share of partnership income has been viewed more similar to investment income (e.g., dividends and interest) than business income. Section 1402 (a)(13) reflects this line of reasoning, providing that a limited partner's share of partnership income is not subject to self-employment tax. However, based on this

---

[20] §§ 1361 through 1379.

[21] Reg. § 301.7701-3.

approach, it was not clear whether a member of an LLC was to be treated like a limited partner, in which case the LLC's income would escape employment taxes. Hoping to eliminate this potential loophole, proposed regulations created new rules to test limited partners as well as LLC members. Under the proposed regulations, a limited partner or LLC member must treat his or her share of income as self-employment income if any of the following tests are met:[22]

1. The individual has personal liability for the debts of or claims against the business by reason of being a partner. This rule should rarely apply to a member of an LLC.
2. The individual has authority to contract on behalf of the entity.
3. The individual participates in the entity's trade or business for more than 500 hours during the year.
4. Substantially all of the activities of the entity involve the performance of services in the fields of health, law, engineering, architecture, accounting, actuarial science, or consulting.

Although these proposals provide needed guidance, they were heavily criticized. As a result, Congress intervened in 1997, passing legislation that postponed their implementation.[23] Since that time there has been no further action and the treatment of LLCs for purposes of self-employment taxes is still unresolved.

## Tax–Exempt Organizations

Since inception, U.S. tax laws have exempted from federal income taxation charitable and religious organizations as well as a variety of nonprofit associations. The vast majority of tax-exempt organizations obtain their tax exempt status from § 501(c)(3). Under this provision, corporations that are organized and operated exclusively for religious, charitable, scientific, literary, or educational purposes are exempt, assuming certain requirements are met. It is often said that these organizations are twice blessed since not only are they exempt from tax but contributions they receive are deductible.

Although tax-exempt entities usually do not pay tax, there are exceptions. If a nonprofit organization conducts a business unrelated to the purpose for which its exemption was granted, any income resulting from that business would be subject to tax. The tax is referred to as the unrelated business income tax (UBIT). The UBIT rules are designed to prevent unfair competition that would otherwise arise between taxable and nontaxable entities that carry on the same business. If the tax-exempt entity is organized as a corporation, its tax on unrelated business taxable income is computed in the same manner as a regular corporation. Also note that if unrelated business income comprises a substantial portion of the organization's income, it could lose its tax-exempt status.

### Example 8

HHH Corporation is a nonprofit organization that operates a health agency. It collects dues from all of its members that number over 50,000. The dues income is nontaxable. Each month it e-mails a monthly newsletter to its members. Recently, several companies expressed interest in advertising in its newsletter. Would the advertising income be considered unrelated business income?

Yes. Even though the corporation is a nonprofit organization, the advertising income would be taxable since the sale of ads is sufficiently commercial in nature to constitute a business activity that is carried on regularly (e.g., monthly). Moreover, if the advertising income comprised a substantial portion of the organization's income, it could lose its tax-exempt status.

---

[22] Prop. Reg. § 1.1402(a)-2(h).

[23] See § 935 of the Tax Reform Act of 1997.

**Example 9**

The Mudville Little League Baseball Organization is a tax-exempt organization. Every spring it holds a car wash to raise money for its operation. Is the income subject to tax?

No. The income from the car wash is exempt because the activity is not regularly carried on as a business.

As the examples might suggest, whether an otherwise tax-exempt organization has unrelated taxable income is often unclear. The point to grasp at this level is that even those organizations that might seem exempt—churches, universities, foundations and the like—may produce taxable income and, if the amount is substantial, they may lose their tax-exemption.

## ✓ Check Your Knowledge

### Review Question 1

Section 1 of the Internal Revenue Code imposes a tax on all individuals. If taken literally, this would mean that the United States taxes not only Oprah Winfrey but also Fidel Castro and Elton John. Are these foreign citizens subject to U.S. tax?

The U.S. income tax generally applies to the worldwide income of U.S. citizens and resident aliens. As a result, it would not apply to Mr. Castro and Mr. John since they are not citizens and do not live in the United States. The key question for an alien is whether the individual could be considered a resident. Whether a foreign citizen is considered a resident is normally based on the period of time he or she is present in the United States. For this purpose, an alien who is a mere transient (e.g., a foreigner who vacations in the United States) is not a resident.

Although foreign citizens such as Castro and John usually are not subject to U.S. tax, they can be. Nonresident aliens are taxed on their income from U.S. sources. Based on this rule, income earned from a job or a business in the United States is subject to U.S. tax. In addition, nonresident aliens who receive investment income from U.S. sources, such as dividends on U.S. stocks, normally must pay U.S. taxes on such income.

### Review Question 2

Child actors and actresses have made millions of dollars from their movie appearances (e.g., Hannah Montana).

**a.** Must these children file their own returns and report the income, or do their parents simply include it on their return?

Although there are some special rules that can apply, parents normally do not report the income of their children on their return. A child is treated as a taxable entity, separate and distinct from his or her parents. Consequently, if a child's income exceeds the filing requirement threshold, he or she must usually file a return.

**b.** Do you think there could be any advantage derived from the fact that a child is a separate taxpayer?

Besides all of the other things that children are—both good and bad—they can also be mini-tax shelters. Since they are separate taxpayers, they have their own set of tax rates and other tax characteristics. Therefore, to the extent that parents are able to shift income from the parents' high bracket to the child's low bracket (and still control the use of the income), taxes can be saved. These opportunities and some limitations that restrict such schemes are discussed more fully in Chapter 4 and Chapter 5.

### Review Question 3

After all these years, Bob decided to start his own business: Bob's Bar and Grill. He has even convinced his wife, Jane, to help. Bob has everything ready but still must decide what form the business should take. Originally, he did not even think about it. Bob simply thought he would operate the business as a sole proprietorship.

**a.** If Bob does pursue this course, will he need to file a separate return for the business?

A sole proprietorship is not considered a separate taxable entity. Instead, all of the information related to the proprietorship is included on the individual's personal tax return. The results of operation are summarized on Schedule C. The net profit or loss is transferred from Schedule C to page 1 of Form 1040. In addition, since such income is also subject to self-employment tax, the net profit is also transferred to Schedule SE, where the special computation is made. It is important to note that either Bob or Jane can be the proprietor—but not both. If Jane is to be the proprietor, she must own the business. If Jane wishes to compensate Bob, she can pay him a salary or wages. However, if Bob and Jane both wish to be owners, they must use another form of business.

**b.** After Bob and Jane talked to their attorney, it was clear that they did not want to be a general partnership (where each and every partner is liable for partnership obligations) or a sole proprietorship. Why?

Typically, individuals want to protect their personal assets from the liabilities of risky ventures. While insurance may provide some protection, most individuals want the added safety of limited liability that only the corporate or LLC form offers. A *limited* partnership allows some partners protection, but this business form requires that there must be at least one *general* partner (who would have unlimited liability).

**c.** At first Bob and Jane thought they would be a corporation. But according to their accountant, this new thing called an LLC allows business owners to achieve what he believes is tax nirvana. What is all the fuss about LLCs? Can you not get the same thing with S corporations? What do you think? How are LLCs taxed? What form of business organization seems best for Bob and Jane's business?

The beauty of an LLC is that all of the owners have limited liability yet the entity is usually taxed like a partnership. As a result, all of the income, as well as any loss, flows through to the partners. The significance of this treatment is twofold. First, if any loss occurs, it can be used to offset any other income Bob and Jane may have. If a C corporation is chosen, early losses do not provide any benefit until the business starts to make money. The NOL carryback feature for corporations is useless, because the business is brand new. Moreover, if it is like most businesses, Bob and Jane's operation will experience losses—at least until the clientele develop a love for Bob's cooking. The second attraction of an LLC is the fact that its income avoids the double tax that can occur with C corporations. But why opt for an LLC? Is not this same treatment available with an S corporation? In this regard, the LLC is virtually identical to an S corporation, but there are many differences that some argue make the LLC more attractive. The only difference that can be gleaned from the discussion above is that an S corporation is limited to 100 shareholders while a partnership or LLC can have an unlimited number of owners. This may be irrelevant for Bob and Jane but could be extremely important for some businesses (e.g., a large public accounting firm). Another difference concerns the type of owner allowed. For example, an S corporation can generally have only individuals (and no nonresident aliens) as shareholders, but there are no restrictions on the type of partner or member that a partnership or an LLC can have. This too may be unimportant for Bob and Jane but there are still other considerations too technical to touch on here.

As a practical matter, prior to the advent of the LLC, most advisers would have suggested that Bob and Jane choose to be an S corporation. Since 1986 S corporations have generally been the most popular form of conducting business—at least when there were no more than the maximum shareholders allowed—because they were the only form of business that offered limited liability to all of its owners and a single level of tax. But the advent of the LLC changes all of this. As time passes, it will be interesting to see if LLCs become more popular than S corporations. In any event, they provide yet one more option for the business owner to select.

# Tax Formula

Computing an income tax liability is normally uncomplicated, requiring only a few simple mathematical calculations.[24] These steps, referred to as the tax formula, are shown in Exhibits 3-2 and 3-3. The tax formula is presented here in two forms: the simpler general formula that establishes the basic concepts as applicable to corporate taxpayers (Exhibit 3-2) and the more complex formula for individual taxpayers (Exhibit 3-3). The formulas in Exhibits 3-2 and 3-3 are useful references while studying the various aspects of Federal income tax law in the subsequent chapters. To make such reference easier, both formulas are reproduced on the inside back cover of the text.

The tax formula for each type of entity is incorporated into the Federal income tax forms. Exhibit 3-2 may be compared with Form 1120 (the annual income tax return for corporations) and Exhibit 3-3 with Form 1040 (the return for individuals). These forms are included in Appendix B at the back of the text.

Examination of the two formulas reveals the importance of tax terms such as *gross income, deductions, and exemptions.* Each of these terms and countless others used in the tax law have very specific meanings. Indeed, as later chapters will show, taxpayers often have been involved in litigation solely to determine the definition of a particular term. For this reason, close attention must be given to the terminology used in taxation.

## Analyzing the Tax Formula

**LO.4**
Define many of the basic terms used in the tax formula such as gross income, adjusted gross income, taxable income, exclusion, deduction, and credit.

### Income

The tax computation begins with a determination of the taxpayer's total income, both taxable and nontaxable. As the formula in Exhibit 3-3 suggests, income is defined very broadly to include income from any source.[25] The list of typical income items in Exhibit 3-4 illustrates its comprehensive nature. A specific definition of income is developed in Chapter 5

**EXHIBIT 3.4 Partial List of Items Included in Gross Income**

| | |
|---|---|
| Alimony and separate maintenance payments | Income in respect of a decedent |
| Annuities | Interest |
| Awards | Pensions and other retirement benefits |
| Bonuses | Prizes and gambling or lottery winnings |
| Commissions | Pro rata share of income of a partnership |
| Debts forgiven to debtor by a creditor | Pro rata share of income of an S corporation |
| Dividends from corporations | Punitive damages |
| Employee expense reimbursements | Rewards |
| Fees and other compensation for personal services | Royalties |
| Gains from illegal transactions | Salaries and wages |
| Gains from transactions in property | Social Security benefits (zero or a portion) |
| Gross profit from sales | Tips and gratuities |
| Hobby income | Trade or business income |
| Income from an interest in an estate or trust | Unemployment compensation |
| Income from rental operations | |

[24] §§ 1 and 63.

[25] § 61(a).

**EXHIBIT 3.5 Partial List of Exclusions from Gross Income**

- Amounts received from employer-financed health and accident insurance to the extent of expenses
- Amounts received from health, accident, and disability insurance financed by the taxpayer
- Amounts received under qualified educational assistance plans
- Certain specified employee fringe benefits
- Child support payments received
- Contributions by employer to employer-financed accident and health insurance coverage
- Dependent care assistance provided by employer
- Gifts and inheritances
- Improvements by lessee to lessor's property
- Interest on most state and local government debt
- Meals and lodging furnished for the convenience of one's employer
- Personal damage awards (physical injury or sickness)
- Premiums paid by employer on group-term life insurance (for coverage up to $50,000)
- Proceeds of life insurance paid on death
- Proceeds of borrowing
- Qualified transportation plan benefits
- Scholarship and fellowship grants (but only for tuition, fees, books, and supplies)
- Social Security benefits (within limits)
- Veteran's benefits
- Welfare payments

## Exclusions

Although the starting point in calculating the tax is determining total income, not all of the income identified is taxable. Over the years, Congress has specifically exempted certain types of income from taxation, often in an attempt to accomplish some specific goal.[26] In tax terminology, income exempt from taxation and thus not included in a taxpayer's gross income is referred to as an "exclusion." Exhibit 3-5 shows a sample of the numerous items that can be excluded when determining gross income. Exclusions are discussed in detail in Chapter 6.

## Gross Income

The amount of income remaining after the excludable items have been removed is termed *gross income.* When completing a tax return, gross income is usually the only income disclosed, because excluded income normally is not reported.

### Example 10

E is divorced and has custody of her only child. E's income for the current year is from the following sources:

| | |
|---|---|
| Salary | $34,000 |
| Alimony from former spouse | 12,000 |
| Child support for child | 6,000 |
| Interest from First Savings & Loan | 1,200 |
| Interest on U.S. Government Treasury Bonds | 1,600 |
| Interest on State of Texas Bonds | 2,000 |
| Total | $56,800 |

Even though E's total income is $56,800, her gross income for tax purposes is only $48,800 because the child support and the interest income from the State of Texas are excluded. All the other items are included in gross income. Note that the interest from the Federal government is taxable, even though interest from state and local governments is generally excluded from gross income.

[26] See Chapter 6 for a discussion of the social and economic reasons for excluding certain items of income from taxation.

## Deductions

*Deductions* are those items that are subtracted from gross income to arrive at taxable income. The deductions normally allowed may be classified into two major groups:

1. *Business and Production-of-Income Expenses*—deductions for expenses related to carrying on a trade or business or some other income-producing activity, such as an investment.[27]
2. *Certain Personal Expenses*—deductions for a few expenses of an individual taxpayer that are primarily personal in nature, such as charitable contributions and medical expenses.[28]

Observe that the Code allows a deduction only for business or investment expenses. Personal expenses—other than a handful of special items—are not deductible. As someone once said, the Code's treatment of deductions is relatively simple: the costs of earning a living are deductible but the costs of living are not. The problem is determining into which category the expense falls.

A trade or business is an activity that is entered into for profit and involves significant taxpayer participation, either personally or through agents. It typically involves providing goods or services to customers, clients, or patients. If the activity qualifies as a trade or business, all the costs normally associated with operating the business are generally deductible. In most cases, it is easy to determine whether a taxpayer is engaged in a trade or business, but not always. For example, consider a taxpayer who travels around the world looking for antiques and incurs $10,000 of travel expenses but ultimately sells one item for a $100 profit. In this situation, the taxpayer might argue that he has a $9,900 loss from the activity that he should be able to offset against other income. On the other hand, it could easily be argued that the taxpayer was not really trying to make a profit. In such case, the IRS may deny the taxpayer's deduction. In these and similar situations, the determination of whether the taxpayer is truly in a trade or business must be based on all the facts and circumstances.

It should also be noted that the law takes the view that an individual who is employed is in the business of providing services. This is an extremely important assumption since it enables employees to deduct their business expenses (e.g., professional dues, subscriptions, and similar costs).[29]

Although business expenses are deductible, the line between a deductible business expense and a nondeductible personal expense is not always clear. For this reason, the Code often contains additional rules or requires certain conditions to be met to ensure that the expense is truly for business. For example, the Code addresses the personal element of business meals and entertainment that are not reimbursed by limiting the deduction to only 50 percent of their cost. Similarly, expenses related to education, travel, transportation, moving or a home office are not deductible unless they meet a laundry list of requirements. Most of these special rules are discussed in detail in Chapter 8.

The rental of real estate is generally not considered to be a trade or business, unless the tenants are transient (i.e., stay for short periods of time, as in a hotel or motel) or there are extraordinary services provided to tenants (e.g., a nursing home). Nevertheless, the expenses are normally deductible as expenses related to an income-producing activity and are classified as deductions for adjusted gross income.

As one might suspect at this point, Congress is quite cautious in granting deductions. There are rules, rules, and more rules that try to ensure that only true business expenses are deductible. The tax law is particularly concerned about deduction of losses (i.e., the excess of deductions over revenues) from activities in which the taxpayer has an interest. The problem became particularly acute in the 1970s and 1980s, when certain activities were designed primarily to generate tax losses (tax shelter limited partnerships and rental real estate were the biggest culprits). In an attempt to eliminate widespread abuse, Congress enacted the so-called *passive loss* rules in 1986. These highly complex rules generally limit the deduction of losses from activities, including rental real estate, in which the taxpayer is a mere investor and does not materially participate. The passive loss rules are covered in detail in Chapter 12.

---

[27] §§ 162 and 212.

[28] §§ 170 and 213.

[29] See Reg. § 1.162-6 and *David J. Primuth*, 54 T.C. 374 (1970).

## Classifying Deductions

A comparison of the general tax formulas used by corporations and by individuals reveals some differences in the treatment of deductions. For a corporate taxpayer, all deductions are subtracted directly from gross income to arrive at taxable income. In contrast, the individual formula divides deductions into two groups:[30] one group of deductions is allowed to reduce gross income, resulting in what is referred to as *adjusted gross income* (A.G.I.), while a second group is subtracted from A.G.I. As explained more fully below, the first group of deductions is generally composed of certain business expenses and other special items. The deductions in this group are referred to as deductions *for* adjusted gross income. The second group of expenses consists of two categories of allowable deductions: (1) deductions *from* adjusted gross income, and (2) deductions for personal and dependency exemptions. Deductions from adjusted gross income, normally referred to as *itemized deductions*, may be deducted only if they exceed a stipulated amount known as the *standard deduction* (e.g., in 2011 $5,800 for single taxpayers and $11,600 for married taxpayers filing jointly). The deduction for any personal and dependency exemptions claimed (e.g., $3,700 per exemption in 2011) is deductible regardless of the amount of other deductions.

Dividing deductions into two groups is done primarily for administrative convenience. Congress substantially reduced the number of individuals who claim itemized deductions because such deductions need to be reported only if they exceed the taxpayer's standard deduction. This reduction in the number of tax returns with itemized deductions significantly reduced the IRS audit procedures involving individual taxpayers. In recent years, only about 35 percent of taxpayers have itemized their deductions. Since corporate taxpayers have only business deductions, no special grouping was needed and thus the term *adjusted gross income* does not exist in the corporate formula.

## Adjusted Gross Income

The amount of an individual taxpayer's adjusted gross income (A.G.I.) serves two primary purposes. First, it is simply a point of reference used for classifying deductions: deductions are classified as either for or from A.G.I. Second, the calculation of many deductions, credits and other tax items is made with reference to A.G.I. For example, medical expenses are deductible only if they exceed 7.5 percent of A.G.I., while personal casualty losses may be deducted only if they exceed 10 percent of A.G.I. In addition, recent changes in the tax law make A.G.I. even more important for some taxpayers. As explained below, most itemized deductions and the deduction for exemptions are reduced if adjusted gross income exceeds certain levels.

### Example 11

This year proved to be very difficult for T; his divorce became final, and shortly thereafter he became very sick. For the year, he earned $45,000 and paid $5,000 in alimony to his ex-wife and $10,000 for medical expenses that were not reimbursed by insurance. T's A.G.I. is $40,000 ($45,000 – $5,000) because alimony is a deduction for A.G.I. As computed below, T's medical expense deduction is limited to $7,000 because he is allowed to deduct only the amount that exceeds 7.5% of his A.G.I.

| | | |
|---|---|---|
| Medical expenses (unreimbursed) | | $10,000 |
| Adjusted gross income | $40,000 | |
| Times: | × 7.5% | |
| Threshold | $ 3,000 | (3,000) |
| Deductible medical expenses | | $ 7,000 |

## Deductions for Adjusted Gross Income

Code § 62 specifically lists the deductions that are subtracted from gross income to determine A.G.I. This listing is a potpourri of items, as illustrated in Exhibit 3-6. Over the years, this

30 § 62.

**EXHIBIT 3.6 List of Deductions for Adjusted Gross Income**

- Alimony and separate maintenance payments paid
- Attorney fees and court costs related to unlawful discrimination cases
- Certain deductions of life tenants and income beneficiaries of property
- Certain portion of lump-sum distributions from pension plans subject to the special averaging convention
- Certain required repayments of supplemental unemployment compensation benefits
- Contributions to health savings accounts
- Contributions to pension, profit sharing, and other qualified retirement plans on behalf of a self-employed individual
- Contributions to the retirement plan of an electing Subchapter S corporation on behalf of an employee/shareholder
- Deduction for domestic production activities
- Deductions attributable to property held for the production of rents and royalties (reported on Schedule E)
- Educator expenses
- Individual retirement account contributions (within limits)
- Losses from the sale or exchange of property
- Moving expenses
- One-half of any self-employment tax
- Penalties for premature withdrawal of deposits from time savings accounts
- Reforestation expenses
- Reimbursed trade or business expenses of employees (only if the employee adequately accounts to the employer under an accountable plan in which case neither the reimbursement nor the expense is reported (see Chapter 8; see also expenses of statutory employees)
- State and local official's deductible expenses
- Statutory employee's deductions (life insurance salespersons, traveling salespersons and certain others report income and deductions on Schedule C; see Chapters 7 and 8)
- Student loan interest
- Trade or business deductions of self-employed individuals (including deductions claimed on Schedule C and unreimbursed expenses of qualified performing artists)
- Tuition payments up to $4,000 for some students

group of deductions has gone by various names. For example, practitioners often refer to this category of deductions as being "above the line"—the line being A.G.I. Some commentators and authors label these as deductions from gross income. For years, the Form 1040 listed these deductions as "adjustments" to income, although this label is no longer used (see Form 1040 in Appendix B). This text will use the "deduction for" terminology. Classification of a deduction as one for A.G.I. is significant for numerous reasons, as explained fully in Chapter 7. The most important of these reasons, however, is that unlike itemized deductions, deductions for A.G.I. need not exceed a minimum level before they are subtracted when computing taxable income.

## Itemized Deductions and the Standard Deduction

Itemized deductions are all deductions other than the deductions for A.G.I. and the deduction for personal and dependency exemptions.[31] While deductions for A.G.I. are deductible without limitation, itemized deductions are deducted only if their total exceeds the taxpayer's *standard deduction.* For example, if in 2011 T has total itemized deductions of $3,900 and his standard deduction amount is $5,800, he normally would claim the standard deduction in lieu of itemizing deductions. In contrast, if T's itemized deductions were $7,000, he would no doubt elect to itemize in order to maximize his deductions.

The standard deduction was introduced along with the concept of adjusted gross income and deductions *for* and *from* A.G.I. as part of the overall plan to eliminate the need for every

[31] § 63.

taxpayer to list or itemize certain deductions on his or her return. As suggested above, by allowing the taxpayer to claim some standard amount of deductions in lieu of itemizing each one, the administrative problem of verifying the millions of deductions that otherwise would have been claimed has been eliminated. The standard deduction also simplifies return preparation since most individuals no longer have to determine the amount of most of the deductions to which they are entitled. For this reason, the amount of the standard deduction is theoretically set at a level that equals or exceeds the average person's expenditures for those items qualifying as deductions from A.G.I. Consequently, the great majority of taxpayers claim the standard deduction in lieu of itemizing deductions.

After changes in 2008, the standard deduction is the sum of the following components:

1. Basic standard deduction
2. Increase for individuals who are age 65 or over and/or blind

### Basic Standard Deduction

The basic amount of each taxpayer's standard deduction differs depending on his or her filing status.[32] The amounts for each filing status are adjusted annually for inflation. For 2010 and 2011, the amounts are shown below:

| | Standard Deduction Amount | |
|---|---|---|
| *Filing Status* | *2010* | *2011* |
| Single | $ 5,700 | $ 5,800 |
| Unmarried head of household | 8,400 | 8,500 |
| Married persons filing a joint return (and surviving spouse) | 11,400 | 11,600 |
| Married persons filing a separate return | 5,700 | 5,800 |

### Additional Standard Deduction for Elderly or Blind Taxpayers

Congress has long extended some type of tax relief to the elderly and blind to take into account their special situations. Currently, an unmarried taxpayer who is either blind or age 65 at the close of the taxable year is allowed to increase his or her basic standard deduction by an additional $1,450 (2011).[33] If an unmarried taxpayer is *both* blind and 65 or older, he or she is allowed to increase the standard deduction by $2,900. If a taxpayer is married, he or she is allowed only $1,150 (2011) for each status for a maximum increase on a joint return of $4,600 [($1,150 × 2 for the husband = $2,300) + ($1,150 × 2 for the wife = $2,300)].

#### Example 12

In 2011, S, single, celebrated her sixty-fifth birthday. Instead of using the $5,800 standard deduction amount allowed for single taxpayers for 2011, S will be allowed a standard deduction of $7,250 ($5,800 basic standard deduction + $1,450 additional standard deduction).

If S were married filing a joint return for 2011, the standard deduction amount allowed would be $12,750 ($11,600 + $1,150). If both S and her husband were 65 or older, the standard deduction would be $13,900 [$11,600 standard deduction + (2 × $1,150 additional standard deduction)].

Both age and blindness are determined at the close of the taxable year. Guidelines are provided for determining whether an individual is legally blind, and specific filing requirements must be met.[34] An individual is considered to have attained age 65 on the day *preceding*

[32] § 63(c) contains the standard deduction amounts for 1988. The amounts for subsequent years are adjusted for inflation and announced by the IRS annually. Filing status is discussed in Chapter 4.

[33] § 63(f).

[34] §§ 151(d) and 151(d)(3). A taxpayer is legally blind if he or she cannot see better than 20/200 in the better eye with corrective lenses, or the taxpayer's field of vision is not more than 20 degrees. A statement prepared by a physician or optometrist must be attached to the return when a taxpayer is less than totally blind. Reg. § 1.151-1(d)(2).

his or her sixty-fifth birthday.[35] Thus, if a taxpayer's sixty-fifth birthday is January 1, 2012, he or she is considered to be 65 on December 31, 2011.

## Limitations on Use of Standard Deductions

Not all individuals are entitled to the full benefit of the standard deduction.[36] For example, a married person filing a separate return is not allowed a standard deduction if his or her spouse itemizes. This prevents a married couple from increasing their total deductions by having one spouse claim all of the itemized deductions and the other spouse claiming the standard deduction. Nonresident aliens are also denied use of the standard deduction. In addition, the standard deduction is limited for an individual who is claimed as a dependent on another taxpayer's return. This limitation is discussed in Chapter 4.

## Itemized Deductions

As explained above, itemized deductions simply are those deductions that are not deductible for A.G.I. The majority of itemized deductions are for selected personal, family and living expenses that Congress believed should be allowed for various policy reasons. These include medical expenses, state and local property, income and sales taxes, home mortgage interest, charitable contributions and casualty and theft losses. A partial list of itemized deductions is provided in Exhibit 3-7. In addition to these, a special subset of itemized deductions, so-called "miscellaneous itemized deductions" are allowed as discussed below.

**EXHIBIT 3.7** **Partial List of Itemized Deductions**

Medical expenses (amount in excess of 7.5 percent of A.G.I.):
- Prescription drugs and insulin
- Medical insurance premiums
- Fees of doctors, dentists, nurses, hospitals, etc.
- Medical transportation
- Hearing aids, dentures, eyeglasses, etc.

Investment interest (to extent of investment income)

Casualty and theft losses (amount in excess of 10 percent of A.G.I.)

Wagering losses (to the extent of wagering income)

Certain state, local, and foreign taxes:
- State, local, and foreign income taxes
- State, local, and foreign real property taxes
- State and local personal property taxes
- State and local sales taxes

Mortgage interest on personal residences (limited)

Mortgage insurance on personal residences

Charitable contributions (not to exceed 50 percent of A.G.I.)

Miscellaneous itemized deductions (amount in excess of 2 percent of A.G.I.):
- Costs of preparation of tax returns
- Fees and expenses related to tax planning and advice
- Investment counseling and investment expenses
- Certain unreimbursed employee business expenses (including travel and transportation, professional dues, subscriptions, continuing education, union dues, and special work clothing)

[35] Reg. § 1.151-1(c)(2).

[36] See § 63(c)(6) for this exception and others.

**Miscellaneous Itemized Deductions.** Itemized deductions are also allowed for a group of other expenses referred to as *miscellaneous itemized deductions.* Miscellaneous itemized deductions include the deductions for unreimbursed employee business expenses (e.g., dues to professional organizations, subscriptions to professional journals, travel and others that are not reimbursed under an accountable plan), tax return preparation fees and related costs, and certain investment expenses (e.g. safety deposit boxes, investment advice).[37] The classification of an expense as a miscellaneous itemized deduction is extremely important because a limitation is imposed on their deduction. Only the portion of miscellaneous itemized deductions exceeding 2 percent of adjusted gross income is deductible. Congress imposed this limitation in hopes of simplifying the law. The 2 percent floor is intended to relieve taxpayers of the burden of recordkeeping (unless they expect to incur substantial expenditures) and relieve the IRS of the burden of auditing these expenditures.

### Example 13

R, single, is employed as an architect. This year his wages were $50,000. His itemized deductions for the year were interest on his home mortgage, $5,000; charitable contributions, $900; tax return preparation fee, $300; and unreimbursed professional dues, $800. R's total itemized deductions are computed as follows:

| | |
|---|---|
| Miscellaneous itemized deductions: | |
| Tax return preparation fee | $ 300 |
| Professional dues | 800 |
| Total miscellaneous itemized deductions | $ 1,100 |
| A.G.I. limitation (2% × $50,000) | (1,000) |
| Total deductible miscellaneous itemized deductions | $ 100 |
| Other itemized deductions: | |
| Interest on home mortgage | 5,000 |
| Charitable contributions | 900 |
| Total itemized deductions | $ 6,000 |

Because R's itemized deductions of $6,000 exceed the standard deduction for single persons, $5,800 (2011), he will deduct the entire $6,000. Note that only $100 of R's miscellaneous itemized deductions is deductible, whereas all of his other itemized deductions are deductible.

## Exemptions

Congress has always recognized the need to insulate from tax a certain amount of income required by the taxpayer to support himself and others. For this reason, every individual taxpayer is entitled to a basic deduction for himself and his dependents. This deduction is called an *exemption*. For 2011, an individual taxpayer is entitled to a deduction of $3,700 for each *personal* and *dependency* exemption.[38] *Personal exemptions* are those allowed for the taxpayer. Generally, every taxpayer is entitled to claim a personal exemption for himself or herself. However, taxpayers *cannot* claim a personal exemption on their own return if they can be claimed as a dependent on another taxpayer's return.[39] If husband and wife file a joint return, they are treated as two taxpayers and are therefore entitled to claim two personal exemptions. *Dependency exemptions* may be claimed for qualifying individuals who are supported by the taxpayer.[40] All the special rules governing deductions for exemptions are discussed in detail in Chapter 4.

[37] An employee's business expenses are treated as reimbursed under §62 only if the employee adequately accounts for the expense to his or her employer (e.g., submits documentation) under the accountable plan rules. In such case the employee reports neither income nor expense and the expense is essentially the employer's. Otherwise the employee reports the income and claims the expense as a miscellaneous itemized deduction. See Reg. §1.62-2 and Chapter 8.

[38] § 151(d)(1). For 1989 the exemption was $2,000. For years *after* 1989, the amount has been indexed for inflation.

[39] § 151(d)(2).

[40] § 152.

### Taxable Income and Tax Rates

After all deductions have been identified, they are subtracted from gross income to arrive at taxable income. Taxable income is the tax base to which the tax rates are applied to determine the taxpayer's gross tax liability (i.e., the tax liability before any credits or prepayments).

The tax rate schedule to be used in computing the tax varies, depending on the nature of the taxable entity. For example, one set of tax rates applies to all regular corporations (see inside back cover of text). In contrast, individuals use one of four tax rate schedules (see inside front cover) depending on their filing status, of which there are four. These are:

1. Unmarried individuals (i.e., single) but not surviving spouses or heads of household
2. Heads of household
3. Married individuals filing jointly and surviving spouses
4. Married individuals filing separately

These tax rate structures are all graduated with six rates: 10, 15, 25, 28, 33, and 35 percent. Although the rates in each schedule are identical, the degree of progressivity differs. For example, in 2011 the 28 percent marginal rate applies to single taxpayers when income exceeds $83,600, but this rate does not apply to married individuals filing jointly until income exceeds $139,350. Filing status and rate schedules are discussed in Chapter 4.

#### Example 14

H and W are married and file a joint return for 2011. They have A.G.I. of $151,000, two dependents, and itemized deductions of $31,400. Their taxable income is $104,800, computed as follows:

| | | |
|---|---|---|
| Adjusted gross income | | $ 151,000 |
| Minus: Itemized deductions | $31,400 | |
| Personal exemptions ($3,700 × 4) | + 14,800 | − 46,200 |
| Equals: Taxable income | | $ 104,800 |

The tax for a married couple filing jointly on this amount computed using the rate schedules is $18,450.00 as shown below.

| | |
|---|---|
| Tax on $69,000 | $ 9,500.00 |
| Plus: Tax on excess at 25% [($104,800 − $69,000 = $35,800) × .25] | 8,950.00 |
| Equals: Total tax | $18,450.00 |

### Credits

Unlike a deduction, which reduces income in arriving at taxable income, a credit is a direct reduction in tax liability. Normally, when the credit exceeds a person's total tax, the excess is not refunded—hence, these credits are referred to as *nonrefundable* credits. In some instances, however, the taxpayer is entitled to receive a payment for any excess credit. This type of credit is known as a *refundable* credit.

**EXHIBIT 3.8** Partial List of Tax Credits

| | |
|---|---|
| Foreign tax credit | Credit for the elderly |
| Child tax credit | Credit for producing fuel from a nonconventional source |
| Earned income credit | Credit for increasing research activities |
| Child and dependent care credit | Welfare to work credit |
| Credit for adoption expenses | Work opportunity credit |
| Hope scholarship credit | Low income housing credit |
| Lifetime learning credit | Credit for rehabilitating certain buildings |

Credits have frequently been preferred by Congress and theoreticians because they affect all taxpayers equally. In contrast, the value of a deduction varies with the taxpayer's marginal tax rate. However, credits often have complicated rules and limitations. A partial list of tax credits is included in Exhibit 3-8.

### Prepayments

**LO.4**
Define many of the basic terms used in the tax formula such as gross income, adjusted gross income, taxable income, exclusion, deduction, and credit.

Attempting to accelerate the collection of revenues for the war effort in 1943, Congress installed a "pay-as-you-go" system for certain taxes. Under this system, income taxes are paid in installments as the income is earned.

Prepayment, or advance payment, of the tax liability can be made in several ways. For individual taxpayers, the two most common forms of prepayment are Federal income taxes withheld from an employee's salaries and wages and quarterly estimated tax payments made by the taxpayer. Certain corporate taxpayers must make quarterly estimated tax payments as well. Quarterly estimated tax payments are required for taxpayers who have not prepaid a specified level of their anticipated Federal income tax in any other way, and there are penalties for failure to make adequate estimated prepayments.

These prepayments serve two valuable purposes. As suggested above, prepayments allow the government to have earlier use of the tax proceeds. Secondly, prepayments reduce the uncertainty of collecting taxes since the government, by withholding at the source, gets the money before the taxpayer has a chance to put it to a different use. In effect, the government collects the tax while the taxpayer has the wherewithal (ability) to pay the tax.

### Other Taxes

There are several types of other taxes that must be reported and paid with the regular Federal income tax. A partial list of these taxes is included in Exhibit 3-9. Two deserve special mention.

**Self-Employment Tax.** As explained in Chapter 1, self-employed individuals as well as general partners in partnerships are, like employees, required to pay FICA taxes (commonly known as self-employment taxes). Since the tax is paid on income from sole proprietorship and partnership businesses carried on by individual partners, it is convenient for the IRS to collect this tax along with the income tax on Form 1040. The individual calculates the tax on Schedule SE and claims the income tax deduction for one-half of the self-employment tax paid on page 1 of Form 1040.

**Alternative Minimum Tax.** In 1969 there was an outcry by the media and others that the rich did not pay their fair share of taxes. Indeed, the House Ways and Means Committee Report indicated that in 1964 over 1,100 returns with adjusted gross incomes over $200,000 paid an average tax of 22 percent. Moreover, it reported that there were a significant number of cases where taxpayers with economic income of $1 million or more paid an effective tax amounting to less than 5 percent of their income. As might be expected, faced with such facts Congress decided to take action. However, instead of risking the wrath of their constituents by simply repealing the various loopholes that enabled these taxpayers to avoid taxes, Congress elected to take a politically cautious approach: a direct tax on the loopholes. In effect, the taxpayer simply added up all of the loopholes and paid a flat tax on them. As a result, the minimum tax was born. The whole thrust of this new tax was to ensure that all individuals paid a minimum tax on their income. It currently applies to all taxpayers, individuals, corporations, and fiduciaries.

**EXHIBIT 3.9** **Partial List of Other Taxes**

Alternative minimum tax
Self-employment tax
Social security tax on tip income not reported to employer
Tax on premature withdrawal from an Individual Retirement Account
Tax from recapture of investment credit
Uncollected employee F.I.C.A. and R.R.T.A. tax on tips

Over the years, the minimum tax evolved into a monster and was adorned with its current name, the alternative minimum tax (AMT). Despite the changes and increased complexity, it remains basically the same. The mathematical steps for computing the AMT are relatively simple:

|   |   |
|---|---|
|   | Regular taxable income |
| ± | Adjustments and preferences |
|   | Alternative minimum taxable income |
| − | Exemption (subject to phase-out) |
|   | Tax base |
| × | Rate |
|   | Tentative alternative minimum tax |
| − | Regular tax |
|   | Alternative minimum tax |

As the formula above illustrates, the taxpayer starts with taxable income and then adds certain income that is excluded for regular tax purposes and adds back certain deductions that are normally allowed. These modifications to regular taxable income are referred to as *preference items* and *adjustments.* In this regard, it is important to recognize that the AMT effectively functions as an entirely separate system with its own rules. For example, while most interest from state and local bonds is not taxable, such interest is taxable for AMT purposes if the bonds are used to fund some private activity such as a downtown mall. Similarly, deductions that are usually allowed for regular tax purposes, such as exemptions, miscellaneous itemized deductions, and state and local taxes, are not allowed in computing the AMT. In effect, there are two rules for some items: one rule for regular tax purposes and another for AMT purposes. After taking into account all of the special adjustments required under this alternative system, the new result is called alternative minimum taxable income. This amount is then reduced by an allowable exemption to arrive at the tax base. For 2011, the exemption amounts are $74,450 for joint filers ($37,225 for those filing separately) and $48,450 for single and head-of-household taxpayers. The exemption is reduced by 25% for each dollar by which AMTI exceeds certain levels (e.g. $150,000 for joint filers, $112,500 for singles). A two-tier rate structure is then applied to the tax base (26 percent on the first $175,000 and 28 percent on the excess). The product is referred to as the tentative AMT. This amount is compared to the regular tax, and the taxpayer pays the higher. Technically, the excess of the tentative AMT over the regular tax is the AMT, but the bottom line is that the taxpayer pays the higher amount.

## Example 15

H and W are married with four children. For 2011, they filed a joint return, reporting gross income of $400,000 and regular taxable income of $180,000. Various adjustments required under the AMT were $40,550. Using the 2011 exemption and 2011 regular tax rates, the couple must pay an AMT of $4,102, computed as follows:

|   |   |   |
|---|---|---|
|   | Regular taxable income | $180,000 |
| ± | Adjustments | 40,550 |
|   | Alternative minimum taxable income | $220,550 |
| − | Exemption [$74,450 − $17,637 (25% × ($220,550 − $150,000 = 70,550))] | (56,813) |
|   | Tax base | $163,737 |
| × | Rate | ×26% |
|   | Tentative alternative minimum tax | $ 42,572 |
| − | Regular tax (2011 rates) | (38,470) |
|   | Alternative minimum tax | $ 4,102 |

Note that the AMT is only $4,102, but the taxpayer must pay a total of $42,572 (regular tax of $38,470 + AMT of $4,102).

There is no good rule of thumb as to when the AMT is triggered. For the vast majority of taxpayers it is simply not an issue. These individuals are not subject to the tax since they have low to moderate taxable incomes with few adjustments, causing them to fall below the exemption amounts. It is typically high-income taxpayers who have substantial adjustments, and other taxpayers who are successful in avoiding the regular tax, that fall prey to the AMT. Obviously the key lies in the nature of the adjustments. For now it is sufficient to say that beyond the few preferences and adjustments mentioned above there are several more such as those relating to depreciation, depletion, and stock options. Full coverage of the AMT is deferred until Chapter 13. Nevertheless, even at this early juncture it is important to recognize that the AMT exists and often alters what appears to be very favorable tax treatment for some items. More importantly, the net of the AMT has started catching far more taxpayers than Congress ever intended.

## ✓ CHECK YOUR KNOWLEDGE

### Review Question I

It's time for "Tax Jeopardy." Here are the answers; supply the questions.

**a.** The type of expenses all taxpayers can deduct.

What are business expenses? Around tax time, there is a single question that can be heard reverberating across the land: What can I deduct? The answer is business expenses. All taxpayers are allowed to deduct the ordinary and necessary expenses incurred in carrying on a trade or business. The vast majority of all deductions fall into this category. Note also that this rule allows the deduction of employee business expenses. In addition, taxpayers are entitled to deduct expenses related to investment activities (e.g., investment advice or repairs and maintenance on rental property).

**b.** The type of expenses taxpayers normally cannot deduct.

What are personal expenses? Although business expenses are deductible, personal expenses normally are not deductible. For example, the costs of food, shelter, clothing, and personal hygiene cannot be deducted. However, there are some exceptions.

**c.** Five notable exceptions to the rule that personal expenses are not deductible. (Hint: they are all reported on Schedule A of Form 1040, found in Appendix B of this book.) What are the following?

1. Medical expenses (but only if they exceed 7.5 percent of A.G.I.)
2. Taxes
   - State and local income or sales taxes but not both
   - Real estate taxes
   - Personal property taxes
3. Interest
   - Home mortgage interest
   - Student loan interest (maximum of $2,500)
   - Investment interest (but only to the extent of investment income)
4. Charitable contributions
5. Casualty and theft losses

**d.** The type of business expenses that are deductible as itemized deductions.

What are unreimbursed employee business expenses? For example, if an employee pays for a business meal and his or her employer reimburses the cost of the meal, the expense is deductible in arriving at A.G.I. if the employer includes the reimbursement in the employee's gross income. Technically, if the employee adequately accounts to the employer under the accountable plan rules, the employee has no income for the reimbursement nor any deduction for the expense (see Chapter 8). However, when the expense is not reimbursed, it is allowable only as a miscellaneous itemized deduction subject to the 2 percent floor. Other common examples of employee business expenses that are frequently deductible as miscellaneous itemized deductions are unreimbursed professional expenses (e.g., subscriptions, dues, license fees), union dues, and special clothing (when deductible).

**e.** The only type of tax-exempt income reported on the return. (Hint: see page 1 of Form 1040.)

What is tax-exempt interest income (reported on line 8b of page 1 of Form 1040)?

**f.** Something the individual tax formula has that the corporate tax formula does not have.

What is adjusted gross income? What is the standard deduction? What are exemptions?

**g.** A benefit received by the elderly and blind.

What is the increased standard deduction for taxpayers who are age 65 or over or who are blind?

**h.** Deductions that are deductible for individuals even if the taxpayer does not itemize deductions.

What are deductions for A.G.I.? In addition, deductions for exemptions are permitted regardless of whether the taxpayer itemizes. However, exemption deductions are not deductions for A.G.I.

**i.** A deduction that may be claimed by virtually all individual taxpayers.

What is the exemption deduction, or the standard deduction? As explained above, however, certain persons are not entitled to a standard deduction. For example, a married person filing a separate return must itemize if his or her spouse does. In addition, as fully explained in Chapter 4, taxpayers cannot claim a personal exemption on their own return if they can be claimed as a dependent on another taxpayer's return.

**j.** A loss from this activity may not be deductible.

What are losses from rental real estate and any other activity in which the taxpayer does not materially participate? Before losses from an activity can be deducted (e.g., a loss that passes through from a partnership or a loss from renting a duplex), they must run through the gauntlet of tests prescribed by the passive loss rules covered in Chapter 12.

**k.** A separate tax intended to close loopholes.

What is the alternative minimum tax?

## Review Question 2

Mabel, single, just reached the age of 65 and was somewhat relieved because she remembered hearing of the tax she would save as a 65-year-old senior. What tax savings can Mabel *expect?*

*Perhaps none.* The only benefit for being 65 years old is an additional standard deduction ($1,450 for unmarried taxpayers for 2011). If Mabel itemizes her deductions rather than claiming the standard deduction, she receives no benefit. If she does not itemize, her standard deduction for 2011 is $7,250 (the basic standard deduction of $5,800 plus the extra $1,450)

## Review Question 3

Dick and Jane just learned that they are expecting their first child. What tax benefits can they expect after Junior is born?

*Many.* First are the dependency exemption deduction ($3,700 for 2011) and the child tax credit ($1,000 for 2011). In addition, Dick and Jane can look forward to a credit for any job-related child care expenses that they pay.

## Review Question 4

Are deductions of a sole proprietor deductible *for* or *from* adjusted gross income? (Hint: see lines 23 through 27 on Page 1 of Form 1040 and Schedule C in Appendix B of this book.)

The trade or business expenses of a sole proprietor or someone who is self-employed are deductible for A.G.I. Note that these are not shown as one of the deductions for A.G.I.

on Page 1 of Form 1040. Instead, they are netted against the sole proprietor's income on Schedule C, and this net profit is included in the taxpayer's total income reported on Page 1 of Form 1040.

### Review Question 5

A sole proprietor's income generally is subject to self-employment tax. Is the deduction for one-half of the self-employment tax deducted for or from adjusted gross income? Is it reported on Schedule C or Form 1040?

This is a deduction for A.G.I. and is reported as a deduction for A.G.I. on page 1 of Form 1040 (and not Schedule C).

## Introduction to Property Transactions

The tax provisions governing property transactions play a very important part in our tax system. Obviously, their major purpose is to provide for the tax treatment of transactions involving a sale, exchange, or other disposition of property. However, the basic rules covering property transactions can also impact the tax liability in other indirect ways. For example, the amount of the deduction granted for a charitable contribution of property may depend on what the tax result would have been had the property been sold rather than donated. As this example suggests, a basic knowledge of the tax treatment of property transactions is helpful in understanding other facets of taxation. For this reason, an overview of property transactions is presented here. Chapters 14, 15, 16, and 17 examine this subject in detail.

The tax consequences of any property transaction may be determined by answering the following three questions:

1. What is the amount of gain or loss *realized*?
2. How much of this gain or loss is *recognized*?
3. What is the *character* of the gain or loss recognized?

Each of these questions is considered in the following sections.

### Gain or Loss Realized

**LO.5**
Calculate the gain or loss on the disposition of property and explain the tax consequences, including the special treatment of capital gains and losses.

A realized gain or loss results when a taxpayer sells, exchanges, or otherwise disposes of property. In the simple case where property is purchased for cash and later sold for cash, the gain or loss realized is the difference between the purchase price and the sale price, adjusted for transaction costs. The determination of the realized gain or loss is more complicated when property other than cash is received, when liabilities are involved, or when the property was not acquired by purchase. As a result, a more formal method for computing the gain or loss realized is used. The formulas for computing the gain or loss realized are shown in Exhibits 3-10, 3-11, and 3-12. As these exhibits illustrate, the gain or loss realized in a sale or other disposition is the difference between the *amount realized* and the *adjusted basis* in the property given up.

**EXHIBIT 3.10 Computation of Amount Realized**

| | |
|---|---|
| | Amount of money received (net of money paid) |
| *Add:* | Fair market value of any other property received |
| | Liabilities discharged in the transaction (net of liabilities assumed) |
| *Less:* | Selling costs |
| Equals: | **Amount realized** |

**EXHIBIT 3.11** **Determination of Adjusted Basis**

***Basis at time of acquisition:***

For purchased property, use cost

Special rules apply for the following methods of acquisition:

Gift

Bequest or inheritance

Nontaxable transactions

***Add:*** Capital improvements, additions

***Less:*** Depreciation and other capital recoveries

Equals: **Adjusted basis in property**

**EXHIBIT 3.12** **Computation of Gain or Loss Realized**

Amount realized from sale or other disposition

***Less:*** Adjusted basis in property (other than money) given up

Equals: **Gain or loss realized**

## Amount Realized

The amount realized is a measure of the economic value received for the property given up. It generally includes the amount of any money plus the fair market value of any other property received, reduced by any selling costs.[41] In determining the amount realized, consideration must also be given to any liabilities from which the taxpayer is relieved or which the taxpayer incurs. From an economic standpoint, when a taxpayer is relieved of debt, it is the same as if cash were received and used to pay off the debt. In contrast, when a taxpayer assumes a debt (or receives property that is subject to a debt), it is the same as if the taxpayer gave up cash. Consequently, when a sale or exchange involves the transfer of liabilities, the amount realized is increased for the net amount of any liabilities discharged or decreased for the net amount of any liabilities incurred.

## Adjusted Basis

The adjusted basis of property is similar to the concept of "book value" used for accounting purposes. It is the taxpayer's basis at the time of acquisition—usually cost—increased or decreased by certain required modifications.[42] The taxpayer's basis at the time of acquisition, or original basis, depends on how the property was acquired. For purchased property, the taxpayer's original basis is the property's cost. When property is acquired by gift, inheritance, or some form of tax-deferred exchange, special rules are applied in determining the original basis. Once the original basis is ascertained, it must be increased for any capital improvements and reduced by depreciation and other capital recoveries. The adjusted basis represents the amount of investment that can be recovered free of tax.

[41] § 1001(b).

[42] §§ 1011 through 1016.

### Example 16

This year, L sold 100 shares of M Corporation stock for $41 per share for a total of $4,100. He received a settlement check of $4,000, net of the broker's sales commission of $100. L had purchased the shares several years ago for $12 per share for a total of $1,200. In addition, he paid a sales commission of $30. L's realized gain is $2,770, computed as follows:

| | |
|---|---|
| Amount realized ($4,100 − $100) | $4,000 |
| Less: Adjusted basis ($1,200 + $30) | − 1,230 |
| Gain realized | $2,770 |

### Example 17

During the year, T sold his office building. As part of the sales agreement, T received $20,000 cash, and the buyer assumed the mortgage on the building of $180,000. T also paid a real estate brokerage commission of $7,000. T originally acquired the building for $300,000 in 1990, but since that time had deducted depreciation of $230,000 and had made permanent improvements of $10,000. T's gain realized is computed as follows:

| | | |
|---|---|---|
| Amount realized: | | |
| Cash received | $ 20,000 | |
| Liability assumed by buyer | +180,000 | |
| Selling expenses | −7,000 | |
| | | $193,000 |
| Less: Adjusted basis | | |
| Original cost | $300,000 | |
| Depreciation claimed | −230,000 | |
| Capital improvements | + 10,000 | |
| | | − 80,000 |
| Gain realized | | $113,000 |

## Gain or Loss Recognized

The gain or loss *realized* is a measure of the economic gain or loss that results from the ownership and sale or disposition of property. However, due to special provisions in the tax law, the gain or loss reported for tax purposes may be different from the realized gain or loss. The amount of gain or loss that affects the tax liability is called the *recognized* gain or loss.

Normally, all realized gains are recognized and included as part of the taxpayer's total income. In some instances, however, the gain recognition may be permanently excluded. For example, an individual is generally allowed to exclude up to $250,000 of gain realized on the sale of a personal residence ($500,000 for married taxpayers). Other gains may be deferred or postponed until a subsequent transaction occurs.

### Example 18

M exchanged some land in Oregon costing $10,000 for land in Florida valued at $50,000. Although M has realized gain of $40,000 ($50,000 − $10,000), assuming certain requirements are satisfied, this gain will not be recognized, but rather postponed. This rule was adopted because the taxpayer's economic position after the transaction is essentially unchanged. Moreover, the taxpayer has not received any cash or wherewithal with which she could pay any tax that might result.

Chapter 15 contains a discussion of the more common types of property transactions in which the recognition of an individual taxpayer's realized gains are postponed.

Any loss realized must be specifically allowed as a deduction before it is recognized. Individuals generally are allowed to deduct *three* types of losses. These are:

1. Losses incurred in a trade or business (e.g., an uncollectible receivable of an accrual basis taxpayer)
2. Losses incurred in an activity engaged in for profit (e.g., sale of investment property such as stock at a loss)
3. Casualty and theft losses

Losses in the first two categories generally are deductions for adjusted gross income. Casualty and theft losses from property used in an individual's trade, business, or income-producing activity also are allowed as deductions for adjusted gross income. However, casualty and theft losses from personal use property are classified as itemized deductions and are deductible only to the extent they exceed $100 per casualty or theft and 10 percent of A.G.I. Other than casualty and theft losses, all other losses from dispositions of personal use assets are *not* deductible. For example, if a taxpayer sold his personal residence for a loss, the loss would not be deductible. The rules governing the deductibility of losses in the first three categories are covered in Chapter 10. The special rules governing the deduction of "capital" losses are introduced below and covered in greater detail in Chapter 16.

## Character of the Gain or Loss

From 1913 through 1921, all includible income was taxed in the same manner. Since 1921, however, Congress has provided special tax treatment for "capital" gains or losses. As a result, in determining the tax consequences of a property transaction, consideration must be given to the character or nature of the gain or loss—that is, whether the gain or loss should be classified as a *capital* gain or loss or an *ordinary* gain or loss. Any *recognized* gain or loss must be characterized as either an ordinary or a capital gain or loss.

### Capital Gains and Losses

Although capital gains and losses arise in numerous ways, they normally result from the sale or exchange of a *capital asset.* Any gain or loss due to the sale or exchange of a capital asset is considered a capital gain or loss.

Capital assets are defined in § 1221 of the Code as being anything *other* than the following:

1. Inventory, or other property held primarily for sale to customers in the ordinary course of a trade or business
2. Depreciable property or real property used in a trade or business of the taxpayer
3. Trade accounts or notes receivable
4. Certain copyrights, literary, musical, or artistic compositions, and letters or memoranda held by the person whose personal efforts created them, and certain specified other holders of these types of property
5. U.S. government publications acquired other than by purchase at the price at which they are sold to the general public

The term *capital assets*, therefore, includes most passive investments (e.g., stocks and bonds) and most personal use assets of a taxpayer. However, property used in a trade or business is not a capital asset but is subject to special tax treatment, as discussed later in this chapter.

### Treatment of Capital Gains

Except for a short period between 1913 and 1922, the tax law consistently has taxed gains from the sale of certain "capital assets" at rates that are substantially lower than those that apply to other income. Most recently, the special advantage is justified on the grounds that it encourages greater investment and savings. Regardless of the rationale, the hard fact is that the rules necessary to carry out the objective create an incredible layer of complexity to the tax laws. To illustrate, simply consider that capital gains qualifying for special treatment could now be taxed at one of five different rates (28%, 25%, 15%, 10% or 0%).

**Holding Period.** The exact treatment of a capital gain or loss depends primarily on how long the taxpayer held the asset or what is technically referred to as the taxpayer's *holding period.* The holding period is a critical element in determining which of the rates will apply. As might be expected, the longer the holding period is, the lower the applicable tax rate will be. A *short-term* gain or loss is one resulting from the sale or disposition of an asset held *one year or less.* A *long-term* gain or loss occurs when an asset is held for *more than one year.* However, after this initial classification, individuals must subdivide the long-term group into additional subgroups: (1) the 28% group for long-term capital gains resulting from the sales of *collectibles* (e.g., antiques, coins, stamps) and *qualified small business stock* (note that only 50% of this gain is taxed if the holding period exceeds 60 months, making the effective tax rate 14%); (2) the 25% group for long-term capital gains (and only gains) from the sale of depreciable real estate (e.g., office buildings, warehouses, apartment buildings) held for more than one year but only to the extent of the depreciation claimed on such property; and (3) the 15% group for other (most) long-term capital gains.

The effect of the rules is to require taxpayers to assign their capital gains and losses into one of four different groups and net the amounts to determine the net gain or loss in each group as shown below.

| | *Short-term* | *Long-term* | | |
|---|---|---|---|---|
| Holding period (months) | ≤ 12 | Collectibles > 12 & § 1202 stock > 60 | Realty > 12 | > 12 |
| | Ordinary | 28% | 25% | 15% |
| Gains | $xx,xxx | $x,xxx | Gains only | $xx,xxx |
| Losses | (xxx) | (x,xxx) | — | (x,xxx) |
| Net gain or loss | ???? | ???? | Gain only | ???? |

As a practical matter, the capital gains of most individuals arise from the sales of stocks and bonds and mutual fund transactions. Rarely do individuals have gains from collectibles, § 1202, stock or depreciable realty. Consequently, for most individuals, the classification and netting process is much easier than it might appear.

## Applicable Capital Gains Rates

Generalizations about the treatment of capital gains and losses are difficult because the actual treatment can be determined only after the various groups (i.e., the four groups above) are combined, or netted, to determine the overall net gain or loss during the year. The details of this netting process are quite complex and left to Chapter 16. Suffice it to say here that the treatment of the net gains of each group—*before any netting between groups*—can be summarized as follows:

1. A net short-term capital gain (NSTCG) generally receives no special treatment and is taxed as ordinary income at the taxpayer's regular tax rate (up to 35%).
2. A net 28% capital gain (N28CG) is taxed at a maximum rate of 28%.
3. A net 25% gain (N25CG) from dispositions of realty is taxed at a maximum rate of 25% (generally only to the extent of any depreciation claimed). The balance of any gain is part of the 15% group.
4. A net 15% gain (N15CG) is taxed at a maximum rate of 15%. However, if the taxpayer's taxable income *including* the net 15% gain would be taxed at 15% or less, a special rule applies. In this case, the net gain in this group is taxed at a rate of 0%. For example, if a joint filer has $60,000 of ordinary taxable income and $9,000 of N15CG, his total taxable income normally is taxed at no greater than a 15% rate. Therefore, the N15CG is taxed at a 0% rate.

In applying these rules, it should be emphasized that they operate to set only the maximum rate at which the particular type of gain will be taxed. If the taxpayer's tax using the regular rates would be lower, the regular rates are used. For example, if the taxpayer is in the 15% tax bracket and has a 28% gain, the 15% rate would apply instead of the 28% rate.

### Example 19

During the year, T, who is in the 35% tax bracket, reported the following capital gains and losses.

| | Short-term | Long-term 28% | Long-term 15% |
|---|---|---|---|
| Gains | $10,000 | $4,000 | $10,000 |
| Losses | (4,000) | — | (3,000) |
| | $ 6,000 | $4,000 | $ 7,000 |

In this case, T has a NSTCG of $6,000, a N28CG of $4,000, and a N15CG of $7,000. As explained in Chapter 16, no further netting of these transactions occurs. T's NSTCG of $6,000 receives no special treatment and is taxed as ordinary income. T's N28CG is taxed at 28% while his N15CG is taxed at 15%.

## Dividends Taxed at Capital Gain Rates

Beginning in 2003 and through 2012, most dividends received are taxed at the same rate that historically has been reserved for long-term capital gains rates.[43] Currently, the rate is 15% and 0% for dividends that would otherwise be taxed at an ordinary rate of 15% or lower. The qualifying dividend is not subject to the capital gain and loss netting process. As a result, the dividends are subject to capital gains treatment regardless of whether the taxpayer has other capital gains or losses. The details related to calculating the tax on these dividends are presented in Chapter 16.

### Example 20

During 2011, S, single, sold stock he had held for several years. He sold 100 shares of L for a $500 long-term capital loss and 200 shares of G for a $3,200 long-term capital gain. S also received qualified dividends of $370 for the year. S is single and has no dependents. Assume her taxable income including the above transactions is $86,670. The following calculations demonstrate the application of the favorable 15 percent capital gains rate.

| | |
|---|---|
| Gain on Evergreen Solar | $ 3,200 |
| Loss on Gateway | (500) |
| Net capital gain | $ 2,700 |
| Dividend income | 370 |
| Amount subject to 15% capital gains ratc | $ 3,070 |
| S's taxable income is taxed as follows: | |
| Amount subject to 15% capital gains rate | $ 3,070 |
| Amount treated as ordinary income ($86,670 − $3,070) | $83,600 |
| S's tax is calculated as follows: | |
| Tax on ordinary income of $83,600 (see inside front cover) | $17,025 |
| Tax on gains and dividends at 15% ($3,070 × 15%) | 461 |
| Total tax | $17,486 |

[43] § 1(h)(11).

### Treatment of Capital Losses

While capital gains receive favorable treatment, such is not the case with capital losses. As can be seen in *Example 20*, capital losses are first netted with capital gains within the same group. A net capital loss from a particular group can then be combined with net capital gains from the other groups. As a general rule, the long-term groups are netted together before considering any short-term items. If after netting all of the groups together, the taxpayer has an overall net capital loss, the loss is deductible up to an annual limit of $3,000. The deductible capital loss is a deduction for adjusted gross income. Any losses in excess of the annual $3,000 limitation are carried forward to the following year where they are treated as if they occurred in such year. In effect, an unused capital loss can be carried over for an indefinite period.

#### Example 21

During the year, B reported the following capital gains and losses.

| | Short-term | Long-term 28% | Long-term 15% |
|---|---|---|---|
| Gains | $10,000 | $3,000 | $5,000 |
| Losses | (18,000) | (4,000) | (3,000) |
| | ($8,000) | ($1,000) | $2,000 |

B's only other taxable income included his salary of $50,000. He had no other deductions for A.G.I. After netting all of his gains and losses, B has a net capital loss of $7,000. T may deduct only $3,000 of the net capital loss in determining his A.G.I. Therefore, his A.G.I. is $47,000 ($50,000 – $3,000). The unused capital loss of $4,000 ($7,000 – $3,000) is carried forward to future years when it is treated as if it arose in the subsequent year. In such case, the loss can be used against other capital gains or ordinary income just as it was this year.

Details of capital gain and loss treatment and the capital loss carryover rules are discussed in Chapter 16.

### Corporate Taxpayers

The taxation of capital gains for corporate taxpayers differs somewhat from that for individuals. Most important, the capital gains of a corporation normally receive no special treatment but are taxed as ordinary income. In addition, the capital losses of a corporation can never offset ordinary income but can be carried back three and forward five years to offset other capital gains. There are a number of other differences which are considered in a full discussion of a corporation's capital gains and losses in Chapter 19.

## Trade or Business Property

Depreciable property and real property used in a trade or business are not capital assets, but are subject to several special provisions. Nevertheless, gain on the sale of these assets may ultimately be treated as capital gain while losses may be treated as ordinary losses. These rules are quite complex and considered in Chapter 17.

## ✓ Check Your Knowledge

Try the following true-false questions.

### Review Question I

An individual always receives preferential treatment for his or her capital gains.

*False.* An individual can receive special treatment only for long-term capital gains. Short-term capital gains are treated just like ordinary income.

## Review Question 2

J is interested in the stock market. This year she realized a $1,000 short-term capital gain and an $8,000 capital loss from stock she held for two years. She will report a $1,000 short-term capital gain and carry over the $8,000 long-term capital loss.

*False.* She first nets the short-term gain of $1,000 against her $8,000 15% loss, resulting in an overall long-term capital loss of $7,000. She may deduct $3,000 of this loss as a deduction for A.G.I. The remaining loss is carried over to the following year, when it will be treated as if she had realized a long-term (28%) capital loss of $4,000.

## Review Question 3

K makes $500,000 a year and plays the stock market. So far this year she has realized a 15% capital gain of $3,000. It is now December 31. Should K sell stock and recognize a $3,000 15% loss?

Who knows? If she recognizes a $3,000 loss, the loss is offset against the gain and therefore reduces income that would have been taxed at a 15 percent rate. This would produce a tax benefit from the loss of only $450 ($3,000 × 15%). If she waits and uses the loss against ordinary income, it will produce a tax benefit of $1,050 (35% × $3,000), or $600 ($1,050 – $450) more. However, if she postpones the loss until some subsequent year hoping to use it to offset income taxed at a higher rate, she will lose the time value of the $450.

## Review Question 4

A corporation normally receives no special treatment for its long-term capital gains.

*True.* The long-term capital gains of a corporation normally are treated in the same manner as ordinary income.

## Review Question 5

John Doe is the typical American taxpayer. He is married, has a dog and two kids. He also owns two cars: a brand new Ford and a 1996 Chevrolet. He bought the Ford for $17,000 and the Chevy for $10,000. Both of the cars were used for personal purposes. This year John and his family moved to New York and decided they did not need the cars, so he sold them. He sold the Chevy for only $3,000. The story on the Ford was different. The Ford happened to be a Mustang convertible, and because Mustangs were in demand and were on back order, a car nut was willing to give him $19,000, a $2,000 premium for not having to wait. How will these sales affect John's taxable income? Explain whether the taxpayer has a gain or loss, its character, and in the case of a loss whether it is deductible for or from A.G.I.

John reports a capital gain of $2,000. The first step is to determine John's gain or loss *realized.* In this case, the determination is simple. On the sale of the Chevy, John realized a loss of $7,000 ($3,000 – $10,000), and on the sale of the Mustang he realized a gain of $2,000 ($19,000 – $17,000). The second step is to determine whether he *recognizes* the gain and loss realized. John must recognize the gain. As a general rule, all income is taxable unless the taxpayer can point to a specific provision that specifically exempts the income from tax. In this case, there is no exclusion. On the other hand, the $7,000 loss is not deductible. Although all income is normally taxable, only those items specifically authorized are deductible. Only three types of losses are deductible: (1) losses incurred in carrying on a trade or business; (2) losses incurred in an activity engaged in for profit (e.g., investment losses); and (3) casualty and theft losses. In this case, the loss on the sale of the Chevy is purely personal, and therefore no deduction is allowed. Thus John is not allowed to net the loss against the gain but must report only the gain of $2,000. While this may seem like a surprising result, understand that tax is a one-way street: as a general rule, all income is taxable and only those expenses and losses specifically allowed are deductible. The final step is determining the character of the gain, that is, whether the gain is capital gain or ordinary income. In order for a taxpayer to have a capital gain, there must be a sale or exchange of a capital asset. The Code defines a capital asset as essentially everything but inventory and real or depreciable property used in a trade or business. In this case, the car is not used in business and it does not represent inventory, so it is a capital asset. As a result, John reports a capital gain of $2,000.

**Review Question 6**

Indicate whether the following assets are capital assets.

**a.** 2,000 boxes of Frosted Flakes held by a grocery store
**b.** A crane used in the taxpayer's bungee-jumping business
**c.** A warehouse owned by Wal-Mart
**d.** IBM stock held for investment
**e.** The personal residence of Jane Doe

The Code generally defines a capital asset as essentially everything but inventory, business receivables, and real or depreciable property used in a trade or business. Based on this definition, the Frosted Flakes are not a capital asset since they are held as inventory by the grocery; the crane is not a capital asset since it is depreciable property used in a business; and the warehouse is not a capital asset since it is real property used in a business. The personal residence and IBM stock are both capital assets since they are neither inventory nor property used in a trade or business.

# Tax Planning Considerations

## Choice of Business Form

One of the major decisions confronting a business from a tax perspective concerns selecting the form in which it conducts its operations. A taxpayer could choose to operate a business as a sole proprietorship, a partnership, a limited liability company, an S corporation, or a regular C corporation. Each of these entities has its own tax characteristics that make it more or less suitable for a particular situation. The following discussion highlights a number of the basic factors that should be considered.

Perhaps the most important consideration in choosing a business form is the outlook for the business. A business that expects losses will typically opt for a business form different from the one that expects profits. A key advantage of a conduit entity (i.e., partnership or S corporation) applies in years in which a business suffers losses. Like income, losses flow through to the owners of the entity and generally can be used to offset other income at the individual level. In contrast, losses suffered by a regular C corporation are bottled up inside the corporate entity and can benefit only the corporation. Losses of a regular corporation generally are carried back two years and carried forward 20 years to offset income that the corporation has in prior or subsequent years.

A profitable business may also benefit from choosing the proper form of organization. To illustrate, consider a business that is generating taxable income of $1 million per year. If the taxpayer conducts the business as a sole proprietorship or through one of the conduit entities, the top tax rate applied to the income is 35 percent. Similarly, if a C corporation is used to operate the business, the top rate is 35 percent. However, for most corporations—those with taxable incomes not exceeding $10 million—the top rate is 34 percent. Moreover, tax savings may also be generated at lower levels of income. This possibility can be seen in the tax rate schedules for corporations and individuals. A quick comparison reveals that the first $50,000 of income of a corporate taxpayer is taxed at a 15 percent rate, whereas married taxpayers filing jointly receive the benefits of a 15 percent (or lower) rate on a maximum of $69,000 (for 2011). Obviously, the tax-wise individual might try to structure the activities so that the best of both worlds could be obtained. Consider a business that produces taxable income of $90,000. If a corporation is used, the company could pay a deductible salary of $50,000 to the owner (assuming it is a reasonable amount), leaving $40,000 of taxable income in the corporation. By so doing, the maximum tax rate paid on the income would be 15 percent. Had the business been operated as a sole proprietorship or an S corporation, $21,000 ($90,000 – $69,000), the amount of taxable income in excess of $69,000, would have been taxed at a 25 percent rate (married filing jointly) or 10 percentage points higher. This may seem appealing, but it is a very simplistic analysis and leaves vital elements out of the equation. For example, this scheme completely ignores the problem of double taxation; it assumes that the taxpayer will be able to withdraw the $34,000 ($40,000 – $6,000 corporate income tax) left in the corporation at a later time in a deductible fashion so as to avoid the second tax. Unfortunately, doing so is not as easy as it may appear, and this plan as well as any other requires careful analysis. Suffice it to say here, however, that careful planning at the outset of a new business can save the taxpayer substantial taxes in the future.

A possible disadvantage of partnerships and S corporations concerns the treatment of certain fringe benefits. As explained in Chapter 6, the Code contains a host of fringe benefits that generally are deductible by the employer and nontaxable to the employee. For example, a corporation is entitled to deduct the costs of group-term life insurance provided to an employee, and the benefit (i.e., the payment of the premiums) is not treated as taxable compensation to the employee but is tax-free. Note that if the employee purchases the insurance directly, it is purchased with compensation that has been previously taxed. As a result, the employee acquires the benefit with after-tax dollars. The favorable tax treatment of fringe benefits is generally available only to employees of a business. Unfortunately, partners and shareholders in S corporations who work in the business are not considered employees for this purpose and consequently cannot obtain many of the tax-favored fringe benefits. In contrast, shareholders in regular C corporations who work in the business are treated as employees and are therefore able to take advantage of the various benefits. Consideration should also be given to payroll and self-employment taxes.

## Itemized Deductions versus Standard Deduction

A typical complaint of many taxpayers is that they have insufficient deductions to itemize and therefore cannot benefit from any deductions they have in a particular year. Nevertheless, with a little planning, not all of those deductions will be wasted. Taxpayers in this situation should attempt to bunch all their itemized deductions into one year. By so doing, they may itemize one year and claim the standard deduction the next. By alternating each year, total deductions over the two-year period are increased. This could be accomplished simply by postponing or accelerating the payment of expenses. Cash basis taxpayers have this flexibility because they are entitled to deduct expenses when paid.

### Example 22

X, a widow age 61, sold her home and moved to an apartment. Due to the sale of the house, she anticipates that the only itemized deduction she would have in the future would be charitable contributions to her church as follows.

| | *2011* | *2010* |
|---|---|---|
| Charitable contributions. . . . . . . . . . . . . . . . . . . . . . . . . . . . | $5,800 | $5,800 |

If the pattern above continues, X will not receive any tax benefit from her charitable contributions since they do not exceed the standard deduction for single taxpayers, $5,800 (2011). However, what would happen if X simply shifted the payment of the charitable contributions from one year to the other by paying it either earlier or later. In such case, total itemized deductions in one year would be $11,600 ($5,800 + $5,800) and she could itemize, while in the other year she could claim the standard deduction. As a result, she would obtain total deductions over the two-year period of $16,400 ($10,600 + $5,800), or 4,800 ($16,400 – $11,600) more than if she merely claimed the standard deduction in both years.

## Employee Business Expenses

Most employee business expenses are typically paid by the employer, either through direct payment or reimbursement according to the accountable plan rules. Under these rules, employees must "adequately account" to their employers for their expenses by submitting a record, with receipts and other substantiation and return in excess advance or allowance, if any.[44] When this is done, it is as if the employee had no expense at all. Essentially, it is the employer's deduction. This approach, as set forth in the Regulations, is equivalent to treating the expenses as deductible for A.G.I.[45] Note that the net effect on A.G.I. is zero.

[44] Regs. § 1.62-2 and § 1.162-17. See also Chapter 8.

[45] § 62(b) and Reg. § 1.62-2.

On the other hand, if an employer requires employees to incur some business expenses, the employee can claim them only to the extent he or she itemizes and has miscellaneous itemized deductions in excess of 2 percent of A.G.I. The result is the same if an employee does not adequately account for an expense under the accountable plan rules. The amount received from the employer is included in gross income and the expense is reported as a miscellaneous itemized deduction. When this occurs, the employee may receive little or no tax benefit from the expenses.

In reviewing the employee's compensation package, employers might consider changing their reimbursement policies. If an employer adopts more generous reimbursement policies in lieu of compensation increases, the employees may benefit.

**Example 23**

E, single, is an employee with gross income of $50,000. She typically has annual employee business expenses of $1,000 that are not reimbursed. Since E does not itemize, she derives no tax benefit from the expenses.

If, instead of the above arrangement, E received a salary of $49,000 and the $1,000 of expenses were reimbursed, she would be in the same economic position before tax. However, she would pay $250 ($1,000 × 25% marginal tax on her salary) less in Federal income taxes.

## Problem Materials

### DISCUSSION QUESTIONS

**3-1** *Taxable Entities.* List the classes of taxable entities under the Federal income tax. Identify at least one type of entity that is not subject to the tax.

**3-2** *Double Taxation.* It has been stated that corporate earnings are subject to double taxation by the Federal government. Elaborate.

**3-3** *Fiduciary.* In some regards, the fiduciary is a conduit for Federal income tax purposes. Explain.

**3-4** *Partnership and S Corporation Returns.* The partnership and S corporation tax returns are often referred to as information returns only. Explain.

**3-5** *Income from Partnerships.* Y is a general partner in the XYZ Partnership. For the current calendar year, Y's share of profits includes his guaranteed compensation of $55,000 and his share of remaining profits, which is $22,000. What is the proper income tax and payroll tax (F.I.C.A. or self-employment tax) treatment of each of the following to Y for the current calendar year?

**a.** The guaranteed compensation of $50,000

**b.** The remaining income share of $22,000

**3-6** *Income from S Corporations.* K is the president and chief executive officer of KL, Inc., an S corporation that is owned equally by individuals K and L. K receives a salary of $83,000, and her share of the net income, after deducting executive salaries, is $50,000. What is the proper income tax and payroll tax (F.I.C.A. or self-employment tax) treatment of each of the following to K for the current calendar year?

**a.** The salary, assuming it is reasonable in amount

**b.** The net income of $50,000 that passes through to K

**c.** The $3,600 that the company paid for group employee medical insurance for K and her family

**3-7** *Tax Formula.* Reproduce the tax formula for individual taxpayers in good form and briefly describe each of the components of the formula. Discuss the differences between the tax formula for individuals and that for corporations.

**3-8** *Gross Income.* How is gross income defined in the Internal Revenue Code?

**3-9** *Deductions.* Distinguish between deductions *for* and deductions *from* adjusted gross income.

**3-10** *Standard Deduction.* What is the standard deduction? Explain its relationship to itemized deductions. Which taxpayers are entitled to additional standard deductions?

**3-11** *Itemized Deductions.* List seven major categories of itemized deductions. How and when are these reduced? Is the standard deduction reduced? If so, under what circumstances?

**3-12** *Employee Business Expenses.* Expenses incurred that are directly related to one's activities as an employee are trade or business expenses. True or False?

**3-13** *Additional Standard Deduction.* H and W are married and are 74 and 76 years of age, respectively. They also paid real property taxes on their home of $1,500. The couple does not itemize. Assuming they have gross income of $40,000 for 2011 and file a joint return, determine their taxable income.

**3-14** *Exemptions.* Differentiate between personal exemptions and dependency exemptions. Which taxpayers are denied a personal exemption?

**3-15** *Credits.* There are numerous credits that are allowed to reduce a taxpayer's Federal income tax liability. List at least four such credits.

**3-16** *Credits.* Credits of equal amount affect persons in different tax brackets equally, whereas deductions of equal amount are more beneficial to taxpayers in higher tax brackets. Explain.

**3-17** *Prepayments.* What is meant by the concept of "wherewithal to pay" for tax purposes? How do prepayments of an individual's income taxes in the form of withholding and quarterly estimates represent the application of this concept?

**3-18** *Alternative Minimum Tax.* What is the alternative minimum tax? Explain what is meant by *alternative* and *minimum* in this context.

**3-19** *Amount Realized.* What is meant by "the amount realized in a sale or other disposition"? How is the amount realized calculated?

**3-20** *Adjusted Basis.* Describe the concept of adjusted basis. How is the basis in purchased property determined?

**3-21** *Gain or Loss Realized.* Reproduce the formula for determining the gain or loss realized in a sale or other disposition of property.

**3-22** *Gain or Loss Recognized.* Differentiate between the terms "gain or loss realized" and "gain or loss recognized."

**3-23** *Losses.* Which losses are deductible by individual taxpayers?

**3-24** *Capital Assets.* Define the term "capital asset."

**3-25** *Holding Period.* The determination of the holding period is important in determining the treatment of capital gains and losses. What is the difference between a long-term holding period and a short-term holding period?

**3-26** *Capital Gains.* Briefly explain the favorable treatment given to capital gains and when such treatment applies.

**3-27** *Capital Losses of Individuals.* There are "limitations" on the capital loss deduction for individuals. Identify these limitations.

**3-28** *Capital Losses of Corporations.* What is the limitation on the deduction for capital losses of a corporate taxpayer?

**3-29** *Carryover of Excess Capital Losses.* Excess capital losses of individuals may be offset against gains for other years. Specify the carryover and/or carryback period for such excess losses.

## YOU MAKE THE CALL

**3-30** Shortly after Murray began working in the tax department of the public accounting firm of Dewey, Cheatham and Howe, he was preparing a tax return and discovered an error in last year's work papers. In computing the gain on the sale of the taxpayer's duplex, the preparer had failed to increase the amount realized by the $50,000 mortgage assumed by the buyer. Apparently, the mistake was overlooked during the review process. Upon discovering the mistake, Murray went to his immediate supervisor, Norm (who actually prepared last year's return), and pointed out the error. Norm, knowing that the client would probably flip if he found out he had to pay more tax, told Murray "let's just wait and see if the IRS catches it. Forget it for now." What should Murray do?

## PROBLEMS

**3-31** *To Whom Is Income Taxed?* In each of the following separate cases, determine how much income is to be taxed to each of the taxpayers involved:

**a.** Alpha Partnership is owned 60 percent by W and 40 percent by P, who agree to share profits according to their ownership ratios. For the current year, Alpha earned $12,000 in ordinary income. The partnership distributed $3,000 to W and $2,000 to P.

**b.** Beta Trust is managed by T for the benefit of B. The trust is required to distribute all income currently. For the current year, Beta Trust had net ordinary income of $5,500 and made cash distributions to B of $7,000.

**c.** Gamma Inc., a C corporation, is owned and operated by its two equal owners, H and K. This year the corporation reported earned income—before any distributions to its owners—of $24,000. On May 4, the corporation declared a dividend, distributing $1,350 to H and $1,350 to K.

**3-32** *Selecting a Form of Doing Business.* Which form of business—sole proprietorship, partnership, S corporation, limited liability company, or regular corporation—is each of the following taxpayers likely to choose? An answer may include more than one business form.

**a.** Edmund and Gloria are starting a new business that they expect to operate at a net loss for about five years. Both Edmund and Gloria expect to have substantial incomes during those years from other sources.

**b.** Robin would like to incorporate her growing retail business for nontax reasons. Because she needs all of the net profits to meet personal obligations, Robin would like to avoid the corporate "double tax" on dividends.

**3-33** *Income from C Corporations.* M is the president and chief executive officer of MN, Inc., a corporation that is owned solely by M. During the current calendar year, MN, Inc. paid M a salary of $80,000, a bonus of $22,000, and dividends of $30,000. The corporation's gross income is $350,000, and its expenses excluding payments to M are $225,000.

**a.** Compute the corporation's taxable income and determine its gross income tax. See inside back cover for corporate tax rates.

**b.** Assuming M's only other income is interest income of $12,500, determine M's A.G.I.

**c.** Does this situation represent double taxation of corporate profits? Explain.

**3-34** *Income from Partnerships.* J is a one-fourth partner in JKLM Partnership. The partnership had gross sales of $880,000, cost of sales of $540,000, and operating expenses excluding payments to partners of $145,000 for the current calendar year. Partners' compensation for services of $90,000 ($45,000 to J) were paid, and distributions of $120,000 ($30,000 to J) were made for the year.

**a.** Determine the partnership's net income for tax reporting purposes.

**b.** Determine the amount of income J must report from the partnership for the year.

**c.** Determine how much of the income in (b) is self-employment income.

**3-35** *Income from Fiduciaries.* G created a trust for the benefit of B to be managed by T. For the current year, the trust had gross income of $45,000, income-producing deductions of $1,900, and cash distributions to B of $12,500.

**a.** Determine the taxable income of the trust.

**b.** Assuming B's only other income is interest of $22,300, determine B's A.G.I.

**3-36** *Tax Treatment of Various Entities.* Office Supplies Unlimited is a small office supply outlet. The results of its operations for the most recent year are summarized as follows:

| | |
|---|---|
| Gross profit on sales | $95,000 |
| Cash operating expenses | 43,000 |
| Depreciation expense | 16,500 |
| Compensation to owner(s) | 20,000 |
| Distribution of profit to owner(s) | 5,000 |

In each of the following situations, determine how much income is to be taxed (i.e., to be included along with any other income in calculating taxable income) to each of the taxpayers involved.

**a.** The business is a sole proprietorship owned by T.
**b.** The business is a partnership owned by R and S with an agreement to share all items equally. S is guaranteed a salary of $20,000 (see above).
**c.** The business is a corporation owned equally by U and K. K is employed by the business and receives a salary of $20,000 (see above).

**3-37** *Gross Income.* The following represent some of the more important items of income for Federal tax purposes. For each, indicate whether it is fully includible in gross income, fully excludable from gross income, or partially includible and partially excludable.

**a.** Alimony received from a former spouse
**b.** Interest from state and local governments
**c.** Money and other property inherited from a relative
**d.** Social security benefits
**e.** Tips and gratuities
**f.** Proceeds of life insurance received upon the death of one's spouse

**3-38** *Classifying Deductions.* The following represent some of the more important deductions for Federal tax purposes. For each, indicate whether it is deductible for A.G.I. or as an itemized deduction.

**a.** Alimony paid to one's former spouse
**b.** Charitable contributions
**c.** Trade or business expenses of a self-employed person
**d.** Expenses of providing an apartment to a tenant for rent
**e.** Interest incurred to finance one's principal residence
**f.** Reimbursed trade or business expenses of an employee
**g.** Unreimbursed business expenses of an employee

**3-39** *Determining Adjusted Gross Income and Taxable Income.* Fred and Susan are married and file a joint income tax return. Neither is blind or age 65. They have two children whom they support, and the following income and deductions for 2011:

| | |
|---|---|
| Gross income | $57,200 |
| Deductions for A.G.I. | 1,200 |
| Total itemized deductions | 8,900 |
| Credits and prepayments | 3,050 |

Determine Fred and Susan's adjusted gross income and taxable income for the calendar year 2011.

**3-40** *Tax Formula.* The following information is from the 2011 joint income tax return of Gregory and Stacy Jones, both of good sight and under 65 years of age.

| | |
|---|---|
| Gross income | $67,400 |
| Adjusted gross income | 58,550 |
| Taxable income | 29,250 |
| Number of personal exemptions | 2 |
| Number of dependency exemptions | 2 |

Determine the amount of the Jones's deductions for A.G.I. and the amount of their itemized deductions.

**3-41** *Tax Formula.* Complete the following table of independent cases for Zac Williams for 2011. Zac is 31 years old and is single. He has perfect eyesight. He does not own a car, truck, motorcycle or motor home. He rents an apartment, and it is not located in a federally declared disaster area.

| | A | B | C |
|---|---|---|---|
| Gross income | $50,000 | $ ??? | $ ??? |
| Deductions for A.G.I. | (???) | (8,000) | (7,000) |
| Adjusted gross income (A.G.I.) | $42,000 | $78,000 | ??? |
| Itemized deductions | (???) | (4,650) | (7,350) |
| Standard deduction | (???) | (???) | (???) |
| Exemptions | 2 | 1 | 1 |
| | (???) | (???) | (???) |
| Taxable income | $25,600 | $ ??? | $64,650 |

**3-42** *Worldwide Income Subject to Tax.* T, a U.S. citizen, has income that was earned outside the United States. The income was $20,000, and a tax of $2,000 was paid to the foreign government. Determine the general treatment of this income and the tax paid under the following circumstances:

**a.** The tax paid was on income earned on foreign investments, and the U.S. tax attributable to this income is $2,800.

**b.** Same as (a), except the U.S. tax attributable to this income is $1,800.

**c.** Same as (a), except the income is from services rendered while absent from the United States for 13 successive months.

**3-43** *Alternative Minimum Tax.* L is single, has no dependents, and uses the cash method and the calendar year for tax purposes. The following information was derived from L's records for 2011:

| | |
|---|---|
| Taxable income (regular income tax) | $74,200 |
| AMT adjustments and preferences | 70,200 |

Although L has substantial gross income and deductions, she does not itemize. Calculate L's regular income tax using the tax rates for 2011 and her alternative minimum tax, if any.

**3-44** *Asset Classification.* For each of the assets in the list below, designate the appropriate category using the symbols given:

C - Capital asset

T - Trade or business asset (§ 1231)

O - Other (neither capital nor § 1231 asset)

**a.** Personal residence

**b.** Stock in Xerox Corporation

**c.** Motor home used for vacations

**d.** Groceries held for sale to customers

**e.** Land held for investment

**f.** Land and building held for use in auto repair business

**g.** Trade accounts receivable of physician's office

**h.** Silver coins held primarily for speculation

**3-45** *Gain or Loss Realized.* During the current year, W disposed of a vacant lot which he had held for investment. W received cash of $12,000 for his equity in the lot. The lot was subject to a $32,000 mortgage that was assumed by the buyer. Assuming W's basis in the lot was $23,000, how much is his realized gain or loss?

**3-46** *Adjusted Basis.* M owns a rental residence that she is considering selling, but she is interested in knowing her exact tax basis in the property. She originally paid $39,000 for the property. M has spent $8,000 on a new garage, $2,500 for a new outdoor patio deck, and $4,500 on repairs and maintenance. M has been allowed depreciation on the unit in the amount of $7,500. Based on this information, calculate M's basis in the rental residence.

**3-47** *Gain or Loss Realized, Adjusted Basis.* This year S sold her rental house. She received cash of $6,000 and a vacant lot worth $30,000. The buyer assumed the $36,000 mortgage loan outstanding against S's property. S had purchased the house for $52,000 four years earlier and had deducted depreciation of $12,000. How much are S's amount realized, her adjusted basis in the house sold, and her gain or loss realized in this transaction?

**3-48** *Capital Gain and Loss.* Individual D is in the 35% tax bracket. This year he executed the following transactions.

| Transaction | Sales Price | Adjusted Basis | Holding Period |
|---|---|---|---|
| Sale of 100 shares of XYZ | $2,000 | $1,000 | 15 months |
| Sale of land held for investment | 9,000 | 3,000 | 19 months |
| Sale of silver held for speculation | 5,000 | 7,000 | 23 months |
| Sale of personal jewelry | 4,000 | 6,000 | 60 months |

Determine the tax consequences (e.g., gain, loss, applicable tax rates) of these transactions.

**3-49** *Excess Capital Loss.* This year, T, an individual taxpayer, had a short-term capital gain of $4,000 and a capital loss of $9,000 from stock he held for four years. How much is T's allowable capital loss deduction for the year? What is the treatment of the short-term gain?

**3-50** *Individual's Tax Computation.* Richard Hartman, age 29, single with no dependents, received a salary of $32,670 in 2011. During the year, he received $1,300 interest income from a savings account and a $1,500 gift from his grandmother. At the advice of his father, Richard sold stock he had held as an investment for five years, for a $3,000 gain. He also sustained a loss of $1,000 from the sale of land held as an investment and owned for four months. Richard had itemized deductions of $5,250. For 2011 compute the following for Richard:

**a.** Gross income
**b.** Adjusted gross income
**c.** Taxable income
**d.** Income tax before credits and prepayments (use the appropriate 2011 tax rate schedule located on the inside front cover)
**e.** Income tax savings that would result if Richard made a deductible $2,000 contribution to a qualified Individual Retirement Account

**3-51** *Tax Treatment of Income from Entities.* The G family—Mr. G, Mrs. G, and G Jr.—owns interests in the following successful entities:

1. X Corporation is a calendar year regular corporation owned 60 percent by Mr. G and 15 percent by G Jr. During the year, it paid salaries to Mr. G of $80,000 to be its president and to G Jr. of $24,000 to be a plant supervisor. The company earned a net taxable income of $75,000, and paid dividends to Mr. G and G Jr. in the amounts of $42,000 and $10,500, respectively.
2. Mrs. G owned a 60 percent capital interest in a retail outlet, P Partnership. The partnership earned a net taxable income of $60,000 and made distributions during the year of $72,000. The profit and the distributions were allocated according to relative capital interests.
3. Mr. G and G Jr. each own 25 percent interest in H Corporation, an electing S Corporation. The corporation is a start-up venture and generated a net tax loss of $28,000 for the calendar year. No dividend distributions were made by H. Both Mr. G and G Jr. have bases in their H Corporation stock of $30,000.
4. G Jr. is the sole beneficiary of G Trust created by Mrs. G's father. The trust received dividends of $16,000 and made distributions of $4,500 to G Jr.

Determine the amount of income or loss from each entity that is to be reported by the following:

**a.** Mr. and Mrs. G on their joint calendar year tax return
**b.** G Jr. on his calendar year individual return
**c.** X Corporation
**d.** P Partnership
**e.** H Corporation
**f.** G Trust

**3-52** *Comprehensive Taxable Income Computation.* Indy Smith, single, is an anthropology professor at State University. The tax records that he brought to you for preparation of his return revealed the following items.

| | |
|---|---|
| *Income* | |
| Salary from State University | $68,250 |
| Part-time consulting | 5,000 |
| Dividend income | 1,250 |
| Reimbursement of travel to Denver by State University | 200 |
| *Expenses* | |
| Interest on personal residence | $ 9,800 |
| Travel expenses related to consulting | 1,000 |
| Tax return preparation fee | 500 |
| Safe deposit box to hold bonds | 50 |
| Travel and lodging to present academic paper in Denver related to his teaching position | 450 |

In addition, Indy claims a dependency exemption for his father for whom he provides 60 percent support (including 60 percent of housing costs). Compute Indy's final tax liability for calendar year 2011.

**3-53** *Comprehensive Taxable Income Computation.* Eli and Lilly have been happily married for 30 years. Eli, 67, is a research chemist at Pharmaceuticals Inc. Lilly, 64, recently retired but stays busy managing the couple's investments, including a duplex. The majority of the couple's income is derived from Eli's employment, from which he received a salary of $95,000 this year. Other income includes interest on corporate bonds of $5,600 and interest on State of Illinois bonds of $1,000. In addition, rents collected from the duplex were $10,000 while rental expenses (e.g., maintenance, utilities, depreciation) were $6,000. During the year, the company transferred Eli to a new division located in nearby suburb about 55 miles north of his old office. As a result, the couple decided to move so that Eli would not have such a long commute. They paid deductible moving expenses of $2,000. The couple also paid the following expenses: unreimbursed medical expenses, $7,400; interest on the home mortgage, $11,300; property taxes on the home, $3,000; charitable contributions, $4,000; and rental of safe deposit box, $100. Determine the couple's taxable income for 2011.

**3-54** *Alternative Minimum Tax.* H and W are married and filed a joint return for 2011. The couple has five children between the ages of 3 and 13. Their records for the current year reveal the following:

| | |
|---|---|
| Salary income (their only income) | $165,000 |
| State and local taxes (property and income) | 40,000 |
| Miscellaneous itemized deductions (after 2% of A.G.I. limitation) | $5,000 |

Using the 2011 tax rates, compute the alternative minimum tax, if any.

**3-55** *Losses.* This year, B and J formed a partnership to operate a bar and grill. B was the brains behind the venture and J supplied the bulk of the financing. B contributed $30,000 to the partnership, receiving a 30 percent interest while J contributed $70,000 for a 70 percent interest. B received 30 percent of the profits and losses and J received 70 percent. During the year, B worked his fingers to the bone, running the business. J did little, sitting back and watching his investment. For the year, the partnership reported a $30,000 loss (revenues $60,000, deductible expenses $90,000). Can B and J use their share of the loss as a deduction to offset other income they might have on their own individual tax return (Form 1040) such as the salary income of their spouses? Explain.

## TAX RETURN PROBLEMS

- *CONTINUOUS TAX RETURN PROBLEMS* See Appendix I, Part 1.

## TAX RESEARCH PROBLEMS

**3-56** *Using the Internal Revenue Code.* Locate a copy of the *Internal Revenue Code of 1986*. Read §§ 61 through 65, 67, 151, and 152. Read the titles of §§ 71 through 135, 161, and 162.

**a.** Describe how Congress defined "gross income."

**b.** Why is the "exemption deduction" properly called a deduction from adjusted gross income?

**c.** A taxpayer is self-employed and incurs an ordinary and necessary expense in his business endeavor. What is the authority for deducting the expense? Why is it considered a deduction *for* adjusted gross income?

**d.** A taxpayer pays alimony to her former husband. Within limits, it is deductible *for* adjusted gross income. Why?

4

# Personal and Dependency Exemptions; Filing Status; Determination of Tax for an Individual; Filing Requirements

## Learning Objectives

Upon completion of this chapter you will be able to:

- LO.1 Identify the types of exemptions that may be claimed.
- LO.2 Explain the requirements to claim an exemption for dependents.
- LO.3 Describe the child tax credit.
- LO.4 Apply the rules to determine the taxpayer's filing status.
- LO.5 Compute the tax liability of an individual taxpayer using the tax rate schedules and the tax tables.
- LO.6 Explain the special approach used in computing the tax liability of certain children.
- LO.7 Describe the filing requirements for individual taxpayers.
- LO.8 Explain when taxes must be paid and the penalties that apply for failure to pay on a timely basis.
- LO.9 Describe the statute of limitations as it applies to the filing of tax returns.

## Chapter Outline


Introduction 4-2
Personal and Dependency Exemptions 4-2
  Personal Exemptions 4-2
  Exemptions for Dependents 4-3
  Exemption for Qualifying Child 4-3
  Exemption for Qualifying Relative 4-4
  Provisions Common to all Dependency Exemptions 4-9
  Children of Divorced or Separated Parents 4-11
  Phase-Out of Personal and Dependency Exemptions 4-12
  Child Tax Credit 4-12
Filing Status 4-14
  Evolution of Filing Status 4-14
  Married Individuals 4-16
  Head of Household 4-17
Computation of Tax for Individual Taxpayers 4-22
  Tax Tables 4-22
  Tax Rate Schedules 4-25
  Special Tax Computation Rules 4-26
  Determination of Net Tax Due or Refund 4-31
Filing Requirements 4-32
  Due Dates for Filing Returns 4-35
  Penalties 4-36
  Claim for Refund 4-40
  Statute of Limitations 4-41
  Indexation and the Federal Income Tax 4-43
Appendix 4-45
  Tax Return Illustrations 4-45
Problem Materials 4-54

## Introduction

As seen in Chapter 3, numerous factors must be considered in the determination of an individual's net tax liability. Beginning in this chapter and continuing through Chapter 18, a detailed examination of these factors is conducted. This chapter is devoted to five particular concerns of individual taxpayers:

1. Personal and dependency exemptions;
2. Child tax credit;
3. Filing status;
4. Calculation of the tax liability using the tax rate schedules and tax tables; and
5. Filing requirements.

## Personal and Dependency Exemptions

**LO.1**
Identify the types of exemptions that may be claimed.

Since the inception of the income tax, policymakers have recognized the need to protect from tax some minimum amount of income that could be used for the support of the taxpayer and those who depend on him. The device used to accomplish this objective is the deduction allowed for exemptions. There are two types of exemptions for which deductions are allowed: personal exemptions and exemptions for a child or other dependent.[1] Taxpayers may deduct the *exemption amount* for each of their exemptions. The exemption amount for 2011 is $3,700.[2] Each type of exemption is discussed below.

### Personal Exemptions

There are *two* types of personal exemptions:

1. Exemption for the taxpayer
2. Exemption for the taxpayer's spouse

Each individual taxpayer normally is entitled to one personal exemption. When a *joint return* is filed by a married couple, *two* personal exemptions may be claimed. This occurs not because one spouse is the dependent of the other, but because the husband and wife are each entitled to his or her own personal exemption. If a married individual files a *separate return*, however, a personal exemption may be claimed for his or her spouse only if the spouse has no gross income and is not claimed as a dependent of another taxpayer.[3]

#### Disallowance of Personal Exemption

A taxpayer is denied a personal exemption if he or she qualifies as a dependent of another taxpayer (see discussion below).[4] This rule prevents two taxpayers (e.g., a child and his or her parent) from benefiting from two exemptions for the same person.

**Example 1**

J is 21 years of age and a full-time college student. J receives a partial scholarship and works part-time, but the majority of his support is received from his parents. Assuming

---

[1] §§ 151(a), 151(b), and 151(c).

[2] Since 1985 the exemption amount has been increased to reflect price level changes based on changes in the consumer price index. The exact amount is announced by the IRS in the fall of the preceding year. For instance, the exemption amount for 2012 will be announced by December 15, 2011. §§ 1(f) and 151(d)(3). If the exemption amount had been adjusted for inflation since 1948, when it was $600, it would have been about $5,428 for 2010 (calculated using the Bureau of Labor Statistics inflation calculator based on the Consumer Price Index, http://data.bls.gov/cgi-bin/cpicalc.pl). Also see Steurle, "Decline in the Value of the Dependent Exemption," 62 *Tax Notes* 109 (October 4, 1993).

[3] § 151(b).

[4] § 151(d)(2).

J is eligible to be claimed as a dependent on his parents' return, he is not entitled to a personal exemption deduction on his own return. This rule applies *regardless* of whether J's parents actually claim an exemption for him.

## EXEMPTIONS FOR DEPENDENTS

**LO.2**
Explain the requirements to claim an exemption for dependents.

For as long as most remember, an individual qualified as a taxpayer's dependent if he or she met one set of rules. Ironically, in an attempt toward simplicity in 2005, Congress added a second set of rules under which an individual might be considered a dependent. Section 152 now defines a dependent as either:

1. A qualifying child, or
2. A qualifying relative.

## EXEMPTION FOR QUALIFYING CHILD

An individual is considered a *qualifying child* and can be claimed as a dependent of the taxpayer if he or she satisfies all of the following tests.[5]

1. *Relationship Test.* The individual and the taxpayer must meet one of the following relationship tests:

   - Natural child, stepchild, adopted child, certain foster children
   - A sibling or step-sibling
   - A descendant of one of the above

   Note that the scope of these rules goes far beyond the conventional definition of a taxpayer's "child." For example, a taxpayer's brother or sister is considered his or her child as are his nieces or nephews. Similarly, a taxpayer's "children" include a grandchild as well as great grandchildren and other descendants.

2. *Residence Test.* The "child" must have the *same principal place of abode* (i.e., residence) as the taxpayer for more than one half of the taxable year. Temporary absences are permissible if due to special circumstances such as education, illness, business, vacation, or military service. Note that a child could live more than half of the taxable year with more than one person where several people, including the child, live together. For example, the child could live with his mother, grandmother and grandfather. Thus this test could be met with respect to more than one person.
3. *Age Requirement.* The "child" must also meet one of the conditions concerning age:

   - Has not reached age 19 by the close of the taxable year.
   - Has not reached age 24 *and* is considered a full-time student at a qualifying educational institution. For this purpose, "full-time" is whatever is considered full-time under the rules and regulations of the institution. The individual must meet the full-time condition for any part of five calendar months during the calendar year.
   - Is permanently and totally disabled at any time during the year. The age limitation does not apply to these individuals.
   - The qualifying child must be younger than the taxpayer.

4. *Joint Return Test.* The "child" must not have filed a joint return with his or her spouse except to claim a refund (i.e., the tax due was zero before prepayments).
5. *Citizenship or Residency Test.* The "child" must be a U.S. citizen, resident or national, or a resident of Canada or Mexico.
6. *Not Self-Supporting Test.* To be a "qualifying child" the "child" may not be self-supporting; that is, the child must not have provided more than one-half of his or her own support. For this purpose, scholarships received from an educational institution are not considered an amount spent on support.

[5] § 152(c).

### Tie Breaker Rules

Application of the tests above could result in an individual being a "qualifying child" for more than one taxpayer. For example, if a 10-year-old child lived with his father, grandmother and uncle in the same residence during the year, the father, grandmother, or uncle could potentially claim the child as a dependent since the child meets the relationship, age and residence test with respect to each. Such a situation is not surprising in an age when family structures are often unconventional due to divorce and remarriage, absentee parents, child-bearing by unmarried individuals, and multi-generational households. When a child is a qualifying child for more than one taxpayer and the parties cannot agree as to who will claim an exemption, the following tie-breaker rules apply.[6]

- If only one of the taxpayers is the child's parent, the parent claims the exemption for the child.
- If both taxpayers are the child's parents and they do not file a joint return, the parent with whom the child resided for the longest period of time during the tax year claims the exemption for the child. Note that this tie-breaker rule must be used. The parents cannot agree between themselves as to whom will claim the exemption.
- If the child resides with both parents for the same period of time during the tax year and the parents do not file a joint return, the parent with the highest adjusted gross income claims the exemption for the child.
- If none of the taxpayers are the child's parent, the taxpayer with the highest adjusted gross income for the tax year claims the exemption for the child.

#### Example 2

For the current year, M and D, mom and dad, provide a home in which they live with their son, P, and P's daughter, G. P is unmarried, 23 years of age and a full-time student. P earned $6,000 for the year, which is less than 50% of his total support. M and D may claim an exemption for P—he is their qualifying child since he meets all of the tests (age, residence and relationship). Under the tie-breaking rules, P, as parent, would be able to claim an exemption for his daughter G; however, P cannot claim G as a dependent because P is, himself, a dependent. In this case, M and D could claim an exemption for their granddaughter G because she is a qualifying child with respect to them.

## Exemption for Qualifying Relative

The second type of dependent is a *qualifying relative*—generally a relative or member of the taxpayer's household that depends on the taxpayer for support. In contrast to the definition for qualifying children, this term permits exemptions for a broader class of individuals but only if the taxpayer provides for their support and the prospective dependent meets an income test.

Technically, an individual is considered a *qualifying relative* only if he or she is *not* a qualifying child and meets the following requirements each of which is discussed in detail below.[7]

1. *Support Test.* The taxpayer must provide more than 50 percent of the dependent's total support.
2. *Gross Income Test.* The dependent's gross income must be less than the exemption amount.

---

[6] § 152(c)(4).

[7] § 152(d).

3. *Relationship or Member of the Household Test.* The dependent must be a relative of the taxpayer or a member of the taxpayer's household for the entire taxable year.
4. *Joint Return Test.* The dependent must not have filed a joint return with his or her spouse.
5. *Citizenship or Residency Test.* The dependent must be a U.S. citizen, resident or national, or a resident of Canada or Mexico.

Although an individual could conceivably be a qualifying relative and a qualifying child, the Code makes it clear that in such case the individual is treated as a qualifying child, and therefore, he or she cannot be claimed as a dependent by someone under the qualifying relative rules.

## Support Test

To satisfy the support requirement, the taxpayer must provide more than half of the amount spent for the dependent's total support.[8] Total support includes not only amounts expended by others on behalf of the dependent but also any amounts spent by the dependent. Note that only the amount *actually spent* for support is relevant. Income and other funds available to the dependent for spending are ignored unless they are spent.

### Example 3

During the year, C paid $10,000 to maintain her father, F, in a nursing home that provides all of his needs. No other amounts were spent for his support. C made these payments, even though her father could afford them since he has cash in the bank and tax-exempt bonds valued at $200,000. Although F has funds available for providing his own support, they are not considered in applying the support test because the funds were not spent. Consequently, the support test is satisfied.

Support is generally measured by the cost of the item to the individual providing it. However, when support is provided in a noncash form, such as the use of property or lodging, the amount of support is the fair market value or fair rental value.

What constitutes an item of support is not always clear. If, for example, a child receives a stereo or car, are these items considered support, or do only necessities qualify? The

**EXHIBIT 4.1 Partial List of Support Items**

| | |
|---|---|
| Automobile | Lodging |
| Care for a dependent's pet | Medical care |
| Charitable contributions by or on behalf of dependent | Medical insurance premiums |
| Child care | Singing lessons |
| Clothing | Telephone |
| Dental care | Television |
| Education | Toys |
| Entertainment | Transportation |
| Food | Utilities |
| Gifts | Vacations |

[8] § 152(d)(1)(c).

Regulations provide some guidance as to the nature of support, indicating that it includes food, shelter, clothing, medical and dental care, education, recreation, and transportation.[9] Support is not limited to these items, however. Examination of the numerous cases and rulings reveals a hodgepodge of qualifying expenditures as well as some that are not. For example, the costs for boats, life insurance, and lawn mowers are not considered support. Additionally, the value of any services performed for the dependent by the taxpayer is ignored.[10] Exhibit 4-1 presents a sampling of those items that constitute support.

The determination of support also is complicated by several items accorded special treatment. For example, scholarships and fellowships received by the taxpayer's child or stepchild are not considered support items. Accordingly, such amounts are not treated as being provided by either the taxpayer or the dependent.[11]

### Example 4

J was the recipient of an athletic scholarship that covered 100% of her tuition, books, supplies, room, and board. In addition, J was paid a small cash allowance. J's parents also provided her with $4,000 cash to be used for clothing, entertainment, and miscellaneous expenses.

The scholarship package, which was related to J's continued scholastic activity, was valued at $19,500 per year. Nevertheless, assuming the other four tests are met, J's parents are entitled to a dependency exemption, since the scholarship is not included in her support and she is not self-supporting.[12]

Although social security benefits generally are not taxable income to the recipient, they are considered as support provided by the person covered by social security. Thus, social security benefits are included in determining support to the extent they are spent for support.[13] State welfare payments are considered provided by the state, and therefore are not treated as provided by the parent or any other taxpayer. This is true even though the parent is entrusted to oversee the prudent expenditure of the funds.[14]

### Example 5

F received support during the current year from various sources, including amounts contributed by his son, S. The amounts spent toward F's support were provided as follows:

| | |
|---|---|
| F's social security benefits | $ 7,500 |
| Taxable interest income | 900 |
| Amount provided by S | 4,100 |
| Total | $12,500 |

S is not entitled to a dependency exemption for F because he did not provide more than 50% of F's total support ($4,100 is not greater than 50% of $12,500).

[9] Reg. § 1.152-1(a)(2)(i).

[10] *Markarian v. Comm.*, 65-2 USTC ¶9699, 16 AFTR2d 5785, 352 F.2d 870 (CA-7, 1965).

[11] Reg. § 1.152-1(c). Note that G.I. Bill benefits are not treated as scholarships and therefore are included as support items provided by the recipient.

[12] Any part of a scholarship providing benefits other than tuition, fees and supplies, is *includible* in the recipient's gross income to the extent of those benefits. See Chapter 6 for a discussion of taxable scholarships.

[13] Reg. § 1.152-1(a)(2)(ii).

[14] See Rev. Rul. 71-468, 1971-2 C.B. 115 and *N. Williams*, T.C. Memo 1996-126. A similar result was reached related to state payments for the care of a mentally retarded child. See *Trail*, T. C. Memo 1993-221, *aff'd* at 73 AFTR2d ¶ 94-931 (CA-5, 1994).

### Example 6

This year K received social security benefits of $8,000, $5,500 of which was immediately deposited in a savings account. The amounts spent toward K's support were provided as follows:

| | |
|---|---|
| K's social security benefits spent | $ 2,500 |
| Taxable interest income | 600 |
| Amount provided by K's brother, B | 4,000 |
| Total | $ 7,100 |

Assuming the other tests are met, B is entitled to a dependency exemption for K since he provided more than one-half of her support expenditures ($4,000 is > 50% of $7,100).

In many instances, an individual who is not self-supporting is supported by more than one taxpayer. Generally, no dependency exemption is allowed for such persons because no *one* individual provides more than 50 percent of the total support provided. However, an exemption may be allowed under what is referred to as a "multiple support agreement."

## Multiple Support Agreements

A dependency exemption for a qualifying relative may be assigned to a taxpayer under a multiple support agreement if all of the following tests are met:[15]

1. No one person contributed over half the support of the individual.
2. Over half the support was provided by a group, all of whose members are qualifying relatives of the individual.
3. The citizenship, joint return, and gross income requirements are met by the individual.
4. The dependency exemption is assigned by agreement to a group member *who contributed more* than 10 percent of the total support.

The assignment is effective only if each of the members contributing more than 10 percent signs a declaration to the effect that he or she will not claim the exemption. This declaration is made on Form 2120 (see Appendix), which is then filed with the return of the taxpayer claiming the exemption.

### Example 7

M is single and received her support of $12,000 for the current year from the following sources:

| | *Amount* | *Percentage* |
|---|---|---|
| Social security benefits | $ 4,000 | 33.33% |
| Taxable interest income | 800 | 6.67 |
| From D, M's daughter | 4,700 | 39.17 |
| From S, M's son | 1,500 | 12.50 |
| From G, M's grandchild | 1,000 | 8.33 |
| | $12,000 | 100.00% |

[15] § 152(c).

Together, D, S, and G contribute more than 50% of M's support for the year ($7,200 > 50% of $12,000). If a multiple support agreement is executed, either D or S may be allowed the exemption deduction. G is not eligible since he did not contribute more than 10% of the total support. Also, note that S may claim M as a dependent even though D provided more of M's support.

### Gross Income Test

The second test that must be satisfied before an individual (other than a qualifying child) may be claimed as a dependent concerns his or her gross income. A dependency exemption generally is not allowed for a person whose gross income equals or exceeds the exemption amount ($3,700 for 2011).[16] In applying this test, the technical definition of "gross income" must be heeded.[17] It does not include items that are excluded from income. Accordingly, a person whose only sources of income are excluded from gross income (e.g., social security and municipal bond interest) may qualify as a dependent.

It also should be noted that gross income is not always synonymous with includible gross receipts. Regulation § 1.61-3 indicates that gross income for a merchandising business generally means the total sales less the cost of goods sold *plus* any income from investments or other sources. The importance of this distinction between gross receipts and gross income is demonstrated in the following example.

#### Example 8

T provides 60% of the support for his single brothers, F and R, for the 2011 calendar year. F's sole source of income is from the sale of fireworks. During the year, he sold fireworks costing $4,000 for $6,500. R's sole source of income is derived from rental property. During the year, he collected rents of $4,200 while incurring expenses of $1,700 for repairs, maintenance, and interest. Although F and R each earned $2,500 (F: $6,500 – $4,000 = $2,500; R: $4,200 – $1,700 = $2,500), F's gross income was $2,500, whereas R's was $4,200. As a result, T can only claim an exemption for F, since F's *gross income* of $2,500 was less than the $3,700 exemption amount for 2011.

### Relationship or Member of the Household Test

The third of the five hurdles that must be cleared before an individual can be claimed as a dependent concerns the individual's relationship to the taxpayer. Regardless of the amount of support that the taxpayer provides for another person, no exemption is allowed unless the prospective dependent is properly related to the taxpayer.[18] Apparently the authors of the dependency rules believed that the tax law should not grant an exemption unless there is some obligation on the part of the taxpayer to support an individual. Such an obligation normally exists between relatives or others who are members of the taxpayer's household. Therefore, to qualify as a dependent, an individual must satisfy one the qualifying relationship tests below. All of these are *familial* (i.e., related by blood, marriage, or adoption) except one. These are:

1. A child or descendant of a child (other than one who would be considered a "qualifying child" under the tests discussed earlier)
2. A brother, sister, stepbrother, or stepsister
3. The father or mother, or an ancestor of either (e.g., a grandparent)
4. A stepfather or stepmother
5. A niece or nephew[19]

---

[16] § 151(c)(1)(A). Note that there is no relief from the gross income test for qualifying relatives. Under prior law, this relief was reserved for children of the taxpayer.

[17] See Chapters 5 and 6 for detailed discussion of "gross income."

[18] § 152(a). Note: Recall that there is no dependency exemption for a spouse. The exemption for a spouse is the *personal* exemption.

[19] A niece or nephew must be a daughter or son of a brother or sister of the taxpayer. § 152(a)(6).

6. An aunt or uncle[20]
7. A son-in-law, daughter-in-law, father-in-law, mother-in-law, brother-in-law, or sister-in-law
8. Any person who lives in the taxpayer's home and is a member of the taxpayer's household for the entire *taxable* year. Even though such a person is not legally related to the taxpayer (i.e., a familial relative), he or she is treated the same as one who satisfies one of the legal relationships as long as he or she lives with the taxpayer the entire taxable year; for this purpose, temporary absences due to illness, school, vacation, business, or military service are ignored; in addition, a person cannot be claimed as a dependent if the relationship with the taxpayer violated local law (e.g., cohabitation).[21]

A relationship created by marriage does not cease upon divorce or the death of the spouse. Thus, for tax purposes, a divorce would not terminate an individual's relationship with his or her mother-in-law.[22] Additionally, if a dependent dies before the close of the tax year, the taxpayer may still claim a dependency exemption.

### Example 9

This year F provided all the support for several individuals, none of whom had income in excess of the exemption amount. Each person and his or her status as a relative is shown below:

1. S, F's 25-year-old son, living in Los Angeles and attending UCLA. S is a relative; a son is a familial relative and such persons need not live in the home.
2. B, F's 29-year-old brother who moved in with F on November 1 after leaving the military. B is a relative; a brother is a familial relative and such persons need not live in the home.
3. C, F's 27-year-old cousin who moved in with F on October 1 after being unemployed for 10 months. C is not a relative; a cousin is not considered a familial relative and, therefore, qualifies only if he lives with the taxpayer the entire taxable year.
4. BL, the brother of F's former wife. BL is a relative; BL is F's brother-in-law, a familial relative; such a relationship continues to exist whether F is divorced or his wife dies.
5. Z, a friend who has been living with F since December 1 of the prior year. Z is a "relative"; a person who lives with the taxpayer the *entire* taxable year qualifies as a relative even though such person is not related by blood or marriage.

### Joint Return Test

The dependent must not have filed a joint return with his or her spouse. This requirement is discussed further below.

### Citizenship or Residency Test

The dependent must be a U.S. citizen, resident or national, or a resident of Canada or Mexico. Additional exceptions exist as noted below.

## Provisions Common to All Dependency Exemptions

As is apparent from the discussion above, there are several important differences in the definitions of a qualifying child and a qualifying relative. For example, there is no gross income test or support test applicable to a "child" of the taxpayer. In a sense, these conditions

[20] An aunt or uncle must be a sister or brother of the father or mother of the taxpayer. § 152(a)(7). For example, the person married to your mother's sister would be her brother-in-law, but he would not qualify as your uncle for purposes of this definition. Technically, such a person would be your "uncle-in-law," a relationship not defined in Code § 152.

[21] § 152(d)(2)(h).

[22] Reg. § 1.152-2(d).

are assumed to be met where the individual is the child of the taxpayer. Notwithstanding these differences, it is important to note that—as may be apparent–there are some rules common to both types of dependents. Each of these is considered in greater detail below. Exhibit 4-2 also compares the two provisions.

### No Joint Return

A taxpayer normally cannot claim a dependency exemption for a married individual if such person files a joint return.[23] This is true for both a qualifying child and a qualifying relative. This rule appears to reflect a presumption that married taxpayers usually rely on themselves for support rather than others. Note, however, that if a joint return is filed solely for a refund (i.e., the tax is zero and all withholding is refunded), the return is ignored and the individual may be claimed as a dependent (assuming the other tests are met).[24] Also observe that the test is met as long as a joint return is *not* filed. If the married individual files a separate return, he or she may still be claimed as a dependent. In certain situations, parents of newlyweds and others may find it beneficial for their child to file a married, separate return.

#### Example 10

B and C were married on December 21, 2011. B, a budding 25-year-old attorney, earned $48,000 for the year. C, age 23, is a full-time graduate student. Because C was fully supported by her parents, she was eligible to be claimed as a dependent on her parents' return. However, C's parents may not claim C as a dependent if B and C elect to file a joint return. The family must determine whether they are better off if: (l) B and C file a joint return and C claims her exemption on their joint return; or (2) B and C each file married filing separately and they relinquish C's exemption to her parents. A partial analysis would suggest the first alternative is far superior. If a joint return is filed, all of B's income would be taxed at 15% or less (see inside front cover of text for rates). Alternatively, the filing of separate returns would cause a substantial portion of B's taxable income to be taxed at 25%. In this case, it would appear that the additional tax caused by filing separate returns would more than offset any savings to be derived from shifting the exemption to C's parents.

#### Example 11

D and E were married on December 28, 2011. During 2011, D, age 22, attended State University full time. In addition, she worked part-time, earning $10,500 for the year. E, age 21, was also a full-time student, fully supported by his parents. E had no income. In this case, E's parents are entitled to claim an exemption for E even if D and E elect to file a joint return. The joint return requirement would not be violated because the couple owes no tax (the couple's standard deduction eliminates their taxable income). Consequently, under the IRS view, they would be filing merely to obtain a refund of any withholding and not filing an actual return.

It should be emphasized that the fact that a person files his or her own tax return does not bar another taxpayer (who otherwise meets all the necessary tests) from claiming him or her as a dependent. This is true as long as the dependent does not file a joint return for any reason other than to claim a refund of the entire amount of taxes withheld. Otherwise, the joint return test would not be met and the dependency exemption would be denied.

---

[23] § 151(c)(2).

[24] Rev. Rul. 54-567, 1954-2 C.B. 108.

### Citizenship or Residency Test

A dependent must be a citizen or national (e.g., an American Samoan) of the United States or a resident of the United States, Canada, or Mexico. In addition, an adopted child of a citizen qualifies, even though not a resident, if he or she was a member of the taxpayer's household for the entire taxable year. For example, if a taxpayer's employment results in his relocation to London where he adopts a British child, this rule enables the taxpayer to claim the child as a dependent even though the child is not a U.S. citizen or resident.

### Taxpayer Not a Dependent

A person who is a dependent cannot claim others as dependents. For example, if a child is a dependent of his or her parents, the child cannot claim his or her own children as dependents.

### Social Security Number

In order to claim an exemption for a dependent, the taxpayer must list the dependent's Social Security number on the tax return. If the number is not listed or is listed incorrectly, the exemption may be disallowed and a $50 penalty may be imposed. More importantly, the taxpayer's filing status (head of household, surviving spouse) or child credit could be affected. Since it usually takes about two weeks to obtain a social security number, obtaining one by the extended due date of the return normally does not present a problem.[25]

**EXHIBIT 4.2 Qualifying Child vs. Qualifying Relative**

| *Test* | *Qualifying Child* | *Qualifying Relative* |
|---|---|---|
| Relationship | Yes *(child and siblings, their descendants)* | Yes *(familial & certain nonrelatives)* |
| Residence | Yes *(> ½ taxable year)* | No *(but see support)* |
| Age | Yes *(< 19; < 24 & full-time student)* | No *(but see income)* |
| Tie-breaker | Yes *(parent first)* | No *(but see multiple support agreement)* |
| Support | No *(not self supporting)* | Yes *(>½ spent)* |
| Income | No | Yes *(but not child if < 19; < 24 & full-time student)* |
| Joint return | Cannot file joint return | Cannot file joint return |
| Citizenship | Yes | Yes |

## Children of Divorced or Separated Parents

If a married couple with children is divorced or separated, special rules may apply in determining who claims exemptions for the children.[26] These rules operate when the couple is:

- Legally separated under a decree of divorce or separate maintenance
- Separated under a written separation agreement; or
- Lived apart at all times during the last six months of the calendar year.

In these situations, if over half of a child's support is provided by one parent or collectively by both parents and the child is in custody of one or both parents for more than half of the year, the parent with custody for the greater portion of the year may claim the exemption. Thus, the custodial parent ordinarily receives the exemption regardless of the amount paid by either parent.

In certain situations, the divorced couple may be better served if the noncustodial parent claims the exemption. Consequently, if the conditions above are met, the custodial parent may surrender his or her right to the exemption to the noncustodial parent. To accomplish this, the release must be evidenced in a signed declaration that the custodial parent will not claim the exemption. For this purpose, the custodial parent must complete Form 8332. The

[25] The year that this requirement became effective the number of exemptions dropped 7 million below what had been expected, resulting in about $2.8 billion in additional tax revenue. Interestingly, more than 48 percent of the drop was attributable to single taxpayers. See IRS Pub. 1500 (August 1991).

[26] § 152(e).

custodial parent then transfers the form to the noncustodial parent who must attach the form or statement to his or her return.

## Phase–Out of Personal and Dependency Exemptions

From 1989 through 2009, high-income taxpayers receive reduced benefits from their personal and dependency exemptions. Taxpayers were required to reduce their deduction for personal and dependency exemptions by 2 percent for each $2,500 or fraction thereof ($1,250 for married persons filing separate returns) by which a taxpayer's A.G.I. exceeded the applicable threshold. However, the phase-out expired in 2009 but is scheduled to return in 2013.

## Child Tax Credit

**LO.3**
Describe the child tax credit.

Although most credits are covered in Chapter 13, the child tax credit is addressed briefly here because it is so closely tied with exemptions.[27] Under § 24, the amount of the child tax credit is $1,000 for each *qualifying child*.[28] For example, if a taxpayer had four children, the potential credit would be $4,000 ($1,000 × 4). The definition of a qualifying child for purposes of the child credit piggybacks on the uniform definition of a child used in determining a taxpayer's dependency exemption (discussed earlier in this chapter). In other words, a *qualifying child* for the child credit is a *qualifying child* as that expression is defined for determining a taxpayer's dependents but with certain modifications. A qualifying child for the child credit is any person who meets the following conditions.

- The individual is a *qualifying child* as defined in § 152 relating to dependents (age, relationship, residence tests).
- The individual has not attained the age of 17 by the close of the calendar year.
- The individual is a U.S. citizen.

To summarize, a taxpayer normally can claim the $1,000 credit for each child under age 17. Also note that as mentioned above, if a divorced or separated taxpayer waives his or her right to an exemption, the child credit is also waived and transferred to the noncustodial spouse.

**Example 12**

M and D are the proud parents of a 16-year-old daughter, C. The parents file jointly, reporting gross income of $37,825 for 2011. After claiming a standard deduction of $11,600 and three exemptions of $3,700 each, their taxable income is $15,125. Their tax on $15,125 (using the Tax Tables) is $1,513. After claiming their child tax credit of $1,000 for C, the couple's gross income tax before prepayments is $513.

### Phase–Out of Credit

Like many other tax benefits, the child tax credit is phased out for higher income taxpayers. Specifically, the allowable credit is reduced by $50 for each $1,000 (or fraction thereof) of A.G.I. in excess of specified thresholds. The thresholds are $75,000 for unmarried taxpayers and $110,000 for married taxpayers filing jointly ($55,000 for those filing separately).[29]

**Example 13**

R and S have two daughters, L and M (both under age 17). R and S are married and file jointly, reporting A.G.I. of $117,100 for 2011. The child tax credit for two qualifying

[27] § 24.

[28] §§ 24(c)(1)(C) and 32(c)(3)(B).

[29] § 24(b). For purposes of this phase-out, adjusted gross income is increased by the amount of the foreign earned income exclusions under §§ 911, 931, and 933.

children is generally $2,000, but R and S must reduce their credit by $400 ($50 × 8, since $117,100 exceeds $110,000 by $7,000 and a fraction) to $1,600.

## Refundable Child Tax Credit

As a general rule, most credits are limited to the taxpayer's tax liability for the year. For example, if the taxpayer's tax liability before the child credit is $5,000 and the child credit is $3,000, the taxpayer's regular tax usually would be reduced to $2,000. If the taxpayer's regular tax liability before the credit is $3,000 and the child credit is $4,000, the credit would reduce the tax to zero and *normally* the $1,000 balance of the credit would not be used and the taxpayer would not receive a refund of the unused credit. However, the law permits a portion of the unused child credit to be refunded. In other words, in the situation above, all or a portion of the unused credit of $1,000 would be refunded. The amount of the refundable credit depends on several variables, including the number of children, the taxpayer's earned income, other credits and some additional factors. The actual calculation of the amount of refundable credit can be found in Chapter 13 in the discussion of refundable credits.

## ✓ Check Your Knowledge

Try these 10 true-false questions concerning exemptions. If the statement is false, explain why. Assume all tests are met unless otherwise implied.

### Review Question 1

All individuals are entitled to claim a personal exemption.

*False.* An individual who may be claimed as a dependent on another taxpayer's return cannot claim a personal exemption. This prohibits two different taxpayers from claiming two separate exemptions for the same person.

### Review Question 2

Certain people who are normally considered relatives (e.g., cousins) do not qualify as relatives for purposes of the exemption tests.

*True.* A cousin is not a familial relative.

### Review Question 3

An individual, such as a cousin, can qualify as a "relative" even though he or she is not a familial relative.

*True.* An individual who lives in the taxpayer's home the entire taxable year is treated as a relative even though such person and the taxpayer would not be "related" under the statutory definition.

### Review Qucstion 4

T takes care of his mom. He satisfies the support test if he provides more than 10 percent of her total support.

*False.* A taxpayer must generally provide more than 50 percent of an individual's support in order to claim the individual as a dependent. However, an individual who provides more than 10 percent of a person's support may be able to claim a dependency exemption under a multiple support agreement.

### Review Question 5

In determining whether T provides more than 50 percent of his mom's support, her savings of over $100,000, and any earnings from themz, are not counted except to the extent they are actually spent.

*True.* Funds available for an individual's support are ignored in applying the support test. Only amounts spent (or the value of support items provided, such as lodging) are considered.

### Review Question 6

T's mom has no income other than social security benefits of $5,000 and interest from City of Duluth bonds of $6,000. T may claim an exemption for her mom.

*True.* A dependency exemption normally cannot be claimed for an individual if such person's gross income exceeds the exemption amount. For this purpose, gross income includes only income that is subject to tax. In this case, T's mom's income from social security is excluded as is the interest from the municipal bonds.

### Review Question 7

T's 25-year-old son lives with him. This year he earned $5,000 from his paper route. T may not claim an exemption for his son.

*True.* T is not a qualifying child since he fails the age test (not less than 19 nor a full-time student less than 24). He also is not a qualifying relative because he fails the gross income test since he earns more than the exemption amount and is neither less than 19 nor a full-time student less than 24. Had T been a full-time student less than 24, he would have qualified as either a qualifying child or a qualifying relative.

### Review Question 8

In the case of a divorced couple with children, the custodial parent normally receives the exemption for the children even if the noncustodial parent provides all of the child support.

*True.* The custodial parent is entitled to the exemption unless he or she releases it to the noncustodial parent. This treatment generally follows from the uniform definition of a qualifying child that requires a child to have lived with the taxpayer for more than one-half of the taxable year.

### Review Question 9

H and W are married with three children ages 15, 16, and 17. The couple can normally claim a child tax credit of $3,000.

*False.* The child tax credit is generally available for dependent children less than 17 years old. Therefore the couple can usually claim a credit of $2,000 ($1,000 × 2).

# Filing Status

## Evolution of Filing Status

**LO.4**
Apply the rules to determine the taxpayer's filing status.

The tax rates that are applied to determine the taxpayer's tax liability depend on the taxpayer's filing status. From 1913 to 1948, there was only one set of tax rates that applied to individual taxpayers. During this period, each taxpayer filed a separate return, even if he or she were married. For example, if both a husband and wife had income, each would file a separate return, reporting their respective incomes. This system, however, proved inequitable due to the differing state laws governing the ownership of income (or property).

In the United States, the rights that married individuals hold in property are determined using either the common law or community property system. There are ten community property states: Alaska, Arizona, California, Idaho, Louisiana, Nevada, New Mexico, Texas, Washington, and Wisconsin. In a community property state, income generated through the personal efforts of either spouse is generally owned *equally* by the community (i.e., the husband and wife). In common law states, income belongs to the spouse that earns the income. The differing treatments of income by community property and common law states produced the need for a special rate schedule for married taxpayers.

### Married Status

The category of married couples filing jointly and its unique rate schedule were added to the law because of an inequity that existed between married couples in community property states and non-community property jurisdictions (separate or common law property states). As noted above, earnings derived from personal services performed by married persons in community property states generally are owned jointly by the two spouses. Accordingly, both husband and wife in a community property state would file returns showing one-half of their earned income, even though only one may have been employed. Note that the total income of the couple would be split equally between the husband and wife regardless of who earned the income. If a couple in a non-community property state relied on one spouse's earnings, the employed spouse filed a return showing the entire amount of those earnings.

Since the tax rates are progressive, a married couple in a non-community property state would bear a larger tax burden than one in a community property state if only one spouse was employed outside the home or one spouse earned substantially more than the other. To eliminate this inequity, Congress elected to grant the benefits of income splitting to all married couples. This was accomplished by authorizing a new tax schedule for married persons filing jointly. A joint return results in the same amount of tax as would be paid on two "married, filing separate" returns showing half the total income of a married couple.

## Example 14

L and M are married and reside in California with their two children. L is an executive with a major corporation and M works in the home. Under state law, L's salary of $70,000 is owned equally by L and M. Each may file a separate return and report $35,000 of the salary.

## Example 15

S and T are married and reside in Virginia with their two children. S is an executive with a major corporation and T works in the home. S earns a salary of $70,000. If S were to file a separate return, she would report the entire $70,000 salary on that return. Since the tax rate schedules for individuals are progressive, S would pay a higher tax than the total paid by L and M in *Example 15*. Consequently, the total tax burden on S and T would be greater than that on L and M. By filing a joint return, S and T are placed in a position equivalent to that of L and M.

### Head-of-Household Status

Introduction of the joint return in 1948 was not viewed by the public as merely a solution to a problem caused by differing state laws. Many saw it as a tax break for those who had family obligations. As a result, single parents and other unmarried taxpayers with dependents tried to persuade Congress that they should be entitled to some tax relief due to their family responsibilities. Their arguments were based on the fact that they suffered a greater tax burden than single-earner married couples. In 1957, a tax reduction was allowed in the form of a new tax rate schedule for taxpayers who qualify as a *head of household.* The rates were designed to be lower than the original rates, which applied to all taxpayers, but *higher* than the rates for married persons filing jointly.

### Single Status

The most recent change in the overall tax rate structure was the addition of a separate tax rate schedule for single persons. This change was made because a single person was paying a higher rate of tax on the same income than married persons filing jointly and heads of households. The reduced rates for single taxpayers still are higher than those for a head of household, but lower than those in the original rate structure. As a result of this final change, the original tax rate structure that once applied to all taxpayers now applies only to married persons filing separately.

### Summary

The Federal income tax on individuals is based on four tax rate schedules. Taxpayers must file under one of the following classifications, listed in order from lowest to highest in tax rates:

1. Married filing jointly (including surviving spouses)
2. Head of household
3. Single
4. Married filing separately

The 2011 tax rate schedules for these classifications are reproduced on the inside front cover of this text.[30]

## Married Individuals

Marital status is determined on the last day of an individual's taxable year. A person is married for tax purposes if he or she is married under state law, regardless of whether he or she is separated or in the process of seeking a divorce.[31]

### Joint Return

A husband and wife generally may file a return using the rates for married persons filing jointly.[32] If a joint return is filed, husband and wife are jointly and severally (individually) liable for any tax, interest or penalties related to *that* joint return. As a result, one spouse may be held liable for paying the entire tax, even though the other spouse earned all the income. For this reason, a spouse should be cautious in signing a joint return. However, under the *innocent spouse rule*, a spouse will not be held liable for tax and penalties attributable to misstatements by the other spouse in two instances. The first provision allows relief if the innocent spouse establishes that he or she did not know and had no reason to know of the understatement, that it is inequitable to hold him or her liable for the deficiency, and that he or she elected the benefits of this provision within two years after the date collection activities began. The second provision limits the liability of a spouse to only the portion of the deficiency properly allocable to him or her if he or she is no longer married to, is legally separated from, or is no longer living with the spouse with whom the joint return was filed.[33]

### Surviving Spouse

To provide relief in those situations where a spouse dies and must continue to support the couple's children, the law permits use of the joint return rates for a short period. A so-called *surviving spouse* may use the lower rates in the first or second taxable year after the year of his or her spouse's death. Technically, a taxpayer qualifies as a surviving spouse if he or she meets two tests. First, the spouse must have died within the two taxable years preceding the current taxable year. Second, the taxpayer must provide over half the cost of maintaining a home in which he or she and a *dependent* son, stepson, daughter, or stepdaughter live.[34] In determining whether the child is a dependent, the following modifications are made when applying the qualifying individual or qualifying relative tests.

- For purpose of determining whether the child is a dependent under the "qualifying relative" standard, the gross income test is ignored.
- In applying either test, the fact that the individual files a joint return is ignored.
- In applying either test, the fact that a dependent is ineligible to have dependents is ignored.

Remarriage terminates surviving spouse status. Of course, a joint return can be filed with the new spouse.

#### Example 16

H and W were married and had two children, S and D. In 2011, H died. After H's death, W continued to provide a home and all the support of S and D. As a result, W is entitled to claim S and D as dependents. For the year of death, 2011, W normally will file a joint return with her deceased husband, H. In the following two years, 2012 and

[30] The 2011 tax tables had not been issued by the IRS at the date of publication of this text. However, the 2010 tax tables are reproduced in Appendix A.

[31] Special rules apply to a taxpayer whose spouse dies during the year. See §§ 7703(a)(1) and 6013(a)(2).

[32] § 6013(a). However, a special rule applies if the spouse is a nonresident alien. See § 6013(g). Also, both spouses must have the *same* taxable year.

[33] § 6015(b) and (c).

[34] § 2(a).

2013, W may file as a surviving spouse since she provides a home for a dependent child. As a surviing spouse, she may use the same rates as married persons filing jointly. In subsequent years, W may file as a head of household if she meets all the other requirements.

### Separate Returns

Normally, it will be advantageous for married persons to file a joint return because it is simpler to file one return than it is to file two, and the tax will be as low or lower than the tax based on the rules for married persons filing separately. In some situations, a taxpayer may prefer to file a separate return. For example, a person may wish to avoid liability for the tax on the income —especially any unreported income—of his or her spouse. Similarly, a husband and wife who are separated and are contemplating divorce may wish to file separate returns.

Separate returns may be to the taxpayers' advantage in certain circumstances. Although rare, use of the separate rate schedules may result in a lower total tax than by using the rates applicable to a joint return. Filing of separate returns may also prove beneficial when the filing of a joint return would prevent another taxpayer (e.g., a parent) from claiming a dependency exemption deduction for either the husband or the wife (*see Example 10 above*). State income tax laws may also make filing separately beneficial.

## Head of Household

Head-of-household rates may be used if the taxpayer satisfies two conditions. First, the taxpayer must be unmarried (and not a surviving spouse) or considered unmarried (i.e., an abandoned spouse) on the last day of the tax year. Second, the taxpayer must provide more than one-half of the cost of maintaining as his or her home a household which is the principal place of abode for more than one-half the year of

1. A qualifying child, or
2. A dependent familial relative[35]

As might be expected, the same individuals that are considered "relatives" for exemption purposes generally qualify as relatives when applying the head-of-household rules (e.g., children, grandchildren, parents, grandparents). However, there is an exception. Even though a person who is not truly related to the taxpayer but who lives in the taxpayer's home for the entire taxable year is treated as a relative for purposes of the dependency exemption, such is not the case here. In order for the taxpayer to qualify for head-of-household status, the individual living in the home must be a familial relative.[36] Exhibit 4-3 gives a listing of those who are normally considered relatives for purposes of meeting both the head-of-household and dependency rules. Note that they are all the same except for the nonfamilial relative.

An individual normally enjoys head of household status *only* if he or she is the taxpayer's dependent *and* lives in the taxpayer's household. Two exceptions exist to this general rule.

1. A parent must be a dependent but need not live in the taxpayer's home; however, the taxpayer still must pay more than half of the cost of keeping up a home for his or her mother or father.

For example, the taxpayer qualifies if he or she paid more than half the cost of the parent's living in a nursing home and the parent is a dependent.

2. An *unmarried qualifying child* of the taxpayer need not be a dependent. This exception permits a divorced parent to qualify as head-of-household even though the former other parent claims the exemption for the child.

---

[35] § 2(b)(1).

[36] §§ 2(b)(3), 152(a)(9), and 152(c).

**EXHIBIT 4.3** **Relatives for Dependency and Head-of-Household Tests**

| Relative | For Dependency Exemption | For Head-of-Household Test |
|---|---|---|
| Qualifying child | Yes | Yes |
| Familial relative | Yes | Yes |
| Other individuals—person who lives in taxpayer's home entire taxable year | Yes | No |

## Example 17

D, an unmarried individual, lives in Seattle and pays more than half of the cost of maintaining a home in Reno for her dependent parents. Although her parents do not live with her in Seattle, D qualifies for the head-of-household rates.

## Example 18

R is divorced and maintains a household for herself and her 10-year-old daughter. Although R is the custodial parent, she allows her former husband to claim the exemption for the child. R still qualifies for the head-of-household rates.

## Example 19

M is divorced. At the beginning of the year, M's son, S, started medical school and moved in with his mom to save money. M pays all of the cost of maintaining the home and also provides more than one-half of S's support. S is 25 years old and earned $46,000 during the year. M cannot claim head of household because S is neither a qualifying child nor a qualifying relative. S is not a qualifying child because he is too old. To be a qualifying child, S must be less than 19 or a full-time student less than 24. S is also not a qualifying relative since his income is too high (i.e., $46,000 exceeds the amount of the personal exemption).[37]

It should be noted that a person for whom a dependency exemption is claimed solely under a multiple support agreement (e.g., the taxpayer did not provide over half the cost of maintaining the home) is not considered a qualifying relative and the agreement *cannot* qualify the taxpayer as a head of household. In addition, a nonresident alien cannot be a head of household.[38]

### Costs of Maintaining a Home

In determining whether a taxpayer qualifies for head-of-household status, it is necessary to determine whether he or she pays more than half of the cost of maintaining a home for the taxable year. This determination must also be made for surviving spouse filing status. The costs of maintaining the home include the costs for the mutual benefit of the occupants and

[37] Prior to 2005, M would have qualified for head of household treatment since the child of a taxpayer was not required to be a dependent.

[38] *Supra*, footnote 36.

include such expenses as property taxes, mortgage interest, rent, utilities, insurance, repairs, upkeep, and *food* consumed on the premises. The cost of maintaining a home does not include clothing, educational expenses, medical expenses, or transportation.[39]

## Abandoned Spouse Provision

Without a special provision, an individual whose spouse has simply abandoned him or her might be forced to file using the high rates for married individuals filing separately. Aware of this problem, Congress has provided that a married individual who files a separate return may file as head of household if he or she qualifies as an *abandoned spouse*. To qualify, the individual must provide more than half the cost of maintaining a home that houses him or her and a child for whom a dependency exemption deduction is *either* claimed or could be claimed by the taxpayer except for the fact that the exemption was assigned to the non-custodial parent.[40] The child must live in the home with the taxpayer for more than half the taxable year and the taxpayer's spouse must not live in the home at any time during the last six months of the year. If each of these requirements is met, an abandoned spouse qualifies as a head of household.

### Example 20

M and N are married with six children. In October, M stormed out of the house, saying he would never return. N was hopeful that M would return and consequently had not taken action to obtain a divorce by the end of the year. Although M and N are eligible to file a joint return, M indicated that he would not. Consequently, N's filing status is married filing separately. She does not qualify as an abandoned spouse since her husband lived in the home during the last six months of the year. In the following year, however, N could qualify and file as head of household.

## Single

Single filing status is defined by exception. A single taxpayer is anyone who is unmarried and does not qualify as a head of household or surviving spouse. Even though single rates are somewhat lower, they may not be used by married persons filing separately.[41]

## Marriage Tax Penalty

A well-known tax phenomenon faced by couples contemplating marriage is the possibility of a marriage tax penalty. Whether matrimony is for better or for worse on the couple's tax return depends on a number of factors, such as how much each earns as well as whether either individual brings dependents into the marriage.

Joint filing originally was intended as a benefit to married couples. Prior to 1969, the joint return schedule was designed to tax one-half of total marital income at the tax rates applicable to single individuals. The resultant tax was then doubled to produce the married couple's tax liability. Note that this procedure produces a perfect split of a single earner's income between two spouses so that it is taxed at a lower marginal rate. While this approach is quite beneficial for married taxpayers, single taxpayers felt that they were paying an unjustifiable "singles penalty." To illustrate, consider the situation of a single taxpayer with taxable income of $24,000. In 1965, this taxpayer owed $8,030 of income tax, with the last dollar of income taxed at a 50 percent marginal tax rate. A married couple with the same 1965 taxable income owed only $5,660 (more than $2,000 less) and faced a marginal tax rate of only 32 percent.

In 1969 Congress attempted to alleviate the singles penalty by enacting a new (and lower) rate schedule for single taxpayers. While this action did reduce (but not eliminate) the singles penalty, it also created a marriage penalty for certain individuals as shown in the example below.

---

[39] Reg. § 1.2-2(d).

[40] § 2(c) and § 7703(b). An adopted child of the taxpayer is considered a son or daughter for this test.

[41] Single filing status is referred to in Code § 1(c) as "Unmarried individuals (Other Than Surviving Spouses and Heads of Households)."

## Example 21

H is currently single and his only source of income is his salary of $90,000. He is considering marrying his girlfriend, W. As shown below, for 2011 his tax as a single taxpayer after considering his standard deduction and one exemption is $16,250.00. If H marries W and W has no taxable income, their tax on a joint return with its wider brackets and double the standard deduction and exemption amounts would be $10,000.00 or $6,250.00 less ($16,250.00 – $10,000.00). Observe that in this situation where there is one earner, there is a singles penalty. In other words, for the same amount of income ($90,000), those who are single pay more than those who are married. But now consider what happens if W also has a $90,000 salary, the same as H. If W and H remain single, they both will pay a tax of $16,250.00 for a combined total of $32,500.00. However, if they marry, their combined taxable income remains the same at $161,000 (2 × $80,500) but their tax on a joint return is $33,149.50 or $649.50 more. Here, where there are two high-income earners both with about the same income, there is a marriage tax penalty.

| Filing Status | *2011 H One earner Single* | *2011 H & W One earner Married* | *2011 H & W Two earners Married* |
|---|---|---|---|
| Gross income of H | $ 90,000 | $ 90,000 | $ 90,000 |
| Gross income of W | — | — | $ 90,000 |
| Gross income | $ 90,000 | $ 90,000 | $180,000 |
| Standard deduction | ($ 5,800) | ($11,600) | ($ 11,600) |
| Exemption(s) | ($ 3,700) | ($ 7,400) | ($ 7,400) |
| Taxable income | $80,500 | $ 71,000 | $ 161,000 |
| Tax | $16,250.00 | $ 10,000.00 | $ 33,149.50 |

| | *H Single* | *H & W Married* | *H & W Married* |
|---|---|---|---|
| Tax | $16,250.00 | $10,000.00 | $33,149.50 |
| Tax for two singles (2 × $16,250.00) | | | (32,500.00) |
| Singles penalty ($16,250.00 – $10,000.00) | | $ 6,250.00 | |
| Marriage penalty ($33,149.50 – $32,500.00) | | | $ 649.50 |

As a general rule, if a couple marries and only one spouse has income (or there is a large disparity between their incomes), marriage will be beneficial due to the splitting effect (i.e., the married, one earner effect above). In contrast, if a couple marries and they have similar incomes, there may be a marriage tax penalty (i.e., the married, two earners effect above).

### Tax Reform and the Marriage Penalty

One of the goals of changes made in 2001 was to reduce the marriage tax penalty. The specific provisions are summarized as follows:

- The standard deduction for a married couple was increased to an amount which is exactly double that for a single individual.
- The tax brackets were adjusted in a way to reduce the marriage penalty. First, the 10 percent bracket for married couples ($17,000) is double that for single individuals ($8,500). Next, the 15 percent bracket was adjusted to an amount which is double that for single taxpayers. Note, however, that the higher tax brackets were not adjusted and will remain in the same proportions that they were before for married persons compared to unmarried persons (retaining an element of marriage penalty). Absent these changes, the married rates would be 167 percent of the single rates. Without action, these rates are scheduled to return in 2013.

**EXHIBIT 4.4** **Determination of Filing Status**

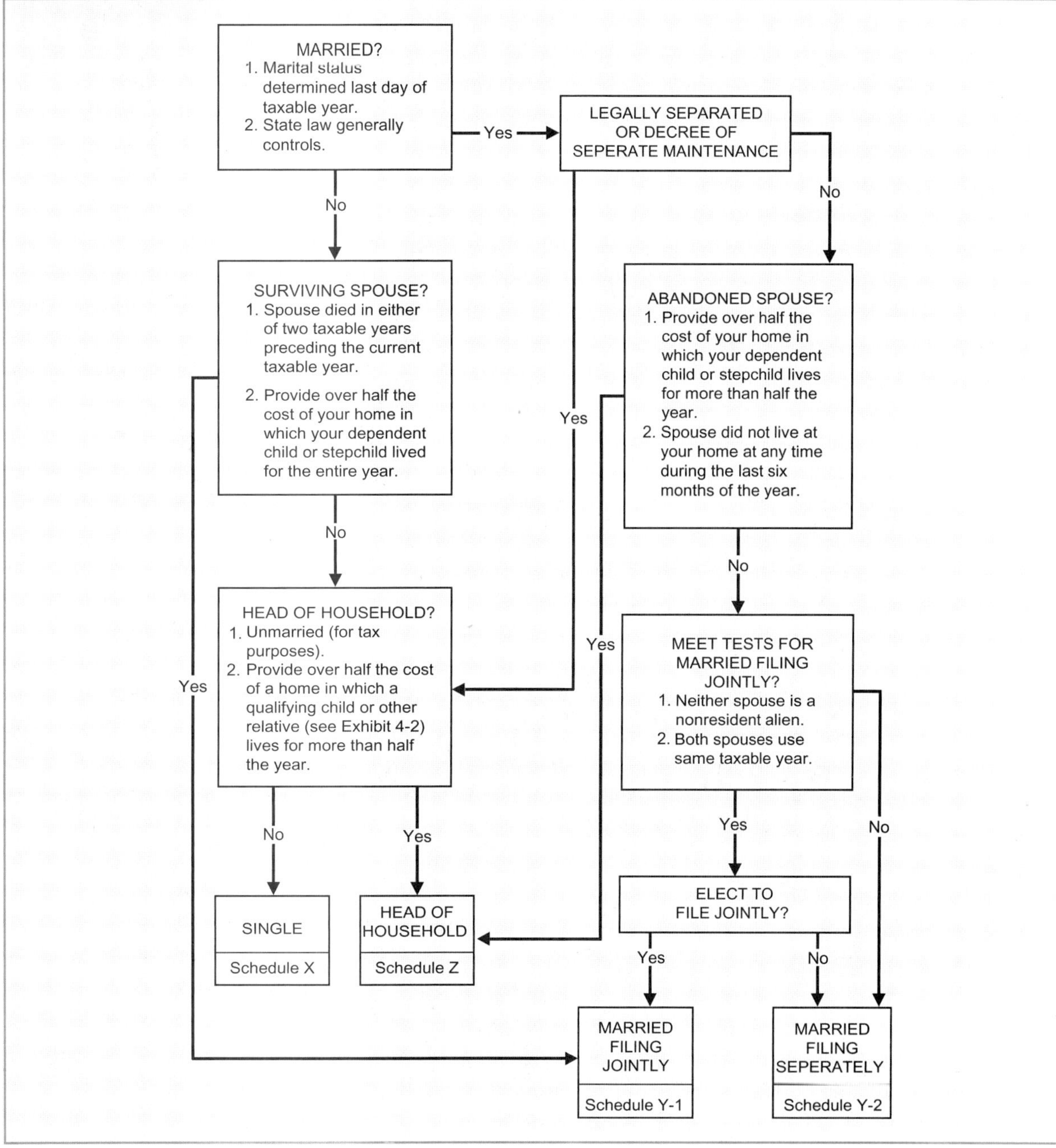


## ✓ Check Your Knowledge

### Review Question 1

List the available rate schedules in the order of their progressivity (highest to lowest tax rates).

Married filing separately, single, head of household, and married filing jointly (including surviving spouses).

### Review Question 2

H died in 2009, survived by his wife, W, and two young children, S and D. What rate schedule may W use in 2011 assuming she has not remarried?

She should be able to file as a surviving spouse and use the joint return rate schedule for the two taxable years after her husband's death (2010 and 2011). A taxpayer qualifies as a surviving spouse if his or her spouse has died in either of the two taxable years preceding the current year (i.e., 2009 or 2010 in this case) and he or she provides over half the cost of a home in which he or she and a dependent child live. In this case, H died in 2009, and it appears that W provides a home in which she and her dependent children live.

### Review Question 3

Q, divorced, is alive and well in Los Angeles. She has a 19-year-old daughter who attends school full-time at Arizona State. Q provides all her daughter's support, including payment of her dorm bill each month. Can Q file as a head of household? What additional questions must be asked before this question can be answered?

An individual can normally file as a head of household if he or she provides over *one-half* the cost of maintaining a home in which a qualifying child or a dependent familial relative lives for more than *one-half* of the taxable year. In this case, it is not completely clear whether the half-and-half test is met. As a general rule, the relative must live in the home of the taxpayer one-half of the year. Here Q's daughter may only live in Q's home during the summer months, and it would therefore appear that Q could not qualify. However, temporary absences due to special circumstances such as those due to education, business, vacation, and military service are ignored. Since the daughter's absence is temporary, the test is satisfied. Note that Q's daughter need not be a dependent since this requirement is relaxed in the case of an unmarried child of the taxpayer.

## Computation of Tax for Individual Taxpayers

**LO.5**
Compute the tax liability of an individual taxpayer using the tax rate schedules and the tax tables.

Once filing status and taxable income have been determined, the tax computation for most individuals is fairly straightforward. The gross tax is computed using the tax tables or the tax rate schedules. This amount is then reduced by any tax credits available to the taxpayer and any tax prepayments in arriving at the tax due or the refund. Children under age 19 with unearned income and all persons claimed as dependents are subject to special rules in the computation of their income tax.

### Tax Tables

The vast majority of individuals must determine their tax using *tax tables*, which are provided by the IRS along with the instructions for preparing individual income tax returns. The tables are derived directly from the rate schedules to simplify compliance and reduce taxpayer errors. The tax for any particular range of taxable income is determined by using the mid-point of the range and the appropriate rate schedule. For example, the tax in the 2010 tables for a single taxpayer with taxable income of $23,010 is $3,035 which is the tax computed on $23,025 using the tax rate schedules (see Exhibit 4-5 for an excerpt and Appendix A for the complete 2010 Tax Tables). The tables cover taxpayers in each filing status with taxable incomes less than $100,000. A taxpayer who qualifies generally is required to use the tax tables.[42]

[42] § 3.

## EXHIBIT 4.5 Excerpts From Tax Tables for 2010

| If line 43 (taxable income) is— At least | But less than | And you are— Single | Married filing jointly * | Married filing separately | Head of a household |
|---|---|---|---|---|---|
| | | Your tax is— | | | |
| **23,000** | | | | | |
| **23,000** | **23,050** | 3,035 | 2,616 | 3,035 | 2,856 |
| **23,050** | **23,100** | 3,043 | 2,624 | 3,043 | 2,864 |
| **23,100** | **23,150** | 3,050 | 2,631 | 3,050 | 2,871 |
| **23,150** | **23,200** | 3,058 | 2,639 | 3,058 | 2,879 |
| **23,200** | **23,250** | 3,065 | 2,646 | 3,065 | 2,886 |
| **23,250** | **23,300** | 3,073 | 2,654 | 3,073 | 2,894 |
| **23,300** | **23,350** | 3,080 | 2,661 | 3,080 | 2,901 |
| **23,350** | **23,400** | 3,088 | 2,669 | 3,088 | 2,909 |
| **23,400** | **23,450** | 3,095 | 2,676 | 3,095 | 2,916 |
| **23,450** | **23,500** | 3,103 | 2,684 | 3,103 | 2,924 |
| **23,500** | **23,550** | 3,110 | 2,691 | 3,110 | 2,931 |
| **23,550** | **23,600** | 3,118 | 2,699 | 3,118 | 2,939 |
| **23,600** | **23,650** | 3,125 | 2,706 | 3,125 | 2,946 |
| **23,650** | **23,700** | 3,133 | 2,714 | 3,133 | 2,954 |
| **23,700** | **23,750** | 3,140 | 2,721 | 3,140 | 2,961 |
| **23,750** | **23,800** | 3,148 | 2,729 | 3,148 | 2,969 |
| **23,800** | **23,850** | 3,155 | 2,736 | 3,155 | 2,976 |
| **23,850** | **23,900** | 3,163 | 2,744 | 3,163 | 2,984 |
| **23,900** | **23,950** | 3,170 | 2,751 | 3,170 | 2,991 |
| **23,950** | **24,000** | 3,178 | 2,759 | 3,178 | 2,999 |
| **24,000** | | | | | |
| **24,000** | **24,050** | 3,185 | 2,766 | 3,185 | 3,006 |
| **24,050** | **24,100** | 3,193 | 2,774 | 3,193 | 3,014 |
| **24,100** | **24,150** | 3,200 | 2,781 | 3,200 | 3,021 |
| **24,150** | **24,200** | 3,208 | 2,789 | 3,208 | 3,029 |
| **24,200** | **24,250** | 3,215 | 2,796 | 3,215 | 3,036 |
| **24,250** | **24,300** | 3,223 | 2,804 | 3,223 | 3,044 |
| **24,300** | **24,350** | 3,230 | 2,811 | 3,230 | 3,051 |
| **24,350** | **24,400** | 3,238 | 2,819 | 3,238 | 3,059 |
| **24,400** | **24,450** | 3,245 | 2,826 | 3,245 | 3,066 |
| **24,450** | **24,500** | 3,253 | 2,834 | 3,253 | 3,074 |
| **24,500** | **24,550** | 3,260 | 2,841 | 3,260 | 3,081 |
| **24,550** | **24,600** | 3,268 | 2,849 | 3,268 | 3,089 |
| **24,600** | **24,650** | 3,275 | 2,856 | 3,275 | 3,096 |
| **24,650** | **24,700** | 3,283 | 2,864 | 3,283 | 3,104 |
| **24,700** | **24,750** | 3,290 | 2,871 | 3,290 | 3,111 |
| **24,750** | **24,800** | 3,298 | 2,879 | 3,298 | 3,119 |
| **24,800** | **24,850** | 3,305 | 2,886 | 3,305 | 3,126 |
| **24,850** | **24,900** | 3,313 | 2,894 | 3,313 | 3,134 |
| **24,900** | **24,950** | 3,320 | 2,901 | 3,320 | 3,141 |
| **24,950** | **25,000** | 3,328 | 2,909 | 3,328 | 3,149 |
| **25,000** | | | | | |
| **25,000** | **25,050** | 3,335 | 2,916 | 3,335 | 3,156 |
| **25,050** | **25,100** | 3,343 | 2,924 | 3,343 | 3,164 |
| **25,100** | **25,150** | 3,350 | 2,931 | 3,350 | 3,171 |
| **25,150** | **25,200** | 3,358 | 2,939 | 3,358 | 3,179 |
| **25,200** | **25,250** | 3,365 | 2,946 | 3,365 | 3,186 |
| **25,250** | **25,300** | 3,373 | 2,954 | 3,373 | 3,194 |
| **25,300** | **25,350** | 3,380 | 2,961 | 3,380 | 3,201 |
| **25,350** | **25,400** | 3,388 | 2,969 | 3,388 | 3,209 |
| **25,400** | **25,450** | 3,395 | 2,976 | 3,395 | 3,216 |
| **25,450** | **25,500** | 3,403 | 2,984 | 3,403 | 3,224 |
| **25,500** | **25,550** | 3,410 | 2,991 | 3,410 | 3,231 |
| **25,550** | **25,600** | 3,418 | 2,999 | 3,418 | 3,239 |
| **25,600** | **25,650** | 3,425 | 3,006 | 3,425 | 3,246 |
| **25,650** | **25,700** | 3,433 | 3,014 | 3,433 | 3,254 |
| **25,700** | **25,750** | 3,440 | 3,021 | 3,440 | 3,261 |
| **25,750** | **25,800** | 3,448 | 3,029 | 3,448 | 3,269 |
| **25,800** | **25,850** | 3,455 | 3,036 | 3,455 | 3,276 |
| **25,850** | **25,900** | 3,463 | 3,044 | 3,463 | 3,284 |
| **25,900** | **25,950** | 3,470 | 3,051 | 3,470 | 3,291 |
| **25,950** | **26,000** | 3,478 | 3,059 | 3,478 | 3,299 |
| **26,000** | | | | | |
| **26,000** | **26,050** | 3,485 | 3,066 | 3,485 | 3,306 |
| **26,050** | **26,100** | 3,493 | 3,074 | 3,493 | 3,314 |
| **26,100** | **26,150** | 3,500 | 3,081 | 3,500 | 3,321 |
| **26,150** | **26,200** | 3,508 | 3,089 | 3,508 | 3,329 |
| **26,200** | **26,250** | 3,515 | 3,096 | 3,515 | 3,336 |
| **26,250** | **26,300** | 3,523 | 3,104 | 3,523 | 3,344 |
| **26,300** | **26,350** | 3,530 | 3,111 | 3,530 | 3,351 |
| **26,350** | **26,400** | 3,538 | 3,119 | 3,538 | 3,359 |
| **26,400** | **26,450** | 3,545 | 3,126 | 3,545 | 3,366 |
| **26,450** | **26,500** | 3,553 | 3,134 | 3,553 | 3,374 |
| **26,500** | **26,550** | 3,560 | 3,141 | 3,560 | 3,381 |
| **26,550** | **26,600** | 3,568 | 3,149 | 3,568 | 3,389 |
| **26,600** | **26,650** | 3,575 | 3,156 | 3,575 | 3,396 |
| **26,650** | **26,700** | 3,583 | 3,164 | 3,583 | 3,404 |
| **26,700** | **26,750** | 3,590 | 3,171 | 3,590 | 3,411 |
| **26,750** | **26,800** | 3,598 | 3,179 | 3,598 | 3,419 |
| **26,800** | **26,850** | 3,605 | 3,186 | 3,605 | 3,426 |
| **26,850** | **26,900** | 3,613 | 3,194 | 3,613 | 3,434 |
| **26,900** | **26,950** | 3,620 | 3,201 | 3,620 | 3,441 |
| **26,950** | **27,000** | 3,628 | 3,209 | 3,628 | 3,449 |
| **27,000** | | | | | |
| **27,000** | **27,050** | 3,635 | 3,216 | 3,635 | 3,456 |
| **27,050** | **27,100** | 3,643 | 3,224 | 3,643 | 3,464 |
| **27,100** | **27,150** | 3,650 | 3,231 | 3,650 | 3,471 |
| **27,150** | **27,200** | 3,658 | 3,239 | 3,658 | 3,479 |
| **27,200** | **27,250** | 3,665 | 3,246 | 3,665 | 3,486 |
| **27,250** | **27,300** | 3,673 | 3,254 | 3,673 | 3,494 |
| **27,300** | **27,350** | 3,680 | 3,261 | 3,680 | 3,501 |
| **27,350** | **27,400** | 3,688 | 3,269 | 3,688 | 3,509 |
| **27,400** | **27,450** | 3,695 | 3,276 | 3,695 | 3,516 |
| **27,450** | **27,500** | 3,703 | 3,284 | 3,703 | 3,524 |
| **27,500** | **27,550** | 3,710 | 3,291 | 3,710 | 3,531 |
| **27,550** | **27,600** | 3,718 | 3,299 | 3,718 | 3,539 |
| **27,600** | **27,650** | 3,725 | 3,306 | 3,725 | 3,546 |
| **27,650** | **27,700** | 3,733 | 3,314 | 3,733 | 3,554 |
| **27,700** | **27,750** | 3,740 | 3,321 | 3,740 | 3,561 |
| **27,750** | **27,800** | 3,748 | 3,329 | 3,748 | 3,569 |
| **27,800** | **27,850** | 3,755 | 3,336 | 3,755 | 3,576 |
| **27,850** | **27,900** | 3,763 | 3,344 | 3,763 | 3,584 |
| **27,900** | **27,950** | 3,770 | 3,351 | 3,770 | 3,591 |
| **27,950** | **28,000** | 3,778 | 3,359 | 3,778 | 3,599 |
| **28,000** | | | | | |
| **28,000** | **28,050** | 3,785 | 3,366 | 3,785 | 3,606 |
| **28,050** | **28,100** | 3,793 | 3,374 | 3,793 | 3,614 |
| **28,100** | **28,150** | 3,800 | 3,381 | 3,800 | 3,621 |
| **28,150** | **28,200** | 3,808 | 3,389 | 3,808 | 3,629 |
| **28,200** | **28,250** | 3,815 | 3,396 | 3,815 | 3,636 |
| **28,250** | **28,300** | 3,823 | 3,404 | 3,823 | 3,644 |
| **28,300** | **28,350** | 3,830 | 3,411 | 3,830 | 3,651 |
| **28,350** | **28,400** | 3,838 | 3,419 | 3,838 | 3,659 |
| **28,400** | **28,450** | 3,845 | 3,426 | 3,845 | 3,666 |
| **28,450** | **28,500** | 3,853 | 3,434 | 3,853 | 3,674 |
| **28,500** | **28,550** | 3,860 | 3,441 | 3,860 | 3,681 |
| **28,550** | **28,600** | 3,868 | 3,449 | 3,868 | 3,689 |
| **28,600** | **28,650** | 3,875 | 3,456 | 3,875 | 3,696 |
| **28,650** | **28,700** | 3,883 | 3,464 | 3,883 | 3,704 |
| **28,700** | **28,750** | 3,890 | 3,471 | 3,890 | 3,711 |
| **28,750** | **28,800** | 3,898 | 3,479 | 3,898 | 3,719 |
| **28,800** | **28,850** | 3,905 | 3,486 | 3,905 | 3,726 |
| **28,850** | **28,900** | 3,913 | 3,494 | 3,913 | 3,734 |
| **28,900** | **28,950** | 3,920 | 3,501 | 3,920 | 3,741 |
| **28,950** | **29,000** | 3,928 | 3,509 | 3,928 | 3,749 |
| **29,000** | | | | | |
| **29,000** | **29,050** | 3,935 | 3,516 | 3,935 | 3,756 |
| **29,050** | **29,100** | 3,943 | 3,524 | 3,943 | 3,764 |
| **29,100** | **29,150** | 3,950 | 3,531 | 3,950 | 3,771 |
| **29,150** | **29,200** | 3,958 | 3,539 | 3,958 | 3,779 |
| **29,200** | **29,250** | 3,965 | 3,546 | 3,965 | 3,786 |
| **29,250** | **29,300** | 3,973 | 3,554 | 3,973 | 3,794 |
| **29,300** | **29,350** | 3,980 | 3,561 | 3,980 | 3,801 |
| **29,350** | **29,400** | 3,988 | 3,569 | 3,988 | 3,809 |
| **29,400** | **29,450** | 3,995 | 3,576 | 3,995 | 3,816 |
| **29,450** | **29,500** | 4,003 | 3,584 | 4,003 | 3,824 |
| **29,500** | **29,550** | 4,010 | 3,591 | 4,010 | 3,831 |
| **29,550** | **29,600** | 4,018 | 3,599 | 4,018 | 3,839 |
| **29,600** | **29,650** | 4,025 | 3,606 | 4,025 | 3,846 |
| **29,650** | **29,700** | 4,033 | 3,614 | 4,033 | 3,854 |
| **29,700** | **29,750** | 4,040 | 3,621 | 4,040 | 3,861 |
| **29,750** | **29,800** | 4,048 | 3,629 | 4,048 | 3,869 |
| **29,800** | **29,850** | 4,055 | 3,636 | 4,055 | 3,876 |
| **29,850** | **29,900** | 4,063 | 3,644 | 4,063 | 3,884 |
| **29,900** | **29,950** | 4,070 | 3,651 | 4,070 | 3,891 |
| **29,950** | **30,000** | 4,078 | 3,659 | 4,078 | 3,899 |
| **30,000** | | | | | |
| **30,000** | **30,050** | 4,085 | 3,666 | 4,085 | 3,906 |
| **30,050** | **30,100** | 4,093 | 3,674 | 4,093 | 3,914 |
| **30,100** | **30,150** | 4,100 | 3,681 | 4,100 | 3,921 |
| **30,150** | **30,200** | 4,108 | 3,689 | 4,108 | 3,929 |
| **30,200** | **30,250** | 4,115 | 3,696 | 4,115 | 3,936 |
| **30,250** | **30,300** | 4,123 | 3,704 | 4,123 | 3,944 |
| **30,300** | **30,350** | 4,130 | 3,711 | 4,130 | 3,951 |
| **30,350** | **30,400** | 4,138 | 3,719 | 4,138 | 3,959 |
| **30,400** | **30,450** | 4,145 | 3,726 | 4,145 | 3,966 |
| **30,450** | **30,500** | 4,153 | 3,734 | 4,153 | 3,974 |
| **30,500** | **30,550** | 4,160 | 3,741 | 4,160 | 3,981 |
| **30,550** | **30,600** | 4,168 | 3,749 | 4,168 | 3,989 |
| **30,600** | **30,650** | 4,175 | 3,756 | 4,175 | 3,996 |
| **30,650** | **30,700** | 4,183 | 3,764 | 4,183 | 4,004 |
| **30,700** | **30,750** | 4,190 | 3,771 | 4,190 | 4,011 |
| **30,750** | **30,800** | 4,198 | 3,779 | 4,198 | 4,019 |
| **30,800** | **30,850** | 4,205 | 3,786 | 4,205 | 4,026 |
| **30,850** | **30,900** | 4,213 | 3,794 | 4,213 | 4,034 |
| **30,900** | **30,950** | 4,220 | 3,801 | 4,220 | 4,041 |
| **30,950** | **31,000** | 4,228 | 3,809 | 4,228 | 4,049 |
| **31,000** | | | | | |
| **31,000** | **31,050** | 4,235 | 3,816 | 4,235 | 4,056 |
| **31,050** | **31,100** | 4,243 | 3,824 | 4,243 | 4,064 |
| **31,100** | **31,150** | 4,250 | 3,831 | 4,250 | 4,071 |
| **31,150** | **31,200** | 4,258 | 3,839 | 4,258 | 4,079 |
| **31,200** | **31,250** | 4,265 | 3,846 | 4,265 | 4,086 |
| **31,250** | **31,300** | 4,273 | 3,854 | 4,273 | 4,094 |
| **31,300** | **31,350** | 4,280 | 3,861 | 4,280 | 4,101 |
| **31,350** | **31,400** | 4,288 | 3,869 | 4,288 | 4,109 |
| **31,400** | **31,450** | 4,295 | 3,876 | 4,295 | 4,116 |
| **31,450** | **31,500** | 4,303 | 3,884 | 4,303 | 4,124 |
| **31,500** | **31,550** | 4,310 | 3,891 | 4,310 | 4,131 |
| **31,550** | **31,600** | 4,318 | 3,899 | 4,318 | 4,139 |
| **31,600** | **31,650** | 4,325 | 3,906 | 4,325 | 4,146 |
| **31,650** | **31,700** | 4,333 | 3,914 | 4,333 | 4,154 |
| **31,700** | **31,750** | 4,340 | 3,921 | 4,340 | 4,161 |
| **31,750** | **31,800** | 4,348 | 3,929 | 4,348 | 4,169 |
| **31,800** | **31,850** | 4,355 | 3,936 | 4,355 | 4,176 |
| **31,850** | **31,900** | 4,363 | 3,944 | 4,363 | 4,184 |
| **31,900** | **31,950** | 4,370 | 3,951 | 4,370 | 4,191 |
| **31,950** | **32,000** | 4,378 | 3,959 | 4,378 | 4,199 |

* This column must also be used by a qualifying widow(er).

## Example 22

William W. Bristol was single for 2010 and had no dependents. Bill's only income was wages of $27,410 and taxable interest of $350. Since his itemized deductions totaled only $1,650, Bill claims the $5,700 standard deduction allowed for single taxpayers in 2010. Federal income tax of $2,820 was withheld from Bill's salary. Bill's taxable income and tax for 2010 are calculated as follows:

| | | | |
|---|---|---|---|
| Salary | | | $27,410 |
| Taxable interest | | | + 350 |
| Equals: | Adjusted gross income | | $27,760 |
| Less: | Standard deduction for 2010 | $5,700 | |
| | Personal exemption for 2010 | 3,650 | – 9,350 |
| Equals: | Taxable income | | $18,410 |
| Tax on $18,410 from Tax Table for 2010 (See Appendix A) | | | $ 2,345 |
| Less: | Income tax withheld | | – 2,820 |
| Equals: | Tax due or (refund) | | ($ 475) |

A completed Form 1040EZ for William W. Bristol, based on the information in this example, is shown in the Appendix at the end of the chapter.

## Example 23

Clyde F. and Delia C. Cooper were married during all of 2010 and had income from the following sources:

| | | |
|---|---|---|
| Salary, Clyde | | $33,445 |
| Federal income tax withheld | $1,170 | |
| Part-time salary, Delia | | 23,600 |
| Federal income tax withheld | 780 | |
| Interest from City Savings | | 950 |
| Interest from U.S. Government Treasury bond | | 550 |

Clyde and Delia are the sole support for their two children, ages 2 and 7. During 2010 they paid job-related child care expenses of $3,500 and made deductible contributions of $4,000 to their Individual Retirement Accounts ($2,000 each). Their itemized deductions for the year do not exceed their standard deduction for 2010 of $11,400. The Coopers' taxable income and tax for 2010 are calculated as follows:

| | | |
|---|---|---|
| Salary ($33,445 + $23,600) | | $ 57,045 |
| Plus: Taxable interest ($950 + $550) | | +1,500 |
| Less: Contributions to IRAs | | –4,000 |
| Equals: Adjusted gross income | | $ 54,545 |
| Less: Standard deduction for 2010 | $11,400 | |
| Exemptions for 2010 ($3,650 × 4) | 14,600 | –26,000 |
| Equals: Taxable income | | $ 28,545 |
| Tax on $28,145 for 2010 (See Appendix A) | | $ 3,441 |
| Less: Child care credit (.20 × $3,500) | | –700 |
| Child tax credit (2 × $1,000) | | –2,000 |
| Equals: Net tax | | $ 741 |
| Less: Income tax withheld ($1,170 + $780) | | –1,950 |
| Equals: Tax due or (refund) | | ($ 1,209) |

A completed Form 1040A using this information is included in the Appendix at the end of the chapter.

## TAX RATE SCHEDULES

Taxpayers who are unable to use the tax tables must use the tax rate schedules in computing their income tax. These schedules contain the rates provided in § 1 of the Internal Revenue Code. The 2010 tax rate schedules are included, along with the 2010 tax tables, in Appendix A. The 2011 tax rate schedules are summarized in Exhibit 4-6. The tax rate schedules for 2011 also are reproduced on the inside front cover of this text.

**EXHIBIT 4.6** **Individual Tax Rate Schedules for 2011**

**2011 Tax Rates Single**

*If taxable income is*

| *Over* | *But not over* | *The Tax is* | *% on + Excess* | *Of the Amount over* |
|---|---|---|---|---|
| $ 0 | $ 8,500 | $ 0.00 | 10% | $ 0 |
| 8,500 | 34,500 | 850.00 | 15% | 8,500 |
| 34,500 | 83,600 | 4,750.00 | 25% | 34,500 |
| 83,600 | 174,400 | 17,025.00 | 28% | 83,600 |
| 174,400 | 379,150 | 42,449.00 | 33% | 171,850 |
| 379,150 | | 110,016.50 | 35% | 379,150 |

**2011 Tax Rates Married Filing Jointly**

*If taxable income is*

| *Over* | *But not over* | *The Tax is* | *% on + Excess* | *Of the Amount over* |
|---|---|---|---|---|
| $ 0 | $ 17,000 | $ 0.00 | 10% | $ 0 |
| 17,000 | 69,000 | 1,700.00 | 15 | 17,000 |
| 69,000 | 139,350 | 9,500.00 | 25 | 69,000 |
| 139,350 | 212,300 | 27,087.50 | 28 | 139,350 |
| 212,300 | 373,650 | 47,513.50 | 33 | 212,300 |
| 379,150 | | 102,574.00 | 35 | 379,150 |

**2011 Tax Rates Head of Household**

*If taxable income is*

| *Over* | *But not over* | *The Tax is* | *% on + Excess* | *Of the Amount over* |
|---|---|---|---|---|
| $ 0 | $ 12,150 | $ 0.00 | 10% | $ 0 |
| 12,150 | 46,250 | 1,215.00 | 15% | 12,150 |
| 46,250 | 119,400 | 6,330.00 | 25% | 46,250 |
| 119,400 | 193,350 | 24,617.50 | 28% | 119,400 |
| 199,350 | 379,150 | 45,323.50 | 33% | 193,350 |
| 379,150 | | 106,637.50 | 35% | 379,150 |

**2011 Tax Rates Married, Filing Separate**

*If taxable income is*

| *Over* | *But not over* | *The Tax is* | *% on + Excess* | *Of the Amount over* |
|---|---|---|---|---|
| $ 0 | $ 8,500 | $ 0.00 | 10% | $ 0 |
| 8,500 | 34,500 | 850.50 | 15% | 8,500 |
| 34,500 | 69,675 | 4,750.00 | 25% | 34,500 |
| 69,675 | 106,150 | 13,543.75 | 28% | 69,675 |
| 106,150 | 189,575 | 23,756.75 | 33% | 106,150 |
| 189,575 | | 51,287.00 | 35% | 189,575 |

A typical example illustrating the use of the tax rate schedules is given below.

### Example 24

R, single, has taxable income of $175,000 for 2011. R's gross tax liability is $42,647, computed using the rate schedules as follows:

| | |
|---|---|
| Tax on $174,400 . . . . . . . . . . | $42,449.00 |
| Plus: Tax on income above $174,400 [($175,000 − $174,400 = $600) × 33%] . . . . . . | 198.00 |
| Tax liability . . . . . . . . . . | $42,647.00 |

### Tax Reform and the Tax Rates

One of the major changes made by the Bush administration in 2001 was to cut the tax rates for individual taxpayers. Before the change, there were five brackets: 15%, 28%, 31%, 35% and 39.6%. The new law created the six brackets that currently exist: 10%, 15%, 25%, 28%, 33% and 35%. The lower brackets were scheduled to expire in 2010. However, in 2010 Congress extended them to remain through 2012 when they revert back to the former rates. Consequently, without Congressional action, tax rates are scheduled to increase in 2013. Note that all of the tax brackets (i.e., their widths) are adjusted for inflation annually.

## Special Tax Computation Rules

Unfortunately, the computation of the income tax is not always as straightforward as shown in *Example 24* above. For certain individuals, special rules must be followed.

### Persons Claimed as Dependents

**LO.6**
Explain the special approach used in computing the tax liability of certain children.

As one might deduce from the brief introduction to tax rates, one of the most fundamental principles of tax planning concerns minimizing the marginal tax rate that applies to the taxpayer's income. The significance of this principle is easily understood when it is recognized that Federal marginal tax rates have at times exceeded 90 percent. Even with the reduction of marginal rates to their current levels, minimizing the tax rate can provide benefits.

Historically, one of the most popular techniques to minimize the tax rate has been to shift income to a taxpayer in a lower tax bracket such as a child. As discussed in Chapter 5, this could be accomplished most easily by giving the child income-producing property. For example, a parent might establish a savings account for a child. In this way, the income would be taxed to the child at his or her low rate rather than the parents' high rate. In addition, this strategy—absent any special rules—takes advantage of the personal exemption and standard deduction available to a child.

Congress has long recognized the tax-saving potential inherent in such plans. For this reason, it is not surprising that it has taken steps to limit the opportunities. These are:

1. **Personal exemption.** A taxpayer who can be claimed as a dependent on another taxpayer's return is not entitled to a personal exemption. This rule effectively prohibits all children from claiming a personal exemption. Observe that *without this rule*, a child could currently receive up to $3,700 (2011) of income tax-free due to the exemption.
2. **Standard deduction.** The standard deduction available to a taxpayer who can be claimed as a dependent on another taxpayer's return is limited to the *greater* of $950 or $300 plus his or her earned income—but not to exceed the standard deduction amount ($5,800 for single taxpayers in 2011). Without this rule, a child could receive unearned income such as interest of up to $5,800 tax-free.

3. **Kiddie tax.** As explained further below, the investment income (technically referred to as unearned income) of most children is generally taxed as if the parent received it to the extent it exceeds \$1,900.[43] Absent this provision, affectionately known as the *kiddie tax*, a parent could shift up to \$34,500 of taxable income to the child in 2011, who would pay taxes at a rate of 15 percent or less.

The effect of these provisions is to severely limit the success of any schemes designed to shift income to children.

## Example 25

V, age 15, lives at home and may be claimed as a dependent on her parents' return. Several years ago, V's grandfather died, leaving her with a tidy sum to help send her to college. For 2011 V received interest income of \$3,225. Her taxable income is computed as follows:

| | | |
|---|---|---|
| Adjusted gross income | | \$3,225 |
| Less: Standard deduction | \$950 | |
| Personal exemption | +0 | −950 |
| Taxable income | | \$2,275 |

Note that, in computing V's taxable income, her standard deduction is limited to \$950 (the larger of \$300 plus her earned income, \$300, or \$950). The limitation is imposed because she is eligible to be claimed as a dependent on another taxpayer's return. For the same reason, she is not allowed to claim her own personal exemption deduction. In addition, a portion of her income is subject to the kiddie tax as explained below.

## Example 26

Assume the same facts in *Example 25*, except that V also earns \$2,000 from a part-time job. V's taxable income is determined as follows:

| | | |
|---|---|---|
| Adjusted gross income: | | |
| Earned income | \$ 2,000 | |
| Interest income | +3,225 | \$ 5,225 |
| Less: Standard deduction (\$2,000 earned income + \$300) | \$ 2,300 | |
| Personal exemption | +0 | −2,300 |
| Taxable income | | \$ 2,925 |

As in *Example 25*, because V is a dependent, she is not allowed to claim her personal exemption deduction, nor may she claim the full standard deduction of \$5,800. Note, however, that her standard deduction has increased because of her earned income. Her standard deduction is now \$2,300 (the *larger* of \$300 plus her earned income of \$2,000, or \$950). In effect, V is able to shelter income from tax with the standard deduction to the extent it is earned from personal services (plus another \$300).

[43] § 1(g). The annual threshold is adjusted for inflation and is twice the standard deduction for dependents.

### Kiddie Tax

The *kiddie tax* extends to children who at the close of the taxable year are either under 19 or are full-time students under the age of 24. However, the kiddie tax does not apply to the student group if their earned income exceeds one-half of the amounts spent on their support. For this purpose, scholarships received by a child are not included in the individual's total support. In addition, the kiddie tax does not apply if the child files a joint return or has no living parents.

The kiddie tax rules are triggered only when the affected child has *net unearned income*. For this purpose, unearned income generally includes investment income such as dividends, interest, capital gains, rents, royalties and income received from a trust. Net unearned income is unearned income in excess of $1,900 in 2011.[44] In short, most "children" who have unearned income exceeding the annual threshold, $1,900 in 2011, must compute their tax using a special procedure. The effect of this calculation is that the first $950 of unearned income is offset by the standard deduction and the second $950 of unearned income is taxed at the child's rates (currently 10 percent). Any unearned income exceeding $1,900 is taxed at the parents' top rates.

#### Example 27

J is 18 years old. In 2011, he received interest income from a savings account and earned income from his paper route. The table below shows several sample calculations of J's taxable income assuming various amounts of earned and unearned income. In addition. the amount taxed at his rates and his parents' rates is computed.

| | *A* | *B* | *C* | *D* |
|---|---|---|---|---|
| Unearned income | $1,950 | $ 500 | $1,950 | $ 3,200 |
| Earned income | 350 | 750 | 700 | 5,700 |
| Total | $2,300 | $1,250 | $2,650 | $ 8,900 |
| Standard deduction: | | | | |
| Greater of $950 or earned income + $300 not to exceed $5,700 standard deduction | –950 | –1,050 | –1,000 | –5,700 |
| Personal exemption | — | — | — | — |
| Taxable income (a) | $1,350 | $ 200 | $1,650 | $ 3,200 |
| Taxed at parents' rates | | | | |
| Unearned income > $1,900 (b) | $ 50 | $ 0 | $ 50 | $ 1,300 |
| Taxed at child's rates [(a) – (b)] | $1,300 | $ 200 | $1,600 | $ 1,900 |

In case B, there is no net unearned income because J's unearned income was less than $1,900. J has net unearned income in cases A, C, and D. In each case, the amount taxed at his parents' rate is the amount by which the child's unearned income exceeded $1,900. Any other income is taxed at the regular rates for the child.

When the child has net unearned income, the tax must be computed as if such income had been the parents' income. The child is required to pay the tax computed using his or her

[44] § 1(i)(4).

parents' rates except in rare cases where the tax computed in the normal manner is greater (in which case the higher tax must be paid). The tax computation cannot be completed until the parents' taxable income is known.

Although the thrust of the kiddie tax is to tax income that would be taxed at a 10 or 15 percent rate at a higher rate, determination of the child's actual tax is somewhat complicated.[45] The tax is computed on Form 8615 using the following approach:

| | |
|---|---|
| Taxable income from parents' return | $xxx |
| Add: Net unearned income of child (children) | +xxx |
| Equals: Total income taxed at parents' rate | $xxx |
| Tax on total income taxed at parents' rate | $xxx |
| Minus: Tax on parents' income | −xxx |
| Equals: Parental tax on child's net unearned income | $xxx |
| Add: Tax on child's remaining taxable income at child's rate | +xxx |
| Equals: Total tax on child's taxable income | $xxx |

The first step in this process requires the calculation of the parental tax. This is accomplished by combining the income of the parents with the net unearned income of the child and then calculating the total tax on this combined income as if the parents had reported all the income. Then, by subtracting the tax on the parents' income (from the parents' return), the amount of tax that the parents would have paid on the child's net unearned income is determined. This *parental tax* is, therefore, the tax that the parents would have paid on the net unearned income had they reported it directly.

The final part of the calculation involves determining the tax on the child's remaining taxable income at the child's tax rate of 10 percent (or higher). This tax is added to the parental tax to arrive at the child's total tax.

In those situations where the parents are divorced, the parental tax is computed using the taxable income of the custodial parent (or joint income if he or she has remarried). Where the parents file separate returns, the tax is computed using the greater of the parents' two taxable incomes.

In computing the tax on the parent *including* the child's net unearned income, such income is not considered when computing any of the parents' deductions or credits (e.g., the deduction for miscellaneous itemized deductions, which is limited to the amount that exceeds two percent of adjusted gross income).

Where there is more than one child under 18 with net unearned income, the parental tax must be computed using the net unearned income of all children. As shown below, the tax so computed is then allocated pro rata based on each child's relative contribution to total net unearned income.

$$\frac{\text{Child's net unearned income}}{\text{All children's net unearned income}} \times \text{Parental tax} = \text{Child's share of parental tax}$$

[45] If the child has dividend income or long-term capital gains, such income continues to be taxed at the favorable rates at the parents' level. See Form 8615.

## Example 28

In 2011, T, age 15, received $5,300 in interest from a savings account. Similarly, his sister, V, age 6, had $2,500 of interest income. Since T and V are under 19 and have net unearned income of $3,400 ($5,300 – $1,900) and $600 ($2,500 – $1,900), respectively, their tax must be computed in the special manner. The children's parents had income of $105,000. In addition, due to special medical problems of the father, they incurred $12,875 of medical expenses. The couple also has other itemized deductions of $10,000. T's tax is computed as follows:

| | |
|---|---|
| 1. Tax on parents computed in the normal manner: | |
| Adjusted gross income | $105,000 |
| Deductions: | |
| Medical expenses [$12,875 – (7.5% × $105,000 = $7,875)] | –5,000 |
| Other itemized deductions | –10,000 |
| Exemptions (4 × $3,700) | –14,800 |
| Taxable income computed in the normal manner | $ 75,200 |
| Tax [$9,500 + 25% ($75,200 – $69,000 = $6,200)] | $ 11,050 |
| 2. Tax on parents including net unearned income of all children: | |
| Parents' taxable income computed in the normal manner | $ 75,200 |
| Net unearned income of children: | |
| ($3,400 + $600) | +4,000 |
| Taxable income including net unearned income | $ 79,200 |
| Tax [$9,500 + 25% ($79,200 – $69,000 = $10,200)] | $ 12,050 |
| 3. Parental tax: | |
| Tax on parents including net unearned income | $ 12,050 |
| –Tax on parents computed in the normal manner | –11,050 |
| = Parental Tax | $ 1,000 |
| 4. T's share of parental tax [$1,000 × ($3,400 ÷ $4,000)] = | $ 850 |
| 5. Tax on T excluding net unearned income: | |
| Interest income | $ 5,300 |
| – Net unearned income | –3,400 |
| – Standard deduction (as limited for dependents) | –950 |
| – Exemption deduction (none for dependents) | –0 |
| Taxable income | $ 950 |
| Tax (10% × $950) | $ 95 |
| 6. Total tax on T: | |
| Tax on T excluding net unearned income | $ 95 |
| + Parental Tax | +850 |
| = T's total tax | $ 945 |

The total parental tax of $1,000 is the product of the net unearned income of $4,000 ($3,400 + $600) and the parents' marginal tax rate of 25%. Note that the parents' medical expense deduction is computed without net unearned income of the children (i.e., the percentage limitation is based on $105,000 rather than $109,000).

### Election to Report Child's Income on Parents' Return

In order to simplify the return filing process, parents may elect to include on their own return the unearned income of a child if certain conditions are satisfied.[46] Note that this is contrary to the normal procedure where the child files his or her own return and pays the tax computed with respect to the parents' rates. This election eliminates the hassle of filing separate returns for each child. However, the election can only be made where the child is under age 19, his or her income is more than $950 and less than $9,500 in 2010, and it consists *solely* of interest and dividends. The election is not available if estimated taxes have been paid or taxes have been withheld on dividend or interest income (i.e., the child is subject to back-up withholding).

Although making the election may make it easier to file, it may not be wise. Inclusion of the child's income, increases the parents' A.G.I. and therefore may reduce the deductions and credits that are phased-out based on A.G.I.

## DETERMINATION OF NET TAX DUE OR REFUND

Once the tax is determined using the tax tables, tax rate schedules, or the special tax computation procedures described above, it is reduced by the amount of any credits or prepayments. The primary prepayments are the Federal income tax withheld from the taxpayer's salary or wages by an employer, quarterly estimated tax payments, and the estimated tax paid when an extension of time to file a return is requested. Estimated tax payments and extensions of time to file are discussed later in this chapter.

Numerous credits are allowed in computing the Federal income tax. The credit most frequently encountered on an uncomplicated income tax return is the child care credit. This and other credits are discussed in detail in Chapter 13.

## ✓ CHECK YOUR KNOWLEDGE

### Review Question 1

What are the top and bottom tax rates for individuals?

It depends on the year. For 2011, the lowest rate is 10 percent and the highest rate is 35 percent (on taxable income over $379,150 for Married Filing Jointly, Single or Head of Household).

### Review Question 2

Several years ago Grandma gave her grandchild K, now 17, $20,000 to be used for her college education. All of the money was invested in stock. This year K's dad, acting on her behalf, sold some of the stock for a $4,050 short-term capital gain. K's parents are in the 35 percent tax bracket.

**a.** Compute K's taxable income and K's tax.

| | |
|---|---|
| Income (unearned) | $4,050 |
| Standard deduction: | |
| Greater of $950 or $300 plus earned income | –950 |
| Exemption | 0 |
| Taxable income | $3,100 |

K's personal exemption and standard deduction are limited since she can be claimed as a dependent on her parent's return. Consequently, she is not entitled to an exemption, and her standard deduction is $950 since she has no earned income. K is also subject to the kiddie tax since she is less than 19. In computing K's tax, the amount of unearned income in excess of $1,900 is $2,150 ($4,050 – $1,900), which must be taxed at her parents' rates while the remainder is taxed at her rates. Thus her tax is $848 [(35% × $2,150) + ($950 × 10%)].

**b.** Assume there were no kiddie tax. How much unearned income could be shifted to a dependent child and taxed at the child's 15 percent or lower rate rather than the parents'rate?

---

[46] § 1(g)(7). The parents use Form 8814 for this purpose. If the child file his or her own return, the child uses Form 8615 to compute the tax.

The 10 percent bracket for 2011 extends from taxable income of $1 to $8,500 and the 15 percent bracket extends from $8,501 to $34,500 for single taxpayers. Plus, another $950 escapes tax all together due to the child's standard deduction.

## Filing Requirements

**LO.7**
Describe the filing requirements for individual taxpayers.

Individual taxpayers with extremely low levels of income are not required to file a Federal income tax return. In general, a taxpayer is not required to file an income tax return for the year if his or her gross income is less than the *total* of his or her standard deduction (including the additional amount for the elderly but not the blind) *plus* personal exemptions (but not dependency exemptions).[47] These taxpayers generally are not liable for any Federal income tax. The filing requirement is based on gross income, so taxpayers who have gross incomes exceeding specified thresholds *must* file even if they owe no Federal income tax. A partial list of filing requirements for 2011 and how they are computed is illustrated in Exhibit 4-7.

In addition to the general requirement for filing (gross income is at least as much as the taxpayer's standard deduction + personal exemptions), certain individuals *must* file returns. These include:

1. Any taxpayer who has self-employment income of $400 or more
2. An individual who is claimed as a dependent on another taxpayer's return *and* who has unearned income at least equal to his or her minimum standard deduction (i.e., generally $950, but increased by the additional amount for elderly or blind taxpayers)[48]
3. Any person who receives any advance payments of earned income credit

### Form 1040

The individual taxpayer is required to file Form 1040, along with related forms and schedules. A complicated return involves many forms and schedules in addition to the Form 1040, whereas a simpler return may require only a few or no attached schedules.

Two simplified forms are provided for taxpayers with uncomplicated tax calculations. The Form 1040EZ is available for taxpayers who are single or married filing jointly and have no dependents. To qualify, the taxpayer's income normally must consist only of salaries and wages plus interest income of $1,500 or less. The only allowable deductions on this form are the personal exemption amount and the standard deduction.

The Form 1040A is available for a large number of taxpayers who do not itemize their deductions and have no income other than salaries and wages, dividends, interest, and unem-

**EXHIBIT 4.7 Gross Income Filing Requirements for 2011**

| | *Personal Exemption* | + | *Standard Deduction* | + | *Elderly Standard Deductions* | = | *2011 Gross Income* |
|---|---|---|---|---|---|---|---|
| Single person < 65 | $3,700 | | $ 5,800 | | — | | $ 9,500 |
| Single person ≥ 65 | 3,700 | | 5,800 | | $1,450 | | 10,950 |
| Head of household < 65 | 3,700 | | 8,500 | | — | | 12,200 |
| Head of household ≥ 65 | 3,700 | | 8,500 | | 1,450 | | $13,650 |
| Married filing jointly, both < 65 | 7,400 | | 11,600 | | — | | 19,000 |
| Married filing jointly, both ≥ 65 | 7,400 | | 11,600 | | 2,300 | | 21,300 |
| Married filing separately | 3,700 | | | | | | 3,700 |
| Surviving spouse < 65 | 3,700 | | 11,600 | | — | | 15,300 |
| Surviving spouse ≥ 65 | 3,700 | | 11,600 | | 1,150 | | 16,450 |
| Dependents | | | | | | | Special Rules |

[47] § 6012(a)(1).

[48] § 6012(a)(1)(C)(i). As stated earlier, certain children under the age of 19 are not required to file a tax return *if* their parents *elect* to include the child's income on their return and pay the appropriate additional tax.

ployment compensation. This form provides for deductions for individual retirement account (IRA) contributions, personal and dependency exemptions, and the earned income credit.

## Example 29

Jeremy S. Allen, a registered nurse, and Shelly R. Allen, an air traffic controller, are married and file a joint income tax return for 2010. They are the sole support of their three children: William, Susan, and Gregory (all under age 17). The following information is from their records for 2010:

| | | |
|---|---|---|
| Salaries and wages, Jeremy | | $32,875 |
| Federal income tax withheld | $1,700 | |
| Salaries and wages, Shelly | | 44,900 |
| Federal income tax withheld | 2,400 | |
| Interest income—Mercantile National Bank | | 1,800 |
| Interest income—U.S. Treasury Bonds | | 700 |
| Interest income—Ben Franklin Savings | | 500 |
| Itemized deductions are as follows: | | |
| Unreimbursed prescription drugs | | 200 |
| Hospitalization insurance | | 700 |
| Unreimbursed fees of doctors, hospitals, etc. | | 2,100 |
| Real estate taxes on residence | | 1,200 |
| State income taxes paid | | 3,400 |
| Interest paid on original home mortgage | | 8,500 |
| Investment interest | | 400 |
| Charitable contribution—First Church | | 1,300 |
| Charitable contribution—Home State University | | 200 |
| Preparation of prior year's tax return | | 275 |

The Allens' adjusted gross income is $80,775 ($32,875 + $44,900 + $3,000 interest income) since there were no deductions for A.G.I. The deductible amount of their itemized deductions is $15,000, summarized as follows:

| | |
|---|---|
| Medical expenses exceeding $6,058 [$3,000 < (7.5% × $80,775 = $6,058)] | $ 0 |
| Deductible taxes ($1,200 + $3,400) | 4,600 |
| Qualifying home mortgage interest | 8,500 |
| Investment interest | 400 |
| Charitable contributions | 1,500 |
| Miscellaneous itemized deductions exceeding $1,616 [$275 < (2% × $80,775 = $1,616)] | 0 |
| Total itemized deductions | $15,000 |

The Allens' taxable income, gross tax, and tax refund for 2010 are determined as follows:

| | | | |
|---|---|---|---|
| Adjusted gross income | | | $ 80,775 |
| Less: | Itemized deductions | $ 15,000 | |
| | Personal and dependency exemptions ($3,650 × 5) | +18,250 | −33,250 |
| Equals: Taxable income | | | $ 47,525 |
| Gross Tax (from 2010 Tax Table) | | | $ 6,291 |
| Less: | Prepayments ($1,700 + $2,400) | | −4,100 |
| | Child tax credit (3 × $1,000) | | −3,000 |
| Equals: Tax due or (refund) | | | ($ 809) |

The Allens' completed 2010 tax return is shown in the Appendix at the end of the chapter. It consists of a Form 1040 plus Schedules A and B.

The more common tax forms and schedules used by individual taxpayers are listed in Exhibit 4-8. Copies of these forms are contained in Appendix B at the end of the text.

### EXHIBIT 4.8 List of Common Forms and Schedules Used by Individual Taxpayers

| | |
|---|---|
| **Form 1040** | **U.S. Individual Income Tax Return** |
| *Accompanying Schedules:* | |
| Schedule A | Itemized deductions |
| Schedule B | Interest and dividend income |
| Schedule C | Profit (or loss) from business or profession |
| Schedule D | Capital gains and losses |
| Schedule E | Supplemental income schedule (rents, royalties, etc.) |
| Schedule F | Farm income and expenses |
| Schedule R | Credit for the elderly |
| Schedule SE | Computation of social security self-employment tax |
| *Accompanying Forms:* | |
| Form 2106 | Employee business expenses |
| Form 2210 | Underpayment of estimated tax by individuals |
| Form 2441 | Credit for child and dependent care expenses |
| Form 3800 | General business credit |
| Form 3903 | Moving expense adjustment |
| Form 4562 | Depreciation |
| Form 4684 | Casualties and thefts |
| Form 4797 | Supplemental schedule of gains and losses |
| Form 6251 | Alternative minimum tax computation |
| Form 6252 | Computation of installment sale income |
| Form 8582 | Passive activity losses |
| Form 8615 | Computation of tax for children under age 19 who have investment income of more than $1,900 |
| Form 8814 | Parents' election to report child's interest and dividends |
| *Other Common Forms:* | |
| Form 1040A | U.S. Individual Income Tax Return |
| Form 1040EZ | Income tax return for single filers with no dependents |
| Form 4868 | Application for automatic extension of time to file |

## DUE DATES FOR FILING RETURNS

**LO.8**
Explain when taxes must be paid and the penalties that apply for failure to pay on a timely basis.

The day on which a Federal return must be filed with the IRS depends upon what type of return is involved. Generally the tax returns must be filed on or before the due dates, which are as follows:[49]

| *Type of Return* | *Due Date* |
|---|---|
| Annual Individual Income Tax Returns | Fifteenth day of the fourth month following the close of the tax year (April 15 for calendar year individuals) |
| Annual C Corporation and S Corporation Income Tax Returns | Fifteenth day of third month following the close of the tax year (March 15 for calendar year corporations) |
| Annual Partnership, Estate, and Trust Income Tax Returns | Fifteenth day of the fourth month following the close of the year (April 15 for calendar year entities) |
| Estate Tax Returns | Nine months after the date of the descedent's death |
| Gift Tax Returns | April 15 (All gift tax returns are for a calendar year) |

Any return that is mailed via the U.S. Postal Service is deemed to be delivered when mailed, so any return postmarked on or before the above due dates is timely filed. If any of these due dates fall on Saturday, Sunday, or a legal holiday, the return must be filed on the succeeding day that is not a Saturday, Sunday, or legal holiday.

### Extension of Time to File

The Internal Revenue Code provides extensions of time for filing returns. The extension must be requested on or before the due date of the return. Currently, there is an *automatic* six-month extension for filing the individual income tax return (Form 1040). Thus the extended due date for calendar year individuals is October 15. If the taxpayer desires to use the six-month extension, he or she simply fills out Form 4868 and mails it to the IRS by the original due date along with a check covering the estimated balance due. It should be noted that an extension of time to file is not an extension of time to pay. There is *no extension* of time to pay the tax due.[50] The penalty for failing to pay the tax due is discussed below.

The extensions for other taxpayers are designed so that the extended due date is one month before the extended due date for individuals. Thus C corporations and S corporations are entitled to a six-month extension for filing their returns, resulting in an extended due date for calendar year corporations of September 15. Partnerships and trusts are entitled to a five-month extension, resulting in an extended due of September 15 if the calendar year is used.

### Interest

Whenever a taxpayer fails to pay the amount of tax owed by the due date of the return, interest is charged. To encourage payment, the rate is 3 percentage points higher than the Federal short-term rate. For the quarter January 1–March 31, 2011, the annual interest rate charge on such a deficiency is 3 percent (0% + 3%), compounded daily on the unpaid balance. Interest is generally charged from the day the tax is due (e.g., the due date of the return) and continues until the tax is paid.[51]

[49] § 6072(a).

[50] Reg. § 1.6081-4(a).

[51] § 6601(a). The rate is based on the federal short-term rate. Generally, the government pays interest to taxpayers in the case of overpayments, beginning on the due date for the tax (usually the due date for the tax return). The rate of interest is the same as that on underpayments for non-corporate taxpayers. See § 6621.

## PENALTIES

Around April 15, it is not uncommon to hear procrastinating taxpayers ask what happens if they neither file their returns nor pay their taxes on time. When either of these occurs, taxpayers not only have to pay interest but also penalties. There are three types of penalties that may apply:[52]

1. A penalty for *failure-to-file a return* by the due date;
2. A penalty for *failure-to-pay* at least 90 percent of the *tax* by the due date; and
3. A penalty for *failure to pay estimated taxes* during the course of the year.

If the taxpayer owes nothing or is entitled to a refund, these penalties do not apply even if he or she does not file a return. On the other hand, if the taxpayer has an amount due, any one or all three of these penalties could be imposed. In addition, since these penalties are technically additions to and part of the total tax liability, any interest that must be paid effectively includes *interest on the penalties*. Finally, if the taxpayer wants to obtain a refund, there are time limits for claiming it. Each of these possibilities is discussed below.

### Failure-to-File

Taxpayers who do not file their returns by the due date (e.g., April 15) or fail to obtain a proper extension on such date are subject to the *failure-to-file penalty*. Under § 6651, the penalty is 5 percent of the amount of tax due for each month the return is not filed.[53] The penalty cannot exceed a maximum of 25 percent (e.g., 5% × 5 months). For this purpose, any fraction of a month is counted as a full month. To illustrate how harsh this rule can be, consider a taxpayer who owes $10,000 and his return is postmarked one day late. Even though the return is only one day late, the failure-to-file penalty is 5 percent for an entire month on the amount due or $500 (5% × 1 month × $10,000 amount due)!

To deal with the administrative costs of handling small penalties, a minimum penalty exists. If the return is more than 60 days late, the minimum penalty is $135 or 100% of the tax due, whichever is less.[54] For example, a taxpayer who owes $300 and files her return on June 16 would normally owe a penalty of $45 (5% × 3 months × $300) but the minimum penalty is $135 (the lesser of $135 or the tax due of $300).

Taxpayers who fail to file their returns may not be penalized in certain situations. The penalty is not imposed if the failure was due to reasonable cause and not willful neglect. In addition, since the penalty is based on the amount due no penalty results if there is no amount due. Because of this rule taxpayers who are entitled to a refund are not penalized for filing late since there is no amount due.

### Failure-to-Pay Penalty

Filing a return is not enough to avoid penalty. Section 6651 also imposes a *failure-to-pay* penalty if a taxpayer does not pay at least 90 percent of the total tax on or before the due date of the return.[55] In other words, the IRS does not assess a penalty if an extension of time to file is properly obtained and the tax due is less than 10 percent of the total tax shown on the return (i.e., gross tax after credits but before any withholding and estimated tax payments). The penalty can also be avoided if the failure is due to reasonable cause and not willful neglect. If the taxpayer does not meet either test, the *failure-to-pay* penalty is one-half of 1 percent (.5% or .005) per month (or any fraction of a month) up to a maximum 25 percent of the amount due.[56] Note that if the taxpayer files an extension and pays 90 percent of the tax by the due date, the taxpayer must still pay interest on any tax due but avoids both the failure-to-pay and failure-to-file penalties.

---

[52] Technically, the Internal Revenue Code does not refer to these as penalties but as "additions to the tax." See §§ 6651 and 6654.

[53] § 6651(a)(1). If the failure to file is fraudulent, the penalty is 15 percent per month up to a maximum of 75 percent. § 6551(f).

[54] § 6651(a)(1)

[55] § 6651(a)(2)

[56] § 6651(a)(2)

### Example 30

As the time approached for filing his tax return, W was too busy to file. Accordingly, on April 15 he requested an automatic extension of time to file until October 15. W estimated that his total tax would be $6,000, and he had prepaid taxes of $5,300 in the form of withholding. Therefore, when he filed his request for an extension, he paid $700 ($6,000 – $5,300). By filing a timely extension, he is treated as filing a return and avoids the failure-to-file a return penalty. When he finally did file his return on June 15, W's earlier estimate proved wrong and the return showed a total tax of $7,000 and a tax due of $1,000 [$7,000 total tax due – $6,000 ($5,300 withholding + $700 payment with the extension)]. W is required to pay a penalty for failure-to-pay since the total paid by the due date, $6,000 is less than 90 percent of the tax due, $6,300 (90% × $7,000). The amount of the penalty is based on the total amount due that was unpaid on April 15, $1,000 ($7,000 – $6,000 paid) and not the amount short of the 90 percent requirement ($300). In addition, assuming the current rate of interest on underpayments is 10%, W must pay interest of about $17 ($1,000 amount due at 10% annually, compounded daily until June 15 for 61 days).

**Interaction of Failure-to-Pay and Failure-to-File Penalties.** When both the failure-to-file and failure-to-pay penalties apply, the penalty for failure-to-file to file is reduced by the amount of the penalty for failure to pay.

### Example 31

K forgot to file her Federal tax return for the most recent calendar year. When she finally filed the return on November 1 (7 months late), her return showed a gross tax of $6,200 and a tax due after withholding of $800. Assuming the current rate of interest on underpayments is 3%, K must pay not only her tax due of $800 but also late penalties of $208 ($28 + $180) and interest on the tax and penalties of $16, for a total of $1,024, as computed below.

| | | |
|---|---|---|
| Tax due | | $800 |
| Penalties: | | |
| Failure to pay ($800 × .005 × 7) | | 28 |
| Failure to file: | | |
| Failure-to-file penalty ($800 × .05 × 5) | $200 | |
| Reduced by failure-to-pay penalty ($800 × .005 × 5) | (20) | 180 |
| Total tax and penalties | | $1,008 |
| Interest on tax and penalties ($1008 × 3% × 199/365) | | 16 |
| Total due | | $1,024 |

Note that the minimum failure-to-file penalty is not triggered here since the penalty of $180 computed in the normal manner exceeds the minimum penalty of $135 (the lesser of the total tax due, $800, or $135).

## Estimated Tax Payments

The last of the three "late" penalties is the penalty for failure to pay estimated taxes.[57] This penalty should be distinguished from the *failure-to-file* and *failure-to-pay* penalties that begin

[57] § 6654

to run as of the due date of the return. The estimated tax penalty applies if the taxpayer fails to pay sufficient taxes *during the year*. In essence, the law sets forth a series of intermediate due dates for estimated tax payments during the tax year.

The estimated tax penalty is a product of the "pay-as-you-go" system for collection of taxes. Under this system, taxpayers are required to prepay Federal income taxes periodically during the year. Prepayments are made through withholding from certain types of income (e.g., salary and wages) and by making estimated tax payments. Failure to make adequate payments during the year results in a penalty that is computed much like interest.

As a practical matter, estimated tax penalties do not affect the vast majority of individuals. For those receiving only salaries and wages, withholding is usually sufficient to cover the required payments. However, those taxpayers with other income may need to make up the shortfall by making estimated tax payments. Regardless of the causes, if the amount of taxes paid during the year is insufficient, the penalty may apply.

**Imposition of the Estimated Tax Penalty.** Individual taxpayers avoid the estimated tax penalty if total prepayments (estimated taxes and withholding) equal or exceed the *required annual payment*, which is the lesser of:[58]

1. 90% of the tax shown on the return, or
2. 100% of the tax shown on the return for the individual for the preceding year. If A.G. I. in the prior year exceeded $150,000, the payment must be 110% of the prior year's tax.
3. The annualized income installment

For this purpose, the tax due includes the self-employment tax as well as the alternative minimum tax and certain other taxes. If the total amounts paid are less than the amount due, an *underpayment* exists and the penalty must be calculated and paid as explained below. However, there is no estimated tax penalty if the underpayment is less than $1,000.[59]

## Example 32

For 2010, T, a single individual, reported an adjusted gross income of $165,000, a taxable income of $140,000, and a tax liability (after credits) of $40,000. In 2011 his tax liability is $60,000. Under the general rules T must have paid the lesser of 90% of the current year's tax, $54,000, or 100% of last year's tax, $40,000, to avoid the underpayment penalty. However, because T's adjusted gross income exceeded $150,000 in the prior year, 2010, he is subject to the 110% rule regarding his estimated tax payments for the current year, 2011. As a result, he can avoid underpayment penalties with respect to 2011 only if he pays the lesser of the following:

| | | |
|---|---|---|
| 1. | 90% of the current year's tax of $60,000 | $54,000 |
| 2. | 110% of last year's tax of $40,000 | 44,000 |

Thus, if T pays at least $44,000 on a timely basis during 2011, he will not be subject to any penalty for failing to pay estimated taxes.

The required payment is due in four equal installments or 25 percent on each due date. Although it is convenient to say that the payments are made on a quarterly basis, this is not quite the case. For calendar year taxpayers, the amounts are due on April 15, June 15, September 15, and January 15.

Whether the payments are adequate is determined at the end of each "quarter." For this purpose, withholding is treated as if it occurred proportionately throughout the year. For example, if a taxpayer had withholding of $3,650, he or she would be treated as if $10 was withheld each day. At the end of each quarter, the payments to date are compared to the

[58] § 6654(d)

[59] § 6654(e)(1)

amount required to be paid. If the proper amount has not been paid, an underpayment exists and a penalty must be paid.

The penalty is assessed on the amount of the underpayment at the same rate as the interest that is charged on tax deficiencies. This penalty is separate from the failure-to-pay penalty as well as the interest which is charged. As noted earlier, interest and the failure-to-pay penalty apply to underpayments of tax due as of the due date of the return (e.g., April 15, 2012). In contrast, the estimated tax penalty is charged from the date each estimated tax installment was due (e.g., April 15, June 15, September 15 of *2011* and January 15, 2012) until the tax is paid (or, if the tax is paid late, the due date of the return).

## Example 33

For 2010 and 2011 G's gross tax was $12,000 and $16,000, respectively. G's withholding for 2011 was $6,500 and his estimated tax payments were $1,500 on April 15 and June 15 and $500 on September 15 and January 15. G's underpayment is determined as follows:

| | *Payment Due Date* | | | |
|---|---|---|---|---|
| | *4/15* | *6/15* | *9/15* | *1/15* |
| Percentage due | 25% | 50% | 75% | 100% |
| 90% of current year's tax ($16,000 × .90 × percentage due) | $ 3,600 | $ 7,200 | $ 10,800 | $14,400 |
| 100% of prior year's tax ($12,000 × percentage due) | $ 3,000 | $ 6,000 | $ 9,000 | $12,000 |
| Payments to date: | | | | |
| Withholding | $ 1,625 | $ 3,250 | $ 4,875 | $ 6,500 |
| Estimated tax payments | +1,500 | +3,000 | +3,500 | +4,000 |
| Total | $ 3,125 | $ 6,250 | $ 8,375 | $10,500 |

G's payments are adequate for the first quarter and the second quarter, since the payments up to each date exceed the lesser of the two required amounts (the prior year's tax in both cases). As of the third payment date, G is underpaid by $625 ($9,000 − $8,375); and as of the last payment date, he is underpaid by $1,500 ($12,000 − $10,500). The penalty is computed based on these amounts from the due date until the day they are paid (or April 15, if earlier).

Assuming the current rate of penalty is 10% and G does not pay his tax early, G's penalty would be $58, which is the penalty on $625 from September 15 through January 15 [$625 × .1 × 122 days/365 days) = $21] *plus* that on $1,500 from January 15 through April 15 [$1,500 × (.1 × 90 days/365 days) = $37].

The penalty for failure to make adequate estimated tax payments is calculated on Form 2210 (see Appendix for a sample form). Unless a taxpayer can reduce the penalty by applying the annualized income installment or otherwise, he or she may simply let the IRS calculate this penalty and assess a deficiency for it. In addition, the IRS may waive the underpayment penalty in the event of a casualty or unusual circumstances where it might be inequitable to impose the additional tax. The IRS may also waive the penalty for retired taxpayers who are at least age 62 or disabled where the underpayment was due to reasonable cause rather than willful neglect.

### Annualized Income Installment

If income for a year is earned disproportionately during the year, the taxpayer may be able to avoid penalty for one or more of the first three payments under the *annualized income installment* method.[60] Under this method, no penalty is imposed when the payment to date

[60] § 6654(d).

exceeds the tax which would be due on the income for the months preceding the payment date determined on an annualized basis.

### Example 34

F, a calendar year individual, is engaged in a seasonal business that earns most of its income during the fourth quarter. F is able to demonstrate that the income was earned as follows:

| | Payment Due Date | | | |
|---|---|---|---|---|
| | 4/15 | 6/15 | 9/15 | 1/15 |
| Months preceding payment | 3 | 5 | 8 | 12 |
| Net income earned for the months preceding the payment | $10,000 | $18,000 | $25,000 | $50,000 |
| Annualized amount [Net income × (12/months to date)] | $40,000 | $43,200 | $37,500 | $50,000 |

To apply this exception, the tax on the annualized income is determined. There is an underpayment only if the estimated tax payments are less than the appropriate portion of the tax on the annualized income.

The required payment for April 15 is the fraction 3 months ÷ 12 months times the tax on $40,000. If the tax on $40,000 is $8,000, F has no underpayment for the first payment so long as she paid $2,000 ($8,000 × 3/12) or more. If she had paid less, the underpayment would be the amount by which $2,000 exceeded the payments. A similar process would be followed for each quarter.

To apply the annualized income installment calculations, a taxpayer completes a worksheet that accompanies the Form 2210. If this method is used to the benefit of the taxpayer for one payment, it must be used for *all* four payments.

### Other Penalties

As mentioned in Chapter 2, many other penalties exist to ensure proper compliance with the tax laws. For example, the Code provides for an accuracy-related penalty of 20 percent of the amount of understatement due to negligence or intentional disregard of the rules (e.g., failing to report income), or substantial valuation misstatements.[61] In addition, severe penalties, both civil and criminal, exist for fraud.[62]

## Claim for Refund

The vast majority of taxpayers actually overpay their taxes and are entitled to a refund. For example, the IRS reported in 2007 that of the 143 million returns filed about 107.7 million (about 75 percent) claimed a refund. On average, this represented a refund of about $2,488 per return. While most people routinely file their returns and receive their refund checks, others procrastinate. Unfortunately, some people assume it makes no difference how late they file if they wish to recover a refund. That can be a costly mistake. As a general rule, the Code requires taxpayers to file a tax return to claim a refund within two years of paying the tax, *deemed* to be April 15 in most cases.[63] Taxpayers who file a timely return, but subsequently realize that they overpaid, have a bit longer—three years from the due date of the return.

[61] § 6653 (a)(1)

[62] § 6653(b)

[63] See § 6511 and § 6513

**Example 35**

With April 15, 2009 just a few days away, C made a few quick calculations regarding his 2008 tax liability and determined that his tax was $12,000. Knowing that he had $14,000 withheld and did not owe any tax, C did not file a return. C continued to put off filing a return until one day he received a letter from the IRS. In the letter dated November 2011, the IRS explained that based on information available to it C owed a tax of $1,500. In response, C finally filed a correct return on May 1, 2012, showing that he did in fact owe $12,000 in tax and the government should refund him his overpayment of $2,000 ($14,000 – $12,000). C is not entitled to any of the $2,000 refund. Since C did not file a timely return on April 15, 2009, the time for filing a refund claim expired two years from the date the tax was paid, April 15, 2011. By procrastinating, C lost his entire refund. Had he filed a timely return, the date for claiming the refund would have been three years after the return was filed or April 15, 2012.

The two year rule applies if the taxpayer did not file a return.[64] If a return was filed, a claim for a refund can be filed by the later of three years from the date of filing the original return (April 15 if filed before such date), or two years from the time the tax was paid. In situations where a return has been filed, the claim for refund usually arises from the filing of an amended individual income tax return (i.e., Form 1040X—see Appendix).

**Example 36**

K filed a timely return for 2010 on March 12, 2011. The total tax on the return was $5,500, and after withholding of $4,700, K owed $800. K's return was audited and she was required to pay a deficiency of $200 on June 3, 2012. K may file a claim for refund for any part of the tax of $5,700 ($5,500 on the original return plus the additional tax of $200) until April 15, 2014 (three years from the date filed). A claim for up to $200 could be filed up until June 3, 2014 (two years from the date the $200 was paid).

## Statute of Limitations

**LO.9**
Describe the statute of limitations as it applies to the filing of tax returns.

Even in the administration of the Federal tax laws, all things must finally come to an end. As the U.S. Supreme Court has stated:

> Congress has regarded it as ill advised to have an income tax system under which there would never come a day of final settlement and which required both a taxpayer and the Government to stand ready forever and a day to produce vouchers, prove events, and recall details of all that goes into an income tax contest.[65]

Accordingly, there are certain time periods within which the IRS must take action *against* a taxpayer. If the Service does not take action within the prescribed time period, it is *barred* from pursuing the matter further. Technically the period in which an action must be commenced is called the Statute of Limitations. If the Statute of Limitations runs (expires) without any action on the part of the IRS, then the government is prohibited from assessing additional taxes for the expired periods.

Under the general rule, the IRS has three years from the date a return is filed to assess an additional tax liability against the taxpayer. If the tax return is filed before its due date, the three-year period for assessment begins *on* the due date.

---

[64] *Comm. v. Lundy*, 116 116 S. Ct. 647, 77 AFTR2d 406, 96-1 USTC 50,035 (USSC, 1996).

[65] *Rothensies v. Electric Storage Battery Co.*, 47-1 USTC ¶9106, 35 AFTR 297, 329 U.S. 296, 301 (USSC, 1946).

**EXHIBIT 4.9** **Interest and Penalties**

| Description | Violation | Amount |
|---|---|---|
| Interest on underpayments | Insufficient payment on due date; applies to tax and penalties | 3% + Federal short-term rate until paid |
| Failure to file | Tax return or extension not filed by due date | 5% per month of amount due (maximum 25%)<br>If more than 60 days late, minimum penalty is the smaller of $135 or 100% of the tax due |
| Failure to file (fraud) | Tax return or extension not filed by due date because of fraud | 15% per month of amount due (maximum 75%) |
| Failure to pay tax | Fail to pay 90% of tax due on due date | 0.5% per month of amount due (maximum 25%) |
| Failure to pay estimated taxes | Failure to pay 25% of required annual payment on 4/15, 6/15, 9/15 or 1/15 | 3% + Fed short-term rate until paid |
| Accuracy Related | Negligence or disregard of rules or regulations | 20% of tax underpayment |
| Fraud | | 75% of tax underpayment |
| Claim for refund | Filed later that 2 years after tax paid or 3 years after return filed | Loss of refund |

### Example 37

R, a calendar year taxpayer, files a 2011 income tax return (due April 15) on March 8, 2012. The IRS will be prevented from assessing R additional taxes for 2011 any time after April 15, 2015.

### Example 38

Refer to *Example 37*. If R files a 2011 income tax return on October 15, 2012, the IRS may assess additional taxes for 2011 at any time through October 15, 2015.

There are several important exceptions to the three-year time period for assessing additional taxes. First, if the taxpayer has filed a false or a fraudulent return with the intention to *evade* the tax, then the tax may be assessed (or a proceeding may be initiated in court without assessment) at *any time* in the future. Similarly, if the taxpayer fails to file a return, the Statute of Limitations will not begin to run. Interestingly, a willful failure to file, a negligent failure to file, or an innocent failure to file are all treated the same. Thus, under any of these circumstances there is no limit to the time in which the IRS may make an assessment or begin a court proceeding against the taxpayer.

In the case of a *substantial omission of income* from a tax return, the Statute of Limitations is extended to six years. A substantial omission is defined as an omission of income in excess of 25% of the gross income *reported* on the return.[66] If the omission of gross income was committed with the intent of evading the tax, however, the assessment period would be unlimited.

---

[66] § 6501(e).

**EXHIBIT 4.10 Periods Within Which Assessments Must Be Made**

| *Circumstances of Return* | *Period of Assessment* |
|---|---|
| Normal return had been filed | Three years from date of filing or due date, whichever is later |
| Return filed with substantial omission of gross income | Six years from date of filing or due date, whichever is later |
| No return is filed | No time limit |
| False or fraudulent return | No time limit |

**Example 39**

T, a calendar year taxpayer, unintentionally failed to include $8,000 of dividends in his 2010 tax return filed on April 15, 2011. If the $8,000 omitted is more than 25% of the gross income reported on T's 2010 return, the IRS may assess an additional income tax liability against him at any time until after April 15, 2017.

The periods within which assessments must be made are summarized in Exhibit 4-10, which follows.

## Indexation and the Federal Income Tax

Inflation has significant effects on a progressive tax rate structure stated in terms of a *constant* dollar. Taxpayers whose *real* incomes remain constant will have increasing levels of income, stated in terms of *nominal* dollars. Accordingly, their incomes will *creep up* into higher tax brackets. As an illustration, assume a taxpayer who earned $100,000 in 2007 is entitled to an annual raise at least equal to any increase in the Consumer Price Index (approximately four percent increase in 2007). Although his 2008 salary will creep up to $104,000, his before tax income in terms of 2007 prices remains at $100,000. At first glance, the taxpayer is as well off in 2008 as he was in 2007. Note, however, that the salary increase will be taxed at his marginal tax bracket, in which case he would have less after-tax income in real terms in 2008 than he had in 2007. Over time, this *bracket creep*, as it has been labeled, results in a larger portion of the taxpayer's earnings being paid to the Federal government. In effect, unlegislated tax increases occur.

For many years, Congress simply ignored the bracket creep phenomenon, choosing instead to allow the hidden tax increases to occur. As might be expected, this was a very palatable approach to politicians, particularly considering the alternative. The concerns of the few who objected were mollified in part by tax reduction packages enacted in 1981 and 1986. Both the Economic Recovery Tax Act of 1981 and the Tax Reform Act of 1986 directly reduced tax rates. These specific tax rate adjustments have since been followed by a permanent remedy for bracket creep: indexation.

Congress began adding the concept of indexation to the tax law in 1985. In 1986 it specified the amounts of the standard deduction, exemption amounts, and tax brackets for 1987 and 1988 (and the exemption amount for 1989). Thereafter, each of these amounts and many others have been annually adjusted for price level changes as measured by the Consumer Price Index.[67]

[67] See §§ 1(f), 1(g)(4), 639(c)(4), and 151(d)(3).

## ✓ CHECK YOUR KNOWLEDGE

### Review Question 1

Z, age 16, earned $2,000 from umpiring baseball games and refereeing soccer matches during the year. Z—rather Z's parents—wants to know whether he is required to file a tax return since this was his only income.

A taxpayer normally is not required to file a return if his or her income is less than the sum of the personal exemption amount and the standard deduction. However, this general rule does not apply to an individual who can be claimed as a dependent on another return since he or she is not entitled to claim a personal exemption and the standard deduction may be limited. In this case, all of Z's income is earned income and is therefore offset by his standard deduction of $2,300 (in 2011 the greater of $950 or $300 plus earned income). Consequently, it seems that there is no need for him to file a return. However, even though he is not subject to the income tax, he still must consider self-employment taxes (assuming the income is self-employment income). A return is required if a taxpayer has self-employment income of at least $400. As a result, Z must file a return.

### Review Question 2

After spending three years on the auditing staff of a large accounting firm, Norm took a job as controller of a small construction company. On the first day of the job, Norm looked around his new office and noticed a bunch of tax forms on the corner of his desk. One looked like the 1040 for his boss, and the others were corporate and partnership returns related to the company. At first he panicked. But then he realized that it was only the end of February and he had until April 15 to figure out what needed to be done. Should Norm relax?

Doubtful. Although returns for calendar year individuals and partnerships are normally due on April 15, the returns for C corporations or S corporations are due on March 15.

### Review Question 3

As always, April 15 arrived and T had not even begun to prepare his tax return. Not to worry, he thought. He could simply file for an extension.

**a.** Assume T does not file for an extension and files his return late. Are there any penalties?

Maybe. A failure-to-file and a failure-to-pay penalty may be imposed. Both penalties apply only if there is a tax due. If T is entitled to a refund, there is no penalty. The failure-to-file penalty is 5 percent per month on the balance due, not to exceed 25 percent.

**b.** How long is the extension?

An automatic extension of six months until October 15 is available.

**c.** Is an extension for time to file the return also an extension of time to pay the tax?

No. If T does not pay a sufficient amount of his tax by April 15, he faces penalties and interest imposed on the balance due.

**d.** Assuming T's gross tax liability before withholding is $10,000, how much must he pay by April 15 in order to avoid penalty?

T must pay 90 percent of the gross tax, or $9,000, by April 15. Otherwise, a penalty of ½ of 1 percent per month is imposed (up to a maximum of 25 percent) on the entire underpayment from the due date of the return (April 15).

**e.** Assume that T's net tax due for the year is $10,000 and he never files a return or a proper extension. What is the maximum failure-to-file and failure-to-pay penalty that can be assessed (ignore any potential fraud penalty and interest)?

The maximum failure-to-file and failure-to-pay penalty in this case is $4,750 (47.5% × $10,000). The failure-to-file penalty is 5 percent per month up to a maximum of 25 percent reduced by .5 percent per month for any month in which the failure-to-pay penalty also applies. Thus, the maximum failure-to-file penalty when the failure-to-pay penalty also applies is 22.5 percent [(5 × 5% = 25%) – (5 × .05 = 2.5%)]. The maximum failure-to-pay penalty is .5 percent per month up to a maximum of 25 percent. Adding the two penalties together produces a maximum penalty for failure to file the return and failure to pay the tax of 47.5 percent (22.5% + 25%) of the amount due.

**f.** If T fails to pay his tax and he is subject to penalties, how does interest work? Must he pay interest on just the tax due or on both the tax and the penalties?

He pays interest not only on the tax due but also on the penalties since the penalties are considered an additional tax.

## Review Question 4

Penalties for failing to file a return and failing to pay at least 90 percent of the tax due by the due date must be distinguished from penalties for failure to adequately make estimated tax payments during the year (underpayment penalties). Try the following true-false questions concerning estimated tax payments.

**a.** T finally filed her 2010 tax return and is now worrying about 2011. As a general rule, an individual taxpayer must pay 22.5 percent of her 2011 tax (even though she has no idea what it will be) 15 days after the end of each quarter (i.e., April 15, July 15, October 15, and January 15).

*False.* Although it is true that the taxpayer must normally pay 90 percent of the current tax due during the year (or 22.5 percent per installment), the installments are due on April 15, June 15, September 15, and January 15. Notwithstanding the fact that these payments are not truly paid on a quarterly basis, most people refer to them as "quarterly" estimated tax payments.

**b.** In lieu of paying 90 percent of their tax liability, individual taxpayers may avoid the underpayment penalty by paying 90 percent of last year's tax liability.

*False.* Penalty can be avoided if the taxpayer pays 90 percent of the current year's tax or 100 percent of last year's tax. However, the 100 percent rule is increased to 110 percent if the taxpayer's adjusted gross income in the prior year exceeded $150,000.

**c.** T earns a salary but also does some tinkering in the stock market. In October she realized that she should have paid estimated taxes throughout the year given what her income was going to be. Asking her employer to withhold an extra $36,500 in taxes during October, November, and December will help solve T's estimated tax problems for April, June, and September.

*True.* Withholding is treated as being paid ratably throughout the year. Therefore the additional $36,500 is not simply applied to the later due dates. Instead, T is treated as having paid $100 per day each day of the year. For example, she is treated as having paid an additional $10,500 (105 × $100) on April 15.

## Review Question 5

T filed her 2010 tax return on March 15, 2011. The IRS is barred from assessing a deficiency after

**a.** March 15, 2013
**b.** March 15, 2014
**c.** March 15, 2015
**d.** April 15, 2014
**e.** April 15, 2015

**d.** The statue of limitations runs out on April 15, 2014, three years from the later of the due date or the date of filing.

# Appendix

## Tax Return Illustrations

The following pages provide realistic examples of uncomplicated tax returns for individual taxpayers. The information from *Examples 22, 23, and 29* of this chapter is used.

Form **1040EZ**

Department of the Treasury—Internal Revenue Service

**Income Tax Return for Single and Joint Filers With No Dependents** (99) **2010**

OMB No. 1545-0074

**Name, Address, and SSN**

See separate instructions.

PRINT CLEARLY

| Your first name and initial | Last name | Your social security number |
|---|---|---|
| William W. | Bristol | 187 52 5034 |
| If a joint return, spouse's first name and initial | Last name | Spouse's social security number |
| | | |
| Home address (number and street). If you have a P.O. box, see instructions. 651 South Hampton | Apt. no. | ▲ Make sure the SSN(s) above are correct. ▲ |
| City, town or post office, state, and ZIP code. If you have a foreign address, see instructions. Blue Springs, MO 64015 | | Checking a box below will not change your tax or refund. |

**Presidential Election Campaign** (see page 9) Check here if you, or your spouse if a joint return, want $3 to go to this fund . . ▶ ☐ **You** ☐ **Spouse**

## Income

Attach Form(s) W-2 here.

Enclose, but do not attach, any payment.

You may be entitled to a larger deduction if you file Form 1040A or 1040. See *Before You Begin* on page 4.

| Line | Description | | Amount |
|---|---|---|---|
| 1 | Wages, salaries, and tips. This should be shown in box 1 of your Form(s) W-2. Attach your Form(s) W-2. | 1 | 27,410 |
| 2 | Taxable interest. If the total is over $1,500, you cannot use Form 1040EZ. | 2 | 350 |
| 3 | Unemployment compensation and Alaska Permanent Fund dividends (see page 11). | 3 | |
| 4 | Add lines 1, 2, and 3. This is your **adjusted gross income.** | 4 | 27,760 |
| 5 | If someone can claim you (or your spouse if a joint return) as a dependent, check the applicable box(es) below and enter the amount from the worksheet on back. ☐ **You** ☐ **Spouse** If no one can claim you (or your spouse if a joint return), enter $9,350 if **single;** $18,700 if **married filing jointly.** See back for explanation. | 5 | 9,350 |
| 6 | Subtract line 5 from line 4. If line 5 is larger than line 4, enter -0-. This is your **taxable income.** ▶ | 6 | 18,410 |

## Payments, Credits, and Tax

| Line | Description | | Amount |
|---|---|---|---|
| 7 | Federal income tax withheld from Form(s) W-2 and 1099. | 7 | 2,345 |
| 8 | Making work pay credit (see worksheet on back). | 8 | |
| 9a | **Earned income credit (EIC)** (see page 13). | 9a | |
| b | Nontaxable combat pay election. 9b | | |
| 10 | Add lines 7, 8, and 9a. These are your **total payments and credits.** ▶ | 10 | 2,820 |
| 11 | **Tax.** Use the amount on **line 6 above** to find your tax in the tax table on pages 27 through 35 of the instructions. Then, enter the tax from the table on this line. | 11 | 2,345 |

## Refund

Have it directly deposited! See page 18 and fill in 12b, 12c, and 12d or Form 8888.

| Line | Description | | Amount |
|---|---|---|---|
| 12a | If line 10 is larger than line 11, subtract line 11 from line 10. This is your **refund.** If Form 8888 is attached, check here ▶ ☐ | 12a | 475 |
| ▶ b | Routing number x x x x x x x x x ▶ c Type: ☐ Checking ☐ Savings | | |
| ▶ d | Account number x x x x x x x x x x x x x x x x x | | |

## Amount You Owe

| Line | Description | | Amount |
|---|---|---|---|
| 13 | If line 11 is larger than line 10, subtract line 10 from line 11. This is the **amount you owe.** For details on how to pay, see page 19. ▶ | 13 | |

## Third Party Designee

Do you want to allow another person to discuss this return with the IRS (see page 20)? ☐ **Yes.** Complete the following. ☑ **No**

Designee's name ▶ Phone no. ▶ Personal identification number (PIN) ▶

## Sign Here

Under penalties of perjury, I declare that I have examined this return, and to the best of my knowledge and belief, it is true, correct, and accurately lists all amounts and sources of income I received during the tax year. Declaration of preparer (other than the taxpayer) is based on all information of which the preparer has any knowledge.

Joint return? See page 6.

Keep a copy for your records.

| Your signature | Date | Your occupation | Daytime phone number |
|---|---|---|---|
| | | Restaurant Manager | 816 229-1207 |
| Spouse's signature. If a joint return, **both** must sign. | Date | Spouse's occupation | |

## Paid Preparer Use Only

| Print/Type preparer's name | Preparer's signature | Date | Check ☐ if self-employed | PTIN |
|---|---|---|---|---|
| Firm's name ▶ | | | Firm's EIN ▶ | |
| Firm's address ▶ | | | Phone no. | |

For Disclosure, Privacy Act, and Paperwork Reduction Act Notice, see page 36. Cat. No. 11329W Form **1040EZ** (2010)

Form **1040A** Department of the Treasury—Internal Revenue Service
**U.S. Individual Income Tax Return** (99) **2010** IRS Use Only—Do not write or staple in this space.

OMB No. 1545-0074

**Name, Address, and SSN**

See separate instructions.

PRINT CLEARLY

| Your first name and initial | Last name | Your social security number |
|---|---|---|
| Clyde F. | Cooper | 234 56 7850 |
| If a joint return, spouse's first name and initial | Last name | Spouse's social security number |
| Delia C. | Cooper | 345 67 8901 |
| Home address (number and street). If you have a P.O. box, see instructions. 1234 Fine Street | Apt. no. | ▲ Make sure the SSN(s) above and on line 6c are correct. |
| City, town or post office, state, and ZIP code. If you have a foreign address, see instructions. Desirable, OK 66987 | | Checking a box below will not change your tax or refund. |

**Presidential Election Campaign** ▶ Check here if you, or your spouse if filing jointly, want $3 to go to this fund . . . . . . . ▶ ☐ You ☐ Spouse

**Filing status**
Check only one box.

1 ☐ Single
2 ☑ Married filing jointly (even if only one had income)
3 ☐ Married filing separately. Enter spouse's SSN above and full name here. ▶
4 ☐ Head of household (with qualifying person). (See instructions.) If the qualifying person is a child but not your dependent, enter this child's name here. ▶
5 ☐ Qualifying widow(er) with dependent child (see instructions)

**Exemptions**

6a ☑ **Yourself.** If someone can claim you as a dependent, **do not** check box 6a.
b ☑ **Spouse**

Boxes checked on 6a and 6b: 2

c **Dependents:**

If more than six dependents, see instructions.

| (1) First name Last name | (2) Dependent's social security number | (3) Dependent's relationship to you | (4) ✓ if child under age 17 qualifying for child tax credit (see page 16) |
|---|---|---|---|
| Gary Cooper | 777 99 6451 | Son | ☑ |
| Debra Cooper | 564 99 8765 | Daughter | ☑ |
| | | | ☐ |
| | | | ☐ |
| | | | ☐ |
| | | | ☐ |

No. of children on 6c who:
• lived with you: 2
• did not live with you due to divorce or separation (see instructions):
Dependents on 6c not entered above:

d Total number of exemptions claimed. Add numbers on lines above ▶ 4

**Income**

Attach Form(s) W-2 here. Also attach Form(s) 1099-R if tax was withheld.

If you did not get a W-2, see page 20.

Enclose, but do not attach, any payment. Also, please use Form 1040-V.

|  |  | |  |  |
|---|---|---|---|---|
| 7 | Wages, salaries, tips, etc. Attach Form(s) W-2. | | 7 | 57,045 |
| 8a | **Taxable** interest. Attach Schedule B if required. | | 8a | 1,500 |
| b | **Tax-exempt** interest. **Do not** include on line 8a. | 8b | | |
| 9a | Ordinary dividends. Attach Schedule B if required. | | 9a | |
| b | Qualified dividends (see instructions). | 9b | | |
| 10 | Capital gain distributions (see instructions). | | 10 | |
| 11a | IRA distributions. 11a | **11b** Taxable amount (see instructions). | 11b | |
| 12a | Pensions and annuities. 12a | **12b** Taxable amount (see instructions). | 12b | |
| 13 | Unemployment compensation and Alaska Permanent Fund dividends. | | 13 | |
| 14a | Social security benefits. 14a | **14b** Taxable amount (see instructions). | 14b | |
| 15 | Add lines 7 through 14b (far right column). This is your **total income.** ▶ | | 15 | 58,545 |

**Adjusted gross income**

|  |  | | |  |  |
|---|---|---|---|---|---|
| 16 | Educator expenses (see instructions). | 16 | | | |
| 17 | IRA deduction (see instructions). | 17 | 4,000 | | |
| 18 | Student loan interest deduction (see instructions). | 18 | | | |
| 19 | Tuition and fees. Attach Form 8917. | 19 | | | |
| 20 | Add lines 16 through 19. These are your **total adjustments.** | | | 20 | 4,000 |
| 21 | Subtract line 20 from line 15. This is your **adjusted gross income.** ▶ | | | 21 | 54,545 |

**For Disclosure, Privacy Act, and Paperwork Reduction Act Notice, see separate instructions.** Cat. No. 11327A Form **1040A** (2010)

Form 1040A (2010) Page **2**

| Section | Line | Description | | Amount | Line | Amount |
|---|---|---|---|---|---|---|
| **Tax, credits, and payments** | 22 | Enter the amount from line 21 (adjusted gross income). | | | 22 | 54,545 |
| | 23a | Check if: ☐ **You** were born before January 2, 1946, ☐ Blind; ☐ **Spouse** was born before January 2, 1946, ☐ Blind. **Total boxes checked** ▶ 23a ☐ | | | | |
| | b | If you are married filing separately and your spouse itemizes deductions, see page 30 and check here ▶ 23b ☐ | | | | |
| | 24 | Enter your **standard deduction** (see instructions). | | | 24 | 11,400 |
| | 25 | Subtract line 24 from line 22. If line 24 is more than line 22, enter -0-. | | | 25 | 43,145 |
| | 26 | **Exemptions.** Multiply $3,650 by the number on line 6d. | | | 26 | 14,600 |
| | 27 | Subtract line 26 from line 25. If line 26 is more than line 25, enter -0-. This is your **taxable income.** ▶ | | | 27 | 28,545 |
| | 28 | **Tax,** including any alternative minimum tax (see instructions). | | | 28 | 3,441 |
| | 29 | Credit for child and dependent care expenses. Attach Form 2441. | 29 | 700 | | |
| | 30 | Credit for the elderly or the disabled. Attach Schedule R. | 30 | | | |
| | 31 | Education credits from Form 8863, line 23. | 31 | | | |
| | 32 | Retirement savings contributions credit. Attach Form 8880. | 32 | | | |
| | 33 | Child tax credit (see instructions). | 33 | 2,000 | | |
| | 34 | Add lines 29 through 33. These are your **total credits.** | | | 34 | 2,700 |
| | 35 | Subtract line 34 from line 28. If line 34 is more than line 28, enter -0-. | | | 35 | 741 |
| | 36 | Advance earned income credit payments from Form(s) W-2, box 9. | | | 36 | |
| | 37 | Add lines 35 and 36. This is your **total tax.** ▶ | | | 37 | 741 |
| | 38 | Federal income tax withheld from Forms W-2 and 1099. | 38 | 1,950 | | |
| | 39 | 2010 estimated tax payments and amount applied from 2009 return. | 39 | | | |
| If you have a qualifying child, attach Schedule EIC. | 40 | Making work pay credit. Attach Schedule M. | 40 | | | |
| | 41a | **Earned income credit (EIC).** | 41a | | | |
| | b | Nontaxable combat pay election. 41b | | | | |
| | 42 | Additional child tax credit. Attach Form 8812. | 42 | | | |
| | 43 | American opportunity credit from Form 8863, line 14. | 43 | | | |
| | 44 | Add lines 38, 39, 40, 41a, 42, and 43. These are your **total payments.** ▶ | | | 44 | 1,950 |
| **Refund** | 45 | If line 44 is more than line 37, subtract line 37 from line 44. This is the amount you **overpaid.** | | | 45 | 1,209 |
| Direct deposit? See instructions and fill in 46b, 46c, and 46d or Form 8888. | 46a | Amount of line 45 you want **refunded to you.** If Form 8888 is attached, check here ▶ ☐ | | | 46a | 1,209 |
| | ▶ b | Routing number x x x x x x x x x ▶ **c** Type: ☐ Checking ☐ Savings | | | | |
| | ▶ d | Account number x x x x x x x x x x x x x x x x x | | | | |
| | 47 | Amount of line 45 you want **applied to your 2011 estimated tax.** | 47 | | | |
| **Amount you owe** | 48 | **Amount you owe.** Subtract line 44 from line 37. For details on how to pay, see instructions. ▶ | | | 48 | |
| | 49 | Estimated tax penalty (see instructions). | 49 | | | |

**Third party designee** Do you want to allow another person to discuss this return with the IRS (see instructions)? ☐ **Yes.** Complete the following. ☑ **No**

Designee's name ▶ Phone no. ▶ Personal identification number (PIN) ▶

**Sign here** Under penalties of perjury, I declare that I have examined this return and accompanying schedules and statements, and to the best of my knowledge and belief, they are true, correct, and accurately list all amounts and sources of income I received during the tax year. Declaration of preparer (other than the taxpayer) is based on all information of which the preparer has any knowledge.

Joint return? See page 13. Keep a copy for your records.

| Your signature | Date | Your occupation | Daytime phone number |
|---|---|---|---|
| | | Professional Model | |
| Spouse's signature. If a joint return, **both** must sign. | Date | Spouse's occupation | |
| | | Programmer | |

**Paid preparer use only**

| Print/type preparer's name | Preparer's signature | Date | Check ▶ ☐ if self-employed | PTIN |
|---|---|---|---|---|
| Firm's name ▶ | | | Firm's EIN ▶ | |
| Firm's address ▶ | | | Phone no. | |

Form **1040A** (2010)

Form **2441**

Department of the Treasury
Internal Revenue Service (99)

## Child and Dependent Care Expenses

▶ Attach to Form 1040, Form 1040A, or Form 1040NR.
▶ See separate instructions.

1040 / 1040A / 1040NR — 2441

OMB No. 1545-0074

**2010**

Attachment Sequence No. **21**

Name(s) shown on return: CLYDE F & CORDELIA C COOPER

Your social security number: 234 56 7890

**Part I** **Persons or Organizations Who Provided the Care—**You **must** complete this part.
(If you have more than two care providers, see the instructions.)

| 1 (a) Care provider's name | (b) Address (number, street, apt. no., city, state, and ZIP code) | (c) Identifying number (SSN or EIN) | (d) Amount paid (see instructions) |
|---|---|---|---|
| HAPPY TRAILS PRESCHOOL | 2391 BRONCO STREET<br>DESIRABLE, OK 66789 | 44-5678656 | 3,500 |
| | | | |

Did you receive dependent care benefits?
- **No** ▶ Complete only Part II below.
- **Yes** ▶ Complete Part III on the back next.

**Caution.** If the care was provided in your home, you may owe employment taxes. If you do, you cannot file Form 1040A. For details, see the instructions for Form 1040, line 59, or Form 1040NR, line 58.

**Part II** **Credit for Child and Dependent Care Expenses**

2 Information about your **qualifying person(s)**. If you have more than two qualifying persons, see the instructions.

| (a) Qualifying person's name — First | Last | (b) Qualifying person's social security number | (c) **Qualified expenses** you incurred and paid in 2010 for the person listed in column (a) |
|---|---|---|---|
| GARY | COOPER | 777 99 6451 | 1,750 |
| DEBRA | COOPER | 564 99 8765 | 1 750 |

| Line | Description | | Amount |
|---|---|---|---|
| 3 | Add the amounts in column (c) of line 2. **Do not** enter more than $3,000 for one qualifying person or $6,000 for two or more persons. If you completed Part III, enter the amount from line 31 | 3 | 3,500 |
| 4 | Enter your **earned income**. See instructions | 4 | 33,445 |
| 5 | If married filing jointly, enter your spouse's earned income (if your spouse was a student or was disabled, see the instructions); **all others**, enter the amount from line 4 | 5 | 23,600 |
| 6 | Enter the **smallest** of line 3, 4, or 5 | 6 | 3,500 |
| 7 | Enter the amount from Form 1040, line 38; Form 1040A, line 22; or Form 1040NR, line 37. — 7: 54,545 | | |
| 8 | Enter on line 8 the decimal amount shown below that applies to the amount on line 7 | 8 | X.20 |

**If line 7 is:**

| Over | But not over | Decimal amount is |
|---|---|---|
| $0— | 15,000 | .35 |
| 15,000— | 17,000 | .34 |
| 17,000— | 19,000 | .33 |
| 19,000— | 21,000 | .32 |
| 21,000— | 23,000 | .31 |
| 23,000— | 25,000 | .30 |
| 25,000— | 27,000 | .29 |
| 27,000— | 29,000 | .28 |
| $29,000— | 31,000 | .27 |
| 31,000— | 33,000 | .26 |
| 33,000— | 35,000 | .25 |
| 35,000— | 37,000 | .24 |
| 37,000— | 39,000 | .23 |
| 39,000— | 41,000 | .22 |
| 41,000— | 43,000 | .21 |
| 43,000— | No limit | .20 |

| Line | Description | | Amount |
|---|---|---|---|
| 9 | Multiply line 6 by the decimal amount on line 8. If you paid 2009 expenses in 2010, see the instructions | 9 | 700 |
| 10 | Tax liability limit. Enter the amount from the Credit Limit Worksheet in the instructions. — 10: | | 3,641 |
| 11 | **Credit for child and dependent care expenses.** Enter the **smaller** of line 9 or line 10 here and on Form 1040, line 48; Form 1040A, line 29; or Form 1040NR, line 46 | 11 | 700 |

**For Paperwork Reduction Act Notice, see your tax return instructions.** Cat. No. 11862M Form **2441** (2010)

Form **1040** Department of the Treasury—Internal Revenue Service
**U.S. Individual Income Tax Return** **2010** (99) IRS Use Only—Do not write or staple in this space.

For the year Jan. 1–Dec. 31, 2010, or other tax year beginning , 2010, ending , 20 OMB No. 1545-0074

**Name, Address, and SSN**

See separate instructions.

PRINT CLEARLY

| Your first name and initial | Last name | Your social security number |
|---|---|---|
| Jeremy S. | Allen | 123 45 9875 |
| If a joint return, spouse's first name and initial | Last name | Spouse's social security number |
| Shelly R. | Allen | 456 85 2447 |
| Home address (number and street). If you have a P.O. box, see instructions. | Apt. no. | ▲ Make sure the SSN(s) above and on line 6c are correct. |
| 8473 Smithson Place | | |
| City, town or post office, state, and ZIP code. If you have a foreign address, see instructions. | | Checking a box below will not change your tax or refund. |
| Boring, OR 97832 | | |

**Presidential Election Campaign** ▶ Check here if you, or your spouse if filing jointly, want $3 to go to this fund . . . . . ▶ ☐ You ☐ Spouse

**Filing Status**

Check only one box.

1 ☐ Single
2 ☑ Married filing jointly (even if only one had income)
3 ☐ Married filing separately. Enter spouse's SSN above and full name here. ▶
4 ☐ Head of household (with qualifying person). (See instructions.) If the qualifying person is a child but not your dependent, enter this child's name here. ▶
5 ☐ Qualifying widow(er) with dependent child

**Exemptions**

6a ☑ **Yourself.** If someone can claim you as a dependent, **do not** check box 6a . . . . . Boxes checked on 6a and 6b: 2
b ☑ **Spouse**

c **Dependents:**

| (1) First name Last name | (2) Dependent's social security number | (3) Dependent's relationship to you | (4) ✓ if child under age 17 qualifying for child tax credit (see page 15) |
|---|---|---|---|
| William Alle | 789 65 4321 | Son | ☑ |
| Susan Allen | 456 65 9876 | Daughter | ☑ |
| Gregory Alle | 321 72 9347 | Son | ☑ |
| | | | ☐ |

If more than four dependents, see instructions and check here ▶ ☐

No. of children on 6c who:
• **lived with you**: 3
• **did not live with you due to divorce or separation (see instructions)**:
**Dependents on 6c not entered above**:

d Total number of exemptions claimed . . . . . . . . . . . . **Add numbers on lines above** ▶ 5

**Income**

**Attach Form(s) W-2 here. Also attach Forms W-2G and 1099-R if tax was withheld.**

If you did not get a W-2, see page 20.

Enclose, but do not attach, any payment. Also, please use **Form 1040-V.**

|  |  | |  |  |
|---|---|---|---|---|
| 7 | Wages, salaries, tips, etc. Attach Form(s) W-2 | | 7 | 77,775 |
| 8a | **Taxable** interest. Attach Schedule B if required | | 8a | 3,000 |
| b | **Tax-exempt** interest. **Do not** include on line 8a | 8b | | |
| 9a | Ordinary dividends. Attach Schedule B if required | | 9a | |
| b | Qualified dividends | 9b | | |
| 10 | Taxable refunds, credits, or offsets of state and local income taxes | | 10 | |
| 11 | Alimony received | | 11 | |
| 12 | Business income or (loss). Attach Schedule C or C-EZ | | 12 | |
| 13 | Capital gain or (loss). Attach Schedule D if required. If not required, check here ▶ ☐ | | 13 | |
| 14 | Other gains or (losses). Attach Form 4797 | | 14 | |
| 15a | IRA distributions 15a | b Taxable amount | 15b | |
| 16a | Pensions and annuities 16a | b Taxable amount | 16b | |
| 17 | Rental real estate, royalties, partnerships, S corporations, trusts, etc. Attach Schedule E | | 17 | |
| 18 | Farm income or (loss). Attach Schedule F | | 18 | |
| 19 | Unemployment compensation | | 19 | |
| 20a | Social security benefits 20a | b Taxable amount | 20b | |
| 21 | Other income. List type and amount | | 21 | |
| 22 | Combine the amounts in the far right column for lines 7 through 21. This is your **total income** ▶ | | 22 | 80,775 |

**Adjusted Gross Income**

| Line | Description | Line | Amount | Line | Amount |
|---|---|---|---|---|---|
| 23 | Educator expenses | 23 | | | |
| 24 | Certain business expenses of reservists, performing artists, and fee-basis government officials. Attach Form 2106 or 2106-EZ | 24 | | | |
| 25 | Health savings account deduction. Attach Form 8889 | 25 | | | |
| 26 | Moving expenses. Attach Form 3903 | 26 | | | |
| 27 | One-half of self-employment tax. Attach Schedule SE | 27 | | | |
| 28 | Self-employed SEP, SIMPLE, and qualified plans | 28 | | | |
| 29 | Self-employed health insurance deduction | 29 | | | |
| 30 | Penalty on early withdrawal of savings | 30 | | | |
| 31a | Alimony paid **b** Recipient's SSN ▶ | 31a | | | |
| 32 | IRA deduction | 32 | | | |
| 33 | Student loan interest deduction | 33 | | | |
| 34 | Tuition and fees. Attach Form 8917 | 34 | | | |
| 35 | Domestic production activities deduction. Attach Form 8903 | 35 | | | |
| 36 | Add lines 23 through 31a and 32 through 35 | | | 36 | |
| 37 | Subtract line 36 from line 22. This is your **adjusted gross income** ▶ | | | 37 | 80,775 |

**For Disclosure, Privacy Act, and Paperwork Reduction Act Notice, see separate instructions.** Cat. No. 11320B Form **1040** (2010)

Form 1040 (2010) Page 2

| Section | Line | Description | Line | Amount |
|---|---|---|---|---|
| **Tax and Credits** | 38 | Amount from line 37 (adjusted gross income) | 38 | 80,775 |
| | 39a | Check if: ☐ **You** were born before January 2, 1946, ☐ Blind. ☐ **Spouse** was born before January 2, 1946, ☐ Blind. **Total boxes checked ▶ 39a** ☐ | | |
| | b | If your spouse itemizes on a separate return or you were a dual-status alien, check here ▶ 39b☐ | | |
| | 40 | **Itemized deductions** (from Schedule A) **or** your **standard deduction** (see instructions) | 40 | 15,000 |
| | 41 | Subtract line 40 from line 38 | 41 | 65,775 |
| | 42 | **Exemptions.** Multiply $3,650 by the number on line 6d | 42 | 18,250 |
| | 43 | **Taxable income.** Subtract line 42 from line 41. If line 42 is more than line 41, enter -0- | 43 | 47,525 |
| | 44 | **Tax** (see instructions). Check if any tax is from: a ☐ Form(s) 8814 b ☐ Form 4972 | 44 | 6,291 |
| | 45 | **Alternative minimum tax** (see instructions). Attach Form 6251 | 45 | |
| | 46 | Add lines 44 and 45 ▶ | 46 | 6,291 |
| | 47 | Foreign tax credit. Attach Form 1116 if required — 47 | | |
| | 48 | Credit for child and dependent care expenses. Attach Form 2441 — 48 | | |
| | 49 | Education credits from Form 8863, line 23 — 49 | | |
| | 50 | Retirement savings contributions credit. Attach Form 8880 — 50 | | |
| | 51 | Child tax credit (see instructions) — 51 | | |
| | 52 | Residential energy credits. Attach Form 5695 — 52: 3,000 | | |
| | 53 | Other credits from Form: a ☐ 3800 b ☐ 8801 c ☐ — 53 | | |
| | 54 | Add lines 47 through 53. These are your **total credits** | 54 | 3,000 |
| | 55 | Subtract line 54 from line 46. If line 54 is more than line 46, enter -0- ▶ | 55 | 3,291 |
| **Other Taxes** | 56 | Self-employment tax. Attach Schedule SE | 56 | |
| | 57 | Unreported social security and Medicare tax from Form: a ☐ 4137 b ☐ 8919 | 57 | |
| | 58 | Additional tax on IRAs, other qualified retirement plans, etc. Attach Form 5329 if required | 58 | |
| | 59 | a ☐ Form(s) W-2, box 9 b ☐ Schedule H c ☐ Form 5405, line 16 | 59 | |
| | 60 | Add lines 55 through 59. This is your **total tax** ▶ | 60 | 3,291 |
| **Payments** | 61 | Federal income tax withheld from Forms W-2 and 1099 — 61: 4,100 | | |
| | 62 | 2010 estimated tax payments and amount applied from 2009 return — 62 | | |
| | 63 | Making work pay credit. Attach Schedule M — 63 | | |
| If you have a qualifying child, attach Schedule EIC. | 64a | **Earned income credit (EIC)** — 64a | | |
| | b | Nontaxable combat pay election — 64b | | |
| | 65 | Additional child tax credit. Attach Form 8812 — 65 | | |
| | 66 | American opportunity credit from Form 8863, line 14 — 66 | | |
| | 67 | First-time homebuyer credit from Form 5405, line 10 — 67 | | |
| | 68 | Amount paid with request for extension to file — 68 | | |
| | 69 | Excess social security and tier 1 RRTA tax withheld — 69 | | |
| | 70 | Credit for federal tax on fuels. Attach Form 4136 — 70 | | |
| | 71 | Credits from Form: a ☐ 2439 b ☐ 8839 c ☐ 8801 d ☐ 8885 — 71 | | |
| | 72 | Add lines 61, 62, 63, 64a, and 65 through 71. These are your **total payments** ▶ | 72 | 4,100 |
| **Refund** | 73 | If line 72 is more than line 60, subtract line 60 from line 72. This is the amount you **overpaid** | 73 | 809 |
| | 74a | Amount of line 73 you want **refunded to you.** If Form 8888 is attached, check here ▶ ☐ | 74a | 809 |
| Direct deposit? See instructions. | ▶ b | Routing number x x x x x x x x x ▶ c Type: ☐ Checking ☐ Savings | | |
| | ▶ d | Account number x x x x x x x x x x x x x x x x x | | |
| | 75 | Amount of line 73 you want **applied to your 2011 estimated tax** ▶ — 75 | | |
| **Amount You Owe** | 76 | **Amount you owe.** Subtract line 72 from line 60. For details on how to pay, see instructions ▶ | 76 | |
| | 77 | Estimated tax penalty (see instructions) — 77 | | |

**Third Party Designee** Do you want to allow another person to discuss this return with the IRS (see instructions)? ☐ **Yes.** Complete below. ☑ **No**

Designee's name ▶ Phone no. ▶ Personal identification number (PIN) ▶

**Sign Here**

Joint return? See page 12. Keep a copy for your records.

Under penalties of perjury, I declare that I have examined this return and accompanying schedules and statements, and to the best of my knowledge and belief, they are true, correct, and complete. Declaration of preparer (other than taxpayer) is based on all information of which preparer has any knowledge.

| Your signature | Date | Your occupation | Daytime phone number |
|---|---|---|---|
| | | Registered Nurse | |
| Spouse's signature. If a joint return, **both** must sign. | Date | Spouse's occupation | |
| | | Air Traffic Controller | |

**Paid Preparer Use Only**

| Print/Type preparer's name | Preparer's signature | Date | Check ☐ if self-employed | PTIN |
|---|---|---|---|---|
| Firm's name ▶ | | | Firm's EIN ▶ | |
| Firm's address ▶ | | | Phone no. | |

Form **1040** (2010)

**SCHEDULE A (Form 1040)**

Department of the Treasury
Internal Revenue Service (99)

# Itemized Deductions

▶ Attach to Form 1040. ▶ See Instructions for Schedule A (Form 1040).

OMB No. 1545-0074

**2010**

Attachment Sequence No. **07**

Name(s) shown on Form 1040: *Jeremy S & Shelly R Allen*

Your social security number: *123 45 9875*

|  |  |  | |  | |  |
|---|---|---|---|---|---|---|
| **Medical and Dental Expenses** | | **Caution.** Do not include expenses reimbursed or paid by others. | | | | |
| | 1 | Medical and dental expenses (see instructions) | 1 | *3,000* | | |
| | 2 | Enter amount from Form 1040, line 38 [2] *80,775* | | | | |
| | 3 | Multiply line 2 by 7.5% (.075) | 3 | *6,058* | | |
| | 4 | Subtract line 3 from line 1. If line 3 is more than line 1, enter -0- | | | 4 | *0* |
| **Taxes You Paid** | 5 | State and local **(check only one box):** a ☐ Income taxes, **or** b ☐ General sales taxes | 5 | *3,400* | | |
| | 6 | Real estate taxes (see instructions) | 6 | *1,200* | | |
| | 7 | New motor vehicle taxes from line 11 of the worksheet on back (for certain vehicles purchased in 2009). Skip this line if you checked box 5b | 7 | | | |
| | 8 | Other taxes. List type and amount ▶ | 8 | | | |
| | 9 | Add lines 5 through 8 | | | 9 | *4,600* |
| **Interest You Paid** | 10 | Home mortgage interest and points reported to you on Form 1098 | 10 | *8,500* | | |
| **Note.** Your mortgage interest deduction may be limited (see instructions). | 11 | Home mortgage interest not reported to you on Form 1098. If paid to the person from whom you bought the home, see instructions and show that person's name, identifying no., and address ▶ | 11 | | | |
| | 12 | Points not reported to you on Form 1098. See instructions for special rules | 12 | | | |
| | 13 | Mortgage insurance premiums (see instructions) | 13 | | | |
| | 14 | Investment interest. Attach Form 4952 if required. (See instructions.) | 14 | *400* | | |
| | 15 | Add lines 10 through 14 | | | 15 | *8,900* |
| **Gifts to Charity** | 16 | Gifts by cash or check. If you made any gift of $250 or more, see instructions | 16 | *1,500* | | |
| If you made a gift and got a benefit for it, see instructions. | 17 | Other than by cash or check. If any gift of $250 or more, see instructions. You **must** attach Form 8283 if over $500 | 17 | | | |
| | 18 | Carryover from prior year | 18 | | | |
| | 19 | Add lines 16 through 18 | | | 19 | *1,500* |
| **Casualty and Theft Losses** | 20 | Casualty or theft loss(es). Attach Form 4684. (See instructions.) | | | 20 | |
| **Job Expenses and Certain Miscellaneous Deductions** | 21 | Unreimbursed employee expenses—job travel, union dues, job education, etc. Attach Form 2106 or 2106-EZ if required. (See instructions.) ▶ | 21 | | | |
| | 22 | Tax preparation fees | 22 | *275* | | |
| | 23 | Other expenses—investment, safe deposit box, etc. List type and amount ▶ | 23 | | | |
| | 24 | Add lines 21 through 23 | 24 | *275* | | |
| | 25 | Enter amount from Form 1040, line 38 [25] *80,775* | | | | |
| | 26 | Multiply line 25 by 2% (.02) | 26 | *1,616* | | |
| | 27 | Subtract line 26 from line 24. If line 26 is more than line 24, enter -0- | | | 27 | *0* |
| **Other Miscellaneous Deductions** | 28 | Other—from list in instructions. List type and amount ▶ | | | 28 | |
| **Total Itemized Deductions** | 29 | Add the amounts in the far right column for lines 4 through 28. Also, enter this amount on Form 1040, line 40 | | | 29 | *15,000* |
| | 30 | If you elect to itemize deductions even though they are less than your standard deduction, check here ▶ ☐ | | | | |

**For Paperwork Reduction Act Notice, see Form 1040 instructions.** Cat. No. 17145C **Schedule A (Form 1040) 2010**

**SCHEDULE B (Form 1040A or 1040)**

Department of the Treasury Internal Revenue Service (99)

# Interest and Ordinary Dividends

▶ Attach to Form 1040A or 1040. ▶ See instructions on back.

OMB No. 1545-0074

2010

Attachment Sequence No. 08

Name(s) shown on return: Jeremy S & Shelly R Allen

Your social security number: 123 45 9875

## Part I Interest

(See instructions on back and the instructions for Form 1040A, or Form 1040, line 8a.)

**Note.** If you received a Form 1099-INT, Form 1099-OID, or substitute statement from a brokerage firm, list the firm's name as the payer and enter the total interest shown on that form.

| | | | Amount |
|---|---|---|---|
| 1 | List name of payer. If any interest is from a seller-financed mortgage and the buyer used the property as a personal residence, see instructions on back and list this interest first. Also, show that buyer's social security number and address ▶ | | |
| | Mercantile Bank | 1 | 1,800 |
| | U.S. Treasury Bonds | | 700 |
| | Ben Franklin Savings | | 500 |
| 2 | Add the amounts on line 1 | 2 | 3,000 |
| 3 | Excludable interest on series EE and I U.S. savings bonds issued after 1989. Attach Form 8815 | 3 | |
| 4 | Subtract line 3 from line 2. Enter the result here and on Form 1040A, or Form 1040, line 8a ▶ | 4 | 3,000 |

**Note.** If line 4 is over $1,500, you must complete Part III.

## Part II Ordinary Dividends

(See instructions on back and the instructions for Form 1040A, or Form 1040, line 9a.)

**Note.** If you received a Form 1099-DIV or substitute statement from a brokerage firm, list the firm's name as the payer and enter the ordinary dividends shown on that form.

| | | | Amount |
|---|---|---|---|
| 5 | List name of payer ▶ | 5 | |
| 6 | Add the amounts on line 5. Enter the total here and on Form 1040A, or Form 1040, line 9a ▶ | 6 | |

**Note.** If line 6 is over $1,500, you must complete Part III.

## Part III Foreign Accounts and Trusts

(See instructions on back.)

| | | Yes | No |
|---|---|---|---|
| | You must complete this part if you **(a)** had over $1,500 of taxable interest or ordinary dividends; **(b)** had a foreign account; or **(c)** received a distribution from, or were a grantor of, or a transferor to, a foreign trust. | | |
| 7a | At any time during 2010, did you have an interest in or a signature or other authority over a financial account in a foreign country, such as a bank account, securities account, or other financial account? See instructions on back for exceptions and filing requirements for Form TD F 90-22.1 | | ✓ |
| b | If "Yes," enter the name of the foreign country ▶ | | |
| 8 | During 2010, did you receive a distribution from, or were you the grantor of, or transferor to, a foreign trust? If "Yes," you may have to file Form 3520. See instructions on back | | ✓ |

**For Paperwork Reduction Act Notice, see your tax return instructions.** Cat. No. 17146N **Schedule B (Form 1040A or 1040) 2010**

# Problem Materials

## DISCUSSION QUESTIONS

**4-1** *Exemptions.* Distinguish between personal and dependency exemptions.

**4-2** *Dependency Exemption for a Qualifying Child.* List the requirements that must be met in order for one to claim a dependency exemption for a *qualifying child.*

**4-3** *Relationship.* In addition to a natural child, which other *children* are included in the definition of a *qualifying child?*

**4-4** *Tie-breaking.* Determine who gets the dependency exemption for D in each of the independent cases below. Assume that the parties cannot agree if more than one person could claim the exemption. Also assume that any tests that are not addressed (e.g., citizenship) are met. F's other support (> $3,000) is provided by S.

- **a.** Q provides a home in which she lives with her daughter, C, and C's son, D. C is 25 years of age and has gross income of $6,500 for the current year.
- **b.** R provides a home in which she lives with her son, E, and E's son, D. E is 18 years of age and has gross income of $6,500 for the current year.
- **c.** S provides a home in which she lives with her daughter, F, and F's daughter, D. F is 25 years of age and has gross income of $3,000 for the current year.

**4-5** *Tests for Dependency Exemptions.* List and briefly describe the five tests that must be met before a taxpayer is entitled to a dependency exemption for an individual other than a qualifying child. Must all five tests be met?

**4-6** *Support.* Describe the concept of support, including examples of support items.

**4-7** *Support—Special Items.* With respect to the support test, discuss the treatment of each of the following items: athletic scholarships, social security survivors' benefits paid to an orphan, and aid to dependent children paid by the state government.

**4-8** *Gross Income Test.* Explain the gross income test. Must all dependents for whom a dependency exemption is claimed meet this test?

**4-9** *Gross Income Test—Dependency Exemption.* M provides more than half of the support for her father, F, who is single for tax purposes. F's other support is in the form of interest income of $5,000 and social security benefits of $9,000.

- **a.** May M claim a dependency exemption for supporting F in the current year?
- **b.** Would your answer differ if F's interest income were only $1,500?

**4-10** *Relationship Test—Dependency Exemption.* Assuming Q provides more than 50 percent of their support and the dependent meets the gross income, relationship, and citizenship tests, which of the following relatives may be claimed as a dependent?

- **a.** Widow of Q's deceased son
- **b.** Q's husband's brother
- **c.** Daughter of Q's husband's brother
- **d.** Q's mother's brother
- **e.** Q's grandmother's brother
- **f.** Q's great grandson

**4-11** *Joint Return Test—Dependency Exemption.* K and L were married in 2011 and elected to file a joint return. K had interest income of $5,000 and a salary of $30,000 for the year. L had interest income of $2,250 and received the remainder of her support from her mother and K.

- **a.** If L's mother provided more than 50 percent of L's support, can she claim a dependency exemption for L?
- **b.** If not, under what circumstances could the exemption be claimed?

**4-12** This year P, 25, was accepted to medical school. P is a single parent. To save money, she and her one-year-old baby, B, moved in with P's mom and dad, M and D. The four lived together from May through December. May anyone claim an exemption for B? If so, whom?

**4-13** *Community Property Law.* How does the treatment of earned income differ between a community property state and a non community property (i.e., separate property) state for Federal income tax purposes? Why?

**4-14** *Filing Status, Tax Schedules.* List the four sets of rate schedules that apply to individual taxpayers. Refer to them by filing status and schedule designation (e.g., Schedule Z). Which taxpayers must use the rate schedules rather than the tax rate tables?

**4-15** *Determination of Marital Status.* Married taxpayers are subject to a separate set(s) of tax rates. When is marital status determined? What authority (state or federal) controls marital status?

**4-16** *Exceptions—Marital Status.* In certain instances, a person who is married may use the rates for unmarried persons. In another instance, a single person may use the rates for married persons filing jointly. Elaborate.

**4-17** *Head of Household—Requirements.* What are the specific requirements for head-of-household status? List at least ten relatives who may qualify the taxpayer for head-of-household filing status.

**4-18** *Head of Household—Divorced Parents.* May a divorced parent with custody of a child qualify as a head of household even though his or her former spouse is entitled to the dependency exemption for the child? Explain.

**4-19** *Head of Household—Taxpayer's Home.* Must the person who qualifies a taxpayer as a head of household (i.e., the taxpayer's child or other dependent) live in the taxpayer's home? Are there any exceptions to this rule?

**4-20** *Costs of Maintaining Home.* Which of the following expenses are included in determining the cost of a home when determining whether a taxpayer qualifies as a head of household?

**a.** Food consumed on the premises
**b.** Transportation for a dependent to and from school
**c.** Clothing for a dependent
**d.** Property taxes on residence
**e.** Rent paid on residence

**4-21** *Abandoned Spouse.* M is married and lives with her dependent son, S. M receives child support sufficient to provide 65 percent of S's support from S's father, who lived in a nearby city for the entire year. M provides more than one-half of the cost of providing the home in which she and S live.

**a.** What is M's filing status and what is the number of exemption deductions that she may claim?
**b.** How would your answers differ if M agreed to let S's father claim the dependency exemption for S?

**4-22** *Tax Tables.* Are taxpayers required to use the tax tables? Which taxpayers are ineligible to use the tables?

**4-23** *Limited Standard Deduction.* W is 16 years old, single, and claimed as a dependent by his parents. His 2011 A.G.I. is \$6,150, and he claims the standard deduction. Given W's taxable income below, what is the character of his income, earned or unearned?

**a.** Taxable income \$5,200
**b.** Taxable income \$3,700
**c.** Taxable income \$350.

**4-24** *Kiddie Tax.* G is 13 years old and claimed as a dependent by her parents. G's top marginal tax rate is 10 percent and her parents' is 25 percent. Calculate G's taxable income and the rate at which it will be taxed in the following instances:

**a.** Interest of \$1,050
**b.** Interest of \$1,950
**c.** Interest of \$900 and wages of \$5,000
**d.** Interest of \$3,500 and wages of \$500

**4-25** *Filing Requirements.* Which individuals are exempted from filing a Form 1040 (or equivalent Form 1040A or Form 1040EZ)?

**4-26** *Due Date.* P is a calendar year taxpayer with taxable income of $45,000 and a tax due of $350 for the current year.

a. When is P's tax return due if P is an individual?

b. Assume P is a corporation and uses a fiscal year ending June 30, when is its annual income tax return due?

**4-27** *Extensions.* Q is a calendar year individual taxpayer with taxable income of $25,000 and a tax refund of $150 for the current year.

a. If Q is unable to file on time, she may request an automatic extension of time to file her tax return. How long is the maximum extension period?

b. If Q is unable to complete her return by the extended due date and she has an appropriate reason, how long of an additional extension can she request?

c. How much is Q's penalty if she fails to file an extension?

**4-28** *Due Dates for Estimated Tax Payments.* R is a calendar year taxpayer whose estimated tax liability for the current year is $4,000. What are the amounts and the due dates of R's estimated tax payments?

**4-29** *Amount of Estimated Tax Payments.* H is a calendar year taxpayer who estimates his Federal income tax to be $5,500 and his self-employment tax to be $4,500 for 2011. For 2010, H's Federal income tax was $4,950, and his self-employment tax was $3,975. What is the amount of estimated tax that H must pay on each due date to avoid a penalty for failure to make adequate estimated tax payments?

**4-30** *Penalties and Interest.* J is a calendar year individual whose gross tax for 2011 is $10,000. J had taxes of $5,750 withheld and made estimated tax payments of $500 each due date. She submitted $1,350 along with her request for an automatic extension on April 15. The remaining $900 was paid when J's tax return was filed on July 9. J's 2010 tax totaled $9,950.

a. Does J owe a penalty for failure to file for 2011?

b. Does J owe a penalty for failure to pay for 2011? If so, for what period?

c. Does J owe a penalty for failure to make adequate estimated tax payments for 2012? If so, over what period?

d. Does J owe interest on any of the amounts paid? If so, for what period?

**4-31** *Statute of Limitations.* What is the importance of the Federal Statute of Limitations to the taxpayer? To the IRS? Generally, how long is the statute of limitations on tax matters?

**4-32** *Six-Year Statute of Limitations.* Under what circumstances will the regular three-year statutory period for assessments be extended to six years?

**4-33** *Indexation and the Individual Income Tax.* Congress has provided for indexation of certain deductions. What items are subject to indexation? What index is to be used as an estimate of price-level changes?

## PROBLEMS

**4-34** *Exemptions.* In each of the following situations determine the proper number of personal and dependency exemptions available to the taxpayer. Unless otherwise implied, assume that all tests are satisfied.

a. R's mother, age 85, lives in his home. R figures that including the value of the lodging, he provides support of about $6,000. The remainder of her support is paid for with her social security benefits of $4,000.

b. This year D sent his father, F, monthly checks of $200, or $2,400 for the year. F used these checks along with $2,300 of rental income ($4,400 of rents less $2,100 of expenses) to pay all of his support.

c. H and W are married with one daughter, D, age 7. D models children's clothing and earned $4,000 of wages this year. D also has a trust fund of $50,000 established by her grandparents. All of D's wages were saved and none were used to pay for her support. Similarly none of the funds of the trust were used to pay for D's support.

d. Professor and Mrs. Smith participated in the foreign exchange student program at their son's high school. In December of 2010 a student, Hans, arrived from Germany, spent the spring of 2011 with the Smiths, then returned to Germany.

e. B and C are happily married with one son, S. S, age 20, is a full-time student at the University of Cincinnati. S worked as a painter during the summer to help put himself through school. He earned wages of $4,000, $2,500 of which was used to pay for his room and board at school and $1,500 for miscellaneous living expenses (e.g., gas for his car, dates, laundry, etc.). He lived with his parents during the summer. The value of their support including meals and lodging was $5,000. He also received a National Merit Scholarship, which paid for his tuition of $8,000.

**4-35** *Personal and Dependency Exemptions.* In each of the following situations determine the proper number of personal and dependency exemption deductions available to the taxpayer.

**a.** A is single and 44 years of age. He provides full support for his mother, who is 67 and lives in a small retirement community in A's hometown.

**b.** D and K are married and file a joint return for the year. D is 67 years of age and K is 62. They have no dependents.

**c.** E and O are married and file a joint return for the year. They provide all the support for their two younger children for the entire year. E and O also provided all the support for their oldest child (age 19) for the eight months she was a full-time student. After graduating from high school, she accepted a job that paid $3,000 in salary. Nevertheless, her parents contributed more than one-half of her support for the entire year.

**4-36** *Married Dependents.* In November of this year Jim Jenkins married his college sweetheart, Kate Brown. Jim was 27 and Kate was 25. Jim had graduated two years ago. Kate was in graduate school and had one more year left. The majority of Kate's support this year was provided by her parents. Jim earned $16,250 during the year while Kate received $950 of interest from her savings account. Assume Kate's parents are in the 25 (2011) percent tax bracket and would give the couple any tax savings to be derived from claiming Kate as a dependent.

**a.** May Kate's parents claim an exemption for Kate if the couple files a joint return?

**b.** Would the couple be better off filing separate returns (and thus receiving any taxes saved by Kate's parents) or filing a joint return? Show all computations you must make to determine your answer.

**4-37** *Multiple Support Agreements.* G's support is provided as follows:

| | |
|---|---|
| Social security benefits | $3,600 |
| Taxable interest income | 800 |
| Support from: | |
| A, G's oldest son—Cash for trip to Europe | 1,600 |
| B, G's daughter—Fair value of lodging and cash | 2,300 |
| C, G's youngest son—Cash | 700 |
| Total | $9,000 |

**a.** Who is entitled to a dependency exemption for G in the absence of any agreement as to who gets the deduction?

**b.** Who may claim a dependency exemption for G under a multiple-support agreement?

**c.** How would your answer to (b) differ if A contributed $650 instead of $1,600?

**4-38** *Children of Divorced Parents.* For each of the following, determine whether M or F is entitled to the dependency exemption in 2011 for their only child, S. M and F were divorced in 2008 and M has custody, except when F has visitation privileges. Together, M and F provide 100 percent of S's support.

**a.** M was granted the dependency exemption under the divorce decree. F pays child support for the year totaling $1,500. Total support expenditures for S are $5,600.

**b.** No mention of the dependency exemption was made in the divorce decree. F pays child support for S of $3,400, and the total support for S is $6,500.

**c.** F paid child support of $2,800 for the year. M signed Form 8332, indicating that she will not claim a dependency exemption for S. The total support for S for the year was $5,500.

**4-39** *Filing Status and Standard Deduction.* Determine the most beneficial filing status and the standard deduction for each of the following taxpayers for 2011:

**a.** M is a 54-year-old unmarried widow whose spouse died in 2008. During all of 2011 M's 15-year-old son, for whom she claims a dependency exemption, lives with her.

**b.** S is a 67-year-old bachelor who lives in New York City. S pays more than half the cost of maintaining a home in Tampa, Florida for his 89-year-old mother. He is entitled to a dependency exemption under a multiple-support agreement executed by his brother, his sister, and himself.

**c.** R is a widower whose wife died in 2010. R maintained a household for his three dependent children during 2011 and provided 100 percent of the cost of the household.

**d.** J is divorced and has custody of his 9-year-old child. J provides more than half the cost of the home in which he lives with his child, but his ex-wife is entitled to the dependency exemption for the child for the current year.

**4-40** *Head of Household.* Indicate whether the taxpayer would be entitled to file using the head-of-household rate schedule.

**a.** Y is divorced from her husband. She maintains a home in which she and her 10-year-old son live. Her ex-husband pays child support to her that she uses to provide all of the support for the child. In addition, Y has relinquished her right to claim her son as a dependent to her former spouse.

**b.** C is divorced from his wife. He provides 75 percent of the support for his mother, who lives in a nursing home. His mother receives $5,000 of interest income annually.

**c.** J's grandson, G, had a falling-out with his parents and moved in with him early this year. J did not mind because he had grown lonely since his wife died three years ago. G is 17 years old and earned $5,000 this year as a part-time grocery clerk. G's total support was $12,000.

**d.** B's wife died four years ago and he has not remarried. Last year his 26-year old daughter, D, graduated from Arizona State University and moved to Hawaii with the intention of living there permanently. Unfortunately, D was unable to earn enough money to make ends meet and had to rely on checks from dad. B paid for D's own apartment and provided the majority of her support.

**e.** M's wife died last year. This year he maintains a home for himself and his 25-year-old daughter, E, who is temporarily away from home while attending graduate school in a nearby city. While going to school, E rents an apartment but then returns home during the summer and on holidays. M not only pays for all of the costs associated with his home but also the E's cost of living in the apartment. E earned $8,000 as a teaching assistant. Nevertheless, M provided the majority of E's support.

**f.** F's husband died this year. She continues to provide a home for her two children, ages 6 and 8.

**4-41** *Dependent's Personal Exemption and Standard Deduction.* K is 16 years old and is claimed as a dependent on her parents' income tax return. She earned wages of $2,800 and collected interest of $1,450 for the year. What is the amount of K's taxable income for the year?

**4-42** *Dependent's Personal Exemption and Standard Deduction.* B is 20 years old and is claimed as a dependent on his sister's tax return. B earned $3,000 from a part-time job during the year. What is B's taxable income?

**4-43** *Tax Tables.* S earned a salary during 2010 of $56,015. She is single, claims the standard deduction, and has no dependents for the year. Her only other income was taxable interest income of $560. Determine S's taxable income and her Federal income tax. (**Note:** This tax table computation is for 2010 because the 2011 tax tables will not be available until late 2011. See Appendix for the 2010 tax tables.)

**4-44** *Tax Rate Schedules.* W and T were married and filed a joint return for 2011. Their adjusted gross income for the year was $141,950. Their total itemized deductions were $12,700 and they were entitled to three personal and dependency exemptions. Neither W nor T is 65 or older and both have good sight. Determine W and T's taxable income and their Federal income tax liability before prepayments and credits for 2011.

**4-45** *Application of the Kiddie Tax.* For each of the following situations, determine the child's taxable income and the amounts that would be taxed at the child's and parents' rates for the 2011 tax year.

**a.** When J's rich uncle died, he left her GM corporate bonds. This year J received $3,000 of interest from these bonds, her only income. J is seven years old and her parents claim an exemption for her.

**b.** L, age 13, works in his father's music store on weekends. During the year, he earned $1,200 from this job. In addition, L had $2,500 of interest income attributable to a gift from his grandfather. L's father claims an exemption for him.

**c.** Same as (b) except L's earned income was $6,600 and interest income was $2,850.

**4-46** *Computation of the Kiddie Tax.* G's great aunt gave her a certificate of deposit that matures in ten years when she is 21. The certificate pays interest of $4,000 annually. G's parents file a joint return. Their 2011 taxable income is $131,500. Compute G's tax.

**4-47** *Failure-to-File Penalty.* T, overwhelmed by other pressing concerns, simply forgot to file his tax return for 2010 until July 20, 2011. When filed, T's 2010 return showed a tax due before withholding and estimated taxes of $10,000.

**a.** Will T be penalized for failure to file his return if the total income taxes withheld by his employer were $11,000?

**b.** Assuming T's employer withheld $9,000, what is the amount of the failure-to-file penalty, if any?

**4-48** *Failure-to-Pay Penalty.* On April 13, 2012, R, a calendar year taxpayer, sat down to prepare his 2011 tax return. Realizing that he simply did not have time to accumulate all of his records, R decided to file for an extension. R's tax liability for the previous year, 2010, was $8,000. During 2011 R's employer withheld $2,500 and R paid estimated taxes of $500. R estimates that his final gross tax liability for 2011 will be $12,000.

**a.** Assuming R obtains an extension to file his 2011 return, when will his return normally be due?

**b.** Based on the facts above, what amount must R pay by April 15 to avoid a failure-to-pay penalty?

**c.** R completed and filed his return on July 20, 2012. Unfortunately, his initial estimate of his tax was low and his final tax (before withholding and estimated tax payments) was $15,000. Assuming R paid the amount determined in part (b) above, what is the amount of the failure-to-pay penalty, if any?

**4-49** *Estimated Taxes and Underpayment Penalty.* K works as a salesperson for the National Hospital Supply Corporation, selling surgical and other hospital supplies. He receives a salary plus a percentage commission on sales over a certain threshold. In the current year 2011 K's tax liability before prepayments was $20,000. His 2010 tax liability was $12,000. In each year his A.G.I. was less than $150,000.

**a.** What is the lowest required tax installment (including withholding) that K can make and avoid the penalty for underpaying his taxes during the year? (Ignore the annualized income installment.)

**b.** Assume that K paid estimated taxes of $1,000 on each due date. In addition, K's employer withheld a total of $3,000 during the year. K filed and paid the balance of his liability on April 15, 2012. Assume the applicable interest rate charged on underpayments for each period in 2011 is 10 percent. Compute K's penalty, if any, for failure to pay estimated taxes. Compute the penalty for the first installment only.

**c.** Assume that K works solely for commissions and that he had no income through March 31, 2011 because he decided to take a winter vacation. Income for the remainder of the year was sufficient to generate a tax liability before prepayments of $20,000. What implications do these facts have on the calculation of the underpayment penalty for 2011?

**4-50** *Penalties for Inadequate Estimated Tax Payments.* Z is a calendar year individual whose gross tax for 2011 is $40,000. Z had taxes of $8,000 withheld and did not make estimated tax payments. Z's tax due was paid with his timely filed return on April 15, 2012. His 2010 tax was $35,000 on adjusted gross income of $148,000.

**a.** Calculate Z's penalty for failure to make adequate estimated tax payments, if any.

**b.** Does Z owe interest on any of the amounts paid? If so, for what period?

**c.** Same as (a) above, except Z's adjusted gross income for 2010 was $160,000.

**4-51** *Penalties and Interest.* Y filed her tax return for 2010 on April 15, 2011. Upon discovering an inadvertent error, Y filed an amended return and submitted additional tax of $1,250.

**a.** Does Y owe a penalty for failure to pay? If so, how much?

**b.** Does Y owe interest on the $1,250 paid with the amended return? If so, how much?

**4-52** *Statute of Limitations.* T, a calendar year taxpayer, filed her 2010 Federal income tax return on January 29, 2011 and received a tax refund check for overpaid 2010 taxes on May 17, 2011.

**a.** Assuming that T did not file a false return or have a substantial omission of income, what is the last date on which the IRS may assess an additional income tax liability against her for the 2010 tax year?

**b.** If T unintentionally had a substantial omission of income from her 2010 return, what is the last day on which the IRS may assess her an additional 2010 income tax liability?

**c.** If T had never bothered to file her 2010 tax return, what is the last day on which the IRS may assess her an additional 2010 income tax liability?

## TAX RETURN PROBLEMS

■ *CONTINUOUS TAX RETURN PROBLEMS* See Appendix I, Part 1.

**4-53** *Form 1040EZ.* Samuel B. White was single for 2010 and had no dependents. Sam's only income was wages of $21,150 and taxable interest of $465. Federal income tax of $930 was withheld from Sam's salary.

Calculate Sam's Federal income tax and his tax due or refund for 2010. A Form 1040EZ may be completed based on this information. Supply fictitious occupation, social security number, and address. (**Note:** Use the 2010 tax forms since the 2011 forms may not be available)

**4-54** *Form 1040A.* Charles D. and Alice A. Davis were married during all of 2010 and had income from the following sources:

| | |
|---|---|
| Salary, Charles | $47,100 |
| Federal income tax withheld | 1,425 |
| Part-time salary, Alice | 16,700 |
| Federal income tax withheld | 880 |
| Interest from Home Savings | 320 |
| Interest from U.S. Government Bonds | 430 |

Charles and Alice provide the sole support of their two children (both under age 17). During the year, they paid job-related child care expenses of $2,200. Their itemized deductions for the year are insufficient for them to itemize, but a deductible $2,000 was deposited in each of their individual retirement accounts.

Calculate the Federal income tax and the tax due (or refund) for Mr. and Mrs. Davis, assuming they file a joint return. Use the 2010 tax tables since the 2011 tables may not be available. A Form 1040A may also be completed. Supply fictitious information for the address, occupations, social security numbers, and children's names. (**Note:** Use 2010 tax forms since the 2011 forms may not be available)

**4-55** *Form 1040.* William A. Gregg, a high school educator, and Mary W. Gregg, a microbiologist, are married and file a joint income tax return for 2010. Neither William nor Mary is over 50 years old, and both have excellent sight. They provide the sole support of their three children: Barry, Kimberly, and Rachel (all under age 17). The following information is from their records for 2010:

| | |
|---|---|
| Salaries and wages, William | $34,550 |
| Federal income tax withheld | $2,320 |
| Salaries and wages, Mary | 44,800 |
| Federal income tax withheld | 4,360 |
| Interest income—Home Savings and Loan | 690 |
| Interest income—City Bank | 220 |
| Tax-exempt interest income | 1,400 |
| Itemized deductions as follows: | |
| Hospitalization insurance | 320 |
| Unreimbursed fees of doctors, hospitals, etc | 740 |
| Unreimbursed prescription drugs | 310 |
| Real estate taxes on residence | 1,350 |
| State income taxes paid | 1,440 |
| State sales taxes paid | 720 |
| Interest paid on original home mortgage | 8,430 |
| Charitable contribution—Faith Church | 1,720 |
| Charitable contribution—State University | 200 |
| Quarterly estimated taxes paid | 3,500 |

Calculate the 2010 Federal income tax and the tax due (or refund) for the Greggs assuming they file a joint return. Form 1040, along with Schedules A and B, may be completed. Supply fictitious information for the address and social security numbers. (**Note:** Use 2010 tax forms since the 2011 forms may not be available)

## TAX RESEARCH PROBLEMS

**4-60** *Nonresident Alien Spouse.* C is a citizen of the United States who resides indefinitely in Europe. C is married to N, a citizen of Greece. C has $32,000 of gross income subject to United States tax and would like to file jointly with N. Can C accomplish this goal? If so, what steps are necessary? How is the income of N treated?

***Research aids:***
Code § 6013(g) and Reg. § 1.6013-6.

**4-61** Much to Ted's surprise, his employer, a major hotel chain, asked him to manage the company's premier resort property in Cabo San Lucas, Mexico for the entire calendar year. Ted accepted and was paid $110,000 in compensation for the assignment, visiting the U. S. for only two weeks during the year. Ted's only other income is interest income of $20,000. Ted is single, claims the standard deduction and has no dependents. He is a U. S. citizen. Calculate Ted's tax due and refund assuming he uses the foreign earned income exclusion rather than the foreign tax credit. Ted's tax paid to Mexico was $8,500.

***Research aids:***
Code §§ 901 and 911(a).

# Gross Income

# PART 2

**CHAPTER 5** Gross Income

**CHAPTER 6** Gross Income: Inclusions and Exclusions

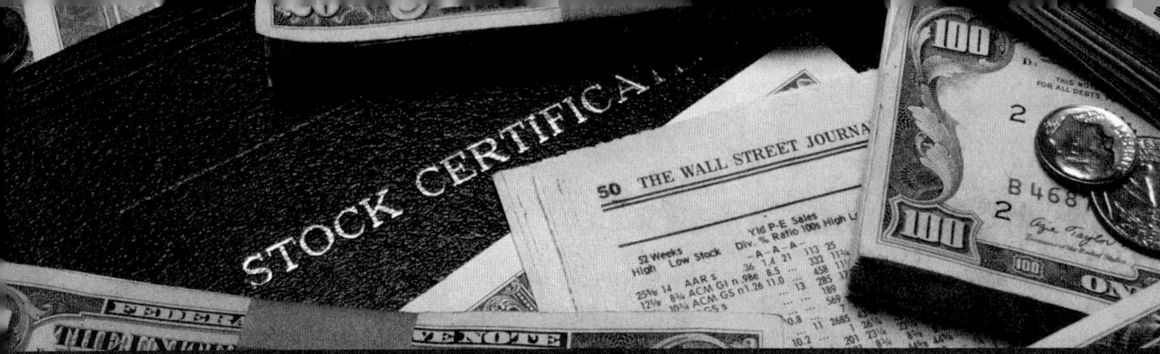


# 5

# Gross Income

## Learning Objectives

Upon completion of this chapter you will be able to:

LO.1 Define income for tax purposes and explain how it differs from the definitions given to it in accounting or economics.

LO.2 Explain the concept of the taxable year and identify who is eligible to use fiscal years.

LO.3 Apply the cash and accrual methods of accounting to determine the tax year in which items are reported.

LO.4 Determine the effect of a change in accounting method.

LO.5 Describe some of the special rules governing the treatment of prepaid income, interest income, interest-free loans, and income from long-term contracts.

LO.6 Identify which taxpayer is responsible for reporting income and paying the taxes on such income.

## Chapter Outline


Introduction 5-2
Gross Income Defined 5-2
  Economic Concept of Income 5-3
  Accounting Concept of Income 5-5
  Income for Tax Purposes: The Judicial Concept 5-5
Refinements of the Gross Income Definition 5-6
  Form-of-Benefit Principle 5-7
  Return of Capital Doctrine 5-8
  Indirect Economic Benefits 5-10
Reporting Income: Tax Accounting 5-12
  Accounting Periods 5-12
  Accounting Methods 5-14
  Cash Method of Accounting 5-15
  Accrual Method of Accounting 5-20
  Changes in Accounting Methods 5-21
Accounting for Income: Special Rules 5-24
  Claim of Right Doctrine 5-24
  Prepaid Income 5-26
  Interest Income 5-29
Identification of the Taxpayer 5-33
  Income from Personal Services 5-34
  Income from Property 5-34
  Unearned Income of Children 5-34
  Interest-Free and Below-Market Loans 5-35
  Income from Community Property 5-38
Tax Planning 5-40
  Timing Income Recognition 5-40
  Income-Splitting Techniques 5-40
  Excluded Economic Income 5-41
Problem Materials 5-42

## Introduction

Determination of the final income tax liability begins with the identification of a taxpayer's gross income. Before that can be done, however, one obviously must understand what constitutes *income* for tax purposes. The primary purpose of this chapter is to examine the income concept and thus provide some general guidelines regarding what is and what is not subject to taxation. As a practical matter, income is normally easy to spot. Salary, interest, dividends, rents, gains from the sales of property, and most other items that one customarily thinks of as income are in fact income for tax purposes. In fact, these represent the bulk of all income that is reported. But what if a taxpayer is lucky enough to receive an inheritance, a gift, or a scholarship? Are these taxable? What about court-awarded damages? And if a taxpayer borrows $1,000, is there income? What happens if Publishers Clearing House gives you $10 million? Is the IRS as happy as you are? And how do hurricane victims treat their government aid? Is their relief taxable? The list of possible income items goes on and on. Fortunately, these items are more the exception than the rule. In any event, newcomers to tax should understand that there are no hard and fast rules that can be applied to every conceivable situation. The Supreme Court clearly stated the problem in a case concerning the income status of embezzled funds:

> In fact, no single conclusive criterion has yet been found to determine in all situations what is sufficient gain to support the imposition of an income tax. No more can be said in general than that all relevant facts and circumstances must be considered.[1]

Notwithstanding the Court's observations, three important generalizations developed in this chapter are

1. "Income" is broadly construed for tax purposes to include virtually any type of gain, benefit, or profit that has been realized.
2. Although the scope of the income concept is broad, certain types of income are exempted from taxation by statute, administrative ruling, or judicial decree.
3. Taxpayers who realize income may not be required to recognize and report it immediately but may be able to postpone recognition until some time in the future.

To sum up, there are three basic questions to address concerning income:

1. Did the taxpayer have income?
2. If the taxpayer had income, was it realized?
3. If the taxpayer has realized income, must it be recognized now or is it permanently excluded or perhaps temporarily deferred and reported at some future date?

The first part of this chapter examines the concept of income. Once one is sensitive to the concept of income, consideration must be given to *if and when* the income must be reported as well as *who* must report it. The latter part of the chapter focuses on the timing of income recognition and the identification of the reporting entity.

## Gross Income Defined

The definition of income found in the Internal Revenue Code reflects the language of the constitutional amendment empowering Congress to impose taxes on income.[2] Section 61(a) of the Code defines *gross income* as follows:

---

[1] *Comm. v. Wilcox*, 46-1 USTC ¶9188, 34 AFTR 811, 327 U.S. 404 (USSC, 1946).

[2] See Chapter 1.

*Sec. 61. Gross income defined.*

*(a) General definition.*

*Except as otherwise provided in this subtitle, gross income means all income from whatever source derived, including (but not limited to) the following items:*

1. *Compensation for services, including fees, commissions, fringe benefits, and similar items;*
2. *Gross income derived from business;*
3. *Gains derived from dealings in property;*
4. *Interest;*
5. *Rents;*
6. *Royalties;*
7. *Dividends;*
8. *Alimony and separate maintenance payments;*
9. *Annuities;*
10. *Income from life insurance and endowment contracts;*
11. *Pensions;*
12. *Income from discharge of indebtedness;*
13. *Distributive share of partnership gross income;*
14. *Income in respect of a decedent; and*
15. *Income from an interest in an estate or trust.*

Despite the statute's detailed enumeration of income items, the list is not comprehensive. The items specified are only a sample of the more common types of income. Taxable income includes many other economic benefits not identified above.

As a practical matter, Code § 61 furnishes little guidance for determining whether a particular benefit should be treated as income. The statute provides no criteria or factors that could be used for assessment. For example, the general definition does not provide any clue as to whether a gift or an inheritance constitutes taxable income. Similarly, the statute is not helpful in determining whether income arises upon the discovery of buried treasure. These and similar issues, as will be seen, are often answered by reference to other, more specific, sections of the Code. On the other hand, many questions cannot be resolved by reference to the statute or the regulations. In situations where clear statutory guidance is absent, the difficult task of ascertaining how far the definitional boundary of income extends falls to the courts. To this end, the courts have utilized the meanings given income in both economics and accounting to mold a workable definition of income for tax purposes.

**LO.1**
Define income for tax purposes and explain how it differs from the definitions given to it in accounting or economics.

## Economic Concept of Income

Economists define income as the amount that an individual could have spent for consumption during a period while remaining as well off at the end of the period as at the beginning of the period. This concept of income may be expressed mathematically as the sum of an individual's consumption during the period plus the change in the individual's net worth between the beginning and end of the period.[3] Note that an increase in net worth is actually savings. Thus income can be defined as $I = C + S$ where I is income, C is consumption and S is savings.

[3] The economic definition of income given here is often referred to as the Haig-Simons definition as derived from the following works: Robert M. Haig, "The Concepts of Income—Economic and Legal Aspects," *The Federal Income Tax* (New York: Columbia University Press, 1921); Henry C. Simons, *Personal Income Taxation* (Chicago: University of Chicago Press, 1921).

## Example 1

K's records revealed the following assets and liabilities as of December 31, 2011 and 2012:

| | 12-31-11 | 12-31-12 |
|---|---|---|
| Assets (fair market value) | $100,000 | $140,000 |
| Liabilities | (20,000) | (30,000) |
| Net worth | $ 80,000 | $110,000 |

During the year, K spent $25,000 on rent, food, clothing, entertainment, and other items. From an economic perspective, K's income for 2012 is $55,000 determined as follows:

| | |
|---|---|
| Consumption | $25,000 |
| Change in net worth ($110,000 – $80,000) | 30,000 |
| Economic income | $55,000 |

There are two key aspects of an economist's definition. The first is the emphasis on a change in net worth. According to the economist, a taxpayer has income under any circumstances that cause his or her net worth to increase. Note that this view is extremely broad. Taxpayers who receive an inheritance, are the beneficiaries of a life insurance policy, discover buried treasure, or have their debts cancelled have all had an increase in net worth and would therefore have income using this definition. Some may object to this comprehensive approach. It is nevertheless consistent with § 61, which states that income includes *all* income regardless of its source.

The second and perhaps more critical aspect of the economist's definition from a tax perspective is the notion that consumption and the change in net worth must be computed using market values on an accrual basis rather than on a realization basis. For example, economists include in income any increase in the value of an individual's shares of stock during the period, even though the shares are not sold and the individual does not *realize* the increase in value. In addition, economists would include in income the rental value of one's car or home, as well as the value of food grown for personal use, since such items constitute consumption. Gifts and inheritances would also be considered income by an economist since these items would affect an individual's net worth. Although the economist's approach to income is theoretically sound, it has significant drawbacks from a practical view.

For practical application, the meaning given to income must be objective to minimize controversies. The economist's reliance on market values to measure net worth and consumption violates this premise. Few assets have readily determinable and accurate values. Valuation of most assets would be a subjective determination. For example, an individual may be able to value shares of stock by referring to an active publicized market, but how is the value of a closely held business or work of art to be computed? The difficulty in making such valuations would no doubt lead to countless disputes and administrative hassles. These practical problems of implementing the economic concept of income have caused the courts to adopt a different interpretation.

It should be pointed out, however, that the economist's approach to measuring income—the so-called net worth method—is sometimes used when the IRS decides that the taxpayer's records do not adequately reflect income.[4] Application usually occurs where the taxpayer has not maintained records, or has falsified or destroyed any records that were kept. In these situations, the IRS reconstructs income by determining the change in net worth during the year and adding estimated living expenses.

Before leaving the economist's definition of income, a final observation is warranted. Over the years, some have argued that the income tax does not encourage savings and, therefore, the U.S. should switch to a consumption tax such as a national retail sales tax. Observe, however, that a similar result could be obtained under the current income tax law if taxpayers were given a deduction for savings. This can be demonstrated mathematically by simply manipulating the terms of the income equation above:

---

[4] *Holland v. U.S.*, 54-2 USTC ¶9714, 46 AFTR 943, 348 U.S. 121 (USSC, 1954). Net worth, however, is to be determined using the tax basis in assets and not their fluctuating market values [*S. Bedeian*, 54 T.C. 295 (1970)].

$$I = C + S$$
$$C = I - S$$

In recent discussions of tax reform, it is not surprising that this concept has surfaced. Only time will tell what changes will be made.

## Accounting Concept of Income

The principle of realization distinguishes the accountant's concept of income from that of the economist. Under this principle, accountants recognize income when it is *realized.* Income is generally considered realized when (l) the earnings process is complete, and (2) an exchange or transaction has taken place.[5] Normally, some type of *conversion* occurs that substantially changes the taxpayer's relationship to the asset. To illustrate, consider a taxpayer who discovers oil on his property. He may have "income" in the economic sense (at least to the extent that the value of his property and his net worth have increased). But he has not realized that increase in net worth and does not have income in the accounting sense until he converts his discovery into another asset (e.g., he sells the property or the oil). Observe that these two criteria provide the objective determination of value traditionally believed necessary for the work that accountants perform. As a result, accounting income usually does not recognize changes in market values of assets during a period (as would economic income) unless such changes have been realized.

## Income for Tax Purposes: The Judicial Concept

The landmark decision of the Supreme Court in *Eisner v. Macomber* in 1918 provided the first glimpse of how the concept of income would be interpreted for tax purposes.[6] In this case, the court embraced the realization principle of accounting, indicating that income must be *realized* before it can be taxed. As later decisions suggested, the primary virtue of the realization principle is not that it somehow yields a better or more theoretically precise income figure. Rather, it provides an objective basis for measuring income, eliminating the problems that would arise if income were determined using subjective valuations. In short, the realization principle is a well-entrenched part of the tax law because it makes the law so much easier to administer.

A second issue addressed by the *Eisner* decision concerned the scope of the income concept. How far did it reach? Did income include gifts, scholarships, court-awarded damages, a personal secretary, and other types of benefits? In essence, the Court again followed the accounting approach, stating that income was restricted to gains realized from property or personal services.

Hence, finding a $10 bill, receiving a prize or award, or profiting from a cancelled debt would not have been taxable under *Eisner*, since the benefits were obtained without any effort by the taxpayer. Later decisions, however, expanded the concept of income by rejecting the notion that only gains derived from capital or labor are recognized. The courts have taken what is often referred to as an "all-inclusive" approach; that is, *all* gains are presumed to be taxable except those specifically exempted. The Supreme Court's opinion in *Glenshaw Glass Co.* provides the definition of income that is perhaps most commonly accepted today.[7] This case involved the treatment of punitive damages awarded to Glenshaw Glass for fraud and antitrust violations of another company. In holding that such awards were income, the Court stated:[8]

> Here we have instances of undeniable accessions to wealth, clearly realized, and over which the taxpayer has complete dominion. The mere fact that the payments were extracted from wrongdoers as punishment for unlawful conduct cannot detract from their character as taxable income to the recipients.

Thus, income for tax purposes is construed to include any type of gain, benefit, profit, or other increase in wealth that has been realized and is not exempted by statute. Note that the

---

[5] "Basic Concepts and Accounting Principles Underlying Financial Statements of Business Enterprises," *Accounting Principles Board Statements No. 4* (New York: American Institute of Certified Public Accountants, 1970), ¶134.

[6] 1 USTC ¶32, 3 AFTR 3020, 252 U.S. 189 (USSC, 1920).

[7] 55-1 USTC ¶9308, 47 AFTR 162, 348 U.S. 426 (USSC, 1955).

[8] *Ibid.*

courts have adopted key elements of both the economic and accounting definition of income: income is any increase in the taxpayer's *net worth* (i.e., wealth) that has been *realized.* Also note that, even though it all sounds very technical and precise, the rule, like so many rules in taxation, may be difficult to apply in a given situation. For example, if a tenant paints the walls of her apartment or plants some gladiolus in the garden, has the landlord realized income? Arriving at a solution for this and any particular set of facts can be quite frustrating, but one can generally take heart that these are rare and, moreover, a common sense approach generally works: if it seems as if the taxpayer is better off, there is probably income.

It should be emphasized that even though a taxpayer may have "income" that has in fact been realized, this by itself does not guarantee that it will be taxed. In tax parlance, the question still remains as to whether the taxpayer must "recognize" the income (i.e., report the income for tax purposes). There are *three* relatively common exceptions to the general rule that all income must be recognized immediately:

1. *Excluded Income.* Income that has been realized need not be recognized if it is specifically exempted from taxation by virtue of some provision in the Code. For example, as discussed in Chapter 6, interest income from state and local bonds is specifically excluded under § 103 while gifts and inheritances (which obviously increase net worth) are excluded under § 102. In these cases, the income permanently escapes tax and normally creates a difference between taxable income and financial accounting income. It should be noted that, notwithstanding the Code's all-inclusive concept of income, the tax base is far from comprehensive because of the numerous exclusions and exemptions that have crept into the law over the years.[9]
2. *Accounting Methods.* A taxpayer may be able to defer recognition of income to a subsequent year by following some particular method of accounting (e.g., the installment sales method or the completed contract method).
3. *Nontaxable Exchanges.* Income realized on a sale or exchange may be deferred under a special nonrecognition rule. For example, a taxpayer who swaps one parcel of land costing $10,000 for another parcel worth $50,000 is not required to recognize the $40,000 gain under the like-kind exchange rules. The theory underlying nonrecognition in this and similar situations is that the taxpayer has not liquidated his investment to cash but has continued it, albeit in another form. In effect, the law is willing to defer the tax until such time when the taxpayer does in fact convert the asset to cash and has the wherewithal to pay the tax. It is important to note, however, that in these and similar cases, the gain is only *deferred*; it does not escape tax permanently as is the case with excluded income.

In summary, income for tax purposes can generally be defined as any increase in wealth (net worth) or consumption that has been realized. In addition, such income normally must be recognized unless it is specifically excluded or postponed due to an accounting rule or deferral provision. A list of some of the common types of income—both taxable and nontaxable—can be found in Exhibit 3-3 and Exhibit 3-4 in Chapter 3.

Before leaving this subject, one final observation should be made. It is important to understand that this definition of gross income is the same for all types of taxpayers. In other words, § 61 and its many interpretations not only applies to individual taxpayers but also applies equally to business entities such as C corporations, S corporations, partnerships, and LLCs as well as trusts and estates.

## Refinements of the Gross Income Definition

As one might imagine, in the early years of the tax law, when there were few specific rules, people found it easy to take the position that Congress never intended to tax their particular type of "income." To support such contentions, taxpayers, never lacking for imagination, often concocted ingenious arguments explaining why they should escape tax. In one

[9] For an excellent discussion of the concept of income and the notion of a comprehensive tax base see Boris Bittker, "A Comprehensive Tax Base as a Goal of Income Tax Reform," 80 *Harvard Law Review* 925 (1967).

memorable case, a taxpayer who received a gift (gifts are specifically excluded from income) argued that the income from the gifted property was also exempt since the income was merely an extension of the gift. Unfortunately, the court did not accept this gift-that-keeps-on-giving theory and taxed the income. But this was typical of the development of the tax law. As the courts dealt with this and other income issues, their decisions set a number of precedents that shaped and refined the concept of income. Because of their significance, some of the principles established by early court decisions were given statutory effect; that is, the rule evolving from the decision was subsequently enacted as part of the law, or codified. For example, § 102(b) now provides that income from gifted property is not part of the gift and is fully taxable.

Other court rulings have been incorporated into the Regulations either directly or by way of reference. Several of these rulings, however, have not found their way into the Code or Regulations. Nevertheless, they provide authoritative guidance for the determination of taxable income. This section examines three major principles that are relevant to the income concept. These concern:

1. *Form of Benefit.* Must income be realized in a particular form, such as cash, before it becomes taxable?
2. *Return of Capital.* Does gross income mean gross receipts or net gain after allowance for a tax-free recovery of the taxpayer's capital investment?
3. *Indirect Economic Benefits.* Are benefits provided by an employer (such as a company car) taxable where they are not intended as compensation?

## Form-of-Benefit Principle

Many taxpayers erroneously believe that income need be reported only when cash is received. The Regulations clearly state, however, that gross income includes income realized in any form.[10] Thus, income is not limited to receipts of cash but also extends to receipts of property, services, and *any other economic benefits.* For example, taxpayers may realize income when their debts are cancelled or they purchase property at a price less than its fair market value—a so-called *bargain purchase.* In situations where income is received in a form other than cash, a cash-equivalent approach is adopted.[11] Under this method, the measure of income is its fair market value at the time of receipt.

### Example 2

Several years ago on the television show *60 Minutes*, a segment was devoted to what the commentators implied was a tax travesty. In truth, it was a sad tale. According to the story, a generous employer who wanted to reward his employees for their long years of service gave them stock in the company. At that time, the stock had a value of about $100 per share. The employees, as one might guess, were extremely pleased. Unfortunately, a sudden turn of events caused the value of the shares to plummet. By the close of the year, the stock was practically worthless. Some employees still holding the stock were upset but accepted their misfortune graciously. On April 15, however, those still holding the stock found themselves in tax shock. What was the problem? As may be apparent from the discussion of the form-of-benefit principle, the employees were required to report compensation income equal to the value of stock at the time of receipt, $100 per share. This meant that many employees had to report thousands of dollars of income even though the stock was currently worthless. They had income without any way to pay the tax. Although the employees might be able to claim a deduction for worthless stock, it might not provide total relief since such loss would be a capital loss, the deduction of which is limited.

---

[10] Reg. § 1.61-1(a).

[11] Reg. § 1.446-1(a)(3).

### Example 3

Borrower B owed Lender L $10,000, evidenced by a note payable due in six months. If L allows B to cancel the note for a payment of $9,000, B must normally recognize gross income of $1,000.

## RETURN OF CAPITAL DOCTRINE

The return of capital doctrine is best illustrated by a simple loan transaction. When a taxpayer lends money and it is later repaid, no income is recognized since the repayment represents merely a *return of capital* to the taxpayer. Although there is no statutory provision to this effect, it is a well-recognized rule. Moreover, the taxpayer's net worth has not increased (one asset, a receivable, has simply been replaced by another, cash). However, any interest on the loan that is paid to the taxpayer would be income.

### Sale or Disposition

The application of the return of capital doctrine is not limited to loans. One of the first refinements made to the income concept concerned the use of the return of capital principle to determine the income from a sale of property. In 1916 the Supreme Court held that the total proceeds received on a sale were not to be treated as income.[12] Rather, the portion of the proceeds representing the taxpayer's capital (i.e., adjusted basis) could be recovered tax free. Thus, it is the return of capital doctrine that allows the taxpayer to determine the income upon a sale or disposition of property by reducing the amount realized (cash + the fair market value of other receipts such as property) by the adjusted basis of the property. Using this approach—now contained in § 1001(a)—the taxpayer's income on dispositions of property is limited to the *gain* realized.

### Example 4

R sold XYZ stock for $10,000. He purchased the stock for $6,000. R's realized gain is $4,000 ($10,000 amount realized – $6,000 adjusted basis) rather than the gross amount of the sales price, $10,000, since the return of capital doctrine permits him to recover his $6,000 investment tax free.

The return of capital doctrine also stands for the important proposition that gross income is not the same as gross receipts. This is reflected in Regulations, which provide that in the manufacturing, merchandising, or mining business, *gross income* means total sales less costs of goods sold.[13]

### Damages

The return of capital doctrine may also apply to amounts awarded for injury inflicted upon the taxpayer.

### Example 5

In *Edward H. Clark*, the Clarks overpaid their taxes by about $19,000 due to a mistake made by an attorney in the preparation of their return. The attorney subsequently reimbursed the Clarks for the overpayment.[14] The Court allowed the Clarks to exclude the reimbursement since there was no economic gain but merely a recovery of their

[12] *Doyle v. Mitchell Bros.*, 1 USTC ¶17, 3 AFTR 2979, 247 U.S. 179 (USSC, 1918). See also *Southern Pacific Company v. Lowe*, 1 USTC ¶19, 247, 3 AFTR 2989, 247 U.S. 330 (USSC, 1918).

[13] Reg. § 1.61-3(a).

[14] 40 BTA 333 (1939); See also Rev. Rul. 81-277, 1981-2 CB 14.

capital. In *Inaja Land Co., Ltd.*, the taxpayer received payments from the city of Los Angeles to compensate it for damages caused by the city's diversion of polluted waters into the taxpayer's fishing area.[15] The court granted an exclusion on the return of capital theory but required the taxpayer to reduce its basis in the property by the amount received.

Section 104, discussed in detail in the following chapter, specifically excludes from income the amount of any damages awarded for personal physical injury or physical sickness on the grounds that the amount received represents a return of the personal capital destroyed. In many cases, amounts are also awarded to penalize the party responsible for the wrongdoing. These so-called punitive damages are normally taxable.[16] Similarly, where the damages awarded represent reimbursement for lost profits, the amounts are considered taxable since they are merely substitutions for income.[17]

### Example 6

After ten consecutive losing seasons as head football coach at Trample University and a swing at his offensive line coach, Coach F was fired. Shortly thereafter, F developed an ulcer, which forced him to have surgery. It was subsequently determined that the operation had been improperly performed. F sued the university for lost wages and the court awarded him $25,000. The $25,000 is fully taxable since it represents a substitution of income. F also sued the surgeon for $200,000 for malpractice and won. If the $200,000 represents damages awarded for physical injury, the amount is excluded under §104. However, if the award represents punitive damages, it is taxable.

Damages awarded to businesses are generally subject to the same tests applied to individuals. Awards or settlements for antitrust violations or patent infringements are examples of substitutions for income and thus are taxable. This is true for both actual and punitive damages. Compensation for damages to property are taxable to the extent that amounts received exceed the adjusted basis of the assets. Where the award is for damages to the goodwill of the business, the entire amount is usually taxable since the taxpayer normally does not have any recoverable basis in the goodwill.[18]

### Example 7

M left her car running and ran inside the bank to make a deposit. When she came back, she stopped in shock as she watched her car plunge through the front of a furniture store. The furniture store ultimately received $50,000 in damages for property for which it had a basis of $35,000. The store realized a gain of $15,000. This gain must be recognized unless certain special rules concerning involuntary conversions discussed in Chapter 15 are followed.

### Other Considerations

The scope of the return of capital doctrine extends beyond situations involving damages and simple sales transactions. Numerous Code sections are grounded on this principle, and often contain detailed rules for ascertaining how a receipt should be apportioned between capital and income. For example, amounts received under a life insurance policy are not taxable on

[15] 9 T.C. 727, (1947).

[16] § 104(a)(2); but see § 104(c) for an exception if only punitive damages can be awarded.

[17] *Phoenix Coal Co. v. Comm.*, 56-1 USTC ¶9366, 49 AFTR 445, 231 F.2d 420 (CA-2, 1956).

[18] *Raytheon Production Corp. v. Comm.*, 44-2 USTC ¶9424, 32 AFTR 1155, 144 F.2d 100 (CA-1, 1944).

the theory that the proceeds—at least in part—represent a return of the taxpayer's premium payments.[19] Similarly, where the taxpayer purchases an annuity (i.e., an investment which makes a series of payments to the investor in the future), the return of capital doctrine provides that each payment is in part a tax-free return of capital.[20] In addition, somewhat intricate provisions exist to determine whether a corporate distribution represents a distribution of earnings (i.e., a dividend) or a tax-free return of the taxpayer's investment.[21] The special rules governing life insurance, annuities, and dividends are covered in detail in Chapter 6.

## Indirect Economic Benefits

Another refinement to the otherwise all-inclusive definition of gross income concerns certain benefits provided by employers for employees. Early rulings and decisions exempted benefits conferred to employees that did not represent compensation and were provided for the convenience of the employer. For example, in 1919, the IRS ruled that lodging furnished seamen aboard ship was not taxable.[22] Similarly, in 1925, the Court of Claims held that the value of quarters provided an Army officer was not includible in income.[23] Explanations offered for exempting the lodging from income emphasized that the employee was granted the benefit solely because the employer's business could not function properly unless an employee was furnished that benefit on the employer's premises. The Court also observed that the benefits were not designed as a form of compensation for the employee, but rather were an outgrowth of business necessity. These early holdings established the view that certain benefits an employee receives indirectly from his or her employer are nontaxable. Current law grants an exclusion only if the employee can demonstrate that the benefit served a business purpose of the employer other than to compensate the employee.[24]

### Example 8

In the following situations an employee is permitted to exclude the benefit received under the rationale discussed above.

1. An employer provides the employee with a place to work and supplies tools and machinery with which to do the work. Similarly, an employee is not taxed when his or her secretary types a letter.
2. An employer provides tuition-free, American-style schools for its overseas employees.
3. An employer provides an executive with protection in response to threats made by terrorists.
4. An employer requires its employees to attend a convention held in a resort in Florida and pays the travel costs of the employees.

It is often difficult to determine whether a particular benefit represents compensation or, alternatively, serves the business needs of the employer. For example, free parking places and similar fringe benefits provided by an employer could arguably fall into either category, depending upon the circumstances. After many years of controversy concerning the taxation of fringe benefits, Congress addressed the problem in 1984. To emphasize that fringe benefits are taxable, Congress modified the listing of typical income items found in § 61 to specifically include "fringe benefits and similar items." However, several exceptions exempting certain benefits still exist. These exceptions are discussed in Chapter 6 concerning exclusions.

---

[19] § 101.

[20] § 72.

[21] §§ 301 and 316.

[22] O.D. 265, 1 C.B. 71 (1919).

[23] *Jones v. U.S.*, 1 USTC ¶129, 5 AFTR 5297, 60 Ct. Cls. 552 (1925). Section 119, discussed in Chapter 6, currently provides specific rules that must be satisfied before meals and lodging may be excluded.

[24] *George D. Patterson v. Thomas*, 61-1 USTC 9310, 7 AFTR2d 862, 289 F.2d 108 (CA-2, 1960).

## Check Your Knowledge

### Review Question 1

After exploring the cavernous pits of his patient's mouth, Dr. Will Floss, a dentist, concluded that the gentleman had to have a root canal. Floss explained to the patient the nature of the work and that it could very well be the first in a series of expensive steps required to put his teeth back in working order. He estimated the total cost at $5,000. At that moment, the patient, a wily floor-covering dealer, immediately recalled Floss's need for new carpeting. As a result, he suggested that he would be happy to make a deal: carpeting, pad, and installation in exchange for the dental work. The two agreed, the teeth were repaired, and the carpeting was installed. Is there a tax problem here?

The issue is whether either party must report income. Many individuals think that barter transactions, exchanges of property for services or property other than cash, are not taxable. However, taxpayers who believe bartering escapes the eye of the tax collector are in for a rude awakening by the IRS. Barter transactions are fully taxable under the form-of-benefit principle. It makes no difference whether the taxpayer's net worth is increased by cash or property. In either case, the taxpayer is better off and must recognize income. Here the dentist recognizes income equal to the value of the services rendered, $5,000, and the carpet salesman has revenue equal to the value of services received.

### Review Question 2

Several years ago, Intel Corporation, a leading manufacturer of computer chips in the United States, sued another chip manufacturer, American Micro, for using its patented technology. The courts awarded Intel millions of dollars for the infringement. Another situation, perhaps more well-known, was the McDonalds coffee debacle. In this case, a jury awarded 79-year-old Stella Liebeck of Albuquerque, New Mexico $200,000 in compensatory damages and another $2.7 million in punitive damages for severe burns she suffered when she spilled McDonald's coffee in her lap. (Liebeck and McDonald's ultimately settled for unknown amounts out of court.) In a comparable story, Theresa Burke and more than 8,000 other women employees of the Tennessee Valley Authority claimed unlawful discrimination in the payment of salaries on the basis of sex. The TVA had increased the salaries in certain male-dominated pay schedules, but not in certain female-dominated pay schedules. Moreover, the TVA lowered salaries in the latter. The female employees asked for and were awarded back pay, costs, and attorney's fees. Burke and the other women each received amounts in settlement according to a formula based on their length of service and rates of pay. What tax treatment might be proposed for these taxpayers?

The basic question in all of these situations is the same: does Intel, Liebeck, or Burke have taxable income? The key is recognizing that the amounts received may be taxable or nontaxable depending on the application of the return of capital doctrine and perhaps other provisions of the Code. The problem that Intel faces is demonstrating that the award for the patent infringement is not merely a replacement of lost income. It would appear that the corporation would have a difficult time overcoming a long string of cases that indicates that patent infringement awards are taxable. Nevertheless, there is no certainty in these matters without knowledge of all of the facts and a great deal of research. On the other hand, Liebeck probably had an easier time excluding her compensatory damages for her physical injury since they represent a return of her personal capital. However, the treatment of the punitive damages, although clearly taxable now, was not as clear under prior law. And what about Ms. Burke? It would seem that the knife could cut either way. On the one hand, the amounts received reimbursed her for back pay and arguably should be taxable as a substitution of income. On the other hand, the amounts could be viewed as a nontaxable reimbursement for a personal injury, sexual discrimination. If this seems difficult, it was. The courts struggled with the issue. The Sixth Circuit Court of Appeals held that the amounts were not taxable, but that decision was reversed by the Supreme Court. In 1996, Congress clarified the treatment, providing in § 104 that emotional distress does not constitute physical injury or physical sickness, thereby making damages from sex or age discrimination taxable.

### Review Question 3

There is little doubt that the CEOs of Chrysler and GM, receive the use of a company car. The same can probably be said for the owners of every car dealership in the country as well as their salespeople. (If only accountants could receive such a deal!) Assume that each individual can drive the car for only 3,000 miles, after which he or she must evaluate the experience then exchange the old car for a new one and do it all over again. This is a nice arrangement: use a Jeep Grand Cherokee one month and a Chrysler Town and Country Van the next. Great benefits, but what are the tax consequences?

Once again the question concerns income. Is the value of the use of the company car taxable? Can the taxpayers argue that their use (including all personal trips) is not compensation but simply an incidental benefit that they must endure in order to evaluate the car? Does the indirect benefit rule apply? Is there a special provision that exempts fringe benefits of this nature? In a long line of cases, it has been established that the value of a car provided by an employer is compensation to the extent of the employee's personal use. The twist on the basic fact pattern—the required evaluation—may, however, suggest a different conclusion. The fringe benefit rules enacted in 1984 and discussed more fully in Chapter 6 do allow an exclusion for certain full-time automobile salespeople who use demonstration vehicles in the sales area in which the automobile dealer's sales office is located. Note that this rule applies only to salespeople. Thus an owner or executive would not qualify for an exclusion under this exception unless he or she also is considered a salesperson. There may be another escape hatch for executives and other management personnel, however, buried in the Regulations concerning product testing.[25] These Regulations allow the employee to exclude the benefit if the employee receives goods for testing and evaluation if a laundry list of requirements is met. The key point to remember here is not necessarily knowing the specific answer to this question but recognizing that an important theory exists—the indirect benefit doctrine—that is a valuable weapon on which the taxpayer can sometimes rely to avoid taxation of what at first glance has all the characteristics of taxable income.

## Reporting Income: Tax Accounting

Once the taxpayer has realized an item of taxable income, he or she must determine *when* the income should be reported. This determination, however, requires an understanding of the nature of accounting periods and accounting methods that may be used for tax purposes. This section examines some of the fundamental rules of tax accounting and how they govern the timing of income recognition.

### Accounting Periods

**LO.2**
Explain the concept of the taxable year and identify who is eligible to use fiscal years.

Taxable income is usually computed on the basis of an annual accounting period commonly known as the taxable year.[26] There are two types of taxable years: a calendar year and a fiscal year. A calendar year is a 12-month period ending on December 31, whereas a fiscal year generally is any period of 12 months ending on the last day of any month other than December.[27] Any taxpayer may use a calendar year. Fiscal years may be used only by taxpayers who maintain adequate books and records. A taxpayer filing his or her *first* return may adopt either a calendar year or a fiscal year without IRS consent simply by filing a return. After adoption, however, any change does require IRS consent.[28]

#### Income from Partnerships, S Corporations, and Fiduciaries

Reporting income derived from an interest in a partnership, an S corporation, or an estate or trust presents a special problem. As explained in Chapter 3, income realized by a partnership or an S corporation is not taxable to either of these because they are not treated as separate taxable entities. Rather, the partnership or S corporation merely serves as a conduit through which the income flows. Consequently, partners or S shareholders report their distributive shares of the entity's income in their taxable year within which (or with which) the

[25] Reg. § 1.132-5(n).

[26] § 441(a) and (b).

[27] Reg. § 1.441-1(d) and (e). The taxpayer may elect to end the tax year on a particular day of the week rather than a date, resulting in a tax year that varies in length between 52 and 53 weeks. See Reg. § 1.441-2.

[28] A request for a change is made on Form 1128. The initial selection of, or a change in, tax year may result in a short tax year, in which case the tax may have to be computed on an annualized basis. See §§ 442 and 443.

partnership or S corporation tax year ends. Partners or S shareholders must report their share of the income regardless of the amounts distributed to them.

### Example 9

DEF Company, a fiscal year taxpayer, is a partnership owned equally by D, E, and F. For the taxable year ending September 30, 2011, the company had net income of $90,000. During the 12-month period ending on September 30, 2011, D withdrew $20,000 from his capital account. For his year ending December 31, 2011, D must report his share of partnership income, $30,000 (of $90,000), even though he only received a distribution of $20,000. Note that any income earned by the partnership from October 2011 through December 2011 is not reported until D files his 2012 tax return, which is normally due on April 15, 2013.

Income realized by a trust or an estate is generally taxed to the beneficiaries to the extent it is actually distributed or required to be distributed. Income that is not taxed to the beneficiaries is taxed to the estate or trust.

## Limitation on Fiscal Years

One effect of allowing fiscal years for reporting is to enable certain taxpayers to *defer* the taxation of income. For instance, in Example 9 above, the choice by the partnership to use a fiscal year creates an opportunity for D. Note that D's share of the partnership's income for October 2011 through December 2011 is not reported until D files his 2012 tax return, which is normally filed on April 15, 2013. A small corporation that primarily provides personal services could obtain a similar deferral.

### Example 10

G&H Inc., a law firm, is a regular C corporation owned by two attorneys, G and H. The corporation reports using a fiscal year ending on January 31. During 2011 the corporation paid G and H small salaries. Just before the close of its taxable year ending January 31, 2012, the corporation paid a bonus to G and H equal to its taxable income. By deducting the bonus, the corporation reports no income for its taxable year ending January 31, 2012, and G and H defer reporting the bonus until they file their 2012 tax return on April 15, 2013.

In 1986, Congress felt that the use of fiscal years to create deferral of income as shown above was improper. As a result, provisions were enacted that restrict the use of fiscal years by partnerships, S corporations, and so-called personal service corporations (i.e., corporations where the principal activity is the performance of services, substantially all of which are performed by employees who are also the owners of the business). Although certain exceptions enable these entities to use a fiscal year on a limited basis, as a general rule, these taxpayers normally must use the calendar year.[29]

## Annual Accounting and Progressive Rates

The use of an annual accounting period in combination with other features of the taxation process causes numerous difficulties. For example, consider the effect of the tax system's use of both an annual accounting period and a progressive tax rate structure. Each year the taxpayer computes his or her taxable income for that period and applies a progressive rate structure to the income of that year. If income varies from one year to the next, taxes paid on the *total* income of those two years are likely to exceed the total taxes that would have resulted had the taxpayer earned the income equally each year. The problems that occur with so-called incoming-bunching are illustrated below.

[29] §§ 441(i), 444, 706(b), and 1378.

## Example 11

Taxpayer R is a salesperson whose income is derived solely from commissions. Taxpayer S earns a salary. Both taxpayers are single. In 20X1 and 20X2 R's taxable income was $80,000 and $20,000 respectively, while S had taxable income of $50,000 each year. The tax effect on R and S (rounded to the nearest dollar and using 2011 tax rates) is as follows:

| | *R (Single)* | | *S (Single)* | |
|---|---|---|---|---|
| | *Taxable Income* | *Tax* | *Taxable Income* | *Tax* |
| 20X1 . . . . . . . . . . . . . . . . . . . . | $ 80,000 | $16,125 | $ 50,000 | $ 8,625 |
| 20X2 . . . . . . . . . . . . . . . . . . . . | 20,000 | 2,575 | 50,000 | 8,625 |
| Total . . . . . . . . . . . . . . . . . | $100,000 | $18,700 | $100,000 | $17,250 |

Note that although R and S have the same total income of $100,000 for the two-year period, R's total tax bill of $18,700 exceeds S's bill of $17,250 by $1,450.

As the above example demonstrates, the use of an annual accounting period may create inequities. Here R could reduce his tax bite if he could defer some of his income from one year to the next so as to split his income between years as equally as possible. Occasionally, Congress has responded by enacting special provisions. For example, where a taxpayer has a loss during the year, the net operating loss rules allow the taxpayer to utilize the loss by permitting it to be carried back or forward to profitable years.[30] Without these carryback and carryover provisions, the taxpayer would receive no benefit from any losses realized. Unfortunately, Congress has not always acted. Gamblers can deduct their losses but only to the extent of their winnings. So if they have winnings in one year and losses in another, they are out of luck.

## Accounting Methods

**LO.3**
Apply the cash and accrual methods of accounting to determine the tax year in which items are reported.

Once a tax year is identified, the taxpayer must determine in which period a transaction is to be reported. The year in which a particular item becomes part of the tax calculation is not a trivial matter. The time of recognition can make a substantial difference in the taxpayer's total tax liability not only because of the time value of money but also because factors affecting the tax calculations may change from year to year. For instance, tax rates may go up or down from one year to the next. Such change does not necessarily take an act of Congress. A taxpayer may simply marry, divorce, incorporate, or change from a taxable to tax-exempt entity. In such case, deferral of income to the low-rate year and acceleration of deductions to the high-rate year could produce significant savings. Similarly, Congress may completely revise the treatment of an item. For example, in 1993 Congress raised the top tax rate from 31 to 39.6 percent, eliminated the deduction for business club dues, dropped the amount of the deduction for business meals and entertainment from 80 to 50 percent, eliminated the deduction for certain moving expenses, increased the Medicare tax, increased the amount of social security benefits that are subject to tax, and raised the amount of business equipment that may be expensed from $10,000 to $17,500. Changes like these have become an annual rite in the tax area, consequently making timing critical.

The rules that determine when a particular item is reported are generally referred to as accounting methods. The Code identifies four permissible methods of accounting:[31]

1. The cash receipts and disbursements method
2. The accrual method
3. Any other method permitted by the Code (e.g., a method for a specific situation such as the completed contract method or the use of LIFO to value inventories)[32]
4. Any combination of the three methods above permitted by the Regulations

[30] § 172.See Chapter 10 for a discussion of the net operating loss rules.

[31] § 446(c).

[32] Reg. § 1.446-1(c)(1)(iii).

The term *accounting method* is not limited to the overall method of accounting used by the taxpayer (e.g., the cash or accrual method). It generally includes the treatment of *any particular item* if such treatment affects *when* the item will be reported. For example, the use of LIFO to value inventories would be considered an accounting method since the use of this method determines when the cost of a product will become part of cost of goods sold.

It should be emphasized that the taxpayer is not required to adopt one overall method of accounting. For example, a taxpayer with inventories generally must use the accrual method to account for inventories and related sales. However, the same taxpayer could use the cash method to report interest income or other items. This approach (referred to as the *hybrid method*) is completely acceptable as long as the taxpayer applies the same methods consistently.

Taxpayers are generally allowed to select the methods of accounting they wish to use. In all cases, however, the IRS has the right to determine if the method used *clearly reflects income*, and, if not, to make the necessary adjustments.[33] For example, assume that each year a taxpayer changes the way it computes the amount of overhead that it capitalizes as part of inventory (e.g., on the basis of direct labor hours one year, machine hours the next). In such case, the IRS might require the taxpayer to use one method consistently so that income would not be distorted from year to year but would be clearly reflected.

### Tax Methods versus Financial Accounting Methods

At first glance, many people—particularly accountants—would no doubt conclude that a method of accounting that conforms with generally accepted accounting principles (GAAP) would be regarded as clearly reflecting income.[34] Although this is ordinarily true, it is not always the case.[35] Conflicts sometimes exist because the objectives of the income tax system differ from that of financial accounting. The primary goal of financial accounting is to provide useful information to management, shareholders, creditors, and other interested parties. In contrast, the goal of the income tax system is to ensure that revenues are fairly collected. Due to these different goals, the tax law may disregard fundamental accounting principles. Perhaps the most obvious example can be found in the tax law's allowance of the cash method of accounting. Despite its failure to properly match revenues and expenses, the cash method is normally tolerated because from an administrative view it is simple and objective. Such administrative concerns often dictate a different approach for tax purposes. For example, an accrual basis taxpayer is often required to report prepaid income when received rather than when earned. Although this practice violates the matching principle, it ensures that the tax is imposed when the taxpayer has the cash to pay it.

The operation of differing objectives can also be seen in the use of estimates. One of the major responsibilities of financial accountants is to ensure that financial statement users are not misled. This demand normally encourages accountants to be conservative, which in turn may cause them to understate rather than overstate income. Although the government does not want taxpayers to overstate income, it certainly does not want to endorse principles that would tend toward understatement. Thus, the tax law generally does not allow taxpayers to estimate future expenses such as bad debts or warranty costs and deduct them currently, as is the case with financial accounting. Instead, the deduction is allowed only when there is objective evidence that a cost has been incurred. The government frowns on estimates of expenses, presumably because taxpayers would tend to overstate them.

Reporting of prepaid income and the treatment of estimated expenses are just two examples of where financial accounting principles deviate from tax accounting. The key point to recognize is that a particular item may be treated one way for financial accounting purposes and another way for tax purposes. As a practical matter, this may mean that two sets of books are maintained, or what is perhaps more likely, one set based on financial accounting principles to which adjustments must be made to arrive at taxable income.

## Cash Method of Accounting

### General Rule

Virtually all individuals—as well as many corporations, partnerships, trusts, and estates—use the cash method of accounting. Its prevalence is no doubt attributable to the fact that it is

---

[33] § 446(b).

[34] Reg. § 1.446-1(a)(2).

[35] For an excellent example, see *Thor Power Tool Co.*, 79-1 USTC ¶9139, 43 AFTR2d 79-362, 439 U.S. 522 (USSC, 1979).

easy to use. Under the cash method, taxpayers simply report items of income and deduction in the year in which they are received or paid.[36] In effect, the cash method allows taxpayers merely to refer to their checkbooks to determine taxable income.

In using the cash method, items of income need not be in the form of cash but need only be capable of valuation in terms of money. Under this rule, sometimes termed the *cash equivalent doctrine*, the taxpayer reports income when the equivalent of cash is received.[37] Thus, where property or services are received, the fair market value of these items serves as the measure of income.

Due to the cash equivalent doctrine, reporting of income arising from notes and accounts receivable differs. Notes received by a cash basis taxpayer are usually considered property and hence constitute income equal to the value of the note.[38] Where a promise to pay is *not* evidenced by a note (e.g., credit sales resulting in accounts receivable), income is normally not recognized by a cash basis taxpayer until payment is received.[39] This treatment results because unsupported promises to pay normally are not considered as having a fair market value.

### Constructive Receipt Doctrine

Taxpayers using the cash method of accounting have substantial control over income recognition since they may control the timing of the actual receipt of cash. If the requirement calling for *actual* receipt were strictly adhered to, the cash basis taxpayer could easily frustrate the purpose of progressive taxation. For example, taxpayers could select the year with the lowest tax rate and simply cash their salary or dividend checks or redeem their interest coupons in that year. To curtail this practice, the doctrine of constructive receipt was developed. Under this principle, a taxpayer is *deemed* to have received income even though such income has not actually been received. It should be noted that there is no corresponding doctrine for deductions (i.e., there is no constructive payment doctrine).

The constructive receipt doctrine is currently expressed in Regulation § 1.451-2(a) as follows:

> Income, although not actually reduced to the taxpayer's possession, is constructively received by him in the taxable year in which it is credited to his account, set apart for him or otherwise made available so that he could have drawn upon it during the taxable year if notice of intention to withdraw had been given. However, income is not constructively received if the taxpayer's control of its receipt is subject to substantial limitations or restrictions.

As the Regulation indicates, the taxpayer is treated as having received income when three conditions are satisfied:

1. The taxpayer has control over the amount without substantial limitations and restrictions
2. The amount has been set aside or credited to the taxpayer's account
3. The funds are available for payment by the payer (i.e., the payer's ability to make payment must be considered)

Some of the common situations to which the rule is applied are illustrated in the following examples.

#### Example 12

B refereed a basketball game on Saturday night, December 31, 2011 and did not receive the check for his services until after the banks had closed. He cashed the check on January 3, 2012. B must report the income in 2011. In the case of a check, a taxpayer is deemed to have received payment in the year the check is received rather than when it is cashed.[40]

---

[36] Reg. § 1.446-1(c)(1)(i).

[37] Reg. § 1.446-1(a)(3).

[38] *A.W. Wolfson*, 1 B.T.A. 538 (1925).

[39] *Bedell v. Comm.*, 1 USTC ¶359, 7 AFTR 8469, 30 F.2d 622 (CA-2, 1929).

[40] *C.F. Kahler*, 18 T.C. 31 (1952).

### Example 13

T mailed a check on December 29, 2011, which S received in January 2012. S is not in constructive receipt of the check since it was not available to him for his immediate use and enjoyment. However, if S requested that T mail him the check so that he receives it in 2012, or if S could have received the check by merely appearing in person and claiming it, S would be deemed to have received the payment in 2011.

### Example 14

When G made a deposit on January 15, 2012, the bank updated her passbook on December 31, 2011 to show that $200 of interest was credited to her account for the last quarter of 2011. G withdrew the interest on January 31. G must report the interest in 2011. Interest credited to the taxpayer's account is taxable when credited, regardless of whether it is in the taxpayer's possession, assuming that it may be withdrawn.[41]

### Example 15

B Corporation mailed dividend checks dated December 20 on December 28, 2011. R, a shareholder in B, received her check on January 4, 2012. R reports the dividend income in 2012 as long as the payer customarily pays dividends by mail so that the shareholder receives it after the end of the year.[42]

### Example 16

R's secretary received several checks for services that R had performed. Payments received by a taxpayer's agent are considered constructively received by the taxpayer.[43]

### Example 17

A taxpayer who agrees not to cash a check until authorized by the payer has not constructively received income if the payer does not have sufficient funds in the bank to cover the check.[44]

## Limitations on the Use of the Cash Method

As a method of accounting, the cash method's principal advantage lies in its simplicity and objectivity. If a taxpayer uses the cash method, taxable income is easily computed merely by

---

[41] Reg. § 1.451-2(b).

[42] *Ibid.*; *S.L. Avery*, 4 USTC ¶1277, 13 AFTR 1168, 292 U.S. 210 (USSC, 1934). See also *H.B. McEuen v. Comm.*, 52-1 USTC ¶9281, 41 AFTR 1169, 196 F.2d 127 (CA-5, 1952).

[43] *T. Watson*, 2 TCM 863 (1943).

[44] *A.V. Johnston*, 23 TCM 2003, T.C. Memo 1964-323.

referring to cash receipts and disbursements. Moreover, the amount of taxable income computed in this manner is incontrovertible—it is not open to question or dispute and is readily verifiable. Unlike the accrual method, whether income has been "earned" or expenses have been "incurred" are simply not issues under the cash method.

On other counts, the cash method scores poorly, ranking a distant second to the accrual method. From an accounting perspective, the cash method is entirely inappropriate since income and expense are recognized without regard to the taxable year in which the economic events responsible for the income or expense actually occur. Similarly, when some parties to a transaction use different methods of accounting, there may be a mismatching of income and deductions. For example, an accrual basis corporation could accrue expenses payable to a cash basis individual. In such case, the corporation could obtain deductions without ever having to make a disbursement and, moreover, without the individual taxpayer recognizing any offsetting income.

While the above are clearly shortcomings, the major flaw found in the cash method is that it is easily abused. Taxpayers have often secured benefits by merely timing their transactions appropriately: recognizing income in one year, deductions in the next, or what is more likely, deductions in years in which the taxpayer is in a high tax bracket and income in years in which the taxpayer is in a low tax bracket.

To attack these problems, Congress has limited the use of the cash method of accounting. The following entities are normally prohibited from using the cash method:[45]

1. Regular C corporations;
2. Partnerships that have regular C corporations as partners (other than certain personal service corporations described below); and
3. *Tax shelters*, generally defined as any enterprise (other than a regular C corporation) in which interests have been offered for sale in any offering required to be registered under Federal or State security agencies.

Despite these general restrictions, Congress believed that the simplicity of the cash method justified its continued use in certain instances. For example, Congress felt that it would be costly for small businesses to switch to the accrual method. Similarly, it recognized that the accrual method would create undue complexity for farming businesses if such a method were required to account for growing crops and livestock. In addition, Congress believed that personal service corporations, which have traditionally used the cash method, should be allowed to continue their use. Accordingly, the following entities are allowed to use the cash method.[46]

1. Any corporation or partnership whose average annual *gross receipts* for *all* preceding years do not exceed $5 million. This test is satisfied for any prior year only if the average annual gross receipts[47] for the three-year period ending with such year does not exceed $5 million. Once this average *exceeds* $5 million, the corporation cannot use the cash method for the following year.
2. Certain farming businesses.
3. Qualified personal service corporations. A regular C corporation is qualified if substantially all of the activities consist of performing services in eight fields, including health, law, engineering, architecture, accounting, actuarial science, performing arts, or consulting, *and* at least 95 percent of its stock is held by the employees who are providing such services.[48]

**Example 18**

Dr. C and Dr. D, both heart surgeons, own 100% of the stock of Cardiac Care Corporation. The corporation provides the latest in diagnostic testing and treatments,

[45] § 448(a).

[46] § 448(b).

[47] Gross receipts include total sales (net of returns and allowances but not reduced by costs of goods sold) and amounts received for services, interest, rents, royalties, and annuities. For sales of capital assets and real or depreciable property used in trade or business, gross receipts are reduced by the taxpayer's adjusted basis in such property. See Temp. Reg. § 1.448-1T(f)(2)(iv).

[48] § 448(d)(2).

including open heart surgery and rehabilitation. Because all of the corporations's services are in the area of health and more than 95% of the stock is owned by the doctors who are providing the services, the corporation may use the cash method of accounting.

## Example 19

C's Video Rentals, a regular C corporation, started business in 20X1. Since that time it has grown to 20 locations and had annual gross receipts as follows:

| *Year* | *Gross Receipts* | *Average Annual Gross Receipts** |
|---|---|---|
| 20X1 | $ 4,000,000 | $4,000,000 |
| 20X2 | 2,000,000 | 3,000,000 |
| 20X3 | 6,000,000 | 4,000,000 |
| 20X4 | 10,000,000 | 6,000,000 |

$$^*\frac{\text{Current} + \text{Prior two years}}{3 \text{ (or if less, years in existence)}}$$

It initially adopted the cash method in 20X1. It was able to use the cash method through 20X4 because the average annual gross receipts for all prior years did not exceed $5 million. Note that although its gross receipts were $6,000,000 in 20X3, its *average annual* gross receipts for that year were only $4,000,000 [($4,000,000 + $2,000,000 + $6,000,000) ÷ 3]. Consequently, the cash method could be used for 20X4. It will be denied use of the cash method for 20X5 since the average annual gross receipts for 20X4 exceed $5 million [($2,000,000 + $6,000,000 + $10,000,000) ÷ 3 = $ 6,000,000].

It should be noted that the above exceptions do not apply to tax shelters. Any enterprise considered a tax shelter must use the accrual method. In addition, as discussed below, if the taxpayer maintains inventories, special rules apply.

### Accounting for Inventory

As noted above, most businesses—other than large C corporations—are permitted to use the cash method. However, an important exception exists for taxpayers with inventories. According to the longstanding rule of Regulation §1.471-1 "[I]n order to reflect taxable income correctly, inventories ... are necessary in every case in which the production, purchase, or sale of merchandise is an income producing factor." Regulation § 1.446-1(c)(2) adds that in any case in which it is necessary to use an inventory the accrual method of accounting must be used with regard to purchases and sales ... In short, if a business sells "inventory," taxpayers must capitalize the cost of inventory purchases and can expense such costs only when the item is sold. Just as important, if not more so, businesses with inventories also must accrue and recognize income at the time of sale—regardless of when the cash is received. Both halves of the accrual requirement are significant since both effect the amount of income that the taxpayer ultimately reports in a particular year.

The reasoning behind the regulatory scheme requiring inventories is anchored in the matching principle that ensures income will be clearly reflected. The rationale was eloquently stated by the Appellate Court in *Knight-Ridder Newspapers Inc.*, a case involving whether a cash-basis corporation should inventory its costs of newsprint and ink.[49]

[49] 84 -2 USTC ¶9827, 54 AFTR 2d 84-6120, 743 F.2d 781 (CA-11, 1984).

> According to accounting wisdom the income realized from the sale of merchandise is most *clearly measured* by matching the cost of the merchandise with the revenue from its sale. In order to achieve such matching of revenue and cost, it is necessary to keep an inventory account reflecting the costs of merchandise, raw materials, and manufacturing expenses. These costs are not deducted immediately when paid but are deferred until the year when the resulting merchandise is sold.
>
> *To make the matching complete, the taxpayer must report income on the accrual method.* That method helps to ensure that income from the sale (like the inventory costs) is reflected in the year of the sale. For example, if the sale is made on credit, the accrual method nevertheless treats the income as accrued and reflects it when the sale occurs. The prophetic skills of the accrual shaman permit it to recognize both income and deductions in the same year.
>
> By contrast, the primal cash method is unable to achieve such a mystical joinder [matching] of inventory deductions and credit sale income. To be sure, the cash method could theoretically operate in tandem with inventories. The beast could conceivably close its eyes to deductions until the year of the sale. It could never learn, however, to prophesy future cash payments. If there were a credit sale, the beast could not grasp income and deductions simultaneously in its rugged paw. The goal of matching costs and revenues would fail.

While the inventory rule seems relatively simple and necessary to guarantee the clear reflection of income of a cash basis taxpayer, it is has led to a great deal of controversy. These issues are discussed in further detail in Chapter 10.

## ACCRUAL METHOD OF ACCOUNTING

Taxpayers using the accrual method of accounting report income in the year in which it is considered earned under the so-called *all-events test*. Under this test, income is earned when all the events have occurred that fix the right to receive such income and the amount of income can be determined with reasonable accuracy.[50] As the courts have consistently observed in cases involving the all-events test, the "objective is to determine at what point in time the seller acquired an unconditional right to receive payment under the contract."[51]

### Example 20

Sellco Corporation manufactures a special machine used in a process to convert oranges into orange juice. On December 15, 2011, Sellco sold a machine to B Inc. According to the terms of the sales agreement, B was given a 30-day period for testing and acceptance. As of the end of 2011, B had not indicated its acceptance. Sellco would not accrue the income from the sale in 2011 because it did not have an unconditional right to receive the income. The first prong of the all-events test, a fixed right to receive income, is not met. The sale was contingent on satisfaction of certain conditions—test and acceptance—and since these conditions had not been met at the close of 2011 the sale was not completed and Sellco had no right to the income. If B subsequently rejected the machine, this would clearly mean delay or a complete loss of the sale.[52]

In most situations involving a sale of merchandise, the right becomes fixed when the goods are shipped, when the product is delivered or accepted or when title passes, as long as the method is consistently used.[53]

### Example 21

In *Hallmark Cards*, the greeting card giant, a calendar year accrual basis taxpayer, shipped Valentine cards before year end but deferred income from the sales to the

[50] Reg. § 1.451-1(a).

[51] *Hallmark Cards, Inc. v. CIR*, 90 T.C. 26, 33 (1988).

[52] See *Webb Press Co. v. CIR*, 3 BTA 247 (1925) (acq.).

[53] *Lucas v. North Texas Lumber Co.*, 2 USTC ¶484, 8 AFTR 10276, 281 U.S. 11 (USSC, 1929). See also Reg. §1.446-1(c)(1)(ii).

following year. Early shipment was necessary to deal with certain production and shipping problems related to supplying cards in a timely manner to its customers (more than 20,000 retailers at over 35,000 locations). Contracts with the customers specified that title and risk of loss passed to customers on January 1. The IRS argued that Hallmark should accrue the income when the cards were shipped since it had a fixed right to the income, therefore meeting the all-events test. Notwithstanding the fact that the items had been delivered to customers prior to year end, the Court held that Hallmark was *not* required to accrue the income upon shipment. The Court explained that "passage of title and risk of loss to buyer" did not occur under the contract until January 1 and therefore Hallmark could postpone recognition since it did not have a fixed right to the income.[54]

As the two examples above illustrate, the terms of the agreement are critical in determining whether the taxpayer has an unconditional right to the income. Other facts may also be important such as doubts concerning whether the receivable can be collected or disputes or other uncertainties relating to the amount of the liability. If the agreement requires a particular act, such as submitting a bill, and such act is viewed as simply ministerial, the requirement may be ignored in determining whether the taxpayer has a "right" to the income.

### Example 22

In 1996, in *Charles Schwab Corp.*, the discount securities broker asserted that its commission income accrued on the settlement date.[55] However, the Tax Court ultimately agreed with the government that the income should be accrued on the trade date. According to the Court, the broker's "essential service" was "execution of trades," and the subsequent settlement activities were merely "of a ministerial nature."

As discussed above, the accrual method normally *must* be used in accounting for sales, purchases, and inventories if inventories are an income-producing factor. However, the taxpayer who must use the accrual method in this instance may still account for other items of income and expense using the cash method. The accrual method, as noted earlier, must be used by regular C corporations and partnerships with C corporations as partners unless one of several exceptions is satisfied.

There are several special rules relating to the accrual method of accounting that cause variations in the normal scheme. For example, dividends would normally accrue under the all-events test on the date of record. An exception exists, however, so that dividends are reported when received.[56] In addition to this exception, others exist that are discussed later in this chapter.

## Changes in Accounting Methods

Taxpayers are initially given great freedom in the methods of accounting they may use. However, once a particular method has been adopted (e.g., when it is first used to account for an item), it may not be changed unless consent is granted by the IRS. Taxpayers seeking a change must apply for permission by filing Form 3115, Application for Change in Accounting Method, anytime during the tax year when the change is to become effective.[57] The IRS does not rubber-stamp these requests. Permission is granted only if the taxpayer is willing to make any adjustments required by the IRS. Under §481, the IRS is authorized to

**LO.4**
Determine the effect of a change in accounting method.

[54] *Supra*, Footnote 51, *Hallmark Cards, Inc. v. CIR*, 90 T.C. 26, 33 (1988).

[55] *Charles Schwab Corp. v. CIR*, 107 T.C. 282 (1996).

[56] Reg. § 1.451-2(b), *Tar Products Corp. v. Comm.*, 42-2 USTC ¶9662, 29 AFTR 1190, 130 F.2d 866 (CA-3, 1942).

[57] Some changes may be made automatically without consent, thereby avoiding the user fee for filing Form 3115.

require adjustments if a change in method would result in the omission of income or the duplication of deductions.

### Example 23

T, Inc. operates a computer consulting company. It has always used the cash method to account for its income from services. In 2011, it decided that it should switch to the accrual method. At the end of 2010, T's outstanding receivables were $10,000. If T were allowed to switch to the accrual method and no adjustment were required, the $10,000 would escape taxation. The $10,000 would not be taxed in 2010 since T was on the cash basis in that year and no collections were made. Similarly, the $10,000 would not be taxed in 2011 because T is on the accrual method in that year and the income did not accrue in 2011 but rather 2010. Thus, without an adjustment, the $10,000 of income would be omitted from both the 2010 and 2011 returns, never to be taxed.

## Accounting for the Adjustment

Taxpayers are normally required to report any adjustment attributable to a change in method in the year of the change and pay any additional tax due (or receive a refund).[58] In certain situations, this may create a severe hardship for the taxpayer (e.g., the required inclusion of several years' income in a single year). Moreover, taxpayers may be reluctant to change from an erroneous method of accounting to a correct method and simply wait for the IRS to detect their mistake. However, § 481(c) allows the IRS to alter this approach. The IRS has used this authority to develop a system that encourages taxpayers to switch from an erroneous method they may be using to a correct method.[59]

Under the revised approach of Revenue Procedure 97-27, the treatment of the adjustment depends primarily on whether the taxpayer voluntarily or involuntarily changes the accounting method. If the change is voluntary, the adjustment is spread over a four-year period (the year of the change and the three subsequent years). If the change is involuntary (e.g., the taxpayer is under examination and is not allowed under the rules of Revenue Procedure 97-27 to make a change) and the adjustment is positive, the entire adjustment is included in the earliest tax year under examination. However, a taxpayer may elect to use a one-year adjustment period if the entire adjustment is less that $ 25,000.

### Example 24

J has operated a small hardware store as a sole proprietorship since 2000. In August, 2013 the IRS audited J's 2011 tax return and determined that J had failed to use the accrual method of accounting for inventories. Instead, J had expensed all of his inventory as it was acquired. Consequently, the IRS required J to change his method of accounting. Based on a physical count and valuation of his inventory, the IRS determined that J had understated his income in prior years by $300,000. Assuming J is not allowed to voluntarily change his accounting method during the examination, he must report all $300,000 in income in 2011. Had J voluntarily made the change prior to examination or had he qualified under the special relief provisions to voluntarily make the change while under examination, he could have spread the adjustment over four years: $75,000 of income in 2011—the year of the change—and $75,000 in each of the three following years, 2012, 2013, and 2014.

[58] *Ibid.*

[59] Rev. Proc. 97-27, 1997-1, C.B. 680, as modified by Rev. Proc. 2002-19, 2002-1 C.B. 696.

### Example 25

During 2011, R asked for and obtained permission to change from the cash method to the accrual method. This change resulted in a negative income adjustment of $20,000. Because this adjustment is less than $25,000, R can take into account the entire adjustment in 2011.

Changes in accounting method are not to be confused with correction of errors. Errors such as mathematical mistakes or the improper calculation of a deduction or credit can be corrected by the taxpayer without permission of the IRS by simply filing an amended return. Alternatively, the IRS may discover the mistake and require the taxpayer to make a correction. However, if the statute of limitations has run on a return containing an error, no correction can be made. In these cases, the taxpayer's income is forever over- or understated, as the case may be.

## ✓ CHECK YOUR KNOWLEDGE

### Review Question 1

On Sunday, December 31, 1961 in Green Bay, Wisconsin, Paul Hornung, All-American quarterback from Notre Dame, star of the Green Bay Packers and later a sports analyst, won a Corvette for being the most valuable player in the NFL championship game.[60] After the game, the editor of *Sport* magazine, the sponsor of the award, gave nothing to Hornung to evidence his ownership of the car, which was being held at a dealership in New York. Hornung picked up the car on January 3, 1962 in New York. What are the tax concerns here?

There is little question that Hornung must report income (although that was uncertain in 1961). The important issue to be resolved is when. Was Hornung in constructive receipt of the car that snowy afternoon in December 1961? Although Hornung, wanting to report the income in 1961, argued that he had received the car, the court disagreed. In a decision that should be mandatory reading for its witty analysis, the court explained that the basis of constructive receipt is unfettered control over the date of actual receipt. In this case, the facts indicated that Hornung did not have such control. He did not receive the car or even the keys or title to the car in 1961. Moreover, the car was in a dealership that was not only 1,000 miles away but was also closed. In addition, the car had not been set aside for Hornung's use and delivery was not solely up to him. Accordingly, the doctrine of constructive receipt was inapplicable.

### Review Question 2

Mr. Mike, an accountant, is the proud owner of Maggie, a West Highland terrier. Shortly after Mike acquired Maggie, he discovered the need to take her to get the appropriate shots. It did not take long for Mike to pick a vet. He elected to use one of his long-time clients for whom he prepares tax returns, Nonhuman Companion Inc. that operates a chain of veterinary clinics throughout Arizona and California. Mike's visit to the vet was the first time he had actually been to his client's office. While there, he noticed that the clinic provided not only veterinarian and kennel services but also a great variety of food, toys, and pet paraphernalia for sale. To his best recollection, the corporation used the cash method of accounting. Is this the correct method?

There are two rules concerning accounting methods that come into play here. First, a corporation is normally required to use the accrual method of accounting. However, several exceptions may apply. The accrual requirement is waived if the corporation is an S corporation or its average annual gross receipts are less than $5 million for all preceding tax years. If neither of these exceptions applies, the corporation could possibly use the cash method if it is considered a personal service corporation, since it provides services in the

---

[60] *Paul V. Hornung*, 47 T.C. 428 (1967).

health field. Interestingly, the IRS has addressed this question and ruled that veterinarian services fall within the definition of "personal" services (i.e., health services). Never-theless, there could be a concern that "substantially all the activities" do not consist of performing "health" services. The second rule that operates in this situation concerns accounting for inventory. A business normally must use the accrual method to account for inventory even if it otherwise qualifies to use the cash method. The IRS has held that a partnership that provided veterinary services was required to switch from the cash method to the accrual method when more than 50 percent of the partnership's receipts were from merchandise (pet food, supplies, and drugs).[61]

### Review Question 3

X Inc., an accrual basis calendar year taxpayer, filed a lawsuit against the U.S. government for breach of contract. X was awarded a judgment of $100,000 by the Court of Appeals for the Fifth Circuit for the alleged breach in 2010. The income was fully taxable. The government tried to appeal the decision to the Supreme Court, filing a petition for writ of certiorari. The writ and appeal were denied in 2011. No appropriation was made by the U.S. government for payment of the claim during 2010. When should X report the income?

X should accrue the income if the all-events test is met. The test is met when X has an unconditional right to the income. Here, the taxpayer's right to the income is not fixed until the Supreme Court denied the government's appeal in 2011. Such a condition is not simply ministerial in nature. In determining whether X's right was fixed, the fact that Congress did not make an appropriation for the payment of such sum in 2010 is irrelevant since the judgment became an acknowledged liability of the government in 2011.[62]

### Review Question 4

In light of the decision in *Hallmark Cards*, Greetings Inc., an accrual basis calendar year taxpayer changed the terms of its contracts for sales of Valentine cards this year so that passage of title and risk of loss to buyer did not occur under the contract until January 1. In the past, Greetings had accrued the income when the cards were shipped. Indicate whether the following statements are true or false and if false explain why.

- **a.** Greetings' change in the terms of its contracts constitutes a change in accounting method.
- **b.** Greetings must seek permission from the IRS to change its method.
- **c.** Any omission of income that results in Greetings' change must be reported in the year of the change

Statements (a) and (b) true. Any change which affects the time when income will be reported is considered a change in accounting method and permission must be obtained from the IRS to ensure there is not an omission of income or duplication of deduction. In this case, the change shifts incomes it normally reports in one year to the next year. Statement (c) is false. Assuming Greetings receives permission to change, it is normally permitted to spread the income adjustment over four years.

## Accounting for Income: Special Rules

**LO.5**
Describe some of the special rules governing the treatment of prepaid income, interest income, interest-free loans, and income from long-term contracts.

### Claim of Right Doctrine

Occasionally income may be received before the taxpayer's rights to such income have been clearly established. The tax difficulty posed in these instances concerns whether the taxpayer should report the income currently or wait until the proper claims to the income have been identified. For these situations, the courts have established a rule of law termed the *claim of right doctrine*. Under this rule, if a taxpayer actually or constructively *receives* income under a claim of right (i.e., the taxpayer claims the income is rightfully his or hers) and such income is not restricted in use, it must be included in gross income.[63] In other words, earnings received

[61] Technical Advice Memorandum 9218008.

[62] Rev. Rul. 70-151, 1970-1 C.B. 116.

[63] *North American Oil Consolidated v. Burnet*, 3 USTC ¶943, 11 AFTR 16, 286 U.S. 417 (USSC, 1932).

must be included in income if the taxpayer has an *unrestricted claim*, notwithstanding the possibility that the income may be subsequently relinquished if the taxpayer's claim is later denied.

## Example 26

Television station WXYZ received $100,000 from KLM Company to air the firm's commercials during a local talk show in the month of December. During this month, the ratings dropped sharply when the star of the show quit. Shortly thereafter, KLM contacted the station, indicating that it wanted to discontinue its sponsorship and requesting return of $75,000 of the payment. In view of their interpretation of the agreement, the station continued to air the firm's commercials and retained the $100,000. KLM brought suit to recover the $75,000. Under the claim of right doctrine, WXYZ must include the entire $100,000 in income even though it may have to repay the amount or a portion thereof to KLM. The amount is included because WXYZ received the money and could use the amount without restriction.

The claim of right doctrine applies to both cash and accrual basis taxpayers. As previously discussed, income is usually reported by an accrual basis taxpayer only when all the events have occurred that fix the taxpayer's right to receive such income. However, in the case of contested income, the taxpayer's rights to such amounts have not been fixed, and under the all events test he or she would not report it. The all-events test notwithstanding, the claim of right doctrine carves out an exception to this rule for contested income the taxpayer has *received*. An accrual basis taxpayer who *receives* contested income under a claim of right without restrictions on its use must report the amount in income even though his or her rights to the income have not been fixed.[64] Alternatively, if the accrual basis taxpayer has *not received* the contested income, it will not be included because his or her rights thereto have not been fixed.[65] Thus, an *accrual basis* taxpayer's reporting of contested income depends on whether or not the taxpayer has received it.

## Example 27

RST, Inc, an accrual basis taxpayer, shipped parts to MNO Corporation and sent MNO a bill for $25,000. MNO used the parts and reported that they did not perform according to specifications. If MNO had paid the $25,000 and subsequently sued to recover the purchase price, RST would be required to include the $25,000 in income since the amount was received and the claim of right doctrine applies (i.e., RST has an unrestricted claim to the income). On the other hand, if MNO had not paid the $25,000, RST would not be required to accrue the income because the amount was *not* received and the all-events test has not been satisfied (i.e., RST's rights to the income have not been fixed).

The claim of right doctrine has been used in many differing instances to cause the inclusion of income in the year received. Some examples where the rule has been applied to make the income taxable are

1. Contingent legal fees that must be returned upon a reversal by an appellate court;[66]
2. Illegal income and gains (e.g., embezzled amounts);[67] and
3. Bonuses and commissions that were improperly computed and had to be subsequently repaid.[68]

---

[64] *Ibid.*

[65] Reg. § 1.446-1(c)(1)(ii).

[66] *Michael Phillips v. Comm.*, 56-2 USTC ¶10,067, 50 AFTR 718, 238 F.2d 473 (CA-7, 1956).

[67] *James v. U.S.*, 61-1 USTC ¶9449, 7 AFTR2d 1361, 366 U.S. 213 (USSC, 1961).

[68] *U.S. v. Lewis*, 51-1 USTC ¶9211, 40 AFTR 258, 340 U.S. 590 (USSC, 1951).

The claim of right doctrine does not apply where the taxpayer receives the income but recognizes an obligation to repay.[69] For example, a landlord would not be required to report the receipt of a tenant's security deposit as income because the deposit must be repaid upon the tenant's departure if the apartment unit is undamaged.

In those situations where the taxpayer repays an amount that previously had been included in income, a deduction is allowed. Section 1341 provides a special rule for computing the deduction, which ensures that the tax benefit of the deduction is the equivalent to the tax paid on the income in the prior year.

## Prepaid Income

Over the years, a web of exceptions and special rules have developed regarding the reporting of prepaid income by an *accrual basis* taxpayer. Absent these rules, the accrual basis taxpayer (in accordance with the all-events test) would defer recognition of prepaid income until it becomes earned, as is the case in financial accounting. For tax purposes, however, accrual basis taxpayers often report prepaid income in the year received. This treatment normally results from application of the claim of right doctrine, which requires income recognition when the taxpayer receives earnings under an unrestricted claim. For example, accrual basis taxpayers must report prepaid rental income when received (not when earned) since the taxpayer accepts the money under a claim of right without restrictions on its use. Unfortunately, no general rule is completely reliable to determine when prepaid income must be reported. Rather, the reporting procedure depends on the type of income received. As discussed below, special rules exist for prepaid income from rents, interest, services, warranties, goods, dues, subscriptions, and similar items. Note, however, these rules apply to *accrual basis* taxpayers only. A *cash basis* taxpayer reports all of these prepaid items of income in the year the cash is received.

### Prepaid Interest, Rents, and Royalties

Several types of advance payments are included in income when received without question. For example, prepaid interest is income when received.[70] Prepaid rent and lump-sum payments, such as bonuses or advance royalties received upon execution of a lease or other agreement, are also income when received.[71] As subsequently explained, however, the term *rent* does not include payments for the use or occupancy of rooms or space where their use is ancillary to the services provided to the user of the property (e.g., hotels, motels, and convalescent homes are not considered as having received rents).[72] Because of the significant service element, these prepayments are reported using the rules applying to prepaid service income. Prepaid rents must be distinguished not only from services but also from lease or security deposits. Amounts received from a lessee that are refundable provided the lessee complies with the terms of the lease are not income since the lessor recognizes an obligation to repay.[73] The deposits become income only when the lessor becomes entitled to their unrestricted use upon the lessee's violation of the agreement.

### Prepaid Service Income

Over the years, the treatment of advance payments for services—prepaid service income—has been quite controversial. Disputes between the IRS and taxpayers began when the IRS argued that the claim of right doctrine required accrual basis taxpayers to report prepayments for services as income in the year received. The IRS took this approach notwithstanding the fact that the taxpayer had not performed the services. After a great deal of litigation, the government relented and permitted limited deferral in certain circumstances. These rules were recently revised in 2004, with the issuance of Rev. Proc. 2004-34.[74]

Rev. Proc. 2004-34 now permits two acceptable methods of accounting for advanced payments for services. These are: a "full-inclusion method" and a "deferral method."

---

[69] *Comm. v. Turney*, 36-1 USTC ¶9168, 17 AFTR 679, 82 F.2d 661 (CA-5, 1936).

[70] *Franklin Life Insurance v. U.S.*, 68-2 USTC ¶9459, 22 AFTR2d 5180, 399 F.2d 757 (CA-7, 1968).

[71] *South Dade Farms, Inc. v. Comm.*, 43-2 USTC ¶9634, 31 AFTR 842, 138 F.2d 818 (CA-5, 1943); *W.M. Scott*, 27 B.T.A. 951.

[72] Rev. Proc. 2004-34, 2004-22 I.R.B. 991.

[73] *Clinton Hotel Realty Corp. v. Comm.*, 42-2 USTC ¶9559, 29 AFTR 758, 128 F.2d 968 (CA-5, 1942).

[74] Rev. Proc. 2004-34, 2004-22 IRB 991 (effective for tax years ending after 5/5/04) superseding Rev. Proc. 71-21, 1971-2 C.B. 549.

The full-inclusion option is the easiest and the least desirable: all of the payments are reported in the year of receipt regardless of how the payments are reported for financial accounting purposes. In contrast, under the deferral method, taxpayers generally must report advanced payments as income in the year of receipt to the extent the payments are included in the revenues of the taxpayer's financial statements.[75] The balance of the advanced payments are deferred and reported as income in the following year. Thus, book income normally equals taxable income in the first year but may differ in subsequent years. This technique, unlike the previous approach, permits at least one year of deferral regardless of the length of the contract.

## Example 28

Murray Inc.—a calendar-year, accrual-method taxpayer—is in the business of providing ballroom dance lessons. On October 29 of year 1, Murray received $4,800 for a 48-month contract under which Murray would provide up to 96 lessons. Murray provides 8 lessons in year 1, 48 lessons in year 2, and 40 lessons in year 3. In its audited financial statements, the company reports the income as the lessons are provided. Therefore, for financial accounting purposes, Murray reports $400 ($4,800 × 8/96) in year 1. Similarly, under the deferral method of Rev. Proc. 2004-34, Murray would also report $400 of income for tax purposes since this procedure permits deferral equal to that reported for financial statement purposes. In year 2, for financial statement purposes, Murray would report $2,400 (48/96 × $4,800) based on the number of lessons provided. However, in year 2 for tax purposes, Murray would report the remaining balance of the advanced payment, $4,400, as income.

The advance payment rules allowing limited deferral for prepaid service income also apply to prepaid rental income if the occupancy or use of property is ancillary to the provision of services to the user of the property.[76] According to the procedure, advance payments for the use of hotel rooms or other quarters, booth space at a trade show, campsite space at a mobile home park, and recreational or banquet facilities are not considered rents but rather services. Note that this treatment permits hotels, motels and the like to enjoy the deferral provision as outlined above for services.

### Advance Payments for Goods

Normally, an accrual basis taxpayer reports advance payments for sales of merchandise when they are earned (e.g., when the goods are shipped). This treatment enables the taxpayer to defer recognition of the prepayments. However, this approach is allowed only if the taxpayer follows the same method of reporting for financial accounting purposes.[77]

## Example 29

C Corporation, a calendar year taxpayer, manufactures kitchen appliances. In late December 2011, it received $50,000 for kitchen appliances that it will produce and ship in May 2012. The corporation may postpone recognition of the income until 2012, assuming that such income is also reported on the financial accounting income statement in 2012.

---

[75] If "applicable" financial statements (a certified audited financial statement used for credit purposes, reporting to shareholders, or any other substantial nontax purpose) have not been prepared, the amount of the payment earned is reported in the first year. Rev. Proc. 2004-34 (4.06), 2004-22 I.R.B. 991.

[76] Rev. Proc. 2004-34 identifies other types of prepayments that do and do not qualify as an advanced payment for which limited deferral is permitted.

[77] Reg. § 1.451-5(b). See Reg. § 1.451-4(c)(1) for certain situations where the prepayments must be reported earlier.

## Long-Term Contracts

Section 460 contains special rules for the reporting of income from long-term contracts. A long-term contract is defined as any contract for the manufacture, building, installation, or construction of property that is not completed within the same taxable year in which it was entered into. However, a *manufacturing* contract is still not considered long-term unless it also involves either (1) the manufacture of a unique item not normally carried in finished goods inventory (e.g., a special piece of machinery), or (2) items that normally require more than 12 months to complete. If a manufacturing contract does not qualify as a long-term contract, deferral may still be available under the rules regarding advance payments for goods discussed above. Note that contracts for services normally do not qualify for treatment as long-term contracts.

The tax law has long allowed taxpayers who enter into a long-term contract to use the percentage of completion method or the completed contract method (subject to certain limitations) to account for advance payments.[78] The percentage of completion method requires the taxpayer to recognize a portion of the gross profit on the contract based on the estimated percentage of the contract completed. In contrast, the completed contract method allows the taxpayer to defer income recognition until the contract is complete and acceptance has occurred. When available, taxpayers usually opt to use the completed contract method in order to postpone recognition of income. In some extreme cases, however, taxpayers have been able to postpone income for many years on the claim that the contract was not complete.

Over the years, Congress became concerned about the opportunities for deferral as well as the potential for abuse. Consequently, it took various steps, slowly but surely limiting the use of the completed contract method. These actions culminated with the virtual repeal of the method in 1989. As a result, long-term contracts currently entered into normally must be accounted for using the percentage of completion method.[79] However, there are two situations where the completed contract method can still be used. These include:[80]

1. *Home construction contracts.* Contracts in which 80 percent of the costs are related to buildings containing four or fewer dwelling units. Special rules apply to contracts if the buildings contain more than four units (i.e., so-called residential construction contracts).[81]
2. *Contracts of small businesses.* Construction contracts that are completed within two years of commencement and are performed by a contractor whose average annual gross receipts for the three preceding tax years do not exceed $10 million.

When using the percentage of completion method, the portion of the total contract price reported during the year and matched against current costs is computed as follows

$$\text{Total contract price} \times \frac{\text{Direct and allocable indirect costs incurred this period}}{\text{Total estimated costs of contract}}$$

Note that if less than 10 percent of the contract's costs have been incurred, the taxpayer may elect to defer reporting until the year in which the 10 percent threshold is reached.[82]

### Example 30

In October 2011, W Corporation entered into a contract to build a hotel to be completed by May 2013. The contract price was $1 million. The company's estimated total costs of construction were $800,000. W's average annual gross receipts exceed $10 million, and it is therefore required to use the percentage of completion method. Total costs incurred during 2011 were $600,000. In 2012, the contract was completed at a total cost of $840,000. The income reported in 2011 and 2012 is computed below:

[78] Reg. § 1.451-3.

[79] § 460(a).

[80] § 460(e).

[81] A 70 percent of completion method may be used for certain residential construction contracts.

[82] § 460(b)(5).

| | 2011 | 2012 |
|---|---|---|
| Revenue recognized | $ 750,000* | $ 250,000 |
| Current costs | (600,000) | (240,000) |
| Total | $ 150,000 | $ 10,000 |

$$^{*}\frac{\$600,000}{\$800,000} = 75\% \times \$1,000,000$$

Any contract for which the percentage of completion method is used is subject to the special *look-back* provisions.[83] Under these rules, once the contract is complete, annual income is recomputed based on final costs rather than estimated costs. Interest is then paid to the taxpayer if there was an overstatement of income. Conversely, the taxpayer must pay interest if income was understated.

## Example 31

Same facts as in Example 30, above. Based on total actual costs of $840,000, W's 2011 income should have been $114,000, computed as follows:

| | 2011 |
|---|---|
| Revenue recognized | $714,000* |
| Current costs | (600,000) |
| Total | $114,000 |

$$^{*}\frac{\$600,000}{\$840,000} = 71.4\% \times \$1,000,000$$

Because the contract was in reality only 71.4% complete and not 75% complete, W overstated income in 2011 by $36,000 ($150,000 – $114,000). Consequently, the IRS is required to pay the taxpayer interest on the overpayment of the related tax.

### Prepaid Dues and Subscriptions

Amidst much controversy concerning the reporting of prepaid income, Congress provided specific rules for the reporting of prepaid dues and subscriptions. Section 455 permits the taxpayer to elect to recognize prepaid subscription income (amounts received from a newspaper, magazine, or periodical) ratably over the subscription period. Section 456 provides that taxpayers may elect to report prepaid dues ratably over the membership period.

## INTEREST INCOME

The period in which a taxpayer recognizes interest income usually follows the basic tax accounting rules for cash and accrual basis taxpayers. In some cases, however, these taxpayers must observe special provisions that may cause reporting to vary from the normal pattern.

### General Rules

As a general rule, cash basis taxpayers recognize interest income when received, while accrual basis taxpayers recognize the income when it is earned. As previously noted, both accrual and cash basis taxpayers that receive interest before it is earned (prepaid interest) must report the income when it is received.

---

[83] § 460(b)(2). The lookback rule is elective if the cumulative income (loss) determined using estimated contract price and cost is within 10 percent of actual.

### Example 32

T operates a small business that manufactures pottery dishes. When one of her customers was unable to pay her bill, T accepted a $10,000 note, dated October 1, 2011, payable with 6% interest on October 1, 2012. Assuming T is a cash basis taxpayer, she will report $600 of interest income ($10,000 × 6%) when received in 2012. If T uses the accrual method, she would include $150 ($10,000 × 3/12 × 6%) in her gross income for 2011 and $450 ($10,000 × 9/12 × 6%) when received in 2012. Had the customer paid all of the interest, $600, in 2011 as a showing of good faith, T would report the entire $600 in 2011 regardless of whether she is a cash or accrual basis taxpayer.

In many instances, a taxpayer will purchase an interest-bearing instrument between payment dates. When this occurs, it is assumed that the purchase price includes the interest accrued to the date of the purchase. Thus, when the buyer later receives the interest payment, the portion accrued to the date of purchase is considered a non-taxable return of capital that reduces the taxpayer's basis in the instrument. On the other hand, the seller must include as interest income the amount accrued to the date of the purchase, regardless of the seller's method of accounting.

### Example 33

S owned a $1,000, 12% AT&T bond that paid interest semiannually on November 1 and May 1. He purchased the bond at par several years ago. On September 1, 2011, S sold the bond for $1,540 including $40 of the accrued interest ($1,000 × 12% × 4/12). S must report $40 of interest income accrued to the date of sale. In addition, S will report a capital gain of $500 ($1,540 – $40 interest – $1,000 basis). The result is the same if S is a cash or accrual basis taxpayer.

### Example 34

Assume B purchased for $1,540 the bond that S sold in the example above. On November 1, B receives an interest payment of $60 ($1,000 × 12% × 6/12). B treats the interest accrued to the date of purchase, $40, as a nontaxable return of basis. Thus, B's basis is reduced to $1,500 ($1,540 – $40). The remaining $20 of interest is included in B's gross income.

In practice, the broker's statement normally reflects the interest accrued to the date of the sale or purchase.

## Discount

When accounting for interest income, any discount relating to the debt instrument—the excess of the face value of the obligation over the purchase price—must be considered. Discount typically results when the rate at which the instrument pays interest is less than the market rate. In such case, the discount essentially functions as a substitute for interest. Consistent with this view, the tax law attempts to ensure that the discount is treated as interest income and is normally reported currently. Special provisions have been introduced over the years to clarify the reporting of the discount income as well as to prohibit taxpayers from converting the discount income into capital gain.

### Example 35

During 2009, T purchased a $10,000, 8% corporate bond for $8,000, or a $2,000 discount. In 2011 the bond matured and the taxpayer redeemed the bond for its par value of $10,000. The redemption is treated as an exchange, and the taxpayer recognizes a long-term capital gain of $2,000 ($10,000 redemption price – $8,000 basis). In this case, the taxpayer has converted the discount of $2,000, which from an economic view is ordinary interest income, to capital gain. Moreover, the taxpayer has deferred the reporting of such income from the time it accrues to the time the bond is sold. To eliminate this opptunity, the discount generally must be amortized and included in gross income as it accrues. These rules are discussed in greater detail in Chapter 16.

The tax treatment of discount depends in part on when it arises. The discount often occurs at the time the instrument is issued. For example, certain instruments such as U.S. Savings Bonds, Treasury bills, and so-called zero coupon bonds do not bear interest and are usually *issued* at discounts. Other debt obligations that do bear interest (such as corporate bonds) also may be issued at a discount, usually if the coupon rate is set lower than the current rate. Discount could also result after the instrument is issued. For example, where interest-bearing instruments are issued at par, discount may arise upon a subsequent purchase. The specific treatment of discount is examined below.

## Non-Interest-Bearing Obligations Issued at a Discount

The Code provides special rules for non-interest-bearing obligations that are issued at a discount and redeemable for a fixed amount that increases over time. The instruments to which these rules would normally apply are Series E and EE U.S. Savings Bonds. Series E Bonds were issued between 1941 and 1980, having maturities up to 40 years. Beginning in 1980, these bonds were replaced by Series EE Bonds. Beginning in 2001, Series EE Bonds are inscribed with the special legend "Patriot Bonds" inspired by the tragedy of September 11, 2001. Series EE bonds earn 90 percent of five-year Treasury security yields. They do not pay interest but are sold at a discount (half their face value), and are available in denominations ranging from $50 through $10,000. They generally have maturities of 20 years. The bonds are normally redeemable at any time up until the final maturity date at a price that increases with the passage of time. No interest payments are made while the bond is held. The holder's interest income is represented by the difference between the redemption price and purchase price. Note, however, that Series EE savings bonds stop increasing in value after 20 years. Bonds issued after May 1, 2005 have a fixed rate of interest revised each year in May and again in November. For example, for bonds issued on or after May 1, 2010, the rate was 1.40 percent (up from 0.70 on May 1, 2009 and 1.40 on May, 1, 2008).

For reporting purposes, taxpayers may elect to include in income the annual increase in the redemption price of the bond.[84] In essence, this election allows a cash basis taxpayer to use the accrual method with respect to these bonds. If income is not reported on an annual basis, the taxpayer reports the entire difference between the redemption and issue prices as income when the bond is redeemed.

### Example 36

S purchased Series EE Bonds with a face value of $10,000 at a cost of $8,000. The redemption price of the bonds increases during the year by $100. If S elects to report the income annually, she will include $100 in her gross income. Alternatively, S could wait until she redeems the bond to report the income. For example, if S later redeemed the bonds for $9,500, she would report $1,500 income (the difference between the redemption price of $9,500 and her cost of $8,000) at the time of redemption.

[84] § 454(a).

The taxpayer may make the election to report the interest annually at any time. When the election is made, all interest previously deferred on all Series E and EE Bonds must be reported. This procedure effectively allows the taxpayer to choose the year in which the interest income is to be reported. However, once the election is made, it applies to *all* Series E and EE Bonds subsequently acquired. Should the taxpayer desire to change to reporting the income at redemption, consent from the IRS is required.[85]

As discussed in Chapter 6, certain taxpayers who cash in Series EE Bonds and use the proceeds for educational expenses may be able to exclude the interest.

## Government Obligations

Special rules also govern the treatment of the discount arising upon the purchase of short-term government obligations such as Treasury bills.[86] Typically, a taxpayer purchases a short-term Treasury bill at a discount and redeems it for par value shortly thereafter. In this instance, Code § 454(b) applies to cash basis taxpayers to ensure that the gain on the redemption—in effect, the discount—is treated as ordinary interest income. Specifically, any gain realized by cash basis taxpayers from the sale or redemption of non-interest-bearing obligations issued by governmental units that have a fixed maturity date that is one year or less from the date of issue is always ordinary income. This ordinary income is reported *in the year* of sale or redemption. In contrast, accrual basis taxpayers are required to amortize the discount (i.e., include it in income) on a *daily* basis under Code § 1281(a).

### Example 37

On December 1, 2010, B, a cash basis calendar year taxpayer, purchased a $10,000 non-interest-bearing Treasury bill. She purchased the bill at 97 ($9,700) and redeemed the bill on March 1, 2011 at par. B recognizes a $300 gain ($10,000 – $9,700) on the redemption, and the entire gain is treated as ordinary income in 2011. The same result would occur if B had *sold* the Treasury bill for $10,000 on January 15, 2011. Note that if B were an accrual basis taxpayer, the $300 discount would have been included in income on a daily basis. Consequently, a portion of the income would be reported in 2010 and the remainder in 2011.

## Original Issue Discount

When interest-bearing obligations such as corporate bonds are *issued* at a discount, a complex set of provisions operates to prevent taxpayers from not only deferring the discount income but also converting it to capital gain as depicted in *Example 35*. These rules apply only to discount that arises when the bonds are originally issued. This discount is technically referred to as *original issue discount* (OID) and is determined as follows:

| | |
|---|---|
| Redemption price | $x,xxx |
| – Issue price | – xxx |
| = Original issue discount | $x,xxx |

The thrust of the provisions is to require the holder of the bond to amortize the discount into income during the period the bond is held. A complete discussion of the treatment of OID is provided in Chapter 16.

[85] As of September 1, 2004, investors are no longer able to exchange EE/E bonds for HH bonds.

[86] Special rules also apply to Treasury Inflation-Protection Bonds (TIPs) and Treasury Inflation-Indexed Securities.

## ✓ Check Your Knowledge

### Review Question 1

For financial accounting purposes, prepaid income is generally reported as it is earned. Does the same treatment apply for tax purposes? Explain the treatment of prepaid interest, rents, royalties, services, and advance payments for goods.

As a general rule, prepaid income must be reported when received. This is obviously true for cash basis taxpayers and surprisingly true for accrual basis taxpayers. The unusual treatment for accrual basis taxpayers stems from the claim of right doctrine, which requires recognition of income whenever the amount has been received and the taxpayer does not recognize an obligation to repay. This treatment applies to prepaid interest, rents, and royalties. It does not apply to prepaid service income (including prepaid rents if the property's use is secondary to the services provided) where the reporting follows that for books in the first year with the balance reported in the second year. It also does not apply to advance payments for goods, which are normally reported in the same manner as they are for financial accounting purposes (the normal accrual method).

A close look at the reporting requirements for prepaid income reveals that cash basis taxpayers report prepaid income when it is received and this approach is consistent with the cash method of accounting. In contrast, accrual basis taxpayers report—subject to certain exceptions—prepaid income as if they were on the cash basis. The table below summarizes the law's schizophrenic approach to prepaid income and—as seen in Chapter 7—prepaid expenses.

| | Prepaid Income | Prepaid Expenses |
|---|---|---|
| Cash basis taxpayer | Report in year received<br>*Consistent with cash method* | Deduct over appropriate period<br>*Treat as if on accrual basis* |
| Accrual basis taxpayer | Report in year received<br>*Treated as if on cash basis* | Deducted over appropriate period<br>*Consistent with accrual method* |

### Review Question 2

After the changes made during the 1980s, some commentators pronounced the use of the completed contract method dead. Is this true? Are there any circumstances under which the completed contract method can be used?

The completed contract may be dead for large construction companies that build mammoth projects such as airplanes, stadiums, dams, office towers, and the like. But it is alive and well for the majority of construction companies. The completed contract method may be used by any home builder (regardless of size) and small construction companies (those with average annual gross receipts of less than $10 million).

### Review Question 3

During the autumn of 1986, it became clear that the Reagan administration and Congress planned to cut tax rates from a top rate of 50 percent to something around 28 percent. As a result, the papers and financial press were filled with planning ideas. Some advisers suggested that people who had cash sitting in money market accounts should buy Treasury bills. Why?

An investment in Treasury bills allows the taxpayer to defer the interest until the bonds are redeemed. Consequently, many advisers suggested purchasing Treasury bills at a discount during the fall of 1986 with the idea of redeeming them when income tax rates dropped in 1987.

# Identification of the Taxpayer

**LO.6**
Identify which taxpayer is responsible for reporting income and paying the taxes on such income.

A final consideration in the taxation of income concerns identification of the taxpayer to whom the income is taxed. Generally, this is not a mind-boggling task. The person who receives the income usually must pay the tax. As discussed below, however, receipt or nonreceipt of income does not always govern who must report it.

## Income from Personal Services

In the famous case of *Lucas v. Earl*, the Supreme Court was required to determine whether Mr. Earl was taxable on earnings from personal services despite a legally enforceable agreement made with his wife in 1901 that the earnings would be shared equally.[87] At the time of this decision, such agreements effectively split income between a husband and wife; this resulted in a reduced tax liability since each individual was treated as a separate taxable entity and a progressive income tax rate structure existed. The Court eliminated the usefulness of this technique, however, by holding that the income is taxable to the taxpayer who earns it. Thus, anticipatory assignments of income that one has a *right* to receive are an ineffective device to escape taxation. In explaining what has become the assignment of income doctrine, the Court gave birth to the well-known *fruit of the tree* metaphor. According to Justice Holmes, the fruit (income) must be attributed to the tree from which it grew (Mr. Earl's services).

Section 73 directly addresses the treatment of a child's earnings. This provision indicates that amounts received for the services of a child are included in the *child's* gross income. Thus, a parent or a guardian who collects income earned by a child would not report the income; rather the income would be reported by the child since he or she earned it. As discussed in Chapter 4, however, the *unearned* income of a child under age 18 may be reported on his or her parents' tax return and taxed at the parents' rates.

## Income from Property

The assignment of income doctrine also applies when income from property is received. Under this rule, income from property is included in the gross income of the taxpayer who owns the property. This principle was derived from another famous case, *Helvering v. Horst.*[88] In this case, Mr. Horst clipped the interest coupons from bonds he owned and gave them to his son, who later collected them. The Supreme Court held Mr. Horst taxable since he owned and controlled the source of income (i.e., the bonds). Accordingly, income from property can be effectively assigned only if the taxpayer relinquishes ownership of the property.

## Unearned Income of Children

Perhaps the most fundamental principle in tax planning concerns minimizing the marginal tax rate that applies to the taxpayer's income. The significance of this principle is easily understood when one realizes that Federal marginal tax rates have at times exceeded 90 percent. Although the current disparity between the top and bottom rates, 25 percent (35% – 10%), is not as great as in some years, the potential for significant tax savings still exists.

Minimizing the tax rate is normally accomplished by shifting income to a lower bracket taxpayer. As discussed above, the assignment of income doctrine makes it virtually impossible for taxpayers to shift income arising from services. Opportunities do exist, however, for shifting income through transfers of property. The most popular technique in this regard has traditionally involved transferring income-producing property to a child. In this manner, not only is the tax rate applying to the income reduced, but the income also stays within the family unit, normally to be used as the parent directs.

As part of the tax overhaul in 1986, Congress took steps to reduce tax avoidance opportunities available through income shifting to a child. This was accomplished by enacting a special provision affectionately referred to as the "kiddie" tax.[89] The thrust of this rule—as explained in Chapter 4—is to tax the *unearned* income of a child under the age of 19 (or less than 24 if a full-time student) as if it were the parents' income and thus at the parents' rates. By limiting the tax to unearned rather than earned income, Congress was taking direct aim at parents and others who shifted income by making gifts of property. Accordingly, shifting techniques based on gifts of property such as bonds and rental property that produce unearned income (e.g., interest and rents) are now severely limited.

## Interest-Free and Below-Market Loans

To be successful in shifting income to another, the assignment of income doctrine generally requires that the taxpayer transfer the income-producing property itself, not merely the

[87] 2 USTC ¶496, 8 AFTR 10,287, 281 U.S. 111 (USSC, 1930).

[88] 40-2 USTC ¶9787, 24 AFTR 1058, 311 U.S. 112 (USSC, 1940).

[89] § 1(i).

income from the property. Thus, shifting income requires a completed gift of the property. Taxpayers, however, are understandably reluctant to forever relinquish ownership and control of the property. For this reason, taxpayers have attempted to design techniques that enable them to retain ownership of the property yet shift income.

Prior to 1984, a popular method of shifting income from one family member to another, or from a corporation to its shareholders (or employees), used interest-free loans. Under the typical arrangement, a father who was in the 50 percent tax bracket would make a loan to his son who was in a far lower bracket. Upon receipt of the loan, the son would invest the funds. As a result, any income earned on the investment would be taxed to the son at a lower rate than would have been paid had the father received the income directly. This arrangement could secure substantial tax savings, particularly if there was a great disparity between the tax rates of the two family members.

The success of this tax-saving technique was attributable to the terms of the loan agreement. These terms required the son to repay the loan on demand *without interest*. Had the father charged interest, he would still have income attributable to the amount loaned, and no income shifting would have occurred. By not charging interest, however, the interest income that the father would have earned was successfully shifted to the son and tax savings resulted. In addition, the interest that was not charged, a valuable benefit for the son, was not considered a taxable gift. Moreover, this arrangement was extremely appealing because it did not require the father to part with the property forever. Since he had only loaned the funds to his son, he could demand repayment of the funds at any time.

The IRS viewed interest-free loans as a tax avoidance device designed to circumvent the assignment of income rules. After much controversy, Congress eliminated this opportunity in 1984 by enacting Code § 7872, which imputes interest income to the lender where the actual interest is considered inadequate.

## Treatment of Below-Market Loans

In general, § 7872 applies to loans when the interest charged is below the current market rate of interest. As pictured below, when such a loan is made, the treatment is determined *assuming* that the borrower pays the "foregone interest" to the lender at the market rate, which the lender is then deemed to transfer back to the borrower:[90]

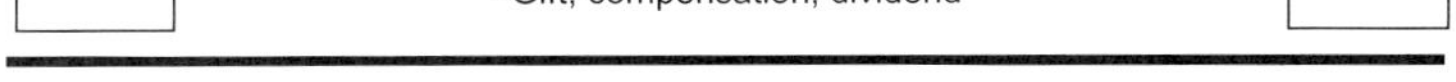


This hypothetical scenario results in the following tax consequences:

1. The borrower may be allowed a deduction for the interest hypothetically paid to the lender, while the lender reports the fictitious payment as *interest income*.
2. The lender treats the hypothetical payment to the borrower as either compensation, dividend, or gift depending on the nature of the loan. The borrower treats the payment as either compensation, dividend, or gift as the case may be. In determining the character of the lender's hypothetical payment, the Code classifies loans into three types based on the relationship between the lender and the borrower.
   - *Gift loans*—those where the forgone interest is in the nature of a gift;
   - *Compensation-related loans*—those made by an employer to an employee or an independent contractor; and
   - *Corporation-shareholder loans*—those made by a corporation to a shareholder.[91]

The thrust of these rules is to treat the borrower as having paid the foregone interest, which is funded by the lender through compensation, dividends, or gift.

---

[90] See § 7872(e)(2) for definition of foregone interest.

[91] In this regard, Prop. Reg. § 1.7872-4(d)(2) indicates that a payment to a shareholder-employee is presumed to be a dividend if the corporation is (1) closely held and such person owns more than 5 percent of its stock, or (2) publicly held and such person owns ½ of one percent of the stock.

## Example 38

Lender L loaned $500,000 to Borrower B payable on demand without interest. Assume the foregone interest is $15,000. Thus, the interest hypothetically paid by B and which must be imputed to L is $15,000. The following table shows the effect on L and B, assuming the loan is

1. A gift loan.
2. A compensation-related loan.
3. A corporation-shareholder loan.

| Lender L | | | | Borrower B | | | |
|---|---|---|---|---|---|---|---|
| *Interest Income* | *Gift Made* | *Comp. Expense* | *Dividend Paid* | *Interest Expense* | *Gift Received* | *Comp. Income* | *Dividend Received* |
| (1) $15,000 | $15,000 | | | $(15,000) | $15,000 | | |
| (2) 15,000 | | $(15,000) | | (15,000) | | $15,000 | |
| (3) 15,000 | | | $15,000 | (15,000) | | | $15,000 |

The first situation reveals the effects where the interest forgone by the lender is considered a gift (e.g., loans between family members). In this case, income shifting is prohibited since L does not avoid taxation on the income from the loan. Rather, he or she is deemed to receive an interest payment from B on the amount loaned. In addition, L is treated as having made a taxable gift to B of $2000 ($15,000 gift − $13,000 annual exclusion). On the other hand, B is entitled to exclude the $15,000 gift from income. B's hypothetical interest payment may or may not be deductible, depending on whether it is treated as investment interest, business interest, or personal interest (see Chapter 11 for a discussion of interest).

The second situation assumes that the loan is made by an employer to an employee, and, thus, the hypothetical payment by the lender is considered compensation. In this case, the lender is treated as having received interest income that is offset by a deduction for compensation expense to B. Note, however, that if B is an employee, L would be responsible for employment taxes and withholding. The effect on the borrower, B, depends on whether the hypothetical interest payment is deductible. If so, there generally will be no effect since such deduction offsets B's compensation income.

The third situation demonstrates the undesirable consequences that a corporation encounters when its deemed payment is considered a dividend rather than compensation. This problem would normally arise where the loan is made to an individual who is both a shareholder and an employee of the corporation. In this situation, like the second situation above, L (a corporation) has income from the deemed payment. In contrast to the second situation, however, L receives no offsetting deduction since dividend payments are not deductible. The effect on B again depends on whether the hypothetical interest is deductible.

These provisions govern not only the treatment of gift, compensation-related, and corporate shareholder loans, but also any other type of below-market loan designed to achieve tax avoidance or affect the tax liability of the lender or the borrower.

### Example 39

During the year, J joined a country club. The club requires each member to loan the club $10,000 without interest. Assuming interest rates are currently 8 percent, the club is effectively receiving annual dues of $800 from each member. More important from the member's standpoint, the dues are paid with tax-free dollars.

Had J received the $800 directly, she would be required to pay taxes. By making the loan to the club, she has effectively converted taxable income to tax-exempt income. Under Code § 7872, however, this arrangement would not be effective since J would be treated as having received the $800 income and would have no offsetting deduction for the payment to the club.

### Exempt Loans

To restrict the application of § 7872 to predominantly abusive situations, Congress carved out several exceptions to the rules described above. Under the first exception, § 7872 does not apply to *gift* loans as long as the loans outstanding during the year do not exceed $10,000 *and* the borrower does not use the loan proceeds to purchase or carry income-producing assets. Without this latter requirement, income of small amounts could still be shifted. The effect of this provision is to exempt small loans where income shifting is absent.

Congress also granted compensation-related and corporation-shareholder loans an exemption from the onerous rules of § 7872 if they do not exceed $10,000. The exemption does not apply to these loans, however, if tax avoidance is one of the principal purposes of the loan.

### Interest Income Cap

Another special rule imposes a limit on the amount of imputed interest income for loans between individuals. Generally, if the amount of outstanding loans does not exceed $100,000 and their principal purpose is not tax avoidance, the deemed interest payment by the borrower to the lender is limited to the borrower's investment income. This rule follows from the theory that the amount of income shifted by the lender is limited to that which the borrower actually earns. In addition, to enable loans where tax avoidance is obviously not a motive, the lender is treated as having no imputed interest income if the borrower's investment income does not exceed $1,000. However, the lender is still deemed to have made a gift of the forgone interest.

### Example 40

L has a son, B, who earns a salary and has $800 investment income. During the year, L loaned B $90,000 without interest to purchase a home. Interest imputed at the IRS rate is $15,000. L has no imputed interest income since the loan is less than $100,000 and investment income is less than $1,000. However, L is charged with a taxable gift of $2,000 ($15,000 – $13,000 exclusion). Note that if B had $7,000 of investment income, L also would have been charged with interest income of $7,000.

### Loans to Qualified Continuing Care Facility

Older individuals who must enter a continuing care facility may be required to make an interest free or below-market-rate loan to the facility as a condition of admission. Absent any special rule, the § 7872 requirement to impute interest would saddle these individuals with taxable interest income without cash. Section 7872(g) creates an important exception, exempting loans made to "qualified continuing care facilities" if the contractual provisions meet certain requirements.

## INCOME FROM COMMUNITY PROPERTY

In the United States, the rights that married individuals hold in property are determined using either the common law or community property system. The community property system developed in continental Europe and was adopted in several states having a French or Spanish origin. The ten states currently recognizing the community property system are Alaska, Arizona, California, Idaho, Louisiana, Nevada, New Mexico, Texas, Washington, and Wisconsin. The remaining 40 states use the common law system, which originated in England.

The community property system categorizes property into two types: separate property, which is considered belonging separately to one of the spouses, and community property, which is considered owned equally by each spouse. In general, separate property consists only of those assets owned before marriage or acquired by gift or inheritance while married. All property acquired during a marriage except by gift or inheritance is community property.

*Income* from separate property may be community property or separate property depending on the state of jurisdiction. In Texas, Louisiana, and Idaho, income from separate property is community property. Accordingly, for Federal tax purposes each spouse is responsible for one-half of the income. In the other seven states, income from separate property is separate property and must be reported by the person owning the property. Income from personal services is generally treated as belonging to the community. The following example illustrates how these differing rules must be taken into account.

### Example 41

A husband and wife elect to file separate returns. The husband received a $30,000 salary and $1,000 of dividends on stock he had purchased prior to the couple's marriage. The husband also receives $500 of taxable interest from a certificate of deposit that he had purchased in his own name while married. The wife's income would vary depending on the state in which she lived:

| | Texas | Arizona | Common Law States |
|---|---|---|---|
| Salary | $15,000 | $15,000 | $0 |
| Dividends | 500 | 0 | 0 |
| Interest | 250 | 250 | 0 |
| Wife's income | $15,750 | $15,250 | $0 |

### Community Income Where Spouses Live Apart

The treatment of community income can create financial problems, particularly where spouses live apart during the year and are later divorced before the end of the taxable year. For example, consider R and S, who were married but lived apart during the first half of the year before their divorce became final. Under these circumstances, the property settlement should consider the accrued tax liability that arises due to any community income. Accounting for the liability may be difficult or impossible, however, if one of the spouses has abandoned the other. In such cases, the abandoned spouse becomes liable for the tax on income earned by a spouse who cannot be located to share the financial responsibility. To eliminate these difficulties, special provisions were enacted.

Section 66 provides that a spouse will be taxed only on the earnings attributed to his or her personal services if during the year the following requirements are satisfied:

1. The two married individuals live apart at all times.
2. The couple does not file a joint return with each other.
3. No portion of the earned income is transferred between the spouses.

This rule only applies to income from personal services and not income from property.

### Example 42

M and N, residents of Texas, decided in November 2009 to obtain a divorce, which became final on March 31, 2011. N earns $2,000 each month and M is unemployed. N has a savings account that yielded $200 of taxable interest during the first three months of 2011. Assuming the two live apart during all of 2011 and none of the earned income is transferred between them, N will report all of the $6,000 ($2,000 × 3) attributable to her personal services and $100 of the interest. M will report his $100 share of the taxable interest.

## ✓ Check Your Knowledge

### Review Question 1

In 1960 18-year-old Randy Hundley signed a contract to play baseball for the Chicago Cubs.[92] The contract provided for a bonus of $110,000 (a grand sum in those days) to be paid over a five-year period at a rate of $22,000 per year: $11,000 to Randy and $11,000 to his father, Cecil. The payment to Randy's father was pursuant to an oral agreement the two had made when Randy was 16. According to the agreement, Cecil, a former semiprofessional baseball player and coach, acted as Randy's coach and business manager in exchange for 50 percent of any bonus that Randy might receive if he should obtain a baseball contract.

At about the same time that the Cubs were striking a deal with Hundley, the Philadelphia Phillies reached an agreement with Richie Allen, another future star.[93] According to this arrangement, Allen was to receive a $70,000 bonus: $30,000 paid to him over five years and $40,000 paid to his mother. How should the bonuses be treated? Should they both be treated the same?

The question in both cases is whether the child has effectively split the income between himself and his parent or merely made an anticipatory assignment of income. If the latter is true, all of the income would be taxed to the child and none to the parent. In both cases, the IRS argued that the payment to Randy's father and Richie's mother should be treated as being first made to the child and then followed by a nondeductible gift. Despite the similarity of the cases, the Court believed that the services provided by Hundley's father were instrumental in his son's success, whereas Allen's mother made no tangible contribution. As a result, Hundley was allowed to deduct the payment to his father as a business expense and, therefore, split the income between them. In contrast, no deduction was allowed to Allen and he was required to pay taxes on the entire bonus.

### Review Question 2

M wants to shift income to her 19-year-old daughter (who is not a student) so that it will be taxed at the daughter's 10 percent rate rather than at M's 35 percent rate. M plans on loaning her daughter $10,000 interest-free for this purpose. Will her plan to shift income to the daughter work?

As a general rule, interest-free loans can no longer be used successfully to shift income, since interest income must be imputed to the lender. In this case, M would be treated as having

---

[92] *Cecil Randolph Hundley, Jr.*, 48 T.C. 339 (1967). [93] *Richard A. Allen*, 50 T.C. 466 (1968).

received an interest payment from her daughter, thus defeating the entire plan. At first blush, some might believe that because the loan is less than $10,000, the de minimis rule operates and M is not required to impute interest; this is a typical misconception. It is true that imputation is not required if the loan is less than $10,000, but only if the borrower does not invest the loan amount in income-producing property. Of course, if the borrower does not invest in income-producing property there is no income and nothing is shifted. Therefore, the $10,000 de minimis rule does not create any opportunity. In this particular case, the $100,000 rule also would come into play. This exception provides that the maximum amount of interest to be imputed to the lender is equal to the net investment income of the borrower (zero, if net investment income is less than $1,000). This provision does provide a small opportunity. If the daughter invests the $10,000 to produce $900 of interest income, no income would be imputed to M and $900 would be successfully shifted. M would be treated as having made a gift of $900 to her daughter, but there would be no gift tax because of the annual exclusion of $13,000 in 2010.

# Tax Planning

## Timing Income Recognition

The proper timing of income recognition can reap great benefits for the taxpayer. As a general rule, postponement of income recognition is wise since the tax on such income is deferred. The major advantage of tax deferral is that the taxpayer has continued use of the real funds that otherwise would have been used to pay taxes. Deferral of the tax is in essence an interest-free loan from the government.

When considering deferral, attention must be given to the marginal tax rates that may apply to the income. For example, taxpayers often postpone income until their retirement years, when they are usually in a lower tax bracket. Although deferral may be wise in this situation, it may be unwise where tax rates rise by operation of law or because of the taxpayer's increase in earnings. Ideally, the taxpayer should attempt to level out taxable income from one year to the next and equalize the tax rate that applies annually (to avoid the situation of R in *Example 11* and duplicate that of S).

The opportunities for most individuals to postpone income are limited, particularly in light of the constructive receipt doctrine. Several techniques do exist, however, as outlined below:

1. Installment sales of property enable the taxpayer not only to avoid the bunching of income in a single year but also to defer the tax.
2. Income on Series E and EE bonds, Treasury bills, and certain certificates of deposit may be deferred until they are redeemed.
3. Investments in Individual Retirement Accounts (IRAs), Keogh plans, and qualified retirement plans are all made with before-tax dollars (since these contributions are deductible), and earnings on these investments are not taxed until they are withdrawn.
4. Deferred compensation arrangements may be suitable, as in the case of a professional athlete, celebrity, or executive. (See Chapter 18.)

## Income-Splitting Techniques

As stressed earlier, the most fundamental rule in tax planning concerns minimizing the marginal tax rate that applies to the taxpayer's income. Minimizing the applicable rate is usually accomplished through use of some type of income splitting or shifting technique.

### Example 43

Mr. and Mrs. J pay taxes at a rate of 35% in 2011. The couple helps support Mr. J's 67-year-old retired mother, M, by giving her $5,000 annually. Such gifts do not entitle the couple to claim M as a dependent. In providing M's support through gifts, the couple is using after-tax dollars. That is, the couple would have to earn $7,692 to provide M with $5,000 in support [$7,692 – (35% of $7,692) = $5,000]. Instead, the couple could transfer income-producing property to M to provide the needed support. By so doing, the income would not be subject to tax because M could utilize her own exemption and standard deduction. In 2011, M may claim an exemption deduction of $3,700 and a standard deduction of $7,250 ($5,800 regular + $1,450 addition for unmarried 65 years of age or over) for total deductions of $10,950. Providing support in this manner would be far less expensive than making outright gifts of $5,000 annually Although this arrangement requires the couple to give up the property permanently (since any type of reversionary interest would cause the income to be taxed back to the couple), in many family situations, M would probably give the property back when she no longer needs it or when she dies. In addition, other techniques are available that can circumvent the problem of permanently departing with the property.

The above example demonstrates how income can be shifted successfully. Where income is to be shifted to children, however, the taxpayer must contend with the "kiddie" tax.

The "kiddie" tax clearly limits opportunities for shifting unearned income to children. However, it does not eliminate them. Recall that the "kiddie" tax applies generally applies to children less than 19 or those that are full-time students less than 24. However, the "kiddie" tax does not apply until unearned income exceeds $1,900 (in 2011). Consequently, for a child subject to the kiddie tax, the first $950 of unearned income bears no tax because of the standard deduction, and the next $950 is taxed at the child's rates. Although the "kiddie" tax severely curtails the amount of tax that could otherwise be saved through shifting income to children, taxpayers attempting to shift modest amounts of income are not affected.

For taxpayers wanting to shift more unearned income to their children, other techniques are available. One way of coping with the "kiddie" tax is by making investments with income that is deferred until the child is no longer subject to the tax. For example, the taxpayer could give a child Series EE savings bonds. The income from these bonds can be deferred by not electing to report the accumulated interest until after the child has turned 24 (or 19 if he or she is not a student). Interest thereafter would be reported annually. Similarly, discount bonds—those *without* original issue discount—could be purchased. In this case, the interest is not reported until the bond is sold.

The "kiddie" tax applies to unearned income and not earned income. As a result, earned income can be successfully shifted by paying the child for performing some task. Of course, shifting does not occur unless the payment is deductible by the parent. Such payments, when made by a parent directly to a child under 18, have the added benefit of not being subject to social security taxes.

## Excluded Economic Income

In arranging one's affairs, it should be observed that certain "economic" income does not fall within the definition of income for tax purposes and thus can be obtained tax-free.

### Example 44

Taxpayer R received a gift from her rich uncle of $100,000, which she is considering investing in either a condominium or corporate stocks. The condominium in which she is interested is the one in which she currently lives and rents for $8,000 annually. In lieu of purchasing the condominium, she could continue to rent and invest the $100,000 in preferred stocks paying dividends of 10% annually, or $10,000 of income per year. Assume that R pays taxes at a marginal rate of 30%. The return after taxes on the preferred stock will be 7%, or $7,000. The return from the investment in the condominium is represented by the rent that she does not pay of $8,000, which is nontaxable. In essence, the condominium pays a dividend-in-kind (i.e., shelter), which is tax-exempt. Consequently, R would obtain a higher yield on her investment by purchasing the condominium. Note that income for tax purposes does not include the value of the condominium which would be considered income in the economic sense because the use of the condominium's shelter represents consumption. This same type of analysis applies to all types of investments in consumer goods that provide long-term benefits, such as washers and refrigerators.

## Problem Materials

### DISCUSSION QUESTIONS

**5-1** *Economic versus Tax Concept of Income.* It has been said that the income tax discriminates against the person who lives in a rented home as compared with the person who owns his or her own residence. Comment on the truth of this assertion and why such discrimination may or may not be justified.

**5-2** *Net Worth Method.* Explain the circumstances in which the economist's approach to measuring income might be used for tax purposes and what specific steps might be taken to implement such an approach.

**5-3** *What Is Income?* Listed below are several items that may or may not constitute income for purposes of economics and income taxes. Indicate whether each item would be considered income for each of these purposes, including comments on why differences, if any, might exist.

**a.** Beef raised and consumed by a cattle rancher.
**b.** Interest received on state or local bonds.
**c.** Air transportation provided by an airline to one of its flight attendants.
**d.** Appreciation of XRY stock from $1,000 to $6,000 during the year.
**e.** Proceeds collected from an insurance company for a casualty loss and reinvested in similar property.
**f.** A loan obtained from a friend.
**g.** $105 received from sale of stock purchased one year ago for $100; inflation during the past year averaged five percent.
**h.** A gift received as a Christmas present.

**5-4** *Cash Equivalent Doctrine.* A financial newsletter recently reported the many advantages that may be obtained from belonging to a barter club or organization. Would tax benefits be included among these advantages (e.g., no taxable income realized on the exchange of services)?

**5-5** *Return of Capital Doctrine—General.* Explain the return of capital doctrine and discuss three situations in which the doctrine operates.

**5-6** *Indirect Benefits.* A, an assistant manager for a department store, often is required to work overtime to help mark down merchandise for special sales. On these occasions, her employer pays the cost of her evening meal. Does the meal constitute income? Explain.

**5-7** *Annual Accounting Period-Planning.* Briefly explain the notion of "income bunching" and why it is a problem.

**5-8** *52-53 Week Year.* At first glance, it may appear that the "52-53 week" taxable year is one of those accounting practices that has no real world application. Using the Internet, determine if any well-known company uses the 52-53 week accounting period as its taxable year.

**5-9** *Relationship between Tax and Financial Accounting Methods.* Does conformity with generally accepted accounting principles satisfy the requirement of § 446(c) that income must be clearly reflected? Explain, including some illustrations where income for tax purposes will differ from that for financial accounting purposes.

**5-10** *Cash Basis Taxpayer's Receipt of Notes.* Does a cash basis taxpayer recognize income when a note is received or when collections are made?

**5-11** *Constructive Receipt Doctrine.* Discuss the planning opportunities related to the cash method of accounting and how these are affected by the constructive receipt doctrine.

**5-12** *Accrual Method of Accounting*. Address the following questions:

**a.** When does a taxpayer using the accrual method of accounting normally report income?

**b.** Under what circumstances is an accrual basis taxpayer treated like a cash basis taxpayer for purposes of reporting income?

**5-13** *Change in Accounting Method*. T Corporation is considering altering the way in which it accounts for a particular item.

**a.** If T wishes to make the change, how should it proceed?

**b.** Explain the Section 481 adjustment and how T must account for it.

**5-14** *Changing Accounting Methods: Procedures*. F files the tax returns for his three-year-old son, S. Up until this year, F had always reported the interest on S's Series EE savings bonds annually. F now wishes to report the interest income when the bonds are redeemed (e.g., when the child reaches age 18). Can F change the way he reports the interest? If so, how?

**5-15** *What Is an Accounting Method?* This year, T hired a new accountant, A. As part of A's routine review procedures, A determined that T's previous accountant had improperly computed the gross profit percentage to be used in recognizing income on an installment sale. Based on the previous accountant's calculation, 40 percent of each year's receipts were to be included in income, whereas according to A's calculation the proper percentage was 50 percent. Explain what A should do upon finding the discrepancy.

**5-16** *Claim of Right*. Consider the questions below.

**a.** Is the application of the claim of right doctrine limited to situations that involve only contested income? Explain.

**b.** Explain the difference between the claim of right and constructive receipt doctrines.

**5-17** *Prepaid Rent*. In light of the tax treatment, if landlords of apartment complexes had a choice, should they characterize an initial $500 payment from their tenants as a security deposit or as a payment of the last month's rent in advance? Explain.

**5-18** *Prepaid Services*. Identify several types of services where the accrual basis provider will not be permitted to defer any prepayments of income related to such services. Explain.

**5-19** *Long-Term Contracts*. Indicate which method of accounting for long-term contracts—completed contract or percentage of completion—the taxpayer may use in the following situations. Assume each contract is considered a long-term contract unless otherwise implied.

**a.** A contract to build an office building. The taxpayer's annual gross receipts for the past five years have exceeded $11 million.

**b.** A contract to build a home to be finished next year. The taxpayer's annual gross receipts for the last five years have exceeded $11 million.

**c.** A contract to build a high-rise apartment complex containing 120 units. The contractor's average gross receipts are $11 million.

**d.** A contract to manufacture 15,000 seats for a football stadium. The taxpayer has several contracts for this type of seat. Average gross receipts are $12 million.

**e.** A contract to manufacture a special part for NASA's space shuttles. Average annual gross receipts were $12 million.

**5-20** *Taxpayer Identification—Family Trusts*. In recent years, many taxpayers have fallen victim to vendors of the so-called family trust tax shelter. Under this arrangement the taxpayer signs a contractual agreement entitling the trust to all of the taxpayer's income which is subsequently distributed to the beneficiaries of the trust. Explain how this arrangement is supposed to save taxes and why it fails.

**5-21** *Income Reporting by Partnerships and S Corporations*. Absent special rules, explain how partners and shareholders in S corporations might defer the reporting of income by having their respective entities select fiscal years for reporting rather than calendar years.

**5-22** *Income from Community Property*. Under what circumstances will knowledge of the community property system be relevant? Is it necessary for persons residing in common law states to understand the community property system?

**5-23** *Planning—Timing Income Recognition.* Although it is generally desirable to defer income recognition and the related taxes. when would acceleration of income be preferred?

**5-24** *Planning—Income Splitting.* How might R, who operates a shoe store as a sole proprietorship, reduce the taxes that are imposed on his family using income-splitting techniques?

**5-25** *"Kiddie" Tax.* R has been advised that due to changes in the tax law over the years he can no longer save taxes by shifting income to his children.

- **a.** Explain the origin of such advice.
- **b.** What techniques currently exist to shift income successfully to children and other low-bracket family members?

## YOU MAKE THE CALL

**5-26** In the last episode in the adventures of Dr. Will Floss, the tax-evading dentist identified earlier in this chapter, he was found exploring the cavities of his patient's mouth. As may be remembered, Dr. Floss had just made a deal with a patient whereby he exchanged a root canal for some carpet complete with pad and installation. Floss's accountant, Al, was faced with a dilemma. After dumping his records on Al's desk, Floss had proudly proclaimed that it was another great year. Al could remember his exact words: "Made over $200,000 but reported only $50,000. Not bad," said Floss. "Am I glad I talked to Dr. Moller!" Unfortunately, Al had to lower the boom on Floss's plan, explaining to him that he was required to report his barter income. However, Floss has stated flatly that he will not report the income. "If Moller doesn't report his, I'm not reporting mine," insists Floss. What should Al the accountant do about his client Floss and his friend Moller? If Floss goes to another accountant, does Al have any responsibilities?

## PROBLEMS

**5-27** *What Is Income?* In each of the following situations indicate whether taxable income should be recognized.

- **a.** Q purchased an older home for $20,000. Shortly after its purchase, the area in which it was located was designated a historical neighborhood, causing its value to rise to $50,000.
- **b.** R, a long-time employee of XYZ Inc., purchased one of the company's cars worth $7,000 for $3,000.
- **c.** I borrowed $10,000 secured by property that had an adjusted basis of $3,000 and a fair market value of $15,000.
- **d.** S, a 60 percent shareholder in STV Corporation, uses a company car 70 percent of the time for business and 30 percent for personal purposes. The rental value of the car is $200 per month.

**5-28** *What Is Income?* In each of the following situations indicate whether taxable income should be recognized.

- **a.** R discovered oil on his farm, causing the value of his land to increase by $100 million.
- **b.** While jogging, L found a portable stereo radio valued at $200.
- **c.** E agreed to rent his lake cottage to F for $1,000 during the summer. After living there for two weeks, E and F agreed that E would only charge $700 if F made certain improvements.
- **d.** D borrowed $100,000, $20,000 each from S, T, U, V, and W. He gave them each a one-year note bearing interest at a rate of 25 percent. At the end of the year, D borrowed $200,000 from X, promising to pay him back in one year plus 30 percent interest. D used part of the $200,000 from X to pay the interest due to S, T, U, V, and W. D also convinced them to extend the original notes for another year. D has no intention of ever repaying the principal of the notes.

**5-29** *What Is Income?* In each of the following situations indicate whether taxable income should be recognized.

**a.** L sued her former employer for sex discrimination evidenced in his compensation policy. She was awarded $100,000, $39,000 of which represented reimbursement for mental anguish.

**b.** M, a sales clerk for a department store, purchased a microwave oven from the store's appliance department. The store has a policy allowing employees a 10 percent discount. This discount results in $45 savings to M.

**c.** R received a bottle of perfume and a case of grapefruit from her boss at the annual Christmas party. The items were valued at $25.

**5-30** *Constructive Receipt.* When would a cash basis taxpayer recognize income in the following situations? Assume the taxpayer reports on a calendar year.

**a.** R, a traveling salesperson, was out of town on payday, December 31. He picked up his check when he arrived back on January 3.

**b.** C owns a bond with interest coupons due and payable on December 31. C clipped the coupons and redeemed them on January 7.

**c.** R is an officer and controlling shareholder in XYZ Corporation. In December the corporation authorized bonuses for all officers. The bonus was paid in February of the following year.

**5-31** *Constructive Receipt.* For each of the following situations, indicate whether the taxpayer has constructively received the income.

**a.** R received a bonus as top salesperson of the year. He received the check for $20,000 at 10 p.m. on December 31 at a New Year's Eve party. All the banks were closed.

**b.** On January 3, D received the check for January's rent of her duplex. The envelope was postmarked December 31.

**c.** On December 25, C Corporation rewarded its top executive, E, with 100 shares of stock for a job well done. E was unable to find a buyer until March 15 of the following year.

**d.** Immediately after receiving her check on December 31, Z went to her employer's bank to cash it. The bank would not cash it since the employer's account was overdrawn.

**5-32** *Constructive Receipt.* For each of the following situations, indicate whether the taxpayer has constructively received the income.

**a.** X Corporation declared a dividend on December 15 and mailed dividend checks on December 28. R received her check for $200 on January 4.

**b.** F owns a small apartment complex. His son, S, lives in one of the units and manages the complex. Several tenants left their January rent checks with S during the last week of December. S delivered the checks to his father in January.

**c.** This year, the cash surrender value of L's life insurance policy increased by $500. In order to obtain the value, L must cancel the policy.

**5-33** *Changes in Accounting Method.* JB and his sons have operated a small "general store" in Backwoods, Idaho, since 1990. This year, JB hired a new accountant, who immediately told him he should be using the accrual method to account for his inventories and related sales and receivables. The receivables were primarily attributable to sales of seed to farmers as well as appliances. JB has always used the cash method of accounting, reporting all of his income when he receives it and deducting all costs when paid. According to the accountant, as of the close of the current year, JB had $70,000 in receivables outstanding (none of which had been reported in income), inventory of $130,000 (all expensed), and outstanding accounts payable for recent purchases of inventory of $20,000.

**a.** If the IRS audits JB and requires him to change his method of accounting, what is the adjustment amount and when will JB report it?

**b.** Same as (a) except JB voluntarily changes his method of accounting prior to the audit.

**c.** If JB changes to the accrual method of accounting to account for inventories and sales, may he continue to report other items of income (e.g., interest income) and expense (e.g., supplies) using the cash method?

**5-34** *Advanced Payments for Goods.* HIJ Furniture, an accrual basis company for both tax and financial accounting purposes, normally does not sell the items displayed in its showrooms, nor does it keep those items in stock. Instead, it obtains partial payment from the customer and orders the items directly from the manufacturer. During the current year, HIJ collected $60,000 with respect to furniture sales still on order at the close of the year. (The partial payments collected by HIJ do not exceed their cost for the items ordered.) Must HIJ report any of the $60,000 as income this year?

**5-35** *Percentage of Completion.* THZ Corporation is a large construction company. This year it contracted with the city of Old York to build a new performing arts center for a price of $5,000,000. Estimated total costs of the project were $4,000,000. Annual costs incurred were as follows:

| | |
|---|---|
| 2012 | $2,000,000 |
| 2013 | 500,000 |
| 2014 | 1,000,000 |
| Total | $3,500,000 |

a. What method(s) of accounting may the corporation use to report income from the project?
b. How much income would be reported each year under the percentage of completion method?
c. Would any interest be due to (or from) the IRS as a result of this contract? If so, compute for the first year only, assuming the taxpayer is in the 34 percent tax bracket and the interest rate is 10 percent.

**5-36** *U.S. Savings Bonds.* This year S purchased U.S. Government Series EE Bonds for $700. The redemption value of the bonds at the end of the year was $756. What options are available to S with respect to reporting the income from the bonds?

**5-37** *Contested Income.* In 2011, GLX Company, an accrual basis taxpayer, received $10,000 for supplying running shoes to T for sale in his sporting goods store. During 2011, T claimed the shoes had defective soles and requested GLX to refund the $10,000 payment.
a. Must GLX report any of the $10,000 as income in 2011?
b. Had GLX not received payment in 2011, would your answer in (a) change?

**5-38** *Deposits and Prepaid Rents.* Q owns several duplexes. From each new tenant she requires a $150 security deposit and $300 for the last month's rent. The deposit is refundable assuming the tenant complies with all the terms of the lease. During the year, Q collected $1,000 in deposits and $2,400 of prepaid rents for the last month of occupancy. In addition, she refunded $400 to previous tenants but withheld $300 due to damages. How much must Q include in income assuming she is an accrual basis taxpayer?

**5-39** *Prepaid Service Income: Accrual Method.*
a. LL Corporation, a calendar year and accrual basis taxpayer, is engaged in the lawn care business, providing fertilizer treatments. It sells one-, two- and three-year contracts. Each contract provides that the customer will receive four treatments (fall, winter, spring and summer). An analysis of its customer contracts revealed that it received $200,000 during the fall for a one-year contract. Each of these customers will receive one treatment in 2011 and three treatments in 2012. In its financial accounting statements, the company reports the income as services are performed. What amount of income must the corporation report in 2011 and 2012?
b. Same as (a) above except the contracts are for two years. The customers will receive one treatment in 2011, four treatments in 2012 and three treatments in 2013.
c. A professional basketball team that reports on the calendar year and uses the accrual method collected $700,000 in pre-season ticket sales in August and September of 2011. Of its 41-game home season, 15 games were played *prior to the end* of the year. In its financial statements, the organization reports the income as the games are played. What amount must be included in income in 2011?
d. A posh resort hotel in Florida reports on the calendar year and uses the accrual method. During 2011, it collected $10,000 in advance payments for rooms to be rented during January and February 2012. What amount of income must be included in 2011 and 2012?

**5-40** *Income from Transferred Property.* E's grandmother owns several vending machines on campus. To help him through college, she allows E to collect and keep all the receipts from the machines. During the year, E spent approximately two hours a month to collect $5,000. Who must report the income and what is the amount to be included?

**5-41** *Partnership Income.* QRS, a partnership, had taxable income of $120,000 for the fiscal year ended September 30, 2011. For the first quarter ending December 31, 2011, taxable income was $30,000. During 2011, Q, a partner with a 30 percent interest in profits and losses, withdrew $1,000 per month for a total of $12,000. What is Q's taxable income from QRS for 2011?

**5-42** *Reporting Interest Income.* On November 1, 2010, G received a substantial inheritance and promptly made several investments. Indicate in each of the following cases the amount of interest income that he must report and the period in which the income is properly reported, assuming that G uses (1) the cash method of accounting, or (2) the accrual method of accounting. G reports using the calendar year.

**a.** G purchased a $10,000, 90-day U.S. Treasury bill at 99. The bill matured on January 30, 2011, when G redeemed it at par.

**b.** G purchased $100,000 of AFN Inc. 10 percent bonds for $95,000. The bonds were issued at par in 2003. The bonds pay interest semiannually on March 1 and September 1. On March 1, 2011, G received an interest payment of $5,000.

**5-43** *Interest-Free Loans.* This year Dr. W, an orthopedic surgeon, and her husband, H, an attorney, established a trust for their five-year-old daughter, D. In conjunction with setting up the trust, the couple loaned the trust $200,000 payable on demand without interest. Assuming the interest that should have been charged under the applicable rate was $23,000, explain the effect of the loan on all of the parties.

**5-44** *Shareholder Advances.* In 2000, J started ACC Corporation, a construction company. J owns all of the stock of the corporation and is also its president. Like many owners of closely-held corporations, J pretty much treats the corporation's checkbook as his own. He often asks the bookkeeper to make out checks to him that he ostensibly uses for business purposes. Over time, J does repay the amounts used for personal purposes, or turns in receipts for amounts used for business. In the meantime, the bookkeeper charges these checks to a special account titled "J Suspense." Upon the accountant's review this year, he noted that the account showed a balance of $15,000 (indicating an amount due from J). Explain the tax consequences.

**5-45** *Interest-Free Loans.* F is chief executive officer of CVC Corporation and has taxable income in excess of $200,000 annually. During the year, he loaned his 20-year-old son, S, $30,000, payable on demand without interest. S promptly invested the $30,000 and earned $1,200, which was his only income during the year.

**a.** Assuming the interest that should have been charged under applicable rate is $3,000, compute the effect of the loan on the taxable income of both F and S.

**b.** Would F be able to shift income to his son if he had made a loan of only $9,000?

**5-46** *Code § 7872: Exceptions.* For each of the following independent cases, indicate the income and gift tax consequences for both the lender and the borrower.

**a.** J loaned his 25-year-old son, K, $8,000 interest-free, which K used to purchase a car. K had $400 investment income from a savings account for the year.

**b.** Same as (a) except K decided to invest the money in a certificate of deposit yielding $800 of interest income producing a total net investment income of $1,200 for the year.

**c.** G loaned her 29-year-old daughter, D, $50,000 interest-free to help her acquire a franchise for a fast-food restaurant. All of D's funds were invested in the business and consequently she had no investment income for the year.

**d.** P Corporation loaned its sole shareholder, Q, $150,000 interest-free.

**e.** Same as (d) except Q owns no stock in P but is simply a key employee.

**5-47** *Cash Method Eligibility*. Given the facts below, indicate whether the taxpayer may use the cash method for 2011 in the following situations.

**a.** Sweatshirt Corporation, a publicly traded corporation: annual gross receipts for 2008 and previous years were $1 million annually; gross receipts for 2009 were $3 million; and for 2010, $8 million.

**b.** Dewey, Cheatham, and Howe, a national public accounting firm, operated as a partnership. Annual gross receipts for the past five years have exceeded $50 million.

**c.** McSwane, McMillan, and McClain, Inc., an architectural firm, operated as a regular C corporation. Annual gross receipts for the past two years have exceeded $7 million. McSwane, McMillan, and McClain own all of the stock and perform services for the firm.

**d.** Buttons and Bows, Inc., an S corporation.

**e.** A trust established for John Doe.

**f.** Plantation Office Park, a publicly traded limited partnership: annual gross receipts have never exceeded $2 million. The partnership is a tax shelter.

**5-48** *Accrual Method of Accounting*. Frank's Casing Crew and Rental Tools Inc. uses the accrual method of accounting and reports using the calendar year. The corporation sells oil pipes, leases equipment used in oil fields, and provides crews necessary to operate the leased equipment. The company's customers are primarily large oil companies. The company's contracts provide that payment is due when it sends the customer an invoice that includes all supporting documentation (i.e., job tickets, equipment tickets, and third party charges). In 2011, the company finished several jobs but did not invoice the customers until after year-end because it had not yet received a third party's invoice. When should the corporation report the income from these contracts?

**5-49** *Accrual Method of Accounting*. N Corporation operates a chain of coffee shops in various locations throughout Indiana. It uses the accrual method of accounting and reports using the calendar year. In 2012, its expenses exceeded its revenue resulting in a net operating loss (NOL). Like federal law, Indiana's state law, permits corporations to carry back an NOL to prior years where it can be used to offset such year's taxable income, enabling the corporation to obtain a refund of previously paid Indiana state income taxes. (Note that state income taxes are deductible business expenses so a recovery of such expenses is taxable income.) The Indiana Department of Revenue has the right to examine any refund claim before determining whether to allow the claim and the refund amount. In 2013, the corporation filed the proper forms to carry back the NOL, seeking a refund of part of the state income taxes it had paid in previous years. In 2014, N received a refund of $100,000. When should N report the income?

**5-50** *Accrual Method of Accounting*. Giant Corp. operates retail stores throughout the country. It uses the accrual method of accounting and reports using the calendar year. Each store offers film processing. Customers wanting film developed put the film in an order envelope and place the envelope in a drop box. Finished prints are produced primarily by Giant's own processing labs but also unrelated labs. The labs develop the film using highly specialized equipment and a complex chemical process, normally returning the finished prints within two days of when their couriers pick up the film. The finished prints are held for customer pick-up at the stores. Customers are not required to buy the prints unless they are completely satisfied. Store employees review the unsold prints on hand every 30 days and remind customers by phone or mail that their prints are available. Finished prints that are unclaimed after 120 days or customer rejects are discarded. Giant owns the finished prints until either a customer purchases them or they are discarded. Only a small percentage of customers do not purchase the finished prints. Upon audit, the IRS asserted that Giant should have to report the income when the stores receive the finished prints. Indicate whether the agent is correct or incorrect and explain the reasons for your answer.

**5-51** *Shifting Income to Children.* Mr. and Mrs. D wish to shift income to their seven-year-old son, C, to be used for his college education. Explain whether the following would serve their goals or, alternatively, how they affect any technique designed to shift income.

**a.** Paying C an allowance for making his bed and picking up his clothes.
**b.** Paying C for helping to wash cars at his dad's car wash.
**c.** Buying C Series EE Savings Bonds.
**d.** Arranging to have Mrs. D's employer pay C part of her salary.
**e.** The social security rules.
**f.** The rules governing personal exemptions.

## TAX RETURN PROBLEMS

■ *CONTINUOUS TAX RETURN PROBLEMS* See Appendix I, Part 1.

## CUMULATIVE PROBLEM

**5-52** David K. Gibbs, age 37, and his wife, Barbara, age 33, have two children, Chris and Ellen, ages 2 and 12. David is employed as an engineer for an oil company, and his wife recently completed a degree in accounting and will begin working for a public accounting firm next year. David has compiled the following information for your use in preparing his tax return for 2010.

1. For the current year, David received a salary of $70,000. His employer withheld Federal income taxes of $9,000 and the appropriate amount of FICA taxes.
2. At the annual Christmas party, he received a card indicating that he would receive a bonus of $3,000 for his good work during the year. The bonus check was placed in his mailbox at work on December 30. Since David was out of town for the holidays, he did not pick up the bonus check until January 2.
3. A bond issued by AM&T Inc. was sold on May 30, 2010 for $9,700, $700 of which represented interest accrued to the date of the sale. The Gibbs had purchased the bond (issued at par value of $10,000 on March 1, 1999) in 2006 for $10,000.
4. The couple has a $500 U.S. Savings Bond, which they purchased for $300 and gave to their daughter several years ago. The proper election to report the income from the bond annually was made. The bond's redemption value increased $30 this year.
5. David was an instant winner in the state lottery and won $50.
6. The Gibbs sold 100 shares of stock in JB Corporation for $10,000 on May 1, 2010. They had purchased the stock on June 1, 2003 for $14,000.
7. During the year, Barbara prepared a number of tax returns for which she received $5,000. Her only deductible expense incurred in performing these services was $100 for some tax software.
8. The couple's itemized deductions were medical expenses of $7,468, interest on their home mortgage of $8,500, state income taxes $3,750, property taxes on their home of $5,000, and charitable contributions of $2,000.

Compute Mr. and Mrs. Gibbs' Federal income tax liability (or refund) for 2010. If a tax return is required by your instructor, prepare Form 1040, including Schedules A and B.

## TAX RESEARCH PROBLEMS

**5-53** During the year, J, a college accounting professor, received complimentary copies of various textbooks from numerous publishers. J gives some of these books to students and the school library. J also keeps some of the books for his personal use and reference. A few times during the year J sold an unwanted text to a wholesale book dealer who periodically checked with him and other professors for texts. Must J report any income related to receipt of these books?

**5-54** R recently became a member of a religious order. As a member, she was subject to the organization's complete control. The organization often required its members to terminate their employment in order to work in other jobs consistent with the organization's philosophy. For example, the organization supplied personnel to missions, hospitals, and schools. The organization also requires all members to take an oath of poverty and pay over all their earnings to it. Members' living expenses are paid for by the organization out of its own funds. Is R taxed on her earnings?

**5-55** In each of the following cases, indicate who is responsible for reporting the income.

**a.** Dr. A instructed the hospital for which he worked to pay his salary to his daughter C.

**b.** R, a famous entertainer, agreed to perform at a concert gratuitously (without fee) for the benefit of a charitable organization.

**c.** In a contest for the best essay on why education is important, T, age 25, won the right to designate a person under 17 to receive $1,000.

**5-56** M owed her good friend, F, $20,000. In addition, M planned on making a charitable contribution to her church of $10,000. Instead of using cash to pay her friend and to make the contribution, M is considering transferring stock to each in the appropriate amount. The stock is currently worth $100 per share. M had purchased the 300 shares of stock several years ago for $6,000 ($20 per share). Will M realize any income if she transfers the stock rather than paying cash?

**5-57** Sam Sellit is a salesperson for Panoramic Pools of St. Louis, a construction company that builds and sells prefabricated swimming pools. Over the past several years, Sam has progressed to become the top salesperson for the St. Louis franchise. Sam has done so well that he is considering purchasing his own franchise and starting a company in San Antonio. This year he contacted the home office in Pittsburgh about the possibility of opening up his own shop. The vice president in charge of expansion, Greg Grow, suggested that the two of them meet at the company's annual meeting of franchisees in Orlando. Greg knew that Sam, although not a franchisee, would be attending because he was the top salesperson in the St. Louis office, and the company invites the top salesperson from each office as well as his or her spouse to attend the meeting.

While at the four-day meeting (Tuesday through Friday) in Orlando, Sam and his wife, Sue, met with Greg and discussed the potential venture. In addition, Greg allowed Sam and Sue to attend the parts of the meeting that were only for franchisees so that they could get a glimpse of how the company operated. Of course, while they were in Orlando, Sam and his wife visited all of the tourist attractions. On Tuesday, there were no meetings scheduled and everyone spent the day at Disney World and Epcot Center. On Thursday afternoon, no meetings were scheduled and the couple went with Greg and his wife to Sea World. Sam attended meetings for several hours on Friday while his wife played golf. The couple stayed over through Sunday and continued their sightseeing activities.

The company picked up the tab for the couple's trip, reimbursing Sam $3,500 which included the costs of air fare, meals, lodging, and entertainment. What are the tax consequences to Sam?

**5-58** Large Corporation manufactures computers. Its total sales of computers last year were well over $100 million. With each computer it offers a three-year warranty, covering parts and labor. The company estimates the future costs of warranty work related to current-year sales and defers the recognition of income until such time that it expects the warranty work will be done. Currently, the corporation reports 60 percent of the warranty income in the year of sale because the majority of warranty work occurs shortly after the computer has been sold. Thirty percent of the warranty income is reported in the second year of the warranty, and the remaining 10 percent is reported in the last year of the warranty. The company's estimates were based on sophisticated statistical techniques. Such techniques have produced estimates that appear extremely accurate based on the past ten years of data. No insurance is purchased to cover the warranty risk. Upon audit this year, the IRS agent indicated that the company cannot defer the warranty income and assessed a large tax deficiency. Advise the taxpayer as to whether it should pay the additional tax or pursue the matter in court.

**5-59** Several years ago, R started his own delivery company, RT Haulers Inc. (RTH). The corporation is an accrual basis taxpayer. The corporation grew quickly, in part because of the excellent service that it was able to offer. Historically, the company has accrued its income when its services were completed. If the customer objected to the manner in which the services were performed (e.g., late delivery, damaged goods), RTH gave the client a credit against any future services that it might provide. RTH is now considering changing its agreements with customers to provide for a seven day acceptance period during which the customer could reject the services, in which case the customer would not have any obligation to pay. Advise the client regarding when its income should be reported, specifically addressing how the change in terms might impact the reporting of future service revenues.

**5-60** Basinger Hauling is a trucking company that does business primarily on the west coast and in Mexico and Canada. Its headquarters are in Portland, Oregon. The company generally pays its drivers a specific rate, depending on a variety of factors such as miles driven, load weight, weather, unloading, fuel costs and the like. The company treats eight percent of each driver's compensation as a reimbursement for meals and lodging. Consequently, the company does not pay employment taxes (social security and Medicare) on the portion considered a reimbursement and does not include the reimbursement on the driver's W-2 form, reporting the amount representing wage income. Advise the client regarding this practice.

# 6

# Gross Income: Inclusions and Exclusions

## Learning Objectives

Upon completion of this chapter you will be able to:

- LO.1 Explain the important distinction between taxable and nontaxable income.
- LO.2 Explain the tax treatment of common items of investment income: dividends, interest, and annuities.
- LO.3 Identify various types of employee compensation and fringe benefits and explain their tax treatment.
- LO.4 Explain the treatment of gifts, inheritances, alimony and child support.
- LO.5 Describe the treatment created for unique items of income such as life insurance, debt cancellation, scholarships, and government transfers.

## Chapter Outline


Introduction 6-2
Investment Income 6-2
  Dividends 6-3
  Interest 6-6
  Annuities 6-10
  529 Plans: Qualified Tuition Programs 6-14
Employee Compensation and Other Benefits 6-17
  Reimbursement of Employee Expenses 6-19
  Employer Gifts 6-19
  Employer Awards 6-19
  Social Security Benefits 6-20
  Unemployment Benefits 6-22
  Employee Insurance 6-22
  Employer-Provided Meals and Lodging 6-26
  Child and Dependent Care Assistance 6-28
  Adoption Assistance Programs 6-28
  Educational Assistance Plans 6-28
  Section 132 Fringe Benefits 6-29
  Military Personnel 6-34
  Reparations to Holocaust Victims 6-34
Personal Transfers between Individuals 6-34
  Gifts and Inheritances 6-35
  Alimony and Separate Maintenance 6-35
Transfers by Unrelated Parties 6-40
  Life Insurance Proceeds and Other Death Benefits 6-40
  Employee Death Benefits 6-42
  Prizes and Awards 6-42
  Scholarships and Fellowships 6-43
  Cancellation of Indebtedness 6-44
  Government Transfer Payments 6-47
Business Gross Income 6-48

Agreement not to Compete and Goodwill 6-48
Business Interruption Insurance Proceeds 6-48
Damages Awarded 6-49
Lease Cancellation Payments 6-49
Leasehold Improvements 6-50
Contributions to Capital 6-51
Miscellaneous Items 6-51
Fees Received 6-51
Asset Discovery 6-51
Car Pool Receipts 6-51
Income Tax Refunds 6-51
Temporary Living Costs 6-52
Damages Awarded to Individuals 6-52
Tax Planning 6-53
Investments 6-53
Employee Benefits 6-54
Employee Versus Self-Employed 6-55
Divorce 6-56
Problem Materials 6-57


## Introduction

**LO.1**
Explain the important distinction between taxable and nontaxable income.

While the tax law makes it clear that any type of gain, benefit, profit, or other increase in wealth is potentially taxable, in reality not all income is within the grasp of the IRS. As a practical matter, there are a number of special rules that must be observed before the final treatment of any particular benefit can be determined. For example, Congress has specifically exempted several types of income from tax such as interest on state and local bonds, scholarships, gifts, and inheritances. In addition, special provisions exist that clarify the treatment of a long list of possible income items such as annuities, alimony, and employee benefits. Because of these rules, the concept of income is not quite as comprehensive as perhaps suggested in Chapter 5. As a result, any particular item initially identified as "income" might ultimately fall into one of the following three categories:

- Taxable (i.e., totally includible)
- Nontaxable (i.e., excluded in full)
- Taxable in part and nontaxable in part

The fact that some income does escape tax provides a huge opportunity. For this reason, tax advisers go to great lengths to identify methods that will convert taxable income into nontaxable income. In some cases, it may be as simple as changing a label or altering the nature of the payment. Regardless of how it is done, the benefits can be significant. For example, assume an employee pays federal and state income taxes at a combined rate of 30 percent. If a $1.00 of the employee's taxable compensation can be converted to a nontaxable fringe benefit of $1.00, it is the equivalent of giving the employee $1.42 [$1/(1– 30%)], a significant increase in after-tax income. Think of the advantage that can be obtained if this principle is applied on a grand scale to an employer with thousands of employees! The magic of exclusions is the subject of this chapter.

This chapter examines the more frequently encountered sources of income. To provide some order and logic to the presentation, the various sources of income are grouped and discussed as follows:

- Investment income (dividends, interest, annuities)
- Employee compensation and fringe benefits
- Personal transfers (gifts, inheritances, alimony)
- Transfers by unrelated individuals (life insurance, prizes, scholarships)
- Business income
- Miscellaneous items

## Investment Income

As shown in Exhibit 6-1, the vast majority of the income reported by individuals comes in some form of employee compensation such as salaries and wages (68.01 percent of all

**EXHIBIT 6.1** **Sources of Income 2006**

| *Type of Income* | *Percent of Returns Showing* | *Percent of All Income Reported* |
|---|---|---|
| Salaries and wages | 84.09%* | 68.01% |
| Taxable interest | 45.09 | 2.77 |
| Pensions, annuities, individual retirement accounts | 24.61 | 7.17 |
| Dividends | 22.85 | 2.48 |
| Qualified dividends | 19.21 | 1.71 |
| Net capital gain | 13.03 | 9.04 |
| Business or profession net income | 11.71 | 4.11 |
| Social Security benefits | 9.93 | 1.80 |
| Net capital loss | 6.24 | −.23 |
| Partnership and S corporation net income | 5.51 | 5.30 |
| Unemployment compensation | 5.33 | .33 |
| Tax-exempt interest | 4.36 | .91 |
| Rent and royalty net income | 4.18 | .99 |
| Business or profession net loss | 3.94 | −.61 |
| Rent and royalty net loss | 3.87 | −.74 |
| Farm net income less loss | 1.41 | −.19 |
| Sales of property other than capital assets, net gain less loss | 1.29 | .05 |
| Estate or trust net income less loss | .43 | .21 |

*Preliminary estimates based on samples taken from 138,394,754 individual returns filed in 2006.
**Source**: Statistics of Income, 2006 Individual Income Tax Returns, Table 1.3, Fall 2008. Publication 1304 Internal Revenue Service, Washington, D.C. 2008.

reported income for 2006). However, as Exhibit 6-1 also shows the income of many individuals is also likely to contain some type of investment income.

Common examples of investment income—sometimes referred to as unearned income—include

- Dividends
- Interest
- Annuities
- Rents

**LO.2**
Explain the tax treatment of common items of investment income: dividends, interest, and annuities.

For the most part, these income items present little problem for taxpayers. Each is usually fully taxable as ordinary income. In addition, to make reporting and compliance easier, those who pay dividends, interest, and annuities during the taxable year normally must report such payments to both the taxpayer and the IRS on the appropriate Form 1099. Nevertheless, special rules often apply in determining not only the amount of income that must be reported but also when it must be reported. The treatment of each is discussed below.

## Dividends

Today it is not uncommon for even the smallest investor to own stock in a corporation or an interest in a mutual fund. Those who do are likely to obtain part of their investment return in the form of dividends. One of the high-profile debates surrounding the Jobs and Growth Tax Relief Reconciliation Act of 2003 concerned the taxation of dividends. The original proposal of the administration called for the complete exclusion for dividends in order to address the potential problem of double taxation. However, the final legislation did not adopt such a sweeping measure. Instead, the Act reduced the tax rates imposed on dividends to what they are for capital gains. As recently extended through 2012, the rate is normally 15 percent but drops to 0 percent for taxpayers whose income falls in the 10 or 15 percent ordinary income tax brackets. To emphasize, for low-bracket taxpayers (e.g., married taxpayers with taxable income less than $65,100), dividends as well as long-term capital gains are tax free![1] The reduced rate generally applies to so-called *qualified dividends*. Qualified dividends include dividends paid with respect to stock of all domestic corporations. For domestic stock, It makes no difference whether it is publicly traded or closely held. In addition, the reduced rate generally applies to dividends from foreign corporations but only if the stock is readily tradable on an established U.S. securities market. Also, to secure the special rate the taxpayer must hold the stock for more than 60 days during a 120 day window that begins 60 days before the stock goes ex-dividend. This requirement helps prevent taxpayers from exploiting the preferential treatment for dividends. To illustrate the possible injustice, consider a taxpayer who buys a stock a few days before the ex-dividend date, receives a $1,000 dividend and then sells the stock. Assuming the value of the stock drops in direct proportion to the amount of the dividend, a sale immediately after the ex-dividend date would produce a $1,000 short-term capital loss. It appears that the $1,000 dividend is offset by the $1,000 loss and the net effect is zero. However, the dividend is taxed at 15 percent and the loss may offset ordinary income that is taxed at 35 percent. In such case, the taxpayer is better-off by $200 ($350 – $150). The holding period rule requires taxpayers to be at risk for at least 61 days if they want to use this scheme.[2]

Note that this change represents a major philosophical shift that has little precedent in tax history. Dividends received by individuals have historically been taxed as ordinary income with little or no special treatment. Although a small exclusion for dividends once existed, dividends have otherwise been treated the same as ordinary income. It should also be observed that there is no special treatment for interest income.

### Corporate Dividends

The vast majority of all distributions made by corporations to their shareholders are considered dividends and are fully taxable as ordinary income. Technically, however, a distribution made by a corporation is treated as a *dividend* only to the extent that it is out of the corporation's current or accumulated *earnings and profits*, or *E&P* as it is commonly called.[3] Amounts not considered dividends because the distribution exceeds E&P are treated as nontaxable returns of capital to the extent of the shareholder's basis in the stock. In effect, the nondividend portion of the distribution is applied to and reduces the basis of the stock. Should the return of capital distribution exceed the shareholder's basis, the excess is capital gain. In applying these rules, all distributions by corporations are deemed to be distributions of E&P to the extent thereof.

#### Example 1

C, Inc. distributes $100,000 to shareholders when its current E&P is $60,000 and it has no accumulated E&P. T, a 10% shareholder, has a basis in C, Inc. stock of $3,000. T receives $10,000, of which $6,000 (10% × $60,000) is from C's current E&P. Thus, T has a $6,000 taxable dividend; the $3,000 equal to his basis in the stock is a nontaxable return of investment, and the remaining $1,000 is capital gain. T's basis in the stock after the distribution will be zero.

As noted above, for individual taxpayers dividends are fully taxable as ordinary income but are taxed at favorable rates.[4]

Dividends received by corporate taxpayers are treated differently than dividend received by individuals. As explained in Chapter 3, in order to prevent multiple taxation of dividends, corporate taxpayers are entitled to a special dividends-received deduction. This special deduction (discussed more fully in Chapter 19) normally entitles the corporation to deduct

---

[1] § 1(h)(11)

[2] The holding period is extended for preferred stock. For other special rules see §1(h)(11).

[3] §§ 301 and 316.

[4] Special rules apply to the rare distribution of noncash property (e.g., land). See §§ 301(b) and (d).

70 percent of the dividend received.[5] The favorable tax rates, 15 or 0 percent, do not apply to dividends received by a corporation.

The most critical variable in determining the treatment of a corporate distribution is the amount of the corporation's earnings and profits. The actual computation of E&P can be quite complex but the theory underlying it is relatively simple. The calculation attempts to measure the amount the corporation can pay out without impairing its capital account. In this regard, it is quite similar to the financial accounting concept of retained earnings. However, the two are not identical. Current E&P generally represents taxable income as adjusted for certain specified items.[6] Accumulated E&P is the sum of current E&P reduced by distributions. Using this information, a corporation determines the amount of its distribution that is considered a dividend (e.g., 60%) and reports this information to the shareholder on Form 1099-DIV or similar statement.

### Mutual Fund Dividends

Millions of taxpayers now invest in stocks, bonds, and other securities indirectly through mutual funds. Mutual funds typically buy and sell investments realizing gains and losses as well as collect earnings from investments such as interest on bonds or dividends on stock.[7] Like corporations, mutual funds make distributions. However, the treatment of these distributions differs somewhat from regular corporate dividends in that they are generally characterized to reflect the nature of the income realized by the mutual fund. Mutual fund distributions are normally characterized as either *ordinary dividends* or *capital gain dividends*.[8] Ordinary dividends represent the individual's share of the fund's earnings from its own investments such as interest or dividends as well as any short-term gains the fund may realize. An individual reports all ordinary dividends as dividend income. The mutual fund designates the portion that represents "qualified dividend" income which is taxed at the 15 and 0 percent rates. Capital gain dividends represent the capital gains and losses actually realized by the mutual fund during the year. All capital gain dividends are treated as *long-term* capital gains. Corporate taxpayers are entitled to the dividends-received deduction for ordinary dividends but not capital gain dividends. Each fund reports the information regarding its distributions to its shareholders on Form 1099-DIV.

A few funds retain their capital gains, in which case they are required to pay tax on such amounts. Nevertheless, these gains are allocated to the shareholders who must include them in income as capital gain.[9] In such case, shareholders may claim a credit for any tax paid by the fund and increase their basis in their shares for the amount included in income less the tax paid.

### Other "Dividends"

There are a number of other distributions that taxpayers receive that are often called dividends. Technically, however, these are not "dividends" in the tax sense but receive special treatment. Some of these are listed below.

1. In some instances, earnings on deposits with banks, credit unions, investment companies, and savings and loan associations are referred to as dividends when they actually possess all the characteristics of interest. These dividends are reported as interest.[10]
2. Mutual insurance companies distribute amounts referred to as dividends to owners of unmatured life insurance policies. These dividends are treated as a nontaxable return of a portion of the insurance premium paid.[11]
3. Cooperatives distribute patronage dividends to cooperative members. These dividends are treated as a return of part of the original price paid for items purchased by members.[12]

---

[5] §§ 243 through 246. Generally, the deduction is a percentage of the dividends received from a domestic corporation determined as follows: (1) 70% when the stock ownership percentage (SOP) is less than 20%, (2) 80% when the SOP is 20% or more but less than 80%, and (3) 100% when the SOP is 80% or more.

[6] E&P is not defined in the Code. See § 312 and the related regulations.

[7] Funds are taxed like trusts, deducting income distributed and paying tax on income retained. Distributed income generally retains its character as either ordinary income or capital gain.

[8] Reg. § 1.852-4(a) and (b).

[9] § 852(b)(3)(D).

[10] Reg. § 1.61-7(a).

[11] § 316(b)(1).

[12] § 1385(b).

4. As noted above, dividends from regulated investment companies (mutual funds) that represent gains on sales of investments from the fund are treated as long-term capital gains.[13]

### Stock Dividends

From time to time, a corporation may make a distribution of its own stock. These so-called stock dividends are normally declared as a means to reduce the selling price of the stock or as simply a gesture of goodwill to the shareholders. As a practical matter, when a corporation distributes its own stock, it is not distributing an asset of the business; indeed, the corporation's assets remain completely intact and only the number of shares outstanding changes. From the shareholder's point of view, assuming all shareholders receive their proportionate shares of the stock distributed, they have essentially received nothing because their interest in corporate assets remains unchanged. Since the effect is to leave both the corporation and the shareholder in the same economic position as they held prior to the distribution, the stock dividend—a misnomer in this case—is nontaxable.[14] On the other hand, if the distribution is structured so that the shareholder's interest does change (e.g., the shareholder can elect to take stock or cash), the stock distribution is taxable.[15]

If the distribution of stock is nontaxable, the only responsibility of the shareholder is to determine the basis of the "new" and the "old" stock. Note that only the shareholder's per-share basis is altered. Total basis for all of the stock owned remains the same. Technically, the shareholder must allocate a portion of the basis of the original stock to the distributed stock. The basis is allocated between the old and the new in proportion to the relative values of the old and new stock on the date of the distribution.[16] When the old shares are identical to the new shares (e.g., a common on common stock dividend), the basis for each share is determined simply by dividing the basis of the old stock by the total number of shares held by the shareholder after the distribution. The holding period of the old shares carries over to the new shares.[17]

#### Example 2

V owns 100 shares of Z common with a basis of $2,200 ($22 per share). He receives 10 shares of Z common as a stock dividend. If V did not have the right to receive cash or other assets in lieu of the stock, he has no taxable income from this transaction and his $2,200 basis is allocated among the 110 shares of common for a $20 per share basis ($2,200 ÷ 110).

#### Example 3

Q owns 100 shares of S common with a basis of $2,200. She receives 10 shares of S preferred as a stock dividend. The market value is $4,000 ($40 per share) for common and $1,000 ($100 per share) for preferred. If Q did not have the right to receive cash or other assets in lieu of the stock, she has no taxable income since her proportionate interest did not change. Her basis for the preferred stock is $440 [$1,000 ÷ ($4,000 + $1,000 = $5,000 total value) = 20% × $2,200] and her basis for the common stock is $1,760 [either ($2,200 − $440) or ($4,000 ÷ $5,000) × $2,200].

## INTEREST

The second most common item of income appearing on individual tax returns is interest (see Exhibit 6-1). More than 45 percent of all returns filed in 2006 reported some type of taxable

---

13 § 1382(b).
14 § 305(a).
15 § 305(b).
16 § 307(a).
17 § 1223(5).

interest. As a general rule, interest income is taxable. This is true regardless of its source (a bank, business, friend, or relative) or the form of the interest-bearing instrument (savings account, bond, or note). However, there are two notable exceptions to this rule: (1) the exclusion for interest on certain state and local government obligations, and (2) the exclusion for interest on educational savings bonds.

### Interest on State and Local Government Obligations

From the inception of the Federal income tax law, interest on obligations of a state, a territory, a U.S. possession, or any of their political subdivisions has been *nontaxable*.[18] From time to time and even currently this exclusion has been criticized as an unwarranted loophole. Critics often characterize this exclusion as simply a tax shelter existing primarily for the rich. In truth, however, this treatment stems from an uncertainty about whether taxing this interest would be unconstitutional and also from political pressure exerted by the affected governments.[19] The exclusion is exceedingly beneficial to these governments because it means they can pay a lower interest rate and still attract investors, especially those investors who are subject to taxes at the highest marginal rates.

#### Example 4

K, Inc. invests $10,000 in corporate bonds that pay 13% annually and $10,000 in state bonds that pay 9% annually. If K, Inc.'s marginal tax rate is 34%, its after-tax earnings on the corporate bonds are less than its earnings on the state bonds.

| | *Corporate Bonds* | *State Bonds* |
|---|---|---|
| Annual interest income | $1,300 | $900 |
| Federal income tax (34%) | 442 | 0 |
| After-tax income | $ 858 | $900 |

If K's marginal tax rate is 15%, however, its after-tax earnings for the corporate bonds increase to $1,105 ($1,300 – $195).

A break-even point between taxable and nontaxable rates of return may be calculated with the following formula:

$$\text{Taxable interest rate} \times (1 - \text{Marginal tax rate}) = \text{Tax-free rate}$$

Applying the numbers in the example above when K, Inc.'s tax rate is 34 percent, the breakeven point for the taxable bond is

$$13\% \times (1 - 0.34 = 0.66) = 8.58\%$$

Thus, at the 34 percent marginal tax rate, a 13 percent taxable return is equal to an 8.58 percent tax-exempt return.

The formula can be converted to compute the break-even point for the tax-exempt bond as follows:

$$\text{Tax-free rate} \div (1 - \text{Marginal tax rate})$$

or

$$9\% \div (1 - 0.34 = 0.66) = 13.6\%$$

[18] § 103(a); § 103(c).

[19] The constitutional issue now seems to be moot. See *South Carolina v. Baker*, 109 S.Ct. 1355 (1988) where the Supreme Court noted that there was no constitutional prohibition barring the Federal government from taxing such interest. See also *National Life Insurance Co.*, 1 USTC ¶314, 6 AFTR 7801, 277 U.S. 508 (USSC, 1928), where the Supreme Court originally indicated that Federal taxation of *interest* paid by state and local governments was unconstitutional.

**EXHIBIT 6.2 Comparison of Taxable versus Tax-Free Investments**

| | *If your tax-free investment is yielding:* | | | | | |
|---|---|---|---|---|---|---|
| | 4.50% | 5.00% | 5.50% | 6.00% | 6.50% | 7.00% |
| Marginal Tax Bracket* | *Your taxable equivalent yield is:* | | | | | |
| 15% | 5.29% | 5.88% | 6.47% | 7.06% | 7.65% | 8.24% |
| 28% | 6.25% | 6.94% | 7.64% | 8.33% | 9.03% | 9.72% |
| 31% | 6.52% | 7.25% | 7.97% | 8.70% | 9.42% | 10.14% |
| 36% | 7.03% | 7.81% | 8.59% | 9.38% | 10.16% | 10.94% |
| 40.0% | 7.50% | 8.33% | 9.16% | 10.0% | 10.83% | 11.67% |

*Based on combined federal and state

Thus, at the 34 percent marginal tax rate, a 9 percent tax-exempt return is equal to a 13.6 percent taxable return.

A comparison of the effective yield on tax-free versus taxable investments is provided in Exhibit 6-2. Given current market conditions, the effective yield on tax-exempt securities will be difficult to match with taxable investments. For example, if a taxpayer is in the 28 percent bracket and the current yield on tax-exempt securities is five percent, the after-tax return on taxable securities would be greater as long as the yield exceeded 6.94 percent.

Over the years, Congress has reacted to the criticism that this exclusion subsidizes the wealthy (i.e., those subject to the highest tax rates) and has also reacted to the increasing number and complexity of financial offerings developed by state and local governments. Originally, these governments sold securities to fund public projects. More recently, however, bonds have been issued to fund business construction and other industrial development projects. When this occurs, a governmental unit retains ownership of the facilities and leases them to a business. Because the interest rate on these bonds is lower than it would be on bonds issued by the corporation, the negotiated lease payments can be lower. Congress has curtailed the tax-exempt status of these so-called industrial development bonds. With certain specified exceptions, interest on industrial development bonds is taxable income.[20]

In addition to the limitations imposed on industrial development bonds, there are still other restrictions intended to curb the use of state and local bonds to finance business activities. For example, tax-exempt bonds can no longer be issued to finance airplanes, gambling facilities, liquor stores, health clubs, sky boxes, or other luxury boxes. Nor can the bonds be issued to finance the acquisition of farmland or existing facilities, with certain exceptions.

## Gain on Sale of Tax-Exempt Bonds

It should be noted that any exclusion on state and local obligations is for *interest* income received by the bondholder. Thus, *gain* on the sale of tax-exempt securities that does not represent interest is taxable income.[21]

### Example 5

On January 1 of the current year N purchased at par a $30,000, 10-year tax exempt municipal bond, yielding 8%. On September 30 of the following year, she sold the bond for $32,000 plus accrued interest of $800. Although the accrued interest is tax-exempt, N must report $2,000 of capital gain ($32,000 – $30,000) subject to tax of up to 15%.

[20] § 103 (b).

[21] *Willcuts v. Bunn*, 2 USTC ¶640, 9 AFTR 584, 282 U.S. 216 (USSC. 1931). (See footnote 17.)

### Educational Savings Bonds

In 1988, Congress took steps to help taxpayers finance the rising costs of higher education by offering a special tax break for those who save to meet such expenses. Code § 135 generally provides that accrued interest on Series EE savings bonds issued after 1989 is exempt from tax when the accrued interest and principal amount of such bonds are used to pay for *qualified educational expenses* of the taxpayer or the taxpayer's spouse or dependents (but only if these relationships are satisfied in the year of the redemption). For this purpose, qualified education expenses include those for tuition or fees to attend college or certain schools offering vocational education. Costs that otherwise qualify must be reduced by any scholarships or fellowships that may be received, as well as any employer-provided assistance.

The interest exclusion is allowed only to the extent that the taxpayer uses the proceeds of the bond redemption to pay qualified educational expenses during the year that he or she redeems a bond. If the redemption proceeds received during the year exceed the amount of education expenses paid during the same year, the amount of the interest exclusion must be reduced proportionately. The amount of the exclusion may be computed as follows:

$$\frac{\text{Qualified educational expenses paid during the year}}{\text{Total redemption proceeds of qualified bonds during the year}} \times \text{Accrued interest} = \text{Exclusion}$$

#### Example 6

Mr. and Mrs. T purchased Series EE savings bonds in 2011 for $4,000. On June 2, 2022 they cashed in the bonds and received $10,000, $6,000 representing accrued interest and $4,000 representing their original investment. Three months later on September 2, they paid tuition of $9,000 for their dependent daughter, D, who attends a private university. In November, D received a scholarship of $1,000 for being an outstanding accounting major. Only $8,000 ($9,000 tuition − $1,000 scholarship) of D's expenses are considered qualified educational expenses. Since this amount represents only 80% ($8,000/$10,000) of the total redemption proceeds, Mr. and Mrs. T may exclude only 80% of the $6,000 accrued interest, or $4,800.

Note that to qualify for the exclusion, the savings bonds need not be transferred directly to the educational institution. The exclusion applies to interest on *any* post-1989 Series EE savings bond that is realized during the taxable year as long as the taxpayer pays sufficient qualified educational expenses during the same taxable year.

The special exclusion is designed to benefit only those who have moderate incomes. To achieve this objective, the exclusion is gradually reduced once the taxpayer's A.G.I. (as determined in the taxable year when the bonds are redeemed) reaches a certain level. The 2011 income level at which the phase-out begins depends on the taxpayer's filing status as shown below.

| *Filing Status* | *Phase-out Range Modified A.G.I.** |
|---|---|
| Single (including heads of household) | $ 71,100 – $ 86,100 |
| Married filing jointly | $106,650 – $136,650 |

*Adjusted annually for inflation

The reduction of the exclusion otherwise allowed is computed as follows:

$$\frac{\text{Excess A.G.I.}}{\$15{,}000\ (\$30{,}000 \text{ for joint returns})} \times \text{Otherwise excludable interest} = \text{Reduction}$$

Married taxpayers filing separately are not eligible for the exclusion. Taxpayers who are married must file a joint return to secure the exclusion.

## Example 7

Mr. and Mrs. B have an A.G.I., after proper modifications, of $115,100, before the exclusion. As a result, the amount of any interest that would otherwise be nontaxable must be reduced by one third:

$$\frac{(\$116{,}650 \text{ A.G.I} - \$106{,}650 \text{ threshold} = \$10{,}000)}{(\$136{,}650 - \$106{,}650 = \$30{,}000 \text{ phase-out range})}$$

Assume the couple redeemed qualified bonds this year with accrued interest of $10,000. Only 90% of the proceeds of the bonds (i.e., interest and principal) were spent on qualifying education expenses. They could exclude $6,000 of the interest, computed as follows:

| | |
|---|---|
| Excludable interest (90% × $10,000) | $ 9,000 |
| Exclusion phase-out (1/3 × $9,000) | – 3,000 |
| Amount of interest excluded | $ 6,000 |

Note that the exclusion would not be available to the couple if their A.G.I. in the year they redeemed the bonds exceeded the phase-out range (e.g., $136,650 for 2011).

Without any special provision, taxpayers with high incomes might try to circumvent the income limitation to obtain the exclusion. For example, a father earning an income of $150,000 might give $10,000 to his 10-year-old daughter who would then be instructed to buy the bonds. When the daughter started college, she would redeem the bonds to pay for her tuition. Absent any restrictions, the daughter could secure 100 percent of the available exclusion since she would have little or no income. To prevent such schemes, the exclusion is available only for bonds that are *issued* to individuals who are at least 24 years old. In addition, the exclusion is available only to the original purchaser of the bond or his or her spouse. This rule prohibits gifts of qualified bonds.

## Example 8

Mr. and Mrs. C have an A.G.I. of $150,000. Assume they currently hold qualified Series EE bonds with $10,000 of accrued interest. To avoid the income limitation, the bonds are given to Mr. C's father, GF, who has little income. This year, GF cashes the bonds in and pays for his grandson's tuition. The payment is sufficient to qualify the grandson as GF's dependent. Even though the redemption proceeds are used to pay for education expenses of the taxpayer's dependent, no exclusion is available for the interest since GF was not the original purchaser of the bond. Had GF originally purchased the bonds for his grandson, the exclusion would be allowed (assuming his grandson is his dependent).

## ANNUITIES

An annuity is a type of investment contract normally between an individual and an insurance company. In its simplest form, the annuity contract requires the insurance company to pay a fixed amount of money to be paid to the purchaser (the annuitant) beginning at a particular date (the starting date) and continue at specific intervals for either a certain period of time or for life. Annuities are quite common in a number of situations. For example, retirees often receive their retirement benefits (i.e., their pensions) in the form of an annuity. In this case, employees and employers contribute to a retirement fund while the individual is employed. Upon retirement, the employee is usually given the choice of receiving his or her pension in the form of a lump-sum distribution or the accumulations are used to buy an annuity. The annuity option is often selected. Annuities are also a popular investment among elderly taxpayers. These taxpayers, often fearing that they may outlive their assets, purchase an annuity that will provide a steady stream of income until they die. Indeed, the aging of the population–the graying of America–is making annuities far more popular than ever before.

When the annuity is purchased by an individual, the insurance company invests the amount received and the investment income increases the value of the account. Under the terms of the contract, the individual has the right to cancel the annuity. When this occurs, the insurance company pays the individual the value of the investment normally reduced by penalties for early cancellation referred to as surrender charges. These charges can run as high as ten percent of the amount withdrawn and are an important consideration when investing in an annuity. In most cases, however, insurance companies allow withdrawals of a certain percentage of the account annually without having to pay any surrender charge. The tax treatment of these withdrawals is discussed below.

The income earned on the investment is tax-deferred. This means the income is taxable but not during the current year when it is earned. Instead, the income is taxable at some future date when the annuitant receives cash payments. Until then, the income is automatically reinvested in full, without payment of Federal income taxes, to earn tax-deferred income. Observe that the income is not taxed currently because the individiual has not received it either directly or constructively. It is not treated as constructively received since it is not available unless the taxpayer cancels the policy–a substantial restriction on its use.

The tax deferral feature of annuities make them particularly attractive for persons considering retirement. Annuity payments are commonly scheduled to begin on retirement when the recipients' marginal tax rates are lower. Because of the lower rates, these individuals usually pay less total taxes in addition to receiving the benefits from tax deferral.

### Taxation of Annuities

The taxation of annuities reflects the cost recovery principle. As discussed in Chapter 5, the portion that is a return of capital is nontaxable.[22] Determination of the portion that represents income and the portion that is a nontaxable return of capital generally depends on whether the amounts are received before or after the starting date for periodic payments.

**Amounts Received Before Starting Date** Cash withdrawals, including loans, before the annuity starting date are normally taxable to the extent of the earnings accumulated in the account. Amounts in excess of the earnings are treated as a nontaxable return of capital until the taxpayer's cost has been completely recovered. Additional amounts are taxable.[23]

**Early Withdrawals of Annuities** To discourage investors from withdrawing funds before the starting date, a 10 percent penalty is assessed on the deferred income. The penalty is waived if the taxpayer has reached age 59½ or is disabled.[24]

#### Example 9

When S was 50, he purchased an annuity from an insurance company for $10,000. The annuity was to start when S became 65. At age 55, he requested and received an $8,000 distribution from the account. At the time of the distribution, the annuity had grown by $7,000 and had a total cash value of $17,000. Since the withdrawal is before the starting date and before he reached age 59 1/2 the distribution is taxable to the extent of the accumulated earnings and a 10 percent penalty is imposed. Of the $8,000 received, $7,000 ($17,000 – $10,000) is attributable to earnings and taxable and the remaining $1,000 is a nontaxable return of capital. The penalty imposed is $700 (10% × the income recognized of $7,000).

---

[22] § 72(b)(1).

[23] Special rules may apply depending on the type of annuity. See Pension and Annuity Income, IRS Publication 575 (Revised 2010) p. 14.

[24] See § 72(q)(2). The penalty provision does not apply to contracts issued before August 14, 1982.

**Amounts Received on or after Starting Date** The treatment of periodic payments beginning on or after the starting date differs from that for amounts received before the starting date. In these situations, the portion that is a return of capital is the product of the exclusion ratio (investment in the contract ÷ expected return) and the amount received as shown in the following formula

$$\frac{\text{Investment in the contract}}{\text{Expected return from the contract}} \times \text{Amount received currently} = \text{Excluded portion}$$

The taxable portion is the amount received currently less the portion that is a return of capital (i.e., the excluded portion). When the annuity will be received over a stipulated number of years, the expected return from the contract is the amount to be received each year (or month) multiplied by the number of years (or months) payments are to be received.

### Example 10

W invests $20,000 in a single-premium deferred annuity. At the end of 15 years, W elects to receive the $20,000 principal plus interest over the next ten years. She receives $7,000 in the current year and will receive $7,000 each of the following nine years. W's nontaxable return of capital each year is $2,000 computed as follows

$$\frac{\$20,000}{\$7,000 \times 10 \text{ years} = \$70,000} \times \$7,000 = \$2,000$$

W's taxable income each year is $5,000 ($7,000 – $2,000).

### Example 11

Refer to *Example 10*. If W receives only three payments in the first year totaling $1,750 ($7,000 × 3/12), the computation remains the same except the amount received currently is $1,750 (instead of $7,000). Consequently, her nontaxable return of capital in the first year is $500 [($20,000 ÷ $70,000) × $1,750] and her taxable income is $1,250 ($1,750 – $500).

Note that the solution to *Example 10* is the same if W had simply divided the $20,000 principal by the 10 years (and to *Example 11* if W adjusted the annual amount to months). This is not true, however, when the annuity payments are received over the individual's life. For these situations, the Regulations provide several tables based on contract payment terms and the annuitant's age.[25] These tables must be used by those taxpayers making post-June 1986 contributions to the annuity contract. A portion of these tables is reproduced in Exhibit 6-3.

When the payments will be received over the life of the annuitant, the expected return from the contract is the amount to be received each year multiplied by the multiple that corresponds to the annuitant's age in the table. It also is important to note that the portion of any annuity payment to be excluded from gross income cannot *exceed* the unrecovered investment in the contract immediately before the receipt of the payment.[26] In other words, the exclusion ratio remains the same until the investment is fully recovered at which time subsequent receipts are fully taxable. In addition, if the annuitant dies before the entire investment is recovered, the amount of the *unrecovered investment* is allowed as a *deduction* on his or her final tax return.[27] The deduction is not a miscellaneous itemized deduction subject to the 2% floor.

[25] Reg. § 1.72-9.

[26] § 72(b)(2). For annuities beginning before July 2, 1986, the exclusion ratio remains the same for life regardless of whether the investment is recovered and no deduction is allowed for any unrecovered investment.

[27] § 72(b)(3).

**EXHIBIT 6.3** **Ordinary Life Annuities—One Life—Expected Return Multiples**

| Age | Multiple | Age | Multiple | Age | Multiple |
|---|---|---|---|---|---|
| 21 | 60.9 | 58 | 25.9 | 95 | 3.7 |
| 22 | 59.9 | 59 | 25.0 | 96 | 3.4 |
| 23 | 59.0 | 60 | 24.2 | 97 | 3.2 |
| 24 | 58.0 | 61 | 23.3 | 98 | 3.0 |
| 25 | 57.0 | 62 | 22.5 | 99 | 2.8 |
| 26 | 56.0 | 63 | 21.6 | 100 | 2.7 |
| 27 | 55.1 | 64 | 20.8 | 101 | 2.5 |
| 28 | 54.1 | 65 | 20.0 | 102 | 2.3 |
| 29 | 53.1 | 66 | 19.2 | 103 | 2.1 |
| 30 | 52.2 | 67 | 18.4 | 104 | 1.9 |

## Example 12

T, 65 years old, purchased a single-premium immediate life annuity on January 1, 2011 for $11,400. It will pay $100 a month for the rest of her life (i.e., annual payment of $1,200). From *Exhibit 6-3*, her multiple is 20.0. T's nontaxable return of capital each year is $570 computed as follows:

$$\frac{\$11,400}{\$1,200 \times 20 = \$24,000} \times \$1,200 = \$570$$

T's taxable income is $630 ($1,200 – $570). The $570 is considered a return of capital until T recovers her $11,400 investment. Note that if she lives 21 years, the total amount she excludes is limited to $11,400 ($570 × 20 years = $11,400). Thus, T's taxable income for year 21 is the entire $1,200 received. In contrast, if she lives just 15 years, the total amount she excludes is $8,550 ($570 × 15 years), and the unrecovered amount of $2,850 ($11,400 – $8,550) is allowed as a deduction on T's final tax return.

As noted above, employers with qualified pension or profit-sharing plans (see Chapter 18) purchase annuity contracts for their employees' retirement. The taxable income to the employee is dependent on the employee's total *after-tax* investment in the annuity. After-tax funds generally exclude contributions, for example, to certain Individual Retirement Accounts (when individuals are allowed a deduction for the contribution) and to qualified employer retirement plans (since these contributions are made from amounts that are excluded from gross income in the current year). Investments that are not from after-tax funds are ignored in determining the individual's capital investment in the annuity. In some situations, employees may not have invested any after-tax funds in the employer's plan. Consequently, their basis in the annuity contract is zero and all amounts are included in gross income when received by them. In all other instances, calculations for return of capital and taxable income are identical to the procedure outlined in the above paragraphs.

### Simplified Treatment for Annuities from Qualified Plans

As a general rule, the method above must be used for purchased commercial annuities and certain other annuities. However, many, if not most annuities, come from retirement plans. The method to be used for an annuity from a qualified retirement plan depends on when the annuity started. If the

**EXHIBIT 6.4 Monthly Payments Table**

| *Age of Distributee* | *Number of Payments* |
|---|---|
| 55 and under | 360 |
| 56–60 | 310 |
| 61–65 | 260 |
| 66–70 | 210 |
| 71 and over | 160 |

annuity payments started before November 19, 1996, the method above must be used. For annuities starting after November 18, 1996, a simplified method must be used.[28]

A taxpayer using the simplified method will find the computations less onerous than those previously described for computing the exclusion ratio under § 72. Under this method, the total number of monthly annuity payments expected to be received is based on the distributee's age at the annuity starting date. Consequently, the life expectancy tables (such as Exhibit 6-3) can be ignored. Instead, Exhibit 6-4 is used, and is applicable whether the annuity is single life or joint and survivor type.[29]

The portion of each monthly annuity payment that is nontaxable is determined using the following formula:

$$\frac{\text{Investment in the contract}}{\text{Number of monthly payments}} = \text{Nontaxable return of capital}$$

### Example 13

H, an employee, retired on January 1, 2011 at the age of 65. He started receiving retirement benefits in the form of a joint and 50% survivor annuity to be paid for the joint lives of H and W (his spouse), who is 60. H contributed $52,000 (after-tax contributions) to the plan and will receive a retirement benefit of $2,000 a month. Upon H's death, W will receive a survivor retirement benefit of $1,000 each month. The nontaxable portion of each monthly annuity payment to H is calculated as follows:

$$\frac{\$52,000 \text{ investment}}{260 \text{ payments (see Exhibit 6-4)}} = \$200 \text{ nontaxable return of capital}$$

Should H die prior to receiving his entire investment of $52,000, W will likewise exclude $200 from her $1,000 monthly payment. As explained earlier, after 260 annuity payments have been made, any additional payments will be fully taxable. Should both H and W die prior to receiving 260 payments, a deduction is allowed in the amount of the unrecovered investment in the last income tax return.

## 529 Plans: Qualified Tuition Programs

To help families fund the increasing costs of higher education, Congress created several tax-favored savings arrangements. The most popular plans are contained in § 529 that was enacted in 1996. There are actually two types of 529 plans: (1) prepaid tuition plans and

[28] § 74(d). The simplified method cannot be used by (1) those 75 or older on the starting date whose annuity payments are guaranteed for at least 5 years and (2) annuities from a nonqualified plan such as a private annuity.

[29] A single life annuity pays a fixed amount at regular intervals for the remainder of one person's life. A joint and survivor annuity pays a fixed amount at regular intervals to one individual for life, and on his or her death, the payments continue over the life of a designated person such as a spouse or child.

(2) savings plans. Every state has either a prepaid tuition or a savings plan and some states have both. Similar to Educational Savings Bonds, the income from these savings programs is nontaxable if used for higher education expenses.

### Prepaid Tuition Plans

Under a prepaid tuition plan, an individual buys tuition credits or certificates that can be redeemed to pay tuition at a later date. These plans enable parents to freeze the cost of future tuition to the price currently charged by the institution. States typically offer a "units" plan that allows parents to buy units of tuition (e.g., a set number of credit hours or a certain percentage of the college's tuition). Some states offer "contract" plans that permit the purchase of contracts for one to five years of tuition. Individuals normally are allowed to contribute to either arrangement in a lump sum or in installments. There is no deduction allowed for such purchases.

Without special treatment, the difference between cost of the tuition credits and the value of the credits when used would represent taxable income. However, § 529 permits taxpayers to exclude this benefit.

#### Example 14

Shortly after H and W had their first son, S, they decided to start saving for his college education. Betting that the costs of tuition would continue to increase, they opted for a prepaid tuition plan. They purchased 15 hours of college credit from their alma mater, State University, at a cost of $200 per hour. This year S began his freshman year at State when the cost of tuition was $350 per hour. H and W used the prepaid credits to pay for the first semester's tuition. Although H and W have income of $150 ($350 – $200) per credit, it is nontaxable.

Depending on its terms, the plan may also permit prepayment of fees, books, supplies, equipment and room and board. Prepaid tuition plans can be offered only by eligible educational institutions which include colleges and universities as well as proprietary and vocational institutions (e.g., trade schools). Prepaid tuition plans are not restricted to those residing in the state where the university is located. For example, an individual living in Illinois, can invest in a prepaid tuition plan of Indiana University. If a child does not attend the school at which the plan was established, all is not lost. The contributions may be withdrawn without penalty, assuming the funds are used at another school. If not, the 10 percent penalty would apply to any earnings. In these situations, universities provide some type of return on the individual's investment (e.g., 2 percent per year). It should be mentioned that many private universities, almost 300 (2009), have joined together so that any tuition prepaid can be used at any member college (see Independent 529 Plan at *www.independent529plan.org*).

### 529 College Savings Plans

A 529 savings plan (or simply a 529 plan as it is commonly called) is much different than a prepaid tuition plan. A 529 plan is simply a tax favored savings account for any person that the donor wants to name as a beneficiary. Contributions are made to 529 accounts where they normally can be invested in one or more mutual funds offered by the plan. Contributions are not deductible for federal income tax purposes. However, some states allow a deduction or a credit. The amount that can be contributed is not limited by the tax law but only by the plan itself, and these amounts can be substantial. For example, in 2011 the plan for Indiana state universities, CollegeChoice, allows contributions of up to almost $300,000 for one individual. In addition, Indiana provides a 20 percent credit of contributions but not to exceed $1,000 per year. Earnings attributable to the account are nontaxable. In other words, contributions to the plan grow tax-free for as long as money stays in the plan. Distributions from the account are nontaxable to the extent they are used to pay for qualified higher education expenses. Section 529(e)(3) defines qualified expenses as those for tuition, books, supplies, computer equipment and technology, Internet access, equipment required for enrollment or attendance and certain expenses incurred for special needs beneficiaries. Expenses for room and board also qualify if the student attends at least half-time. However, the amount cannot exceed that normally charged for housing owned or operated by the university. Amounts withdrawn which are not considered qualified are subject to 10 percent penalty. In addition, taxpayers may utilize the qualified tuition deduction ($4,000 in 2011) to deduct the amount of a distribution from a qualified tuition plan that is used for qualified expenses and is not attributable to earnings (e.g., amounts contributed). Contributions must be made by the close of the taxable year

**Example 15**

This year, F withdrew $1,000 from a qualified tuition plan to pay her undergraduate tuition at State University. F does not claim a credit for the amount spent. If the $1,000 consists of $800 of contributions to the plan and $200 of earnings, a deduction for the $800 of contributions may be claimed for A.G.I. by F. Furthermore, the $200 of earnings is excluded from F's income.

What happens if there is a downturn in the market and the plan drops in value? If this occurs–as it did in the market crash of 2008–the contributor can deduct a loss but only if the account is liquidated; that is, everything in the account must be withdrawn. If the total withdrawals are less than the amount the individual contributed (i.e., the basis for the account), a deduction is allowed for the difference. Unfortunately, the loss is deductible only as a miscellaneous itemized deduction. In addition, the funds cannot be reinvested too soon. If the distributions are rolled over to another 529 account for that or another related beneficiary within 60 days of their withdrawal, there is not a taxable transaction and no deduction would be allowed.

In a 529 plan, the named beneficiary has no rights to the funds. The donor has complete control, deciding when withdrawals are taken and for what purpose. Most plans allow the donor to reclaim the funds at any time desired, no questions asked. However, as noted above, the earnings portion of the "non-qualified" withdrawal are subject to income tax and an additional 10 percent penalty tax. Amounts contributed can be withdrawn at any time without penalty.

In situations where an account balance is not used (e.g., student did not finish, qualified expenses did not exhaust the account balance), the unused amount can be rolled over without penalty to an account for another member of the taxpayer's family.

### 529 Plans versus Prepaid Tuition Plans

There are a number of differences between 529 savings plans and prepaid tuition plans. Perhaps the most important is that there is no guarantee that the amount saved in a 529 savings plan will equal the amount of tuition in the future. Poor investments in the account can produce insufficient returns or even losses. A 529 savings plan does permit the participant to use the savings at a variety of institutions, but a prepaid tuition plan may be limited by the plan's institutions. However, as noted above, many prepaid tuition plans provide a guaranteed return if a child decides not to attend the college from which the prepaid tuition credits were purchased. Many savings plans include the ability to save for other college expenses whereas prepaid tuition plans are often limited to tuition and fees.

### Gift and Estate Tax Considerations

Contributions to either a prepaid tuition plan or a 529 savings plan are considered gifts and, therefore, could be subject to the gift tax if they exceed the annual exclusion of $13,000 (2011). However, for purposes of contributions to 529 plans, a taxpayer may elect to have a contribution to a plan treated as if it had been made ratably over five years. In so doing, the amount may come under the annual exclusion. For example, a contributor could give $65,000 to a plan and treat the transfer as if he or she had made gifts of $13,000 per year over the next five years. A gift tax return must be filed for amounts contributed in excess of the exclusion. If the contributor should die before the five-year period has elapsed, the balance is included in his or her estate.

**Example 16**

In 2011 G made a $65,000 contribution to Indiana University's qualified tuition plan for the benefit of her grandson. She elected to treat the transfer as being made over a five-year period. In 2013, G died. In 2011, 2012, and the year of death, G may exclude $13,000 annually. The remaining $21,000 [$60,000 − (3 × $13,000 = $39,000)] would be included in her gross estate.

The current gift tax law also permits an unlimited exclusion for tuition paid on someone's behalf if it is paid directly to an educational institution. This latter rule is not extended to payments made to qualified prepaid tuition plans. Consequently, only the basic $13,000 (2011) exclusion applies. For example, this prohibition bars a grandmother from prepaying a grandchild's tuition for four years (e.g., over $100,000 for some schools) and quickly removing substantial amounts from her estate tax-free.

The law also clarifies the estate tax treatment of amounts accumulated in prepaid tuition plans. Such amounts are not included in an individual's taxable estate (i.e., neither the estate of the parent nor that of the student).

### Interaction with HOPE and Lifetime Learning Credits

As discussed in Chapter 13, there are two credits related to education: (1) the HOPE credit available for the first four years of college, and (2) the Lifetime Learning credit for undergraduate, graduate and other educational courses. Interestingly, the statute makes it clear that taxpayers receiving qualified tuition plan distributions are also eligible to claim either the HOPE or Lifetime Learning credit for a taxable year as long as the income portion of the distributions is not used for the same expenses for which a credit is claimed.

## Employee Compensation and Other Benefits

**LO.3**
Identify various types of employee compensation and fringe benefits and explain their tax treatment.

By far the most important source of income for individual taxpayers is compensation from their employment. As seen earlier in Exhibit 6-1, preliminary statistics from 2006 indicate that salaries and wages represent more than 68 percent of all income reported on returns. While the bulk of employee compensation consists of salaries and wages, compensation includes all payments received for personal services such as commissions, bonuses, tips, vacation pay, severance pay, jury fees, and director's fees.[30] In addition, employers typically provide a variety of fringe benefits for their employees such as health and life insurance, child care, discounts on merchandise or services, parking, and contributions to retirement plans.

Although most forms of compensation are taxable, Congress has exempted certain benefits (e.g., health insurance, group-term life insurance), hoping the exclusion would encourage employers to provide such benefits for their employees. It is important to emphasize that these benefits are typically exempt not only from income tax but also from social security and medicare taxes. The power of the exclusion feature is shown in the following example.

**Example 17**

T recently began working for B Corporation, which provides each of its employees with a number of fringe benefits. Among these benefits is payment of the premium on a health insurance policy for T and his family at an annual cost of $2,000 (a nontaxable fringe benefit). However, T may elect to receive $2,000 in cash instead. Assume that T's marginal tax rate is 15% and that he would buy the health insurance in any event. The table below compares the two options:

[30] § 61(a)(1) and Reg. § 1.61-2(a). See Chapter 18 for the treatment of stock received for services.

| | *Salary* | *Premium Payment* |
|---|---|---|
| Amount | $2,000 | $2,000 |
| Income tax (15% × $2,000) | (300) | — |
| FICA (7.65% × $2,000) | (153) | — |
| After tax | $1,547 | $2,000 |

Observe that T is much better off if he elects to have the employer pay for his health care. Electing the cash option would leave T with $453 less to pay for a similar insurance policy. Moreover, the employer is probably able to secure a better insurance rate than T could individually.

As the above example demonstrates, structuring a compensation package to include nontaxable fringe benefits provides a significant advantage to an employee. In effect, the employee is able to secure a particular benefit with before-tax or pre-tax rather than after-tax dollars. Employers also benefit because not only can they deduct the cost of the benefit just like cash compensation but they normally reduce their compensation cost since they are not required to pay social security, medicare, or unemployment taxes on such amounts.

Exhibit 6-5 provides a listing of the common examples of compensation grouped by whether they are ordinarily taxable or nontaxable.

Most employee fringe benefit plans must meet rigid rules to enable the employer to deduct contributions to the plans and for employees to exclude these amounts. Basically, the plans must (1) not discriminate in favor of highly compensated employees, (2) be in writing, (3) be for the exclusive benefit of the employees, (4) be legally enforceable, (5) provide employees with information concerning available plan benefits, and (6) be established with the intent that they will be maintained indefinitely. In addition, several eligibility and benefit

**EXHIBIT 6.5** **Taxable and Nontaxable Employee Compensation**

| *Generally included in gross income* | *Generally excluded from gross income* |
|---|---|
| Salaries, wages | Premiums paid on |
| Commissions | • Group-term life insurance (up to $50,000 coverage) |
| Bonuses | • Health, accident, disability or long-term care insurance |
| Garnished wages | Life insurance proceeds |
| Tips | Meals and lodging if for employer's convenience |
| Director's fees | Adoption assistance |
| Jury fees | Educational assistance plans (undergraduate and graduate) |
| Severance pay | Child or dependent care |
| Reimbursements for | Benefits otherwise deductible by the employee (i.e., working condition fringe benefits) |
| Business transportation and travel | |
| Business entertainment | Qualified employee discounts |
| Indirect moving expenses | No-additional cost services |
| Educational expenses | De minimus benefits |
| Employer gifts | Parking |
| Employer awards | Use of company facilities or services |
| | Qualified retirement planning services |
| | Supper money |
| | Tuition reduction by educational institutions |

tests provide detailed rules that must be met to ensure that employer costs are nontaxable income for employees. Additional employment benefits involving stock option, profit-sharing, and pension plans are discussed in Chapter 18.

## Reimbursement of Employee Expenses

Employers often reimburse employees for their business-related expenses. Commonly reimbursed items include expenses for transportation, out-of-town travel, entertainment, and moving expenses. Such reimbursements are generally considered taxable. However, the employee usually has an offsetting expense that is deductible for A.G.I., so the effect on the tax return is usually a wash.[31] This is not always the case, however. If the employee is over-reimbursed or reimbursed for nondeductible expenses, there is a net increase in A.G.I. The effects of under-reimbursements and other aspects of reporting reimbursed expenses is considered in Chapter 8.

## Employer Gifts

Although § 102(a) allows taxpayers to exclude gifts from gross income, amounts transferred from an employer to an employee in the form of cash or other property are not excludable as a gift.[32] In effect, employers are prohibited from disguising compensation as a nontaxable gift. Consequently, employers interested in providing nontaxable benefits must look to other sections of the Code that offer exclusions. For example, as discussed below, an employee can exclude certain employee achievement awards (e.g., golf clubs for productivity)[33] and certain insignificant or de minimis fringe benefits such as inexpensive holiday gifts (e.g., a turkey at Thanksgiving).[34]

## Employer Awards

It is quite common for an employer to award an employee for some type of achievement. An employee might receive a gold watch for many years of faithful service, a gift certificate for low absenteeism, or a free dinner for a great idea dropped in the suggestion box. For many years, employees argued that such awards were gifts rather than compensation and, therefore, were not taxable. Congress addressed this problem in two ways. As discussed above, the rules governing gifts were amended to make it clear that employers generally cannot make nontaxable gifts to employees. At the same time, Congress created a special rule allowing employees to exclude awards from their employer if certain conditions are met.

Employer awards to employees, other than de minimis fringe benefits (discussed later in this chapter), are generally treated as compensation with two exceptions: if they are provided (l) for length-of-service or safety achievements, or (2) under a nondiscriminatory qualified award plan. To be nontaxable, the awards must be made with tangible personal property. No exclusion is available for cash payments or their equivalents. A gift certificate is permissible but only if it allows the employee to acquire tangible personal property.[35] The award must be given as part of a meaningful presentation and under conditions and circumstances that do not create a significant likelihood of the payment of disguised compensation. Also, no exclusion for the length-of-service award is available if it or a similar award is made within the individual's first five years of employment with the employer. To be nontaxable, safety awards cannot have been made to more than 10 percent of a company's eligible employees. All employees are considered to be eligible except those in managerial, professional, and clerical positions.[36]

Qualifying awards are deductible by the employer and nontaxable by the employee if the amount does not exceed the statutory limits. Under these limitations, the cost of property

---

[31] This is only true if the reimbursement is made pursuant to an "accountable plan." See Chapter 8 for a complete discussion.

[32] § 102(c). See Lisa B. Williams 2005-1 USTC 50,163, 95 AFTR 2d 2005-764, 120 Fed. Appx. 289 (CA-10, 2005).

[33] §§ 74(c) and 274(j).

[34] § 132(e).

[35] Prop. Reg. § 1.274-8(c)(2) also makes taxable such items as vacations, meals, lodging, event tickets, and securities.

[36] See §§ 74(c) and 274(j).

cannot exceed $400 per employee annually for length-of-service and safety achievements or $1,600 annually for all qualified plan awards, including length-of-service and safety achievements. For example, an employee achievement award (other than a qualified plan award) that costs the employer $390 and has a fair market value of $440 would be fully excluded from the employee's gross income. Excess costs are taxable income to the extent of the *greater* of (l) the nondeductible cost to the employer due to the limitations, or (2) the property's market value in excess of the limitations. This taxable income must be reported on the employee's Form W-2.

### Example 18

R, Inc. pays $525 ($640 market value) J for a brooch that it awards to L in recognition of her 15 years of service to the company. No other awards are given to L during the year. R's deduction is limited to $400, and L has taxable income of $240 (the greater of $525 – $400 = $125 and $640 – $400 = $240). The $240 will appear on L's Form W-2 as taxable income.

## Social Security Benefits

When most taxpayers collect social security benefits, these benefits can be excluded from gross income. This treatment can be traced to an early IRS ruling that granted the exclusion with little explanation in 1941.[37] Interestingly, the exclusion was allowed notwithstanding the fact that there was no statutory authority for it. In 1984, however, Congress apparently felt that this gracious treatment, while proper for those whose primary source of income was social security, was not appropriate for higher-income taxpayers. As a result, it created § 86 to address its concern.

Under the 1984 legislative formula, the social security benefits of most taxpayers continued to be nontaxable. However, upper-income taxpayers could have as much as 50 percent of their social security benefits taxed. Note that the effect of this provision is to tax these amounts—at least that portion representing the taxpayer's contributions—twice; first when included as gross wages and second when included as social security benefits are received. On the other hand, the portion received representing the contribution by the employer and any earnings on the amounts contributed are not taxable at all.

The treatment created in 1984 continued until 1993 when the Clinton administration, with the backing of Congress, increased the amount that could be taxed from 50 to 85 percent.[38] The thrust of the current rules is quite simple. As long as income remains below a certain threshold, social security benefits are completely nontaxable. But as income increases, the amount of social security that may be taxed increases. Unfortunately, the actual calculation of the amount that must be included in gross income is unduly cumbersome. The effect of the revised provisions is to establish two income thresholds:

| | *Married Filing Jointly* | *Married Filing Separately* | *Unmarried Taxpayers* |
|---|---|---|---|
| Modified A.G.I. threshold #1 | $32,000 | $0 | $25,000 |
| Modified A.G.I. threshold #2 | 44,000 | 0 | 34,000 |

Notice that in determining whether a taxpayer's level of income warrants taxation of his or her social security benefits, an expanded notion of income referred to as *modified adjusted gross income* is used. Modified adjusted gross income is generally computed as follows:

| | |
|---|---|
| | Adjusted gross income |
| + | ½ of social security benefits |
| + | Tax-exempt income |
| + | Foreign earned income exclusion |
| | Modified A.G.I. |

[37] Rev. Rul 70-217,1970-1 C.B. 12.

[38] § 86.

Taxpayers whose modified A.G.I. is less than the first threshold ($32,000 for married filing jointly) are not taxed on their social security benefits. Those whose modified A.G.I. falls between the two thresholds ($32,000 – $44,000 for married filing jointly) must include the lesser of one-half of their social security benefits or one-half of the excess of their modified A. G.I. over the specified threshold. For those taxpayers whose modified A.G.I. *exceeds* the first threshold (e.g., $32,000 for married filing jointly), the calculation can be made using the following schedules:

**Married filing jointly**

If modified A.G.I. is

| Over | But not over | Amount taxed: |
|---|---|---|
| $32,000 | $44,000 | Step 1:<br>Lesser of<br>**(1)** 50% of benefits, or<br>**(2)** 50% × (Modified A.G.I. – $32,000) |
| $44,000 | | Step 2:<br>Lesser of<br>**(1)** Step 1 amount, not to exceed $6,000, + 85% × (Modified A.G.I. – $44,000), or<br>**(2)** 85% of benefits |

**Unmarried taxpayers**

If modified A.G.I. is

| Over | But not over | Amount taxed: |
|---|---|---|
| $25,000 | $34,000 | Step 1:<br>Lesser of<br>**(1)** 50% of benefits, or<br>**(2)** 50% × (Modified A.G.I. – $25,000) |
| $34,000 | | Step 2:<br>Lesser of<br>**(1)** Step 1 amount, not to exceed $4,500, + 85% × (Modified A.G.I. – $34,000), or<br>**(2)** 85% of benefits |

## Example 19

George and Mildred, happily married for 45 years, received the following income:

| | |
|---|---|
| Dividend income | $50,000 |
| Social security benefits | 16,000 |

Here the couple's modified A.G.I. is $58,000 [$50,000 + (50% × $16,000 = $8,000)]. Because the couple's $58,000 modified A.G.I. exceeds the second threshold of $44,000, the 85% rule is triggered. Their taxable social security is $13,600, computed as follows:

**Step 1 amount**

| | | |
|---|---|---|
| Lesser of (1) or (2) | | |
| (1) 50% × social security of $16,000 | $ 8,000 | |
| (2) 50% × ($58,000 – $32,000 = $26,000) | $13,000 | |
| Step 1 amount | | $ 8,000 |

**Step 2 amount**

| | | |
|---|---|---|
| Lesser of (1) or (2) | | |
| (1) Step 1 amount ($8,000), not to exceed $6,000, + | $ 6,000 | |
| 85% × ($58,000 – $44,000 = $14,000) | 11,900 | |
| | $17,900 | |
| (2) 85% × benefits of $16,000 | $13,600 | |
| Step 2 amount and taxable social security benefits | | $13,600 |

**Example 20**

Assume the same facts as in Example 19 above except that dividend income amounts to \$30,000. Because the couple's \$38,000 modified A.G.I. [\$30,000 + (50% × \$16,000)] falls below the second threshold (\$44,000), their taxable social security is \$3,000, computed as follows:

| | | |
|---|---|---|
| Lesser of | | |
| 50% × social security of \$16,000 | \$8,000 | |
| or | | |
| 50% × (\$38,000 − \$32,000 = \$6,000) | \$3,000 | |
| Step 1 amount and taxable social security benefits | | \$3,000 |

As indicated above, the base or threshold amount is zero for married filing separately. Consequently, married taxpayers who elect to file separately automatically expose social security benefits to taxation.

Taxpayers whose social security benefits are subject to taxation should give consideration to shifting money out of municipal bonds and into other investment vehicles such as growth stocks that do not pay dividends or into Series EE U.S. savings bonds, which generally do not produce taxable income until they are redeemed.

## Unemployment Benefits

In any dynamic economy, the forces at work often leave individuals without a job. For example, in the United States, weekly unemployment claims during 2008 surged, ranging from about 300,000 to 750,000. During 2008 and 2009, the unemployment rate was 4.9% in January of 2008, reached 10.2 percent by October 2009 and was still hovering around 9 percent at this writing. In order to help those workers who have lost their jobs through no fault of their own, Congress created the unemployment insurance system as part of the Social Security Act in 1935. Under this system, employers, not employees, are subject to Federal and State unemployment taxes, which they are entitled to deduct as ordinary business expenses. These taxes are then used to provide benefits for the unemployed, thus allowing them a period of time that they can seek a new job without major financial distress.

Prior to 1979, unemployment benefits received were not taxable. In 1979, however, Congress reversed direction and opted to tax such benefits. Apparently it believed that the exclusion might actually reduce the incentive to work, making unemployment more, rather than less, attractive. Currently, unemployment benefits received under a government program are fully taxable.[39]

## Employee Insurance

Over the years, Congress has created several exclusions for employer-provided life, health, accident, and disability insurance. The continuation for these exclusions can generally be found in the Congressional desire to ensure that all individuals are adequately protected against unforeseen hardships. As a result, it is quite common for employers to provide some type of group insurance for employees. Premiums for insurance coverage may be paid by the employer only, by the employee only, or by both the employer and employee under some

[39] § 85(a). For 2009, \$2,400 of unemployment benefits are nontaxable.

shared cost arrangement. Generally, employer-paid premiums for health, accident, and disability insurance are deductible business expenses and are excluded from the employee's gross income. On the other hand, life insurance premiums paid by the employer generally are included by the employee and deductible by the employer. As may be expected, however, there are exceptions.

### Life Insurance Premiums and Proceeds

Employer-paid life insurance premiums are nontaxable by an employee but *only* for the first $50,000 of *group-term life insurance* protection.[40] Premiums paid by an employer for any other type of life insurance are fully included in each employee's gross income. In order to qualify as group insurance, the employer's plan generally must not discriminate. The employer must provide coverage for all employees with a few permitted exceptions based on their age, marital status, or factors related to employment. Examples of employment-related factors are union membership, duties performed, compensation received, and length of service.[41] Acceptable discrimination, however, is limited by the Regulations. Thus, employers may establish eligibility requirements that exclude certain types of employees, such as those who work part-time, who are under age 21, or who have not been employed at least six months. But omitting older employees or those with longer service records generally is not permitted.

When group-term insurance protection exceeds $50,000, the employee generally must include in income the premium attributable to the amount of coverage over $50,000. The actual amount to be included is set forth in the Regulations rather than actual premiums paid. The taxable amount for each $1,000 of insurance in excess of $50,000 is based on the employee's age as of the last day of his or her tax year. These amounts (which were recently lowered by the Treasury) are shown in Exhibit 6-6.[42]

**EXHIBIT 6.6** **Imputed Costs of Excess Group-Term Life Insurance**

| | Includible Income per $1,000 | |
|---|---|---|
| Employee's Age | Monthly | Annually |
| Under 25 | $0.05 | $ 0.60 |
| 25 to 29 | 0.06 | 0.72 |
| 30 to 34 | 0.08 | 0.96 |
| 35 to 39 | 0.09 | 1.08 |
| 40 to 44 | 0.10 | 1.20 |
| 45 to 49 | 0.15 | 1.80 |
| 50 to 54 | 0.23 | 2.76 |
| 55 to 59 | 0.43 | 5.16 |
| 60 to 64 | 0.66 | 7.92 |
| 65 to 69 | 1.27 | 15.24 |
| 70 and over | 2.06 | 24.72 |

**Source:** Reg. § 1.79-3, effective July 1, 1999.

40 § 79(a)(1). The $50,000 limit is eliminated for retired employees who are disabled.

41 Reg. §§ 1.79-0 and 1.79-1(a)(4).

42 Reg. § 1.79-3. Beginning in 1988, the cost of group-term life insurance that an employee must include in his or her gross income must also be treated as wages for social security withholding purposes.

### Example 21

BC, Inc. provides all full-time employees with group-term insurance. Records for three of the employees show the following information. All three were employed by BC for the full year.

| Employee | Age | Insurance Coverage | Coverage in Excess of $50,000 |
|---|---|---|---|
| D | 56 | $80,000 | $30,000 |
| E | 38 | 62,000 | 12,000 |
| F | 35 | 40,000 | 0 |

D's taxable income is $154.80 ($5.16 × $30,000 ÷ $1,000). E's taxable income is $12.96 ($1.08 × $12,000 ÷ $1,000). F has no taxable income from group-term life insurance, since the coverage does not exceed $50,000.

As explained further within, regardless of whether life insurance is provided by the employer, proceeds received by a beneficiary on the death of the insured ordinarily are excludable from gross income.[43]

## Health Insurance Benefits

As a general rule, all medical insurance benefits are excluded from income regardless of who pays the premiums.[44] Any reimbursement of medical costs simply reduces the amount of medical expenses that can be itemized (as deductions from A.G.I.—discussed in Chapter 11).[45] However, in some instances the expenses are paid in one year but reimbursement is not received until a later year. Taxpayers have a choice when this occurs. One, they may anticipate the reimbursement and not deduct any of the reimbursable expenses. This decision means the reimbursement is nontaxable when received. Alternatively, these taxpayers may choose to itemize all medical costs in the year paid even though reimbursement is expected. This decision means the reimbursement is included in gross income when received to the extent a *tax benefit* was obtained for the prior year's deduction.[46] Since only the amount of medical expenditures that exceed 7.5 percent of A.G.I. provides a tax benefit (i.e., reduces an individual's taxable income), it is possible that part of the reimbursement is nontaxable.

### Example 22

J pays $4,000 medical expenses in 2011 and receives reimbursement of $1,100 in 2011 and $2,900 in 2012 from the insurance company. J's 2011 A.G.I. is $20,000, and her other itemized deductions exceed the standard deduction for the year. If J chooses to deduct all unreimbursed medical expenses in 2011, her itemized deduction is $2,900 ($4,000 − $1,100 reimbursed in 2011) and her *tax benefit* is $1,400 [$2,900 − (7.5% × $20,000 A.G.I. = $1,500)]. Thus, only $1,400 of the $2,900 reimbursement received in 2012 is included in gross income. Alternatively, if J decides to forgo the deduction in 2011, she has no taxable income in 2012. In this example, the important factors in J's decision are (l) her marginal tax rates for both years, and (2) the present value to her of the tax deferral for one year.

If medical coverage is financed by the employer, any reimbursement in excess of medical expenses incurred by an employee for himself or herself, a spouse, and dependents is included

[43] § 101(a)(1).

[44] § 106.

[45] §§ 105(b) and 213.

[46] § 111 (a).

in gross income.[47] These excess amounts, however, are not included if the premiums were paid by the individual.

Many businesses finance their own medical benefit plans from company funds (instead of through insurance). These companies must establish plans that do not discriminate in favor of certain officers, shareholders, or highly paid employees. If the plan is discriminatory, individuals in these three categories must report taxable income equal to any medical reimbursement they received that is not available to other employees.[48] Thus, the purpose is to encourage businesses to extend medical coverage to all of their employees.

## Qualified Long-Term Care Benefits

Under prior law, benefits received under long-term care insurance policies were not necessarily excluded. Current law makes it clear that insurance contracts for long-term care that provide services for chronically-ill individuals and meet a number of other requirements are considered an accident and health insurance contract. As a result, taxpayers can exclude benefits received under such policies. However, the amount of the exclusion from gross income for 2011 is the greater of $300 per day or the actual cost of the care.[49]

Qualified long-term care services generally include necessary diagnostic, preventive, therapeutic, curing, treating, mitigating and rehabilitative services, and maintenance or personal care services that are required by a chronically-ill individual and provided pursuant to a plan of care prescribed by a licensed health care practitioner.[50] A chronically-ill individual is generally a person who is unable to perform at least two activities of daily living (e.g., eating, toileting, transferring, bathing, dressing, and continence) for a period of at least 90 days due to a loss of some type of functional capacity.

### Example 23

In 2011, L, 93, broke her hip and was confined to a nursing home for 30 days. The nursing home charged L $200 per day for a total of $6,000. L's long-term care insurance policy pays 90 percent of the amount charged by the home after a 10-day waiting period. In October, L received an insurance reimbursement of $3,600 [90% × ($200 × 20 days). L may exclude the entire $3,600 received since it is less than the maximum allowable exclusion of $300 per day. In addition, she can deduct the unreimbursed amount of $2,400 ($6,000 − $3,600) as a medical expense subject to the 7.5 percent of A.G.I. limitation (see Chapter 11).

Employees normally can exclude from income the value of employer-provided coverage under a long-term care plan. However, there is no exclusion if the coverage is provided through a cafeteria plan. Furthermore, long-term care services cannot be reimbursed on a tax-free basis under a flexible spending account.

## Accident and Disability Insurance Benefits

As a general rule, all amounts received under an *employer-financed* accident or disability plan are taxable, with few exceptions. However, when payments are for permanent loss or use of a function or member of the body or for permanent disfigurement of the employee, employee's spouse or dependent, they are nontaxable.[51] Moreover, to be excludable, the payments must be computed with reference to the *nature* of the injury, and not on the *time* the employee is absent from work (i.e., a wage substitute).

### Example 24

G lost two fingers while making repairs to her automobile. She received $20,000 from her employer-provided accident insurance policy. The $20,000 is nontaxable to G because the payment was solely for loss of a function or member of the body.

---

[47] § 105(b).

[48] § 105(h).

[49] § 7702B(d)(4).

[50] § 7702B(c).

[51] §§ 105(a) and (c).

In contrast with employer-financed disability plans, all disability income is *nontaxable* if the taxpayer paid for the disability coverage.[52] Consequently, those employees with long-term disabilities may incur substantial tax costs if their disability income is received from employer-financed plans.

### Example 25

After graduation from high school, R was employed by WW Manufacturing Company. The company's employee benefits included disability insurance. R's disability insurance premiums averaged $250 annually. After 15 years with WW, R became seriously ill. The illness left him permanently disabled. After a three-month wait, required by the insurance company, R began receiving $800 monthly disability income. Whether the $800 is taxable income depends on who paid the $250 annual premium on the disability policy. If WW paid the premium, the $800 monthly disability income is taxable income. If R paid the premium, the $800 is nontaxable. If R paid a portion of the premium, for example 40%, then that portion, $320 (40% × $800), is nontaxable, and the remaining $480 is attributable to the employer's contribution and is, therefore, taxable income.

## Employer-Provided Meals and Lodging

As explained in Chapter 5, early rulings and decisions exempted certain benefits given to employees when they did not serve as compensation but rather were for the "convenience of the employer." A classic example of this principle can be found in the working relationship between many apartment owners and their managers. Typically, owners require their managers to live on the premises without charge so that they are immediately available should they be needed. While this is an obvious benefit to employees, the tax law allows employees to exclude the value of the housing because in this case it is not primarily a means of compensation but serves some overriding purpose of the employer. In 1954, Congress codified this principle for meals and lodging in § 119.

Under § 119, the value of meals and lodging provided by an employer to an employee and the employee's spouse and dependents is excluded from income if

1. Provided for the *employer's convenience*;
2. Provided on the employer's *business premises*; and
3. In the case of lodging, the employee is *required* to occupy the quarters in order to perform employment duties.[53]

Generally, meals and housing furnished to employees without charge are considered to be for the employer's convenience if a substantial noncompensatory business purpose exists.[54] The regulations provide some guidance in this regard, indicating that meals are usually considered noncompensatory if there are insufficient eating facilities in the vicinity of the employer's premises (e.g., an employee working on an oil rig in the North Sea) or the employee must be available for emergency calls during the meal period (a 911 operator). The regulations also specifically provide that meals provided to wait staff, and other food service employees are noncompensatory. Beyond the examples in the regulations, there are numerous court decisions on the subject. For example, the Tax Court found that there were substantial business reasons to provide meals and lodging to the manager of a motel who is on 24-hour call.[55] But, if the employee has the option to receive other compensation instead, the value of the meals and lodging is included in income.[56]

---

[52] § 104(a)(3) and Reg. § 1.104-1(d).

[53] § 119(a)(2) and Reg. § 1.119-1(b).

[54] Reg. §§ 1.119-1(a)(2) and (b).

[55] *J.B. Lindeman*, 60 T.C. 609 (1973), acq.

[56] Reg. § 1.119-1(c)(2).

### Example 26

Z is a warden at a state prison in Northern Arizona. She must be on duty from 8:00 a.m. until 5:00 p.m. Monday through Friday. Z is given the choice of residing at the prison free of charge (value of $12,000 per year), or of residing elsewhere and receiving a cash allowance of $1,000 per month in addition to her regular salary. If she elects to reside at the prison, the value to Z of the lodging furnished by the prison will be taxable because her residence at the prison is not required in order for her to perform properly the duties of her employment.

Nontaxable meals and lodging must be furnished on the employer's premises. The term *business premises* has been interpreted to be either the primary place of business (e.g., the hotel, restaurant, or construction site) or elsewhere as long as it is near the place of business and where a significant portion of the business is conducted.[57] However, employer-owned housing located two blocks from the primary place of business, a motel, was disallowed because it was not considered to be on the employer's premises.[58] This contrasts with employer-owned housing located across the street from the primary place of business, a hotel, that was held to be on the premises.[59] Apparently, taxpayer success in this second case was based on the amount of business conducted in the home rather than its location.

Over the years, there has been a great deal of controversy about application of the exclusion where the employer did not provide the meals but rather reimbursed the employee for his or her meal cost. The landmark case in the area is *Kowalski*, which dealt with a New Jersey state trooper who was given meal allowances under the condition that he eat in his assigned duty area and remain on call.[60] In denying the exclusion, the Supreme Court explained that it applied only to meals in kind and not to cash reimbursements. Despite the apparent clarity of this decision, controversy still arises over this issue.

Interestingly, the *Kowalski* court indicated in a footnote that its decision was not intended to address the treatment of so-called supper money, the term used to describe meal money given to employees who are required to work overtime. The IRS had historically allowed taxpayers to exclude such amounts.[61] This exclusion, as discussed later in this chapter, is now preserved in the Regulations as a de minimis fringe benefit. These rules specifically allow taxpayers to exclude supper money which is provided to overtime workers on an occasional basis.[62]

### Example 27

F Inc., a furniture retailer, has an exhibit each year at the local home show convention. Three of F's employees are asked to put in 12-hour days during the week-long convention. To help ease their burden, F provides each of the three employees $8 per day to cover the cost of their dinner. The $56 ($8 × 7 days) each employee receives is considered "supper money" and is therefore excluded as a de minimis fringe benefit.

In addition, § 119 explains that meals provided to all employees will be excludable if provided to more than one-half of all employees for the convenience of the employer. This rule is important for employers as well since it enables employers to deduct all of such costs (e.g. the cost of a company cafeteria) and avoid employment taxes that otherwise would apply.

---

[57] Rev. Rul. 71-411, 1971-2 C.B. 103.

[58] *Comm. v. Anderson*, 67-1 USTC ¶9136, 19 AFTR2d 318, 371 F.2d 59 (CA-6, 1966), cert. denied.

[59] *J.B. Lindeman*, 60 T.C. 609 (1973), acq.

[60] *Kowalski v. Comm.*, 77-2 USTC ¶9748, 40 AFTR2d 6128, 434 U.S. 77 (USSC, 1977).

[61] O.D. 514, 2 C.B. 90 (1920).

[62] Reg. § 1.132-6.

## Child and Dependent Care Assistance

A touchy issue over the years has been the treatment of child care expenses. Arguably, a taxpayer should be extended some tax relief because such costs are inevitable if he or she is to be gainfully employed. Currently, the tax law underwrites the cost of child care under these circumstances in two ways. Employees who receive reimbursements for their child care expenses or whose employer provides child care in kind (e.g., a day care facility) may exclude up to $5,000 annually.[63] In addition, the law allows gainfully employed individuals a limited credit for their child care expenses (20–35% of $3,000 – $6,000 of expenses depending on the taxpayer's income and the number of children).[64] While this might suggest that the taxpayer may be able to secure two benefits, the law effectively prohibits this by reducing any expenses that qualify for the credit by the amount of any benefits that are excluded. In order to claim either the exclusion or the credit, a laundry list of special rules must be followed. These are discussed in connection with the child care credit in Chapter 13.

**Example 28**

J works for the U.S. Group, Inc. J routinely drops off her two young children at a day care facility provided by her employer. This year the value of the service is worth approximately $5,000. J normally may exclude the full $5,000 from income. Had J paid $5,000 for child care which her employer reimbursed, she could also exclude the $5,000. However, in such case, the amount of her qualifying expenses for purposes of the child care credit would be zero ($5,000 expense – $5,000 exclusion). Alternatively, J could report the $5,000 as income and claim a credit equal to 20–35% of the maximum allowable expenses of $6,000. See Chapter 13 for a complete discussion.

## Adoption Assistance Programs

To encourage adoptions, Code § 137 allows an employee an exclusion in 2011 of $13,170 per child for qualified adoption expenses paid or incurred by an employer. The exclusion begins to be phased out for taxpayers with modified A.G.I. above $185,210 and is not available once modified A.G.I. reaches $225,210. The law also provides a nonrefundable adoption credit of up to $13,170 per child adopted. A detailed discussion of the adoption credit and its interaction with the exclusion is contained in the discussion of nonbusiness credits in Chapter 13. It is worth noting here that when the adoption involves a "special needs" child, the full credit may be claimed even if there were no adoption expenses incurred.

### Foster Care Payments

Under § 131, taxpayers are entitled to exclude "qualified foster care payments" made if they are eligible foster care providers. The definition of qualified payments includes payments made by either a state or local governmental agency or any "qualified foster care placement agency" that is licensed or certified by a state or local government or an entity designated by a state or local government to make payments to foster care providers. This enables payments from for-profit agencies contracting with state and local governments to provide nontaxable foster care payments to foster care providers. Prior to this change, payments made by licensed, private providers to qualified foster care providers were taxable.

## Educational Assistance Plans

Employers often assist their employees in furthering their education by providing them with financial assistance. To encourage such initiatives, Congress enacted § 127. This provision grants an annual exclusion of up to $5,250 for employer-provided educational assistance (i.e., tuition, fees, books, supplies and equipment). The exclusion applies to reimbursements or direct payment of expenses related to both undergraduate and graduate level courses.

[63] § 129(a)(1).

[64] § 21.

## Section 132 Fringe Benefits

In 1984, Congress attempted to tackle what was a growing controversy over fringe benefits. During that time, more and more employers were finding innovative ways to reward their employees with benefits that many aggressive taxpayers argued were nontaxable fringe benefits. Congress responded to these potential abuses by inserting a clause in the definition of gross income in § 61, stating that all fringe benefits were taxable. At the same time, however, § 132 was added and it not only sanctioned the exclusion for certain benefits that historically had escaped tax, but also created guidelines for evaluating others. It should be emphasized that the amendment to include fringe benefits as income reinforces the principle that *all* benefits are taxable unless the Code specifically excludes them. Unfortunately, this concept apparently was lost on Senator Tom Daschle who was nominated to be Secretary of Health and Human Services in 2009. During his vetting, it came to light that he had failed to report the value of a car and driver provided by his employer as income in the amounts of $73,031, $89,129 and $93,096 in 2005, 2006 and 2007, respectively. In addition, he omitted more than $80,000 of income from consulting!

An overview of the nontaxable fringe benefits now provided under § 132 is given in Exhibit 6-7. These additional employee benefits include the following:

1. Working condition fringe benefits
2. No-additional-cost services
3. Qualified employee discounts
4. De minimis fringe benefits
5. On-premises athletic facilities
6. Qualified transportation fringe benefits
7. Qualified moving expense reimbursement
8. Qualified retirement planning services

Furthermore, employees of educational institutions receive special treatment under § 117 for reduction in tuition costs.

### Working Condition Fringe Benefits

This exclusion provides that fringe benefits are nontaxable to the extent that employees could deduct the costs if they reimbursed their employer or otherwise paid the costs.[65] For example, if an accounting firm paid $100 for an employee's membership dues to the AICPA and $50 for a subscription to *The Wall Street Journal*, the employee could exclude the amounts since such costs could be deducted by the employee as routine business expenses had he or she paid them directly. Similarly, many businesses furnish some of their employees with company-owned automobiles. Expenses related to the business usage of the cars are deductible by employers and are excluded from income by the employees. In contrast, personal use of the cars, which includes commuting between the employees' home and work, is taxable compensation (unless it is nontaxable under the de minimis rule discussed later in this section).[66] This income is reported as other compensation, and thus not subject to withholding taxes.[67] If, however, employees reimburse their employers for all personal use of the automobiles, there is no auto-related taxable compensation. These benefits need not be provided to all employees (i.e., they may be reserved for officers, owners, and highly paid employees).

In addition to the above exclusions, the working condition fringe allows an exclusion for payments made for education by an employer if the employee could have deducted the cost as a business expense under § 162 (e.g., the education enabled the taxpayer to improve his skills used in his business and was not necessary to meet the minimum education requirement imposed by the job). This rule supplements the exclusion for employer-provided educational assistance of $5,250 but only in those cases where the educational costs would have been deductible had they been paid by employee. For example, if an employee could meet the tests

---

[65] Such costs would have been deductible as business expenses under § 162 or as depreciation under § 167. § 132(d); Reg. § 1.132-5.

[66] § 61(a)(1) and Reg. § 1.61-2(d)(1).

[67] Reg. § 1.6041-2 and Ltr. Rul. 8122017. Although not subject to withholding taxes, this income is subject to social security taxes.

**EXHIBIT 6.7** **Nontaxable Fringe Benefits under § 132**

| *Type of Benefit* | *Conditions* | *Examples* |
|---|---|---|
| No additional cost service—§ 132(b) | Company incurs no substantial additional cost<br>Service sold in normal course of business<br>Same-line-of-business limitations<br>Reciprocal agreements allowed<br>Must be nondiscriminatory | Airplane tickets<br>Hotel rooms<br>Telephone services |
| Qualified employee discount—§ 132(c) | Offered for sale in normal course of business<br>Same-line-of-business limitation<br>Merchandise discounts limited to employer's gross profit<br>Service discounts limited to 20% of normal price<br>Must be nondiscriminatory<br>Not applicable to investment property or real estate | Retail items |
| Working condition fringes—§ 132(d) | Nontaxable to extent employee would have deducted the cost had he or she paid for the property or service | Company car<br>Club memberships<br>Professional dues and subscriptions<br>Seminar expenses |
| De minimus fringes—§ 132(e) | Benefits are so small that accounting for them is unreasonable or administratively impractical | Employee picnics<br>Cocktail parties<br>Holiday gifts<br>Occasional use of:<br>Copying machine<br>Typing services<br>Meals<br>Coffee and donuts |
| Qualified transportation fringes—§ 132(f) | Valuation of parking: amount a person would pay in an arm's-length transaction to obtain parking at the same site<br>Available only to employees—not "partners" and "independent contractors" | Up to $230 per month:<br>Transit passes and<br>Vanpooling combined<br>Up to $230 per month:<br>Parking |
| Qualified bicycle commuting reimbursement | Reimbursements by an employer for employee expenses related to a bicycle used regularly for commuting | Up to $20 per month<br>Bicycle tires<br>Repairs, storage |
| Moving expense reimbursement—§ 132(g) | Reimbursements or payments by an employer to an employee for qualified moving expenses (i.e., those that would be deductible under § 217) | Moving expenses in connection with:<br>Beginning employment<br>Changing job locations |
| Athletic facilities—§ 132(j)(4) | Located on employer's premises<br>Operated by employer<br>Substantially all use is by employees, spouses, and children | Tennis court<br>Golf course<br>Gym<br>Pool |
| Qualified retirement planning services—§ 132(m)(1) | Any retirement planning services provided to an employee/spouse by an employer maintaining a "qualified" employer plan (i.e., pension plans) | Advice and information on retirement income planning<br>Does not apply to:<br>Tax preparation<br>Accounting services<br>Legal or brokerage services |

for deducting the expenses related to a graduate degree (e.g., an M.B.A.), financial assistance provided by an employer could be excluded.

## No-Additional-Cost Services

Some employers allow employees to use company facilities or services without charge or for a minimal maintenance fee. For example, an airline may allow its employees to fly stand-by for free because it loses nothing since the seat would have otherwise not been used. In this and similar situations, § 132(b) permits the employee to exclude the benefit as long as the company incurs *no substantial additional cost* as a result of the employee's usage. However, unlike the working condition fringe benefit, the exclusion is not allowed if the benefit discriminates in favor of officers or other highly compensated employees.

There are literally thousands of benefits that could qualify as no-additional-cost services. They range from use of company meeting rooms to free tickets in the entertainment industry for seats that would otherwise be empty. Note that the exclusion is limited to services sold in the normal course of business in which the employee works. For example, the value of a hotel room is nontaxable if used by an employee (and/or a spouse or dependent children) who works in the employer's hotel business. It is taxable, however, if the employee works for another line of business of an employer with diversified interests such as hotels and auto rentals. Those employees identified with more than one line of business (e.g., an accountant) may exclude the benefits received from all of them. The exclusion is extended to benefits provided under a written reciprocal agreement by another employer that is in the same line of business.[68] Thus, the hotel employee has nontaxable income for free use of a hotel room provided by another company that has a qualified reciprocal agreement with the employer.

## Qualified Employee Discounts

It is common practice for companies to allow employees to purchase inventory items at a discount. For example, a department store may allow its employees to purchase merchandise at the selling price less a stipulated discount. Such discounts seldom result in taxable income unless they discriminate in favor of highly compensated employees.[69] The exclusion, however, is not available for discounts on investment property or on residential or commercial real estate.

The rules governing nondiscrimination, the requirement that items must be offered for sale in the normal course of business and line of business, and the rules governing coverage of spouses and dependent children discussed above for nontaxable services also pertain to nontaxable discounts. In contrast with services, however, discounts under reciprocal agreements are taxable income. The merchandise discount exclusion is limited to the employer's normal profit (i.e., the discount may not exceed the employer's gross profit). In the case of employer services, the discount may not exceed 20 percent of the price charged to customers. Any discount beyond that amount is taxable income to the employee.

### Example 29

V, an employee of an auto mechanic business, has her automobile repaired by the company. Accounting records show the following information for the parts and service necessary to repair V's car:

| | *Normal Selling Price* | *Firm's Cost* | *V's Cost* |
|---|---|---|---|
| Parts | $200 | $120 | $112 |
| Service | 90 | 81 | 70 |

V's taxable income for the parts is $8 ($120 – $112) and for the service is $2 [($90 – $70 = $20) – ($90 × 20% = $18)].

[68] § 132(i). The line of business limitation is relaxed in certain instances if a special excise tax is paid.

[69] § 132(c).

## De Minimis Fringe Benefits

Exclusion of employee benefits also extends to items of minimal value such as the occasional use of a company's photocopy machines, other equipment, or typing services; annual employee picnics, cocktail parties, or occasional lunches; and inexpensive holiday gifts such as a turkey at Thanksgiving. No dollar amount is specified in determining what qualifies as de minimis. The general guideline is that the value of these benefits is so small that accounting for them is unreasonable or administratively impractical.[70] The exclusion also covers discounts on food served in an eating facility provided by an employer *if* (1) the facility is located on or near the employer's business premises, (2) its revenue equals or exceeds its direct operating costs, and (3) the nondiscriminatory rules discussed above are met.[71] In addition, as noted earlier, supper money—cash meal allowances—given occasionally to employees who are required to work overtime may be excluded as a de minimis fringe benefit.

Under the 1997 Act, meals provided on the employer's premises for the convenience of the employer (and excluded from an employee's income under Code § 119) are now considered a de minimis fringe benefit under Code § 132. As a result, employers will be able to deduct the entire cost of the provided meals and they no longer will be subject to the 50 percent disallowance rule that normally applies for meals and entertainment (see Chapter 8).

## Employer-Provided Transportation Benefits

Historically, employers have often reimbursed employees for their costs of commuting to and from work. When Congress finally addressed the treatment of such benefits in 1984, it grandfathered the practice of excluding such items. Thus was born the "qualified transportation fringe." The components of this exclusion and their amounts in 2011 are:

- Commuting to work in a qualified commuter vehicle (i.e., a vehicle that seats at least six people, excluding the driver such as a van) and transit passes, subway tokens, vouchers; maximum total exclusion for both when summed is $230 per month.
- Qualified parking (parking on or near the employers premises); maximum exclusion of $230 per month.
- Qualified bicycle commuting reimbursement (e.g., reimbursements for costs relating to using a bicycle for commuting such as the cost of the bicycle, repairs, and storage); maximum exclusion is $20 per month.

Amounts received in excess of these limits are included in gross income for both income and employment tax purposes.

### Example 30

For each month in 2011, Employer M provides a transit pass valued at $255 to Employee D. D does not reimburse M for any portion of the pass. Because the value of the monthly transit pass exceeds the statutory limit by $25, D is subject to both income and employment taxes on the $25 excess.

Note that if an employer offers cash in lieu of free parking, those who elect to take cash are taxed while those who opt for parking are not. Also note that in determining whether an amount can be excluded, any payments made by the employee to the employer must be considered. Payments by employees for qualified transportation fringes must also be considered in determining if the value of the benefit exceeds the statutory limit.

[70] § 132(e).

[71] § 132(e)(2).

> **Example 31**
>
> Employer P provides qualified parking with a value of $250 per month to its employees, but P charges the employees $30 per month. Because the net benefit of $220 ($250 − $30) is less than the exclusion amount of $230 per month, no amount is includible in the employee's gross income.[72]

### Qualified Moving Expense Reimbursement

Section 132 also excludes reimbursements received by employees for qualified moving expenses. These expenses, as discussed in Chapter 8, are those that would be deductible such as the cost of the moving van and transportation to the new location.[73]

### On-Premises Athletic Facilities

Section 132 also authorizes an exclusion for the value of the use of athletic facilities provided on the employer's premises primarily for current or retired employees, their spouses, and their dependent children. Facilities that qualify for the exclusion include gyms, golf courses, swimming pools, tennis courts, and running and bicycle paths. Resorts are not qualifying facilities. Although the athletic facility must be located on premises owned or leased by the employer, it need not be located on the employer's business premises. Because the nondiscrimination rules are not applicable to on-premises athletic facilities, they may be made available to executives only.[74]

### Employer-Provided Retirement Advice

In order to help employees adequately prepare for retirement, § 132 provides that "qualified retirement planning services" are an excludable fringe benefit.[75] The exclusion is granted for retirement planning services provided to an employee and his or her spouse by an employer that maintains a qualified pension plan. For example, General Motors might pay a financial planning firm to meet with their employees regarding retirement planning. The exclusion is not intended to apply to services that may be related to tax preparation, accounting, legal, or brokerage services. In an earlier ruling, the IRS concluded that financial counseling services provided to family members of terminally ill employees and survivors of deceased employees were taxable income.[76] Presumably, the value of such services would not be taxable under current fringe benefit rules.

### Qualified Tuition Reduction by Educational Institutions

A common and extremely valuable fringe benefit offered by educational institutions to their employees is a tuition reduction or tuition waiver. For example, a child of a university faculty member might pay only a portion of the tuition normally charged to other students. Since 1984, § 117(d) has blessed these arrangements and granted an exclusion for a "qualified tuition reduction." Such reductions qualify only if they are offered by a nonprofit educational institution and do not discriminate in favor of highly compensated employees. Therefore, most plans offer benefits not only to faculty but also to all other employees of the institution (e.g., advisors, librarians, secretaries, maintenance personnel). This exclusion is available to the employee, a spouse, and dependent children and is extended to these individuals even if the employee is retired, disabled, or deceased.[77]

As a general rule, the exclusion applies only to tuition waivers for undergraduate education. However, the exclusion also is extended to tuition waivers for graduate students if they are engaged in teaching or research (e.g., teaching or research assistants).[78]

It should be emphasized that the regulations indicate that only the benefit in excess of the portion representing reasonable compensation for the graduate student's services can be excluded. Moreover, the amount received for services cannot be excluded solely because all candidates for the degree are required to perform such services.

---

[72] Notice 94-3. p. 15.

[73] § 132(g).

[74] § 132(j)(4) and Reg. § 1.132-1T(e)(5).

[75] § 132(a)(7).

[76] Letter Ruling 199929043.

[77] § 117(d)(1).

[78] § 117(d) is subject to the compensation limitation in 117(c).

### Example 32

F is a doctoral student at State University. As part of her doctoral program she is required to teach one of the basic accounting courses each semester. For her efforts, she receives free tuition worth $17,000. Assuming other adjunct professors receive $3,000 for providing like services, F may only exclude $14,000. She must report $3,000 because it represents compensation for services.

### Military Personnel

Military personnel are employees subject to most of the same provisions as nonmilitary employees. As a result, all compensation is normally taxable. However, the character and tax treatment of some military benefits differ from those of nonmilitary employee benefits. Examples of taxable compensation are active duty and reservist pay, reenlistment bonuses, lump-sum severance and readjustment pay, and retirement pay. Examples of nontaxable benefits are allowances for subsistence, uniforms, and quarters; extra allowances for housing and living costs while on permanent duty outside the United States, and family separation allowances caused by overseas duty; moving and storage expenses; compensation received by *enlisted* service members (up to the highest monthly enlisted pay plus any hostile fire or imminent danger pay received for commissioned officers) for active duty in an area designated by the President as a combat zone (e.g., Iraq); and all pay while a prisoner of war or missing in action.[79] Benefits provided to military veterans by the Veterans Administration also are nontaxable. Examples of these are allowances for education, training, and subsistence; disability income; pensions paid to veterans or family members; and grants for specially equipped vehicles and homes for disabled veterans. In addition, bonuses paid from general welfare funds by state governments to veterans are nontaxable.

Military deployed in combat zones, qualified hazardous duty areas, or certain contingency operations may deposit up to $10,000 of their pay into a special Department of Defense savings account during a single deployment. Interest accrues on the account at an annual rate of 10 percent and compounds quarterly. Although federal income earned in hazardous duty zones is tax-free, interest accrued on earnings deposited into these accounts is taxable.

### Reparations to Holocaust Victims

Over the years, countries and businesses that benefited from forced labor or property confiscation during the Holocaust have made restitution payments to those who suffered and returned property to the rightful owners. To ensure that the victims, their heirs and estates receive the full benefit of the payments undiminished by taxes, Congress granted an exclusion for reparation payments received after January 1, 2000. In addition, confiscated property that is returned is deemed to have a basis equal to its fair market value.[80]

## Personal Transfers between Individuals

**LO.4**
Explain the treatment of gifts, inheritances, alimony and child support.

While the bulk of all income is derived from the fruits of one's labor or invested capital, there are a number of items that still have significance for which special rules exist. Among these are the provisions covering the treatment of certain transfers between individuals, specifically gifts, inheritances, child support, and alimony. With the exception of alimony, each of these is nontaxable. In each case, the recipient does not include the amount in income and the payer is not entitled to a deduction.

[79] The TRA of 1986 consolidated existing military benefits and provided the Treasury with the authority to expand the list.

[80] § 803(a), Economic Growth and Tax Relief Reconciliation Act of 2001, P.L. 107-16

## Gifts and Inheritances

Section 102 excludes the value of property received as a gift, bequest, devise, or inheritance from gross income.[81] This exclusion is normally justified on the theory that there is merely a redistribution of the donor's or decedent's after-tax income.

While gifts are nontaxable, it is not always easy to determine whether an amount received represents a gift or compensation. The problem was clearly revealed in the landmark case of *Comm. v. Duberstein*.[82] In this case, Duberstein, a businessman from Dayton, Ohio, provided the names of potential customers to Berman, an entrepreneur from New York City. The names proved to be very valuable to Berman and, to show his appreciation, he gave Duberstein a Cadillac. Although Berman's company deducted the cost of the car on its tax return as a business expense, Duberstein considered the Cadillac a gift and therefore nontaxable. The issue was ultimately reviewed by the Supreme Court, which announced its now famous distinction between gifts and compensation. According to the court, a gift is made out of a detached and disinterested generosity and not as a reward for past services or made in expectation of future services. Based on the Court's view, Berman intended the car to be remuneration for services rendered and consequently ruled that Duberstein had taxable compensation.

The exclusion for gifts does not extend to income earned on the property.[83] For example, the value of bonds inherited or received as a gift is nontaxable, but any interest income earned on the bonds by the new owner is taxable unless specifically exempted by the Code (e.g., interest on tax-exempt bonds issued by a municipality).

## Alimony and Separate Maintenance

As may be clear by now, virtually nothing is left untouched by the tax law and that includes the area of matrimonial disputes. Indeed, given the divorce rate in the United States (generally thought to be between 40 and 50 percent of first marriages), it should not be surprising that a thriving part of many tax practices relates to the tax consequences of divorce and separation. That this can be is attributable to the fact that a major element in the dissolution of many marriages is the financial arrangement of the settlement.

Typically, a divorcing couple must first split up their property and establish separate households. Under most state laws, each spouse is entitled to the property he or she brought into the marriage and an equal share of property accumulated during the marriage. In addition to the property settlement, the divorce decree may require one of the spouses to pay support for the children (i.e., child support), and in many cases make support payments—normally referred to as alimony or separate maintenance payments-to the ex-spouse. For tax purposes, the obvious questions concern the treatment of the property settlement, child support, and alimony. The general rules governing these transfers are quite straightforward:

- *Property Settlement*. The division of the property (i.e., the transfer of property from one spouse to the other in exchange for the release of that spouse's marital claim) is a nontaxable event.[84] Neither spouse has income for the property received or a deduction for the property transferred. Consistent with this approach, the basis of the property received by either spouse under the property settlement remains the same, leaving any built-in gain or loss unchanged.[85]
- *Alimony*. Amounts designated as alimony (or equivalent payments) are considered a mere reallocation or sharing of the payer's income and, therefore, are taxable to the recipient and deductible by the payer.[86]
- *Child Support*. Amounts paid for child support, often covered in a separate agreement, are nontaxable to the recipient (regardless of how the money is used) and nondeductible to the payer.

---

[81] § 102(a).

[82] 60-2 USTC ¶9515, 5 AFTR2d 1626, 363 U.S. 278 (USSC, 1960).

[83] Reg. § 1.102-1(a). Amounts paid out of an estate or trust may be taxable under certain circumstances. However, the end result should protect the exclusion for the gift or inheritance. See § 663.

[84] § 1041(b)(2). Prior to 1985, transfers between spouses were taxable. See *U.S. v. Thomas Crawley Davis*, 62-2 USTC S ¶9509, 9 AFTR2d 1625, (USSC, 1962).

[85] § 1041(b)(2).

[86] § 215(a) and 71(a)(1).

### Example 33

H and W are divorced, and W was awarded custody of their only child. Pursuant to the divorce decree, this year H transferred his various investments in stock to W worth $24,000 (basis to H of $16,000). In addition, H paid W $18,000 in alimony and $10,000 in child support. Neither H nor W is affected by the transfer of stocks. H's basis of $16,000 carries over to W so that her basis is also $16,000. Thus the built-in appreciation of $8,000 shifts to W. H is entitled to deduct all $18,000 of the alimony as a deduction for A.G.I. while W must report the $18,000 as taxable income. H is not entitled to deduct the $10,000 paid as child support, but W is allowed to exclude the $10,000 from income.

Due to the drastically different tax treatments of these transfers, characterization of a particular payment as alimony, child support, or part of the property settlement is obviously crucial in structuring a divorce settlement. As might be expected, without some rules and coordination, a paying spouse might want to call something alimony while the recipient spouse may feel that it is either child support or part of the property settlement. Moreover, the two parties, despite their failure in marriage, may be able to work out a financial arrangement that works well for both but unfairly reduces the government's rightful share. To help eliminate controversy, a number of special rules must be observed when dealing in this area. In this regard, these rules normally do not apply to divorces occurring before 1985.[87]

## Alimony

Prior to 1942, there was no specific statute governing the treatment of alimony or child support. As early as 1917, however, the Supreme Court ruled that alimony did not fall within the definition of income and, consequently, the recipient avoided tax. From the payer's perspective, the payments were not deductible since there was no provision that authorized the deduction. In some cases, this treatment could produce an inequitable result. For example, consider a taxpayer who earns $150,000 and is required to pay alimony of $100,000 to his ex-wife. Assuming the taxpayer pays taxes at a rate of 50 percent, he would have only $75,000 after-tax to meet his $100,000 alimony obligation! Because alimony seriously reduced the taxpayer's ability to pay, Congress believed it was more appropriate to view the payments of alimony as simply a splitting of the payer's income. Consequently, the law was changed to make payments of alimony deductible by the payer and taxable to the recipient.

Under current law, payments qualify as alimony or separate maintenance only if[88]

1. They are made in *cash*;
2. They are made as a result of a divorce or separation under a *written decree* of separate maintenance or support;
3. They are *required* under a decree or a written instrument incident to a divorce or separation;
4. The spouses or court do *not* elect that they be designated as not qualifying as alimony;
5. The husband and wife do not live together nor do they file a joint return together; and
6. Payments cease with the death of the *recipient*.

Payments meeting these requirements, however, are not treated as alimony if the divorce or separation agreement clearly states they are not alimony for Federal income tax purposes. Note that this provision gives the parties a great deal of flexibility in structuring the divorce.

---

[87] These rules apply to a pre-1985 divorce decree *only if* both parties expressly agree. Ltr. Rul. 8634040.

[88] § 71(a) and (b) and Reg. § 1.71-1.

As noted above, payments only qualify as alimony if they are in cash. However, the payments need not be made directly to the ex-spouse.[89] Specifically, the following types of payments qualify as alimony:

1. Payments made in cash, checks, and money orders payable on demand.
2. Payments of cash by the ex-husband to the ex-wife's creditors in accordance with the terms of the divorce or separation instrument such as payments of the ex-wife's mortgage (i.e., on house ex-wife owns), taxes, rent, medical and dental bills, utilities, tuition, and other similar expenses.
3. Premiums paid by the ex-husband for term or whole life insurance on the ex-husband's life made pursuant to the terms of the divorce or separation instrument, provided the ex-wife is the owner of the policy.
4. Payments of cash to a third party on behalf of the ex-wife, if they are made at the written request of the ex-wife, such as a contribution to a charitable organization.

However, the following *do not* qualify as alimony or separate maintenance payments:[90]

1. Assets transferred as a part of the property settlement, such as a home, car, stocks and bonds, life insurance policies, annuity contracts, etc.
2. Any payments to maintain property owned by the ex-husband and used by the ex-wife, including mortgage payments, real estate taxes, insurance premiums, and improvements. Such payments increase the ex-husband's equity in the property.
3. Fair rental value of residence owned by ex-husband but used exclusively by ex-wife.
4. Repayment by the ex-husband of a loan previously made to him by his ex-wife as part of the general settlement.[91]
5. Transfers of services (i.e., professional or otherwise).[92]
6. Voluntary payments not required by the divorce or separation agreement.
7. Payments made prior to a divorce or separation.

### Example 34

D and G are divorced. The divorce decree requires D to transfer personal assets valued at $30,000 to G, to pay G $2,400 per year until G remarries or dies, and to pay G $50,000 over a period of 12 years. During the year. D pays G the following amounts:

1. $1,000 separate maintenance, voluntarily made prior to their separation or divorce
2. $2,400 separate maintenance, made in accordance with the divorce agreement
3. $30,000 of personal assets, transferred in accordance with the divorce agreement
4. $6,000 of the $50,000 to be paid over 12 years

G's alimony is $8,400 ($2,400 + $6,000). The $1,000 separate maintenance is not alimony because it was paid voluntarily and before any divorce or separate maintenance agreement was made. The $30,000 transfer of personal assets is not alimony since it is a property settlement. Since G has taxable alimony of $8,400, D has a deduction for A.G.I. of $8,400.

### Limitations on Front Loading

Absent some limitations, *both* spouses might be better off if what is really a property settlement is treated as deductible alimony. To illustrate, consider the following example.

---

[89] Temp. Reg. § 1.71-1T(b).

[90] Temp. Reg. § 1.71-1T(b), Questions 5 and 6.

[91] Reg. § 1.71-1(b)(4).

[92] Temp. Reg. § 1.71-1T(b), Question 5.

### Example 35

H and W are in the process of negotiating the terms of their divorce. It is anticipated that after the divorce, H will be in the 50% bracket while W will pay taxes at a rate of 20%. If H pays $10,000 to his wife and the amount is *not* considered alimony, the after-tax cost of the payment to the husband is $10,000 while the after-tax benefit to the wife is $10,000. On the other hand, if the payment is considered deductible alimony, H could increase the payment to W to $20,000 and it would have the same $10,000 after-tax cost as the first payment. However, in such case, W would receive $16,000 after-tax, $6,000 more even though she has to pay taxes. As a result, both H and W are inclined to characterize any payment that is made as alimony.

As the above example illustrates, depending on the tax rates of the parties, a divorcing couple may be inclined to characterize a payment as alimony regardless of its actual substance. This is particularly true for the spouse required to make the payments since the value of the alimony deductions up front is normally far greater than their value if deferred to later years.

When an arrangement like this might provide an advantage, the divorce agreement normally calls for large "alimony" payments for the first few years followed by smaller payments later. As a practical matter, however, the large payments made initially that are purportedly alimony are in all likelihood simply part of what is a disguised property settlement. To prevent this so-called front loading, Congress created special rules.[93]

The front loading rules are triggered when there is a significant drop in alimony in either the second or third year after the divorce. If such a drop occurs, the alimony is *recaptured,* that is, the payment is no longer treated as alimony. As a result, the payer must include the amount in income and the recipient who previously reported the payment as income is entitled to a deduction. Unfortunately, the actual calculation of the amount to be recaptured is quite cumbersome.

Alimony paid in the first and second years must be recaptured in the third year if, during this three years, alimony payments decreased by more than $15,000. Amounts recaptured are included in gross income by the payor and deductible by the payee in arriving at A.G.I. To compute the recapture, the years must be considered in reverse order. Thus, the recapture formula for the second post-separation year is (1) total payments made in the second year less (2) payments made in the third year less (3) $15,000. The recapture formula for the first year is similar with one exception. In the second step, an *average* is computed of the second-year payments (less excess payments for that year, determined in the preceding computation above) plus the third-year payments.

### Example 36

Alimony payments by W to H for the first three years after divorce are $25,000, $20,000, and $15,000. Since payments did not decrease by more than $15,000, no recapture is required. Both W's deductions for A.G.I. and H's taxable income are $25,000 the first year, $20,000 the second year, and $15,000 the third year.

[93] § 71(f).

### Example 37

Alimony payments by M to F for the first three years after divorce are $50,000, $20,000, and $0. Since payments decrease by more than $15,000, recapture is required in the third year. As computed below, the recapture for the second year is $5,000 and for the third year is $27,500.

| | |
|---|---|
| Drop from year 2 to year 3: | |
| Total payments made in second year | $20,000 |
| −Payments made in third year | 0 |
| Drop from year 2 to year 3 | $20,000 |
| −$15,000 allowance | (15,000) |
| Year 3 recapture amount | $ 5,000 |
| Drop from year 1 to year 2: | |
| Total payments made in first year | $50,000 |
| −(Year 2 + year 3 payments − year 3 recapture)/2 | (7,500)* |
| Drop from year 1 to year 2 | $42,500 |
| −$15,000 allowance | (15,000) |
| Recapture amount | $27,500 |

*($20,000 + $0 − $5,000 = $15.000)/2 = $7,500

M's deduction for A.G.I. and F's taxable income are $50,000 the first year and $20,000 the second year. In the third year, the recaptures exceed payments: thus, M's taxable income and F's deduction for A.G.I. is $32,500 ($5,000 + $27,500).

The recapture rules do not apply for post-1984 divorce instruments if payments:

1. Cease because of the death of either spouse during the three-year period;
2. Cease because the payee remarries during the three-year period;
3. Are made under a support agreement, and thus do not qualify as alimony; or
4. Are a fixed portion of income to be paid for at least three years and based on revenues from a business, from property, or from employee or self-employment compensation.

### Child Support

If there are children, it is reasonable to assume that a portion of the husband's payments will be for their care and support. Amounts that qualify as child support are nondeductible personal expenses for the husband and nontaxable income to the wife.[94] Funds qualify as child support *only* if:

1. A specific amount is fixed or is contingent on the child's status (e.g., reaching a certain age);
2. Paid solely for the support of minor children; and
3. Payable by decree, instrument, or agreement.

If all three requirements are not met, the payments are treated as alimony with no part considered to be child support.[95] All other factors are irrelevant to the issue. For example, the intent of the parties involved, the actual use of the funds, and state or local support laws have no bearing on whether payments qualify as child support. Also, even though state law may be to the contrary, a minor child is anyone under age 21.[96]

---

[94] Reg. § 1.71-1(e).

[95] See § 71(c)(2) and Temp. Reg. § 1.71-1T, Questions 16 and 17. Also, see *Arnold A. Abramo*, 78 T.C. 154 (1983) acq. and *Comm. v. Lester*, 61-1 USTC ¶9463, 7 AFTR2d 1445,366 U.S. 299 (USSC, 1961).

[96] *W.E. Borbonus*, 42 T.C. 983 (1964).

### Example 38

A divorce decree states that B is to pay $300 per month as alimony and support of two minor children. The agreement also states that the payments will decrease by one-third (1) if the former spouse dies or remarries, and (2) as each child reaches 21 years of age. This type of agreement meets the contingency rule for child support. Consequently, $100 per month qualifies as alimony and $200 per month qualifies as child support.

Once child support is established, no payments are considered to be alimony until all past and current child support payments are made.[97]

### Example 39

A divorce decree states that H is to pay $100 per month as alimony and $200 per month as support of two minor children. The first payment was due October 1. H paid $150 in October, $300 in November, and $350 in December. These payments are allocated between child support and alimony as follows:

| | Payment | Child Support | Alimony |
|---|---|---|---|
| October | $150 | $150 | $ 0 |
| November | 300 | 250 | 50 |
| December | 350 | 200 | 150 |
| Total | $800 | $600 | $200 |

The above allocation is made even if H or state law stipulates that payments are to cover alimony first.

## Transfers by Unrelated Parties

**LO.5**
Describe the treatment created for unique items of income such as life insurance, debt cancellation, scholarships, and government transfers.

The last section clearly revealed that the income concept can be quite broad and could, without special rules, encompass benefits normally derived from personal relationships. This section discusses a hodgepodge of provisions that are loosely associated in that the benefits are received from unrelated or third parties. These include life insurance, prizes and awards, scholarships, cancellation of debts, and government transfer payments.

## Life Insurance Proceeds and Other Death Benefits

### Life Insurance

Since its inception the tax law has contained an exclusion for life insurance proceeds received by a beneficiary after an insured person's death.[98] Congress apparently wanted to encourage individuals to buy life insurance to provide adequate resources for their survivors and, at the same time, provide tax-free funds in a time of need.

[97] Reg. § 1.71-1(e).

[98] § 101(a)(1). Insurance proceeds are also taxable if the policy is an investment contract with little or no *insurance risk* or the owner of the policy does not have an *insurable interest* in the insured. In addition to the insured, a spouse, dependents, business partners, and in some instances, creditors and employers are considered to possess the requisite insurable interest.

Many life insurance policies allow the beneficiary to take the life insurance proceeds in either a lump-sum payment or installments. The exclusion applies in either situation. However, the beneficiary is entitled to exclude only the face amount of the policy. Any excess (e.g., investment earnings while the proceeds were left with the insurance company) are taxable.

### Example 40

This year W's husband, H, died. Under the terms of a life insurance policy, W is to receive $500,000. Alternatively, W can elect to receive $55,000 per year for the next 10 years. If W takes the lump sum payment, she can exclude the entire $500,000. If she elects to take the installment payout of $55,000 annually, $50,000 of each payment is a nontaxable return of the life insurance proceeds, but the remaining $5,000 is taxable income [$55,000 – ($500,000/10)].

Although life insurance proceeds are normally nontaxable, there are several special rules that should be observed.

**Cashing-In the Policy Before Death** Some life insurance policies, notably whole-life, enable the holder to cash the policy in before the taxpayer's death. Any amount received in excess of the premiums paid is taxable. No loss is recognized if the premiums paid exceed the amount received. The 1996 tax legislation provides, however, tax-favored treatment for accelerated death benefits.

Over the past several years, many terminally-ill individuals (e.g., AIDS patients) have surrendered their life insurance policies or sold the policies to a third party in exchange for the death benefits. These death benefits would then be used to pay for medical and other expenses. Although life insurance benefits that are payable on account of death are normally nontaxable, the treatment of accelerated death benefits, often referred to as "viatical settlements," was somewhat unclear. Congress clarified their treatment by adding Code § 101(g). This section provides that accelerated death benefits (i.e., surrender of the policy to the insurer for a lump sum or sale to a third party) generally may be excluded if the individual is chronically or terminally ill. While the exclusion for terminally ill individuals is unlimited, the exclusion for a chronically ill individual (who is not also terminally ill) is restricted to the amount of long-term care services actually incurred.

An individual is considered terminally ill if he or she has been certified by a physician as having an illness or physical condition that can reasonably be expected to result in death in 24 months or less. A chronically-ill individual is generally a person who is unable to perform at least two activities of daily living (e.g., eating, toileting, transferring, bathing, dressing, and continence) for a period of at least 90 days due to a loss of functional capacity.

### Example 41

C is 60 years old and has smoked two packs of cigarettes a day since he was a young man. Three years ago, C was diagnosed with lung cancer. His condition recently took a turn for the worse and his physician now expects that C will live less than a year. C owns a life insurance policy with a face value of $150,000. In order to pay for his medical expenses and home nursing care, C has elected to surrender the policy to his insurance provider for a lump sum of $130,000. Because C is expected to die in 24 months or less, the accelerated death benefit of $130,000 is excluded from his gross income.

**Substitute for Taxable Income** In some instances, life insurance is used to protect a creditor against a bad debt loss on the death of the insured. However, the fact that the debt is offset by life insurance proceeds on the death of the insured does not cause otherwise taxable income to be nontaxable. For example, amounts equal to unreported interest due on the debt are taxable interest income.[99] Similarly, proceeds offsetting debt that was previously written off as uncollectible, or proceeds representing gain not previously reported, are included in gross income.[100]

**Transfer for Valuable Consideration** If a policy is transferred to another party in exchange for valuable consideration, any *gain* from the proceeds on the insured's death is taxable income.[101] Gain is defined as the insurance proceeds less the owner's basis. Basis is the total purchase price plus all premiums paid by the subsequent owner after the transfer.

**Example 42**

XY Corporation purchased a $15,000 life insurance policy from S, the insured, for $7,300. The corporation made five annual premium payments of $600 each on the policy. S died at the end of the fifth year and XY collected $15,000 insurance. since XY's basis in the policy is $10,300 [($600 × 5 payments) + $7,300], its taxable income is $4,700 ($15,000 – $10,300).

There are four exceptions to *Example 43*. All gain is nontaxable if the purchaser is (1) a partner of the insured, (2) a partnership in which the insured is a partner, (3) a corporation in which the insured is a shareholder or officer, or (4) the insured.[102]

## Employee Death Benefits

Upon the death of an employee, it is not uncommon for employers to provide the employee's family with some type of compensation for their loss. These amounts are fully taxable to the beneficiaries and cannot be excluded as gifts.

## Prizes and Awards

The tax law provides no escape for those fortunate enough to receive prizes and awards. Prizes and awards are fully taxable. This is true regardless of the reason for the award. While this was not always the case, since 1986 winners of the Nobel Prize are taxed the same as those who win the grand prize from Publisher's Clearinghouse. Similarly, winners of sweepstakes, lotteries, employer service awards, contests, door prizes, and raffles held by charitable organizations have taxable income to the extent the fair market value of the winnings exceeds the cost of entering the contests.[103]

Taxpayers who have won a prize or award may avoid taxation if they immediately transfer the prize or award to charity. Although this may seem unnecessary given that taxpayers are entitled to a charitable contribution deduction, the deduction is generally limited to 50 percent of the taxpayer's A.G.I. Consequently, if the taxpayer received a $100,000 award that he or she wanted to donate to charity, an outright contribution might not necessarily offset the income. This treatment is available only for prizes and awards that are

[99] *Landfield Finance Co. v. Comm.*, 69-2 USTC ¶9680, 24 AFTR2d 69-5744, 418 F.2d 172 (CA-7, 1969), aff'g. 69-1 USTC ¶9175, 23 AFTR2d 69-601, 296 F. Supp. 1118 (DC, 1969).

[100] *St. Louis Refrigerating & Cold Storage Co. v. Comm.*, 47-2 USTC ¶9298, 35 AFTR 1477, 162 F.2d 394 (CA-8, 1947), aff'g. 46-2 USTC ¶9320, 34 AFTR 1574, 66 F. Supp. 62 (DC, 1946) and Rev. Rul. 70-254, 1970-1 C.B. 31.

[101] § 101(a)(2).

[102] § 101(a)(2)(B).

[103] Reg. § 1.74-1(a)(2). For the determining the value of property won, see *Lawrence W. McCoy*, 38 T. C. 841(1962), acq. and *Reginald Turner*, 13 TCM 462, T.C. Memo. 1954-38.

made in recognition of religious, charitable, scientific, educational, artistic, literary, or civic achievements, but only if

1. The recipient was selected without any direct action on his or her part to enter the contest or proceeding;
2. The recipient is not required to perform substantial future services as a condition of receiving the prize or award; and
3. The prize or award is given by the payor to a governmental unit or tax-exempt organization as designated by the recipient.[104]

When these rules are met, the award has no impact on the winner's tax liability; it is neither taxable income nor a deductible charitable contribution.

### Example 43

After twenty years of medical research at the MNO Institute, E gained an international reputation for her computer studies of protein structures. As a result, she was recently awarded the Nobel Prize in Medicine. E gave the award, which amounted to $375,000, to the American Cancer Society. Because all of the conditions for exclusion are satisfied, the $375,000 prize is excludable from E's gross income.

## Scholarships and Fellowships

Although scholarships and fellowships are considered to be prizes and awards, Congress has elected to specifically exempt them from the above provisions in order to promote and lower the cost of education. To this end, § 117 generally allows an exclusion of scholarships and fellowships for those individuals who are candidates under the following conditions:

- The individual is a candidate for a degree (either undergraduate or graduate).
- The degree granting organization is a qualified educational institution, that is, the organization has a faculty, curriculum, and an organized student body (e.g., obtaining a degree at correspondence schools would not qualify).
- The amount received is a scholarship. It must aid the individual in his or her pursuit of study or research and not represent compensation for services.
- The amounts received are used for tuition and related expenses, including fees, books, supplies, equipment, and other expenses that are required for either enrollment or attendance (but not room and board).

### Example 44

C holds a Ph.D. in chemistry from the University of Michigan. This year the Gemini Foundation, a nonprofit research institution, awarded C a post-doctoral fellowship of $30,000 to do research for a semester at the University of Texas with a noted scientist. C must include the fellowship as taxable income since he is not a candidate for a degree.

As a practical matter, most scholarships easily meet these requirements. A few potential difficulties should be mentioned, however.

It should be emphasized that amounts received for room and board cannot be excluded; however, they are considered earned income for purposes of determining the individual's standard deduction, which should facilitate an offsetting deduction.

[104] § 74(b).

### Example 45

J, a junior majoring in engineering at Private University, was awarded a $10,000 scholarship during the current year. She used the funds to pay the following school-related expenses: tuition $6,000, technology fee $100, athletic fee $25, books $875, room and board $2,500, and notebooks, pencils, and other supplies, $100. J used the remaining $400 to purchase a set of software products (word processor, spreadsheet, data base, presentation) that several of her professors said would be useful in their courses. J must report $2,900 of taxable income, representing the room and board of $2,500, and the equipment that was not required of $400. Assuming J had no other sources of income, her standard deduction would be equal to her earned income, which in this case is the $2,900 spent on room and board and the suggested equipment. As a result, J's standard deduction would offset her $2,900 of taxable income.

In some situations, amounts that are characterized as scholarships may be considered compensation for services rendered or to be rendered. In such case, the amounts received are taxable even if a current employment relationship does not exist. For example, a scholarship that was awarded a beauty contest winner was considered taxable, since much like an employee, she participated in a televised pageant and was expected to perform promotional services in the future.[105]

Note, however, that amounts received by an employee may qualify for exclusion under an educational assistance plan or as a working condition fringe benefit, as discussed earlier in this chapter. Similarly, employees of educational institutions, including graduate students engaged in teaching or research activities, are entitled to exclude any tuition reductions. In addition, amounts paid for education that are related to the taxpayer's employment may be deductible if certain conditions are met, as described in Chapter 8.

## Cancellation of Indebtedness

When a taxpayer borrows money, no income must be recognized since there has been no increase in the taxpayer's net worth. On the other hand, if a lender reduces or cancels a taxpayer's debt, there is a corresponding increase in net worth. In such case, the taxpayer is normally required to include the amount of debt forgiveness in gross income.[106] However, in certain situations the taxpayer may be able to exclude this so-called cancellation of debt income. Some of these include:

- The cancellation represents a gift or bequest (e.g., a father forgives his son's debt).
- The cancellation occurs when the taxpayer is insolvent or bankrupt.
- The cancellation represents a renegotiation of the purchase price.
- The cancellation of student loans.
- The cancellation is of debt related to the taxpayer's principal residence.

### Bankruptcy or Insolvency

If the taxpayer is *solvent* at the time a debt is cancelled, there is normally no exclusion and income must be recognized to the extent of the debt forgiveness. On the other hand, if the taxpayer is *bankrupt* or *insolvent* (liabilities exceed the value of the assets), the IRS does not add to the taxpayer's financial woes with more taxable income but provides a reprieve under § 108.

When a debt is cancelled pursuant to a bankruptcy proceeding, there is no taxable income.[107] However, the taxpayer is required to reduce certain tax attributes that normally would produce tax savings in the future. For example, the taxpayer must reduce any net operating loss carryovers by the amount of debt forgiveness. As a result, the taxpayer would

---

[105] Rev. Rul. 68-20, 1968-1 C.B. 55.

[106] § 61(a)(12).

[107] § 108(a)(1)(A).

lose the benefit of deducting the NOL in the future. In this sense, the income is not truly excluded but rather deferred. However, any debt reduction that exceeds the attributes identified below is ignored entirely, and the related income forever escapes tax. The attributes that must be reduced are:

1. Net operating losses (NOLs) and any NOL carryovers
2. General business credit carryovers
3. Minimum tax credit
4. Capital losses (current and carryovers)
5. Basis of the taxpayer's property (generally depreciable realty)
6. Passive activity loss and credit carryovers
7. Foreign tax credit carryovers

While the attributes normally must be reduced in the order shown, the taxpayer may elect to reduce the basis of property first (i.e., shift number 5 to number 1). By so doing, the taxpayer gives up a deferred deduction (i.e., the depreciation related to the property) for perhaps an immediate deduction (e.g., an NOL as soon as income is produced).

If the taxpayer is not bankrupt when the debt is cancelled, but insolvent, the approach is generally the same as shown above.[108] However, to the extent the taxpayer becomes solvent, taxable income results. Thus, an insolvent taxpayer reduces the attributes identified above until solvency results and the balance is included in gross income.

### Example 46

XYZ Inc. has assets of $375,000, liabilities of $500,000, and an NOL carryover of $100,000. If creditors forgive $90,000 of debt, none of the forgiveness will generate taxable income because, as shown below, XYZ is insolvent both before and after the debt cancellation. XYZ would be required to reduce the NOL carryover by $90,000 (from $100,000 to $10,000).

| | *Before* | *After* |
|---|---|---|
| Total assets | $ 375,000 | $375,000 |
| Total liabilities | (500,000) | (410,000) |
| Insolvent | $(125,000) | $ (35,000) |

If, on the other hand, the creditors forgive $140,000 of debt, XYZ will be solvent after the cancellation (i.e., $375,000 − $360,000 = $15,000). Consequently, the firm would report $15,000 of the forgiveness as taxable income in such case. In addition, XYZ would reduce the NOL carryover by $100,000 to zero.

## Qualified Real Property Business Indebtedness

As explained above, if a business's debt is cancelled, the taxpayer normally must recognize income unless the business is bankrupt or insolvent. To provide relief to those engaged in the real estate business (other than corporations), Congress created a special exception. Under § 108, a taxpayer may elect to exclude the income resulting from the cancellation of indebtedness incurred or assumed in connection with real property used in a trade or business (*qualified real property business indebtedness*). This is true even though the taxpayer is neither bankrupt nor insolvent. The cancellation of debt income does not escape tax, however. The taxpayer must reduce the basis of the depreciable property for any income that is excluded. As a result, the taxpayer forgoes future deductions. The maximum amount of exclusion may not exceed the excess of the outstanding principal amount of the debt over the fair market value of the property.

---

[108] § 108(a)(1)(B).

### Example 47

During 2003 T acquired an office building in Houston for $800,000. He borrowed $700,000 of the purchase price by giving First Bank of Houston a note payable with interest at a rate of 14%. The note was secured by the building. By 2011 the value of the building had dropped to $400,000. At that time, the balance on the note was $600,000. Instead of foreclosing and taking the property, the bank agreed it would be better to leave the real estate in the hands of T and renegotiate the terms of the note so that T could handle the payments. As a result, the bank reduced the principal of the note from $600,000 to $400,000. T may elect to exclude the cancellation of debt income of $200,000, but he must reduce the basis of the property by $200,000.

### Seller Reduction of Purchaser's Debt

Another situation where § 108 allows the taxpayer to exclude cancellation of debt income relates to sales where the seller provides the financing for the buyer. If the seller/lender cancels the debt, the buyer may exclude the benefit but must reduce the basis of the property.[109] In effect, the Code treats the transaction as a renegotiation of the purchase price. Note that the result is identical to that discussed above for qualified real property business indebtedness. This rule does not apply if the buyer is bankrupt or insolvent.

### Example 48

Several years ago, B purchased an apartment building from S for $1,000,000. B gave S $200,000 cash and signed a note payable to S for the $800,000 balance. The note was secured by the building. B has recently fallen on hard times and may default on the note, which has a current balance of $700,000. S, not wanting to become a landlord again and not sure that he could find another buyer, reduced the note's principal to $400,000. Since S provided the financing and B is solvent, B may exclude the $300,000 cancellation of debt income but must reduce his basis in the building by $300,000.

### Cancellation of Debt on a Principal Residence

Until recently, the cancellation of debt related to a taxpayer's personal residence resulted in taxable income unless the taxpayer was bankrupt or insolvent. However, the rise in foreclosures led to a change in the law. Beginning in 2007, income realized as a result of modification of the terms of a mortgage (e.g., a restructuring) or a foreclosure on a principal residence can be excluded. The taxpayers basis in the residence must be reduced by the amount of the exclusion. Note that the taxpayer need not be bankrupt or insolvent to take advantage of this rule. The new provision generally applies to debt of up to $2,000,000 ($1,000,000 for married filing separately) used to acquire, construct or improve the taxpayer's principal residence. When the debt was the result of a refinancing, the amount of the exclusion is limited to the amount of debt that was refinanced. The rule does not apply to home equity loans or debt forgiven related to a second home, a credit card loan, a car loan or any other type of loan. The new rule applies to qualified debt forgiven in 2007 and before January 1, 2013. The exclusion is claimed on Form 982.

### Example 49

Several years ago, R purchased a residence for $115,000, paying $10,000 and financing the balance. R lost his job and was no longer able to make payments on the mortgage that at the time had a balance of $100,000. After discussions with the holder of the mortgage, the debt was reduced to $80,000. Although R is neither bankrupt nor

[109] § 108(e)(5)(A).

insolvent, he can exclude the $20,000 cancellation of debt income. Had the lender foreclosed on the home and sold it for $80,000 in complete satisfaction of the $100,000 debt, the $20,000 of forgiveness also can be excluded.

### Cancellation of Student Loans

Code § 108(f) allows individuals to exclude from income the amount of certain student loans that have been cancelled. This exclusion normally applies only if the loan is issued by the government and the forgiveness is contingent on the student's fulfilling a public service work requirement.

## Government Transfer Payments

Many government transfer payments are excluded from income. For example, earlier discussion in this chapter revealed that all or a portion of Social Security benefits are excluded from income. Since medicare benefits are considered to be Social Security, they also are nontaxable. Supplementary medicare payments received as reimbursement of medical expenses deducted in a prior year are taxable, however, to the extent the taxpayer received a *tax benefit* in that year.[110]

Worker's compensation received as a result of a work-related injury is excluded from income.[111] Similar to the typical accident insurance policy discussed earlier in this chapter, worker's compensation provides the injured employee with a fixed amount for the permanent loss or use of a function or member of the body. For example, an individual who loses a hand, fingers, or hearing in a work-related accident receives a nontaxable amount, according to a schedule of payments. This exclusion is extended to compensation received by the survivors of a deceased worker. Other worker's compensation benefits are taxable unless the requirements for accident or health plans, previously discussed, are met.

Both state and Federal government transfer payments that are classified as public assistance (e.g., food stamps) or paid from a general welfare fund (e.g., welfare payments) are nontaxable.[112] Among others, these include payments to foster and adoptive parents, to individuals who are blind, to victims of crimes, for disaster relief, (e.g., hurricane or flood relief) to reduce energy costs for low-income groups, and for urban renewal relocation payments.[113]

Benefits to participants in government programs designated to train or retrain specified groups are frequently nontaxable. Whether these benefits are nontaxable or not is dependent upon the primary purpose of the programs. Thus, if the objective of the program is to provide unemployed or under-employed individuals with job skills that enhance their employment opportunities, amounts received are nontaxable.[114] But, if the primary purpose is to provide compensation for services, participants are government employees with taxable wages.[115]

Most government transfer payments to farmers are included in income.[116] For example, gross income from farming includes government funds received for trees, shrubs, seed, and certain conservation expenditures, and for reducing farm production.[117] If materials are received instead of cash, their fair market value is taxable income. In addition, taxpayers receiving government funds under qualifying conservation cost-sharing plans may elect to exclude the reimbursement of capital improvements. However, the capitalized cost of the projects must be reduced by the excluded amount.[118]

---

[110] Rev. Rul. 70-341, 1970-2 C.B. 31.

[111] § 104(a)(1).

[112] Rev. Rul. 71-425 1971-2 C.B. 76.

[113] See generally § 139. Rev. Ruls. 78-80, 1978-1 C. B. 22; 74-153, 1974-1 C.B. 20; 77-323, 1977-2 C. B. 18; 74-74, 1974-1 C.B. 18; 76-144, 1976-1 C.B. 17; 78-180, 1978-1 C.B. 136; and 76-373, 1976-2 C.B. 16.

[114] Rev. Ruls. 63-136, 1963-2 C.B. 19; 68-38, 1968-1 C.B. 446; 71-425, 1971-2 C.B. 76; and 72-340, 1972-2 C.B. 31.

[115] Rev. Rul. 74-413, 1974-2 C.B. 333.

[116] Reg. § 1.61-4(a)(4).

[117] *R. L. Harding*, 29 TCM 789, T.C. Memo. 1970-179 andRev. Rul. 60-32, 1960-1 C.B. 23.

[118] See § 126 and Temp. Reg. § 16A.126-1.

## Business Gross Income

The amount to be included in gross income for proprietorships, partnerships, and corporations is total revenues plus net sales less cost of goods sold. This same concept is applicable even if the business conducted is illegal or if the activities do not qualify as a trade or business but constitute a hobby. Many of the other includible and excludable business gross income items are discussed earlier in this chapter. Additional income items peculiar to business that deserve discussion are classified as (A) generally includible in, or (B) generally excludable from, gross income.

### A. *Generally Includible in Gross Income*

- Agreement not to compete
- Goodwill
- Business interruption insurance proceeds
- Damages awarded
- Lease cancellation payments

### B. *Generally Excludable from Gross Income*

- Leasehold improvements (unless made in lieu of rent)
- Contributions to capital

### Agreement not to Compete and Goodwill

The sale of a business often contains an agreement that the seller will not compete with the buyer in the same or similar business within a particular area or distance. In such case, the seller must treat any amount assigned to the agreement as ordinary income. The purchaser may amortize (deduct) this amount over 15 years on a straight-line basis regardless of its useful life.

When the net selling price of the business exceeds the fair market value of all identifiable net assets, the business generally is considered to possess *goodwill*. That is, its potential value exceeds its net assets because of the business name, location, reputation, or other intangible factor. Goodwill is considered a capital asset and, consequently any amounts received for goodwill are normally treated as capital gain. As provided in the Revenue Reconciliation Act of 1993, acquired goodwill can be amortized ratably over a period of 15 years. If the contract includes a single amount for both goodwill *and* a noncompetition agreement, the entire amount is treated as goodwill. In negotiating the sale, the seller should consider the tradeoffs involved in an allocation of the sales price between the covenant not to compete and goodwill. As a general rule, a seller will normally prefer to allocate more of the sales price to assets that produce capital gain, such as goodwill, than to those that produce ordinary income, such as a covenant not to compete.

**Example 50**

On January 1 of the current year, Ralph purchased all of the assets of Ed's Bowling Alley (a sole proprietorship) for $500,000. Included in the purchase contract is $60,000 allocable to goodwill and $45,000 to a covenant that prohibits Ed from opening another bowling alley in the next five years. Ed will report $60,000 as a long-term capital gain (taxed at no more than 15%) and the $45,000 as ordinary income. On the other hand, Ralph may amortize the amount paid for goodwill over 15 years (i.e., $60,000 ÷ 15 years = $4,000 per year), and the amount paid for the covenant not to compete over 15 years, notwithstanding it has a useful life of only five years ($45,000 ÷ 15 = $3,000 per year).

### Business Interruption Insurance Proceeds

Some businesses carry insurance policies that provide for the loss of the use of property and of net profits sustained when the business property cannot be used because of an unexpected event such as fire or flood. The Regulations state that the insurance proceeds are included in gross income regardless of whether they are a reimbursement for the loss of the use of property or of net profits.[119] Similarly, insurance proceeds that are to reimburse the business for overhead expenses during the period of interruption are taxable.[120]

### Example 51

Jordan Manufacturing, Inc. (JMI) was the victim of arson during the current year. The fire destroyed the main office building and the company's warehouse and its contents. JMI received a check for $1.5 million from its insurance company covering the projected lost profit for six months during which operations at JMI ceased. Since the profits which were not generated would be taxed, the payment representing the lost profit is fully included in JMI's gross income.

## Damages Awarded

Cash may be awarded by the courts or by insurance companies for damages suffered by businesses because of patent infringement, cancellation of a franchise, injury to a business's reputation (see later discussion concerning professional reputation), breach of contract, antitrust action, or unfair competition. The treatment of the damages depends on whether they are compensatory (i.e., those amounts making the taxpayer whole) or punitive (i.e., those amounts that serve as a penalty). Punitive damages are fully taxable.[121] On the other hand, compensatory awards may be used *first* to offset any litigation expenses or other expenditures in obtaining the award.[122] *Second*, funds that represent a recovery of capital when damages are awarded because of a loss in value to a business's goodwill or other assets are used to offset or write down the capitalized asset costs.[123] Remaining damages generally are considered to be a reimbursement for a loss of profits and are included in gross income.[124] An exception to the latter classification occurs when compensatory damages are awarded in an antitrust suit. While the punitive damages in these cases are taxable, the compensatory damages are taxable only to the extent that losses sustained by the business resulted in a tax benefit.[125]

### Example 52

Several years ago, Good Corporation contracted with Bad Corporation to build a condominium project. Good later identified defects in the construction and sued Bad. This year the court awarded Good $1,000,000; $750,000 for compensatory damages and $250,000 for punitive damages. Good incurred legal fees of $150,000. Good must treat the $250,000 punitive damages as ordinary taxable income. The compensatory damages are first reduced by the costs incurred to secure the award, $150,000. The remaining $600,000 is used to reduce the basis of the property, and any excess would be taxable.

## Lease Cancellation Payments

Early termination of lease agreements may result in a lease cancellation payment. Either a lessor or a lessee may receive these payments, depending on which party cancelled the lease.

---

[119] Reg. § 1.1033(a)-2(c)(8).

[120] Rev. Rul. 55-264, 1955-1 C.B. 11.

[121] *Comm. v. Glenshaw Glass Co.*, 55-1 USTC ¶9308, 47 AFTR 162,348 U.S. 426 (USSC, 1955).

[122] *State Fish Corp.*, 49 T.C. 13 (1967), mod'g. 48 T. C. 465 (1967).

[123] *Farmers' and Merchants Bank of Cattletsburg, Ky. v. Comm.*, 3 USTC ¶972,11 AFTR 619,59 F.2d 912 (CA-6, 1932) and *Thomson v. Comm.*, 69-1 USTC ¶9199,23 AFTR2d 69-529,406 F.2d 1006 (CA-9, 1969).

[124] *Durkee v. Comm.*, 1950-1 USTC ¶9283,35 AFTR 1438, 162 F.2d 184 (CA-6, 1947),*rem'g.* 6 T.C. 773 (1946).

[125] § 186 and Reg. § 1.186-1.

In *Hort*, the Supreme Court held that lease cancellation funds received by a lessor are a substitute for rent.[126] Consequently, these receipts are taxable income. Amounts received by a lessee on cancellation of a lease are considered proceeds from the sale of the lease.[127] Thus, the gain is included in gross income. Whether the gain is ordinary or capital depends on the use of the property (see discussion in Chapter 16).

**Example 53**

Alice owns a 50-unit apartment complex in Manhattan. Nancy, who rents one of Alice's units, has decided to purchase her own house. Consequently, Nancy paid Alice $1,100 in return for cancelling her lease. Alice must treat the payment as a substitute for rental income and, therefore, must include the amount as ordinary income.

**Example 54**

This year Alice decided to convert her 50-unit apartment complex into a medical clinic for use by physicians and dentists. She paid one of her tenants $2,000 to cancel the lease. Because the lease agreement represents a capital asset to the tenants (i.e., the lease on a residence is a personal asset), the tenant will treat the $2,000 as capital gain.

## Leasehold Improvements

A lessee often makes improvements to leased real estate. These may range from minor improvements up to the construction of a building on the leased land. If these improvements are made in lieu of rent payments, they are included in the lessor's gross income.[128] Otherwise, the lessor has no taxable income either at the time the improvements are made or at the time the lease is terminated, even if the improvements substantially increase the property's value.[129] The lessor's only taxable income from these improvements will occur indirectly on the sale of the property to the extent the improvements result in a higher net selling price.

**Example 55**

For the past 10 years W had leased land to X. During the current year the lease expired and W became the owner of a three-stall garage (FMV $19,000) that X had constructed on the property seven years previously. Assuming the improvements were not made in lieu of rent, the FMV of the garage is not currently included in W's gross income.

Under § 110, a retail tenant that receives cash or rent reductions from the lessor of retail space does not include such amounts in income if the cash (or equivalent) is used for qualified construction or improvement to the space. In order to qualify for the exclusion, the tenant must have a short-term lease (i.e., a lease of retail space for 15 years or less). The amount excluded cannot exceed the amount spent by the tenant for the improvement.

From time to time, lessors will make improvements on their property in order to attract lessees. If a lessor abandons a leasehold improvement in the year the lease terminates, the lessor is allowed a deduction equal to the landlord's adjusted basis of the improvement [§ 168(i)(8)]. This rule does not apply where the improvement is demolished in which case the landlord simply increases the basis of the property (§ 280B).

[126] *Hort v. Comm.*, 41-1 USTC ¶9354, 25 AFTR 1207, 313 U.S. 28 (USSC, 1941).

[127] § 1241.

[128] Reg. § 1.109-1.

[129] § 109.

## Contributions to Capital

Cash or other property received by a business in exchange for an ownership interest are nontaxable transactions for the business. These transfers are treated as contributions to capital and not income.[130] Contributions to capital that are not in exchange for an ownership interest also are nontaxable.

# Miscellaneous Items

As stated in the first paragraph of this chapter, gross income includes *all* income unless specifically exempted. Although this chapter is not intended to discuss every income item, some additional items are classified for discussion purposes as miscellaneous.

## Fees Received

Ordinarily, fees received for services performed are included in gross income. Thus, fees paid to corporate directors, jurors, and executors are reported as miscellaneous gross income. However, if executor fees are paid regardless of whether the taxpayer performs any services, they may qualify as nontaxable gifts.[131]

## Asset Discovery

Cash or other assets found by a taxpayer are taxable income even if found accidentally, with no effort expended in discovering them.[132] For example, taxpayers were held to have taxable income equal to cash found in a used piano they had purchased.[133]

## Car Pool Receipts

One type of earned income is nontaxable. Vehicle owners operating car pools for fellow commuters may exclude all the revenues received.[134] Car pool expenses are *personal* commuting expenses, and therefore are not deductible. If, however, the car pool activities are sufficient to qualify a taxpayer as being in a trade or business, all revenues are taxable. How much activity constitutes a trade or business is a question of fact not easily answered, but in this type of situation, the definition of trade certainly requires considerably more activity than a single automobile or small van making one round trip daily.

## Income Tax Refunds

All state and local income tax refunds are nontaxable except to the extent the taxpayer received a *tax benefit* in a prior year.[135] A corporation receives a tax benefit for all business expenses, including state and local income taxes, unless the corporation incurs a net operating loss for the year of deduction. State and local income taxes paid by individuals, however, provide a tax benefit only if the taxpayer itemized these deductions in the year paid. There is no tax benefit for the expense if the standard deduction was used instead of itemized deductions. In addition, the taxable amount of a state and local income tax refund is affected by the amount of state and local sales tax that the taxpayer could have otherwise deducted. Under current law, a taxpayer is entitled to deduct the larger of state and local income taxes or state and local sales taxes (see Chapter 11). The amount of the refund is taxable only to the extent that the state income taxes deducted exceeded the amount of state sales tax that the taxpayer could have otherwise deducted.[136]

---

130 §§ 118 and 721.

131 Rev. Rul. 57-398, 1957-2 C.B. 93.

132 Rev. Rul. 53-61, 1953-1 C.B. 17.

133 *Cesarini v. Comm.*, 70-2 USTC ¶9509, 26 AFTR2d 70-5107. 428 F.2d 812 (CA-6, 1970).

134 Rev. Rul. 55-555, 1955-2 C.B. 20.

135 § 111(a).

136 See *Taxable and Nontaxable Income*, IRS Publication 525 (2006), p. 20.

### Example 56

John and Lori Hansen are married and live in Kokomo, Indiana. The couple filed a joint return for 2011. Their total itemized deductions, including state income taxes withheld by their employers of $7,000, amounted to $18,100 in 2011. The couple could have deducted state and local sales taxes of $6,000 but deducted the state and local income taxes since the $7,000 amount was larger. On June 12, 2012, the Hansens received a refund from the State of Indiana for $2,500 as a result of overpaying their 2011 Indiana income taxes. Because the Hansens received a tax benefit by deducting the state income taxes on their 2011 Federal income tax return of only $1,000 ($7,000 state income tax – $6,000 state sales tax), they must include the $1,000 refund in gross income on their 2012 Federal income tax return.

## Temporary Living Costs

If an individual receives insurance proceeds to cover temporary living costs incurred because the principal residence was destroyed or damaged by fire, flood, or other casualty, the funds are nontaxable to the extent they are offset by *extra* living costs.[137] These funds also may be excluded if the government prevented the individual from using an undamaged residence because of the existence or threat of a casualty. Extra living costs are limited to those additional costs actually incurred for temporarily housing, feeding, and transporting the taxpayer and members of the household. Typical qualifying costs are hotel or apartment rent and utilities, extra costs for restaurant meals, and additional transportation necessitated by having to live outside the immediate area of the residence.

## Damages Awarded to Individuals

More and more often people are suing or being sued. Each year millions of lawsuits are filed in state and federal courts. Most of these cases have financial implications. Some of these are settled out of court while others go on. In many situations, individuals receive damages compensating them for their loss (compensatory damages) and, in some, damages are awarded to penalize or punish the wrongdoer (punitive damages). Section 104(a) provides the treatment of compensatory and punitive damages.

### Compensatory Damages

For many years, Section 104(a)(2) provided that damages awarded on account of personal injuries and sickness were nontaxable. Historically, the treatment was justified on the grounds that the amounts received represent a return of human capital. According to the theory, injured parties are no better off since the damages merely restored them to their original state. However, controversies arose in applying this exclusion to certain awards such as those involving age, sex, and race discrimination. Taxpayers artfully argued that these awards were related to personal injuries, hoping to qualify for an exclusion. The seriousness of the situation could be seen in a class action suit brought by hundreds of IBM employees that had been laid off who argued for the exclusion of their severance pay on the grounds that such payments were made in part to allay future claims of discrimination.

To address these concerns, § 104 was amended in 1996 to make it clear that only damages awarded on account of physical injury and sickness are not taxable.[138] In addition, § 104 explains that *emotional distress* is not considered a physical injury or sickness unless such distress had its origins from physical injury or sickness. Emotional distress includes physical symptoms such as insomnia, headaches or stomach disorders that may result from such emotional distress. According to the Committee Reports, this rule bars an exclusion for any damages received based on a claim of employment discrimination or injury to reputation

[137] § 123.

[138] But see *Marrita Murphy* 2006-2 USTC, ¶50,476, 98 AFTR 2d 2006-6088, 460 F3d 79, (CA-DC, 2006) where the appellate court recently held that this provision was unconstitutional.

accompanied by a claim of emotional distress. Thus it appears that awards made due to employment discrimination based on age, sex, race or similar factors would be fully taxable. The fact that the individual suffered emotional distress that produced physical symptoms would not enable the taxpayer to qualify for the exclusion. However, the law does explain that damages actually used to pay for medical expenses related to emotional distress are nontaxable.

**Example 57**

In July of 2009 K filed a sex discrimination lawsuit against Statewide University after being denied promotion to associate professor with tenure. In November of 2011 the parties entered into an out-of-court settlement pursuant to which the university awarded K $80,000 in lost wages, $5,000 for medical expenses related to emotional distress and $40,000 of punitive damages. Of the $125,000 she received, only the $5,000 payment for medical expenses would be excluded from K's gross income. Amounts allocated to lost wages and punitive damages are taxable.

### Punitive Damages

Historically, punitive damages normally have been taxable. At times, however, courts have reached differing opinions about the treatment of punitive damages related to cases involving damages awarded for physical injury or sickness. One theory allowed the taxpayer to exclude punitive damages related to physical injury or sickness since the compensatory damages were nontaxable. The other theory took the view that all punitive damages were taxable. Section 104(a)(2) now makes it clear that all punitive damages are taxable even if they are related to physical injury or sickness.

# Tax Planning

## INVESTMENTS

Tax-planning strategy must be viewed in terms of each taxpayer's own financial position. When considering investments, both the after-tax return and the risk involved must be evaluated. Before-tax income frequently is lower for tax-exempt and tax-deferred investments than it is for taxable investments with the same degree of risk. Consequently, tax-exempt investments should be most attractive to those in the higher tax bracket. They may not be beneficial to those in the lower bracket. Tax-deferred investments should be most attractive to those expecting a lower tax bracket when the deferral period ends. In addition, investors must consider whether any gains will be taxed as ordinary income or capital gains (see Chapter 16), and whether capital gains will be needed to offset capital losses.

Taxpayers have a variety of investment opportunities available to them. In order to arrive at informed investment decisions, comparative evaluations are necessary. However, such evaluations must be viewed with caution. The very nature of this type of analysis means that tentative assumptions must be made about the future. For example, when comparing a possible stock purchase with an annuity purchase, assumptions must be made about (1) future cash flows for the two investments, (2) future marginal tax rates, and (3) the discount rate to be used in determining the present value of the expected cash flows. A decision should never be based on a simple nonmathematical tax comparison of the total of annual dividends plus capital gains for the stock, as opposed to the total deferred ordinary income for the annuity. A tax adviser should always remember that while taxation is a very important factor, it is just one of several that must be considered.

On the death of an insured person, life insurance companies ordinarily allow beneficiaries to receive the proceeds in one lump sum, or in installments for a stipulated period or over the beneficiary's life. Tax concerns aside, some beneficiaries may elect to leave the proceeds with the insurance company simply because they like the security of receiving a periodic payment from an established financial institution. Each installment contains a ratable portion of the proceeds plus interest. This interest is taxable income. Thus, life insurance proceeds received in installments are treated the same as annuities.

**Example 58**

M is the sole beneficiary of her husband's $60,000 life insurance policy. She elects to receive the proceeds in monthly installments for 10 years. Her monthly installment is $500 plus interest on the unpaid principal. In the current year, she receives $6,000 plus $3,700 interest. Her taxable interest income is $3,700.

One feature of life insurance that has enticed many investors over the years is its tax-free cash build-up. Taxpayers have taken advantage of this by borrowing against the policy—in effect receiving use of the income without having to pay tax on it. To discourage the purchase of life insurance as a tax-sheltered investment vehicle, special rules have been established. As a result, taxpayers must closely scrutinize the type of insurance they purchase with respect to its tax treatment. Under the revised rules, a taxpayer who receives amounts before age 59½, including loans, from certain single premium and other investment-oriented life insurance contracts (modified endowment contracts) is treated as receiving income first and then a recovery of basis. In addition, the recipient is subject to an additional 10 percent income tax on the amounts received that are includible in gross income. This provision affects only "modified endowment contracts" entered into on or after June 21, 1988.

An investor who desires nontaxable income may choose to purchase assets such as:

1. Qualifying state and local government bonds to obtain the full interest income exclusion
2. Stocks in companies with net income for accounting purposes, but no earnings and profits for tax purposes, to obtain the full exclusion for distributions that are treated as a return of capital

Investors who wish to defer income may choose to:

1. Exchange Series E or EE bonds that are maturing for Series HH bonds in order to continue deferring the accrued interest on the surrendered E or EE bonds
2. Purchase annuities (or to elect that life insurance proceeds be received as annuities) to obtain the deferral of all interest income until received
3. Purchase assets that are expected to appreciate, such as stocks, real estate, and collectables, to obtain the deferral of all appreciation until it is realized

If the taxpayer does not dispose of the assets, the deferral becomes permanent. That is, no one recognizes the income and the assets are inherited at their market values, including the deferred income.

## Employee Benefits

Company fringe benefits can provide employees with tax consequences that range from excellent savings to actual disadvantages. From a tax viewpoint, the best fringe benefits are those that are deductible by the employer and convert otherwise taxable income to nontaxable income for the recipient. For example, most employee benefits that are provided in lieu of additional salary convert taxable compensation to nontaxable benefits.

**Example 59**

W is a new employee of Z Corporation. Her compensation package is $20,000. However, she may choose to receive (a) $20,000 salary and no benefits, or (b) $19,000 salary and Z will pay premiums of $600 for medical insurance and $400 for group-term life insurance. If W chooses the first option, she has $20,000 taxable income, but if she selects the second option, she has $19,000 taxable income.

Another very valuable type of fringe benefit is one that is nontaxable income if provided by the employer but is a nondeductible expenditure if paid by the employee. Most fringe benefits are of this type. These include premiums paid for group-term life insurance up to $50,000, qualifying meals and lodging on the premises, supper money, company parking, use of company facilities, and employee discounts. All of these benefits are deductible costs by the employer but nontaxable income to the employee when the necessary requirements discussed in this chapter are met. If, however, the employees pay these costs instead of the employer, there is no tax deduction for them.

A third type of fringe benefit includes expenditures that are deductible expenses, when paid by individuals, but are subject to restrictions. For example, health insurance premiums are deductible for employees who itemize their deductions but *only* to the extent that all qualifying medical expenditures exceed 7.5 percent of A.G.I. (see Chapter 11). Thus, employer-paid health insurance represents different tax savings to different employees.

**Example 60**

L's compensation includes a salary of $30,000 plus employer-paid health insurance premiums of $600. L's taxable income is $30,000 since the $600 is nontaxable. If the company policy is changed so that L pays the $600 health insurance premiums and the company increases his salary to $30,600, the tax effect on L depends on his individual tax situation.

1. If L does not itemize medical expenses, he has taxable income of $30,600 salary and no deduction for the $600.
2. If L itemizes deductions and his medical expenditures before the health insurance premiums exceed 7.5% of A.G.I., he still has taxable income of $30,600 salary but now has a deduction of $600.

Assume L has a 25% marginal tax rate. In situation 1 above, his tax benefit from employer-paid health insurance premiums is $150 ($600 × 25%). In the second situation, L appears to receive no tax benefit when his company pays the health insurance premiums. However, his A.G.I. is $600 higher when L pays the premium. Since medical expenses equal to 7.5% of A.G.I. are not deductible, this increases the nondeductible portion by $45 ($600 × 7.5%). Thus, at the 25% tax rate, his tax increases by $11.25 ($45 × 25%).

Some employer-provided benefits can be a disadvantage to employees. Recall, for example, that disability income is taxable if the premiums were paid by the employer but nontaxable if they were paid by the individual. The best tax-planning advice when employers pay disability insurance premiums is for employees to convince employers to provide another benefit and let employees pay their own disability premiums.

Considerable leeway in tax planning is available to those employees who are allowed to select their own fringe benefits. Simply looking at the cost of each benefit to the company, however, is inadequate. Each employee should carefully evaluate personal needs and the tax effect of each desirable benefit before selection is made.

## Employee Versus Self-Employed

The tax advantages of many fringe benefits are available only if an employer/employee relationship exists. For example, sole proprietors are not considered employees of their proprietorships so many fringe benefits are not available to them. Similarly, partners in partnerships and members of LLCs are not considered employees and, therefore, some benefits are not available to them. In contrast, owners of C corporations can be employees of the corporation and are entitled to fringe benefits. This situation creates an incentive to operate some businesses as corporations rather than as proprietorships or partnerships or LLCs.

One of these fringe benefits, employer-furnished meals and lodging, has been of interest to closely held businesses for years. Farming represents a particularly good example of a business that requires someone to be available on the property 24 hours a day. When the working owner lives on the farm, a business deduction plus an employee exclusion for the cost of meals and lodging provided to the farmer can be significant.

**Example 61**

A farm owned by M has the following information for the current year:

| | |
|---|---|
| Gross income | $130,000 |
| Cost of food consumed by M | 2,000 |
| Cost of lodging used by M | 4,200 |
| Salary to M | 20,000 |
| Other farm expenses | 85,000 |

If the farm is a proprietorship, net farming income is $25,000 ($130,000 – $20,000 – $85,000) and M has an A.G.I. of $45,000 ($25,000 + $20,000).[139] Similar results occur if the farm is a partnership, except M will report only his share of the $25,000. In contrast, if the farm is a corporation, net income is $18,800 ($130,000 – $2,000 – $4,200 – $20,000 – $85,000) and M has an A.G.I. of $20,000. Thus, M, the proprietor, has $45,000 A.G.I. compared with a combined income of $38,800 ($18,800 + $20,000) for the M Corporation and M, the employee.

Although the above example seems to result in a tax advantage for the corporate farm, such a conclusion is over-simplified. Other tax factors are important. For example, corporate net income is taxed to the corporation currently and again as dividend income to shareholders when distributed to them (see Chapter 20). Another important factor is that individuals and corporations are subject to different tax rates. Also, if farming losses occur, the results may be very unfavorable with a corporate entity. The important point to remember is that the tax advantage achieved with the corporation for meals and lodging (and other employee benefits) is just one of the necessary ingredients when evaluating whether a business should be incorporated.

## Divorce

Insufficient attention usually is given to tax planning during separation and divorce. Of course, favorable tax results are easier to accomplish when the individuals are parting amicably, but good results still can occur amid animosity. The more disparate the husband's and wife's tax brackets, the greater the benefits to be achieved. This is because payments classified as alimony or separate maintenance are deductible by the payor and are taxable income to the recipient. In contrast, all other asset transfers are neither deductible expenses nor taxable income.

**Example 62**

H and W are divorced. H's marginal tax rate is 35% while W's is 15%. Every $10 of alimony costs H $6.50 after taxes [$10 paid – $3.50 tax savings ($10 × 35%)] and is worth $8.50 to W after taxes [$10 received – $1.50 tax due ($10 × 15%)]. Thus, H pays $6.50 for W to receive $8.50. If W requires $425 after taxes each month, she must receive $500 if the payments qualify as alimony [$500 – ($500 × 15% = $75)] or $425 if they do not. On the surface, it seems that H would rather pay $425 a month than $500 but $500 in alimony results in an after-tax cost of $325 [$500 – ($500 × 35% = $175)] for a monthly savings of $100 ($425 – $325). Naturally, the closer the two marginal rates, the less there is in tax savings.

[139] Technically, a proprietor's salary is not a farming expense but is shown in the example for comparison purposes. Thus, net income is $45,000 ($130,000 – $85,000) and M's A.G.I. is $45,000.

# Problem Materials

## DISCUSSION QUESTIONS

**6-1** *Basic Concepts.* Determine whether each of the following statements is true or false. If false, rewrite the statement so that it is true. Be prepared to explain each statement.

**a.** Receipts are included in gross income only if specifically listed in the Code.

**b.** Tax returns show (1) gross receipts from all sources, less (2) excludable income, which equals (3) taxable income.

**c.** Interest earned on tax-exempt municipal bonds is nontaxable income regardless of whether it is received by an individual or by a corporation.

**6-2** *Investment—Stocks versus Bonds.* C has $10,000 to invest but is uncertain whether to purchase H, Inc. stocks or tax-exempt bonds issued by the State of Illinois. List the relevant types of information that C must obtain or estimate in order to make a mathematical calculation of her after-tax return on the two investments she is considering.

**6-3** *Investments—Bonds.* D, Inc. bonds are selling for $1,000 each with an interest rate of 7 percent. Tax-exempt bonds issued by the State of Kentucky are selling for $1,000 each with an interest rate of 3 percent. Which bond provides a taxpayer with the higher after-tax return when the marginal tax rate is

**a.** 35 percent?

**b.** 15 percent?

**6-4** *Investments—Dividend Income.* Corporate distributions may qualify as dividends, return of capital, or stock dividends. Explain the tax treatment of each of these three distributions. What determines whether a distribution is a dividend, a return of capital, or a stock dividend?

**6-5** *Employee Benefits.* Z, Inc. owns and operates several businesses, including six hotels and two real estate agencies. R, an employee of Z, spends three nights free of charge in one of Z's hotels in Indiana. Is the value of the lodging nontaxable to R, assuming the information below? Explain.

**a.** R works for one of the real estate agencies.

**b.** R tends bar in one of the hotels in Maine.

**c.** R is a tax accountant in Z's corporate headquarters where the tax records of all of Z's businesses are maintained.

**6-6** *Employee Benefits—Comparison.* Compare the tax treatment for each of the items listed below assuming they are paid by (1) the employer, or (2) the employee.

**a.** Parking in the company lot during working hours

**b.** Health insurance premiums

**c.** Disability insurance premiums

**d.** Meals eaten in the company cafeteria when the employee must remain on the premises for job reasons

**6-7** *Employee Benefits—Meals and Lodging.* Employer-provided meals and lodging that qualify as nontaxable income can be an exceedingly valuable employee benefit.

**a.** When do employer-provided meals and lodging qualify as nontaxable income?

**b.** List at least 10 types of occupations in which employer-provided lodging and/or meals could qualify for the exclusion. Explain why these occupations are appropriate for the exclusion.

**6-8** *Employee Benefits.* Over the years, the list of employee benefits that qualify as deductible expenses by the employer and nontaxable income for the employee has expanded. Assume Congress is interested in further expanding the list of benefits available for this special tax treatment. Prepare a list for Congress of at least three items not discussed in this chapter that would provide many employees with valuable benefits. Explain why these three would be logical additions.

**6-9** *Gifts.* How can gifts to family members reduce the family's income tax liability?

**6-10** *Alimony and Child Support.* A husband and wife who are obtaining a divorce disagree whether certain periodic payments should be classified as alimony or child support.

**a.** What difference does it make how the payments are classified?

**b.** What if the agreement states the payments are for both alimony and child support without making a specific distinction in dollar allocation between the two?

**c.** List three types of compromise offers that could be made by the husband to reach an allocation that might satisfy both the husband and wife. Explain the tax consequences of each of the three possible solutions.

**6-11** *Alimony.* A husband (H) and wife (W) are obtaining a divorce. He agrees to pay alimony of $25,000 in each of the two years after the divorce to enable her to attend graduate school. No alimony will be paid after the second year.

**a.** What are his deductible and her taxable amount of alimony for each of the two years, and what are the tax effects in year three?

**b.** How could the payment schedule be restructured to maximize his deductions?

**c.** How could the payment schedule be restructured to minimize her taxable income?

**6-12** *Prizes and Awards.* Contest winners must report the value of prizes won as taxable income.

**a.** What arguments could the taxpayer use to convince the IRS and the courts that the values of the prizes are less than their retail selling prices?

**b.** Are any prizes or awards ever nontaxable? Explain.

**6-13** *Scholarships and Fellowships.* CPA firms are interested in encouraging practical research that explores accounting issues with an objective of developing better accounting methods for the profession. Assume the XY firm decides to establish a fund that will support individual research efforts. Recipients of these grants will be selected based on the quality of their past work and on a written proposal of a specific research project to be completed with funds from the XY firm. Do recipients of these grants have taxable or nontaxable income? Explain.

**6-14** *Distributions from 529 Savings Plans.* During the year, G withdrew $18,000 from a 529 plan for his daughter. He used the most of the money to pay for the following costs associated with her first year of college: tuition $10,000, fees $1,000, apartment rental $3,000, computer $1,600, books $400, appliances and furniture $505 and bedding $200. How will the $18,000 be treated?

**6-15** *Goodwill versus Agreement Not to Compete.* A preliminary agreement covering the sale/purchase of a dental practice includes an allocation of $40,000 to goodwill and the agreement that the seller will not practice dentistry within a five-mile radius for five years.

**a.** What are the tax consequences of this $40,000 allocation?

**b.** What advice should a tax adviser give the seller?

**c.** What advice should a tax adviser give the buyer?

**6-16** *Damages Awarded.* As the result of a newspaper article, V claims his character was damaged beyond repair, he lost his job, and he incurred medical expenses for psychiatric care. His lawsuit requested that the court award him the following amounts: $500,000 for personal injury due to slander; $30,000 in lost wages; and $5,000 for psychiatric care.

**a.** What are the tax consequences to V if he is awarded the $535,000?

**b.** V decides to accept an out-of-court settlement of $150,000. The newspaper and its insurer are willing to allocate the $150,000 in any manner that V requests. How should V have the amount allocated?

## PROBLEMS

**6-17** *Basic Concepts.* Calculate the amount to be included in gross income for the following taxpayers.

**a.** T is self-employed as a beautician. Her records show

| *Receipts* | |
|---|---|
| Services | $21,000 |
| Product sales | 3,000 |

| *Expenditures* | |
|---|---|
| Cost of products sold | 1,800 |
| Cost of supplies used | 2,600 |
| Utilities | 2,400 |
| Shop and equipment rent | 3,600 |
| Other expenses | 1,000 |

**b.** R owns rental property. His records show

| | |
|---|---|
| Gross rents | $6,000 |
| Depreciation expense | 4,200 |
| Repair expense | 2,100 |
| Miscellaneous expense | 300 |

**c.** S is an employee with the following tax information:

| | |
|---|---|
| Gross salary | $15,000 |
| Social security (FICA) taxes withheld (rounded for simplicity) | 1,000 |
| Federal income tax withheld | 2,200 |
| Health insurance premiums withheld | 500 |
| Net salary received in cash | 11,300 |
| Employer's share of social security taxes | 1,000 |

**6-18** *Investments—Cash Dividends.* Three years ago, Z purchased 50 shares of L common stock for $6,000. Although Z is married, the stocks are recorded in his name alone. The current market value of these shares totals $7,200. He and Mrs. Z file a joint return and neither of them owns any other stock. Mr. Z wants to know what effect each of the following totally separate situations has upon (1) his taxable income and (2) his basis in each share of stock.

**a.** L distributes a cash dividend and Z receives $330.

**b.** L distributes cash as a return of capital and Z receives $330.

**6-19** *Investments—Stock Dividends.* A, who is single, purchased 100 shares of N Corporation common stock four years ago for $12,000. The stock has a current fair market value of $14,400. A asks how each of the following separate situations affects her (1) taxable income and (2) basis in each share of stock.

**a.** N distributes common stock as a dividend and A receives ten shares.

**b.** N distributes nonconvertible preferred stock as a dividend and A receives 10 shares. The preferred stock has a current fair market value of $100 per share.

**6-20** *Investments—Cash Dividends.* D, Inc. had accumulated earnings and profits at January 1 of the current year of $20,000. During the taxable year, it had current earnings and profits of $10,000. On December 31 of the current year, D, Inc. made a cash distribution of $40,000 to its sole shareholder, G. G paid $25,000 for his stock three years ago.

**a.** How will G treat the $40,000 he received on December 31?

**b.** Assume G sold all of his stock for $36,000 on January 1 of the following year. Compute his capital gain.

**6-21** *Investments—Interest.* Mr. K died at the beginning of the year. Mrs. K received interest during the year from the following sources:

| | |
|---|---|
| Corporate bonds | $1,100 |
| Bank savings account | 200 |
| Personal loan to a friend | 500 |
| City of Maryville bonds (issued to build a new high school) | 600 |

In addition to the above, Mrs. K was the beneficiary of her husband's $50,000 life insurance policy. She elected to receive the $50,000 proceeds plus interest over the next 10 years. She receives $7,500 in the current year and will receive a like amount each of the following nine years. Calculate the taxable portion of the interest income received by Mrs. K during the year.

**6-22** *Educational Savings Bonds Requirements.* H and W have twin sons, S and T, and two daughters, D and E. The couple purchased Series EE savings bonds, hoping to take advantage of the interest exclusion for their children's education. This year, they cashed in some of the bonds, receiving \$5,000. Of this amount, \$2,000 represented interest. For each of the following independent situations, indicate how much, if any, of the exclusion is allowed this year.

**a.** D enrolled at Michigan State University and paid tuition of \$4,000. To help defray some of these expenses, she used an academic scholarship of \$1,000.

**b.** While on her way to the first day of class, D fell and broke her leg. She withdrew from classes and received all of her money back.

**c.** S is 25 and entered the Ph.D. program at the University of Texas this year. As a teaching assistant, he receives a salary of \$7,000 during the year. His parents paid \$1,000 of his tuition.

**d.** H and W paid for all of T's tuition to attend Arizona State University. The couple's A.G.I. for this year was \$110,000. When the couple purchased the particular bonds used to pay for T's tuition, their A.G.I. was \$55,000.

**e.** E, 22, redeemed bonds this year, receiving \$5,000. E used all of the proceeds to pay for her tuition. She received the bonds as a gift from her parents last year. E's A.G.I. for this year is \$3,000.

**6-23** *Investments—Annuities.* P is single, 65 years old, and retired. On August 1, 2000 he purchased a single-premium deferred life annuity for \$40,000 using after-tax funds. This year, P received \$5,000 in annuity benefits. He will receive a like amount each year for the rest of his life. (**Note:** In answering the following questions, use the information in Exhibit 6-3 of this chapter.)

**a.** Calculate P's taxable income from the annuity for the current year.

**b.** Calculate P's taxable income from the annuity for year 5.

**c.** Calculate P's taxable income from the annuity for year 22.

**d.** Assume P lives just 15 more years. Calculate the deduction that would be allowed on P's final tax return.

**e.** Assume the annuity was purchased by P and his employer jointly. P contributed \$12,000 in after-tax funds, and the employer contributed \$28,000. Calculate P's taxable income from the annuity for the current year.

**6-24** *Annuities.* A, age 62, retired after 30 years of service as an employee of the XYZ Corporation. He started receiving retirement benefits in the form of a single life annuity on January 1 of the current year. A's total after-tax contributions to the plan amounted to \$39,000, and his retirement benefit is \$1,500 per month.

**a.** Determine A's nontaxable portion of each monthly payment, assuming he elects the simplified safe-harbor method.

**b.** Assume A lives another 25 years. Will there be a time period in which A will be required to fully include the monthly payments in gross income? If so, when?

**6-25** *529 Savings Plan.* Z is a dependent beneficiary of a 529 savings plan established by her parents. During the current year, Z received a \$20,000 distribution and used it to pay \$20,000 for tuition at a private university. Z's parents contributed \$60,000 to the plan and earnings from investments total an additional \$20,000.

**a.** How much of the \$20,000 distribution may Z exclude from gross income?

**b.** Assume Z elects to join the work force rather than attend college and the entire \$80,000 accumulated in the plan is distributed to Z's parents. How much is included in the parent's gross income?

**6-26** *529 College Savings Plan.* V, who is divorced, transfers \$45,000 to Eastern University's 529 savings plan for the benefit of his son, W, in 2011. W received no other gifts during 2011.

**a.** Compute V's taxable gift for 2011 (assume no election was made).

**b.** Assume V elects to treat the contribution as a gift made over five years. Does V owe any gift taxes?

**c.** Assume V dies in 2014. How much of the \$45,000 contribution made in 2011 will be included in V's gross estate?

**6-27** *Investments—Life Insurance.* L is 65 years old and retired. Her husband died early in the year. L was the beneficiary of his $20,000 life insurance policy. L elected to receive $5,200 annually for five years rather than receive a single payment of $20,000 immediately. Calculate L's taxable income from the first payment.

**6-28** *Social Security Benefits.* X, who is single and retired, has the following income for the current year:

| | |
|---|---|
| Taxable interest | $12,000 |
| Dividend income | 10,000 |
| Tax-exempt bond interest | 8,000 |
| Social security benefits | 7,200 |

**a.** Compute the taxable portion of X's social security benefits.

**b.** Assume the above information remains the same, except X's taxable interest amounted to $10,000. Compute the taxable portion of his social security benefits.

**6-29** *Group-Term Life Insurance.* E, age 55, is Vice President of QRS, Incorporated. His salary for the year amounted to $75,000. Employees at QRS receive group-term life insurance coverage equal to twice their annual salaries. Determine E's taxable income from his group-term life insurance protection for the year.

**6-30** *Employee Benefits.* Determine the (1) deductible employer amount, and (2) taxable employee amount for each of the following employer-provided benefits.

**a.** Reimbursement of expenses paid by an employee to entertain a client of the business, $200.

**b.** Bonus paid an employee when a sales quota was met, $300.

**c.** Watches given employees at Christmas, $18 each.

**d.** The company provides free parking on its premises for its employees. The fair value of this parking is $500 per month, as evidenced by the fact that a commercial parking lot located across the street from the company's property charges $500 per month to park in its lot.

**e.** Supper money of $15 paid to an employee for each of 10 nights that she worked past 6 p.m., $150.

**6-31** *Employee Benefits.* Determine the (1) deductible employer amount, and (2) taxable employee amount for each of the following employer-provided benefits.

**a.** Premiums of $700 paid on $70,000 of group-term life insurance for a 52-year-old woman employee.

**b.** Ten percent employee discounts are allowed on the retail price of all merchandise purchased from the employer. During the year, sales to employees totaled $18,000 ($20,000 retail price − $2,000 discount) for merchandise that cost the employer $14,000. The employer reported the $18,000 as sales and the $14,000 as cost of goods sold.

**c.** The employer company reimburses employees who use public transportation, such as a bus or train, to get to work. The maximum amount the company is willing to reimburse an employee for this expense is $200 per month.

**6-32** *Employee Benefits—Medical Insurance.* F's $400 annual health insurance premium is paid by his employer. During the year, F received $870 reimbursement of medical expenses; $650 for this year's expenses and $220 for last year's expenses. Determine F's taxable income from the reimbursement in the current year if

**a.** F never itemizes any medical expenses.

**b.** F deducted medical expenses from his A.G.I. this year of $900 and last year of $450.

**6-33** *Tax Benefit Rule.* During 2010 K had adjusted gross income of $30,000. A list of itemized deductions available to K in preparing her 2010 return is shown below:

| | |
|---|---|
| State income taxes paid | $2,000 |
| Property taxes on residence | 600 |
| Charitable contributions | 400 |
| Medical expenses | 2,500 |
| Interest paid on residence | 1,200 |

K is single, and her son M, who is 8 years old, lives with her. She qualifies as a head of household. In 2011 K received $2,500 from an insurance company for reimbursement of her 2010 medical expenses. Is K required to include any of the $2,500 reimbursement in her gross income in 2011?

**6-34** *Fringe Benefits versus Compensation.* P is a 46-year-old professor at Z University, a private school in the Midwest. P is married and has triplets who are freshmen at Z University. Among others, P is provided with the following fringe benefits during the current year:

Group-term life insurance coverage of $75,000. Premium cost to Z University is $300.
Tuition reduction of $30,000 for the triplets.

**a.** How much does the group-term life insurance cost Professor P? Assume his marginal tax bracket is 31 percent.
**b.** Would P be equally well off if the university simply paid him an additional $300 in compensation to cover the term insurance?
**c.** Is the tuition reduction for the triplets taxable?
**d.** Assuming tuition remains constant, how much will Professor P save in tuition payments by remaining on the faculty at Z University until the triplets graduate?
**e.** What would be the result for the current year if the university increased Professor P's salary by $30,000 a year to pay for the triplets' tuition?

**6-35** *Unemployment Compensation and Disability Income.* Mr. and Mrs. B are married filing jointly. Mrs. B was permanently disabled the entire year and Mr. B was unemployed part of the year. Both are 55 years old. Their receipts for the year were

| | |
|---|---|
| Disability income—Mrs. B | $ 6,200 |
| Social security income—Mrs. B. | 1,000 |
| Salary—Mr. B. | 16,500 |
| Unemployment compensation—Mr. B | 4,500 |

Calculate their taxable income for the year, assuming the disability insurance premiums were paid
**a.** Entirely by Mrs. B.
**b.** Entirely by Mrs. B's employer.

**6-36** *Damages Awarded and Disability Income.* D works for the XYZ Tool and Die Shop. On March 1, 2011 a stamping press that D was operating malfunctioned, resulting in the loss of the index finger on his right hand. D, claiming the machine was not properly maintained, sued XYZ for the following damages:

| | |
|---|---|
| Medical expenses during D's one-week stay in the hospital | $ 8,000 |
| Loss of D's finger | 50,000 |
| Punitive damages | 5,000 |
| Total | $63,000 |

On April 1, 2012 the court awarded D $63,000.
**a.** Assuming D did not deduct the $8,000 of medical expenses he incurred in 2011, what portion of the $63,000 settlement is included in D's gross income in 2012?
**b.** D did not return to work for three months. During this time period, he received $3,000 in disability income payments. Assuming D paid the annual premium on the disability insurance, how much of the $3,000 is taxable income to D?

**6-37** *Meals and Lodging.* Mr. and Mrs. G own and operate a small motel near Big Mountain resort area. Their only employees are two maids and one cook. The rest of the work is done by Mr. and Mrs. G. In order to be on 24-hour call, they live in a home next to the motel. The home is owned by the business. Both Mr. and Mrs. G eat most of their meals in the motel restaurant. Answer the questions below assuming the business is (1) a corporation, or (2) a partnership.

**a.** Are any of the costs for the meals and lodging deductible by either the business or Mr. and Mrs. G?

**b.** Is the value of the meals and lodging included in Mr. and Mrs. G's gross income?

**c.** Answer the questions in (a) and (b) again, but assume Mr. and Mrs. G paid the business for all their meals in the restaurant and for rent of the home.

**6-38** *Adoption Assistance.* R and L are married and file a joint return. R is the controller of a tool and die firm and is paid a salary of $140,000. L is a grade school teacher and earns $27,500. Other income received during the current year includes $1,000 in interest on State of Indiana bonds owned by R and $2,500 in dividends on Procter & Gamble stock that L owns. R and L, who have no children of their own, incurred $9,000 in qualified adoption expenses (i.e, adoption fees, attorney fees and court costs) to adopt a 2-year-old "special needs" child. These expenses were covered by R's employer under the company's adoption assistance program.

**a.** Determine R and L's A.G.I. for the current year.

**b.** Assuming the couple elects the standard deduction, compute their taxable income for the current year.

**6-39** *Transportation Fringes.* How much is includible in the employee's gross income in each of the following scenarios?

**a.** Employee A receives a transit pass each month from Employer X valued at $95.

**b.** Employer Y provides free parking each month to employee B valued at $300.

**c.** Employer Z provides parking each month to employee C valued at $250. Employee C pays Employer Z $40 per month for this parking fringe.

**d.** Employer Q reimburses employee R $15 a month for storage of his bike while at work.

**6-40** *Employer-Provided Parking.* Employer G operates a factory in a rural area in which no commercial parking is available. G provides ample parking for its employees on the business premises, free of charge.

**a.** What guidance does the Internal Revenue Service provide for determining the value of free parking?

**b.** Given the facts presented above, what value would the IRS place on the free parking provided by Employer G?

**6-41** *Military Compensation.* After graduating from high school last year, K, who is single, joined the U.S. Air Force. Her military compensation for 2011 is

| | Cash | Market Value |
|---|---|---|
| Salary | $50,000 | |
| Military housing | | $2,500 |
| Computer training on the job | | 1,800 |
| Uniforms | | 800 |
| Meals on the base | | 3,600 |
| Reimbursement of moving expenses | 500 | |

Calculate K's taxable income for the year.

**6-42** *Inheritances.* In each of the following independent situations. determine how much, if any, the taxpayer must include in gross income.

**a.** At the beginning of this year, a taxpayer inherited rental property valued at $87,000 from his grandmother. Rental income from the property after the transfer of title totaled $6,000, and rental expenses were $5,200.

**b.** A taxpayer inherited $50,000 from her employer. She was his housekeeper for ten years and was promised she would be provided for in his will if she continued employment with him until his death.

**c.** A taxpayer lent $15,000 to a friend. To protect the loan, the taxpayer had his friend make him beneficiary on her $20,000 life insurance policy. Six months later the friend died and the taxpayer received $20,000 from the insurance company.

**6-43** *Gifts.* In each of the following independent situations, determine how much, if any, the taxpayer must include in gross income.

**a.** A taxpayer often visits her uncle in a nursing home. In addition, she manages his investment portfolio for him. To show his gratitude, he has given her stock valued at $5,000. He has also implied that if she continues these activities, he will transfer other shares of stock to her.

**b.** A taxpayer saved a child's life during a fire. The child's parents gave him land valued at $5,000 to show their gratitude. They paid $2,200 for the land several years ago.

**c.** Taxpayer's employer gave him $1,200 in recognition of his 20 years of service to the company. The employer deducted the $1,200 as a business expense.

**6-44** *Awards.* In each of the following independent situations, determine how much, if any, the taxpayer must include in gross income.

**a.** The taxpayer, a professional basketball player, was voted as the outstanding player of the year. In addition to the honor, he received an automobile with a sticker price of $16,000. He drove the car for six months and sold it for $12,000. The taxpayer's employer also gave him a gold watch worth $1,200. He wears the watch. Both donors deducted their respective costs for the automobile and the watch as business expenses. The costs of the automobile and watch were $13,500 and $800, respectively.

**b.** The taxpayer was selected by the senior class as the most outstanding classroom teacher. The high school presented her with a $1,000 check in recognition of her significant accomplishments. She used the money to take a well-earned vacation to Cancun.

**c.** M, Inc. gave T a watch in recognition of her 20 years of service to the company. The watch cost the employer $400.

**6-45** *Child Support and Alimony.* Determine the effect on A.G.I. for the husband (H) and wife (W) in each of the following *continuous* situations. H and W are divorced and do not live in a community property state. They have three children.

**a.** H pays W $400 per month as alimony and support of the three children.

**b.** W discovers her attorney did not word the agreement correctly. H and W sign a statement that the *original* agreement is retroactively amended to hold that H pays $100 per month as alimony to W and $300 per month as support of the three children. All other language remains unchanged. What is the effect of this change on future and past payments?

**c.** Assume the original agreement contained the wording in (b) above. In the first year, H makes only 10 of the 12 payments for a total of $4,000. In the second year, H pays the $800 balance due for the prior year and makes all 12 payments of $400 each on time.

**d.** On their divorce, W was awarded an automobile. H is required to pay the loan outstanding on the car, $94 per month for 20 months. During the year, H pays $94 for 12 months. This includes $130 interest and $998 loan principal.

**e.** H owns the home in which W and the children live free of charge. H's mortgage payments are $360 per month for the next 20 years. During the year, his expenses on the home are $2,900 interest, $800 property taxes, $340 insurance, $280 loan principal, and $218 repairs. The rental value of the home is $425 per month.

**f.** In addition to the monthly alimony and support payments above, H is to pay W $30,000 over a period of 11 years. H pays $2,500 of this amount the first year and $3,600 the second year.

**g.** H inherits considerable property. As a result, he voluntarily increases the alimony to $150 and child support to $450 per month. He makes 12 payments of $600 each during the year.

**6-46** *Alimony.* Determine the effect on A.G.I. for the husband (H) and wife (W) in each of the three years. W is to pay H alimony of $100,000 as follows:

| Year | Amount |
|---|---|
| 1. | $56,000 |
| 2. | 26,000 |
| 3. | 18,000 |

**6-47** *Divorce—Property Settlement.* Husband (H) and wife (W) are divorced this month. The divorce agreement states that all jointly owned property will be transferred as follows:

| | Cost | Market Value | Transferred to |
|---|---|---|---|
| Home | $35,000 | $65,000 | W |
| Investments | 3,000 | 5,000 | W |
| Cash | 7,000 | 7,000 | H and W equally |

W will occupy the home and H will rent an apartment. Determine the recognized gain or loss and the basis of the assets to H and W after the transfer. Explain.

**6-48** *Divorce—Property Settlement.* H and W, who live in Michigan (a common law state), decided to end their troubled 30-year marriage. Pursuant to the divorce decree, the following assets are transferred from H to W on March 1, 2011:

| | Basis to H | Market Value |
|---|---|---|
| Stocks (purchased by H on April 10, 2005) | $300,000 | $400,000 |
| Land (purchased by H on June 2, 2002) | 200,000 | 500,000 |

In addition to the above, H transferred a life insurance policy on his life with a face value of $200,000 to W, who assumed responsibility for the annual premium.
W sold the stocks for $500,000 on November 1, 2011 and the land for $550,000 on December 1, 2011. H died on December 20, 2011.

**a.** Determine W's gain on the sale of the stocks and land in 2011.

**b.** Are any of the life insurance proceeds taxable to W? Explain.

**6-49** *Accelerated Death Benefits.* T, a wife and mother of three, was diagnosed with throat cancer. Due to the complications from chemotherapy treatments, she resigned from her teaching position at a private university in Chicago on June 1. Having been certified by her medical doctor on July 7 as terminally ill, T is considering selling her life insurance policy with a face value of $200,000 to a viatical "settlement provider" (VSP) for a lump sum.

**a.** Assuming T has paid $15,000 in premiums, how much must she include in her gross income if she sells her policy to VSP for $150,000 on August 1?

**b.** Does your answer change if T lives longer than 24 months from the date of certification?

**c.** If T dies 8 months later, how much must VSP include in its gross income? (Assume VSP paid additional premiums of $10,000 after purchasing the policy.)

**6-50** *Employee Fringe Benefits.* For each of the following independent situations, indicate whether the fringe benefit the employee receives is taxable or nontaxable. Explain your answer.

**a.** C is a ticket agent for North Central Airways. The airline has a nondiscriminatory policy that allows its employees to fly without charge on a standby basis only. The last week in July, C took a vacation and flew from Kansas City to San Francisco. The value of the round-trip ticket was $400.

**b.** Assume that C [in part (a) above] also stayed, without charge, for the entire week at a hotel in San Francisco that North Central Airways owns. The value of a week's stay in the hotel was $2,000.

**c.** Assume in part (a) above that C was unable to obtain an empty seat on North Central the last week in July. Consequently, utilizing the qualified reciprocal arrangement that North Central has with South Shore Airlines, C flew free to San Francisco on South Shore. The value of the round-trip ticket was $400.

**d.** M is a sales clerk for J-mart department store. The store has a nondiscriminatory policy whereby its employees may purchase inventory items at a discount. In June,

M purchased a microwave oven for $250 that J-mart sells to its customers for $300. J-mart's gross profit rate is 20 percent.

e. F is a CPA and works for a public accounting firm. On F's behalf, the firm paid $375 in subscription fees for three professional accounting journals.

f. Officers of the XYZ Corporation are provided free parking space in a public parking garage located across the street from the firm's office building. The monthly cost of the parking space to XYZ is $300 for each officer.

**6-51** *Unrelated Party Transfers.* In each of the following independent situations, determine how much, if any, the taxpayer must include in gross income.

a. Taxpayer has been very active as a volunteer hospital worker for many years. In the current year, the city named her as the Outstanding Volunteer of the Year. She later discovered that she was nominated for the award by two nurses at the hospital. The honor included a silver tray valued at $400. In addition, the two nurses collected $700 from hospital personnel and gave her a prepaid one-week vacation for two people.

b. Taxpayer, an undergraduate degree candidate, was selected as one of five outstanding sophomore students in accounting by the Institute of Management Accountants. Selection was based on an application submitted by eligible students. The winner received $15,000. Although there was no stipulation of how the money was to be used, the award was given with the expectation that the money would be used for tuition, books, and fees in the student's junior and senior years.

c. Taxpayer won the bowling league award for the highest total score over a five-week period. Taxpayer received a trophy valued at $65 and $100 cash.

d. Taxpayer purchased church raffle tickets in her eight-year-old son's name and gave the tickets to him. One of the tickets was drawn. The prize was a $600 color television.

e. Taxpayer receives a $20,000 grant from the National Association of Chiefs of Police to conduct a research study on crowd control. The grant stipulates that the research period is for eight months and that $8,000 of it is for travel and temporary living costs.

f. An accounting student accepted an internship with a CPA firm and is paid $3,000. The stated purpose of the internship is to provide students with a basic understanding of how accounting education is applied. It is believed this understanding will help students in remaining course work and later job selection. Although the faculty believes internships would benefit all students, only 40 percent of the accounting majors participate in the program.

**6-52** *Businesses.* In each of the following independent situations, determine how much, if any, the taxpayer must include in gross income.

a. A taxpayer sold a beauty shop operated as a proprietorship for $60,000. The assets were valued as follows: tangible assets, $45,000; agreement not to compete, $10,000; and goodwill, $5,000. The seller's basis for the tangible assets is $45,000 but there is no basis for the other two assets.

b. The building in which a drug store is located is damaged by fire. The store had to be closed for two weeks while repairs were made. As a result, the insurance company paid the store $50,000 for lost profits during the period and $15,000 to cover overhead expenses.

c. E, Inc. leases land to V, Inc. The agreement states that the lease period is for five years and the annual lease payment is $1,000 per month. Under the terms of the lease, V immediately constructs a storage building on the land for $40,000. E receives $12,000 from V each year for three years. At the end of the third year, V cancels the lease and pays a cancellation penalty of $6,000. At this time, the building's market value is $30,000. Thus, in the third year, E received $18,000 cash and a building worth an additional $30,000. Determine E's taxable income from the lease for each of the three years.

d. A corporation accepted $100,000 from an insurance company as an out-of-court settlement of a lawsuit for patent infringement.

**6-53** *Debt Cancellation.* DEF, Inc. is in the van conversion business. Due to stiff competition and a declining economy in the region served by DEF, the company has incurred significant operating losses during the past year. As of December 31 of the current year, DEF's financial statements reflect the following pertinent information:

| | |
|---|---|
| Total assets | $ 750,000 |
| Total liabilities | 1,000,000 |
| Tax attributes | |
| Adjusted basis of depreciable assets | 300,000 |
| NOL carryover | 100,000 |
| Capital loss carryover | 25,000 |

In an attempt to rescue the company from going out of business, DEF's suppliers have agreed to forgive $180,000 of indebtedness.

**a.** Assuming DEF is not in bankruptcy proceedings, what are the tax consequences to the corporation resulting from the cancellation of the debt?

**b.** Would your answer to part (a) change if DEF makes an election under Code § 108(b)(5)?

**c.** Would your answer to part (a) change if the $180,000 of debt is cancelled under bankruptcy proceedings?

**d.** Assume that the facts in the problem remain the same, except that DEF has total assets of $1 million and total liabilities of $750,000. What impact does the cancellation of $180,000 in debt now have on DEF?

**6-54** *Debt Cancellation: Principal Residence.* Five years ago, J and his wife decided that it was time to quit renting and buy a new home. They had little cash. Nevertheless they shopped around and found the perfect home. Although it was beyond their price range, they could afford it by virtue of an ultra low-interest rate. Thus they bought the home for $110,000, paying $10,000 down and financing the remaining $100,000 with an adjustable rate mortgage. This year the rate was adjusted in accordance with the terms of the agreement. As a result, J was no longer able to make his mortgage payments. J considered refinancing to get a lower fixed rate but this was not an option. There was a steep penalty for refinancing. Moreover, the value of the home had actually dropped and no one was willing to refinance a mortgage that was more than the value of their home. Fortunately, the bank did not want to become the owner of the home given the current market and agreed to reduce the debt to $90,000. What are the tax consequences to J?

**6-55** *Miscellaneous Items.* In each of the following independent situations, determine how much, if any, the taxpayer must include in gross income.

**a.** A taxpayer's round trip mileage to and from work is 50 miles. Five fellow employees live near him and pay to ride with him. The taxpayer's records for the current year show $3,900 receipts and $3,120 automobile expenses.

**b.** While walking across campus, a taxpayer found a diamond ring. She notified the authorities on campus and paid $10 for an ad in the lost-and-found section of the newspaper. When six weeks went by with no response, she had the ring appraised. It was valued at $1,200. After six more weeks with no response, she sold the ring for $850.

**c.** A taxpayer was injured on the job and was out of work for most of the year. He received the following government benefits during the year: $800 in food stamps; $1,500 worker's compensation for the injury; and $1,800 in welfare payments.

**d.** A taxpayer sued her neighbor for malicious slander. The court awarded her $30,000 for personal injury due to indignities suffered as a result of the slander; $3,500 in lost income; and $200 reimbursement for medical expenses incurred. The taxpayer does not itemize deductions.

**6-56** *Ordinary v. Capital Gain Income.* In each of the following scenarios, determine the amount (if any) and type of income to be included in gross income by the recipient:

**a.** Denise acquired all of the net assets of Mary's CPA firm. Mary operated the practice as a sole proprietorship. The purchase price includes $20,000 allocable to goodwill and $15,000 allocable to a covenant not to compete for five years.

**b.** Ernie rents an apartment from Doug. Because Ernie is being transferred to another city by his employer, he paid Doug $800 to cancel his lease.

c. Mary Ann owns an apartment complex in Jacksonville, Florida. In an effort to convert the apartment into an office building, she pays Jean, one of her tenants, $900 to cancel the apartment lease.

d. John, who is single and lives in Detroit, had total itemized deductions in 2010 of $6,000 including $700 of state income taxes withheld by his employer. John could have deducted state and local sales taxes of $600. On May 14, 2011, John received a refund from the State of Michigan for $200 due to overpaying his Michigan income taxes in 2010.

**6-57** *Miscellaneous Fringe Benefits.* In each of the following independent situations answer true if the ending sentence is correct and false if the ending sentence is incorrect.

a. During the current year, A withdraws $2,000 from a qualified tuition plan to pay his undergraduate tuition at Ivy Tech. Of the $2,000 received, $1,600 represents contributions to the plan and $400 represents earnings. *The $400 of earnings is excluded from A's income.*

b. B is employed at the Tire Rack Company. She works the day shift and her two children, ages 3 and 4, stay at the company's day care facility. The current year's value of this service is approximately $4,000. *B may exclude the full $4,000 from income.*

c. C works for Ever Green, Inc. During the evenings C attends State University where she is working on her undergraduate degree in Marketing. During the current year Ever Green paid C's tuition ($3,000) and her textbooks ($800) out of the company's nondiscriminatory educational assistance program. *C may exclude the full $3,800 from income.*

d. D is an employee of Night Line, Inc. where he is covered under the company's qualified pension plan. During the current year D, who is 64 years old, and his wife attended several seminars related to retirement planning that were sponsored by Night Line. The value of this service is approximately $1,500. *The $1,500 will be reported on D's Form W-2 as taxable income.*

## TAX RETURN PROBLEMS

• *CONTINUOUS TAX RETURN PROBLEMS* See Appendix I, Part 1.

## CUMULATIVE PROBLEMS

**6-58** H, age 45, and W, age 43, are married with two dependent children: M, age 18, and N, age 19. Both are full-time students at a local university. H, who is president of a local bank, is paid a salary of $150,000. He also is the sole proprietor of a jewelry store that had a net profit for 2010 of $75,000. W, a registered nurse at a large hospital, is paid a salary of $50,000. In addition to the above income, H and W received the following during 2010:

a. $3,000 cash dividend on ABC, Inc. stock, which they own jointly. They paid $25,000 for the stock three years ago and it has a current market value of $40,000. ABC, Inc. has $300,000 of current and accumulated E&P.

b. $750 in interest on State of Michigan bonds that H owns.

c. $7,000 in interest on corporate bonds that H and W purchased two years ago at face value for $100,000.

d. W received a check for $400 from her employer in recognition of her outstanding service to the hospital during the past 10 years.

e. The bank provides H with $90,000 of group term life insurance protection. The bank provides all full-time employees with group term insurance.

f. 1,000 shares of XYZ common as a stock dividend. Prior to the distribution, H and W owned 9,000 shares of common with a basis of $15,000. H and W did not have the right to receive cash or other assets in lieu of the stock.

g. Because W must be available should an emergency arise, she is required to eat her lunches in the hospital cafeteria. The value of the free meals provided by her employer during 2010 was $1,100.

h. H's grandfather passed away in February 2010, leaving H a 400-acre farm in southern Illinois valued at $500,000. H rented the land to F, a neighboring farmer, for $13,000.

i. In order to drain off the excess surface water from 10 acres, F (see h above) installed drainage pipe at a cost of $1,500.

**j.** W sold 50 shares of DEF stock for $100 per share. She bought the stock four years ago for $1,800.

**k.** H received a dividend check for $280 from the MNO Mutual Life Insurance Company. H purchased the policy in 1984, and W is the primary beneficiary.

**l.** H and W's only itemized deductions were interest on their home mortgage, $18,000; property taxes on their home, $4,000; and charitable contributions, $6,000.

**m.** The hospital withheld $11,000 of Federal income taxes on W's salary and the appropriate amount of FICA taxes. The bank withheld $30,000 in Federal income taxes from H's salary and the appropriate amount of FICA taxes. Furthermore, H's quarterly estimated tax payments for 2010 total $35,000.

*Part I: Computation of Federal Income Tax.* Calculate H and W's 2010 Federal income tax liability (or refund) assuming they file a joint return.

Part II: Tax Planning Ideas. H and W are very concerned about the amount of Federal income tax they now pay. Because they want to send M and N on to graduate school, they have come up with the following strategies, which they hope will reduce their family's total tax liability.

**1.** In 2011 M and N will begin working at the jewelry store two nights a week and on Saturdays throughout the school year and 20 hours a week during the summer months. Each child will be paid $4,500 for services during the year.

**2.** On January 1, 2011 H and W will sell their corporate bonds for $100,000 and invest the cash proceeds in Series EE savings bonds. H and W will use the bonds to pay for M and N's qualified educational expenses.

**3.** On January 1, 2011 H and W will gift their stock in ABC, Inc. to M and N equally.

**4.** Beginning in 2011 H will instruct the farmer who is leasing his Illinois farm to pay the $13,000 in rent directly to M and N (i.e., $6,500 each).

H and W have asked for your opinion concerning the above strategies. For each idea, explain why it will or will not reduce the family's total tax liability. Assuming H and W implement only the strategies that will reduce taxes, how much will the family save in taxes in 2011 compared to 2010 (**Note:** Calculate the 2011 tax using the tax law and rates applicable to 2010 and assume all other data from Part I above is the same.)

**6-59** A and B are married with two children, ages 15 and 16. A, who is 45 years old, is president of Greenville Savings & Loan (a large financial institution located in Greenville, Michigan). During 2010 his salary amounted to $400,000. Additional information pertaining to A and B's financial affairs for 2010 is summarized below:

**a.** A and B purchased 1,000 shares of GHI, Inc. common stock on January 1, 2010 for $22,000. On May 1, 2010 A and B received 100 shares of GHI, Inc. common as a stock dividend. They did not have the right to receive cash or other assets in lieu of the stock.

**b.** On November 15, 2009 A and B purchased a small farm (50 acres) five miles from Greenville for $50,000. Although A and B originally planned to move to the farm when A retires, they ended up selling it on October 20, 2010 to a large real estate developer for $200.000.

**c.** On August 1, 2010 A and B redeemed Series EE bonds that had matured for $30,000. They originally purchased the bonds for $14,000. During the period they held the bonds, A and B never elected to include in income the annual increase in the redemption price.

**d.** B's father passed away on September 1, 2010. She inherited $100,000, which they deposited in a savings account at the Greenville Savings & Loan. The interest on the deposit amounted to $2,000 for the year.

**e.** Greenville Savings & Loan provided A with the following benefit package:

| *Fringe Benefit* | *Annual Cost to Greenville S & L* |
|---|---|
| Health insurance premium | $2,400 |
| Accident and disability premium | 600 |
| Parking space | 190 |
| Group-term life insurance of $150,000 | 800 |

**f.** A and B's only itemized deductions were mortgage interest on their personal residence, $40,000; state and local taxes, $30,000; and charitable contributions, $8,000.

**g.** The Greenville Savings & Loan withheld $100,000 of Federal income taxes on A's salary and the appropriate amount of payroll taxes. In addition, A's quarterly estimated tax payments for 2010 total $40,000.

*Part I: Calculation of Taxable Income and Tax Due.* Compute A and B's taxable income and Federal income tax liability for 2010 assuming they file a joint return.

*Part II: Tax Planning Suggestions.* Assume that A and B come to you on July 1, 2010 seeking your advice on ways in which they can reduce their 2010 Federal income tax liability. They provide you with the following additional information:

1. The real estate developer, who is interested in acquiring A and B's 50 acres, is willing to defer the purchase date to June 16, 2011. What would you recommend A and B do? Explain your answer.
2. A and B would like to get the best return possible on the money they will receive from the sale of their farm. Two options they are considering are (1) invest the proceeds in corporate bonds paying 7% annually and (2) purchase State of Michigan bonds paying 5 1/2% annually. What would you recommend A and B do? Explain your answer.
3. A and B have been informed that the Series EE bonds that mature on August 1, 2010 can be exchanged for Series HH bonds that pay interest semiannually. What would you recommend A and B do? Explain your answer.

## TAX RESEARCH PROBLEMS

**6-60** *Divorce.* J and M are obtaining a divorce after ten years of marriage. They have two children. A draft of the divorce agreement and property settlement between them states that they will have joint custody of the children. They plan to live in the same general area and each child will live half of each year with each parent. Since J's A.G. I. is $40,000 and M's $15,000, he will pay her $100 per month for each child ($2,400 per year) and $500 per month for her support. The $500 ceases on his or her death, her remarriage, or when her A.G.I. equals his. In addition, J agrees to continue to pay premiums of $50 per month on his life insurance policy payable to her. All jointly owned property will be distributed as follows:

| | *Basis* | *Market Value* | *Transfer to* |
|---|---|---|---|
| Home | $50,000 | $80,000 | M |
| Furnishings | 20,000 | 15,000 | M |
| Investments | 10,000 | 30,000 | J |

Each will keep his or her individually owned personal items and an automobile. This is an amicable divorce and they both request your advice. Their objective is to maximize total tax benefits without making too many changes to the agreement. Use tax-planning techniques when possible in responding to the following questions.

**a.** Who will be able to claim the children as dependents?

**b.** What is each one's filing status for the current year if neither one remarries?

**c.** Does the $500 per month qualify as alimony? Does the $50 per month qualify as alimony?

**d.** J expects to make the $500 and $50 payments for three months while legally separated before the divorce. What are the tax effects during this period?

**e.** What is the tax effect of the distribution of jointly owned property to J and to M?

**f.** What tax planning advice could you give to J and M that would decrease their combined tax liability?

**6-61** *Meals and Lodging.* H and W are married with three children. The children are 8, 10, and 15 years old. H and W are purchasing a 500-acre farm, which they will manage and operate themselves. In addition, they will employ one full-time farmer year round and several part-time people at peak times. H will be responsible primarily for management of the operations, the crops, and the dairy herd and other farm animals. W will be responsible primarily for the garden, the chickens, providing meals for the family and farm hands, and maintaining the family home. The children are assigned farm chores to help their parents after school and on weekends.

The taxpayers prefer to operate the farm as a partnership but, after all factors are considered, are willing to incorporate the farm if it seems to provide greater benefits. Presently, they ask for detailed information about the residence on the farm and the groceries that will be purchased to feed them and their employees on the farm. Some of their specific questions are listed below.

**a.** What are the benefits and requirements covering meals and lodging provided by the business?

**b.** Is it possible to meet the requirements and obtain all or at least some of the benefits if the farm is operated as a proprietorship or partnership, or must it be operated as a corporation?

**c.** If full benefits are obtained, are any adjustments required for the children, for personal entertainment and meals shared with friends and relatives in the farm home, or any other personal use? If any adjustments are required, which ones, and are they made at cost or market value?

**d.** If full benefits are obtained, exactly what qualifies? For example, do all groceries qualify, including supplies that are not eaten, such as freezer bags to store frozen foods from the garden, soap, and bathroom supplies? Do all expenses for the home qualify, such as utilities, insurance, and repairs?

**e.** Should the business or should H and W own the home?

**f.** Is it acceptable for H and W to purchase the food and be reimbursed by the business?

**6-62** *Discharge of Indebtedness.* T, who is single, purchased a new home in 1979 from the XYZ Construction Co. for $55,000. She received a 7.25 percent mortgage from the Federal Savings and Loan Association (FS&L). Currently, the home's fair market value is approximately double its original purchase price. Since interest rates have risen significantly in recent months, FS&L wants to rid itself of the low 7.25 percent mortgage. Lending to others at a much higher interest rate would clearly enhance FS&L's profits. Consequently, during the current year FS&L sent a letter to T offering to cancel the mortgage (which had a remaining principal balance of $35,000) in return for a payment of $29,000. T took advantage of the prepayment opportunity, thus receiving a discount equal to the difference between the remaining principal balance of $35,000 and the amount paid by T of $29,000, or $6,000.

**a.** Although T is pleased she no longer has a monthly mortgage payment, she is concerned about the possible tax consequences resulting from the discharge of indebtedness. T has come to you for your advice.

**b.** Assume that the fair market value of T's residence has declined to $25,000 due to the construction of a nearby land fill operation. Does this fact change your answer?

**6-63** *Compensatory Damages.* T. J. Taxpayer, CLU, has owned an insurance agency in Santa Rosa, California since 1980. As an independent agent, he represented five companies selling auto, home, commercial, and life insurance. Because of his excellent reputation in the community, T. J. has built a very successful agency. Last year, T. J. applied for an agency license from the American Life Insurance Co. in order to broaden his life insurance business. In reviewing his application, American requested a credit report from Federal Credit. Federal Credit provided copies to American Life as well as other insurance companies.

The credit report contained numerous false accusations. In addition to questioning Taxpayer's integrity, the report stated that T. J. seldom returned phone calls from clients and lacked understanding of basic insurance practices and concepts. As a result, American Life denied T. J. a license to sell its life insurance. Because the report adversely affected his ability to work with existing clients and to attract new business, T. J.'s profits declined considerably.

T. J. sued Federal Credit for libel, claiming that the credit report was issued with intent to damage his business or professional reputation. The jury found that Federal Credit had committed libel and awarded him \$100,000 in compensatory damages. T. J. has heard conflicting comments from various sources about whether the \$100,000 is taxable and comes to you for help. What advice would you give T. J. Taxpayer concerning the taxability of the \$100,000?

**6-64** *Sex Discrimination.* Alice Johnson has worked for the AMAX Corporation for ten years. In March 2009, after talking with various company employees, Alice came to the realization that there was a significant pay differential between men and women. In fact, she discovered that the corporation had modified its compensation package in 2008 whereby the salaries of employees in certain male-dominated pay schedules were increased but those in certain female-dominated pay schedules were either unchanged or reduced.

As a result, Alice Johnson brought suit (under Title VII of the Civil Rights Act of 1964) in District Court against the AMAX Corporation alleging unlawful discrimination in the payment of wages based upon gender. Alice sought back pay from the company in the amount of \$10,000 to eliminate the discrimination. Rather than incur substantial costs in litigating the issue, AMAX reached an out-of-court settlement with Alice on January 15, 2011. The settlement requires AMAX to pay Alice back pay of \$8,000 and to develop gender-neutral pay schedules.

Is the \$8,000 subject to tax?

# Deductions and Losses

PART 3

CHAPTER 7 Overview of Deductions and Losses

CHAPTER 8 Employee Business Expenses

CHAPTER 9 Capital Recovery: Depreciation, Amortization, and Depletion

CHAPTER 10 Certain Business Deductions and Losses

CHAPTER 11 Itemized Deductions

CHAPTER 12 Deductions for Certain Investment Expenses and Losses

# 7

# Overview of Deductions and Losses

## Learning Objectives

Upon completion of this chapter you will be able to:

LO.1 Recognize the general requirements for deducting expenses and losses.

LO.2 Define the terms *ordinary*, *necessary*, and *reasonable* as they apply to business deductions.

LO.3 Recognize tax accounting principles with respect to deductions and losses.

LO.4 Describe the importance of properly classifying expenses as deductions *for* or *from* adjusted gross income.

LO.5 Classify expenses as deductions *for* or *from* adjusted gross income.

LO.6 Explain the proper treatment of employee business expenses.

LO.7 Recognize statutory, administrative, and judicial limitations on deductions and losses.

LO.8 Explain tax planning considerations for optimizing deductions.

## Chapter Outline

Introduction 7-2
- Deduction Defined 7-2

Deductions for Expenses:
- General Requirements 7-3
- General Rules:
  - Code §§ 162 and 212 7-3
- Related to Carrying on a Business or an Income-Producing Activity 7-4
- Ordinary and Necessary Expenses 7-7
- Reasonable Expenses 7-8
- Paid or Incurred During the Taxable Year 7-8
- Employee Business Expenses 7-9

Accounting for Deductions 7-9
- Cash Method of Accounting 7-9
- Accrual Method of Accounting 7-13
- Relationship to Financial Accounting 7-17

Deductions for Losses 7-18

Classification of Expenses 7-19
- Importance of Classification 7-19
- Deductions for A.G.I 7-20
- Itemized Deductions 7-20
- Self-Employed Versus Employee 7-21

Limitations on Deductions 7-24
- Hobby Expenses and Losses 7-24
- Personal Living Expenses 7-26
- Capital Expenditures 7-28
- Business Investigation Expenses and Start-up Costs 7-31
- Public Policy Restrictions 7-34
- Lobbying and Political Contributions 7-36

Expenses and Interest Relating to Tax-Exempt Income 7-37
Related Taxpayer Transactions 7-38
Payment of Another Taxpayer's Obligation 7-41
Substantiation 7-42
Tax Planning Considerations 7-42
Maximizing Deductions 7-42
Timing of Deductions 7-43
Expenses Relating to Tax-Exempt Income 7-43
"Points" on Mortgages 7-43
Hobbies 7-44
Problem Materials 7-44


## Introduction

As explained in Chapter 3, the income tax is imposed on taxable income, a quantity defined as the difference between gross income and allowable deductions.[1] The concept of gross income was explored in Chapters 5 and 6. This chapter and the following four chapters examine the subject of deductions.

There is little doubt that when it comes to taxation, the questions asked most frequently concern deductions. What is deductible? Can this expense be deducted? How much can I deduct? This is a familiar refrain around taxpaying time, and rightfully so, since any item that might be deductible reduces the tax that otherwise must be paid. Many of the questions concerning deductions are easily answered by merely referring to the basic criteria. On the other hand, many items representing potential deductions are subject to special rules. The purpose of this chapter is to introduce the general rules that are in fact used for determining the answer to that age-old question: Is it deductible?

### Deduction Defined

In the preceding chapters, the definition given for income was described as being "all-inclusive" (i.e., gross income includes *all* items of income except those specifically excluded by law). Given this concept of income, it might be assumed that a similarly broad meaning is given to the term deduction. Deductions, however, are defined narrowly. Deductions are only those *particular* expenses, losses, and other items for which a deduction is authorized.[2] The significance of this apparently meaningless definition is found in the last word—"authorized." *Nothing is deductible unless it is allowed by the Code.* It is a well-established principle that before a deduction may be claimed the taxpayer must find some statutory provision permitting the deduction. The courts consistently have affirmed this principle, stating that a taxpayer has no constitutional right to a deduction. Rather, a taxpayer's right to a deduction depends solely on "legislative grace" (i.e., Congress has enacted a statute allowing the deduction).[3]

Although a taxpayer's deductions require statutory authorization, this does not mean that a particular deduction must be specifically mentioned in the Code. While several provisions are designed to grant the deduction for a specific item, such as § 163 for interest expense and § 164 for taxes, most deductions are allowed because they satisfy the conditions of some broadly defined category of deductions. For example, no specific deduction is allowed for the advertising expense of a restaurant owner, but the expense may be deductible if it meets the criteria required for deduction of *business expenses.*

The remainder of this chapter examines those provisions authorizing several broad categories of deductions: § 162 on trade or business expenses, § 212 on expenses of producing income, and § 165 on losses. In addition to these deduction-granting sections, several provisions that expressly deny or limit deductions for certain items are considered. The rules provided by these various provisions establish the basic framework for determining whether a deduction is allowed. Once the deductibility of an item is determined, an additional problem exists for individual taxpayers—the deduction must be classified as either a deduction *for* adjusted gross income or a deduction *from* adjusted gross income (itemized deduction). The classification process is also explained in this chapter.

---

[1] § 63.

[2] § 161.

[3] *New Colonial Ice Co. v. Helvering*, 4 USTC ¶1292, 13 AFTR 1180, 292 U.S. 435 (USSC, 1934).

# Deductions for Expenses: General Requirements

**LO.1**
Recognize the general requirements for deducting expenses and losses.

Given that the taxpayer can deduct only those items that are authorized, what deductions does Congress in fact allow? The central theme found in the rules governing deductions is relatively straightforward: those expenses and losses incurred in business and profit-seeking activities are deductible while those incurred in purely personal activities are not. The allowance for business and profit-seeking expenses stems in part from the traditional notion that income is a *net* concept. From a conceptual perspective, income does not result until revenues exceed expenses. It generally follows from this principle that it would be unfair to tax the revenue from an activity but not allow deductions for the expenses that produced it.

In light of the Code's approach to deductions, many commentators have aptly stated that the costs of *earning* a living are deductible while the costs of living are not. Although this is a good rule of thumb, it is also an over-generalization. As will become clear, the Code allows deductions not only for the costs of producing income, but also for numerous personal expenses such as interest on home mortgages, property taxes, medical expenses, and charitable contributions. To complicate matters further, the line between personal and business expenses is often difficult to draw. For this reason, the various rules governing deductions must be examined closely.

## General Rules: Code §§ 162 and 212

Two provisions in the Code provide the authority for the deduction of most expenses: § 162 concerning trade or business expenses and § 212 relating to expenses for the production of income. Numerous other provisions of the Code pertain to deductions. These other provisions, however, normally build on the basic rules contained in §§ 162 and 212. For this reason, the importance of these two provisions cannot be overstated.

Section 162(a) on trade or business expenses reads, in part, as follows:

> *Sec. 162. Trade or business expenses.*
>
> **(a)** *In general.*
> *There shall be allowed as a deduction all the ordinary and necessary expenses paid or incurred during the taxable year in carrying on any trade or business, including:*
>
> **(1)** *a reasonable allowance for salaries or other compensation for personal services actually rendered;*
>
> **(2)** *expenses (including amounts expended for meals and lodging other than amounts which are lavish or extravagant under the circumstances) while away from home in the pursuit of a trade or business;*
>
> **(3)** *rentals or other payments required to be made as a condition to the continued use or possession, for purposes of the trade or business, of property to which the taxpayer has not taken or is not taking title or in which he has no equity.*

Although § 162(a) specifically enumerates three items that are deductible, the provision's primary importance lies in its general rule: ordinary and necessary expenses of carrying on a trade or business are deductible.

Section 212 contains a general rule very similar to that found in § 162. Section 212, in part, reads as follows:

> *Sec. 212. Expenses for the production of income.*
>
> *In the case of an individual, there shall be allowed as a deduction all the ordinary and necessary expenses paid or incurred during the taxable year—*
>
> **(1)** *for the production of income*
>
> **(2)** *for the management, conservation, or maintenance of property held for the production of income…*

Production of income expenses are normally those related to investments, such as investment advisory fees and safe deposit box rentals.

An examination of the language of §§ 162 and 212 indicates that a deduction is allowed under either section if it meets *four* critical requirements. The expense must have all of the following properties:

1. It must be related to carrying on a trade or business or an income-producing activity.
2. It must be ordinary and necessary.
3. It must be reasonable.
4. It must be paid or incurred during the taxable year.

It should be emphasized, however, that satisfaction of these criteria does not ensure deductibility. Other provisions in the Code often operate to prohibit or limit a deduction otherwise granted by §§ 162 and 212. For example, an expense may be ordinary, necessary, and related to carrying on a business, but if it is also related to producing tax-exempt income, § 265 prohibits a deduction. This system of allowing, yet disallowing, deductions is a basic feature in the statutory scheme for determining deductibility.

## Related to Carrying on a Business or an Income-Producing Activity

### The Activity

Whether an expense is deductible depends in part on the type of activity in which it was incurred. A deduction is authorized by § 162 only if it is paid or incurred in an activity that constitutes a trade or business. Similarly, § 212 permits a deduction only if it is paid or incurred in an activity for the production or collection of income. The purpose of each of these requirements is to deny deductions for expenses incurred in an activity that is *primarily personal* in nature. For example, the costs incurred in pursuing what is merely a hobby, such as collecting antiques or racing automobiles, normally would be considered nondeductible personal expenditures. Of course, this assumes that such activities do not constitute a trade or business.

The Code does not provide any clues as to when an activity will be considered a trade or business or an income-producing activity rather than a personal activity. Over the years, however, one criterion has emerged from the many court cases involving the issue. To constitute a trade or business or an income-producing activity, the activity must be *entered into for profit.*[4] In other words, for the taxpayer's expenses to be deductible, they must be motivated by his or her hope for a profit. For this reason, taxpayers who collect antiques or race automobiles can deduct all of the related expenses if they are able to demonstrate that they did so with the hope of producing income. In such case, they would be considered to be in a trade or business. If the required profit motive is lacking, however, expenses of the activity generally are not deductible except to the extent the activity has income.

As may be apparent, the critical question in this area is what inspired the taxpayer's activities. The factors to be used in evaluating the taxpayer's motivation, along with the special provisions governing activities that are not engaged in for profit—the so-called hobby loss rules—are considered in detail later in this chapter.

A profit motive is the only requirement necessary to establish existence of an *income-producing* activity. However, the courts have imposed an additional requirement before an activity qualifies as a *trade or business*. Business status requires both a profit motive and a sufficient degree of taxpayer involvement in the activity to distinguish the activity from a passive investment. No clear guidelines have emerged indicating when a taxpayer's activities rise to the level of carrying on a business. The courts, however, generally have permitted business treatment where the taxpayer has devoted a major portion of time to the activities or the activities have been regular or continuous.[5]

**Example 1**

C owns six rental units, including several condominiums and townhouses. He manages his rental properties entirely by himself. His managing activities include seeking new tenants, supplying furnishings, cleaning and preparing the units for occupancy,

[4] *Doggett v. Burrett*, 3 USTC ¶1090, 12 AFTR 505, 65 F.2d 192 (CA-D.C., 1933).

[5] *Grier v. U.S.*, 55-1 USTC ¶9184, 46 AFTR 1536, 218 F.2d. 603 (CA-2, 1955).

advertising, and bookkeeping. In this case, C's involvement with the rental activities is sufficiently continuous and systematic to constitute a business.[6] If the rental activities were of a more limited nature, they might not qualify as a trade or business. The determination ultimately depends on the facts of the particular situation.[7]

## Example 2

H owns various stocks and bonds. Her managerial activities related to these securities consist primarily of maintaining records and collecting dividends and interest. She rarely trades in the market. These activities are those normally associated with a passive investor, and accordingly would not constitute a trade or business under § 162 (they would be considered an income-producing activity under § 212).[8] On the other hand, if H had a substantial volume of transactions, made personal investigations of the corporations in which she was interested in purchasing, and devoted virtually every day to such work, her activities could constitute a trade or business.[9] Again, however, the answer depends on the facts.

### Distinguishing between §§ 162 and 212

Prior to enactment of § 212, many investment-related expenses were not deductible because the activities did not constitute a business. The enactment of § 212 in 1942, allowing for the deduction of expenses related to production or collection of income, enabled the deduction of investment-oriented expenses. This expansion of the deduction concept to include so-called nonbusiness or investment-related expenses eliminates the need for an activity to constitute a business before a deduction is allowed. As a result, the issue of deductibility (*assuming* the other requirements are met) is effectively reduced to a single important question: Is the expense related to an activity engaged in for profit?

It may appear that the addition of § 212 completely removed the need for determining whether the activity resulting in the expense constitutes a business or is merely for the production of income. However, the distinction between business and production of income expenses remains important. For example, the classification of the expense as a deduction for or from adjusted gross income may turn on whether the expense is a trade or business expense or a production of income expense. Production of income expenses (other than those related to rents or royalties) are usually miscellaneous itemized deductions that can be deducted only to the extent they *exceed* two percent of adjusted gross income. In contrast, most business expenses are deductions for adjusted gross income and are deductible in full.

## Example 3

Refer to *Example 2*. In the first situation, where H is considered a passive investor, her investment related expenses (e.g., subscriptions to stock advisory services and investment newsletters) would be miscellaneous itemized deductions and deductible only to the extent they exceed 2% of adjusted gross income. In the second situation, however, the same type of expenses would be deductions for adjusted gross income since H's trading activities qualify as a trade or business.

---

[6] *Edwin R. Curphey*, 73 T.C. 766 (1980).

[7] *Ibid.*

[8] *Higgins v. Comm.*, 41-1 USTC ¶9233, 25 AFTR 1160, 312 U.S. 212 (UCSC, 1941).

[9] *Samuel B. Levin v. U.S.*, 79-1 USTC ¶9331, 43 AFTR2d 79-1057, 597 F.2d 760 (Ct. Cls., 1979). But see *Joseph Moller v. U.S.*, 83-2 USTC ¶9698, 52 AFTR2d 83-633 (CA-FC, 1983) where, for purposes of the home office deduction, the court held that the taxpayer's management of his substantial investment portfolio could not be a trade or business regardless of how continuous, regular, and extensive the activities were. But see Chapter 16 and discussion of traders in securities and § 475(f)

Another reason for ascertaining whether the activity constitutes a business relates to the use of the phrase "trade or business" in other Code Sections. The phrase "trade or business" appears in at least 60 different Code Sections, and the interpretation given to this phrase often controls the tax treatment. For example, whether an activity is an active business or a passive investment affects the tax consequences related to losses (deductible or limited), bad debts (short-term capital loss versus ordinary loss), property sales (capital gain or loss versus ordinary gain or loss), expenses for offices in the home (deductible versus nondeductible), and limited expensing of depreciable property (allowed versus disallowed).[10]

### The Relationship

Before an expense is deductible under §§ 162 or 212, it must have a certain relationship to the trade or business or income-producing activity. The Regulations require that business expenses be directly connected with or pertain to the taxpayer's trade or business.[11] Similarly, production of income expenses must bear a reasonable and proximate relationship to the income-producing activity.[12] Whether an expenditure is directly related to the taxpayer's trade or business or income-producing activity usually depends on the facts. For example, the required relationship for business expenses normally exists where the expense is primarily motivated by business concerns or arises as a result of business, rather than personal, needs.[13]

#### Example 4

While driving from one business to another, T struck a pedestrian with his car. He paid and deducted legal fees and damages in connection with the accident that were disallowed by the IRS. The Court found that the expenses were not directly related to, nor did they proximately result from, the taxpayer's business. The accident was merely incidental to the transportation and was related only remotely to the business.[14]

Whether a particular item is deductible often hinges on whether the expense was incurred for business or personal purposes. Consider the case of a law enforcement officer who is required to keep in top shape to retain his employment. Is the cost of a health club membership incurred for business or personal purposes? Similarly, can a disc jockey who obtains dentures to improve his speech deduct the cost as a business expense? Unfortunately, many expenses—like these—straddle the business-personal fence and the final determination is difficult. In both of the cases above, the Court denied the taxpayers' deductions on the theory that such expenses were inherently personal.

Another common question concerns expenses paid or incurred prior to the time that income is earned. In the case of § 212 expenses, it is not essential that the activity produce income currently. For example, expenses may be deductible under § 212 even though there is little likelihood that the property will be sold at a profit or will ever produce income.[15] Deductions are allowed as long as the transaction was entered into for profit.

---

[10] See §§ 165, 166, 1221, 280A, and 179.

[11] Reg. § 1.162-1(a).

[12] Reg. § 1.212-1(d).

[13] *U.S. v. Gilmore*, 63-1 USTC ¶9285, 11 AFTR2d 758, 372 U.S. 39 (USSC, 1963).

[14] *Julian D. Freedman v. Comm.*, 62-1 USTC ¶9400, 9 AFTR2d 1235, 301 F.2d. 359 (CA-5, 1962); but see *Harold Dancer*, 73 T.C. 1103 (1980), where the Tax Court allowed the deduction when the taxpayer was traveling between two locations of the *same* business. Note how the subtle change in facts substantially alters the result!

[15] Reg. § 1.212-1(b).

**Example 5**

B purchased a vacant lot three years ago as an investment. During the current year she paid $200 to have it mowed. Although the property is not currently producing income, the expense is deductible since it is for the conservation or maintenance of property held for the production of income.

## Ordinary and Necessary Expenses

**LO.2**
Define the terms *ordinary, necessary,* and *reasonable* as they apply to business deductions.

The second test for deductibility is whether the expense is ordinary and necessary. An expense is *ordinary* if it is normally incurred in the type of business in which the taxpayer is involved.[16] This is not to say that the expense is habitual or recurring.[17] In fact, the expense may be incurred only once in the taxpayer's lifetime and be considered ordinary. The test is whether other taxpayers in similar businesses or income-producing activities would customarily incur the same expense.

**Example 6**

P has been in the newspaper business for 35 years. Until this year, his paper had never been sued for libel. To protect the reputation of the newspaper, P incurred substantial legal costs related to the libel suit. Although the taxpayer has never incurred legal expenses of this nature before, the expenses are ordinary since it is common in the newspaper business to incur legal expenses to defend against such attacks.[18]

It is interesting to note that the "ordinary" criterion normally becomes an issue in circumstances that are, in fact, unusual. For example, in *Goedel*,[19] a stock dealer paid premiums for insurance on the life of the President of the United States, fearing that his death would disrupt the stock market and his business. The Court denied the deduction on the grounds that the payment was not ordinary but unusual or extraordinary.

A deductible expense must be not only ordinary, but also *necessary*. An expense is necessary if it is appropriate, helpful, or capable of making a contribution to the taxpayer's profit-seeking activities.[20] The necessary criterion, however, is rarely applied to deny a deduction. The courts have refrained from such a practice since to do so would require overriding the judgment of the taxpayer.[21] The courts apparently feel that it would be unfair to judge *currently* whether a previous expenditure was necessary at the time it was incurred.

It should be emphasized that not all necessary expenses are ordinary expenses. Some expenses may be appropriate and helpful to the taxpayer's business but may not be normally incurred in that particular business. In such case, no deduction is allowed.

**Example 7**

W was an officer in his father's corporation. The corporation, unable to pay its debts, was adjudged bankrupt. After the corporation was discharged from its debts, W decided to resume his father's business on a fresh basis. To reestablish relations with old customers and to solidify his credit standing, W paid as much of the old debts as he could. The Supreme Court held that the expenses were necessary in the sense that they

[16] *Deputy v. DuPont*, 40-1 USTC ¶9161, 23 AFTR 808, 308 U.S. 488 (USSC, 1940).

[17] *Dunn and McCarthy, Inc. v. Comm.*, 43-2 USTC ¶9688, 31 AFTR 1043, 139 F.2d 242 (CA-2, 1943).

[18] *Welch v. Helvering*, 3 USTC ¶1164, 12 AFTR 1456, 290 U.S. 111 (USSC, 1933).

[19] 39 B.T.A. 1 (1939).

[20] *Supra*, Footnote 18. See also *Comm. v. Heininger*; 44-1 USTC ¶9109, 31 AFTR 783, 320 U.S. 467 (USSC, 1943).

[21] *Supra*, Footnote 18.

were appropriate and helpful in the development of W's business. However, the Court ruled that the payments were not ordinary because people do not usually pay the debts of another.[22]

## Reasonable Expenses

The third requirement for a deduction is that the expense be reasonable in amount. An examination of § 162(a) reveals that the term "reasonable" is used only in conjunction with compensation paid for services (e.g., a reasonable allowance for salaries). The courts have held, however, that reasonableness is implied in the phrase "ordinary and necessary."[23] In practice, the reasonableness standard is most often applied in situations involving salary payments made by a closely held corporation to a shareholder who also is an employee. In these situations, if the compensation paid exceeds that ordinarily paid for similar services—that which is reasonable—the excessive payment may represent a nondeductible dividend distribution.[24] Dividend treatment of the excess occurs if the amount of the excessive payment received by each employee closely relates to the number of shares of stock owned.[25] The distinction between reasonable compensation and dividend is critical because characterization of the payment as a dividend results in double taxation (i.e., it is taxable to the shareholder-employee and not deductible by the corporation).

### Example 8

B and C own 70 and 30% of XYZ Corporation, respectively. Employees in positions similar to that of B earn $60,000 annually while those in positions similar to C's earn $20,000. During the year, the corporation pays B a salary of $130,000 and C a salary of $50,000. The excessive payment of $100,000 [($130,000 + $50,000) – ($60,000 + $20,000)] is received by B and C in direct proportion to their percentage ownership of stock (i.e., B's salary increased by $70,000 or 70% of the excessive payment). Because the payments are in excess of that normally paid to employees in similar positions and the excessive payment received by each is closely related to his stockholdings, the excessive payment may be treated as a nondeductible dividend.

Some of the factors used by the IRS when considering the reasonableness of compensation are:[26]

1. Duties performed (i.e., amount and character of responsibility)
2. Volume and complexity of business handled (i.e., time required)
3. Individual's ability and expertise
4. Number of available persons capable of performing the duties of the position
5. Corporation's dividend policies and history

## Paid or Incurred During the Taxable Year

Sections 162 and 212 both indicate that an expense is allowable as a deduction only if it is "paid or incurred during the taxable year." This phrase is used throughout the Code in sections concerning deductions. Use of both terms, "paid" and "incurred," is necessary because the year in which deductions are allowable depends on the method of accounting used by the taxpayer.[27] The term *paid* refers to taxpayers using the cash basis method of accounting while the term *incurred* refers to taxpayers using the accrual basis

---

[22] *Supra*, Footnote 18.

[23] *Comm. v. Lincoln Electric Co.*, 49-2 USTC ¶9388, 38 AFTR 411, 176 F.2d 815 (CA-6, 1949).

[24] Reg. § 1.162-7(b)(1).

[25] Reg. § 1.162-8.

[26] Internal Revenue Manual 4233, § 232.

[27] § 461(a).

method of accounting. Accordingly, the year in which a deduction is allowed usually depends on whether the cash or accrual basis method of accounting is used. Each of these methods is discussed in detail in a later section.

## Employee Business Expenses

The definition of *trade or business* also includes the performance of services as an employee. In other words, an employee is considered to be in the business of being an employee.[28] As a result, the ordinary and necessary expenses incurred by an employee in connection with his or her employment are deductible under § 162 as business expenses. Examples of deductible expenses typically incurred by employees include union dues, dues to trade and professional societies, subscriptions to professional journals, small tools and supplies, medical exams required by the employer, and work clothes and uniforms as well as their maintenance (where required as a condition of employment and not suitable for everyday use).[29] Expenses such as travel, entertainment, and education may also be deducted as employee business expenses under certain conditions explained in Chapter 8. As explained later in this chapter, employee business expenses—other than those that are reimbursed—are considered miscellaneous itemized deductions and thus are deductible only to the extent they exceed 2 percent of A.G.I.

# Accounting for Deductions

**LO.3**
Recognize tax accounting principles with respect to deductions and losses.

Identifying the taxable year in which a taxpayer can claim a deduction is extremely important for a number of reasons. No doubt the most important of these is the time value of money. Taxpayers normally want to claim their deductions and obtain the accompanying tax savings as soon as possible. In contrast, the government is concerned about zealous taxpayers who, in its view, prematurely deduct their expenses. When an expense is deductible generally depends on whether the taxpayer uses the cash or accrual method of accounting. However, the natural friction between taxpayers and the government over when an expense should be deducted has led to a somewhat confusingly intricate set of rules filled with exceptions. Interestingly, the effects of the various exceptions often make the accrual method look like the cash method and vice versa.

## Cash Method of Accounting

### General Rule

For those taxpayers eligible to use the cash method (as discussed in Chapter 5), expenses are deductible in the taxable year when the expenses are actually paid.[30] However, there are numerous exceptions to this rule that are designed to restrict the flexibility a cash basis taxpayer would otherwise have in reporting deductions. Without these restrictions, a cash basis taxpayer could choose the year of deductibility simply by appropriately timing the cash payment. Before examining these restrictions, it is important to understand when the taxpayer is considered to have paid the expense.

### Time of Payment

Determining when a cash basis taxpayer has paid an expense usually is not difficult. A cash basis taxpayer "pays" the expense when cash, check, property, or service is transferred. Neither a promise to pay nor a note evidencing such promise is considered payment. Consequently, when a cash basis taxpayer buys on credit, no deduction is allowed until the debts are paid. However, if the taxpayer borrows cash and then pays the expense, the expense is deductible when paid. For this reason, a taxpayer who charges expenses to a credit card is deemed to have borrowed cash and made payment when the charge is made. Thus, the

---

[28] See *Lloyd U. Noland, Jr. v. Comm.* 59-2 USTC ¶9600, 4 AFTR 2d 5031, 269 F2d 108, (CA-4, 1959) holding that "every person who works for compensation is engaged in the business of earning his pay, and that expense which is essential to the continuance of his employment is deductible..."

[29] Rev. Rul. 70-474, 1970 C.B. 35.

[30] Reg. § 1.446-1(a)(1).

deduction is claimed when the charge is actually made and not when the bank makes payment or when the taxpayer pays the bill.[31] If the taxpayer uses a "pay-by-phone" account, the expense is deductible in the year the financial institution paid the amount as reported on a monthly statement sent to the taxpayer.[32] When the taxpayer pays by mail, payment is usually considered made when the mailing occurs (i.e., dropping it in the post-office box).[33]

### Restrictions on Use of Cash Method

Under the general rule, a cash basis taxpayer deducts expenses when paid. Without restrictions, however, aggressive taxpayers could liberally interpret this provision to authorize not only deductions for routine items, but also deductions for capital expenditures and other expenses that benefit future periods (e.g., supplies, prepaid insurance, prepaid rent, and prepaid interest). To preclude such an approach, numerous limitations have been imposed.

**Inventories** One of the more fundamental restrictions applying to cash basis taxpayers concerns inventories. For example, if no limitation existed, a cash basis owner of a department store could easily reduce or eliminate taxable income by increasing purchases of inventory near year-end and deducting their cost. To prevent this possibility, the Regulations require taxpayers to use the accrual method for computing sales and costs of goods sold if inventories are an income-producing factor.[34] In such cases, inventory costs must be capitalized, and accounts receivable and accounts payable (with respect to cost of goods sold) must be created. The taxpayer could continue to use the cash method for other transactions, however. It is also important to note that there are two relief provisions for small business owners that allow them to elect out of the accrual method and the requirement to account for inventories. As discussed in Chapter 10, taxpayers with average gross receipts of no more than $1 million, and certain taxpayers with average annual gross receipts of more than $1 million and up to $10 million may use the cash method of accounting even when inventory is an income producing factor.[35]

**Capital Expenditures** Provisions of both the Code and the Regulations limit the potential for deducting capital expenditures. As discussed later in this chapter, Code § 263 specifically denies the deduction for a capital expenditure; such costs as those for equipment, vehicles, and buildings normally are recovered through depreciation, as discussed in Chapter 9. Special rules exist requiring taxpayers to capitalize certain costs as part of their inventory under the uniform capitalization rules of § 263A. The "unicap" rules are discussed in Chapter 10.

The Regulations—at least broadly—deal with other expenditures that are not capital expenditures per se but that do benefit future periods. According to the Regulations, any expenditure resulting "in the creation of an asset having a useful life which extends *substantially beyond the close of the taxable year* may not be deductible when made, or may be deductible only in part."[36] In this regard, the courts agree that "substantially beyond" means a useful life of more than one year.[37] Perhaps the simplest example of this rule as so interpreted concerns payments for supplies. Assuming the supplies would be exhausted before the close of the following tax year, a deduction should be allowable when payment is made.

### Prepaid Expenses in General

One of the most troublesome issues related to both the cash and accrual methods of accounting concerns prepaid expenses. If prepayments are made for regularly recurring expenses and the payments result in the creation of an asset having a life extending substantially beyond the taxable year of payment, the treatment historically has not always been clear. Unfortunately, the *one-year rule* described above was not necessarily applied to all expenses uniformly.

---

[31] Rev. Rul. 78-39, 1978-1 C.B. 73.

[32] Rev. Rul. 80-335, 1980-2 C.B. 170.

[33] See Rev. Rul. 73-99, 1973-1 C.B. 412 for clarification of this general rule.

[34] Reg. § 1.446-1(c)(2).

[35] Rev. Proc. 2000-22, Rev. Proc. 2001-10, and Rev. Proc. 2002-28. See full discussion of inventory in Chapter 10.

[36] Reg. § 1.446-1(a)(1).

[37] *Martin J. Zaninovich*, 69 T.C. 605, rev'd in 80-1 USTC ¶9342, 45 AFTR2d 80-1442, 616 F.2d 429 (CA-9, 1980).

**12-Month Rule** The problems with prepaid expenses became acutely apparent in *U.S. Freightways Corporation.*[38] Here an accrual basis calendar-year trucking company claimed a deduction for permits, licenses and fees paid in order for its trucks to operate legally in certain locations. In 1993, the company paid $4,308,460 for licenses, many of which expired in 1994 rather than 1993. Similarly, in 1993, the company paid premiums of $1,090,602 for liability and property insurance for the 1-year period from July 1, 1993, to June 30, 1994. Relying on the one-year rule, the corporation expensed all of the prepayments. However, the government denied the deduction, asserting that the 12-month rule existed solely for cash basis taxpayers and did not apply to accrual basis taxpayers. The Seventh Circuit disagreed and extended the rule to accrual basis taxpayers.

To address the confusion resulting from *U.S. Freightways* and similar cases, the government issued Regulations in early in 2004 to address the capitalization of intangibles.[39] Among these lengthy provisions is the government's own 12-month rule. Under these Regulations, taxpayers—both cash and accrual—are entitled to claim an immediate deduction for prepaid expenses (e.g. prepaid insurance) if the rights or benefits do not extend beyond the earlier of

- 12 months after the first date on which the taxpayer realizes the benefit or
- The end of the taxable year following the year in which payment was made

This rule generally is consistent with prior law that enables cash basis taxpayer to claim deductions for prepaid expenses for supplies, service and other non-capital expenditures. It should be emphasized that the rule applies to both cash and accrual taxpayers. However, as discussed below, accrual taxpayers must meet the all events and economic performance tests before a deduction can be claimed. Specific items are discussed below.

### Prepaid Insurance and Prepaid Rent

Prepayments of insurance and rent follow the 12-month rule. If the 12-month rule does not apply, the prepayment cannot be deducted when paid and must be amortized over the term for which the insurance is provided or the term of the lease.[40]

#### Example 9

On December 1, 2011, Blue Inc., a cash basis taxpayer, paid a $12,000 insurance premium to obtain a property insurance policy with a one-year term that begins on February 1, 2012. Although the policy is only for one year, the payment does not meet the 12-month rule since the benefit attributable to the $12,000 payment extends beyond the end of the taxable year following the taxable year in which the payment was made. The corporation must capitalize the payment and amortize it over the policy period. Thus the corporation's deduction is $0 in 2011, $11,000 in 2012 and $1,000 in 2013.

#### Example 10

Same facts as above except the policy has a term beginning on December 15, 2011. The 12-month rule applies since the benefit does not extend more than 12 months beyond December 15, 2011 (the date when the benefit is first realized by the corporation) nor beyond the close of the tax year following the year in which the payment was made (December 31, 2012). Thus the corporation may deduct the entire $12,000 prepayment in the year paid, 2011.

---

[38] 2001-2 USTC 50,731, 88 AFTR2d 2001-6703, 270 F3d 1137 (CA-7, 2001)).

[39] Reg. § 1.263-(a)(4).

[40] See Reg. 1.263(a)-4(f)(8), Examples 1, 2 and 10.

### Example 11

WRK Corporation, a cash basis taxpayer, leases space at a monthly rate of $2,000. In December of 2011, the corporation prepays its rent for the first six months of 2012 in the amount of $12,000. The corporation may deduct the entire $12,000 in 2011 since the benefits received for the prepayment do not extend beyond 12 months. (Note as discussed below accrual basis taxpayers would be required to amortize this expense over the term because the economic performance test delays deduction until the property is used.)

### Other Prepayments

Perhaps the Service's current view of the proper treatment of most prepayments is best captured in a ruling concerning prepaid feed. In this ruling, the taxpayer purchased a substantial amount of feed prior to the year in which it would be used.[41] The purchase was made in advance because the price was low due to a depressed market. The IRS granted a deduction for the prepayment because there was a business purpose for the advanced payment, the payment was not merely a deposit, and it did not materially distort income. Based on this ruling and related cases, prepayments normally should be deductible if the asset will be consumed by the close of the following year, there is a business purpose for the expenditure, and there is no material distortion of income.

### Prepaid Interest

The Code expressly denies the deduction of prepaid interest. Prepaid interest must be capitalized and deducted ratably over the period of the loan.[42] The same is true for any costs associated with obtaining the loan. The sole exception is for "points" paid for a debt incurred by the taxpayer to purchase his or her *principal* residence. In this regard, the IRS has ruled that points incurred to refinance a home must be amortized over the term of the loan.[43] However, an Appeals Court case allowed a taxpayer to deduct the amount of points paid on refinancing a home. The proceeds were used to pay off a three-year, temporary loan that was made to allow the borrower time to secure permanent financing for the home.[44] The court stated that, since the temporary loan was merely an integrated step in securing permanent financing for the taxpayer's residence, the points were deductible currently.

### Example 12

K desires to obtain financing for the purchase of a new house costing $100,000. The bank agrees to make her a loan of 80% of the purchase price, or $80,000 (80% of $100,000) for thirty years at a cost of two points (two percentage "points" of the loan obtained). Thus, she must pay $1,600 (2% of $80,000) to obtain the loan. Assuming it is established business practice in her area to charge points in consideration of the loan, the $1,600 in points (prepaid interest) is deductible. However, if the house is not the principal residence of the taxpayer, then the prepaid interest must be deducted ratably over the 30-year loan period.

---

[41] Rev. Rul. 79-229, 1979-2 C.B. 210. See also, *Kenneth Van Raden*, 71 T.C. 1083 (1979), aff'd in 81-2 USTC ¶9547, 48 AFTR2d 81-5607, 650 F.2d 1046 (CA-9, 1981).

[42] § 461(g).

[43] Rev. Rul. 87-22, 1987-1 C.B. 146. See also Rev. Proc. 94-27, 1994-1 I.R.B. 15.

[44] *James R. Huntsman*, 90-2 USTC ¶50,340, 66 AFTR2d 90-5020, 905 F.2d 1182 (CA-8, 1990). In an *Action on Decision* issued on February 11, 1991, the IRS ruled that although it will not appeal the *Huntsman* decision, it will not follow this decision outside the Eighth Circuit.

## ACCRUAL METHOD OF ACCOUNTING

An accrual basis taxpayer deducts expenses when they are incurred. For this purpose, an expense is considered incurred when the all events test is satisfied and economic performance has occurred.[45]

### All Events Test

Two requirements must be met under the all-events test: (1) all events establishing the existence of a liability must have occurred (i.e., the liability is fixed); and (2) the amount of the liability can be determined with reasonable accuracy. Therefore, before the liability may be accrued and deducted it must be fixed and determinable.

> **Example 13**
>
> In *Hughes Properties, Inc.*, an accrual basis corporation owned a gambling casino in Reno, Nevada that operated progressive slot machines that paid a large jackpot about every four months.[46] The increasing amount of the jackpot was maintained and shown by a meter. Under state gaming regulations, the jackpot amount could not be turned back until the amount had been paid to a winner. In addition, the corporation had to maintain a cash reserve sufficient to pay all the guaranteed amounts. At the end of each taxable year, the corporation accrued and deducted the liability for the jackpot as accrued at year-end. The IRS challenged the accrual, alleging that the all events test had not been met, and that the amount should be deducted only when paid. It argued that payment of the jackpot was not fixed but contingent, since it was possible that the winning combination may never be pulled. Moreover, the Service pointed out the potential for tax avoidance: the corporation was accruing deductions for payments that may be paid far in the future, and thus—given the time value of money—overstated the amount of the deduction. The Supreme Court rejected these arguments, stating that the probability of payment was not a remote and speculative possibility. The Court noted that not only was the liability fixed under state law, but it also was not in the interest of the taxpayer to set unreasonably high odds, since customers would refuse to play and would gamble elsewhere.

The all events test often operates to deny deductions for certain estimated expenditures properly accruable for financial accounting purposes. For example, the estimated cost of product guarantees, warranties, and contingent liabilities normally may not be deducted—presumably because the liability for such items has not been fixed or no reasonable estimate of the amount can be made.[47] However, the courts have authorized deductions for estimates where the obligation was certain and there was a reasonable basis (e.g., industry experience) for determining the amount of the liability.

### Economic Performance Test

The condition requiring *economic performance* was introduced in 1984 due to Congressional fear that the all events test did not prohibit so-called premature accruals. Prior to 1984, the courts—with increasing frequency—had permitted taxpayers to accrue and deduct the cost of estimated expenditures required to perform certain activities *prior* to the period when the activities were actually performed. For example, in one case, a strip-mining operator deducted the estimated cost of backfilling land that he had mined for coal.[48] The court allowed the deduction for the estimated expenses in the current year even though the back filling was not started and completed until the following year. According to the court, the liability satisfied the all-events test since the taxpayer was required by law to backfill the land and a reasonable estimate of the cost of the work could be made. A similar decision involved a taxpayer that was a self-insurer of its liabilities arising from claims under state and Federal

---

[45] § 461(h).

[46] *Hughes Properties, Inc.*, 86-1 USTC ¶9440, 58 AFTR2d 86-5015, 106 S. Ct. 2092 (USSC, 1986).

[47] *Bell Electric Co.*, 45 T.C. 158 (1965).

[48] *Paul Harrold v. Comm.*, 52-1 USTC ¶9107, 41 AFTR 442, 192 F.2d 1002 (CA-4, 1951).

worker's compensation laws.[49] Under these laws, the taxpayer was obligated to pay a claimant's medical bills, disability payments, and death benefits. In this situation, the taxpayer was allowed to accrue and deduct the estimated expenses for its obligations even though actual payments would extend over many years. In Congress' view, allowing the deduction in these and similar cases prior to the time when the taxpayer actually performed the services, provided the goods, or paid the expenses, overstated the true cost of the expense, because the time value of money was ignored. Perhaps more importantly, Congress recognized that allowing deductions for accruals in this manner had become the foundation for many tax shelter arrangements. Accordingly, the economic performance test was designed to defer the taxpayer's deduction until the activities giving rise to the liability are performed.

The time at which economic performance is deemed to occur—and hence the period in which the deduction may be claimed—depends on the nature of the item producing the liability. A taxpayer's liabilities commonly arise in three ways, as summarized below.

1. *Liability of Taxpayer to Provide Property and Services.* When the taxpayer's liability results from an obligation to provide goods or services to a third party (e.g., perform repairs), economic performance occurs when the taxpayer provides the goods or services to the third party.
2. *Liability for Property or Services Provided to the Taxpayer.* When the taxpayer's liability arises from an obligation to pay for services, goods, or the use of property provided to (or to be provided to) the taxpayer (e.g., consulting, supplies, and rent), economic performance occurs when the taxpayer receives the services or goods or uses the property. Note that in this case, economic performance occurs when the taxpayer *receives* the consideration bargained for, while in the situation above it occurs when the taxpayer *provides* the consideration. Under a special rule, a taxpayer may treat services or property as being provided when the taxpayer makes *payment* to the person providing the services or property *if* the taxpayer can reasonably expect the person to provide the services or property within 3½ months after the date of payment.[50]
3. *Liabilities for which Payment Represents Economic Performance.* There are a number of liabilities for which economic performance is deemed to occur only when the taxpayer actually makes payment. This rule for so-called "payment liabilities" effectively places the taxpayer on the cash basis for these liabilities. These include the following:

   - Refunds and rebates
   - Awards, prizes, and jackpots
   - Premiums on insurance
   - Provision of work to the taxpayer under warranty or service contracts
   - Taxes
   - Liabilities arising under a worker's compensation act or out of any tort, breach of contract, or violation of law, including amounts paid in settlement of such claims

**Example 14**

In 2011 C, an accrual basis corporation, contracted with P, a partnership, to drill 50 gas wells over a five-year period for $500,000. Absent the economic performance test, C could accrue and deduct the $500,000 fee in 2011 because the obligation is fixed and determinable. However, because economic performance has not occurred (i.e., the services have not been received by C), no deduction is permitted in 2011. Rather, C may deduct the expense when the wells are drilled.

---

[49] *Crescent Wharf & Warehouse Co. v. Comm.*, 75-2 USTC ¶9571, 36 AFTR2d 75-5246, 518 F.2d 772 (CA-5, 1975).

[50] § 1.461-4(d)(6)(ii).

### Example 15

Same facts as above. Although P is obligated to perform services for C for $500,000 over the five-year period (i.e., the obligation is fixed and determinable), P cannot prematurely accrue the cost of providing these services because economic performance has not occurred. Deduction is permitted only as the wells are drilled.

### Example 16

C Corporation, a calendar year, accrual method taxpayer, owns several casinos across the country. Each contains progressive slot machines. These machines provide a guaranteed jackpot that increases as money is gambled through the machine until the jackpot is won or until a maximum predetermined amount is reached. On July 1, 2011, the guaranteed jackpot amount on one of C's slot machines reaches the maximum predetermined amount of $100,000. On February 1, 2012, the $100,000 jackpot is won by B. Although the all-events test is met in 2011 when the amount of the liability becomes fixed (i.e., guaranteed) and determinable, economic performance does not occur for prizes until payment is actually made. As a result, C is not allowed to accrue the deduction in 2011 but must wait and claim the expense when it pays the jackpot in 2012. (Note this rule reverses the decision in *Hughes Properties, Inc.* However, the deduction may still be allowed under the recurring item exception discussed below.)

Note that even though payment of an expense may make it ripe for accrual, other rules may require deferral of the deduction.

### Example 17

On December 10, 2011, T Inc., an accrual basis calendar year taxpayer, paid a painting contractor $15,000 to paint the interior of its office building. T anticipated that the painting would be completed by February 15 of 2012. Since the painting services are to be provided within 3 ½ months after the date of payment, economic performance is deemed to have occurred when the payment is made and T may deduct the $15,000 expense in 2011.

### Example 18

Kidco Products Corporation, a calendar year E accrual method taxpayer, manufactures car seats for children. On July 1, 2011 it purchased an insurance policy from INS Inc. for $360,000 under which INS must satisfy any liability arising during the next three years for any claims attributable to defects in the manufacturing. Although economic performance occurs when Kidco pays the premium, it has created an asset with a life that extends substantially beyond 2011. Under cash-basis principles, such expenses cannot be deducted currently but must be amortized. Consequently, Kidco should amortize the insurance premium over the term of the policy, deducting $60,000 ($360,000/36 × 6 months) in 2011 and the remaining $300,000 over the next 30 months.

### Example 19

WNDE Corporation leases space at a monthly rate of $2,000. In December of 2011, the corporation prepays its rent for the first six months of 2012 in the amount of $12,000. If WNDE is a cash basis taxpayer, it could deduct the $12,000 in 2011 under the 12-month rule *(See Example 10 above)*. However, if WNDE uses the accrual method, economic performance for the rent does not occur until the corporation uses the property and, therefore, it cannot use the 12 month rule but must deduct the rental expense over the period it uses the property, 2012.

### Economic Performance and Recurring Item Exception

To prohibit the disruption of normal business and accounting practices, certain recurring expenses are exempted from the economic performance rules. The expense may be accrued and deducted under the recurring item exception if all of the following conditions are met.[51]

1. The all-events test is satisfied.
2. Economic performance does in fact occur within eight and one-half months after the close of the taxable year or the filing of the return if earlier.
3. The item is recurring in nature, and the taxpayer consistently treats such items as incurred in the taxable year.
4. The item is immaterial or accrual in the earlier year results in a better match against income than accruing the item when economic performance occurs.

The recurring item exception does not apply to liabilities arising under a worker's compensation act or out of any tort, breach of contract, or violation of law.

### Example 20

M Corporation, a calendar year, accrual method taxpayer, manufactures and sells automobile mufflers. Under the terms of an agreement with D Corporation, one of its distributors, D is entitled to a discount on future purchases (i.e., a rebate) from M based on the amount of purchases made by D from M during any calendar year. During 2011, purchases by D entitled it to future rebates of $20,000. M paid $12,000 of the rebate in January 2012 and the remaining $8,000 in October 2012. M filed its 2011 tax return on March 15, 2012. Although the all events test has been met in 2011 (i.e., the fact of the liability is fixed and the amount can be determined with reasonable accuracy), no deduction is allowed until economic performance occurs. Normally, economic performance for rebates is deemed to occur when the rebate is paid. Therefore, the expense would usually be deductible by M in 2012. However, under the recurring item exception M should be able to accrue $12,000 of the $20,000 in 2011 because all of the conditions are met: (1) the all events test is met, (2) economic performance occurs in a timely manner (i.e., the January payment occurs before the earlier of the filing of the tax return or 8½ months after the close of the year), (3) the item is recurring, and (4) accrual in the earlier year results in a better match against income. The remaining $8,000 is not eligible for the recurring item exception because economic performance (payment of the $8,000 liability) did not occur until October, which is beyond both the filing of the return and the 8½-month window.

### Real Property Taxes

The addition of the economic performance test and the recurring item exception posed a problem for a great number of taxpayers who incur real property taxes.

[51] § 461(h)(3).

### Example 21

Oldco Corporation uses the accrual method and reports on the calendar year. It owns a warehouse in a state where the lien date (i.e., the date on which the corporation technically becomes liable) for real property taxes for 2011 is January 1, 2012. Payment is due in two installments, 40 percent due on June 1 and the remaining 60 percent due on December 1. Shortly after the close of 2011, the corporation received its bill for its 2011 taxes of $100,000, paying $40,000 on June 1, 2012 and $60,000 on December 1, 2012. For financial accounting purposes, the corporation accrues the entire $100,000 expense in 2011. For tax purposes, however, economic performance for taxes does not occur until payment is made. Therefore, accrual normally is not allowed until the payment is made (2012) unless the recurring item exception applies. In this case, the recurring item exception would apply. However, the corporation could deduct only the portion paid by the earlier of the filing of its tax return or September 15 (8½ months after the close of the taxable year). If the corporation delayed filing its return until the extended due date, September 15, it could accrue and deduct on its 2011 tax return the $40,000 paid on June 1. However, if it filed its return by March 15, none of the taxes could be accrued under the recurring item exception.

Recognizing the problem illustrated *Example 18* above, Code § 461(c) was created. Under this provision, taxpayers can elect to accrue real property taxes ratably over the period to which the taxes relate. Note that if the taxpayer makes the election, the treatment for tax purposes is consistent with that for financial accounting.

### Example 22

Same facts as *Example 21*. If the corporation makes the election under § 461(c), it may accrue and deduct the entire $100,000 in 2011 because all of the taxes related to such period.

## Relationship to Financial Accounting

As may be apparent from the discussion above, the rules for accruing expenses for tax accounting purposes do not necessarily produce the same result as those for financial accounting. Differences often occur, particularly in the treatment of estimated expenses. As noted in Chapter 5, such differences are justified given the differing goals of financial and tax accounting. Financial accounting principles adopt a conservative approach in measuring income to ensure that income is not overstated and investors are not misled. Accordingly, financial accounting embraces the matching principle that encourages the accrual of estimated expenditures. In contrast, the objective of the income tax system is to ensure that taxable income is objectively measured so as to minimize controversy. Consistent with this view, the tax law allows a deduction only when a liability is actually fixed and economic performance has occurred. Estimates of future expenses are not sufficient to warrant a deduction for tax purposes (unless the recurring item exception should apply). Note, however, that these different accounting techniques produce differences only in *when* the expense is taken into account. The total amount of expense to be accounted for is not affected. Common examples of these so-called timing differences include:

- *Depreciation.* As discussed in Chapter 9, depreciation for tax purposes differs substantially from that for financial accounting purposes. Although the total amount of depreciation is often the same in both cases, the amount expensed in any one period may differ significantly.
- *Bad Debts.* For tax purposes, bad debts normally may be deducted only in the year they actually become worthless. In contrast, financial accounting permits use of the reserve method, which allows an estimate of future bad debts related to current

year sales to be charged against current year income. The tax treatment of bad debts is discussed fully in Chapter 10.

- *Vacation Pay.* For financial accounting purposes, vacation pay accrues as it is earned by the employees. For tax purposes, however, vacation pay may be accrued and deducted only if it is paid within 2½ months following the close of the taxable year.
- *Warranty costs.* For financial accounting purposes, warranty costs are normally estimated and matched against current year sales. For tax purposes, no deduction is allowed until the warranty work is actually performed (unless the recurring item exception applies).

Timing differences should be distinguished from permanent differences. As seen throughout this text, there are a number of situations in which an expense for financial accounting purposes is not allowed as a deduction for tax purposes. For example, fines and penalties are expenses that must be taken into account in determining financial accounting income, as are expenses related to tax-exempt income. However, tax deductions for such costs are not allowed. Similarly, expenses for business meals and entertainment may be fully expensed for financial accounting but only 50 percent of such costs can be deducted for tax purposes.

The rules governing the accrual of deductions are summarized in Exhibit 7-1.

**EXHIBIT 7.1 Requirements for Accrual of Deduction**

Requirements

- All events test is met.
  All events have occurred that fix the fact of the liability.
  The amount of the liability can be determined with reasonable accuracy.
- Economic performance has occurred as follows:

| *Event Producing Liability* | *Time When Economic Performance Occurs* | *Example* |
|---|---|---|
| Taxpayer obligated to provide goods or services to a third party | When the taxpayer provides the property or services | Taxpayer to perform repairs, warranty work |
| Goods or services provided or to be provided to the taxpayer | When taxpayer actually receives the goods or services | Taxpayer buys supplies, contracts for consulting |
| Property provided or to be provided to the taxpayer | When taxpayer uses the property | Taxpayer rents property |
| Obligations to pay refunds, rebates, awards, prizes, insurance, warranty or service contracts, taxes | When taxpayer makes payment | Refunds, rebates, etc. |
| Claims under worker's compensation, tort, breach of contract | When taxpayer makes payment | Taxpayer incurs product liability |
| Real property taxes | When taxpayer makes payment unless he or she elects special accrual rule | Real estate taxes |

## Deductions for Losses

The general rules concerning deduction of losses are contained in § 165. This provision permits a deduction for any loss sustained that is not compensated for by insurance. The deductions for losses of an individual taxpayer, however, are limited to

1. Losses incurred in a trade or business
2. Losses incurred in a transaction entered into for profit
3. Losses of property not connected with a trade or business if such losses arise by fire, storm, shipwreck, theft, or some other type of casualty

Note that personal losses—other than those attributable to a casualty—are not deductible. For example, the sale of a personal residence at a loss is not deductible.

Before a loss can be deducted, it must be evidenced by a closed and completed transaction. Mere decline in values or unrealized losses cannot be deducted. Normally, for the loss to qualify as a deduction, the property must be sold, abandoned, or scrapped, or become completely worthless. The amount of deductible loss for all taxpayers cannot exceed the taxpayer's basis in the property. Special rules related to various types of losses are discussed in Chapter 10.

## Classification of Expenses

Once the deductibility of an item is established, the tax formula for individuals requires that the deduction be classified as either a deduction *for* adjusted gross income or a deduction *from* adjusted gross income (itemized deduction).[52] In short, the deduction process requires that two questions be asked. First, is the expense deductible? Second, is the deduction for or from adjusted gross income (A.G.I.)? Additional aspects of the first question are considered later in this chapter. At this point, however, it is appropriate to consider the problem of classification.

The classification process arose with the introduction of the standard deduction in 1944. The standard deduction was introduced to simplify filing for the majority of individuals by eliminating the necessity of itemizing primarily personal deductions such as medical expenses and charitable contributions. In addition, the administrative burden of checking such deductions was eliminated. Although these objectives were satisfied by providing a blanket deduction in lieu of itemizing actual expenses, a new problem arose. The standard deduction created the need to classify deductions as either deductions that would be deductible in any event (deductions for A.G.I.), or deductions that would be deductible only if they exceeded the prescribed amount of the standard deduction (deductions from A.G.I.).

### Importance of Classification

**LO.4**
Describe the importance of properly classifying expenses as deductions *for* or *from* adjusted gross income.

The classification problem is significant for several reasons. First, itemized deductions may be deducted only to the extent they exceed the standard deduction. For this reason, a taxpayer whose itemized deductions do not exceed the standard deduction would lose a deduction if a deduction for A.G.I. is improperly classified as a deduction from A.G.I. This would occur because deductions for A.G.I. are deductible without limitation.

A second reason for properly classifying deductions concerns the treatment of miscellaneous itemized deductions. As part of the tax overhaul in 1986, Congress limited the deduction of miscellaneous itemized deductions—defined below—to the amount that exceeds 2 percent of A.G.I. This limitation is extremely important. Under prior law, taxpayers who itemized deductions could misclassify a deduction for A.G.I. as an itemized deduction with little or no effect, since the expense would be deductible either one place or the other. Under the current scheme, however, misclassification of a deduction for A.G.I. as a miscellaneous itemized deduction would subject the expense to the 2 percent floor, possibly making it wholly or partially nondeductible.

A third reason for properly classifying deductions concerns A.G.I. itself. Limitations on deductions such as medical expenses and charitable contributions are expressed in terms of the taxpayer's A.G.I. For example, miscellaneous itemized deductions are deductible only to the extent they exceed 2 percent of A.G.I., medical expenses are deductible only to the extent they exceed 7.5 percent of A.G.I., and charitable contributions are deductible only to the extent of various limitations (50, 30, or 20 percent) based on A.G.I.

Adjusted gross income for Federal income tax purposes also serves as the tax base or the starting point for computing taxable income for many state income taxes. Several states do not allow the taxpayer to itemize deductions. Consequently, misclassification could result in an incorrect state tax liability.

Still another reason for properly classifying expenses concerns the self-employment tax. Under the social security and Medicare programs, self-employed individuals are required to make an annual contribution based on their net earnings from self-employment. Net earnings

---

[52] § 62.

from self-employment include gross income from the taxpayer's trade or business less allowable trade or business deductions attributable to the income. Failure to properly classify a deduction as a deduction for A.G.I. attributable to self-employment income results in a higher self-employment tax.

## DEDUCTIONS FOR A.G.I

**LO.5**
Classify expenses as deductions *for* or *from* adjusted gross income.

The deductions for A.G.I. are specifically identified in Code § 62. It should be emphasized, however, that § 62 merely classifies expenses; it does *not* authorize any deductions. Deductions *for* A.G.I. are:

1. Trade or business deductions except those expenses incurred in the business of being an employee (e.g., expenses of a sole proprietorship or self-employment normally reported on Schedule C of Form 1040)
2. Trade or business deductions of a "statutory employee," generally including traveling salespersons, full-time life insurance salespersons, agent-drivers, commission-drivers and homeworkers. Statutory employees (discussed in detail in Chapter 8) generally report both their income (i.e., wages) and their business expenses on Schedule C much like a sole proprietor.
3. Three categories of employee business deductions:
   a. Expenses that are reimbursed by an employee's employer (and the reimbursement is included in the employee's income);[53]
   b. Expenses incurred by a qualified performing artist (see below); and
   c. Expenses incurred by an official of a state or local government who is compensated on a fee basis
4. Losses from sale or exchange of property
5. Deductions attributable to rents or royalties
6. Educator expenses (K–12 teachers)
7. Deductions for reservists, performing artists, fee-basis government officials
8. Deductions for certain tuition and fees
9. Student loan interest expense
10. Deduction for certain legal expenses
11. Deductions for contributions to Individual Retirement Accounts or Keogh retirement plans
12. Alimony deductions
13. Deductions for penalties imposed for premature withdrawal of funds from a savings arrangement
14. Deduction for 50 percent of self-employment tax paid by self-employed persons
15. Deduction for contributions to Medical Savings Accounts (MSAs) and Health Savings Accounts (HSAs)
16. Moving expenses
17. Deduction for 100 percent of self-employed health insurance premiums
18. Certain other deductions

All of the above are deductible for A.G.I., while all other deductions are from A.G.I. (i.e., itemized deductions).

## ITEMIZED DEDUCTIONS

As seen above, only relatively few expenses are deductible for A.G.I. The predominant expenses in this category are the deductions incurred by taxpayers who are self-employed

[53] Reimbursements must be made under an "accountable plan." Chapter 8 discusses in detail the proper reporting for these reimbursements.

(i.e., those carrying on as a sole proprietor). All other expenses are deductible from A.G.I. as itemized deductions.

Itemized deductions fall into two basic categories: those that are *miscellaneous itemized deductions* and those that are not. The distinction is significant because miscellaneous itemized deductions are deductible only to the extent they exceed two percent of A.G.I. Miscellaneous itemized deductions are all itemized deductions *other than* the following:

1. Interest
2. Taxes
3. Casualty and theft losses
4. Medical expenses
5. Charitable contributions
6. Gambling losses to the extent of gambling gains
7. Deduction where annuity payments cease before investment is recovered
8. Certain other deductions

The miscellaneous itemized deductions category is comprised primarily of *unreimbursed* employee business expenses, investment expenses, and deductions related to taxes such as tax preparation fees. Examples of these (assuming they are not reimbursed by the employer) include:

1. Employee travel away from home (including meals and lodging)
2. Employee transportation expenses
3. Outside salesperson's expenses [unless those individuals qualify as a "statutory employee" in which case they are allowed to report their income (i.e., wages) and expenses on a separate Schedule C and avoid the two percent of A.G.I. limitation]
4. Employee entertainment expenses
5. Employee home office expenses
6. Union dues
7. Professional dues and memberships
8. Subscriptions to business journals
9. Job-seeking expenses (in the same business) or employment-seeking expenses
10. Education expenses
11. Investment expenses, including expenses for an investment newsletter, investment advice, and rentals of safety deposit boxes
12. Tax preparation fees or other tax-related advice including that received from accountants or attorneys, tax seminars, and books about taxes

With respect to item 12 above, expenses related to tax preparation and resolving tax controversies normally are reported as miscellaneous itemized deductions. However, the IRS allows taxpayers who own a business, farm, or rental real estate or have royalty income to allocate a portion of the total cost of preparing their tax return to the cost of preparing Schedule C (trade or business income), Schedule E (rental and royalty income), or Schedule F (farm income) and deduct these costs "for" A.G.I.[54] The same holds true for expenses incurred in resolving tax controversies, including expenses relating to IRS audits or business or rental activities.

## Self-Employed Versus Employee

**LO.6**
Explain the proper treatment of employee business expenses.

Under the current scheme of deductions for and from A.G.I., an important—and perhaps inequitable—distinction is made based on whether an individual is an employee or self-employed. As seen above, employees generally deduct all unreimbursed business expenses as itemized deductions. In contrast, self-employed taxpayers (i.e., sole proprietors or partners)

[54] Rev. Rul. 92-29, 1992-1 C.B.20.

deduct business expenses for A.G.I. At first glance, the difference appears trivial, particularly for those taxpayers who itemize their deductions. Recall, however, that an employee's business expenses are treated as miscellaneous itemized deductions and thus are deductible only to the extent that these and all other miscellaneous itemized deductions collectively exceed 2 percent of the taxpayer's A.G.I. Due to this distinction, deductibility often depends on the employment status of the taxpayer.

### Example 23

T is an accountant. During the year she earns $30,000 and pays dues of $100 to be a member of the local CPA society. These were her only items of income and expense. If T practices as a self-employed sole proprietor (e.g., she has a small firm or partnership), the dues are fully deductible for A.G.I. However, if T is an employee, none of the expense is deductible since it does not exceed the 2% floor of $600 (2% × $30,000). If T's employer had reimbursed her for the expense and included the reimbursement in her income, the expense would have been completely deductible, totally offsetting the amount that T must include in income. If T is employed, but at the same time does some accounting work on her own, part-time, the treatment is unclear.

The logic for the distinction based on employment status is fragile at best. According to the committee reports, Congress believed that it was generally appropriate to disallow deductions for employee business expenses because employers reimburse employees for those expenses that are most necessary for employment. In addition, Congress felt that the treatment would simplify the system by relieving taxpayers of the burden of record keeping and at the same time relieving the IRS of the burden of auditing such deductions.

### Reimbursed Expenses

The classification and treatment of an employee's deductible business expenses can vary depending on whether they are reimbursed. If the employee is not reimbursed, the unreimbursed business expenses are deductible as miscellaneous itemized deductions. If the employee is reimbursed and he or she properly accounts to the employer according to the "accountable plan" rules, neither the amount of the reimbursement nor the expense is reported on the return.[55] The accountable plan rules, which are discussed in detail in Chapter 8, generally require employees to substantiate their expenses (e.g., provide documentation such as receipts). If the accountable plan rules are not followed or a plan does not exist, the reimbursement is treated as wages subject to employment taxes and the expense is deducted as a miscellaneous itemized deduction.

### Example 24

Professor K is employed by State University in the finance department. The department has a policy of reimbursing up to $50 for each faculty member's costs of subscribing to finance journals. During the year, K spent $75 on subscriptions. He submitted the receipt for $50 of his expenses and was reimbursed by his employer. Assuming the employer's reimbursement policy meets the accountable plan requirements and K has adequately accounted for the expense, the $50 reimbursement is not included in K's wages and K claims no deduction. K may deduct the remaining $25 as a miscellaneous itemized deduction. In this situation, there is no effect on A.G.I. The transaction is a "wash" economically for K and is, therefore a "wash" on K's tax return.

---

[55] See Reg. § 1.62-2. Note also that the employer is not required to file an information return when there is an accountable plan.

## Example 25

Same as above except the plan did not meet the accountable plan standard. In this case, the employer would include the reimbursement of $50 in K's wages (e.g., his W-2) and K could deduct the $50 of expenses along with the other $25 as miscellaneous itemized deductions. Of course, if K does not itemize or his miscellaneous itemized deductions do not exceed the 2 percent floor, he would not benefit from the deduction. Observe that in this situation where the accountable plan rules are not met, the transaction is not a "wash" from a tax point of view. The amount K receives is reduced by employment taxes on the $50 and he may or may not be able to deduct the $50 of his subscriptions.

### Expenses of Performing Artists

Most employee business expenses were relegated to second-class status in 1986 as they became subject to the 2 percent limitation. However, one group of employees, the struggling performing artists, escaped this restriction. These actors, actresses, musicians, dancers, and the like are technically employees but exhibit many attributes of the self-employed. They often work for several employers for little income yet incur relatively large unreimbursed expenses as they seek their fortunes. For these reasons, "qualified performing artists" are permitted to deduct their business expenses *for* A.G.I. To qualify, the individual must perform services in the performing arts as an employee for at least two employers during the taxable year, earning at least $200 from each. In addition, the individual's A.G.I. before business deductions cannot exceed $16,000. Lastly, the artist's business deductions must exceed 10 percent of his or her gross service income, otherwise they too are considered miscellaneous itemized deductions.

## Example 26

Z is an actress. This year she worked in two Broadway productions for two different employers, earning $7,000 from each for a total of $14,000. Her expenses, including the fee to her agent, were $2,000. She may deduct all of her expenses for A.G.I.

### Self-Employed or Employee?

The above discussion illustrates the importance of determining whether an individual is self-employed or is treated as an employee. However, whether an individual is self-employed or is an employee is often difficult to determine. An employee is a person who performs services for another individual subject to that individual's direction and control.[56] In the employer-employee relationship, the right to control extends not only to the result to be accomplished but also to the methods of accomplishment. Accordingly, an employee is subject to the will and control of the employer as to both what will be done and how it will be done. In the case of the self-employed person, the individual is subject to the control of another only as to the end result, and not as to the means of accomplishment. Generally, physicians, lawyers, dentists, veterinarians, contractors, and subcontractors are not employees. An insurance agent or salesperson may be an employee or self-employed, depending on the facts. The courts have developed numerous tests for differentiating between employees and self-employed persons. Each of the following situations would suggest that an employer-employee relationship exists.[57]

1. Complying with written or oral instructions (an independent contractor need not be trained or attend training sessions)
2. Regular written or oral reports on the work's status

[56] Reg. § 31.3401(c)-1(a).

[57] Rev. Rul. 87-41, 1987-1 C.B. 296. This Revenue Ruling actually contains 20 questions.

3. Continuous relationship—more than sporadic services over a lengthy period
4. Lack of control over the place of work
5. No risk of profit or loss; no income fluctuations
6. Regular payment—hourly, weekly, etc. (an independent contractor might work on a job basis)
7. Specified number of hours required to work (an independent contractor is master of his or her own time)
8. Unable to delegate work—hiring assistants not permitted
9. Not independent—does not work for numerous firms or make services available to general public

## Limitations on Deductions

**LO.7**
Recognize statutory, administrative, and judicial limitations on deductions and losses.

Some provisions of the Code specifically prohibit or limit the deduction of certain expenses and losses despite their apparent relationship to the taxpayer's business or profit-seeking activities. These provisions operate to disallow or limit the deduction for various expenses unless such expenses are specifically authorized by the Code. As a practical matter, these provisions have been enacted to prohibit abuses identified in specific areas. Several of the more fundamental limitations are considered in this chapter.

### Hobby Expenses and Losses

As previously discussed, a taxpayer must establish that he or she pursues an activity with the objective of making a profit before the expense is deductible as a business or production of income expense. When the profit motive is absent, the deduction is governed by § 183 on activities not engaged in for profit (i.e., hobbies). Section 183 generally provides that hobby expenses of an individual taxpayer or S corporation are deductible only to the extent of the gross income from the hobby. Thus, the tax treatment of hobby expenses substantially differs from profit-seeking expenses if the expenses of the activity exceed the income, resulting in a net loss. If the loss is treated as arising from a profit-motivated activity, then the taxpayer ordinarily may use it to reduce income from other sources.[58] Conversely, if the activity is considered a hobby, no loss is deductible. Note, however, that hobby expenses may be deducted to offset any hobby income.

#### Profit Motive

The problem of determining the existence of a profit motive usually arises in situations where the activity has elements of both a personal and a profit-seeking nature (e.g., auto racing, antique hunting, coin collecting, horse breeding, weekend farming). In some instances, these activities may represent a profitable business venture. Where losses are consistently reported, however, the business motivation is suspect. In these cases all the facts and circumstances must be examined to determine the presence of the profit motive. The courts have held that the taxpayer simply is required to pursue the activity with a bona fide intent of making a profit. The taxpayer, however, need not show a profit. Moreover, the taxpayer's expectation of profit need not be considered reasonable.[59] The Regulations set out nine factors to be used in ascertaining the existence of a profit motive.[60] Some of the questions posed by these factors are:

1. Was the activity carried on in a businesslike manner? Were books and records kept? Did the taxpayer change his or her methods or adopt new techniques with the intent to earn a profit?
2. Did the taxpayer attempt to acquire knowledge about the business or consult experts?

[58] The limitations imposed on losses from passive activities should not be applicable in this situation since the taxpayer materially participates in the activity. See discussion in Chapter 12 and § 469.

[59] Reg. § 1.183-2(a).

[60] Reg. § 1.183-2(b).

3. Did the taxpayer or family members devote much time or effort to the activity? Did they leave another occupation to have more time for the activity?
4. Have there been years of income as well as years of loss? Did the losses occur only in the start-up years?
5. Does the taxpayer have only incidental income from other sources? Is the taxpayer's wealth insufficient to maintain him or her if future profits are not derived?
6. Does the taxpayer derive little personal or recreational pleasure from the activity?

An affirmative answer to several of these questions suggests a profit motive exists.

### Presumptive Rule

The burden of proof in the courts is normally borne by the taxpayer. Section 183, however, shifts the burden of proof to the IRS in hobby cases where the taxpayer shows profits in any three of five consecutive years (two of seven years for activities related to horses).[61] The rule creates a presumption that the taxpayer has a profit motive unless the IRS can show otherwise. An election is available to the taxpayer to postpone IRS challenges until five (or seven) years have elapsed from the date the activity commenced. Making the election allows the taxpayer sufficient time to have three profitable years and thus shift the burden of proof to the IRS. This election must be filed within three years of the due date of the return for the taxable year in which the taxpayer first engages in the activity, but not later than 60 days after the taxpayer has received notice that the IRS proposes to disallow the deduction of expenses related to the hobby. The election automatically extends the statute of limitations for each of these years, thus enabling a later challenge by the IRS. It should be emphasized that this presumptive rule only shifts the burden of proof. Profits in three of the five (or two of seven) years do not absolve the taxpayer from attack.

#### Example 27

T enjoys raising, breeding, and showing dogs. In the past, she occasionally sold a dog or puppy. In 2010 T decided to pursue these activities seriously. During the year, she incurred a loss of $4,000. T also had a loss of $2,000 in 2011. If T made no election for any of these years (i.e., within three years of the start of the activity), the IRS may assert that T's activities constitute a hobby. In this case, the burden of proof is on T to show a profit motive, since she has not shown a profit in at least three years. If T made an election, then the IRS is barred from assessing a deficiency until five years have elapsed. Five years need to elapse to determine whether T will have profits in three of the five years and, if so, shift the burden of proof to the IRS in any litigation that may occur. If an election is made, however, the period for assessing deficiencies for all years is extended until two years after the due date of the return for the last taxable year in the five-year period.[62] In T's case, an election would enable the IRS to assess a deficiency for 2010 and subsequent years up until April 15, 2017, assuming T is a calendar year taxpayer. If an election were not made, the statute of limitations would normally bar assessments three years after the return is due (e.g., assessments for 2010 would be barred after April 15, 2014).

### Deduction Limitation

If the activity is considered a hobby, the related expenses are deductible to the extent of the activity's gross income as reduced by *otherwise allowable deductions.*[63] Otherwise allowable deductions are those expenses relating to the hobby that are deductible under other sections of the Code regardless of the activity in which they are incurred. For example, property taxes are deductible under § 164 without regard to whether the activity in which they are

[61] § 183(d).

[62] § 183(d)(4).

[63] § 183(b). On classification of the deductions, see Rev. Rul. 75-14, 1975-1 C.B. 90 and Senate Finance Committee Report on H.R. 3838, S. Rep. No. 99-313 (5/29/86), p. 80, 99th Cong., 2nd. Sess.

incurred is a hobby or a business. Similarly, interest on debt secured by the taxpayer's principal or secondary residence is deductible regardless of the character of the activity. Consequently, any expense otherwise allowable is deducted *first* in determining the gross income limitation. Any other expenses are deductible to the extent of any remaining gross income (i.e., other operating expenses are taken next, with any depreciation deductions, taken last). Otherwise allowable deductions are fully deductible as itemized deductions, while other deductible expenses are considered miscellaneous itemized deductions and are deductible only to the extent they exceed 2 percent of A.G.I. (including the hobby income).

## Example 28

R, an actor, enjoys raising, breeding, and racing horses as a hobby. His A.G.I. excluding the hobby activities is $68,000. He has a small farm on which he raises the horses. During the current year, R won one race and received income of $2,000. He paid $2,300 in expenses as follows: $800 property taxes related to the farm and $1,500 feed for horses. R calculated depreciation with respect to the farm assets at $6,500. As a result, R has a net loss from the activity of $6,800 ($2,000 – $2,300 – $6,500). If the activity is *not* considered a hobby but rather a trade or business, R would report the loss on Schedule C and assuming it is not a passive loss, he could use it to offset his other income. However, if the activity is considered a hobby and R itemizes deductions, he would compute his deductions as follows:

| | | |
|---|---|---|
| Gross income | $2,000 | |
| Otherwise allowable deductions: | | |
| Taxes | (800) | $ 800 |
| Gross income limitation | $1,200 | |
| Feed expense: | | |
| $1,500 limited to remaining gross income | | 1,200 |
| Total | | $2,000 |

Note that because depreciation is taken last, there is no deduction for this item.

R would include $2,000 in gross income, increasing his A.G.I. to $70,000. Of the $2,000 in deductible expenses, the property taxes of $800 are deductible in full as an itemized deduction. The remaining $1,200 is considered a miscellaneous itemized deduction. In this case, none of the $1,200 is deductible since this amount does not exceed the 2% floor of $1,400 (2% of $70,000). No deduction is allowed for the remaining feed expense of $300 ($1,500 – $1,200) due to the gross income limitation.

## Example 29

Assume the same facts as in *Example 25* except that R's expense for property taxes is $2,400 instead of $800. In this case, because the entire $2,400 is deductible as an otherwise allowable deduction and exceeds the gross income from the hobby, none of the feed expense is deductible. Thus, R would include $2,000 in gross income and the $2,400 of property taxes would be fully deductible from A.G.I.

## Personal Living Expenses

Just as the Code specifically authorizes deductions for the costs of pursuing income—business and income-producing expenses—it denies deductions for personal expenses. Section 262 prohibits the deduction of any personal, living, or family expenses. Only those personal expenditures expressly allowed by some other provision in the Code are deductible. Some of the personal expenditures permitted by other provisions are medical expenses, contributions, qualified residence interest, and taxes. Normally, these expenses are classified as itemized deductions. These deductions and their underlying rationale are discussed in Chapter 11.

The disallowance of personal expenditures by § 262 complements the general criteria allowing a deduction. Recall that the general rules of §§ 162 and 212 permit deductions for ordinary and necessary expenses *only where a profit motive exists.* As previously seen in the discussion of hobbies, however, determining whether an expense arose from a personal or profit motive can be difficult. Some of the items specifically disallowed by § 262 are:

1. Expenses of maintaining a household (e.g., rent, utilities)
2. Losses on sales of property held for personal purposes
3. Amounts paid as damages for breach of promise to marry, attorney's fees, and other costs of suits to recover such damages
4. Premiums paid for life insurance by the insured
5. Costs of insuring a personal residence

## Legal Expenses

Legal expenses related to divorce actions and the division of income-producing properties are often a source of conflict. Prior to clarification by the Supreme Court, several decisions held that divorce expenses incurred primarily to protect the taxpayer's income-producing property or his or her business were deductible.[64] The Supreme Court, however, has ruled that deductibility depends on whether the expense arises in connection with the taxpayer's profit-seeking activities. That is, the *origin* of the expense determines deductibility.[65] Under this rule, if the spouse's claim arises from the marital relationship—a personal matter—then no deduction is allowed. Division of income-producing property would only be incidental to or a consequence of the marital relationship.

### Example 30

R pays legal fees to defend an action by his wife to prevent distributions of income from a trust to him. Because the wife's action arose from the marital relationship, the legal expenses are nondeductible personal expenditures.[66]

Legal expenses related to a divorce action may be deductible where the expense is for advice concerning the tax consequences of the divorce.[67] The portion of the legal expense allocable to counsel on the tax consequences of a property settlement, the right to claim children as dependents, and the creation of a trust for payment of alimony are deductible.

## Contingent Attorney Fees

Over the years, there has been a great deal of controversy regarding the treatment of contingent attorney fees incurred in securing a damages award. To illustrate, assume a taxpayer receives an award of fully taxable punitive damages of $10 million and the attorney is to receive a contingent fee of 40 percent of that amount or $4 million. In this situation, the taxpayer typically asserted that the fees represent a splitting of the income and, therefore, he or she should be taxed only on the net amount received or $6 million. Conversely, the government argued that the full $10 million is included in gross income and the $4 million of attorney fees were a miscellaneous itemized deduction subject to the two percent limitation and the one percent cutback. But more importantly, since the attorney fees were classified as miscellaneous itemized deductions, they were not allowed in computing the alternative

---

[64] *F.C. Bowers v. Comm.*, 57-1 USTC ¶9605, 51 AFTR 207, 243 F.2d 904 (CA-6, 1957).

[65] *Supra*, Footnote 13, Also, compare *Comm. v. Tellier*, 66-1 USTC ¶9319, 17 AFTR2d 633, 383 U.S. 687 (USSC, 1966) with *Boris Nodiak v. Comm.*, 66-1 USTC ¶9262, 17 AFTR2d 396, 356 F.2d 911 (CA-2, 1966).

[66] *H.N. Shilling, Jr.*, 33 TCM 1097, T.C. Memo 1974-246.

[67] Rev Rul. 72-545, 1972-2 C.B. 179.

minimum tax (AMT). As a result, an AMT often resulted. In effect, the taxpayer paid tax on $10 million when he or she had only received $6 million.

Congress addressed this problem in 2004. Attorney's fees and court costs incurred for certain legal actions are deductible for A.G.I. This rule applies to most legal actions, but not necessarily all.[68] Apparently, certain types of tort actions, such as defamation, would not fall within the statute unless they occur within the employment context. By classifying these expenses as deductions for A.G.I., the AMT problem is eliminated since the AMT limitations generally apply only to certain itemized deductions.[69]

## Capital Expenditures

A capital expenditure is ordinarily defined as an expenditure providing benefits that extend beyond the close of the taxable year. It is a well-established rule in case law that a business expense, though ordinary and necessary, is not deductible in the year paid or incurred if it can be considered a capital expenditure.[70] Normally, however, a capital expenditure may be deducted ratably over the period for which it provides benefits. For example, the Code authorizes deductions for depreciation or cost recovery, amortization, and depletion where the asset has a determinable useful life.[71] Capital expenditures creating assets that do not have a determinable life, however, generally cannot be deducted. For example, land is considered as having an indeterminable life and thus cannot be depreciated or amortized. The same is true for stocks and bonds. Expenditures for these types of assets are recovered (i.e., deducted) only when there is a disposition of the asset through sale (e.g., cost offset against sales price), exchange, abandonment, or other disposition.

As a general rule, assets with a useful life of one year or less need not be capitalized. For example, the taxpayer can write off short-lived assets with small costs such as supplies (e.g., stationery, pens, pencils, calculators), books (e.g., the Internal Revenue Code), and small tools (e.g., screwdrivers, rakes, and shovels).

### Goodwill

Like land, goodwill is an example of an asset that does not have a determinable useful life. Because of this indeterminate life, acquired goodwill historically has been treated as a capitalized asset that could not be depreciated. The only way a taxpayer could receive a current tax benefit from acquired goodwill was to identify components separate and apart from goodwill that had an ascertainable value and limited useful life (e.g., client files and subscription lists). If a taxpayer was successful in establishing the requisite valuation and limited life for a goodwill component, the taxpayer could depreciate the cost of the intangible asset over its useful life using the straight-line method (known as amortization). However, in practice, taxpayers often faced challenges by the IRS, and many attempts to depreciate goodwill components were unsuccessful.

Congress enacted Code § 197 to reduce the uncertainty surrounding the depreciation of goodwill and its identifiable components. Effective August 10, 1994, the cost of acquiring intangible assets (including acquired goodwill) may, at the election of the taxpayer, be amortized over a 15-year period. If the election is not made, the cost of acquiring goodwill and related intangibles must be capitalized and no amortization will be allowed.

---

[68] § 62 (a)(20) extends the deduction for actions in connection with unlawful discrimination claims, certain claims against the federal government, and private causes of action under the Medicare Secondary Payer law. Unlawful discrimination actions include those that claim violations of the Civil Rights Acts of 1964 and 1991, the Congressional Accountability Act of 1995, the National Labor Relations Act, the Family and Medical Leave Act of 1993, the Fair Housing Act, the Americans with Disabilities Act of 1990, and various whistle-blower statutes.

[69] The Jobs Act does apply to cases settled prior to October 23, 2004. The Supreme Court settled the issue for these cases, reversing pro-taxpayer decisions in the Sixth and Ninth Circuits, indicating that there had been an invalid assignment of income and, therefore the legal expenses were miscellaneous itemized deductions. See *Comm. v. John W. Banks II and Comm. v. Sigitas J. Banaitis*, (combined) 2005-1 USTC ¶50,595, AFTR 2d 2005-659, (USSC, 2005), rev'g *Banks II*, 92 2003-6298, 2003-2 USTC ¶50,675,AFTR 2d, 345 F3d 373 (CA-6, 2003), and rev'g *Banaitis*, 92 AFTR 2d 2003-5834, 2003-2 USTC ¶50,638; 340 F3d 1074 (CA-9, 2003).

[70] *Supra*, footnote 18.

[71] §§ 167, 168, 169, 178, 184, 188, and 611 are examples.

### Example 31

B has decided to purchase a newspaper business in a small town for $100,000. It can be determined that $80,000 of the purchase price is allocable to the assets of the business and $20,000 is attributable to goodwill (subscription lists and other intangibles). B may be able to recover all $100,000 of the cost through deductions for depreciation and amortization.

## Capital Expenditures versus Repairs

The general rule of case law disallowing deductions for capital expenditures has been codified for expenditures relating to property. Code § 263 provides that deductions are not allowed for any expenditures for new buildings or for permanent improvements or betterments made to increase the value of property.[72] Additionally, expenditures substantially prolonging the property's useful life, adapting the property to a new or different use, or materially adding to the value of the property are not deductible.[73] Conversely, the cost of incidental repairs that do not materially increase the value of the property nor appreciably prolong its life, but maintain it in a normal operating state, may be deducted in the current year.[74] For example, costs of painting, inside and outside, and papering are usually considered repairs.[75] However, if the painting is done in conjunction with a general reconditioning or overhaul of the property, it is treated as a capital expenditure.[76]

### Example 32

L operates his own limousine business. Expenses for a tune-up such as the costs of spark plugs, points, and labor would be deductible as routine repairs and maintenance since such costs do not significantly prolong the car's life. In contrast, if L had the transmission replaced at a cost of $600, allowing him to drive it for another few years, the expense must be capitalized.

## Acquisition Costs

As a general rule, costs related to the acquisition of property must be capitalized. For example, freight paid to acquire new equipment or commissions paid to acquire land must be capitalized. In addition, Code § 164 requires that state and local general sales taxes related to the purchase of property be capitalized. The costs of demolition or removal of an old building prior to using the land in another fashion must be capitalized as part of the cost of the land.[77] Costs of defending or perfecting the title to property, such as legal fees, are normally capitalized.[78] Similarly, legal fees incurred for the recovery of property must be capitalized unless the recovered property is investment property or money that must be included in income if received.[79]

## INDOPCO and the Long-Term Benefit Theory

Interestingly, one of the most important and widely debated tax developments to occur in recent years concerns the capital expenditure area. The controversy stems from a Supreme Court decision involving the treatment of costs incurred by a target company as part of a friendly takeover. In 1977, Unilever approached one of its suppliers, INDOPCO, about the possibility of a takeover to which INDOPCO agreed. During the acquisition process, INDOPCO paid an investment banking company, Morgan Stanley, about $2.2 million for

[72] § 263(a).

[73] Reg. § 1.263(a)-1(b).

[74] Reg. § 1.162-4.

[75] *Louis Allen*, 2 BTA 1313 (1925).

[76] *Joseph M. Jones*, 57-1 USTC ¶9517, 50 AFTR 2040, 242 F.2d 616 (CA-5, 1957).

[77] § 280B.

[78] Reg. § 1.263(a)-2.

[79] Reg. § 1.212-1(k).

advice and a fairness opinion and another $500,000 to its own legal counsel for services related to the takeover. The IRS ultimately denied deduction of the expenses (as well as amortization) on the grounds that the expenses were capital in nature. In 1992, the Supreme Court concurred with the IRS, believing that INDOPCO would receive long-term benefits from the acquisition, including the opportunity for synergy with Unilever and the future availability of Unilever's financial and business resources.[80]

The effect of the INDOPCO decision would not be so great if it were confined to costs incurred as part of a friendly takeover. However, the IRS has used the broad language of the court to capitalize any expense to which it can associate any long-term benefit. In this regard, it is important to understand that the Supreme Court indicated that the long-term benefits need not be associated with any specific identifiable asset. As long as the expenditure leads to the permanent betterment of the business as a whole, capitalization may be in order. For example, the IRS has used this approach to deny a deduction for the costs of removing asbestos insulation from equipment if the removal is part of a general plan of rehabilitation, despite the fact that the expense did not extend the life of the asset.[81] Instead, the taxpayer was required to capitalize the expenditure on the grounds that the firm would derive long-term benefits from safer working conditions and reduced risk of liability. In another ruling concerning advertising costs, the IRS, while allowing a current deduction, warned that in certain instances advertising could produce long-term benefits, in which case such expenses must be capitalized.[82] In short, the INDOPCO decision has increased the tension between taxpayers and the IRS in the capital expenditure arena.

Over time, the intensity of the controversy and the level of uncertainty produced by INDOPCO escalated to an intolerable level. In response to the criticism, the IRS issued final regulations in 2004 to reign in the scope of INDOPCO and its "long-term-benefit" theory.[83] The regulations are quite extensive. There are over 50 pages and more than 80 examples all aimed at resolving whether a particular cost related to an intangible should be capitalized. Although a full discussion of these regulations is beyond the scope of this text, they are required reading whenever a taxpayer incurs an expense related to an intangible. Specifically, the regulations address amounts paid to

- *Acquire* an intangible (e.g., purchase a customer list, lease, patent, copyright, franchise, trademark, trade name, assembled workforce, or goodwill; most of these must be amortized over 15 years under § 197)
- *Create* an intangible (e.g., costs for prepaid items such as prepaid rents and insurance, membership privileges such as membership in a trade association, rights from governmental agencies such as the exclusive rights obtained from the local government by a cable television company to serve a particular region, contract rights and contract terminations such as the rights to renew or renegotiate, licenses, and covenants not to compete)
- *Create* or enhance a separate and distinct intangible
- *Facilitate* the acquisition or creation of an intangible (e.g., legal expenses for negotiating commercial property lease, drafting agreements)
- *Facilitate* the acquisition of a trade or business, a change in the capital structure of a business entity, and certain other transactions (e.g., legal expenses to issue debt, payments to investment banker and outside legal counsel for evaluating alternative investments, performing due diligence, structuring the transaction, preparing SEC filings, and obtaining necessary regulatory approvals, hostile takeover defenses).

These regulations should bring to a close a period of great uncertainty that was not envisioned when the Supreme Court decided the INDOPCO case in 1992.

## Environmental Remediation Costs

Under Code § 198 which took effect on August 5, 1997, a taxpayer may elect to treat certain environmental remediation expenditures that would otherwise be chargeable to a capital account as deductible in the year paid or incurred. To qualify for this special treatment, the

[80] *INDOPCO, Inc. v. Comm.*, 92-1 USTC ¶50,113, 69 AFTR2d 92-694, 503 U.S. 79 (USSC, 1992).

[81] *Norwest Corporation*, 108 T.C. No. 15 (1997).

[82] Rev. Rul. 92-80, 1992-2 C.B. 57.

[83] Reg. § 1.263(a)-4 and -5.

expense must be incurred in connection with the abatement or control of hazardous substances at a qualified contaminated site. Prior to the enactment of this provision, the IRS took the view that costs incurred to clean-up the environment were controlled by the long-term benefit theory of INDOPCO and, therefore, were capital expenditures for which no deduction was allowed. The effect of § 198, then, is to override the IRS's reliance on the long-term benefit theory to deny deductions with respect to environmental remediation costs.

### Elections to Capitalize or Deduct

Various provisions of the Code permit a taxpayer to treat capital expenditures as deductible expenses, as deferred expenses, or as capital expenditures. For example, at the election of the taxpayer, expenses for research and experimentation may be deducted currently, treated as deferred expenses and amortized over at least 60 months, or capitalized and included in the basis of the resulting property.[84]

## Business Investigation Expenses and Start-up Costs

Another group of expenses that arguably may be considered capital expenditures are those incurred when seeking and establishing a new business, such as costs of investigation and start-up. Business investigation expenses are those costs of seeking and reviewing prospective businesses prior to reaching a decision to acquire or enter any business. Such expenses include the costs of analysis of potential markets, products, labor supply, and transportation facilities. Start-up or pre-opening expenses are costs that are incurred after a decision to acquire a particular business and prior to its actual operations. Examples of these expenses are advertising, employee training, lining up distributors, suppliers, or potential customers, and the costs of professional services such as attorney and accounting fees.

For many years, the deductibility of expenses of business investigation and start-up turned solely on whether the taxpayer was "carrying on" a business at the time the expenditures were incurred. Notwithstanding some modifications, the basic rule still remains: when the taxpayer is in the same or similar business as the one he or she is starting or investigating, the costs of investigation and start-up are wholly deductible in the year paid or incurred.[85] The deduction is allowed regardless of whether the taxpayer undertakes the business.[86] However, this rule often forces taxpayers to litigate to determine whether a business exists at the time the expenses are incurred. Prior to the enactment of § 195, if the taxpayer could not establish existence of a business, the expenditures normally were treated as capital expenditures with indeterminable lives.[87] As a result, the taxpayer could only recover the expenditure if and when he or she disposed of or abandoned the business.

In 1980 Congress realized that the basic rule not only was a source of controversy but also discouraged formation of new businesses. For this reason, special provisions permitting deduction of these expenses under certain conditions were enacted.[88] Before examining these provisions, it should be emphasized that the traditional rule continues to be valid. Thus, if a taxpayer can establish that the investigation and start-up costs are related to a similar existing business of the taxpayer, a deduction is allowed.

> **Example 33**
>
> S owns and operates an ice cream shop on the north side of the city. A new shopping mall is opening on the south side of the city, and the developers have approached her about locating a second ice cream shop in their mall. During 2011 S pays a consulting firm $1,000 for a survey of the potential market on the south side. Because S is in the ice cream business when the expense is incurred, the entire $1,000 is deductible regardless of whether she undertakes the new business.

---

[84] § 174. See §§ 175 and 180 for other examples.

[85] *The Colorado Springs National Bank v. U.S.*, 74-2 USTC ¶9809, 34 AFTR2d 74-6166, 505 F.2d 1185 (CA-10, 1974).

[86] *York v. Comm.*, 58-2 USTC ¶9952, 2 AFTR2d 6178, 261 F.2d 421 (CA-4, 1958).

[87] *Morton Frank*, 20 T.C. 511 (1953).

[88] § 195(a).

### Amortization Provision

Section 195 sets out the treatment for the start-up and investigation expenses of taxpayers who are *not* considered in a similar business when the expenses are incurred *and* who actually enter the new business. Eligible taxpayers may elect to deduct up to $5,000 of business investigation and start-up expenses in the tax year in which the business begins. If the §195 expenses exceed $5,000, the excess must be amortized over the 180-month period (15 years) beginning with the month in which the business begins.[89] If the expenses exceed $50,000, the $5,000 allowance is reduced one dollar for each dollar in excess of $50,000. Expenses for research and development, interest payments, and taxes are not considered start-up expenditures.[90] Thus, these costs are not subject to §195 and may be deducted under normal rules.

#### Example 34

J, a calendar year, cash basis taxpayer, recently graduated and received $10,000 from his uncle as a graduation gift. J paid an accountant $1,200 in June to review the financial situation of a small restaurant he desired to purchase. In December, J purchased the restaurant and began actively participating in its management. J may deduct the entire $1,200 for the current year since it does not exceed $5,000.

#### Example 35

S, a famous bodybuilder, has decided to build his first health spa. While the facility is being constructed, a temporary office is set up in a trailer next to the site. The office is nicely decorated and contains a small replica of the facility. S hired a staff who will manage the facility but at this time are calling prospective customers. Elaborate brochures have been printed. All of these costs, including the salaries paid to the staff, the printing of the brochures, and the costs of operating the trailer such as depreciation and utilities, are start-up costs. Assuming the total start-up costs were less than $50,000, the taxpayer could expense the first $5,000 and amortize the balance over 180 months.

#### Example 36

Same facts as above except S incorporated and the corporation incurred $23,000 of start-up and investigation expenses. The corporation was formed in July of this year and adopted the calendar year. In this case, the corporation could deduct $5,000 immediately and amortize the remaining balance of $18,000 over 15 years (180 months) beginning in July. This would result in amortization of $100/month for 180 months. The deduction for start-up and investigation expenses for 2011 would be $5,600 computed as follows:

| | |
|---|---|
| First-year allowance | $5,000 |
| Amortization ($18,000/180 = $100/month × 6 months) | 600 |
| Total deduction in first year | $5,600 |

In 2012, the corporation would continue to amortize the remaining expenses, resulting in a deduction of $1,200 ($100/month × 12).

---

[89] § 195 expenses incurred prior to October 23, 2004 are amortized over 60 months.

[90] § 195(c)(1).

## Example 37

In March, 2011 LMN, LLC was formed and incurred start-up and investigation expenses of $52,000. LMN's immediate expensing allowance of $5,000 must be reduced one dollar for each dollar of § 195 expense exceeding $50,000. In this case, the allowance is reduced by $2,000 ($52,000 – $50,000) to $3,000. Thus LMN may deduct $3,000 plus amortization of the remaining $49,000, resulting in a deduction of $5,720 computed below.

| | | |
|---|---|---|
| First-year allowance [$5,000 – ($52,000 – $50,000 = $2,000)] | | $3,000 |
| Amortization: | | |
| Total expense . . . . . . . . . . . . . . . . . . . . . . . . . . . . . . . . . | $52,000 | |
| First-year allowance . . . . . . . . . . . . . . . . . . . . . . . . . . . . . | (3,000) | |
| Amortizable balance. . . . . . . . . . . . . . . . . . . . . . . . . . . . . | $49,000 | |
| Amortization ($49,000/180 = $272/month × 10 months) . . . | | 2,720 |
| Total § 195 expense deduction in first year. . . . . . . . . . . . . . . . | | $5,720 |

Note that if LMN had incurred $55,000 or more of § 195 expenses, the $5,000 immediate write-off would be reduced to zero and all $55,000 of the expenses would be amortized over 180 months.

As suggested above, the taxpayer must enter the business to qualify for amortization. Whether the individual is considered as having entered the business normally depends on the facts in each case.

If the taxpayer (who is not in a similar, existing business) does not enter into the new business, the investigation and start-up expenses generally are not deductible. The Tax Court, however, has held that a taxpayer may deduct costs as a loss suffered from a transaction entered into for profit if the activities are sufficient to be considered a "transaction."[91] The IRS has interpreted this rule to mean that those expenditures related to a *general search* for a particular business or investment are not deductible.[92] Expenses are considered general when they are related to whether to enter the transaction and which transaction to enter. Once the taxpayer has focused on the acquisition of a *specific* business or investment, expenses related to an unsuccessful acquisition attempt are deductible as a loss on a transaction entered into for profit.

## Example 38

L, a retired army officer, is interested in going into the radio business. He places advertisements in the major trade journals soliciting information about businesses that may be acquired. Upon reviewing the responses to his ads, L selects two radio stations for possible acquisition. He hires an accountant to audit the books of each station and advise him on the feasibility of purchase. He travels to the cities where each station is located and discusses the possible acquisition with the owners. Finally, L decides to purchase station FMAM. To this end, he hires an attorney to draft the purchase agreement. Due to a price dispute, however, the acquisition attempt collapses. The expenses for advertising, auditing, and travel are not deductible since they are related to the taxpayer's general search. The legal expenses are deductible as a loss, however, since they occurred in the taxpayer's attempt to acquire a specific business.

### Job-Seeking Expenses

The tax treatment of job-seeking expenses of an employee is similar to that for expenses for business investigation. If the taxpayer is seeking a job in the same business in which he or she is presently employed, the related expenses are deductible as miscellaneous itemized

[91] *Harris W. Seed*, 52 T.C. 880 (1969).

[92] Rev. Rul. 77-254, 1977-2 C.B. 63.

deductions subject to the 2 percent floor.[93] The deduction is allowed even if a new job is not obtained. No deduction or amortization is permitted, however, if the job sought is considered a new trade or business or the taxpayer's first job.

**Example 39**

B, currently employed as a biology teacher, incurs travel expenses and employment agency fees to obtain a new job as a computer operator. The expenses are not deductible because they are not incurred in seeking a job in the profession in which she was currently engaged. Moreover, the expenses are not deductible even though B obtained the new job. However, the expenses would be deductible if she had obtained a new job in her present occupation.

## Public Policy Restrictions

Although an expense may be entirely appropriate and helpful, and may contribute to the taxpayer's profit-seeking activities, it is not considered necessary if the allowance of a deduction would frustrate sharply defined public policy. The courts established this long-standing rule on the theory that to allow a deduction for expenses such as fines and penalties would encourage violations by diluting the penalty.[94] Historically, however, the IRS and the courts were free to restrict deductions of any type of expense where, in their view, it appeared that the expenses were contrary to public policy—even if the policy had not been clearly enunciated by some governmental body. As a result, taxpayers were often forced to go to court to determine if their expense violated public policy.

Recognizing the difficulties in applying the public policy doctrine, Congress enacted provisions specifically designed to limit its use.[95] The rules identified and disallowed certain types of expenditures that would be considered contrary to public policy. Under these provisions no deduction is allowed for fines, penalties, and illegal payments.

### Fines and Penalties

A deduction is not allowed for any fine or similar penalty paid to a government for the violation of any law.[96]

**Example 40**

S is a salesperson for an office supply company. While calling on customers this year, he received parking tickets of $100. None of the cost is deductible because the violations were against the law.

**Example 41**

Upon audit of T's tax return, it was determined that he failed to report $10,000 of tip income from his job as a maitre d', resulting in additional tax of $3,000. T was also required to pay the negligence penalty for intentional disregard of the rules. The penalty—20% of the tax due—is not deductible.

---

[93] Rev. Rul. 75-120, 1975-1 C.B. 55, as clarified by Rev. Rul. 77-16, 1977-1 C.B. 37.

[94] *Hoover Motor Express Co., Inc. v. U.S.*, 58-1 USTC ¶9367, 1 AFTR2d 1157, 356 U.S. 38 (USSC, 1958).

[95] S. Rep. No. 91-552, 91st Cong., 1st Sess. 273-75 (1969). Note, however, that the Tax Court continues to utilize the doctrine despite Congress's attempt to restrict its use—see *R. Mazzei*, 61 T.C. 497 (1974).

[96] § 162(f).

### Example 42

This year the Federal Drug Administration fined C Inc., a drug manufacturing company, $5,000,000 for failure to maintain adequate quality control. The fine is not deductible because the practices were in violation of Federal law.

Fines include those amounts paid in settlement of the taxpayer's actual or potential liability.[97] In addition, no deduction is allowed for two-thirds of treble damage payments made due to a violation of antitrust laws.[98] Thus, one-third of this antitrust "fine" is deductible.

## Illegal Kickbacks, Bribes, and Other Payments

The Code also disallows the deduction for four categories of illegal payments:[99]

1. Kickbacks or bribes to U.S. government officials and employees if illegal
2. Payments to governmental officials or employees of *foreign* countries if such payments would be considered illegal under the U.S. Foreign Corrupt Practices Act

### Example 43

R travels all over the world, looking for unique items for his gift shop. Occasionally when going through customs in foreign countries, he is forced to "bribe" the customs official to do the necessary paperwork and get him through customs as quickly as possible. These so-called grease payments to employees of foreign countries are deductible unless they violate the Foreign Corrupt Practices Act. In general, such payments are not considered to be illegal.

3. Kickbacks, bribes, or other illegal payments to any other person if illegal under generally enforced U.S. or state laws that provide a criminal penalty or loss of license or privilege to engage in business
4. Kickbacks, rebates, and bribes, although legal, made by any provider of items or services under Medicare and Medicaid programs

Those kickbacks and bribes not specified above would still be deductible if they were ordinary and necessary. The payment, however, may not be necessary and thus will be disallowed if it controverts public policy.

Kickbacks generally include payments for referral of clients, patients, and customers. However, under certain circumstances, trade discounts or rebates may be considered kickbacks.

### Example 44

M, a life insurance salesperson, paid rebates or discounts to purchasers of policies. Since such practice is normally illegal under state law, the rebate is not deductible.[100]

---

[97] § 162(g).

[98] Reg. § 1.162-21(b).

[99] § 162(c).

[100] *James Alex*, 70 T.C. 322 (1978).

### Expenses of Illegal Business

The expenses related to an illegal business are deductible.[101] Similar to the principle governing taxation of income from whatever source (including income illegally obtained), the tax law is not concerned with the lawfulness of the activity in which the deductions arise. No deduction is allowed, however, if the expense itself constitutes an illegal payment as discussed above. In addition, Code § 280E prohibits the deduction of any expenses related to the trafficking in controlled substances (i.e., drugs).

## LOBBYING AND POLITICAL CONTRIBUTIONS

Although expenses for lobbying and political contributions may be closely related to the taxpayer's business, Congress has traditionally limited their deduction. These restrictions usually are supported on the grounds that it is not in the public's best interest for government to subsidize efforts to influence legislative matters.

### Lobbying

Prior to 1962, no deduction was permitted for any type of lobbying expense. In 1962, however, Congress altered its position slightly with the addition of § 162(e), which carved out a narrow exception for certain lobbying expenses. This provision allowed a deduction for the expenses of appearing before or providing information to governmental units on legislative matters of *direct interest* to the taxpayer's business. Similarly, a deduction was permitted for expenses of providing information to a trade organization of which the taxpayer was a member where the legislative matter was of direct interest to the taxpayer and the organization. The portion of dues paid to such an organization attributable to the organization's allowable lobbying activities was also deductible. Beginning in 1994, however, these rules for deducting lobbying expenses are even more restrictive. Lobbying expenditures are now deductible only if incurred for the purpose of influencing legislation at the *local* level. Therefore, the expense of influencing national and state legislation (including the costs of hiring lobbyists to represent the taxpayer in these matters) is not deductible. This prohibition is extended to the costs of any direct communication with executive branch officials in an attempt to influence official actions or positions of such official.

The taxpayer must have a direct interest in the local legislation before lobbying expenses may be deducted. Although the definitional boundaries of the term "direct" are vague, a taxpayer is considered as having satisfied the test if it is reasonable to expect that the local legislative matter affects or will affect the taxpayer's business. However, a taxpayer does not have a direct interest in the nomination, appointment, or operation of any local legislative body.[102]

The deduction for lobbying *does not* extend to expenses incurred to influence the general public on legislative matters, elections, or referendums.[103] Expenses related to the following types of lobbying are not deductible:

1. Advertising in magazines and newspapers concerning legislation of direct interest to the taxpayer.[104] However, expenses for "goodwill" advertising presenting views on economic, financial, social, or similar subjects of a general nature, or encouraging behavior such as contributing to the Red Cross, are deductible.[105]
2. Preparing and distributing to a corporation's shareholders pamphlets focusing on certain legislation affecting the corporation and urging the shareholders to contact their representatives in Congress.[106]

---

[101] See *Max Cohen v. Comm.*, 49-2 USTC ¶9358, 176 F.2d 394 (CA-10, 1949) and *Neil Sullivan v. Comm.*, 58-1 USTC ¶9368, AFTR2d 1158, 356 U.S. 27 (USSC, 1958).

[102] Reg. § 1.162-20(b).

[103] § 162(e)(2).

[104] Rev. Rul. 78-112, 1978-1 C.B. 42.

[105] Reg. § 1.162-20(a)(2).

[106] Rev. Rul. 74-407, 1974-2 C.B. 45, as amplified by Rev. Rul. 78-111, 1978-1 C.B. 41.

### Example 45

T owns a restaurant in Austin, Texas. Legislation has been introduced by the City Council to impose a sales tax on food and drink sold in Austin, to be used for funding a dome stadium. T places an ad in the local newspaper stating reasons why the legislation should not be passed. He goes to the City Council and testifies on the proposed legislation before several committees. He pays dues to the Austin Association of Restaurant Owners organization, which estimates that 60% of its activities are devoted to lobbying for local legislation related to restaurant owners. T may deduct the cost of travel and 60% of his dues since the local legislation is of direct interest to him. He may not deduct the ad since it is intended to influence the general public.

### Political Contributions

No deduction is permitted for any contributions, gifts, or any other amounts paid to a political party, action committee, or group or candidate related to a candidate's campaign.[107] This rule also applies to indirect payments, such as the payments for advertising in a convention program and admission to a dinner, hall, or similar affair where any of the proceeds benefit a political party or candidate.[108]

## Expenses and Interest Relating to Tax-Exempt Income

Section 265 sets forth several rules generally disallowing deductions for expenses relating to tax-exempt income. These provisions prohibit taxpayers from taking advantage of the tax law to secure a double tax benefit: tax-exempt income and deductions for the expenses that help to produce it. The best known rule prohibits the deduction for any *interest* expense or nonbusiness (§ 212) expense related to tax-exempt *interest* income.[109] Without this rule, taxpayers in high tax brackets could borrow at a higher rate of interest than could be earned and still have a profit on the transaction.

### Example 46

D, an investor in the 25% tax bracket with substantial investment income, borrows funds at 9% and invests them in tax-exempt bonds yielding 7%. If the interest expense were deductible, the after-tax cost of borrowing would be 6.75% [(100% – 25% = 75%) × 9%]. Since the interest income is nontaxable, the after-tax yield on the bond remains 7%, or .25 percentage points higher than the effective cost of borrowing. Section 265, however, denies the deduction for the interest expense, thus eliminating the feasibility of this arrangement. It should be noted, however, that business (§ 162) expenses (other than interest) related to tax-exempt interest income may be deductible.

If the income that is exempt is not interest, none of the related expenses are deductible.[110]

### Example 47

A company operating a baseball team paid premiums on a disability insurance policy providing that the company would receive proceeds under the policy if a player were injured. Because the proceeds would not be taxable, the premiums are not deductible even though the expenditure would apparently qualify as a business expense.[111] Note,

[107] § 162(e).

[108] § 276.

[109] § 265(2).

[110] § 265(1).

[111] Rev. Rul. 66-262, 1966-2 C.B. 105.

however, that such expenses would enter into the calculation of net income for financial accounting purposes.

As a practical matter, it would appear difficult to determine whether borrowed funds (and the interest expense) are related to carrying taxable or tax-exempt securities. For example, an individual holding tax-exempt bonds may take out a mortgage to buy a residence instead of selling the bonds to finance the purchase price. In such case, it could be inferred that the borrowed funds were used to finance the bond purchase. Generally, the IRS will allow the deduction in this and similar cases unless the facts indicate that the primary purpose of the borrowing is to carry the tax-exempt obligations.[112] The facts must establish a *sufficiently direct relationship* between the borrowing and the investment producing tax exempt income before a deduction is denied.

**Example 48**

K owns common stock with a basis of $70,000 and tax-exempt bonds of $30,000. She borrows $100,000 to finance an investment in an oil and gas limited partnership. The IRS will disallow a deduction for a portion of the interest on the $100,000 debt because it is presumed that the $100,000 is incurred to finance all of K's portfolio including the tax-exempt securities.[113]

**Example 49**

R has a margin account with her broker. This account is devoted solely to the purchase of taxable investments and tax-exempt bonds. During the year, she buys several taxable and tax-exempt securities on margin. A portion of the interest expense on this margin account is disallowed because the borrowings are considered partially related to financing of the investment in tax-exempt securities.[114]

### Business Life Insurance

Absent a special rule, premiums paid on insurance policies covering officers and employees of a business might be deductible as ordinary and necessary business expenses. However, to ensure that the taxpayer is not allowed to deduct expenses related to tax-exempt income (i.e., life insurance proceeds), a special provision exists. Under § 264, the taxpayer is not allowed any deduction for life insurance premiums paid on policies covering the life of any officer, employee, or any other person who may have a financial interest in the taxpayer's trade or business, if the taxpayer is the *beneficiary* of the policy. Thus, premiums paid by a business on a key-person life insurance policy where the company is beneficiary are not deductible. Note that this differs from the financial accounting treatment, where the premiums would be considered routine operating costs that should be expensed in determining net income. In contrast, payments made by a business on group-term life insurance policies where the employees are beneficiaries are deductible.

## Related Taxpayer Transactions

Without restrictions, related taxpayers (such as husbands and wives, shareholders and their corporations) could enter into arrangements creating deductions for expenses and losses, and

[112] Rev. Proc. 72-18, 1972-1 C.B. 740, as clarified by Rev. Proc. 74-8, 1974-1 C.B. 419, and amplified by Rev. Rul. 80-55, 1980-2 C.B. 849.

[113] *Ibid.*

[114] *B.P. McDonough v. Comm.*, 78-2 USTC ¶9490, 42 AFTR2d 78-5172, 577 F.2d 234 (CA-4, 1978).

not affect their economic position. For example, a husband and wife could create a deduction simply by having one spouse sell property to the other at a loss. In this case, the loss is artificial because the property remains within the family and their financial situation is unaffected. Although the form of ownership has been altered, there is no substance to the transaction. To guard against the potential abuses inherent in transactions between related taxpayers, Congress designed specific safeguards contained in § 267.

## Related Taxpayers

The transactions that are subject to restriction are only those between persons who are considered "related" as defined in the Code. Related taxpayers are:[115]

1. Certain family members: brothers and sisters (including half-blood), spouse, ancestors (i.e., parents and grandparents), and lineal descendants (i.e., children and grandchildren)
2. Taxpayer and his or her corporation: an individual and a corporation if the individual owns either directly or *indirectly* more than 50 percent of the corporation's stock[116]
3. Personal service corporation and an employee-owner: a corporation whose principal activity is the performance of personal services that are performed by the employee-owners (i.e., an employee who owns either directly or indirectly *any* stock of the corporation)
4. Certain other relationships involving regular corporations, S corporations, partnerships, estates, trusts, and individuals

In determining whether a taxpayer and a corporation are related, the taxpayer's direct and indirect ownership must be taken into account for the 50 percent test. A taxpayer's indirect stock ownership is any stock that is considered owned or "constructively" owned but not actually owned by the taxpayer. Section 267 provides a set of constructive ownership rules, also referred to as *attribution rules*, indicating the circumstances when the taxpayer is considered as owning the stock of another. Under the constructive ownership rules, a taxpayer is considered owning indirectly[117]

1. Stock owned directly or indirectly by his or her family as defined above
2. His or her proportionate share of any stock owned by a corporation, partnership, estate, or trust in which he or she has ownership (or of which he or she is a beneficiary in the case of an estate or trust)
3. Stock owned indirectly or directly by his or her partner in a partnership

In using these rules, the following limitations apply: (1) stock attributed from one family member to another *cannot* be reattributed to members of his or her family, and (2) stock attributed from a partner to the taxpayer *cannot* be reattributed to a member of his or her family or to another partner.[118]

### Example 50

H and W are husband and wife. HB is H's brother. H, W, and HB own 30, 45, and 25% of X Corporation, respectively. H is considered as owning 100% of X Corporation, 30% directly and 70% indirectly (25% through HB and 45% through W, both by application of attribution rule 1 above). W is considered as owning 75% of X Corporation, 45% directly and 30% indirectly through H by application of attribution rule 1 (note that HB's stock cannot be attributed to H and reattributed to W). HB is considered as owning 55% of X Corporation, 25% directly and 30% indirectly through H by application of attribution rule 1 and the reattribution limitation.

---

[115] § 267(b).

[116] A partner and a partnership in which the partner owns more than a 50 percent interest are treated in the same manner. See § 707(b).

[117] § 267(c).

[118] § 267(c)(5).

### Losses

The taxpayer is not allowed to deduct the loss from a sale or exchange of property directly or indirectly to a related taxpayer (as defined above).[119] However, any loss disallowed on the sale may be used to offset any gain on a subsequent sale of the property by a related taxpayer to an unrelated third party.[120]

#### Example 51

A father owns land that he purchased as an investment for $20,000. He sells the land to his daughter for $15,000, producing a $5,000 loss. The $5,000 loss may not be deducted because the transaction is between related taxpayers. If the daughter subsequently sells the property for $22,000, she will then realize a $7,000 gain ($22,000 sales price – $15,000 basis). However, the gain may be reduced by the $5,000 loss previously disallowed, resulting in a recognized gain of $2,000 ($7,000 realized gain – $5,000 previously disallowed loss). If the daughter had sold the property for only $19,000, the realized gain of $4,000 ($19,000 – $15,000) would have been eliminated by the previous loss of $5,000. The $5,000 loss previously disallowed is used only to the extent of the $4,000 gain. The remaining portion of the disallowed loss ($1,000) cannot be used. Had the father originally sold the property for $19,000 to an outsider as his daughter subsequently did, the father would have recognized a $1,000 loss ($19,000 sales price – $20,000 basis). Note that the effect of the disallowance rule does not increase the basis of the property to the related taxpayer by the amount of loss disallowed.

The results of these transactions are summarized below.

| | | |
|---|---|---|
| *Original sale between related parties* | | |
| Sales price | $15,000 | |
| Adjusted basis | (20,000) | |
| Disallowed loss | ($ 5,000) | |
| *Subsequent sale* | 1 | 2 |
| Sales price | $ 22,000 | $ 19,000 |
| Adjusted basis | (15,000) | (15,000) |
| Realized gain (loss) | $ 7,000 | $ 4,000 |
| Usage of disallowed loss | (5,000) | (4,000) |
| Recognized gain | $ 2,000 | $ 0 |

#### Example 52

S owns 100% of V Corporation. She sells stock with a basis of $100 to her good friend T for $75, creating a $25 loss for S. T, in turn, sells the stock to V Corporation for $75, thus recouping the amount he paid S with no gain or loss. The $25 loss suffered by S, however, is not deductible because the sale was made *indirectly* through T to her wholly owned corporation.

### Unpaid Expenses and Interest

Prior to enactment of § 267, another tax avoidance device used by related taxpayers involved the use of different accounting methods by each taxpayer. In the typical scheme, a taxpayer's corporation would adopt the accrual basis method of accounting while the taxpayer reported on a cash basis. The taxpayer could lend money, lease property, provide services, etc., to the corporation and charge the corporation for whatever was provided. As an accrual basis

[119] § 267(a)(1).

[120] § 267(d).

taxpayer, the corporation would accrue the expense and create a deduction. The cash basis individual, however, would report no income until the corporation's payment of the expense was actually received. As a result, the corporation could accrue large deductions without ever having to make a disbursement and, moreover, without the taxpayer recognizing any offsetting income. The Code now prohibits this practice between "related taxpayers" as defined above. Code § 267 provides that an accrual basis taxpayer can deduct an accrued expense payable to a related cash basis taxpayer *only* in the period in which the payment is included in the recipient's income.[121] This rule effectively places all accrual basis taxpayers on the cash method of accounting for purposes of deducting such expenses.

### Example 53

B, an individual, owns 100% of X Corporation, which manufactures electric razors. B uses the cash method of accounting while the corporation uses the accrual basis. Both are calendar year taxpayers. On December 27, 2011 the corporation accrues a $10,000 bonus for B. However, due to insufficient cash flow, X Corporation was not able to pay the bonus until January 10, 2012. The corporation may not deduct the accrued bonus in 2011. Rather, it must deduct the bonus in 2012, the year in which B includes the payment in his income.

### Example 54

Assume the same facts as above, except that B owns only a 20% interest in X. In addition, X is a large law firm in which B is employed. The results are the same as above because B and X are still related parties: a personal service corporation and an employee-owner.

## Payment of Another Taxpayer's Obligation

As a general rule, a taxpayer is not permitted to deduct the payment of a deductible expense of another taxpayer. A deduction is allowed only for those expenditures satisfying the taxpayer's obligation or arising from such an obligation.

### Example 55

As part of Q's rental contract for his personal apartment, he pays 1% of his landlord's property taxes. No deduction is allowed because the property taxes are the obligation of the landlord.

### Example 56

P is majority stockholder of R Corporation. During the year, the corporation had financial difficulty and was unable to make an interest payment on an outstanding debt. To protect the goodwill of the corporation, P paid the interest. The payment is not deductible, and P will be treated as having made a contribution to the capital of the corporation for interest paid.

---

[121] § 267(a)(2).

An exception to the general rule is provided with respect to payment of medical expenses of a dependent. To qualify as a dependent for this purpose, the person needs only to meet the relationship, support, and citizen tests.[122] If the taxpayer pays the medical expenses of a person who qualifies as a dependent under the modified tests, the expenses are treated as if they were the taxpayer's expenses and are deductible subject to limitations applicable to the taxpayer.

### SUBSTANTIATION

The Code requires that taxpayers maintain records sufficient to establish the amount of gross income, deductions, credits, or other matters required to be shown on the tax return.[123] As a practical matter, record keeping requirements depend on the nature of the item. With respect to most deductions, taxpayers may rely on the "*Cohan* rule."[124] In *Cohan*, George M. Cohan, the famous playwright, spent substantial sums for travel and entertainment. The Board of Tax Appeals (predecessor to the Tax Court) denied any deduction for the expenses because the taxpayer had no records supporting the items. On appeal, however, the Second Circuit Court of Appeals reversed this decision, indicating that "absolute certainty in such matters is usually impossible and is not necessary."[125] Thus, the Appeals Court remanded the case to make some allowance for the expenditures. From this decision, the "*Cohan* rule" developed, providing that a reasonable estimation of the deduction is sufficient where the actual amount is not substantiated. In 1962, however, Congress eliminated the use of the *Cohan* rule for travel and entertainment expenses and established rigorous substantiation requirements for these types of deductions. Substantiation for other expenses, however, is still governed by the *Cohan* rule. Despite the existence of the *Cohan* rule, records should be kept documenting deductible expenditures since estimates of the expenditures may be substantially less than actually paid or incurred.

## Tax Planning Considerations

### MAXIMIZING DEDUCTIONS

**LO.8**
Explain tax planning considerations for optimizing deductions.

Perhaps the most important step in minimizing the tax liability is maximizing deductions. Maximizing deductions obviously requires the taxpayer to identify and claim all the deductions to which he or she is entitled. Many taxpayers, however, often overlook deductions that they are allowed because they fail to grasp and apply the fundamental rules discussed in this chapter. To secure a deduction, the taxpayer needs only to show that the expense paid or incurred during the year is ordinary, necessary, and related to a profit-seeking activity. Notwithstanding the special rules of limitation that apply to certain deductions, most deductions are allowed because the *taxpayer* is able to recognize and establish the link between the expenditure and the profit-seeking activity. The taxpayer is in the best position to recognize that an expenditure relates to his or her trade or business, not the tax practitioner. Practitioners typically lack sufficient insight into the taxpayer's activities to identify potential deductions. Thus, it is up to the taxpayer to recognize and establish the relationship between an expenditure and the profit-seeking activity. Failure to do so results in the taxpayer's paying a tax liability higher than what he or she is required to pay.

The taxpayer should maximize not only the absolute dollar amount of deductions, but also the value of the deduction. A deduction's value is equal to the product of the amount of the deduction and the taxpayer's marginal tax rate. Because the taxpayer's marginal rate fluctuates over time, the value of a deduction varies depending on the period in which the deduction is claimed. When feasible, deductions should normally be accelerated or deferred to years when the taxpayer is in a higher tax bracket. In timing deductions, however, the time value of money also must be considered. For example, in periods of inflation, the deferral of a deduction to a high-bracket year may not always be advantageous, since a deduction in the future is not worth as much as one currently.

[122] § 213(a)(1).

[123] Reg. § 1.6001-1(a).

[124] *Cohan v. Comm.*, 2 USTC ¶489, 8 AFTR 10552, 39 F.2d 540 (CA-2, 1930).

[125] *Ibid.*

An individual taxpayer's timing of itemized deductions is particularly important in light of the standard deduction and the floor on miscellaneous itemized deductions. Many taxpayers lose deductions because their deductions do not exceed the standard deduction in any one year. These deductions need not be lost, however, if the taxpayer alternates the years in which he or she itemizes or uses the standard deduction. For example, in those years where the taxpayer itemizes, all tax deductible expenditures from the prior year should be deferred while expenditures of the following year should be accelerated. By so doing, the taxpayer bunches itemized deductions in the current year to exceed the standard deduction. In the following year, the taxpayer would use the standard deduction. Itemized deductions are considered in detail in Chapter 11.

Maximizing deductions also requires shifting of deductions to the taxpayer who would derive the greatest benefit. For example, if two sisters are co-obligors on a note, good tax planning dictates that the sister in the higher tax bracket pay the deductible interest expense. In this case, either sister may pay and claim a deduction.

## Timing of Deductions

In the previous section, the importance of maximizing the absolute amount of deductions was emphasized. However, because of the time value of money it is equally important to consider the timing of deductions.

### Example 57

R, who pays Federal, state, and local taxes equal to 50% of his income, makes a cash expenditure of $10,000. If the $10,000 is deductible immediately, R will realize a tax benefit of $5,000 ($10,000 × 50%). Moreover, because the tax savings were realized immediately, the present value of the benefit is not diminished. On the other hand, if R is not able to deduct the $10,000 for another five years, the benefit of the deduction is substantially reduced. Specifically, assuming the annual interest rate is 10%, the present value of the $5,000 tax savings decreases to $3,105 ($5,000 × [1 ÷ (1 + 0.10)5]), a decrease of almost 38%.

As the above example illustrates, accelerating a deduction from the future to the present can substantially increase its value. Awareness of the provisions permitting acceleration of deductions allows taxpayers to arrange their affairs so as to reap the greatest rewards. For example, a taxpayer may choose an investment that the tax law allows him or her to deduct immediately rather than an investment that must be capitalized and deducted through depreciation over the asset's life.

## Expenses Relating to Tax-Exempt Income

Although expenses related to tax-exempt income are not deductible, expenses related to tax-deferred income are deductible.[126] For example, income earned on contributions to Individual Retirement Accounts is not taxable until the earnings are distributed (usually at retirement). If the taxpayer borrows amounts to contribute to his or her Individual Retirement Account, interest paid on the borrowed amounts may be deductible (if the general rules for deductibility are met) because the income to which it relates is only tax-deferred, not tax-exempt.

## "Points" on Mortgages

"Points" paid to secure a mortgage to acquire or improve a principal residence normally are deductible in the year paid or incurred. In some cases, however, the points are not paid out of independent funds of the taxpayer but are withheld from the mortgage proceeds. For

[126] *Hawaiian Trust Co., Ltd. v. U.S.*, 61-1 USTC ¶9481, 7 AFTR2d 1553, 291 F.2d 761 (CA-9, 1961). See also Letter Rul. 8527082 (April 2, 1985).

example, where a lender is charging two points on a $50,000 loan, or $1,000 (2% of $50,000), the $1,000 is withheld by the lender as payment while the remaining $49,000 ($50,000 – $1,000) is advanced to the borrower. The Tax Court has ruled that in these situations, the taxpayer has not prepaid the interest (as represented by the points) and thus must amortize the points over the term of the loan.[127] To avoid this result and obtain a current deduction, the taxpayer should pay the points out of separate funds rather than having them withheld by the lender. This requirement will be met if the cash paid by the borrower up to and at the closing (including down payments, escrow deposits, earnest money, and amounts paid at closing) is at least equal to the amount deducted for points.[128] In this regard, the IRS has ruled that points paid by the seller on behalf of a borrower will be treated as paid directly from the funds deposited by the borrower.[129] Thus, the borrower will be entitled to a deduction. However, in determining the basis of the residence, the borrower must subtract the amount of seller paid points from the purchase price.

### HOBBIES

Several studies suggest that the factor on which the hobby/business issue often turns is the manner in which the taxpayer carries on the activity.[130] For business treatment, it is imperative that the taxpayer have complete and detailed financial and nonfinancial records. Moreover, such records should be used in decision making and in constructing a profit plan. The activity should resemble a business in every respect. For example, the taxpayer should maintain a separate checking account for the activity, advertise where appropriate, obtain written advice from experts and follow it, and acquire some expertise about the operation.

Although the taxpayer is not required to actually show profits, profits in *three* of *five* consecutive years create a substantial advantage for the taxpayer. Where the profit requirement is satisfied, it is presumed that the activity is not a hobby and the IRS has the burden of proving otherwise. For this reason, the cash basis taxpayer might take steps that could convert a loss year into a profitable year. For example, in some situations it may be possible to accelerate receipts and defer payment of expenses. However, the taxpayer should be cautioned that arranging transactions so nominal profits occur has been viewed negatively by the courts.

## Problem Materials

### DISCUSSION QUESTIONS

**7-1** *General Requirements for Deductions.* Explain the general requirements that must be satisfied before a taxpayer may claim a deduction for an expense or a loss.

**7-2** *Deduction Defined.* Consider the following:

- **a.** It is often said that income can be meaningfully defined while deductions can be defined only procedurally. Explain.
- **b.** The courts are fond of referring to deductions as matters of "legislative grace." Explain.
- **c.** Although deductions may only be defined procedurally, construct a definition for a deduction similar to the "all inclusive" definition for income.
- **d.** Will satisfaction of the requirements of your definition ensure deductibility? Explain.

**7-3** *Business versus Personal Expenditures.* Consider the following:

- **a.** If the taxpayer derives personal pleasure from an otherwise deductible expense, will the expense be denied? Explain.
- **b.** Name some of the purely personal expenses that are deductible, and indicate whether they are deductions for or from A.G.I.

**7-4** *Business versus Investment Expenses.* Two Code sections govern the deductibility of ordinary and necessary expenses related to profit-motivated activities. Explain why two provisions exist and the distinction between them.

---

[127] *Roger A. Schubel*, 77 T.C. 701 (1982).

[128] Rev. Proc. 92-12, 1992-3, I.R.B. 27.

[129] Rev. Proc. 94-27, 1994 I.R.B. 15, 6.

[130] See, for example, Burns and Groomer, "Effects of Section 183 on the Business Hobby Controversy," *Taxes* (March 1980) pp. 195–206.

**7-5** *An Employee's Business.* Is an employee considered as being in trade or business? Explain the significance of your answer.

**7-6** *Year Allowable.* The year in which a deduction is allowed depends on whether the taxpayer is a cash basis or accrual basis taxpayer. Discuss.

**7-7** *Classification of Expenses.* F is a self-employed registered nurse and works occasionally for a nursing home. G is a registered nurse employed by a nursing home. Their income, exemptions, credits, etc. are identical. Explain why a deductible expense, although paid in the same amount by both, may cause F and G to have differing tax liabilities.

**7-8** *Above- and Below-the-Line Deductions.* At a tax seminar, F was reminded to ensure that he properly classified his deductions as either above- or below-the-line. After the seminar, F came home and scrutinized his Form 1040 to determine what the instructor meant and why it was important. Despite his careful examination of the form, F could not figure out what the instructor was talking about or why it was important. Help F out by explaining the meaning of this classification scheme.

**7-9** *Performing Artists.* V hopes to become a movie star someday. Currently, she accepts bit parts in various movies, waiting for her break. What special tax treatment may be available for V?

**7-10** *Classification of Deductions.* J and K are both single, and each earns $30,000 of income and has $2,000 of deductible expenses for the current year. J's deductions are for A.G.I. while K's deductions are itemized deductions.

**a.** Given these facts, and assuming that the situation of J and K is identical in every other respect, will their tax liabilities differ? Explain.

**b.** Same as (a) except their deductions are $7,000.

**7-11** *Constructive Distributions.* D owns all of the stock of DX Inc., which manufactures record jackets. Over the years, the corporation has been very successful. This year, D placed his 16- and 14-year-old sons on the payroll, paying them each $10,000 annually. The boys worked on the assembly line a couple of hours each week. Explain D's strategy and the risks it involves.

**7-12** *Disguised Distributions.* E owns all of the stock of EZ Inc., which operates a nursery. During the past several years, the company has operated at a deficit and E finally sold all of his stock to C. C drew a very low salary before he could turn things around. Now the business is highly profitable, and C is paying himself handsomely. As C's tax adviser, what counsel if any should be given to C?

**7-13** *Income and Expenses of Illegal Business.* B is a bookie in a state where gambling is illegal. During the year, he earned $70,000 accepting bets. His expenses included those for rent, phone, and utilities. In addition, he paid off a state legislator who was a customer and who obviously knew of his activity.

**a.** Discuss the tax treatment of B's income and expenses.

**b.** Same as (a) except B was a drug dealer.

**7-14** *Permanent and Timing Differences.* Financial accounting and tax accounting often differ in the manner in that certain expenses are treated. Identify several expenditures that, because of their treatment, produce permanent or timing differences.

**7-15** *Capital Expenditures.* Can a cash basis taxpayer successfully reduce taxable income by purchasing supplies near year-end and deducting their cost?

**7-16** *Independent Contractor versus Employee.* Briefly discuss the difference between an independent contractor (self-employed person) and an employee and why the distinction is important.

**7-17** *Hobby Expenses.* Discuss the factors used in determining whether an activity is a hobby and the tax consequences resulting from its being deemed a hobby.

**7-18** *Public Policy Doctrine.* A taxpayer operates a restaurant and failed to remit the sales tax for August to the city as of the required date. As a result, he must pay an additional assessment of 0.25 percent of the amount due. Comment on the deductibility of this payment.

**7-19** *Constructive Ownership Rules.* Explain the concept of constructive ownership and the reason for its existence.

**7-20** *Expenses Relating to Tax-Exempt Income.* Discuss what types of expenses relating to tax exempt income may be deductible.

**7-21** *Substantiation.* Explain the Cohan rule.

## PROBLEMS

**7-22** *General Requirements for Deduction.* For each of the following expenses identify and discuss the general requirement(s) (ordinary, necessary, related to business, etc.) upon which deductibility depends.

**a.** A police officer who is required to carry a gun at all times lives in New York. The most convenient and direct route to work is through New Jersey. The laws of New Jersey, however, prohibit the carrying of a gun in the car. As a result, he must take an indirect route to the police station to avoid New Jersey. The indirect route causes him to drive ten miles more than he would otherwise. The cost of the additional mileage is $500. (**Note:** commuting expense from one's home to the first job site generally is a nondeductible personal expense.)

**b.** The current president of a nationwide union spends $10,000 for costs related to reelection.

**c.** The taxpayer operates a lumber business. He is extremely religious and consequently is deeply concerned over the business community's social and moral responsibility to society. For this reason, he hires a minister to give him and his employees moral and spiritual advice. The minister has no business background although he does offer solutions to business problems.

**d.** The taxpayer operates a laundry in New York City. He was recently visited by two "insurance agents" who wished to sell him a special bomb policy (i.e., if the taxpayer paid the insurance "premiums," his business would not be bombed). The taxpayer paid the premiums of $500 each month.

**7-23** *Accrual Basis Deductions.* In each of the situations below assume the taxpayer uses the accrual method of accounting and indicate the amount of the deduction allowed.

**a.** R sells and services gas furnaces. As part of his sales package, he agrees to turn on and cut off the buyer's furnace for five years. He normally charges $80 for such service, which costs him about $50 in labor and materials. Based on 2011 sales, R sets up a reserve for the costs of the services to be performed, which he estimates will be $9,000 over the next five years.

**b.** At the end of 2011, XYZ, a regular corporation, agreed to rent office space from ABC Leasing Corp. Pursuant to the contract, XYZ paid $10,000 on December 1, 2011 for rent for all of 2012.

**c.** RST Villas, a condominium project in a Vermont ski resort, reached an agreement with MPP Pop-Ins providing that MPP would provide maid services in 2012 for $20,000. RST transferred its note payable for $20,000 at the end of 2012 to MPP on December 1, 2011.

**7-24** *Economic Performance.* KKO Printing, a calendar year, accrual method taxpayer, leases a number of copying machines. As part of the lease, it typically purchases a one-year maintenance contract covering service on the machines. On July 20, 2011, KKO paid $6,000 for a one-year service contract that runs from July 1, 2011 through June 30, 2012. Ignoring the recurring item exception, when may KKO deduct the expense?

**7-25** *Recurring Items.* M Corporation is an accrual basis taxpayer and uses the calendar year for both financial accounting and tax purposes. The corporation manufactures car stereo equipment and provides a one-year warranty. Based on an analysis of its sales for 2011, it estimates that its warranty expense for equipment sold in 2011 will be $500,000. For financial accounting purposes, M plans to accrue the expense in 2011. The corporation is in the process of finishing its 2011 tax return, which it plans on filing by the extended due date, September 15, 2012. According to the company's latest figures, as of August 31, it had incurred $200,000 in parts and labor costs in honoring warranties on 2011 sales. How should the corporation treat the $500,000 estimated warranty cost on its 2011 tax return?

**7-26** *Accrual of Real Property Taxes.* M Inc. owns a chain of hamburger restaurants located all across the country. In one state where the company has several outlets, it paid real property taxes of $12,000 for the period October 1, 2010 through September 30, 2011 on January 10, 2012. M is an accrual basis taxpayer and uses a calendar year-end for reporting.

**a.** When is M entitled to a deduction for the real estate taxes assuming it has not made an election under § 461(c) and the recurring item exception does not apply?

**b.** Same as (a) except the M makes an election under § 461(c).

**7-27** *Accrual versus Cash Method of Accounting.* D operates a hardware store. For 2011, D's first year of operation, D reported the following items of revenue and expense:

| | |
|---|---|
| Cash receipts | $140,000 |
| Purchase of goods on credit | 90,000 |
| Payments on payables | 82,000 |

By year-end, D had unsold goods on hand with a value of $25,000.

**a.** Using the cash method of accounting, compute D's taxable income for the year.

**b.** Using the accrual method of accounting, compute D's taxable income for the year.

**c.** Which method of accounting is required for tax purposes? Why?

**7-28** *Prepaid Interest.* In each of the following cases, indicate the amount of the deduction for the current year. In each case, assume the taxpayer is a calendar year, cash basis taxpayer.

**a.** On December 31, P, wishing to reduce his current year's tax liability, prepaid $3,000 of interest on his home mortgage for the first three months of the following taxable year.

**b.** On December 1 of this year, T obtained a $100,000 loan to purchase her residence. The loan was secured by the residence. She paid two points to obtain the loan bearing a 6 percent interest rate.

**c.** Same as (b) except the loan was used to purchase a duplex, which she will rent to others. The loan was secured by the duplex.

**7-29** *Prepaid Rent.* This year F, a cash basis taxpayer, secured a ten-year lease on a warehouse to be used in his business. Under the lease agreement he pays $12,000 on September 1 of each year for the following twelve months' rental.

**a.** Assuming F pays $12,000 on September 1 for the next 12 months' rental, how much, if any, may he deduct? How would your answer change if F were an accrual basis taxpayer?

**b.** In order to secure the lease, F also was required to pay an additional $12,000 as a security deposit. How much, if any, may he deduct?

**7-30** *Prepaid Expenses.* D, a cash basis taxpayer, operates a successful travel agency. One of her more significant costs is a special computer form on which airline tickets are printed as well as stationery on which itineraries are printed. Typically, D buys about a three-month supply of these forms for $2,000. Knowing that she will be in a lower tax bracket next year. D would like to accelerate her deductions to the current year.

**a.** Assuming that D pays $12,000 on December 15 for forms that she expects to exhaust before the close of next year, how much can she deduct?

**b.** Same as above except D purchases the larger volume of forms because D's supplier began offering special discounts for purchases in excess of $3,000.

**7-31** *Expenses Producing Future Benefits.* B took over as chief executive officer of Pentar Inc., which specializes in the manufacture of cameras. As part of his strategy to increase the corporation's share of the market, he ran a special advertising blitz just prior to Christmas that cost more than $1,000,000. The marketing staff estimates that these expenditures could very well increase the company's share of the market by 10 percent over the next three years. Speculate on the treatment of the promotion expenses.

**7-32** *Capital Expenditure or Repair.* This year, Dandy Development Corporation purchased an apartment complex with 100 units. At the time of purchase, it had a 40 percent vacancy rate. As part of a major renovation, Dandy replaced all of the carpeting and painted all of the vacant units. Discuss the treatment of the expenditures.

**7-33** *Identifying Capital Expenditures.* K, a sole proprietor, made the following payments during the year. Indicate whether each is a capital expenditure.

**a.** Sales tax on the purchase of a new automobile
**b.** Mechanical pencil for K
**c.** Mops and buckets for maintenance of building
**d.** Freight paid on delivery of new machinery
**e.** Painting of K's office
**f.** Paving of dirt parking lot with concrete
**g.** Commissions to leasing agent to find new office space
**h.** Rewiring of building to accommodate new equipment

**7-34** *Hobby Expenses—Effect on A.G.I.* C is a successful attorney and stock car racing enthusiast. This year she decided to quit watching the races and start participating. She purchased a car and entered several local races. During the year, she had the following receipts and disbursements related to the racing activities:

| | |
|---|---|
| Race winnings . . . . . . . . . . . . . . . . . . . . . . . . . . . . . . . | $3,000 |
| Property taxes . . . . . . . . . . . . . . . . . . . . . . . . . . . . . . . | 2,800 |
| Fuel, supplies, maintenance . . . . . . . . . . . . . . . . . . . . . . . | 1,000 |

Her A.G.I. exclusive of any items related to the racing activities is $100,000.

**a.** Indicate the tax consequences assuming the activity is not considered to be a hobby.
**b.** Assuming the activity is treated as a hobby, what are the tax consequences?
**c.** Assuming the activity is deemed a hobby and property taxes are $4,000, what are the tax consequences?
**d.** What is the critical factor in determining whether an activity is a hobby or a business?
**e.** What circumstances suggest the activity is a business rather than a hobby?

**7-35** *Hobby-Presumptive Rule.* In 2010 R, a major league baseball player, purchased a small farm in North Carolina. He grows several crops and maintains a small herd of cattle on the farm. During 2010 his farming activities resulted in a $2,000 loss, which he claimed on his 2010 tax return, filed April 15, 2011. In 2011 his 2010 return was audited, and the IRS proposed an adjustment disallowing the loss from the farming activity, asserting that the activity was merely a hobby.

**a.** Assuming R litigates, who has the burden of proof as to the character of the activity?
**b.** Can R shift the burden of proof at this point in time?
**c.** Assume R filed the appropriate election for 2010 and reported losses of $3,000 in 2011 and profits of $14,000 in 2012, $5,000 in 2013, and $6,000 in 2014. What effect do the reported profits have?

**7-36** *Hobby Losses and Statute of Limitations.* Assume the same facts as in Problem 7-35. When does the statute of limitations bar assessment of deficiencies with respect to the 2010 tax return?

**7-37** *Investigation Expenses.* H currently operates several optical shops in Portland. This year he traveled to Seattle and Tacoma to discuss with several doctors the possibility of locating optical shops adjacent to their practices. He paid travel costs to Seattle of $175 and to Tacoma of $200. The physicians in Seattle agreed to an arrangement and H incurred $500 in legal fees drawing up the agreement. The physicians in Tacoma did not agree, and H did not pursue the matter further.

In the following year, H decided to enter the ice cream business. He sent letters of inquiry to two major franchisers of ice cream stores and subsequently traveled to the headquarters of each. He paid $400 for travel to Phoenix for discussions with P Corporation and $500 for travel to Santa Fe for discussions with S Corporation. He also paid an accountant $2,400 to evaluate the financial aspects of P and $3,000 for S. H decided to acquire a franchise from S Corporation. He paid an attorney $800 to review the franchising agreement.

**a.** Discuss the tax treatment of H's expenses associated with the attempt to expand his optical shop business.

**b.** Discuss the tax treatment of the expenses incurred in connection with the ice cream business, assuming H acquires the Y franchise and begins business.

**c.** Same as (b). Discuss the treatment of these costs if H abandons the transaction after being informed that there is no franchise available in his city.

**7-38** *Investigation Expenses.* P incurred significant expenses to investigate the possibility of opening a Dowell's Hamburgers franchise in Tokyo, Japan. Her expenditures included hiring a local firm to perform a feasibility study, travel, and accounting and legal expenses. Her 2011 expenditures total $25,000. With respect to this amount:

**a.** Assuming this was P's first attempt at opening a business of her own, how much may she deduct in 2011 if she decides not to acquire the franchise?

**b.** Assuming this was P's first attempt at opening a business of her own, how much may she deduct in 2011 if she decides to acquire the franchise?

**c.** Assuming P was already in the fast-food business (she owns a Dowell's franchise in Toledo, Ohio), how much may she deduct in 2011 to acquire the franchise?

**7-39** *Capital Expenditures.* Consider the following:

**a.** A corporate taxpayer reimbursed employees for amounts they had loaned to the corporation's former president, who was losing money at the racetrack. Comment on the deductibility of these payments as well as those expenditures discussed in Example 7 of this chapter (relating to payments of debts previously discharged by bankruptcy) in light of the rules concerning capital expenditures.

**b.** How are expenditures such as land and investment securities recovered?

**c.** How are the costs of expenditures for goodwill recovered?

**d.** Distinguish between a capital expenditure and a repair.

**7-40** *Classification of Deductions.* M works as the captain of a boat. His income for the year is $20,000. During the year, he purchased a special uniform for $100. Indicate the amount of the deduction and whether it is for or from A.G.I. for the following situations:

**a.** M's boat is a 50-foot yacht, and he operates his business as a sole proprietorship (i.e., he is self-employed).

**b.** M is an employee for Yachts of Fun Inc.

**c.** M is an employee for Yachts, which reimbursed him $70 of the cost (included in his income on Form W-2).

**7-41** *Computing Employee's Deductions.* T is employed as a supervisor in the tax department of a public accounting firm in Manhattan. She took the job after working on the tax staff at a commercial tax preparation firm. She lives in a condominium on the upper east side. Every day she takes the subway to and from work. She loves living in New York. T's total income for the year consisted of compensation of $80,000 and alimony of $2,100. This year she incurred the following expenses:

| | |
|---|---|
| AICPA dues | $ 400 |
| New York State Society of CPAs dues | 315 |
| State of New York CPA license | 345 |
| Subscriptions to tax journals | 225 |
| Continuing education course on new tax law | 600 |
| New business suits | 700 |
| Cleaning of suits | 389 |
| Legal fee for preparation of will ($230 related to tax planning) | 1,500 |
| Legal fee to collect alimony | 250 |
| Job hunting expenses (resumes and employment agency fee) | 150 |
| Subway expenses | 456 |
| Safe deposit box (holds investment documents) | 90 |
| Annual fee on brokerage account | 130 |
| Qualified residence interest | 6,000 |

T's employer reimbursed her $100 for the AICPA dues (included in her income).

**a.** Compute T's taxable income.

**b.** Assuming T expects her expenses to be about the same for the next several years, what advice can you offer?

**7-42** *Computing Employee's Deductions.* Z, single, is employed as a nurse at a local hospital. Z's records reflect the following items of income and expense for 2011:

| | |
|---|---|
| Gross wages | $20,000 |
| Expenses: | |
| Employee travel expenses, not reimbursed | 1,100 |
| Cost of commuting to and from work, reimbursed (included in gross wages) | 520 |
| Charitable contributions | 700 |
| Interest and taxes on personal residence | 3,900 |
| Nurse's uniform, reimbursed (included in gross wages) | 250 |

**a.** What is Z's A.G.I.?

**b.** What is Z's total of itemized deductions?

**7-43** *Interest.* Mr. E operates a replacement window business as LLC. He uses the cash method of accounting. On November 1, 2011 he secured a loan in order to purchase a new warehouse to be used in his business. Information regarding the loan and purchase of the warehouse is shown below. All of the costs indicated were paid during the year.

| | |
|---|---|
| Term | 20 years |
| Loan origination fee | $ 2,000 |
| Points | 6,000 |
| One year's interest paid in advance | 20,000 |
| Legal fees for recording mortgage lien | 500 |

What amount may E deduct in 2011?

**7-44** *Insurance.* Hawk Harris owns and operates the Waterfield Mudhens, a franchise in an indoor soccer league. Both Hawk and the corporation are cash basis, calendar year taxpayers. During 2011 the corporation purchased the following policies:

| *Policy Description* | *Cost* | *Date Paid* |
|---|---|---|
| Two-year fire and theft effective 12/1/11 | $2,400 | 12/15/11 |
| One-year life insurance policy on Jose Greatfoot, star forward; the corporation is beneficiary; effective 11/1/11 | 1,000 | 11/1/11 |
| One-year group-term life insurance policy covering entire team and staff; effective 1/1/12 | 9,000 | 11/15/11 |
| One-year policy for payments of overhead costs should the team strike and attendance fall; effective 11/1/11 | 3,600 | 9/1/11 |

In addition to the policies purchased above, the corporation is unable to get insurance on certain business risks. Therefore, the corporation has set up a reserve—a separate account—to which it contributes $5,000 on February 1 of each year. How much may the corporation deduct for 2011?

**7-45** *Life Insurance.* The Great Cookie Corporation is owned equally by F and G. Under the articles of incorporation, the corporation is required to purchase the stock of each shareholder upon his or her death to ensure that it does not pass to some undesirable third party. To finance the purchase, the corporation purchased a life insurance policy on both F and G, naming the corporation as beneficiary. The annual premium is $5,000. Can the corporation deduct the premiums?

**7-46** *Business Life Insurance.* L, 56, has operated her sole proprietorship successfully since its inception three years ago. This year she has decided to expand. To this end, she borrowed $100,000 from the bank, which would be used for financing expansion of the business. The bank required L to take out a life insurance policy on her own life that would serve as security for the business loan. Are the premiums deductible?

**7-47** *Public Policy-Fines, Lobbying, etc.* M is engaged in the construction business in Tucson. Indicate whether the following expenses are deductible.

**a.** The Occupational Safety and Health Act (OSHA) requires contractors to fence around certain construction sites. M determined that the fences would cost $1,000 and the fine for not fencing would be only $650. As a result, he did not construct the fences and paid a fine of $650.

**b.** M often uses Mexican quarry tile on the floors of homes that he builds. To obtain the tiles, he drives his truck across the border to a small entrepreneur's house and purchases the materials. On the return trip he often pays a Mexican customs official to "expedite" his going through customs. Without the payment, the inspection process would often be tedious and consume several hours. This year he paid the customs officials $200.

**c.** M paid $100 for an advertisement supporting the administration's economic policies, which he felt would reduce interest rates and thus make homes more affordable. In addition, he paid $700 for travel to Washington, D.C. to testify before a Congressional Committee on the effects of high interest rates on the housing industry. While there, he paid $100 to a political action committee to attend a dinner, the proceeds from which went to Senator Q.

**7-48** *Limitations on Business Deductions.* This is an extension of *Problem 7-22(d)*. In that problem, you are asked to determine if the case contains expenditures that are ordinary, necessary, and reasonable under the provisions of Code § 162. Assume the positive criteria of § 162 are met (i.e., the expenditures are ordinary, necessary, and reasonable). Are there any additional provisions in § 162 that will cause the expenditures to be disallowed?

**7-49** *Related Taxpayers—Sale.* E sold stock to her son for $8,000. She purchased the stock several years ago for $11,000.

**a.** What amount of loss will E report on the sale?

**b.** What amount of gain or loss will the son report if he sells the stock for $12,000 to an unrelated party?

**c.** If the son sells for $10,000?

**d.** If the son sells for $4,000?

**7-50** *Related Taxpayers—Different Accounting Methods.* G, a cash basis, calendar year taxpayer, owns 100 percent of XYZ Corporation. XYZ is a calendar year, accrual basis taxpayer engaged in the advertising business. G leases a building to the Corporation for $1,000 per month. In December, XYZ accrues the $1,000 rental due. Indicate the tax treatment to XYZ and G assuming the payment is

**a.** Made on December 30 of the current year; or

**b.** Made on April 1 of the following year.

**c.** Would your answers above change if G owned 30 percent of XYZ?

**7-51** *Constructive Ownership Rules.* How much of RST Corporation's stock is B considered as owning?

| Owner | Shares Directly Owned |
|---|---|
| B. | 20 |
| C, B's brother. | 30 |
| D, B's partner. | 40 |
| E, B's 60-percent-owned corporation | 100 |
| Other unrelated parties | 10 |

**7-52** *Expenses of Another Taxpayer.* B is the only child of P and will inherit the family fortune. P, who is in the 28 percent tax bracket, is willing to give B and his wife $500 a month. Comment on the advisability of P paying the following directly in lieu of making a gift.

**a.** Medical expenses of B, who makes $20,000 during the year; P (the father) provides 55 percent of B's support.

**b.** Interest and principal payments on B's home mortgage, on which B and his wife are the sole obliges.

**c.** Same as (b) except that P is also an obligee on the note.

**7-53** *Losses.* This year was simply a financial disaster for Z. Indicate the effects of the following transactions on Z's taxable income. Ignore any limitations that may exist.

**a.** After the stock market crash, Z sold her stock and realized a loss of $1,000.

**b.** Z sold her husband's truck for $3,000 (basis $2,000) and her own car for $5,000 (basis $9,000). Both vehicles were used for personal purposes.

**c.** Z's $500 camera was stolen.

**d.** The land next to Z's house was rezoned to light industrial, driving down the value of her home by $10,000.

**7-54** *Planning Deductions.* X, 67, is a widow, her husband having died several years ago. Each year, X receives about $30,000 of interest and dividends. Because the mortgage on her home is virtually paid off, her only potential itemized deductions are her contributions to her church and real estate taxes. Her anticipated deductions are:

| Year | Contribution |
|---|---|
| 2011 | $2,000 |
| 2012 | 3,000 |
| 2013 | 1,000 |

What tax advice can you offer X?

**7-55** *Timing Deductions.* T currently figures that Federal, state, and local taxes consume about 30 percent of his income at the margin. Next year, however, due to a tax law change his taxes should increase to about 40 percent and remain at that level for at least five or six years. Assuming T buys a computer for $4,000 and he has the option of deducting all of the cost this year or deducting it ratably through depreciation over the next five years, what advice can you offer?

**7-56** *Classification and Deductibility.* In each of the following independent situations, indicate for the current taxable year the amounts deductible *for* A.G.I., *from* A.G.I., or *not deductible* at all. Unless otherwise stated, assume all taxpayers use the cash basis method of accounting and report using the calendar year.

**a.** M spent $1,000 on a life insurance policy covering her own life.

**b.** G is an author of novels. His wife attempted to have him declared insane and have him committed. Fearing the effect that his wife's charges might have on him and his book sales, G paid $11,000 in legal fees, resulting in a successful defense.

**c.** Taxpayer, a plumber employed by XYZ Corporation, paid union dues of $100.

**d.** Q Corporation paid T, its president and majority shareholder, a salary of $100,000. Employees in comparable positions earn salaries of $70,000.

**e.** L operates a furniture business as a sole proprietorship. She rents a warehouse (on a month-to-month basis) used for storing items sold in her store. In late December, L paid $2,000 for rental of the warehouse for the month of January.

**f.** M is a self-employed security officer. He paid $100 for uniforms and $25 for having them cleaned.

**g.** N is a security officer employed by the owner of a large apartment complex. He pays $150 for uniforms. In addition, he paid $15 for having them cleaned. His employer reimbursed him $60 of the cost of the uniforms (included in his income on Form W-2).

**h.** K owns a duplex as an investment. During the year, she paid $75 for advertisements seeking tenants. She was unable to rent the duplex, and thus no income was earned this year.

**i.** P paid $200 for subscriptions to technical journals to be used in his employment activities. Although P was fully reimbursed by his employer, his employer did not report the reimbursement in P's income.

**7-57** *Classification and Deductibility.* In each of the following independent situations, indicate for the current taxable year the amounts deductible *for* A.G.I., *from* A.G.I., or *not deductible* at all. Unless otherwise stated, assume all taxpayers use the cash basis method of accounting and report using the calendar year.

**a.** O paid the interest and taxes of $1,000 on his ex-wife's home mortgage. The divorce agreement provided that he could claim deductions for the payments.

**b.** P paid an attorney $1,500 in legal fees related to her divorce. Of these fees, $600 is for advice concerning the tax consequences of transferring some of P's stock to her husband as part of the property settlement.

**c.** R paid $10,000 for a small warehouse on an acre of land. He used the building for several months before tearing it down and erecting a hamburger stand.

**d.** H and his wife moved into the city and no longer needed their personal automobiles. They sold their Chevrolet for a $1,000 loss and their Buick for a $400 gain.

**e.** C is employed as a legal secretary. This year he paid an employment agency $300 for finding him a new, higher-paying job as a legal secretary.

**f.** X operates his own truck service. He paid $80 in fines for driving trucks that were overweight according to state law.

**g.** T, an employee, paid $175 to an accountant for preparing her personal income tax returns.

**7-58** *Classification and Deductibility.* In each of the following independent situations, indicate for the current taxable year the amounts deductible for A.G.I., from A.G.I., or not deductible at all. Unless otherwise stated, assume all taxpayers use the cash basis method of accounting and report using the calendar year.

**a.** B sold stock to his mother for a $700 loss. B's mother subsequently sold the stock for $400 less than she had paid to B.

**b.** Same as (a) but assume the mother sold the stock for $500 more than she had paid to B.

**c.** D operates three pizza restaurants as a sole proprietorship in Indianapolis. In July he paid $1,000 in air fares to travel to Chicago and Detroit to determine the feasibility of opening additional restaurants. Because of economic conditions, D decided not to open any additional restaurants.

**d.** T owns and operates several gun stores as a sole proprietorship. In light of gun control legislation, he traveled to the state capital at a cost of $80 to testify before a committee. In addition, he traveled around the state speaking at various Rotary and Kiwanis Club functions on the pending legislation at a cost of $475. T also placed an advertisement in the local newspaper concerning the merit of the legislation at a cost of $50. He pays dues to the National Rifle Association of $100.

**e.** D is employed as a ship captain for a leisure cruise company. He paid $1,000 for rent on a warehouse where he stores smuggled narcotics, which he sells illegally.

**f.** M, a plumber and an accrual basis taxpayer, warrants his work. This year he estimates that expenses attributable to the warranty work are about 3 percent of sales, or $3,000.

**g.** G, a computer operator, pays $75 for a subscription to an investment newsletter devoted to investment opportunities in state and municipal bonds.

**7-59** *Employee Business Expenses: Planning.* J is employed as a salesman by Bigtime Business Forms Inc. He is considering the purchase of a new automobile that he would use primarily for business. Are there any tax factors that J might consider before purchasing the new car?

## TAX RETURN PROBLEMS

- *CONTINUOUS TAX RETURN PROBLEMS* See Appendix I, Part 1.

## CUMULATIVE PROBLEMS

**7-60** Tony Johnson (I.D. No. 456-23-7657), age 45, is single. He lives at 5220 Grand Avenue, Brooklyn, NY 10016. Tony is employed by RTI Corporation, which operates a chain of restaurants in and around New York City. He has supervisory responsibilities over the managers of four restaurants. An examination of his records for 2010 revealed the following information.

1. During the year, Tony earned $33,000. His employer withheld $2,200 in Federal income taxes and the proper amount of FICA taxes. Tony obtained his current job through an employment agency to which he paid a $150 fee. He previously was employed as a manager of another restaurant. Due to the new job, it was necessary to improve his wardrobe. Accordingly, Tony purchased several new suits at a cost of $600.
2. On the days that Tony works, he normally eats his meals at the restaurants for purposes of quality control. There is no charge for the meals, which are worth $2,000.
3. He provides 60 percent of the support for his father, age 70, who lived with Tony all year and who has no income other than social security benefits of $7,000 during the year. Tony provided more than one-half of the cost of maintaining the home.
4. Dividend income from Chevron Corporation stock that he owned was $350. Interest income on savings was $200.
5. Tony and other employees of the corporation park in a nearby parking garage. The parking garage bills RTI Corporation for the parking. Tony figures that his free parking is worth $1,000 annually.
6. Tony subscribes to several trade publications for restaurants at a cost of $70.
7. During the year, he paid $200 to a bank for a personal financial plan. Based on this plan, Tony made several investments, including a $2,000 contribution to an individual retirement account, and also rented for $30 a safety deposit box in which he stores certain investment related documents.
8. Tony purchased a new home, paying three points on a loan of $70,000. He also paid $6,000 of interest on his home mortgage during the year. In addition, he paid $650 of real property taxes on the home. He has receipts for sales taxes of $534.
9. While hurrying to deliver an important package for his employer, Tony received a $78 ticket for violating the speed limit. Because his employer had asked that he deliver the package as quickly as possible, Tony was reimbursed $78 for the ticket, which he paid.

Compute Tony's taxable income for the year. If forms are used for the computations, complete Form 1040 and Schedule A.

**7-61** Wendy White (I.D. No. 526-30-9001), age 29, is single. She lives at 1402 Pacific Beach Ave., San Diego, CA 92230. Wendy is employed by KXXR television station as the evening news anchor. An examination of her records for 2010 revealed the following information.

1. Wendy earned $150,000 in salary. Her employer withheld $22,000 in Federal income taxes and the proper amount of FICA taxes.
2. Wendy also received $10,000 in self-employment income from personal appearances during the year. Her unreimbursed expenses related to this income were: transportation and lodging, $523; meals, $120; and office supplies, $58.
3. Wendy reports the following additional deductions: home mortgage interest, $6,250; charitable contributions, $1,300; state and local income taxes, $3,100; and employment-related expenses, $920.

Compute Wendy's taxable income for 2010 and her tax due (including any self-employment tax). If forms are used for the computations, complete Form 1040, Schedule A, Schedule C, and Schedule SE.

## TAX RESEARCH PROBLEMS

**7-62** T and two associates are equal owners in LST Corporation. The three formed the corporation several years ago with the idea of capitalizing on the fitness movement. After a modest beginning and meager returns, the corporation did extremely well this year. As a result, the corporation plans on paying the three individuals salaries that T believes the IRS may deem unreasonable. T wonders whether he can avoid the tax consequences associated with an unreasonable compensation determination by paying back whatever amount is ultimately deemed a dividend.

**a.** What would be the effect on T's taxable income should he repay the portion of a salary deemed a dividend?

**b.** Would there be any adverse effects of adopting a payback arrangement?

Partial list of research aids:

*Vincent E. Oswald*, 49 T.C. 645.
Rev. Rul. 69-115,1969-1 C.B. 50.

**7-63** C, a professor of film studies at State University, often meets with her doctoral students at her home. In her home, C has a room that she uses solely to conduct business related to the classes she teaches at the university. In the room she and her students often review the movies the students have made to satisfy requirements in their doctoral program. Can C deduct expenses related to her home office?

**7-64** R moved to St. Louis in 2010 and purchased a home. After living there for a year, his family had grown and required a much larger home. On August 1, 2011 they purchased their dream house, which cost far more than their first home. Shortly before he closed on the new residence, he put his first house on the market to sell. After two months had passed, however, he had received no offers. Fearing that he would be unable to pay the debt on both homes, R decided to rent his old home while trying to sell it. Surprisingly, he was able to rent the house immediately. However, in order to secure the party's agreement to rent monthly, he was required to perform a few repairs costing $500. Seven months after he had rented the home, R sold it. During the rental period, R paid the utilities and various other expenses. R has come to you for your advice on how these events in 2011 would affect his tax return.

**7-65** In November 2011 B, employed as a life insurance salesperson for PQR Insurance Company in Newark, New Jersey, purchased a personal computer for use in his work. B has come to you for help in deciding how to handle this purchase on his 2011 tax return. He, of course, wants to expense the full price of the computer under Code § 179. B relates the following salient information to you with respect to this purchase:

1. B files a joint return with his wife, L. They have a combined A.G.I. of $65,000 before considering this item. They have sufficient qualified expenditures to itemize deductions on Schedule A, but they have no miscellaneous itemized deductions.
2. B paid $3,000 for the laptop computer, which will be used 100 percent for business use.
3. B bought the computer to analyze client data. He figures this will help him increase his sales because he can analyze the results of various insurance options at the client's home or office (all personalized, of course).
4. PQR does not provide B with company-owned computing equipment. In fact, they refused to pay for B's computer because the expense of providing computers for all of PQR's agents would be too great.

How should B treat this purchase on his 2011 tax return?

**7-66** On January 28, 2011 S comes to you for tax preparation advice. She has always prepared her own return, but it has become somewhat complicated and she needs professional advice.

During your initial interview, you discover that S is a teacher at a high school in Chicago, Illinois. She is also the coach of the golf team. In 2009 S decided she wanted to be a professional golfer. So, when she was 32 years old, she began a part-time apprenticeship program with the Professional Golfers' Association of America (PGA), where she was an unpaid assistant to the pro at a local country club. Then, in 2010 she became a member of the PGA and began her professional career.

S has not made much money as a professional golfer. In fact, her expenses exceeded her income in both 2009 and 2010 ($4,000 loss in 2009; $3,500 loss in 2010). Believing she was actively engaged in a trade or business (she kept separate records for her golf activities, practiced about 10 hours each week, and worked with a pro whenever she could), S deducted her golf-related expenses on Schedule C and reported her losses from this activity on her prior returns.

The IRS has challenged S's 2009 and 2010 loss deductions, calling them nondeductible "hobby" losses. Is the IRS correct in this matter? Would she win if the matter is taken to court? What planning steps can S take to ensure that any future losses are deductible trade or business losses?

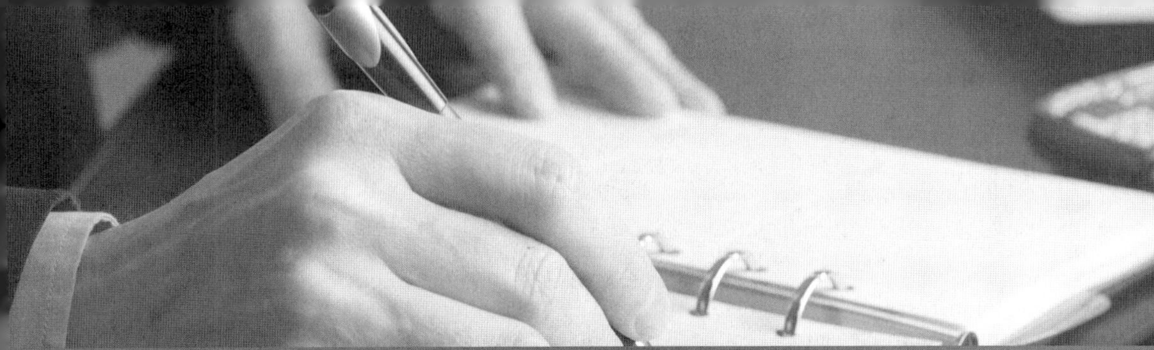

# 8 Employee Business Expenses

## Learning Objectives

Upon completion of this chapter you will be able to:

- LO.1 Discuss the rules governing the deduction of several common expenses incurred by employees and self-employed persons
- LO.2 Recognize when educational expenses are deductible
- LO.3 Explain the rules concerning the deduction of moving expenses
- LO.4 Describe when expenses of maintaining a home office are deductible
- LO.5 Distinguish between deductible transportation expenses and nondeductible commuting costs
- LO.6 Understand the differences between deductible travel expenses and deductible transportation costs
- LO.7 Determine when entertainment expenses can be deducted
- LO.8 Describe the 50 percent limitation on the deduction of meals and entertainment
- LO.9 Explain the special record-keeping requirements for travel and entertainment expenses
- LO.10 Discuss the two types of reimbursement arrangements: accountable and nonaccountable plans

## Chapter Outline


Introduction 8-2
Education Expenses 8-2
Requirements for Deduction 8-3
Travel as a form of Education 8-4
Types and Classification of Education Deductions 8-4
Deduction for Qualified Tuition and Related Expenses 8-5
Relationship to Education Credits and Qualified Prepaid Tuition 8-6
Deduction for Expenses of Primary and Secondary School Teachers 8-8
Moving Expenses 8-9
Distance Requirement 8-9
Time Test 8-10
Deductible Moving Expenses 8-10
Classifying and Reporting the Moving Expense Deduction 8-12
Home Office Expenses 8-13
Requirements for Deductibility 8-13
Amount Deductible 8-16
Daycare and Storage Use 8-17
Residential Phone Service 8-18
Transportation Expenses 8-19
Deductible Transportation Versus Nondeductible Commuting 8-19

Computing Car Expenses 8-24
Classification of Transportation and Travel Expenses 8-26
Travel Expenses 8-26
Away-from-Home Test 8-27
Combined Business and Pleasure Travel 8-28
Foreign Conventions 8-32
Cruise Ships 8-32
Entertainment Expenses 8-33
Deduction Requirements 8-33
Entertainment Facilities 8-37
Exceptions to Directly-Related-to and Associated-with Tests 8-37
Fifty Percent Limitation on Entertainment and Meal Expenses 8-38
Limitations on Deductions for Tickets 8-39
Business Gifts 8-40
Travel and Entertainment Record Keeping Requirements 8-41
Reporting Business Expenses and Losses 8-44
Sole Proprietors and Self-Employed Persons 8-44
Statutory Employees 8-44
Employees 8-46
Tax Planning Considerations 8-50
Moving Expenses 8-50
Travel and Entertainment Expenses 8-50
Problem Materials 8-53


## Introduction

Over the years, many rules have been developed to govern the deductibility of specific business expenses. These rules normally augment the general requirements of § 162 (identified in Chapter 7) by establishing additional criteria that must be satisfied before a deduction may be claimed. As a practical matter, the primary purpose of many of these rules is to prohibit taxpayers from deducting what are in reality personal expenditures. For example, consider a taxpayer who uses a room at home to work or a taxpayer who takes a customer to lunch. In both cases, the expenses incurred very well may be genuine business expenses and deductible under the general criteria. On the other hand, such expenses could simply be *disguised* personal expenditures. As these examples suggest, some of the expenses that are likely to be manipulated are those often incurred by employees in connection with their employment duties. Such common employee expenses as those for travel and entertainment, education, moving, and home offices have long been the source of controversy. Of course, such costs are incurred by a self-employed person as well as by employees and raise similar problems. This chapter examines the special provisions applicable to these items.

## Education Expenses

Historically, the tax law has taken the view that most education expenses are personal and, therefore, not deductible. For example, an art appreciation course for the taxpayer's cultural enrichment is purely personal in nature. Consequently, its cost is not deductible.[1] Similarly, no deduction is granted for expenses of a college education as a business expense on the theory that they are costs of preparing the taxpayer to enter a new business—not the costs of carrying on a business. Therefore, such general education expenses are nondeductible capital expenditures for which no amortization is allowed. Other education expenses, however, such as those incurred by an accountant to attend a seminar on a new tax law, are considered essential costs of pursuing income and are deductible like other ordinary and necessary business expenses. To ensure that deductions are permitted only for education expenses that serve current business objectives and are not personal or capital in nature, special tests must be met.

**LO.2**
Recognize when educational expenses are deductible.

The Regulations allow a deduction if the education expenses satisfy *either* of the following conditions *and* are not considered personal or capital in nature, as discussed below.[2]

1. The education maintains or improves skills required of the taxpayer in his or her employment or other trade or business.
2. The education meets the express requirements imposed by either the individual's employer or applicable law, and the taxpayer must meet such requirements to retain his or her job, position, or rate of compensation.

---

[1] As discussed below, beginning in 2002, § 222 permits a deduction for qualified expenses.

[2] Reg. § 1.162-5(a).

Education expenses that meet either of these conditions are still not deductible if they are considered personal or capital expenditures under either of the following two tests:[3]

1. The education is necessary to meet the minimum educational requirements of the taxpayer's trade or business.
2. The education qualifies the taxpayer for a new trade or business.

## Requirements for Deduction

### Maintain Skills

For the expense to qualify under the first criterion, the education must be related to the taxpayer's present trade or business and maintain or improve the skills used in such business. The taxpayer must be able to establish the necessary connection between the studies pursued and the taxpayer's current employment. For example, a personnel manager seeking an M.B.A. degree was allowed to deduct all of her education expenses when she ingeniously related each course taken to her job (e.g., a computer course enabled her to be more effective in acquiring information from and communicating with computer personnel).[4] In contrast, the U.S. Tax Court denied the deductions of a research chemist's cost of an M.B.A., indicating that courses such as advanced business finance, corporate strategy, and business law were only remotely related to the skills needed for his job.[5]

Refresher and continuing education courses ordinarily meet the skills maintenance test.

**Example 1**

T repairs appliances. To maintain his proficiency, he often attends training schools. The costs of attending such schools are deductible because the education is necessary to maintain and improve the skills required in his job.

### Required by Employer or Law

Once the minimum education requirements are met to obtain a job, additional education may be required by the employer or by law to retain the taxpayer's salary or position. Costs for such education are deductible as long as they do not qualify the taxpayer for a new trade or business.

**Example 2**

This year, R took a new job as a high school instructor in science. State law requires that teachers obtain a graduate degree within five years of becoming employed. Expenses for college courses for this purpose are deductible even though they lead to a degree since such education is mandatory under state law.

### New Trade or Business

If education prepares the taxpayer to enter a new trade or business, no deduction is permitted. In this regard, a mere change of duties usually is not considered a new business.[6] For example, a science teacher may deduct the cost of courses enabling him or her to teach art since the switch is a mere change in duties. The taxpayer becomes qualified for a new occupation if the education

---

[3] Reg. §§ 1.162-5(b)(2) and (3).

[4] *Frank S. Blair, III*, 41 TCM 289, T.C. Memo 1980-488.

[5] *Ronald T. Smith*, 41 TCM 1186, T.C. Memo 1981-149.

[6] Reg. § 1.162-5(b)(3).

enables the taxpayer to perform substantially different tasks, regardless of whether the taxpayer actually uses the skills acquired.

> **Example 3**
>
> R was hired as a trust officer in a bank several years ago. His employer now requires that all trust officers must have a law degree. R may not deduct the cost of obtaining a law degree because the degree qualifies him for a new trade or business.[7] No deduction is allowed even though it is required by his employer and R does not actually engage in the practice of law.

### Minimum Education

Expenses of education undertaken to gain entry into a business or to meet the minimum standards required in a business are not deductible. These standards are determined in light of the typical conditions imposed by the particular job. For example, the Tax Court denied a $21,000 deduction for the cost of a Northwestern University "MBA" because the degree not only enabled her to meet the minimum education requirements for her position at Merrill Lynch and Raymond James but also prepared her for a new trade or business.[8] In contrast, the Tax Court permitted a salesman for a dental manufacturing company to deduct the cost of his Pepperdine MBA.[9] In this case, the Court found that the employer did not have a minimum education requirement and that the MBA did not qualify the taxpayer for a new trade or business or a promotion. As these two recent cases suggest, if the government can demonstrate that the employer has a minimum education requirement either to begin the job or obtain a promotion, it will deny the deduction for any education that enables the taxpayer to meet such requirement.

The minimum education requirement also operates to prohibit the deduction of such expenses as those for a review course for the bar or C.P.A. exam and fees to take such professional exams.[10] Similarly, education expenses related to a pay increase or promotion may not be deductible under this rule if the increase or promotion was the primary objective of the education. However, as discussed below, a special provision allows a deduction for qualified tuition expenses.

## Travel as a Form of Education

Prior to 1986, travel in and of itself was considered a deductible form of education when it was related to a taxpayer's trade or business. For example, an instructor of Spanish could travel around Spain during the summer to learn more about the Spanish culture and improve her conversational Spanish. In such case, the travel cost would have been deductible since it was related to the taxpayer's trade or business. In 1986, Congress became concerned that many taxpayers were using this rule to deduct what were essentially the costs of a personal vacation. Moreover, Congress believed that any business purpose served by traveling for general education purposes was insignificant. To eliminate possible abuse, no deduction is allowed simply because the travel itself is educational.[11] Deductions are allowed for travel only when the education activity otherwise qualifies and the travel expense is necessary to pursue such activity. For example, a deduction for travel would be allowed where a professor of French literature travels to France to take courses that are offered only at the Sorbonne.

## Types and Classification of Education Deductions

Education expenses normally deductible include costs of tuition, books, supplies, typing, transportation, and travel (including meals, lodging, and similar expenses). Typical education expenses are for college or vocational courses, continuing professional education programs, professional development courses, and similar courses or seminars.

---

7 Reg. § 1.162-5(b)(3)(ii), Ex.1.

8 *Will M. McEuen III*, TC Summary Opinion 2004-107. See also *Veronica L. Foster*, TC Summary Opinion 2008-22.

9 *Daniel Allemeir* TC Memo 2005-207.

10 Rev. Rul. 69-292, 1969-1 C.B. 84.

11 § 274(m)(2).

The costs of transportation between the taxpayer's place of work and school are deductible. If the taxpayer goes home before going to school, however, the expense of going from home to school is deductible, but only to the extent that it does not exceed the costs of going directly from work. The cost of transportation from home to school on a nonworking day represents nondeductible commuting.

Unreimbursed educational expenditures of an employee are treated as miscellaneous itemized deductions subject to the 2 percent floor. In contrast, if an employer reimburses an employee for such expenses under an *accountable plan* (discussed later in this chapter), the reimbursement is excludable from gross income. Any reimbursement not made under an accountable plan must be included in the employee's gross income, and qualifying deductions must be treated as miscellaneous itemized deductions. Finally, education expenses incurred by a self-employed person are deductible *for* A.G.I.

## Deduction for Qualified Tuition and Related Expenses

The general rules governing the deduction of education expenses normally prohibit taxpayers from deducting the costs of obtaining a college education since such expenses are considered personal (i.e., incurred to meet minimum education requirements). However, to help subsidize the increasing cost of higher education, Congress created a special provision. Section 222 allows a deduction for *qualified tuition and related expenses* incurred in connection with enrollment or attendance at an *eligible educational institution.* Normally, the amount of the deduction is $4,000 and is available to all taxpayers since it may be claimed for A.G.I. However, the deduction can be reduced or eliminated depending on the taxpayer's filing status and adjusted gross income as follows:

| *A.G.I. Joint Returns* | *A.G.I. Other Taxpayers* | *Amount of Deduction* |
|---|---|---|
| $ 0–$130,000 | $ 0–$65,000 | $4,000 |
| $130,001–$160,000 | $65,001–$80,000 | $2,000 |
| >$160,000 | >$80,000 | $ 0 |

Note that there is no phase-out of the deduction, but rather a cliff effect. If A.G.I. exceeds the applicable dollar limit, the deduction is either reduced or disallowed in its entirety. The deduction can be claimed for expenses of the taxpayer, the taxpayer's spouse, and the taxpayer's dependents. Consistent with this approach, the law prohibits taxpayers who are eligible to be claimed as dependents from claiming the deduction. In addition, married taxpayers must file jointly in order to claim the deduction. Finally, to prohibit a double benefit, the deduction is not allowed if the taxpayer or any other person claims the Hope Scholarship credit or the Lifetime Learning credit (see below) with respect to that individual for that particular year. Moreover, if the taxpayer receives distributions from a 529 plan or an educational savings account that are nontaxable (see below), the deduction must be reduced by such amounts.[12]

Only qualified tuition and related expenses may be deducted. This definition normally encompasses the tuition and fees charged by most universities. It should be noted, however, that fees for course-related books, supplies, and equipment normally do not qualify unless—according to the IRS—the fees must be paid *to the institution* as a condition of enrollment or attendance. For example, a student activity fee, a special technology or lab fee charged by a university should qualify. On the other hand, qualified expenses do not include the cost of: insurance, medical expenses (including student health fees), room and board, transportation, or similar personal, living, or family expenses. This is true even if the fee must be paid to the institution as a condition of enrollment or attendance. In addition, qualified tuition and related expenses generally do not include expenses that relate to any course of instruction or other education that involves sports, games or hobbies, or any noncredit course unless the course is part of the student's degree program. Note that both undergraduate and graduate courses qualify and it makes no difference whether the course is part of a program that leads to a degree.

[12] See *Tax Benefits for Higher Education*, IRS Publication 970 (Rev. 2006, p. 33).

Only qualified expenses paid to *eligible educational institutions* are deductible. An eligible education institution is defined as any accredited post secondary institution that offers credit toward a bachelor's degree, an associate's degree or other recognized post-secondary credential. Thus tuition for most colleges and universities as well as junior colleges qualify. Some vocational institutions (e.g., trade schools) and proprietary for-profit organizations may qualify as well.

### Example 4

In August 2011, Mr. and Mrs. Smith paid the tuition for their son's attendance at State University to obtain a graduate degree in accounting. Tuition was $1,900. In December 2011, the Smiths paid the tuition for the second semester of $2,300. The second semester began in January 2012. Mr. and Mrs. Smith have an A.G.I. of $125,000. The son is a graduate student and, consequently, the expenses do not qualify for the Hope Scholarship credit discussed below. In addition, because their A.G.I. exceeds $125,000, the couple is not entitled to claim the Lifetime Learning credit. While the credits are not available, a deduction is allowed since the expenses are paid during the year and are for education for such year or education that begins within three months after the close of the year. The deduction is limited to $4,000 and may be claimed for A.G.I.

### Example 5

This year R started law school. He is a part-time student and has a part-time job. He paid tuition of $12,000 for the year. He may deduct $4,000 of the tuition for A.G.I. Alternatively, he could elect to use the Lifetime Learning credit of $2,000 ($10,000 maximum qualified expenses × 20%). However, as noted above, he can either deduct the expenses or claim the credit but not both. If his marginal rate was 25%, the $4,000 deduction would be worth only $1,000 so in this case, he would be better off claiming the credit.

## Relationship to Education Credits and Qualified Prepaid Tuition

In addition to the deduction for education expenses, the Code provides other benefits for education related expenses. There are two credits related to education: (1) the Hope Scholarship credit, and (2) the Lifetime Learning credit. Special benefits are also extended to Educational Savings Accounts and Qualified Tuition Programs (§ 529 plans). These credits and tax-favored savings arrangements, discussed in detail in Chapters 13 and 18, are designed to help middle America fund the ever-increasing cost of higher education.

The Hope Scholarship credit and the Lifetime Learning credit are both available for education expenses paid on behalf of the taxpayer, the taxpayer's spouse, or a dependent. For 2009 and 2010, Hope Scholarship credit is 100 percent of the first $2,000 of education expenses and 25 percent of the next $2,000 of expenses for each student. Thus the maximum credit is $2,500 [(100% × $2,000 = $2,000) + (25% × $2,000 = $500)] per year per student. The Hope Scholarship credit generally can be claimed only for the first four years of post-secondary education (e.g., college). The Lifetime Learning credit can be claimed for 20 percent of up to $10,000 of qualified tuition and fees annually. Thus the maximum credit per taxpayer return would be $2,000. In contrast to the Hope Scholarship credit, the Lifetime Learning is available for virtually any type of education for an unlimited number of years. For any one particular student, a taxpayer could elect *either* the Hope credit or a Lifetime Learning credit but not both. Note that the Hope credit is per child and not per taxpayer. The Lifetime Learning credit is per return. As noted above, if the taxpayer elects either credit, the deduction is not allowed. Both credits are phased out for high-income earners. For the Hope credit, the phase-out in 2011 runs from $80,000 to $90,000 ($160,000 to $180,000 for joint filers). For the Lifetime Learning credit, the phase-out in 2011 runs from $51,000 to $61,000 ($102,000 to $122,000 for joint filers). See Chapter 13 for a complete discussion.

The tax law also provides favorable treatment for two savings arrangements: (1) Educational Savings Accounts (Coverdell Accounts described in §530) and (2) Qualified Tuition Programs (so-called § 529 plans). Contributions to these plans are not deductible. However, income on amounts contributed are nontaxable when earned. In addition, amounts distributed from the plans are nontaxable if such amounts are used for certain expenses for higher education. As noted above, to prevent a double benefit, taxpayers cannot deduct qualified education expenses that have been used to figure the tax-free portion of a distribution from an education savings account or a 529 plan.[13]

It is important to note that the law prevents taxpayers from trying to double dip; that is, the law specifically prohibits taxpayers from claiming both a deduction and a credit for the same education expenses. For example, if a CPA spends $300 to attend a continuing education course, he could claim a deduction of $300 as a business expense under § 162, qualified tuition under § 222, or as the basis for the Lifetime Learning credit of $60. Observe, however, that due to limitations, differing phase-out amounts, definitions of qualifying expenditures, and the interaction with other educational provisions such as the exclusion for educational assistance of § 127 and the working condition fringe benefit rules of § 132, a single expense could be covered by multiple provisions and results in mind-boggling complexity.

## Example 6

J recently completed his undergraduate degree at the University of Texas and took a job with a brokerage firm in Dallas. The firm agreed to reimburse him for a portion of the cost of an M.B.A. program. In January, J enrolled as a part-time student in the M. B.A. program at a local university. This year he paid tuition of $22,250 and the firm reimbursed him $8,250 of this amount. In addition, J withdrew $1,000 from an Educational Savings account to help pay the tuition. He paid for the remaining $13,000 from a student loan.

Under the educational assistance rules of § 127(see Chapter 6), J could exclude $5,250 reimbursement for the coursework (both undergraduate and graduate courses qualify) and neither he nor his employer would be required to pay FICA or Medicare taxes on this amount. J also could exclude $1,000 withdrawn from the Educational Savings Account since it was used for qualified higher education expenses. Note that J could not deduct the amount for which he was reimbursed or the withdrawal since both were excluded. The treatment of the remaining $16,000 ($22,250 – $5,250 – $1,000) is not clear. In order to exclude the $3,000 balance reimbursed by his employer as a working condition fringe benefit under § 132, the expense must qualify as a deductible business expense under § 162. The IRS might take the position that none of the remaining amount paid is deductible under § 162 since J has not met the minimum education requirement of the brokerage firm and, therefore, the $3,000 reimbursement would not qualify for exclusion. In any event, J could deduct $4,000 as a qualified tuition expense under § 222. (Observe, that to exclude the $3,000 reimbursement as a working condition fringe under § 132, the item must be deductible under § 162—not § 222.) J could utilize the Lifetime Learning credit instead of the deduction. If it is assumed that he could not exclude the additional reimbursement under §132 and he did not deduct *any* amount under § 222, he could claim a Lifetime Learning credit of $2,000 (20% × up to $10,000). Whether J utilizes the amount paid as a basis for claiming the credit or as a deduction under § 222 depends on any phase-outs and his tax bracket. However, he cannot use the expenses for claiming both the deduction and the credit. Also note that the new § 222 deduction is a deduction for AGI and not a miscellaneous itemized deduction subject to the 2% floor.

[13] The reduction is normally equal to the amount of earnings that are nontaxable because they were used to pay qualified education expenses. However, for 529 plans, the amount representing the recovery of contributions to the program that are used for education expenses could be deducted subject to the $4,000 limitation. See footnote 12

## Deduction for Expenses of Primary and Secondary School Teachers

In 2002, the Bush administration reached out to the teaching profession by creating a special deduction. The deduction originated from a 1996 National Education Association study which found that the average kindergarten–12th grade teacher spent approximately $400 per year out of their personal funds for unreimbursed classroom supplies (e.g., a first grade teacher may incur expenses for the decoration of his or her classroom). Although such expenses were deductible, because they were miscellaneous itemized deductions, it was unlikely that most teachers could deduct such expenses. In supporting the deduction, President Bush asserted that if a businessperson could deduct a meal, "a teacher certainly ought to be able to deduct the cost of pencils or a Big Chief tablet." To this end, §62(a)(2)(D) allows a deduction of up to $250 per year for unreimbursed business expenses incurred in connection with books, supplies, computer equipment, other equipment and supplementary materials used in the classroom. The deduction is for A.G.I. and, therefore, all qualifying teachers benefit. Qualifying teachers are defined as "eligible educators" who for at least 900 hours during a school year is a kindergarten–12th grade teacher, instructor, counselor, principal or aide. The educator is eligible only if he or she works at a school that provides elementary or secondary education (kindergarten–12th grade).

### ✓ Check Your Knowledge

For each of the following situations, indicate whether the expenditures are deductible as education expenses.

**Review Question 1**

Last June, D graduated magna cum laude from the University of Virginia. This fall he entered Johns Hopkins Medical School, paying tuition of thousands of dollars.

The costs of medical school are not deductible under § 162 as business expenses for two reasons. First, the education is necessary to meet the minimum educational requirements to become a doctor. Second, the education qualifies the taxpayer to carry on a new trade or business. Nevertheless, D could deduct a portion under § 222 as qualified tuition or claim the Lifetime Learning credit, but not both.

**Review Question 2**

H, a practicing tax accountant, is taking a series of correspondence courses to become a certified financial planner.

As may be clear by now, very little is black or white in the tax law; here is yet another case. The IRS would probably take the position that the expenses are not deductible because the education qualifies the taxpayer to carry on a new trade or business. From the accountant's perspective, however, the course work simply improves or maintains the skills that he is already using in his business. It would appear that the education does not necessarily enable the taxpayer to do anything that he could not do before except to hold himself out as a certified financial planner. The accountant would deduct the expense. In addition, the Lifetime Learning credit and qualified tuition deduction may also be available if the courses are taken at an eligible educational institution (e.g., as part of a university sponsored program).

**Review Question 3**

Ms. McClain, an elementary school teacher, took a sabbatical to Ireland, where she studied the art of storytelling.

Whether her expenses are deductible ultimately depends on the facts and circumstances. As noted above, changes made in 1986 aimed to eliminate deductions for travel that were primarily personal in nature. In this case, the taxpayer appears to be pursuing that which might not be available at home. Assuming she spent a reasonable amount of time studying and researching, the expense would be deductible. In contrast, consider an architect who travels all over Europe simply taking pictures of classic architectural styles that he may incorporate in his work. Without more, a court would probably view his trip as merely a disguised vacation and deny a deduction for his travel expenses. As in the previous question, the Lifetime Learning credit and qualified tuition deduction may also be available if the courses are taken at an eligible educational institution (e.g., as part of a university sponsored program).

## Moving Expenses

For many years, moving expenses were viewed as nondeductible personal expenses. In 1964, however, Congress revised its position, believing that moving expenses necessitated by the taxpayer's employment should be regarded as a deductible cost of earning income. To this end, Code § 217 was enacted, expressly authorizing a deduction for moving expenses. Section 217 allows self-employed individuals and employees to deduct moving expenses incurred in connection with beginning employment or changing job locations. To ensure that the deduction is allowed only for moves required by the taxpayer's employment, the taxpayer must satisfy *both* a distance test and a time test in order to qualify for the deduction.

**LO.3**
Explain the rules concerning the deduction of moving expenses.

### Distance Requirement

The thrust of § 217 is to allow a taxpayer to deduct moving expenses only if there is a change in job location *and* the new location is sufficiently far away that it essentially requires the taxpayer to uproot and move his or her residence. This idea is captured in a somewhat misleading 50-mile distance test. The taxpayer does not satisfy the requirement simply by moving 50 miles to a new residence in connection with a new job location. If this were the case, the taxpayer could meet the requirement by simply moving his office down the hall and at the same time moving his residence 50 miles. Instead, the distance test is constructed to determine if the taxpayer's commute to the new job site *without the move* would have increased at least 50 miles. Technically, the condition is satisfied if the distance between the old residence and the new job site is at least 50 miles greater than the distance between the old residence and the old job site. Note that both distances are measured from the taxpayer's *former residence*. Thus, if the taxpayer's old commute was four miles, the new commute (absent a move) would have to be at least 54 miles (54 – 4 = 50) before the test is satisfied.

### Example 7

During the year, R was promoted to district sales manager, requiring her to move from Tucson to Phoenix. To determine whether the 50-mile test is met, the distances shown below must be compared.

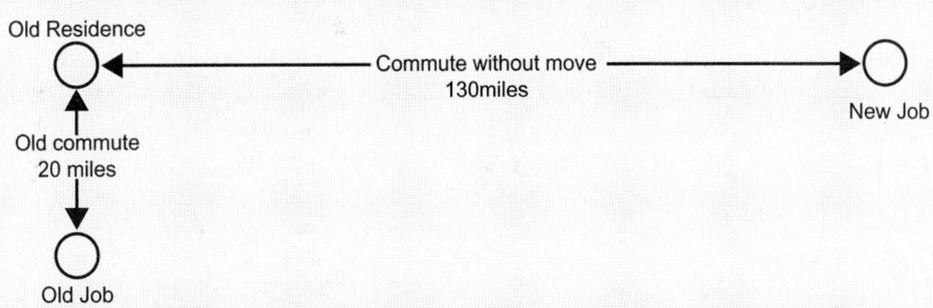


Since the distance between R's old residence and new job (AC = 130 miles) exceeds the distance between R's old residence and old job (AB = 20 miles) by at least 50 miles (130 – 20 = 110), the distance requirement is satisfied. In this case, it is quite clear that if the taxpayer had not moved, her commute would have increased significantly (110 miles). Consequently, § 217 grants her a deduction for the costs of moving her residence to a place where the commute is more reasonable. In applying the test, note that the location of the new residence is irrelevant.

If the taxpayer has no old job site, the distance test is satisfied if the new job site is 50 miles from the old residence.[14]

## Time Test

If taxpayers were not required to maintain employment at the new job site for a minimum amount of time, they could move from place to place, taking temporary jobs in each location to justify the deduction of what in effect are personal travel expenses. To prohibit this possibility, the second test generally requires the taxpayer to work for a *sustained period* of time upon arrival at the new job location. This condition is met if the taxpayer is a *full-time* employee in the area of the new job location for at least 39 weeks during the 12-month period immediately following arrival.[15] Alternatively, the taxpayer may satisfy the test by being an employee or self-employed on a *full-time* basis for at least 78 weeks during the 24-month period after arrival. Note, however, that—like the first test—39 of these 78 weeks must be during the first 12-month period. In either case, the taxpayer need not work for the same employer or for 39 weeks in a row. The time requirement is waived if the taxpayer dies, becomes disabled, is involuntarily dismissed, or is transferred by the new employer.[16]

**Example 8**

N, an accountant, left his job in Boston to take a new job with a firm in Orlando. After working for the firm for eight months, he became dissatisfied and quit to open his own practice as a sole proprietor. Due to the poor economy, N closed the business after six months and moved to Denver. N may not deduct his expenses of moving to Orlando. since he was employed for only 32 weeks (eight months) during the 12-month period after arrival in Orlando, he does not meet the 39-week test for employees. Similarly, he does not meet the alternative 78-week test since he was employed or self-employed only 56 weeks (14 months) of the 24-month period in Orlando after his arrival. Whether the costs of moving to Denver are deductible depends on whether either of the tests can be satisfied.

In many instances, taxpayers do not know by the end of the tax year whether they will be able to satisfy the time test. Accordingly, the law permits the taxpayer to claim the deduction on the assumption that the test will be satisfied. If the test is subsequently failed, the taxpayer must increase income in the year of failure by the amount of the previous deduction. In lieu of claiming the deduction prior to satisfaction of the test, the taxpayer may wait until the test is satisfied and file an amended return for the year of the moving expense.

## Deductible Moving Expenses

For many years, taxpayers were allowed to deduct a variety of moving expenses. These included not only direct expenses such as the cost of moving the taxpayer's personal belongings and the cost of traveling to the new location but also a limited amount of indirect expenses. For example, a taxpayer could deduct expenses for house-hunting trips, temporary living at the new location, and expenses related to disposing of the taxpayer's former residence. In 1993, however, Congress eliminated the deduction for all indirect moving expenses. Currently, only direct moving expenses are deductible. They are:[17]

1. Costs of moving household goods and personal belongings; and
2. Costs of traveling from the old location to the new location.

---

[14] § 217(c)(1).

[15] § 217(c)(2).

[16] § 217(d).

[17] §§ 217(b)(1)(A) and (B).

### Costs of Moving Household Goods and Personal Belongings

This category of direct moving expenses includes the following:[18]

- Packing, crating, and transporting the taxpayer's personal possessions (e.g., the cost of hiring a moving company or renting a truck)
- Storage and insurance of goods and personal effects while "in-transit" (i.e., any consecutive 30-day period after the day the items are moved from the former home and before they are delivered to the new home)
- Connecting and disconnecting utilities required by the moving of the taxpayer's appliances
- Moving a pet or shipping a car

Losses on dispositions of club memberships, expenses of refitting rugs and drapes, mortgage prepayment penalties (perhaps deductible as interest), and similar expenses are not deductible.

### Costs of Traveling

Once the taxpayer's furniture and other items are out the door, the taxpayer's household must follow. Only the costs of moving a taxpayer's family members (including pets) are deductible. Those for such nonfamily members as servants, chauffeurs, governesses, or nurses do not qualify. The following travel expenses are deductible:

- Transportation costs. The taxpayer may use actual expenses (i.e., the costs of oil, gasoline, tolls, and parking—but not those for general repairs or maintenance) or 19 cents per mile in 2011.
- Lodging expenses. The taxpayer may deduct the costs of lodging incurred in traveling to the new location. No deduction is allowed for any meal expenses related to the move.[19]

### Nondeductible Expenses

As noted above, in 1993 Congress eliminated the deduction for so-called "indirect" moving expenses. As a result, expenses for the following are no longer deductible:

- House-hunting trips
- Temporary living at the new job location (e.g., an apartment or motel)
- Sale, purchase, or lease of a residence (e.g., appraisals, attorney's fees, points, or payments to a lessor to cancel a lease)
- Meals

#### Example 9

L, who was employed as a professional basketball player in Cleveland, was traded to the Miami Heat during the year. Although he had lived in Cleveland for years, L decided to move permanently to Miami. Prior to the move, L made several trips to Miami to look for a new home. After finding just the right one, he hired a moving company to pack and move all of his personal belongings. During the summer, he drove to Miami. Upon arrival, however, complications arose and he was not able to move in immediately. He ended up staying at a hotel for three weeks before he was able to take possession. L incurred the following expenses in making the move:

| | |
|---|---|
| Costs of traveling to Miami to look for a house | $ 900 |
| Costs of moving van (including costs of $500 for packing and crating) | 15,000 |
| Costs of storage in Miami | 1,000 |
| Transportation costs (3,000 miles @ 19 cents per mile) | 570 |
| Three-week hotel stay (meals and lodging) | 3,000 |
| Real estate commission on sale of former residence | 30,000 |

[18] Reg. § 1.217-2(b)(3).

[19] § 217(b)(1)(B).

L is allowed to deduct only the direct expenses related to the move: the van, storage, and transportation, for a total of $16,570 ($15,000 + $1,000 + $570). The indirect expenses, house-hunting, temporary living, and selling expenses are not deductible. However, L may treat the costs of selling his home as a reduction in the amount realized on the sale of the home, decreasing any gain realized or increasing any loss realized. Note that if L's new employer reimburses L for any of the expenses, he must include the reimbursement in income.

## Classifying and Reporting the Moving Expense Deduction

Moving expenses of an employee or a self-employed person are deductible for A.G.I. All moving expenses are reported on Form 3903.

In many cases, the employer will either pay the moving expenses directly or reimburse the employee for such expenses. When the latter occurs, the employee excludes the payment from gross income as a qualified fringe benefit under § 132. However, the exclusion is allowed only to the extent that the moving expenses meet the requirements for deductibility. It is not unusual for the employer to pay for a number of moving expenses that are not deductible (e.g., house-hunting and temporary living expenses); in such case, these amounts are included in the employee's W-2 as other income. Similarly, no exclusion is allowed for any moving expenses actually deducted by the employee in the prior year.

## ✓ Check Your Knowledge

### Review Question 1

After 15 years with the firm, J was finally promoted to partner. The substantial raise that came along with the promotion enabled him to build the house of his dreams. The new home is nestled in the woods near Lake Lemon, 60 miles from his old condo in the city. His new commute is 58 miles. Will J be able to deduct his moving expenses?

*No.* The distance requirement focuses on what would have happened to the taxpayer's commute had he not moved. As a general rule, J's commute absent the move must have increased by at least 50 miles. In other words, the distance between the old home and the *new job site* must exceed the distance between the old home and the *old job site* by at least 50 miles. Note that in order to satisfy this requirement there normally must be a change in job location. In this case, his commute without the move does not increase since the job location did not change. Therefore, his moving expenses are not deductible.

### Review Question 2

Mitch's three grueling years in law school finally paid off. This year he graduated from Harvard and took a job with a firm in Memphis for $80,000 a year. He does not itemize his deductions. Can he deduct any of his moving expenses?

*Yes.* Deduction of moving expenses normally requires the taxpayer to change job sites. However, if the taxpayer is not currently employed and has no former job site, the distance test is met if the new job site is at least 50 miles from the taxpayer's old residence. Also note that because moving expenses are deductible for A.G.I., Mitch can claim the deduction even though he does not itemize.

### Review Question 3

Grandma and Grandpa retired this year and moved from Detroit to Florida at a cost of $15,000. Both took part-time jobs at a local fast-food restaurant. Can they deduct their moving expenses?

*No.* In order to meet the time test, the taxpayer must be employed on a *full-time* basis for 39 weeks of the 12-month period immediately following arrival at the new location.

### Review Question 4

Indicate whether the following moving expenses are deductible.

- **a.** Rental of moving truck
- **b.** Boxes to pack household items
- **c.** Brake job for car while en route to new location
- **d.** 51 cents per mile for each mile driven to the new job location
- **e.** Meals on the three-day, 900-mile trip to the new location
- **f.** Trip to look for a new house after the new job was secured but before the move

Only (a) and (b) are deductible. Unusual costs incurred in traveling to the new location such as repairs are not deductible. In lieu of deducting actual transportation expenses, 19 cents per mile is allowed. Meals and house-hunting trips are not deductible.

## Home Office Expenses

It is currently estimated that more than 39 million Americans—39 percent of the labor force—work at home either full or part time. However, simply working at home does not automatically enable a taxpayer to write off the costs of owning or renting. Very narrow standards must be met before a deduction is permitted.

At one time, expenses relating to use of a portion of the taxpayer's home for business purposes were deductible without limitation when they were merely appropriate and helpful in the taxpayer's business. In 1976, however, Congress felt that the appropriate and helpful test was insufficient to prevent the deduction of what were really personal expenses. For example, under the helpful test, a university professor who was provided an office by his employer could convert personal living expenses into deductions by using a den or some other room in his residence for grading papers. In such a situation, it was unlikely that any additional expense was incurred due to the business use. To prevent the deduction of disguised personal expenses, Congress enacted § 280A, severely limiting the deduction of expenses related to the home. Section 280A generally disallows deduction of any expenses related to the taxpayer's home except those otherwise allowable, such as qualified residence interest and taxes, and those for *certain* business and rental use (the exception for rental use is discussed in Chapter 12).

### Requirements for Deductibility

**LO.4**
Describe when expenses of maintaining a home office are deductible.

Under the business use exception, a deduction is allowed for a home office if a portion of the home is "exclusively" used on a "regular" basis for any of three types of business use:[20]

1. As the principal place of business for *any* business of the taxpayer;
2. As a place of business used regularly by patients, clients, or customers in meeting or dealing with the taxpayer in the normal course of his or her trade or business; or
3. In connection with the taxpayer's trade or business when the office is located in a separate structure.

Beyond these basic requirements applicable to all taxpayers, there is one additional test that must be met if the taxpayer is an employee. Employees are entitled to claim a home office deduction only if the home office is for the *convenience of the employer.* Each of these prerequisites is considered below.

#### Exclusive Use

Under prior law, a taxpayer might write off his whole kitchen just because he opened his briefcase there. The exclusive use requirement was intended to put an end to such

[20] § 280A(c).

shenanigans. A deduction is allowed only when the space in the home is devoted solely to business use. The authors of § 280A apparently did not believe a deduction should be allowed where the space was used for both personal and business purposes. The exclusive use requirement does not mean that the home office must be physically separated from the remainder of the home. It is not necessary that the portion of the room be marked off by a permanent partition. It is sufficient if the home office activities are confined to a particular space in a room that is used only for business purposes.[21] To what extent, if any, the IRS will permit personal activities to be carried on in the home office (e.g., making personal phone calls, reading for pleasure, taking care of investments as well as business) is not clear. In any event, the taxpayer should be reminded that the key word is *exclusive.* Two exceptions to the exclusive use test, storage and daycare use, are discussed below.

### Regular Use

Section 280A also requires the home office to be used on a regular basis. Fortunately, the Code and Regulations have not adopted precise rules that require the taxpayer to punch a time clock every time he or she steps into the home office. Currently, there is no requirement to keep track of the hours spent in the office. The little guidance that does exist on the issue can be found in IRS publications. The Service does not specifically define *regular* but does explain that occasional or incidental use does not meet the regular use test even if that part of the home is used for no other purpose.[22]

### Convenience of the Employer

As noted above, if the taxpayer is an employee, he or she must jump one additional hurdle before claiming the home office deduction. An employee must work at home for the *convenience of the employer.* To meet this condition, the home office must be more than appropriate and helpful. The U.S. Tax Court has suggested that satisfaction of this test requires the taxpayer to show that he or she was unable to do the work performed at home at the employer's office.[23] For example, the Second Circuit has held in *Weissman* that this standard is met if the employer does not provide the employee with space to properly perform his or her employment duties.[24] In this case, a college professor who shared an office and did extensive research at home satisfied the test because in the Court's view the home office was necessitated by lack of suitable working space on campus.

### Principal Place of Any Business

A taxpayer satisfies the first business use test if the home office is the principal place of business for *any* business of the taxpayer. Most taxpayers, as employees, fail this test since their only business is that of being an employee and the principal location of that business is at the employer's office. This rule is not foolproof, however. In one decision, the court held that the principal place of business of a taxpayer employed as a concert musician was his home practice room rather than where he gave performances.[25] In contrast, employees who have a *second* business (e.g., selling cosmetics or vitamins) or self-employed persons who operate these activities out of their home normally satisfy the first business use test as long as they can show that the home is in fact the principal place of business.

For years, taxpayers and the IRS squabbled over when a home office constituted a taxpayer's *principal* place of business.[26] The leading case was the Supreme Court's 1993 decision in *Nader E. Soliman.*[27] Soliman was an anesthesiologist who worked for three hospitals. However, none of the hospitals provided him an office so he spent 10 to 15 hours a week at his home office doing his billing and scheduling. To Soliman's chagrin, the IRS denied his deductions for his home office expenses. Upon review, the U.S. Tax Court was more sympathetic, allowing the deductions on the grounds that the home office was essential to Soliman's business, he had spent substantial time there, and there was no other location

---

[21] *George Weightman*, 42 TCM 104, T.C. Memo 1981-301.

[22] § 280A(c)(1). See *Business Use of Your Home*, IRS Publication 587 (2007), p. 3.

[23] *Robert Chauls*, 41 TCM 234, T.C. Memo 1980-471.

[24] *Weissman v. Comm.*, 85-1 USTC ¶9106, 55 AFTR2d 85-539, 751 F.2d (CA-2, 1984).

[25] *Drucker v. Comm.*, 83-2 USTC ¶9550, AFTR2d 83-5804 (CA-2, 1983); but see *Popov v. Comm.*, T.C. Memo 1998-374.

[26] For example, see *Rudolph Baie*, 74 T.C. 105 (1980).

[27] *Comm. v. Soliman*, 93-1 USTC ¶50,014 (USSC, 1993), rev'g Nader E. Soliman, 94 T.C. 20 (1990).

available to perform the office function of the business. Although the Fourth Circuit agreed with the U.S. Tax Court, the Supreme Court did not. The high court stated that it is not sufficient that the work done in the home office is essential to the business. The court explained that to satisfy the principal place of business test, the home office must be the most important place of business as compared to all the other locations where the taxpayer carries on business. In determining whether the home office is the *most important place of business*, the court identified two factors that should be considered: (1) the relative importance of the functions performed at each of the business locations, and (2) the amount of time spent at each location. In this case, the court believed that the hospital, where Soliman performed his services and treated patients, was his most important place of business.

As might be expected, a huge backlash erupted after the *Soliman* decision since it operated to deny the home office deduction to millions of taxpayers. Most affected were those who performed essential business functions in their homes but who spent most of their time at the locations of their clients and customers (e.g., salespeople, consultants, repair people, personal trainers, caterers, etc.). In response, Congress acted in 1997 to restrict the scope of *Soliman*. Although the tests of *Soliman* can still apply, the taxpayer may now meet the principal place of business test if both of the following conditions are met:

1. The office is used by the taxpayer to conduct *administrative and management activities* of a trade or business; and
2. There is no other fixed location of the trade or business where the taxpayer conducts *substantial* administrative and management activities of the trade or business.

Under the new test, taxpayers who manage or administer their businesses out of a home office should be allowed a deduction even if the taxpayer conducts substantial non-administrative or nonmanagement business activities at a fixed location of the business outside the home. For example, this new approach would allow taxpayers like the doctor in *Soliman* a deduction for their home office expenses even though they conduct significant activities away from home at a fixed location (e.g., surgery at a hospital). Similarly, outside salespeople who spend the majority of their time calling on customers can claim the deduction if they use their home office to conduct administrative activities such as receiving orders, setting up appointments, or writing-up orders. In some cases, taxpayers may have an office available to perform administrative activities but opt to perform these tasks at home. In such case, the test is still met assuming the taxpayer does not actually perform substantial management or administrative activities at the other location. At all times, however, it must be emphasized that in the case of an employee, the *convenience of the employer test* must still be met. For this reason, an *employee* may be denied the deduction of expenses for a home office used for administrative activities if suitable space is available for performing such duties at the employer's office.

## Example 10

T is a manufacturer's representative. He promotes the products of several companies, selling to both wholesalers and retailers all over the state of Ohio. None of the companies he represents provide him an office, so he maintains an office at home. T spends an average of 30 hours a week visiting customers and 12 hours a week working in his home office. Under the *Soliman* rule, T would not be allowed to deduct the costs of maintaining a home office since his clients' premises would be his most important place of business.[28] Using the revised approach, however, T could claim the deduction since he conducts management activities in the home and there is no other fixed location where he conducts substantial management activities related to his business.

It should be emphasized that taxpayers who cannot qualify for the home office deduction under the principal place of business test may still find relief if they meet one of the

[28] Notice 93-12, 1993-1 C.B. 202; see also, Rev. Rul. 94-24, 1994-1 C.B. 87 for how the IRS will apply the *Soliman* tests.

other—more liberal—tests discussed below (i.e., regularly meet with clients or separate structure tests).

### Trade or Business

No deduction is permitted for home office expenses if the activities to which they relate do not constitute a business.[29]

> **Example 11**
>
> B, an engineer, regularly uses a room in his home exclusively for evaluating his investments. No deduction is permitted since the activity does not constitute a business.

### Meeting Place

The second exception for business use is less restrictive than the first. Under this exception, the home office qualifies if clients regularly meet with the taxpayer there. Interestingly, in *John W. Green*, the taxpayer ingeniously argued that this exception should be satisfied where he regularly received phone calls in his home office. Although a majority of the U.S. Tax Court agreed with the taxpayer, the decision was reversed on appeal. The Appellate Court believed that the statute required that the taxpayer *physically* meet with clients in the home office.[30]

### Separate Structure

The third exception for business use is the least restrictive of the three. If a separate structure is the site of the home office, it need be used only in connection with the taxpayer's work (e.g., a converted detached garage or barn).

## Amount Deductible

If the taxpayer qualifies for the home office deduction, an allocable portion of expenses related to the home may be deducted. The allocation of expenses generally must be based on square footage. Typical expenses include utilities, depreciation, insurance, security systems, repairs (e.g., furnace repair), interest, taxes, and rent. It should be emphasized that the home office deduction is limited to the gross income from the home business as reduced by allowable deductions. This computation is very similar to that for determining deductible hobby expenses. The taxpayer may deduct expenses equal to the extent of gross income reduced by (1) expenses allowable without regard to the use of the dwelling unit (e.g., interest—assuming it is a primary or secondary residence—and taxes), and (2) business or rental expenses incurred in carrying on the activity other than those of the home office (e.g., supplies and secretarial expenses).[31] Any home office expenses that are not deductible due to this limitation may be carried over and used to offset income from the business which led to the deduction, even if the taxpayer does not use the unit in the business in subsequent years.

When the taxpayer is self-employed (i.e., a sole proprietor), all of the taxpayer's expenses, including those attributable to the home office, are deductible for A.G.I. In contrast, if the taxpayer is an employee, the *otherwise allowable* expenses (e.g., interest and taxes) are deductible in full as itemized deductions. The other business expenses, including the home office expenses, are considered miscellaneous itemized deductions and are subject, along with other miscellaneous itemized deductions, to the 2 percent floor. All expenses for business use of a home office must be reported on Form 8829 (see Appendix B for a sample form).

---

[29] S. Rep. No. 94-938, 94th Cong., 2d Sess. 147-49 (1976).

[30] 78 T.C. 428 (1982).

[31] See § 280A(c)(5).

### Example 12

K maintains a qualifying home office. During this year, she earned only $2,000 from the home office activities. Her expenses included the following: interest and taxes allocable to the home office, $600; secretarial services, miscellaneous supplies and postage, $900; and expenses directly related to the home office including insurance, utilities, and depreciation, $1,700. K's potential deduction is $2,000 computed as follows:

| | | |
|---|---|---|
| Gross income | $2,000 | |
| Otherwise allowable deductions: | | |
| Interest and taxes | (600) | $ 600 |
| Other business expenses | (900) | 900 |
| Gross income limitation | $ 500 | |
| Home office expenses: | | |
| $1,700 limited to remaining gross income | | 500 |
| Total potential deduction | | $2,000 |

Whether the $2,000 of deductible expenses are deductible for or from A.G.I. depends on whether K is self-employed or an employee. If K is self-employed, the entire $2,000 is deductible for A.G.I. If the taxpayer is an employee, the $600 of interest and taxes allocable to the home office are deductible as itemized deductions. The remaining $1,400 is considered a miscellaneous itemized deduction subject (along with other miscellaneous itemized deductions) to the 2% floor. The home office expenses that are not deductible this year, $1,200 [($600 + $900 + $1,700 = $3,200) – $2,000], may be carried over to the following years to be offset against future home office income.

## Daycare and Storage Use

The home office rules for taxpayers who use their home as a daycare center or as a place to store inventory or product samples of a home-based business receive special attention from the Code. In both cases, the normal rules apply except that the exclusive use test is relaxed.

### Daycare Use

If a portion of the taxpayer's home doubles as both a living space and a daycare center it would appear that no deduction would be allowed since the exclusive use test would not be satisfied. When the home is used as a daycare center, however, the exclusive use test does not apply.[32] Instead, the expenses attributable to the room are prorated between personal and daycare use based on the number of hours of use per day. Thus, if the taxpayer uses a family room for daycare 40 percent of the time, 40 percent of the expenses allocable to that room would be deductible. A portion of the home qualifies for this special treatment if the taxpayer uses the home to provide daycare services for children, individuals over age 65, or those who are physically or mentally incapable of taking care of themselves.

### Storage Use

If the taxpayer regularly uses part of the home to store product samples or goods sold at retail or wholesale *and* the home is the sole fixed location of that business, expenses related to the storage space are deductible.[33] More important, the space need not be used exclusively for this purpose. However, the space should be a specific area (e.g., a particular part of a basement or closet).

[32] § 280A(c)(4).

[33] § 280A(c)(2).

## Residential Phone Service

For many years, taxpayers who used their home phone for business or income-producing purposes deducted a portion of the basic charge for local service on the grounds that it was business-related. In 1988, however, Congress saw the issue differently. Apparently, in 1988, it believed that the cost of basic phone service to a taxpayer's residence would have been incurred in any event—without regard to any business that the taxpayer might otherwise conduct. As a result, a taxpayer may not deduct any charge (including taxes) for local phone service for the *first* phone line provided to any residence. Presumably, the same rationale would apply to cell phones, in which case only the costs associated with a second telephone number would be deductible. The taxpayer may still deduct the costs of long-distance phone calls or optional phone services such as call waiting or call forwarding, when such costs are related to business. In addition, taxpayers may deduct the costs of additional phone lines into the home that are used for business (e.g., a separate line for a fax machine or modem).

### ✓ Check Your Knowledge

#### Review Question 1

Indicate whether the following taxpayers would be allowed to deduct expenses attributable to a home office.

**a.** T is on the tax staff of a public accounting firm. From time to time, he brings home returns and does a little work in his home office. In addition, he does most of his technical reading in the home office.

T would not be allowed a deduction since he does not meet the principal place of business or convenience of the employer tests. He fails the first of these tests since his principal place of business is his employer's office. He fails the convenience of the employer test since the employer provides him an office and he could do at the office what he does at home. His work at home appears to be for his own convenience.

**b.** R is a decorator. She works out of an office in her home. She spends about 10 hours per week visiting her client's homes and another 10 visiting businesses that carry furniture and home accessories. The remainder of her 40-hour week is spent at her home office doing sketches, ordering, keeping books, and the like.

R may deduct her home office expenses since she conducts management activities in the home and there is no other fixed location used by her to perform substantial management activities related to her business.

**c.** J operates a floral shop in town. He grows the plants for his shop in a greenhouse behind his home.

Even though the principal place of J's business is arguably at J's shop, J would still qualify for the deduction under the separate structure exception.

#### Review Question 2

With the kids starting college, income from their regular jobs was not enough, so this year N and her husband started a small blind and drapery operation. They run it out of an office in their home. N orders the fabric and sews the drapes while her husband installs. In their first year of business, the couple had gross income of $2,000. Interest and taxes allocable to the home office were $600. Various supplies and equipment, including a file cabinet, table, Rolodex, sewing machine, and scissors, cost $1,000. Depreciation, utilities, insurance, and similar expenses allocable to the home office were $900. According to their friend Norm, they should be able to deduct all $1,900 since they are all ordinary and necessary business expenses. Is Norm correct? How much can they deduct?

Norm is only partially right. Section 280A limits the deduction of home office expenses. Home office expenses are essentially deductible to the extent of net income from the business before taking into account the home office expenses (other than the interest and taxes). The home office expenses cannot create a loss from the activity. As a result, the couple can deduct $400 ($2,000 – $1,000 – $600), and the couple's net income from the business after the home office deductions is zero. Note that § 280A limitations do not apply to the $1,000 of expenses for items directly used in the business. These costs relate directly to the business (rather than the home) and, therefore, are fully deductible (or depreciable, as explained in Chapter 9).

## Transportation Expenses

If there ever was a contest for the most popular tax deduction or at least the one that arouses the most attention, it would be easy to pick the winner. Virtually everyone who tumbles out of bed each morning and makes the daily trip to work has the same question at tax time: can I deduct the costs of getting there and getting back? In a world where commuting is routine for millions of taxpayers, it would seem that the answers would be clear-cut. But this is not necessarily the case.

Before examining the deduction for transportation expenses, the distinction between transportation expenses and travel expenses should be explained. In tax jargon, transportation and travel are not synonymous. Travel expenses are broadly defined to include not only the costs of transportation but also related expenses such as meals, lodging, and other incidentals when the taxpayer is in a travel status. As discussed below, the taxpayer is in travel status when he or she is *away from home overnight* on business.[34] In contrast, transportation expenses are defined narrowly to include only the actual costs of transportation—expenses of getting from one place to another while in the course of business when the taxpayer is *not* away from home overnight.[35] Transportation expenses normally occur when the taxpayer goes and returns on the same day. The most common transportation expense is the cost of driving and maintaining a car, but the term also includes the cost of traveling by other forms of transportation such as bus, taxi, subway, or train.[36]

### Example 13

M is an architect in Cincinnati. At various times during the year, he drove to Cleveland to inspect one of his projects. He often ate lunch and dinner in Cleveland before returning home. M is allowed to deduct only the costs of transportation. The costs of the meals are not deductible since he was not away from home overnight. Had he spent the night in Cleveland and returned the next day, the costs of meals and lodging as well as transportation would be deductible.

The deduction for transportation is allowed under the general provisions of §§ 162 and 212. Therefore, to qualify for deduction, the transportation expense must be ordinary, necessary, and related to the taxpayer's trade or business or income-producing activity. Personal transportation, of course, does not qualify for deduction. Like many other expenses, however, the boundary between business and personal transportation is often difficult to identify. Some of the common problem areas are discussed below.

### Deductible Transportation Versus Nondeductible Commuting

**LO.5**
Distinguish between deductible transportation expenses and nondeductible commuting costs.

The cost of transportation or commuting between the taxpayer's home and his or her place of employment may appear to be a necessary business expense. It is settled, however, that commuting expenses generally are nondeductible personal expenses. This rule derives from the presumption that the commuting expense arises from the taxpayer's *personal preference* to live away from the place of business or employment. The distance is irrevelant.[37] Moreover, this presumption persists even though there often is no place to live within walking distance of

[34] § 162(a)(2).

[35] Reg. § 1.62-1(g).

[36] *Ibid.*

[37] *Roger A. Green*, TC Summary Opinion 2008-80.

employment, much less one that is suitable or within the taxpayer's means. The fact that the taxpayer is forced to live far away from the place of employment is irrelevant and does not alter the personal nature of the expenses.

### Example 14

In *Sanders v. Comm.*, the taxpayers were civilian employees working on an Air Force base.[38] Despite the fact that they were not allowed to live on the base next to their employment and could only live elsewhere and commute, the transportation costs were not deductible. The Court found it impossible to distinguish between these expenses and those of a suburban commuter, both being personal in origin.

### Example 15

In *Tauferner v. Comm.*, the taxpayer worked at a chemical plant that was located 20 miles from any community due to the dangers involved.[39] The taxpayer was denied deductions for his commuting even though he lived in the nearest habitable spot. Arguably, the nature of his job—not personal convenience—produced additional transportation costs. Nevertheless, the Court did not believe that such hardship changed the personal character of the expenses.

While the costs of commuting normally are not deductible, there are several exceptions. These exceptions are discussed below.

## Commuting with Tools and Similar Items

The fact that the taxpayer hauls tools, instruments, or other equipment necessary in pursuing business normally does not cause commuting expenses to be deductible. The Supreme Court has ruled that only the *additional* expenses attributable to carrying the tools are deductible.[40] The IRS determines the taxpayer's "additional expenses" by applying the so-called "same mode" test.[41] Under this test, a deduction is allowed for the extra cost of commuting by one mode with the tools over the cost of commuting by the same mode without the tools. Thus, a carpenter who drives a truck would not be allowed a transportation deduction simply by loading it with tools since carrying the tools created no additional expense. The fact that tools may have caused the carpenter to drive a truck, which is more expensive than some other type of transportation, is irrelevant under the IRS view. The courts, however, have rejected this test in certain cases.[42]

### Example 16

M plays third trumpet in the Dallas orchestra. During the year, his employer indicated that they did not need the third trumpet and that M would have to switch to his second instrument, the tuba, to retain his job. If, in order to transport the tuba, M had to change from driving to work in a small car costing $3 per day to driving to work in a van costing $5 per day, the IRS would not allow a deduction for the additional cost. Under the same mode test, the cost of driving the van with the tuba is the same as without the tuba. The courts, however, may allow a deduction for the $2 increase in cost. On the other hand, if M rented a trailer to carry the tuba at a cost of $2 per day,

---

38 71-1 USTC ¶9260, 27 AFTR2d 71-832, 439 F.2d 296 (CA-9, 1971).

39 69-1 USTC ¶9241, 23 AFTR2d 69-1025, 407 F.2d 243 (CA-10, 1969).

40 *Fausner v. Comm.*, 73-2 USTC ¶95-15, 32 AFTR2d 73-5202, 413 U.S. 838 (USSC, 1973).

41 Rev. Rul. 75-380, 1975-2 C.B. 59.

42 *J.F. Grayson*, 36 TCM 1201, T.C. Memo 1977-304. See also *H.A. Pool*, 36 TCM 93, T.C. Memo 1977-20.

the IRS would allow the deduction because the cost of driving the van with the tuba is now $2 more than without the tuba.

The IRS view on the treatment of local transportation is summarized in Exhibit 8-1.

## Commuting between Two Jobs

The transportation cost of going from one job to a second job is deductible.[43] The deduction is limited to the cost of going *directly* from one job to the other.

**EXHIBIT 8.1** **When Are Local Transportation Expenses Deductible?**

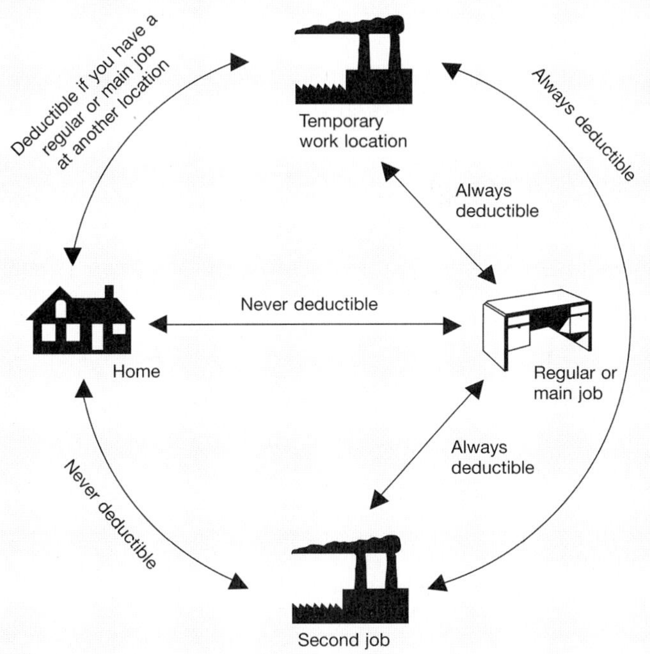


**Home:** The place where you reside. Transportation expenses between your home and your main or regular place of work are personal commuting expenses.

**Regular or main job:** Your principal place of business. If you have more than one job, you must determine which one is your regular or main job. Consider the time you spend at each, the activity you have at each, and the income you earn at each.

**Temporary work location:** A place where your work assignment is realistically expected to last (and does in fact last) one year or less. Unless you have a regular place of business, you can only deduct your transportation expenses to a temporary work location outside your metropolitan area.

**Second job:** If you regularly work at two or more places in one day, whether or not for the same employer, you can deduct your transportation expenses of getting from one workplace to another. If you do not go directly from your first job to your second job, you can only deduct the transportation expenses of going directly from your first job to your second job. You cannot deduct your transportation expenses between your home and a second job on a day off from your main job.

**Source:** *Travel, Entertainment, Gift and Car Expense*, IRS Publication 463 (Rev. 2010), p. 14.

[43] *Supra*, Footnote 39.

### Example 17

R works for X Corporation on the morning shift and for Y Corporation on its afternoon shift. The distances he drives are diagrammed below.

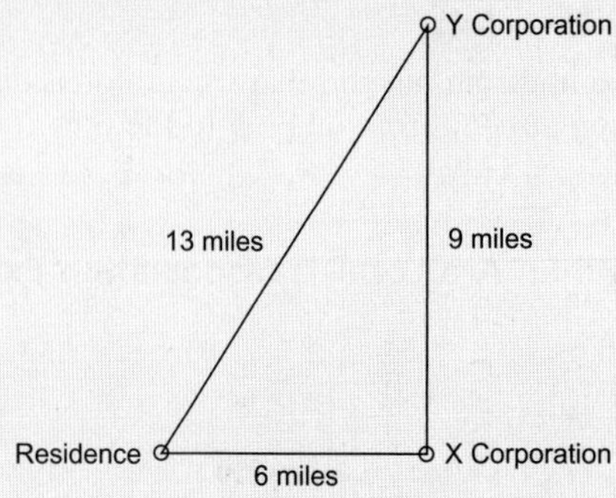


If R leaves X and goes home to eat lunch before going to Y, he actually drives 19 miles to get to Y, or 10 more miles than if he had driven directly (19 – 9). However, only the cost of driving directly, 9 miles, is deductible.

## Commuting to a Temporary Assignment

Individuals are often assigned to work at a location other than where they regularly work. When a taxpayer commutes to a *temporary work location*, the commuting expenses are deductible transportation costs if either of the following tests are satisfied:

1. The temporary assignment is *within* the general area of the taxpayer's employment and he or she otherwise has a *regular* place of business (e.g., an office);[44] or
2. The temporary assignment is *outside* the general area of the taxpayer's employment (i.e., his or her tax home).[45]

### Example 18

C is an auditor for a public accounting firm that has its office in downtown Chicago. C works about 30% of the time in her employer's office, and the remaining 70% is spent at various clients' offices around the city. C may deduct the costs of commuting between her residence and a client's office because the client's office is a temporary work location and C otherwise has a regular place of business (i.e., her employer's office).

### Example 19

M is a carpenter. He works for a construction company that builds houses in subdivisions in various areas of Houston. Most of his assignments are located within about 25 miles of downtown Houston. During the year, M worked at two different locations, one on the north side of Houston and the other on the west side. Although M is assigned to temporary work locations, he is not allowed to deduct any of his commuting expenses because he does not otherwise have a regular place of business.

---

[44] Rev. Rul. 99-7, 1999-1 C.B. 361.

[45] *Ibid.*

## Example 20

Assume the same facts as above except that M was temporarily assigned to a job in Galveston, 60 miles from Houston. He drove to Galveston daily and returned home in the evenings. Under these circumstances, M may deduct the cost of driving the entire 120-mile round trip from his home to Galveston. Observe that when the temporary assignment is beyond the general vicinity of employment, the taxpayer need not have a regular place of business.[46] The following diagram illustrates this approach.

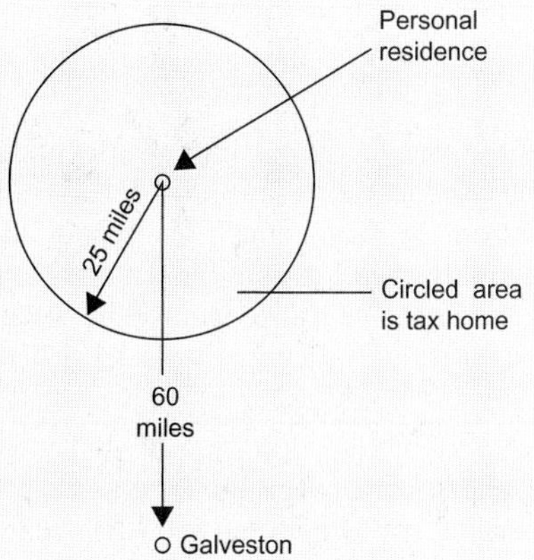


The IRS draws an important distinction between temporary and regular work locations. A work location is temporary if employment at the location is realistically expected to last and does in fact last for one year or less.[47] In contrast, a work location is considered a *regular* place of business if—as one might expect—the taxpayer performs services there on a regular basis. According to the IRS, a taxpayer may have more than one regular place of business even though he or she does not perform services at that location every week or on a set schedule. When the taxpayer commutes to these different locations on a "regular" basis, the costs of commuting would not be deductible because such locations are not temporary.

## Example 21

Dr. T, a podiatrist, has an office on both the north side and south side of Indianapolis. In addition, she performs services at a clinic and a hospital with which she is associated. T may not deduct the costs of transportation between her residence and these various locations because each is considered a regular place of business and not a temporary work location. As discussed below, however, the costs of going between two business locations (e.g., a clinic and a hospital) are deductible.

### Transportation between Job Sites

While the transportation costs between a taxpayer's home and the first and last job sites generally are considered nondeductible commuting expenses, transportation costs between two job sites are deductible.[48] Accordingly, once the taxpayer arrives at the first job site any business travel thereafter usually is deductible.

[46] See *Estate of David B. Lease, Deceased*, TC Summary Opinion 2008-11.

[47] *Ibid.*

[48] Rev. Rul. 55-109, 1955-1 C.B. 261 and Rev. Rul. 99-7, 1999-1 C.B. 361.

### Example 22

R is employed as a tax accountant and works primarily in his employer's office downtown. R drives 34 miles round-trip from his home to the office. After arriving at work one day, R drove 6 miles to a client's office and returned to his employer's office. In this case, R may deduct the cost of driving 12 miles.

### Example 23

Assume R drives 17 miles to work in the morning. In the afternoon, he drives 15 miles to a client's office where he conducts some business. From the client's office he drives 9 miles home. In this situation, R may deduct the cost of driving 15 miles because transportation between two job sites is deductible. In addition, it appears that he may deduct the cost of driving 9 miles since transportation between the taxpayer's residence and a temporary work location (i.e., the client's office) is deductible.

Although transportation expenses between the taxpayer's home and work normally are not deductible, the rule concerning travel between job sites creates a favorable exception for taxpayers who maintain a separate trade or business at home. For these taxpayers, the transportation from the first job site—the home—and the second job site in the same trade or business would be deductible.

### Example 24

V is a landscape engineer and works out of his home. Transportation costs from his home to a client's place of business are deductible since the expenses are incurred in traveling from his principal place of business to a job site.[49]

## Computing Car Expenses

Deductions relating to driving and maintaining a car may be computed using actual expenses or a standard mileage rate (automatic mileage method). Under either method, if the car is used for both business and personal purposes, only the car expenses attributable to business or income production are deductible.

### Actual Expenses

Actual car expenses normally deducted include the costs for gas, oil, repairs, insurance, depreciation, interest on loans to purchase the car (other than that of an employee), taxes, licenses, garage rent, parking fees, and tolls. Calculating actual expenses usually requires determining the portion of the nondeductible expenses attributable to personal use. Under the actual expense method, the total actual expense is allocated based on mileage.

### Example 25

R, self-employed, drove 20,000 miles during the year: 16,000 on business and 4,000 for personal purposes. Total actual expenses were as follows:

[49] See *Raymond Garner*, 42 TCM 1181, T.C. Memo 1981-542, and *Joe J. Adams*, 43 TCM 1203, T.C. Memo 1982-223. See also, *Charles Walker*, 101 T.C. 36 (1993) and Rev. Rul. 94-47, 1994-2 C.B. 18.

| General expenses: | |
|---|---|
| Gas | $1,200 |
| Maintenance (oil, repairs) | 200 |
| Insurance | 1,100 |
| Interest expense | 600 |
| Depreciation | 1,900 |
| Total | $5,000 |

| Other business expenses: | |
|---|---|
| Tolls incurred on business trips | $ 10 |
| Parking fees when calling on clients | 90 |
| Total | $ 100 |

Since R used the car 80% (16,000 ÷ 20,000) for business, he may deduct 80% of the general expenses, $4,000 (80% × $5,000). In addition, he may deduct the entire $100 cost for the parking and tolls since they were incurred solely for business purposes, for a total deduction of $4,100. Note that the nonbusiness portion of the interest expense would not be deductible, assuming it is not attributable to a loan secured by his first or second home. If R were an employee, *none* of the interest would be deductible because business interest of an *employee* is not deductible.

### Standard Mileage Rate

The automatic mileage method allows a deduction of 51 cents per mile (2011) for *all* business miles driven during the year.[50] The business portion of expenses for interest (if self-employed), state and local property taxes, parking, and tolls also may be added to the amount computed using the mileage rate. Other expenses such as depreciation, insurance, and maintenance are built into the mileage rate and cannot be added.

## Example 26

Same facts as in Example 25. R's deduction using the standard mileage rate would be $8,740, as computed below.

| | |
|---|---|
| Business mileage (16,000 × $0.51) | $8,160 |
| Interest ($600 × 80%) | 480 |
| Parking and tolls | 100 |
| Total | $8,740 |

Note that in arriving at the deduction, gas, maintenance, insurance, and depreciation are not added to the amount computed using the standard rate since they are built into the rate. Conversely, interest (if self-employed), parking, and tolls are added since they are not included in the rate.

Taxpayers who lease their cars may also use the standard mileage rate. If a taxpayer elects to use the rate for a leased car, it must be used for the entire lease period.[51]

The standard mileage rate may be used *only* if it is adopted in the first year the car is placed in service. In addition, the following conditions must be satisfied:[52]

[50] Rev. Proc. 2010-51, 2010-51 IRB 883.

[51] Prop. Reg. § 1.274-5(g).

[52] *Ibid.*

1. The car must not be one of two or more cars being used simultaneously in a business, such as in a fleet operation. When a taxpayer alternates in using different cars on different occasions, the cars are treated as one and the mileage is combined.
2. The car must not be for hire, such as a taxi.
3. Additional first-year depreciation or depreciation using an accelerated method must not have been claimed in a prior year.

If these conditions are met, the taxpayer may switch methods from year to year. However, use of the standard mileage method precludes the taxpayer from using the Modified Accelerated Cost Recovery System (MACRS) for computing depreciation in a subsequent year, and depreciation must be computed under one of the alternative methods (e.g., straight-line).[53] Note that selecting the actual method in the first year generally *prohibits* the taxpayer from ever using the standard mileage rate for that automobile.

Taxpayers who use the standard mileage rate are required to reduce the adjusted basis of their automobiles just as if they had claimed depreciation. The rate per mile varies by year as shown below.[54]

| Year | Depreciation Per Mile |
|---|---|
| 2011 | 22¢ |
| 2010 | 23¢ |
| 2008–2009 | 21¢ |
| 2007 | 19¢ |
| 2005–2006 | 17¢ |
| 2003–2004 | 16¢ |
| 2001–2002 | 15¢ |
| 2000 | 14¢ |
| 1994–1999 | 12¢ |

### Classification of Transportation and Travel Expenses

The *unreimbursed* transportation and travel expenses of an employee are treated as miscellaneous itemized deductions subject to the 2 percent floor. In contrast, if an employee is reimbursed for such expenses under a qualified arrangement known as an *accountable plan* (discussed later in this chapter), the reimbursement is excludable from gross income. Any reimbursement not made under such a plan must be included in the employee's gross income, and any qualifying deductions must be treated as miscellaneous itemized deductions. If the expenses are incurred by a self-employed person, the expenses are deductible for A.G.I. An employee reports the expenses on Form 2106, a copy of which is reproduced in the last section of this chapter.

Travel and transportation expenses related to property held for the production of income are also considered miscellaneous itemized deductions unless the income is rents or royalties, in which case the deductions would be for A.G.I. In addition, the deduction for meals may be limited to 50 percent of their cost. This limitation is discussed in detail with entertainment expenses later in this chapter.

## Travel Expenses

**LO.6**
Understand the differences between deductible travel expenses and deductible transportation costs.

Section 162 of the Code provides for the deduction of travel expenses while "away from home" in the pursuit of a trade or business.[55] A similar deduction is allowed for travel expenses connected with income-producing activities not constituting a business.[56] The definition of travel expenses is not as narrow as that of transportation expenses. Travel expenses include not only the costs of transportation but also the costs of meals (but limited to

[53] *Supra*, footnote 47.

[54] For previous rates see *Travel, Entertainment, Gift and Car Expenses*, IRS Publication 463 (Rev. 2007) p. 25.

[55] *Supra*, Footnote 34.

[56] §§ 212(1) and (2).

50 percent of actual costs, as discussed later), lodging, cleaning and laundry, telephone, and other similar expenses related to travel.[57] Whether these additional expenses such as meals and lodging are deductible depends on whether the taxpayer is considered "away from home."

## Away-from-Home Test

The taxpayer must be *away from home* before travel expenses are deductible. The "away from-home" test poses two questions: for what period does the taxpayer need to be away from home, and where is the taxpayer's home for tax purposes? With respect to the first question, the Supreme Court has ruled that the away-from-home test generally requires the taxpayer to be away from home *overnight.*[58] Later interpretations of this decision have indicated that the taxpayer will be considered to be "overnight" when it is reasonable for the taxpayer to stop for needed sleep or rest. A trip where the taxpayer leaves and returns the same day is not travel and, consequently, only the transportation cost would be deductible. Meals eaten during the trip, lodging, etc., would not be deductible.

The second and more critical aspect of the away-from-home test concerns the determination of the taxpayer's *tax home.* The IRS and the Tax Court have defined the term *tax home* to mean the business location of the taxpayer or the general vicinity of the taxpayer's employment, regardless of the location of the taxpayer's personal residence.[59] The Court of Appeals in several circuits, however, has held that "home" should be interpreted in the normal fashion (i.e., as the place where the taxpayer normally maintains his or her residence;[60] *see Example 28*). The interpretation problems usually arise when taxpayers live in one location but also conduct substantial business at another location where they often stay because it is impractical to return to the residence. To illustrate, consider a construction worker who lives with his family in Milwaukee but obtains a job to work on the construction of a nuclear power plant near Chicago. During the week, he stays in a motel in Chicago and eats his meals. The issue here is the location of the taxpayer's tax home. If the taxpayer normally works in Chicago, the IRS would take the position that the taxpayer's tax home is in Chicago and deny the deductions for meals and lodging. On the other hand, if the taxpayer normally works in Milwaukee and takes a job in Chicago, he may be able to secure a deduction for his Chicago expenses if he could demonstrate that the Chicago job is only a *temporary* assignment. The IRS permits taxpayers to deduct travel expenses incurred away from the principal place of business if an assignment away from home is temporary and not indefinite. Under § 162(a), assignments in a single location lasting a year or more are not temporary but indefinite.[61] Consequently, if a taxpayer anticipates an assignment to last more than a year or it actually exceeds one year, none of the taxpayer's travel expenses are deductible (not even those for the first 12 months).

### Example 27

D is employed as an engineer, living and working in Kansas city. D's employer assigned her to a job in El Paso that D expected to complete in five months. In reality, D lived and worked in El Paso for ten months before completing the job and returning to Kansas city. Because she realistically expected the assignment to last for one year or less and it in fact did not exceed this period, D may deduct her travel expenses for the entire ten months. What would be the result if at the end of four months it became clear that D's stay in El Paso would exceed a year? In such case, the IRS takes the position that she would be able to treat the first four months as temporary and deduct her expenses for those months. However, the expenses for the remainder of the job assignment would not be deductible.

[57] Reg. § 1.162-2(a).

[58] *U.S. v. Correll*, 68-1 USTC ¶9101, 20 AFTR2d 5845, 389 U.S. 299 (USSC, 1967).

[59] G.C.M. 23672, 1943 C.B. 66, superseded by Rev. Rul. 74-291, 1974-1 C.B. 42.

[60] For example, see *Rosenspan v. U.S.*, 71-1 USTC ¶9241, 27 AFTR2d 71-707, 438 F.2d 905 (CA-2, 1971).

[61] *Supra*, Footnote 44 and Rev. Rul 93-86, 1993-2 C. B. 71. Federal employees providing services related to investigating or prosecuting a Federal crime are not subject to this rule. See § 162(a), last sentence.

### Example 28

In *Joseph Cornelius*,[62] Mr. Cornelius, a computer system administrator, lived and worked in Austin, Texas. In 2001, his employer closed its Austin office and he became unemployed. Subsequently, he was offered work by a systems company on an "as needed" basis and was immediately assigned to work on a client in Boulder, Colorado. The assignment lasted from March, 2002 to April 2003. While in Boulder, he stayed in a hotel and shared a condominium. After Boulder, he took another assignment in New Jersey that lasted from April 2003 to July 2005. While in New Jersey he lived in a hotel and shared an apartment. During the time he was on both assignments, he continued to rent his apartment in Austin and periodically returned to visit family and friends. On his 2002 and 2003 tax returns, Mr. Cornelius deducted expenses for meals and lodging while on assignment on the theory that he was away from home on business temporarily. However, upon audit, the IRS denied the deductions and assessed deficiencies of $16,445 and $19,420 for the two years in question. At trial, the Court understood how Mr. Cornelius could believe his assignments to be "temporary," as that word is commonly used. Still, it denied the deductions since both assignments exceeded a year and by law could not be considered temporary. Moreover, deductions for traveling back and forth between Austin and Boulder and Austin and New Jersey were treated as being for personal purposes and disallowed.

If the taxpayer has no principal place of employment, the tax home is normally his regular place of abode.[63] However, if the taxpayer has no permanent place of residence, the courts have consistently denied the taxpayer's deductions for meals and lodging since there is no "home" to be away from. This rule has been applied to itinerant construction workers and salespeople whom the courts view as being *at home* wherever their work may take them.[64]

The purpose of the away-from-home provision is to reduce the burden of the taxpayer who, because of business needs, must maintain two places of abode and consequently incurs additional and duplicate living expenses. The rule is based on the principle that a taxpayer normally lives and works in the same general vicinity. Thus, when taxpayers choose to live in an area other than where they work, the resulting expenses normally are considered personal. This rule often is difficult to apply in particular situations. For this reason, the deduction of travel expenses ultimately depends on the facts.

### Example 29

C works at a testing laboratory in a remote mountain area of New Mexico, 70 miles from his home. His residence, however, is the closest place to the laboratory to live. C normally commutes to work but sometimes stays at the testing facilities' quarters overnight when he works overtime. In this situation, the IRS would not allow a deduction for travel expenses since C's tax home is at the testing laboratory, and when staying there he is not away from home. Some Appellate Courts, however, may permit the deduction for meals and lodging since he is away from his residence.[65]

## Combined Business and Pleasure Travel

As discussed above, travel costs are deductible only while away from home in pursuit of business or income-producing activities. When traveling away from home, however, taxpayers often combine business with pleasure with the hope that they can deduct what is really

[62] TC Summary Decision 2008-42.

[63] Criteria exist for determining whether a taxpayer has a regular place of abode. See Rev. Rul. 73-529, 1973-2 C.B. 37.

[64] *George H. James v. U.S.*, 62-2 USTC ¶9735, 10 AFTR2d 5627, 308 F.2d 204 (CA-9, 1962).

[65] For example, see *Lee E. Coombs*, 79-2 USTC ¶9719, 45 AFTR2d 80-444, 608 F.2d 1269 (CA-9, 1979).

a personal vacation. With an eye to this possibility, the Regulations provide special guidance as to how much can be deducted in this situation. The rules governing combined business and pleasure travel differ depending on whether the taxpayer is traveling inside or outside of the United States.

### Domestic Travel

The taxpayer who travels within the United States (all 50 states and the District of Columbia) may deduct *all* of the costs of travel to and from the destination if the trip is *primarily* for business.[66] If the trip is primarily for business, the taxpayer will not lose all or even a part of the deduction merely because he or she takes a personal side-trip or extends the trip for a short vacation. However, the costs of any personal side-trips are not allowed. Travel which is primarily for personal purposes is not deductible even though some business is conducted. Note that the taxpayer either deducts *all* of the *to-and-from* travel expenses or deducts *none* of them—there is no allocation. Of course, any travel expenses (e.g., meals and lodging) directly related to business upon arriving at the destination qualify.

#### Example 30

F, a CPA, flew from Dallas to Denver to attend a conference. The air fare was $500. Meals and lodging for the three days she attended were $150 and $230, respectively. Upon conclusion of the meeting, F drove to the mountains and skied for two days before returning home. The travel to the mountains, including meals and lodging, cost $600. F may deduct all of the air fare, $500, because costs of transportation are fully deductible without allocation when the trip is primarily for business. In addition, F may deduct 50% of the meal costs, $75 (50% × $150), and $230 for lodging because these travel expenses are directly related to business. The expenses of $600 for the ski trip are nondeductible personal expenses.

#### Example 31

Assume the same facts as in *Example 29*, except that F skied for five days. Here the trip may be treated as primarily personal thus preventing any deduction of the $500 air fare. Fifty percent of the expenses for meals and all of the lodging costs while at the convention on business are still deductible.

Obviously the most troublesome question concerning domestic travel is whether the nature of the trip is primarily business or pleasure. The Regulations, Rulings, and reported decisions offer little guidance—saying only that the answer depends on the facts and circumstances in each case. Among the factors normally considered, the amount of time devoted to business as compared to personal activities is often decisive. Another factor emphasized is the type of location where the business occurs (e.g., a resort hotel or a more businesslike setting). As might be expected, the IRS casts a doubtful eye on deductions for meetings in resort areas, believing that the alleged business trip is merely a disguised vacation. In this regard, Congress took action concerning travel expenses related to nonbusiness conventions (e.g., investment and tax seminars), completely disallowing their deduction after 1986.[67] However, if it can be clearly shown that the expenses were incurred for *business* purposes, the deduction is not disallowed merely because the meeting occurs at a resort.

---

[66] Reg. § 1.162-2(b)(1).

[67] § 274(h)(7). For an interesting case, *see Carl Jones*, 131 TC 3 (2008), where the taxpayer was denied travel deductions incurred to take a course on day trading.

### Example 32

This year, Dr H, a surgeon, attended a week-long course on arthroscopic surgery in Miami. His wife accompanied him and attended a seminar on personal financial planning. H may deduct his costs of transportation as well as the travel expenses incurred after arriving in Miami because the expenses are related to business. None of his wife's expenses are deductible because they relate not to her trade or business but to investments and taxes.

## Travel Expense of Spouse and Dependents

The IRS has always taken a dim view of taxpayers who combine business travel with pleasure and in the process deduct the cost of taking their families with them. For years, the Service attacked this abuse with a longstanding regulation that denied the deduction of a family member's travel expenses unless the taxpayer could demonstrate that the family member's presence served a bona fide business purpose.[68] Apparently this ammunition was incapable of adequately policing the problem. Consequently, Congress provided the IRS more help with new legislation in 1994.[69] Currently, no deduction is allowed for any travel expenses paid or incurred with respect to a spouse, dependent, or other individual accompanying the taxpayer (or an officer or employee of the taxpayer) on business unless (1) the individual is an employee of the person paying or reimbursing the expenses, (2) the travel of such individual has a bona fide business purpose, and (3) such expenses are otherwise deductible. The rule does not apply to deductible moving expenses.

### Example 33

T is the owner and president of TDI Corporation, which owns seven car dealerships in and around Des Moines. This year General Motors held a meeting for all of its dealers in Maui, and T took his wife and 18-year-old daughter. TDI reimbursed T for all of his traveling expenses including those of his wife and daughter. TDI is not allowed to claim a deduction for the travel expenses of T's wife and daughter unless they are both employees of the company and it can establish that their presence had a bona fide business purpose. Note that T and TDI may be able to overcome the first requirement by employing both his wife and daughter. Satisfying the second test is more difficult. In this regard, the regulations provide that performance of incidental services does not cause a family member's expenses to qualify. The courts, however, have allowed a deduction for a spouse's expenses when the facts have shown that the spouse's presence enhanced the image of the taxpayer or the spouse acted as a business assistant.[70]

## Foreign Travel

When the taxpayer travels outside the United States, the travel expenses must satisfy more stringent requirements for deduction. Generally, the costs of transportation to and from the foreign destination and other travel expenses must be allocated between business (or income-producing activities) and personal activities. If the travel is *primarily* business, the costs of transportation are fully deductible without allocation if *one* of the following conditions is satisfied:[71]

1. *Travel outside the United States does not exceed one week* (seven consecutive days). In counting the days out of the United States, the day of departure from the United

[68] Reg. § 1.162-2(c); Rev. Rul. 55-57, 1955-1 C.B. 315.

[69] § 274(m).

[70] See *Fraser Wilkins*, 72-2 USTC ¶9707, 30 AFTR2d 72-5639, 348 F. Supp. 1282 (D.Ct. Neb., 1972); *Pierre C. Warwick*, 64-2 USTC ¶9864, 14 AFTR2d 5817, 236 F. Supp. 761 (D.Ct. Va., 1974).

[71] § 274(c); Reg. § 1.274-4.

States is excluded while the day of return to the United States is included. (For example, leaving on Sunday and returning on the following Sunday is exactly seven days.)

2. *More than 75 percent of the days on the trip were devoted to business.* A day is treated as a business day if during any part of the day the taxpayer's presence is required at a particular place for a business purpose. Moreover, the day is considered a business day even though the taxpayer spends more time during normal working hours on nonbusiness activity than on business activity. Weekends, holidays, or other "standby" days that fall between the taxpayer's business days are also considered business days. However, such days are not business days if they fall at the end of the taxpayer's business activities and the taxpayer merely elects to stay for personal purposes. The day of departure and the day of return are both treated as business days.
3. Taxpayer has no substantial control over arranging the business trip.
4. Personal vacation is not a major consideration in making the trip.

If the travel is not primarily for business or fails to satisfy one of the above conditions, an *allocation* of the to-and-from travel expenses must be made. In such cases, the deductible travel expenses are determined by the following allocation formula:

$$\frac{\text{Business days on trip}}{\text{Total days on trip}} \times \begin{array}{c}\text{Total}\\ \text{to-and-from}\\ \text{Travel Expenses}\end{array} = \begin{array}{c}\text{Deductible}\\ \text{to-and-from}\\ \text{Travel Expenses}\end{array}$$

A deduction for the to-and-from travel expenses is not allowed if the trip is primarily personal. However, travel costs (e.g., meals and lodging) directly related to business upon arriving at the destination are deductible.

### Example 34

B, an executive, arranged a trip to Japan primarily for business. He left Chicago for Tokyo on July 1 and returned on July 20. During his trip, he spent 15 days on business (including the two travel days) and five days sight-seeing. His air fare was $1,000 and his lodging plus 50% of the meal costs totaled $100 per day. Unless B can show that a personal vacation was not a major consideration for the trip, he must allocate his expenses because none of the other conditions are satisfied. In such case, B may deduct $2,250 [(15 business days ÷ 20 total days = 75%) × $3,000 total expenses]. If B had returned July 8 or spent one less day sight-seeing, no allocation would be required since he would have been out of the United States less than a week or would have spent more than 75% of his time on business activities.

## Luxury Water Travel

When lawmakers lowered the boom on entertainment and meal expenses in 1986, they also took a swipe at unhurried business people who travel by cruise ships, ocean liners, and other luxury water transportation. As a general rule, deductions for transportation by water are limited to *twice* the highest per diem amount allowed to Federal employees while away from home but serving in the 48 contiguous states.[72] For example, the highest Federal per diem for travel from October 1, 2009 through December 31, 2009 was $411 in Manhatten, New York so the daily limit on luxury water travel would be $822.

### Example 35

To conduct a business meeting in London, T traveled by ocean liner, taking five days at a total cost of $3,000. If the top per diem rate for Federal employees serving in the United States is $411 per day, T's deduction is limited to $4,110 ($411 × 2 × 5).

[72] § 274(m)(1).

## Foreign Conventions

Notwithstanding the restrictions imposed on deductions related to foreign travel, substantial abuse existed until 1976. Most of this abuse involved travel to foreign conventions, seminars, cruises, etc., which if properly scheduled amounted to government-subsidized vacations. To eliminate this possibility, specific safeguards were enacted. Currently, no deduction is allowed for travel expenses to attend a convention, seminar, or similar meeting *outside* of North America *unless* the taxpayer establishes the following:[73](1) the meeting is directly related to the active conduct of his or her trade or business, and (2) it is as reasonable to hold the meeting outside North America as within North America. North America includes the United States, its possessions, Canada, Mexico, the Trust Territory of the Pacific Islands, Bermuda and qualifying Caribbean countries.

**Example 36**

B, a professor of international business, traveled to Spain to present a paper on tax incentives for exports at the International Accounting Convention. Since it is as reasonable to hold an international meeting in Spain as in North America, and presentation of the paper is directly related to B's business, she may deduct her travel expenses subject to the normal rules for travel outside the United States.

## Cruise Ships

No deduction is allowed for the cost of attending a meeting conducted on a cruise ship unless the following requirements are met:[74] (1) the ship is a vessel registered in the United States and it sails *only* between ports in the United States or its possessions; (2) the meeting is directly related to the taxpayer's business; and (3) certain detailed information regarding the cruise is submitted with the return. For qualifying cruises, the maximum deduction is $2,000 per calendar year for each taxpayer. An employer, however, may deduct the cost of sending an individual to a foreign convention or on any type of cruise if the amount is included in the employee's income.

## Check Your Knowledge

### Review Question 1

Try the following true-false questions. F is director of sales for QVS in Los Angeles but chooses to live 90 miles away in Santa Barbara. Each day he drives to and from work. Once in a while he will leave the office to call on a customer and then return. F may not deduct his cost to commute but can deduct the cost of driving to make calls.

*True.* As a general rule, commuting is not deductible regardless of the distance traveled. However, the cost of going from one job site to another site is deductible.

### Review Question 2

A taxpayer must have a regular work location in order to deduct the costs of commuting to a temporary work assignment outside his tax home.

*False.* In order to deduct the cost of commuting to a work location *within* the taxpayer's tax home, the taxpayer must have a regular place of business. The same requirement does not apply to commuting outside the taxpayer's tax home.

### Review Question 3

The costs of depreciation and insurance for an automobile vary significantly depending on the type of car and driver. Consequently, these items are not reflected in the standard mileage

[73] See § 274(h)(1), (3), and (6).

[74] § 274(h)(2).

rate; however, the taxpayer can add the appropriate amount of depreciation and insurance expense to the amount computed using the standard rate in computing deductible automobile expenses.

*False.* Depreciation and insurance are included in the rate.

### Review Question 4

T is the district manager for Mississippi Catfish, a fast-food chain with more than 100 stores. He lives in New Orleans. On Monday he traveled to Baton Rouge and returned the same day. On Tuesday he traveled to Houston, spent the night, and returned on Wednesday. T may deduct the costs of lunch both in Baton Rouge and in Houston.

*False.* In order to deduct the costs of meals and lodging, the taxpayer must be in a travel status (i.e., away from home overnight). Thus T cannot deduct the cost of lunch on his day trip to Baton Rouge. He is allowed to deduct the cost of his lunch while in Houston since he was there overnight.

### Review Question 5

This year, Dr. F, an ophthalmologist, attended a four-day meeting of his professional organization in Cancun. He remained another three days to lie on the beach and fish. Dr. F may deduct 4/7 of his airfare.

*False.* If the trip is primarily for business, the taxpayer is allowed to deduct all of the transportation costs to and from the destination.

## Entertainment Expenses

Perhaps no single deduction has created as much controversy as that for entertainment expenses. The difficulty lies in the fact that there is no simple way to distinguish entertainment expenses incurred out of business necessity from those incurred for personal purposes. The problem is the "dual personality" of entertainment. Entertainment can be purely for fun and amusement. Or it can be used to break the ice with a potential customer, to relax, or to create an engaging atmosphere for closing the sale or getting the contract. Over the years, Congress and various administrations have continually struggled to devise the proper test that would prohibit taxpayers from deducting what might be a personal expenditure.

The Kennedy administration was the first to have some success in limiting the entertainment deduction. In 1961, President Kennedy recommended abolishing the deduction for entertaining customers at parties, nightclubs, etc., as well as disallowing the deduction for country club dues. Although Kennedy's suggestions were not enacted, Congress did move to make it more difficult to deduct entertainment expenses with the enactment of Code § 274. This provision—discussed below—still stands as the major hurdle that must be overcome before entertainment expenses may be deducted. Under § 274, entertainment expenses must not only satisfy the normal criteria for business and income-producing expenses but also several additional requirements, including certain record keeping standards. Despite these additional conditions, the so-called *Kennedy rules* still were viewed by many to be inadequate.

President Carter's administration ventured into the battle over entertainment deductions in 1977, blasting the taxpayer's right to deduct the cost of what is now the infamous "three-martini lunch." The Carter attacks were generally unsuccessful, however. It was not until President Reagan's term that the entertainment deduction was drastically curtailed. Present law now presumes that virtually every entertainment and meal expense contains a personal element that is not deductible. As discussed below, only 50 percent of the cost of allowable meals and entertainment is currently deductible.

### Deduction Requirements

**LO.7**
Determine when entertainment expenses can be deducted.

To be deductible, an entertainment expense must survive the gauntlet of tests applied to all potential deductions by § 162 and then pass the special requirements of § 274. Section 162 first demands that the expense must be reasonable, ordinary, and necessary, and incurred in carrying on a trade or business.

### Example 37

D is a sales representative of M Corporation, a manufacturer of cookware. Twice a month, she takes buyers from the leading retail department stores to lunch where they discuss the corporation's new products. Business meals are customary, appropriate, and helpful in commissioned sales and thus are deductible.

As a practical matter, most entertainment expenses satisfy the ordinary and necessary tests with little difficulty. It is the additional requirements of § 274 that provide the greatest obstacles.

The restrictions contained in § 274 apply to any expense related to an activity customarily considered to provide entertainment, amusement, or recreation.[75] The provision applies to expenses for entertaining guests such as those for the following: food, liquor, sporting events, movie and theater productions, social, athletic and country clubs, yachts, hunting and fishing trips, and company-provided vacations. Business gifts also are governed by this provision.[76] It should be emphasized that expenses ostensibly for other purposes also are subject to the requirements of § 274 if they are of an entertaining nature.

### Example 38

A national magazine desiring publicity often sends the company president flying in a hot air balloon emblazoned with the corporation's logo. Although the expense is for advertising, § 274 applies since the activity constitutes entertainment.

As might be expected, when the IRS questions the taxpayer about his or her deductions for entertainment, the auditor does not ask whether the taxpayer had a good time. Unfortunately, the agent is concerned with whether the taxpayer has satisfied either of two principal tests. Under § 274, no deduction is allowed unless the taxpayer can adequately substantiate that the entertainment expense is *either* "directly related to" or "associated with" the taxpayer's business or falls within one of ten exceptions.

## Directly-Related-to Expenses

The Regulations set forth what the taxpayer must establish for an entertainment expenditure to be considered *directly related* to the taxpayer's business or income-producing activity. Expenses are treated as directly related under the so-called *general test* if the taxpayer shows all of the following:[77]

1. More than a general expectation of deriving some income or other specific benefit (other than goodwill) existed as a result of making the expenditure; no resulting benefit must be shown, however.
2. Business was actually discussed or engaged in during the entertainment.
3. The combined business and entertainment was principally characterized by business.

### Business Benefit

Prior to the enactment of § 274, entertainment deductions were liberally granted where they were shown to promote the customer's goodwill. Section 274 rejects this prior standard. Under current law, the taxpayer must have more than just a general expectation of deriving some income or some specific business benefit. Although this standard is hardly the epitome of clarity, it is clear that the likelihood of a benefit must be greater than a remote possibility.

---

[75] § 274(a)(1).

[76] § 274(d).

[77] Reg. § 1.274-2(c)(3).

**Example 39**

T, an insurance salesperson, sees his old college chum, C, in a bar. T buys his buddy a few drinks and then takes him to a ball game, using an extra ticket T has. Before the night is over, T mentions that if C ever needs insurance he should give T a call. In this case, T's prospect of a business benefit is slight, too distant, and thus not directly related. It simply creates goodwill, which is insufficient to obtain a deduction. However, T may be able to benefit from hindsight. If C later calls him about insurance, T could rightfully claim the deduction.

### Actively Engage in Business

Under the general test, the taxpayer must actually discuss or engage in business. This means that at some point during the entertainment—at halftime, during the intermission, between innings—the taxpayer must forsake the merriment of the moment and get down to business, negotiating, dealing, or bargaining with respect to a bona fide business transaction. Since this is obviously difficult to police, the Regulations have given the IRS two helpful presumptions.[78] First, it is presumed that no business can take place if the taxpayer is not present. If the taxpayer is at home mowing the lawn while the client is enjoying the game using tickets given to him by the taxpayer, the implication is that no business can take place. (In such case, the taxpayer may be able to deduct the cost of the tickets as a business gift as discussed below.) Second, it is presumed that no business can take place where there are substantial distractions. The Regulations insist that such distractions are present at night clubs, sporting events, social gatherings, cocktail lounges, theaters, and wherever the taxpayer meets with a group including not only business associates but others. Despite these presumptions, a deduction is still allowed if the taxpayer can establish to the contrary that he or she actively engaged in the discussion of business. As a practical matter, most taxpayers take advantage of this latitude, claiming the deduction and hoping that they will never be called upon to justify it.

**Principal Character Is Business** During the entertainment, business must predominate. This does not mean that the taxpayer must spend more time on business than enjoying the activity. It does mean that the business aspects must be more than incidental. As above, the Regulations rest on the rebuttable presumption that the primary character of certain activities—those on a hunting or fishing trip, a yacht or pleasure boat—is not business.

The Regulations also specify several other situations where the entertainment expense will be considered directly related. For example, entertainment is directly related if it is provided in a clear business setting—a setting where the guest recognizes the taxpayer's business motive (e.g., a hospitality room provided by a book publisher at a convention of accounting professors).[79] Expenditures for entertainment provided for those who render services for the taxpayer also are regarded as directly related. For example, a vacation trip awarded by a manufacturer to the retailer selling a number of its products qualifies.[80]

### Associated-with Expenses

It is often difficult to qualify the entertainment under the directly-related-to test, generally due to the presumption regarding distractions or simply because the taxpayer could not squeeze in any business during the show or game. However, the entertainment may still qualify for deduction if it satisfies the *associated-with test.* Entertainment expenses are considered *associated with* the taxpayer's business if the entertainment is immediately before or after a substantial business discussion.[81] The key distinction between associated-with and directly-related-to expenses concerns when the business activity occurs. The associated-with test allows the business to occur immediately preceding or following the entertainment while the directly-related-to standard requires business during the entertainment. Note that to satisfy the "immediately preceding or following" requirement it is sufficient that the entertainment

[78] Reg. § 1.274-2(c)(7).

[79] Reg. § 1.274-2(d)(4).

[80] Reg. § 1.274-2(d)(5).

[81] *Supra*, Footnote 71; Reg. § 1.274-2(d).

merely takes place on the same day as business. In some cases, the entertainment may be on the day before or after the business activity.

### Example 40

B operates a chain of sporting goods stores in Dallas. Before school begins each fall, he invites area coaches to one of his stores, where he presents his new lines of equipment. Immediately afterward, he takes them to a Cowboys football game. B may deduct the costs of tickets to the game since there was substantial business activity immediately before the entertainment. Note that due to the distractions presented by the game no deduction would be permitted if B merely took the coaches to the game and discussed business there.

## Business Meals

For many years, taxpayers were allowed to deduct the cost of meals with business associates regardless of whether they satisfied the directly-related-to or associated-with requirements. More importantly, the costs could be deducted even if business was not discussed. The effect of these rules was to allow a deduction for entertaining that created goodwill. In 1986, Congress believed that this favorable treatment was no longer justified and therefore tightened the rules.

Currently, expenses for meals, like other entertainment expenses, are not deductible unless they satisfy the directly-related-to or associated-with tests.[82] Under these criteria, the business meal is not deductible unless there is a substantial and bona fide business discussion either before, after, or during the meal.[83] In addition, the taxpayer or an employee of the taxpayer normally must be present at the meal.[84] For example, if the taxpayer merely reserves a table for dinner at a restaurant for a customer, but neither the taxpayer nor one of his or her employees attends the dinner, no deduction is allowed. For purposes of this rule, an independent contractor who performs significant services for the taxpayer such as an attorney or accountant is considered an employee.

A common question regarding the deduction for business meals concerns the costs of the taxpayer's own meals. From a purely theoretical view, the cost would presumably be a nondeductible personal expense since the taxpayer has to eat in any event. In *Richard A. Sutter*, the U.S. Tax Court took just such a view in disallowing a taxpayer's deduction for his own meals at business lunches.[85] The Court said:

> We think the presumptive nondeductibility of personal expenses (the taxpayer's meals) may be overcome only by clear and detailed evidence as to each instance that the expenditure in question was *different from or in excess* of that which would have been made for the taxpayer's personal purposes (emphasis supplied).

Despite the Court's holding, the IRS has been quite gracious. The Service permits the taxpayer to deduct the *entire cost* of his or her own meal except in abusive situations where it is evident that a substantial amount of personal expenditures are being deducted.[86] Where abuse is apparent, the IRS would invoke the *Sutter* rule and allow a deduction only to the extent it exceeds the amount the taxpayer would normally spend.

Another common question concerns the costs of entertaining those who are not directly involved in the business activities to which the entertainment relates. The portion of any entertainment expense attributable to the customer's and the taxpayer's spouses is deductible where the purpose is business rather than personal or social.[87] For example, when the taxpayer entertains a business client and it is impractical to entertain the client without the spouse, the expenses of both the taxpayer's spouse and the client's spouse are deductible. Any expenses of other persons not closely connected with those who attended the business discussion are not deductible.

---

[82] An individual who is away from home on business and eats alone need not satisfy these tests.

[83] §§ 274(a) and (b).

[84] § 274(k)(1)(B).

[85] 21 T.C. 170 (1953).

[86] Rev. Rul. 63-144, 1963-2 C.B. 129.

[87] Reg. § 1.274-2(d)(4).

## ENTERTAINMENT FACILITIES

For many years, the costs of owning and maintaining such status symbols as airplanes, luxury skyboxes, yachts, and hunting and fishing lodges could be subsidized by deducting them as entertainment expenses. Typically, taxpayers would deduct expenses like depreciation, utilities, maintenance, insurance, and salaries (e.g., that of the yacht's captain) that were allocable to business usage of the property. In 1978, however, Congress imposed severe restrictions. Currently, costs such as those listed above that are related to *any entertainment facility* are not deductible.[88] Additional special rules apply to expenses incurred in using a luxury skybox.[89]

These rules governing entertainment facilities do not prohibit the deduction of out-of-pocket expenses incurred while at the entertainment facility. Expenses for such items as food or beverage would be deductible, assuming they meet the directly-related-to or associated-with tests. In addition, the various exceptions of § 274 discussed below may enable an employer to deduct expenses connected with entertainment facilities. For example, an employer may deduct the costs of vacation condominiums, swimming pools, tennis courts, and similar facilities if such entertainment facilities are provided primarily for employees.[90]

### Club Dues

For years, the tax law contained an exception to the facility rule that allowed taxpayers to deduct their dues or fees paid for a membership in country clubs, etc., if the club was primarily used for business. In the never-ending attack on entertainment expenses, Congress eliminated the deduction for club dues in 1993. Currently no deduction is allowed for the cost of membership in any club organized for business, pleasure, recreation, or any other social purpose.[91] The new rule extends not only to country club dues but to all types of clubs, including luncheon, social, athletic, airline, and hotel clubs. The prohibition does not apply to dues paid to civic organizations, such as the Kiwanis or Rotary Club, or to professional organizations, such as the bar association, as long as the principal purpose of the organization is not entertainment. Note that specific expenses incurred at a club such as a business meal continue to be deductible to the extent that they satisfy any other applicable requirements.

## EXCEPTIONS TO DIRECTLY-RELATED-TO AND ASSOCIATED-WITH TESTS

In certain innocent situations, entertainment and meal expenses need not meet either the directly-related-to or associated-with requirements. These include expenses for the following:[92]

1. Food and drink furnished on the business premises primarily for employees (e.g., costs of a holiday office party)
2. Recreational or social activities, including facilities primarily for employees (e.g., a summer golf outing, a company health club, an annual picnic)
3. Entertainment and meal expenses for an employee if the employee reports their value as taxable compensation (e.g., a company-provided vacation for the top salesperson)
4. Entertainment and meal expenses at business meetings of employees, stockholders, and directors (e.g., refreshments at a directors' meeting)
5. Costs of items made available to the general public (e.g., soft drinks at a grand opening, free ham to the first 50 customers)
6. Costs of entertainment and meals sold to customers (e.g., costs of food sold at an event)

---

[88] § 274(a)(1)(B); Reg. § 1.274-2(e)(2).

[89] § 274(l)(2).

[90] § 274(e)(5).

[91] § 274(a)(3).

[92] § 274(e)(1)-(9).

## Fifty Percent Limitation on Entertainment and Meal Expenses

**LO.8**
Describe the 50 percent limitation on the deduction of meals and entertainment.

Opponents of the deduction for entertainment and meal expenses have long argued that, despite their business relationship, such expenses are inherently personal and should not be deductible. These same critics typically declare that business persons should not be able to live high-on-the-hog at the expense of the government. In 1986 the critics got their way, cutting the deduction to 80 percent of the actual cost. In 1993, they did it again, slashing the deduction even further.[93]

Currently, § 274(n) generally limits the amount that can be deducted for meals and entertainment to 50 percent of their actual cost. In effect, 50 percent of the cost is disallowed. For employees whose entertainment expenses are *not reimbursed*, the 50 percent limitation is applied before the 2 percent floor for itemized deductions.

### Example 41

B, an employee, pays $3,000 for business entertainment for which he is not reimbursed. B's A.G.I. is $50,000 for the year and he has no other miscellaneous itemized deductions. B's deduction is $500, computed as follows:

| | |
|---|---|
| Total unreimbursed entertainment expenses | $3,000 |
| Less 50% reduction (50% × $3,000) | (1,500) |
| Miscellaneous itemized deductions | $1,500 |
| Less 2% of A.G.I. (2% × $50,000) | (1,000) |
| Itemized deduction | $ 500 |

Expenses subject to the 50 percent limitation include the costs of taxes, tips, and parking related to a meal or an entertainment activity. In contrast, the costs of transportation to and from the activity are not subject to limitation.

### Example 42

B is the agent of G, who recently signed a lucrative contract with the Milwaukee Bucks. After successfully negotiating G's contract, B and G took a cab to a local restaurant where they toasted their success. After dinner, they walked to a nearby nightclub. For the night, B spent $207 for the following:

| | *Limited Expenses* | *Other* |
|---|---|---|
| Meal | $120 | |
| Tax | 12 | |
| Tips | 30 | |
| Cover charge | 38 | |
| Cab | | $7 |
| Total | $200 | $7 |

The cost of the cab ride, $7, is not subject to limitation and thus can be deducted in full. Of the remaining $200, only $100 is deductible (50% of $200).

[93] § 274(n). Taxpayers subject to the hours of work limitations of the Department of Transportation (e.g., pilots and flight attendants, truck operators) and workers at remote seafood processing facilities (e.g., Alaskan whale boat captains) may deduct a greater portion.

It should be emphasized that the percentage reduction rule applies to meals while away from home overnight on business as well as the traditional quiet business meal. The 50 percent limitation does not apply in several situations, thus allowing the taxpayer to deduct the meal or entertainment in full. These exceptions are discussed below.

### Reimbursed Expenses

When the taxpayer is reimbursed for the meal or entertainment, the limitation is imposed on the party making reimbursement, not the taxpayer.[94]

> **Example 43**
>
> N, a sales representative for Big Corporation, took a customer to lunch after he secured a large order. He paid $30, for which he was totally reimbursed. N includes the $30 in income and may deduct the entire $30. The corporation can deduct only $15 (50% of $30).

If an employee has a reimbursement or expense allowance arrangement with the employer, but under the arrangement the full amount of business expenses is not reimbursed, special problems arise. These problems are considered along with record keeping requirements later in this chapter.

### Excludable Fringe Benefit

The 50 percent limitation does not apply where the food or beverage provided is excludable as a de minimis employee fringe benefit (e.g., holiday turkeys, hams, fruitcakes, etc., given to employees, subsidized cafeterias, or to meals provided on the employer's premises for the convenience of the employer).[95]

### Code § 274(e) Exceptions

The percentage reduction rule generally is not imposed on entertainment and meal costs which are exempted from the directly-related-to and associated-with tests noted above.[96] For example, there is no reduction required for the deductible costs of an annual employee Christmas party, summer golf outings, or company-provided vacations treated as compensation. Similarly, the costs of promotional items made available to the general public (e.g., 100 baseball tickets given by a radio to the first 100 callers) or the salaries of comedians paid by a nightclub are not subject to the 50 percent limitation.

### Charitable Sporting Event

The costs of tickets to a sporting event are not subject to the reduction rule if the event is related to charitable fund-raising.[97] Specifically, the event must be organized for the primary purpose of benefiting a tax-exempt charitable organization, must contribute 100 percent of the proceeds to the charity, and must use volunteers for substantially all work performed in putting on the event. For example, the cost of tickets to attend a golf or tennis celebrity tournament sponsored by the local chapter of the United Way would normally satisfy these requirements and would be fully deductible. Tickets for high school, college, or other scholastic events (e.g., a football game or theater tickets) do not qualify for this exception on the grounds that volunteers do not do all the work (e.g., coaches, their assistants, and other paid individuals provide substantial work such as coaching and recruiting).

## Limitations on Deductions for Tickets

In the entertainment fracas of 1986, lawmakers also struck a blow at the deductible costs of tickets. This deduction is limited to the face value of the ticket (e.g., 50% of the normal ticket price).[98] This rule is aimed at amounts paid to a ticket scalper in excess of the regular price of

---

94 §§ 274(n)(2) and 274(e)(3).

95 § 274(n)(2)(B).

96 § 274(n)(2).

97 § 274(n)(2)(C).

98 § 274(l)(1).

the ticket. Such excess is not deductible. The rule also makes nondeductible any fee paid to a ticket agency for arranging tickets. Note, however, that this rule does not apply to tickets to qualified charitable fundraisers.

## Business Gifts

In hopes that their generosity will someday be rewarded, taxpayers often make gifts to customers, clients, and others with whom they have a business relationship. Such business connected gifts are deductible under the general rules of § 162. Under prior law, taxpayers wanting to create goodwill could shower their business associates with gifts and deduct these instruments of goodwill. Moreover, the recipient of such bounty could arguably exclude the presents. Currently, § 274(b) curbs such practice by limiting the deduction for business gifts to $25 per donee per year.[99] For this purpose, the following items *are not* considered gifts:

1. An item costing $4 or less imprinted with the taxpayer's name (e.g., pens)
2. Signs, display racks, or other promotional materials to be used on the business premises of the recipient

Incidental costs such as engraving, mailing, and wrapping are not considered part of the cost of an item for purposes of the $25 limit. However, husband and wife are treated as *one* recipient for purposes of the $25 limitation.

### Example 44

J, a saleswoman of hospital supplies, computes her deduction for business gifts during the year in the following manner.

| *Description of Gift* | *Amount* | *Deduction* |
|---|---|---|
| H, head of purchasing at St. Jude hospital: | | |
| Perfume | $10 | |
| Solar calculator | 30 | |
| Total | $40 | $25 |
| Dr. Z: | | |
| Box of golf balls | $18 | |
| Gift wrap | 2 | |
| Total | $20 | 20 |
| Total business gift deduction | | $45 |

Assuming J is an employee, she may deduct the $45 as a miscellaneous itemized deduction.

### Employee Achievement Awards

When a business expresses its gratitude for an employee's performance with a gift, special rules allow amounts greater than $25 to be transferred. The effect of these rules is to allow an employer to make and deduct gifts of up to $1,600 to an employee who is allowed to *exclude* the amount of the gift. The Code generally allows an employer to deduct up to $400 per employee for an *employee achievement award.*[100] An employee achievement award is defined as an item of tangible personal property (e.g., a television or watch, not cash or a gift

[99] § 274(b).

[100] § 274(j).

certificate) transferred to the employee for *length of service* or for *safety* achievement. To help ensure that such awards are not merely disguised compensation, the award must be transferred as part of a meaningful presentation. When the employer has a qualified plan in effect—a nondiscriminatory written plan where the average annual award to all employees does not exceed $400—a deduction of up to $1,600 for a particular award is allowed.

## Travel and Entertainment Record Keeping Requirements

Travel and entertainment expenses (including business gifts) are not deductible unless the taxpayer properly substantiates the expenses.[101] The *Cohan* rule permitting a deduction for an unsupported but reasonable estimation of an expense does not apply in regard to travel and entertainment.[102]

**LO.9**
Explain the special record-keeping requirements for travel and entertainment expenses.

Section 274(d) specifically requires the taxpayer to substantiate each of the following five elements of an expenditure for travel or entertainment:

1. Amount
2. Time
3. Place
4. Business purpose
5. Business relationship (for entertainment only)

In most cases, each item must be supported by adequate records such as a diary, account book, or similar record, *and* documentary evidence including receipts or paid bills. Where adequate records have not been maintained, the taxpayer's personal statement will suffice—but only if there is other corroborating evidence, such as the testimony of the individual who was entertained.[103] Congress has indicated that oral evidence would have the least probative value of any evidence and has also authorized the IRS to ask certain additional questions concerning substantiation on the return (see Part II, lines 19–21 of Form 2106, discussed below). In addition, the legislative history makes it clear that the IRS and the courts will invoke the negligence and fraud penalties in those cases where the taxpayer claims tax benefits far in excess of what can be justified.

A receipt is necessary only for lodging expenses and any other expenses of $75 or more. Cancelled checks, without other evidence, may not be sufficient. In the well-known blizzard case of 1975, the importance of properly substantiating each element of the expense was made clear.[104] In this case, the taxpayer did not keep a diary or other record of his substantial travel and entertainment expenses, but he presented the District Court with over 1,700 bills, chits, and memos, as well as 20 witnesses. The District Court allowed the deduction holding that the virtual "blizzard" of bills, etc., met the required tests. The Appellate Court, however, disagreed, indicating that the District Court did not determine whether the elements of each expense were substantiated. Lacking sufficient information on the specific purpose of each expenditure, deductions were denied. A written statement of the purpose is unnecessary, however, where the business purpose or business relationship is obvious from other surrounding facts.

In lieu of substantiating the *amount* of meals and lodging expenses while away from home on business, employees and self-employed individuals may elect to compute the deduction using a standard daily allowance rate. For example, in 2011 the standard meal and incidental expense rate (M&IE rate) is usually $46 per day and is reduced by the 50 percent limit on meals. The standard lodging rate is $77 per day. These rates vary depending on location and time of year. For example, for 2011 the lodging rate in Indianapolis is $152 per day ($61 M&IE) while in Manhattan it is $263 (for 1/1/11–3/31/11) ($71 M&IE).[105]

---

[101] § 274(d).

[102] Reg. § 1.274-5T(a)(4).

[103] Reg. § 1.274-5(c)(3).

[104] *Cam F. Dowell, Jr. v. U.S.*, 75-2 USTC ¶9819, 36 AFTR2d 75-6314, 522 F.2d 708 (CA-5, 1975), *vac'g. and rem'g.* 74-1 USTC ¶9243, 33 AFTR2d 74-739, 370 F. Supp. 69 (D.Ct. Tex., 1974).

[105] Rev. Proc. 2010-39, 2010-42 IRB 459. See the website for the U.S. General Services Administration at www.gsa.gov. Note also that a standard meal and snack rate exists for day care providers. See Rev. Proc. 2003-22, 2003-1 CB 577.

## ✓ Check Your Knowledge

### Review Question 1

P, the public defense attorney of South City, occasionally takes all of his staff to lunch. Q, an attorney in private practice, occasionally takes all of her staff to lunch. Can P and Q deduct the costs of the meals?

Too bad, P. This question illustrates the relatively rare situation when the taxpayer's entertainment expenses may fail the ordinary and necessary criterion or perhaps be considered lavish or extravagant. Q, the attorney in private practice, would have no trouble deducting her expenses. However, the IRS denied (with the U.S. Tax Court's support) a public defender's deduction since public defenders do not commonly take their staffs to lunch!

### Review Question 2

To illustrate the problems with entertainment expenses, consider the case of Danville Plywood Corporation,[106] a custom manufacturer of plywood. In 1981, Danville sponsored a four-day excursion for 116 people to the Super Bowl in New Orleans. The so-called Super Bowl Sales Seminar cost $103,444 including tickets, airfare, food, and lodging. On its 1981 tax return, the corporation claimed a deduction for the entire amount, euphemistically calling it "advertising expense." The list of attendees included 55 customers, 37 of their spouses, and two of their children. The remainder consisted of a few employees of the corporation and their spouses, as well as the owner, a few of his friends, and two of his children. According to the corporation, the goal of the seminar was to have discussions with the customers over a period of days in order to ascertain how Danville could do a better job as well as cut down on the travel expenses its salespeople incurred on customer visits. In the past, customers had rarely participated in plant visits so the corporation thought some type of sales meeting held in conjunction with a sporting event might boost attendance. In preparation for the trip, the company instructed its employees regarding some new products and provided other information that they were to share with the customers during the Super Bowl or a side trip to the French Quarter. The company also arranged a display showing some of its products in an area adjacent to the lobby of the hotel where everyone stayed. However, when Danville invited its guests, the letter made no reference to business meetings of any kind, nor did the company reserve rooms where business could be conducted. The corporation did hold a dinner in the hotel for all of its guests, but other individuals were also present. Danville had sponsored a similar trip to the 1980 Super Bowl and had deducted about $98,000. Was Danville able to deduct the expenses of all of the attendees?

Unfortunately, Danville got sacked on this play and none of the costs were deductible. In denying the deduction, the court emphasized that the expenses not only had to meet the tests of § 162 (i.e., ordinary and necessary business expenses) but also had to pass the rigorous requirements of § 274. The court found little difficulty in concluding that these tests were not met. It found incredible the corporation's attempt to deduct not only the expenses of the president's children but also those of the customers, explaining that their presence did not serve a bona fide business purpose. The court felt similarly about the president's friends as well as the spouses of both the customers and the employees. With respect to the customers and employees, it noted that there was little if any business discussed—a few idle conversations at most. Moreover, the letters to the customers never mentioned the possibility of business discussions or meetings. Nor were meeting rooms reserved for such purpose. In addition, the court believed that such trips were not commonplace in the industry. Based on these observations, the court concluded that the central focus of the trip was entertainment, not business. Unfortunately, it appears that Danville could have won this contest if it had a better game plan. For example, the deduction may have been secured if only the company's correspondence had properly explained the business nature of the weekend and it had actually conducted a business meeting in a separate

---

[106] *Danville Plywood Corp. v. U.S.*65 AFTR 2d 90-982, 899 F2d 3, 90-1 USTC ¶50,161 (CA-FC, 1990) aff'g 63 AFTR 2d 89-1036, 16 Cl Ct 584, 89-1 USTC ¶9248 (Cl Ct, 1989). Contrast with *Townsend Industries, Inc. v. U.S.*.92 AFTR 2d 2003-6096 342 F3d 890 (CA-8, 2003) rev'g 90 AFTR 2d 2002-6588 (Southern D. Ct. IA, 2002), where a fishing trip for employees had "a bona fide business purpose" for the trip and it enabled informal conversation about employer's business.

room devoted to such purpose. No doubt, it also did not sit well with the IRS that the corporation was so aggressive that it deducted the expenses of the children and the friends. Simply bypassing these deductions may have saved the day.

### Review Question 3

Although there appears to be one test after another that taxpayers must meet before they deduct entertainment expenditures, there are some basic requirements. Describe them.

The entertainment must be either directly related or associated with business. This means that a taxpayer must discuss business either before, after, or during the entertainment activity.

### Review Question 4

D, an attorney in Indianapolis, is an avid Hoosier fan. Somehow he managed to obtain season tickets to the IU basketball games. From time to time, he is unable to attend a game, so he calls a client and surprises him or her with a pair of tickets. Can D deduct the cost of the tickets for his clients?

D can continue to make his friends happy. As a general rule, no deduction is allowed unless the taxpayer or his representative (e.g., an employee) is present, since business cannot take place. However, D could deduct up to $25 as a business gift.

### Review Question 5

E runs an advertising firm and is constantly taking people to lunch. Just yesterday he took the ad director at Channel 12 to dinner at his favorite gourmet restaurant. They both had drinks, salad, prime rib, dessert, and coffee: a total of $30 each. When E eats alone, he typically eats a value meal at the local fast-food place. Can E deduct the cost of his client's meal? Can he deduct the entire cost of his own meal or only the amount in excess of what he normally spends?

E can eat, drink, and be merry. As long as E and his friend discussed business in between bites or the meal followed or preceded a business meeting, he can deduct the entire $60 subject to the 50 percent limitation.

### Review Question 6

This year F was admitted to the partnership of her accounting firm. Not only was F required to contribute $50,000 to the partnership but she was also required to join a country club. She joined the plush Meridian Lakes Country Club at a cost of $25,000. In addition, she must pay monthly dues of $300. Assuming F uses the club exclusively for business, can she deduct the membership and dues?

Sorry, F, but it is the price of being a partner. The Code denies a deduction for the costs of both the membership and the club dues.

### Review Question 7

True or False: Taxpayers are generally allowed to deduct only 50 percent of their unreimbursed travel and entertainment expenses.

*False.* Do not be fooled. A typical mistake is to lump travel and entertainment together. Only meals and entertainment expenses are subject to the 50 percent rule. Travel (other than meals) is not subject to the limitation.

### Review Question 8

G&H, a public accounting firm, provides continuing education for its tax staff at a resort in Florida. During the week, the employees spend hour upon hour in seminars devoted to the tax law. The firm pays for the meals and lodging of the participants. Is G&H entitled to deduct the entire costs of the meals or only 50 percent?

The 50 percent limitation normally applies to the costs of all meals and entertainment. However, the limitation does not apply if any of the various exceptions contained in § 274(e) apply. One of these concerns business meetings of employees. Consequently, the firm is allowed to deduct 100 percent of the meal costs.

### Review Question 9

This year the School of Business at X University created an annual award of $100 given to three staff members (e.g., secretaries) for outstanding performance during the year. The School's bookkeeper is uncertain as to whether taxes are to be withheld on such awards. How should the awards be handled?

Unfortunately, what appears to be an award of $100 is probably closer to $60 since the award is fully taxable and both income and employment taxes must be withheld. No exclusion is available since the award is given in cash and is not for length of service or safety.

## Reporting Business Expenses and Losses

### Sole Proprietors and Self-Employed Persons

Sole proprietors and self-employed persons are not treated as separate taxable entities. Rather, their income and expenses are compiled and reported simply as a part of their individual return. This information is reported on Schedule C or C-EZ of Form 1040. Page 1 of Schedule C appears below. An examination of Schedule C reveals that it is relatively straightforward and self-explanatory. The net income or loss as reported on line 31 of Schedule C is transferred to Page 1 of Form 1040 and is added to the taxpayer's income. The net income or loss on Schedule C also is used in the computation of self-employment tax. Accordingly, the net amount on Schedule C must also be transferred to Schedule SE.

### Statutory Employees

Before examining the reporting requirements for employees, attention must be given to a subset of workers commonly referred to as *statutory employees*. These are individuals who work in four occupational groups (described below) and are not otherwise employees under the usual common law tests. Rather, under a specific statutory provision, they are treated as employees for purposes of FICA (and sometimes FUTA) and are subject to favorable rules concerning the reporting of their income and deductions.[107] Statutory employees include.[108]

- Life insurance salespersons who work full-time for a single life insurance company selling life insurance or annuity contracts.
- Traveling salespersons who work full-time for one person to solicit orders for merchandise from customers for resale or supplies for use by the customers in their businesses (e.g., a manufacturers representative, salesmen that regularly call on customers and get paid a commission)
- Agent-drivers or commission-drivers that distribute meat, vegetable, fruit or bakery products, beverages (other than milk) or laundry or dry cleaning services (e.g., a delivery man that distributes bakery products)
- Individual who work off the premises of the person for whom the services are performed (e.g., at home or the home of another) according to furnished specifications on material provided and the products are returned to the principal (e.g., garment workers who make clothing, quilts, bedspreads and similar items at home and return them to the person for whom they performed the work; people who address envelopes at home or provide typing or transcribing services).[109]

To be considered statutory employees, these individuals also must perform all of the work (no delegation of a significant portion), have no substantial investment in facilities (vehicles excluded) and have a regular and recurring relationship with the business for which they are providing services.

---

[107] § 3121(d).

[108] See reference in § 3509(d)(3)concerning withholding to the workers identified in § 3121(d)(3).

[109] For an example of the reach of this rule, *see Laverne S. VanZant* TCS 2007-195.

**SCHEDULE C (Form 1040)**

Department of the Treasury
Internal Revenue Service (99)

# Profit or Loss From Business

**(Sole Proprietorship)**

**▶ Partnerships, joint ventures, etc., generally must file Form 1065 or 1065-B.**
**▶ Attach to Form 1040, 1040NR, or 1041. ▶ See Instructions for Schedule C (Form 1040).**

OMB No. 1545-0074
**2010**
Attachment Sequence No. **09**

Name of proprietor | **Social security number (SSN)**

A Principal business or profession, including product or service (see instructions) | **B Enter code from pages C-9, 10, & 11** ▶

C Business name. If no separate business name, leave blank. | **D Employer ID number (EIN), if any**

E Business address (including suite or room no.) ▶
City, town or post office, state, and ZIP code

F Accounting method: **(1)** ☐ Cash **(2)** ☐ Accrual **(3)** ☐ Other (specify) ▶

G Did you "materially participate" in the operation of this business during 2010? If "No," see instructions for limit on losses ☐ **Yes** ☐ **No**

H If you started or acquired this business during 2010, check here . . . ▶ ☐

## Part I Income

| | | | |
|---|---|---|---|
| 1 | Gross receipts or sales. **Caution.** See instructions and check the box if:<br>• This income was reported to you on Form W-2 and the "Statutory employee" box on that form was checked, or<br>• You are a member of a qualified joint venture reporting only rental real estate income not subject to self-employment tax. Also see instructions for limit on losses. . . ▶ ☐ | 1 | |
| 2 | Returns and allowances | 2 | |
| 3 | Subtract line 2 from line 1 | 3 | |
| 4 | Cost of goods sold (from line 42 on page 2) | 4 | |
| 5 | **Gross profit.** Subtract line 4 from line 3 | 5 | |
| 6 | Other income, including federal and state gasoline or fuel tax credit or refund (see instructions) | 6 | |
| 7 | **Gross income.** Add lines 5 and 6 ▶ | 7 | |

## Part II Expenses. Enter expenses for business use of your home **only** on line 30.

| | | | | | | | |
|---|---|---|---|---|---|---|---|
| 8 | Advertising | 8 | | 18 | Office expense | 18 | |
| 9 | Car and truck expenses (see instructions) | 9 | | 19 | Pension and profit-sharing plans | 19 | |
| | | | | 20 | Rent or lease (see instructions): | | |
| 10 | Commissions and fees | 10 | | a | Vehicles, machinery, and equipment | 20a | |
| 11 | Contract labor (see instructions) | 11 | | b | Other business property | 20b | |
| 12 | Depletion | 12 | | 21 | Repairs and maintenance | 21 | |
| 13 | Depreciation and section 179 expense deduction (not included in Part III) (see instructions) | 13 | | 22 | Supplies (not included in Part III) | 22 | |
| | | | | 23 | Taxes and licenses | 23 | |
| | | | | 24 | Travel, meals, and entertainment: | | |
| | | | | a | Travel | 24a | |
| 14 | Employee benefit programs (other than on line 19) | 14 | | b | Deductible meals and entertainment (see instructions) | 24b | |
| 15 | Insurance (other than health) | 15 | | 25 | Utilities | 25 | |
| 16 | Interest: | | | 26 | Wages (less employment credits) | 26 | |
| a | Mortgage (paid to banks, etc.) | 16a | | 27 | Other expenses (from line 48 on page 2) | 27 | |
| b | Other | 16b | | | | | |
| 17 | Legal and professional services | 17 | | | | | |

| | | | |
|---|---|---|---|
| 28 | **Total expenses** before expenses for business use of home. Add lines 8 through 27 ▶ | 28 | |
| 29 | Tentative profit or (loss). Subtract line 28 from line 7 | 29 | |
| 30 | Expenses for business use of your home. Attach **Form 8829** | 30 | |
| 31 | **Net profit or (loss).** Subtract line 30 from line 29.<br>• If a profit, enter on both **Form 1040, line 12,** and **Schedule SE, line 2,** or on **Form 1040NR, line 13** (if you checked the box on line 1, see instructions). Estates and trusts, enter on **Form 1041, line 3.**<br>• If a loss, you **must** go to line 32. | 31 | |

32 If you have a loss, check the box that describes your investment in this activity (see instructions).

• If you checked 32a, enter the loss on both **Form 1040, line 12,** and **Schedule SE, line 2,** or on **Form 1040NR, line 13** (if you checked the box on line 1, see the line 31 instructions). Estates and trusts, enter on **Form 1041, line 3.**

• If you checked 32b, you **must** attach **Form 6198.** Your loss may be limited.

32a ☐ All investment is at risk.
32b ☐ Some investment is not at risk.

**For Paperwork Reduction Act Notice, see your tax return instructions.** Cat. No. 11334P **Schedule C (Form 1040) 2010**

Statutory employees report their income and expenses in a unique manner. They receive a Form W-2 that reports their wages or commissions. In recognition of their special treatment, box 13 of the W-2 for "Statutory Employee" is checked. The wages or commissions earned by the statutory employee that are reported on the W-2 are subject to FICA taxes but withholding of income taxes is optional. More significant is the manner in which a statutory employee reports the W-2 income and related expenses. They are not considered employees subject to the normal rules governing the reporting of deductions.[110] Even though a statutory employee receives a W-2, he or she reports that income and the related expenses on Schedule C. The net amount is not subject to self-employment taxes as is normally the case since the employer withheld FICA. By reporting the expenses in this fashion, a statutory employee effectively deducts these expenses for A.G.I. and avoids the need to itemize deductions as well as the floor on miscellaneous itemized deductions (MIDs). Avoiding classification as MIDs is extremely important in light of the alternative minimum tax (AMT), which denies deductions for MIDs, making the taxpayer more vulnerable to the AMT (see Chapter 13).

Although statutory employee status provides substantial benefits, unfortunately employers do not always cooperate. Sometimes they are reluctant to check the magic box on the W-2, making the individual reluctant to claim the benefits of being a statutory employee for risk of an audit. Nevertheless, this is not a choice the employer has and it seems that the statutory employee should be able to report the W-2 correctly.

## EMPLOYEES

Both the treatment and reporting of an employee's business expenses vary significantly depending on whether the expenses are reimbursed. As explained in Chapter 7, employee business expenses that are *not* reimbursed are treated as miscellaneous itemized deductions, and are therefore deductible only to the extent that total miscellaneous itemized deductions exceed 2 percent of A.G.I. On the other hand, expenses reimbursed under an accountable plan (discussed below) are *not deductible* by the employee, *but* the reimbursement is excludable from his or her gross income. In such case, there is no effect on the taxpayer's return. This latter treatment normally applies to most employee expense accounts, including those arrangements where the employer reimburses an employee for a particular expense as well as those where the employer gives the employee a fixed allowance (e.g., a per diem amount such as $15 per day for meals and $25 per day for lodging). It should be emphasized, however, that even though an expense may appear to be reimbursed in the normal sense, it may not be treated as reimbursed for determining whether the expense is deductible from A.G.I. or the reimbursement is excludable from gross income.

### Accountable and Nonaccountable Plans

**LO.10**
Discuss the two types of reimbursement arrangements: accountable and nonaccountable plans.

Since 1989, an employee's business expenses are treated as reimbursed only if his or her employer has a reimbursement or allowance arrangement that qualifies as an *accountable plan.* An arrangement generally qualifies as an accountable plan if the employee properly substantiates the expenses to the employer, and, in the case of advances or allowances, is required to return to the employer any amount in excess of that which is substantiated.[111] If the arrangement does not meet the accountable plan requirements, it is considered a *nonaccountable plan.* As might be expected, the tax treatment of payments under the two different plans differs drastically.

Reimbursements or advances made under an accountable plan are treated far more favorably than those under a nonaccountable plan. Amounts paid under an accountable plan are normally excluded from gross income, not reported on the employee's Form W-2, and are exempt from employment taxes (i.e., social security and unemployment). In contrast, reimbursements and advances made under a nonaccountable plan must be reported in the employee's gross income, included on Form W-2, and are subject to employment taxes. More importantly, the expenses for which the employee is reimbursed under a nonaccountable plan must be claimed as miscellaneous itemized deductions subject to the 2 percent floor. In contrast, in the case of an accountable plan, consistent with the fact that the reimbursement is

[110] Statutory employees are not considered employees for purposes of § 62 that identifies the deductions that are for A.G.I. See IRS acknowledgement in Rev. Rul. 90-93, 1990-2 CB 33 concerning a full-time life insurance salesman.

[111] Temp. Reg. § 1.62-2T.

not included in income, the expense is not deducted—at least in the normal sense. Instead, the expense, like the reimbursement, is not reported. As the IRS puts it, there is "no deduction since [the employee's] expenses and reimbursements are equal." In effect, the employer claims the deduction rather than the employee.

Under either plan, the employee normally summarizes employee business expenses on Form 2106 (shown on pp. 8–51 and 8–52). When this form is properly completed, expenses not considered reimbursed flow to Schedule A and are deducted as miscellaneous itemized deductions. The reporting of employee business expenses is summarized in Exhibit 8-2, which follows.

Under an accountable plan, an employee who substantiates his or her expenses and returns any excess reimbursement reports neither the reimbursements nor the expenses because there is a complete wash. See Exhibit 8-2 Item 1.) *However*, if the employee fails to return any excess reimbursement, a different accounting is required. In this case, the excess reimbursement is treated as *if* paid under a nonaccountable plan. Therefore, the employer must report the *excess* in the employee's Form W-2 as well as pay the related employment taxes. On the other side, the employee must include the excess in gross income. (See Exhibit 8-2, Item 3).

### Example 45

R is a sales representative for C Corporation and has an expense account arrangement. Under this arrangement, R fills out an expense report every two weeks, documenting all of his expenses, and submits it for reimbursement. This year R submitted travel expenses of $5,000, all of which were reimbursed. Assuming this is an accountable plan and R has properly substantiated expenses of $5,000, there is nothing included on his Form W-2 and none of the expenses are reported on his return. In effect, there is no effect on R because the reimbursement and expenses wash. (See Exhibit 8-2 Item 1.)

### Example 46

Assume the plan in *Example 44* was not properly structured and did not require R either to substantiate his expenses or to return any excess reimbursement. In this case, the arrangement would be a nonaccountable plan. Consequently, the $5,000 reimbursement would be included as income in R's Form W-2 and he could deduct the $5,000 as a miscellaneous itemized deduction. In this case, the income and deduction do not necessarily wash (e.g., if R does not itemize), and R ends up with taxable income that economically he does not have. (See Exhibit 8-2 Item 4. The Form 2106 shown on pp. 8–51 and 8–52 reveals how this information would be reported.)

As the above examples illustrate, most employers should opt to establish reimbursement arrangements that meet the accountable plan requirements so that employees are not unduly penalized. Nevertheless, as noted above, even if the employer has an accountable plan, the employee must still substantiate any expenses and return any reimbursements in excess of the expenses substantiated to avoid unfavorable treatment.

## Substantiation

A plan generally satisfies the substantiation requirement if the employee meets the normal rules for substantiation of expenses. For example, travel and entertainment expenses must be substantiated under the special rules of § 274(d) discussed earlier in this chapter. Note that an employee whose reimbursement is based on some type of fixed allowance (e.g., a per diem for meals and lodging or a mileage allowance) is *deemed* to have substantiated the amount of his or her expenses up to the amount set by the IRS for per diem, mileage, or other expense allowances.[112] Generally, the only

[112] See Temp. Regs. §§ 1.62-2T(e)(2) and 1.274-5T(g).

**EXHIBIT 8.2** **Reporting Travel, Transportation, Meal, and Entertainment Expenses and Reimbursements**

| **Type** *of Reimbursement or Other Expense Allowance Arrangement* | **Employer** *Reports on Form W-2* | **Employee** *Shows on Form 2106* | **Employee** *Claims on Schedule A* |
|---|---|---|---|
| 1. **Accountable** | | | |
| *Adequate accounting and excess returned* | *Not reported* | *Not shown* | *Not claimed* |
| 2. *Per diem or mileage allowance (up to government rate)* | *Not reported* | *All expenses and reimbursements only if excess expenses are claimed. Otherwise, form is not filed* | *Expenses the employee can prove and which exceed the reimbursements received* |
| *Adequate accounting and excess returned* | | | |
| 3. *Per diem or mileage allowance (exceeds government rate)* | *Excess reported as wages in Box 1. Amount up to the government rate is reported only in a Box 13—it is not reported in Box 1* | *All expenses, and reimbursements equal to the government rate, only if expenses in excess of the government rate are claimed.*[1] *Otherwise, form is not filed* | *Expenses the employee can prove and which exceed the government rate*[2] |
| *Adequate accounting up to the government rate only and excess not returned* | | | |
| 4. **Nonaccountable** | *Entire amount is reported as wages in Box 1.*[3] | All expenses[1] | *Expenses the employee can prove*[2] |
| *Adequate accounting or return of excess either not required or required but not met* | | | |
| 5. *No reimbursement* | *Normal reporting of wages, etc.* | All expenses[1] | *Expenses the employee can prove*[2] |

[1]These amounts are subject to income tax withholding and to all employment taxes such as FICA and FUTA.
[2]Any allowable expense is carried to line 20 of Schedule A and deducted as a miscellaneous itemized deduction.
[3]These amounts are subject to the applicable limits including the 50 percent limit on meals and entertainment expenses and the two percent of adjusted gross income limit on the total miscellaneous itemized deductions.
**Source:** Travel, Entertainment, Gift and Car Expense, IRS Publication 463 (Rev. 2008), p. 30.

expense substantiation for such plans is the number of business miles traveled and the number of days away from home spent on business. Due to this rule, employees who receive allowances within the IRS guidelines will have no reimbursements in excess of their substantiated expenses and, therefore, will not have any excess to return.

### Example 47

K works as an accountant for a public accounting firm in Tampa. This year she attended a continuing education course in Jacksonville. The firm gives its employees a meal allowance of $12 per diem, which is within the IRS guidelines. K attended the course for five days. When she returned from the trip, she submitted her expense report requesting reimbursement for meals of $60 (5 × $12). In reality, K, wanting to save as much as she could, spent only $40 on meals. Although K has actually received $20 more than she spent ($60 – $40), she does not have to return the excess because she is deemed to have substantiated expenses of $60.

If an employee has expenses that the employer did not reimburse, the employee should file Form 2106 to claim a deduction for the unreimbursed expenses. Proper completion of this form results in the unreimbursed expenses being claimed as miscellaneous itemized deductions on Schedule A. (See Exhibit 8-2 Item 2.)

### Example 48

Under an accountable plan, T is reimbursed 40 cents per mile for all business miles driven. For the year, he received $1,000. After consulting his records, T determined that his actual expenses exceed 40 cents per mile for a total of $1,200. None of the reimbursement is included on T's Form W-2 because this is an accountable plan and the allowance does not exceed the government rate. T should report the $1,200 of expenses on lines 1–6 of Form 2106. The $1,000 reimbursement is entered on line 7 and subtracted from the $1,200 expense amount to leave $200. The $200 (the amount for which T did not receive a reimbursement) flows through to Schedule A and is treated as a miscellaneous itemized deduction. (See line 10 of Form 2106 and Exhibit 8-2, Item 2).

### Example 49

J's employer pays her a flat $100 per month to cover her car expenses. The employer does not have an accountable plan. Thus the employer must include the $100 as income in J's Form W-2, and J may deduct her car expenses as miscellaneous itemized deductions. (See Exhibit 8-2, Item 4.)

In certain instances, the employer may give the employee a per diem allowance that exceeds the Federal government allowable rate (e.g., 60 cents per mile instead of the allowable standard mileage rate). In such cases, special reporting rules apply.[113] Similarly, special allocation rules must be observed when the amount of the reimbursement covers only a portion of the employee's expenses.[114]

[113] *Supra*, Footnote 101, p. 11.

[114] Reg. § 1.62-1(f).

# Tax Planning Considerations

## Moving Expenses

Upon retirement, many individuals move to another location. Normally, the moving expenses would not be deductible. If the taxpayer can obtain a *full-time* job at the new location, however, the costs of moving become deductible. In this regard, the taxpayer must be sure to satisfy the 39- or 78-week test.

## Travel and Entertainment Expenses

The rules governing deductions for combined business and pleasure travel permit some vacationing on business trips without jeopardizing the deduction. As long as the trip is primarily for business, the entire cost of traveling to the business/vacation destination is deductible. Although the expenses of personal side-trips are not allowed, these expenses may be incidental to the major costs of getting to the desired location. For example, a taxpayer living in New York can deduct a major portion of the cost of a vacation in Florida—the cost of getting there—by properly scheduling business in Miami. In those situations where vacation time exceeds time spent on business, the taxpayer must be prepared to establish that the trip would not have been taken *but for* the business need.

When traveling, the taxpayer may also be able to deduct the expenses of a spouse if a business purpose for the spouse's presence can be established. Even where a spouse's travel expenses are clearly not deductible, only the *incremental* expense attributable to the spouse's presence is not allowed. When an automobile is used for transportation, there is no incremental expense. In the case of lodging, the single room rate would be fully deductible and only the few extra dollars added for a double room rate, if any, would not be deductible.

The importance of adequate records for travel and entertainment expenses cannot be over-emphasized. However, the *actual* cost of travel expenses need not be proved when a per diem or a fixed mileage allowance arrangement exists between the employee and the employer. In these situations, the other elements of the expense—time, place, and business purpose—must still be substantiated by the employer and employee. Moreover, the taxpayer must substantiate the cost of travel where the employee is "related" to the employer (an employee is considered related when he or she either owns more than 10 percent of a corporate employer's stock or is the employer's spouse, brother, sister, ancestor, or lineal descendant). Notwithstanding the relaxation of the substantiation requirements for travel costs, it is advisable to maintain receipts and other records to substantiate the other elements of the expenditure.

The taxpayer should get in the habit of contemporaneously recording the required elements for each expenditure. Although a bothersome task, this must be done to secure deductions for travel and entertainment expenses. *Each* element of each expenditure must be established.

With respect to vehicle expenses, the taxpayer cannot simply deduct the expenses and hope that he or she will never be asked to produce evidence supporting the deduction. Form 2106 (Part II, line 21) specifically asks whether the taxpayer has proper written evidence. Thus, failure to maintain such documentation would mean that the taxpayer could not answer this question in the affirmative, increasing the probability of audit. Of course, indicating that such evidence exists when it in fact does not could subject the taxpayer to negligence or fraud penalties.

Form **2106**

Department of the Treasury
Internal Revenue Service (99)

# Employee Business Expenses

▶ See separate instructions.

▶ Attach to Form 1040 or Form 1040NR.

OMB No. 1545-0074

**2010**

Attachment Sequence No. **129**

| Your name | Occupation in which you incurred expenses | Social security number |
|---|---|---|
| | | |

**Part I** **Employee Business Expenses and Reimbursements**

| **Step 1 Enter Your Expenses** | | **Column A** Other Than Meals and Entertainment | **Column B** Meals and Entertainment |
|---|---|---|---|
| **1** Vehicle expense from line 22 or line 29. (Rural mail carriers: See instructions.) | 1 | | |
| **2** Parking fees, tolls, and transportation, including train, bus, etc., that **did not** involve overnight travel or commuting to and from work | 2 | | |
| **3** Travel expense while away from home overnight, including lodging, airplane, car rental, etc. **Do not** include meals and entertainment | 3 | | |
| **4** Business expenses not included on lines 1 through 3. **Do not** include meals and entertainment | 4 | | |
| **5** Meals and entertainment expenses (see instructions) | 5 | | |
| **6** **Total expenses.** In Column A, add lines 1 through 4 and enter the result. In Column B, enter the amount from line 5 | 6 | | |

**Note:** *If you were not reimbursed for any expenses in Step 1, skip line 7 and enter the amount from line 6 on line 8.*

**Step 2 Enter Reimbursements Received From Your Employer for Expenses Listed in Step 1**

| | | | |
|---|---|---|---|
| **7** Enter reimbursements received from your employer that were **not** reported to you in box 1 of Form W-2. Include any reimbursements reported under code "L" in box 12 of your Form W-2 (see instructions) | 7 | | |

**Step 3 Figure Expenses To Deduct on Schedule A (Form 1040 or Form 1040NR)**

| | | | |
|---|---|---|---|
| **8** Subtract line 7 from line 6. If zero or less, enter -0-. However, if line 7 is greater than line 6 in Column A, report the excess as income on Form 1040, line 7 (or on Form 1040NR, line 8) | 8 | | |
| **Note:** *If* ***both columns*** *of line 8 are zero, you cannot deduct employee business expenses. Stop here and attach Form 2106 to your return.* | | | |
| **9** In Column A, enter the amount from line 8. In Column B, multiply line 8 by 50% (.50). (Employees subject to Department of Transportation (DOT) hours of service limits: Multiply meal expenses incurred while away from home on business by 80% (.80) instead of 50%. For details, see instructions.) | 9 | | |

| | | |
|---|---|---|
| **10** Add the amounts on line 9 of both columns and enter the total here. **Also, enter the total on Schedule A (Form 1040), line 21** (or on **Schedule A (Form 1040NR), line 9**). (Armed Forces reservists, qualified performing artists, fee-basis state or local government officials, and individuals with disabilities: See the instructions for special rules on where to enter the total.) ▶ | 10 | |

**For Paperwork Reduction Act Notice, see your tax return instructions.** Cat. No. 11700N Form **2106** (2010)

Form 2106 (2010) Page **2**

## Part II Vehicle Expenses

**Section A—General Information** (You must complete this section if you are claiming vehicle expenses.)

| | | | (a) Vehicle 1 | (b) Vehicle 2 |
|---|---|---|---|---|
| 11 | Enter the date the vehicle was placed in service | 11 | / / | / / |
| 12 | Total miles the vehicle was driven during 2010 | 12 | miles | miles |
| 13 | Business miles included on line 12 | 13 | miles | miles |
| 14 | Percent of business use. Divide line 13 by line 12 | 14 | % | % |
| 15 | Average daily roundtrip commuting distance | 15 | miles | miles |
| 16 | Commuting miles included on line 12 | 16 | miles | miles |
| 17 | Other miles. Add lines 13 and 16 and subtract the total from line 12 | 17 | miles | miles |

| | | | |
|---|---|---|---|
| 18 | Was your vehicle available for personal use during off-duty hours? | ☐ Yes | ☐ No |
| 19 | Do you (or your spouse) have another vehicle available for personal use? | ☐ Yes | ☐ No |
| 20 | Do you have evidence to support your deduction? | ☐ Yes | ☐ No |
| 21 | If "Yes," is the evidence written? | ☐ Yes | ☐ No |

**Section B—Standard Mileage Rate** (See the instructions for Part II to find out whether to complete this section or Section C.)

| | | | |
|---|---|---|---|
| 22 | Multiply line 13 by 50¢ (.50). Enter the result here and on line 1 | 22 | |

**Section C—Actual Expenses**

| | | | (a) Vehicle 1 | | (b) Vehicle 2 | |
|---|---|---|---|---|---|---|
| 23 | Gasoline, oil, repairs, vehicle insurance, etc. | 23 | | | | |
| 24a | Vehicle rentals | 24a | | | | |
| b | Inclusion amount (see instructions) | 24b | | | | |
| c | Subtract line 24b from line 24a | 24c | | | | |
| 25 | Value of employer-provided vehicle (applies only if 100% of annual lease value was included on Form W-2—see instructions) | 25 | | | | |
| 26 | Add lines 23, 24c, and 25 | 26 | | | | |
| 27 | Multiply line 26 by the percentage on line 14 | 27 | | | | |
| 28 | Depreciation (see instructions) | 28 | | | | |
| 29 | Add lines 27 and 28. Enter total here and on line 1 | 29 | | | | |

**Section D—Depreciation of Vehicles** (Use this section only if you owned the vehicle and are completing Section C for the vehicle.)

| | | | (a) Vehicle 1 | | (b) Vehicle 2 | |
|---|---|---|---|---|---|---|
| 30 | Enter cost or other basis (see instructions) | 30 | | | | |
| 31 | Enter section 179 deduction and special allowance (see instructions) | 31 | | | | |
| 32 | Multiply line 30 by line 14 (see instructions if you claimed the section 179 deduction or special allowance) | 32 | | | | |
| 33 | Enter depreciation method and percentage (see instructions) | 33 | | | | |
| 34 | Multiply line 32 by the percentage on line 33 (see instructions) | 34 | | | | |
| 35 | Add lines 31 and 34 | 35 | | | | |
| 36 | Enter the applicable limit explained in the line 36 instructions | 36 | | | | |
| 37 | Multiply line 36 by the percentage on line 14 | 37 | | | | |
| 38 | Enter the **smaller** of line 35 or line 37. If you skipped lines 36 and 37, enter the amount from line 35. Also enter this amount on line 28 above | 38 | | | | |

Form **2106** (2010)

# Problem Materials

## DISCUSSION QUESTIONS

**8-1** *Requirements for Education Expenses.* J has been told that, as a practical matter, most education expenses are considered nondeductible personal expenses. Under what conditions. if any, may J deduct expenses for education?

**8-2** *Education: Degrees, Promotion, and Employer Assistance.* Y is currently employed as the manager of a fast-food restaurant, earning $29,000. In order to improve her upward mobility in the company, Y decides that she should go to college and earn her degree.

**a.** Can Y deduct any of the cost of obtaining her bachelor's degree in business?

**b.** Same as above, except Y already has her bachelor's degree and now decides to take courses which could lead to her receiving an M.B.A.

**c.** What is the effect on Y if her employer pays for her education costs this year of $6,000? Answer for both a bachelor's degree and an M.B.A.

**8-3** *Expenses of Education.* F, vice president of sales for a large corporation, is in the executive M.B.A. program at the University of Michigan. F lives in Chicago and travels to Ann Arbor and Detroit to take certain courses.

**a.** F's employer reimburses F for the tuition, which is $30,000 per year. Explain how F will treat the reimbursement and the expense. What if F was not reimbursed?

Indicate whether the following expenses incurred by F would be deductible:

**b.** Meals and lodging when he stays overnight

**c.** Transportation costs from Chicago and back

**d.** Books

**e.** Secretarial fees for typing term projects

**f.** Copying expenses

**g.** Value of vacation time used to take classes

**h.** Tutor

**8-4** *Qualifying Educational Expenses.* Indicate whether education expenses would be deductible in the following situations:

**a.** J is currently an elementary school teacher. State law requires beginning teachers to have a bachelor's degree and to complete a master's degree within five years after first being hired. This year he took two courses toward the master's degree.

**b.** R is a full-time engineering student and has a part-time job as an engineer with a firm that will employ him as an engineer when he graduates.

**c.** C is an airline pilot and is presently taking lessons to become a helicopter pilot.

**d.** H retired from the finance department of the Army and now is getting his M.B.A. He plans to get a job with a financial institution.

**8-5** *Moving Expenses.* Address the following:

**a.** What two tests must be satisfied before moving expenses may be deducted?

**b.** What moving expenses are deductible?

**c.** Are moving expenses deductible *for* or *from* adjusted gross income?

**8-6** *Moving Expenses: Real Estate Commissions.* B's employer transferred him during the year. As a result, B sold his home in North Dakota and moved to New York, where he lives in an apartment. He does not plan to move into a new home. B's real estate commissions were $6,000. B has asked how he should treat the real estate commissions.

**8-7** *Home Office Expenses.* The enactment of the restrictive rules related to home office deductions caused many commentators to conclude that the home office deduction had been essentially eliminated. Which particular requirement(s) of § 280A prompted such a conclusion?

**8-8** *Computing Car Expenses.* Briefly answer the following:

**a.** With respect to a business car, can the taxpayer claim depreciation in addition to the expense determined using the standard mileage rate?

**b.** Can a taxpayer switch to the automatic mileage method after using MACRS to compute depreciation? If so, when does the car become fully depreciated?

**8-9** *Transportation vs. Travel.* Explain the distinction between transportation expenses and travel expenses.

**8-10** *U.S. Travel vs. Foreign Travel.* Compare and contrast the rules governing travel in the United States to those rules governing travel outside of the United States.

**8-11** *Limitations on Entertainment and Meals.* T is employed by KL Publishing Corporation. He is a sales representative with responsibility for college textbook sales in Alabama, Florida and Georgia. T lives in Atlanta. For each of the following situations, indicate whether T's or the corporation's deduction for entertainment or meals would be limited, and if so, how?

**a.** T flew to Birmingham on a Tuesday night. After checking in at the hotel, he caught a cab to his favorite restaurant where he ate by himself. The cost of the meal was $20, including a $1 tax and a $3 tip. The cost of the cab ride was $10. The next day he called on a customer.

**b.** Same as (a), except that T's employer reimbursed him under an accountable plan for all of his costs.

**c.** Same as (a), but further assume that T's A.G.I. for the year was $30,000 and that he has other miscellaneous itemized deductions of $700.

**d.** At the year-end Christmas party for employees, the corporation gave T a 10-pound, honey-baked ham, costing $40. The cost of the party (excluding the ham), which was held at a local restaurant, was $300.

**e.** During the annual convention of college marketing professors in New Orleans, the corporation rented a room in the convention hotel for one night and provided hors d'oeuvres. The room cost $200 while the food and drink cost $1,000.

**8-12** *Statutory Employees.* L was an education consultant for ALS. Her duties required her to visit schools, collect data and input the data into a software template provided by ALS. Upon completion, she e-mailed the information to ALS. Is she a statutory employee? Regardless of your answer, explain the benefits of being so classified.

**8-13** *Entertainment Expenses.* Distinguish between entertainment expenses that are considered "directly related to" the taxpayer's business and those that are "associated with" the taxpayer's business.

**8-14** *Business Meals.* Can the taxpayer deduct the cost of his or her own meal when he or she pays for the lunch of a customer and no business is discussed?

**8-15** *Entertainment Facilities.* Under what circumstances are expenses related to an entertainment facility deductible?

**8-16** *Substantiation of Travel and Entertainment Expenses.* What information must the taxpayer be prepared to present upon the audit of his or her travel and entertainment expenditures? Does the taxpayer need to maintain records if he or she has a per diem arrangement with the employer?

**8-17** *Foreign Convention.* Dr. B recently learned that a world famous plastic surgeon will be making a presentation concerning her area of expertise at a convention of physicians in Switzerland. If B attends, can she deduct the costs of airfare, meals, lodging, and registration? Explain.

**8-18** *Cruise Ship Seminars.* The American Organization of Dental Specialists is offering a seven-day seminar on gum disease aboard a cruise ship. Dr. D, a dentist. would like to attend. If D attends, can he deduct his expenses?

**8-19** *Reporting Reimbursements.* R is regional sales manager for a large steel manufacturing corporation. His job requires him to travel extensively to call on customers and salespeople. As a result, he incurs substantial expenses for airfare, hotel, meals, and entertainment, for which he is reimbursed. Under what conditions may R simply ignore reporting the reimbursements and the expenses for tax purposes?

**8-20** *Reporting Employee Business Expenses.* T is a salesperson for Classy Cosmetics Inc. During the year, she incurred various business expenses for which she was reimbursed under an accountable plan. Discuss the problems T encounters when reporting the reimbursements and expenses in the following situations, assuming an adequate accounting was made.

**a.** T was reimbursed $3,800 for expenses totaling $3,000.

**b.** T was on a per diem of $25 per day for lodging and $15 per day for meals. She received $2,000 under the per diem arrangement for expenses totaling $2,200.

**8-21** *Per Diem Arrangement.* A1 was recently hired by a public accounting firm as a staff accountant. When A1 is out of town on business (e.g., staff training or an audit at a client's place of business), the firm gives him $12 a day for dinner. A1 normally spends $5 and banks the rest. What are the tax consequences?

**8-22** *Substantiation Requirements.* Indicate whether each of the following is required in order to properly substantiate a deduction:

**a.** Purpose of an entertainment expenditure

**b.** Date of entertainment expenditure

**c.** Receipt for business meal with client, which cost $15

**d.** Receipt for lodging at Motel Cheap, which cost $12

**e.** Description of what the taxpayer wore on the day he lunched with client

**f.** Diary detailing information normally required for substantiation of entertainment expenses

**g.** Canceled check for $12 for tickets to baseball game that was attended with customer

**h.** Social security number of client entertained

## YOU MAKE THE CALL

**8-23** The unfortunate experience of Danville Plywood Corporation and its deduction for the Super Bowl trip described earlier in this chapter raises another issue. The corporation booked what clearly seemed to be entertainment expenses as advertising expenses, perhaps with the hope that the expense would be forever buried. Assume that you were the accountant on the job, noted this, and proposed a reclassification entry to the client who objected. What action should you take?

## PROBLEMS

**8-24** *Education Expenses.* Indicate the amount, if any, of deductible education expenses in each of the following cases. Comment briefly on your answer and state whether the deduction is deductible *for* or *from* adjusted gross income:

**a.** C is employed as a plumber, but is training to become a computer programmer. During the year, he paid $500 for tuition and books related to a college course in programming.

**b.** E is a licensed nurse. During the year, she spent $300 on courses to become a registered nurse.

**c.** R paid a $1,000 fee to take the C.P.A. exam and $3,000 for a C.P.A. review course. R currently is employed by a public accounting firm.

**d.** R is an IRS agent. This year, he began taking courses toward a law degree emphasizing tax. Tuition and books cost for the year cost $20,000.

**e.** H is a high school instructor teaching European history. On a one-year sabbatical leave from school, he traveled to Europe, taking slides which he planned on using in his classes. The trip cost $7,000, including $1,000 for meals.

**8-25** *Moving Expenses.* In May of the current year. M found a new job, forcing him to move from Tulsa to Seattle. On June 1, the moving company picked up all of M's possessions. M and his family stayed in a hotel on June 1, left the morning of June 2, and arrived in Seattle on June 4. They incurred the following expenses.

1. Airfare and meals for him and his wife while traveling to Seattle to look for a new house, \$260 and \$50 respectively. They failed to find a home. Consequently, they moved into an apartment, from which they continued their search.
2. Lodging in Tulsa on the day they moved out of their house, \$70.
3. Expenses on the way to Seattle included meals, \$80, and lodging, \$100.
4. Mileage to Seattle, 2,000 miles.
5. Car repair on trip to Seattle, \$175.
6. Moving van, \$4,000.
7. Storage charges for furniture that would not fit in the apartment: \$3 per day for the period June 5–July 31.
8. Temporary living expenses for period June 5–July 31: apartment, \$10 per day; meals, \$20 per day; and cleaning and laundry, \$25.
9. Realtor's commission on sale of old home. \$1,000.

Compute M's moving expense deduction (Form 3903 may be helpful).

**8-26** *Home Office.* In each of the following independent situations, indicate whether the taxpayer is entitled to deduct expenses related to the home office:

**a.** C, a dermatologist employed by a hospital, also owns several rental properties. He regularly uses a bedroom in his home solely as an office for bookkeeping and other activities related to management of the rental properties.

**b.** R, an attorney employed by a large law firm, frequently brings work home from the office. She uses a study in her home for doing this work as well as paying bills, sorting coupons and conducting other personal activities.

**c.** M is a research associate employed by the Cancer Research Institute. His duties include designing and carrying out experiments, reviewing data, and writing articles and grant proposals. His employer furnishes M a laboratory but due to insufficient space cannot provide an office for him. Thus, for about three hours each day, M uses a portion of his bedroom (where he and his wife sleep) to do the writing, reviewing, and other related activities.

**d.** T is a self-employed tax consultant. He has an office downtown and a home office. He occasionally meets with his clients in the home office since it is often more convenient for the clients to meet there.

**e.** S, an artist, converted a detached garage to a studio for painting. She sells her paintings at her own gallery located in town.

**f.** D has four toddlers. Since her home is virtually a nursery already, she decided to turn her family room into a daycare center.

**8-27** *Home Office.* R is considering purchasing a home priced somewhat over her budget. Her brother has suggested that converting a room to a home office would enable her to deduct a substantial part of the costs related to the home, thus making the purchase feasible. R is a sales manager for X Corporation, which transfers its middle management employees frequently.

Comment on the following advice given to R by her brother:

**a.** Establishing a home office is an effective method for reducing the costs of home ownership by the amount of the tax benefits received.

**b.** There are no disincentives for claiming the home office deduction.

**8-28** *Home Office Computations.* T is employed as a law professor at State University. Outside of her university work she teaches continuing education courses for attorneys and occasionally provides legal services. T does all her work for these outside pursuits in her home office. Income and expenses relating to these were

| | |
|---|---|
| Income: | |
| Fees for services | $2,000 |
| Expenses: | |
| Depreciation on home office furniture and computer | 400 |
| Miscellaneous supplies, books, etc. | 500 |
| Expenses attributable to home office: | |
| Depreciation | 500 |
| Insurance and utilities | 700 |
| Taxes | 300 |
| Interest | 700 |

Determine the tax consequences resulting from T's part-time activities.

**8-29** *Deductible Moving Expenses.* Indicate whether the following expenses qualify as deductible moving expenses:

**a.** Costs of meals and lodging while en route to new location.
**b.** Insurance on household and personal effects being transported—an option provided by the moving company.
**c.** Costs of driving the family car to new location.
**d.** Costs of storing items that would not fit in apartment at the new location; the apartment served as a temporary residence until a home was purchased.
**e.** Costs of new carpeting and wallpaper to prepare old home to be sold.
**f.** Real estate commission on sale of former residence.
**g.** Loss on sale of residence.
**h.** Payment of six months' rent to settle lease obligation at old location; the lease had six more months to run.
**i.** Cost of appraisal of new home required as part of loan application.

**8-30** *Moving Expenses: Time Test.* On September 1, 2011, L left her former employment in Indianapolis to seek her fortune in Cincinnati. Indicate whether L could deduct the cost of her moving expenses to Cincinnati under the following conditions.

**a.** L found a teaching job with the public school system for which she worked ten months, September through June. After school was out, L took a three-month vacation. She then decided to leave Cincinnati and move to Atlanta.
**b.** Same as (a) except L found a job as a tutor and was considered self-employed.
**c.** L moved to take a new position as product manager with P&G Corporation. After working three months, she and her new employer had a falling out over what she considered unethical advertising. She quit her job and moved to New York.

**8-31** *Moving Expenses: Distance Test.* P is an accountant for L Corporation. This year, his employer moved from its downtown Manhattan location to a new office in New Jersey. As a result, P decided to move to be closer to the office.

**a.** Assuming P did not change jobs, is he allowed to deduct any moving expenses?
**b.** Regardless of your answer to (a), indicate whether P satisfies the distance test in light of the following information:
- Old office building to new building: 60 miles
- Old home to new home: 65 miles
- New home to old office: 51 miles
- Old home to old office: 30 miles
- New home to new office: 15 miles
- Old home to new office: 58 miles

**8-32** *Standard Mileage Rate.* R, self-employed, leases her car. She elects to compute her deduction for car expenses using the standard mileage rate. Indicate whether the following expenses may be deducted in addition to expenses computed using the standard rate:

**a.** Depreciation
**b.** Interest on car loan
**c.** Insurance
**d.** Parking while calling on customers
**e.** Parking tickets incurred while on business
**f.** Major overhaul
**g.** Personal property taxes on car
**h.** Tolls

**8-33** *Transportation Expenses.* Indicate the amount, if any, deductible by the taxpayer in each of the following cases. (Ignore the floor on miscellaneous itemized deductions.)

**a.** R works in downtown Denver, but chooses to live in the mountains 90 miles away. During the year, he spent $2,700 for transportation expenses to and from work.

**b.** Q, a high school basketball coach, liked to scout his opposition. On one Friday afternoon, he left school and drove 40 miles to attend the game of the team he played next. On the way, he stopped for a meal ($5). He watched the game and returned home.

**c.** R, a carpenter, commutes to work in a truck. He drives the truck in order to carry the tools of his trade. During the year, R's total transportation costs were $5,000. R estimates that his costs of transportation without the tools would have been $4,000, since he otherwise would have taken public transportation.

**d.** G, an attorney, works downtown. She is on retainer, however, with a client who has offices two miles from her home. G often stops at the client's office before going to work. The distance between these locations is as follows: home to office, 20 miles; home to client, 2 miles; and client to office, 22 miles. During the year, G drove directly to work 180 days and via the client's office 50 days.

**8-34** *Transportation to Temporary Assignments.* For each of the following cases, indicate the number of business miles driven by the taxpayer. (Ignore the floor on miscellaneous itemized deductions.)

**a.** K is employed as a salesperson for Midwest Surgical Supply Company. The company's offices are in downtown Chicago. K's sales territory is the northwest side of Chicago and the adjacent suburbs. During Monday through Thursday, K drives directly from her residence to call on various customers. She sees each customer about once a month. On Friday of each week, she goes directly from her home to her office downtown to turn in orders, attend the weekly sales meeting, and do any other miscellaneous work. A portion of K's trip diary appears below.

| | | *Odometer Reading* | | |
|---|---|---|---|---|
| *Date* | *Destination* | *Begin* | *End* | *Mileage* |
| 3-17 | Springmill Clinic | 470 | 482 | 12 |
| | Dr. J | 482 | 485 | 3 |
| | Home | 485 | 500 | 15 |
| 3-18 | Office | 500 | 530 | 30 |
| | Home | 530 | 560 | 30 |

**b.** F, an electrician, works for EZ Electrical. He lives and works in the Los Angeles area. For 200 days of this year, he was assigned to do the wiring on a 30-story office building in downtown Los Angeles. His mileage from his home to the building was 20 miles. For 50 days during the year, he was assigned to a job in San Diego. Most of F's assignments are 20 miles closer than San Diego. F commuted 70 miles from his home to San Diego. Although the company's headquarters are in downtown Los Angeles, F goes there only on rare occasions.

**8-35** *Travel Expenses.* Indicate the amount, if any, deductible by the taxpayer in each of the following situations. (Ignore the floor on miscellaneous itemized deductions.)

**a.** P, a steelworker, obtained a job with XYZ Corporation to work on a nuclear reactor 200 miles from his residence. P drove to the site early on Monday mornings and returned home late Friday nights. While at the job site he stayed in a boarding house. P anticipates that the job will last for eight months. During the year, he traveled 4,000 miles in going to and from the job. Other expenses while away from home included the following: meals, $1,000; lodging, $900; and laundry, $75.

**b.** Same as (a), except P anticipates the job to last for more than a year.

**c.** W plays professional football for the Minnesota Vikings. He has an apartment in St. Paul but he and his wife's permanent personal residence is in Tucson. During the season, W usually stays in St. Paul. In the off-season he returns to Tucson. Expenses for the year include travel between St. Paul and Tucson, $2,000; apartment in St. Paul, $1,800; meals while in St. Paul, $900.

**d.** R took a trip to New York primarily for business. R's husband accompanied her. She spent two weeks on business and one week sight-seeing in the city. Her train fare was $400 and meals and lodging cost $30 and $50 per day, respectively. R's husband incurred similar expenses.

**e.** L flew from Cincinnati to Chicago for $300 round-trip. She spent one day on business and four days shopping and sight-seeing. Her meals and lodging cost $30 and $50 per day, respectively.

**8-36** *Car Expense Computation.* E, a salesperson for T Corporation, incurred the following expenses for transportation during the year:

| | |
|---|---|
| Gas and oil | $ 1,200 |
| Repairs | 200 |
| Insurance | 700 |
| Interest on car loan | 400 |
| Depreciation | 2,000 |
| License | 100 |

In addition, he spent $70 on parking while calling on customers. E drove the car 20,000 miles during the year, 18,000 for business.

**a.** Compute E's deduction, assuming the standard mileage rate is elected.

**b.** Compute E's deduction, assuming he claims actual expenses.

**8-37** *Travel Outside of the United States.* S, an executive for an automotive company, traveled to Paris this year for business meetings with a European subsidiary. Prior to the trip, she thought that the meetings presented an ideal opportunity for her to vacation in Paris as well as to conduct business. For this reason, she scheduled the trip. S's airfare to Paris was $1,000 and her daily meals and lodging were $30 and $50 respectively. Given the additional facts below, indicate the amount, if any, of the deduction that S may claim.

**a.** S's trip was primarily business. She spent two days on business (including travel days) and four days sight-seeing.

**b.** Her itinerary revealed the following:

| | |
|---|---|
| *Thursday May 1:* | Depart New York, arrive Paris |
| *Friday, May 2:* | Business 9–11 a.m.; remainder of day sight-seeing in Paris |
| *Saturday and Sunday, May 3–4:* | Tour French countryside |
| *Monday and Tuesday, May 5–6:* | Business 9–5 |
| *Wednesday–Sunday, May 7–11:* | Tour Germany |
| *Monday, May 12:* | Business 9–5 |
| *Tuesday, May 13:* | Depart Paris, arrive New York |

**c.** Same as (a) except the travel was to Paris for the International Car Exposition, a foreign convention.

**d.** Same as (a) except the business meetings took place on a luxury liner cruising the Caribbean.

**e.** Same as (a) except S had no control over arranging the trip.

**f.** Same as (a) except the trip was primarily personal.

**8-38** *Entertainment Expenses.* R is president of X Corporation, a company that manufactures and distributes office supplies. During the year, he and the company incurred various expenses relating to entertainment. In each of the following situations, indicate the amount of the deduction for entertainment expenses. Briefly explain your answer and classify the deduction as either *for* or *from* adjusted gross income. (Assume all the substantiation requirements are satisfied.)

**a.** R and his wife took a potential customer and his wife to a night club to hear a popular singer. Tickets for the event cost $10 each. R was unable to discuss any business during the evening.

**b.** After agreeing in the afternoon to supply S's company with typing paper, R took S to a baseball game that evening. Tickets were $8 each. X Corporation reimbursed R $16 for the tickets under an accountable plan.

**c.** R and S, a client, went to lunch at an expensive restaurant. R paid the bill for both his meal, $30, and S's meal, $40. No business was discussed during lunch.

**d.** X Corporation purchased a vacation condominium for use primarily by its employees. Expenses relating to the condominium, including depreciation, maintenance, utilities, interest, and taxes, were $7,000.

**e.** R joined an exclusive country club this year. The membership fee, which is not refundable, was $1,000. In addition, R paid annual dues of $3,600. During the year, R used the club 100 days, 70 days for entertainment directly related to business and 30 days for personal use.

**f.** R gave one of the company's best customers a $100 bottle of wine.

**g.** X Corporation gave one of its retailers 1,000 golf balls ($1 each) to distribute for promotional purposes. X Corporation's name was imprinted on the balls.

**8-39** *Convention and Seminar Expenses.* Dr. F, a pediatrician, is employed at a hospital located in Chicago. He also operates his own practice. During the year, he attended the following seminars and conventions. In each case, he incurred expenses for registration, travel, meals, and lodging. Indicate whether such expenses would be deductible assuming he attended.

**a.** "The Care and Feeding of Newborns," a seminar in Honolulu sponsored by the American Family Medical Association.

**b.** While Dr. F was attending the meeting above, his wife attended a concurrent seminar entitled "Tax Planning for Physicians and their Spouses."

**c.** "The Economics of a Private Practice: Make Your Investment Count," sponsored by the American Management Corporation in Chicago.

**d.** "Investing and Inside Information," sponsored by the National Association of Investment Specialists in Orlando.

## CUMULATIVE PROBLEMS

**8-40** George (445-42-5432) and Christina Campbell (993-43-9878) are married with two children, Victoria, 7, and Brad, 2. Victoria and Brad's social security numbers are 446-75-4389 and 449-63-4172, respectively. They live at 10137 Briar Creek Lane, Tulsa, OK 74105. George is the district sales representative for Red Duck, a manufacturer of sportswear. His principal job is to solicit orders of the company's products from department stores in his territory, which includes Oklahoma and Arkansas. The company provides no office for him. Christina is a maker of fine quilts which she sells in selected shops in the surrounding area. The couple uses the cash method of accounting and reports on the calendar year. Their records for the year reveal the following information:

**1.** George received a salary of $65,000 and a bonus of $5,000. His employer withheld Federal income taxes of $5,000 and the proper amount of FICA taxes.

**2.** Christina's income and expenses of her quilting business, Crazy Quilts, include

| | |
|---|---|
| Quilt sales | $7,000 |
| Costs of goods sold | 600 |
| Telephone (long-distance calls) | 100 |

Christina makes all of the quilts at home in a separate room that is used exclusively for her work. This room represents 10 percent of the total square footage of their home. Expenses related to operating the entire home include utilities, $2,000; and insurance, $500. Depreciation attributable solely to the home office is $800. Christina computes her deduction relating to use of her car using actual expenses, which included gas and oil, $900; insurance, $300; and repairs, $100. The car is fully depreciated. Her daily diary revealed that, for the year, she had driven the car a total of 20,000 miles, including the following trips:

| *Trip Description* | *Miles* |
|---|---|
| Home to sales outlets and return | 10,000 |
| Between sales outlets | 2,000 |
| Miscellaneous personal trips | 8,000 |

3. George incurs substantial expenses for travel and entertainment, including meals and lodging. He is not reimbursed for these expenses. This is the second year that George has used the standard mileage rate for computing his automobile expenses. During the year he drove 50,000 miles; 40,000 of these were directly related to business. Expenses for parking and tolls directly related to business were $90. Total meal and lodging costs for days that he was out of town overnight were $600 and $1,200, respectively. Entertainment expenses were $400.
4. This is George's second marriage. He has one child, Ted (age 11), from his first marriage to Hazel, who has custody of the child. He provides more than 50 percent of the child's support. The 2003 divorce agreement between George and Hazel provides that George is entitled to the exemption for Ted. George paid Hazel $4,800 during the year, $1,600 as alimony and the remainder as child support. Ted's Social Security number is 122-23-3221.
5. The couple's other income and expenses included the following:

| | |
|---|---|
| Dividends (IBM stock owned separately by George) | $ 400 |
| Interest on redeemed Treasury bills | 700 |
| Interest on City of Reno bonds | 566 |
| Interest paid on home mortgage | 10,000 |
| Real property taxes on home | 900 |
| Safety deposit box fee | 50 |
| State income taxes | 4,000 |

6. Both taxpayers elect to give to the Presidential campaign fund.

Compute the couple's tax liability for the year. If forms are used, complete Form 1040 for the year, including Schedules A, B, C, SE, and Form 2106. Ignore any alternative minimum tax.

## TAX RESEARCH PROBLEMS

**8-41** *Travel Away from Home.* M is a traveling salesperson who lives with his family in Cincinnati. His sales territory consists of Indiana, Illinois, and Kentucky. Most of his business, however, is in the Louisville area. For this reason, he normally travels to Louisville weekly and spends three or four days there living in a hotel. He also spends considerable time traveling throughout his territory. M completes the paperwork and other tasks incidental to his work at his home in Cincinnati. M's wife has a good job in Cincinnati and consequently M has never considered moving to Louisville. May M deduct the costs of traveling between his residence in Cincinnati and Louisville (including the costs of meals and lodging while in Louisville)?

**8-42** *Business Gifts.* R is product manager for a large pharmaceutical company. At the annual Christmas party, he handed out $50 gifts (checks from his personal account) to each of the 10 employees that work in his division under his supervision. R's group had been highly successful during the year and he felt that each person contributed to the division's profitability. He also gave his secretary $100. What amount, if any, may R deduct?

9

# Capital Recovery: Depreciation, Amortization, and Depletion

## Learning Objectives

Upon completion of this chapter you will be able to:

LO.1 Explain the concept of cost recovery and the various cost recovery methods used for tax purposes, including depreciation, amortization and depletion.

LO.2 Describe the requirements that must be met to claim deductions for depreciation.

LO.3 Calculate depreciation for tax purposes, using the modified cost recovery system.

LO.4 Describe the special election under Section 179, allowing immediate expensing of certain property.

LO.5 Identify the restrictions on depreciation of listed property, including automobiles, trucks, computers and other items.

LO.6 Distinguish amortization from depreciation and identify assets subject to amortization.

LO.7 Determine the current depletion deduction for various assets.

LO.8 Explain the options available in selecting the appropriate tax treatment of research and experimentation expenditures.

LO.9 Explain the tax treatment of certain expenditures incurred in farming and ranching activities.

## Chapter Outline


Introduction 9-2
Depreciation and Amortization for Tax Purposes 9-2
General Rules for Depreciation Deductions 9-2
Historical Perspective 9-4
Modified Accelerated Cost Recovery System 9-5
An Overview of MACRS 9-5
Property Subject to MACRS 9-5
Classes of Property 9-6
Calculating Depreciation 9-9
Other Methods 9-16
Changes in Depreciation 9-19
Limited Expensing Election: Code § 179 9-21
Additional First-Year (Bonus) Depreciation 9-23
Limitations for Automobiles 9-25
Limitations for Personal Use 9-30
Other Considerations 9-36
Amortization 9-37
Goodwill and Covenants not to Compete 9-38
Five-Year Elective Amortization 9-39
Leasehold Improvements 9-39
Depletion 9-39

Computing the Depletion Deduction 9-39
Research and Experimental Expenditures 9-42
Research and Experimental Expenditures Defined 9-42
Alternative Tax Treatments 9-42
Other Related Provisions 9-44
Expenses of Farmers and Ranchers 9-44
Expenses Related to Livestock 9-44
Soil and Water Conservation, Fertilizer, Land Clearing 9-44
Development Expenses 9-45
Tax Planning Considerations 9-45
Depreciation and After-Tax Cash Flow 9-45
Accelerating Depreciation with Cost Segregation 9-46
Goodwill Amortization Rule Benefits Buyers and Sellers 9-47
Problem Materials 9-48


## Introduction

**LO.1**
Explain the concept of cost recovery and the various cost recovery methods used for tax purposes, including depreciation, amortization and depletion.

The concept of capital recovery originated with the basic premise that income does not result until revenues exceed the capital expended to produce such revenues. For example, consider the situation where a taxpayer purchases an asset at a cost of $1,000 and subsequently sells it. Generally, the sale produces no income unless the asset is sold for a price exceeding $1,000. This result derives from the principle that the taxpayer first must *recover* his or her $1,000 of capital invested (basis) before he or she can be considered as having income. Here, the recovery occurs as the taxpayer offsets the basis of the asset against the amount realized on the sale. This same principle operates when an asset, instead of being sold and providing a readily identifiable benefit, provides benefits indirectly (e.g., a machine used for many years as part of a process to manufacture a product). In this case, the cost of the asset or the capital invested is *recovered* by offsetting (deducting) the asset's cost against the revenues the asset helps to produce. Thus, in the absence of a sale or other disposition of an asset, capital recovery usually occurs when the taxpayer is permitted to deduct the expenditure. Certain capital expenditures such as research and experimental costs are recovered in the year of the expenditure since the tax law allows immediate deduction. For other types of capital expenditures, the taxpayer is allowed to deduct or recover the cost over the years for which the asset provides benefits.

This chapter examines the various cost allocation methods allowed by the Code. These are depreciation, amortization, and depletion. Although each of these methods relates to a process of allocating the cost of an asset over time, different terms for the same process are used because each method relates to a different type of property. Depreciation concerns *tangible property*, amortization concerns *intangible property*, and depletion concerns *natural resources*. Tangible property means any property having physical existence (i.e., property capable of being touched such as plant, property, and equipment). Conversely, intangible property has no physical existence but exists only in connection with something else, such as the goodwill of a business, stock, patents, and copyrights. There are two types of tangible property: real property and personal property. Real property (or *realty*) is land and anything attached to the land such as buildings, curbs, streets, fences, and other improvements. Personal property is property that is not realty and is usually movable. The concept of personal property or *personalty* should be distinguished from property that a person owns and uses for his or her benefit—usually referred to as *personal-use* property.

In addition to the cost recovery methods mentioned above, this chapter discusses the tax treatment of other capital expenditures such as those for research and experimentation, and certain expenses of farmers.

## Depreciation and Amortization for Tax Purposes

**LO.2**
Describe the requirements that must be met to claim deductions for depreciation.

### General Rules for Depreciation Deductions

The Code allows as a depreciation deduction a reasonable allowance for the exhaustion, wear and tear, and obsolescence of property that is either used in a trade or business or held for the production of income.[1] This rule makes it clear that not all capital expenditures for property

[1] § 167(a).

are automatically eligible for depreciation. Rather, like all other expenditures, only those that satisfy the initial hurdles can be deducted.

### Exhaustion, Wear and Tear, and Obsolescence

Only property that wears out or becomes obsolete can be depreciated. As normally construed, this requirement means that depreciation is allowed only for property that has a *determinable life.*[2] Property such as land that does not wear out and that has no determinable life cannot be depreciated. Similarly, works of art cannot be amortized or depreciated since they normally have an indefinite life. In contrast, intangible assets with definite lives, such as patents, copyrights, and licenses that cover a fixed term, can be amortized.

### Business or Income-Producing Property

Like other expenses, no deduction is allowed for depreciation unless the property is used in a trade or business or an income-producing activity. Property used for personal purposes cannot be depreciated. In many instances, however, a single asset may be used for *both* personal purposes and profit-seeking activities. In these cases, the taxpayer is permitted to deduct depreciation on the portion of the asset used for business or production of income.

#### Example 1

N is a salesperson who uses his car for both business and personal pur- poses. He purchased the car this year for $18,000. During the year, N drove the car 50,000 miles: 40,000 miles for business and 10,000 miles for personal purposes. Under these circumstances, 80% (40,000 ÷ 50,000) of the cost of the car is subject to depreciation in the current year. Note that the business-use percentage may vary from year to year. If so, the depreciation allowed each year will vary accordingly.

Property held for the production of income, even though not currently producing income, may still be depreciated. For example, a duplex held out for rental that is temporarily vacant may still be depreciated for the period during which it is not rented. Similarly, if the taxpayer's trade or business is suspended temporarily, rather than indefinitely, depreciation can be continued despite the suspension of activity.

### Depreciable Basis

The basis for depreciation is the adjusted basis of the property as used for computing gain or loss on a sale or other disposition.[3] This is usually the property's cost. Where property used for personal purposes *is converted* to use in business or the production of income, the basis for depreciation purposes is the lesser of the fair market value or the adjusted basis at the time of conversion.[4] This ensures that no deduction is claimed for declines in value while the property was held for personal purposes.

#### Example 2

R purchased a home computer for $1,000 while attending college. He used it solely for personal purposes. After graduation, R went into the consulting business and began using the computer for business purposes. At the time he converted the computer to business use, its value was $400. R may compute depreciation using a basis of $400 (the lesser of the adjusted basis, $1,000, or its value, $400, at the time of conversion).

---

[2] Reg. §§ 1.167(a)-2 and 1.167(a)-3.

[3] § 167(g).

[4] Reg. § 1.167(g)-1.

### Commencement of Depreciation

The date on which depreciation begins can be quite important. Depreciation may not begin until an asset is *placed in service*. This is not necessarily the time when the asset is purchased. According to the Regulations, an asset is placed in service when it is in a "state of readiness and availability for the assigned function" of the activity.[5] For those assets acquired for a new business, the depreciation period starts when the business begins.

**Example 3**

In 1981, William and Lois Walsh[6] leased a building and immediately began making substantial repairs and improvements to prepare it to open as a restaurant. Although the restaurant did not open until 1982, the couple claimed depreciation deductions in 1981 that were denied by the IRS. At trial, the taxpayers asserted that their restaurant business began in 1981 when they acquired assets for use in the restaurant and executed a lease for the premises. Although the taxpayers purchased the assets in 1981, the court denied the taxpayers' 1981 depreciation deductions. According to the court, the restaurant had not yet begun to function as a going concern and to perform those activities for which it was organized. For this reason, the assets had not been placed in service until the restaurant opened in 1982.

## Historical Perspective

Prior to 1981, taxpayers could compute depreciation using either of two approaches: (1) the facts-and-circumstances method or (2) the Class Life System. Depreciation methods such as straight-line, declining balance, and sum-of-the-years'-digits were available for most assets under each system. The facts-and-circumstances method enabled taxpayers to choose useful life and salvage value estimates for depreciable assets based on their experience and judgment of all surrounding facts and circumstances. There were no predetermined or prescribed guidelines. Conflicts often arose between taxpayers and the IRS over useful life selections because taxpayers were motivated to employ short useful lives in order to maximize the present value of tax savings from depreciation deductions.

As an alternative to the facts-and-circumstances system, the Class Life System became part of the law in 1971. It was developed primarily to minimize IRS-taxpayer conflicts over useful life estimates. The system prescribed depreciable life ranges for numerous categories of assets. For example, office furniture and fixtures could be depreciated using lives from 8 years to 12 years under the Class Life System.[7] Taxpayers electing this system were not challenged by the IRS. However, IRS-taxpayer conflicts were not eliminated because many taxpayers continued to employ the facts-and-circumstances system, seeking depreciable lives that were shorter than those available with the Class Life System.

In 1981, the facts-and-circumstances system and Class Life System were all but eliminated for assets placed in service after 1980. In the Economic Recovery Tax Act of 1981 (ERTA), Congress substantially revised the method for computing depreciation by enacting Code § 168 and the Accelerated Cost Recovery System (ACRS). Altered several times since 1981, the current version of this system is known as the Modified Accelerated Cost Recovery System (MACRS). An alternative to MACRS, called the Alternative Depreciation System (ADS), is also available.

A major benefit of MACRS and ADS is the elimination of previous areas of dispute between taxpayers and the IRS. Under these systems, the taxpayer is required to choose from a small set of predetermined options regarding depreciable life and depreciation method. Salvage value is ignored in all cases. Thus, depreciation calculations are more uniform for all taxpayers.

It should be emphasized, however, that some assets may not be depreciated using either of these systems. For this reason, the facts-and-circumstances approach and the Class Life System have continuing validity in certain instances.

---

[5] Reg. §§ 1.46-3(d)(1) and § 1.167(a)-11(e)(1)(i).

[6] William J. Walsh, TC Memo 1988-242.

[7] Rev. Proc. 77-10, 1977-1 C.B. 548.

# Modified Accelerated Cost Recovery System

## An Overview of MACRS

> **LO.3**
> Calculate depreciation for tax purposes, using the modified cost recovery system.

Once it is determined that property is eligible for depreciation, the amount of the depreciation deduction must be computed. Under current law, taxpayers are required to calculate depreciation for most property using the Modified Accelerated Cost Recovery System (MACRS) or what is sometimes referred to as the General Depreciation System or GDS. As suggested earlier, MACRS is a radical departure from traditional approaches to depreciation. Under MACRS, useful lives for assets are termed *recovery periods* and are prescribed by statute. Regardless of the effects of nature and outside forces, each asset is deemed to have a particular useful life of 3, 5, 7, 10, 15, 20, 27.5, or 39 years. In addition, salvage value is ignored under MACRS. By assuming there is no salvage value, taxpayers can depreciate the basis of each asset to zero. With these rules, possibilities for abuse using unrealistic values for useful life and salvage value are essentially eliminated. Finally, certain assumptions—so-called *accounting conventions*—exist regarding about how much depreciation is allowed for the year of acquisition and disposition (e.g., a half-year or something more or less).

The basic machinery of MACRS that is used to compute depreciation can be summarized as follows:

1. The system establishes eight classes or categories of property (e.g., three-year property).
2. For each class of property, a specific useful life and depreciation method are prescribed (e.g., for three-year property the useful life is three years and either the 200 percent declining-balance or straight-line method must be used).

To actually compute depreciation, taxpayers must first determine when the asset is placed in service, whether the property is subject to MACRS, then—based on the property's classification—determine the applicable method, recovery period, and accounting convention. These elements of the depreciation calculation are discussed below.

## Property Subject to MACRS

Taxpayers generally must use MACRS to compute depreciation for all *tangible* property, both real and personal, new or used.[8] MACRS is not used to amortize *intangible* assets such as patents or copyrights, which are amortized using the straight-line method. In addition, MACRS may not be used with respect to the following property:[9]

1. Property depreciated using a method that is not based on years (e.g., the units-of production or income forecast methods)
2. Automobiles if the taxpayer has elected to use the standard mileage rate (such an election precludes a depreciation deduction)
3. Property for which special amortization is provided and elected by the taxpayer in lieu of depreciation (e.g., amortization of pollution control facilities)
4. Certain motion picture films, video tapes, sound recordings, and public utility property
5. Generally, any property that the taxpayer—or a party related to the taxpayer—owned or used (e.g., leased) prior to 1987

As a practical matter, MACRS is mandatory for all tangible property. But as explained below, the taxpayer has several alternatives under MACRS, including the option to elect out entirely and use the Alternative Depreciation System. In addition, in lieu of depreciation, the taxpayer may be allowed to expense up to $500,000 (2010 and 2011) annually of certain assets placed in service during the year. Observe, however, that there are no elections available enabling the taxpayer to use the facts-and-circumstances method typically used for financial accounting purposes. Exhibit 9-1 identifies the depreciation methods and accounting conventions available under the MACRS and ADS systems.

---

[8] § 168(a).

[9] § 168(f).

**EXHIBIT 9.1 Depreciation Methods and Accounting Conventions Under MACRS and ADS**

| 8 MACRS Property Classes | Modified Accelerated Cost Recovery System (MACRS): Use MACRS Property Class Life | Alternative Depreciation System (ADS): Use ADS Life | Accounting Convention[1] |
|---|---|---|---|
| 3-year, 5-year, 7-year, 10-year[2] | Choices: 200% DB, 150% DB, or SL[3] | SL | Half-year or mid-quarter |
| 15-year, 20-year | Choices: 150% DB or SL | Choices: 150% DB or SL | Half-year or mid-quarter |
| Residential rental real estate | 27.5 years SL | 40 years SL | Mid-month |
| Nonresidential real estate | 39 years SL | 40 years SL | Mid-month |

**Notes:**

**(1)** Taxpayers do *not* have the option of choosing either the half-year or mid-quarter convention. As explained later in this chapter, either the half-year or mid-quarter convention is *required* depending on the timing of asset purchases during the year.

**(2)** Under certain conditions, $500,000 (2010 and 2011) immediate expensing under Code § 179 is available for most 3-, 5-, 7-, and 10-year assets (i.e., depreciable tangible personal property).

**(3)** Abbreviations:
DB = declining balance
SL = straight-line

## Classes of Property

As indicated in Exhibit 9-1, all property subject to MACRS is assigned to one of eight classes.[10] Classification is important because the recovery periods, methods, and accounting conventions to be used in calculating depreciation can vary among the different classes of property. Property is assigned to a particular class based on its *class life* as prescribed in Revenue Procedure 87-56.[11] This Revenue Procedure, an excerpt of which is provided in Exhibit 9-2, specifies not only the class lives of various assets but also the recovery periods to be used for both MACRS and ADS. Note that the "General Depreciation System" column of Exhibit 9-2 pertains to MACRS. Exhibit 9-3 provides examples of property in each of the eight MACRS property classes.

In examining Exhibit 9-2, it is important to emphasize that many classes of assets and their descriptions are omitted. Only by examining Revenue Procedure 87-56 can one truly appreciate its scope. Nevertheless, it is impossible to identify the useful life of every asset. For this reason, as can be seen in Exhibit 9-2, Revenue Procedure 87-56 divides assets into two major categories: *Specific Depreciable Assets Being Used in All Business Activities* (such as computers and automobiles) and *Depreciable Assets Used in the Following Activities*. Thus if a particular asset is not assigned a recovery period—a common occurrence, its life is determined by the activity in which it is used.

### Example 4

FunSpot Inc. operates a chain of bowling alleys all over New Jersey. During the year, it purchased furniture, computers, automatic pin-setters, bowling balls and shoes. In determining the recovery period of these assets, the only assets to which a specific life has been assigned are the furniture (Asset Class .11, 7 years) and the computers (Asset Class .12, 5 years). The life of the pin-setters, bowling balls and shoes would be determined based on the activity in which they are used, (Asset Class 80.0, 7 years).

---

[10] § 168(e).

[11] 1987-2 C.B. 674, as modified by Rev. Proc. 88-22, 1988-1 C.B. 785. For class lives, see *How to Depreciate Property*, IRS Publication 916, (Rev. 2006) p. 101.

**EXHIBIT 9.2 Excerpt from Revenue Procedure 87-56**

| Asset Class | Description of Assets Included | Class Life (in Years) | Recovery Periods (in Years) General Depreciation System | Recovery Periods (in Years) Alternative Depreciation System |
|---|---|---|---|---|
| | **SPECIFIC DEPRECIABLE ASSETS USED IN ALL BUSINESS ACTIVITIES, EXCEPT AS NOTED:** | | | |
| 00.11 | **Office Furniture, Fixtures, and Equipment:** Includes furniture and fixtures that are not structural components of a building. Includes such assets as desks, files, safes, and communications equipment. Does not include communications equipment that is included in other classes . . . . . . . . . . . . . . | 10 | 7 | 10 |
| 00.12 | **Information Systems:** Includes computers and their peripheral equipment . . . . . . . . . | 6 | 5 | 5 |
| 00.13 | **Data Handling Equipment, Except Computers:** Includes only typewriters, calculators, adding and accounting machines, copiers, and duplicating equipment . . . . . . . . . . . . | 6 | 5 | 6 |
| 00.21 | **Airplanes (Airframes and Engines), Except Those Used in Commercial or Contract Carrying of Passengers or Freight, and All Helicopters (Airframes and Engines)** . . . . . . . . . . . . . . . | 6 | 5 | 6 |
| 00.22 | **Automobiles, Taxis** . . . . . . . . . . . . . . . . . . . . . . . . . . . . . | 3 | 5 | 5 |
| 00.23 | **Buses** . . . . . . . . . . . . . . . . . . . . . . . . . . . . . . . . . . . . . . | 9 | 5 | 9 |
| 00.241 | **Light General Purpose Trucks:** Includes trucks for use over the road (actual unloaded weight less than 13,000 pounds). . . . . . . . . . . . . . . . . . . . . . . . . . . . . | 4 | 5 | 5 |
| 00.242 | **Heavy General Purpose Trucks:** Includes heavy general purpose trucks, concrete ready mix trucks, and ore trucks, for use over the road (actual unloaded weight 13,000 pounds or more). . . . . . . . . . . . . . . . . . . . . . . . . . | 6 | 5 | 6 |
| | **DEPRECIABLE ASSETS USED IN THE FOLLOWING ACTIVITIES:** | | | |
| 01.1 | **Agriculture:** Includes machinery and equipment, grain bins, and fences but no other land improvements, that are used in the production of crops or plants, vines, and trees; livestock; the operation of farm dairies, nurseries, greenhouses, sod farms, mushroom cellars, cranberry bogs, apiaries, and fur farms; the performance of agriculture, animal husbandry, and horticultural services. . . . . . . . . . . . . . . . | 10 | 7 | 10 |
| 01.11 | **Cotton Ginning Assets**. . . . . . . . . . . . . . . . . . . . . . . . . . | 12 | 7 | 12 |
| 01.21 | **Cattle, Breeding or Dairy** . . . . . . . . . . . . . . . . . . . . . . . . . | 7 | 5 | 7 |
| 01.4 | **Single-Purpose Agricultural or Horticultural Structures** . . . . . | 15 | 10 | 15 |
| 15.0 | **Construction** Includes assets used in construction by general building, special trade, heavy and marine construction contractors, operative and investment builders, real estate subdividers and developers, and others except railroads. . . . . . . . . . . . . . . . . . . . . . . . . . . . | 6 | 5 | 6 |
| 20.1 | **Manufacture of Grain and Grain Mill**. . . . . . . . . . . . . . . . . | 17 | 10 | 17 |
| 27.0 | **Printing, Publishing, and Allied Industries** . . . . . . . . . . . . . | 11 | 7 | 11 |

**EXHIBIT 9.2** **Excerpt from Revenue Procedure 87-56 (continued)**

| Asset Class | Description of Assets Included | Class Life (in Years) | Recovery Periods (in Years) General Depreciation System | Recovery Periods (in Years) Alternative Depreciation System |
|---|---|---|---|---|
| 36.0 | **Manufacture of Electronic Components, Products, and Systems** | 6 | 5 | 6 |
| 37.11 | **Manufacture of Motor Vehicles** | 12 | 7 | 12 |
| 39.0 | **Manufacture of Athletic, Jewelry and Other Goods:** Includes assets used in the production of jewelry; musical instruments; toys and sporting goods; motion picture and television films and tapes; pens, pencils, office and art supplies, brooms, brushes, caskets, etc. | 12 | 7 | 12 |
| 45.0 | **Air Transport** | 12 | 7 | 12 |
| 48.2 | **Radio and Television Broadcastings:** Includes assets used in radio and television broadcasting, except transmitting towers | 6 | 5 | 6 |
| 48.42 | **CATV-Subscriber Connection and Distribution Systems** | 10 | 7 | 10 |
| 79.0 | **Recreation** | 10 | 7 | 10 |
| | Includes assets used in the provision of entertainment services on payment of a fee or admission charge, as in the operation of bowling alleys, billiard and pool establishments, theaters, concert halls, and miniature golf courses. Does not include amusement and theme parks and assets which consist primarily of specialized land improvements or structures, such as golf courses, sports stadia, race tracks, ski slopes, and buildings which house the assets used in entertainment services | 10 | 7 | 10 |
| 80.0 | **Theme and Amusement Parks** | 12.5 | 7 | 12 |

**EXHIBIT 9.3** **Examples of MACRS Property**

| MACRS Property Class | Examples |
|---|---|
| 3 years | Special tools, race horses, tractors, and property with a class life of 4 years or less |
| 5 years | Automobiles, trucks, computers and peripheral equipment (such as printers, external disk drives, and modems), typewriters, copiers, R&E equipment, and property with a class life of more than 4 years and less than 10 years |
| 7 years | Office furniture, fixtures, office equipment, most machinery, property with a class life of 10 years or more but less than 16 years, and property with no assigned class life |
| 10 years | Single-purpose agricultural and horticultural structures, assets used in petroleum refining and manufacturing of tobacco and certain food products, and property with a class life of 16 years or more but less than 20 years |
| 15 years | Land improvements (such as sidewalks, roads, parking lots, irrigation systems, sewers, fences, and landscaping), service stations, billboards, telephone distribution plants, and property with a class life of 20 years or more but less than 25 years |
| 20 years | Municipal sewers and property with a class life of 25 years or more |
| 27.5 years | Residential rental real estate, including apartment buildings, duplexes, etc. |
| 39 years | Nonresidential real estate, including office buildings, warehouses, factories, and farm buildings |

## CALCULATING DEPRECIATION

Under MACRS, depreciation is a function of *three* factors: the recovery period, the method, and the accounting convention.

### Recovery Periods

As seen in Exhibit 9-1, recovery periods run various lengths of time depending on the class of property.[12] In examining the different classes, several features should be observed. First, certain property is assigned to a class without regard to its class life. The most notable example of this is cars, which are assigned to the five-year class (see asset class 00.22 in Exhibit 9-2). Note also that the current structure provides different recovery periods for real property, depending on whether it is residential (27.5 years) or nonresidential (39 years) real estate. As a result, when a building is used for both residential and nonresidential purposes (e.g., a multilevel apartment building with commercial space on the bottom two floors) it must be classified as one or the other. For this purpose, realty qualifies as residential real estate if 80 percent of the gross rents are for the dwelling units.[13]

### Depreciation Method

The depreciation method to be used—like the recovery period—varies depending on the class of the property. A closer look at Exhibit 9-1, however, reveals that the variation is actually between real and personal property. Real property is depreciated using the straight-line method, while personal property is depreciated using either straight-line or a declining balance method. If a declining-balance depreciation method is elected, a switch to straight-line is made in the first year in which a larger depreciation would result. *Example 5* illustrates this procedure, and the IRS depreciation tables presented later in this chapter incorporate the switch to straight-line.

### Accounting Conventions

For assets placed in service or disposed of during the year, an assumption is made regarding the amount of depreciation that is allowed for the year (e.g., a half-year).[14] These assumptions are referred to as depreciation or accounting conventions. The conventions apply only in the years of acquisition and disposition. The applicable convention generally depends on the type of property: realty or personalty. As discussed further below, they are:

| *Type of Property* | *Convention* |
|---|---|
| Real property | Mid-month convention |
| Tangible personal property | Half-year convention |
| Tangible personal property | Mid-quarter convention |

### Half-Year Convention

The half-year convention applies to all property *other than* nonresidential real property and residential rental property. From a practical perspective, the half-year convention applies to *all depreciable tangible personal property.* Under the half-year convention, one-half year of depreciation is allowed regardless of when the asset is placed in service or sold during the year (e.g., ½ × the annual depreciation as normally computed).[15] Since only one-half year's depreciation is allowed in the first year, the recovery period is effectively extended one year so that the remaining one-half may be claimed.

#### Example 5

On March 1, 2011 T purchased a car to be used solely for business for $10,000. It was his only acquisition during the year. The car had an estimated useful life of four years and an estimated salvage value of $2,000. Although these estimates might be used for financial accounting purposes, under MACRS, salvage value is ignored and T is

---

[12] § 168(c).

[13] § 168(e)(2).

[14] § 168(d).

[15] § 168(d)(4).

required to use the recovery period, depreciation method, and accounting convention prescribed for five-year property, the class to which cars are assigned under MACRS. T elects to compute his depreciation using the 200% declining-balance method (switching to straight-line where appropriate), a five-year recovery period, and the half-year convention. The 200% declining-balance rate would be 40% (200% × straight-line rate, 15 or 20%). The declining balance method would be used until 2014, when a switch to straight-line maximizes the depreciation deduction. Due to the half-year convention, the cost is actually recovered over six years rather than the five-year recovery period. Depreciation would be computed as follows:

| *Year* | *Depreciation Method* | *Basis for Depreciation Computation* | *Rate* | *Depreciation* |
|---|---|---|---|---|
| 2011 | 200% D.B. | $10,000 | 20%* | $ 2,000 |
| 2012 | 200% D.B. | 8,000 | 40% | 3,200 |
| 2013 | 200% D.B. | 4,800 | 40% | 1,920 |
| 2014 | 200% D.B. | 2,880 | 40% | 1,152** |
| 2015 | S.L. | 1,730 | 1.0/1.5 | 1,152*** |
| 2016 | S.L. | 1,730 | 0.5/1.5 | 576 |
| | | | | $ 10,000 |

*Half-year allowance (40% × ½ = 20%).

**Note that straight-line depreciation is the same ($2,880 × 2/5).

***Declining-balance depreciation would have been $692 ($1,730 × 40%); since straight-line depreciation over the remaining 1.5 years is $1,152 and greater than $692, the switch to straight-line is made.

## Example 6

Same facts as above except the property was sold on December 20, 2013. In computing depreciation for personal property in the year of sale or disposition, the half-year convention must also be used. Thus, depreciation for 2013 would be $960 ($4,800 × 40% × ½).

To simplify the computation of depreciation, the IRS provides optional tables as shown in Exhibit 9-4 to Exhibit 9-7.[16] The percentages (or rates) shown in the tables are the result of combining the three factors used in determining depreciation—method, rate, and convention—into a single, composite percentage to be used for each class of property.[17]

## Example 7

The depreciation rates shown in Exhibit 9-4 for 5-year property for the year that it is placed in service and for the following year is determined as follows:

*Year 1*

| | |
|---|---|
| Straight-line rate (1/5) | 20% |
| × Declining-balance rate | × 200% |
| 200% declining-balance rate | 40% |
| × Half-year allowance | × ½ |
| Depreciation rate per table | 20% |

[16] Rev. Proc. 87-57, 1987-2 C.B. 687.

[17] Depreciation percentages in the tables are rounded to one-hundredth of a percent for recovery property with a recovery period of less than 20 years, and one-thousandth of a percent for all other property. See Rev. Proc. 87-57 *supra.*

| *Year 2* | |
|---|---|
| Basis of asset remaining (100% – 20%). . . . . . . . . . . . . . . . . . . . . . . . . . | 80% |
| × 200% declining-balance rate . . . . . . . . . . . . . . . . . . . . . . . . . . . . . . . . . | × 40% |
| Depreciation rate per table . . . . . . . . . . . . . . . . . . . . . . . . . . . . . . . . . . . | 32% |

In studying Example 7 above, note how the table percentage for the second year, 32 percent, is derived. This percentage takes into account the requirement of the declining-balance method that the annual rate must be applied to the cost of the asset less previous depreciation [i.e., the second-year percentage of 32 percent is the product of the annual rate of 40 percent and the balance of the asset not yet depreciated, 80% (100% – 20%)]. Similarly, the

**EXHIBIT 9.4** **MACRS Accelerated Depreciation Percentages Using the Half-Year Convention for 3-, 5- and 7-Year Property**

| | *Property Class* | | |
|---|---|---|---|
| *Recovery Year* | *3-Year* | *5-Year* | *7-Year* |
| 1 | 33.33% | 20.00% | 14.29% |
| 2 | 44.45 | 32.00 | 24.49 |
| 3 | 14.81 | 19.20 | 17.49 |
| 4 | 7.41 | 11.52 | 12.49 |
| 5 | | 11.52 | 8.93 |
| 6 | | 5.76 | 8.92 |
| 7 | | | 8.93 |
| 8 | | | 4.46 |

**Source:** Rev. Proc. 87-57, Table 1.
Appendix C has additional depreciation tables.

**EXHIBIT 9.5** **MACRS Depreciation Percentages for Residential Rental Property**

| | *Recovery Year* | | | | | |
|---|---|---|---|---|---|---|
| *Month Placed in Service* | *1* | *2* | *3–26* | *27* | *28* | *29* |
| 1 | 3.485% | 3.636% | 3.636% | 3.636% | 1.970% | 0.000% |
| 2 | 3.182 | 3.636 | 3.636 | 3.636 | 2.273 | 0.000 |
| 3 | 2.879 | 3.636 | 3.636 | 3.636 | 2.576 | 0.000 |
| 4 | 2.576 | 3.636 | 3.636 | 3.636 | 2.879 | 0.000 |
| 5 | 2.273 | 3.636 | 3.636 | 3.636 | 3.182 | 0.000 |
| 6 | 1.970 | 3.636 | 3.636 | 3.636 | 3.485 | 0.000 |
| 7 | 1.667 | 3.636 | 3.636 | 3.637 | 3.636 | 0.152 |
| 8 | 1.364 | 3.636 | 3.636 | 3.637 | 3.636 | 0.455 |
| 9 | 1.061 | 3.636 | 3.636 | 3.637 | 3.636 | 0.758 |
| 10 | 0.758 | 3.636 | 3.636 | 3.637 | 3.636 | 1.061 |
| 11 | 0.455 | 3.636 | 3.636 | 3.637 | 3.636 | 1.364 |
| 12 | 0.152 | 3.636 | 3.636 | 3.637 | 3.636 | 1.667 |

**Source:** IRS Publication No. 534. Appendix C of this book has additional depreciation tables.

**EXHIBIT 9.6** **MACRS Depreciation Percentages for Nonresidential Real Property Placed in Service after May 12, 1993**

| | *Recovery Year* | | |
|---|---|---|---|
| *Month Placed in Service* | *1* | *2–39* | *40* |
| 1 | 2.461% | 2.564% | 0.107% |
| 2 | 2.247 | 2.564 | 0.321 |
| 3 | 2.033 | 2.564 | 0.535 |
| 4 | 1.819 | 2.564 | 0.749 |
| 5 | 1.605 | 2.564 | 0.963 |
| 6 | 1.391 | 2.564 | 1.177 |
| 7 | 1.177 | 2.564 | 1.391 |
| 8 | 0.963 | 2.564 | 1.605 |
| 9 | 0.749 | 2.564 | 1.819 |
| 10 | 0.535 | 2.564 | 2.033 |
| 11 | 0.321 | 2.564 | 2.247 |
| 12 | 0.107 | 2.564 | 2.461 |

**Source:** IRS Publication No. 534.
Appendix C of this book has additional depreciation tables.

**EXHIBIT 9.7** **MACRS Accelerated Depreciation Percentages Using the Mid-Quarter Convention for 3- and 5-Year Property**

**3-Year Property:**

| | *Quarter Placed in Service* | | | |
|---|---|---|---|---|
| *Recovery Year* | *1* | *2* | *3* | *4* |
| 1 | 58.33% | 41.67% | 25.00% | 8.33% |
| 2 | 27.78 | 38.89 | 50.00 | 61.11 |
| 3 | 12.35 | 14.14 | 16.67 | 20.37 |
| 4 | 1.54 | 5.30 | 8.33 | 10.19 |
| **5-Year Property:** | | | | |
| 1 | 35.00 | 25.00 | 15.00 | 5.00 |
| 2 | 26.00 | 30.00 | 34.00 | 38.00 |
| 3 | 15.60 | 18.00 | 20.40 | 22.80 |
| 4 | 11.01 | 11.37 | 12.24 | 13.68 |
| 5 | 11.01 | 11.37 | 11.30 | 10.94 |
| 6 | 1.38 | 4.26 | 7.06 | 9.58 |

**Source:** Rev. Proc. 87-57. Appendix C has additional depreciation tables.

percentages given for declining-balance methods also incorporate a switch to the straight-line method whenever the straight-line rate would yield a higher depreciation amount. Because these various considerations are already reflected in the tables, depreciation is computed by simply applying the appropriate percentage to the *unadjusted basis* of the property. The general formula for computing depreciation can be expressed as follows.

Unadjusted basis of the property × Recovery percentage = Annual depreciation

## Example 8

Same facts as in *Example 5*. Depreciation computed using the table in Exhibit 9-4 would be the same as above, computed as follows:

| Year | Unadjusted Basis | × | Accelerated Recovery Percentage | Annual Depreciation |
|---|---|---|---|---|
| 2011 | $10,000 | | 20.00% | $ 2,000 |
| 2012 | 10,000 | | 32.00 | 3,200 |
| 2013 | 10,000 | | 19.20 | 1,920 |
| 2014 | 10,000 | | 11.52 | 1,152 |
| 2015 | 10,000 | | 11.52 | 1,152 |
| 2016 | 10,000 | | 5.76 | 576 |
| | | | 100.00% | $10,000 |

*Example 8* illustrates the basic steps necessary to compute annual depreciation. These steps are as follows:

1. Identify the *depreciable basis* of the asset (generally its cost): $10,000 in *Example 8*.
2. Determine the MACRS *property class:* five-year property in *Example 8*.
3. Identify the *depreciation convention* (either half-year or mid-quarter for personal property; mid-month for real estate): half-year convention in *Example 8*.
4. Determine the *recovery period* and *method.* See Exhibit 9-1 for a summary of the available choices: five-year 200 percent declining balance in *Example 8*.
5. Locate the *appropriate table* based on the depreciation convention, recovery period, and method: Exhibit 9-4 for the 5-year property (car) in *Example 8*. (Note the depreciation convention is already reflected in the table percentages for the year of acquisition, but *not* for the year of disposition.)
6. Choose the *table percentages* relating to the recovery period of the asset: five-year property percentages for *Example 8* (i.e., 20 percent, 32 percent, etc.).
7. Multiply the table percentages by the depreciable (cost) basis of the asset to *compute annual depreciation* amounts: $10,000 multiplied by 20 percent provides $2,000 of depreciation for 2011 in *Example 8*.

When using the depreciation tables, a special adjustment must be made if there is a disposition of the property before its cost is fully recovered. As noted above, under the half-year convention the taxpayer is entitled only to a half-year of depreciation in the year of disposition. Therefore, where the half-year convention applies and the property is used for only a portion of the disposition year, only one-half of the amount of depreciation determined using the table is allowed.

## Example 9

Same facts as *Example 8* except the taxpayer sold the property on December 1, 2013. Since the taxpayer did not hold the property the entire taxable year and the half-year convention is in effect, only one-half of the amount of depreciation using the table is allowed. Therefore, depreciation for 2013 would have been $960 ($10,000 × 19.2% × ½). Note that this is the same result as obtained in *Example 6* above.

### Mid-Month Convention

This convention applies only to real property (i.e., nonresidential real property and residential rental property).[18] Under the mid-month convention, one-half month of depreciation is allowed for the month the asset is placed in service or sold and a full month of depreciation is allowed for each additional month of the year that the asset is in service.[19] For example, if a calendar year taxpayer places a building in service on April 3, the fraction of the annual depreciation allowed is 8.5/12 (half-month's depreciation for April and eight months' depreciation for May through December).

#### Example 10

The first-year depreciation rate for residential rental realty that is placed in service in April is determined as follows:

| | |
|---|---|
| Straight-line rate (1/27.5) | 3.636% |
| × Mid-month convention | × 8.5/12 |
| Depreciation rate per table | 2.576% |

Due to the mid-month convention, the recovery period must be extended one month to claim the one-half month of depreciation that was not claimed in the first month. For example, the entire cost of residential rental property is recovered over 331 months (27½ years is 330 months + 1 additional month to claim the half-month of depreciation not claimed in the first month). As a result, depreciation deductions are actually claimed over either 28 or 29 years depending on the month in which the property was placed in service. This can be seen by examining the composite depreciation percentages for real property reflecting the mid-month convention given in Exhibit 9-5 and Exhibit 9-6.

#### Example 11

S purchased a duplex as an investment for $110,000 on July 17, 2011. Of the $110,000 cost, $10,000 is allocated to the land. The estimated useful life of the duplex is 30 years—the same period as her mortgage—and the estimated salvage value is $15,000. Despite these estimates, under MACRS salvage value is ignored and S is required to use the recovery period, depreciation method, and convention prescribed for residential rental property, the class to which the duplex is assigned. Therefore, S uses a 27.5-year life, the straight-line method, and the mid-month convention. Using the table in Exhibit 9-5, depreciation for the first year would be $1,667 ($100,000 × 1.667%).

When using the depreciation tables, an adjustment must be made if there is a disposition of the real property before its cost is fully recovered. This adjustment is similar to that required where the half-year convention applies, but not identical. In the year of disposition, the taxpayer may deduct depreciation only for those months the property is used by the taxpayer. In addition, under the mid-month convention, the taxpayer is entitled to only a half-month of depreciation for the month of disposition.

#### Example 12

Same facts as *Example 11* except the taxpayer sold the property on May 22, 2012. Depreciation for 2012 would be $1,363 ($100,000 × 3.636% × 4.5/12).

---

[18] § 168(d)(2).

[19] § 168(d)(4)(B).

### Mid-Quarter Convention

The mid-quarter convention applies only to *personal property*. However, it applies only if more than 40 percent of the aggregate bases of all personal property placed in service during the taxable year is placed in service during the last three months of the year.[20] Property placed in service and disposed of during the same taxable year is not taken into account. Also not taken into account is any amount immediately expensed under § 179 (discussed below) or property used for personal purposes. If the 40 percent test is satisfied, the mid-quarter convention applies to *all* personal property placed in service during the year (regardless of the quarter in which it was actually placed in service).

**Example 13**

During the year, K Company, a calendar year taxpayer, acquired and placed in service the following assets:

| *Assets* | *Acquisition Date* | *Cost* |
|---|---|---|
| Office furniture . . . . . . . . . . . . . . . . . . . . . | March 28 | $20,000 |
| Machinery . . . . . . . . . . . . . . . . . . . . . . . . . | October 9 | 80,000 |
| Warehouse . . . . . . . . . . . . . . . . . . . . . . . . | February 1 | 90,000 |

Of the total *personal* property placed in service during the year, more than 40% [\$80,000 ÷ (\$20,000 + \$80,000)] occurred in the last quarter (i.e., October through December). As a result, K must use the mid-quarter convention for computing the depreciation of both the furniture and the machinery.

When applicable, the mid-quarter convention treats all personal property as being placed in service in the middle of the quarter of the taxable year in which it was actually placed in service.[21] Therefore, one-half of a quarter's depreciation—in effect one-eighth (½ × ¼) or 12.5 percent of the annual depreciation—is allowed for the quarter that the asset is placed in service or sold. In addition, a full quarter's depreciation is allowed for each additional quarter that the asset is in service. For example, personal property placed in service on March 3 would be treated as having been placed in service in the middle of the first quarter and the taxpayer would be able to claim 3½ quarters—3.5/4 or 87.5 percent—of the annual amount of depreciation. The percentages of the annual depreciation allowed under the mid-quarter convention for a year in which an asset is placed in service are

| | *Quarter Placed in Service* | | | |
|---|---|---|---|---|
| | *First January–March* | *Second April–June* | *Third July–September* | *Fourth October–December* |
| Percentage of annual depreciation allowed . . | 87.5% | 62.5% | 37.5% | 12.5% |

The above chart illustrates that where an asset is placed in service in the first quarter and the mid-quarter convention applies, the taxpayer is allowed to deduct 87.5 percent of the annual depreciation. In contrast, for personal property placed in service during the fourth quarter only 12.5 percent of the annual depreciation may be deducted. Note that the recovery period must be extended by one year so that the balance of the depreciation not claimed in the first year may be deducted. Composite depreciation percentages to be used for 3-year and 5-year property where the mid-quarter convention applies are provided in Exhibit 9-7. Appendix C has depreciation tables for all categories of personal property under the mid-quarter convention.

[20] § 168(d)(3).

[21] *Ibid.*

### Example 14

In 2011 T, a calendar year taxpayer, purchased five trucks to use in his business at a cost of $20,000 each. These purchases were his only acquisitions of personal property during the year. Four of the trucks were purchased in December while the other truck was purchased in January. Since more than 40% of the property placed in service during the year was placed in service in the last quarter ($80,000 ÷ $100,000 = 80%), the mid-quarter convention applies in computing depreciation. Thus, the depreciation allowed on the truck purchased in January would be limited to 87.5% of a full year's depreciation, and the depreciation allowed on the three trucks purchased in December would be limited to 12.5% of a full year's depreciation. Since a full year's depreciation would be 40% of cost (straight-line rate of 20% per year × 200% declining-balance = 40%), the depreciation for the January purchase would be limited to 35% of cost (40% × 87.5%), or $7,000 (35% × $20,000). Similarly, the depreciation for the December purchases would be limited to 5% of cost (40% × 12.5%), or $4,000 (5% × $80,000). Total depreciation under the mid-quarter convention is limited to $11,000 ($4,000 + $7,000). These amounts are easily computed using the tables in Exhibit 9-7.

Note that had the mid-quarter convention not applied, the depreciation percentage would have been 20%—reflecting the half-year allowance for 5-year property (40% × ½ = 20%), or $20,000 ($100,000 × 20%). Due to the timing of the acquisitions, T's depreciation for the year is reduced by $9,000 ($20,000 – $11,000).

When using the depreciation tables, a special adjustment must be made if there is a disposition of the property before its cost is fully recovered. This adjustment is similar to that for the half-year and mid-month conventions. As noted above, under the mid-quarter convention, the taxpayer is entitled to only one-half of a quarter's depreciation—in effect one-eighth (½ × ¼) or 12.5 percent of the annual depreciation—for the quarter that the asset is sold. In addition, a full quarter of depreciation is allowed for each quarter that the asset is in service. For example, if property was sold on August 2, the taxpayer could claim 2½ quarters—2.5/4 or 62.5 percent—of the annual amount of depreciation. The percentages of annual depreciation allowed under the mid-quarter convention for the year an asset is sold are

| | *Quarter Property Sold* | | | |
|---|---|---|---|---|
| | *First* January–March | *Second* April–June | *Third* July–September | *Fourth* October–December |
| Percentage of annual depreciation allowed . . | 12.5% | 37.5% | 62.5% | 87.5% |

### Example 15

Same facts as in *Example 14* above, except the truck acquired in January 2011 was sold on August 9, 2013. Since T did not hold the property the entire taxable year and the mid-quarter convention is in effect, only 62.5% of the amount of depreciation using the table is allowed. Therefore, using the table in Exhibit 9-7, T's depreciation for this truck would have been $1,950 ($20,000 × 15.6% × 62.5%).

## Other Methods

The accelerated depreciation methods prescribed by MACRS are normally desirable since they allow taxpayers to recover their costs more rapidly than the straight-line method. However, there may be circumstances where the slower-paced straight-line method may be more advantageous. For example, if the taxpayer is currently in the 10 or 15 percent tax bracket, he or she may want to defer depreciation deductions to years when he or she is in a higher tax bracket. By doing this, the taxpayer may be able to maximize the present value of the tax savings from depreciation deductions (depending upon the taxpayer's discount rate).

Perhaps a more common reason for using straight-line depreciation concerns the alternative minimum tax (AMT). As discussed briefly in Chapter 3 and in detail in Chapter 13, the AMT is an alternative system for computing the tax, using certain modifications. For AMT purposes, depreciation is generally computed using a method slower than MACRS (e.g., 150% rather than 200% declining balance). This difference can lead to an AMT liability. To avoid this, taxpayers often elect to use a straight-line method for regular tax purposes. If a taxpayer elects to use the straight-line method in lieu of the accelerated method, two different approaches are available: straight-line under MACRS, or straight-line under ADS.

## MACRS Straight-Line

Although it may seem inconsistent, the *Modified Accelerated Cost Recovery System* offers taxpayers a straight-line method of depreciation.[22] If the taxpayer so elects, the straight line method is used in conjunction with all of the other rules that normally apply under MACRS; that is, the taxpayer simply uses the straight-line method (in lieu of the accelerated method) along with the applicable recovery period and accounting convention. The depreciation percentages to be used where the taxpayer elects the straight-line method are contained in Exhibit 9-8 (half-year convention property) for 3-, 5-, and 7-year property. Appendix C has straight-line depreciation tables for all categories of personal property under the half-year convention. The depreciation percentages for the straight-line method when the mid-quarter convention applies can be found in Revenue Procedure 87-57.[23]

### Example 16

On June 1, 2011 L purchased 5-year property (to which the half-year convention applies) for $50,000. Using the table in Exhibit 9-8, depreciation for the year would be $5,000 ($50,000 × 10%). Depreciation for 2012 would be $10,000 (20% × $50,000). If L sold the property on January 22, 2013, depreciation would be $5,000 ($50,000 × 20% × ½).

**EXHIBIT 9.8** **MACRS and ADS Straight-Line Depreciation Percentages Using the Half-Year Convention for 3-, 5-, and 7-Year Property**

| Recovery Year | Property Class: 3-Year | 5-Year | 7-Year |
|---|---|---|---|
| 1 | 16.67% | 10.00% | 7.14% |
| 2 | 33.33 | 20.00 | 14.29 |
| 3 | 33.33 | 20.00 | 14.29 |
| 4 | 16.67 | 20.00 | 14.28 |
| 5 | | 20.00 | 14.29 |
| 6 | | 10.00 | 14.28 |
| 7 | | | 14.29 |
| 8 | | | 7.14 |

**Source:** Rev. Proc. 87-57
Appendix C has additional depreciation tables.

[22] § 168(b)(3)(C).

[23] 1987-2 C.B. 687.

The election to use the straight-line method is made annually by class (recall the straight-line method must be used for realty). For example, if in 2011 the taxpayer makes the election for 7-year property, *all* 7-year property placed in service during the year must be depreciated using the straight-line method. The election does not obligate the taxpayer to use the straight-line method for any other class. Similarly, the taxpayer need not use the straight-line method for such class of assets placed in service in the following year.

## Alternative Depreciation System

The Alternative Depreciation System (ADS) is an option for taxpayers.[24] This system is similar to MACRS in two ways: salvage value is ignored, and the same averaging conventions must be followed. The major differences between MACRS and ADS are the longer recovery periods provided by ADS for most assets and in some cases, slower rates of depreciation. The recovery period to be used for ADS is normally the property's class life. The class life—which is usually longer than the MACRS life—is used unless no class life has been prescribed for the property or a specific class life has been designated in Code § 168. For example, as shown in Exhibit 9-2, the ADS class life for copiers (asset class 00.13) is six years, whereas the MACRS life is five years. Thus, depreciation under ADS would be computed using a six-year life, whereas depreciation for MACRS would be computed using a five-year life. The recovery periods to be used for ADS are summarized in Exhibit 9-9.

Taxpayers electing ADS for real property are restricted to straight-line depreciation. Thus, an office building (nonresidential real property) would be depreciated using straight-line and a 40-year recovery period under ADS. The ADS depreciation percentages for real property are found in Exhibit 9-10.

In contrast, either straight-line or 150 percent declining balance depreciation may be chosen for depreciable tangible personal property. The ADS straight-line depreciation percentages for such property, which in fact have class lives of three, five and seven years, are the same as those for MACRS straight-line and can be found in Exhibit 9-8.

Taxpayers have as many as four options for depreciating personal property—straight line or accelerated depreciation over the MACRS recovery period, or straight line over a longer ADS recovery period. Accelerated depreciation options are 200 percent or 150 percent declining balance. For example, the ADS option for a copier consists of straight-line over six years. The MACRS alternatives allow for a five-year write-off using either 200 percent or 150 percent declining balance or straight line. Which of these four choices would be best for depreciating the

**EXHIBIT 9.9 Alternative Depreciation System Recovery Periods**

**General Rule:** Recovery period is the property's class life unless

1. There is no class life (see below), or
2. A special class life has been designated (see below).

| *Type of Property* | *Recovery Period* |
|---|---|
| Personal property with no class life | 12 years |
| Nonresidential real property with no class life | 40 years |
| Residential rental property with no class life | 40 years |
| Cars, light general-purpose trucks, certain technological equipment, and semiconductor manufacturing equipment | 5 years |
| Computer-based telephone central office switching equipment | 9.5 years |
| Railroad track | 10 years |
| Single-purpose agricultural or horticultural structures | 15 years |
| Municipal wastewater treatment plants, telephone distribution plants | 24 years |
| Low-income housing financed by tax-exempt bonds | 27.5 years |
| Municipal sewers | 50 years |

[24] § 168(g).

**EXHIBIT 9.10** ADS Straight-Line Depreciation Percentages for Real Property Using the Mid-Month Convention

| Month Placed in Service | Recovery Year 1 | 2–40 | 41 |
|---|---|---|---|
| 1 | 2.396% | 2.500% | 0.104% |
| 2 | 2.188 | 2.500 | 0.312 |
| 3 | 1.979 | 2.500 | 0.521 |
| 4 | 1.771 | 2.500 | 0.729 |
| 5 | 1.563 | 2.500 | 0.937 |
| 6 | 1.354 | 2.500 | 1.146 |
| 7 | 1.146 | 2.500 | 1.354 |
| 8 | 0.938 | 2.500 | 1.562 |
| 9 | 0.729 | 2.500 | 1.771 |
| 10 | 0.521 | 2.500 | 1.979 |
| 11 | 0.313 | 2.500 | 2.187 |
| 12 | 0.104 | 2.500 | 2.396 |

**Source:** Rev. Proc. 87-57, Table 13.

copier? In general, the taxpayer should select the depreciation method that maximizes the present value of tax savings from depreciation deductions. For taxpayers who expect their future marginal tax rate to either remain constant or decline, the fastest depreciation method over the shortest time period will maximize the present value of tax savings from depreciation.

The mechanics of the election to use ADS—except for real property—are identical to those of MACRS discussed above. Except for real property, the taxpayer may elect to use ADS on a class-by-class, year-by-year basis.[25] For realty, the election is made on a property-by-property basis. In addition, the taxpayer *must* use ADS straight-line for depreciating the following:[26]

- Certain "listed property" that is not used predominately for business (see discussion below)
- Foreign use property (i.e., property used outside the U.S. more than half of a taxable year)
- Property leased to a tax-exempt entity
- Property leased to foreign persons (unless more than 50 percent of the income is subject to U.S. tax)
- Property financed by the issuance of tax-exempt bonds (i.e., tax-exempt bond-financed property).

ADS is also used for computing depreciation for purposes of the alternative minimum tax (discussed in Chapter 13) and a corporation's earnings and profits (discussed in Chapter 20).

## Changes in Depreciation

There are many situations where the taxpayer incorrectly computes depreciation, resulting in too much or too little depreciation. For example, a corporation may discover it mistakenly classified an asset initially and the wrong recovery period was used. Similarly, the IRS may change the recovery period of an asset. In 2003, the Service ruled that the life of canopies at gas stations that protect the pumps and customers from inclement weather are 5-year rather

[25] § 168(g)(7).

[26] § 168(g)(1).

than 15-year property.[27] When the taxpayer is entitled to additional depreciation, the IRS permits a change in accounting method and the taxpayer may deduct all of the unclaimed depreciation for years that are closed by the statute of limitations as well as open years. This is normally done through a § 481(a) adjustment that reduces income in the year of the change (a single year adjustment).[28] If the adjustment increases the taxpayer's income, the increase is normally spread over four years.

## ✓ CHECK YOUR KNOWLEDGE

### Review Question 1

Indicate whether the following statements concerning tax depreciation are true or false.

**a.** During the year, Mr. L purchased a computer that he uses to track how his stocks and bonds are doing. L can depreciate the computer even though it is not used in a trade or business.

*True.* An asset generally may be depreciated to the extent that it is used in a trade or business or an income-producing activity. Since the computer is used to monitor investments, an income-producing activity, it is depreciable. Thus if L uses the computer 30 percent of the time to monitor his stocks and bonds and 70 percent for playing solitaire (i.e., personal use), 30 percent of the cost of the computer could be depreciated.

**b.** Land and goodwill are never depreciable or amortizable since neither has a determinable life.

*False.* Assets without a determinable life normally cannot be depreciated or amortized. Under normal circumstances, neither of these assets would be considered as having a determinable life and, therefore, neither could be depreciated. However, § 197 of the Code creates a specific exception to this rule for goodwill, allowing taxpayers to amortize goodwill over 15 years. Land normally is not depreciable.

**c.** This year Z Corporation purchased a new car to be used in its business. For financial accounting purposes, the company computed depreciation assuming the car had an estimated useful life of three years and an approximate salvage value of $1,000. In computing depreciation for tax purposes, the company will also use a three-year life and a salvage value of $1,000.

*False.* The computation of tax depreciation ignores the asset's actual useful life and salvage value. For tax purposes, a car is deemed to have a five-year life and salvage value is always ignored. Note that because different depreciation methods are used annual depreciation for financial accounting will normally differ from tax depreciation.

### Review Question 2

In November of this year, Park and Ride Inc., a calendar year taxpayer, purchased five new vans to use in its limousine service for $100,000. In February, the company closed on the acquisition of a new maintenance facility. Indicate whether the following are true or false.

**a.** Assuming the cost of the maintenance facility was $50,000, the corporation must use the mid-quarter convention to depreciate the facility.

*False.* The mid-quarter convention applies only to personal property and not realty. The mid-month convention must be used in computing depreciation for realty. The mid-quarter convention must be used for the vans.

**b.** Assuming the cost of the maintenance facility was $500,000, the corporation must use the *half-year* convention in depreciating the vans.

*False.* The mid-quarter convention applies if more than 40 percent of the *personal property* placed in service during the year is placed in service during the last three

---

[27] Rev. Rul. 2003-54, 2003-23 I.R.B. 982.

[28] Rev. Proc. 96-31, 1996-1 C.B. 714. But see *Brookshire Brothers Holding, Inc.*, 320 F.3d 507 (CA-5, 2003) where the court held that it was not a change in accounting method and the government was barred from reducing depreciation in closed years. See also *Green Forest Manufacturing Inc.*, T.C. Memo 2003-75.

months. For purposes of making this calculation, only personal property—the vans—is considered and the realty (i.e., the maintenance facility) is ignored. Moreover, any personal property that is expensed under § 179 (discussed below) is also ignored. In this case, all of the personal property was placed in service during the last quarter of the year and, therefore, the corporation must use the mid-quarter convention.

### Review Question 3

During the year, C Corporation purchased equipment that qualifies as five-year property. Due to other purchases of personal property during the year, the mid-quarter convention must be used in computing depreciation. Compute the first-and second-year depreciation rates that should be used assuming the asset was placed in service in February. Check your answers by using the table in Exhibit 9-7.

The depreciation rates are 35 percent for the first year and 26 percent for the second year, which are computed as follows:

*Year 1:*

| | |
|---|---|
| Straight-line rate (1/5) | 20% |
| × Declining-balance rate | × 200% |
| 200 percent declining-balance annual rate | 40% |
| Mid-quarter percentage | × 87.5% |
| | 35% |

*Year 2:*

| | |
|---|---|
| Basis of asset remaining (100% − 35%) | 65% |
| × 200 percent declining-balance annual rate | × 40% |
| Depreciation rate per table | 26% |

### Review Question 4

On February 15 of this year, K Corporation purchased a warehouse for $250,000 ($50,000 allocable to the land). For financial accounting purposes, the building is treated as having a 40-year life and a salvage value of $20,000.

**a.** Compute the depreciation deduction for the year.

Depreciation for the year is $4,494 as computed below. Note that the useful life and the salvage value that are used for financial accounting purposes are irrelevant for tax purposes.

| | |
|---|---|
| Unadjusted basis of the building | $200,000 |
| × Recovery percentage for month placed in service (February) | × 2.247% |
| Depreciation | $ 4,494 |

**b.** Assuming the corporation sold the building on March 10 of the following year, compute the depreciation deduction for the year.

| | |
|---|---|
| Unadjusted basis of the building | $ 200,000 |
| × Recovery percentage for second year | × 2.564% |
| × Mid-month convention in year of disposition | × 2.5/12 |
| Depreciation | $ 1,068 |

## Limited Expensing Election: Code § 179

**LO.4** Describe the special election under Section 179, allowing immediate expensing of certain property.

When Congress introduced ACRS in 1981, it also created § 179. This provision allows taxpayers (other than estates or trusts) to *elect* to treat the cost of qualifying property as a currently deductible expense rather than a capital expenditure subject to depreciation. Initially, the maximum amount that could be expensed under § 179 was $5,000. Over the years, Congress has gradually increased that amount and in 2010 and 2011 it is $500,000 (adjusted annually for inflation). This measure was intended primarily to stimulate investment; however, its corollary effect was to eliminate the need for maintaining depreciation records where the taxpayer's annual acquisitions were not substantial.

Although the maximum amount that can be expensed by a taxpayer is $250,000 for 2010 and 2011, two limitations may restrict the amount that the taxpayer may otherwise expense:

1. *Acquisitions of Eligible Property Exceeding $2,000,000* (2010 and 2011). When the aggregate cost of *qualifying* property placed in service during the year exceeds $2,000,000 (in 2010 and 2011), the $500,000 amount must be reduced $1 for each $1 of cost in excess of $2,000,000. For example, taxpayers purchasing $2,010,000 of property could expense up to $490,000 [$500,000 – ($2,010,000 – $2,000,000 = $10,000)] of the cost while taxpayers purchasing in excess of $2,500,000 ($2,000,000 + $500,000) could not benefit from § 179 at all.
2. *Taxable Income Limitation.* The § 179 deduction cannot exceed the amount of taxable income derived from all of the taxpayer's trades or businesses (including wage income).[29] Any amount that cannot be deducted due to this limitation can be carried over indefinitely to following years to be used against future taxable income. Note, however, that the $500,000 maximum amount that can be expensed in subsequent years is not increased by the carryover amount. Also observe that the taxpayer has another option regarding the amount not deducted due to the limitation. Instead of carrying over the amount the taxpayer has the option of not reducing the property's basis by the carryover amount so it can be depreciated along with the rest of the property's cost.

As explained later in this chapter, additional limitations on the use of § 179 apply in the case of luxury automobiles, sports utility vehicles (SUVs) and "listed" property.

In applying § 179, the taxpayer may elect to expense all or a portion of an asset so long as the total amount expensed does not exceed the dollar limitation. If only a portion of an asset is expensed, the remaining portion is subject to depreciation.

### Example 17

T Corporation purchased 5-year property for $100,000 and 7-year property for $550,000 during the current year. Both assets are eligible to be expensed subject to the limitations of § 179. Assume T expects its future marginal tax rate to remain constant. To maximize the present value of the tax savings from limited expensing and depreciation deductions, T should expense $500,000 of the 7-year property rather than the 5-year property since the cost of the 5-year property could be recovered more quickly, thus resulting in higher depreciation deductions in the current year. Assuming T elects to expense $500,000 of the 7-year property, its deduction for such property would be $507,145 computed as follows:

| | | |
|---|---|---|
| Original cost | $ 550,000 | |
| – Expensed portion | – 500,000 | $ 500,000 |
| Remaining depreciable basis | $ 50,000 | |
| × Depreciation percentage | × 14.29% | |
| Depreciation deduction | $ 7,145 | 7,145 |
| Total deduction | | $ 507,145 |

In addition to the deductions for the 7-year property, the taxpayer could claim a deduction for *depreciation* of the 5-year property.

## Eligible Property

Only property that satisfies certain requirements is eligible for expensing. To qualify, the property may be new or used and must be:[30]

1. Recovery property;
2. Property that would have qualified for the investment credit (e.g., most property other than buildings and their components);

[29] Taxable income is computed with § 1231 gains and interest from working capital but not deductions allowable for § 179, one half of self-employment tax, net operating loss carrybacks or carryforwards and deductions suspended under other Code sections (e.g., passive losses, partnership or S corporation losses limited for lack of basis). Note that taxable income presumably reflects depreciation for the § 179 property without considering § 179. [See § 179(b)(3)(C) and Reg. § 1.179-2(c)(1) and -(2)(c)(5)].

[30] §§ 179(d)(1) and (2).

3. Property used in a trade or business, as distinguished from property held for the production of income; and
4. Property acquired by purchase from someone who is generally not a "related party" under § 267 (e.g., gifted or inherited property usually does not qualify nor would property acquired from a spouse or parent).

Certain property is designated as *ineligible* for expensing. Such property includes:

1. Property used predominantly to furnish lodging or in connection with furnishing lodging unless the business is a hotel or motel that provides accommodations used primarily by transients. Presumably, this rule prohibits taxpayers who provide long-term rentals (e.g., apartments, duplexes, etc.) from expensing such items as furniture and appliances.
2. Air conditioning and heating units;
3. Property that is primarily used by a tax-exempt organization; and
4. Property used outside the U.S. (But there are a number of exceptions).

### Recapture

Without any special rule, taxpayers could use an asset in business for a short period (e.g., one day), expense it for tax purposes, then convert it to nonbusiness use. To prohibit this possible abuse, a special rule applies. If the property is converted to *nonbusiness* use *at any time*, the taxpayer must *recapture* the benefit derived from expensing.[31] For this purpose, a sale does not trigger recapture. Recapture requires the taxpayer to *include* in income the difference between the amount expensed and the MACRS deductions that would have been allowed for the actual period of business use.

#### Example 18

On January 1, 2010 F purchased a computer for $5,000. He used it for business for one year, then gave it to his teenage son as a graduation present and bought himself another computer. F may expense the entire $5,000 cost of the computer. However, in 2012 he must recapture and include in income the difference between the expensed amount and the deduction computed under MACRS, $4,000 [$5,000 expensed − MACRS deduction of $1,000 ($5,000 × 20%)]. Note that the net effect in this case is to allow F a deduction equal to what he otherwise could have claimed under MACRS, $1,000.

## Additional First-Year (Bonus) Depreciation

The sagging economy recently prompted Congress to turn to a tool that it often has used for stimulation: additional first-year or so-called bonus depreciation. The amount of the deduction depends on when the property is placed in service. For property placed in service between January 1, 2008 and September 8, 2010, the bonus depreciation is equal to 50% of the adjusted basis of new qualified property.[32] For property placed in service after September 8, 2010 through December 31, 2011, the deduction is generally 100 percent of the cost of the property. For 2012, the deduction drops to 50 percent. Thus, if a business purchases qualified property for $10,000 or $100,000 or $10,000,000 during the magic period, it will be able to write-off the entire cost of the property. Bonus depreciation is in addition to any amount expensed under § 179 and regular depreciation.[33] Of course, § 179 and regular depreciation would only apply in those situations where the 100 percent write-off rule does not apply (e.g., before September 8, 2010 and after December 31, 2011 or used property).

[31] § 179(d)(10).

[32] § 168(k)

[33] Bonus depreciation can be used for purposes of the alternative minimum tax but not in computing the earnings and profits of a corporation.

## Qualified Property

Section 168(k)(2) provides that qualified property is generally all newly acquired depreciable propertyother than buildings. Only new property qualifies. Used property does not qualify. In other words, to qualify, the propertys first or original use must commence with the taxpayer after December 31, 2007 and before January 1, 2011. For this purpose, capital expenditures incurred to recondition or rebuild property meet this requirement. In contrast, the cost of reconditioned or rebuilt property acquired by the taxpayer is considered used property and does not qualify. Technically, qualified property includes:

- Property eligible for MACRS depreciation with a recovery period of 20 years or less (business and investment property);
- Certain water utility property (as defined in Code § 168(e)(5));
- Computer software (except software acquired in connection with the acquisition of a business unless such software is available to the general public and is not substantially modified); and
- Qualified leasehold improvement property (as extended for 2011 only). A qualified leasehold improvement is an interior improvement made under a lease of commercial property (such as an office building or warehouse), and placed in service more than three years after the building was first placed in service. Certain structural improvements do not qualify, and neither do expansions.

In light of these rules, certain property is not eligible. Bonus depreciation cannot be used for residential and nonresidential real estate since the lives of these properties (27.5 and 39 years respectively) exceed 20 years. Intangibles are not subject to MACRS and, thus, do not qualify for the additional allowance. Section 197 intangibles such as goodwill, covenants not to compete, and customer lists acquired in connection with the purchase of a business also would not be eligible. In addition, property that must be depreciated using the alternative depreciation system (ADS) does not qualify. As discussed below, under the special depreciation limitations of § 280F for so-called listed property (e.g., automobiles), ADS is required if qualified business used does not exceed 50 percent. Similarly, ADS must be used for tangible property (e.g., a machine) used predominantly outside of the U.S. However, if the taxpayer merely elects to use ADS for certain property, bonus depreciation can still be claimed

## Computation of Bonus Depreciation

There is no limitation on the amount of bonus depreciation that may be claimed. Taxpayers may claim bonus depreciation for all *qualified* property. In addition, taxpayers may claim both bonus depreciation and § 179 expensing. When both amounts are claimed for the same property, the bonus depreciation is equal to 50 percent of the adjusted basis of the property *after the reduction for the amount expensed under § 179.* The effect is to reduce the amount of bonus depreciation that may be claimed since the basis is smaller. Regular depreciation is computed after the basis of the property is reduced by both the § 179 amount and the 50 percent additional allowance.

### Example 19

In March 2009, X Corporation purchased two heavy-duty machines. Each machine cost $300,000. The corporation elected to expense $250,000 of the cost of one machine and take advantage of the additional 50 percent allowance for both machines. The machinery is 5-year property. Regular depreciation, § 179 expense and bonus depreciation for the first year would be computed as shown below.

| | Machine #1 | | Machine #2 | |
|---|---|---|---|---|
| Adjusted basis | $300,000 | | $300,000 | |
| § 179 expensed portion | (250,000) | $250,000 | — | |
| Remaining depreciable basis | $50,000 | | $300,000 | |
| Additional allowance | x 50% | | x 50% | |
| Bonus depreciation | $25,000 | 25,000 | $150,000 | $150,000 |
| Remaining depreciable basis | $25,000 | | $150,000 | |
| Regular depreciation | x 20% | | x 20% | |
| Regular depreciation | $5,000 | 5,000 | $ 30,000 | 30,000 |
| Total deduction | | $280,000 | | $180,000 |

A comparison of the *bonus depreciation* for both machines reveals different amounts deducted even though the costs of the machines were the same. This occurs because of the special ordering rule. The rule requires that the property's basis for computing bonus depreciation must first be reduced by any amount expensed under § 179. Had the machines been new property purchased in 2011, the entire $600,000 cost could be deducted immediately.

The full amount of bonus depreciation may be claimed regardless of whether the mid-quarter convention applies. Note also that a taxpayer may elect *not* to claim the additional 50 percent allowance. This may be done simply by computing depreciation in the normal fashion.

### Bonus Depreciation and § 179 Compared

Bonus depreciation and § 179 expensing allowance are subject to special limitations that are similar but not identical. Bonus depreciation

- is not limited to the taxable income from the business;
- does not phase-out based on the amount of property placed in service during the year;
- is allowed for investment property and § 179 applies only to business property;
- can be claimed on purchases from related parties while § 179 cannot;
- can be used by estates and trusts which are not allowed to elect § 179;
- cannot be used for used property while § 179 can.

## Limitations for Automobiles

**LO.5**
Identify the restrictions on depreciation of listed property, including automobiles, trucks, computers and other items.

Over the years, Congress has become more and more concerned about taxpayers who effectively use the benefits of the tax law to reduce the cost of what are essentially personal expenses. For example, a taxpayer may justify the purchase of a luxury rather than standard automobile on the grounds that the government is helping to defray the additional cost through tax deductions and credits allowed for the purchase. In 1984 Congress enacted Code § 280F to reduce the benefits of depreciation and limited expensing for certain automobiles and other properties that are often used partially for personal purposes. In addition, the record keeping requirements for travel and entertainment were tightened and extended to certain property used for personal purposes.

Section 280F sets forth a special set of limitations for *passenger automobiles.* A passenger automobile is defined as any four-wheeled vehicle manufactured primarily for use on public streets, roads, and highways that weighs 6,000 pounds or less unloaded. For purposes of § 280F, the term *passenger automobiles* does not include vehicles for hire, such as taxis, rental trucks, and rental cars.[34] Ambulances and hearses directly used in a trade or business are also unaffected by the § 280F limitations. Temporary regulations create certain exceptions to the definition of passenger automobile. Excluded is any "qualified nonpersonal use vehicle" defined as any vehicle which, by reason of its nature (i.e., design or modification), is not likely to be used more than a *de minimis* amount for personal purposes.[35] This category would

[34] § 280F(d)(5).

[35] Regs. § 1.274-5T(k)(2)).

include police and fire vehicles, ambulances, qualified moving vans, and delivery and utility repair trucks.

For passenger automobiles, trucks and vans, § 280F generally imposes a ceiling on the amount of annual depreciation and first-year expensing deductions. The *maximum* depreciation and/or § 179 expense is shown in Exhibit 9-11 for automobiles and Exhibit 9-12 for trucks and vans. The limits for a particular auto are determined by the year the auto is placed in service by the taxpayer. The annual limits for autos placed in service in 2011 are found in the 2011 column in Exhibit 9-11.[36] For example, in 2011 the deduction for depreciation and § 179 expensing cannot exceed $3,060 for the year placed in service and $4,900 for the second year of service. However, if the taxpayer used bonus depreciation in 2008–2011, the first year deduction amounts for passenger vehicles as well trucks and vans are increased by $8,000. However, the later year amounts remain the same.

**EXHIBIT 9.11** **Section 280F Depreciation Limits for Autos**

| | *Limits for Autos Based on Year Placed in Service* |
|---|---|
| | *2011* |
| First year of service | $3,060* |
| Second year of service | 4,900 |
| Third year of service | 2,950 |
| Thereafter | 1,775 |

*Increase by $8,000 to $11,060 if bonus depreciation claimed.

The 2011 limitations under § 280F restrict the annual depreciation amounts for autos costing $15,300 or more (assuming 200 percent declining-balance depreciation was claimed). The $15,300 amount reflects the $3,060 first-year depreciation limitation ($15,300 × 20% regular depreciation rate for five-year property).

Where the car is used less than 100 percent of the time for business—including the portion of time the car is used for production of income purposes—the maximum amounts given above must be reduced proportionately.

## Example 20

T purchased a car for $20,000 in 2011. She used it 60% of the time for business purposes and 20% of the time traveling to her rental properties. Depreciation and limited expensing may not exceed $2,448 (80% × $3,060) for the first year, $3,920 (80% × $4,900) for the second year, and so on. If bonus depreciation is claimed, depreciation and limited expensing would be limited to $8,848 [80% × ($3,060 + $8,000 = $11,060)] for the first year and remains the same $3,920 (80% × $4,900) for the second year.

If the property's basis has not been fully deducted by the close of the normal recovery period (i.e., normally the extended recovery period of six years), a deduction for the *unrecovered basis* is allowed in subsequent years. Deductions for the property's unrecovered basis are limited to $1,775 (2011) annually until the entire basis is recovered.

[36] Rev. Proc. 2010-18, 2010-9 IRB 427.

## Example 21

On December 1, 2011 R purchased a new automobile for $18,000 which he uses solely for business. R's regular depreciation for the first year initially is $3,600 but is limited to $3,060 as shown below:

| | | |
|---|---|---|
| Original cost | $18,000 | |
| Depreciation percentage | x 20% | |
| Depreciation before limitation | | $3,600 |
| Limitation | | $3,060 |

The calculation of regular depreciation for the first year and subsequent years is summarized below.

In examining the schedule below, note that the recovery period is extended from six to eight years due to the limitations. Also, understand that the unadjusted depreciable basis used for computing depreciation is $18,000 for each year even though only $3,060 of the depreciation was deducted in the first year.

| | 1<br>**2011** | 2<br>**2012** | 3<br>**2013** | 4<br>**2014** | 5<br>**2015** | 6<br>**2016** | 7<br>**2017** | 8<br>**2018** |
|---|---|---|---|---|---|---|---|---|
| Unadjusted basis | $18,000 | $18,000 | $18,000 | $18,000 | $18,000 | $18,000 | $18,000 | $18,000 |
| Depreciation Percentage | 20.00% | 32.00% | 19.20% | 11.52% | 11.52% | 5.76% | | |
| MACRS depreciation | $ 3,600 | $ 5,760 | $ 3,456 | $ 2,074 | $ 2,074 | $ 1,037 | $ 1,775 | $ 1,775 |
| Limit | $ 3,060 | $ 4,900 | $ 2,950 | $ 1,775 | $ 1,775 | $ 1,775 | $ 1,775 | $ 1,775 |
| Deduction | $ 3,060 | $ 4,900 | $ 2,950 | $ 1,775 | $ 1,775 | $ 1,037 | $ 1,775 | $ 728 |
| Cumulative depreciation | $ 3,060 | $ 7,960 | $10,910 | $12,685 | $14,460 | $15,497 | $17,272 | $18,000 |
| Adjusted basis | $14,940 | $10,040 | $ 7,090 | $ 5,315 | $ 3,540 | $ 2,503 | $ 728 | 0 |

### Trucks, Vans, and SUVs

Responding to criticisms that the limitations for passenger automobiles did not fairly reflect the higher price that must be paid for trucks and vans, the IRS created a separate set of limitations for these vehicles as shown in Exhibit 9-12.

For this purpose, a vehicle qualifies as a truck or van if it is built on a truck chassis. Since most Sport Utility Vehicles (SUVs) are built on a truck chassis these higher limits would apply, assuming these vehicles do not have a gross vehicle weight exceeding 6,000 pounds. If the weight exceeds 6,000 pounds, special rules apply as discussed below.

**EXHIBIT 9.12 Section 280F Depreciation Limits for Trucks and Vans**

| *Year* | *2011* |
|---|---|
| 1 | $3,260* |
| 2 | 5,200 |
| 3 | 3,250 |
| Thereafter | 1,875 |

*Increase by $8,000 to $11,260 if bonus depreciation claimed.

### Leasing

Without any special rule, the taxpayer could lease a car and circumvent the limitations on depreciation since the restrictions would appear to apply only to the deduction for depreciation and not lease payments. For instance, in *Example 21* above, the taxpayer might lease the car for $400 per month and claim a deduction of $4,800 for the year—far in excess of the amount allowed for depreciation after the first year. To prohibit this possibility, lessees may deduct the amount of the lease payment (applicable to business or income-producing use)—but must *include* certain amounts in income to bring their deductions for use of the car in line for owners. In practice, these inclusion amounts are not actually added to income but simply reduce the deduction for the lease payment.

The amount that the taxpayer must include in income is generally based on the automobile's fair market value and is determined in the following manner.[37]

1. Using the value of the automobile for the taxable year in which the auto is first used under the lease, identify the annual inclusion amount from the table found in Exhibit 9-14. Note that for the last year of the lease, the dollar amount for the preceding year is used unless the lease term begins and ends in the same year.
2. Prorate the dollar amount for the number of days of the lease term included in the taxable year.
3. Multiply the prorated dollar amount by the business and investment use for the taxable year.

**EXHIBIT 9.14** **Dollar Amounts for Passenger Automobiles (that are not Trucks or Vans) with a Lease Term Beginning in Calendar Year 2011**

| *Fair Market Value of Passenger Automobile* | | *Tax Year During Lease* | | | | |
|---|---|---|---|---|---|---|
| *Over* | *Not Over* | *1st* | *2nd* | *3rd* | *4th* | *5th & Later* |
| $ 18,500 | $ 19,000 | 3 | 8 | 11 | 13 | 16 |
| 19,000 | 19,500 | 4 | 9 | 13 | 15 | 18 |
| 19,500 | 20,000 | 4 | 10 | 15 | 17 | 20 |
| 20,000 | 20,500 | 5 | 11 | 16 | 19 | 23 |
| 20,500 | 21,000 | 5 | 12 | 18 | 21 | 25 |
| 21,000 | 21,500 | 6 | 13 | 19 | 24 | 26 |
| 21,500 | 22,000 | 6 | 14 | 21 | 26 | 29 |
| 22,000 | 23,000 | 7 | 16 | 23 | 29 | 32 |
| 23,000 | 24,000 | 8 | 18 | 27 | 32 | 37 |
| 24,000 | 25,000 | 9 | 20 | 30 | 36 | 42 |
| 25,000 | 26,000 | 10 | 23 | 33 | 40 | 46 |
| 26,000 | 27,000 | 11 | 25 | 36 | 44 | 51 |
| 27,000 | 28,000 | 12 | 27 | 40 | 48 | 55 |
| 28,000 | 29,000 | 13 | 29 | 43 | 52 | 60 |
| 29,000 | 30,000 | 14 | 31 | 47 | 55 | 65 |
| 30,000 | 31,000 | 15 | 34 | 49 | 60 | 69 |
| 31,000 | 32,000 | 16 | 36 | 53 | 63 | 73 |
| 32,000 | 33,000 | 17 | 38 | 56 | 68 | 77 |
| . | | | | | | |
| . | | | | | | |
| . | | | | | | |
| 240,000 | And up | 230 | 506 | 752 | 902 | 1,040 |

**Source:** Rev Proc 2011-21, 2011-12 IRB. This table extends to values of $240,000 and up.

[37] § 280F(c) and Reg. § 1.280F-7(a). Note that these limitations do not apply to cars leased for 30 or fewer days or to lessors who regularly engage in the auto-leasing business.

Taxpayers who lease trucks and vans do not use the tables above for passenger auto-mobiles but must use separate tables designed specifically for these two categories.

## Example 22

On April 1, 2011, M, a calendar year taxpayer, signed a three-year lease on a new passenger automobile with a value of $26,800. For 2011 and 2012, M used the car exclusively in his business. During 2013 and 2014, his business use dropped to 40%. The amounts that M must include in income for 2011 through 2014 are computed as follows:

| Tax Year | Dollars Amount | Proration | Business Use% | Inclusion Amount |
|---|---|---|---|---|
| 2011 | $11 | 275/365 | 100% | $8 |
| 2012 | 25 | 366/366 | 100% | 25 |
| 2013 | 36 | 365/365 | 40% | 14 |
| 2014 | 36 | 90/365 | 40% | 4 |

Observe that dollar amounts are based on the value of the car in the first year of the lease. Subsequent declines in the car's value are ignored. Also note that in computing the inclusion amount for 2014, the $71 amount for the preceding year (2013) is used instead of $52 per the table because the lease did not begin and end in the same year.

### Deducting SUVs

As noted above, a truck or van—including an SUV or minivan—is *not* treated as a passenger automobile subject to annual depreciation limits if it has *a gross vehicle weight* (GVW) of more than 6,000 pounds. "GVW" is the weight of the vehicle plus its maximum load (typically printed on the inside of the driver's door).[38] This exception was created for taxpayers who need to use large vehicles in their businesses such as farmers, construction workers and others—but not white-collar professionals. However, without further limitations, any taxpayer would be able to expense "heavy" SUVs (assuming they were used for business). When the limited expensing amount was raised to $100,000 ($500,000 in 2011) this enabled taxpayers to deduct the entire cost of a qualified SUV. For example, the taxpayer could expense the entire cost of a Porsche Cayenne or a Hummer H2 that weigh about 7,000 pounds and cost more than $100,000, assuming they were used entirely for business. Believing that many of these SUVs were in reality luxury automobiles, Congress decided to close what had become the so-called Hummer loophole.

As revised, §179 now limits the first-year write-off for vehicles considered SUVs. The maximum amount that can be expensed in the first year is limited to $25,000. Taxpayers may still claim regular depreciation for the balance. Note that the $25,000 amount is not reduced for personal use (as are the other limitations as seen in Example 20).

The $25,000 allowance applies only to SUVs as defined in §179(b)(6)(B). This provision defines an SUV as any four-wheeled vehicle that is primarily designed or that can be used to carry passengers over public streets, roads, or highways and that weighs more than 6,000 pounds unloaded gross weight and not more than 14,000 pounds gross vehicle weight. Thus heavier vehicles, weighing 14,000 pounds or more (e.g., refrigerated trucks) are not subject to the $25,000 limitation. Similarly, to ensure that the $25,000 limitation does not apply to heavy pickup trucks, vans and small buses (and thereby allowing the taxpayer to expense up to $500,000 of their cost), the following vehicles are not considered SUVs.

- A vehicle designed to have a seating capacity of more than nine persons behind the driver's seat.
- A vehicle equipped with a cargo area of at least six feet in interior length which is an open area or is designed for use as an open area but is enclosed by a cap and is not readily accessible directly from the passenger compartment.

[38] PLR 9520034.

- A vehicle having an integral enclosure, fully enclosing the driver compartment and load carrying device, and does not have seating rearward of the driver's seat.
- A vehicle having no body section protruding more than 30 inches ahead of the leading edge of the windshield.

Note that the exceptions would permit deductions for large pick-up trucks weighing more than 6,000 pounds under the cargo area exception or because it as no seats behind the driver. Similarly, cargo vans should qualify under the exception.

**Example 23**

In 2011, T purchased a Lexus LX 470 for $65,000. The SUV has a GVW exceeding 6,000 pounds and is used 100% for business. In such case, the § 179 deduction is $25,000 and regular depreciation would be $8,000 [20% × ($65,000 – $25,000 = $40,000)] for a total deduction of $33,000 ($25,000 + $8,000). If T were in the 35% tax bracket, the deduction would save him $11,550. Note that the limitation on the § 179 deduction is $25,000 and there is no limit on depreciation since the SUV is not a passenger automobile because it weighs more than 6,000 pounds.

**Example 24**

Same facts as in *Example 23* except the SUV is used 80% of the time for business. There is no reduction for the $25,000 allowance as is required for the luxury automobile limitations. Thus the § 179 amount is still $25,000. However, depreciation must be adjusted for personal use. The depreciable basis would be 80% of the $65,000 cost or $52,000. The taxpayer could expense $25,000 and claim regular depreciation of $5,400 (20% × ($52,000 – $25,000 = $27,000)) for a total depreciation deduction of $30,400.

Below is a list of some SUVs with GVWs more than 6,000 pounds:

| *SUV* | |
|---|---|
| BMW X5 | Land Rover Discovery |
| Cadillac Escalade | Land Rover Range Rover |
| Chevrolet Suburban | Lexus LX 470 |
| Chevrolet Tahoe | Lexus GX 470 |
| Dodge Durango | Lincoln Navigator |
| Ford Expedition | Mercedes-Benz M Class |
| Ford Excursion | Mercedes-Benz G 500 |
| Hummer H2 | Porsche Cayenne |
| Hummer H1 | Toyota Land Cruiser |
| GMC Yukon | Toyota Sequoia |

## Limitations for Personal Use

Section 280F also restricts the amount of depreciation that may be claimed for so-called listed property that is not used predominantly—more than 50 percent—for business. If the property is not used more than 50 percent *for business* in the year it is placed in service, the following restrictions are imposed:[39]

1. Limited expensing under § 179 is not allowed.

[39] § 280F(b).

2. MACRS may *not* be used in computing depreciation. Property not qualifying must be depreciated using the straight-line method of ADS and the asset's class life (except in the case of certain property such as automobiles and computers, where the life to be used is specifically prescribed as five years).

Note that these restrictions are imposed if the property is not used primarily for business in the *first* year. Subsequent usage in excess of 50 percent does not permit the taxpayer to amend the earlier return or later use accelerated depreciation or limited expensing. On the other hand, if qualified usage initially exceeds 50 percent but subsequently drops to 50 percent or below, benefits previously secured must be relinquished. The recapture of these benefits is discussed below. Exhibit 9-15 identifies the depreciation methods available for listed property.

**EXHIBIT 9.15 Depreciation Methods Available for Listed Property**

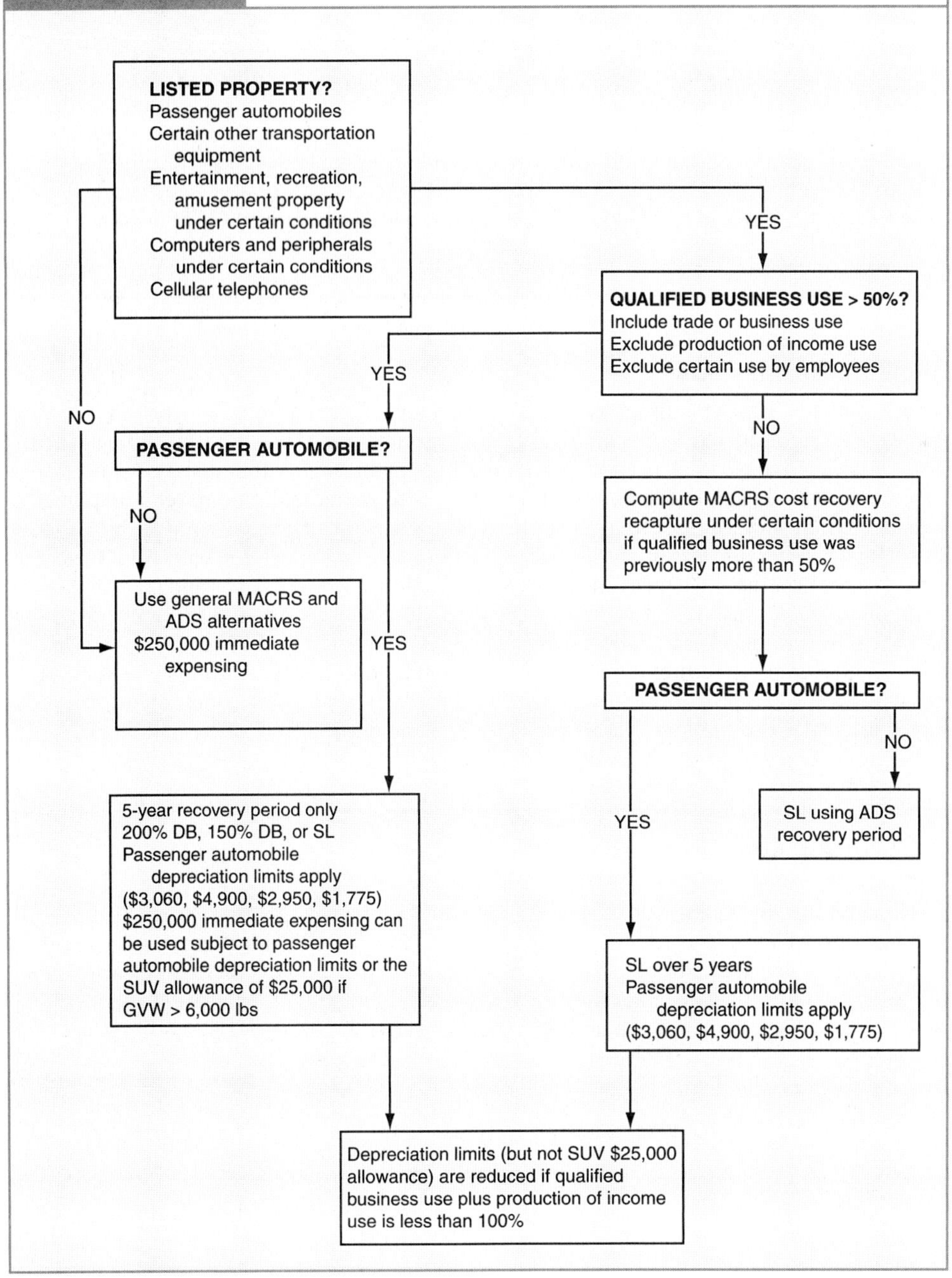

These restrictions apply only to *listed property*. Listed property includes the following:[40]

1. Passenger automobiles (as defined above)
2. Any other property used as a means for transportation (e.g., motorcycles and trucks)
3. Any property generally used for purposes of entertainment, recreation, or amusement (e.g., yacht, photography equipment, video recorders, and stereo equipment) *unless* used exclusively at a regular business establishment (e.g., at the office or at a home office) or in connection with the taxpayer's principal trade or business
4. Any computer or peripheral equipment *unless* used exclusively at a regular business establishment
5. Any cellular telephones and similar communications equipment

### Example 25

K, self-employed, purchased a car for $20,000 in 2011. She uses her car 40% of the time for business and the remaining time for personal purposes. Since the property is a car, the limitations on depreciation are first reduced in light of the personal usage. In the first year, depreciation would initially be limited to $1,224 ($3,060 maximum allowed × 40% business use). In addition, since the car is listed property and is not used more than 50% for business, K must use ADS to compute depreciation. Therefore, depreciation in the first year is $800 ($20,000 cost × 40% business use = $8,000 × 10% ADS rate).

## Qualified Business Use

In determining whether the property is used more than 50 percent for business, only *qualified business use* is considered.[41] Generally, qualified business use means any use in a trade or business of the taxpayer.[42] Thus, for this test *only*, use in an activity that does not constitute a trade or business is ignored (e.g., use of a computer to monitor the taxpayer's investments does not count toward the 50 percent threshold since the activity is not a business).[43] Additionally, an employee's use of his or her own property in connection with employment is not considered business use unless it is for the *convenience of the employer* and is *required as a condition of employment*.[44] According to the Regulations, these two requirements generally have the same meaning for § 280F as they have for § 119 relating to the exclusion for meals or lodging.[45] Given this interpretation, a mere statement by the employer expressly requiring the employee to use the property is insufficient. Ordinarily, the property is considered required only if it enables the employee to properly perform the duties of his or her employment.

### Example 26

T is employed by X, a newspaper company, to deliver papers in a rural area where the homes are widely scattered. The company does not provide T with a car and does not require T to own a car for employment. Since the car enables T to properly perform his duties and is for the convenience of X, T's use should qualify for purposes of the 50% test even though he is not explicitly required to own a car.

---

[40] § 280F(d)(4).

[41] § 280F(b)(1) and (2).

[42] § 280F(d)(6).

[43] Temp. Reg. § 1.280F-6T(d)(2).

[44] § 280F(d)(3).

[45] Temp. Reg. § 1.280F-6T(a)(2).

### Example 27

J is a budget analyst in the accounting department of a large construction firm. She owns a personal computer that is identical to the one she uses at work. Instead of staying late at the office, J occasionally brings home work for which she uses her computer. J's use of her computer for her work is not qualified business use.

The IRS takes a very narrow view regarding what satisfies the convenience-of-the-employer and condition-of-employment tests. In one instance, the Service held that a professor's use of her home computer for writing related to her research—which was required for continued employment—did not satisfy the tests.[46] Although the Service agreed that the use of the computer was related to her work, it found no evidence that employees who did not use home computers were professionally disadvantaged. The Service also felt that her employer did not explicitly require use of the home computer before she was hired. Apparently, the Service will require taxpayers to demonstrate that the work could not properly be performed without the computer or at least that they will be professionally disadvantaged if they do not use the computer. In addition, under the IRS view, taxpayers will be obliged to show that use of the computer was mandatory and not optional.

The reach of this and other rulings goes farther than it first appears. As brought out by the Service, a literal interpretation of the statute indicates that if an employee does not satisfy the convenience-of-the-employer and condition-of-employment tests, *none* of the employee's use is treated as business use. This view does *not* mean that the employee is merely relegated to using ADS for depreciation. Rather, with no business use, the employee is prohibited from claiming any deductions relating to the listed property. Only time will tell whether this interpretation is consistent with Congressional intent.

In those cases where qualified business use exceeds 50 percent, any usage for the production of income or other business purposes is included in determining the percentage of the asset that may be depreciated using MACRS. Similarly, if business use is 50 percent or less, the usage for production of income or other nonqualified business purposes is still included in determining the percentage of the asset that may be depreciated using ADS. Note that depreciation is still allowed where the 50 percent test is not met, assuming there is business or investment usage.

### Example 28

V, a financial consultant, operates her business as an independent contractor. She purchased a car for $20,000. She uses the car 25% of the time for business and 55% for production of income activities (e.g., managing her rental properties) that do not qualify as a business. V must use ADS since business usage is only 25%. Although the time spent for the production of income cannot be counted toward the 50% test, it may be considered in the depreciation computation. Thus, V's depreciation would be $1,600 [$20,000 × (55% + 25%) × 10%]. It should be noted that where the listed property is an automobile, the limitations on depreciation also apply. Here the depreciation limitation in 2010 is $2,448 [(55% + 25%) × $3,060]; note that the production of income usage is considered in making the proper reduction]; thus it does not restrict the amount of the depreciation deduction. Had the usage percentages been reversed (i.e., 55% for business), the depreciation and limited expensing deduction would still have been limited to $2,448.

## Employer-Provided Cars

The qualified business use rules directly address the problems of the company-owned car and other company-owned property used by employees. In the case of automobiles, employers typically provide company-owned cars to their employees principally for use in the employer's business. Normally, however, the employee also uses the car for personal purposes if only to

---

[46] Letter Ruling 8615024.

commute to work. Under prior law, the employer claimed deductions and credits for the car without limitation (i.e., 100 percent of the car's basis was taken into account) while employees were required to treat the personal use as compensation. In most cases, the compensation income was avoided as long as the employee reimbursed the company for the value of the personal use, which the company in turn reported as income. Section 280F now prescribes specific rules governing depreciation where listed property is used by someone *other than* the owner—such as an employer-provided automobile. The following discussion examines these rules as they apply to employer-provided automobiles; however, such rules extend to other listed property as well.

Where an employee uses an automobile, an *employer* is able to secure 100 percent qualified business use—and thus depreciate the entire cost of the automobile—in one of four ways.[47]

1. The employee's actual business usage is disregarded and the *entire value* of using the vehicle is included in the employee's income.
2. The employee's actual business usage is combined with inclusion of the value of any personal use by the employee as income.
3. The employee's actual business usage is combined with a reimbursement arrangement where the employee reimburses the employer for any personal use (i.e. a fair rent is paid).
4. The use falls under one of four exceptions.

Conditions 2 and 3 cannot be applied to qualify the use of a person owning greater than a 5 percent interest in the business (e.g., the company president, who is also a 30 percent shareholder). In this case, the employer can depreciate the car based only on the employee's actual business usage.

Before looking at several examples of these rules, it should be noted that each requires a valuation of the vehicle's use to the employee. The value can be determined using a facts-and-circumstances approach (e.g., considering such variables as geographic location, make and model, etc.) or one of several safe harbors provided by Temporary Regulations.[48] For example, the Regulations provide a table (i.e., a lease value table) based on the car's total value which provides values for personal use. Another alternative that can be used to value personal use under certain circumstances is the standard mileage allowance.

## Example 29

During 2011, X Corporation provided T, an employee, with a new car costing $10,000. T drove the company car 15,000 miles, 9,000 miles or 60% for business purposes, and 6,000 miles or 40% for personal purposes. X Corporation may use any of the first three alternatives to account for the car.

*Alternative No. 1.* Under this full inclusion method, the employee's actual use is disregarded and the employee must include 100% of the value of the car's use in income, $7,650 (15,000 × 51 cents—the standard mileage rate for 2011)[49] just as if it were salary (i.e., X Corporation includes it on T's Form W-2 and withholds income and FICA taxes). Therefore, all of T's use qualifies and X may depreciate 100% of the car using MACRS. T may then deduct any substantiated business use as a miscellaneous itemized deduction subject to the 2% floor. One advantage of this method for the employer is that it shifts all of the substantiation burden to the employee.

*Alternative No. 2.* Under this partial inclusion method, only T's personal use is treated as income, or $3,060 (6,000 × 51 cents). X could depreciate the car in the same manner as above. T may be better off under this method since the amount of compensation is reduced. This may have an effect on the amount of deductions or credits T may otherwise claim (e.g., the 2% floor on miscellaneous itemized deductions would be smaller due to the lower amount of income). In this case, X must be able to substantiate the employee's actual business use.

*Alternative No. 3.* Under the rental reimbursement method, T would pay X Corporation for his personal use, $3,060. X could depreciate the car in the same manner as above. T would be worse off in this situation. Each dollar of reimbursement costs T one

[47] Temp. Reg. § 1.280F-6T(d)(4)(iv).

[48] Temp. Reg. § 1.61-2T(d)(2)(iii).

[49] See Chapter 8 for discussion of standard mileage rate.

dollar, while inclusion of the value of the personal use costs the employee only the tax on the value. Again, X must be able to substantiate the employee's actual business use.

*Five Percent Owner.* If T owns 5% or more of the business (i.e., X Corporation), the only alternative is to compute depreciation using T's actual business mileage. In this case, X could depreciate 60% of the car using MACRS. Had T's business usage been 50% or less, X would be required to use ADS to compute depreciation.

Additional rules for determining qualified business usage exist for other situations. For example, leasing the property to a 5 percent owner of the business or a related person is not considered qualified business use. Similarly, special rules are provided for aircraft.

### Recapture Provisions

If the 50 percent test is satisfied in the year property is placed in service but failed prior to the time when the cost of the asset would be completely recovered using the listed property recovery rules, the taxpayer is required to relinquish the benefits of MACRS. Technically, the taxpayer must recompute the depreciation in the prior years using ADS and include in income the excess of the depreciation actually claimed over the ADS amounts. Depreciation in future years is computed using the straight-line method.

## Example 30

In 20X1 G purchased a car for $10,000 and used it entirely for business. Depreciation for 20X1 was $2,000 ($10,000 × 20%). In 20X2 G's business usage dropped to 40%. Since G's business usage is no longer greater than 50%, he must recapture the benefits of accelerated depreciation. Depreciation using the straight-line method in 20X1 would have been $1,000 ($10,000 × 10%). Thus, G must include $1,000 ($2,000 original depreciation—$1,000 straight-line depreciation) in income in 20X2. Depreciation for 20X2 and all subsequent years must be computed using the straight-line method.

### Recordkeeping Requirements

Not only has Congress severely restricted tax benefits for listed property, it also has imposed strict record keeping requirements for such property. The substantiation rules contained in Code § 274(d), which were formerly reserved solely for travel and entertainment expenses, now extend to expenses related to "listed property." For listed property, the taxpayer is required to substantiate the following:[50]

1. The amount of each expenditure related to the property, including the cost of acquisition, maintenance, and repairs
2. The date of the use of the property
3. The amount of each business or investment use as well as total use [the number of miles—in the case of a car or other means of transportation—or the amount of time that the property was used for other listed property (e.g., a computer)]
4. The purpose of the use of the property

In those cases where the overall use of the property for a taxable year can be definitely determined without entries, nonbusiness use need not be recorded. For example, in the case of a car, total miles can be determined by comparing the odometer readings at the beginning and the end of the taxable year. Consequently, the taxpayer needs to make entries only for business and investment use.

[50] Temp. Reg. § 1.274-5T(b)(6).

## ✓ Check Your Knowledge

### Review Question I

This year Y purchased new property. Indicate whether the following questions are true or false.

**a.** Assuming the property is a duplex that Y rents to others, she may not expense any of the cost.

*True.* Only eligible property may be expensed. As a general rule, only personal property such as machinery and equipment are eligible. Buildings are normally not eligible.

**b.** Assuming the property is machinery costing \$520,000, Y may expense \$500,000, and the \$20,000 balance may be carried over to the following years to be expensed to the extent the maximum amount is not used in such years.

*False.* Y may expense \$500,000, and the balance is subject to depreciation in the current year.

**c.** Assuming the property is a \$20,000 passenger automobile that is used 70 percent for business, Y may deduct \$14,000.

*False.* Depreciation and expensing for automobiles are limited. The maximum amount of depreciation or expense claimed in the year the automobile is placed in service is limited to \$2,142 (\$3,060 × 70%).

**d.** Assuming the property is a \$40,000 car that is used 30 percent for business, Y may deduct \$918 (\$3,060 × 30%).

*True.* If the property is listed property and qualified business use does not exceed 50 percent, the taxpayer is not allowed to expense any of the car and must use straight-line depreciation. Therefore, Y's potential deduction is \$1,200 (\$40,000 × 30% × 10%) but is limited to \$918.

**e.** If the property is listed property, such as a passenger automobile or a computer, and the property is not used more than 50 percent of the time for business, the restrictions of § 280F do not affect the total amount of cost deducted but simply alter the time when it is deducted.

*True.* The total depreciation is not changed. If the property is restricted and qualified business use does not exceed 50 percent, the taxpayer is simply forced to use the straight-line method in lieu of the accelerated methods of MACRS and the expensing allowance of § 179 that are normally available.

## Other Considerations

### Anti-Churning Rules

In some cases, a taxpayer's depreciation deductions under MACRS would be higher than those that the taxpayer may currently have. For this reason, Congress believed that some taxpayers would engage in transactions that might enable them to secure the advantages of MACRS.

#### Example 31

In 1980 H acquired an apartment building as an investment that she chose to depreciate using the straight-line method over 35 years. H made this decision because the use of accelerated depreciation caused a portion of any gain from the subsequent sale of such property to be treated as ordinary income rather than favorable capital-gain. With the elimination of favorable capital-gain treatment in 1986, there no longer was any disincentive to use the accelerated method. Therefore, H created a plan to benefit from the change. She sold the property to her son, who immediately leased it back to her. The rental payments to be paid by H were structured in light of the higher depreciation deductions (27.5-year life instead of 35 years) that her son would be able to take as the new owner of the property.

Sales, exchanges, and other dispositions of assets such as that illustrated above are referred to as "churning" transactions—exchanges of used property solely to obtain the benefits of MACRS.

The thrust of the anti-churning rules is to preclude the use of MACRS for property placed in service prior to the enactment of either version of MACRS, unless the property is transferred in a transaction where not only the owner changes but also the user.[51] In *Example 31* the anti-churning rules prohibit H's son from using MACRS since ownership did not truly change.

There are three sets of rules designed to police churning. For practical purposes these provisions should be given close review whenever the taxpayer is involved in a leasing or nontaxable transaction. For example, a taxpayer would typically be subject to the anti-churning rules in the following situations:

1. Sale followed by immediate leaseback
2. Like-kind exchange
3. Formation and liquidation of a corporation or partnership, including transfers of property to and distributions from these entities

### Expensing Costs of Qualified Film and Television Productions

Over the years, production of American film projects has migrated to foreign locations often lured by tax and other incentives offered by foreign countries. To encourage producers to bring feature film and television production projects back to the U.S., Congress created § 181 in 2004. Section 181 allows immediate deduction for costs of qualified film or television productions. To qualify, one condition requires that at least 75 percent of the total compensation expended on the production is for services performed in the U.S.. The special expensing allowance is limited to smaller productions in that it does not apply if the aggregate production costs exceed $15 million. In other words, if the total costs exceed $15 million, none can be expensed. Instead the amount must be capitalized and amortized. The $15 million amount is increased to $20 million if a significant amount of the production expenditures are incurred in areas eligible for designation as a low-income community or eligible for designation by the Delta Regional Authority as a distressed county or isolated area.

### Property Leased to Tax-Exempt Entities

For a variety of reasons, tax-exempt entities, such as schools, hospitals, or government organizations, lease property from taxable entities rather than purchase it. One incentive for this type of transaction is that the taxable entity can benefit from depreciation deductions, whereas the tax-exempt entity cannot. Thus, a tax plan might be devised under which a taxable lessor and a tax-exempt lessee "share" the tax benefits of the depreciation deductions. This would be accomplished through discounted lease payments. The taxable lessor would be willing to accept discounted lease payments "in exchange" for receiving all of the tax benefits from depreciation deductions. To reduce the incentive for this type of tax plan, depreciation of "tax-exempt use property"—most property leased to a "tax-exempt entity"—must be depreciated using ADS with special rules to determine the applicable recovery period.[52] This rule applies regardless of the tax planning motives of the lessor and lessee. The result of the rule is to lower the present value of the tax savings from the depreciation deductions. There are several types of leasing transactions that are exempted from the rule. For example, the rule does not apply to "short-term leases."

## Amortization

**LO.6** Distinguish amortization from depreciation and identify assets subject to amortization.

As previously discussed, MACRS does not apply to intangible property. Therefore, intangibles are subject to the rules existing prior to enactment of ACRS and MACRS. Generally, intangibles are amortized using the straight-line method over their estimated useful life. Special amortization and depreciation rules apply to certain expenditures, however.

[51] § 168(e)(4).

[52] § 168(g)(1)(C).

## Goodwill and Covenants not to Compete

As mentioned in Chapter 6, buyers of a going concern often pay an amount in excess of the fair market value of the concern's tangible assets. This excess purchase price normally is attributable to intangible assets such as goodwill and/or a covenant not to compete. The tax treatment for such intangible assets was changed dramatically by the Revenue Reconciliation Act of 1993 for acquisitions occurring after August 10, 1993. Acquisitions taking place on or before August 10, 1993 continue to be treated under prior law, which held that goodwill could not be amortized because it was considered as having an unlimited life. Thus, recovery of a taxpayer's basis in goodwill could occur only when the business was subsequently sold or abandoned. In contrast, a covenant not to compete usually has an ascertainable life because the seller typically agrees to refrain from conducting similar business or some other activity for a certain number of years. As a result, prior law held that any cost attributable to the covenant may be amortized over the appropriate period using the straight-line method.

Under prior law, taxpayers attempted to allocate the purchase price to assets other than goodwill since goodwill could not be amortized. In this regard, accountants were quite creative, assigning the purchase price to a variety of intangibles such as covenants not to compete, favorable contracts, customer lists, accounting control systems, and a long list of other items. As long as the taxpayer was able to establish that the intangible was separate and distinct from goodwill and had a determinable useful life, the taxpayer was entitled to amortize the cost. For example, a taxpayer might allocate a substantial portion of the purchase price of a business to a covenant not to compete and amortize the cost over three years, producing a significant benefit where otherwise there would be no benefit at all if the cost were allocated to goodwill.

### Post–August 10, 1993 Acquisitions

As might be expected, the IRS did not sit idly by and allow taxpayers to do as they pleased. In case after case, the IRS challenged the taxpayer's allocation, and there was a great deal of controversy and litigation. To put an end to the disputes and clear up the uncertainty, Congress enacted § 197. Effective for acquisitions after August 10, 1993 all "Section 197 intangibles" must be amortized over 15 years. (A taxpayer may elect to have the rules of § 197 apply to intangibles acquired after July 15, 1991.) Much like MACRS, § 197 forces the taxpayer to use the 15-year period even if the useful life is actually more or less than 15 years. Section 197 intangibles include a number of items such as goodwill, going-concern value, covenants not to compete, information bases such as customer or subscription lists, know-how, customer-based intangibles, governmental licenses and permits (e.g., liquor licenses, taxicab medallions, landing or takeoff rights, regulated airline routes, television or radio licenses), franchises, trademarks, and trade names.

To further prohibit the deduction of an intangible obtained as part of an acquisition, special rules govern disposition. No loss is allowed on the disposition of an intangible if the business retains other intangible assets acquired in the same or a series of related transactions. Instead, any remaining basis is reallocated among the bases of other § 197 intangibles. Although losses are not recognized, the same treatment does not apply to gains.

If § 197 intangibles are sold at a gain, the gain is recognized. The tax character of the entire gain is ordinary income if the intangible is held one year or less. Gains from sales of intangibles held more than one year are treated as gains from sales of § 1245 property. As explained in Chapter 17, gains from dispositions of § 1245 property are "recaptured" and treated as ordinary income up to the amount of amortization on the intangible deducted through the time of sale. Any excess gain is a § 1231 gain.

#### Example 32

Buyer allocates $150,000 to intangible assets in a purchase. Under § 197 Buyer would claim $10,000 per year for 15 years as an amortization deduction. The deduction would not be affected by breaking the $150,000 into separate portions for goodwill, a covenant not to compete, or any other specifically identified intangibles.

Assume that the purchase occurred on January 1, 2011. Buyer will claim a $10,000 deduction every year for 15 years through 2025. Assume that Buyer allocates $105,000 to goodwill and the remaining $45,000 to a covenant not to compete that would expire on January 1, 2014. From 2011 through 2013. Buyer claims an annual amortization deduction of $3,000 ($45,000/15) on the covenant and $7,000 ($105,000/15) on the goodwill. Note that the covenant not to compete is amortized over 15 years regardless of its economic life. On January 1, 2014, Buyer will have an unrecovered basis of $36,000 on the covenant, which has expired [$45,000 – $9,000 amortization ($3,000 amortization per year for three years)]. However, Buyer must add the $36,000 unrecovered basis to the basis of goodwill and continue to deduct $10,000 per year as amortization of the goodwill.

A number of anti-churning rules exist to prohibit taxpayers from creating and amortizing goodwill and going-concern value. Other intangibles are not covered by these rules.

## Five-Year Elective Amortization

To accomplish certain economic and social objectives, Congress has enacted various optional five-year (60-month) amortization procedures from time to time over the last 40 years. During certain periods, a five-year amortization election (in lieu of regular depreciation) has been available for expenditures made in connection with child care facilities (§ 188), pollution control facilities (still an option under § 169), railroad rolling stock (§ 184), and rehabilitation of low-income housing [§ 167(k)]. In 2006, Congress passed legislation allowing five-year amortization of costs of creating or acquiring musical works or copyrights (§167(g)).

## Leasehold Improvements

Taxpayers often lease property and improve the property while leasing it. In this situation, the lessee is entitled to recover the investment in the improvement.[53] After 1986, the cost of any leasehold improvement made by a lessee is normally depreciated in the normal manner without regard to the term of the lease. However, under §168(e)(6), property owners are allowed to depreciate improvements they make for tenants, such as interior walls or lighting fixtures, over 15 years rather than the current 39 years. This special rule applies to property placed in service before 2011. They must use the straight-line method. Similarly, tenants who make their own improvements receive the same benefit. Any unrecovered cost at the end of the lease term would increase the taxpayer's basis for determining gain or loss. The recovery of the costs of acquiring a lease is determined under special rules in Code § 178.

# Depletion

**LO.7**
Determine the current depletion deduction for various assets.

A taxpayer who invests in natural resources that are exhausted over time is entitled to recover his or her capital investment. Depletion is the method of recovering this cost and is similar to depreciation.[54] Depletion usually is claimed for investments in oil, gas, coal, copper, and other minerals. Land is not subject to depletion.

To qualify for depletion, the taxpayer must have an economic interest in the mineral deposits.[55] Typically, both the owner of the land who leases the property and the operator to whom the land is leased have the requisite interest since they both receive income from the severance or extraction of the minerals.

## Computing the Depletion Deduction

Taxpayers generally are permitted to compute their depletion deduction using either the cost or percentage (statutory) depletion method. The taxpayer computes both cost and percentage depletion and is required to claim the higher amount.[56]

---

[53] § 168(i)(8); also see § 178(a) when the lease permits renewals.

[54] § 611.

[55] Reg. § 1.611-1(b).

[56] § 613(a); Reg. § 1.611-1(a).

## Cost Depletion

Using cost depletion, the taxpayer recovers the actual investment (adjusted basis in the natural resource) as the mineral is produced. The following formula is used:[57]

$$\frac{\text{Annual cost}}{\text{depletion}} = \frac{\text{Unrecovered adjusted basis}}{\text{Estimated recoverable units}} \times \frac{\text{Number of units sold}}{\text{during the year}}$$

This formula generally matches the cost of the investment against the revenues produced.

### Example 33

A coal producer, T, paid $150,000 to acquire the mineral rights in a property which contains coal. He estimates that 90,000 tons of coal are recoverable from the property. During the year, 58,000 tons of coal were produced and 30,000 were sold. T's cost depletion would be $50,000 computed as follows:

$$\frac{\$150{,}000\text{ basis}}{90{,}000\text{ units}} \times \frac{30{,}000}{\text{units sold}} = \frac{\$50{,}000}{\text{depletion}}$$

Similar to depreciation, total cost depletion can never exceed the taxpayer's adjusted basis in the property.

## Percentage Depletion

For large oil and gas producers, cost depletion is the only depletion method allowed. However, both cost depletion and percentage depletion are available to small "independent" oil and gas producers as well as royalty owners.[58] Both cost depletion and percentage depletion are also allowed for *all* producers of certain types of minerals (e.g., gold, silver, gravel).

Under the percentage depletion method, the taxpayer's depletion deduction is computed *without reference* to the taxpayer's cost of the investment. Rather, percentage depletion is based on the amount of income derived from the property.[59] For this reason, the taxpayer may deduct percentage depletion in excess of the adjusted basis of the investment. Thus, the taxpayer is entitled to a deduction for percentage depletion as long as the property continues to generate income.

To compute percentage depletion, a percentage specified in the Code (see Exhibit 9-16) is applied to the *gross* income from the property. The resulting product is the amount of percentage

**EXHIBIT 9.16 Summary of Various Percentage Depletion Rates**

| *Natural Resource* | *Percentage Rate* |
|---|---|
| 1. Gravel, sand, and other items | 5 |
| 2. Shale and clay used for sewer pipes; or brick and clay, shale, and slate used for lightweight aggregates | 7.5 |
| 3. Asbestos, coal, sodium chloride, etc. | 10 |
| 4. Gold, silver, oil and gas, oil shale, copper, and iron ore from deposits in the United States | 15 |
| 5. Sulfur and uranium and a series of minerals from deposits in the United States | 22 |
| 6. Metals, other than those subject to 22% or 15% rate | 14 |

[57] Reg. § 1.611-2(a).

[58] § 613A(c).

[59] § 613.

depletion unless limited. For oil and gas properties, percentage depletion is generally limited to the taxpayer's *taxable* income before depletion. Percentage depletion is limited to 50 percent of the taxpayer's taxable income from mineral properties. Gross income is the value of the natural resource when severed from the property before any processing. Taxable income from the property is the difference between income and operating expenses including overhead.

## Example 34

Assume the same facts in *Example 33* and that the 30,000 tons sold were sold for $10 per ton (gross income of $300,000). Further, operating expenses attributable to the coal operation were $260,000. Percentage depletion is computed as follows:

| | |
|---|---|
| Gross income | $300,000 |
| Statutory percentage for coal | × 10% |
| Percentage depletion before limitation | $ 30,000 |
| Taxable income limitation: | |
| Gross income | $300,000 |
| Less: Operating expenses | – 260,000 |
| Taxable income before depletion | $ 40,000 |
| Limitation percentage | × 50% |
| Percentage depletion limit | $ 20,000 |
| Percentage depletion allowable | $ 20,000 |

In this situation, T would use cost depletion of $50,000 as computed in *Example 33* because it exceeds allowable percentage depletion.

## Example 35

Assume the same facts in *Example 34* except that barrels of oil are being produced, rather than tons of coal. Cost depletion computations are the same as in *Example 33*. Percentage depletion is computed as follows:

| | |
|---|---|
| Gross income | $300,000 |
| Statutory percentage for oil | × 15% |
| Percentage depletion before limitation | $ 45,000 |
| Gross income | $300,000 |
| Less: Operating expenses | – 260,000 |
| Taxable income before depletion | $ 40,000 |
| Percentage depletion limit | $ 40,000 |
| Percentage depletion allowable | $ 40,000 |

T would use cost depletion of $50,000 (computed in *Example 33*) rather than percentage depletion of $40,000 because cost depletion is larger.

Whether percentage or cost depletion is used, the taxpayer must reduce the property's basis (but not below zero) by the amount of depletion claimed. Note that once the basis of the property is reduced to zero, only percentage depletion may be claimed (when the taxpayer is permitted to take percentage depletion), and *no* adjustment is made to create a negative basis.

## Research and Experimental Expenditures

**LO.8**
Explain the options available in selecting the appropriate tax treatment of research and experimentation expenditures.

At first glance, it may appear that the proper tax treatment for research and development expenses requires their capitalization as part of a project's cost. This approach seems appropriate since these costs normally yield benefits only in future periods. Under this theory, the capitalized costs could be recovered over the period during which the project provides benefits or when the project is disposed of or abandoned. Upon closer examination, however, it becomes apparent that this approach is fraught with problems. Since it is difficult to establish any direct relationship between costs of research and development and the actual period benefited, it may be impossible to determine the appropriate period for recovery. For example, establishing a useful life for a scientific discovery that has numerous applications and which continually contributes to later research would be guesswork at best. A similar problem exists for unsuccessful efforts. Although a particular effort may not prove fruitful, it may at least indicate what does not work and thus lead to other, perhaps successful, research. In such case, it is not clear whether the costs should be written off or capitalized as part of the subsequent project.

Due to the administrative difficulties inherent in these determinations, the IRS historically granted research and experimental costs favorable treatment by generally allowing the taxpayer to deduct the expenses as incurred or to capitalize the expenses and amortize them over whatever period the taxpayer desires. Although this approach encountered difficulties in the courts, Congress eliminated the problems with enactment of special provisions in 1954.

### Research and Experimental Expenditures Defined

The Code provides separate rules for research and experimental costs.[60] It should be emphasized that the provisions apply to research and *experimental* costs, not to research and development costs. The term *experimental* was used instead of *development* to limit the special treatment to laboratory costs.[61] Qualified costs generally include those incident to the development or improvement of a product, a formula, an invention, a plant process, an experimental or pilot model, or similar property. Research and experimental costs do *not* include expenditures for ordinary testing or inspection of materials or products for quality control, efficiency surveys, management studies, consumer surveys, advertising, or promotion. Costs of obtaining a patent, such as legal fees, qualify. However, the costs of acquiring an existing patent, model, or process are not considered research and experimental costs. Expenditures for depreciable property do not qualify but the depreciation allowable on the property is eligible for special treatment.

### Alternative Tax Treatments

Three alternative methods may be used to account for research and experimental expenditures. The expenses may be deducted as they are paid or incurred, deferred and amortized, or capitalized. Immediate deduction usually is the preferred method since the present value of the tax benefit is greater using this method. Deferral may be preferable in two instances, however. If the taxpayer's income is low in the current year, the tax benefit of the deduction might be increased by deferring the deduction to high-income years when the taxpayer is in a higher marginal tax bracket. Deferral also may be better if an immediate deduction creates or adds to a net operating loss since such losses may be carried over and used only for a limited period of time. The general rule for selecting the best alternative is to choose the one that maximizes the present value of the tax savings from the research and experimental expenditures.

#### Expense Election

The taxpayer can elect to deduct all research and experimental expenditures currently.[62] Note, however, that expenditures for depreciable property cannot be expensed currently.[63] If the taxpayer adopts this method in the first tax year in which research and experimental expenses are incurred, the method must be used for all such expenditures in all subsequent

[60] § 174.

[61] Reg. § 1.174-2(a).

[62] § 174(a).

[63] § 174(c).

years, unless permission is secured to change methods of part or all of the expenditures.[64] The IRS does not need to approve the method the taxpayer adopts initially. Consent is required, however, if the taxpayer wishes to change methods.

### Deferral Option

Research and experimental expenditures may be deferred and amortized at the election of the taxpayer.[65] The expenses must be amortized ratably over a period not less than 60 months beginning in the period in which benefits from the expenditures are first realized. It should be emphasized that costs of depreciable property are not deferred expenses; rather, the depreciation expense must be capitalized and amortized over 60 months. Also, if the taxpayer elects to defer the expenditures and a patent is subsequently obtained, the cost must be amortized over the life of the patent, 20 years (17 before June 8, 1995). If the deferral method is initially elected, the taxpayer must use this method for all future expenses in subsequent tax years unless permission to change methods is obtained.[66]

### Election to Capitalize

A taxpayer who does not elect either to amortize research and experimental expenditures over 60 months or to deduct them currently must capitalize them. Capitalizing the expenditure increases the basis of the property to which the expense relates. No deduction is permitted for the capital expenditure until the research project is considered worthless or abandoned. A disposition of the research project such as a sale or an exchange enables the taxpayer to offset the capitalized expenditures—the basis of the project—against any amount realized.

#### Example 36

L Corporation, a drug manufacturer, is an accrual basis, calendar year taxpayer. During 2011 the corporation performed research to improve various cold and flu medications. On December 1, 2011 a new cold and flu product line was successfully introduced on the market. In connection with this project, L incurred the following costs:

| | |
|---|---|
| Lab equipment (5-year property) | $50,000 |
| Salaries | 90,000 |
| Laboratory materials | 5,000 |

If L Corporation elects to expense the research and experimental costs, it may deduct $105,000 in 2011 as follows:

| | |
|---|---|
| MACRS depreciation on lab equipment (20% of $50,000) | $ 10,000 |
| Salaries | 90,000 |
| Laboratory materials | 5,000 |
| Total deductions | $105,000 |

Note that only the depreciation on the lab equipment may be deducted as a research and experimental cost, not the entire cost of the equipment. If L Corporation elects to defer the expense, its monthly amortization beginning December 1, 2011 would be

$$\frac{\$105,000}{60} = \$1,750$$

*Alternatively,* L could capitalize all the expenses as an asset (including the $10,000 of depreciation) and receive no deduction until a later disposition or abandonment.

[64] § 174(a)(2).

[65] § 174(b).

[66] § 174(b)(2).

### Other Related Provisions

Several other provisions exist relating to the treatment of research and experimental expenditures, such as a tax credit for research and experimentation. Generally, the credit is 20 percent of the current year's expenditures after adjustments (see Chapter 13).[67] Taxpayers electing the credit are generally required to reduce their research and experimentation expenses by 50 percent of the credit for purposes of computing the amount to either be expensed, deferred, or capitalized.[68] Special rules also exist for contributions of research property by corporations (see Chapter 11).[69]

## Expenses of Farmers and Ranchers

**LO.9**
Explain the tax treatment of certain expenditures incurred in farming and ranching activities.

Special provisions exist for certain types of expenditures incurred by those engaged in farming and ranching. The rules examined below generally differ from the treatment of expenses that normally would be considered capital expenditures subject to depreciation.

### Expenses Related to Livestock

Costs of acquiring animals used for breeding, dairy, work, or sport are treated as capital expenditures and are depreciable under MACRS unless such animals are primarily held for sale and would be appropriately included in inventory. If a farmer raises his or her own livestock, however, expenses incurred such as feed normally can be deducted as paid, assuming the taxpayer uses the cash basis method of accounting.[70] This rule is in sharp contrast to that applying to other self-production costs. Costs incurred by farmers and others in constructing their own equipment and buildings must be capitalized and depreciated.

### Soil and Water Conservation, Fertilizer, Land Clearing

Farmers often incur expenses for soil and water conservation. Examples of these expenses are the costs of leveling or terracing the soil to control the flow of water, irrigation and drainage ditches, ponds, dams, eradication of brush, and planting windbreaks. Although normal tax rules would require these expenses to be capitalized, Code § 175permits a deduction when such expenses are paid or incurred as long as such expenses are consistent with a conservation plan approved by the Soil Conservation Service of the Department of Agriculture. To encourage these practices and still restrict the availability of this benefit, the Code requires that the taxpayer be engaged in the business of farming. In addition, the annual deduction for these expenses is limited to 25 percent of the taxpayer's gross income from farming. This limitation prohibits a taxpayer from using the deductions to reduce nonfarm income. Expenditures exceeding this limitation may be carried over to subsequent years.

Like soil and water conservation expenditures, Code § 180 provides that the cost of fertilizer, lime, and other materials used to enrich farmland can be deducted in the year paid or incurred by those engaged in the business for farming. There is no limitation imposed on the amount of the deduction.

Taxpayers engaged in the farming business must capitalize expenses of clearing land in preparation for farming. These expenses include any cost of making the land suitable for farming such as those for removing and eradicating brush or tree stumps and the treating or moving of earth. Routine brush clearing and other ordinary maintenance related to the land may be expensed, however.

---

[67] § 41.

[68] § 280C(c).

[69] § 170.

[70] Reg. § 1.162-12

## Development Expenses

Expenses incurred in the development of farms and ranches prior to the time when production begins may be capitalized or expensed at the election of the taxpayer.[71] Examples of these expenses are costs of cultivation, spraying, pruning, irrigation, and management fees.

The expensing of development and other farm-related costs prior to the period in which the farm begins to produce income provides an attractive device for high-bracket taxpayers who have no interest in farming—to shelter their income from other nonfarm sources. These and other tax advantages offered by farming in the 1960s brought such an influx of "urban cowboys" to the farming industry that several farm groups protested and demanded protection. Congress first responded to these groups in 1969. Currently, this provision prohibits the immediate expensing of any amount attributable to the planting, cultivation, maintenance, or development of any citrus or almond grove. Any of these development costs that are incurred in the first four years of the grove's life must be capitalized.

Congress adopted additional safeguards in 1976. Section 447 generally requires that corporations (and partnerships having a corporate partner) engaged in the business of farming must use the accrual method of accounting. Since this provision was intended to protect small farmers and family-owned farms, the following are not treated as corporations: (1) S corporations; (2) family-owned corporations (at least 50 percent of the stock is owned by family members); and (3) any corporation that did not have gross receipts exceeding $1 million in any prior year. In addition, farming syndicates may deduct the costs of feed, seed, fertilizer, and similar farm supplies only as they are actually used.[72] A farming syndicate generally is defined to include partnerships and S corporations where the sale of their interests is specifically regulated by state or local securities laws, or more than 35 percent of their losses during any period are allocated to limited partners or persons who do not actively participate in the management of the business.

In 1986 the prohibition against the deduction of prepaid farming expenses was extended to all farmers that prepay more than 50 percent of their expenses such as feed, seed, and fertilizer.[73] Farmers cannot deduct such expenses until the items are consumed or used. Several exceptions exist, however.

# Tax Planning Considerations

## Depreciation and After-Tax Cash Flow

Many taxpayers, when analyzing an investment, fail to consider the tax aspects. For example, a taxpayer who looks solely to the cash flow projections of investing in a rental property might overlook the effect of depreciation. The depreciation deduction does not require an outlay of cash, but does produce a tax benefit.

### Example 37

In January of the current year, L purchased a duplex for $80,000, which she rented to others. Of the $80,000 purchase price, $70,000 was allocable to the building and $10,000 was allocable to the land. L financed the purchase with a $5,000 downpayment and a mortgage calling for monthly payments of interest and principal of $400. During the year, L rented the property for $7,000. Expenses for the year were as follows:

| | |
|---|---|
| Mortgage interest | $ 4,000 |
| Taxes | 1,200 |
| Insurance | 500 |
| Maintenance and utilities | 300 |
| Depreciation (MACRS: $70,000 × 3.485%) | 2,440 |
| Total expenses | $ 8,440 |

[71] *Ibid.*

[72] § 464.

[73] § 464(f).

The net taxable loss from the real property would be

| | |
|---|---|
| Rental income | $ 7,000 |
| Less: Rental expenses | − 8,440 |
| Net taxable loss | $ 1,440 |

Note that the taxable loss contains depreciation expense of $2,440, a noncash expenditure. Assuming L is in the 28 percent tax bracket, the net cash flow from the project would be computed as follows:

| | | | |
|---|---|---|---|
| Cash inflow: | | | |
| Rental income | | | $7,000 |
| Tax saving from loss ($1,440 × 28%) | | | 403 |
| Total cash inflow | | | $7,403 |
| Cash outflow: | | | |
| Total expenses | | $ 8,440 | |
| Less: Depreciation | | − 2,440 | |
| | | $ 6,000 | |
| Debt service | | | |
| Mortgage payments ($400 × 12) | $ 4,800 | | |
| Less: Interest (included in expenses above) | − 4,000 | + 800 | |
| Total cash outflow | | | (6,800) |
| After-tax cash flow | | | $ 603 |

Therefore, L has a positive cash flow of $603 on the project notwithstanding the taxable loss that she suffered of $1,440.

Under certain circumstances, limitations are imposed on the deduction of losses from rental property. These limitations are discussed in Chapter 12.

## Accelerating Depreciation with Cost Segregation

Prior to 1981, some taxpayers used a technique called "component depreciation" to accelerate real estate depreciation deductions. These taxpayers separated the costs of their depreciable buildings into various components with useful lives shorter than the rest of the building. For example, structural components such as wiring, plumbing, and roofing were depreciated over periods of 10 or 15 years rather than the much longer periods typically associated with the useful life of the building shell.

While the introduction of ACRS and MACRS prohibited component depreciation, it did not eliminate a similar but different technique referred to as "cost segregation." In 1997, the Tax Court, in a the seminal case on cost segregation, *Hospital Corporation of America (HCA)*, permitted HCA for purposes of depreciation to segregate the costs of components constituting real property (§ 1250 property) and tangible personal property (§ 1250 property).[74] As a result, HCA was able to depreciate a long list of improvements as 5-year property rather than 39-year property, producing huge tax savings. Shortly after the *HCA* decision, the IRS grudgingly acquiesced and announced that cost segregation did not constitute component depreciation.[75] As a result, this subtle distinction permitted what has become the widespread use of cost segregation.

[74] 109 TC 21 (1997).

[75] AOD 1999-008 9/08/1999 and Announcement 99-116, 1999-52 I.R.B. 763. See also Reg. § 1.446-1T and CCA 199921045

The importance of cost segregation cannot be overemphasized. Consider the benefits of reclassifying $100,000 of property from a 39 to a 5 year recovery period. Depreciation as 39-year property using the required straight-line method produces an annual deduction of about $2,600 per year for 39 years. In contrast, depreciation as 5-year property using double declining balance results in the entire cost being deducted over six years ($20,000, $32,000, $19,200, $11,500, $11,500 and $5,760). Reclassifying $100,000 from 39 to 5-year property produces about $16,000 in net-present-value savings, assuming a 5% discount rate and a 35% marginal tax rate. It is no wonder that a whole niche business involving cost segregation has developed.

Examples of assets that taxpayers should segregate from the cost of the building and depreciate over five or seven years include movable partitions, computers, separate fire protection systems, manufacturing equipment and built-in desks and cabinets. Properties reclassified from 39 to 5 year property in *HCA* included carpeting, vinyl wall and floor coverings, electrical distribution system and a number of other items. A rule of thumb for identifying these separate depreciable assets is to assess whether the items would be removed if the business were to relocate. If so, the removable assets can have their own depreciation schedules.

Land improvements represent another set of costs that should be separated since they can be depreciated over 15 years. These include parking lots, landscaping, sewers and irrigation systems.

To segregate costs successfully, taxpayers or their advisers should work closely with building contractors to document the costs of fast-depreciating assets. Early involvement with the contractor or architect could even lead to building designs that maximize the number of separate depreciable assets while not reducing the productive use of the building.

## Goodwill Amortization Rule Benefits Buyers and Sellers

Prior to August 10, 1993 the goodwill portion of the cost of acquiring a business provided no tax benefit to the buyer until the buyer later sold the business because the basis assigned to goodwill could not be amortized. Now that goodwill can be amortized over 15 years, its value is greater because the present value of a series of tax deductions received throughout a 15-year period is higher than the present value of a single deduction received many years in the future (assuming constant or declining marginal tax rates over time). Buyers and sellers will share this increase in value as they negotiate purchase/sale prices of their businesses.

Typically, buyers and sellers have some flexibility regarding the allocation of purchase price between goodwill (a capital asset that produces capital gain for the seller) and other intangibles. Two factors encourage increased allocations to goodwill. First, the seller will recognize capital gain income instead of ordinary income (assuming the allocation choice is between goodwill and a covenant not to compete). Second, for buyers concerned about earnings per share, goodwill may be preferable to payments for a covenant not to compete due to the treatment of goodwill under generally accepted accounting principles (GAAP). Under GAAP, goodwill normally is not amortized unless it is found to be impaired. Thus, as long as there is no reduction in the value of goodwill, no amortization is required. In contrast, the covenant may be amortized over its economic life. Buyers not concerned about GAAP should be indifferent between allocations to goodwill versus a covenant not to compete because *all* intangibles are amortizable over 15 years for tax purposes. Thus, at best, increased allocations to goodwill could benefit both buyers and sellers of businesses. At worst, increased goodwill allocations will neither help nor harm buyers or sellers.

## Problem Materials

### DISCUSSION QUESTIONS

**9-1** *Requirements for Depreciation.* Indicate the basic requirements that must be satisfied before property may be depreciated.

**9-2** *Depreciation and Amortization: Eligible Property.* Indicate whether a taxpayer could claim deductions for depreciation or amortization of the following property:

**a.** Land used in the taxpayer's farming business.
**b.** A duplex—the taxpayer lives in one half while he rents the other half out.
**c.** The portion of the taxpayer's residence that she uses as a home office.
**d.** The taxpayer's former residence, which he listed for rental temporarily until he is able to sell it. The residence was listed in late November and was not rented as of the end of the taxable year.
**e.** A mobile home that the taxpayer initially purchased and used while he was in college and this year began renting to several students.
**f.** The costs attributable to goodwill and a covenant not to compete.
**g.** An automobile used for business. The taxpayer accounts for his deductible car expenses using the standard mileage rate.

**9-3** *Definitions: Cost Allocation Methods and Types of Property.* Explain the terms depreciation, amortization, and depletion. Include in your discussion an explanation of tangible and intangible property as well as personal and real property.

**9-4** *Depreciation Systems.* Briefly describe the depreciation systems (e.g., MACRS) for computing tax depreciation that one may encounter in practice.

**9-5** *Ineligible Property.* What types of property are not depreciated using MACRS? How can the taxpayer avoid MACRS?

**9-6** *Depreciation Methods and MACRS Statutory Percentages.*

**a.** Indicate the first-year depreciation percentage applicable to office furniture and show how it is determined.
**b.** Same as (a) except the property is an apartment building.

**9-7** *MACRS and Straight-Line Depreciation.* Assuming a taxpayer desires to use the straight-line method of depreciation, what alternatives, if any, are available?

**9-8** *Alternative Depreciation System.* Typically, all depreciation is computed using MACRS. However, Code § 168 also establishes an alternative depreciation system (ADS). As a practical matter, when will use of ADS be most likely?

**9-9** *Depreciating Recovery Property.* During the year, X purchased land and a building for a total of $500,000 and furniture for the building for $100,000. He intends to lease the building. Indicate whether the following factors are taken into account in computing the depreciation of these assets.

**a.** Each asset's useful life as estimated by the taxpayer in light of industry standards.
**b.** Salvage value.
**c.** The month in which the property was placed in service.
**d.** The use of the building by the lessee.
**e.** The taxpayer is a corporation.
**f.** The property is used for investment rather than business use.
**g.** The acquisition cost of the building including the land.
**h.** The lessee.

**9-10** *Half-Year Convention.* Indicate whether the following statements are true or false regarding the half-year convention.

**a.** Depreciation can be claimed for the *entire* year if the asset has been in service for more than six months.
**b.** The half-year convention applies to *all* property placed in service during the year.
**c.** The half-year convention applies *both* in the year of acquisition and the year of disposition of the asset.
**d.** The convention must be considered when expensing an asset under Code § 179.

**9-11** *Acquiring a Business.* L has worked as a salesperson in the outdoor advertising business for ten years. This year he decided to go into business for himself. To this end he purchased all of the assets of Billboards Unlimited Corporation for $2 million. The value of the tangible assets such as the office building, furniture, and equipment was $1.4 million. Explain how L will recover the cost of his investment.

**9-12** *Luxury Cars.* Indicate whether the following statements are true or false. If false, explain why.

**a.** W purchased a new car used solely for business for $12,000. The limitations imposed by Code § 280F on deductions related to automobiles do not alter what W could claim in the year of acquisition.

**b.** P Corporation is a distributor of hospital supplies. During the year, it purchased a $20,000 car for its best salesperson. Section 280F does not alter the total amount of depreciation deducted while P owns the car. Section 280F alters only the timing of the depreciation deductions.

**9-13** *Leasing and Luxury Automobiles.* D is a manufacturer's representative for several different companies. His sales territory covers all of Indiana, Kentucky and Ohio. Recently, he decided it was time to get rid of his old car, which had just passed the 100,000-mile mark. Many of his friends have told him that he should lease his next car rather than buy it. Assuming D plans on using the car exclusively for business, briefly discuss the tax factors that should be considered in making the decision.

**9-14** *Listed Property.* Indicate whether the following statements are true or false. If false, explain why.

**a.** J is a part-time photographer. This year she purchased a camera that cost $1,000 for her videocassette recorder. Thirty percent of her usage was for business while the remainder was personal. J may use the accelerated depreciation recovery percentages of MACRS.

**b.** P, a proprietor of a lighting store, purchased computer equipment for $10,000 which he uses 50 percent of the time for business. Under Code § 280F, the maximum deduction for depreciation and limited expensing in the first year is $500, while without § 280F the deduction would be $5,000.

**c.** C purchased computer equipment that he uses 60 percent of the time for managing his investments and 35 percent of the time in connection with a mail-order business he operates out of his home. C may claim straight-line depreciation deductions based on 95 percent of the cost of the asset.

**d.** G is employed as a research consultant for RND Corporation, a research institute. G uses the company's computer at the office but often takes home work, which she does on her home computer. G's use of her home computer for work done for her employer is considered qualified business use.

**e.** T is a college professor who uses a computer, for which he properly claims deductions, to write textbooks in his home office. It is unnecessary for T to maintain records on business usage of the computer.

**9-15** *Employer-Provided Automobiles.* WS Corporation, a large clothing manufacturer, provides a company car for each of its salespeople. Indicate whether the following statements are true or false. If false, explain why.

**a.** An employee must generally include the value of any personal use of the automobile as income; however, he or she is allowed to depreciate the car to the extent of any business use and to deduct any other business-related operating expenses.

**b.** This year B, an employee, used a new company-owned vehicle 55 percent of the time for personal purposes and 45 percent of the time for business. The corporation can only depreciate 45 percent of the car, and, since qualified business use is less than 50 percent, it cannot use limited expensing and must use straight-line depreciation.

**c.** This year C, an employee, used a company car, driving it 50,000 miles: 40,000 for business and 10,000 for personal purposes. Under the arrangement with C, the company includes $27,500 (50,000 × 55 cents) in C's W-2 as additional income. C may deduct any business expenses incurred related to operation of the car.

**d.** Assuming WS charges all of its employees the standard mileage rate for each mile of personal use, the corporation may ignore any personal use of the cars by its salespeople and depreciate 100 percent of the cost of the cars.

**e.** WS Corporation also provides a car for its chief executive officer, C, who owns 10 percent of the company's stock. All of C's use is for business except for commuting to work, which represents 60 percent of the car's use. C reimburses the company for the personal use. WS may claim accelerated depreciation for the car based on 40 percent of the car's cost.

**9-16** *Amortization.* How are the costs of patents, copyrights, and goodwill recovered?

**9-17** *Leasing Restrictions.* Address the following:

**a.** Construct a numerical example illustrating why a tax-exempt entity would rather lease than buy.

**b.** R acquired a ten-year ground lease on three acres on which it constructed a small office building. Explain how R will recover its cost of the building.

**9-18** *Depreciation—Allowed or Allowable.* R inherited her mother's personal residence in 1979 and converted it to rental property. Her basis for depreciation was $100,000. The residence had an estimated useful life of 30 years. This year, R sold the residence for $170,000. During the time R held the property, she never claimed a deduction for depreciation on the residence. What amount of gain will R report upon the sale?

**9-19** *Salvage Value.* How is salvage value used in computing the depreciation deduction using MACRS?

**9-20** *Depreciable Basis and Limited Expensing.* Explain how the taxpayer's depreciable basis may be affected by the amount expensed under the limited expensing election of § 179.

**9-21** *Anti-Churning Rules.* Explain the purpose of the anti-churning rules and when they normally will apply.

**9-22** *Component versus Composite Depreciation.* Answer the following:

**a.** Distinguish component depreciation from composite depreciation.

**b.** May the taxpayer use either method? Explain.

**9-23** *Mid-Quarter Convention.* T Company, a calendar year taxpayer, purchased $300,000 of equipment on December 3 of this year.

**a.** Under what circumstances will the mid-quarter convention apply in computing depreciation of the equipment?

**b.** Assume that T can purchase the equipment at any time during the year. How will T time the acquisitions if it wants to maximize the firm's depreciation deductions for the year?

**9-24** *Determining Recovery Periods: Special Considerations.* During the year, the WJ LLC opened a gas station that also had a convenience food store. The controller is trying to determine how these new items should be depreciated for tax purposes.

**a.** After reading *Iowa 80 Group and Subs v. U.S.* 95 AFTR 2d 2005-2367, 371 F. Supp. 2d 1036 (D.Ct. Southern District of Iowa, 2004), explain the alternatives that might be available and how the court ruled. For fun, see http://www.iowa80truckstop.com/tour1.htm

**b.** What happened in *Iowa 80* on appeal?

**c.** What can you conclude about using the standard procedures for determining depreciation outlined in this chapter?

**9-25** *Depletion.* Address the following:

**a.** Briefly describe how cost and percentage depletion are computed and determine which is used in a particular year.

**b.** Assuming the taxpayer has completely recovered her depletable cost basis (e.g., her basis is zero), is she entitled to further depletion deductions?

**9-26** *Farming Expenses.* N plans on stepping down from his position as president of a large energy company in five years. At that time, he and his wife would like to move to the country where they would retire and perhaps operate a small dairy farm. N has spotted some land through which a sparkling creek runs. His accountant has suggested that he purchase the land now and begin to operate it despite initial losses. Explain the rationale behind the accountant's advice.

## PROBLEMS

**9-27** *Depreciation of Converted Personal-Use Property.* F purchased a mobile home to live in while at college. The home cost $50,000. When he graduated, he left the home in the trailer park and rented it. At the time he converted the home to rental property, it had a fair market value of $15,000.

**a.** What is F's basis for depreciation?

**b.** F now lives 75 miles away from his alma mater. Can he deduct the cost of traveling back to check on his rental property (including those trips on which he also attended a football game)?

**9-28** *MACRS Accelerated Depreciation.* In 2011 T, a calendar year taxpayer, decided to move her insurance business into another office building. She purchased a used building for $700,000 (excluding the land) on March 15. T also purchased new office furniture for the building. The furniture was acquired for $200,000 on May 1. Compute MACRS depreciation. Ignore first-year expensing and bonus depreciation. MACRS depreciation tables are located in the Appendix.

**a.** Compute T's depreciation deduction for 2011.

**b.** Compute T's depreciation deduction for 2012.

**c.** Assuming that T sold the office building and the furniture on July 20, 2013, compute T's depreciation for 2013.

**d.** Answer (a), (b), and (c) above assuming that the furniture was purchased on October 20.

**9-29** *Mid-Quarter Convention.* Q Corporation anticipates purchasing $300,000 of office furniture and fixtures (seven-year property) next year. This will be Q's only personal property acquisition for the year. Q Corporation management is willing to purchase and place the property in service any time during the year to accelerate its depreciation deductions. In addition, management wants to depreciate the property as rapidly as possible. MACRS depreciation tables are located in the Appendix. Ignore limited expensing.

**a.** Compute depreciation for the first two years of ownership assuming *all* of the property is purchased and placed in service on February 2.

**b.** Compute depreciation for the first two years of ownership assuming *all* of the property is purchased and placed in service on December 6.

**c.** Compute depreciation for the first two years of ownership assuming $177,000 (59%) of the property is purchased and placed in service on February 2 and $123,000 (41%) is purchased and placed in service on December 6.

**d.** Based on the results of (a) through (c) above, what course of action do you recommend for Q Corporation?

**9-30** *MACRS Straight-Line Depreciation.* G Corporation operates a chain of fast-food restaurants. On February 7, 2011 the company purchased a new building for $1,000,000 (excluding the land). In addition, on May 5, 2011 G purchased a used stove for $5,000 and refrigeration equipment for $30,000 (both seven-year property). G does not elect to use the limited-expensing provision. The company does elect to compute depreciation using the straight-line method under MACRS. MACRS depreciation tables are located in Appendix. Ignore limited expensing and bonus depreciation.

**a.** Why might G elect to use the straight-line method?

**b.** Assuming G elects to use the straight-line method and a seven-year recovery period for depreciating the stove applies, can it use MACRS accelerated recovery percentages for the refrigeration equipment? For the building?

**c.** Compute G's depreciation for the stove and building in 2011 assuming it elects the straight-line method for the seven-year property.

**d.** Compute the depreciation for the stove and building in 2012.

**e.** If G does not dispose of either the stove or building, what is the final (i.e., last year's) depreciation deduction for the stove and the building?

**f.** Assuming G disposes of both the stove and the building on October 18, 2012, what is the depreciation for each of these assets in 2012?

**9-31** *ADS Depreciation.* P retired several years ago to live on a small farm. To supplement his income, he cuts wood and sells it in the nearby community. This year he purchased a used light duty truck to haul and deliver the wood. He used the truck 20 percent of the time for business. Assuming the truck cost $9,000, compute P's depreciation for the year.

**9-32** *Section 179 Election.* Although K is currently a systems analyst for 3L Corporation, her secret desire is to write a best-selling novel. To this end, she purchased a computer for $3,000 this year. She used the computer only for writing her novel. Can she deduct the entire cost of her computer this year even though she has not yet received any income from the novel? Next year?

**9-33** *Limitations on § 179 Expensing.* In each of the following situations, indicate whether T may elect to use the limited-expensing provisions of § 179. Assume the acquisition qualifies unless otherwise indicated.

**a.** T is a corporate taxpayer.

**b.** This year, T purchased a $600,000 building and $50,000 of equipment.

**c.** T suffered a net operating loss of $40,000 this year before consideration of the § 179 deduction.

**d.** T purchased the asset on the last day of the taxable year.

**9-34** *Limited-Expensing Election: Eligible Property.* For each of the following assets, indicate whether the taxpayer may elect to expense a portion or all of the asset's cost.

**a.** A $40,000 car used 75 percent of the time for business purposes and 25 percent of the time for personal purposes.

**b.** A home computer used by the taxpayer to maintain records and perform financial analyses with respect to her investments.

**c.** An apartment building owned by a large property company.

**d.** A roll-top desk purchased by the taxpayer's father, who gave it to the taxpayer to use in her business.

**9-35** *Limited-Expensing Election Calculations.* N, a single taxpayer, purchased copying equipment to use in his business. He purchased the equipment new on June 3 of the current year for $550,000. N elects to expense the maximum amount allowable with respect to the equipment.

**a.** What portion of the cost of the equipment may N expense for this year?

**b.** Compute N's depreciation deduction for the current year.

**c.** Answer parts (a) and (b) assuming that the cost of the equipment was $2,040,000.

**9-36** *Leasing Automobiles.* On May 27, 2011 J signed a three-year lease on a new Corvette with a list price of $40,000. His lease payments are $600 a month beginning on June 15. Assuming J is self-employed and uses the car exclusively for business, how does the lease affect his taxable income in 2011 and 2012?

**9-37** *Section 280F Calculations.* In the current year, H purchased a new automobile for $30,000. The first-year expensing election is not made. Use the most current limits from Exhibit 9-11 in responding to the questions below.

**a.** Assuming the car is used solely for business, prepare a depreciation schedule illustrating the amount of annual depreciation to which H is entitled assuming he holds the car until the entire cost is recovered.

**b.** Assume the same facts as (a) except the car is used 80 percent of the time for business and 20 percent of the time for personal purposes. Compute the current year's depreciation deduction.

**c.** Same as (b) except the car is used 70 percent of the time for business, 10 percent of the time for production of income activities, and 20 percent of the time for personal purposes.

**d.** Same as (a) except the car is used 40 percent of the time for business and 60 percent of the time for personal purposes.

**9-38** *SUV Limitations.* On March 7, 2011, C, an attorney, purchased an SUV for $40,000. The SUV had a gross vehicle weight exceeding 6,000 pounds. She expects to use the vehicle 80 percent of the time for business. C wishes to maximize her deductions related to the vehicle. Ignore bonus depreciation.

**a.** Compute C's depreciation and § 179 expense for 2011.

**b.** Same as (a) except the SUV cost $30,000.

**c.** Assume C plans to purchase a pickup truck rather than the SUV. She plans to buy a pickup truck that is available in three body styles (regular cab, extended cab and crew cab) and three bed lengths (5.5-foot, 6.5-foot and 8-foot). The truck has a gross vehicle weight exceeding 6,000 pounds. What tax advice may be appropriate, assuming C plans to use the truck like the SUV?

**d.** Would the answer to (a) change if the vehicle weighed more than 14,000 pounds? If so, how?

**9-39** *Section 280F Calculations.* M purchased a new automobile for $30,000. The first year expensing election is not made. The car is used solely for business. M is in the 25 percent tax bracket. The present value factors for a 10 percent discount rate are as follows: year 1, .91; 2, .83; 3, .75; 4, .68; 5, .62; 6, .56; 7, .51; 8, .47; 9, .42; 10, .39; 11, .35; 12, .32; 13, .29; 14, .26; 15, .24; 16, .22; 17, .20.

**a.** Prepare a depreciation schedule.

**b.** Compute the total tax savings M will receive throughout the recovery period from depreciation deductions.

**c.** Using an after-tax discount rate of 10 percent, compute the present value of tax savings from depreciation deductions under § 280F.

**d.** Using an after-tax discount rate of 10 percent, compute the present value of tax savings from depreciation deductions under MACRS as if § 280F were repealed.

**e.** Compare the results of (b) and (c) above. What impact does discounting have in assessing the tax benefits of depreciation?

**f.** Compare the results of (c) and (d) above. What is the discounted after-tax cost of the § 280F limitations for this taxpayer?

**9-40** *Research and Experimental Expenditures.* ABC Corporation is developing a new process to develop film. During the year, the company had the following expenditures related to research and development:

| | |
|---|---|
| Salaries | $60,000 |
| Laboratory equipment (5-year property) | 30,000 |
| Materials and supplies | 10,000 |

Compute ABC's deduction for research and experimental expenditures under each of the alternative methods.

**9-41** *Depletion.* DEF Company produces iron ore. It purchased a property for $100,000 during the year. Engineers estimate that 50,000 tons of iron ore are recoverable from the property. Given the following information, complete DEF's depletion deduction and undepleted cost basis for each year.

| Year | Units Sold (tons) | Gross Income | Taxable Income before Depletion |
|---|---|---|---|
| 1 | 15,000 | $300,000 | $124,000 |
| 2 | 20,000 | 400,000 | 50,000 |
| 3 | 10,000 | 250,000 | 90,000 |

**9-42** *Depletion.* Assume the same facts in *Problem 9-41* except that barrels of oil are being produced rather than tons of iron ore. Compute DEF's depletion deduction and undepleted cost basis for each year.

## CUMULATIVE PROBLEMS

**9-43** David and Lauren Hammack are married with one child, Jim, age 12. The couple lives at 2006 Rolling Drive, Indianapolis, IN 46222. David is a product manager for G&P Corporation, a food company. Lauren operates a clothing store as a sole proprietorship (employer identification number 35-1234567). The couple uses the cash method of accounting except where the accrual method is required. They report on the calendar year.

David earned a salary of $60,000 during the year. G&P also provides health insurance for David and his family. Of the total insurance premium, the company paid $750. Income taxes withheld from David's salary were $7,000. The couple paid $9,000 in estimated taxes in four equal installments during the year. Last year's tax liability was $5,000.

Lauren's father died on June 20. As a result, Lauren received $40,000 as beneficiary of a life insurance policy on her father. In addition, her father's will provided that she receive all of his shares of IBM stock. The stock was distributed to her in October when it was worth $30,000.

On August 1 of this year, the couple purchased a six-month Treasury Bill for $9,700. They redeemed it on February 1 of the following year for its face value, $10,000. In addition, the couple purchased a previously issued AT&T bond with the face value of $1,000 for $890 on June 1. The bond pays interest at 6 percent per year on January 1 and July 1. On July 1 they received an interest payment of $30, which was also reported on Form 1099-INT, sent to them shortly after year-end. The couple plans on reporting any accrued market discount in taxable income when they sell or redeem the bond, in some future year.

Each year, Lauren travels to Paris to attend the annual fashion shows for buyers. When scheduling her trip for this year, Lauren decided to combine business with pleasure. On Thursday, March 6, Lauren departed for Paris, arriving on Friday morning. Friday afternoon was devoted to business discussions with several suppliers. Since the shows began on Monday, she spent the weekend touring Paris. After attending the shows Monday through Wednesday, she returned to Indianapolis on Thursday, arriving late that night. The cost of her round-trip air fare to Paris was $500. Meals were $30 per day and lodging was $100 per day for Friday through the following Wednesday.

In addition to running her own shop, Lauren teaches an M.B.A. course in retailing at the local university. She received a $5,400 salary for her efforts this year. The university withheld $429 in FICA taxes, but did not make additional tax withholdings related to the salary. The school is ten miles from her office. Normally, she goes home from her office to get dinner before she goes to the school to teach (16 miles from her home). According to her log, she made 80 trips from home to school. In addition, the log showed that she had driven 20,000 miles related to her clothing business. She uses the standard mileage rate to compute her automobile expenses.

Lauren's records, which she maintains for her business using the cash method of accounting, reveal the following additional information:

| | |
|---|---|
| Sales | $120,000 |
| Cost of goods sold | (50,000) |
| Gross profit | $ 70,000 |
| Advertising | 6,000 |
| Insurance | 1,400 |
| Rent | 9,000 |
| Wages | 15,000 |
| Employment taxes | 2,000 |

The insurance included (1) a $200 premium paid in September for coverage of her car from October through March of the following year; and (2) a $1,200 payment for fire insurance for June 1 through May 31 of the following year. Similarly, rent expense includes a $4,500 payment made on November 1 for rent from November through April. She has a five-year lease requiring semiannual rental payments of $4,500 on November 1 and May 1.

During the year, David purchased a new automobile for $30,000, which he uses 60 percent of the time for business (i.e., "qualified business usage" is 60 percent). His actual operating expenses, excluding depreciation, were $3,000.

In addition to the information provided earlier in this problem, the couple paid the following amounts during the year:

| | |
|---|---|
| State income taxes | $5,500 |
| County income taxes | 500 |
| Real estate taxes | 2,400 |
| Mortgage interest on their home | 3,600 |
| Charitable contributions | 2,000 |

David and Lauren's social security numbers are 445-54-5565 and 333-44-5789, respectively. Their son Jim's social security number is 464-57-4681.

Compute David and Lauren's tax liability for the year. Make all computations (including any special elections required) to minimize the Hammacks' tax liability based on current tax law. If a tax return is to be prepared for this problem, complete the following forms: 1040 (including Schedules A, C, and SE), and 2106. There is no alternative minimum tax liability. (Note: If the § 280F limitations apply to any auto depreciation, you should use the most current numbers from Exhibit 9-11.)

**9-44** Michelle Kay purchased a small building on February 1 of the current year for $650,000. In addition, she paid $15,000 for land. Ms. Kay obtained a $640,000 mortgage for the acquisition. She and five of her employees use the property solely to store and sell a variety of gift items under the business name of "Michelle's Gifts." The following information pertains to the business:

| | |
|---|---|
| Sales | $950,000 |
| Cost of goods sold | 625,000 |
| Wages for employees ($20,000 each) | 100,000 |
| Payroll taxes for five employees | ? |
| Depreciation | ? |
| Advertising | 25,000 |
| Mortgage interest | 60,000 |
| Legal services | 20,000 |
| Real estate taxes | 4,000 |
| Fire insurance | 3,000 |
| Meals and entertainment | 2,500 |

During the year, Ms. Kay purchased the following assets for the business. She wants to depreciate all business assets as rapidly as the law allows.

| | *Cost* | *Month/Day of Acquisition* |
|---|---|---|
| Personal computer | $14,000 | March 31 |
| Printer for computer | 2,000 | April 2 |
| Office furniture and fixtures | 20,000 | April 29 |
| Machinery (7-year property) | 30,000 | May 12 |

Michelle Kay was divorced from Benjamin Kay two years ago. The divorce decree stipulates that Benjamin Kay would receive the dependency exemption for their son, Eric (now 12 years old), even though Eric lives full-time with Ms. Kay in a home she maintains. During the year, Ms. Kay provided 25 percent of Eric's support and Mr. Kay provided 75 percent. Ms. Kay received $15,000 of alimony and $10,000 of child support from Mr. Kay during the year. Ms. Kay's social security number is 333-46-2974. Her address is 567 North Hollow Drive, Grimview, IL 48124. For business purposes, her employer ID number is 66-2869969. She uses the cash method of accounting for all purposes.

Unrelated to her business, Ms. Kay paid the following amounts during the year:

| | |
|---|---|
| Estimated federal income taxes | $16,000 |
| State income taxes | 3,500 |
| County income taxes | 1,500 |
| Real estate taxes | 2,000 |
| Mortgage interest on her home | 5,600 |
| Charitable contributions | 2,900 |
| Deductible contribution to individual retirement account (Note: This is a deduction for A.G.I. It is one of the "adjustments to income" on page 1 of Form 1040.) | 2,000 |
| Health insurance for Ms. Kay | 1,000 |

Compute Ms. Kay's tax liability for the year based on current tax law. (Hint: Ms. Kay's adjusted gross income is less than $100,000.) If a tax return is to be prepared for this problem, complete the following forms: 1040 (including Schedules A, C, and SE) and 4562. There is no alternative minimum tax liability. For grading purposes, attach a sheet to Schedule C showing supporting calculations for payroll taxes.

## TAX RESEARCH PROBLEMS

**9-45** *Depreciation.* S is a land developer. During the year, he finished construction of a complex containing a new shopping mall and office building. To enhance the environment of the complex, substantial landscaping was done including the planting of many trees, shrubs, and gardens. In addition, S acquired a massive sculpture that served as the focal point of the complex. S also purchased numerous pictures, which were hung in the shopping center and office building. Can S claim depreciation deductions for any of the items noted above?

**9-46** *Amortization.* During the year, the metropolis of Burnsberg accepted bids from various cable television companies for the right to provide service within its city limits. The accepted bid was submitted by Cabletech Inc. in the amount of $500,000. For this amount, the city granted the company a license to operate for 10 years. The terms of the agreement further provided that the company's license would be renewed if the city was satisfied with the services provided. May Cabletech amortize the cost of the license?

# 10

# Certain Business Deductions and Losses

## Learning Objectives

Upon completion of this chapter you will be able to:

- LO.1 Determine when a deduction is allowed for a bad debt.
- LO.2 Understand the different tax treatment for business and nonbusiness bad debts.
- LO.3 Explain what constitutes a deductible casualty or theft loss.
- LO.4 Compute the amount of the deduction for casualty and theft losses.
- LO.5 Determine the net operating loss deduction and explain how it is treated.
- LO.6 Explain the basic tax accounting requirements for inventories.
- LO.7 Identify the costs that must be capitalized as part of inventory and the role of the uniform capitalization rules in making this determination.
- LO.8 Explain how inventory costs are assigned to costs of goods sold using the FIFO and LIFO assumptions.
- LO.9 Explain the special deduction related to domestic production activities.

## Chapter Outline


Introduction 10-2
Bad Debts 10-2
    Treatment of Business Versus Nonbusiness Bad Debts 10-2
    General Requirements 10-4
    Deduction Methods 10-5
Casualty and Theft Losses 10-7
    General Rules 10-7
    Casualty and Theft Defined 10-8
    Loss Computation 10-8
    Casualty Gains and Losses 10-10
    Year Deductible 10-11
Net Operating Losses 10-13
    Carryback and Carryforward Years 10-14
    Net Operating Loss Computation 10-15
    Recomputing Taxable Income for Year to Which Net Operating Loss is Carried 10-18
Inventories 10-19
    Exceptions to the Inventory Requirement 10-20
    Inventory Accounting in General 10-22
    Costs to be Inventoried 10-22
    Allocating Inventoriable Costs 10-25
    Dollar Value LIFO 10-26
    The LIFO Election 10-29
    Lower of Cost or Market 10-29
    Qualified Production Activities Deduction 10-30
Tax Planning Considerations 10-36
    Casualty and Theft Losses 10-36
    Bad Debts 10-37
    Net Operating Losses 10-37
Problem Materials 10-37

## Introduction

The rules governing the treatment of expenses and losses discussed in Chapter 7 set forth the general requirements that must be met if the taxpayer wishes to claim a deduction. As already seen, the basic test—whether the item was incurred in carrying on business or profit-seeking activities—is often just the initial hurdle in obtaining a deduction. Other provisions in the Code may impose additional conditions or limitations that must be considered. This chapter examines some of the special rules that relate to certain business losses and expenses of the taxpayer, including the provisions for bad debts, casualty losses, the net operating loss deduction, and inventories.

## Bad Debts

**LO.1**
Determine when a deduction is allowed for a bad debt.

Loans are made for a variety of reasons. Some are made in connection with the taxpayer's trade or business while others are made for purely personal purposes. People also make loans hoping to make a profit. Regardless of the motive, with the extension of credit comes the possibility—as every lender knows—that the loan will never be repaid. When the borrower, in fact, cannot repay the loan, the taxpayer has what is termed a *bad debt* and may be entitled to a deduction. For tax purposes, a bad debt is considered a special form of loss subject to the specific rules of Code § 166. This provision governs the treatment of all types of bad debts: those that arise from the sale of goods or services such as accounts receivable, as well as those resulting from a direct loan of money. Moreover, § 166 applies regardless of the form of the debt (e.g., a secured or unsecured note receivable or a mere oral promise to repay).[1]

### Treatment of Business Versus Nonbusiness Bad Debts

The tax treatment of a bad debt vastly differs depending on whether it is a *business* or *nonbusiness* bad debt. Business bad debts generally may be deducted without limitation. In contrast, nonbusiness bad debts are deductible only as *short-term* capital losses and are therefore subject to the limitation on deductions of capital losses (i.e., to the extent of capital gains plus $3,000).[2] Congress provided this distinctive treatment for nonbusiness bad debts in part to ensure that investments cast in the form of loans are handled in virtually the same manner as other investments that become worthless. As a general rule, an investment in a company's stock or bonds that becomes worthless also receives capital loss treatment.

Another difference between business and nonbusiness bad debts concerns the method allowed to claim a deduction. For some debts, it may be apparent that a portion of the loan will become uncollectible but determination of the exact amount must await final settlement. In the case of a nonbusiness bad debt, there is no deduction for partial worthlessness.[3] A deduction is postponed until the ultimate status of the debt is determined.

**Example 1**

R loaned his neighbor $5,000 in 2010. During 2011 his neighbor declared bankruptcy, and it is estimated that R will recover no more than 20 cents on the dollar or a maximum of $1,000 from the debt. Although R can establish that he has a bad debt of at least $4,000 ($5,000 – $1,000), no deduction is permitted in 2011 since the debt is nonbusiness, and it is partially worthless. If in 2012 R settles for $500, he will realize a

[1] Notes issued by a corporation (with interest coupons or in registered form) that are considered capital assets in the hands of the taxpayer are treated as worthless securities, as discussed in Chapter 12.

[2] § 166(d)(1)(B). See Chapter 16 for a detailed discussion of capital gains and losses.

[3] Reg. § 1.166-5(a)(2).

loss of $4,500. Assuming he has no capital gains or other capital losses, he may deduct $3,000 of this loss as a *short-term* capital loss and carry over the remaining $1,500 ($5,000 – $3,000 – $500) to the following year. On the other hand, if the debt had arisen from R's *business*, R could deduct $4,000 in 2011 based on his estimate of the uncollectible amount, and the $500 remainder of the loss in 2012, all against ordinary income.

Because of their significantly different treatments, the determination of whether a particular debt is a business or nonbusiness bad debt has produced substantial controversy.

## Business Bad Debts

**LO.2**
Understand the different tax treatment for business and nonbusiness bad debts.

Business bad debts are defined as those that arise in connection with the taxpayer's trade or business.[4] To qualify, the loan must be closely related to the taxpayer's business activity. Simply making a loan to a business associate does not make the loan business-related; it must support the business activity. Common business bad debts include the following:

1. Uncollectible accounts receivable (for accrual basis taxpayers only)
2. Loans to suppliers to ensure a reliable source of materials
3. Loans to customers, clients, and others to preserve business relationships or nurture goodwill
4. Loans to protect business reputation
5. Loans or advances to employees
6. Loans by employees to protect their employment
7. Loans made by taxpayers in the business of making loans

It is important to note that C corporations are not subject to the nonbusiness bad debt rules.[5] All loans made by a C corporation are deemed to be related to its trade or business. Thus, any bad debt of a corporation is considered to be a *business* bad debt.

## Nonbusiness Bad Debts

A nonbusiness bad debt is defined as any debt other than one acquired in connection with the taxpayer's trade or business.[6] From a practical perspective, nonbusiness bad debts are simply those that do not qualify as business bad debts.

The most common nonbusiness bad debts are losses on personal loans, such as those made to friends or relatives. As suggested above, however, nonbusiness bad debt treatment also extends to loans that are made to make a profit and that essentially function as investments. For example, a loan to an acquaintance to start a new business is in effect an investment and thus a nonbusiness debt. Similarly, a loan to a business to protect an investment in such enterprise would be considered a nonbusiness debt. For instance, an investor may loan funds to a struggling corporation in which he owns stock, hoping that the infusion of cash might sustain it and save the original investment.

Although the dividing line between business and nonbusiness bad debts usually is clear, controversy typically arises in several common situations. One troublesome area involves taxpayers who frequently make loans to make a profit but who do not make such loans their full-time occupation. In such cases, the Service takes the view that the taxpayers are not in the business of making loans and thus any bad debts are not business bad debts. These situations can become even more difficult when the taxpayer devotes substantial time and energy to establishing and developing the business.

[4] § 166(d)(2).

[5] § 166(d)(1).

[6] § 166(d)(2).

## Example 2

In *Whipple v. Comm.*, Whipple had made sizable cash advances to the Mission Orange Bottling Co., one of several enterprises that he owned.[7] He spent considerable effort related to these enterprises but received no type of compensation, either salary, interest, or rent. When these advances subsequently became worthless, Whipple deducted them as a business bad debt. The Supreme Court held that the loans made by the shareholder to his closely held corporation were nonbusiness bad debts even though Whipple had worked for the company. According to the Court:

> Devoting one's time and energies to the affairs of a corporation is not of itself, and without more, a trade or business of the person so engaged. Though such activities may produce income, profit or gain in the form of dividends—this return is distinctive to the process of investing—as distinguished from the trade or business of the taxpayer himself. When the only return is that of an investor, the taxpayer has not satisfied his burden of demonstrating that he is engaged in a trade or business.

Despite the Court's holding in *Whipple*, taxpayers have achieved limited success where they have shown that they were in the business of organizing, promoting, and financing businesses.

The other prominent area of controversy concerns a situation common to many new struggling corporations: loans made to corporations by employees who are also shareholders. Here, the issues are similar to that above. Is the taxpayer making the loan to protect an investment or to protect his or her job (i.e., the business of being an employee)? When employee-shareholders have been able to show that a loan was made to protect their jobs rather than their investment, they have been able to secure business bad debt treatment.

Although the deduction is normally unlimited, in the case of an employee, the loss is considered an employee business expense and therefore treated as a miscellaneous itemized deduction subject to the 2% floor.[8]

## General Requirements

To be deductible, the debt must not only be partially or totally worthless but must also represent a bona fide debt and have a basis.[9]

### Bona Fide Debt

A debt is considered bona fide if it arises from a true debtor-creditor relationship. For this relationship to exist, there must be a promise to repay a fixed and determinable sum, and the obligation must be enforceable under local law.

The question of whether there is valid debtor-creditor relationship usually arises when it appears that the taxpayer made the loan with little expectation of being repaid. This is typically the case when there is a close relationship between the taxpayer and the borrower. For example, loans to relatives or friends are likely to be viewed as nondeductible gifts rather than genuine debts. Such treatment is most likely where the lender makes little attempt to enforce repayment of the loan—a common occurrence when the borrower is a child or parent. In a similar fashion, advances to a closely held corporation that are not repaid may be considered nondeductible contributions to capital. On the other hand, loans made by a corporation may be something other than what they purport to be. For example, a loan to a shareholder may be treated as a disguised dividend distribution while a loan to an employee could be considered compensation.

---

[7] 63-1 USTC ¶9466,11 AFTR2d 1454, 373 U.S.193 (USSC, 1963).

[8] *Graves v. Comm.*, 2007-1 USTC ¶50,252, 99 AFTR 2d 2007-950, 220 Fed. Appx. 601 (CA-9, 2007). Note that miscellaneous itemized deductions are not deductible for purposes of the alternative minimum tax in which case the taxpayer may not benefit from the deduction.

[9] Reg. §§ 1.166-1(c) and (e).

To determine whether a bona fide debtor-creditor relationship exists requires an assessment of all of the facts and circumstances related to the debt. Besides the relationship of the parties, factors typically considered are (1) whether the debt is evidenced by a note or some other written instrument (in contrast to a mere oral promise to repay that has not been reduced to writing); (2) whether the debt is secured by collateral; (3) whether the debt bears a reasonable interest rate; and (4) whether a fixed schedule for repayment has been established.

### Basis

A taxpayer may deduct a loss from a bad debt only if he or she has a basis in the debt.[10] For this reason, cash basis taxpayers who normally do not report income until it is received are not entitled to deductions for payments they cannot collect. Their loss is represented by the unrecovered expenses incurred in providing the goods or services. Conversely, accrual basis taxpayers who engage in credit transactions usually report income as it is earned. Accordingly, they may deduct bad debts for those amounts previously included in income. Uncollectible loans (as distinguished from accounts receivable) made by either cash or accrual basis taxpayers may be deducted, assuming the taxpayer has a basis for the loan.

**Example 3**

R is an orthodontist and uses the cash method of accounting. This year he completed some dental work for B for $3,000, which he never collected. In addition, he loaned $1,000 to a material supplier who left the country. Assuming both debts are worthless, R may deduct only the loan to the supplier for $1,000. No deduction is allowed for the uncollected $3,000 since R does not report the amount as income until he collects it and, therefore, has no basis in the debt. However, any expenses incurred in doing the dental work (i.e., materials. etc.) are deductible.

### Worthlessness

Whether a debt is worthless ultimately depends on the facts. The Regulations indicate that a taxpayer does not have to undertake legal action to enforce payment or obtain an uncollectible judgment with respect to the debt to prove its worthlessness.[11] It is sufficient that the surrounding circumstances suggest that legal action would not result in recovery. Among the circumstances indicating a debt's worthlessness are the debtor's bankruptcy or precarious financial position, consistent failure to pay when requested, or poor health or death. As noted above, a *business* bad debt need not be totally worthless before a deduction is allowed. When events occur which suggest that the debt will not be recoverable in full, a deduction for partial worthlessness is granted.

## Deduction Methods

As a general rule, deductions for bad debts must be claimed using the specific charge-off method.[12] This method—often called the direct write-off method—allows a deduction only in the year when the debt actually becomes worthless. The reserve method, which allows deductions for estimated bad debts and is typically used for financial accounting purposes, was repealed for all businesses except certain financial institutions and service businesses by the Tax Reform Act of 1986.

The direct write-off method provides some flexibility in accounting for business bad debts. When the facts indicate that a specific debt is *partially* worthless, the portion considered uncollectible may be deducted, but only if such portion is actually written off the taxpayer's books for financial accounting purposes.[13] Any remaining portion of the debt that later becomes worthless can be deducted in subsequent years. Using this approach, taxpayers need not wait until the debt becomes totally worthless before any deduction is claimed. Alternatively, taxpayers can wait until the debt becomes totally worthless and claim the entire

[10] Reg. §§ 1.166-1(d) and (e).

[11] Reg. §§ 1.166-2(a) and (b).

[12] § 166(a).

[13] Reg. § 1.166-3(a).

deduction at that time. Note that when the debt is totally worthless (in contrast to partially worthless), there is no requirement that the debt actually be written off the taxpayer's books.

**Example 4**

K Company is a major supplier of lumber to homebuilders. One of its customers, which owed the company $10,000, fell on hard times in 2011 and declared bankruptcy. Because this event suggests that the debt is partially worthless, a deduction is permitted. K estimated that it would recover $7,000 of the debt, and therefore claimed a $3,000 bad debt deduction in 2011. The $3,000 amount was also charged off the taxpayer's books as required. In 2013 K Company actually received $1,000 and deducted the remainder of the loss, $6,000 ($10,000 – $3,000 previously deducted – $1,000 actually received). Alternatively, K may opt to claim no deduction for 2011 and deduct the entire $9,000 loss in 2013. Note that when the debt becomes totally worthless in either case, the taxpayer is not required to write the debt off its books for financial accounting purposes. The company should take heed, however. If the IRS later determines that the debt is partially worthless, no deduction would be allowed since the debt was not written off on the books.

### Experience Method for Service Businesses

Although the 1986 Act ostensibly eliminated the reserve method of accounting for bad debts, it provided an equivalent—but not identical—technique for service businesses. If a business uses the *accrual method* to account for income from services, the business is not required to accrue any amount that, *based on experience*, it knows will not be collected.[14] Businesses can take advantage of this exception only if they do not charge interest or a late charge on the amount billed. The experience method is available only for businesses that (1) have average annual gross receipts of less than $5,000,000 or (2) perform services in the following eight areas: health, law, engineering, architecture, accounting, actuarial science, performing arts, or consulting.

As a practical matter, the actual use of this technique may be limited, since most service businesses are allowed and often do use the cash method rather than the accrual method of accounting. Service businesses usually are exempt from the rule requiring use of the accrual method,[15] falling under the exceptions for sole proprietorships, S corporations, qualifying partnerships, personal service corporations, or taxpayers with gross receipts that generally do not exceed $5 million.

✓ CHECK YOUR KNOWLEDGE

### Review Question I

Over the years Dr. D has done extremely well financially and has made a number of investments. Several years ago, her good friend T started a small amusement park with such attractions as a water slide and a miniature golf course. Needing some venture capital, T convinced D to lend the new business $50,000, which he would repay to D in three years with 15 percent interest. This year the note came due and T was unable to repay because his business had failed. How will D treat the bad debt?

D's loan did not arise during the ordinary course of business but rather was in the nature of an investment. Therefore, the debt is considered a nonbusiness bad debt and is deductible as a short-term capital loss (limited annually to $3,000 plus capital gains).

[14] § 448(d)(5).

[15] Subject to certain exceptions, § 448 requires corporations, partnerships with corporate partners, or tax shelters to use the accrual method of accounting.

### Review Question 2

T worked for P Corporation for 25 years. When the company began struggling this year, she worked without pay. The company finally went out of business this year, owing T six months of back pay. Does T have a business or nonbusiness bad debt?

*Neither.* Although most taxpayers would believe that they have a deductible loss, such is not the case. As a cash basis taxpayer, which T no doubt is, no deduction is allowed because she has no basis in her debt. Had she reported the income (i.e., had she been on the accrual basis), the IRS would be happy to allow a bad debt deduction.

### Review Question 3

At the close of current year, Z Corporation, a lumber company, estimated that based on current year sales about $30,000 of its accounts receivable would be uncollectible. Therefore, in accordance with generally accepted accounting principles, the company adjusted its reserve account, charging bad debt expense for $22,000. May Z claim a $22,000 bad debt deduction for tax purposes?

For most businesses, the reserve method is not permitted for tax purposes. Since 1986 the law has generally required the use of the direct write-off method. Under this method, a taxpayer can claim a deduction for a bad debt only when the debt actually becomes totally or partially worthless. This requirement is relaxed for service businesses that are allowed to use a method based on their experience. Consequently, since Z is not a service business, it is not allowed to deduct $22,000 but only the amount that represents debts that are actually worthless.

# Casualty and Theft Losses

## General Rules

Unfortunately, as everyone knows, disaster may strike at any moment. Hurricanes hit, volcanoes erupt, and rivers overflow. Thieves steal, and people are mugged. The list of possible calamities is endless. Luckily, Congress has recognized that when such events occur they may seriously impair a taxpayer's ability to pay taxes. For this reason, taxpayers are generally allowed to deduct losses arising from casualty or theft. The special rules governing this deduction are the subject of this section.

The Code generally provides that an individual's losses arising from casualty or theft are deductible regardless of the activity in which the losses are incurred. An individual's casualty and theft losses related to profit-seeking activities may be deducted under the general rules, which provide that losses incurred in a trade or business or a transaction entered into for profit are deductible.[16] In addition, § 165(c)(3) expressly allows a deduction for losses related to property used for *personal* purposes where the loss arises from fire, storm, shipwreck, theft, or other casualty.

A deduction is allowed only for casualty losses related to property owned by the taxpayer; no deduction is allowed for damages the taxpayer may be required to pay for inflicting harm upon the person or property of another.[17] Further, the casualty must damage the property itself. A casualty that indirectly reduces the resale value of the property normally does not create a deductible loss (e.g., a mud slide near the taxpayer's residence).[18] Any expenses of cleanup, or similar expenses such as repairs to return the damaged property to its condition prior to the casualty, are usually deductible as part of the casualty loss. Incidental expenses that arise from the casualty, such as the cost of temporary housing or a rental car, are considered personal expenses and are not deductible as part of the casualty loss.

---

[16] §§ 162 and 212.

[17] *Robert M. Miller*, 34 TCM 528, T.C. Memo 1975-110.

[18] *Pulvers v. Comm.*, 48 T.C. 245, aff'd. in 69-1 USTC ¶9272, 23 AFTR2d 69-678, 407 F.2d 838 (CA-9, 1969).

## Casualty and Theft Defined

### Casualties

**LO.3**
Explain what constitutes a deductible casualty or theft loss.

The Code permits a deduction for losses arising not only from fire, storm, or shipwreck, but also from other casualties. While the terms *fire*, *storm*, and *shipwreck* are easily construed and applied, such is not the case with the phrase "other casualty." Interpretation and application of this phrase is a continuing subject of conflict. The courts and the IRS generally have agreed that to qualify as a casualty the loss must result from some *sudden, unexpected, or unusual event, caused by some external force.*[19] Losses deductible under these criteria include those resulting from earthquakes, floods, hurricanes, cave-ins, sonic booms, and similar natural causes.[20] On the other hand, losses resulting from ordinary accidents or normal everyday occurrences (e.g., breakage due to dropping) are not considered unusual and consequently are not deductible.[21] Similarly, no deduction is allowed for losses due to a gradual process, since such losses are not sudden and unexpected.[22] For this reason, losses suffered because of rust, corrosion, erosion, disease, insect infestation, or similar types of *progressive deterioration*, generally are not deductible. Unfortunately, the casualty criteria are vague, and the taxpayer may be forced to litigate to determine if his or her loss is sufficiently sudden or unusual to qualify. For example, the IRS has ruled that termite damage does not occur with the requisite swiftness to be deductible.[23] The courts, however, have found the necessary suddenness to be present in several termite cases and have allowed a deduction for the resulting losses.[24]

### Thefts

Losses of business or personal property due to theft are deductible. The term *theft* includes, but is not limited to, larceny, embezzlement, and robbery.[25] If money or property is taken as the result of kidnapping, blackmail, threats, or extortion, it also may be a theft. Seizure or confiscation of property by a foreign government does not constitute a casualty or theft loss but may be deductible if incurred in profit-seeking activities.[26] Losing or misplacing items is not considered a theft but may qualify as a casualty if it results from some sudden, unexpected, or unusual event.[27]

**Example 5**

H slammed a car door on his wife's hand, dislodging the diamond from her ring, never to be found. The Tax Court held that the loss was deductible as an "other" casualty.[28]

## Loss Computation

The loss computation is the same whether the casualty or theft relates to property connected with profit-seeking activities or personal use.[29] As explained below, however, limitations on the amount of deductible loss may differ depending on the property's use.

**LO.4**
Compute the amount of the deduction for casualty and theft losses.

The *amount* of the loss is the difference between the fair market value immediately before the casualty and the fair market value immediately after the casualty as reduced by any insurance reimbursement. Of course, when the property is completely destroyed or stolen, the loss is simply the fair market value of the property as reduced by any insurance reimbursement. Although appraisals are the preferred method of establishing fair market values, costs of repairs to restore the property to its condition immediately before the casualty may be sufficient under certain circumstances.[30]

For many years, a controversy existed concerning the deductibility of insured casualty losses for which taxpayers chose not to file a claim. The problem typically arises when

---

19 *Matheson v. Comm.*, 2 USTC ¶830,10 AFTR 945, 54 F.2d 537 (CA-2, 1931).

20 *Your Federal Income Tax*, IRS Publication 17 (Rev. Nov. 96), p. 190.

21 *Diggs v. Comm.*, 60-2 USTC ¶9584, 6 AFTR2d 5095, 281 F.2d 326 (CA-2, 1960).

22 *Supra*, Footnote 18.

23 Rev. Rul. 63-232, 1963-2 C.B. 97.

24 *Rosenberg v. Comm.*, 52-2 USTC ¶9377, 42 AFTR 303, 198 F.2d 46 (CA-8, 1952).

25 Reg. § 1.165-8(d).

26 *W.J. Powers*, 36 T.C. 1191 (1961).

27 Rev. Rul. 72-592, 1972-2 C.B. 101.

28 *John P. White*, 48 T.C. 430 (1967).

29 Reg. § 1.165-7(a).

30 Reg. § 1.165-7(a)(2)(ii).

taxpayers avoid filing a claim for fear that their insurance coverage may be cancelled or its cost may increase. When this occurs, the Treasury is effectively acting as an insurance company, partially subsidizing the taxpayer's loss. In 1986 Congress eliminated the controversy for *nonbusiness* property by providing that no deduction is permitted for casualty losses of insured property unless a timely insurance claim is filed.[31]

The amount of the deductible loss generally is limited to the lesser of the property's adjusted basis or fair market value (decline in value if a partial casualty).[32] The lesser of these two amounts is then reduced by any insurance reimbursements. There are two exceptions to this general rule, however. First, for property used in a trade or business or for the production of income that is *completely* destroyed or stolen, the deductible loss is the property's adjusted basis reduced by insurance reimbursements. Second, losses to property *used for personal* purposes are deductible only to the extent they exceed a $100 floor. The $100 floor does not apply to property used in a trade or business or for the production of income. The $100 floor applies to each event, not each item. Further, if spouses file a joint return, they are subject to a single $100 floor. If spouses file separately, each one is subject to a $100 floor for each casualty.[33]

In 1982, Congress added a further limitation on the deduction for casualty or theft losses of property used for personal purposes. In addition to the $100 floor on personal losses, only total losses (after reduction by the $100 floor) in excess of 10 percent of adjusted gross income are deductible.[34] This limitation does not apply to property used in a trade or business or an income-producing activity. The computation of the casualty and theft loss deduction is summarized in Exhibit 10-1.

**EXHIBIT 10.1** **Computation of Casualty and Theft Loss Deduction**

Smaller of

1. Decline in value; or
2. Adjusted basis*

Less:

- Insurance reimbursement
- $100 floor/casualty if personal
- 10% of A.G.I. if personal

Equals: Deductible casualty loss

*Adjusted basis, not decline in value, is used used if business or income property is completely destroyed or stolen.

## Example 6

R had four casualties during the year:

| Casualty | Property | Adjusted Basis | Fair Market Value Before Casualty | Fair Market Value After Casualty |
|---|---|---|---|---|
| 1. Accident | Business car | $ 3,000 | $ 9,000 | $ 5,000 |
| 2. Robbery | Ring | 500 | 800 | 0 |
| | Suit | 95 | 75 | 0 |
| 3. Tornado | Residence | 50,000 | 60,000 | 57,000 |
| 4. Fire | Business computer | 3,000 | 4,000 | 0 |

[31] § 165(h)(4)(E).

[32] Reg. § 1.165-7(b)(i).

[33] Reg. § 1.165-7(b)(4)(iii).

[34] § 165(h)(2). The 10 percent floor is waived for losses in federally declared disasters (§ 165(h)(3)).

R received a $600 insurance reimbursement for his loss on the residence. The deductible loss for each casualty is as follows:

1. The loss for the business car is $3,000 [lesser of the decline in value $4,000 ($9,000 – $5,000) or the adjusted basis of $3,000]. The deduction is *for* A.G.I. unless it is related to R's business as an employee, in which case the deduction would be an itemized deduction.
2. The loss for the ring and suit is $475. The loss for the ring is $500 [lesser of decline in value of $800 ($800 – $0) or the adjusted basis of $500]. The loss for the suit is $75 [lesser of decline in value of $75 ($75 – $0) or the adjusted basis of $95]. The total loss attributable to the robbery is $575 ($500 + $75). This loss must be reduced by the $100 floor to $475 ($575 – $100). Note that the $100 floor is applied to the event, not to each item of loss. The loss, subject to the ten percent overall limitation, is deductible *from* A.G.I.
3. The loss on the residence is $2,300 [lesser of decline in value of $3,000 ($60,000 – $57,000) or the adjusted basis of $50,000, reduced by the insurance reimbursement of $600 and the $100 floor]. The loss, subject to the ten percent overall limitation, is deductible *from* A.G.I. Assuming R's A.G.I. is $20,000, $775 is deductible [$2,300 + $475 – $2,000 (10% × $20,000)].
4. The loss for the computer is $3,000. Since the computer is used for business and is completely destroyed, the loss is the adjusted basis of the property regardless of its fair market value. The loss is deductible *for* A.G.I.

## Casualty Gains and Losses

When the claims for some casualties are settled, the insurance reimbursement may exceed the taxpayer's adjusted basis for the property resulting in a gain. As discussed in Chapter 15, the Code provides some relief in this case, permitting the taxpayer to postpone recognition of the gain if the insurance proceeds are reinvested in similar property. When the gain must be recognized, however, Code § 165(h) sets forth special treatment.

Under § 165(h), all gains and losses arising from a casualty unrelated to business or a transaction entered into for profit—*personal casualty gains and losses*—must first be netted. For this purpose, the personal casualty loss is computed after the $100 floor but before the 10 percent limitation. If personal casualty gains exceed personal casualty losses, each gain and each loss is treated as a gain or loss from the sale or exchange of a capital asset. The capital gain or loss would be long-term or short-term depending on the holding period of the asset. In contrast, if losses exceed gains, the net loss is deductible as an itemized deduction to the extent it exceeds 10 percent of the taxpayer's A.G.I.

### Example 7

This year T had three separate casualties involving personal use assets.

| | | | Fair Market Value | |
|---|---|---|---|---|
| *Casualty* | *Property* | *Adjusted Basis* | *Before Casualty* | *After Casualty* |
| 1. Accident | Personal car | $ 12,000 | $ 8,500 | $ 6,000 |
| 2. Robbery | Jewelry | 1,000 | 4,000 | 0 |
| 3. Hurricane | Residence | 60,000 | 80,000 | 78,000 |

T received insurance reimbursements as follows: (1) $900 for repair of the car; (2) $3,200 for the theft of her jewelry; and (3) $1,500 for the damages to her home. If T does not elect (under § 1033) to purchase replacement jewelry, her personal casualty gain exceeds her personal casualty losses by $300, computed as follows:

1. The loss for the car is $1,500 [(lesser of $2,500 decline in value or the $12,000 adjusted basis = $2,500) – $900 insurance recovery – $100 floor].

2. The loss from the residence is $400 [(lesser of $2,000 decline in value or the $60,000 adjusted basis = $2,000) – $1,500 insurance recovery – $100 floor].

T must report each separate gain and loss as a gain or loss from the sale or exchange of a capital asset. The classification of each gain and loss as short-term or long-term depends on the holding period of each asset.

**Example 8**

Assume the same facts as in Example 7 except the loss for the personal car was not insured. In this case the loss on the car is $2,400 and the personal casualty losses exceed the gain by $600 ($2,400 + $400 – $2,200). T must treat the $600 net loss as an itemized deduction subject to the limitation of 10% of A.G.I.

## Year Deductible

A casualty loss usually is deductible in the taxable year in which the loss occurs.[35] A theft loss is deductible in the *year of discovery*. If a claim for reimbursement exists and there is a reasonable prospect of recovery, the loss must be reduced by the amount the taxpayer *expects* to receive.[36] If later receipts are less than the amount originally estimated and no further reimbursement is expected, an amended return is *not* filed. Instead, the remaining loss is deductible in the year in which no further reimbursement is expected. If the casualty loss deduction was reduced by the $100 floor in the prior year, the remaining loss need not be further reduced. However, the remaining loss is subject to the 10 percent limitation of the later year.

**Example 9**

G's diamond bracelet was stolen on December 4, 2011. Her loss was $700 before taking into account any insurance reimbursement. She expects the insurance company to reimburse her $400 for the loss. In 2011 G may deduct $200 ($700 loss less the expected reimbursement of $400 and reduced by the $100 floor) subject to the 10% limitation for 2011. If G actually receives only $300 in the following year, she may deduct an additional $100 (the difference between the expected reimbursement of $400 and the $300 received) subject to the 10% limitation for 2012. If the reimbursement was greater than that expected, the excess is included in gross income.

A special rule exists for the reporting of casualty losses sustained within an area designated by the President as a "disaster area." This rule permits the taxpayer to accelerate the tax relief provided for casualty losses by electing to deduct the disaster loss in the taxable year immediately preceding the year of the disaster loss.[37] In addition, the loss is not subject to the 10 percent floor.

**Example 10**

F, a calendar year taxpayer, suffered a loss in a "disaster area" from a flood on March 4, 2011. F may elect to deduct the loss on his 2010 return. If he has not filed the 2010 return by the casualty date, he may include the loss on the original 2010 return. If the 2010 return has been filed prior to the casualty, an amended return or refund claim is required. Alternatively, F could claim the loss on his 2011 return.

35 Reg. § 1.165-7(a).

36 Reg. § 1.165-1(d)(2)(i).

37 § 165(i).

## ✓ CHECK YOUR KNOWLEDGE

### Review Question 1

While acting like a couch potato and channel surfing one rainy day, S felt a drop on the end of his nose. Then, all of a sudden, water started gushing out of the ceiling. S later determined that squirrels had eaten a hole in his roof. Can S claim a casualty loss deduction for any damage caused by the squirrels? What must S demonstrate before he can claim a casualty loss deduction?

In order to claim a deduction for an "other casualty," S must establish that the damage is sudden, unexpected, and unusual. As can be imagined, these standards are often difficult to apply. In this case, the IRS has ruled that no deduction was allowed since it is common knowledge that squirrels are destructive and because the roof holes caused by the rodents were not unexpected or unusual.[38]

### Review Question 2

In 2005 B purchased a music box as a Christmas present for his wife at a cost of $1,000. This year the box was stolen. It turned out that the music box was an antique worth more than $5,000. Because of the deductible on his homeowner's insurance policy, B received only $400 for his loss.

**a.** Before considering *any* limitation, what is the amount of B's casualty loss deduction?

In the case of a casualty of personal use property, a taxpayer is generally allowed to deduct the lesser of the property's value or basis as reduced by any insurance reimbursement. As a result, B is allowed to deduct a loss of $600 ($1,000 – $400).

**b.** After B found out that his loss in the eyes of the tax law was only $600, he went crazy. He said it was ridiculous to allow a deduction of only $600 when in fact his economic loss was really $4,600 ($5,000 – $400). Is B right or wrong?

B's belief that he has a $4,600 loss rather than a $600 loss is based on the value of the property. It is true that he has had an economic loss of $4,600, but he never had to recognize the increase in value from $1,000 to $5,000 as income for tax purposes. Therefore, the loss is measured from his basis.

**c.** Answer (a) assuming the music box had been worth only $700.

In this case, the deduction would be $300 [(lesser of fair market value, $700, or basis, $1,000) – $400]. Note that B would probably believe this is unfair since he paid $1,000 for the box and was reimbursed only $400. However, the starting point for measuring the loss is the value; Congress did not want to allow a deduction for the loss in value that is not attributable to the casualty since to do so would allow the taxpayer to deduct a personal expense.

**d.** Even though B has a casualty loss, he will probably not receive any tax relief. Why?

Despite the loss, the deduction for *personal* casualty losses is subject to two limitations. The amount of the casualty (as measured above) must exceed the $100 floor per casualty and 10 percent of the taxpayer's A.G.I. After the 10 percent floor was added to the law in 1982, reported casualty loss deductions fell by 97 percent. Because of this limitation, a personal casualty loss must be almost catastrophic before a taxpayer receives any tax relief.

**e.** Answer (a) and (c) assuming that B was in the business of selling music boxes.

If the property is used in a trade or business, the taxpayer is entitled to a deduction equal to the basis of the property reduced by an insurance reimbursement. Consequently, in (a), where the box is worth $5,000 and has a basis of $1,000, the deduction would be $600 (adjusted basis $1,000 – insurance reimbursement $400). The same rationale provided for the solution in (b) above applies here. The deduction is limited since the taxpayer has never recognized the appreciation as income. In (c), where the box is worth

---

[38] Ltr. Rul. 8133097.

$700 and has a basis of $1,000, the taxpayer is also allowed a deduction for $600 (rather than $300 as was the case when the property was used for personal purposes). Note that even though the value of the property is less than its basis, the business taxpayer is allowed to deduct the entire basis in the property. This treatment is allowed since the taxpayer would have been able to deduct the $1,000 in any event because the property is used in a trade or business. For example, the taxpayer would be able to claim a deduction when the property was sold or if the property was depreciable, through depreciation.

### Review Question 3

Checkers Pizza delivers. This year one of its cars was stolen. Does the $100 floor and 10 percent of A.G.I. limitation apply in determining the amount of its casualty loss?

The $100 floor and 10 percent rule do not apply to casualties of property used in a trade or business or an income-producing activity. These limitations apply only to casualties of personal use property.

### Review Question 4

During 2011, the Smiths' house was destroyed by a hurricane. As a result, the Smiths moved into a motel until their home was rebuilt six months later. The cost of their motel stay was $2,700. May the couple deduct the $2,700 cost as a casualty loss?

No deduction is allowed. This is considered an incidental personal expense and is not deductible as part of the casualty loss.

## Net Operating Losses

**LO.5**
Determine the net operating loss deduction and explain how it is treated.

As someone once said, life is not always a bed of roses. This chapter, at least in part, is a testimonial to that. Debts do go bad, lightning may strike, and casualties can happen. Perhaps taxpayers can take some consolation in that in both of these cases, the government shares in the taxpayer's misfortune and provides some relief. Unfortunately, this section also dwells on the negative. For some taxpayers, income does not always exceed deductions. Businesses are not always profitable and catastrophic events may give rise to large expenses. In those lean or rotten years, the taxpayer may actually have a negative taxable income, usually referred to as a loss. When this happens, as might be expected, the taxpayer to his or her joy does not have to pay taxes. More importantly, the taxpayer may be able to use the loss to reduce his or her tax in a previous or subsequent year. This section examines this possibility.

In a year during which the taxpayer's deductions exceed gross income, the taxpayer is allowed to use the excess deductions to offset taxable income of prior or subsequent years.[39] Technically, the excess of deductions over income, as modified for several complex adjustments, is referred to as the taxpayer's *net operating loss* (NOL).[40] The Code generally permits the taxpayer to carry back the NOL two years and forward 20 years to redetermine taxable income.[41]

Allowance of the net operating loss deduction reduces the inequity that otherwise exists due to the use of an annual reporting period and a progressive tax rate structure. For example, consider a situation involving two taxpayers, R and S, who over a two-year period have equivalent taxable incomes of $100,000 each. R earned $50,000 each year while S earned $300,000 in the first year and had a loss of $200,000 in the second year. Without the NOL

---

[39] § 172.

[40] § 172(c).

[41] § 172(b)(1). Pre-1998 NOLs are carried back three and forward 15 years. NOLs arising in 2001 and 2002 and those of a small business attributable to federally declared disasters may be carried back five rather than two years. For an NOL arising in 2008 and 2009, businesses may elect to carry it back either 3, 4 or 5 years, instead of the normal 2-year carryback period.

provisions, S would *not* be able to offset his $200,000 loss against his $300,000 income and consequently would pay a substantially greater tax than R. Such a result clearly would be unfair since both taxpayers had identical taxable incomes over the two-year period. The NOL provision partially eliminates this inequity by allowing a loss in one year to offset income in other years.

## Carryback and Carryforward Years

As mentioned above, under the general rules, an NOL resulting in the current year is carried back two years and forward 20 years. The loss is first carried back to the second prior year (i.e., the earliest year first) and taxable income is recomputed for that year. If any loss remains after reducing that year's tax liability to zero, the remaining loss is carried to the first prior year. If a loss still remains, the taxpayer carries it forward to the first year after the loss and so on up to the 20th year following the loss year. For example, a loss occurring in 2011 would be applied to taxable income of these years as follows: 2009, 2010, 2012, 2013, ... , 2031, 2032.[42]

The taxpayer may *elect* to forego the carryback period and carry forward the loss instead.[43] The election is made simply by attaching a statement to the tax return for the year to indicate the taxpayer's intention of forgoing the carryback period. This election must be made by the due date of the return (including extensions) in which the net operating loss is reported. The election *cannot* be subsequently claimed or revoked by filing an amended return. This election normally is appropriate only where the taxpayer expects future profits. If future profits are anticipated, the taxpayer must determine whether carrying the loss back or forward will yield the greater tax benefit. This decision is often difficult since the taxpayer may be unable to predict the future with any certainty.

When the taxpayer carries the loss back to a prior year, the loss deduction is claimed on an amended return for the earlier year (Form 1040X). For this purpose, the statute-of-limitations period for returns of the earlier years normally is extended to three years after the due date (including extensions) of the return in which the loss was originally reported.[44] Alternatively, the loss may be claimed using Form 1045 (Form 1139 for corporations) for a so-called quick refund. This form must be filed *after* the return of the loss year is filed and *within* one year after the *close* of the loss year. If the taxpayer fails to file Form 1045, an amended return (Form 1040X) may still be filed.

### Example 11

B, a calendar year taxpayer, reported a loss for 2011. He filed his 2011 return April 15, 2012. Under normal conditions, B must file an amended return for 2009 (the year to which the loss is carried) by April 15, 2013 (three years after April 15, 2010, the due date for the 2009 return). The Code, however, extends the period for filing an amended return for 2009 until April 15, 2015, three years after the due date of the return for the loss year. Alternatively, B may claim the loss using Form 1045 by filing the form before December 31, 2012, one year after the close of the loss year.

Where the taxpayer carries the loss forward, the loss deduction is claimed on the subsequent year's normal return (Form 1040).

If the taxpayer has losses occurring in two or more years, the loss occurring in the earliest year is used first. When the loss from the earliest year is absorbed, the losses from later years may be claimed.

---

[42] Subject to certain limitations, taxpayers who have an NOL for any tax year ending after December 31, 2007, and beginning before Jan. 1, 2010 may elect to carry the NOL for 2, 3, 4 or 5 years. See 172(b)(1)(H)(ii).

[43] § 172(b)(3)(c).

[44] § 6511(d)(2).

## Net Operating Loss Computation

The term *net operating loss* (NOL) is defined as the excess of the deductions allowed over gross income, computed with certain modifications.[45] The purpose of the modifications is twofold. First, the net operating loss provisions are designed to permit a taxpayer a deduction for his or her true *economic* loss. Thus, certain artificial deductions that do not require cash outlays (such as the deductions for personal and dependent exemptions) are added back to negative taxable income. Second, the net operating loss provisions were enacted to provide relief only in those cases where there is a business or casualty loss. As a practical matter, a net operating loss is caused by one of the following:

- Loss from operating a sole proprietorship (e.g., a loss on Schedule C)
- Loss from rental operations in which the taxpayer actively participates subject to certain limitations
- Share of an S corporation or partnership loss
- A casualty or theft loss

Since the NOL provisions generally allow only for the carryback or carryforward of losses attributable to business or casualty, restrictions are imposed on the amount of nonbusiness expenses that may be deducted in computing the NOL. As will be seen, it is these limitations on the deduction of nonbusiness expenses and losses that make the computation of the NOL deduction so complex.

The net operating loss deduction of an individual taxpayer is computed by making the following modifications in computing taxable income:[46]

1. Any net operating loss deduction carried forward or carried back from another year is not allowed.
2. The deduction for personal and dependent exemptions is not allowed.
3. Deductions for capital losses and nonbusiness expenses are limited as explained below.

To determine the extent of any deduction for capital losses and nonbusiness expenses, gross income must be classified into *four* categories: (1) capital gains from business; (2) other income from business; (3) capital gains not from business; and (4) other income not from business. With income so classified, the following rules are applied with respect to nonbusiness expenses and capital losses in the following order:[47]

1. Nonbusiness capital losses may be deducted to the extent of any nonbusiness capital gains; thus, any excess is added back to taxable income.
2. Nonbusiness expenses may be deducted to the extent of any nonbusiness income, including any excess of nonbusiness capital gains over nonbusiness capital losses (as determined in step l); thus, any excess is added back to taxable income.
3. Business capital losses may be deducted to the extent of any business capital gains; any excess business capital losses may be deducted to the extent of any excess of nonbusiness capital gains over nonbusiness capital losses and nonbusiness expenses (as determined in step 2).

A general formula for computing the NOL deduction is set forth in Exhibit 10-2. As may be surmised from the previous discussion and the formula, the critical first step when actually calculating the deduction is classifying income and deductions and gains and losses as either business or nonbusiness. Exhibit 10-3 identifies and classifies the most common items appearing on tax returns.

---

[45] *Supra*, Footnote 39.

[46] § 172(d)(1) through (4).

[47] § 172(d)(4).

### EXHIBIT 10.2 Computation of Net Operating Loss

Taxable loss shown on return

Add back:

- Exemptions
- Nonbusiness deductions
  - Less:
    - Nonbusiness ordinary income
    - Nonbusiness net capital gain
- Nonbusiness capital losses
  - Less:
    - Nonbusiness capital gains
- Business capital losses
  - Less:
    - Nonbusiness net capital gains
    - Less: (Nonbusiness deductions − nonbusiness income)

Equals: Net Operating Loss Deduction

### EXHIBIT 10.3 Calculation of Net Operating Loss Deduction: Classification of Business and Nonbusiness Income and Expenses

| Business income | Nonbusiness income |
|---|---|
| Salaries and wages | Interest income |
| Schedule C income | Dividends |
| Rental income | Pension income |
| Farm income | Annuity income |
| Partnership and S corporation income if not passive | Partnership and S corporation income if passive |
| Gains from sale of business assets | Gain from sale of capital assets not used in business (such as stocks) |

| Business deductions | Nonbusiness expenses |
|---|---|
| Schedule C expenses | Standard deduction |
| Rental expenses | Itemized deductions including medical, interest, taxes, contributions |
| Farm expenses | |
| Partnership and S corporation loss if not passive | Partnership and S corporation loss if passive |
| Casualty or theft losses (business and personal) | IRA contribution |
| Loss on sale of § 1244 stock | Contribution to self-employed retirement plan |
| Miscellaneous itemized deductions for business | Alimony |
| Moving expenses | |

## Example 12

In 2011 G quit his job and opened a car repair shop. G's filing status is married, filing jointly, and he reported the following income and deductions for the year:

| | |
|---|---|
| *Income* | |
| Business income | $ 40,000 |
| Salary from previous job | 10,000 |
| Business capital gains—long term | 7,000 |
| Business capital losses—long term | (2,000) |
| Nonbusiness capital gains—long term | 5,000 |
| Nonbusiness capital losses—long term | (3,000) |
| Interest income on nonbusiness investments | 1,000 |
| *Expenses* | |
| Business expenses | 70,000 |
| Casualty loss on personal car | 5,100 |
| Interest on home mortgage | 8,000 |

Taxable income is computed as follows:

| | | |
|---|---|---|
| Net business loss ($40,000 − $70,000) | | ($30,000) |
| Salary | | 10,000 |
| Interest earned | | 1,000 |
| Net long-term capital gain | | 7,000 |
| Adjusted gross income (loss) | | ($12,000) |
| Less: Itemized deductions | | |
| Casualty loss | $5,000* | |
| Mortgage interest paid | 8,000 | (13,000) |
| Less: Personal exemptions ($3,700 × 2) | | (7,400) |
| Taxable income (loss) | | ($32,400) |

*$5,100 − $100 floor. Note that the 10 percent limitation does not apply since A.G.I. is a negative number.

Following Exhibit 10-2, G's NOL for 2011 is computed as follows:

| | | | |
|---|---|---|---|
| Taxable income (loss) | | | ($32,400) |
| Modifications | | | |
| Add back: | | | |
| Personal exemptions | | | 7,400 |
| Excess nonbusiness expenses: | | | |
| Mortgage interest | | $8,000 | |
| Nonbusiness income: | | | |
| Interest | $1,000 | | |
| Nonbusiness net capital gain ($5,000 − $3,000) | + 2,000 | (3,000) | 5,000 |
| Net operating loss for 2011 | | | ($20,000) |

Computation of the real dollar loss or economic loss results in a similar deduction:

| | |
|---|---|
| Business loss | ($30,000) |
| + Salary | 10,000 |
| + Business capital gains | 5,000 |
| − Casualty loss | (5,000) |
| Net operating loss | ($20,000) |

Note that the nonbusiness income (capital gains of $2,000 and interest income of $1,000) is not considered in this computation of economic loss since it is offset by nonbusiness expenses.

## RECOMPUTING TAXABLE INCOME FOR YEAR TO WHICH NET OPERATING LOSS IS CARRIED

Once the net operating loss deduction is computed, it is carried to the appropriate year and used in the recomputation of taxable income for that year. The net operating loss deduction is a deduction *for* A.G.I. As a result, the deduction may have an effect on the amount of the deduction for certain items such as medical expenses, which are based on the taxpayer's A.G.I. All expenses based on A.G.I. except charitable contributions must be *recomputed* in determining the revised taxable income.[48] The net operating loss deduction also may have an effect on any tax credits originally claimed. For example, if a year 2013 net operating loss deduction completely eliminates the taxable income of 2011, any credit originally claimed in 2011 becomes available for use in another year.

After the effect on the tax of the earliest year is computed, the amount of any loss remaining to be carried forward must be determined. In other words, a computation is required to determine how much of the net operating loss is absorbed in the year to which it is carried and how much may be carried to subsequent years. Although this calculation is somewhat similar to that explained above, additional nuances exist making the computation somewhat complex. For this reason, further reference should be made to the Regulations and Form 1045.

### ✓ CHECK YOUR KNOWLEDGE

During 2011, T opened his own computer store, specializing in sales of multimedia. He operated the business as an S corporation. Upon his first crack at computing his taxable income for the year, T determined that he had a negative taxable income of $15,000.

**Review Question 1**

Assuming T has a net operating loss for the year, how is it treated?

An NOL is generally carried back two years and forward 20 years. The 2011 loss is carried back to the second prior year (i.e., the earliest year, 2009), where taxable income is recomputed and a refund claim is filed. If any loss remains after reducing the taxable income of 2009 to zero, the loss is carried forward to the first prior year (i.e., 2010). If a loss still remains, T may carry it forward for up to 20 years, after which any remaining loss expires and is lost. Alternatively, T may elect not to carry the loss back but to carry the loss forward for 20 years. Carrying forward the loss may make more sense if he expects to be in a tax bracket in the future that is higher than past years. In such case, the loss would produce greater benefit.

**Review Question 2**

A review of T's tax return reveals that his negative taxable income of $15,000 includes several items of income and deductions. For example, his only income other than that related to his business was interest and dividends of $5,000. Indicate whether the following deductions would be allowed in computing T's NOL deduction and, if so, how much could be used.

- **a.** Personal exemption
- **b.** Dependency exemption
- **c.** Net loss from S corporation operations (sales less operating expenses)
- **d.** Casualty loss to personal residence from earthquake damage
- **e.** Interest expense on the mortgage on his personal residence of $7,000
- **f.** Net capital loss $8,000 ($3,000 offsets ordinary income and $5,000 carried over)

In computing his NOL deduction, T must make certain adjustments to negative taxable income to arrive at the taxpayer's true economic loss that the law allows to be carried over. No deduction is allowed for personal or dependency exemptions since these are artificial deductions. Thus, the exemption deduction must be added back to negative taxable income.

---

[48] Reg. § 1.172-5(a)(3)(ii).

The net loss from his business (i.e., the S corporation) does reduce taxable income in calculating the NOL, so there is no adjustment. The casualty loss is also allowable in computing the NOL. Nonbusiness expenses such as mortgage interest and taxes are considered personal expenses and can be deducted only to the extent of nonbusiness income. So, only $5,000 of the $7,000 expense is deductible, requiring an addback of $2,000. Finally, a capital loss can generally be used only to offset capital gains. Thus, the $3,000 deduction attributable to the capital loss is not allowed and must be added back.

## Inventories

As might be expected, taxpayers who buy or produce merchandise for subsequent sale are not allowed to deduct the costs of the merchandise *at the time* the goods are produced or purchased. Instead, such costs normally must be capitalized (i.e., inventoried) and deducted when the goods are sold. The following example illustrates what might occur if taxpayers were not required to capitalize the costs of inventory.

### Example 13

C Corporation began business in 2011 and purchased 10,000 gizmos at $10 each for a total of $100,000. In 2011 the corporation sold 6,000 gizmos for $120,000. In 2012 the corporation made no further purchases and sold the remaining 4,000 gizmos for $80,000. Gross profit reported with and without inventories is computed below:

| | *No Inventories* | | *Inventories* | |
|---|---|---|---|---|
| | *2011* | *2012* | *2011* | *2012* |
| Sales | $120,000 | $80,000 | $120,000 | $80,000 |
| Cost of good sold: | | | | |
| Beginning inventory | — | — | — | $40,000 |
| + Purchases | $100,000 | — | $100,000 | — |
| – Ending Inventory | — | — | (40,000) | — |
| Costs of goods sold (4,000 @ $10) | $100,000 | — | $ 60,000 | $40,000 |
| Gross profit | $ 20,000 | $80,000 | $ 60,000 | $40,000 |

Although the total income for the two-year period is the same under either method ($100,000), when it is reported differs significantly. The use of inventories produces higher income and higher taxes in the first year because only the costs of goods actually sold are deducted.

**LO.6**
Explain the basic tax accounting requirements for inventories.

As the preceding example shows, the lack of inventories causes a mismatching of revenues and expenses and with it the possibility of widely fluctuating incomes. Without inventories, the income reported in any one year would in most cases represent a distorted picture—not a clear reflection—of how well the firm was doing. Perhaps what is more crucial, at least from the Treasury's point of view, is that taxpayers would be able to postpone the payment of taxes if inventories were not required. Note in Example 13 that absent inventories, the taxpayer is able to defer $40,000 ($60,000 – $20,000) of income and the corresponding tax from 2011 to 2012. Congress recognized these possibilities at an early date and in 1918 took corrective action that is still intact today. Currently, Code § 471 provides the following:

> Whenever in the opinion of the Secretary the use of inventories is necessary in order clearly to determine the income of any taxpayer, inventories shall be taken by such taxpayer on such basis as the Secretary may prescribe as conforming as nearly as may be to the best accounting practice in the trade or business and as most clearly reflecting income.

With the enactment of § 471, Congress delegated its rulemaking authority concerning inventories to the IRS. The IRS has responded with a number of regulations indicating when inventories are necessary as well as what methods are acceptable for tax purposes.

The Regulations require taxpayers to maintain inventories whenever the production, purchase, or sale of merchandise is an income-producing factor.[49] As a practical matter, this means virtually all manufacturers, wholesalers, and retailers must keep track of inventories while service businesses are usually exempt. Note that inventories are required regardless of the taxpayer's method of accounting. Cash basis taxpayers must account for inventories as do accrual basis taxpayers. However, the mandatory use of the accrual method for purchases and sales does not prohibit taxpayers from using the cash method to account for other items such as advertising costs or interest income.[50]

## Exceptions to the Inventory Requirement

While the inventory rule seems relatively straightforward, it has led to a significant amount of controversy. To understand the problem, it is necessary to recall that where inventory exists, the taxpayer not only must capitalize inventory costs, it also must accrue income from credit sales. The difficulty stems from the requirement that only those items representing merchandise *inventory* must be capitalized. In contrast, under Regulation §1.162-3 materials and supplies that are considered *incidental* to the primary function of the business may be expensed currently. In contrast, *nonincidental* materials and supplies can be deducted only as they are consumed—much like inventory. Therefore, according to these rules, if a taxpayer can successfully argue that items are merely incidental materials or supplies, the items can be expensed immediately and the taxpayer may defer recognition of income from their sale until cash is received. On the other hand, if the IRS can prove that the items are inventory, the items must be capitalized and the income from their sale must be accrued. Note how much is at stake in the definition of inventory. If the items are considered incidental, the taxpayer wins the entire battle: deductions now and income in the future. If the items are nonincidental, the IRS secures a partial victory in that nonincidental items cannot be deducted immediately but only as they are consumed; however, income is still deferred. But if the items are considered inventory, the IRS has won the entire war since such characterization not only prevents an immediate write-off of the items' costs but also forces the taxpayer to accrue income currently. The difficulty is that there is no clear definition of inventory.

The problem is particularly acute with service providers. In *Wilkinson-Beane*, a mortuary provided funeral services, including supplying the caskets.[51] The taxpayer did not separately bill for the caskets but merely charged a flat fee for the services. Consistent with this approach, the taxpayer did not treat the caskets as inventory even though the costs represented 15.1 percent of total cash receipts. Unfortunately for the taxpayer, the court held that the caskets must be capitalized and any income forthcoming from the services to be accrued. A different approach was taken in the recent decision in *Osteopathic Medical Oncology and Hematology P.C.*[52] In this situation, the taxpayer provided chemotherapy treatment for cancer patients. In so doing, it used certain drugs. The IRS argued that the drugs were inventory and, therefore, the taxpayer could not expense the drugs and had to report the income when the treatments were provided (rather than when the cash was received—usually much later). However, the Tax Court sided with the taxpayer, ruling that the drugs were not inventory but rather an indispensable and inseparable part of the service of treating patients.

Due to the growing controversy about the definition of inventory and the ensuing problems, the government reacted. In 2000, the IRS began to relax its position on the mandatory use of inventories and at the same time the mandatory use of the accrual method. In a series of Revenue Procedures, the IRS has carved out two major exceptions, allowing taxpayers with inventories to escape the clutch of the accrual method. As may be grasped from the discussion above, the exceptions are of huge importance primarily because they permit the taxpayers—at least small businesses—to defer income.

1. *Gross Receipts of $1,000,000 or Less.* Taxpayers with average annual gross receipts of $1,000,000 or less are not required to use the accrual method for inventories. This does not mean that taxpayers can simply expense inventory purchases. Instead, as

---

[49] Reg. § 1.471-1 and Reg. § 1.446-1(a)(4)(i).

[50] Reg. § 1.446-1(c)(1)(iv).

[51] 70-1 USTC ¶9173, 25 AFTR 2d 70-418 420 F.2d 352 (CA-1, 1970).

[52] 113 T.C. 376.

discussed above, the items must be accounted for as nonincidental materials and supplies and expensed as they are used or consumed. While the treatment of inventory *costs* is essentially the same whether the costs are treated as inventory or nonincidental materials and supplies, the treatment of *income* significantly differs. Taxpayers who fall under this exception need not recognize accounts receivable income until they collect the receivables. In other words, they may defer the recognition of income until they receive payment for the merchandise.[53]

2. *Gross Receipts Less Than $10,000,000.* The above rule carves out a special exception only for small businesses: taxpayers with gross receipts of $1,000,000 or less. Revenue Procedure 2002-28 extends the same rule discussed above to taxpayers with average annual gross receipts exceeding $1,000,000 but less than $10,000,000 but only if their principal business activity is providing services or is not in certain industries, including manufacturing, wholesale, retail and information industries (e.g., newspapers, books, periodicals, database publishers and sound recording industries) or they meet certain other exceptions. These businesses also need not use the accrual method for purchases and sales but inventory must be accounted for as nonincidental materials and supplies and expensed as they are used or consumed. Note that this rule does not override § 448 discussed above. Farming businesses, C corporations having gross receipts exceeding $5,000,000 and partnerships with a tainted C corporation partner do not qualify for this exception. This rule should benefit small businesses primarily in service businesses.[54]

### Example 14

Golf Accessories Inc. (GAI) sells a variety of items for golfers, such as golf balls, tees, headcovers, ball marks, towels, clothing, training tapes and devices. The company sells direct to the public through its Internet site as well as to golf shops around the country. It has average annual gross receipts (e.g., sales) of $700,000. GAI began the year with $80,000 of merchandise on hand. During the year it purchased $300,000 of new merchandise, and at the end of the year had $70,000 on hand. Sales during the year were $650,000 but at the end of the year it had $40,000 of receivables outstanding. It also collected $15,000 of the receivables outstanding from the prior year. Because GAI averages gross receipts of less than $1,000,000 it need not use the accrual method to account for purchases and sales. As a result, it has revenues of $625,000 ($15,000 + $650,000 − $40,000) and costs of good sold of $310,000 ($80,000 + $300,000 − $70,000). Note that under the exception GAI is able to defer the $40,000 of income from the uncollected receivables until it is collected next year—a very valuable benefit. Also note that the inventory costs were still capitalized and could not be expensed until the items were sold or consumed.

### Example 15

Same facts as above except GAI Inc. had average annual gross receipts of $4,000,000. Under these revised circumstances, the company would not qualify for the first exception since its gross receipts exceed $1,000,000. Moreover, it also would not qualify for the second exception even though its gross receipts are less than $10,000,000 since it is in one of the prohibited businesses of retail and wholesale trade.

[53] Rev. Proc. 2000-22, 2000-1 C.B. 1008 *modified* and *superseded* by Rev. Proc. 2001-10, I.R.B. 2001-2, 272. Note that Rev. Proc. 2001-10 eliminated the book conformity requirement.

[54] Rev. Proc. 2002-28, 2002-18 I.R.B. 2002-18, 815 clarifying and implementing Notice 2001-76, I.R.B. 2001-52, 613. See Rev. Proc. 2002-28 for exceptions where the principal business activity is the provision of services or fabrication or modification of or property to meet customer specifications.

**Example 16**

Same facts as in *Example 14* above except that GAI Inc. had average annual gross receipts of $8,000,000 and provided heating and air conditioning services. GAI meets the requirements of the second exception in that it is in the business of providing services and its gross receipts are less than $10,000,000. It would appear that GAI could avoid use of the accrual method and defer income from credit sales. However, if GAI is a C Corporation, it must still use the accrual method in accounting for purchases and sales because its gross receipts exceed $5,000,000.

## Inventory Accounting in General

A close reading of § 471 reveals that Congress has given the IRS two criteria to be followed in determining what inventory accounting methods are acceptable for tax purposes: (1) the method should conform as nearly as possible to the best accounting practice used in the taxpayer's trade or business; and (2) the method should clearly reflect income. Because of these requirements, the tax rules for inventory are quite similar to those used for financial accounting. Nevertheless, it is important to recognize that the IRS is the ultimate authority on determining what method represents the "best accounting practice" as well as what method most clearly reflects income. Consequently, as will be seen, taxpayers are sometimes required to adopt methods that vary from generally accepted accounting principles and cause differences between book income and taxable income.

There are three steps that must be followed in accounting for inventories and computing costs of goods sold: (1) identifying what costs (e.g., direct and indirect) are to be inventoried or capitalized; (2) evaluating the costs assigned to the ending inventory and determining whether reduction is necessary to reflect lower replacement costs (i.e., lower of cost or market); and (3) allocating the costs between ending inventory and costs of goods sold (e.g., specific identification, FIFO, LIFO). Each of these steps is discussed below.

## Costs to be Inventoried

**LO.7**
Identify the costs that must be capitalized as part of inventory and the role of the uniform capitalization rules in making this determination.

The first step in determining costs of goods sold and ending inventory is identifying the costs that should be capitalized as part of inventory. Without guidance, taxpayers no doubt would be inclined to expense as many costs as possible. However, over the years, the IRS with help from Congress has established strict guidelines concerning what can be deducted currently (i.e., period costs) and what must be capitalized (i.e., product costs). The most recent development in this continuing debate was the enactment of the *uniform capitalization rules* (unicap) in 1986. As discussed below, the unicap provisions narrow further what the taxpayer is able to treat as a period cost.

As a general rule, the costs that must be capitalized depend on whether the taxpayer manufactures the goods (e.g., a producer of razor blades) or purchases the items for later resale (e.g., a wholesaler or a retailer such as a department store). When merchandise is bought for resale, the taxpayer must capitalize as a cost of inventory the invoice price less trade discounts plus freight and other costs of acquisition. Cash discounts may be deducted from the inventory cost or reported as a separate income item. In addition, certain retailers and wholesalers are subject to the unicap rules that require capitalization of particular indirect costs as discussed below. For manufactured items, inventory cost includes costs of raw materials, direct labor, and certain indirect costs. The unicap rules apply to all manufacturers.

Many of the problems concerning inventory involve the treatment of indirect costs. Various methods have been devised to account for these costs. For example, under the *prime costing* method only the costs of direct materials and direct labor are capitalized; all indirect costs are expensed. Another method, often advocated by cost accountants, is the *variable* or *direct costing* approach. This method capitalizes only those costs varying with production and expenses all fixed costs. Despite the acceptance of these methods for managerial and internal reporting, the IRS has outlawed their use.

Determining which costs should be included in inventory has been a continuing source of irritation in the tax law. Prior to 1973, questions were often resolved on a case-by-case method, resulting in confusion and inconsistency. In 1974, the IRS addressed the problems by issuing regulations requiring all manufacturers to use the *full absorption costing method.*[55] The full absorption method requires the capitalization of direct costs of material and labor as well as the capitalization of certain indirect expenses. However, retailers and wholesalers were not subject to the full absorption rules, and, therefore, were not required to capitalize any indirect costs. The full-absorption rules seemed to work but apparently not well enough and were essentially replaced in 1986 by the enactment of § 263A containing *the uniform capitalization rules* (UNICAP).

The UNICAP rules attempt to provide standard guidelines regarding the capitalization of expenditures for all types of taxpayer and all types of activities. The UNICAP rules apply to *all* manufacturers. In addition, they apply to any retailers and wholesalers (resellers) if their average annual gross receipts for the past three years exceed $10 million. For tax purposes, the UNICAP rules generally replace the full-absorption costing method. However, in practice, many manufacturers continue to use the full-absorption method modified to meet the UNICAP requirements. UNICAP requires more expenses to be capitalized than full-absorption so it is sometimes referred to as the super-absorption method. To be clear, for covered taxpayers, UNICAP requirements must be met and traditional full-absorption methods often used for financial accounting purposes do not meet these standards unless modified.

Section 263A requires the capitalization of direct material, direct labor costs, and, most important, any indirect costs that, in the words of the Regulations, "directly benefit or are incurred by reason of the performance of a production or resale activity."[56] The effect of these rules is to require taxpayers to capitalize many costs that they may have otherwise deducted. The Regulations require covered taxpayers to categorize all costs into three categories and treat them as follows.

| Category | Treatment |
|---|---|
| 1. Production and resale activities | Capitalize |
| 2. General administration | Do not capitalize (expense) |
| 3. Mixed service costs (benefit both production/resale and administration) | Allocate between production and administration |

As seen in the more detailed breakdown in Exhibit 10-4, the Regulations classify costs as (1) those that benefit only production and resale activities (must capitalize); (2) those that benefit only policy and management functions (do not capitalize); (3) those that benefit both production and resale activities and policy and management functions, referred to as mixed service costs (capitalized by using any reasonable basis to allocate costs between production and policy functions). In addition, interest expense is subject to special rules. Taxpayers are required to develop reasonable bases for cost allocations. In this regard, the Regulations provide several straightforward allocation techniques.[57]

A threshold question with respect to UNICAP (as well as the special deduction for domestic production activities discussed below) is whether a taxpayer is a manufacturer. If the taxpayer is a manufacturer, § 263A applies regardless of the size of the taxpayer's business. If the taxpayer is not a manufacturer, § 263A only applies if the taxpayer's average gross receipts are greater than $10 million. In this regard, gross receipts includes those from all sources, not merely gross receipts from the sale of inventory. Because of the differing treatment between the two groups, a major concern is whether the manufacturing activities of a business are sufficient to cause it to be treated as a manufacturer. For example, are businesses that assemble some products that they sell considered manufacturers? Is a grocery store that uses a portion of its space to prepare foods for consumption on the premises or for takeout considered a manufacturer? As these examples suggest, a clear distinction between manufacturers and resellers does not always exist.

---

[55] Reg. § 1.471-11. Absorption costing is currently used for financial statement purposes.

[56] Reg. § 1.263A-1T(b)(2)(ii).

[57] For example, Reg. § 1.263A-3(d) for a discussion of the simplified resale method and the same method using used in conjunction with the historic absorption ratio.

**EXHIBIT 10.4** **Capitalizable Costs for Uniform Capitalization**

| ***Direct costs*** | Unicap |
|---|---|
| Direct material | C |
| Direct labor | C |
| ***Indirect costs*** | |
| Repairs/maintenance (equipment and facilities) | C |
| Utilities (equipment and facilities) | C |
| Rent (equipment and facilities) | C |
| Indirect labor | C |
| Indirect material and supplies | C |
| Small tools and equipment | C |
| Quality control and inspection | C |
| Taxes other than income taxes | C |
| Depreciation and depletion for books | C |
| Depreciation and depletion: excess tax | C |
| Insurance (facilities, contents, equipment) | C |
| Current pension costs | C |
| Past service pension costs | C |
| Bidding expenses—successful bids | C |
| Engineering and design | C |
| Warehousing, purchasing, handling and general and administrative related to such functions | C |
| ***Policy and Management*** | |
| Marketing, selling, advertising, and distribution | E |
| Bidding expenses-unsuccessful bids | E |
| Research and experimental expenses | |
| Losses | E |
| Depreciation on idle equipment or facilities | E |
| Income taxes | C |
| Strike costs | E |
| ***Interest*** | * |
| ***Mixed Service Costs*** | |
| Administrative/coordination of production or resale | C |
| Personnel department | C |
| Purchasing department | C |
| Materials handling and warehousing | C |
| Accounting and data servicing departments | C |
| Data processing | C |
| Security services | C |
| Legal department providing services to production | C |
| Overall management and policies | E |
| General business planning | E |
| Financial accounting | E |
| General financial planning | E |
| General economic analysis and forecasting | E |
| Internal audit | E |
| Shareholder and public relations | E |
| Tax department | E |

C: Capitalize
E: Expense currently

*Capitalized if the produced property has a life of 20 years or more, if the property has an estimated production period of more than two years, or if the production period exceeds one year and the cost exceeds $1 million. Does not apply to property acquired for resale.

## Allocating Inventoriable Costs

LO.8
Explain how inventory costs are assigned to costs of goods sold using the FIFO and LIFO assumptions.

After total product costs for the year have been identified, these costs along with the cost of beginning inventory must be allocated between the goods sold during the year and ending inventory. If each item sold could be identified (e.g., a car or jewelry) or all items had the same cost, there would be little difficulty in determining the cost of items sold and those still on hand. As a practical matter, these conditions rarely exist. Consequently, the taxpayer must make some assumptions regarding which costs should be assigned to costs of goods sold. Like financial accounting, the tax law does not require the cost flow assumption to be consistent with the physical movement of goods. There are several acceptable approaches for allocating costs: specific identification, first-in first-out (FIFO), last-in first-out (LIFO), and weighted averaged.

### Example 17

K Corporation's inventory records revealed a beginning inventory of 300 units acquired at a cost of $3 per unit. This year the corporation purchased 400 units for $4 per unit, and it sold 500 units for $5,000. Gross profit using FIFO and LIFO are computed below:

| | *FIFO* | *LIFO* |
|---|---|---|
| Sales (500 units @ $10) | $5,000 | $5,000 |
| Costs of goods sold: | | |
| Beginning inventory (300 @ $3) | $ 900 | $ 900 |
| Purchase (400 @ $4) | 1,600 | 1,600 |
| Goods available | $2,500 | $2,500 |
| Ending inventory: | | |
| FIFO (200 @ $4) | (800) | |
| LIFO (200 @ $3) | | (600) |
| Costs of goods sold | $1,700 | $1,900 |
| Gross profit | $3,300 | $3,100 |

If K uses FIFO it is assumed that goods are used in the order that they are purchased (i.e., the first goods in are the first goods to be sold). Thus, the ending inventory consists of the most recent purchases, $800 (200 at $4 per unit). The effect of FIFO is to assign the oldest costs to costs of goods sold. In contrast, LIFO assumes that the last goods purchased are the first sold. As a result, under LIFO the most recent costs are assigned to costs of goods sold and the oldest costs to ending inventory. Thus, ending inventory under LIFO is $600 (200 at $3).

The preceding example illustrates the principal advantage of LIFO. In periods of rising prices, LIFO matches current costs against current revenue. From a financial accounting perspective, it can be reasoned that this produces a better measure of current income since both revenues and costs are stated on a comparable price basis, thereby reducing the inflationary element of earnings.[58] From a tax perspective, LIFO appears preferable because taxable income is typically lower and the corresponding tax is reduced. In effect, taxable income is not "overstated" by fictitious gains. Interestingly, LIFO became part of the tax law

[58] Arguably, income results only to the extent that the sales price exceeds what it will cost to buy a replacement item for the merchandise sold. LIFO approximates this approach.

in 1939 for just this reason—to help businesses reduce the "paper profits" that conventional methods were yielding and that were being taxed at wartime rates of close to 80 percent.

It must be noted, however, that the advantage of LIFO is lost to the extent that sales in any one year exceed purchases (*see Example 17* above). In this case, the lower prices of goods purchased in previous periods are charged to costs of goods sold. This dipping into the past LIFO layers creates inventory profits, the specific problem that LIFO was designed to address. In a worst case scenario, a company that adopted LIFO in 1942 might unexpectedly liquidate all of its LIFO layers, matching 1942 costs with 2011 revenues. This would no doubt lead to an unforeseen tax liability with little "real" income to pay the tax. This is a significant risk when LIFO is used. At the same time, it may represent an opportunity. Companies may be able to create income, if desirable, by liquidating LIFO layers (e.g., to absorb an expiring net operating loss).

## Dollar Value LIFO

As a practical matter, applying the LIFO procedure to specific goods can be quite cumbersome and costly. In contrast to the simple one-item example above, most firms have hundreds or thousands of individual inventory items, and the number of units purchased and sold each period may amount to hundreds of thousands or more. Pricing each separate unit at the oldest costs and properly accounting for the liquidation of any LIFO layers might be a recordkeeping nightmare. Moreover, the major advantage of LIFO could be lost if old LIFO layers had to be liquidated because a specific item was discontinued or replaced. To address the problems of specific-goods LIFO, variations of LIFO have been developed. Perhaps the most widely used version of LIFO is the dollar-value method.

The dollar-value method reaches the desired result—eliminating the inflationary element of earnings attributable to inventory—in a unique way. Ending inventory is priced using the prices at the time LIFO was originally adopted (base-year). This value is then compared to beginning inventory to determine if there is a real increase or decrease in the pool of dollars invested in inventory. If there is no real change (i.e., ending inventory at base-year prices is the same as beginning inventory at base-year prices), the effect is to charge costs of goods sold with an amount reflecting current prices. On the other hand, if there is a real increase in inventory in terms of base-year dollars, the increase is valued at current prices and added to beginning inventory as a separate LIFO layer to determine ending inventory.

### Example 18

T Corporation had an ending inventory on December 31, 2010 of 10,000 units at a cost of $20,000. During the year, T sold the original units and purchased another 10,000 units for $24,000. On December 31, 2011 ending inventory valued at current prices was $24,000. In such case, costs of goods sold would be $20,000, computed as follows:

| | |
|---|---|
| Beginning inventory | $20,000 |
| Purchases | 24,000 |
| Ending inventory | (24,000) |
| Costs of goods sold | $20,000 |

But what if, as the facts suggest, prices have increased by 20%? If so, the real amount invested in inventory has not changed ($24,000 ÷ 120% = $20,000). Consequently, valuing ending inventory at current-year prices of $24,000 (as above) effectively assigns the oldest costs of $20,000 to costs of goods sold, resulting in an inflationary profit of $4,000. Dollar-value LIFO eliminates this artificial gain—the objective of LIFO—by restating ending inventory at base-year prices. In this case, ending inventory would be restated at $20,000 ($24,000 ÷ 120%). This restatement would yield a cost of goods sold of $24,000, and would properly match current-year costs against current-year revenues.

The important difference between dollar-value and specific-goods LIFO is that increases and decreases in inventory are measured in terms of dollars rather than physical units. This

**EXHIBIT 10.5** **Double-Extension Dollar-Value LIFO Computation of Ending Inventory**

***Step 1.*** *Extension #1*. Value ending inventory at current-year prices (actual cost of most recent purchases, average cost, or other acceptable method).

***Step 2.*** *Extension #2*. Value ending inventory at base-year prices.

***Step 3.*** Compute current-year quantity increase or decrease by comparing beginning and ending inventories at base-year prices.

|   |   |
|---|---|
|   | Ending inventory at base-year price (Step 2) |
| − | Beginning inventory at base-year price |
|   | Curent-year quantity increase (decrease) at base-year price |

***Step 4.*** Calculate current-year price index.

$$\text{Index} = \frac{\text{Ending inventory at current-Year price (Step)}}{\text{Ending inventory at base-year price (Step 2)}}$$

***Step 5.*** Compute the quantity increase or decrease to be added to or subtracted from beginning inventory.

a. For a quantity increase: convert the increase measured at base-year prices (Step 3) to current year's prices using the current-year price index (Step 4).

$$\begin{matrix}\text{Quantity increase at} \\ \text{Base-year price} \\ \text{(Step 3)}\end{matrix} \times \begin{matrix}\text{Index} \\ \text{(Step 4)}\end{matrix} = \begin{matrix}\text{New} \\ \text{LIFO} \\ \text{layer}\end{matrix}$$

b. For a quantity decrease: a current-year decrease consumes the layer(s) of inventory in LIFO fashion (i.e., the decrease must be subtracted from the most recently added layer). Previous layers are peeled off at the prices at which they were added.

***Step 6.*** Ending LIFO inventory is the beginning inventory increased by the new LIFO layer [Step 5(a)] or decreased by any liquidation of LIFO layers [Step 5(b)].

approach allows goods to be easily combined into pools and effectively treated as a single unit. Consequently, the likelihood of liquidating LIFO layers is reduced.

Although there are various methods of dollar-value LIFO, the most frequently used is the *double-extension method.*[59] The steps to be used in applying the double-extension method are summarized in Exhibit 10-5 and applied to the following example.

## Example 19

In 2011 T Corporation elected to value inventories using double-extension dollar-value LIFO. Beginning inventory for 2010 consisted of the following:

| Date | Pool Items | *Ending Quantity* | *Current Cost Per Unit* | *Total at Current Cost* |
|---|---|---|---|---|
| 1-1-2011 | A | 3,000 | $3 | $ 9,000 |
|  | B | 4,000 | 6 | 24,000 |
| Total base-year cost |  |  |  | $ 33,000 |

[59] Taxpayers may use the link-chain method or certain simplified procedures. See Code §§ 472(f) and 474 and the applicable regulations.

Inventory information for 2011–2013 and the computation of ending inventory using the steps in Exhibit 10-5 are shown below.

*Steps 1 and 2:* Double extend ending inventory.

| | | Ending Inventory at Current-Year Prices | | | Ending Inventory at Base-Year Prices | |
|---|---|---|---|---|---|---|
| Date | Pool Items | Ending Quantity | Current Cost Per Unit | Total at Current Cost | Base-Year Cost Per Unit | Total at Base-Year Cost |
| 12-31-2011 | A | 2,000 | $ 4 | $ 8,000 | $3 | $ 6,000 |
| | B | 5,000 | 7 | 35,000 | 6 | 30,000 |
| | | | | $ 43,000 | | $ 36,000 |
| 12-31-2012 | A | 6,000 | $ 5 | $ 30,000 | $3 | $ 18,000 |
| | B | 7,000 | 9 | 63,000 | 6 | 42,000 |
| | | | | $ 93,000 | | $60,000 |
| 12-31-2013 | A | 4,000 | $ 6 | $ 24,000 | $3 | $ 12,000 |
| | B | 5,000 | 10 | 50,000 | 6 | 30,000 |
| | | | | $ 74,000 | | $ 42,000 |

*Step 3:* Determine quantity increase (decrease) at base-year price.

| | 2011 | 2012 | 2013 |
|---|---|---|---|
| Ending inventory base-year price . . . . . . . . . . . | $ 36,000 | $ 60,000 | $ 42,000 |
| Beginning inventory base-year price . . . . . . . . . | (33,000) | (36,000) | (60,000) |
| Quantity increase at base-year price. . . . . . . . . | $ 3,000 | $ 24,000 | ($18,000) |

*Step 4:* Calculate current-year price index.

| | 2011 | 2012 | 2013 |
|---|---|---|---|
| Index = $\frac{\text{Ending inventory at current-year price}}{\text{Ending inventory at base-year price}}$ | $\frac{\$43,000}{\$36,000}$ | $\frac{\$93,000}{\$60,000}$ | Decrease: use index at which units were added |
| | 1.19 | 1.55 | 1.55 |

*Step 5:* Compute quantity increase (decrease) to adjust beginning inventory.

| | 2011 | 2012 | 2013 |
|---|---|---|---|
| Quantity increase at base-year price | $ 3,000 | $24,000 | ($18,000) |
| × Index | ×1.19 | ×1.55 | ×1.55 |
| = Increase or decrease to beginning inventory | $ 3,570 | $37,200 | ($27,900) |

*Step 6:* Compute ending inventory.

| | 2011 | 2012 | 2013 |
|---|---|---|---|
| Base-year. . . . . . . . . . . . . . . . . . . . . . . . | $33,000 | $33,000 | $33,000 |
| 2011 layer . . . . . . . . . . . . . . . . . . . . . . . | 3,570 | 3,570 | 3,570 |
| 2012 layer . . . . . . . . . . . . . . . . . . . . . . . | — | 37,200 | 9,300* |
| Total ending inventory . . . . . . . . . . . . . . | $36,570 | $73,770 | $45,870 |

*$37,200 − $27,900 = $9,300

## THE LIFO ELECTION

Taxpayers may elect to use LIFO by filing Form 970 with the tax return for the year in which the change is made. Unlike most other changes in accounting method, prior approval by the IRS is not required. Conversely, the LIFO election cannot be revoked unless consent is obtained. As explained below, the lower of cost or market procedure may not be used with LIFO. Consequently, in the year LIFO is elected, all previous write-downs to market must be restored to income. For many years, the IRS required that all of the income due to the change had to be reported in the year of the change. In 1981, Congress expressed its disfavor with this view and enacted Code § 472(d). This provision allows the taxpayer to spread the adjustment equally over three years, the year of the change and the two following years. Nevertheless, if substantial write-downs have been made, there may be a considerable cost to elect LIFO.

Another ramification of the LIFO election concerns the *conformity requirement*. Under § 472(c), taxpayers who use LIFO for tax purposes must also use LIFO in preparing financial reports to shareholders and creditors. Failure to comply with this rule terminates the LIFO election and requires the taxpayer to change the method of accounting for inventory. As a result, taxpayers not conforming may be forced to give back any income tax savings previously obtained with LIFO.

The conformity requirement appears to have stifled the use of LIFO, presumably because during periods of rising prices it produces lower income and earnings per share than other inventory methods. This is true notwithstanding the tax savings that are available with LIFO and the relaxation of the rule over the years. The Regulations now permit the taxpayer to disclose income using an inventory method other than LIFO if the disclosure is made in the form of a footnote to the balance sheet or a parenthetical on the face of the balance sheet.[60] No comparative disclosures are allowed on the face of the income statement.

## LOWER OF COST OR MARKET

In certain instances, the value of an inventory item may have dropped below the cost allocated to such items. When this occurs, financial accounting has traditionally abandoned the historical cost principle and allowed businesses to write-down their inventories to reflect the decline in value. The tax law has adopted a similar approach. Under the Regulations, taxpayers may value inventory at either (1) cost, or (2) the lower of cost or market.[61] However, the lower of cost or market approach may not be used if the LIFO method is used. Note that the lower of cost or market procedure deviates from the normal rule that losses are not deductible until they are realized.

In the phrase the *lower of cost or market*, "market" generally means replacement cost, or in the case of manufactured products, reproduction cost. When the rule is applied, the value of each similar item must be compared to its cost, and the lower is used in computing ending inventory.

### Example 20

J's inventory records reveal the following:

| Item | FIFO Cost | Market | Lower of Cost or Market |
|---|---|---|---|
| A | $ 3,100 | $ 3,500 | $ 3,100 |
| B | 5,100 | 3,000 | 3,000 |
| C | 6,000 | 7,500 | 6,000 |
| | $14,200 | $14,000 | $12,100 |

If J elects to value inventories at cost, the inventory value is $14,200. Alternatively, if the lower of cost or market approach is elected, the inventory is valued at $12,100. This value is used because unsimilar items cannot be aggregated for tax purposes. For financial accounting purposes, J could combine the various items. Consequently, a difference may arise between book and taxable income.

[60] Reg. § 1.472-2(e).

[61] Reg. § 1.471-2(c).

The approach used above is that prescribed in the Regulations for normal goods. Note that these rules only allow a write-down to replacement cost. What if the firm believes that it will ultimately sell the item for less than what it would cost to replace it? Financial accountants refer to estimated sales price less costs of disposition as net realizable value. For tax purposes, a write-down below this value is allowed only for what are often referred to as "subnormal" goods.[62]

Subnormal goods are those items in inventory that cannot be sold at normal prices because of damage (e.g., a dent in a file cabinet), imperfections (e.g., a thousand sweatshirts with the logo improperly spelled), shop wear, changes of style, odd or broken lots, and so on. The Regulations allow the taxpayer to value these "subnormal" goods at a bona fide selling price less direct costs of disposition. However, this lower value is acceptable *only* if the goods are actually offered for sale at such price 30 days after the inventory date (e.g., cars with severe hail-damage are actually on the lot with a sales price slashed below replacement cost within 30 days of when inventory is taken).

### Example 21

In the landmark decision of *Thor Power Tool Co.*,[63] the taxpayer manufactured power tools consisting of 50 to 200 parts. Thor followed the common practice of producing additional parts at the same time it manufactured the original tool. This practice helped the company to avoid expensive retooling and special production runs as replacement parts were actually required. When accounting for these spare parts, the company initially capitalized their costs and—consistent with GAAP—subsequently wrote them down to reflect the decline in their expected sales price. The Supreme Court ultimately denied the write-down because Thor could not show that the parts (i.e., the excess inventory) were a subnormal good, and even if they had, the company had not actually offered the parts for sale at the lower price. The effect of this decision is to prohibit companies from writing down the value of slow-moving inventory.

## Qualified Production Activities Deduction

Over the years, Congress has adopted a number of measures that it hoped would attract, create and maintain manufacturing jobs in the U.S. For the most part, these provisions were designed to encourage businesses to increase its exports. Most of these approaches, however, resulted in a permanent reduction of U.S. tax and were held to constitute an illegal export subsidy under the U.S. trade agreements with the World Trade Organization. Congress addressed the problem with a different tactic in the *American Jobs Creation Act of 2004* (Jobs Act) with the creation of § 199.

In short, the law now provides direct tax breaks for domestic production activities. The focus has shifted to what companies are doing in the United States, not what they are exporting or moving overseas. Section 199 allows taxpayers to claim a special deduction relating to production and manufacturing activity undertaken in the U.S. and Puerto Rico, regardless of whether the items are exported. When fully effective in 2010, eligible taxpayers will be able to claim a deduction equal to 9 percent of the taxpayer's *qualified production activities income* (QPAI) or if less, the taxpayer's taxable income (modified A.G.I. in the case of an individual). The deduction percentage allowed has been phased in as follows:

| Year | Deduction Percentage |
|---|---|
| 2005–2006 | 3% |
| 2007–2009 | 6 |
| 2010 and thereafter | 9 |

[62] See Reg. § 1.471-2(c). Note that reduction of net realizable value by an allowance for a normal profit margin is not allowed for tax purposes.

[63] 79-1 USTC ¶9139, 43 AFTR2d 79-362, 439 U.S. 522 (USSC, 1979).

All taxpayers are entitled to the deduction (C corporations, S corporations, partnerships, sole proprietorships, estates and trusts). For individual taxpayers, the deduction is for A.G.I. but is not deductible in computing self-employment tax. The effect of the deduction is to reduce a corporation's effective tax rate by about 3 percent (35% × 9% = 3.15%).

## Limitations on Deduction

There are two critical limitations impacting the deduction. QPAI cannot exceed the taxable income limitation and the § 199 deduction itself cannot exceed 50 percent of the employer's wages.

**Taxable Income Limitation** As noted above the deduction is generally 9 percent of QPAI or if smaller, the taxpayer's taxable income. For individual taxpayers, A.G.I. with certain modifications is substituted for taxable income. The taxable income limitation normally applies when a taxpayer has current losses from activities other than production sufficient to offset production income or no current income because of a carryback or carryforward of losses. In such case, the taxpayer receives no benefit from the manufacturing deduction, either currently or by an increase in its NOL carryback or carryforward.

For pass-through entities, the taxable income limitation is determined at the owner or beneficiary level. Therefore, partnerships, S corporations, trusts and estates must separately state the amount of QPAI that flows through to the owners or beneficiaries.

**W-2 Wages Limitation** The § 199 deduction itself cannot exceed 50 percent of the W-2 wages of the employer for the taxable year. W-2 wages are defined as the sum of wages and elective deferrals [e.g., contributions to 401(k) plans that must be reported on Form W-2]. Fiscal year taxpayers use the W-2 wages for the calendar year that ends within the taxpayer's fiscal year Wages include production and non-production employees, as well as key executive officers and staff, in-house counsel, and research and marketing staff. Only wages that are related to domestic production gross receipts are considered in computing the limitation. In addition, in a concession to the film industry, any compensation for services performed in the U.S. by actors, directors and producers is considered W-2 wages.

### Example 22

H and W are married and file a joint return. Each owns and operates a separate business. H has a tax practice with 10 employees. W's business manufactures handcrafted baskets, pottery, ceramics and matching accessories. W's business has about 25 employees directly involved in production and 10 others including herself that are involved in administration, accounting, marketing and similar support functions. Without a special rule, W could count the wages paid by H to his employees in determining the wage limitation. However, § 199 makes it clear that in determining the wage limitation, only the wages related to domestic production gross receipts are considered. Thus only the wages paid to W's employees are taken into account since the wages paid to H's employees are not related to production activities. Also note that the wages of not only those involved directly in the manufacturing process are counted but also those paid to support personnel. Finally observe that the result would be the same if both activities were carried on within a single C or S corporation or partnership.

With respect to partnerships, S corporations and other flow-through entities, the partners, S shareholders and beneficiaries are treated as having paid qualified wages in an amount equal to that owner's allocable share of the wages paid by the entity.

Wages do not include the Schedule C earnings of sole proprietors or the Schedule F earnings of farmers. In addition, wages do not include payments made to partners in partnerships for services rendered (so-called guaranteed payments). In light of this rule, it would appear that "one-person" sole proprietorships do not qualify for the deduction because the income from such businesses is not paid to the owner in the form of wages. This may encourage "one-person" operations to be conducted in the form of an S corporation that pays its owner/sole-employee wages.

### Example 23

Red Flag Inc. manufactures and sells flags. For 2010, it has qualified production activities income (QPAI) of $2,000,000 and taxable income of only $500,000 due to losses from rental activities. The § 199 deduction normally would be $180,000 (9% × $2,000,000) but due to the taxable income limitation the deduction is limited to $45,000 (9% × $500,000 taxable income). The deduction is limited to 9% of the lesser of QPAI or taxable income. Moreover, the deduction cannot exceed 50% of wages paid.

### Example 24

Organic Farms Inc. has QPAI and taxable income of $10,000,000 in 2013. Organic's W-2 wage expense for the year is $1,500,000. The normal deduction would be $900,000 (9% of $10,000,000) but is limited to $750,000 (50% × wages of $1,500,000).

### Example 25

Carl's Custom Cabinets operates as a single member LLC. Carl produces all of the cabinets himself and has no employees. The LLC reports Schedule C net income of $100,000. The amount of the § 199 deduction is zero since Carl's LLC paid no wages. If the $100,000 net income included a $20,000 payment to an independent contractor, the deduction would still be zero since he paid no W-2 wages. The same result would occur if Carl's business was engaged in farming rather than cabinetry.

## Qualified Production Activities Income (QPAI)

QPAI and the § 199 deduction are computed in the following manner:

  Domestic production gross receipts
− Allocable costs of goods sold
− Directly allocable deductions
− Ratable allocation of other deductions not directly allocable to another class of income
= Qualified production activities income (QPAI) not to exceed taxable income
× 9% in 2010 and thereafter
= Qualified production activities deduction not to exceed 50% of W-2 wages

The starting point for computing QPAI is "domestic production gross receipts" (DPGR). DPGR means the gross receipts derived from the following:[64]

1. Any lease, rental, license, sale, exchange, or other disposition of:
   - *Qualifying production property* (QPP) that is manufactured, produced, grown or extracted by the taxpayer in whole or in significant part within the U.S. According to the Regulations, the qualifying activities also include constructing, building, installing, manufacturing, developing or improving property. QPP includes tangible personal

[64] §199(c)(4). For purposes of § 199, the term United States includes Puerto Rico (§ 199(d)(8)). Thus DPGR attributable to activities in Puerto Rico qualify.

property, computer software and certain sound recordings. Production includes farming, food storage, and food processing.
- Certain *qualified films* produced by the taxpayer, including copyrights, trademarks and other intangibles created in production of the film.
- Electricity, natural gas and potable (drinking) water produced in the U.S.

2. Construction performed in the U.S. (including not only erection but also substantial renovation of residential or nonresidential buildings); and
3. Engineering or architectural services performed in the U.S. for construction projects in the U.S.

### Example 26

XBX Corporation sells a CD-ROM disk in a plastic case that contains a video game to be played on a computer. XBX also provides technical support. The CD-ROM and the case are tangible personal property but the computer game on the disk is considered computer software. If the disk was manufactured in China, the case was manufactured in Mexico and the software was developed in California, the proceeds of the sale must be allocated between qualified DPGR (the software) and nonqualified gross receipts (the CD-ROM and the case). Note also that computer software qualifies even though it might not be be operated on a computer (e.g., a video game for a video game player (e.g., Play-station, Xbox, Gameboy)). In addition, observe that in selling the game the company has also sold a service (technical support), the price of which is embedded in the total price of the item. Receipts from services do not qualify as DPGR. A special de minimis rule permits the taxpayer to ignore the receipts attributable to the services if they are less than five percent of the receipts received from the property.

### Example 27

Same facts as in *Example 26* except the game may be played on demand online for a fee. According to the Regulations, such fees are not considered qualified DPGR. As might be expected, businesses question whether such interpretation is appropriate since the software is produced in the same way but simply delivered differently.

Note that the definition of DPGR is quite broad, extending the benefits of § 199 to a wide variety of activities. In fact, some of these activities normally are not associated with manufacturing. For example, § 199 blesses receipts from engineering and architectural services, publishing and related advertising, motion picture production, television production, musical recording production, traditional or cable broadcasting, home construction, the writing of machine-readable computer code and meat packing. However, § 199 identifies certain gross receipts that do not qualify, including those from the

1. Sale of food and beverages prepared by the taxpayer at a retail establishment (e.g., restaurants); but, wholesale sales of such prepared items do qualify.
2. Transmission or distribution of electricity, natural gas, or potable (drinkable) water.
3. Property leased, licensed, or rented by the taxpayer for use by any related person.

**De Minimus 5% Rule** One major simplification addresses the calculation of DPGR where the taxpayer has receipts from both qualifying and nonqualifying activities (e.g., U.S. and foreign production or manufacturing and services). If the taxpayer earns less than five percent of total gross receipts from nonqualifying activities (including interest, dividends, royalties and all other nonqualifying receipts), it may treat all of its gross receipts as domestic production gross receipts and no allocation is required. The reverse is also true. If less than five percent of total gross receipts are from domestic production activities, all of the taxpayer's gross receipts may be treated as non-DPGR. This rule enables taxpayer to avoid the complex provisions of § 199. In this regard, it should be emphasized that § 199 is not optional.

**DPGR: Item-By-Item Determination** In many cases, a product represents the combination of several components only some of which may be qualified property (e.g., manufactured in the U.S). For example, televisions, cars, computers or similar products may consist of components manufactured in the U.S. or elsewhere. In these situations, DPGR must be determined on an item-by-item basis and not by division, product line or transaction.[65] Generally this requires that the taxpayer drill down and perform an analysis of each component of the property to determine its origin even though doing so can be unduly burdensome and costly. This approach is often referred to as the "shrinkback rule" because the taxpayer must "shrink back" the product to the largest component that does qualify. The government believes that if this approach was not used, taxpayers might otherwise receive benefits for gross receipts that do not qualify.

### Example 28

Since 1930 CH Inc. has operated a shoe manufacturing business in Maine. Historically, everything was "made in the U.S.A." However, last year, CH hired a new CEO who brought in new ideas, including changes in the company's traditional manufacturing practices. Under the new approach, the company continues to manufacture leather and rubber soles but imports the shoe's uppers (the parts of the shoe above the sole). CH manufactures shoes for sale by sewing or otherwise attaching the soles to the imported uppers. In determining CH's DPGR from the shoe sales, the gross receipts from the sale of the entire shoe would not qualify. However, under the shrinkback rule, the soles would be considered the item and the sales receipts allocable to the soles would qualify as DPGR.

**Expense Allocation** After DPGR is determined, allocable costs are subtracted to arrive at QPAI. As may be seen in the formula, if a taxpayer is in a "manufacturing" business, the taxpayer's QPAI theoretically will equal its taxable income. Indeed, for many businesses, particularly small ones, this should be the case. For example, if a company only manufactures envelopes in the U.S., its taxable income and QPAI should be the same. since all of its taxable income relates to manufacturing. This also would be the case for a contractor that only builds homes in the U.S. Similarly, an architectural firm whose sole source of income is from providing architectural services should have identical amounts of taxable income and QPAI. On the other, because this is often not the case, the key to calculating the correct deduction amount is a proper allocation of items of gross receipts, expense, losses, and deductions for determining QPAI.

The Regulations contain three methods for allocating expenses. Two of these are simplifed methods for small businesses while the third applies to all other taxpayers (or small businesses if they choose).

1. *Small Business Simplified Overall Method.* Taxpayers with gross receipts less than $5 million may allocate all costs, including costs of goods sold, based on gross receipts. This also applies to taxpayers with gross receipts less than $10 million if they are eligible to use cash-method of accounting.
2. *Simplified Deduction Method.* Taxpayers with less than $25 million gross receipts may allocate non-costs of good sold expenses based on gross receipts.
3. *Section 861 method.* This method uses the principles relating to determining the source of taxable income for purposes of the foreign tax credit (i.e., whether taxable income derives from activities within or outside the United States). The § 861 method is mandatory for taxpayers with greater than $25 million gross receipts; it is voluntary for other taxpayers.

---

[65] Reg. § 1.199-3(d)(1)

### Example 29

G Inc. manufactures razor blades in a plants in Columbus, Ohio and Munich, Germany. The blades from both factories are sold all over the world. Gross receipts from the sales of blades from the Columbus operation qualify as DPGR for purpose of calculating the production deduction since they are derived from the sale of qualifying production property—tangible personal property (the razor blades)—that is manufactured by the taxpayer, G, entirely in the U.S. Note that all of the gross receipts qualify as domestic notwithstanding the fact that a portion could be attributable to sales in foreign countries (e.g., Canada and Mexico).

### Example 30

Same facts as above. For the current year, the company reported taxable income of $4,000,000. Total wages for all employees were $6,000,000. The company's records reveal the additional information below. Based on this information the production deduction is $360,000 computed as follows:

| | | | | |
|---|---|---|---|---|
| Qualifying domestic production gross receipts | | $15,000,000 | | |
| Allocable costs: | | | | |
| Costs of good sold | $4,000,000 | | | |
| Directly allocable expenses | 3,000,000 | | | |
| Indirect expenses | 1,000,000 | | | |
| Total allocable costs | | (8,000,000) | | |
| Qualified production activities income | | $7,000,000 | | |
| Taxable income before the production deduction | | $4,000,000 | | |
| Lesser of QPAI $7,000,000 or taxable income $4,000,000 | | | $4,000,000 | |
| 2011 rate | | | × 9% | |
| Tentative production deduction | | | $ 360,000 | |
| Wage limitation (50% × $6,000,000 wages) | | | $3,000,000 | |
| Production deduction (lesser of tentative production deduction or wage limitation) | | | | $360,000 |

Note that the production deduction is permitted for AMT purposes. However, the taxable income limitation is based on AMTI rather than taxable income.

**Unresolved Issues** Unfortunately, the artificial simplicity of the examples above masks the many obstacles that make application of § 199 troublesome. To appreciate the difficulty, simply consider the basic requirements that must be met in order to secure the deduction: *qualified property must be manufactured, produced, grown, or extracted by the taxpayer in whole or in significant part within the U.S.* At the start, § 199 provides no definition of manufacturing or production. Does assembly of vacuum cleaners or conversion of orange concentrate into orange juice constitute production? What about mixing water and concentrate to produce soft drinks or French Vanilla coffee? When McDonald's sells a hamburger is it providing a service or is it combining inputs to manufacture a product? While the Regulations address some of these issues, many are still unresolved.

Still another complication involves the complexity in distinguishing between qualified and nonqualified gross receipts and the problem of allocating expenses between them. The already famous "Starbucks footnote" found in the Conference Report acknowledges the difficulty.

**Example 31**

Coffee Inc. operates a chain of coffee shops all over the world. It buys coffee beans and roasts and packages them at its own central processing facility. It distributes the packages of roasted coffee to its own retail stores which the stores brew for selling to customers. In addition, the stores sell the packaged coffee directly to consumers and to other retail stores. How are the gross receipts from a single sale of coffee classified? How much is attributable to the qualifying production activity, the roasting of the beans, and how much is attributed to the nonqualifying activity, the processing in the retail establishment. An even more daunting question concerns how the various costs of operating the company are to be allocated between these activities. According to the footnote, only the sales receipts attributable to the off-site roasting function can be taken into account in computing QPAI. The balance of the receipts is not qualified. Note also that the rule creates an incentive for a company like Starbucks to increase the amount that its factory charges its retail store in order to increase the amount of factory gross receipts and thus increase the deduction.

There are many other issues worthy of consideration but are beyond the scope of this overview. The Regulations issued in October 2005 do provide guidance on how to solve some of these problems but not all. In any event, it should be emphasized that § 199 can have a major impact not simply on the accounting systems that must be designed to capture the required information but also on how a company structures itself and conducts its business.

# Tax Planning Considerations

## Casualty and Theft Losses

Much of the controversy surrounding casualty losses results from insufficient documentation of the loss. For this reason, taxpayers should give careful attention to accumulating the evidence necessary to establish the deduction. Such evidence would include, where appropriate, pictures, eyewitnesses, police reports, and newspaper accounts. The taxpayer also should gather evidence regarding the value of the property damaged or destroyed. In situations where an item is not repaired or replaced, an appraisal may be the only method of adequately valuing the loss.

In some cases, a taxpayer may suffer a casualty loss and in seeking insurance reimbursement incur appraisal costs. Even if the casualty loss is not deductible due to the 10 percent limitation, the appraisal costs are deductible as a cost of preparing the tax return and are therefore claimed as a miscellaneous itemized deduction.

Taxpayers often measure the amount of their casualty losses by the amount paid for repairs that are necessary to bring the property back to its condition before the casualty. This method of measuring may be inappropriate, however, if the repairs do not restore the property to its same condition before the casualty. In such case, an additional loss representing the decline in value should be claimed.

The rules for determining the deductible casualty loss have important implications for the amount of insurance that a taxpayer should maintain.

**Example 32**

T purchased a home in Boston for $70,000 15 years ago. This year, the home burned to the ground and the taxpayer received a $70,000 reimbursement from the insurance company. The cost of rebuilding the house was $200,000. Although T's economic loss was $130,000 ($200,000 – $70,000), none of the loss is deductible as a casualty loss. The casualty loss deduction is the *lesser* of the decline in value, $200,000, or the taxpayer's adjusted basis, $70,000, less the insurance reimbursement. Since the insurance reimbursement of $70,000 completely offset T's basis, there is no deductible loss.

## Bad Debts

It is not uncommon for family members or friends to make loans to each other that are never repaid. This often occurs when a son or daughter is embarking on a business venture in which a parent is willing to invest. If the taxpayer wishes to claim a deduction if the debt is not paid, steps should be taken upon making the loan to ensure that the loan is not considered a gift. For example, the taxpayer should document the transaction in such a way that it is clear that both parties intend that repayment of the loan will occur. The best method of documenting the parties' wishes is to have a formal note drafted. Such a note would lend support to the argument that a debtor-creditor relationship existed between the parties. The note also should have a definite payment schedule, and each payment should be made on time. Collateral could be included as well. In addition, the note should call for a reasonable amount of interest. Failure to charge adequate interest could cause the imputed interest rules discussed in Chapter 5 to operate.

**Example 33**

In 2011 F loaned his friend K $10,000 to start a chocolate chip cookie business. The business struggled along, requiring K to ask F for another $5,000, which he gladly loaned her. The business failed after six months. If F documented the loans and sought repayment, he may claim a deduction for a nonbusiness bad debt. If he failed to do so, any deduction may be disallowed.

## Net Operating Losses

When a taxpayer suffers a net operating loss, a decision must be made whether to carry the loss back or elect to carry it forward only. Due to the time value of money, a carryback is usually more advantageous since an immediate tax refund can be obtained. However, this gain must be weighed against the future benefits to be obtained by a carryforward. If the taxpayer expects to be in a higher tax bracket in the future, the present value of the higher savings may be greater than the value of an immediate refund.

# Problem Materials

### DISCUSSION QUESTIONS

**10-1** *Business vs. Nonbusiness Bad Debts.* R is employed as the chief executive officer of XYZ Corporation. Believing the company's future to be bright, he has acquired 75 percent of XYZ's stock. During the year, R loaned XYZ $10,000. Explain the tax consequences assuming XYZ is unable to repay all or a portion of the loan.

**10-2** *Bad Debt Requirements.* Under what circumstances, if any, is a cash basis taxpayer allowed to claim a deduction for a bad debt? An accrual basis taxpayer?

**10-3** *Identifying Bad Debts.* For each of the following situations, indicate whether the taxpayer would be able to claim a deduction for a bad debt.

**a.** Several years ago, F advanced $30,000 to his wholly owned corporation, which was experiencing financial difficulties. Last year he loaned it another $10,000. No notes were executed and no payments have been made. During the current year, the company declared bankruptcy.

**b.** E quit his old job as a salesperson to become a sales manager for K Corporation this year. As part of his arrangement with K, he was to receive a $10,000 bonus if the company reached $1 million in sales for the year. Sales for the year were $900,000, and K Corporation did not pay E a bonus.

**c.** B and C each own 50 percent of ABC Incorporated. Over the years, ABC made loans to C. When C died he was penniless. He owed the company $20,000.

**10-4** *Is There a Bad Debt?* Several years ago, R's son, S, got into the restaurant business. R loaned S $10,000 to help him get the business going. No note was signed nor was any interest charged. The business was initially a huge success but as time passed, it began having financial problems. This year the son's business failed.

**a.** Can R claim a bad debt deduction? If so, is the debt a business or nonbusiness bad debt and how much is the deduction?

**b.** Same as (a) except R obtained a signed note from his son.

**10-5** *Bad Debt of Related Party.* H loaned her son $10,000 to enter the car repair business. If the son subsequently abandons the business and does not repay the loan, what are the tax consequences to H?

**10-6** *Casualty Losses.* Explain the rationale underlying the rules (lower of basis or value with certain exceptions) for computing the amount of the deduction for a casualty loss.

**10-7** *Casualty Losses.* During the year, R had various losses. Explain whether each of the following would qualify as a casualty loss.

**a.** Loss of stove due to electrical fire.

**b.** Damage to water pipes from freezing temperatures in Southern California.

**c.** Loss of tree from Dutch elm disease.

**d.** Ruined carpeting from clogged sewer line.

**e.** Hole in his suit from cigarette ashes he dropped; ruined shirt from pen leaking.

**f.** Damage to both his and his neighbor's car while R's son drove R's car.

**g.** Luggage and contents seized by a foreign government during a European vacation.

**10-8** *Theft Loss Calculation.* If taxpayers could plan their taxes to account for thefts of their own personal use property (e.g., theft of their stereo and television), would they want the burglar to take all the property at once or take some property the first time and return for more later?

**10-9** *Net Operating Losses in General.* Comment on each of the following:

**a.** The purposes of the net operating loss deduction.

**b.** The rationale underlying the complex calculation of the net operating loss deduction.

**c.** How a net operating loss occurring in 2011 is utilized (i.e., the carryover process).

**10-10** *Inventoriable Costs: § 263A.* HHG operates a chain of retail appliance stores. The company has grown tremendously over the past several years. It expects that its gross receipts will exceed $10 million this year. What are the implications of this growth for the company's method of accounting for inventories?

**10-11** *LIFO vs. FIFO.* During the 1970s, there was a tremendous shift from the FIFO method of inventory to LIFO. Nevertheless, not every company shifted to the LIFO method. Discuss why some might shift to LIFO although others might not.

## PROBLEMS

**10-12** *Treatment of Bad Debts.* AAA Computer Company, an accrual basis corporation, installed a new computerized accounting system for a customer and billed him $1,500 in June, 2011. When aging its accounts receivable at year-end, the company found that the customer was experiencing financial difficulties.

**a.** Assuming the company estimated that only $1,000 of the account would be collected, what is the amount of the bad debt deduction, if any, that it can claim in 2011?

**b.** Would the answer to (a) change if the debt were a nonbusiness bad debt?

**c.** In 2012 the company actually collected $200 and the remainder of the debt was worthless. What is the amount of the bad debt deduction, if any, that it can claim in 2012?

**10-13** *Bad Debts and Accounting Methods.* Dr. D, a dentist, performed a root canal for a patient and charged him $300. The patient paid $100, then left town, never to be seen again. What is the amount of bad debt deduction, if any, that D may claim assuming that she is a cash basis taxpayer?

**10-14** *Uncollectible Loan.* Several years ago, L loaned his old high-school friend B $5,000 to help him start a new business. Things did not go as well as B planned, and late in 2011 B declared bankruptcy. L expects to collect 40 cents on the dollar. In 2012 all of B's affairs were settled and L received $1,000. What are the tax consequences to L in 2011 and 2012?

**10-15** *Personal Casualty.* When the waters of the Mississippi began to overflow their banks and flood the surrounding area, M was forced to leave her home and head for higher ground. On December 2, she returned to her home to find that it had been vandalized as well as damaged from the flood. After cleaning up, she determined that the following items had been stolen or damaged:

| Item | Adjusted Basis | FMV Before | FMV After | Insurance Reimbursement |
|---|---|---|---|---|
| Fur coat | $6,000 | $7,000 | $0 | $7,000 |
| Computer | 4,000 | 3,000 | 0 | Uninsured |
| Couch | 1,200 | 800 | See below | 500 |
| Van | 7,000 | 5,000 | | |

The couch had been damaged and M had it reupholstered for $700. The insurance company reimbursed her for the amounts shown on December 27. Under M's insurance policy, the company did not reimburse her for loss on the car until 45 days had passed. M expected to recover $4,000 but, after several delays, finally received a check for $2,000 on April 25, 2012. While she was waiting for reimbursement for her van, she rented a car at a total cost of $700. Although M received value for the coat, she did not replace it. In addition to the losses shown above, her real estate broker advised that even though her house had not been damaged by the flood, the value had dropped by $20,000 since it was evident that it was located in an area prone to flooding.

**a.** Compute M's casualty loss deduction, assuming her A.G.I. in 2011 was $18,000 and in 2012, $20,000.

**b.** Assume the loss occurred on January 2, 2012 and the location was officially designated a disaster area by the President. Explain when the loss could be deducted.

**10-16** *Casualty Loss: Business and Investment Property.* H is a private detective. While sleuthing this year, his car was stolen. The car, which was used entirely for business, was worth $7,000 and had an adjusted basis of $12,000. H received no insurance reimbursement for his car. Also this year, his office was the victim of arson. The fire destroyed only a painting that had a basis of $1,500 and was worth $3,000. H received a reimbursement of $800 from his insurance company for the painting. H suffered yet another misfortune this year as his rental property was damaged by a flood, the first in the area in 70 years. Before the casualty, the property—which had greatly appreciated in value—was worth $90,000 and afterward only $40,000. The rental property had an adjusted basis of $30,000. He received $20,000 from the insurance company, the maximum amount for which homes in a flood plain could be insured. Compute H's casualty loss deduction assuming his A.G.I. is $30,000. Can a casualty loss create a net operating loss?

**10-17** *Casualty Gains and Losses.* This year, C's jewelry, which cost $10,000, was stolen from her home. Luckily, she was insured and the insurance company reimbursed her for its current value, $19,000. In addition, while she was on vacation all of her camera equipment was stolen. The camera equipment had cost her $3,500 and was worth $3,100. She received no reimbursement since she carried a large deductible on such items. C's A.G.I. for the year was $15,000.

**a.** What is the effect of the casualty losses on C's taxable income?

**b.** Same as above except the jewelry was worth $11,000.

**10-18** *Casualty and Theft Loss Computation.* In each of the following cases, compute the taxpayer's casualty loss deduction (before percentage limitations) and indicate whether it is deductible *for* or *from* adjusted gross income.

**a.** While G was at the theater, his house (adjusted basis $60,000, fair market value $80,000) was completely destroyed by fire. The fire also completely destroyed both his skiing equipment (cost $300, fair market value $90) and a calculator (adjusted basis \$110, fair market value \$80) used for business. He was reimbursed for \$30,000 with respect to the house.

b. B owned a duplex which she rented. A tornado demolished the roof but did not damage the remainder of the duplex. The duplex's value before the tornado was \$45,000 and after the tornado was \$40,000. B's adjusted basis in the property was \$30,000. The President declared the entire city a "disaster area."

c. Assume the same facts in (b) except that instead of B's duplex being partially damaged it was her personal cabin cruiser, and she received a \$2,000 reimbursement from the insurance company.

d. L backed his car out of the garage and ran over his 10-speed bicycle (cost \$400, fair market value \$300). The bicycle is worthless.

**10-19** *NOL Items.* Indicate whether the following items can create a net operating loss for an individual taxpayer.

a. Business capital loss
b. Nonbusiness bad debt
c. Casualty loss
d. Interest expense on mortgage secured by primary residence
e. Employee business expenses
f. Contribution to Individual Retirement Account
g. Alimony
h. Personal exemption

**10-20** *Items Considered in Computing an NOL.* Indicate whether the following items are considered in computing the net operating loss deduction for an individual.

a. Salary
b. Capital gain on the sale of investment property
c. Interest income
d. Interest on a mortgage on a primary residence

**10-21** *Net Operating Loss Computation.* R, a single taxpayer, operates a bicycle shop. For the calendar year 2011 he reports the following items of income and expense:

| | |
|---|---|
| Gross income from business | \$150,000 |
| Business operating expenses | 210,000 |
| Interest income from investments | 7,000 |
| Casualty loss | 4,000 |
| Interest expense on home mortgage | 9,000 |
| Long-term capital gains (nonbusiness) | 3,000 |
| Long-term capital loss (nonbusiness) | 5,000 |
| Long-term capital gains (business) | 1,000 |

The casualty loss represented the uninsured theft of R's personal auto worth \$4,100 (\$9,000 adjusted basis).

a. Compute R's net operating loss for 2011.
b. Assuming R carries the loss back to 2009, when must the corrected return for 2009 be filed?

**10-22** *Net Operating Loss Computation.* V, married with two dependents, owns a hardware store. For the current year, her records reveal the following:

| | |
|---|---|
| Gross income from sales | \$180,000 |
| Business operating expenses | 230,000 |
| Royalties from investment | 6,000 |
| Nonbusiness expenses | 9,000 |
| Long-term capital gain (nonbusiness) | 5,000 |
| Long-term capital gain (business) | 3,000 |
| Long-term capital loss (business) | 3,500 |

What is V's net operating loss?

**10-23** *Valuing Inventories.* Chapters Inc., a large publishing house, prints a variety of titles, some of which are best sellers and others of which are duds. Because it is very difficult for Chapters to estimate with any accuracy which books will be successful, and because the marginal cost of printing an additional book is small, it typically prints 5,000 more copies than it expects to sell. Books that are not sold within a year of release are stored. The company's experience has shown that 95 percent of the books stored are never sold. Consequently, the company writes off any excess copies once they are delivered to storage. This practice appears permissible for financial accounting purposes. Can the same procedure be used for tax purposes?

**10-24** *Applying Lower of Cost or Market.* Fitness Galore specializes in selling physical fitness equipment. The company's inventory at the close of this year revealed the following:

| *Mercandise* | *Cost* | *Replacement Cost* |
|---|---|---|
| Weight machines | $40,000 | $43,000 |
| Stationary bicycles | 10,000 | 8,000 |
| Stair climbers | 24,000 | 27,000 |

**a.** Compute the company's inventory assuming it uses the lower of FIFO cost or market.

**b.** Assume the company adopts LIFO next year. Explain the tax consequences.

**10-25** *Double Extension Dollar-Value LIFO.* Unwound Sound has recently engaged a CPA to evaluate its inventory procedures and determine if it should change from using FIFO to LIFO to account for inventories. The company's inventory records for 2010 and 2011 are shown below. Assume that the company had adopted double-extension dollar-value LIFO in 2010, and compute the ending inventory for:

**a.** 2010

**b.** 2011

| | *1-1-2010* | | *12-31-2011* | |
|---|---|---|---|---|
| *Inventory Pool* | *Units* | *Cost Per Unit* | *Units* | *Cost Per Unit* |
| Records | 5,000 | $2 | 3,000 | $2 |
| Tapes | 4,000 | 3 | 6,000 | 4 |
| Compact discs | 2,000 | 6 | 5,000 | 7 |

| | *12-31-2011* | |
|---|---|---|
| *Inventory Pool* | *Units* | *Cost Per Unit* |
| Records | 2,000 | $3 |
| Tapes | 3,000 | 5 |
| Compact discs | 4,000 | 7 |

**10-26** *LIFO Pooling.* As shown in *Problem 10-25* above, the inventory of Unwound Sound consists of records, tapes, and compact discs. Over the last 15 years, the components of the company's inventory have changed dramatically. Whereas once the company only carried records, now it also carries tapes and CDs. Unwound Sound expects that in the very near future it will discontinue selling records. Assuming the company uses LIFO, explain the advantages of having one single pool containing all three items rather than three different pools.

**10-27** *Accounting for Inventories.* VE Trucking Inc., an S Corporation and a cash-basis taxpayer, buys and transports sand and gravel for its customers, primarily contractors and developers. The contractors and developers use the materials in the construction of foundations for streets, houses, buildings and other construction projects. Normally, a customer contacts VE and orders a load of sand or gravel which VE subsequently buys from another source. VE then picks up the materials and delivers them to the customer's job site. VE bills the customer a flat sum, representing the costs of the materials and transportation. To determine the amount of the charge, the total cost is marked up for a reasonable profit. Because VE acquires and delivers the sand and gravel to its customers during the same business day, it does not possess any sand and gravel at the beginning or end of its business day. VE has been very profitable over the past ten years, averaging annual earnings of about $4,000,000 on annual revenues of about $15,000,000.

**a.** Must VE use the accrual method? If so, will the accrual method have any impact given that VE has no materials at the beginning and end of each business day?

**b.** Same as (a) except VE has average annual gross receipts of $8,000,000.

**c.** Same as (b) except VE is a C corporation

**d.** Same as (a) except VE has average annual gross receipts of $700,000.

**10-28** *Production Deduction.* For each of the following situations, explain how the facts affect application and determination of the § 199 deduction related to qualified production activities.

**a.** BAH is a strategic management and technology consulting firm that provides advisory services to companies around the world.

**b.** AMZ Inc. sells books and other products over the Internet throughout the world. All of its products that are purchased for resale are manufactured or produced by U.S. companies in the U.S.

**c.** MSFT Inc. distributes software written by its employees.

**d.** RYL Inc., located in Detroit, is a construction company that primarily builds residential homes. It also is in the business of selling and assembling prefabricated steel buildings used primarily by businesses. The materials for these metal buildings are supplied by another corporation. RYL simply pours the foundation and bolts the materials in place. In addition, RYL's engineers and architects provide consulting services. One of RYL's subsidiaries is in the remodeling business.

**e.** CSC is currently a single member limited liability company operated by Jim Smith. The LLC has seven employees. It is in the advertising business, producing commercials for television, radio, the Internet, and print media.

**f.** PNA Inc. operates several restaurants in Houston. Its menu consists primarily of soup and sandwiches. The company's baked products such as bread and cookies are also popular. In fact, PNA has its own central baking operation that produces bread and other pastry items that are sold to some of the finest restaurants in the area.

**10-29** *Domestic Production Gross Receipts.* OMG owns and operates grocery stores throughout Chicago. In addition to its retail outlets, it has its own bakery, ice-making, meat-processing and egg-farming businesses. Answer the following questions concerning the company's domestic production gross receipts (DPGR).

**a.** OMG is primarily a reseller. Will it qualify for the § 199 deduction?

**b.** Many OMG stores have their own bakery that bakes bread, cakes, and similar items that are sold at the store to its retail customers. Do the receipts qualify as DPGR?

**c.** Many stores have contracts to provide fresh baked goods daily to area restaurants. Would receipts from sales to these wholesale customers qualify as DPGR?

**d.** Many of the baked goods sold to retail customers at OMG stores such as bread are baked off-site at a central baking facility and transported to their stores. Would receipts from sales to its retail customers qualify as DPGR?

**e.** In some instances, dough may be made or bread may be partially baked at a central baking facility and then transported to the stores for final baking. Would receipts from sales to its retail customers qualify as DPGR?

**f.** OMG has a construction division that builds the company's stores as well as strip malls in which the stores are located and serve as anchors. It leases the space in the strip malls to other businesses. Does OMG have any qualifying DPGR from these activities?

## TAX RESEARCH PROBLEMS

**10-30** R has had several minor automobile accidents in the last two years. During the current year, R demolished his car (value, $7,000; adjusted basis, $8,000) when he ran into a telephone pole. He used the car solely for business. R decided not to report the accident to the insurance company and claim his reimbursement because he believes his insurance rates will be raised if he does. Will R's deduction of his unreimbursed casualty loss be allowed?

**10-31** T, a cash basis taxpayer, paid a swimming pool contractor, C, the sum of $10,000 in advance for improvements that C agreed to make to T's personal residence. C performed part of the contract and then ceased activity, leaving much of the work uncompleted. T seeks advice concerning whether she may claim a deduction for a bad debt.

**10-32** Ten years ago Mac and Beth left the stress of city life and moved to a beautiful home near Davenport overlooking the Mississippi River. Mac took a job as a dealer at a local riverboat gambling casino while Beth became a full-time mom. The couple was happily raising their four children until 2010, the year of the great flood. Their home, although several miles from the river, suffered thousands of dollars of water damage. Other homes in their small subdivision that were on somewhat lower ground had far worse damage. Mac and Beth and their neighbors were quite shocked that this could happen to them since they lived in an area where it had not flooded for over 100 years. But then some were calling this the 100-year flood. After cleaning up, several of the owners decided to move, not willing to take any more chances. Unfortunately, those people who were able to sell their homes sold them for far less than what they thought they were worth, presumably because they lived in what was now perceived as a flood-prone area. Although Mac was not planning on selling his home, he did decide it was time to refinance his mortgage, the second time in 18 months. As part of the process, he got an appraisal that revealed that the value of his home had dropped substantially from the last time it was appraised. In 2007, when he refinanced for the first time, it appeared that he had made a great investment since he had purchased the house for $150,000 and the house was appraised at a value of $225,000. However, the most recent appraisal revealed that the house was worth only $120,000. What is the amount of the couple's casualty loss deduction, if any?

**10-33** In 1987, Michael Malone, a professor of computer science and a specialist in digital technology, realized that it was only a short time before the computer would change the way people lived. Although he was 49 and quite happy with his $70,000 annual salary, he decided that this was an opportunity he just could not pass up. In 1986, he formed a new corporation, investing virtually all of his accumulated wealth, $200,000, in exchange for 51 percent of its stock. Three other individuals contributed additional cash for the remaining 49 percent of the stock. In the first few years of operation, the corporation was immensely successful. In 1988 Mike retired from the university and turned all of his attention to the business. All went well. In fact, things went so well that, by 1995, Mike turned over the supervision of everyday operations to several trusted employees; he began spending more time at the golf course and less time at the office. He was completely content working 20 hours a week and drawing an annual salary of $70,000. That income combined with his pension from the university of $20,000 a year was more than enough to keep him happy. During 2009, however, the competition in the computer business became fierce and the corporation had cash flow problems. As a result, Michael loaned the corporation $150,000 to keep it afloat. Unfortunately, the corporation was not able to survive and declared bankruptcy in 2011. How should Michael treat the worthless loan?

# 11

# Itemized Deductions

## Learning Objectives

Upon completion of this chapter you will be able to:

LO.1 Identify the personal expenses that qualify as itemized deductions.

LO.2 Explain the rules regarding deductible medical expenses and compute the medical expense deduction.

LO.3 Distinguish between deductible taxes and nondeductible fees or other charges.

LO.4 Explain the rules regarding deductible state income taxes.

LO.5 Distinguish between currently deductible and nondeductible interest expenses.

LO.6 Explain the requirements for the deductibility of charitable contributions and compute the contribution deduction.

LO.7 Identify the personal expenditures that qualify as either miscellaneous itemized deductions or other itemized deductions.

## Chapter Outline


Introduction 11-2
Medical Expenses 11-2
- In General 11-2
- When Deductible 11-3
- Deduction Limitations 11-4
- Special Items and Equipment 11-5
- Special Care Facilities 11-6
- Long-Term Care Costs 11-7
- Medical Travel and Transportation 11-7
- Medical Insurance Costs and Reimbursements 11-8
- Health Savings Accounts and Medical Savings Accounts 11-9
- Health Insurance Costs of Self-Employed Taxpayers 11-12

Personal Casualty and Theft Losses 11-13
- Year Deductible 11-13
- Reporting Casualty Losses 11-13

Taxes 11-13
- General Requirements for Deductibility 11-14
- Income Taxes 11-15
- Deduction for State and Local General Sales Tax 11-16
- Property Taxes 11-17
- Reporting Deductions for Taxes 11-19

Interest Expense 11-20
- Limitations on Deductions of Interest Expense 11-20
- Classification of Interest Expense 11-29
- When Deductible 11-33
- Where Reported 11-34

Charitable Contributions 11-35
- Deduction Requirements 11-35
- Limitations on Deductions 11-37
- Contribution Carryovers 11-45

Miscellaneous Itemized Deductions 11-46
- Other Itemized Deductions 11-47

| | | | |
|---|---|---|---|
| Tax Planning Considerations | 11-48 | Charitable Contributions | 11-49 |
| Maximizing Personal Deductions | 11-48 | Miscellaneous Deductions | 11-49 |
| Medical Expenses | 11-48 | Problem Materials | 11-50 |


## Introduction

**LO.1**
Identify the personal expenses that qualify as itemized deductions.

Although the vast majority of deductions are those for trade or business expenses, a taxpayer's deductions are not confined to these alone. As noted in Chapter 7, since 1942 Congress has also allowed taxpayers to deduct expenses relating to profit-seeking activities—thus creating a *second* category of so-called investment or nonbusiness expenses. In addition, despite the fact that Code § 262 expressly prohibits the deduction of personal expenditures, Congress has created various exceptions. As a result, a *third* category of deductible expenses exists, which contains such personal items as medical expenses, casualty losses, interest on home mortgages, taxes on real and personal property, charitable contributions, and tax return preparation costs. The last four chapters have focused primarily on business expenses. This chapter continues the discussion of the three types of deductions by examining the specific statutory and administrative authority relating to personal itemized deductions. As defined in Chapter 3, these personal expenses are deducted by a taxpayer only if (1) they exceed the available standard deduction, or (2) the taxpayer is not eligible for the standard deduction.

Before considering these deductions in detail, it should be emphasized that a particular type of expense (e.g., interest) does not necessarily receive the same treatment in all situations. More often than not, the expense is treated differently depending on whether it is business, investment, or personal in nature. For example, the deductibility of interest expense generally depends on whether it is related to a loan that was used to make a business, investment, or personal expenditure. In contrast, real property taxes are deductible regardless of whether the property is used for business, investment, or personal purposes. The character of the expense may also affect the deduction's classification. Generally, trade or business expenses (other than the unreimbursed expenses of an employee) and expenses related to producing rents or royalties are deductions *for* A.G.I., while other expenses are *itemized deductions* which may or may not be subject to the 2 percent floor.

## Medical Expenses

### In General

**LO.2**
Explain the rules regarding deductible medical expenses and compute the medical expense deduction.

Deductible medical expenses include amounts paid for the diagnosis, cure, relief, treatment, or prevention of disease of the taxpayer, his or her spouse, and dependents.[1] The status of a person as the taxpayer's spouse or dependent must exist *either* at the time the medical services are rendered *or* at the time the expenses are paid.[2] A spousal relationship does not exist if the taxpayer is legally separated from his or her spouse under a decree of separate maintenance because the two parties are not considered married.[3] For purposes of dependency status, however, *both* the gross income test and the joint return test are waived.[4]

**Example 1**

T pays all the medical expenses of his mother, M, during the current year. Although M had gross income in excess of the exemption amount ($3,700 in 2011) for the current year, all other dependency tests are met by T. Even though T cannot claim M as a dependent, he will be allowed to deduct all medical expenses paid on her behalf (assuming T itemizes his deductions and they exceed the percentage limitations imposed on medical deductions).

---

1 See §§ 213(a) and 213(d)(1).

2 Reg. § 1.213-1(e)(3).

3 § 143(a).

4 See Reg. § 1.213-1(a)(3)(i) and Chapter 4 for a discussion of the dependency tests.

Medical expenses for children of divorced parents are deductible by the parent who pays for them, regardless of which parent is entitled to the dependency exemption. Additionally, if a taxpayer is entitled to a dependency exemption under a multiple support agreement, the taxpayer will be allowed to deduct any medical expenses which he or she actually pays on behalf of the claimed dependent.[5]

Medical expenses also include payments for treatment affecting any part or function of the body,[6] expenditures for certain medicines and drugs,[7] expenses paid for transportation primarily *for* and *essential* to the rendition of the medical care,[8] and payments made for medical care insurance for the taxpayer, his or her spouse, and dependents.[9] Again, the term *dependent* includes any person who would otherwise qualify as the taxpayer's dependent even though the gross income or separate return tests are not met, and any person claimed as a dependent under a multiple support agreement.

Partial lists of deductible and nondeductible medical expenses are presented in Exhibits 11-1 and 11-2. The most recent addition to the list of nondeductible medical expenses involves cosmetic surgery or other similar procedure. Cosmetic surgery is defined as any procedure that is directed at improving the patient's appearance and does not meaningfully promote the proper function of the body or prevent or treat disease. Thus, the costs of face lifts, liposuction, hair transplants, and other similar elective procedures undertaken primarily to improve the taxpayer's physical appearance are not deductible. However, deductions are allowed for procedures necessary to ameliorate a congenital deformity, a personal injury arising from an accident or trauma, or a disfiguring disease.

## WHEN DEDUCTIBLE

In computing the medical expense deduction for a given tax year, the taxpayer is allowed to take into account *only* those medical expenses *actually paid* during the taxable year,

**EXHIBIT 11.1 Partial List of Deductible Medical Expenses[10]**

- Fees paid for doctors, surgeons, dentists, osteopaths, ophthalmologists, optometrists, chiropractors, chiropodists, podiatrists, psychiatrists, psychologists, and Christian Science practitioners
- Fees paid for hospital services, therapy, nursing services (including nurse's meals while on duty), ambulance hire, and laboratory, surgical, obstetrical, diagnostic, dental, and X-ray services
- Meals and lodging provided by a hospital during medical treatment, and meals and lodging provided by a center during treatment for alcoholism or drug addiction
- Medical and hospital insurance premiums
- Medicines and drugs, but only if prescribed by doctor (includes vitamins, iron, and pills or other birth control items)
- Special foods and drinks prescribed by doctor, but only if for the treatment of an illness
- Special items, including braces for teeth or limbs, false teeth, artificial limbs, eyeglasses, contact lenses, hearing aids, crutches, wheelchairs, and guide dogs for the blind or deaf
- Smoking cessation programs
- Transportation expenses for needed medical care, including air, bus, boat, railroad, and taxi fares

[5] See § 213(d)(5) and Reg. § 1.213-1(a)(3)(i). Medical expenses taken into account under § 21 in computing a credit for the care of certain dependents are not allowed to be treated as deductible medical expenses. See § 213(e) and Reg. § 1.213-1(f) and Chapter 13 for a discussion of the tax credit allowed under § 21.

[6] § 213(d)(1)(A) and Reg. § 1.213-1(e)(1)(i).

[7] § 213(d)(2) and Reg. § 1.213-1(e)(2).

[8] § 213(d)(1)(B) and Reg. § 1.213-1(e)(1)(iv).

[9] § 213(d)(1)(C) and Reg. § 1.213-1(e)(4).

[10] See *Your Federal Income Tax*, IRS Publication 17 (Rev. 2010), p. 142.

**EXHIBIT 11.2 Partial List of Nondeductible Expenditures**[11]

Accident insurance premiums
Bottled water
Care of a normal and healthy baby by a nurse*
Cosmetic surgery (with limited exceptions)
Diaper service
Funeral and burial expenses
Health club dues
Household help*
Illegal operation or treatment
Maternity clothes
Social activities, such as dancing lessons, for the general improvement of health, even though recommended by doctor
Toothpaste, toiletries, cosmetics, etc.
Trip for general improvement of health
Vitamins for general health

***Note:** A portion of these expenditures may qualify as expenses for the child or dependent care tax credit allowed under § 21. See Chapter 13 for further discussion of this credit.

regardless of when the illness or injury that occasioned the expenses occurred, and regardless of the method of accounting used by the taxpayer in computing his or her taxable income (i.e., cash or accrual).[12] Consequently, if the medical expenses are incurred but not paid during the current tax year, the deduction for such expenses will not be allowed *until* the year of payment. The IRS has ruled, however, that the use of a bank credit card to pay for medical expenses *will* qualify as payment in the year of the credit card charge regardless of when the taxpayer actually repays the bank.[13]

The *prepayment* of medical expenses does not qualify as a current deduction unless the taxpayer is required to make the payment as a condition of receiving the medical services.[14] Accordingly, the IRS has ruled that a taxpayer's nonrefundable advance payments required as a condition for admission to a retirement home or institution for future lifetime medical care are deductible as expenses in the year paid.[15]

**Example 2**

As a prerequisite for prenatal care and the delivery of her child, M prepays $3,150 to her doctor on November 15, 2011. Even though much of the prenatal care and the delivery of the child does not occur until 2012, M will be allowed to treat the prepayment as a medical expenditure in 2011.

## DEDUCTION LIMITATIONS

The medical expense deduction was created by Congress with the stated social objective of providing individual taxpayers relief from a heavy tax burden during a period of medical emergency and thereby encouraging the maintenance of a high level of public health.

[11] *Ibid.*

[12] Reg. § 1.213-1(a)(1).

[13] Rev. Rul. 78-39, 1978-1 C.B. 73.

[14] See *Robert S. Basset*, 26 T.C. 619 (1956). Absent such a prohibition, a taxpayer could maximize the tax benefits of medical deductions simply by timing the year of payment.

[15] Rev Rul. 75-303, 1975-2 C.B. 87.

However, the deduction was designed to provide relief for only those expenditures in excess of a normal or average amount. Currently, the medical expense deduction is allowed only to the extent medical expenditures exceed 7.5 percent of the taxpayer's adjusted gross income. This limitation ensures that only extraordinary medical costs will result in a deduction.

In addition to the percentage limitation imposed on the medical expense deduction, it is important to note that most of the everyday type of expenditures incurred by an individual for items incident to his or her general health and hygiene are excluded from the definition of qualifying medical expenses. For example, medicine and drug expenditures are deductible only if they are for insulin and *prescribed* drugs.[16] Over-the-counter medicines and drugs such as aspirin, cold remedies, skin lotions, and vitamins are not deductible. Other nondeductible expenditures are listed in Exhibit 11-2.

### Example 3

F had adjusted gross income of $30,000 for 2011 and paid the following medical expenses:

| | |
|---|---|
| Doctors | $ 500 |
| Dentist | 600 |
| Hospital | 1,300 |
| Medical insurance premiums | 800 |
| Medicines and drugs: | |
| Prescription drugs | 300 |
| Nonprescription medicines | 150 |

Assuming F is not reimbursed for any of the medical expenditures during 2011, her medical expense deduction is computed as follows:

| | |
|---|---|
| Medical insurance premiums | $ 800 |
| Fees paid doctors and dentist | 1,100 |
| Hospital costs | 1,300 |
| Prescription drugs only | 300 |
| Total medical expenses taken into account | $ 3,500 |
| Less: 7.5% of $30,000 (A.G.I.) | −2,250 |
| Allowable medical deduction for 2011 | $ 1,250 |

## Special Items and Equipment

The term *medical care* includes not only the diagnosis, treatment, and cure of disease, but the mitigation and prevention of disease as well. Thus, a taxpayer's expenditures for special items such as contact lenses, eyeglasses, hearing aids, artificial teeth or limbs, and ambulance hire would also qualify as medical expenditures.[17] Similarly, the cost of special equipment (e.g., wheelchairs and special controls or other equipment installed in an auto for use by a physically handicapped person) purchased *primarily* for the prevention or alleviation of a physical or mental defect or illness will be allowed as medical deductions. If the purchase of special equipment qualifies as a medical expenditure, the cost of its operation and maintenance is also a deductible medical expense.[18]

---

[16] § 213(b) and Reg. § 1.213-1(b)(2)(i).

[17] Reg. § 1.213-1(e)(1)(ii). The IRS has ruled that the costs to acquire, train, and maintain a dog that assists a blind or deaf taxpayer are deductible medical expenses (see Rev. Rul. 55-216, 1955-1 C.B. 307 and Rev. Rul. 68-295, 1968-1 C.B. 92). In the Committee Reports for the Technical and Miscellaneous Revenue Act of 1988, Congress indicated its approval of this IRS position and stated that similar costs incurred with respect to a dog *or* other service animal used to assist individuals with *other physical disabilities* would also be eligible for the medical expense deduction.

[18] *Supra*, Footnote 10.

Capital expenditures generally are not deductible for Federal income tax purposes (i.e., depreciation is allowed only for property or equipment used in a taxpayer's trade or business or other income-producing activity). However, if a capital expenditure would otherwise qualify as a medical expense (i.e., it is incurred primarily for medical care), it will not be disqualified as a deduction. If the capital expenditure is for the permanent improvement or betterment of property such as the taxpayer's home, *only* the amount of the expenditure which *exceeds* the increase in value of the property improved will qualify as a medical expense.[19]

> **Example 4**
>
> After suffering a heart attack, T is advised by his physician to install an elevator in his residence rather than continue climbing the stairs. If the cost of installing the elevator is $18,000 and the increase in the value of his residence is determined to be only $7,000, the difference of $11,000 will be deductible by T as a medical expense in the year paid. Annual operating costs (i.e., utilities) and maintenance of the elevator also qualify as deductible medical expenses.

In two specific situations, any increase in value of the improved property is ignored (or deemed to be zero) for purposes of measuring the medical expense deduction. First, if permanent improvements are made to property *rented* by the taxpayer, the *entire* costs are deductible (subject to the 7.5% floor).[20] Likewise, the entire cost of certain home-related capital expenditures incurred by a physically handicapped individual qualifies as a medical expense. Qualifying costs include expenditures for (1) constructing entrance or exit ramps to the residence; (2) widening doorways at entrances or exits to the residence; (3) widening or otherwise modifying hallways and interior doorways to accommodate wheelchairs; (4) railings, support bars, or other modifications to bathrooms to accommodate handicapped individuals; (5) lowering of or other modifications to kitchen cabinets and equipment to accommodate access by handicapped individuals; and (6) adjustment of electrical outlets and fixtures.

## Special Care Facilities

Expenses paid for emergency room treatment or hospital care of the taxpayer, his or her spouse, or dependents qualify for the medical deduction.[21] However, the deductibility of expenses for care in an institution other than a hospital depends upon the medical condition of the individual *and* the nature of the services he or she receives. If the *principal reason* an individual is in an institution (such as a nursing home or special school) is the availability of medical care, the *entire cost* of the medical care qualifies as a medical expenditure. This includes the cost of meals and lodging as well as any tuition expenses of special schools.[22]

> **Example 5**
>
> T enrolled his dependent son, S, in a special school for children with hearing impairments. If the principal reason for S's attendance at the school is his medical condition *and* the institution has the resources to treat or supervise training of the hearing impaired, the entire cost of S's attendance at the school qualifies as a medical expense. This includes tuition, meals and lodging, and any other costs that are incidental to the special services furnished by the school.

[19] Reg. § 1.213-1(e)(1)(iii).

[20] Rev. Rul. 70-395, 1970-2 C.B. 65.

[21] This includes the cost of meals and lodging incurred as an in-patient of a hospital. See Reg. § 1.213-1 (e)(1)(v).

[22] Reg. § 1.213-1(e)(1)(v)(a). See also *Donald R. Pfeifer*, 37 TCM 817, T.C. Memo 1978-189; *W.B. Counts*, 42 T.C. 755 (1963); Rev. Rul. 78-340, 1978-2 C.B. 124; and Rev. Rul. 58-533, 1958-2 C. B. 108.

If an individual's medical condition *is not* the principal reason for being in an institution, only that part of the cost of care in the institution which is attributable to medical care will qualify as a medical expense.[23]

> **Example 6**
>
> T placed her dependent father, F, in a nursing home after F suffered a stroke and partial paralysis. Of the $6,000 total nursing home expenses, only $2,500 is attributable to the medical care and nursing attention furnished to F. If F is not in the nursing home for the principal reason of the medical and nursing care, only $2,500 will be deductible by T.

## Long-Term Care Costs

As life expectancy has increased and the population aged, more and more people have incurred costs related to long-term care. Costs of long-term care include expenses not only for medicine and medical treatment but also a variety of services (e.g., help in eating, dressing, using the bathroom, bathing, taking medications, going places, grooming and the like). Prior to 1996, it was unclear whether the costs of long-term care qualified as a medical expense. The IRS commonly challenged such costs as personal and denied their deduction. Tax legislation passed in 1996 clarified the treatment of such expenses by providing that the costs for qualified long-term care services provided to a chronically-ill taxpayer (or his or her spouse or dependents) that are not reimbursed, as well as the premiums paid for long-term care insurance that meets certain requirements, are eligible for deduction as medical expenses.

Qualified long-term care services generally include necessary diagnostic, preventive, therapeutic, curing, treating, mitigating and rehabilitative services, and maintenance or personal care services that are required by a chronically-ill individual and provided pursuant to a plan of care prescribed by a licensed health care practitioner. A chronically-ill individual is generally a person who is unable to perform at least two activities of daily living (e.g., eating, toileting, transferring, bathing, dressing, and continence) for a period of at least 90 days due to a loss of functional capacity.

The amount deductible for insurance premiums is subject to limitations, but also is adjusted annually for inflation. The limits for 2011 are as follows:

| *Age before close of tax year* | *Limitation* |
|---|---|
| 40 or less | $ 340 |
| More than 40 but less than 50 | 640 |
| More than 50 but less than 60 | 1,270 |
| More than 60 but less than 70 | 3,390 |
| More than 70 | 4,240 |

Amounts paid to relatives for long-term care services normally are not eligible for deduction unless such person is a licensed professional with respect to the services that he or she is providing.

In addition, § 7702B allows an income exclusion for long-term care benefits received by an individual. For 2011, the exclusion from gross income is the greater of $300 per day or the actual cost of the care.

## Medical Travel and Transportation

Expenses paid for transportation to and from the office of a doctor or dentist or to a hospital or clinic usually are deductible as medical expenses. This includes amounts paid for bus, taxi, train, and plane fares, as well as the out-of-pocket expenses for use of the taxpayer's personal

[23] Reg. § 1.213-1(e)(1)(v)(b). This *excludes* meals and lodging and any other expenses not directly attributable to the medical care or treatment.

vehicle (i.e., gas and oil, parking fees, and tolls). If the taxpayer uses his or her personal automobile for medical transportation and does not want to calculate actual expenses, the IRS allows a deduction. For 2011, the deduction is 19 cents a mile *plus* parking fees and tolls paid while traveling for medical treatment.[24]

Travel costs include *only* transportation expenses and the cost of lodging. For these expenses to qualify as a medical deduction, a trip beyond the taxpayer's locale *must* be "primarily for and essential to medical care."[25] Meal costs are deductible only if provided by a hospital or similar institution as a necessary part of medical care. Thus, meals consumed while en route between the taxpayer's home and the location of the medical care are not deductible.

If an individual receives medical treatment as an outpatient at a clinic or doctor's office, the cost of lodging while in the new locality may be deductible—but not the cost of meals. The cost of lodging will qualify as a medical expense if (1) the lodging is not lavish or extravagant under the circumstances; and (2) there is no significant element of personal pleasure, recreation, or vacation in the travel away from home. If deductible, the amount of lodging costs includible as a medical expense may not exceed *$50* for *each night* for each individual.[26] It is important to note that travel costs of a companion (including parents or a nurse) are included as medical expenses if the individual requiring medical treatment could not travel alone, or if the companion rendered medical treatment en route.[27] Thus, the lodging costs of such a person while in the new locality should also be treated as a part of any medical expenses (subject to the $50 per night limitation).

### Example 7

At the advice of a doctor, T travels with his three-year-old daughter, D, from Lincoln, Nebraska to Houston, Texas. D has a rare blood disease and a hospital in Houston is the nearest facility specializing in treatment of her disorder. The transportation costs and lodging for both T and his daughter while en route to and from Houston are deductible. If they stay at a nearby hotel while D receives treatment as an outpatient, the costs of lodging (but not meals) incurred in Houston—up to $100 per night—are also deductible.

## Medical Insurance Costs and Reimbursements

Amounts paid for medical care insurance for the taxpayer, his or her spouse, and dependents qualify as medical expenses. If premiums are paid under an insurance contract which offers coverage beyond medical care (e.g., coverage for loss of life, limb, or sight, or loss of income), only the portion of the premiums paid that is attributable to medical care is deductible. To be deductible, however, the medical care portion of the premiums paid must either be separately stated in the contract itself, or included in a separate bill or statement from the insurer.[28]

Taxpayers receiving reimbursements for medical expenses in the *same year* in which the expenses were paid must reduce any medical expense deduction to a net amount. However, if the reimbursement is for medical expenses in a prior year, the income tax treatment of the reimbursement depends upon whether the taxpayer claimed a medical expense deduction for the year in which the expenses were actually paid. If no medical expense deduction was taken in the year in which the expenses were paid (e.g., taxpayer used the standard deduction or total medical expenses did not exceed the required percentage of A.G.I.), any reimbursement for such expenses will not be included in gross income. If the taxpayer claimed a deduction for the medical expenses in the prior year, however, the reimbursement must be included in gross income to the extent of the *lesser* of: (1) the previous medical expense deduction, or (2) the excess of the taxpayer's itemized deductions over his or her standard deduction. The inclusion in gross income of all or a part of the reimbursement is in accordance with the tax benefit rule.

[24] Rev. Proc. 2010-51, I.R.B. 2010-51.

[25] See § 213(d)(2), Reg. § 1.213-1(e)(1)(iv), and *Comm. v. Bilder*, 62-1 USTC ¶9440, 9 AFTR2d 1355, 369 U.S. 499 (USSC, 1962).

[26] § 213(d)(2).

[27] See Rev. Rul. 75-317, 1975-2 C.B. 57.

[28] Reg. § 1.213-1(e)(4). Participants in the Federal Medicare program are entitled to treat as medical care insurance premiums the amounts withheld for voluntary doctor-bill insurance.

### Example 8

T has adjusted gross income of $30,000 for 2011. During the year, T pays the following medical expenses:

| | |
|---|---|
| Hospitalization insurance premiums . . . . . . . . . . . . . . . . . . . . . . . | $1,900 |
| Doctor and dental bills . . . . . . . . . . . . . . . . . . . . . . . . . . . . . . | 800 |
| Eyeglasses . . . . . . . . . . . . . . . . . . . . . . . . . . . . . . . . . . . . . . | 175 |
| Medical transportation . . . . . . . . . . . . . . . . . . . . . . . . . . . . . . | 25 |

T's medical expense deduction is computed as follows:

| | |
|---|---|
| Total medical expenses . . . . . . . . . . . . . . . . . . . . . . . . . . . . . . | $ 2,900 |
| Less: 7.5% of $30,000 (A.G.I.) . . . . . . . . . . . . . . . . . . . . . . . | − 2,250 |
| Medical expense deduction for 2011 . . . . . . . . . . . . . . . . . . . . . | $ 650 |

T's itemized deductions (including the $650 medical expense deduction) for 2011 exceeded his standard deduction by $1,500. In 2012, T received $400 as a reimbursement from his insurance company. T must include the *entire* $400 in gross income for 2012. If T had received the $400 reimbursement in 2011, his medical expense deduction would have been limited to $250.

### Example 9

Assume the same facts as in *Example 8* except that the medical expense reimbursement was $900 instead of $400. If the reimbursement was received in 2012, T would be required to include only $650 in gross income—the amount of the medical expenses included in his itemized deductions. If the amount by which T's itemized deductions exceeded his standard deduction was *less* than $650 for 2011, he would include in gross income for 2012 only so much of the reimbursement represented by the prior year's itemized deductions in excess of the standard deduction amount. However, if T had used the standard deduction in 2011, none of the $900 reimbursement would be included in 2012 gross income because T received no tax benefit in 2011.

The situations illustrated in *Examples 8 and 9* occur quite often because taxpayers are *not required* to reduce a current year's medical expense deduction by *anticipated* insurance reimbursements. Notice that this can result in a taxpayer receiving reimbursements early in the next tax year and not being required to pay income taxes on the reimbursement until April 15 of the following year.

## Health Savings Accounts and Medical Savings Accounts

During the past fourteen years, Congress has taken several steps to make health care more affordable. Chief among these was the creation of Medical Savings Accounts (also known as Archer MSAs) and Health Savings Accounts (HSAs).[29] These accounts enable individuals to pay for unreimbursed medical expenses on a before tax basis. For those familiar with flexible spending accounts for medical expenses (now used by many employers and their employees), MSAs and HSAs are virtually identical without the use it or lose it rule. For those familiar with Individual Retirement Accounts, MSAs and HSAs are quite similar.

[29] See §§ 220 and 223

### Example 10

In 2011, H set up an HSA for his family. H can contribute up to $6,150 to the HSA and claim the amount as a deduction for A.G.I. Any amounts withdrawn from the account that are used to pay for medical expenses are nontaxable. As a result, income funneled through HSAs to pay medical expenses is never subject to tax. Amounts not withdrawn from the HSA can earn income and such income normally is not taxable as long as it remains in the account or is withdrawn to pay medical expenses. In order to obtain this favorable tax treatment, H has a health insurance policy that meets several requirements. The policy has a high "deductible," meaning that he must pay for the first $2,400 of medical expenses incurred by his family (i.e., the individual must report medical expenses to the plan and pay $2,400 before the insurance starts paying). The policy also limits the total costs that H could incur to $11,900 thus providing his family with catastrophic protection. Most importantly for H, because the plan has such a high deductible, the cost of the plan is much less than most and he is able to afford coverage that he otherwise might not be able obtain.

Congress first introduced MSAs in 1996 as an experiment, restricting both the number that could be created and those who were eligible to use them. After a lukewarm reception, a bipartisan effort expanded the concept of MSAs and created HSAs which debuted in 2004. HSAs are a vast improvement over MSAs and very well may become an important tool in the fight against the rising costs of health care.[30] The plans are intended to hold down costs by giving consumers a tax incentive to shop for the best price for health services and to forgo procedures they do not need. At this point, it is difficult to determine whether this theory will work. However, recent reports suggest that there is growing interest in HSAs as more and more employers are offering them to their employees in lieu of traditional plans.[31] As interest in HSAs grow, interest in MSAs has dropped. For this reason, the following discussion focuses on HSAs.

Section 223 permits individuals to deduct for A.G.I. a limited amount of contributions to an HSA. Similarly, § 106(b) allows individuals to exclude limited contributions to such accounts made on their behalf by their employers. Amounts contributed to the HSA may be invested and the earnings are nontaxable. Distributions from the account are nontaxable as long as they are used for medical expenses that normally would be deductible under § 213 other than those for health insurance.

Note that no deduction is allowed for expenses paid for with dollars out of the HSA. However, the deduction for amounts *contributed* and the exclusion for amounts distributed essentially provide the same benefit. The end result of these rules effectively enables an individual to pay for medical expenses not covered by insurance with dollars that have never been subject to tax. Observe that if the taxpayer pays for unreimbursed medical expenses using dollars that do not come from the HSA, they normally are not deductible due to the 7.5 percent limitation. In such case, the payments are effectively made with after-tax dollars.

### Example 11

Assume M is in the 30% tax bracket with an adjusted gross income of $60,000. He is covered by health insurance that pays for most but not all of his medical expenses. During the year, M contributed $1,000 to an HSA. Later during the year he withdrew the entire $1,000 to pay for medical expenses related to knee surgery that were not covered by his insurance. As shown by the following analysis (ignoring exemptions and the standard deduction and assuming M itemized deductions), by using an HSA, M

[30] MSAs are available only to employees of certain small businesses and to self-employed persons and the number of MSAs were restricted. HSAs are available to all individuals and the required health plan is far more flexible.

[31] Individuals covered by other medical insurance plans are not eligible for HSAs.

saves $300, the tax that otherwise would have been paid on the amounts used to pay for the unreimbursed medical expenses.

| | *Employee Pays* | *HSA Pays* | |
|---|---|---|---|
| Income | $60,000 | $ 60,000 | |
| Deduction for contribution to HSA | — | (1,000) | |
| Adjusted gross income | $60,000 | $ 59,000 | |
| Medical expense deduction [$1,000 − (7.5% × $60,000)] | 0 | — | |
| Income | $60,000 | $ 59,000 | |
| Tax @ 30% | (18,000) | (17,700) | |
| Cost of medical expense | (1,000) | — | (HSA pays) |
| After-tax income | $41,000 | $ 41,300 | |

Another advantage of contributions provided by an employer to an HSA is that they are not subject to FICA or FUTA taxes.

### Penalty for Distributions Not Used for Medical Expenses

If the taxpayer withdraws amounts from the HSA and uses them for something other than qualified medical expenses before age 65 (or death or disability), a penalty equal to 10 percent of the amount withdrawn is imposed. Amounts withdrawn after age 65 are not subject to penalty but will be taxed as ordinary income to the extent they are not used to pay for medical expenses.

### Eligible Individuals

HSAs may be established only by eligible individuals. A person is eligible if he or she is:

- Covered under a high deductible health plan (HDHP). A HDHP is a plan that for 2011 has an annual deductible of at least $1,200 and an annual limitation on out-of-pocket expenses (other health care premiums) not greater than $5,950. These limits are doubled to $2,400 and $11,900 for family coverage.
- Not covered by any other health care plan that is not an HDHP
- Not eligible for Medicare (i.e., has not reached the age of 65)
- Not claimed as a dependent on another person's tax return

### Deductible Contributions

In 2011, annual contributions to HSAs are generally limited to $3,050 for singles and $6,150 for families. Individuals from age 55–64 are entitled to make "catch-up" contributions up to $1,000.

**EXHIBIT 11.3** **Health Savings Accounts High Deductible Health Plan (HDHP) Requirements and Contribution Limitations 2011**

| | ***Individual*** | ***Family*** |
|---|---|---|
| Minimum Deductible | $1,200 | $2,400 |
| Maximum Out-Of-Pocket Expenses | 5,950 | 11,900 |
| Maximum Contribution deduction | 3,050 | 6,150 |

### Treatment of HSAs at Death

If the taxpayer dies before using the amount in the HSA, the treatment of the balance for both income tax and estate tax purposes depends on who is the beneficiary of the account.[32]

- *Surviving spouse as beneficiary.* If the surviving spouse is the beneficiary, the surviving spouse has no income and treats the account as his or her own.
- *Beneficiary other than surviving spouse.* If the surviving spouse is not the beneficiary but another person is the beneficiary (e.g., a son or daughter), the account stops being an HSA, and the beneficiary must include in taxable income the fair market value of the HSA in the year of the owner's death. Such person would be able to exclude from gross income the amount of any qualified medical expenses for the decedent that are paid by the beneficiary within one year after the date of death as well as deduct any estate taxes that may be paid that are attributable to such amounts.
- *Estate.* If no beneficiary is named or the estate is the beneficiary, the value of the HSA is included on the decedent's final income tax return; however, such amount is *not* reduced by final medical expenses of the decedent paid after death.

Upon death, any balance in the HSA is included in the decedent's gross estate subject to estate taxes. Such amount would be subject to estate taxes unless it passes to the surviving spouse and therefore, qualifies for the marital deduction.

### Recordkeeping and Filing Requirements

Taxpayers with HSAs must file Form 8889 with their Form 1040 if there was any activity in the HSA during the year. Activity includes both distributions (e.g., to pay medical expenses) as well as contributions by the taxpayer or spouse or the employer of either. In addition, HSA owners must keep records sufficient to show that: (1) any distributions were used exclusively for qualified medical expenses; (2), the qualified medical expenses had not been previously paid or reimbursed from another source; and (3) the medical expenses had not been taken as an itemized deduction in any year.

## Health Insurance Costs of Self-Employed Taxpayers

Self-employed individuals are allowed to treat the amounts paid for health insurance on behalf of a self-employed individual, his or her spouse, and dependents as a deductible business expense.[33] A more than two percent owner-employee of S Corp. stock can deduct 100% of the amount paid for medical insurance for himself, spouse and dependents [§ 162 (l)(5)]. The deduction is allowed in determining adjusted gross income (i.e., a deduction *for* A.G.I.) rather than being treated as an itemized medical expense deduction subject to the 7.5 percent floor. No deduction is allowable to the extent it *exceeds* the taxpayer's net earnings from self-employment.[34] Thus, the deduction cannot create a loss. More important, the deduction does not reduce the income base for which the taxpayer is liable for self-employment taxes.

### Example 12

K, a self-employed individual, paid $2,600 for health insurance for himself, his wife, and their two children. K had no employees during the year. K is entitled to deduct the entire $2,600 in determining adjusted gross income, provided the deduction does not exceed his net earnings from self-employment, and his A.G.I. before the deduction is at least $2,600.[35]

---

[32] § 223(f)(8).

[33] § 162(l).

[34] § 162(l)(2)(A).

[35] § 162(l)(3).

Absent a special rule, self-employed individuals who are also employees might be tempted to opt out of an employer-provided medical insurance plan. By so doing, the 7.5 percent floor on medical expenses could be avoided and taxpayers could deduct a portion of what normally would be nondeductible premium payments. To prevent this course of action, the deduction is not allowed if a self-employed individual or spouse is eligible to participate in a health insurance plan of an employer.[36]

## Personal Casualty and Theft Losses

As discussed in Chapter 10, Congress has provided for a deduction of losses related to property used for *personal* purposes where the loss arises from fire, storm, shipwreck, or other casualty, or theft.[37] Like the medical expense deduction, the deduction for personal casualty and theft losses is designed to provide relief for only extraordinary losses. Thus, an individual taxpayer's deduction for personal casualty and theft losses is allowed only to the extent such losses exceed $100 per occurrence *and* the sum of all losses (after reduction by the $100 floor) for a given tax year exceeds 10 percent of the taxpayer's adjusted gross income. These deduction limitations were discussed and illustrated in Chapter 10.

### Year Deductible

A personal casualty loss is generally deductible in the taxable year in which the loss occurs. Recall, however, that a theft loss is deductible only in the year of discovery. If a claim for insurance reimbursement (or any other potential recovery) exists and there is a reasonable prospect of recovery, the loss must be reduced by the amount *expected* to be received.[38] If later receipts are *less* than the amount originally estimated and no further reimbursement is expected, an amended return is not filed. Instead, the remaining loss is deductible in the year in which no further reimbursement is expected. Most important, if the casualty loss deduction claimed in the prior year was reduced by the $100 floor and exceeded the 10 percent A.G.I. limitation, the remaining loss is not further reduced. However, the remaining loss is subject to the 10 percent limitation of the later year.[39]

### Reporting Casualty Losses

Individual taxpayers are required to report and compute casualty losses on Form 4684,[40] which is to be filed with Form 1040. The casualty loss deduction, if any, is reported with other itemized deductions on Schedule A, Form 1040.

## Taxes

Code § 164 is the statutory authority that permits taxpayers to deduct several types of taxes for Federal income tax purposes. If the taxes are related to an individual taxpayer's trade or business or income-producing activity, the deduction is generally allowed in arriving at adjusted gross income. However, both the IRS and the courts have taken the position that state, local, and foreign *income* taxes are deductible by an individual taxpayer *from* his or her adjusted gross income—even though it could be argued that such taxes are related to his or her trade or business. Likewise, if *property* taxes are related to personal use property (e.g., residence, car, etc.), such taxes are generally deductible only if the individual itemizes his or her deductions. If taxes are deductible by taxpayers other than individuals, the deductions simply reduce gross income to taxable income.[41]

---

36 § 162(l)(2)(B).

37 § 165(c)(3) Special rules apply to casualties and thefts occurring in Federally declared disaster areas.

38 Reg. § 1.165-1(d)(2)(i).

39 *See Example 9* of Chapter 10.

40 See Appendix B for a sample of this form.

41 See the later section in this chapter entitled "Reporting Deductions for Taxes."

The types of taxes specifically allowed as deductions under § 164 are:

1. State, local, and foreign real property taxes;
2. State and local personal property taxes;
3. State and local general sales taxes;
4. State, local, and foreign income, war profits, and excess profit taxes; and
5. The generation-skipping transfer tax.[42]

The generation-skipping transfer tax is imposed on income distributions from certain trusts. Discussion of this tax is beyond the scope of this text. However, each of the other types of deductible taxes is discussed in detail below.

## General Requirements for Deductibility

**LO.3**
Distinguish between deductible taxes and nondeductible fees or other charges.

A tax is deductible *only* if (1) it is imposed on the taxpayer's income or property; and (2) it is paid or incurred by the taxpayer in the taxable year for which a deduction is being claimed. Even if these two requirements are met, deductions for certain Federal, state, and local taxes are expressly denied. Exhibit 11-4 contains a list of nondeductible taxes.

In addition to the nondeductible taxes listed in Exhibit 11-4, deductions for *fees* (whether or not labeled as taxes) paid by taxpayers usually are denied *unless* the fees are incurred in the taxpayer's trade or business or for the production of income. Fees paid or incurred in connection with a trade or business, if ordinary and necessary, are deductible as business expenses under § 162. Similarly, fees related to the production of income generally are deductible expenses under § 212.[43]

**EXHIBIT 11.4 Nondeductible Taxes[44]**

***Nondeductible federal taxes:***

- Federal income taxes (including those withheld from an individual's pay)
- Social security or railroad retirement taxes withheld from an individual by his or her employer (includes self-employment taxes)
- Social security and other employment taxes paid on the wages of the taxpayer's employee who performed domestic or other personal services
- Federal excise taxes or customs duties unless they are connected with the taxpayer's business or income-producing activity
- Federal estate and gift taxes

***Nondeductible state and local taxes:***

- Motor vehicle taxes (unless they qualify as ad valorem taxes on personal property)
- Inheritance, legacy, succession, or estate taxes
- Gift taxes
- Per capita or poll taxes
- Cigarette, tobacco, liquor, beer, wine, etc., taxes

---

[42] § 164(a).

[43] See Chapter 7 for a discussion of the requirements that must be met in order to deduct business and nonbusiness expenses of this nature.

[44] See § 275, Reg. § 1.164-2, and *Your Federal Income Tax*, IRS Publication 17 (Rev. 2010), pp. 147–150.

The IRS distinguishes a "tax" from a "fee" by looking to the *purpose* of the charge.[45] If a particular charge is imposed upon the taxpayer for the purpose of *raising revenue* to be used for public or government purposes, the IRS will consider the charge to be a tax. However, if the charge is imposed because of either *particular acts or services* received by the taxpayer, such charge will be considered as a *fee*. Thus, fees for driver's licenses, vehicle registration and inspection, license tags for pets, hunting and fishing licenses, tolls for bridges and roads, parking meter deposits, water bills, sewer and other service charges, and postage fees are not deductible *unless* related to the taxpayer's trade or business, or income-producing activity.[46]

Since most individual taxpayers use the cash receipts and disbursements method of accounting for tax purposes, the following discussion of income and property tax deductions concentrates on cash-basis taxpayers and the requirement that taxes be *paid* in the year of deduction. Bear in mind throughout this discussion, however, that accrual method taxpayers are allowed a deduction for taxes in the tax year in which the obligation for payment becomes fixed and determinable (i.e., the all-events test is met).

## INCOME TAXES

**LO.4**
Explain the rules regarding deductible state income taxes.

Most state, local, or foreign income taxes paid or accrued by a taxpayer are deductible in arriving at taxable income. For individual taxpayers, however, a deduction for state and local income taxes is allowed only if the taxpayer itemizes his or her deductions. Furthermore, as explained below, in lieu of deducting state and local income taxes, taxpayers can deduct state and local sales taxes (i.e., deduct either but not both).

Although the income taxes may be related solely to the individual's business income (e.g., income from a sole proprietorship or partnership), or income from rents and royalties, these taxes are considered personal in nature. Since income taxes paid to a foreign country or a U.S. possession may either be deducted as an itemized deduction or claimed as a credit against the U.S. income tax, an individual who does not itemize deductions should elect to claim foreign income taxes as credits.[47]

Cash-basis taxpayers are allowed to deduct state and local income taxes *paid* during the taxable year, including those taxes imposed on interest income that is exempt from Federal income taxation. Amounts considered paid during the taxable year include:

1. State and local income or foreign taxes withheld from an individual's salary by his or her employer;
2. Estimated payments made by the taxpayer under a pay-as-you-go requirement of a taxing authority; and
3. Payments made in the current year on an income tax liability of a prior year.

### Example 13

During 2011, Z, a cash basis taxpayer, had $1,500 of Illinois state income taxes withheld by her employer. In 2011, she paid the remaining $450 in state income taxes due on her 2010 Illinois tax return, and also paid $300 in estimated state income tax payments during 2011. If Z itemizes her deductions for Federal income tax purposes, she is entitled to a $2,250 ($1,500 + $300 + $450) state income tax deduction for 2011.

If a cash basis taxpayer receives a refund of state, local, or foreign income taxes in the current year, the refund must be included in the current year's gross income to the extent a deduction in an earlier tax year provided a tax benefit.[48]

---

[45] See § 275 and Reg. § 1.164-2.

[46] *Your Federal Income Tax*, IRS Publication 17 (Rev. 2010), p. 147.

[47] § 27.

[48] § 111. Special rules apply when married taxpayers file separate state or Federal income tax returns. See *Your Federal Income Tax*, IRS Publication 17 (Rev. 2010), p. 146.

### Example 14

Assume the same facts as in *Example 13*. While preparing her 2011 Illinois state income tax return in early 2012, Z determined she had overpaid the state tax liability by $375. She received a refund of the entire overpayment on August 10, 2012. If Z claimed the total $2,250 state income taxes paid as a deduction on her 2011 Federal income tax return and her itemized deductions exceeded the standard deduction amount by at least $375, she must include the entire refund in gross income on her 2012 Federal income tax return.

In determining the amount of the refund that must be included in income, the IRS further explains that the amount is limited to the excess of the tax deducted for the year over the state and local sales taxes that the taxpayer chose not to deduct for that same year.[49]

### Example 15

In preparing his 2010 income tax return, H elected to deduct $12,000 of state income tax instead of $11,000 of state sales tax. During 2011, H received a refund of his state income tax of $2,500. The amount of state income tax refund that H must include in gross income for 2011 is $1,000 ($12,000 – $11,000) since he could have deducted the state sales tax.

## Deduction for State and Local General Sales Tax

Taxpayers are currently allowed to deduct state and local sales and use taxes instead of state and local income taxes.[50] The sales tax deduction was elimated in 1986 but was resurrected in 2004 when states without income taxes but high sales taxes wanted equitable treatment. Although scheduled to expire at the end of 2009, Congress extended the deduction for both 2010 and 2011.

The sales tax deduction is classified as an itemized deduction but not a miscellaneous itemized deduction. It is subject to the itemized deduction cutback discussed in a later part of this chapter. In addition, the deduction for state and local sales and use taxes is not allowed for alternative minimum tax purposes.

Only "general" sales taxes are deductible. Section 164(b)(5)(B) defines a general sales tax as a tax imposed at one rate with respect to the sale at retail of a broad range of classes of item. In determining whether a tax is a "general" sales tax, the fact that it does not apply to food, clothing, medical supplies and motor vehicles, or applies at a different rate is disregarded. If other items are taxed at a different rate, such taxes are not deductible. If the rate of tax on a motor vehicle exceeds the general rate, the excess is disregarded. If the amount of the general sales tax is separately stated, to the extent it is paid by the consumer, the amount is treated as a tax imposed on and paid by the consumer.

Taxpayers may deduct their actual sales taxes as substantiated by accumulated receipts or use IRS-published tables. These tables are contained in Appendix A of this text. The tables take into account the number of exemptions, "available" income (A.G.I. increased by any tax-exempt income such as social security and tax-exempt interest) and rates of state and local general sales taxation. Since sales tax rates vary from state to state (and even by localities

[49] These basic rules for inclusion must be modified in several other situations. For example, when a taxpayer receives a state income tax refund for 2010 and the last estimated tax payment of the 2010 state taxes was made in 2011, the portion of the refund attributable to the 2011 payment reduces the deduction for state income taxes.

[50] See § 165(b)(5). According to the IRS, the sales tax deduction was claimed on approximately 11.2 million tax returns filed in 2006. Only time will tell if Congress decides to continue its current extension of this deduction.

within a state), there are 51 different tables for the 50 states and the District of Columbia. The tables extend to available income as high as $200,000.

The tables include only general *state* sales taxes and do not include any additional *local sales taxes*. Another table may be used to determine the amount of local sales taxes that may be added to the table amount. In addition to the amount determined using the tables, taxpayers may add the taxes on cars, motorcycles, motor homes, recreational vehicles, sport utility vehicles, trucks, vans, and off-road vehicles, aircraft, boats, homes (including mobile and prefabricated), or home-building materials, if the tax rate was the same as the general sales tax rate. Tax commentators have suggested that the sales taxes on other high-priced unusual purchases such as expensive furniture, high-definition plasma televisions or the like arguably could be added. However, the IRS limits the additions to those noted above.[51] Special rules apply when a taxpayer lives in more than one state during the year. A portion of the tables appears below.

**2010 Optional State and Certain Local Sales Tax Tables**

| Income At least | Income But less than | Alabama 4.0000% | | | | | | Arizona[1] 6.1863% | | | | | | Arkansas 6.0000% | | | | | |
|---|---|---|---|---|---|---|---|---|---|---|---|---|---|---|---|---|---|---|---|
| | Exemptions | 1 | 2 | 3 | 4 | 5 | Over 5 | 1 | 2 | 3 | 4 | 5 | Over 5 | 1 | 2 | 3 | 4 | 5 | Over 5 |
| $0 | $20,000 | 235 | 287 | 324 | 353 | 378 | 413 | 253 | 297 | 326 | 349 | 368 | 395 | 302 | 359 | 397 | 427 | 452 | 487 |
| 20,000 | 30,000 | 336 | 409 | 460 | 501 | 535 | 583 | 408 | 476 | 522 | 558 | 588 | 630 | 472 | 559 | 618 | 664 | 702 | 756 |
| 30,000 | 40,000 | 385 | 468 | 525 | 570 | 609 | 663 | 487 | 567 | 622 | 664 | 700 | 749 | 558 | 659 | 728 | 782 | 827 | 890 |
| 40,000 | 50,000 | 426 | 516 | 579 | 629 | 670 | 730 | 555 | 646 | 708 | 756 | 795 | 851 | 630 | 745 | 822 | 883 | 933 | 1004 |
| 50,000 | 60,000 | 463 | 559 | 626 | 680 | 724 | 788 | 616 | 717 | 785 | 837 | 881 | 943 | 695 | 821 | 906 | 972 | 1027 | 1105 |
| 60,000 | 70,000 | 495 | 597 | 669 | 725 | 773 | 840 | 671 | 781 | 855 | 912 | 960 | 1026 | 754 | 890 | 982 | 1053 | 1113 | 1197 |
| 70,000 | 80,000 | 525 | 633 | 708 | 767 | 817 | 889 | 724 | 842 | 921 | 982 | 1033 | 1105 | 809 | 954 | 1053 | 1129 | 1193 | 1283 |
| 80,000 | 90,000 | 553 | 666 | 744 | 806 | 858 | 933 | 773 | 898 | 982 | 1048 | 1102 | 1178 | 860 | 1014 | 1118 | 1199 | 1267 | 1362 |
| 90,000 | 100,000 | 579 | 696 | 778 | 842 | 897 | 974 | 819 | 951 | 1040 | 1109 | 1167 | 1247 | 908 | 1070 | 1180 | 1266 | 1337 | 1437 |
| 100,000 | 120,000 | 613 | 736 | 821 | 889 | 946 | 1028 | 881 | 1022 | 1117 | 1191 | 1252 | 1338 | 971 | 1144 | 1261 | 1353 | 1428 | 1535 |
| 120,000 | 140,000 | 659 | 790 | 881 | 953 | 1014 | 1100 | 965 | 1118 | 1222 | 1302 | 1369 | 1462 | 1058 | 1245 | 1372 | 1471 | 1553 | 1669 |
| 140,000 | 160,000 | 699 | 836 | 932 | 1008 | 1071 | 1162 | 1038 | 1202 | 1313 | 1399 | 1471 | 1571 | 1133 | 1333 | 1468 | 1574 | 1661 | 1785 |
| 160,000 | 180,000 | 739 | 882 | 982 | 1062 | 1128 | 1223 | 1111 | 1287 | 1405 | 1496 | 1572 | 1679 | 1207 | 1420 | 1564 | 1676 | 1769 | 1900 |
| 180,000 | 200,000 | 774 | 923 | 1027 | 1110 | 1179 | 1278 | 1178 | 1362 | 1487 | 1584 | 1664 | 1777 | 1274 | 1498 | 1649 | 1767 | 1865 | 2003 |
| 200,000 or more | | 947 | 1123 | 1246 | 1344 | 1425 | 1542 | 1508 | 1741 | 1898 | 2020 | 2121 | 2262 | 1605 | 1883 | 2072 | 2219 | 2341 | 2512 |

| Income At least | Income But less than | California[2] 8.2500% | | | | | | Colorado 2.9000% | | | | | |
|---|---|---|---|---|---|---|---|---|---|---|---|---|---|
| | Exemptions | 1 | 2 | 3 | 4 | 5 | Over 5 | 1 | 2 | 3 | 4 | 5 | Over 5 |
| $0 | $20,000 | 326 | 379 | 414 | 441 | 464 | 495 | 122 | 141 | 154 | 164 | 172 | 184 |
| 20,000 | 30,000 | 523 | 605 | 660 | 702 | 737 | 786 | 185 | 213 | 232 | 247 | 259 | 276 |
| 30,000 | 40,000 | 624 | 721 | 785 | 835 | 876 | 934 | 216 | 249 | 271 | 288 | 302 | 321 |
| 40,000 | 50,000 | 710 | 820 | 892 | 949 | 995 | 1061 | 243 | 279 | 304 | 322 | 338 | 360 |
| 50,000 | 60,000 | 788 | 908 | 989 | 1051 | 1102 | 1174 | 267 | 306 | 333 | 353 | 370 | 393 |
| 60,000 | 70,000 | 859 | 989 | 1076 | 1144 | 1199 | 1277 | 288 | 331 | 359 | 381 | 399 | 424 |
| 70,000 | 80,000 | 926 | 1066 | 1159 | 1231 | 1291 | 1374 | 309 | 354 | 384 | 407 | 426 | 453 |
| 80,000 | 90,000 | 988 | 1136 | 1236 | 1312 | 1376 | 1464 | 327 | 375 | 406 | 431 | 451 | 479 |
| 90,000 | 100,000 | 1047 | 1204 | 1308 | 1389 | 1456 | 1549 | 345 | 395 | 428 | 453 | 474 | 504 |
| 100,000 | 120,000 | 1125 | 1292 | 1404 | 1490 | 1562 | 1662 | 368 | 421 | 456 | 483 | 505 | 536 |
| 120,000 | 140,000 | 1231 | 1413 | 1535 | 1629 | 1706 | 1815 | 400 | 456 | 494 | 523 | 547 | 581 |
| 140,000 | 160,000 | 1324 | 1519 | 1649 | 1750 | 1833 | 1949 | 427 | 487 | 527 | 558 | 583 | 619 |
| 160,000 | 180,000 | 1417 | 1625 | 1763 | 1870 | 1959 | 2082 | 454 | 518 | 560 | 593 | 619 | 657 |
| 180,000 | 200,000 | 1501 | 1720 | 1866 | 1979 | 2072 | 2203 | 479 | 545 | 590 | 624 | 652 | 691 |
| 200,000 or more | | 1921 | 2195 | 2378 | 2520 | 2637 | 2800 | 601 | 682 | 735 | 777 | 811 | 858 |

## Example 16

A family of four living in Arkansas has available income of $51,800 for 2010. If the election is made to claim a deduction for their general sales taxes rather than state and local income taxes, the family will be allowed a deduction of $1,165 ($972 from the Optional State Sales Tax Table above + $193 from the Local Sales Tax Tables located in Appendix A of this text). If the taxpayers paid a sales tax of $450 on a new truck purchased in 2010, the sales tax table amounts would be increased to $1,615 ($1,165 + $450). Note that the 2010 Optional Sales Tax Tables were used here because the 2011 tables were not available at the publication date of this text.

Since the addition of the sales tax deduction in 2004, the taxpayers in the seven states that do not impose an income tax—Alaska, Florida, Nevada, South Dakota, Texas, Washington and Wyoming—have an additional itemized deduction. As a result, taxpayers in these states, who may not have been able to itemize their deductions, now may be able to itemize. For taxpayers in the other 43 states, which levy at least some form of state or local income tax, they will be forced to make a decision about whether an election should be made.

## PROPERTY TAXES

Personal property taxes paid to a state, local, or foreign government are deductible *only* if they are *ad valorem* taxes.[52] Ad valorem taxes are taxes imposed on the *value* of property. Quite often, state and local taxing authorities impose a combination tax and fee on personal property. In such cases, only that portion of the charge based on value of the property will qualify as a deductible tax.[53]

---

[51] 164(b)(5)(H)

[52] § 164(b)(1) and Reg. § 1.164-3(c).

[53] § 164(b)(2)(E). States known to include some ad valorem tax as part of auto and boat registration fees are Arizona, California, Colorado, Indiana, Iowa, Maine, Massachusetts, Nevada, New Hampshire, Oklahoma, Washington, and Wyoming.

### Example 17

State A imposes an annual vehicle registration charge of 60 cents per hundredweight. X, a resident of the state, paid $24 in 2011 for the registration of his personal automobile. Since this charge is not based on the value of the auto, X has not paid a deductible tax.

### Example 18

State B imposes an annual vehicle registration charge of 1% of value plus 50 cents per hundredweight. Y, a resident of the state, owns a personal use automobile having a value of $10,000 and weighing 4,000 pounds. Of the $120 [(1% × $10,000) + ($0.50 × 40 hundredweight)] total registration charge paid by Y, only $100 would be deductible as a personal property tax.

Real property (real estate) taxes are generally deductible only if imposed on property owned by the taxpayer and paid or accrued by the taxpayer in the year the deduction is claimed. If real property taxes are imposed on jointly held real estate, each owner may claim his or her portion of the taxes. For example, if cash basis, married taxpayers file separate Federal income tax returns and real property taxes are imposed on jointly held real estate, each spouse may claim *half* of the taxes paid.

If real estate is sold during the year, the deduction for real estate taxes *must be apportioned* between the buyer and seller according to the number of days in the year each held the property, regardless of which party actually paid the property taxes.[54] The taxes are apportioned to the seller up to (but not including) the date of sale, and to the buyer beginning with the date of sale.

### Example 19

The real property tax year in Colorado County is April 1 to March 31. X, the owner on April 1, 2011 of real property located in Colorado County, sells the real property to Y on June 30, 2011. Y owns the real property from June 30, 2011 through March 31, 2012. The real property tax is $730 for the county's tax year April 1, 2011 to March 31, 2012. For purposes of § 164(a), $180 (90 ÷ 365 × $730 = $180 taxes for April 1, 2011 through June 29, 2011) of the real property tax is treated as imposed on X, the seller. The remaining $550 (275 ÷ 365 × $730 = $550 taxes for June 30, 2011 through March 31, 2011) of such real property tax is treated as imposed on Y, the purchaser.[55]

When both buyer and seller of real property are cash-basis taxpayers and only one of the parties *actually* pays the real property taxes for the period in which both parties owned the property, *each* party to the transaction is entitled to deduct the portion of the real property taxes based on the number of days he or she held the property. As a practical matter, real property taxes are usually allocated during the closing process, and the details are provided in the closing statement for real property sales. A taxpayer need only acquire the closing statement to ascertain the proper allocation and how the sales price has been affected by the allocation.

Unless the actual real property taxes are apportioned between buyer and seller as part of the sale/purchase agreement, adjustments for the taxes must be made to determine the

---

[54] § 164(d) and Reg. § 1.164-6(b).

[55] Reg. § 1.164-6(b)(3), *Example 1*.

amount realized by the seller, as well as the buyer's cost basis of the property.[56] The treatment of the adjustments depends upon which party actually paid the real estate taxes.

**Example 20**

Assume that buyer and seller are both cash basis, calendar year taxpayers, and real estate taxes for the entire year are to be paid at the end of the year. Real property is sold on October 1, 2011 for $30,000, and B, the buyer, pays the real estate taxes of $365 on December 31, 2011. The real estate taxes attributable to and deductible by B are $92 (92 ÷ 365 × $365). The remaining $273 ($365 − $92) of the taxes will be apportioned to and deductible by S, the seller. As a result of this apportionment, the seller must increase the amount realized from the sale to $30,273, and the buyer will have an adjusted cost basis for the property of $30,273.

**Example 21**

Assume the same facts as in *Example 20*, except that the real property taxes are payable in advance for the entire year and that S, the seller, paid $365 in January 2011. The real estate taxes are apportioned in the same manner, and the buyer, B, will be entitled to deduct $92. However, B must adjust his cost basis of the property to $29,908 ($30,000 purchase price − $92 taxes paid by seller). The seller, S, is entitled to deduct $273 of the taxes and reduce his amount realized from the sale to $29,908.

Real property taxes assessed against local benefits of a kind tending to increase the value of the property assessed (e.g., special assessments for paved streets, street lights, sidewalks, drainage ditches, etc.) are not deductible.[57] Instead, the property owner simply adds the assessed amount paid to his or her cost basis of the property. However, if assessments for local benefits are made for the purpose of maintenance or repair, or for the purpose of meeting interest charges with respect to such benefits, they are deductible.[58] If an assessment is in part for the cost of an improvement and in part for maintenance, repairs or for interest charges, only *that* portion of the tax assessment relating to maintenance, repairs, or interest charges will be deductible. Unless the taxpayer can show the allocation of the amounts assessed for the different purposes, *none* of the amount paid is deductible.[59]

## Reporting Deductions for Taxes

Deductible state and local taxes are reported on different forms depending on the taxpaying entity claiming the deduction. Corporations report their deductions for these taxes on Form 1120. Fiduciaries (trusts and estates) report deductible taxes on Form 1041. Partnerships and S corporations report deductible taxes on Forms 1065 and 1120S, respectively. Individuals report deductible taxes on Form 1040, but the particular schedule used depends upon whether the taxes are business expenses or personal itemized deductions.

An individual's deduction for taxes (other than income taxes) related to his or her trade or business is reported on Schedule C of Form 1040 (Schedule F for farmers and ranchers). Deductible taxes (other than income taxes) related to rents and royalties are reported on Schedule E. All other deductible taxes, including state and local general sales taxes or state and local income taxes on business income or income from rents or royalties, are reported by an individual taxpayer on Schedule A of Form 1040.

---

[56] Reg. § 1.164-6(d); Reg. § 1.1001-1(b); and Reg. § 1.1012-1(b). A similar result should occur if buyer and seller are using different accounting methods.

[57] § 164(c)(1), Reg. § 1.164-2(g), and Reg. § 1.164-4(a).

[58] § 164(c)(1) and Reg. § 1.164-4(b)(1).

[59] Reg. § 1.164-4(b)(1).

## Interest Expense

Interest expense is an amount paid or incurred for the use or forbearance of money.[60] Under the general rule of Code § 163(a), all interest paid or accrued on indebtedness within the taxable year is allowed as a deduction. As with most general rules in the tax law, however, there are limitations imposed on the deduction of certain interest expense as well as the complete disallowance of deductions for interest related to certain items. These restrictions are discussed below.

### Limitations on Deductions of Interest Expense

**LO.5**
Distinguish between currently deductible and nondeductible interest expenses.

Prior to 1987, interest expense for most taxpayers was totally deductible. As part of the tax reform package of 1986, however, Congress substantially limited the deduction for interest. Over the years, Congress became concerned that by allowing a deduction for all interest expense the tax system encouraged borrowing and, conversely, discouraged savings. This problem was exacerbated by the fact that the "economic" income arising from the ownership of housing and other consumer durables is not subject to tax. For example, when a taxpayer purchases a residence, the return on the investment—the absence of having to pay rent for the item—is not subject to tax. Had the taxpayer invested in assets other than housing or other durables, the return (e.g., interest or dividends) would have been fully taxable. In those situations where the investment is financed by borrowing, allowing a deduction is equivalent to allowing a deduction for expenses related to tax-exempt income—which is expressly prohibited under Code § 265. The net result of this system is to provide an incentive to consume rather than save.

In rethinking the approach to interest in 1986, Congress believed that it would not be advisable to impute income on investments in durables and tax it. However, Congress did feel that it was appropriate and practical to address situations where consumer expenditures are financed by borrowing. Accordingly, Congress enacted rules that prohibit the deduction for personal interest (other than certain home mortgage interest and interest on certain education loans). As a result, interest expenses on personal auto loans, credit card purchases, etc., are no longer deductible.

In eliminating the deduction for personal interest, Congress effectively established *six* categories of interest expense, each of which is subject to its own special set of rules. The different categories of interest expense are (1) personal interest, (2) qualified residence interest, (3) trade or business interest, (4) investment interest, (5) passive-activity interest, and (6) qualified student loan interest. As explained in detail below, interest (other than qualified residence interest) is classified according to how the loan proceeds are *spent*. Consequently, taxpayers are required to determine the nature of an expenditure from loan proceeds before the amount of the interest deduction can be determined.

#### Personal Interest

Today, taxpayers are not allowed to deduct any *personal interest*. Personal interest is defined as all interest arising from personal expenditures *except* the following:[61]

1. Interest incurred in connection with the conduct of a trade or business (other than the performance of services as an employee);
2. Investment interest;
3. Qualified residence interest;
4. Interest taken into account in computing the income or loss from passive activities;
5. Interest on qualified education loans; and
6. Interest related to payment of the estate tax liability where such tax is deferred.

The effect of these rules is to severely limit the deduction for interest on consumer debt. For example, if a taxpayer borrows $3,000 from the bank and uses it to take a Caribbean cruise,

[60] *Old Colony Railroad v. Comm.*, 3 USTC ¶880, 10 AFTR 786, 284 U.S. 552 (USSC, 1936).

[61] § 163(h)(1).

none of the interest on the loan is deductible. Similarly, interest and finance charges would not be deductible on the following:

1. Automobile loans;
2. Furniture and appliance loans;
3. Credit card debt;
4. Life insurance loans;
5. Loans from qualified pension plans [including § 401(k) plans]; and
6. Delinquent tax payments and penalties.

It should be emphasized that interest incurred by an *employee* in connection with his or her trade or business is treated as consumer interest and is not deductible. In contrast, interest incurred by a self-employed person in his or her trade or business is fully deductible.

**Example 22**

K sells cosmetics for Fantastic Faces, Incorporated. Her job involves calling on department stores all over the state of Ohio and soliciting their orders. She uses her car entirely for business. Interest on her car loan for the year was $2,000. Since K is an employee, none of the interest is deductible.

**Example 23**

R is a real estate agent working for Bungalow Brokers. All of his compensation is based on the number of homes he sells during the year. He uses his car entirely for business. Under the employment tax rules (§ 3508), real estate agents and direct sellers are not considered employees where their remuneration is determined by sales. Since R would not be considered an employee, all of the interest on his car loan would be deductible.

**Example 24**

P is a reporter for the *News-Gazette*. She purchased a portable computer for $1,000, charging it on her bank credit card. She uses the computer entirely for business. Finance charges attributable to the purchase are $25. Even though the finance charges are incurred in connection with P's business, they are not deductible since she is an employee.

### Qualified Residence Interest

The elimination of the deduction for personal interest in 1986 did not extend to interest on most home mortgages. As a general rule, interest on any debt *secured* by a taxpayer's first or second home is deductible. The interest is normally deductible whether the interest is on an original, second, or refinanced mortgage. Moreover, the interest is deductible regardless of how the taxpayer uses the money as long as the debt is *secured* by a mortgage on his or her primary or secondary residence. Unfortunately, tucked behind these seemingly simple rules are several complex restrictions.

**Qualifying Indebtedness** Technically, only "qualified residence interest" is deductible. There are two types of qualified residence interest:[62]

1. Interest on *acquisition indebtedness:* Interest on debt that is incurred in acquiring, constructing, or improving a qualified residence *and* that is secured by such residence.
2. Interest on *home equity indebtedness:* Interest on debt secured by a qualified residence to the extent that the debt does not exceed the property's fair market value reduced by its acquisition debt.[63]

Note that in both cases, the crucial element in determining whether the interest qualifies is whether the debt is secured by a residence. Unsecured debt and debt secured by other property does not qualify even though the debt proceeds may be used to acquire a personal residence.

### Example 25

J borrowed $50,000 from her pension plan and $10,000 from her father to buy a new home. None of the interest on the debt is deductible because neither of the debts is secured by the residence. This is true even though the borrowed amounts were used to buy a residence.

Also observe that in the case of both acquisition and home equity debt, the debt must be secured by a *qualified* residence. A qualified residence is the taxpayer's principal home and one other residence of the taxpayer.[64] This rule effectively allows taxpayers to deduct the interest on only two homes: their first home and a second of their choosing. A taxpayer with more than two homes must designate which is the second home when the return is filed. Different homes can be selected each year.

### Example 26

After winning the New York State lottery, T retired from her job and purchased a home in Tampa, Florida. She also purchased a motor home and a condominium in Vail, Colorado. All purchases were debt-financed and secured by the property. Within certain dollar limitations, T can treat the interest paid on her home in Tampa *and* the interest paid on *either* the motor home *or* the condominium as qualified residence interest.

### Example 27

Assume the same facts as above except that T converted the condominium into rental property at the advice of her tax accountant. In this case, the condominium will not qualify as T's secondary residence.[65]

[62] § 163(h)(3).

[63] Interest relating to home equity loans is not deducitble for purposes of the alternative minimum tax unless the loan proceeds are used for improvements. See § 56(e).

[64] § 163(h)(4).

[65] This does not mean that a taxpayer's interest expense on rental property is not deductible. As discussed later, however, losses from rental property (including interest expense) may be subject to deduction limitations.

In determining the deductibility of interest on a second home, special rules must be considered if the taxpayer *rents* it out. These rules are examined in conjunction with vacation homes discussed later in this chapter. If the second home is not rented out, no personal use is actually needed in order to meet the qualified residence test.

Congress also took steps to ensure that a taxpayer could not convert nondeductible interest into qualified residence interest simply by pitching a tent on the property and calling it a second home (e.g., vacant land or a car). In determining whether the debt is incurred with respect to a qualified residence, the term *residence* includes a vacation home, condominium, mobile home, boat, or recreational vehicle as long as the property contains basic living accommodations (i.e., sleeping space, toilet, and cooking facilities).

**Limitations on Deductible Amount** To prevent taxpayers from taking undue advantage of the deductibility of home mortgage interest, Congress imposed limits on the maximum amount of debt qualifying under either definition. The aggregate amount of debt that can be treated as acquisition indebtedness for any taxable year cannot exceed $1 million ($500,000 in the case of a married individual filing a separate return),[66] whereas the aggregate amount of debt that will be treated as home equity indebtedness for any taxable year cannot exceed $100,000 ($50,000 if married and filing separately).[67] Collectively, the total amount of debt in any one year on which the interest paid or accrued will be treated as qualified residence interest cannot exceed $1.1 million.

### Example 28

During the current year, T purchases a principal residence in Boston for $900,000 and a vacation home in Tampa for $500,000. Mortgages secured by both properties total $1.3 million. T may treat *only* the interest paid on $1 million of acquisition indebtedness as qualified residence interest. In addition, he may treat $100,000 of the loans as home equity indebtedness and, therefore, the related interest is deductible as qualified residence interest. Whether interest on the balance of the debt, $200,000, is deductible depends on how the funds are used.

### Example 29

C purchased his present residence several years ago at a cost of $1.9 million. The present balance on his home mortgage is $800,000 and the property is valued at $2.5 million. This year, C borrowed $300,000 secured by a second mortgage on his home. Even though the total indebtedness does not exceed $1.1 million, C may deduct the interest on the $800,000 unpaid acquisition indebtedness and the interest on only $100,000 of the home equity mortgage. Any excess interest paid during the year will be treated as personal interest.

It is important to note that the interest paid on qualifying home equity indebtedness is allowed as a deduction *regardless* of how the taxpayer uses the loan proceeds. Thus, the obvious reason for the $100,000 limit on qualifying home equity debt is to impose a limit on the amount of an interest deduction the taxpayer may claim on loan proceeds used for personal purposes.

---

[66] Any qualified residence indebtedness incurred before October 14, 1987—whether it is acquisition debt, home equity debt, or a combination of both —is to be treated as acquisition debt and is not subject to the $1 million limitation. If the property is later refinanced, however, the new indebtedness is subject to this limitation. § 163(h)(3)(D).

[67] § 163(h).

### Example 30

K purchased her present residence 10 years ago at a cost of $70,000. The present balance on her home mortgage is $40,000 and the property is appraised at a value of $150,000. This year, K borrowed $80,000 secured by a second mortgage on her home. She used the loan proceeds to purchase new clothes and a new automobile, and to take a vacation to Hawaii. The interest on the $80,000 loan is deductible since it is qualified residence interest. The fact that K used the loan proceeds for personal purposes is irrelevant. Also note that K's original cost of $70,000 is not used to limit the amount of her $80,000 home equity loan.

**Refinancing** As mortgage interest rates rise and fall, homeowners often refinance their original home loans to get a better rate. During the past 25 years, refinancing has been quite common as the rates on 30-year fixed mortgages have been as high as about 18 percent in 1982 and as low as about 3.25 percent in 2010. Any attempt to refinance acquisition indebtedness should be undertaken with caution. A qualifying residence's acquisition debt is *reduced* by principal payments and *cannot be increased* unless the loan proceeds are used for home improvements. Thus, the acquisition debt can be refinanced only to the extent that the principal amount of the refinancing does not exceed the principal amount of the acquisition debt immediately before the refinancing.[68] The interest paid on any excess refinanced debt will not be treated as acquisition indebtedness. However, any excess may be treated as home equity indebtedness. As noted above, the total qualifying indebtedness (acquisition and home equity) cannot exceed the value of the residence.

### Example 31

In 1970, G purchased her California bungalow for $25,000. The house is now worth $350,000. G paid off the mortgage on the home several years ago. This year, G mortgaged her house for $120,000 and subsequently loaned the money to her grandson to enable him to buy his first home. None of the loan qualifies as acquisition debt because the balance of acquisition debt refinanced was zero. However, G may deduct interest on $100,000 of the loan, which qualifies as home-equity debt.

### Example 32

R purchased his present residence in 1999 for $250,000 and borrowed $210,000 on a 11% mortgage secured by the property. In 2011, R refinanced the balance of his mortgage, $190,000, by securing a new mortgage of $230,000 at 5%. Unless R used the additional loan proceeds to substantially improve the residence, only $190,000 of the new mortgage constitutes acquisition indebtedness, and the corresponding interest is therefore deductible. In addition, the $40,000 balance of the debt may be treated as home-equity debt. In such case, the interest on the entire $230,000 mortgage would be deductible as qualified residence interest.

## Qualified Mortgage Insurance

Many individuals who purchase homes are required to buy mortgage insurance. The insurance is intended to provide funds to pay off the mortgage balance or help meet the payments on a mortgage as they fall due in the case of the individual's death or disability. Mortgage insurance is typically required when the loan has a loan to value ratio of 80 percent or greater

[68] § 163(h)(3)(B).

(i.e., the down payment is less than 20% of the home's value). Such insurance is often called private mortgage insurance (PMI) for conventional loans, because a private institution rather than the federal government backs the loan.

Under the Tax Relief and Health Care Act of 2006, taxpayers were allowed to deduct premiums paid in 2007 for qualified mortgage insurance.[69] Congress extended this deduction through the year 2010 by the Mortgage Forgiveness Debt Relief Act of 2007. Premiums on mortgage insurance provided by VA, FHA, RHA, and private mortgage insurance normally qualify. In addition, the insurance qualifies only if it is on acquisition indebtedness on a qualified residence.

The deduction is subject to phase-out. The phase-out begins when the taxpayer's A.G.I. exceeds $100,000 and is complete once A.G.I. is greater than $109,000. For example, a taxpayer with $1,500 of qualified premiums and A.G.I. of $103,000 will be limited to a deduction of $1,000 [$1,500 – ($3,000/$9,000 × $1,500 = $500)].

## Trade or Business Interest

While the taxpayer normally cannot deduct interest of a personal nature, interest related to a trade or business expenditure is totally deductible. Perhaps the most common example of business interest is that arising from loans used to acquire fixed assets such as buildings and equipment that are used in the business. Business interest also includes that attributable to loans used to acquire an interest in an S corporation or a partnership in which the taxpayer materially participates. Recall, however, that interest incurred in connection with performing services as an employee is not considered business interest, and thus is considered non-deductible personal interest.

As explained below, the fact that a business incurs interest expense does not necessarily mean that such interest is classified as business interest. If interest expense incurred by a business arises from an investment considered unrelated to the business, it will not be business interest (e.g., a closely held corporation purchases stock on margin).

## Investment Interest

The fourth category of interest expense subject to limitation is investment interest. This limitation is imposed on taxpayers, other than regular corporations, who have paid or incurred interest expense to purchase or carry investments.[70] Common examples include interest on loans to purchase unimproved land and interest incurred on margin accounts used to purchase stocks and other securities. Congress imposed the investment interest limitation to eliminate what it perceived was an unfair advantage to certain wealthy investors. For example, consider the taxpayer who borrows to acquire or carry investments that produce little or no income currently but pay off handsomely when the investment is sold. This is commonly the hoped-for result with investments in such assets as growth stock or land. Without any restrictions, the taxpayer would be able to claim an immediate deduction for interest expense yet postpone any income recognition until the property was ultimately sold. Moreover, the income that the taxpayer would realize on the sale would normally be favorable capital gain. Congress apparently felt that this mismatching of income and expense was unwarranted and reacted by limiting the taxpayer's deduction for investment interest to the taxpayer's current investment income.

Before examining the investment interest limitation, the definition of investment interest should be clarified. *Investment interest* is generally any interest expense on debt used to finance property held for investment. It does not include, however, qualified residence interest or any interest related to a passive activity. As discussed in Chapter 12, interest related to a passive activity is allocated to the passive activity and is taken into account in computing the activity's income or loss. As a result, such interest is effectively limited by the passive-loss rules. Note, however, that any interest incurred by a passive activity that is related to its portfolio income (i.e., interest and dividend income) would normally be considered investment interest subject to the investment interest limitation. Because rental activities are usually treated as a passive activity, interest expense allocable to a rental activity is normally subject to the passive-loss rules.

The annual deduction for investment interest expense is limited to the taxpayer's *net investment income*, if any, for the tax year.[71] Any investment interest that exceeds the

---

[69] § 163(h)(4)(E)(i).

[70] § 163(d).

[71] § 163(d)(1).

limitation and is disallowed may be carried forward until it is exhausted. Operationally, the disallowed interest is carried forward to the subsequent year, where it is combined with current year interest and is once again subject to the net investment income limitation. (Note that a sale of the financed property does not trigger the allowance of any disallowed interest.)

**Net Investment Income** Net investment income is the excess of the taxpayer's investment income over investment expenses. For this purpose, *investment income* is generally defined as the gross income from property held for investment. Common examples of investment income include:

1. Interest;
2. Royalties;
3. Ordinary income from the recapture of depreciation or intangible drilling costs under §§ 1245, 1250, and 1254;
4. Portfolio income under the passive loss rules; and
5. Income from a trade or business in which the taxpayer did not materially participate (but which is not a passive activity, e.g., a working interest in an oil or gas property).

Note that income from rental property and income from a passive activity (other than portfolio income) are not considered investment income. As noted above, any interest expense incurred in rental or passive activities is allocated to those activities and is used in computing the passive income or loss of such activity.[72] For example, mortgage interest on rental property would be deductible only to the extent of passive income. It is also important to note that qualified dividends (i.e., those taxed at a rate of 15 percent) and a net long-term capital gain from the disposition of an asset producing investment income (e.g., stocks or bonds) normally is not included in investment income. However, a taxpayer currently facing a limitation on the deduction for investment interest expense because of a limited amount of investment income may elect to include all or a part of the dividends or gain as investment income. Basically, such an election results in the dividends or the net capital gain being taxed as ordinary income in order to increase the electing taxpayer's ordinary deduction for investment interest expense.

Investment expenses are generally all those deductions (except interest) that are directly connected with the production of the investment income. Any investment expenses that are considered miscellaneous itemized deductions are considered only to the extent they exceed the 2 percent floor. For this purpose, the 2 percent floor is first absorbed by all other miscellaneous expenses.

### Example 33

G's records for 2011 revealed the following information:

| | |
|---|---|
| Salary | $ 40,000 |
| Dividends and interest | 3,500 |
| Share of partnership income: | |
| Partnership ordinary income | 700 |
| Portfolio income: | |
| Dividends | 50 |
| Interest | 80 |
| Rental income from duplex | 15,000 |
| Rental expenses | (14,000) |
| Adjusted gross income | $ 45,330 |

[72] § 163(d)(4)(E). See Chapter 12 for a detailed discussion of the passive loss rules.

| | |
|---|---|
| Qualified residence interest | $ 8,000 |
| Real estate taxes on home | 4,000 |
| Property tax on land held for investment | 1,000 |
| Miscellaneous itemized deductions: | |
| Safety deposit box rental | 50 |
| Financial planner | 1,500 |
| Fee to maintain brokerage account | 100 |
| Unreimbursed employee business expenses | 725 |

G is a limited partner in the partnership and thus treats the partnership as a passive activity. G also paid $7,700 of interest expense on the land held for investment. G's net investment income is computed as follows:

| | | | |
|---|---|---|---|
| Investment income: | | | |
| Dividends and interest | | $3,500 | |
| Partnership income: | | | |
| Portfolio income: | | | |
| Dividends | | 50 | |
| Interest | | 80 | |
| Total investment income | | | $ 3,630 |
| Investment expenses: | | | |
| Property tax on land | | $1,000 | |
| Safe deposit box rental | | 50 | |
| Financial planner | | 1,500 | |
| Fee to maintain brokerage account | | 100 | |
| Miscellaneous itemized deductions disallowed 2% floor (2% × $45,330) | $ 907 | | |
| Unreimbursed employee business expenses | (725) | | |
| Investment expenses classified as miscellaneous itemized deductions disallowed | | (182) | |
| Total investment expenses | | | (2,468) |
| Net investment income | | | $ 1,162 |

For 2011, G may deduct $1,162 of investment interest expense (*not* subject to the itemized deduction cutback rule). The balance of $6,538 ($7,700 – $1,162) is carried over to the next year, 2012, and is treated as if it were paid in 2011. There is no limit on the carryover period. Note that in computing investment expenses, only investment expenses exceeding the 2% floor are allowed. In computing the disallowed portion, investment expenses are deemed to come last. Also note that rental income is not considered investment income.

## Passive Activity Interest

Deductions attributable to so-called *passive activities* (e.g., those in which a taxpayer does not participate in a material fashion) are subject to special rules. Interest expense incurred by a passive activity itself (e.g., a limited partnership), or by investment in a passive activity, is treated as a deduction relating to the passive activity and is limited by the passive loss rules.[73] The passive activity loss rules are discussed in Chapter 12.

[73] § 163(d)(3)(B).

### Interest on Student Loans

One of several measures enacted by Congress to help taxpayers finance the cost of higher education concerns the treatment of interest on student loans. As noted earlier, without a special rule, interest paid on loans to help pay college tuition and the like would be nondeductible personal interest. Currently, § 221 authorizes a deduction for interest on qualified educational loans. The maximum amount of interest that can be deducted annually is limited to $2,500.

If the interest qualifies for deduction, it is deductible *for* adjusted gross income. Therefore taxpayers are not required to itemize in order to benefit from the deduction.

**Student Loan Interest Deduction Phase-Out** Like many relief provisions, the deduction for interest on qualified educational loans is not extended to high-income taxpayers. To accomplish this objective, the maximum deduction is phased out once the taxpayer's A.G.I. (computed with certain modifications) exceeds $120,000 for joint returns ($60,000 for other returns). The reduction occurs over a $30,000 income range for married filing jointly ($15,000 for all others), producing a complete phase-out as follows:

$$\frac{\text{Reduction of deductible}}{\text{Portion of student loan interest}} = \frac{\text{Deductible Amount of Interest}}{\text{(\$2,500 maximum in 2010)}} \times \frac{\text{Modified A.G.I.} - \text{threshold}}{\text{Income range}}$$

| | *Modified A.G.I. Phase-Out Begins* | *Modified A.G.I. Phase-Out Complete* |
|---|---|---|
| Married filing jointly | $120,000 | $150,000 |
| Other taxpayers | 60,000 | 75,000 |

For this purpose, modified A.G.I. is A.G.I. before the exclusions for (1) foreign earned income and housing; (2) income from American Samoa, Guam and the Northern Mariana Islands; and after the exclusions for (1) Series EE savings bonds interest used to pay for education; (2) employer provided adoption benefits; (3) social security; (4) the deduction for contributions to IRAs; and (5) the deduction for losses on passive activities.

**Example 34**

In 2011, S, single, graduated from Notre Dame with a law degree. During the year, she paid student loan interest of $5,000 and reported adjusted gross income before consideration of the interest of $66,000. Since S's adjusted gross income exceeds the $60,000 threshold for single taxpayers by $6,000 (40% of the $15,000 range), the maximum allowable deduction is reduced in 2011 to $1,500 [$2,500 – ($6,000/$15,000 × $2,500 = $1,000)]. Therefore, S may deduct $1,500 of the $5,000 interest for adjusted gross income.

Only interest on qualified education loans is deductible. Such loans are defined as any debt (other than a loan from a related party) incurred to pay qualified educational expenses for the taxpayer, the taxpayer's spouse, or other individuals who were the taxpayer's dependents at the time the debt was incurred. No deduction is allowed for interest paid by the taxpayer if the taxpayer is claimed as a dependent on another's return. For example, a child who pays interest on his student loans could not deduct the interest if his parents claim an exemption for him. Married taxpayers must file a joint return to claim the deduction.

Interest is deductible only if the education is furnished to an eligible student. An eligible student is generally one who is enrolled in a degree, certificate, or other program leading to a recognized credential at an eligible institution of higher education. In addition, the student must have been attending at least half-time (i.e., one-half of the normal full-time work load for the course of study that the student is pursuing).

Qualified educational expenses include the costs of attendance at an eligible educational institution. They include tuition, fees, room and board, and related expenses, such as books and supplies. Such amounts must be reduced by any amounts excluded under § 127 concerning employer educational assistance plans, § 135 concerning interest excluded on Series EE bonds, or § 530 excluding distributions from education IRAs (see discussion in Chapter 6).

## Classification of Interest Expense

The different rules for different types of interest expense force taxpayers to classify and allocate their interest expense among appropriate categories. The classification procedure established by the Treasury is very straightforward in principle. Under the Temporary Regulations, interest is generally classified according to how the loan proceeds are spent—that is, the character of the expenditure determines the character of interest.[74] The type of collateral that may secure the loan is irrelevant in the classification process—except in the case of the qualified residence interest which is deductible regardless of how loan proceeds are spent.[75]

**Example 35**

This year, T pledged IBM stock held as an investment as collateral for a loan which he uses to purchase a personal car. Any interest expense on the loan is considered nondeductible personal interest since the debt proceeds were used for personal purposes. The fact that the debt is secured by investment property is irrelevant. If the loan were secured by T's primary residence, the interest could be deductible as qualified residence interest.

The classification scheme demands that the taxpayer trace how any loan proceeds were used. To simplify this task, specific rules exist for debt proceeds that are (1) deposited in the borrower's account, (2) disbursed directly by the lender to someone other than the borrower, or (3) received in cash.

### Proceeds Deposited in the Borrower's Account

In most cases, taxpayers borrow money, deposit it in an account, and write checks for various expenditures. Since money is fungible (that is, one dollar cannot be distinguished from another) it would be impossible without special rules to determine how the loan proceeds were spent, and therefore, how the related interest should be allocated. The Temporary Regulations create such rules.[76]

The first presumption created by the Regulations concerns the treatment of interest on funds that have not been spent. To the extent borrowed funds are deposited and not spent, interest attributable to such a period is considered *investment interest* regardless of whether the account bears interest income.[77]

**Example 36**

On November 1, K borrowed $1,000 which she intends to use to fix up her boat. She deposited the $1,000 in a separate account. No expenditures were made during the remainder of the year. In this case, K is subject to the interest allocation rules since the interest expense is considered attributable to an investment, and is therefore, investment interest.

---

74 Temp. Reg. § 1.163-8T.

75 Temp. Reg. § 1.163-8T(c)(1). For purposes of the alternative minimum tax, however, qualified housing interest is deductible only if the debt is spent on the residence. See Chapter 13 for further discussion.

76 Temp. Reg. § 1.163-8T(c)(4).

77 *Ibid.*

### Example 37

Same as above except K makes several personal expenditures during the next three months. Interest must be allocated between investment interest and personal interest.

### Example 38

A borrows $100,000 on January 1 and deposits it in a separate account where it remains until April 1 when he purchases an interest in a limited partnership for $20,000. On September 1, R purchases a new car for $30,000. Interest expense attributable to the $100,000 is allocated in the following manner:

| | Debt Proceeds | | |
|---|---|---|---|
| *Period* | *Investment Interest* | *Passive Interest* | *Personal Interest* |
| 1/1–3/31 | $100,000 | | |
| 4/1–8/31 | 80,000 | $20,000 | |
| 9/1–12/31 | 50,000 | 20,000 | $30,000 |

## Commingled Funds

In most situations, a taxpayer has one account in which all amounts are deposited. When this occurs, all expenditures from the account after the loan is deposited are deemed to come first from the borrowed funds.

### Example 39

On October 1, B borrowed $1,000 to purchase a snowplow attachment for the front of his truck. He plans to make some extra money this winter by plowing driveways and parking lots. B deposited the $1,000 in his only checking account. On October 20, he bought the attachment for $1,500. Prior to October 20, he wrote $700 in checks for groceries and other personal items. Of the $1,000 loan, $700 is deemed to have been spent for personal items while the remaining $300 is allocated to the snow plow. Consequently, B may deduct only the interest expense on $300.

If proceeds from more than one loan are deposited into an account, expenditures are treated as coming from the borrowed funds in the order in which they were deposited (i.e., first-in, first-out).

### Example 40

Dr. T has a personal checking account with a current balance of $3,000. On November 1, T obtained a $1,000 one-year Loan (Debt A) from her bank, which it credited to her personal account. She planned to use the loan to purchase a small copier for her dental practice. After shopping, T determined she would need additional funds. Therefore, on November 30 she obtained another $1,000 loan (Debt B). On December 12, T wrote a check for $800 to pay for her husband's Christmas present, a diamond ring. On

December 19, she wrote a check for $2,100 to purchase the copier. These transactions are summarized as follows:

| Date | Transaction | |
|---|---|---|
| 11/1 | Borrowed (Debt A) | $1,000 |
| 11/30 | Borrowed (Debt B) | 1,000 |
| 12/12 | Purchased ring | (800) |
| 12/19 | Purchased copier | (2,100) |

For purposes of determining the deduction for the interest on the loan, $800 of Debt A is deemed to be used for personal purposes (i.e., the ring purchase) and $200 toward the copier. All of Debt B is used for the copier. Thus, interest attributable to $800 of Debt A is nondeductible personal interest while that attributable to $200 is totally deductible. All of the interest on Debt B is deductible business interest. This may be summarized as follows:

| | 11/1 Debt A $1,000 | | 11/30 Debt B $1,000 | | |
|---|---|---|---|---|---|
| Expenditure | Personal | Business | Personal | Business | Other |
| $ 800 ring | $800 | | | | |
| 2,100 copier | | $200 | | $1,000 | $900 |

## Thirty-Day Rule

In lieu of allocating the debt proceeds in the above manner, an alternative method is available. A borrower can elect to treat any expenditure made from any account within 30 days before or 30 days after debt proceeds are deposited in any account of the borrower as having been made from the proceeds of that loan.[78]

### Example 41

C borrowed and deposited $5,000 in his checking account on December 1. On December 23, he wrote a check for $6,000 for his estimated income taxes. On December 29, he wrote a check for $5,000 for furniture for his business. Under the normal allocation rule, the entire $5,000 proceeds from the debt would be considered spent for personal purposes. Under the 30-day rule, however, C may treat the $5,000 as used to purchase the furniture since the proceeds were spent within 30 days of deposit. Also note that if C actually purchased the furniture for his business in November, he could still elect to treat that expenditure as being made from the December 1 loan proceeds regardless of which checking account (business or personal) was used to deposit the loan proceeds or from which the expenditure was made.

## Loan Proceeds Received Indirectly

In many transactions, a borrower incurs debt without receiving any loan proceeds directly. For example, if the taxpayer borrowed $100,000 from a bank to purchase a building, the bank typically disburses the $100,000 directly to the seller rather than to the borrower. Similarly, the borrower may purchase the building and assume the seller's $100,000 mortgage. In this and similar situations, the borrower is treated as having received the proceeds and used them to make the expenditure for the property, services, or other purpose.[79]

## Loan Proceeds Received in Cash

When the borrower receives the loan proceeds in cash, the taxpayer may treat any cash expenditure made within 30 days before or 30 days after receiving the cash as made from the loan.

[78] See Temp. Reg. § 1.163-8T(c)(5)(i) as modified by Notice 89-35, 1989-1 CB 675.

[79] Temp. Reg. § 1.163-8T(c)(3).

### Debt Repayments, Refinancings, and Reallocations

Loans that are used for several purposes present a unique problem when a portion of the loan is repaid. In this case, repayments must be applied in the following order:[80]

1. Personal expenditures;
2. Investment expenditures and passive activity expenditures (other than rental real estate in which the taxpayer actively participates);
3. Rental real estate expenditures;
4. Former passive activity expenditures; and
5. Trade or business expenditures.

**Example 42**

R borrows $10,000, $6,000 of which is used to purchase a personal automobile and $4,000 of which is used to invest in land. On June 1 of this year she paid $7,000 on the loan. Of the $7,000 repayment, $6,000 reduces the portion of the loan allocated to personal expenditures and the remaining $1,000 reduces the portion allocated to investment.

If the taxpayer refinances an old debt, interest on the new debt is characterized in the same way as that on the old debt.

**Example 43**

In 2010, S borrowed $10,000 at an annual interest rate of 14%. He used $8,000 to purchase a new boat and $2,000 to purchase a computer to use in his business. This year, he borrowed $6,000 from another bank at 10% to pay off the balance of the old loan. At the time the original loan was paid off, $4,000 of the $6,000 balance was allocated to the boat purchase and $2,000 was allocated to the computer purchase. The new debt will be allocated in the same manner as the old debt.

If the taxpayer borrows to finance a business asset, the debt must be recharacterized whenever the asset is sold or the nature of the use of the asset changes.

**Example 44**

Several years ago B, a traveling salesperson, borrowed $12,000 to buy a car that he used entirely for business. This year, B gave his car to his wife who uses it solely for personal use. The loan and interest thereon must be reclassified.

### Computation and Allocation of Interest Expense

The special rules governing the taxpayer's deduction for interest expense do not affect its computation. Interest is computed in the normal manner. However, allocation of the interest expense among the different categories does present certain difficulties. As a general rule, interest expense accruing on a debt for any period is allocated in the same manner as the debt. Interest which accrues on interest—that is, compound interest—is allocated in the same manner as the original interest.[81]

---

[80] *Ibid.*

[81] Temp. Reg. § 1.163-8T(c)(2).

### Example 45

On January 1, R borrowed $100,000 at an interest rate of 10%, compounded semi-annually. She deposited the loan in a separate account and on July 1 used the funds to purchase a yacht. On December 31, R paid the accrued interest of $10,250, computed as follows:

| *Period* | *Principal* | | *Rate* | | *Time* | | *Interest* |
|---|---|---|---|---|---|---|---|
| 1/1–6/30 | $100,000 | × | 10% | × | 6/12 | = | $ 5,000 |
| 7/1–12/31 | 105,000 | × | 10% | × | 6/12 | = | 5,250 |
| | | | | | | | $10,250 |

Under the allocation rules, R's loan is classified as an investment loan from January 1 through June 30 and, therefore, the interest accruing for that period of $5,000 is investment interest. In addition, the interest expense which accrues on this $5,000 from July 30 through December 31 of $250 ($5,000 × 10% × 612) is considered investment interest for a total of $5,250. This $250 of "compound interest" accruing from July 31 through December 31 is allocated to the investment category even though the original loan has been assigned to a new category for the same period. The remaining $5,000 of interest expense accruing from July 1 through December 31 ($100,000 × 10% × 612) is personal interest.

To simplify the allocation of interest expense, the taxpayer may use a straight-line method. Using this technique, an equal amount of interest is allocated to each day of the year. For this purpose, the taxpayer may treat a year as consisting of twelve 30-day months.

### Example 46

Assume the same facts as in *Example 45* above, except that R elects to allocate the interest expense on a straight-line basis, treating the year as consisting of twelve 30-day months. As a result, interest expense of $5,125 (180/360 × $10,250) would be investment interest while the remaining $5,125 of interest expense would be personal interest.

## When Deductible

The taxpayer's method of accounting generally controls the timing of an interest expense deduction. Accrual method taxpayers generally may deduct interest over the period in which the interest accrues, regardless of when the expense is actually paid. However, cash-basis taxpayers must *actually* pay the interest before a deduction is allowed. Many situations arise in which the "actual payment" requirement imposed on cash-basis taxpayers delays the timing of a deduction. Other situations concern measurement of the amount of interest actually paid. The most common of these situations are briefly discussed below.

### Interest Paid in Advance

If interest is paid in advance for a time period that extends beyond the end of one tax year, *both* accrual method and cash-basis taxpayers generally are required to spread the interest deduction over the tax years to which it applies.[82] An important exception is made for cash-basis individual taxpayers who are required to pay interest "points" in connection with indebtedness incurred to *purchase* or *improve* the taxpayer's principal residence (i.e., taxpayer's home).[83] The term *points* is often used to describe charges imposed on the borrower under such descriptions as "loan origination fees," "premium charges," and

[82] § 461(a).

[83] § 461(g).

"maximum loan charges." Such charges usually are stated as a percentage (point) of the loan amount. If the payment of any of these charges is *strictly* for the use of money *and* actual payment of these charges is made out of *separate funds* belonging to the taxpayer, an interest deduction is allowed in the year of payment.[84]

> **Example 47**
>
> R borrowed $15,000 from State Bank to make improvements on his home. The loan is payable over a 10-year period, and the bank charged R a loan origination fee of $300 (2 points). If R pays the $300 charge from separate funds, it is currently deductible as an interest expense (assuming R itemizes his deductions). However, if the $300 charge is added to the amount of the loan, R has not currently paid interest. Instead, R will be required to treat the charge as note-discount interest (see discussion below).

### Note-Discount Interest

Taxpayers often sign notes calling for repayment of an amount greater than the loan proceeds actually received. This occurs when the creditor subtracts (withholds) the interest from the face amount of the loan and the taxpayer receives the balance, or when the face amount of the note simply includes add-on interest. In either case, cash-basis taxpayers are not allowed a deduction until the tax year in which the interest is actually paid. Accrual-method taxpayers are allowed to deduct the interest over the tax years in which it accrues.

### Graduated Payment Mortgages

A creature of the high interest rate mortgage market of recent years, graduated payment mortgages provide for increasing payments in the early years of the mortgage until the payments reach some level amount. Under these plans, the payments in the early years are less than the amount of interest owed on the loan. The unpaid interest is added to the principal amount of the mortgage and future interest is computed on this revised balance. As should be expected, cash-basis taxpayers may deduct *only* the interest actually paid in the current year; the increases in the principal balance of the mortgage are treated much the same as note-discount interest.

### Installment Purchases

Individual taxpayers who purchase personal property or pay for educational services under a contract calling for installment payments in which carrying charges are separately stated but the interest charge cannot be determined are allowed to *impute* an interest expense. The imputed expense is allowed whether or not a payment is actually made during the tax year, and is computed at a rate of 6 percent of the *average unpaid balance* of the contract during the year.[85] The average unpaid balance is the sum of the unpaid balance outstanding on the first day of each month of the tax year, divided by 12 months. Credit card and revolving charge account finance charges are generally much greater than 6 percent. Fortunately, these charges are usually stated separately at a *predetermined* interest rate (e.g., finance charge of 10% of unpaid monthly balance). Recall, however, that this type of interest expense is generally personal interest and thus nondeductible!

## Where Reported

Like the deductions for taxes, the appropriate tax form or schedule on which deductible interest is reported depends upon the entity entitled to the deduction and the nature of the indebtedness to which the interest relates. A corporation's deductible interest is reported on its annual tax return Form 1120. Estates and trusts report interest deductions on Form 1041; partnerships and S corporations claim interest deductions on Forms 1065 and 1120S,

---

[84] See *Roger A. Schubel*, 77 T.C. 701 (1982), and *James W. Hager*, 45 TCM 123, T.C. Memo 1982-663. Note, however, that this interest deduction is subject to the rules regarding qualified residence interest.

[85] § 163(b)(1).

respectively. Individuals claiming a deduction for interest expense must report the amount on the appropriate schedule of Form 1040. If the interest is related to business indebtedness—and the business is self-employment—the individual will claim his or her deduction on Schedule C (Schedule F for farmers and ranchers). Interest on debt incurred in connection with the production of rents or royalties is reported on Schedule E. Deductible interest on indebtedness incurred for personal use must be reported as an itemized deduction on Schedule A (with the exception of qualifying student loan interest which is deductible for A.G.I.). However, any individual who has refinanced his or her home, or is otherwise subject to the limitations imposed on qualified residence interest, should see IRS Publication 936 for instructions in computing the home mortgage interest deduction.

An individual's current deduction for investment interest expense should be calculated on Form 4952 (see Appendix B), and any disallowed deduction reported as a carryover amount. The deductible amount from Form 4952 should be transferred to and claimed as a deduction on the individual's Schedule E, Form 1040, if the interest relates to the production of royalties; otherwise, the deductible amount is reported on Schedule A. Partnerships and S corporations are not allowed to deduct investment interest expense in determining income or loss. Instead, these conduit entities are required to set out and separately report each partner's or shareholder's share of *both* investment interest expense *and* net investment income for the current year. Each partner or shareholder must claim his or her deduction subject to the previously described limitations. Recall, however, that a partner that is a regular corporation will not be subject to the investment interest expense limitation.

## Charitable Contributions

To encourage the private sector to share in the cost of providing many needed social services, Congress allows individuals, regular corporations, estates, and trusts deductions for charitable contributions (or gifts) of money or other property to certain qualified organizations. Partnerships and S corporations are not allowed to deduct charitable contributions. Instead, these conduit entities pass the contributions through to the partners and shareholders who must claim the deduction on their own Federal income tax returns.[86]

Code § 170 contains the rules regarding deductions for charitable contributions made by individuals and regular corporations. Code § 642(c) sets forth the rules regarding the amount and timing of charitable contribution deductions claimed by estates and trusts. The rules related to the measurement, timing, and qualification of contribution deductions claimed by individuals and corporations are discussed below. A discussion of the percentage limitations imposed on current deductions by individual taxpayers is also included. The specific rules regarding limitations imposed on a corporation's annual charitable contribution deduction are discussed in Chapter 19.

### Deduction Requirements

**LO.6**
Explain the requirements for the deductibility of charitable contributions and compute the contribution deduction.

Individual taxpayers are allowed a deduction for contributions of cash or other property *only if* the gift is made to a qualifying donee organization. Additionally, individuals are required to actually pay cash or transfer property before the close of the tax year in which the deduction is claimed. An exception to the payment requirement is made in the case of contribution deductions which, due to deduction limitations, have been carried over from prior years. The deduction limitations and carryover rules are discussed later in this chapter.

In addition to these basic considerations, Congress added two extremely important limitations in 2007 that will have widespread effect. First, no deduction is allowed for contributions of cash, check or any other type of monetary gift unless the taxpayer has some type of bank record such as a cancelled check, credit card statement or receipt from the charity verifying the contribution. Note that this rule applies to any contribution of money, regardless of amount. Thus, there is no de minimis exception to the new substantiation requirements for gifts of cash to charity.[87] Second, a charitable contribution for clothing and household goods will be permitted only if the items are "in good used condition or better." In

---

[86] See §§ 702(a)(4) and 1366(a)(1).

[87] Section 170(f)(17), introduced by the Pension Protection Act of 2006. As a result of these requirements, taxpayers are likely to make more contributions by check.

this regard, the IRS is authorized to deny deductions for items of minimal value (e.g., used socks and underwear). Unfortunately, the new law provides no guidance as to what is good condition for used items or how the new rule might be enforced.[88]

## Qualifying Donees

To be deductible, contributions of cash or other property must be made to or for the use of one of the following:[89]

1. A state, a U.S. possession, a political subdivision of a state or possession, the United States, or the District of Columbia, if the contribution is made solely for public purposes;
2. A community chest, corporation, trust, fund, or foundation that is organized or created in, or under the laws of, the United States, any state, the District of Columbia, or any possession of the United States *and* is organized and operated exclusively for religious, charitable, scientific, literary, or educational purposes or for the prevention of cruelty to children or animals;
3. A war veterans' organization;
4. A nonprofit volunteer fire company or civil defense organization;
5. A domestic fraternal society operating under the lodge system, but only if the contribution is to be used for any of the purposes stated in item 2 above; and
6. A nonprofit cemetery company, if the funds are to be used solely for the perpetual care of the cemetery as a whole, and not for a particular lot or mausoleum crypt.

If the taxpayer has not been informed by the recipient organization that it is a qualifying donee, he or she may check its status in the *Cumulative List of Organizations* (IRS Publication 78). This publication contains a frequently updated listing of organizations which have applied to and received tax-exempt status from the IRS. To be a qualifying donee, however, the organization is not required to be listed in this publication.

## Disallowance Possibilities

Direct contributions to needy or worthy individuals are not deductible. In addition, contributions to qualifying organizations must not be restricted to use by a specific person; if so, deductions generally are disallowed.

### Example 48

F contributed cash of $10,000 to his son, S. S is a missionary for a church that is a qualified organization, and the gift proceeds were used exclusively by S to further the charitable work of the church. F is not entitled to a charitable contribution deduction since the gift was not made to a qualifying donee. Similarly, F would be denied a deduction if he made the gift to the church but restricted the use of the funds only for his missionary son.[90]

A taxpayer's contribution to a qualified organization that is motivated by the taxpayer's expectation and receipt of a significant economic benefit will not be deductible as a charitable contribution. The receipt of an unexpected and indirect economic benefit as a result of the gift should not disqualify the taxpayer's deduction, however.

---

[88] See § 170(f)(16) and other limitations applying to such items as "taxidermy property," conservation easements and certain other property

[89] See § 170(c).

[90] *White v. U.S.*, 82-1 USTC ¶9232, 49 AFTR2d 82-364, 514 F. Supp. 1057 (D.Ct. Utah, 1981). For a similar result, see *Babilonia v. Comm.*, 82-2 USTC ¶9478, 50 AFTR2d 82-5442 (CA-9, 1982).

**Example 49**

T donated two parcels of land to a nearby city for use as building sites for new public schools. The location of the building sites was such that the city had to construct two access roads through the taxpayer's remaining undeveloped land in order to make use of the gifted property. Construction of the access roads significantly enhanced the value of T's remaining acreage, and as a result, his charitable contribution deduction may be denied.[91]

Apparently, because Congress does not believe that the benefit received by a taxpayer is of great significance, 80 percent of the amount paid by a taxpayer to a college or university that either directly or indirectly entitles the taxpayer to purchase tickets to the institution's athletic events is allowed as a deduction.[92] However, any amount actually paid for the tickets will not be deductible.

## Limitations on Deductions

Unlike the requirement that an individual's medical expenses and casualty losses *exceed* some minimum percentage of adjusted gross income (referred to as the *floor* amount) *before* any deductions are allowed, deductions for charitable contributions are subject to *ceiling* limitations (i.e., not to *exceed* a percentage of A.G.I.). Generally, an individual's current deduction for charitable contributions is limited to 50 percent of the taxpayer's adjusted gross income. A 30 percent ceiling limitation is imposed on an individual's contributions of *certain appreciated property*, and a 20 percent overall limitation is imposed on an individual's contributions to *certain qualifying organizations*.

Under the general rule, the amount of a taxpayer's charitable deduction (before any percentage limitation) is the *sum* of money *plus* the fair market value of any property other than money which is contributed to a qualifying donee. However, both the gift of property to certain organizations and the gift of certain types of property other than money may result in a deduction of an amount *less than* the property's fair market value. These exceptions to the general rule are explained below, followed by a discussion of the various percentage limitations imposed on an individual's deduction for charitable contributions.[93]

### Contributions Other Than Money or Property

No charitable contribution deduction is allowed for the value of time or services rendered to a charitable organization.[94] Likewise, no deduction is allowed for any "lost income" associated with the rent-free use of a taxpayer's property by a qualifying charity. However, *unreimbursed* (out-of-pocket) *expenses* incurred by the taxpayer in rendering services to a charitable institution or allowing rent-free use of property by such an organization *qualify* as charitable contributions.[95] For example, a taxpayer is allowed a deduction for the cost and upkeep of uniforms required to be worn while performing the charitable services, but only if the uniforms are not suitable for everyday use. Similarly, a taxpayer is generally allowed to deduct amounts paid for transportation to and from his or her home to the place where the charitable services are performed.[96] This includes the costs for gasoline, oil, parking, and tolls incurred by a taxpayer using his or her own vehicle in connection with the charitable services. In lieu of deducting the actual expenses for gasoline and oil, a taxpayer is allowed to use a

---

91 See *Ottawa Silica Co. v. U.S.*, 83-1 USTC ¶9169, 51 AFTR2d 83-590, 699 F.2d 1124 (CA-Fed. Cir., 1983) where, under similar circumstances, the taxpayer's claimed contribution deduction was disallowed.

92 See § 170(m).

93 Regular corporations are subject to an overall limitation of 10 percent of taxable income, determined without regard to certain deductions. See Chapter 19 for more details.

94 Reg. § 1.170A-1(g).

95 *Ibid.*

96 The Tax Reform Act of 1986 added § 170(k) to the Code to disallow a deduction for travel expenses related to charitable services where there is a significant element of personal pleasure, recreation, or vacation in such travel.

standard mileage rate in calculating the cost of using an automobile in charitable activities. In 2011, the rate is 14 cents per mile.[97] In either case, no deduction is allowed for insurance, depreciation, or the costs of general repairs and maintenance.

## Example 50

T is the scoutmaster of a local troop of the Boy Scouts of America. During the current year, T incurred the following expenses in rendering his services to this charitable organization:

| | |
|---|---|
| Cost and upkeep of uniforms | $ 80 |
| Gasoline and oil expenses | 200 |
| Parking and tolls | 30 |
| Estimated value of rent-free use of den in home | 1,000 |
| Estimated value of services (500 hours @ $50 per hour) | 25,000 |
| Total | $26,310 |

T is entitled to a $310 charitable contribution deduction for his out-of-pocket expenses ($80 + $200 + $30) incurred in rendering the charitable services as a scoutmaster. No deduction is allowed for the estimated value of his services or the rent-free use of his home.

## Example 51

Assume the same facts as in *Example 50*, except that T drove his automobile 3,000 miles in connection with the charitable services. If he did not keep records of the actual expenses for gasoline and oil, T could use the standard mileage rate of 14 cents per mile. In this case, he will be allowed to deduct $530 [(3,000 miles × $0.14 per mile for charitable use of auto = $420) + $30 for parking and tolls + $80 related to uniforms].

### Fair Market Value Determination

The IRS defines fair market value as "the price at which the property would change hands between a willing buyer and a willing seller, neither being under any compulsion to buy or sell and both having reasonable knowledge of relevant facts."[98] Determination of this amount usually means the taxpayer must make an educated guess or incur the cost of an independent appraisal. Since the IRS requires that the taxpayer attach a statement to his or her return when a deduction exceeding $500 is claimed for a charitable gift of property (Form 8283, Noncash Charitable Contributions), many taxpayers seek independent appraisals to support their claimed deductions. Independent appraisals are *required*—and the donee must *attach* a summary of the appraisal to his or her return—if the claimed value of the contributed property exceeds $5,000.[99] Appraisal fees are not deductible as contributions. However, they are deductible by individuals as miscellaneous itemized deductions (subject to the 2% floor).[100]

### Ordinary Income Property

The term *ordinary income property* is used to describe any property which, if sold, would require the owner to recognize gain *other than* long-term capital gain. For example, ordinary

97 See § 170(j) and Rev. Proc. 2010-51, I.R.B. 2010-51.

98 Reg. § 1.170-1(c)(1).

99 § 6050L. A donee charity that sells or otherwise disposes of such property within two years of the donation *must* report the disposition (and amount received, if any) to the IRS and the donor.

100 Under § 212(3), individuals are allowed to deduct expenses associated with the determination of their tax liability. This includes appraisal fees paid in valuing property contributions.

income property includes a donor/taxpayer's property held primarily for sale to customers in his or her trade or business (i.e., inventory items), a work of art created by the donor, a manuscript prepared by the donor, letters and memoranda prepared by or for the donor, and a capital asset held by the taxpayer for not more than one year (i.e., short-term capital gain property). Musical compositions can be treated as capital assets for purposes of determining the character of the gain or loss on a sale or exchange but are considered ordinary income property for purposes of determining the amount of the contribution. Thus a contribution of song by the composer would normally result in a deduction equal to the song's basis which is usually little or nothing.[101] The term also includes property which, if sold, would result in the recognition of ordinary income under any of the depreciation recapture provisions.[102]

The charitable deduction (without regard to any percentage limitations) for the gift of ordinary income property is equal to the property's fair market value *reduced* by the amount of ordinary income that would be recognized if the property had been sold at its fair market value (this amount is often called the *ordinary income potential)*.[103]

### Example 52

F donated 100 shares of IBM stock to his church on December 15, 2011. F had purchased the stock for $9,000 on August 7, 2011 and it was worth $12,000 on the date of the gift. Since F would have recognized a short-term capital gain if the stock had been sold on December 15, 2011 (i.e., holding period not more than one year), the stock is ordinary income property. As a result, F's charitable contribution deduction is limited to $9,000 ($12,000 fair market value – $3,000 ordinary income potential).

In most cases, the charitable deduction for ordinary income property will be limited to the taxpayer's adjusted basis in the property since its fair market value is reduced by the *unrealized appreciation* in value (fair market value – adjusted basis), which would not result in long-term capital gain if the property were sold. There are, however, three important instances when this would not be the case. First, the charitable deduction for *any property* which, if sold, would result in a *loss* (i.e., adjusted basis > fair market value) is limited to the property's fair market value.

### Example 53

J donated 1,000 shares of Intel stock to the University of Alabama that he purchased several years ago for $40,000 but that were now worth only $15,000. J may claim a charitable contribution deduction only for the stock's fair market value of $15,000. Note that the property does not qualify as either capital gain property or ordinary income property (since he would have recognized a capital loss on the sale). J would have been better off had he sold the property, recognized the loss and donated the proceeds from the sale.

Second, any depreciable property held by the taxpayer for more than one year and used in his or her trade or business is *§ 1231 property*. The amount of gain from the sale of such property that exceeds any depreciation recapture is referred to as "§ 1231 gain." Potential § 1231 gains are treated as long-term capital gains for purposes of measuring a taxpayer's charitable contribution deduction.[104] As such, any unrealized appreciation in the value of property that is attributable to § 1231 gain will not be considered ordinary income potential for purposes of the limitation described above.

The remaining exception entitles C corporations to increase their deduction for contributions of certain ordinary income items by one-half of the unrealized ordinary income in

[101] See §§ 170(e)(1)(A) and 1221(b)(3).

[102] See § 170(e)(1), Reg. §§ 1.170A-4(b)(1) and (b)(4).

[103] § 170(e)(1). For an application of this rule, see *William Glen*, 79 T.C. 208 (1982).

[104] § 170(e)(3)..

the property. The enhanced deduction, which is limited to twice the property's basis, is available for contributions of the following:[105]

- Contributions of inventory or depreciable property used in business that is used by the charitable organization for the care of children, the ill, or the needy. For example, gifts of drugs and medical supplies by pharmaceutical companies to a charity would qualify. Gifts of food inventory (by any entity) and book inventory to schools also qualify but are subject to additional rules.
- Contributions of "scientific property or apparatus" constructed or assembled by the taxpayer that is held as inventory and is donated within two years of its manufacture to an educational institution for use in research or for research training in physical or biological sciences. For example, a computer manufacturer's contribution of computers to a university for use in research or by its students in computer science courses would qualify.
- Contributions of computer software, computers, peripheral equipment, and fiber optic cable for computer use to a school, organizations formed to support elementary and secondary education and certain public libraries.

### Example 54

ELI Corporation manufactures insulin and gives $1,000,000 of the drug (basis $700,000) to hospitals around the country to be used for charitable purposes. Normally, the deduction would be limited to the property's adjusted basis of $700,000. However, because the hospitals will use it for the care of children and those who are needy, the deduction is $850,000 [$700,000 + $150,000 (50% × ($1,000,000 − $700,000 = $300,000 unrealized ordinary income))] If the basis had been $100,000, the tentative deduction would be $550,000 ($100,000 + $450,000 (50% × $900,000) but it would be limited to $200,000 (2 × adjusted basis of $100,000).

## Capital Gain Property

Any property which, if sold by the donor/taxpayer, would result in the recognition of a long-term capital gain or § 1231 gain is *capital gain property*.[106] A taxpayer is generally allowed to claim the fair market value of such property as a contribution deduction. There are two important exceptions to this rule, however. *First*, if capital gain property is contributed to or for the use of a private nonoperating foundation [as defined in § 509(a) such as the Gates Foundation], the donor must *reduce* the contribution deduction by the *entire* amount of any long-term capital gain or § 1231 gain that would be recognized if the property were sold at its fair market value.[107] In effect, this exception treats the contribution of capital gain property to private nonoperating foundations exactly like contributions of ordinary income property, since the donor must reduce the contribution deduction to the basis of the property.

### Example 55

G donates land worth $10,000 to a private nonoperating foundation on November 17, 2011. G had purchased the land for $4,000 on August 23, 2007. G's charitable contribution deduction must be reduced to $4,000 ($10,000 fair market value − entire $6,000 appreciation).

It is important to note that this limitation *generally* does not apply to donations of capital gain property to public charities.

---

[105] Reg. § 170A-4(b)(4).

[106] § 170(e)(1).

[107] § 170(e)(1)(B)(ii). An exception is provided for contributions of publicly traded stock to private foundations. Taxpayers making such contributions are allowed to deduct the full fair market value of such stock.

### Example 56

Assume the same facts as in *Example 55*, except that G donated the land to her alma mater, State University (a public charity). G's charitable contribution would be $10,000 because the reduction requirement applies only to contributions to private foundations.

The *second* exception to the general rule that taxpayers are allowed to claim a deduction for the fair market value of contributed capital gain property involves contributions of tangible personalty.[108] If tangible personalty is contributed to a public charity (i.e., a university, museum, church, etc.) and the property is put to an *unrelated use* by the donee organization, the charitable contribution must be reduced by the entire amount of the property's unrealized appreciation in value (i.e., to the property's basis). For purposes of this limitation, the term *unrelated use* means that the property could not be used by the public charity in its activities for which tax-exempt status had been granted. For example, if antique furnishings are donated to a local museum that either stores, displays, or uses the items in its office in the course of carrying out its functions, the use of such property is a related use.[109] Thus, if the taxpayer can reasonably anticipate that the tangible personalty donated to the charitable organization will be put to a related use, this limitation will not be applicable.[110]

### Example 57

J contributes a painting to the local university. He had purchased the painting in 1995 for $10,000, and it was appraised at $60,000 on the date of the gift. The painting was placed in the university's library for display and study by art students. J's charitable contribution will be measured at $60,000 (the painting's fair market value) since the property was not put to an unrelated use. This is true even if the university later sells the painting.

### Example 58

R donates her gun collection to the YWCA (a public charity). R had paid $8,000 for the collection 10 years ago, and the guns were appraised at $18,000 on the date of the gift. The YWCA immediately sold the collection for $18,000 to a local gun dealer. Although the property had appreciated by $10,000, R's charitable contribution must be reduced to $8,000 (the property's basis) since the property was not (and most likely could not be) put to a related use.

## Fifty Percent Limitation

An individual's deduction for contributions made to public charities may not exceed 50 percent of his or her adjusted gross income for the year.[111] This "ceiling" deduction limitation applies to contributions made to the following types of public charities:[112]

1. A church or a convention or association of churches;
2. An educational organization that normally maintains a regular faculty and curriculum;

---

108 As described in Chapter 9, tangible personalty is all tangible property *other than* realty (i.e., land, buildings, structural components).

109 Reg. § 1.170A-4(b)(3). Under § 170(e)(7), if tangible personal property worth more than $5,000 is contributed and later sold by the charity, the donor may be required to include certain amounts in income.

110 Reg. § 1.170A-4(b)(3)(ii).

111 § 170(b) and Reg. § 1.170A-8(b).

112 § 170(b)(1).

3. An organization whose principal purposes or functions are providing medical or hospital care (hospitals) or medical education or medical research (medical schools);
4. An organization that receives support from the government and is organized and operated exclusively to receive, hold, invest, and administer property for the benefit of a college or university;
5. A state, a possession of the United States, or any political subdivision of any of the foregoing, or the United States or the District of Columbia;
6. An organization that normally receives a substantial part of its support from a government unit (described in item 5 above) or from the general public; and
7. Certain types of private foundations discussed below.

Private foundations are organizations that, by definition, do not receive contributions from the general public. Examples of well-known private foundations include the Ford, Carnegie, Cullen, and Mellon Foundations. For charitable deduction purposes, private foundations are classified as either operating or nonoperating foundations. Contributions to *all* private operating foundations are subject to the 50 percent ceiling limitation.[113] The 50 percent limit also applies to contributions to certain private, nonoperating foundations if the organizations:

1. Distribute the contributions they receive to public charities and private operating foundations *within* two and one-half months following the year the contributions were received; or
2. Pool all contributions received into a common fund, and distribute *both* the income and the principal from the fund to public charities.

An individual's contributions of cash and ordinary income property to public charities, private operating foundations, and the above described nonoperating foundations that exceed the 50 percent limitation are carried forward and deducted in subsequent years. The carryover rules are discussed in a later section of this chapter. Contributions of capital gain property *and* contributions to private nonoperating foundations (other than those described above) are subject to *either* the 30 percent or 20 percent limitation. These limitations are discussed below.

### Thirty Percent Limitation

There are *two* situations in which the 30 percent limitation may apply. The first situation involves the following types of contributions:

1. Contributions for the *use* of any charitable organization;
2. Contributions to veterans' organizations, fraternal societies, and not-for-profit cemetery companies; *and*
3. Contributions to most private nonoperating foundations.

The annual deduction for these contributions is limited to the *lesser of*:

1. Thirty percent of adjusted gross income, *or*
2. An amount equal to 50 percent of adjusted gross income, *reduced* by contributions qualifying for the 50 percent limitation.[114]

#### Example 59

R has adjusted gross income of $50,000 for the current year and contributes $5,000 cash to his church and $20,000 cash to the Veterans of Foreign Wars. R's deduction for the contribution to his church will not be limited because it does not exceed 50% of A.G.I. (i.e., $5,000 < $25,000). However, only $15,000 of the contribution to the

[113] See § 4942(j) for the requirements for classification as a private operating foundation. For all practical purposes, an operating foundation is recognized as a public charity.

[114] See § 170(b)(1)(C).

veterans' organization will be allowed as a deduction for the current year because this donation is subject to the 30% limitation.

| | | |
|---|---|---|
| Contribution to church . . . . . . . . . . . . . . . . . . . . . . . . . . . . . | | $ 5,000 |
| Plus: Lesser of | | |
| (1) | 30% × $50,000 = $15,000 | |
| | or | |
| (2) | 50% × $50,000 = $25,000, reduced by $5,000 gift to church = $20,000 | |
| | | 15,000 |
| Total contribution deduction . . . . . . . . . . . . . . . . . . . . . . . . . | | $20,000 |

## Example 60

Assume the same facts in *Example 59*, except that the contribution to the church was $20,000 and the contribution to the veterans' organization was $8,000. Again, the contribution to the church will not be limited because it does not exceed 50% of A.G.I. However, the contribution to the veterans' organization will be limited to $5,000, computed as follows:

| | | |
|---|---|---|
| Contribution to church . . . . . . . . . . . . . . . . . . . . . . . . . . | | $20,000 |
| Plus: Lesser of | | |
| (1) | 30% × $50,000 = $15,000 | |
| | or | |
| (2) | 50% × $50,000 = $25,000, reduced by $20,000 gift to church = $5,000 | |
| | | 5,000 |
| Total contribution deduction . . . . . . . . . . . . . . . . . . . . . . | | $25,000 |

Note that it is not the 30% of A.G.I. Limitation that causes R's contribution to the veterans' organization to be limited. Instead, it is the fact that the overall limitation on the annual contribution deduction amount is 50% of adjusted gross income, and the contribution to the public charity is considered first.

The *second* situation in which the 30 percent limitation may apply involves contributions of capital gain property. The annual deduction allowed for contributions of capital gain property that have not been reduced by the unrealized appreciation will generally be limited to 30 percent of the taxpayer's adjusted gross income.[115] As in the first situation discussed above, these contributions subject to the 30 percent limit are considered only after the amount of contributions allowed under the 50 percent limitation has been determined. Contributions in excess of the 30 percent limit can be carried forward and deducted in subsequent years.

## Example 61

K has adjusted gross income of $30,000 for the 2011 tax year. The only contribution made by K in 2011 consisted of stock worth $10,000, which she had purchased for $4,000 in 2007. The stock was given to her church. Although the contribution does not exceed 50% of her adjusted gross income, K's deduction is limited to $9,000 (30% × $30,000 A.G.I.) since the stock is capital gain property. The $1,000 excess contribution can be carried over to subsequent years.

[115] § 170(b)(1)(C)(i).

**Example 62**

Assume the same facts as in *Example 61*, except that K's 2011 adjusted gross income is \$40,000 and she also gave \$14,000 cash to her church. In this case, her deduction for the gift of the stock is limited to \$6,000 (50% × \$40,000 A.G.I. = \$20,000 − \$14,000 cash contribution) since the 50% overall limitation is applied before the 30% limitation. The remaining \$4,000 (\$10,000 fair market value of stock − \$6,000 deduction allowed) will be carried forward to subsequent years.

When capital gain property has been contributed, the 30 percent limitation can be avoided if the taxpayer *elects* to reduce his or her claimed deduction for the capital gain property by the property's unrealized appreciation.[116] This may result in a larger deduction in the current year since the reduced amount will be subject to a higher ceiling limitation (i.e., 50 percent of A.G.I. rather than 30 percent). It is important to note that this election, if made, applies to all contributions of capital gain property made during the year.

**Example 63**

T has adjusted gross income of \$50,000 for the current year and contributes stock worth \$23,000 to the American Heart Association (a public charity). T had purchased the stock for \$19,000 two years earlier. Assuming this is T's only contribution for the current year, he can either claim his deduction subject to the 30% limitation and carry over any excess, or *elect* to reduce the claimed deduction by the capital gain property's unrealized appreciation and forgo any carryover. T's deduction choices are:

1. \$15,000 current deduction (30% × \$50,000 A.G.I.) and \$8,000 (\$23,000 − \$15,000) contribution carryover; or
2. \$19,000 current deduction (\$23,000 − \$4,000 unrealized appreciation) and no carryover.

Obviously, the decision to reduce a current deduction by the property's unrealized appreciation *or* to claim the deduction subject to the 30 percent limit and carry over any excess amount will depend on several factors. Among the factors to be considered are:

1. The difference between the capital gain property's fair market value and its adjusted basis to the taxpayer (i.e., unrealized appreciation);
2. The taxpayer's current marginal income tax bracket compared to his or her anticipated future marginal tax rates; and
3. The expected remaining life of the taxpayer and his or her anticipated future contributions.

### Twenty Percent Limitation

The 50 percent ceiling limitation imposed on an individual's annual charitable contribution deduction is an "overall" limitation. The 30 percent limitation applies to most contributions of capital gain property and to contributions of cash and ordinary income property contributed to nonqualifying private nonoperating funds. However, a more severe restriction is imposed on deductions for contributions of capital gain property to such private nonoperating foundations. In addition to the required *reduction* of the contribution by any unrealized appreciation in value, the deduction allowed for contributions to *private charities* (i.e., organizations not included in the seven categories listed earlier) is limited to the *lesser of*:

1. Twenty percent of adjusted gross income; or

---

[116] § 170(b)(1)(c)(iii).

2. An amount equal to 50 percent of adjusted gross income, and reduced by contributions qualifying for the 50 percent and 30 percent limitations, including any amount in excess of the 30 percent limitation.[117]

Like excess contributions to public charities, any contributions to private nonoperating foundations that exceed the 20 percent limitation are carried forward and deductible subject to the 20 percent limit, in subsequent years.[118]

### Example 64

D contributed $8,000 to his church (a public charity) and land worth $15,000 to a private nonoperating foundation in 2011. D had purchased the land for $11,000 in 2006. His adjusted gross income for the year is $20,000. D's contribution deduction for 2011 is $10,000 [$8,000 contribution to church + $2,000 of the eligible $11,000 contribution to private foundation ($15,000 market value – $4,000 unrealized "appreciation" = $11,000)]. The deduction allowed for the contribution to the private foundation is limited to the *lesser of:*

1. $4,000 (20% × $20,000 A.G.I.); or
2. $2,000 [(50% × $20,000 A.G.I. = $10,000) – $8,000 contribution qualifying for the 50% limitation].

Note that D's total contribution deduction of $10,000 does not exceed 50 percent of his current adjusted gross income. If D had contributed $10,000 or more to his church, *none* of the $11,000 contribution to the private foundation would have been allowed. In either case, the excess contributions can be carried over to subsequent years.

## Contribution Carryovers

An individual's contributions that exceed either the 20 percent limitation, the 30 percent limitation, or the 50 percent overall limitation may be carried over for five years.[119] All excess contributions due to the 20 and 30 percent limitations will *again* be subject to these limitations in the carryover years.[120] Although contribution carryovers are treated as having been made in the year to which they are carried, contributions *actually* made in the carryover year must be claimed before any carryover amounts are deducted.[121]

### Example 65

In 2011, D contributes $10,000 cash to State University (a public charity). Her adjusted gross income for 2011 is $15,000. D's contribution deduction for 2011 is limited to $7,500 (50% × $15,000 A.G.I.) and she may carry over the remaining $2,500 to 2012. If she does not make contributions in 2012 that exceed the 50% limitation, D can claim the $2,500 carryover as a deduction. If the contributions actually made in 2012 exceed 50% of D's 2012 adjusted gross income, she must carry over the 2012 excess contributions *and* the $2,500 carryover from 2011.

### Example 66

Assume the same facts as in *Example 65*, except that D's contribution was a capital gain property worth $10,000 instead of cash. Her 2011 deduction would be limited to $4,500

[117] § 170(b)(1)(B)(i).

[118] § 170(d)(1).

[119] § 170(d)(1)(A) and Reg. § 1.170A-10(a).

[120] Reg. § 1.170A-10(b)(2).

[121] Reg. § 1.170A-10(c)(1).

(30% × $15,000 A.G.I.) and she would have a $5,500 contribution carryover. Since this carryover resulted from the 30% limitation, it will be subject to the 30% limit in any carryover year. Thus if D has adjusted gross income of $10,000 and does not make contributions in 2012, she can claim a deduction of $3,000 (30% × $10,000 A.G.I.) and carry over the remaining $2,500.

All charitable contribution carryovers are applied on a first-in, first-out basis in determining the amount of any carryovers deductible in the current year.[122] Since such carryovers will expire if not deducted within five succeeding tax years, taxpayers obviously should limit actual contributions until the carryovers are used.

## Miscellaneous Itemized Deductions

**LO.7**
Identify the personal expenditures that qualify as either miscellaneous itemized deductions or other itemized deductions.

As discussed in Chapter 7, two major changes regarding miscellaneous itemized deductions were introduced into the tax laws in 1986. Perhaps the most significant change involves the inclusion in this category of all *unreimbursed* employee business expenses. Prior to 1987, an employee's unreimbursed travel and transportation expenses were allowed as deductions in arriving at adjusted gross income. Since 1986, *both* unreimbursed employee expenses *and* those not reimbursed under an accountable plan must be treated as miscellaneous itemized deductions.[123] Additionally, an employee's unreimbursed costs for business entertainment and meals (whether or not incurred in connection with travel) must first be reduced by a 50 percent disallowance since only 50 percent of these costs qualify for deduction.[124] It is also important to remember that interest on any indebtedness to finance an employee's business expenses is treated as *nondeductible* personal interest expense.

The second major change involves the introduction of a deduction *floor* on the total of all expenses in this category similar to the approach taken for medical and casualty loss deductions. After 1986, miscellaneous itemized deductions are deductible only to the extent they *exceed* 2 percent of A.G.I.[125] The obvious intent of this change in the law is to limit the number of taxpayers who will be able to deduct miscellaneous itemized deductions—and thereby reduce the administrative cost of policing such deductions. Exhibit 11-5 contains a partial list of items qualifying as miscellaneous itemized deductions.

### Example 67

T has $40,000 of adjusted gross income in 2011. His unreimbursed employee business expenses and other miscellaneous itemized deductions include:

| | |
|---|---|
| Unreimbursed business travel expenses | $ 90 |
| Subscription to *The Wall Street Journal* | 110 |
| Professional dues | 250 |
| Safe deposit box rental | 50 |
| Tax return preparation fee | 250 |
| Total | $750 |

Since T's total miscellaneous itemized deductions of $750 do not exceed $800 (2% × $40,000 A.G.I.), he will not be able to claim any deduction for these expenses.

[122] Reg. § 1.170A-10(b)(2).

[123] Reg. § 1.62-2.

[124] § 274(n).

[125] § 67(a).

**EXHIBIT 11.5** **Partial List of Miscellaneous Itemized Deductions**

Reimbursed employee expenses under
- A nonaccountable plan

Unreimbursed employee expenses for
- Travel away from home (lodging and 50% of meals)
- Transportation expenses
- Entertainment expenses (after 50% reduction)
- Home office expenses
- Outside salesperson's expenses
- Professional dues and memberships
- Subscriptions to business journals
- Uniform costs, cleaning, and maintenance expenses
- Union dues

Investment expenses for
- Investment advice
- Investment newsletter subscriptions
- Management fees charged by mutual funds
- Rentals of safe deposit boxes

Qualifying education expenses

Job seeking expenses (in the same business)

Tax determination expenses for
- Appraisal costs incurred to measure deductions for medical expenses (capital improvements), charitable contributions, and casualty losses
- Tax return preparation fees
- Tax advice, tax seminars, and books about taxes

## Other Itemized Deductions

The final category of itemized deductions includes certain personal expenses and losses that cannot be classified in any of the other categories discussed thus far. Some of the items in this category—referred to as "Other Miscellaneous Itemized Deductions"—are discussed in other chapters.

1. Unrecovered investment in an annuity where the taxpayer's death prevents recovery of the entire investment. As discussed in Chapter 6, this deduction is allowed on the taxpayer's final tax return.
2. Impairment-related work expenses of persons with disabilities.
3. Amortizable premium on bonds purchased before October 23, 1986. Amortization of bond premium is discussed in Chapter 16.
4. Gambling losses to the extent of gambling winnings.

It is important to note that each of these items may be subject to its own unique set of limitations (e.g., gambling losses). Unlike miscellaneous itemized deductions, however, these deductions *are not* subject to the two percent limit.

## Tax Planning Considerations

### MAXIMIZING PERSONAL DEDUCTIONS

Each year the taxpayer must choose between taking the standard deduction and itemizing actual deductions. If the standard deduction is chosen, then legitimate itemized deductions are lost. If the taxpayer chooses to itemize actual deductions, then the standard deduction is lost. One technique used to minimize the loss of personal deductions is to shift actual itemized deductions from one year to another (to the extent allowed by law) so that they are high in one year and low in the next.

#### Example 68

S is single and has itemized deductions that are expected to be constant in 2011 and 2012 as follows:

| | |
|---|---|
| Mortgage interest | $ 400 |
| Dental expense (deductible portion) | 1,400 |
| State and local taxes | 350 |
| Charitable contributions | 1,350 |
| Total | $3,500 |

S cannot itemize actual deductions in 2011 or 2012 because actual deductions are less than the standard deduction for single status (assumed to be $4,000 in each year for illustration purposes). Over the two-year period, S will deduct $8,000 for personal expenses by claiming the standard deduction. However, if S were able to shift $1,000 of elective dental expenses from 2012 into 2011, and to accelerate the 2012 charitable contribution into 2011, then she would receive a greater tax benefit in the two-year period for personal expenses. Actual expenses in each year would be:

| | *2011* | *2012* |
|---|---|---|
| Mortgage interest | $ 400 | $ 400 |
| Dental expense (deductible portion) | 2,400 | 400 |
| State taxes | 350 | 350 |
| Charitable contributions | 2,700 | 0 |
| Total | $5,850 | $1,150 |

Although actual personal expenses still total $7,000 over the two-year period, S now has itemized deductions of $5,850 in 2011 and a standard deduction of $4,000 in 2012. During the two-year period S will deduct $9,850 for personal expenses and will receive $1,850 more in deductions than if personal expenses had not been shifted.

### MEDICAL EXPENSES

The dependency exemption under a multiple support agreement should be assigned to the taxpayer who pays the medical expenses of the dependent. The medical expenses are deductible only by the family member entitled to the dependency exemption and only if that family member actually pays on behalf of the claimed dependent. Medical expenses paid by other family members on behalf of the dependent will not be allowed as deductions.

Often expenditures incurred in the care of an ill or handicapped child may qualify for either a medical expense deduction or for the child care credit (discussed in Chapter 13). When this happens, the tax liability should be computed under each alternative to determine which is more advantageous. Usually the choice depends on the taxpayer's marginal tax rate as compared to the credit percentage rate. The choice will also depend on the 7.5 percent threshold and whether the taxpayer is itemizing or taking the standard deduction.

**Example 69**

In 2011, T and W spend \$2,000 for care of their handicapped child. The \$2,000 qualifies both as a medical expense and for the child care credit. T and W have other medical expenses that exceed the 7.5% threshold amount. T and W file a joint tax return, and their marginal tax rate is 31%. The applicable percentage for the child care credit is 20%. If T and W are able to itemize deductions, they will receive a \$620 tax benefit (\$2,000 × 31%) for claiming the expenditure as a medical expense, whereas they will receive only a \$400 tax benefit (\$2,000 × 20%) if they claim the expenditure for the child care credit. If T and W are not able to itemize deductions or if they cannot exceed the 7.5% medical expense threshold amount, then the expenditure should be claimed for the child care credit.

## Charitable Contributions

When a taxpayer makes noncash donations of property having a fair market value lower than the adjusted tax basis, it may be more advantageous to sell the property and donate the proceeds. If the property is held for investment, the sale will yield a deductible capital loss in addition to the charitable deduction. No loss will result, however, if the property itself is donated. To recognize a loss when selling depreciated property, the property must be held for investment or business use rather than for personal use.

**Example 70**

T owns 100 shares of X Corporation stock that he bought for \$5,000 in 2009. The stock currently has a fair market value of \$2,000. If T donates the stock to a qualified charity, he will only be entitled to a \$2,000 charitable deduction. If T sells the stock and donates the \$2,000 proceeds to a qualified charity, he will be entitled to a \$3,000 capital loss as well as a \$2,000 charitable deduction.

## Miscellaneous Deductions

Because certain miscellaneous itemized deductions are deductible only to the extent that they aggregately exceed 2 percent of the adjusted gross income, it is important that expenses that can be properly classified into another, nonlimited category be identified and separated. For example, if a taxpayer supplements his or her regular salary with self-employed consulting income, it may be proper to deduct some of the cost of professional publications, professional journals, and educational expenses on Schedule C rather than as a miscellaneous itemized deduction.

Some unreimbursed employee business expenses that are not presently deductible because of the 2 percent limit might be converted into deductible reimbursed employee business expenses by agreement with the employer.

**Example 71**

K incurs \$500 of unreimbursed employee business expenses each year for subscriptions to professional journals. Her miscellaneous itemized deductions do not exceed the 2 percent limit; she is therefore unable to deduct any of this expense. K's employer agrees, as part of next year's compensation increase, to reimburse her for this \$500 of employee business expenses. In effect, K is using pre-tax dollars for the professional subscriptions and the result is equivalent to \$500 of increased wages offset by a fully deductible \$500 of employee business expenses.

## Problem Materials

### DISCUSSION QUESTIONS

**11-1** *Medical Expenses and Dependency Status.* Under what circumstances is a taxpayer entitled to deduct medical expenses attributable to other people?

**11-2** *Medical Expenses.* F and M are the divorced parents of three minor children. M, the custodial parent, has proposed to F that the current child-support payments be increased in order to pay the expected dental costs of having braces put on their oldest son's teeth. F's tax advisor has suggested that F agree to pay these costs directly to the dentist rather than increasing the support payments. From a tax perspective, why has F's advisor made this suggestion?

**11-3** *Medical Expenses.* K and her two brothers currently provide more than half the support of their mother. For the past several years, they have taken turns claiming a dependency exemption deduction for their mother under a multiple support agreement. This year, K will be entitled to the exemption, and her mother needs money for cataract surgery and new eyeglasses. K's accountant has suggested that she can double up on the tax benefits by directing her share of her mother's support toward these expenses. How is this possible?

**11-4** *Medical Expenses.* For the past several years, L's total itemized deductions have barely exceeded his standard deduction amount, and this pattern is not expected to change in the near future. L is currently faced with elective surgery to repair a hernia, and the procedure is not covered under his health insurance policy. Strictly from a tax perspective, and assuming that this ailment is not life-threatening, what advice would you give to L concerning the timing of the surgery?

**11-5** *Prepaid Medical Expenses.* What is the requirement imposed on taxpayers who wish to deduct prepaid medical expenses? What potential abuse is prevented by this requirement?

**11-6** *Medical Deductions—Percentage Limitation.* The only medical expenditures made by taxpayer T during 2011 were for prescription drugs costing $1,800 and new eyeglasses costing $250. If T has adjusted gross income of $20,000 for the year and itemizes his deductions, how much, if any, medical expense deduction will he be allowed?

**11-7** *Medical Travel Expenses.* W resides in Gary, Indiana and suffers from chronic bronchitis. At the advice of her doctor, W spends three months each year in Flagstaff, Arizona. Under what circumstances would W be entitled to claim the costs incurred for these trips as deductible medical expenses? If deductible, which costs?

**11-8** *Casualty Losses.* Taxpayer F has adjusted gross income of $20,000 during the current year and he asks you the following questions regarding the deductibility of damages to his home caused by a recent hurricane. (**Hint:** See Chapter 10 for discussion of limitations on casualty loss deductions.)

**a.** If F does not have home insurance, how much must his loss be before any deduction is available?

**b.** If F repairs the damage himself, what amount can he deduct for the value of his time?

**c.** If the area in which he resides is declared a disaster area, what options are available to F as to when and how to claim a deduction for the casualty loss?

**11-9** *Taxes versus Fees.* What is the distinction between a deductible tax and a fee? If an individual taxpayer paid appraisal fees in connection with the determination of his personal casualty loss and charitable contribution deductions, would these payments be deductible?

**11-10** *Deductible Income Taxes.* Which income taxes are deductible by an individual taxpayer? Does it make any difference whether the taxes are paid directly by the taxpayer as opposed to being withheld from his or her salary and paid by an employer to the appropriate taxing authority?

**11-11** *Filing Status and State Income Taxes.* If married taxpayers file separate state or Federal income tax returns, how is the Federal tax deduction for state income taxes determined?

**11-12** *State and Local Sales Tax Deduction.* Your brother has called you for advice concerning the deductibility of the $1,460 state sales taxes that he paid on the purchase of his new Ford F250 truck. What other information would you need from you brother to properly answer his question?

**11-13** *Personal Property Taxes.* What is an ad valorem tax? What difference does it make to a taxpayer if he or she pays a tax on nonbusiness property and the tax is based on weight or model year as opposed to value?

**11-14** *Real Estate Tax Apportionment.* How are real estate taxes apportioned between the buyer and seller in the year real property is sold? What effect does the apportionment have on the seller if the buyer pays the real estate taxes for the entire year?

**11-15** *Special Tax Assessments.* Under what circumstances can a property owner claim a deduction for a special tax assessment?

**11-16** *Personal Interest.* What is the current limitation imposed on the deductions of personal interest? What impact do you suppose this restriction might have on debt-financed consumer purchases?

**11-17** *Deductible Interest.* Your neighbor has come up with an excellent tax plan and he asks you for advice on structuring his scheme. He plans to give each of his five children a $10,000 promissory note, due in 20 years and bearing interest at 10 percent per year. The interest will be paid annually and he plans to claim a $5,000 interest expense deduction. Do you see any flaws in this plan? What advice would you give to your neighbor?

**11-18** *Classifying Interest Expenses.* The local bank has just introduced a new loan program entitled "Home Equity Credit Line" under which individuals can either borrow funds or finance credit card purchases based on the equity they have in their homes. What is the tax incentive offered by this arrangement?

**11-19** *Investment Interest Expense.* What is the investment interest expense limitation? Which taxpayers are not subject to this limitation? What is the purpose of the limitation?

**11-20** *Types of Interest Expense.* D is a spender, not a saver. In fact, he spends money he doesn't even have. This year he borrowed more than $50,000 and paid interest of close to $7,000. D was shocked when his accountant told him that only certain types of interest were deductible.

**a.** Identify the different types of interest expense and explain the treatment of each.
**b.** How will D classify the interest expense that he paid?

**11-21** *Charitable Contribution Requirements.* What are the basic requirements imposed on an individual taxpayer's deduction for charitable contributions?

**11-22** *Contributions of Ordinary Income Property.* What is ordinary income property? Does this contribution deduction limitation apply to all taxpayers? Explain.

**11-23** *Contributions of Capital Gain Property.* Under what circumstances must a taxpayer reduce his or her contribution deduction by the unrealized appreciation in value of capital gain property donated to a qualifying charity? How might this limitation be avoided?

**11-24** *Contribution Deduction Percentage Limitations.* What are the percentage limitations imposed on an individual taxpayer's annual charitable contribution deduction? In what order must these percentage limitations be applied to current contributions?

**11-25** *Contribution Carryovers.* Which excess contributions may be carried forward by an individual taxpayer? For how many years? In determining the amount of his or her contribution deduction for the current year, how must the taxpayer treat the carryovers from prior years?

**11-26** *Miscellaneous Itemized Deductions.* E's employer has offered her the option of a $50 monthly pay raise or a reimbursement plan to cover her current subscriptions to professional journals ($200) and her dues to professional organizations ($350). E files a joint return with her husband, and they expect their adjusted gross income to be $50,000 for the upcoming year. Assuming that their only miscellaneous itemized deductions are from E's subscriptions and professional dues, is this a good offer? Explain.

## PROBLEMS

**11-27** *Medical Expense Deduction.* R, an unmarried taxpayer, has adjusted gross income of $20,000 for 2011. During the year, he paid the following amounts for medical care: $300 for prescription medicines and drugs, $600 for hospitalization insurance, and $1,100 to doctors and dentists. R filed an insurance reimbursement claim in December 2011 and received a check for $1,200 on January 24, 2012.

**a.** Assuming R itemizes deductions, determine the deduction allowed for the medical expenses paid in 2011.

**b.** What effect does the insurance reimbursement have on R's deduction for 2011? How should the reimbursement be treated in 2011 if R's itemized deductions for 2011 (including the medical expense deduction) were $4,500 greater than his standard deduction?

**c.** How should the reimbursement be treated in 2012 if R's itemized deductions for 2011 were $400 greater than his standard deduction?

**11-28** *State Income Taxes.* During 2011, K paid $500 in estimated state income taxes. An additional $400 in state income taxes was withheld from her salary by K's employer and remitted to the state. K also received a $200 refund check during 2011 for excess state income taxes paid in 2010. She had claimed a deduction for $750 of state income taxes paid in 2010. K uses the cash method of accounting and has adjusted gross income of $50,000 for the year.

**a.** If K itemizes her deductions, how much may she claim as a deduction for state income taxes on her 2011 Federal tax return?

**b.** If K's itemized deductions for 2010 were $1,900 greater than her standard deduction, how must the $200 refund be treated for Federal income tax purposes?

**11-29** *General Sales Tax Deduction.* Rob and Lisa are married and file a joint return for 2010. They have three dependent children ages 7, 9, and 12 and the family lived in Orlando Florida for the entire year. For each of the questions below, assume that the couple has A.G.I. of $87,900 and no other available income.

**a.** Using the 2010 optional sales tax tables located in Appendix A of this text, determine the couple's state sales tax deduction for 2010.

**b.** How would your answer in (a) above change if Rob and Lisa also paid $1,250 sales tax on the purchase of a new car and an additional $350 on the purchase of new furniture?

**c.** Assume that the family lived in Georgia rather than Florida for the entire year. Also assume that Rob and Lisa paid $3,200 in state income taxes in 2010. How does this additional information change your answer to (b) above?

**11-30** *Real Estate Tax Apportionment.* S sells her home located in Blue Springs, Missouri, on March 1, 2011. Blue Springs assesses real property taxes at the beginning of each calendar year for the entire year, and the property tax becomes a personal liability of the owner of real property on January 1. The tax is payable on April 1, 2011. Buyer B paid $80,000 for the home on March 1, 2011 and also paid the $1,200 real estate taxes on April 1. Both S and B are cash basis, calendar year taxpayers.

**a.** How much of the $1,200 in real estate taxes is deductible by S? What adjustment must S make to the amount she realized from the sale?

**b.** How much of the $1,200 in taxes is deductible by B? How will he treat any of the taxes paid which are attributable to S?

**11-31** *Interest Expense Limitations.* Indicate in each of the following cases the amount of interest expense, if any, that the taxpayer is allowed to deduct.

**a.** During the year, H used his bank credit card to purchase a new tablet computer for his teenage daughter. Finance charges for the year were $70.

**b.** Over the years, G has consistently borrowed against her insurance policies because of their low rates. This year, she paid interest of $1,100 on the loans.

**c.** D has three residences. His principal residence is in Newark, New Jersey. On the Newark home, he has a mortgage of $300,000 on which he paid interest of $18,000 for the year. He also owns a summer home in Martha's Vineyard, a beautiful island off the southern coast of Massachusetts. He has a $200,000 mortgage on his summer home and this year paid $10,000 of interest. His third residence is a condominium in Aspen, Colorado on which he has a $120,000 mortgage. This year he paid $8,000 of interest expense on the condominium's mortgage.

**d.** B owns a home in Denver that she purchased in 1999 for $95,000. The current balance on B's mortgage loan is $60,000 and the property is worth $150,000. During the year, B obtained a second mortgage on her home, receiving $20,000 which she used to pay off her two outstanding car loans. Interest on the first mortgage was $4,000 while interest on the second mortgage was $1,000.

**e.** M is a heavy trader of stocks and bonds, using his margin account frequently. This year, interest expense charged on his margin purchases was $5,200. M's investment income was $2,400.

**f.** R is an employee of a television repair shop. He uses his own truck solely for business, making customer service calls. During the year, he paid $1,450 interest on a loan on his truck.

**11-32** *Investment Interest Expense.* R, a cash basis, single taxpayer, paid $17,000 of investment interest expense during 2011. R uses the calendar year for tax purposes and reports the following investment income: $1,500 interest income, and $3,500 dividends.

**a.** How much of the investment interest expense is deductible by R in 2011?

**b.** What must R do with any investment interest expense deduction which is disallowed for 2011?

**11-33** *Investment Interest Expense Limitation.* L is an engineer. This year, she borrowed $300,000 and purchased 40 acres south of Houston. For the year, L paid interest of $30,000 on the loan. Her tax records revealed the following additional information:

| | |
|---|---|
| Income: | |
| Salary | $50,000 |
| Qualifying dividends | 8,000 |
| Share of partnership income: | |
| Ordinary loss | (3,000) |
| Portfolio income: | |
| Interest | 1,000 |
| Rental income | 8,000 |
| Expenses: | |
| Rental expenses | 7,000 |
| Qualified residence interest | 10,000 |
| Property tax on land | 5,000 |
| Investment publications | 400 |
| Professional dues, licenses, and subscriptions | 1,100 |

The items noted concerning the partnership result from L's limited partnership interest in Country Homes, a real estate development. The rental income is derived from a four-unit apartment complex that is currently filled with tenants with one-year leases. The related rental expenses include $2,000 of interest expense on the debt to acquire the apartments. Compute L's deduction for investment interest expense this year, assuming that she includes the qualifying dividends in the calculation of net investment income.

**11-34** *Interest Expense—Note Discount.* Taxpayer T signed a note for $2,000 on August 30, 2011, agreeing to pay back the loan in 12 equal installments beginning September 30, 2011. The 12 percent interest charge ($2,000 × 12% = $240) was subtracted from the face amount of the note and T received $1,760, all of which was used to purchase furniture for his business. T uses the calendar year as his taxable year.

**a.** If T is a cash-basis taxpayer and he makes the four payments scheduled for 2011, what is his deduction for interest on the note in 2011? In 2012?

**b.** Would your answers to (a) change if T were an accrual method taxpayer? Explain.

**11-35** *Charitable Contributions.* Determine the amount of the charitable deduction (without regard to percentage limitations) allowed in each of the following situations:

**a.** Rent-free use of building for three months allowed for the United Way fund drive. The building normally rents for $900 per month, and the owner paid $1,100 for utilities during this period.

**b.** Gift of General Motors stock valued at $9,000 to State University. Taxpayer purchased the stock five months ago for $11,000.

**c.** Donation of stamp collection valued at $4,000 to local museum for display to the general public. Taxpayer had paid $1,000 for the stamps many years ago.

**d.** Gift of paintings to local hospital to be placed on the walls of a remodeled floor. The paintings were painted by the donor and were appraised at $20,000.

**e.** Donation of Civil War relics to American Heart Association to be sold at its current fund-raising auction. Taxpayer paid $1,000 for the relics ten years ago and an expert appraiser valued them at $7,000 on the day of the gift.

**11-36** *Contribution Deductions—Percentage Limitations.* J contributed $10,000 to the University of Southern California and a long-term capital asset worth $10,000 (basis of $5,000) to a private nonoperating foundation during 2011. Assuming his adjusted gross income for the year is $24,000, answer the following:

**a.** What is the amount of J's contribution deduction for 2011?

**b.** How must any excess contributions be treated?

**c.** If J had come to you for advice before making the gifts, what advice would you have offered?

**11-37** *Contribution Deductions—Percentage Limitations.* During 2011 R donated land to her church (a public charity) to be used as a building site for a new chapel. R had purchased the land as an investment in 2003 at a cost of $10,000. The land was appraised at a fair market value of $30,000 on the date of the gift. Assuming R's adjusted gross income for 2011 is $60,000, answer the following:

**a.** If R made no additional charitable contributions during 2011, what is the amount of her contribution deduction for the year?

**b.** If R contributed cash of $20,000 to her church in addition to the land, what is the amount of her charitable contribution deduction for 2011?

**c.** Calculate the amount of R's excess contributions from (a) and (b) and explain how these amounts are to be treated.

**11-38** *Contribution Deductions—Percentage Limitations.* T, a single taxpayer, had adjusted gross income of $20,000 for 2011. During the year, T contributed cash of $1,000 and Xerox Corporation stock worth $10,000 to his church (a public charity). T inherited the stock during 2008 when it was valued at $8,000.

**a.** Calculate T's total contribution deduction for 2011.

**b.** How must any excess contributions be treated?

**c.** If T does not anticipate being able to itemize his deductions in any future years, what might he do in 2011 to increase his current contribution deduction?

**11-39** *Miscellaneous Itemized Deductions.* R, single, has the following miscellaneous itemized deductions for the current year:

| | |
|---|---|
| Unreimbursed employee business expenses | $1,350 |
| Professional dues and subscriptions | 650 |
| Job-seeking expenses | 800 |
| Tax return preparation fee | 250 |
| Safe-deposit box rental (for stocks and bonds) | 50 |

Assume that R itemizes his deductions for the current year.

**a.** What is the amount of R's deduction for the above items if his adjusted gross income is $70,000 for the current year?

**b.** What is the amount of R's deduction for these items if his adjusted gross income is $100,000 for the current year?

**11-40** *Calculating Itemized Deductions.* Robert and Jean Snyder have an adjusted gross income of $30,000 for 2011. Their expenses for 2011 are:

| | |
|---|---|
| Prescription drugs | $ 300* |
| Medical insurance premiums | 900 |
| Doctor and dental bills paid | 1,400* |
| Eyeglasses for Robert | 155 |
| Hospital and clinic bills paid | 450* |
| Property taxes paid on home | 900 |
| State income taxes paid: | |
| Remaining 2010 tax liability | 125 |
| Withheld from wages during year | 1,850 |
| State and local sales taxes paid: | |
| Amount paid on new automobile | 800 |
| Amount paid on new wide screen television | 280 |
| Personal property taxes paid | 100 |
| Interest on home mortgage** | 4,750 |
| Interest paid on personal auto loan | 1,100 |
| Interest paid on credit card purchases | 400 |
| Interest paid on E.F. Hutton margin account*** | 120 |
| Cash contributions to church | 2,000 |
| Fair market value of Hightech Corp. stock contributed to church (purchased for $1,000 three years ago) | 5,000 |
| Labor union dues paid by Robert | 200 |
| Qualifying education costs paid by Jean | 300 |
| Safe deposit box rental (for stocks and bonds) | 50 |
| Fee paid accountant for preparation of 2009 state and Federal tax returns | 350 |

*These amounts are net of insurance reimbursements received during 2011.
**This mortgage was created at the time the home was purchased.
***This investment interest expense is related to the production of $1,500 of net investment income.

The Snyders drove their personal automobile 500 miles for medical and dental treatment and an additional 1,000 miles in connection with charitable services performed for their church. Assuming Robert and Jean are both under age 40, lived in Virginia for the entire year, and plan to file a joint income tax return, determine their total itemized deductions. If a tax form is used for the computations, complete Schedule A (Form 1040).

## TAX RESEARCH PROBLEMS

**11-41** Sam Simpson transferred stock, real estate, and his principal residence to his former wife, Shirley, under the terms of the property settlement agreement. In exchange, Shirley agreed to pay Sam $250,000 down and another $750,000 at 10 percent per year for 10 years. Can Shirley deduct any of the interest she expects to pay over the next 10 years? Explain.

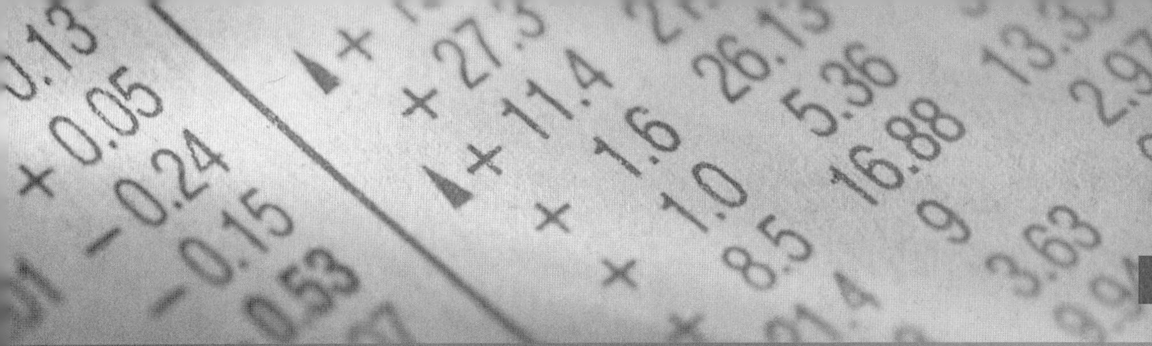

12

# Deductions for Certain Investment Expenses and Losses

## Learning Objectives

Upon completion of this chapter you will be able to:

LO.1 Discuss the basic rules governing the deduction of investment expenses.

LO.2 Describe the structure of a tax shelter.

LO.3 Explain the at-risk rules.

LO.4 Explain the passive loss rules.

LO.5 Understand the special treatment for interest expense related to a passive activity.

LO.6 Discuss the restrictions imposed on deductions related to vacation homes.

## Chapter Outline


Introduction 12-2
Introduction to Tax Shelters 12-2
  Structure of a Tax Shelter 12-3
  Elements of a Tax Shelter 12-3
At-Risk Rules 12-6
  At-Risk Computation 12-7
Passive Activity Loss Limitations 12-9
  General Rule 12-9
  Taxpayers Subject to Limitations 12-13
  Passive Activities 12-14
  Definition of an Activity 12-14
  Rental Versus Nonrental Activities 12-18
  Material Participation 12-20
  Recharacterized Passive Income 12-24
Passive-Activity Interest Expense 12-25
Rental of Residence
  (Vacation Home Rentals) 12-28
  Basic Rules 12-28
  Allocation of Expenses 12-31
Problem Materials 12-34

## Introduction

**LO.1**
Discuss the basic rules governing the deduction of investment expenses.

Since 1942 Congress has generally allowed taxpayers to deduct expenses and losses incurred in connection with investment activities. As explained in Chapter 7, Code § 212 currently authorizes the deduction of investment-oriented expenses. This provision specifically allows a deduction for expenses incurred for the production or collection of income or for the management, conservation, or maintenance of property held for the production of income. Deductible investment expenses typically include such items as fees paid to rent a safety deposit box to hold securities, cost of financial advice, and travel expenses incurred in managing property. Expenses incurred in operating rental property such as those for maintenance, depreciation, utilities, and insurance are also deductible under § 212. Similarly, deductions for interest expense incurred by taxpayers to finance their investments also are deductible under § 212, although certain restrictions apply (as discussed in Chapter 11). Most important, the law generally allows the deduction of losses flowing through to the taxpayer from investments in partnerships and S corporations. Specific investment expenses incurred by the taxpayer are normally classified as miscellaneous itemized deductions and are subject to the two percent limitation and the deduction cutback. However, expenses related to property held for the production of rents or royalties are deductible *for* A.G.I. In addition, losses flowing from a partnership or S corporation are generally deductible for A.G.I.

For many years, the general rules adequately governed the deduction of most investment expenses and losses. In time, these rules became insufficient to police growing abuse. As a result, Congress enacted special provisions to restrict investment-type deductions where it found the general rule to be lacking. This chapter examines four additional measures: the at-risk rules, the passive activity limitations, the restrictions on the deduction for interest expense related to passive activities, and the provisions related to the rental of vacation homes.

## Introduction to Tax Shelters

Historically, the tax law has generally allowed taxpayers to use deductions from one activity to offset the income of another. Similarly, most credits could be used to offset tax attributable to income from any of the taxpayer's activities.

### Example 1

R earns $50,000 annually working as vice president of marketing at Plentiful Products, Inc. Over the years, he has accumulated a modest portfolio of stocks which generates dividends of about $10,000 a year. In addition, he is a 10% limited partner in a partnership that owns an apartment complex consisting of 200 units. During the year, the apartment complex had operating expenses that exceeded rental income, creating a $100,000 loss. Prior to 1987, R could use his share of the loss, $10,000, to offset his other income, both salary and dividends. Assuming R's marginal tax rate was 30%, the loss produced tax savings of $3,000.

The above example illustrates the essentials of what is now a well-publicized phenomenon: under prior law, an individual could reduce his or her tax liability—even eliminate it—by investing in "tax shelters" that produced losses which could be offset against other income. The attraction of such losses for taxpayers wishing to avoid taxes was so great that the tax shelter business grew into a thriving industry.

**LO.2**
Describe the structure of a tax shelter.

A tax shelter is simply an investment which takes advantage of certain tax rules to enhance its rate of return. Like any investment, there is an outlay of cash (or credit) for something that hopefully will yield income year after year and produce gain on its disposition. The ultimate reward or potential loss is usually commensurate with the risk that the investor is willing to assume. It is the tax treatment of the various pieces of the investment that converts an ordinary investment to a potential tax shelter. For example, in the broadest sense, an investment in municipal bonds may be considered a type of tax shelter because the return paid on the investment—the interest—is tax exempt. In the real world, however, the term *tax shelter* is usually not associated with tax-exempt bonds—tax-favored probably would be a more appropriate label. The words "tax shelter" typically conjures up images of complex investments that—as in Example 1—throw off losses to "shelter" the investor's other income.

## Structure of a Tax Shelter

In the heyday of the industry, a tax shelter was organized as a limited partnership. From a tax perspective, the partnership form is the perfect structure for the shelter because it is not a separate taxable entity. Instead, a partnership acts as a conduit, enabling the tax benefits produced by the activity to flow through to the investing partners. Operating losses from the partnership's business flow through to the partners who may be able to offset the losses against their other income. Long-term capital gains realized by the partnership flow through, retaining their favorable character to be reported by the partners on their own returns. Special credits generated by the partnership's activity (e.g., the rehabilitation and low-income housing credits) might pass through to the partners to be used to reduce the tax on other taxable income. Observe the vital role that the flow-through characteristic of a partnership plays in a tax shelter. Such results could not be obtained with a C corporation. A C corporation, which is a separate taxable entity, pays taxes on its own income which may be taxed again when distributed to the shareholders as a dividend. More important, at least in a tax shelter sense, the losses of a C corporation can only be used by the corporation to offset its own income and, therefore, produce no benefits to the investing shareholders. For these reasons, tax shelters are not organized as C corporations. Indeed, it is not surprising that as tax shelters became more popular, the IRS tried to halt their growth by arguing that tax shelters posing as limited partnerships were not really partnerships but—because of their limited liability and their close resemblance to a corporation—were corporations. However, the government had little success with this theory and had to devise other techniques to eliminate the perceived abuse.

Promoters of tax shelters historically used limited partnerships—rather than general partnerships—as the vehicle of choice. The promoter, the one who put the deal together and got a fee for his efforts, normally acted as the general partner. To lure an investor, the promoter had to limit an individual's exposure to risk. By structuring the investment as a "limited" partnership, individuals could invest and limit the possibility of financial loss to the amount of their investment. Any liability in excess of that borne by the limited partners was the responsibility of the general partner. This ceiling on an individual's exposure was an extremely attractive feature in the promotion of tax shelters, paving the way for otherwise wary investors to make a financial commitment to the activity.

## Elements of a Tax Shelter

Most tax shelters are constructed to offer three basic benefits: tax deferral, conversion of ordinary income into capital gain, and leverage. Each of these characteristics on its own can produce significant benefits. But when the three are combined into a single package, the result is almost too good to be true.

### Deferral

Deferral is one of the most important tools in tax planning. Postponing the time at which taxes must be paid is the equivalent of an interest-free loan from the government. To illustrate, consider a taxpayer who can defer the payment of $10,000 of taxes for a five-year period. Assuming an after tax rate of return of ten percent, the present value of the tax payment is only $6,210 [$10,000 × $(1/(1.10)^5)$]. In this case, postponing payment of tax saves $3,790, a decrease of almost 38 percent!

A typical tax shelter achieves deferral through a mismatching of revenues and expenses. Mismatching occurs because of the timing of income and deductions. Normally a tax shelter produces deductible expenses prior to the period in which the investment produces income in sufficient amounts to offset the deductions. In the appropriately structured tax shelter, taxpayers may be able to use these excess deductions, in effect losses from the shelter, to offset income from other sources thus producing immediate benefits. Most tax shelters were built around this same modus operandi: deduct expenses now while the gain accrues and is not taxed until later. This approach, "deduct now, pay later," is still the foundation of many current tax planning ideas.

### Example 2

R, S, and T formed a partnership for the purpose of breeding cattle. Each contributed $15,000 for a one-third interest. The partnership uses the cash to purchase a herd of cattle consisting primarily of cows, heifers and a few bulls. The partnership's only cash expenses during the year were the costs for breeding and maintaining the cattle totaling $45,000. No income was produced since none of the cattle were sold. Assuming the partnership uses the cash method of accounting and ignoring depreciation, the partnership has a loss of $45,000 which is allocated equally among R, S and T. As a result, R, S and T each have a $15,000 deduction for the losses attributable to their investment in the partnership, and this loss—prior to 1987—could be offset against income from other sources. Assuming each is in the 50% tax bracket (federal, state and local), each saves taxes of $7,500 ($15,000 × 50%).

[Note: while a 50% tax rate might seem high today, that has not always been the case. From 1965–1986, the top federal rate was 70%. Even in 2011, a taxpayer living in New York City could pay a combined rate of almost 50% (35% federal + 8.97% state + 3.876% city = 47.846%).]

Note in the above example that the tax savings occur because the cash method of accounting results in a mismatching of expenses and revenues. Had the partnership been required to use the accrual method or simply prohibited from deducting the expenses until the partnership *sold* the cattle, revenue and expenses would have been properly matched—at least in the financial accounting sense—and no tax savings would result (unless the cattle are later sold at a loss). It also should be emphasized that the taxes saved in this situation are not permanently avoided but only *deferred* until the future when the cattle are sold.

### Example 3

Refer to the situation in *Example 2* where expenses during the first year of operations were $45,000, producing a $45,000 deductible loss. Now assume that the cattle that were born and raised are sold for $45,000 on the first day of the next accounting period. If there were no other expenses, the partnership would have income of $45,000, each partner reporting $15,000. Since each partner is in the 50% tax bracket each pays taxes of $7,500. Note that the taxes paid in this period are the same as the taxes saved in the prior period. Thus, the taxpayer has not escaped $7,500 in taxes; nevertheless, the taxpayer has benefited since he deferred payment of the tax for one year. In addition, the taxpayer has benefited even though he had no gain or loss on the transaction as a whole ($45,000 income was equal to the $45,000 cost of breeding and raising). Of course, whether the taxpayers are happy with the result depends on the return that they could have otherwise received had the $45,000 been invested elsewhere.

The cattle example typifies the classic tax shelter but there were many more. Taxpayers could invest in partnerships created to explore for oil and gas, produce a movie or broadway show, buy art masters from which lithographs and prints could be made, or lease equipment (e.g., railroad boxcars, barges, cable TV systems, houseboats, executive jets and any other item someone might be willing to rent). Perhaps the shelter of all shelters is real estate. Here the partnership buys an office or apartment building for which current depreciation deductions can be claimed even though the value of the building is holding or increasing. Despite their differences, all tax shelters had one common thread: claim deductions this year for expenses that add value that will not be taxed until next year.

While deferral is a huge advantage, the opportunities increase dramatically when the element of conversion can be added to the mix.

## Conversion

The second element of the successful tax shelter involves conversion. Conversion is a two-step process. The first step concerns the treatment of deductions arising from the tax shelter activity. These expenses are deductible and reduce ordinary operating income that would otherwise be taxed at ordinary tax rates. The second step is where the conversion takes place.

When the tax shelter activity is sold, any gain on the sale is taxed as long-term capital gain, which is taxed at the far more favorable capital gain rates.

### Example 4

Recall *Example 3* where the cattle were purchased, bred and raised at a cost of $45,000. Assume now that the cattle are sold after they were held for more than two years—the holding period necessary for cattle if gain is to qualify for long-term capital gain treatment. Given this additional fact, the $45,000 gain would be treated as long-term capital gain and thus each partner would (using the tax rates in effect today) pay taxes at a capital gains rate of 20%, producing a tax of $3,000 (20% × $15,000) for each of the partners. Contrast the tax paid on the gain, $3,000, with the $7,500 of taxes saved from deducting the costs (50% × $15,000 share of the loss = $7,500). Most important, note that there was no real economic gain on the transaction: the cattle cost $45,000 to raise and then were sold for $45,000. However, because of the difference between the tax rates applying to ordinary income and capital gains, each partner is better off by $4,500 ($7,500 − $3,000). Note that in the previous example the $7,500 of taxes initially saved by each partner were entirely recouped by the government when the cattle were sold. In this situation, however, the government recoups only $3,000 of the original savings because the ordinary income was converted to capital gain. Thus, in this case, the taxpayer has not only benefited from deferral—deductions now, income later—but also earned $4,500 from the conversion of ordinary income into capital gain.

## Leverage

The third element of most tax shelters is leverage. In physics, a strategically placed lever provides a mechanical benefit, enabling people to lift more than they would be able to with their own physical strength. The principle is the same in the world of finance. In investing, borrowing money enables an individual to obtain a larger return than otherwise could be obtained. For example, assume an individual purchases land for $100,000, $10,000 of her own money and $90,000 borrowed from a lender. If the investment is sold a year later for $120,000, there has been a 20 percent return on the total $100,000 investment. But for the individual investor, after paying back the lender $90,000 and $10,000 for the use of the money (i.e., interest), the $20,000 remaining means that she has doubled her money, a return of 100 percent! In tax terminology, the term *leverage* means that by borrowing money, a taxpayer can obtain a disproportionately large benefit from a small investment. The most common use, sometimes referred to as "tax leverage" concerns depreciation. For example, a tax shelter partnership might purchase a railroad boxcar for $25,000 down and finance the balance with a $75,000 note (i.e., the leverage). The law allows depreciation on the entire $100,000 not just the $25,000—creating much larger depreciation deductions than could have been obtained had depreciation been allowed only on the amount not borrowed.

### Example 5

Assume the same facts as in the previous examples concerning the cattle breeding tax shelter except that the partnership acquired the original herd using an initial investment of $5,000 each—$15,000 total—and $30,000 of funds borrowed from the bank for which the partners are personally liable. Note the result when the taxpayer leverages a small investment with borrowed funds: each taxpayer receives a deductible loss providing a tax saving of $7,500 ($45,000 deduction × 1/3 = $15,000 × 50%) which is more than his $5,000 original investment!

Note in the example above that by using leverage the taxpayers are able to generate $45,000 of deductions for an investment of only $15,000. In the language of tax shelters, this means that the taxpayers got a 3:1 write-off, $3 of deduction for each $1 invested. If the taxpayer is in the 50 percent tax bracket, a $3 deduction produces a benefit of $1.50 in tax savings at a cost of $1—clearly a miracle. When tax shelters were at the peak of their popularity, some investments boasted far greater benefits, 5:1, 10:1 and higher.

While the principle of leverage can work miracles, it can also spell disaster. If a taxpayer invests in a tax shelter where the write-off is 10:1, this means that the deal is highly leveraged—a large amount is being borrowed. If the investment goes sour, the lender still must be repaid. In such cases, the cost of the deductions could result in a severe financial loss. However, tax shelter promoters usually solved this problem by using a magical tool: *nonrecourse financing*.

A nonrecourse note is a loan for which the borrower bears no liability for the debt. If the borrower defaults on the loan, the lender can foreclose on the property (i.e., the collateral). However, if the funds derived from foreclosure and sale of the property are not sufficient to satisfy the loan obligation, the lender is out of luck—there is no recourse against the borrower. In a partnership, if the financing for the tax shelter activity was provided using nonrecourse debt (e.g., an office building or other real estate), the investing partners were only liable for the debt to the extent of their investment. As might be imagined, promoters took advantage of this phenomenon. In the most outrageous deals, the promoter would overstate the value of the investment and then act as the banker, providing the financing, all nonrecourse. The investors' cash investment would cover any real costs of the promoter and the nonrecourse financing simply served to create deductions.

### Example 6

P put together a limited partnership to create deductible losses for the investors. Ten doctors invested $10,000 each for a partnership interest. The partnership used the $100,000 to buy a building from P for $1,000,000. The partnership signed a nonrecourse note to P for $900,000, payable with interest only for 20 years and a balloon payment of $900,000 at the end of the term. Before consideration of depreciation, operation of the office building broke even. The partnership proceeded to depreciate the property (a noncash expenditure), producing net losses that could be passed through and deducted by the partners. At the end of 20 years, the partnership might default on the note. In this case, P would take back his property and each partner would have received essentially $100,000 of deductions at a cost of $10,000. If the partners were in the 50% tax bracket, the deductions would be worth $50,000 and the arrangement would have provided a terrific return on the partners' investments. On the other side of the deal, P would pocket the $100,000 for his trouble. Note that the value of the building could have been whatever the partnership wanted to set, $1 million, $1.5 million, $2 million, or whatever, since the debt was nonrecourse and no one was ever going to pay!

In order to prevent what it considered the harmful and excessive use of tax shelters, Congress took action—albeit indirect—with enactment of the at-risk rules in 1976 and the passive loss rules in 1986. Perhaps fearing that it would alienate certain constituencies, Congress opted not to eliminate or limit the provisions on which shelters are built (e.g., special benefits for low-income housing and rehabilitation of old and historic buildings). Instead, the new legislation, placed limitations on the losses created by these special provisions.

## At-Risk Rules

**LO.3**
Explain the at-risk rules.

As can be seen in *Example 6*, the linchpin that held many tax shelters together was nonrecourse financing. From the outset, the government believed that investors should not be entitled to deductions unless they actually incurred a cost—something that was not necessarily present when a tax shelter was structured with nonrecourse financing. Consequently, to eliminate the possibility of artificial deductions, as part of the Tax Reform Act of 1976, Congress enacted § 465 and the so-called at-risk rules. Section 465 generally limits the deductions of individuals and closely held businesses to the amount which they could actually lose from the investment—the amount at-risk. Consequently, to secure the deduction, investors generally must commit personal funds to the venture's activities or be personally liable for debt incurred by the venture in carrying on its activities. The at-risk rules were subsequently amended in the Revenue Act of 1978 and the Tax Reform Act of 1986.

Initially, the at-risk rules were limited to four specific types of activities: (1) holding, producing, or distributing motion picture films or tapes; (2) farming; (3) leasing personal property; and (4) oil and gas exploration and development. As the list suggests, all of these were ripe for sheltering income. In 1978, legislation extended the rules to cover all other activities with one blatant omission: real estate. Real estate was added in 1986 but a huge exception was created in 1987. This exception essentially allowed real estate ventures to escape the at-risk limitations when they were financed using funds from a third-party commercial lender. Consequently, as the law currently reads, the at-risk rules apply to all trade or business or the production of income activities operated by individuals and closely held businesses. Real estate placed in service before 1987 (e.g., an office building or an apartment complex) is exempt as is a separate activity that involves the leasing of equipment by a closely held C corporation. It is important to realize that the at-risk rules cover *any* trade or business or investment activity. Unlike the passive loss rules discussed below, they are not limited to those investments that produce portfolio income or loss, or to those that produce passive income or loss.

## At-Risk Computation

Under § 465(a), the at-risk provisions limit the deduction of losses incurred in an activity to the amount *at-risk* in the activity at the close of the tax year. Any loss in excess of the amount at-risk cannot be deducted in the current year but can be carried forward and used when there is an increase in the amount at-risk. The following formula can be used to compute the amount at-risk (see Form 6198):

| | |
|---|---|
| | Beginning at-risk balance |
| + | Contributions of cash and property (adjusted basis) |
| + | Increases in recourse debt (taxpayer is personally liable and the lender has no interest in the venture) |
| + | Increases in debt for which the taxpayer has pledged property which is not used in the activity as security |
| + | Increases in qualified nonrecourse debt related to realty |
| + | Income (taxable and tax-exempt) |
| − | Cash or property withdrawals or distributions |
| − | Nondeductible expenses related to tax-exempt income |
| − | Decreases in qualified nonrecourse debt related to realty |
| − | Decreases in recourse debt (T/P personally liable) |
| − | Losses |
| = | Amount at-risk |

Observe that the calculation attempts to measure the amount of the taxpayer's economic investment that could be lost from the activity. Accordingly, a taxpayer's at-risk basis includes cash and other assets committed to the activity. Similarly, adjustments are made for income that is retained within the activity and not distributed since such amounts represent additional investments that might be lost. In addition, the at-risk amount includes amounts borrowed for use in the activity for which the taxpayer is personally liable for repayment—recourse debt—as well as amounts borrowed for which the taxpayer has pledged property as security (other than property used in the activity). Finally, as discussed further below, Congress appeased the real estate industry by including in the amount at-risk certain nonrecourse debt related to the holding of real property. Note that while the taxpayer's at-risk basis increases as these items increase, conversely, the at-risk amount is reduced as these items decrease (e.g., amounts are withdrawn, losses are incurred, recourse debt is reduced).

### Example 7

In 2012, G started a business, designing web pages and providing connections to the Internet. He operated the business as a sole proprietorship. His first step was to purchase a server from a computer manufacturer for $100,000. He gave the company $10,000 cash and agreed to pay the manufacturer $90,000 over the next 10 years. In addition, he put up 20 shares of stock that he owned in his father's business worth $20,000 as collateral. The company agreed to accept the stock and equipment as security for the loan. G also borrowed $150,000 from the local bank. The bank required S to sign a note for the loan for which he is personally liable for repayment. During 2012, he contributed another $50,000 of his own money to keep the business running. For 2012 the business turned a small profit of $30,000 and G left the money in the business for working capital. G's at-risk basis includes, the $50,000 of his own money contributed to the business, the $10,000 used to purchase the equipment, the $20,000 of stock that he pledged to secure the equipment loan, the debt of $150,000 for which he is personally obligated, and the $30,000 of income that he left in the business for a total of $260,000. It does not include the $90,000 to be paid to the manufacturer since the note is nonrecourse and the property is used in the business. Note that the pledged property is included since the property is not used in the business as is the case with the equipment.

In the second year of operations, 2012, the business turned sour and produced a loss of $10,000. In addition, G withdrew $50,000 for personal use. He also made a $20,000 payment on the principal of the loan. Since G's at-risk basis is $260,000 the loss is not limited and G may use the loss to offset his other income (assuming he satisfies the passive loss rules discussed later in this chapter). G must adjust his beginning at-risk basis of $260,000 by reducing it for the loss of $10,000, the distribution of $50,000 and the $20,000 payment of the debt, leaving an at-risk basis of $180,000.

While the at-risk rules went a long way to eliminate abusive tax shelters, one industry was able to escape—real estate. After much controversy, the real estate lobby convinced Congress to provide relief for real estate deals to the extent that they used arm's length, third-party commercial financing (e.g., savings and loan provides loan and charges interest at a reasonable market rate). Consequently, a taxpayer's at-risk amount includes so-called qualified nonrecourse financing. Section 465(b)(6) sets forth the specific requirements.

1. The financing is secured by the real property used in the activity.
2. No person is personally liable for the debt (nonrecourse debt).
3. The amounts are borrowed from a person who is regularly engaged in the lending business (e.g., a commercial lender such as a bank or savings and loan or a federal, state, or local governmental unit).
4. The lender is not related to the taxpayer. Note that financing made by a lending institution that has an equity interest in the venture is permissible if the loan is commercially reasonable and similar to those made to unrelated parties.
5. The lender is not the seller of the property or the promoter of the deal (i.e., receives a fee for the taxpayer's investment) or related to the seller or promoter.

## Example 8

J was one of 10 investors to contribute $100,000 to Silver Queen Partnership. Each investor received a 10% partnership interest. The partnership used the cash and $900,000 borrowed from First National Bank to purchase an office building for $1,000,000. The debt was secured by a mortgage on the building and was payable over 20 years with interest at 7%, the current market rate. None of the partners were personally liable on the obligation. This year J's share of the partnership's loss was $200,000. J's at-risk amount is $190,000, including the $100,000 cash contribution and 10% of the $900,000 nonrecourse loan. The loan is considered qualified nonrecourse financing since it was borrowed from an unrelated commercial lender and not the seller. Although J's share of the loss is $200,000, her deduction is limited to the amount she has at-risk, $190,000, and the balance is carried over. Her at-risk basis is reduced to zero and she may not deduct the $10,000 carryover until her amount at-risk increases.

Despite the at-risk rules, wily tax shelter promoters were able to structure investments that could avoid them. As might be expected, many of these deals involved real estate since real estate was effectively exempt if the financing was properly structured. To the chagrin of Congress, the tax shelters industry continued to grow. Perhaps one of the most revealing testimonials of the popularity of tax shelters can be found on the cover of the February 1986 issue of *Money* magazine. The cover pictured three highly successful individuals, and indicated that each had made more than a million dollars but paid no taxes. In light of this and other similar reports, it is not surprising that taxpayer confidence in the fairness of the tax system had badly eroded. Many taxpayers had come to believe that tax was paid only by the naive and the unsophisticated. This belief, in turn, was leading to noncompliance and providing incentives for expansion of the tax shelter market, often diverting investment capital from productive activities to those principally or exclusively servicing tax avoidance goals. Consequently, Congress took aim at tax shelters again in 1986 and enacted yet another hurdle to be cleared before losses could be deducted: the passive loss rules of § 469. These rules go beyond the at-risk provisions, placing far-reaching restrictions on when deductions, losses, and credits of a passive activity can be used to offset the income of another activity. Although these restrictions were designed principally for losses from a limited partnership interest, they also limit losses from rental activities, as well as losses from any trade or business in which the taxpayer does not materially participate.

## Passive Activity Loss Limitations

### General Rule

**LO.4**
Explain the passive loss rules.

The thrust of § 469 is to divide a taxpayer's income into three types: (1) wages, salaries, and other income from activities in which the taxpayer materially participates (e.g., income from an S corporation that the taxpayer owns and operates); (2) portfolio income (e.g., interest, dividends, capital gains and losses); and (3) passive income—the sort deemed to be produced by most tax shelters and rental activities. Expenses related to passive activities can be deducted only to the extent of income from *all* such passive activities. Any excess expenses of these passive activities—the passive activity loss— may not be deducted against portfolio income or wages, salaries, or any other income from activities in which the taxpayer materially participates. Losses that cannot be used are held in suspension and carried forward to be used to offset passive income of future years.[1] Suspended losses from a passive activity can be used in full to offset portfolio or active income *only* when the taxpayer disposes of his or her entire interest in the activity. Upon disposition, any current and suspended losses (including any loss realized on the disposition) are used to offset income in the following order:[2]

1. Any gain on the disposition of the interest
2. Any *net* income from all passive activities (after taking into account any suspended losses)
3. Any other income or gain (i.e., active and portfolio income)

Observe that this special ordering rule requires the taxpayer to use up the suspended losses against gain on the disposition and any passive income (net of any passive losses) before offsetting such losses against active or portfolio income. Without this rule, a taxpayer would use all of the suspended loss against active income, thus freeing up the passive gain on the disposition to absorb other passive losses.

[1] Suspended losses are carried forward to the following year, where they are treated as if they were incurred in such year. Temp. Reg. § 1.469-1T(f)(4)(B). Special limitations apply to farm losses of noncorporate taxpayers that receive subsidies (§ 461(j)).

[2] § 469(g). To date, Regulations have not been issued on dispositions, leaving many unanswered questions. See Erickson, "Passive Activity Disposition," *The Tax Adviser* (May 1989), p. 338. See TAM 9742002 where the taxpayer did not have to offset current and suspended losses from sold activities with passive income from only those activities that produced net incomes.

### Example 9

T owned and operated her own construction company as a sole proprietorship. For the year, the company had net income of $120,000. T has a substantial portfolio that produced dividends of $15,000 and a short-term capital loss from the sale of stock of $7,000. In addition, her investment in LP1, a limited partnership, produced a passive loss. T's share of the loss was $30,000. Her investments in LP2 and LP3, two other limited partnerships, generated passive activity income. T's share of the income was $5,000. Under the capital gain and loss provisions, T may deduct $3,000 of the capital loss and carry over the remaining $4,000. The $30,000 passive loss is deductible only to the extent of passive income, which is $5,000. In effect, income and loss from the passive activities are netted, and the net loss attributable to LP1, $25,000, is carried over to the following year.

### Example 10

Same facts as above. T held on to her investment in LP1 until this year, when she sold her entire interest, producing a gain of $40,000. Total suspended losses attributable to her investment in LP1 were $70,000. Net income from LP2 was $30,000 for the year while LP3 produced a net loss of $10,000. T may deduct the entire $70,000 loss: $40,000 against the gain, $20,000 against the net passive income from LP2 and LP3 ($30,000 – $10,000), and $10,000 against any other income.

As a practical matter, many taxpayers will have investments in several passive activities, some that produce income and some that produce losses. If the taxpayer has losses from more than one activity, the suspended loss for *each* activity must be determined in the event that the taxpayer subsequently disposes of one of the activities. The suspended loss of each activity is determined by allocating the total loss disallowed for the year, including any suspended losses, pro rata among the loss activities using the following formula:[3]

$$\text{Total disallowed loss for year} \times \frac{\text{Loss for this activity}}{\text{Total losses from all activities with losses}} = \begin{array}{c}\text{Suspended loss}\\ \text{for this activity}\end{array}$$

Note that this fraction simply represents the percentage of losses attributable to a particular activity. For example, if a loss from a particular activity represents 10 percent of all losses, 10 percent of the disallowed loss is allocated to such activity and carried over to the following year. Alternatively, it could be said that the particular activity absorbs 10 percent of any passive income. In effect, each loss activity absorbs this fraction of any passive income from other activities.

[3] Temp. Reg. § 1.469-1T(f)(2).

## Example 11

T owns an interest in three passive activities: A, B, and C. For 2011, activity B reports income of $2,000 while activities A and C report losses of $10,000, $6,000 from A and $4,000 from C. T is allowed to deduct the passive losses from A and C to the extent of the passive income from B. Thus he may deduct $2,000 of the losses. The remaining loss of $8,000 cannot be used to offset T's income from other sources (e.g., wages, dividends, or interest income) but must be suspended and carried forward to the following year. The suspended loss of $8,000 must be allocated between the loss activities pro rata. Since 60% ($6,000/$10,000) of the net loss was attributable to A, the suspended loss for A is $4,800 (60% × $8,000). Similarly, the suspended loss for C is $3,200 [($4,000/$10,000) × $8,000]. Alternatively, the loss activities could be viewed as absorbing the passive income. Using this approach, the suspended losses would be computed somewhat differently but with the same result.

| | *A* | *C* | *Total* |
|---|---|---|---|
| Loss for the year. . . . . . . . . . . . . . . . . . . . . . | $ (6,000) | $ (4,000) | $ (10,000) |
| Loss absorbed: | | | |
| $2,000 × ($6,000/$10,000). . . . . . . . . . . | 1,200 | — | 1,200 |
| $2,000 × ($4,000/$10,000). . . . . . . . . . . | — | 800 | 800 |
| Suspended loss. . . . . . . . . . . . . . . . . . . . . . . | $ (4,800) | $ (3,200) | $ (8,000) |

These losses are carried over and treated as if they were a deduction in the following year.

## Example 12

Assume the same facts as in *Example 11*. The income and loss for 2012 of the three activities is shown below.

| *Activity* | *Current Net Income (Loss)* | *Carryforward from Prior Years* | *Total* |
|---|---|---|---|
| A | $ (5,200) | $ (4,800) | $ (10,000) |
| B | 12,000 | — | 12,000 |
| C | (1,800) | (3,200) | (5,000) |
| Total | $ 5,000 | $ (8,000) | $ (3,000) |

The total passive loss disallowed in 2012 is $3,000. The $3,000 disallowed loss is allocated among the activities with total losses (taking into account both current operations and losses suspended from prior years) as follows:

| *Activity* | *Total Disallowed Loss* | × | *Percentage of Total Loss* | = | *Allocable Portion of Loss* |
|---|---|---|---|---|---|
| A | $3,000 | × | $10,000/($10,000 + $5,000) | = | $2,000 |
| C | 3,000 | × | 5,000/($10,000 + $5,000) | = | 1,000 |

In making the allocation, the disallowed loss is allocated based on an activity's net loss *including* suspended losses (e.g., $10,000 for A) rather than the loss that actually occurred in the current year (e.g., $5,200 for A).

## Example 13

J has three passive activities: R, S, and T. The suspended losses and current income and losses for each activity for 2011 are shown below. In addition, J sold activity S for a $10,000 gain in 2011. Because there has been a complete disposition of S, J is able to deduct all of the suspended losses for S as shown below.

| | *R* | *S* | *T* |
|---|---|---|---|
| Suspended loss | $ (9,000) | $(12,000) | $(15,000) |
| Current income (loss) | (5,000) | (6,000) | (7,000) |
| Total | $(14,000) | $(18,000) | $(22,000) |
| Gain on disposition of S | | 10,000 | |
| Excess loss of S deducted against other income | | $ (8,000) | |

J must first offset the suspended and current losses of $18,000 from activity S against the $10,000 gain on the sale of S. The next step is to offset the $8,000 balance of losses against any net passive income for the year. In this case, the activities have no income, and thus none of the loss is absorbed by passive income. At this point, the remaining loss of $8,000 is no longer considered passive and can be used to offset any active or portfolio income that J may have.

## Example 14

K has three passive activities: X, Y, and Z. The suspended losses and current income and losses for each activity for 2011 are shown below. In addition, in 2011, K sold activity Y for a $21,000 gain. K is able to deduct all of the suspended losses of Y as shown below.

| | *X* | *Y* | *Z* |
|---|---|---|---|
| Suspended loss | $ (7,000) | $(10,000) | $(18,000) |
| Current income (loss) | (8,000) | (6,000) | 8,000 |
| Total | $(15,000) | $(16,000) | $(10,000) |
| Gain on disposition of Y | — | 21,000 | — |
| | $(15,000) | $ 5,000 | $(10,000) |
| Loss absorbed: | | | |
| $5,000 × ($15,000/$25,000) | 3,000 | | |
| $5,000 × ($10,000/$25,000) | | | 2,000 |
| Suspended loss | $(12,000) | | $ (8,000) |

K must first offset Y's current and suspended losses of $16,000 against the $21,000 gain on the sale. Note that the balance of the gain ($5,000) is considered passive income that can be combined with the net losses (the sum of current income or loss and suspended losses) from the other passive activities for the year.[4]

Rules similar to those for passive losses apply to tax credits produced by passive activities (e.g., the low-income housing credit, rehabilitation credit, research credit, and jobs credit). Passive credits can be used *only* to offset any tax attributable to passive income. Any unused credit may be carried forward to the next taxable year to offset future taxes arising from

[4] § 469(g)(1)(A) and Temp. Reg. § 1.469-2T(c)(2)(i)(A)(2).

passive income. In contrast to passive losses, however, credits being carried over are not fully triggered when a passive activity is sold. In the year of disposition, like any other year, the credit can be used only if there is tax attributable to passive income (including gain on the sale of the activity). If the credit cannot be used, it can continue to be carried over to offset tax from other passive activities. However, the credit is subject to its own rules concerning carryover and expiration.

**Example 15**

T invested in a limited partnership that rehabilitated a historic structure. In 2011, T sold his interest, realizing a gain of $5,000. At that time, T had suspended losses of $20,000 and credits of $10,000. T is able to use $5,000 of the losses to offset the gain and the other $15,000 to offset other active or portfolio income. None of the credit can be used, however, because there is no income from the passive activity. Had T sold the property for a gain of $50,000, he would have had $30,000 of passive income. Assuming T is in the 28% tax bracket, he could have used $8,400 ($30,000 × 28%) of the credit. The remaining credit of $1,600 may be carried over to offset tax that may arise from passive income.

## Taxpayers Subject to Limitations

The passive loss rules apply to individuals, estates, trusts, personal service corporations, and certain closely held C corporations.[5] Partnerships and S corporations are not subject to the limitations per se. However, their activities flow through to the owners who are subject to limitation.

The passive loss rules generally do not apply to regular C corporations. Presumably, their immunity is based on the theory that individuals generally do not benefit from losses locked inside the corporate form. Congress, however, did not want taxpayers to be able to circumvent the passive loss rules merely by incorporating. Absent a special rule, a taxpayer could utilize corporate immunity to shelter income derived from personal services. Taxpayers would simply incorporate as a personal service corporation and acquire tax shelter investments at the corporate level. The losses produced by the tax shelters would offset not only the service income but also income from any investments made at the corporate level. Consequently, the passive loss rules apply to *personal service corporations* (PSC). A PSC is one where the principal activity is the performance of personal services and such services are primarily performed by employee-owners who, *in the aggregate*, own more than 10 percent of the stock of the corporation either directly or indirectly (e.g., through family members). Common examples of personal service corporations are professional corporations such as those of doctors, accountants, attorneys, engineers, actors, architects, and others where personal services are performed.

Without additional restrictions, any taxpayer—not just one who derives income from services—could incorporate his or her portfolio and offset the investment income with losses from tax shelters. To prohibit this possibility, the passive loss rules also apply in a limited fashion to all closely held C corporations (i.e., a regular C corporation where five or fewer individuals own more than 50 percent of the stock either directly or indirectly). Note that some personal service corporations that might escape the tests above may still be subject to the rules due to their status as closely held corporations. A closely held corporation may not use passive losses to offset its portfolio income. However, such corporations may offset losses from passive activities against the income of any active business carried on by the corporation.[6]

[5] § 469(a)(2).

[6] § 469(e)(2).

### Example 16

R and his two brothers own Real Rustproofing Corporation. For 2012, the corporation suffered a loss from operations of $10,000. In addition, it received interest income from short-term investments of working capital of $20,000. The corporation also had a passive loss from a real estate venture of $30,000. In determining taxable income, the passive activity limitation rules apply since the corporation is closely held (i.e., five or fewer individuals own more than 50%). As a result, none of the loss can be deducted since the loss cannot offset portfolio income of the corporation and the corporation did not have any income from operations. Had the corporation had $50,000 of operating profit, the entire loss could be deducted since passive losses can be used by a closely held corporation to offset active income—but not portfolio income.

## Passive Activities

Assuming the taxpayer is subject to the passive activity rules, the most important determination is whether the activity in which the taxpayer is engaged is *passive*. The characterization of an activity as passive generally depends on the level of the taxpayer's involvement in the activity, the nature of the activity, or the form of ownership. Section 469(c) provides that the following activities are passive:

1. Any activity (other than a working interest in certain oil and gas property) that involves the conduct of a trade or business in which the taxpayer *does not materially participate*; and
2. *Any* rental activity regardless of the level of the taxpayer's participation.

Given these definitions, several questions must be addressed to determine whether a particular endeavor of the taxpayer is a passive activity.

1. What is an activity?
2. Is the activity a rental or nonrental activity?
3. What is material participation?

Unfortunately, none of these questions are easily answered. An exceedingly complex set of Regulations exists that, in large measure, creates intricate definitions designed to prohibit wily taxpayers from deducting their passive losses. The basic rules are considered below.

## Definition of an Activity

The definition of an activity serves as the foundation for the entire structure of the passive loss rules. Virtually all of the important determinations required in applying the passive loss rules are made at the activity level. Perhaps the most significant of these concerns the taxpayer's level of participation. As discussed later in this chapter, if the taxpayer participates for more than 500 hours per year in a nonrental activity, he or she is deemed to materially participate in the activity, and the activity is therefore not passive. As the following example illustrates, this 500-hour test requires an unambiguous definition of an activity.

### Example 17

Mr R. Rock owns and operates 10 restaurants in 10 different cities. In addition, in each of those 10 cities he owns and operates 10 movie theaters. R spends 80 hours working in each restaurant during the year for a total of 800 hours. R spends 70 hours working in each movie theater for a total of 700 hours. If *each* restaurant and each movie theater are treated as separate activities, it would appear that R would not be treated as a material participant in any one of the businesses because he devoted only a minimum amount of his time during the year, 80 or 70 hours, to each. On the other hand, if all the restaurants are aggregated and deemed a *single activity*, R's total participation in all the restaurants, 800 hours would, in fact, be considered material. A similar conclusion could be reached for the movie theaters. In addition, if the restaurants are adjacent to the movie theaters (or in fact are concession stands in the theaters), it might be appropriate to treat the restaurant operation and the movie theater operation as a single activity.

The definition of an activity is not only important for the material participation test, but it is also significant should there be a disposition. As noted above, a complete disposition of an activity enables a taxpayer to deduct any suspended losses of the activity.

## Example 18

Same facts as in *Example 17* above. Also assume that there are suspended losses for each restaurant. If each restaurant is treated as a separate activity, a sale of one of the restaurants would enable R to deduct the suspended loss for that restaurant. In contrast, if the restaurant is not considered a separate activity, none of the loss would be recognized on the tax return for the year of sale.

*Examples 17 and 18* demonstrate not only the importance of the definition of an activity but also the problems inherent in defining what constitutes an activity.

The authors of § 469 obviously anticipated the difficulty in defining an activity and therefore provided no working definition in the Code. As a result, the formidable task of defining an activity fell in the laps of those who write the Regulations. Defining an activity would not be difficult if all taxpayers were engaged in a single line of business at one location. As a practical matter, this is not always the case. Some taxpayers, such as Mr. Rock in *Example 17*, are involved in several lines of business at multiple locations. Consequently, any definition of an activity had to consider such situations. In fixing the scope of an activity, the Treasury feared that a narrow definition would allow taxpayers to generate passive income at will that could be used to offset passive losses. For example, if Mr. Rock were able to treat each restaurant as a separate activity, he could easily manipulate his participation at each restaurant to obtain passive or active income as he deemed most beneficial. To combat this problem, the IRS initially designed a broad definition that generally required a taxpayer to aggregate various endeavors into a single activity. By establishing a broad definition that treats several undertakings as a single activity, the IRS made the material participation test easier to meet, resulting in active rather than passive income. Unfortunately, the initial definition was quite complicated, as evidenced by the Temporary Regulations, which contained 196 pages of intricate rules and examples devoted to the subject.[7] In a refreshing change of direction, however, the IRS allowed these Temporary Regulations to expire, creating a far simpler approach all contained in only four pages![8]

### Appropriate Economic Unit

Under the final regulations, taxpayers are required to treat one or more trade or business activities or one or more rental activities as a single activity if the activities constitute an *appropriate economic unit* for measuring gain or loss.[9] Whether two or more activities constitute an appropriate economic unit (AEU) is determined by taking into account all of the relevant facts and circumstances. Five factors are to be given the greatest weight in making the determination. These are as follows:

1. Similarities and differences in *types* of business;
2. The extent of common control;
3. The extent of common ownership;

---

[7] Temp. Reg. § 1.469-4T(a)(2).

[8] Reg. § 1.469-4.

[9] Reg. § 1.469-4(c)(1).

4. Geographical location; and
5. Interdependencies between activities (e.g., they have the same customers or same employees, are accounted for with a single set of books, purchase or sell goods between themselves, or involve products or services that are normally provided together).

A taxpayer may use *any* reasonable method of applying the relevant facts and circumstances.

### Example 19

C operates several businesses as a sole proprietor. These include a bakery and a movie theater at a shopping mall in Santa Fe and a bakery and a movie theater in Albuquerque. Reasonable groupings, depending on the facts and circumstances. may be as follows:

- A single activity
- A movie theater activity and a bakery activity
- A Santa Fe activity and an Albuquerque activity
- Four separate activities

### Consistency Requirement

To ensure that taxpayers do not bounce from one grouping to another to fit their needs, a consistency requirement is imposed. Once the activities have been grouped in a particular manner, the grouping may not be changed unless the original grouping was clearly inappropriate or there has been a material change in the facts and circumstances that makes the original grouping inappropriate.[10] For instance, in *Example 19* above, once one of the groupings is selected, the taxpayer is required to continue using the grouping unless a material change in the facts and circumstances makes it clearly inappropriate.

In addition, to prevent a taxpayer from misusing the facts-and-circumstances approach, the IRS has the power to regroup activities if the taxpayer's grouping fails to reflect one or more appropriate economic units and one of the primary purposes of the taxpayer's grouping is to circumvent the passive loss rules.[11]

### Activities Conducted through Conduit Entities

As a practical matter, many taxpayers will conduct activities through a partnership or an S corporation. In this case, the grouping is done at the partnership or S corporation level. Partners and S corporation shareholders then determine whether they should aggregate the entity activities with those they conduct directly or through other partnerships or S corporations.[12]

### Grouping of Rental and Nonrental Activities

Rental activities and nonrental activities normally may *not* be grouped together and treated as a single activity. This rule is consistent with the basic provision that all rental activities are passive regardless of the taxpayer's participation. Therefore, it makes sense that rental and nonrental activities should not be aggregated. The practical significance of the rule is to prohibit taxpayers from sheltering active income with passive rental losses. Nevertheless, the Regulations do carve out an exception, allowing aggregation of rental and nonrental activities whenever either activity is *insubstantial* in relation to the other or the owners of the business activity have the same proportionate ownership interest as they have in the rental activity (e.g., 40% in one and 40% in the other).[13]

---

[10] Reg. § 1.469-4(g). In Notice 2008-64, 2008-31 IRB 268, the IRS proposed that taxpayers should be required to report any changes in groupings on the return.

[11] Reg. § 1.469-4(h).

[12] Reg. § 1.469-4(j).

[13] Reg. § 1.469-4(d).

### Example 20

PB&K, an accounting firm, operates its practice out of an office building that it owns. The firm occupies two floors of the building and leases the other three floors to third parties. This year, 90% of the firm's income is from its accounting practice and 10% is from rental of the office space. Because the rental operation is insubstantial in relation to the nonrental operation, the rental and nonrental operations are aggregated into a *single nonrental* activity. Note that in this case any net loss on the rental activity is effectively combined with the income of the accounting operation.

### Example 21

H and W, husband and wife, equally own Sliders, an S corporation that owns and operates 25 restaurants throughout the Midwest. Sliders is quite profitable. Several years ago, the company decided it should buy an airplane to enable it travel easily to its various locations. On the advice of their attorney, H formed Airmax, a single member LLC that purchased and leases out the plane. Sliders rents the plane on a long-term basis from Airmax. The S corporation pays the LLC a fair rent for use of the plane but because of depreciation and interest, the LLC annually reports a net rental loss from its operations. The LLC does not provide any services with respect to providing the plane so it is considered a rental activity and therefore is deemed to be passive. Absent any special rule, H would not be able to offset the losses of Airmax against the income from Sliders. However, under the Regulations, H may elect to group the LLC rental activity and the S corporation restaurant business as a single activity. This grouping election is permitted because the LLC and the S corporation have identical ownership. Alternatively, had there not been identical ownership, H may have been able to group the airplane leasing activity with the restaurant business assuming the rental activity is insubstantial to the restaurant activity.

It should also be noted that the rental of real property and the rental of personal property cannot be grouped unless the personal property is provided in connection with the real property.[14]

### Example 22

T owns a small apartment building with eight units that he rents completely furnished. In addition, the building contains a small room with coin-operated laundry facilities. As a general rule, the laundry rental and apartment rental cannot be aggregated because the rental of real property cannot be grouped with the rental of personal property. In this case, however, the rental income and laundry income can be grouped since the personal property is provided in connection with the real property.

Rental and nonrental operations normally must be separated because they are subject to different rules. For example, rental activities are always passive, whereas nonrental activities are passive only if the taxpayer does not materially participate in such activities. In addition, owners of rental real estate are normally entitled to deduct up to $25,000 of rental losses annually without limitation, whereas there is no comparable rule for nonrental activities. Although rentals and nonrental activities are usually separated, certain exceptions may allow aggregation. As discussed above, if either activity is insubstantial to the other, aggregation can occur or if the owners own the same proportionate interest in each activity, they may be grouped.

[14] Reg. § 1.469-4(e).

## RENTAL VERSUS NONRENTAL ACTIVITIES

Under the general rule described above, all rental activities are deemed to be passive, *regardless* of whether the taxpayer materially participates. Congress adopted this view based on the belief that there is seldom any significant participation in rental activities. Therefore, it created a presumption that all rental activities would be passive. For this purpose, a rental activity is defined as any activity whereby a taxpayer receives payments that are principally for the use of property owned by the taxpayer (e.g., apartments or equipment).

Observe that this blanket rule effectively classifies many rental activities as passive even though an owner might render significant services in connection with the rental. For example, renting video tapes would be considered passive under the general rule even though the owner might perform substantial services. This approach would be unfair to those who participate yet suffer losses. Moreover, the rule creates a huge planning opportunity for those seeking passive income given that many rental businesses are profitable. Recognizing these problems, the authors of the Regulations identified six situations where what is normally a rental is to be treated as a nonrental activity.[15]

1. *1–7 Days Rental.* The activity is not a rental if the average rental period is seven days or less. Under this exception, short-term rentals of such items as cars, hotel and motel rooms, or videocassettes are not considered rental activities.

2. *8–30 Days Rental.* The activity is not a rental if the average rental period is 30 days or less and significant services are performed by the owner of the property. In determining whether *significant services* are provided, consideration is given to the type of service performed and the value of the services relative to the amount charged for the use of the property. In this regard, the Regulations indicate that telephone service and cable television are to be ignored as are those services commonly provided in connection with long-term rentals of commercial and residential property (e.g., janitorial services, repairs, trash collection, cleaning of common areas, and security services provided by landlords of shopping malls and centers). Unfortunately, the Regulations provide few other clues as to what constitutes significant services.

**Example 23**

T owns and rents a resort condominium in Florida. He provides telephone, cable, trash removal, cleaning of the common areas, and daily maid and linen service. The cost of the maid and linen services is less than 10% of the amount charged to tenants occupying the apartments. In determining whether significant services are provided, the telephone, cable, trash, and cleaning services are disregarded. Moreover, according to the Regulations, the maid and linen services would not be considered significant in this case. Because there are no significant services under the Regulations' view, the activity would be considered a rental (*assuming* the average rental use exceeds seven days) and, therefore, a passive activity.

3. *Extraordinary Services.* The activity is not a rental if extraordinary personal services are provided by the owner of the property. Services are considered extraordinary if the use of the property is merely incidental to the services performed.

**Example 24**

Nathan Hale Military Academy, a private college preparatory school, provides housing for its students. The school's rental of such facilities would be considered incidental to the educational services provided and thus be treated as a nonrental activity.

---

[15] Temp. Reg. § 1.469-1T(e)(3)(ii).

4. *Incidental Rentals.* The activity is not a rental activity if the rental of the property is merely incidental to the nonrental activity.

The Temporary Regulations identify two situations when this rule applies.[16]

- *Investment Property.* An activity is not considered a rental if the rental property is held primarily for investment. Two tests must be met. First, the principal purpose for holding the property must be for the expectation of gain from appreciation due to market changes and not due to improvements to the property. Second, the gross rental income from the property is insignificant; that is, the rent must be less than two percent of the lesser of (1) the unadjusted basis of the property or (2) the fair market value of the property.

### Example 25

S owns land that she is holding for future appreciation. She purchased the land for $500,000 and it is currently worth $800,000. To defray the costs of holding the land, she leases it to a rancher for grazing his cattle. The rent is $9,000 per year. Since the rent is less than $10,000 (2% of the lesser of the basis of the property $500,000 or its fair market value of $800,000), the two percent test is met. Because S is holding the property primarily as an investment and her rental income is insignificant (it is less than the two percent threshold), the rental is considered incidental and would not be automatically treated as a rental activity for purposes of the passive loss rules. On the other hand, if S bought the land intending to build a shopping center on it, the rental would not be considered incidental since the land is not considered held primarily for appreciation. In such case, the activity is deemed to be a rental.

- *Property Normally Used in a Trade or Business.* A rental is not considered a rental activity if the property is normally used by the taxpayer in a business and occasionally is rented to others when it is not needed in the business. The property qualifies as business property only if (1) the property is used in the business during the current year (or two of the last five) and (2) the two percent test is met (i.e., gross rental income from the property is less than two percent of the lesser of the unadjusted basis of the property or the fair market value of the property).

### Example 26

P, a farmer, owns land that he uses for farming. This year a nearby country club, Roaring Fork Golf and Country Club, is hosting the U.S. Open. P rented a portion of his land to the club to be used for a parking lot for the month of June for $3,000. The allocable cost of the land is $200,000 and it is currently worth $500,000. The rental income is considered incidental and not passive since the property is normally used in P's farming business and the $3,000 rent is less than $4,000 (2% of the lesser of the basis of the property $200,000 or its fair market value of $500,000). The result would be the same if P had rented the property to another farmer or for some other purpose.

5. *Nonexclusive Use.* The activity is not a rental activity if the taxpayer customarily makes the property available during defined business hours for the nonexclusive use of various customers. For example, this exception would apply to a golf course that sells annual memberships but which is also open to the public on a daily basis.

---

[16] Temp. Reg. § 1.469-1T(e)(3)(vi)(B).

6. *Property Made Available for Use in a Nonrental Activity.* The activity is not a rental activity if the taxpayer owns an interest in a partnership, S corporation, or joint venture to which the property is rented. For example, if T rents equipment to a partnership in which he is a partner, the rental is treated as a nonrental activity.

Similarly, rental of property to a C corporation in which the taxpayer materially participates is not considered a rental.

### Example 27

Mr. F, an attorney, owns and operates F&H Corporation, a law firm. This year F and his wife leased a building that they owned jointly to F&H Inc. The corporation was the sole tenant. Mr. F would like to treat the rent as passive and use it to absorb the couple's passive activity losses. Unfortunately, the regulations provide that rental to a C corporation in which the taxpayer materially participates is a nonrental activity. Therefore, the amounts received for leasing the building are not considered passive income.[17]

As noted above, any activity constituting a "rental" is a passive activity. Note, however, that those activities not classified as rentals (i.e., nonrental activities) may still be considered passive. Whether a *nonrental* activity is a passive activity depends on whether the taxpayer has materially participated in the activity.

## Material Participation

Material participation serves a crucial role in the application of the passive loss rules. It is the criterion that distinguishes between "passive" and "active" nonrental activities. The Code provides that an individual meets the material participation test only if he or she is involved in the operation of the activity on a regular, continuous, and substantial basis. Without further guidance, applying this nebulous criterion would essentially be left to the subjective interpretation of the taxpayer. However, the Regulations establish objective standards that look to the actual number of hours spent in the activity.

Under the regulatory scheme, a taxpayer materially participates in an activity if he or she meets any of seven tests.[18]

1. *More Than 500 Hours.* An individual materially participates if he or she spends more than 500 hours in the activity during the taxable year. Apparently the authors of the Regulations believed that this threshold (e.g., about 10 hours per week) appropriately distinguished those who truly were involved in the business from mere investors. Note that the work of a spouse is counted if it is work typically done by owners. For example, if B owned an S corporation that suffered losses (e.g., a football team), he would materially participate if he devoted more than 500 hours to the activity. However, if he spent only 300 hours and hired his wife as a receptionist who spent 250 hours, the test is not met because her work is not normally done by owners.

2. *Substantially All of the Participation.* The individual and his or her spouse materially participate if they are the sole participants or their participation constitutes substantially all of the participation of all individuals (including nonowners and nonemployees) who participate in the activity. This test, as well as the next, takes into account the fact that not all businesses require 500 hours to operate during the year. For example, if S operates a snow removal service by himself and spends only 50 hours in the activity this year because of light snow, the test is met because he was the sole participant.

---

[17] See *Remy Fransen, Jr.*, 99-2 USTC ¶50,882 (CA-5, 1999), aff'g 98-2 USTC ¶50,776 (D.C., E.D. La., 1998) where the Court upheld the validity of Reg. § 1.469-2(f)(6), recharacterizing the activity as active and not passive. See also *Schwalbach*, 111 T.C. No. 9 (1998).

[18] Temp. Reg. § 1.469-5T(a).

3. *More Than 100 Hours and Not Less Than Anyone Else.* An individual materially participates if he or she participates for more than 100 hours and no other individual spends more time on the activity. For example, assume that S, above, occasionally hires E to help him remove snow. If S spent 160 hours and E 140, S qualifies because he spent more than 100 hours and not less than anyone else. Had S spent only 60 and E 40, S arguably would not qualify under either this or the previous test.

4. *Participation in Several Activities.* An individual materially participates if his or her total participation in all *significant participation activities* (SPAs) exceeds 500 hours. A "significant participation activity" is defined as a trade or business in which the taxpayer participates more than 100 hours, but fails the other six tests for material participation. Thus a taxpayer must spend more than 100 hours in each activity and greater than 500 in all. The rule derives from the view that an individual who spends more than 500 hours in several different activities should be treated the same as those who spend an equivalent amount of time on a single activity.

## Example 28

T spends 140 hours overseeing his car wash, 160 hours supervising his quick-lube operation, and 499 hours managing his gas station. Each activity qualifies as a SPA because T spends more than 100 hours in each. More importantly, T is treated as materially participating in each because the total hours in all SPAs exceeds 500. However, if T spent two more hours in his gas station, then he would not be a material participant in either the car wash or quick-lube business. This occurs because the gas station would no longer be a SPA since the activity by itself satisfies the more-than-500-hours test. As a result, T's total hours in all SPAs, 300 (160 + 140), would not exceed the 500-hour benchmark. Obviously, this is a strange result.

The Regulations provide what at first glance is a curious treatment of SPAs. As expected, losses from SPAs failing to meet the 500-hour test are passive and generally not deductible. However, income from SPAs failing to meet the 500-hour test is *not* passive. Note that the IRS obtains the best of both worlds when a taxpayer is unable to combine his or her SPAs to get over the 500-hour threshold: passive loss but not passive income. This "heads I win, tails you lose" approach was designed to prevent taxpayers from creating passive income that could be used to absorb passive losses by spending small amounts of time in unrelated activities that are profitable.[19]

5. *Prior Participation.* An individual materially participates if he or she has materially participated (by tests 1 through 4) in an activity for five of the past ten years. This test prevents the taxpayer from moving in and out of material participation status. For example, D and son are partners in an appliance business that D started 30 years ago. D has essentially retired, leaving the day-to-day operations to his son. Without a special rule, D could tailor his participation year by year to obtain passive or nonpassive income as fits his needs.

6. *Prior Participation in a Personal Service Activity.* An individual materially participates in a personal service activity if he or she has materially participated in the activity for at least three years. Like the previous test, this rule eliminates the flexibility those working for personal service businesses have in tailoring their participation to obtain passive or nonpassive income as they need. For example, if a general partner in a law firm retired and converted her interest to a limited partnership interest, she would still be treated as a material participant in that law firm.

[19] See Reg. § 1.469-2T(f)(2).

7. *Facts and Circumstances.* An individual materially participates if, based on the facts and circumstances, he or she participates in the activity on a regular, continuous, and substantial basis.

### Rental Real Estate Exception

An extremely important exception to the passive activity rules is carved out in § 469(i) for rental real estate activities of the small investor. In many cases, the rental real estate held by a taxpayer is a residence that is used part-time, was formerly used, or may be used by the taxpayer in the future. Relief was provided for this type of rental real estate because it is often held to provide financial security to individuals with moderate incomes. In such a case, these individuals share little common ground with the tax shelter investors. The relief is provided solely to individuals and certain trusts and estates. Regular C corporations are ineligible.

Under the exception, a taxpayer who *actively* participates (in contrast to materially participates) may deduct up to $25,000 of losses attributable to rental real estate annually. The $25,000 allowance is reduced by 50 percent of the excess of the taxpayer's A.G. I. over $100,000. This relationship may be expressed as follows:

$$\text{Reduction in \$ 25,000 allowance} = 50\% \ (\text{A.G.I} - \$100,000)$$

Based on this formula, high-income taxpayers (i.e., those with A.G.I. of $150,000 or more) cannot take advantage of this provision. A.G.I. for this purpose is computed without regard to contributions to individual retirement accounts, taxable social security, and any net passive losses that might be deductible. Any portion of the rental loss that is not deductible may be carried over and deducted subject to the same limitations in the following years.

#### Example 29

L moved to a new home this year. Instead of selling his old home, L decided to rent it out to supplement his income. For the year, rents were $3,000 while expenses including maintenance, depreciation, interest, utilities, and taxes were $10,000. L's A.G.I. is $40,000. L may deduct the $7,000 loss for A.G.I. Had L's A.G.I. been $140,000, he could have deducted only $5,000 and carried over $2,000 to the following year. This computation is illustrated below.

| | | |
|---|---|---|
| Loss allowance | | $ 25,000 |
| Phase-out: | | |
| A.G.I. | $ 140,000 | |
| Threshold | (100,000) | |
| Excess A.G.I. | $ 40,000 | |
| Rate | × 50% | |
| Phase-out | | (20,000) |
| Maximum loss allowed | | $ 5,000 |

It should be emphasized that the taxpayer can use this exception only if the property is considered rental real estate. It cannot be used for losses from rental of personal property. More important, the real estate is not considered a "rental" activity where the rental period is either 1 to 7 days or between 8 and 30 days and significant services are performed.[20] For example, consider the typical investor who owns a vacation condominium. If the average rental of the condominium is 1 to 7 days, the condominium is not considered rental property and the $25,000 exception does not apply. The result is the same if the average rental period is between 8 and 30 days and significant services are provided. Note that even though the

[20] For an excellent discussion of this topic and issue see Bomyea and Marucheck, "Rental of Residences," *The Tax Adviser* (September 1990), p. 543.

$25,000 exception is not available in either case, all is not necessarily lost. In both situations, the condominium is treated as a nonrental activity. In such case, the taxpayer will be able to deduct all losses if there is material participation.[21]

## Example 30

M lives in Orlando, where she practices law. M owns a condominium, which she rents out on a daily basis to tourists. M runs ads in the local newspaper, makes arrangements for the rental, and cleans the unit as needed. In this case, it appears that the activity is not a rental business because of the short-term rental. As a result, the $25,000 exception for rentals does not apply. However, M still may be able to deduct a loss. Since the property by definition is not a rental activity due to the short-term rental period, it is—by default—a nonrental activity. Accordingly, the loss would be deductible if she materially participates in the activity. For example, if M spent more than 100 hours in the activity and more than anyone else or met any of the other six material participation tests, the loss would be deductible.

As noted above, the Code draws a distinction between material and active participation. The primary difference concerns the taxpayer's degree of involvement in operations. For example, a taxpayer is actively involved if he or she participates in management decisions such as approving new tenants, deciding on rental terms, approving capital or repair expenditures, or if he or she arranges for others to provide services such as repairs. In all cases, the taxpayer is not treated as actively participating in the activity if less than a 10 percent interest is owned. On the other hand, the taxpayer is not presumed to actively participate if the interest is 10 percent or more. The above standard still must be satisfied.

### Real Estate Professional Exception

Under the basic rules described above, taxpayers who are engaged in the rental real estate business (e.g., owners of warehouses, shopping centers, or office buildings) cannot deduct losses from such business activities since the law presumes that virtually all long-term rental real estate activities are passive. Note that this treatment occurs regardless of the amount of time and energy spent by the taxpayer in such activities. The level of the taxpayer's participation is irrelevant. After much debate, however, Congress finally agreed in 1994 that the passive loss rules were aimed at passive investors in real estate and not those who were in the real estate business. For this reason, it took steps to enable these individuals to deduct losses arising from these activities. This special relief is granted only if the individual can pass certain tests that effectively establish that he or she is truly in the real estate business.

Generally, an individual can take advantage of the exception for real estate professionals if he or she spends more than half of their working hours in the real estate business and the number of hours spent exceeds 750. Technically an individual is *eligible* to deduct losses from rental real estate if both of the following conditions are met:[22]

1. Services representing more than 50 percent of the total personal services performed by the individual in all trades or businesses during the tax year are performed in *real property trades or businesses* in which the taxpayer materially participates during the year. For this purpose, real property trades or businesses include real property development, redevelopment, construction, acquisition, conversion, rental, operation, management, leasing, and brokerage. In the case of a closely held C corporation, this test is met if more than 50 percent of the gross receipts of such corporation are derived from real property businesses in which the corporation materially participates.
2. The individual performs more than 750 hours of services in *real property trades or businesses in which he or she materially participates.*

[21] See *Steven D. Rapp*, T.C. Memo 1999-249, 78 TCM 175 and *Walter A. Barniskis*, T.C. Memo 1999-258, 78 TCM 226.

[22] § 469(c)(7). For an interesting example, see *Edward C. Hanna* T.C. Summary Opinion 2006-57.

If a joint return is filed, the special relief is available if either spouse separately satisfies the requirements. Note that for this purpose, the couple *cannot* aggregate their hours.

Observe that satisfaction of these two tests merely opens the door for possible deduction of losses. In order to treat the losses as nonpassive, the taxpayer must still meet the material participation requirements (e.g., spend more than 500 hours in the activity). For this purpose, each activity is normally treated as a separate activity. However, the taxpayer may elect to aggregate such activities.[23] In most cases, it would seem that those who are eligible and who elect to aggregate their real property businesses should be able to meet the material participation tests. It should also be emphasized that personal services as an *employee* in a real property business are not treated as performed in the real property business unless the individual owns at least 5 percent of the business.

**Example 31**

G graduated from the Vanderbilt law school in 1961 and has been practicing his trade ever since. Over the years, however, he has accumulated a number of properties. As a result, he is increasingly spending more time being a real estate magnate and less time being a lawyer. Currently, he owns, operates, and manages a small shopping center and several duplexes. Each of these rental activities produces a loss, primarily due to depreciation. According to G's detailed diary of how he spends his time, he worked 40 hours a week for 50 weeks during the year for a total of 2,000 hours. Assuming G elects to aggregate his interests in each of the rental real estate activities and treat them as a single activity, the majority, 1,100 hours, was devoted to his real estate ventures. The other 900 hours related to his law practice. In this case, G meets both tests that enable him to treat the rental operations as nonrental activities: (1) more than 50% of his personal services were performed in real property businesses, and (2) his 1,100 hours of service in these businesses exceeded the 750-hour threshold. Although the rental taint is removed, this does not necessarily mean G is allowed to deduct the losses. He must still satisfy the material participation tests. Whether this final requirement is met depends on whether G elects to aggregate all of the activities. If so, his 1,100 hours of participation is greater than the 500 hours required and he would be entitled to deduct all of the losses.

## Recharacterized Passive Income

As is evident throughout the passive loss Regulations, the IRS was concerned that taxpayers might create passive income which could be used to absorb otherwise nondeductible passive losses. Nowhere is this more evident than in the recharacterization rules. In certain situations, income that is characterized under the general rules as passive is recharacterized under a special rule and treated as active. An example of the type of recharacterization that can occur was discussed earlier in connection with SPAs. As noted in that discussion, income from SPAs that fail to meet the 500-hour test would normally be treated as passive, but under the special recharacterization rule it is treated as active. There are several other situations when this might occur. Consequently, before it can be concluded that income is passive, the recharacterization rules must be considered. These rules operate to convert the following types of income to nonpassive (i.e., active) or portfolio income rather than passive income.[24]

1. *Significant Participation Activities:* Income from "significant participation activities" that fail to meet the 500-hour test is nonpassive.
2. *Rental of Nondepreciable Property:* Income from rental activities is active if less than 30 percent of the basis of the property rented is depreciable (e.g., rental of land). This

[23] The aggregation election is made by filing a statement with the taxpayer's *original* income tax return for the taxable year pursuant to Reg. § 1.469-9(g). The statement must contain a declaration that the taxpayer is a qualifying taxpayer for the taxable year and is making the election pursuant to § 469(c)(7). Merely, aggregating the rental operations on Schedule E is not sufficient. For an excellent example of what not to do, see *Karl Jahina, et ux. v. Commissioner*, TC Summary Opinion 2002-150.

[24] Temp. Reg. § 1.469-2T(f).

rule makes not only rental income nonpassive but also gain on a sale of the activity or property used in it. However, losses are passive.

3. *Developer Sales of Rental Property:* Rental income, including gain on the sale of rental property, if (1) gain on the sale is included in income during the taxable year; (2) rental of the property commenced less than 24 months before the date of disposition; and (3) the taxpayer performed sufficient services that enhanced the value of the rental property.
4. *Self-Rented Property:* Income from rental of property to an activity in which the taxpayer materially participates, other than related C corporations.
5. *Licensing of Intangible Property:* Royalty income from a pass-through entity that the taxpayer acquired after the entity created the intangible property.
6. *Equity-Financed Lending Activity:* Income from the trade or business of lending money if certain conditions are satisfied.

### Example 32

Dr. S owns a dental practice that he operates through a corporation, Family Dentistry, Inc. He also has substantial passive losses derived from two rental properties, an apartment and shopping center. Hoping to generate some passive income to absorb such losses, he purchased a building and leased it to his corporation for $25,000 this year. The corporation uses the building to house the doctor's dental practice. The self-rental rule treats the rental income received by Dr. S as portfolio income since S materially participates in the corporation to which the property is rented.[25]

In a similar move, S and his brother, B, formed an LLC to establish a trailer park. The LLC purchased the land for $300,000 and made depreciable improvements on the land of $100,000. Any rental income derived from the park is treated as portfolio income rather than passive income since the basis of the depreciable property (unadjusted for depreciation) is less than 30% of the basis of all the property used in the rental activity ($100,000/$400,000 = 25%). Any gain on the sale of the partnership interest would also be treated as portfolio income. Note that this recharacterization rule is usually triggered when the bulk of the rental property's cost is in the land rather than the improvements.

## Passive-Activity Interest Expense

**LO.5** Understand the special treatment for interest expense related to a passive activity.

One aspect related to the passive loss rules that requires special attention is the treatment of interest expense. As discussed in Chapter 11, Congress has imposed severe limitations on the deduction of interest. Interest expense incurred by a taxpayer to finance an investment in a passive activity is subject to the passive loss rules and is not considered investment interest. Similarly, interest expense incurred by an activity that is considered passive (e.g., a partnership if the taxpayer is a limited partner) is subject to the passive loss rules.[26]

### Example 33

In 2011, Dr. P borrowed $50,000 and invested it by acquiring an interest in a limited partnership that produces movies. Interest on the loan for the year is $5,000. P can deduct the interest only to the extent of any passive income that he may have.

[25] *Krukowski*, 114 T.C. 366 (2000).

[26] § 163(d)(3)(B).

### Example 34

Assume the partnership above incurs interest expense related to loans obtained to acquire equipment used in its operations. For the partnership, the interest is treated as a normal deduction and is used in arriving at the partnership's net income or loss from operations. For 2011, the partnership suffered a net loss including deductions for interest expense. Dr. P is allowed to deduct his share of the loss only to the extent he has passive income from other activities.

## ✓ Check Your Knowledge

Try the following true-false questions.

### Review Question 1

This year T's tax records revealed that he had income consisting of a salary of $90,000, dividends of $10,000, and a capital gain from the sale of stock of $5,000. In addition, he received a Schedule K-1 from a partnership in which he is a limited partner. According to the K-1, his share of the partnership's loss for the year was $50,000. T can deduct $15,000 of this loss (i.e., to the extent of his passive dividend and capital gain income).

*False.* While a taxpayer is entitled to deduct passive losses to the extent of passive income, passive income does not include dividends, interest, capital gains, and the like, which are considered portfolio income.

### Review Question 2

A passive loss that cannot be deducted in the current year is generally suspended. The suspended loss is deductible only in the year in which the property to which the loss relates is sold, since the sale affirms the fact that the taxpayer has actually suffered an economic loss.

*False.* The above is true for the most part, but suspended passive losses are not frozen to thaw only when the taxpayer sells his or her interest. Passive losses that cannot be deducted in a particular year are carried over to the following year and treated as if they occurred in that subsequent year. Accordingly, the suspended loss can be deducted to the extent that the taxpayer has passive income in the following year. In addition, the taxpayer is allowed to deduct the suspended losses whenever the property to which the loss relates is sold.

### Review Question 3

A capital gain from the sale of stock in an S corporation in which the taxpayer does not materially participate is considered portfolio income.

*False.* Capital gains are normally considered portfolio income, but when such gain arises from the sale of the taxpayer's interest in a passive activity, it is treated as passive income.

### Review Question 4

The passive loss rules do not apply to regular C corporations since the losses do not flow through and are not available to the individual shareholders.

*False.* The passive loss rules do apply to personal service corporations and closely held corporations (i.e., corporations where five or fewer individuals own more than 50 percent of the stock). Personal service corporations must play by the same rules applicable to individuals. Closely held corporations, however, are allowed to offset passive losses against income from operations *other than* portfolio income.

### Review Question 5

Moe, Larry, and Curly pooled all of their savings to start a new restaurant, Stooges. Stooges is operated as an S corporation, and its stock is owned equally by the threesome. In its first year, the restaurant produced a loss. Depending on the circumstances, Moe may be able to deduct his share of the loss this year while Larry and Curly may not be able to deduct their shares.

*True.* Whether a deduction is allowed for the loss depends on whether the taxpayer materially participates in the activity. Moe may be actively involved on a daily basis, and Larry and Curly may be passive investors. In such a case, only Moe would be able to deduct the loss currently.

### Review Question 6

D operates a small bed-and-breakfast motel. Most of his customers rent rooms for one or two days. D's operation is not considered a rental activity for purposes of the passive-loss rules.

*True.* An activity is not considered a rental for purposes of the passive-loss rules if the average period of customer use is seven days or less.

### Review Question 7

T owns a duplex and rents it out. She normally signs six-month leases with her tenants. Any loss related to the rental is considered a passive loss and is not deductible regardless of T's participation.

*True.* This activity is considered a rental since the average period of customer use exceeds 30 days and T does not provide any extraordinary services. Losses on long-term rental real estate are normally not deductible except to the extent of passive income unless the taxpayer can qualify under one of two exceptions. First, she is permitted to deduct up to $25,000 of losses from rental real estate if she actively participates and her adjusted gross income is less than $150,000. In addition, a special exception allows individuals who spend more than 50 percent of their time in real property businesses and more than 750 hours in such businesses to treat the activities as nonrental and deduct any losses if they materially participate in such activities.

### Review Question 8

Several years ago, Q purchased an interest in a limited partnership. This year his share of the partnership's loss was $10,000. Assuming Q's adjusted gross income is $80,000, he may deduct the loss since it is less than $25,000.

*False.* The loss would be treated as a passive loss since Q does not materially participate in the partnership activity. The de minimis exception that enables a taxpayer to deduct up to $25,000 of passive losses annually applies only to losses from rental real estate activities in which the taxpayer actively participates.

### Review Question 9

B opened her first Planet Jupiter Cafe five years ago in Aspen. Now she has five restaurants, each located in a different resort. Since each store is located in a separate city, she must treat each store as a separate activity.

*False.* A taxpayer is required to treat one or more activities as a single activity if the activities constitute an appropriate economic unit (AEU). The Regulations give the taxpayer a great deal of flexibility in determining what constitutes an AEU. Thus, the taxpayer could treat each as a separate activity, combine all and treat as a single activity, or use some other grouping that may be appropriate under the Regulations.

### Review Question 10

B is a college professor who recently got involved in a mail-order smoke alarm business. This year he spent about 100 hours in the activity, taking orders and arranging to fill them. B materially participates in the business.

*True.* Under the general rule, a taxpayer is considered a material participant if he or she spends more than 500 hours in the activity during the year. Although B does not meet the general rule, he does meet an alternative test; that is, his participation constitutes substantially all of the participation in the activity. Therefore the activity is not a passive activity.

### Review Question 11

G owns two businesses, a convenience grocery store and a dry cleaners. For the last several years, the grocery has not done as well as G had hoped and she has lost money. This year, G did not play as much golf as usual and spent about 400 hours trying to turn the business around. She spent about 300 hours at the cleaners. Each business has a number of full-time employees. G may offset any loss attributable to the grocery store against the profits from her dry cleaners.

*True.* The restaurant and the dry cleaners are considered significant participation activities since G spends more than 100 hours in each. If the total participation in all SPAs exceeds 500 hours, the taxpayer is deemed to materially participate in each of the activities. In this case, the total participation in all SPAs exceeds the 500-hour threshold, and G is therefore deemed to materially participate in each of the activities. Thus, she can use the loss in the grocery activity to offset the income from the cleaning business.

### Review Question 12

Same as above, except G spends 100 hours at the cleaners, 300 hours at the grocery, and the remaining time at the beach. G may offset any loss attributable to the grocery against the profits from her dry cleaners.

*False.* In this case, G's combined participation in the SPAs does not exceed 500 hours. This is the "heads we win, tails you lose" situation: the loss is passive, the income is nonpassive, and the two cannot be combined.

### Review Question 13

J borrowed $100,000 to purchase an interest in the Lockwood Limited Partnership, which operates several apartment complexes. This year J paid $8,000 interest on the loan to acquire his interest. In addition, J's share of the partnership's losses was $10,000. J has no passive income. The loss is a passive loss and cannot be deducted, but the interest is treated as investment interest and is deductible to the extent of J's investment income.

*False.* J simply treats the $8,000 of interest expense as another operating expense of the partnership, increasing the loss from $10,000 to $18,000. None of the loss, including the interest, is deductible.

## Rental of Residence (Vacation Home Rentals)

**LO.6**
Discuss the restrictions imposed on deductions related to vacation homes.

Section 280A imposes restrictions on the deduction of expenses related to rental of a residence if the taxpayer is considered as using the residence primarily for personal purposes rather than for making a profit. These restrictions are aimed at the perceived abuse existing in the area of vacation home rental. Prior to the enactment of § 280A, many felt that personal enjoyment was the predominant motive for purchasing a vacation home. Any rental of the vacation home served merely to minimize the personal expense of ownership and not to produce income.

### Basic Rules

In 1976, Congress prescribed an objective method for ascertaining the purpose of the rental activity as well as the amount of the deduction. According to this approach, the expenses incurred by the taxpayer in owning and operating the home (e.g., interest, taxes, maintenance, utilities, and depreciation) must first be allocated between personal use and rental use. The deductibility of the expenses allocated to each then depends on whether the home is considered the taxpayer's *residence or rental property*. This latter determination is made based on the owner's personal use and the amount of rental activity.[27]

1. *Nominal Rentals:* If the residence is rented out fewer than 15 days, all rental income is excluded from gross income and no deduction is allowed for rental expenses. Otherwise allowable deductions, such as those for qualified residence interest, real estate taxes, and casualty losses may be deducted *from* A.G.I.

---

[27] §§ 280A(c)(5) and 280A(d) through (g).

2. *Used as a "Residence":* If the taxpayer uses the vacation home for more than 14 days or 10 percent of the number of days the property is actually rented out, whichever is greater, the home is treated as his or her residence and deductions are restricted as explained below. A typical taxpayer caught by this rule is the owner of a vacation home who uses it for more than two weeks and rents it out to defray the cost.
   a. *Expenses Allocable to the Rental Use:* These expenses are deductible to the extent of gross income less otherwise allowable deductions. Any deductions in excess of gross income can be carried over and deducted to the extent of any future income. These expenses are deductible *for* A.G.I. since they are related to rental use. Note that the passive-loss rules do not apply since the property is used as a residence and not a rental.
   b. *Expenses Allocable to Personal Use:* Since these expenses are considered personal, they may be deducted only if they are specifically authorized by the Code. Allocable property taxes are deductible without limitation as an itemized deduction since such expenses are fully deductible regardless of the activity in which they are incurred. Interest expense *may* be deductible as an itemized deduction. Allocable interest is normally qualified residence interest since the home—*in this case*—is considered the taxpayer's residence (e.g., because it is used more than 14 days). However, if the home is not the primary or secondary residence of the taxpayer (e.g., the taxpayer has several vacation homes), no deduction would be available. The other operating expenses are not deductible.

3. *Used as "Rental Property":* If the taxpayer does not use the property extensively (i.e., more than the greater of 14 days or 10 percent of the number of days rented out), then the property is effectively treated as rental property.
   a. *Expenses Allocable to the Rental Use:* These expenses are deductible subject only to the restrictions on passive losses. If the property's average rental period is either (1) 1–7 days or (2) 8–30 days *and* significant services are provided, the property is not rental property under the passive loss rules. Thus, the treatment of any loss depends on whether the taxpayer materially participates in this "nonrental activity." If the taxpayer materially participates, any loss would not be passive and would therefore be fully deductible. If the property is considered a rental (e.g., perhaps under the facts-and-circumstances test or if the rental is 8–30 days and no significant services are provided) and the taxpayer is considered as having met the active participation standard, the taxpayer may qualify for the rental exception under the passive loss rules. This would allow the taxpayer to deduct up to $25,000 in losses annually. Any deductions would be for A.G.I.
   b. *Expenses Allocable to Personal Use:* As noted above, since these expenses are personal, they may be deducted only if they are specifically authorized by the Code. In this case, property taxes would continue to be fully deductible. On the other hand, none of the interest expense would be deductible as qualified residence interest since the vacation home is not considered a "residence" (because the taxpayer did *not* use it more than 14 days). However, the excess interest expense would be treated as investment interest and could be deducted to the extent of investment income. Other operating expenses would not be deductible.

This treatment is summarized in Exhibit 12-1.

For purposes of the owner use test, the number of days a unit is rented out does not include any day the unit is used for personal purposes. The unit is generally treated as used for personal purposes on any day where the owner or a member of his or her family uses it for any portion of the day for personal purposes or the unit is rented at less than a fair rental.[28] A day on which the taxpayer spends at least two-thirds of the time at the unit (or if less than two-thirds then at least eight hours) on repairs is not counted as a personal day. This is true even though individuals who accompany the taxpayer do not perform repairs or maintenance.[29]

---

[28] § 280A(d)(2).

[29] Prop. Reg. § 1.280A-1(e)(4) and § 280A(d)(2).

**EXHIBIT 12.1** **Vacation Homes—Summary of § 280A Rules**

| Character of vacation home: | Residence | Rental property |
|---|---|---|
| Characterization: | | |
| Personal use exceeding the greater of | Yes | No |
| **1.** 14 days, or | | |
| **2.** 10 percent of days rented out | | |
| Expenses allocable to rental use: | Limited to gross income by § 280A | Limited by passive-loss rules<br>Rental exception may apply |
| Expenses allocable to personal use: | | |
| Taxes | Deductible | Deductible |
| Interest | Qualified residence interest | Investment interest |
| Other | Not deductible | Not deductible |

## Example 35

In 1985, Floyd Toups and his wife purchased a vacation home for $120,000. The unit was one of 155 individually owned "cottages" located at Callaway Gardens, a favorite vacation resort in Pine Mountain, Georgia, about 70 miles south of Atlanta. The units were marketed and managed by a development company that received 50% of the net rental income for its services. Each owner was entitled to rent-free use of the cottage for no more than 14 days during the year. On their 1988, 1989, and 1990 returns, the Toupses took the position that the cottage, which was generating losses, was a *non-rental* activity since the average period of customer use of the cottage was seven days or less, and accordingly the Toupses deducted the losses on their Schedule C on the grounds that they materially participated in the activity. However, the IRS disagreed and assessed deficiencies exceeding $3,000 for each year. In the Tax Court, the Toupses attempted to justify their position, explaining that they had spent 341 hours each year in activities related to the rental of the unit. They listed 13 activities, which they believed supported their claim. According to the couple they (1) provided funds for the purchase; (2) prepared an annual budget; (3) prepared a cash flow analysis; (4) provided a rental agency for renting their unit; (5) marketed the resort and rental of the cottage; (6) met with other owners; (7) established rental rates for the cottages with other owners; (8) inspected the cottage and common areas at least twice a year; (9) reviewed monthly reports received from the rental agent; (10) reviewed other correspondence from the rental agent; (11) reviewed advertising brochures about the resort received from the rental agent; (12) received and deposited net revenues received from the rental; and (13) issued checks for expenses of the cottage. The Tax Court agreed that the property was not "rental property" under the passive-loss rules and, therefore, did not qualify for the $25,000 allowance available for rental real estate. Unfortunately, the court did not agree with the taxpayers' claim that they materially participated in the activity. The court found that the activities of the taxpayer did not constitute material participation because they were not involved in the day-to-day operation of their cottage or in its management. The activities of the taxpayers were considered to be activities of an investor, and therefore their losses were passive.[30]

[30] *Floyd A. and Joanna Toups*, 66 T.C.M. 370, T.C. Memo 1993-359.

**EXHIBIT 12.2 Vacation Homes—Expense Allocation Rules**

| *Type of Expense* | *Personal Use* | *Rental Use* |
|---|---|---|
| | | Gross rental receipts |
| Directly related (advertising, brokers' fees) | None allocated | − Directly related expenses Sch. E |
| | | Gross rental income |
| Otherwise allowable (qualified residence interest, taxes, etc.) | Itemized deduction* | − Otherwise allowable Sch. E |
| | | Limit on indirect rental expenses |
| Indirect (maintenance, depreciation, utilities, etc.) | Not deductible | − Indirect expenses Sch E** |

***Interest allocated to personal use:**

**(1)** if the property is treated as a residence, deductible as qualified residence interest;
**(2)** if not a residence, the interest may be deductible as investment interest to the extent of investment income.
Taxes allocated to personal use are fully deductible in either case.

****Indirect expenses allocated to rental use:**

**(1)** if the property is treated as a residence, such expenses are limited to remaining rental income;
**(2)** if not a residence but a rental, passive loss rules apply unless not considered a rental (i.e., average customer use does not exceed seven days);
**(3)** if rental for passive loss purposes, limited to passive income and $25,000 allowance may be available;
**(4)** if not a rental for passive activity purposes, loss deductible if materially participate

## Allocation of Expenses

As discussed above, the treatment of expenses incurred in operating a vacation home varies depending on whether the expenses are allocated to rental or personal use. Consequently, the critical first step in applying the vacation home rules is allocation of the expenses. Once expenses are properly allocated between rental and personal use, the appropriate limitations can be applied.

Vacation home expenses can be classified as either direct and indirect. Direct expenses are those that are *not* related to the general operation or maintenance of the unit but which are incurred to obtain tenants.[31] For example, advertising, brokers' fees, office supplies, and depreciation on office equipment used in the rental activity are considered directly related to the rental. These direct expenses reduce gross rental receipts to arrive at gross rental income. All other expenses are considered indirect expenses—including otherwise allowable deductions such as interest and taxes—and must be allocated *between* personal and rental use.

In allocating the expenses between personal and rental use, two different methods are used. Under the so-called *Bolton* approach, otherwise allowable deductions such as interest and taxes are assumed to *accrue daily* regardless of use.[32] Consequently, the fraction for allocating these items to the rental use was:

$$\text{Otherwise allowable deduction} \times \frac{\text{Number of rental days}}{365} = \text{Portion attributable to rental use}$$

In contrast, expenses such as utilities, maintenance, and depreciation are considered a *function of use.* As a result, the fraction used for allocating these items to the rental use was:

$$\text{Operating expenses} \times \frac{\text{Number of rental days}}{\text{Rental} + \text{Personal days}} = \text{Portion attributable to rental use}$$

The method of allocating expenses and their treatment is summarized in Exhibit 12-2 top.

Note that the court's approach in *Bolton* (which uses a denominator of 365 rather than total personal and rental days used) allocates less interest and taxes to the rental portion and, therefore, more to the residential or personal portion. This approach enables the taxpayer to

[31] Prop. Reg. § 1.280A-3(d)(2).

[32] *Dorance D. Bolton*, 77 T.C. 104 (1982), aff'd. at 82-2 USTC ¶9699, 51 AFTR2d 83-305 (CA-9, 1982).

deduct a larger amount of expenses allocable to the rental. At the same time, this method increases the amount of the itemized deduction for interest and taxes. The end result is that a larger deduction can be secured using the *Bolton* approach. Unfortunately, the IRS continues to oppose *Bolton* so taxpayers must proceed with caution.[33] The example below follows *Bolton*.

## Example 36

A owns a condominium in a ski resort. During the year, A uses the condominium as a secondary residence for 30 days and rents it out for 90 days. The condominium is not used the remainder of the year. During the year, A's rental agent, R, collected rents of $5,000. The agent's standard fee was 30% of rents; therefore the charge was $1,500 and R sent Form 1099 to A showing net rental income of $3,500. Total expenses for the entire year include maintenance and utilities of $1,000, interest of $6,200, taxes of $1,100, and $2,000 depreciation on the entire cost of the unit.

A's use for 30 days is more than 14 days, the greater of 14 or 9 days (10% of the 90 days rented). Therefore, the unit is treated as a residence. For this reason, expenses attributable to the rental are deductible to the extent of gross income as reduced by otherwise allowable deductions (the interest and taxes). Deductions are computed and deducted in the *following order:*

| | |
|---|---|
| Gross rental receipts | $ 5,000 |
| Deduct directly related expenses (brokerage fee) | –1,500 |
| Gross rental income | $ 3,500 |
| Deduct allocable portion of otherwise allowable deductions: | |
| Interest and taxes [$7,300 × (90 ÷ 365)] | –1,800 |
| Gross income limitation | $ 1,700 |
| Deduct allocable portion of deductions other than those otherwise allowable and depreciation: | |
| Utilities and maintenance [$1,000 × 90 ÷ (30 + 90)] | –750 |
| Gross income limitation | $ 950 |
| Deduct allocable portion of depreciation: | |
| Depreciation [$2,000 × 90 ÷ (30 + 90)] = $1,500 but limited to $950 balance of gross income | –950 |
| Net income | $ 0 |

All of the above deductions are *for* A.G.I. The balance of interest and taxes not allocated to the rental use, $5,500 ($7,300 – $1,800), is deductible if the taxpayer itemizes deductions. Note that the interest in this case is qualified residence interest since the unit is treated as A's residence. The deduction for maintenance and utilities is not limited by gross income since all of these expenses attributable to the rental activity are deductible. The $250 ($1,000 – $750) remaining balance of maintenance and utilities would not be deductible in any case since it represents the expenses attributable to personal use. Of the remaining depreciation balance of $1,050 ($2,000 – $950), $550 ($1,500 – $950) attributable to the rental is not deductible due to the gross income limitation but may be carried over to subsequent years. The other $500 of depreciation is not deductible since it is the portion attributable to personal use. Also note that only the $950 of depreciation allowed is treated as a reduction in the basis of A's condominium.

[33] § 280A(e). The IRS continues to take the position that all expenses should be allocated based on use. See *Residential Rental Property*, IRS Publication 527 (2006), p. 8.

## Example 37

Assume the same facts as in *Example 36*, except that A used the condominium for 10 days rather than 30. Also assume that the rental is on a three-month basis to locals and no services are provided. In such case, the condominium would be treated as rental property rather than as a residence since A stayed less than 14 days. In addition, the $25,000 rental exception of the passive loss rules would apply since there is a long-term rental and no significant services are provided. A's deduction would be computed as follows:

| | |
|---|---|
| Gross rental receipts | $ 5,000 |
| Deduct directly related expenses (brokerage fee) | −1,500 |
| Gross rental income | $ 3,500 |
| Deduct allocable portion of otherwise allowable deductions ($7,300 × 90 ÷ 365) | −1,800 |
| Deduct allocable portion of utilities and maintenance [$1,000 × 90 ÷ (90 + 10)] | − 900 |
| Deduct allocable portion of depreciation ($2,000 × 90 ÷ (90 + 10)] | −1,800 |
| Loss | $ (1,000) |

In this case, a loss is created that may offset any other income of the taxpayer under the $25,000 rental loss exception. In contrast to *Example 36* above, however, the balance of the interest expense, $5,500 ($7,300 − $1,800), would not be deductible as qualified residence interest since the property does not qualify as a residence. Nevertheless, the taxpayer may be able to deduct the amount as investment interest to the extent of any net investment income that he or she may have from other investments. Lacking investment income, the taxpayer would be better off using the condominium more, in order that he could qualify it as a second residence and deduct the interest. The balance of the other expenses would not be deductible.

The vacation home rules, as discussed above, could operate to eliminate legitimate deductions for those taxpayers who convert their personal residence for rental during the year. In these cases, the owner usually uses the residence for more than 14 days and thus deductions are limited. However, § 280A(d) provides relief for taxpayers in these situations. The provision accomplishes this goal by not counting as personal use days any days of personal use during the year immediately before (or after) the rental period begins (or ends). This rule, often referred to as the *qualified rental period exception*, applies only if the rental period is at least a year (or if less than a year, the house is sold at the end of the rental period).

## Example 38

B lived in her home from January through July. In August, she moved into a condominium and decided to convert her old home to rental property. B was able to find a tenant who leased the old home for a year. Under the normal rules of § 280A, B's deductions related to the old home would be limited to gross income since her personal use exceeded 14 days. The relief measure of § 280A(d) removes this limitation because the seven months of personal use preceding the one-year rental period are not counted as personal use days. As a result, B would treat the lease as a rental activity and could deduct expenses subject to the passive loss rules, possibly qualifying for the $25,000 exception.

## ✓ CHECK YOUR KNOWLEDGE

### Review Question 1

During the Olympics held in Atlanta during 1996, many Georgians left town and rented their homes out for the two weeks the games were in town. It was rumored that some of the mansions were rented for more than $100,000 during this time. How would these temporary landlords treat the income?

Under § 280A, if the home is rented out for less than 15 days, all of the rental income is excluded and none of the expenses allocable to the rental period are deductible. Consequently, these temporary landlords received a real windfall because they were allowed to exclude all of the income.

### Review Question 2

T owns a condominium in Vail. This year his rental agent was able to rent it out for 100 days (most guests stayed for six days). Unfortunately, he was able to use the condo for personal purposes for only one week in January because of a skiing accident in which he broke his shoulder. Interest expense and taxes allocable to the personal use were $500. The net loss attributable to the rental during the remainder of the year was $4,000. What amount can T deduct? Is the property considered rental property subject to the passive loss rules?

Since the personal use was nominal (i.e., not more than the greater of ten percent of the number of days rented or two weeks), the property is not considered a residence. Moreover, it is not considered rental property under the passive loss rules since the average rental period was less than eight days. Thus, it is considered a nonrental activity with the treatment dependent on whether T materially participates in the activity. Since he does not materially participate, the loss is a passive loss and is not deductible unless he has other passive income. The interest attributable to the period of personal use is not qualified residence interest since the unit did not qualify as a residence. Instead the interest is treated as investment interest and is deductible to the extent of investment income.

### Review Question 3

W owns a condominium in St. John in the Caribbean. She rented it out for seven months (one month at a time) during the year but used it personally for the entire month of January. Can W treat the activity as a rental activity and take advantage of the $25,000 de minimis exception that would allow her to deduct a loss from the property?

*No.* If a taxpayer uses a home for more than two weeks or 10 percent of the number of days the unit is rented, she treats the home as a residence. In this case, the taxpayer used the home 31 days for personal purposes, thereby exceeding the threshold and converting the property to a residence. Any interest is deductible as qualified residence interest, assuming this is a first or second home. On the other hand, rental expenses can be deducted only to the extent of rental income. The excess expenses may be carried over and deducted in subsequent years to the extent the unit generates income. The passive loss rules do not apply, and the $25,000 allowance is not available.

## Problem Materials

### DISCUSSION QUESTIONS

**12-1** *Tax Shelters and the Solution.* In 1982, T purchased for $10,000 an interest in Neptune III, a limited partnership created by Dandy Development Company to finance and build a 25-story office building in downtown Houston. T, who was in the 50 percent tax bracket, hoped that this investment would significantly cut her taxes.

- **a.** Explain the features of the investment that during that period made such investments attractive and might produce the benefits desired by T.
- **b.** Explain what steps Congress took in 1986 to eliminate the benefits of investments in such activities as Neptune III. Comment in some detail on the approach used by Congress to accomplish its objective.
- **c.** What steps might you have suggested had you been advising Congress on the restriction of tax shelter?

**12-2** *Effect of Code § 469.* D owns and operates several ski rental shops in Vail, Aspen, Beaver Creek, and Steamboat Springs. Over the years, the shops have had their ups and downs, with profits in some years, losses in others. Recently, D has spent less and less time at the shop, letting his employees do most of the work.

a. What is the significance should the business be characterized as a passive activity?
b. Should D worry about his business being treated as a passive activity? When is an activity considered passive?
c. Does the fact that D's business is a rental operation have any bearing on the nature of the activity?
d. What are the aggregation or grouping rules and why might they be important in D's case?

**12-3** *Taxpayers Subject to § 469.* Dr. R has been quite successful over the years. She left St. James hospital in 1981 and started her own sports medicine practice, The Sports Institute Inc., a regular C corporation. After building this operation into a thriving practice, she branched out. In 1990, she and a good friend opened their own restaurant, The Diner, a partnership. In 1993, her college roommate persuaded R to invest and buy stock in a new venture, Compatible PCS, a corporation that manufactured personal computers. Compatible PCS was owned by R and three other individuals and operated as a regular C corporation until this year, when it converted to S status. Dr. R's other investments include a single family house that she rents out, a limited partnership interest in an oil and gas operation, and a limited partnership interest in a business that develops land into shopping centers. Explain how R is affected by the passive loss rules.

**12-4** *Definition of an Activity and Planning.* D owns several businesses, including an indoor soccer facility, a gas station adjacent to the soccer facility (he bought it with the intention of someday expanding the soccer facility), and a fast-food restaurant across the street from the soccer facility. Within the soccer facility, he has rented space to a local soccer retail store. He also rents space in the facility to another company, which operates a small bar and restaurant. In any one year, each business may be profitable or may have losses. For simplicity, assume each business is operated as a sole proprietorship.

a. Assuming one of the businesses is profitable, would D prefer passive or active income?
b. Assuming one of the businesses has losses, would D prefer a passive or active loss?
c. Discuss the passive loss rules, how they might apply to D, and what planning might be considered. Identify as many questions as possible that might be asked in determining how the passive loss rules apply to D.

**12-5** *Aggregating Activities.* Aggregation of activities may be required for purposes of the material participation tests.

a. Explain the general rules concerning aggregation and their purpose.
b. Explain when this rule is beneficial and when it is detrimental for the taxpayer.

**12-6** *Rental Activities and Material Participation.* T owns a 10-unit apartment complex. He not only manages the apartments but also performs all of the routine maintenance and repairs as well as keeping the books. Most of the leases that he signs with tenants are for one year. This year the complex produced a loss of $30,000. How will T treat the loss, assuming his adjusted gross income from other sources is $90,000?

**12-7** *Recharacterization.* Briefly explain the purpose of the recharacterization rules and why they must not be overlooked when dealing with passive activities.

**12-8** *Credits from a Passive Activity.* P is considering rehabilitating a home in a historic neighborhood. She hopes to qualify for both the rehabilitation credit and the low-income housing credit.

a. Assuming she qualifies, explain how she will compute the amount of credit that she may claim.
b. P's accountant has explained the limitations that apply to losses and has indicated to P that any losses on the rental that are denied currently will ultimately be allowed once P sells the property. Can the same be said of credits?

**12-9** *Grouping Activities.* Urged by their accountants to reduce their tax liability, a group of orthopedic surgeons invested in real estate that produced passive losses. Prior to 1986, these losses did in fact serve as tax shelters. After 1986, however, the passive loss rules significantly restricted the tax benefits of the investments. Consequently, the accountants prodded the doctors to form a partnership to acquire and operate X-ray equipment. The doctors do not participate in the X-ray partnership, and, therefore, any income produced by the partnership is passive income. Most of the income from operation of the partnership is derived from services provided to the doctors themselves. Will this scheme successfully produce passive income that can be used to absorb passive losses?

**12-10** *Interest Expense.* This year Dr. Z purchased a 20 percent interest in a partnership that is building an office building in downtown Dallas. To finance the acquisition, he used his line of credit at the bank and borrowed $100,000. As a result, he paid $10,000 in interest during the year.

**a.** How will Dr. Z treat the interest expense?

**b.** After the building was completed, the partnership secured permanent financing. This year the partnership paid mortgage interest of $700,000, of which $14,000 represented Dr. Z's allocable share. How will Dr. Z treat the interest?

## PROBLEMS

**12-11** *Identifying Activities.* For each of the following situations, indicate the number of activities in which the taxpayer participates.

**a.** S owns and operates an ice cream store in Southwoods Mall. He is also a camera buff and owns a camera shop in the same mall.

**b.** T owns a small "strip" shopping center that houses 10 businesses, including T's own video store. This year T received $40,000 in income from renting out space in the shopping center and grossed $60,000 from her video store.

**c.** O owns five greeting card stores spread all around Denver.

**d.** P owns 10 gas stations throughout the state of Georgia. Each station not only sells gas but also sells groceries. Seven of the stations derive 60 percent of their income from gas sales and 40 percent from food sales. Two of the stations derive 55 percent of their income from food sales and 45 percent from gas sales. One station also provides auto repair services and derives one-third of its income from each operation.

**e.** E owns a beer distributorship and ten liquor stores throughout Minneapolis. Sixty percent of the distributorship sales are to the liquor stores.

**12-12** *Combining Activities.* T owns a 70 percent interest in each of three partnerships: a radio station (WAKO), a minor league baseball team (the Harrisville Hippos), and a video and film company (Dynamite Productions) that produces short subjects for television, including advertisements. In any particular year, one business may be profitable while another may be unprofitable. Each business is at a different location. Each business also prepares its own financial statements and has its own management, although T participates extensively in the management of all three partnerships. Any financing needed for the three partnerships is usually obtained from Second National, a local bank. The radio station broadcasts all of the Hippo games, and the production company often prepares material for local television spots on the Hippos. Occasionally, some employees in one partnership assist the other partnership in periods of peak activity or emergency. Explain how the passive loss rules apply to T in this case.

**12-13** *Material Participation.* During the week, A is a mild-mannered reporter for the local paper. On the weekends, he is a partner with his brother-in-law, B, in a small van-conversion operation in Elkhart. The two typically work seven or eight hours on most Saturdays during the year. This year, the partnership suffered a loss of $10,000.

**a.** How will A treat the loss?

**b.** What planning might you suggest?

**12-14** *Participation Defined.* Three recent Purdue graduates—C, D, and E—formed their own lawn treatment company. Each of the three participates on a part-time basis because each is otherwise employed on a full-time basis. In this, their first year of operations, C spent 40 hours, D spent 70 hours, and E contributed 80 hours. E's wife also kept the books for the partnership. Explain whether C, D, and E satisfy the material participation test.

**12-15** *Material Participation.* F is an accountant with a large C.P.A. firm. She also has an interest in two partnerships: a night club and a family-owned drugstore. F maintains the accounting records for each partnership, spending 200 hours working for the night club and 400 hours for the drugstore.

**a.** How will F treat any losses that the partnerships might have?

**b.** How will F treat any income that the partnerships might have?

**12-16** *Material Participation.* In 1986, H started his own replacement window business, Sting Construction, an S corporation. Up until 1999 H had been the sole shareholder. In 1999 he sold 90 percent of his stock to J and K, who continued the business. From time to time, H still provides advice to J and K. This year, H spent 300 hours working for the company. J and K each devoted 1,500 hours to the business. Unfortunately, the corporation suffered a loss this year because of a downturn in the economy. How will H treat the loss?

**12-17** *Rental or Nonrental Activities.* Indicate whether the following are rental or nonrental activities.

**a.** P owns an airplane. She has an arrangement with a flying club at a small airport to lease the plane out on a short-term basis to its students. Most of the time the plane is rented for two to three hours.

**b.** Q owns a condominium in Aspen that he rents out during the year. The average stay is one week. Q has arranged to provide daily maid and linen service for the unit. In addition, his monthly condominium fee pays for maintenance of the common areas.

**c.** S and his wife, T, own White Silver Sands, a posh resort on the coast of Florida. As part of its package, the resort provides everything a vacationer could want (daily maid service, free use of the golf, tennis, and pool facilities, an on-site masseuse, etc.). The average stay is two weeks.

**d.** Z owns a duplex near the University of Texas that she normally rents out to students on a long-term basis. The average stay is nine months. Z provides typical landlord services such as repairs and maintenance.

**e.** B owns Quiet Quarters, a retirement home for the elderly. The home's staff includes a physician and several nurses.

**f.** C owns and operates Body Beautiful, a fitness club. The club has over 1,000 members. who have use of the club daily from 6 a.m. to 11 p.m.

**g.** D owns a 200-acre parcel of land on the outskirts of Lubbock. The land is worth $700,000 (basis $200,000). During the year, D leased the land to a local car enthusiast who used it as a raceway. D collected rents of $5,000.

**12-18** *Passive Activities.* G is the head chef for Half-Way Airlines, making a salary of $70,000 a year. In addition, his portfolio income is about $20,000 a year. Over the years, G has made numerous investments and has been a participant in many ventures. Indicate whether the passive activity rules would apply in each of the following situations:

**a.** A $10,000 loss from G's interest in Flimsy Films, a limited partnership. G is a limited partner.

**b.** A $5,000 loss from G's interest as a shareholder in D's Bar and Grill, an S corporation. G and his wife operate the bar. Each spent 300 hours working there in the current year.

**c.** G and his friend, F, are equal partners in a partnership that produces and markets a Texas-style barbecue sauce. G leaves the management of the day-to-day operations to F. However, G spent 130 hours working in the business during the current year. For the year, the partnership had income of $15,000. Assume that this is G's only investment.

**d.** Same as (c) except G has an ownership interest in three other distinctly different activities (e.g., construction and consulting). He spends 130 hours in each of the four activities.

**e.** G is a 10 percent partner in a restaurant consulting firm. The firm operates the business on the bottom floor of a three-story building it owns. The firm leases the other two floors to a law firm and a real estate company. The consulting side of the business reported a $100,000 profit from consulting, $5,000 in interest income, and had a loss from the rental operation.

**f.** G is the sole owner of Try, Inc., a regular C corporation that produces G's special salad dressing. The corporation had an operating profit of $4,000. In addition, Try, Inc. had interest income of $5,000 and a $7,000 loss from its investment in a real estate limited partnership in which it was a limited partner.

**12-19** *Passive-Activity Limitations.* M is a successful banker. Two years ago, M's 27-year-old son, J, asked his dad to become his partner in opening a sporting goods store. M agreed and contributed $50,000 for a 50 percent interest in the partnership. J operates the store on his own, receiving little advice from his father. Information regarding M's financial activities reveals the following for the past two years:

| *Year* | *Salary* | *Interest Income* | *Partnership Income (Loss)* |
|---|---|---|---|
| 2011 | $100,000 | $20,000 | $(40,000) |
| 2012 | 100,000 | 20,000 | 12,000 |

All parties are cash basis, calendar year taxpayers. Answer the following questions.

**a.** How did M's investment in the partnership affect his A.G.I. in 2011?

**b.** How did M's investment in the partnership affect his A.G.I. in 2012?

**c.** Would your answer to (b) change if the partnership had a loss in 2012 and the income shown was from M's interest as a limited partner in a real estate venture?

**d.** On January 1, 2013, M sold his interest in the partnership to his son for a $40,000 gain. What effect?

**12-20** *Passive-Activity Limitations: Rental Property.* L, single, is the chief of surgery at a local hospital. During the year, L earned a salary of $120,000. L owns a four-unit apartment building that she rents out unfurnished. The current tenants have one-year leases, which expire at various times. This year, the property produced a loss of $30,000 due to accelerated depreciation. L is actively involved in the rental activity, making many of the decisions regarding leases, repairs, etc.

**a.** How much of the loss may L deduct?

**b.** Would the answer to (a) change if L materially participated?

**12-21** *Rental Real Estate.* M and H are real estate moguls. Together they have created a number of partnerships that own more than 50 shopping malls as well as a few office buildings, apartments, and warehouses. Most of their lease agreements with their mall tenants are tied to the tenant's gross receipts. Unfortunately, with the downturn in the economy, several of the mall projects have produced substantial losses. How will M and H treat their share of the losses?

**12-22** *Suspended Losses.* When tax shelter activity was at its highest, G was one of its biggest proponents. Currently, she still owns an interest in several limited partnerships. She is now considering what she should do in light of the passive loss rules. To help her make this decision, she has put together her best guess as to the performance of her investments over the next two years. These are shown below.

| *Activity* | *2011* | *2012* |
|---|---|---|
| X | $(7,000) | $(2,000) |
| Y | (3,000) | (9,000) |
| Z | 6,000 | 1,000 |

a. Determine the amount of suspended loss for each activity at the end of 2011 and 2012.
b. Assume the same facts as in (a) above, except assume that in 2012 G sells the Y activity for a $4,000 gain. Explain the effect of the disposition on any suspended losses G might have, including the amount of suspended losses to be carried forward to 2013.

**12-23** *Characterizing Income.* Indicate whether the income in the following situations is passive or nonpassive:

a. Ten years ago, T purchased a strip of land for $300,000. Shortly thereafter, he built an office building on the land for $100,000. He currently leases the entire building to a large corporation on a ten-year lease for $90,000 annually. This year he sold the building for $700,000.
b. Q owns a real estate development business that she operates as an S corporation. In 2010, she purchased a vacant lot for $100,000. Q proceeded to put in roads, sewers, and other amenities at a cost of $50,000. Shortly thereafter, she contracted for the construction of a warehouse at a cost of $1 million. Upon completion of the building in September 2010, Q began leasing the space. It was completely leased by June 2011. In December 2012, she sold the property for $2 million.
c. T owns 100 percent of the stock of Z Corporation, an S corporation that operates a construction company. This year T purchased and leased a crane to the corporation. T received total rents of $10,000.
d. X operates a travel agency and an office supply store to which she devotes 300 and 100 hours, respectively. The travel agency produced a profit of $10,000 while the office supply business sustained a loss of $40,000.

**12-24** *Rental versus Nonrental Activities.* Identify rental activities that would not be considered "rental activities" for purposes of the passive loss rules.

**12-25** *Vacation Home Rental.* S owns a condominium in Florida, which he and his family use occasionally. During the year, he used the condominium for 20 days and rented it for 40 days. The remainder of the year, the condominium was vacant. S compiled the following information related to the condominium for the entire year:

| | |
|---|---:|
| Rental income | $1,000 |
| Expenses: | |
| Interest on mortgage | 3,650 |
| Maintenance | 900 |
| Depreciation | 6,000 |

a. Compute the tax effect of the rental activity on S.
b. Assuming S only used the condominium personally for ten days, compute the tax effect.
c. Assuming S only rented the condominium for 14 days, compute the tax effect.

**12-26** *Vacation Home-Personal Use Days.* Indicate the number of personal use days in each of the following situations:

a. Saturday morning, March 3, S drove to Vail to replace a water heater in his vacation home. He arrived in Vail at 9 a.m. and skied until late afternoon, when he retired to his condominium at 6 p.m. After dinner, he worked on replacing the water heater until midnight, when he went to sleep. The following morning he awoke and went skiing until 5 p.m., when he returned home.
b. Same as (a) except S's wife and family accompanied him. S's family also skied but did not perform any repairs or maintenance related to the vacation home.
c. T owns a duplex, which he rents. On February 1 of this year, the one-year lease of the tenant living upstairs expired and she moved. Unable to rent the upstairs unit, T moved in on December I and remained through the end of the year.

**12-27** *Participation in Real Estate.* When D reached age 60 several years ago, he decided to cut back on the number of hours he devoted to his dental practice. He figured that the income from a mini-warehouse, a trailer park, and a duplex that he owned would sufficiently supplement the income that he derived from his practice. Unfortunately, this year all of these rental activities produced losses. Assuming D has no passive income, indicate whether each of the following statements is true or false. If false, explain why.

**a.** D is not allowed to deduct the losses since rental real estate activities are considered passive regardless of the taxpayer's participation.

**b.** D is allowed to deduct the losses if most of his working hours are spent managing the real estate properties.

**c.** Assuming D works 700 hours managing the properties and his wife spends 200 hours helping him, the couple will be able to deduct the losses on their joint return.

**12-28** *At-Risk Computation.* Ajax Construction builds apartments and condominiums. It has developed a unique construction technique. It created forms in the shape of a U in which concreted is poured. The U forms are then inverted and set on top of each other to form the walls and floors of a building. A crane is needed to hoist a U out of the concrete forms and stack it on top of another U. The owners of Ajax Construction, A and B, formed the AB Partnership to purchase the crane and other heavy equipment that would be rented to Ajax and other parties. The partnership is formed on January 1, 2011 by equal partners A and B who each contribute $100,000. The AB Partnership reports on a calendar year and is engaged in activities subject to §465. The following transactions occurred during 2011 and 2012:

| | |
|---|---|
| 7/01/2011 | AB Partnership borrows $120,000 from a bank using a recourse note. |
| 10/01/2011 | AB Partnership acquires equipment at a cost of $400,000 by giving a nonrecourse note to the vendor. |
| 12/01/2011 | AB Partnership reduces the recourse note balance to $30,000 and the nonrecourse note balance to $380,000. |
| 12/31/2011 | AB Partnership reports a taxable loss of $420,000 for 2008. |
| 12/31/2011 | Partners A and B each withdraw $40,000 from the partnership. |
| 4/01/2012 | Partners A and B each contribute $50,000 to the partnership. |
| 12/31/2012 | AB Partnership reports taxable income of $120,000 |

**a.** Computer partner A's amount at risk on 12/31/2011.

**b.** Compute partner A's amount at risk on 12/31/2012.

**12-29** *At-Risk: Real Estate.* Kingsmill is a limited partnership. The partnership has three equal partners and it deals exclusively in rental real estate. S is the only general partner. On January 1, all three capital accounts were zero. No changes in the accounts occurred during the year. The partnership incurred losses of $75,000 during the year. As of the close of the year, the partnership had liabilities in the form of $20,000 of accounts payable and a $30,000 nonrecourse mortgage obtained from a commercial lender.

**a.** What losses can the partners claim as deductions on their returns for the year?

**b.** Would the result be the same if the partnership were engaged in equipment leasing rather than rental real estate?

# Alternative Minimum Tax and Tax Credits

PART 4

CHAPTER 13 The Alternative Minimum Tax and Tax Credits

# 13

# The Alternative Minimum Tax and Tax Credits

## Learning Objectives

Upon completion of this chapter you will be able to:

LO.1 Explain the tax policy reasons underlying the Alternative Minimum Tax (AMT) system.

LO.2 Understand the conceptual framework of the AMT system and understand the terminology necessary to communicate AMT issues or concerns to a tax professional.

LO.3 Determine the amount of AMT adjustments, preferences, and exemptions, and calculate the alternative minimum taxable income, the tentative minimum tax, and the AMT.

LO.4 Complete Form 6251, Alternative Minimum Tax—Individuals.

LO.5 Explain the tax policy reasons for enacting recent tax incentives in the form of tax credits rather than deductions.

LO.6 Distinguish between nonrefundable tax credits subject to dollar limitations and refundable tax credits, which have no such limitations.

LO.7 Understand the components of the general business credit and be able to calculate the amount of credit allowable with respect to separate components.

LO.8 Identify and calculate the nonbusiness tax credits, including the child tax credit, the dependent care credit, the educational tax credits, the earned income credit, and the minimum tax credit.

LO.9 Understand and apply the tax credit carryover, carryback, and recapture rules.

## Chapter Outline


Introduction 13-2
Alternative Minimum Tax 13-3
- Policy Objectives 13-3
- Overview of AMT 13-3
- AMT Rates and Exemptions 13-5
- Adjustments and Tax Preference Items in General 13-7

AMT Adjustments 13-7
AMT Adjustments Applicable to All Taxpayers 13-7
AMT Adjustments Applicable Only to Individuals 13-10
Adjustment Applicable Only to Corporations 13-13

Special Tax Shelter Loss Adjustments 13-14
Tax Preference Items 13-15
Alternative Minimum Tax Computations 13-17
Minimum Tax Credit 13-19
AMT Refundable Tax Credit 13-23
Income Tax Credits 13-25
Overview of Tax Credits 13-26
General Business Credit 13-28
Investment Credit 13-29
Work Opportunity Credit 13-33
Alcohol Fuel Credit 13-34
Research and Experimental (R&E) Credit 13-34
Low-Income Housing Credit 13-38
Disabled Access Credit 13-38
Empowerment Zone Employment Credit 13-39
Credit for Employer-Provided Child-Care 13-39
Other Components of the General Business Credit 13-40
General Business Credit Carryover Rules 13-41
Foreign Tax Credit 13-42
Nonbusiness Credits 13-43
Child Tax Credit 13-43
Child and Dependent Care Credit 13-44
Education Credits 13-49
Credit for Adoption Expenses 13-52
Credit for the Elderly and Permanently Disabled 13-53
Credit for Interest on Certain Home Mortgages 13-54
Refundable Credits 13-55
Tax Withheld at the Source 13-55
Earned Income Credit 13-55
Refundable Child Tax Credits 13-59
Other Refundable Credits 13-61
Problem Materials 13-61


## Introduction

As may be abundantly clear at this point, the U.S. tax system is replete with rules whose purpose is not simply to raise revenue but also to shape the behavior of its citizens.[1] These so-called tax incentives—*or tax preferences*—are sprinkled throughout the Code, and they come in several forms. There are exclusions, deductions, and credits that stimulate economic activity and/or modify social behavior. For example, accelerated depreciation stimulates the acquisition of machinery and equipment, and percentage depletion boosts investment in natural resources. Research is encouraged through a quick write-off as well as a credit. There are also credits to attract investment in low-income housing and the rehabilitation of old buildings. Still other credits exhort taxpayers to use certain fuels, buy electric cars, and hire certain people. Even more tax benefits await those who invest in empowerment zones, enterprise communities, and small corporations.

Unfortunately, using the Code to solve some of the country's ills has created problems of its own. As the number of tax preferences began to grow, astute tax advisers and promoters saw an opportunity. They began to structure business and investment deals—all perfectly legal—that took advantage of the favorable treatment extended to particular investments. In fact, tax professionals did their jobs so well that it was not unusual to find wealthy individuals with large economic incomes who paid little or no income tax. Indeed, in 1966, it was determined that 154 individuals with adjusted gross incomes in excess of $200,000 were able to completely escape tax by using the various incentives. Although the revenue lost from these high-income, no-tax individuals was slight, concerns started to surface. By the late 1960s, Congress recognized that an increasing number of people were losing faith in the system, believing that it was unfairly tipped in favor of the rich. Finally, amidst cries that only the poor and middle class paid taxes, the Johnson administration responded.

In 1969, legislation was enacted to guarantee that all wealthy individuals paid at least some amount of Federal income tax. The method adopted, however, was circuitous. Instead of repealing the tax preferences that created the opportunities, Congress chose to add another layer of taxation: the minimum tax. Since 1969, the minimum tax has come a long way, steadily growing in scope and importance. The first part of this chapter takes a look at these complex provisions.

The second part of this chapter is devoted to the world of credits. Over the years, Congress has established a number of credits that attempt to accomplish a variety of

[1] See "Goals of Taxation" discussion in Chapter 1.

objectives. In addition to the business credits noted above, there are also several credits reserved for individuals. For example, there are credits to aid individuals with child care, help the elderly and disabled, encourage individuals to get off welfare and go to work and to conserve energy. Each of the common credit provisions is discussed below.

# Alternative Minimum Tax

## Policy Objectives

Since its enactment in 1969, the minimum tax has gone through a virtual metamorphosis. Substantial revisions occurred in 1976, 1978, 1981, and 1982, and a complete overhaul took place in 1986. Throughout, however, the rationale behind the tax has remained virtually unchanged. The policy underlying the minimum tax was well-summarized in the following excerpt from the Senate Finance Committee Report on the Tax Reform Act of 1986:

**Reasons for Change**

> The committee believes that the minimum tax should serve one overriding objective: to ensure that no taxpayer with substantial economic income can avoid significant tax liability by using exclusions, deductions, and credits. Although these provisions may provide incentives for worthy goals, they become counterproductive when taxpayers are allowed to use them to avoid virtually all tax liability. The ability of high-income individuals and highly profitable corporations to pay little or no tax undermines respect for the entire tax system and, thus, for the incentive provisions themselves. In addition, even aside from public perceptions, the committee believes that it is inherently unfair for high-income individuals and highly profitable corporations to pay little or no tax due to their ability to utilize various tax preferences.[2]

Guided by these goals, Congress revised the AMT to ensure that the tax liability is at least a minimum percentage of a broad-based concept of income, less related expenses and certain personal or unavoidable expenditures. The intent of the legislation is to increase tax levies on certain wealthy taxpayers.

Under the current AMT rules, taxpayers must make a completely separate tax calculation to determine the *tentative minimum tax*; if the tentative minimum tax is greater than the regular tax liability, the taxpayer will have to pay the higher amount. The upshot of these rules is that the separate tax calculations force taxpayers to keep a separate set of books just to compute the AMT.

## Overview of AMT

The AMT applies to all of the separate taxable entities: individuals, estates, trusts, and regular C corporations. Partnerships and S corporations are not subject to the AMT per se; but if either has items of AMT significance, such items flow through to the partners or shareholders, who must consider them in calculating their own AMT. Consequently, these flow-through entities, like any other taxpayer, cannot ignore the AMT. The Taxpayer Relief Act of 1997 significantly impacted the AMT system. One ramification is discussed here and the others have been integrated with their related rules discussed later in this chapter. In an attempt at simplification, the new law exempts "small corporations" from the AMT for taxable years beginning after December 31, 1997.[3] For this purpose, a small corporation is one that has less than $5,000,000 in average annual gross receipts for the first three-taxable year period (or portion thereof) of the corporation beginning after December 31, 1993. Subsequent to the first three-taxable year period the corporation's average gross receipts for all three-taxable-year periods ending before the current taxable year cannot exceed $7,500,000.[4]

---

[2] Senate Finance Committee Report. H.R. 3838, Page 518, U.S. Government Printing Office, May 29, 1986.

[3] § 55(e).

[4] See § 448 and Chapter 5. This test is the same as the one applied in determining whether a corporation must use the accrual method of accounting. Note that once a corporation is classified as a small corporation, special rules apply when the gross receipts exceed $7,500,000 because the corporation will lose its status as a small corporation [§ 55(e)].

**EXHIBIT 13.1 The Alternative Minimum Tax Formula**

| | | | |
|---|---|---|---|
| Start with: | Regular taxable income | | $ xxx,xxx |
| Plus/Minus: | AMT adjustments (see Exhibit 13-3) | ± | xx,xxx |
| Equals: | AMT adjusted taxable income | | $ xxx,xxx |
| Plus: | Sum of tax preference items (see Exhibit 13-5) | + | xx,xxx |
| Equals: | Alternative minimum taxable income (AMTI) | | $ xxx,xxx |
| Less: | Exemption amount (adjusted for phase-out) | − | xx,xxx |
| Equals: | AMT base (taxable excess) | | $ xxx,xxx |
| Times: | AMT rate | × | xx% |
| Equals: | Gross alternative minimum tax | | $ xx,xxx |
| Less: | AMT foreign tax credit | − | x,xxx |
| Equals: | Tentative minimum tax (TMT) | | $ xx,xxx |
| Less: | Regular tax liability | − | x,xxx |
| Equals: | Alternative minimum tax (AMT) | | $ xx,xxx |

The basic formula for computing the AMT, like the basic formula for determining taxable income, is relatively uncomplicated. As can be seen from Exhibit 13-1, the calculation starts with the taxpayer's final taxable income computed in the normal fashion.[5] This amount, regular taxable income, is increased by any *tax preferences* and further modified—increased or decreased—by certain *adjustments* (see Exhibits 13-3 and 13-5 for a list and brief explanation). The resulting amount is termed *alternative minimum taxable income* (AMTI). However, AMTI is not the amount subject to tax. AMTI is further reduced by an *exemption* to arrive at the tax base or "taxable excess." The appropriate rate is then applied to produce the gross AMT. This amount is reduced by an available AMT foreign tax credit to yield the *tentative minimum tax*. Finally, the tentative minimum tax (TMT) is compared to the regular tax and the taxpayer pays the higher. Technically, the excess of the tentative minimum tax over the regular tax is the AMT, but as can be seen from the formula, the effect is to require the taxpayer to pay the higher amount.[6] It is important to observe that, in computing the AMT, the general business tax credits normally cannot be used to reduce the TMT.[7] This can be quite a surprise for taxpayers who have a large general business credit that wipes out their regular tax liability but does nothing to shield them from the AMT. Lastly, to prevent more individual taxpayers from paying the AMT, the non-business credits can offset both the regular tax and the AMT.[8]

---

[5] § 55(b)(2).

[6] § 55(a).

[7] The empowerment zone credit can offset 25 percent of the tentative minimum tax as authorized by § 38(c)(2)(A).

[8] For tax years 2000 through 2011, most of the nonrefundable personal credits may be offset against the regular tax and the AMT. The credits include the following: credit for the elderly and disabled, adoption expense credit, child tax credit, credit for interest paid or accrued on certain home mortgages of low-income persons, credit for higher education expenses (the American Opportunity Tax Credit), credit for elective deferrals and IRA contributions (saver's credit), non-business energy property credit for energy-efficient improvements to a principal residence, residential energy efficient property credit for photovoltaic, solar hot water, and fuel cell property added to a residence, and first-time home buyer credit for the District of Columbia.

The last issue that is not revealed in the AMT formula concerns some Congressional largess. In an attempt to protect taxpayers from being taxed under both the regular tax system and the AMT system, Congress introduced the minimum tax credit. As explained later, the minimum tax credit provision essentially allows the alternative minimum tax paid in one year to be used (with some modifications) as a credit in subsequent years against the taxpayer's regular tax liability.

### Example 1

K is single and has taxable income of $92,500, on which she is required to pay a regular income tax of $19,517 (2011). In computing her regular taxable income, she utilized regular tax incentives that resulted in $55,000 of AMT adjustments (including her personal exemption) and $35,000 of AMT tax preference items. K's alternative minimum taxable income is $182,500 ($92,500 + $55,000 + $35,000).

As might be suspected, it is not the AMT formula that causes problems. The difficulty lies in the determination of the various adjustments and preferences that must be computed to arrive at AMTI. The next several sections examine each of the items entering into the AMT calculation.

## AMT Rates and Exemptions

### Tax Rates

Until 1993, the AMT was computed with two flat rates, one rate for corporations and a different rate for noncorporate taxpayers. But the increase in individual tax rates by the Revenue Reconciliation Act of 1993 (RRA) apparently necessitated a change in this approach for individuals, estates, and trusts. Consequently, these entities must use a two-tier rate system. Today, the rates for individuals, estates, and trusts are:

| *If the AMT base is* | | | |
|---|---|---|---|
| Over | But not over | Tax liability is | Of the amount over |
| $ 0 | $ 175,000 | 26% | $ 0 |
| 175,000 | — | $45,500 + 28% | 175,000 |

In addition, to help ensure that taxpayers are not snared by the AMT due to the new lower rates on capital gains, Congress conformed the AMT and regular tax. The new lower rates for unrecaptured § 1250 gain (25%) and long-term capital gains (15%) now apply for AMT purposes.[9] In contrast, the rate for corporate taxpayers is a flat 20 percent.

### AMT Exemption

In order to shield taxpayers with small amounts of tax preferences from the AMT, the Code provides an exemption. As shown in Exhibit 13-2, the exemption amount varies depending on the entity and, in the case of an individual, his or her filing status. Although the exemption is designed to reduce the reach of the AMT, the substantial reduction in the regular tax rates in 2001 without corresponding cuts in the AMT rates have resulted in more and more taxpayers paying the AMT, the exemption notwithstanding. Consequently, in the last several years Congress has enacted specific legislation, on an annual basis, to increase the exemption to minimize the AMT's impact.[10]

The exemption provides little or no protection for high income taxpayers. Presumably, Congress did not want high income taxpayers to benefit from the exemption. Consequently, the law provides that the exemption is reduced as the taxpayer's income increases.

[9] § 55(b)(3).

[10] § 55(d).

**EXHIBIT 13.2** **Alternative Minimum Tax Exemptions and Phase-Out Levels for 2002–2011**

| *Taxpayer* | *Exemption Amount* | | *Phase-Out Begins* | *Phase-Out Complete* |
|---|---|---|---|---|
| | 2002* | 2011 | 2011 | 2011 |
| Married filing jointly | $45,000 | $74,450 | $150,000 | $447,800 |
| Single individuals[11] | 33,750 | 48,450 | 112,500 | 306,300 |
| Married filing separately | 22,500 | 37,225 | 75,000 | 223,900 |
| Estates and trusts | 22,500 | 22,500 | 75,000 | 165,000 |
| C corporations | 40,000 | 40,000 | 150,000 | 310,000 |

*For 2012, the exemption amounts are scheduled to decline to 2002 levels shown above, but it is anticipated that tax legislation will extend the higher exemption amounts through 2012 or beyond.

Specifically, the exemption amount for each taxpayer is reduced (but not below zero) by 25 cents for each $1 of AMTI exceeding a certain threshold. These thresholds are identified in Exhibit 13-2. Note that the phase-out rule completely eliminates the exemption as AMTI increases beyond a certain amount. For example, the $74,450 exemption for married taxpayers is completely eliminated when AMTI reaches $433,800 [($447,800 – $150,000 = $297,800) × .25 = $74,450]. The various points at which the phase-out is complete are also shown in Exhibit 13-2.

## Example 2

Assume the same facts as in *Example 1*. Since K is single, her initial AMT exemption is $48,450. However, because K's AMTI of $182,500 exceeds the $112,500 threshold for single individuals by $70,000, her exemption amount must be reduced by $17,500 ($70,000 × 0.25). Thus, the allowable exemption for the year is $30,950 ($48,450 – $17,500).

K's AMT is $19,886, computed as follows:

| | |
|---|---|
| Regular taxable income | $ 92,500 |
| Plus: AMT adjustments | +55,000 |
| AMT adjusted taxable income | $ 147,500 |
| Plus: AMT preference items | +35,000 |
| AMTI | $ 182,500 |
| Less: exemption amount [$48,450 – 25% ($182,500 – $112,500)] | –30,950 |
| AMTI base | $ 151,550 |
| Times: AMT rate | × 26% |
| Gross AMT | $ 39,403 |
| Less: AMT foreign tax credit | – 0 |
| Tentative AMT | $ 39,403 |
| Less: regular tax liability | –19,517 |
| AMT | $ 19,886 |

[11] § 59(j). The exemption amount for children subject to the "kiddie tax" is earned income plus $6,800. The phase-out range is the same as that for single individuals. Rev. Proc. 2010-40, 2010-46, I.R.B. 663.

## Adjustments and Tax Preference Items in General

Once taxable income is determined, the search for AMTI can begin. As noted above, there are two types of modifications that must be made to regular taxable income to arrive at AMTI: adjustments and preferences. Although both of these modifications serve a similar purpose (i.e., provide a more "realistic" measure of the taxpayer's economic income), they are not identical. *Preferences* generally require only an add-back to income. For example, one tax preference item requires the taxpayer to add back certain private activity bond income that was excluded from regular tax gross income under § 103. In contrast, *adjustments* generally call for the complete substitution of some special AMT treatment for the regular tax treatment. For instance, instead of using the regular tax rules to compute depreciation, the taxpayer must use the slower-paced methods for the AMT. Note that, when this occurs, depreciation for regular tax purposes may be more or less than AMT depreciation, resulting in either a positive or a negative adjustment. In short, AMT adjustments may increase or decrease taxable income whereas preferences only increase taxable income.

Another important distinction between adjustments and preferences concerns their effect on the taxpayer's basis in property. Adjustments, such as those for AMT depreciation, usually cause the property's basis for AMT purposes to differ from that for regular tax purposes. Consequently, when the taxpayer later disposes of the property, gain or loss for AMT purposes will normally not be the same as the gain or loss reported for regular tax purposes.[12] As might be imagined, this system effectively requires the taxpayer to maintain a separate set of records for AMT purposes. These separate records are used to compute the annual adjustments as well as the adjustment when the asset is subsequently sold. Note that adjustments can generally be thought of as timing differences between regular taxable income and AMTI. In early years the adjustment normally produces an increase in AMTI. In later years, however, the trend reverses and a negative adjustment is required, actually reducing AMTI.

Although adjustments affect a property's basis, preferences do not. This approach makes accounting for preferences somewhat easier than it is for adjustments. In many cases, only a side calculation is necessary to determine the preference. The preference amount is then simply added to taxable income in the determination of AMTI. Generally, tax preference items are analogous to permanent differences between the regular tax and the minimum tax.

## AMT Adjustments

AMT adjustments can be classified into four groups. As shown in Exhibit 13-3, not all adjustments apply to all taxpayers; some apply to all taxpayers while others apply only to individuals or only to corporations.[13] In addition, there are special adjustments concerning losses from tax shelters. Although all of the adjustments are listed in Exhibit 13-3, only the more common adjustments are discussed below.

## AMT Adjustments Applicable to All Taxpayers

### Depreciation

For AMT purposes, depreciation of property *placed in service after 1986* must be computed using the Alternative Depreciation System (ADS) with an exception for personal property discussed below.[14] This substitution of ADS for the taxpayer's normal method (e.g., MACRS) creates a difference between AMT depreciation and regular tax depreciation, and an adjustment must be made. The amount of the AMT adjustment is merely the difference between regular tax and AMT depreciation, which may be positive or negative as illustrated below.

As discussed in Chapter 9, depreciation under ADS is computed using the straight-line method, the appropriate convention, and the ADS life (the class life for personal property and 40 years for real property). While this same approach generally applies for AMT purposes, there is an exception for tangible personal property. For personal property placed in service after 1998, Congress simplified the depreciation system and the AMT adjustments by allowing the MACRS recovery periods to be used for AMT purposes. The 150 percent declining-balance method does not apply to assets for which the taxpayer has elected the straight-line method for regular tax purposes. The allowable methods of depreciation for

---

[12] § 56(b)(1)(F).

[13] § 56.

[14] § 56(a)(1).

**EXHIBIT 13.3 AMT Adjustments**

| *Applicable to All Taxpayers* | | *Brief Explanation* |
|---|---|---|
| § 56(a)(1) | Depreciation | Use ADS or 150% DB |
| § 56(a)(2) | Mining exploration and development costs | Capitalize and amortize over 10 years |
| § 56(a)(3) | Income reported on the completed contract method | Use percentage completion |
| § 56(a)(4) | Alternative tax net operating loss deduction | Recompute with AMT rules |
| § 56(a)(5) | Pollution control facilities | MACRS with straight line method |
| § 56(a)(6) | Gains or losses on asset dispositions | Differing AMT basis |
| § 56(a)(7) | Alcohol fuel credit | Do not include as income |
| *Applicable Only to Individuals* | | |
| § 56(b)(1)(A) | Itemized deductions | No taxes, misc. itemized deductions; adjust interest, adjust medical |
| § 56(b)(1)(E) | Standard deduction | Not allowed |
| § 56(b)(1)(E) | Personal dependent exemptions | Not allowed |
| § 56(b)(1)(D) | Income tax refunds | Do not include |
| § 56(b)(2) | Circulation and research expenditures | Capitalize and amortize |
| § 56(b)(3) | Incentive stock options | Include spread (FMV − option price) |
| *Applicable Only to Corporations* | | |
| § 56(c) | ACE (adjusted current earnings) | Add 75% (ACE − AMTI) |
| *Specialized Tax Shelter Loss Adjustments* | | |
| § 56(b) | Passive activity losses | Recompute with AMT rules |
| § 56(a) | Farm shelter losses | Deduct in following year, if income |

**EXHIBIT 13.4 Allowable Depreciation Methods for AMT and Regular Tax Purposes for Property Placed in Service after 1998**

| *Method* | *Depreciable Life* | *Regular Tax* | *AMT* | *AMT-ACE* |
|---|---|---|---|---|
| 200% DB | Recovery period | ✔ | | |
| 150% DB | Recovery period | ✔ | ✔ | ✔ |
| Straight line | Recovery period | ✔ | | |
| Straight line | Class life | ✔ | ✔ | ✔ |

regular tax and AMT purposes are shown in Exhibit 13-4. The exhibit reveals that there are four methods of depreciation available for regular tax purposes, two of which are also suitable for AMT purposes. Two observations should be made that are not obvious from this table. The first concerns realty: note that even though the straight-line method must be used for both AMT and regular tax purposes, an adjustment is still necessary since the AMT class life is longer than the normal recovery period (40 years vs. 27.5 or 39 years).[15] The second

[15] § 168(g)(2)(C)(iii).

concerns avoidance of the AMT adjustment. Observe that the taxpayer can avoid the AMT adjustment by electing regular tax depreciation, which uses a slower rate (150% declining-balance or straight-line).[16]

## Example 3

T placed an asset costing $100,000 in service on February 5, 2011. Assume the asset is "3-year property" and has an ADR class life of 3 years. The effect on the minimum tax is computed below assuming that the 150 percent declining-balance method was used for AMT purposes.

| | *2011* | *2012* | *2013* | *2014* |
|---|---|---|---|---|
| Regular tax deduction (200%) | $ 33,330 | $ 44,450 | $ 14,810 | $ 7,410 |
| AMT deduction (150%) | – 25,000 | – 37,500 | – 25,000 | – 12,500 |
| Effect of adjustment on AMTI | $ 8,330 increase | $ 6,950 increase | ($10,190) decrease | ($5,090) decrease |

Note that in the first two years regular depreciation exceeds what is allowed for AMTI—requiring the taxpayer to increase AMTI—a positive adjustment. In the third year, however, the trend reverses itself, and AMT depreciation is greater than what was actually deducted for regular tax purposes. Consequently, the taxpayer is allowed to decrease AMTI—a negative adjustment. Also note that the differences in regular and AMT depreciation cause the property's basis for AMT purposes to be different from the regular tax basis. Accordingly, if the property is sold, the amount of gain or loss for AMT and regular tax purposes may differ.

Recognizing the burdensome task of maintaining one set of depreciation books for each tax system, Congress took steps to coordinate the two. As shown in Exhibit 13-4, taxpayers may eliminate the AMT adjustment by electing the appropriate method for regular tax purposes.[17] For example, the taxpayer could, for regular tax purposes, elect to use the 150 percent declining balance method, which would be the same as AMT depreciation. Alternatively, if the taxpayer elects to use the ADS life and the straight-line method for regular tax purposes, that same method must be used for the AMT. Either approach eliminates the AMT adjustment.

## Example 4

Assume the same facts as in *Example 3* above, except T elects to use the 150 percent modification. In this case, the need for an AMT adjustment is eliminated, as shown below.

| | *2011* | *2012* | *2013* | *2014* |
|---|---|---|---|---|
| Regular tax depreciation (150%, ADS life) | $ 25,000 | $ 37,500 | $ 25,000 | $ 12,500 |
| AMT depreciation (150%, ADS life) | – 25,000 | – 37,500 | – 25,000 | – 12,500 |
| AMT adjustment | $ 0 | $ 0 | $ 0 | $ 0 |

[16] The Tax Reform Act of 1997 allows AMT depreciation to be computed using the same recovery periods as are used for regular tax purposes. For property placed in service prior to 1999, the AMT required tangible personal property to be depreciated over the longer Alternative Depreciation System class life of the property. See §56(a)(1)(A)(i).

[17] §§ 168(g)(7) and 56(a)(1)(A)(ii).

### Section 179 Limited Expensing

Given the elaborate scheme to curtail accelerated depreciation deductions for AMT purposes, it is surprising that the election to expense property under § 179 does not give rise to an AMT adjustment. Currently, first-year § 179 expensing deductions are allowed for both AMT and regular tax purposes.[18]

### Mining Exploration and Development Costs

For regular tax purposes, mining exploration and development costs related to mineral property are currently expensed. For AMT purposes, however, such costs must be capitalized and amortized ratably over a 10-year period.[19]

### Long-Term Contracts

As explained in Chapter 5, for regular tax purposes, taxpayers normally must use the percentage of completion method to account for long-term contracts. However, the Code carves out two exceptions. The completed contract method may be used to account for home construction contracts and by small contractors who have gross receipts less than $10 million. AMT treatment is similar, but it is not identical. For AMT purposes, there is no exception for small contractors. Consequently, the percentage of completion method must be used for computing AMTI in all cases except in accounting for home construction contracts.[20]

### Pollution Control Facilities

While taxpayers are permitted to amortize expenditures related to pollution control facilities over 60 months for regular tax purposes, the AMT requires use of ADS.[21]

### Alternative Tax Net Operating Loss (ATNOL) Deduction

An ATNOL is allowed as a deduction for minimum tax purposes.[22] The procedure for computing the ATNOL parallels its cousin, the regular tax NOL, but the ATNOL must be determined taking into consideration all of the AMT adjustments and tax preference items. In addition, the amount of the ATNOL is *limited* to 90 percent of the AMTI determined without regard to this deduction. Note, however, as part of the Job Creation and Worker Assistance Act of 2002, taxpayers are entitled to deduct 100 percent of the AMT NOLs generated in 2001 or 2002 as well as any AMT NOLs that are carried forward into 2001 or 2002. Also, an election to forgo the NOL carryback period for regular tax purposes is likely to control the treatment for the ATNOL.[23]

## AMT Adjustments Applicable Only to Individuals

All of the adjustments applicable only to individual taxpayers are listed in Exhibit 13-3. Each of these is discussed below. But first it is important to note that the IRS, while routinely taking the position that the AMT and the regular tax system are two distinct and separate systems, has issued regulations governing the computation of AMTI for noncorporate taxpayers. These regulations provide that, in determining the AMTI of noncorporate taxpayers, all references to the taxpayer's A.G.I. or modified A.G.I. in determining the amount of items of income, exclusion, or deduction in the AMT system must be treated as references to the taxpayer's modified A.G.I. as determined for regular tax purposes.[24] For example, in the AMT system the medical expense deduction is subject to a 10 percent limitation just as the regular tax medical expense deduction is limited to a 7½ percent limitation. The important but apparently inconsistent point is that the limitation for the AMT system is not subject to 10 percent of AMTI (as it should be if the AMT were a separate system), but rather the regulation specifies that the AMT limitation will be subject to 10 percent of the taxpayer's regular tax system A.G.I. The purported goal of the regulations is to reduce the complexity

[18] See Footnote 2, *supra*, page 552, note 5.

[19] §§ 616 and 617; but see Footnote 52, *infra*, for the election under § 59(e) that allows taxpayers to avoid an AMT adjustment with respect to these expenditures.

[20] § 56(a)(3).

[21] § 169 and § 56(a)(5).

[22] § 56(a)(4).

[23] *Branum v. Comm.*, 94-1 USTC ¶50, 163, (CA-5, 1994).

[24] Reg. § 1.55-1(e).

and to ease the record keeping burdens that are imposed on noncorporate taxpayers under a completely separate and parallel system that would require a computation of a separate adjusted gross income for alternative minimum tax purposes.

## Itemized Deductions

For the most part, itemized deductions allowed for regular tax purposes are also allowed for AMT purposes (sometimes referred to as alternative minimum tax deductions, or ATIDs). However, there are several important exceptions and modifications. These adjustments differ from those above (e.g., depreciation) in that they serve to increase the tax base as permanent adjustments instead of merely altering the timing of the item.

Two itemized deductions are totally disallowed for AMT purposes:[25]

1. Miscellaneous itemized deductions (MIDs). For example, unreimbursed employee business expenses and tax preparation expenses are not allowed for the AMT.[26]
2. Itemized deductions related to the payment of any tax. For example, state, local, and foreign income taxes and real and personal property taxes are not allowed as deductions for AMT purposes.

In computing the itemized deductions allowed for AMT purposes, the limitations for regular tax purposes normally apply (e.g., the 10% limitation on personal casualty losses or the 50% limitation for charitable contributions).[27] In addition, as noted below, special rules exist for medical expenses and interest.

ATIDs generally include the following:[28]

1. Medical expenses, but *only in excess* of 10 percent of taxpayer's regular tax A.G.I.
2. Interest expense, but only for:
   a. Qualified housing interest
   b. Investment interest expense to the extent of net investment income
3. Charitable contributions
4. Theft, casualty, and wagering losses
5. Estate tax deductions resulting from reporting income in respect of a decedent under § 691
6. Impairment-related work expenses
7. Bond premium amortization deductions

The above list is self-explanatory with the exception of the amount of interest that will be allowed as an ATID. Several new terms and concepts regarding the deduction for interest were developed and incorporated into the alternative minimum tax system. *Qualified housing interest* is interest paid or accrued on indebtedness incurred after June 30, 1982, in acquiring, constructing, or substantially rehabilitating property that is a principal residence (within the meaning of Code § 121) or qualified dwelling, including a secondary residence.[29] For indebtedness incurred *before* July 1, 1982, a deduction can be taken for interest paid or accrued on a debt that, at that time, was secured by a qualified dwelling without regard for the purpose or use of the proceeds of the indebtedness. The essence of these rules is that interest on second mortgages on homes—home equity loans—established after 1982 is not deductible for AMT purposes as qualified housing interest *unless* the proceeds are used to improve the principal residence.

---

[25] § 56(b)(1)(A).

[26] Beginning in 1998, employee business expenses relating to service as an official of a state or local government or political subdivision thereof are deductible for A.G.I. provided the official is compensated on a fee basis. Thus, these expenses become deductible for the AMT system.

[27] In future years, however, any deduction phase out under § 68 will not apply for AMT purposes. See § 68 and § 56(b)(1)(F).

[28] See § 67(b) for a complete list of itemized deductions that are allowed as ATIDs. Also note that a standard deduction is not allowed for AMT purposes.

[29] A qualified dwelling is a house, apartment, condominium, or mobile home (not used on a transient basis). Qualified dwelling for AMT is a narrow definition and differs from that of Code § 280A(f)(1), which broadly defines a dwelling unit as a house, apartment, condominium, mobile home, boat, or similar property.

When interest rates fall, taxpayers often refinance their homes, and a question arose about the interest paid on a loan (new loan) the proceeds of which were used to pay off the original qualified housing indebtedness (old loan). The TRA of 1986 resolved the issue by allowing an interest expense deduction for AMT purposes on the new loan used to refinance the principal residence, but only to the extent that the new loan does not exceed the outstanding balance of the old loan.[30]

Investment interest expense is allowed as an ATID, but only to the extent of qualified *adjusted* net investment income.[31] The adjustment in computing the net investment income is required for AMT purposes as a result of including a portion of the tax-exempt interest income from specified private activity bonds (SPAB) as a tax preference item that increases the AMTI (see *Example 10* for details relating to the tax-exempt income preference item). If exempt interest income from SPABs is included as a preference item for AMT purposes, the interest expense incurred with respect to it will be allowed as a deduction for AMT purposes. These adjustments for tax-exempt income and its related interest expenses are also allowed in computing the "adjusted" net investment income for AMT purposes.

### Circulation and Research Expenditures

For regular tax purposes, § 173 allows newspapers, magazines and other periodicals to immediately deduct circulation expenditures (i.e., costs incurred to establish, maintain, or increase circulation). However, for AMT purposes, circulation expenditures must be capitalized and amortized over a three year period. The same rule applies to research and experimental expenditures, except the amortization period is ten years.[32] However, the Revenue Reconciliation Act of 1989 repealed the AMT adjustment for research expenses of individuals who materially participate in the activity in which research expenses are incurred.[33] As with other adjustments that create a disparity between basis for regular tax and basis for AMT, *separate records must be maintained* to determine the allowable amortization deduction in subsequent years or the gain or loss on disposition or abandonment.

### Gains from Incentive Stock Options (ISOs)

For regular tax purposes, the bargain element of ISOs (i.e., the difference between the fair market value of the stock and the option price) is *not* required to be included in income either at the time the option is granted or when the option is exercised.[34] However, an income adjustment may be required for the AMT. Assuming the stock acquired is not subject to substantial risk of forfeiture, the adjustment to AMTI is equal to the amount by which the value of the share at the time of exercise exceeds the option price. If the stock is disposed of in the option year, however, this income adjustment is not required because the income attributable to the bargain element will be reported under the regular tax system in the same year.

#### Example 5

D receives an incentive stock option to purchase 1,000 shares of her employer's stock at $50 per share. Three years after the receipt of the option, D exercises her option when the stock is selling for $70 per share. When D exercises the option, she has an AMT adjustment of $20,000 ($70,000 – $50,000).

Since the AMT adjustment amount computed above increases the AMTI, an upward basis adjustment in the stock of an equal amount is allowed for AMT purposes. This disparity in the stock's basis for regular tax and the AMT requires an *extra set of books* to determine the amount of gain recognized upon a subsequent disposition of the stock for AMT purposes.

---

[30] § 56(e)(1). See the Tax Reform Act of 1986.

[31] See Chapter 11 for a discussion of the investment interest deduction limitation.

[32] § 56(b)(2)(A)(ii). See Footnote 52, *infra*, for an optional tax accounting method for research and experimental expenditures.

[33] § 56(b)(2)(D). The repeal is effective for taxable years beginning after December 31, 1990.

[34] See Chapter 18 for a discussion of ISOs and § 83.

**Example 6**

Assume the same facts as in *Example 5* and that D holds the stock until it further increases in value to $85,000. If D sells the stock for $85,000, she has a $35,000 gain for regular tax purposes ($85,000 – $50,000). However, for AMT purposes, the gain is $15,000 ($85,000 - AMT basis of $70,000). To reflect the difference in the regular tax and AMT gain, D makes a negative adjustment to AMTI of $20,000 ($35,000 regular tax gain - $15,000 AMT gain) which potentially reduces her tentative AMT in the year of the sale.[35]

### Standard Deduction Not Allowed

Individuals are not permitted to take into account the standard deduction in computing the alternative minimum taxable income.[36]

### Personal Exemptions

Personal exemptions authorized under § 151 are not allowed as deductions in computing the AMTI.[37]

### Adjustment to Income for Tax Refunds

Generally, taxpayers who itemize deductions must report a refund of a prior year's state or local income tax as gross income in the year of receipt.[38] However, since itemized deductions for all tax expenditures are not allowed for AMT purposes, the refund or recovery in *all cases* is excluded from AMTI.

## Adjustment Applicable Only to Corporations

The only adjustment applicable solely to corporate taxpayers[39] is the adjustment based on a corporation's adjusted current earnings—commonly referred to as the *ACE adjustment.*[40] The ACE adjustment, like the minimum tax itself, was the Congressional response to what seemed an increasingly frequent phenomenon: corporations were reporting substantial earnings for financial accounting purposes yet paying little or no income tax. Curiously, this occurred despite the existence of the AMT. To address the problem, Congress created the ACE adjustment. This special adjustment is designed to ensure that all corporations pay some minimum tax on economic income.

In theory, the ACE adjustment is relatively simple. It requires a corporation to compare its economic income to taxable income to determine the amount of economic income, if any, that escaped tax. Part of this elusive income is then included in the corporation's AMTI. Technically, the ACE adjustment is equal to 75 percent of the difference between *adjusted current earnings* and AMTI.[41] In this calculation, adjusted current earnings essentially serve as a substitute for economic income. The actual computation of adjusted current earnings is

---

[35] Taxpayers that have exercised ISOs, properly reported the income for AMT purposes and paid an AMT in the year of exercise, traditionally have looked to the minimum tax credit to reduce the regular tax imposed on the gain from the sale of the stock for regular tax purposes. The AMT rules were designed so that the gain in the regular tax system makes the regular tax larger than the tentative minimum tax and allows the minimum tax credit to reduce the regular tax imposed in excess of the tentative minimum tax. This approach works when the stock appreciates in value but it is flawed if the stock is disposed of after it has decreased in value. There may not be a gain on the disposition in the regular tax system and the taxpayer will not benefit from the minimum tax credit. This situation has been addressed by Congress and is discussed later in this chapter under the refundable minimum tax credit rules.

[36] § 56(b)(1)(E).

[37] *Ibid.*

[38] See § 56(b)(1)(D) and Chapter 6 for an exception based on the tax benefit rule.

[39] Recall, however, that small corporations are exempt from the AMT system. *See supra*, Footnote 3.

[40] This adjustment *does not* apply to certain corporations, including S corporations, regulated investment companies, real estate investment trusts, or real estate mortgage investment conduits. § 56(g)(6).

[41] § 56(g)(1).

quite technical. It begins with AMTI, to which a laundry list of adjustments are made.[42] A discussion of the various adjustments is beyond the scope of this text. Suffice it to say that their collective purpose is to yield the corporation's economic income so its true ability to pay tax can be determined.

### Example 7

T Corporation has AMTI of $200,000 without regard to the ACE adjustment. T's adjusted current earnings are determined to be $400,000. T's regular income tax liability is $41,750. T has an ACE adjustment of $150,000, AMTI of $350,000, a tentative AMT of $70,000, and AMT of $28,250, computed as follows:

| | |
|---|---|
| AMTI before ACE | $ 200,000 |
| Plus: Ace adjustment [($400,000 − $200,000) × 75%] | + 150,000 |
| AMTI | $ 350,000 |
| Less: Exemption amount (completely phased out) | − 0 |
| AMTI base | $ 350,000 |
| Times: AMT rate | × 20% |
| Gross AMT | $ 70,000 |
| Less: AMT foreign tax credit | − 0 |
| Tentative AMT | $ 70,000 |
| Less: Regular tax liability | − 41,750 |
| AMT | $ 28,250 |

This portion of the alternative minimum tax system has been crafted to make certain the AMT is imposed on corporate taxpayers having an economic ability to pay.

## Special Tax Shelter Loss Adjustments

Certain losses that may be deductible for regular tax are *denied* for purposes of the AMT. Specifically, tax shelter farm losses and passive-activity losses allowed as deductions for regular tax purposes must be recomputed under the AMT system, taking into account all of the AMT tax accounting rules.[43] Clearly, a separate set of books will be required for each activity. The amount of the AMT adjustment required by the statute is the difference between the loss allowed for the regular tax system and the loss allowed under the AMT system.

### Tax Shelter Farm Losses

Noncorporate taxpayers and personal service corporations are not allowed to deduct losses from a tax shelter farm activity in computing AMTI.[44] For the AMT system, the disallowed loss will be treated as a deduction allocable to such activity in the *first* succeeding taxable year, and will be allowed to offset income from that activity in any succeeding year. Under this rule, each farm is treated as a separate activity. In the year that the taxpayer disposes of his or her entire interest in any tax shelter farm activity, the amount of previously disallowed loss related to that activity is allowed as a deduction for the year under the AMT system.

### Passive-Activity Losses

As discussed in Chapter 12, there are limitations on the use of losses from passive activities to offset other income of the taxpayer for regular tax purposes.[45] For AMT purposes, similar rules apply, except for AMT purposes a loss generated from a passive activity must be

[42] § 56(g)(4).

[43] These rules are specified in §§ 56 and 57.

[44] § 58(a).

[45] See Chapter 12 for a discussion of passive losses.

recomputed to reflect the AMT rules. This means that depreciation, certain intangible drilling and development costs, certain percentage depletion, and other adjustments and preferences must be reflected in computing the loss for AMT purposes.[46] Because of the differences in the treatment of such items, the amount of suspended losses relating to an activity may differ for minimum tax and regular tax purposes and may require that two sets of books be kept in order to track the passive-loss carryover on each activity.[47]

### Example 8

C has $200,000 of salary income, $50,000 of gross income from passive activities, and $170,000 of deductions from passive activities for the current year. C's passive activity loss is $120,000 for regular tax purposes. Because the recomputed expenses for AMT purposes are only $130,000, the passive-activity loss is $80,000 for AMT purposes. For regular tax purposes, the taxpayer has taxable income of $200,000 and a suspended passive loss in the amount of $120,000 ($170,000 passive deductions – $50,000 passive income). For minimum tax purposes, the taxpayer has AMTI of $200,000 and a suspended passive loss of $80,000 ($130,000 – $50,000).

As illustrated in the example above, the recomputed passive loss using the AMT rules can be significantly different from the regular tax passive loss with respect to an activity. In fact, in some situations it is possible to have a regular tax passive-loss amount *and* an AMT passive income amount on the same activity!

### Example 9

Assume that taxpayer C in the example above had passive-activity deductions of $80,000 for regular tax purposes and $40,000 for minimum tax purposes. C would have regular taxable income of $200,000 and a suspended passive loss of $30,000 ($80,000 – $50,000) for regular tax purposes. For AMT purposes, C has alternative minimum taxable income of $210,000 [$200,000 salary + ($50,000 – $40,000)] and no suspended passive loss for minimum tax purposes.

## Tax Preference Items

Since tax preference items are required to be identified and computed for both corporate and noncorporate taxpayers, all the current preference items are listed in Exhibit 13-5; however, only the most common items are explained below.[48]

**EXHIBIT 13.5 AMT Tax Preference Items**

Percentage depletion in excess of cost basis on certain mineral properties
Certain intangible drilling and development costs
Specified tax-exempt interest
Exclusion for gain on sale of certain small business stock

[46] § 58(b).

[47] P.L. 99-514, Tax Reform Act of 1986, Conference Committee Report, Act § 701.

[48] § 57 sets forth all of the tax preference items and the specifics of each calculation.

### Excess Depletion

The amount of the preference item is the excess (if any) of the percentage depletion claimed for the taxable year over the adjusted basis of the property at the end of the taxable year (determined without regard to the depletion deduction for the taxable year).[49] This computation must be made for each unit of property.

### Intangible Drilling and Development Costs

In general, the amount of the tax preference is equal to the intangible drilling costs (IDC) incurred and deducted on productive oil, gas, and geothermal wells reduced by the sum of:

1. The amount allowed as if the IDCs had been capitalized and amortized over a ten-year period, and
2. Sixty-five percent of the net income for the year from these properties.[50]

If the intangible drilling and development costs are capitalized and amortized in accord with special rules contained in § 59(e), they are not treated as a preference item.[51]

### Private Activity Bond Interest

This preference item pertains to interest income on specified private activity bonds (SPABs) issued after August 7, 1986.[52] The term *private activity bond* means any bond issued if 10 percent of the proceeds of the issue is used for private business use in any trade or business carried on by any person that is not a governmental unit. Where interest income on SPABs is includible in AMTI under the above rule, the regular tax rule of Code § 265 (denying deductions for expenses and interest relating to tax-exempt income) does not apply, and expenses and interest incurred to carry SPABs are deductible for minimum tax purposes.

#### Example 10

Taxpayer P is required to include in AMTI $10,000 of otherwise tax-exempt interest income on SPABs as a preference item. She incurred $900 of interest expense on a temporary loan in order to purchase the bonds. Code § 265 disallows a deduction of this $900 for regular tax purposes, but it is deductible for minimum tax purposes.

### Gain on the Sale of Qualified Small Business Stock

As explained in detail in Chapter 16, the Revenue Reconciliation Act of 1993 created a special incentive to encourage taxpayers to invest in the stock of qualified small businesses (i.e., stock of a C corporation with gross assets of $50 million or less at the time the stock was issued and that was held by the original owner for more than five years prior to sale). Under this special rule, a taxpayer is entitled to exclude 50 percent of the gain on the sale of the stock. However, what Congress gives with the right hand it takes away with the left. Seven percent of this exclusion (or 3.5% of the entire gain) is treated as a tax preference item.[53]

---

[49] § 57(a)(1). This preference was repealed for certain independent producer and royalty interest owners of oil and gas properties for taxable years beginning after 1992.

[50] § 57(a)(2)(E)(ii). The CNEPA of 1992 repealed this preference item for taxpayers (other than certain integrated oil and gas companies) for years beginning after December 31, 1992. However, the repeal of the excess IDCs preference "may not result in more than a 40 percent reduction in the amount of the taxpayer's AMTI computed as if the present-law excess IDC preference had not been repealed."

[51] Code § 59(e) was enacted to provide relief to taxpayers that are subject to the AMT, but through proper planning want to maximize the regular tax deductions and at the same time minimize the impact of the AMT. This section provides an election to capitalize "qualified expenditures" and deduct them ratably over a 10-year period (three years in the case of circulation expenditures). Qualified expenditures include IDCs, circulation, research and experimentation, and mining exploration and development costs.

[52] § 57(a)(5)(C)(iv).

[53] § 57(a)(7), as amended by the Tax Relief, Unemployment Insurance Reauthorization and Job Creation Act of 2010. The rule is applicable for tax years beginning before 2013.

### Example 11

On October 31, 2011, J sold qualified small business stock and recognized a gain of $80,000. Only 50 percent of the gain, $40,000, is subject to regular tax, and the remaining $40,000 is excluded. For AMT purposes, J has a tax preference of $2,800 (7% × $40,000).

## ALTERNATIVE MINIMUM TAX COMPUTATIONS

Before the alternative minimum tax calculations can be made, the taxpayer's current taxable income and Federal income tax liability must first be determined. As shown in Exhibit 13-1, a taxpayer's AMT liability is the excess of the tentative minimum tax over the regular tax liability. To further examine this interaction, a factual situation is presented below in *Example 12*, where the taxpayer's regular tax liability is determined. The same facts are then used to compute the ATIDs in *Example 13* and the taxpayer's AMT liability in *Example 14*.

### Example 12

T is a married taxpayer filing a joint return for 2011. He had the following items of income, expenses, and regular tax liability for the year:

| | | |
|---|---|---|
| Income: | | |
| Salary | $88,000 | |
| Interest | 12,000 | |
| Adjusted gross income | | $100,000(1) |
| Itemized deductions: | | |
| Medical expenses [$9,500 total – (7.5% of $100,000 A.G.I.)] | $ 2,000 | |
| Real property taxes on home | 12,000 | |
| Real property taxes on mountain range property | 8,000 | |
| Personal property taxes | 4,000 | |
| Interest expense: | | |
| Residence interest | 20,000(2) | |
| Investment interest on mountain range property ($12,000 total, but limited to) | 4,000(3) | |
| Charitable contributions | 10,000 | |
| Casualty loss [$13,000 total – (10% of A.G.I.)] | 3,000 | |
| Miscellaneous itemized deductions [$11,000 total – (2% of A.G.I.)] | 9,000 | |
| Total itemized deductions | | – 72,000 |
| Personal exemptions (2 × $3,700) | | – 7,400 |
| Taxable income | | $20,600 |
| Regular tax | | $ 2,240 |

(1) Although not required to be included in his taxable income, T exercised an incentive stock option for $20,000 when the fair market value of the stock was $80,000.

(2) Residence interest includes $18,000 of qualified housing interest (interest on mortgage to acquire home) and $2,000 of interest on a home equity loan to buy a boat.

(3) The mountain range property was acquired as a speculative investment and was 90 percent debt-financed. Recall that interest on investment indebtedness is allowed as a deduction under § 163(d) to the extent of net investment income. Net investment income = $12,000 interest – $8,000 property taxes = $4,000. Thus the $12,000 interest expense is limited to $4,000.

## Example 13

Refer to *Example 12*. T's 2011 alternative tax itemized deductions (ATIDs) and the resulting AMT adjustments are determined as follows:

| | *Allowed ATIDs for AMT* | *Allowed Itemized Deductions for Regular Tax* | *AMT Adjustments* |
|---|---|---|---|
| Medical expenses (in excess of 10% of A.G.I.) .... | $ 0* | $ 2,000 | $ 2,000 |
| Itemized deductions for taxes (not allowed) ..... | 0 | 24,000 | 24,000 |
| Qualified housing interest .................. | 18,000 | 18,000 | 0 |
| Home equity loan ........................ | 0 | 2,000 | 2,000 |
| Other qualified interest (limited to net investment income, = $12,000) .................. | 12,000** | 4,000 | (8,000)** |
| Casualty losses ......................... | 3,000 | 3,000 | 0 |
| Charitable contributions .................... | 10,000 | 10,000 | 0 |
| Miscellaneous itemized deductions (not allowed) .. | 0 | 9,000 | 9,000 |
| Totals ............................... | $ 43,000 | $ 72,000 | $ 29,000 |

*$9,500 does not exceed 10% of $100,000, or $10,000.
**The real property taxes on the investment mountain property are not deductible for AMT purposes. See § 56(b)(1)(C)(v).

Note that the computations for ATIDs are similar to those in *Example 12* for itemized deductions except (1) the reduction in medical expenses is 10% of the regular tax A.G.I. rather than 7.5%, (2) deductions for state and local taxes are not allowed, (3) the miscellaneous itemized deductions are not allowed, (4) the interest on the home equity loan to purchase the boat is not allowed and (5) in the calculation of net investment income, the real property taxes on the mountain property are excludable for AMT purposes. The differences between the ATIDs allowed for AMT purposes and the itemized deductions allowed for regular tax purposes result in AMT adjustments. These adjustments are added back to T's regular taxable income to arrive at AMT adjusted taxable income and are reported on Form 6251, Computation of Alternative Minimum Tax for Individuals.

## Example 14

Refer to *Examples 12 and 13*. T's alternative minimum tax (AMT) 2011 is computed as follows:

| | | |
|---|---|---|
| Regular taxable income ................. | | $ 20,600 |
| Plus: | Net adjustment for itemized deductions ........ | + 29,000(1) |
| | Net adjustment for exercise of ISO ........ | + 60,000(2) |
| | Adjustment for personal exemptions ........ | + 7,400 |
| AMT adjusted taxable income ........ | | $117,000 |
| Plus: | Tax preference items ........ | + 0 |
| Alternative minimum taxable income (AMTI) ........ | | $117,000 |
| Less: | Exemption amount 2011 (married filing jointly) ........ | – 74,450 |
| AMT base (taxable excess) ........ | | $ 42,550 |
| Times: | AMT rate ........ | × 26% |

| | |
|---|---|
| Gross alternative minimum tax . . . . . . . . . | $ 11,063 |
| Less: AMT foreign tax credit . . . . . . . . . | – 0 |
| Tentative minimum tax . . . . . . . . . | $ 11,063 |
| Less: Regular tax liability . . . . . . . . . | – 2,240 |
| AMT liability for 2011 . . . . . . . . . | $ 8,823 |

| | |
|---|---|
| (1) Regular tax itemized deductions | $72,000 |
| ATIDs allowed for AMT | (43,000) |
| Disallowed itemized deductions increase in the AMTI | $29,000 |
| (2) Stock FMV when ISO exercised | $80,000 |
| Option price | (20,000) |
| Excess is AMT adjustment that increases AMTI | $60,000 |

Since the tentative minimum tax of $11,063 *exceeds* his $2,240 regular tax liability (computed in *Example 12*), T must pay the difference of $8,823 for 2011 because of the alternative minimum tax. Note that T must pay a total of $11,063 in taxes for 2011 ($2,240 regular income tax + $8,823 alternative minimum tax).

The previous example illustrates an unfortunate consequence of the strict application of the AMT provisions. The tax benefits of longstanding regular-tax incentive provisions such as home ownership (e.g., deductibility of interest and real property taxes) and medical expenses are either decreased or totally eliminated by the AMT. Although Congress continues to support the objectives of these incentives, their use by individuals to avoid all or most of their Federal income tax liability is not the intent of the law. Recent changes to the AMT are an attempt to minimize such perceived abuses. As illustrated in *Example 14*, because of the limited definition of ATIDs and the decreasing Federal income tax rates, it is possible that many unsuspecting individuals (like T) will be subject to the AMT.[54] Consequently, tax planning to avoid or minimize the AMT is becoming more important for a growing number of taxpayers. As an adjunct to planning for the impact of the AMT, it should be remembered that each taxpayer has the responsibility to maintain adequate records to support the accuracy of the amounts of tax preferences and adjustments used in the AMT computation [as required by Reg. § 1.57-5(a)].

A completed Form 6251, based on the facts from *Examples 12, 13, and 14*, is contained in Exhibit 13-6. The 2010 form is used because the 2011 form was not available at the publication date of this text.

## Minimum Tax Credit

Although the second half of this chapter is devoted entirely to credits, it is perhaps best to cover credits related to the AMT at this point. The first of these is the credit for the AMT.

One significant feature of the AMT system is that many taxpayers are required to pay the AMT on income from certain investments long before they would have had to pay the regular income tax on the same income. For example, taxpayers with substantial investments in depreciable personal property are *denied* the tax reduction benefits of MACRS for purposes of computing the AMT.[55] Likewise, a taxpayer who exercises an ISO must recognize income for AMT purposes to the extent the fair market value of the stock exceeds its option price, but for regular income tax purposes the taxpayer does not recognize income until the stock acquired with the ISO is sold. Without some form of relief, a taxpayer could be subject to the AMT in one year and the regular tax in a later year on the same item.

---

[54] *N. Holly v. Comm.*, T.C. Memo 1998-55.

[55] Recall that depreciable personal property placed in service after 1986 can be depreciated using either the 150 percent declining balance or the ADS straight-line method over the asset's class life for AMT purposes.

**EXHIBIT 13.6** **Form 6251 Alternative Minimum Tax for Individuals**

Form **6251** | **Alternative Minimum Tax—Individuals** | OMB No. 1545-0074

Department of the Treasury Internal Revenue Service (99)

▶ See separate instructions.

▶ Attach to Form 1040 or Form 1040NR.

**2010** Attachment Sequence No. **32**

Name(s) shown on Form 1040 or Form 1040NR: *MR. AND MRS. T*

Your social security number: *324 91 0070*

**Part I Alternative Minimum Taxable Income** (See instructions for how to complete each line.)

| | |  |  |
|---|---|---|---|
| 1 | If filing Schedule A (Form 1040), enter the amount from Form 1040, line 41 (minus any amount on Form 8914, line 6), and go to line 2. Otherwise, enter the amount from Form 1040, line 38 (minus any amount on Form 8914, line 6), and go to line 7. (If less than zero, enter as a negative amount.) | 1 | *28,000* |
| 2 | Medical and dental. Enter the **smaller** of Schedule A (Form 1040), line 4, **or** 2.5% (.025) of Form 1040, line 38. If zero or less, enter -0- | 2 | *2,000* |
| 3 | Taxes from Schedule A (Form 1040), lines 5, 6, and 8 | 3 | *24,000* |
| 4 | Enter the home mortgage interest adjustment, if any, from line 6 of the worksheet on page 2 of the instructions | 4 | *2,000* |
| 5 | Miscellaneous deductions from Schedule A (Form 1040), line 27 | 5 | *9,000* |
| 6 | If Form 1040, line 38, is over $166,800 (over $83,400 if married filing separately), enter the amount from line 11 of the **Itemized Deductions Worksheet** on page A-11 of the instructions for Schedule A (Form 1040) | 6 | ( ) |
| 7 | If filing Schedule L (Form 1040A or 1040), enter as a negative amount the sum of lines 6 and 20 from that schedule | 7 | ( ) |
| 8 | Tax refund from Form 1040, line 10 or line 21 | 8 | ( ) |
| 9 | Investment interest expense (difference between regular tax and AMT) | 9 | *(8,000)* |
| 10 | Depletion (difference between regular tax and AMT) | 10 | |
| 11 | Net operating loss deduction from Form 1040, line 21. Enter as a positive amount | 11 | |
| 12 | Alternative tax net operating loss deduction | 12 | |
| 13 | Interest from specified private activity bonds exempt from the regular tax | 13 | |
| 14 | Qualified small business stock (7% of gain excluded under section 1202) | 14 | *60,000* |
| 15 | Exercise of incentive stock options (excess of AMT income over regular tax income) | 15 | |
| 16 | Estates and trusts (amount from Schedule K-1 (Form 1041), box 12, code A) | 16 | |
| 17 | Electing large partnerships (amount from Schedule K-1 (Form 1065-B), box 6) | 17 | |
| 18 | Disposition of property (difference between AMT and regular tax gain or loss) | 18 | |
| 19 | Depreciation on assets placed in service after 1986 (difference between regular tax and AMT) | 19 | |
| 20 | Passive activities (difference between AMT and regular tax income or loss) | 20 | |
| 21 | Loss limitations (difference between AMT and regular tax income or loss) | 21 | |
| 22 | Circulation costs (difference between regular tax and AMT) | 22 | |
| 23 | Long-term contracts (difference between AMT and regular tax income) | 23 | |
| 24 | Mining costs (difference between regular tax and AMT) | 24 | |
| 25 | Research and experimental costs (difference between regular tax and AMT) | 25 | ( ) |
| 26 | Income from certain installment sales before January 1, 1987 | 26 | |
| 27 | Intangible drilling costs preference | 27 | |
| 28 | Other adjustments, including income-based related adjustments | 28 | ( ) |
| 29 | **Alternative minimum taxable income.** Combine lines 1 through 28. (If married filing separately and line 29 is more than $216,900, see page 8 of the instructions.) | 29 | *117,000* |

Taxable income before exemptions ($20,600 + $7,400 = $28,000)

**Part II Alternative Minimum Tax (AMT)**

30 Exemption. (If you were under age 24 at the end of 2009, see page 8 of the instructions.)

| **IF your filing status is . . .** | **AND line 29 is not over . . .** | **THEN enter on line 30 . . .** |
|---|---|---|
| Single or head of household | $112,500 | $46,700 |
| Married filing jointly or qualifying widow(er) | 150,000 | 70,950 |
| Married filing separately | 75,000 | 35,475 |

If line 29 is **over** the amount shown above for your filing status, see page 8 of the instructions. — **30** *74,450*

2011 Exemption

| | |  |  |
|---|---|---|---|
| 31 | Subtract line 30 from line 29. If more than zero, go to line 32. If zero or less, enter -0- here and on lines 34 and 36 and skip the rest of Part II. | 31 | *42,250* |
| 32 | • If you are filing Form 2555 or 2555-EZ, see page 9 of the instructions for the amount to enter.<br>• If you reported capital gain distributions directly on Form 1040, line 13; you reported qualified dividends on Form 1040, line 9b; **or** you had a gain on both lines 15 and 16 of Schedule D (Form 1040) (as refigured for the AMT, if necessary), complete Part III on the back and enter the amount from line 55 here.<br>• **All others:** If line 31 is $175,000 or less ($87,500 or less if married filing separately), multiply line 31 by 26% (.26). Otherwise, multiply line 31 by 28% (.28) and subtract $3,500 ($1,750 if married filing separately) from the result. | 32 | *11,063* |
| 33 | Alternative minimum tax foreign tax credit (see page 9 of the instructions) | 33 | |
| 34 | Tentative minimum tax. Subtract line 33 from line 32 | 34 | *11,063* |
| 35 | Tax from Form 1040, line 44 (minus any tax from Form 4972 and any foreign tax credit from Form 1040, line 47). If you used Schedule J to figure your tax, the amount from line 44 of Form 1040 must be refigured without using Schedule J (see page 11 of the instructions) | 35 | *2,240* |
| 36 | **AMT.** Subtract line 35 from line 34. If zero or less, enter -0-. Enter here and on Form 1040, line 45 | 36 | *8,823* |

**For Paperwork Reduction Act Notice, see page 12 of the instructions.** Cat. No. 13600G Form **6251** (2010)

In order to limit the possibility of double taxation under the two tax systems, Congress introduced an AMT credit. Basically, the AMT paid in one year may be used as a credit against the taxpayer's *regular* tax liability in subsequent years. The credit may be carried forward indefinitely until used; however, the credit cannot be carried back *nor*, until recently, could it be used to offset any future AMT liability.[56]

## Example 15

In 2010, J paid an alternative minimum tax, and his AMT credit after making the appropriate adjustments was $20,000. In 2011, J's regular tax liability before considering the minimum tax credit, is $45,000 and his *tentative* minimum tax is $40,000. Since J's regular tax exceeds his tentative minimum tax, there is no AMT for 2011. In computing his final tax liability, J is entitled to use the minimum tax credit against his regular tax liability but only to the extent that it does not create an AMT (i.e., bring his regular tax liability below his tentative minimum tax). Consequently, he may use $5,000 of the credit, reducing his regular tax liability to $40,000, as shown below. The remaining $15,000 of the minimum tax credit may be carried forward indefinitely.

| | | |
|---|---|---|
| Regular tax liability | | $45,000 |
| Minimum tax credit: | | |
| Limitation | | |
| Regular tax | $ 45,000 | |
| Tentative minimum tax | – 40,000 | |
| Allowable minimum tax credit | | – 5,000 |
| Total tax due | | $40,000 |

Note that the minimum tax credit effectively converts the AMT from a permanent out-of-pocket tax to a prepayment of regular tax to the extent the AMT is attributable to deferral or timing preferences and adjustments rather than to exclusion items.[57]

For noncorporate taxpayers, the minimum tax credit for any year is the amount of the taxpayer's *adjusted net minimum tax* for all tax years after reduction for the minimum tax credit utilized for all such prior years. The adjusted net minimum tax, generally the amount of the minimum tax credit, is the difference between the AMT actually paid and the amount of AMT that would have been paid if only exclusion items were taken into account. The exclusion items are listed below.

1. Itemized deductions or standard deduction
2. Personal exemptions
3. Percentage depletion treated as a preference
4. Tax-exempt interest treated as a preference
5. The preference amount computed on the sale of the § 1202 stock.

[56] § 53(a). See next section for discussion of AMT refundable credit.

[57] § 53(d)(1)(B)(iv) authorizes corporate taxpayers to use the entire minimum tax liability as the minimum tax credit.

## Example 16

J is married and files a joint return for the current year on which she reports $79,200 of taxable income and claims the standard deduction. In computing her taxable income, J excluded $56,000 of tax-exempt interest from SPABs, which creates a $56,000 AMT preference item, and she claimed a $100,000 deduction for research expenses from an activity in which she does not materially participate, which creates a $90,000 AMT adjustment for research and experimental expenditures. J's minimum tax credit to be carried forward is $29,616, as computed below.

The amount of AMT actually required to be paid is $38,574, determined as follows:

| | | |
|---|---|---|
| Regular taxable income | | $ 79,200 |
| Plus: | AMT adjustment for research expenses | + 90,000 |
| | AMT adjustment for personal exemptions | + 7,400 |
| | AMT adjustment for standard deduction | + 11,600 |
| | AMT preference item for SPAB income | + 56,000 |
| AMTI | | $ 244,200 |
| Less: | Exemption amount 2011 [$74,450 – 23,550 phase-out ($244,200 – $150,000 = $94,200 × 0.25)] | – 50,900 |
| AMT base | | $ 193,300 |
| Tentative minimum tax [$45,500 + 28% ($193,300 – $175,000)] | | $ 50,624 |
| Less: | Regular tax liability for 2011 | – 12,050 |
| AMT liability for current year | | $ 38,574 |

The amount of AMT that would have been required to be paid if only exclusion items were taken into account is determined as follows:

| | | |
|---|---|---|
| Regular taxable income | | $ 79,200 |
| Plus: | AMT adjustment for personal exemptions | + 7,400 |
| | AMT adjustment for standard deduction | + 11,600 |
| | Tax preference item for SPAB income | + 56,000 |
| AMTI | | $ 154,200 |
| Less: | Exemption amount (no phase-out) [$74,450 – $1,050 phase-out ($154,200 – $150,000 = $4,200 × .25)] | – 73,400 |
| | AMT base | $ 80,800 |
| Times: | AMT rate | × 26% |
| Tentative AMT | | $ 21,008 |
| Less: | Regular tax liability | –12,050 |
| AMT using only exclusions | | $ 8,958 |

The minimum tax credit is computed as follows:

| | |
|---|---|
| AMT liability for current year | $ 38,574 |
| AMT using only exclusion items | – 8,958 |
| Minimum tax credit | $ 29,616 |

The $29,616 minimum tax credit may be carried forward and used to offset (reduce) the regular tax liability in subsequent years.

## AMT Refundable Tax Credit

As part of the Tax Relief and Health Care Act of 2006, Congress created an AMT refundable credit. The relief provided by this credit is intended primarily for individuals who had minimum tax credits but could not use them. This problem normally occurred when individuals exercised ISOs at a profit and subsequently sold the stock when the price had significantly declined. Taxpayers in these situations normally paid an AMT on the profit in the year of the exercise, producing an AMT credit. However, because of the diminution in value of the stock at the time of the sale, little or no gain was recognized for regular tax purposes and the AMT credit could not be used. As a result, such individuals ended up with large minimum tax credits that they may not be able to use for many years to come.

### Example 17

During the height of the bull market in 2000, T was working for a high-tech company. While there, she exercised an ISO to buy her employer's stock worth $1,000,000 for $9,000. As a result, T had an AMT adjustment of $991,000 and paid an AMT of $277,000. This in turn created a minimum tax credit (MTC) of $277,000. Consistent with the AMT rules, T's AMT basis in the acquired stock was $1,000,000 ($9,000 cost plus the $991,000 adjustment). In 2002, the company went bankrupt. For regular tax purposes, the worthless stock is deemed to have been sold for $0 (basis $9,000), resulting in a long-term capital loss of $9,000. For AMT purposes, the rules are the same but because her basis is $1,000,000, she has an AMT capital loss of $1,000,000. Unfortunately, she has no AMT capital gains and all she can deduct for AMT purposes in the current year is the same amount that she can deduct for regular tax purposes, $3,000.[58] Although the MTC of $277,000 can be used to offset the regular tax in excess of the TMT in subsequent years, she may receive little or no benefit from the MTC in the future.

To address the problem illustrated above, Congress created a special credit. Beginning in 2007, § 53(e) generally allows taxpayers that have long-term unused minimum tax credit carryovers to claim a *refundable* AMT credit for each taxable year prior to 2013. For taxable years after 2007 the AMT refundable credit amount each year is the greater of:

**A.** 50 percent of the long term unused minimum tax credit for the year, or

**B.** The amount (if any) of the AMT refundable credit determined for the taxpayer's preceding year.

The long-term unused minimum tax credit for a tax year is the portion of the MTC available at the beginning of the third tax year immediately preceding the current year. For example, for the tax year 2011, the available credit would be that which existed at the beginning of 2008. In applying the rules, the credits are treated as allowed on a FIFO basis. Note also that the credit is available for only individual taxpayers. In addition, because it is refundable, this credit reduces both the AMT liability and the regular tax liability and the remainder of the credit amount being paid to the taxpayer as a refund.

### Example 18

Refer to the facts in the previous example and assume that T has a MTC carryover at the beginning of 2008 of $277,000. In addition, assume that T is married to H, has two children in college, files a joint return and takes the standard deduction. The couple's only income is T's salary of $124,300 from which T's employer withheld $18,000 in federal income tax. The couple's regular tax liability for 2011 is $16,975 and they have no AMT liability for the year and no other credits are allowable. As a result, T's AMT refundable credit amount is $138,500 (50% × $277,000). In this case, $16,975 (the

[58] See *Merlo v. Comm.*, 126 TC 205 (2006).

amount of the couple's regular tax) is treated as a nonrefundable credit and the remaining $121,525 is treated as a refundable credit. T's refund for the year will also include the $18,000 of federal income tax that she had withheld from her salary, for a total refund of $139,525.

### Example 19

Refer to the facts in previous two examples to compute the AMT refundable credit for 2012. Assume that the couple's only income is T's salary of $124,300 from which T's employer withheld no federal income tax. Assume the couple's regular tax liability for 2012 is $16,725 and they have no AMT liability for the year and no other credits are allowable. The couple's AMT refundable credit amount is $138,500 as computed below. The AMT refundable credit amount is the greater of:

**A.** 50% of the long-term unused minimum tax credit for the year $138,500 (50% × $277,000) or

**B.** The amount of the credit for the preceding year, $138,500 in 2011.

In 2012 $16,725 is treated as a nonrefundable credit and the $121,775 is treated as a refundable credit, providing a refund to the couple of $121,775.

## ✓ Check Your Knowledge

### Review Question 1

After completing his tax return for the year, C has a regular tax liability of $30,000, a tentative minimum tax of $45,000, and an alternative minimum tax of $15,000. How much does C actually owe the IRS?

C owes $45,000 in taxes, consisting of a regular tax liability of $30,000 and an AMT liability of $15,000.

### Review Question 2

True-False. Jack is a professional golfer, earning more than $800,000 on the tour this year. After deducting expenses, taxable income for the year is $500,000. He and his wife are entitled to a $74,450 (2011) exemption in computing their alternative minimum tax liability.

*False.* The exemption phases out once their AMTI exceeds $150,000 and is completely phased out when AMTI reaches $447,800. Based on the size of his earnings, it would appear that his AMTI exceeds $447,800 so that the exemption would provide no benefit.

### Review Question 3

True-False. In determining AMTI, the taxpayer begins with taxable income and then adds back all of the deductions allowed by so-called loopholes. There are no negative adjustments.

*False.* Although the effect of the AMTI is to fill in the loopholes, adjustments may be positive or negative (e.g., when AMT depreciation exceeds regular tax depreciation). All tax preference items are positive.

### Review Question 4

True-False. Steelco Corporation acquired several new copying machines for its offices and depreciated them under MACRS, using the 200 percent declining-balance method and a five-year recovery period. For AMT purposes, Steelco must use the straight-line method and a six-year class life. (**Hint:** See Revenue Procedure 87-56 and Exhibit 9-2).

*False*. Steelco may use the recovery period of five years, but is only allowed to use 150 percent declining-balance in computing depreciation for personal property for AMT purposes.

### Review Question 5

Fred and Ethel are married with two children. Fred is a partner in a public accounting firm. Ethel recently retired as a traveling salesperson for an athletic shoe manufacturer. After completing their return, Fred and Ethel realized that they may have to pay the alternative minimum tax. Indicate whether an adjustment is required for AMT purposes for the following items that the couple reported for regular tax purposes.

**a.** Personal exemptions for Fred and Ethel
**b.** Dependent exemptions for their children
**c.** Social security benefits that were nontaxable, $10,000
**d.** Contribution to individual retirement account, $2,000
**e.** Fred's membership dues to the Indiana C.P.A. Society reimbursed by his employer, $200
**f.** Straight-line depreciation on their newly acquired duplex, which they are currently renting out, $6,000
**g.** State income taxes, $10,000
**h.** Property taxes on their personal residence, $4,000
**i.** Tax-exempt interest from City of Indianapolis bonds used to finance its downtown mall, $2,000 (the bonds were issued after August 7, 1988)
**j.** State income tax refund, $500
**k.** Interest on the mortgage on their personal residence, $22,000
**l.** Interest on a second mortgage on their residence (proceeds used to add a porch), $3,600
**m.** Ethel's unreimbursed travel and entertainment expenses related to her employment, $1,000
**n.** Alimony to Fred's ex-wife, Luci, $4,000

An adjustment is required for (a) and (b) (exemptions not allowed), (f) (40- vs. 39-year life), (g) and (h) (taxes), (i) (private activity bond), (j) (no AMT income for tax refunds), and (m) (miscellaneous itemized deduction). No adjustment is required for (c), (d), (e) (reimbursed employee business expense deductible for A.G.I.), (k) (qualified housing interest), (l) (home equity loan used for improvement to house is qualified housing interest), or (n) (no adjustment required).

### Review Question 6

GHI Construction Corporation, a calendar year taxpayer, specializes in building warehouses. Its annual gross receipts average about $8 million. The corporation began work on a building in November 2011 and finished construction in February 2012. The contract was approximately 40 percent complete as of the close of the year. For regular tax purposes, the corporation uses the completed contract method. Consequently, it reported all of the income from the contract, $100,000, in 2012.

**a.** What is the amount of the AMT adjustment for 2011, if any?

**b.** Assume that the AMT attributable to the above contract was $8,000 (20% × $40,000) and that GHI paid this amount as AMT when it filed its 2011 tax return. In 2012, GHI reported the entire $100,000 profit for regular tax purposes. Is the $40,000 of profit earned in 2011 taxed twice, once under the AMT system when it is included as a $40,000 adjustment in 2011 and once under the regular tax system when it is included in the $100,000 reported in 2012?

*No*. The AMT paid in 2011 may be credited against the regular tax in 2012. The minimum tax credit ensures that the income is not taxed twice. Note that in this case the AMT effectively operates to accelerate the income tax paid on a portion of the $100,000 profit.

## Income Tax Credits

One reason tax credits are popular is that a credit is viewed as providing a more equitable benefit than a comparable deduction. This is because a credit is a direct reduction of the tax liability, while a deduction merely reduces the amount of taxable income. This difference is illustrated in *Example 20*.

**Example 20**

Hi is in the 36% tax bracket, and Lo is in the 15% tax bracket. A credit of $100 is worth the *same* to both taxpayers since it reduces the tax liability of each by $100. On the other hand, a deduction of $100 provides a *different* benefit for each: $36 (36% × $100) for Hi and only $15 (15% × $100) for Lo.

The results from *Example 20* can be generalized for tax policy as (1) all taxpayers receive the *same dollar benefit* from credits, regardless of marginal tax rates; (2) taxpayers with higher marginal tax rates benefit more from tax deductions than do those with lower marginal rates; and (3) taxpayers receive more benefit from tax credits than from tax deductions of the same amount. In addition, the argument has been made that credits are of more benefit to those with lower incomes. This is based on the reasoning that the $100 tax saved has more relative value for those with low incomes than it has for those with high incomes. However, this line of reasoning is questionable since taxable income is just one inexact measure of a person's economic situation.

## Overview of Tax Credits

In recent years, the number of tax credits has been significantly increased by Congress. Most of them have been enacted into law to achieve a specified social, economic, or political goal. These goals range from encouraging taxpayers to engage in scientific research (the research credit) and the conservation of energy (energy tax credits) to providing compensatory tax reductions for those individuals who may carry greater burdens than others (credits for the elderly and for individuals with low earned incomes).

As the table in Exhibit 13-7 illustrates, the credit provisions are divided into *six* major groups. Technically these are all subparts of Part IV - Credits Against Tax contained in Subchapter A of the Code. Subpart A consists of nonrefundable individual tax credits and Subpart B contains certain other nonrefundable credits. All of these nonrefundable credits may be used to reduce the tax liability, but *only* to the extent of the "regular tax liability." Subpart C contains the *refundable* credits. Subpart D consists of 13 separate credits, which are combined to form the "general business credit." The minimum tax credits are contained in Subpart G. And finally, the credit to holders of clean renewable energy bonds is in Subpart H. A quick look at the Exhibit reveals that Congress has gone wild on credits. While some of the credits have widespread applicability, many apply to a very limited group of taxpayers.

### Limitation on Nonrefundable Credits

The nonrefundable credits may be used to reduce only the taxpayer's regular tax liability as that quantity is defined in §26. Under § 26, a taxpayer's "regular tax liability" does not include (1) the alternative minimum tax (§ 55); (2) the additional tax imposed on distributions from certain annuities [§ 72(m)]; (3) the additional tax imposed on distributions from educational IRAs [§ 530(d)]; (4) the accumulated earnings tax (§ 531); (5) the personal holding company tax (§ 541); (6) the tax on certain capital gains of S corporations (§ 1374); or (7) the tax on passive income of S corporations (§ 1375). Thus, the nonrefundable credits cannot be used to offset penalty taxes imposed by the Code (e.g., personal holding company tax, accumulated earnings tax, etc.). The practical impact of defining the "regular tax liability" in this manner is that the regular tax credits cannot offset the alternative minimum tax. Note, however that for taxable years 2002 through 2009 Congress generally has authorized the nonrefundable personal credits to offset the AMT as well as the regular tax liability.[59]

For taxpayers to whom two or more credits apply, generally the Code specifies an ascending order for the use of nonrefundable credits. Nonrefundable credits are to be used to reduce the § 26 tax liability in the following order: §§ 21, 22, 25A, 25, 25B, 24, 27, 23, 29, 30,

[59] *Huntsberry v. Comm.*, 83 T.C. 742. But see Footnote 8 for an amendment to § 26(a) that allows personal credits to offset the AMT for the years 2000 through 2009

## EXHIBIT 13.7 Table of Tax Credits

| | *Code Section* | *Specific Credit* | *Termination Date* |
|---|---|---|---|
| *Subpart A:* | § 21 | Child and Dependent Care Credit | None |
| | § 22 | Credit for the Elderly | None |
| | § 24 | Child Tax Credit | None |
| | § 25 | Credit for Interest on Certain Home Mortgages | None |
| | § 25A | Hope and Lifetime Learning Credits | None |
| | § 25B | IRA Contribution Credit | None |
| | § 25C | Residential Energy Property Credit | 12/31/2011 |
| | § 25D | Residential Alternative Energy Credit | 12/31/2016 |
| | § 25F | Employer Provided Childcare Credit | 12/31/2012 |
| *Subpart B:* | § 27 | Possession and Foreign Tax Credit | None |
| | § 30 | Credit for Qualified Electric Vehicle | 12/31/2011 |
| | § 30B | Alternative Motor Vehicle Credit | 12/31/2014 |
| | § 30C | Alternative Motor Vehicle Refueling Property Credit | 12/31/2011 |
| | § 30D | New Qualified Plug-In Electric Drive Motor Vehicles | 12/31/2014 |
| *Subpart C:* | § 31 | Credit for Taxes Withheld on Wages | None |
| | § 32 | Earned Income Credit | None |
| | § 33 | Credit for Taxes Withheld at Source on Nonresident Aliens and Foreign Corporations | None |
| | § 34 | Credit for Certain Uses of Gasoline and Special Fuels | None |
| | § 35 | Health Insurance credit | None |
| | § 36 | Credit for Adoption Expenses | 12/31/2011 |
| *Subpart D:* | § 38 | General Business Credit (including) | |
| | | **1.** Alcohol Fuels Credit (§ 40) | 12/31/2011 |
| | | **2.** Research Credit (§ 41) | 12/31/2011 |
| | | **3.** Low-Income Housing Credit (§ 42) | None |
| | | **4.** Enhanced Oil Recovery Credit (§ 43) | None |
| | | **5.** Disabled Individual Access Credit (§ 44) | None |
| | | **6.** Renewable Electricity Production (§ 45) | None |
| | | **7.** Indian Employment Credit (§ 45A) | 12/31/2011 |
| | | **8.** Employer Social Security Credit (§ 45B) | None |
| | | **9.** Credit for Clinical Testing of Certain Drugs (§ 45C) | None |
| | | **10.** New Markets Tax Credit (§ 45D) | 12/31/2012 |
| | | **11.** Small Employer Pension Plan Start Up Costs (§ 45E) | 12/31/2012 |
| | | **12.** Employer Provided Child Care Credit (§ 45F) | 12/31/2012 |
| | | **13.** Railroad Track Maintenance Credit (§ 45G) | 12/31/2011 |
| | | **14.** Credit for production of low sulfur diesel fuel (§ 45H) | None |
| | | **15.** Credit for producing oil and gas from marginal wells (§ 45I) | None |
| | | **16.** Credit for production from advanced nuclear power facilities (§ 45J) | None |
| | | **17.** Credit for producing fuel from a non-conventional source (§ 45K) | None |
| | | **18.** New Energy Efficient Home Credit (§ 45L) | 12/31/2011 |
| | | **19.** Energy Efficient Appliance Credit (§ 45M) | 12/31/2011 |
| | | **20.** Mine Rescue Team Training Credit (§ 45N) | 12/31/2011 |

| | *Code Section* | *Specific Credit* | *Termination Date* |
|---|---|---|---|
| | | **21.** Agricultural Chemical Security Credit (§ 45O) | 12/31/2012 |
| | | **22.** Differential Wage Payment Credit (§ 45P) | None |
| | | **23.** Carbon Dioxide Sequestration (§ 45Q) | None |
| | | **24.** Rehabilitation Credit (§ 47) | None |
| | | **25.** Energy Credit (§ 48) | 12/31/2016 |
| | | **26.** Qualifying Advanced Coal Project Credit (§ 48A) | None |
| | | **27.** Qualifying Gasification Project Credit (§48B) | None |
| | | **28.** Work Opportunity Credit (§ 51) | 8/31/2011 |
| | | **29.** Empowerment Zone Employment Credit (§ 1396) | 12/31/2011 |
| *Subpart G:* | § 53 | Credit for Prior Year Minimum Tax Liability | None |
| | § 53(e) | AMT Refundable Credit | 12/31/2012 |
| *Subpart H:* | § 54 | Credit to holders of Clean Renewable Energy Bonds | 12/31/2010 |

30A, 38 and 53.[60] This order is important because some of the credits may be carried forward or back and utilized in different tax years, while others "fall through the cracks" (i.e., provide no tax benefit) if they exceed the § 26 tax liability in the year they originate.

### Refundable Credits

Refundable credits—listed in Exhibit 13-7 under Subpart C—are accounted for *after* the nonrefundable ones and may be applied against *any* income tax imposed by the Code-including the penalty taxes. As the name suggests, refundable credits may result in the taxpayer receiving a refund check for an amount in excess of any Federal taxes paid or withheld. In a sense, these credit provisions may result in a "negative income tax."

Due to the magnitude and relative importance of the business credits, they are examined first. A discussion of the tax credits available only to individual taxpayers immediately follows.

## General Business Credit

As shown in Exhibit 13-7, the general business credit actually consists of a variety separate credits that are commonly available to business. Each of these credits is separately computed under its own set of rules. The various credits are then combined to determine the current year's total business credit. The credits are combined in order to determine an overall limitation on the amount of credit that can be used.

In order to prevent taxpayers from using business credits to avoid paying all income taxes, the general business credit is limited each year by the taxpayer's *net regular tax liability*. The net regular tax liability is the § 26 tax liability reduced by the credits allowed in §§ 21 through 30A. In addition, taxpayers with a net regular tax liability exceeding $25,000 are subject to an additional limitation. The business credit is limited to $25,000 *plus* 75 percent of

[60] The order in which credits are absorbed can be pieced together by reading §§ 25(e), 23(b), 25B(g) and 53(c).

the net regular tax liability in excess of \$25,000.[61] It should also be recalled that the business credits normally are not allowed to offset the AMT. Generally, credits arising in tax years beginning after December 31, 1997 that are unused because of these limits can be carried back one year and then forward 20 years, applied on a first-in, first-out basis.[62]

### Example 21

In 2011, F has a potential general business credit of \$92,000 and a net regular tax liability of \$100,000. The maximum allowable business credit for 2011 is \$81,250 [\$25,000 + (75% × \$75,000 = \$56,250)]. The unused credit of \$10,750 (\$92,000 – \$81,250) is subject to the carryover rules.

When the general business credit is limited and two or more components of the credit are applicable, special ordering rules as specified in § 38(d) apply to determine which credits will be utilized currently and which credits will be subject to the carryback and carryover rules.

The common rules for computing the separate components of the general business credit beginning with the investment tax credit, are detailed in the following sections.

## Investment Credit

In 1962, Congress enacted the investment tax credit in hopes of stimulating the economy by encouraging taxpayers to purchase certain assets—generally tangible personal property used in a trade or business. Although application of the provision became quite difficult, the essence of the law was simple. It allowed a credit equal to a particular percentage of the cost of the property. For example, taxpayers who purchased equipment at a cost of \$100,000 might be entitled to a credit equal to 10 percent of the cost, or \$10,000—but only as long as they met a host of requirements.

Since its enactment, the investment tax credit has had a tortuous history, in the law one year and out the next. It most recently was part of the Code in 1985 before it fell victim to the Tax Reform Act of 1986. In order to partially offset the significant loss of Federal tax revenues resulting from the 1986 tax rate reductions, Congress terminated the regular investment tax credit for assets placed in service after December 31, 1985. However, Congress allowed certain portions of the old credit to continue as the investment credit (IC). Under current law, the IC is made up of distinct parts: (1) the credit for rehabilitation expenditures and, (2) the energy credit. Each part of the IC is computed separately under its own specific rules. The actual amount of each part of the IC is the function of two factors: the taxpayer's basis in property qualifying for the credit, and the rate of the credit. The two components of the IC—the rehabilitation and energy credits—are discussed below.[63]

### Rehabilitation Investment Credit

The Economic Recovery Tax Act of 1981 grafted onto the regular investment credit an additional tax credit designed to encourage the restoration of buildings constructed prior to 1936. The credit represents a unique tax incentive for the restoration of old buildings.

With an emphasis on urban renewal, the rehabilitation investment credit is limited to substantial *rehabilitation expenditures* (excluding the purchase price) of *commercial buildings* and *historic structures*.[64] *Substantial* is defined to mean qualifying expenditures that exceed the greater of (1) the property's basis, or (2) \$5,000. To prevent destruction of these buildings, the amended legislation requires that:

1. Fifty percent or more of the existing external walls of the buildings is retained in place as external walls;

---

[61] § 38(c)(1). Married taxpayers filing separate returns are limited to \$12,500 plus 75 percent of the tax liability in excess of \$12,500 [§ 38(c)(4)].

[62] § 39(a). Note that credits arising in years prior to 1998 generally could be carried back three years and then forward for 15 years.

[63] Credits for qualifying advanced coal projects and for qualifying gasification projects were added to the energy credit in 2005 but are of limited application and are not discussed in this chapter.

[64] § 47(a).

2. Seventy-five percent or more of the external walls of the building is retained in place as internal or external walls; and
3. Seventy-five percent or more of the existing internal structural framework of the building is retained in place.

If these requirements are met, the credit is available for qualified expenditures on *both* non-residential real property and residential rental property or an addition or improvement to either type of property. However, if the rehabilitation credit is taken, the property *must* be depreciated under the straight-line method over the MACRS recovery period or the alternative depreciation system.[65]

The rate of rehabilitation credit is:

| *Rate* | *Type of Structure* |
|---|---|
| 10% | Commercial building originally placed in service prior to 1936 |
| 20 | All certified historic structures[66] |

## Example 22

On January 3, 2011, R purchases a commercial building that was constructed in 1920. In addition to the $300,000 of the purchase price allocated to the building, the entire core of the building is renovated at a cost of $600,000. R's rehabilitation credit is $60,000. computed as follows:

| | |
|---|---|
| Qualified investment. . . . . . . . . . . . . . . . . . . . . . . . . . . . . . . . . . . . . . . | $600,000 |
| Rate of credit. . . . . . . . . . . . . . . . . . . . . . . . . . . . . . . . . . . . . . . . . | × 10% |
| Current credit (before limitations). . . . . . . . . . . . . . . . . . . . . . . . . . . . . | $ 60,000 |

In some instances, rehabilitation expenditures also qualify for the energy investment credit (discussed below). When this occurs, taxpayers *must choose* between the two credits because both credits cannot be claimed for the same expenditure.[67]

### Energy Investment Credit

Recognizing the need for energy conservation, Congress added the *energy credit* provisions to the Code. The objective of this credit is to encourage taxpayers to decrease energy consumption or change the type of energy used.

The credit is 10 percent for qualified microturbine property and 30 percent for solar energy property, qualified fuel cell property and qualified small wind energy property.[68] "Energy property" for which the credit is allowed includes subject to a number of limitations:

- Equipment that uses solar energy to generate electricity, to heat or cool (or provide hot water for use in) a structure, to provide solar process heat and in certain cases to illuminate a room
- Equipment used to produce, distribute, or use energy from a geothermal deposit
- Qualified fuel cell property or qualified microturbine property
- Qualified small wind energy property

[65] § 47(c)(2)(B).

[66] § 47(c)(3).The designation as a certified historic structure is made by the Secretary of the Interior.

[67] § 48(a)(2).

[68] § 48.

### Example 23

S is the owner of a deluxe print shop. In March 2011, S installed four solar panels to heat water to be used in a photographic development process. The panels, pumps, valves, storage tanks, control system, and installation cost a total of $80,000. S's energy tax credit is $8,000.

| | |
|---|---|
| Qualified investment | $80,000 |
| Rate of credit | × 30% |
| Current credit (before limitations) | $24,000 |

## Basis Reduction of Qualified Property

At one time, taxpayers were allowed to take a full 10 percent IC or any applicable energy tax credit and still recover their entire cost basis of qualifying property under ACRS. In 1986, Congress decided that this treatment was too liberal with respect to rehabilitation property and required the basis of the property to be reduced by the amount of IC taken with respect to the property.[69] A similar rule requires that the basis of energy property be reduced by *one-half* of the amount of the IC taken on such energy property.[70]

### Example 24

Refer to the facts in *Example 22*, where R's rehabilitation credit is $60,000. R purchased the property for $300,000 and incurred $600,000 of rehabilitation expenditures. R's basis in the rehabilitated property is $840,000 ($300,000 + $600,000 – $60,000).

### Example 25

Refer to the facts in *Example 23*, where S's energy tax credit is $24,000. S purchased the solar property for $80,000. S's basis in the energy property is $68,000 [$80,000 – ($24,000 × 50%)].

The investment credit calculations discussed here provide the background for computing the recapture of IC on early dispositions required by the Code.[71] The amount of IC recapture should be an economic consideration in planning the disposition of any asset upon which the IC was claimed.

## Investment Credit Recapture

When taxpayers place qualified investment property into service, they claim the full amount of IC regardless of how long they intend to use the property. However, if an asset ceases to be qualified property during a five-year period (due to a sale or other disposition, or a change in the purpose or use of the asset), taxpayers are required to recapture a portion of the "unearned" IC. The recapture percentages illustrated in Exhibit 13-8 must be used to calculate the amount of unearned credit that is recaptured as an additional tax in the year of

[69] § 50(c)(1). Note that for determining the amount and character of gain on the disposition of the property, the downward basis adjustment is treated as a deduction allowed for depreciation. Accordingly, the amount of the basis adjustment will be subject to the § 1245 depreciation recapture rules discussed in Chapter 7.

[70] § 50(c)(3).

[71] § 50(a).

**EXHIBIT 13.8 Investment Tax Credit Recapture Percentages**[72]

| *If qualified property ceases to be qualified property—* | *The recapture percentage is:* |
|---|---|
| Before one full year, after placed in service | 100% |
| After one year, within two full years | 80 |
| After two years, within three full years | 60 |
| After three years, within four full years | 40 |
| After four years, within five full years | 20 |

early disposition. As a general rule, 20 percent of the credit is "earned" for each full year the property is held. For example, a qualified rehabilitation property placed in service on December 20, 2010 qualified for the rehabilitation credit in 2010 and was taken on the taxpayer's return for the year. However, none of the credit was *earned* until December 21, 2011. On that date, 20 percent of the credit allowed in 2010 was earned and thus no longer subject to recapture.

### Example 26

Assume that the commercial building (acquired on January 3, 2011) in *Example 22* was sold by R on September 1, 2012. The IC recapture is computed as follows:

| *Property* | *IC Claimed* | × | *Recapture Percentage* | = | *Amount Recaptured* |
|---|---|---|---|---|---|
| Commercial bldg. | $60,000 | × | 80% | = | $48,000 |

This amount is reported on Form 4255 and is treated as an additional tax imposed on the taxpayer in the year in which an early disposition occurs. Because the building's basis was originally decreased by the entire credit claimed, its basis is increased by the amount of the recapture for purposes of computing the gain or loss to be recognized on the sale.[73]

In addition to sales and exchanges (including like-kind exchanges), dispositions generally include gifts, dividend distributions from corporations, cessation of business usage, and involuntary conversions.[74] Even though the recaptured IC is referred to as an "other tax" on Form 1040, the amount recaptured will not be treated as a tax for purposes of determining the amount of nonrefundable tax credits allowed under § 26.[75]

The recapture rules do not apply to transfers by reason of death or to assets transferred in certain corporate acquisitions.[76] The recapture rules also will not apply to transfers of property between spouses, even if the transfer is made incident to divorce.[77] Finally, property is not treated as ceasing to be qualified property when a mere change in the form of conducting the trade or business occurs, so long as the property continues to be qualified property in the new business and the taxpayer retains a substantial interest in this trade or business.[78]

### Investment Credit Carryovers

Like the other components of the general business credit, the IC allowed in tax years beginning after December 31, 1997 but not utilized because of the tax liability limitation can

[72] § 50(a)(1)(B).

[73] § 50(c)(2). A similar rule applies to energy property, but only one-half of the amount of recapture is added to the basis of the property.

[74] Reg. § 1.47-2.

[75] § 50(a)(5)(C).

[76] § 50(a)(4).

[77] § 50(a)(5)(B).

[78] § 50(a)(4) and Reg. § 1.47-3(f).

be carried forward for 20 years. Finally, in determining the extent to which an investment credit is used in a taxable year, the regular investment credit is deemed to be used *before* the rehabilitation credit and the energy credit.[79]

## Work Opportunity Credit

For many years Congress has tried to spur employment by granting businesses a tax credit for hiring new workers that otherwise had a hard time finding employment. Since 1979, businesses have been able to claim the credit if they hire individuals from certain targeted groups. The targeted groups have been most recently redefined to include:[80]

- Recipients of a state law providing assistance for needy families with minor children,
- Qualified veterans,
- Qualified ex-felons,
- High-risk youth,
- Vocational rehabilitation referrals,
- Qualified summer youth employees,
- Qualified food stamp recipients, or
- Qualified SSI recipients.
- A long term family assistance recipient.
- Unemployed veterans
- Disconnected youth

To be eligible, each individual must obtain certification from a designated local agency, specifying that the individual meets the established criteria and therefore qualifies as a member of one of the targeted groups.

### Amount of Credit

The work opportunity tax credit is 40 percent of the first $6,000 of first-year wages paid to a qualified individual.[81] Thus, the maximum credit is $2,400 for each new employee. Note that, without any restriction, the employer would be able not only to claim a credit for the wages paid to the employee but also to deduct those wages. However, employers who elect to take the credit must reduce their wage expense by the amount of the credit; this eliminates the potential windfall. Note also that, as part of the general business credit, the § 38 rules limiting the amount of the credit ($25,000 + 75% of the tax liability in excess of $25,000) are applicable, as are the one-year carryback and 20-year carryover rules.

### Special Rule for Qualified Summer Youth Employees

Employers are allowed to claim the jobs credit for wages paid for the summer employment of teenagers that are members of economically disadvantaged families. These individuals must be 16 or 17 years of age on the hiring date and must not have worked previously for the employer. To qualify for the credit, the services must be attributable to any 90-day period between May 1 and September 15. The summer youth employment credit is 40 percent of the first $3,000 of eligible wages, for a maximum credit of $1,200 per youth.[82] If a summer youth employee continues to work after the 90-day period, his or her wages may qualify for the general targeted jobs credit previously discussed. However, certification of this employee as a member of a second target group must be determined as of the date of the second certification rather than on the basis of the employee's original certification as a qualified summer youth employee. In addition, the $6,000 wage limit for the targeted job credit must be reduced by the qualified summer wages.

---

[79] See § 38(d).

[80] §§ 51(d) and 51(c)(4).

[81] See § 51(i) for other limitations based on the number of hours worked.

[82] § 51(d)(12)(B).

### Example 27

On July 29, 2011, the owners of a farm hired 10 youths that were certified as qualified summer employees to help harvest crops. The owners paid the youths $150 a week for eight weeks (through September 22). The amount of targeted jobs credit in 2011 without regard to additional certifications is $4,200, computed in the following manner:

| | |
|---|---|
| Qualifying wages ($150 × 10 youths × 7 weeks) | $10,500 |
| Percent of credit | × 40% |
| Amount of credit | $ 4,200 |

The wage expense deduction attributable to the youths' salaries would be $7,800, computed as follows:

| | |
|---|---|
| Total wages paid ($150 × 10 youths × 8 weeks) | $12,000 |
| Reduced by allowable credit | – 4,200 |
| Allowable wage expense | $ 7,800 |

Note that the eighth week does not qualify for the credit since it occurs after the September 15 cutoff date.

### Special Rules for a Long Term Family Assistance Recipient

The former Welfare to Work Credit has been combined with the Work Opportunity Credit. For individuals that receive assistance for more than 18 months under a State program funded under part A of Title IV of the Social Security Act, the credit amount for the first year of employment is up to 40% on the first $10,000 of wages. Also, an additional 50% credit is available for wages paid up to $10,000 in the second year of employment. The maximum credit per new employee over the two year period is $9,000.[83]

## Alcohol Fuel Credit

The fourth component of the general business credit is the alcohol fuel credit. To foster the production of gasohol, an income tax credit for alcohol and alcohol-blended fuels applies to fuel sales and uses before January 1, 2012. The alcohol fuel credit is computed and reported on Form 6478. Generally, for 2011 the credit is $0.45 per gallon of alcohol used in a qualified alcohol mixture or as a straight alcohol fuel.[84] Although taxpayers are entitled to a credit, they must include an amount equal to the credit claimed in income.[85]

## Research and Experimental (R&E) Credit

The fifth component of the general business credit is the research credit—commonly referred to as the R&E credit. Created in 1981 and amended several times since, the R&E credit provisions generally allow taxpayers a credit equal to 20 percent of their *incremental* expenditures that constitute either (1) qualified research expenditures or (2) basic research payments.[86] The method for identifying what qualifies as an incremental expenditure is considered in detail below, as are the types of qualifying research. First, however, the relationship of the R&E credit and the deduction for R&E must be addressed.

[83] 51(e).

[84] § 40. A similar credit applies to small ethanol producers.

[85] § 87.

[86] § 41(a). This credit will terminate for amounts paid or incurred after 12/31/2011 [§ 41(h)].

### Impact of R&E Credit on Current Deductions

The research credit is the second part of Congress's two-prong approach for stimulating research. The first part of this plan, as might be recalled from Chapter 9, allows taxpayers either to deduct research and experimental expenditures immediately or capitalize the expenditures and amortize them over 60 months. As might be expected, taxpayers are not allowed to have their research cake and eat it too—they must reduce their R&E deduction for the amount of R&E credit determined for the year.[87] For those taxpayers who normally expense R&E costs, this means that their deduction for R&E is simply smaller. For those taxpayers who capitalize and amortize the costs, the amount capitalized is reduced. Note that if the credit is not utilized by the taxpayer within the 20-year carryover period, a deduction equal to the amount of the expiring credit is allowed in the year following the expiration of the tax credit carryover period.[88]

Without additional rules, the cutback of the deduction for the credit could prove unduly harsh for taxpayers subject to the AMT, which generally does not allow the use of credits. For this reason taxpayers are allowed to *elect* to claim a reduced credit.[89] This election effectively enables the taxpayer to trade a credit that is not allowed to reduce the AMT for a deduction that could be used to reduce the AMT.

### Qualified Research Expenditures

The R&E credit is allowed for both in-house research and contract (outside) research. *Qualified research expenditures* are those incurred in carrying on a trade or business for in-house research expenses (e.g., wages, supplies, rental of equipment, overhead) and 65 percent of *contract research expenses* (those paid to any person other than an employee of the taxpayer for qualified research).[90] To be eligible for the credit, the expenditures must meet the same criteria that must be met for their deduction. As a general rule, these criteria extend special treatment only for research and development in the experimental or laboratory sense. This includes (1) the development of an experimental or pilot model, plant process, formula, invention, or similar property, and (2) the improvement of such types of property already in existence.[91] In addition, the expenditures must be technological in nature *and* must relate to establishing a new or improved function, or improving the performance, reliability, or quality of a product.[92] Finally, the credit is *denied* for certain expenditure items,[93] including:

1. Research undertaken outside the United States
2. Research conducted in the social sciences or humanities
3. Ordinary testing or inspection of materials or products for quality control
4. Market and consumer research
5. Research relating to style, taste, cosmetic, or seasonal design
6. Advertising and promotion expenses
7. Management studies and efficiency surveys
8. Computer software for internal use of the taxpayer
9. Research to locate and evaluate mineral deposits, including oil and gas
10. Acquisition and improvement of land and of certain depreciable or depletable property used in research (including the annual depreciation deduction)

### Amount of Credit

The 20 percent credit is extended only to taxpayers who increase their research activities. As shown in the formula in Exhibit 13-9, this is accomplished by allowing a credit only for qualified research expenditures for the current year that exceed the taxpayer's base amount.[94]

---

[87] § 280C(c).

[88] § 196. The deduction allowed is 50 percent of the expired R&E credits attributable to taxable years beginning before 1990.

[89] § 280C(c)(3).

[90] § 41(b)(4). The trade or business requirement may be met by certain start-up companies even though they are not currently in business.

[91] Reg. § 1.174-2(a).

[92] § 41(d)(1)(B).

[93] § 41(d)(4).

[94] § 41(a)(1).

**EXHIBIT 13.9** **Calculation of R&E Credit**

R&E Credit = 20% × (qualified R&E expenditures − base amount)

Base amount = Fixed-base percentage × Average gross receipts for four previous years

$$\text{Fixed} - \text{base percentage}^* = \frac{\text{Total research expenses}(1984-1988)}{\text{Total gross receipts}(1984-1988)}$$

*Subject to special rules for start-up companies and limited to a maximum of 16 percent.

The base amount is a fixed percentage of the taxpayer's average gross receipts for the four previous years.[95] As a result, those taxpayers who continually increase their research benefit the most from this special incentive.

The fixed-base percentage is computed differently for firms with a history of doing research than for firms that do not have such a history. For taxpayers reporting both qualified research expenses and gross receipts during each of at least three years from 1984 to 1988, the "fixed-base percentage" is the ratio that its total qualified research expenses for the 1984 to 1988 period bears to its total gross receipts for this period, subject to a maximum ratio of 16 percent. "Start-up companies" and those taxpayers not meeting the R&E expenditures and gross receipt requirements above are assigned a fixed-base percentage of 3 percent for the first five years in which qualified research expenditures are incurred.[96]

## Example 28

Assume R Corporation reported the following research expenditures and gross receipts:

| | *1986* | *1987* | *1988* |
|---|---|---|---|
| Research expenditures ..... | $ 90,000 | $100,000 | $110,000 |
| Gross receipts ........... | 700,000 | 900,000 | 800,000 |

| | *2007* | *2008* | *2009* | *2010* | *2011* |
|---|---|---|---|---|---|
| Research expenditures..... | $120,000 | $130,000 | $ 140,000 | $ 150,000 | $ 180,000 |
| Gross receipts........... | 700,000 | 800,000 | 1,000,000 | 1,100,000 | 1,200,000 |

R Corporation's R&E credit for 2011 is computed as follows:

1. Fixed-base percentage = $300,000/$2,400,000 = .125
2. Base amount = .125 × $3,600,000/4 = $112,500
3. Qualified R&E expenditures for 2011 = $180,000
4. R&E Credit = 20% × ($180,000 − $112,500) = $13,500

Note that R's fixed-base percentage is based on the research activity and gross receipts during 1984–1988, whereas the average annual gross receipts number is based on receipts for the four previous years, 2007–2010 ($700,000 + $800,000 + $1,000,000 + $1,100,000 = $3,600,000). Also note that in 2011, R must reduce its current deduction for research expenditures by $13,500, or if the deferred asset method of accounting is used, the $180,000 R&E costs must be reduced to $166,500 ($180,000 − $13,500) before being capitalized and amortized over a period of not less than 60 months.

---

[95] § 41(c).

[96] Special rules apply to start-up companies after the sixth taxable year in which they incur qualified research expenditures. See § 41(c)(3)(B).

## Basic Research Expenditures

The second category of expenditures qualifying for the research credit is the *incremental* amount of *basic research payments* made to universities and other qualified organizations.[97] Basic research means any original investigation for the advancement of scientific knowledge not having a specific commercial objective. The term "basic research payment" means any amount paid in cash during the taxable year by a corporation to a qualified organization for basic research, but only if such payment is made pursuant to a written agreement and the basic research is to be performed by the qualified organization. Qualified organizations include educational institutions, certain scientific research organizations, and certain grant organizations.

The R&E credit applies to the *excess* of corporate cash expenditures in a year over the qualified organization base period amount. The qualified organization base period amount is the *sum* of (l) the minimum basic research amount, plus (2) the maintenance-of-effort amount. The *maintenance-of-effort amount* prevents the corporation from shifting its historical charitable contribution to any qualifying educational organization over to a creditable basic research payment. It is an amount equal to the *average* nondesignated university contributions paid by the corporation during the base period, increased by the cost of living adjustment for the calendar year over the amount of nondesignated university contributions paid by the taxpayer during that year. Any portion of the basic research payment that does not exceed the qualified organization base period amount will be treated as contract research expenses for computing the incremental qualified research expenditures discussed above under "qualified research expenditures" above.[98]

## Alternative Incremental Credit

For taxable years beginning after June 30, 1996, a taxpayer may make an election to compute the research credit utilizing three tiers of reduced fixed base percentages and reduced credit rates.[99] This election may be beneficial for companies that have average gross receipts increasing at a faster rate than the increases in qualified research expenditures. This election is mentioned here only to round out the discussion of this credit but further analysis of the election is beyond the scope of this text.

## Alternative Simplified Credit for Qualified Research Expenses

The Tax Relief and Health Care Act of 2006 allows taxpayers, at their election, to compute the research credit under a third method. This method is referred to as the alternative simplified credit. Under this approach, a taxpayer can claim an amount equal to 12 percent of the amount by which qualified research expenses exceed 50 percent of the average qualified research expenses for the three preceding tax years. If the taxpayer has no qualified research expenses for any of the preceding three tax years, then the credit is equal to six percent of the qualified research expenses for the current tax year. As with the alternative incremental credit, an election to calculate the research credit using the alternative simplified credit is effective for all succeeding tax years unless revoked with the consent of the IRS.[100]

## Credit Limitations

As part of the general business credit, the tax liability limitation ($25,000 + 75% of the tax liability in excess of $25,000) applies, as do the one-year carryback and 20-year carryover rules. Additional limitations are imposed in an effort to prevent the research credit from being exploited by tax shelter promoters. For individuals with ownership interests in unincorporated businesses (i.e., partners of a partnership), trust or estate beneficiaries, or S corporation shareholders, any allowable pass-through of the credit cannot exceed the *lesser of* (1) the individual's net regular tax liability limitation discussed earlier, or (2) the amount of tax attributable to the individual's taxable income resulting from the individual's interest in the entity that earned such credit.

The final unique characteristic of the R&E credit is applicable to changes in business ownership. Special rules apply for computing the credit when a business changes hands, under

---

97 § 41 (e)(2).

98 § 41(e)(1)(B).

99 § 41(c)(4). These percentages were increased for years beginning after 2006.

100 § 41(c)(5).

which qualified research expenditures for periods prior to the change of ownership generally are treated as transferred with the trade or business that gave rise to those expenditures.[101]

## Low-Income Housing Credit

The next component of the general business credit is the low-income housing credit. This credit is available for low-income housing that is constructed, rehabilitated, or acquired after 1986. The credit is claimed over a 10-year period, with an annual credit of approximately 9 percent of the qualifying basis of low-income units placed in service. If federal subsidies are used to finance the project, the credit is limited to approximately 4 percent.[102] For property placed in service after 1987, the exact percentage is determined by the IRS on a monthly basis. The percentages for any month are calculated to yield, over a 10-year credit period, amounts of credit that have a present value equal to (1) 70 percent of the qualified basis of new buildings that are not federally subsidized for the tax year, and (2) 30 percent of the qualified basis of existing buildings and new buildings that are federally subsidized.[103]

### Example 29

In March 2011, H, an individual, constructed and placed in service a qualified low-income housing project. The qualified basis of the project was $1 million. The 70% present value credit for buildings placed in service in March 2011 is 7.78%.[104] Thus, the annual credit that H could claim is $77,800.

Each year, the sum of allowed low-income housing credits is subject to a nationwide cap. The cap amount is allotted among all of the states so that each state will have a cap on the amount of low-income housing credits it can authorize. A credit allocation from the appropriate state credit authority must be received by the owner of the property eligible for the low-income housing credit. The credit is available on a per-unit basis; thus, a single building may have some units that qualify for the credit and some that do not. In order to qualify, a low-income housing project must meet a host of exacting criteria throughout a 15-year compliance period.[105]

## Disabled Access Credit

Another component of the general business credit is the disabled access credit. This credit was established in 1994 primarily as a relief measure for those businesses that are required under the Americans with Disabilities Act of 1990 to make improvements that make existing facilities accessible to the disabled. Under Code § 44, an eligible small business can elect to take a nonrefundable tax credit equal to 50 percent of the amount of the eligible access expenditures for any taxable year that exceed $250 but do not exceed $10,250. An eligible small business is defined as one having gross receipts for the preceding taxable year that did not exceed $1,000,000, or having no more than 30 full-time employees during the preceding taxable year. Eligible access expenditures are defined as amounts paid or incurred by an eligible small business to comply with applicable requirements of the Disabilities Act. Eligible access expenditures generally include amounts paid or incurred for the following:

1. Removing architectural, communication, physical, or transportation barriers that prevent a business from being accessible to, or usable by, individuals with disabilities
2. Providing qualified interpreters or other effective methods of making aurally delivered materials available to individuals with hearing impairments

---

[101] § 41(f)(3).

[102] § 42(b)(1).

[103] § 42(b)(2)(B). A formula for making such computations is provided in Rev. Rul. 88-6, 1988-1 C.B. 3.

[104] Rev. Rul. 2011-6, IRB 2011-10.

[105] See §§ 42(g) and 42(l).

3. Providing qualified readers, taped texts, and other effective methods of making visually delivered materials available to individuals with visual impairments
4. Acquiring or modifying equipment or devices for individuals with disabilities
5. Providing other similar services, modifications, materials, or equipment

In cases where the eligible business is being conducted as a partnership or an S corporation, the dollar limitations are applied at both the entity and the owner level. Any portion of the unused general business credit attributable to the disabled access credit may not be carried back to any taxable year ending before 1990.

**Example 30**

J, a sole proprietor, had gross receipts of $700,000 last year and incurred $5,250 of eligible access expenditures this year. J's disabled access credit for this year is $2,500 [($5,250 − $250) × 50%].

As is the case with other components of the general business credit, the depreciable basis of assets acquired subject to the credit using access expenditures must be reduced by the amount of credit claimed with respect to those expenditures. Alternatively, any current deduction attributable to the access expenditures must be reduced by the amount of credit claimed.[106]

## Empowerment Zone Employment Credit

To help rebuild distressed urban and rural areas, the RRA of 1994 created several tax incentives. The hope is that these incentives will encourage businesses to locate in these areas and hire individuals who live there. The goal is carried out in § 1396, which authorizes the Secretary of Housing and Urban Development and the Secretary of Agriculture to identify 95 *enterprise communities* and 29 *empowerment zones* where the tax benefits will be offered. The regions must meet certain criteria concerning population, size (urban areas cannot exceed 20 square miles and rural areas cannot exceed 1,000 square miles), and poverty (a minimum rate of 20 percent).[107]

Businesses that operate within the designated areas are entitled to a variety of benefits. Perhaps the most important of these is the empowerment zone employment credit (EZEC). All employers located in an empowerment zone are entitled to a 20 percent credit for the first $15,000 of wages paid to full-time as well as part-time employees who are residents of the empowerment zone. The maximum credit per employee is $3,000 per year. If an employer is entitled to both a work opportunity credit (WOC) and an EZEC, the first $6,000 of wages paid qualify for the higher WOC of 40 percent, and the next $9,000 qualify for the EZEC of 20 percent. Thus, the payment of $15,000 of wages could enable the employer to claim a credit as high as $4,200 ($6,000 × 40% = $2,400) + ($9,000 × 20% = $1,800). Of course, the employer's deduction for wages must be reduced by the amount of credits allowed.

Like the WOC, the EZEC is part of the general business credit and is consequently subject to the tax liability limitation as well as the carryback and carryover rule. Unlike the WOC, the EZEC can offset 25 percent of the employer's AMT liability.

## Credit for Employer-Provided Child-Care

To encourage employers to provide quality child care for its employees, Congress established a special credit in 2002. The credit is considered a part of the general business credit and will expire for tax years beginning after 12/31/2012.

Under new § 45F, employers may claim a credit equal to 25 percent of the cost of qualified child care expenditures and 10 percent of qualified child care resource and referral expenditures. The maximum total amount of credit is limited to $150,000 per year. In addition, the

[106] § 44(c)(7).

[107] §§ 1391(a), 1391(d)(1)(A), 1391(g) and 1396.

basis of any property is reduced by the amount of credit claimed. Similarly, any other deduction or credit must be reduced by the amount of credit claimed.

Qualifying expenditures include the costs of (1) building, acquiring, rehabilitating or expanding property that is used as part of a *qualified child care facility* of the taxpayer for its employees, (2) operating such facilities, and (3) a contract with a qualified child care facility. A qualified child care facility is a facility whose principal use is to provide child care assistance and meets the requirements of all applicable laws and regulations of the state and local government in which it is located, including the licensing requirements applicable to a child care facility. The definition does not include a facility which is the principal residence of the taxpayer, any employee of the taxpayer, or the operator of the facility. Thus day care centers will be qualified only if they are separate and distinct from the operator's personal residence.

In addition, expenses incurred in providing child-care resource and referral services are eligible for a 10 percent credit. Usage of a facility cannot favor high-income earners, and at least 30 percent of the children in the center must be children of employees. Finally, if the facility is no longer used as a child care center or there is a disposition of the taxpayer's interest (e.g., the taxpayer sells the property), § 45F(d)(2) requires the taxpayer to recapture (i.e., pay back to the government) a percentage of the tax savings from prior years as shown below.

| *If the Recapture Event Occurs in Years* | *Percentage Recapture* |
|---|---|
| 1–3 | 100% |
| 4 | 85 |
| 5 | 70 |
| 6 | 55 |
| 7 | 40 |
| 8 | 25 |
| 9–10 | 10 |
| 11 | 0 |

## OTHER COMPONENTS OF THE GENERAL BUSINESS CREDIT

There are several other credits that make up the general business credit:

- *Indian Employment Credit.* Added by the RRA of 1994 to encourage the hiring of Native Americans, the Indian employment credit (authorized in § 45A) generally entitles employers conducting businesses located on Indian reservations to claim a credit of 20 percent for up to $20,000 of wages and insurance benefits paid to employees who are members of an Indian tribe and who work and live on the reservation. This credit is set to expire after 2009, but may be extended.

- *Employer Social Security Credit.* This credit represents a relief measure (or perhaps a peace offering) for the restaurant industry, which presumably was detrimentally impacted by the 1994 cut in the deduction for business meals from 80 to 50 percent. Section 45B allows employers operating food and beverage establishments to claim a credit against their income tax liability for their FICA obligation (7.65%) on tips in excess of those treated as wages for purposes of satisfying the minimum wage provisions. To prevent a double benefit, no deduction is allowed for any FICA taxes taken into account in determining the credit.

- *Renewable Electricity Production Credit.* Section 45 provides a credit for taxpayers who produce electricity from qualified wind energy or certain other renewable resources from facilities placed in service after 2003.

- *Enhanced Oil Recovery Credit.* This is a special credit directed at owners of oil and gas properties requiring secondary or tertiary methods of production.

- *Orphan Drug Credit.* The credit for qualified clinical testing expenses for certain drugs for rare diseases or conditions has been made a permanent part of the general business credit. The credit is equal to 50 percent of the qualified clinical testing expenses for the taxable year.

- *Credit for Plan Start-up Costs of Small Employers.* Small employers with no more than 100 employees receive a tax credit for some of the costs of establishing new retirement plans. The credit equals 50 percent of the start-up costs incurred to create or maintain a new employee retirement plan. The credit is limited to $500 in any tax year and it may be claimed for qualified costs incurred in each of the three years beginning with the tax year in which the plan becomes effective [Code § 45E(b).]
- *Alternative Motor Vehicle Credit.* Perhaps the credit of greatest interest to individuals is that for purchases of personal or business automobiles. Section 30B offers an incentive to purchase energy efficient cars. The alternative motor vehicle credit is only available for purchases of qualified fuel cell motor vehicles:
    - Fuel cell vehicle (FCV). The credit can be as much as $12,000 for vehicles powered by fuel cells. However, the cost of these vehicles can be well over $100,000. FCVs are propelled by electric motors that are somewhat like batteries. Fuel cells create their own electricity through an electrochemical reaction between hydrogen and oxygen taken from the air.
- *Energy Efficient Appliance Credit.* Manufacturers can qualify for a credit for producing energy efficient dishwashers, clothes washers, and refrigerators. The credit depends on the type of appliance and how much energy it saves. The maximum tax credit is $100 per dishwasher or clothes washer, and $175 per refrigerator. Appliances eligible for the credit include only those produced by the taxpayer during the calendar year in the U.S. that exceed the average amount of production by the taxpayer in the U.S. during the three prior calendar years. Details are contained in § 45M. Currently, the credit is available only for property placed in service after 2005 and before 2012.
- *Savers Credit.* Section 25B allows low and middle-income taxpayers a nonrefundable tax credit of up to $2,000 of qualified retirement savings contributions. This credit is discussed in Chapter 18.
- *Non-business Energy Property Credit.* Section 25C allows individuals to claim annual nonrefundable credits for amounts spent to make energy improvements to their homes. The credit is generally 30% of amounts paid for "qualified energy efficient improvements" and "residential energy property expenditures." The credit is available for expenses for such items as insulation, exterior doors and windows (including skylights), and properly coated metal as well as certain energy efficient heating and air conditioning units. However, the total non-business energy credits claimed by taxpayers for 2009, 2010 and 2011 cannot exceed $1,500. Expenses must be made on or in connection with a dwelling unit located in the U.S., owned and used by the taxpayer as his principal residence and originally placed in service by the taxpayer. Currently, the credit is available for expenditures made before 2012.
- *Residential Energy Efficient Property (REEP) Credit.* Section 25D also allows individuals annual nonrefundable credit for the purchase of property for their homes that is energy efficient. Qualifying property includes certain photovoltaic property (i.e., property that uses solar power to generate electricity in a home), solar-powered water heaters and certain fuel cell property. Each of the credits is generally 30% of the cost of the property. The credit is set to expire in 2016.

In addition to those credits that make up the general business credit, there are still other credits available to business, but they are of limited applicability and are not discussed in this text. The foreign tax credit available to both businesses and individuals, is discussed briefly below.

## General Business Credit Carryover Rules

Recall that the carryback period is one year and the carryforward period is 20 years for business credits incurred in years beginning after 1997. If the business credit carryover cannot be used within the stipulated time period, the credit expires. Without special rules, this would be a double loss for taxpayers who claimed the full investment tax credit percentages or other credits and who decreased the basis of property for MACRS computations. Not only have they lost the credit but they also were unable to depreciate the full cost of the assets. Because of this possibility, taxpayers are allowed to take a deduction equal to the amount of the previous reductions from basis stipulated by the expired IC or other credits. This deduction may be taken in the year *following* the expiration of the tax credit carryover period.[108]

### Example 31

Q originally claimed an IC of $10,000 and reduced the basis in the assets by $5,000. After the expiration of the carryforward period, an unused IC of $3,000 expires. In the first taxable year after the expiration of the credit carryover period, Q may deduct $1,500 (½ of $3,000). This amount equals the original decrease in basis for the expired investment credit.

## Foreign Tax Credit

The new emphasis on the global economy and global investing is making the treatment of foreign income and foreign taxes a concern for far more taxpayers than ever before. As explained in Chapter 3, U.S. citizens (including U.S. corporations) and resident aliens must pay U.S. taxes on their worldwide income: income earned in the United States as well as income from foreign sources. In many cases, they pay not only U.S. taxes but also foreign taxes on the same income. To alleviate the burden of two taxes on the same income, § 27 generally allows taxpayers to claim a credit for income taxes paid or accrued to a foreign country. Alternatively, taxpayers may elect to claim a deduction for the taxes. Also note that if the taxpayer elects to use the $92,900 (2011) earned income exclusion (see Chapter 3), any foreign taxes paid on such income cannot be claimed as a credit.

Although the taxpayer is normally allowed a credit for any foreign taxes paid, the amount of the credit may be limited in some cases. As a general rule, the credit for the foreign taxes cannot exceed the U.S. tax that would otherwise be paid on the same income. For example, assume a U.S. taxpayer earns $10,000 while living abroad and pays a foreign tax on such income of $3,000. If the U.S. tax on such income is only $2,000, the taxpayer's credit is limited to $2,000, and she consequently pays a foreign tax of $3,000 and no U.S. tax because her $2,000 U.S. tax liability is reduced to zero by the $2,000 FTC. Note that, without the limitation, the United States could effectively lose $1,000 of taxes on other U.S. income that it would otherwise receive. As this example illustrates, the limitation is generally triggered when the foreign tax rate exceeds the U.S. tax rate. The actual limitation is computed using the following formula:

$$\frac{\text{Foreign source taxable income}}{\text{Worldwide taxable income*}} \times \text{U.S. tax before credits} = \text{Foreign tax credit limitation}$$

*U.S. source taxable income + Foreign source taxable income + Personal exemptions

Any unused foreign tax credits may be carried back two years and carried forward five years. However, the credits may be carried over only to years where the foreign tax credit limitation has not been exceeded.

### Example 32

This year Mr. and Mrs. T took their financial consultants' advice on global investing. As a result, they received $10,000 of dividends from several foreign stocks. The couple's taxable income including the dividends was $92,600, producing a tax before credits of $15,400. The maximum foreign tax credit would be computed as follows:

$$\frac{\$10,000}{\$92,600 + \$7,400 = \$100,000} \times \$15,400 = \$1,540$$

---

[108] § 196.

One caveat is in order before leaving the foreign tax credit. Although the above rules normally apply, taxpayers must be careful. Not only are the rules complex (they are applied separately to different classes of income), but tax treaties with a particular country may provide special rules for income earned in that country by U.S. citizens. Such treaties must be examined when dealing with foreign income.

# Nonbusiness Credits

In addition to the numerous business credits discussed thus far, there are several nonbusiness credits available to individual taxpayers only. These credits include (1) the child tax credit, (2) the child and dependent care credit, (3) the Hope (the American Opportunity Tax Credit) and Lifetime learning credits, (4) the credit for adoption expenses, (5) the credit for the elderly, (6) the credit for interest on certain home mortgages, and (7) the earned income credit and other refundable credits. Each of these credits is discussed below.

## CHILD TAX CREDIT

Section 24 currently allows most taxpayers to claim a special credit of $1,000 for each qualifying child. As a general rule, the credit is nonrefundable. Importantly, however, a portion of the credit may be refundable. The refundable child tax credit is discussed later in this Chapter along with other refundable credits.

In order to be considered a qualifying child, the individual in question must meet the following conditions:

- The individual must be the child of the taxpayer. For this purpose, a stepson or stepdaughter or an eligible foster child qualifies as a child. Descendants of these individuals are also treated as a qualifying child.
- The child must not have attained the age of 17 before the close of the taxable year.
- The taxpayer is eligible to claim a dependency exemption for the child.
- The child is a citizen, or a national of the U.S., or a resident of the U.S.

Like many of the other tax relief provisions contained in the Code, the benefits of the credit are not extended to wealthy individuals. To accomplish this policy objective, the credit is reduced by $50 for each $1,000 (or part thereof) of adjusted gross income (computed with certain modifications) exceeding the levels of income shown in Exhibit 13-10 below.

**EXHIBIT 13.10** **Child Tax Credit Phase-Out**

| Taxpayer | Phase-Out begins When Modified A.G.I. Exceeds | Phase-Out Ends when Modified A.G.I. Exceeds | | | |
|---|---|---|---|---|---|
| | | *One child* | *Two children* | *Three children* | *Four children* |
| Single | $ 75,000 | $ 86,000 | $ 98,000 | $ 110,000 | $122,000 |
| Married filing jointly | $110,000 | $121,000 | $133,000 | $ 145,000 | $157,000 |

Modified A.G.I. is A.G.I. determined before any exclusion for foreign earned income and foreign housing costs and income from certain possessions. These thresholds are not indexed for inflation. In order to claim the credit, the taxpayer must disclose the TIN of each qualifying child on the return and the taxable year of the taxpayer must include a 12 month period.

## Example 33

H and W are married with three children. At the close of 2011, the children, X, Y, and Z, were ages 12, 16 and 18 respectively. H and W claim a dependency exemption for each of the children. This year H and W reported adjusted gross income of $114,200. H and W may claim a child credit for X and Y since they are both dependents and did not attain the age of 17 before the close of the year. The amount of the credit is limited to $1,750 determined as follows:

| | | |
|---|---|---|
| Tentative credit for each child | | $1,000 |
| Qualifying children | | × 2 |
| Total credit before phase-out | | $2,000 |
| Reduction: | | |
| Adjusted gross income | $114,200 | |
| Threshold for joint return | (110,000) | |
| Excess adjusted gross income | $ 4,200 | |
| Reduction [($4,200/$1,000 = 4.2 rounded up to 5) × $50] | | (250) |
| Child credit allowed for children | | $1,750 |

The amount of the child tax credit that can be claimed by a taxpayer for any taxable year shall not exceed the excess of the sum of the § 26 regular tax liability plus the AMT over the sum of the credits allowed by the Child and Dependent Care Credit (§ 21), the Credit for the Elderly (§ 22), the Credit for Interest on Certain Home Mortgages (§ 25), Residential Energy Credit (§ 25C) and the foreign tax credit (§ 27). The nonrefundable portion of the child tax credit may be claimed against both regular and AMT tax liability.

## Child and Dependent Care Credit

The emergence of the working wife and two-earner couples during the post-World War II era produced a new tax issue. The dilemma concerned the treatment of the costs for the care of children and other dependents. The question posed was whether taxpayers who were forced to pay such costs in order to work should be entitled to deduct them as business expenses. Early court cases denied a deduction for these expenses on the grounds that they were personal in nature. In the court's view, the expenses stemmed from a personal choice by married couples to employ others to discharge their domestic duties, a purely personal expense. Congress, however, became sensitive to the issue in the late 1960s and responded with a limited deduction in 1971. After several alterations and amendments, the deduction received a complete makeover and was converted into a credit in 1976—a far better deal for those who did not itemize. It now appears that, almost 20 years after its creation, the credit is a permanent part of the tax law, presumably justified as both a relief measure for those who have differing abilities to pay and as a stimulant that reduces the costs of entering the work force.

As the statute is now drawn, taxpayers are able to claim a credit for a portion of their child and dependent care expenses if they meet two requirements: (l) the taxpayer maintains a household for a qualifying individual and (2) the expenses—so-called *employment-related expenses*—are incurred to enable the taxpayer to be gainfully employed.[109] Each of these requirements and the computation of the credit are discussed below.

### Qualifying Individual

What many believe is simply a credit for child care actually has a far broader scope. True to its name, the *child and dependent care credit* is available not only to those who have children but also to those who take care of other dependents, such as an aging parent or other relative.

[109] § 21.

A taxpayer (or in the case of divorced parents, only the custodial parent) can claim the credit only if he or she maintains a household for one of the following individuals:[110]

- A dependent under the age of 13 (e.g., taxpayer's child)
- An incapacitated dependent
- An incapacitated spouse

Note that the year in which a dependent turns 14 is an important factor in determining the applicability of the credit. First, if the individual becomes 13 during the year, he or she normally qualifies only for the part of the year he or she was under 13. Second, once the individual reaches age 14, expenses do not qualify unless the individual is incapable of self-care.

## Employment-Related Expenses

Only certain expenses that enable the taxpayer to be gainfully employed or *seek* gainful employment qualify for the credit.[111] The work can be either full-time or part-time, but it must be work. Volunteer work for a nominal salary does not constitute gainful employment. For example, expenses for a baby-sitter while the taxpayer works at a church or hospital do not qualify. Note, however, that expenses incurred when one spouse works and the other attends school on a full-time basis are eligible.

Only certain types of expenses qualify as employment-related expenses. The expenses generally must be for the care of the qualifying individual (e.g., the cost of a baby-sitter). In this regard, the costs of household services qualify if the expenses are attributable at least in part to the care of a qualifying individual. Thus the IRS generally takes the position that the costs of a maid, nanny, or cook can qualify, but not those of a gardener or chauffeur. Eligible expenses normally do not include amounts paid for food, clothing, or entertainment. Similarly, the costs of transportation to a place for care do not qualify unless the qualifying individual is incapacitated. In addition, educational expenses incurred for a child in the first or higher grade level do not qualify. Observe, however, that the costs of pre-school or nursery school are eligible for the credit.

As a general rule, expenses for services both inside and outside the home qualify for the credit. However, there are several notable exceptions for the outside services:

- Care provided by a dependent care facility (e.g., a day care center) qualifies only if the facility provides care for more than six individuals.[112]
- Services outside the home for qualifying individuals other than a dependent under 13 (e.g., nursing home services for a spouse or an over-13-year-old dependent who is incapable of self-care) are eligible only if the individual spends at least eight hours a day in the employee's household.[113]
- Overnight camps do not qualify (day camps, however, can qualify).[114]

A final note on eligible expenses concerns payments made to relatives. Can the credit be claimed if the taxpayer simply pays his mother to baby-sit while he works? Payments to individuals do qualify as long as the individual is not a dependent of the taxpayer.[115] Thus payments to a child's grandparents would probably qualify since the grandparents normally are not dependents. Conversely, payments to a child's older brothers or sisters normally would not qualify since such individuals would be dependents. However, payments to the taxpayer's child can qualify if the child is not a dependent and is at least 19 years of age.

## Computation of the Credit

The credit is generally computed by multiplying the applicable percentage times employment-related expenses. A general formula for the calculation is shown in Exhibit 13-11.

[110] §§ 21(b)(1) and 21(e)(5).

[111] § 21(b)(2).

[112] § 21(b)(2)(C).

[113] § 21(b)(2)(B).

[114] Last sentence of § 21(b)(2)(A).

[115] § 21(e)(6).

**EXHIBIT 13.11 Computations of the Child and Dependent Care Credit**

| | |
|---|---|
| | Employment-related expenses |
| | Lesser of: |
| | 1. Amount paid, |
| | 2. Earned income or imputed earned income if full-time student or incapacitated spouse, or |
| | 3. \$3,000 (if one qualifying individual) or \$6,000 (if more than one) |
| × | Applicable percentage (20–35%) |
| = | Child and dependent care credit |

## Applicable Percentage

The applicable percentage begins at 35 percent but is reduced (but not below 20 percent) by one percentage point for each \$2,000 (or fraction thereof) that the taxpayer's adjusted gross income exceeds \$15,000. For example, the rate for a taxpayer with an A.G.I. of \$17,001 is 33 percent, one point reduction for the first \$2,000 over \$15,000 and another point reduction for the fractional part of the next \$2,000. Based on this scheme, taxpayers with adjusted gross incomes exceeding \$43,000 have a rate of 20 percent.[116]

## Limitations on Employment-Related Expenses

The Code imposes several limitations on the amount of expenses eligible for the credit. The first limitation simply sets a maximum dollar amount of expenses that may be taken into account in computing the credit. These amounts are based on the number of qualifying individuals: \$3,000 for one qualifying individual and \$6,000 for two or more individuals.[117] Thus, the maximum credits would be \$1,050 (35% × \$3,000) and \$2,100 (35% × \$6,000). As explained below, however, these amounts may be reduced. The computation of the credit requires a three-step approach, as illustrated in the following example.

### Example 34

F is a widower and maintains a household for his two small children. He incurs \$5,000 of employment-related expenses and reports A.G.I. of \$27,300 for the current year. F's child care credit is determined as follows:

***Step 1:*** Determining the applicable percentage:

| | |
|---|---|
| Adjusted gross income | \$27,300 |
| Less: Ceiling on 35% rate | (15,000) |
| Adjusted gross income over \$15,000 limit | \$12,300 |

Divided by \$2,000 and rounded up: (\$12,300 ÷ \$2,000) = 6.15%
Rounded up to 7%

| | |
|---|---|
| Maximum rate | 35% |
| Percentage reduction | (7%) |
| Allowable percentage | 28% |

[116] § 21(a)(2).

[117] § 21(c).

**Step 2:** Determine the allowable employment-related expenses:

| | |
|---|---|
| Lesser of $5,000 paid or $6,000 limit | $ 5,000 |

**Step 3:** Determine the dependent care credit:

| | |
|---|---|
| Allowable employment-related expenses | $ 5,000 |
| Times: Applicable percentage | × 28% |
| Dependent care credit | $ 1,400 |

## Earned Income Limitation

In addition to the $3,000 and $6,000 limitations, employment-related expenses are limited to the individual's earned income for the year.[118] For this purpose, earned income generally includes such items as salaries, wages, and net earnings from self-employment, but not investment income such as dividends and interest.

The earned income limitation is a bit more cumbersome for married couples. If an individual is married, a joint return is required to claim the credit, and the amount of the exclusion may not exceed the lesser of the taxpayer's earned income or the earned income of the taxpayer's spouse.[119] In addition, in determining the lesser earned income for married couples, special rules apply if one spouse is either a *full-time student*[120] or an incapacitated person. The student or incapacitated spouse will be deemed to have earned income of $250 a month if there is one qualified dependent or $500 a month if there are two or more qualified dependents for each month a taxpayer is incapacitated or is a full-time student. This deemed income does not increase A.G.I. when determining the applicable percentage. These rules are illustrated in the following example.

### Example 35

B and G are married, have one dependent child, age 9, incur employment-related expenses of $2,700, and have A.G.I. of $22,500 for the current taxable year. G is employed full-time and earns $27,000 a year. B returned to graduate school and was a full-time student for 10 months during the year. He was not employed during the year.

**Step 1:** The applicable percentage is determined to be 31% [35% − ($22,500 − $15,000 = $7,500 ÷ $2,000 = 3.75%, rounded up to 4%)].

**Step 2:** The allowable employment-related expenses are $2,500. This is determined by the lesser of three amounts: (1) the $2,700 spent, (2) the $3,000 limit, and (3) B's deemed earned income of $2,500 ($250 for one dependent × 10 months).

**Step 3:** Determine the dependent care credit:

| | |
|---|---|
| Allowable employment-related expenses | $ 2,500 |
| Applicable percentage (35% − 4%) | × 31% |
| Dependent care credit | $ 775 |

---

[118] § 21(d)(1).

[119] § 21(e)(2) and 21(d)(2).

[120] § 21 (d)(2). For this purpose, a full-time student is defined exactly the same as for the dependency test (i.e., for at least five months, partial months count as full months).

### Filing Requirements for the Child and Dependent Care Credit

In order to claim the credit for taxable years beginning after 1996, married couples must file a joint return and the taxpayer ID numbers of *both* the day care service provider and of the child must be disclosed on the return.

### Relationship to Other Credits

The child and dependent care credit is nonrefundable and is used to offset the tax liability determined under § 26. It is the *first* credit to be used in reducing an individual's tax liability, and there is no carryover or carryback available for unused credits.

### Relationship to Dependent Care Assistance Programs

Congress has addressed the problem of child and dependent care in two ways: the child care credit and the exclusion for dependent care assistance. As mentioned in Chapter 6, since 1981 employers have been allowed to establish qualified dependent care assistance plans.[121] These plans allow employers a current deduction for contributions to the plans and allow employees to exclude from gross income up to $5,000 of payments (e.g., reimbursements) received under the plan to the extent that the expenses would qualify as employment-related expenses for purposes of the child and dependent care credits. If the taxpayer elects to exclude a reimbursement for care, the limit on the amount of employment-related expenses that qualify for the credit ($3,000 or $6,000) is reduced dollar for dollar by the amount excluded.[122] Whether the taxpayer is better off using the exclusion or the credit requires careful analysis of the taxpayer's situation, and some tax planning may be in order.

### Example 36

H and W are married with two children. H works full-time as an accountant, and he estimates his earnings for the year will be $50,000. W is employed part-time and estimates her earnings will be $20,000 for the year. H and W estimate that they will incur $4,000 of qualified employment-related expenses for the year. H and W are in the 28 percent tax bracket.

At the beginning of H's employer's plan year, H has a decision to make. He can elect to have $1,000 excluded from his gross income in accordance with his employer's qualified dependent care assistance plan, which will be distributed to him as a reimbursement for qualified expenses, or he can elect to have the $1,000 included in his gross income as part of his salary. If the couple elects not to exclude the reimbursement, the child care credit is $800 (20% × $4,000), and they must pay taxes of $280 on the $1,000 of income, a net benefit of $520 ($800 − $280). On the other hand, if the couple elects to exclude the reimbursement, they pay no income tax on the $1,000 reimbursement, and their credit and net benefit is $800, computed as follows:

| | |
|---|---|
| Employment-related expenses | $4,000 |
| Dollar limit: maximum allowable expenses for two individuals | $6,000 |
| Reduction for employer-provided dependent care excluded from income | (1,000) |
| Limit on expenses eligible for credit | $5,000 |
| Amount of credit (20% × lesser of $4,000 or $5,000) | $ 800 |

Note that only the dollar limit eligible for the credit is reduced by the excluded income. The employment-related expenses total of $4,000 is still eligible for the credit.

[121] See § 129 and the discussion in Chapter 6.

[122] § 21(c).

## EDUCATION CREDITS

A major thrust of the Tax Reform Act of 1997 was to provide tax incentives to help reduce the cost of higher education and life-long learning. The law added six different provisions directed at this policy objective. Unfortunately, these rules often conflict and can be quite complex.

Taxpayers planning for the cost of educational programs or college degrees now must consider the following tax incentives:

- The exclusion for interest on Series E bonds.[123]
- The deductibility of certain interest on student loans.[124]
- Participation in qualified state tuition programs (529 plans).[125]
- Distributions from regular IRAs to pay educational expenses.[126]
- Establishing an education IRA.[127]
- The Hope scholarship credit or the American Opportunity Tax Credit.[128]
- The Lifetime Learning credit.[129]

Section 25A contains two credits, the Hope Scholarship credit and the Lifetime Learning credit, that are directly aimed at subsidizing the costs of pursuing undergraduate and graduate degrees as well as vocational training. While there are two credits, for any one particular student, a taxpayer could elect either the Hope credit or a Lifetime Learning credit but not both. Like most of the other tax incentives created in 1997, these credits are phased out at specific income levels and, therefore, are not available to high income or wealthy taxpayers. The following discussion first looks at each credit individually and then at requirements common to each credit.

### Hope Scholarship Credit

The Hope Scholarship Credit was enhanced in 2009 by the enactment of new Code § 25A(i) and is referred to as the American Opportunity Tax Credit through 2011. The Hope Credit was originally born out of Congressional desire to enable all students to continue to pursue their education once they have completed high school. The credit is allowed for qualified tuition and certain related expenses for post secondary education furnished to an eligible student. For 2011 under the American Opportunity Tax Credit (AOTC), a taxpayer may elect to claim a credit for 100 percent of the first $2,000 of qualifying expenses and 25 percent of the next $2,000 of expenses for each student. Thus the maximum credit is $2,500 per year per student (e.g., the taxpayer whose triplets enroll at the local state college could claim a maximum credit for the year of $7,500). In its initial form, the Hope credit could be used only for the first two years of post-secondary education. However, to help underwrite the cost of a college education, the AOTC extended eligibility to four taxable years. In addition, 40 percent of the credit is refundable unless the taxpayer could be subject to the kiddie tax (i.e., the child is a full-time student less than 24 and whose earned income does not exceed one-half his or her support).[130]

The credit is available only for expenses paid on behalf of the taxpayer, the taxpayer's spouse, or a dependent. In the case of a dependent's expenses, the eligible student is not

---

[123] See § 135 and Chapter 6.

[124] § 222. With respect to tax incentives directed toward students, also see § 117 (exclusion for scholarships and fellowships) and § 127 (employer paid educational expenses).

[125] § 529.

[126] § 72(t).

[127] § 530.

[128] § 25A and § 25A(i).

[129] *Ibid.*

[130] The American Opportunity Tax Credit is scheduled to expire after 2012, and the original Hope Credit rules will be reinstated. For 2013 the Hope Credit is nonrefundable and the credit amount is equal to 100 percent of the first $1,200 of qualifying expenses and 50 percent of the next $1,200 of expenses for each student. Thus the maximum credit is $1,800 per year per student. The Hope credit can be claimed for only two taxable years. In addition, it is permitted only if the student has not completed the first two years of post-secondary education as of the beginning of the taxable year. Normally, these rules should provide a credit for each student on $1,800 per year for two years for a total benefit of $3,600.

entitled to claim a credit if he or she is claimed as a dependent by the parent or another taxpayer. Instead, if a parent or other taxpayer claims a student as a dependent, any qualified tuition and related expenses paid by the student are treated as paid by the parent and the parent benefits from the credit![131]

The credit is generally available only for expenses paid during the taxable year for education that begins during such year. For this purpose, education that begins during the first three months of the next year is treated as having started in the previous year. This special three-month rule allows a credit for prepaid expenses. Observe that these rules require careful planning to take advantage of the full credit. Because the credit is tied to the taxable year rather than the typical academic year (i.e., a year that begins with the fall semester and ends with the spring semester), taxpayers may lose some of the credit's benefits without taking advantage of the prepayment privilege.

### Example 37

H is a typical high school graduate who enrolled for the 2010 fall semester of a local two-year community college. He plans to finish in the spring semester of 2012. The school charges $2,000 tuition per semester. Assuming H elects to claim the credit in 2010 and 2011, he can claim a total credit for the two years of $4,500 ($2,000 for fall 2010 + $2,500 for spring and fall of 2011. In such case, he does not benefit from the entire $5,000 ($2,500 per year) credit available. In order to avoid this result, H should prepay his 2011 tuition in December of 2010. Since prepayments qualify for the credit as long as the education occurs within the first three months of the following year, he would be eligible for the full $2,500 credit in 2010. He should also prepay in 2011 his tuition for the spring 2012 semester so that he will have paid at least $4,000 in 2011.

Note that qualifying expenses paid with loan proceeds are eligible for both credits in the year the expenses are paid, not when the loan is repaid.

## Eligible Student

Expenses qualify for the credit only if they are for an eligible student. An eligible student is one who is enrolled in a program leading to a degree, certificate or other recognized educational credential at an eligible education institution. In addition, the student must carry one-half the load that a normal full-time student carries for at least one academic period per year. For example, if a student goes part-time during the spring semester (i.e., presumably one academic period) and carries one-half the full time load, his expenses for the summer and fall semesters will qualify even if he takes less than one-half the full time load during these later periods. Note also that the credit is not available for students that have been convicted of a federal or state felony offense consisting of the possession or distribution of a controlled substance.

## Qualified Tuition and Expenses

Qualified tuition and related expenses include tuition and fees required for the enrollment or attendance at an eligible institution. Expenses also include course materials. However, expenses that do not directly relate to the student's education such as student activity fees, athletic fees, insurance expenses, transportation, or other expenses unrelated to an individual's academic course of instruction do not qualify for either credit. Similarly, expenses related to courses involving sports, games, or hobbies do not qualify unless such course is part of the individual's degree program. In addition, neither the AOTC nor the Lifetime Learning credit is available for expenses incurred for room and board.

For both the AOTC and the Lifetime Learning credit, the amount of qualifying expenses must be reduced by amounts covered by excludable scholarships or educational assistance plans.[132] However, amounts withdrawn from a qualified prepaid tuition plan and used to pay eligible expenses qualify for the credit.

---

131 § 25A(g)(3).

132 § 25(g)(2).

### Eligible Institutions

Only expenses paid to eligible institutions qualify for the credit. While most colleges and universities would be considered eligible, other providers of courses may also qualify. Technically, an eligible institution includes accredited post-secondary educational institutions offering credit toward a bachelor's degree, an associate's degree, or another recognized post-secondary credential. Certain proprietary institutions and post-secondary vocational institutions also are eligible. The bright line test is whether the institution is eligible to participate in Department of Education student aid programs.

**Phase-Out for High Income Taxpayers** The AOTC (like the Lifetime Learning credit discussed below) is not extended to high income taxpayers. To accomplish this objective, the total maximum credit allowed for all eligible students is phased out once the taxpayer's modified adjusted gross income exceeds certain thresholds. For 2011, the thresholds for the AOTC differ from those for the Lifetime Learning credit. For the AOTC, the phase-out begins at $160,000 for joint returns and $80,000 for other returns. The reduction occurs over a $20,000 *income range* for joint filers and $10,000 for other taxpayers. If the taxpayer is married, a joint return must be filed to claim the credits. The formula for determining the phase-out and the levels at which a complete phase-out occurs is shown below.

**EXHIBIT 13.12** **Phase-Out of AOTC and the Lifetime Learning Credit for 2011**

$$\text{Reduction of total allowable credits} = \text{Allowable credits} \times \frac{\text{Modified A.G.I.}^{*} - \text{threshold}}{\text{Income range}}$$

| *Credit* | *Taxpayer* | *Modified A.G.I.* Phase-Out begins* | *Modified A.G.I.* Phase-Out complete* |
|---|---|---|---|
| AOTC | Married filing joint | $160,000 | $180,000 |
| | Other taxpayers | 80,000 | 90,000 |
| Lifetime Learning | Married filing joint | $102,000 | $122,000 |
| | Other taxpayers | 51,000 | 61,000 |

*Modified A.G.I. is A.G.I. increased by income earned outside the U.S. which normally is excluded under § 911. The income phase-out threshold amounts are indexed annually for inflation.

### Example 38

M, a single mother, has modified A.G.I. of $81,000. In 2011, M's daughter, D, begins studying for her bachelor's degree as a full-time student at City University. On September 1, M pays $5,000 in qualified tuition for D's first semester. Without the income limitations, M would be entitled to the maximum AOTC of $2,500 (100% of $2,000 plus 25% of $2,000). However, taking into account the income limitations, M's credit is reduced as shown below.

$$\text{Reduction of total allowable credits} = \$2,500 \times \frac{\$81,000 - \$80,000}{\$10,000} = \$250$$

Thus, M is entitled to a $2,250 ($2,500 – $250) credit.

### Lifetime Learning Credit

In addition to the AOTC, § 25A creates the Lifetime Learning credit. This credit can be claimed for 20 percent of qualified tuition and fees incurred during the taxable year on behalf of the taxpayer, the taxpayer's spouse, or any dependents. Up to $10,000 of qualified tuition and fees per taxpayer return are eligible for the credit (i.e., the maximum credit per return is $2,000). For any one particular student, a taxpayer could elect either the AOTC or a Lifetime Learning credit but not both.

In contrast to the AOTC, a taxpayer may claim the Lifetime Learning credit for a unlimited number of taxable years. Also in contrast to the AOTC, the maximum amount of the Lifetime Learning credit that may be claimed on a taxpayer's return is not related to the number of students in the taxpayer's family. The key variable is the amount of qualified expenses incurred during the year and not the number of eligible individuals.

### Qualified Tuition and Related Expenses for Lifetime Learning Credit

Qualified tuition and fees for purposes of the Lifetime Learning credit are defined in the same manner as for the AOTC but with several important additions. As noted above, the AOTC is available only for four taxable years and ceases after the year the student has completed four years of post-secondary education. In contrast, the Lifetime Learning credit—true to its name—applies not only to these same expenses but also such expenses incurred in any taxable year during the taxpayer's lifetime. For example, the Lifetime Learning credit would be applicable to expenses incurred in obtaining an undergraduate degree (all four years or whatever is required) or a graduate degree (e.g., a law degree, a medical degree, an M.B.A., and similar graduate degrees). In addition, the definition of qualified tuition and expenses is expanded for the Lifetime Learning credit to include any course of instruction at an eligible educational institution to acquire or improve job skills of the taxpayer. Thus expenses need not be incurred in a degree program but could be simply a continuing education course (e.g., a C.P.A. takes a course on the new tax law). Note, however, that for the course to qualify it must be provided by a qualifying educational institution (e.g., one that is eligible to participate in student aid programs of the Department of Education).

Like the AOTC, the amount of qualifying expenses for the Lifetime Learning credit must be reduced by amounts covered by scholarships or educational assistance plans (assuming such amounts are excludable from gross income). Expenses taken into account for the AOTC cannot be taken into account for the Lifetime Learning credit.

These credits are automatically available to the taxpayer unless the taxpayer elects not to take the credit with respect to the qualified tuition and related expenses of an individual for any taxable year. Previously, the taxpayer had to elect to claim the credit.[133]

### Interaction of AOTC, Lifetime Learning Credit, Education IRAs and Series EE Savings Bonds

Special rules exist to prohibit the taxpayer from obtaining multiple benefits from the credits and nontaxable withdrawals from education individual retirement accounts. For each eligible student in each taxable year, the taxpayer must elect one of the three tax benefits: (1) the AOTC, (2) the Lifetime Learning credit, or (3) the exclusion from gross income for withdrawals from education IRAs. The election is separate for each student. Thus a parent could elect the AOTC for one child, the Lifetime Learning credit for another child, and the exclusion for IRA withdrawals for a third child. Any educational expenses taken into account for purposes of the credits or the IRA withdrawal cannot again be taken into account in determining the exclusion for interest on Series EE savings bonds that are used to pay for educational expenses.

## Credit for Adoption Expenses

To encourage adoptions, § 36C provides a maximum refundable credit of $13,170 per child for qualified adoption expenses paid or incurred by the taxpayer through 2011. Qualified adoption expenses are reasonable and necessary adoption fees, court costs, attorney's fees and

[133] § 25A(e), as amended by the 2001 Tax Act, makes the credits applicable to the taxpayer unless the taxpayer *elects out* of the credit provisions.

other expenses that are directly related to the legal adoption of an eligible child. An eligible child is an individual (1) who has not attained age 18 as of the time of the adoption, or (2) who is physically or mentally incapable of caring for himself or herself. No credit is allowed for expenses incurred (1) in violation of state or federal law, (2) in carrying out any surrogate parenting arrangement, or (3) in connection with the adoption of a child of the taxpayer's spouse. The credit is phased out ratably for taxpayers with modified adjusted gross income above $185,210, and is fully phased out at $225,210 of modified A.G.I. For these purposes modified A.G.I. is computed by increasing the taxpayer's A.G.I. by the amount otherwise excluded from gross income of citizens or residents living abroad.

The $13,170 limit is a per child limit, not an annual limitation. If adoption expenses are paid during a tax year prior to the tax year in which the adoption is final, the credit is allowed for the year the adoption is made final. If adoption expenses are paid during or after the tax year in which the adoption is finalized, the credit is allowed for the tax year in which the expense is paid. For example, in the case of an adoption which is finalized in 2011, if a taxpayer pays or incurs $3,500 of otherwise allowable qualified adoption expenses with respect to the child in year 2010 and $9,500 of otherwise allowable qualified adoption expenses with respect to that same child in 2011, then the taxpayer would receive a $3,500 credit with respect to expenses incurred in 2010 and a $9,670 credit with respect to expenses incurred in 2011 (both credits are allowed on the 2011 tax return).

When the adoption credit is attributable to amounts chargeable to a capital account (e.g., the costs of constructing an elevator at the taxpayer's house to accommodate a wheelchair that is required as a condition of the adoption), the taxpayer is not allowed additional basis in the house to the extent of the adoption credit allowed. An ordering rule specifies that qualified adoption expenditures not chargeable to a capital account (the legal fees) are allowed for the credit before any amounts that are chargeable to a capital account.

A special rule applies to the adoption of a child with special needs. "Special needs" include the child's ethnic background, age, or membership in a minority or sibling group, or the presence of such factors such as medical conditions or physical, mental or emotional handicaps. In the case of a special needs child, $13,170 is allowed as an adoption credit regardless of whether the taxpayer has qualified adoption expenses. The credit for a special needs child is only allowed if the adoption becomes final and the credit is only allowed in the year in which the adoption becomes final.[134]

### Interaction with the Exclusion for Qualified Adoption Expenses

A companion but separate $13,170 exclusion from gross income is also available to employees for qualified adoption expenses paid by the employer in accordance with a qualified adoption assistance program.[135]

Adoption expenses paid or reimbursed under an adoption assistance program may not be taken into account in determining the adoption credit. A taxpayer may, however, satisfy the requirements of the adoption credit *and* the exclusion with different expenses paid or incurred by the taxpayer and the employer, respectively. For example, in the case of an adoption that costs $14,000 with $7,000 of expenses paid by the taxpayer and $7,000 paid by the taxpayer's employer under an adoption assistance program, the taxpayer may qualify for the adoption credit and the exclusion.

There are special rules that apply to the adoption of foreign children, with no credit allowed until the year in which the adoption is final.

In order to claim the adoption credit, married couples must file a joint return and include the child's taxpayer I.D. number on the tax return claiming the adoption credit.[136] Recall that this credit can be used to offset the tentative minimum tax. This credit has been made a refundable credit for the years 2010 and 2011.

## Credit for the Elderly and Permanently Disabled

A nonrefundable tax credit is available to certain taxpayers who are either 65 years of age or older or are permanently and totally disabled.[137] The credit is 15 percent of an individual's

[134] § 36C(a)(3) – formerly § 23(a)(3).

[135] § 137.

[136] § 23(f).

[137] Limited rules apply to taxpayers who are under 65 years old if they are certain governmental retirees subject to the Public Retirement System and elect to have this section apply [see § 22(c)].

earned and investment income that does not exceed the taxpayer's appropriate § 22 amount.[138] The maximum § 22 amount is:

1. $5,000 for single individuals
2. $5,000 for a joint return where only one spouse is at least 65 years old
3. $7,500 for a joint return where both spouses are 65 years or older
4. $3,750 for a married individual filing separately

The maximum amount from above is then reduced by excludable pension and annuity income received during the year, including social security and railroad retirement benefits, and by one-half of the taxpayer's A.G.I. that exceeds:

1. $7,500 for unmarried individuals
2. $10,000 if married filing jointly
3. $5,000 if married filing separately

### Example 39

P is single, 65 years old, and has A.G.I. of $8,300 from interest and dividends. During the taxable year, she also received social security of $1,500. Her credit for the elderly is computed as follows:

| | | |
|---|---|---|
| Maximum § 22 amount | | $ 5,000 |
| Less: Social security received | $1,500 | |
| 50% of A.G.I. over $7,500 ($8,300 − $7,500 = $800 × 50%) | + 400 | (1,900) |
| Section 22 amount available for credit | | $ 3,100 |
| Multiply by rate | | × 15% |
| Amount of credit | | $ 465 |

There are a number of additional special rules, and because these rules are quite complicated, individuals are allowed to file their return with a request that the IRS compute their tax liability and tax credit. However, few people are able to take advantage of the credit for the elderly since social security receipts commonly exceed the maximum § 22 amount.

The credit for the elderly or permanently disabled is limited to the § 26 tax liability reduced by the child and dependent care credit. Like the child and dependent care credit, this credit is nonrefundable and may not be carried back or forward.

## Credit for Interest on Certain Home Mortgages

In order to help provide financing for first-time home buyers, Congress has created several special programs. One of these allows state and local governments to issue mortgage credit certificates (MCCs).[139] Taxpayers who receive such certificates are allowed to claim a nonrefundable credit for a specified percentage of interest paid on mortgage loans on their principal residence. Each certificate must specify the principal amount of indebtedness that qualifies for the credit as well as the applicable percentage rate of the credit. The credit percentage may differ with each certificate but must be between 10 and 50 percent. If the credit exceeds 20 percent, the maximum credit is limited to $2,000. Of course, the amount of the taxpayer's interest deduction must be reduced by the amount of the credit claimed during the year. Any credit that cannot be used may be carried over for three years.

---

[138] § 22(a).

[139] § 25.

**Example 40**

After saving for years, R and his wife, W, decided to buy their first house. In order to finance the purchase, R applied for and received from the state an MCC. The certificate specifies that the rate is 15% and the maximum loan amount is $70,000. The couple purchased a house for $75,000 and obtained a loan of $65,000 from a savings and loan. For the year, R and W paid interest of $5,000 on the loan. They may claim a credit of $750 ($5,000 × 15%). In addition, they may deduct interest of $4,250 ($5,000 − $750).

While the credit can provide a significant benefit, it is not available to everyone. Under the MCC program, state and local governments are limited in the volume of credits they may dispense and in the individuals to whom they may be issued. Taxpayers are eligible to receive a certificate only if they meet certain narrowly defined criteria. For example, the purchaser's income cannot generally exceed 115 percent of the area's median gross income, the price of the home cannot exceed 90 percent of the average purchase price of homes in the area, and the homes may be available only in targeted areas. Still other constraints exist that restrict the credit's use.

# Refundable Credits

Refundable credits are those credits that are recoverable even though an individual has no income tax liability in the current year. They are treated as payments of taxes. Included in this category are the credit for taxes withheld at the source (§ 31), the earned income credit (§ 32), the credit for tax withheld at the source on nonresident aliens and foreign corporations (§ 33), the gasoline and special fuels credit (§ 34) and the AMT refundable credit (§ 53(e)).

Refundable credits may be used to offset all taxes imposed by the Code, including penalty taxes. This result is accomplished by combining all the refundable credits and accounting for them after all the nonrefundable credits have been used to offset the § 26 tax liability.

## Tax Withheld at the Source

The first and most important of the refundable credits is styled "Credit for Tax Withheld on Wages" and obviously includes the amount withheld by an employer as a tax on wages earned.[140] However, the credit has broader application with respect to certain taxes withheld by the payor at the source of payment, including:

1. Tax on pensions and annuities withheld by the payor
2. Overpaid FICA taxes (in cases where a taxpayer has two or more employers in the same year)
3. Amounts withheld as backup withholding in cases where the taxpayer fails to furnish a taxpayer identification number to the payor of interest or dividends[141]
4. Quarterly estimated tax payments

## Earned Income Credit

In 1975, Congress introduced the earned income credit to eliminate some of the disincentives that discouraged low-income taxpayers with children from working.[142] The credit was specifically designed to alleviate the increasing burden of social security taxes. In many cases, income taxes were not a concern for these low-income taxpayers since they were protected by personal and dependent exemptions as well as the standard deduction. However, they were

---

[140] §§ 31(a) and 3401.

[141] §§ 31(c) and 3406.

[142] § 32(a).

not exempt from social security taxes. Consistent with its purpose, the credit is refundable (e.g., the taxpayer would receive the credit amount even if he or she is not required to pay income taxes since it is viewed as a refund of the social security taxes).

Since its creation, the earned income credit has been the subject of a great deal of Congressional tinkering. The most recent round of adjustments was introduced by the Clinton administration in 1993. These changes not only increased the benefits of the credit but also expanded its coverage. Beginning in 1994, the credit may apply even if the taxpayer does not have children.

## Computation of the Credit

The starting point for determining the credit is determination of the taxpayer's earned income. As might be expected, *earned income* consists of wages, salaries, tips, and other employer compensation plus earnings from self-employment included in gross income for the taxable year. Taxpayers may elect to treat combat zone compensation that is otherwise excluded from gross income under § 112 as earned income.[143] Earned income does not include pension and annuity income even if provided by an employer for past services. Amounts received similar to compensation that are excluded are not treated as earned income. For example, excludable dependent care benefits, the value of meals and lodging furnished for the convenience of the employer, excludable educational assistance benefits and salary deferrals [contributions to a § 401(k) plan] are not included in earned income.

The initial credit is computed by multiplying the earned income of the taxpayer (limited by a ceiling amount) by a statutory percentage; however, this initial credit amount is phased out as the taxpayer's income increases above a phase-out amount. As can be seen from Exhibit 13-13, the maximum amounts of earned income that qualify for the credit as well as the statutory credit percentages vary depending on the number of children the taxpayer has.[144] Observe that the credit for an individual with no children is essentially designed to give the taxpayer back the FICA taxes on the first \$6,070 wages (7.65% rate × \$6,070). The maximum credits for eligible individuals for 2011 are shown in Exhibit 13-13.

As noted above, the credit begins to phase out once the taxpayer's income increases above the phase-out amount. The credit is reduced if *either* the earned income or the A.G.I. of the taxpayer exceeds certain specified amounts shown in Exhibit 13-14.[145]

The phase-out is computed by multiplying the applicable phase-out rate by the excess of A.G.I. or earned income (whichever is greater) over the phase-out amounts. The credit can be computed using the following formula:

Maximum credit
  Applicable percentage × earned income (not to exceed the ceiling amounts)
− Reduction
  Applicable percentage × (larger of earned income or A.G.I. − phase-out amount)
= Earned income credit

**EXHIBIT 13.13** **Earned Income Credit: Credit Percentages and Maximum Credits**

| *Number of Qualifying Children* | *Credit Percentage* | *Ceiling on Earned Income* | *Maximum Credit* |
|---|---|---|---|
| 0 | 7.65% | $ 6,070 | $ 464 |
| 1 | 34.00 | 9,100 | 3,094 |
| 2 | 40.00 | 12,780 | 5,112 |
| 3 or more | 45.00 | 12,780 | 5,751 |

[143] § 32(c)(2)(B)(vi).

[144] § 32(b)(1).

[145] Rev. Proc. 2011-12, 2011-2, IRB 297.

**EXHIBIT 13.14 Earned Income Credit: Phase-Outs**

| | | Other than Joint Filers | | Joint Filers | |
|---|---|---|---|---|---|
| Qualifying Children | Phase-Out Percentage | *Threshold Phaseout Starts at* | *Completed Phaseout Level* | *Threshold Phaseout Starts at* | *Completed Phaseout Level* |
| 0 | 7.65% | $ 7,590 | $13,660 | $12,670 | $18,740 |
| 1 | 15.98 | 16,690 | 36,052 | 21,770 | 41,132 |
| 2 | 21.06 | 16,690 | 40,964 | 21,770 | 46,044 |
| 3 or more | 21.06 | 16,690 | 43,998 | 21,770 | 49,078 |

For example, the maximum 2011 earned income credit for an unmarried taxpayer with one child is $3,094 ($9,100 × 34%). This credit is completely eliminated when the taxpayer's modified A.G.I. or earned income exceeds $36,052 [15.98% × ($36,052 − $16,690 = $19,362) = $3,094]. The levels at which the credit is completely phased out are shown in Exhibit 13-14.

## Example 41

D and M are married, file a joint return for 2011, and maintain a household for their dependent son, who is three years old. D has earned income of $20,000 and M has none. The couple own investments that produce $2,475 of includible income for the year and have an A.G.I. of $22,475 ($20,000 + $2,475). The earned income credit is computed as follows:

| | |
|---|---|
| Maximum credit (34% × $9,100) | $3,094 |
| Less: Reduction for A.G.I. over $21,770 ($22,475 − $21,770 = $705 × 15.98%) | − 113 |
| Earned income credit | $2,981 |

To help taxpayers compute the credit, the IRS provides a worksheet and an earned income credit table to aid taxpayers in determining the correct amount of the earned income credit. The worksheet and table are included with the instructions for completing Form 1040 and Form 1040A.[146]

As a refundable credit, qualified individuals may receive tax refunds equal to their earned income credit even in years when they have no tax liability.[147]

## Example 42

Y has earned income and A.G.I. of $10,000, has three exemptions (including two qualified children), and files as head of household. As a result, she has no income tax liability for the year. However, she is entitled to a tax refund equal to the earned income credit of $4,000 ($10,000 × 40%) plus any taxes (other than FICA taxes) withheld from her wages. She may also qualify for a refundable child tax credit (see the next section and *Example 43*).

[146] § 32(f) Note that the earned income credit table prepared annually by the IRS reflects the credit based on a midpoint of each $25 increment of an income range.

[147] The taxpayer is required to reduce his or her earned income credit by the amount of the alternative minimum tax imposed on that individual.

### Eligibility Requirements

Because the earned income credit was a mechanical calculation under the former rules, some wealthy taxpayers inadvertently qualified for the earned income credit in years in which they reported a small amount of earned income. To preclude such taxpayers from taking advantage of the earned income credit, a major change was made. The earned income credit is now disallowed for taxpayers that have too much investment income. Taxpayers are not allowed to claim the earned income credit if they have more than $3,150 of disqualified income.[148] The definition of disqualified income includes:

- Interest
- Dividends
- Tax-exempt interest
- The net income from rents or royalties not derived in ordinary course of a trade or business
- Capital gain net income
- The excess of aggregate passive income over aggregate passive losses

Finally, in an attempt to cut down on fraud and abuse relating to this credit, the taxpayer identification number required to be disclosed on the return means a Social Security number issued to an individual by the Social Security Administration.

Until 1993, the earned income credit was available only to taxpayers who had children. In a major change, the RRA of 1993 extended the earned income credit to certain individuals without children. In so doing, the law significantly broadened the availability of the credit. In either situation, if the taxpayer is married a joint return must be filed as a requirement to obtain the EIC.[149] The eligibility requirements for taxpayers with and without children are set forth below.

### Taxpayers without Children

Taxpayers without a qualifying child are eligible to claim the credit if the taxpayer meets three conditions:[150]

1. The taxpayer (or the spouse of the taxpayer) must be at least 25 years old and not more than 64 years old at the end of the taxable year.
2. The taxpayer is not a dependent in the same year the credit is claimed.
3. The taxpayer has a principal residence in the United States for more than one-half of the taxable year.

### Taxpayers with Children

Taxpayers are entitled to claim the credit if they have a qualifying child. The child need not be a dependent but must meet the following tests:

1. *Relationship.* The individual must be a child, stepchild, foster child, a legally adopted child of the taxpayer, or a descendant of any such individual. A married child does not meet this test unless the taxpayer can claim the child as a dependent.
2. *Age.* The child must be either (1) less than 19 years old at the close of the calendar year, (2) less than 24 years old and a full-time student at the close of the calendar year, or (3) permanently and totally disabled any time during the year.
3. *Residency.* The child must share the same principal place of abode as the taxpayer for more than one-half of the taxable year, and that abode must be located in the United States.

Assuming all of the above requirements are met and the taxpayer properly identifies the child on the return (i.e., name, age, taxpayer identification number), the credit is allowed.

---

148 See § 32(i) and Rev. Proc. 2011-12, 2011-2, IRB 297.

149 § 32(d).

150 § 32(c)(1)(A)(ii).

## REFUNDABLE CHILD TAX CREDITS

Taxpayers who qualify for the regular child credit may also qualify for a refundable Child Tax Credit which is authorized in § 24(d). Any amount allowed as a refundable credit will reduce the Child Tax Credit (CTC) that would otherwise be allowed under § 24.

One of the principal policy goals of the Child Tax Credit for low-income taxpayers is to offset not only the taxpayer's regular income tax but also the employee's share of FICA (or for those who are self-employed, one-half of the taxpayer's self-employment tax). To accomplish this goal, a portion of the Child Tax Credit was made refundable.

The overall limit on the amount of the CTC that will be refundable is the amount of the CTC determined as if the tax liability limitation did not apply. Recall that the CTC is limited to an amount not to exceed the excess of the sum of the § 26 regular tax liability plus the AMT over the sum of the credits allowed by the Child and Dependent Care Credit (§ 21), the Credit for the Elderly (§ 22), the credit for Interest on Certain Home Mortages (§ 25), the Hope and Lifetime Learning credit (§ 25A) and the foreign tax credit (§ 27). Generally this limitation will be equal to the full CTC computed by multiplying the per child amount by the number of qualifying children.

The amount of the refundable Child Tax Credit for 2011 is the lesser of:

1. The child credit allowed without regard to the tax liability limitation of § 26, or
2. The amount by which the nonrefundable personal credits allowed would increase if the tax liability limitation were increased by 15 percent of the taxpayer's earned income in excess of $3,000.

Referred to as the 15 percent rule, the CTC is refundable to the extent that the nonrefundable personal credits allowed would increase if the tax liablity limitation was increased by 15 percent of the taxpayer's earned income in excess of $3,000. For purposes of computing earned income as applicable to the refundable CTC, combat pay excludable from gross income under §112, is treated as earned income.

Taxpayers with three or more children may calculate the refundable portion of the credit using the excess of their social security taxes (i.e., the taxpayer's share of the FICA taxes and one-half of self-employment taxes) over the earned income credit if this calculation results in a greater amount than computed under the 15 percent rule.

### Example 43

D, a single parent, is raising two children at home and earns a salary in 2011 of $22,000. The CTC is the only nonrefundable personal tax credit that D is entitled to.

| | |
|---|---|
| Income | $22,000 |
| Standard deduction | (8,500) |
| Personal exemptions | (11,100) |
| Taxable income | $ 2,400 |
| Tax on $2,400 | $ 240 |
| Earned income credit [$5,112 – (21.06% × ($22,000 – $16,690))] | $ 3,994 |
| FICA paid (7.65% × $22,000) | $ 1,683 |

The refundable portion of the CTC is the lesser of:

| | |
|---|---|
| 1. The CTC as if the tax liability limitation did not apply | $ 2,000 |
| *or* | |
| 2. Increased tax liability and nonrefundable credit allowed | $ 2,000 |
| $2,850 [15% × (22,000 – 3,000)] limited to $2,000 (amount of child credit) | |
| Less tax liability and nonrefundable credit allowed before this calculation | –240 |
| Nonrefundable credit increase | $ 1,760 |
| Refundable portion of the child tax credit | $ 1,760 |

If D's tax liability were increased by $2,850, D's tax liability would be $3,115 ($2,850 + $240) and the amount of nonrefundable credits would go from $240 to $2,000. This is an increase of $1,760 which is D's allowable refundable portion of the CTC for 2011.

Thus D's refundable portion of the CTC is $1,760. D's nonrefundable CTC is $240 and will be allowed to reduce her regular tax liability.

D's total tax refund is computed as follows:

| | | |
|---|---|---|
| Tax liability | | $ 240 |
| Less: CTC | | (240) |
| Tax liability before refundable credits | | $ 0 |
| Less: Refundable credits: | | |
| CTC | $1,760 | |
| EIC | 3,994 | (5,754) |
| Total refund | | $5,754 |

## Example 44

H and W have three children and earned income of $30,450. For 2011 their tax liability would be $35. The CTC is the only nonrefundable personal credit that H and W are entitled to.

| | |
|---|---|
| Income | $30,450 |
| Standard deduction | (11,600) |
| Personal exemptions | (18,500) |
| Taxable income | $ 350 |
| Tax on $350 | $ 35 |
| Earned income credit [$5,751 – $1,828 (21.06% × ($30,450 – $21,770))] | $ 3,923 |
| FICA paid (7.65% × $30,450) | $ 2,329 |

The refundable portion of the CTC is the lesser of:

| | |
|---|---|
| 1. The CTC as if the tax liability limitation did not apply | $ 3,000 |
| *or* | |
| 2. Increased tax liability and nonrefundable credit allowed | $ 3,000 |
| $4,118 [15% × (30,450 – 3,000)] limited to 3,000 (amount of child credit) | |
| Tax liability and nonrefundable credit allowed before this calculation | –35 |
| Nonrefundable credit increase | $ 2,965 |
| Refundable portion of the child tax credit | $ 2,965 |

If H & W's tax liability were increased by $4,118, their tax liability would be $4,153 ($4,118 + $35) and the amount of the nonrefundable credits would go from $35 to $3,000. This increase of $2,965 is H and W's allowable refundable portion of the CTC for 2011.

Since H and W have at least three children, they should compute the excess of their FICA taxes over their EIC and compare it to $2,965. In this case, there is no excess and H and W will be able to treat $2,965 as the refundable portion of their CTC. Thus their nonrefundable CTC is $35 ($3,000 – $2,965).

H and W's total refund is $5,146, computed as follows:

| | | |
|---|---|---|
| Tax liability | | $ 35 |
| Less: CTC | | (35) |
| Tax liability before refundable credits | | $ 0 |
| Less: Refundable credits: | | |
| CTC | $2,965 | |
| EIC | 3,923 | (6,888) |
| Total refund | | $6,888 |

Although the total amount of the child credit is the same whether or not part of it is treated as a refundable credit, it is advantageous for taxpayers to claim a refundable credit rather than a nonrefundable child credit. As noted above, nonrefundable credits are subtracted from the total tax for the year and may *only* reduce the regular tax and the AMT tax to zero; any excess is not refunded. In contrast, refundable credits are treated as tax payments, and are added to the amounts of federal income taxes that have been withheld and any estimated tax payments that have been made. If this sum is more than the total tax due, the excess is refunded.

## Other Refundable Credits

Three other refundable credits are allowed. Code § 33 allows as a credit the amount of tax withheld at the source for nonresident aliens and foreign corporations. Code § 34 provides an income tax credit for the amount of excise tax paid on gasoline, where the gasoline is used on a farm, for other nonhighway purposes, by local transit systems, and by operators of intercity, local, or school buses. Finally, Code § 35 provides that an overpayment of taxes resulting from filing an amended return will be treated as a refundable credit.

# Problem Materials

## DISCUSSION QUESTIONS

**13-1** *Alternative Minimum Tax.* It has been said that a taxpayer must maintain a second set of books to comply with the AMT system. Why is the extra set of books necessary?

**13-2** *Alternative Minimum Tax.* The AMT requires taxpayers to keep an extra set of books for several adjustment items. What action can a taxpayer take to minimize the recordkeeping requirements with respect to depreciation deductions?

**13-3** *Alternative Minimum Tax.* Assume a taxpayer has a regular tax liability of $25,000, a tentative AMT of $28,000, and an AMT of $3,000 for the current year. How much does the taxpayer actually owe the IRS?

**13-4** *Alternative Minimum Tax.* A taxpayer has an AMT liability of $50,000 and a general business credit of $50,000. He is not concerned about paying the AMT because he thinks the general business credit can be used to offset the AMT. Is he correct? What if the taxpayer were a corporation?

**13-5** *Alternative Minimum Tax.* Is it safe to assume that only wealthy individuals who have low taxable incomes are subject to the alternative minimum tax? Are any taxpayers whose marginal rates exceed 26 percent subject to the alternative minimum tax? Explain.

**13-6** *Alternative Minimum Tax.* G will be subject to the alternative minimum tax in 2011 but not in 2012. G's property tax on her residence is due November 15, 2011. If she defers payment of the property tax until 2012, she must pay a 5 percent penalty. When should G pay the property tax? Explain.

**13-7** *Alternative Minimum Tax.* Some interest expense can be taken as an itemized deduction for regular tax purposes but different rules control the interest expenses allowable as an AMT itemized deduction. Explain the differences in these rules and note which rules are more restrictive.

**13-8** *Alternative Minimum Tax.* Is the § 179 (first-year expensing) deduction allowed as a deduction for the AMT system?

**13-9** *Credits vs. Deductions.* Assume taxpayers have a choice of deducting $1,000 for A.G.I. or taking a $250 tax credit for the current year. Which taxpayers should choose the deduction? Why?

**13-10** *Rehabilitation and Energy Credits.* A taxpayer purchased an old train station, which was placed in service in 1935, for $20,000. He plans to tear the building down and erect a new office building for $100,000. Will any of this qualify for the rehabilitation or energy investment credit? What tax advice could you give the taxpayer for his consideration in maximizing these credits?

**13-11** *Rehabilitation and Energy Credit.* When a taxpayer claims a rehabilitation credit, what impact does the credit have on the basis of the property for cost recovery purposes? What is the impact on the basis when a business energy credit is claimed? What if the disabled access credit is claimed?

**13-12** *IC Recapture.* Explain two possible consequences if a taxpayer claims an investment credit on property and then makes an early disposition of the property.

**13-13** *Minimum Tax Credit.* If a taxpayer pays an AMT in the current year, what consequences does that payment have on the AMT liability that may be owed in subsequent years? What impact does the payment of the AMT in the current year have on the regular tax liability in subsequent years?

**13-14** *Dependent Care Credit.* A husband and wife both work and employ a babysitter to watch the children during their work hours. How much of the babysitter's salary qualifies for the child and dependent care credit if:

**a.** The babysitter performs cooking and cleaning services while she is watching the children.

**b.** The babysitter also performs services around the house including gardening, bartending, and chauffeuring.

**13-15** *Earned Income Credit.* A husband and wife with A.G.I. and earned income of $7,000 maintained a household for their son but were unable to claim him as a dependent because he was 20 years old and earned $3,500. Can the son or his parents qualify for the earned income credit? Explain.

**13-16** *Research Credit.* An entrepreneur works in a garage during 2010 doing research for a new patent. He spends $15,000 on the research in 2010. In January 2011, he forms an S corporation and applies for the patent, which is granted in 2010. How much credit for research expenditures will the taxpayer be allowed and in what year?

**13-17** *Work Opportunity Credit.* The purpose of the work opportunity credit is to encourage the employment of certain groups of people with high unemployment rates. The credit has not quite achieved the desired objectives. What changes should be made to the present credit to increase its effectiveness?

## PROBLEMS

**13-18** *Alternative Minimum Tax—Computation.* T is single and has taxable income of $56,550 and a regular tax liability of $10,263 for the current year. T uses the standard deduction for regular tax purposes and has $60,000 of positive adjustments (excluding the adjustment for the standard deduction) for AMT purposes.

**a.** Determine T's tentative minimum tax and her AMT.

**b.** Determine the amount that T actually has to pay the IRS this year.

**13-19** *Alternative Minimum Tax—Computation.* V and W are married and file a joint return for the current year. They have no other dependents and they take the standard deduction. V and W's taxable income is $94,250 and their regular tax liability is $15,813. They have $60,000 of AMT preference items and $32,050 of AMT positive adjustments. Determine V and W's tentative AMT and their AMT liability.

**13-20** *AMT and Qualified Small Business Stock.* T is an avid investor, always looking for that one stock that will make him rich and famous. On January 4, 1997, BC Corporation, a fast food chain, went public, and T thought this could be the one. He purchased 10,000 shares of stock for $100,000. One of the benefits from buying this initial offering was that BC's stock was eligible for treatment as qualified small business stock. After enduring the ups and downs of the market, T sold 5,000 shares of the stock for $250,000 on January 9, 2011.

**a.** Determine the gain recognized on the sale of the BC stock and the amount included in T's regular taxable income.

**b.** Determine the amount of tax preference or adjustment, if any, that T must take into account in computing his alternative minimum tax.

**13-21** *Alternative Minimum Tax—Charitable Contribution Preference.* During the year, J contributed stock to the local university. He had purchased the stock in 1984 for $10,000, and it was appraised at $60,000 on the date of gift. The stock was sold shortly after the contribution was made, and a painting was purchased by the university with the proceeds from the sale. The university placed the painting in its Art Building for display and study by art students. J's A.G.I. in the year of contribution is $300,000.

**a.** Determine J's allowable charitable contribution deduction for the regular tax system.

**b.** Based solely on these facts, determine any AMT adjustments or preference items that apply to J.

**13-22** *Alternative Minimum Tax—Computation.* B is single and reports the following items of income and deductions for the current year:

| | |
|---|---:|
| Salary | $ 50,000 |
| Net long-term capital gain on sale of investment property | 200,000 |
| Medical expenses | 17,500 |
| Casualty loss | 4,500 |
| State and local income taxes | 15,000 |
| Real estate taxes | 20,000 |
| Charitable contributions (all cash) | 15,000 |
| Interest on home mortgage | 12,000 |
| Interest on investment loans (unimproved real property) | 10,000 |

The only additional transaction during the year was the exercise of an incentive stock option of her employer's stock at an option price of $12,000 when the stock was worth $100,000. Compute B's tax liability and AMT, if any.

**13-23** *Alternative Minimum Tax.* Refer to the facts in *Problem 13-22* and assume B holds the stock acquired by exercising her ISO for two years and sells it for $105,000. Determine the amount of gain that must be reported for regular tax purposes and the gain that must be reflected in the AMT calculations in the year the stock was sold.

**13-24** *Alternative Minimum Tax—Cost Recovery Adjustment.* In 2011, T placed a light-duty truck in service at a cost of $40,000. T uses the applicable MACRS method of depreciation for all his assets and does not elect the § 179 first-year expensing option. Identify and calculate the minimum tax adjustment that must be made for AMT purposes in 2011.

**13-25** *Alternative Minimum Tax—Cost Recovery.* Refer to the facts in *Problem 13-24*, but assume the truck that was placed in service this year at a cost of $40,000 was a heavy-duty truck. Identify and calculate the minimum tax adjustment that must be made for AMT purposes in 2011.

**13-26** *Alternative Minimum Tax—Cost Recovery Adjustment.* In January 2011, A purchases residential rental property for $200,000, excluding the cost of the land. For regular tax purposes, the 2011 depreciation on the building is $6,970. For AMT purposes, depreciation is $4,792. Determine the AMT adjustment for cost recovery for 2011 and 2012.

**13-27** *Alternative Minimum Tax—Computation.* O is married to G and they file a joint return for 2011. O and G have A.G.I. of $70,000. One of the deductions from gross income was $50,000 of percentage depletion. Cost depletion on their gold mine was zero because the cost basis of the property was reduced to zero by prior years' depletion deductions. They do not itemize deductions. Determine O and G's tax liability for 2011.

**13-28** *Alternative Minimum Tax.* T is an unmarried entrepreneur. In 2003, he purchased several rental properties and leased them to tenants on long-term leases. In 2011, T has $100,000 of rental losses on his real estate activities in which he actively participates and income of $100,000 from his brokerage business. T also has a $25,000 general business credit carryover from 2010. Determine T's tax liability for 2011, assuming he does not itemize his deductions.

**13-29** *Minimum Tax Credit.* Refer to the facts in *Problem 13-22* and determine the minimum tax credit, if any, that is available to offset the regular tax liability in 2012.

**13-30** *General Business Credit—Limited by Tax Liability.* K's tax liability before credits is $35,000. She earned a general business credit of $40,000. Determine K's tax liability after credits and any general business credit carryback or carryforward that may exist.

**13-31** *Energy Credit.* In May of the current year, J invested $60,000 in a solar system to heat water for a production process.

**a.** Determine the amount of business energy credit available to J.

**b.** Determine the basis of the energy property that J must use for cost recovery purposes.

**13-32** *Rehabilitation Credit.* During the current year, T incurred $300,000 of qualified rehabilitation expenditures with respect to 75-year-old property. Prior to these expenditures, T had a $100,000 cost basis in the depreciable building.

**a.** Determine the amount of rehabilitation credit available to T.

**b.** Determine the basis of the rehabilitated property that T must use for cost recovery purposes.

**13-33** *Rehabilitation Credit—Computation.* During the current year, K incurred $200,000 of qualified rehabilitation expenditures with respect to property constructed in 1930. The entire block where his property is located has been designated as a Certified Historical District.

**a.** Determine the amount of credit allowable to K if his structure is recognized as a historical structure.

**b.** Assuming that K paid $180,000 for his building in the current year and that he would claim MACRS depreciation, calculate his adjusted basis in the building at the end of the year. Assume that the property was placed in service in July of the current year.

**13-34** *IC Recapture.* Assume D claimed a business energy credit of $30,000 for property placed in service on December 18, 2008 and that D sold this property on January 7, 2009. Determine the amount, if any, of IC recapture that D should report as an additional tax in 2011.

**13-35** *IC Recapture.* Assume L claimed rehabilitation credit of $80,000 on property placed in service on February 18, 2008 and that L exchanged this rehabilitated property for like-kind property (a § 1031 exchange) on March 17, 2011. Determine the amount of IC recapture that L should report as an additional tax in 2011, if any.

**13-36** *Research and Experimentation Credit.* M, a sole proprietor, has been in business only two years but is very successful. He has average annual gross receipts of $150,000 for this period and incurred $40,000 in qualified R&E expenses this year.

**a.** Determine M's R&E credit for the current year.

**b.** Determine the current deduction for R&E expenditures that M is entitled to, assuming he elects to deduct R&E expenditures currently.

**13-37** *Disabled Access Credit—Computation.* P Corp. had gross receipts of $500,000 last year and incurred $9,000 of eligible access expenditures to build a wheelchair ramp this year.

**a.** Determine P's disabled access credit.

**b.** Determine the basis of the wheelchair ramp that will be eligible for cost recovery deductions.

**13-38** *Child Tax Credit.* H and W are married with three children. At the close of 2011, the children, A, B, and C, were ages 2, 6, and 8, respectively. H and W claim a dependency exemption for each of the children. This year H and W reported adjusted gross income of $125,000. Determine the allowable child tax credit for H and W.

**13-39** *Child Tax Credit.* M is a single mom raising one child, age 16, at home. M may claim a dependency exemption for her child. This year M earned $70,000 as salary and had investment income of $12,500. Determine the allowable child tax credit for M.

**13-40** *Dependent Care Credit.* V and J are married and file a joint return for the current year. Because they both work, they had to pay a babysitter $5,200 to watch their three children (ages 7, 8, and 9). V earned $17,000 and J earned $21,200 during the year. They do not have any other source of income nor do they claim any deductions for adjusted gross income. Determine the allowable dependent care credit for V and J.

**13-41** *Dependent Care Credit.* M and B are married, have a son three years old, and file a joint return for the current year. They incurred $500 a month for day care center expenses. During the year, B earned $23,000 but M did not work outside the home. They do not have any other source of income nor do they claim any deductions for adjusted gross income. Determine the allowable dependent care credit for the year if:

**a.** M enrolled as a full-time student in a local community college on September 6 of the current year.

**b.** M was in school from January through June, and from September through December of the current year.

**13-42** *Dependent Care Credit.* C is a single parent raising a son who is eight years old. During the current year, C earned $19,500 and paid $3,000 to a sitter to watch her son after school. Determine C's dependent care credit for the current year.

**13-43** *Hope Scholarship Credit.* D is a single dad and has modified A.G.I. of $52,000. This year D's son begins studying for his bachelor's degree as a half-time student at Arapahoe County Community College. On September 1, D pays $2,500 in qualified tuition for his son's first semester. Determine the amount of Hope credit available to D.

**13-44** *Hope Scholarship Credit.* H and W are married and have twins who are attending the State University as freshmen this year. State University is on the semester system and charges $1,000 tuition per semester. H and W pay State University $2,000 this year. H and W have adjusted gross income of $83,000.

**a.** Determine the allowable Hope Scholarship credit for H and W.

**b.** If H and W ask your advice in terms of maximizing the Hope Scholarship credit, what advice would you give them?

**13-45** *Earned Income Credit.* R is 43, divorced, and maintains a household for his 7-year-old dependent daughter. R was laid off in 2010 and his unemployment benefits have run out. During 2011, he worked at part-time jobs earning $5,500. He has no other sources of income.

**a.** Determine R's allowable earned income credit.

**b.** Determine R's tax payment due or his refund, assuming that nothing was withheld from his wages and that he did not make any quarterly estimated tax payments.

**13-46** *Earned Income Credit.* S, who is 24 and a single parent, maintains a household for her 3-year-old dependent daughter and her 10-month-old son. S earned $16,000 during this calendar year. S has no other source of income and does not itemize her deductions.

**a.** Determine S's allowable earned income credit.

**b.** Determine S's tax payment due or her refund, assuming that $200 was withheld from her wages and that she did not make any quarterly estimated tax payments.

**13-47** *Additional Child Tax Credit.* H and W have four children and earned $24,000 for 2011. H and W paid $1,836 in FICA taxes but neither had any income tax withheld from their wages. Determine the amount of refund they should receive from the IRS.

**13-48** *Integrative Credit Problem.* J, who is 32 and a single parent, maintains a household for his six-year-old dependent son. J earned $20,000 and paid $3,000 in child care payments during the calendar year. J did not have any Federal income tax withheld from his check. Determine the amount of J's refund from the IRS, if any, or the amount that J must pay the IRS, if required.

**13-49** *Credit for the Elderly.* P and D are 66 years old, married, and file a joint return. The only sources of income they have are dividend income of $14,000 and social security of $2,500.

**a.** Determine the allowable credit for the elderly for the current year.

**b.** Determine the tax payable or refund due, assuming that no withholding was made on the dividends and that no quarterly estimated payments were made.

## CUMULATIVE PROBLEMS

**13-50** R and S, married and the parents of two children ages 10 months and 6 years, file a joint return. R is a college professor of civil engineering and teaches at State University. R applied for a one-year visiting professorship with International Engineering Corpora-tion (IEC) and was selected for the position. The visiting professor position was available from July 1 to May 31 of the following year and required R to relocate his family from Detroit to Los Angeles at a total cost of $6,500 during the last week in June. IEC reimbursed R only $5,000 for these expenses. R rented his Detroit home for the last six months of the calendar year at a net loss of $6,000 for regular tax purposes. Due to the longer life of the residential real property for AMT purposes, and therefore a smaller cost recovery deduction, the net loss for AMT purposes was only $4,000.

S was employed by the government and was able to get a temporary transfer to Los Angeles. S earned $12,000 for the calendar year. During the calendar year, R and S paid $6,000 in child care expenses.

R and his family incurred expenses of $2,500 a month to rent a furnished apartment (assume $1,000 a month was attributable to R and $1,000 a month was attributable to S) for the last six months of the calendar year. R and his family incurred expenses of $800 a month for food during the last six months of the year (assume 25% of the food is specifically attributable to R and that 25% is attributable to S). In addition, R incurred transportation expenses, parking fees, and laundry expenses of $2,500, and he spent $1,200 on lunches on work days during the last half of the year. S incurred transportation expenses of $500 and took her lunch to work with her. R earned $25,000 from State University for teaching half of the calendar year and $60,000 from IEC for practicing half of the year. Together, R and S had $12,000 of Federal income tax withheld from their paychecks.

During the year, R and S also incurred the following expenses:

| | |
|---|---|
| Unreimbursed medical expenses | $7,000 |
| Charitable contribution of stock to State University (adjusted basis $1,000) | 5,000 |
| State and local income taxes | 4,000 |
| Real estate taxes on lake property | 3,000 |
| Real estate taxes on principal residence (one-half year) | 2,000 |
| Interest on principal residence (one-half year) | 4,800 |

The couple also had these additional income items:

| | |
|---|---|
| State tax refund from previous year | $1,500 |
| Interest income from private activity bonds | 7,000 |

R and S have a minimum tax credit carryover from last year of $5,000. Determine R and S's tax liability for the year.

## TAX RESEARCH PROBLEMS

**13-51** *Rehabilitation Credit.* Taxpayer S, a real estate developer, rehabilitated an old commercial building and was entitled to an investment credit based on the rehabilitation expenses incurred. Prior to placing the new offices into service, S is approached by P, who is interested in purchasing the building. As an inducement to get P to buy the property, S offers to transfer the IC to P. That is, S agrees not to claim the credit on his tax return with the expectation that P can claim the credit instead. Will P be allowed to take credit on her tax return in the year she places the office building into service?

**13-52** *Dependent Care Credit.* B is a single parent and his child is enrolled in a public school. The school administrators have scheduled a supervised trip to Dearborn, Michigan for one full week for the students to see Greenfield Village and the Henry Ford Museum. Total trip cost per student is $800. If B pays for his child to make the trip, will he be entitled to a child care credit for the expenditures? If so, how much of the costs will qualify?

**13-53** *Alternative Minimum Tax.* This year T was the victim of his company's restructuring and downsizing. Midway through the year his employer, ABC Corporation, offered him early retirement on the condition that he would provide consulting services when needed. The offer proved so lucrative that T accepted. T ended up working for the company for the first six months of the taxable year and earned $50,000 during this period. Prior to his retirement he exercised an incentive stock option he had received several years earlier. At the time he exercised the option, the market price of the stock was $140,000 and the purchase price under the option was $50,000. After he retired, T began a new business of building toys for disabled children. He materially participated in the business and incurred a loss of $60,000, which he properly reported on Schedule C of his Form 1040 tax return. T is married and files a joint return with his wife. The couple paid $18,000 in qualified housing interest and $6,000 in real estate taxes, and made a $25,000 cash contribution to Children's Hospital during the year. Determine T's regular tax liability and AMT, if any.

**13-54** *Child Care Credit.* K recently divorced and decided to go back to school full-time to get her Masters of Taxation at Central University. She has a four-year-old child who attends nursery school at a cost of $4,000 per year. As a single parent, K finds it difficult just to get by. However, she maintains her home using her alimony payments, some dividend and interest income, and her child support. She also works as a volunteer for 10 hours a week at the library and receives $15 per week. This year she attended school for 11 months. Is K eligible for the child care credit?

# Property Transactions

PART 5

**CHAPTER 14** Property Transactions: Basis Determination and Recognition of Gain or Loss

**CHAPTER 15** Nontaxable Exchanges

**CHAPTER 16** Property Transactions: Capital Gains and Losses

**CHAPTER 17** Property Transactions: Dispositions of Trade or Business Property

14

# Property Transactions: Basis Determination and Recognition of Gain or Loss

## Learning Objectives

Upon completion of this chapter you will be able to:

LO.1 Explain the basic computation used to determine gain or loss realized from the disposition of property.

LO.2 Understand the general rule concerning when a gain or loss realized is recognized.

LO.3 Compute the amount realized from a sale or other disposition.

LO.4 Understand how the adjusted basis of property is determined.

LO.5 Identify the most common types of adjustments to basis of property.

LO.6 Understand how liabilities affect the amount realized and adjusted basis.

LO.7 Define an installment sale and identify taxpayers eligible to use the installment method of reporting gain.

LO.8 Compute the amount of gain required to be recognized in the year of installment sale and the gain to be reported in any subsequent year.

LO.9 Explain the limitations imposed on certain installment sales, including:

- The imputed interest rules.
- Related-party installment sales.
- Gain recognition on the disposition of installment obligations.
- Required interest payments on deferred Federal income taxes.

LO.10 Identify various transactions in which loss recognition is prohibited.

## Chapter Outline

Introduction 14-2
Determination of Gain or Loss 14-2
  Introduction 14-2
  General Rule of Recognition 14-3
  Computing Amount Realized 14-4
Basis Determination Rules 14-6
  Property Acquired by Purchase 14-6
  Property Acquired by Gift 14-7
  Property Acquired from a Decedent 14-9
  Property Acquired in a Nontaxable Exchange 14-10
  Property Converted from Personal Use to Business Use 14-11
  Property Converted from Business Use to Personal Use 14-11
  Adjustments to Basis 14-12
Effect of Liabilities on Amount Realized and Adjusted Basis 14-13
Concepts Related to Realization and Recognition 14-13
  Sale or Other Disposition 14-13
  Allocations of Purchase Price and Basis 14-18

Installment Sale Method 14-19
General Rules 14-19
Election out of Installment Reporting 14-20
Gain Reported Under the Installment Method 14-21
Limitations on Certain Installment Sales 14-23
Reporting Gain on Installment Sales 14-26
Disallowed Losses 14-27
Wash Sales 14-27
Sales Between Related Parties 14-28
Tax Planning Considerations 14-29
Gift Versus Bequest 14-29
Charitable Transfers Involving Property Other than Cash 14-29
Changes in the Use of Property 14-29
Sales to Related Parties 14-30
Use of Installment Sales 14-30
Problem Materials 14-30

## Introduction

Section 61(a)(3) of the Code provides that gross income includes gains derived from dealings in property. Similarly, § 165 allows a deduction, subject to limitations, for losses incurred in certain property transactions. The term *dealings in property* includes sales, exchanges, and other types of acquisitions or dispositions of property. This chapter examines the determination of the amount of gains and losses from dealings in property. Specific rules regarding gain recognition are addressed, as are the gain-deferral possibilities associated with certain installment sales. Various limitations on the deductibility of losses also are addressed.

Other topics dealing with property transactions are examined in the next three chapters. Chapter 15 deals with certain nontaxable exchanges. Chapter 16 covers the special treatment accorded gains and losses from sales or exchanges of capital assets. The unique rules governing the disposition of property used in a trade or business, including depreciable property, are examined in Chapter 17.

## Determination of Gain or Loss

### Introduction

**LO.1**
Explain the basic computation used to determine gain or loss realized from the disposition of property.

Determining the gain or loss realized in a property transaction is usually a simple computation. It is the mathematical difference between the amount realized in a sale or other disposition and the adjusted basis of the property surrendered (See Exhibit 14-1). The amount realized is a measure of the consideration received in the transaction. It represents the economic value *realized* by the taxpayer.

*Sale or other disposition* essentially refers to any transaction in which a taxpayer realizes benefit in exchange for property. It is not necessary that there be a sale transaction or that cash be received for gain or loss to be realized by the taxpayer surrendering property other than cash.

The adjusted basis of purchased property is generally cost, plus or minus certain adjustments. Computing gain or loss realized is similar to determining gain or loss for accounting purposes, and adjusted basis is similar in concept to book value. However, the

**EXHIBIT 14.1 Computation of Gain or Loss Realized**

| | |
|---|---|
| | Amount realized (See Exhibit 14-3) |
| – | Adjusted basis |
| = | Gain or loss realized |

adjusted basis of a property will not always be, and frequently is not, equal to its book value for accounting purposes.

In effect, the adjusted cost, or adjusted basis, of a given property is the amount that can be recovered tax-free upon its disposition. For example, if property is sold for exactly its cost, as adjusted, there is no gain or loss realized. This concept is referred to as the *recovery of capital or recovery of basis* principle. If a taxpayer receives more than the adjusted basis in exchange for property, gain is realized only to the extent of that excess. The adjusted basis is recovered tax-free. The following examples illustrate this concept:

**Example 1**

K transferred 30 acres of land to ZX Company for $42,000 cash. K had purchased the 30 acres five years earlier for $35,000, which is his adjusted basis. As a result of this "sale or other disposition," K has a realized gain of $7,000 ($42,000 – $35,000). His $35,000 basis in the land is recovered tax-free.

**Example 2**

In 2009, L purchased 300 shares of W Corporation stock for $3,600 cash, including brokerage fees. When the market outlook for W Corporation's product began to weaken in 2011, L sold her shares for $3,100. The broker deducted a commission of $48 and forwarded $3,052 cash to her. L has a realized loss on this transaction of $548 ($3,052 – $3,600) in 2011.

**Example 3**

R transferred 200 shares of C Corporation stock worth $4,000 and $2,000 cash for an auto he will use for personal purposes. The C Corporation stock had been purchased two years earlier for $4,600. R realizes a loss of $600 [($6,000 – $2,000) – $4,600] on the "sale or other disposition" of the stock.

## General Rule of Recognition

**LO.2**
Understand the general rule concerning when a gain or loss realized is recognized.

Any gain or loss realized must be recognized unless some provision of the Internal Revenue Code provides otherwise. A *recognized gain* is reported on a tax return. For example, a gain on the sale of stock generally is recognized in full in the year of sale (i.e., the gain is reported on a tax return, included in gross income, and considered in determining the tax liability for the year). In determining taxable income, the recognized gain is either offset against losses for the year or included in the computation of taxable income.[1]

A *recognized loss* also is generally given its full tax effect in the year of realization. Depending on the type of loss, it may be either offset against gains or deducted against other forms of income in determining taxable income. Some losses, however, are not deductible[2] and others are limited.[3] For example, losses on the sale of property used for personal purposes are disallowed. Certain other losses are deferred to later tax years. Some examples of nontaxable exchanges are listed in Exhibit 14-2.

[1] Capital gains must be offset by capital losses, and only net capital gains are included in taxable income. See the discussion of capital gains and losses in Chapter 16.

[2] Losses on certain sales to related parties are disallowed under § 267, and losses on the sale of personal use property are not allowed under § 165(c).

[3] The deduction for capital losses is limited under § 1211(b).

**EXHIBIT 14.2 Partial List of Nontaxable Exchanges**

| Types of Transaction | Action Required | Tax Result |
|---|---|---|
| Casualty, theft, condemnation (involuntary conversion) | Reinvest in similar property | Gain may be deferred see Chapter 15 and § 1033 |
| Like-kind exchange | Exhchange directly for like-kind property | Gain or loss is deferred* see Chapter 15 and § 1031 |
| Formation of a corporation or subsequent stock issues | Transfer property in exchange for stock by controlling shareholders | Gain or loss is deferred* see § 351 |
| Corporate reorganizations | Examples include mergers, consolidations, divisions, recapitalizations | Gain or loss is deferred* see § 368 |
| Partnership formation | Transfer property in exchange for a partnership interest | Gain or loss is deferred* see § 721 |

*When gain or loss is deferred, the deferral is only until the replacement property is sold or otherwise transferred (i.e., the deferred gain or loss is recognized along with any subsequent gain or loss when the replacement property is sold).

## Computing Amount Realized

**LO.3**
Compute the amount realized from a sale or other disposition.

The amount realized from a sale or other disposition of property includes the amount of money received plus the fair market value of any other property received in a transaction. Other property includes both tangible and intangible property.

### Example 4

P received $20,000 and a motor home worth $80,000 in exchange for a sailing yacht that she had used for personal enjoyment. P's amount realized on the disposition of the yacht is $100,000 ($20,000 + $80,000).

The amount realized also includes any debt obligations of the buyer, and if the contract provides for inadequate interest or no interest, interest must be imputed and the sales price reduced accordingly.

### Example 5

Y sold his vintage Dodge automobile to C for $10,000 and a note payable from C to Y for $15,000 plus interest compounded monthly at 9%. Y's amount realized in this transaction is $25,000, the down payment plus the value of C's note.

### Example 6

Z sold a parcel of real estate for $100,000. Her basis in the land was $60,000. The sales contract called for $10,000 to be paid upon transfer of the property and the remaining $90,000 to be paid in full two years later.

Since no interest was provided for in the contract, interest must be imputed on the buyer's $90,000 obligation (in this case, 9% interest, compounded semiannually, is used).[4] Accordingly, the sales price is reduced to $85,471 [$10,000 cash down payment + $75,471 (the discounted present value of the $90,000 payment in two years)]. Z will report an amount realized of $85,471 and a gain realized of $25,471 ($85,471 − $60,000 basis). When Z collects the $90,000, she must report interest income of $14,529 ($90,000 face value − $75,471 present value on date of sale).

The amount realized also includes the amount of any existing liabilities of the seller discharged in the transaction. Specifically, it includes any debts assumed by the buyer and any liabilities encumbering the property transferred that remain with the property in the buyer's hands.[5] Exhibit 14-3 illustrates the computation of *both* the amount realized and the gain or loss realized from the sale or other disposition of property.

## Example 7

B purchased a rental house for $40,000 in 2004. She paid $8,000 down and signed a mortgage note for the balance. During the years she owned the property, B deducted depreciation totaling $16,000 and made principal payments on the note of $4,000, leaving a mortgage balance of $28,000.

During 2011, B sold the house for $62,000. The buyer paid $34,000 cash and assumed the $28,000 mortgage liability. B's amount realized is $62,000 ($34,000 cash + $28,000 relief of liability), and her adjusted basis is $24,000 ($40,000 cost reduced by $16,000 depreciation). Her gain realized is therefore $38,000 ($62,000 amount realized − $24,000 adjusted basis).

### EXHIBIT 14.3 Computation of Amount Realized and Gain or Loss Realized

| **Amount realized:** | | |
|---|---|---|
| Amount of money received | | $xxx,xxx |
| Add: | Fair market value of other property received | + x,xxx |
| | Liabilities discharged: | |
| | Liabilities assumed by the buyer | +xx,xxx |
| | Liabilities encumbering the property transferred | + x,xxx |
| Less: | Selling expenses | −xx,xxx |
| | Amount of money given up | − x,xxx |
| | Liabilities incurred: | |
| | Liabilities assumed by the taxpayer | −xx,xxx |
| | Liabilities encumbering the property received | − x,xxx |
| Equals: | Amount realized | $xxx,xxx |
| Less: | ***Adjusted basis*** in property other than money given up | − xx,xxx |
| Equals: | ***Gain or loss realized*** | $xxx,xxx |

[4] The actual rate is determined with reference to current market rates and is announced periodically by the IRS. For transactions involving $2.8 million or less, the rate cannot exceed 9 percent compounded semiannually.

[5] Reg. § 1.1001-2. Also, see the following discussion of the effect of liabilities in property transactions.

Any expenses of selling the property reduce the amount realized. Selling costs include many costs, paid by the seller, associated with offering a property for sale and transacting the sale. For example, selling costs include advertising expenses, appraisal fees, sales commissions, legal fees, transfer taxes, recording fees, and mortgage costs of the buyer paid by the seller.

## Basis Determination Rules

**LO.4**
Understand how the adjusted basis of property is determined.

The adjusted basis of property may be determined in several ways, depending on how the property is acquired and whether any gain or loss is being deferred in the transaction. Various methods of acquiring property and their specific basis determination rules are discussed below.

### Property Acquired by Purchase

#### Cost Basis

In a simple purchase transaction, basis is the cost of the property acquired. Cost is the amount of money paid and the fair market value of any other property transferred in exchange for a given property.[6] The cost basis includes any payments made by the buyer with borrowed funds and any obligations (i.e., promissory notes) of the buyer given to the seller or any obligations of the seller assumed by the buyer in the exchange.[7]

Any costs of acquiring property are included in basis. For stock and securities, commissions, transfer taxes, and other acquisition costs are included. For other property, many types of acquisition costs, including commissions, legal fees related to purchase, recording fees, title insurance, appraisals, sales taxes, and transfer taxes, are added to basis.[8] Any installation and delivery costs also are part of basis.

**Example 8**

C purchased a new machine for his auto repair business during the year. He paid $16,500 for the machine, $8,500 of which was made possible by a bank loan. In addition, C paid state sales taxes of $660, delivery charges of $325, and installation charges of $175. C's cost basis in the equipment is $17,660 ($16,500 purchase price + $660 sales taxes + $325 delivery charges + $175 installation charges).

Periodic operating costs such as interest and taxes are generally deducted in the year paid. However, a taxpayer may elect to *capitalize* (i.e., include in basis) certain taxes and interest related to unproductive and unimproved real property or related to real property during development or improvement rather than take a current tax deduction.[9]

**Example 9**

T purchased a small parcel of unimproved land near a lake known for its excellent fishing. She uses the property as a weekend retreat and plans someday to build a log cabin. T annually pays $150 for local property taxes but does not itemize deductions. T should elect to capitalize the property taxes paid each year as a part of her basis in the land.

[6] Reg. § 1.1012-1(a).

[7] § 1001 and *Crane v. Comm.*, 47-1 USTC ¶9217, 35 AFTR 776, 331 U.S. 1 (USSC, 1947).

[8] § 1012 and Reg. § 1.1012-1(a).

[9] § 266 and Reg. § 1.266-1(b)(1).

### Identification Problems

Generally, the adjusted basis of property sold or otherwise transferred is easily traced to the acquisition of the property and certain subsequent events. However, identification of cost may be difficult if a taxpayer has multiple homogeneous assets. For example, if a taxpayer owns identical shares of stock in a corporation that were acquired in more than one transaction and sells less than his or her entire investment in that stock, it is necessary to identify which shares are sold. For tax purposes, the owner must use the *first-in, first-out* (FIFO) method of identification if it is impossible to identify which shares were sold. Specific identification of the shares sold is appropriate if the shares can be identified.[10]

#### Example 10

K purchased the following lots of G Corporation stock:

| | | |
|---|---|---|
| 50 shares | Purchased 1/10/08 | Cost \$5,500 |
| 75 shares | Purchased 8/15/08 | Cost \$9,000 |
| 40 shares | Purchased 6/18/10 | Cost \$4,600 |

K sold 60 shares of her G Corporation stock in 2011 for \$8,700. Unless she can specifically identify the shares sold, her basis will be determined using the FIFO method. Therefore, her basis in 50 shares sold is \$5,500 and her basis in 10 shares sold is \$1,200 [10 shares × \$120 (\$9,000 ÷ 75 shares)]. Her total gain is \$2,000.

#### Example 11

Assuming the same facts in *Example 10*, the gain would be different if K could specifically identify the shares sold. If she directed her broker to deliver to the buyer the shares purchased on 8/15/08, referring to them by certificate number and date of purchase, her gain would be \$1,500 [\$8,700 sale price − \$7,200 (\$120 basis per share × 60)].

## Property Acquired by Gift

Generally, the basis of property received by gift is the same as the basis was to the donor.[11] This basis is *increased* by that portion of the gift tax paid by the donor, which is attributable to the appreciation in the property's value, if any, up to the date of the gift. A property's taxable value is its fair market value on the date of gift reduced by any gift tax exclusion, marital deduction or charitable deduction taken on the gift. The appreciation is measured by the difference between the taxable value of the property and the donor's adjusted basis in the property immediately before the gift.[12] The appropriate increase in basis for a given property is determined using the following formula:[13]

$$\frac{\text{Fair market value date of gift} - \text{Donor's basis date of gift} = \text{Appreciation}}{\text{Taxable gift}} \times \text{Gift taxes paid}$$

In making the adjustment for the gift tax, the amount of increase cannot exceed the amount of the tax. Also observe that there is an adjustment for gift tax only if the property had appreciated in the donor's hands at the time of the gift.

---

[10] Reg. § 1.1012-1(c).

[11] § 1015(a).

[12] See § 1015(d)(6) and Reg. § 1-1015-5(c)(3). For gifts made before 1977, the entire amount of the gift taxes paid could be used for the gift tax adjustment, but the adjusted basis could not exceed the property's taxable value at the time of the gift.

[13] See § 1015(d)(2) and Reg. § 1-1015-5(c)(3), Example 1. If there is more than one gift on the annual gift tax return, the gift tax is allocated among the gifts proportionately based on the amount of the taxable gift.

## Example 12

On March 7, 2009, Ann received 10 acres of undeveloped land as a gift from her Uncle Carl. On the date of the gift, the land had a value of $112,000 and Carl's adjusted basis in the land was $82,000. On his gift tax return, Carl reported a taxable gift of $100,000 (fair market value $112,000 – annual exclusion $12,000) and paid gift taxes of $41,000. Since Ann received the land, she has held it for investment. Now she is thinking about selling the property. If Ann sells the property, her basis in the land, including an adjustment for gift taxes, is $94,300 as determined below.

| | |
|---|---|
| Appreciation at date of gift: | |
| Fair market value of property | $112,000 |
| Adjusted basis | (82,000) |
| Appreciation | $ 30,000 |
| Donee's basis calculation: | |
| Donor's adjusted basis | $ 82,000 |
| Gift tax attributable to appreciation | |
| Gift tax $41,000 × ($30,000 appreciation at date of gift / $100,000 taxable gift) | 12,300 |
| Donee's adjusted basis | $ 94,300 |

If Ann sells the land for $154,300, her taxable gain would be $60,000 ($154,300 – $94,300). If Ann sells the land for $74,300, her deductible loss would be $20,000 ($74,300 – $94,300). Note that since the property had appreciated as of the date of the gift, the basis for determining gain and loss is the same.

### Loss Limitation Rule

If the fair market value of the property *at the time of the gift* is less than the donor's basis (i.e., it has a built-in loss), special rules must be applied to determine the basis for the donee. The special rule is designed to prevent shifting of the loss to the taxpayer (e.g., a family member), who would obtain the greatest benefit. Perhaps the clearest expression of the rules in this case is as follows: the basis for *determining gain* is the donor's basis, while the basis for *determining loss* is the lower of either (1) the donor's basis or (2) the property's fair market value at the date of the gift.[14] Due to the way the rule for determining loss is stated, the donee will not recognize any gain or loss if the property is disposed of for any amount that is *less than* the donor's basis *but greater than* the value of the property at the date of the gift. These rules are illustrated in the following examples.

## Example 13

S received 200 shares of X Corporation stock as a gift from his uncle. The stock had a basis to the uncle of $32,000 and a fair market value on the date of the gift of $29,000. Gift taxes of $1,400 were paid on the transfer.

This year, S sold all of the shares for $24,000. His loss realized on the sale is $5,000 ($24,000 sale price – $29,000 fair market value at date of gift). Note that S was not permitted to add any of the $1,400 gift taxes to his basis since such adjustments are allowed only if the taxable value is more than the donor's basis on the date of the gift (i.e., the property appreciated in the donor's hands).

[14] § 1015(a). It also should be noted that total depreciation claimed using the gain basis for computation cannot exceed the property's fair market value at date of gift. Reg. § 1.167(g)-1.

### Example 14

Assuming the same facts as in *Example 13*, if S's stock had been sold for $36,000, his realized gain would have been $4,000 ($36,000 sales price – $32,000 gain basis). There is no adjustment for gift taxes paid because the property did not appreciate in the donor's hands.

### Example 15

Assuming the same facts as in *Example 13*, if S had sold his stock for $31,000 he would not realize gain or loss on the sale. His basis for gain is $32,000 (the donor's basis) and his basis for loss is limited to $29,000 (fair market value on the date of the gift). Since the $31,000 sales price does not exceed the gain basis and is not less than his loss basis, neither gain nor loss is realized on the sale.

Application of these special rules illustrates *three* important points. First, *any gain* realized by the donee on a subsequent sale of the property is limited to the amount of gain that the donor would have realized had he or she sold it at the donee's sales price. Second, *any loss* allowed on a subsequent sale of the property is limited to the decline in the property's value that occurs while owned by the donee. Third, although the payment of a gift tax may be required as a result of the gift, the donee is not allowed to adjust the donor's basis in the property by any gift taxes paid because there is no appreciation in value of the property in the donor's hands (i.e., the taxable value of the property at the time of the gift is less than the donor's basis).

## Property Acquired from a Decedent

The adjusted basis of property acquired from a decedent generally is its fair market value on the date of the decedent's death.[15] This also is the value used in determining the taxable estate for estate tax purposes.[16] The fiduciary (executor or administrator) of the estate may, however, *elect* to value the estate for estate tax purposes six months after the date of death.[17] This election is available only if (1) the estate is required to file a Federal estate tax return (Form 706), and (2) the alternate valuation reduces *both* the gross estate and the Federal estate tax.[18] If the fiduciary elects to use this alternate valuation date, the fair market value on the later date must also be used as the income tax basis to the heir or estate.[19]

### Example 16

D inherited some gold jewelry from his grandmother several years ago. The fair market value of the jewelry on the date of her death was $4,000 and its adjusted basis to the grandmother was $3,050. If D sells the jewelry this year for $4,350, his realized gain will be $350 ($4,350 sale price – $4,000 basis).

[15] § 1014(a).

[16] § 2031(a).

[17] § 2032(a).

[18] § 2032(c).

[19] § 1014(a)(2).

**Example 17**

If D, from the previous example, sells the jewelry for $3,000, he will have a realized loss of $1,000 ($3,000 – $4,000).

Exceptions to this basis rule are provided for *income in respect of a decedent* under § 691[20] and for certain property acquired by the decedent by gift. Income in respect of a decedent (often referred to as IRD) includes all items of income that the decedent had earned or was entitled to as of the date of death, but which were not included in the decedent's final income tax return under his or her method of accounting. For example, if a cash basis individual performed all the services required to earn a $3,000 consulting fee but had not collected the fee before his or her death, the $3,000 would be income in respect of a decedent. All IRD items are includible in the decedent's gross estate at fair market value for Federal estate tax purposes. Whoever receives the right to collect these items of income must report them in the same manner as the decedent would have been required to report them had he or she lived to collect the income. As a result, IRD items generally are fully included in the gross income of the recipient when received.[21]

If appreciated property was acquired by the decedent by gift within one year before his or her death and the property passes *back* to the donor or the donor's spouse, the recipient's adjusted basis is the decedent's adjusted basis.[22]

**Example 18**

H transferred a parcel of lake-front real estate to his elderly grandmother when the property had an adjusted basis to H of $3,000 and a fair market value of $40,000. No gift taxes were paid on the transfer.

H's grandmother died three months after the gift and left the lake-front property to H in her will. H's basis in the property is $3,000 (the rules used for gifted property apply rather than those for inherited property). If his grandmother had lived for more than a year after the gift was made, H's basis would have been determined under the general rule for property acquired from a decedent.

Another exception is provided in the case of real property subject to special use valuation for Federal estate tax purposes. In such cases, the basis to the heir is the special value used for estate tax purposes. This special use valuation applies only to certain real property used in a trade or business and held by the heir more than 10 years.[23]

## Property Acquired in a Nontaxable Exchange

Most nontaxable exchanges provide deferral, rather than permanent nonrecognition of gain or loss. The mechanism for such deferral is typically an adjustment to the basis in some replacement property.[24] This adjustment is a reduction in basis in the case of a deferred gain and an increase in basis in the case of a deferred loss.

The specific rules for determining the basis of property acquired in nontaxable transactions, along with the requirements of each nontaxable transaction, are discussed in various parts of this text. Several such transactions are discussed in the next chapter. The following example illustrates one such transaction:

[20] § 1014(c).

[21] § 691(a)(1).

[22] § 1014(e).

[23] § 2032A(b).

[24] See, for example, § 1031(d), dealing with like-kind exchanges.

### Example 19

T exchanged a five-acre residential lot for a 100-acre tract of farmland. He realized a $70,000 gain on the exchange because the farmland was worth $90,000 and his basis in the residential lot was $20,000. Since T met all the requirements for nonrecognition of gain in a like-kind exchange under § 1031, his basis in the farmland is $20,000 ($90,000 fair market value – $70,000 deferred gain).

## Property Converted from Personal Use to Business Use

Losses on the disposition of personal use properties are clearly not deductible. Absent some provision to the contrary, business owners could simply convert personal use assets to business use before disposing of them in order to generate business deductions for losses on their sale. Accordingly, when property is converted from personal use to trade or business use, its basis is limited for determining realized loss and for depreciation purposes. For each of those purposes, fair market value on the date of conversion is used as the property's basis if it is less than its adjusted basis.[25]

### Example 20

J owned a single-family home that had been her personal residence for five years. When J discontinued use of the house as her residence, she converted it to rental property. J's original basis in the property was $90,000, and the property was worth $70,000 on the date of conversion. J must determine any depreciation using the fair market value of $70,000, since it is less than her $90,000 adjusted basis. If the property is later sold, J's *gain basis* will be the original $90,000 adjusted basis reduced by the depreciation allowed after the conversion. Her *loss basis* will be the lower fair market value on the date of conversion, $70,000, reduced by the allowed depreciation. Note that if J was hoping to deduct her loss of $20,000 on the property by converting it to business use, she is out of luck since the basis for loss is $70,000. Also observe the similarity to the basis rules that would have applied if J had received the residence as a gift (see *Examples 13, 14*, and *15*).

## Property Converted from Business Use to Personal Use

Once property is converted from business use to personal use, it is treated as personal use property. Any loss on the disposition of such property would, therefore, be disallowed; and, in the event that the property was subsequently converted back to business use, the limitations discussed above would apply.

### Example 21

W has a photocopier used exclusively for business. The copier cost $4,000 and depreciation of $1,800 has been allowed, making its basis $2,200. If W converts the copier to personal and family use and later sells it for $500, no loss will be deductible. Of course, if W had immediately sold the copier at a loss rather than converting it to personal use, he would have a business loss.

---

[25] Reg. §1.167(g)-1.

## Adjustments to Basis

**LO.5**
Identify the most common types of adjustments to basis of property.

Regardless of the method used in determining a property's basis initially, certain adjustments are made to that basis. Generally, the adjustments can be broken down into three groups. Basis is *increased* by *betterments* or *improvements*[26] and *reduced* by *depreciation allowed* or *allowable*[27] and by *other capital recoveries.*[28]

Depreciation reduces basis regardless of whether it is actually deducted by the taxpayer. The *allowable depreciation* is determined using the straight-line method if no method is adopted by the taxpayer.[29]

Various types of *capital recoveries* also reduce a property's adjusted basis. The following are some of the specific items that reduce basis:

1. Certain dividend distributions that are treated as a return of basis[30]
2. Deductible losses with respect to property, such as casualty loss deductions[31]
3. Credits for rehabilitation expenditures related to older commercial buildings and certified historic structures[32]

Numerous other events have an impact on a property's adjusted basis. Many of them are discussed in the remaining chapters of this text, which deal with specific types of transactions.

Exhibit 14-4 summarizes the rules for determining a property's adjusted basis.

**EXHIBIT 14.4** **Determination of Adjusted Basis**

| *Method of Acquisition* | *Basis* | *Exceptions* |
|---|---|---|
| ***General Rule*** | | |
| Acquired by purchase | Purchase cost | See special rules |
| ***Special Rules*** | | |
| Acquired by gift | Donor's basis + gift tax paid adjustment, if any | If fair market value at date of gift is less than donor's basis use fair market value to determine loss |
| Acquired from a decedent | Fair market value at date of death (or alternate valuation date, if elected) | **1.** Income in respect of a decedent<br>**2.** Property given to the decedent by the donor/heir within one year of decedent's death<br>**3.** Property subject to special § 2032A |
| Converted from personal use | Adjusted basis before conversion | For determining loss and depreciation, use fair market value date of conversion if lower than original adjusted basis |
| Acquired in a nontaxable exchange | Fair market value less any gain not recognized or plus any loss deferred | |

***Note***: The basis as determined under any of the above methods is subject to adjustments as provided by other provisions of the Code. Basis is increased by betterments or improvements and reduced by depreciation allowed or allowable and by other capital recoveries.

[26] § 1016(a)(1).

[27] § 1016(a)(2).

[28] See following examples.

[29] § 1016(a)(2).

[30] § 1016(a)(4).

[31] See Reg. § 1.1016-6 and Rev. Rul. 74-206, 1974-1 C.B. 198.

[32] See §§ 46(a), 48(q), and 1016(a)(22).

## Effect of Liabilities on Amount Realized and Adjusted Basis

**LO.6**
Understand how liabilities affect the amount realized and adjusted basis.

Liabilities can affect not only the seller's amount realized but also the buyer's adjusted basis. As noted above, the amount realized in a sale or other disposition of property includes the amount of any liabilities of the seller assumed by the buyer plus any liabilities encumbering the transferred property that remain with the property.[33] In addition, the amount realized from a transaction is reduced by any liabilities assumed by the seller plus any liabilities encumbering property received in the transaction that remain with the property. Similarly, the basis of any property received includes the portion of the cost represented by the liabilities assumed by the seller or encumbering the property.[34]

### Example 22

B exchanges a vacant lot with an adjusted basis of $20,000 for a mountain cabin worth $75,000. B's vacant lot has a fair market value of $50,000 and is subject to a $15,000 mortgage. The mountain cabin B receives is subject to a mortgage of $40,000. B assumes the $40,000 mortgage on the mountain cabin and the other party to the exchange assumes the $15,000 mortgage on the vacant lot.

B's amount realized on this exchange is $50,000 ($75,000 fair market value of cabin received + $15,000 mortgage on vacant lot assumed by the other party – $40,000 mortgage on the mountain cabin assumed by B). If this exchange does not qualify for tax deferral, B has a realized and recognized gain of $30,000 ($50,000 amount realized – $20,000 adjusted basis of the vacant lot given up); and his basis in the mountain cabin is $75,000 (i.e., its fair market value).

### Example 23

D, the other party to the exchange in *Example 22*, had an adjusted basis in her mountain cabin of $65,000. D's amount realized on the exchange is $75,000 ($50,000 fair value of vacant lot received + $40,000 mortgage assumed by B – $15,000 mortgage on the vacant lot). If the exchange does not qualify for tax deferral, D has a realized and recognized gain of $10,000 ($75,000 amount realized – $65,000 adjusted basis in the mountain cabin given up); and her basis in the vacant lot is $50,000 (i.e., its fair market value).

The amount realized on a sale or exchange of property is affected by liabilities even though neither the buyer nor the seller is personally obligated for payment.[35] The rationale for such treatment is that the owner benefits from the nonrecourse liabilities as owner of the property because his or her basis in the property, or some other property, is properly increased because of the liability.[36]

## Concepts Related to Realization and Recognition

### Sale or Other Disposition

Realization of gain or loss occurs upon any sale or other disposition of property. Whether such an event has occurred generally is not difficult to ascertain. A typical sale or exchange obviously constitutes a sale or other disposition, but other transactions in which the taxpayer

[33] Reg. § 1.1001-2(a)(1).

[34] *Crane v. Comm.*, 47-1 USTC ¶9217, 35 AFTR 776, 331 U.S. 1 (USSC, 1947). Such liabilities are not included if they are contingent or not subject to valuation. Rev. Rul. 78-29, 1978-1 C.B. 62.

[35] *Ibid.*

[36] See *Tufts v. Comm.*, 83-1 USTC ¶9328, 51 AFTR2d 1983-1132, 461 U.S. 300 (USSC, 1983) for an excellent discussion of nonrecourse liabilities and their impact on basis.

surrenders property other than cash also may be so classified. The timing of such realization is determined according to the taxpayer's method of accounting. Under the accrual method, realization generally occurs when a transaction is closed and the seller has an unqualified right to collect the sales price.[37] Under the cash method, the taxpayer realizes gain or loss upon the receipt of cash or cash equivalents.[38] In any case, a sale is consummated and realization occurs if beneficial title or possession of the burdens and benefits of ownership are transferred to the buyer.[39]

### Transactions Involving Certain Securities

Generally, a sale or other disposition occurs any time a taxpayer surrenders property in exchange for some consideration. Accordingly, if a taxpayer exchanges securities of one type for securities of another type, a taxable event has occurred.[40]

#### Example 24

F exchanged X Corporation 12% bonds with a face value of $100,000 for Z Corporation 9% bonds with a face value of $120,000. Each group of bonds was worth $105,000 at the time of the exchange. If the X Corporation bonds that F exchanged had a basis of $100,000, he has a $5,000 gain on the exchange.

Several exceptions to this scheme do exist. In some instances, the exchange of *substantially identical* bonds of state or municipal governments has been declared a nontaxable transfer.[41] The condition of being substantially identical is usually determined in terms of rate of return and fair market value. If the bonds received do not meet this test, the exchange may be taxable.[42]

It is clearly established that converting bonds into stock under a conversion privilege contained in the bond instrument does not result in the recognition of gain.[43] Similarly, the conversion of stock into some other stock of the same corporation pursuant to a right granted under the stock certificate does not result in recognition of gain or loss.[44]

### Transfer Related to Taxpayer's Debt

When property is transferred to a creditor, the transfer may or may not be a disposition. The mere granting of a lien against property to secure a loan is not a disposition.[45] The transfer of property in satisfaction of a liability, however, is a taxable disposition.[46] Similarly, the loss of property in a foreclosure sale[47] and the voluntary transfer of mortgaged property to creditors in satisfaction of debt[48] are dispositions of property.

#### Example 25

M purchased a commercial property for $20,000, paying $4,000 down and signing a note secured by a mortgage for the $16,000 difference. Three years later, when M had

[37] See *Alfred Scully*, 20 TCM 1272, T.C. Memo 1961-243 (1961), and Rev. Rul. 72-381, 1972-2 C.B. 581.

[38] See, for example, *Comm. v. Union Pacific R.R. Co.*, 36-2 USTC ¶9525, 18 AFTR 636, 86 F.2d 637 (CA-2, 1936).

[39] *Ibid.*

[40] Rev. Rul. 60-25, 1960-1 C.B. 283, and Rev. Rul. 78-408, 1978-2 C.B. 203.

[41] *Motor Products Corp. v. Comm.*, 44-1 USTC ¶9308, 32 AFTR 672, 142 F.2d 449 (CA-6, 1944), and Rev. Rul. 56-435, 1956-2 C.B. 506.

[42] See *Emery v. Comm.*, 48-1 USTC ¶9165, 36 AFTR 741, 166 F.2d 27 (CA-2, 1948), and Rev. Rul. 81-169, 1981-25 I.R.B. 17. Also, see *Mutual Loan and Savings Co. v. Comm.*, 50-2 USTC ¶9420, 39 AFTR 1034, 184 F.2d 161 (CA-5, 1950) for an example of nonrecognition where the state Supreme Court held the new bonds with a lower interest rate to be a mere continuation of the original issue.

[43] Rev. Rul. 57-535, 1957-2 C.B. 513.

[44] Ltr. Rul., 2-23-45, ¶76,130 P-H Fed. 1945.

[45] See *Dorothy Vickers*, 36 TCM 391, T.C. Memo 1977-90.

[46] *Carlisle Packing Co.*, 29 B.T.A. 514 (1933), and Rev. Rul. 76-111, 1976-1 C.B. 214 (1976).

[47] *O'Dell & Sons Co., Inc.*, 8 T.C. 1165 (1947).

[48] *Estate of Delman*, 73 T.C. 15 (1979).

reduced the balance on the note to $7,000, the lender accepted 300 shares of T Corporation stock in satisfaction of the obligation. The T Corporation stock had a fair market value of $7,000 and an adjusted basis to M of $5,000. By transferring the stock to satisfy the liability, there is a disposition of the stock and M has a $2,000 realized gain. Note that this result is the same as if M had sold the stock for $7,000 cash and paid the balance on the note.

### Example 26

K purchased a warehouse for use in her business for $30,000, paying $5,000 down and signing a nonrecourse note (K is not personally liable) secured by a mortgage lien for the $25,000 difference. Over a three-year period, K's business suffered a decline and as a result she was able to make payments of only $3,000 on the note. During the same three-year period, K deducted depreciation of $12,000, thereby reducing her basis in the warehouse to $18,000.

After the three years, K reduced the size of her business substantially and voluntarily transferred the warehouse to the lender. Upon the transfer, K's amount realized from the discharge of the remaining indebtedness is $22,000 ($25,000 original note – $3,000 payments). Since her basis in the warehouse was $18,000, K has a $4,000 realized gain on the disposition of the property.

## Abandonment

The abandonment of property used in a business or income-producing activity, whether depreciable or not, results in realization of loss to the extent of the property's adjusted basis. A loss deduction is allowed if the taxpayer takes action that demonstrates that he or she has no intention of retrieving the property for use, for sale, or other disposition in the future.[49]

### Example 27

While working in a logging operation, R's truck became unoperational, and it was clear that the cost of having the truck moved to a repair site exceeded its value. R abandoned the truck with no intention of seeking its return. If R has a $2,500 adjusted basis in the truck, he is entitled to an abandonment loss deduction of $2,500.

## Demolition

No deduction is allowed for expenses related to the demolition of a building or for a loss where the adjusted basis of the building exceeds any salvage value. Both the cost of the demolition and any disallowed loss are added to the basis of the land on which the building stood.[50]

### Example 28

T purchased a rezoned commercial lot with a small house for $75,000. The structure was worth $2,000. In order to expedite construction of a new car wash, T simply razed the house at a cost of $1,500. No deduction is allowed for the loss of the house or the razing cost, and T's basis in the vacant lot is $76,500 ($73,000 lot + $2,000 house + $1,500 demolition costs).

---

[49] Reg. §§ 1.165-2 and 1.167(a)-8.

[50] § 280B.

### Spousal Transfers

The transfer of property to one's spouse while married or upon dissolution of the marriage does not constitute a taxable event. This is true even if the transfer is in exchange for the release of marital rights under state law or for other consideration. This rule applies to *any* transfer made to one's spouse during the marriage or within *one year* after the marriage is terminated. It also applies to later transfers to a former spouse if the transfers are made incident to the divorce (e.g., under a provision of the divorce decree).[51] In a consistent manner, the basis of the transferred property for the transferee (recipient) is the same as the transferor's basis.[52]

Note that this nonrecognition provision applies to all transfers between spouses—including the sale of property at a fair market price. Also, the transferor is required to provide the transferee with records needed to determine the basis and holding period of the property.[53]

**Example 29**

H and W divorced this year. Under the terms of their agreement, H received stock with a basis of $16,000 and a value of $10,000. W received the house with a basis of $80,000, valued at $96,000 and subject to a mortgage of $60,000. No gain or loss is recognized by either party regardless of who owned the property before the transfer. H and W have bases in their separate properties of $16,000 and $80,000, respectively.

**Example 30**

Under an option provided in their divorce agreement, W (from the previous example) sold the house to H six months later (subject to the mortgage obligation) for $36,000. W still recognizes no gain and H's basis in the residence is $80,000.

### Gift or Bequest

A transfer of property by gift or bequest generally does not constitute a sale or other disposition. Accordingly, there is no gain or loss recognized by the donor or decedent, respectively. An exception exists, however, in the case of a sale of property at a price below its fair market value. In such a *part-gift* and *part-sale*, the donor recognizes gain *only* to the extent the sales price exceeds the adjusted basis of the property transferred.[54]

**Example 31**

M sold her personal automobile to her brother for $4,000. She had a basis of $12,000 in the auto which was worth $6,000 on the date of sale. M has made a gift of $2,000 in this part-sale/part-gift transaction and she recognizes no gain or loss.

**Example 32**

Assume the same facts above, except that M's basis in the auto had been reduced to $3,000 from depreciation deductions allowed in prior years. Although M has still made a $2,000 gift in this transaction, she must now recognize a $1,000 gain on the sale ($4,000 amount realized – $3,000 adjusted basis).

---

[51] §§ 1041(a) and (c).

[52] § 1041(b)(2).

[53] Temp. Reg. § 1.1041-1T(e).

[54] Reg. § 1.1015-4(d).

If the donee/buyer pays some cash and assumes debt of the donor/seller, or takes the property subject to encumbrances, the amount of the liabilities must be included by the donor/seller in the amount realized from the transaction.[55] Even if no cash changes hands, the part-gift and part-sale rules apply if there are liabilities associated with the transfer. Accordingly, if the donee assumes liabilities that exceed the donor's basis in the transferred property, the donor has taxable gain to the extent the liabilities exceed such basis.[56] Also, the donee/purchaser will take as his or her basis in the property acquired the *greater* of the basis under the gift rules or the purchase (cost) basis.

## Example 33

F gave a duplex rental unit to her grandson for his 18th birthday so he could develop property management skills. The duplex had a basis to F of $22,000 and a fair market value on the date of the gift of $40,000. The property was subject to a mortgage of $25,000, for which the grandson is now responsible. F has an amount realized on the gift transaction of $25,000 (transfer of the mortgage). Since the adjusted basis of the duplex was $22,000, F has a $3,000 taxable gain. If no gift taxes were paid, the grandson's basis in the duplex will be $25,000, the greater of the basis under the gift rules ($22,000) or the purchase (cost) basis.

## Example 34

If the property in the previous example had been subject to a mortgage of only $8,000, the general rule would have applied, and F would not have recognized gain or loss. The exception only applies when the discharged liabilities exceed the adjusted basis of the gifted property. Note also that the grandson's basis in the duplex would be $22,000, the same basis F had in the property.

### Transfer of Property to Charities

The transfer of property to a charity generally is not treated as a sale or other disposition. Accordingly, no gain or loss is realized or recognized. However, an exception is provided for *bargain sales* of property to charities that result in a charitable contribution deduction to the seller. In such a case, the adjusted basis of the transferred property must be allocated between the sale portion and the contribution portion based on the fair market value of the property—and any resulting gain must be recognized.[57]

## Example 35

P sold land to her church for $30,000. P had an adjusted basis in the land of $25,000. The land was appraised at $50,000 at the time of the bargain sale. P is entitled to a charitable contribution deduction of $20,000 ($50,000 fair market value – $30,000 sale price). She also has taxable gain of $15,000 on the sale ($30,000 amount realized – the $15,000 pro rata share of the adjusted basis allocable to the sale portion [($30,000 sale price ÷ $50,000 fair market value) × $25,000 basis]).

---

[55] *Reginald Fincke*, 39 B.T.A. 510 (1939).

[56] *Levine Est. v. Comm.*, 80-2 USTC ¶9607, 46 AFTR2d, 80-5349, 634 F.2d 12 (CA-2, 1980).

[57] § 1011(b); Reg. § 1.1011-2(a).

A charitable contribution of encumbered property is also treated as a bargain sale. The amount realized includes the amount of cash and the fair market value of any other property received plus the amount of the liabilities transferred. Accordingly, the property's adjusted basis must be allocated between the sale portion (represented by the amount realized) and the contribution portion.[58] This is true even if no cash or other property is received by the taxpayer.[59]

### Example 36

E made a gift of land to his alma mater. The land had a fair market value of $50,000 and was subject to a $22,000 mortgage which was assumed by the university. If the land is a long-term capital asset, E is entitled to a charitable contribution deduction of $28,000 ($50,000 fair market value reduced by the $22,000 mortgage).[60]

Additionally, E's $20,000 adjusted basis in the property must be allocated between the contribution of $28,000 and the amount realized of $22,000. The basis allocated to the sale portion is $8,800 [$20,000 basis × ($22,000 amount realized ÷ $50,000 fair market value)]. The result of the bargain sale is a taxable gain to E of $13,200 ($22,000 amount realized – $8,800 allocated basis).

## Allocations of Purchase Price and Basis

Properties purchased in a single transaction are often sold separately. In such a situation, the total basis must be allocated between the various items in order to determine gain or loss on the independent sales. Generally, relative fair market values at the time of acquisition are used to allocate the total basis among the various properties.[61] Similarly, allocation is necessary when a single sale involves properties acquired at different times in separate transactions. It may be necessary to allocate the sales price to individual assets; in such a situation, the relative fair market values on the date of sale are used for the allocation. Generally, an allocation in the sale agreement between buyer and seller will sufficiently establish the relative values unless it is shown that such assigned values were arbitrary or unreasonable.[62]

### Example 37

T purchased a commercial lot in 2004 for $30,000 and built a warehouse on the site in 2005 at a cost of $60,000. During the six years he used the warehouse in his business, T deducted depreciation of $32,000. The property was sold this year for $110,000. T must allocate the $110,000 sale price between the building and the land to determine the gain or loss on each. If $40,000 is allocated to the land and $70,000 is allocated to the building based on relative fair market values, T has a gain of $10,000 ($40,000 – $30,000) and $42,000 [$70,000 – ($60,000 – $32,000)], respectively, on the properties.

### Sale of a Business

When a business operated as a sole proprietorship is sold, the sale is treated as a sale of each of the individual assets of the business. Accordingly, allocations of sales price and basis must be made to the individual assets of the business.[63] The various gains and losses have separate impact, according to their character, on the taxable income of the owner.

[58] See Reg. § 1.1011-2(a).

[59] *Winston Guest*, 77 T.C. 9 (1981) and Rev. Rul. 81-163, 1981-1 C.B. 433.

[60] See Chapter 11 for a discussion of charitable contributions involving long-term capital gain property.

[61] See, for example, *Fairfeld Plaza, Inc.*, 39 T.C. 706 (1963), and Rev. Rul. 72-255, 1972-1 C.B. 221.

[62] See *John B. Resler*; 38 TCM 153, T.C. Memo 1979-40.

[63] See Rev. Rul. 55-79, 1955-1 C.B. 370, and *Williams v. McGowan*, 46-1 USTC ¶9120, 34 AFTR 615, 152 F.2d 570 (CA-2, 1945).

### Example 38

F has owned and operated a dress shop for 12 years. F's increased interest in her grandchildren and in fishing prompted her to sell the shop and retire. The sales agreement with the buyer allocated the total sales price to the individual assets as follows:

| | *Value per Sales Agreement* | *F's Adjusted Basis* |
|---|---|---|
| Inventory | $16,000 | $18,000 |
| Furniture and fixtures | 14,000 | 6,000 |
| Leasehold and leasehold improvements | 20,000 | 3,000 |
| Goodwill | 0 | 0 |
| Total | $50,000 | $27,000 |

F has a $2,000 loss on the sale of inventory, and gains on the furniture and fixtures of $8,000 and on the leasehold and improvements of $17,000, each of which has its separate impact on taxable income.

The sale of an interest in a partnership or in a corporation that operates a business is generally treated as the sale of such interest, rather than of the underlying assets. Therefore, no allocation is necessary and gain or loss is recognized on the sale of the interest. For each type of entity, major exceptions to this treatment exist and are discussed in a later chapter.[64]

## Installment Sale Method

**LO.7**
Define an installment sale and identify taxpayers eligible to use the installment method of reporting gain.

The general rule of Federal taxation is that all gains or losses are recognized in the year of sale or exchange. This rule could place a severe burden on taxpayers who sell their property for something other than cash, particularly deferred payment obligations. Without some relief, taxpayers would be required to pay their tax liability before obtaining the sale proceeds with which they could pay the tax. If the tax is substantial, a requirement to pay before sufficient cash collections occur might necessitate the sale of other assets the taxpayer wished to retain.

Because of the potential hardship placed on taxpayers from reporting gain without the corresponding receipt of cash, Congress enacted the installment sale method of reporting in 1926. The installment method has been significantly modified over the years, with each modification further restricting *both* the types of gains and the taxpayers eligible for its use. The eligibility requirements are discussed below.

### General Rules

The installment method is used to report *gains*—not losses—from qualifying installment sales of property. An *installment sale* is defined as any sale of property whereby the seller will receive at least one payment after the close of the tax year in which the sale occurs. Unfortunately, not all gains from installment sales qualify for installment reporting.

#### Ineligible Sales

The installment method cannot be used for reporting gains from sales of the following:[65]

1. Property held for sale in the ordinary course of the taxpayer's trade or business (e.g., inventories)
2. Stocks or securities that are traded on an established securities market

In addition, the portion of any gain from the sale of depreciable property that must be reported as ordinary income under the depreciation recapture rules is not eligible for installment reporting. These rules are discussed in Chapter 17.

[64] See Chapter 19 for a discussion of corporate taxation, and Chapter 22 for partnership taxation.

[65] §§ 453(b), (i), and (l). See § 453(l)(2) for certain limited exceptions.

### Mandatory Reporting Requirement

Generally, gains from eligible sales *must* be reported under the installment method regardless of the taxpayer's method of accounting.[66] Thus, the installment method is considered to be *mandatory* rather than elective. However, Congress recognized the fact that for some taxpayers the installment method of reporting would not be the relief measure that it was intended to be. Consequently, taxpayers are allowed to *elect out* of the installment method simply by reporting the entire gain in the year of sale.[67]

## Election out of Installment Reporting

There are various reasons why a taxpayer might wish to elect not to use the installment method of reporting gain from the sale of property. Such reasons might include the following:

1. The taxpayer's income in the year of sale is quite low and income is expected to be higher in subsequent years.
2. The taxpayer might have a large capital loss with which to absorb the capital gain in the year of sale.
3. The taxpayer might have an expiring net operating loss.
4. It might be necessary for the taxpayer to report the gain in order to utilize a tax credit carryover.
5. The burden of complying with the installment sale rules might outweigh the advantage of the installment reporting of the gain.

If a taxpayer *elects not to use* the installment method for a given sale, the amount of gain must be computed under his or her usual method of accounting (i.e., cash or accrual) and reported in the year of sale.[68] A cash basis taxpayer must use the *fair market value* of any installment obligation received in determining the amount realized from the installment sale.[69] On the other hand, an accrual basis taxpayer must account for an installment obligation at its *face value* in computing the amount realized.[70]

### Example 39

S, a cash basis taxpayer, sold land to B on May 15, 2011. S received $100,000 cash and a note from B payable in five equal annual installments of $80,000 (i.e., face value), bearing a 9% interest rate. The note has a value of $300,000 and S has a $75,000 basis in the land. If S elects not to use the installment method, his gain to be reported in 2011 is computed as follows:

| | |
|---|---|
| Amount realized: | |
| Cash received | $100,000 |
| FMV of installment obligations | 300,000 |
| | $400,000 |
| Less: Basis of land | (75,000) |
| Gain to be reported in 2011 | $325,000 |

In addition to the interest income that S will recognize when the installment payments are collected, he must recognize additional income on the collection of each installment payment as follows:

| | |
|---|---|
| Amount realized (installment payment) | $ 80,000 |
| Less: Basis in each installment ($300,000 FMV of note ÷ 5 installments) | (60,000) |
| Ordinary income to be reported | $ 20,000 |

[66] § 453(a).

[67] See § 453(d) and Temp. Reg. 15a.453-1(d)(2)(ii).

[68] *Ibid.*

[69] § 1001(b).

[70] Rev. Rul. 79-292. 1979-2 C.B. 287.

**Example 40**

Assume the same facts as in *Example 39*, except that S is an accrual basis taxpayer. His gain to be reported in the year of sale is computed as follows:

| | |
|---|---|
| Amount realized: | |
| Cash received | $100,000 |
| Face value of installment obligations | 400,000 |
| | $500,000 |
| Less: Basis in land | (75,000) |
| Gain to be reported in 2011 | $425,000 |

In this case, S will not be required to report any income other than the interest received as each of the payments are collected because his basis in each installment obligation is $100,000 (i.e., its face amount).

## Gain Reported Under the Installment Method

**LO.8**
Compute the amount of gain required to be recognized in the year of installment sale and the gain to be reported in any subsequent year.

The following *six* factors must be taken into account by a taxpayer using the installment method of reporting gain:

1. The gross profit on the sale
2. The total contract price
3. The gross profit percentage
4. The payments received in the year of sale
5. The gain to be reported in the year of sale
6. The gain to be reported in the following years

### Determining Gross Profit

A taxpayer's gross profit is nothing more than the total gain that will be reported (excluding interest) from the installment sale. It is determined by subtracting the *sum* of the seller's adjusted basis and expenses of sale from the selling price:[71]

| | |
|---|---|
| Selling price | $xxx,xxx |
| Less: Adjusted basis in property plus selling expenses | −xx,xxx |
| Gross profit on sale | $ xx,xxx |

### Determining the Total Contract Price

The total contract price is the total amount of cash (excluding interest) that the seller expects to collect from the buyer over the term of the installment sale. It is usually equal to the selling price less any liabilities of the seller that are transferred to the buyer. However, if the liabilities assumed by the buyer *exceed* the seller's adjusted basis in the property and the selling expenses, the excess must be treated as a *deemed payment* received in the year of sale. Because a deemed payment is treated as cash collected in the year of sale, it must be added to the contract price.[72]

---

[71] Temp. Reg. § 15a.453-1(b)(2)(v).

[72] § 453A(a)(2) and Temp. Reg. § 15a.453-1(b)(2)(ii).

### Determining Gross Profit Percentage

The taxpayer's gross profit percentage is the percentage of each dollar received that must be reported as gain. It is equal to the gross profit divided by the total contract price.[73]

$$\frac{\text{Gross profit}}{\text{Total contract price}} = \text{Gross profit percentage}$$

### Determining Payments Received in Year of Sale

Payments received in the year of sale include the following:[74]

1. Money received at the time of closing the sale, including any selling expenses *paid* by the buyer
2. Deemed payments (i.e., excess of seller's liabilities transferred over the property's adjusted basis plus selling expenses)
3. The fair market value of any third-party obligations received at the time of closing and the fair market value of any other property received
4. Installment payments received in the year of sale, excluding interest income

### Gain Reported in Year of Sale

Gain reported in the year of sale is computed as follows:

$$\frac{\text{Gross profit}}{\text{Total contract price}} \times \text{Payments received} = \text{Recognized gain}$$

### Gain Reported in Following Years

Gain to be reported in the years following the year of sale equals the taxpayer's gross profit percentage multiplied by the principal payments received on the purchaser's note in that year.

#### Example 41

T sold a 70-acre tract of land that she had held as an investment on March 1, 2011. The facts concerning the sale are as follows:

| | | |
|---|---|---|
| Sales price: | | |
| Cash payment | $120,000 | |
| Mortgage assumed by buyer | 200,000 | |
| Buyer's notes payable to T | 480,000 | $800,000 |
| Less: Selling expenses | $ 50,000 | |
| T's basis in land | 250,000 | (300,000) |
| Gross profit on sale | | $500,000 |

The contract price is $600,000 ($800,000 sales price − $200,000 debt assumed by buyer). Assuming the $120,000 payment is the only payment received in 2011, T's gain to be reported for the year is computed as follows:

$$\frac{\$\ 500{,}000\ \text{(gross profit)}}{\$\ 600{,}000\ \text{(contract price)}} \times \$\ 120{,}000 = \$\ 100{,}000 \text{ gain to be recognized}$$

As T collects the remaining $480,000 of the total contract price, she will report the remaining $400,000 gross profit from the sale (i.e., $480,000 × 5/6 gross profit percentage = $400,000).

[73] § 453(c) and Temp. Reg. § 15a.453-1(b)(2)(i).

[74] Temp. Reg. § 15a.453-1(b)(3)(i).

## Example 42

Assume the same facts as in *Example 41*, except that T's basis in the land is only $100,000. In this case, the gross profit on the sale is $650,000 [$800,000 − ($50,000 + $100,000)]. T's payments received in the year of sale are computed as follows:

| | | |
|---|---|---|
| Cash payment | | $120,000 |
| Plus: deemed payment received: | | |
| Mortgage assumed by buyer | $200,000 | |
| Less: Selling expense | (50,000) | |
| T's basis in land | (100,000) | 50,000 |
| Total payments received in 2011 | | $170,000 |

The total contract price is $650,000 ($800,000 selling price − $200,000 mortgage transferred + $50,000 excess of mortgage assumed over T's basis in property and selling expenses). T's gain to be reported in 2011 is computed as follows:

$$\frac{\$\ 650{,}000\ \text{(gross profit)}}{\$\ 650{,}000\ \text{(contract price)}} \times \$\ 170{,}000\ \text{payments} = \$\ 170{,}000$$

Note that the excess of the mortgage transferred over T's basis in the land and the selling expenses (i.e., the deemed payment) causes the gross profit percentage to become 100%. This adjustment to *both* the total contract price and the payments received in the year of sale must be made to ensure that the entire gain from the sale is ultimately reported by the seller. As a result, all payments received by T in subsequent years (excluding interest) will be reported as gain from the sale [$650,000 total gross profit − $170,000 gain reported in year of sale = $480,000 gain to be reported in subsequent years ($480,000 buyer's notes × 100%)].

## Limitations on Certain Installment Sales

**LO.9**
Explain the limitations imposed on certain installment sales, including:

- The imputed interest rules.
- Related-party installment sales.
- Gain recognition on the disposition of installment obligations.
- Required interest payments on deferred Federal income taxes.

As mentioned earlier, the installment sales provisions have been modified over the years to limit or stop perceived taxpayer abuse of what was intended to be simply a relief from immediate taxation of all gain from deferred payment sales. These modifications have created the following problem areas:

1. Imputed interest rules
2. Related-party rules
3. Gain recognition on dispositions of installment note
4. Required interest payments on deferred taxes

Each of these problem areas is discussed below.

### Imputed Interest Rules

Without some limitation, a taxpayer planning a deferred payment sale of a capital asset could require the buyer to pay a higher sales price in return for a lower than prevailing market rate of interest on the deferred payments, thereby converting into capital gain what would have been ordinary (interest) income. The imputed interest rules were designed to prevent just such a scheme. Under these rules, any deferred payment sale of property with a selling price exceeding $3,000 must provide a *reasonable* interest rate.[75] Thus, in a deferred payment sale

[75] See §§ 483 and 1274.

providing little or no interest, the selling price must be *restated* to equal the sum of payments received on the date of the sale and the discounted present value of the future payments. The difference between the face value of the future payments and this discounted value (i.e., the imputed interest) generally must be reported as interest income under the accrual method of accounting, regardless of the taxpayer's regular accounting method.[76]

If the sales contract does not provide for interest equal to the *applicable Federal rate* (AFR), interest will be imputed at that rate.[77] The AFR is the interest rate the Federal government pays on borrowed funds, and the actual rate varies with the terms of the loan. Loans are divided into short-term (not over three years), mid-term (over three years but not over nine years), and long-term (over nine years).[78]

## Example 43

S, a cash basis taxpayer, sold land held as an investment on July 1, 2011 for $1 million cash and a non-interest-bearing note (face value of $4 million) due on July 1, 2013. At the time of the sale, the short-term AFR was 10% (compounded semiannually). Because the sales contract did not provide for interest of at least the AFR, the selling price must be restated and interest must be imputed at 10% (compounded semi-annually).

| Sale price: | |
|---|---|
| Cash payment. . . . . . . . . . . . . . . . . . . . . . . . . . . . . . . . . . . . . . . . | $1,000,000 |
| Present value of $4,000,000 note due July 1, 2013 (0.8227 × $4,000,000) | 3,290,800 |
| Recomputed sale price . . . . . . . . . . . . . . . . . . . . . . . . . . . . . . . . . . | $4,290,800 |

S must use this recomputed sale price in determining the total contract price, gross profit percentage, gain to be reported in the year of sale, and gain to be reported (excluding interest) when the $4 million deferred payment is received. In addition, S must report $164,540 of imputed interest income in 2011, computed as follows:

| *Period* | *Present Value* | × | *10% Compounded Semiannually* | = | *Imputed Interest* |
|---|---|---|---|---|---|
| 7/1/11 to 12/31/11 | $3,290,800 | × | 0.05 | = | $164,540 |

S must also compute and report her imputed interest for 2012 and 2013. When the $4 million note payable is collected on July 1, 2013, S will report only the gain on the sale remaining after that portion reported in 2011.

### Related-Party Sales

Generally, installment sales between related parties are subject to the same rules as other such sales *except* (1) when the related-party purchaser resells the property before payment of the original sales price;[79] and (2) when the property sold is depreciable property.[80] The primary purpose of the *resale* rule is to prevent a related-party seller from deferring his or her gain on the first sale while the related-party purchaser enjoys the use of proceeds from its resale.

76 See §§ 1272(a), 1273(a), and 1274(a). Also see §§ 483 and 1274(c) for various exceptions to this requirement.

77 § 1274(d)(1).

78 These three Federal rates are published monthly by the IRS.

79 § 453(e).

80 § 453(g).

## Example 44

M plans to sell a capital asset (basis \$40,000) to B, an unrelated party, for \$200,000. Instead of selling the asset to B, she sells it to her son, S, for \$10,000 cash and a \$190,000 note due in five years and bearing a reasonable interest rate. Shortly after his purchase, S sells the asset to B for \$200,000.

Without the resale rule, M would report a gain of \$8,000 in the year of sale, computed as follows:

$$\frac{\$200{,}000 - \$40{,}000}{\$200{,}000} \times \$10{,}000 = \$8{,}000$$

M would have a deferred gain of \$152,000 (\$160,000 gross profit – \$8,000 gain reported in year of sale). More importantly, S would have a cost basis of \$200,000 in the asset and report no gain on the subsequent resale to B. The net result of the two transactions is a \$152,000 deferred gain and the immediate use of the sales proceeds by a family member.

Under the resale rule, any proceeds collected by the related-party purchaser on the subsequent sale are treated as being collected by the related-party seller. Consequently, M must report her \$152,000 deferred gain when S resells the property, even though she has not yet collected the \$190,000 note.

For purposes of the resale rule, the term *related party* includes the spouse, children, grandchildren, and parents of the seller.[81] Any controlled corporation, partnership, trust, or estate in which the seller has an interest is also considered related under these rules.[82] It is also important to note that the resale rule does not apply when the second sale occurs (1) more than two years after the first sale, or (2) after the death of the related-party seller.[83]

The installment method is generally not allowed to be used to report a gain on the sale of depreciable property to an entity controlled by the taxpayer.[84] This rule is designed to prevent a related-party seller from deferring gain on a sale that will result in the purchaser's being able to use a higher (cost) basis to claim depreciation deductions. For this purpose, a *controlled entity* is a partnership or corporation in which the seller owns a more than 50 percent direct or indirect interest. Indirect ownership includes any interest owned by the seller's spouse and certain other family members.[85] It is important to note that this rule is based on a presumption that the related-party installment sale is motivated by tax avoidance. Thus, the related-party seller can use the installment method of reporting the sale if he or she can establish that tax avoidance *was not* the principal motive of the transaction. This makes such a sale subject to a facts and circumstances review and approval of the Internal Revenue Service.

### Dispositions of Installment Obligations

After deciding to report a deferred payment sale under the installment method, rather than *electing out*, sellers ordinarily collect the payments in due course and report the remaining gain in full. However, if this process is interrupted by a sale, gift, or other transfer of some or all of the installment obligations, rules require that any unreported gain be reported at the time of the transfer. Consequently, if an installment obligation is satisfied at other than its face value or is distributed, transmitted, sold, or otherwise disposed of, the taxpayer is generally required to recognize gain or loss.

The amount of gain or loss is the difference between the obligation's basis and *either* the amount realized, if the obligation is satisfied at an amount other than its face value because it is sold or exchanged, *or* its fair market value when distributed, transmitted, or disposed of, if the transfer is not a sale or exchange.[86] The obligation's basis is its face amount less the amount of gain that would have been reported if the obligation had been satisfied in full.[87]

[81] §§ 453(f) and 267(b).

[82] §§ 453(f) and 318(a).

[83] § 453(e)(2).

[84] *Supra*, Footnote 80.

[85] §§ 1239(b) and (c).

[86] § 453B(a).

[87] § 453B(b).

Taxable dispositions include most sales and exchanges. Also included are gifts, transfers to trusts, distributions by trusts and estates to beneficiaries, distributions from corporations to shareholders, net proceeds from the pledge of an installment obligation, and cancellation of the installment obligation.

The obvious purpose of the disposition rules is to prevent the seller from *either* shifting the income to another taxpayer (e.g., by gift) *or* enjoying the use of the sales proceeds prior to gain recognition (e.g., by pledging an installment obligation for borrowed funds). However, there are several exceptions to the requirement of immediate gain recognition. Transfers of installment obligations upon the death of the seller, transfers incident to divorce, transfers to or distributions from a partnership, certain transfers to controlled corporations, and certain transfers incident to corporate reorganization are among the exceptions to these rules.[88]

### Required Interest Payments on Deferred Taxes

Another rule designed to reduce the benefits of installment reporting for certain taxpayers is the requirement to pay interest to the government on the deferred taxes. This rule applies if *two conditions* are met. First, the taxpayer must have outstanding installment obligations from the sale of property (other than farming property) for more than $150,000. Second, the outstanding obligations from such sales must exceed $5 million at the close of the tax year.[89] Only the deferred taxes attributable to the installment obligations in *excess* of $5 million are subject to this annual interest payment. The interest must be calculated using the tax underpayment rate in § 6621.

**Example 45**

T has $9 million of installment obligations outstanding on December 31, 2011. These obligations arose from the sale of a vacant lot located in the downtown area of Chicago. T's gross profit percentage on the installment sale was 40%. Assuming the underpayment rate in § 6621 is 10% and T's 2011 marginal tax rate is 35%, the required interest payment on the deferred taxes is computed as follows:

| | |
|---|---|
| Outstanding installment obligations | $9,000,000 |
| Less: Amount not subject to rule | (5,000,000) |
| Excess installment obligations | $4,000,000 |
| Times: Gross profit percentage | × 40% |
| Deferred gross profit | $1,600,000 |
| Times: T's marginal tax rate | × 35% |
| Deferred Federal income taxes | $ 560,000 |
| Times: § 6621 underpayment rate | × 10% |
| Required interest payment | $ 56,000 |

Because taxpayers are allowed to have up to $5 million of installment obligations outstanding without being subject to the required interest payment rule, it is apparent that only those taxpayers with one or more substantial installment sales need be concerned with this rule.

## Reporting Gain on Installment Sales

Taxpayers reporting gain on the installment sale method should attach Form 6252, Computation of Installment Sale Income, to the tax return for the year of sale and each subsequent year in which a payment is collected. A sample of this form is contained in Appendix B.

---

88 See §§ 453B(c), (d), and (g).

89 § 453A.

# Disallowed Losses

**LO.10**
Identify various transactions in which loss recognition is prohibited.

Various limitations exist regarding gain and loss recognition in certain property transactions. Several such limitations have already been discussed. Recall that any losses on the sale of personal use assets are disallowed. Similarly, losses on the sale of property acquired by gift are limited to the decline in its value subsequent to the transfer by gift. This results because the basis for determining loss is the fair market value on the date of gift, if that fair market value is less than the donor's basis (which would otherwise be the donee's basis).[90] Likewise, a loss on the disposition of property that has been converted from personal use to business use is limited to the decline in its value subsequent to the conversion. In determining any loss on such a disposition, the adjusted basis is the lesser of the taxpayer's adjusted basis or the fair market value on the date of conversion.[91]

There are several other limitations on the deductibility of losses arising from sales or other dispositions of property. As discussed in Chapter 7, losses incurred in sales between related taxpayers are not deductible. Also, certain losses incurred from the sale of stock or securities will not be allowed as a deduction.

## Wash Sales

A *wash sale* occurs when a taxpayer sells stock or securities at a loss and reinvests in substantially identical stock or securities within 30 days before or after the date of sale. Any loss realized on such a wash sale is not deductible.[92] In essence, a taxpayer who has a wash sale has not had a *change* in economic position—thus the transaction resulting in a loss is ignored for tax purposes. The loss is, however, taken into consideration in determining the adjusted basis in the new shares.[93]

### Example 46

C, a calendar year taxpayer, owns 400 shares of X Corporation stock (adjusted basis of $9,000), all of which he sells for $5,000 on December 28, 2011. On January 7, 2012. C purchases another 400 shares of X Corporation stock for $5,500. C's realized loss of $4,000 in 2011 will not be deductible because it resulted from a wash sale. Instead, his basis in the 400 shares purchased in 2012 is increased to $9,500 ($5,500 purchase price + $4,000 disallowed loss).

The *numbers* of shares purchased and sold are not always the same. When the number of shares reacquired is less than the number sold, the deduction for losses is disallowed only for the number of shares purchased.[94]

### Example 47

Assume the same facts as in *Example 46*, except that C purchased only 300 shares of X Corporation stock for $4,125. Because C replaced only 300 of the shares previously sold at a loss, only 75% (300 ÷ 400) of the $4,000 realized loss is disallowed. Consequently, C will report a $1,000 loss ($4,000 × 25%) in 2011 and will have a basis of $7,125 ($4,125 purchase price + $3,000 disallowed loss) in the 300 shares purchased.

When the number of shares repurchased is greater than the number of shares sold, none of the loss is deductible and the basis in a number of shares equivalent to the number of shares sold is affected by the disallowed loss.[95]

[90] § 1015(a).

[91] Reg. § 1.165-9(b).

[92] § 1091(a).

[93] § 1091(d).

[94] Reg. § 1.1091-1(c).

[95] Reg. § 1.1091-1(d).

Any loss also will be disallowed if the "substantially equivalent" stock or securities are acquired by certain related parties. For example, the U.S. Supreme Court held that the wash sale provisions apply if replacement stock is acquired by a taxpayer's spouse *and* they file a joint return for the tax year of the loss.[96]

## Sales Between Related Parties

The Code places numerous limitations on gain or loss recognition from transactions between certain related parties. The purpose of such restrictions is to prevent related taxpayers from entering into various property transactions solely for the tax reduction possibilities. For example, a father could sell land to his daughter at a loss, deduct the loss, and the property would still remain within the family unit. Similarly, a taxpayer could sell depreciable property to her spouse and report a long-term capital gain on their joint return. For many years thereafter, she and her husband could claim ordinary deductions for depreciation on this higher basis. To control such potentially abusive situations, Congress enacted Code §§ 267 and 1239.

Section 267 disallows deductions for any losses that result from the sale or exchange of property between related parties.[97] Such losses may, however, be used by the related purchaser to offset any gain realized from a subsequent disposition of the property.[98] For purposes of § 267, related parties include the following:[99]

1. Members of an individual's family—specifically, brothers and sisters (including by half blood), spouses, ancestors (i.e., parents and grandparents), and lineal descendants (i.e., children and grandchildren)
2. A corporation owned more than 50 percent in value by the taxpayer (directly or indirectly)
3. Two corporations owned more than 50 percent in value by the taxpayer (directly or indirectly) if either corporation is a personal holding company or a foreign personal holding company in the tax year of the transaction
4. Various partnership, S corporation, grantor, fiduciary, and trust relationships with regular corporations and individual taxpayers

**Example 48**

M sells stock (adjusted basis of $10,000) to her daughter, D, for its fair market value of $8,000. D sells the stock two years later for $11,000. M's $2,000 loss is disallowed as a deduction. However, D's realized gain of $3,000 ($11,000 sales price – $8,000 cost basis) is reduced by the $2,000 previously disallowed loss, and she will report only $1,000 of gain.

Note the similarity between the results in *Example 48* and the situation that would result if D had received the stock as a gift from M. First, D's basis for gain would be $10,000 (M's basis) if the stock had been received as a gift; its subsequent sale for $11,000 would have resulted in the same $1,000 recognized (reported) gain. Although the disallowance of a loss deduction might discourage many related-party transactions, some taxpayers prefer to sell rather than give property to a related party in order to avoid paying state or Federal gift taxes.

Section 1239 provides that any gain realized from the sale of depreciable property between specified related parties will be taxed as ordinary income.[100] In effect, this statute precludes the possibility that any gain on the sale might be taxed as a long-term capital gain since the sale results in a higher basis in the depreciable property to a related party. Furthermore, recall that such related-party sales of depreciable property are not eligible for installment sale treatment.[101] Transactions subject to § 1239 treatment are discussed in Chapter 19.

[96] *Helvering v. Taft*, 40-2 USTC ¶9888, 24 AFTR 1976, 311 U.S. 195 (USSC, 1940).

[97] § 267(a)(1).

[98] § 267(d).

[99] See §§ 267(b) and (c).

[100] § 1239(a).

[101] § 453(g).

# Tax Planning Considerations

## Gift Versus Bequest

In devising a plan for transferring wealth from one family member to another, several considerations related to the income tax, the transfer taxes, and the wishes of the parties involved must be evaluated. If there is a desire to transfer properties, there are relative advantages and disadvantages to lifetime transfers as opposed to testamentary transfers (transfers by will). Some of the specific factors that should be considered are as follows:

1. The income tax rate of each individual (decedent and heirs) relative to the estate and gift tax rates.
2. Whether the property is highly appreciated. If so, a testamentary transfer may be preferred since the property's basis to the heirs or the estate will be its fair market value at date of death or alternate valuation date. If the property is gifted, its basis will be the donor's basis increased by a fraction of any gift taxes paid. If the property has declined in value, only the *original owner* (donor) can benefit from any tax loss by disposing of the property to an unrelated party, due to the basis for determination of loss under § 1015(a).
3. Whether the property is expected to appreciate rapidly in the foreseeable future. If so, a current gift might be considered because the amount subject to gift taxes would be the current market value. If the property were held until death, the higher fair market value at that time would be used in calculating estate taxes. This action is, of course, speculative in nature.
4. Whether the transferee is likely to hold the property for a long period of time. If so, the basis considerations are not as important as they would be if the property were to be sold immediately upon its receipt.
5. Whether the property is income-producing property. If the property produces income, and the owner (donor) is in a high income tax bracket, a lifetime transfer could result in the profits being taxed at a lower tax rate to another family member. If the donee is in a significantly lower income tax bracket, substantial income tax savings can be accomplished.

These factors, as well as the health of the parties involved and other personal considerations, must all be considered. It is possible that the personal factors will outweigh the tax factors, or that significant amounts of taxes cannot be saved.

## Charitable Transfers Involving Property Other than Cash

Taxpayers who are considering making major charitable transfers and who have property other than cash that they would consider transferring must consider both the effects of any gain or loss if property is sold and the effects of any allowable charitable deduction. If a property has declined in value, its owner may benefit from selling the property and deducting the loss and later contributing the cash proceeds to the charity.

Planning can be even more important when the property is appreciated, since in certain instances a charitable deduction is allowed equal to the fair market value of the property. This is true when the property is long-term capital gain property that is used in the exempt function of the charity, is intangible, or is real estate (see Chapter 11). In such a case, the taxpayer will avoid paying tax on the property's unrealized appreciation and still receive full benefit from the charitable deduction.

## Changes in the Use of Property

A taxpayer who converts business property to personal use when its value is less than its adjusted basis should consider selling the asset in order to trigger a deduction for the loss. Also, a taxpayer who buys property that he or she intends to use in a business should think carefully before using the asset for personal purposes. For example, a taxpayer who purchases a new auto and drives it for personal purposes for two years before converting it to business use must use the fair value upon conversion—if less than adjusted basis—in determining both depreciation and any loss on disposition.

## Sales to Related Parties

Care must be exercised to avoid the undesirable effects of transactions between related parties. If a loss on the sale of property to a related party is disallowed, the tax benefit of a loss deduction is permanently lost unless the value of the property subsequently increases. The only way to generate a tax deduction for the loss is for the original owner to sell the property to an unrelated party. Also, characterizing gain on the sale of depreciable property as ordinary income under § 1239 should normally be avoided.

## Use of Installment Sales

Installment sale treatment provides an excellent opportunity for deferring the tax on gain (other than depreciation recapture) when a taxpayer is willing to accept an installment obligation in exchange for property. Actually, installment reporting may provide such attractive tax deferral and tax savings possibilities that the taxpayer is induced to accept an installment obligation, even though he or she would not do so otherwise. In short, this is a tax variable that must be considered by a prudent taxpayer in planning sales of property.

A taxpayer may benefit in at least two ways from the installment method. First, benefits accrue from the deferral of the tax. The time value of money works to the taxpayer's benefit, assuming the sales contract provides for a fair rate of interest. The second benefit from installment reporting is the spreading of the gain over more than one tax year. If the gain on a sale is unusual and moves the taxpayer into a higher tax bracket, spreading the gain over several years tends to allow the overall gain to be taxed in lower tax brackets.

It is important to remember, however, that taxpayers may face several limitations on certain installment sales. First, if a reasonable interest rate is not provided in the deferred payment sale, the seller will be required to impute interest at the appropriate Federal rate. Second, a taxpayer unaware of the rules relating to related-party sales may find that he or she is required to report all the gain on such a sale long before the actual collection of cash from the installment obligations. Third, taxpayers with installment obligations must be informed of the rules requiring immediate gain recognition on certain dispositions of such obligations. These rules include treating borrowed funds as collections on the installment notes if such notes are used as collateral for a loan. Finally, taxpayers with significant amounts of installment obligations outstanding at the end of a particular tax year (i.e., in excess of $5 million) may find that the required interest payment on the deferred income taxes is greater than the interest currently being collected.

# Problem Materials

### DISCUSSION QUESTIONS

**14-1** *Realization versus Recognition.* In a few sentences, distinguish realization from recognition.

**14-2** *Return-of-Capital Principle.* What is the return-of-capital principle?

**14-3** *Computing Amount Realized.* Reproduce the formula for computing the amount realized in a sale or exchange.

**14-4** *Impact of Liabilities.* What impact do liabilities assumed by the buyer or liabilities encumbering property transferred have on the amount realized? How are they treated if both parties to the transaction incur new liabilities?

**14-5** *Cost Basis.* How does one determine cost basis for property acquired? How is this basis affected if property other than money is transferred in exchange for the new property?

**14-6** *Gift Basis.* Reproduce the formula for the general rule for determining basis of property acquired by gift.

**14-7** *Gift Basis Exception.* When does the general rule for determining basis of property acquired by gift *(Question 14-6)* not apply?

**14-8** *Basis of Inherited Property.* The basis of property acquired from a decedent is generally fair market value at date of death. What are the two exceptions to this rule (do not include property subject to special-use valuation)?

**14-9** *Basis Adjustments.* List the three broad categories of adjustments to basis.

**14-10** *Transfers Pursuant to Divorce.* In general, do transfers of property in a divorce action result in the realization of gain or loss? Under what circumstances might gain recognition be required?

**14-11** *Part-Sale/Part-Gift.* When does a bargain sale to a donee (part-gift) result in gain to the donor? Does the assumption of the donor's liabilities by the donee have any impact? Explain.

**14-12** *Bargain Sales.* How is a bargain sale of property to a charitable organization treated for tax purposes?

**14-13** *Allocating Sales Price.* Allocations are generally necessary when a sole proprietorship is sold as a unit. What method is normally used for such allocation? What impact does the sales agreement have if it allocates the price to the individual assets?

**14-14** *Installment Sales Method—General Rules.* What is the purpose of the installment sale method of reporting gains? Is it an elective provision? How does one elect out of the installment sale method? What sales do not qualify for installment sale treatment?

**14-15** *Installment Sales Method—Key Terms.* Explain how each of the following factors related to an installment sale is determined.

**a.** Gross profit on deferred payment sale
**b.** Total contract price
**c.** Gross profit percentage
**d.** Payments received in the year of sale
**e.** Gain to be reported in the year of sale

**14-16** *Imputed Interest Rules.* Under what circumstances must a taxpayer impute interest income from an installment sale? How is the applicable Federal rate (AFR) determined?

**14-17** *Related-Party Installment Sales.* Under what circumstances will a taxpayer be faced with the related-party installment sale rules? Explain how a resale of the property by the related party purchaser before the seller has collected the balance of the installment obligation affects the seller.

**14-18** *Dispositions of Installment Obligations.* Your neighbor has $30,000 of installment obligations from a recent sale of land held for investment. He asks you for advice concerning his planned gift of these obligations to his children to be used for their future college expenses. An examination of Form 6252 attached to his most recent tax return reveals a gross profit percentage of 60 percent and a reasonable market rate of interest related to these installment obligations. What tax advice would you give regarding this plan?

**14-19** *Wash Sale.* What is a wash sale? How is a wash sale treated for tax purposes?

**14-20** *Timing of Recognition.* Under what circumstances is a realized gain actually recognized? What event generally controls the timing of gain recognition?

## PROBLEMS

**14-21** *Sale Involving Liabilities.* C sold a cottage in which his basis was $32,000, for cash of $12,000 and a note from the buyer worth $28,000. The buyer assumed an existing note of $30,000 secured by an interest in the property.

**a.** What is C's amount realized in this sale?
**b.** What is C's gain or loss realized on this sale?

**14-22** *Exchange Involving Liabilities.* D exchanged a mountain cabin for a leisure yacht and $30,000 cash. The yacht was worth $25,000 and was subject to liabilities of $10,000, which were assumed by D. The cabin was subject to liabilities of $32,000, which were assumed by the other party.

**a.** How much is D's amount realized?

**b.** Assuming D's basis in the cabin was $42,000, what is his gain or loss realized?

**14-23** *Identification of Stock Sold.* T purchased the following lots of stock in Z Corporation:

| | | |
|---|---|---|
| 50 shares | 1/12/02 | Cost $1,200 |
| 100 shares | 2/28/07 | Cost $3,000 |
| 75 shares | 10/16/08 | Cost $2,500 |

T sold 75 shares on January 16, 2011 for $2,800. His only instruction to his broker, who actually held the shares for T, was to sell 75 shares.

**a.** How much gain or loss does T recognize on this sale?

**b.** How could this result be altered?

**14-24** *Sale of Property Acquired by Gift.* J received 1,000 shares of Exxon stock as a gift from her grandmother in 2007, when the stock was worth $50,000. The stock had a basis to the grandmother of $10,000, and gift taxes of $16,000 were paid on the $40,000 taxable value of the gift.

**a.** How much gain does J recognize when she sells the stock for $80,000 (net of commissions) during the current year?

**b.** What would be your answer if the sale price were $35,000 (net of commissions)?

**c.** What would be your answer if the sale price were $19,000 (net of commissions)?

**14-25** *Sale of Property Acquired by Gift.* In 2008, F gave his son, S, 100 shares of IBM stock, which at that time were worth $30,000. F paid a gift tax on the transfer of $5,000. Assuming F had purchased the stock in 2004 for $40,000, what are the tax consequences to S if he sells the stock for the following amounts?

**a.** $25,000

**b.** $37,000

**c.** $45,000

**14-26** *Sale of Inherited Property.* D inherited two acres of commercial real estate from her grandmother, who had a basis in the property of $52,000, when it had a fair market value of $75,000. For estate tax purposes, the estate was valued as of the date of death, and estate and inheritance taxes of $8,250 were paid by the estate on this parcel of real estate.

**a.** How much gain or loss will be realized by D if she sells the property for $77,000?

**b.** What would be your answer if the sale price were $66,000?

**14-27** *Basis of Inherited Property.* H inherited a parcel of real estate from his father. The property was valued for estate tax purposes at $120,000, and the father's basis was $45,000 immediately before his death. H had given the property to his father as a gift six weeks before his death. The proper portion of the gift taxes paid by H are included in his father's basis.

**a.** What is H's basis in the real estate?

**b.** What would be your answer if H had given the property to his father two years before his father's death?

**14-28** *Basis of Converted Property.* K converted his 2005 sedan from personal use to business use as a delivery vehicle in his pizza business. The auto had an adjusted basis to K of $4,200 and a fair market value on the date of the conversion of $2,400. K properly deducted depreciation on the auto of $900 over two years before the auto was sold.

**a.** How much is K's gain or loss if he sells the auto for $800?

**b.** What would be your answer if the auto were sold for $3,500?

**14-29** *Part-Sale/Part-Gift.* G sold a personal computer to his son for $2,000. The computer was worth $3,000, and G had a basis in the unit of $2,200. G has made a gift of $1,000 in this part-sale/part-gift.

**a.** How much gain, if any, must G recognize on this sale?

**b.** Would your answer differ if G's basis had been $1,700?

**14-30** *Bargain Sale to Charity.* F sold a parcel of land to the city to be used as a location for a new art museum. The land had a market value of $70,000 and was sold for $40,000. F's adjusted basis in the property was $35,000. How much is F's charitable contribution deduction on this transfer? How much gain does F recognize on this sale?

**14-31** *Installment Sale.* On July 1, 2011, G sold her summer cottage (basis $70,000) for $105,000. The sale contract provided for a payment of $30,000 at the time of sale and payment of the $75,000 balance in three equal installments due in July 2012, 2013, and 2014. Assuming a reasonable interest rate is charged on this deferred payment sale, compute each of the following:

**a.** Gross profit on the sale
**b.** Total contract price
**c.** Gross profit percentage
**d.** Gain to be reported (excluding interest) in 2011
**e.** Gain to be reported (excluding interest) in 2012
**f.** Gain to be reported in 2011 if G elects not to use the installment method

**14-32** *Imputed Interest on Installment Sale.* On January 1, 2011, S sold a 100-acre tract of land for $200,000 cash and an $800,000 non-interest-bearing note due on January 1, 2014. On the date of sale, the land had a basis of $400,000. Assuming the applicable Federal rate is ten percent compounded semiannually, calculate the following:

**a.** Gain, excluding interest, to be reported in 2011
**b.** The imputed interest to be reported by S for 2011
**c.** Gain, excluding interest, to be reported in 2014

**14-33** *Wash Sale.* R purchased 500 shares of Y Corporation common stock for $12,500 on August 31, 2010. She sold 200 shares of this stock for $3,000 on December 21, 2011. On January 7, 2012, R purchased an additional 100 shares of Y Corporation common stock for $1,600.

**a.** What is R's realized loss for 2011?
**b.** How much of the loss realized can R report in 2011?
**c.** What is R's adjusted basis in the 100 shares purchased on January 7, 2012?

**14-34** *Related-Party Sale.* J sold 2,000 shares of T Corporation stock, in which he had an adjusted basis of $3,000, to his brother, F, for $1,200.

**a.** How much of the realized loss is recognized (reported) by J?
**b.** How much gain or loss to F if he subsequently sells the stock for $1,000? For $2,000?

**14-35** *Property Settlements.* H was divorced from W this year. H was required to transfer stock, which was his separate property, to W in satisfaction of his obligation for spousal support. The stock was worth $5,700 and had an adjusted basis to H of $2,900.

**a.** How much gain, if any, does H recognize on the transfer?
**b.** How much gain or loss does W recognize? What is her basis in the property received?

**14-36** *Property Tax Allocation.* J purchased a rental property during the current year for $45,000 cash. He was required to pay all of the property taxes for the year of sale, and under the law of the state $47 is allocable to the period before J purchased the property (see Chapter 11).

**a.** How much is J's property tax deduction if the total payment made during the tax year of acquisition is $700?
**b.** What is J's adjusted basis in the property?

**14-37** *Sales of Inherited Properties.* Each of the following involves property acquired from a decedent. None of the properties include income in respect of a decedent. Determine the gain or loss for each.

| Case | Decedent's Basis | Death Taxes Paid | Fair Market Value(*) | Sales Price |
|---|---|---|---|---|
| A | $3,000 | $600 | $4,000 | $6,000 |
| B | 6,000 | 600 | 4,000 | 5,000 |
| C | 6,000 | 400 | 4,000 | 3,000 |

*Date of decedent's death.

**14-38** *Nontaxable Dividends.* M owned 300 shares of X Corporation common stock, in which her basis was $6,000 on January 1, 2011. With respect to her stock, during 2011 M collected dividends of $600 and tax-free distributions of $400. What is M's basis in the stock as of December 31, 2011?

## TAX RESEARCH PROBLEMS

**14-39** *Gain Realized from Transferred Debt.* H owns a small office building and commercial complex, which he purchased for $175,000 in 2005. H invested $20,000 and signed a nonrecourse note secured by an interest in the property for the difference. The note provided for 9 percent interest, compounded annually and payable quarterly.

After six years, H decided his property was not as good an investment as he had originally thought. He found a buyer who offered him $1,000 cash for the property, subject to the existing liabilities. H eventually accepted the offer and sold the property. During the six years he owned the property, H made timely interest payments and no payments of principal. He was allowed depreciation deductions of $34,000, using the straight-line method of depreciation and a 39-year recovery period.

***Required:***

1. How much is H's gain or loss realized on this sale?
2. Would your answer differ if H's building was only worth $150,000 and instead of selling the building he had voluntarily transferred it to the obligee on the note?

***Partial list of research aids:***

Reg. § 1.1001-2.
*Crane v. Comm.*, 47-1 USTC ¶9217, 35 AFTR 776, 331 U.S. 1 (USSC, 1947).
*Tufts v. Comm.*, 83-1 USTC ¶9328, 51 AFTR2d 1983-1132, 461 U.S. 300 (USSC, 1983).
*Millar v. Comm.*, 78-2 USTC ¶9514, 42 AFTR2d 78-4276, 577 F.2d 212 (CA-3, 1978).

**14-40** *Bargain Sale to Charity.* K sold a mountain cabin for $55,000 to State University (her alma mater) for use in an annual fund-raising auction. The cabin was worth $85,000. K had purchased the cabin five years earlier as an investment for $40,000, and no depreciation has been allowed.

***Required:***

1. What is K's charitable contribution deduction and her gain or loss realized on this bargain sale?
2. Would your answers differ if the property were a painting instead of a mountain cabin?

***Research aids:***

§ 170(e)(1).
§ 1011(b).
Reg. §§ 1.170A-4(a)(2) and (c)(2).
Reg. § 1.1011-2.

# 15 Nontaxable Exchanges

## Learning Objectives

Upon completion of this chapter you will be able to:

LO.1 Understand the rationale for deferral of gains and losses on certain property transactions.

LO.2 Explain how gain or loss deferral is accomplished through basis adjustments.

LO.3 Apply the nonrecognition rules to the sale of a principal residence.

LO.4 Describe how the nonrecognition rules apply to involuntary conversions of property.

LO.5 Explain the tax consequences of a like-kind exchange of business or investment property.

LO.6 Identify other common nontaxable transactions.

LO.7 Recognize tax planning opportunities related to the more common types of gain-deferral transactions available to individual taxpayers.

## Chapter Outline


Introduction 15-2
Types of Nontaxable Exchanges 15-3
Sale of a Personal Residence 15-3
- Computation of Basis of Residence and Gain or Loss Realized 15-3
- Section 121 Exclusion of Gain 15-4
- Frequency Limitation: One Sale Every Two Years 15-7
- Exceptions to Ownership, Use, and Frequency Tests 15-7

Involuntary Conversions 15-15
- Involuntary Conversion Defined 15-16
- Replacement Property 15-18
- Replacement Period 15-19
- Election Required 15-20
- Amount of Gain Recognized 15-21

Like-Kind Exchanges 15-24
- Qualified Property 15-24
- Like-Kind Property 15-25
- Receipt of Property Not of a Like-Kind (Boot) 15-28
- Basis in Property Received 15-30
- Exchange Requirement 15-33
- Treatment Mandatory 15-35
- Holding Period 15-36

Other Nontaxable Transactions 15-38
- Changes in form of Doing Business 15-38
- Certain Exchanges of Stock in Same Corporation 15-38
- Certain Exchanges of U.S. Obligations 15-38
- Repossession of Real Property 15-38
- Certain Exchanges of Insurance Policies 15-38

Tax Planning Considerations 15-39
Current Recognition Versus Deferral 15-39
Current Gain Resulting in Future Reductions 15-39
Importance of Capital Budgeting in Decision Making 15-39
Problem Materials 15-39

# Introduction

"If I could show you a perfectly legal way to pyramid your wealth to $1 million without paying tax, would you be interested?" Although this sounds like it came straight out of the con artist's guide to tax scams, its source is far more reputable.[1] More important, the assertion is entirely true. If a taxpayer is able to make the right investments—obviously a big if—the Internal Revenue Code is willing to lend a helping hand. The key to this wonderland without taxes can be found in the provisions concerning nontaxable exchanges, the subject of this chapter.

By now, the basic recipe for determining the tax treatment of any sale or exchange is fairly familiar. Whenever a taxpayer disposes of property, three questions must be addressed: (1) what is the gain or loss *realized*, (2) how much of this realized gain or loss is *recognized*, and (3) what is its character. This chapter focuses on the second of these questions, examining a handful of property transactions—such as the sale of a residence or a like-kind exchange—where all or at least a portion of the gain or loss realized is not recognized.

**LO.1**
Understand the rationale for deferral of gains and losses on certain property transactions.

As a general rule, any gain or loss realized on a sale or other disposition of property must be recognized unless an exception is specifically provided. For the most part, this means taxpayers must include all of their realized gains and losses in determining their taxable income. However, there are a number of transactions that the Code has singled out for *nonrecognition*. In many cases, the property sold or exchanged is replaced with new property. For example, a taxpayer might trade in an old business car for a new one. When this occurs, any gain or loss realized is usually not taxed—at least immediately—on the theory that the taxpayer's economic situation has not changed sufficiently to warrant taxation. Nonrecognition is deemed appropriate since the taxpayer has not liquidated her investment to cash but has continued it, albeit in another form. In substance, the taxpayer's investment has remained intact. For these situations, Congress is willing to allow a taxpayer to postpone the tax (or perhaps defer the deduction for a loss) until such time when the taxpayer does in fact convert the asset to cash and has the wherewithal to pay the tax.

**LO.2**
Explain how gain or loss deferral is accomplished through basis adjustments.

When the recognition of a gain or loss is deferred, it is normally recognized later, when the replacement property from the deferred transaction is sold in a taxable transaction. This deferral is usually achieved by building the gain or loss not recognized into the basis of the replacement property.

### Example 1

D exchanged a vacant lot in San Jose that had been held for investment for unimproved farmland near Fresno. The city lot had cost $35,000 fifteen years earlier and had not been improved. Both the city lot and the rural property were worth $120,000. D recognizes no gain on the exchange and his basis in the farmland is $35,000.[2] Of course, if D later sells the farm for $130,000, his recognizable gain will be $95,000, the gain on the farm of $10,000 plus the gain deferred from the city lot of $85,000.

It is important to observe that nonrecognition can take one of two forms: permanent exclusion or temporary deferral. The world of permanent exclusions, first introduced in Chapter 6, is relatively small. It includes such items as interest paid on state and local

[1] Robert J. Bruss, "Real Estate Exchange Provides a Way to Build Net Worth," *The Palm Beach Post*, February 19, 1989, p 57H.

[2] See discussion of § 1031 following.

government bonds, insurance proceeds paid on account of death, gifts, inheritances, scholarships, child support, and a number of fringe benefits. On the other side of the ledger, losses and expenses that are personal in nature (other than casualty losses) are generally disallowed. Note that if nonrecognition is permanent, the gain or loss never affects taxable income.

One instance in which the permanent exclusion of gain is allowed in property transactions is upon the sale of one's principal residence. This benefit, which was widely expanded by the *Taxpayer Relief Act of 1997*, allows a taxpayer who has owned and used his or her residence for two years to simply avoid tax on part or all of any gain.

**Example 2**

F, an elderly widow, sold her personal residence of 30 years for $292,000 (basis $121,000) and moved into a rented unit in a retirement community. Under Code § 121, F is allowed to exclude her gain of $171,000 from gross income. Since the gain is excluded, F will never be required to pay tax on the gain from that residence.[3]

## Types of Nontaxable Exchanges

There are several types of nontaxable exchanges allowed under the Internal Revenue Code. Three are discussed in detail in this chapter. The sale of a personal residence is covered initially. Separate discussions of the deferral of gain on involuntary conversions and the deferral of gain or loss on like-kind exchanges follow. Then several other types of nontaxable transactions are discussed briefly.

## Sale of a Personal Residence

**LO.3**
Apply the nonrecognition rules to the sale of a principal residence.

While one's home may be one's castle, in the United States it is also a tax shelter. The tax law contains several provisions that encourage home ownership. Two of these, the deductions for interest and property taxes, were discussed in Chapter 11. A third, considered in detail below, concerns the sale of a residence. The effect of these provisions, whether intended or not, is to provide what is clearly a tax bonanza. If an individual sells a residence, any gain may be totally excluded from income up to $250,000 ($500,000 for certain married persons filing jointly) if the taxpayer qualifies under § 121. Gain in excess of the limit will generally be recognized.

**Example 3**

T sold his principal residence for $400,000 on July 22, 2011. He has lived in the home since 2000. His basis in the property was $225,000 and his realized gain on the sale is $175,000 ($400,000 – $225,000). T may exclude all of the $175,000 in gain from his taxable income.

### Computation of Basis of Residence and Gain or Loss Realized

The calculation of the gain recognized on the sale of the house begins in the normal fashion. It starts with the sales price, which is then reduced by selling expenses to determine the amount realized. The sales price is usually easy to determine. Selling expenses are generally those costs paid to bring about the sale of the property. Although they are not directly

[3] See discussion of § 121 following.

deductible, they do reduce the potential gain. A few of the more common selling expenses incurred when selling a home are:

- Realtor's commission
- Advertising
- Surveys
- Buyer's points paid by the seller
- Inspection fees (termites, radon, etc.)
- Legal fees
- Title fees (abstracts, certificate, opinion)
- Transfer taxes
- Mortgage title insurance
- Escrow fees

## Gain or Loss Realized

The amount of the gain or loss realized is merely the difference between the amount realized and the adjusted basis. In computing the basis of the home, improvements the owner has made should be included. These include anything that adds value to the house and prolongs its useful life. Some of these are:

- Additions (rooms, porch, deck)
- Roof, siding, insulation
- Appliances, attic fan, grill
- Landscaping, sprinkling system
- Garage
- Basement improvement
- Shed
- Flooring (carpeting, tile, vinyl)
- Fences
- Air conditioning, furnaces, water heaters
- Alarm system
- Basketball goal post
- Solar or geothermal heating
- Driveway, walks
- Curtains
- Well
- Mailbox, house numbers
- Septic system
- Sewer assessment
- Smoke detector

## Gain or Loss Recognized

The next concern, and no doubt the most important, is the determination of the amount of the gain or loss to be recognized. Losses are not subject to any special provision. Accordingly, since a personal residence is not held for either trade or business or investment purposes, any recognized loss is not deductible.[4] While losses are not deductible, gains receive far more favorable treatment. As explained below, if certain requirements are met, most homeowners will be able to exclude all or at least part of their gain.

# SECTION 121 EXCLUSION OF GAIN

On the sale of a principal residence, § 121 generally allows a taxpayer to exclude any gain realized up to a maximum of $250,000 ($500,000 for married taxpayers). Any realized gain in excess of this threshold is taxable as capital gain. This relief provision applies to taxpayers of all ages and as frequently as every two years. To obtain this special treatment, taxpayers must meet several requirements as discussed below.

## Principal Residence

The exclusion applies only to the sale of the taxpayer's *principal* residence. Most taxpayers have one residence, and if they move, they simply change their principal residence. However, it is sometimes difficult to determine which residence is the *principal residence* for taxpayers with multiple residences. This is a facts and circumstances determination. Some of the factors to be considered are the amount of time each residence is used, the taxpayer's place of employment, where other family members live, the addresses used (for things like tax returns, driver's licenses, car and voter registration, bills and correspondence), and the location of banks, religious organizations and recreational clubs.[5]

The exclusion only applies if the property is a *residence*. A residence not only includes a conventional home but also a condominium, a cooperative apartment, a mobile home, and a fully equipped recreational vehicle (e.g., plumbing, kitchen, sleeping facilities) notwithstanding that it is a means of transportation.[6] The residence also includes the land on which

---

[4] § 165(c).

[5] Reg. § 1.121-1.

[6] See Reg. § 1.121-1(b)(1) and (e)(2), § 280A(f)(1)(A); Prop Reg § 1.280A-1(e)(7), Ex (2) and *Ronald Haberkorn* 75 T.C. 259 (1980). See also *Richard Dougherty*, T.C. Memo 1994-597, T.C. Memo ¶94597 where a 32-foot charter cruiser that berthed six was considered a home.

the residence sits and any gain attributable to the land is eligible for exclusion.[7] Land adjacent to the home qualifies if it is regularly used by the owner as part of the residential property, and it is sold along with the home or within two years before or after the sale of the home.[8]

It is not that uncommon for the seller of a home to also sell property that is technically not part of the residence such as furniture, lawn equipment, pool table, hot tub, or similar property. Unless such personalty is treated as a fixture under local law it is not considered part of the residence and, therefore, is not eligible for the exclusion. In most cases, however, sales of such items would result in nondeductible losses.

## Ownership and Use Tests

The § 121 exclusion is applicable to the sale of a residence only if the residence was *owned* by the taxpayer and *used* as his or her principal residence for at least two of the five years preceding its sale.[9] Observe that the five year window permits taxpayers to use the exclusion even though the property is not owned or used by the taxpayer at the time of the sale. The taxpayer merely needs to meet both tests at some time during the five year period.

The ownership and use requirements are two separate tests. Normally, the period of ownership is not an issue.[10] However, whether the taxpayer *uses* the property as a *principal residence* for the requisite two years during the five-year window can be a bit more troubling. Whether this test is met depends on the fact and circumstances. In this regard, recall that an individual can only have one principal residence at any given time.

### Example 4

Y purchased a home in Miami 1988 and lived in it until she took a new job in Orlando on April 30, 2007. From May 1, 2007 until the Miami house was sold on May 1, 2011, it was used by Y only on occasional days off since she lived in a rented apartment in Orlando. In determining whether the exclusion is available, Y has met the ownership test because she owned it for two of the five years prior to its sale. However, she fails the use test because she did not use the house as her principal residence for two of the five years before its sale. Since she did not meet both tests, she does not qualify for the § 121 exclusion.

If, taking into account all facts and circumstances, the house, and not the apartment, had been Y's principal residence, she would have qualified. She would have to be able to demonstrate that she lived in the house, with only temporary visits to the apartment.

In applying the use test, short temporary absences, such as for vacation or other seasonal absence are counted as periods of use. For this purpose, temporary rental of the property is ignored.

### Example 5

T purchased his home in South Bend in 1999. He used the house as his principal residence until January 31, 2009, when he moved to Chicago. Upon moving, T rented his house to tenants until April 18, 2011, when he sold it. T is eligible for the exclusion because he has owned and used the house as his principal residence for at least two of the five years preceding the sale.

---

[7] But see where a taxpayer who moved his house and sold the land was not entitled to the exclusion for the land. See also IRS Publication 523 (2008) p. 3.

[8] Reg. § 1.121-1(b)(3).

[9] § 121(a).

[10] See Reg. § 1.121-1(c)(3) allowing the exclusion where the residence is owned by grantor trusts and disregarded entities such as a single member LLC.

**Example 6**

B owned and used her house in Houston as her principal residence from 1989 to the end of 2005. On January 4, 2006, she moved to Denver. Shortly thereafter, B's son moved into the house in March 2006 and used the residence until it sold on July 1, 2011. B may not exclude gain from the sale because she did not use the property as her principal residence for at least two years out of the five years preceding the sale. Use by the son is not counted as the mother's use.

### Maximum Exclusion

The maximum amount excludable with respect to any sale or exchange is $250,000. This amount is doubled to $500,000 for most married taxpayers filing joint returns. In such cases, the ownership requirement only needs to be met by one spouse. So if either spouse meets the ownership test and both spouses meet the use test, the $500,000 exclusion applies.[11] However, if only one spouse satisfies the use test, the exclusion is allowable but limited to $250,000 (or the sum of the amount excludable by each spouse individually).

**Example 7**

H and W sold their jointly owned and occupied family residence on June 3, 2011, for $650,000. Their basis in the property, that they had owned for thirty years, was $125,000, so their gain was $525,000. If H and W file a joint return for their calendar year 2011, they may exclude $500,000 of the gain and must recognize a long-term capital gain of $25,000.

**Example 8**

Q purchased a home for use as her principal residence in 1993. On March 31, 2008, Q was transferred by her employer, so she moved away, rented an apartment and left her residence unused. When Q sells the residence at a gain of $200,000 on March 1, 2011, she may exclude the entire gain. During the five years preceding the sale—March 1, 2006 to February 28, 2011—Q *owned* the property for all five years and *used* it as her principal residence for 25 months (i.e., more than the requisite two years).

**Example 9**

L purchased a residence for use as his principal residence for $123,000 on July 12, 2009. Presented with an attractive offer on the property, L sold the residence on February 2, 2011 for $198,000 (net of selling costs). L must report a long-term capital gain of $75,000 since L does not meet the two of five year tests.

[11] § 121(b)(1) and (2).

### Example 10

F purchased a new personal residence in 1990 for $40,000 and lived in it until June 30, 2000. The house was rented out until January 1, 2008, with depreciation of $8,500 being claimed. On January 2, 2008, F moved back into the house and occupied it as her principal residence until February 5, 2011, when it was sold for $280,000. Since F owned and lived in the home for at least two of the five years preceding the sale, she may exclude up to $250,000 of gain (see subsequent discussions of "depreciation recapture" and "rental and other nonqualified use").

## Frequency Limitation: One Sale Every Two Years

The benefits of the § 121 exclusion are so great that without some prohibition taxpayers might utilize the provision in unintended ways. One could easily envision a taxpayer selling one principal residence and excluding the gain, buying and selling another residence and excluding the gain, and continuing this pattern, using the exclusion as a tax shelter. To restrict this possibility, the Code imposes a limitation on the frequency with which the exclusion may be used. The exclusion cannot be used for sales occurring within two years of its last use. In other words, the law allows the exclusion for one sale every two years. To ensure that this rule does not unfairly penalize taxpayers who may be forced to sell their homes before the two-year period has elapsed, special rules concerning sales for unforeseen circumstances exist and are discussed below.[12]

### Example 11

M purchased a residence for use as her principal residence for $70,000 on January 2, 2006, and lived in it until March 15, 2008. On March 16, 2008, M rented the original residence and purchased and moved into another residence costing $85,000. Upon retiring, M sold the original residence for $90,000 on December 31, 2009, and excluded most of her gain on the sale (see subsequent discussion of depreciation recapture). Even though M would otherwise be eligible to exclude any gain on the sale of the other residence on March 16, 2010, due to this one sale every two years rule, M will not be eligible until January 1, 2012 (see subsequent discussion related to electing out of § 121).

## Exceptions to Ownership, Use, and Frequency Tests

At times, taxpayers may be forced to sell their homes due to events beyond their control. For example, an individual may be forced to take a job in another location or move because of health reasons. In these and similar situations, taxpayers may run afoul of the ownership and use requirement or the frequency limitation. Without relief, any realized gain on the sale of the house would be *fully* taxable notwithstanding the fact that there was nothing the taxpayer could do to avoid the sale. Recognizing this problem, § 121 provides some relief.[13] Taxpayers who fail the two-year ownership and use requirement or the one-sale-every-two-year rules may qualify for a *portion* of the exclusion if the sale were due to unforeseen circumstances. In many cases the reduced exclusion would be more than sufficient to offset any appreciation that occurred.

[12] § 121(b)(3).

[13] § 121(c).

## Computation of the Reduced Exclusion

The portion of the exclusion allowed is the percentage of the required 24 months for which the taxpayer satisfies the ownership and use test or if lower the number of months used since the last sale.[14]

$$\underset{(\$250,000 \text{ or } \$500,000)}{\text{Exclusion}} \times \frac{\text{Lesser of time owned and used or time since last sale}}{\text{24 months}} = \begin{matrix}\text{Reduced}\\ \text{Exclusion}\end{matrix}$$

### Example 12

H and W have one son, S, who was recently diagnosed to have a rare disease. After living in their home only six months, the couple sold their home in Kansas City and moved to Memphis to obtain special treatment only available at St. Jude's Children's Research Hospital. H and W do not meet the ownership and use test since they did not own and use the home as their principal residence for two of the five years prior to the sale. However, because the sale is due to unforeseen circumstances, they qualify for a reduced exclusion of $125,000 [(6/24 = 25%) × $500,000].

This rule is often misconstrued. Taxpayers are *not* entitled to a portion of the exclusion just because they meet the ownership and use test for a few months. For example, if a taxpayer owns and uses the home for only 8 of the 24 months required, he or she is *not* automatically entitled to one-third of the exclusion. The reduced exclusion is granted only if the sale is due to unforeseen circumstances. If a taxpayer simply decides to sell before meeting the tests (e.g., because of market conditions) and without cause, the entire gain is taxable.

### Unforeseen Circumstances

The Code provides that the reduced exclusion is available only if due to:[15]

- Change in place of employment
- Health concerns
- Unforeseen circumstances

**Change in Place of Employment** Under a safe harbor provided by the Regulations, the reduced exclusion is available due to a change in employment if the new place of business is at least 50 miles farther from the old residence than was the old job.[16] This is the same test that must be met to deduct moving expenses (the taxpayer's new commute without the move would exceed the old commute by more than 50 miles). If the taxpayer was not employed and moves to obtain employment, the distance between the new job and the residence sold must be at least 50 miles.

The tests regarding employment can be met by the:

- Taxpayer
- Taxpayer's spouse
- Member of the taxpayer's household
- Co-owner of the residence

**Health Reasons** A reduced exclusion is also allowed for sales due to health reasons (i.e., the sale enables the taxpayer "to obtain, provide, or facilitate the diagnosis, cure mitigation, or treatment of diseases, illness or injury").[17] If a physician recommends a change of location for health reasons, the test should be met. In contrast, sales that are merely beneficial to the general health or well-being of an individual do not qualify.

---

[14] § 121(c)(1).

[15] § 121(c)(2).

[16] Reg. § 1.121-3(c)(2).

[17] Reg. § 1.121-3(d).

**Unforeseen Circumstances** If an event occurs that could not reasonably have been anticipated *before* purchasing the residence, the reduced exclusion can be used. According to the Regulations, unforeseen circumstances include:[18]

- Involuntary conversion of the residence
- Natural or man-made disasters
- Acts of war or terrorism resulting in a casualty to the residence
- Death
- Unemployment so as to qualify for unemployment compensation
- Change in employment or self-employment status that results in the taxpayer's inability to pay housing costs and reasonable basic living expenses for the taxpayer's household
- Divorce
- Multiple births resulting from the same pregnancy

If a safe harbor is not met, the reduced exclusion may still be available.[19] The Regulations identify a number of other factors to be considered.

### Example 13

F purchased a personal residence on March 15, 2010 for $125,000. F must have been living right—he was transferred by his employer to his favorite city, received a big raise, and sold his house in two weeks time for $200,000 (on September 15, 2011). Even though F did not meet the two of five years test, he may exclude his entire $75,000 gain. Because the sale was related to a change of place of employment, F can exclude up to $187,500 [$250,000 × (18 months/24 months)].

### Effects of Marriage

In applying the two of five year test, a widow or widower (who has not remarried) selling a residence is treated as having owned and occupied a residence for the period of time it was owned and occupied by his or her deceased spouse.[20]

**EXHIBIT 15.1** **Section 121 Exclusion Basics**

**Taxpayer Qualifies If**

- The residence was *owned* and *used as a principal residence* for two of the five years preceding the sale

  *and*

- No gain was excluded under § 121 in a qualifying sale made within the two years preceding the sale

**Maximum Amount Excluded**

- Generally $250,000
- $500,000 for married taxpayers filing jointly if either spouse meets the ownership test and both spouses meet the use test
- A fraction of these amounts is allowed if the sale is related to a change in the taxpayer's work location, health, or other qualifying unforeseen circumstances

---

[18] Reg. § 1.121-3(e).

[19] In PLR 200403049, the IRS found that hostilities between the taxpayers and their neighbors concerning a household member released from rehabilitation qualified as unforeseen circumstances for purposes of § 121.

[20] § 121(e)(1) and (2).

### Example 14

R married S on November 27, 2009, and moved into a home that had been owned and occupied by S since 1998. S died on March 15, 2010, leaving the residence to R. Since R is deemed to have owned and lived in the residence since 1998, she qualifies for the $250,000 exclusion when the residence is sold on February 12, 2011.

Homes owned by one spouse before marriage or held as separate property during a marriage could also present problems in applying the two of five year rule. To prevent inequities, if a property is transferred to a spouse or former spouse in a transaction that is tax-free under § 1041 (e.g., in a divorce), the transferee is deemed to have owned the residence for the period of time it was owned by the transferor.

### Example 15

D lived in a residence owned as separate property by his spouse, E, for the duration of their four-year marriage. Upon their divorce, D received the residence. Fifteen months after the divorce, D married G and sold the residence (on December 24, 2011), realizing a gain of $280,000. D lived in the residence four years and is deemed to have owned the residence all of the five years preceding the sale. He may, therefore, exclude gain of $250,000 and recognize long-term capital gain of $30,000. D and G cannot exclude $500,000 since G does not meet the residential use test with respect to the residence.

When a spouse dies, the exclusion normally would be limited to that for single taxpayers, $250,000. However, the law provides relief in these situations. A surviving spouse (who has not remarried) qualifies for the $500,000 exclusion if the following conditions are satisfied:

1. All the requirements for the larger exclusion were met at the time of death (i.e., at least one spouse meets the two year ownership test and both spouses meet the two year use test) and
2. The sale occurs within two years of the date of death.

## Incapacitated Taxpayers

A taxpayer who purchases a residence and is soon forced to move to a rest home or similar facility may never be able to meet the time requirement for the § 121 exclusion. Fortunately, if a person in this situation lives in the residence for at least one year, he or she will be treated as having lived in that residence during any period of time that he or she has lived in a licensed facility for incapacitated individuals.[21] Thus, anyone who purchases a home, lives in it one year, and spends at least a year in a rest home while still owning the home will meet all the tests for § 121.

## Involuntary Conversions

For purposes of § 121, an involuntary conversion of a qualifying residence is treated as the sale of that residence.[22] Thus, a person who meets the ownership and use tests can exclude at least a portion of any gain from the destruction, theft, or condemnation of his or her residence. Involuntary conversions are discussed in detail later in this chapter.

## Depreciation Recapture

In some situations, a residence qualifying for the Section 121 exclusion may have been used as a rental property or business property (e.g., the taxpayer had a home office). In such case, the taxpayer may have depreciated the property. To be able to depreciate a property, resulting in

[21] § 121(d)(9).

[22] § 121(d)(5)(A).

a basis reduction, and subsequently exclude any gain is too good to be true. Realizing this, Congress requires that the gain be recognized to the extent of any depreciation allowed after May 6, 1997.[23]

### Example 16

P purchased a home for use as a residence in 2001 for $60,000 and made improvements costing $18,000 in 2007. On June 30, 2010, P retired, moved out and converted the house to rental property. Between that date and the day the property was sold for $200,000, September 30, 2011, P claimed depreciation of $3,600, making the basis in the property $74,400 [$60,000 + $18,000 – $3,600]. P's realized gain is $125,600 ($200,000 – $74,400). P must recognize $3,600 of the gain and may exclude the remaining $122,000 under § 121.

### Example 17

Assume the same facts as in the prior example, except the sales price is $77,000. P's gain is $2,600 ($77,000 – $74,400). Since the gain realized is less than the depreciation claimed after May 6, 1997, none of the gain may be excluded under § 121. P must, therefore, recognize a $2,600 gain (i.e., the lesser of the gain realized or the depreciation claimed).

When only a portion of a dwelling was used for business purposes, including use as an office in the home, gain is recognized only to the extent of the depreciation recapture that is required.[24] Any additional gain qualifies for the exclusion, subject to the dollar limitation.

### Example 18

B purchased a residence for use as his principal residence for $125,000 in 1991. After the children moved out, he converted a bedroom (ten percent of the residence) to a business office. Depreciation of $1,350 was claimed over three years before the residence was sold during the current year for $375,000. The total gain realized is $251,350 [$375,000 – ($125,000 – $1,350)]. One way to look at the sale would be to treat the sale as that of two separate properties.

| | *Business* 10% | *Personal* 90% |
|---|---|---|
| Sales price | $ 37,500 | $ 337,500 |
| Adjusted basis | (11,150)* | (112,500) |
| Gain | $ 26,350 | $ 225,000 |

*$125,000 × 10% – $1,350

Fortunately, the IRS chose not to require this two separate sales approach, and B is required to recognize gain of only $1,350. The remaining gain of $250,000 ($251,350 – $1,350) qualifies for exclusion since B owned and occupied the residence for the required period.

[23] § 121(e)(6).

[24] Temp. Reg. § 1.121-2.

### Rental and Other Nonqualified Use

Before 2009, individuals who owned rental property could convert it to a personal residence in order to exclude all or a portion of their gain on a subsequent sale.

#### Example 19

J, a resident of Illinois, purchased a vacation home in Florida in 1998 for $120,000. After many years of renting it out, he moved into the home on December 19, 2007 and made it his personal residence. At the time of conversion, he had deducted depreciation of $20,000 on the property. After living in the home for the required two years, he sold the residence on December 29, 2009 for $210,000. J realized a gain of $110,000 [$210,000 – (120,000 – $20,000 = $100,000)]. He recognized gain of $20,000 due to the depreciation recapture rule. However, prior to 2009, the remaining $90,000 was excluded under § 121.

To eliminate the possibility described above, § 121 was amended in 2008. Currently, any gain allocable to periods of nonqualified use after 2008 is not eligible for exclusion. The portion of the gain attributable to nonqualified use is computed as follows:

$$\begin{matrix}\text{Gain realized} \\ (\text{net of depreciation})^{25}\end{matrix} \times \frac{\text{Aggregate periods of nonqualified use}}{\text{Total time owned}} = \text{Taxable Gain}$$

The key factor in determining the amount of gain that could be taxed is the taxpayer's nonqualified use. Nonqualified use is generally any period during which the property is not used as the principal residence of the taxpayer or spouse (or former spouse). For this purpose, the numerator does not include nonqualified use prior to 2009. On the other hand, the denominator is the total time owned, including that before 2009. Periods during which the property is vacant or used by relatives are considered periods of nonqualified use. Note also that if the property appreciates in value after a taxpayer makes the property his or her principal residence, the gain is still potentially taxable even though the appreciation occurred while the taxpayer used the property as a personal residence.

#### Example 20

B, single, was a long-time resident of Cincinnati. On January 1, 2009, he purchased a condominium in South Carolina for $400,000. He used the condo as rental property for two years. He claimed $20,000 of depreciation deductions, reducing his basis in the home to $380,000. On January 1, 2011, B moved to Florida and moved into the condo converting it to his principal residence. After living there for three years, on January 1, 2014 B sold the condo for $700,000 and moved out. His gain realized would be $320,000 [($700,000 – ($400,000 – $20,000 = $380,000)]. The $20,000 of gain attributable to the depreciation is included in income.[26] Of the remaining $300,000 gain (the amount remaining after depreciation recapture), 40 percent of the gain (2 years / 5 years), or $120,000 is allocated to nonqualified use and is taxable as long-term capital gain. The remaining 60 percent of the gain, $180,000, is attributable to qualified use and can be excluded.

---

[25] § 121(b)(4)(D) provides that the gain potentially ineligible for the exclusion is the gain remaining after applying depreciation recapture rule.

[26] Gain attributable to the depreciation would be taxed at a maximum rate of 25 percent (unrecaptured straight-line depreciation on § 1250 property). See Chapter 17.

> **Example 21**
>
> R bought an investment property on January 1, 2007 and rented it until January 1, 2010 when he began occupying it as his principal residence for the next three years. He sold the property on January 1, 2013, realizing a gain. The two years prior to January 1, 2010 are disregarded for determining nonqualified use (but included for purposes of the ownership test). Thus he has one year of nonqualified use (disregard 2007 and 2008) and six years of total ownership. Thus, 16.67 percent (1/6) of the gain (after accounting for depreciation) is taxable.

Although the above examples measure use in terms of years, presumably the regulations will require taxpayers to keep track of their use and its type in terms of months or perhaps days.

The nonqualified use rule was aimed at taxpayers who purchase rental property, rent the property out and then convert it to a personal residence. That is, the rule is designed for taxpayers who formerly used their residence as rental property. For this reason, nonqualified use that occurs after the taxpayer's last use of the property as a principal residence and is within five years prior to the sale is disregarded. This rule allows homeowners to move out of their principal residence and convert it to nonqualified use property (e.g., rental) and still be eligible for the full exclusion assuming the other requirements of § 121 are met.

> **Example 22**
>
> T purchased a home in Nantucket on June 1, 2009. She used it as her personal residence for two years until June 1, 2011 and then converted it to rental property. On June 1, 2014, she sold the home. The nonqualified rental use is disregarded since it occurred after T had used it as her residence and within five years prior to the sale. While she would be required to recognize income to the extent of any depreciation deducted, the remaining gain would be eligible for the exclusion. Note that the special rule gives taxpayers up to three years to sell the home after moving out without having the exclusion reduced. Had T sold her home on June 1, 2015, she would not have qualified for the exclusion because she did not use it as her personal residence for 2 of the last 5 years.

In identifying nonqualified use, certain periods when the homeowner did not live in the residence are ignored. These include absences due to government service (e.g., service in the military, intelligence community or U.S. Foreign Service), change of employment, health conditions and other unforeseen circumstances.

> **Example 23**
>
> Before shipping off to military duty in Europe, H purchased a home in Maryland. He rented the property for the five years that he was stationed overseas. The rental use is not considered nonqualified use since it was attributable to military service.

### Sale After a Like-Kind Exchange

The $250,000 or $500,000 exclusion is so attractive that without certain restrictions, it could be easily abused. For example, owners of rental property might be interested in exchanging a rental property for another rental property in a tax-deferred exchange (see subsequent coverage in this chapter), later converting the replacement property to a principal residence, and then (after at least two years) selling the replacement property and taking advantage of the exclusion. This possibility remains, but the § 121 exclusion will not apply to a property unless five years have passed since the like-exchange occured.

### Example 24

B owned a duplex that he rented to college students. He purchased it for $240,000 in 1991. Depreciation of $98,000 was claimed, reducing B's basis to $142,000. On November 16, 2007, B exchanged the duplex for a residential property worth $450,000 that was used as rental property. In October 2008, the tenant moved out and B moved into the residence. Under the general rule, B would qualify for the § 121 exclusion in October 2010. However, the special rule for like-kind exchange property applies. As a result, B will not qualify until November 16, 2012 (five years after the exchange).

If B sells the property, after November 15, 2012, for $490,000, the gain realized is $348,000 [$490,000 – ($240,000 – $98,000)]. B can exclude $250,000. However, if the sale had occurred earlier, none of the gain is excludable.

## Interaction of Sections 121 and 1031

Occasionally, a like-kind exchange may involve property that not only qualifies for tax-deferral under the like-kind exchange provisions of Section 1031 but also qualifies for the residence exclusion of Section 121. For example, a taxpayer may have used a house as a principal residence from 2004 through 2008, rented out the house from 2009 through 2010 and then exchanged the house for cash and new property that will be rented. The IRS has provided guidance for the tax consequences of such exchanges, allowing taxpayers to exclude any otherwise excludable gain and to generally defer any other excess gain.[27]

## Electing Out

Taxpayers may find themselves in a position where they may have two or more residence sales within a two year period. However, as noted above, the exclusion cannot be used within two years of its last use. In such case, a taxpayer normally wants to apply the exclusion to the sale producing the most gain. Section 121 provides such flexibility by allowing a taxpayer to elect not to have § 121 apply to an otherwise qualifying sale. The election is made by reporting the gain on the tax return for the year of the sale.[28] Presumably (unless future guidance provides otherwise) the election can be made on an amended return.

### Example 25

S purchased her first residence in Chicago on May 1, 2004. She lived there until she was transferred by her employer to Phoenix on August 1, 2008. She did not immediately sell her Chicago residence but decided to rent it to an old friend. In Phoenix, she purchased a second residence which she occupied beginning on September 1, 2008. On December 15, 2010, S sold the second residence in Phoenix, realizing a gain of $5,000. Then on January 31, 2011, she sold her original Chicago residence at a gain of $177,000 ($2,000 of which is attributable to depreciation allowed). Only $175,000 can qualify for exclusion due to the depreciation claimed.

Both residences meet the two of five years ownerships and use tests. If S excludes the $5,000 gain from the second residence in 2010, she cannot exclude the $175,000 gain from the original residence in 2011 because of the one sale every two years rule. It would, therefore, be in her best interest to elect out of the benefits of § 121 exclusion with respect to the $5,000 gain, in order to take advantage of the § 121 exclusion with respect to the $175,000 gain. This would be done by including the $5,000 gain in her 2010 income.

---

27 Rev. Proc. 2005-14 IRB No. 2005-7.

28 See § 121(f) and I.R.S. Publication 523, p.2.

## ✓ Check Your Knowledge

### Review Question 1

True-False. Helen excluded $250,000 of gain from the sale of her primary residence which was sold on August 4, 2009. Helen cannot exclude her $23,000 gain from the sale of another primary residence on November 1, 2011, even though she has owned and used this home for more than two years.

*False.* Since more than two years transpired from the first sale to the second sale, Helen qualifies to exclude gain on both sales. The fact that the sale was in the second tax year after the original sale is not determinative.

### Review Question 2

True-False. Mick purchased a residence on March 1, 2007 and lived in it until July 31, 2008. He rented it from August 1, 2008 until June 30, 2010 (claiming depreciation of $7,000), and then lived in it again from July 1, 2010 until it was sold on June 1, 2011. Mick cannot exclude any of his gain of $40,000 under § 121.

*False.* Mick qualifies for the § 121 exclusion because he lived in the residence more than two years during the five years preceding the sale (i.e., June 1, 2006 to May 31, 2011). Specifically, he lived there 28 (17 + 11) months. However, Mick can only exclude $33,000, since the first $7,000 of the $40,000 gain must be recognized due to the depreciation claimed.

### Review Question 3

Lin purchased a residence on June 1, 2010, for $235,000. On December 1, 2011, she sold the residence for $295,000, so she could move to a nearby city where she was transferred by her employer. How much gain, if any, may Lin exclude under § 121?

*All $60,000.* Even though Lin did not meet the two of five years ownership and use requirements, she qualifies for a reduced exclusion limit since the sale is related to a change in the place of employment. The reduced limit if $187,500 [$250,000 × (18 months/24 months)].

### Review Question 4

J and K were married on June 1, 2010, and K moved into the home that J had owned and occupied for ten years. On September 1, 2011, J and K sold the residence, recognizing a gain of $295,000. How much of the gain may J and K exclude on their joint return for 2011?

*Only $250,000.* In order to qualify for the increased $500,000 exclusion, both husband and wife must have used the residence for two of the five years preceding the sale. K only lived there for 15 months.

### Review Question 5

After living together for ten years, L and M finally married on June 1, 2010. After their marriage, the couple continued to live in L's home. L never retitled the property and held it separately primarily for estate planning purposes. On September 1, 2011, L sold the residence, recognizing a gain of $360,000. How much of the gain may L and M exclude on their joint return for 2011?

*All $360,000.* In order to qualify for the increased $500,000 exclusion, only one spouse must have owned the residence for two of the preceding five years, but both husband and wife must have used the residence for two of the five years. They must file a joint return, but there is no requirement that the property be jointly owned or that they be married during the two years that they lived there.

## Involuntary Conversions

Taxpayers occasionally lose their property from casualty or theft or are forced to sell their property because of some type of condemnation proceeding. When an *involuntary conversion* like this occurs, the taxpayer usually receives some form of compensation such as insurance proceeds or a condemnation award. In some cases, the compensation may actually cause the

**LO.4**
Describe how the nonrecognition rules apply to involuntary conversions of property.

taxpayer to realize a gain from the "loss." Without any special rule, the tax resulting from this gain could produce a real hardship since the taxpayer typically uses the compensation received to acquire a replacement property. Recognizing that taxpayers may not have the wherewithal to pay the tax in this situation—which was totally beyond their control—Congress provided some relief. Special rules allow taxpayers to defer any gain realized from an involuntary conversion if they acquire qualified replacement property within a specified period of time.

> **Example 26**
>
> J operates a fishing boat in Miami. Unfortunately, the boat was totally destroyed when Hurricane Charley hit the Florida coast. J's basis in the boat was $40,000 (cost of $60,000 less depreciation of $20,000). Luckily, J was insured. He filed an insurance claim and received $75,000 based on the fair market value of the boat. As a result, he realized a gain of $35,000 ($75,000 – $40,000). J may defer the entire gain if he reinvests at least $75,000 in similar-use property within the allowable period.

## Involuntary Conversion Defined

An involuntary conversion is defined in the Code as the compulsory or involuntary conversion of property "as a result of its destruction in whole or in part, theft, seizure, or requisition or condemnation or threat or imminence thereof."[29] The terms *destruction* and *theft* have the same basic meaning as when they are used for casualty and theft losses. The IRS has ruled, however, that the destruction of property for purposes of § 1033 need not meet the *suddenness* test, which has been applied to casualty loss deductions.[30]

Typical involuntary conversions involve accidents, natural disasters, and other events beyond the control of the taxpayer. This has been found to include damages caused by other parties such as poisoning of cattle by contaminated feed and destruction of crops and soil by chemicals.[31] In each case, the taxpayer was allowed to defer recognition of gain upon the receipt of damages by reinvesting in qualified property.

### Seizure, Requisition, or Condemnation

It is not as simple to determine what qualifies as a "seizure, or requisition or condemnation" as it is to identify theft or destruction. The property must be taken without the taxpayer's consent and the taxpayer must be compensated.[32]

Not all types of forced dispositions will qualify. For example, the courts have found that a foreclosure sale[33] and a sale after continued insistence by a Chamber of Commerce[34] did not constitute involuntary conversions. Similarly, the IRS has ruled that the condemnation of rental properties due to structural defects or sanitary conditions does not constitute an involuntary conversion since the sale was made to avoid making property improvements necessary to meet a housing ordinance.[35] Generally, a transfer must be made to an authority that has the power to actually condemn the property, and the property must be taken for a public use.

In the case of the conversion of part of a single economic unit, § 1033 applies not only to the condemned portion, but also to the part not condemned if it is *voluntarily sold.* When a truck freight terminal was rendered virtually useless because the adjoining parking lot for the trucks was condemned, a single economic unit was found to exist and § 1033 applied to the sale of the terminal as well as the condemnation of the parking area.[36] In a similar situation when a shopping center was partially destroyed by fire and the owner chose to sell the entire

---

[29] § 1033(a).

[30] Rev. Rul. 59-102, 1959-1 C.B. 200.

[31] Rev. Rul. 54-395, 1954-2 C.B. 143 and Ltr. Rul. 9615041.

[32] See, for example, *Hitke v. Comm.*, 62-1 USTC ¶9114, 8 AFTR2d 5886, 296 F.2d 639 (CA-7, 1961).

[33] See *Cooperative Publishing Co. v. U.S.*, 40-2 USTC ¶9823, 25 AFTR 1123, 115 F.2d 1017 (CA-9, 1940), and *Robert Recio*, 61 TCM 2626, T.C. Memo. 1991-215.

[34] *Davis Co.*, 6 B.T.A. 281 (1927), acq. VI-2 C.B. 2.

[35] Rev. Rul. 57-314, 1957-2 C.B. 523.

[36] *Harry Masser*, 30 T.C. 741 (1958), acq. 1959-2 C. B. 5; Rev. Rul. 59-361, 1959-2 C.B. 183.

shopping center rather than reconstruct the destroyed portion, the IRS ruled that no conversion existed with respect to the remaining portion since the undamaged portion could still be used and the damaged portion repaired. The fire insurance proceeds, but not the sale proceeds, qualified for deferral under § 1033.[37]

### Threat or Imminence of Condemnation

The possibility of a condemnation may very well cause a taxpayer to sell property before the actual condemnation occurs. For example, a farming corporation may discover that its property is being considered as the site for a new airport and sell the property. Section 1033 extends deferral to these *voluntary* sales to someone other than the condemning authority if they are due to the *threat or imminence* of condemnation. It should be emphasized that newspaper reports, magazine articles, or rumors that property is being considered for condemnation are not sufficient.[38] Threat or imminence exists only after officials have communicated that they intend to condemn the property and the owner has good reason to believe they would.

#### Example 27

LSA Corporation has owned a department store in downtown Indianapolis for more than 50 years. The property has a value of about $2 million and a basis of only $400,000 (since the building is completely depreciated). Recently, the corporation learned that the city fathers, in an attempt to revive the downtown area, plan to build a new mall that may result in the condemnation of the building. Fearing that interest rates may rise before the city gets around to condemning the property, the corporation sold the building to another investor, who wanted to try to preserve the building as a historic structure. The corporation quickly used the sales proceeds to build another store in a nearby suburb. Unfortunately, the corporation's sale may not qualify for deferral since it has not been officially notified that the building will be condemned. The threat or imminence does not exist merely because the city is considering plans that may lead to condemnation. Nevertheless, the corporation may be able to produce evidence that clearly suggests otherwise.

As noted above, the sale to a third party after the threat exists is permissible.[39] If the third party realizes gain when the property is later sold to the condemning authority, the new transaction may also qualify for involuntary conversion treatment if the proceeds are reinvested in qualified property after the condemnation of the property, even though the threat existed before the property was acquired.[40]

#### Example 28

T has owned and operated a successful automobile dealership for many years. This year he received legal notice from the City of New Orleans indicating that it planned to condemn his showroom and car lot for use as the site of a new convention center in approximately five years. As a result, T began searching for an acceptable new location. After finding a suitable location, T sold the old property to a person who could use it for just four or five years.

T's sale and reinvestment qualifies for involuntary conversion treatment and his gain can be deferred so long as all other requirements are met. When the property is finally purchased by the city, the new owner can also qualify for involuntary conversion treatment if he or she realizes a gain and the proceeds are reinvested in qualifying property within the replacement period.

---

[37] Rev. Rul. 78-377, 1978-2 C.B. 208, distinguishing Rev. Rul. 59-361, Footnote 27.

[38] Rev. Rul. 58-557, 1958-2 C.B. 402.

[39] *Creative Solutions, Inc. v. U.S.*, 63-2 USTC ¶9615, 12 AFTR2d 5229, 320 F.2d 809 (CA-5, 1963); Rev. Rul. 81-180, 1981-2 C.B. 161.

[40] Rev. Rul. 81-181, 1981-2 C.B. 162.

## Replacement Property

To qualify for deferral of gain on an involuntary conversion, the taxpayer must reinvest in property that is *similar or related in service* or *use* to the property that is converted.[41] The IRS and taxpayers often disagree as to what qualifies as replacement property. It is clear, however, that the new property must replace the converted property, and therefore, property that was already owned by the taxpayer will not qualify.[42]

Generally, the replacement property must serve the same functional use as that served by the converted property. This *functional use* test requires that the character of service or use be the same for both properties.

**Example 29**

N owned and operated a bowling alley for many years. This year the bowling alley burned down, and N replaced it with a billiard parlor. The billiard parlor is not qualified replacement property since the services provided by each are not functionally equivalent. Although they both provide recreational services, the IRS believes bowling balls and billiard balls are not the same.[43]

When tangible trade or business personalty is destroyed in a Presidentially declared disaster area, the taxpayer is given more flexibility. The destroyed property may be replaced with *any* tangible trade or business personalty.[44]

A different and more liberal test has been applied to rental properties involved in involuntary conversions. This test is the *taxpayer use* test, which basically requires that the replacement property be used by the taxpayer/lessor as rental property regardless of the lessee's use.[45]

**Example 30**

Several years ago J purchased 30 acres of land and built a large warehouse that he leased to an appliance store. This year the warehouse site was condemned, and J used the proceeds to purchase a gas station that he currently leases to an oil company. The gas station is qualified replacement property since both properties are rental properties. The fact that the tenants use the properties for different purposes is irrelevant. From the owner's perspective each property is being used in the same way.

### Control of Corporation

The replacement property in an involuntary conversion may be controlling stock in a corporation owning property that is "similar or related in use or service."[46] Control consists of owning at least 80 percent of all voting stock plus at least 80 percent of all other classes of stock.[47]

### Condemned Real Estate

Congress provided special relief in the situation where real property is condemned by an outside authority. A more liberal interpretation of "similar or related in use" is allowed for the replacement of condemned real property if it is held by the taxpayer for use in a trade or business or for investment. The Code provides that the *like-kind* test shall be applied.[48] This is the test used for § 1031 like-kind exchanges. As explained later in this chapter, these rules allow

---

[41] § 1033(a).

[42] § 1033(a)(1)(A)(i).

[43] Rev. Rul. 76-319, 1976-2 C.B. 242.

[44] § 1033(h).

[45] Rev. Rul. 71-41, 1971-1 C.B. 223.

[46] § 1033(a)(2)(A).

[47] § 1033(a)(2)(E)(i).

[48] § 1033(g)(1). The similar or related in use test must be applied if the real property is destroyed or the replacement property is stock in a controlled corporation.

nonrecognition whenever a taxpayer exchanges real estate for real estate regardless of the real estate's use. Thus, if the taxpayer's unimproved real estate (e.g., raw land) is condemned and replaced with improved real estate (e.g., shopping center), deferral would be granted.

### Conversion of Livestock

Section 1033 includes certain special provisions related to sales of livestock. Livestock sold because of disease[49] or solely because of drought, flood or other weather-related conditions[50] are considered involuntarily converted. Furthermore, if livestock are sold because of soil contamination or environmental contamination and it is not feasible for the owner to reinvest in other livestock, then other farm property, including real property, will qualify as replacement property.[51]

### Property Acquired from a Related Party

Congress was concerned that the replacement property would conveniently be acquired from a related party. In order to prevent this, C corporations, partnerships with C corporations as partners, and other taxpayers deferring gains in excess of $100,000, will not be allowed the deferral under § 1033 if the replacement is purchased from a related party. For this purpose, a related party includes certain close family members and most entities where there is more than 50 percent control.[52]

## Replacement Period

The taxpayer is entitled to deferral only if reinvestment in the replacement property occurs within the proper time period. The replacement period usually begins on the date of disposition of the converted property; but in the case of condemnation or requisition, it begins at the earliest date of threat or imminence of the requisition or condemnation. The replacement period ends on the last day of the second taxable year after the year in which a gain is first realized,[53] but may be extended by the IRS if the taxpayer can show reasonable cause for being unable to replace within the specified time limit.[54] In the case of condemned real property used in a trade or business or held for investment, the replacement period is extended. The extension is one year, causing the replacement period to remain open until the end of the third taxable year after the first year in which gain is first realized.[55] These time periods are diagrammed below.

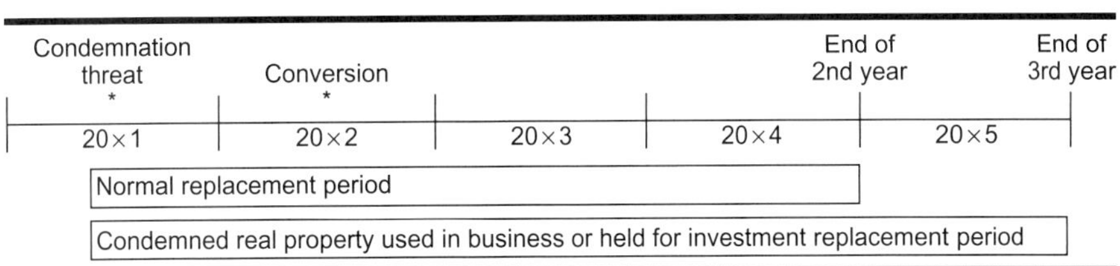


### Example 31

E's rental house was condemned for public use by the county during 2011. Her basis in the residence was $32,000 and the county paid her $46,000. E's replacement period begins the day of the condemnation, or threat thereof. The replacement period normally ends at the close of the second taxable year after the year of the conversion. However, in the case of realty that has been held for productive use in business or for investment and which has been condemned, the replacement period is extended to the close of the third taxable year. In this case, the replacement period ends on December 31, 2014.

---

[49] § 1033(d).

[50] § 1033(e).

[51] § 1033(f).

[52] § 1033(i).

[53] § 1033(a)(2)(B).

[54] Reg. § 1.1033(a)-2(c)(3).

[55] § 1033(g)(4).

### Example 32

If the residence in the previous example had been used as E's personal residence, the replacement period would end on December 31, 2013. As noted above, the replacement period is extended only for real estate held for productive use in a trade or business or for investment, so the usual two-year rule applies.

Earlier reference was made to specific provisions dealing with replacement property upon the destruction of one's principal residence. A special reinvestment period is also provided. When the destruction is in a Presidentially declared disaster area, the reinvestment period is extended to the last day of the fourth year following the year in which gain is first realized.[56]

### Example 33

U's principal residence was destroyed in an earthquake. U's insurance policy included limits of $100,000 for the residence, $40,000 for contents, and an additional $20,000 for U's prized musical instruments. U realized gains on the residence and musical instruments and a small loss on the contents. The region affected by the earthquake was declared a disaster area by the President and U's insurer paid the maximum amounts under the policy. U may defer his gain on the structure and musical instruments by reinvesting $120,000 in similar (residence or contents) property. The reinvestment must take place by the end of U's fourth taxable year after receiving the insurance settlement.

## Election Required

As a general rule, taxpayers are allowed to elect whether or not they want to defer any gain realized from an involuntary conversion. The election is made simply by not reporting any of the deferred gain on the tax return for the year in which the gain is realized. However, deferral of gain is mandatory if the property is converted directly into property that is similar or related in use.[57]

### Example 34

G owned 100 acres of land next to an airport. He had farmed the land for 25 years. All of that changed this year when the city condemned G's land to expand the airport. Pursuant to the condemnation agreement, the city transferred similar farmland to G. In this case, nonrecognition is mandatory since there was a direct conversion into similar property. Had the city paid G for the land, G would have had the option to elect deferral or recognize any gain realized.

The return for the year of conversion must include detailed information relating to the involuntary conversion,[58] and if the taxpayer has not yet reinvested when the return is filed, he or she is required to notify the IRS when replacement property has been acquired or that no replacement will occur.[59] If after an election has been made under § 1033 *and* the

[56] § 1033(h)(1)(B).

[57] § 1033(a).

[58] Reg. § 1.1033(a)-2(c)(2).

[59] Reg. § 1.1033(a)-2(c)(5).

taxpayer fails to reinvest all of the required amount within the allowable period, the tax return for the year (or years) in which gain was realized must be *amended to include the recognized gain* and the tax deficiency must be paid.[60]

### Statute of Limitations

The statute of limitations is extended for involuntary conversions when the taxpayer elects to defer his or her gain but has not replaced the property by the time the return for the year of the conversion is filed. The IRS may audit the transaction and assess a deficiency any time within three years after the taxpayer notifies the IRS that he or she has replaced the converted property or has failed to replace the property triggering the recognition of gain.[61]

## Amount of Gain Recognized

No gain is recognized by an electing taxpayer on an involuntary conversion if the amount reinvested in replacement property equals or exceeds the amount realized from the converted property (i.e., the taxpayer does not "cash out" on the transaction). If the amount reinvested is less than the amount realized, the taxpayer has "cashed out" on the transaction and *must* recognize gain to the extent of the amount *not* reinvested (see Exhibit 15-2).[62] No gain is recognized in a direct conversion.[63]

The *amount reinvested* is the *cost* of the replacement property. The property may not have been acquired by gift, inheritance, or any other method resulting in other than a cost basis.[64] The cost basis would include the amount of any debt incurred in the purchase.

The taxpayer will determine his or her basis in property acquired in an involuntary conversion by taking into consideration the deferred gain. In the case of a direct conversion, the basis of the replacement property is the same as the basis in the converted property. In conversions into money and other property, the basis in the replacement property is its cost *reduced* by the amount of gain realized but not recognized (see Exhibit 15-2).[65]

**EXHIBIT 15.2 Involuntary Conversion: Computation of Recognized Gain and Basis of Replacement Property**

1. Gain realized

| | |
|---|---|
| | Amount realized (net proceeds) |
| Less: | Adjusted basis |
| | Gain (loss) realized |

2. Gain recognized

| | |
|---|---|
| | Amount realized |
| Less: | Cost of replacement property |
| | Gain recognized (not to exceed gain realized)* |

3. Basis of replacement property

| | |
|---|---|
| | Cost of replacement property |
| Less: | Gain not recognized |
| | Adjusted basis of replacement property |

*If this amount is negative, the taxpayer has reinvested more than the amount realized and no gain is recognized.

---

[60] Special rules extend the statute of limitations. § 1033(a)(2)(C): Reg. § 1.1033(a)-2(c)(5).

[61] § 1033(a)(2)(C).

[62] § 1033(a)(2)(A).

[63] § 1033(a)(1).

[64] Reg. § 1.1033(a)-2(c)(4).

[65] § 1033(b); Reg. § 1.1033(b)-1.

## Example 35

M owned a rented industrial equipment warehouse that was adjacent to a railway. The warehouse was destroyed by fire on January 15, 2011, and M received $240,000 from her insurance carrier on March 26, 2011. Her basis in the warehouse was $130,000. M constructed a wholesale grocery warehouse on the same site since the predicted demand for such space was superior to equipment storage. The new warehouse was constructed at a cost of $280,000 and was completed May 7, 2012.

Leased (rental) property is subject to the more liberal *taxpayer use* test, rather than the *functional use* test that is applied to other properties. Therefore, the new warehouse meets the similar or related in use test since it is rental property to M.

As calculated below, M reports no gain on her 2011 return since she reinvested a sufficient amount within the reinvestment period, which ends December 31, 2013. She is required to give the IRS the details of the conversion with her 2011 return and provide a description of the replacement property when it is completed. The basis in the replacement property is $170,000 (cost of $280,000 – the gain not recognized of $110,000).

| | |
|---|---|
| Amount realized | $ 240,000 |
| Less: Adjusted basis | (130,000) |
| Gain (loss) realized | $ 110,000 |
| Amount realized | $ 240,000 |
| Less: Cost of replacement property | (280,000) |
| Gain recognized (not to exceed gain realized) | None |
| Cost of replacement property | $ 280,000 |
| Less: Gain not recognized | (110,000) |
| Adjusted basis of replacement property | $ 170,000 |

## Example 36

Assume the same facts as in *Example 30*, except that M reinvested $200,000. In this case she would be required to recognize a gain since she did not reinvest all of the insurance proceeds of $240,000. As a result, her recognized gain would be $40,000 and her basis in the replacement property would be $130,000, calculated as follows:

| | |
|---|---|
| Amount realized | $ 240,000 |
| Less: Cost of replacement property | –200,000 |
| Gain recognized (not to exceed gain realized) | $ 40,000 |
| Cost of replacement property | $ 200,000 |
| Less: Gain not recognized ($110,000 – $40,000) | –70,000 |
| Adjusted basis of replacement property | $ 130,000 |

### Conversion of Personal Residence

Section 1033 also applies to the involuntary conversion of a principal residence. Taxpayers that qualify may elect to use § 121 instead of, or along with, § 1033 for the involuntary conversion of a personal residence.[66]

### ✓ CHECK YOUR KNOWLEDGE

Over the last several years, Rock and Roller Blades Inc. opened two new roller skating rinks to capitalize on the in-line skating craze. In February 2011, however, one of the rinks was destroyed by fire. At that time, the building had a basis of $300,000. The insurance proceeds awarded to the company amounted to $360,000.

#### Review Question 1

If the corporation uses the insurance proceeds to build a new indoor soccer facility, will the soccer facility be considered qualified replacement property?

*Probably not.* In order to qualify for deferral, the replacement property must be similar to or related in service or use to the converted property. This generally means that the replacement property must provide the same functional use as the converted property. Based on the IRS ruling that a billiard parlor is not functionally equivalent to a bowling alley, it would appear that a soccer facility does not provide the same services as a roller rink.

#### Review Question 2

By what date must the calendar year corporation invest in qualified replacement property?

The corporation must reinvest by the close of the second taxable year following the year in which the conversion takes place, in this case December 31, 2013. The extended replacement period for business or investment realty only applies if the property is condemned.

#### Review Question 3

Assuming the corporation immediately erects another roller rink at the cost of $390,000 and elects to defer any gain realized, the company's gain (or loss) recognized will be:

**a.** $60,000
**b.** $30,000
**c.** $90,000
**d.** $0
**e.** $30,000 loss
**f.** None of the above

The answer is (d). As shown in the following computations, the corporation is allowed to defer the entire gain realized since it reinvested all of the insurance proceeds.

| | |
|---|---|
| Amount realized | $ 360,000 |
| Less: Adjusted basis | −300,000 |
| Gain (loss) realized | $ 60,000 |

| | |
|---|---|
| Amount realized | $ 360,000 |
| Less: Cost of replacement property | −390,000 |
| Gain recognized (not to exceed gain realized) | None |

#### Review Question 4

Same facts as in Question 3. The basis of the replacement property is:

**a.** $300,000
**b.** $390,000
**c.** $370,000
**d.** $0
**e.** $360,000
**f.** None of the above

---

[66] § 121(d)(4).

The answer is (f). The basis is $330,000, determined as follows:

| | |
|---|---|
| Cost of replacement property | $390,000 |
| Less: Gain not recognized | −60,000 |
| Adjusted basis of replacement property | $330,000 |

## Like-Kind Exchanges

**LO.5**
Explain the tax consequences of a like-kind exchange of business or investment property.

Section 1031 of the Code provides that a taxpayer may exchange certain types of property *in kind* without the recognition of a taxable gain or loss. Specifically, no gain or loss is recognized when qualifying property is exchanged *solely* for other qualifying property that is of like-kind.

**Example 37**

E traded in his automobile that was worth $4,500 and was used entirely for business purposes and also paid $15,000 cash for a new auto worth $19,500. E's basis in the old auto was $8,200, based on an original cost of $16,000 less depreciation of $7,800. E recognizes no gain or loss on the transaction since it is a qualifying like-kind exchange. His basis in the new auto is $23,200 ($8,200 basis of trade-in + $15,000 cash paid).

If property other than like-kind property—commonly called *boot*—is received in the exchange, a gain may be recognized.[67] Losses, however, are never recognized.

In order for a transaction to qualify as a nontaxable exchange, it must meet four separate requirements:

1. Both the property exchanged and the property received must be held for business or investment purpose.
2. Both the items exchanged and received must not be specifically excluded from § 1031 treatment.
3. The properties are like-kind.
4. There must be an exchange.

Each of these requirements are discussed below.

### Qualified Property

#### Holding Purpose

In order to qualify for like-kind exchange treatment, a property must be held *either* for use in a trade or business *or* for investment. A qualified exchange may, however, involve the transfer of investment property for trade or business property, or vice versa.[68] No personal use properties qualify.

It is important to note that it is the taxpayer's purpose for holding that is critical. The purposes or plans of the other party to the exchange are irrelevant. For example, if the taxpayer held the property exchanged for business or investment, the taxpayer has met the holding-purpose requirement even if the other party plans to sell the property, has a contract to sell it before the exchange, or is helped by the taxpayer in finding a buyer.

[67] § 1031(b).

[68] Reg. § 1.1031(a)-1(a).

### Excluded Properties

Certain properties are specifically excluded from like-kind exchange treatment. These are:[69]

- Inventory or other property held primarily for sale
- Stocks, bonds, or notes
- Other securities or evidences of indebtedness
- Partnership interests
- Interest in trusts (e.g., the beneficiary's interest)
- Livestock of different sexes

Whether an item is inventory (i.e., held primarily for sale to customers in the ordinary course of a trade or business) is discussed in Chapter 16. Several courts have interpreted the phrase *held for sale* to include any property that is acquired in an exchange only to be resold shortly thereafter.[70]

> **Example 38**
>
> K exchanged a parcel of real estate held for investment for another parcel and immediately offered the parcel received for sale. The parcel was sold on the installment basis. Since K held the new property for sale rather than for use in a trade or business or for investment, the entire gain realized on the exchange must be recognized at the time of the exchange.

## Like-Kind Property

The term like-kind is not defined in the Code. However, the Regulations provide that "the words like-kind have reference to the nature or character of the property and not to its grade or quality."[71] This interpretation has been applied to allow exchanges of realty for realty and personalty for personalty. Exchanges of realty for personal property (nonrealty) or vice versa, are not considered exchanges of like-kind property and are fully taxable.

### Real Estate

Generally, any exchange of realty for realty will meet the like-kind test. It is immaterial whether the real property is improved or unimproved.[72] No distinction is made between improved or unimproved, productive or unproductive, or similar differences since these relate to the grade or quality of the property and are to be specifically ignored. The IRS has ruled that a lease of real property with a remaining term of at least 30 years will be treated as real property for purposes of determining whether a like-kind exchange has occurred.[73] Accordingly, a realized loss from the exchange of property that had declined in value for a lease interest in that property with a life of 30 years or more resulted in a nondeductible (nonrecognized) loss.[74] Recall that condemned real estate in an involuntary conversion is also subject to the like-kind test.

---

[69] § 1031(a)(2).

[70] Ethel Black, 35 T.C. 90 (1960); *George M. Bernard*, 26 TCM 858, T.C. Memo. 1967-176.

[71] Reg. § 1.1031(a)(1)(A).

[72] Reg. § 1.1031(a)-1(b). It is also important to note that § 1250 may supersede § 1031 and cause the recognition of gain. Effectively, § 1250 property (generally depreciable realty) must be acquired in an amount at least as great as the § 1250 recapture potential—§ 1250(d)(4)(C). See Chapter 17 for a discussion of § 1250 recapture of depreciation.

[73] Rev. Rul. 76-301, 1976-2 C.B. 241.

[74] *Century Electric Co. v. Comm.*, 51-2 USTC ¶9482, 41 AFTR 205, 192 F.2d 155 (CA-8, 1951).

## Tangible Depreciable Personalty

In determining the meaning of "like-kind" for personalty, the IRS, with some support, has adopted a much narrower interpretation than its view toward realty.[75] This stems from the fact that personalty includes a far greater variety of assets than realty. From the Service's perspective, adoption of a lenient "like-kind" test for personalty would enable exchanges that violate the spirit of § 1031 (e.g., a car for a horse, a railroad boxcar for an airplane). As noted earlier, deferral is granted on the theory that the taxpayer's economic position has not changed sufficiently to warrant taxation. In the government's opinion, this principle would be seriously undermined if taxpayers were permitted to exchange any type of personalty. Thus, a restrictive approach is understandable. Unfortunately, this approach (i.e., determining whether replacement property represents a continuing interest or a conversion to a wholly new endeavor) is very subjective and difficult to implement.

Notwithstanding support for its position, the IRS became concerned about what it believed could be endless debate over what personalty was like-kind. Consequently, the government issued new Regulations in 1991.[76] These Regulations put taxpayers on alert that the government would continue to take its narrow view of whether one item of personalty is considered the equivalent of another, but, at the same time, offered safe harbors that would provide the taxpayer with some certainty.

Under the current Regulations, personal property qualifies for § 1031 treatment if the properties are either:

1. Like-kind or
2. Like-class.

The definition of "like-kind" remains the same, nebulous as it may be. In contrast, the *like-class* definition offers a more practical approach to determine if properties have the requisite similarity. The like-class definition utilizes a two class system: (1) General Asset Classes and (2) Product Classes. If the properties are within the same General Asset Class or the same Product Class, they are considered like-class and, therefore, like-kind for § 1031 purposes. Note that if the properties meet the like-class standard, they are considered like-kind regardless of whether the exchanged properties would be considered like-kind under general § 1031 standards. The like-class system is significant in that it provides taxpayers the certainty they need before engaging in a transaction. This is particularly true given the absence of authority on like-kind characterizations for personal property.

The General Asset Classes are identified and defined in Revenue Procedure 87-56. There are 13 classes of assets, as shown in Exhibit 15-3. If two assets fall in the same class, they are considered like-class. For instance, a computer, printer, monitor, and modem used in a trade or business would qualify as like-class properties since they are all part of the information systems class (General Asset Class .12). Note that these classes are quite narrow. For example, an automobile and a light-duty truck would not be considered like-class since they are not in the same Class. Recall, however, that these classes serve only as safe harbors in which taxpayers have guaranteed like-kind treatment.[77]

If a General Asset Class is not provided for a particular asset, the Product Classes are to be used to determine if the exchanged properties are like-class. Observe that it is possible—but not likely—that the properties may be in two different General Asset Classes but in the same Product Class. In such case, the items are not like-class since the Product Classes cannot be used if the properties can be found in the General Asset Classes which were designed by the government.

Assets are within the same Product Class if they have the same four-digit product code as listed in the *North American Industrial Classification System* (NAICS) *Manual* published by the Department of Commerce.

[75] In *California Federal Life Insurance Co.*, 50 AFTR 2d 82-5271, 680 F2d 85, 82-2 USTC ¶9464 (CA-9, 1982), aff'g 76 TC 107 (1981) the courts upheld the government's argument that Swiss francs and U.S. double-eagle gold coins were not like-kind. In explaining its holding, the Ninth Circuit noted that it was Congressional concern for lenient interpretation of the like-kind standard that prompted it to amend § 1031 to say that livestock of different sexes are not like-kind. According to the Ninth Circuit, in so acting, Congress was suggesting that personal property was to be accorded different treatment.

[76] Reg. § 1.1031(a)-2(b)(1).

[77] PLR 200450005 provides that sport utility vehicles (SUVs) and passenger automobiles are like-kind. Note, however, that for depreciation purposes heavy SUVs are not subject to the depreciation limitations applicable to passenger automobiles under § 280F.

**EXHIBIT 15.3** General Asset Classes: Revenue Procedure 87-56

| Asset Class | Class Number |
|---|---|
| 1. Office furniture, fixtures, and equipment | .11 |
| 2. Information systems (computers and peripheral equipment) | .12 |
| 3. Data handling equipment, except computers | .13 |
| 4. Airplanes and helicopters (airframes and engines), except those used in commercial or contract carrying of passengers or freight | .21 |
| 5. Automobiles, taxis | .22 |
| 6. Buses | .23 |
| 7. Light general-purpose trucks | .241 |
| 8. Heavy general-purpose trucks | .242 |
| 9. Railroad cars and locomotives | .25 |
| 10. Tractor units for use over the road | .26 |
| 11. Trailers and trailer-mounted containers | .27 |
| 12. Vessels, barges, tugs, and similar water-transportation equipment, except those used in marine construction | .28 |
| 13. Industrial steam and electric generation and/or distribution systems | .4 |

As noted above, if the property does not qualify as like-class under the safe harbors created by the Regulations, it may still be treated as like-kind. The IRS historically has allowed like-kind exchange treatment for personal property when the properties were substantially the same. The courts have ruled that livestock used in a trade or business, but not held for sale, may qualify as like-kind. However, the Code does explain that livestock of different sexes are not like-kind.[78] While it may be obvious that a bull is not a cow, the treatment of bullion-type coins (e.g., decorative gold coins) has created a great deal of controversy. For some investors, collecting and trading gold and silver coins is a popular investment strategy. The IRS has ruled that an exchange of gold bullion held for investment for silver bullion held for the same purpose is not a like-kind exchange since gold and silver are intrinsically different minerals.[79] On the other hand, bullion-type coins of different countries constitute like-kind property.[80] Currency exchanges are not like-kind exchanges. Similarly, legal tender coins (currency) are not of like-kind with bullion-type noncurrency coins.[81]

## Intangibles

The like-class rules apply only to tangible depreciable personalty. There are no like classes for intangible personal property. Whether intangibles such as patents and copyrights are like-kind depends on the nature of the property to which the rights relate. For example, copyrights on two novels are like-kind; but a copyright on a novel and a copyright on a song are not like-kind.[82] Similarly, the IRS has ruled that the contracts of professional athletes are like-kind.

## Multiple Property Exchanges

In some cases an exchange may involve more than one property. When this occurs, as in an exchange of one business for another, the Regulations provide a somewhat complex set of rules. The effect of these rules is that the various assets are matched with those of the same kind or class. Note that if two businesses are exchanged, the IRS guidelines provide that the

---

[78] § 1031(e). Apparently, if male calves could be exchanged for female calves, a breeding herd of females could be built up more quickly and sold for capital gain treatment.

[79] Rev. Rul. 82-166, 1982-2 C.B. 190.

[80] Rev. Rul. 76-214, 1976-1 C.B. 218.

[81] Rev. Rul. 79-143, 1979-1 C.B. 264; *California Federal Life Insurance Co. v. Comm.*, 82-2 USTC ¶9464, 50 AFTR2d 82-5271, 680 F.2d 85 (CA-9, 1982), aff'g. 76 T.C. 107 (1981). It is interesting that the Revenue Ruling states that U.S. gold coins are currency, while the courts in these cases state that they are more like "other property" than "money."

[82] Reg. § 1.1031(a)-2(c)(3), *Examples 1* and *2*.

goodwill and going concern values of similar businesses are not considered like-kind properties."[83]

### Property Outside the United States

Generally, real property located outside the U.S. is not like-kind with respect to real property located within the U.S. Similarly, personal property used predominately outside the U.S. is not like-kind with respect to personalty used predominantly within the U.S. In determining where property is predominately used, the two years before the exchange are considered for the property given up and the two years after the exchange are considered for the property received.[84]

## Receipt of Property Not of a Like-Kind (Boot)

As a general rule, an exchange is nontaxable only if property is exchanged *solely* for like-kind property. But in many cases, taxpayers wanting to make an exchange do not have like-kind property of equal values. Consequently, one of the parties typically throws in cash or some other non-like-kind property—commonly called *boot*—to equalize the values exchanged. Fortunately, the receipt of boot does not totally disqualify the transaction. Instead, § 1031(b) provides that the taxpayer must recognize any gain realized to the extent of any boot received. For these purposes, *boot* includes any money received in the exchange *plus* the fair market value of any property that is either nonqualified or not like-kind. Under § 1031(c), the receipt of boot does not cause the recognition of any realized losses in such an exchange.[85]

**Example 39**

J transferred a vacant lot held as an investment and worth $8,000 to another party in exchange for a similar lot worth $6,000. J received $2,000 cash in addition to the new lot. J's basis in her old lot was $5,500. J's realized gain is $2,500 ($8,000 amount realized – $5,500 basis). If she holds the new lot as an investment, J still must recognize gain on this exchange in the amount of $2,000 because she received *cash boot* of $2,000.

**Example 40**

If J's basis in the property given up in the prior example had been $6,500, her realized gain would have been $1,500 ($8,000 amount realized – $6,500 basis). Although she received $2,000 of boot, J's recognized gain is $1,500 (recognized gain is *never* more than the realized gain).

**Example 41**

If J's basis in the vacant lot exchanged in the previous two examples had been $9,000, she would have a realized loss of $1,000 and a recognized loss of zero. Losses in like-kind exchanges are never recognized.

### Liabilities as Boot

In many exchanges, a taxpayer transfers property encumbered by indebtedness (e.g., land subject to a mortgage) or has liabilities assumed as part of the exchange agreement. When a taxpayer is relieved of a liability, the tax law takes the view that such relief is the equivalent of

[83] Reg. § 1.1031(a)-2(c)(2).

[84] § 1031(h).

[85] If a note is received as boot, the gain may be reported using the installment sales rules. See § 453(h)(6) and (7).

receiving cash and paying off the liability. In essence, the party assuming the liability is treated as having paid cash for the property. Consistent with this view, any liabilities from which the taxpayer is relieved in a like-kind exchange are treated as boot received (or boot paid in the case of the party assuming the debt).[86] Note that without these rules, taxpayers could mortgage property shortly before the exchange, receive cash, and then transfer the property along with liability without having to recognize any gain. The treatment of liability relief as boot thwarts such plans.

### Example 42

Wanting to move his business out of the city, R exchanged his downtown warehouse encumbered by a mortgage of $200,000 for a new suburban building worth $700,000. R's basis in the warehouse was $600,000. As a result, R realized a gain of $300,000 ($700,000 + $200,000 = $900,000 amount realized − $600,000 basis). Although R received only the building, the relief of the $200,000 liability is treated as boot received. Therefore, R must recognize a gain of $200,000.

### Relief and Assumption of Liabilities

If both parties to the exchange assume a liability (e.g., the taxpayer is relieved of a liability of $100,000 but also incurs a liability of $90,000), the process becomes a bit more confusing. In this case, the taxpayer first nets the assumption and the relief. If the taxpayer has net relief (i.e., net decrease in liabilities), such amount is treated as boot received, which in turn may trigger gain recognition.[87] If the taxpayer has net incurred (i.e., net increase in liabilities), such amount is treated as boot paid and no gain is recognized. Note that liabilities are the only type of boot paid or received that can be netted. Other types of boot are not netted. But what if a taxpayer receives cash and incurs liabilities? Can the taxpayer offset any cash received (and the gain that goes with it) by any liabilities incurred? And what if a taxpayer is relieved of liabilities? Can the taxpayer offset any liability relief by giving cash? The Regulations have addressed these possibilities. A taxpayer cannot offset boot received by liabilities incurred. However, liability relief can be offset by boot given (since the taxpayer could presumably pay off the debt with the boot, thereby reducing the liability relief).[88] These various situations are addressed in the next three examples.

### Example 43

S exchanged a tractor worth $11,000 for a similar tractor worth $9,000, both held for use in his landscaping business. The tractor given up was subject to a secured obligation of $8,000 and S incurred a liability secured by the new tractor of $6,000. S's basis in the tractor given up was $6,500, his cost of $13,500 less depreciation allowed of $7,000. S's realized gain on this exchange is $4,500, computed as follows:

| | |
|---|---|
| Fair market value of property received | $ 9,000 |
| Plus: Liabilities encumbering the property transferred | +8,000 |
| Less: Liabilities assumed by tax payer | −6,000 |
| Amount realized | $11,000 |
| Less: Adjusted basis of property given up | −6,500 |
| Gain realized | $ 4,500 |

S's recognized gain is $2,000 since his net liability relief ($8,000 liability relief − $6,000 liability assumed) is treated as boot.

---

86 § 1031(d).

87 See Reg. §§ 1.1031(b)-1(c) and 1.1031(d)-2. It is important to note that liabilities incurred in anticipation of a like-kind exchange will not qualify for this netting treatment. See Prop. Reg. § 1.1031(b)-1(c).

88 Reg. 1.1031(d)-2, Ex. 2.

## Example 44

Use the facts in *Example 43*, but assume that instead of receiving a $9,000 tractor and incurring a $6,000 liability, S received a tractor worth $7,500 and paid $4,500 cash. S's realized gain is $4,500 computed as follows:

| | |
|---|---|
| Fair market value of property received | $ 7,500 |
| Plus: Liabilities encumbering the property transferred | +8,000 |
| Less: Amount of money given up | −4,500 |
| Amount realized | $11,000 |
| Less: Adjusted basis of property given up | −6,500 |
| Gain realized | $ 4,500 |

S's recognized gain is $3,500, the amount of his liability relief ($8,000) less the other boot paid ($4,500 cash).

## Example 45

If S had received a tractor worth $3,000 and incurred no liabilities and paid no cash in the transaction, his realized gain is still $4,500, computed as follows:

| | |
|---|---|
| Fair market value of property received | $ 3,000 |
| Plus: Liabilities encumbering the property transferred | +8,000 |
| Amount realized | $11,000 |
| Less: Adjusted basis of property given up | −6,500 |
| Gain realized | $ 4,500 |

The amount of boot received is $8,000, the amount of his liability relief. The recognized gain is $4,500, since the gain is recognized to the extent of boot received, but never more than the gain realized.

## BASIS IN PROPERTY RECEIVED

Exhibit 15-4 presents two ways of computing the basis of property received in a like-kind exchange. The first method (Method 1), prescribed by the Code, is based on the notion that the like-kind property received in the exchange is merely a continuation of the taxpayer's investment in the like-kind property given up. Thus, the basis of the property received should be the same as the property given up—a so-called *substituted* basis. This basis is *increased* by any gain recognized and by any additional consideration given or to be paid in the future, or *decreased* by the fair market value of any boot received and by any liabilities transferred.[89] The second method is derived from the basis determination method used for replacement property in involuntary conversions and sales of principal residences. Under this method, the fair market value of the like-kind property received (i.e., its cost if purchased) is *reduced* by a deferred gain or *increased* by deferred loss in determining its basis. This adjustment is made so that if the newly acquired property is later sold, any realized gain or loss that is not recognized (deferred amount) from the previous like-kind exchange will be automatically considered in the computation of the realized gain or loss. Under either method, the basis of any boot received is its fair market value.

[89] § 1031(d).

**EXHIBIT 15.4** **Basis of Property Received in a Like-Kind Exchange**

**Method 1:**

| | | | |
|---|---|---|---|
| Adjusted basis of property given up | | | $xxx,xxx |
| Plus: | Gain recognized | $xx,xxx | |
| | Boot paid | x,xxx | |
| | Liabilities assumed by the taxpayer | xx,xxx | |
| | Liabilities encumbering the property received | xx,xxx | + xx,xxx |
| | | | $xxx,xxx |
| Less: | Boot received | $xx,xxx | |
| | Liabilities assumed by the other party (transferee) | xx,xxx | |
| | Liabilities encumbering the property transferred | xx,xxx | −xx,xxx |
| Basis of property received | | | $xxx,xxx |

**Method 2:**

| | | |
|---|---|---|
| Fair market value of like-kind property received | | $xxx,xxx |
| Less: | Deferred gain (realized gain − recognized gain) | −xx,xxx |
| Plus: | Realized loss (deferred) | + xx,xxx |
| Basis of property received | | $xxx,xxx |

## Example 46

J operates a charter flight business out of Ft. Lauderdale. This year he put together a deal with one of his flying buddies whereby he traded his old plane, with a basis of $40,000, for another smaller plane worth $53,000 and a hangar to park it in, worth $7,000. J's realized gain is $20,000 [($53,000 + $7,000 = $60,000) − $40,000]. Since the hangar is realty, it is treated as boot. Thus, J must recognize a gain of $7,000 (lesser of the gain realized or boot received). The basis of the boot received, the hangar, is its fair market value of $7,000. J's basis in the new plane is $40,000, computed as follows:

**Method 1:**

| | |
|---|---|
| Adjusted basis of property given up | $ 40,000 |
| Plus: gain recognized | 7,000 |
| Less: boot received | −7,000 |
| Basis of property received | $ 40,000 |

**Method 2:**

| | |
|---|---|
| Fair market value of like-kind property received | $ 53,000 |
| Less: Deferred gain ($20,000 − $7,000) | −13,000 |
| Basis of property received | $ 40,000 |

At first glance, the basis calculations may not make sense. In the substituted basis computation, the basis of the new property is initially the same as the property given up, $40,000. However, any gain recognized, in this case $7,000, must be added to ensure that upon subsequent sale of the property such gain is not taxed again. The sum of these two amounts ($40,000 + $7,000 = $47,000) represents the basis for the like-kind property and the boot received. A portion of this total is then allocated to the boot by subtracting the value of the boot, $7,000. In effect, the basis assigned to the boot is its $7,000 value, leaving the remaining $40,000 to be assigned to the like-kind property. Note how a subsequent sale of the like-kind property for its $53,000 value would cause the taxpayer to recognize the previously postponed gain of $13,000 ($53,000 − $40,000). This same result is accomplished in a much more obvious manner in the second calculation, where the deferred gain is simply subtracted from the value of the property. The following example is a comprehensive review of the like-kind exchange rules.

## Example 47

E exchanged a rental house for T's rental condominium. E's house was worth $36,000 and her adjusted basis was $27,000. The house was not subject to any liabilities. T's condominium was worth $82,000 and was subject to a mortgage of $54,000. T also transferred $8,000 worth of Alpha Corp. stock to E in order to equalize the transaction. T's adjusted basis in his condominium and the Alpha stock were $64,000 and $5,600, respectively. The gains realized by E and T are computed as follows:

| E | | |
|---|---|---|
| Fair market value of property received | | |
| Rental condominium (like-kind property) | | $ 82,000 |
| Alpha Corp. stock (boot received) | | +8,000 |
| | | $ 90,000 |
| Less: Liabilities (mortgage) assumed by taxpayer | | −54,000 |
| Amount realized | | $ 36,000 |
| Less: Adjusted basis of rent house given up | | −27,000 |
| Gain realized | | $ 9,000 |

| T | | |
|---|---|---|
| Fair market value of rental house received | | $ 36,000 |
| Plus: Liabilities discharged (assumed by E) | | +54,000 |
| Amount realized | | $ 90,000 |
| Less: Adjusted basis of properties given up: | | |
| Rental condominium | $64,000 | |
| Alpha Corp. stock (boot paid) | 5,600 | −69,600 |
| Gain realized | | $ 20,400 |

E's gain recognized is $8,000, the amount of boot (stock) received. The amount of boot received by T is $54,000 (the amount of liabilities discharged), which is reduced by his boot paid of $8,000 (fair market value of Alpha stock). Therefore, T's net liabilities discharged are $46,000. T's recognized gain, however, is $20,400, since recognized gain never exceeds realized gain. T's recognized gain consists of $2,400 ($8,000 fair market value − $5,600 basis) for the taxable exchange of the Alpha stock, and the remaining $18,000 is attributable to the exchange of his house.

E and T's bases in their like-kind property received are determined as follows:

| | | *E's Condominium* | *T's House* |
|---|---|---|---|
| Adjusted basis of like-kind property given up | | $27,000 | $64,000 |
| Plus: | Gain recognized | +8,000 | +20,400 |
| | Boot paid | +0 | +5,600 |
| | Liabilities assumed | +54,000 | +0 |
| Less: | Boot received | −8,000 | −0 |
| | Liabilities discharged | −0 | −54,000 |
| Basis of property received | | $81,000 | $36,000 |

E's basis in the Alpha Corp. stock is $8,000, its fair market value.[90] E and T could have computed their bases in the like-kind property received by using the alternative method (Method 2) discussed previously.

[90] Reg. §§ 1.1031(d)-1(c) and 1.1031(d)-1(d).

| | E | T |
|---|---|---|
| Fair market value of like-kind property received: | | |
| Rental house | | $ 36,000 |
| Rental condominium | $ 82,000 | |
| Less: Deferred gain | −1,000 | −0 |
| Basis of like-kind property received | $ 81,000 | $ 36,000 |

## Exchange Requirement

Generally, the determination of whether an exchange has occurred is not difficult. All that is required is a reciprocal transfer of qualifying properties. An exchange of one real estate investment for another would normally qualify. Similarly, a trade-in of a business auto along with some cash for another auto is a qualifying exchange. However, an argument can be made for collapsing seemingly independent transactions that might appear to be an exchange in substance.[91]

### Example 48

B, a traveling salesperson, "sold" his business auto to a car dealership for $3,200 cash. Shortly thereafter, he purchased another auto from the same dealer for $12,000 cash. The IRS could collapse the *two* transactions (sale and purchase) between the same parties in *one* like-kind exchange. Thus, if B's basis in the old vehicle was $6,000, his loss would be disallowed, and his basis in the new auto would be $14,800 ($12,000 fair market value of new auto + $2,800 deferred loss).

### Three-Corner Exchanges

It is not always easy for two parties with properties of equal value, both of which are suitable to the other party, to get together. Even so, it may be possible for a taxpayer who cannot find an exchange partner to qualify for like-kind treatment through a three-corner exchange.

Several forms of multiple-party exchanges have qualified for like-kind exchange treatment. The IRS has ruled that when three property owners entered into an exchange in which each gave up and received qualifying property, like-kind exchange treatment was appropriate.[92] However, a three-corner exchange must be part of a single, integrated plan.[93]

### Example 49

X, Y and Z each own rental property. They exchange the properties as follows:

X gets Y's property, Y gets Z's property, and Z gets X's property. X, Y, and Z pay or receive boot in order to equalize the difference in the values of the properties.

This three-party transaction qualifies as a like-kind exchange under §1031. Each party receiving boot must recognize gain up to the amount of the boot received.

---

[91] Rev. Rul. 61-119, 1961-1 C.B. 395.

[92] Rev. Rul. 57-244, 1957-1 C.B. 247; Rev. Rul. 73-476, 1973-2 C.B. 300.

[93] Rev. Rul. 75-291, 1975-2 C.B. 332; Rev. Rul. 77-297, 1977-2 C.B. 304.

Perhaps a more common situation involves a taxpayer who is willing to "sell" property but does not want to recognize gain. In this situation, the interested buyer purchases like-kind property identified by the "seller" and then exchanges it for the seller's property.

**Example 50**

C owned rental property worth $70,000 (adjusted basis of $34,000), which she was willing to dispose of only if she could do so without recognizing any gain. B wanted to purchase C's property, but in order that C might defer her potential gain of $36,000, he agreed to purchase another rental property of equal value that was suitable to C. As long as she receives no boot, C would recognize no gain and her basis in the replacement property would be $34,000 ($70,000 fair market value of property received – $36,000 deferred gain). B will not qualify for § 1031 treatment since he purchased the property specifically for the exchange and thus never held it for business use or investment.[94] However, B will not have any realized gain or loss as a result of the transaction since his amount realized of $70,000 (fair market value of rental property received from C) is equal to his cost basis of the property given up.

### Delayed Exchanges

The property to be accepted by the taxpayer in a like-kind exchange need not be received *simultaneously* with the transfer of his or her property. Delayed exchanges are popularly referred to as *Starker* exchanges, after a 1979 case in which a taxpayer transferred significant real property in exchange for a promise by a corporation to deliver the replacement property over five years.[95] These exchanges qualify currently for tax deferral only if specific timing requirements are met. In order to qualify for nonrecognition treatment, the property to be acquired must be:

1. Identified within 45 days after the date the taxpayer surrenders the property; and
2. Received within 180 days of the transfer, but no later than the due date (including extensions) of the tax return for the year of transfer.[96]

**Example 51**

R has agreed to purchase any real property worth $120,000 that is acceptable to S if S will immediately transfer his commercial parking lot, which is adjacent to R's store, to R. S agrees to the plan. S later identifies a duplex worth $120,000 and directs R to purchase it for him. This delayed exchange will qualify under § 1031 if the duplex is specified as the replacement property within 45 days and is transferred to S within 180 days of the transfer of the parking lot to R. Note how the taxpayer has effectively sold the property for $120,000 cash and then reinvested the cash without having to pay tax.

Delayed exchanges are frequently expedited by an escrow company that holds money that is to be used to purchase a property for the transferor. It is possible that a property would be identified within 45 days but, due to circumstances beyond the taxpayer's control, cannot be acquired. To prevent this misfortune, the taxpayer may identify one or more additional properties within the 45-day period to be acquired if the acquisition of the first property cannot be completed.[97]

---

[94] *Biggs v. Comm.*, 81-1 USTC ¶9114, 47 AFTR2d 81-484, 632 F.2d 1171 (CA-5, 1980).

[95] *Starker v. U.S.*, 79-2 USTC ¶9541, 44 AFTR 2d 79-5525, 602 F.2d 1341 (CA-9, 1979).

[96] § 1031(a)(3).

[97] Reg. § 1.1031(k)-1. Also see Rev. Proc. 2000-37, 2000 I.R.B. 40, where the IRS provides a safe harbor for exchanges that occur through an intermediary in a reverse order.

### Related-Party Exchanges

For many years, related parties used a clever device to reduce gain on the sale of appreciated property. At the heart of the scheme were the substituted basis rules applied in like-kind exchanges. These rules effectively enabled the taxpayer to create a high basis for what otherwise was low-basis property that the taxpayer planned to sell.

> **Example 52**
>
> T owns all of the stock of D Corporation, which is planning to sell 100 acres of land for $700,000 (basis $100,000). Accordingly, D anticipates that it will recognize a gain of $600,000. To minimize the gain on the sale, however, T transfers one of his real estate investments worth $700,000 (basis $500,000) to the corporation in exchange for the land and subsequently sells the land. T's gain on the sale of the land is only $200,000 ($700,000 – $500,000) since the like-kind exchange rules enabled him to substitute the higher basis of his realty, $500,000, as the basis for the land.

To put an end to the so-called basis-swapping illustrated in *Example 47*, Congress created a special rule. If a taxpayer exchanges property with a *related party* and either taxpayer disposes of the transferred property within two years, the like-kind exchange rules do not apply to the original exchange and any deferred gain must be recognized in the year of the subsequent disposition.[98] For this purpose, the definition of a related party is the same as that used for the loss disallowance rules of §§ 267 and 707(b)(1), which generally includes the taxpayer's family (spouse, brothers, sisters, ancestors, lineal descendants) and certain entities (e.g., corporations and partnerships) in which the taxpayer owns more than a 50 percent interest.

> **Example 53**
>
> Assume the same facts as in *Example 47* above. Under current law T's plan would not work since T and his corporation are considered related parties and he sold the property within two years of the exchange. As a result, both T and D must recognize their deferred gains on the original exchange in the year of the sale. T recognizes a gain of $200,000 ($700,000 – $500,000) and D recognizes a gain of $600,000 ($700,000 – $100,000). T recognizes no gain on the sale itself because his basis in the land is now treated as $700,000 (i.e., his cost) since the original transaction became taxable. Note that T's plan would have worked had T been patient and sold the land more than two years after the exchange.

## Treatment Mandatory

Like-kind exchange treatment is mandatory. Therefore, no gain or loss is recognized on any transaction that meets the like-kind exchange requirements even if the taxpayer desires otherwise. Since the provision applies to losses as well as gains, like-kind treatment may work to the disadvantage of a taxpayer, and it may be to his or her benefit to avoid exchange status.

> **Example 54**
>
> This year B swapped her rental property in Malibu worth $200,000 (basis $230,000) for rental property in Vail worth $175,000 and cash of $25,000. B has realized a loss of $30,000 ($200,000 – $230,000). Although she received boot of $25,000, none of the loss is recognized. In this case, B would probably be better off selling the Malibu property and purchasing the Vail property so that she could recognize her loss.

[98] § 1031(f).

## Holding Period

The holding period of like-kind property received in a § 1031 exchange includes the holding period of the property given up on the exchange.[99] This also applies to the holding period of replacement property in an involuntary conversion. However, the holding period of any property received as boot in a § 1031 exchange *begins* on the date of its receipt. In effect, when boot received is property other than money (or liability relief), it is treated as if the taxpayer received money (equal to the property's fair market value) and used it to purchase the property. Consequently, the property's holding period starts on the day of the exchange *and* the basis of the property is its fair market value.

## ✓ Check Your Knowledge

### Review Question 1

This year H retired. He decided to continue to live in Chicago but wanted to get rid of his rental property (fair market value $240,000, basis $140,000) and buy a condominium in Florida. H is now entertaining an offer to sell the property to a real estate mogul who loves the property and is hot to buy. What would you advise?

Without good advice, most taxpayers would sell the property, recognize a $100,000 gain, and pay a capital gains tax of up to $25,000, leaving them with as little as $72,000 to invest. There is a much better approach. H is a perfect candidate for a delayed like-kind exchange. He could "sell" the property and have the buyer transfer the funds to an escrow agent, who would hold the money while H identifies the property in Florida he wants. He must do this within 45 days after the sale. As long as he closes on the new property within 180 days of the transfer (but no later than the due date of the return for the year of the transfer, including extensions), the like-kind exchange provisions will apply and H does not have to recognize the gain!

### Review Question 2

At the outset of this chapter, it was indicated that there is a way to pyramid one's wealth to $1 million without ever having to pay tax. How could this be done?

The first step is to make wise investments (typically real estate). If the investor desires to sell after the property has appreciated, he or she may "sell" the property using the delayed like-kind exchange technique just as H did in the previous question. The effect is to invest in replacement property without having to pay any tax. If H can continue to invest successfully, he never has to pay tax along the way to $1 million (and beyond). Note that H does not necessarily have to find a property of equal value, assuming the amount escrowed is reinvested in like-kind property. As long as all of the cash is used and none passes to H, he does not recognize any gain. Thus, H could effectively use the property as a down payment for new property and use additional leverage to accelerate the process.

Note that the property must be qualifying property. Since like-kind exchange treatment does not apply to stocks and bonds, this scheme would not work with respect to stock market investments.

### Review Question 3

True-False. This year D swapped her billiard parlor building for a bowling alley building. The transaction qualifies as a like-kind exchange.

*True.* Although the properties are not considered similar or related in use according to the functional use test applied to involuntary conversion rules, the two investments are considered like-kind property since they are both realty.

### Review Question 4

True-False. During the year, E exchanged her personal residence for a rental house. The swap qualifies as a like-kind exchange.

---

[99] § 1223(1).

*False.* The properties exchanged must be held for productive use or investment. In this case, E is not holding her home for investment, and therefore the exchange is taxable.

### Review Question 5

True-False. Under the like-kind exchange rules, a taxpayer must receive cash before any gain realized is recognized.

*False.* Although this may appear to be true, the taxpayer is taxed whenever boot is received. Any property other than the like-kind property received is treated as boot. For example, the boot could take the form of stock, a note, or even liability relief.

### Review Question 6

True-False. This year, F swapped her investment land for a friend's land and $10,000 of cash. As a result, F realized a $20,000 loss. F may recognize a loss of $10,000.

*False.* Losses are never recognized on a like-kind exchange even if the taxpayer receives boot.

### Review Question 7

True-False. G sold her rental property in Galveston for $100,000 and realized a $25,000 gain. Two months later, she used the $100,000 plus an additional $50,000 to purchase another rental property on Padre Island for $150,000. G does not recognize gain since she has not liquidated her investment but continued it in another rental property.

*False.* Although G seems to have met the spirit of the law, there must, as a general rule, be a direct exchange in order to qualify for nonrecognition under the like-kind exchange provisions. Note that G could have postponed the gain had she taken advantage of the delayed like-kind exchange rules or had she simply had the buyer of her property buy the Padre Island property and then done an exchange.

### Review Question 8

During the year, Fred traded one of his buddies a tractor used solely in his construction business for another tractor for the same use. On the date of the trade, the old tractor had an adjusted basis of $3,000. He received in exchange $500 in cash and a smaller tractor with a fair market value of $2,800. Fred should recognize a gain on the exchange of:

**a.** $800
**b.** $500
**c.** $300
**d.** $0
**e.** None of the above

The answer is (c). Fred realized a gain of $300 [($2,800 + $500 = $3,300) – $3,000]. Since he received boot of $500, he must recognize the lesser of the gain realized, $300, or the boot received, $500.

### Review Question 9

Assuming the same facts as above, the basis of the new tractor to Fred would be:

**a.** $3,300
**b.** $3,000
**c.** $2,800
**d.** $2,300
**e.** None of the above

The answer is (c), as determined below.

**Method 1:**

| | |
|---|---|
| Adjusted basis of property given up | $3,000 |
| Plus: Gain recognized | 300 |
| Less: Boot received | –500 |
| Basis of property received | $2,800 |

**Method 2:**

| | |
|---|---|
| Fair market value of like-kind property received. | $2,800 |
| Less: Deferred gain | –0 |
| Basis of property received | $2,800 |

## Other Nontaxable Transactions

### CHANGES IN FORM OF DOING BUSINESS

**LO.6**
Identify other common nontaxable transactions.

Several provisions in the Internal Revenue Code are intended to allow mere changes in the form of carrying on a continuing business activity without the recognition of gain or loss. Section 721, for example, allows the transfer of property to a partnership in exchange for a partnership interest without the recognition of taxable gain or loss. Section 351 allows a similar treatment when property is transferred to a corporation solely in exchange for its stock by persons possessing control, and § 355 provides for nontaxability in certain corporate reorganizations. These specific topics are addressed in subsequent chapters.

### CERTAIN EXCHANGES OF STOCK IN SAME CORPORATION

No gain or loss is recognized by the shareholder who exchanges common stock for common stock or preferred stock for preferred stock in the same corporation under § 1036. The exchange may be voting stock for nonvoting stock, and it is immaterial whether the exchange is with another shareholder or with the issuing corporation.[100] If the exchange is not solely in kind, the rules of § 1031(b) (applicable to like-kind exchanges) are applied to determine the amount of any gain recognized.[101]

### CERTAIN EXCHANGES OF U.S. OBLIGATIONS

Gain may be deferred in the case of certain exchanges of U.S. obligations between the taxpayer and the U.S. Government. Section 1037 applies to exchanges of bonds of the government issued under Chapter 31 of Title 31 (the Second Liberty Bond Act). The Treasury regulations for § 1037 discuss the application of this section.

### REPOSSESSION OF REAL PROPERTY

Section 1038 provides that the seller of real property will recognize a gain on the repossession of real property only to the extent the sum of the money and other property besides the repossessed realty received exceeds the gain from the transaction previously reported. This provision applies only to repossessions to satisfy debt obligations received in exchange for the sold property (e.g., foreclosure for nonpayment of mortgage). Such purchase-money obligations must be secured by an interest in the property. If any part of these obligations has previously been deducted as a bad debt, the amount of such deductions is included in income in the year of the repossession.

### CERTAIN EXCHANGES OF INSURANCE POLICIES

Section 1035 allows the deferral of gain on the exchange of a life insurance contract for another insurance policy. Additionally, it allows certain exchanges involving annuity contracts and endowment contracts.

[100] Reg. § 1.1036-1(a).

[101] Reg. § 1.1036-1(b).

# Tax Planning Considerations

## Current Recognition Versus Deferral

**LO.7**
Recognize tax planning opportunities related to the more common types of gain-deferral transactions available to individual taxpayers.

A basic concept in tax planning, as discussed in earlier chapters, is the deferral of tax payments. Each of the provisions discussed in this chapter (as it relates to gains) is a perfect example of such a deferral. A taxpayer is usually better off by deferring any gain—unless he or she expects to be in a much higher effective tax bracket in the later year when the deferred gain would be recognized. Of course, a taxpayer is *always* better off if he or she can avoid tax altogether, as is the case under § 121. However, if a loss is deferred under § 1031, taxes are accelerated. Thus, if the adjusted basis of business or investment property being disposed of exceeds its fair market value, the nonrecognition treatment of § 1031 should be avoided.

## Current Gain Resulting in Future Reductions

In each case of deferred gain, the mechanism is a reduced basis in the replacement property. If this replacement property is depreciable property, the depreciation deductions will also be smaller. It may be advantageous to report a large gain *currently* if the tax cost is low, and reap the benefit of the larger depreciation deductions in later years.

### Example 55

W plans to dispose of a building that would result in capital gain if sold, and acquire similar property in a different location. W could defer gain by arranging an exchange, but his basis in the new property would be low. W also has a large capital loss carryforward that he has been deducting at the rate of $3,000 per year.

If W sells the property, the gain would offset the capital loss carryforward and he would pay no tax. His basis in the new building would be its cost, resulting in larger future depreciation deductions.

## Importance of Capital Budgeting in Decision Making

In any decision of whether to defer taxes when subsequent tax years are affected, capital budgeting techniques are appropriate in making the decision. When considering possible investment opportunities, a taxpayer must *compare* current investment requirements and tax effects with the future returns from the investment and their tax effects. Some form of present-value analysis will help the taxpayer to make a sound decision. A similar analysis should be applied in deciding the appropriateness of entering into any nontaxable (tax-deferred) transaction.

# Problem Materials

## Discussion Questions

**15-1** *Repair versus Improvement.* H owned her personal residence for ten years before she had to incur a cost of $4,000 due to a leaking roof. Is this roof maintenance a nondeductible repair or a capitalized improvement? Explain.

**15-2** *Principal Place of Residence.* V lived in Milwaukee and worked in Chicago for many years. Finally, V rented an apartment in Chicago, where she stayed on weeknights. Weekends and holidays were spent in Milwaukee. Where is V's *principal* place of residence for purposes of § 121?

**15-3** *Section 121 Exclusion.* List the two principal requirements that must be met before one can qualify for the § 121 exclusion upon the sale of a residence.

**15-4** *Limit on Amount of Exclusion.* What is the maximum amount of gain that can be excluded under § 121?

**15-5** *Loss on Sale of Personal Assets.* Y sold his principal residence and realized a $12,000 loss. What is the proper tax treatment of this loss?

**15-6** *Conversion of Residence.* Y purchased a property to be used as a rental on September 15, 1998. Y moved into this house on May 1, 2011 so it would qualify for the § 121 exclusion.

**a.** Can the residence eventually qualify for the § 121 exclusion?
**b.** If so, how long must Y live in it before the gain can qualify for the exclusion?
**c.** Can the entire gain be excluded?

**15-7** *Two of Five Years Test.* F sold her primary residence on June 2, 2011, and excluded her $22,500 gain. She purchased and moved into another primary residence on August 5, 2011. On what date can F first qualify for the § 121 exclusion with respect to the second residence?

**15-8** *One Sale Every Two Years Rule.* G sold a qualifying residence on June 2, 2009, and excluded his $22,500 gain on his calendar year 2009 return. G had previously purchased and moved into another residence on December 7, 2008. On what date may G first qualify for the § 121 exclusion with respect to the second residence?

**15-9** *Sale Due to Unanticipated Events.* S purchased her dream home on April 17, 2010 for $120,000. Then, much to her surprise, she was given a promotion and transferred by her employer. So she sold the home on January 2, 2011, for $170,000.

**a.** Does S qualify for the exclusion of gain under § 121?
**b.** If so, what is the maximum amount S can exclude?
**c.** Under what other circumstances might S be able to qualify for this partial exclusion?

**15-10** *Conversion of Rental Property.* R lives in the suburbs of Miami. Several years ago, he bought a condo on the beach. He rented the condo out for several years. During this time, the property appreciated substantially. He is now considering selling his suburban home, converting the condo into his personal residence and then selling it to take advantage of the exclusion for gains on the sale of a personal residence. What advice would you give R?

**15-11** *Marriage and § 121.* D gave E a one-half interest in D's home of 10 years as a wedding gift. E moved into the home after the wedding. Eighteen months later, on December 2, 2011, the residence was sold at a gain of $314,500. How much of the gain may be excluded by D and E on their joint return for 2011?

**15-12** *Divorce and § 121.* F and G lived in a home that was F's separate property during the duration of their five-year marriage. Upon their divorce, G received title to the property. How much, if any, of the $200,000 gain may G exclude upon the sale of the house one year later?

**15-13** *Death of a Spouse and § 121.* X and Y were married on November 14, 2011, after which Y moved into the home that had been owned and occupied by X for more than 30 years. Upon X's death, Y inherited the home that had cost $40,000 and was worth $300,000. How much gain must Y recognize when she sells the home one year after X's death for $315,000?

**15-14** *Condemnation.* What is required in order to have "threat or imminence" of condemnation?

**15-15** *Replacement Property under § 1033.* How does the concept of "similar or related in service or use" differ between an owner/user of property and an owner/lessor?

**15-16** *Replacement Period.* B's beauty salon was destroyed by fire on April 21, 2011. The building was covered by current value insurance, and B realized a gain of $70,000. When must B reinvest in order to defer this gain under § 1033?

**15-17** *Making the § 1033 Election.* How does a taxpayer elect to defer gain under § 1033 in involuntary conversions?

**15-18** *Interaction of §§ 121 and 1033.* G and H had an amount realized of $800,000 and a gain of $520,000 in 2011 on the insurance recovery from the fire that totally destroyed their residence of ten years. May the taxpayers use both the residence exclusion and the involuntary conversion rules to avoid gain recognition?

**15-19** *Ineligible Property.* Property "held for sale" is not eligible for like-kind exchange treatment. Elaborate.

**15-20** *Real Property under § 1031.* K proposes to exchange a downtown office building she holds as rental property for a 450-acre ranch in Virginia that she would operate as a horse ranch. Will this transaction qualify for like-kind exchange treatment?

**15-21** *Personal Property under § 1031.* What constitutes personal property of "like-kind"?

**15-22** *Boot.* What is the meaning of "boot" in § 1031 like-kind exchanges?

**15-23** *Liabilities.* Are liabilities discharged always treated as boot received in a like-kind exchange under § 1031? Explain.

**15-24** *Basis of Property Received.* How is the basis in the property received in a like-kind exchange under § 1031 determined? What is the basis in any boot received?

**15-25** *§ 1031 Elective or Mandatory.* Is like-kind exchange treatment elective with the taxpayer? If not, how could such treatment be avoided if the taxpayer was so inclined?

**15-26** *Holding Period.* In the current year, R received a rental house and 300 shares of IBM common stock in exchange for a vacant lot he had held as an investment since April 16, 2006. When does the holding period for the rental house begin? For the IBM stock?

## PROBLEMS

**15-27** *Calculation of Gain Realized.* M, single. purchased a residence on May 1, 1998 for $195,000. M lived in the residence until June 1, 2002 and from December 1, 2008, until it was sold on May 6, 2011. In between, the property was rented. The following information was derived from M's records:

| | |
|---|---|
| Purchase closing costs . . . . . . . . . . . . . . . . . . . . . . . . . . . . . . . . | $ 1,450 |
| Depreciation claimed while the property was rented . . . . . . . . . . . | 12,250 |
| Addition of family room (January 2006) . . . . . . . . . . . . . . . . . . . . | 23,500 |
| Painting of interior (April 2008) . . . . . . . . . . . . . . . . . . . . . . . . . | 4,200 |

The property sold for $289,000, and M incurred realtor's commissions of $16,340 and other closing costs of $2,300. The depreciation claimed after May 6, 1997 was $12,250.

**a.** How much is M's basis in the residence at the time of the sale?
**b.** How much is M's gain realized on the sale?
**c.** How much is M's gain recognized?
**d.** How would the answer to "c" differ if any of the rental period had been after December 31, 2008?

**15-28** *Section 121 Exclusion.* P and Q, who are married, sold their residence of 19 years on February 12, 2011. The house had cost $120,000 and improvements of $22,000 had been made. The house sold for $750,000. Selling costs of $37,500 were incurred and deferred maintenance costs of $4,500 were paid weeks before the sale. P and Q have taxable income not including this gain of $70,000 on their joint return for the year.

**a.** How much is P and Q's gain realized on this sale?
**b.** How much of that gain, if any, must be recognized? How will it be taxed?

**15-29** *Section 121 Exclusion.* Four years ago C bought a sail boat for $225,000. Immediately after the purchase he moved in and it became his principal residence. He keeps the sail boat in a slip near Sarasota but often sails off for weeks at a time. This year he decided to sell the boat. In preparation for sale, he made improvements costing $22,300 and repairs totaling $32,000. He sold the boat for $345,000. How is this sale treated on C's income tax return for the calendar year of sale?

**15-30** *Section 121 Exclusion with Depreciation.* V owned a house that cost $200,000 in which she lived from July 1, 1997 until June 30, 2010. From July 1, 2010 until September 30, 2010, the home was rented, and depreciation of $8,000 was claimed. How will the sale of the residence for $325,000 on October 1, 2011 be treated?

**15-31** *Limitation on Amount Excluded.* In each of the following situations, determine the maximum amount that may be excluded under § 121.

- **a.** H and W sold their home on October 31, 2011. The home was owned as separate property and lived in by W for six years. H lived in the home since they were married three years ago.
- **b.** K owned a rental property which she rented to J for several years. Upon marrying J on June 1, 2010, K moved into the house. The house was sold on August 1, 2011. and J and K file a joint return for 2011.
- **c.** L, an unmarried individual, purchased and moved into a residence on March 15, 2010 for $650,000. On June 16, 2011, L sold the residence for $825,000 because she was transferred to a new work location.

**15-32** *Sale of Principal Residence—Costs.* U received and accepted an offer to purchase her principal residence for $78,000 on March 12 and completed the sale on May 8 (all in the current year). She later purchased a replacement residence. Specify whether each of the following is properly classified as a nondeductible expense, a selling expense, an addition to the basis of the residence that was sold, or none of these.

- **a.** New garage built during February of the current year at a cost of $12,500 because the city requires that every residence that is sold in the subdivision have a garage.
- **b.** Real estate transfer taxes of $780 assessed by the city government.
- **c.** Steam cleaning of carpets for $125 on April 22 and paid for upon completion.
- **d.** Painting interior of residence completed and paid for in February.
- **e.** Commissions of $4,680 paid to listing and selling real estate brokers.

**15-33** *Sale Due to Unanticipated Events.* Q purchased a new residence on April 17, 2009 for $720,000. Upon receiving a very lucrative offer of employment, Q moved to another city and sold the residence on January 17, 2011, for $1,000,000. How much gain must Q recognize on this sale?

**15-34** *Sale of Principal Residence.* During the current year, H and W ended their stormy marriage of 20 years. They had jointly owned a residence valued at $330,000 with a basis of $95,000. As part of their divorce settlement, H sold his interest in the home to W for $165,000. Assuming that there were no selling costs or fixing-up expenses, answer the following:

- **a.** How much gain must H recognize?
- **b.** What is W's basis in the residence?

**15-35** *Rental Use.* K purchased a house for $200,000 on May 1, 2000. She rented the house to tenants from May 1, 2000 to May 1, 2009 and deducted depreciation of $50,000. On May 1, 2009, she moved into the home and used it as her residence until May 1, 2011. On April 30, 2015, she sold the home for $400,000. What is the amount gain recognized on the sale of the home?

**15-36** *Involuntary Conversion.* The business office of K, a real estate broker, was destroyed by fire on August 22, 2011.

- **a.** By what date must K reinvest to avoid recognizing gain from the insurance proceeds received as a result of the fire?
- **b.** What type of property must K purchase to avoid recognition?
- **c.** Would your answers differ if, rather than being destroyed by fire, the office building had been condemned by the state for highway right of way?

**15-37** *Involuntary Conversion.* L owned a leased warehouse that was totally destroyed by fire on October 31, 2011. The building had a basis to L of $45,000 and his insurance paid the replacement cost of $75,000. L completed construction of a new warehouse on the same land on December 2, 2013 at a cost of $80,000.

**a.** How much gain must L recognize on this conversion?

**b.** What is L's basis in the replacement warehouse?

**c.** Summarize L's reporting requirements.

**d.** How would your answers to parts (a), (b), and (c) differ if L had invested only $65,000 in the replacement property?

**15-38** *Involuntary Conversion.* Complete the following table involving certain involuntary conversions in which the taxpayer elects to defer gain. The property is converted into cash and the cash is invested in qualifying replacement property in each case. Each case is independent of the others.

| Case | Amount Realized | Adjusted Basis | Amount Reinvested | Gain Recognized | Basis in Replacement |
|---|---|---|---|---|---|
| A | $3,000 | $1,600 | $1,200 | $______ | $______ |
| B | 3,000 | 1,300 | 1,400 | $______ | $______ |
| C | 6,000 | 4,000 | 5,500 | $______ | $______ |
| D | 7,500 | 3,400 | 7,900 | $______ | $______ |
| E | 8,400 | 9,000 | 8,700 | $______ | $______ |

**15-39** *Involuntary Conversion Replacement Period.* For each of the following involuntary conversions, state the beginning and ending dates of the permissible replacement period.

**a.** The city of Knoxville announced plans to condemn D's rental property on March 15, 2010 and completed condemnation proceedings on June 12, 2011 for $330,000.

**b.** Same facts as in part (a), except that the property was D's principal residence.

**c.** A fire destroyed G's bike shop on November 7, 2010. G received an insurance settlement on April 12, 2011.

**15-40** *Involuntary Conversion—Condemned Real Estate.* The city of Orange Grove condemned T's automobile parts warehouse for use as a community park. Plans to condemn the property were announced on June 14, 2010, instituted on December 12, 2010, and completed on May 1, 2011. T's basis in the warehouse was $235,000, and the condemnation award was $366,000.

**a.** Describe the type of property with which T must replace this warehouse in order to qualify for involuntary conversion treatment.

**b.** Specify the reinvestment period during which T must reinvest in order to qualify for involuntary conversion treatment.

**c.** Determine the amount of gain that T must recognize and T's basis in the replacement property, which costs $387,000.

**15-41** *Involuntary Conversion—Destroyed Residence.* B's residence and contents were totally destroyed when a nearby gas main burst. The gas company paid B $90,000 for the building (with a basis of $65,000) and $35,000 for the contents as follows:

| | Fair Value | Adjusted Basis |
|---|---|---|
| Clothing, personal effects | $10,000 | $22,000 |
| Furniture and fixtures | 8,000 | 16,500 |
| Appliances, utensils, etc. | 7,000 | 11,000 |
| Art collection | 10,000 | 4,500 |

**a.** What requirements must be met for B to defer all of his gain under § 1033?

**b.** How would your answer differ if the loss had been caused by a fire which was a Presidentially declared disaster and the payments were made by B's insurer (the art collection was not separately listed in the insurance policy)?

**15-42** *Interaction of §§ 121 and 1033.* B's home was totally destroyed by fire on May 22, 2011. B, an unmarried individual, received $1,050,000 for the house which had cost $700,000 five years earlier.

**a.** How much gain may B exclude under § 121?

**b.** Can B defer the remaining gain, if any, under § 1033? If so, how much is the minimum amount that B must reinvest in order to exclude all of the gain?

**c.** Assuming that B reinvests $760,000 in another personal residence, what is the amount of gain B must recognize and what is his basis in the replacement residence?

**15-43** *Like-Kind Exchange.* F traded in an automobile that was used 100 percent of the time for business for a new auto for the same use. F had fully depreciated the old auto. The auto received was worth $12,000 and F paid $5,000 cash in addition to giving up her old auto.

**a.** How much gain must F recognize on the trade-in?

**b.** What is F's adjusted basis in the new auto?

**15-44** *Like-Kind Exchange.* T transferred his farmland (100 percent business) to V in exchange for a parcel of unimproved urban real estate held by V as an investment. The farm was valued at $400,000 and was subject to a mortgage obligation of $260,000. T's basis in the farm was $340,000. The urban real estate was valued at $450,000 and was subject to a mortgage of $310,000.

**a.** How much gain must T recognize on this exchange?

**b.** What is T's basis in the urban real estate received?

**15-45** *Like-Kind Exchange.* Refer to Problem 15-44. Assume that V had a basis of $360,000 in the urban real estate transferred to T.

**a.** How much gain must V recognize on the exchange?

**b.** What is V's basis in the farm property received?

**15-46** *Like-Kind Exchange.* B exchanged undeveloped land worth $245,000 with C for developed land worth $225,000 and DEF corporation stock worth $20,000. B's adjusted basis in the land was $176,000. C's adjusted bases in the land and stock were $243,000 and $17,500, respectively.

**a.** How much gain or loss must B recognize in this exchange, and what are his bases in the land and stock received?

**b.** How much gain or loss must C recognize in this exchange, and what is her basis in the land received?

**15-47** *Like-Kind Exchange.* F exchanged undeveloped land worth $45,000 with G for land worth $42,000 and a personal automobile worth $3,000. F's adjusted basis in the land was $36,000. G's adjusted bases in the land and automobile were $39,500 and $2,500, respectively.

**a.** How much gain or loss must F recognize in this exchange, and what are his bases in the land and automobile received?

**b.** How much gain or loss must G recognize in this exchange, and what is her basis in the land received?

**15-48** *Like-Kind Exchange: Installment Reporting.* D entered into an agreement on December 15, 2010 under which he will immediately receive an apartment complex worth $300,000 and an installment obligation of the buyer for $200,000 with interest at 12 percent annually. D is to give up another apartment complex in which he has a basis of $320,000.

**a.** What is the minimum gain that D must recognize on this exchange in 2010?

**b.** How much gain must D report when he receives his first principal installment of $20,000 (plus accrued interest) in 2011?

**15-49** *Like-Kind Exchanges.* Complete the following table for exchanges that qualify for like kind exchange treatment under § 1031.

| *Case* | *Adjusted Basis of Property Given Up* | *FMV of Property Received* | *Cash Boot Received* | *Cash Boot Paid* | *Gain or Loss Recognized* | *Basis of Property Received* |
|---|---|---|---|---|---|---|
| A | $3,000 | $2,500 | $ 0 | $ 0 | $______ | $______ |
| B | 5,000 | 5,000 | 0 | 1,000 | $______ | $______ |
| C | 4,000 | 6,000 | 1,000 | 0 | $______ | $______ |
| D | 7,000 | 5,900 | 600 | 0 | $______ | $______ |
| E | 5,000 | 4,000 | 2,500 | 0 | $______ | $______ |
| F | 3,000 | 3,200 | 200 | 0 | $______ | $______ |
| G | 4,000 | 3,600 | 500 | 0 | $______ | $______ |

## TAX RESEARCH PROBLEMS

**15-50** *Exchange of Businesses.* T has owned and operated a taxi service (T's Taxi) for many years, but he now wishes to move to a new city. If T sells his business, he will have a substantial gain. Through a business broker, T has arranged to exchange his business for a limousine service (U's Limos) in the other city. In order to strike the deal, U insists that T sign a covenant-not-to-compete that U and T value at $25,000. The balance sheets (representing fair market values) of the two businesses are as follows:

| | *T's Taxi* | *U's Limos* |
|---|---|---|
| Automobiles | $700,000 | $750,000 |
| Computers and data handling equipment | 60,000 | 30,000 |
| Covenant-not-to-compete | 25,000 | |
| Goodwill | 65,000 | 60,000 |
| Totals | $850,000 | $840,000 |

In order to equalize the transaction, U will pay T $10,000 cash. T's bases are as follows: in the automobiles, $675,000; in the computers, etc., $65,000; and in the covenant and goodwill, $0. T has asked you to determine the tax effect of this proposed exchange before he completes it.

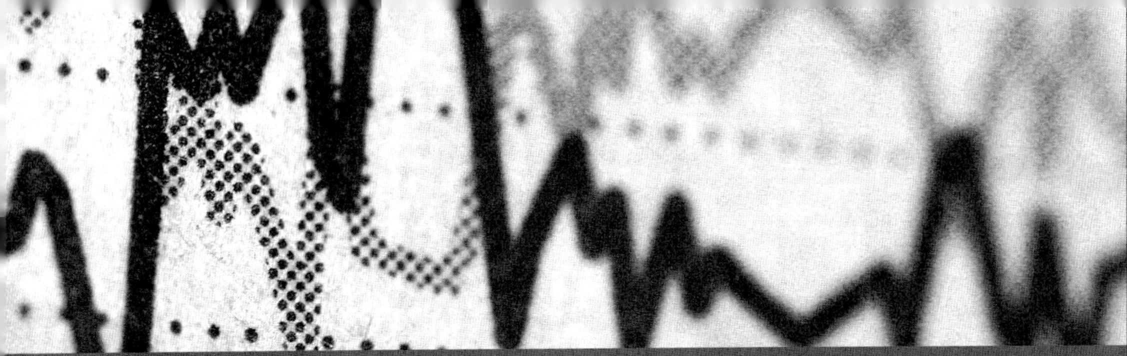

16

# Property Transactions: Capital Gains and Losses

## Learning Objectives

Upon completion of this chapter you will be able to:

LO.1 Discuss the rationale for preferential treatment of capital gains.

LO.2 Explain the conditions that must be met to obtain capital gain treatment.

LO.3 Define a capital asset and use this definition to distinguish capital assets from other types of property.

LO.4 Explain the holding period rules for classifying a capital asset transaction as either short-term or long-term.

LO.5 Apply the capital gain and loss netting process to a taxpayer's capital asset transactions and explain their treatment.

LO.6 Explain the differences in tax treatment of the capital gains and losses of a corporate taxpayer versus those of an individual taxpayer.

LO.7 Identify various transactions to which capital gain or loss treatment has been extended.

LO.8 Discuss the tax treatment of investments in corporate bonds and other forms of indebtedness.

## Chapter Outline


Introduction 16-2
General Requirements for Capital Gain 16-3
Capital Assets 16-4
  Definition of a Capital Asset 16-4
  Inventory 16-5
  Copyrights, Artistic Works, Letters and Similar Items 16-5
  Federal Publications 16-6
  Disposition of a Business 16-6
Sale or Exchange Requirement 16-7
  Worthless and Abandoned Property 16-7
  Certain Casualties and Thefts 16-9
  Other Transactions 16-10
Holding Period 16-10
  Stock Exchange Transactions 16-11
  Special Rules and Exceptions 16-11
Treatment of Capital Gains and Losses 16-13
  The Process in General 16-13
  Netting Process 16-14
  Dividends Taxed at Capital Gain Rates 16-18
  Corporate Taxpayers 16-19
  Calculating the Tax 16-20
  Reporting Capital Gains and Losses 16-24
Capital Gain Treatment Extended to Certain Transactions 16-25
  Patents 16-25
  Lease Cancellation Payments 16-26
Incentives for Investments in Small Businesses 16-26

Losses on Small Business Stock: § 1244 16-26
Qualified Small Business Stock (§ 1202 Stock) 16-27
Rollover of Gain on Certain Publicly Traded Securities 16-30
Dealers and Developers 16-30
Dealers, Investors and Traders of Securities 16-31
Subdivided Real Estate 16-32
Other Related Provisions 16-33
Nonbusiness Bad Debts 16-33
Franchise Agreements, Trademarks, and Trade Names 16-33
Short Sales 16-34
Options 16-35
Corporate Bonds and Other Indebtedness 16-37
Original Issue Discount 16-38
Market Discount 16-41
Conversion Transactions 16-41
Bond Premium 16-42
Tax Planning Considerations 16-42
Timing of Capital Asset Transactions 16-42
Section 1244 Stock 16-43
Problem Materials 16-44


## Introduction

**LO.1**
Discuss the rationale for preferential treatment of capital gains.

The final piece of the property transaction puzzle concerns the treatment of the taxpayer's recognized gains and losses. In the infancy of the tax law, solving this puzzle was relatively easy. Taxpayers who sold or otherwise disposed of property needed only to determine their gain or loss realized and how much, if any, they had to recognize. The actual treatment of the gain or loss recognized—or more precisely, the rate at which it was taxed—was identical to that for other types of income. The simplicity of treating all income and loss the same was short-lived, however, lasting a mere eight years, from 1913 to 1921. Since 1921, the taxation of property transactions has been complicated by the additional need to determine not only the amount of the taxpayer's gain but also its character. Virtually all of this complication can be traced to one source: Congress's desire to provide some type of preferential treatment for capital gains.

Whether capital gains should be taxed more leniently than wages and other types of income is the subject of what seems to be a never-ending debate. When the first income tax statute was enacted, there was nothing in the definition of income to indicate that gains on dealings in property were taxable. Seizing on the omission, taxpayers relied on somewhat abstract tax theory and ingeniously argued that a gain on a sale of property (e.g., a citrus grove) was not the same as income derived from such property (e.g., sale of the fruit) and should not be taxed at all. Moreover, taxpayers who sold property and reinvested in similar property argued that they had not altered their economic position and that taxation was therefore not appropriate. While detractors cried "nonsense!" champions of favorable treatment offered additional justification, explaining that capital gain is often artificial, merely reflecting increases in the general price level. Perhaps the most defensible argument can be found in the Ways and Means Committee Report that accompanied the Revenue Act of 1921. As the following quotation shows, Congress believed that the progressive nature of the tax rates was unduly harsh on capital gains, particularly when the rate (at that time) could be as high as 77 percent.

> The sale of … capital assets is now seriously retarded by the fact that gains and profits earned over a series of years are under present law taxed as a lump sum (and the amount of surtax greatly enhanced thereby) in the year in which the profit is realized. Many of such sales … have been blocked by this feature of the present law. In order to permit such transactions to go forward without fear of a prohibitive tax, the proposed bill … adds a new section [providing a lower rate for gains from the sale or dispositions of capital assets].[1]

Although the top rate is currently much lower than it has been historically, the bunching effect is still cited as one of the major justifications for lower rates for capital gains. Proponents also reason that taxing capital gains at low rates encourages taxpayers to make riskier investments and also helps stimulate the economy by encouraging the mobility of capital. Without such rules, taxpayers, they believe, would tend to retain rather than sell their assets.

[1] House Rep. No. 350, 67th Cong. 1st Sess., pp. 10–11, as quoted in Seidman, *Legislative History of the Income Tax Laws, 1938–1961*, 813 (1938).

Of course, opponents of special treatment are equally vocal in their objections to the benefits extended capital gains. They reject the proposition that capital gain should not be taxed. They maintain that income is income regardless of its form. Opponents also doubt the stimulus value of preferential treatment and complain about the uneven playing field that such treatment creates. Finally, opponents offer one argument for which there is no denial. As will become all too clear in this and the following chapter, the special treatment reserved for capital gains and losses creates an inordinate amount of complexity in the tax law.

Despite the various objections, Congress has generally sided with those in favor of preferential treatment. But, as history shows, there is little agreement on exactly what that treatment should be. From 1922 to 1933, taxpayers were given the option of paying a flat 12.5 percent tax on their capital gains and the normal rate on ordinary income. From 1934 to 1937, the treatment was altered to allow an exclusion for capital gains ranging from 20 to 80 percent, depending on how long the asset was held. After some tinkering with the exclusion in 1938, Congress moved again in 1942. This time it replaced the exclusion with a deduction equal to 50 percent of the gain. The 50 percent deduction—increased in 1978 to 60 percent—made capital gains the most popular game in town for almost 45 years. In 1986, however, Congress had a complete change of heart. After lowering the top rate on ordinary income to 28 percent, it apparently believed that special treatment for capital gains was no longer needed. Accordingly, favorable capital gain treatment was repealed. This period of low rates, however, proved to be only temporary, as Congress raised the top rate to 31 percent in 1991 and 39.6 percent in 1993. The increase prompted Congress to resurrect favorable treatment for capital gains, in this case providing that the gains of an individual would be taxed at a maximum rate not to exceed 28 percent. In 2003, Congress decided, once again, to improve the tax advantage extended to capital gains. Under the new rules, capital gains qualifying for special treatment can be taxed at one of four different rates (28 percent, 25 percent, 15 percent, 10 percent, or 0 percent).

The current rates applying to capital gains, like their predecessors, can produce substantial savings. The table below illustrates the benefit of the 15 percent capital gains rate.

| *Ordinary Rate* | *Capital Gains Rate* | *Differential Rate* | *Percentage Savings* |
|---|---|---|---|
| 35.0% | 15% | 20.0% | 57.14% |
| 33.0 | 15 | 18.0 | 54.55 |
| 28.0 | 15 | 13.0 | 46.43 |
| 25.0 | 15 | 10.0 | 40.00 |
| 15.0 | 0 | 15.0 | 100.00 |
| 10.0 | 0 | 10.0 | 100.00 |

It should be emphasized that the 15 percent rate is 0 percent for 2008 through 2012 for taxpayers whose gains would be taxed at 15 or 10 percent if they were ordinary income. For example, assume a single taxpayer has taxable income of $15,000, all of which is net capital gain. The tax rate on the $15,000 is 0 percent since it would have been taxed at 10 and 15 percent had it been ordinary income (i.e., it falls in the 10 and 15 percent brackets).

As is apparent from the table above, capital gain treatment is extremely desirable. But as the remainder of this chapter explains, this favorable treatment is not extended to just any gain. The taxpayer must jump through a few hoops, turn a couple of cartwheels, and clear innumerable hurdles before he or she reaches the pot of gold at the end of the capital gains rainbow.

## General Requirements for Capital Gain

**LO.2**
Explain the conditions that must be met to obtain capital gain treatment.

A gain or loss is considered a capital gain or loss and receives special treatment only if each of several factors is present. The asset being transferred must be a *capital asset* and the disposition must constitute a *sale or exchange*. In addition, the exact treatment of any net gain or loss can be determined only after taking into consideration the *holding period* of the property transferred. Each of these factors is discussed below.

# Capital Assets

## Definition of a Capital Asset

**LO.3**
Define a capital asset and use this definition to distinguish capital assets from other types of property.

In order for a taxpayer to have a capital gain or loss, the Code generally requires a sale or exchange of a *capital asset*. Obviously, the definition of a capital asset is crucial. Sales involving property that qualifies as a capital asset are eligible for a reduced tax rate while sales of assets that have not been so blessed may not be as lucky.

The Internal Revenue Code takes a roundabout approach in defining a capital asset. Instead of defining what a capital asset is, the Code identifies what is not a capital asset. Under § 1221, all assets are considered capital assets unless they fall into one of five excluded classes. The following are *not* capital assets:

1. Inventory or property held primarily for sale to customers in the ordinary course of a trade or business
2. Accounts and notes receivable acquired in the ordinary course of a trade or business for services rendered or from the sale of inventory
3. Depreciable property and land used in a trade or business
4. Copyrights, literary, musical,[2] or artistic compositions, letters or memoranda, or similar property held by the creator, or letters or memoranda held by the person for whom the property was created; in addition, such property held by a taxpayer whose basis is determined by reference to the creator's basis (e.g., acquired by gift), or held by the person for whom it was created
5. Publications of the United States Government that are received from the Government by any means other than purchase at the price at which they are offered to the public, and which are held by the taxpayer who received the publication or by a transferee whose basis is found with reference to the original recipient's basis (e.g., acquired by gift)

Before looking at some of these categories, one should appreciate the statutory scheme and the rationale behind it.

As noted above, the Code starts with the very broad premise that all property held by the taxpayer is a capital asset. Thus the sale of a home, car, jewelry, clothing, stocks, bonds, inventory, and plant, property, and equipment used in a trade or business would produce, *at least initially*, capital gain or loss since all assets are by default capital assets. However, § 1221 goes on to alter this general rule with several significant exceptions. It specifically excludes from capital asset status inventory, property held for resale, receivables related to the sales of services and inventory, and certain literary properties. As may be apparent, the purpose of these exclusions, as the Supreme Court has said, "is to differentiate between the 'profits and losses arising from the everyday operation of business' on the one hand... and 'the realization of appreciation in value accrued over a substantial period of time' on the other."[3] In essence, the statute is generally drawn to deny capital gain treatment for income from regular business operations. Income that is derived from the taxpayer's routine personal efforts and services is also treated as ordinary income and in effect receives the same treatment as wages, interest, and all other types of income.

Based on the above analysis, it might seem strange that § 1221 also excludes from capital asset status a class of assets that most people would consider capital assets: the fixed assets of a business (depreciable property and land used in a business). Although it is true that these assets are not "pure" capital assets, as will be seen in Chapter 17, these assets can, if certain tests are met, sneak in the back door and receive capital gain treatment. Also observe that this rule does not exclude intangibles from capital asset treatment even though they may be amortizable. For example, goodwill is a capital asset even though it may be amortized.

One final note: it should be emphasized that the classification of an asset as a capital asset may affect more than the character of the gain or loss on its sale. For example, the amount of a

[2] Beginning May 18, 2006 taxpayers may elect to treat musical compositions or copyrights in musical works as capital assets but only for sales or exchanges of such items and not charitable contributions. See §1221(b)(3).

[3] *Malat v. Riddell*, 66-1 USTC ¶9317, 17 AFTR2d 604, 383 U.S. 569 (USSC, 1966).

charitable contribution deduction also may be affected in certain instances. For example, generally the amount of a charitable contribution of property is its value but only if its sale would have produced long-term capital gain. Otherwise the amount of the contribution is normally the adjusted basis of the property. For this reason, whether the contributed property is a capital asset is critical. For example, authors and artists can deduct only the adjusted basis of art objects or manuscripts (usually little or nothing) because such assets are not capital assets.[4]

## Inventory

The inventory exception has been the subject of much litigation and controversy. Whether property is held primarily for sale is a question of fact. The Supreme Court decided in *Malat v. Riddell*[5] that the word "primarily" should be interpreted as used in an ordinary, everyday sense, and as such, means "principally" or of "first importance." As a practical matter, such interpretations provide little guidance. In many cases, it simply boils down to whether the court views the taxpayer as a "dealer" in the particular property or merely an investor. Unfortunately, the line of demarcation is far from clear.

The determination of whether an item is inventory or not frequently arises in the area of sales of real property. In determining whether a taxpayer holds real estate, or a particular tract of real estate, primarily for sale, the courts seem to place the greatest emphasis on the frequency, continuity, and volume of sales.[6] Other important factors considered by the courts are subdivision and improvement,[7] solicitation and advertising,[8] purpose and manner of acquisition,[9] and reason for and method of sale.[10]

## Copyrights, Artistic Works, Letters and Similar Items

Should authors and artists be entitled to favorable capital gains treatment on the sale of their works? Should the sale of game show formats like Jeopardy or scripts for television or radio programs produce capital gain to their creators? Prior to 1950, sale of such works were granted lucrative tax treatment even though the property was attributable to the creator's personal efforts.[11] However, amidst growing concerns about the extension of low rates to such transactions, Congress reacted. Section 1223(3) now bars capital asset status to "a copyright, a literary, musical, or artistic composition, a letter or memorandum, or similar property" if the property was created by the taxpayer's personal efforts. In the case of letters, memoranda, and similar property, the disqualification also applies to the person for whom the work was prepared or produced.[12] In addition, a person receiving these items by gift from the creator or the person for whom the work was created is denied capital gain treatment.

The term similar property includes theatrical productions, radio programs, newspaper cartoon strips, manuscripts, diaries, corporate archives, financial records and other property eligible for copyright protection.[13] It is important to emphasize, however, that this provision does not include patents, inventions or other designs that may be protected only under patent law. Thus inventors get favorable capital gain for their creative genius!

Surprisingly, in 2006, Congress created an exception to this rule, allowing taxpayers to elect to treat musical compositions or copyrights in musical works sold as capital assets. This exception extends favorable capital gain treatment to the creators of musical compositions (i.e., song writers). This election is available for compositions or copyrights sold or exchanged

---

[4] See § 170(e)(1) and Chapter 11 for a discussion of these charitable contribution limitations.

[5] *Supra*, Footnote 2.

[6] See, for example, *Houston Endowment, Inc. v. U.S.*, 79-2 USTC ¶9690, 44 AFTR2d 79-6074, 606 F.2d 77 (CA-5, 1979) and *Reese v. Comm.*, 80-1 USTC ¶9350, 45 AFTR2d 80-1248, 615 F.2d 226 (CA-5, 1980).

[7] See, for example, *Houston Endowment, Inc.*, and *Biedenharn Realty Co., Inc. v. U.S.*, 76-1 USTC ¶9194, 37 AFTR2d 76-679, 526 F.2d 409 (CA-5, 1976).

[8] See, for example, *Houston Endowment, Inc.*

[9] See, for example, *Scheuber v. Comm.*, 67-1 USTC ¶9219, 19 AFTR2d 639, 371 F.2d 996 (CA-7, 1967), and *Biedenharn Realty Co., Inc. v. U.S.*

[10] See, for example, *Voss v. U.S.*, 64-1 USTC 9290, 13 AFTR2d 834, 329 F.2d 164 (CA-7, 1964).

[11] For examples, see *Julius H. Marx* 29 T.C. 88 (1957) and *Jack Benny* 25 T.C. 197 (1955).

[12] This expansion was added in 1969 to prevent public officials (e.g., Presidents, Congressmen) from deducting the value of the memorabilia they had collected in office and then contributed to libraries, universities and museums.

[13] Reg. § 1.1221-1(c)(1) and (2).

in a taxable year beginning after May 17, 2006. It should be noted that musical compositions are not treated as capital assets for purposes of the charitable contributions rules. Thus the deduction for contributions of compositions is not the value, but rather the basis of the property, which is usually little or nothing.

### Example 1

J is an amateur artist who loved to paint desert landscapes. This year she sold one of her paintings through an art dealer in Santa Fe for $2,000. J has ordinary income on the sale because artistic compositions such as paintings are not capital assets. The result would be the same had J painted the picture for her daughter, D, and D sold the picture. Even though D did not paint the picture herself, it was prepared for her and capital asset status is denied for both the creator and the one for whom it was prepared.

### Example 2

B returned from a trip around the world and decided to write a book. This year she died and her son, S, inherited the manuscript which he sold several years later for a gain of $10,000. S would have long-term capital gain because the manuscript is a capital asset since S's basis is not determined in reference to B's basis but is automatically fair market value as of the date of death.

## Federal Publications

Publications of the U.S. government (e.g., the Congressional Record) that are given to a taxpayer by the government are not capital assets. This provision was enacted in 1976 primarily to prohibit Presidents, Congressmen, Cabinet members and others from securing charitable contribution deductions for gifts to libraries and museums of items that they collected while working for the government. By denying capital asset treatment for these items, the amount of the contribution is limited to the taxpayer's basis rather than its value.[14] As a result, little or no deduction is available for the contributions.

## Disposition of a Business

The treatment of the sale of a business depends on the form in which the business is operated and the nature of the sale. If the business is operated as a sole proprietorship, the sale of the proprietorship business is not, as one taxpayer argued, a sale of a single integrated capital asset.[15] Rather, it is treated as a separate sale of each of the assets of the business. Accordingly, the sales price must be allocated among the various assets and gains and losses determined for each individual asset. Any gain or loss arising from the sale of inventory items and receivables would be treated separately as ordinary gains and losses. Gains and losses from the sale of depreciable property and land used in the business would be subject to special treatment discussed in Chapter 17 and may qualify for capital gain treatment. Finally, gains and losses from capital assets would of course be treated as capital gains and losses.

If the business is operated in the form of a corporation or partnership, the sale could take one of two forms: (1) a sale of the owner's interest (e.g., the owner's stock or interest in the partnership) or (2) a sale of all the assets by the entity followed by a distribution of the sales proceeds to the owner. An owner's interest—stock or an interest in a partnership—is a capital asset. Consequently, a sale of such interest normally produces capital gain or capital loss (although there are some important exceptions for sales of a partnership interest). On the

[14] See § 170(e)(1). The addition of this rule overturned the holding in Rev. Rul. 75-342 1997-2 CB 341 that such assets were capital assets.

[15] *Williams v. McCowan*, 46-1 USTC ¶9120, 34 AFTR 615, 152 F.2d 570 (CA-2, 1945); Rev. Rul. 55-79, 1955-1 C.B. 370.

other hand, a sale of assets by the entity would be treated in the same manner as the sale of a sole proprietorship, a sale of each individual asset.

## ✓ CHECK YOUR KNOWLEDGE

### Review Question 1

Lois Price operates an office supply store, Office Discount, and owns the property listed below. Indicate whether each of the following assets is a capital asset. Respond yes or no.

- **a.** Refrigerator in her home used solely for personal use
- **b.** The building that houses her business
- **c.** A picture given to her by a well-known artist
- **d.** 100 shares of Chrysler Corporation stock held as an investment
- **e.** Furniture in her office
- **f.** A book of poems she has written
- **g.** The portion of her home used as a qualifying home office
- **h.** 1,000 reams of paper held for sale to customers
- **i.** Goodwill of the business

The following are capital assets: (a), (d), and (i). The other assets are not capital assets, including inventory (item h), real or depreciable property used in a trade or business (items b, e, g), literary or artistic compositions held by the creator (item f), or property received by gift from the creator (item c). Note that the Code does not exclude intangible assets from capital assets status. For example, internally generated (i.e., not previously purchased) goodwill that is sold as part of a sale of a business is treated as a capital asset.

### Review Question 2

Slam-Dunk Corporation manufactures collapsible basketball rims in Houston, Texas. Because of its tremendous growth, Mr. Slam and Ms. Dunk, the owners of the company, brought in a highly skilled executive to manage it, the famous Sam Jam. As part of the employment agreement, the company agreed to buy Sam's house if it should terminate his contract. Slam and Dunk did not get along with Sam and his creative management techniques. Consequently, the corporation dismissed Sam after two years and purchased his house at Sam's original cost of $300,000. Needing the cash, the corporation decided to unload the house immediately. Unfortunately, in the depressed housing market of Houston, the corporation sold the house for only $200,000. Explain the tax problems associated with the sale by the corporation. What important issue must be resolved and why?

In this situation, the corporation has realized a loss of $100,000. The critical issue is determining whether the loss is an ordinary or capital loss. The treatment, as explained below, is quite different. If the loss is ordinary, the corporation may deduct the entire loss in computing taxable income. In contrast, if the loss is a capital loss, the corporation can deduct the loss only to the extent of any capital gains that it has during the year or a three-year carryback and five-year carryforward period. The determination turns on the definition of a capital asset.

# Sale or Exchange Requirement

Before capital gain or loss treatment applies, the property must be disposed of in a "sale or exchange." In most cases, determining whether a sale or exchange has occurred is not difficult. The requirement is met by most routine transactions and as a practical matter is often overlooked. Nevertheless, there are a number of situations when a sale or exchange does not actually occur but the Code steps in and creates one, thus converting what might have been ordinary income or loss to capital gain or capital loss. Several of these are considered below.

## WORTHLESS AND ABANDONED PROPERTY

When misfortune strikes, leaving the taxpayer with worthless property, the taxpayer normally has a loss equal to the adjusted basis of the property. Note, however, that the loss in these situations does not technically arise from a sale or exchange, leaving the taxpayer to wonder how the loss is to be treated.

### Worthless Securities

The Code has addressed this problem with respect to worthless securities (e.g., stocks and bonds). In the event that a qualifying security becomes worthless at any time during the taxable year, the resulting loss is treated as having arisen from the sale or exchange of a capital asset on the last day of the taxable year.[16] Losses from worthlessness are then treated as either short-term or long-term capital losses depending on the taxpayer's holding period.

#### Example 3

After receiving a hot tip, N bought 200 shares of Shag Carpets, Inc. for $2,000 on November 1, 2010. Just three months later, on February 1, 2011, N received a shocking notice that the company had declared bankruptcy and her investment was worthless. Because of the worthlessness, N is treated as having sold the stock for nothing on the last day of her taxable year, December 31, 2011. Because the sale is deemed to occur on December 31, 2011 (and not February 1), N is treated as if she actually held the stock for more than a year. As a result, she reports a $2,000 long-term capital loss.

The sale or exchange fiction applies only to qualifying securities. To qualify, the security must be (1) a capital asset and (2) a security as defined by the Code. Under § 165, the term *security* means stock, stock rights, and bonds, notes, or other forms of indebtedness issued by a corporation or the government. When these rules do not apply (e.g., property other than securities), the taxpayer suffers an ordinary loss. Whether a security actually becomes worthless during a given year is a question of fact, and the burden of proof is on the taxpayer to show that the security became worthless during the year in question.[17]

### Worthless Securities in Affiliated Corporations

The basic rule for worthless securities is modified for a corporate taxpayer's investment in securities of an affiliated corporation. If securities of an affiliated corporation become worthless, the loss is treated as an ordinary loss and the limitations that normally apply if the loss were a capital loss are avoided.[18] A corporation is considered affiliated to a parent corporation if the parent owns at least 80 percent of the voting power of all classes of stock and at least 80 percent of each class of nonvoting stock of the affiliated corporation. In addition, to be treated as an affiliated corporation for purposes of the worthless security provisions, the defunct corporation must have been truly an operating company. This test is met if the corporation has less than 10 percent of the aggregate of its gross receipts from passive sources such as rents, royalties, dividends, annuities, and gains from sales or exchanges of stock and securities. This condition prohibits ordinary loss treatment for what are really investments.

#### Example 4

Toy Palace Corporation is the parent corporation for more than 100 subsidiary corporations that operate toy stores all over the country. Each subsidiary is 100 percent owned by Toy Palace. This year the store in Chicago, TPC Inc., declared bankruptcy. As a result, Toy Palace's investment in TPC stock of $1 million became totally worthless. Toy Palace is allowed to treat the $1 million loss as an ordinary loss since TPC was an affiliated corporation (i.e., Toy Palace owned at least 80 percent of TPC's

---

[16] § 165(g).

[17] *Young v. Comm.*, 41-2 USTC ¶9744, 28 AFTR 365, 123 F.2d 597 (CA-2, 1941). Code § 6511(d) extends the statute of limitations from three years to seven years because of the difficulty of determining the specific tax year in which stock becomes worthless.

[18] § 165(g)(3).

stock and TPC was an operating corporation). Observe that without this special rule, Toy Palace would have a $1 million capital loss that it could deduct only if it had capital gains currently or within the three-year carryback or five-year carryforward period.

### Abandoned Property

While the law creates a sale or exchange for worthless securities, it takes a different approach for abandoned business or investment property. When worthless property (other than stocks and securities) is abandoned, the abandonment is not considered a sale or exchange.[19] Consequently, any loss arising from an abandonment is treated as an ordinary loss rather than a capital loss, a much more propitious result. Note, however, that the loss is deductible only if the taxpayer can demonstrate that the business or investment property has been truly abandoned and not simply taken out of service temporarily.

## Certain Casualties and Thefts

Still another exception to the sale or exchange requirement involves *excess* casualty and theft gains from the involuntary conversion of *personal use assets.* As discussed in Chapter 10, § 165(h) provides that if personal casualty or theft gains *exceed* personal casualty or theft losses for any taxable year, each such gain and loss must be treated as a gain or loss from the sale or exchange of a capital asset. Each separate casualty or theft loss must be reduced by $100 before being netted with the personal casualty or theft gains.

### Example 5

T had three separate casualties involving personal-use assets during the year:

| | | | Fair Market Value | |
|---|---|---|---|---|
| *Casualty* | *Property* | *Adjusted Basis* | *Before Casualty* | *After Casualty* |
| 1. Accident | Personal car | $12,000 | $ 8,500 | $ 6,000 |
| 2. Robbery | Jewelry | 1,000 | 4,000 | 0 |
| 3. Hurricane | Residence | 60,000 | 80,000 | 58,000 |

T received insurance reimbursements as follows: (1) $900 for repair of the car; (2) $3,200 for the theft of her jewelry; and (3) $21,500 for the damages to her home. Assuming T does not elect (under § 1033) to purchase replacement jewelry, her personal casualty gain exceeds her personal casualty losses by $300, computed as follows:

1. The loss for the car is $1,500 [(lesser of $2,500 decline in value or the $12,000 adjusted basis = $2,500) – $900 insurance recovery – $100 floor].
2. The gain for the jewelry is $2,200 ($3,200 insurance recovery – $1,000 adjusted basis).
3. The loss from the residence is $400 [(lesser of $22,000 decline in value or the $60,000 adjusted basis = $22,000) – $21,500 insurance recovery – $100 floor].

T must report each separate gain and loss as a gain or loss from the sale or exchange of a capital asset. The classification of each gain and loss as short-term or long-term depends on the holding period of each asset.

It is important to note that this exception *does not* apply if the personal casualty losses exceed the gains. In such case, the *net* loss, subject to the 10 percent limitation, is deductible *from*

[19] Reg. §§ 1.165-2 and 1.167(a)-8.

A.G.I. Recall, however, that casualty and theft losses are among those itemized deductions that are not subject to the deduction cutback rule imposed on high-income taxpayers. (See Chapter 11 for a discussion of this cutback rule.)

### Example 6

Assume the same facts in *Example 5* except the insurance recovery from the hurricane damage to the residence was only $11,500. In this case, the loss from the hurricane is $10,400 ($22,000 – $11,500 – $100), and the personal casualty losses exceed the gain by $9,700 ($1,500 + $10,400 – $2,200). T must treat the $9,700 net loss as an itemized deduction subject to the 10% of A.G.I. limitation, but not subject to the cutback rule.

### Other Transactions

There are still other situations where the sale or exchange requirement is an important consideration. For example, foreclosure, condemnation, and other involuntary events are treated as sales even though they may not qualify as such for state law purposes. Similarly, as discussed in greater detail later in this chapter, the collection of the face value of a corporate bond (i.e., bond redemption) at maturity is treated as a sale or exchange.

## Holding Period

**LO.4**
Explain the holding period rules for classifying a capital asset transaction as either short-term or long-term.

The exact treatment of a capital gain or loss depends primarily on how long the taxpayer held the asset or what is technically referred to as the taxpayer's *holding period.* The holding period is a critical element in determining which of the various tax rates will apply. As might be expected, the longer the holding period is, the lower the applicable tax rate will be. A *short term* gain or loss is one resulting from the sale or disposition of an asset held *one year or less.*[20] A *long-term* gain or loss occurs when an asset is held for *more than one year.*

In computing the holding period, the day of acquisition is not counted but the day of sale is. The holding period is based on calendar months and fractions of calendar months, rather than on the number of days.[21] The fact that different months contain different numbers of days (i.e., 28, 30, or 31) is disregarded.

### Example 7

P purchased 10 shares of EX, Inc. on March 16, 2011. Her gain or loss on the sale is short-term if the stock is sold on or before March 16, 2012, but long-term if sold on or after March 17, 2012.

### Example 8

T purchased 100 shares of FMC Corp. stock on February 28, 2011. His gain or loss will be long-term if he sells the stock on or after March 1, 2012.

The holding period runs from the time property is acquired until the time of its disposition. Property is generally considered *acquired* or *disposed* of when title passes from one party to another. State law usually controls the passage of title and must be consulted when questions arise.

[20] § 1222.

[21] Rev. Rul. 66-7, 1966-1 C.B.188.

## Stock Exchange Transactions

The holding period for securities traded on a stock exchange is determined in the same manner as for other property. The trade dates, rather than the settlement dates, are used as the dates of acquisition and sale.

Generally, both cash and accrual basis taxpayers must report (recognize) gains and losses on stock or security sales in the tax year of the trade, even though cash payment (settlement) may not be received until the following year. This requirement is imposed because the installment method of reporting gains is not allowed for sales of stock or securities that are traded on an established securities market.[22]

> **Example 9**
>
> C, a cash basis calendar year taxpayer, sold 300 shares of ARA stock at a gain of $5,000 on December 29, 2011. The settlement date was January 3, 2012. C must report the gain in 2011 (the year of trade).

## Special Rules and Exceptions

Section 1223 contains a number of special provisions that must be used for determining the holding period of certain properties. The rules address the holding period of property acquired (1) in a tax-deferred exchange; (2) by gift; (3) by inheritance; (4) in a wash sale; (5) as a stock dividend; or (6) by exercising stock rights or options.

### Property Acquired in Tax-Deferred Transaction

The holding period of property received in an exchange *includes* the holding period of the property given up in the exchange if the basis of the property is determined by reference, in whole or in part, to the basis in that property given up (e.g., a substituted basis in a like-kind exchange).[23] This rule applies only if the property exchanged is a capital asset or a § 1231 asset (e.g., real or depreciable property used in a trade or business) at the time of the exchange. For this purpose, an involuntary conversion–where the taxpayer normally purchases replacement property for that which was involuntarily converted—is treated as an exchange.[24]

As suggested above, this rule commonly can be found operating when there is a like-kind exchange. For example, if a taxpayer purchased land on May 16, 1981 and swapped it for other land in 2011, the taxpayer's holding period for the new land would begin in 1981 since the basis of the new land is the same as the old land, $50,000, (i.e., the basis of the new land was "determined by reference" to the property given up). Normally, if any gain or loss is deferred, the holding period of the replacement property includes the holding period of the property that was converted or exchanged.

> **Example 10**
>
> In 2010, the city of Milwaukee condemned 10 acres of M's farm land (a § 1231 asset) in order to build an exit for an interstate highway. M had acquired the land on May 1, 1997 for $20,000. M received $120,000 for the land and therefore realized a gain of $100,000. On July 7, 2012, M replaced the property by purchasing new land for $120,000. As a result, he was able to defer all of the realized gain, producing a basis for the new property of $20,000 ($120,000 cost less $100,000 deferred gain). Since an involuntary conversion is treated as an exchange, M's holding period begins on the date that he acquired the original property, May 1, 1997.

---

[22] § 453(k)(2). See Chapter 14 for a detailed discussion of the installment sale method.

[23] § 1223(1).

[24] § 1223(1)(A).

### Property Acquired by Gift

Another exception provides that if a taxpayer's basis in property is the same basis as another taxpayer had in that property, in whole or in part, the holding period will include that of the other person.[25] Therefore, the holding period of property acquired by gift generally will include the holding period of the donor. This will not be true, however, if the property is sold at a loss and the basis in the property for determining the loss is fair market value on the date of the gift. If the donee's basis is fair market at the date of the gift, the donee's holding period begins on the date of the gift.

**Example 11**

G received a gold necklace from her elderly grandmother as a birthday gift on August 31, 2011. The necklace was worth $5,200 at that time and had a basis to the grandmother of $1,300. Grandmother had bought the necklace in 1977. Contrary to her grandmother's wishes, G sold the family heirloom for $5,000 on December 13, 2011. G will recognize a gain of $3,700 ($5,000 – $1,300). Her holding period began in 1977 since her $1,300 basis is determined (under § 1015) by reference to her grandmother's basis, *and* her holding period includes the time the necklace was held by her grandmother.

**Example 12**

If G's grandmother had a basis in the necklace of $6,000, G's basis for determining loss would be $5,200, the fair market value at the date of the gift (see discussion in Chapter 14). Because G's basis is *not* determined by reference to her grandmother's basis, the grandmother's holding period is not added to G's holding period and the holding period begins on the date of the gift. Since G only held the necklace for three months, she will have a $200 short-term capital loss ($5,200 basis – $5,000 sales price).

### Property Acquired from a Decedent

A special rule is provided for the holding period of property acquired from a decedent. The holding period formally begins on the date of death. However, the Code provides that, if the heir's basis in the property is its fair market value under § 1014 and the property is subsequently sold after the decedent's death, the property is deemed to have a long-term holding period.[26]

**Example 13**

P sold 50 shares of Xero Corp. stock for $11,200 on July 27, 2011. The stock was inherited from P's uncle who died on May 16, 2011, and it was included in the uncle's Federal estate tax return at a fair market value of $12,000. Since P's basis in the stock ($12,000) is determined under § 1014, the $800 loss on the sale will be a capital loss from property deemed to be held more than 12 months. This would be the case even if P's uncle had purchased the stock within days of his death. The decedent's prior holding period is irrelevant.

### Other Holding Period Rules

There are various other provisions that contain special rules for determining holding periods. The holding period of stock acquired in a transaction in which a loss was disallowed under

---

[25] § 1223(2).

[26] § 1223(9).

the "wash sale" provisions (§ 1091) is added to the holding period of the replacement stock.[27] Also, when a shareholder receives stock dividends or stock rights as a result of owning stock in a corporation, the holding period of the stock or stock rights includes the holding period of the stock already owned in the corporation.[28] The holding period of any stock acquired by exercising stock rights, however, begins on the date of exercise.[29]

The holding period of property acquired by exercise of an option begins on the day after the option is exercised.[30] If a taxpayer sells the property acquired by option within one year after exercising the option, then he or she will have a short-term gain or loss.

**Example 14**

N owned an option to purchase ten acres of land. She had owned the option more than one year when she exercised it and purchased the property. Her holding period for the property begins on the day after she exercises the option. Had she sold the option, her gain or loss would have been long-term. If she had sold the property immediately, her gain or loss would have been short-term.

The holding period of a commodity acquired in satisfaction of a commodity futures contract includes the holding period of the futures contract. However, the futures contract must have been a capital asset in the hands of the taxpayer.[31]

## Treatment of Capital Gains and Losses

The Taxpayer Relief Act of 1997 and the amendments of the Jobs and Growth Tax Relief Reconciliation Act of 2003 significantly cut the tax rates on capital gains but not without introducing an inordinate amount of complexity. The adventure begins below.

### The Process in General

**LO.5**
Apply the capital gain and loss netting process to a taxpayer's capital asset transactions and explain their treatment.

The first step in determining the treatment of a taxpayer's capital gain or loss is identifying the applicable holding period. Once the holding period is determined, the gain or loss can normally be assigned to an appropriate group to determine its taxation. Historically, there have only been two groups: short-term and long-term. However, beginning in 1997, the law made the classification process a bit more cumbersome, producing the following groups for individual taxpayers.

- *Short-Term Group.* Gains and losses from properties held not more than one year
- *Long-Term Group.* Generally gains and losses from properties held more than one year. However, individual taxpayers must subdivide the long-term group into additional subgroups according to the rate at which they are to be taxed. The long-term group includes:

  1. The 28% group (28CG and 28CL)
     - Capital gains and losses from collectibles (e.g., works of art, antiques, gold and silver bullion, etc.).[32]

---

[27] § 1223(3); Reg. § 1.1223-1(d).

[28] § 1223(5); Reg. § 1.1223-1(e).

[29] § 1223(6); Reg. § 1.1223-1(f).

[30] See, for example, *Helvering v. San Joaquin Fruit & Inv. Co.*, 36-1 USTC ¶9144, 17 AFTR 470, 297 U.S. 496 (USSC, 1936), and *E.T. Weir*, 49-1 USTC ¶9190, 37 AFTR 1022, 173 F.2d 222 (CA-3, 1949).

[31] § 1223(8); Reg. § 1.1223-1(h).

[32] § 1(h)(1)(C) and (h)(4).

- Capital gains from qualified small business stock (taxable portion of § 1202 gains discussed below).

2. The 25% group (25CG)
   - Capital *gains* (and only gains) from the sales of depreciable real estate (e.g., office buildings, warehouses, apartment buildings) that are held for more than 12 months but only to the extent of any unrecaptured straight-line depreciation on such property. (See Chapter 17 for discussion of depreciation recapture.)
3. The 15% group (15CG and 15CL)
   - Capital gains and losses from the dispositions of other capital assets held more than 12 months.

The effect of the rules is to require taxpayers to assign their capital gains and losses into one of four different groups and net the amounts to determine the net gain or loss in each group as shown below.

| | *Short-Term* | *Long-Term* | | |
|---|---|---|---|---|
| Holding period (months) | ≤12<br>Ordinary | Collectibles & § 1202 stock > 12<br>28% | Realty > 12<br>25% | > 12<br>15% |
| Gains | $xx,xxx | $x,xxx | Gains only | $xx,xxx |
| Losses | (xxx) | (x,xxx) | — | (x,xxx) |
| Net gain or loss | ???? | ???? | Gain only | ???? |

The capital gains of most individuals arise from sales of stocks and bonds and mutual fund transactions. Rarely do individuals have gains from collectibles, § 1202 stock, or depreciable realty. Consequently, for most individuals, the classification and netting process is much easier.

## Netting Process

Generalizations about the treatment of capital gains and losses are difficult because the actual treatment can be determined only after the various groups (i.e., the four groups above) are combined, or netted, to determine the overall net gain or loss during the year. This process is described below.[33]

### Netting within Groups

The first step in the netting process is to combine the gains and losses within each group to produce one of the following:

1. Net short-term capital gain or net short-term capital loss (NSTCG or NSTCL).
2. Net 28% capital gain or net 28% capital loss (N28CG or N28CL).
3. Net 15% capital gain or net 15% capital loss (N15CG or N15CL).

Note that the first step requires no netting in the 25% group since this group initially contains only gains.

### Netting between Groups

The second step requires the combination of the net capital loss positions in any particular group against any net capital gain positions. The treatment of these different groups is explained below.

1. *Short-Term Capital Gains and Losses.* A NSTCG receives no special treatment and is taxed as ordinary income. If a NSTCL results, it may be used to offset net gains of the long-term group in the following order: (1) the net 28% gain; (2) any 25% gain; and (3) the net 15% gain. Any remaining NSTCL not absorbed by the capital gains in the groups above is deductible subject to limitations on the deduction of capital losses discussed below.
2. *28% Group.* A N28CG is taxed at a maximum 28%.[34] Any net loss in the 28% group (N28CL) is applied in the following order: (1) 25% gain; (2) net 15% gain; and (3)

[33] § 1(h)(1).

[34] § 1(h)(1)(C). Note that 28% gains are taxed at the lower rates (10%, 15%, 25%), if such brackets are not filled by the taxpayer's other taxable income.

NSTCG. Any remaining N28CL that is not absorbed is deductible subject to limitations on the deduction of capital losses discussed below.

3. *25% Group.* The 25% group generally includes *only* capital *gains* from the sales of depreciable real estate held for more than 12 months. Such gains are only included to the extent of any unrecaptured straight-line depreciation on such property. The net 25% capital gain (N25CG) is taxed at a maximum rate of 25%.[35] Note that there can be no net loss in the 25% group.
4. *15% Group.* A N15CG is taxed at a maximum of 15%. However, if the taxpayer's tax bracket (determined by *including* the N15CG) is only 10 or 15%, the net gain falling into these brackets is taxed at 0%.[36] Any N15CL is applied in the following order: (1) the net 28% gain; (2) any 25% gain; and (3) any NSTCG. Any remaining N15CL not absorbed is deductible subject to limitations on the deduction of capital losses discussed below.

It should be noted that the three *long-term* groups (the 28%, 25% and 15% groups) are always netted together before taking into accounting any short-term items. Also observe that Congress has generally given taxpayers the best possible treatment of net capital losses in that a NSTCL offsets the net capital gain from the highest taxed group, then the next highest taxed and so on.

## Example 15

During the year, T, who is in the 35 percent tax bracket, reported the following capital gains and losses.

| | | Long-Term | |
|---|---|---|---|
| | *Short-Term* | *28%* | *15%* |
| Gains | $10,000 | $5,000 | $8,000 |
| Losses | (4,000) | (1,000) | (1,000) |
| Net | $ 6,000 | $4,000 | $7,000 |

In this case, T first nets the items within each group. She nets the $10,000 STCG and $4,000 STCL to arrive at a NSTCG of $6,000; she nets a $5,000 28CG and a $1,000 28CL to produce a N28CG of $4,000; and she nets the $8,000 15CG and the $1,000 15CL, resulting in a N15CG of $7,000. No further netting of these groups can occur since each group contains a positive amount. T's NSTCG of $6,000 receives no special treatment and is taxed as ordinary income. T's N28CG is taxed at 28% while her N15CG is taxed at 15%.

## Example 16

This year, L, who is in the 28% tax bracket, reported the following capital gains and losses:

| | | Long-Term | |
|---|---|---|---|
| | *Short-Term* | *28%* | *15%* |
| Gains | $10,000 | $5,000 | $8,000 |
| Losses | (15,000) | (1,000) | (1,000) |
| Net | ($5,000) | $4,000 | $7,000 |

35 § 1(h)(1)(B). Note that 25% gains are taxed at the lower rates (10% or 15%) if such brackets are not filled by the taxpayer's other taxable income.

36 § 1(h)(1)(D) and (E). The 0% rate was extended through 2012 by the Tax Relief, Unemployment Insurance Reauthorization, and Job Creation Act of 2010. Note that this is not the case with 25% and 28% gains, which would be taxed at the normal 10 or 15% rate.

| | Short-Term | Long-Term 28% | Long-Term 15% |
|---|---|---|---|
| Netting | 5,000 | (4,000) | (1,000) |
| Net | $ 0 | $ 0 | $6,000 |

Here L has a NSTCL of $5,000 which is netted *first* against N28CG of $4,000, reducing it to zero. The remaining NSTCL of $1,000 would next be offset against N25CG, if any. In this case, there is no N25CG, therefore the remaining NSTCL of $1,000 is offset against the N15CG of $7,000, reducing it to $6,000 which would be taxed at a rate of 15%.

## Example 17

This year, X, who is in the 35% tax bracket, reported the following capital gains and losses:

| | Short-Term | Long-Term 28% | Long-Term 25% | Long-Term 15% |
|---|---|---|---|---|
| Gains | $14,000 | $1,000 | $1,000 | $6,000 |
| Losses | (4,000) | (9,000) | — | (1,000) |
| Net | $10,000 | ($8,000) | $1,000 | $5,000 |
| Netting | (2,000) | 8,000 | (1,000) | (5,000) |
| Net | $ 8,000 | $ 0 | $ 0 | $ 0 |

Here X has a N28CL of $8,000 which is netted first against the 25CGs of $1,000, reducing this group to zero. X next uses the remaining $7,000 N28CL to offset his $5,000 N15CG, reducing it to zero. The remaining N28CL of $2,000 ($7,000 – $5,000) is offset against NSTCG, producing a NSTCG of $8,000 which is treated as ordinary income. Note that the effect of the rules is to net the long-term groups before considering any short-term items. Absent these rules, X would prefer to use the N28CL loss against the NSTCG which would leave $5,000 to be taxed at 15% and $2,000 to be taxed as ordinary income, a far more beneficial result. X must net the long-term groups first.

### Treatment of Capital Losses

While capital gains receive favorable treatment, such is not the case with capital losses. As can be seen above, capital losses are first netted with capital gains within the same group (rather than reducing ordinary income). A net capital loss from a particular group can then be combined with net capital gains from the other groups. If after netting all of the groups together, the taxpayer has an overall net capital loss, the loss is deductible against ordinary income. This deduction is limited to the lesser of (1) $3,000 ($1,500 in the case of a married individual filing a separate return) or (2) the net capital loss. In either case, the capital loss deduction cannot exceed taxable income before the deduction.[37] The deductible capital loss is a deduction *for* adjusted gross income. Any losses in excess of the annual $3,000 limitation are carried forward to the following year where they are treated as if they actually occurred in such year. In effect, an unused capital loss can be carried over for an indefinite period.[38] However, should the taxpayer die, any unused capital loss is normally lost.

If the netting process results in a NSTCL and either a N28CL or N15CL or both, the NSTCL is applied first toward the maximum $3,000 limit. For example, if the taxpayer has a NSTCL of $5,000 and a N15CL of $4,000, the NSTCL is used first. Any NSTCL in excess of

[37] § 1212(b).

[38] Reg. § 1.211-1(b)(4)(i).

the $3,000 limit along with any other unused losses may be carried forward to subsequent years indefinitely. In this case, the NSTCL carryover retains its character to be treated just as if it had occurred in the subsequent year. The N15CL or N28CL are both carried over as N28CLs. In other words, any long-term capital loss carryover is carried over as a 28CL. In the example above, $3,000 of the $5,000 NSTCL would be used first against ordinary income and the $2,000 remaining would be carried over as a STCL while the $4,000 N15CL would be carried over as a 28CL. In the absence of a NSTCL or, if after deducting any existing NSTCL, the taxpayer has not reached the annual $3,000 limit for the capital loss deduction, the taxpayer uses any other net capital losses (e.g., the excess of N15CL over N28CG and N25CG or the excess of N28CL over 25 CG and N15CG) to reduce ordinary income up to the $3,000 limit.[39] In this regard, the order in which the remaining net capital losses are used is irrelevant since any remaining losses (i.e., the long-term losses) are carried over as a N28CL which is treated as if it occurred in the subsequent year.

## Example 18

During the year, B reported the capital gains and losses revealed below. B's only other taxable income included his salary of $50,000. He had no other deductions for A.G.I. The combination of gains, losses, and ordinary income is shown in the following table.

| | | Long-Term | |
|---|---|---|---|
| | *Short-Term* | *28%* | *15%* |
| Gains | $ 10,000 | $ 5,000 | $ 9,000 |
| Losses | (18,000) | (7,000) | (6,000) |
| Net | ($ 8,000) | ($ 2,000) | $ 3,000 |
| Netting (long-term against long-term) | | 2,000 | (2,000) |
| | | $ 0 | $ 1,000 |
| Netting (long-term against short-term) | 1,000 | | (1,000) |
| | ($ 7,000) | | $ 0 |
| Deduction | 3,000 | | |
| Carryover | ($ 4,000) | | |

B first nets the long-term items, that is, the N28CL of $2,000 is netted against the N15CG of $3,000. This produces a N15CG of $1,000 ($3,000 – $2,000). B then combines the $8,000 NSTCL and the remaining N15CG of $1,000, leaving a NSTCL of $7,000. In determining his A.G.I., B may deduct only $3,000 of the NSTCL. Therefore his A.G.I. is $47,000 ($50,000 – $3,000). The unused NSTCL of $4,000 ($7,000 – $3,000) is carried forward to future years as a STCL where it is treated as if it arose in the subsequent year.

## Example 19

This year, Q reported the capital gains and losses as shown below. He had no other deductions for A.G.I. The combination of gains, losses, and ordinary income is revealed in the following table.

| | | Long-Term | |
|---|---|---|---|
| | *Short-Term* | *28%* | *15%* |
| Gains | $ 1,000 | $ 5,000 | $ 4,000 |
| Losses | (2,000) | (3,000) | (9,000) |
| Net | ($ 1,000) | $ 2,000 | ($ 5,000) |

[39] § 1211(a).

| | Short-Term | Long-Term 28% | Long-Term 15% |
|---|---|---|---|
| Netting (long-term against long-term) | 0 | (2,000) | 2,000 |
| Net | ($ 1,000) | $ 0 | ($ 3,000) |
| Deduction | 1,000 | | 2,000 |
| Carryover | $ 0 | | ($ 1,000) |

Here Q has a NSTCL of $1,000 and a net $5,000 N15CL. He first combines the long-term groups, using $2,000 of the $5,000 N15CL to offset the N28CG of $2,000, reducing it to zero. The remaining $3,000 normally would be netted against 25CG if there were any. No further netting is allowed. Therefore, J first uses the NSTCL of $1,000 and then $2,000 of the $3,000 N15CG remaining toward the $3,000 offset against ordinary income. The remaining N15CL of $1,000 is carried over and is treated as a *28CL*. It should be emphasized that the N15CL of $1,000 does not retain its character but becomes a capital loss in the 28% group. Note that the carryover rule is quite favorable. If next year J had $1,000 of N28CG and $1,000 of N15CG, the carryover would wipe out the N28CG, leaving the most favorable gain to be taxed.

## Example 20

W's records for 2010 and 2011 revealed substantial ordinary income and the following capital gains and losses:

| | Short-Term | Long-Term 28% | Long-Term 15% |
|---|---|---|---|
| 2010 gains | $ 1,000 | $ 5,000 | $ 4,000 |
| 2010 losses | (2,000) | (9,000) | (9,000) |
| | $ (1,000) | $ (4,000) | $ (5,000) |
| 2011 | $ 10,000 | $ 12,000 | $ 15,000 |

In 2010, there can be no further netting. Therefore, W first uses the NSTCL of $1,000 against ordinary income and then uses $2,000 of the $9,000 in long-term losses, leaving a long-term capital loss carryover of $7,000. Note that it makes no difference which long-term loss is used (i.e., the 28% loss or the 15% loss) since all long-term capital loss carryovers are treated as 28CLs.

In 2011, W treats the $7,000 long-term capital loss carryover as a N28CL. As a result, W would report a N28CG of $5,000 ($12,000 – the $7,000 loss carryover), N15CG of $15,000 and a NSTCG of $10,000.

## Dividends Taxed at Capital Gain Rates

In negotiations related to the *Jobs and Growth Tax Relief Reconciliation Act of 2003*, Congress and the Bush administration considered a number of alternative statutory schemes to reduce or eliminate the double taxation of corporate dividends. In the end, Congress opted to reduce the tax on dividends as well as capital gains. These measures were part of what are commonly referred to as the "Bush tax cuts."

Beginning in 2003, qualifying dividends are taxed at capital gains rates:[40] 15 percent generally and in 2008–2012, 0 percent for dividends that would otherwise be taxed at an ordinary rate of 15 percent or lower. Qualified dividends are not included in the capital gain and loss netting process but are simply added to the net capital gain for purposes of computing the tax. As a result, the dividends are taxed at capital gains rates regardless of whether the taxpayer has other capital gains or losses.[41]

*Qualified dividends* are dividends from domestic corporations or qualified foreign corporations but only if the stock meets a holding period requirement.[42] *Qualified foreign corporations* generally include those that are incorporated in possessions of the United States, those subject to a treaty with the U.S. (involving the exchange of tax information by the governments) and others, the stocks of which are traded on a U.S. stock exchange (certain foreign corporations that are not subject to U.S. tax are not included). The holding period test requires the taxpayer to hold the stock for more than 60 days during a 120 day window that begins 60 days before the stock goes ex-dividend. This requirement helps prevent taxpayers from exploiting the preferential treatment for dividends. To illustrate the possible injustice, consider a taxpayer who buys a stock a few days before the ex-dividend date, receives a $1,000 dividend and then sells the stock. Assuming the value of the stock drops in direct proportion to the amount of the dividend, a sale immediately after the ex-dividend date would produce a $1,000 short-term capital loss. It appears that the $1,000 dividend is offset by the $1,000 loss and the net effect is zero. However, the dividend is taxed at 15 percent and the loss may offset ordinary income that is taxed at 35 percent. In such case, the taxpayer is better-off by $200 ($350 − $1500). The holding period rule requires taxpayers to be at risk for at least 61 days if they want to use this scheme.[43]

## CORPORATE TAXPAYERS

**LO.6**
Explain the differences in tax treatment of the capital gains and losses of a corporate taxpayer versus those of an individual taxpayer.

The capital gains and losses of corporate taxpayers are treated a bit differently from those of individual taxpayers. Corporations separate all of their capital gains and losses into only two groups: short-term and long-term (holding period of more than one year). Unlike individuals, there is no further subdividing of the long-term group. Items within the groups are then netted, producing one of the following: NLTCG, NLTCL, NSTCG or NSTCL. If the taxpayer has a NSTCG and a NLTCG, no further netting is allowed. However, if the taxpayer has either a NSTCL and NLTCG or a NSTCG and a NLTCL, these results can be combined to produce a final position. This can be illustrated as follows:

| | *Short-Term* | *Long-Term* | *Result* |
|---|---|---|---|
| Holding period (months) | ≤ 12 | >12 | |
| Gains | $xx,xxx | $xx,xxx | |
| Losses | (xxx) | (x,xxx) | |
| Net gain or loss | ???? | ???? | |
| Possibilities | NSTCG | NLTCG | No further netting |
| | NSTCG | NLTCL | NLTCL or NSTCG |
| | NSTCL | NLTCG | NSTCL or NLTCG |
| | NSTCL | NLTCL | No further netting |

A corporate taxpayer receives no special treatment for either a NSTCG or NLTCG.[44] They are treated just like ordinary income. If after netting, the corporation has a NSTCL or a NLTCL,

[40] § 1(h)(11). The 0% rate was extended through 2012 by the *Tax Relief, Unemployment Insurance Reauthorization, and Job Creation Act of 2010.*

[41] Like other long-term capital gains, dividends qualifying for capital gain treatment are not investment income for purposes of the investment interest limitation. However, a taxpayer can elect to treat the dividends as investment income and forego the capital gain treatment. See § 1(h)(11)(D)(i).

[42] § 1(h)(11)(B).

[43] The holding period is extended for preferred stock. For other special rules see § 1(h)(11).

[44] For tax years ending after May 22, 2008 and beginning before May 22, 2009, NLTCGs from the sale of certain timber by a C Corporation are taxed at a maximum rate of 15 percent. See § 1201(b).

such losses receive special treatment. Unlike an individual taxpayer, a corporation is not allowed to offset capital losses against ordinary income. A corporate taxpayer's capital losses can be used only to reduce its capital gains.[45] Any excess losses are first carried back to the three prior years as *short-term capital losses* and offset against any net short-term capital gains and then any net long-term capital gains. Absent any capital gains in the three prior years, or if the loss carried back exceeds any capital gains, the excess may be carried forward for five years.[46] If the loss is not used at the end of the five year period, it is lost.

### Example 21

An examination of C Corporation's records for 2011 revealed $200,000 of net ordinary taxable income, a long-term capital loss of $9,000 and a short-term capital gain of $2,000. The corporation nets the loss against the gain to produce a NLTCL of $7,000. The corporation cannot offset the loss against ordinary income and, therefore, reports $200,000 of taxable income (undiminished by the NLTCL). Instead the NLTCL is carried back to the third prior year, 2008, as a STCL where it can be used to first offset any NSTCG and then any NLTCG. If there are no capital gains in 2008, the corporation would carryover the loss, now a STCL of $7,000, to 2009 to use against capital gains. This process would continue until the loss is entirely used or it expires at the end of 2016. Note that when the loss is used in prior years, an immediate refund can be obtained.

## Calculating the Tax

Section 1(h) provides a special tax calculation to ensure that an individual's capital gains will not be taxed at a rate greater than the applicable preferred rate (i.e., in 2011 the 28%, 25%, 15%, 10% or 0% rate). This calculation can only reduce the tax, not increase it.

### Example 22

H and W are married. For 2011, their sole source of income was a 15CG of $89,500 from the sale of assets held four years. Their taxable income is computed as follows:

| | |
|---|---|
| 15CG | $89,500 |
| Standard deduction | (11,600) |
| Exemption deduction (2 × $3,700) | (7,400) |
| Taxable income | $70,500 |

The 10% and 15% tax brackets for taxpayers filing jointly in 2011 extend to $69,000 at which point any dollar of income in excess of that amount is taxed at 25%. Since all of the couple's income is from capital gain, however, none of it is taxed at the 15% or 25% ordinary brackets. The effect of the special capital gains calculation is to tax the portion of the N15CG that falls into the 10% and 15% bracket at a 0% rate and the portion that falls into the 25% bracket at 15%. Therefore, $69,000 of the N15CG is taxed at 0% and the remaining $1,500 ($70,500 – $69,000) is taxed at 15%. The total tax is $225 [($69,000 × 0% = $0) + ($1,500 × 15% = $225)].

[45] § 1212(a).

[46] *Ibid.*

## EXHIBIT 16.1 Tax Computation Involving Capital Gains

**Step 1.** Calculate the regular income tax using the regular rates on the taxpayer's taxable income

**Step 2.** Determine the tax on the *ordinary income*

a. Select the greater of—
- Ordinary taxable income (taxable income – net capital gain), or
- The lesser of—
  - The maximum amount that would be taxed at 15 percent, or
  - Taxable income – the adjusted net capital gain

b. Compute the regular income tax on this amount

**Step 3.** Determine the tax on the *net capital gain* by adding the following together

a. *Tax on 0 Percent Gains*—0 percent of the portion of the adjusted net capital gain that would have been taxed at 10 or 15 percent when added to ordinary income [i.e., the lesser of (1) the adjusted net capital gain or (2) the maximum amount that would normally be taxed at 10 or 15 percent minus the amount of ordinary income].

b. *Tax on 15 Percent Gains*—15 percent of (the adjusted net capital gain minus any 0 percent gains).

c. *Tax on 25 Percent Gains*—The lesser of
- 25 percent of the 25 percent gains, or
- If less, (1) 10 or 15 percent (respectively) of the amount of the 25 percent gains that, when added to ordinary income and any 0 percent gains, would be taxed at 10 or 15 percent*, plus (2) 25 percent of any remaining 25 percent gains.

d. *Tax on 28 Percent Gains*—The lesser of
- 28 percent of the 28 percent gains, or
- If less, (1) 10 or 15 percent (respectively) of the amount of the 28 percent gains that, when added to ordinary income, any 0 percent gains, and any 25 percent gains, would be taxed at 10 or 15 percent**, plus (2) 28 percent of any remaining 28 percent gains.

**Step 4.** Add the tax on the ordinary income (Step 2) to the tax on the net capital gain (Step 3) to get the total capital gains tax.

**Step 5.** The final tax is the lesser of the taxes computed in Step 1 and Step 4.

*This is the amount that would otherwise be taxed at 10 or 15 percent when added to ordinary income and any 0 percent gains (or stated differently, it is the maximum amount that would be taxed at 10 or 15 percent minus the amount of ordinary income and the amount of 0 percent gains).

**This is the amount that would otherwise be taxed at 10 or 15 percent when added to ordinary income, any 0 percent gains, and any 25 percent gains (or, stated differently, it is the maximum amount that would be taxed at 15 percent minus the amount of ordinary income and the amount of 0 percent gains).

It may be clear from the above example that whenever an individual's *ordinary* taxable income exceeds the amount that would be taxed at 10 or 15 percent (e.g., $69,000 in 2011 for a joint return, $46,250 for head of household and $34,500 for single), none of the N15CG is taxed at 0 percent. In such case, the taxpayer computes the tax liability by first calculating the regular tax on ordinary taxable income and adding to that a tax of 15 percent on the N15CG. On the other hand, if ordinary taxable income does not exceed the amount that is taxed at 10 or 15 percent, a portion of the N15CG is taxed at the 0 percent rate until the 10 and 15 percent brackets are exhausted. A similar approach applies for N25CGs and N28CGs.

Before proceeding, it is important to understand some statutory terms. The first term is *net capital gain*—the excess of the net long-term capital gain over the net short-term capital loss for a year. If there is no net short-term capital loss, the net capital gain is simply the net gain from the 15 percent group, the 25 percent group, and the 28 percent group combined. If there is a short-term loss, it is the excess of the combined long-term gains minus the net short-term capital loss. The second term is *adjusted net capital gain*—the net capital gain reduced (but not below zero) by the 25 percent gain and the net 28 percent gain (reduced by any net short-term capital loss).

The actual steps to compute the capital gains tax are built into Schedule D of Form 1040. They are also summarized in Exhibit 16-1.

## Example 23

J and K are married and file a joint return for 2011. They have taxable income of $84,000, including a N15CG of $15,000. Thus they have ordinary taxable income of $69,000. Their tax is computed as follows:

*Step 1:* Regular tax on $84,000 = $13,250 as computed below

| | |
|---|---|
| Tax on $69,000 (10% and 15% brackets) | $ 9,500 |
| Plus: Tax on excess at 25% [($84,000 – $69,000) × 25%] | +3,750 |
| Equals: Total tax | $13,250 |

*Step 2a:* Ordinary income = $69,000 ($84,000 – $15,000)

*Step 2b:* Regular tax on ordinary income of $69,000 = $9,500

*Step 3:* Tax on the net capital gain = $2,250 as computed below

**a.** Tax on 0% Gains = 0% of zero (All of the net capital gain would have been taxed at a rate exceeding 15% since V's ordinary income plus 25% gains and 28% gains equaled or exceeded $69,000—the limit of the 15% bracket)
**b.** Tax on 15% Gains = 15% × $15,000 = $2,250
**c.** Tax on 25% Gains = 25% of zero
**d.** Tax on 28% Gains = 28% of zero

*Step 4:* Total capital gains tax = $11,750 ($9,500 + $2,250)

*Step 5:* The final tax is $11,750. The *savings* is $1,500 ($13,250 – $11,750). Note that this $1,500 is the 10% difference (25% – 15%) on the $15,000 gain.

## Example 24

V is single for 2011 and has taxable income for the year of $100,000 including the following:

| | |
|---|---|
| Loss from stock held 11 months | ($2,000) |
| Gain from stamps held for investment 3 years | 3,000 |
| Gain from land held 9 years | 16,000 |
| Loss from stock held 2 years | (3,000) |

V would summarize his gains and losses as follows:

| | | Long-Term | |
|---|---|---|---|
| | *Short-Term* | *28%* | *15%* |
| | ($2,000) | $3,000 | $16,000 |
| | — | — | (3,000) |
| | ($2,000) | $3,000 | $13,000 |
| Netting | 2,000 | (2,000) | |
| | $ 0 | $1,000 | $13,000 |

The loss is a STCL since it was held for not more than a year. The gain on the sale of the stamps is treated as a 28CG since it is a collectible. Collectibles are treated as 28CGs even though they may have been held more than 12 months. The gain and loss from the land and stock are both classified as 15% items since they were held more than 12 months. Thus V's overall capital gain is $14,000, consisting of a N28CG of $1,000 and a N15CG of $13,000. V's tax is computed as follows:

*Step 1:* Regular tax on $100,000 = $21,617 as computed below

| | |
|---|---|
| Tax on $82,400 (10%, 15% and 25% bracket) | $17,025 |
| Plus: Tax on excess at 28% [($100,000 – $83,600) × 28%] | 4,592 |
| Equals: Total tax | $21,617 |

*Step 2a:* Ordinary income = $86,000 ($100,000 – $14,000)

*Step 2b:* Regular tax on ordinary income of $86,000 = $17,697

| | |
|---|---|
| Tax on $82,400 | $17,025 |
| Plus: Tax on excess at 28% [($86,000 – $83,600) × 28%] | 672 |
| Equals: Total tax | $17,697 |

*Step 3:* Tax on the net capital gain = $2,230 ($280 + $1,950)

**a.** Tax on 0% Gains = 0% of zero (All of the net capital gain would have been taxed at a rate exceeding 15% since V's ordinary income exceeded $34,000—the limit of the 15% bracket)

**b.** Tax on 15% Gains = 15% × $13,000 = $1,950

**c.** Tax on 25% Gains = 25% of zero

**d.** Tax on 28% Gains = 28% × $1,000 = $280

*Step 4:* Total capital gains tax = $19,927 ($17,697 + $2,230)

*Step 5:* The final tax is $19,927 (the lesser of *Step 1* or *Step 4*). The difference between the regular tax and the capital gains tax is $1,690 ($21,617 – $19,927). Note that this $1,690 is the 13% difference (28% – 15%) on $13,000 (13% × $13,000 = $1,690). There is no capital gain difference on the 28 percent gain since the ordinary rate and the capital gain rate are the same.

### Example 25

Same as *Example 22*, except V's total taxable income is $40,000.

*Step 1:* Regular tax on $40,000 = $6,125

| | |
|---|---|
| Tax on $34,500 | $4,750 |
| Plus: Tax on excess at 25% [($40,000 – $34,500) × 25%] | 1,375 |
| Equals: Total tax | $6,125 |

*Step 2a:* Ordinary income = $26,000 ($40,000 – $14,000)

*Step 2b:* Regular tax on $26,000 = $3,475 ($8,500 × 10% + $17,500 × 15%)

*Step 3:* Tax on the net capital gain = $925 ($0 + $675 + $250)

**a.** Tax on 0% Gains = $0 [$8,500 × 0%—The N15CG is taxed at 0% to the extent the limit on the 15% tax bracket exceeds the ordinary income ($34,500 – $26,000 = $8,500)]

**b.** Tax on 15% Gains = $675 [($13,000 – $8,500 = $4,500) × 15%—The adjusted net capital gain reduced by the portion taxed at 0% multiplied by 15%]

**c.** Tax on 25% Gains = 25% of zero

**d.** Tax on 28% Gains = 25% × $1,000 = $250 [Since ordinary income plus the 0% gains, 15% gains, and 25% gains are more than the limit on the 15% tax bracket ($26,000 + $13,000 + $1,000 > $34,500) but less than the top of the 25% bracket amounts, the 28% gains are taxed at 25%.]

*Step 4:* Total capital gains tax = $4,400 ($3,475 + $925)

*Step 5:* The final tax is $4,400 (the lesser of *Step 1* or *Step 4*). The difference between the regular tax and the capital gains tax is $1,725 ($6,125 – $4,400). Note that this savings of $1,725 is the sum of the 15% difference (15% – 0%) on $8,500 or $1,275 and the 10% difference (25% – 15%) on $4,500 ($13,000 – $8,500) or $450. Observe that there is no difference on the 28% gain that was taxed at the ordinary income rate.

## Reporting Capital Gains and Losses

Individual taxpayers report any capital gains or losses on Schedule D of Form 1040.[47] This form is designed to facilitate the netting process, with one part used for reporting short-term gains and losses and another part used to report long-term transactions. A third part of the form is available for the second step of the netting process in the event the taxpayer has either NSTCGs and NLTCLs *or* NLTCGs and NSTCLs.

Regular corporations must report capital gains and losses on Schedule D of Form 1120 in much the same manner as individual taxpayers. Partnerships and S corporations must also report capital gains and losses on a separate schedule (Schedule D of Form 1065 for partnerships and Schedule D of Form 1120S for S corporations). However, these conduit entities are limited to the *first* step of the netting process. Each owner (partner or S corporation shareholder) must include his or her share of the results from the entity with the appropriate capital transactions being netted on the owner's Schedule D, Form 1040.

[47] See Appendix for a sample of this form.

## ✓ Check Your Knowledge

### Review Question 1

For 2011, Ms. Reyes earned a salary of $70,000 from her job as an art curator. In addition, she sold stock, realizing the following capital gains and losses:

| | |
|---|---|
| 15CG | $10,000 |
| 15CL | (7,000) |
| STCL | (11,000) |

In 2012, she changed jobs, becoming a tax accountant and earning a salary of $300,000. In addition, she realized a 15CG of $12,000.

Compute Ms. Reyes's adjusted gross income for 2011 and 2012 and indicate the amount, if any, that is eligible for preferential treatment as long-term capital gain.

Her adjusted gross incomes for 2011 and 2012 are $67,000 and $307,000, respectively. After netting her capital gains and losses in 2011, Ms. Reyes has a net capital loss of $8,000, all of which is short-term. The deduction for capital losses of an individual is generally limited to $3,000. As a result, her adjusted gross income is $67,000 ($70,000 – $3,000). She is entitled to carry over the remainder of her short-term loss of $5,000. In 2012, she nets the $5,000 short-term capital loss against her $12,000 15CG to produce a N15CG of $7,000. The $7,000 is combined with her other $300,000 of salary income to produce an adjusted gross income of $307,000. Of this amount, her N15CG of $7,000 is taxed at a preferred rate of 15 percent.

### Review Question 2

True-False. This year Mr. and Mrs. Simpson retired. The couple's only income was a capital gain from the sale of stock held three years. Assuming the Simpsons file a joint return, all $100,000 of their taxable income is taxed at a rate of 15 percent.

*False*. The tax computation operates to ensure that the 15CG is taxed at 0 percent to the extent that ordinary income does not absorb the 10 and 15 percent brackets. For 2011 the 15 percent bracket for a joint return extends to taxable income of $69,000. Therefore, $69,000 is taxed at a 0 percent rate and the remaining $31,000 is taxed at a 15 percent rate.

The Simpsons should have considered making the sales in two separate years (perhaps 2011 and 2012) if they have no other income in either year. That would allow them to double the benefit of the 0 percent rate.

### Review Question 3

True-False. An individual taxpayer is generally entitled to deduct any capital loss recognized during the current year to the extent of any capital gains recognized plus $3,000. Any capital loss in excess of this amount retains its character and may be used in subsequent years until it is exhausted.

*True*.

## Capital Gain Treatment Extended to Certain Transactions

**LO.7** Identify various transactions to which capital gain or loss treatment has been extended.

The Internal Revenue Code contains several special provisions related to capital asset treatment. In some instances the concept of capital asset is expanded and in others it is limited. Some of the provisions merely clarify the tax treatment of certain transactions.

### Patents

Section 1235 provides that certain transfers of patents shall be treated as transfers of capital assets held for more than one year. This virtually assures that a long-term capital gain will result if the patent is transferred in a taxable transaction, because the patent will have little, if any, basis since the costs of creating it are usually deducted under §174 (research and experimental expenditures) in the tax year in which such costs are incurred. Any transfer, other than by gift, inheritance, or devise, will qualify as long as *all substantial rights* to the patent are transferred. All substantial rights have been described as all rights that have value at the time of the transfer. For example, the transfer must not limit the geographical coverage within the country of issuance or limit the time application to less than the remaining term of the patent.[48]

The transferor must be a *holder* as defined in § 1235(b). The term *holder* refers to the creator of the patented property or to an individual who purchased such property from its creator if such individual is neither the employer of the creator nor related to such creator.[49]

The sale of a patent will qualify for § 1235 treatment even if payments are made over a period that ends when the purchaser's use of the patent ceases or if payments are contingent on the productivity, use, or disposition of the patent.[50] It also is important to note that §§ 483 and 1274, which require interest to be imputed on certain sales contracts, do not apply to amounts received in exchange for patents qualifying under § 1235 that are contingent on the productivity, use, or disposition of the patent transferred.[51]

**Example 26**

K, a successful inventor, sold a patent (in which she had a basis of zero) to Bell Corp. The sale agreement called for K to receive a percentage of the sales of the property covered by the patent. All of K's payments received in consideration for this patent will be long-term capital gain regardless of her holding period.

### Lease Cancellation Payments

Section 1241 allows the treatment of payments received in cancellation of a lease or in cancellation of a distributorship agreement as having been received in a sale or exchange. Therefore, the gains or losses will be treated as capital gains or losses if the underlying assets are capital assets.[52]

## Incentives for Investments in Small Businesses

Congress has frequently provided incentives for investment in general or for specific investments. The Subchapter S election, for example, was intended to remove any impediment for small business owners who were not incorporating because they believed there was a double tax on corporate profits. Other incentives provide special treatment upon the disposition of certain business interests. The following sections deal with various prominent examples.

### Losses on Small Business Stock: § 1244

Losses on dispositions (e.g., sale or worthlessness) of corporate stock are generally classified as capital losses. For a year in which a taxpayer has no capital gains, the deduction for capital losses would be limited to $3,000 annually. In contrast, a loss on the disposition of a sole proprietorship would be recognized upon the disposition of the assets used in the business. Losses on the sale of many (if not most) of the assets would be treated as ordinary losses, thereby avoiding (or partially avoiding) the $3,000 limit. Similarly, proper planning could result in ordinary loss treatment upon the disposition of interests in businesses operated in the partnership form.

Without special rules, the limitation on deductions for capital losses might discourage investment in new corporations. For example, if an individual invested $90,000 in stock of a new corporate venture, deductions for any loss from the investment, absent off-

---

[48] Reg. § 1.1235-2(b).

[49] For definition of "relative," see § 1235(d).

[50] § 1235(a).

[51] §§ 483(d)(4) and 1274(c)(4)(E). See Chapter 14 for a discussion of the imputed interest rules.

[52] See Chapter 17 for treatment if the asset is a § 1231 asset.

setting gains, would be limited to $3,000 annually.[53] Thus, where the stock becomes worthless it could take the investor as long as 30 years to recover the investment. This restriction on losses also is inconsistent with the treatment of losses resulting from investments by an individual in his or her sole proprietorship or in a partnership. In the case of a sole proprietorship or a partnership, losses generally may be used to offset the taxpayer's other income without limitation. For example, assume a sole proprietor sank $150,000 into a purchase of pet rocks that he ultimately sold for only $100,000. In such case, he would have an ordinary loss of $50,000, all of which could be used to offset other ordinary income. Assume the same individual invested $150,000 in a corporation that had the same luck. If the taxpayer could at best sell the stock for $100,000, he would realize a capital loss of $50,000. Obviously the sole proprietor is in a much better position. To eliminate these problems and encourage taxpayers to invest in small corporations, Congress enacted § 1244 in 1958.

Under § 1244, losses on "Section 1244 stock" generally are treated as ordinary rather than capital losses.[54] Ordinary loss treatment normally is available *only to individuals* who are the original holders of the stock. If these individuals sell the stock at a loss or the stock becomes worthless, they may deduct up to $50,000 annually as an ordinary loss. Taxpayers who file a joint return may deduct up to $100,000 regardless of how the stock is owned (e.g., separately or jointly). When the loss in any one year exceeds the $50,000 or $100,000 limitation, the excess is considered a capital loss.

### Example 27

T, married, is one of the original purchasers of RST Corporation's stock, which qualifies as § 1244 stock. She separately purchased the stock two years ago for $150,000. During the year, she sold all of the stock for $30,000, resulting in a $120,000 loss. On a joint return for the current year, she may deduct $100,000 as an ordinary loss. The portion of the loss exceeding the limitation, $20,000 ($120,000 – $100,000), is treated as a long-term capital loss.

Stock issued by a corporation (including preferred stock issued after July 18, 1984) qualifies as § 1244 stock only if the issuing corporation meets certain requirements. The most important condition is that the corporation's total capitalization (amounts received for stock issued, contributions to capital, and paid-in surplus) must not exceed $1 million at the time the stock is issued.[55] This requirement effectively limits § 1244 treatment to those individuals who originally invest the first $1 million in money and property in the corporation.

### Example 28

In 2009, F provided the initial capitalization for MNO Corporation by purchasing 700 shares at a cost of $1,000 a share for a total cost of $700,000. In 2011, G purchased 500 shares at a cost of $1,000 per share or a total of $500,000. All of F's shares otherwise qualify as § 1244 stock. Only 300 of G's new shares qualify for § 1244 treatment, however, since 200 of the 500 purchased caused the corporation's total capitalization to exceed $1 million.

## Qualified Small Business Stock (§ 1202 Stock)

As part of the *Revenue Reconciliation Act of 1993*, Congress created a new tax incentive to stimulate investment in small business. By virtue of this special rule, individuals who start their own C corporations or who are original investors in C corporations (e.g., initial public offerings) may be richly rewarded for taking the risk of investing in such enterprises.

[53] A taxpayer can offset any capital losses against capital gains, if any.

[54] § 1244(a).

[55] § 1244(c)(3)(A).

### Exclusion

Under § 1202, noncorporate investors (i.e., individuals, partnerships, estates, and trusts) are allowed to exclude up to $10 million (or if greater, 10 times the invested capital) of the gain on the sale of *qualified small business stock* (QSB stock or § 1202 stock) held for more than five years.[56] The exclusion is normally 50 percent of the gain. However, that amount is increased to 75 percent for stock acquired after February 17, 2009 and before September 28, 2010. Amazingly, the exclusion is 100 percent for gain related to stock acquired after September 27, 2010 and before January 1, 2012. The balance of this gain is treated as a 28 percent gain. The effect of this provision is to impose a maximum effective tax of 14 percent (50% × 28% maximum capital gain rate), or 7 percent, or 0 percent on the gains from such investments,[57] a far lower rate than the 35 percent that may apply to other types of income received by the taxpayer.

**Example 29**

On October 31, 2004, N purchased 1,000 shares of Boston Cod Corporation for $10,000. The stock was part of an initial public offering of the company's stock that was designed to raise $30 million to open another 200 fast fish restaurants. On December 20, 2011, N sold all of her shares for $50,000. As a result, she realized a capital gain of $40,000, her only gain or loss during the year. Since N was one of the original investors and the stock qualified as § 1202 stock at the time of its issue (assets at that time were less than $50 million), she is entitled to exclude 50 percent of her gain, or $20,000. The maximum tax on the $20,000 gain is $5,600 ($20,000 × 28%). Note that if the taxpayer is in a bracket lower than 28% (e.g., 25%, 15% or 10%), the gain would be taxed at that rate.

In the netting process, only the § 1202 gain remaining after the exclusion is taken into account.

**Example 30**

Assume the same facts as above, but assume that in addition to the $40,000 gain on § 1202 stock, N also has other long-term capital gains of $10,000 and short-term capital losses of $5,000. N first applies the 50% exclusion and then nets the remainder with the other capital gains and losses. Therefore, N's net capital gain for the year is $25,000 [($40,000 − $20,000 = $20,000) + $10,000 − $5,000].

**Example 31**

Assume N has a gain on § 1202 stock of $40,000 and a short-term capital loss of $23,000. N first applies the 50% exclusion and then nets the remaining gain with the capital loss. As a result, N has a net capital loss of $3,000 ($20,000 − $23,000).

### Rollover Provision

An individual who realizes a gain on the sale of QSB stock held for more than six months can defer recognition of the gain by reinvesting in other QSB stock within 60 days of the sale.

---

[56] Special rules apply for computing the exclusion on the sale of stock in a specialized small business investment company (see following discussion). The latest change was made by the *Tax Relief, Unemployment Insurance Reauthorization, and Job Creation Act of 2010.*

[57] § 1h. Recall that the § 1202 gain on the sale of qualified small business stock is excluded from the adjusted net capital gain. Therefore, the 15 percent rate does not apply.

Note that the stock qualifies for the rollover provision if it is held more than six months (not five years). The individual must recognize gain to the extent that the amount reinvested is less than the sales price of the original stock. If the taxpayer uses the rollover provision, the basis in the newly acquired QSB stock is reduced by the deferred gain. The holding period of the new QSB stock includes the holding period of the old QSB stock.

### Example 32

D purchased Netbrowser stock two years ago, for $10,000. The stock qualified as § 1202 stock. After rising dramatically, the stock started to fall so D sold it for $14,000 before he lost all of his profit. He realized a $4,000 gain on the sale. D wanted to preserve the special treatment for § 1202 stock so 45 days after the sale, he reinvested in MMX Inc., another issue of § 1202 stock, for $15,000. D recognizes no gain on the sale since his holding period of two years exceeded the required six months and he reinvested all $10,000 received from the sale of § 1202 stock. His basis in the replacement stock is $11,000 ($15,000 – $4,000) and the two-year holding period of the old stock attaches to the new. Had D reinvested only $13,000, he would have recognized a gain of $1,000 ($14,000 – $13,000) and have a basis in the replacement stock of $10,000 ($13,000 – deferred gain of $3,000). Note that this rollover provision enables the taxpayer to move in and out of positions in QSB stock so long as QSB is repurchased.

## § 1202 Requirements

Stock qualifies as § 1202 stock if it is issued after August 10, 1993 and meets a long list of requirements.

1. At the time the stock is issued, the corporation issuing the stock must be a *qualified small business*. A corporation is a qualified small business if:
   - The corporation is a domestic C corporation
   - The corporation's gross assets do not exceed $50 million at the time the stock was issued (i.e., cash plus the fair market value of contributed property measured at the time of contribution plus the adjusted basis of other assets)
2. The seller is the original owner of the stock (i.e., the stock was acquired directly from the corporation or through an underwriter at its original issue)
3. During substantially all of the seller's holding period of the stock, the corporation was engaged in an active trade or business other than the following:
   - A business involving the performance of providing services in the fields of health, law, engineering, architecture, accounting, actuarial science, performing arts, consulting, athletics, financial services, brokerage services, or any other business where the principal asset is the reputation or skill of one or more of its employees
   - Banking, insurance, financing, leasing, or investing
   - Farming
   - Businesses involving the production or extraction of products eligible for depletion
   - Business of operating a hotel, motel, or restaurant
4. The corporation generally cannot own:
   - Real property with a value that exceeds 10 percent of its total assets unless such property is used in the active conduct of a trade or business (e.g., rental real estate is not an active trade or business)
   - Portfolio stock or securities with a value that exceeds 10 percent of the corporation's total assets in excess of its liabilities

Note that the active trade or business requirement and the prohibition on real estate holdings severely limit the exclusion. These conditions effectively grant the exclusion to corporations engaged in manufacturing, retailing, or wholesaling businesses.

The new provision also imposes a restriction, albeit a liberal one, on the amount of gain eligible to be excluded on the sale of a particular corporation's stock. The maximum amount of gain that may be excluded on the sale of one corporation's stock is the *larger* of:

1. $10 million, reduced by previously excluded gain on the sale of such corporation's stock; or
2. 10 times the adjusted basis of all qualified stock of the corporation that the taxpayer sold during the tax year.

This exclusion is extremely attractive, but it should be remembered that whatever Congress gives it can also take away. And that is exactly what Congress has done with § 1202 stock. For purposes of the alternative minimum tax, § 57 provides that 7% of the amount excluded from gross income under § 1202 (i.e., 3.5% of the total gain) is a tax preference item. In addition, the excluded gain is generally not considered investment income for purposes of determining the investment interest limitation.

### Rollover of Gain on Certain Publicly Traded Securities

Another creature of the 1993 Act encourages investment in small businesses owned by disadvantaged taxpayers. Individuals and C corporations that recognize gain on the sale of publicly traded securities are allowed to defer recognition of such gain if they reinvest the proceeds from the sale in common stock or a partnership interest in a *specialized small business investment company* (SSBIC).[58] The reinvestment must occur within 60 days of the sale. An SSBIC is generally any corporation or partnership licensed by the Small Business Administration under § 301 of the Small Business Investment Act of 1958 (as in effect on May 13, 1993). This typically includes investment companies that finance small businesses owned by disadvantaged taxpayers.

The maximum amount of gain that a taxpayer may exclude per year is generally limited to $50,000 (or, if smaller, $500,000 reduced by any previously excluded gain). These limits are increased to $250,000 and $1 million, respectively, for C corporations. Note that the special deferral privilege is not available for partnerships, S corporations, estates, or trusts.

The operation of the deferral provision is virtually identical to the rollover rules for gains on the sale of a residence and involuntary conversions. As a general rule, the taxpayer must recognize gain to the extent that the sales proceeds are not properly reinvested. Any gain deferred reduces the basis of the stock acquired.

**Example 33**

G sold 4,000 shares of IBM stock for $200,000, realizing a long-term capital gain of $40,000. Less than a week later, G used the entire $200,000 plus additional cash of $15,000 to purchase an interest in the P Partnership, an SSBIC. G may exclude the gain of $40,000 since she reinvested at least $200,000 in qualified property within 60 days. Her basis in the partnership interest would be $175,000 ($215,000 cost − $40,000 deferred gain).

## Dealers and Developers

Since property held primarily for sale to customers in the ordinary course of a trade or business (or inventory) is generally excluded from the definition of a capital asset, any gain or loss on the sale of inventory is generally treated as ordinary gain or loss. For taxpayers who would otherwise benefit from capital gain treatment, this is an obstacle. In certain instances, Congress has provided special relief.

---

[58] § 1202(g).

## Dealers, Investors and Traders of Securities

With the arrival of the Internet and the ease in which individuals can buy and sell securities (e.g., computerized trading, day traders), the need for taxpayers and practitioners to understand the potential problems has significantly increased. Important differences in the tax treatment exist, depending on whether the taxpayer is an investor, trader or dealer.[59]

### Dealers

A dealer is a taxpayer who purchases securities from customers or sells securities to customers in the ordinary course of business. The securities held by a dealer represent inventory held primarily for resale. Dealers are distinguished from traders in two ways: (1) they have customers and (2) their income is primarily based on a mark-up on the buying and selling of securities, rather than obtaining profit from price fluctuations. Dealers report ordinary income or ordinary loss from their business transactions, using the mark-to-market provisions discussed below.

The difficulty with the tax treatment of dealers is that they not only hold stocks and bonds for sale to customers as part of their regular business operations, but they also invest in stocks and bonds for their own account. As may be apparent, the potential for abuse is great. Since long-term capital gain and ordinary loss are generally preferred, securities dealers have the natural tendency to classify the assets to provide the greatest tax benefit. On the other hand, the IRS wants to do just the opposite. To eliminate the potential controversy and prohibit taxpayers from using their hindsight, Congress enacted § 1236. This provision simply requires the dealer to indicate that a particular security is held for investment (and is therefore a capital asset) by the end of the day on which it was acquired. If the security is not properly identified on a timely basis, the dealer must characterize any gain or loss as ordinary.

### Investors

In contrast to dealers, investors are not conducting a trade or business. Their income is normally derived from the price movement of the securities as well as dividends and interest. Most individuals are investors. The basic rules discussed in this chapter concerning capital gains and losses (including the wash sales provisions) apply to investors. Investors report their gains and losses on Schedule D. On the expense side, because investors are not carrying on a trade or business, their expenses may be restricted in some way. For example, the investment interest provisions of § 163(d) limit the deduction of investment interest to investment income. Similarly, the home office deduction is not extended to investors since it is allowed only for those carrying on a trade or business. Likewise, § 179 concerning limited expensing is allowed only for property used in a business. Moreover, any expenses that are deductible are treated as investment expenses and characterized as miscellaneous itemized deductions subject to the 2% limitation as well as the 2% cutback rule. And perhaps the most significant problem for investors is the elimination of the deduction of these expenses for purposes of the alternative minimum tax (AMT).

### Traders

The tax treatment of a trader's transactions can differ significantly from those of an investor. For this reason, it is important to draw the distinction. Unfortunately, there is not a clear line of demarcation between the two. A trader is one whose stock and security transactions are so regular and continuous as to rise to the level of a trade or business. In this regard, the distinguishing factors are the individual's intent and the frequency or regularity of trades.

Although traders are treated as conducting a business, they do not have inventory and do not have clients. Therefore, their gains and losses on the sales of securities are still treated as capital gains and capital losses and reported on Schedule D, the same as an investor. Similarly, dividend and interest income are still treated as investment income, reported on Schedule B. But expenses are treated much differently. Traders may deduct their expenses such as margin account interest, management fees, home office expenses and others as deductions for A.G.I. on Schedule C. This solves the limitations associated with miscellaneous itemized deductions, the 2% cutback rule and the AMT. Notwithstanding the fact that traders are in a trade or business they are not subject to self-employment tax. Dividends, interest from securities and gain or loss from the sale of capital assets, are not

---

[59] For an excellent discussion, see Robison and Mark, "On-Line Transactions Intensify Trader vs. Investor Question," *Practical Tax Strategies* (February, 2001).

considered self-employment income. In addition to these rules, traders are entitled to special treatment not extended to investors: the use of the mark-to-market rules.

### Traders and Mark-to-Market Provisions

Traders are given an important option unavailable to investors. Taxpayers who are considered traders (but not investors) may take advantage of the mark-to-market (MTM) rules of § 475. Under the MTM rules, traders who make the § 475(f) election are deemed to have sold all of their stocks and securities for their fair market value on the last business day of the taxable year. As a result, traders must recognize all gains and losses as of that date. Traders report their gains and losses on Schedule C. Due to the deemed sale, the basis of the securities is increased to fair market value and used as the basis for subsequent transactions. Although making the MTM election eliminates the opportunity to defer income beyond year end, it offers at least one huge advantage. Section 475(d)(3) provides that the gains and losses recognized on the deemed sales are treated as ordinary income or ordinary losses. This rule is extremely important since it allows traders (who make the election) to avoid the limitation on the deduction of capital losses.[60] By making the election, losses can be used to offset all other taxable income without limitation. Moreover, as business losses, they could add to or create a net operating loss that can be carried back two years and forward for twenty years. Also, the wash sales rules do not apply.

Although the MTM election converts capital losses to ordinary losses, it also converts capital gains to ordinary income. As a practical matter, this is of little significance since the income of most traders would be short-term capital gain which is treated as ordinary income. However, traders who want to preserve the possibility of long-term capital gain treatment for certain securities may do so by taking advantage of another special rule. Section 475(f)(1)(B) permits a trader to segregate trader transactions from investor transactions by using separate accounts for each.

For the § 475(f) election to be effective for a particular tax year, a statement must be filed with the IRS no later than the due date (without extensions) for the tax return for the immediately preceding year. Thus, an election for 2011 must be filed no later than the due date of the 2010 return, April 15, 2011. The election is a change in accounting method so those rules (see Chapter 5) must be observed.

## Subdivided Real Estate

The dealer vs. investor debate also raises its ugly head for taxpayers selling land. Is the land held for investment or primarily for resale?

It is not uncommon for a taxpayer to hold land for investment for many years and then subdivide or improve it just before selling it. If the subdivision and improvements are significant, the property will probably be deemed to be held primarily for sale to customers in a trade or business. If the activities are minor, the land probably retains its character as a capital asset. As was pointed out earlier in this chapter, the determination usually is made based on the frequency, continuity, and volume of sales, but development activities are also very important.

In an attempt to prevent disputes, Congress created a safe harbor that guarantees capital gain treatment where there is a limited amount of subdivision activity. This rule allows the taxpayer, as someone once said, to subdivide and conquer the ordinary income problem. Under § 1237, real estate is not treated as held primarily for sale if all of the following conditions are met:[61]

1. The tract of land has been held at least five years prior to the sale (except in the case of inheritance).
2. The taxpayer has made no substantial improvements to the property that increase the value of the lots sold while the property was owned.
3. The parcel sold, or any part thereof, had not previously been held by the taxpayer primarily for resale.
4. No other real property was held by the taxpayer primarily for sale during the year of the sale.

---

[60] To appreciate the mark-to-market election, see L.S. Vines 126 T.C. 279 (2006).

[61] § 1237(a).

Even if the requirements are met, the taxpayer may still be required to report a portion of the gain as ordinary income. If five or fewer lots are sold from the same tract of land, the entire gain is capital gain. However, in the year that the sixth lot is sold, all lots sold in that year and later years become the target of § 1237(b). This special rule provides that 5 percent of the sales price (not gain) is ordinary income.[62] In addition, any selling expenses reduce the ordinary income portion of the gain (limited to the amount of ordinary income), rather than the amount treated as capital gain.[63]

**Example 34**

Twenty years ago X bought 100 acres 20 miles south of Tulsa for $100,000. This year he retired and decided to sell the land. In order to sell the property, he subdivided it into 10 lots of 10 acres each. This year X sold 5 lots for $310,000 and paid a real estate commission of $10,000. As a result, he recognized a gain of $250,000 ($310,000 − $10,000 − $50,000 basis). Since he sold only 5 lots, the gain on each sale is treated as long-term capital gain. Had X sold 6 lots for the same total price, 5% of his selling price, $15,500 (5% × $310,000), would be considered ordinary income and he could reduce this amount by the selling expenses of $10,000, for net ordinary income on the sale of $5,500.

Note that § 1237 applies to property that has been subdivided, but it is of no help where significant improvements have been made to the property.

## Other Related Provisions

### Nonbusiness Bad Debts

Bad debt losses from nonbusiness debts are deductible as short-term capital losses. Nonbusiness bad debts are deductible only in the year they become totally worthless since no deduction is allowed for partially worthless debts.[64] These rules and others related to the allowable deduction for bad debts were discussed in Chapter 10.

### Franchise Agreements, Trademarks, and Trade Names

Section 1253 includes specific guidelines for the treatment of both the transferee and the transferor of payments with respect to franchise, trademark, and trade name agreements. The transfer of such rights is *not* treated as the sale or exchange of a capital asset by the transferor *if* he or she retains significant power, right, or continuing interest with respect to the property.[65] Capital gain and loss treatment also is denied for periodic payments that are contingent on the productivity, use, or sale of the property.[66]

"Significant power, right, or continuing interest" is defined in the Code by example. Some of the characteristics listed in the Code as indicative of such power, right, or interest retained by the transferor of the franchise are as follows:[67]

1. The right to terminate the franchise at will;
2. The right to disapprove any assignment;
3. The right to prescribe quality standards;
4. The right to require that the transferee advertise only products of the transferor;

---

62 § 1237(b)(1).

63 § 1237(b)(2).

64 See § 166(d) and related discussion in Chapter 10.

65 § 1253(a).

66 § 1253(c).

67 § 1253(b)(2).

5. The right to require that the transferee acquire substantially all of his or her supplies or equipment from the transferor; and
6. The right to require payments based on the productivity, use, or sale of the property.

The transferee is allowed current deductions for amounts paid or accrued that are contingent on the productivity, use, or sale of the property transferred.[68] Other payments must be at least partially deferred. They generally are amortized over 15 years.[69]

### Example 35

M, Inc. and R enter into a franchise agreement that allows R to operate a hamburger establishment using the trade name and products of M, Inc. According to the contract, M, Inc. has retained all six rights that are listed above. R is required to pay M $50,000 upon entering the contract and 2% of all sales. The term of the contract is 25 years with provision for renewals. R must also pay for any supplies provided by M. Both the $50,000 payment and the percentage royalty payment are ordinary income to M, Inc.

R may treat the royalty payments to M, Inc. as ordinary deductions incurred in his trade or business. The initial fee of $50,000 is amortized equally over 10 years beginning with the year in which the payment is made.

## SHORT SALES

Investors who believe that the price of a security will fall rather than rise may bank on their belief by using short sales. Selling short essentially means selling shares that are not actually owned. To accomplish this, the seller typically borrows shares from a broker, sells such shares, and agrees to return an equivalent number of substantially identical shares to the broker within a certain period of time. For example, an investor may sell 100 shares of borrowed stock for $100 per share, or $10,000. If the stock price falls to $80 per share, the investor can purchase 100 shares in the market for $8,000, replace the 100 borrowed shares, and have a tidy profit of $2,000. Of course, if the price goes up to $110, it costs the investor $11,000 to *cover* the short position and a loss is realized.

The tax consequences of short sales are triggered at the time the seller replaces the borrowed shares (i.e., the short position is closed or covered). No gain or loss is recognized until this time.[70] The character of the gain or loss realized depends on whether the asset involved (normally stock) is a capital asset. Determination of the holding period is more confusing. If the replacement securities have been held for a year or less before the *short sale* or are acquired after the sale, the gain or loss realized on closing the position is short term.[71] Moreover, if the taxpayer does not use such stock to replace the borrowed shares, the holding period of such securities starts again, beginning on the date the short position was closed.[72] If the replacement property has been held for more than a year prior to the short sale, the gain or loss recognized on closing is long-term, regardless of the holding period of the actual shares used to close the short position.

### Example 36

On March 15, 2010, T purchased 100 shares of S stock for $4,000. On February 15, 2011, T sold 100 shares of S stock short for $5,000. On June 15, 2011, T closed out her short position by delivering the March 15, 2010 shares. Because T held the replacement shares less than one year before she shorted the stock (March 15, 2010 to February 15, 2011), she reports a $1,000 short-term capital gain.

[68] § 1253(d)(1).

[69] § 197(d)(1)(F).

[70] Reg. § 1.1233-1(a)(1).

[71] § 1233(b).

[72] *Ibid.*

### Example 37

Same facts as *Example 34*, except T closed out her position by purchasing 100 new shares on June 15, 2011 for $6,500. In addition, she sold the original shares on August 15, 2011 for $7,000. T reports a capital loss of $1,500 ($5,000 – $6,500) upon covering her short position, and it is short-term since she held substantially identical stock less than a year before she shorted the stock (March 15, 2010 to February 15, 2011). In addition, T reports a *short-term* capital gain on the sale of the original stock of $3,000 ($7,000 – $4,000) even though she has held the stock for more than one year (March 1, 2010 to August 15, 2011). The holding period for the original stock begins again on the date the short sale was closed by virtue of the fact that she owned such stock less than one year before the short sale.

### Constructive Sale Treatment for Appreciated Financial Positions

For many years, investors often wanted to lock in their gain positions without having to recognize them for tax purposes. To accomplish this, an investor would sell stock short and close out the position at a later time. This was referred to as selling short against the box. The tax benefit of this technique was eliminated in 1997. Now, if a taxpayer undertakes a short sale or similar disposition of property that he or she owns, the taxpayer must treat the short sale as the disposition of the underlying property and recognize gain as if the underlying property had been sold.[73]

### Example 38

P owns 200 shares of BDF Corporation that was purchased at a cost of $24 per share. On November 14 of the current year, P sold 50 shares of BDF short for $50 per share. P is treated as selling the shares for $2,500 on November 14 and must recognize a gain of $1,300 ($2,500 – $1,200).

This rule does not apply if the transaction is closed within 30 days after the close of the year of the short sale or similar disposition.

## Options

Options of one variety or another have become commonplace in the business and investment world. They can be used in a variety of ways (e.g., an option to buy a house or buy land), but they are probably best known as a technique—sometimes a speculative one—to invest in the stock and commodities markets. The popularity of options has skyrocketed since the Chicago Board Options Exchange began organized trading in listed options in 1973. Currently, listed options on hundreds of securities can be bought and sold just like the securities themselves. One need only glance at the daily quotes in the *Wall Street Journal* or similar financial resource on the Internet to appreciate this everyday phenomenon. This growth in the use of options requires tax advisers to have some appreciation of how they work and how they are taxed.

For some, however, options are shrouded in a cloud of mystery, an esoteric investment tool too sophisticated for the common investor. In reality, the basic operation of options is not that complicated. An option simply gives the holder the right to buy or sell a specific asset at a certain price by a specified date. A taxpayer who owns an option may either exercise the option, sell the option, or allow it to expire. The tax treatment of these actions is just as straightforward as the operation of the option itself.

[73] § 1259.

### Treatment of Option Buyer

If the taxpayer exercises the option, the amount paid for the option is treated as a capital expenditure and added to the taxpayer's basis for the property. If the taxpayer sells the option or allows it to expire, the tax treatment depends on the nature of the underlying property.[74] In other words, if the taxpayer sells the option, the sale is treated as a sale of the option property. Therefore, any gain or loss recognized is a capital gain or loss only if the option property is a capital asset.

#### Example 39

On May 1, J purchased for $500 an option to buy 100 shares of Wells Fargo common stock at a price of $100 per share at any time before August 2nd. On August 1, when Wells Fargo was trading at $130 per share, J exercised his option and bought 100 shares for $10,000. Although J is immediately better from his purchase, he has no income. The basis of his stock is $10,500 (the $500 cost of the option + the $10,000 cost of the stock) and the holding period begins on August 2nd.

#### Example 40

On January 2, Compaq common stock was trading at what K thought was a bargain price of $65 per share. Consequently, K purchased for $700 an option to buy 100 shares of Compaq at a price of $80 on or before March 15. After the corporation reported its earnings, the stock value jumped, and by March 1 the price was bouncing between $95 and $100 per share. The value of K's option had also increased, and he sold it for $3,000. Since the option property, the stock, is a capital asset, K reports a short-term capital gain of $2,300 ($3,000 – $700).

#### Example 41

Same facts as *Example 38*, except Compaq's earnings were disappointing and the value of the stock as well as the value of K's option decreased. On March 15, the stock was trading at $60 per share and K decided to let the option expire. K recognizes a short-term capital loss of $700.

Options are generally billed as a way to secure a potentially large profit from a relatively small investment with a known risk. The option buyer knows in advance that the most that can be lost is the amount paid for the option. There are generally two types of options: puts and calls. A *call* is simply the shorthand term given to an option that gives the holder the right to purchase a particular security at a fixed price. All of the discussion and examples above deal with call options. For example, if an individual believes the price of IBM will rise from $50 to $70 over the next several months, she might purchase a call that enables her to buy 1,000 shares at a price far lower than the $50,000 that would be required to actually buy the stock. The ultimate tax treatment of the call depends, as explained above, on whether the taxpayer sells or exercises the option or allows it to lapse.

### Treatment of Option Writer (Seller)

In any option agreement, there are two parties, the party who buys the option and the person who "writes," or sells, the option. Individuals who write, or sell, call options obligate themselves to deliver a certain number of shares at a particular price in exchange for the

---

[74] § 1234(a). Note that the lapse of an option is treated as a sale or exchange [§ 1234(b)].

payment of some amount referred to as the call premium. If the call is written by a person who owns the underlying stock (a "covered" call), the individual can deliver such stock if the call is exercised. If the writer does not own the stock (a "naked" call), the stock must be purchased to meet the obligation—a very risky situation. Writers of covered calls generally view the call premium as an additional source of income or as a hedge against a possible decline in the value of the stock. If the buyer exercises the call, the writer of the option adds the premium to the amount realized in determining the gain or loss realized on the stock sold. The gain or loss is long-term or short-term depending on the holding period of the underlying stock. If the buyer allows the call to expire, the writer of the call treats the premium received for the option as a short-term capital gain regardless of the actual holding period.[75] The gain is reported at the time the option expires.

**Example 42**

After discussing it with her broker, W decided to write call options on her 100 shares of Colgate that she bought several years ago for $3,000. She deposited the stock with her broker and instructed him to write a call that allows an investor to purchase 100 shares of Colgate at $40 per share at a premium of $5 per share. Within a few business days, W's account was credited with $500 for writing the call. If the call is not exercised, W has a $500 short-term capital gain. If the call is exercised, W sells her stock and realizes a long-term capital gain of $1,500 ($4,000 + $500 − $3,000).

### Puts

To understand puts, one has to mentally shift gears. Puts are the exact opposites of calls. Whereas a buyer of a call buys the right to purchase stock at a fixed price, a buyer of a put buys the right to sell stock at a fixed price. As in short sales, the buyer of a put typically believes that the price of the underlying stock will drop. If the put is sold, the taxpayer reports a short-term capital gain or loss regardless of the holding period. If the put is exercised (i.e., the taxpayer does in fact sell the underlying stock), the amount realized on the sale is decreased by the premium paid for the put. If the put lapses, a loss is allowable as of the date the option expires. As a practical matter, most puts are bought with the intention of selling them.

**Example 43**

After seeing reports on television that the airline industry was falling on hard times, P believed the current $47 price on Boeing stock would fall. He immediately called his broker and bought a put at a price of $200 on March 4. The put enables him to sell 100 shares of the stock at a price of $45 per share before August 24. The price did in fact fall and bottomed at $40 per share. As a result, his put, that is, his right to sell the stock at $45, became more valuable, and he sold the put for $500. P must report a short-term capital gain of $300 ($500 − $200).

## Corporate Bonds and Other Indebtedness

**LO.8**
Discuss the tax treatment of investments in corporate bonds and other forms of indebtedness.

Investments in corporate bonds and other forms of indebtedness present several unique problems that must be considered by taxpayers who choose this form of investment. Under the general rules, mere collection of principal payments does not constitute a sale or exchange and, therefore, a capital gain or capital loss cannot result. However, the Code creates an exception for certain forms of debt. This special rule provides that any amounts received by the holder on

[75] If the writer of the call is in the trade or business of granting options, the gain would be ordinary rather than capital gain. § 1234(b).

retirement of any debt are considered as amounts received in exchange for the debt.[76] Consequently, capital gain or loss is normally recognized when the debt is redeemed or sold for more or less than the taxpayer's basis in the debt.

### Example 44

B purchased a $1,000, 10% bond issued by Z Corporation for $990. Assuming the bond is held to maturity and redeemed by the corporation, B will recognize a capital gain of $10. If B had sold the bond prior to redemption for $995, he would recognize a capital gain of $5.

A second and more difficult problem to be considered concerns the *interest element* that may be inherent in the purchase price of a corporate bond. For example, if the rate at which a bond pays interest—the stated rate—is less than the current market rate, the bond will sell for less than its face value, or at a discount. In this case, the *discount* effectively functions as a substitute for interest income. Conversely, if the stated rate exceeds the market rate, the bond will sell for more than its face value, or at a premium. Here, the *premium* essentially reduces the amount of interest income. Without special rules, the proper amount of interest income would not be captured and reported in a timely manner.

### Example 45

Several years ago when interest rates were 10%, T purchased a $10,000, 8% corporate bond for $8,000, or a $2,000 discount. This year the bond matured and T redeemed the bond for its par value of $10,000. Under normal accounting procedures, the redemption is treated as an exchange and the taxpayer would recognize a long-term capital gain of $2,000 ($10,000 – $8,000). In this case, the taxpayer would have converted the discount of $2,000, which from an economic view is ordinary interest income, to capital gain. Moreover, this income would be deferred until T sold the bond.

The example above illustrates the problems that the special tax rules governing bond transactions address. The provisions ensure that any premium or discount is not treated as part of the capital gain or loss realized on disposition of the bond, but rather is treated as an *adjustment* to the taxpayer's interest income received from the bond. In addition, the Code provides rules for determining how much of the premium or discount will affect interest income and *when* the additional interest income (in the case of discount) or the interest expense (in the case of premium) will be reported.

The Code provides a separate set of rules governing the treatment of premium and discount. In the case of discount, the rules differ depending on when the discount arises. One set applies when the bonds were *originally issued* at a discount (the "original issue discount" provisions) and another set applies if the discount arises when the bonds are purchased later in the open market (the "market discount" rules). The rules governing premium are the same regardless of when the premium arises.

## Original Issue Discount

When corporate bonds are *issued* at a price less than the stated redemption price at maturity (i.e., the bond's face value), the resulting discount is referred to as *original issue discount*, or more commonly OID. The amount of OID is easily computed as follows:

| | | |
|---|---|---|
| | Redemption price (face value) | $x,xxx |
| – | Issue price | –xxx |
| = | Original issue discount | $x,xxx |

[76] § 1271.

The OID provisions generally require the holder of the bond to amortize the discount and include it in income during the period the bond is held.[77] For purposes of computing the gain or loss on disposition of the bond, the holder must increase the basis of the bond by the amount of any amortized discount. Any gain or loss on the disposition of the bond normally is capital gain. However, if at the time of issue there was an intention to call the bond before maturity, any gain on the bond is treated as ordinary income to the extent of any unamortized discount.[78]

Before examining the amortization methods, it should be emphasized that the Code furnishes a de minimis rule that may exempt the debt from the OID amortization requirements. OID is considered to be zero when the bond discount is less than one-fourth of one percent of the redemption price at maturity multiplied by the number of complete years to maturity.[79] This may be expressed as follows:

| | | |
|---|---|---|
| | Redemption price at maturity. . . . . . . . . . . . . . . . . . . . . . . . | $x,xxx |
| × | Percentage. . . . . . . . . . . . . . . . . . . . . . . . . . . . . . . . . . . | x 0.25% |
| × | Number of complete years to maturity . . . . . . . . . . . . . . . | xx |
| = | De minimis amount . . . . . . . . . . . . . . . . . . . . . . . . . . . . | $x,xxx |

In most cases, new bond issues do not create OID because the stated interest rate is set near the market rate so that the amount of discount that arises, if any, does not exceed the de minimis amount. As a result, no amortization is required.

For bonds issued after July 1, 1982, the discount is amortized into income using a technique similar to the effective interest method used in financial accounting.[80] To determine the includible OID, the OID attributable to an accrual period must be computed. This is done by multiplying the *adjusted issue price* at the beginning of the *accrual period* by the *yield to maturity* and reducing this amount by any interest payable on the bond during the period. The adjusted issue price is the bond's original issue price as increased for previously amortized OID. The accrual period is generally the six-month period ending on the anniversary date of the bond (date of original issue) and six months before such date. The yield to maturity must be determined using present value techniques or may be found in bond tables designed specifically for this purpose.[81]

Once the OID attributable to the entire bond period is computed, this amount is allocated ratably to each day in the bond period. The bondholder's includible OID is the sum of the daily portions of OID for each day during the taxable year that the owner held the bond.

## Example 46

On July 1, 2011, R purchased 100 newly issued 30-year, 8% bonds with a face value of $1,000 for $800 each or $80,000. The bonds pay interest semiannually on July 1 and December 31. The OID rules apply since the $200 discount per bond exceeds the de minimis amount of $75.

| | | |
|---|---|---|
| | Redemption price at maturity | $ 1,000 |
| × | Percentage | x 0.25% |
| × | Number of complete years to maturity | x 30 |
| = | De minimis amount | $ 75 |

Using present value calculations, the annual yield to maturity for this bond is 10.14% (or 5.07% semiannually). The OID that R must include in income in 2011 and 2012 for all of the bonds is computed in the aggregate as follows:

---

77 §§ 1271–1275.

78 § 1271(a)(2).

79 § 1273(a)(3).

80 § 1272(a). For bonds issued after July 1, 1982, and before January 1, 1985, the accrual period is one year.

81 Given the issue price, the redemption price, and the number of periods to maturity, the yield to maturity may be approximated by reference to appropriate present-value tables.

| | 7/1–12/31 2011 | 1/1–6/30 2012 | 10/1–12/31 2012 |
|---|---|---|---|
| Adjusted issue price | $80,000 | $80,056** | $80,115 |
| Semiannual yield | x 5.07% | x 5.07% | x 5.07% |
| Total effective interest | $ 4,056 | $ 4,059 | $ 4,062 |
| Less: Interest received | −4,000* | −4,000 | −4,000 |
| Includible OID | $ 56 | $ 59 | $ 62 |

*$100,000 × 4% = $4,000
**$80,000 + $56 = $80,056

R would include the amount of OID in income in addition to the interest income actually received. Note that the issuer of the bond would include in its annual deduction for interest expense the amount of OID that must be amortized.

### Example 47

Assume the same facts as above, except that R sells all of the bonds for $85,000 on July 1, 2012. Assuming there was no intention to call the bonds when issued, R will report a capital gain of $4,885 ($85,000 – $80,115).

Additional computations are required when the purchase price exceeds the original issue price as increased by OID amortized by previous holders. As a practical matter, the issuer of the bond is obligated to provide the taxpayer a Form 1099-OID, Statement of Original Issue Discount, disclosing the amount of interest income to be reported annually. For those who do not receive such a form, the IRS provides a special publication with the necessary information.

For bonds issued before July 2, 1982, the OID is generally included in the income of the holder ratably over the term of the bond (i.e., a straight-line method is used).[82]

### Example 48

Assume the bond in *Example 46* was issued prior to July 2, 1982. The original issue discount included annually would be $667 ($20,000 ÷ 30).

Although the OID rules are to apply to virtually all debt instruments, there are several notable exceptions:[83]

1. U.S. Savings Bonds (which are treated as discussed in Chapter 5)
2. Tax-exempt state and local obligations (although the discount income is not included as taxable income, the taxpayer increases the basis of the instrument)
3. Debt instruments that have a fixed maturity date not exceeding one year [unless held by certain parties identified in § 1281(b), including accrual basis taxpayers]
4. Obligations issued by individuals before March 2, 1984
5. Nonbusiness loans between individuals of $10,000 or less

In 1984, the coverage of the OID rules was substantially extended to help curb abuses that occurred when a taxpayer sold property and received a note in exchange. The application of the OID rules in this area was discussed in Chapter 14 in conjunction with unstated interest.

[82] § 1272(a); for bonds issued before May 28, 1969, special rules apply. See § 1272(b).

[83] §§ 1272(a)(2) and 1274(c)(2).

## MARKET DISCOUNT

As previously noted, without special rules, amortization of discount would not be required where the security was treated as having no OID (e.g., where the discount on the bond when originally issued was small). For example, if a bond having a $10,000 face value bearing 10 percent interest over a 30-year term was issued for $9,500, there would be no OID since the discount is less than $750 (0.25% × 30 × $10,000). In subsequent years, however, interest rates might rise, causing the bond to sell at a substantially greater discount (i.e., lower value), say $8,000 (e.g., if rates rose to 14 percent the bond's price might fall to $8,000). In such case, an investor could purchase the bond and ultimately report the built-in appreciation as capital gain—the $2,000 rise from the discounted price to face value at maturity—notwithstanding the fact that a portion of the increase in value actually represents interest income. Moreover, the investor could borrow amounts to purchase the investment and obtain an immediate deduction for interest on the debt, although the income from the bond was deferred until it was redeemed or sold. This highly publicized and extremely popular investment technique was foreclosed by the Deficit Reduction Act of 1984 for newly issued bonds.

Changes made in 1993 make the rules applicable to *all* bonds purchased after April 30, 1993. Code § 1276 provides that any gain on the disposition of a bond is treated as ordinary income to the extent of any accrued *market discount*. Market discount, in contrast to OID, is measured at the time the purchaser acquires the bond. Hence, market discount is the excess of the stated redemption price over the basis of the bond immediately after *acquisition*.[84] Like OID, market discount is considered to be zero if it is less than one-fourth of one percent of the stated redemption price multiplied by the number of complete years to maturity after acquisition. The portion of market discount that is considered ordinary income upon disposition of the bond is computed assuming the discount accrues ratably over the number of days from the purchase of the bond to the bond's maturity date.

### Example 49

On January 1, 2010, T purchased a bond issued in 2009 having a face value of $10,000 for $8,000. The bond matures four years later on January 1, 2014. The market discount on the bond is $2,000, the difference between the stated redemption price of $10,000 and the taxpayer's $8,000 basis in the bond immediately after acquisition (assuming there was no OID). The $2,000 is deemed to accrue on a daily basis over the 1,460 days remaining on the bond's term. Assuming T sells the bond for $9,000 on January 2, 2011, her gain is $1,000, of $500 of which is ordinary interest income [$2,000 × (365 ÷ 1,460)] and the remaining $500 is long-term capital gain.

In lieu of using the daily method of computing the accrued market discount, the taxpayer may use the effective interest method similar to that used for amortizing OID. In addition, the taxpayer may elect to report accrued market discount in taxable income annually rather than at the date of disposition. If this election is made, the taxpayer increases the basis of the bond by the amount of market discount included in income.

Congress also enacted provisions limiting the taxpayer's interest deduction on loans to purchase market discount bonds. Section 1277 requires the taxpayer to defer the deduction for interest expense until that time when income from the bond is reported.

## CONVERSION TRANSACTIONS

The original issue discount and market discount provisions exist in order to prevent taxpayers from converting ordinary interest income into capital gain when the interest element is in the form of a discount. In certain instances, taxpayers may still be able to avoid this treatment by structuring the transactions somewhat differently. Congress refers to these as *conversion transactions*.

---

[84] § 1277(a)(2). If the bond also has OID, the market discount is reduced by the amortized portion of OID.

*Conversion transactions* are certain investments on which the return is attributable to the time value of money, or for which the sales price of the investment is known at the time the investment is made. Upon the sale or disposition of such investments, any gain is treated as ordinary income, rather than capital gain, to the extent of a return on the investment calculated at 120 percent of the applicable federal rate.[85] Any gain in excess of the ordinary income or any loss realized on the investment is treated as capital gain or loss, assuming the contract is a capital asset to the taxpayer.

## Bond Premium

The treatment of premium depends in part on whether the interest income on the bond is taxable.[86] When the interest income is taxable, the taxpayer *may* elect to amortize and deduct the premium as interest expense and concomitantly reduce the basis in the bond. The interest expense in this case is considered investment interest and is, therefore, deductible as an itemized deduction to the extent of net investment income. If the taxpayer does not elect to amortize the premium, the unamortized premium is simply included as part of the taxpayer's basis in the bond and thus decreases the gain or increases the loss on disposition of the bond.

If the interest income on the bond is tax-exempt, the premium *must* be amortized and the bond's basis decreased. No deduction is allowed for the amortized premium since it merely represents an adjustment in the amount of nontaxable income received by the holder. In other words, no deduction for the premium is allowed since it represents interest expense related to producing tax-exempt income. Note that by requiring amortization of the premium, the taxpayer is prohibited from securing a deduction for the premium in the form of a capital loss or a reduced gain on the disposition of the bond.

### Example 50

V purchased a $1,000 tax-exempt bond for $1,100. If V holds the bond to maturity, all of the premium will be amortized and his basis in the bond will be $1,000. Therefore, on redemption of the bond for $1,000, no gain or loss is recognized. However, if amortization of the premium was not required, V would report a capital loss of $100 on redemption of the bond.

The method to be used for amortizing premium depends on when the bond was issued. If the bond was issued before September 28, 1985, the premium is amortized using the straight-line method over the number of months to maturity. Premium on bonds issued on or after that date must be amortized based on the bond's yield to maturity determined when the bond was issued.

# Tax Planning Considerations

## Timing of Capital Asset Transactions

A taxpayer with investments that he or she may wish to sell should pay careful attention to the timing of those sales, particularly near the end of a year. Since the netting process takes into consideration only the sales for the year under consideration plus any capital loss carryovers, the year into which a particular transaction falls may have significant impact on the total amount of taxes paid. The taxpayer must also consider market conditions, since he or she may believe that waiting to sell a particular asset may cost more than paying any additional tax.

Strictly from a tax planning perspective, a taxpayer should consider timing the recognition of year-end capital gains and losses using the following strategy:

---

[85] § 1258.

[86] § 171.

1. *No Capital Gains or Losses Currently*—recognize up to $3,000 STCL or LTCL to take advantage of the annual capital loss deduction.
2. *Currently Have STCG*—recognize either STCL or LTCL to offset the STCG and more, if possible, to take advantage of the capital loss deduction.
3. *Currently Have LTCG*—recognize either LTCL or STCL to offset the LTCG and more, if possible, to take advantage of the capital loss deduction.
4. *Currently Have STCL*—if less than $3,000, recognize more STCL or LTCL to take advantage of the capital loss deduction. If more than $3,000, recognize either STCG or LTCG to offset the STCL in excess of $3,000.
5. *Currently Have LTCL*—if less than $3,000, recognize more LTCL or STCL to take advantage of the capital loss deduction. If more than $3,000, recognize either STCG or LTCG to offset the LTCL in excess of $3,000.

The current tax rate differential between ordinary income and capital gains for noncorporate taxpayers (including flow-through entities) makes it far more important to distinguish between ordinary income and capital gain. Taxpayers should carefully plan in order to secure the benefit of this rate differential, which can be as great as 20 percent (35% – 15%).

## Section 1244 Stock

The importance of § 1244 should not be overlooked when making an investment.

### Example 51

Dr G is extremely successful and consequently is often approached by friends, promoters, and others asking her to make an investment in one deal or another. If G loans $30,000 to a friend to start a business which ultimately fails, the loss would be governed by the worthless-security rules and thus treated as a capital loss. In such case, Dr. G's annual loss deduction is limited to the extent of her capital gains plus $3,000. If G has no capital gains (which are not necessarily easily found), it could take her as long as ten years to deduct her loss. However, if the investment had been in the form of § 1244 stock, the entire $30,000 loss would be deductible in the year incurred.

Under § 1244, the taxpayer is allowed to deduct up to $50,000 ($100,000 in the case of a joint return) of loss *annually*. Any loss in excess of this amount is treated as a capital loss and is subject to limitation. In light of these rules, a taxpayer who anticipates a loss on § 1244 stock that exceeds the annual limitation should attempt to limit the loss recognized in any one year to $50,000 (or $100,000).

### Example 52

C, a bachelor, invested $200,000 in Risky Corporation several years ago, receiving 1,000 shares of § 1244 stock. It now appears that Risky, true to its name, will fail and that C will receive at best $100,000 for his investment. If C sells all of his shares this year, $50,000 of the loss is completely deductible as an ordinary loss under § 1244, while the remaining $50,000 of the loss would be a capital loss of which only $3,000 could be deducted (assuming he has no capital gains). C should sell half of his shares this year and half of his shares next year. By so doing, his loss for each year will be $50,000. In such case, neither loss would exceed the annual limitation, and therefore both would be deductible in full.

## Problem Materials

### DISCUSSION QUESTIONS

**16-1** *Capital Asset Defined.* Define a capital asset. How would you describe the way a capital asset is defined?

**16-2** *Sale of a Business.* How is the sale of an operating business treated? Discuss the sale of sole proprietorships, partnerships, and corporations in general.

**16-3** *Holding Period.* Explain the holding period requirements that must be met to secure favorable capital gain treatment. How does one determine the holding period for purchased property?

**16-4** *Holding Period.* What is the rule for determining the holding period for property acquired by gift?

**16-5** *Holding Period.* What is the holding period of property acquired from a decedent?

**16-6** *Holding Period—Stock Exchange Transactions.* T placed an order with her stock broker to sell 100 shares of Kent Electronics, Inc. stock on December 23, 2011. Because the sale order was received after the close of the market on the 23rd, the sale was executed at 9:00 A.M. on December 30, 2011. T received a settlement check from the brokerage house on January 5, 2012. What is the date of sale and what is the last date of T's holding period?

**16-7** *Holding Period—Worthless Securities.* D purchased 1,000 shares of H, Inc. for $4,450 in a speculative investment on October 25, 2010. Weeks later, on January 5, 2011, D received notice that the H, Inc. stock was worthless. What are the amount and character of D's loss in 2011?

**16-8** *Capital Gain and Loss Netting Process.* Describe the three possible results of the capital gain and loss netting process. How are the gains treated for tax purposes?

**16-9** *Capital Gains Tax.* D is single and has taxable income for the current year of $72,000, including a $7,000 capital gain on the sale of stock held for two years. Describe how D will determine the tax on his income for the year.

**16-10** *Capital Loss Deduction: Individuals.* How is the capital loss deduction limited for individual taxpayers?

**16-11** *Capital Gains and Losses: Corporations.* The tax rules governing a corporation's capital gains and losses differ somewhat from those for an individual.

**a.** Explain how a corporation treats capital gains and losses and how this treatment differs from that of an individual.

**b.** Some commentators are fond of saying that corporations rarely have capital gains and losses to worry about. Why might this be true?

**16-12** *Capital Loss Carryover.* Capital losses in excess of the annual limit can be carried forward to the subsequent year. How long may losses be carried forward by individual taxpayers? What is the character of the loss carryover and what happens if net losses from each of the groups (short-term, 28 percent, and 15 percent) are carried forward?

**16-13** *Patents.* What is necessary for a patent to qualify for capital gain or loss treatment under § 1235?

**16-14** *Ordinary v. Capital Loss Treatment.* What are the tax consequences to P, a bachelor, of a $70,000 loss occurring on June 1 of the current year attributable to the following:

**a.** An uncollectible nonbusiness loan to XYZ Corporation

**b.** Worthless bonds of XYZ Corporation acquired on November 30 of the prior year

**c.** The sale of XYZ stock qualifying as § 1244 stock when acquired two years ago

**16-15** *Section 1244 Stock.* When is a taxpayer's stock considered § 1244 stock? Why is the designation significant?

**16-16** *Section 1202 Exclusion.* S purchased qualified small business stock in U Corp. on October 27, 2011 for $35,000 with hopes to later qualify for the Section 1202 exclusion.

- **a.** What two major requirements must U Corp. meet throughout S's holding period?
- **b.** What is the first day on which S may sell the stock and qualify for the Section 1202 exclusion?
- **c.** What is the rollover provision and why is it important?

**16-17** *Rollover of Gain on Sales of Publicly Traded Securities.* Q sold common stock in K Corp., a publicly traded corporation, for $140,000, realizing a gain of $60,000.

- **a.** How much must Q reinvest in a corporation or partnership that is licensed by the Small Business Administration under § 301(d) of the Small Business Investment Act of 1958 (as in effect on May 13, 1994) in order to defer all of the $60,000 gain?
- **b.** By what day must Q reinvest to qualify for this gain rollover (deferral)?

**16-18** *Dealers, Traders and Investors.* In September 2010, R decided to try his luck in the stock market. Using a recent inheritance and borrowing funds on margin, he started investing. On a tip, one of his purchases was 10,000 shares of Overpriced Corp. He paid $70 per share at a total cost of $700,000. By December, 2010, the stock price had slipped to $30 per share. The prices of his other investments also were falling. All of this was happening and he was paying interest on his margin account as well.

- **a.** Would R be considered a dealer? Why or why not?
- **b.** If R is a dealer, how could R guaranteed that a particular investment will not be subject to capital gain or loss treatment?
- **c.** If R is an investor, how will his gains or losses be treated for tax purposes? His expenses?
- **d.** If R is a trader, how will his gains or losses be treated for tax purposes? His expenses?
- **e.** What is the mark-to-market election? Is R eligible for the mark-to-market election?
- **f.** If R can make the election, when must it be made and what effect will it have? Explain the effect of the election on any unrealized gains and losses he may have, expenses that he may incur such as margin interest and home office costs, and other concerns such as self-employment taxes and the alternative minimum tax.

**16-19** *Dealers in Securities.* How does a dealer in securities guarantee that a particular "investment" will qualify for capital gain or loss treatment?

**16-20** *Original Issue Discount—Deep Discount Bonds.* Financial consulting services often advise investment in so-called *deep discount bonds* (e.g., a $1,000 par value bond maturing in 10 years with coupon rate of six percent that sells at a discounted price of $400). Explain how such an investment could provide any tax savings in light of the original issue discount rules.

**16-21** *Bond Premium.* This year, G purchased a $1,000 bond for $1,100. The bond matures in 2017 and pays interest at a rate of 10 percent. Interest is paid semiannually on February 1 and August 1. Explain the treatment of the premium on the bond if the bond was issued by:

- **a.** General Motors
- **b.** City of Sacramento

## PROBLEMS

**16-22** *Identifying Capital Assets.* Which of the following items are capital assets?

- **a.** An automobile held for sale to customers by Midtown Motors, Inc.
- **b.** An automobile owned and used by Sherry Hartman to run household errands
- **c.** An automobile owned and used by Windowwashers, Inc.
- **d.** The private residence of Robert Hamilton
- **e.** Letters from a famous U.S. President written to Jane Doe (Jane Doe has the letters.)
- **f.** A warehouse owned and used by Holt Packing Company
- **g.** Gold bullion
- **h.** A country and western ballad written by W. Nelson.

**16-23** *Identifying Capital Assets.* Which of the following properties are capital assets? Briefly explain your answers.

**a.** A house built by a home-building contractor and used by her as her principal residence

**b.** A house, 80 percent of which is used as a residence and 20 percent of which is used to store business inventory

**c.** The same house in (b) above, used as stated for 10 years, and now used exclusively as a residence

**d.** Undeveloped land held for investment by a real estate broker

**e.** Stock held for investment by a stock broker

**16-24** *Capital Gain Netting Process.* D sold the following capital assets during 2011:

| Description | Date Acquired | Date Sold | Sales Price | Adjusted Basis |
|---|---|---|---|---|
| 100 shares XY Corp. | 1/10/89 | 1/12/11 | $14,000 | $1,000 |
| 50 shares LM Inc. | 9/14/10 | 1/12/11 | 1,900 | 4,000 |
| 140 shares CH Corp. | 11/20/10 | 4/10/11 | 3,400 | 3,000 |
| Gold necklace | 4/22/97 | 6/30/11 | 5,000 | 1,300 |
| Personal auto | 5/10/05 | 8/31/11 | 4,000 | 6,500 |

Explain the effects of the transactions above on D's taxable income and final tax liability.

**16-25** *Calculation of Capital Gains Tax.* Refer to the facts in *Problem 16-24* above. Assuming D, single, also has taxable income of $77,000 (net of her standard deduction and exemption), compute her tax liability.

**16-26** *Capital Gain Netting Process.* Each of the following situations deals with capital gains and losses occurring during the current year for an individual taxpayer. For each case, determine the change in adjusted gross income and the maximum tax to be imposed on any gain.

**Note:** N15CG(L) = Net 15 percent capital gain or (loss)
NSTCG(L) = Net short-term capital gain or (loss)

| Case | N15CG(L) | NSTCG(L) |
|---|---|---|
| A | $1,200 | $1,200 |
| B | 1,600 | (1,000) |
| C | (1,200) | 1,800 |
| D | 4,500 | (800) |
| E | 2,400 | 1,800 |

**16-27** *Gain and Losses on Property Acquired by Gift.* In each of the following independent situations, assume that the taxpayer received the capital asset as a gift on March 19, 2011, that the donor had held the property since 2006, and that the property was sold during 2011. No gift taxes were payable on the transfer. Determine the gain or loss recognized in each case.

| Case | Date of Sale | Sales Price | Donor's Basis | FMV Date of Gift |
|---|---|---|---|---|
| A | 4/19 | $1,000 | $ 400 | $ 600 |
| B | 6/3 | 1,000 | 1,400 | 1,200 |
| C | 11/20 | 1,000 | 900 | 1,100 |

**16-28** *Capital Gains and Losses.* K, a single individual, earned salaries and wages of $59,000 and interest $2,000 and dividends of $1,700 for the current year. In addition, K sold the following capital assets:

| | |
|---|---|
| 100 shares of GHJ common stock, held 14 months . . . . . . . . . . . | $3,400 gain |
| 1955 Ford pickup, used five years for personal purposes . . . . . . . | 4,500 gain |
| 30 acres of land, held three years for investment. . . . . . . . . . . . | 6,200 loss |

a. Compute K's net capital gain or loss.
b. Compute K's adjusted gross income.

**16-29** *Capital Gains and Losses.* L, a single individual, earned salaries and wages of $57,000 and interest of $3,000 and dividends of $3,700 for the current year. In addition, L sold the following capital assets:

| | |
|---|---|
| 10 shares LMN common stock, held ten months | $1,400 gain |
| 1990 Dodge sedan, used four years for personal purposes | 2,600 loss |
| 10 acres of land, held six years for investment | 9,200 loss |

a. Compute L's overall capital gain or loss.
b. Compute L's adjusted gross income.

**16-30** *Capital Gains Tax.* During her calendar year 2011, G, a single individual with no dependents, had the following capital gains and losses:

| *Asset* | *Gain/Loss* | *Holding Period* |
|---|---|---|
| 200 shares of Western Airlines | $1,400 loss | 11 months |
| Land held for appreciation | 12,300 gain | 8 years |
| Silver vases held for appreciation | 1,800 loss | 15 months |

a. Assuming G's taxable income (properly calculated) is $34,000, calculate G's gross tax.
b. Same as above, except G's taxable income is $75,000.

**16-31** *Capital Gains Tax.* R is a single, calendar year taxpayer. During 2011, R recognized a $20,000 15 percent capital gain from the sale of stock held for three years. Calculate R's tax liability (before credits and prepayments) for each of the following levels of taxable income, assuming that the net capital gains have been included in the taxable income numbers.
a. $44,000
b. $104,000
c. $600,000

**16-32** *Capital Gains Tax.* H and J are married, calendar year taxpayers who elect to file jointly. They have no dependents and do not itemize their deductions. Their income and deductions for 2011 are summarized below.

| | |
|---|---|
| Salaries and wages | $105,500 |
| Interest income | 16,900 |
| Qualifying dividends received | 4,600 |
| Short-term capital loss | 5,000 |
| Long-term capital gains (held > 12 months) | 20,000 |

Determine H and J's tax liability (before credits and prepayments).

**16-33** *Effective Tax Rate on Net Capital Gains.* T is an unmarried, calendar year taxpayer. He provides more than one-half the support of his elderly mother, who is living in a nearby nursing home. T's income and deductions for 2011 are summarized below.

| | |
|---|---|
| Salary | $152,950 |
| Interest income | 14,550 |
| Itemized deductions | 12,800 |
| Personal and dependency exemptions | 2 |

a. Calculate T's taxable income and income tax liability (before credits and prepayments) for the year.
b. How would your answers to (a) above change if T also had a $20,000 capital gain during the year from the sale of stock held 15 months?
c. Is the additional income tax from the capital gain limited to $3,000 ($20,000 × 15%)? If not, explain why.

**16-34** *Tax Treatment of Dividends as Capital Gain.* P and H, married, cash basis, calendar year taxpayers who file a joint return have the following income and expenses for 2011:

| | |
|---|---|
| Salaries and wages | $91,900 |
| Qualifying dividends | 4,000 |
| Long-term capital gains | 5,000 |
| Short-term capital gains or (losses) | 0 |
| Itemized deductions | 31,700 |
| Dependents—None | |

**a.** Calculate the federal income tax for P and H for the year.
**b.** How would you answer differ if P and H also had short-term capital losses of $10,000?

**16-35** *Netting Process and Capital Losses.* T, an unmarried taxpayer, sold the following capital assets during her calendar year 2011:

| | *Date Acquired* | *Date Sold* | *Sales Price* | *Adjusted Basis* |
|---|---|---|---|---|
| 100 shares CZ Corp. | 1/10/11 | 9/17/11 | $14,000 | $18,000 |
| 75 shares PC, Inc. | 7/6/11 | 9/17/11 | 5,200 | 4,300 |
| Silver coins (held as a collector) | 12/2/06 | 11/20/11 | 2,000 | 5,000 |

Complete each of the following requirements based on T's taxable income of $37,000 before capital gains and losses:
**a.** T's net 15 percent capital gain or loss
**b.** T's net 28 percent capital gain or loss
**c.** T's net short-term capital gain or loss
**d.** T's capital loss deduction in arriving at adjusted gross income
**e.** T's capital loss carryover to 2012 (describe amount and character)
**f.** How would your answers to (d) and (e) differ if T's basis in the PC stock had been $1,000?

**16-36** *Capital Loss and Carryover.* N earned a salary of $59,000 and interest and dividends of $6,500 for the current year. N also has the following capital gains and losses for the current year:

| | |
|---|---|
| 30 shares MNO common stock, held ten months | $ 400 gain |
| 50 shares NOP common stock, held four years | 3,600 loss |
| Long-term capital loss carryforward from prior year | 11,600 loss |
| 10 acres of land, held six years for investment | 9,200 gain |

**a.** Compute L's overall capital gain.
**b.** Compute L's adjusted gross income.

**16-37** *Capital Gains and Losses.* Each of the following independent cases involves capital gains and losses occurring during the calendar year for an unmarried individual taxpayer.

**Note:** N15CG(L) = Net 15 percent capital gain or (loss)
NSTCG(L) = Net short-term capital gain or (loss)

| *Case* | *N15CG(L)* | *NSTCG(L)* |
|---|---|---|
| A | $1,200 | $(4,300) |
| B | (5,000) | 200 |
| C | (1,200) | (2,300) |
| D | (7,000) | 200 |
| E | (5,000) | (200) |

**a.** Determine the amount deductible in arriving at adjusted gross income in each case for the current year.
**b.** Which, if any, of the above case(s) generate(s) a capital loss carryover to the following year? Give the amount and character.

**16-38** *Capital Loss Deduction and Capital Loss Carryover.* W, an unmarried calendar year individual, had numerous capital asset transactions during the years listed. Determine the amount deductible in each year and the amount and character of any carryover.

| Year | N15CG(L) | NSTCG(L) |
|---|---|---|
| 2011 | $(8,000) | $1,000 |
| 2012 | (1,500) | (2,000) |
| 2013 | 0 | (4,000) |
| 2014 | 2,000 | (3,000) |

**16-39** *Capital Loss Deduction and Capital Loss Carryover.* M, an unmarried calendar year individual, had numerous capital asset transactions during the years listed. Determine the amount deductible in each year and the amount and character of any carryover.

| Year | N15CG(L) | NSTCG(L) |
|---|---|---|
| 2011 | $1,000 | $(5,000) |
| 2012 | (6,000) | 0 |
| 2013 | 3,000 | (3,000) |
| 2014 | (3,000) | (3,000) |

**16-40** *Capital Loss Carryovers.* For her calendar year 2010, H, a single individual with no dependents, had unused short-term capital losses of $10,000. For 2011, her gains and losses were as follows:

| Asset | Amount | Holding Period |
|---|---|---|
| Corporate stock | $ 1,400 loss | 11 months |
| Land held for appreciation | 14,300 gain | 8 years |
| Miniature dolls held as a collector | 1,800 gain | 25 months |

After completing the netting process, how much are H's 15 percent gains and 28 percent gains?

**16-41** *Requirements for § 1244 Stock.* During the year, X, who is single, sold stock and realized a loss. For each of the following situations, indicate whether § 1244 would apply to the taxpayer's stock loss. Unless otherwise indicated, Code § 1244 applies.

**a.** The stock was that issued to X when she incorporated her business several years ago.

**b.** The stock was that of General Motors Corporation and was purchased last year.

**c.** X inherited the stock from her grandfather, who had started the company ten years ago.

**d.** X is a corporate taxpayer.

**e.** X acquired her stock interest in 2004. The other four owners had acquired their interest for $250,000 each in 1999.

**f.** The loss was $60,000.

**16-42** *Section 1244 Stock Computation.* S is a bachelor. During the year, he sold stock in X Corporation that qualifies as § 1244 stock at a loss of $70,000. In addition, S sold stock in Y Corporation, realizing a $4,000 15 percent capital gain. Compute the effect of these transactions on S's A.G.I.

**16-43** *Short Sales.* K purchased 400 shares of Intel common five years ago for $7,000. During the current year, she sold short 200 shares for $17,500. Her plan is to either buy new shares to cover the short sale or deliver 200 of the original shares in one year. Assuming the stock drops, and as planned, K purchases 200 shares for $16,000 to cover the short sale, how are these transactions treated for tax purposes?

**16-44** *Worthless Securities.* Several years ago, T was persuaded by his good friend W to invest in her new venture, Wobbly Corporation. T purchased 100 shares of Wobbly stock from W for $60,000. He also purchased Wobbly bonds, which had a face value of $20,000 for $18,000. This year, Wobbly declared bankruptcy and T's investment in Wobbly became worthless. What are the tax consequences to T?

**16-45** *Sale of Stock.* B owned 50 percent of the stock in a small incorporated dress shop. The business was successful for several years until a new freeway diverted nearly all of the traffic away from the location. The shop was moved, but to no avail, and the stock continued to quickly decline in value. Other than small interest payments, the income of the business came exclusively from sales of women's apparel.

The total paid-in capital of the corporation was $250,000, all in the form of cash. B's basis in the stock was always $125,000. In an attempt to prevent further losses, the shop was sold to a larger competitor during 2011. B received $50,000 for all of her stock.

**a.** How will B report the loss on the joint return she files with her husband for 2011?

**b.** How would your answer to (a) differ if the stock became totally worthless rather than being sold in 2011?

**16-46** *Worthless Securities.* Y purchased 30 shares of BCD Corporation common stock on March 2, 2010, for $2,475. On February 26, 2011, Y was notified by her broker that the stock was worthless.

**a.** What are the amount and character of Y's loss?

**b.** Could this loss qualify as an ordinary deduction under § 1244? Explain.

**16-47** *Section 1202 Exclusion.* E purchased qualified small business stock in P, Inc. on October 27, 2004 for $75,000. The stock continued to qualify until E sold it for $400,000 on December 15, 2011.

**a.** How much is E's gain realized upon this sale?

**b.** How much of this gain may E exclude from gross income?

**c.** What is the maximum amount of tax that E could pay on this gain (assuming no change in tax rates)?

**d.** How could E avoid recognizing the gain realized?

**16-48** *Rollover of Gain on Sale of Publicly Traded Securities.* R sold common stock in L Corp., a publicly traded corporation, on March 13, 2011 for $160,000, realizing a gain of $40,000. On April 1, 2011, R reinvested $200,000 in M Partnership, a partnership licensed by the Small Business Administration under § 301(d) of the Small Business Investment Act of 1958 (as in effect on May 13, 1993).

**a.** How much gain must R recognize on the sale of the L Corp. stock?

**b.** What is R's basis in his interest in M Partnership?

**16-49** *Combining the Exclusion and Rollover.* Y sold common stock in X Corp., a publicly traded corporation, on October 1, 2005 for $200,000, realizing a gain of $35,000. On October 15, 2005, Y reinvested $250,000 in N, Inc., a corporation licensed by the Small Business Administration under § 301(d) of the Small Business Investment Act of 1958 (as in effect on May 13, 1993), the stock of which is qualified small business stock. On December 1, 2011, Y sold all of the N, Inc. stock for $625,000.

**a.** How much is Y's gain realized on the sale of the N, Inc. stock?

**b.** How much of this gain is excludable from gross income?

**16-50** *Lease Cancellation Payment.* L rents a house to T for $450 per month under a two-year lease. When T is transferred, he offers L $675 to terminate the lease. If L accepts, what is the tax treatment of the transaction to L and T?

**16-51** *Franchise Agreements.* J entered into a franchise agreement with Box, Inc. under which J will operate a fast food restaurant bearing the trademark and using the products of Box. Box retained "significant power, right and continuing interest" related to the franchise agreement.

J made an initial payment under the contract of $40,000, which entitles him to the rights under the contract for 15 years with indefinite extensions at the agreement of both parties. J also is required to pay for all supplies used plus a royalty of 1.5 percent of gross sales. J's sales were $112,000 during the first year. All of the payments described, totaling $41,680, were made during the current year.

**a.** How will J report these payments on his cash basis tax return for the current year?

**b.** How would Box, Inc. treat the payments from J on its return for the current year? The corporation reports on the cash basis.

**16-52** *Original Issue Discount.* On January 1, 2011, B purchased from XYZ Corporation a newly issued, $1 million, 30-year, 4 percent bond for $300,000. The bond produces a semiannual yield to maturity of 7 percent. Interest is paid semiannually on January 1 and July 1. What is B's income with respect to the bond in 2011 and 2012?

**16-53** *Market Discount.* D purchased a $10,000, 7 percent bond, for $6,350, on January 1, 2010. The bond was issued at par on January 1, 2009 and matures January 1, 2014. On January 1, 2011, D sold the bond for $8,000. What is D's income from the sale?

**16-54** *Conversion Transaction.* J purchased a non-interest-bearing financial instrument on June 1, 2010 for $60,000. It was purchased subject to a contract that allows J to redeem the instrument for $66,000 on May 31, 2011, but it may not be redeemed early. The applicable federal rate is 5 percent throughout J's holding period. What are the amount and character of J's gain recognized in 2011?

**16-55** *Comprehensive Capital Gain Problem.* P is an unmarried full-time investor with no dependents. Her income for the year 2011 is as follows:

| | |
|---|---|
| Taxable interest income | $25,900 |
| Excludable municipal bond interest | 8,600 |
| Qualifying dividends | 11,650 |
| Consulting fees | 6,400 |
| Social security benefits | 8,400 |

Although P does not have sufficient deductions to itemize, her records reveal the following:

| | |
|---|---|
| Investment expenses | $ 850 |
| Expenses related to consulting | 1,200 |

In addition to the above, P recognized the following gains and losses during the year:

| | |
|---|---|
| Loss on sale of 100 shares of A, Inc., held three years | $(1,200) |
| Loss on sale of personal automobile | (1,800) |
| Sales price of 100 shares of B Corp., sold short | 8,200 |
| (This short sale was closed the following year with newly purchased shares costing $9,600. P owned no B Corp. stock at the time of the short sale.) | |
| Gain on sale of unimproved land held as an investment for six years | 45,000 |

Calculate P's adjusted gross income, taxable income, and gross income tax based on the above for 2011. Begin by calculating P's self-employment tax.

**16-56** *Investors vs. Traders.* M has a large portfolio of stocks. It seems that she is always buying and selling one stock or another. During the year, she realized gains of $300,000 and losses of $500,000 on sales of stocks that she held for less than a year. At the end of the year, she had unrealized gains of $150,000 and unrealized losses of $375,000. In managing her portfolio, she paid $12,000 of investment expenses. She also has paid $10,000 in margin interest. She conducts all of these activities online in her home office. This year she purchased a new computer for $3,000. Explain the tax treatment of her income and expenses (including how they would be reported (e.g., forms) as well as any related effects (e.g., self-employment taxes, alternative minimum tax) if she is considered:

**a.** An investor.
**b.** A trader who has not made the § 475(f) mark-to-market election.
**c.** A trader who has made the § 475(f) mark-to-market election.

## TAX RESEARCH PROBLEMS

**16-57** *Transfer of Patents.* G has just completed a successful invention of a new automotive fuel conservation device. He is willing to sell his patent rights for all areas of the United States east of the Rocky Mountains.

In the current year, G entered into an agreement with a marketing firm, giving it exclusive rights to market his invention anywhere east of the Rockies. In exchange, he received a principal sum and is to receive royalties based on sales volume.

Is G entitled to capital gain treatment on this sale under § 1235? Would it make any difference if the transferee of the patent was given exclusive rights to the patent and was given the right to "sublease" the patent?

**Research aids:**

*Kueneman v. Comm.*, 80-2 USTC ¶9616, 46 AFTR2d 80-5677, 628 F.2d 1196 (CA-9, 1980).
*Klein Est v. Comm.*, 75-1 USTC ¶9127, 35 AFTR2d 75-457, 507 F.2d 617 (CA-7, 1974).
*Rouverol v. Comm.*, 42 T.C. 186 (1964), non. acq., 1965-2 C.B. 7.

**16-58** *Sale of Subdivided and Improved Real Property.* D, a full-time physician, has owned 15 acres of unimproved suburban real estate for 10 years. The property was originally purchased for $30,000 and has been held solely for investment. D is now interested in selling the property and has several alternatives. She has come to you for advice concerning the tax treatment of these alternatives. What is the proper tax treatment of each of the following?

**a.** A sale of the entire acreage to an unrelated party in a single transaction for $150,000.

**b.** Recording the property with the county as 30 single residential lots, adding roads and improvements at a cost of $100,000, and selling the lots for $25,000 each.

**c.** Recording the property with the county as 30 single residential lots, and then selling them to an unrelated developer in a single transaction for $190,000.

**d.** Recording the property with the county as 30 single residential lots and then selling them for $190,000 in a single transaction to a partnership in which D is a 40 percent partner. The partnership then adds roads and improvements at a cost of $100,000 and sells the lots for $25,000 each.

# 17

# Property Transactions: Dispositions of Trade or Business Property

## Learning Objectives

Upon completion of this chapter you will be able to:

LO.1 Trace the historical development of the special tax treatment allowed for dispositions of trade or business property.

LO.2 Define § 1231 property.

LO.3 Apply the § 1231 gain and loss netting process to a taxpayer's § 1231 asset transactions.

LO.4 Explain the purpose of the depreciation recapture rules.

LO.5 Compute depreciation recapture under § 1245.

LO.6 Compute depreciation recapture under § 1250.

LO.7 Explain the additional recapture rule applicable only to corporate taxpayers.

LO.8 Identify tax planning opportunities related to sales or other dispositions of trade or business property.

## Chapter Outline


Introduction 17-2
Section 1231 17-2
  Historical Perspective 17-2
  Section 1231 Property 17-3
  Other § 1231 Property 17-4
  Section 1231 Netting Process 17-6
  Look-Back Rule 17-10
  Applicability of Lower Rates 17-11
Depreciation Recapture 17-13
  Historical Perspective 17-13
  When Applicable 17-14
  Types of Depreciation Recapture 17-14
  Full Recapture—§ 1245 17-15
  Partial Recapture—§ 1250 17-17
  Additional Recapture—Corporations 17-27
  Other Recapture Provisions 17-33
Related Business Issues 17-35
  Installment Sales of Trade or Business Property 17-35
  Intangible Business Assets 17-35
  Dispositions of Business Assets and the Self-Employment Tax 17-36
Tax Planning Considerations 17-36
  Timing of Sales and Other Dispositions 17-36
  Selecting Depreciation Methods 17-36
  Installment Sales 17-37
  Sales of Businesses 17-37
  Dispositions of Business Assets and the Self-Employment Tax 17-37
Problem Materials 17-38

## Introduction

As is no doubt clear by now, the treatment of property transactions is a complex story that seeks to answer three questions: (1) What is the gain or loss realized? (2) How much is recognized? and (3) What is its character? This chapter, the final act in the property transaction trilogy, addresses the problems in determining the character of gains or losses on the dispositions of *property used in a trade or business.*

In an uncomplicated world, it might seem logical to assume that gains or losses from property dispositions—be it stock, equipment, buildings, or whatever—would be treated just like any other type of income or deduction. But, as shown in the previous chapter, treating all items alike apparently was not part of the grand plan. Congress forever changed the process with the institution of preferential treatment for capital gains in 1921. Since that time taxpayers have been required to determine not only the gain or loss realized and recognized but also whether a disposition involved a capital asset. It is important to understand that these rules did not simply tip the scales in favor of capital gain. In the interest of fairness and equity, they also established a less than friendly environment for capital losses. The limitations on the deductibility of capital losses is clearly a major disadvantage, particularly considering that ordinary losses are fully deductible. The end result of Congress's handiwork was the creation of a system in which the preferred result is capital gain treatment for gains and ordinary treatment for losses. This chapter contains the saga of what happens when Congress attempts to provide taxpayers with the best of both worlds.

## Section 1231

The road to tax heaven—capital gain and ordinary loss—begins at § 1231 (in tax parlance properly pronounced as "twelve thirty-one"). While § 1231 can be a completely bewildering provision, its basic operation is relatively simple. At the close of the taxable year, the taxpayer nets all gains and losses from so-called § 1231 property (e.g., land and depreciable property used in a trade or business). If there is a net gain, it is treated as a long-term capital gain. If there is a net loss, it is treated as an ordinary loss. In short, § 1231 allows taxpayers to have their cake and eat it, too. Unfortunately, this is accomplished only with a great deal of complexity, much of which makes sense only if the historical events that shaped § 1231 are considered.

### Historical Perspective

**LO.1**
Trace the historical development of the special tax treatment allowed for dispositions of trade or business property.

At first glance, it seems that the productive assets of a business—its property, plant, and equipment—would be perfect candidates for capital gain treatment and would therefore be considered capital assets. Indeed, that was exactly the case initially. From 1921 to 1938, real or depreciable property used in business was in fact treated as a capital asset. At that time, the classification of such property as a capital asset seemed not only appropriate but desirable—particularly as the economy grew during the early 1920s and taxpayers were realizing gains. However, the opposite became true with the onset of the Great Depression. As the economy deteriorated, businesses that had purchased assets at inflated prices during the booming 1920s found themselves selling such properties at huge losses during the depression-plagued 1930s. To make matters worse, the tax law treated such losses as capital losses, severely limiting their deduction. But Congress apparently had a sympathetic ear for these concerns. Hoping that a change would help stimulate the economy, Congress enacted legislation that removed business properties from the list of capital assets. The legislative history to the Revenue Act of 1938 provides some insight into Congressional thinking, explaining that "corporations will not, as formerly, be deterred from disposing of partially obsolescent property, such as machinery or equipment, because of the limitations imposed ... upon the deduction of capital losses."[1] With the 1938 changes in place, business got the ordinary loss treatment it wanted but at the same time was saddled with ordinary income treatments for its gains.

[1] House Ways and Means Committee, H.R. Rep. 1860, 75th Cong., 3d Sess. (1938).

Although these rules worked well during the Depression years as businesses were reporting losses, they produced some unduly harsh results once the country moved to a wartime economy. By 1942, the build-up for World War II had the economy humming and inflation had once again set in. Businesses that earlier had sold assets for 10 cents on the dollar now found themselves realizing gains. Of course, under the 1938 changes these gains no longer benefited from preferential treatment but were taxed at extraordinarily high tax rates (88 percent for individuals and 40 percent for corporations). The shipping industry was particularly hard hit by the new treatment. Shippers not only had gains as the enemy destroyed their insured ships but also profited when they were forced to sell their property to the government for use in the war. Other businesses that had their factories and equipment condemned and requisitioned also felt the sting of higher ordinary rates. Although these companies could have deferred their gains had they replaced the property under the involuntary conversion rules of § 1033, qualified reinvestment property was in short supply, making § 1033 virtually useless. Understanding the plight of business, Congress once again came to the rescue. In 1942, Congress enacted legislation generally reinstating capital gain treatment but preserving ordinary loss treatment.

The changes in 1942 stemmed primarily from a need to provide relief for those whose property was condemned for the war effort. But in the end they went much further. For consistency, capital gain treatment was extended not only to condemnations of a business property but to other types of involuntary conversions as well. Under the new rules, casualty and theft gains from business property and capital assets also received capital gain treatment. In addition, the new legislation unexpectedly extended capital gain treatment to regular sales of property, plant, and equipment. Apparently, Congress felt that capital gain treatment was also appropriate for taxpayers who were selling out in anticipation of condemnation or simply because wartime conditions had made operations difficult. While Congress thought capital gain treatment was warranted for these gains, it also knew that other businesses had not profited from the war and were still suffering losses from their property transactions. Accordingly, it acted to preserve ordinary loss treatment. The end result of these maneuvers was the enactment of § 1231, an extremely complex provision that provides taxpayers with the best of all possible tax worlds: capital gain and ordinary loss.

The product of Congressional tinkering in 1942 still remains today. To summarize, real and depreciable property used in a trade or business is specifically denied capital asset status. But this does not necessarily mean that such property will be denied capital gain treatment. As explained at the outset, § 1231 generally extends capital gain treatment to gains and losses from these assets if the taxpayer realizes a net gain from all § 1231 transactions. On the other hand, if there is a net loss, ordinary loss treatment applies. But this summary lacks a great deal of precision. The specific rules of § 1231 are described below.

## Section 1231 Property

**LO.2**
Define § 1231 property

The special treatment of § 1231 is generally granted only to certain transactions involving assets normally referred to as *§ 1231 property*.[2] Section 1231 property includes a variety of assets, but among them the most important is *real or depreciable property that is used in the taxpayer's trade or business* and that is held for more than one year.[3] This definition takes in most items commonly identified as a business's fixed assets, normally referred to as its property, plant, and equipment. For example, the reach of § 1231 includes depreciable personal property used in business, such as machinery, equipment, office furniture, and business automobiles. Similarly, realty used in a business, such as office buildings, warehouses, factories, and farmland, is also considered § 1231 property.

[2] As explained below, § 1231 also applies to involuntary conversions of pure capital assets held more than one year that are used in a trade or business or held for investment. Involuntary conversions by theft or casualty of personal assets are not included under § 1231 but are subject to a special computation.

[3] The holding period is determined in the same manner as it is for capital assets. See § 1223 discussed in Chapter 16.

The Code specifically excludes the following assets from § 1231 treatment:

1. Property held primarily for sale to customers in the ordinary course of a trade or business, or includible in inventory, if on hand at the close of the tax year;
2. A copyright; a literary, musical, or artistic composition; a letter or memorandum; or similar property held by a taxpayer whose personal efforts created such property or by certain other persons; or
3. A publication of the United States Government received from the government other than by purchase at the price at which the publication is offered to the general public.[4]

Note that the excluded assets are also excluded from the definition of a capital asset. As a result, gains or losses on the disposition of inventory, property held primarily for resale, literary compositions, and certain government publications always yield ordinary income or ordinary loss.

One of the critical conditions for § 1231 treatment requires that the property be used in a trade or business. Although this test normally presents little difficulty, from time to time it has created problems, particularly for those with rental property. As an illustration, consider the common situation of a taxpayer who sells rental property such as a house, duplex, or apartment complex. Is the property sold a capital asset or § 1231 property? If a taxpayer sells rental property at a gain, the gain would normally receive capital gain treatment regardless of whether the property is a capital asset or § 1231 property. On the other hand, if the taxpayer sells the rental property at a loss, § 1231 treatment is usually far more desirable. Although the Code does not provide any clear guidance on the issue, the courts have generally held that property used for rental purposes is considered as used in a trade or business and is therefore eligible for § 1231 treatment.[5]

## Other § 1231 Property

From time to time, Congress has been convinced that particular industries deserve special tax relief. As a result, it has added a number of other properties to the § 1231 basket. Those eligible for capital gain and ordinary loss are:

1. Timber, coal, and iron ore to which § 631 applies;[6]
2. Unharvested crops on land used in a trade or business and held for more than one year;[7] and
3. Certain livestock.[8]

### Timber

Under § 631, the mere cutting of timber by the owner of the timber, or by a person who has the right to cut the timber and has held the timber or right more than one year, is to be treated, at his or her election, as a sale or exchange of the timber that is cut during the year. The timber must be cut for sale or for use in the taxpayer's trade or business. In such case, the taxpayer would report a § 1231 gain or loss and potentially receive capital gain treatment for what otherwise might be considered the taxpayer's inventory—a very favorable result. It may appear that the timber industry has secured an unfair advantage, but timber's eligibility is arguably justified on the grounds that the value of timber normally accrues incrementally as it grows over a long period of time.

The amount of gain or loss on the "sale" of the timber is the fair market value of the timber on the first day of the taxable year minus the timber's adjusted basis for depletion. For all subsequent purposes (i.e., the sale of the cut timber), the fair market value of the timber as of the beginning of the year will be treated as the cost of the timber. The term *timber* not only

---

[4] § 1231(b)(1).

[5] See, for example, *Mary Crawford*, 16 T.C. 678 (1951) A. 1951-2 C.B. 2, and *Gilford v. Comm.*, 53-1 USTC ¶9201, 43 AFTR 221, 201 F.2d 735 (CA-2, 1953).

[6] § 1231(b)(2).

[7] § 1231(b)(4).

[8] § 1231(b)(3).

includes trees used for lumber and other wood products, but also includes evergreen trees that are more than six years old when cut and are sold for ornamental purposes (e.g., Christmas trees).[9]

> **Example 1**
>
> B owned standing timber that he had purchased for $250,000 three years earlier. The timber was cut and sold to a lumber mill for $410,000 during 2011. The fair market value of the standing timber as of January 1, 2011 was $320,000. B has a § 1231 gain of $70,000 if he makes an election under § 631 ($320,000 fair market value of the timber on the first day of the taxable year less its $250,000 adjusted basis for depletion). The remainder of his gain on the *actual* sale of the timber, $90,000 ($410,000 selling price − $320,000 new "cost" of the timber), is ordinary income. Any expenses incurred by B in cutting the timber would be deductible as ordinary deductions.

An election under § 631 with respect to timber is binding on all timber owned by the taxpayer during the year of the election *and* in all subsequent years. The IRS may permit revocation of such election because of significant hardship. However, once the election is revoked, IRS consent must be obtained to make a new election.[10]

Section 631 also applies to the sale of timber under a contract providing a retained economic interest (i.e., a taxpayer sells the timber, but keeps the right to receive a royalty from its later sale) for the taxpayer in the timber. In such a case, the transfer is considered a sale or exchange. The gain or loss is recognized on the date the timber is cut, or when payment is received, if earlier, at the election of the taxpayer.[11]

### Coal and Iron Ore

When an owner disposes of coal or domestic iron ore under a contract that calls for a retained economic interest in the property, the disposition is treated as a sale or exchange of the coal or iron ore. The date the coal or ore is mined is considered the date of sale and since the property is § 1231 property, the gain or loss will be treated under § 1231.[12]

The taxpayer may not be a co-adventurer, partner, or principal in the mining of the coal or iron ore. Furthermore, the coal or iron ore may not be sold to certain related taxpayers.[13]

### Unharvested Crops

Section 1231 also addresses the special situation where a farmer sells land with unharvested crops sitting upon the land. In this case, it seems logical that the farmer should allocate the sales price between the crops and the land to ensure ordinary income or loss for the sale of the farmer's inventory and capital gain or ordinary loss on the sale of the land. While this may be the theoretically correct result, Congress wanted to eliminate potential controversy over the allocation. Accordingly, for administrative convenience it brought the entire transaction into the § 1231 fold in 1951. Currently, whenever land used in a trade or business and unharvested crops on that land are sold at the same time to the same buyer, the gain or loss is subject to § 1231 treatment as long as the land has been held for more than a year.[14] It is worth noting that the benefits of § 1231 were not extended to farmers free of charge. At the same time, Congress eliminated the current deduction for production expenses. The law now provides that any expenses related to the production of crops cannot be deducted currently but must be capitalized as part of the basis of the crops.[15] Such treatment, in a year when land and crops are sold, reduces the farmer's capital gain on the sale rather than any other ordinary income.

---

[9] § 631(a).

[10] *Ibid.*

[11] § 631(b).

[12] § 631(c).

[13] §§ 631(c)(1) and (2).

[14] § 1231(b)(4).

[15] § 268.

### Example 2

F sold 100 acres of land used in his farming business just days before the corn on the land was harvested. For the "package" deal, he received $600,000, including an estimated $70,000 for the unharvested crops that he figured had cost $20,000 to produce. F had purchased the land in 2000 for $200,000. In determining the character of his gain, F is not required to allocate the sales price between the crops and the land since he sold both at the same time to the same buyer, therefore qualifying for § 1231 treatment. He will recognize a § 1231 gain of $380,000 computed as follows:

| | |
|---|---|
| Sales price . . . . . . . . . . . . . . . . . . . . . . . . . . . . . . . | $600,000 |
| Adjusted basis ($200,000 + $20,000) . . . . . . . . . . | −220,000 |
| § 1231 gain . . . . . . . . . . . . . . . . . . . . . . . . . . . . . . | $380,000 |

Note that F has effectively turned the $50,000 ($70,000 − $20,000) profit from the sale of his crops from ordinary income into potential capital gain.

### Livestock

Livestock that are used for breeding and other income producing purposes are depreciable assets much like machinery and thus qualify for § 1231 treatment. In many situations, however, livestock are used for these purposes for only a short period of time and then sold. If this is the farmer's or rancher's normal practice, the IRS is inclined to argue that the animals are held primarily for resale, in which case the law specifically denies § 1231 treatment. To help end this controversy, Congress specifically made all livestock (other than poultry) used for draft, breeding, dairy, or sporting purposes eligible for § 1231 treatment if they are held for over a year.[16] In the case of cattle and horses, the holding period is extended to two years. Note that this treatment is extremely beneficial since the taxpayer effectively gets capital gain from animals pulled out of the breeding process and sold. Moreover, the farmer or rancher is allowed to deduct the costs of raising such animals currently against ordinary income. The extension of the holding period for cattle and horses was in part, an attempt to cut back on the benefits of this favorable treatment.

## Section 1231 Netting Process

**LO.3**
Apply the § 1231 gain and loss netting process to a taxpayer's § 1231 asset transactions

The treatment of § 1231 gains or losses ultimately depends on the outcome of a netting process that is far more complicated than outlined earlier.[17] As can be seen from the flowchart in Exhibit 17-1, the taxpayer must first identify all of the gains and losses that enter into the netting process. These include gains and losses from what has been described above as § 1231 property. Also, the § 1231 "bucket" includes *involuntary conversions* of certain *capital assets*. Surprisingly, gains or losses recognized from casualties, thefts, or condemnations of capital assets that are used in a trade or business or held for investment are part of the § 1231 netting process. Involuntary conversions of capital assets that are held for *personal use* are not considered under § 1231 but are subject to special rules.

After identifying all of the § 1231 transactions, the taxpayer must segregate the § 1231 gains and losses arising from casualty and theft from those attributable to sale, exchange, and condemnation. The end result is that there are two sets of § 1231 transactions:

1. Involuntary conversions due to casualty and theft of:
   - § 1231 property
     - Real and depreciable property used in business and held more than one year
     - Timber, coal, iron ore, unharvested crops, and livestock
   - Capital assets
     - Used in a trade or business or held for investment in connection with business and held more than one year

---

[16] § 1231(b)(3).

[17] § 1231(a).

2. Sales and exchanges of:
   - § 1231 property
     - Real and depreciable property used in business
     - Timber, coal, iron ore, unharvested crops and livestock

   Involuntary conversion due to condemnation of:
   - § 1231 property
     - Real and depreciable property used in business and held more than one year
     - Timber, coal, iron ore, unharvested crops, and livestock
   - Capital assets
     - Used in a trade or business or held for investment in connection with business and held more than one year

**EXHIBIT 17.1** **Section 1231 Netting Process**

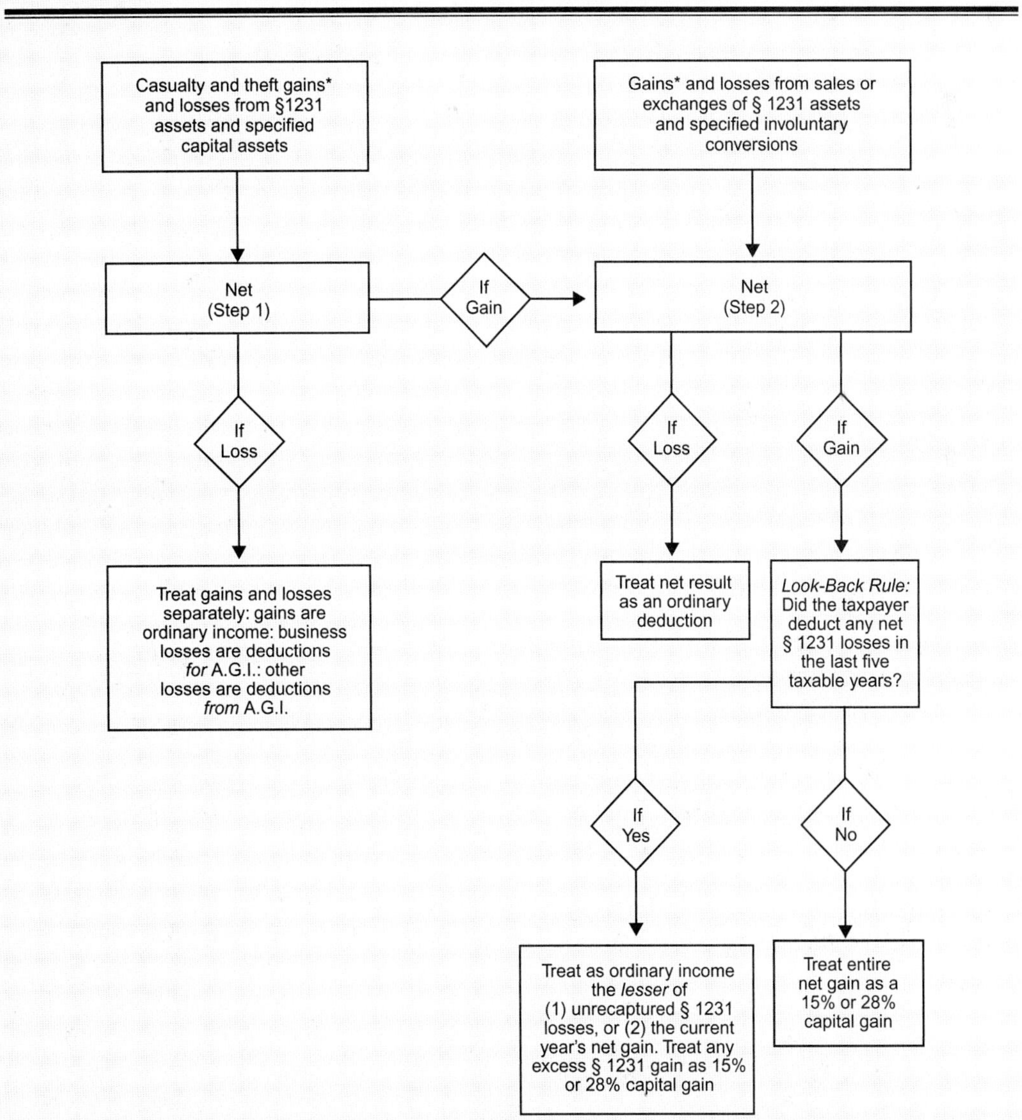


* Gains remaining after reduction for any depreciation recapture

Within each of these two categories, each gain and loss is assigned to one of the three *potential* long-term capital gain groups and netted just as if they had been 28%, 25% or 15% capital gains or losses (see Chapter 16). This means that each § 1231 gain or loss is assigned to one of the following categories: (1) 15% group for § 1231 gains and losses (15G or 15L); (2) 25% group for unrecaptured § 1250 depreciation on gains from § 1231 assets (25G discussed below); and (3) 28% group for gains and losses from collectibles (28G or 28L). Once all of the appropriate transactions have been poured into the § 1231 process, the netting process can begin. There are three steps.

1. First, all of the gains and losses in the first category of § 1231 transactions (casualties and thefts) are netted. Specifically, gains and losses within the 15% and 28% groups are netted to arrive at one of the following: (1) a net gain or loss on 15% § 1231 assets (N15G or N15L); and (2) a net gain or loss on 28% § 1231 assets (N28G or N28L). Any net loss positions are then combined with the net gain positions using the rules discussed for netting the three groups for capital asset transactions:

   - A N28L first offsets 25G, then N15G.
   - A N15L first offsets a N28G, then 25G.
   - There can be no net loss in the 25G group since this group contains only gains.

   This netting process is summarized as follows:

*Section 1231 Gains and Losses from Casualty and Theft*

| | *Collectibles* | *Unrecaptured Depreciation* | *Other* |
|---|---|---|---|
| | *28%* | *25%* | *15%* |
| Gains | $x,xxx | Gains only | $xx,xxx |
| Losses | (x,xxx) | – | (x,xxx) |
| Net gain or loss | ???? | Gain only | ???? |
| Possibilities: | | | |
| 1 | N28G | 25G | N15G |
| 2 | N28G | 25G | N15L |
| 3 | N28L | 25G | N15G |
| 4 | N28L | 25G | N15L |

If the netting process results in a net gain position(s) (e.g., a N28G, N25G, and a N15G) the net gains from casualties and thefts become § 1231 gains and become part of the second category of other § 1231 transactions (each assigned to either the 28%, 25%, or 15% groups).

## Example 3

During the year, T, who is in the 35% tax bracket, reported the following § 1231 gains and losses from casualties of § 1231 assets (including casualties of capital assets used in a trade or business) and netted them as shown below.

*Section 1231 Gains and Losses*

| | *Collectibles* | *Unrecaptured Depreciation* | *Other* |
|---|---|---|---|
| | *28%* | *25%* | *15%* |
| Gains | $10,000 | $4,000 | $ 2,000 |
| Losses | (4,000) | — | (7,000) |
| Net gain or loss | $ 6,000 | $4,000 | ($ 5,000) |
| Netting | (5,000) | — | 5,000 |
| To Section 1231 Other | $ 1,000 | $4,000 | $ 0 |

T has a N28G of $1,000 and a N25G of $4,000. Since the end results are net gains, each net gain is assigned to its appropriate group in the second category of other § 1231 transactions.

If a net loss results, the casualty and theft gains and losses are removed from the § 1231 process and treated separately. The gains are treated as ordinary income, and the losses on business use assets are deductible for A.G.I. Any other casualty and theft losses are deductible from A.G.I.

2. The second step of the process is to combine any net casualty or theft gains from the first step with the gains or losses in the second set of § 1231 transactions. In this regard, the net casualty and theft gains must be assigned to the appropriate group (15%, 25%, or 28% group) in the second category of § 1231 transactions (sales and exchanges of § 1231 assets and certain condemnations). For example, if the taxpayer had a net 15% gain from § 1231 casualties, this gain would become a 15% gain in the second category of § 1231 transactions. These transactions are then netted just as if they had been 28%, 25%, or 15% capital gains or losses to determine if there is a net gain or loss.

3. The final step in the § 1231 netting process is to characterize the gain or loss resulting from netting the transactions in the second step. If the net result is a loss, the net loss is treated as an ordinary deduction for A.G.I. It is not treated as a capital loss. If the net result is a gain (e.g., a N25G and a N15G), these gains are normally treated as capital gains and become part of the capital gain and loss netting process.

The § 1231 netting process is illustrated in Exhibit 17-1 above and the following examples.

## Example 4

During the current year, D sold real estate used in her business for $45,000. She had purchased the property several years ago for $36,000. D also sold a business car (held for more than 15 months) at a loss of $1,200. D's gain on the real estate is computed as follows:

| | |
|---|---|
| Selling price | $45,000 |
| Less: Adjusted basis | (36,000) |
| Gain realized and recognized | $ 9,000 |

D nets the gain and loss as follows:

| | |
|---|---|
| 15% Gain from sale of § 1231 asset | $ 9,000 |
| 15% Loss from sale of § 1231 asset | (1,200) |
| Net 15% § 1231 gain for year | $ 7,800 |

D's net 15% § 1231 gain of $7,800 is treated as a 15% capital gain. If she had other capital gains or losses during the year, they will be subject to the capital gain and loss netting process discussed in Chapter 16.

## Example 5

During the year R, a sole proprietor, sold a business computer for $32,000. His basis at the time of the sale was $44,000. He also sold land used in his business at a gain of $1,400 and had an uninsured theft loss of works of art used to decorate his business offices (i.e., capital assets held in connection with a trade or business). R had purchased the artwork for $1,500 and it was valued at $5,000 before the burglary. All of the assets were acquired more than 12 months ago.

R nets his gains and losses as follows:

**Step 1:** The net loss from the casualty is $1,500 (adjusted basis). Since R has a net 15% casualty loss, it is not treated as a § 1231 loss. Instead, the loss is treated as an ordinary loss (which is fully deductible for A.G.I. since the art works were business property).

**Step 2:** Combine gains and losses from sales of § 1231 assets:

| | |
|---|---|
| 15% loss from sale of business computer | ($12,000) |
| 15% gain from sale of business land | 1,400 |
| Net § 1231 loss for year | ($10,600) |

**Step 3:** A net § 1231 loss is treated as an ordinary deduction. Thus, R's $10,600 loss can be used to offset other ordinary income.

Note that the theft loss of the works of art is included in the first step of the netting process even though these items are capital assets. This loss would have offset, dollar for dollar, any casualty or theft gains (net of depreciation recapture) from § 1231 assets as well as any casualty or theft gains from other capital assets held in connection with R's business. Also note that the current year's deductible § 1231 loss may result in a change in the character of any net § 1231 gains in the next five years due to the look-back rule.

## Look-Back Rule

For many years, taxpayers took advantage of the § 1231 netting process. For example, assume a taxpayer in the 35 percent tax bracket currently owns two § 1231 assets, both held for 15 months. One asset has a built-in gain of $10,000 and the other has a built-in loss of $9,000. If both assets are sold during the year, the loss offsets the gain and the taxpayer pays a capital gain tax of $150 [($10,000 – $9,000 = $1,000) × 15%]. If the taxpayer had sold the assets in different years, the loss would *not* have reduced the gain, and the tax after both transactions would have been $1,500 in one year ($10,000 × 15%) and $3,150 ($9,000 × 35%) of savings in the other year, for a net tax savings of $1,650 ($3,150 – $1,500). As might be imagined, taxpayers carefully planned their transactions to maximize their tax savings.

In an effort to prevent taxpayers from cleverly timing their § 1231 gains and losses to ensure that § 1231 losses reduced ordinary income and not potential capital gain, Congress enacted the so-called *look-back* rule in 1984. Under this rule, a taxpayer with a net § 1231 gain in the current year must report the gain as ordinary income to the extent of any *unrecaptured net* § 1231 losses reported in the past five taxable years.[18] In recapturing the § 1231 gains, recapture occurs in the following order: 28% gains, 25% gains, and 15% gains. Unrecaptured net § 1231 losses are simply the *net* § 1231 losses that have occurred during the past five years that have not been previously recaptured (i.e., the excess of net § 1231 losses of the five preceding years over the amount of such loss that has been recaptured in the five prior years).

### Example 6

Assume the same facts in *Example 5* and that R's 2010 net § 1231 loss of $10,600 is the only loss he has deducted in the past five years. In 2011, R has a net 15% § 1231 gain of $15,000. R is subject to the look-back rule since in the prior year he reported a § 1231 loss of $10,600 that has not been recaptured. He must report $10,600 of ordinary income and $4,400 of net 15% § 1231 gain. Should R have a § 1231 gain in the following year, he will not be subject to the look-back rule again since he has recaptured all prior year's net § 1231 losses.

[18] § 1231(c).

## Applicability of Lower Rates

Five potential tax rates apply to long-term capital gains while six rates can apply to ordinary income, which includes short-term capital gains.

To ensure that the appropriate rate is applied, the following process should be followed.

- The first step is to complete the § 1231 netting process.
  - If there is a net § 1231 loss, that loss must be treated as an ordinary loss and it is left out of the capital gain and loss netting process entirely.
  - If there is a net § 1231 gain, it is treated as a long-term capital gain and is entered into the capital gain and loss netting process in the next step. In order to do this, a determination must be made as to which part of the gain, if any, is 25% gain, and which part, if any, is 15% gain.
- Netting of capital gains and losses occurs in each of the various groups of assets.
  - Short-term gains are netted against short-term losses and long-term gains are netted against long-term losses.
  - Within the long-term netting process, gains and losses are further broken down in the various sub-groups with 15% gains and losses, and 28% gains and losses being netted. Since there are no 25% losses, the 25% gains are not reduced.
  - The net gains and losses from these three groups are netted against one another as prescribed in Chapter 16 (e.g., 28% losses are first offset against 25% gains, then 15% gains, and 15% losses are first offset against 28% gains, then 25% gains).
- Short-term gains and losses are netted/combined with long-term gains and losses. Short-term losses are first netted against 28% gains, then 25% gains, and finally 15% gains. Net long-term losses are netted against short-term gains.
- The net results are subject to the capital gains tax.
  - Short-term gains are treated like ordinary income
  - Long-term gains are subject to tax at the appropriate specified capital gains rates (0%, 10%, 15%, 25%, and 28%)
  - Losses are subject to the $3,000 annual limit with the excess being carried forward.

Numerous possibilities exist, therefore, for any net § 1231 gain. Perhaps, the gain would be offset by capital losses, receiving no favorable treatment at all. However, if the § 1231 gain survives the netting process to be included in a net capital gain, it is subject to the preferred rates right along with any other long-term capital gains with surviving unrecaptured § 1250 gain being treated as 25% gain and any other surviving gain treated as 15% gain.

## ✓ Check Your Knowledge

### Review Question 1

Indicate whether the following gains and losses are § 1231 gains or losses or capital gains and losses or neither. Make your determination prior to the § 1231 netting process and assume any holding period requirement has been met.

**a.** Gain on the sale of General Motors stock held as a temporary investment by Consolidated Brands Corporation.

**b.** Gain on the sale of a four-unit apartment complex owned by Lorena Smith. This was her only rental property.

**c.** Loss on the sale of welding machinery used by Arco Welding in its business.

**d.** Loss on theft of welding machinery used by Arco Welding in its business.

**e.** Gain on sale of diamond bracelet by Nancy Jones.

**f.** Income from sale of electric razors by Razor Corporation, which manufactures them.

**g.** Gain on condemnation of land on which Tonya Smith's personal residence is built.

**h.** Gain on condemnation of land owned by Tonya Smith's business.

**i.** Loss on sale of personal automobile.

*Answer.* The § 1231 hodgepodge contains not only gains and losses from § 1231 property but also those from involuntary conversions by casualty, theft, or condemnation of capital assets that are used in a trade or business or held as an investment in connection with a trade or business.

**a.** The sale of the GM stock is not included in the § 1231 pot since it is a sale of a capital asset and not an involuntary conversion.

**b.** The rental property is generally considered property used in a trade or business and thus § 1231 property even if the owner owns only a single property.

**c.** The welding machinery is depreciable property used in a business and is therefore considered § 1231 property.

**d.** The theft of the welding machinery is also a § 1231 transaction. Note, however, that in processing the § 1231 gains and losses, the casualties must be segregated from the sales.

**e.** The sale of the diamond bracelet produces capital gain since it is a pure capital asset and not trade or business property.

**f.** The razors are inventory and are therefore neither capital assets nor § 1231 property.

**g.** The condemnation of the land near the residence is considered a personal involuntary conversion gain. Since the land is not held in connection with a trade or business, it does not qualify as § 1231 property, but it is a capital asset.

**h.** The condemnation of the land held for business does enter into the § 1231 hodgepodge as a regular § 1231 gain.

**i.** Although the personal automobile is a capital asset, no loss is allowed from the sale.

## Review Question 2

During his senior year at the University of Virginia, Bill decided that he never wanted to leave Charlottesville. After some thought, he opened his own hamburger joint, Billy's Burgers. That was 20 years ago and Bill has had great success, owning a number of businesses all over Virginia and North Carolina. Not believing in corporations, Bill and his wife, Betty, operate all of these as partnerships.

**a.** Information from the partnerships and his own personal records revealed the following transactions during the current year:

1. Sale of one of 50 apartment buildings that one of their partnerships owns: $50,000 gain (ignore depreciation)
2. Sale of restaurant equipment: $20,000 loss
   Assuming both assets have been held for several years, how should Bill and Betty report these transactions on their current year return?

*Answer.* Under § 1231, the taxpayer generally nets gains and losses from the sale of § 1231 property. If a net gain results, the gain is treated as a long-term capital gain, while a net loss is treated as an ordinary loss. For this purpose, § 1231 property generally includes real or depreciable property used in a trade or business. In this case, both the apartment complex and the restaurant equipment are § 1231 property and both are in the 15 percent group. As a result, the couple should net the gain and loss and report a 15 percent capital gain of $30,000.

**b.** The couple's records for the following year revealed several gains and losses:

1. Office building burned down: $20,000 loss
2. Crane for bungee jumping business stolen: $35,000 gain (assume no depreciation had been claimed)
3. Parking lot sold: $14,000 loss
4. Exxon stock sold: long-term capital loss of $10,000
5. Condemnation of Greensboro land held for use in the business: $15,000 gain.

Assuming each of the assets was held for several years, determine how much 15 percent capital gain or loss as well as the amount of ordinary income or loss that Bill and Betty will report for the year.

*Answer.* The § 1231 netting process requires the taxpayer to separate § 1231 casualty gains and losses from other § 1231 transactions (sometimes referred to as regular § 1231 items). The casualty loss on the office building and the casualty gain on the crane are both considered § 1231 15 percent casualties since they involve § 1231 property (i.e., real or depreciable property used in business). Note that the condemnation—even though it is an involuntary conversion—is not treated as a § 1231 casualty. The casualty items are netted to determine whether there is a net gain or loss. Here, there is a net casualty 15 percent gain of $15,000 ($35,000 – $20,000). This net gain is then combined with any "regular" § 1231 items, in this case the $14,000 loss on the sale of the parking lot (real property used in a business) and the $15,000 gain on the condemnation of the land (a capital asset). Note that both "regular" § 1231 items are also in the 15 percent group. After netting these items, the partnership has a net gain of $16,000. This $16,000 net § 1231 gain is treated as a 15 percent capital gain and is combined with $10,000 15 percent capital loss on the sale of the stock. The end result is a $6,000 15 percent capital gain. This process can be summarized as follows (see also Exhibit 17-3):

| Transaction | 15% § 1231 Casualties | 15% § 1231 Regular | Capital Gains and Losses Short-term | 15% |
|---|---|---|---|---|
| 1. Office burned | $(20,000) | | | |
| 2. Crane stolen | 35,000 | | | |
| 3. Parking lot sold | | $(14,000) | | |
| 4. Exxon stock sold | | | | $(10,000) |
| 5. Condemnation of land | ______ | 15,000 | | |
| Net casualty | $15,000 → | 15,000 | | |
| Net § 1231 gain | | $16,000 → | | 16,000 |
| Net 15% capital gain | | | | $ 6,000 |

**c.** Same as in (b), except Bill and Betty reported a net § 1231 loss of $3,000 in the previous year.

*Answer.* In this case, the look-back rule applies, causing $3,000 of the net 15 percent § 1231 gain to be treated as ordinary income. As a result, the couple's 15 percent capital gain from the § 1231 netting process is $13,000 and their net 15 percent capital gain is only $3,000.

## Depreciation Recapture

### Historical Perspective

For many years, taxpayers have taken advantage of the interaction of § 1231 and the depreciation rules to secure significant tax savings. Prior to 1962 there were no substantial statutory restrictions on the depreciation methods that could be adopted. Consequently, a taxpayer could quickly recover the basis of a depreciable asset by selecting a rapid depreciation method such as declining balance and using a short useful life. If the property's value did not decline as quickly as its basis was being reduced by depreciation deductions, a gain was ensured if the property was disposed of at a later date. The end result could be quite beneficial.

### Example 7

During the current year, T purchased equipment for $1 million. After two years, T, using favorable depreciation rules, had claimed and deducted $600,000 of depreciation, leaving a basis of $400,000. Assume that the property did not truly depreciate in value and T was able to sell it in the third year for its original cost of $1 million. In such case T would report a gain of $600,000 ($1,000,000 – $400,000). Except for time value of money considerations, it appears that the $600,000 gain and the $600,000 of depreciation are simply a wash. However, the depreciation reduced ordinary income that would be taxed at ordinary rates while the gain would be a § 1231 gain and likely taxed at capital gain rates. As an illustration of the savings that could be achieved, assume that the law at this time provided for a top capital gain rate of 20% and the taxpayer's ordinary income was taxed at a 40%. In this case the depreciation would offset ordinary income and provide tax savings of $240,000, but the $600,000 gain on the sale would be treated as a capital gain and produce a tax of only $120,000. Thus, even though the taxpayer has had no economic gain or loss with respect to the property—he bought and sold the equipment for $1,000,000—he was able to secure a tax benefit of $120,000 ($240,000 – $120,000).

The above example clearly illustrates how taxpayers used rapid depreciation and the favorable treatment of § 1231 gains to effectively convert ordinary income into capital gain. In fact, this strategy—deferring taxes with quick depreciation write-offs at ordinary rates and giving them back later at capital gains rates—was the foundation of many tax shelter schemes.

**LO.4**
Explain the purpose of the depreciation recapture rules.

Legislation to limit these benefits came in a number of forms, but the most important was the enactment of the so-called *depreciation recapture* rules. These rules strike right at the heart of the problem, generally treating all or some portion of any gain recognized as ordinary income, based on the amount of depreciation previously deducted. Thus, in the above example, the taxpayer's $600,000 gain, which was initially characterized as a § 1231 gain, is treated as ordinary income because of the $600,000 of depreciation previously claimed. In this way, all of the tax savings initially given away by virtue of the ordinary depreciation deductions are recaptured. In this regard, it may be useful to think of a gain as consisting of two parts: the gain attributable to depreciation and the gain attributable to holding the asset (resulting from appreciation and inflation). "Depreciation gains" normally are treated as ordinary income while "holding gains" are § 1231 gains and potentially taxed as long-term capital gains. Unfortunately, much like § 1231 in general, the recapture rules can become quite complex. The operations of the specific provisions are discussed below.

## When Applicable

Before specific recapture rules are examined, there are two very important points to keep in mind. First, depreciable assets held for one year or less do not qualify for § 1231 treatment. Thus, any gain from the disposition of such assets is always reported as ordinary income. Second, the depreciation recapture rules *do not apply* if property is disposed of at a *loss*. Remember that losses from the sale or exchange of depreciable assets are treated as § 1231 losses if the property is held more than a year. In addition, casualty or theft losses of such property are included in the § 1231 netting process. Any loss from a depreciable asset held one year or less is an ordinary loss regardless of whether it was sold, exchanged, stolen, or destroyed.

## Types of Depreciation Recapture

There are essentially *three* depreciation recapture provisions in the Code. These are:

1. Section 1245 Recapture—commonly called the *full recapture rule*, and applicable primarily to depreciable personalty (rather than realty)

2. Section 1250 Recapture—commonly called the *partial recapture rule*, and applicable to most depreciable realty if a method of depreciation other than straight-line was used
3. Section 291 Recapture—commonly called the *additional recapture rule*, and applicable *only* to corporate taxpayers

These depreciation recapture provisions affect the character—not the amount—of the gain. Losses are not affected. Each of these recapture rules is discussed below.

## FULL RECAPTURE—§ 1245

**LO.5**
Compute depreciation recapture under § 1245.

The recapture concept was first introduced with the enactment of § 1245 by the Revenue Act of 1962. Section 1245 generally requires any gain recognized to be reported as ordinary income to the extent of *any* depreciation allowed on § 1245 property after 1961.

### Definition of § 1245 Property

The recapture of depreciation under § 1245 applies only to *§ 1245 property*, normally *depreciable personal property*.[19] Because the definition of personal property itself is so broad, § 1245 generally covers a wide variety of depreciable assets such as:

- Machinery and equipment used in production of goods and services
- Office furniture and equipment
- Automobiles, vans, trucks, and other transportation equipment
- Livestock used for breeding or production
- Intangibles such as patents, copyrights, trademarks, and goodwill that have been amortized under § 197 or otherwise.

Essentially the amortization is treated the same as depreciation, just like any portion of the cost of a depreciable asset that is expensed under § 179 is treated as depreciation allowed.[20] It is important to understand that § 1245 applies only if the property is depreciable or amortizable. Consequently, it pertains only to property that is used in a trade or business and property held for the production of income. For example, livestock that are considered inventory are not subject to depreciation and are therefore not § 1245 property, although any gain or loss from the disposition of inventory is ordinary income.

Although the above definition is usually sufficient, § 1245 property actually includes a number of other assets besides depreciable personalty, including the following:[21]

1. Property used as an integral part of manufacturing, production, or extraction, or in furnishing transportation, communications, electrical energy, gas, water, or sewage disposal services.
   a. However, any portion of a building or its structural components is not included.
   b. A research facility or a facility for the bulk storage of commodities related to an activity listed above is included.
2. A single-purpose agricultural or horticultural structure (e.g., greenhouses).
3. A storage structure used in connection with the distribution of petroleum or any primary product of petroleum (e.g., oil tank).
4. Any railroad grading or tunnel bore.
5. Certain other property that is subject to a special provision allowing current deductibility or rapid amortization (e.g., pollution control facilities and railroad rolling stock).

---

[19] § 1245(a)(3).

[20] See § 197(f)(7) for intangibles and § 1245(a)(3)(D) for expensed property and certain other properties subject to unique expensing rules.

[21] The definition parallels that of § 38 property, which qualified for the investment tax credit. § 48(a)(1).

## Operation of § 1245

Section 1245 generally requires any gain recognized to be treated as ordinary income to the extent of *any* depreciation allowed.[22] To state the rule in another way: any gain on the disposition of § 1245 property is ordinary income to the extent of the *lesser* of the gain recognized or the § 1245 recapture potential, generally the depreciation claimed and deducted. Although both statements say the same thing, the latter helps focus attention on two points and eliminates some misconceptions. First, a taxpayer is never required to report more income than the amount of gain realized regardless of the amount of depreciation claimed and deducted (i.e., regardless of the amount of recapture potential). For example, if the taxpayer realizes a gain of $10,000 and has deducted depreciation of $15,000, the taxpayer reports only $10,000 of income, all of which would be ordinary. Note that the depreciation recapture rules do not affect the amount of gain or loss, only the character of any gain to be recognized. Second, using the term *recapture potential* helps emphasize that sometimes the amount that must be recaptured may include more than mere depreciation.

Section 1245 *recapture potential* includes *all* depreciation or amortization allowed (or allowable) with respect to a given property—regardless of the method of depreciation used. This is why § 1245 is often called the full recapture rule. Recapture potential also includes adjustments to basis related to items that are expensed (e.g., under § 179 expense election) or where tax credits have been allowed under various sections of the Code.[23]

To summarize, determining the character of gain on the disposition of § 1245 property is generally a three-step process:

1. Determine the amount of gain to be recognized, if any.
2. The gain is ordinary income to the extent of the *lesser* of the gain recognized or the § 1245 recapture potential (all depreciation allowed or allowable).
3. Any recognized gain in excess of the recapture potential retains its original character, usually § 1231 gain.

Recall that there is no § 1245 depreciation recapture when a property is sold at a loss, so any loss is normally a § 1231 loss.

### Example 8

T owned a printing press that he used in his business. Its cost was $6,800 and T deducted depreciation in the amount of $3,200 during the three years he owned the press. T sold the press for $4,000 and his realized and recognized gain is $400 ($4,000 sales price − $3,600 adjusted basis). T's recapture potential is $3,200, the amount of depreciation taken on the property. Thus, the entire $400 gain is ordinary income under § 1245.

### Example 9

Assume the same facts as in *Example 8*, except that T sold his press for $7,000. In this case, T's realized and recognized gain would be $3,400 ($7,000 − $3,600). The ordinary income portion under § 1245 would be $3,200 (the amount of the recapture potential), and the remaining $200 of the gain is a § 1231 gain. Note that in order for any § 1231 gain to occur, the property must be sold for more than its original cost since all of the depreciation is treated as ordinary income.

---

[22] § 1245(a).

[23] See § 1245(a)(2) for a listing of these adjustments and their related Code sections, including the basis adjustment related to the earned portion of any investment credit.

**Example 10**

Assume the same facts as in *Example 8*, except that the printing press is sold for $3,000 instead of $4,000. In this case, T has a loss from the sale of $600 ($3,000 – $3,600 adjusted basis). Because there is a loss, there is no depreciation recapture. All of T's loss is a § 1231 loss.

### Exceptions and Limitations

In many ways, § 1245 operates much like the proverbial troll under the bridge. It sits ready to spring on its victim whenever the proper moment arises. Section 1245 generally applies whenever there is a transfer of property. However, § 1245 does identify certain situations where it does not apply, most of which are nontaxable events. For example, there is no recapture on a transfer by gift or bequest since both of these are nontaxable transfers.[24]

In involuntary conversions and like-kind exchanges, the depreciation recapture under § 1245 is limited to the *gain recognized*.[25] Similarly, in nontaxable business adjustments such as the formation of partnerships, transfers to controlled corporations, and certain corporate reorganizations, § 1245 recapture is limited to the gain recognized under the controlling provisions.[26] In any situation where recapture is not triggered, it is generally not lost but carried over in some fashion.

## Partial Recapture—§ 1250

**LO.6**
Compute depreciation recapture under § 1250.

As originally enacted in 1961, the concept of recapture as set forth in § 1245 generally applied only to personalty. Gains derived from dealing in realty were not subject to recapture. In 1963, however, Congress eliminated this omission by enacting § 1250, a special recapture provision that applied to most buildings. Since 1963, § 1245 has generally been associated with depreciation recapture for personal property while § 1250 served that role for buildings. Although the two provisions are similar, § 1250 is far less damaging. Specifically, § 1250 calls for the recapture of only a *portion* of any *accelerated* depreciation allowed with respect to *§ 1250 property*. Note that while §§ 1250 and 1245 are essentially the same—they both convert potential capital gain into ordinary income—§ 1250 differs from § 1245 in several important ways: (1) it applies only if an accelerated method is used; (2) it does not require recapture of all the depreciation deducted but only a portion—generally only the *excess of accelerated depreciation over what straight-line would have been*; and (3) it applies to a different type of property, *buildings and their components*, rather than personal property. These basic concepts are illustrated in the following example and discussed further below.

**Example 11**

T purchased an office building in 1979 for $600,000. In 1979, depreciation generally was computed using either the straight-line or accelerated method based on the estimated useful life of the property and estimated salvage value, all determined by the taxpayer. T depreciated the building over its estimated useful life of 40 years, using an accelerated method and no salvage value. This year, T sold the building for $900,000. At the time of sale, accelerated depreciation actually deducted was $500,000. Straight-line depreciation using the same facts would have been $300,000. The building is § 1250 property since it is realty acquired after 1969. As determined below, T recognizes a gain of $800,000, $200,000 is recaptured as ordinary income under § 1250 and the $600,000 balance is § 1231 gain.

[24] §§ 1245(b)(1) and (2). Recapture of depreciation under § 1245 is required, however, to the extent § 691 applies (relating to income in respect to a decedent).

[25] § 1245(b)(4).

[26] § 1245(b)(3). See Chapter 19 for further discussion of nontaxable business adjustments.

| | | |
|---|---|---|
| Amount realized | | $900,000* |
| Adjusted basis | | |
| Cost | $600,000 | |
| Depreciation (accelerated) | (500,000) | |
| Adjusted basis | | (100,000) |
| Gain on sale | | $ 800,000 |
| Depreciation recapture under § 1250 | | |
| Accelerated depreciation actually deducted | $500,000 | |
| Hypothetical straight-line depreciation | (300,000) | |
| Section 1250 recapture reported as ordinary income | | $ 200,000 |
| Section 1231 gain | | $ 600,000 |

*A separate allocation and calculation would be required to determine any gain or loss on the land and is ignored here for simplicity.

Note that under the partial recapture rule of § 1250 only the excess of the actual amount of accelerated depreciation deducted ($500,000) over what the straight-line depreciation would have been ($300,000), a difference of $200,000, is recaptured. This excess is treated as ordinary income. Had the property been § 1245 property, all $500,000 would have been recaptured. Also observe that under § 1250 none of the straight-line depreciation, $300,000 is recaptured. However, this unrecaptured depreciation on § 1250 property is taxed at a maximum rate of 25% as discussed below.

As noted in the example, § 1250 does not recapture the straight-line depreciation. In enacting § 1250 Congress wanted to ensure that ordinary income treatment would be applied only to what were truly excess depreciation deductions. Gain not attributable to excess depreciation was considered attributable to a rise in price levels and was eligible for relief provided for capital gains and not subject to recapture.

## Section 1250 Property

Section 1250 property is generally any real property that is depreciable and is not covered by § 1245.[27] For the most part, § 1250 applies to all of the common forms of real estate such as office buildings, warehouses, apartment complexes, and low-income housing. As a practical matter, sales of these properties rarely produce recapture because the law has required the straight-line method for depreciation since 1986. However, Section 1250 property also includes 15- and 20-year realty which is depreciated using the 150 percent declining balance and, therefore, is capable of creating excess depreciation. This category includes such assets as multi-purpose agricultural structures (e.g., barns), land improvements (roads, sidewalks, fences, landscaping, shrubbery, docks), gas stations, convenience stores and more. As explained earlier, nonresidential real estate (e.g., warehouses and office buildings) placed in service after 1980 and before 1987 for which an accelerated method was used is covered by the full recapture rule of § 1245.[28]

## Depreciation of Real Property

Section 1250 applies only if an accelerated method of depreciation is used. If the straight-line depreciation method is used, § 1250 does not apply and there is no depreciation recapture for noncorporate taxpayers.[29] For this reason, a critical first step in determining the relevance of § 1250 is determining how the taxpayer has depreciated the realty.

**Realty Placed in Service before 1987** Prior to 1987, taxpayers could choose to use either an accelerated or straight-line method to compute depreciation for realty. This was an extremely important decision. It affected not only the amount of depreciation the taxpayer claimed but also the character of any gain on a subsequent disposition of the property. For

[27] § 1250(c).

[28] It is important to note, however, that such properties are § 1250 property if the optional straight-line method is used. § 1245(a)(5).

[29] As explained within, corporate taxpayers are still required to recapture 20 percent of any straight-line depreciation under § 291. Also, any unrecaptured straight-line depreciation is taxed at a maximum rate of 25 percent.

example, a taxpayer could accelerate depreciation deductions but only at the possible expense of recapture. Alternatively, the taxpayer could accept the slower-paced straight-line method and avoid the § 1250 recapture rules. But the Tax Reform Act of 1986 ended this flexibility and at the same time simplified the law. Taxpayers who place realty in service *after 1986* must use the straight-line method for residential and nonresidential realty. As a result, the recapture rules of § 1250 do not apply to residential and nonresidential realty acquired after 1986. However, much of the existing inventory of real property was acquired before 1987 and may therefore be subject to § 1250, depending on the depreciation method used.

**Realty Placed in Service from 1981 through 1986** For real property acquired between the beginning of 1981 and the end of 1986, the taxpayer could either use the accelerated depreciation method allowed under ACRS or elect an optional straight-line method. In most cases, a taxpayer would select the accelerated method. If an accelerated method is used for *residential* realty acquired during 1981 through 1986, § 1250 applies, requiring recapture of the excess depreciation. However, as noted earlier, if an accelerated method is used for *nonresidential* realty acquired during 1981 through 1986, the property is considered § 1245 and the full recapture rule applies.

By the close of 2005, realty acquired during 1981 through 1986 became fully depreciated since the lives were 15, 18 or 19 years during this time. As a result, there is no § 1250 recapture for residential realty since there is no excess depreciation (i.e., total accelerated depreciation would be identical to total straight-line depreciation). Similarly, there is no § 1250 recapture for nonresidential realty if the straight-line method was used. However, to reiterate, if the accelerated method was used in depreciating nonresidential realty acquired during these tainted years, 1981–1986, § 1245 applies and all of the accelerated depreciation is recaptured.

**Realty Placed in Service before 1981** All depreciable real property acquired before 1981 is classified as § 1250 property. For such property acquired before 1981 (non-ACRS property), taxpayers were required to estimate useful lives and salvage values. Although various methods could be used, there were restrictions.[30] In those situations where an accelerated method was used, § 1250 applies subject to certain limitations. As discussed further below, none of the excess depreciation produced by realty for years after 1963 and before 1970 is subject to recapture. In the case of *low-income housing* and other *residential* real estate, excess depreciation resulting after 1969 and before 1976 is no longer recaptured. After 1975, excess depreciation on low-income housing is exempt from recapture if the property is held more than 16 2/3 years.

## Summary of § 1250 Application

The significance of § 1250 has declined considerably over the years. Subject to certain unusual situations (e.g., certain low-income housing, certain Liberty Zone property, etc.), the following general observations can be made about the current status of § 1250:

- For residential and nonresidential realty acquired after 1986, there is no § 1250 recapture because the straight-line method must be used for such property and no excess depreciation results.
- For *residential* realty acquired during 1981–1986 there is no § 1250 recapture since these assets are fully depreciated and there is no excess depreciation.
- For *nonresidential* realty acquired during 1981–1986 for which the straight-line method was used, there is no recapture under § 1250, but § 1245 requires full-recapture if an accelerated method was used for the property.
- The reach of § 1250 is usually limited to realty acquired during 1970–1980. And much of this property, which at this point is 27–37 years old, has turned over and in the hands of the new buyer § 1250 does not apply.

Although the traditional recapture rules of § 1250 may not apply, gains on § 1250 property are not guaranteed the benefits of favorable capital gain rates. As explained further below, such gains may be taxed at a rate of up to 25 percent to the extent of any unrecaptured straight-line depreciation.

---

[30] § 167(j).

## Operation of § 1250

The two critical factors in determining the amount, if any, of *§ 1250 recapture* are the gain realized *and* the amount of *excess depreciation.* Excess depreciation refers to depreciation deductions in excess of that which would be deductible using the straight-line method. For property held one year or less, all depreciation is considered excess depreciation.[31]

As a general rule, § 1250 requires recapture of the excess depreciation, that is, the excess of accelerated over straight-line. Consequently, even if the taxpayer uses an accelerated method to compute the amount of depreciation deducted on the return, the hypothetical amount of straight-line depreciation must still be computed in order to determine the excess of accelerated over straight-line when the property is sold. In determining the hypothetical amount of straight-line depreciation, the taxpayer uses the same life and salvage value, if any, that were used in computing accelerated depreciation.[32] Because of this approach, a taxpayer who uses the straight-line method would have no excess depreciation and no recapture. Because the § 1250 recapture rule applies only to any excess depreciation claimed by a taxpayer, it is sometimes referred to as the partial recapture rule. However, it should be emphasized that beginning in 1997, the unrecaptured § 1250 depreciation (e.g., the straight-line depreciation) on § 1250 property held more than 12 months is subject to a special 25 percent tax rate (assuming it survives the § 1231 netting process).

Determining the taxation of any gain recognized on the disposition of § 1250 property is a four-step process:

1. Determine the amount of gain to be recognized, if any.
2. The gain is ordinary income to the extent of the *lesser* of the gain recognized or the § 1250 recapture potential (generally the excess depreciation allowed).[33]
3. Any recognized gain in excess of the recapture potential is usually treated as § 1231 gain.
4. Any gain recognized on § 1250 property held more than 12 months that is due to depreciation that is not recaptured and which survives the applicable netting processes is taxed at a maximum rate of 25 percent to the extent of any unrecaptured depreciation. Any additional gain is generally 15 percent gain.

Two other considerations should be noted. If § 1250 property is held for a year or less, all depreciation (not just the excess) is recaptured.[34] In addition, there is no § 1250 depreciation recapture when a property is sold at a loss, so any loss is normally a § 1231 loss.

## Unrecaptured § 1250 Gain

As may be apparent from step 3 above, under § 1250, taxpayers are required to recapture depreciation only if an accelerated method is used to depreciate the property. Consequently, individual taxpayers never recapture depreciation on § 1250 property if the straight-line method is used. Without some special rule, any gain attributable to straight-line depreciation for § 1250 property held more than 12 months would normally qualify for taxation at a 15 percent rate. Congress felt this treatment was too generous and created a special rule for *unrecaptured § 1250 gain.* The unrecaptured § 1250 gain is the lesser of (1) the gain recognized, or (2) the depreciation allowed after each (the gain recognized and the depreciation allowed) is reduced by any § 1250 recapture. The resulting amount will equal the amount of straight-line depreciation that was claimed or would have been claimed had the straight-line method been used (or, if less, the gain recognized minus the § 1250 recapture).

---

[31] § 1250(b).

[32] § 1250(b)(5).

[33] See § 1250(a) and discussion following dealing with recapture of only a portion of the excess depreciation for certain properties.

[34] § 1250(b)(1).

### Example 12

About 10 years ago, F purchased some residential rental property for $100,000. This year he sold the property for $110,000. He had claimed straight-line depreciation of $30,000 over this time, resulting in a basis of $70,000 (do not attempt to verify this amount). As a result, F recognized a gain of $40,000. Since the property is realty and a straight-line depreciation method was used there is no § 1250 recapture. Consequently, the entire gain is a § 1231 gain. However, the § 1231 gain will be treated as a 25% gain to the extent of any straight-line depreciation claimed. Therefore, $30,000 of the gain is a 25% § 1231 gain while $10,000 is a 15% § 1231 gain (i.e., in the capital gain netting process these will be 15% and 25% long-term gains, respectively). If F had sold the property for $90,000, he would have had a gain of $20,000, all of which would have been a 25% gain (i.e., the lesser of the gain realized, $20,000, or the unrecaptured straight-line depreciation, $30,000).

### Example 13

Same facts and $110,000 sales price from *Example 12* above, except that F also has a $400 gain on the sale of K Corporation stock held 26 months. F is single and has taxable income, excluding these transactions, of $68,000. F's tax would be computed as follows (using the 2010 tax rates for single taxpayers):

| | | |
|---|---|---|
| Regular tax on $68,000: | | |
| Tax on $16,750 | $1,675 | |
| Tax on excess at 15% [($68,000 – $16,750 = $51,250) × 15%] | 7,688 | |
| | | $ 9,363 |
| Tax on 15% gains (15% × $10,400) | | 1,560 |
| Tax on 25% gains (25% × $30,000) | | 7,500 |
| Total tax | | $18,423 |

## Combined Results

The net gain from the disposition of § 1250 property can be treated as ordinary income subject to the regular tax rate, 15 percent capital gain, and/or 25 percent capital gain (and rarely 28 percent capital gain). Each step in the netting and tax calculation processes has been covered. *Examples 14 through 17* and *Comprehensive Example 19* illustrate how they work in combination.

### Example 14

During the current year, L sold a small office building for $38,000. The building cost $22,000 in 1980, and she had deducted depreciation of $12,000 using an accelerated method ($10,000 was assigned to the land and was not depreciable). Straight-line depreciation would have been $10,600. L's gain recognized on the sale is $28,000 ($38,000 amount realized – $10,000 adjusted basis). Of that amount, $1,400 ($12,000 – $10,600 = $1,400 excess depreciation) is ordinary income under § 1250 and the remainder, $26,600, is § 1231 gain. Of the $26,600 § 1231 gain, the unrecaptured depreciation of $10,600 ($12,000 – $1,400) is a 25% gain. The $16,000 excess of the amount realized over the original basis is 15% gain.

## Example 15

M purchased a rental duplex during 1986 for $60,000 (not including any value assigned to land). He deducted $60,000 depreciation using the 19-year realty ACRS tables. Depreciation using the straight-line recovery percentages for 19-year realty would have resulted in total depreciation of $60,000 (the duplex is fully depreciated under each method). This year on May 3 M sold the property for $87,000. His gain is reported as follows:

| | | |
|---|---|---|
| Sales price | | $ 87,000 |
| Less: Adjusted basis | | |
| Cost | $60,000 | |
| Depreciation allowed | (60,000) | (-0-) |
| Gain to be recognized | | $87,000 |
| Accelerated depreciation claimed and deducted | | $60,000 |
| Straight-line depreciation (hypothetical) | | (60,000) |
| Excess depreciation subject to recapture | | $ -0- |
| Character of gain: | | |
| Ordinary income (partial recapture) | | $ -0- |
| § 1231 gain subject to 25% rate | | 60,000 |
| § 1231 gain subject to 15% rate | | 27,000 |
| Total gain recognized | | $87,000 |

First, observe that the property is residential property (rather than nonresidential property) so it is subject to §1250 that requires recapture of the excess of accelerated depreciation over straight line. In this case, however, there is no excess depreciation since the rental property is fully depreciated. Thus, without a special rule, the gain not recaptured under § 1250 might be subject to the 15% capital gains rate. However, the depreciation that has not been recaptured, $60,000, is carved out and is considered a 25% § 1231 gain. Also observe that the $60,000 of 25% § 1231 gain is the amount of straight-line depreciation. The remaining gain (i.e., the amount above the original cost) of $27,000 is a 15% § 1231 gain.

## Example 16

Assume the same facts as in *Example 15*, except that M elected to recover his basis in the duplex using the 19-year straight-line method. Consequently she still recognizes gain of $87,000 computed as follows:

| | | | |
|---|---|---|---|
| Sales price | | | $ 87,000 |
| Less: | Adjusted basis | | |
| | Cost | $60,000 | |
| | Depreciation (straight-line) | (60,000) | |
| | | | (-0-) |
| Gain | | | $(87,000) |

None of the gain is subject to § 1250 recapture since M used straight-line depreciation (a requirement after 1986). However, the amount representing the unrecaptured depreciation (i.e., the straight-line depreciation) of $60,000 is considered a 25% § 1231 gain and the $27,000 balance is considered a 15% § 1231 gain.

**Example 17**

Assume the same facts as in *Example 15*, except that the property is an office building rather than a duplex. In this case, because the property is nonresidential real property and the accelerated method was used, the asset is treated as § 1245 property rather than § 1250 property. Thus, M is subject to full rather than partial depreciation recapture. All of the $60,000 depreciation is recaptured and treated as ordinary income. The balance of the gain, $27,000 is treated as a 15% § 1231 gain.

### History of § 1250

Over the years, § 1250 has been changed frequently, with a general trend toward an expanded scope. The rules explained above apply only to depreciation allowed on nonresidential property after 1969 and residential property (other than low-income housing) after 1975. Only a *portion* of any other excess depreciation on § 1250 property is included in the recapture potential. The following percentages are applied to the gain realized in the transaction or the excess depreciation taken during the particular period, whichever is less:

1. For all excess depreciation taken after 1963 and before 1970, 100 percent less 1 percent for each full month over 20 months the property is held.[35] Any sales after 1979 would result in no recapture of pre-1970 excess depreciation since this percentage, when calculated, is zero.
2. For all excess depreciation taken after 1969 and before 1976, as follows:
   a. In the case of low-income housing, 100 percent less 1 percent for each full month the property is held over 20 months.
   b. In the case of other residential rental property (e.g., an apartment building) and property that has been rehabilitated [for purposes of § 167(k)], 100 percent less 1 percent for each full month the property is held over 100 months.[36]

All sales from this group of real property after August 1992 will have no recapture of excess depreciation claimed before 1976.

3. For excess depreciation taken after 1975 on low-income housing and property that has been rehabilitated [for purposes of § 167(k)], 100 percent less 1 percent for each full month the property is held over 100 months.[37]

In summary, 100 percent of the excess depreciation allowed with respect to § 1250 property after 1975 is subject to recapture unless it falls into one of the above categories. Any gain recognized to the extent of any unrecaptured depreciation will be considered 25% gain. The rules for the various categories are set forth in § 1250(a).

### Exceptions and Limitations under § 1250

Generally, the exceptions and limitations that apply under § 1245 also apply under § 1250. Thus, gifts, inheritances, and most nontaxable exchanges are allowed to occur without triggering recapture.[38] This exception is extended to any property to the extent it qualifies as a principal residence and is subject to deferral of gain under § 1034 or nonrecognition of gain under § 121.[39] In such nontaxable exchanges, the excess depreciation (that is not recaptured) taken prior to the nontaxable exchange on the property transferred carries over to the property received or purchased.[40] Similarly, in the case of gifts and certain nontaxable transfers in which the property is transferred to a new owner with a carryover basis, the excess

[35] § 1250(a)(3).

[36] § 1250(a)(2).

[37] § 1250(a)(1).

[38] §§ 1250(d)(1) through (d)(4).

[39] § 1250(d)(7).

[40] Reg. §§ 1.1250-3(d)(5) and (h)(4).

depreciation carries over to the new owner.[41] In the case of inheritances in which basis to the successor in interest is determined under § 1014, no carryover of excess depreciation occurs.[42]

Certain like-kind exchanges and involuntary conversions may result in the recognition of gain solely because of § 1250 if insufficient § 1250 property is acquired. Since not all real property is depreciable, it is possible that the replacement property would not be § 1250 property and would still qualify for nonrecognition under the appropriate rules of §§ 1033 or 1034. In such situations, gain will be recognized to the extent the amount that would be recaptured exceeds the fair market value of the § 1250 property received (property purchased in the case of an involuntary conversion).[43]

### Example 18

D completed a like-kind exchange in the current year in which he transferred an apartment complex (§ 1250 property) for rural farmland (not § 1250 property). The apartment had cost D $175,000 in 1980 and depreciation of $89,000 has been taken under the 200% declining-balance method. D would have deducted $62,000 under the straight-line method.

The farm land was worth $200,000 at the time of the exchange. There were no improvements on the farm property. D's realized gain on the exchange is $114,000 ($200,000 amount realized – $86,000 adjusted basis in property given up). If there had been no § 1250 recapture, then D would have had no recognized gain. Because the property acquired was not § 1250 property, § 1250 supersedes (overrides) § 1031. D has a recognized gain of $27,000 [($89,000 – $62,000), the amount of excess depreciation], which is all ordinary income under § 1250.

Exhibit 17-2 provides an overview of the handling of sales and exchanges of business property. Exhibit 17-3 provides a chart that may be useful in summarizing property transactions. Note that for purposes of this Exhibit 17-3, no distinction is made between 15%, 25% and 28% § 1231 gains and losses or 15%, 25% and 28% capital gains and losses. A comprehensive example of sales and exchanges of trade or business property is presented below.

### EXHIBIT 17.2 Stepwise Approach to Sales or Exchange of Trade or Business Property—An Overview

**Step 1:** Determine the amount of gain to be recognized, if any. There is no recapture in the case of losses.

**Step 2:** Calculate any depreciation recapture on the disposition of § 1245 property and § 1250 property sold or exchanged at a taxable *gain* during the year.

**Step 3:** For any remaining gain (after recapture) on depreciable property held for more than one year, add to other § 1231 gains and losses and complete the § 1231 netting process.

- The § 1231 gain must be broken down into the portions that qualify as 15%CG and 25%CG (and rarely 28%CG).

**Step 4:** Complete the netting process for capital assets, taking into consideration the net § 1231 gain, if any.

- The § 1231 gain is combined with other long-term capital gains and losses (with separate netting for 15%CG, 25%CG, and 28%CG. Then the long-term capital gain or loss is combined with the short-term capital gain or loss.

---

41 Reg. §§ 1.1250-3(a), (c), and (f).

42 Reg. § 1.1250-3(b).

43 § 1250(d)(4)(C). A similar rule is provided for rollovers (deferral) of gains from low-income housing under § 1039 [see § 1250(d)(8)].

**EXHIBIT 17.3** **Summary of Property Transactions**

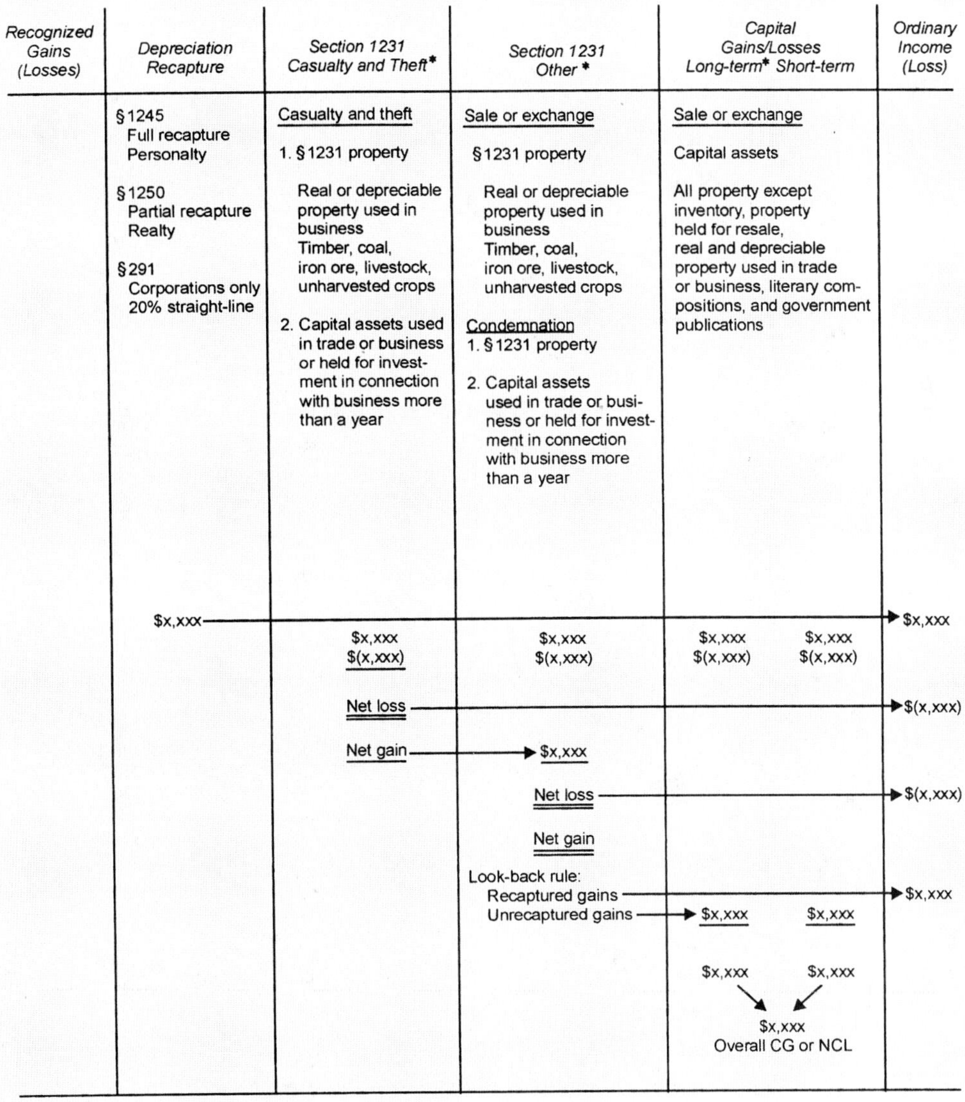


* These catagories must be subdivided into 15%, 25% and 28% groups.

## Example 19

Ted and Carol Smith sold the following assets during the current year:

| Description | Holding Period | Selling Price | Adjusted Basis | Recognized Gain (Loss) |
|---|---|---|---|---|
| Land and building (straight-line depreciation) | 3 years | $14,000 | $9,000 | $5,000 |
| Cost, $13,000 | | | | |
| Depreciation allowed, $4,000 | | | | |
| Photocopier | 14 months | 2,600 | 2,000 | 600 |
| Cost, $2,500 | | | | |
| Depreciation allowed, $500 | | | | |
| Business auto | 2 years | 1,800 | 1,920 | (120) |
| Cost, $4,000 | | | | |
| Depreciation allowed, $2,080 | | | | |

In determining the tax consequences of these sales, the Smiths must start with gains and losses from § 1231 transactions. The ultimate treatment of the gains, the character of the gain and any possible depreciation recapture must be considered.

- On the sale of the land and the building, there is no depreciation recapture for the building since straight-line depreciation was used. However, there is unrecaptured depreciation of $4,000 which is accounted for as a 25% § 1231gain. The balance of the gain on the land and building, $1,000, is a 15% § 1231 gain.
- On the sale of the photocopier, $500 of the § 1231 gain of $600 is recaptured and treated as ordinary income. The balance of the gain, $100, is a 15% § 1231 gain.
- On the sale of the automobile, there is no recapture since it is sold at a loss. The $120 loss is treated as a 15% § 1231 loss. This information can be summarized as follows:

| | Section 1231 Gains and Losses | | |
|---|---|---|---|
| | Collectibles | Unrecaptured Depreciation | Other |
| | 28% | 25% | 15% |
| Land and building | | $4,000 | $1,000 |
| Photocopier | | | 100 |
| Automobile | | | (120) |
| Capital gains from § 1231 | $0 | $4,000 | $ 980 |

In this situation, the Smiths net the various groups, resulting in net gains in each of the groups as shown above. These amounts are then combined with the appropriate capital gain groups to determine the final treatment. Note that if the Smiths had unrecaptured § 1231 losses, they would first offset the 28% gains, then 25% gains, and finally 15% gains. The information is summarized in Exhibit 17-3.

## Example 20

Assume that the Smiths, from the previous example, had the following capital asset transactions during the same year:

| Description | Holding Period | Selling Price | Adjusted Basis | Description of Gain or (Loss) |
|---|---|---|---|---|
| 100 shares XY Corp. | 4 months | $ 3,200 | $4,200 | $(1,000) STCL |
| 100 shares GB Corp. | 3 years | 3,200 | 4,600 | (1,400) LTCL |
| 1 acre vacant land | 5 years | 12,000 | 5,000 | 7,000 LTCG |

Taking into consideration the § 1231 gains from *Example 18*, the Smith's summarize their transactions as follows.

| | Short-Term | Capital Gains and Losses | | |
|---|---|---|---|---|
| | | Collectibles | Unrecaptured Depreciation | Other |
| | Ordinary | 28% | 25% | 15% |
| Capital gains from § 1231 | | $0 | $4,000 | $ 980 |
| XY stock loss | (1,000) | | | |
| GB stock loss | | | | (1,400) |
| Vacant land gain | | | | 7,000 |
| | $(1,000) | $0 | $4,000 | $6,580 |
| Netting | 1,000 | | (1,000) | |
| Total | $ 0 | $0 | $3,000 | $6,580 |

Ted and Carol Smith would report a $3,000 N25CG and a $6,580 N15CG.

A Form 4797 and Schedule D containing the information from *Examples 18* and *19* are included in Exhibit 17-4 which follows. In using the forms, it should be pointed out that neither the Form 4797 nor Schedule D Parts I, II, and III (i.e., the form for reporting capital gains and losses) require the taxpayer to distinguish 25% gains from 28% or 15% gains. The 25% distinction comes into play only when the taxpayer computes the tax as can be seen on Schedule D, Part IV, Lines 25 and 47. The tax is computed assuming the taxpayers have taxable income of $126,830 (including the capital gains).

## Additional Recapture—Corporations

**LO.8**
Identify tax planning opportunities related to sales or other dispositions of trade or business property

Corporations generally compute the amount of § 1245 and § 1250 ordinary income recapture on the sales of depreciable assets in the same manner as do individuals. However, Congress added Code § 291 to the tax law in 1982 with the intent of reducing the tax benefits of the accelerated cost recovery of depreciable § 1250 property available to corporate taxpayers. For sales or other taxable dispositions of § 1250 property, corporations must treat as ordinary income 20 percent of any § 1231 gain *that would have been* ordinary income if § 1245 rather than § 1250 had applied to the transaction.[44] The effect of this provision is to require the taxpayer to recapture 20 percent of any straight-line depreciation that has not been recaptured under some other provision. Technically, the amount that is treated as ordinary income under § 291 is computed in the following manner:

| | |
|---|---|
| Amount that would be treated as ordinary income under § 1245 | $xx,xxx |
| Less: Amount that would be treated as ordinary income § 1250 | (x,xxx) |
| Equals: Difference between recapture amounts | $xx,xxx |
| Times: Rate specified in § 291 | ×20% |
| Equals: Amount that is treated as ordinary income | $xx,xxx |

[44] § 291(a)(1).

**EXHIBIT 17.4** **Completed Form 4797**

Form **4797**

Department of the Treasury
Internal Revenue Service (99)

**Sales of Business Property**
**(Also Involuntary Conversions and Recapture Amounts Under Sections 179 and 280F(b)(2))**
▶ **Attach to your tax return.** ▶ **See separate instructions.**

OMB No. 1545-0184
**2010**
Attachment Sequence No. **27**

Name(s) shown on return: *TED AND CAROL SMITH*
**Identifying number**: *467-42-6030*

| | | |
|---|---|---|
| 1 | Enter the gross proceeds from sales or exchanges reported to you for 2009 on Form(s) 1099-B or 1099-S (or substitute statement) that you are including on line 2, 10, or 20 (see instructions) | 1 | |

**Part I** **Sales or Exchanges of Property Used in a Trade or Business and Involuntary Conversions From Other Than Casualty or Theft—Most Property Held More Than 1 Year** (see instructions)

| 2 (a) Description of property | (b) Date acquired (mo., day, yr.) | (c) Date sold (mo., day, yr.) | (d) Gross sales price | (e) Depreciation allowed or allowable since acquisition | (f) Cost or other basis, plus improvements and expense of sale | (g) Gain or (loss) Subtract (f) from the sum of (d) and (e) |
|---|---|---|---|---|---|---|
| *AUTO* | *3-1-06* | *10-2-10* | *1,800* | *2,080* | *4,000* | *(120)* |
| | | | | | | |
| | | | | | | |
| | | | | | | |

| | | | |
|---|---|---|---|
| 3 | Gain, if any, from Form 4684, line 43 | 3 | |
| 4 | Section 1231 gain from installment sales from Form 6252, line 26 or 37 | 4 | |
| 5 | Section 1231 gain or (loss) from like-kind exchanges from Form 8824 | 5 | |
| 6 | Gain, if any, from line 32, from other than casualty or theft. | 6 | *5,100* |
| 7 | Combine lines 2 through 6. Enter the gain or (loss) here and on the appropriate line as follows: | 7 | *4,980* |
| | **Partnerships (except electing large partnerships) and S corporations.** Report the gain or (loss) following the instructions for Form 1065, Schedule K, line 10, or Form 1120S, Schedule K, line 9. Skip lines 8, 9, 11, and 12 below. **Individuals, partners, S corporation shareholders, and all others.** If line 7 is zero or a loss, enter the amount from line 7 on line 11 below and skip lines 8 and 9. If line 7 is a gain and you did not have any prior year section 1231 losses, or they were recaptured in an earlier year, enter the gain from line 7 as a long-term capital gain on the Schedule D filed with your return and skip lines 8, 9, 11, and 12 below. | | |
| 8 | Nonrecaptured net section 1231 losses from prior years (see instructions) | 8 | |
| 9 | Subtract line 8 from line 7. If zero or less, enter -0-. If line 9 is zero, enter the gain from line 7 on line 12 below. If line 9 is more than zero, enter the amount from line 8 on line 12 below and enter the gain from line 9 as a long-term capital gain on the Schedule D filed with your return (see instructions) | 9 | *4,980* |

**Part II** **Ordinary Gains and Losses** (see instructions)

10 Ordinary gains and losses not included on lines 11 through 16 (include property held 1 year or less):

| | | | | | | |
|---|---|---|---|---|---|---|
| | | | | | | |
| | | | | | | |
| | | | | | | |
| | | | | | | |

| | | | |
|---|---|---|---|
| 11 | Loss, if any, from line 7 | 11 | ( ) |
| 12 | Gain, if any, from line 7 or amount from line 8, if applicable | 12 | |
| 13 | Gain, if any, from line 31 | 13 | *500* |
| 14 | Net gain or (loss) from Form 4684, lines 35 and 42a | 14 | |
| 15 | Ordinary gain from installment sales from Form 6252, line 25 or 36 | 15 | |
| 16 | Ordinary gain or (loss) from like-kind exchanges from Form 8824. | 16 | |
| 17 | Combine lines 10 through 16 | 17 | *500* |
| 18 | For all except individual returns, enter the amount from line 17 on the appropriate line of your return and skip lines a and b below. For individual returns, complete lines a and b below: | | |
| a | If the loss on line 11 includes a loss from Form 4684, line 39, column (b)(ii), enter that part of the loss here. Enter the part of the loss from income-producing property on Schedule A (Form 1040), line 28, and the part of the loss from property used as an employee on Schedule A (Form 1040), line 23. Identify as from "Form 4797, line 18a." See instructions | 18a | |
| b | Redetermine the gain or (loss) on line 17 excluding the loss, if any, on line 18a. Enter here and on Form 1040, line 14 | 18b | *500* |

**For Paperwork Reduction Act Notice, see separate instructions.** Cat. No. 13086I Form **4797** (2010)

EXHIBIT 17.4 **Completed Form 4797–Continued**

Form 4797 (2010) TED AND CAROL SMITH Page **2**

**Part III Gain From Disposition of Property Under Sections 1245, 1250, 1252, 1254, and 1255** (see instructions)

| 19 (a) Description of section 1245, 1250, 1252, 1254, or 1255 property: | (b) Date acquired (mo., day, yr.) | (c) Date sold (mo., day, yr.) |
|---|---|---|
| A LAND/BUILDING | 7-14-98 | 11-21-10 |
| B PHOTOCOPIER | 6-12-08 | 8-31-10 |
| C | | |
| D | | |

| These columns relate to the properties on lines 19A through 19D. ▶ | | Property A | Property B | Property C | Property D |
|---|---|---|---|---|---|
| 20 Gross sales price (**Note:** *See line 1 before completing.*) | 20 | 14,000 | 2,600 | | |
| 21 Cost or other basis plus expense of sale | 21 | 13,000 | 2,500 | | |
| 22 Depreciation (or depletion) allowed or allowable | 22 | 4,000 | 500 | | |
| 23 Adjusted basis. Subtract line 22 from line 21 | 23 | 9,000 | 2,000 | | |
| 24 Total gain. Subtract line 23 from line 20 | 24 | 5,000 | 600 | | |
| 25 **If section 1245 property:** | | | | | |
| a Depreciation allowed or allowable from line 22 | 25a | | 500 | | |
| b Enter the **smaller** of line 24 or 25a | 25b | | 500 | | |
| 26 **If section 1250 property:** If straight line depreciation was used, enter -0- on line 26g, except for a corporation subject to section 291. | | | | | |
| a Additional depreciation after 1975 (see instructions) | 26a | | | | |
| b Applicable percentage multiplied by the **smaller** of line 24 or line 26a (see instructions) | 26b | | | | |
| c Subtract line 26a from line 24. If residential rental property **or** line 24 is not more than line 26a, skip lines 26d and 26e | 26c | | | | |
| d Additional depreciation after 1969 and before 1976 | 26d | | | | |
| e Enter the **smaller** of line 26c or 26d | 26e | | | | |
| f Section 291 amount (corporations only) | 26f | | | | |
| g Add lines 26b, 26e, and 26f | 26g | 0 | | | |
| 27 **If section 1252 property:** Skip this section if you did not dispose of farmland or if this form is being completed for a partnership (other than an electing large partnership). | | | | | |
| a Soil, water, and land clearing expenses | 27a | | | | |
| b Line 27a multiplied by applicable percentage (see instructions) | 27b | | | | |
| c Enter the **smaller** of line 24 or 27b | 27c | | | | |
| 28 **If section 1254 property:** | | | | | |
| a Intangible drilling and development costs, expenditures for development of mines and other natural deposits, mining exploration costs, and depletion (see instructions) | 28a | | | | |
| b Enter the **smaller** of line 24 or 28a | 28b | | | | |
| 29 **If section 1255 property:** | | | | | |
| a Applicable percentage of payments excluded from income under section 126 (see instructions) | 29a | | | | |
| b Enter the **smaller** of line 24 or 29a (see instructions) | 29b | | | | |

**Summary of Part III Gains.** Complete property columns A through D through line 29b before going to line 30.

| | | |
|---|---|---|
| 30 Total gains for all properties. Add property columns A through D, line 24 | 30 | 5,600 |
| 31 Add property columns A through D, lines 25b, 26g, 27c, 28b, and 29b. Enter here and on line 13 | 31 | 500 |
| 32 Subtract line 31 from line 30. Enter the portion from casualty or theft on Form 4684, line 37. Enter the portion from other than casualty or theft on Form 4797, line 6 | 32 | 5,100 |

**Part IV Recapture Amounts Under Sections 179 and 280F(b)(2) When Business Use Drops to 50% or Less** (see instructions)

| | | (a) Section 179 | (b) Section 280F(b)(2) |
|---|---|---|---|
| 33 Section 179 expense deduction or depreciation allowable in prior years | 33 | | |
| 34 Recomputed depreciation (see instructions) | 34 | | |
| 35 Recapture amount. Subtract line 34 from line 33. See the instructions for where to report | 35 | | |

Form **4797** (2010)

## EXHIBIT 17.5 Completed Schedule D

**SCHEDULE D (Form 1040)**

Department of the Treasury
Internal Revenue Service (99)

# Capital Gains and Losses

▶ Attach to Form 1040 or Form 1040NR. ▶ See Instructions for Schedule D (Form 1040).
▶ Use Schedule D-1 to list additional transactions for lines 1 and 8.

OMB No. 1545-0074
**2010**
Attachment Sequence No. **12**

Name(s) shown on return: TED AND CAROL SMITH

Your social security number: 467 | 42 | 6030

**Part I** **Short-Term Capital Gains and Losses—Assets Held One Year or Less**

| | (a) Description of property (Example: 100 sh. XYZ Co.) | (b) Date acquired (Mo., day, yr.) | (c) Date sold (Mo., day, yr.) | (d) Sales price (see page D-7 of the instructions) | (e) Cost or other basis (see page D-7 of the instructions) | (f) Gain or (loss) Subtract (e) from (d) |
|---|---|---|---|---|---|---|
| 1 | 100 SHS XY CORP | 6-1-10 | 10-15-10 | 3,200 | 4,200 | (1000) |
| | | | | | | |
| | | | | | | |
| | | | | | | |
| | | | | | | |

| | | | |
|---|---|---|---|
| 2 | Enter your short-term totals, if any, from Schedule D-1, line 2 . . . . . | 2 | |
| 3 | **Total short-term sales price amounts.** Add lines 1 and 2 in column (d) . . . . . | 3 | 3,200 |
| 4 | Short-term gain from Form 6252 and short-term gain or (loss) from Forms 4684, 6781, and 8824 | 4 | |
| 5 | Net short-term gain or (loss) from partnerships, S corporations, estates, and trusts from Schedule(s) K-1 . . . . . | 5 | |
| 6 | Short-term capital loss carryover. Enter the amount, if any, from line 10 of your **Capital Loss Carryover Worksheet** on page D-7 of the instructions . . . . . | 6 | ( ) |
| 7 | **Net short-term capital gain or (loss).** Combine lines 1 through 6 in column (f) . . . . . | 7 | (1000) |

**Part II** **Long-Term Capital Gains and Losses—Assets Held More Than One Year**

| | (a) Description of property (Example: 100 sh. XYZ Co.) | (b) Date acquired (Mo., day, yr.) | (c) Date sold (Mo., day, yr.) | (d) Sales price (see page D-7 of the instructions) | (e) Cost or other basis (see page D-7 of the instructions) | (f) Gain or (loss) Subtract (e) from (d) |
|---|---|---|---|---|---|---|
| 8 | 100 SHS XY CORP | 6-1-07 | 11-1-10 | 3,200 | 4,600 | (1,400) |
| | VACANT LAND | 6-1-07 | 12-1-10 | 12,000 | 5,000 | 7,000 |
| | | | | | | |
| | | | | | | |
| | | | | | | |

| | | | |
|---|---|---|---|
| 9 | Enter your long-term totals, if any, from Schedule D-1, line 9 . . . . . | 9 | |
| 10 | **Total long-term sales price amounts.** Add lines 8 and 9 in column (d) . . . . . | 10 | 15,200 |
| 11 | Gain from Form 4797, Part I; long-term gain from Forms 2439 and 6252; and long-term gain or (loss) from Forms 4684, 6781, and 8824 . . . . . | 11 | 4,980 |
| 12 | Net long-term gain or (loss) from partnerships, S corporations, estates, and trusts from Schedule(s) K-1 . . . . . | 12 | |
| 13 | Capital gain distributions. See page D-2 of the instructions . . . . . | 13 | |
| 14 | Long-term capital loss carryover. Enter the amount, if any, from line 15 of your **Capital Loss Carryover Worksheet** on page D-7 of the instructions . . . . . | 14 | ( ) |
| 15 | **Net long-term capital gain or (loss).** Combine lines 8 through 14 in column (f). Then go to Part III on the back . . . . . | 15 | 10,580 |

**For Paperwork Reduction Act Notice, see Form 1040 or Form 1040NR instructions.** Cat. No. 11338H **Schedule D (Form 1040) 2010**

**EXHIBIT 17.5** **Completed Schedule D–Continued**

Schedule D (Form 1040) 2010 *TED AND CAROL SMITH* Page **2**

**Part III** **Summary**

| | | | |
|---|---|---|---|
| **16** Combine lines 7 and 15 and enter the result . . . . . . . . . . . . . . . . . . | 16 | *9,580* | |
| If line 16 is:<br>• A **gain**, enter the amount from line 16 on Form 1040, line 13, or Form 1040NR, line 14. Then go to line 17 below.<br>• A **loss**, skip lines 17 through 20 below. Then go to line 21. Also be sure to complete line 22.<br>• **Zero**, skip lines 17 through 21 below and enter -0- on Form 1040, line 13, or Form 1040NR, line 14. Then go to line 22. | | | |
| **17** Are lines 15 and 16 **both** gains?<br>☐ **Yes.** Go to line 18.<br>☐ **No.** Skip lines 18 through 21, and go to line 22. | | *3,000* | |
| **18** Enter the amount, if any, from line 7 of the **28% Rate Gain Worksheet** on page D-8 of the instructions . . . . . . . . . . . . . . . . . . . . . . . . . . . ▶ | 18 | | |
| **19** Enter the amount, if any, from line 18 of the **Unrecaptured Section 1250 Gain Worksheet** on page D-9 of the instructions . . . . . . . . . . . . . . . . . . . . . . ▶ | 19 | | |
| **20** Are lines 18 and 19 **both** zero or blank?<br>☐ **Yes.** Complete Form 1040 through line 43, or Form 1040NR through line 40. Then complete the **Qualified Dividends and Capital Gain Tax Worksheet** on page 39 of the Instructions for Form 1040 (or in the Instructions for Form 1040NR). **Do not** complete lines 21 and 22 below.<br>☐ **No.** Complete Form 1040 through line 43, or Form 1040NR through line 40. Then complete the **Schedule D Tax Worksheet** on page D-10 of the instructions. **Do not** complete lines 21 and 22 below. | | | |
| **21** If line 16 is a loss, enter here and on Form 1040, line 13, or Form 1040NR, line 14, the **smaller** of:<br>• The loss on line 16 or<br>• ($3,000), or if married filing separately, ($1,500) } . . . . . . . . . . . . . . | 21 | ( | ) |
| **Note.** When figuring which amount is smaller, treat both amounts as positive numbers. | | | |
| **22** Do you have qualified dividends on Form 1040, line 9b, or Form 1040NR, line 10b?<br>☐ **Yes.** Complete Form 1040 through line 43, or Form 1040NR through line 40. Then complete the **Qualified Dividends and Capital Gain Tax Worksheet** on page 39 of the Instructions for Form 1040 (or in the Instructions for Form 1040NR).<br>☐ **No.** Complete the rest of Form 1040 or Form 1040NR. | | | |

**Schedule D (Form 1040) 2010**

## Example 21

This year K Corporation sold residential rental property for $500,000. The property was purchased for $400,000 in 1986. Assume that K claimed ACRS depreciation of $140,000 (i.e., do not attempt to verify this estimate). Straight-line depreciation would have been $105,000. K Corporation's depreciation recapture and § 1231 gain are computed as follows:

| | | | |
|---|---|---|---|
| ***Step 1:*** | Compute realized gain: | | |
| | Sales price | | $500,000 |
| | Less: Adjusted basis | | |
| | Cost | $400,000 | |
| | ACRS depreciation | (140,000) | (260,000) |
| | Realized gain | | $240,000 |
| ***Step 2:*** | Compute *excess* depreciation: | | |
| | Actual depreciation | | $140,000 |
| | Straight-line depreciation | | (105,000) |
| | Excess depreciation | | $ 35,000 |
| ***Step 3:*** | Compute § 1250 depreciation recapture: | | |
| | *Lesser* of realized gain of $240,000 | | |
| | or | | |
| | Excess depreciation of $35,000 | | |
| | § 1250 depreciation recapture | | $ 35,000 |
| ***Step 4:*** | Compute depreciation recapture if § 1245 applied: | | |
| | *Lesser* of realized gain of $240,000 | | |
| | or | | |
| | Actual depreciation of $140,000 | | |
| | Depreciation recapture if § 1245 applied | | $140,000 |
| ***Step 5:*** | Compute § 291 ordinary income: | | |
| | Depreciation recapture if § 1245 applied | | $140,000 |
| | § 1250 depreciation recapture | | (35,000) |
| | Excess recapture potential | | $105,000 |
| | Times: § 291 rate | | × 20% |
| | § 291 ordinary income | | $ 21,000 |
| ***Step 6:*** | Characterize recognized gain: | | |
| | § 1250 depreciation recapture | | $ 35,000 |
| | Plus: § 291 ordinary income | | 21,000 |
| | Ordinary income | | $ 56,000 |
| | Realized gain | | $240,000 |
| | Less: Ordinary income | | (56,000) |
| | § 1231 gain | | $184,000 |

Note that without the additional recapture required under § 291, K Corporation would have reported a § 1231 gain of $205,000 ($240,000 total gain – $35,000 § 1250 recapture). If the property had been subject to § 1245 recapture, K Corporation would have only a $100,000 § 1231 gain ($240,000 – $140,000 § 1245 recapture). Section 291 requires that the corporation report 20% of this difference ($205,000 – $100,000 = $105,000 × 20%), or $21,000, as *additional* recapture. Note that this is 20% of the straight-line depreciation that is normally not recaptured on the disposition of non-residential or residential real estate.

### Example 22

Assume the same facts as in *Example 21*, except that the property is an office building rather than residential realty *and* straight-line depreciation was elected. An individual taxpayer would report the entire gain of $205,000 [$500,000 – ($400,000 basis – $105,000 straight-line depreciation)] as a § 1231 gain. However, the corporate taxpayer must recapture $21,000 (20% × $105,000 depreciation) as ordinary income under § 291. The remaining $184,000 ($205,000 – $21,000) would be a § 1231 gain.

## OTHER RECAPTURE PROVISIONS

There are several other recapture provisions that exist. They include the recapture of farmland expenditures,[45] recapture of intangible drilling costs,[46] and recapture of gain from the disposition of § 126 property (relating to government cost-sharing program payments for conservation purposes).[47] Another type of recapture is investment credit recapture.[48] This is discussed in detail in Chapter 13.

## ✓ CHECK YOUR KNOWLEDGE

### Review Question 1

True-False. This year T sold equipment for $6,000 (cost $15,000, depreciation $10,000), recognizing a gain of $1,000 ($6,000 – $5,000). To ensure that all of the ordinary deductions obtained from depreciation are recaptured, T must report ordinary income of $10,000 and a capital loss of $9,000, ultimately producing net income of $1,000.

*False.* This novel approach may seem consistent with Congressional intent, but it is incorrect. Under § 1245 any gain realized is treated as ordinary income to the extent of any depreciation allowed. As a result, the entire $1,000 is ordinary income. It may be useful to think of the depreciation recapture as an adjustment to the depreciation claimed. Depreciation of $10,000 was claimed, but the value of the equipment dropped by $9,000 ($15,000 cost – $6,000 sales price). T claimed an ordinary depreciation deduction of $10,000, and recognized ordinary income of $1,000, for a net ordinary deduction of $9,000.

### Review Question 2

True-False. This year L sold a machine and recognized a small gain. Assuming L claimed straight-line depreciation, there is no depreciation recapture.

*False.* The machine is § 1245 property since it is depreciable personalty. Under the full recapture rule of § 1245, all depreciation is subject to recapture regardless of the method used.

### Review Question 3

Several years ago Harry purchased equipment at a cost of $10,000. Over the past three years he claimed and deducted depreciation of $6,000. Assuming that Harry sold the equipment for (1) $7,000, (2) $13,000, or (3) $1,000, determine the amount of gain or loss realized and its character (i.e., ordinary income or § 1231 potential capital gain).

| | *1* | *2* | *3* |
|---|---|---|---|
| Amount realized | $ 7,000 | $13,000 | $ 1,000 |
| Adjusted basis ($10,000 – $6,000) | –4,000 | –4,000 | – 4,000 |
| Gain (loss) recognized | $ 3,000 | $ 9,000 | $(3,000) |

[45] § 1252.

[46] § 1254.

[47] § 1255.

[48] § 47.

The equipment is § 1245 property since it is depreciable personalty. As a result, the full recapture rule operates and any gain recognized is ordinary income to the extent of any depreciation deducted. In the first case, the entire $3,000 is ordinary income (the lesser of the gain recognized, $3,000, or the recapture potential, $6,000). In the second situation, $6,000 is ordinary income (the lesser of the gain recognized, $9,000, or the recapture potential, $6,000) and $3,000 is § 1231 gain. In the final case, § 1245 does not apply because the property is sold at a loss. Therefore, Harry has a § 1231 loss that is potentially an ordinary loss. Its ultimate treatment depends on the outcome of the § 1231 netting process.

### Review Question 4

True-False. In 1990, Sal purchased an office building to rent out. This year she sold the building, recognizing a large gain. The entire gain is a § 1231 gain since there is no recapture under either § 1245 or § 1250.

*True.* The office build is § 1250 property. The recapture rules of § 1250 apply only when the taxpayer uses an accelerated method, in which case the excess of accelerated depreciation over straight-line is treated as ordinary income. However, since 1987 taxpayers have been required to use the straight-line method in computing depreciation on real estate. As a result, § 1250 is inapplicable and Sal's gain retains its original § 1231 character. Nevertheless, the gain will not be treated as a 15 percent gain to the extent of any unrecaptured § 1250 depreciation (i.e., all of the straight-line depreciation) but rather 25 percent gain.

### Review Question 5

True-False. In 1997, Z Corporation purchased an office building to rent out. This year the corporation sold the building, recognizing a large gain. The entire gain is a § 1231 gain since there is no recapture under either § 1245 or § 1250.

*False.* There is no recapture under § or § 1250. However, under § 291, corporate taxpayers are required to recapture up to 20 percent of any straight-line depreciation. The 25 percent rate does not apply to corporate taxpayers.

### Review Question 6

True-False. In 1986, the Rose Partnership purchased a new office building to use as its headquarters. This year the partnership sold the building, recognizing a gain of $100,000. The partnership claimed and deducted accelerated depreciation of $40,000. Straight-line depreciation would have been $40,000. The partnership will report ordinary income of zero and § 1231 gain of $100,000.

*False.* This would be true if the building were § 1250 property, but § 1250 does not apply. Nonresidential real estate such as this office building that was acquired from 1981 through 1986 is treated as § 1245 property and is subject to the full recapture rule if accelerated depreciation was used. In this case, the taxpayer opted for accelerated depreciation, so $40,000 is ordinary income and the remaining $60,000 is a 15% § 1231 gain.

### Review Question 7

In 1984, the Daisy Partnership purchased a new apartment complex to rent out. This year the partnership sold the building, recognizing a gain of $100,000. The partnership claimed and deducted straight-line depreciation of $35,000. Accelerated depreciation would have been $40,000. The partnership will report ordinary income of $35,000 and § 1231 gain of $65,000.

*False.* In contrast to question 6, the property is residential real estate and is consequently treated as § 1250 property. The partial recapture rule of § 1250 applies only if the taxpayer actually uses an accelerated method. In this case the taxpayer used straight-line, so the recapture rules of § 1250 are not triggered. As a result, the entire $100,000 gain is a § 1231 gain. However, the gain will be a 25 percent gain to the extent of any unrecaptured § 1250 gain (i.e., the $35,000 straight-line depreciation).

# Related Business Issues

## Installment Sales of Trade or Business Property

As discussed in Chapter 14, gains on sales of trade or business property may be deferred using the installment sale method. However, depreciation recapture does not qualify for installment sale treatment. Thus, ordinary income from depreciation recapture must be reported in the year of sale—*regardless* of whether the seller received any payment in that year.[49] Consequently, only the § 1231 gain from such sales will qualify for installment gain deferral.

### Example 23

During the year, K sold a rental house for $90,000. According to the terms of the sale, K received $30,000 down and the balance in two equal installments of $30,000 over the next two years. K had purchased the house in 1986 for $60,000 and deducted $20,000 of accelerated depreciation. Had she used the straight-line method, the straight-line depreciation would have been $15,000. K realizes a gain of $50,000 and has $5,000 of § 1250 recapture, computed as follows:

| | |
|---|---|
| Amount realized | $90,000 |
| Adjusted basis ($60,000 − $20,000) | −40,000 |
| Gain realized | $50,000 |
| Accelerated depreciation on residential real estate acquired before 1987 | $20,000 |
| Hypothetical straight-line depreciation | −15,000 |
| Excess depreciation | $ 5,000 |

K must report all of the depreciation recapture, $5,000, as ordinary income in the year of the sale. In addition, she must report $15,000 of the remaining gain of $45,000 as a § 1231 gain under the installment sale rules for the year of sale, computed as follows:

$$\frac{\text{Remaining gain, \$45,000}}{\text{Contract price, \$90,000}} \times \text{\$30,000 Payment received} = \text{\$15,000 Gain recognized}$$

Note that in computing the gross profit ratio, only the remaining gain is used in the numerator and not the entire $50,000 gain realized, as would normally be the case.

## Intangible Business Assets

Historically, many purchased intangible assets were not subject to amortization for tax purposes. This was because the life of the assets was indefinite and the amortization deduction was indeterminable. However, § 197 currently allows the amortization (over 15 years) of most *purchased* intangibles acquired after August 11, 1993. No amortization is allowed, of course, for intangibles *developed* by the taxpayer.

For years, conventional thinking was that goodwill and similar intangibles were capital assets. A taxpayer who purchased or developed goodwill and similar intangibles generally recognized capital gain (or loss) to the extent the proceeds of the sale of a business were allocated to them.

All this became much more complex with the passage of § 197. Section 197(e) stipulates that upon the sale or disposition of § 197 assets, they are to be treated as depreciable property.

Private Letter Ruling [PLR] 200243002 brought clarity to this change. Under this ruling, intangible assets that are not subject to amortization are still treated as capital

[49] § 453(i). See Chapter 14 for a detailed discussion of installment reporting.

assets. This applies to assets placed in service on or before August 11, 1993, and any self developed goodwill and other intangibles (with no basis). However, intangibles purchased after August 11, 1993 (i.e. amortizable "§ 197 intangibles") are to be treated as depreciable assets and upon sale they are subject to § 1245 and § 1231 treatment.

Under § 1245, any gain recognized will be ordinary income to the extent of amortization allowed. Any remaining gain or loss will be subject to the netting process under § 1231 and whatever treatment is required after the netting process.

### Dispositions of Business Assets and the Self-Employment Tax

Gains and losses on the disposition of business assets do not increase or decrease self-employment income. So, even though gains are ordinary income for income tax purposes to the extent of depreciation recapture under § 1245 and § 1250, these amounts are not included in self-employment income.

## Tax Planning Considerations

### Timing of Sales and Other Dispositions

**LO.8**
Identify tax planning opportunities related to sales or other dispositions of trade or business property

Timing the sale of trade or business properties is very important and, from a tax perspective, can be critical. In the simplest case, if a taxpayer has a tax loss or is in a lower tax bracket, any contemplated sales at a gain should be considered to take advantage of the favorable tax result under § 1231. If tax rates are particularly high in the current year, loss transactions should be considered. Any net § 1231 loss is treated as an ordinary deduction for A.G.I. and avoids the $3,000 deduction limit imposed on net capital losses.

In addition, a net § 1231 gain qualifies as a long-term capital gain. For high-income taxpayers with no capital asset transactions or with a net capital gain in the current year, the net § 1231 gain qualifies for the maximum capital gains tax rate of 15 percent. The benefit can be even greater for a taxpayer with substantial capital losses for the year. Because the losses in excess of $3,000 would otherwise be suspended, any net § 1231 gain that would be offset by these losses can be currently recognized at no additional tax cost.

If a taxpayer has recognized or could recognize a § 1231 gain for the year and benefit from § 1231 treatment, additional sales of § 1231 property at a loss should be avoided. Because such losses must be netted against the gains, the favorable treatment of the gains is lost.

The look-back rule must be considered whenever a taxpayer is contemplating the timing of sales of § 1231 gain and loss assets. If no § 1231 losses have been recognized in the past five years, the gain assets should be sold in the current year to receive the favorable treatment of net § 1231 gains. The loss assets can then be sold in the next year and be treated as ordinary losses. This plan will not work, however, if the loss assets are sold first.

Finally, the timing of casualty and theft gains and losses should be considered. Obviously, a taxpayer cannot control the timing of such losses—not legally, anyway. However, the § 1033 gain deferral rules discussed in Chapter 15 may offer some tax planning opportunity. Because this deferral provision is generally elective, the taxpayer should consider existing § 1231 gains or losses before making a decision to defer gain. For example, a taxpayer with substantial capital losses may decide not to defer a capital gain or § 1231 gain under § 1033 even though the involuntarily converted asset is to be replaced. Immediate recognition of the gain will not have any negative tax consequences because it can be offset by the existing capital losses. The replacement property will have a higher (cost) basis for future depreciation. This plan is much more important to corporate taxpayers because excess capital losses can be carried forward only five years.

### Selecting Depreciation Methods

The accelerated cost recovery system provides taxpayers with several choices of depreciation methods and conventions. For example, a taxpayer with depreciable personalty may elect to use the straight-line method and either the class life or a longer alternative life. For real estate, an alternative 40-year life may be used.

### Effect of Recapture

Generally, a taxpayer should adopt the most rapid method of depreciation available because this results in a deferral of income taxes. Unless tax rates are expected to change significantly in the near future, the tax benefits produced by large depreciation deductions currently allow the taxpayer the use of the money that would otherwise have been used to pay income taxes. In addition, the availability of the like-kind exchange and involuntary conversion provisions eliminates the risk of depreciation recapture when the taxpayer plans to continue in business. It is also important to remember that, for noncorporate taxpayers, there is no depreciation recapture possibility for real estate placed in service after 1986. Because only the straight-line depreciation method can be used, there will be no excess depreciation. However, the unrecaptured § 1250 depreciation is taxed at 25 percent.

### Section 179

As discussed in Chapter 9, any § 179 expense amount is treated as depreciation allowed. As a result, the comments above may also apply in deciding whether to claim the option to expense the cost of qualifying property. If more than one qualifying asset is placed in service during the year and their total cost exceeds the annual limit (or reduced limit), the taxpayer must select the assets to be expensed. Obviously, only the assets not expected to be sold should be considered for this option. Given the time value of money, however, it seems unlikely that any taxpayer should forgo the § 179 expense option—unless the additional record keeping is considered to outweigh the current tax benefit.

## Installment Sales

Installment sales provide an excellent tax deferral possibility. Caution must be exercised, however, if trade or business property is to be sold under a deferred-payment arrangement. Because any depreciation recapture must be reported as income in the year of sale regardless of the amount of money received, taxpayers should require a cash down payment sufficient to pay any income taxes resulting from the depreciation recapture.

## Sales of Businesses

The sale of a business typically involves some recognition of intangible assets, whether it be goodwill, or some similar asset, or other assets such as customer lists. The buyer is generally entitled to amortize the intangibles over 15 years. The seller may have ordinary income, capital gain, and/or § 1231 gain.

The IRS generally is required to recognize agreements between the buyer and the seller as to the value of the various assets in the sale of a business so long as they are reasonable. Thus in negotiating the value of the underlying assets, the buyer should consider the possible deductions related to the purchased assets. For depreciable assets and purchased intangibles, the deductions come in the form of depreciation and amortization. With respect to these assets, the buyer should also evaluate the effects of the depreciation recapture of the assets if they are to be sold in a short period of time.

## Dispositions of Business Assets and the Self-Employment Tax

Gains on the disposition of business assets do not increase self-employment income. Similarly, losses do not reduce self-employment income. Generally speaking, foregoing allowable depreciation is not really optional since the basis of the depreciable assets must be reduced by depreciation allowed or allowable. So a taxpayer who does not feel like he or she needs the deduction, and realizes that the resulting gain if the asset is sold at a gain will be depreciation recapture, should claim it anyway!

**Example 24**

D purchased a machine for $4,000 in the current year. The machine qualifies for expensing under § 197. D is uncertain as to whether she should claim the entire $4,000 since she expects to sell the machine for $3,200 the next tax year. Her dilemma involves the fact that the $4,000 is an ordinary deduction and the $3,200 is an ordinary gain. Why not just depreciate the machine? The reason is that by claiming the entire amount, she defers the tax on $3,200 for a year—assuming no change in her marginal tax rate.

Taxpayers paying self-employment tax should normally depreciate assets as rapidly as possible since the depreciation allowed will reduce the self-employment tax, but the future gain on the disposition of the asset is not includible in self-employment income.

**Example 25**

D, in the prior example, can deduct the full $4,000, reducing her income tax and her self-employment tax. However, when she sells the machine the next year, the gain is subject only to income tax (as ordinary income).

# Problem Materials

## DISCUSSION QUESTIONS

**17-1** *Section 1231 Assets.* What are § 1231 assets? What is the required holding period? Does the § 1231 category of assets include § 1245 and § 1250 assets as well? Elaborate.

**17-2** *Excluded Assets.* What type of property is excluded from § 1231 treatment?

**17-3** *Section 1231 Netting Process.* Briefly describe the § 1231 netting process. Are personal use assets included in this process?

**17-4** *Net § 1231 Gains.* What is the appropriate tax treatment of net § 1231 gains? Are they offset by short-term capital losses? Can they be offset by capital loss carryovers from prior years?

**17-5** *Net § 1231 Losses.* What is the appropriate tax treatment of net § 1231 losses? Are they subject to any annual limitation? Can they be used to create or increase a net operating loss for the year?

**17-6** *Certain Casualty or Theft Gains and Losses.* Which casualty or theft gains and losses are included in the § 1231 netting process? What is the proper treatment of a net casualty or theft gain? What is the proper treatment of a net casualty or theft loss?

**17-7** *Section 1231 Look-Back Rule.* Describe how the § 1231 look-back rule operates. Why do you think Congress enacted such a rule?

**17-8** *Section 1245 Property.* What category of trade or business property is subject to § 1245? What depreciable real property has been included in this category?

**17-9** *Full Depreciation Recapture—§ 1245.* What is meant by § 1245 recapture potential? Why is this rule sometimes called the full recapture rule? What is the lower limit of § 1245 recapture?

**17-10** *Section 1245 Recapture Potential.* During the current year Z sold a vacuum used in his pool-cleaning business. The vacuum had cost $3,600 three years ago, and he had expensed the entire amount under § 179.

**a.** How much is the § 1245 recapture potential with respect to this vacuum?

**b.** If the vacuum was sold for $900, what is the character of the gain?

**17-11** *Asset Classification.* When will the sale or other disposition of depreciable equipment be subject to both § 1231 and § 1245? What is the appropriate treatment of any loss from the sale of such equipment?

**17-12** *Section 1245 Property.* F gave property with § 1245 recapture potential to his daughter, D. Will F be required to recapture any of the depreciation previously claimed? How must D characterize any gain she might recognize on a subsequent disposition of the property?

**17-13** *Section 1245 Recapture Potential.* What happens to the § 1245 recapture potential when property is disposed of in a like-kind exchange?

**17-14** *Section 179 Expense Treatment.* Explain the proper tax treatment of any gain recognized on the disposition of an asset that the taxpayer had earlier elected to expense under § 179. Does this mean that any amounts ever deducted under § 179 will always be subject to recapture? Explain.

**17-15** *Section 1250 Property.* Is land included in the definition of § 1250 property? Is any real property depreciated under the straight-line method included in this definition?

**17-16** *Section 1250 Property.* Is nonresidential real estate acquired after 1980 always § 1250 property? Explain.

**17-17** *Section 1250 Property.* Why will depreciable real property placed in service after 1986 never be subject to § 1250 recapture? How is the unrecaptured depreciation treated?

**17-18** *Section 1250 Recapture Potential.* Why is § 1250 sometimes called the partial recapture rule? Will the § 1250 recapture potential ever simply disappear? Explain.

**17-19** *Section 1250 Recapture Potential.* This year Y sold a duplex that she had rented out for several years. The house had cost $40,000 20 years earlier and depreciation expense of $27,000 has been claimed. Straight-line depreciation would have been $24,500.

**a.** How much is the § 1250 recapture potential with respect to the duplex?

**b.** If the duplex was sold for $75,000, what is the character of Y's gain and how is it taxed?

**17-20** *Additional Recapture—§ 291.* Briefly describe the additional depreciation recapture rule of § 291.

**a.** Which taxpayers are subject to this rule?

**b.** Compare this to the special rate for unrecaptured depreciation on § 1250 property for individual taxpayers.

**17-21** *Section 291 Recapture.* Can a corporation that has always elected to use the straight-line depreciation method for all real property ever be subject to additional recapture under § 291? Explain.

**17-22** *Reporting § 1231 Transactions.* What tax form does a taxpayer use to report the results of § 1231 transactions? How is any depreciation recapture reported on this form?

**17-23** *Planning § 1231 Transactions.* Under what circumstances should a taxpayer with an in voluntary conversion gain from business property consider not electing to defer the gain under § 1033?

**17-24** *Planning § 1231 Transactions.* A taxpayer plans to trade in depreciable property in order to acquire new property but is quite disappointed to find that his old equipment is worth less than its unrecovered cost basis. He is currently in the top marginal tax bracket and has no capital gains or losses or other § 1231 transactions for the year. What tax advice would you offer this taxpayer concerning the planned exchange?

**17-25** *Installment Sales and Depreciation Recapture.* Briefly describe how recapture is reported when either § 1245 property or § 1250 property is disposed of in an installment sale. What tax planning should a taxpayer undertake concerning such sales?

## PROBLEMS

**17-26** *Characterizing Assets.* Indicate whether the following gains and losses are § 1231 gains or losses or capital gains and losses or neither. Make your determination prior to the § 1231 netting process.

**a.** Printing press used in A's business; held for three years and sold at a loss.
**b.** Goodwill sold as part of the sale of B's business
**c.** Vacant lot used five years as a parking lot in C's business; sold at a gain
**d.** House, 80 percent of which is D's home and 20 percent of which is used as a place of business; held 15 years and sold at a gain
**e.** Camera used in E's business; held for 10 months and sold at a gain
**f.** Land used by F for 10 years as a farm and sold at a loss
**g.** Personal residence sold at a loss

**17-27** *Section 1231.* During the year H sold the following assets, both of which had been held for several years:

| Asset | Gain (Loss) |
|---|---|
| Vacant land held for investment | $52,000 |
| Equipment used in his business | (12,000) |

Determine how much capital gain or loss and the amount of ordinary income or loss that H will report for the year. At what rate will the gain, if any, be taxed?

**17-28** *Section 1231 Netting.* G operates the Corner Bar and Grill as a sole proprietorship. During the year he sold the following assets, all of which had been held for several years:

| Asset | Gain (Loss) |
|---|---|
| IBM stock | $(12,000) |
| Land and building used in the business | 34,000 |
| Equipment used in the business | (3,000) |

The building had been acquired in 1993. Straight-line depreciation claimed and deducted with respect to the building was $8,000. Straight-line depreciation on the equipment was $4,000. Determine how much capital gain or loss as well as the amount of ordinary income or loss that G will report for the year and explain how they will be taxed.

**17-29** *Involuntary Conversions and § 1231.* Assume the same facts as in *Problem 17-28*. In addition, G's records revealed the following information:

- A portion of the grill's parking lot was condemned by the city when it decided to expand the adjacent street. G pocketed the cash and recognized a gain of $5,000.
- A pool table was destroyed as part of a barroom brawl. G realized a casualty loss of $2,000.

Determine how much capital gain or loss as well as the amount of ordinary income or loss that G will report for the year. At what rate will the recognized gain, if any, be taxed?

**17-30** *Section 1231 Hodgepodge.* For 30 years Rae has operated The General Store, a hardware store in Columbus. Rae runs the business as a sole proprietorship. During the year, she recognized the following gains and losses from assets held several years:

1. Uninsured warehouse burned down: $10,000 loss
2. Equipment stolen: $190,000 gain (ignore depreciation)
3. Parking lot sold: $120,000 gain
4. IBM stock sold: capital loss of $70,000
5. Condemnation of land: $1,000 gain

Determine how much capital gain or loss as well as the amount of ordinary income or loss that Rae will report for the year. At what rate will the gain, if any, be taxed?

**17-31** *Section 1231 Lookback.* J has recognized the following § 1231 gains and losses in the current year (2011) and since the inception of his business:

| Year | Net § 1231 Gain (Loss) |
|---|---|
| 2011 | $50,000 |
| 2010 | 12,000 |
| 2009 | (35,000) |
| 2008 | 0 |
| 2007 | 65,000 |
| 2006 | (13,000) |

How will J treat the $50,000 gain for the current year?

**17-32** *Section 1231—Timber.* A owns timber land that she purchased in 1991. During the current calendar tax year, the timber was cut and A elected § 631 treatment for the gain. Her cost assignable to the timber was $25,000 and its fair market value on January 1 of this year was $40,000. The actual sales price of the cut timber when it was sold was $55,000.

a. How much is A's gain or loss recognized and what is its character?
b. Can A deduct the costs of cutting the timber?

**17-33** *Section 1231—Unharvested Crops.* This year L sold her farmland, which she had owned for 20 years. L had made minor improvements to the farm and had used straight-line depreciation to depreciate them. No personal property was sold with the farm.

The sales price was $80,000 and L's adjusted basis was $36,000. The unharvested crops on the land represented $8,000 of the sales price, and L had spent $3,200 in producing the crop to the point of sale.

a. How does L report the gain or loss from the sale of the farm?
b. If L has no other sales of trade or business property or of capital assets, how much of the gain is included in her taxable income?

**17-34** *Section 1245 Recapture.* During the current year, D sold a drill press he had used in his wood shop business for three years. D had purchased the press for $820 and had deducted depreciation of $476. Straight-line depreciation would have been $410. Determine the amount and character of gain or loss to D under each of the following circumstances below:

a. The press is sold for $500.
b. The press is sold for $100.
c. The press is sold for $900.

**17-35** *Section 1245 Recapture.* This year N sold three different pieces of equipment used in her business:

| Description | Holding Period | Sales Price | Cost | Depreciation Allowed |
|---|---|---|---|---|
| Processing machine | 3 years | $1,200 | $1,400 | $600 |
| Work table | 4 years | 1,600 | 1,300 | 500 |
| Automatic stapler | 2 years | 500 | 900 | 300 |

What are the amount and character of N's gain or loss from these transactions?

**17-36** *Section 1245 Recapture.* Fill in the missing information for each of the three independent sales of § 1245 assets identified below. Enter a dollar amount or n/a (for not applicable) in each blank space.

| | Assets | | |
|---|---|---|---|
| | A | B | C |
| Sales price | $105 | $ 90 | $ |
| Cost | 100 | 125 | 100 |
| Depreciation allowed | 30 | | 30 |
| Depreciation recapture | | | 20 |
| § 1231 gain or (loss) | | (10) | |

**17-37** *Basis Reductions.* Dr. T purchased a treadmill for use in his cardiology practice for $13,000 on August 14, 2009. T claimed § 179 expense of $10,000 and depreciation of $429 in 2009. The depreciation for 2010 and 2011 is $735 and $524, respectively. T sold the treadmill on January 13, 2011 for $3,500,

**a.** What are the amount and character of T's gain on the sale?

**b.** What would be your answer if the unit had been sold for $13,500?

**17-38** *Section 1250 Recapture.* Fill in the missing information for each of the three independent sales of § 1250 assets identified below. Enter a dollar amount or n/a (for not applicable) in each blank space.

| | Assets | | |
|---|---|---|---|
| | X | Y | Z |
| Sales price | $100 | $ | $200 |
| Cost | 135 | 100 | 100 |
| Depreciation allowed | 55 | | 30 |
| Straight-line depreciation | | 20 | |
| Depreciation recapture | 0 | 10 | |
| § 1231 gain or (loss) | | 30 | 120 |

**17-39** *Real Property Acquired after 1986.* V sold an office building in the current year that she had purchased for $60,000 two years earlier. Depreciation of $4,127 was claimed before the building was sold for $75,000. Determine V's gain, its character and the rate at which it will be taxed?

**17-40** *Depreciation Recapture.* K purchased a warehouse on January 18, 1986 for $50,000 ($10,000 allocable to the land and $40,000 allocable to the building). The property was 19-year realty and was depreciated using the 175 percent declining balance method and mid-month convention. The unit was sold on January 15 of the current year for $120,000 ($30,000 allocable to the land and $90,000 allocable to the building). At the time the property was sold, the building was fully depreciated (i.e., K deducted depreciation of $40,000 while holding the property).

**a.** Determine K's gain, its character and the rate at which it will be taxed.

**b.** If K had used the straight-line method and a 19-year life under ACRS, the depreciation deductions would have been the same, $40,000. Determine K's gain, its character and the rate at which it will be taxed.

**c.** What would be your answer to (b) if K were a corporation?

**17-41** *Depreciation Recapture.* Happy Acres operates a small organic farm. In the current year, it sold some of its land including a barn for $500,000. The company purchased the property seven years earlier for $300,000. The barn is used for multiple purposes (storage of hay, tractors, equipment, animals). For MACRS, multi-purpose agricultural buildings are considered 20-year property and are depreciated using the 150% declining balance method (§ 168(b)(2)(A)). Assume accelerated depreciation deducted was $125,000 and straight-line depreciation would have been $105,000. For the following questions, ignore the land.

**a.** Compute the amount of gain realized and its character.

**b.** What amount of the gain, if any, is taxed at 25 percent?

**c.** What would your answer to (a) be if the company is a corporation?

**17-42** *Depreciation Recapture.* JWP Development, an LLC, built a hotel in downtown Chicago in 1980 at a cost of $700,000. It depreciated the building using an accelerated method over a useful life of 40 years. This year it sold the building for $1,000,000. At the time of the sale, the company had deducted accelerated depreciation of $400,000. Straight-line depreciation on the building would have been $150,000. (Do not try to verify these amounts.)

**a.** What is the amount of the company's gain and what is its character?

**b.** What amount of the gain, if any, will be taxed at a 25 percent rate?

**c.** If the company had used the straight-line method, what would be the amount and character the gain? At what rate would the gain be treated?

**d.** What would be your answer to (a) if JWP were a corporation?

**17-43** *Installment Sales and Recapture.* Assume the same facts as in Problem 17-42 except that Z sold the property under an installment contract with $100,000 down and $100,000 in each of the next nine years along with reasonable interest. How much gain would Z report in the year of sale and the following year and what is its character?

**17-44** *Unrecaptured § 1250 Gain.* B purchased a small warehouse for $45,000 in 2007. This year he sold the property for $62,000. He had deducted straight-line depreciation of $6,500 on the property prior to the sale. What is the amount of gain, if any, and how will it be taxed?

**17-45** *Twenty-five Percent Gains.* V had the following gains and losses for the current year:

| | |
|---|---|
| § 1250 recapture . . . . . . . . . . . . . . . . . . . . . . . . . . . . . . . . . . | $2,000 |
| Net § 1231 gains . . . . . . . . . . . . . . . . . . . . . . . . . . . . . . . . . . | 6,000 |
| Net short-term capital loss. . . . . . . . . . . . . . . . . . . . . . . . . . . . | (3,000) |

V's § 1231 gain was from a building that was held 15 years. The total depreciation allowed was $5,000. How much are V's *15 percent gains* and *25 percent gains*, respectively?

**17-46** *Section 1231 Gain and Look-Back Rule.* R sold land and a building used in farming for many years at a gain of $30,000 during 2011. No other sales or dispositions of § 1231 assets were made during the year. The § 1250 depreciation recapture for the building was zero and the unrecaptured depreciation was $1,000.

**a.** How is R's gain to be reported if he had a net § 1231 gain of $10,000 in 2008, a net § 1231 loss of $12,000 in 2009, and no § 1231 transactions in 2010?

**b.** How would your answer to (a) differ if the sale of the property had resulted in a loss of $7,500?

**17-47** *Section 1231 and Depreciation Recapture.* Fill in the missing information for each of the separate sales of § 1231 assets indicated below. Enter a dollar amount or n/a (for not applicable) in each blank space.

| | *Land* | *Building* | *Machine* | *Machine* |
|---|---|---|---|---|
| Sales price . . . . . . . . . . . . . . . . . . . . . | $100 | $ ___ | $90 | $ ___ |
| Cost . . . . . . . . . . . . . . . . . . . . . . . . . | 140 | 100 | 125 | 100 |
| Depreciation allowed . . . . . . . . . . . . | 0 | 30 | ___ | 30 |
| Straight-line depreciation. . . . . . . . . . | 0 | 20 | ___ | ___ |
| Depreciation recapture . . . . . . . . . . . | ___ | ___ | ___ | ___ |
| § 1231 gain or (loss). . . . . . . . . . . . . | ___ | 30 | (10) | 5 |

**17-48** *Depreciation Recapture and the § 1231 Netting Process.* T had three § 1231 transactions during the current year. All of the assets were held for several years.

**a.** Theft of electric cart used on business premises. The cart was worth $600, originally cost $800, and had an adjusted basis of $425.

**b.** Sale of equipment used in manufacturing. The equipment sold for $5,500, originally cost $8,000, and had an adjusted basis of $4,250.

**c.** Sale of land and a small building used for storage. The property was sold for $60,000, originally cost $56,000, and had an adjusted basis of $42,500. Straight-line depreciation was claimed on the building.

Determine the amount of ordinary income or loss and capital gain or loss that T must report from these transactions for the current year.

**17-49** *Section 1231 Transactions.* K has the following business assets that she is interested in selling in either 2011 or 2012.

| | Fair Market Value | Basis |
|---|---|---|
| Manufacturing equipment | $220,000 | $400,000 |
| Factory building | 350,000 | 220,000 |
| Land used for factory | 450,000 | 120,000 |

Straight-line depreciation of $60,000 was claimed on the factory. K has never sold any other § 1231 assets.

**a.** What are the tax results if K sells the land and building in 2011 and the equipment in 2012?

**b.** What are the tax results if K sells the equipment in 2011 and the land and building in 2012?

**c.** What are the tax results if K sells all the assets in 2011?

**17-50** *Comprehensive Problem for Capital Asset and Trade or Business Property Transactions.* T owned a number of apartment units and sold several properties related to that trade or business during the current year as follows:

| Description | Holding Period | Sales Price | Cost | Depreciation Allowed | Method |
|---|---|---|---|---|---|
| Apartment unit, including land (straight-line depreciation = $2,400) | 3 years | $65,000 | $24,000 | $3,000 | DB |
| Lawn tractor | 5 years | 1,000 | 3,000 | 2,600 | SL |
| Spray painter | 2 years | 500 | 1,400 | 600 | SL |

During a severe winter storm, T also lost a depreciable motor scooter used in his business. The scooter, which was owned by T for two years and used exclusively in the business, had cost $2,600 and had an adjusted basis of $1,750.

In addition, T sold several capital assets during the current year as follows:

| Description | Holding Period | Sales Price | Adjusted Basis |
|---|---|---|---|
| 100 shares LM Corp. | 16 months | $2,000 | $1,000 |
| 75 shares PL, Inc. | 8 months | 1,600 | 6,000 |
| Silver ingots | 6 years | 2,600 | 6,000 |

Assuming T has never deducted § 1231 losses before, calculate the following amounts based on the above information:

**a.** The amount of § 1245 recapture and § 1250 recapture, if any.

**b.** The net § 1231 gain or loss.

**c.** The capital gain or loss and the rate at which it is taxed.

**d.** The net short-term capital gain or loss.

**e.** The overall impact of the above transactions on T's adjusted gross income.

**17-51** *Netting Gains and Losses.* G had the following gains and losses for the current calendar year:

| | |
|---|---|
| DFG Corporation stock held 3 years | $4,000 |
| Gold held 6 years | (5,000) |
| Sale of business building: | |
| § 1250 recapture | 1,500 |
| § 1231 gain | 7,000 |

Depreciation of $7,500 had been claimed on the building. What is the character of these gains in calculating the capital gains tax?

**17-52** *Capital Gains Tax.* C, an unmarried head of household, has the following gains and losses for the current taxable year:

| | |
|---|---|
| GHJ, Inc. stock held 16 months | ($3,000) |
| Land held for investment 15 years | 4,000 |
| Sale of business real estate held 15 years: | |
| § 1250 recapture | 1,800 |
| Net § 1231 gain | 7,250 |

Depreciation claimed on the real estate was $7,800. C's taxable income (properly calculated and including the information above) is $121,900. How much is C's income tax for the current calendar year?

**17-53** *Comprehensive Problem with Sales of Business Use Assets.* O and P are married. They have no dependents and elect to file jointly for the current year. They recently decided to retire, sell their home, and try renting for a while. Their income and related transactions for the year follow:

| | |
|---|---|
| Ordinary income from business | $ 45,200 |
| Interest income | 10,100 |
| Sale of personal residence of 20 years: | |
| Sales price | $760,000 |
| Selling costs | 43,000 |
| Adjusted basis | 195,000 |
| Sale of business: | |
| § 1245 recapture | 15,000 |
| § 1250 recapture | 26,000 |
| § 1231 gain | 90,000 |
| Gain on sale of stock held 5 years | 16,000 |
| Itemized deductions (after 2 percent cutback) | 23,400 |

O and P had claimed depreciation on the § 1245 property and the § 1250 property in the amount of $25,000 and $56,000, respectively. Calculate O and P's adjusted gross income, taxable income, and gross income tax for the current year.

**17-54** *Sections 1231 and 1245 Property.* The terms § 1231 property and § 1245 property are often used interchangeably. However, there are times when a specific asset can be classified as (1) *both* § 1231 and § 1245 property; (2) only § 1231 property; or (3) only § 1245 property. Based on the values assigned to the letters below, indicate the appropriate classification for each of the following mathematical expressions.

Let X = asset's original cost
Y = depreciation claimed
Z = asset's adjusted basis
T = amount realized on sale

**a.** If T Z, asset is § _________ property.
**b.** If T > X, asset is § _________ property.
**c.** If X > T < Z, asset is § _________ property.
**d.** If Y > T > Z, asset is § _________ property.

**17-55** *Section 1231 and § 1250 Property.* It is possible that (1) *both* § 1231 and § 1250 apply to the sale of depreciable real property, (2) only § 1250 applies, or (3) only § 1231 applies. Based on the values assigned to the letters below, indicate which Code sections apply for each of the following mathematical expressions.

Let X = asset's original cost
Y = depreciation claimed
Z = asset's adjusted basis
T = amount realized on sale
S = amount of straight-line depreciation

**a.** If Y > S and T Z, § ________ applies.
**b.** If Y > S and T > X, § ________ applies.
**c.** If Y = S, § ________ applies.
**d.** If Y > S and (T − Z) (Y − S), § ________ applies.

**17-56** *Sale of Property Converted from Personal Use—Comprehensive Problem.* L owned and used a house as her personal residence since she purchased it in 2006 for $110,000. On February 11, 2009, when it was worth $85,000, L moved out and converted the property into a rental property. She rented the house until December 15, 2011, when it was sold for $104,500.

**a.** Determine L's depreciation deductions for the rental property from the time it was converted in 2009 until it was sold in 2011. Ignore land value.
**b.** What are the amount and character of L's gain or loss to be recognized from the sale?

**17-57** *Sale of Property Converted to Personal Use—Comprehensive Problem.* Z purchased a computer system with peripherals for $14,500 on August 12, 2008. The system was used exclusively in his business. In October 2011, when the computer was worth $8,200, Z closed the business and began using the unit for personal purposes.

**a.** Determine Z's depreciation deductions for the computer system from the time it was purchased until it was converted to personal use, assuming that he elected the maximum § 179 expensing option for other assets placed into service in 2008.
**b.** Assume the computer system was sold for $5,400 on May 15, 2011 rather than being converted to personal use. What are the amount and character of Z's loss?

## TAX RESEARCH PROBLEMS

**17-58** *Capital Assets versus § 1231 Assets.* R inherited a residence that had been used exclusively by her grandmother as a principal residence for 30 years. Upon receiving the property, R immediately offered the property for rent and rented to several tenants. After several months, R encountered an interesting potential business venture that would require a substantial capital investment. After an agonizing decision, she proceeded to sell her inherited rental unit. The unit was sold at a loss and R deducted the loss under § 1231. Since she had no § 1231 gains, the loss was deducted as an ordinary deduction. Is the treatment R chose the appropriate treatment for the loss? Does the character of the property to her grandmother carry over to R, resulting in disallowance of the loss or capital loss treatment?

***Research aids:***

*Campbell v. Comm.*, 5 T.C. 272 (1945).
*Crawford v. Comm.*, 16 T.C. 678 (1951), acq. 1951-2 C.B. 2.

**17-59** *Business Use of Personal Residence.* J purchased a home in March 1990 for $120,000. Twenty percent of its cost was attributable to the land. From the date of purchase until March 2006, 20 percent of the house was used as a home-office, the costs of which were properly deducted annually (including depreciation). The home was used exclusively as J's residence from April 2006 until the house was sold for $325,000 on November 15, 2010.

**a.** J used the straight line method and the normal useful life of 32.5 years (applicable at the time, it would be 39 years for property placed in service currently). What amount of depreciation did he claim over the 15-year period that the property was used as a home-office?
**b.** Is there any depreciation recapture to be reported if gain is reported on the sale?
**c.** Is there depreciation recapture to be reported if all or part of the gain is excluded?

# Employee Compensation and Retirement Plans

PART 6

**CHAPTER 18** Employee Compensation and Retirement Plans

18

# Employee Compensation and Retirement Plans

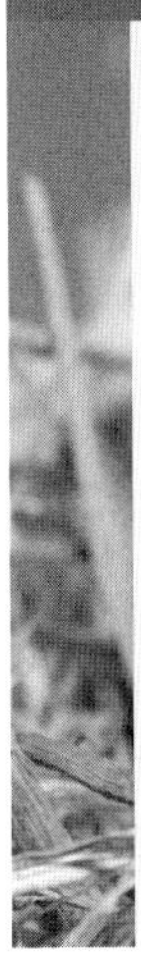

## Learning Objectives

Upon completion of this chapter you will be able to:

LO.1 Distinguish between taxable and nontaxable employee fringe benefits.

LO.2 Explain the tax treatment of the receipt of property for services.

LO.3 Explain the advantages and disadvantages of qualified retirement plans.

LO.4 Distinguish between a defined benefit plan and a defined contribution plan.

LO.5 Explain the requirements associated with qualified retirement plans.

LO.6 Explain the special qualified plans available for self-employed individuals.

LO.7 Describe various qualified plans for employees such as 401(k) plans and individual retirement accounts.

LO.8 Describe nonqualified deferred compensation plans.

LO.9 Determine the tax consequences of the issuance and exercise of both nonqualified and qualified stock options.

## Chapter Outline


Introduction 18-2
Taxation of Current Compensation 18-2
Statutory Fringe Benefits 18-2
Deferred Compensation 18-3
Receipt of Property for Services 18-4
General Rule of § 83 18-4
The § 83(B) Election 18-5
Qualified Retirement Plans for Corporations 18-6
Tax Benefits of Qualified Plans 18-6
Taxability of Qualified Plan Lump-Sum Distributions 18-7
Additional Taxes on Premature or Excess Distributions 18-8
Rollover Contribution 18-8
Plan Loans 18-9
Types of Qualified Plans 18-10
Qualification Requirements 18-13
Existence of a Qualified Trust 18-13
Anti-Discrimination Rules 18-13
Scope of Plan Participation and Coverage 18-14
Vesting Requirements and Forfeitures 18-15
Funding and Contribution Limitations 18-15
Top Heavy Plans 18-17
Deductibility of Contributions by Employer 18-17
Determination Letters 18-17
Qualified Plans for Self-Employed Individuals 18-17
Contribution Limitations 18-18
Qualified Plans for Employees 18-19

Cash or Deferred Arrangements [§ 401(k) Plans] 18-19
Individual Retirement Accounts 18-22
Traditional IRA 18-22
Roth IRAs 18-27
Credit for Contributions to Plans by Low-Income Individuals 18-28
Education IRAs (Coverdell Education Savings Accounts) 18-29
Simplified Employee Pensions 18-31
Retirement Planning Using Nonqualified Deferred Compensation 18-31
Constructive Receipt 18-31
Treatment of Nonqualified Deferred Compensation Plans 18-32
Unfunded Deferred Compensation Plans 18-33
Funded Deferred Compensation Plans 18-34
Stock Options 18-34
Option Exercise 18-35
Incentive Stock Options 18-35
Holding Period Requirements 18-36
Qualification Requirements 18-37
Nonqualified Stock Options 18-38
Stock Appreciation Rights 18-38
Tax Planning Considerations 18-39
Planning for Retirement Income 18-39
Advantages of IRAs 18-40
Spousal IRAs 18-40
What Is an Active Participant? 18-40
Making a Nondeductible Contribution to an IRA 18-40
Problem Materials 18-42

## Introduction

For a large majority of individual taxpayers, compensation received for services rendered as an employee is the most significant, if not the only, source of taxable income. Because of this significance, the topic of taxation of employee compensation is of primary interest to the taxpaying public. Employee compensation consists not only of cash wage and salary payments but an incredible variety of compensation "packages" designed to accommodate the needs and desires of employer and employee alike.

The tax consequences to both the employer and employee of various types of employment compensation are examined in this chapter. Because the concept of compensation includes provisions for employee retirement income, the chapter also includes a discussion of the numerous types of retirement income plans available to both employees and self-employed taxpayers.

## Taxation of Current Compensation

**LO.1**
Distinguish between taxable and nontaxable employee fringe benefits.

Under the broad authority of § 61, a taxpayer's gross income includes all compensation for services rendered including wages, salaries, fees, fringe benefits, sales commissions, customer tips, and bonuses. Compensatory payments may be made in a medium other than cash. For example, payment for services rendered may be made with property, such as marketable securities. In such cases, the fair market value of the property is the measure of the gross compensation income received.[1]

Payment for services performed by Taxpayer A for Taxpayer B could consist of services performed by Taxpayer B for Taxpayer A. For example, a lawyer might agree to draft a will for a carpenter, who in turn agrees to repair the lawyer's roof. As a result of such a *service swap*, both taxpayers must recognize gross income equal to the value of the services received.[2]

### Statutory Fringe Benefits

As a general rule, any economic benefit bestowed on an employee by his or her employer that is intended to compensate the employee for services rendered represents gross income. This is

[1] Reg. § 1.61-2(d).

[2] *Ibid.*

true whether the benefit is in the form of a direct cash payment or an indirect noncash benefit that nonetheless improves the recipient's economic position.

Certain indirect or *fringe benefits*, however, are excludable from gross income under specific statutory authority. The following is a list of nontaxable fringe benefits and the authority for their exclusion from income. The details of these exclusions are discussed in Chapter 6.

1. Employer payment of employee group-term life insurance premiums (up to $50,000 of coverage)—§ 79
2. Employer contributions to employee accident or health plans—§ 106
3. Amounts paid to an employee under an employer's medical expense reimbursement plan—§ 105(b)
4. Employee meals or lodging furnished for the convenience of the employer—§ 119
5. Amounts received under an employer's group legal services program—§ 120
6. Amounts received under an employer's educational assistance program—§ 127
7. Amounts received under an employer's dependent care assistance program—§ 129
8. No-additional-cost services, qualified employee discounts, working condition fringes, and de minimis fringes—§ 132

The length of the above list demonstrates Congressional tolerance for the use of innovative fringe benefits to attract employees. Employers who want to design the most flexible compensation package for employees who have differing compensation needs may use a *cafeteria plan* of employee benefits. Under a cafeteria plan, an employee is allowed to choose among two or more benefits consisting of both cash and statutory nontaxable benefits.[3]

## Deferred Compensation

Deferral of compensation can be accomplished under a variety of methods that includes both "qualified" and "nonqualified" plans. A qualified plan is one that meets the requirements of Code § 401(a) and offers the employer a current deduction for money set aside for the eventual benefit of the employee. In this manner, the employees are not taxed on the amount set aside until it is distributed to them, and the income earned on the funds is exempt from tax. A nonqualified plan, on the other hand, does not possess all the specialized tax benefits, but offers a plan that is easier to administer and allows for discrimination among employees. Some of the more popular types of each of these plans are listed in Exhibit 18-1.

The purpose of deferred compensation plans is to allow employees to receive income at a later date when, presumably, they will have much less income. The employee's tax objective in participating in such an arrangement is to ensure that they will be taxed only when payments are received under the plan or agreement. The employer's tax objective is to offer a vehicle that will attract and compensate key personnel while obtaining a current tax deduction for any funds set aside for these employees.

Changes in the tax law, specifically the 1986 Tax Reform Act, reduced some of the glamour of deferred arrangements through its repeal of the capital gains differential and compression of the individual-corporate tax rate structure. However, subsequent legislation has reinstated a modest resurgence in plan activity due to the prospects of a widening capital gain differential and a probable increase in tax rates. Nevertheless, while the 1986 Act reduced the tax benefits of qualified plans, it is still possible to achieve both deferral of taxation and capital gains treatment on the eventual distribution of funds to the employee. However, most deferred compensation arrangements are not ordinarily utilized as vehicles to recharacterize the form of income.

While numerous deferred compensation arrangements focus on tax benefits, most qualified plans are flexible and have a wide range of purposes other than reducing an employee's tax liability. For example, a retirement benefit program can have a substantial psychological impact on an employee's morale because it offers an effortless program of saving for the future. In addition, a nonqualified deferred compensation arrangement can be

---

[3] § 125.

**EXHIBIT 18.1** **Types of Deferred Compensation Plans**

*Qualified Plans*

Defined Contribution Plans
Defined Benefit Plans
Money Purchase Plans
Stock Bonus Plans
Employee Stock Ownership Plans
Cash or Deferred Arrangements (401k)
Simplified Employee Plans
Individual Retirement Accounts
Incentive Stock Options
SIMPLE Plans

*Nonqualified Plans*

Restricted Stock
Deferred Payments
Rabbi Trusts
Secular Trusts
Nonqualified Stock Options

tailored to attract and compensate new executives for benefits they may have forfeited when they left their former employer. Finally, both qualified and nonqualified deferred compensation plans can provide other benefits, such as disability guarantees, death benefits, income security, and plan loans, to safeguard and preserve the well-being of the company's most valued asset—its employees.

## Receipt of Property for Services

**LO.2**
Explain the tax treatment of the receipt of property for services.

From a corporate employer's point of view, any form of employee compensation that somehow strengthens that employee's commitment to the corporation is highly desirable. One such type of compensation is a payment made in the capital stock of the corporation itself. Such payment converts the employee into a stockholder and gives him or her an equity interest in the future prosperity of the corporation.

When stock in the corporate employer is used to compensate employees, it is typical for the employment contract to provide that the employee must continue to work for the corporation for some stated time period before he or she is given unrestricted ownership of the stock. If the employee leaves the job before the period expires, the stock received will be forfeited. In this situation, the tax consequences of the compensatory payment to both employee and employer are governed by § 83.

### General Rule of § 83

If in connection with the performance of services, property of any type is transferred to any person other than the person for whom such services are performed, § 83(a) provides that the fair market value of such property shall be included in the gross income of the person performing such services. If the recipient made any payment for the property, only the excess of the property's value over the amount of such payment is includible gross income. Such inclusion shall occur in the first taxable year in which the rights of the person having the beneficial interest in such property are *transferable* or are not subject to a *substantial risk of forfeiture*, whichever is applicable. If the property received for services is not immediately transferable by the recipient or is subject to risk of forfeiture, it is referred to as *restricted property*.

Regulation § 1.83-3(c)(1) explains that a substantial risk of forfeiture exists when the ownership of the transferred property is conditioned, directly or indirectly, upon the future performance (or refraining from performance) of substantial services by the recipient. The Regulation also states that the existence of a substantial risk of forfeiture can only be determined by examining the facts and circumstances of the specific situation.

Under §83(h), a taxpayer that pays for services using property is entitled to a deduction equal to the fair market value of the property. The deduction must be taken in the taxable year in which (or with which) ends the taxable year in which the value of the property is recognized as gross income to the recipient.

**Example 1**

Corporation M is on a fiscal year ending June 30. On November 1, 2008, the corporation gave employee E, a calendar year taxpayer, 100 shares of its own stock worth $100 per share as compensation for E's services to Corporation M. If E leaves M's employ for any reason during the three-year period beginning on November 1, 2008, he must return the shares. On November 2, 2011, E is still employed and the risk of forfeiture of the stock lapses. On this date the stock is worth $120 per share. For his taxable year 2011, E must include $12,000 in gross income; his tax basis in his shares will also be $12,000. Corporation M has a deduction of $12,000 for its fiscal year ending June 30, 2012.

The Regulations make it clear that a deduction is available to the transferor of the property only if the transfer is an expense meeting the deductibility requirements of § 162 or § 212. If the transfer constitutes a capital expenditure, it must be capitalized rather than deducted.[4]

**Example 2**

Refer to the facts in *Example 1*. If the shares were transferred to E because E performed organizational services for Corporation M, the corporation must capitalize the $12,000 amount included in E's gross income.

## THE § 83(B) ELECTION

Section 83(b) gives a taxpayer who has performed services for *restricted* property an interesting option. Within 30 days of the receipt of the property, the taxpayer may choose to include its fair market value in his or her current year's gross income. This election accelerates the recognition of gross income to the taxpayer. However, the election could be beneficial if the property were rapidly appreciating in value and consequently would have a higher fair market value on the date the risk of forfeiture or other restrictions are scheduled to lapse.

**Example 3**

In 2009, employee Z receives property worth $10,000 as payment for services rendered. The property is subject to a substantial risk of forfeiture, but Z elects to include the $10,000 value in her 2009 gross income. In 2011, when the risk of forfeiture lapses, the property is worth $25,000. However, Z has no gross income attributable to the property in 2011. Z will have a $10,000 basis in her stock, and Z's employer has a $10,000 deduction for its taxable year that includes December 31, 2009.

[4] Reg. § 1.83-6(a)(4).

The election is not without risk. If the property depreciates during the forfeiture period, the election leads to a larger gross income inclusion as well as acceleration of tax recognition. And more costly still, if the property is in fact forfeited, the taxpayer receives no deduction for the original gross income inclusion.[5] Obviously, the decision to use the § 83(b) election requires a careful analysis of both the current and expected future value of the property, current and future marginal tax rates, and the nature of the restriction involved.

## Qualified Retirement Plans for Corporations

**LO.3**
Explain the advantages and disadvantages of qualified retirement plans.

Historically, Congress has viewed with favor the establishment of employer retirement plans as part of a total compensation package offered to employees. The existence of an employer designed and administered plan encourages the young employee to think seriously about his or her retirement years and offers the employee a most convenient way to provide financially for such retirement.

Congress provided an extremely attractive set of tax benefits available to *qualified* employer retirement plans as part of the Internal Revenue Code of 1954. Since the enactment of the 1954 Code, the scope of the benefits has been periodically expanded, and Congress has made different forms of qualified plans available to an ever-increasing number of individual taxpayers. Before examining the various types of qualified plans and the specific features of each, it will be useful to analyze the two basic tax benefits associated with qualified plans for employees—the tax-free nature of employer contributions and the tax-free growth of these contributions.

### Tax Benefits of Qualified Plans

When an employer makes a current contribution to a *qualified* retirement plan on behalf of an employee, §§ 402(a) and 403(a) provide that the value of the contribution is not includible gross income to the employee, even though the employee has obviously received additional compensation in the form of the contribution. In contrast, if the contribution was made by the employer to a *nonqualified* retirement plan in which the employee had a vested interest, the employee would have additional gross income equal to the value of the contribution. As a result, the net amount saved toward retirement by the employee participating in a nonqualified plan is less than the amount saved by the employee participating in a qualified plan.

The second major benefit of qualified retirement plans is that the earnings generated by employer contributions are nontaxable. Sections 401(a) and 501(a) provide that a trust created to manage and invest employer contributions to a qualified retirement plan is exempt from tax.

The effect of these two benefits on the total amount of savings available to an employee at retirement is illustrated in Exhibit 18-2. The exhibit compares two retirement plans, A and B.

**EXHIBIT 18.2** **Comparison of Nonqualified versus Qualified Retirement Plans' Year-End Values of Employer Contributions**

| | *Nonqualified Plan A* | *Qualified Plan B* |
|---|---|---|
| Year 1 | $ 7,500 | $ 10,000 |
| Year 2 | 15,675 | 21,200 |
| Year 15 | 220,208* | 372,800** |

*$7,500 × 29.361 (factor for the sum of an annuity of $1.00 at 9% for 15 years)
**$10,000 × 37.280 (factor for the sum of an annuity of $1.00 at 12% for 15 years)

[5] § 83(b)(1).

The plans are identical in every respect but one—A is a nonqualified personal savings plan while B is a qualified employer's trust. The exhibit is based on the following assumptions:

1. The employer will make an annual $10,000 contribution to the plan on behalf of the employee.
2. The employee has a 25 percent marginal tax rate. Therefore, the net amount saved by the employee in Plan A is only $7,500 ($10,000 – $2,500 tax on the current compensation represented by the contribution). The net amount saved in Plan B is $10,000.
3. Funds invested in both plans can earn a 12 percent before-tax return. The earnings from Plan A are taxable to the employee so that the plan's after-tax rate of return is 9 percent. Plan B is in the form of a qualified trust and therefore its earnings are tax-exempt.

The difference in the amounts available to an employee after 15 years of participation in either plan is dramatic. It is not difficult to understand why qualified retirement plans have become such an attractive fringe benefit to employees concerned with providing for their retirement years. However, before the analysis presented in Exhibit 18-2 is complete, it is necessary to examine the general rule as to the taxability of benefits paid out of a qualified plan upon an employee's retirement.

When an employee begins to withdraw funds from a nonqualified retirement savings plan, such funds represent *after-tax* dollars, and he or she will not be taxed on these funds a second time. In comparison, benefits received by an employee out of a qualified plan funded solely by employer contributions are fully taxable to the employee. It is important to understand that the retirement dollars available under Plan A of Exhibit 18-2 are excludable (as a return of capital), while the retirement dollars available under Plan B are fully includible in the recipient's gross income.

## Taxability of Qualified Plan Lump-Sum Distributions

If an employee who has made no contributions to the employer's qualified retirement plan receives a distribution from the plan, the employee has no investment in the distribution and therefore must include the entire amount in adjusted gross income.[6] When the distribution is made by a series of payments (i.e., an annuity), the taxability of the distribution is spread over a number of years.[7] If the distribution is made in a lump sum, all the retirement income is taxed in one year.[8] Given the progressive rate structure of the Federal income tax, the normal tax on a large lump sum distribution could be prohibitive.

To mitigate this problem, Congress provided two relief provisions that benefit the recipient of a lump-sum distribution from a qualified retirement plan. First, an employee could treat the portion of a distribution attributable to the employee's participation in the retirement plan prior to 1974 as long-term capital gain.[9] The Tax Reform Act of 1986 generally repealed such capital gain treatment. However, a taxpayer who was age 50 before January 1, 1986 (or a person who receives it on his or her behalf) may elect to utilize this relief provision. In such case, the long-term capital gain portion of a distribution will be taxed at a flat 20 percent rate.[10] Note that in 2012, individuals who turned 50 before 1986 would be 77 years old at this point.

A second relief provision is a special procedure for computing the amount of current tax on a lump sum distribution.[11] A taxpayer who was age 50 before January 1, 1986 may elect to use a 10-year forward averaging computation based on 1986 income tax rates for distributions received after 1986.[12] The calculation is made on Form 4792 (2010).

---

[6] If the employee has made contributions to the plan, he or she will have an investment in the plan, which may be recovered tax-free under the rules of § 72.

[7] § 402(a).

[8] § 402(e)(1).

[9] § 402(a)(2), repealed by the Tax Reform Act of 1986.

[10] Tax Reform Act of 1986, Act § 1122(h)(3).

[11] § 402(e).

[12] Tax Reform Act of 1986, Act § 1122(h)(5) A special 5-year averaging rule was repealed for tax years after 1999.

Under pre-2000 law, the averaging computation could be elected only for lump sum distributions received on or after the taxpayer had reached 59½ years of age, and a taxpayer could only make one such election.[13] Note that those who were born before 1936 continue to be eligible for ten-year averaging even after the five-year averaging is repealed.

## Additional Taxes on Premature or Excess Distributions

Congress intended for the tax-favored status of qualified plans to serve as an inducement for taxpayers to provide for a source of retirement income. Therefore, if a taxpayer makes a premature withdrawal from a qualified plan, a 10 percent penalty tax is imposed on the amount of the distribution included in the taxpayer's gross income.[14] However, the Code does permit penalty-free withdrawal from IRAs before age 59½ if any of the distributions are:

- On account of death or permanent disability.
- In the form of annuity payments over the taxpayer's lifetime.
- For medical expenses of the individual, his or her spouse and dependents that exceed 7.5 percent of A.G.I.
- For medical insurance of the individual, his or her spouse and dependents (without regard to the 7.5% of A.G.I. floor) if the individual has received unemployment compensation for at least 12 weeks, and the withdrawal is made in the year such unemployment compensation is received or the following year.
- For qualified education expenses. For this purpose, the term qualified higher education expenses is defined in § 529(e)(3) and generally means tuition, fees, books, supplies, and equipment required for enrollment or attendance at an eligible educational institution. It also includes the reasonable costs of room and board. In order to qualify, the expenses must be for education furnished to the taxpayer, the taxpayer's spouse, or any child or grandchild of the taxpayer or the taxpayer's spouse at an eligible education institution. Such expenses are reduced by amounts excluded from gross income that are used for such education.
- For first-time homebuyer expenses. The penalty waiver applies only to the first $10,000 withdrawn during the taxpayer's lifetime. The withdrawals must be used within 120 days of withdrawal to acquire, construct, or reconstruct a home that is the principal residence of the individual, his or her spouse, or any child, grandchild, or ancestor of the individual or spouse. Acquisition costs include any usual settlement, financing, or other closing costs. Although the name of the law suggests that it applies only to the purchase of a taxpayer's first home (and therefore is a once-in-a-lifetime opportunity), such is not the case. A first time homebuyer is defined as an individual (or if married, such individual's spouse) who had no present ownership interest in a principal residence during the two-year period ending on the date of acquisition. Thus, as long as the taxpayer has not owned a home in the past two years, withdrawals may be made from an IRA to help pay for the "new" home even though it is not the taxpayer's first home.
- To reservists called to active duty for at least 179 days.

## Rollover Contribution

There are many situations in which taxpayers receive lump-sum distributions from qualified plans prior to retirement. For example, a taxpayer who quits his job with his current employer to accept a position with a new employer may have a right to a distribution from his current employer's qualified plan. Any taxpayer who receives a qualified plan distribution but

[13] § 402(e)(4)(B).

[14] § 72(t).

does not need additional disposable income can exclude the distribution from gross income (and thus avoid both the income tax and any penalty tax on the distribution) by making a *rollover contribution* of the distributed funds. A rollover contribution must be made into another qualified employer plan, a Keogh plan, or an IRA, and it must be made within 60 days of the receipt of the distribution.[15] Note that in the case of a withdrawal, an employer is normally required to withhold 20 percent of the distribution as an estimated tax payment. However, withholding can be avoided if the amount is rolled directly into another qualified retirement plan, Keogh plan, or an IRA on a timely basis.[16] Failure to observe these rules can create a severe hardship and may lead to a penalty.

**Example 4**

T is 45 years old. This year his employer laid-off 200 employees and, unfortunately, T lost his job. T decided to take a lump-sum distribution from his retirement plan of $200,000. Absent a direct rollover, T's employer will withhold $40,000 (20% × $200,000) and T will receive $160,000. Note that in order to avoid taxation on the $200,000 as well as the ten percent early withdrawal penalty, T must rollover the entire $200,000 to a qualified plan, even though he only received $160,000. Consequently, he would have to find an additional $40,000 to go along with the $160,000 to avert a catastrophe!

## Plan Loans

Plan participants can avoid making taxable withdrawals from qualified plans while indirectly utilizing their retirement funds by borrowing money from their qualified plans. There is a very complex limit on the amount of a plan loan. In very general terms, a plan loan to a participant is limited to the lesser of (1) one-half the participant's vested accrued benefit (but not less than $10,000) or (2) $50,000. Any amount of a loan in excess of this limit is considered a taxable distribution.[17] Currently, owners of any small business (those with fewer than 100 employees) are generally permitted to make participant loans.

**Example 5**

R and S are members of P's small business qualified plan. R has accrued vested benefits of $14,000, and S has accrued vested benefits of $80,000. R can borrow up to $10,000 even though this amount exceeds 50% of his vested benefits. If S, on the other hand, borrows $62,000 from the fund, $22,000 will be treated as a taxable distribution to her because this exceeds 50% of her benefits (which is more severe than the $50,000 ceiling violation).

In order to avoid being treated as a taxable distribution, a loan must be repaid in quarterly installments with interest within five years of the loan. However, if a taxpayer uses the loan to purchase a principal residence, any reasonable repayment period is allowed. The treatment of the interest expense depends on how the loan proceeds were used and whether the taxpayer is a key employee. If the plan loan is secured by the residence, the interest is qualified residence interest and is fully deductible as an itemized deduction. If the loan is used

[15] § 402(a)(5).

[16] § 3405(c)(2).

[17] § 72(p).

for investment purposes, the interest is considered investment interest and is normally deductible to the extent of any investment income. Unlike regular employees, key employees are not allowed to deduct any interest on plan loans.

## TYPES OF QUALIFIED PLANS

**LO.4**
Distinguish between a defined benefit plan and a defined contribution plan.

Qualified plans fall into two basic categories, defined benefit plans and defined contribution plans. A *defined benefit plan* is one designed to systematically provide for the payment of definitely determinable benefits to retired employees for a period of years or for life. The focus of the plan is on the eventual retirement benefit to be provided. The amount of the benefit is usually based on both an employee's compensation level and years of service to the company. Defined benefit plans are commonly referred to as pension plans. The current amount of employer contributions that are required to fund future pension benefits under a given plan must be determined actuarially.[18]

*Defined contribution plans* provide for annual contributions to each participating employee's retirement account. Upon retirement, an employee will be entitled to the balance accumulated in his or her account. Defined contribution plans are designed to allow employees to participate in the current profitability of the business. Generally, in profitable years, an employer will make a contribution to a qualified trust and such contribution will be allocated to each employee's retirement account. However, contributions may be made to a qualified profit sharing plan without regard to current or accumulated profits of the employer corporation.[19] Although the employer may have the discretion as to the dollar amount of an annual contribution, such contributions must be recurring and substantial if the plan is to be qualified.[20]

While most defined contribution plans constitute "profit sharing plans," other types of defined contribution arrangements exist. These arrangements include *money purchase plans*, *stock bonus plans*, and *employee stock ownership plans*. Each of these is briefly discussed below.

In an effort to encourage small businesses to establish qualified retirement plans, Congress enacted a special credit as part of the 2001 Tax Act. The credit is 50 percent of up to $1,000 (i.e., $500 maximum credit) of the administrative and retirement education costs incurred during the first three years of the plan to create or maintain the plan. The special credit is only available to businesses that did not employ, in the previous year, more than 100 employees with compensation of at least $5,000.

### Money Purchase Plans

A money purchase plan is a defined contribution plan that is treated like a defined benefit plan. The employer's annual contribution is determined by a specific formula that involves either a percentage of compensation of covered employees or a flat dollar amount. Under a money purchase plan, unlike a defined benefit plan, a definite pension amount is not guaranteed. Rather, a participant's retirement benefit will be determined by his or her vested account balance at retirement.

Because an employee's account balance will be fashioned according to a definite formula under a money purchase plan, a certain amount of flexibility is permitted in structuring the plan's contribution formula.

**Example 6**

Under a company's money purchase plan formula, an employer is required to contribute to the plan 3% of an employee's compensation plus an extra 1% for each year of prior service up to a maximum of 10%. Thus, an employee with 12 years of service would receive a contribution equal to 13% [3 + (12 limited to 10)] of his covered compensation. A new employee would receive only 3%.

---

[18] Reg. § 1.401-1(b)(1)(i).

[19] § 401(a)(27).

[20] Reg. § 1.401-1(b)(1)(ii).

Note that under a money purchase plan an employer is required to make a contribution. If an employer fails to make these required contributions under the plan, the employer will be subject to certain excise taxes. This minimum funding standard does not apply to stock bonus or profit-sharing plans.[21]

### Stock Bonus Plans

A stock bonus plan is another type of deferred compensation arrangement in which the employer establishes a plan in order to contribute shares of the company's stock. A stock bonus plan is subject to the same requirements as a profit sharing plan; therefore, a stock bonus plan must have a predetermined formula for allocating and distributing the stock among the employees. All benefits paid from the plan must be distributed in the form of the employer company's stock. An exception is made for fractional shares distributed from the plan, which may be paid in the form of cash.[22]

### Employee Stock Ownership Plans

Another variety of qualified plans is the Employee Stock Ownership Plan (ESOP). As the name suggests, the major purpose of the ESOP legislation was to encourage stock ownership by all employees by giving employers and employees a host of tax incentives. Supporters of ESOPs believe in the fundamental principle that ownership of a business by its employees can help cure many of the ills of a market-based economy. A major proponent of this principle, former Senator Russell Long, now deceased, endlessly extolled the virtues of ESOPs, saying that they could eliminate all of what is wrong with capitalism. According to Long and his followers, ESOPs increase worker productivity, improve labor relations, promote economic justice, provide a source of low-cost capital and are basically a savior for our economic system. On the other hand, critics of ESOPs say such claims are merely snake oil. Regardless of the view, ESOPs are now plentiful and have been a part of the system for more than 25 years.

Technically, an ESOP is a defined contribution plan. Like other qualified plans, a company that wants an ESOP first establishes a trust to which it makes annual contributions. The employer contributes either cash or its own stock. If the employer contributes cash, the ESOP uses the cash to purchase stock or securities of the sponsoring employer (rather than stocks or bonds of other companies). Regardless of how the stock or securities are obtained, they are then allocated to individual employee accounts within the trust using some type of formula. For example, the allocation may be in proportion to the employee's compensation or according to years of service or some combination of compensation and years of service. As a result, the company's employees—rather than outsiders—wind up owning a portion or all of the company. Any income earned by the ESOP is treated like that in other plans; that is, the income is completely tax-exempt. When the employee retires, he or she typically sells his or her shares of stock back to the trust and receives cash.

The tax benefits of this arrangement, once huge, have been whittled back by Congress over the years. Nevertheless, ESOPs still offer significant advantages. If the employer contributes stock, it receives a deduction for the value of the stock contributed.[23] Since it costs the employer little or nothing to issue the stock, the employer increases its cash flow by the taxes saved from the deduction. If the employer contributes cash that is subsequently used by the ESOP to purchase stock from the employer, the same benefit is obtained.

#### Example 7

This year P Corporation established an ESOP. Under the terms of the plan, P transferred 30,000 shares of unissued stock valued at $90,000 to the trust. Under § 1032, the issuance of the stock is nontaxable to P. However, P is entitled to a deduction for the value of the stock contributed, $90,000. Assuming P's marginal rate is 34 percent, the contribution provides tax savings of $30,600 ($90,000 × 34%) with little or no cash drain.

---

[21] § 412(h)(1).

[22] Regs. § 1.401-1(b)(1)(iii).

[23] § 1032.

The deductibility of contributions to an ESOP becomes even more attractive in the case of a *leveraged* ESOP. In a leveraged ESOP, the ESOP typically borrows money from a lender (e.g., a bank) and uses the cash to purchase the sponsoring corporation's stock. In subsequent years, the company makes contributions to the ESOP that are used to repay the interest and principal on the loan. When the contributions are used to pay the loan, such contributions are deductible. Observe that the effect is to allow the company to deduct the payments of not only the interest but also the principal. This feature makes the ESOP a very attractive form of debt financing for the employer. Similarly, the Code allows the company to deduct any dividends paid on ESOP stock which are used to repay the loan or which are passed through to the employees (a special feature of ESOPs).

Another significant benefit of the ESOP—no doubt the one that attracts the most attention—is the tax-free rollover permitted by § 1042. If the conditions of this provision are met, a shareholder who sells stock to an ESOP and who has owned the stock for at least three years may defer recognition of any gain realized on the sale by reinvesting in other stocks or bonds. This enables a retiring owner to get out of the business at the cost of one capital gains tax (rather than two taxes in most cases) that is deferred until the replacement property is sold.

## SIMPLE Plans

As a general rule, retirement plan coverage is lower for small employers than among medium and larger employers. Congress believed that one of the reasons for this result stemmed from the complexity of the rules relating to establishment of tax-qualified retirement plans as well as the high costs associated with complying with those rules. In an effort to encourage small employers to adopt retirement plans for its employees, Congress created a simplified retirement plan option known as SIMPLE (the Savings Incentive Match Plan for Employees).[24]

Under a SIMPLE plan, employers with 100 or fewer employees and no other employer-sponsored retirement plan are permitted to establish a savings incentive match plan for their employees. Deductible contributions may be made either to individual IRA accounts established for each employee or to accounts established as part of a 401(k) plan. One of the key benefits of adopting a SIMPLE plan is that those plans which satisfy the SIMPLE plan contribution requirements are not required to satisfy the nondiscrimination and top-heavy requirements that other qualified plans must continue to meet.

Under a SIMPLE plan, an employer generally must either match elective employee contributions dollar-for-dollar up to 3 percent of compensation or make a 2 percent of compensation contribution on behalf of each eligible employee. The limitation on employee contributions is reflected in the table below. Contributions to a SIMPLE account are deductible by the employer and excluded from the employee's income. Distributions are generally taxed under the rules applicable to IRAs. All employees with W-2 income of at least $5,000 annually must be allowed to participate.

The annual contribution limit to a SIMPLE plan is as follows:

| *Year* | *Amount* |
|---|---|
| Prior to 2002 | $ 6,000 |
| 2002 | 7,000 |
| 2003 | 8,000 |
| 2004 | 9,000 |
| 2005–2006 | 10,000 |
| 2007–2008 | 10,500 |
| 2009 and thereafter | 11,500 |

### Catch-up Contributions

A SIMPLE plan can permit participants who are age 50 or over at the end of the calendar year to make catch-up contributions. The catch-up contribution limit for 2010 and 2011 is

---

[24] §§ 1421 and 1422 of the Small Business Job Protection Act of 1996 amending § 401(k) and § 408(p).

$2,500. The amount of a catch-up contribution that a participant can make for a year cannot exceed the lesser of the following amounts:

- The catch-up contribution limit; or
- The excess of the participant's compensation over the salary reduction contributions that are not catch-up contribution.

## Qualification Requirements

**LO.5**
Explain the requirements associated with qualified retirement plans.

In order for a retirement plan to be *qualified* and therefore eligible for preferential tax treatment, it first must comply with a long list of requirements set forth in §§ 401 through 415. These requirements are extremely complex and can prove burdensome to the employer wishing to establish a qualified plan for his or her employees. The rigorous requirements are intended to ensure that a qualified retirement plan operates to benefit a company's employees in an impartial and nondiscriminatory manner.

The current requirements for plan qualification came into the law in 1974 with the enactment of the Employees Retirement Income Security Act (ERISA). Prior to ERISA, many qualified plans were designed to benefit only those employees who were officers of the company, shareholders, or highly compensated executives. Since the passage of ERISA, such discriminatory plans are no longer qualified.

### Existence of a Qualified Trust

Under § 401 and the accompanying Treasury Regulations, contributions made as part of a qualified plan must be paid into a domestic (U.S.) trust, administered by a trustee for the exclusive benefit of a company's employees. The plan must be in written form and its provisions must be communicated to all employees. The plan must be established by the employer. Any type of employer—sole proprietor, partnership, trust, or corporation—may establish a plan.

### Anti-Discrimination Rules

A retirement plan will not qualify if the contributions to or benefits from the plan discriminate in favor of the *prohibited group*. The prohibited group is defined as employees who are highly compensated or who are officers or shareholders of the company. If a plan provides for contributions or benefits to be determined under an equitable and reasonable formula, the fact that the prohibited group receives a greater dollar amount of contributions or benefits than employees in the nonprohibited group will not constitute discrimination.[25]

The Small Business Job and Protection Act of 1996 substantially simplified the definition of a "highly compensated employee." Currently, a highly compensated employee is a 5 percent owner during the current or prior year, or an employee with compensation during the prior year over $110,000 (2011). Employers may also elect to limit the pool of highly compensated employees to anyone who satisfies the basic definition and is in the top 20 percent of employees by compensation.[26]

An important aspect of the statutory antidiscrimination rules for qualified plans is the fact that such plans may be integrated with public retirement benefits.[27] Under the integration rules, the calculation of plan benefits may take into account the extent to which an employee is covered by social security or a state retirement program. In effect, an employer can credit a portion of its social security contribution toward the amount it is required to contribute to the qualified plan. Without any limitations, integration could be used to pay substantially more benefits to a highly compensated employee. For example, assume H owns a corporation that has two employees, H who earns $150,000 and L who earns $20,000. Also assume that the corporation's qualified plan contribution rate was 6.2 percent of compensation. Using integration and ignoring current limitations, the corporation would not be required to contribute any amounts for L since all of its required contribution is met by its payment for L's social security. On the other hand, it would contribute 6.2 percent for H for every dollar above the

---

[25] §§ 401(a)(4) and (5).

[26] § 414(q).

[27] § 401(a)(5).

social security wage base, $106,800 in 2011. As might be expected, special rules exist to prohibit such abuse. Nevertheless, integration can be used in a limited fashion to increase the benefits to highly compensated employees at the expense of other employees.

## Scope of Plan Participation and Coverage

A qualified retirement plan must provide that a substantial portion of a company's employees are eligible to participate in the plan. Specifically, any employee who has reached age 21 must be eligible to participate after completing one year of service for the employer.[28] The plan may not exclude an employee from participation on the basis of a maximum age.[29]

In addition to these *minimum* and *maximum* age and service conditions, a qualified plan must meet complex minimum coverage requirements. A qualified plan must satisfy one of the following three minimum coverage tests: the *percentage test*, the *ratio test*, or the *average benefits test*.[30]

Under the percentage test, a plan must benefit 70 percent or more of all of the employer's non-highly compensated employees. For this test, all eligible employees are considered to benefit under the plan. A plan that has no coverage requirements or highly compensated employees will automatically satisfy this test.

### Example 8

P Corporation has two divisions, R and S. P Corporation adopts a plan that covers only the employees of division S. If R division has 2 highly compensated and 20 non-highly compensated employees and S division has 18 highly compensated and 80 non-highly compensated employees, P satisfies the percentage test. This is because the plan covers 80% [80% of (20 + 80)] of the nonhighly paid employees.

The ratio test requires that the plan benefit a classification of employees that does not allow more than a reasonable difference between the percentage of an employer's highly compensated employees who are covered and a similarly computed percentage for non-highly compensated employees. In other words, the ratio test allows the percentage test to be proportionately reduced.

### Example 9

Assume the same facts as *Example 8*. Because only 90% of the highly compensated employees are covered (18 of 20), only 90% of the percentage test must be met. Thus, the plan would meet the ratio test if as few as 63% of the non-highly compensated employees are covered (90% of 70%).

A plan will satisfy the average benefits test if (1) it benefits employees under a classification that the IRS finds does not discriminate and (2) the average benefit percentage for non-highly compensated employees is at least 70 percent of the average benefit percentage for highly compensated employees. The average benefit percentage, with respect to any group of employees, is the sum of all employer contributions and benefits under the plan provided to the group, expressed as a percentage of pay for all group members. An employer may compute the average benefit percentage based on either the current plan year or on a rolling average of three plan years that includes the current year. Once the employer makes this choice, it must obtain IRS consent to revoke it.[31]

---

[28] § 410(a)(1). The plan may defer participation for two years if it provides immediate 100 percent vesting.

[29] § 410(a)(2).

[30] § 410(b)(1).

[31] § 410(b)(2)(C).

### The 50/40 Rule

While this rule is not a separate coverage rule, the 50/40 rule deserves attention because of the significance of the law involved. Basically, a plan will lose its qualification unless on each day of the plan year, it benefits the lesser of (1) 50 employees or (2) 40 percent of all employees of the employer. The 50/40 requirement applies separately to each qualified plan, and the Regulations exempt certain plans from this rule.[32]

## Vesting Requirements and Forfeitures

Once an employee is participating in an employer-sponsored retirement plan, he or she may not be entitled to any benefits under the plan for a certain period of time. After the requisite period of time, the employee's benefits *vest* and become nonforfeitable regardless of his or her continued employee status.

Under a qualified plan, vesting for non-top heavy employees must occur according to one of two statutory schedules designed to guarantee that an employee obtains a right to plan benefits within a reasonable time.[33] These two schedules are often referred to as "Cliff" vesting and "Graded" vesting.

### Cliff Vesting

This schedule derived its name from the tendency, before ERISA, of some employers to push off the employment "cliff" (terminate) those employees just about to become vested in the retirement plan. Effective for years beginning after 1988, plans are no longer permitted to be more restrictive than five-year cliff vesting. Beginning in 2002, the cliff vesting must be complete within three years. Under three-year cliff vesting, an employee would not be entitled to any vesting before completing three years of service. At the end of the third year, the employer would have to vest the employee 100 percent in his or her accrued benefit attributable to employer contributions.[34]

### Graded Vesting

The second permissible non-top heavy vesting schedule is graded vesting. Under such a schedule, employees must become proportionately vested over a two- to six-year vesting period. Under six-year graded vesting, a plan must provide at a minimum the following:

| | |
|---|---|
| 20% | vesting after two years service; |
| 40% | vesting after three years service; |
| 60% | vesting after four years service; |
| 80% | vesting after five years service; and |
| 100% | vesting after six years service. |

Under this schedule, the potential for discrimination diminishes because vesting occurs at a more gradual rate and, after three years of service, all employees are entitled to some vesting.[35]

If an employee leaves the job before some or all of the retirement benefits have vested, he or she forfeits the right to such benefits. Previous employee contributions toward these forfeited benefits are not returned to the employer, but instead transfer to remaining plan participants in a nondiscriminatory manner.[36]

## Funding and Contribution Limitations

Qualified retirement plans must be *funded*. Consequently, an employer is required to make current payments into a qualified trust. For a defined benefit plan, an actuarially determined minimum current contribution is required by statute.[37] For a defined contribution plan, the annually determined contribution must be *paid* to the trustee. Because of these rules, an employer must back up its promises to the employees with actual plan contributions.

---

32 § 401(a)(26) and Prop. Regs. § 1.401(a)(26)-2.

33 § 411(a)(2).

34 § 411(a)(2)(A).

35 § 411(a)(2)(B).

36 Rev. Rul. 71-149, 1971-1 C.B. 118.

37 § 412.

The Code limits the amount of contributions or benefits that are provided for employees. If these amounts should be exceeded, the plan will terminate.[38] In addition, § 404 establishes a limit on the amount that an employer may deduct. Sometimes the deductibility issue may have an impact on the amount that an employer may contribute on behalf of an employee. The maximum amounts that can be contributed to various plans are shown in Exhibit 18.3 below.

**EXHIBIT 18.3** **Maximum Annual Inflation-Adjusted Dollar Amounts**

| *Plan Type* | *2010* | *2011* |
|---|---|---|
| Defined Benefit Plan | $195,000 | $195,000 |
| Defined Contribution Plan | 49,000 | 49,000 |
| Annual Compensation Limit | 245,000 | 245,000 |
| Cash or Deferred (401k) | 16,500 | 16,500 |
| Highly Compensated Employees | 110,000 | 110,000 |
| SIMPLE Contribution Limit | 11,500 | 11,500 |

### Defined Contribution Plans

Under a defined contribution plan, the maximum contribution that can be made to the account of an employee is limited to the lesser of the following:

1. $49,000 (in 2011); or
2. 100 percent of the employee's compensation (subject to limits described in Exhibit 18-3 above).

#### Example 10

S is a participant in Summa Inc.'s qualified profit sharing plan. If S's annual salary is $275,000, her employer can make a maximum annual contribution for 2011 on her behalf of $49,000 (the *lesser* of $49,000 or 100% of S's first $245,000 of compensation).

#### Example 11

If S's current salary is $35,000, the annual contribution is limited to $35,000 (the *lesser* of $49,000 or 100% of S's compensation).

### Defined Benefit Plans

Under a defined benefit plan, the maximum annual benefit that can accrue to a participant is limited to the lesser of the following:[39]

1. $195,000 for 2011; or
2. 100 percent of the participant's average compensation for his or her three most highly compensated consecutive years of service with the employer.

Section 401(a)(17) was amended in 1993 to reduce the annual compensation limit to $150,000. Proposed regulations provide illustrations of how these new compensation limits affect *average compensation* for defined benefit plans.[40]

---

[38] §§ 415(a) and (b).

[39] § 415(b)(1)(A).

[40] Prop. Regs. § 1.401(a)(17)-1(b).

The limit is indexed annually for inflation, and adjustments to this figure are to be made if benefit payments are to begin before or after Social Security retirement age. Adjustments will be downward if payments begin before Social Security retirement age and upward if they begin after that age. The amount of the adjustment is determined actuarially based upon a straight-life annuity.[41] The current limitation is $195,000 for 2011.

## Top Heavy Plans

Section 416 contains additional requirements for qualified status of retirement plans that are deemed to be "top heavy." A *top heavy plan* is one in which more than 60 percent of the cumulative benefits provided by the plan are payable to *key employees*. Key employees include officers of the employer and highly compensated owner-employees. If a top heavy plan exists, § 416 provides an extra measure of assurance that the plan does not discriminate against non-key employees. To maintain qualified status a top heavy plan *must provide* a more rapid vesting schedule (generally 100% vesting after three years of service) and a minimum benefit to *all* employees regardless of social security or similar public retirement benefits.

## Deductibility of Contributions by Employer

Section 404(a) allows a deduction for employer contributions to qualified retirement plans if the contributions represent an ordinary and necessary business expense. In addition, § 404 contains complex rules that limit the dollar amount of the annual deduction. (Note that the statutory limitations on employer deductions are independent of the previously discussed limitations on the amount of contributions.) For example, the deduction for an employer's contribution to a qualified profit sharing plan is subject to a general limitation of 25 percent of total annual compensation paid to participating employees.[42] If an employer makes a contribution that exceeds this percentage limitation, the excess may be carried forward and deducted in succeeding years (subject to the percentage limitation for each succeeding year).[43]

## Determination Letters

At this point, it should be obvious to the beginning tax student that the qualification rules for employer-sponsored plans are many and complex. As a result, employers are well advised to request a determination letter from the IRS before a plan is put into effect. Such determination letter is a *written approval* of the plan verifying that the plan, as described to the IRS, complies with all requirements for qualified status. If a plan treated by an employer as qualified is disqualified in an IRS audit, the employer could be liable for a considerable amount of unwithheld income and payroll taxes on employer contributions.

# Qualified Plans for Self-Employed Individuals

**LO.6**
Explain the special qualified plans available for self-employed individuals.

Unincorporated taxpayers who earn money through self-employment are often precluded from retirement benefits afforded employees. To mitigate this result, Keogh (H.R. 10) plans were developed whereby contributions to such a plan are tax deductible, earnings accrue tax-free, and the self-employed individual is not taxed on any of the benefits until retirement. While Keogh plans provide substantial benefits, there are specific requirements that must be followed.

A self-employed individual who establishes an employer qualified retirement plan for his employees is not an employee eligible for participation in the plan. Self-employed individuals include sole proprietors and the partners in a business partnership. These taxpayers, however, may use the *Keogh* rules to obtain the tax benefits of a qualified plan.[44] A Keogh plan must

---

41 § 415(b)(2)(B).

42 § 404(a)(3).

43 *Ibid.*

44 See § 410(c)(1). It is interesting to note that retirement plans for self-employed individuals often are referred to as Keogh *or* H.R. 10 plans. Actually, the descriptions are interchangeable since H.R. 10 designated the legislative bill introduced by Congressman Keogh and passed by Congress in 1962.

**EXHIBIT 18.4 Special Definitions for KEOGH Plans**

| | |
|---|---|
| *Earned Income* | Self-employment income reduced by the self- employment tax deduction *and* the amount of the allowable Keogh deduction. |
| *Net Earnings from Self-Employment* | Earnings from self-employment without regard to the self-employment tax deduction or the allowable Keogh deduction. |
| *Modified Net Earnings from Self-Employment* | Net earnings from self-employment reduced by the self-employment tax deduction. |
| *Self-Employment Tax Deduction* | One-half of the self-employment taxes due for the year. |

benefit both the self-employed taxpayer and his or her employees in a nondiscriminatory manner under the wide range of rules for qualified plans previously discussed. In addition, the top heavy rules of § 416 apply to Keogh plans.[45]

To be eligible for a Keogh plan, the sole proprietor or partner must be an individual who satisfies one of the following conditions:[46]

1. Has "earned income" for the taxable year;
2. Would have had "earned income" for the year, but the trade or business being carried on had no net profits; or
3. Has been self-employed for any prior taxable year.

Generally, net earnings from self-employment will be the gross income from the trade or business less any related deductions; plus any distributive share of income or loss (if any) from a partnership. More specific definitions that are required for the tax computations are found in Exhibit 18-4.

## Contribution Limitations

Annual contributions to Keogh plans are generally subject to the same limitations that apply to employer plans. For a defined contribution plan, the annual contribution by a self-employed taxpayer is limited to the lesser of $49,000 (2011) or 100 percent of *earned income*.[47] As seen in Exhibit 18-4, earned income is net earnings from self-employment as reduced by the deduction for self-employment taxes as well as the deduction for the allowable Keogh contribution, so the computation is a circular one.[48] The computation of the allowable contribution can best be expressed in the following formula:

| | |
|---|---|
| | Net Earnings from Self-Employment (NE) |
| − | Self-Employment Tax Deduction |
| | Modified Net Earnings from Self-Employment (MNE) |
| − | Allowable Contribution (AC) |
| | Earned Income (EI) |
| × | 100% |
| = | Allowable Contribution (AC) |

The results of this formula can now be restated in the form of the equation found in Exhibit 18-5. Notice that the solution to this equation demonstrates that the actual limit on a self-employed taxpayer's annual contribution to a defined contribution Keogh plan is just 50 percent of *modified net earnings*. For individuals who have self-employment income but no liability for employment taxes (e.g., they have exceeded the maximum FICA through other employment), the allowable contribution will be 50 percent of their *net earnings* from self-employment not to exceed the dollar limit for the year.

---

[45] § 416(i)(3).

[46] § 415(c)(1)(B).

[47] §§ 415(c)(1) and (3)(B).

[48] § 401(c)(2).

**EXHIBIT 18.5** **Circular Computation of Allowable KEOGH Contribution**

$$AC = 1.00(EI) = 1.00(MNE-AC) = 1.00MNE-1.00AC$$
or
$$2.00AC = MNE$$
thus
$$AC = [MNE/2.00 = .50MNE\ (50\%\ of\ MNE)]$$

### Example 12

During the current year, Mr. T earned $75,924 and paid $7,848 in self-employment taxes. The maximum contribution T can make to his defined contribution plan is 100% of $72,000 [$75,924 – (½ of $7,848)] less the contribution itself. Therefore, the maximum contribution is $36,000 [100% of ($75,924 – $3,924 – $36,000)]. Note that this contribution is actually 50% of the modified net earnings of $72,000.

A different limitation applies to a Keogh plan if it is purely a discretionary profit sharing plan as opposed to the defined contribution plan discussed above. In this case, § 404(a)(3) limits the deductible contribution to only 15 percent of *modified net earnings* from self-employment. Once again, because the computation is a circular one, a calculation similar to Exhibit 18-5 would be necessary. While the computation is not illustrated, the results of such a determination indicate that the actual limit is 13.043 percent of *modified net earnings* (net earnings if no self-employment taxes are paid) from self-employment.

Many individuals do not want to be locked into maximum contributions of 50 percent of modified net earnings that are required annually by a defined contribution plan. To provide some flexibility, most individuals have a combination of plans:

1. A purely discretionary profit sharing plan and
2. A defined contribution plan.

The sum of the two contributions would be the maximum allowable but the portion to be contributed to the profit sharing plan would be optional each year.

## Qualified Plans for Employees

Since the establishment of employer-qualified plans as part of the Internal Revenue Code of 1954, Congress has expanded the scope of the law to provide similar plans for individual taxpayers who are not covered by an employer plan or who wish to supplement their employer plan.

**LO.7**
Describe various qualified plans for employees such as 401(k) plans and individual retirement accounts.

### Cash or Deferred Arrangements [§ 401(k) Plans]

Cash or deferred arrangements (CODAs), also known as salary reduction plans or 401(k) plans, have attained enormous popularity because these plans offer all the tax advantages of a qualified retirement plan and allow employees to exclude from their taxable wages or salaries the amount contributed to the plan. However, such amounts are still subject to FICA and Medicare taxes. Contributions made on behalf of the employee can come in the form of bonuses paid to the employee, additional salary, or an agreement by the employee to reduce his or her normal salary.[49]

[49] Regs. § 1.401(k)-1(a).

One of the major benefits of a 401(k) plan is the flexibility it offers an employee. For example, a plan may be designed to allow an employee to defer up to 6 percent of his or her compensation. If the employee elects, he can defer 6 percent, or any smaller amount such as 1, 2, or 3 percent. This gives employees greater control of their taxable income in as much as they may choose annually how much they want in salary and how much they want to defer in trust. In addition, loans from the trust are available to the plan participants.

The amount that an employee may elect to defer under a 401(k) plan may not exceed $16,500 for 2011 as shown in the table below.[50] While this figure is adjusted annually for inflation, it must be reduced by contributions to other retirement plans such as tax sheltered annuities and simplified employee plans. Any amounts in excess of this limit must be included in the individual's gross income. Furthermore, the limitations apply to the plan year and not to the calendar year of the individual. Thus, a CODA on a noncalendar year (e.g., 2009 and 2010) could theoretically allow an employee on a calendar year to defer up to $33,000 ($16,500 + $16,500), for example, in a single year.

*Section 401(k) Plan Contributions Limitations*

| *Year* | *Amount* |
|---|---|
| 2001 | $10,500 |
| 2002 | 11,000 |
| 2003 | 12,000 |
| 2004 | 13,000 |
| 2005 | 14,000 |
| 2006 | 15,000 |
| 2007 and 2008 | 15,500 |
| 2009 and thereafter | 16,500 |

## Employer Contributions

One of the major benefits of a 401(k) plan to an employer is that it provides a low-cost method of financing retirement benefits to the employee. Thus, amounts that would have been paid in salaries or wages can now be directed toward the retirement plan. The offsetting administrative expenses of initiating and operating the plan should be relatively low so that they do not detract from its overall benefits. When establishing a 401(k), contributions made to the trust should be treated as employer contributions as opposed to employee contributions. This is necessary to ensure the exclusion from income that is available only to contributions made by the employer.[51]

### Example 13

An employee's election form to fund a 401(k) plan should not state that she elects to contribute $5,000 of her salary to a 401(k) plan. Instead, the election should request that the employer reduce her salary by $5,000 in exchange for the employer's agreement to fund a 401(k) plan by the amount of $5,000.

An employer is entitled to take a deduction for a contribution to a CODA of up to 25 percent of an employee's compensation. This 25 percent limit is reduced by the employee's actual contribution. Compensation for this purpose is net compensation after considering the employee's contribution.

[50] § 402(g)(5).

[51] § 414(h)(1).

## Example 14

E, an employee of Z Corporation, desires to make an elective contribution of $8,000 to a qualified CODA. If E's compensation for the year is $110,000, the available contribution that Z Corporation can make for the year is determined as follows:

| | |
|---|---|
| Compensation | $110,000 |
| Less: E's contribution | (8,000) |
| Net Compensation | $102,000 |
| Employer limit | × 25% |
| Maximum Contribution | $ 25,500 |
| Less: E's contribution | (8,000) |
| Available Contribution | $ 17,500 |

### Catch-up Adjustment for Individuals Over Age 50

The Pension Protection Act of 2006 made permanent a provision that allows taxpayers over the age of 55 to make additional elective deferrals in excess of the otherwise permissible limits. These additional amounts—commonly called catch-up contributions—can be contributed to § 401(k) plans, § 403(b) plans, SEPs, and SIMPLE plans. These additional deferrals may be made without regard to the qualification requirements or limitations that usually apply to these provisions. The amount of the catch-up adjustments (by year) are illustrated in the table below:

| *Year* | *§ 401(k)* | *§ 403(b)* | *SEPs* | *SIMPLE* | *IRAs* |
|---|---|---|---|---|---|
| 2011 | 5,500 | 5,500 | 5,500 | 2,500 | 1,000 |
| 2010 | 5,500 | 5,500 | 5,500 | 2,500 | 1,000 |

### Plan Requirements

In order to secure the benefits of a CODA, specific requirements must be satisfied. While a detailed explanation is beyond the scope of this coverage, a synopsis of these rules summarizes their features.[52]

1. A CODA must meet the qualification requirements of a profit sharing or stock bonus plan including its participation and coverage requirements.
2. A CODA must provide for an election by each eligible participant to have their employer make payments to a qualified trust or directly to them in cash.
3. Amounts held under a qualified CODA are restricted as to when the funds may be distributed to the employee, and the employee's right to those benefits must be nonforfeitable.
4. Under complicated rules, amounts available for tax deferral may not discriminate in favor of highly compensated employees.[53]

### Roth 401(k) Plans

Beginning in 2006, taxpayers may create a Roth 401(k), 403(b) or similar plans. Amounts contributed to such plans (i.e., salary reductions), like those to Roth IRAs, would not be deferred but would be reported on a participant's Form W-2. For most purposes, these Roth 401(k) plans are identical to Roth IRAs with certain limited differences. For example distributions for first-time home-buyers before age 59½ are not permitted tax-free. In addition, there is no income limitation imposed on a Roth 401(k). Taxpayers may establish Roth 401(k) plans regardless of their adjusted gross income.

---

[52] § 401(k)(2) and (3).

[53] Regs. § 1.401(k)-1(a)(4)(iv).

## Individual Retirement Accounts

Prior to 1974, the benefits of qualified retirement plans were generally limited to employees of companies that opted to incur the expense of establishing plans. In 1974, however, Congress decided to provide an incentive for retirement savings in situations where there was no employer-provided plan and created the Individual Retirement Account (IRA). Since their creation, IRAs have been immensely popular.

The basic operation of a conventional IRA then and now mirrors that for employer-provided plans. Under the IRA provisions, an individual is generally entitled to make an annual tax-deductible contribution to the IRA. The contribution is a deduction for A.G.I., making it available to those who do not itemize deductions as well as those who do. Contributions are then invested and the income earned on such investments is not taxable currently. However, when amounts are withdrawn from the IRA they are fully taxable (both the earnings and the amounts representing the contributions). From an investment perspective, the tremendous advantages of the IRA relative to a traditional savings arrangement are the same as discussed earlier for employer-provided retirement plans. As explained above, the benefits of an IRA can be traced to two key factors: (1) the amounts invested are before-tax, providing a greater initial investment and (2) the tax is deferred until the amounts are withdrawn, resulting in greater earnings over the life of the investment.

The popularity of the IRA and the need to stimulate savings for retirement has caused Congress to expand the IRA concept over the years. Currently, there are three types of savings arrangements that bear the IRA name. They are:

1. The traditional or conventional IRA (discussed above).
2. The Roth IRA
3. The Educational IRA

Unfortunately, even though each of these savings vehicles is called an IRA, their treatment can be quite different.

## Traditional IRA

The traditional IRA is currently the most common type of IRA since they have been in existence since 1974. Individuals are permitted to make three types of contributions to a traditional IRA.

1. Deductible contributions
2. Nondeductible contributions
3. Rollover contributions (i.e., contributions of amounts withdrawn from other qualified retirement plans)

### Deductible Contributions to a Traditional IRA

As a general rule, an individual who is not covered by an employer-sponsored retirement plan can deduct contributions to a traditional IRA. Only contributions of money are allowed. Contributions of property cannot be made. The maximum contribution was increased to $5,000 in 2008 and has remained at that amount (see the table below). $5,000 per year (2011). However, the deduction cannot exceed the taxpayer's compensation for the year.[54] In addition, taxpayers over 70½ cannot make contributions to a traditional IRA.

*Increase in IRA Contribution Limit*

| *Year* | *Amount* |
|---|---|
| 2002–2004 | $3,000 |
| 2005–2007 | 4,000 |
| 2008 and thereafter | 5,000 |

Similar to the § 401(k) rules discussed earlier, individuals age 50 and over are permitted to make additional annual IRA contributions. The catch-up contribution is limited to $1,000 for 2006 and thereafter.

[54] § 219(b)(l).

### Example 15

H and W are married with two kids, Z and K. H's mom, M, also lives with the family. This year, Z, 14, received $500 of interest income from a savings account and earned $1,500 from sacking groceries at the local supermarket. K, 17, earned $5,000 delivering pizzas. M, age 75, earned $7,000 from a part-time job at a fast-food restaurant and had $40,000 of interest and dividends. Since Z's earned income is only $1,500, the maximum amount that he can deduct for contributions to an IRA is limited to $1,500 (his compensation). In contrast, K is able to contribute and deduct the maximum amount of $5,000 (2011) since she has compensation of at least $5,000. On the other hand, M cannot make contributions to an IRA since she is more than 70½ years old.

### Example 16

Assume the same facts as *Example 15* except that M is 55 years old. In this case, her contribution to an IRA is limited to $6,000 for 2011. This includes the $5,000 that was available because of her compensation, as well as the $1,000 additional *catch-up adjustment* due to her age.

## Deduction Phase-out Rules for Plan Participants

If a taxpayer or his or her spouse is an active participant in an employer-sponsored retirement plan *and* has A.G.I. in excess of a specified *applicable dollar amount*, the maximum deductible amount is phased out.[55] The applicable dollar amounts differ depending on which of following four categories the taxpayer is in:

1. Files jointly and is an active participant in an employer-sponsored plan.
2. Files jointly, is not active in another employer-sponsored plan but has a spouse that is active in an employer-sponsored plan.
3. Files married filing separately and is active in an employer-sponsored plan.
4. Files as a single or head of household taxpayer and is active in another employer-sponsored plan.

The applicable dollar amounts at which the phase-out begins and the IRA deduction ends are shown for each group in Exhibit 18-6. Note that the applicable dollar amounts increase over the next several years (except in the latter two cases). Also observe that if A.G.I. exceeds the applicable dollar amount by more than $10,000, none of the contribution is deductible. For excess A.G.I. amounts between $0 and $10,000, the phase-out is proportional. For example,

**EXHIBIT 18.6 Applicable Dollar Amount Phase-out Ranges**

| | *Joint Filer Who Is Active Participant* | *Single or Head of Household Who Is Active Participant* | *Joint Filer Who Is Inactive but Active Spouse* | *Married Separate Who Is Active Participant* |
|---|---|---|---|---|
| 2011 | $90,000–$110,000 | $56,000–$66,000 | $169,000–$179,000 | $0–$10,000 |
| 2010 | $89,000–$109,000 | $56,000–$66,000 | $167,000–$177,000 | $0–$10,000 |

[55] § 219(g) and (g)(3)(B).

if the excess A.G.I. is $4,000, the taxpayer loses 40 percent of the $5,000 deduction or $2,000. The amount of the phase-out can be computed using the following formula:

$$\frac{\text{A.G.I.} - \text{Applicable Dollar Amount}}{\$10,000} \times \text{IRA Deduction} = \text{Reduction in Dedcutible Allowance}$$

### Example 17

Q, a single taxpayer, is a salesperson for C Corporation. She actively participates in her employer's qualified retirement plan. In 2010, her compensation and A.G.I. were $28,000. Even though she participates in her employer's plan, she may make a contribution to an IRA. Her maximum deductible contribution is $5,000 (2010) since her A.G.I. did not exceed the applicable dollar amount of $56,000 (2010). In 2011, her compensation and A.G.I. increased to $60,000. Since she participates in an employer plan and her A.G.I. exceeds the applicable dollar amount of $56,000 (2011), the amount that she can deduct is subject to the phase-out rules. Her maximum deductible IRA contribution for 2011 is $3,000 [$5,000 (2011 maximum contribution amount) – $2,000 phase-out as calculated below].

$$\frac{\$60,000 \text{ A.G.I.} - \$56,000 \text{ Applicable Dollar Amount}}{\$10,000} = 40\% \times \$5,000 \text{ (2011 amount)}$$

$$= \text{Reduction in Deductible Allowance in the amount of } \$\ 2,000$$

### Example 18

T, who works as an accountant for a small corporation is single and age 38. He received compensation of $70,000 in 2011. T's employer does not maintain a retirement plan. Since T is not an active participant in a qualified plan, he is not subject to the phase-out rules and can deduct contributions to a traditional IRA of up to $5,000.

## Special Rules for Married Couples

Traditional IRAs provide a special rule for married couples where one spouse is the major breadwinner. Each spouse may make a deductible IRA contribution of up to $5,000 (2011) provided the couple's *combined* compensation exceeds the amount of the contributions. In effect, this allows a married couple to contribute up to $10,000 even though only one spouse works (assuming the working spouse has A.G.I. of at least $10,000).

### Example 19

H and W are married. H had compensation income of $22,000 while W had no compensation and stayed at home taking care of the family's children. Although W had no compensation for the year, she may make a deductible IRA contribution of $5,000 to her own account in addition to H's contribution to his account since their combined compensation of $22,000 exceeded their total contributions for theyear of $10,000.

As noted above, if one spouse is an active participant in an employer-provided plan but the other spouse is not, the nonworking spouse may still contribute to a traditional deductible IRA but the nonworking spouse's contribution is subject to phase-out if the couple's A.G.I. exceeds $169,000 in 2011. The active participant's phase-out begins at $90,000 for 2011.

### Example 20

H and W are married. W is covered by a qualified plan sponsored by her employer. H is not employed. The couple files a joint return for 2011 reporting A.G.I. of $135,000. Even though H is married to an active participant in a qualified plan, he may make a deductible IRA contribution of $5,000 since the applicable dollar amount for the spouse of an active participant begins at $169,000. On the other hand, W may not make a deductible IRA contribution since the couple's A.G.I. exceeds the $90,000 applicable dollar amount for married plan participants in 2011 by more than $10,000.

### Example 21

Assume the same facts as the *Example 20* above except that the couple's A.G.I. is $195,000. In this case, neither spouse could make a deductible contribution because their A.G.I. exceeds the applicable dollar amounts ($169,000 and $90,000) by more than $10,000 for each spouse.

## Nondeductible IRA Contributions to a Traditional IRA

Individuals are permitted to make *nondeductible* contributions to their IRAs. These contributions can be made only to the extent that the maximum deduction for IRA contributions is not claimed (i.e., $5,000 or 100 percent of compensation).[56] Note that there is no phase-out or compensation income limitation that applies to nondeductible contributions.

### Example 22

G, single, had compensation and A.G.I. for 2010 of $64,000. G is covered by his employer's qualified plan. Since G's A.G.I. exceeds the threshold by $9,000 ($64,000 – $55,000) his maximum deductible contribution is $500 [$5,000 – (90% × $5,000)]. However, he is still permitted to make nondeductible contributions of $4,500 ($5,000 – 500).

## Excess Contributions

Since the earnings generated by contributions into an IRA are tax deferred, taxpayers might be tempted to contribute amounts in excess of the contribution limit. To prohibit this possibility, a 6 percent penalty tax is imposed on any excess contribution left in an IRA after the close of the taxable year.

## Rollover Contributions

As alluded to earlier, one reason for establishing an IRA is for the purpose of *rolling over* a lump-sum distribution from a qualified retirement plan. In addition, individuals who receive distributions from an IRA may also make rollovers of distributions into another IRA. By rolling over a distribution to an IRA, the taxpayer avoids taxation as well as any early withdrawal penalty.

Rollovers generally take one of two forms: (1) the distribution is paid to the plan participant who then must roll the distribution into an IRA within 60 days; or (2) the distribution is paid directly to the IRA. Failure to transfer the funds to an IRA within the 60-day period makes the distribution taxable and also subject to the early withdrawal penalty. Note that by having the distribution paid directly to the IRA, the participant avoids the provision that requires the employer to withhold 20 percent of the distribution as an estimated tax payment.

---

[56] § 408(o).

It should also be noted that taxpayers who choose to roll over a lump-sum distribution forego the right to use any beneficial capital gain or forward averaging rules for computing the tax on the distribution when it is ultimately withdrawn from the IRA.

### Due Date for Contributions

An IRA can be established during the year or after year-end. Contributions can be made to a traditional IRA at any time during the year or by the due date for filing a return for that year, not including extensions. For most people, this means contributions for 2010 must be made by April 15, 2011. In addition, if a contribution is made between January 1 and April 15, 2011 the taxpayer should designate the year targeted for that contribution (2010 or 2011). As discussed below, the due date for creating and contributing to a SEP-IRA is the extended due date.

### Withdrawals from a Traditional IRA

Income earned in an IRA is tax-exempt, regardless of the deductibility of the contributions to the IRA.[57] When funds are withdrawn from an IRA, an amount of the withdrawal proportionate to any unrecovered nondeductible contributions in the account is not subject to tax; the balance of the withdrawal is fully includible in gross income.[58]

#### Example 23

In the current year, taxpayer A, age 61, withdrew $9,000 from his IRA, after which the account balance was $26,000. A has made $1,500 of unrecovered nondeductible contributions to the IRA. The nontaxable portion of the withdrawal is $386, computed as follows:

$$\frac{\$1{,}500 \text{ (nondeductible contributions)}}{\$26{,}000 + \$9{,}000 \text{ (account balance before withdrawal)}} \times \$9{,}000 \text{ withdrawal} = \$386$$

For subsequent years, A's unrecovered nondeductible contribution balance is $1,114 ($1,500 − $386).

For years 2010 through 2012, taxpayers, age 70½ or older, can take advantage of a special rule for withdrawals that are contributed to charities. These individuals can withdraw and donate up to $100,000 per year from their IRAs to qualifying charitable organizations and exclude such amounts from gross income. Consistent with the exclusion, no deduction is allowed for the contribution. Without the rule, the amount withdrawn could be taxable and there might not be an offsetting contribution deduction (e.g., the taxpayer does not itemize).

### Distribution Requirements

Without special rules, IRA owners might postpone distributions for as long as possible, hoping to take advantage of tax deferral to build their estate. However, the law requires taxpayers to take the entire IRA balance or start taking periodic distributions from their IRAs no later than April 1 of the year following the year in which the taxpayer reaches age 70½. The minimum distribution is generally based on either the life expectancy of the taxpayer or the joint life expectancies of the taxpayer and his or her spouse or another designated beneficiary. If a taxpayer has multiple IRA accounts, the minimum distribution amount is computed for each account but can be satisfied from a single account. The actual calculation of the required distribution is somewhat complex and beyond the scope of this text. However, it is important to note that if the distributions received are less than the required distribution amount, a penalty equal to 50 percent of the shortage may apply. Special rules apply to IRAs that are inherited. Note that Roth IRAs are not subject to these distribution requirements while the individual is alive; however, those who inherit a Roth IRA are subject to minimum distribution rules.

---

[57] § 408(c).

[58] § 408(d).

## Roth IRAs

The 1997 Tax Act created a nondeductible IRA called the Roth IRA. Under this plan honoring Senator Roth of Delaware, individuals may make nondeductible contributions of up to $5,000 annually. However, the $5,000 maximum contribution limit is reduced to the extent of any contributions to another IRA in the same taxable year. In addition, the maximum annual contribution that can be made to a Roth IRA is phased out for single individuals with A.G.I. between $107,000 and $122,000 and for joint filers with A.G.I. between $169,000 and $179,000. The increase in contribution limits for the Roth IRA closely follows the traditional IRA over the next several years.

A Roth IRA is an IRA which is designated at the time of establishment as a Roth IRA. The major benefits of a Roth IRA are that distributions from a Roth IRA are generally not taxable, and unlike a deductible or nondeductible IRA, contributions to a Roth IRA may be made even after the individual for whom the account is established reaches the age of 70½.

Technically, only qualified distributions are nontaxable. A qualified distribution is any distribution that:

- Is made after the taxable five-year period beginning with the first taxable year in which the individual made a contribution to a Roth IRA and
- Meets *one* of the following conditions:
    1. Is made on or after the date on which the individual attains age 59½
    2. Is made to a beneficiary (or to the individual's estate) on or after the death of the individual
    3. Is attributable to the individual being disabled
    4. Is a distribution for first-time homebuyer expenses (see earlier discussion)
    5. Is used for certain education expenses

Note that there are no minimum distribution rules for Roth IRAs while an individual is alive. However, those who inherit a Roth IRAs are required to take minimum distributions.

Distributions from a Roth IRA that are *not* qualified distributions are includible in income to the extent they are not attributable to contributions. In addition, these distributions are subject to the 10 percent early withdrawal tax that also applies to other IRAs. An ordering rule applies for purposes of determining what portion of a distribution is not a qualified distribution and is includible in income. Under the ordering rule, distributions from a Roth IRA are treated as made from contributions *first*. For purposes of determining the amount of contributions, all of an individual's Roth IRAs are treated as a single Roth IRA. Thus, no portion of a distribution from a Roth IRA is treated as attributable to earnings until the total of all distributions from a Roth IRA exceeds the sum of all contributions as well as rollover contributions. In effect, a taxpayer can make withdrawals of previous *contributions* without penalty or tax at any time—even within the mandatory five-year holding period.

### Example 24

L first opened a Roth IRA at his bank on November 1, 2009, making a contribution of $5,000. He continued to make $5,000 contributions in 2010, 2011, 2012, and 2013. On May 1, 2013, L celebrated his 65th birthday, retired and took a distribution of $11,000 from his Roth IRA to take a trip to Europe. Under the ordering rule, the $11,000 withdrawal represents his contributions in 2009 ($5,000), 2010 ($5,000), and 2011 ($1,000) and, therefore, is neither taxable nor subject to the 10 percent penalty that otherwise applies to distributions during the five-year holding period. Note that he can begin withdrawing distributions in excess of previous contributions (without penalty) once the five-year holding period requirement is met in 2014. Observe that the five-year holding period begins in 2009, the first taxable year that L contributed to the Roth IRA.

### Conversion of Traditional IRA to Roth IRA

The lure of tax-free earnings and tax-free distributions forever is so strong that individuals who have traditional IRAs may want to convert them to Roth IRAs. Graciously, Congress has blessed such conversions. The law permits individuals to convert traditional IRAs to Roth IRAs if certain requirements are met.

All individuals are entitled to convert their traditional IRAs to Roth IRAs. Technically, the conversion is accomplished by transferring the assets from a traditional IRA and reinvesting them (within 60 days) in a Roth IRA. This is normally referred to as a "conversion contribution." There is no minimum or maximum amount that must be converted. Most importantly, on conversion any previously untaxed amounts in the traditional IRA are taxable as ordinary income. The 10% penalty for withdrawal before age 59½ does not apply. After conversion, the taxpayer's A.G.I. includes the taxable portion of the conversion for all purposes (e.g., 2% floor on miscellaneous itemized deductions, 7.5% floor on medical expenses). The conversion must be completed by December 31 of the year in question.

**Example 25**

C, single, age 48, has an A.G.I of $70,000 for 2011. As of May 1, he had accumulated $200,000 in his traditional IRA that he is wants to convert. C's A.G.I. for conversion purposes is $70,000, the amount of his A.G.I. before considering any taxable income resulting from the conversion. The amounts in the IRA represent deductible contributions, nontaxable earnings and funds from a prior rollover from his 401(k) plan. Assuming C converts the traditional IRA, he will have taxable income of $70,000. There is no penalty for early withdrawal.

## Credit for Contributions to Plans by Low-Income Individuals

To encourage low and middle-income taxpayers to save for their retirement, the 2001 Tax Act created a nonrefundable credit for contributions to certain retirement saving plans (§ 25B). Credits are available for contributions to § 401(k) plans, § 403(b) plans, § 457 state and local government plans, SIMPLE plans, SEP plans, traditional IRAs, and Roth IRAs. The credit is in addition to the deduction to which the taxpayer is normally entitled. The amount of the credit is generally equal to 50 percent of the individual's retirement savings contributions not to exceed $2,000. Thus the maximum credit is $1,000 (50% × $2,000). On a joint return, the maximum credit would be $2,000, however, the credit decreases as the taxpayer's income increases. The allowable credit percentage is a function of the taxpayer's modified adjusted gross as follows:

Modified Adjusted Gross Income Credit Determination (2011)

| *Joint Return* | | *Head of Household* | | *All Others* | | |
|---|---|---|---|---|---|---|
| *Over* | *Not Over* | *Over* | *Not Over* | *Over* | *Not Over* | *Percentage* |
| $ 0 | $34,000 | $ 0 | $25,500 | $ 0 | $17,000 | 50% |
| 34,000 | 36,500 | 25,500 | 27,375 | 17,000 | 18,250 | 20% |
| 36,500 | 56,500 | 27,375 | 42,375 | 18,250 | 28,250 | 10% |
| 56,500 | | 42,375 | | 28,250 | | 0% |

The credit is *not* available to the following individuals:

1. Individuals who have not attained the age of 18 by the close of the tax year;

2. Individuals for whom a dependency exemption my be claimed; and
3. Full-time students.

**Example 26**

T, single, graduated from college last year and took a job with a national accounting firm. His adjusted gross income for the year was $24,000. If T contributes $5,000 to a Roth IRA, he may claim a credit of $200 for 2011 (10% credit percentage × $2,000 ceiling amount). Had T been a full-time college student for the year, he would not have been eligible for the credit.

## Education IRAs (Coverdell Education Savings Accounts)

In an effort to encourage savings and provide a vehicle to promote higher education, the Tax Reform Act of 1997 created a special type of IRA known as an education IRA or Coverdell Education Savings Account (CESA).[59] Although the creation of such an account has nothing to do with retirement planning, as the name might suggest, the tax treatment of this arrangement is very similar to that for nondeductible contributions to traditional or Roth IRAs—thus its classification as an IRA.

Currently, taxpayers may make *nondeductible* contributions of up to $2,000 in cash per year into a CESA for certain qualified beneficiaries. This amount decreases to $500 in years beginning in 2012. A CESA is a trust account that is created for the purpose of paying *qualifying higher education* expenses. A qualified beneficiary is any individual under the age of 18 years, or any special needs child regardless of age. Qualifying higher education expenses include tuition, fees, books, supplies and equipment required for enrollment that are incurred during the taxable year for a student who attends an eligible education institution. The term also includes amounts contributed to a prepaid tuition plan. In certain circumstances, *room and board* are also included in these expenses. An eligible educational institution means any post-secondary education courses (e.g., undergraduate or graduate courses) as well as the cost of elementary, secondary, private and parochial schools.

Similar to retirement IRAs, earnings on the amounts contributed to a CESA are not taxed as they accumulate. Withdrawals from a CESA are totally nontaxable to the extent that they are used exclusively for the purpose of paying qualifying higher education expenses. Furthermore, no contribution may be made during a taxable year in which a contribution is made by *anyone* to a qualified prepaid tuition program on behalf of the same beneficiary. Note also that for any year in which an exclusion from gross income is claimed with respect to distribution from an education IRA, neither a Hope credit nor a Lifetime Learning credit may be claimed with respect to education expenses incurred during that year on behalf of the same beneficiary.

### Contribution Limit

The $2,000 annual contribution limit, computed at the donor level, is phased out ratably for contributors with A.G.I. (computed with certain modifications) between $95,000 and $110,000 ($190,000 and $220,000 for contributors filing joint returns). The term "Modified A.G.I." means A.G.I. increased by income earned outside the U.S. that normally is excluded under § 911. Individuals with modified A.G.I. greater than the upper phase-out range are not allowed to make contributions to an education IRA established on behalf of any other individual. The contribution phase-out computation is shown in Exhibit 18.7.

---

[59] § 530.

**EXHIBIT 18.7 Phase-out for CESAs**

$$\text{Reduction of the } \$2{,}000 \text{ Contribution} = \$2{,}000 \text{ Contribution} \times \frac{\text{Modified A.G.I.} - \text{threshold}}{\text{Income Range}}$$

| | *Modified A.G.I. Phase-out Begins* | *Modified A.G.I. Phase-out Complete* |
|---|---|---|
| Married filing jointly: | $190,000 | $220,000 |
| Other taxpayers: | $ 95,000 | $110,000 |

## Multiple CESAs for a Single Beneficiary

Taxpayers contributing more than $2,000 per year to an a CESA for a single beneficiary are subject to a penalty. Section 4973 imposes a six percent excise tax on excess contributions. An excess contribution consists of two parts:

1. The amount by which contributions to all CESAs for a single beneficiary exceed $2,000, plus
2. The amount contributed during the year to a qualified tuition plan.

Note that this rule prohibits a taxpayer from contributing to both a qualified tuition plan and a CESA without penalty. These rules do not appear to prohibit parents from contributing $2,000 to a CESA for one child while the grandparents contribute to a prepaid tuition plan. Moreover, there is no rule requiring that the person contributing be related to the beneficiary. Similarly, there is no restriction on the number of CESAs an individual may establish as long as each has a different beneficiary.

## Distributions

Distributions from a CESA that are used to pay qualifying education expenses are generally nontaxable. In reality, this general rule is a bit more complex. Technically, distributions from a CESA are deemed to consist of a proportionate part of both the original contributions and the earnings on such contributions. Distributions representing contributions are always nontaxable. Distributions of earnings are excludable from gross income only to the extent that the distribution does not exceed qualified higher education expenses incurred by the beneficiary during the year the distribution is made. In effect, all of the earnings on a CESA are nontaxable as long as they are used for qualified education expenses. Distributions of earnings in excess of qualified expenses cause a ratable portion of the entire distribution to be taxable. In addition, an excise tax of 10 percent is imposed on the portion not used for education.

## Rollovers

If any balance remains in a CESA at the time a beneficiary becomes 30 years old, such amount *must* be distributed, and the amount representing the account's earnings will be taxable. In addition, the distribution will be subject to a 10 percent penalty tax because the distribution was not for educational purposes. Prior to the time the beneficiary reaches 30, the 1997 Act allows tax-free (and penalty-free) transfers and rollovers of account balances from one CESA benefiting one beneficiary to another education IRA benefiting a different beneficiary (as well as redesignations of the named beneficiary), provided that the new beneficiary is a member of the family of the old beneficiary. For this purpose, a family member includes the beneficiary's spouse or a familial relative described in the rules governing dependency exemptions. These would include a child, sibling, parent and certain other individuals. For example, if the taxpayer's son did not fully utilize the amount in the CESA, the unused balance could be converted to an account for his daughter or his grandchild.

## Gift and Estate Tax Treatment

Contributions made to CESAs are considered completed gifts and qualify for the annual exclusion. Distributions are not treated as gifts nor is a rollover to another beneficiary and, therefore, not subject to gift tax. Amounts in a CESA are not includible in the estate of any individual. If a beneficiary dies and the interest passes to a spouse, the spouse simply becomes the beneficiary of the CESA. If the interest passes to someone other than a spouse, the CESA terminates at death and the account balance is includible in the beneficiary's income (e.g., a child).

### SIMPLIFIED EMPLOYEE PENSIONS

The concept of a Simplified Employee Pension (SEP) was added to the law in 1978 to provide employers with a way to avoid the fearsome complexities involved in establishing and maintaining a qualified retirement plan. By following the relatively simple rules of § 408(k), which are designed to prevent discrimination in favor of the prohibited group, an employer may establish a SEP. This qualified plan allows the employer to make contributions directly into an employee's existing IRA, thereby avoiding the necessity of a qualified trust.

The annual limit on SEP contributions is the lesser of 25 percent of employee compensation (subject to compensation limits) or $49,000 (2011). Employer contributions to a SEP are excludable from an employee's gross income.[60]

SEPs are not available just to employees. An individuals with earnings from self-employment also may create a SEP-IRA, even if he or she is an employee elsewhere and covered by an employer's retirement plan. Like other IRAs, a SEP-IRA can be created after the end of the year. Unlike traditional IRAs, the SEP-IRA may be created by the *extended* due date of the tax return. For example, if a self-employed person extends his or her return until October 15, he or she has until October 15 to create and fund a SEP. Observe that this rule differs significantly from Keogh plans. A Keogh plan must be established before the close of the tax year while SEPs can be established after year-end. Thus SEPs, like other IRAs, are one of the few tax planning tools that can be implemented after the tax year has come to a close.

The computation of the maximum amount that a self-employed person can contribute is—like Keogh plans—a bit complicated. The 25 percent limit is applied to net profit reduced by the deduction for half of the self-employment tax as well as the deduction for the SEP-IRA contribution itself. Thus, the calculation is circular. Ignoring the deduction for self-employment taxes, the maximum deduction would be 20 percent of self-employment income.

## Retirement Planning Using Nonqualified Deferred Compensation

**LO.8**
Describe nonqualified deferred compensation plans.

For many years employers have designed total compensation packages for valued employees that combined both a current compensation element and a *deferred* compensation element. A *nonqualified* deferred compensation arrangement typically is one in which the employee is compensated for current services rendered by the employer's promise to pay a certain amount at some future date. Although nonqualified deferred compensation plans do not receive the favorable tax treatment given to qualified plans, such arrangements are often attractive to employers because of their flexibility. Many employers find that what may be lost in tax benefits is more than made up in the savings derived from not having to comply with restrictive rules concerning the discrimination, participation, vesting, and funding that apply to qualified plans. The two questions that must be answered about a deferred compensation arrangement are:

1. When is the employee taxed on deferred compensation that is earned currently but will be received in a later year?
2. When is the employer entitled to a business deduction for deferred compensation that will be paid in a later year?

Note that if a plan is a qualified plan, an employer is entitled to a current deduction for contributions and the employee is taxed on such contributions only when they are distributed. For nonqualified plans, however, the timing of the deduction and income is not quite as clear.

In order to completely answer the first question, an examination of the constructive receipt doctrine is necessary. To thoroughly answer the second, an examination of funded and unfunded plans is required.

### CONSTRUCTIVE RECEIPT

The Regulations state that income (both current and deferred) is to be included in gross income for the taxable year in which it is actually or constructively received by the taxpayer.[61] Thus for a

[60] § 402(h).

[61] Regs. § 1.451-1(a).

cash basis taxpayer, all items that constitute gross income (whether in the form of cash, property, or services) are to be included for the taxable year in which they are actually or constructively received. Consequently, the question to be resolved is whether deferred compensation is constructively received in the taxable year when it is authorized or in the year of actual receipt.

A mere promise to pay, not represented by notes or secured in any way, is not regarded as a receipt of income under the cash receipts and disbursements method. This should not be construed to mean that under the cash receipts and disbursements method income may be taxed only when realized in cash. Income, although not actually received, is constructively received by an individual in the taxable year during which it is credited to his account or set aside for him so that he may draw upon it at a later date.[62] Thus, under the doctrine of constructive receipt, a taxpayer may not deliberately turn his back upon income, nor may a taxpayer, by a private agreement, postpone receipt of income from one year to another.

Income is not constructively received if the taxpayer's control of its receipt is subject to substantial limitations or restrictions. Consequently, if a corporation credits its employees with bonus stock, but the stock is not available to those employees until some future date, the mere crediting on the books of the corporation does not constitute constructive receipt. In most cases, speculating whether an employer would have been willing to relinquish a payment earlier or determining a taxpayer's control over funds is not an easy task. As a result, in each case involving a deferral of compensation (especially nonqualified plans), the determination of whether the constructive receipt doctrine is applicable must be made on a fact-and-circumstances basis.

### Example 27

T, a football player, entered into a two-year contract to play football for the California Cauliflowers. In addition to his salary, as an inducement for signing the contract, T would be paid a signing bonus of $150,000. Although T could have demanded and received his bonus at the time of signing the contract, T's attorneys suggested that the $150,000 be transferred to an escrow agent to be held for five years and then paid to T over the next five years as an annuity. If T should die, the escrow account would become part of his estate. Because the bonus is set aside for T, the $150,000 bonus must be included in T's gross income in the year in which the club unconditionally paid the amount to the escrow agent. The employer's obligation for payment terminated when the amount of the bonus was fixed at $150,000 and irrevocably set aside for T's sole benefit.[63]

## Treatment of Nonqualified Deferred Compensation Plans

Persuaded by corporate scandals at companies such as Enron, the *American Jobs Creation Act of 2004* imposes new restrictions and limitations on the design of nonqualified deferred compensation plans.[64] Under the new law, in order for deferred compensation to be excluded from gross income, the deferred compensation plan must meet specific guidelines. These guidelines include: (1) a distribution requirement, (2) an acceleration of benefits requirement, and (3) certain election requirements.

### Restrictions on Distributions

Under Code § 409A(a)(2)(A), a nonqualified deferred compensation plan may not permit distributions from the plan earlier than:

- The participant's separation from service, as determined by the IRS, subject to a special rule for separation from service of any "specified employee";
- The date the participant becomes "disabled";
- The participant's death;
- A time specified, or a schedule fixed, under the plan at the date of the deferral of the compensation;

---

[62] Regs. § 1.451-2(a).

[63] Rev. Rul. 55-527, 1955-2 C.B. 25.

[64] § 409A.

- To the extent allowed by the IRS, a change in the ownership or effective control of the corporation, or in the ownership of a substantial portion of the corporation's assets; or
- The occurrence of an "unforeseeable emergency" as defined in §409A(a)(2)(B)(ii).

Additionally, specified employees (referred to as "key employees") of publicly traded corporations generally may not receive their distributions earlier than six months after separation. A key employee is defined as an officer with compensation greater than $160,000 in 2011 (adjusted for inflation and limited to 50 employees); 5 percent owners; and 1 percent owners with compensation greater than $170,000. Furthermore, taking a distribution with a "haircut" (i.e., forfeiture of a portion of the account balance in exchange for access to the plan account) is no longer a distribution option.

### Acceleration of Benefits

Section 409A does not permit a plan to allow for the acceleration of benefits. However, under the anticipated IRS regulations, a nonqualified deferred compensation plan would not violate the prohibition on accelerations in certain limited situations. For example, a plan could provide that upon separation from service of a participant, account balances less than $10,000 will be automatically distributed (except in the case of specified key employees).

### Election Requirements

Under the new law, the flexibility of a participant to change his or her deferral elections generally must be made in the tax year preceding the year in which the services are performed, or within 30 days of becoming eligible for plan participation. If the award is performance-based (e.g., an incentive bonus), the election must be made no later than six months before the end of the performance period.

In addition to the above rules, a deferred compensation plan may not provide that the deterioration in the financial status of the employer will trigger payment of the deferred compensation. Offshore Rabbi trusts and Rabbi trusts that are convertible into Secular trusts (protecting the assets from general creditors) are also prohibited under the new law.

### Effective Date of New Rules

The new rules generally apply to amounts deferred after December 31, 2004. If a plan fails to meet the requirements, or is not operated in accordance with any of these three requirements, all compensation earned and deferred must be included in income for the first tax year that the nonqualified deferred compensation plan fails to meet the requirements, to the extent not subject to a "substantial risk of forfeiture" and not previously included in gross income.[65] A 20 percent penalty will also be imposed on the amount required to be included in income. Interest will also be assessed on the underpayment, at the underpayment rate plus one percentage point. Any compensation that becomes taxable will be subject to income tax withholding.

## Unfunded Deferred Compensation Plans

If an employer contractually promises to pay deferred compensation to an employee and does not set aside current funds in some type of trust arrangement, the employee is put in the position of an unsecured creditor of the employer. If the employee is a cash basis taxpayer and does not have any current right to payment under the deferred compensation plan, there is no constructive receipt of the compensation and thus no current taxable income to the employee. The employee will not be taxed until the year in which the deferred compensation is actually paid.[66]

From the employer's point of view, such unfunded arrangements are attractive because they do not require any current cash outflow from the business. However, neither a cash basis nor an accrual basis employer may take a deduction for deferred compensation until the deferred amount is includible in the employee's gross income.[67]

---

[65] § 409A(a)(1)(A)(i).

[66] Rev. Rul. 69-649, 1969-2 C.B. 106.

[67] Rev. Rul. 69-650, 1969-2 C.B. 106.

### Funded Deferred Compensation Plans

Employees who agree to a nonqualified deferred compensation arrangement normally prefer that their employers secure the promise of future compensation by transferring current funds into an independent trust for the employee's benefit. While these employees desire the protection of a funded plan, they do not wish to subject those funds to current taxation. Therefore, innovative methods have been devised to allow deferral of an employee's income under a funded method by making the employee's interest in those funds forfeitable. To this end, an employer can establish one of many types of trusts. Two of the more common nonqualified arrangements are the *Rabbi trust* and the *Secular trust*. The rules of § 83, discussed earlier in the chapter, apply to these funded deferred compensation plans.[68]

#### Rabbi Trusts

Rabbi trusts are so named because the first IRS ruling that approved this arrangement involved a fund established by a congregation for its rabbi. In the typical Rabbi trust arrangement, the rights of employees are forfeitable, so an employee will not recognize taxable income until he or she actually receives a distribution from the trust. If a deferred compensation arrangement provides that employees' rights in the retirement fund eventually become nonforfeitable (i.e., vested), an employee must recognize taxable income in the year his or her rights vest. In both cases, the employer will receive a deduction only in the taxable year in which the deferred compensation is includible in the gross income of the employee.[69]

> **Example 28**
>
> As part of a deferred compensation arrangement, employer X agrees to place $10,000 annually into a trust account for employee Y. Y's rights to the trust funds are forfeitable until he completes 10 years of service for X. In the year in which Y's risk of forfeiture lapses, the value of the trust funds is included in Y's gross income. Subsequent payments into the fund by X are fully taxable to Y.[70]

A disadvantage of the Rabbi trust is that if the employer gets into financial difficulty, the trust assets are subject to the claims of the employer's creditors. In addition, any income that is generated by the trust will be taxable to the employer.

#### Secular Trusts

Designed in 1988, the Secular trust is a variation of the Rabbi trust.[71] Under a Secular trust, the employee receives a vested interest in the full amount of the transfer to the trust. Because the employee has a nonforfeitable interest, the employee is taxed immediately on the transfer of funds to the trust even though he or she has not actually received the funds. In return for the transfer, the employer receives an immediate deduction. The advantage of this arrangement is that the trust assets are not subject to the claims of the employer's creditors. The disadvantage, of course, is that the funds are immediately taxable to the employee. A Secular trust differs from a Rabbi trust, because the assets of the Rabbi trust will not be protected from the creditors of the employer in the event of bankruptcy.

## Stock Options

**LO.9**
Determine the tax consequences of the issuance and exercise of both nonqualified and qualified stock options.

As an alternative to the payment of compensation in the form of corporate stock, corporate employers may issue *options* to purchase stock at a specified price to employees whom the company wants to retain. As a general rule, stock options have no value on the date they are issued because the option price is equal to or greater than the market price of the stock. Consequently, the options will have value to the recipient (and become a cost to the employer) *only if* the market price of the shares increases.

---

68 § 402(b).

69 § 404(a)(5).

70 Reg. § 1.402(b)-1(b).

71 PLR8841023.

If an option has no value upon date of grant to an employee, the employee obviously has not received taxable income. However, in certain unusual cases options may have a value at date of grant. If such value can be determined with reasonable accuracy under criteria provided in Regulation § 1.83-7(b)(2), the value represents compensation income to the recipient of the option. If an option is actively traded on an established market, it is deemed to have an ascertainable value at date of grant.[72]

### Example 29

Corporation C grants employee D an option to purchase 100 shares of C common stock for $11 a share at any time over the next ten years. If C stock is selling at $9 per share, D's option has no readily ascertainable value. Therefore, D has no taxable income at date of grant, and a zero-tax basis in the option. If, however, D's option is actively traded on an established market and as a result can be valued at $5, D has received taxable compensation of that amount, and will have a $5 basis in the option.

### Option Exercise

When the owner of a stock option that had no ascertainable value at date of grant exercises the option, the difference between the option price and the market price (bargain element) of the stock purchased represents ordinary income to the owner. If the option had an ascertainable value at date of grant, so that the recipient recognized taxable income upon receipt of the option, no additional income is recognized when the option is exercised.[73]

### Example 30

In 2008, employee M received certain stock options as part of her compensation from Corporation Q. At date of grant, the options had no ascertainable value. However, in 2011 M exercised the options and purchased 1,000 shares of Q stock, market value $90 per share, for the option price of $60 per share. In 2011 M must recognize $30,000 of ordinary income ($30 per share bargain element × 1,000 shares). M's tax basis in her shares is $90,000.

From the employer's point of view, the value of a stock option can be taken as a deduction under the previously discussed rule of § 83(h). Generally, an employer will receive a deduction at date of grant if the option has a readily ascertainable value. If the option has no value at date of grant, the deduction will equal the income recognized by the owner of the option when the option is exercised.

## Incentive Stock Options

In the past, Congress has experimented with a variety of *qualified stock options*—options afforded preferential tax treatment under § 421. Currently there is only a single type of qualified option, the Incentive Stock Option (ISO) of § 422A.[74]

Under § 421(a), the exercise of an ISO will not result in any income recognition to the owner. Correspondingly, the corporate employer who issued the option will never receive any deduction for the spread between option and market price at date of exercise. If and when the stock received upon exercise is sold, the employee will realize capital gain equal to the difference between the option price and selling price. The difference in tax consequences between a nonqualified stock option and an ISO is presented in the example below.

---

[72] Reg. § 1.83-7(b)(1).

[73] Reg. § 1.83-7(a).

[74] The rules of § 422A apply to options granted on or after January 1, 1976 and outstanding on January 1, 1981.

## Example 31

Employee T was granted an option in 2005 to purchase one share of his corporate employer's stock at any time within the two succeeding calendar years. At the time the option was granted, the option price was $150 and the market price was $140. Assume that T exercised the option in 2007 when the stock had a market price of $200, and the stock acquired was sold in 2011 for $375. The tax consequences for each tax year would be as follows:

| | *Nonqualified Stock Option* | *Incentive Stock Option* |
|---|---|---|
| 2005 | None | None |
| 2007 | Market price of $200 – $150 option price = $50 ordinary income and $200 basis in purchased stock ($150 cost + $50 income recognized). Employer deduction = $50 | No income and $150 basis in purchased stock |
| 2011 | Sale price of $375 – $200 basis = $175 capital gain | Sale price of $375 – $150 basis = $225 capital gain |

It should be noted that § 83 will apply to a tax-free transfer of an incentive stock option in determining a taxpayer's AMTI. Under § 83(a), the taxpayer will include in AMTI the excess of the stock's fair market value at the first time it is transferable over the amount paid for the stock under the option. See Chapter 13 for a discussion of the alternative minimum tax (AMT).

### Holding Period Requirements

For the beneficial rule of § 421(a) to apply, an individual may not dispose of the stock purchased upon exercise of the ISO within two years from the date of the granting of the option and within one year from the date of exercise.[75] Additionally, the individual must be an employee of either the corporation granting the ISO or a parent, subsidiary, or successor corporation from the date of grant until the day three months before the date of exercise.[76]

If an individual violates the holding period requirement by disposing of his or her stock too quickly after purchase, § 421(b) provides that the *compensation income* (ordinary income) the individual did not recognize at date of exercise must be recognized in the year of disposition. Any gain so recognized increases the cost basis of the stock.[77] In such a situation the employer will be entitled to a corresponding deduction.

## Example 32

Beta Corporation grants an ISO to employee Z on November 1, 2005. The option allows Z to purchase 500 shares of Beta stock at $3 per share. Z exercises the option on December 1, 2010, when Beta stock is selling for $7 per share. Z sells his 500 shares on March 1, 2011 for $9 per share. Because of the premature disposition (less than one year from date of exercise), Z must recognize $2,000 ordinary income [500 shares × $4 bargain price ($7 market price – $3 option price)] and a $1,000 capital gain in 2011. Additionally, Beta Corporation may claim a $2,000 deduction in 2011.

If the amount realized on a premature sale is less than the value of the stock at date of exercise, only the excess of the amount realized over the option price is recognized as ordinary income.[78]

[75] § 422A(a)(1).

[76] § 422A(a)(2).

[77] Reg. § 1.421-5(b)(2).

[78] § 422A(c)(2).

> **Example 33**
>
> Refer to the facts in *Example 32*. If Z sold his Beta stock for \$6 rather than \$9 a share, his ordinary income (and Beta's deduction) would be limited to \$1,500 [500 shares × \$3 bargain price (\$6 selling price − \$3 option price)].

## Qualification Requirements

An employee stock option must meet a number of statutory requirements set forth in § 422A(b) to qualify as an ISO. The primary requirements are as follows:

1. The option is granted pursuant to a plan that specifies the total number of shares that may be issued under options and the class of employees eligible to receive the options. The shareholders of the corporation must approve the plan within twelve months before or after the date the plan is adopted.
2. The options are granted within ten years of the date of adoption or the date of shareholder approval, whichever is earlier.
3. The option price is not less than the market value of the stock at date of grant.
4. The option must be exercised within ten years of date of grant.
5. The option can only be exercised by the recipient employee during his or her lifetime and can only be transferred at the employee's death.
6. The recipient of the option does not own stock possessing more than 10 percent of the total combined voting power of all classes of stock of the employer corporation or of its parent or subsidiary corporation.[79]

A major restriction on the use of ISOs is the statutory requirement that the value of stock with respect to which ISOs are *exercisable* shall not exceed \$100,000 per calendar year per employee. For purposes of this requirement, the value of the stock is determined at date of grant.[80]

> **Example 34**
>
> In calendar year 2010, Corporation Q granted Employee F an ISO to purchase 1,000 shares of Q stock with a current aggregate value of \$200,000. In calendar year 2011, Corporation Q granted Employee F a second ISO to purchase 1,200 shares of Q stock with a current aggregate value of \$300,000. If Employee F decides to exercise any of her ISOs in 2011, she may only purchase 500 (500/1,000 × \$200,000 = \$100,000 limit) shares through exercise of her 2009 option or 400 shares through exercise of her 2011 option (400/1,200 × \$300,000 = \$100,000 limit).

### Exclusion from Wages

The *American Jobs Creation Act of 2004* eliminated the uncertainty as to employer withholding obligations upon the exercise of statutory stock options. The Act provides a specific exclusion from the FICA/FUTA payroll tax withholding obligations for remuneration on account of the transfer of stock pursuant to the exercise of an incentive stock option or under an employee stock purchase plan, or any disposition of such stock.[81] The new law also provides that federal income tax withholding is not required on a disqualifying disposition of stock acquired from ISO and employee stock purchase plans (ESPP), nor when compensation is recognized in connection with an ESPP discount.

---

79 § 422A(c)(6) waives this requirement in certain cases.

80 § 422A(b)(7).

81 §§ 3121(a)(22), 3306(b)(19), 421(b), and 423(c).

## Nonqualified Stock Options

A Nonqualified Stock Option (NQSO), also referred to as a nonstatutory stock option, is generally any option that does not meet the statutory requirements in the Code to be treated as an Incentive Stock Option (ISO). NQSOs are often used as implements of deferred compensation because the corporation can avail itself of a tax deduction without a cash outlay and the options themselves can be issued with more flexible terms than ISOs. The only major disadvantage of using an NQSO is the potential for income recognition to the employee. That potential is, in turn, dependent upon whether the option has a readily ascertainable fair market value.

### Readily Ascertainable Fair Market Value

If an option is actively traded on an established exchange (e.g., American Stock Exchange or Chicago Board of Options Exchange), it is deemed to have a readily ascertainable fair market value. An option that is not traded on an established exchange will not have a readily ascertainable fair market value unless it can be measured with reasonable accuracy. The Regulations support this presumption with detailed conditions for determining value.[82]

Determining value is important because, if the option has a readily ascertainable fair market value at the time of grant, the employee will be taxed immediately. Any gain or loss that accrues after the time of the grant will be recognized as capital gain or loss on the disposition of the underlying stock. When gain is recognized, the employee's basis in the stock includes any amounts paid for the stock plus the amount that was recognized as ordinary income at the time of the grant. The corporate employer takes a deduction in the same year (and for the same amount) income is recognized by the employee.[83] It is important to notice that the result of these options is conditioned on establishing a value for the option and not establishing a value for the stock of the corporation.

### No Readily Ascertainable Fair Market Value

If an option does not have a readily ascertainable fair market value, the transaction will remain "open," and the employee will not be taxed when the option is granted. Instead, the employee recognizes ordinary income when the option is exercised. The amount of income to be recognized is the spread between the value of the stock purchased and the price paid at the date of exercise. Any appreciation in the stock after the exercise date will be recognized as capital gain. The corporate employer takes a corresponding tax deduction in the same year and to the extent of ordinary income recognized by the employee.

**Example 35**

On January 1, 2011, R Corporation grants S, an employee, the option to purchase 1,000 shares for $12 per share on or before August 15, 2012. At the time of the grant, R stock is valued at $20 per share. On June 3, 2012, when the value of R stock is $35, S exercises the option and acquires the stock for $12,000 (1,000 × $12). On November 1, 2012, S sells the stock for $48,000 (1,000 × $48). If the option granted has no readily ascertainable fair market value, S will recognize $23,000 ($35,000 – $12,000) of ordinary income and a $13,000 ($48,000 – $35,000) capital gain, both in 2012. R takes a deduction of $23,000 in 2012. If on the other hand, the option has a readily ascertainable value (for example $8 per share), S must recognize $8,000 of ordinary income in 2011 (the grant date) and a capital gain of $28,000 in 2012 (the sale date). R will take an $8,000 deduction in 2011.

## Stock Appreciation Rights

Occasionally, NQSOs can create a problem for employees when they generate taxable income without providing resources to pay the tax. Unfortunately, when this occurs, some employees find it necessary to sell the stock to raise the capital, and this defeats the purpose of providing

[82] Regs. § 1.83-7(b)(2).

[83] Regs. § 1.421-6(c), (d), (e), and (f).

equity compensation. To ameliorate this dilemma, some employers wrap an NQSO with a Stock Appreciation Right (SAR).

An SAR is a type of right (similar to an option) that entitles the employee to a cash payment equal to the difference between the fair market value of one share of the common stock of the corporation on the date of the *exercise* of the SAR over its fair market value on the date it was *granted*. An employee need not own any stock of the corporation to receive an SAR, and SARs are granted without cost to the employee. An SAR cannot be exercised before one year after it was granted and must be exercised by the fifth year, or the SAR will be deemed exercised and cash will be paid to the employee. An SAR is not included in taxable income until the year the right is exercised. The IRS has ruled that an employee who receives an SAR will not be in constructive receipt of income in the year it was granted.[84]

## Tax Planning Considerations

The area of employment compensation and retirement planning offers tremendous opportunity for creative tax planning. During a taxpayer's productive years, he or she needs to be able to analyze and appreciate the tax consequences of the various types of compensation alternatives that may be offered. The taxpayer must be aware of the tradeoff between types of compensation that will be taxed currently and fringe benefits that may not be taxable upon receipt. Sophisticated forms of compensation such as § 83 property and incentive stock options should be considered in designing a specialized compensation package.

Taxpayers should also appreciate the necessity for long-range retirement planning. An understanding of the different tax consequences of qualified and nonqualified retirement plans is essential to effective planning for post-employment years. Exhibit 18-8 contains a comparison of the plans discussed in this chapter.

### Planning for Retirement Income

One of the central features of an individual's financial plan should be a provision for some source of retirement income. As the life span of the average American lengthens, the number of prospective retirement years increases. As a result, many individuals realize that some amount of current investment is necessary in order to ensure that their retirement years can be a period of financial security.

In analyzing a particular retirement plan, two basic questions must be answered:

1. Are payments into the plan deductible for Federal income tax purposes by the taxpayer?
2. To what extent are retirement benefits received from a plan includible in the recipient taxpayer's gross income?

**EXHIBIT 18.8** **IRA Deductions for Active Participants in Qualified Plans for 2011**

| *A.G.I. before IRA Deduction* | *Single or Head of Household* | *Filing Jointly or Widower* | *Married, Filing Separately* |
|---|---|---|---|
| $ 0–$ 10,000 | full | full | partial |
| $10,000–$ 55,000 | full | full | NONE |
| $55,000–$ 66,000 | partial | full | NONE |
| $66,000–$176,000 | NONE | partial | NONE |
| $177,000 + | NONE | NONE | NONE |

*Locate income and filing status. If the word *full* appears, a $5,000 deduction is available in 2011; if *NONE* appears, no deduction is available; and if *partial* appears, a prorated amount is deductible.

[84] Rev. Rul. 80-300. 1980-2 C.B. 165.

## Advantages of IRAs

IRAs used to be among the best retirement saving plans around until Congress clipped some of their more generous features in 1986. Today they are still a useful part of many retirement portfolios; however, some limitations will apply.

Prior to 1987, IRAs were available to anyone who had not reached the age of 70½. Contributions were allowable up to the $3,000 annual limit and were fully tax deductible. Today, these rules apply to only two types of people:

- Those who are not eligible for an employer-sponsored retirement plan; or
- Those whose incomes fall below specified levels.

For individuals with company retirement plans, deductible IRAs are still available, provided certain tests can be satisfied. The first test of IRA deductibility is income. A taxpayer may still make a fully deductible IRA contribution as long as A.G.I. does not exceed certain levels. Exhibit 18-8 provides a list of eligible individuals and the limitations on IRA deductions.

### Example 36

H and W have A.G.I. of $169,000 and file a joint tax return. Their table amount indicates they are entitled to a partial deduction. To determine their deduction, subtract their A.G.I. from the limit for that particular row ($176,000 – $169,000 to get $7,000). Next, divide that amount ($7,000) by $10,000 to get a percentage ($7,000/$10,000 = 70%). This is the percentage of the IRA base, $5,000, that may be deducted. Accordingly, H and W may deduct $3,500.

*Note* that the taxpayers may still *contribute* the full $5,000, but cannot deduct the extra $1,500.

## Spousal IRAs

Holding a job is not a prerequisite to opening and deducting an IRA. A nonworking spouse may start a *spousal IRA*, as long as both taxpayers file jointly and the combined total of both spouse's earned income equals $10,000. When these two requirements are met, each spouse may make contributions to an IRA. Together, they may contribute as much as $10,000 in any single year. No more than $5,000 of that amount, however, may go to either account. If the combined total earned income is less than $10,000, the deduction is not lost. The combined total of the IRA's is limited to the amount of combined income (limited to $5,000 per spouse).

## What Is an Active Participant?

As discussed earlier, an individual may not be eligible for a deductible IRA if he or she is an active participant or eligible to participate in a pension or profit sharing plan. As a general rule, the IRS considers a taxpayer an active participant in a defined plan if the plan's guidelines state that the taxpayer is covered, even if they decline to participate. As a result, just being eligible for a plan makes the taxpayer an active participant.

If an individual is not sure if he is an active participant, he can look at his W-2 form, provided by his employer. It provides a box for the taxpayer's employer to check. If this box is blank, additional research may be necessary. Exhibit 18-9 provides aid in determining whether a taxpayer is eligible to participate.

## Making a Nondeductible Contribution to an IRA

Even if a taxpayer is not eligible, for whatever reason, to make deductible contributions to an IRA, a nondeductible contribution is available. Whether a taxpayer should make a nondeductible IRA contribution depends on the circumstances. Some of the following pros and cons should be considered before a taxpayer makes a decision.

The most obvious pro is that even though a taxpayer may not deduct his or her annual IRA contribution, the earnings from IRA investments accumulate and compound tax-deferred. This means a faster fund build-up compared to a taxable savings account. (See Exhibit 18-10 for a similar comparison.)

## EXHIBIT 18.9 Active Participation

Participation in any of the following plans can make a taxpayer an active participant and not eligible to deduct IRA contributions.

- Qualified pension, profit sharing, or stock bonus plans, including Keogh plans
- Qualified annuity plans simplified employee pension plans (SEPs)
- Retirement plans for Federal, state, or local government employees
- Certain union plans [so-called § 501(c)(18) plans]
- Tax-sheltered annuities for pubic school teachers and employees of charitable organizations.
- § 401(k) plans

## EXHIBIT 18.10 Comparison of Corporate Retirement Plans

| *Description* | *Corporate Plan* | *Keogh [HR 10]* | *Roth or Traditional IRA* | *SEP* | *CODA (401(k))* | *Funded* | |
|---|---|---|---|---|---|---|---|
| | | | | | | *Rabbi* | *Secular* |
| **Qualified** | Yes | Yes | Yes | Yes | Yes | No | No |
| **Participation** | 21 years old or > 1 year = 100% vested | 21 years old or > 1 year = 100% vested | Limited by AGI | 21 years old or 3 out of 5 year's service | 1 year's service | No Requirements | |
| **Limitations** | 100% \| $49,000 or 100% of $220,000 \| 100% average. | 100% \| $49,000 or 13.043% of $220,000 \| 100% average. | $4,000 or 100% Earned Income | $49,000 or 15% Earned Income | $16,500 (for 2011) | No limitations if paid as reasonable compensation | |
| **Vesting** | 3 years Cliff or 6 years Graded | 3 years Cliff or 6 years Graded | 100% | 100% | 100% of employee's contribution | Subject to claims of creditors | 100% |
| **Premature Distributions** | Rollover or 10% Penalty | Rollover or 10% Penalty | Rollover or 10% Penalty | Rollover or 10% Penalty | Rollover or 10% Penalty | Taxable only if not previously taxed | |
| **Lump-Sum 10-Year Averaging Available if Born Before 1936** | Yes | Yes | No, taxed as Ordinary Income or Tax free | No, taxed as Ordinary Income | Yes | Not available: in some cases funds previously taxed | |
| **Date Plan Must Be Established** | By last day of plan year | By last day of plan year | Regular tax due date | Regular tax due date | By last day of plan year | By last day of plan year | |
| **Required Date to Contribute** | Extended due date | Extended due date | Regular due date | Regular due date | Extended due date | Year end | |
| **Employee Loans from the Plan** | Yes | None: Owner-Employees | None | None | Limited | Yes, but very risky | Yes |

The most obvious con is that once money is put into an IRA, it is locked in until the taxpayer attains the age 59½. Otherwise, the taxpayer is subject to pay a 10 percent penalty for early withdrawal. The penalty applies to the deductible portion of the IRA contribution and to any earnings that may have accumulated tax-deferred in the account. However, no penalty applies when nondeductible contributions are withdrawn.

Many investment counselors suggest tax-free bonds as a reasonable alternative to making a nondeductible IRA contribution. The earnings from the bonds are tax-free and are not subject to a penalty if the taxpayer needs to withdraw any of the money. Moreover, a taxpayer is not limited to investing $5,000 ($10,000 for spousal IRAs).

Bonds, however, come with two potential drawbacks. First, a taxpayer can possibly get locked into the bonds until maturity. If interest rates rise, the value of the bonds generally declines, and a taxpayer would potentially have to sell the bonds at a loss. Second, depending on the market, the yields on bonds are sometimes low compared to the after-tax yields of other securities. So, potentially, bonds can be a very poor investment.

# Problem Materials

## DISCUSSION QUESTIONS

**18-1** *Taxation of Barter Transactions.* Your friend who is a practicing dentist tells you that he filled a tooth for a friend's child "for no payment" because the friend had prepared the dentist's income tax return for the previous year. Must the dentist recognize taxable income because of this arrangement? Explain.

**18-2** *Taxation of Fringe Benefits.* Define the term *fringe benefit*. As a general rule are fringe benefits taxable?

**18-3** *Taxation of Fringe Benefits.* Every year, Employer E gives each employee the choice of a turkey or ham as a Christmas "gift." Is the value of this fringe benefit taxable to the employees? Would your answer be different if each employee received a Christmas bonus of $500 cash?

**18-4** *Fringe Benefits—Cafeteria Plans.* What is a cafeteria plan of employee benefits?

**18-5** *Reasons for Stock Options.* How does a corporation benefit from compensating valuable employees with shares of stock in the corporation rather than a cash wage or salary?

**18-6** *Receipt of Restricted Property for Services.* What factors should a taxpayer consider when deciding to make an election under § 83(b) with regard to restricted property?

**18-7** *ISO Plans.* An ISO (incentive stock option) allows the recipient both a deferral of income and a conversion of ordinary income into capital gain. Explain.

**18-8** *Funded versus Unfunded Deferred Compensation Arrangements.* Why would an employee normally prefer a funded rather than an unfunded deferred compensation arrangement? Which would the employer normally prefer?

**18-9** *Deferred Compensation and the Constructive Receipt Doctrine.* Explain the doctrine of constructive receipt as it relates to a cash basis employee who has a deferred compensation arrangement with his or her employer.

**18-10** *Tax Advantages of Qualified Retirement Plans.* Discuss the tax advantages granted to qualified retirement plans.

**18-11** *Defined Benefit versus Defined Contribution Plans.* Differentiate between a defined benefit retirement plan and a defined contribution retirement plan.

**18-12** *Retirement Plan Qualification Requirements.* Any employee of Trion Ltd. Partnership can participate in the company's pension plan after they have been employed by Trion for 36 consecutive months. Can Trion's plan be a qualified retirement plan? Discuss.

**18-13** *The Meaning of Vested Benefits.* Explain the concept of vesting as it relates to qualified retirement plans. How does it differ from the concept of participation?

**18-14** *Profit-Sharing Plans versus Pension Plans.* Many small, developing companies will choose to establish a qualified profit-sharing plan rather than a pension plan. Why?

**18-15** *Spousal IRAs.* Discuss the purpose of a spousal IRA (individual retirement account).

**18-16** *Lump-Sum Distribution Rollovers.* Why might an employee who receives a lump-sum distribution from a qualified retirement plan choose to roll over the distribution into an IRA? What are the negative tax consequences of doing so?

**18-17** *Roth IRAs versus Traditional IRAs.* In 1998, Congress provided taxpayers wanting to establish an IRA a choice. Taxpayers may now use either a Roth IRA or a traditional IRA or both.

**a.** Identify the major differences between Roth IRAs and traditional IRAs.

**b.** Identify circumstances when a Roth IRA may be preferred over a traditional IRA and vice versa.

**18-18** *Education IRAs.* One of the tax incentives created for higher education in 1998 was the Education IRA.

**a.** Explain how an education IRA works.

**b.** Compare an education IRA to a qualified prepaid tuition and how it relates to the Hope and Lifetime Learning credits.

## PROBLEMS

**18-19** *Receipt of Restricted Property for Services.* D, a calendar year taxpayer, is an employee of M Corporation, also on a calendar year for tax purposes. In 2011, M Corporation transfers 100 shares of its own common stock to D as a bonus for his outstanding work during the year. If D quits his job with M within the next three years, he must return the shares to the corporation. At date of transfer, the shares are selling on the open market at $35 per share. Three years later, when the risk of forfeiture lapses, the stock is selling at $100 per share.

**a.** Assume D does not make the election under § 83(b). How much income must he recognize in 2011 because of his receipt of the stock? In 2014 when his restriction lapses?

**b.** Assume D does elect under § 83(b). How much income must he recognize in 2011? In 2014?

**c.** Refer to questions (a) and (b). In each case how much of a deduction may M Corporation claim and in which year should the deduction be taken?

**18-20** *Tax Consequences of a Nonqualified Stock Option Plan.* In 2011, Z Corporation grants a nonqualified stock option to employee M. The option allows M to purchase 100 shares of Z Corporation stock for $20 per share at any time during the next four years. Because the current market value of Z stock is $22 per share, the option has a readily ascertainable value of $200 ($2 per share bargain element × 100 shares) at date of grant. M exercises the option in 2012 when the market value of the Z stock has increased to $28 per share.

**a.** How much income does M recognize in 2011 because of the receipt of the option?

**b.** How much income does M recognize in 2012 upon exercise of the option?

**c.** What amount of deduction is available to Corporation Z because of the option granted to M? In what year is the deduction claimed?

**18-21** *Tax Consequences of a Nonqualified Stock Option Plan.* In 2011, X Corporation grants a nonqualified stock option to E, a valued employee, as additional compensation. The option has no value at date of grant, but entitles E to purchase 1,000 shares of X stock for $20 per share at any time during the next five years. E exercises the option in 2012, when X Corporation's stock is selling on the open market at $48 per share.

**a.** How much income does E recognize in 2011 because of her receipt of the option?

**b.** How much income does E recognize in 2012 upon exercise of the option?

**c.** What amount of deduction is available to X Corporation because of the option granted to E? In what year is the deduction claimed?

**18-22** *Nonqualified Stock Option Plans.* Refer to the facts in *Problems 18-20* and*18-21*. In each case, what tax basis does the employee have in the purchased corporate stock?

**18-23** *Incentive Stock Options (ISO) versus Nonqualified Stock Options.* Refer to the facts in *18-21*. If the stock option issued by X corporation had been an ISO rather than a nonqualified option, how much income would E recognize in 2012 upon option exercise?

**18-24** *Incentive Stock Option Plans.* In May 2010, employee N exercised an ISO that entitled him to purchase 50 shares of Clay Corporation common stock for $120 a share. The stock was selling on the open market for $210 per share. N sold the 50 shares in 2013 for $390 per share.

**a.** How much income must N recognize in 2010 upon exercise of the option?

**b.** How much income must N recognize in 2013 upon sale of the Clay stock?

**18-25** *Incentive Stock Options—Early Disposition of Stock.* Refer to the facts in *Problem 18-24*. What would be the tax consequences if N sold the Clay stock in August 2010 for $250 per share? For $190 per share?

**18-26** *Tax Computation on Lump Sum Distributions.* T participated in his employer's qualified profit sharing plan from 1981 until his retirement at age 64 in the current year. T made no contributions to the plan. In the current year, T received a lump sum distribution of $75,000 from the plan.

**a.** How much of the distribution is taxable to T in the current year?

**b.** As far as the tax treatment is concerned, what options are available?

**18-27** *Tax Computation on Lump-Sum Distributions.* In the current year, Mrs. Z, age 61, retired after a 35-year career with the same corporate employer. She received her entire $51,000 account balance from her employer's qualified profit sharing plan. In the current year, Mrs. Z and her husband will file a joint return on which they will report $21,000 of other taxable income (net of all deductions and exemptions). As far as the tax treatment is concerned, what options are available?

**18-28** *Qualified Pension Plan—Maximum Annual Benefits.* During his last three years as president of R Corporation, G was paid $200,000 in 2009, $230,000 in 2010, and $280,000 in 2011 as total compensation for his services. These were the three highest compensation years of his employment. What is the maximum retirement benefit payable to G from the corporation's qualified pension plan (a defined benefit plan)?

**18-29** *Qualified Profit Sharing Plans—Maximum Annual Contribution.* In the current year, Mr. W, a corporate vice president, earned a base salary of $350,000. His corporate employer maintains a qualified retirement plan that provides for an annual contribution equal to 10 percent of each employee's base level of compensation. Based on these facts. compute the maximum current-year contribution to Mr. W's retirement account.

**18-30** *Additional Taxes on Plan Distributions.* In the current year, Mr. L, age 51 and in perfect health, resigns as President of Meta Industries, Inc. Mr. L receives a $300,000 lump sum distribution from Meta's qualified retirement plan. Before consideration of this distribution, Mr. L's taxable income for the year is over $200,000. If Mr. L decides not to "roll over" the contribution into another qualified plan or IRA, compute the net after-tax amount of the distribution that Mr. L will be able to spend.

**18-31** *Maximum Annual Contributions to Keogh Plans.* H is a self-employed business person with several employees. He has established a profit-sharing plan for himself and his employees. The annual net earned income from his business is $132,000. What is the maximum amount of a deduction available to H for his contribution to the plan for the year?

**18-32** *Maximum Annual Contributions to IRAs.* H and W file a joint tax return. W is a lawyer with current-year earned income of $180,000. H works part-time as a landscape architect and earned $22,000 in the current year.

**a.** Assume that W is an active participant in the firm's qualified profit-sharing plan. How much may W and H contribute to their IRAs for the current year? How much of the contribution is deductible?

**b.** Assume neither H nor W is an active participant in a qualified retirement plan. How does this assumption change your answers to (a) above?

**18-33** *Maximum Deductible Contributions to IRAs.* In the current year, Ms. A, a single taxpayer, contributed $1,400 to her IRA. She also is an active participant in her employer's qualified money purchase pension plan. Ms. A's adjusted gross income (before any deduction for her IRA contribution) is $29,640. How much of the IRA contribution is deductible in 2011?

**18-34** *Taxability of IRA Distributions.* Taxpayer B, age 66, makes his first withdrawal of $8,800 from his IRA in the current year and uses the money to make a down payment on a sailboat. At the end of the year, B's IRA balance is $36,555. During previous years, B had made nondeductible contributions to the IRA totaling $13,400. Based on these facts, what amount of the $8,800 withdrawal must B include in current-year gross income?

**18-35** *Simplified Employee Pensions.* Z is an employee of a company that has established a SEP. Z's current-year salary is $18,000.

**a.** How much may Z's employer contribute to her IRA during 2011?

**b.** May Z make any additional deductible contribution herself to her IRA?

## TAX RESEARCH PROBLEMS

**18-36** *Current versus Deferred Compensation.* Roy Hartman is a 55-year-old executive of the Robco Oil Tool Corporation. The corporation does not have any type of qualified pension or profit-sharing plan, nor does it intend to adopt one in the near future. However, in an effort to ensure the continuing services of Mr. Hartman, Robco Corporation has offered him a choice between two different compensation arrangements. One pays $40,000 additional annual salary; and the other provides for $50,000 a year deferred compensation for 10 years beginning when Roy retires at age 65. Currently, Hartman's marginal tax rate is 31 percent. Roy does not expect to be in a lower tax bracket within his last 10 years of employment or after retirement. Since he does not need the $28,800 which would remain after paying current taxes on the $40,000 additional annual salary, Mr. Hartman asks you to evaluate his alternative compensation proposals. Assuming a 10 percent pre-tax return on savings will prevail over the entire 20-year period (10 years before and 10 years after retirement), and assuming that he would save the entire $28,800 annual after-tax salary under the $40,000 additional annual compensation arrangement, which alternative would you recommend? Why?

**18-37** *Qualified Retirement Plans.* Shelly Carol is the sole shareholder of Gills Corporation. The corporation has been in business since 1989 manufacturing dog food. Profits have averaged about $300,000 per year for the past five years. Shelly projects that with the purchase of additional manufacturing equipment costing $700,000, he can double his production of dog food, resulting in additional profits of $200,000. Unfortunately, Shelly does not have the funds readily available to make the additional capital purchases, so in order to implement the plan he intends to borrow the entire $700,000.

*Required:*

1. How can Gills Corporation achieve its goal of financing the capital improvements while providing an incentive benefit to its employees?

2. Assume that Gills Corporation's payroll is approximately $600,000 and that Shelly intends to set aside $100,000 for the benefit of the employees. Compare the plan selected in (1) above with an ordinary pension or profit-sharing plan.

3. What are some of the disadvantages that Shelly should consider in using the plan established in (1)?

***Research aids:***

§ 401(a)(28)(C)
§ 404(a)(3)
§ 404(a)(9)
§ 409(h)
§ 4975(e)(7)

# Corporate Taxation

PART 7

**CHAPTER 19** Corporations: Formation and Operation

**CHAPTER 20** Corporate Distributions, Redemptions and Liquidations

**CHAPTER 21** Taxation of Corporate Accumulations

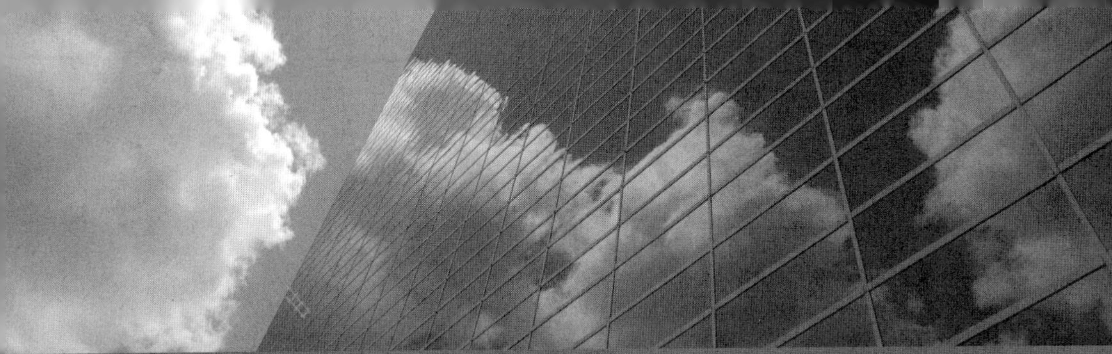

19

# Corporations: Formation and Operation

## Learning Objectives

Upon completion of this chapter you will be able to:

LO.1 Define a corporation for Federal income tax purposes.

LO.2 Compare and contrast corporate and individual taxation.

LO.3 Compute the corporate income tax, including the tax for personal service corporations.

LO.4 Describe the corporate tax forms and filing requirements.

LO.5 Describe the requirements for qualifying a transfer to a corporation for tax-free treatment.

LO.6 Explain the basic tax consequences of forming a new corporation, including:

- Determination of the gain or loss recognized by the shareholders and the corporation.
- Determination of the basis of the shareholder's stock in the corporation and the corporation's basis in the property received.

## Chapter Outline


Introduction 19-2
What is a Corporation? 19-2
- Associations 19-2
- Limited Liability Companies 19-3
- Sham Corporations 19-3

Comparison of Corporate and Individual Income Taxation 19-4
- Gross Income 19-5
- Deductions 19-5
- Dividends-Received Deduction 19-6
- Organizational Expenditures 19-10
- Net Operating Loss 19-11
- Charitable Contributions 19-12
- Capital Gains and Losses 19-15
- Sales of Depreciable Property 19-16
- Transactions between Corporations and Their Shareholders 19-17
- Deduction Attributable to Domestic Production 19-18

Computation of Corporate Income Tax 19-18
- Corporate Surtax 19-18
- Personal Service Corporations 19-20
- Alternative Minimum Tax 19-20
- Tax Credits 19-20
- Accounting Periods and Methods 19-20

Corporate Tax Forms and Filing Requirements 19-21
- Filing Requirements 19-22

Estimated Tax Payments 19-22
Example of Corporate Tax Return 19-22
Corporate Formation 19-29
Transfer of Property 19-29
By One or More Persons 19-29
Solely for Stock 19-30
Control 19-30
Receipt of Boot 19-30
Assumption of Liabilities 19-31
Effect of § 351 on the Transferee Corporation 19-33
Basis to Shareholders 19-33
Basis to Transferee Corporation 19-34
Depreciation Recapture 19-34
Capital Contributions 19-36
Made by Shareholders 19-36
Made by Nonshareholders 19-37
Problem Materials 19-37


## Introduction

As discussed in Chapter 3, there are several types of taxable entities. The individual taxpayer has already been discussed at length. Various aspects of the corporate entity are covered in this chapter and the next two chapters. S corporations, partnerships, and fiduciaries are covered in later chapters.

## What is a Corporation?

**LO.1**
Define a corporation for Federal income tax purposes.

A corporation is an artificial "person" created by state law. The state may impose restrictions on the issuance of shares and the type of business conducted. The state also specifies the requirements for incorporation, such as the filing of articles of incorporation, the issuance of a corporate charter, and the payment of various fees (e.g., franchise taxes).

Federal tax law provides that a tax will be imposed upon the taxable income of every corporation. For this purpose, a *corporation* is a business entity organized under a Federal or state statute, if the statute refers to the entity as incorporated or as a corporation, body corporate, or body public.[1] This definition includes entities such as insurance companies, state-statute authorized joint-stock companies or associations, banks with any FDIC-insured deposits, businesses wholly owned by state or political subdivisions, and business entities, such as publicly traded partnerships, that are treated as corporations. The regulations also classify a list of specified foreign entities as corporations.

### Associations

Historically, an association that was not treated as a corporation under state or Federal law (e.g., a partnership) could be classified as a corporation for Federal income tax purposes and thus be inadvertently exposed to the disadvantages of the regular (C) corporate form of doing business. The aspects that were addressed in determining whether an association should be classified and taxed as a corporation included:[2]

1. Continuity of life,
2. Centralized management,
3. Limited liability, and
4. Free transferability.

If three of these four characteristics were satisfied, an entity would be taxed as a corporation, even if the entity was treated differently under state law. For example, a limited liability partnership (LLP) or a limited liability company (LLC) could be treated as a corporation for tax purposes if it had, along with limited liability, two of the other three characteristics (e.g., centralized management and no restrictions on the transfer of interests).

[1] § 7701(a)(3).

[2] Reg. § 301.7701-2.

It is important to note what could happen to any anticipated tax benefits if an organization was unexpectedly classified as an association. For example, if the owners of a real estate business expected losses in the early years of operations, the corporate tax entity would not be the best choice of business form unless the organization qualified for and elected S corporation status. If the business was treated as a partnership or an S corporation, the losses flowed through to the owners and could be deductible on their personal tax returns, subject to the passive activity loss rules. However, if the entity was classified as an association and was thereby taxable as a regular corporation, the losses simply accumulated at the corporate level in the form of net operating loss carryovers, the tax benefit of which expired at the end of 20 years.[3] Obviously, if the organization's owners did not think that the business was a corporation, they certainly would not file the required election to be treated as an S corporation for Federal income tax purposes. Thus, unless the organization qualified as a partnership for tax purposes, any anticipated tax benefits would *either* be lost or, at best, unduly delayed.

Naturally, the above classification rules led to a great number of conflicts between the IRS and taxpayers. To simplify this process, the IRS issued regulations in 1998 that replace the old rules for classifying entities with a "check-the-box" system.[4] Under the new rules, an entity organized as a corporation under state law, or an entity classified under the Code as a corporation, will be treated as a corporation and will not be allowed to make an election. However, any other business entity (e.g., an LLC) that has at least two members may elect to be treated as a corporation or a partnership for tax purposes (an entity with only one member will be treated as a corporation or a sole proprietorship). In general, existing entities will continue to operate as they are as long as there is a reasonable basis for the current classification. These rules greatly simplify the process of selecting the form of business in which the owners wish to operate.

An important exception to the classification rules, however, is the so-called *publicly traded partnership* (PTP). A partnership meeting the definition of a PTP will be treated *and* taxed as a regular corporation. Basically, a partnership is a PTP if it (1) is a limited partnership, (2) was organized after December 17, 1987 and (3) has interests that are traded on an established securities market or are readily tradeable on a secondary market. Certain exceptions exist for PTPs in existence on December 17, 1987 and for those with income consisting primarily of interest, dividends, rental income from real property and gains from the sale of such property, gains from the sale of capital or § 1231 assets, and income and gains from development, mining or production, refining, transportation, or marketing of any mineral or natural resource (see Chapter 22 for further discussion).

## Limited Liability Companies

The "check-the-box" rules eliminate the need for LLCs to create artificial features (e.g., limits on centralized management, restrictions on transferability, limits on life of the entity) to receive the desired entity classification. Under a default system, a newly formed LLC will automatically be classified as a partnership if it has at least two members unless it affirmatively elects to be taxed as a corporation. Thus, LLCs can easily and effectively provide limited liability to their members while still being treated as a partnership for Federal tax purposes.

## Sham Corporations

In some instances, the IRS will ignore the fact that an entity is considered a corporation as defined by its state law. This may happen when a corporation's only purpose is to reduce taxes of its owners or to hold title to property. If the corporation has no real business or economic function, or if it conducts no activities, it may be a "sham," or "dummy," corporation.[5] Generally, as long as there is a business activity carried on, a corporation will be considered a separate taxable entity.[6]

---

[3] See § 172(b)(1)(B).

[4] Reg. § 301.7701-1.

[5] See *Higgins v. Smith*, 40-1 USTC ¶9160, 23 AFTR 800, 308 U.S. 473 (USSC, 1940).

[6] *Moline Properties, Inc.*, 43-1 USTC ¶9464, 30 AFTR 1291, 319 U.S. 436 (USSC, 1943).

**Example 1**

M owns a piece of real estate. To protect it from his creditors, M forms X Corporation and transfers the land to it in exchange for all of X Corporation's stock. The only purpose of X Corporation is to hold title to the real estate, and X Corporation conducts no other business activities. It is properly incorporated under state law. The IRS is likely to designate X Corporation as a sham corporation and to disregard its corporate status. Any income and expenses of X Corporation will be considered as belonging to M.

If X Corporation had conducted some business activities (such as leasing the property and collecting rents), it is likely that it will not be considered a sham corporation.

Generally the IRS, but not the taxpayer, is allowed to disregard the status of a corporation. The courts have frequently agreed that if a taxpayer has created a corporation, he or she should not be allowed to ignore its status (i.e., in order to reduce taxes). However, the Supreme Court has ruled that a taxpayer could use a corporate entity as the taxpayer's agent in securing financing.[7] Thus, under certain conditions, taxpayers may use a corporation for a business purpose and not have it treated as a corporation for Federal tax purposes.

## Comparison of Corporate and Individual Income Taxation

**LO.2**
Compare and contrast corporate and individual taxation.

A corporation's taxable income is computed by subtracting various deductions from its gross income. Although this appears to be the same basic computation as for individual taxpayers, there are numerous important differences. In order to highlight these differences, Exhibits 19-1 and 19-2 contain the tax formulas for corporate and individual taxpayers.

**EXHIBIT 19.1 Tax Formula for Corporate Taxpayers**

| | |
|---|---|
| **Income (from whatever source)** | $xxx,xxx |
| Less: Exclusions from gross income | −xx,xxx |
| **Gross income** | $xxx,xxx |
| Less: Deductions | −xx,xxx |
| **Taxable income** | $xxx,xxx |
| Applicable tax rates | xx% |
| **Gross tax** | $ xx,xxx |
| Less: Tax credits and prepayments | −x,xxx |
| **Tax due (or refund)** | $ xx,xxx |

[7] *Jesse C. Bollinger*, 88-1 USTC ¶9233, 61 AFTR2d 88-793, 108 S.CT. 1173 (USSC, 1988).

**EXHIBIT 19.2** **Tax Formula for Individual Taxpayers**

| | | | |
|---|---|---|---|
| **Total income (from whatever source)** | | | $xxx,xxx |
| Less: Exclusions from gross income | | | −xx,xxx |
| **Gross income** | | | $xxx,xxx |
| Less: Deductions for adjusted gross income | | | −xx,xxx |
| **Adjusted gross income** | | | $xxx,xxx |
| Less: | **1.** The larger of | | |
| | **a.** Standard deduction | $x,xxx | |
| | *or* | *or* | −x,xxx |
| | **b.** Total itemized deductions | $x,xxx | |
| | **2.** Number of personal and dependency exemptions × exemption amount | | −x,xxx |
| **Taxable income** | | | $xxx,xxx |
| Applicable tax rates (from Tables or Schedules X, Y, or Z) | | | xx% |
| **Gross income tax** | | | $ xx,xxx |
| Plus: | Additional taxes (e.g., self-employment taxes and recapture of tax credits) | | +x,xxx |
| Less: | Tax credits and prepayments | | −x,xxx |
| **Tax due (or refund)** | | | $ xx,xxx |

## Gross Income

The definition of gross income is the same for both corporations and individuals.[8] However, there are some differences in the exclusions from gross income. For example, capital contributions to a corporation (i.e., purchase of corporate stock by shareholders) are excluded from gross income.[9]

## Deductions

Corporations have no "Adjusted Gross Income." Thus, for corporations there are no "deductions for A.G.I." or "deductions from A.G.I." All corporate expenditures are either deductible or not deductible. All allowable deductions are subtracted from gross income in arriving at taxable income.

Although corporations are considered to be "persons" under the tax law, they are not entitled to the following "personal" deductions that are available for individuals:

1. Personal and dependency exemptions
2. Standard deduction
3. Itemized deductions

All activities of a corporation are considered to be business activities. Therefore, corporations usually deduct all their losses since they are considered business losses.[10] In

---

[8] § 61(a).

[9] § 118(a).

[10] § 165(a). Like individuals, certain corporations are subject to the passive-loss rules discussed in Chapter 12.

addition, corporations do not have to reduce their casualty losses by either the $100 statutory floor or by 10 percent of adjusted gross income. (Corporations have no A.G.I., as mentioned.)

Corporations do not have "nonbusiness" bad debts, since all activities are considered business activities. All bad debts of a corporation are business bad debts.[11]

Several deductions are available only for corporations.[12] These are deductible in addition to the other business deductions and include the dividends-received deduction and the amortization of organizational expenditures.

## Dividends-Received Deduction

No doubt the most salient tax aspect of operating a business in the corporate form is that double taxation occurs when corporate profits are distributed in the form of dividends to the shareholders. The corporation is not allowed a deduction for the dividends paid, and an individual shareholder is not entitled to an exclusion. Therefore, when one corporation is a shareholder in another corporation, *triple* taxation might occur. To alleviate this, Congress provided corporations with a deduction for dividends received.[13]

Generally, the dividends-received deduction (DRD) is 70 percent of the dividends received from taxable domestic (U.S.) corporations.[14] However, a corporation that owns at least 20 percent—but less than 80 percent—of the dividend-paying corporation's stock is allowed to deduct 80 percent of the dividends received.[15] In addition, members of an *affiliated group* are allowed to deduct 100 percent of the dividends that are received from another member of the same group. A group of corporations is generally considered affiliated when at least 80 percent of the stock of each corporation is owned by other members of the group.[16]

### Taxable Income Limitation

The 70 percent dividends-received deduction may not exceed 70 percent of the corporation's taxable income computed without the deduction for dividends received, net operating loss carrybacks or carryforwards, and capital loss carrybacks.[17] However, if the dividends-received deduction adds to or creates a net operating loss for the current year, the 70 percent of taxable income limitation does not apply.

Like the dividends-received deduction percentage, the taxable income limitation percentage becomes 80 rather than 70 percent if the dividend-paying corporation is at least 20 percent owned by the recipient corporation. In the unlikely event a corporation receives dividends subject to *both* the 70 and 80 percent rules, a special procedure must be followed. First, the 80 percent limitation is applied by treating the "70 percent dividends" as other income. The 70 percent limitation is then applied by treating the "80 percent dividends" as if they had not been received.[18]

Exhibit 19-3 contains a format for the computation of the 70 percent dividends-received deduction, and *Example 2*, *Example 3*, and *Example 4* illustrate this computational procedure.[19]

---

[11] § 166.

[12] § 241.

[13] §§ 243 through 246.

[14] § 243(a)(1).

[15] § 243(c).

[16] §§ 243(a)(3), 243(b)(5), and 1504.

[17] § 246(b)(2).

[18] § 246(b)(3).

[19] To apply the 80 percent rules, simply substitute 80 for 70 percent in this exhibit and accompanying examples.

**EXHIBIT 19.3** **Computation of Corporate Dividends-Received Deduction**

**Step 1:** Multiply the dividends received from taxable domestic (U.S.) corporations by 70 percent.* This is the *tentative* dividends-received deduction (DRD).

**Step 2:** Compute the tentative taxable income for the current year, using the tentative DRD (from Step 1):

Total revenues (including dividend income)
Less: Total expenses
Equals: Taxable income (before DRD)
Less: Tentative DRD (Step 1)
Equals: Tentative taxable income (loss)

*If* the tentative taxable income is *positive*, the taxable income limitation may apply. Go to Step 3.

*If* the tentative taxable income is *negative*, there is no taxable income limitation. The dividends-received deduction is the amount computed in Step 1.

**Step 3:** Compute the taxable income limitation:

Taxable income (before DRD) (Step 2)
Add: Any net operating loss carryovers from other years that are reflected in taxable income
Add: Any capital loss carrybacks from later years that are reflected in taxable income
Equals: Taxable income, as adjusted
Multiply by 70 percent
Equals: Taxable income limitation

**Step 4:** Compare the tentative DRD (Step 1) to the taxable income limitation (Step 3). Choose the *smaller* amount. This is the corporate dividends-received deduction.

*To apply the 80 percent rules, simply substitute 80 for 70 percent in Steps 1 and 3 above.

## Example 2

R Corporation has the following items of revenue and expenses for the year:

| | |
|---|---|
| Dividends received from domestic corporations | $40,000 |
| Revenue from sales | 60,000 |
| Cost of goods sold and operating expenses | 54,000 |

The dividends-received deduction is computed as follows:

**Step 1:** $40,000 dividends received
×70%

$28,000 *tentative* DRD

| | | |
|---|---|---|
| **Step 2:** | Dividend income | $ 40,000 |
| | Revenue from sales | +60,000 |
| | Total revenues | $100,000 |
| | Less: Total expenses | −54,000 |
| | Taxable income (before DRD) | $ 46,000 |
| | Less: Tentative DRD | −28,000 |
| | Tentative taxable income | $ 18,000 |

Since tentative taxable income is positive, the taxable income limitation may apply. Go to Step 3.

**Step 3:** Compute the taxable income limitation:

| | |
|---|---|
| Taxable income (before DRD) | $46,000 |
| Multiply by 70% | ×70% |
| Taxable income limitation | $32,200 |

**Step 4:** Compare the tentative DRD ($28,000) to the taxable income limitation ($32,200). Choose the *smaller* amount ($28,000). In this case, R Corporation's dividends-received deduction is $28,000 (not subject to limitation).

## Example 3

Assume the same facts as in *Example 2* except that the revenue from sales is $50,000. The dividends-received deduction is computed as follows:

**Step 1:** $40,000 dividends received
×70%
$28,000 *tentative* DRD

**Step 2:**

| | |
|---|---|
| Dividend income | $ 40,000 |
| Revenue from sales | +50,000 |
| Total revenues | $ 90,000 |
| Less: Total expenses | −54,000 |
| Taxable income (before DRD) | $ 36,000 |
| Less: Tentative DRD (Step 1) | −28,000 |
| Tentative taxable income | $ 8,000 |

Since tentative taxable income is *positive*, the taxable income limitation may apply. Go to Step 3.

**Step 3:** Compute the taxable income limitation:

| | |
|---|---|
| Taxable income (before DRD) | $ 36,000 |
| Multiply by 70% | ×70% |
| Taxable income limitation | $ 25,200 |

**Step 4:** Compare the tentative DRD ($28,000) to the taxable income limitation ($25,200). Choose the smaller amount ($25,200). In this case, R Corporation's dividends-received deduction is $25,200 (limited to 70% of taxable income).

## Example 4

Assume the same facts as in *Example 2* except that the revenue from sales is $41,000. The dividends-received deduction is computed as follows:

**Step 1:** $40,000 dividends received
×70%

$28,000 *tentative* DRD

| **Step 2:** | | |
|---|---|---|
| | Dividend income | $40,000 |
| | Revenue from sales | +41,000 |
| | Total revenues | $81,000 |
| | Less: Total expenses | −54,000 |
| | Taxable income (before DRD) | $27,000 |
| | Less: Tentative DRD | −28,000 |
| | Tentative taxable income | ($1,000) |

Because the tentative taxable income (loss) is *negative*, there is no taxable income limitation. The dividends-received deduction is $28,000.

The taxable income limitation discussed above *does not* apply to dividends received from affiliated corporations that are subject to the 100 percent dividends-received deductions.[20]

### Other Restrictions on Dividends-Received Deduction

The dividends-received deduction will be limited if the purchase price of the stock was debt-financed or the stock was refinanced and any portion of the debt remains unpaid during the period dividends are received on that stock.[21] In taxable years before 1984, a corporation could increase its cash flow and decrease its tax liability by purchasing stock with borrowed funds. Under prior law, the interest paid on the debt was fully deductible, whereas the dividends were only partially taxable because of the dividends-received deduction. Currently, corporations must reduce the dividends-received deduction if the stock was debt-financed. The dividends-received deduction for debt-financed stock equals the 70 percent deduction multiplied by the percentage of the stock price that is *not* debt-financed.[22]

## Example 5

T Corporation purchased 100 shares of XYZ stock for $100,000. T borrowed $60,000 of the purchase price. Therefore, the corporation used $40,000 of its own funds or 40% of the purchase price. The dividends-received deduction for dividends from XYZ will be limited to 28% (70% × 40%). As T Corporation *reduces* the debt, the dividends-received deduction will increase. For instance, if T reduces the debt to $50,000 before the next dividends are received from XYZ, the dividends-received deduction *increases* to 35% (70% × 50% of stock price no longer debt-financed). When the debt is retired, the dividends-received deduction is restored to the full 70%.

[20] § 246(b)(1).

[21] § 246A.

[22] § 246A(a)(1); 80 percent in the case of any dividends received from a 20 percent or more owned corporation. This limitation does not apply to dividends that are eligible for the 100 percent dividends-received deduction.

The dividends-received deduction may also cause a reduction in the basis of the stock. If a corporation receives an *extraordinary dividend* within the first two years that the stock is owned, the basis of the stock must be reduced by the nontaxable portion of the extraordinary dividend.[23] An extraordinary dividend is any dividend that equals or exceeds 10 percent of the taxpayer's basis of common stock, or 5 percent of the basis of preferred stock.[24] If the taxpayer can prove the fair market value of the stock, then the taxpayer can use such value instead of basis to determine if the dividend is extraordinary.

**Example 6**

P Corporation purchases 100 shares of Y Corporation common stock on January 1, 2010 for $100,000. On December 31, 2010 Y Corporation declares and pays a $30,000 dividend to P. Since the dividend exceeds 10% of the basis of the stock, it is an extraordinary dividend. P Corporation must reduce its basis of the Y Corporation stock by $21,000 (70% × $30,000), the amount of the dividends-received deduction.

## Organizational Expenditures

When a corporation is formed, various expenses directly related to the organization process are incurred, such as attorneys' fees, accountants' fees, and state filing charges. Although some of the attorneys' and accountants' fees may be ordinary and necessary business expenses which do not benefit future periods (and are therefore deductible), most of these expenditures will benefit future periods and are therefore capitalized as *organizational expenditures.* These organizational expenditures are intangible assets that have value for the life of the corporation.

Generally, assets with indefinite lives may not be amortized for Federal income tax purposes. However, Congress has given corporations the option of expensing some of the organization expenditures and amortizing the remainder. The amount that can be expensed is limited to $5,000 reduced by the amount of the expenditures over $50,000. The amortizable amount is amortized over 180 months.[25] The 180-month period starts in the month in which the corporation begins business.

The Regulations give the following examples of organizational expenditures:[26]

1. Legal services incident to the organization of the corporation, such as drafting the corporate charter, by-laws, minutes of organizational meetings, and terms of original stock certificates
2. Necessary accounting services
3. Expenses of temporary directors and of organizational meetings of directors or stockholders
4. Fees paid to the state of incorporation

The Regulations also give several examples of items that are *not* considered organizational expenditures, such as costs of issuing stock.[27] The costs of issuing stock are considered to be selling expenses, and therefore are reductions in the proceeds from selling the stock. They reduce stockholders' equity and do not create any tax deduction.

[23] § 1059(a).

[24] Amounts distributed to corporate shareholders on certain preferred stock or as part of a partial liquidation or non-pro rata redemption that are treated as dividends are also considered extraordinary dividends. See Chapter 20 for a discussion of redemptions and partial liquidations.

[25] See § 248.

[26] Reg. § 1.248-1(b)(2).

[27] Reg. § 1.248-1(b)(3).

### Example 7

N Corporation was formed and began business on July 1, 2011 and incurred and paid qualifying organizational expenditures of $8,600. N Corporation has chosen to use the calendar year for tax purposes. On its first tax return (2011), N Corporation will expense $5,000 and claim an amortization deduction of $120, computed as follows:

$$\frac{\text{Organizational expenditures}}{\text{180 months}} = \text{Amortization per month}$$

$$\frac{\$3,600}{\text{180 months}} = \$20 \text{ Amortization per month}$$

$$\$20 \times 6 \text{ months in 2010 (July–December)} = \underline{\underline{\$120}}$$

The amortization deduction for organizational expenditures for 2012 will be $240 ($20 per month × 12 months).

An election to amortize organizational expenditures is made by attaching a statement to the corporation's first tax return.[28] If the election is not made, the organizational expenditures may not be amortized.

## Net Operating Loss

Corporations, like individuals, are entitled to deduct net operating loss carryovers in arriving at taxable income. As discussed in Chapter 8, numerous modifications are considered in computing an individual's net operating loss. However, only two modifications are considered in computing a corporation's net operating loss. These two modifications are the net operating loss deductions[29] and the dividends-received deduction.[30] Net operating loss deductions for each year are considered separately. Therefore, the net operating loss deductions for other years are omitted from the computation of the current year's net operating loss. The modification relating to the dividends-received deduction is that the 70 percent (or 80 percent) taxable income limitation is ignored (i.e., the dividends-received deduction is allowed in full).

A corporate net operating loss may be carried back two years and carried forward 20 years.[31] The loss is first carried back to the earliest year. Any unabsorbed loss is carried to the first prior year, the first year after the loss was created, and then forward until the loss is completely used or the 20-year period expires.

A corporation may elect not to carry the loss back.[32] If a corporation makes this election, the loss would be carried forward for 20 years. No loss would be carried back. This election is irrevocable.[33]

### Example 8

T Corporation had the following items of revenue and expense for 2011:

| | |
|---|---|
| Revenue from operations | $42,000 |
| Dividends received from a less than 20% owned corporation | 40,000 |
| Expenses of operations | 63,000 |

[28] Reg. § 1.248-1(c).

[29] § 172(d)(1).

[30] § 172(d)(5).

[31] § 172(b)(1) A five year carryback period was available for NOLs created in both 2008 and 2009.

[32] § 172(b)(3)(C).

[33] *Ibid.*

T Corporation's net operating loss for 2011 is computed as follows:

| | |
|---|---|
| Revenue from operations | $ 42,000 |
| Dividend income | 40,000 |
| Total revenue | $82,000 |
| Less: Total expenses | −63,000 |
| Less: Dividends-received deduction (ignore the taxable income limitation) | −28,000 |
| Net operating loss (negative taxable income) | ($ 9,000) |

The 2011 net operating loss is carried back two years to 2009. If T Corporation's taxable income for 2009 is $3,000, the 2011 net operating loss is treated as follows:

| | |
|---|---|
| 2009 taxable income | $3,000 |
| Less: NOL carryback | −9,000 |
| NOL carryover to 2010 | ($6,000) |

A corporate net operating loss is carried back by filing either Form 1120X (Amended U.S. Corporation Income Tax Return) or Form 1139 (Corporation Application for Tentative Refund). T Corporation should receive a refund of its 2009 income tax paid.

## Charitable Contributions

A corporation's charitable contribution deduction is much more limited than the charitable contribution deductions of individuals. As with individuals, the charitable contributions must be made to qualified organizations.[34] The amount that can be deducted in any year is the amount actually donated during the year plus, *if the corporation is on the accrual basis*, any amounts that are authorized during the year by the board of directors, provided the amounts are actually paid to the charity by the 15th day of the third month following the close of the tax year.[35]

### Example 9

C Corporation donated $3,000 cash to United Charities (a qualified charitable organization) on June 3, 2011. On December 20, 2011 the board of directors of C Corporation authorized a $2,500 cash donation to United Charities. This $2,500 was actually paid to United Charities on March 12, 2012. C Corporation uses the calendar year as its accounting period.

If C Corporation is a *cash basis* corporation, only the $3,000 contribution to United Charities made in 2011 may be deducted in 2011. The additional $2,500 authorized contribution may not be deducted until 2012.

If C Corporation is an *accrual basis* corporation, then $5,500 ($3,000 + $2,500) may be deducted in 2011.

*Note:* If the $2,500 donation authorized on December 20, 2011 had been paid after March 15, 2012, the $2,500 contribution deduction would not be allowed until 2012.

[34] § 170(c).

[35] §§ 170(a)(1) and (2).

### Contributions of Ordinary Income Property

The amount deductible when property is contributed generally is the fair market value of the property at the time it is donated. There are, however, several exceptions to this general rule. One exception involves donations of *ordinary income property*.[36] The Regulations define ordinary income property as property that would produce a gain *other than* long-term capital gain if sold by the contributing corporation for its fair market value. The charitable contribution deduction for ordinary income property generally may not exceed the corporation's basis in the property.

> **Example 10**
>
> G Corporation donates some of its inventory to a church. The inventory donated is worth $5,000 and has an adjusted basis to G Corporation of $2,000. G Corporation's deduction for this contribution is $2,000, its adjusted basis in the inventory.

There is an exception that permits corporate taxpayers to claim contribution deductions in excess of the basis of the ordinary income property. A corporation is allowed to deduct its basis *plus* one-half of the unrealized appreciation in value (not to exceed twice the basis) of any inventory item donated to a qualifying charity and used solely for the care of the ill, the needy, or infants.[37] This rule also applies in two other situations: (1) the gift to a college or university of a corporation's newly manufactured scientific equipment if the donee is the original user of the property and at least 80 percent of its use will be for research or experimentation;[38] and (2) computer equipment donated to a primary or secondary school (i.e. grades K through 12), provided the property is not more than two years old.[39] In either case, the corporation is required to obtain a written statement from the charity indicating that the use requirement has been met.

### Contributions of Capital Gain Property

As discussed in Chapter 11, there are limitations on an individual's deduction for contributions of appreciated property (property which has increased in value). In *two* situations, a corporation also is limited in the amount of deduction when appreciated long-term capital gain property is contributed.[40] The *first* situation is when tangible personal property donated to a charity is put to a use that is not related to the charity's exempt purpose. The *second* situation in which a limitation will apply is the donation of appreciated property to certain private foundations. The limitation applied in these cases is that the fair market value of the property must be reduced by the unrealized appreciation (i.e., the deduction is limited to the property's adjusted basis). For other types of capital gain property, the contributions deduction is the fair market value of the property.

> **Example 11**
>
> L Corporation donated a painting to a university. The painting was worth $10,000 and had an adjusted basis to L Corporation of $9,000. If the painting is placed in the university for display and study by art students, this is considered a use related to the university's exempt purpose.[41] The limitation mentioned above would not apply, and L Corporation's charitable contribution deduction would be $10,000, the fair market value of the painting.
>
> If, however, the painting is immediately sold by the university, this is considered to be a use that is not related to the university's exempt purpose. L Corporation's contribution deduction would be limited to $9,000, its basis in the painting ($10,000 fair market value − $1,000 unrealized appreciation).

---

[36] Reg. § 1.170A-4(b)(1).

[37] § 170(e)(3).

[38] § 170(e)(4).

[39] § 170(e)(6).

[40] § 170(e)(1).

[41] Reg. § 1.170A-4(b)(3).

## Annual Deduction Limitations

In addition to the limitations based on the type of property contributed, there is a maximum annual limitation. The limitation is 10 percent of the corporation's taxable income before certain deductions.[42] The 10 percent limitation is based on taxable income without reduction for charitable contributions, the dividends-received deduction, net operating loss carrybacks, and capital loss carrybacks. Amounts contributed in excess of this limitation may be carried forward and deducted in any of the five succeeding years.[43] In no year may the total charitable contribution deduction exceed the 10 percent limitation. In years in which there is both a current contribution and a carryover, the current contribution is deductible first. At the end of the five-year period, any carryover not deducted expires.

### Example 12

M Corporation has the following for tax year 2011:

| | |
|---|---|
| Net income from operations | $100,000 |
| Dividends received (subject to 70% rules) | 10,000 |
| Charitable contributions made in 2011 | 8,000 |
| Charitable contribution carryforward from 2010 | 5,000 |

M Corporation's contribution deduction for 2011 is limited to $11,000, computed as follows:

| | |
|---|---|
| Net income from operations | $ 100,000 |
| Dividends received | +10,000 |
| Taxable income without the charitable contribution deduction and the dividend-received deduction | $110,000 |
| Multiply by 10% limitation | ×10% |
| Maximum contribution deduction for 2011 | $ 11,000 |

Taxable income for the year will be $92,000, computed as follows:

| | | |
|---|---|---|
| Net income from operations | | $100,000 |
| Dividends received | | +10,000 |
| | | $110,000 |
| Less: Special corporate deductions: | | |
| Charitable contributions (maximum) | $ 11,000 | |
| Dividends received (70% of $10,000) | +7,000 | |
| Total special deductions | | −18,000 |
| M Corporation's 2011 taxable income | | $ 92,000 |

[42] § 170(b)(2).

[43] § 170(d)(2).

**Example 13**

Based on the facts in *Example 12*, M Corporation has a $2,000 charitable contribution carryover remaining from 2010. The first $8,000 of the $11,000 allowed deduction for 2011 is considered to be from the current year's contributions, and the $3,000 balance is from the 2010 carryover. Thus, the remaining (unused) $2,000 of the 2010 contributions must be carried over to 2012.

## CAPITAL GAINS AND LOSSES

Like individuals, corporate taxpayers receive special treatment for capital gains and losses. The definition of a capital asset, the determination of holding period, and the treatment of net short-term capital gains are the same for corporations as they are for individuals. Prior to 1988, corporate taxpayers could obtain favorable treatment for their net long-term capital gains by electing to tax such gains at an alternative rate. For example, in 1986, the alternative tax rate was 28 percent while the top rate applying to ordinary income was 46 percent. Beginning in 1988, however, a corporation's net long-term capital gain is taxed in the same manner as ordinary income. Although such treatment suggests that there is no reason to distinguish capital gains and losses from ordinary income, such is not the case. Like an individual, a corporation's deduction for capital losses is limited.

Net capital losses of corporations may *only* be used to offset corporate capital gains.[44] A corporation is never permitted to reduce income from operations or investment by a capital loss. As a result, corporations may not deduct their excess capital losses for the year. Instead, a corporation may carry back the excess capital losses for three years and forward for five years,[45] and use them to offset capital gains in those years. The losses are *first* carried back three years. They may reduce the amount of capital gains reported in the earliest year. Any amount not used to offset gain in the third previous year can offset gain in the second previous year and then the first previous year. If the sum of the capital gains reported in the three previous years is less than the capital loss, the excess is carried forward. Losses carried forward may be used to offset capital gains recognized in the succeeding five tax years. Losses unused at the end of the five-year carryforward period expire.

**Example 14**

B Corporation has income, gains, and losses as follows:

| | 2008 | 2009 | 2010 | 2011 |
|---|---|---|---|---|
| Ordinary income | $100,000 | $100,000 | $100,000 | $100,000 |
| Net capital gain (or loss) | 4,000 | 3,000 | 2,000 | (10,000) |
| Total income | $104,000 | $103,000 | $102,000 | $ 90,000 |

B reported taxable income in years 2008, 2009, and 2010 of $104,000, $103,000, and $102,000, respectively, since net capital gains are added into taxable income. In 2011, B must report $100,000 taxable income because capital losses are nondeductible. However, B Corporation is entitled to carry the net capital loss back to years 2008, 2009, and 2010 and file a claim for refund of the taxes paid on the capital gains for each year. Because the 2011 capital loss carryback ($10,000) exceeds the sum of the capital gains in the prior three years ($9,000), B has a $1,000 capital loss carryforward. This loss carryforward can be used to offset the first $1,000 of capital gains recognized in years 2012 through 2016.

[44] § 1211(a).

[45] § 1212(a).

Corporations treat all capital loss carrybacks and carryovers as short-term losses. At the present, this has no effect on the tax due and it is often immaterial whether the carryover is considered long-term or short-term. However, if Congress ever reinstates special treatment for corporate long-term capital gains, keeping short-term and long-term carryovers separate will once again have meaning.

## Sales of Depreciable Property

Corporations generally compute the amount of § 1245 and § 1250 ordinary income recapture on the sales of depreciable assets in the same manner as do individuals. As discussed in Example 15, however, Congress added Code § 291 to the tax law in 1982 with the intent of reducing the tax benefits of the accelerated cost recovery of depreciable § 1250 property available to corporate taxpayers. As a result, corporations must treat as ordinary income 20 percent of any § 1231 gain which would have been ordinary income if Code § 1245 rather than § 1250 had applied to the transaction. In effect, a corporation must recapture 20 percent of the straight-line depreciation claimed on residential or nonresidential realty. Similar rules apply to amortization of pollution control facilities and intangible drilling costs incurred by corporate taxpayers.

### Example 15

C Corporation sells residential rental property for $500,000 in 2011. The property was purchased for $400,000 in 1986, and C claimed ACRS depreciation of $120,000. Straight-line depreciation would have been $65,000. C Corporation's depreciation recapture and § 1231 gain are computed as follows:

| | | | |
|---|---|---|---|
| **Step 1:** | Compute realized gain: | | |
| | Sales price | | $500,000 |
| | Less: Adjusted basis | | |
| | Cost | $400,000 | |
| | ACRS depreciation | −120,000 | −280,000 |
| | Realized gain | | $220,000 |
| **Step 2:** | Compute *excess* depreciation: | | |
| | Actual depreciation | | $120,000 |
| | Straight-line depreciation | | −65,000 |
| | Excess depreciation | | $ 55,000 |
| **Step 3:** | Compute § 1250 depreciation recapture: | | |
| | *Lesser* of realized gain of $220,000 | | |
| | or | | |
| | Excess depreciation of $55,000 | | |
| | §1250 depreciation recapture | | $ 55,000 |
| **Step 4:** | Compute depreciation recapture if § 1245 applied: | | |
| | *Lesser* of realized gain of $220,000 | | |
| | or | | |
| | Actual depreciation of $120,000 | | |
| | Depreciation recapture if §1245 applied | | $120,000 |

| | | |
|---|---|---|
| **Step 5:** | Compute § 291 ordinary income: | |
| | Depreciation recapture if § 1245 applied | $120,000 |
| | § 1250 depreciation recapture | −55,000 |
| | Excess recapture potential | $ 65,000 |
| | Multiplied by § 291 rate | ×20% |
| | § 291 ordinary income | $ 13,000 |
| **Step 6:** | Characterize recognized gain: | |
| | § 1250 depreciation recapture | $ 55,000 |
| | Plus: § 291 ordinary income | +13,000 |
| | Ordinary income | $ 68,000 |
| | Realized gain | $220,000 |
| | Less: Ordinary income | −68,000 |
| | § 1231 gain | $152,000 |

## Transactions between Corporations and Their Shareholders

As discussed in Chapter 7, no deduction is allowed for a loss incurred in a transaction between related parties.[46] A corporation may be subjected to this rule. For example, a loss on the sale of the property from a corporation to a shareholder who owns more than 50 percent of the corporation is nondeductible. In such case, the unrecognized loss must be suspended and may be used by the shareholder to offset gain when the property is sold. A corporation also may be subjected to the prohibition of deductions for *accrued* but *unpaid* expenses incurred in transactions between related parties. For example, an accrual basis corporation will be denied a deduction for accrued expenses payable to cash basis related parties *until* the amount actually is paid.[47] In calculating ownership, stock owned by family members and other entities owned by the taxpayer are included.[48] With respect to the matching of income and deduction provisions only, the Tax Reform Act of 1986 expanded the definition of a related party in the case of a *personal service corporation* to include any employee that owns any of the corporation's stock. For this purpose, a personal service corporation is one where the principal activity of the corporation is the performance of personal services *and* such services are substantially performed by employee-owners. This rule applies to firms engaged in the performance of services in the fields of health, law, engineering, architecture, accounting, actuarial science, performing arts, or consulting.

The sale of property at a *gain* between a corporation and its controlling shareholders is not affected by the disallowance rules. Instead, the gain is *reclassified* as ordinary income rather than capital or § 1231 gain if the property is depreciable by the purchaser.[49] For purposes of this rule, a controlling shareholder is defined the same as under the disallowed loss rule (i.e., more than 50 percent ownership).[50] In addition, sales of depreciable property between a corporation and a more than 50 percent shareholder generally are ineligible for the installment method.[51]

---

[46] § 267(a)(1).

[47] § 267(a)(2).

[48] §§ 267(b) and (c).

[49] § 1239(a).

[50] § 1239(c).

[51] § 453(g). The sale can qualify for installment treatment if the taxpayer can prove absence of tax avoidance motive.

### Deduction Attributable to Domestic Production

In an attempt to make U.S. corporations more competitive in the world market, Congress has enacted a special deduction for corporations engaged in production activities within the United States. The deduction is 9 percent times the lesser of *qualified production activity income* or taxable income. Qualified income is gross receipts from domestic production less cost of goods sold, direct expenses allocated to this income and a ratable share of indirect expenses allocated to this income. The deduction may not exceed 50 percent of the taxable wages paid during the year.

## Computation of Corporate Income Tax

**LO.3**
Compute the corporate income tax, including the tax for personal service corporations.

For many years the maximum individual tax rate exceeded the maximum corporate tax rate. The Tax Reform Act of 1986 reversed this situation. This led many advisers to consider entities other than corporations. The Revenue Reconciliation Act of 1993 raised the maximum individual rate, making it once again greater than the maximum corporate rate. This may have the effect of encouraging the formation of corporations. The corporate tax rates for 1993 and subsequent years are as follows:[52]

| *Taxable Income* | *Tax Rate* |
|---|---|
| $ 1–50,000 | 15% |
| 50,001–75,000 | 25 |
| 75,001–10,000,000 | 34 |
| More than $10,000,000 | 35 |

### Corporate Surtax

In an effort to restrict the tax benefit of the lower graduated rates to small corporate businesses with taxable incomes of $100,000 or less, a 5 percent *surtax* is imposed on corporate taxable income in excess of $100,000, up to a maximum surtax of $11,750—the net "savings" of having the first $75,000 of corporate income taxed at the lower rates rather than at 34 percent. For corporations with taxable income in excess of $15 million, an additional surtax is imposed equal to the lesser of $100,000 or 3 percent of the taxable income in excess of $15 million.[53] The purpose of this additional surtax is to eliminate the tax "savings" arising from taxing the first $10 million at 34 percent rather than 35 percent (i.e., 1% of $10 million = $100,000 additional surtax).

#### Example 16

L corporation has taxable income of $120,000 for its 2011 calendar year. Its tax liability is computed as follows:

| | |
|---|---|
| 15% × $50,000 = | $ 7,500 |
| 25% × 25,000 = | 6,250 |
| 34% × 45,000 = | 15,300 |
| Tax liability before surtax | $29,050 |
| Plus: 5% surtax on $20,000 ($120,000 – $100,000) | +1,000 |
| Total tax liability for 2011 | $30,050 |

[52] § 11(b).

[53] *Ibid.*

### Example 17

P Corporation has taxable income of $335,000 for its 2011 tax year. Its tax liability is computed as follows:

| | | | |
|---|---|---|---|
| 15% × | $ 50,000 | = | $ 7,500 |
| 25% × | 25,000 | = | 6,250 |
| 34% × | 260,000 | = | 88,400 |

| | |
|---|---|
| Tax liability before surtax | $102,150 |
| Plus: 5% surtax on $235,000 ($335,000 – $100,000) | +11,750 |
| Total tax liability for 2011 | $113,900 |

Note that the 5% surtax on the $235,000 income in excess of $100,000 completely offsets the benefit of the lower graduated tax rates of 15 and 25%.

### Example 18

R Corporation has taxable income of $20 million for its 2011 tax year. Its tax liability is computed as follows:

| | | | |
|---|---|---|---|
| 15% × | $ 50,000 | = | $ 7,500 |
| 25% × | 25,000 | = | 6,250 |
| 34% × | 9,925,000 | = | 3,374,500 |
| 35% × | 10,000,000 | = | 3,500,000 |

| | | |
|---|---|---|
| Tax liability before surtaxes | | $6,888,250 |
| Plus: | 5% surtax | 11,750 |
| | 3% surtax on $3,333,333 | 100,000 |
| Total tax liability for 2011 | | $7,000,000 |

Note that the combined effect of the 5 and 3% surtaxes results in a flat tax rate of 35% for corporations with taxable income of $18,333,333 or more.

Taking the 5 percent and 3 percent surtaxes into account, a corporate tax rate schedule applicable to *most* corporations would be as follows:

| Taxable Income | Tax Rate |
|---|---|
| $ 1– $ 50,000 | 15% |
| 50,001– 75,000 | 25 |
| 75,001– 100,000 | 34 |
| 100,001– 335,000 | 39 |
| 335,001– 10,000,000 | 34 |
| 10,000,001– 15,000,000 | 35 |
| 15,000,001– 18,333,333 | 38 |
| More than $18,333,333 | 35 |

This rate structure is not available to so-called personal service corporations or to certain related corporations. The specific rules applicable to these corporations are discussed below.

## Personal Service Corporations

As described earlier, a personal service corporation (PSC) is a corporation where the principal activity is the performance of services in the fields of health, law, engineering, architecture, accounting, actuarial science, the performing arts, or consulting, *and* substantially all of the stock is owned by employees, retired employees, or their estates.[54] Apparently concerned that PSCs were being used to shield income from the employee-owners' higher individual tax rates, Congress denied the benefits of the lower tax rates to such corporations for taxable years after 1987. As a result, the taxable income of a PSC is subject to a flat rate of 35 percent.[55]

## Alternative Minimum Tax

As discussed in Chapter 13, corporations are subject to the alternative minimum tax. This tax is computed at a 20 percent rate on alternative minimum taxable income (AMTI) in excess of $40,000.[56] The $40,000 exemption is reduced by 25 percent of the amount of AMTI in excess of $150,000.[57] Consequently, the exemption is completely eliminated for AMTI in excess of $310,000.

Corporations are required to use many of the tax preferences and adjustments that individuals use in arriving at AMTI. However. there is one very important additional adjustment for corporations. The adjustment is 75 percent of the difference between adjusted current earnings (ACE) and alternative minimum taxable income.[58] In general, adjusted current earnings will equal current earnings and profits. The adjustment will be added to taxable income in arriving at AMTI.[59]

In an attempt at simplification, the Taxpayer Relief Act of 1998 exempts small corporations from the AMT. All corporations are exempt their first year of existence. In its second year, a corporation is exempt if its gross receipts for the first year were less than $5,000,000. Starting in its third year, the corporation is exempt if its average annual gross receipts for all prior three year periods are less than $7,500,000. Once a corporation fails this test, it may not claim exemption as a small corporation even if its gross receipts decline to less than $7,500,000. A corporation that fails to meet the $7.5 million gross receipts test becomes subject to the corporate AMT only with respect to preferences and adjustments that relate to transactions and investments entered into after the corporation loses its status as a small corporation. For example, if a corporation fails the test in 2010, it is not required to calculate AMT depreciation for assets placed in service in previous years but only for those placed in service in 2011 (i.e., the year in which they become subject to the AMT).

## Tax Credits

Most of the same tax credits available to individuals are also available to corporations. However, corporations are not entitled to the earned income credit, the child care credit, or the credit for the elderly.[60]

## Accounting Periods and Methods

A corporation is generally allowed to choose either a calendar year or fiscal year for its reporting period.[61] However, a personal service corporation (PSC) must use a calendar year for tax purposes unless it can satisfy IRS requirements that there is a business purpose for a fiscal year.[62] Special rules apply to deductions for year-end payments made by a fiscal year

---

[54] § 448(d)(2).

[55] § 11(b)(2). Note that a PSC is not subject to the 5 or 3 percent surtax since it does not benefit from the lower corporate tax rates.

[56] See §§ 55(b)(1)(B) and (d)(2).

[57] § 55(d)(3)(A).

[58] § 56(g).

[59] See Chapter 13 for a detailed discussion of the required adjustments and tax preferences used in computing the alternative minimum tax.

[60] §§ 32 and 22.

[61] § 441.

[62] § 441(i).

PSC to its employee-owners.[63] Like PSCs, S corporations generally must use a calendar year for tax purposes.[64]

Unlike individuals, most corporations are denied the use of the cash method of accounting for tax purposes. There are three basic exceptions, however. The cash method may be used by the following:

1. Corporations with average annual gross receipts of $5 million or less in all prior taxable years
2. S corporations
3. Personal service corporations[65]

## Corporate Tax Forms and Filing Requirements

**LO.4** Describe the corporate tax forms and filing requirements.

Corporations are required to report their income and tax liability on Form 1120. Page 1 of this form contains the summary of taxable income and tax due the Federal government or the refund due the corporation. There are separate schedules for the computation of cost of goods sold, bad debt deduction, compensation of officers, dividends-received deduction, and tax computation.

In addition to the computational schedules, Form 1120 also has several schedules that contain additional information. For example, Schedule L requires the corporation to provide a balance sheet as prepared for book purposes as of the beginning and end of the year. Form 1120 also contains two schedules of reconciliation, Schedules M-1 and M-2.

Schedule M-1 is a reconciliation of income per books and income per tax return. Both permanent and timing differences will appear in this schedule. For corporations with total assets greater than $10 million, Schedule M-3 is used instead of Schedule M-1.

Schedule M-2 reconciles opening and closing retained earnings. This schedule uses accounting rather than tax data. Corporations without any special transactions will show an increase in retained earnings for net income and a decrease for distributions (i.e., dividends) as the major items in Schedule M-2. The use of these schedules is illustrated in an example of a corporate tax return presented later in this chapter.

**Schedule M-1** **Reconciliation of Income (Loss) per Books With Income per Return**

**Note:** Schedule M-3 required instead of Schedule M-1 if total assets are $10 million or more—see instructions

| | | | | | |
|---|---|---|---|---|---|
| 1 | Net income (loss) per books | 1,389,925 | 7 | Income recorded on books this year not included on this return (itemize): Tax-exempt interest $ 7000 MUNICIPAL BOND INTEREST | 7,000 |
| 2 | Federal income tax per books | 472,575 | | | |
| 3 | Excess of capital losses over capital gains | | | | |
| 4 | Income subject to tax not recorded on books this year (itemize): | | 8 | Deductions on this return not charged against book income this year (itemize): | |
| 5 | Expenses recorded on books this year not deducted on this return (itemize): | | a | Depreciation $ 80,000 | |
| a | Depreciation $ | | b | Charitable contributions $ | |
| b | Charitable contributions $ | | | | |
| c | Travel and entertainment $ KEY EMPLOYEE INS. PREMIUMS | 45,500 | | | 80,000 |
| | | | 9 | Add lines 7 and 8 | 87,000 |
| 6 | Add lines 1 through 5 | 1,908,000 | 10 | Income (page 1, line 28)—line 6 less line 9 | 1,821,000 |

**Schedule M-2** **Analysis of Unappropriated Retained Earnings per Books (Line 25, Schedule L)**

| | | | | | |
|---|---|---|---|---|---|
| 1 | Balance at beginning of year | 650,000 | 5 | Distributions: a Cash | 65,000 |
| 2 | Net income (loss) per books | 1,389,925 | | b Stock | |
| 3 | Other increases (itemize): | | | c Property | |
| | | | 6 | Other decreases (itemize): | |
| | | | 7 | Add lines 5 and 6 | 65,000 |
| 4 | Add lines 1, 2, and 3 | 2,039,925 | 8 | Balance at end of year (line 4 less line 7) | 1,974,925 |

Form **1120** (2010)

[63] § 280H.

[64] § 1378(b). But see § 444 for an exception, and Chapter 23 for further discussion.

[65] § 448.

## Filing Requirements

Form 1120 is required to be filed by the 15th day of the third month following the close of the corporation's tax year.[66] As mentioned previously, a corporation is permitted to elect either a calendar or fiscal year. The decision generally is unaffected by the tax years of its shareholders.[67] The selection is made by filing the first return by the appropriate due date. For calendar year corporations, the due date is March 15. The return must be signed by an officer or other authorized person.[68]

Corporations may obtain an automatic six-month extension of time to file the tax return.[69] The extension covers only the return—not the tax due. The request for extension (Form 7004) must be accompanied by the full amount of estimated tax due. The extension can be terminated by the government on ten days' notice.

## Estimated Tax Payments

Corporations are required to file and pay estimated tax (including any estimated AMT liability).[70] The estimates are due the 15th day of the 4th, 6th, 9th, and 12th months of the tax year. For a calendar year corporation, the payment dates for estimated taxes are April 15, June 15, September 15, and December 15. One-fourth of the estimated tax due is to be paid on each payment date.

To avoid a penalty for underpayment of the estimated tax, at least 100 percent of the corporation's tax due for the year must be paid as estimated taxes. Specifically, the corporation must pay *one-fourth* of this amount—25 percent (100% ÷ 4) of the tax shown on its return—by the due date of each installment.[71] However, the underpayment penalty is normally not imposed where the installment for any period is:

1. At least 25 percent of the tax shown on the prior year's return (if such return was for 12 months and showed a tax liability); or
2. Equal to 100 percent or more of the tax due for each quarter based on annualized taxable income.[72]

A so-called *large* corporation—one with taxable income of $1 million or more in any of its three preceding taxable years—is not allowed to use exception (1) above *except* for its first estimated tax payment of the year.[73] In addition, a corporation whose tax liability for the year is less than $500 is not subject to the underpayment penalty.[74] If a corporation does not qualify for any of the exceptions, its underpayment penalty is computed on Form 2220.

## Example of Corporate Tax Return

The next few pages contain an illustration of a corporation's annual Federal income tax return (Form 1120). This return is based on the following information:

R Corporation is a calendar year, accrual method taxpayer, which operates as a men's clothing store. John Beyond owns 100 percent of R Corporation's stock and is employed as the company's only officer. The corporation had the following items of income and expense for the current year:

[66] § 6072(b).

[67] Although a regular corporation's selection of a calendar or fiscal year is not affected by the tax years of its shareholders, a corporation electing to be treated as a conduit (flow-through) entity under Subchapter S of the Code generally is required to use the calendar year for tax purposes. See Chapter 23 for greater details.

[68] § 6062.

[69] § 6081(b).

[70] § 6655.

[71] § 6655(b).

[72] See §§ 6655(d) and (e) for these exceptions.

[73] § 6655(d)(2).

[74] § 6655(f).

| | |
|---|---|
| Gross sales | $3,900,000 |
| Sales returns | 20,000 |
| Inventory at beginning of year | 120,000 |
| Purchases | 1,100,000 |
| Inventory at end of year | 140,000 |
| Salaries and wages: | |
| Officers | 400,000 |
| Other | 150,000 |
| Rent expenses | 120,000 |
| Interest expense | 50,000 |
| Interest income: | |
| Municipal bonds | 7,000 |
| Other | 10,000 |
| Charitable contributions | 79,000 |
| Depreciation | 110,000 |
| Dividend income | 30,000 |
| Advertising expenses | 50,000 |
| Professional fees paid | 20,000 |
| Taxes paid (state income and payroll taxes) | 40,000 |
| Premiums paid on key employee life insurance policy | 45,500 |

R Corporation timely paid $600,000 in estimated income tax payments based on its prior year's tax liability of $595,200. All dividends received by the corporation qualify for the 70 percent dividends-received deduction. The corporation declared and paid dividends of $65,000 to its sole shareholder. Additional information is provided in the balance sheets in Schedule L.

R Corporation's 2011 tax liability is $612,000 ($1,800,000 × 34%).

*Note:* The sample corporate tax return is shown on 2010 tax forms because the 2011 forms were not available at the publication date of this text.

Form **1120** Department of the Treasury Internal Revenue Service

**U.S. Corporation Income Tax Return**

**For calendar year 2008 or tax year beginning ______________, 2008, ending ______________, 20 ____**

**▶ See separate instructions.**

OMB No. 1545-0123

**2010**

| A Check if: | | | | B Employer identification number |
|---|---|---|---|---|
| 1a Consolidated return (attach Form 851) ☐ | Use IRS label. Otherwise, print or type. | Name | R. CORPORATION | 74 0987650 |
| b Life/nonlife consolidated return ☐ | | Number, street, and room or suite no. If a P.O. box, see instructions. | 123 JONES AVENUE | C Date incorporated 1-1-2008 |
| 2 Personal holding co. (attach Sch. PH) ☐ | | City or town, state, and ZIP code | ANYWHERE, U.S.A. 98765 | D Total assets (see instructions) $ 2,184,925 |
| 3 Personal service corp. (see instructions) ☐ | | | | |
| 4 Schedule M-3 attached ☐ | E Check if: (1) ☐ Initial return (2) ☐ Final return (3) ☐ Name change (4) ☐ Address change | | | |

**Income**

| Line | Description | | | | Line | Amount |
|---|---|---|---|---|---|---|
| 1a | Gross receipts or sales | 3,900,000 | b Less returns and allowances | 20,000 | c Bal ▶ 1c | 3,880,000 |
| 2 | Cost of goods sold (Schedule A, line 8) | | | | 2 | 1,080,000 |
| 3 | Gross profit. Subtract line 2 from line 1c | | | | 3 | 2,800,000 |
| 4 | Dividends (Schedule C, line 19) | | | | 4 | 30,000 |
| 5 | Interest | | | | 5 | 10,000 |
| 6 | Gross rents | | | | 6 | |
| 7 | Gross royalties | | | | 7 | |
| 8 | Capital gain net income (attach Schedule D (Form 1120)) | | | | 8 | |
| 9 | Net gain or (loss) from Form 4797, Part II, line 17 (attach Form 4797) | | | | 9 | |
| 10 | Other income (see instructions—attach schedule) | | | | 10 | |
| 11 | **Total income.** Add lines 3 through 10 ▶ | | | | 11 | 2,840,000 |

**Deductions (See instructions for limitations on deductions.)**

| Line | Description | | Line | Amount |
|---|---|---|---|---|
| 12 | Compensation of officers (Schedule E, line 4) ▶ | | 12 | 400,000 |
| 13 | Salaries and wages (less employment credits) | | 13 | 150,000 |
| 14 | Repairs and maintenance | | 14 | |
| 15 | Bad debts | | 15 | |
| 16 | Rents | | 16 | 120,000 |
| 17 | Taxes and licenses | | 17 | 40,000 |
| 18 | Interest | | 18 | 50,000 |
| 19 | Charitable contributions | | 19 | 79,000 |
| 20 | Depreciation from Form 4562 not claimed on Schedule A or elsewhere on return (attach Form 4562) | | 20 | 110,000 |
| 21 | Depletion | | 21 | |
| 22 | Advertising | | 22 | |
| 23 | Pension, profit-sharing, etc., plans | | 23 | 50,000 |
| 24 | Employee benefit programs | | 24 | |
| 25 | Domestic production activities deduction (attach Form 8903) | | 25 | |
| 26 | Other deductions (attach schedule) PROFESSIONAL FEES | | 26 | 20,000 |
| 27 | **Total deductions.** Add lines 12 through 26 ▶ | | 27 | 1,019,000 |
| 28 | Taxable income before net operating loss deduction and special deductions. Subtract line 27 from line 11 | | 28 | 1,821,000 |
| 29 | **Less:** a Net operating loss deduction (see instructions) | 29a 21,000 | | |
| | b Special deductions (Schedule C, line 20) | 29b | 29c | 21,000 |

**Tax, Refundable Credits, and Payments**

| Line | Description | | | | Line | Amount |
|---|---|---|---|---|---|---|
| 30 | **Taxable income.** Subtract line 29c from line 28 (see instructions) | | | | 30 | 1,800,000 |
| 31 | **Total tax** (Schedule J, line 10) | | | | 31 | 612,000 |
| 32a | 2007 overpayment credited to 2008 | 32a | | | | |
| b | 2008 estimated tax payments | 32b 600,000 | | | | |
| c | 2008 refund applied for on Form 4466 | 32c ( ) | d Bal ▶ 32d | 600,00 | | |
| e | Tax deposited with Form 7004 | | 32e | | | |
| f | Credits: (1) Form 2439 ____ (2) Form 4136 ____ | | 32f | | | |
| g | Refundable credits from Form 3800, line 19c, and Form 8827, line 8c | | 32g | | 32h | 600,000 |
| 33 | Estimated tax penalty (see instructions). Check if Form 2220 is attached ▶ ☐ | | | | 33 | |
| 34 | **Amount owed.** If line 32h is smaller than the total of lines 31 and 33, enter amount owed | | | | 34 | 12,000 |
| 35 | **Overpayment.** If line 32h is larger than the total of lines 31 and 33, enter amount overpaid | | | | 35 | |
| 36 | Enter amount from line 35 you want: **Credited to 2009 estimated tax ▶** | | **Refunded ▶** | | 36 | |

**Sign Here**

Under penalties of perjury, I declare that I have examined this return, including accompanying schedules and statements, and to the best of my knowledge and belief, it is true, correct, and complete. Declaration of preparer (other than taxpayer) is based on all information of which preparer has any know ledge.

▶ *John Beyond* | 3-14-12 ▶ PRESIDENT

Signature of officer | Date | Title

May the IRS discuss this return with the preparer shown below (see instructions)? ☐ **Yes** ☐ **No**

**Paid Preparer's Use Only**

| Preparer's signature ▶ | *Sherry L. Hartman* | Date 3-12-12 | Check if self-employed ☐ | Preparer's SSN or PTIN 454-24-9464 |
|---|---|---|---|---|
| Firm's name (or yours if self-employed), address, and ZIP code ▶ | ROY W. HARTMAN & DAUGHTERS | | EIN | 74 2735841 |
| | 11318 KINGSLAND BLDV, SEALY, TX | | Phone no. | |

**For Privacy Act and Paperwork Reduction Act Notice, see separate instructions.** Cat. No. 11450Q Form **1120** (2010)

Form 1120 (2010) Page 2

**Schedule A** **Cost of Goods Sold** (see instructions)

| | | | |
|---|---|---|---|
| 1 | Inventory at beginning of year | 1 | 120,000 |
| 2 | Purchases | 2 | 1,100,000 |
| 3 | Cost of labor | 3 | |
| 4 | Additional section 263A costs (attach schedule) | 4 | |
| 5 | Other costs (attach schedule) | 5 | |
| 6 | **Total.** Add lines 1 through 5 | 6 | 1,220,000 |
| 7 | Inventory at end of year | 7 | 140,000 |
| 8 | **Cost of goods sold.** Subtract line 7 from line 6. Enter here and on page 1, line 2 | 8 | 1,080,000 |

9a Check all methods used for valuing closing inventory:

(i) ☐ Cost

(ii) ☑ Lower of cost or market

(iii) ☐ Other (Specify method used and attach explanation.) ▶

b Check if there was a writedown of subnormal goods ▶ ☐

c Check if the LIFO inventory method was adopted this tax year for any goods (if checked, attach Form 970) ▶ ☐

d If the LIFO inventory method was used for this tax year, enter percentage (or amounts) of closing inventory computed under LIFO | 9d |

e If property is produced or acquired for resale, do the rules of section 263A apply to the corporation? ☐ Yes ☑ No

f Was there any change in determining quantities, cost, or valuations between opening and closing inventory? If "Yes," attach explanation ☐ Yes ☑ No

**Schedule C** **Dividends and Special Deductions** (see instructions)

| | | (a) Dividends received | (b) % | (c) Special deductions (a) × (b) |
|---|---|---|---|---|
| 1 | Dividends from less-than-20%-owned domestic corporations (other than debt-financed stock) | 30,000 | 70 | 21,000 |
| 2 | Dividends from 20%-or-more-owned domestic corporations (other than debt-financed stock) | | 80 | |
| 3 | Dividends on debt-financed stock of domestic and foreign corporations | | see instructions | |
| 4 | Dividends on certain preferred stock of less-than-20%-owned public utilities | | 42 | |
| 5 | Dividends on certain preferred stock of 20%-or-more-owned public utilities | | 48 | |
| 6 | Dividends from less-than-20%-owned foreign corporations and certain FSCs | | 70 | |
| 7 | Dividends from 20%-or-more-owned foreign corporations and certain FSCs | | 80 | |
| 8 | Dividends from wholly owned foreign subsidiaries | | 100 | |
| 9 | **Total.** Add lines 1 through 8. See instructions for limitation | | | |
| 10 | Dividends from domestic corporations received by a small business investment company operating under the Small Business Investment Act of 1958 | | 100 | 21,000 |
| 11 | Dividends from affiliated group members | | 100 | |
| 12 | Dividends from certain FSCs | | 100 | |
| 13 | Dividends from foreign corporations not included on lines 3, 6, 7, 8, 11, or 12 | | | |
| 14 | Income from controlled foreign corporations under subpart F (attach Form(s) 5471) | | | |
| 15 | Foreign dividend gross-up | | | |
| 16 | IC-DISC and former DISC dividends not included on lines 1, 2, or 3 | | | |
| 17 | Other dividends | | | |
| 18 | Deduction for dividends paid on certain preferred stock of public utilities | | | |
| 19 | **Total dividends.** Add lines 1 through 17. Enter here and on page 1, line 4 ▶ | 30,000 | | |
| 20 | **Total special deductions.** Add lines 9, 10, 11, 12, and 18. Enter here and on page 1, line 29b ▶ | | | 21,000 |

**Schedule E** **Compensation of Officers** (see instructions for page 1, line 12)

**Note:** *Complete Schedule E only if total receipts (line 1a plus lines 4 through 10 on page 1) are $500,000 or more.*

| (a) Name of officer | (b) Social security number | (c) Percent of time devoted to business | Percent of corporation stock owned (d) Common | (e) Preferred | (f) Amount of compensation |
|---|---|---|---|---|---|
| 1 JOHN BEYOND, PRESIDENT | 451-54-6184 | 100 % | 100 % | % | 400,000 |
| 714 ENDEL CIRCLE | | % | % | % | |
| ANYWHERE, U.S.A. 98765 | | % | % | % | |
| | | % | % | % | |
| | | % | % | % | |

| | | |
|---|---|---|
| 2 | Total compensation of officers | 400,000 |
| 3 | Compensation of officers claimed on Schedule A and elsewhere on return | |
| 4 | Subtract line 3 from line 2. Enter the result here and on page 1, line 12 | 400,000 |

Form **1120** (2010)

Form 1120 (2010) Page **3**

**Schedule J** **Tax Computation** (see instructions)

| | | | |
|---|---|---|---|
| 1 | Check if the corporation is a member of a controlled group (attach Schedule O (Form 1120)) ▶ ☐ | | |
| 2 | Income tax. Check if a qualified personal service corporation (see instructions) ▶ ☐ | 2 | |
| 3 | Alternative minimum tax (attach Form 4626) | 3 | 612,000 |
| 4 | Add lines 2 and 3 | 4 | 612,000 |
| 5a | Foreign tax credit (attach Form 1118) — 5a | | |
| b | Credit from Form 8834 — 5b | | |
| c | General business credit (attach Form 3800) — 5c | | |
| d | Credit for prior year minimum tax (attach Form 8827) — 5d | | |
| e | Bond credits from Form 8912 — 5e | | |
| 6 | **Total credits.** Add lines 5a through 5e | 6 | 0 |
| 7 | Subtract line 6 from line 4 | 7 | 612,000 |
| 8 | Personal holding company tax (attach Schedule PH (Form 1120)) | 8 | |
| 9 | Other taxes. Check if from: ☐ Form 4255 ☐ Form 8611 ☐ Form 8697 ☐ Form 8866 ☐ Form 8902 ☐ Other (attach schedule) | 9 | |
| 10 | **Total tax.** Add lines 7 through 9. Enter here and on page 1, line 31 | 10 | 612,000 |

**Schedule K** **Other Information** (see instructions)

| | | Yes | No |
|---|---|---|---|
| 1 | Check accounting method: a ☐ Cash b ☐ Accrual c ☑ Other (specify) ▶ HYBRID | | |
| 2 | See the instructions and enter the: | | |
| a | Business activity code no. ▶ 448110 | | |
| b | Business activity ▶ MEN'S CLOTHING STORE | | |
| c | Product or service ▶ CLOTHING | | |
| 3 | Is the corporation a subsidiary in an affiliated group or a parent-subsidiary controlled group? If "Yes," enter name and EIN of the parent corporation ▶ | | ✓ |
| 4 | At the end of the tax year: | | |
| a | Did any foreign or domestic corporation, partnership (including any entity treated as a partnership), or trust own directly 20% or more, or own, directly or indirect ly, 50% or more of the total voting power of all classes of the corporation's stock entitled to vote? For rules of constructive ownership, see instructions. If "Yes," complete (i) through (v). | | ✓ |

| (i) Name of Entity | (ii) Employer Identification Number (if any) | (iii) Type of Entity | (iv) Country of Organization | (v) Percentage Owned in Voting Stock |
|---|---|---|---|---|
| | | | | |
| | | | | |
| | | | | |
| | | | | |
| | | | | |
| | | | | |

| | | Yes | No |
|---|---|---|---|
| b | Did any individual or estate own directly 20% or more, or own, directly or indirectly, 50% or more of the total voting power of all classes of the corporation's stock entitled to vote? For rules of constructive ownership, see instructions. If "Yes," complete (i) through (iv). | ✓ | |

| (i) Name of Individual or Estate | (ii) Identifying Number (if any) | (iii) Country of Citizenship (see instructions) | (iv) Percentage Owned in Voting Stock |
|---|---|---|---|
| JOHN BEYOND | 451-54-6184 | USA | 100% |
| | | | |
| | | | |
| | | | |
| | | | |

Form **1120** (2010)

Form 1120 (2010) Page **4**

**Schedule K** *Continued*

| | | Yes | No |
|---|---|---|---|
| **5** | At the end of the tax year, did the corporation: | | |
| **a** | Own directly 20% or more, or own, directly or indirectly, 50% or more of the total voting power of all classes of stock entitled to vote of any foreign or domestic corporation not included on **Form 851,** Affiliations Schedule? For rules of constructive ownership, see instructions . If "Yes," complete (i) through (iv). | | ✓ |

| **(i)** Name of Corporation | **(ii)** Employer Identification Number (if any) | **(iii)** Country of Incorporation | **(iv)** Percentage Owned in Voting Stock |
|---|---|---|---|
| | | | |
| | | | |
| | | | |
| | | | |
| | | | |
| | | | |

| | | Yes | No |
|---|---|---|---|
| **b** | Own directly an interest of 20% or more, or own, directly or indirectly, an interest of 50% or more in any foreign or domestic partnership (including an entity treated as a partnership) or in the beneficial interest of a trust? For rules of constructive ownership, see instructions . If "Yes," complete (i) through (iv). | | ✓ |

| **(i)** Name of Entity | **(ii)** Employer Identification Number (if any) | **(iii)** Country of Organization | **(iv)** Maximum Percentage Owned in Profit, Loss, or Capital |
|---|---|---|---|
| | | | |
| | | | |
| | | | |
| | | | |
| | | | |
| | | | |

| | | Yes | No |
|---|---|---|---|
| **6** | During this tax year, did the corporation pay dividends (other than stock dividends and distributions in exchange for stock) in excess of the corporation's current and accumulated earnings and profits? (See sections 301 and 316.) . . . . . . . . . <br>If "Yes," file **Form 5452,** Corporate Report of Nondividend Distributions.<br>If this is a consolidated return, answer here for the parent corporation and on Form 851 for each subsidiary. | | ✓ |
| **7** | At any time during the tax year, did one foreign person own, directly or indirectly, at least 25% of **(a)** the total voting power of all classes of the corporation's stock entitled to vote or **(b)** the total value of all classes of the corporation's stock? . . . . . .<br>For rules of attribution, see section 318. If "Yes," enter:<br>**(i)** Percentage owned ▶ ______ and **(ii)** Owner's country ▶ ______<br>**(c)** The corporation may have to file **Form 5472,** Information Return of a 25% Foreign-Owned U.S. Corporation or a Foreign Corporation Engaged in a U.S. Trade or Business. Enter the number of Forms 5472 attached ▶ ______ | | ✓ |
| **8** | Check this box if the corporation issued publicly offered debt instruments with original issue discount . . . . . . . ▶ ☐<br>If checked, the corporation may have to file **Form 8281,** Information Return for Publicly Offered Original Issue Discount Instruments. | | |
| **9** | Enter the amount of tax-exempt interest received or accrued during the tax year ▶ $ 7,000 | | |
| **10** | Enter the number of shareholders at the end of the tax year (if 100 or fewer) ▶ 1 | | |
| **11** | If the corporation has an NOL for the tax year and is electing to forego the carryback period, check here . . . . . . . ▶ ☐<br>If the corporation is filing a consolidated return, the statement required by Regulations section 1.1502-21(b)(3) must be attached or the election will not be valid. | | |
| **12** | Enter the available NOL carryover from prior tax years (do not reduce it by any deduction on line 29a.) ▶ $ ______ | | |
| **13** | Are the corporation's total receipts (line 1a plus lines 4 through 10 on page 1) for the tax year **and** its total assets at the end of the tax year less than $250,000? . . . . . . . . . . . . . . . . . . . . . .<br>If "Yes," the corporation is not required to complete Schedules L, M-1, and M-2 on page 5. Instead, enter the total amount of cash distributions and the book value of property distributions (other than cash) made during the tax year. ▶ $ | | ✓ |

Form **1120** (2010)

Form 1120 (2010) Page **5**

**Schedule L** **Balance Sheets per Books**

| Assets | Beginning of tax year (a) | (b) | End of tax year (c) | (d) |
|---|---|---|---|---|
| 1 Cash | | 30,000 | | 320,000 |
| 2a Trade notes and accounts receivable | 180,000 | | 210,000 | |
| b Less allowance for bad debts | ( ) | 180,000 | ( ) | 210,000 |
| 3 Inventories | | 120,000 | | 140,000 |
| 4 U.S. government obligations | | | | 100,000 |
| 5 Tax-exempt securities (see instructions) | | | | 104,425 |
| 6 Other current assets (attach schedule) | | | | |
| 7 Loans to shareholders | | | | |
| 8 Mortgage and real estate loans | | | | |
| 9 Other investments (attach schedule) | | 200,000 | | 970,500 |
| 10a Buildings and other depreciable assets | 420,000 | | 420,000 | |
| b Less accumulated depreciation | ( 50,000 ) | 370,000 | ( 80,000 ) | 340,000 |
| 11a Depletable assets | | | | |
| b Less accumulated depletion | ( ) | | ( ) | |
| 12 Land (net of any amortization) | | | | |
| 13a Intangible assets (amortizable only) | | | | |
| b Less accumulated amortization | ( ) | | ( ) | |
| 14 Other assets (attach schedule) | | | | |
| 15 Total assets | | 900,000 | | 2,184,925 |
| **Liabilities and Shareholders' Equity** | | | | |
| 16 Accounts payable | | 150,000 | | 110,000 |
| 17 Mortgages, notes, bonds payable in less than 1 year | | | | |
| 18 Other current liabilities (attach schedule) | | | | |
| 19 Loans from shareholders | | | | |
| 20 Mortgages, notes, bonds payable in 1 year or more | | | | |
| 21 Other liabilities (attach schedule) | | | | |
| 22 Capital stock: a Preferred stock | | | | |
| b Common stock | 10,000 | 10,000 | 10,000 | 10,000 |
| 23 Additional paid-in capital | | 90,000 | | 90,000 |
| 24 Retained earnings—Appropriated (attach schedule) | | | | |
| 25 Retained earnings—Unappropriated | | 650,000 | | 1,974,925 |
| 26 Adjustments to shareholders' equity (attach schedule) | | | | |
| 27 Less cost of treasury stock | | ( ) | | ( ) |
| 28 Total liabilities and shareholders' equity | | 900,000 | | 2,184,925 |

**Schedule M-1** **Reconciliation of Income (Loss) per Books With Income per Return**

**Note:** Schedule M-3 required instead of Schedule M-1 if total assets are $10 million or more—see instructions

| | | | |
|---|---|---|---|
| 1 Net income (loss) per books | 1,389,925 | 7 Income recorded on books this year not included on this return (itemize): Tax-exempt interest $ 7000 MUNICIPAL BOND INTEREST | 7,000 |
| 2 Federal income tax per books | 472,575 | | |
| 3 Excess of capital losses over capital gains | | | |
| 4 Income subject to tax not recorded on books this year (itemize): | | | |
| 5 Expenses recorded on books this year not deducted on this return (itemize): a Depreciation $ b Charitable contributions $ c Travel and entertainment $ KEY EMPLOYEE INS. PREMIUMS | 45,500 | 8 Deductions on this return not charged against book income this year (itemize): a Depreciation $ 80,000 b Charitable contributions $ | 80,000 |
| | | 9 Add lines 7 and 8 | 87,000 |
| 6 Add lines 1 through 5 | 1,908,000 | 10 Income (page 1, line 28)—line 6 less line 9 | 1,821,000 |

**Schedule M-2** **Analysis of Unappropriated Retained Earnings per Books (Line 25, Schedule L)**

| | | | |
|---|---|---|---|
| 1 Balance at beginning of year | 650,000 | 5 Distributions: a Cash | 65,000 |
| 2 Net income (loss) per books | 1,389,925 | b Stock | |
| 3 Other increases (itemize): | | c Property | |
| | | 6 Other decreases (itemize): | |
| | | 7 Add lines 5 and 6 | 65,000 |
| 4 Add lines 1, 2, and 3 | 2,039,925 | 8 Balance at end of year (line 4 less line 7) | 1,974,925 |

Form **1120** (2010)

## Corporate Formation

**LO.5**
Describe the requirements for qualifying a transfer to a corporation for tax-free treatment.

When a corporation is formed, property generally is transferred to the corporation and the transferors receive stock in exchange for their property. If the fair market value of the stock received is more than the transferor's adjusted basis in the property transferred, that person has a *realized gain*. Without any special provisions in the Code, this realized gain would be recognized.[75] However, Congress did not wish to prevent or discourage incorporation because of tax reasons. Moreover, this treatment was justified since the taxpayer had not "cashed in" but continued to have an indirect interest in and control over the property transferred. Therefore, Congress enacted Code § 351 permitting the nonrecognition of gain or loss on incorporation.

Section 351(a) provides that:

> No gain or loss shall be recognized if *property* is transferred to a corporation by *one or more persons solely* in exchange for *stock* in such corporation and immediately after the exchange such person or persons are in *control* of the corporation. (Emphasis added.)

This nonrecognition treatment is mandatory and not optional. Thus, if the transferor meets all the requirements, neither gain nor loss will be recognized. Only by failure to meet prescribed conditions will there be recognition of gain or loss.

### Transfer of Property

The first requirement in § 351(a) is that *property* must be transferred to a corporation. The Code states that property does not include services rendered.[76] From this it is inferred that property includes money,[77] real property, and tangible and intangible personal property.

A person who receives stock in exchange for services is required to recognize income from services rendered. In this case, the corporation is entitled to deduct the amount as an expense or capitalize it depending on the nature of services rendered.

**Example 19**

T incorporates his grocery store. He transfers all the assets for stock. The corporation issues additional stock to S, an attorney, in payment of her fee for legal services rendered in connection with the incorporation. T has neither gain nor loss recognized. S, however, is required to report the value of the stock as income. Note that this is the economic equivalent of paying S cash for her services followed by her investment of the amount received in stock of the corporation. The corporation must capitalize the value of the stock issued to S as an organization expense.

The rule that property but not services can be transferred under § 351 is generally applied to persons who transfer both. Such transferors are required to allocate the stock received between the property and services transferred and report the value of the stock received for services as income. Although the shareholder who contributes services is required to report some income, he or she can generally count *all* of the shares received in the determination of control.

### By One or More Persons

For purposes of § 351(a), the term *persons* includes individuals, trusts, estates, partnerships, associations, corporations, or any combination of these.[78] Examples of transactions that might qualify for nonrecognition under § 351 include:

1. Starting a new business
2. Incorporating a business already in existence

---

[75] § 1001(c).

[76] § 351(d)(1).

[77] Rev. Rul. 69-357, 1969-1 C.B. 101.

[78] Reg. § 1.351-1(a)(1).

3. The formation of a subsidiary corporation by an existing corporation
4. Additional contributions to an existing corporation by an existing shareholder or a new shareholder

## Solely for Stock

Section 351 generally applies only if the transferor receives *solely* stock in exchange for property. The stock received by the transferor must be issued by the transferee (new) corporation. This requirement ensures that nonrecognition is granted only where the transferor has a continuing interest in the assets transferred. Stock may be common or preferred, voting or nonvoting, participating or nonparticipating. Stock rights and warrants are not considered stock since these represent only the right to obtain an equity interest.[79] In addition, preferred stock that is redeemable or whose dividend varies with interest rates or commodity prices is not considered stock.

## Control

One of the conditions imposed by § 351 is that the transferors be in *control* of the corporation immediately after the transfer. Under § 368(c), control exists if the transferor(s) own at least 80 percent of the total voting power and at least 80 percent of the total number of shares of all other classes of stock.[80]

The phrase "*immediately after the exchange*" has raised several questions. The first question is *when* to measure control. Transfers by two or more transferors do not have to be simultaneous to fall under this nonrecognition provision provided the transfers are part of one transaction. Therefore, control is measured at the conclusion of the intended transaction and not after each transfer. Another question that has been raised is whether the transferor must obtain control with the transfer or simply have control afterward. The wording of § 351(a) indicates that the transferor(s) must simply have control *after* the exchange.

### Example 20

B owns all the outstanding stock of R Corporation. In the current year, he transfers real estate to the corporation as an additional capital contribution. B does not receive any additional stock from the corporation. The transfer qualifies, therefore, under § 351. B has control of R Corporation *after* the transfer. He did not have to acquire control as a result of the transfer. B did not receive anything other than stock, but the fact that he did not receive anything is immaterial.

**LO.6**
Explain the basic tax consequences of forming a new corporation, including:
- Determination of the gain or loss recognized by the shareholders and the corporation.
- Determination of the basis of the shareholder's stock in the corporation and the corporation's basis in the property received.

The final question raised by the phrase "immediately after the exchange" concerns the *loss of control* after the transfer. Is it necessary for the transferors to maintain control of the corporation or is it sufficient if they have control momentarily? There is no specified length of time for which the transferor must maintain control. Instead, the courts have looked at whether the loss of control is an integral part of the initial transfer.[81] As long as the transaction in which control is lost is not arranged and enforceable prior to the transfer, the receipt of the corporation's stock should be nontaxable. The subsequent transfer of stock and loss of control will be considered a separate transaction.

## Receipt of Boot

Although § 351(a) states that the transferor(s) may receive only stock, § 351(b) deals with the receipt of property other than stock (e.g., money). This cash and other nonqualified property is referred to as *boot*. The receipt of boot does *not* invalidate the § 351(a) nonrecognition

[79] Reg. § 1.351-1(a)(1)(ii).

[80] See Rev. Rul. 59-259, 1959-2 C.B. 115, for specific rules regarding voting power.

[81] *American Bantam Car Co.*, 11 T.C. 397; aff'd., 49-2 USTC ¶9471, 38 AFTR 820, 177 F.2d 513 (CA-3, 1949).

treatment. Section 351(a) still applies to the extent that stock is received. However, any realized gain must be recognized to the extent that boot is *received* by the transferor.[82] This treatment is similar to the receipt of nonqualifying property in a like-kind (§ 1031) exchange.

The amount of gain recognized is the lesser of the realized gain or the fair market value of the boot received. The receipt of boot does not cause the recognition of loss.[83] The gain recognized may be either long- or short-term. The nature of the gain is determined by the property transferred to the corporation. If the property was a capital asset in the hands of the transferor, the gain is capital. If the property was ordinary income property, the gain is ordinary.

### Example 21

T transfers land to X Corporation in return for all of the common stock and $5,000 cash. T had purchased the land three years ago as a speculative investment for $40,000. At the time of transfer, the land was worth $100,000. The stock received is worth $95,000. The corporation plans on subdividing and selling the property.

T's realized and recognized gains are computed as follows:

| | |
|---|---|
| Value of the stock received | $ 95,000 |
| Plus: Boot (cash) received | +5,000 |
| Amount realized | $100,000 |
| Less: T's adjusted basis in the land | −40,000 |
| Realized gain | $ 60,000 |
| Gain recognized equals *lesser* of | |
| a. Realized gain | $ 60,000 |
| or | |
| b. Boot received | $ 5,000 |

Thus, T's recognized gain is $5,000.

The gain is a long-term capital gain because the land was a capital asset in the hands of T. The fact that the land will be inventory to the corporation is immaterial. If no boot had been received by T, no gain would have been recognized.

## Assumption of Liabilities

Transfers to a corporation often include the transfer of liabilities as well as assets. Normally, the relief of a liability is treated the same as if cash had been received and the liability paid off. In a transaction otherwise qualifying under § 351, such treatment would result in the taxpayer receiving boot and having to recognize gain. However, for § 351 transactions, Code § 357(a) carves out a special *exception.*

The general rule of § 357(a) states that the assumption of the transferor's liability by the transferee corporation will not be considered *boot*. Therefore, under the general rule of this special exception, the assumption of liabilities by the transferee corporation will not cause recognition of gain.

However, there are two exceptions to this general rule. First, if the reason for the transfer of any of the liabilities is *tax avoidance*, then the total amount of the liabilities transferred will be considered as boot received.[84]

---

[82] § 351(b)(1).

[83] § 351(b)(2).

[84] § 357(b).

### Example 22

K transferred land to a corporation in exchange for all of its common stock, worth $85,000. The land cost $40,000 and had a fair market value of $100,000. The day before the § 351 transfer, K mortgaged the land, receiving $15,000. The corporation assumed the $15,000 mortgage. The loan and its transfer were principally entered into to avoid tax. K's realized gain is computed as follows:

| | |
|---|---|
| Fair market value of stock received | $ 85,000 |
| Plus: Liabilities assumed by transferee corporation | +15,000 |
| Amount realized | $100,000 |
| Less: Basis in land transferred | −40,000 |
| Realized gain | $ 60,000 |

Because the primary purpose of the transfer was tax avoidance, the liabilities assumed by the transferee corporation are treated as boot received.

Gain recognized equals *lesser* of

**a.** Realized gain .......... $60,000

*or*

**b.** Boot received .......... $15,000

Thus, K's recognized gain is $15,000.

The second exception to the general rule concerning the assumption of liabilities operates when the amount of the liabilities transferred *exceeds* the adjusted basis of all property (including money) transferred. This situation produces a recognized gain, computed as follows:

| | |
|---|---|
| Liabilities assumed by the transferee corporation | $xx,xxx |
| Minus: Adjusted basis of all property transferred (by that transferor) including money | −xx,xxx |
| Equals: Recognized gain | $xx,xxx |

### Example 23

N transfers land to a corporation in exchange for all of its common stock (worth $50,000). N's adjusted basis in the land is $10,000 and has a fair market value of $90,000. The land is subject to a $40,000 mortgage, which the corporation assumes. N's recognized gain is computed as follows:

| | |
|---|---|
| Liabilities assumed by transferee corporation | $40,000 |
| Minus: Adjusted basis in property transferred | −10,000 |
| Recognized gain | $30,000 |

If tax avoidance is not the motivation, and the basis of the assets equals or exceeds the amount of the liabilities, the transferor will not be treated as having received boot.

## Effect of § 351 on the Transferee Corporation

Section 1032 provides that a corporation will not recognize gain or loss when it issues its own stock in exchange for money or other property. Therefore, gain or loss is not recognized by the transferee corporation in a § 351 transfer.

## Basis to Shareholders

Following a transfer to which § 351 applies, the transferors (shareholders) must determine the basis of the stock and property received. To preserve the gain or loss not recognized on the transfer, the shareholder's basis in any stock received is generally the same as the basis of the property transferred (i.e., a substituted basis). Technically, the basis of the stock and other property received by a shareholder is determined under § 358, computed as follows:

| | | |
|---|---|---|
| Basis of property transferred | | $xxx,xxx |
| Plus: | Gain recognized by transferor | +x,xxx |
| Less: | Money received by transferor | −x,xxx |
| | Fair market value of any other property (except stock) received by transferor | −x,xxx |
| | Liabilities assumed by transferee corporation | −xx,xxx |
| Equals: | Shareholder's (transferor's) basis in stock received | $xxx,xxx |

If several classes of stock are received, the total basis is allocated among the several classes based on the relative fair market value of the stock. The shareholder's basis in any other property (boot) received is its fair market value.[85] The holding period of the stock will include the holding period of the assets transferred to the corporation if the transferred property would have produced a capital or § 1231 gain on sale.[86] Otherwise, the holding period starts with the date of transfer.

### Example 24

J owns MNO, Inc. In the current year, he transfers land and building to the corporation in return for 50 shares of common stock and 10 shares of preferred stock. The corporation also assumes mortgage of $40,000. J's adjusted basis in the land is $10,000 and $90,000 in the building. The land and building together have a current fair market value of $200,000. The common stock has a fair market value of $120,000, and the preferred stock has a value of $40,000.

J's basis in the stock received is

| | | |
|---|---|---|
| Basis of property transferred | | $100,000 |
| Less: | Liabilities assumed by transferee corporation | −40,000 |
| J's basis in the stock received | | $ 60,000 |

The $60,000 total basis is allocated based on the relative fair market value of the stock. Thus, J's basis in each class of stock is computed as follows:

Common Stock :

$$\$60{,}000 \text{ total basis} \times \frac{\$120{,}000 \text{ value of common stock}}{\$160{,}000 \text{ value of all stock}} = \underline{\underline{\$45{,}000}} \text{ basis}$$

Preferred Stock :

$$\$60{,}000 \text{ total basis} \times \frac{\$40{,}000 \text{ value of preferred stock}}{\$160{,}000 \text{ value of all stock}} = \underline{\underline{\$15{,}000}} \text{ basis}$$

85 § 358(a)(2).

86 § 1223.

## Basis to Transferee Corporation

The transferee corporation must also determine the basis of the property it has received from the transferor(s). This is computed under § 362 as follows:

| | |
|---|---|
| Transferor's basis in property | $xx,xxx |
| Plus: Gain recognized to transferor on transfer | +x,xxx |
| Equals: Transferee corporation's basis in property received | $xx,xxx |

If the corporation receives assets under §§ 351 or 118 with a built-in loss, then the corporation's basis in the assets will be their fair market value. As an alternative, the transferor can elect to reduce his or her stock basis by the built-in loss instead of the corporation taking the lower basis.

## Depreciation Recapture

If the transferor has no recognized gain in a § 351 transfer, then there will be no recapture of depreciation.[87] However, the transferee corporation is responsible for recapturing depreciation when the asset is later sold or disposed of in a taxable transaction. If there is gain recognized in a § 351 transfer, the depreciation recapture provisions apply to the recognized gain.

Exhibit 19-4 contains a summary of the computations required in a § 351 transfer. A comprehensive example of § 351 transfers follows Exhibit 19-4.

**EXHIBIT 19.4** **Computation in a § 351 Transfer**

**Step 1:** Compute the amount realized by the transferor [§ 1001(b)].

| | | |
|---|---|---|
| Fair market value of stock received | | $xxx,xxx |
| Plus: Amount of money received | $xx,xxx | |
| Fair market value of other property received | xx,xxx | |
| Liabilities assumed by transferee corporation | xx,xxx | +xx,xxx |
| Less: Amount of money given up (paid) | $xx,xxx | |
| Expenses of transfer | x,xxx | |
| Liabilities assumed by the transferor | x,xxx | −xx,xxx |
| Equals: Amount realized | | $xxx,xxx |

**Step 2:** Compute gain realized by transferor [§ 1001(a)].

| | |
|---|---|
| Amount realized | $xxx,xxx |
| Less: Adjusted basis in property transferred | −xx,xxx |
| Equals: Gain realized | $ xx,xxx |

**Step 3:** If any *boot* was *received*, compute transferor's gain recognized [§ 351 (b)].
Gain recognized equals *lesser* of

**a.** Gain realized,

*or*

**b.** Boot received

If no boot was received, then there is no gain recognized by the transferor.

87 §§ 1245(b)(3) and 1250(d)(3).

**Step 4:** Compute shareholder's basis in stock received (§ 358).

| | | |
|---|---|---|
| Basis of property plus any money transferred | | $ xx,xxx |
| Plus: Gain recognized by transferor | | +x,xxx |
| Less: Money received by transferor | $ x,xxx | |
| Fair market value of any other property (except stock) received by transferor | x,xxx | |
| Liabilities assumed by transferee corporation | x,xxx | −x,xxx |
| Equals: Shareholder's (transferor's) basis in stock received | | $ xx,xxx |

The shareholder's basis in any other property (boot) received is its fair market [see § 358(a)(2)].

**Step 5:** Compute the transferee corporation's basis in the property transferred to it (§ 362).

| | |
|---|---|
| Transferor's basis in property | $ xx,xxx |
| Plus: Gain recognized to transferor on transfer | +xx,xxx |
| Equals: Transferee corporation's basis in property received | $ xx,xxx |

## Example 25

R and S pooled their assets to form a new corporation, T Incorporated. R transferred the following:

1. Land (adjusted basis of $54,000, fair market value of $75,000).
2. A mortgage of $52,000 which the land was subject to.
3. Cash of $7,000.

S transferred a patent (adjusted basis of $24,000, fair market value of $32,000).

R received the following:

| | |
|---|---|
| 50 shares of T Corporation stock, fair market value* | $30,000 |

S received the following:

| | |
|---|---|
| 50 shares of T Corporation stock, fair market value* | $30,000 |
| $1,000 cash | |

*The value of the T Corporation stock is computed as follows:

| | |
|---|---|
| R's investment: | |
| Land, FMV | $75,000 |
| Less: Mortgage | (52,000) |
| Cash paid | 7,000 |
| S's investment: | |
| Patent, FMV | 31,000 |
| Less: Cash received | (1,000) |
| Value of T Corporation stock | $60,000 |

| | R | S |
|---|---|---|
| **Step 1:** Compute amount realized. | | |
| FMV of stock received | $30,000 | $30,000 |
| Plus: Money received | 0 | 1,000 |
| Liabilities assumed by transferee corporation | 52,000 | 0 |
| Less: Amount of money given up | (7,000) | 0 |
| Amount realized | $75,000 | $31,000 |
| **Step 2:** Compute gain realized. | | |
| Amount realized | $75,000 | $31,000 |
| Less: Adjusted basis in property transferred | (54,000) | (24,000) |
| Gain realized | $21,000 | $ 7,000 |
| **Step 3:** Compute gain recognized. | | |
| Gain recognized equals lesser of | | |
| **a.** Gain realized | $21,000 | $ 7,000 |
| **b.** Boot received | 0 | 1,000 |
| Gain recognized is | $ 0 | $ 1,000 |
| **Step 4:** Compute shareholder's basis in property received. | | |
| Basis of property and money transferred ($54,000 + $7,000) | $61,000 | $24,000 |
| Plus: Gain recognized | 0 | 1,000 |
| Less: Money received, | 0 | (1,000) |
| Less: Liabilities assumed by the transferee | (52,000) | 0 |
| Shareholder's basis in stock received | $ 9,000 | $24,000 |
| **Step 5:** Compute corporation's basis in property received. | | |
| Transferor's basis in property | $54,000 | $24,000 |
| Plus: Gain recognized to transferor on transfer | 0 | 1,000 |
| Basis in land received | $54,000 | |
| Basis in patent received | | $25,000 |

# Capital Contributions

## MADE BY SHAREHOLDERS

A corporation recognizes neither gain nor loss on the issuance or sale of its stock.[88] It is immaterial whether the stock is a newly authorized issue, previously unissued stock, or treasury stock that the corporation had previously acquired. If it is treasury stock that was purchased for a price different from its sale price, the difference is merely an increase or decrease in the stockholders' equity. If it is a new sale of stock, the discount or premium also is a stockholders' equity adjustment. The contingent liability associated with issuing par value stock at a discount has no counterpart in tax.[89] The sale of stock at a discount is treated as the issuance of stock for the amount received. This provision, however, does not prevent a

[88] § 1032.

[89] In many states, it is *illegal* for a corporation to issue its own stock below par value.

corporation deducting as an expense the value of stock issued for services. However, no gain or loss is recognized.

The provision against recognizing gain or loss afforded a corporation applies only to the issuance or sale of the corporation's own stock. Sale or exchange of stock in another corporation will be treated as any other sale or exchange of an asset. The difference between cost and sale price will produce realized gain or loss. This general rule applies to stock acquired as a short-term investment as well as stock in related corporations.

In addition to the exclusion of gain or loss on the issuance of stock, contributions to capital are excluded from the corporation's income.[90] This exclusion applies to contributions from shareholders and nonshareholders. Although nonshareholder contributions are not as frequent as shareholder contributions, communities occasionally donate land and/or buildings in return for the relocation of a corporation's facilities.

### MADE BY NONSHAREHOLDERS

There are special rules for contributions by nonshareholders.[91] Property contributed by a nonshareholder will have a *zero* basis. This prevents a corporation from obtaining a tax deduction either through depreciation or expense for the property. The provision was placed in the law because the value of the property is not treated as income to the corporation. This provision also guarantees that any amount received by the corporation upon sale of the property will be a taxable gain. The exclusion from income applies only to the receipt of property by the corporation as a contribution to capital, however.

If the property received by the corporation is money, the above rule does not apply. It is impossible to assign a zero basis to cash. Instead, the corporation is required to reduce the basis of property purchased using the cash by the amount of the contribution.[92] If the corporation does not acquire property with the contributed cash within 12 months, it is required to reduce the basis of property it already owns by the amount of the contribution.

## Problem Materials

### DISCUSSION QUESTIONS

**19-1** *What Is a Corporation?* Although an entity may be a corporation under state law, what characteristics must the entity possess to be treated as a corporation for Federal tax purposes? What difference will it make in the Federal tax classification if the entity possesses *all* or only a few of these characteristics?

**19-2** *Disregard of Corporate Form.* Why might the IRS try to disregard the corporate status of an entity that meets the state law requirements for a corporation? Under what circumstances might shareholders try to use the corporate form but attempt to disregard it for Federal tax purposes?

**19-3** *Corporate vs. Individual Taxation.* What are the differences in income tax treatment of corporations and individuals for the items below?

**a.** Dividends received
**b.** Classification of deductions
**c.** Casualty losses
**d.** Charitable contribution limitations
**e.** Capital loss deduction
**f.** Capital loss carryovers and carrybacks
**g.** Gain on sale of depreciable realty

**19-4** *Dividends-Received Deduction.* Why is a corporation allowed a dividends-received deduction? Under what circumstances is the recipient corporation allowed an 80 percent rather than the usual 70 percent dividends-received deduction?

---

90 § 118.

91 § 362(c)(1).

92 § 362(c)(2).

**19-5** *Limitations on Dividends-Received Deduction.* What are the limitations imposed on a corporation's dividends-received deduction? Under what circumstances can one of these limitations be disregarded?

**19-6** *Charitable Contribution Carryovers.* Under what circumstances must a corporation carry over its qualifying contributions to subsequent years? If contributions are made in the current prior year, which contributions are deducted first? Why do you suppose Congress imposes this ordering of contribution deductions?

**19-7** *Five-Percent Surtax.* Which corporations are subject to the five percent surtax? What is the marginal tax rate on the last dollar of taxable income of a corporation with taxable income of $170,000? What is the flat tax rate imposed on a corporation with taxable income of $335,000?

**19-8** *Property Requirement of § 351.* What constitutes property for purposes of § 351? If an individual receives stock for both property and services, what are the tax consequences?

**19-9** *What Are Transferring Persons?* What types of entities are "persons" for purposes of § 351? When might such "person" or "persons" make use of the § 351 nonrecognition provision?

**19-10** *Solely for Stock.* What is considered stock for purposes of § 351? Why do you suppose Congress imposes as a requirement for nonrecognition treatment the receipt of only stock by the transferor?

**19-11** *Control Requirement.* What is the control requirement for purposes of § 351? What is the meaning of the term "immediately" when used to qualify the control requirement?

**19-12** *Taxable § 351 Transfers.* Under what circumstances may a transferor be subject to gain recognition even though his or her transfer is subject to § 351?

**19-13** *Transfer of Liabilities.* Unlike Code § 1031 transactions (like-kind exchanges), the transfer (discharge) of a liability generally is not treated as boot for purposes of Code § 351. Explain.

**19-14** *Transfer of Liabilities and Tax Avoidance.* A transferor is considering whether to receive some cash in addition to stock when she transfers appreciated property to a corporation, or to mortgage the property for a similar amount of money and then transfer the property and the liability to the corporation. What difference will either alternative make?

**19-15** *Basis of Stock Received.* How does a shareholder determine basis in stock received in a § 351 transfer? If both common stock and preferred stock are received, how is basis in each determined?

**19-16** *Corporation's Basis.* What is the corporation's basis in property received in a § 351 transfer? If due to his current tax situation a transferor will not incur additional income taxes on any gain recognized, would it benefit the corporation to have a partially taxable § 351 transfer? Explain.

**19-17** *Depreciation Recapture.* How do the depreciation recapture rules (i.e., §§ 1245, 1250, 291) apply to a § 351 transfer?

## PROBLEMS

**19-18** *Comparison of Corporate vs. Individual Taxation.* In each of the situations below, explain the tax consequences if taxpayer T were either a corporation or a single individual.

**a.** For the current year, T has gross income of $60,000, including $10,000 dividends from Ford Motor Company. Without regard to taxable income, how much of the dividend income will be subject to tax?

**b.** During the current year, T sustains a total loss of an asset. The asset was valued at $2,000 shortly before the loss and had an adjusted basis of $2,700. If the casualty loss were incurred by T as an individual, it would be a personal rather than business loss. Without regard to any taxable income limitation, what is the measure of the casualty loss deduction?

**c.** During 2011, T had $8,000 of long-term capital gains and $3,000 of short-term capital gains. During 2010, the only prior year with capital asset transactions, T had a short-term capital loss of $6,000. How much of T's 2011 gross income will consist of capital gains?

**d.** T's taxable income for 2011, before any deduction for charitable contributions, is $50,000. If T were an individual, adjusted gross income would be $60,000. If T made cash contributions of $40,000 during the year, what is the maximum amount that could be claimed as a deduction for 2011?

**19-19** *Dividends-Received Deduction.* K Corporation has the following items of revenue and expense for the current year:

| | |
|---|---|
| Sales revenue, net of returns | $100,000 |
| Cost of sales | 30,000 |
| Operating expenses | 40,000 |
| Dividends (subject to 70% rules) | 20,000 |

**a.** What is K Corporation's dividends-received deduction for the current year?

**b.** Assuming that K Corporation's operating expenses were $72,000 instead of $40,000, what is its dividends-received deduction for the current year?

**19-20** *Dividends-Received Deduction.* During 2011 R Corporation (a cash method, calendar year taxpayer) has the following income and expenses:

| | |
|---|---|
| Revenue from operations | $170,000 |
| Operating expenses | 178,000 |
| Dividends (subject to 70% rules) | 40,000 |

**a.** What is R Corporation's 2011 dividends-received deduction?

**b.** Assuming R Corporation's 2011 tax year has not yet closed, what would be the effect on its dividends-received deduction if R accelerated to 2011 $5,000 of operating expenses planned for 2012?

**19-21** *Organizational Expenditures.* G Corporation incurred and paid $6,800 of qualifying organizational expenditures in 2011. Assuming G Corporation makes an election under § 248 to expense and amortize these costs, what is the maximum amount that may be deducted for each of the following years if G Corporation adopts a calendar tax year?

**a.** For 2011, during which G Corporation began business on September 1?

**b.** Calendar year 2012?

**c.** Calendar year 2016?

**19-22** *Charitable Contributions Deductions.* T Corporation has the following for tax year 2011:

| | |
|---|---|
| Net income from operations | $600,000 |
| Dividends received (subject to 70% rules) | 100,000 |

**a.** What is T Corporation's maximum charitable contribution deduction for 2011?

**b.** Assuming T Corporation made charitable contributions of $68,000 during 2011 and had a $10,000 charitable contribution carryover from 2009, how much of its 2009 contributions will be carried over to 2012?

**19-23** *Computation of Corporate Tax Liability.* L Corporation had taxable income of $150,000 for 2011. What is L Corporation's 2011 income tax liability before credits or prepayments?

**19-24** *Corporate Tax Computation.* T Corporation had the following items of income for its calendar year 2011:

| | |
|---|---|
| Net income from operations | $150,000 |
| Dividends received (subject to 70% rules) | 10,000 |
| Charitable contributions | 30,000 |
| Net operating loss carryover from 2010 | 30,000 |
| Long-term capital gains | 8,000 |
| Long-term capital losses | 6,000 |
| Short-term capital gains | 3,000 |
| Capital loss carryover from 2010 | 9,000 |

**a.** Compute T Corporation's 2011 income tax liability before credits or prepayments.
**b.** What is the nature and amount of any carryovers to 2012?

**19-25** *Corporate Formation.* Individuals J and R form the JR Corporation. J transfers land with a basis of $50,000 and a fair market value of $100,000. R transfers all the depreciable property from his former business, which has a basis of $80,000 and a fair market value of $70,000. In order to be an equal shareholder, R also transfers cash of $30,000 to the corporation. J and R each receive 100 shares of JR Corporation stock.
**a.** What is J's realized gain or loss? Recognized gain or loss?
**b.** What is R's realized gain or loss? Recognized gain or loss?
**c.** What basis will J have in the JR Corporation stock?
**d.** What basis will JR Corporation have in the land?
**e.** What basis will R have in the JR Corporation stock?
**f.** What basis will JR Corporation have in the depreciable property?

**19-26** *Corporate Formation.* Individuals K, L, and M form the KLM Corporation. K transfers land with a basis of $30,000, with fair market value of $100,000, and which is subject to a $20,000 mortgage in exchange for 80 shares of KLM common stock. L transfers $50,000 cash and equipment with a basis of $25,000 and fair market value of $40,000 in exchange for 90 shares of KLM common stock. M transfers $18,000 cash and renders services incident to the organization of KLM Corporation in exchange for 30 shares of its common stock.

Net of the mortgage transferred by K and assumed by the corporation, KLM issued 188 shares of common stock in exchange for money and other property with a net fair market value of $188,000 [$80,000 from K ($100,000 fair market value of land − $20,000 mortgage) + $90,000 from L ($50,000 cash + $40,000 fair market value of equipment) + $18,000 cash from M]. The additional 12 shares of common stock issued to M were in exchange for services.
**a.** What is K's realized and recognized gain?
**b.** What basis will K have in the KLM stock?
**c.** What basis will KLM Corporation have in the land?
**d.** How much gain must L recognize?
**e.** What basis will L have in the KLM stock?
**f.** What basis will KLM Corporation have in the equipment?
**g.** How much income, if any, must M recognize?
**h.** What basis will M have in the KLM stock?
**i.** Assume that KLM Corporation incurred and paid $6,800 of organizational costs, in addition to its payment of stock in exchange for M's services incident to organization. If the corporation begins business on October 1, 2011, adopts a calendar tax year, and elects to expense and amortize its organizational expenditures, what amount can KLM Corporation deduct for 2011?

**19-27** *Transfer of Liabilities.* Each of the transfers below qualifies as a § 351 transaction, and in each case the transferee corporation assumes liabilities involved in the transfer. For each transfer, compute the transferor shareholder's recognized gain, the transferor's basis in any stock or securities received, and the transferee corporation's basis in any property received.

**a.** T transfers land with a basis of \$60,000 and subject to a mortgage of \$20,000 in exchange for stock worth \$55,000.

**b.** A transfers machinery with a basis of \$4,000 and subject to a mortgage of \$9,000 in exchange for stock worth \$6,000. The \$9,000 mortgage was created two weeks before the transfer and A used the loan proceeds to take her husband on a vacation trip to Europe.

**c.** Assume the same facts in (b) except that the \$9,000 liability is the balance remaining on a five-year \$40,000 mortgage loan created to acquire the machinery transferred by A.

**d.** X transfers equipment with a basis of \$30,000 and subject to a liability of \$10,000 in exchange for stock worth \$80,000 and a \$20,000 security (bond) maturing in 10 years and paying 15 percent interest annually.

## TAX RESEARCH PROBLEMS

**19-28** *Corporate Formation.* T, an individual taxpayer, plans to incorporate his farming and ranching activities currently operated as a sole proprietorship. His primary purpose of incorporating is to transfer a portion of his ownership in land to his son and daughter. T believes that gifts of stock rather than land will keep his business intact. T's current thought is to incorporate and immediately transfer 40 percent of the corporate stock to his two children. In fact, he has promised his children that he would make the stock gifts as soon as the corporation is created. What potential tax problems might result if T pursues his current plans? Would it make any difference if T received all voting stock and had the new corporation transfer nonvoting stock to the children?

***Research aid*:**

Rev. Rul. 59-259, 1959-2 C.B. 115.

**19-29** *Admission of New Shareholder.* RST Corporation is currently owned by three individuals, R, S, and T. The corporation has a net worth of \$750,000 and has 500 shares (1,000 shares authorized) of common stock outstanding. R owns 200 shares (40 percent), and S and T each own 150 shares (30 percent). Individual E owns land worth \$90,000 which the corporation could use as a new plant site. However, E is not interested in selling the land now because it would result in a large capital gain tax. E is willing to transfer the land to the corporation in exchange for 60 shares of its common stock or securities of equivalent value, but only if the transfer will be nontaxable. How would you advise the parties to structure the transaction?

***Research aids*:**

Rev. Rul. 73-472, 1973-2 C.B. 115.
Rev. Proc. 76-22,1976-1 C.B. 562.
Reg. § 1.351-1(a)(1)(ii).

20

# Corporate Distributions, Redemptions and Liquidations

## Learning Objectives

Upon completion of this chapter you will be able to:

- LO.1 Determine the tax consequences of dividend distributions to shareholders and the distributing corporation.
- LO.2 Compute a corporation's earnings and profits.
- LO.3 Identify the more common types of constructive dividends.
- LO.4 Explain the tax consequences of taxable and nontaxable stock dividends.
- LO.5 Define a redemption and distinguish it from other types of nonliquidating distributions.
- LO.6 Explain the tax consequences of a redemption to a shareholder and the distributing corporation.
- LO.7 Define a liquidation and determine its tax consequences to shareholders and the liquidating corporation.
- LO.8 Discuss the special rules that apply when a corporation liquidates a subsidiary.

## Chapter Outline


Introduction 20-2
Dividends 20-2
  Earnings and Profits 20-2
  Distributions from Earnings and Profits 20-5
  Cash Dividends 20-8
  Property Dividends 20-8
  Constructive Dividends 20-9
  Stock Dividends and Stock Rights 20-9
  Nondeductibility of Dividends To Corporation 20-13
Stock Redemptions 20-13
  In General 20-14
  Redemptions Not Equivalent to Dividends 20-14
  Substantially Disproportionate Redemptions 20-15
  Termination of a Shareholder's Interest 20-17
  Redemption from Noncorporate Shareholder in Partial Liquidation 20-17
  Redemptions of Stock to Pay Death Taxes 20-17
  Constructive Ownership of Stock 20-18

Redemptions through Related Corporations 20-20
Effect of Redemptions on Redeeming Corporation 20-21
Complete Liquidations 20-22
Introduction 20-22
Complete Liquidations: The General Rules 20-22
Liquidation of a Subsidiary 20-25
Problem Materials 20-30


## Introduction

The life cycle of a corporation starts with its formation. This is followed by a period of operation and growth. During the growth stage, the corporation generally makes distributions to its shareholders, called *dividends*. Shareholders not only expect to receive dividends, but also expect their stock to appreciate in value. Following the growth phase, the corporation enters a period of maturity. In the maturity stage profits may stabilize, but eventually business may start to decline. A decline may force the corporation to redeem stock, reorganize, or possibly liquidate.

This chapter deals with the Federal income tax aspects of corporate dividends, redemptions of stock, and liquidations as they relate to both the shareholders and the corporations.

## Dividends

**LO.1**
Determine the tax consequences of dividend distributions to shareholders and the distributing corporation.

A distribution by a corporation of cash or property to a shareholder is income to the shareholder to the extent it is a *dividend.*[1] A dividend is defined as a distribution by a corporation out of either its accumulated earnings and profits since 1913 (the inception of corporate income tax) or its earnings and profits for the current year.[2] If the distribution exceeds the corporation's earnings and profits, the excess is treated as a nontaxable reduction of the shareholder's basis in his or her stock. If the distribution exceeds both the corporation's earnings and profits and the shareholder's adjusted basis in his or her stock, the excess is treated as a gain on the sale of the shareholder's stock.

### Example 1

J purchased 100 shares of M Corporation common stock on January 1, 2004 for $1,000. On February 3, 2011, M Corporation distributed to J $5,000 with respect to its stock, of which $2,300 is a dividend. (The amount of M Corporation's earnings and profits allocable to J is $2,300.)

J is required to include this $2,300 of dividend income in gross income. The remaining $2,700 is applied first to reduce the $1,000 basis of J's stock to zero, and the rest ($1,700) is treated as a gain on the sale of his stock. It will be a long-term capital gain since he has held the stock as an investment for more than one year. J still has the 100 shares of stock, but his basis is reduced to zero.

### Earnings and Profits

**LO.2**
Compute a corporation's earnings and profits.

The term *earnings and profits* (also referred to as "E&P") is not defined in either the Internal Revenue Code or the Regulations. Instead, the effect of certain transactions on earnings and profits is described.[3] From an examination of these transactions, however, it is possible to create a general definition of earnings and profits. Basically, corporate earnings and profits equal taxable income *increased* by nontaxable income and *decreased* by nondeductible expenses. Although earnings and profits are similar to retained earnings as used in financial

[1] § 301.

[2] § 316(a).

[3] § 312.

accounting, there are often significant differences between the two. These differences are caused by differences in the treatment of various items (e.g., stock dividends) for financial accounting purposes as opposed to the items' tax treatment. Therefore, the computation of earnings and profits should be completely independent of any computation of retained earnings.

As mentioned previously, earnings and profits generally consist of taxable income plus nontaxable income minus nondeductible expenses. Exhibit 20-1 contains a partial list of the adjustments that must be made to determine earnings and profits for a taxable year.

Although most are self-explanatory, several items in Exhibit 20-1 require further clarification. For example, while there is an adjustment for tax-exempt interest income, there is no adjustment for the portion of a gain that is realized but not recognized in a like-kind exchange. A gain on the sale of assets affects earnings and profits only to the extent that the gain is recognized.[4]

## Depreciation

The use of accelerated depreciation is not permitted in computing earnings and profits.[5] The corporation generally must use the straight-line method. Specifically, depreciation for E&P purposes must be computed under the Alternative Depreciation System (ADS), using the straight-line method and the property's class life. Because taxable income reflects any accelerated methods used, an adjustment in determining earnings and profits is to *add* to taxable income the excess of the accelerated depreciation over straight-line. In the later years of the asset's class life, the corporation would be required to *subtract* from taxable income the excess of straight-line depreciation over accelerated depreciation.

### Example 2

N Corporation uses the 150% declining balance method to compute the depreciation on its warehouse. (Assume that all other assets are depreciated using the straight-line method and that there are no other adjustments to earnings and profits.) The depreciation claimed on the warehouse for the current year (2011) was $7,350. Straight-line depreciation using ADS on the warehouse would have been $5,000. N Corporation's taxable income for 2011 was $19,000. Earnings and profits for 2011 are computed as follows:

| | | |
|---|---|---|
| Taxable income for 2011 | | $19,000 |
| Plus: Excess of accelerated over straight-line depreciation: | | |
| Accelerated depreciation | $7,350 | |
| Straight-line depreciation | (5,000) | + 2,350 |
| Earnings and profits for 2011 | | $21,350 |

## Code § 179 Expense

If a corporation has elected the immediate expensing option of § 179, E&P adjustments are made for the year in which the asset is expensed and also for the four following years.[6] The effect of a § 179 election on earnings and profits is that the amount expensed is an earnings and profits deduction in equal installments over the five-year period.

---

[4] § 312(f)(1).

[5] § 312(k)(1).

[6] § 312(k)(3)(B).

**EXHIBIT 20.1** Partial List of Adjustments Used in Computing Current Earnings and Profits

**Taxable Income**

*Plus*:

- Tax-exempt interest income
- Deferred gain on installment sales
- Dividends-received deduction
- Excess of accelerated depreciation over straight-line depreciation
- Excess of ACRS depreciation over straight-line depreciation [§ 312(k)(3)]
- Excess of LIFO cost of goods sold over FIFO cost of goods sold
- Four-fifths (4/5) of deduction for immediate expensing of assets under § 179 taken during the current year [§ 312(k)(3)(B)]
- Excess of depletion taken over cost depletion
- Increases in cash surrender value of life insurance when the corporation is the beneficiary (directly or indirectly)
- Proceeds of life insurance when the corporation is the beneficiary (directly or indirectly)
- Net operating loss deductions carried over from other years
- Federal income tax refunds
- Recoveries of bad debts and other deductions, but only if they *are* not included in taxable income under the tax benefit doctrine
- Income based on the percentage-of-completion rather than the completed contract method
- In the year they are reflected in taxable income: charitable contribution carryovers, capital loss carryovers, and other timing differences (since they reduced E§P in the year that they originated)

*Minus*:

- Federal income taxes
- Nondeductible expenses:
  - Penalties and fines
  - Payments to public officials not reflected in taxable income
  - Expenses between related parties not deductible under § 267
  - Interest expense related to the production of tax-exempt income
  - Life insurance premiums when the corporation is the beneficiary (directly or indirectly)
  - Travel, entertainment, and gift expenses that do not meet the substantiation requirements of § 247(d)
  - Fifty percent of meals and entertainment disallowed as a deduction under § 274(n)
- Other expenses disallowed to the corporation as the result of an IRS audit
- Nondeductible losses between related parties under § 267
- Charitable contributions in excess of the 10 percent limitation
- Excess capital losses for the year that are not deductible
- Gains on sales of depreciable property to the extent that accelerated depreciation or ACRS exceeds the straight-line depreciation method used for computing increases in E&P
- Gains on sales of depletable property to the extent that depletion taken exceeds cost depletion
- One-fifth (1/5) of any immediate expensing deduction under §179 taken during the previous four years [§§ 312(k)(3)(B)]
- Foreign taxes paid that have been treated as credits on the corporations tax return

*Equals*: **Current Earnings and Profits**

*Note:* This exhibit does not include the effect of corporate distributions and dividends on E&P, which is discussed later in the chapter.

## Example 3

X Corporation elected to expense a $5,000 asset under § 179 in 2011. X Corporation's taxable income for 2011 was $20,000. Although the entire $5,000 deduction is reflected in X Corporation's taxable income, the amount that affects E&P is $1,000 per year for five years. Therefore, taxable income must be adjusted as follows (assume there are no other adjustments to earnings and profits):

| | |
|---|---|
| 2011 Taxable income | $20,000 |
| Plus: $\frac{4}{5}$ of immediate expensing deduction ($\frac{4}{5}$ of $5,000) | 4,000 |
| 2011 Earnings and profits | $24,000 |

In 2012, through 2015, $1,000 per year ($\frac{1}{5}$ of the 2011 immediate expensing deduction) is subtracted when computing E&P.

### Adjustments to More Accurately Reflect Income

Over the years, Congress has required additional adjustments to be made in the computation of a corporation's earnings and profits in an attempt to have E&P more accurately reflect the corporation's current economic gain or loss.[7] One of the most important of these adjustments affects corporations using the LIFO method of inventory valuation. These firms must adjust E&P for the *difference* between the inventory as valued by LIFO and the value the inventory would have if FIFO had been used.[8]

Another similar adjustment applies to corporations that use the installment method for any asset sale. The corporation's E&P must include the full amount of the gain in the year of sale as if the corporation had not used the installment method.[9]

## DISTRIBUTIONS FROM EARNINGS AND PROFITS

A special approach has been designed for determining whether a distribution is made out of E&P and therefore treated as a dividend. This approach treats E&P as consisting of two distinctly separate pools of earnings from which distributions may be made: current E&P and accumulated E&P. Using this approach, the law creates a presumption that any distribution made during the year is deemed to come *first* from any current E&P that may exist.[10] If distributions during the year *exceed* current E&P, the distribution is treated as having been paid from any accumulated E&P. Note that under this "two-pot" process, it is possible for a distribution to be a taxable dividend out of current E&P even though the corporation has a deficit in accumulated E&P that, in fact, exceeds current E&P. In addition, a distribution may be treated as a taxable dividend even though it is distributed at a time during the year when the firm had a current loss. This result can occur because current E&P is computed at the close of the taxable year, without reduction for any distributions.

## Example 4

T Corporation distributed $10,000 cash on February 1 and $10,000 on November 1. The corporation has $25,000 of current earnings and profits and $15,000 of accumulated earnings and profits. The entire $20,000 distributed is a taxable dividend from current earnings and profits, since distributions are considered to come first from current earnings and profits and then from accumulated earnings and profits.

---

[7] § 312(n).

[8] § 312(n)(5).

[9] § 312(n)(6).

[10] Reg. § 1.316-2(a).

### Example 5

Assume the same facts as in *Example 4* except that there is a deficit in accumulated earnings and profits of $15,000. The $20,000 distributed is still a taxable dividend since there are current earnings and profits of $25,000. Accumulated earnings and profits will still have a deficit of $15,000.

### Example 6

R Corporation made a $15,000 distribution to its shareholders on December 31. R Corporation has $3,000 earnings and profits for the current year and $18,000 accumulated earnings and profits. The entire $15,000 distribution is a taxable dividend. Accumulated earnings and profits are reduced to $6,000 as a result of the distribution.

In applying this basic scheme to determine whether a distribution is in fact a dividend, the following additional rules must be observed:[11]

1. Current E&P is allocated among *all* distributions made during the year on a pro rata basis, as follows:

$$\frac{\text{Amount of the distribution}}{\text{Total current distributions}} \times \begin{matrix}\text{Amount of}\\ \text{current E\&P}\end{matrix} = \begin{matrix}\text{Distribution's share}\\ \text{of current E\&P}\end{matrix}$$

### Example 7

During the current year, P Corporation distributed $12,000 to its shareholders on March 1 and an other $12,000 to its shareholders on October 1. Current E&P was only $10,000. Each distribution would be treated as consisting of $5,000 of current E&P [($12,000 ÷ $24,000) × $10,000]. The balance of each distribution would be deemed to come from any accumulated E&P that may exist at the time of the distribution.

2. Accumulated E&P is allocated among distributions made during the year in *chronological order.*

### Example 8

Same facts as in *Example 7*. In addition, the corporation had accumulated E&P of $7,000. Earnings and profits are allocated as follows:

---

[11] Reg. § 1.316-2.

| | $12,000 March Distribution | $12,000 October Distribution | Total |
|---|---|---|---|
| Current earnings and profits [allocated pro rata to all distributions: ($12,000 ÷ $24,000) × $10,000 current E&P = $5,000] | $ 5,000 | $5,000 | $10,000 |
| Accumulated earnings and profits (allocated in chronological order: first to the March distribution and then to the October distribution) | 7,000 | 0 | 7,000 |
| Taxable dividend | $12,000 | $5,000 | $17,000 |

The entire amount of the March distribution ($12,000) is a taxable dividend, but only $5,000 of the October distribution is a taxable dividend to the shareholders. The remaining $7,000 of the October distribution is a return of capital to the shareholders and will first be applied to reduce their bases in their stock. Any amount in excess of their stock bases will be treated as a gain from the sale of their stock.

This allocation process becomes especially important if there is a change of ownership during the year, since each shareholder is concerned with how much of each distribution he or she receives is taxable as dividends. However, the *total* amount of taxable dividends is not affected by the allocations.

3. If there is a deficit in current E&P for the year (e.g., a current operating loss), it is treated as occurring *ratably* during the year (unless it can be shown that the loss did not occur evenly during the year).[12] Accordingly, the loss is allocated on a daily basis against any accumulated E&P.

## Example 9

T Corporation distributed $10,000 to its shareholders on February 1 and $10,000 to its shareholders on October 1. T Corporation had a $6,000 loss for its current calendar tax year and accumulated earnings and profits from prior years of $20,000. The $6,000 loss is assumed to have occurred evenly throughout the year (assume $500 per month). The tax treatment of the distributions is determined as follows:

*February distribution:* Since there are no current earnings and profits, the distribution is presumed to come from accumulated earnings and profits. Accumulated earnings and profits as of February 1 are considered to be $19,500 [$20,000 – $500 (one month of the current loss)]. The entire February distribution of $10,000 is a taxable dividend since accumulated earnings and profits are applied chronologically.

The balance in accumulated earnings and profits after the February distribution is $9,500 ($20,000 – $500 – $10,000).

*October distribution:* Since there are no current earnings and profits, the next step is to look at accumulated earnings and profits. Accumulated earnings and profits as of October 1 are $5,500 [$9,500 remaining after the February 1 distribution – $4,000 (8 months of current loss @ $500 per month from February through September)]. Therefore, $5,500 of the October distribution is a taxable dividend to the shareholders. The remaining $4,500 is a return of capital to the shareholders. After the October 1 distribution, the balance in accumulated earnings and profits is zero.

At the end of the year, the balance in accumulated earnings and profits is a deficit of $1,500 (the remaining 3 months of current loss at $500 per month).

[12] *Ibid.*

## Cash Dividends

Shareholders are required to include in income the amount of any distribution that is a dividend. If the distribution is cash, the amount of the distribution is simply the amount of the cash. As demonstrated in the above examples, earnings and profits are reduced by the amount of the cash distribution, but not below zero.[13]

## Property Dividends

Corporations make distributions of property as well as distributions of cash. Code § 317(a) defines property as "money, securities, and any other property," but excludes from the definition stock and stock rights in the distributing corporation. Special rules must be followed when a property distribution is made. Basically, the thrust of the property distribution rules is to treat the corporation and shareholders as if the corporation had sold the property and distributed to the shareholders the cash proceeds from the sale.

Code § 311 provides that a corporation must recognize gain—*but not loss*—upon the distribution of property other than its own obligations.[14] Thus, when a corporation distributes property that has a value exceeding its basis, gain must be recognized. In contrast, a corporation is not allowed to recognize loss on a distribution of property whose value is less than its basis. This rule prohibits a corporation and its shareholders from circumventing the gain recognition requirement by distributing loss property that would offset the gain on appreciated property. When the corporation distributes appreciated property and recognizes gain, its E&P is first increased by the gain and then reduced by the fair market value of the property distributed.[15] In contrast, if the corporation distributes depreciated property, no loss is recognized and the corporation decreases its E&P by the basis of the property distributed.[16]

Both corporate and noncorporate shareholders that receive a distribution of property report the fair market value of the property as a dividend to the extent it is out of the corporation's E&P.[17] The shareholder's basis in the property is also its fair market value.[18]

### Example 10

P Corporation distributed land worth $100,000 (basis $20,000) and equipment worth $30,000 (basis $45,000) to its sole shareholder, individual X. The corporation must recognize the $80,000 ($100,000 – $20,000) gain realized on the distribution of the land. Although P also realizes a loss on the distribution of the equipment, the loss is not recognized. Assuming the corporation has adequate E&P, X reports a dividend of $130,000 (the fair market values of the property, $100,000 + $30,000). X's basis in the land and equipment is $100,000 and $30,000, respectively. The net effect of the distribution on the corporation's E&P is to decrease it by $65,000 ($80,000 gain – $100,000 value of the land – $45,000 basis of the equipment).

### Adjustments for Liabilities

The above discussion ignores the possibilities that the property may be distributed subject to a liability or that the shareholder may assume a liability in conjunction with the property distribution. In such case, the rules regarding the amount of the distribution and the adjustment to E&P must be modified to account for any liabilities.[19] When a liability is distributed in connection with property, the amount of the distribution is decreased by the liability. Similarly, the reduction in E&P is decreased (i.e., E&P is increased by the amount of the liability). There is no adjustment to the basis of the property to the shareholder.

[13] § 312(a)(1).

[14] §§ 311(a) and (b).

[15] § 312(b).

[16] § 312(a)(3).

[17] § 301(b)(1).

[18] § 301(d).

[19] § 301(b)(2).

## Constructive Dividends

**LO.3** Identify the more common types of constructive dividends.

In addition to actual distributions of cash and property, a shareholder can be charged with the *constructive receipt* of a dividend. For example, excessive salaries to the shareholder or a member of the shareholder's family can be treated as a dividend. The corporation is limited to deducting only those salaries that are reasonable. The amount in excess of the reasonable standard will be considered a constructive dividend. Other transactions that have given rise to constructive dividends are:

1. Loans to shareholders where there is no intent to repay the amounts loaned
2. Bargain purchases and rentals of corporate property by shareholders
3. Excess payment for corporate use of shareholder property
4. Payment of shareholder's loans or expenses by the corporation
5. Personal use by shareholder of corporate assets

As indicated by the above types of transactions, constructive dividends usually arise in closely held corporations, especially those with only one or two shareholders. Constructive dividends are not planned by the corporations. They usually arise in an IRS audit as the result of lack of formality in dealing with the corporate entity and a lack of transactions at "arm's length" (for fair market value). Therefore, it is possible for a shareholder to be considered as having received a dividend even though the corporation did not declare one.

As with other dividends, the corporation must have sufficient earnings and profits for a constructive dividend to be taxable to the shareholders. Also, the dividends-received deduction is available to corporate shareholders with respect to constructive dividends.

## Stock Dividends and Stock Rights

**LO.4** Explain the tax consequences of taxable and nontaxable stock dividends.

Occasionally, a corporation may want to pay a dividend but does not have sufficient cash or property to distribute. In this situation, the corporation may declare a dividend of its stock or of rights to acquire its stock.

### Stock Dividends

As a general rule, a shareholder does not have any income as the result of receiving a distribution of the distributing corporation's own stock.[20] Instead, the shareholder simply allocates the basis of his or her old stock between the old stock and the new stock. There are several exceptions to this general rule, however. If the shareholder is given a choice between receiving stock or receiving property or money, the distribution will be taxable.[21] It does not matter which form of distribution the shareholder actually selects. The ability to select makes the distribution taxable. In fact, the ability of *any* of the shareholders to select property or stock will make the distribution taxable to all of the shareholders.[22]

Another case in which a stock dividend will be taxable is if the distribution is *disproportionate.*[23] The Code defines *disproportionate* in this situation as the receipt of cash or other property by some shareholders with an increase in the proportionate interests of other shareholders in the corporation. The determination as to whether or not a distribution is disproportionate is made at the end of the distribution or series of distributions and is made based on the result of the transactions.

Distributions of preferred stock to common stockholders are covered by the general rule of nontaxability. However, a distribution or a series of distributions that results in some shareholders receiving common and others receiving preferred is a taxable transaction.[24] In addition, any distribution (e.g., common stock) to a preferred stockholder is taxable.[25] A special rule applies for distributions of convertible preferred stock. The distribution will be taxable unless it can be shown that the result will not be disproportionate[26] (see above for definition of disproportionate).

---

[20] § 305(a).
[21] § 305(b)(1).
[22] Reg. § 1.305-2.
[23] § 305(b)(2).
[24] § 305(b)(3).
[25] § 305(b)(4).
[26] § 305(b)(5).

Taxable stock dividends can be either actual or deemed dividends.[27] Actual dividends require distributions of stock. Deemed-dividend transactions include changes in conversion ratios, changes in redemption price, an excess redemption price over issue price, or any other transaction that increases the proportionate ownership of one or more shareholders. Deemed dividends can be totally unintentional. For example, in a corporate reorganization the issuance of preferred stock with a redemption value greater than its current issue price is a possible taxable stock dividend.[28]

### Nontaxable Stock Dividends

If the taxpayer receives a nontaxable distribution of stock, the basis of the shares received is determined by allocation. The basis of the shares upon which the dividend is received is allocated between the old stock and the new stock based on their relative fair market values at the time of distribution.[29] If the shares received are identical to the shares owned (i.e., both the old and new stock are the same class of common stock), the allocation can be accomplished simply by dividing the basis of the old stock by the total number of shares owned after the distribution. If the type of shares received differs from the shares originally owned (e.g., old stock was common stock and new stock is preferred stock), the allocation of basis between the old stock and new stock is computed based on relative fair market value. The holding period of the new stock includes the holding period of the old stock.[30]

#### Example 11

Q owned 100 shares of common stock of V Corporation. His basis in the V Corporation stock was $1,300 ($13 per share). Q received a stock dividend of 25 additional shares of V Corporation common stock in a nontaxable distribution. Q's $1,300 basis in the old stock is allocated between his old stock (100 shares) and his new stock (25 shares) as follows:

$$\frac{\text{Basis in old stock}}{\text{Number of shares after distribution}} \times \frac{\$1{,}300}{125 \text{ shares}} = \underline{\underline{\$10.40}} \text{ per share}$$

Q's basis in his stock is still $1,300, which is $10.40 per share, since he now has 125 values of V Corporation common stock.

#### Example 12

Assume the same facts as in *Example 11* except that Q received 25 shares of preferred stock instead of common stock. On the date of distribution, the fair market value of V Corporation common stock was $15 per share and the fair market value of V Corporation preferred stock was $5 per share. Q's $1,300 basis in his stock is allocated between the old stock and the new stock as follows:

**Step 1:** Determine fair market value of stock:

| | |
|---|---|
| Fair market value of Q's common stock (100 shares × $15) | $1,500 |
| Fair market value of Q's preferred stock (25 shares × $5) | 125 |
| Total fair market value of Q's stock | $1,625 |

[27] § 305(c).

[28] See Rev. Rul. 83-119, 1983-2 C.B. 57.

[29] Reg. § 1.307-1.

[30] § 1223(5).

**Step 2:** Compute basis in each type of stock based on relative fair market value:

(a) $\frac{\text{Fair market value of Q's common stock}}{\text{Total fair market value of Q's stock}} \times \text{Old basis} = \text{New basis in common stock}$

$\frac{\$1{,}500}{\$1{,}625} \times \$1{,}300 = \underline{\underline{\$1{,}200}}$ New basis in common stock ($12 per share)

(b) $\frac{\text{Fair market value of Q's preferred stock}}{\text{Total fair market value of Q's stock}} \times \text{Old basis} = \text{New basis in preferred stock}$

$\frac{\$125}{\$1{,}625} \times \$1{,}300 = \underline{\underline{\$100}}$ Basis in preferred stock ($4 per share)

A nontaxable stock dividend *does not affect* the earnings and profits of the distributing corporation.[31]

### Taxable Stock Dividends

The recipient shareholder must treat a taxable distribution of stock the same as a property distribution. If the stock distribution is taxable, the shareholder must report dividend income equal to the *lesser* of the fair market value of the stock received or the distributing corporation's earnings and profits.[32] The basis of the stock received is the amount of income reported.[33] The holding period of the shares received would start on the date of distribution. The basis of the original stock is not affected by a taxable stock dividend. Taxable stock dividends have the same effect on the earnings and profits of a corporation as property dividends. However, the distributing corporation does not recognize gain or loss from taxable distribution of its stock.

### Stock Rights

Instead of stock, corporations may distribute stock rights to their shareholders. The taxation of the receipt of stock rights is governed by the same general principles as stock dividends.[34] In determining whether the distribution is taxable, it is often easier to assume that the stock that can be acquired by exercise of the rights was distributed instead of the rights. If the distribution of the stock to which the stock rights apply would have been taxable, the rights are taxable. If a distribution of the related stock would not have been taxable, the rights are not taxable.

## Example 13

N Corporation had 100 shares of common stock and 100 shares of nonvoting preferred stock outstanding. The corporation distributed rights to acquire a new issue of nonvoting preferred stock to all of its existing shareholders. The common shareholders have received a nontaxable distribution, whereas the preferred shareholders have received a taxable distribution. Since the distribution of the new preferred stock to the common shareholders would have been nontaxable, the rights received by the common shareholders are nontaxable. However, since preferred shareholders receive only taxable stock dividends, the rights received by the preferred shareholders also are taxable.

### Nontaxable Stock Rights

If the stock rights are not taxable, there is a basis allocation similar to the one for stock dividends.[35] The basis of the old stock is allocated between the old stock and the new rights based on the relative fair market values at the date of distribution. There is no allocation of basis to the rights if the shareholder allows them to lapse[36] (and consequently no recognized loss on the lapse of the rights). Therefore, although the allocation uses the fair market values as of the date of distribution, the actual allocation generally is not made until the rights are sold or exercised.

[31] § 312(d)(1).
[32] Reg. § 1.305-1(b)(1); Code §§ 301(b) and 316(a).
[33] § 301(d).
[34] § 305(a).
[35] § 307(a).
[36] Reg. § 1.307-1(a).

## Example 14

T Corporation distributed nontaxable stock rights to its shareholders on January 3. C received 100 rights on the 100 shares of common stock he purchased three years ago for $1,000. On the date of distribution, T Corporation's common stock had a value of $15 per share and the rights had a value of $5 each. On March 1, C sold the rights for $7 each. The stock had a value of $17 per share on March 1. C allocates the basis of his old stock between the stock and the rights based on their relative fair market values as of January 3, the date of the distribution. The March 1 value of the stock is irrelevant. The basis allocation is computed as follows:

| | | |
|---|---|---|
| **Step 1:** | Fair market value of C's common stock (100 × $15) | $1,500 |
| | Fair market value of C's stock rights (100 × $5) | 500 |
| | Total fair market value of stock and stock rights | $2,000 |

(a) $$\frac{\text{Fair market value of C's common stock}}{\text{Total fair market value of stock and stock rights}} \times \text{Old basis}$$

$$= \frac{\$1{,}500}{\$2{,}000} \times \$1{,}000 = \underline{\underline{\$750}} \quad (\$7.50 \text{ per share})$$

(b) $$\frac{\text{Fair market value of C's stock rights}}{\text{Total fair market value of stock and stock rights}} \times \text{Old basis}$$

$$= \frac{\$500}{\$2{,}000} \times \$1{,}000 = \underline{\underline{\$250}} \quad (\$2.50 \text{ per stock right})$$

C's gain on the sale of his stock rights is computed as follows:

| | |
|---|---|
| Selling price of stock rights (100 × $7) | $700 |
| Less: Basis in stock rights | –250 |
| Gain on sale of stock rights | $450 |

## Example 15

Assume the same facts as in *Example 14* except that C does not sell the stock rights, but allows them to lapse on June 1. Since the stock rights lapsed, rather than being exercised or sold, there is no basis allocated to them. C has no recognized loss (since the rights have no basis) and the basis of the old shares remains $1,000.

If the taxpayer sells or exercises his or her rights, basis is allocated to the rights. The holding period of the rights includes the holding period of the old stock.[37] The fair market value of stock rights is frequently small in relation to the value of the stock on which it was distributed. As a result, an allocation of basis between the old stock and the new rights would produce a very small basis in the stock rights. For this reason, there is an exception to the rule regarding allocation of basis. If the fair market value of the stock rights is *less than* 15 percent of the value of the stock at the date of distribution, no basis is *required* to be allocated to the rights.[38] The basis of the rights is zero and the basis of the old stock remains unchanged. However, even though the basis of the rights is zero, the holding period of the rights includes the holding period of the old stock.[39] If a taxpayer wishes, he or she may elect to allocate basis to the rights even though there is no requirement to allocate basis to the rights under this 15-percent rule.[40] This election to allocate is made by filing a statement with the taxpayer's tax return for the year in which the rights are received. The election applies to all the stock rights received in the distribution and is irrevocable

[37] § 1223(5).

[38] § 307(b)(1).

[39] § 1223(5).

[40] § 307(b)(2) and Reg. § 1.307-2.

### Example 16

Assume the same facts as in *Example 14* except that the fair market values of the stock and rights on January 3 were \$19 and \$1, respectively. Since the value of the rights (\$100) is less than 15% of the value of the stock (15% of \$1,900 = \$285), no allocation is required. C would have a \$700 gain on the sale of the stock rights since their basis was zero. The gain would be long-term since the holding period of the rights includes the holding period of the stock.

### Example 17

Assume the same facts as in *Example 16* except that C elects to allocate basis between the stock and the stock rights. The basis of the rights is computed as follows:

$$\frac{\text{Fair market value of stock rights}}{\text{Fair market value of stock and stock rights}} \times \text{Old basis}$$

$$= \frac{(100 \text{ rights} \times \$1)}{(100 \text{ rights} \times \$1) + (100 \text{ shares} \times \$19)} \times \underline{\underline{\$1,000}} \text{ Old basis}$$

$$\frac{\$100}{\$2,000} \times \$1,000 = \underline{\underline{\$50}} \text{ basis in stock rights}$$

In this situation, the sale of the rights for \$700 would result in a \$650 gain.

### Taxable Stock Rights

The taxable receipt of stock rights, like a taxable stock dividend, is treated as a property dividend by the shareholder. The shareholder would have dividend income equal to the lesser of the fair market value of the rights on date of receipt or the distributing corporation's earnings and profits.[41] The rights would have a basis equal to the fair market value[42] and the holding period starts on the date of distribution. If the rights lapse, the taxpayer will have a loss equal to the basis of the rights. Stock rights have the same effect on a corporation's earnings and profits as stock dividends. Additionally, the corporation does not recognize gain or loss from taxable distributions of its stock rights.

## Nondeductibility of Dividends to Corporation

A corporation is not permitted a deduction for distributions to its shareholders with respect to its stock. It does not matter whether the distribution is cash, property, stock, or stock rights. As mentioned in Chapter 19, this produces "double taxation." The shareholders are taxed individually on dividends (distributed corporate earnings and profits), but the distributing corporation may not take a corresponding deduction for the dividends.

# Stock Redemptions

**LO.5**
Define a redemption and distinguish it from other types of nonliquidating distributions.

Corporations occasionally will acquire their own shares. Sometimes the acquisition is motivated by a desire to eliminate an issue of stock. In these cases, the corporation might cancel the stock after its acquisition. Alternatively, the corporation might reacquire its own shares in order to issue the shares as additional compensation to hire or retain qualified employees or to acquire additional assets or even a whole business. The stock may be kept as treasury stock until needed. Such an acquisition is called a *stock redemption.* A redemption is defined in the Code as the

[41] Reg. § 1.305-1(b)(1): Code §§ 301(b) and 316(a).
[42] § 301(d).

acquisition by a corporation of its own stock from its shareholders in exchange for cash or other property, regardless of whether the shares are canceled, retired, or held as treasury stock.[43]

## In General

The taxation of the acquisition of the shares from an existing shareholder could take either of two forms. It could be treated as a sale of stock, with the corporation treated as an independent purchaser. This generally would result in a capital gain or loss for the shareholder. Alternatively, the sales price could be treated as a distribution. In this situation, the shareholder would have dividend income to the extent of the corporation's earnings and profits. Generally, the key factor as to whether a stock redemption is treated as a sale or a dividend distribution is whether or not the shareholder's proportionate interest in the corporation is significantly reduced.

As a general rule, if a shareholder's interest is basically the same or nearly the same after a redemption, the redemption is treated as a distribution. The tax treatment is based on whether the distribution is of cash or other property. The taxability of cash and property dividends was discussed previously in this chapter.

There are *five* situations in which stock redemptions are treated as a sale by the shareholder instead of as a dividend distribution. These five situations are as follows:

1. Redemptions not equivalent to dividends [§ 302(b)(1)]
2. Substantially disproportionate redemptions of stock [§ 302(b)(2)]
3. Terminations of shareholders' interests [§ 302(b)(3)]
4. Redemptions from noncorporate shareholders in partial liquidation [§ 302(b)(4)]
5. Distributions in redemption of stock to pay death taxes (§ 303)

In the above five situations, a shareholder recognizes gain or loss equal to the difference between the redemption proceeds and the basis of the stock surrendered.

## Redemptions Not Equivalent to Dividends

**LO.6**
Explain the tax consequences of a redemption to a shareholder and the distributing corporation.

The Code states that a stock redemption is treated as a sale or exchange of the shareholder's stock "if the redemption is not essentially equivalent to a dividend."[44] The Regulations refer to *dividend equivalency* as meaning that the redemption has "the same effect as a distribution without any redemption of stock."[45] Several cases have helped to further clarify this provision. The most significant litigation over this issue was *U.S. v. Davis,*[46] decided by the Supreme Court in 1970. The case involved the redemption of all of the corporation's outstanding preferred stock from the sole shareholder (directly and indirectly)[47] of the corporation. The Court ruled that the redemption was a distribution and not a sale. In reaching this decision, the Court rejected the taxpayer's argument that since there was a business purpose for the issuance and redemption of the preferred stock, the transaction was not equivalent to a dividend. Instead, the Court decided that to meet the requirement of § 302(b)(1), there must be a meaningful reduction in the shareholder's interest in the corporation. There are *no other* relevant considerations. One of the outgrowths of this decision is that no redemption from a sole shareholder will qualify as being "not equivalent to a dividend." A sole shareholder remains a 100 percent owner after *any* redemption. Therefore, there can never be a meaningful reduction in a sole shareholder's interest.

Following the decision in *Davis,* it was generally felt that the "not essentially equivalent to a dividend" exception was effectively canceled. Subsequent litigation has shown that this is not so. Taxpayers have been successful in those cases in which they were able to convince the court that there was a meaningful reduction in their interest in the corporation. Unfortunately, no precise definition of "meaningful reduction" has emerged from the litigation. Consequently, all subsequent taxpayers must prove the significance of the reduction based on the facts and circumstances of each specific case.

---

[43] § 317(b).

[44] § 302(b)(1).

[45] Reg. § 1.302-2(a).

[46] 70-1 USTC ¶9289. 25 AFTR 2d 70-827. 397 U.S. 301 (USSC. 1970).

[47] The provisions regarding constructive ownership of stock are discussed later in this chapter.

When a stock redemption is determined to be essentially equivalent to a dividend, the shareholder's basis in the stock redeemed is *added* to the basis of the stock that was not redeemed.[48]

## Example 18

R owned 1,000 shares (100%) of the common stock of T Corporation. (T Corporation had no other classes of stock outstanding.) R's basis in the stock was $20,000 ($20 per share). T Corporation redeemed 500 shares of R's common stock for $15,000. Since R owned 100% of T Corporation, both before and after the redemption, the redemption was essentially the same as a dividend. (There was no meaningful reduction in R's interest in the corporation.) R, therefore, has a distribution of $15,000, a taxable dividend if T Corporation has sufficient earnings and profits. R's basis of $10,000 ($20 per share) in the 500 shares redeemed is added to the basis in his remaining 500 shares. After the redemption. R's basis in his remaining 500 shares is $20,000 ($40 per share).

## SUBSTANTIALLY DISPROPORTIONATE REDEMPTIONS

A stock redemption is treated as a sale if it is *substantially disproportionate.*[49] In order for a redemption to be substantially disproportionate with respect to a shareholder, the shareholder must, after the redemption, own less than 80 percent of the voting stock owned prior to the redemption and own less than 80 percent of the common stock owned prior to the redemption.[50] By requiring the shareholder's ownership of both *voting* and *common stock* to be less than 80 percent of his or her former ownership, the law prevents redemption of solely preferred stock from meeting the § 302(b)(2) requirements. Redemptions of preferred stock may qualify only if there is also a redemption of common stock. In addition to the above requirements, a shareholder is not eligible for sale or exchange treatment unless the shareholder's ownership of voting stock after the redemption is less than 50 percent of the total voting stock.[51] Basically, satisfaction of these three mathematical tests provides a safe harbor for qualifying a redemption as not equivalent to a dividend (i.e., sale or exchange treatment).

## Example 19

M owned 100 shares of Q Corporation's voting common stock. M's basis in this stock was $500 ($5 per share). Q Corporation had 200 shares of common stock (its only class of stock) issued and outstanding. The corporation redeemed 40 shares of M's stock for $300. The tax treatment of the redemption is determined as follows:

***Test 1:*** Does M own less than 80% of the voting stock that she owned prior to the redemption?

Before the redemption M owned 50% of the voting stock. $\left(\frac{100}{200}\right)$

After the redemption M owned 37.5% of the outstanding voting stock. $\left(\frac{60}{160}\right)$

$$\frac{\text{M's percentage interest in the voting stock after the redemption}}{\text{M's percentage interested in the voting stock prior to the redemption}} = \frac{37.5\%}{50\%} = \underline{\underline{75\%}}$$

(**Alternative Computation:** 80% of 50% = 40%; therefore, Test 1 is met because 37.5% is less than 40%.)

***Test 2:*** Does M own less than 80% of the common stock that she owned prior to the redemption? Since the voting stock in this example is the same as the common stock, Test 2 is a repetition of Test 1. Therefore, Test 2 is also met.

---

[48] Reg. § 1.302-2(c).

[49] § 302(b)(2).

[50] § 302(b)(2)(C).

[51] § 302(b)(2)(B).

***Test 3:*** Is M's ownership of voting stock after the redemption less than 50% of the total voting stock? (This is measured in voting *power* if different classes of stock have unequal voting rights.)

$$\frac{\text{Number of shares of voting stock owned by M after the redemption}}{\text{Total number of shares of voting stock after the redemption}} = \frac{60}{160} = \underline{\underline{37.5\%}}$$

37.5% is less than 50% of the voting stock, so Test 3 is met.

(**Alternative Computation:** 160 shares × 50% = 80 shares; therefore, Test 3 is met since 60 shares is less than 80 shares.)

All three tests must be met in order for a stock redemption to be "substantially disproportionate." Since all three tests are met in this example, the redemption of 40 shares of M's stock meets the requirements of § 302(b)(2) and is, therefore, treated as a sale or exchange of the stock. M's gain is computed as follows:

| | |
|---|---|
| Proceeds from redemption | $300 |
| Less: M's basis in the 40 shares redeemed (40 × $5) | (200) |
| Gain from redemption | $100 |

The gain will be long-term or short-term depending on how long the stock was held.

*Note*: All computations regarding ownership after the redemption were made using 160 shares, the number of shares outstanding after 40 of the 200 originally outstanding shares had been redeemed by Q Corporation.

## Example 20

X owned 150 of the 200 outstanding shares of W Corporation's voting common stock. (W Corporation has no other classes of stock.) The corporation redeemed 100 shares of X's stock. The tax treatment of the redemption is determined as follows:

***Test 1:*** Does X own less than 80% of the voting stock that he owned prior to the redemption?

Before the redemption X owned 75% of the voting stock. $\left(\frac{150}{200}\right)$

After the redemption X owned 50% of the voting stock. $\left(\frac{50}{100}\right)$

$$\frac{50\%}{75\%} = \underline{\underline{67\%}}$$

67% is less than 80%, so Test 1 is met.

***Test 2:*** Does X own less than 80% of the common stock that he owned prior to the redemption? Since the voting stock in this example is the same as the common stock, Test 2 is a repetition of Test 1. Therefore, Test 2 is also met.

***Test 3:*** Is X's ownership of voting stock after the redemption less than 50% of the total voting stock?

$$\frac{50\%}{100\%} = \underline{\underline{50\%}}$$

Exactly 50% is not less than 50%. Therefore, Test 3 is not met.

Because *all three tests* must be met in order for a stock redemption to be "substantially disproportionate," the redemption is treated as a distribution, not a sale. Any proceeds from the redemption are treated as a dividend to the extent of earnings and profits, and X's basis in the 100 shares redeemed is added to the basis in his remaining 50 shares.

To prevent abuses in cases of multiple redemptions, the law requires that the tests be applied at the end of the series of redemptions if the redemptions are all part of one plan. Without this limitation, it would be possible to meet the substantially disproportionate rules after each redemption while leaving the redeeming shareholders' relative interests unaffected at the close of the intended transactions.[52]

**Example 21**

A, B, and C each owned 50 shares (1/3) of F Corporation's common stock. There are no other classes of stock. On January 2, pursuant to an overall plan, the corporation redeemed 40 shares of stock from A. On February 1, pursuant to the same plan, the corporation redeemed 40 shares from B. Finally, on March 3, the corporation redeemed 40 shares from C. Independently, each redemption is disproportionate. However, combining the series, A, B, and C each end up with the same 1/3 ownership of F Corporation. Consequently, the redemptions are not substantially disproportionate.

## Termination of a Shareholder's Interest

The third case in which a redemption can qualify as a sale is if the redemption completely terminates the shareholder's interest.[53] A *complete termination* requires the corporation to redeem all of the shares that the stockholder owns. If a shareholder is completely terminating his or her interest in a corporation in which various close relatives own stock, special rules apply to the termination of the shareholder's interest.[54] These special rules regarding constructive ownership of stock are discussed later in this chapter.

## Redemption from Noncorporate Shareholder in Partial Liquidation

The fourth case in which a redemption can qualify as a sale is a redemption from a noncorporate shareholder in partial liquidation.[55] A *partial liquidation* is a distribution that is not essentially equivalent to a dividend, determined at the corporate level rather than at the shareholder level.[56] To qualify, the distribution must be made in accordance with a plan of partial liquidation and made either in the year the plan is adopted or in the following year.

The Code specifically provides that a distribution in partial liquidation shall include (but not be limited to) distributions attributable to the termination of a business.[57] To satisfy this test, the distribution must be the result of the corporation ceasing to conduct a trade or business that had been in existence for at least five years prior to the distribution. The corporation, following the distribution, must be conducting a trade or business that also has been in existence for at least five years. Neither the continuing nor the terminated business may have been acquired during the five-year period in a transaction in which a gain or loss was recognized.[58] This provision was included to prevent the corporation from purchasing a business in order to convert a dividend into a partial liquidation.

There is no exact definition of a "trade or business." The Regulations state that a trade or business consists of a group of activities that includes every step in the process of earning income.[59] Owning investment assets or real estate used in a trade or business is not a trade or business by itself. The Regulations are helpful but do not eliminate all the questions as to what constitutes a trade or business.

## Redemptions of Stock to Pay Death Taxes

The fifth provision in the Code that classifies a redemption as a sale rather than as a distribution deals with the redemption of stock to pay death taxes.[60] This provision only applies

---

[52] § 302(b)(2)(D).

[53] § 302(b)(3).

[54] § 302(c)(2).

[55] § 302(b)(4).

[56] § 302(e)(1).

[57] § 302(e)(2).

[58] § 302(e)(3).

[59] Reg. § 1.355-1(c).

[60] § 303(a).

to stock included in a decedent's gross estate and was designed to provide a way to obtain cash needed for the administration of an estate. It permits the redemption of stock in an amount equal to the taxes imposed as a result of decedent's death and to the funeral and administration expenses deductible by the estate.[61] There is no restriction in the law that the redemption proceeds actually be used to pay taxes or expenses. The limitation refers simply to the maximum amount that can be redeemed under the provision. The tax treatment of any amount redeemed in excess of the amount of the above expenses is determined by applying the rules previously discussed regarding taxability of stock redemptions.

In order to be eligible to redeem stock using this provision, the value of the stock that the decedent owned in the redeeming corporation must exceed 35 percent of the value of the decedent's gross estate reduced by expenses and losses of the estate.[62] This condition effectively limits the use of this exception to estates of which the stock of the redeeming corporation is a substantial part. It is also possible to use this provision when two or more corporations comprise a substantial part of a decedent's estate. In this situation, if 20 percent or more of the value of the outstanding stock of each of two or more corporations is included in the decedent's gross estate, the corporations are treated as a single corporation for the purpose of determining the 35 percent requirement.[63]

## Constructive Ownership of Stock

As demonstrated above, one of the primary factors distinguishing a stock redemption qualifying for sale or exchange treatment from a dividend distribution is whether there has been a change in the taxpayer's proportionate interest in the corporation. Ownership in a corporation refers to both *actual* and *constructive* ownership.[64]

Under the rules of constructive ownership of stock, a taxpayer is considered to own not only those shares of stock he or she personally owns, but also to own those shares of stock owned by certain relatives and entities in which the taxpayer has an interest. The only family members considered relatives for these constructive ownership rules are the taxpayer's spouse, children, grandchildren, and parents.[65] Excluded from the list are siblings (i.e., brothers and sisters) and grandparents.

### Example 22

F, an individual, owns 60% of the stock of G Corporation. The remaining 40% is owned by S, F's son. F is considered to own 100% of G Corporation, 60% directly and 40% by the application of the constructive ownership rules.

### Example 23

H is married to W. They have one son, C, and a grandchild, G. H owns 100 shares of ABC Corporation. Either W or C can be considered to constructively own H's stock. G is not considered to be a constructive owner of H's stock, since an individual is not considered to constructively own his or her grandparent's stock.

Under the constructive ownership rules (also called the *attribution rules*), a person is deemed to own a proportionate share of the stock owned by a partnership, estate, or trust in which he or she has an interest.[66] Partnerships, estates, and trusts are also deemed to own the stock owned by persons who have an ownership interest in them.[67]

---

[61] Ibid.

[62] § 303(b)(2)(A).

[63] § 302(b)(2)(B).

[64] § 318.

[65] § 318(a)(1).

[66] §§ 318(a)(2)(A) and (B).

[67] §§ 318(a)(3)(A) and (B).

### Example 24

Y and Z are equal (50% each) partners in the YZ Partnership. The YZ Partnership owns 300 shares of A Corporation. Since Y and Z each own one-half of the partnership, they are each considered to constructively own one-half of the 300 shares of A Corporation owned by the YZ Partnership, or 150 shares each.

### Example 25

Assume the same facts as in *Example 24* except that the 300 shares of A Corporation stock are owned by Y instead of by the partnership. Since a partnership is considered to constructively own all of the stock of its partners, the YZ Partnership is deemed to own the entire 300 shares of A Corporation stock. Z does not constructively own any of the stock unless Y and Z are related family members.

In order for there to be attribution (constructive ownership) between a shareholder and a corporation, the shareholder must own, actually or constructively, at least 50 percent of the value of the corporation's stock.[68] Once this requirement is met, a shareholder is deemed to own a proportionate share of the stock owned by the corporation.

### Example 26

C Corporation is owned 60% by B and 40% by W. C Corporation owns 1,000 shares of Z Corporation stock. B constructively owns 600 (1,000 shares × 60%) shares of the Z Corporation stock. W does not constructively own any shares of Z Corporation stock since he does not own at least 50% of C Corporation.

A corporation is deemed to own all of the stock owned by shareholders who have a 50 percent or more interest in the corporation.[69]

There are rules against *double* attribution. Specifically, stock may not be attributed to a family member from a family member and then reattributed to another family member.[70] In addition, stock attributed to an entity from an owner may not then be attributed to another owner.[71] These rules prevent attribution between unrelated individuals.

### Example 27

P has two children, R and S. R owns 100 shares of H Corporation. Therefore, P constructively owns R's 100 shares of H Corporation. Without the rules against double attribution, the 100 shares could be reattributed from P to S, resulting in sibling attribution, which is not authorized by the definition of relatives.

## Complete Termination of Interest

The stock attribution rules could make it very difficult for a redemption by a family-owned corporation to qualify as a complete termination of interest under § 302(b)(3). Any constructively owned stock would prevent the shareholder from qualifying as having completely

[68] § 318(a)(2)(C).

[69] § 318(a)(3)(C).

[70] § 318(a)(5)(B).

[71] § 318(a)(5)(C).

terminated his or her interest. To eliminate this problem, the Code permits the redeeming shareholder to ignore the family attribution rules (but not attribution from other entities) in determining whether there has been a complete termination of the shareholder's interest.[72] To qualify for this provision, the shareholder must not have any interest in the corporation after the redemption other than that of a creditor. Specifically, the shareholder may not be an officer, director, or even an employee of the corporation. In addition, the shareholder must not acquire one of the prohibited interests in the corporation during the 10 years following the redemption. This provision makes it much easier for a shareholder to qualify a redemption as a complete termination of interest.

## Redemptions through Related Corporations

As stated earlier, a stock redemption is defined as the acquisition by a corporation of its own stock. The limitations on sale treatment discussed thus far could be avoided by an individual who controls two or more corporations. Instead of having a corporation redeem its stock, the shareholder could *sell* the stock of one controlled corporation to another controlled corporation. To prevent this type of transaction from avoiding the redemption limitations, Code § 304 reclassifies the "sale" of one controlled corporation's stock to another controlled corporation as a stock redemption.[73] Two different transactions are included in the reclassification provision. First, the sale of stock of a corporation controlled by one or more persons to another corporation controlled by the *same persons* is reclassified as a redemption.[74] Control is defined as ownership of either 50 percent or more of the combined voting power or 50 percent or more of the value of the outstanding stock.[75] The second reclassified transaction is the sale of stock of a parent corporation to its controlled subsidiary.[76]

### Example 28

A, B, and C, unrelated individuals, each own equal shares of T Corporation's outstanding stock. These same individuals own 100% of V Corporation's stock. If either A, B, or C sells shares of T Corporation to V Corporation, the transaction will be treated as a stock redemption.

### Example 29

Individual D owns all of the stock of P Corporation. P Corporation owns all of the stock of S Corporation. If D sells some of her P Corporation stock to S Corporation, the transaction will be treated as a stock redemption.

The fact that a transaction is reclassified as a stock redemption does not mean that the shareholder will be denied sale treatment. Instead, it requires that the selling shareholder meet one of the special rules relating to stock redemptions in § 302 (i.e., being not essentially equivalent to a dividend, substantially disproportionate, a complete termination of an interest, or a partial liquidation from a noncorporate shareholder) to qualify for sale treatment. In measuring the change in ownership under § 302, the stock of the issuing corporation—not the purchasing corporation—is used.[77] In addition, stock owned by attribution is counted.

---

[72] § 302(c)(2).

[73] § 304.

[74] § 304(a)(1).

[75] § 304(c)(1).

[76] § 304(a)(2).

[77] § 304(b)(1).

## Example 30

Individual G owns 80 of the 100 shares of X Corporation and 90 of the 100 shares of Y Corporation. G "sells" 10 shares of X Corporation stock to Y Corporation. Since G controls both corporations, the transaction is reclassified as a redemption. Before the transaction, G owns 80% of X Corporation. After the transaction, G owns 79% of X, computed as follows:

| | |
|---|---|
| Actual ownership (70 × 100 shares) . . . . . . . . . . | 70% |
| Constructive ownership: | |
| (90% ownership of Y corporation × Y Corporation's 10% ownership of × Corporation) . . . . . . . . | 9% |
| Total direct and indirect ownership. . . . . . . . . . | 79% |

Since G's ownership of X Corporation has only declined from 80% to 79%, the redemption does not meet any of the tests for sale treatment. Consequently, G must treat the "sale" proceeds as a dividend.

If the transaction is treated as a dividend rather than a sale, the amount of dividend income is measured by the earnings and profits of *both* the issuing corporation and the purchasing corporation.[78] This deemed dividend is considered as having been paid first from the E&P of the purchasing (acquiring) corporation to the extent thereof, and then from the E&P of the issuing corporation.

## Example 31

Assume the same facts as in *Example 30.* Since the transaction is treated as a dividend, it is considered to come from Y Corporation's E&P first and then, if necessary, from X Corporation's E&P.

## Effect of Redemptions on Redeeming Corporation

In a stock redemption, the stockholders are concerned with whether the redemption is treated for tax purposes as a sale or as a distribution. The redeeming corporation, however, is concerned with whether or not it has income on the redemption and what effect there is on earnings and profits.

### Gain or Loss

The tax effect of redemption distributions on the corporation is identical to that arising from property distributions discussed earlier. As previously explained, the corporation must recognize gain—but not loss—on the distribution of property.[79]

### Effect of Redemption on E&P

The E&P of a corporation must be adjusted to reflect any redemption distributions. First, if the corporation must recognize gain on the distribution under § 311, E&P must be increased for the gain. The amount of the reduction of E&P on account of the distribution depends on whether the distribution qualifies for sale treatment. If the distribution does not qualify for sale treatment but rather is treated as a dividend, the rules discussed earlier for cash and property dividends must be followed. If the redemption qualifies for sale treatment, only a portion of the distribution is charged against E&P. In such case, E&P is reduced by the

[78] § 304(b)(2).

[79] § 311.

redeemed stock's proportionate share of E&P but not by more than the amount of the redemption distribution.[80]

**Example 32**

B Corporation had the following capital accounts on January 2:

| | |
|---|---|
| Common stock | $100,000 |
| Paid-in capital in excess of par | 300,000 |
| Earnings and profits | 500,000 |

The common stock outstanding consisted of 1,000 shares of $100 par value stock. On January 2, B Corporation redeemed 100 shares for $700 per share (a total of $70,000). The corporation therefore redeemed 10% of its stock (100 ÷ 1,000). Of the $70,000 paid for the shares, B Corporation must charge $50,000 to its earnings and profits (10% × $500,000). The remaining $20,000 is charged to the capital accounts [$10,000 to common stock (10% × $100,000) and the remaining $10,000 to paid-in capital in excess of par].

*Note*: This example assumes that this redemption meets the requirements for sale or exchange treatment.

# Complete Liquidations

## Introduction

**LO.7**
Define a liquidation and determine its tax consequences to shareholders and the liquidating corporation.

As discussed earlier in the chapter, in a partial liquidation or stock redemption the corporation redeems only a portion of its stock. In these situations, the corporation continues to operate all or part of its business. In other situations, however, a corporation may wish to terminate its existence by liquidating completely. A complete liquidation of a corporation occurs when, under a plan of complete liquidation, the corporation redeems *all* of its stock using a series of distributions.[81] In addition, the corporation must be in a status of liquidation throughout the life of the liquidation. The Regulations state that a status of liquidation exists when a corporation ceases to be a going concern and is engaged in activities whose sole function is the winding up of the business affairs.[82] There is one set of rules that governs most liquidations and one special set of rules that governs liquidations of a subsidiary.

## Complete Liquidations: The General Rules

### Shareholder Gain or Loss

When a shareholder receives a liquidating distribution, the treatment of the shareholder—except where a parent liquidates a subsidiary—is governed solely by Code § 331. This rule provides that shareholders treat property received in liquidation of a corporation as full payment for their stock. Therefore, the shareholder must recognize gain or loss equal to the difference between the *net* fair market value of the property received (fair market value of the assets received less any liabilities assumed by the shareholder) and the basis of the stock surrendered. Special rules must be followed where a shareholder receives an installment note arising from a sale by the corporation within the 12-month period after the corporation has adopted a plan of liquidation.[83] If the stock was purchased at different times and for different amounts, the gain or loss is computed on each separate lot. The gain or loss normally is capital gain or loss since the shareholder's stock is usually a capital asset.

---

[80] § 312(n)(7).

[81] § 346(a).

[82] Reg. § 1.332-2(c).

[83] § 453(h).

### Basis to Shareholder

When a shareholder uses the general rule of § 331 to determine gain or loss on the liquidation, the shareholder's basis in the property received in the liquidation is its fair market value on the date of distribution.[84]

## Example 33

K owned 100 shares of stock in L Corporation. K's adjusted basis in the stock was $400. L Corporation completely liquidated and distributed to K $200 cash and office equipment worth $700 in exchange for his stock. K's recognized gain is computed as follows:

| | |
|---|---|
| Cash received by K | $200 |
| Fair market value of property distributed to K | 700 |
| Amount realized | $900 |
| Less: K's adjusted basis in his stock | (400) |
| Realized gain | $500 |

K's entire realized gain of $500 is recognized under § 1001(c). K's basis in the cash received is, of course, $200. K's basis in the office equipment received is $700, its fair market value on the date of distribution.

### Gain or Loss to the Liquidating Corporation

A corporation generally must recognize gain *and* loss on the distribution of property as part of a complete liquidation.[85] The gain or loss is computed as if such property were sold to the shareholder for its fair market value.

## Example 34

Sleepwaves Corporation, a waterbed retailer, fell on hard times and decided to dissolve the business. During the year, the corporation adopted a plan of liquidation and completely liquidated. The furniture that the corporation was unable to move in their going-out-of-business sale was distributed to its sole shareholder. This inventory was worth $5,000 (basis $1,000). In addition, the corporation distributed land held for investment worth $8,000 (basis $10,000). The corporation must recognize $4,000 of ordinary income ($5,000 – $1,000) on the distribution of the inventory and a $2,000 capital loss ($8,000 – $10,000) on the distribution of the land.

If the shareholder assumes a corporate liability or takes the property subject to a liability, the fair market value of the property is treated as being no less than the liability.[86] Therefore, where the liability exceeds the value of the property, gain must be recognized to the extent the liability exceeds the basis of the property.

## Example 35

T Corporation's only asset is a building with a basis of $100,000 and which is subject to a liability of $400,000. The low basis is attributable to accelerated depreciation. The property is currently worth $250,000. During 2011, T distributed the land to its sole

[84] § 334(a).

[85] § 336.

[86] § 336(b).

shareholder, R. T Corporation must recognize a gain of $300,000 ($400,000 liability – $100,000 basis). Had the liability been $200,000, T would have ignored the liability and recognized a gain of $150,000 ($250,000 value – $100,000 basis).

The treatment of distributions in liquidation differs from that of nonliquidating distributions in that the corporation is normally allowed to recognize loss on a liquidating distribution. This is not true for all liquidating distributions, however. As with nonliquidating distributions, Congress was concerned that taxpayers might use the loss recognition privilege to circumvent the gain recognition rule. To prohibit possible abuse, § 336(d) provides two exceptions concerning the treatment of losses.

The first exception prohibits the deduction of the loss if certain conditions are satisfied. Section 336(d)(1) provides that the liquidating corporation cannot recognize any loss on the distribution of property to a *related party* if the distribution is either (1) non-pro rata or (2) the property was acquired by the corporation during the five-year period prior to the distribution, either in a nontaxable transfer under § 351 (relating to transfers to a controlled corporation) or as a contribution to capital. For this purpose, a related party is the same as that defined in Code § 267 (e.g., an individual who owns either directly or constructively more than 50 percent of the distributing corporation).

### Example 36

J is the sole shareholder of Z Corporation. In anticipation of the corporation's liquidation, J contributed a dilapidated warehouse to the corporation, with a built-in loss of $100,000 (value $200,000, basis $300,000). Shortly thereafter, Z Corporation distributed the warehouse along with land worth $90,000 (basis $20,000). Absent the special rule, the corporation would recognize a loss of $100,000, which would offset the $70,000 gain on the land that it must recognize ($90,000 – $20,000). Under the exception, however, no loss is recognized since the distribution is to a related party, J, and the property was acquired as a contribution to capital within five years of the liquidation.

The second provision concerning losses limits the amount of loss that can be deducted—assuming the loss is not disallowed entirely under the related-party rule above. Under § 336(d)(2), the amount of loss recognized by a liquidating corporation on the sale, exchange, or distribution of any property acquired in a § 351 transaction or as a contribution of capital is reduced. This rule applies only if the principal purpose for the acquisition was the recognition of a loss by the corporation in connection with the liquidation. It is generally presumed that any property acquired in the above manner during the period starting two years prior to the date on which a plan of liquidation is adopted was acquired for the purpose of recognizing a loss. When the tax-avoidance motive is found, the rule effectively limits the loss deduction to the decline in value that occurs while the property is in the hands of the corporation. In other words, any built-in loss existing at the time of contribution is not deductible. To ensure that any built-in loss is not deducted, the Code provides a special computation. For purposes of determining the *loss* on the disposition of the tainted property, the basis of such property is reduced (but not below zero) by the amount of the built-in loss (i.e., the excess of the property's basis over its value at the time the corporation acquired it). By reducing the basis, any subsequent loss recognized is reduced.

### Example 37

R, S, T, and U own the stock of Q Corporation. Knowing that the corporation planned to liquidate, R contributed land to the corporation with a built-in loss of $100,000 (value $200,000, basis $300,000) in exchange for shares of Q stock that qualified for nonrecognition under § 351. During the liquidation, the corporation sold the property for $160,000. Under the general rule, the corporation would recognize a loss of $140,000 ($160,000 amount realized – $300,000 carryover basis). However, since the property was acquired in a § 351 exchange and the principal purpose of the transaction was to recognize loss on the property in liquidation, the special rule applies. The loss recognized is limited to that which occurred in the hands of the corporation $40,000 ($200,000 value at contribution – $160,000 amount realized). In other words, the loss computed in the normal manner, $140,000, must be reduced by the built-in loss of $100,000. Technically, Q Corporation would compute the loss by reducing its basis in the property by the amount of built-in loss as follows:

| | | | |
|---|---|---|---|
| Amount realized | | | $ 160,000 |
| Adjusted basis: | | | |
| Carryover basis | | $ 300,000 | |
| – Basis reduction: | | | |
| Carryover basis | $300,000 | | |
| –Value at contribution | –200,000 | | |
| Built-in loss | | –100,000 | |
| Adjusted basis | | | (200,000) |
| Loss recognized | | | ($ 40,000) |

## Liquidation of a Subsidiary

**LO.8**
Discuss the special rules that apply when a corporation liquidates a subsidiary.

A parent corporation generally recognizes no gain or loss on property it receives from the liquidation of a subsidiary corporation.[87] In order to qualify to use this provision (Code § 332), the parent corporation must own at least 80 percent of the voting power and this stock must have a value at least equal to 80 percent of the total value of the subsidiary corporation's stock.[88] For purposes of these computations, nonvoting preferred stock is excluded.[89] This minimum amount of stock must be owned on the date of adoption of the plan of liquidation and at all times thereafter until the liquidation is completed. All of the property of the subsidiary must be distributed in complete cancellation of the subsidiary's stock within three years following the close of the tax year in which the first distribution takes place.[90] It also is important to note that Code § 332 is not elective. If the above conditions are met, no gain or loss is recognized.

### Effect on Subsidiary

Under § 337, a subsidiary recognizes no gain or loss on the distribution of its assets to its parent in a liquidation under § 332.[91] This rule only applies to property transferred to the parent corporation in the liquidation. Property transferred to minority shareholders will result in the recognition of gain but not loss.[92]

Ordinarily, when one taxpayer is indebted to another and the debt is canceled, the indebted taxpayer has income to the extent of the debt due to the relief of the indebtedness. Section 337(b) contains an exception to this general rule. The exception states that when a subsidiary corporation is indebted to its parent corporation and the subsidiary liquidates under § 332, no gain or loss is recognized when the subsidiary transfers property to the parent to satisfy the debt.

### Basis of Assets—General Rule

When a subsidiary is liquidated by its parent corporation, the basis of the assets transferred from the subsidiary to the parent must be determined. Generally, the basis of each of the assets transferred is the same for the parent corporation as it had been for the subsidiary.[93] This rule applies not only to property transferred in cancellation of the subsidiary's stock, but also to property transferred in order to satisfy the subsidiary's debt to the parent.[94] The

[87] § 332.
[88] §§ 332(b)(1) and 1504(a)(2).
[89] § 1504(a)(4).
[90] § 332(b)(3).
[91] § 337(a).
[92] §§ 337(a) and 336(d)(3).
[93] § 334(b)(1).
[94] §§ 337(b)(1) and 334(b)(1).

amount of the parent's investment in the subsidiary's stock is ignored. The parent's basis is determined solely by the subsidiary's basis.

**Example 38**

T Corporation had assets with a basis of $1 million and no liabilities. P Corporation bought all of the stock of T Corporation for $1.2 million. Several years later, when T Corporation's assets had a basis of $800,000, P Corporation liquidated T Corporation in a tax-free liquidation under § 332. P Corporation's basis in the assets received from T Corporation is $800,000, the same basis as T Corporation had in the assets. The $400,000 difference between the basis of the assets and P Corporation's basis in the stock of T Corporation is lost.

**Example 39**

Assume the same facts as in *Example 38* except that P Corporation had paid $700,000 (instead of $1,200,000) for T Corporation's stock. P Corporation's basis in the assets received from T Corporation is still $800,000, the same as T Corporation's basis in the assets. In this example, rather than losing a $400,000 investment, P Corporation received a $100,000 tax-free increase in its basis in T Corporation and its assets ($800,000 basis in T Corporation's assets – $700,000 basis that P Corporation had in T Corporation's stock).

As demonstrated above, this carryover of the basis of assets from a subsidiary to its parent can be either beneficial *(Example 39)* or detrimental *(Example 38)* to the parent corporation.

## Basis of Assets—Exception

The carryover basis rule was challenged in the case of *Kimbell-Diamond Milling Co. v. Commissioner:*[95] In this case, Kimbell-Diamond's plant was destroyed by fire. The corporation wished to purchase replacement property to avoid recognizing gain on the involuntary conversion. The only plant that they wanted was owned by a corporation that would not sell. To acquire the asset, Kimbell-Diamond purchased the corporation's stock and then liquidated the corporation. Kimbell-Diamond used the basis of the assets of the liquidated corporation as its basis for the assets. The amount that Kimbell-Diamond paid for the stock of the corporation was *much less* than the liquidated corporation's basis in the assets, so that by using the carryover basis, Kimbell-Diamond received much larger depreciation deductions (and therefore had much smaller taxable income) than if it had actually purchased the plant. Upon review, however, the IRS reclassified the transaction as a purchase of assets, rather than a purchase of stock followed by a separate liquidation. The Tax Court agreed with the IRS that the two transactions should be treated as one. This decision created the *Kimbell-Diamond* exception. Under this exception, if the original purpose of the stock acquisition was to acquire assets, the purchaser's basis in the assets acquired was the cost of the stock rather than the liquidated corporation's basis.

Congress incorporated the Kimbell-Diamond exception into the Internal Revenue Code,[96] effectively allowing an acquiring corporation such as Kimbell-Diamond to select the basis to be used for the subsidiary's assets: either a basis equal to the purchase price of the assets or the same basis as that of the subsidiary. As might be expected, many acquiring corporations attempted to take advantage of this latitude provided by the Code. Consequently, to curb potential abuses, Congress enacted § 338 in 1982. Although § 338 is still a

[95] 14 T.C. 74 (1950), aff'd., 51-1 USTC ¶9301, 40 AFTR 328, 187 F2d 718 (CA-5, 1951).

[96] The Kimbell-Diamond exception was formerly § 334(b)(2).

codification of the *Kimbell-Diamond* exception, its requirements are much more specific than the previous law.

## Code § 338—Purchase of Assets

To qualify for a purchase price basis offered under § 338, the parent corporation must purchase stock having at least 80 percent of the voting power and at least 80 percent of the value of all stock (except nonvoting, nonparticipating, preferred stock).[97] To qualify as a purchase, the stock may not be acquired from a related party, in a transaction that qualifies under Code § 351, or in any transaction that will result in the purchaser using a carryover basis.[98] This acquisition of control may occur in a series of transactions; however, no more than 12 months may elapse between the first purchase and the acquisition of the required 80 percent control.[99]

If the parent corporation meets the purchase requirement, it must elect to treat the acquisition as an asset purchase by the 15th day of the ninth month following the month of acquisition.[100] The election, once made, is irrevocable. Failure to make the election results in the parent being treated as having purchased stock and thus prohibits the subsidiary from adjusting the basis of its assets. After the election, the subsidiary generally increases or decreases the basis of its assets to their fair market value.

Code § 338 does not require a liquidation. As a result, both the parent and the subsidiary may continue to exist. Section 338 takes a *two-step* approach to achieve the basis step-up. First, the subsidiary is treated as having sold in a single transaction all of its assets at fair market value on the close of the acquisition date. Any gain or loss realized on this hypothetical sale must be recognized *and* reported on the subsidiary's final tax return. Second, the subsidiary is treated as a new corporation that is deemed to have purchased all of the assets of the old subsidiary (i.e., the acquired or target corporation) on the day after the date the parent obtained the necessary control. For purposes of determining the subsidiary's new basis in its assets, the deemed purchase price is generally equal to the price the parent corporation paid for the subsidiary's stock adjusted for ownership less than 100 percent (i.e., the portion not owned by the parent) as well as liabilities of the subsidiary and other relevant items.[101] Note that in increasing the purchase price of the stock for liabilities of the subsidiary, such liabilities include the tax liability attributable to income arising from the deemed sale.

### Example 40

During 2011, P Corporation purchased all of the stock of T Corporation for $1 million. T's only asset is land with a basis of $200,000. It had no liabilities. Assuming P makes the appropriate election under § 338, T is deemed to have sold its assets, in this case the land, for its fair market value, $1 million. Thus, T must recognize a gain of $800,000 ($1,000,000 − $200,000). The tax liability arising from the deemed sale is $272,000 ($800,000 × 34%). After the hypothetical sale and repurchase, P's basis in the land is $1,272,000, its purchase price of the stock ($1 million) increased by the liability arising on the deemed sale of $272,000. Note that P, as the new owner of T, bears the economic burden of the tax liability. Consequently, assuming the value of the land is truly $1 million, P would no doubt desire to reduce the purchase price of the stock by the liability that arises with a § 338 election; that is, it probably would try to buy the stock for $728,000 ($1,000,000 − $272,000). If P did buy the stock for $728,000, presumably the gain on the deemed sale would still be $800,000, since the land is considered sold for its value of $1 million. In such case, the tax liability would still be $272,000 and the basis of the land under § 338 would be $1 million ($728,000 purchase price of the stock + $272,000 tax liability). Note that the effect of these rules is to reduce the value of the target subsidiary by an amount equal to the tax liability that would arise if § 338 is elected.

---

[97] § 338(d)(3).

[98] § 338(h)(3).

[99] § 338(d) and (h).

[100] § 338(g).

[101] § 338(a). § 338(b) provides that the basis is the sum of the grossed-up basis of stock purchased during the 12-month acquisition and the basis of stock not purchased during the period, adjusted as necessary.

Under § 338, the subsidiary is considered to have purchased all of its assets from itself at the deemed price. The subsidiary must increase or decrease the basis of its assets so that its new basis in its assets equals the deemed purchase price. The method of allocating the basis among the assets is outlined by the Regulations.[102]

## Allocation of Deemed Purchase Price

The temporary regulations under Code § 338 provide that the deemed purchase price of the stock is to be allocated to the subsidiary's assets using the "residual value" approach.[103] Under this technique, assets must be grouped into seven classes for purposes of making the allocation:

1. *Class I:* Cash, demand deposits, and other cash equivalents
2. *Class II:* Certificates of deposit, U.S. government securities, readily marketable securities, and other similar items
3. *Class III:* Accounts receivable
4. *Class IV:* Inventory
5. *Class V:* All assets other than those in Classes I, II, III, or IV, such as accounts receivable, inventory, plant, property, and equipment
6. *Class VI:* Section 197 intangibles other than goodwill or going concern value
7. *Class VII:* Intangible assets in the nature of goodwill and going-concern value

According to the system, the purchase price is first allocated to Class I assets in proportion to their relative fair market values as determined on the date following the acquisition. Because Class I assets are either cash or cash equivalents, the basis assigned to them is their face value. Once this allocation is made, any excess of the purchase price over the amount allocated to Class I assets is allocated to Class II assets, again based on relative fair market values. Any excess purchase price remaining after making the allocation to Class II assets is allocated to Class III assets based on relative values. Then amounts are allocated to Classes IV, V and VI in order. Any excess of purchase price over amounts allocated to Classes I, II, III, IV, V and VI is allocated to Class VII assets based on relative fair market values. In allocating such excess to Class II through Class VI assets, the amount allocated *cannot exceed the fair market value* of the asset. Thus, any purchase price which remains after the allocation to Class I, II, III, IV, V and VI assets is assigned to Class VII assets—hence the reason for calling this method the *residual* value approach. By limiting the allocation to Class I, II, III, and IV, V and VI assets to the assets' fair market values, the rules generally seek to ensure that corporate taxpayers allocate the proper amount to goodwill.

For the purpose of these allocation rules, the temporary regulations provide that the fair market value of the asset is its gross value computed without regard to any mortgages, liens, or other liabilities related to the property. These rules are illustrated in the following example.

### Example 41

P Corporation purchases from an unrelated person 100% of the stock of T Corporation on June 1, 2011. Assume the purchase price adjusted for all relevant items is $100,000. T's assets at acquisition date are as follows:

| | Basis | Fair Market Value |
|---|---|---|
| Cash | $10,000 | $10,000 |
| Accounts receivable | 20,000 | 20,000 |
| Inventory | 25,000 | 55,000 |
| Total | $55,000 | $85,000 |

The purchase price is first allocated to cash in the amount of $10,000. This leaves $90,000 to be allocated. Since there are no Class II assets, the allocation is to Class III.

[102] § 338(b)(3).

[103] Temp. Reg. § 1.338-6T.

Thus \$20,000 is allocated to the accounts receivable. If the residual approach was not required, the taxpayer might allocate all of the remaining \$70,000 to the inventory, despite the fact that its value is only \$55,000. If this were allowed, the subsequent sale of the inventory would result in a loss. However, since the remaining purchase price (\$70,000) exceeds the fair market value of the Class IV assets, the basis of the assets in this class is their fair market value, \$55,000 for the inventory. This leaves \$15,000 of the purchase price which has not been allocated. It is all assigned to goodwill since there are no Class VII intangibles.

If the parent corporation owns less than 100 percent of the subsidiary, the deemed price must be "grossed up" to take into account the minority interest. The adjustment for a minority interest results in a deemed purchase price called the "grossed-up basis." This grossed-up basis is obtained by multiplying the actual purchase price of the stock by a ratio, the numerator being 100 percent and the denominator equal to the percentage of the subsidiary stock owned by the parent.[104] This computation can be expressed as follows:

$$\text{Grossed-up basis} = \begin{matrix}\text{Parent corporation's basis}\\ \text{in the subsidiary's stock}\\ \text{on the acquisition date}\end{matrix} \times \frac{100\%}{\begin{matrix}\text{Percentage of subsidiary's stock held}\\ \text{by parent on the acquisition date}\end{matrix}}$$

## Example 42

P Corporation purchased 90% of the outstanding stock of T Corporation for \$900,000. T Corporation had only one asset, land with a basis of \$900,000. Assume there are no liabilities or other relevant items that affect the deemed purchase price. Since P owns less than 100% of T, a grossed-up basis must be calculated. The result is \$1 million [\$900,000 purchase price × (100 ÷ 90, the percentage of T owned by P)]. If P elects § 338, T's basis for the land is \$1 million. Note, however, that it is likely that the Regulations require the deemed sales price to be increased by any liabilities of the subsidiary. In such case, the deemed purchase price here would include the tax liability resulting from the fact that P purchased less than 100% of the stock, which in turn causes T to recognize income.

Section 338 not only entitles the subsidiary to a stepped-up basis for its assets, it also treats the subsidiary as a new corporation in every respect. As a result, the subsidiary may adopt any tax year it chooses, unless it files a consolidated return with the parent corporation, in which case it must adopt the parent's tax year. It may adopt new accounting methods if it desires. MACRS depreciation may be used for all of the hypothetically purchased property—the antichurning rules being inapplicable since the old and new subsidiary are considered unrelated. The new subsidiary acquires none of the other attributes of the old subsidiary. The earnings and profits of the old subsidiary are eliminated and any net operating loss carryovers of the old subsidiary are unavailable to the new subsidiary.

In most situations, the target subsidiary has some assets that have appreciated in value (i.e., fair market value exceeds the asset's basis) and other assets where the value is less than the asset's basis. In such cases, the acquiring corporation, desiring the highest possible basis for the assets, might first purchase the appreciated property, then purchase the subsidiary's stock and liquidate the subsidiary under § 332. By so doing, the acquiring corporation would obtain the best of both worlds: a basis for the appreciated property equal to its fair market value and a carryover basis for the other assets. In the latter case, the basis is higher than it would have been had the assets themselves been purchased or the stock purchased followed by an election under § 338. To prohibit the acquiring corporation from effectively selecting the basis that is most desirable for each separate asset, the Code contains the so-called consistency provisions. According to these rules, an acquiring corporation is required to use a

[104] § 338(b)(2). This approach is modified when the parent holds stock not acquired during the 12-month period.

carryover basis for purchased assets unless a § 338 election is made for the acquired corporation. The consistency period begins one year before the date of the first acquisition that comes within § 338 and ends one year after the acquisition date (i.e., the date on which the corporation obtains 80 percent control).

**Example 43**

P Inc. purchased 60% of T Corporation's stock on March 7, 2011 and the remaining 40% on December 4, 2011. The consistency period runs from March 7, 2010 through December 4, 2012. If P acquires any assets of T during this period, it will be required to use carryover basis unless a § 338 election is made.

As mentioned above, § 338 is an elective provision. If the election is not made and the subsidiary is liquidated, § 332, the general rule for the nontaxable liquidation of a subsidiary, applies. If § 332 is used, the parent corporation carries over the subsidiary's basis for its assets, whereas under § 338 the basis of the assets is their deemed purchase price (based upon the parent corporation's investment in the subsidiary).

## Problem Materials

### DISCUSSION QUESTIONS

**20-1** *Dividends.* Define the term *dividend.*

**20-2** *Earnings and Profits.* What are "earnings and profits"? Are earnings and profits the same as "retained earnings"? Why or why not?

**20-3** *Earnings and Profits.* In addition to taxable income, what types of items affect earnings and profits?

**20-4** *Earnings and Profits.* How does the use of an accelerated method of depreciation affect a corporation's earnings and profits?

**20-5** *Earnings and Profits.* How does the § 179 immediate expensing option affect a corporation's earnings and profits?

**20-6** *Distributions.* Is it possible for a distribution to be a taxable dividend even if there is a deficit in accumulated earnings and profits? If so, how?

**20-7** *Cash Dividends.* What is the amount of distribution when cash is distributed?

**20-8** *Property Dividends.* What is the amount of the distribution when property other than cash is distributed?

**20-9** *Property Dividends and Liabilities.* What effect does a liability have on the amount and basis of property distributed if the property is subject to the liability?

**20-10** *Constructive Dividends.* What are constructive dividends? When do they arise?

**20-11** *Effect of Property Dividend on the Corporation.* In what situations must a corporation recognize income as a result of a distribution?

**20-12** *Effect of Property Dividends on Earnings and Profits.* How do property dividends affect earnings and profits?

**20-13** *Stock Dividends.* What is a stock dividend?

**20-14** *Stock Dividends.* In what situations may a stock dividend be taxable? When is it not taxable?

**20-15** *Stock Dividends.* How is the shareholder's basis in a stock dividend determined?

**20-16** *Stock Dividends.* How do stock dividends affect earnings and profits?

**20-17** *Stock Rights.* What are stock rights? How does their tax treatment differ from stock dividends?

**20-18** *Dividends.* What is the effect of a dividend on the distributing corporation's taxable income?

**20-19** *Stock Redemptions.* What is a stock redemption?

**20-20** *Stock Redemptions.* List the situations in which a stock redemption will be treated as a sale of stock.

**20-21** *Constructive Ownership.* What is constructive ownership of stock? How may stock be constructively owned?

**20-22** *Effect of Redemption on Redeeming Corporation.* How do stock redemptions affect the redeeming corporation? In what situations must gain or loss be recognized when stock is redeemed? How do stock redemptions affect earnings and profits?

**20-23** *Complete Liquidations.* What is a complete liquidation?

**20-24** *Code § 331.* Generally explain the treatment of the shareholders in a complete liquidation.

**20-25** *Code § 336.* Generally explain the treatment of the liquidating corporation in a complete liquidation.

**20-26** *Liquidation of a Subsidiary.* What conditions must be met in order for § 332 to apply to the liquidation of a subsidiary?

**20-27** *Liquidation of a Subsidiary—Basis.* What is the general rule for determining the parent corporation's basis in the assets received from its liquidated subsidiary?

**20-28** *Kimbell-Diamond Exception.* What is the *Kimbell-Diamond* exception?

**20-29** *Code § 338—Purchase of Assets.* When does § 338 apply to the liquidation of a subsidiary? How does it differ from the general rule for determining basis in the liquidation of a subsidiary?

## PROBLEMS

**20-30** *Dividends.* A's basis in his 50 shares of Q Corporation stock is $3,000. A purchased the Q Corporation stock in 2006. On November 11, 2011, Q Corporation distributed $8,000 to A with respect to the Q Corporation stock. The portion of Q Corporation's earnings and profits allocable to A is $3,500. What is the tax treatment of the $8,000 distribution to A?

**20-31** *Earnings and Profits.* D Corporation's taxable income for the year was computed as follows:

| | | |
|---|---|---|
| Gross income from operations | | $1,000,000 |
| Less: Operating expenses | | (900,000) |
| Net income from operations | | $ 100,000 |
| Dividend income | | 20,000 |
| Long-term capital gain | $15,000 | |
| Less: Capital loss carryover | (7,000) | 8,000 |
| Income before special deductions | | $ 128,000 |
| Net operating loss carryover | $ 9,000 | |
| Dividends-received deduction | 16,000 | |
| Total of special deductions | | (25,000) |
| Taxable income | | $ 103,000 |

Additional information:

1. The corporation received $5,000 in tax-exempt interest income.
2. Included in operating expenses is depreciation of $130,000. Straight-line depreciation of the depreciable assets would have been $50,000.

Compute the earnings and profits of D Corporation for the current year.

**20-32** *Earnings and Profits.* V Corporation's taxable income for the year included the following items:

1. A $12,000 charitable contributions deduction. Actual charitable contributions made by V Corporation were $20,000, but only $12,000 was deductible this year due to the 10 percent charitable contributions limitation.
2. An 80 percent dividends-received deduction of $8,000. The amount of dividend income received by V Corporation was $10,000.
3. Percentage depletion of $4,000 was deducted by V Corporation. Cost depletion would have been $800.
4. $2,000 of assets purchased by V Corporation this year were expensed using the § 179 immediate expensing option.
5. MACRS depreciation of $1,500 was taken on a new heavy-duty truck (five-year property) purchased this year. The cost of the automobile was $10,000.

Compute the effect of the above items on V Corporation's current earnings and profits.

**20-33** *Distributions.* For each of the following independent situations, compute the amount of dividend income to the shareholder as a result of the distribution(s), and specify the source of each distribution (current and/or accumulated earnings and profits).

***Distributions***

| | *April 1* | *October 1* | *Current E&P* | *Accumulated E&P* |
|---|---|---|---|---|
| a. | $5,000 | $5,000 | $15,000 | $10,000 |
| b. | 9,000 | 9,000 | 15,000 | 10,000 |
| c. | 2,000 | 4,000 | 7,000 | (20,000) |
| d. | 6,000 | 2,000 | 0 | 11,000 |
| e. | 3,000 | 5,000 | (12,000) | 30,000 |
| f. | 3,000 | 2,000 | 1,000 | 0 |
| g. | 1,000 | 3,000 | (6,000) | 8,000 |

**20-34** *Cash and Property Dividends.* A Corporation is owned by J (an individual) and B Corporation. A Corporation declared and paid the following dividends: $10,000 cash and a printing press with a fair market value of $10,000 and an adjusted basis of $6,000. A Corporation's current and accumulated earnings and profits exceed $20,000. Consider each alternative independently.

**a.** If B Corporation received the cash and J received the printing press, how much dividend income would each report?

**b.** If J received the cash and B Corporation received the printing press, how much dividend income would each report?

**c.** What are the tax consequences to A Corporation of the distribution?

**d.** What is the effect of the distribution on corporate earnings and profits?

**20-35** *Property Dividends—Installment Obligations.* G Corporation distributed installment notes with a face value of $20,000 to its shareholders. The gross profit percentage of the notes was 20 percent, and the fair market value of the notes was $18,000 when they were distributed. Compute G Corporation's recognized gain on the distribution of the installment notes.

**20-36** *Stock Dividends.* P owns 100 shares of Z Corporation common stock, which she purchased in 2003 for $50 a share. Z Corporation declared and paid a 100 percent stock dividend to all common stockholders. At the date of record, the selling price of a share of common stock was $200. Immediately following the distribution, the stock was selling for $225 per share.

**a.** How much income must P recognize on the receipt of the 100 shares of common stock as a dividend?

**b.** What is the basis of the dividend shares?

**c.** Assume that P received the dividend on June 1 and sold 50 shares of stock (25 new and 25 old) on July 1 for $150 per share. What is P's recognized gain or loss? Is it long-term or short-term?

**20-37** *Stock Dividends.* R owns 50 shares of A Corporation common stock, which he purchased in 2006 for $100 per share. On January 1 of the current year, A Corporation declared a dividend of one share of new preferred stock for each share of common. The shares were distributed on March 1. On that date, the common stock was selling for $150 per share and the preferred stock had a value of $50 per share.

- **a.** How much income must R recognize on the receipt of the preferred stock?
- **b.** What is R's basis in the preferred stock?
- **c.** On June 1, R sells 25 shares of common stock for $175 per share and 25 shares of preferred stock for $75 per share. What is R's recognized gain or loss? Is it long-term or short-term?

**20-38** *Stock Dividends.* N owns 200 shares of M Corporation preferred stock. She purchased the stock for $200 per share in 2008. On February 1 of the current year, the corporation declared and paid a 50 percent stock dividend. At date of declaration, the preferred stock was selling for $220 per share. Immediately following the distribution (June 1), the preferred stock was selling for $150 per share.

- **a.** How much income will N have as a result of the dividend?
- **b.** What is her basis of the dividend shares?
- **c.** If N sells 25 shares of the old and 25 shares of the new for $180 per share on August 1, what is her recognized gain or loss? Is it long-term or short-term?

**20-39** *Stock Rights.* Y Corporation's profits had taken a deep dive in recent years. To encourage purchase of its stock, the corporation issued one stock right for each share of outstanding common stock. The rights allow the holder to purchase a share of stock for $1. The common stock was selling for $1.50 when the rights were issued (June 1). The value of the stock rights on June 1 were $0.50 each. A owns 1,000 shares of common stock for which he paid $20 per share 10 years ago, and therefore received 1,000 stock rights. A sold 100 rights on July 1 for $175. He exercised 100 rights on August 1 when the stock was selling for $1.80 per share. The remaining rights lapsed on December 30.

- **a.** How much dividend income must A recognize?
- **b.** How much gain or loss must A recognize on the July 1 sale of the stock rights? Is it long-term or short-term?
- **c.** What is A's recognized loss when the remaining rights lapse?
- **d.** What is the basis of the original 1,000 shares on December 31?

**20-40** *Stock Redemptions.* B owned 100 shares (100%) of the common stock of C Corporation. C Corporation has no other classes of stock outstanding. B's basis in his 100 shares was $3,000 ($30 per share). C Corporation redeemed 20 of B's shares for $1,000.

- **a.** What is B's recognized gain or loss on the redemption? What is the character of B's recognized gain or loss?
- **b.** What is B's basis in his remaining shares of C Corporation stock?

**20-41** *Stock Redemptions.* W has owned 500 shares of X Corporation's 1,000 outstanding shares of voting common stock since 1998. X Corporation has no other classes of stock outstanding. W's basis in her 500 shares was $1,500 ($3 per share). X Corporation redeemed 200 shares of W's stock for $800.

- **a.** Is this redemption treated as a sale or a distribution?
- **b.** What is W's recognized gain or loss on the redemption? What is the character of W's recognized gain or loss?
- **c.** What is the basis of W's remaining shares after the redemption?

**20-42** *Stock Redemptions.* Assume the same facts as in *Problem 20-41* except that X Corporation redeemed 100 shares of W's stock instead of 200 shares. Answer the above questions a, b, and c for this situation.

**20-43** *Stock Redemptions.* T Corporation is owned by the following unrelated individuals:

| | |
|---|---|
| K | 60 shares |
| L | 20 shares |
| M | 10 shares |
| N | 10 shares |
| Total | 100 shares |

If T Corporation redeems 30 shares owned by K, will the transaction qualify as a sale? Why or why not?

**20-44** *Stock Redemptions—Constructive Ownership.* Use the same facts as in *Problem 20-43*. Would this redemption qualify as a sale if L is K's son? Why or why not?

**20-45** *Constructive Ownership of Stock.* Q, an individual, owns 20 percent of A Corporation. Mrs. Q owns 60 percent of A Corporation and 50 percent of BC Partnership. R, Q's daughter, owns 30 percent of BC Partnership and 10 percent of A Corporation. What is Q's ownership (directly and indirectly) in A Corporation and BC Partnership, if the constructive ownership rules of § 318 apply?

**20-46** *Constructive Ownership of Stock.* D is a 30 percent partner in DE Partnership. DE Partnership owns 10 percent of F Corporation. Using the § 318 constructive ownership rules, what percentage of F Corporation is D considered to own?

**20-47** *Constructive Ownership of Stock.* G owns 200 shares of H Corporation stock. G is a 50 percent partner in GJ Partnership. Using the § 318 constructive ownership rules, how many shares of H Corporation is the GJ Partnership considered to own?

**20-48** *Liquidations—General Rule (§§ 331 and 336).* S, an individual, owns all of the stock of B Corporation. S purchased the stock 10 years ago for $300,000. S decided to completely liquidate B Corporation, and all of the assets of B Corporation were distributed to S. The balance sheet for B Corporation immediately prior to the liquidation was as follows:

| | | Basis | Fair Market Value |
|---|---|---|---|
| Cash | | $ 40,000 | $ 40,000 |
| Marketable securities | | 40,000 | 80,000 |
| Equipment | $300,000 | | |
| Less: Accumulated depreciation | (150,000) | 150,000 | 200,000 |
| Land | | 520,000 | 880,000 |
| Total assets | | $750,000 | $1,200,000 |
| Retained earnings | | $450,000 | $ 0 |
| Common stock | | 300,000 | 1,200,000 |
| Total equity | | $750,000 | $1,200,000 |

**a.** What is S's recognized gain or loss?
**b.** What is S's basis in the assets received?
**c.** How much, if any, income or loss will B Corporation recognize as a result of the liquidation?

**20-49** *Liquidations (§ 332).* Assume the same facts as in *Problem 20-48* except that the stock is owned by S, Inc.

**a.** How much, if any, gain or loss must S, Inc. recognize?
**b.** What is the basis of the assets received by S, Inc.?
**c.** How much, if any, income must B Corporation recognize as a result of the liquidation?

**20-50** *Section 338 Election.* Assume the same facts as in *Problem 20-48* except that all the stock was purchased by Z Corporation during the past 12 months for $1 million. Assume Z makes a § 338 election and pays taxes at a 34 percent rate.

**a.** What is Z's recognized gain or loss?
**b.** What, if any, income must B recognize?
**c.** What is the total basis of the assets to B after the election?

# 21 Taxation of Corporate Accumulations

## Learning Objectives

Upon completion of this chapter you will be able to:

LO.1 Understand the rationale for the two corporate penalty taxes: the accumulated earnings tax and the personal holding company tax.

LO.2 Identify the circumstances that must exist before the accumulated earnings tax will apply.

LO.3 Recognize when earnings have accumulated beyond the reasonable needs of the business.

LO.4 Explain how the accumulated earnings tax is computed.

LO.5 Indicate when the personal holding company tax applies.

LO.6 Apply the stock ownership and income tests to determine if a corporation is a personal holding company.

LO.7 Explain how the personal holding company tax is computed and how it might be avoided.

## Chapter Outline


Introduction 21-2
Accumulated Earnings Tax 21-3
- An Overview 21-3
- Intent 21-4
- Reasonable Needs of the Business 21-5
- Computation of the Accumulated Earnings Tax 21-10
- Accumulated Earnings Credit 21-12
- Dividends-Paid Deduction 21-14

Personal Holding Company Tax 21-15
- Personal Holding Company Defined 21-16
- PHC Ownership Test 21-17
- Income Test 21-17
- Adjusted Ordinary Gross Income 21-18
- Personal Holding Company Income (PHCI) 21-20
- Computation of the PHC Tax 21-25

Tax Planning 21-28
- Accumulated Earnings Tax 21-28
- Personal Holding Company Tax 21-29

Problem Materials 21-34

## Introduction

**LO.1**
Understand the rationale for the two corporate penalty taxes: the accumulated earnings tax and the personal holding company tax.

In addition to the regular tax, a corporation may be subject to two penalty taxes—the *accumulated earnings tax* and the *personal holding company tax*. As the label "penalty" suggests, the primary goal of these taxes is not to raise revenues but rather to prohibit certain activities. The objective of the accumulated earnings tax and the personal holding company tax is to discourage individual taxpayers from using the corporate entity solely for tax avoidance. These taxes contend with potential abuse by imposing limitations on the amount of earnings a corporation may retain without penalty. The rationale for these taxes is readily apparent when some of the opportunities for tax avoidance using the corporate structure are considered.

Perhaps the best illustration of how the corporate entity could be used to avoid taxes involves the 70 percent dividends-received deduction. As discussed in Chapter 1, this deduction is available only to corporate taxpayers. Nevertheless, individuals could take advantage of the deduction by establishing a corporation and transferring their dividend-paying stocks to it. By so doing, all dividend income would be taxable to the corporation instead of the individual. Using this arrangement, the corporation would pay tax on dividends at an effective rate of 10.5 percent or lower [35% × (100% − 70%)] in 2010. Most individual taxpayers with taxable dividend income would reap substantial tax savings from this arrangement since all individual marginal rates are 10 percent or higher. This is but one of the alluring features of the corporate entity.

Another corporate advantage that individuals previously used to avoid taxes concerned the difference between individual and corporate tax rates. Until the current year, because the highest individual tax rate exceeded the top corporate tax rate, individuals operating a business in the corporate form could benefit by leaving earnings in the corporation and reinvesting at this lower tax rate. The savings obtained by utilizing this disparity, the dividends-received deduction, and other advantages of the corporate entity, illustrate that individuals could achieve wholesale tax avoidance if not for some provision denying or discouraging such plans.

The two penalty taxes were developed to battle avoidance schemes such as those above by attacking their critical component: the accumulation. This can be seen by examining the two previous examples. The fate of both tax savings schemes rests on whether the shareholder can reduce or totally escape the second tax normally incurred when the income is ultimately received. In other words, the success of these arrangements depends on the extent to which double taxation is avoided. Herein lies the role of corporate accumulations. As long as the earnings are retained in the corporation, the second tax is avoided and the taxpayer is well on the way to obtaining tax savings. To foil such schemes, Congress enacted the accumulated earnings tax and the personal holding company tax. Both taxes are imposed on unwarranted accumulations of income—income that normally would have been taxable to the individual at individual tax rates if it had been distributed. By imposing these taxes on unreasonable accumulations, Congress hoped to compel distributions from the corporation and thus prevent taxpayers from using the corporate entity for tax avoidance.

Although these penalty taxes are rarely incurred, each serves as a strong deterrent against possible taxpayer abuse. However, with the reduction in the tax rate on dividends to 15 percent, imposition of these penalties or change in corporate behavior is even less likely. This chapter examines the operation of both the accumulated earnings tax and the personal holding company tax.

Mitigation of the double tax penalty and any resulting tax savings are not achieved solely through corporate accumulations. The effect of double taxation can be reduced or avoided in other ways. The most common method used to avoid double taxation is by making distributions that are deductible. Typical deductible payments include compensation for services rendered to the corporation, rent for property leased to the corporation by the shareholder, and interest on funds loaned to the corporation. All of these payments are normally deductible by the corporation (thus effectively eliminating the corporate tax) and taxable to the shareholder. Avoidance of the double tax penalty does not ensure tax savings, however. All of these payments are taxable to the shareholder; thus, savings through use of the corporate entity may or may not result. For example, savings could occur if the payments are made to shareholders after they have dropped to a tax bracket lower than the one in which they were when the earnings were initially realized by the corporation. In addition, even if the shareholder's tax bracket remains unchanged, deferral of the tax could be beneficial.

### Example 1

L operates a home improvement company, specializing in kitchen renovations. He is in the 35% bracket in 2011. Assume that he incorporates his business in 2011 and it earns \$100,000, of which \$50,000 is paid to him as a salary and \$50,000 is accumulated. In 2011 L saves \$10,000 [(35% – 15%) × \$50,000] in taxes on the \$50,000 not distributed. However, if the \$50,000 accumulated is distributed to L as a salary in 2016 when he is still in the 35% bracket, the \$10,000 of taxes originally saved is lost. Although no taxes have been saved, L continues to benefit because he has been able to postpone the \$10,000 in tax for five years. Assuming his after-tax rate of return is 10%, the present value of the \$10,000 tax is reduced to \$6,209—a savings of \$3,791, or almost 38%. Note that the savings would have increased if the distribution had been made to L when his tax bracket dropped below 35%.

# Accumulated Earnings Tax

The accumulated earnings tax, unlike most taxes previously discussed, is not computed by a corporation when filing its annual income tax return. There is no form to file to determine the tax. Normally, the issue arises during an audit of the corporation. Consequently, the actual tax computation is made only after it has been determined that the penalty must be imposed.

## An Overview

**LO.2**
Identify the circumstances that must exist before the accumulated earnings tax will apply.

The accumulated earnings tax applies whenever a corporation is "formed or availed of" for what is generally referred to as the *forbidden purpose*, that is, "for the purpose of avoiding the income tax with respect to its shareholders ... by permitting earnings and profits to accumulate instead of being ... distributed."[1] Whether a corporation is in fact being used for the forbidden purpose and thus subject to penalty is an elusive question requiring a determination of the taxpayer's *intent*. Without guidance from the law, ascertaining the taxpayer's intent might prove impossible. However, the Code states that the required intent is deemed present whenever a corporation accumulates earnings beyond its reasonable needs unless the corporation can prove to the contrary by a preponderance of evidence.[2] The problems concerning intent are considered in detail below.

Not all corporations risk the accumulated earnings tax. The Code specifically exempts tax-exempt corporations, personal holding companies, and passive foreign investment companies.[3] In addition, the tax normally does not apply to an S corporation since it does not shield shareholders from tax. An S corporation's earnings are taxed to its shareholders annually.

If it applies, the accumulated earnings tax is imposed on the annual increment to the corporation's total accumulated earnings, not on the total accumulated earnings balance. This annual addition is referred to as *accumulated taxable income*. The tax is 15 percent of the corporation's accumulated taxable income.[4] This tax does not replace any other taxes (e.g., the corporate income tax or the alternative minimum tax) but is imposed in addition to these taxes.

### Example 2

In an audit of P Corporation, it was determined that the company had accumulated earnings beyond the reasonable needs of its business. In addition, the corporation's accumulated taxable income was \$150,000. Since evidence of the forbidden purpose is present and the corporation has accumulated taxable income, the accumulated earnings tax must be paid. P Corporation's accumulated earnings tax is \$22,500 (\$150,000 × 15%).

[1] § 532(a).
[2] § 533(a).
[3] § 532.
[4] § 531.

In short, the corporation actually pays the accumulated earnings tax only if the forbidden purpose is found and it has accumulated taxable income. The following sections examine the determination of the taxpayer's intent and the computation of accumulated taxable income.

## INTENT

The accumulated earnings tax is imposed only if the corporation is formed or used for the purpose of avoiding income tax on its shareholders by accumulating earnings.[5] Unfortunately, the Code provides no objective, mechanical test for determining whether a corporation is in fact being used for the forbidden purpose. As a result, application of the accumulated earnings tax rests on a subjective assessment of the shareholders' intent. The Code and regulations offer certain guidelines for making this assessment. Section 533 provides that a corporation is deemed to have been formed or used for the purpose of avoiding tax on its shareholders in two situations:

1. If the corporation has accumulated earnings beyond the reasonable needs of the business; or
2. If the corporation is a mere holding or investment company.

The first situation is the most common cause of an accumulated earnings tax penalty. Consequently, avoidance of the accumulated earnings tax normally rests on whether the corporation can prove that its balance (i.e., the amount in excess of the $250,000 or $150,000 threshold) in accumulated earnings and profits is required by the reasonable needs of the business. Before discussing what constitutes a "reasonable need" of the business, it should be noted that other circumstances may indicate that the forbidden purpose does or does not exist.

According to the Regulations, the following factors are to be considered in determining whether the corporation has been used to avoid tax:[6]

1. Loans to shareholders or expenditures that benefit shareholders personally;
2. Investments in assets having no reasonable connection with the corporation's business; and
3. Poor dividend history.

Although these factors are not conclusive evidence, their presence no doubt suggests improper accumulations.

In determining whether the requisite intent exists, the courts have considered not only the criteria mentioned above but also whether the corporation's stock is widely held. As a general rule, the accumulated earnings tax does not apply to publicly held corporations. Publicly held corporations normally are protected since the number and variety of their shareholders usually preclude the formation of a dividend policy to minimize shareholder taxes. Nevertheless, the tax has been applied to publicly held corporations in which management was dominated by a small group of shareholders who were able to control dividend policy for their benefit.[7] Moreover, in 1984, Congress eliminated any doubts as to whether publicly held corporations are automatically exempt from the penalty tax. Section 532(c) currently provides that the tax be applied without regard to the number of shareholders of the corporation. Thus, the tax may be imposed on a publicly held corporation if the situation warrants.

While publicly held corporations usually are immune from the penalty tax, closely held corporations are particularly vulnerable since dividend policy is easily manipulated to meet shareholders' desires. Indeed, it may be a formidable task to prove that the corporation was not used for tax avoidance in light of the *Donruss* decision.[8] In that case, the Supreme Court held that the tax avoidance motive need not be the primary or dominant motive for the accumulation of earnings before the penalty tax is imposed. Rather, if tax avoidance is but one of the motives, the tax may apply.

---

[5] § 532(a).

[6] § 1.533-1(a)(2).

[7] See *Trico Products*, 42-2 USTC ¶9540, 31 AFTR 394, 137 F.2d 424 (CA-2, 1943). In *Golconda Mining Corp.*, 58 T.C. 139 (1972), the Tax Court held that the tax applied where management controlled 17 percent of the outstanding stock of a publicly held corporation but the Ninth Circuit reversed, suggesting the tax should be applied solely to closely held corporations, 74-2 USTC ¶9845. 35 AFTR2d 75-336, 507 F.2d 594 (CA-9, 1974). Tax applied to publicly held corporation in *Alphatype Corporation v. U.S.*76-2 USTC ¶9730, 38 AFTR2d 76-6019 (Ct. Cls., 1976). In Rev. Rul. 73-305, 1975-2 C.B. 228 the IRS confirmed its position that it will apply the tax to publicly held corporations.

[8] *U.S. v. Donruss*, 69-1 USTC ¶9167, 23 AFTR2d 69-418, 393 U.S. 297 (USSC, 1969).

As a practical matter, it is difficult, if not impossible, to determine the actual intent of the corporation and its shareholders. For this reason, the presumption created by § 533(a) looms large in virtually all accumulated earnings tax cases. Under this provision, a tax avoidance purpose is deemed to exist if earnings were accumulated beyond the reasonable needs of the business.[9] As might be expected, most of the litigation in this area has concerned what constitutes a reasonable need of the business. In fact, many cases do not even mention intent, implying that the accumulated earnings tax will be applied in all cases in which the accumulation exceeds business needs. Except in the unusual case in which a corporation's intent can be demonstrated, a corporation should be prepared to justify the accumulations based on the needs of the business.

## Reasonable Needs of the Business

The Code does not define the term "reasonable needs of the business." Instead it states that the reasonable needs of the business include the *reasonably anticipated needs* of the business.[10] The Regulations clarify the term reasonably anticipated needs.[11] First, the corporation must have specific, definite, and feasible plans for the use of the accumulation. The funds do not have to be expended in a short period of time after the close of the year. In fact, the plans need only require that the accumulations be expended within a *reasonable* time in the future. However, if the plans are postponed indefinitely, the needs will not be considered reasonable. As a general rule, the plans must not be vague and uncertain. If the plans are based on specific studies containing dollar estimates and are approved by the board of directors, the corporation is in a better position to prove that the plans qualify as reasonable business needs.

**LO.3**
Recognize when earnings have accumulated beyond the reasonable needs of the business.

In addition to reasonably anticipated needs, the Code and Regulations identify certain specific reasons for accumulations that are considered to be reasonable needs of the business.[12] Several of these reasons are discussed below.

### Stock Redemptions from an Estate

A corporation is allowed to temporarily accumulate earnings in order to redeem the stock of a deceased shareholder in conjunction with Code § 303(discussed in Chapter 20).[13] The accumulations may commence *only after* the death of a shareholder. The fact that a shareholder dies after accumulations have been made and the corporation redeems his or her stock under § 303 is ignored in evaluating pre-death accumulations.[14] If the shareholder owned stock in two or more corporations, each corporation is entitled to accumulate only a portion of the total redeemable amount unless the estate's executor or administrator has indicated that more shares of one of the corporations will be offered for redemption than will those of another corporation.[15] The requirements of § 303 (relating to redemption of stock to pay death taxes) must be met in order for this provision to apply.

### Product Liability Loss Reserves

The Code also allows accumulations to cover product liability losses.[16] Product liability is defined as damages for physical or emotional harm as well as damages and loss to property as a result of the use of a product sold, leased, or manufactured by the taxpayer.[17] The amount accumulated can cover both actual and reasonably anticipated losses.

### Business Expansion or Plant Replacement

Perhaps the most common reason for accumulating earnings that the Regulations specifically authorize is for *bona fide* expansion of business or replacement of plant.[18] This provision includes the purchase or construction of a building.[19] It also includes the modernization,

[9] § 533(a).

[10] § 537(a)(1).

[11] Reg. § 1.537-1(b).

[12] See § 537(a) and (b), and Reg. § 1.537-2.

[13] § 537(b)(1).

[14] § 537(b)(5).

[15] Reg. § 1.537-1(c)(3).

[16] § 537(b)(4).

[17] § 172(f).

[18] Reg. § 1.537-2(b)(1).

[19] *Sorgel v. U.S.*, 72-1 USTC ¶9427, 29 AFTR2d 72-1035, 341 F. Supp. 1 (D. Ct. Wisc., 1972).

rehabilitation, or replacement of assets.[20] However, this provision does not shield a corporation which has not adequately specified and documented its expansion needs.[21]

### Acquisition of a Business Enterprise

A second reason offered in the Regulations for accumulating earnings is for the acquisition of a business enterprise through the purchase of stock or assets.[22] This provision appears to encourage business expansion, since the Regulations state that the business for which earnings can be accumulated includes any line of business the corporation wishes to undertake, and not just the line of business previously carried on.[23] However, this provision for accumulation is limited by the statement in the Regulations that investments in properties or securities that are *unrelated* to the activities of the business of the corporation are unacceptable reasons for accumulations.[24] The statements in the Regulations raise a question as to the validity of accumulations for diversification. On one hand the corporation can acquire an enterprise or expand its business into any field. On the other hand the acquisition should be related to the corporation's activities. This apparent conflict in the Regulations is reflected in court decisions. A corporation that manufactured automobile clutches was permitted to accumulate income to acquire a business that would make use of the corporation's metal-working expertise, whereas a corporation in the printing business was not permitted to accumulate income to acquire real estate.[25] The extent to which a corporation can diversify is uncertain. It appears that diversification into passive investments is unacceptable whereas diversification into an operating business, no matter how far removed from the original line of business, is acceptable.

### Retirement of Indebtedness

The Regulations also provide for the accumulation of earnings to retire business indebtedness.[26] The debt can be to either a third party or a shareholder as long as it is a bona fide business debt.

### Investments or Loans to Suppliers or Customers

The Regulations state that earnings may be accumulated to provide for investments or loans to suppliers or customers.[27] However, loans to shareholders, friends and relatives of shareholders, and corporations controlled by shareholders of the corporation making the loan indicate that earnings are possibly being accumulated beyond reasonable business needs.[28]

### Contingencies

Although the Regulations do not specifically allow accumulations for contingencies, they do imply approval of such accumulations as long as the contingencies are not unrealistic.[29] Unfortunately, the distinction between realistic and unrealistic contingencies is difficult to define. However, the more specific the need, the more detailed the cash estimate, and the more likely the occurrence, the easier it will be to prove the accumulation is reasonable.

### Redemption of Stock

As noted above, accumulations to redeem stock from a decedent's estate under § 303 constitute a reasonable need of the business. This provision does not cover any other stock redemption. Several cases have held that a redemption may be a reasonable need provided the redemption is for the benefit of the corporation and not the shareholder.[30] For example, the redemption of a dissenting minority shareholder's stock can be for the corporation's benefit

---

[20] *Knoxville Iron*, 18 TCM 251, T.C. Memo 1959-54.

[21] *I.A. Dress Co.*, 60-1 USTC ¶9204, 5 AFTR2d 429, 273 F.2d 543 (CA-2, 1960), aff&g. 32 T.C. 93; *Herzog Miniature Lamp Works, Inc.*, 73-2 USTC ¶9593, 32 AFTR2d 73-5282, 273 F.2d 543, (CA-2, 1973).

[22] Reg. § 1.537-2(b)(2).

[23] Reg. § 1.537-3(a).

[24] Reg. § 1.537-2(c)(4).

[25] *Alma Piston Co.*, 22 TCM 948, T.C. Memo 1963-195; *Union Offset*, 79-2 USTC ¶9550, 44 AFTR2d 79-5652. 603 F.2d 90 (CA-9, 1979).

[26] Reg. § 1.537-2(b)(3).

[27] Reg. § 1.537-2(b)(5).

[28] Reg. §§ 1.537-2(c)(1), (2), and (3).

[29] Reg. § 1.537-2(c)(5).

[30] See *John B. Lambert & Assoc. v. U.S.*, 38 AFTR2d 6207 (Ct. Cls., 1976); *C.E. Hooper, Inc. v. U.S.*, 38 AFTR2d 5417, 539 F.2d 1276 (Ct. Cls.,1976); *Mountain State Steel Foundries, Inc. v. Comm.*, 6 AFTR2d 5910, 284 F.2d 737 (CA-4, 1960); and *Koma, Inc. v. Comm.*, 40 AFTR 712, 189 F.2d 390 (CA-10, 1951).

whereas the redemption of a majority shareholder's stock would be for the shareholder's benefit. It might also be possible to prove that the redemption was necessary to reduce or eliminate disputes over management or conduct of the business.

## Working Capital

Another reason mentioned in the Regulations for a reasonable accumulation of earnings and profits is the need for working capital.[31] This is one of the primary justifications corporations use for the accumulation of earnings. A corporation is permitted to retain earnings to provide necessary working capital. Initially, the courts tried to measure working capital sufficiency by using rules of thumb. A current ratio of 2.5 to 1 generally meant that the corporation had not accumulated income unreasonably.[32] The courts considered a current ratio more than 2.5 to 1 an indication of unreasonable accumulation.

In the 1965 case of *Bardahl Mfg. Corp.*, the Tax Court utilized a formula to compute the working capital needs of a corporation.[33] Under this approach (called the *Bardahl* formula), the working capital needed for one operating cycle is computed. This amount in essence represents the cash *needed* to meet expenses incurred during the operating cycle—the period required for a business to convert cash into inventory, sell the merchandise, convert the customer's accounts receivable into cash, and pay its accounts payable. This necessary working capital is then compared to actual working capital. If necessary working capital is greater than actual working capital, an accumulation of earnings to meet the necessary working capital requirements is justified. If actual working capital is greater than the working capital needed, the corporation must show other reasons for the accumulation of earnings in order to avoid the accumulated earnings tax.

The initial step of the *Bardahl* formula is to calculate the inventory, accounts receivable, and accounts payable cycle ratios. These ratios are computed as follows:

1. *Inventory cycle ratio* $= \dfrac{\text{Average inventory}}{\text{Cost of goods sold}}$
2. *Accounts receivable cycle ratio* $= \dfrac{\text{Average accounts receivable}}{\text{Net sales}}$
3. *Accounts payable cycle ratio* $= \dfrac{\text{Average accounts payable}}{\text{Purchases}}$

The ratios resulting from these calculations represent the cycle expressed as a percentage of the year. In other words, if the accounts receivable cycle ratio is 10 percent, then it normally takes about 36 days (10% × 365) to collect a receivable once it has been generated by a sale.

Instead of using the *average* inventory and the average receivables, a corporation can use *peak values* if it is in a seasonal business. If the corporation uses peak values for the other ratios, it may be required to use peak payables.

Once computed, the three ratios are combined. The result represents the number of days—expressed as a fraction of the year—during which the corporation needs working capital to meet its operating expenses. The operating cycle ratio is computed as follows:

$$\begin{array}{r} \text{Inventory cycle ratio} \\ +\text{Accounts receivable cycle ratio} \\ -\text{Accounts payable cycle ratio} \\ \hline =\text{Operating cycle ratio} \end{array}$$

The operating cycle ratio is multiplied by the *annual operating expenses* to compute the necessary working capital. Operating expenses are defined as the cost of goods sold plus other annual expenses (i.e., general, administrative, and selling expenses). The operating expense category does not include depreciation since depreciation does not require the use of cash. However, the category can include income taxes if the corporation pays estimated taxes and

[31] Reg. § 1.537-2(b)(4).

[32] *J Scripps Newspaper*, 44 T.C. 453 (1965).

[33] *Bardahl Mfg. Corp.*, 24 TCM 1030, T.C. Memo 1965-200.

will make a tax payment during the next operating cycle.[34] Other expenses should be included if they will require the expenditure of cash during the next operating cycle.

The required working capital computed by the *Bardahl* formula is compared to actual working capital to determine if there have been excess accumulations. Since the computed working capital is based on accounting data, it is normally compared to actual working capital (current assets − current liabilities) computed from the corporation's financial statements. There are exceptions to this rule. Financial statements are not used if they do not clearly reflect the company's working capital. The Supreme Court authorized the use of fair market value instead of historical cost to value a firm's current assets in *Ivan Allen Co.*[35] The assets in question were marketable securities that had appreciated. The decision is broad enough to permit the Internal Revenue Service to determine actual working capital based on current value any time there is a significant difference between cost and market.

Any corporation whose actual working capital does not exceed required working capital (per the *Bardahl* formula) should be exempt from the accumulated earnings tax. If the actual working capital exceeds required working capital, the excess is considered an indication of unreasonable accumulations. This excess is compared to the reasonable needs of the business (other than working capital) to determine if the accumulations are unreasonable. To the extent that the corporation has needs, it may accumulate funds. If all of the excess working capital is not needed, the tax is imposed. The tax is based on the accumulated taxable income and not the excess working capital.

## Example 3

K owns and operates K's Apparel, Inc. (KAI). After hearing that a friend's corporation was recently slapped with an accumulated earnings tax penalty, she asked her accountant to determine the vulnerability of her own business. The following is a balance sheet and income statement for 2010 and 2011 for KAI.

**Balance Sheet**

| | *2010* | *2011* |
|---|---|---|
| Current Assets: | | |
| Cash | $ 55,000 | $ 67,000 |
| Marketable securities | 10,000 | 8,000 |
| Accounts receivable (net) | 45,000 | 55,000 |
| Inventory | 30,000 | 20,000 |
| Total Current Assets | $ 140,000 | $ 150,000 |
| Property, plant, and equipment (net) | 300,000 | 425,000 |
| Total Assets | $ 440,000 | $ 575,000 |
| Current Liabilities: | | |
| Notes payable | $ 5,000 | $ 4,000 |
| Accounts payable | 50,000 | 30,000 |
| Accrued expenses | 8,000 | 16,000 |
| Total Current Liabilities | $ 63,000 | $ 50,000 |
| Long-term debt | 37,000 | 40,000 |
| Total Liabilities | $ 100,000 | $ 90,000 |
| Stockholders' Equity: | | |
| Common stock | 10,000 | 10,000 |
| Earnings and profits | 330,000 | 475,000 |
| Total Liabilities and Stockholders' Equity | $ 440,000 | $ 575,000 |

[34] *Empire Steel*, 33 TCM 155, T.C. Memo 1974-34.

[35] *Ivan Allen Co. v. U.S.*, 75-2 USTC ¶9557, 36 AFTR2d 75-5200, 422 U.S. 617 (USSC, 1975).

**Income Statement**

| | | |
|---|---|---|
| Sales | $ 400,000 | $ 500,000 |
| Cost of goods sold: | | |
| Beginning inventory | $ 40,000 | $ 30,000 |
| Purchases | 300,000 | 320,000 |
| Ending inventory | (30,000) | (20,000) |
| Total | $ 310,000 | $ 330,000 |
| Gross profit | $ 90,000 | $ 170,000 |
| Other expenses: | | |
| Depreciation | $ 40,000 | $ 55,000 |
| Selling expenses | 10,000 | 15,000 |
| Administrative | 20,000 | 50,000 |
| Total | $ 70,000 | $ 120,000 |
| Net income before taxes | $ 20,000 | $ 50,000 |
| Income tax expense | (2,000) | (5,000) |
| Net income | $ 18,000 | $ 45,000 |

In addition to this information, K indicated that at the end of 2011 the securities were worth $15,000 more than their book value, or $23,000. K also estimates that her reasonable needs for the current year 2011 amount to $20,000.

Under the *Bardahl* formula, her working capital needs are determined as follows:

***Step 1:*** Operating cycle expressed as a fraction of the year (in thousands):

| | | | | | | | | |
|---|---|---|---|---|---|---|---|---|
| | Inventory cycle | = | Average inventory / Cost of goods sold | = | [(30 + 20) ÷ 2] | ÷ 330 | = | 0.0758 |
| + | Receivable cycle | = | Average receivables / Sales | = | [(45 + 55) ÷ 2] | ÷ 500 | = | 0.1000 |
| − | Payables cycle | = | Average payables / Purchases | = | [(50 + 30) ÷ 2] | ÷ 320 | = | (0.1250) |
| = | Operating cycle expressed as percentage of the year | | | | | | = | 0.0508 |

***Step 2:*** Computation of operating expenses:

| | |
|---|---|
| Operating expenses: | |
| Cost of goods sold | $330,000 |
| Selling expenses | 15,000 |
| Administrative expenses | 50,000 |
| Taxes | 5,000 |
| Total operating expenses | $400,000 |

***Step 3:*** Working capital needs:

| | | |
|---|---|---|
| | Operating expenses (Step 2) | $400,000 |
| × | Operating cycle (Step 1) | × 0.0508 |
| = | Working capital needs | $ 20,320 |

K's working capital needs, $20,320, must be compared to actual working capital using the assets' fair market value. Any excess of actual working capital over required working capital must be compared to the current year's needs to determine if unwarranted accumulations exist. Assuming the marketable securities are actually worth $23,000, the comparison is made as follows:

| | | | |
|---|---|---|---|
| | Actual working capital: | | |
| | Current assets ($150,000 + $15,000) | $165,000 | |
| − | Current liabilities | (50,000) | |
| = | Actual working capital | | $115,000 |
| − | Required working capital (Step 3) | | (20,320) |
| = | Excess working capital | | $ 94,680 |
| − | Reasonable needs | | (20,000) |
| = | Accumulations beyond current needs | | $ 74,680 |

The accumulated earnings tax focuses on whether the corporation has accumulated liquid assets beyond its reasonable needs that could be distributed to shareholders. In this case, actual working capital exceeds required working capital and other needs of the business by $74,680, implying that the accumulated earnings tax applies. If so, the actual penalty tax is computed using accumulated taxable income, as explained below.

## Computation of the Accumulated Earnings Tax

**LO.4**
Explain how the accumulated earnings tax is computed.

The purpose of the accumulated earnings tax is to penalize taxpayers with unwarranted accumulations. To accomplish this, a 15 percent tax is imposed on what the Code refers to as accumulated taxable income. Accumulated taxable income is designed to represent the amount that the corporation could have distributed after funding its reasonable needs. In essence, the computation attempts to determine the corporation's dividend-paying capacity. Exhibit 21-1 shows the formula for computing accumulated taxable income.[36]

**EXHIBIT 21.1 Accumulated Taxable Income[37]**

*Taxable income:*

*Plus:*

1. The dividends-received deduction
2. Any net operating loss deduction that is reflected in taxable income
3. Any capital-loss carryovers from other years that are reflected in taxable income

*Minus:*

1. Federal income taxes for the year, but not the accumulated earnings tax or the personal holding company tax
2. The charitable contributions for the year in excess of the 10 percent limitation
3. Any net capital loss incurred during the year reduced by net capital gain deductions of prior years that have not previously reduced any net capital loss deduction
4. Any net capital gain (net long-term capital gain − the net short-term capital loss) for the year minus the taxes attributable to the gain and any net capital losses of prior years that have not reduced a net capital gain deduction in determining the accumulated earnings tax

Equals: ***Adjusted taxable income***

*Minus:*

1. Accumulated earnings credit (see Exhibit 21-2)
2. Dividends-paid deduction (see Exhibit 21-3)

Equals: ***Accumulated taxable income***

---

[36] § 535.

[37] § 535. Several additional adjustments are required for computing accumulated taxable income of a holding or investment company.

The computation of accumulated taxable income begins with an imperfect measure of the corporation's ability to pay dividends-taxable income. To obtain a more representative measure of the corporation's dividend-paying capacity, taxable income is modified to arrive at what is often referred to as *adjusted taxable income*.[38] For example, the deduction allowed for dividends received is added back to taxable income since it has no effect on the corporation's ability to pay dividends. The same rationale can be given for the net operating loss deduction. In contrast, charitable contributions in excess of the 10 percent limitation may be deducted in determining adjusted taxable income since the corporation does not have the nondeductible amount available to pay dividends. For the same reason, Federal income taxes may be deducted in computing adjusted taxable income.

The deduction for capital gains stems from the assumption that these earnings are used to fund the corporation's needs and consequently may be accumulated with impunity. Capital losses are deductible since these amounts are unavailable for payment of dividends and are not reflected in taxable income. As shown in Exhibit 21-1, however, the deductions for capital gains as well as capital losses must be modified.

Prior to 1984, corporations were entitled to reduce taxable income not only by the amount of their net capital gains (reduced by related taxes) but also by the full amount of their net capital losses, depending on whether a net capital gain or loss occurred. Consequently, there was an advantage in recognizing capital gains in one year and capital losses in another year in order to avoid netting and thus permit both gains and losses to be deductible in full. For example, if the corporation had a capital loss of $1,000 this year and a capital gain of $5,000 next year (ignoring taxes), both could be deducted in full each year in computing adjusted taxable income. However, if they occurred in the same year, the deduction would be limited to $4,000. To eliminate this planning opportunity, corporations are now required to reduce their net capital losses by any net capital gain deductions that have been used to arrive at adjusted taxable income in prior years. Under these rules, it is immaterial in what order or in what year gains and losses are recognized. In effect, taxable income is reduced only by the overall net gain or loss that the corporation has recognized to date.

## Example 4

T Corporation has the following income and deductions for 2011:

| | |
|---|---|
| Income from operations | $ 150,000 |
| Dividend income (from less than 20% owned corporations) | 40,000 |
| Charitable contributions | 25,000 |

T Corporation computes its taxable income as follows:

| | | |
|---|---|---|
| Income from operations | | $ 150,000 |
| Dividend income | | 40,000 |
| Income before special deductions | | $ 190,000 |
| Special deductions: | | |
| Charitable contribution (limited) | $ 19,000 | |
| Dividend-received deduction | 28,000 | |
| Total special deductions | | (47,000) |
| Taxable income | | $ 143,000 |

[38] This term is not found in the Code; it is used here solely for purposes of exposition.

T Corporation's Federal income taxes for 2011 are $39,020. T Corporation's adjusted taxable income is computed as follows:

| | | |
|---|---|---|
| Taxable income | | $143,000 |
| Plus: Dividend-received deduction | | 28,000 |
| | | $171,000 |
| Minus the sum of | | |
| Federal income taxes | $39,020 | |
| Actual charitable contributions for the year minus the charitable contribution deduction reflected in taxable income ($25,000 − $19,000) | 6,000 | (45,020) |
| Equals: Adjusted taxable income | | $125,980 |

Two additional deductions are permitted in computing accumulated taxable income: the accumulated earnings credit and the dividends-paid deduction. The deduction allowed for dividends is consistent with the theory that the tax should be imposed only on income that has not been distributed. The accumulated earnings credit allows the taxpayer to accumulate without penalty $250,000 or an amount equal to the reasonable needs of the business, whichever is greater.

## Accumulated Earnings Credit

In creating the accumulated earnings tax, Congress realized that a corporation should not be penalized for keeping enough of its earnings to meet legitimate business needs. For this reason, in computing accumulated taxable income, a corporation is allowed—in effect—a reduction for the amount out of current year's earnings necessary to meet such needs. This reduction is the *accumulated earnings credit.*[39] Note that despite its name, the credit actually operates as a deduction. As a practical matter, it is this credit that insulates most corporations from the accumulated earnings tax.

Specifically, the credit is the greater of two amounts as described in Exhibit 21-2 and discussed further below. Generally, however, the credit for the current year may be determined as follows:

| | |
|---|---|
| Reasonable business needs (or $250,000 if larger) | $xxx,xxx |
| Less: Beginning Accumulated E&P | (xx,xxx) |
| Accumulated earnings credit | $xxx,xxx |

**EXHIBIT 21.2** **Accumulated Earnings Credit**[40]

The accumulated earnings credit is the greater of

1. *General Rule:* Earnings and profits for the taxable year that are retained to meet the reasonable needs of the business, minus the net capital gain for the year (reduced by the taxes attributable to the gain), or
2. *Minimum Credit:* $250,000 ($150,000 for personal service corporations) minus the accumulated earnings and profits of the corporation at the close of the *preceding* taxable year, adjusted for dividends paid in the current year *deemed* paid in the prior year.

Part 1 of Exhibit 21-2 contains the general rule authorizing accumulations. It permits corporations to accumulate earnings to the extent of their reasonable needs without penalty.[41] In determining the amount of the earnings and profits for the taxable year that have been retained to meet the reasonable needs of the business, it is necessary to consider to what extent the accumulated earnings and profits are available to cover these needs.[42] In effect,

[39] § 535(c).

[40] § 535(c)(1).

[41] *Ibid.*

[42] Reg. § 1.535-3(b)(1)(ii).

prior accumulations reduce the amount that can be retained in the current year. If the corporation's accumulated earnings and profits are sufficient to meet the reasonable needs of the business, *none* of the current earnings and profits will be considered to be retained to meet the reasonable needs of the business.

Part 2 of Exhibit 21-2 is the so-called *minimum credit*.[43] For most corporations the amount of the minimum credit is $250,000. For personal service corporations, the minimum credit is $150,000. Personal service corporations are corporations that provide services in the area of health, law, engineering, architecture, accounting, actuarial science, performing arts, or consulting. The lower credit for personal service corporations reflects the fact that their capital needs are relatively small when compared to retail or manufacturing businesses.

To determine the amount of the minimum credit available for the current year, the base amount, $250,000 ($150,000), must be reduced by the accumulated earnings and profits at the close of the preceding tax year. For purposes of this computation, the accumulated earnings and profits at the close of the preceding year are reduced by the dividends that were paid by the corporation within 2½ months after the close of the preceding year.[44]

## Example 5

X Corporation, a calendar year retail department store, had current earnings and profits for 2011 of $75,000. Its accumulated earnings and profits at the close of 2010 were $200,000. X Corporation has paid no dividends for five years. X Corporation's taxable income for 2011 included a net capital gain of $20,000. [The taxes related to this net capital gain were $6,800 (34% × $20,000).] The reasonable needs of X Corporation are estimated to be $240,000. The amount of X Corporation's current earnings and profits that are retained to meet reasonable business needs is computed as follows:

| | |
|---|---|
| Estimated reasonable needs of X Corporation | $ 240,000 |
| Less: Accumulated earnings and profits as of 12/31/10 | (200,000) |
| Extent to which current earnings and profits are needed to cover the reasonable needs of the business | $ 40,000 |

Even though the current earnings and profits are $75,000, only $40,000 of the current earnings and profits are needed to meet the reasonable needs of the business.

The accumulated earnings credit is the greater of

| | | |
|---|---|---|
| 1. Current earnings and profits to meet the reasonable needs of the business | | $ 40,000 |
| Minus: Net capital gain | $20,000 | |
| Reduced by the taxes attributable to the gain | (6,800) | (13,200) |
| General rule credit | | $ 26,800 |
| or | | |
| 2. $250,000 | | $ 250,000 |
| Minus: Accumulated earnings and profits as of 12/31/10 | | (200,000) |
| Minimum credit | | $ 50,000 |

X Corporation's accumulated earnings credit is $50,000, the greater of the general rule credit ($26,800) or the minimum credit ($50,000).

[43] § 535(c)(2).

[44] § 535(c)(4).

## Example 6

Assume the same facts as in *Example 5*, except that X Corporation is an engineering firm. The general rule credit would still be \$26,800, but the minimum credit would be computed as follows:

| | |
|---|---|
| \$150,000 | \$ 150,000 |
| Minus: Accumulated earnings and profits as of 12/31/10 | (200,000) |
| Minimum credit (the minimum credit cannot be a negative number) | \$ 0 |

In this situation the accumulated earnings credit is \$26,800, the greater of the general rule credit (\$26,800) or the minimum credit (\$0).

Two aspects of the accumulated earnings credit deserve special mention. First, the minimum credit has a very limited role. Since the \$250,000 (or \$150,000 for service corporations) is reduced by the prior accumulations, the minimum credit will always be zero for firms that have greater than \$250,000 of accumulated earnings. In other words, accumulations in excess of \$250,000 must be justified by business needs.

The second aspect involves capital gains. As discussed previously, capital gains (net of related taxes) are subtracted from taxable income in arriving at adjusted taxable income. Therefore, a corporation can accumulate all of its capital gains without the imposition of the accumulated earnings tax. At the same time, however, capital gains are subtracted from business needs in arriving at the general credit (see Exhibit 21-2). As a result, a capital gain may cause accumulations of ordinary income to be subject to the special tax even though the capital gain itself escapes penalty. In effect, the computations are based on the assumption that business needs are funded first from capital gains and then from income from operations.

## Dividends-Paid Deduction

Exhibit 21-1 indicated that both the accumulated earnings credit and the dividends-paid deduction are adjustments in computing accumulated taxable income. Exhibit 21-3 lists the types of dividends that constitute the dividends-paid deduction.

**EXHIBIT 21.3** **Dividends-Paid Deduction**[45]

1. Dividends paid during the taxable year,[46]
2. Dividends paid within 2½ months after the close of the taxable year,[47]
3. Consent dividends,plus[48]
4. Liquidating distributions,[49]

   Equals: **Dividends-Paid Deduction**

To qualify for the dividend deduction, the distribution must constitute a "dividend" as defined in § 316.[50] As previously discussed, § 316 limits dividends to distributions out of current earnings and profits and accumulated earnings and profits since 1913. Property distributions qualify only to the extent of their adjusted basis.[51]

---

[45] §§ 561 through 565.

[46] § 561(a)(1).

[47] § 563(a).

[48] § 565.

[49] § 562(b)(1).

[50] § 562(a).

[51] Reg. § 1.562-1(a).

### Throwback Dividends

The dividends-paid deduction includes not only dividends paid during the year, but also so-called *throwback dividends*, dividends paid during the 2½ months following the close of the tax year.[52] Amounts paid during the 2½-month period *must* be treated as if paid in the previous year.[53] This treatment is mandatory and not elective by the shareholders or the corporation.

### Consent Dividends

In addition to actual dividends paid, the corporation is entitled to a deduction for consent dividends.[54] Sometimes a corporation may have a large amount of accumulated earnings, but insufficient cash or property to make a dividend distribution. In order to avoid the accumulated earnings tax, the corporation may obtain a dividends-paid deduction by using consent dividends—so called because the shareholders consent to treat a certain amount as a taxable dividend on their tax returns even though there is no distribution of cash or property. Not only are the shareholders deemed to receive the amount to which they consent, but they also are treated as having reinvested the amount received as a contribution to the corporation's capital.

To qualify a dividend as a consent dividend, the shareholders must file a consent form (Form 972) with the corporate income tax return. The consents must be filed by the due date (including extensions) of the corporate tax return for the year in which the dividend deduction is requested. Only shareholders who own stock on the last day of the tax year need file consent forms. On the forms, each shareholder must specify the amount of the consent dividend and then include this amount as a cash distribution by the corporation on his or her individual income tax return. Consent dividends are limited to the amount that would have qualified as a dividend under Code § 316 had the dividend been distributed in cash.[55] Only shareholders of common and participating preferred stock may consent to dividends.[56]

### Liquidating Distributions

If the distribution is in liquidation, partial liquidation, or redemption of stock, the portion of the distribution chargeable to earnings and profits is included in the dividend deduction.[57] For partial liquidations and redemptions, this is the redeemed stock's proportionate share of accumulated E&P. For complete liquidations, any amount distributed within the two years following the adoption of a plan of liquidation and that is pursuant to the plan is included in the dividends-paid deduction, but not to exceed the corporation's current earnings and profits for the year of distribution.[58]

## Personal Holding Company Tax

As mentioned earlier in this chapter, the accumulated earnings tax is not the only penalty tax applicable to corporations. Congress has also enacted the personal holding company tax. This tax evolved in 1934 from the need to stop the growing number of individuals who were misusing the corporate entity despite the existence of the accumulated earnings tax. The personal holding company tax was designed to thwart three particular schemes prevalent during that period.

The first two schemes specifically aimed to take advantage of the disparity between individual and corporate tax rates. At that time, the maximum individual tax rates were approximately 45 percentage points higher than the maximum corporate rates. A typical plan used to take advantage of this differential involved the formation of a corporation to hold an individual's investment portfolio. This plan allowed an individual's interest and dividends to become taxable to the corporation rather than to the individual and consequently to be taxed at the lower corporate rates. Another, somewhat more sophisticated, technique enabled the transfer of an individual's service income to a corporation. The blueprint for this plan

[52] § 563.

[53] § Reg.1.563-1.

[54] § 565.

[55] Reg. § 1.565-2(a).

[56] § 565(f).

[57] § 562(b)(1).

[58] § 562(b)(1)(B).

required the formation of a corporation by an individual (e.g., movie star) who subsequently became an employee of the corporation. With the corporation in place, parties seeking the individual's services were forced to contract with the corporation rather than with the individual. The individual would then perform the services, but the corporation would receive the revenue. Finally, the corporation would pay the individual a salary that was less than the revenue earned. Through this plan, the individual succeeded in transferring at least some of the revenue to the corporation, where it would be taxed at the lower corporate rates.

The final scheme was not specifically designed to take advantage of the lower corporate rates. Instead, its attraction grew from the practical presumption that all corporate activities are business activities. Given this presumption, an individual would transfer his or her personal assets (e.g., a yacht, race car, or vacation home) along with other investments to the corporation. Under the veil of the corporation, the expenses relating to the personal assets, such as maintenance of a yacht, would be magically transformed from nondeductible personal expenses to deductible business expenses which could offset the income produced by the investments. In short, by using the corporate form, individuals were able to disguise their personal expenses as business expenses and deduct them.

Although the Internal Revenue Service tried to curb these abuses using the accumulated earnings tax, such attempts often failed. These failures normally could be attributed to the problem of proving that the individuals actually intended to avoid taxes. Aware of this problem, Congress formulated the personal holding company tax, which could be applied without having to prove that the forbidden purpose existed. In contrast to the accumulated earnings tax, which is imposed only after a subjective assessment of the individual's intentions, the personal holding company tax automatically applies whenever the corporation satisfies two objective tests.

Not all corporations that meet the applicable tests are subject to the penalty tax, however. The Code specifically exempts certain corporations. These include S corporations, tax-exempt corporations, banks, life insurance companies, surety companies, foreign corporations, lending and finance companies, and several other types of corporations.[59]

If the personal holding company tax applies, the tax is 15 percent of undistributed personal holding company income.[60] Like the accumulated earnings tax, the personal holding company tax is levied in addition to the regular tax.[61] The personal holding company tax differs from the accumulated earnings tax however, in that the corporation is required to compute and remit any personal holding tax due at the time it files its annual return. Form 1120-PH is used to compute the tax and must be filed with the corporation's annual Form 1120. In those cases where both the accumulated earnings tax and the personal holding company tax are applicable, only the personal holding company tax is imposed.[62]

## Personal Holding Company Defined

**LO.5**
Indicate when the personal holding company tax applies.

The personal holding company tax applies only if the corporation is considered a personal holding company (PHC). As might be expected in light of the schemes prevalent at the time the tax was enacted, a corporation generally qualifies as a personal holding company if it is closely held and a substantial portion of its income is derived from passive sources or services. Specifically, the Code provides that a corporation is deemed to be a personal holding company if it satisfies both of the following tests.[63]

1. *Ownership*—At any time during the last half of the taxable year, more than 50 percent of the value of the corporation's outstanding stock is owned by five or fewer individuals.[64]
2. *Passive income*—At least 60 percent of the corporation's adjusted ordinary gross income consists of personal holding company income (PHCI).[65]

Before each of these tests is examined in detail, the distinction between the personal holding company tax and the accumulated earnings tax should be emphasized. The accumulated earnings tax applies only when it is proven that it was the shareholder's intention to use the

[59] § 542(c).
[60] § 541.
[61] *Ibid.*
[62] § 532(b)(1).
[63] § 542.
[64] § 542(a)(2).
[65] § 542(a)(1).

corporation to shield income from individual tax rates. In contrast, application of the personal holding company tax requires only that two mechanical tests be satisfied. As a result, a corporation may fall victim to the personal holding company tax where there was no intention to avoid tax by misusing the corporation. For example, consider a closely held corporation in the process of liquidating. During liquidation, the corporation may have income from operations and passive income from temporary investments (investments made pending final distributions). If the passive income is substantial—60 percent or more of the corporation's total income—the corporation will be treated as a personal holding company subject to the penalty tax even though there was no intention by the shareholders to shelter the passive income. As this example illustrates, the mechanical nature of the personal holding company tax, unlike the subjective nature of the accumulated earnings tax, presents a trap for those with the noblest of intentions.

## PHC Ownership Test

**LO.6**
Apply the stock ownership and income tests to determine if a corporation is a personal holding company.

As indicated above, the first part of the two-part test for personal holding company status concerns ownership. Apparently it was Congressional belief that the tax-saving schemes described above succeeded primarily in those cases where there was a concentration of ownership. For this reason, the ownership test is satisfied only if five or fewer individuals own more than 50 percent of the value of the corporation's outstanding shares of stock at any time during the last half of the taxable year.[66] As a quick study of this test reveals, a corporation having less than ten shareholders always meets the ownership test since there will always be a combination of five or fewer shareholders owning more than 50 percent of the stock (e.g., $100\% \div 9 = 11\%$; $11\% \times 5 > 50\%$). Thus, it becomes apparent that closely held corporations are extremely vulnerable to the tax.

In performing the stock ownership test, the shareholder's *direct and indirect* ownership must be taken into account.[67] Indirect ownership is determined using a set of constructive ownership rules designed specifically for the personal holding company area.[68] According to these rules, a taxpayer is considered owning indirectly the following:

1. Stock owned directly or indirectly by his or her family, including his or her brothers, sisters, spouse, ancestors, and lineal descendents;[69]
2. His or her proportionate share of any stock owned by a corporation, partnership, estate, or trust in which he or she has ownership (or of which he or she is a beneficiary in the case of an estate or trust);[70] and
3. Stock owned indirectly or directly by his or her partner in a partnership.[71]

In using these rules, the following guidelines must be observed: (1) stock attributed from one family member to another cannot be reattributed to yet another member of the family,[72] (2) stock attributed from a partner to the taxpayer cannot be reattributed to a member of his or her family or to yet another partner,[73] (3) stock on which the taxpayer has an option is treated as being actually owned,[74] and (4) convertible securities are treated as outstanding stock.[75] In addition, Code § 544 contains other rules that may affect an individual's stock ownership.

## Income Test

Although the stock ownership test may be satisfied, a corporation is not considered a personal holding company unless it also passes an income test. In general terms, this test is straightforward: at least 60 percent of the corporation's income must be derived from either passive sources or certain types of services. Unfortunately, the technical translation of this requirement is somewhat more complicated. According to the Code, at least 60 percent of the

[66] § 542(a)(2).

[67] *Ibid.*

[68] § 544.

[69] § 544(a)(2).

[70] § 544(a)(1).

[71] § 544(a)(2).

[72] § 544(a)(5).

[73] *Ibid.*

[74] § 544(a)(3).

[75] § 544(b).

corporation's adjusted ordinary gross income must be *personal holding company income*.[76] This relationship may be expressed numerically as follows:

$$\frac{\text{Personal holding company income}}{\text{Adjusted ordinary gross income}} \geq 60\%$$

As will be seen below, the definition of each of these terms can be baffling. However, the general theme of each term and the thrust of the test should not be lost in the complexity. Personal holding company income is generally passive income, while adjusted ordinary gross income is just that, ordinary gross income with a few modifications. Performing the income test is, in essence, a matter of determining whether too much of the corporation's income (adjusted ordinary gross income) is passive income (personal holding company income).

**Example 7**

K, a high-bracket taxpayer, wished to reduce her taxes. Upon the advice of an old friend, she transferred all of her stocks and bonds to a newly formed corporation of which she is the sole owner. During the year, the corporation had dividend income of $40,000 and interest income of $35,000. In this case, the corporation is treated as a personal holding company because both the stock ownership test and the income test are satisfied. The stock ownership test is met since K owned 100% of the stock in the last half of the year. The income test is also met since all of the corporation's income is passive income—or more specifically, its personal holding company income, $75,000 ($40,000 dividends + $35,000 interest) exceeds 60% of its adjusted ordinary gross income, $45,000 (60% of $75,000).

The technical definitions of adjusted ordinary gross income and personal holding company income are explored below.

## Adjusted Ordinary Gross Income

The first quantity that must be determined is adjusted ordinary gross income (AOGI).[77] As suggested above, the label given to this quantity is very appropriate since the amount which must be computed is just what the phrase implies; that is, it includes only the ordinary gross income of the corporation with certain adjustments. In determining AOGI, the following amounts must be computed: (1) gross income, (2) ordinary gross income, and (3) the adjustments to ordinary gross income to arrive at AOGI. Therefore, the starting point for the calculation of AOGI is gross income.

### Gross Income

The definition of gross income for purposes of the personal holding company provisions varies little from the definition found in § 61. Accordingly, gross income includes all income from whatever source except those items specifically excluded. In addition, gross income is computed taking into consideration cost of goods sold. The only departure from the normal definition of gross income concerns property transactions. Only the net gains from the sale or exchange of stocks, securities, and commodities are included in gross income.[78] Net losses involving these assets do not reduce gross income. Similarly, any loss arising from the sale or exchange of § 1231property is ignored and does not offset any § 1231 gains.

### Ordinary Gross Income

In applying the income test, capital-gain type items are ignored and consequently have no effect on whether the corporation is treated as a personal holding company. Therefore, since the quantity desired is adjusted "ordinary" gross income, the second step of the calculation requires the removal of capital-gain type items from gross income. As seen in Exhibit 21-4, all capital

---

[76] § 542(a)(1).

[77] § 543(b)(2).

[78] Prop. Reg. § 1.543-12(a). Also see Reg. §§ 1.542-2 and 1.543-2.

gains and § 1231 gains are subtracted from gross income to arrive at ordinary gross income.[79] It should be noted that this amount, "ordinary gross income," is not simply a subtotal in arriving at AOGI. As discussed below, ordinary gross income (OGI) is an important figure in determining whether certain types of income are treated as personal holding company income.

**EXHIBIT 21.4** **Ordinary Gross Income[80]**

Gross income
Minus: **a.** Capital gains
**b.** (b) Section 1231 gains
Equals: **Ordinary gross income (OGI)**

## Adjustments to OGI

For many years, OGI generally served as the denominator in the income-test fraction shown above. In 1964, however, modifications were necessary to discourage the use of certain methods taxpayers and their advisors had forged to undermine the income test. The popular schemes capitalized on the fact that $1 of gross rental income could shelter 60 cents of passive personal holding company income. This particular advantage could be obtained even though the rental activity itself was merely a break-even operation. Consequently, a taxpayer could easily thwart the income test and reap the benefits of the corporate entity by investing in activities that produced substantial gross rents or royalties, notwithstanding the fact that these activities were not economically sound investments.

### Example 8

Refer to the facts in *Example 7*. Absent special rules, K could circumvent the income test by purchasing a coin-operated laundry which generated gross rents of more than $50,000 (e.g., $51,000) and transferring it to the corporation. In such case, assuming the rents would not be treated as personal holding income, the personal holding company income would still be $75,000 (dividends of $40,000 + interest of $35,000). However, when the laundry rents are combined with the personal holding company income to form the new AOGI, personal holding company income would be less than 60% of this new AOGI [$75,000 60% × ($40,000 + $35,000 + $51,000) = $75,600]. Although the laundry business might not show a profit, this would be irrelevant to K since she would have gained the advantage of the dividends-received deduction and avoided personal holding company status.

To deter the type of scheme illustrated above, the calculation now requires rental and royalty income to be reduced by the bulk of the expenses typically related to this type of income: depreciation, interest, and taxes. This requirement reduces the ability of the activities to shelter income. For instance, in *Example 8* above, K would be required to reduce the gross rental income by depreciation, interest, and taxes—which would severely curtail the utility of purchasing the laundry business.[81] The specific modifications that reduce ordinary gross income to arrive at adjusted ordinary gross income are shown in Exhibit 21-5.[82] Exhibit 21-6 and Exhibit 21-7 illustrate the adjustments required to be made to gross income from rents and mineral, oil, and gas royalties for purposes of computing adjusted ordinary gross income.

[79] § 543(b)(1).

[80] *Ibid.*

[81] Under current law, it is also likely that the rents would be treated as PHCI, thus further spoiling the plan.

[82] § 543(b)(2).

**EXHIBIT 21.5** **Adjusted Ordinary Gross Income**[83]

Ordinary gross income (OGI)

Minus:

a. Depreciation, property taxes, interest expense, and rents paid related to gross rental income. These deductions may not exceed gross rental income. (Gross rental income is income for the use of corporate property and interest received on the sales price of real property held as inventory.)

b. Depreciation and depletion, property and severance taxes, interest expense, and rents paid related to gross income from mineral, oil, and gas royalties. These deductions may not exceed the gross income from the royalties.

c. Interest on tax refunds, on judgments, on condemnation awards, and on U.S. obligations (only for a dealer in the obligations).

Equals: ***Adjusted ordinary gross income*** **(AOGI)**

**EXHIBIT 21.6** **Adjusted Income from Rents**[84]

Gross rental income

Minus:

a. Depreciation

b. Property taxes

c. Interest expense

d. Rents paid

Equals: **Adjusted income from rents**

**EXHIBIT 21.7** **Adjusted Income from Mineral, Oil, and Gas Royalties**[85]

Gross income from mineral, oil, and gas royalties (including production payments and overriding royalties)

Minus:

a. Depreciation

b. Property and severance taxes

c. Interest expense

d. Rents paid

Equals: **Adjusted income from mineral, oil, and gas royalties**[86]

## Personal Holding Company Income (PHCI)

Following the computation of AOGI, the corporation's personal holding company income must be measured to determine whether it meets the 60 percent threshold. Although personal holding company income can be generally characterized as passive income and certain income from services, the Code identifies eight specific types of income which carry the

[83] § 543(a)(1).

[84] § 543(a)(1).

[85] *Ibid.*

[86] § 543(b)(4).

personal holding company taint.[87] These are listed in Exhibit 21-8. Selected items of PHCI are discussed below.

### Dividends, Interest, Royalties, and Annuities

The most obvious forms of PHCI are those usually considered passive in nature: dividends, interest, royalties, and annuities.[88] Generally, identification and classification of these items present little problem. The most noteworthy exception concerns royalties. Mineral, oil, gas,

**EXHIBIT 21.8** **Personal Holding Company Income (PHCI)**

Dividends, interest, royalties (except mineral, oil, or gas royalties, copyright royalties, and certain software royalties), and annuities.

Plus:

a. Adjusted income from rents, *but* the adjusted income from rents is not added to PHCI *if*
   1. The adjusted income from rents is 50 percent or more of AOGI, and
   2. The dividends paid, the dividends considered paid, and the consent dividends equal or exceed
      i. PHCI computed without the adjusted income from rents
      ii. Minus 10 percent of OGI.

b. Adjusted income from mineral, oil, and gas royalties, *but* the adjusted income from these royalties is not added to PHCI *if*
   1. The adjusted income from the royalties is 50 percent or more of AOGI,
   2. PHCI computed without the adjusted income from these royalties does not exceed 10 percent of OGI, and
   3. The § 162 trade or business deductions equal or exceed 15 percent of AOGI.

c. Copyright royalties, *but* the copyright royalties are not added to PHCI *if*
   1. The copyright royalties are 50 percent or more of OGI,
   2. PHCI computed without the copyright royalties does not exceed 10 percent of OGI, and
   3. The § 162 trade or business deductions related to the copyright royalties equal or exceed 25 percent of
      i. The OGI minus the royalties paid, plus
      ii. The depreciation related to the copyright royalties.

d. Software royalties, *but* these are not added to PHCI *if*
   1. The royalties are received in connection with the licensing of computer software by a corporation which is actively engaged in the business of developing, manufacturing, or production of such software,
   2. The software royalties are 50 percent or more of OGI,
   3. Research and experimental expenditures, § 162 business expenses, and § 195 start-up expenditures allocable to the software business are generally 25 percent or more of OGI computed with certain adjustments, and
   4. Dividends paid, considered paid, and the consent dividends equal or exceed
      i. PHCI computed without the software royalties and certain interest income
      ii. Minus 10 percent of OGI.

e. Produced film rents, but the produced film rents are not added to PHCI if the produced film rents equal or exceed 50 percent of OGI.

f. Rent (for the use of tangible property) received by the corporation from a shareholder owning 25 percent or more of the value of the corporation's stock. This rent is only included in PHCI if PHCI computed without this rent and without the adjusted income from rents exceeds 10 percent of OGI.

g. Income from personal service contracts *but only if*
   1. Someone other than the corporation has the right to designate who is to perform the services or if the person who is to perform the services is named in the contract, and
   2. At some time during the taxable year, 25 percent or more of the value of the corporation's outstanding stock is owned by the person performing the services.

h. Income of estates and trusts taxable to the corporation.

Equals: **Personal holding company income (PHCI)**

[87] § 543.

[88] § 543(a)(1).

copyright, and computer software royalties generally are included in this category of PHCI. However, as seen in Exhibit 21-8, items b, c, and d, these royalties are not treated as PHCI if certain additional tests are satisfied.

### Example 9

B Corporation has three stockholders. Its income consisted of

| | |
|---|---|
| Gross income from a grocery | $52,000 |
| Interest income | 38,000 |
| Capital gain | 6,000 |

B Corporation's OGI (see Exhibit 21-4) is $90,000, computed as follows:

| | |
|---|---|
| Gross income ($52,000 + $38,000 + $6,000) | $96,000 |
| Minus: Capital gains | (6,000) |
| OGI | $90,000 |

In this example, AOGI is the same as OGI since the amounts which are subtracted from OGI to arrive at AOGI are zero (see Exhibit 21-5).

B Corporation's PHCI is $38,000, the amount of the interest income (see Exhibit 21-8). Since the corporation's PHCI ($38,000) is not 60 percent or more of its $90,000 AOGI ($90,000 × 60% = $54,000), it does not meet the income requirement.

Although B Corporation meets the stock ownership requirement since it has only three shareholders, it does not meet *both* the ownership requirement and the income requirement. As a result, it is not a personal holding company and is not subject to the personal holding company tax.

### Example 10

Assume the same facts as in *Example 9* except that B Corporation had received $88,000 of interest income.

B Corporation's OGI and AOGI would be computed as follows:

| | |
|---|---|
| Gross income ($52,000 + $88,000 + $6,000) | $146,000 |
| Minus: Capital gains | (6,000) |
| OGI (also AOGI) | $140,000 |

B Corporation's PHCI is now $88,000, the amount of the interest income. Since the corporation's $88,000 of PHCI is more than 60% of the $140,000 AOGI ($140,000 × 60% = $84,000), it meets the income requirement.

Since B Corporation meets both the ownership requirement and the income requirement, *it is* a personal holding company.

## Adjusted Income from Rents

Rental income presents a special problem for the personal holding company provisions. Normally, rents—generally defined as compensation for the use of property—represent a passive type of income. However, for many corporations, most notably those involved in renting real estate and equipment, rental operations are not merely a passive investment but represent a true business activity. If all rental income were considered personal holding income, closely held corporations involved in the rental business could not escape PHI status. To provide these corporations with some relief, rental income is not treated as PHCI under certain circumstances.

The amount of rental income potentially qualifying as PHCI is referred to as the *adjusted income from rents.*[89] As seen in Exhibit 21-6, adjusted income from rents consists of the corporation's gross rental income reduced by the adjustments required for determining AOGI —depreciation, property taxes, interest expense, and rental payments related to such income (e.g., ground lease payments). The corporation's adjusted income from rents is treated as PHCI unless it can utilize the relief measure suggested above. Specifically, adjusted income from rents is PHCI unless: (1) it is 50 percent or more of the corporation's AOGI, and (2) the corporation's dividends during the taxable year as well as dividends paid within the first 2½ months of the following year *and* consent dividends are not less than the amount by which nonrental PHCI (e.g., dividends and interest) exceeds 10 percent of OGI.[90]

These relationships may be expressed as follows:

1. Adjusted income from rents $\geq$ (50% $\times$ AOGI); *and*
2. Dividends $\geq$ [nonrental PHCI $-$ (10% $\times$ OGI)].

As the latter expression indicates, when rents represent a substantial portion of OGI relative to nonrental PHCI (as typically would be the case where a corporation is truly in the rental "business"), no dividends are required. In other words, as long as nonrental income is not a major portion of the corporation's total income—does not exceed 10 percent of the corporation's OGI—dividends are unnecessary. Otherwise, a corporation in the rental business is forced to make dividend distributions to avoid penalty.

## Example 11

D Corporation had four shareholders in 2011 and therefore met the stock ownership requirement. The following information is available for D Corporation for 2011:

| | |
|---|---|
| Interest income | $ 10,000 |
| Gross rental income | 25,000 |
| Depreciation, property taxes, and interest expense related to rental income | 24,000 |
| Maintenance and utilities related to rental income | 3,000 |
| Dividends paid during 2010 | 8,000 |

OGI (Exhibit 21-4) is $35,000 ($10,000 + $25,000). AOGI (see Exhibit 21-5) is computed as follows:

| | |
|---|---|
| OGI | $ 35,000 |
| Minus: Depreciation, property taxes, and interest expense related to rental income | (24,000) |
| AOGI | $ 11,000 |

D Corporation's adjusted income from rents is computed as follows (see Exhibit 21-6):

| | |
|---|---|
| Gross rental income | $ 25,000 |
| Minus: Depreciation, property taxes, and interest expense related to rental income | (24,000) |
| Adjusted income from rents | $ 1,000 |

Note that in determining AOGI and adjusted income from rents, the maintenance and utility expenses are ignored. Such expenses are also not taken into account in determining gross income or OGI. The next step is to determine if the adjusted income from rents is to be added to PHCI. It is *not* added to PHCI if *both* of the following tests are met.

[89] § 543(b)(3).

[90] *Ibid.*

**Test 1.** (50% test): Is the adjusted income from rents 50% or more of AOGI?

The adjusted income from rents ($1,000) is not 50% or more of AOGI ($11,000), so Test 1 is *not* met.

The adjusted income from rents is excluded from PHCI only if *both* Test 1 and Test 2 are met. Since Test 1 is not met, the adjusted income from rents *is* included in PHCI, and there is no need to go on to Test 2. However, Test 2 is done here for illustrative purposes.

**Test 2.** (10% test): Does the total of the dividends paid, the dividends considered paid, and the consent dividends equal or exceed PHCI (computed without the adjusted income from rents) reduced by 10% of OGI? This test can also be expressed as:

Dividends ≥ [nonrental PHCI − (OGI × 10%)]. Nonrental PHCI is $10,000 (interest income). OGI × 10% = $35,000 × 10% = $3,500. Therefore, nonrent PHCI ($10,000) minus OGI × 10% ($3,500) is $6,500. Since the total dividends ($8,000) were more than $6,500, Test 2 is met.

However, as mentioned above, *both* Test 1 and Test 2 must be met if the adjusted income from rents is to be excluded from PHCI. Therefore, the adjusted income from rents *is part of PHCI.*

D Corporation's PHCI is computed as follows (see Exhibit 21-8):

| | |
|---|---|
| Interest income | $10,000 |
| Adjusted income from rents | 1,000 |
| PHCI | $11,000 |

D Corporation's $11,000 PHCI is more than 60% of the $11,000 AOGI. In this example, in fact, PHCI is 100% of AOGI since all of the income is personal holding company income. D Corporation, therefore, meets *both* the ownership requirement and the income requirement, and thus is a personal holding company.

The rules relating to mineral, oil, gas, copyright, and software royalties are very similar to those discussed above for rents. See Exhibit 21-7 and Exhibit 21-8, items b, c, and d.

### Income from Personal Service Contracts

The shifting of service income to a corporation by highly compensated individuals, such as actors and athletes, is sharply curtailed by the personal holding company provision. The PHC provisions attack the problem by treating service income as PHCI under certain conditions. Generally, amounts received by a corporation for services provided are treated as PHCI if the party desiring the services can designate the person who will perform the services and that person owns 25 percent or more of the corporation's stock[91] (see Exhibit 21-8, item g).

#### Example 12

T Corp., a producer of motion pictures, wanted RK to act in a new movie it was producing. Assume that RK's services could be obtained only by contracting with his wholly owned corporation, RK Inc. Accordingly, a contract is drafted providing that RK Inc. will provide the services of RK to T Corp. for $500,000. All of the income is PHCI to RK Inc. since RK owns at least 25% of the corporation *and* he is actually designated in the contract to perform the services.

Given the general rule, it would appear that virtually all service corporations are likely candidates for the PHC tax. This problem was considered in Revenue Ruling 75-67.[92] According to the facts of the ruling, a corporation's primary source of income was attributable to the services of its only employee, a doctor, who also owned 80 percent of the corporation's stock. In this case, all the facts suggested that the income would be PHCI. The only question was whether the doctor's patients formally designated him as the one to perform the services. Although a formal designation was lacking, it was implicit since the doctor was the only employee of the corporation and the patients never expected someone other than

[91] § 543(a)(7).

[92] Rev. Rul. 75-67, 1975-1 C.B. 169.

the doctor to perform the services. Despite evidence to the contrary, the IRS ruled that the income was not PHCI on the theory that there was no indication that the corporation was obligated to provide the services of the doctor in question. In addition, the ruling emphasized that the services to be performed were not so unique as to prohibit the corporation from substituting someone else to perform them. The Service also relied on the uniqueness rationale in situations involving a CPA who had incorporated his or her practice and a musical composer who had incorporated his or her song-writing activities.[93] Apparently, as long as the services are not so unique as to preclude substitution and there is no formal designation of the individual who will perform the services, a service business can escape PHC status.

## Computation of the PHC Tax

**LO.7**
Explain how the personal holding company tax is computed and how it might be avoided.

The personal holding company penalty tax is 15 percent of the *undistributed personal holding company income*. Undistributed personal holding company income is defined as adjusted taxable income minus the dividends-paid deduction.[94] The computation of adjusted taxable income and undistributed PHCI is shown in Exhibit 21-9.

**EXHIBIT 21.9** **Undistributed Personal Holding Company Income[95]**

***Taxable income***

Plus:
- **a.** Dividends-received deduction.
- **b.** Net operating loss deduction (but not a net operating loss of the preceding year computed without the dividends-received deduction).
- **c.** The amount by which the § 162 (trade or business) deductions and the § 167 (depreciation) deductions related to rental property exceed the income produced by the rental property, unless it can be shown that the rent received was the highest possible and that the rental activity was carried on as a bona fide business activity.

Minus:
- **a.** Federal income taxes (but not the accumulated earnings tax or the personal holding company tax).
- **b.** The amount by which actual charitable contributions exceeds the charitable contributions deduction reflected in net income.
- **c.** Net capital gain reduced by the taxes attributable to the net capital gain.

Equals: ***Adjusted taxable income***

Minus: *Dividends-Paid Deduction*

Equals: ***Undistributed Personal Holding Company Income***

Like the computation of accumulated taxable income, the calculation attempts to determine the corporation's dividend-paying capacity. As a practical matter, the tax is rarely paid because of a deduction allowed for "deficiency dividends," which can be made once it has been determined the PHC tax applies.

### Dividends-Paid Deduction

The dividends-paid deduction for personal holding companies is similar to the one for the accumulated earnings tax. It includes the following types of distributions:

1. Dividends paid during the taxable year;
2. Throwback dividends: dividends paid within 2½ months after the close of the taxable year (but subject to limitation as discussed below);
3. Consent dividends;
4. Liquidating distributions; and
5. Deficiency dividends.

[93] Rev. Rul. 75-290, 1975-1 C.B. 172;Rev. Rul. 75-249, 1975-1 C.B. 171; and Rev. Rul. 75-250, 1975-1 C.B. 179.

[94] § 545(a). The term "adjusted taxable income" is not found in the Code.

[95] § 545.

Note that this list of qualifying distributions is identical to that provided in Exhibit 21-3 for the accumulated earnings tax, except for the special deficiency dividend. In addition, personal holding companies are entitled to a dividend carryover, which is not available for accumulated earnings tax purposes.[96]

**Throwback Dividends** As in the accumulated earnings tax computation, a personal holding company is allowed a deduction for throwback dividends (i.e., dividends paid within 2½ months after the close of the taxable year).[97] However, the PHC throwback dividend differs from that for the accumulated earnings tax in two ways. First, it is included in the dividends-paid deduction only if the corporation makes an election at the time the corporate tax return is filed to treat the dividends as applying to the previous year.[98] Second, the amount treated as a throwback dividend is limited to the smaller of the following:[99]

1. Twenty percent of the dividends actually paid during the taxable year in question; or
2. Undistributed PHCI (computed without the dividends paid during the 2½-month period).

**Consent Dividends** The rules for consent dividends are the same for personal holding companies as for the accumulated earnings tax.[100] As mentioned previously, a consent dividend is an amount that a shareholder agrees to consider as having been received as a dividend even though never actually distributed by the corporation. Consent dividends are limited to shareholders who own stock on the last day of the tax year. Their shares must be either common stock or participating preferred stock. Consent dividends do not include preferential dividends. A shareholder who consents to a dividend is treated as having received the amount as a cash dividend and contributing the same amount to the corporation's capital on the last day of the year.

**Dividend Carryover** A personal holding company is also entitled to a dividend carryover as part of its dividends-paid deduction.[101] If the dividends paid in the two prior years exceed the adjusted taxable incomes (see Exhibit 21-9) for those years, the excess may be used as a dividend carryover (and therefore as part of the dividends-paid deduction) for the year in question.

**Deficiency Dividends** Once a determination has been made that a corporation is subject to the personal holding company tax, the tax can still be abated by the use of a *deficiency dividend*.[102] Following the determination of the personal holding company tax, the corporation is given 90 days to pay a deficiency dividend. A deficiency dividend must be an *actual cash dividend* which the corporation elects to treat as a distribution of the personal holding company income for the year at issue, and it is taxable to the shareholders. It does not reduce the personal holding company income of any year other than the year at issue. A deficiency dividend effectively reduces the amount of the penalty tax. However, interest and penalties are still imposed as if the deduction were not allowed. Thus, the corporation may be able to escape the tax itself—but not any interest or penalties related to such tax. It should also be noted that the deficiency dividend is available *only* to reduce the personal holding company tax. This escape is not available to those corporations subject to the accumulated earnings tax.

---

[96] § 561(a)(3).

[97] § 563.

[98] § 563(b).

[99] *Ibid.*

[100] § 565.

[101] § 564.

[102] § 547.

## Example 13

C Corporation determined that it was a personal holding company and had to file Form 1120-PH. Its records for 2010 reveal the following:

| | |
|---|---|
| Gross profit from operations | $ 150,000 |
| Dividend income | 400,000 |
| Interest income | 350,000 |
| Long-term capital gain | 30,000 |
| Gross income | $ 930,000 |
| Compensation | (30,000) |
| Selling and administrative | (100,000) |
| | $ 800,000 |
| Dividends-received deduction | (280,000) |
| Charitable contributions | (80,000) |
| Taxable income | $ 440,000 |
| Federal income tax @ 34% | $ 149,600 |

Charitable contributions actually made during the year were $90,000, but are limited to $80,000 (10% × $800,000 taxable income before the deductions for contributions and dividends received). C paid dividends of $20,000 in 2011 and $10,000 during the first 2½ months of 2012, which it *elects* to throw back to 2011 in computing the dividends-paid deduction. The personal holding company tax is computed as follows:

| | | |
|---|---|---|
| | Taxable income | $ 440,000 |
| + | Dividends-received deduction | 280,000 |
| – | Excess charitable contributions | (10,000) |
| – | Federal income taxes | (149,600) |
| – | Long-term capital gain net of tax [$30,000 – (34% × $30,000)] | (19,800) |
| | Adjustable taxable income | $ 540,600 |
| – | Dividends paid deduction: | |
| | 2011 | (20,000) |
| | 2012 Throwback (Limited to 20% of 2011 dividends) | (4,000) |
| | UPHCI | $ 516,600 |
| | Times: PHC tax rate | × 15% |
| | PHC tax | $ 77,490 |

C Corporation's tax liability for 2011 is $227,090 ($149,600 regular tax + $77,490 PHC tax). The PHC tax could be avoided by paying a deficiency dividend equal to UPHCI ($516,600). However, the payment of the dividend would not eliminate any penalties or interest that might be assessed on the $77,490 PHC tax due if Form 1120-PH is not filed in a timely manner.

# Tax Planning

## Accumulated Earnings Tax

For taxpayers wanting to use the corporate form to shield their income from individual taxes, the accumulated earnings tax represents a formidable obstacle. Although there is an obvious cost if the tax is incurred, that cost may be far more than expected. This result often occurs because the imposition of the tax for one year triggers an audit for all open years. In addition, the IRS usually takes the position that the negligence penalty of Code § 6653 should be imposed whenever the accumulated earnings tax is applicable. Moreover, in contrast to the personal holding company tax which can normally be averted using the deficiency dividend procedure, the accumulated earnings tax, once levied, cannot be avoided. At the time of the audit, it is too late for dividend payments or consent dividends!

Despite the potential cost of the tax, the rewards from avoidance—or at least the deferral—of double taxation are often so great that the shareholders are willing to assume the risk of penalty. Moreover, many practitioners believe that with proper planning the risk of incurring the accumulated earnings tax is minimal, particularly since the tax is not self-assessed but dependent on the audit lottery. In addition, it is possible to shift the burden of proof to the IRS. The discussion below examines some of the means for reducing the taxpayer's exposure to the accumulated earnings tax.

### Liquid Assets and Working Capital

Normally, the accumulated earnings tax is not raised as an issue unless the corporation's balance sheet shows cash, marketable securities, or other liquid assets that could be distributed easily to shareholders. The absence of liquid assets indicates that any earnings that have been retained have been reinvested in the business rather than accumulated for the forbidden purpose. It is a rare occasion, however, when such assets do not exist. Consequently, most IRS agents routinely assess whether the level of the corporation's working capital is appropriate by applying the *Bardahl* formula.

The courts have made it clear that the *Bardahl* formula serves merely as a guideline for determining the proper amount of working capital. In *Delaware Trucking Co., Inc.*, the court held that the amount needed using the *Bardahl* formula could be increased by 75 percent due to the possibility of increased labor and other operating costs due to inflation.[103] Nevertheless, in those instances where working capital appears excessive, the Internal Revenue Manual directs agents to require justification of such excess. Therefore, the corporation should closely control its working capital to ensure that it does not exceed the corporation's reasonable needs.

One way to reduce working capital is to increase shareholder salaries, bonuses, and other compensation. Since these payments are deductible, double taxation is avoided. This technique also has the benefit of reducing taxable income, which in turn reduces the accumulated earnings tax should it apply. However, this method of reducing working capital may not be feasible if the compensation paid exceeds a reasonable amount. To the extent that the compensation is unreasonable, the payments are treated as dividends and double taxation results. In addition, if the unreasonable compensation is not pro rata among all shareholders, the dividend will be considered preferential and no deduction will be allowed for the dividend in computing adjusted taxable income.

Another method for reducing working capital is for the corporation to invest in additional assets. However, the taxpayer must be careful to avoid investments that are of a passive nature or that could be considered unrelated to the corporation's existing or projected business. With respect to the latter, the courts have ruled that the business of a controlled subsidiary is the business of the parent while the business of a sister corporation normally is not the business of its brother.[104]

### Reasonable Needs

The courts have accepted a variety of reasons as sufficient justification for the accumulation of earnings. On the one hand, the needs deemed reasonable have been both certain and well-

[103] 32 TCM 104, T.C. Memo 1973-29.

[104] For example, see *Latchis Theatres of Keene, Inc. v. Comm.*, 54-2 USTC ¶9544, 45 AFTR 1836, 214 F.2d 834 (CA-1,1954).

defined, such as the repayment of corporate debt. On the other hand, the courts have approved needs as contingent and unknown as those arising from possible damage from future floods.

One contingency that seemingly could be asserted by all corporations as a basis for accumulating funds is the possibility of a business reversal, depression, or loss of major customer. Interestingly, the courts have often respected this justification for accumulations, notwithstanding the fact that it is a risk assumed by virtually all business entities. Acceptance of this need, however, appears to be dependent on the taxpayer's ability to establish that there is at least some chance that a business reversal could occur that would affect the taxpayer. For example, in *Ted Bates & Co.*, the corporation was in the advertising business and received 70 percent of its fees from only five clients.[105] In ruling for the taxpayer, the court held that the corporation was allowed to accumulate amounts necessary to cover its fixed costs for a period following the loss of a major client. Much of the court's opinion was based on its view that the advertising business was extremely competitive and the possibility of losing a client was not unrealistic. A similar decision was reached where a manufacturer sold all its products to one customer and had to compete with others for that customer's business. The court believed that accumulations were necessary to enable the corporation to develop new markets if it lost its only customer. Relying on a possible downturn in business as a basis for accumulations has not always sufficed. In *Goodall*, the company accumulated earnings in light of the prospect that military orders would be lost.[106] The court upheld the penalty tax, indicating that even if the loss occurred, it would not have a significant effect because the corporation's business was expanding.

Although the courts have sustained various reasons for accumulations, a review of the cases indicates that the taxpayer must demonstrate that the need is realistic. This was made clear in *Colonial Amusement Corp.*[107] In this case, the corporation's accumulations were not justified when it wanted to construct a building on adjacent land and building restrictions existed that prohibited construction.

In establishing that a need is realistic, a taxpayer's self-serving statement normally is not convincing. Proper documentation of the need is critical. This is true even when the need is obvious and acceptable. In *Union Offset*, the corporation stated at trial that its accumulations were necessary to retire outstanding corporate debt, a legitimate business need.[108] To the taxpayer's dismay, however, the Tax Court still imposed the tax because the corporation had failed to document in any type of written record its plan to use the accumulations in the alleged manner. In this case, a simple statement in the Board of Directors' minutes concerning the proposed use of the funds would no doubt have saved the taxpayer from penalty.

### S Corporation Election

In those cases where it is difficult to justify accumulations, the shareholders may wish to elect to be treated as an S corporation. Since the earnings of an S corporation are taxed to the individual shareholders rather than the corporation, S corporations cannot be used to shelter income and thus are immune to the accumulated earnings tax. However, the election insulates the corporation only prospectively (i.e., only for that period for which it is, an S corporation). Prior years open to audit are still vulnerable. In addition, the S election may raise other problems. The shareholders will be required to report and pay taxes on the income of the corporation even though it may not be distributed to them. As a result, cash flow problems may occur. Further, because the corporation has accumulated earnings and profits, the excess passive income tax specifically designed for C corporations that have elected S status may apply. In addition, the corporation may be subject to the built-in gains tax.[109] For these reasons, an S election should be carefully considered.

## Personal Holding Company Tax

The personal holding company tax, like the accumulated earnings tax, is clearly a tax to be avoided. Unfortunately, the personal holding company tax differs from the accumulated earnings tax in that it is not reserved solely for those whose intent is to avoid taxes. Rather, it is applied on a mechanical basis, regardless of motive, to all corporations that fall within its

[105] 24 TCM 1346, T.C. Memo 1965-251.

[106] *Robert A. Goodall Estate v. Comm.*, 68-1 USTC ¶9245, 21 AFTR2d 813, 391 F.2d 775, (CA-8.1968).

[107] 7 TCM 546.

[108] 79-2 USTC ¶9550, 603 F.2d 90 (CA-9, 1979).

[109] See Chapter 23 for a discussion of these special taxes that may be imposed on S corporations.

purview. For this reason, it is important to closely monitor the corporation's activities to ensure that it does not inadvertently become a PHC.

One important responsibility of a practitioner is to recognize potential personal holding company problems so that steps can be taken to avoid the tax or the need to distribute dividends. This responsibility not only concerns routine operations but extends to advice concerning planned transactions that could cause the corporation to be converted from an operating company to an investment company. For example, a corporation may plan to sell one or all of its businesses and invest the proceeds in passive type assets. Similarly, a planned reorganization may leave the corporation holding stock of the acquiring corporation. Failure to identify the possible personal holding company difficulty which these and other transactions may cause can lead to serious embarrassment.

Although the thrust of most tax planning for personal holding companies concerns how to avoid the tax, there are certain instances when a planned PHC can provide benefits. Both varieties of personal holding companies, the planned and the unplanned, are discussed below.

## PHC Candidates

All corporations could fall victim to the PHC tax. However, some corporations are more likely candidates than others. For this reason, their activities and anticipated transactions should be scrutinized more carefully than others.

Potential difficulties often concern corporations that are involved in rental activities and those that have some passive income. In this regard, it should be noted that the term "rent" is defined as payments received for the use of property. As a result, "rental companies" include not only those that lease such items as apartments, offices, warehouses, stadiums, equipment, vending machines, automobiles, trucks, and the like, but also those that operate bowling alleys, roller and ice skating rinks, billiards parlors, golf courses, and any other activity for which a payment is received for use of the corporation's property. All of these corporations are at risk since each has rental income which could be considered passive personal holding company income unless it satisfies the special two-prong test for rental companies.

There are several other types of corporations that must be concerned with PHC problems. Investment companies—corporations formed primarily to acquire income producing assets such as stock, bonds, rental properties, partnership interests, and similar investments—clearly have difficulties. Corporations that derive most of their income from the services of one or more of their shareholders also are vulnerable. In recent years, however, the Service has taken a liberal view toward the professional corporations of doctors, accountants, and several others. Another group of corporations that are probable targets of the PHC tax includes those that collect royalty income. The royalty income might arise from the corporation's development and licensing of a product (e.g., patent on a food processor or franchises to operate a restaurant). Other logical candidates for the PHC tax are banks, savings and loans, and finance companies since the majority of their income is interest income from making loans and purchasing or discounting accounts receivable and installment obligations. Banks and savings and loans need not worry, however, since they are specifically excluded from PHC status. Finance companies are also exempt from the penalty tax, but only if certain tests—not discussed here—are met. Consequently, those involved with finance companies should review their situation closely to ensure such tests are satisfied.

## Avoiding PHC Status

In general, if a corporation is closely held and 60 percent of its income is derived from passive sources or specified personal services, the PHC tax applies. Thus, to avoid the PHC tax *either* the stock ownership test or the income test must be failed.

## Stock Ownership Test

The stock ownership test is satisfied if five or fewer persons own more than 50 percent of the stock. This test is the most difficult to fail since it requires dilution of the current shareholders' ownership. Moreover, dilution is very difficult to implement in practice due to the constructive ownership rules. The rules make it virtually impossible to maintain ownership in the family since stock owned by one family member or an entity in which the family member has an interest is considered owned by other family members. Therefore, to fail the ownership test, sufficient stock must be owned by unrelated parties to reduce the ownership of the five largest shareholders to 50 percent or less. Unfortunately, it is often impossible to design an arrangement that meets these conditions yet is still desirable from an economic viewpoint.

### Passive Income Test

The corporation is deemed to satisfy the passive income test if 60 percent of its adjusted ordinary gross income (AOGI) is personal holding company income (PHCI)—income from dividends, interest, annuities, rents, royalties, or specified shareholder services. The potential for failing this test is perhaps more easily seen when this test is expressed mathematically:

$$\frac{\text{PHCI}}{\text{AOGI}} \geq 60\%$$

The steps that can be taken to fail this test fall into three categories: (1) increasing operating income or AOGI, (2) reducing PHCI, and (3) satisfying the exceptions to remove the PHC taint from the income.

### Increasing Operating Income

One way to fail the 60 percent test is to increase the denominator in the income test fraction, AOGI, without increasing the numerator. This requires the corporation to increase its operating income without any corresponding increase in its passive income. Obtaining such an increase is not easy since it is essentially asking that the corporation generate more gross income. This does not necessarily mean that sales must increase, however. The corporation might consider increasing its profit margin. Although this could reduce sales, the resulting increase in gross income could be sufficient to fail the test. Alternatively, the corporation might consider expanding the operating portion of the business. Expansion not only in increases AOGI but also may have the effect of reducing PHCI if the investments generating the PHCI are sold to invest in the expansion.

### Reducing Personal Holding Income

Failing the income test normally is accomplished by reducing personal holding company income. It is sometimes asserted that merely reducing PHCI is not sufficient since both the numerator and the denominator in the test fraction are reduced by the same amounts. (This occurs because AOGI includes PHCI.) A mathematical check of this statement shows that it is incorrect and that a simple elimination of PHCI aids the taxpayer.

#### Example 14

Z Corporation has $100,000 of AOGI, including $70,000 of interest income that is PHCI. Substituting these values into the test fraction reveals that the corporation has excessive passive income.

$$\frac{\text{PHCI}}{\text{AOGI}} = \frac{\$70,000}{\$100,000} = 70\%$$

If Z Corporation simply reduces its interest income by $30,000, the corporation would fail the income test despite the fact that both the numerator and the denominator are reduced by the same amounts.

$$\frac{\text{PHCI}}{\text{AOGI}} = \frac{\$40,000}{\$70,000} = 57.1\%$$

One way a corporation could eliminate part of its PHCI is by paying out as shareholder compensation the amounts that otherwise would be invested to generate PHCI. Alternatively, the corporation could eliminate PHCI by switching its investments into growth stocks where the return is generated from capital appreciation rather than dividends. Of course, the taxpayer would not necessarily want to switch completely out of dividend-paying stocks since the advantage of the dividends-received deduction would be lost.

The corporation could also reduce its PHCI by replacing it with tax-exempt income, capital gains, or § 1231 gains. This would have the same effect as simply eliminating the PHCI altogether.

> **Example 15**
>
> Same as *Example 14* above except the corporation invests in tax-exempt bonds which generate $20,000 of tax-exempt, rather than taxable, interest. In addition, the corporation realizes a $10,000 capital gain instead of taxable interest. The effect of replacing the taxable interest of $30,000 with capital gains of $10,000 and tax-exempt income of $20,000 would produce results identical to those above. This derives from the fact that the tax-exempt interest and capital gains are excluded from both the numerator, PHCI, and the denominator, AOGI, creating fractions identical to those shown above.

### Removing the PHC Taint

In some situations, income which is normally considered PHCI (e.g., rental income) is not considered tainted if certain tests are met. For example, the Code provides escape hatches for rental income; mineral, oil, and gas royalties; copyright royalties; and rents from the distribution and exhibition of produced films. Although additional tests must be met to obtain exclusion for these types of income, there is one requirement common to each. *Generally*, if a corporation's income consists predominantly (50 percent or more) of only one of these income types, exclusion is available. More importantly, this condition can normally be obtained without great difficulty. To satisfy the 50 percent test, the taxpayer should take steps to ensure that a particular corporation receives only a single type of income. This may require forming an additional corporation that receives only one type of income, but by so doing the 50 percent test is met and the PHC tax may be avoided.

With proper control of their income, these corporations will have no difficulty in satisfying the income test since at least 50 percent of their AOGI is from one source. For corporations with rental income, however, dividends equal to the amount that their nonrental PHC income exceeds 10 percent of their OGI still must be paid. Note, however, that if a corporation has little or no nonrental PHC income, no dividends are necessary to meet the test. Also note that each additional dollar of gross rents, unreduced by expenses, decreases the amount of dividend that must be paid.

> **Example 16**
>
> G Corporation has $60,000 of OGI, including $53,000 of rental income and $7,000 of dividend income. In this case, dividends of only $1,000 are necessary since nonrental PHCI exceeds the 10% threshold by only $1,000 [$7,000 – (10% of OGI of $60,000)]. If the taxpayer wants to avoid distributing dividends, consideration should be given to increasing gross rents. Note how an increase of $10,000 in gross rents to $63,000 would increase OGI and concomitantly eliminate the need for a dividend. This increase in gross rents would be effective even if the typical adjustments for depreciation, interest, and taxes reduce the taxpayer's net profit to zero or a loss. This is true because such adjustments are not included in determining OGI, but only AOGI. Thus, an incentive exists for the corporation to invest in breakeven or unprofitable activities as a means to eliminate the dividend.

### Reducing the PHC Tax with Dividends

If the tests for PHC status cannot be avoided, the penalty can be eliminated or minimized by the payment of dividends. Although a similar opportunity exists for the accumulated earnings tax, the treatment of dividends differs in several important respects.

On the one hand, the PHC tax requires quicker action than the accumulated earnings tax. For accumulated earnings tax purposes, all dividends paid within the 2½-month period after the close of the taxable year are counted as paid for the previous year. However, for purposes of the PHC tax, the after-year-end dividends are limited to 20 percent of the amount actually paid during the year. Thus, if no dividends are paid during the year, then none can be paid during the 2½-month period. On the other hand, the PHC tax can almost always be avoided through payment of a deficiency dividend, which is not available for the accumulated earnings tax. The deficiency dividend may come at a high price, however. As previously mentioned, any interest and penalties that would have been imposed had the penalty tax applied must be computed and paid as if the PHC tax were still due.

## Planned Personal Holding Companies

Treatment of a corporation as a personal holding company is normally considered a dire consequence. Yet, in certain cases, PHC status may not be detrimental and at times can be beneficial. Two of these situations are outlined below.

Certain taxpayers seeking the benefits of the corporate form are unable to avoid characterization as a personal holding company. For example, an athlete or movie celebrity may seek the benefits reserved solely for employees, such as group-term life insurance, health and accident insurance, medical reimbursement plans, and better pension and profit-sharing plans. In these situations, if the individual incorporates his or her talents, the corporation will be considered a PHC since all of the income for services will be PHCI. This does not mean that the PHC tax must be paid, however. The PHC tax is levied only upon undistributed PHCI. In most cases, all of the undistributed PHCI can be eliminated through the payments of deductible compensation directly to the individual or deductible contributions to his or her pension plan. As a result, the individual can obtain the benefits of incorporation without concern for the PHC tax. This technique was extremely popular prior to 1982, when the benefits of corporate pension plans were significantly better than those available to the self-employed (i.e., Keogh plans).

Over the years, personal holding companies have been used quite successfully in estate planning in reducing the value of the taxpayer's estate and obtaining other estate tax benefits. Under a typical plan, a taxpayer with a portfolio of securities would transfer them to a PHC in exchange for preferred stock equal to their current value and common stock of no value. The exchange would be tax free under Code § 351. The taxpayer would then proceed to give the common stock to his or her children at no gift tax cost since its value at the time is zero. The taxpayer would also begin a gift program, transferring $10,000 of preferred stock annually to heirs, which would also escape gift tax due to the annual gift tax exclusion. There were several benefits arising from this arrangement.

First and probably foremost, any appreciation in the value of the taxpayer's portfolio would accrue to the owners of the common stock and thus be successfully removed from the taxpayer's estate, avoiding both gift and estate taxes. Second, the corporation's declaration of dividends on the common stock would shift the income to the lower-bracket family members. Dividends on the preferred stock would also be shifted to the extent that the taxpayer has transferred the preferred stock. The dividends paid would in part aid in eliminating any PHC tax. Third, the taxpayer's preferred stock in the PHC would probably be valued at less than the value of the underlying assets for estate and gift tax purposes. Although the IRS takes the position that the value of the stock in the PHC is the same as the value of the corporation's assets, the courts have consistently held otherwise. The courts have normally allowed a substantial *discount* for estate and gift tax valuation, holding that an investment in a closely held business is less desirable than in the underlying shares since the underlying securities can easily be traded in the market while the PHC shares cannot.[110]

---

[110] For example, see *Estate of Maurice Gustane Heckscher*, 63 T.C. 485 (1974). Also, see Chapter 26 for possible limitations on this estate planning technique.

## Problem Materials

### DISCUSSION QUESTIONS

**21-1** *Double Taxation.* List four approaches that corporations use to avoid the effects of double taxation.

**21-2** *Accumulated Earnings Tax.* What is the purpose of the accumulated earnings tax?

**21-3** *Accumulated Earnings Tax.* What is the accumulated earnings tax rate? Why do you suppose Congress chose this particular tax rate?

**21-4** *Accumulated Taxable Income.* What is the difference between accumulated taxable income and taxable income?

**21-5** *Accumulated Earnings Credit.* What is the accumulated earnings credit? How does it affect the accumulated earnings tax?

**21-6** *Dividends-Paid Deduction.* What constitutes the dividends-paid deduction for purposes of the accumulated earnings tax?

**21-7** *Throwback Dividend.* What is a throwback dividend?

**21-8** *Consent Dividends.* What is a consent dividend? What is its purpose?

**21-9** *Intent of Accumulations.* What situations are considered to indicate the intent of a corporation to unreasonably accumulate earnings?

**21-10** *Reasonable Needs.* List six possible reasons for accumulating earnings that might be considered reasonable needs of the business.

**21-11** *Reasonable Needs—The Bardahl Formula.* What is the *Bardahl* formula? How is it used?

**21-12** *Personal Holding Company Tax.* What is the purpose of the personal holding company tax?

**21-13** *Personal Holding Company.* What requirements must be met by a corporation in order for it to be a personal holding company?

**21-14** *Ownership Requirement.* What is the ownership requirement for personal holding companies? What constructive ownership rules apply?

**21-15** *Income Requirement.* What is the income requirement for personal holding companies? What terms must be defined in order to determine if a corporation meets the income requirement?

**21-16** *Income Requirement.* What tests must be met in order to determine whether the adjusted income from rents is included in personal holding company income?

**21-17** *Computing the Personal Holding Company Tax.* How is the personal holding company penalty tax computed?

**21-18** *Adjusted Taxable Income.* How does adjusted taxable income differ from taxable income?

**21-19** *Dividends-Paid Deduction.* How does the dividends-paid deduction for personal holding company tax purposes differ from the dividends-paid deduction for accumulated earnings tax purposes?

**21-20** *Deficiency Dividends.* What is a deficiency dividend? What is its purpose? What effect does it have on the personal holding company tax?

### PROBLEMS

**21-21** *Computing the Accumulated Earnings Tax.* Z Corporation had accumulated taxable income of $180,000 for the current year. Calculate Z Corporation's accumulated earnings tax liability.

**21-22** *Computing Adjusted Taxable Income.* R Corporation has the following income and deductions for the current year:

| | |
|---|---|
| Income from operations | $200,000 |
| Dividend income (from less than 20% owned corporations) | 60,000 |
| Charitable contributions | 40,000 |

Compute R Corporation's adjusted taxable income.

**21-23** *Minimum Accumulated Earnings Tax Credit.* B Corporation, a calendar year manufacturing company, had accumulated earnings and profits at the beginning of the current year of $60,000. If the corporation's earnings and profits for the current year are $270,000, what is B Corporation's minimum accumulated earnings tax credit?

**21-24** *Accumulated Earnings Tax Credit.* Assume the same facts in *Problem 21-23* above, except that B Corporation has estimated reasonable business needs of $170,000 at the end of the current year.

**a.** Compute B Corporation's accumulated earnings tax credit for the current year.

**b.** Would your answer differ if B Corporation was an incorporated law practice owned and operated be one person? If so, by how much?

**21-25** *Computing the Accumulated Earnings Tax.* T Corporation had accumulated earnings and profits at the beginning of 2011 of $300,000. It has never paid dividends to its shareholders and does not intend to do so in the near future. The following facts relate to T Corporation's 2011 tax year:

| | |
|---|---|
| Taxable income | $200,000 |
| Federal income tax | 61,250 |
| Dividends received (from less than 20% owned corporations) | 40,000 |
| Reasonable business needs as of 12/31/11 | 356,850 |

**a.** What is T Corporation's accumulated earnings tax?

**b.** If T Corporation's sole shareholder wanted to avoid the accumulated earnings tax, what amount of consent dividends would be required?

**21-26** *Dividends-Paid Deduction.* J Corporation, a small oil tool manufacturer, projects adjusted taxable income for the current year of $200,000. Its estimated reasonable business needs are $500,000; and the corporation has $380,000 of prior years' accumulated earnings and profits as of the beginning of the current year. Using this information, answer the following:

**a.** Assuming no dividends-paid deduction, what is J Corporation's accumulated earnings tax for the current year?

**b.** If J Corporation paid $50,000 of dividends during the year, what is J Corporation's accumulated earnings tax liability?

**c.** If J Corporation's shareholders are willing to report more dividends than the $50,000 actually received during the year, what amount of consent dividends is necessary to avoid the accumulated earnings tax?

**d.** If the corporation's shareholders are not interested in paying taxes on hypothetical dividends, what other possibility is available to increase the dividends-paid deduction?

**21-27** *Working Capital Needs—The* Bardahl *Formula.* X Corporation wishes to use the Bardahl formula to determine the amount of working capital it can justify if the IRS agent currently auditing the company's records raises the accumulated earnings tax issue. For the year under audit, X Corporation had the following:

| | |
|---|---|
| Annual operating expenses | $285,000 |
| Inventory cycle ratio | .41 |
| Accounts receivable cycle ratio | .61 |
| Accounts payable cycle ratio | .82 |

**a.** How much working capital can X Corporation justify based on the above facts?

**b.** If X Corporation's turnover ratios are based on annual averages, what additional information would you request before computing working capital needs based on the *Bardahl* formula?

**21-28** *Working Capital Needs—Bardahl Formula.* B owns and operates BKA Inc., which is a retail toy store. One Wednesday morning in January 2012, she noticed in the *Wall Street Journal's* tax column an anecdote about a small corporation that was required to pay the accumulated earnings tax. Concerned, B presented the following information to her tax advisor to evaluate her exposure as of the end of 2011.

**Balance Sheet**

| | 2010 | 2011 |
|---|---|---|
| Current Assets: | | |
| Cash | $ 15,000 | $ 30,000 |
| Marketable securities (cost) | 10,000 | 23,000 |
| Accounts receivable (net) | 55,000 | 45,000 |
| Inventory | 30,000 | 50,000 |
| Property, plant, and equipment (net) | 500,000 | 552,000 |
| Total Assets | $610,000 | $700,000 |
| Current Liabilities: | | |
| Accounts payable | $ 13,000 | $ 31,000 |
| Long-term debt | 147,000 | 119,000 |
| Common stock | 50,000 | 50,000 |
| Earnings and profits | 400,000 | 500,000 |
| Total Liabilities and Equity | $ 610,000 | $ 700,000 |

**Income Statement**

| | | |
|---|---|---|
| Sales | | $400,000 |
| Cost of goods sold: | | |
| Beginning inventory | $ 30,000 | |
| Purchases | 220,000 | |
| Ending inventory | (50,000) | |
| Total | | (200,000) |
| Gross profit | | $200,000 |
| Other Expenses: | | |
| Depreciation | $ 70,000 | |
| Selling expenses and administrative | 25,000 | |
| Interest | 5,000 | |
| Total | | (100,000) |
| Net income before taxes | | $100,000 |
| Income taxes | | (25,750) |
| Net income | | $ 74,250 |

B noted that the market value of the securities was $40,000 as of December 31, 2011. In addition, B estimates the future expansion of the business (excluding working capital) will require $25,000. Determine whether the accumulated earnings tax will apply to B.

**21-29** *Personal Holding Company—Income Requirement.* K Corporation is equally owned and operated by three brothers. K Corporation's gross income for the current year is $80,000, which consists of $10,000 of dividend income, interest income of $40,000, and a long-term capital gain of $30,000.

**a.** Calculate ordinary gross income.
**b.** Calculate adjusted ordinary gross income.
**c.** Is K Corporation a personal holding company?

**21-30** *Personal Holding Company—Rent Exclusion.* T Corporation has gross income of \$116,000, which consists of gross rental income of \$86,000, interest income of \$20,000, and dividends of \$10,000. Depreciation, property taxes, and interest expense related to the rental property totaled \$16,000. Assuming T Corporation has seven shareholders and has no dividends-paid deduction, answer the following:

**a.** What is T Corporation's ordinary gross income?
**b.** Adjusted ordinary gross income?
**c.** Does the rental income constitute personal holding company income?
**d.** Is T Corporation a personal holding company?

**21-31** *Personal Holding Company Income.* V Corporation is equally owned by two shareholders. The corporation reports the following income and deductions for the current year.

| | |
|---|---|
| Dividend income | \$30,000 |
| Interest income | 15,000 |
| Long-term capital gain | 10,000 |
| Rental income (gross) | 80,000 |
| Rental expenses: | |
| Depreciation | 10,000 |
| Interest on mortgage | 9,000 |
| Property taxes | 3,000 |
| Real estate management fees | 8,000 |

**a.** Calculate ordinary gross income.
**b.** Calculate adjusted ordinary gross income.
**c.** Calculate adjusted income from rentals.
**d.** Calculate personal holding company income.
**e.** Is V Corporation a personal holding company?
**f.** If V Corporation paid \$3,000 of dividends to each of its two shareholders during the current year, how would this affect your answers to (d) and (e) above?

**21-32** *Items of PHC Income.* Indicate whether the following would be considered personal holding company income.

**a.** Income from the sales of inventory
**b.** Interest income from AT&T bond
**c.** Interest income from State of Texas bond
**d.** Dividend income from IBM stock
**e.** Long-term capital gain
**f.** Short-term capital gain
**g.** Rental income from lease of office building (100% of the corporation's income is from rents)
**h.** Fees paid to the corporation for the services of Jose Greatfoot, internationally known soccer player.

**21-33** *PHC Income Test.* All of the stock of C Corporation is owned by B. Next year, the corporation expects the following results from operations:

| | |
|---|---|
| Sales | \$500,000 |
| Costs of goods sold | 200,000 |
| Other operating expenses | 40,000 |
| Interest income | 10,000 |

What is the maximum amount of dividend income that the corporation can have without being classified as a personal holding company?

**21-34** *Computing the Personal Holding Company Tax.* P Corporation is owned by five individuals. For the current year P had the following:

| | |
|---|---|
| Taxable income . . . . . . . . . . . . . . . . . . . . . . . . . . . . . . . . . . . . . . . | $200,000 |
| Federal income tax . . . . . . . . . . . . . . . . . . . . . . . . . . . . . . . . . . . . | 60,750 |
| Dividends received (from less than 20% owned corporations). . . . . . . | 40,000 |
| Long-term capital gain . . . . . . . . . . . . . . . . . . . . . . . . . . . . . . . . | 10,000 |

Compute P Corporation's personal holding company tax assuming that P meets the income test, P did not pay dividends, and the long-term capital gain was taxed at 34 percent.

**21-35** *Personal Holding Company—Dividend Deduction.* H, a personal holding company, anticipates having undistributed personal holding company income of $120,000 before any dividend deduction for 2011. The company wishes to distribute all of its income to avoid the penalty. Because of cash flow problems, it wishes to pay as much of this dividend as it can in the 2½ months after the close of the tax year.

**a.** What is the *maximum* amount that H can distribute during 2012 to accomplish its task if dividends of $50,000 were paid during 2011?

**b.** What is the *minimum* amount that H must distribute during 2011 and still be able to defer until 2012 the payment of any additional dividends?

**21-36** *Personal Holding Company—Service Income.* J, an orthopedic surgeon, is the sole owner of J Inc. The corporation employs surgical nurses and physical therapists in addition to J. The nurses assist Dr. J on all operations, and the therapists provide all follow-up treatment. J Inc. bills all clients for all services rendered and pays the employees a stated salary. Will any of J Inc.'s fee be personal holding company income?

**21-37** *PHC Dividends—Paid Deduction.* Indicate whether the following distributions would qualify for the personal holding company dividends—paid deduction for 2011. Assume that the corporation is a calendar year taxpayer.

**a.** Cash dividends paid on common stock in 2011.

**b.** Dividend distribution of land (value $20,000, basis $5,000) paid on common stock in 2011.

**c.** Cash dividends paid on common stock March 3, 2012.

**d.** Cash dividends paid on common stock in 2010.

**e.** Consent dividend; the 2011 corporate tax return was filed on March 3, 2012; the consents were filed on May 15, 2012.

**f.** Cash dividend paid in 2014 shortly after it was determined that the corporation was a personal holding company.

**g.** The corporation adopted a plan of liquidation in 2009 and the final liquidating distribution was made during 2011.

**21-38** *Accumulated Earnings Tax Dividends-Paid Deduction.* Indicate whether the distributions identified in *Problem 21-37* would qualify for the accumulated earnings tax dividends-paid deduction for 2010.

**21-39** *Understanding the PHC Tax.* Indicate whether the following statements regarding the personal holding company tax are true or false.

**a.** The PHC tax is self-assessed and, if applicable, must be paid in addition to the regular income tax.

**b.** An S corporation or partnership may be subject to the PHC tax.

**c.** A corporation that can prove that its shareholders did not intend to use it as a tax shelter is not subject to the PHC tax.

**d.** A publicly traded corporation normally would not be subject to the PHC tax.

**e.** A corporation that derives virtually all of its income from leasing operations does not risk the PHC tax, even though such income is normally considered passive.

**f.** Federal income taxes reduce the base on which the PHC tax is assessed.

g. Long-term capital gains are not subject to the PHC tax.
h. A corporation that consistently pays dividends normally would not be subject to the PHC tax.
i. Throwback dividends are available to reduce the corporation's potential liability without limitation.
j. Corporations without cash or property that they can distribute cannot benefit from the dividends-paid deduction.
k. The PHC tax is not truly a risk because of the deficiency dividend procedure.
l. A corporation may be required to pay both the accumulated earnings tax and the personal holding company tax in the same year.

**21-40** *Understanding the Accumulated Earnings Tax.* Indicate whether the statements in *Problem 21-39* are true or false regarding the accumulated earnings tax.

## TAX RESEARCH PROBLEMS

**21-41** H Corporation is owned and operated by William and Wilma Holt. The corporation's principal source of income for the past few years has been net rentals from five adjacent rent houses located in an area that the city has condemned in order to expand its freeway system. The Holts anticipate a condemnation award of approximately $400,000, and a resulting gain of $325,000. Although convinced that they will have the corporation reinvest the proceeds in other rental units, the Holts would like to invest the corporation's condemnation proceeds in a high-yield certificate of deposit for at least three years. They have come to you for advice.

a. What advice would you give concerning the reinvestment requirements of Code § 1033?
b. If H Corporation will have substantial interest income in the next few years, could the § 541 tax be a possibility?
c. If the Holts have considered liquidating the corporation and reinvesting the proceeds in rental units, what additional information would you need in order to advise them?

**21-42** Stacey Caniff is the controlling shareholder of Cotton, Inc., a textile manufacturer. She inherited the business from her father. In recent years earnings have fluctuated between $0.50 and $3.00 per share. Dividends have remained at $0.10 per share for the past ten years with a resulting increase in cash. On audit, the IRS agent has raised the accumulated earnings tax issue. In your discussion with Stacey, she has indicated that the dividends are so low because she is afraid of losing the business (as almost happened to her father during the Depression), of decreased profitability from foreign competition, and of the need to modernize if OSHA were to enforce the rules concerning cotton dust. Evaluate the possibility of overcoming an accumulated earnings tax assessment.

# Flow-Through Entities

PART 8

CHAPTER 22 Taxation of Partnerships and Partners

CHAPTER 23 S Corporations

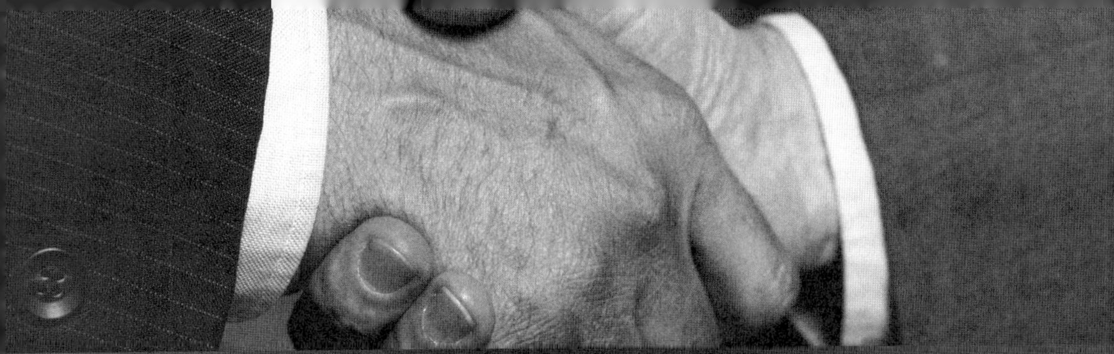

22

# Taxation of Partnerships and Partners

## Learning Objectives

Upon completion of this chapter you will be able to:

LO.1 Define the terms *partner* and *partnership* for federal income tax purposes.

LO.2 Distinguish between the entity theory and the aggregate theory of partnerships.

LO.3 Analyze the tax consequences of forming a new partnership.

LO.4 Determine the tax basis of a partnership interest.

LO.5 Compute partnership taxable income or loss and identify any separately computed items of partnership income, gain, loss, deduction, or credit.

LO.6 Explain how the tax consequences of partnership operations are reported on the tax returns of the partners and how the partners' bases in their partnership interests are adjusted to reflect these tax consequences.

LO.7 Identify the tax consequences of various transactions between a partner and a partnership.

LO.8 Determine the tax consequences of both current and liquidating distributions from a partnership.

LO.9 Analyze the tax consequences of a sale of a partnership interest to both the seller and purchaser.

LO.10 Apply the family partnership rules to partnership interests created by gift.

LO.11 Recognize a termination of a partnership and summarize the tax consequences of the termination to the partners.

## Chapter Outline


Introduction 22-2
Definitions 22-2
What Is a Partnership? 22-2
Electing out of Subchapter K Partnerships 22-3
General and Limited Partnerships 22-3
Entity and Aggregate Theories 22-4
Forming a Partnership 22-4
Contributions of Property 22-5
Effect of Partnership Liabilities on Basis 22-6
Contribution of Services 22-11
Proposed Regulations Change Rules for Services 22-12
Operating the Partnership 22-12
The Partnership's Taxable Year 22-13
Organization Costs and Syndication Fees 22-14
Computation of Partnership Taxable Income 22-15
Reporting of Partnership Items by Partners 22-16

Adjustments to Partner's Basis 22-16
Partners' Distributive Shares 22-17
Substantial Economic Effect 22-18
Allocations with Respect to Contributed Property 22-19
Retroactive Allocations 22-20
Basis Limitation on Loss Deductibility 22-21
Transactions between Partners and Partnerships 22-22
Sales between Partners and Controlled Partnerships 22-23
Partnership Distributions 22-24
Current Distributions 22-24
Liquidating Distributions 22-27
Section 736 Payments 22-32
Dispositions of Distributed Property 22-34
Basis Adjustments to Partnership Property 22-35
Dispositions of Partnership Interests 22-38
Sales of Partnership Interests 22-38
Gifts of Partnership Interests and Family Partnerships 22-45
Death of a Partner 22-46
Partnership Termination 22-47
Technical Terminations 22-47
Effect of Termination 22-48
Problem Materials 22-48


# Introduction

When two or more parties agree to go into business together, they must first decide which form of business to use. Should the business be incorporated or should it operate as a partnership? Although the corporate form predominates for large companies, it is certainly not appropriate for all businesses. Consequently, partnerships are widely used throughout the business world.

Partnerships come in a wide assortment of shapes and sizes. For example, two accountants may form a professional partnership through which to conduct their business, or a family may organize a partnership to manage real estate or operate a corner delicatessen. In contrast, two international corporations may form a partnership to develop a new product or to conduct research. Partnerships may also be used as investment vehicles. For instance, hundreds or thousands of people may invest in partnerships that drill for oil, construct office buildings, or make movies. For whatever reason, when two or more parties decide to pool their resources in order to carry on a profit-making activity, they often choose to do so as partners in a partnership.

The federal tax consequences of business activities that meet the statutory definition of a partnership are governed by the provisions of Subchapter K of the Internal Revenue Code (§§ 701 through 777). This chapter begins with an analysis of this definition and a brief introduction to several other important concepts that underlie Subchapter K. The chapter also includes discussions of the formation and operation of a partnership, the mechanics by which partnership income or loss is allocated to and taken into account by each partner, and the tax consequences of common transactions between partners and partnerships. The more advanced topics of current and liquidating partnership distributions and dispositions of partnership interests are also introduced.

# Definitions

## What Is a Partnership?

**LO.1**
Define the terms *partner* and *partnership* for federal income tax purposes.

The Uniform Partnership Act defines a partnership quite simply as "an association of two or more persons to carry on as co-owners a business for profit."[1] This basic definition is expanded in the Code to include a syndicate, group, pool, joint venture, or any other unincorporated organization.[2] For an organization to constitute a partnership, it must have at least two partners. Note that there are no restrictions on either the maximum number of partners or on the type of entity that may be a partner. Individuals, corporations, trusts, estates, and even other partnerships may join together as partners to carry on a profit-making activity.

[1] Uniform Partnership Act, § 6(1).

[2] § 761(a).

As a practical matter, determining whether an organization qualifies as a partnership is rarely a problem. For example, any organization formed under the Uniform Partnership Act or the Uniform Limited Partnership Act should expect to be treated as a partnership. However, as explained in Chapter 19, certain unincorporated organizations may or may not be treated as partnerships for tax purposes. Under the "check the box" regulations, all business entities incorporated under a state law providing for a separate corporation, a joint stock company, an insurance company, a bank, or certain foreign entities will be classified as corporations for federal tax purposes.[3] All other business entities, known as associations, which are not automatically defined as a corporation can *elect* to be taxed as a corporation. Any association, including any limited liability company having two or more owners and that does not make the election, will be treated as a partnership.[4]

A foreign entity in which all owners have limited liability will be treated as a corporation. A foreign entity in which one or more owners have unlimited liability will be treated as a partnership unless it makes the election to be taxed as a corporation.[5]

Other treasury regulations clarify that certain arrangements are not treated as partnerships for federal tax purposes. A joint undertaking is not a partnership if the only joint activity is the sharing of expenses. For example, if two adjacent property owners share the cost of a dam constructed to prevent flooding, no partnership exists. Similarly, joint ownership of property is not a partnership if the co-owners merely rent or lease the property and provide minimal services to the lessees. In such case, the co-owners are not actively conducting a trade or business. If, however, these co-owners provide substantial tenant services, they may elevate their passive co-ownership to active partnership status.[6]

## Electing out of Subchapter K Partnerships

Section 761(a) allows certain unincorporated organizations that potentially constitute partnerships for federal tax purposes to be excluded from the application of the statutory rules of Subchapter K. An organization may elect out of the statutory rules governing the taxation of partners and partnerships if it is formed for (1) investment purposes only and not for the active conduct of a business, or (2) the joint production, extraction, or use of property. The members of such an organization must be able to compute their separate incomes without the necessity of computing partnership taxable income (i.e., income for the organization as a whole). The election is made by attaching a statement to a properly filed Form 1065 (U.S. Partnership Return of Income) for the first taxable year for which the organization desires exclusion from Subchapter K. The statement must identify all members of the organization and indicate their consent to the election.[7]

## General and Limited Partnerships

There are two types of partnerships: *general* partnerships and *limited* partnerships. The two differ primarily in the nature of the rights and obligations of the partners; the major differences can be summarized as follows:

1. General partnerships are owned solely by general partners, whereas limited partnerships must have at least one general partner and one or more limited partners.
2. General partners have *unlimited liability* for partnership debt, whereas limited partners are usually liable only to the extent of their capital contributions to the partnership.
3. General partners participate in the management and control of the partnership business, whereas limited partners are not allowed to participate in such business.[8]
4. General partners are subject to self-employment taxes on partnership business earnings even if they do not perform services for the partnership, whereas limited partners are not.

---

[3] Reg. §§ 301.7701-1(b) and 301.7701-4.

[4] A limited liability company with only one owner cannot be considered a partnership for tax purposes. Instead, such an entity will be treated as either a corporation or sole proprietorship.

[5] See Reg. §§ 301.7701-1(b) and 301.7701-4.

[6] Reg. § 1.761-1(a).

[7] Reg. § 1.761-2(b)(2).

[8] A limited partner who takes part in the control of the partnership business may become liable to the creditors of the partnership by doing so. Revised Uniform Limited Partnership Act (1976), § 303(a).

Two other types of entities that are usually taxed as partnerships are limited liability companies (LLC) and limited liability partnerships (LLP). In an LLC, all members (i.e., owners) have limited liability. Generally, the partners in an LLP have better liability protection than general partners, but more liability exposure than limited partners. LLP partners usually have unlimited liability, except any particular partner is not personally liable for claims arising from a tort that was committed by a different partner. Nevertheless, the partner committing the tort is personally liability for the claims resulting from his or her actions.

All references throughout the text are to general partners and general partnerships unless otherwise stated.

### Entity and Aggregate Theories

**LO.2**
Distinguish between the entity theory and the aggregate theory of partnerships.

Most rules governing the taxation of partnerships are based on either the entity or aggregate theory of partnerships.[9] According to the *entity theory*, partnerships should be regarded as entities distinct and separate from their owners. As such, partnerships may enter into taxable transactions with partners, may hold title to property in their own names, are not legally liable for debts of partners, are required to file annual returns (Form 1065) that report the results of operations, and can make tax elections concerning partnership activities that apply to all partners.

In contrast, the *aggregate theory* views a partnership as a collection of specific partners, each of which indirectly owns an undivided interest in partnership assets. Under this theory, the partnership itself has no identity distinct from that of its partners. The fact that a partnership is a pass-through rather than a taxable entity, functioning only as a conduit of income to the partners, is a clear reflection of the aggregate theory. The aggregate theory also prevents the recognition of gain or loss on several types of transactions between partners and their partnerships.

The inconsistent application of the entity and aggregate theories throughout Subchapter K certainly complicates the taxation of partners and their partnerships. In extreme cases, a single Code section may contain elements of both theories. In spite of this confusion, taxpayers and their advisers who can determine which theory underlies a particular rule of partnership tax law will gain valuable insight into the proper application of that rule to a specific fact situation.

## Forming a Partnership

**LO.3**
Analyze the tax consequences of forming a new partnership.

The first step in the formation of any partnership is the drafting of a partnership agreement by the prospective partners. A *partnership agreement* is a legal contract stipulating the rights and obligations of the co-owners of the business. Ideally a partnership agreement should be drafted by a competent attorney, should be in writing, and should be signed by each partner. However, even oral partnership agreements between business associates have been respected as binding contracts by the courts.[10]

A partner's *interest in a partnership* is an intangible asset—an equity interest in the partnership business, the exact nature of which is defined in the partnership agreement. Under the typical agreement, each partner has a specified interest in partnership cash and property. The dollar amount of such interest at any time is reflected by the balance in each partner's *capital account* in the equity section of the partnership balance sheet. In addition to his or her capital interest, each partner has an interest in any income or loss generated by the partnership's activities. This interest is usually expressed as a *profit-and-loss sharing ratio* among the partners. If the partners consent, the terms of their agreement may be modified with respect to a particular taxable year at any time before the unextended due date by which the partnership return for such year must be filed.[11]

Partners may certainly agree to share profits and losses in different ratios. They may also agree that these ratios will be independent of the relative amounts of capital to which the partners are entitled.

---

[9] For an interesting historical discussion of the development of these conflicting theories, see Arthur B. Willis, John S. Pennell, and Philip F. Postlewaite, *Partnership Taxation* (Colorado Springs, CO.: Shepard's/McGraw-Hill, Inc.), Chapter 4.

[10] See, for example, *Elrod*, 87 T.C. 1046 (1986).

[11] § 761(c).

### Example 1

Doctors J and K decide to form a general partnership to carry on a medical practice. Both individuals contribute $50,000 of cash to the partnership so that both have an initial capital account balance of $50,000. The partnership will use the cash to purchase equipment and supplies and to lease office space. Doctor J has been in local practice for several years and has an established reputation, while Doctor K recently graduated from medical school. Consequently, the partnership agreement provides that Doctor J will be allocated 65% of profits and losses, while Doctor K will be allocated 35%. The agreement stipulates that J and K will renegotiate this profit-and-loss sharing ratio after three years.

## Contributions of Property

Partners may make initial contributions to partnership capital in the form of cash, property, or a combination of both. When a partner transfers property to a partnership in exchange for an ownership interest, § 721 provides that neither the partner nor the partnership recognizes any gain or loss on the exchange.[12] The partner's tax basis in the transferred property carries over to become the partnership's basis in the property (i.e., a *carryover* basis).[13] The tax basis in the transferring partner's newly acquired partnership interest equals the basis of the transferred property plus any amount of cash contributed to the partnership (i.e., a *substituted* basis).[14] Tax professionals who specialize in the partnership area have coined the term *inside basis* to refer to the tax basis of assets owned by a partnership. In contrast, the term *outside basis* refers to the tax basis of a partner's interest in a partnership. Although neither term is used in the Code or Regulations, they provide a descriptive and easy way to differentiate between these two basis concepts.

The partnership's holding period for contributed assets includes the holding period of the assets in the hands of the contributing partner.[15] If the assets were either capital assets or § 1231 assets to the contributing partner, the partner's holding period for these assets becomes the holding period for his new partnership interest.[16] If the contributed assets were not capital or § 1231 assets, the partner's holding period for his interest begins on the date the interest is acquired.

### Example 2

A contributes § 1231 assets with a fair market value of $25,000 and an adjusted basis of $15,500, and B contributes $25,000 cash to the AB Partnership. The capital accounts on the partnership books are credited to reflect the equal $25,000 contributions of each partner. A does not recognize any gain on the exchange of the appreciated business assets for his interest in the AB Partnership. However, A's initial outside basis in his partnership interest is only $15,500. A's holding period for this interest includes the period of time for which A owned the contributed § 1231 assets. Even though the partnership recorded the contributed assets on its books at their $25,000 fair market value, the partnership's inside basis in these assets is only $15,500. B's initial tax basis in her partnership interest is $25,000, and her holding period for this interest begins on the date of contribution.

[12] This nonrecognition rule does not apply to gain realized on transfer of appreciated stocks and securities to an investment partnership. § 721(b). Also, special rules—beyond the scope of this text—apply to transfers to partnerships with foreign persons and transfers of intangibles to foreign partnerships. See §§ 721(c) and 721(d).

[13] § 723. If contributed property is depreciable, the partnership will continue to use the cost recovery method and life used by the contributing partner. § 168(i)(7).

[14] § 722.

[15] § 1223(2).

[16] § 1223(1).

**LO.4**
Determine the tax basis of a partnership interest.

The above example illustrates two important points. First, a partner's outside basis is not necessarily equal to the balance in his or her capital account on the partnership's financial books and records. The partnership book capital accounts reflect the economic value of contributions to the partnership, while the partners' outside bases in their partnership interests reflect the tax basis of their respective contributions. Second, the tax rules governing contributions to partnerships result in an initial equilibrium between the partners' aggregate outside bases and the total inside basis of partnership assets. In *Example 2*, A and B have aggregate outside bases of $40,500. The AB Partnership has total inside basis in its assets of $40,500 ($25,000 cash + $15,500 carryover basis of its § 1231 assets). This equilibrium reflects the aggregate theory of partnerships under which A and B are considered to own indirect interests in AB's assets. However, it is possible that during the partnership's existence the aggregate outside basis will differ at times from the total inside basis.

A partner may have a divided holding period in his or her partnership interest in two circumstances. If a divided holding period occurs, the portion of a partnership interest to which a holding period relates is based on the relative fair market values of the properties contributed.[17] This will occur if the partner acquired portions of the partnership interest at different times.[18]

**Example 3**

R purchased a 10% interest in Z Partnership for $10,000 on January 1, 2011. She purchased another 5% interest in Z for $5,000 on November 1, 2011. As of January 1, 2012, R has a one-year holding period in two-thirds of her partnership interest ($10,000/$15,000), and a two-month holding period for one-third ($5,000/$15,000) of her interest.

A partner will also have a divided holding period in his or her partnership interest if the partner contributed more than one property for the partnership interest, and these properties had different holding periods in the hands of the partner.[19]

**Example 4**

E contributes cash of $2,000 and a capital asset (basis = $1,000; value = $2,000) held for five years for a 25% interest in Partnership Y. The portion of E's interest attributable to the cash, 50% [$2,000/($2,000 + $2,000)], will have a holding period beginning the day after the contribution. The portion of his interest attributable to the capital asset (50%) has a five-year holding period.

## Effect of Partnership Liabilities on Basis

When a partnership borrows money, the general partners typically have unlimited liability for repayment of the debt to the partnership's creditors. If the partnership itself is unable to repay its debts, each partner must contribute personal funds to satisfy the unpaid balance. As a result, a partner's economic investment in a partnership consists not only of the contribution of cash or property reflected in his or her capital account, but also of the share of partnership debt for which the partner might ultimately be held responsible.

Section 752(a) acknowledges this responsibility by providing that any increase in a partner's share of the liabilities of a partnership or any assumption of a partnership debt by a partner is treated as a contribution of money to the partnership. This constructive cash contribution increases the partner's outside basis in his or her partnership interest.

[17] Reg. § 1.1223-3(b)(1).

[18] Reg. § 1.1223-2(a); for transfers of partnerships interests after September 20, 2000.

[19] Reg. § 1.1223-3(a)(2).

Conversely, § 752(b) provides that any decrease in a partner's share of the liabilities of a partnership or any assumption of a partner's debt by a partnership is treated as a distribution of money from the partnership to the partner. This constructive cash distribution reduces the partner's outside basis.[20]

## Example 5

M and N are equal partners in the M&N Partnership. On January 1 of the current year, both M and N had a $25,000 outside basis in their partnership interests, and the partnership had no debt on its balance sheet. On January 31, the partnership borrowed $15,000 from a local bank and used the funds to buy business assets. Because this transaction increased M and N's respective shares of the partnership's liabilities by $7,500, each was considered to have contributed this amount of cash to the partnership. As a result, their outside bases as of January 31 increased to $32,500.

On June 1, the partnership repaid $6,000 of the outstanding debt. Because this payment decreased M and N's respective shares of partnership debt, each was considered to have received a $3,000 cash distribution from the partnership. As a result, their outside bases as of June 1 decreased to $29,500.

| | *M* | *N* |
|---|---|---|
| January 1 outside basis | $25,000 | $25,000 |
| Plus: Increase in share of partnership debt on 1/31 | 7,500 | 7,500 |
| Less: Decrease in share of partnership debt on 6/1 | (3,000) | (3,000) |
| June 1 outside basis | $29,500 | $29,500 |

Note that in the above example, the inclusion of partnership debt in the partners' outside bases maintained the equilibrium between inside and outside basis. Between January 1 and June 1, M and N's aggregate outside bases increased by a net amount of $9,000. During this same period, the basis of partnership assets also increased by $9,000 ($15,000 debt proceeds – $6,000 cash distribution).

### Partner's Share of Partnership Liabilities

The combined result of § 752(a) and (b) is that on any particular date, a partner's outside basis includes a share of the various debts reflected on the partnership balance sheet as of that date. The Treasury Regulations under § 752 provide a lengthy and complex set of rules for determining a partner's share of partnership liabilities. Under these regulations, each partner's share of any specific debt depends on the classification of the debt itself and whether the partner is a general or limited partner. All partnership debts are classified as either recourse or nonrecourse. A debt is *recourse* if the creditor can look to the personal assets of any general partner to satisfy the unpaid portion of the debt in the event the partnership does not have sufficient assets for repayment. A debt is *nonrecourse* if the creditor cannot look beyond the assets of the partnership for repayment.

A partner's share of recourse debt equals the portion of such debt for which that partner bears the *economic risk of loss*.[21] Because limited partners generally bear no responsibility for the repayment of partnership liabilities, they have no risk of loss with respect to partnership recourse debt. Consequently, no amount of such debt is apportioned to any limited partner. The extent to which general partners are deemed to bear the economic risk of loss for partnership recourse debt is generally determined by using the results from a hypothetical *constructive liquidation scenario*.[22] The basic idea behind these rules is to consider which partners would have to actually satisfy these liabilities if the absolute worst scenario imagi-

[20] § 733.

[21] Reg. § 1.752-2(a).

[22] Reg. § 1.752-2(b). In so-called straight-up partnerships in which the partners' profit-and-loss sharing ratios correspond to the ratios of their respective capital account balances, the application of this analysis has the same result as an apportionment based on loss-sharing ratios.

nable (i.e., all liabilities are due but all partnership assets are worthless) happened to the partnership. The following transactions are assumed to occur, simultaneously, at the end of the partnership's taxable year:

1. All liabilities must be paid immediately in full.
2. All partnership assets, including cash, are assumed to have a fair market value of zero.
3. All partnership assets are sold for no consideration, which results in a recognized loss for each asset equal to the asset's adjusted basis.
4. These losses are allocated to the partners according to the loss sharing ratios in the partnership agreement.
5. The partners reduce their respective capital accounts by the amount of the losses.
6. The partnership liquidates. Consequently, any partner having a negative capital account after step five is deemed to make a cash contribution to the partnership, equal to this negative amount, so that his or her ending capital account will be zero.
7. The partnership is deemed to use this cash to pay off the recourse liabilities of the partnership.
8. Any remaining cash is deemed to be distributed to partners that have positive capital account balances.

The amount of cash that is deemed to be contributed to the partnership under step six is the partner's share of the recourse liabilities.

## Example 6

Individuals W and X are general partners and individuals Y and Z are limited partners in the WXYZ Partnership. Partnership losses are allocated 20% to W, 30% to X, and 25% respectively to Y and Z. As of December 31 of the current year, the partnership has $100,000 of recourse debt. The partnership's balance sheet as of December 31 is as follows:

| | *Basis* | *Fair Market Value* |
|---|---|---|
| Cash | $ 50,000 | $ 50,000 |
| Inventory | 75,000 | 200,000 |
| Machinery and equipment | 75,000 | 150,000 |
| | $200,000 | $400,000 |
| Recourse liabilities | $100,000 | $100,000 |
| W, capital | 20,000 | 60,000 |
| X, capital | 30,000 | 90,000 |
| Y, capital | 25,000 | 75,000 |
| Z, capital | 25,000 | 75,000 |
| | $200,000 | $400,000 |

If the assets were worthless and sold for no consideration, a $200,000 loss would be recognized. In allocating this loss to the partners, the limited partners cannot have a negative capital account since they have limited liability. Therefore, whereas Y and Z would otherwise each be allocated $50,000 of loss ($200,000 × 25%), each is limited to a loss allocation of $25,000. The remaining $150,000 of loss is allocated to W and X based on their relative loss sharing ratios, as follows:

W: $150,000 × 20%/(20% + 30%) = $60,000

X: $150,000 × 30%/(20% + 30%) = $90,000

After allocation of these losses, the capital accounts are as follows:

| | W | X | Y | Z |
|---|---|---|---|---|
| Capital, 12/31 | $ 20,000 | $ 30,000 | $25,000 | $25,000 |
| Loss allocation | (60,000) | (90,000) | (25,000) | (25,000) |
| | $(40,000) | $(60,000) | -0- | -0- |

The WXYZ Partnership is now assumed to liquidate. W and X must contribute $40,000 and $60,000 to the partnership, respectively, to restore their capital accounts to zero. This $100,000 is then used to pay the $100,000 recourse liability. Therefore, W and X are allocated $40,000 and $60,000 of the recourse liability, respectively, while Y and Z are not allocated any of the liability.

If a partnership defaults on the repayment of a nonrecourse debt and partnership assets are insufficient to satisfy the debt, the creditor cannot look to the personal assets of any partner for satisfaction. Therefore, no partner—general or limited—bears any economic risk of loss with regard to partnership nonrecourse debt. As a result, separate rules are provided for the allocation of nonrecourse debt. In general, the Regulations provide that nonrecourse debt is apportioned to all partners based on their profit-sharing ratios. However, an exception is provided to this rule if a partner has contributed property to the partnership encumbered with nonrecourse debt that has a built-in gain. In this case, the contributing partner is first allocated nonrecourse debt to the extent of the lower of 1) the built-in gain on the contributed property, or 2) the excess of the non-recourse debt over the adjusted basis of the contributed property. Any remaining debt is then allocated to all the partners based on their profit-sharing ratios.[23] This apportionment rule reflects the fact that such debt will be repaid from partnership profits and that both general and limited partners alike will pay tax on their allocated shares of such profits.

## Example 7

Individuals G and H are general partners and individuals I and J are limited partners in the GHIJ Partnership. Partnership profits are allocated 10% to G, 20% to H, and 35% respectively to I and J. As of December 31 of the current year, the partnership has $100,000 of nonrecourse debt. This $100,000 debt is attached to property that was contributed by G. At the time of contribution, the property had an adjusted basis to G of $80,000 and a fair market value of $120,000. The first $20,000 of the $100,000 debt is allocated to G as follows:

Lower of

1. the built-in gain on the property, $40,000 ($120,000 – **$80,000**), *or*
2. the excess of the non-recourse debt over the adjusted basis of the contributed property, $20,000 ($100,000 – **$80,000**)

The remaining $80,000 of nonrecourse debt is allocated based on the profit sharing ratios.

In summary, the $100,000 nonrecourse debt is allocated as follows:

| | G | H | I | J |
|---|---|---|---|---|
| Built-in gain | $20,000 | $ 0 | $ 0 | $ 0 |
| Profit ratio | 8,000 | 16,000 | 28,000 | 28,000 |
| | $28,000 | $16,000 | $28,000 | $28,000 |

Consequently, G, H, l, and J may include $28,000, $16,000, $28,000, and $28,000 of the debt respectively in the outside bases of their partnership interests.

[23] Reg. § 1.752-3(a); these regulations also include the concept of minimum gain for allocations of nonrecourse debt, but that discussion is beyond the scope of this book.

## Liabilities Transferred to the Partnership

A partner who contributes property to a partnership in exchange for an ownership interest may negotiate for the partnership to assume a recourse liability of the partner as part of the exchange transaction. Similarly, the property contributed to the partnership may be subject to a nonrecourse liability. In both cases, the rules of § 752 have an impact on the computation of the contributing partner's outside basis.

Any debt from which the contributing partner is relieved of personal liability reduces that partner's basis in his or her new partnership interest. However, this outside basis is also increased by any amount of such debt apportioned to the contributor in his or her capacity as partner. Because this decrease and increase occur simultaneously as the result of a single transaction, only the net increase or decrease is taken into account in computing the contributing partner's basis.[24] The net increase or decrease for the contributing partner's basis can be computed as: amount of liability transferred × (100% – partner's percentage share of debt).

### Example 8

Individual T contributes business assets with an adjusted basis of $50,000 to a partnership in exchange for a 25% general interest in partnership capital, profits, and losses. As part of the contribution, the partnership assumes $12,000 of T's business recourse debt, relieving T of personal liability. The partnership has no other debts. Although T is relieved of the $12,000 debt in her individual capacity, she continues to bear the economic risk of loss for 25% of the debt in her capacity as general partner. Accordingly, T's outside basis in her partnership interest immediately subsequent to her contribution is $41,000 ($50,000 basis of contributed property – $9,000 *net* relief of debt).

| | | |
|---|---|---|
| Basis of contributed property | | $50,000 |
| Less: | Relief of personal liability | (12,000) |
| Plus: | Liability for debt as general partner (25% × $12,000) | 3,000 |
| T's outside basis in partnership interest | | $41,000 |

A partnership's assumption of a contributing partner's debt has tax consequences not only to the contributor but to the other partners as well. The outside bases of the noncontributing partners will increase by the amount of newly assumed debt apportioned to them and decrease by the amount of existing partnership debt apportioned to the newly admitted partner.

### Example 9

Individual L contributes business assets with a fair market value of $23,600 and adjusted basis of $10,000 to a partnership in exchange for a one-third general interest in partnership capital, profits, and losses. As part of the contribution, the partnership assumes $3,600 of L's business recourse debt, relieving L of personal liability. Consequently, L's contribution has a net value of $20,000 ($23,600 – $3,600) and a net basis of $6,400 ($10,000 – $3,600). The partnership has $6,000 of existing debt as of the date of contribution. Immediately after the contribution, the partnership has the following balance sheet:

[24] Reg. § 1.752-1(f).

| | Inside Basis | Fair Market Value |
|---|---|---|
| Contributed assets | $10,000 | $23,600 |
| Existing assets | 30,000 | 46,000 |
| | $40,000 | $69,600 |
| Assumed debt | $ 3,600 | $ 3,600 |
| Existing debt | 6,000 | 6,000 |
| Capital: Partner L (33.3%) | 6,400 | 20,000 |
| Partner M (33.3%) | 12,000 | 20,000 |
| Partner N (33.3%) | 12,000 | 20,000 |
| | $40,000 | $69,600 |

L's outside basis in his new partnership interest is $9,600 ($10,000 basis of contributed property – $2,400 ($3,600 × 66.7%) net relief of the assumed debt + $2,000 ($6,000 × 33.3%) assumption of one-third of existing partnership debt).

Prior to L's admission to the partnership, partners M and N each had $15,000 of outside basis in his partnership interest. This basis number represented a one-half interest in the $24,000 net inside basis of existing partnership assets plus one-half of the $6,000 of existing partnership debt. Upon L's admission, M and N are each apportioned $1,200 of the assumed debt. However, they are each relieved of $1,000 of existing debt. Subsequent to L's admission, their outside bases have each increased to $15,200 ($15,000 + $200 net increase in share of partnership liabilities).

Note that in *Example 9*, the inclusion of $9,600 of total partnership debt in the partners' outside bases maintains the equilibrium between the $40,000 aggregate outside basis (L's $9,600 basis + M's $15,200 basis + N's $15,200 basis) and the $40,000 total inside basis of the partnership assets.

## Contribution of Services

The nonrecognition rule of § 721 does not apply when an incoming partner contributes personal services to a partnership in exchange for an ownership interest. The tax consequences of such an exchange to both parties depend on whether the service partner receives an interest in partnership *capital* or merely an interest in the *future profits* of the partnership business.

### Receipt of a Capital Interest

If a service partner receives an interest in the existing capital of a partnership, the partner must recognize ordinary compensation income to the extent of the value of such interest.[25] The amount of income recognized becomes the partner's initial outside basis in the interest received.[26]

#### Example 10

G agrees to perform services for the AB Partnership in exchange for a 20% interest in partnership capital, profits, and losses. On the date that C is admitted to the partnership, the net value of the partnership assets is $250,000. The value of C's newly acquired interest is $50,000 (20% of $250,000), which equates to the value of the assets

[25] Reg. § 1.721-1(b)(1). The partnership can usually deduct the value of the capital interest given for services as an ordinary business expense. A complete analysis of the tax consequences of this payment by the partnership is beyond the scope of this chapter.

[26] Reg. § 1.722-1.

that C would receive if the partnership were to immediately liquidate and distribute its assets to each partner based on their relative capital account balances. C must recognize $50,000 of compensation income on the exchange and will have a $50,000 outside basis in her partnership interest.

### Receipt of a Profits Interest

The partners in an established partnership may be reluctant to give up any part of their equity in existing partnership assets (i.e., a capital interest) as compensation to a newly admitted service partner. These partners might be more willing to give the service partner an interest in the future profits of the business—profits partially attributable to the new partner's efforts on behalf of the partnership.

**Example 11**

J agrees to perform services for the GHI Partnership in exchange for a 25% interest in future partnership profits and losses. On the date that J is admitted to the partnership, the net value of the partnership's assets is $800,000. However, J is not given an initial capital account and has no legal interest in these assets. If the partnership were to immediately liquidate and distribute its assets to the partners based on their relative capital account balances, J would receive nothing. If the partnership generates income subsequent to J's admission, J will be entitled to 25% of such income.

The tax consequences to a service partner who receives nothing more than an interest in future partnership profits have been the subject of heated debate among tax experts for many years. The courts have also struggled with this issue with confusing and inconclusive results.[27] Currently, the uneasy consensus of opinion is that a service partner does not recognize current income upon the receipt of a profits interest because the interest has no immediate liquidation value. Consequently, the service partner's initial basis in the interest is zero. The partner will, of course, recognize income to the extent of his or her share of future partnership profits.

### Proposed Regulations Change Rules for Services

Proposed regulations issued in 2005 provide that an employer that transfers a capital partnership interest to a service provider would not have to recognize gain or loss on the transaction.[28] Under the proposed regulations, service providers would still recognize income on the receipt of a capital interest (but not a profits interest) and the employer would receive a compensation deduction for the value of the interest (unless the payment is an organization expense). However, this conclusion is reached in a slightly different fashion than existing law. The proposed regulations provide that the value of the partnership interest is its current liquidation value immediately after the transaction. Profits interest would have no liquidation value, so service providers receiving a profits interest would have no income.

## Operating the Partnership

Section 701, the first section in Subchapter K, states that "a partnership as such shall not be subject to the income tax imposed by this chapter. Persons carrying on business as partners shall be liable

[27] See *Sol Diamond*, 56 T.C. 530 (1971), *aff'd* 74-1 USTC ¶9306, 33 AFTR2d 74-852, 492 F.2d 286 (CA-7, 1974), *William G. Campbell*, 59 TCM 236, T.C. Memo 1990-162, *rev'd* 1991-2 USTC ¶50,420 (CA-8, 1991), and Rev. Proc. 93-27, 1993-2 C.B. 343.

[28] Prop. Reg. §§ 1.721-1(b) and 1.83-3(e).

for income tax only in their separate or individual capacities." Even though partnerships are not taxable entities, they are required to file an annual information return, Form 1065 (U.S. Partnership Return of Income).[29] Basically, this return shows the computation of partnership taxable income and how such income is allocated to each partner. Form 1065 is due by the 15th day of the fourth month following the close of the partnership taxable year.[30]

In order to compute its annual taxable income, a newly formed partnership must make a number of initial elections, including the adoption of both an accounting method (or methods) by which to compute income and the partnership taxable year. The fact that these important elections are made by the partnership itself rather than by each partner is a very practical application of the entity theory of partnerships.[31] As a general rule, partnerships are free to elect the cash receipts and disbursements method, the accrual method, or a hybrid method of accounting for tax purposes.[32] As explained in the next section of the chapter, they have much less flexibility in the choice of a taxable year.

## The Partnership's Taxable Year

Income generated by a partnership is included in the taxable income of a partner for the partner's year in which the partnership's taxable year ends.[33] If partnerships had no restrictions as to their choice of taxable year, this simple timing rule could be used to achieve a significant deferral of income recognition.

### Example 12

R and S, calendar year individuals, decide to operate a business as equal partners. The RS Partnership begins business on February 1, 2011. During its first year of operations the partnership generates $3,000 of taxable income each month. If the partnership could adopt a fiscal year ending January 31, its $36,000 of first-year income ($33,000 of which was earned in 2011) would be included in the partners' 2012 tax returns because 2012 is the partners' taxable year in which the partnership's fiscal year ends. For each subsequent year that the RS Partnership remains in existence, eleven months of income earned in one calendar year would not be taxed at the partner level until the following calendar year.

Subchapter K contains a set of complex rules designed to minimize the potential for income deferral through use of a partnership. A partnership must adopt the taxable year used by one or more partners who own more than a 50 percent aggregate interest in partnership capital and profits. If no such *majority interest taxable year* exists, the partnership must adopt the taxable year used by its principal partners (those partners owning at least a 5 percent interest in partnership capital or profits).[34] If the principal partners use different taxable years, the partnership must adopt a taxable year resulting in the least aggregate deferral of income to the partners. The taxable year resulting from the application of these rules is known as the "required taxable year."

Under the *least aggregate deferral method*,[35] all year-ends that any of the partners have must be tested, and the one that produces the least amount of deferral for the partners as a group is the required tax year. The deferral for each partner is computed as the time from the year-end being tested until the next year-end of the partner. The months of deferral are then weighted by each partner's profits interest. The least aggregate deferral method is illustrated by the following example:

---

[29] § 6031.

[30] § 6072. Partnerships may apply for a five month extension of time to file.

[31] § 703(b).

[32] § 446(c). Section 448(a) limits the use of the cash method for a partnership that (1) is a tax shelter, or (2) has a C corporation as a partner. However, § 448(b) provides several important exceptions to this restrictive limitation.

[33] § 706(a).

[34] § 706(b)(1)(A).

[35] Reg. § 1.706-1(b)(3).

### Example 13

M and N are equal corporate partners in the MN Partnership. M has a year-end of March 31 and N has a year-end of November 30. Since M and N each own 50% of the partnership, no partner, or group of partners, that have the same year-end own a more than 50% interest in the partnership. MN Partnership has two principal partners, but the principal partners do not have the same year end. Therefore, the least aggregate deferral method must be used. The two months that must be tested are March and November.

*Test of March 31 Year-End*

| *Partner* | *Year-End* | *Profit Interest* | × | *Months of Deferral* | *Weighted Deferral* |
|---|---|---|---|---|---|
| M | 3/31 | 50% | × | 0 | 0.0 |
| N | 11/30 | 50% | × | 8 | 4.0 |
| | | | | Aggregate Deferral | 4.0 |

*Test of November 30 Year-End*

| *Partner* | *Year-End* | *Profit Interest* | × | *Months of Deferral* | *Weighted Deferral* |
|---|---|---|---|---|---|
| M | 3/31 | 50% | × | 4 | 2.0 |
| N | 11/30 | 50% | × | 0 | 0.0 |
| | | | | Aggregate Deferral | 2.0 |

Therefore, the required year end is November 30 since it produces the least amount of deferral for the partners as a group.

If the partners wish to use a year different from the "required tax year," the Code offers relief from these mechanistic rules by allowing a partnership to adopt any taxable year (without reference to the taxable years of its partners) if it can convince the IRS that there is a valid business purpose for such year.[36] The IRS will generally agree that a partnership has a *business purpose* for adopting a taxable year that conforms to its natural business year. For example, a partnership operating a ski resort might have a natural business year that ends on April 30. The IRS should allow this partnership to adopt this fiscal year for tax purposes, regardless of the taxable years used by the various partners. A partnership can also use a different year-end from its required year-end if it meets the 25 percent test. This test holds that a partnership may change its tax year if at least 25 percent of the taxpayer's annual gross receipts are recognized in the last two months of the tax year to which the partnership wishes to change, and this 25 percent test is met for three consecutive years.[37]

## Organization Costs and Syndication Fees

Any costs incurred to organize a partnership, such as legal fees for drafting the partnership agreement and filing fees charged by the state in which the partnership is formed, must be capitalized and are not deductible as ordinary and necessary business expenses. The partnership must expense the first $5,000 of *organization costs* and amortize the remainder over a period of 180 months, beginning with the month in which the partnership begins business (unless the partnership elects to not do so).[38] The $5,000 amount to be expensed must be reduced (but not below zero) by the amount of organizational costs in excess of $50,000. Any *syndication fees* connected with the issuance and marketing of partnership interests must also be capitalized. These fees may not be amortized and will remain as an intangible asset on the partnership books until the partnership is liquidated.[39]

[36] § 706(b)(1)(B).

[37] Rev. Proc. 2002-39, 2002-22 I.R.B. 1046, provides guidelines for changing from the required tax year because of the business purpose test and the 25 percent gross receipts test. Also see Rev. Rul. 87-57, 1987-2 C.B. 117 for other examples of circumstances that may or may not be considered valid business purposes.

[38] § 709(b).

[39] § 709(a).

## Computation of Partnership Taxable Income

**LO.5**
Compute partnership taxable income or loss and identify any separately computed items of partnership income, gain, loss, deduction, or credit.

Partnership taxable income is computed in the same manner as the taxable income of an individual.[40] However, a partnership must make a separate accounting of any item of income, gain, deduction, loss, or credit that is potentially subject to special treatment at the partner level.[41] Separately stated items include capital gains and losses, § 1231 gains and losses, investment income and expenses, net rental income or loss, and charitable contributions. As a result, partnership taxable income is the net of all items that are not separately stated, which can be narrowly defined as gross receipts from services or gross profits from sales of inventory less deductible business expenses incurred by the partnership during the year. This net number is computed on page 1 of Form 1065 and is labeled *ordinary income (loss)*. In contrast, all separately stated items are listed as such on page 3, Schedule K of Form 1065. (Appendix contains a copy of Form 1065 and accompanying Schedule K.)

The character of any item of partnership income, gain, deduction, or loss is determined with reference to the activities of the partnership rather than the activities of the individual partners.[42] For example, gain on the sale of land held by a partnership as an investment for two years is long-term capital gain. This characterization holds even if some of the partners to whom the gain will be taxed are real estate developers in whose hands the land would have been inventory. Similarly, the gain is long-term even if some of the partners have owned their partnership interests for less than one year.[43]

Section 724 contains three exceptions to the general rule that tax characteristics are determined at the partnership level.

1. In the case of unrealized receivables contributed to the partnership by a partner, any gain or loss recognized when the partnership disposes of the receivables must be treated as ordinary gain or loss.
2. In the case of inventory contributed to the partnership by a partner, any gain or loss recognized on disposition within the five-year period subsequent to contribution must be treated as ordinary gain or loss.
3. In the case of a capital asset contributed to the partnership by a partner, any loss recognized on disposition within the five-year period subsequent to contribution must be treated as capital loss to the extent the basis of the asset exceeded its fair market value at date of contribution.

### Example 14

Three years ago, D exchanged land that he held as an investment ($50,000 fair market value and $65,000 basis) and an inventory asset from his sole proprietorship ($20,000 fair market value and $18,000 basis) for an interest in the DEF Partnership. Both assets had a carryover basis to the partnership under § 723. Both contributed assets were used in the partnership business, and therefore were characterized as § 1231 assets at the partnership level. During the current year, the partnership sold both assets, realizing a $22,000 loss on the sale of the land and a $3,500 gain on the sale of the former inventory asset.

Because the sales took place within the five-year period subsequent to contribution, the partnership must recognize $15,000 of the loss on the land sale (excess of $65,000 contributed basis over $50,000 contributed value) as capital loss and the $7,000 remainder as § 1231 loss. The partnership must recognize the entire gain on the sale of the former inventory as ordinary income. If the sales had taken place after the expiration of the five-year period, both the recognized loss and gain would have been § 1231 in nature.[44]

---

[40] § 703(a).

[41] § 702(a). Reg. § 1.702-1(a)(8)(ii) explains that each partner must be able to take into account separately his or her distributive share of any partnership item that results in an income tax liability different from that which would result if the item were not accounted for separately.

[42] § 702(b).

[43] Rev. Rul. 67-188, 1967-1 C.B. 216.

[44] § 704(c) also requires a special allocation of both loss and gain among the partners. This allocation rule is discussed in a later section of the chapter.

## Reporting of Partnership Items by Partners

**LO.6**
Explain how the tax consequences of partnership operations are reported on the tax returns of the partners and how the partners' bases in their partnership interests are adjusted to reflect these tax consequences.

Partners must take into account their distributive shares of partnership taxable income and any separately stated partnership items in computing their taxable incomes.[45] This passthrough of partnership items to the partners is deemed to occur on the last day of the partnership's taxable year. Consequently, the passthrough items are included in each partner's return for the partner's taxable year within which the partnership year ends.[46]

Each partner's distributive share of every partnership item is reported on a Schedule K-1 for that partner. Partnerships must include a copy of each Schedule K-1 with the annual partnership return filed with the IRS. A second copy is transmitted to each partner. Upon receipt, partners must incorporate the information reported on the Schedule K-1 into their tax returns.

### Example 15

Individual A and Corporation B are calendar year taxpayers and equal partners in the AB Partnership, which uses a September 30 fiscal year end for tax purposes. During December 2011, each partner received a Schedule K-1 showing the following results of partnership operations from October 1, 2010 through September 30, 2011.

| | |
|---|---|
| Ordinary income from business activities (partnership taxable income) | $42,300 |
| Dividend income | 2,300 |
| Net long-term capital loss | (4,000) |
| Investment interest expense | (5,500) |
| Charitable contributions | (1,900) |

Individual A will include his $42,300 share of ordinary business income on Schedule E, his $2,300 share of dividend income on Schedule B, and his $4,000 share of the long-term capital loss on Schedule D of his 2011 Form 1040. Per § 163(d), A's $5,500 share of investment interest expense is deductible only to the extent of his net investment income for 2011. Furthermore, the deductible portion of the interest expense and A's $1,900 share of the charitable contribution must be reported as itemized deductions on Schedule A, Form 1040.

Corporation B will include both its $42,300 share of ordinary business income and its $5,500 share of investment interest expense on page 1, and its $4,000 share of long-term capital loss on Schedule D of its 2011 Form 1120. [Corporations are not subject to the § 163(d) limitation.] B will include its $2,300 share of dividend income on Schedule C (Dividends and Special Deductions) and will compute an appropriate dividends-received deduction. B's $1,900 share of the charitable contribution may be deducted on page 1 of Form 1120 to the extent that the corporation's total charitable contributions for 2011 do not exceed 10% of taxable income.

## Adjustments to Partner's Basis

A partner's distributive share of annual partnership income is determined without reference to actual cash distributions made by the partnership to its partners. If a partner's share of annual partnership income exceeds any cash received from the partnership during the year, the undistributed income will be recorded as an increase in that partner's capital account balance (his or her equity in the partnership) at year-end. On the other hand, in a year in

[45] § 702(a). Section 772(a) provides a simplified reporting system for certain electing *large* partnerships. Large nonservice partnerships with 100 or more members can elect to reduce the number of items that must be separately reported to their numerous partners. See §§ 771 through 777.

[46] § 706(a).

which a partnership operates at a loss, a partner's share of such loss will be recorded as a capital account decrease.

The fluctuating nature of a partnership investment is also reflected in the basis of the partner's interest in the partnership. Outside basis is *increased* by a partner's distributive share of both taxable and nontaxable partnership income.[47] Outside basis is *decreased* by distributions made by the partnership to the partner and by the partner's distributive share of partnership losses and nondeductible current expenditures.[48] These basis adjustments are made in the above order at the end of the partnership taxable year.[49] Even if cash distributions representing advances or draws against a partner's share of current income are made at various dates throughout the year, the effect of these distributions on basis is determined as of the last day of the year.[50]

### Example 16

M owns a 40% interest in the capital, profits, and losses of the KLMN Partnership. Both M and KLMN use a calendar year for tax purposes. At the beginning of the current year, M's outside basis in her partnership interest was $35,000. During the year, M received four cash distributions of $5,000 each as advances against her share of current-year income. At the end of the year, the partnership has $20,000 of nonrecourse debt. M's Schedule K-1 for the current year showed the following distributive shares:

| | |
|---|---|
| Ordinary income | $33,000 |
| Tax-exempt interest income | 4,000 |
| Net long-term capital gain | 8,100 |
| Nondeductible penalty | (1,700) |
| Nondeductible 50% business meals and entertainment | (600) |

As of the last day of the current year, M's outside basis is increased by $8,000 ($20,000 × 40%) for her share of the debt and by $45,100 (her share of partnership taxable and tax-exempt income), decreased by the $20,000 of cash distributions made during the year, and decreased by $2,300 (her share of the partnership nondeductible current expenses). Consequently, M's outside basis as of the first day of the next taxable year is $65,800.

## Partners' Distributive Shares

The income or loss generated by a business conducted in partnership form is measured and characterized at the partnership level, then allocated to the various partners for inclusion on their income tax returns. Each partner's *distributive share* of any item of partnership income, gain, loss, deduction, or credit is determined by reference to the partnership agreement.[51] Consequently, the partners themselves can decide exactly how the profits or losses from their business are to be shared. The sharing arrangement as specified in the partnership agreement can be an equal allocation of profits and losses to each partner or a more elaborate arrangement under which different items of gain or loss are shared in different ratios among different categories of partners.

Although partners certainly have a great deal of flexibility in determining the allocation of partnership income and loss, § 704(b) warns that such allocations must have *substantial economic effect* if they are to be respected by the Internal Revenue Service. If the IRS concludes that the allocation of any partnership item lacks substantial economic effect, it may

[47] § 705(a)(1).

[48] § 705(a)(2).

[49] Reg. § 1.705-1(a).

[50] Reg. § 1.731-1(a)(1)(ii).

[51] § 704(a).

reallocate the item among the partners. Such reallocation will be based upon the partners' true economic interests in the partnership, as determined by the IRS upon examination of all relevant facts and circumstances.

## Substantial Economic Effect

Treasury regulations provide an intricate set of rules for determining whether partnership allocations meet the substantial economic effect test of § 704(b). The basic objective of the regulations is to "ensure that any allocation is consistent with the underlying economic arrangement of the partners. This means that in the event there is an economic benefit or economic burden that corresponds to an allocation, the partner to whom the allocation is made must receive such economic benefit or bear such economic burden."[52] The economic benefit or burden of an allocation equates to the impact of the allocation on a partner's interest in partnership capital. In other words, an allocation of income or loss for tax purposes must correspond to an allocation of dollars to or from a partner's capital account on the partnership books.

The regulations attempt to ensure this correspondence through a three-pronged test for economic effect.[53] Any allocation for tax purposes will have economic effect only if the following three conditions are met:

1. The allocation is reflected in the partners' capital accounts for book purposes.
2. Upon liquidation of the partnership, liquidating distributions of cash and property are made to the partners based upon the balances in their capital accounts.
3. Partners with deficit balances in their capital accounts upon liquidation are unconditionally required to restore such deficit balance to the partnership. (This obligation may be expressly stated in the partnership agreement or imposed by state law.)[54]

### Example 17

The RST Partnership agreement provides that taxable income or loss will be allocated 50% to R and 25% respectively to S and T. The agreement provides that this allocation will be reflected in the partnership capital accounts, that liquidating distributions will be based on capital account balances, and that any partner with a deficit capital account balance must restore the deficit immediately prior to liquidation.

For the current year, the RST Partnership generated $48,000 taxable income, $24,000 of which was reported as R's distributive share on his Schedule K-1 and $12,000 of which was reported as S and T's respective distributive shares on their Schedules K-l. Each partner's capital account was increased by the amount of income reported as his distributive share for tax purposes. Because the allocation meets the three-pronged test, it has economic effect and should be respected by the IRS.

Note that in the above example, the taxable income allocated to each partner matched the increase in each partner's capital account balance for the year. Moreover, upon liquidation of the partnership, the partners will receive an amount of dollars (or property) equal to the balances in their capital accounts. Contrast this result with that in the following example.

---

[52] Reg. § 1.704-1(b)(2)(ii)(a).

[53] The additional requirement that economic effect be *substantial* is discussed in Reg. § 1.704-1(b)(2)(iii). Any discussion of this difficult regulation is beyond the scope of an introductory text.

[54] Reg. § 1.704-1(b)(2)(ii)(c).

**Example 18**

The XYZ partnership agreement provides that taxable income or loss will be allocated 50% to X and 25% respectively to Y and Z. The agreement states that for book purposes income will be allocated equally to each partner. For the current year, the XYZ Partnership generated $48,000 of taxable income, $24,000 of which was reported as X's distributive share on his Schedule K-l and $12,000 of which was reported as Y and Z's respective distributive shares on their Schedules K-l. However, each partner's capital account on the partnership books was increased by $16,000.

In this example, the allocation of taxable income fails to reflect the allocation of dollars to the partners. Because this tax allocation obviously lacks economic effect, the IRS can reallocate the taxable income to the partners based upon its determination of how the partners actually intend to share the economic benefit of the income. The facts of this simple example indicate that X, Y, and Z intend to share the dollars generated by their partnership business equally. Consequently, the IRS will allocate $16,000 of current-year taxable income to each partner.

## Allocations with Respect to Contributed Property

When a partner contributes property to a partnership and the value of such property is more or less than the contributing partner's tax basis in the property, subsequent allocations of taxable income, gain, loss, and deduction with respect to the contributed property will lack substantial economic effect within the meaning of § 704(b).

**Example 19**

M contributed an asset (fair market value $20,000, adjusted basis $14,000) and N contributed $20,000 cash to M&N Partnership in exchange for a one-half interest in partnership capital, profits, and losses. The asset contributed by M was recorded on the partnership books at $20,000 but had a carryover tax basis to the partnership of $14,000. The capital accounts for both M and N were credited with the $20,000 values of their respective contributions. Three months after its formation, the partnership sold the contributed asset for $20,000. For tax purposes, the partnership recognized a $6,000 gain on sale. For book purposes, the partnership realized no gain and made no entry to either partner's capital account.

Because of the initial difference between the contributed *value* and the contributed *basis* of the asset in the above example, the taxable gain on the sale is not equal to the gain realized for book purposes. Consequently, any allocation of the taxable gain to the partners does not have substantial economic effect because the allocation cannot be reflected in book capital accounts.

Section 704(c) solves this problem by mandating a special allocation rule for items of income, gain, loss, and deduction attributable to contributed assets. Essentially, any difference between the amount of the item for tax purposes and for book purposes at the time of contribution must be allocated to the contributing partner when the partnership disposes of the asset. The remainder of the item is allocated for both tax and book purposes according to the sharing ratios specified in the partnership agreement. The application of this special rule to the $6,000 taxable gain recognized in *Example 19* results in an allocation of the entire $6,000 gain to contributing partner M. Note that this amount of gain equals the deferred gain that M was not required to recognize upon the contribution of the appreciated asset to the partnership.

### Example 20

O contributed an asset (FMV $20,000, adjusted basis $26,000) and P contributed $20,000 cash to O&P Partnership in exchange for a one-half interest in partnership capital, profits, and losses. The asset contributed by O was recorded on the partnership books at $20,000 but had a carryover tax basis to the partnership of $26,000. The capital accounts for both O and P were credited with the $20,000 values of their respective contributions. Seven months after its formation, the partnership sold the contributed asset for $17,000. For tax purposes, the partnership recognized a $9,000 loss on sale, while for book purposes it realized only a $3,000 loss (the decline in the value of the asset subsequent to its contribution to the partnership). The first $6,000 of the tax loss must be allocated to contributing partner O. The remaining $3,000 loss is allocated equally between O and P.

Section 704(c) affects the allocation of depreciation deductions attributable to contributed property as well as allocations of gains and losses recognized by the partnership upon disposition of the property. These depreciation deductions are first allocated to the noncontributing partners in an amount equal to their allocable share of book depreciation (depreciation computed on the contributed value of the property). Any remaining tax depreciation is allocated to the partner who contributed the property.

### Example 21

D contributed a depreciable asset (fair market value $60,000, adjusted basis $48,000) and E contributed $120,000 cash to DEF Partnership in exchange for a one-third and a two-thirds interest respectively in partnership capital, profits, and losses. The partnership will depreciate the asset over five years on a straight-line basis. In each year, tax depreciation on the contributed asset is $9,600 (20% of the $48,000 contributed basis), while book depreciation is $12,000 (20% of the $60,000 contributed value). One-third and two-thirds of the book depreciation is allocated to D and E respectively. Each year noncontributing partner E is allocated the first $8,000 of tax depreciation (her two-thirds share of the $12,000 book depreciation). The remaining $1,600 of the annual tax depreciation is allocated to contributing partner D.

## Retroactive Allocations

In addition to the substantial economic effect requirement of § 704(b) and the special allocation rule of § 704(c), the determination of each partner's annual distributive share of partnership income, gain, loss, deduction, or credit must take account of any change in the partner's equity interest in the partnership during the year.[55] This *varying interest rule* was enacted to prevent retroactive allocations of partnership items to new partners who were admitted to the partnership after the items were recognized or incurred.

### Example 22

K and L have been equal partners in the calendar year cash basis K&L Partnership since 2001. On November 1 of the current year, M contributed $100,000 cash in exchange for a one-third interest in partnership capital. The partnership generated a $108,000 operating loss for the current taxable year. The maximum amount of this loss that can be allocated to M under the revised partnership agreement among K, L, and M is $18,049, the portion of the loss attributable to the last 61 days of the year during which M owned an interest in the partnership.

[55] § 706(d)(1).

## Basis Limitation on Loss Deductibility

Under § 704(d), a partner's distributive share of partnership loss is deductible only to the extent of the partner's outside basis in his or her partnership interest as of the end of the partnership year in which the loss was incurred. Any nondeductible portion of a current year loss is carried forward indefinitely into future years and can be deducted if and when sufficient outside basis is restored. This loss limitation rule is applied only after a partner's basis has been increased by any distributive share of current-year partnership income and decreased by any distributions made to the partner for the year.[56]

### Example 23

F is a partner in the calendar year DEFG partnership. At the beginning of the current year, F's outside basis in her partnership interest was $14,500. During the year, F received a $3,000 cash distribution from DEFG. At the close of the year, Schedule K-1 showed that her distributive share of the partnership's current-year operating loss was $20,000, while her shares of current-year dividends and long-term capital gains were $3,400 and $1,300 respectively. F will increase her outside basis by $4,700 (her share of partnership income) and decrease it by the $3,000 cash distribution. Under § 704(d), F may deduct her allocated partnership loss only to the extent of her $16,200 remaining outside basis, thereby reducing her year-end basis to zero. The $3,800 nondeductible portion of F's loss will carry forward into subsequent taxable years.

| | |
|---|---|
| F's January 1 outside basis | $14,500 |
| Plus: Allocated share of income | 4,700 |
| Less: Distributions | (3,000) |
| Deductible share of allocated loss | (16,200) |
| F's December 31 outside basis | -0- |
| F's loss carryforward | $ 3,800 |

If a partner is allocated a distributive share of more than one type of loss and the partner's outside basis is insufficient to absorb the aggregate amount of losses, the § 704(d) limitation is applied proportionately to each type of loss.[57]

### Example 24

Refer to the facts in *Example 23*, but assume that F is allocated a $6,000 § 1231 loss in addition to the $20,000 operating loss. F's currently deductible amounts of each type of loss are computed as follows:

| | |
|---|---|
| Operating loss: | ($20,000 ÷ $26,000) × $16,200 = $12,462 |
| § 1231 loss: | ($6,000 ÷ $26,000) × $16,200 = $3,738 |

The nondeductible $7,538 operating loss and $2,262 § 1231 loss are carried forward into subsequent years.

[56] Reg. § 1.704-1(d)(2).

[57] Reg. § 1.704-1(d)(2).

## Transactions between Partners and Partnerships

**LO.7**
Identify the tax consequences of various transactions between a partner and a partnership.

Under the entity theory, a partner and a partnership are separate and distinct entities that can transact with each other at arm's length. This perspective is adopted in § 707(a), which states that "if a partner engages in a transaction with a partnership other than in his capacity as a member of such partnership, the transaction shall, except as otherwise provided in this section, be considered as occurring between the partnership and one who is not a partner." Because of this general rule, a partner can assume the role of unrelated third party when dealing with the partnership. For example, a partner can lend money to or borrow money from a partnership, rent property to or from a partnership, buy property from or sell property to a partnership, or provide consulting services to a partnership as an independent contractor. The tax consequences of all the above transactions will be determined as if the partnership were dealing with a nonpartner.[58]

The major exception to the general rule of § 707(a) concerns partners who work in the partnership business on a regular and ongoing basis. The point was made earlier in the chapter that general partners are considered self-employed individuals, rather than employees of their partnership. Consequently, partners cannot be paid a salary or wage by the partnership, even if they perform exactly the same duties as nonpartner employees. However, partners who work in a partnership business certainly expect to be compensated for their time and effort. The tax consequences of compensatory payments made by partnerships to partners in their capacities as such are governed by § 707(c). The annual amounts of such payments are typically determined with reference to the extent and nature of the services performed, without regard to the income of the partnership for that year. Such *guaranteed payments* must be recognized as ordinary income by the recipient partner. The partnership will either deduct the guaranteed payment as a § 162 business expense or capitalize it to an appropriate asset account as required by § 263.[59]

### Example 25

P has a one-third interest in the calendar year OPQ Partnership. Unlike partners O and Q, P works in the partnership business on a full-time basis. The partnership agreement provides that for the current year P will receive a monthly guaranteed payment of $4,000 from the partnership. The partnership business generates $175,000 of annual income before consideration of P's guaranteed payment.

Based on the nature of the work performed by P, the partnership may claim a current deduction for the guaranteed payment; accordingly its net income for the year is $127,000 ($175,000 – $48,000 total guaranteed payments), and each partner's one-third distributive share is $42,333. P will report total partnership income for the year of $90,333 ($48,000 guaranteed payment + $42,333 distributive share), while O and Q will each report only their $42,333 distributive shares of income.

### Example 26

Assume the same facts as in *Example 25*, except that the OPQ Partnership generates only $30,000 of annual income before consideration of P's guaranteed payment. In this case, the deduction of the payment results in an $18,000 net *loss* of which each partner's distributive share is $6,000. P will report total partnership income for the year of $42,000 ($48,000 guaranteed payment – $6,000 loss), while O and Q will each report only their $6,000 distributive shares of loss.

[58] Under § 267(a)(2), a payment made by an accrual basis taxpayer to a cash basis related party may not be deducted by the payor until the taxable year in which the payee includes the payment in gross income. Per § 267(e), a partnership and any partner are related parties for purposes of this matching rule. The rule does not apply to § 707(c) guaranteed payments.

[59] Guaranteed payments can also be made with respect to a partner's capital account. Such payments are functionally equivalent to interest, always represent ordinary income to the recipient partner, and will be either deducted or capitalized by the partnership.

From an economic perspective, a guaranteed payment received by a partner is functionally equivalent to a salary received by an employee. Nonetheless, for tax purposes several important differences distinguish the two. An employer is required by law to withhold federal, state, and local income taxes and employee payroll taxes from an employee's salary. Guaranteed payments are not subject to any similar withholding requirement. At the end of each calendar year, employees receive a Form W-2 on which gross annual compensation and various withheld amounts are summarized. Guaranteed payments are reported only as a line item on the recipient partner's Schedule K-1 issued by the partnership. Finally, while cash basis employees must recognize salary payments as gross income in the year the payments are received, guaranteed payments are deemed to be paid to partners on the last day of the tax year, regardless of when they are actually paid during the year.[60]

### Example 27

Refer to the facts in *Example 26*, but assume the OPQ Partnership is on a fiscal year ending September 30. As a result, P actually received three $4,000 guaranteed payments in October, November, and December of the prior calendar year and only nine $4,000 payments during the current calendar year. Notwithstanding, P will report the entire $48,000 of guaranteed payments in the current year because all twelve months of guaranteed payments are deemed to be paid on September 30. Note that this result holds regardless of the amount of any renegotiated guaranteed payment that P may receive during the last three months of the current year.

## Sales between Partners and Controlled Partnerships

Section 707(b) defines two situations in which the general rule of § 707(a) is overridden and the tax consequences of transactions between partners and partnerships are not determined as if the transaction were negotiated at arm's length between independent parties. Both situations involve a sale of property between (1) a partnership and any person owning more than a 50 percent interest in either partnership capital or profits, or (2) two partnerships in which the same persons own more than a 50 percent interest in either capital or profits.[61] If such a sale results in a recognized loss to the seller, such loss is disallowed. If the purchaser of the property subsequently disposes of the property at a gain, the originally disallowed loss may be used to offset such gain.[62]

### Example 28

T owns a 60% interest in the TV Partnership. During the current year, T sells investment land to TV for $100,000; T's basis in the land is $145,000. T may not recognize his $45,000 loss realized on the sale, and TV will take a $100,000 cost basis in the land. If the partnership subsequently sells the land for more than $100,000, T's $45,000 disallowed loss may be used to offset the amount of taxable gain the partnership must recognize. If the partnership sells the land for less than $100,000, T's disallowed loss will have no effect on the amount of the taxable loss the partnership will recognize.

If a sale of property between a partner and a related partnership results in a recognized gain, and the property is *not* a capital asset in the hands of the purchaser, the gain must be characterized as ordinary income.[63]

---

[60] Reg. § 1.707-1(c).

[61] Percentage ownership is determined with reference to the constructive ownership rules of § 267(c) other than paragraph (3) of such section. § 707(b)(3).

[62] § 707(b)(1). Note the similarity to the more general loss disallowance rule of § 267(a)(1).

[63] An almost identical (and therefore redundant) gain characterization rule can be found in § 1239(a).

> **Example 29**
>
> Refer to the facts in *Example 28*, but assume that T's basis in the investment land was $70,000. If the TV Partnership uses the land in its trade or business, rather than holding it as a capital asset, T's $30,000 recognized gain on the sale must be characterized as ordinary income.

## Partnership Distributions

**LO.8**
Determine the tax consequences of both current and liquidating distributions from a partnership.

This next section of this chapter is an analysis of the broad set of rules applicable to partnership distributions to which the specialized provision of § 751(b) does not apply. (Any discussion of disproportionate distributions is beyond the scope of this chapter.) All partnership distributions can be classified as either current or liquidating. A *current distribution* reduces a partner's interest in partnership capital but does not extinguish the interest. In other words, subsequent to the receipt of a current distribution, a partner is still a partner. In contrast, a *liquidating distribution* extinguishes the recipient partner's entire equity interest in the partnership. An ongoing partnership may make liquidating distributions to any of its partners who terminates an interest. When a partnership itself terminates, it will make a final liquidating distribution to all its partners.

The aggregate theory of partnerships predominates in the sections of Subchapter K (§§ 731–737) devoted to distributions. Under this theory, a partner's interest in a partnership represents an indirect ownership interest in partnership assets. Therefore, a partner who receives a distribution of cash or property is merely converting his or her indirect interest in partnership assets to direct ownership of the distributed assets. This change in ownership form should not be a taxable event and should have no effect on the tax basis of the distributed assets. This theorctical foundation is clearly discernible in the set of rules explained in the following paragraphs.

### Current Distributions

#### Cash Distributions

Partners may withdraw cash from their partnerships at various times throughout the partnership's taxable year in order to meet their personal short-term liquidity needs or as advance payments of their anticipated distributive shares of current-year partnership income. Partners may also receive periodic cash distributions as guaranteed payments for ongoing services rendered to the partnership. Finally, partners may receive constructive cash distributions in the form of reductions in their respective shares of partnership liabilities.[64]

Regardless of the nature of a current cash distribution, § 731(a) provides that the recipient partner does not recognize gain upon its receipt. The cash distribution is instead treated as a nontaxable return of capital that reduces the recipient's outside basis in his or her partnership interest.[65] However, the basis of a partnership interest can never be reduced below zero. Consequently, a partner who receives a cash distribution in excess of outside basis must recognize the excess as gain derived from sale of the partnership interest.[66]

Guaranteed payments and other cash distributions representing advances against the recipient's share of current-year partnership income are taken into account as of the last day of the partnership year.[67] This timing rule minimizes the possibility that distributions will trigger gain recognition at the partner level.

[64] § 752(b).

[65] § 733.

[66] § 731(a)(1). This gain is capital gain per § 741.

[67] Reg. § 1.731-1(a)(1)(ii).

### Example 30

Partnership WXYZ and 25% partner Z both use a calendar year for tax purposes. At the beginning of the current year, Z's outside basis was $50,000, and partnership debt totaled $60,000 ($15,000 of which was properly included in Z's outside basis). On July 7, the partnership made a $75,000 cash distribution to Z. As of the last day of the year, partnership debt totaled $80,000. Partnership income for the current year consisted of $109,000 ordinary income and a $5,600 capital loss. Z's outside basis at the end of the year is computed as follows:

| | | |
|---|---|---|
| Basis on January 1 | | $ 50,000 |
| Increased by: | 25% share of ordinary income | 27,250 |
| | 25% share of $20,000 increase in partnership debt | 5,000 |
| Decreased by: | July 7 cash distribution | (75,000) |
| | 25% share of capital loss | (1,400) |
| Basis on December 31 | | $ 5,850 |

The effect of the July 7 distribution is determined as if the distribution had occurred on the last day of the partnership year. Because Z's outside basis is first increased by his distributive share of partnership income and his share of WXYZ's increased debt load, the distribution is treated as a nontaxable return of capital.

If the $75,000 distribution had not been a guaranteed payment or advance against income, its tax effect would have been determined on July 7. Assuming that the partnership debt on this date was still $60,000, Z must recognize a $25,000 capital gain equal to the excess of the distribution over his $50,000 basis. Subsequent to the distribution, Z's outside basis would have been reduced to zero.

## Property Distributions

As a general rule, a current distribution of partnership property to a partner does not cause gain or loss recognition at either the partnership or the partner level.[68] The recipient partner simply takes a *carryover* basis in the distributed property and reduces the outside basis in her partnership interest by a corresponding amount.[69]

### Example 31

S receives a current distribution of property from the STUV Partnership. At date of distribution, the property has a fair market value of $14,000 and an inside basis to the partnership of $7,500. Immediately prior to the distribution, S's outside basis in her partnership interest was $12,000. Neither the partnership nor S recognizes a gain on the distribution. S's basis in the property becomes $7,500 and her outside basis is reduced to $4,500 ($12,000 − $7,500).

Note that in the above example, the $7,500 inside basis of the distributed property (i.e., the carryover basis) was preserved by shifting $7,500 of S's outside basis to the property. If the recipient partner's outside basis is less than the inside basis of the distributed property, the distribution is referred to as a *substituted* basis transaction. In such a situation, the basis of the distributed property in the hands of the partner is limited to his or her outside basis amount.[70]

---

[68] § 731(a) and (b). Section 731(c) provides that certain marketable securities are treated as money rather than property for purposes of § 731(a). Consequently, the distribution of such securities by a partnership may trigger gain recognition to the recipient partner. Discussion of this special rule is beyond the scope of this text.

[69] §§ 732(a)(1) and 733.

[70] § 732(a)(2).

## Example 32

Refer to the facts in *Example 31*. If S's predistribution outside basis had been only $6,000, S's basis in the distributed property would be $6,000 and her postdistribution outside basis would be zero ($6,000 – $6,000). Note that S simply substitutes her outside basis as the basis in the distributed asset.

If a partnership distribution consists of multiple assets and the recipient partner's outside basis is less than the aggregate inside bases of the assets, the outside basis must *first* be reduced by any amount of cash included in the distribution. The remaining basis is allocated between two categories of noncash assets in the following order of priority:

1. To any unrealized receivables and inventory (Category 1) in an amount not to exceed the basis of these assets in the hands of the partnership.[71]
2. To any other distributed properties (Category 2).

Basis is allocated to multiple assets within either of these two categories under a *basis decrease formula*. The basis decrease is first allocated to property with unrealized depreciation (i.e., inside basis greater than fair market value) to the extent of the unrealized depreciation in each property.[72]

## Example 33

J receives a current distribution from the JKL Partnership consisting of the following:

| | JKL Basis | FMV |
|---|---|---|
| Cash | $4,000 | $4,000 |
| Accounts receivable | 0 | 3,000 |
| Inventory | 2,000 | 2,900 |
| Capital asset 1 | 1,000 | 1,500 |
| Capital asset 2 | 3,000 | 1,000 |

Immediately prior to the distribution, J's outside basis in his partnership interest was $8,000. This basis must first be reduced by the $4,000 cash distribution. The $4,000 remaining basis is allocated to the Category 1 assets in an amount not to exceed JKL's inside basis:

| | Partner J's Basis |
|---|---|
| Unrealized receivables | $ 0 |
| Inventory | 2,000 |

Because J's $2,000 remaining outside basis is less than the aggregate inside bases of the Category 2 assets distributed, the basis decrease formula must be used to allocate this amount to the two capital assets received. First, the amount of the basis decrease is computed to be $2,000 by subtracting J's remaining outside basis amount ($2,000) from the aggregate inside bases ($1,000 + $3,000 = $4,000) of these assets. The $2,000 basis decrease is then allocated to any of these assets with unrealized depreciation; in this case only Capital asset 2. Thus J's basis in Capital asset 2 is $1,000 ($3,000 – $2,000). J's resulting basis in each of these assets is reflected below:

| | Inside Basis | FMV | Unrealized Depreciation | Partner J's Basis |
|---|---|---|---|---|
| Capital asset 1 | $1,000 | $1,500 | $ 0 | $1,000 |
| Capital asset 2 | 3,000 | 1,000 | 2,000 | 1,000 |

Subsequent to this distribution, J's outside basis in his partnership interest has been reduced to zero.

[71] An unrealized receivable is any right to payment for goods or services provided to customers in the ordinary course of business that has not been recognized by the partnership as ordinary income. Reg. § 1.732-1(c)(1) and § 751(c).

[72] § 732(c)(3)(A).

If more than one of the distributed assets from the same category has depreciated in value, the basis decrease is allocated based on relative depreciation.

## Example 34

Assume the same facts in *Example 33* above, except that the fair market value of Capital asset 1 is $500 instead of $1,500. In this case, the basis decrease is allocated between the two capital assets based on relative depreciation. J's basis in each of these assets is determined as follows:

| | *Inside Basis* | *FMV* | *Unrealized Depreciation* |
|---|---|---|---|
| Capital asset 1 | $1,000 | $ 500 | $ 500 |
| Capital asset 2 | 3,000 | 1,000 | 2,000 |

| | *J's Basis* |
|---|---|
| *Capital asset 1:* | |
| $1,000 carryover basis – $400 [($500/$2,500) × $2,000 basis decrease] = | $ 600 |
| *Capital asset 2:* | |
| $3,000 carryover basis – $1,600 [($2,000/$2,500) × $2,000 basis decrease] = | 1,400 |

Finally, if the required basis decrease exceeds the unrealized depreciation of the assets, any further decrease is allocated in proportion to the assets relative bases (as previously adjusted).[73]

## Example 35

Assume the same facts as in *Example 34* above, except that the total amount of the required basis decrease is $2,800 instead of $2,500. In this case, the bases of Capital assets 1 and 2 would first be reduced by the existing depreciated amount to $500 and $1,000, respectively. The $300 remaining basis decrease would be allocated between these assets in proportion to these reduced bases. J's basis in each of the capital assets would be computed as follows:

| | *JKL Basis* | *Depreciation* | *Reduced Basis* | *$300 Basis Decrease* | *J's Basis* |
|---|---|---|---|---|---|
| Capital asset 1 | $1,000 | $ 500 | $ 500 | $100 [($500/$1,500) × $300] | $400 |
| Capital asset 2 | 3,000 | 2,000 | 1,000 | 200 [($1,000/$1,500) × $300] | 800 |

There is one exception to the rule that the partnership does not recognize gain or loss on partnership distributions. The IRS has recently ruled that gain may be recognized if appreciated property is given to a partner to satisfy a guaranteed payment obligation. For example, if a partner has an $80,000 guaranteed payment and the partnership uses property with a basis of $60,000 and fair market value of $80,000 to satisfy this obligation, the partnership must recognize gain of $20,000.[74]

## Liquidating Distributions

### Cash Distributions

When a partner's entire interest in a partnership is extinguished upon receipt of a liquidating cash distribution, the partner will recognize capital gain to the extent of any amount of cash in excess of the outside basis in his partnership interest. Conversely, if the cash distribution is less than outside basis, the partner may recognize the amount of unrecovered basis as capital loss.

---

[73] § 732(c)(3)(B).

[74] Rev. Rul. 2007-40, 2007-25 IRB 1426.

### Example 36

C receives a liquidating distribution of $20,000 cash from the ABC Partnership. (This distribution equals the $20,000 value of C's capital account as of the date of distribution.) Because she is no longer a partner, C is relieved of $13,000 of partnership debt. C's total cash distribution is $33,000 ($20,000 actual cash + $13,000 constructive cash in the form of debt relief).

If C's outside basis immediately prior to distribution is $24,500, she must recognize a $8,500 capital gain equal to the excess of the $33,000 cash distribution over this basis.

If C's outside basis immediately prior to distribution is $35,000, she may recognize a $2,000 capital loss equal to the excess of this basis over the $33,000 cash distribution.

## Property Distributions

Liquidating distributions of property generally do not result in gain or loss recognition to either partnership or partner, except as noted in footnote 68 above. When a partnership distributes property as a liquidating distribution, the recipient partner's outside basis (reduced by any amount of cash included in the distribution) is allocated to the distributed property.[75] In most cases, this substituted basis rule defers the recognition of any economic gain or loss realized by the partner upon liquidation.

### Example 37

M receives a liquidating distribution of $6,000 cash and a partnership § 1231 asset with a fair market value of $25,000 and a $14,600 inside basis to the partnership.

Assume M's predistribution outside basis is $40,000. This basis is reduced by the $6,000 cash distribution and the remaining $34,000 basis is substituted as the basis of the distributed asset to M. Neither M nor the partnership recognizes gain or loss because of the distribution.

Assume M's predistribution outside basis is $9,000. This basis is reduced by the $6,000 cash distribution and the remaining $3,000 basis is substituted as the basis of the distributed asset to M. Neither M nor the partnership recognizes gain or loss because of the distribution.

Assume M's predistribution outside basis is only $4,000. M must recognize the $2,000 cash distribution in excess of basis as capital gain. The distributed asset will have a zero basis to M.

If a liquidating distribution includes multiple assets, the recipient partner's outside basis (reduced by any cash distributed) is allocated between two categories of noncash assets in the following order of priority:

1. To any unrealized receivables and inventory (Category 1) in an amount not to exceed the basis of these assets in the hands of the partnership.
2. To any other distributed properties (Category 2).

Unlike the current (nonliquidating) distribution rules that limit the distributee partner's bases in *any* assets to the distributing partnership's inside basis (i.e., a carryover basis), only the bases of unrealized receivables or inventory (Category 1 assets) are subject to this rule in a liquidating distribution. If the distributee partner's outside basis exceeds the partnership's inside basis of any unrealized receivables or inventory distributed, the remaining outside basis must be assigned to any asset received from Category 2.[76] If the partner does not receive any

[75] § 732(b).

[76] § 732(c).

Category 2 assets, then the excess of the outside basis over the inside basis of the Category 1 assets is recognized as a loss by the partner.[77] However, if Category 2 assets are received, the partner can never recognize a loss.

## Example 38

R receives a liquidating distribution from the RST Partnership that consists of the following:

| | *RST Basis* | *FMV* |
|---|---|---|
| Cash | $2,500 | $2,500 |
| Accounts receivable | 0 | 2,000 |
| Inventory | 3,000 | 4,000 |
| Capital asset | 5,000 | 9,000 |

R's predistribution outside basis in his partnership interest was $12,000. This basis must first be reduced by the $2,500 cash distribution. The $9,500 remaining basis is allocated to the Category 1 assets in an amount not to exceed RST's inside basis:

| | *Partner R's Basis* |
|---|---|
| Unrealized receivables | $ 0 |
| Inventory | 3,000 |

The $6,500 remaining basis is allocated to the capital asset (Category 2 asset), even though this substituted basis exceeds the RST Partnership's $5,000 inside basis. In addition, neither R nor the RST Partnership recognizes gain or loss because of the distribution.

## Example 39

N receives a liquidating distribution from the MNOP Partnership that consists of the following:

| | *MNOP Basis* | *FMV* |
|---|---|---|
| Cash | $ 700 | $ 700 |
| Accounts receivable | 0 | 800 |
| Inventory asset 1 | 1,000 | 1,300 |
| Inventory asset 2 | 2,100 | 2,500 |

Immediately prior to the distribution, N's outside basis is $4,000. This basis must first be reduced by the $700 cash distribution. Only $3,100 of the $3,300 remaining basis is allocable to the Category 1 assets.

| | *Partner N's Basis* |
|---|---|
| Unrealized receivables | $ -0- |
| Inventory asset 1 | 1,000 |
| Inventory asset 2 | 2,100 |

N may recognize her $200 unrecovered outside basis as a capital loss.

[77] § 731(a)(2).

Note that in *Example 39* partner N received a liquidating distribution with a total fair market value of $5,300 so that she realized an economic gain upon termination of her partnership interest. The Subchapter K rules governing the tax consequences of partnership property distributions ensure that a partner's economic gain or loss with respect to the distribution is deferred until subsequent disposition of the property.

### Example 40

Refer to the facts in *Example 39*. Although N recognized a $200 tax loss upon receipt of the liquidating distribution, she realized a $1,300 economic gain ($5,300 value of assets received in excess of $4,000 basis in N's liquidated partnership interest). However, N's basis in the distributed assets is only $3,100. If N were to sell the unrealized receivables and inventory for their aggregate value of $4,600, she would recognize a $1,500 taxable gain.

This result is consistent with the aggregate theory of partnerships under which N has not severed her interest in the MNOP Partnership until she no longer owns any interest in partnership *assets*. When N finally sells the distributed MNOP assets, her $1,500 recognized gain on sale netted against her $200 recognized loss upon distribution equates to her $1,300 economic gain attributable to the termination of her partnership interest.

Finally, when a partner receives more than one Category 2 asset in a liquidating distribution, his or her remaining outside basis must be allocated between the assets using one of the following:

1. *Basis decrease formula*—where the sum of the bases of the distributed Category 2 assets *exceeds* the distributee partner's outside basis remaining after reduction for any cash received and basis allocated to any unrealized receivables or inventory (Category 1 assets).
2. *Basis increase formula*—where the sum of the bases of the distributed Category 2 assets is *less* than the distributee partner's outside basis remaining after reduction for any cash received and basis allocated to any unrealized receivables or inventory (Category 1 assets).

### Example 41

After reduction for a distribution of cash and the required allocation of basis to unrealized receivables and inventory received in a liquidating distribution from the RST Partnership, partner T's remaining outside basis of $25,000 must be allocated to the following capital assets:

| | *RST's Basis* | *FMV* |
|---|---|---|
| Capital asset 1 | $10,000 | $20,000 |
| Capital asset 2 | 30,000 | 10,000 |

Because T's $25,000 remaining outside basis is less than the aggregate bases of the Category 2 assets, the basis decrease formula must be used. First, the amount of the basis decrease is computed to be $15,000 by subtracting T's outside basis amount ($25,000) from the aggregate inside bases ($40,000) of these assets. The $15,000 basis decrease is then allocated to any of the assets with unrealized depreciation; in this case only Capital asset 2. T's basis in each of these assets is reflected below:

| | *Inside Basis* | *FMV* | *Unrealized Depreciation* | *Partner T's Basis* |
|---|---|---|---|---|
| Capital asset 1 | $10,000 | $20,000 | $ 0 | $10,000 |
| Capital asset 2 | 30,000 | 10,000 | 20,000 | 15,000 |

Note that even though the depreciation in value of Capital asset 2 is $20,000, the total basis decrease is only $15,000. Thus, the $30,000 inside basis in that asset is reduced to $15,000 in T's hands.

If more than one of the distributed assets from the same category has depreciated in value, the basis decrease is allocated based on relative depreciation.

## Example 42

Assume the same facts in *Example 41* above, except that the fair market value of Capital asset 1 is $5,000 instead of $20,000. In this case, the $15,000 total basis decrease is allocated between the two capital assets based on relative depreciation as follows:

| | *J's Basis* |
|---|---|
| *Capital asset 1:* | |
| $10,000 carryover basis – $3,000 [($5,000/$25,000) × $15,000 basis decrease] = | $ 7,000 |
| *Capital asset 2:* | |
| $30,000 carryover basis – $12,000 [($20,000/$25,000) × $15,000 basis decrease] = | 18,000 |

## Example 43

After reduction for a distribution of cash and the required allocation of basis to unrealized receivables and inventory received in a liquidating distribution from the RST Partnership, partner T's remaining outside basis of $25,000 must be allocated to the following capital assets:

| | *RST's Basis* | *FMV* |
|---|---|---|
| Capital asset 1 . . . . . . . . . . . . . . . . . . . . . . . . . . | $10,000 | $20,000 |
| Capital asset 2 . . . . . . . . . . . . . . . . . . . . . . . . . . | 5,000 | 25,000 |

Because the aggregate bases of the Category 2 assets is *less* than T's remaining outside basis, the basis *increase* formula must be used. First, the amount of the basis increase is computed to be $10,000 by subtracting the aggregate inside bases ($15,000) of these assets from T's outside basis amount ($25,000). The $10,000 basis increase is then allocated to the assets based on relative unrealized appreciation. T's basis in each of these assets is reflected below:

| | *Inside Basis* | *FMV* | *Unrealized Appreciation* | *Basis Increase* |
|---|---|---|---|---|
| Capital asset 1 | $10,000 | $20,000 | $10,000 | $3,333 |
| Capital asset 2 | 5,000 | 25,000 | 20,000 | 6,667 |

T's basis in Capital asset 1 will be $13,333 ($10,000 carryover basis + $3,333 basis increase) and his basis in Capital asset 2 will be $11,667 ($5,000 carryover basis + $6,667 basis increase). Note that the total of T's bases in these assets ($13,333 + $11,667 = $25,000) equals his $25,000 remaining predistribution outside basis.

If only one of the assets in *Example 43* above had unrealized appreciation, it would have been allocated all of the basis increase up to its total fair market value. In the event that the basis increase exceeded the unrealized appreciation, any remaining basis increase amount would be allocated between the assets based on relative fair market values.

### Closing of Partnership Year

When a partner's entire interest in a partnership is liquidated, the partnership taxable year closes with respect to that partner.[78] As a result, the partner may have to include a proportionate share of more or less than 12 months of partnership income in his or her taxable year in which the liquidation occurs.

#### Example 44

The BCD Partnership and partner B both use a calendar year for tax purposes. On September 30, 2011, B received a liquidating distribution from BCD that terminated his interest in the partnership. BCD's taxable year closed with respect to B on September 30. As a result, B will include his proportionate share of BCD's income from January 1 through September 30 (nine months) in his 2011 tax return. BCD's taxable year does not close with respect to the remaining partners, who will include their proportionate shares of BCD's income for the full calendar year on their respective returns.

#### Example 45

Refer to the facts in *Example 44*. If BCD uses a fiscal year ending May 31 for tax purposes, two partnership years (June 1, 2010 through May 31, 2011 and the short year June 1, 2011 through September 30, 2011) ended within partner B's 2011 taxable year. As a result, B will include his proportionate share of BCD's income from June 1, 2010 through May 31, 2011 (12 months) and from June 1, 2011 through September 30, 2011 (four months) in his 2011 tax return.

In *Example 44* and *Example 45*, B's outside basis in his partnership interest immediately prior to the receipt of his liquidating distribution should reflect his distributive share of BCD's income or loss through September 30, 2011.[79] Therefore, B cannot determine the tax consequences of the distribution itself until he receives his final Schedule K-1 from the BCD Partnership.

## Section 736 Payments

The amount of a liquidating distribution paid to a partner who is terminating an interest in an ongoing partnership should theoretically equal the partner's proportionate interest in the value of the partnership assets. In reality, partners may negotiate for and partnerships may agree to pay liquidating distributions in excess of such amount. In such case, § 736 provides that only the portion of the total distribution attributable to the partner's interest in partnership assets is subject to the statutory rules dealing with partnership distributions. The remainder of the distribution (labeled a *§ 736(a) payment*) is not subject to the normal distribution rules. Instead, § 736(a) payments that are determined without regard to the income of the partnership are classified as *guaranteed payments*. Section 736(a) payments determined with reference to partnership income are classified as *distributive shares* of such income.

#### Example 46

R, a 20% general partner in the RSTU Partnership, retired from the partnership business during the current year. As of the date of R's retirement, the partnership had the following balance sheet:

[78] § 706(c)(2)(A)(ii).

[79] § 705(a).

| | Inside Basis | FMV |
|---|---|---|
| Cash | $ 50,000 | $ 50,000 |
| Business assets | 65,000 | 90,000 |
| | $115,000 | $140,000 |
| Debt | $ 5,000 | $ 5,000 |
| Capital: R. | 22,000 | 27,000 |
| Other partners | 88,000 | 108,000 |
| | $115,000 | $140,000 |

Even though R's capital account balance was only $27,000, the other partners agreed to pay R $40,000 cash in complete liquidation of his equity interest. The additional $13,000 payment was in grateful recognition of R's long years of faithful service to the business.

The total liquidating payment to R consisted of $41,000 ($40,000 actual cash + $1,000 relief of 20% of the partnership debt). R's 20% interest in the value of partnership assets was $28,000 (as evidenced by the $27,000 value of his capital account and 20% share of the partnership debt). Therefore, only $28,000 of the liquidating payment is treated as a distribution. If R's outside basis in his partnership interest was $23,000, R must recognize a $5,000 capital gain equal to the excess of the cash distribution over this basis.

The $13,000 § 736(a) payment to R was determined without regard to partnership income. Consequently, it is classified as a guaranteed payment, which R must recognize as ordinary income and the partnership may deduct as a current expense.

### Payments for Unrealized Receivables and Unspecified Goodwill

Section 736 contains a special rule concerning liquidating payments made with respect to a partner's interest in certain partnership assets. Payments made with respect to unrealized receivables must be considered § 736(a) payments rather than distributions.[80] Payments made with respect to goodwill are similarly classified unless the partnership agreement specifies that a withdrawing partner will be paid for his or her share of goodwill. Prior to the enactment of the Revenue Reconciliation Act of 1993, this special rule applied to liquidating payments made to any partner by any partnership. The 1993 Act limited its application to payments made to *general* partners by partnerships in which capital is not a material income-producing factor.[81]

## Example 47

E is a 10% general partner in the Beta Partnership, a professional service partnership in which capital is not a material income-producing factor. During the current year, E had a serious disagreement with the other partners and decided to withdraw from the partnership. As of the date of E's withdrawal, the partnership had the following balance sheet:

| | Inside Basis | FMV |
|---|---|---|
| Cash | $ 35,000 | $ 35,000 |
| Accounts receivable | 0 | 24,000 |

[80] § 751(c) provides that, for § 736 purposes, the term *unrealized receivables* includes only zero basis accounts receivable and not § 1245, § 1250, or other types of ordinary income recapture.

[81] § 736(b)(3). Capital is not a material income-producing factor if substantially all of the partnership's income consists of fees, commissions, or other compensation for personal or professional services performed by individuals.

| | *Inside Basis* | *FMV* |
|---|---|---|
| Business assets | 100,000 | 145,000 |
| | $135,000 | $204,000 |
| Debt | $ 15,000 | $ 15,000 |
| Capital: E | 12,000 | 18,900 |
| Other partners | 108,000 | 170,100 |
| | $135,000 | $204,000 |

After considerable negotiation, the other partners agreed to pay E $20,000 cash in complete liquidation of her equity interest. The partners determined that this was a fair price for E's 10% capital interest because the partnership business has considerable goodwill and going concern value that is not recorded as an asset on its balance sheet. The Beta Partnership agreement does not provide for specific payments with respect to partnership goodwill.

The total liquidating payment to E consisted of $21,500 ($20,000 actual cash + $1,500 relief of 10% of the partnership debt). E's 10% interest in the value of the recorded partnership assets was $20,400 (as evidenced by the value of her $18,900 capital account and 10% share of the partnership debt). However, the $2,400 payment made with respect to E's 10% interest in Beta's unrealized receivables must be classified as a § 736(a) payment. Consequently, only $18,000 of the liquidating payment ($20,400 – $2,400) is treated as a distribution. If E's outside basis in her partnership interest was $13,500, E must recognize a $4,500 capital gain equal to the excess of the cash distribution over this basis.

The $3,500 § 736(a) payment to E represents the value of her 10% interest in Beta's accounts receivable and unspecified goodwill. Because the payment was determined without regard to partnership income, it is classified as a guaranteed payment, which E must recognize as ordinary income and Beta may deduct as a current expense.

## Dispositions of Distributed Property

If a partner who received either a current or liquidating distribution of partnership unrealized receivables subsequently collects the receivables or disposes of them in a taxable transaction, that partner must recognize the excess of the amount realized over the zero basis in the receivables as ordinary income.[82] Similarly, if a partner sells inventory distributed from a partnership within five years of the date of distribution, any gain or loss recognized must be characterized as ordinary gain or loss.[83] A partnership's holding period for a distributed asset is included in the recipient partner's holding period.[84]

### Example 48

Two years ago, G received a current distribution of land from the EFG Partnership, which operates a real estate development business. The land was an inventory asset to EFG and took a carryover basis of $140,000 in G's hands. G held the land as an investment and sold it in the current year for $200,000. Because she sold the land within five years of the date of its distribution by EFG, G must recognize her gain as ordinary income, even though the land was a capital asset in her hands.

[82] § 735(a)(1). This paragraph provides that both gain or loss realized on a partner's disposition of partnership unrealized receivables is characterized as ordinary gain or loss. Except in unusual circumstances, such receivables will have a zero basis in the hands of a distributee partner; consequently, their disposition can only trigger gain recognition.

[83] § 735(a)(2).

[84] § 735(b).

## Basis Adjustments to Partnership Property

Under the general rules governing the tax consequences of partnership distributions, no gain or loss is recognized at either the partnership or the partner level and distributed assets simply take a carryover basis in the hands of the recipient partner. However, in certain circumstances, a partner may be required to recognize either capital gain or loss because of a distribution. In other cases, the inside basis of a distributed partnership asset does not carry over to the recipient partner.

These exceptions to the general rules can be viewed as anomalies that violate the aggregate theory of partnerships. Subchapter K provides a mechanism to correct these anomalies in the form of an adjustment to the inside basis of undistributed partnership property. Specifically, if a partnership has a *§ 754 election* in effect, it is allowed to *increase* the basis of partnership property by (1) any amount of gain recognized by a partner as the result of a distribution, and (2) any reduction of the inside basis of a distributed partnership asset in the hands of the recipient partner.[85]

### Example 49

Partner L received a current distribution from the LMNO Partnership that consisted of $5,000 cash and partnership inventory with an inside basis of $1,500. Because L's predistribution outside basis was only $3,600, L recognized a $1,400 capital gain and took a zero basis in the distributed inventory. If LMNO has a § 754 election in effect, it may increase the inside basis in its remaining assets by $2,900 ($1,400 gain recognized by L + $1,500 reduction in the basis of the distributed inventory).

In *Example 49*, $1,400 of the positive basis adjustment counterbalances the current gain recognized at the partner level by decreasing the amount of future gain the partnership will recognize on a sale of assets (a $1,400 basis increase is equivalent to a $1,400 decrease in gain potential). The remaining $1,500 positive basis adjustment to LMNO's assets compensates for the $1,500 lost basis in the distributed inventory.[86]

A partnership with a § 754 election in effect is required to *decrease* the basis of partnership property by (1) any amount of loss recognized by a partner as the result of a distribution, and (2) any increase in the basis of a distributed partnership asset in the hands of the recipient partner.[87]

### Example 50

Partner E received a liquidating distribution of $5,000 cash from the EFGH Partnership. Because E's predistribution outside basis was $7,000, E recognized a $2,000 capital loss. Partner F received a liquidating distribution from EFGH consisting of a capital asset with an inside basis of $10,000. Because F's predistribution outside basis was $14,500, F took a $14,500 substituted basis in the distributed asset.

If EFGH has a § 754 election in effect, it must decrease the basis in its remaining assets by $6,500 ($2,000 loss recognized by E + $4,500 increase in the basis of the distributed capital asset).

In *Example 50*, $2,000 of the negative basis adjustment counterbalances the current loss recognized at the partner level by decreasing the amount of future loss the partnership will recognize on a sale of assets (a $1,400 basis decrease is equivalent to a $1,400 decrease in loss

---

[85] § 734(b)(1).

[86] The rules for allocating a § 734(b) basis adjustment to specific partnership assets are found in § 755 and the regulations thereunder.

[87] § 734(b)(2).

potential). The remaining $4,500 negative basis adjustment to EFGH's assets compensates for the $4,500 additional basis in the distributed capital asset.

The optional basis adjustment is allocated to the same asset class in which the distributed property falls. For purposes of this adjustment, the partnership's assets are divided into two property classes:

1. Capital assets and § 1231 property (i.e., capital gain property), and
2. All other assets (i.e., ordinary income property).

However, any loss resulting from the distribution of cash, unrealized receivables, and inventory, must be allocated to the partnership's capital gain property. Further, any gain recognized from the distribution of cash must also be allocated to the capital gain property.

For allocations of increases in basis within a class, the increase must be allocated first to any properties in that class with unrealized appreciation. If more than one property has unrealized appreciation, the increase is allocated in proportion to each asset's unrealized appreciation. However, in no case can the allocated increase for an asset exceed that asset's unrealized appreciation. If any increase remains after this allocation, it is allocated to properties within that class in proportion to their fair market values.

The rules are similar for a decrease in basis. The decrease must be allocated first to any properties in that class with unrealized depreciation. If more than one property has unrealized depreciation, the decrease is allocated in proportion to each asset's unrealized depreciation. However, in no case can the allocated decrease for an asset exceed that asset's unrealized depreciation. If any decrease remains after this allocation, it is allocated to properties within that class in proportion to their adjusted bases. The adjusted bases used for this allocation include any adjustments already made as part of the overall allocation process.[88] In no case can the adjusted basis for an asset be reduced below zero. If the bases of all assets within a class have been reduced to zero, any remaining decreases are suspended until the partnership acquires property in that class.[89]

It is important to note that the rules for increases and decreases are similar, except that any remaining adjustment after the initial allocations are based on relative *fair market values* for increases, but on relative *adjusted bases* for decreases.

## Example 51

Refer to the facts in *Example 49*. The § 734 adjustment was $2,900: $1,400 for the gain from the cash distribution and $1,500 due to the reduction in basis for the distributed inventory. The $1,400 for the gain must be allocated to capital gain property. Since inventory is an ordinary asset, the $1,500 for the inventory basis must be allocated to the ordinary income class.

Assume that LMNO Partnership owns the following two capital assets:

| | *Adjusted Basis* | *FMV* | *Unrealized Appreciation* |
|---|---|---|---|
| Capital Asset A | $1,000 | $3,000 | $2,000 |
| Capital Asset B | 1,000 | 1,000 | -0- |

Since the only capital asset with unrealized appreciation is asset A, its basis is increased by $1,400 to $2,400.

Alternatively, assume that LMNO Partnership owns the following two capital assets:

| | *Adjusted Basis* | *FMV* | *Unrealized Appreciation* |
|---|---|---|---|
| Capital Asset A | $1,000 | $2,200 | $1,200 |
| Capital Asset B | 1,000 | 1,800 | 800 |

[88] Reg. § 1.755-1(c)(2).

[89] Reg. § 1.755-1(c)(4).

The $1,400 basis increase is allocated to the assets based on the relative unrealized appreciation. Therefore, asset A receives a basis increase of $840 ($1,200/$2,000 × $1,400). Asset B receives a basis increase of $560 ($800/$2,000 × $1,400). Note that these basis increases are allowed because neither exceeds the unrealized appreciation for the respective asset. Asset A's basis is increased from $1,000 to $1,840, and asset B's basis is increased from $1,000 to $1,560.

## Example 52

Refer to the facts in *Example 50*. The § 734 adjustment was $6,500: $2,000 for the loss recognized and $4,500 for the increase in basis of the capital asset. This results in a $6,500 decrease in the basis of capital assets, because all losses due to distributions are allocated to capital assets, as are adjustments due to the distribution of capital assets.

Assume that LMNO Partnership owns the following two capital assets:

| | *Adjusted Basis* | *FMV* | *Unrealized Depreciation* |
|---|---|---|---|
| Capital Asset A | $12,000 | $ 4,000 | $8,000 |
| Capital Asset B | 10,000 | 12,000 | -0- |

Since the only capital asset with unrealized depreciation is asset A, its basis is decreased by $6,500 to $5,500.

### The Section 754 Election

A partnership will adjust the inside basis of its assets as the result of a distribution to a partner only if it has a § 754 election in effect for the year of the distribution. A partnership makes a § 754 election simply by attaching a statement to that effect to its Form 1065 for the first taxable year for which the election is to be effective. Once made, the election applies for all subsequent years unless the Internal Revenue Service agrees to its revocation.[90]

### Substantial Basis Reduction

Even if a § 754 election is not in effect, the rules discussed above will apply if there is a substantial basis reduction to partnership property as the result of a distribution. A substantial basis reduction occurs if the sum of 1) the partner's loss on the distribution, and 2) the basis increase to the distributed properties is more than $250,000.[91]

## Example 53

Partner B has a basis of $4,000,000 in her partnership interest in Partnership AB. Partnership AB does not have a § 754 election in effect. She receives a liquidating distribution of land from the partnership having a fair market value of $3,500,000 and a basis of $1,800,000. She will recognize no gain or loss on the distribution. Her basis in the land will be $4,000,000 and the basis in her partnership interest will be reduced to zero. Since the basis of the land has increased by more than $250,000 (by $2,200,000, from $1,800,000 to $4,000,000) a substantial basis reduction has occurred. Therefore, Partnership AB will have to reduce the basis of its other properties by $2,200,00 according to the rule § 755.

[90] Reg. § 1.754-1.

[91] See § 734(d)(1). These rules apply for distributions made after October 22, 2004. Different rules apply to electing investment partnerships. A discussion of these rules is beyond the scope of this text.

# Dispositions of Partnership Interests

The most common way for a partner to dispose of a partnership interest is through a liquidating distribution from the partnership itself. There are, however, a number of other types of dispositions, each of which has a unique set of tax consequences to both partner and partnership.

## Sales of Partnership Interests

**LO.9**
Analyze the tax consequences of a sale of a partnership interest to both the seller and purchaser.

Partnership agreements typically place restrictions on the partners' right to sell their equity interests in the partnership to third parties. For example, an agreement might provide that a partner must offer his or her interest to the partnership itself or to the existing partners before offering it to a third-party purchaser. The agreement may also provide that a prospective purchaser must be approved by the general partners or by a majority of all partners. Because of such limits on transferability, partnership interests are considered illiquid assets.

When a partner sells his or her entire interest in a partnership, the partnership's taxable year closes with respect to that partner.[92] The selling partner's outside basis in the partnership interest immediately prior to sale includes his or her distributive share of partnership income or loss through date of sale. The tax consequences of the sales transaction itself to both seller and purchaser are governed by specific rules in Subchapter K.

### Tax Consequences to Seller

Upon sale of a partnership interest, the seller recognizes gain or loss to the extent the amount realized exceeds or is less than the outside basis of the interest. Section 741 contains a general rule that such gain or loss is capital in nature. This rule reflects the entity theory under which a partnership interest represents the partner's equity in the partnership as a whole rather than a proportionate interest in each specific asset owned by the partnership. Literally in mid sentence, § 741 shifts to the aggregate theory by cautioning that the general rule is inapplicable to the extent provided in § 751(a). This subsection applies only if the partnership owns unrealized receivables or inventory, which for convenience' sake tax practitioners have simply labeled *hot assets*.

### Hot Assets

The term *unrealized receivables* includes zero basis trade accounts receivables generated by a cash basis partnership. The term also includes the § 1245 and § 1250 ordinary income recapture potential inherent in depreciable partnership assets.[93] All partnership unrealized receivables are deemed to have a zero tax basis.[94] The term *inventory* includes not only stock in trade and property held primarily for sale to customers in the ordinary course of business, but also any other property that is not a capital asset or a § 1231 asset to the partnership.[95]

**Example 54**

The accrual basis MNO Partnership owns the following assets:

| | Tax Basis | FMV |
|---|---|---|
| Cash | $ 7,000 | $ 7,000 |
| Accounts receivable | 29,000 | 27,000 |
| Stock in trade | 330,000 | 410,000 |

[92] § 706(c)(2)(A)(i). Refer to the discussion of the closing of a partnership year with respect to a partner at 77, *supra*.

[93] § 751(c). The term *unrealized receivables* also includes many esoteric types of ordinary income recapture potential, such as § 1254 recapture of intangible drilling and development costs of oil and gas wells and mining development and exploration expenditures.

[94] Reg. § 1.751-1(c)(5).

[95] § 751 inventory also includes any partnership property that would be inventory if held by a selling or distributee partner [§ 751(d)(2)].

| | | Tax Basis | FMV |
|---|---|---|---|
| Equipment cost | $100,000 | | |
| Accumulated depreciation | (30,000) | 70,000 | 80,000 |
| Other 1231 assets | | 250,000 | 390,000 |
| Total | | $686,000 | $914,000 |

If MNO were to sell its equipment for market value, it would recognize a $10,000 gain, all of which would be recaptured as § 1245 ordinary income. Consequently, the partnership has $10,000 of unrealized receivables.

Both MNO's accounts receivable and stock in trade are inventory assets because accounts receivable are not a capital or § 1231 asset to the partnership.[96]

Under § 751 (a) the amount of gain or loss for the hot assets (unrealized receivables and inventory) is determined by assuming that these assets are sold by the partnership in a fully taxable transaction for cash in an amount equal to the fair market value of the properties. The partner selling his partnership interest is allocated the portion of the ordinary income that would have been allocated to him if these assets had actually been sold by the partnership.[97]

## Example 55

K sold her 10% interest in the KLM Partnership to P for $45,000 cash. KLM used the cash method of accounting and had the following balance sheet as of the date K sold her interest. K's outside basis in her interest was $35,500.

| | Inside Basis | FMV |
|---|---|---|
| Cash | $ 40,000 | $ 40,000 |
| Accounts receivable | 0 | 30,000 |
| Stock in trade | 90,000 | 100,000 |
| Section 1231 assets (no recapture) | 225,000 | 300,000 |
| | $355,000 | $470, 000 |
| Debt | $ 20,000 | $ 20,000 |
| Capital: K. | 33,500 | 45,000 |
| Other partners | 301,500 | 405,000 |
| | $355,000 | $470,000 |

At date of sale, the partnership had both unrealized receivables of $30,000 (zero basis accounts receivable) and $100,000 of inventory.

If the hot assets were sold by the partnership at fair market value the partnership would recognize $40,000 of ordinary income ($130,000 fair market value – $90,000 basis). Ten percent of this income, or $4,000, would be allocated to K. Therefore, on the sale of her partnership interest K must recognize $4,000 of ordinary income under § 751(a).

Subsequent to the application of § 751(a), the amount realized on the sale of K's partnership interest has been reduced to $34,000 ($47,000 total amount realized – $13,000 attributable to hot assets). K's outside basis in her partnership interest has been reduced to $26,500 ($35,500 predistribution basis – $9,000 basis allocated to hot assets). Under the general rule of § 741, K recognizes a $7,500 capital gain on the sale of her partnership interest.

[96] Accounts receivable of a cash basis partnership are both an unrealized receivable and an inventory item for purposes of § 751.

[97] Reg. § 1.751-1(a)(2).

These computations can be summarized as follows:

| | Total | Hot Assets [§ 751(a)] | Other (§ 741) |
|---|---|---|---|
| Amount realized | $ 47,000 | $ 13,000 | $34,000 |
| Adjusted basis | (35,500) | (9,000) | (26,500) |
| Recognized gain/loss | $ 12,500 | $ 4,000 | $ 7,500 |
| | | Ordinary Income | Capital Gain |

In addition to the recognition of ordinary income if the partnership has hot assets, the seller of a partnership interest may also have special tax treatment in three other situations: collectibles gain, § 1250 capital gain, and residual long-term capital gain or loss.

First, if at the time of the sale of a partnership interest (which has been held for more than one year) the partnership holds collectibles with unrealized appreciation, the gain attributable to this appreciation is taxed at 28 percent.[98] A collectible includes any work of art, rug, antique, metal, gem, stamp, coin, or alcoholic beverage.[99]

## Example 56

H and G are individuals that have been equal partners in HG for the last three years. The partnership owns gems that qualify as collectibles that have an adjusted basis of $500 and a fair market value of $1,100. H sells her interest in HG to I. As a result, $300 of H's gain from the sale will be characterized as collectibles gain (50% of the $600 gain that HG would have realized if it sold its collectibles in a fully taxable transaction).

Second, unrecaptured § 1250 gain is taxed at a 25 percent maximum rate. Unrecaptured § 1250(b)(1) required all depreciation to be recaptured as ordinary income. If a partner sells an interest in a partnership, and the partnership has unrecaptured § 1250 gain, then the partner must take into account his or her portion of that gain in computing the tax results.[100]

## Example 57

Assume in *Example 56* above that HG also owns residential rental property. At the time of H's sale, the property had a fair market value of $110,000 and adjusted basis of $60,000. The property's original cost basis was $100,000. Straight-line depreciation of $40,000 had been claimed on the property. At the time of H's sale, one must compute what H's share of unrecaptured § 1250 gain would be if the property was sold. Since the property is realty and straight-line depreciation was used there would be no § 1250 recapture. Consequently, the entire gain ($50,000) would be a § 1231 gain. However, the § 1231 gain would be treated as a 25% gain to the extent of any straight-line depreciation claimed ($40,000). H's share of the 25% gain is $20,000. Consequently, of the total gain recognized by H on the sale of his partnership interest, $20,000 will be 25% gain due to the § 1250 unrecaptured gain.

The collectibles gain and § 1250 unrecaptured gain that are allocable to a partner that has sold his or her partnership interest are together known as the look-through capital gain.[101] The residual long-term capital gain or loss is computed as follows:

Residual long-term capital gain/loss =

§ 741 long-term capital gain or loss (after application of § 751)

− Look-through capital gain or loss.

[98] § 1(h)(6)(B).

[99] § 408 (m)(3).

[100] Reg. § 1.1(h)-1(b)(3)(ii).

[101] § 1(h)(1)(D); Reg. § 1.1(h)-1(b)(1).

## Example 58

G and H are individuals that have been equal partners in Partnership B for the last two years. B owns collectibles with a basis and fair market value of $3,000 and $5,000, respectively. G sells his interest in partnership B to R and has a total recognized gain of $500. After the application of the § 751 hot assets rules, assume that G recognizes ordinary income of $2,000 and § 741 long-term capital loss of $1,500 (i.e., the pre-look through long-term capital loss). G's share of the collectibles gain (i.e., the look-through capital gain) is $1,000 [($5,000 – $3,000) × 50%].

| | |
|---|---|
| Total gain | $ 500 |
| § 751 Hot asset ordinary income | (2,000) |
| Pre-look through long-term capital loss | (1,500) |
| Gain from collectibles | 1,000 |
| Residual long-term capital loss | $(2,500) |

To summarize, G has $2,000 of ordinary income, $1,000 collectibles gain taxed at 28%, and a $2,5000 capital loss.

### Tax Consequences to Purchaser

Section 742 states that the basis of a partnership interest acquired other than by contribution shall be determined under the normal basis rules provided in §§ 1011 and following. Thus, the purchaser of a partnership interest takes a *cost* basis in the interest. The *cost basis* includes the amount of cash and the value of any noncash property paid to the seller plus the amount of any partnership liabilities assumed by the purchaser in his or her role as a new partner.

The fact that a purchaser is given a cost basis in the partnership interest rather than in a proportionate share of partnership assets reflects the entity theory of partnerships. Section 743(a) reinforces this perspective by specifying that the basis of partnership property shall not be adjusted as the result of a transfer of an interest in a partnership by sale or exchange. This general rule typically results in an imbalance between a purchasing partner's outside basis and the inside basis of his or her proportionate share of partnership assets.

## Example 59

P purchased a 10% interest in the accrual basis KLM Partnership from K for $45,000 cash. As of the date of sale, the partnership had the following balance sheet:

| | *Inside Basis* | *FMV* |
|---|---|---|
| Cash | $ 40,000 | $ 40,000 |
| Accounts receivable | 30,000 | 30,000 |
| Stock in trade | 90,000 | 100,000 |
| Depreciable assets | 225,000 | 300,000 |
| | $385,000 | $470,000 |
| Debt | $ 20,000 | $ 20,000 |
| Capital: K (replaced by P) | 36,500 | 45,000 |
| Other partners | 328,500 | 405,000 |
| | $385,000 | $470,000 |

P's cost basis in his new partnership interest is $47,000 ($45,000 cash + 10% of KLM's debt). The transaction between P and K had no effect on the basis of the partnership assets, so that P's aggregate inside basis in 10% of KLM's assets is only $38,500.

The imbalance between P's outside and inside bases in *Example 59* has several negative implications for P. If the partnership sells its entire stock in trade for $100,000, P will be allocated $1,000 of ordinary income (the excess of the $10,000 value of 10 percent of the stock in trade over its $9,000 basis), even though P indirectly paid $10,000 to acquire his share of this asset. Similarly, P will be allocated tax depreciation computed on the $22,500 inside basis of 10 percent of KLM's depreciable assets, even though P indirectly paid $30,000 to acquire his share of these assets.

## Special Basis Adjustment for Purchaser

Strict adherence to the entity theory is relaxed if a purchaser acquires an interest in a partnership with a § 754 election in effect.[102] In this case, § 743(b) provides that any excess of the purchaser's outside basis over the inside basis of his or her proportionate share of partnership assets becomes a *positive* adjustment to that partner's inside basis.[103] Conversely, any excess of a purchaser's inside basis in his or her proportionate share of partnership assets over outside basis becomes a *negative* adjustment to that partner's inside basis.

Any positive or negative adjustment to the inside basis of the partnership property must be allocated to specific assets in such a manner as to reduce the difference between the fair market value and the tax basis of the asset. For purposes of this adjustment, the partnership's assets are divided into two property classes:[104]

1. Capital assets and § 1231 property (i.e., capital gain property), and
2. All other assets (i.e., ordinary income property).

The allocation of the optional basis adjustment between these two classes is based on the gain or loss that would be allocated to the transferee partner based on a hypothetical sale of all the partnership's assets. Therefore, it is possible that a positive adjustment could be made to the capital assets and a negative adjustment to the other assets, or vice-versa.

The adjustment to the ordinary income class is the amount of income, gain, or loss allocated to the transferee partner from the hypothetical sale of all ordinary income property at fair market value for cash. The adjustment to the capital asset class is then the difference in the total adjustment less the adjustment to the ordinary income class. However, any decrease in basis adjustment for the capital asset class cannot reduce the basis of the capital assets below zero. Once the basis of the capital assets is reduced to zero, any remaining negative adjustment must be used to reduce the basis of ordinary income property.[105]

The adjustment to each class must then be allocated to assets within that class. Generally, the adjustment to each item of ordinary income property equals the amount of income, gain, or loss allocated to the transferee partner in a hypothetical sale of the item. The adjustment for each item in the ordinary income class is determined as shown below.

### Example 60

G sells his 25% interest in the JJG Partnership to D on March 15, 2011. JJG Partnership previously made a § 754 election. D paid $50,000 to G and assumed G's share of partnership liabilities. JJG's balance sheet at the date of sale is as follows:

| | *Inside Basis* | *FMV* |
|---|---|---|
| Cash | $ 40,000 | $ 40,000 |
| Accounts receivable | 20,000 | 15,000 |
| Inventory | 42,000 | 50,000 |
| Building | 70,000 | 85,000 |
| Land | 20,000 | 40,000 |
| | $192,000 | $230,000 |
| Debt | $ 30,000 | $ 30,000 |

[102] The § 754 election is discussed at Footnote 88, *supra*.

[103] § 743(b)(1).

[104] § 755.

[105] Reg. § 1.755-1(b).

| | Inside Basis | FMV |
|---|---|---|
| Capital: G (replaced by D) . . . . . . . . . . . . . . . . . . | 40,500 | 50,000 |
| Other partners . . . . . . . . . . . . . . . . . . | 121,500 | 150,000 |
| | $192,000 | $230,000 |

Since the JJG Partnership has a § 754 election in effect, D is entitled to a $9,500 basis adjustment [the excess of his $57,500 outside basis over the $48,000 inside basis of his 25% share of JJG's assets ($192,000 × 25%)]. Note that his outside basis is computed as the $50,000 cash payment plus 25% of the partnership's debt. The $9,500 is labeled as a § 743(b) adjustment.

The § 743(b) adjustment is allocated between classes and among properties based on the allocations of income, gain, or loss that the transferee partner would receive from a hypothetical sale of all partnership assets.

***Allocation between Classes:***

| | D's Allocable Share (25%) | | |
|---|---|---|---|
| *Ordinary Income Property* | *Adjusted Basis* | *FMV* | *Gain/(Loss)* |
| Accounts receivable | $ 5,000 | $ 3,750 | $(1,250) |
| Inventory | 10,500 | 12,500 | 2,000 |
| Total | $ 15,500 | $ 16,250 | $ 750 |

| *Capital Gain Property* | *Adjusted Basis* | *FMV* | *Gain/(Loss)* |
|---|---|---|---|
| Building | $ 17,500 | $ 21,250 | $ 3,750 |
| Land | 5,000 | 10,000 | 5,000 |
| Total | $ 22,500 | $ 31,250 | $ 8,750 |

Therefore, the § 743(b) adjustment is allocated $750 to the ordinary income property and $8,750 to the capital gain property.

***Allocation within Classes:***

If a hypothetical sale occurred, D would be allocated a loss of $1,250 from the sale of the receivables and a gain of $2,000 from the sale of the inventory. D would also be allocated a gain of $3,750 for the building and a gain of $5,000 for the land. Therefore, these amounts are D's basis adjustment for each of these assets.

To summarize, D's allocation of the inside basis of JJG's assets is as follows:

| | *Inside Basis* | *25% of Basis* | *§ 743(b) Adjustment* | *Adjusted Inside Basis* |
|---|---|---|---|---|
| Cash | $40,000 | $10,000 | $ 0 | $10,000 |
| Accounts receivable | 20,000 | 5,000 | (1,250) | 3,750 |
| Inventory | 42,000 | 10,500 | 2,000 | 12,500 |
| Building | 70,000 | 17,500 | 3,750 | 21,250 |
| Land | 20,000 | 5,000 | 5,000 | 10,000 |
| | | | | $57,500 |

Note that D's total outside basis of $57,500 is now equal to his allocation of the inside basis of the partnership's assets.

## Effect of the Adjustment

A § 743(b) special basis adjustment belongs only to the purchasing partner and has no effect on the other partners. Although any benefit of a § 743(b) basis adjustment accrues only to the purchasing partner, the burden of record keeping for the adjustment falls upon the partnership. This disparity is one reason partnerships may be reluctant to make the § 754 election necessary to activate § 743(b). If a partner has a special basis adjustment with respect to an asset disposed of by the partnership in a taxable transaction, the adjustment will be taken into account in calculating that partner's distributive share of gain or loss.

### Example 61

If the JJG Partnership in the previous example sells its inventory for $50,000 and recognizes $8,000 of ordinary income, D's 25% share of that is $2,000. However, D's $2,000 special basis adjustment in the inventory reduces his distributive share of the partnership ordinary income to zero.

If a partner has a special basis adjustment with respect to a depreciable or amortizable asset, the adjustment will generate an additional cost recovery deduction for that partner.[106] Therefore, D can depreciate the $3,750 step-up in basis for the building in *Example 60*.

### Substantial Built-in Loss

Even if a § 754 election is not in effect, the rules discussed above will apply if there is a substantial built-in loss to the partnership immediately after the transfer of the partnership interest. A substantial built-in loss occurs if the partnership's basis in its assets exceeds the fair market value of those assets by more than $250,000.[107]

### Example 62

Partner M sells his 20% partnership interest for $500,000 at a time when the MN partnership has a basis and fair market value in it is assets of $3,000,000 and $2,500,000, respectively. Since the basis of the partnership's assets exceeds the fair market value by more than $250,000 [by $500,000 [($3,00,000 – $2,500,000)], a substantial built-in loss exists. Therefore, even if Partnership MN does not have a § 754 election in effect, the partnership must reduce the acquiring partner's share of the basis in its assets by $100,000, the proportional amount of the $500,000 built-in loss according to §755.

### Special Rule for Built-in-Losses

If the seller of a partnership interest had previously contributed built-in-loss property to the partnership, special rules apply. As explained earlier, if a partner contributes property with built-in losses, § 704(c) requires that when the property is sold, any recognized loss must be allocated to that contributing partner to the extent of the built-in loss, with any remaining loss allocated per the partnership agreement. However, § 704(c)(1)(C) requires that in determining the amount of items allocated to other (non-contributing partners), the basis of the property is assumed to be its fair market value at the time of contribution.[108]

### Example 63

Partner L contributes land to equal partnership LO with a basis of $100 and a fair market value of $80. Therefore, the land has a built-in loss of $20. If the partnership sold the land for $80, the $20 loss would be allocated to L.

Assume that L sells his partnership interest to M for $80. L would recognize a loss of $20 from the sale of his partnership interest. Under previous law, M would "step into the shoes" of L and the first $20 loss from the future sale of the land would be allocated to M. Section 704(c)(1)(C) now requires that the basis of the land be treated as $80 (its fair market value on the date of contribution) for purposes of allocating any tax items to

[106] A § 743(b) basis adjustment to depreciable property is considered a newly purchased asset placed in service in the year in which the adjustment arises. Prop. Reg. § 1.168-2(n).

[107] See § 743(d)(1). These rules apply for distributions made after October 22, 2004.

[108] This provision does not apply to contributions of property made before October 23, 2004.

partners M and O. Thus, if the land was later sold by the partnership for $70, the basis of the land would be $80 (not $100). The sale would create a $10 loss ($70 amount realized less $80 basis), none of which is a built-in loss. The $10 loss would be allocated equally to partners M and O.

The purpose of this rule is to prevent the partners from benefiting from a double loss. If L recognizes a loss of $20 on the sale of the partnership interest and M could recognize another loss of $20 when the land was sold, a double benefit would be created.

## Gifts of Partnership Interests and Family Partnerships

**LO.10**
Apply the family partnership rules to partnership interests created by gift.

Dispositions of partnership interests by gift generally have no income tax consequences to either donor or donee, although the donor may be liable for a gift tax on the transfer. The donee will take a basis in the partnership interest as determined under § 1015.

Transfers of partnership interests by gift usually involve donors and donees who are members of the same family, and therefore often result in the creation of *family partnerships.* Such partnerships can be an effective way to divide the income from a family business among various family members. To the extent the income can be allocated and taxed to individuals in the lower marginal tax brackets, family partnerships can also achieve a significant tax savings.

Not surprisingly, the tax laws restrict the use of family partnerships as income shifting devices. If the income earned by a partnership is primarily attributable to the individual efforts and talents of its partners, any allocation of that income to nonproductive partners would be an unwarranted assignment of earned income. Accordingly, a family member generally cannot be a partner in a personal or professional service business unless he or she is capable of performing the type of services offered to the partnership's clientele.[109]

A family member can be a partner in a business in which capital is a material income-producing factor.[110] In contrast to a service partnership, the mere ownership of an equity interest in a capital intensive partnership entitles a partner to a share of partnership income. Under the general rules of § 704, a partner's allocable share of income does not have to be in proportion to his or her interest in partnership capital as long as the allocation has substantial economic effect. However, § 704(e)(2) provides that in the case of any partnership capital interest *created by gift,* the income allocable to such interest cannot be proportionally greater than the income allocated to the donor's capital.

### Example 64

M creates a partnership with his son S and daughter D by giving each child an equity interest in his business. M is in the highest marginal tax bracket, while his children are in the 15% marginal tax bracket. The initial MSD Partnership balance sheet appears as follows:

| | | |
|---|---|---|
| Contributed business assets | | $300,000 |
| Capital: | M | $200,000 |
| | S | 50,000 |
| | D | 50,000 |
| | | $300,000 |

[109] See *Comm. v. Culbertson,* 337 U.S. 733 (USSC, 1949).

[110] § 704(e)(1). Capital is a material income-producing factor if the operation of the partnership business requires substantial inventories or a substantial investment in plant, machinery, or equipment. Reg. § 1.704-1(e)(1)(iv).

If S and D's interests had not been created by gift, the partnership agreement could allocate any amount of partnership income to S and D as long as the allocation had substantial economic effect. Because the interests were created by gift, the maximum percentage of income allocable to S and D respectively is 16.7% ($50,000 donee's capital ÷ $300,000 total capital of both donor and donees).

Section 704(e)(2) also requires that any allocation of income with respect to donor and donee partners take into account the value of services rendered to the partnership by the donor. This statutory requirement prevents a donor partner from forgoing reasonable compensation from the partnership in order to maximize the amount of income shifted to the donee partners.

**Example 65**

Refer to the facts in *Example 64*. If M performs services for MSD during its first taxable year that are reasonably worth $25,000, he must be compensated for the services before any amount of partnership income may be allocated to S and D. If the partnership earns $145,000 of operating income during its first year, the maximum amount of such income allocable to S and D respectively is $20,000 [16.7% of ($145,000 operating income – $25,000 compensation to M)].

Note that the restrictions illustrated in *Example 64* and *Example 65* technically apply to any partnership interest created by gift, regardless of any familial relationship between donor and donee. Realistically, these restrictions most frequently apply to family partnerships. In order to prevent families from circumventing these restrictions, the statute states that a partnership interest purchased from a family member is considered to have been acquired by gift.[111]

## Death of a Partner

When an individual partner dies, his or her partnership interest passes to a *successor in interest* in the partnership.[112] The partner's gross estate for federal estate tax purposes includes the fair market value of the partnership interest at date of death, and the decedent's successor takes an outside basis in the interest equal to such fair market value.[113] Because the death of a partner causes a closing of the partnership's tax year with respect to that partner, items of income, gain, loss, deduction, or credit attributable to the deceased partner's interest up to date of death will be included on the final tax return of the decedent. Any amounts for the remainder of the partnership's tax year must be reported by the deceased partner's successor in interest.[114]

**Example 66**

Individual Z, who owned a 40% interest in the capital, profits, and loss of the calendar year XYZ Partnership, died on November 3 of the current year. Under the terms of Z's will, all his assets (including his interest in XYZ) passed to his estate. Because the partnership's tax year closes with respect to Z on the date of his death, XYZ's income

[111] § 704(e)(3). For purposes of this rule, a partner's family members include a spouse, ancestors, and lineal descendants.

[112] The successor in interest is named under the decedent partner's will or determined by reference to state intestacy laws if the decedent died without a will.

[113] § 1014(a). Any imbalance between a successor in interest's outside basis and inside basis in the partnership assets is remedied if the partnership has a § 754 election in effect. In such case § 743(b) permits a special adjustment with respect to the inside basis of the partnership assets.

[114] § 706(c)(2)(A)(ii). Prior to 1998, the death of a partner did not cause the partnership's tax year to close with respect to the deceased partner. As a result, income or loss attributable to the interest for the entire year was usually included on the tax return of the successor in interest.

or loss attributable to this interest from January 1 to November 3 will be included in Z's final tax return. Income or loss attributable to this 40% interest for the remainder of the year must be included in the first fiduciary income tax return filed on behalf of Z's estate.

## Partnership Termination

**LO.11**
Recognize a termination of a partnership and summarize the tax consequences of the termination to the partners.

One of the important legal characteristics of the partnership form of business is *limited life*. Under state law, a partnership is dissolved whenever any partner ceases to be associated in the carrying on of the partnership business.[115] From a legal perspective, a partnership's identity, and therefore its existence, is dependent upon the continued association of a particular group of partners. This perspective is consistent with the aggregate theory of partnerships. Nevertheless, it would be totally impractical to require a partnership to close its taxable year and make a final accounting of its business activities every time an existing partner left or a new partner joined the partnership.

Section 708(a) adopts the entity theory by providing that a partnership does not terminate for tax purposes simply because it may be dissolved under state law. In other words, a partnership shall continue in existence as an entity for purposes of Subchapter K even if the association of partners changes. Section 708(b) provides that a partnership shall terminate for tax purposes *only if*:

1. No part of any business, financial operation, or venture is being conducted by the partnership (*natural termination*), or
2. Within a 12-month period there is a sale or exchange of 50 percent or more of the total interest in partnership capital and profits (*technical termination*).

### Technical Terminations

When a partnership ceases to conduct any type of economic activity, its termination for federal tax purposes marks the natural end of its life as a business entity. In contrast, a partnership that is terminated because of a sale or exchange of more than a 50 percent interest may be conducting a vital, ongoing business. Moreover, the partners who were not involved in the sale or exchange may be unaware that the terminating transaction even occurred!

Only sales or exchanges of partnership interests can trigger a technical termination. Other types of dispositions, such as gifts or transfers at death, are ignored. Similarly, changes in the relative ownership interests of partners because of contributions to or distributions from a partnership cannot result in termination. Sales or exchanges will not cause termination unless *at least* a 50 percent cumulative interest in both capital and profits changes hands within a 12-month period.

#### Example 67

Partners A, B, and C have owned equal interests in the capital and profits of the ABC Partnership since 2000.

- On January 12, 2010, A sold her one-third interest to new partner D.
- On July 8, 2010, B sold 10% of his interest to new partner E.
- On November 22, 2010, C gave his one-third interest to new partner F.
- On January 9, 2011, F exchanged this interest for stock in a new corporation; the exchange was nontaxable under § 351.

---

[115] Uniform Partnership Act, § 29.

The January 12 sale did not terminate the ABC Partnership because only a 33.3% interest in capital and profits was sold. The July 8 sale did not terminate the partnership because at that point in time only a 43.3% cumulative interest in capital and profits had been sold within a 12-month period. The November 22 gift did not enter into the termination calculation. The January 9 exchange did result in a termination of the ABC Partnership; within the 12-month period beginning on January 12, 2010, a cumulative 76.6% interest in the partnership was sold or exchanged. If F had delayed his exchange until after January 11, 2011, the transaction would have not triggered a termination.

In determining whether a cumulative 50 percent interest has been sold or exchanged within the crucial 12-month time period, multiple transfers of the *same interest* are counted only once.[116] In *Example 67*, if D (rather than F) had exchanged his one-third interest for corporate stock on January 9, 2011, the exchange would not have resulted in a technical termination.

### EFFECT OF TERMINATION

Upon termination, a partnership's taxable year closes with respect to all its partners. If the partnership and any partner use different taxable years, a bunching of more than 12 months of income may occur.

#### Example 68

The QRS Partnership uses a calendar year for tax purposes, while corporate partner A uses a fiscal year ending June 30. The partnership terminated on March 31, 2011 and closed its taxable year on that date. Because two partnership years (calendar year 2010 and the short taxable year from January 1–March 31, 2011) ended within its fiscal year ending June 30, 2011, Q must include its distributive share of 15 months of partnership income in its taxable income for the year.

Pursuant to a natural termination, a partnership typically will wind up its affairs and distribute all remaining cash and assets to the partners in complete liquidation of their interests.[117] In a technical termination, the partnership contributes all of its assets and liabilities to a new partnership in exchange for an interest in the new partnership. The terminated partnership then distributes interests in the new partnership to the purchasing partner and all other remaining partners.[118] The result of the application of these rules is that the technical termination does not automatically result in adjustments to the bases of the partnership assets because no assets are treated as being distributed.[119]

## Problem Materials

### DISCUSSION QUESTIONS

**22-1** *Partnership versus Corporation.* List both tax and nontax advantages or disadvantages of operating a business as a partnership rather than as a corporation.

**22-2** *General versus Limited Partners.* Distinguish between the legal rights and responsibilities of a general partner and a limited partner.

**22-3** *Aggregate versus Entity Theory.* How does the aggregate theory of partnerships differ from the entity theory of partnerships? Give a specific example of a Subchapter K rule that reflects each theory.

---

[116] Reg. § 1.708-1(b)(2).

[117] Reg. § 1.708-1(b)(1).

[118] Reg. § 1.708-1(b)(1)(iv).

[119] A complete analysis of the potential tax consequences of technical terminations is beyond the scope of an introductory text.

**22-4** *Contributions of Property.* True or false: neither a partner nor a partnership ever recognizes gain or loss on the contribution of property in exchange for a partnership interest. Explain your conclusion.

**22-5** *Partnership Liabilities as Basis.* What is the economic rationale for including a portion of partnership recourse debt in the partners' bases of their partnership interests? What is the rationale for the inclusion of nonrecourse debt?

**22-6** *Contributions of Services.* Distinguish between the tax consequences to a partner who contributes services in exchange for a capital interest in a partnership and one who contributes services in exchange for an interest in future profits.

**22-7** *Organization Costs versus Syndication Fees.* Compare the tax treatment of partnership organization costs to that of syndication fees.

**22-8** *Partnership Taxable Year.* What choices are available to a business partnership when selecting a taxable year?

**22-9** *Basis Adjustments.* Indicate whether each of the following occurrences increases, decreases, or has no effect on a general partner's basis in his partnership interest. Assume all liabilities are recourse liabilities.

**a.** The partnership borrows cash that will be repaid in two years.
**b.** The partnership earns tax-exempt interest on municipal bonds.
**c.** The partnership generates an operating loss for the year.
**d.** The partnership distributes cash to its partners.
**e.** The partnership incurs a nondeductible penalty.
**f.** The partnership makes a principal payment on a mortgage secured by partnership property.
**g.** The partnership recognizes a long-term capital gain on the sale of marketable securities.

**22-10** *Partners' Transactions with Partnerships.* Give three examples of a transaction between a partnership and a partner that will be treated as a transaction between the partnership and a nonpartner for tax purposes. Does such arm's length treatment reflect the aggregate or the entity theory of partnerships?

**22-11** *Partners as Employees.* May a general partner be an employee of the partnership for federal tax purposes? Explain your conclusion.

**22-12** *Current versus Liquidating Distributions.* Explain the difference between a current distribution and a liquidating distribution from a partnership.

**22-13** *Current Distributions.* Is the statement that a partner never recognizes a loss upon the receipt of a current distribution true or false? Explain your conclusion.

**22-14** *Liquidating Distributions.* Under what circumstances will a partner recognize a capital loss upon the receipt of a liquidating distribution?

**22-15** *Closing of Partnership Year.* Partner Z received a liquidating distribution from a calendar year partnership on April 3 of the current year. Explain why Z could not determine the tax consequences of the distribution until the end of the year.

**22-16** *Partnership Goodwill.* Explain the difference in tax consequences to both partner and partnership of liquidating payments with respect to (1) specified and (2) unspecified partnership goodwill.

**22-17** *Sale of a Partnership Interest.* Is the statement that the sale of an interest in a partnership owning hot assets can result in either ordinary gain or loss recognition true or false? Explain your conclusion.

**22-18** *Sale of a Partnership Interest.* Does the fact that a partner recognizes capital gain or loss on the sale of an interest in a partnership with no hot assets reflect the entity or aggregate theory of partnerships?

**22-19** *Tax Consequences to Purchaser.* Explain why the outside basis in a purchased interest in a partnership without a § 754 election in effect is usually different than the purchaser's proportionate share of the inside basis of partnership assets. Does this result reflect the entity or aggregate theory of partnerships?

**22-20** *Family Partnerships.* In what ways does the tax law restrict the use of a family partnership as a device to shift income to individuals in the lower marginal tax brackets?

**22-21** *Death of a Partner.* How is any partnership income, gain, loss, deduction, or credit attributable to a deceased partner's interest allocated between that partner's final tax return and that of the successor in interest? Assume for purposes of your answer that death occurred on August 15th and that both the partnership and the deceased were calendar year taxpayers.

**22-22** *Partnership Terminations.* Distinguish between the dissolution of a partnership under state law and the termination of a partnership for federal tax purposes.

## PROBLEMS

**22-23** *Formation—No Liabilities.* J and G form the JG Partnership and contribute the following business assets:

| *Asset* | *Fair Market Value* | *Basis* | *Contributed by* |
|---|---|---|---|
| Land | $60,000 | $30,000 | J |
| Inventory | 50,000 | 28,000 | G |
| Auto | 10,000 | 14,000 | G |

J and G will share profits and losses equally.

**a.** Calculate each partner's realized and recognized gain or loss.

**b.** Calculate each partner's basis in his or her partnership interest.

**c.** Calculate the partnership's basis in each asset.

**22-24** *Formation—No Liabilities.* The A-E Partnership is being formed by five individuals who each contribute assets in exchange for a 20 percent capital and profit/loss interest. Calculate the following for each partner: (1) recognized gain or loss, (2) each partner's basis in his or her partnership interest, (3) the partnership's basis for each asset, and (4) the holding period of the partnership interest for the partner and the assets for the partnership. Assume all contributed assets will be used in the partnership's trade or business.

**a.** A contributes business furniture with a market value of $10,000. The furniture cost $16,000 when purchased four years ago, and A's adjusted basis in the furniture is $5,000.

**b.** B contributes business equipment with a market value of $10,000. The equipment cost $20,000 when purchased two years ago, and B's adjusted basis in the equipment is $12,000.

**c.** C contributes business inventory with a market value of $10,000. The inventory cost $9,000 when purchased 16 months ago.

**d.** D and E contribute $10,000 cash each.

**22-25** *Formation—Liabilities.* Refer to *Problem 22-24*, but assume that D and E made the following contributions *instead* of cash. How do these new facts change your answers for each partner?

**a.** D contributes land with a market value of $16,000. The land was acquired 10 months ago for $9,000 cash and a $6,000 note payable (recourse debt). The $6,000 note payable is also transferred to the partnership.

**b.** E contributes land with a market value of $18,000. E received the land three years ago as a gift from a relative and has a basis of $5,000. In addition, E transfers an $8,000 mortgage (nonrecourse debt) on the land to the partnership.

**22-26** *Partner's Holding Period.* Individuals X and Y contributed $50,000 each to the equal Z Partnership on January 1, 2011. On July 1, 2011, X contributed land with an adjusted basis of $10,000 and fair market value of $25,000 to Z for an increased interest in the partnership. X had owned the property as an investment for six months. On October 1, 2011, Y contributed land with an adjusted basis of $30,000 and fair market value of $25,000 to Z for an increased interest in the partnership. Y, a dealer in real property, had owned the land for three years. As of December 31, 2011, what are the partners' holding period in their partnership interests?

**22-27** *Allocation of Recourse Debt.* Individuals A and B are general partners and individual L is a limited partner in the ABL Partnership. Partnership losses are allocated 40 percent to A, 35 percent to B, and 25 percent to L. As of December 31 of the current year, the partnership has $50,000 of recourse debt. The partnership's balance sheet as of December 31 is as follows:

| | *Basis* | *Fair Market Value* |
|---|---|---|
| Cash | $ 25,000 | $ 25,000 |
| Receivables | 50,000 | 75,000 |
| Land | 25,000 | 40,000 |
| | $100,000 | $140,000 |
| | | |
| Recourse liabilities | $ 50,000 | $ 50,000 |
| A, capital | 20,000 | 36,000 |
| B, capital | 20,000 | 36,000 |
| L, capital | 10,000 | 18,000 |
| | $100,000 | $140,000 |

How would the $50,000 of recourse debt be allocated to A, B, and L?

**22-28** *Relief of Debt in Excess of Basis.* Corporation C contributed land used in its business to the Beta Partnership in exchange for a 40 percent general interest in partnership capital, profits, and loss. The land had a $320,000 basis to the corporation and an appraised fair market value of $850,000, and was subject to a $635,000 recourse mortgage. Beta assumed the mortgage in the exchange transaction; as of the date of the exchange, Beta had no other liabilities.

**a.** What are the tax consequences to Corporation C of its contribution of the land to Beta? What initial basis does Corporation C have in its partnership interest?

**b.** How would your answers to (a) change if the $635,000 mortgage were nonrecourse rather than recourse?

**c.** How would your answers to (a) change if Beta had $200,000 of other recourse liabilities on its books as of the date of Corporation C's contribution of the land?

**22-29** *Receipt of Partnership Interest for Services.* In return for services rendered to the AX Partnership, T receives a 20 percent unrestricted interest in partnership capital. On the day T receives her interest, the partnership owned the following assets:

| | *Basis* | *Fair Market Value* |
|---|---|---|
| Inventory | $ 5,000 | $10,000 |
| Equipment | 10,000 | 14,000 |
| Land | 15,000 | 21,000 |
| Building | 40,000 | 50,000 |
| Totals | $70,000 | $95,000 |

Assuming the partnership has no liabilities and that before T's admission it is owned 60 percent by partner A and 40 percent by partner X, answer the following questions:

**a.** How much compensation income must be reported by T?

**b.** What is T's basis in the partnership interest received?

**22-30** *Required Taxable Year.* F, G, and H are partners in the FGH Partnership. F, G, and H have profit-sharing ratios of 30 percent, 50 percent, and 20 percent, respectively. F has a year-end of December 31, G of February 28, and H of September 30. What is the required year-end for FGH Partnership?

**22-31** *Computation of Partnership Taxable Income.* N is a 10 percent general partner in the KLMN Partnership. The partnership's records for the current year show the following:

| | |
|---|---|
| Gross receipts from sales | $ 670,000 |
| Cost of sales | (500,000) |
| Operating expenses | (96,000) |
| Net income from rental real estate | 48,000 |
| Dividend income | 10,000 |
| Business meals and entertainment | (6,700) |
| Section 1231 loss | (13,500) |

N's outside basis in his partnership interest was $125,000 at the beginning of the year. During the year, partnership recourse liabilities increased by $55,000; the partnership has no nonrecourse liabilities. KLMN made no distributions during the year to its partners.

**a.** Calculate the partnership's taxable income (Form 1065, page 1) for the current year.
**b.** Calculate N's basis in the partnership at the end of the year.

**22-32** *Organization and Syndication Costs.* The Sigma Limited Partnership was organized during May and June of the current year. During these two months, the partnership paid $40,000 to a law firm to draft the partnership agreement and $10,000 to a CPA to set up an accounting system for the partnership business. The partnership also paid a $2,500 filing fee to the state of Illinois and $18,000 to advertise and market the sale of limited interests to potential investors. Sigma began business in August of the current year and properly adopted a fiscal year ending September 30 for tax purposes. Based on these facts, what portion of the above expenses may be expensed and amortized on Sigma's first Form 1065?

**22-33** *Contributed Property—Allocations.* At the beginning of the current year, S contributed depreciable business property (market value $90,000 and basis $67,200) and T contributed investment land (market value $180,000 and basis $145,000) to form the ST Partnership. S has a one-third interest and T has a two-thirds interest in partnership capital, profits, and loss.

**a.** The ST Partnership will depreciate the property contributed by S on a straight-line basis over six years. Compute the amount of first year tax depreciation on the property and allocate the depreciation between partners S and T.
**b.** Assume the partnership sells the property contributed by S on the first day of the partnership's third taxable year. The amount realized on sale is $65,000. Compute the taxable gain or loss recognized on the sale and allocate the gain or loss between partners S and T.
**c.** How would your answer to (b) change if the amount realized on sale had been $54,000 rather than $65,000?
**d.** During its fourth taxable year, the ST Partnership sells the land contributed by T for $200,000. Compute the taxable gain recognized on sale and allocate the gain between partners S and T.

**22-34** *Sale of Contributed Property—Allocations.* Two years ago, X contributed property, which was part of his proprietorship inventory, to the D Partnership in exchange for a one-third partnership interest. At the date of contribution, the property had a basis of $120,000 and a value of $145,000. The property was used in the partnership's business as a nondepreciable § 1231 asset. The partnership sold the property for $160,000 in the current year.

**a.** Calculate the amount and character of the taxable gain recognized on the sale allocable to X.
**b.** How would the answer for (a) change if the sale occurred six years rather than two years after contribution?
**c.** How would the answer for (a) change if the property had been sold for $100,000 rather than $160,000?

**22-35** *Retroactive Loss Allocations.* On September 1 of the current year, Corporation M contributed $125,000 cash to the calendar year, accrual basis Topper Partnership. For the current year, Topper recognized a $180,000 net operating loss; $82,000 of this loss had accrued as of August 31. In June of the current year, Topper sold marketable securities, recognizing a $63,000 capital gain.

**a.** If Topper does not make an interim closing of its books on August 31, what is the maximum amount of current-year net operating loss and capital gain that can be allocated to Corporation M? Explain your conclusion. (In answering the question, you may assume that any allocation will have substantial economic effect.)

**b.** If Topper does make an interim closing of its books on August 31, what is the maximum amount of current-year net operating loss and capital gain that can be allocated to Corporation M? Explain your conclusion. (In answering the question, you may assume that any allocation will have substantial economic effect.)

**22-36** *Losses—Section 704(d).* Z has a 60 percent interest in the capital, profits, and losses of the Zeta Partnership. Both Z and Zeta are calender year taxpayers. At the beginning of the current year, Z's basis in her partnership interest was $100,000. For the current year, Zeta incurred a $200,000 ordinary loss from its business operation, earned $14,600 of dividend and interest income on its investments, and recognized a $62,000 capital gain on the sale of a partnership capital asset. On March 12 of the current year, Z received a $15,000 cash distribution from Zeta. Assume that there was no change in the amount of Zeta's liabilities during the current year.

**a.** How much of the $200,000 operating loss may Z deduct on her current-year tax return? In answering this question, ignore any impact of the at-risk or passive activity loss limitations.

**b.** Calculate Z's basis in her partnership interest at the end of the year.

**22-37** *Losses—Section 704(d).* Corporation Q owns a 50 percent interest in the capital, profits, and loss of the QRST Partnership. Both Q and QRST are calendar year taxpayers. At the beginning of the current year, Q's outside basis in its partnership interest was $30,000. For the current year, the partnership earned $14,000 of tax-exempt interest on its investment in municipal bonds, incurred a $106,000 ordinary loss from its business operation, and recognized a $42,000 capital loss on the sale of a partnership capital asset. QRST made no distributions to partners during the year and did not change the amount of partnership debt on its books. Based on these facts, how much of the partnership's operating loss and capital loss may Corporation Q deduct in the current year? (In answering this question, assume that Q has sufficient current-year capital gains against which to deduct any amount of partnership capital loss.)

**22-38** *Transactions between Partners and Partnerships.* A calendar year, accrual basis partnership rents property from a calendar year, cash basis partner, paying an arm's-length rent of $4,000 per month. The December rent payment for the current year was not received by the partner until January 5 of the subsequent year. The partnership pays this same partner a guaranteed payment for services rendered to the partnership of $10,000 per month. The December guaranteed payment was not received by the partner until January 10 of the subsequent year.

**a.** In what year should the partnership deduct the December rent payment, and in what year should the partner include this payment in gross income?

**b.** In what year should the partnership deduct the December guaranteed payment, and in what year should the partner include this payment in gross income?

**22-39** *Guaranteed Payments.* B and G are partners in the DR Partnership. B oversees the daily operations of the business and therefore receives compensation of $50,000, regardless of the amount of the partnership's net income. In addition, his distributive share of profits and losses is 50 percent.

**a.** If the partnership had $75,000 ordinary income before any payments to partners, determine the amount and character of B's total income.

**b.** Same as (a), but assume the partnership had $30,000 ordinary income before payments to partners.

**c.** Same as (a), except assume the partnership had $25,000 ordinary income and $50,000 long-term capital gain before payments to partners.

**22-40** *Sale to Related Partnership—Loss.* V, a 60 percent partner, sells land to the partnership for $8,000. V's basis in the land is $9,000.

**a.** Determine (1) V's recognized loss and (2) the partnership's basis in the land after the transaction.

**b.** What are the tax consequences to the partnership if it sells the land six months later for (1) $7,500, (2) $8,600, or (3) $9,300?

**c.** How would your answers to (a) and (b) differ if V were a 40 percent partner?

**22-41** *Sale to Related Partnership—Gain.* During the current year, Corporation J sold investment land with a $400,000 basis to the Kappa Partnership for a selling price of $525,000. Determine the amount and character of Corporation J's recognized gain on the sale under each of the following sets of assumptions.

**a.** Corporation J owns a 75 percent interest in the capital, profits, and loss of Kappa, and Kappa also holds the land as an investment asset.

**b.** Corporation J owns a 35 percent interest in the capital, profits, and loss of Kappa, and Kappa uses the land in its business operation.

**c.** Corporation J owns a 75 percent interest in the capital, profits, and loss of Kappa, and Kappa uses the land in its business operation.

**22-42** *Contribution of Inventory with Built-in Gain.* V is a 40 percent partner in the TUV Partnership. V is a dealer in computer equipment, and V contributes computers to TUV that the partnership will use in its business operations. The computers have a basis to V of $10,000 and a fair market value of $16,000. What are the tax consequences to V and to TUV under the following circumstances?

**a.** TUV sells the computers six months later for $15,000. Assume the basis is the same.

**b.** TUV sells the computers six years later for $3,000. Assume the basis is zero at that time.

**c.** What would your answer be if the facts are the same as in part a, except that TUV also is a dealer in computer equipment?

**22-43** *Contribution of Capital Asset with Built-in Loss.* W is a 20 percent partner in the WXY Partnership. W has owned a parcel of land as an investment for three years. W contributes this land to WXY. WXY is a dealer in land. The land has a basis to W of $120,000 and a fair market value of $100,000. What are the tax consequences to W and to WXY under the following circumstances?

**a.** WXY sells the land six months later for $100,000.

**b.** WXY sells the land six months later for $90,000.

**c.** WXY sells the land six years later for $90,000.

**d.** WXY sells the land six years later for $150,000.

**22-44** *Current Distributions—Proportionate.* X is a 50 percent partner in XY, a calendar year partnership. X had a basis in her partnership interest of $10,000 at the beginning of the year. On October 1, she and the other partner withdrew $15,000 cash each as an advance against their anticipated share of partnership income for the year. The partnership's ordinary, taxable income for the year was $60,000.

**a.** How much gain or loss must X recognize on October 1?

**b.** What is X's distributive share of partnership taxable income for the year, and what is her basis in her partnership interest at the end of the year?

**c.** How would the answers to (a) and (b) change if partnership taxable income had been $6,000 instead of $60,000?

**22-45** *Current Distribution—Proportionate.* During the current year, partner J received a proportionate distribution from HIJK Partnership, consisting of $13,000 cash and land (an investment asset to the partnership). The land had a basis to the partnership of $20,000 and FMV of $33,000. Prior to the distribution, J's basis in his partnership interest was $40,000. The distribution had no effect on J's profit and loss sharing ratio.

**a.** How much gain or loss must J recognize because of this distribution? What basis will J have in the land? What basis will J have in his partnership interest after the distribution?

**b.** Does the partnership recognize any gain on the distribution of the appreciated land to J?

**c.** How would the answer to (a) change if J's basis in his interest prior to distribution had been $25,000 rather than $40,000?

**22-46** *Current Distribution of Inventory.* C received a current proportionate distribution consisting of partnership inventory with an inside basis of $25,000 and a FMV of $31,000. C's predistribution outside basis in his partnership interest was $22,500.

**a.** How much gain or loss must C recognize because of this distribution?

**b.** What basis will C take in the distributed inventory and what will be C's postdistribution outside basis?

**c.** How would your answers to (a) and (b) change if C's predistribution outside basis had been $29,000 rather than $22,500?

**22-47** *Dispositions of Distributed Inventory.* Refer to the facts in *Problem 22-46*.

**a.** What will be the tax consequences to C if he sells the distributed inventory for $30,000 in the first year following the distribution?

**b.** How does your answer to (a) change if C waits for six years and then sells the distributed inventory for $40,000?

**22-48** *Optional Adjustment to Basis—Current Proportionate Distribution.* Refer to *Problem 22-46(b)* and *(c)*. The partnership has a § 754 election in effect. Determine the § 734(b) basis adjustment for the partnership assets.

**22-49** *Basis of Distributed Property—Current Distribution.* R receives a current distribution from the RST Partnership consisting of the following:

| | Inside Basis | Fair Market Value |
|---|---|---|
| Cash | $10,000 | $10,000 |
| Accounts receivable | 0 | 7,500 |
| Inventory | 4,000 | 5,000 |
| Capital Asset 1 | 5,000 | 4,000 |
| Capital Asset 2 | 8,000 | 6,000 |

Immediately prior to the distribution, R's outside basis in her partnership interest was $22,000. What are R's bases in the distributed assets, and what is her basis in his partnership interest after the distribution?

**22-50** *Liquidating Distribution—Proportionate.* Immediately prior to its termination, the FN Partnership owned the following assets:

| | Inside Basis | Fair Market Value |
|---|---|---|
| Cash | $ 40,000 | $40,000 |
| Equipment | 100,000 | 70,000 |
| Accumulated depreciation | (60,000) | |
| Capital asset | 10,000 | 30,000 |

F, a 50 percent owner, receives one-half of all the assets in complete liquidation of her partnership interest. F's outside basis in this interest is $45,000.

**a.** Calculate F's basis for each asset received in the distribution.

**b.** How would your answer to (a) change if F's outside basis in her partnership interest is $95,000?

**22-51** *Basis of Distributed Property—Liquidating Distribution.* After reduction for a distribution of cash and the required allocation of basis to unrealized receivables and inventory received in a liquidating distribution from the HIJ Partnership, Partner J has an outside basis of $100,000. J also receives the following capital assets as part of the liquidating distribution:

| | Inside Basis | Fair Market Value |
|---|---|---|
| Capital asset 1 | $25,000 | $60,000 |
| Capital asset 2 | 50,000 | 20,000 |

What basis does J have in the capital assets?

**22-52** *Section 734 Basis Adjustment.* Partner F received a liquidating distribution of $9,000 cash from the EFG Partnership. F's predistribution outside basis was $12,000.

Assume that EFG has a § 754 election in effect. Partnership EFG owns the following assets after the distribution to F:

| | *Inside Basis* | *Fair Market Value* |
|---|---|---|
| Cash | $20,000 | $20,000 |
| Inventory | 12,000 | 15,000 |
| Capital asset M | 14,000 | 10,000 |
| Capital asset N | 10,000 | 8,000 |

**a.** What is F's gain or loss from the distribution?
**b.** What are the § 734 basis adjustments for the partnership's remaining assets?

**22-53** *Payments to a Retiring Partner.* The balance sheet of RST Partnership shows the following:

| | *Inside Basis* | *Fair Market Value* |
|---|---|---|
| Cash | $120,000 | $120,000 |
| Accounts receivable | 20,000 | 20,000 |
| Inventory | 105,000 | 112,000 |
| § 1231 assets | 4,000 | 57,000 |
| | $249,000 | $309,000 |
| Liabilities | $ 9,000 | $ 9,000 |
| R, capital | 80,000 | 100,000 |
| S, capital | 80,000 | 100,000 |
| T, capital | 80,000 | 100,000 |
| | $249 000 | $309,000 |

During the current year, partners S and T agree to liquidate R's interest in the partnership for $115,000 cash. Capital is a material income-producing factor to the RST Partnership and the partnership has no unrecorded goodwill. R's basis in his interest (including his one-third share of partnership liabilities) is $83,000.
**a.** What are the tax consequences to R of the cash distribution from the partnership?
**b.** What are the consequences to the partnership of the liquidating distribution?

**22-54** *Section 754 Election and Partnership Distributions.* Refer to the facts in *Problem 22-53*. What are the tax consequences to the continuing partnership if a § 754 election is in effect for the year in which R's interest is liquidated?

**22-55** *Sale of a Partnership Interest.* Refer to the facts in *Problem 22-53*. Assume that U, an unrelated party, will purchase R's interest in RST Partnership for a lump sum payment of $115,000.
**a.** What are the tax consequences of the sale to R?
**b.** Compute U's basis in his newly purchased partnership interest.
**c.** What is the effect of U's purchase of R's partnership interest on the inside basis of partnership assets if RST Partnership does not have a § 754 election in effect?

**22-56** *Consequences of a § 754 Election to a Purchasing Partner.* Refer to the facts in *Problem 22-55*. What are the tax consequences to new partner U and to RST Partnership if a § 754 election is in effect for the year in which U purchases R's partnership interest?

**22-57** *Sale of Partnership Interest with Hot Assets.* T, a general partner in the accrual basis TUV Partnership, sells her one-third partnership interest to D at the end of the current year for $50,000 cash. The partnership's balance sheet at the end of the year is as follows:

| | Basis | FMV | | Basis | FMV |
|---|---|---|---|---|---|
| Cash . . . . . . . . . . . | $61,000 | $ 61,000 | T, capital | $30,000 | $ 50,000 |
| Inventory. . . . . . . . | 21,000 | 39,000 | U, capital | $30,000 | $ 50,000 |
| Land . . . . . . . . . . . | 8,000 | 50,000 | V, capital | $30,000 | $ 50,000 |
| | $90,000 | $150,000 | | $90,000 | $150,000 |

**a.** What is T's gain or loss from this sale?
**b.** What basis does D have in her partnership interest?
**c.** If the partnership sells the land for $50,000 immediately after D purchases her interest, what is the tax effect to D?
**d.** What should D request that the partnership do to prevent the result in part (c) from occurring?
**e.** Instead of inventory, assume that the partnership owns collectibles with a basis of $21,000 and fair market value of $39,000. Also, assume that instead of land, the partnership owns a building with a basis of $8,000, fair market value of $50,000, depreciation claimed of $30,000 (of which $20,000 would have been straight-line depreciation). What is T's gain or loss on the sale?

**22-58** *Section 754 Election.* Based on the facts from *Problem 22-57*, what would the tax result be to D upon the sale of the land if the partnership had a § 754 election in effect?

**22-59** *Dispositions of Partnership Interests.* K owns a limited interest in the Kappa Investment Partnership. The interest has a FMV of $50,000 and a basis to K of $37,000. No amount of partnership debt is included in this basis number. What are the tax consequences to K in each of the following situations?
**a.** K exchanges the interest for a general interest in Kappa that is worth $50,000.
**b.** K exchanges the interest for investment land worth $50,000.
**c.** K dies and bequeaths the interest to her nephew.
**d.** K exchanges the interest for newly issued stock in Gamma Inc. Immediately after the exchange, K owns 12 percent of Gamma's outstanding stock.
**e.** K determines that the value of the interest is not $50,000 but is zero. Consequently, she abandons the interest.

**22-60** *Dispositions of Partnership Interests Holding Built-In Loss Property.* C and D create the equal CD Partnership in 2010. C contributes cash of $1,000 and D contributes land (holding period is 5 years) having a basis of $1,400 and a fair market value of $1,000. What are the tax consequences to the partners in the following independent situations? Assume that the partnership has not made a § 754 election.
**a.** The partnership sales the land for $800 on January 15, 2011.
**b.** D sells his partnership to E for $900 on March 15, 2011.
**c.** After D sells the partnership interest to E, the partnership sells the land for $800.

**22-61** *Partnership Termination.* At the beginning of 2011, Beta Partnership was owned by four equal partners. On June 8, 2011, Partner A sold her one-fourth interest to B, one of the other three partners. On November 19, 2011, new partner G contributed cash and property in exchange for a 55 percent interest in partnership capital and profits. On March 31, 2012, G sold a 30 percent interest to a new partner P. Beta and all its partners use the calendar year for tax purposes.
**a.** Do any of the capital transactions described above terminate the Beta partnership?
**b.** What is the effect of any termination on Beta's taxable year?

# 23

# S Corporations

## Learning Objectives

Upon completion of this chapter you will be able to:

LO.1 Identify the requirements necessary to attain S corporation status.

LO.2 Recognize the actions that terminate S status.

LO.3 Compute the taxable income or loss for an S corporation and the impact of S corporate operations on shareholders' taxable income.

LO.4 Determine the shareholders' basis in the S corporation stock and debt, and understand the significance for loss deductions and distributions.

LO.5 Recognize transactions between shareholders and their S corporations that are subject to special treatment.

LO.6 Determine the appropriate taxable year for an S corporation.

LO.7 Explain the unique concepts relevant to family members concerning ownership attribution, compensation, benefits and income allocation.

LO.8 Calculate gain or loss for the S corporation and its shareholders when asset distributions are made and the S corporation (1) has no AE&P or (2) has AE&P.

LO.9 Calculate the special taxes on excessive passive income and on built-in gains.

LO.10 Understand how dispositions of S corporate stock differ from those of C corporate stock.

LO.11 Compare the four business organizations—proprietorships, partnerships, S corporations, and C corporations (see Exhibit 23-6).

## Chapter Outline


Introduction 23-2
S Corporation Eligibility Requirements 23-3
Eligible Corporations 23-3
Shareholder Requirements 23-4
One Class of Stock 23-7
Election of S Corporation Status 23-8
Making the Election: Manner and Period of Effect 23-8
Termination of the Election 23-11
Election after Termination 23-16
Operating the S Corporation 23-16
Determining S Corporation Net Income 23-16
Reporting S Corporation Income 23-21
Allocations to Shareholders 23-28
Losses of the S Corporation 23-30

Determining Shareholder Basis 23-31
Basis in S Corporate Stock 23-31
Basis in S Corporation Debt 23-33
Relationship between an S Corporation and Its Shareholders 23-36
Transactions between S Corporations and Their Shareholders 23-36
Selecting a Taxable Year 23-37
Family Ownership 23-39
Current Distributions of Corporate Assets 23-40
The E&P Question 23-40
S Corporations with no AE&P 23-40
S Corporations With AE&P 23-42
Distributions of Property 23-47
Special Rules Relating to Source of Distributions 23-47
Post-Termination Transactions 23-48
Taxes Imposed on the S Corporation 23-49
Tax on Excessive Passive Income 23-49
Tax on Built-in Gains 23-51
LIFO Recapture 23-54
Estimated Taxes 23-55
Disposition of Ownership Interest 23-55
Worthless Securities 23-56
Corporate Liquidation 23-56
Tax Planning 23-56
Choice of Entity: Comparing S Corporations, C Corporations, Partnerships, and LLCS 23-56
Problem Materials 23-61

## Introduction

Congress added Subchapter S to the Internal Revenue Code in 1958, giving birth to a unique tax entity: the S corporation. The S corporation passes taxable income, losses and other items to its owners, similar to a partnership. However, this entity has all of the nontax (and some tax) characteristics of a corporation. In providing this distinctive treatment, Congressional intent was to allow small businesses to have "the advantages of the corporate form of organization without being made subject to the possible tax disadvantages of the corporation."[1] As this statement suggests, Congress recognized that many taxpayers who normally would incorporate their businesses to secure limited liability were reluctant to do so because of the possibility of double taxation. Accordingly, one of the major objectives of the Subchapter S legislation was to minimize taxes as a factor in the selection of the form of business organization. To accomplish this objective, a complete set of special rules were designed, most of which are contained in Subchapter S.

Although the treatment of S corporations resembles that of partnerships, this goal was not achieved under the 1958 legislation. As originally written, the rules governing S corporations (or Subchapter S corporations as they were initially called) bore little resemblance to partnership rules. Many of these differences were eliminated, however, with the substantial modifications introduced by the Subchapter S Revision Act of 1982. Under the revised rules, Federal income tax treatment of S corporations and their shareholders is similar to that of partnerships and their partners, although there are some significant differences between the two tax entities. The S corporation generally is not subject to the corporate *Federal income tax*. Rather, like a partnership, the S corporation is merely a conduit. The income, deductions, gains, losses, and credits of the S corporation flow through to its shareholders. An S corporation, however, may be subject to a special tax, such as the tax on excessive passive income or on built-in gains.

Even though the Federal income tax treatment of an S corporation resembles that of a partnership, this entity is subject to many rules that apply to regular corporations. For example, since an S corporation is formed in the same manner as a regular corporation (defined as "C" corporations), the basic rules governing organization (i.e., the nonrecognition rules contained in § 351 concerning transfers to a controlled corporation discussed in Chapter 19) of all corporations also apply to S corporations. Similarly, redemptions of an S corporation's stock, as well as liquidation and reorganization of an S corporation, generally are subject to the rules applying to regular corporations. As a practical matter, however, each provision must be closely examined to determine whether special treatment is provided for S corporations.

---

[1] S. Rept. No. 1622, 83rd Cong., 2d Sess., 119 (1954).

# S Corporation Eligibility Requirements

**LO.1**
Identify the requirements necessary to attain S corporation status.

The special tax treatment provided for S corporations is available only if the corporation is a *small business corporation* and its shareholders *consent* to the corporation's election to be taxed under Subchapter S. A small business corporation must:[2]

1. Be an *eligible domestic* corporation;
2. Not have more than 100 shareholders, all of whom must be eligible persons or entities; and
3. Have only *one class of stock* outstanding.

The corporation must meet all of these requirements when it files its S corporation election and at all times thereafter. Failure at any time to qualify as a small business corporation terminates the election, and as of the date of termination, the corporation is taxed as a regular corporation (hereafter referred to as a C corporation).[3]

The phrase *small business corporation* may be a misnomer. As the requirements for this status indicate, the sole restriction on the size of the corporation is the limitation imposed on the *number* of shareholders. Corporations are not denied use of Subchapter S due to the amount of their assets, income, net worth, or any other measure of size. In addition, the S corporation is not required to conduct an active business. Merely holding assets does not bar the corporation from Subchapter S.

## Eligible Corporations

Subchapter S status is reserved for *eligible domestic corporations*.[4] Thus, foreign corporations do not qualify. In addition, certain types of domestic corporations are considered ineligible. These ineligible corporations include insurance companies, banks that use the reserve method of accounting for bad debts, corporations electing the special possessions tax credit under Code § 936 and domestic international sales corporations (DISCs).[5]

It should be emphasized that only corporations or entities that are considered corporations may take advantage of Subchapter S. As a practical matter, this is rarely an issue. A limited liability company (LLC) or other unincorporated entity can qualify as an S corporation if it elects to be treated as a corporation under the check-the-box regulations (see Chapter 19).[6] Under these rules, the entity could only be considered an S corporation if it opts to be taxed as a corporation *and* subsequently makes a valid S election. In other words, an LLC or partnership that elects to be treated as a corporation is treated as a C corporation until the corporation files an S election. An association that wants to be treated as an S corporation must satisfy the S corporation rules for eligible owners, number of owners, and a single class of ownership interest.

Although there once was a restriction about ownership of subsidiaries, S corporations may own stock in *C corporations* without limitation. Thus, S corporations have the freedom to structure their ownership in C corporations to meet the needs of their organization. For example, an S corporation may establish a wholly owned C corporation as a subsidiary to hold a risky business, thereby protecting the assets of the parent. However, S and C corporations cannot file a consolidated return.[7] Thus, the C corporation must file Form 1120 and the S corporation must file Form 1120S.

### Example 1

D Inc., an S corporation, is interested in purchasing T Inc., a C corporation. T operates a hazardous waste disposal business that is quite profitable but also quite risky.

---

[2] § 1361.

[3] § 1362(d)(2). As discussed later, however, a corporation may avoid loss of its election by applying for "inadvertent termination" relief.

[4] § 1361(b); Reg. 301.7701-5(b) includes any U.S. territory as well as states.

[5] § 1361(b)(2).

[6] Rev. Proc. 2004-48, 2004-32 I.R.B.

[7] § 1504(b)(8).

> D would like to structure the acquisition in such a way that it does not expose its current business to the risks associated with T's operation. D may own as little or as much of T stock that it wants since there are no rules prohibiting an S corporation from owning the stock of a C corporation.

While S corporations may own stock of C corporations, the reverse is not allowed. As discussed below, S corporations generally are not allowed to have any corporate shareholders. However, an S corporation may own the stock of another corporation, and treat the wholly-owned corporation as a qualified subchapter S subsidiary (QSub).

### Qualified Subchapter S Subsidiary (QSub)

A QSub is a corporation that is 100 percent owned by an S corporation (i.e., the parent) that elects to treat the subsidiary as a QSub.[8] The QSub is a corporation that exists as a disregarded entity for Federal income tax purposes, but is a separate corporation for most other purposes. By electing to treat the subsidiary as a QSub, the parent corporation agrees to report all of the income and deductions of the QSub along with its own tax items. Note that if a parent S corporation acquires all of the stock of an existing corporation (C or S), it must treat the subsidiary as if it were liquidated for tax purposes when it elects QSub status for the subsidiary.[9] To elect QSub status, the parent files the election on Form 8869. If the parent elects to treat the subsidiary as a QSub, the subsidiary's income and deductions are included in the parent companys tax return (Form 1120S). If the parent does not elect QSub status, the subsidiary's income and deductions should be reported separately on the subsidiary's Form 1120.

## Shareholder Requirements

Subchapter S imposes several restrictions on S corporation shareholders. Not only is the total number of shareholders limited to 100, but certain parties are prohibited from owning stock of the corporation.

### Type of Shareholder

The stock of an S corporation may be owned only by:

1. Individuals who are citizens or resident aliens of the United States,
2. Estates,
3. Certain trusts, and
4. Charitable organizations, pension trusts (not IRAs), and employee stock ownership plans.

Nonresident aliens (i.e., generally foreign citizens residing outside the United States), C corporations, other S corporations, partnerships, and most trusts are *not* allowed to hold stock in an S corporation.

Over the years, rules prohibiting trusts as shareholders have proved unduly inflexible, often intruding on sensible planning. This prohibition has been particularly troublesome in the estate and retirement planning area. For example, an individual may not want to leave the shares of his or her S corporation outright to a young child in his or her will but rather in trust for the benefit of a child. Without special rules, this obviously prudent action would be barred. Consequently, the current provisions allow some freedom in using trusts.

### Eligible Trusts

The list of trusts that are eligible shareholders and a brief description of each follows below. In examining the list, note the concern for the shareholder limitation issue and how the shareholders are counted when an eligible trust holds shares.[10]

---

[8] § 1361(b)(3)(B).

[9] Use Form 8869. The liquidation is nontaxable under §§ 332 and 337.

[10] § 1361(c)(2).

**Grantor Trusts** A grantor trust is a trust that is disregarded under the trust taxation rules because of the power, control and benefits retained by the individual who established the trust (i.e., the grantor). All of the income of a grantor trust (e.g., a revocable trust that is used to avoid probate) is normally taxed to the grantor rather than the trust. If the grantor dies, the S shares normally have to be distributed to the beneficiaries within two years after the death. The grantor is treated as the shareholder for tax purposes. (See Chapter 26 for a discussion of these trusts.) If the grantor is a U.S. citizen or resident who would be eligible to hold the shares directly, the grantor trust may own shares.

**Beneficiary Controlled Trust or Deemed Grantor Trust** A deemed grantor trust is similar to the grantor trust, except the income of the trust is taxed to the beneficiary (rather than the grantor) because of the power that the beneficiary holds over trust property. The beneficiary is treated as the shareholder for tax purposes. As is the case with a grantor trust, the beneficiary, or *deemed grantor*, must be eligible to hold shares directly.

**Qualified Subchapter S Trust (QSST)** A QSST is a trust that has *only one* current income beneficiary (who must be a U.S. citizen or resident) to whom all of the income of the trust must be distributed annually and for which a proper election to be treated as a QSST has been filed in a timely manner. The trust's beneficiary (or legal guardian thereof) must file an election to include all of the trust's share of the S corporation's income, deductions and other tax items directly on the beneficiary's return as if he or she were the shareholder of the trust's stock. The beneficiary must file this election within two months and 16 days from the date the trust acquires the stock.[11] (If the trust owns shares on the date the corporation elects to become an S corporation, the beneficiary must file this election within two months and 16 days after the corporation files its S election. In practice the two elections are often made concurrently.) In addition to this election, there are certain other restrictions on the QSST.

The trust may not distribute any of its income or property to any person other than the current income beneficiary during his or her lifetime. In addition, the trust must distribute (or be required to distribute) all of its income to this beneficiary annually. Note that failure to adhere to these rules properly results in the trust becoming an ineligible shareholder and thus causing loss of the S election. There have been numerous rulings allowing S corporations to continue their tax status after a trust fails to meet one of these rules. See Inadvertent Termination Relief, below.

In practice, the QSST election is often misunderstood. The result has been a multitude of private letter rulings allowing a corporation's S election to take effect, or continue in effect, after a trust has acquired the stock and the beneficiary has failed to make a timely QSST election. Accordingly, the IRS has issued an expedited relief rule for a QSST election that is no more than 24 months late.[12] A trust that qualifies for this provision applies to the IRS Center where the corporation files its returns. Thus it avoids the need for a ruling request and user fee. If the QSST election is not filed within the 24-month period, the corporation must apply for inadvertent termination or inadvertent invalid election relief. Relief is sought from the National Office of the IRS in the form of a letter ruling request, which must be accompanied by a user fee.

For all purposes of subchapter S, the beneficiary of the QSST is treated as the shareholder. This treatment applies to consents, allocations of income, other items, and the 100-shareholder limit.

**Electing Small Business Trust (ESBT)** In contrast to the QSST that has only a single beneficiary, an *ESBT* can have more than one potential current beneficiary (PCB). The trustee can have the right to accumulate or distribute income to any of the PCBs. The trustee must file a timely election for the trust to qualify. A price is paid for use of this trust since all of the income flowing from the S corporation to the trust is taxed to the trust itself (i.e., there is no deduction for distributions of the trust) and such income is taxed at the highest marginal rate (35 percent for ordinary income in 2010 and 2011). In addition, the ESBT must pay tax on any capital gains in the same manner as an individual taxpayer who is in the highest marginal tax bracket. This rule applies both to any capital gains passing through from the S corporation to

[11] Inexplicably, this is one day longer than the grace period in which an S corporation has to file a timely S election.

[12] Rev. Proc. 2003-43, 2003-23 I.R.B. 998.

the trust and to any gain recognized by the trust on the disposition of the S corporation stock. However, a distribution from the trust to a beneficiary is tax-free to the beneficiary and is nondeductible to the trust. In counting shareholders, each PCB is considered to be a shareholder in the S corporation. Thus each PCB must be a U.S. citizen or resident. There may not be enough PCBs to cause the number of shareholders to exceed 100, although with the family attribution rules this situation is not likely to be a frequent cause of concern. However, for administrative purposes, such as consents to the corporation's various elections, the trustee is treated as the shareholder.

**Testamentary Trusts** A testamentary trust is one that is created by the decedent's last will and testament. A testamentary trust may only be an eligible shareholder for two years unless it also qualifies under one of the other trust rules. The estate is treated as the owner of the stock in the case of one or more testamentary trusts that are established (e.g., if three trusts are created, the estate is considered the single owner).

**Charitable Organizations, Pension Trusts, and Employee Stock Ownership Plans** For taxable years beginning after 1997, these organizations (generally tax-exempt) can be shareholders in S corporations. However, individual retirement accounts are not allowed to hold stock in an S corporation.[13]

Charitable organizations and pension trusts may find S corporations unappealing since they must include their share of income from the S corporation as unrelated business taxable income (UBTI). Thus these organizations would be subject to income tax on their income from the S corporation. However, an S corporation may make sufficient cash distributions to enable all shareholders to pay their income taxes on their portions of the S corporation's income. In contrast, these organizations are not subject to taxation on interest or dividend income derived from an investment in a C corporation. In addition, they are normally not taxable on gains from the disposition of stock or securities of a C corporation. However, gain from disposition of S corporation stock is UBTI to the charity. Employee Stock Ownership Plans (ESOPs) may also view investment in an S corporation unattractive since they may lose some special tax breaks to which they are entitled if they own stock in a C corporation. However, the combination of ESOP ownership and S corporation status may be quite attractive for a few corporations with broad-based participation in the ESOP.

**Voting Trusts** A voting trust is a trust created primarily to hold the shares and exercise the voting power of the stock transferred to it. For a voting trust, each beneficiary is treated as a shareholder.

### Number of Shareholders

As a general rule, a corporation does not qualify as an S corporation if the number of shareholders exceeds 100 at any moment during the taxable year. For purposes of counting the number of shareholders in an S corporation, members of a single family are subject to some rather broad attribution rules, which treat a family unit as a single shareholder. Specifically, the law permits six generations of descendants from common ancestors to elect to be treated as a single shareholder, but only for purposes of the shareholder count.[14] Moreover, the six generation limit applies only on the date the corporation files its S election or the date the first family member acquires stock in the corporation, whichever is later. Thereafter the number of generations is limitless. There is no requirement that members of each generation must be living. Thus it is possible to have extended generations of second, third and fourth cousins all be treated as one shareholder. A spouse (or former spouse) of any of the lineal family members is also included in this attribution. However, any of these individuals that holds stock at the time a corporation files an election for S status would have to consent to the election in his or her individual capacity. As a practical matter, few S corporations are troubled by this requirement.

When a permissible trust is a shareholder of the S corporation, the number of shareholders counted depends on the type of trust. As discussed above, all qualifying trusts, *except*

---

[13] There is an extremely narrow exception for certain IRAs that held stock in banking corporations on October 22, 2004. Under a special rule, these IRAs (and no others) are permitted shareholders. See §1361(c)(2)(A).

[14] See §1361(c)(1) and §1361(c)(1)(B)(ii).

ESBTs and voting trusts, represent one shareholder. For ESBTs and voting trusts, each beneficiary is counted as a shareholder.

When stock is held in the name of a nominee, agent, guardian, or custodian, the beneficial owner of the stock is treated as the shareholder.

**Example 2**

XYZ Bank and Trust, a corporation, holds legal title to stock in an S corporation. The XYZ corporation holds the stock for the benefit of R, a minor child. In this case, R, the beneficial owner, is treated as the shareholder rather than XYZ whether the trust qualifies as a QSST, an ESBT, or a deemed grantor trust. As a result, the S corporation is not denied the benefits of Subchapter S because of a corporate shareholder.

**Example 3**

F holds stock in an S corporation as custodian for his two minor children. For purposes of counting shareholders, F is ignored and the children are counted as one shareholder.

## One Class of Stock

In order to minimize the problems of allocating income of the S corporation among shareholders, the corporation is allowed only one class of stock outstanding. Stock that is authorized but unissued does not invalidate the election. For example, an S corporation may have authorized but unissued preferred stock. Similarly, stock rights, options, or convertible debentures may be issued without affecting the election. A corporation that has issued a second class of stock may qualify if the stock is reacquired and cancelled or held as Treasury stock.

Outstanding shares generally must provide identical distribution and liquidation rights to all shareholders. However, differences in *voting rights* are expressly authorized by the Code.[15] This exception enables control of the organization to be exercised in a manner that differs from stock ownership and income allocation.

**Example 4**

R organized MND, an S corporation. MND issued two classes of common stock to R: class A voting and class B nonvoting stock. The rights represented by the stock are identical except for voting rights, and thus do not invalidate the S election. Shortly after the organization of the corporation, R gives the class B nonvoting stock to her two children. Although R has shifted income and future appreciation of the stock to her children (assuming certain other requirements are satisfied), she has retained all of the voting control of the corporation.

### Debt as a Second Class of Stock

In the past, the second class of stock issue has arisen where the IRS or the courts have stepped in and reclassified an S corporation's debt as stock. As discussed in Chapter 19, reclassification might occur when the corporation is thinly capitalized (e.g., the debt to equity ratio exceeds 4:1). If this were to happen to an S corporation, the result would be particularly disastrous since the S corporation might be considered as having two classes of stock,

[15] § 1361(c)(4).

resulting in loss of its S election. To provide S corporations and their shareholders with some certainty in this area, Congress created a safe-harbor for debt meeting certain requirements. Under these rules, an S corporation's *straight debt* will not be classified as a second class of stock if:[16]

1. The interest rate and interest payment dates are not contingent on either the corporation's profits, management's discretion, or similar factors;
2. The debt instrument is written and cannot be converted into stock; and
3. The creditor is an individual, estate or trust, (but only if the trust is a grantor trust, QSST or ESBT) that is eligible to hold stock in an S corporation, or any person that is actively and regularly engaged in the business of lending money (e.g., a bank).

*Straight debt* is defined as any written unconditional promise to pay on demand, or on a specified date, a certain sum of money. Also included as straight debt are any short-term unwritten advances from a shareholder less than $10,000 in the aggregate—if treated as debt by the parties, and if expected to be repaid in a reasonable period of time.[17]

Whether an S corporation has more than one class of stock is determined by the corporate charter, articles of incorporation, bylaws, applicable state law, and binding agreements relating to distributions and liquidation. Unintended unequal distributions will generally not cause a second class of stock, unless they are pursuant to a plan to circumvent the one class of stock rule. The corporation must also correct the situation by making a catch-up distribution or taking some other action to place all shares on an equal footing. For example, excessive compensation paid to an owner-employee may be recharacterized as a distribution by the IRS. However, regulations for § 1361 hold that this type of distribution normally will not result in a second class of stock.[18] The Regulations also permit unequal distributions that occur in states that require the S corporation to withhold state taxes from distributions made to some or all of its shareholders, but only if there is a compensating distribution to shareholders who are not subject to the state withholding. Generally, the facts and circumstances of each situation will be considered. As a practical matter, there is no case or ruling under the current version of Subchapter S in which distributions have caused a corporation to lose its S status.

## Election of S Corporation Status

A corporation that qualifies as a small business corporation is taxed according to the rules of Subchapter S only if the corporation elects to be an S corporation. This election exempts the business from the corporate income tax and all other Federal income taxes normally imposed on corporations except for (1) the tax on excessive passive investment income, (2) the tax on built-in gains, and (3) the investment tax credit recapture tax, which may happen when the corporation has claimed a rehabilitation credit and then disposes of the rehabilitated property. The S corporation may also be required to pay a tax on LIFO recapture income, but that tax is part of the income tax imposed on a C corporation immediately before it converts to become an S corporation. In addition, the corporation is exempt from the personal holding company tax and the accumulated earnings tax. Although the S corporation generally avoids taxation as a regular corporation, most rules governing regular corporations such as those concerning organization, redemptions, and liquidations apply.

### Making the Election: Manner and Period of Effect

In order for a corporation to be taxed according to the rules of Subchapter S, the corporation must file an election on Form 2553. The effective date of the election, as well as the required shareholder consents that must be evidenced on the form, generally depend on when the election is filed. The election must be filed with the IRS center where the S corporation files its tax returns.

---

[16] § 1361(c)(5).

[17] Reg. 1.1361-1(l)(4)(ii)(B).

[18] Reg. § 1.1361-1(l)(2)(vi), Example 3.

### Time of the Election

To be effective for the corporation's current taxable year, the election must be filed within two months and 15 days of the beginning of the corporation's taxable year.[19] Note that well-meaning shareholders or tax professionals trying to ensure a prompt election might file an election before the corporation has actually started its first taxable year. Unfortunately, an election cannot be made before the corporation is in existence and any election filed before such date would be invalid. Since the election must be filed in a particular time period—neither too early nor too late—the starting date is critical. For this purpose, the first taxable year starts on the earliest date that the corporation (1) issues shares; (2) acquires property; or (3) commences business.[20] Once the tax year begins, the election may be filed any time on or before the two months and 15 days deadline. For many years, there was no relief for taxpayers who filed a late election even if there were good reasons for the failure. However, the IRS is now allowed to treat a late election as being timely filed if there is reasonable cause.[21]

**Example 5**

J and B decided to start a publishing corporation in 2010. The corporation issued shares on December 13, 2010 in exchange for $20,000. On January 15, 2011, the corporation opened a bank account and deposited the $20,000. On February 1, 2011, the corporation started operations. In this case, the corporation is considered to have started business on December 13, 2010 (the earliest of the dates that it issued shares, acquired property or commenced business). Consequently, the election is due on or before February 27, 2011 to be treated as timely filed. If the start date was May 1, the election is due on or before July 15. Note that in all of these examples, the third month and the start of the 15-day count begins on the same numerical day as the year began (i.e., February 13, July 1 plus 14 days yields the critical date).

If the corporation does not file a timely election or secure recognition of a late election, it will be considered a C corporation for the taxable year in question and the S election will be effective for the following tax year. Failure to make a timely election can be a crucial blunder. For instance, any losses that occurred during the C year would not flow through and any distributions could be treated as fully taxable dividends. However, since enactment of the legislation specifically enabling the acceptance of late elections, such mistakes have not been quite as costly.

Under current law, the IRS has been reasonable, if not outright lenient, in granting late elections. In 2003, the IRS authorized its Service Centers to accept S elections that are up to a year and six months late as long as the extended due date of the return for the first year of desired S status has not passed and the corporation states a "reasonable cause" for the lateness of the election.[22] The election must include the consent of every person who has been a shareholder from the first day of the first year for which the election is to be effective until the day the corporation files the election with the Service Center. Each shareholder must state that he or she has not filed a tax return that is inconsistent with the corporation's S status.

In 2007, the IRS issued Rev. Proc. 2007-62,[23] which adds to the possibilities for validating late S elections without resorting to a ruling request and user fee. This Revenue Procedure allows the corporation to file Form 2553 along with Form 1120S for the desired S year with the service center. To qualify, the corporation must not have already filed a tax return for the year, and there must be no violations of Subchapter S, except for the failure to file a timely Form 2553.

If the corporation has already filed Form 1120S for its first intended S year, it may file Form 2553 with the Service Center any time up to the day that the election is two years late. In this case all shareholders must state that they have filed returns that are consistent with the S election.

---

[19] §§ 1362(b)(1)(B) and (b)(2) and Reg. § 1.1362-6(a)(2)(ii).

[20] Reg. § 1.1362-6(a)(2)(ii)(c).

[21] § 1362(b)(5).

[22] Rev. Proc. 2003-43, 2003-23 I.R.B. 998.

[23] Rev. Proc. 2007-62, 2007-41 I.R.B. 786.

### Example 6

This year J and B formed a calendar year corporation on May 1, 2010. Unfortunately, J and B were unaware that they needed to file the S election by July 15 (i.e., two months and 15 days after May 1) and their error was not discovered until they visited an accountant in January 2011. Under the current approach, the IRS would accept an election up to September 15, 2011, the extended due date of the return for the first year it desired S status. If the corporation has not already filed its Form 1120S for 2010, it should file its Form 2553 and 1120S simultaneously. If the corporation has already filed Form 1120S, it may file Form 2553 with the Service Center on or before July 15, 2012 (two years after the due date). If the corporation does not meet these qualifications it must apply to the IRS National Office for relief. This request must be in the form of a letter ruling request and requires payment of the user fee.

If an S corporation does not meet these criteria and still wishes to validate a late election, it must apply to the National Office of the IRS for a private letter ruling—a process that can be a very costly (e.g., the IRS fee for the ruling, currently \$14,000, plus the expense of the accounting or law firm that prepares the ruling request). The IRS frequently grants favorable rulings on these requests. The fee is reduced to \$625 if the corporation has no more than \$250,000 of gross receipts. If the corporation has between \$250,000 and \$1,000,000 gross receipts the fee is \$2,000.[24]

It should also be noted that the law instructs the IRS to accept a timely filed but defective election (e.g., second class of stock outstanding) if the reason for the defect is inadvertent. Inadvertence is a higher standard than reasonable cause and only the National Office of the IRS can approve a defective election.[25]

### Shareholder Consent

In order for the election to be valid, the corporation must secure and file the consents of the shareholders along with the election. Consent to the election must be obtained not only from *all* shareholders holding stock (voting and nonvoting) at the time of election, but also from former shareholders who have held stock during the earlier portion of that taxable year.[26] The consent of these former shareholders is required since they will be allocated a share of the income, losses, and other items applicable to the time they held the stock. The IRS may grant an extension for filing the consent for one or more shareholders if reasonable cause can be shown.[27] If a *former* shareholder (whose signature is necessary to validate the election for the desired year) will not or does not sign the consent, the election is effective for the following taxable year. Similarly, if the corporation fails to meet any of the Subchapter S requirements during the pre-election portion of the year, the election is effective for the following taxable year.

### Example 7

At the beginning of 2011, D, E, and F owned the stock of GHI Corporation, a calendar year taxpayer. On February 15, 2011, F sold all of her shares in GHI to C. On March 1, 2011 an S corporation election is desired. In order for the election to be effective for 2011, all shareholders on the date of election (C, D, and E), as well as any shareholders in the pre-election portion of the year (F), must consent. Failure to obtain F's consent would cause the election to become effective for 2012. Consent is required from both C and D even if they are family members and qualify as one shareholder for purposes of the maximum shareholder limit.

---

[24] See Rev. Proc. 2010-1, 2010-1 I.R.B. 1, Appendix A for the most recent schedule of user fees.

[25] § 1362(f).

[26] §§ 1362(a)(2) and (b)(2)(B)(ii).

[27] Reg. § 1.1362-6(b)(3)(iii).

### Election Effective for Subsequent Years

Elections made after the first two months and 15 days of the current taxable year are effective for the following taxable year.[28] When the election becomes effective in the following taxable year, only shareholders holding stock on the date of election must consent. The consent of shareholders who acquire stock after the election is not required.

> **Example 8**
>
> On November 1, 2011, J Corporation filed an S election on Form 2553, including all of the shareholder consents. The election was to be effective for its next taxable year beginning on January 1, 2012. Unknowing to those handling the incorporation, one of the consenting shareholders, V, was a Canadian citizen, living in Vancouver. On December 15, 2011, the corporation discovered the problem and V agreed to sell all of his stock to one of the other shareholders. Since the corporation had a nonresident alien shareholder on the date that the election was filed, the election is not valid. The fact that the problem was corrected before the year in which the election was to be effective is irrelevant. Note, however, that if the corporation recognized the error, it could cure it by filing another Form 2553 by March 15, 2012. As an alternative, the corporation could file—at a cost—a ruling request asking the IRS to accept the inadvertently invalid election. Such requests are granted frequently.

## Termination of the Election

**LO.2**
Recognize the actions that terminate S status.

An election to be taxed as an S corporation is effective until it is terminated. The election may be terminated when the corporation:[29]

1. Revokes the election;
2. Fails to satisfy the requirements; or
3. Receives excessive passive income.

### Revocation

The S corporation election may be revoked if shareholders holding a *majority* of the shares of stock (voting and nonvoting) consent.[30] A revocation filed by the fifteenth day of the third month of the taxable year (e.g., March 15 for a calendar year corporation) normally is effective for the current taxable year.[31] In contrast, if the revocation is filed after this two months and 15-day period has elapsed, it usually becomes effective for the following taxable year.[32] In both situations, however, a date on or after the date of revocation may be specified for the termination to become effective.[33]

> **Example 9**
>
> A calendar year S corporation is owned equally by C, D, and E. On February 12, 2011, C and D consent to revoke the S corporation election. Since C and D own a majority of the outstanding shares of stock, the election is effective beginning on January 1, 2011, unless the revocation specifies February 12, 2010 or some later date.

[28] § 1362(b)(3).
[29] § 1362(d).
[30] § 1362(d)(1)(B).
[31] § 1362(d)(1)(C)(i).
[32] § 1362(d)(1)(C)(ii).
[33] § 1362(d)(1)(D).

### Example 10

Same as *Example 9* above except the revocation was made on May 3, 2011. The election is effective for the following taxable year beginning January 1, 2012. If the revocation had specified, however, that the termination was to become effective May 3, 2011, the S corporation year would end on May 2, 2011.

### Example 11

An S corporation has 100 shares of outstanding stock, 75 owned by J and 25 owned by B. On June 1 of this year, J sold 60 of her 75 shares to D. Since D owns a majority of the outstanding shares, he may cause the corporation to revoke the election, even if J and B are opposed to the revocation. However, the corporation must file the revocation. A statement filed by a shareholder is insufficient to revoke the election.

## Failure to Meet the Eligibility Requirements

If the S corporation fails to satisfy any of the Subchapter S requirements at any time, the election is terminated on the date the disqualifying event occurs.[34] In such case, the corporation is treated as an S corporation for the period ending the day before the date of termination. This often causes the corporation to have two short taxable years: one as an S corporation and one as a C corporation. As a result, the corporation must allocate income and loss for the entire year between the two years. The tax returns for both the short S year and short C year are due two months and 15 days after the end of the C short year, and may be extended for an additional six months.[35]

### Example 12

C, D, and E own a calendar year S corporation. On June 3 of this year, E sold her stock to a corporation. The S corporation's year ends on June 2. The same result would be obtained if the sale had been to a partnership or to an individual who became the 101st shareholder. The S short year includes January 1 through June 2. The C short year is June 3 through December 31. Both returns are due on March 15 of the next year, although they may be extended to September 15.

Unless the S election termination occurs on the first day of the corporation's tax year, the termination year is split into two short periods. There are some special rules governing the allocation of income between the two short periods. The two methods that the corporation may use are the pro-rata allocation and the interim closing method.

Using the pro-rata method, each item required to be reported to the shareholders is assigned equally to each day in the entire tax year.[36] If the corporation uses the interim closing method it must separately account for activities during the S and C portions of the year.[37]

### Example 13

On March 14, 2011, X Corporation terminates its S election. S uses the calendar year for tax purposes. Its income and loss items for 2011 occurred during the following periods.

---

[34] § 1362(d)(2).

[35] § 1362(e)(6)(B).

[36] § 1362(e)(1).

[37] § 1362(e)(3).

| | *S Short Year* | *C Short Year* | *Total* |
|---|---|---|---|
| Ordinary income | $80,000 | $40,000 | $120,000 |
| Long-term capital gain | 16,000 | 0 | 16,000 |
| Dividend income (X holds 20% stock in payor) | 0 | 5,000 | 5,000 |

If the corporation uses the interim closing method, it will report $80,000 of ordinary income and $16,000 of long-term capital gain to the shareholders, who will include these items on their 2011 tax returns. X would include $45,000 income, less a 70% dividends-received deduction of $3,500, on its Form 1120 for the C short year ending December 31, 2011. If the corporation pro rates all of the items, the allocation would be as follows:

| | *S Short Year (73/365)* | *C Short Year (292/365)* | *Total* |
|---|---|---|---|
| Ordinary income | $24,000 | $96,000 | $120,000 |
| Long-term capital gain | 3,200 | 12,800 | 16,000 |
| Dividend income | 1,000 | 4,000 | 5,000 |

The corporation must use the pro-rata method unless it elects to use the interim closing, or there is a change of ownership of 50 percent or more of the corporation's shares within the S termination year.[38] The election is filed with the corporation's Form 1120 for the C short year. The election must be accompanied by consents of all persons who are shareholders at any time during the S short year, as well as all shareholders on the first day of the C short year.[39]

The corporation must annualize its income and tax for the C short year. This is accomplished by grossing up the income as if it were earned ratably for a year of 365 days (366 in a leap year), and then apportioning the tax for the number of days in the C short year.

## Example 14

Refer to *Example 13*, above. Assume that the corporation elects to use the interim closing method. X would report the following annualized income and tax:

| | |
|---|---|
| Ordinary income | $ 40,000 |
| Dividend income | 5,000 |
| Less dividends received deduction | (3,500) |
| Taxable income | $ 41,500 |
| Annualization | (365/292) |
| Annualized taxable income | $ 51,875 |
| Tax on $51,875 | $ 7,969 |
| Annualization | (292/365) |
| Annualized tax | $ 6,375 |

[38] § 1362(e)(6)(D).

[39] Reg. § 1.1362-6(a)(5).

When termination is *inadvertent*, the Code authorizes the IRS to allow a corporation to continue its S status uninterrupted if the disqualifying action is corrected.[40] It is possible, for example, that if stock is transferred to an ineligible shareholder, the IRS might allow the corporation to correct the violation and continue its S status uninterrupted. Inadvertent termination relief can only be granted to a corporation that applies to the IRS National Office and pays the user fee for a letter ruling, except for QSST elections and ESBT elections discussed below.

### Example 15

On the advice of his attorney, a majority shareholder transferred his S corporation shares to an ineligible trust. Neither the attorney nor the shareholder were knowledgeable about the specific rules of Subchapter S. When the shareholder discovered the transfer terminated the S corporation election, the trust transferred the stock to the previous shareholder. The IRS has ruled, under similar circumstances, that the S election was not lost since the termination of the S status was inadvertent, it occurred as the result of advice from counsel, and it was corrected as soon as the violation of S status was discovered.[41]

The same inadvertent termination rules apply to defective (not late) S corporation elections. The corporation must apply for a ruling, disclosing the defect and agreeing to treat the corporation as an S corporation. All shareholders must sign the ruling request, under penalties of perjury. Any of the Subchapter S rules may be violated and cause termination or a defective election. However, a disproportionately high number of these violations have come from the failure to make timely QSST or ESBT elections. Accordingly the IRS has authorized the Service Centers to accept these elections up to two years late, in which case the corporation may avoid the ruling request and user fee.[42]

## Excessive Passive Income

Without special rules relating to passive income, owners of C corporations might convert to S status to avoid problems they face as a C corporation. To illustrate, consider the retiring owner of a C corporation who causes the corporation to sell all of its operating assets. After paying the corporate level tax on the sale, the owner could distribute the after tax proceeds in liquidation, resulting in yet a second tax at the shareholder level. The owner could then take what is left of the original sales price after paying two taxes (one by the C corporation and one by the shareholder on the liquidation) and invest it. Alternatively, the owner could opt not to liquidate and elect S status. Using this latter approach, the tax on the liquidation is avoided, the owner has more capital to invest, yet the investment income is taxed only once—the same as it would have been taxed if the owner held the investments personally. Moreover, the owner need not be concerned with the accumulated earnings tax or the personal holding company tax since these penalty taxes are reserved solely for C corporations. To foil this plan and others, Congress created two provisions that are triggered when evidence of this scheme are present. In short, if an S corporation has E&P accumulated while it was a C corporation (i.e., evidence of conversion) and too much passive income (i.e., investment income), the S corporation will have to pay a corporate level tax and could lose its S election. A later section examines the passive investment income tax.

Under the passive income test, the election is terminated if the corporation has:[43]

1. Passive investment income exceeding 25 percent of its gross receipts for three consecutive years, *and*
2. C corporation accumulated earnings and profits (AE&P) at the end of each of the three consecutive years.

If both of these conditions are satisfied, the termination becomes effective at the beginning of the first year following the end of the three-year period.[44]

---

[40] § 1362(f).

[41] Rev. Rul. 86-110, 1986-38 I.R.B. 4. Also, see Ltr. Ruls. 8550033 and 8608006.

[42] Rev. Proc. 2003-43, 2003-23 I.R.B. 998.

[43] § 1362(d)(3).

[44] § 1362(d)(3)(A)(ii).

As reflected in the second condition above, the excessive passive income test applies only to corporations that were C corporations prior to becoming S corporations. An S corporation might also have earnings and profits if it absorbed a former C corporation in a tax free reorganization, liquidation or QSub election. In addition, the test applies to these former C corporations only if they have AE&P from C years. Accordingly, corporations that have never been C corporations as well as corporations that have distributed all AE&P cannot lose their S election because of passive investment income.

*Passive investment income* generally is defined as gross receipts from royalties, rents, dividends, interest (including tax-exempt interest but excluding interest on notes from sales of inventory and interest derived from a lending business), annuities, and gains on sales or exchanges of stock or securities.[45] For this purpose, rents are not considered passive income if the corporation provides significant services (e.g., room rents paid to a hotel) or if the rents are received in the ordinary course of a rental business.[46] In computing total gross receipts, costs of goods sold, returns and allowances and deductions are ignored. Before 2007, receipts from the sale or exchange of stocks and securities were included to the extent of gains [i.e., gross receipts = amount realized − adjusted basis = gain (but not loss)]. In contrast, receipts from the sale or exchange of capital assets other than stocks and securities are included only to the extent of net gains (i.e., capital gains less capital losses).[47]

## Example 16

OBJ, an S corporation, was a C corporation for several years before it elected to be taxed under Subchapter S beginning in 2010. For 2010 and 2011 the corporation had excessive passive income. In addition, at the close of 2010 and 2011, OBJ reported a balance in its AE&P that was attributable to its years as a C corporation. OBJ's income and expenses for 2012 are shown below. No distributions from its AE&P were made during the year. The corporation's passive investment income and total gross receipts, based on its reported items, are determined as follows:

| | Reported | Gross Receipts | Passive Income |
|---|---|---|---|
| Sales | $200,000 | $200,000 | $ 0 |
| Cost of goods sold | (150,000) | 0 | 0 |
| Interest income | 30,000 | 30,000 | 30,000 |
| Dividends | 15,000 | 15,000 | 15,000 |
| Rental income (passive) | 40,000 | 40,000 | 40,000 |
| Rental expenses | (28,000) | 0 | 0 |
| Gain on sale of stock ($20,000 − $5,000) | 15,000 | 15,000 | 0 |
| Loss on sale of stock ($10,000 − $12,000) | (2,000) | 0 | 0 |
| Total | | $300,000 | $85,000 |
| 25% of gross receipts | | $ 75,000 | |

Because OBJ's passive investment income exceeds 25% of its gross receipts for the third consecutive year and it also has a balance of AE&P at the end of each of those years, the election is terminated beginning on January 1, 2013.

Even though a corporation may avoid having its election terminated by failing the excessive passive income test once every three years, a corporation still may be required to pay a tax on its excessive passive investment income. This tax is explained in detail later in this chapter.

[45] § 1362(d)(3)(D).

[46] Reg. § 1.1362-2(c)(5)(ii)(B)(2).

[47] §§ 1362(d)(3)(C) and 1222(9).

### Election after Termination

When the election is terminated, whether voluntarily through revocation or involuntarily through failure to satisfy the Subchapter S or passive income requirements, the corporation normally may not make a new election until the fifth taxable year following the year in which the termination became effective.[48] The five-year wait is unnecessary, however, if the IRS consents to an earlier election. Consent usually is given in two instances: (1) when the corporation's ownership has changed such that more than 50 percent of the stock is owned by persons who did not own the stock at the time of termination, or (2) when the termination was attributable to an event that was not within the control of the corporation or its majority shareholders.[49] A corporation must apply to the IRS National Office for an early re-election. It must request a ruling and pay the user fee.

**Example 17**

KLZ, an S corporation, was wholly owned by G. The corporation revoked its S election effective on July 17, 2009. KLZ may not make an election until 2014 unless it obtains permission from the IRS. Permission to reelect S status prior to 2014 would ordinarily be denied unless persons other than G acquired more than 50% of the KLZ stock.

## Operating the S Corporation

Once an S election is effective, a corporation officially becomes an S corporation and is subject to a special set of rules governing the measurement and reporting of its income. Under the provisions of Subchapter S, S corporations, like partnerships, are pass-through entities. While S corporations may pay taxes in certain situations (e.g., the passive investment income tax or the built-in gains tax discussed below), they primarily serve as conduits. Items of income, expense, gain, loss, and credit are measured at the S corporation level and then passed through to shareholders who report them on their own returns.[50] The focus of this section is on three questions:

- What items at the corporate level must be reported to the shareholder?
- How much of each item is reported to each shareholder?
- When does the shareholder report the items on his or her own tax return?

### Determining S Corporation Net Income

**LO.3**
Compute the taxable income or loss for an S corporation and the impact of S corporate operations on shareholders' taxable income.

S corporations generally compute net income, gains, and losses in a manner similar to a partnership. The following discussion examines some of the more important aspects that should be considered in measuring S corporation income, particularly the differences between S corporations and partnerships.

#### Elections

Consistent with the partnership provisions, most special elections that must be made in determining the amount of income are made at the S corporation level and not by the shareholder.[51] Among the elections that must be made by the corporation are the corporation's overall method of accounting (e.g., cash or accrual), the inventory method (e.g., FIFO or LIFO), depreciation methods, § 179 limited expensing, the installment method (election out), and deferral of gain on involuntary conversions. The exceptions to this general approach are the same as those for partnerships and affect few taxpayers.

---

[48] § 1362(g).

[49] Reg. § 1.1362-5(a).

[50] § 1366(a).

[51] § 1363(c).

## Payments to a Shareholder-Employee

The treatment of payments to an S shareholder who works for the corporation is markedly different from that of a partner who works for the partnership. S corporation shareholders who work for the corporation are treated as *employees*. As a result, salary paid to a shareholder-employee as well as payroll taxes related to the salary are deductible by the S corporation. In contrast, a partner who works for a partnership is not considered an employee and the payment received for work for the partnership is not technically considered a salary. As discussed in Chapter 22, compensation paid to partners is referred to as a guaranteed payment. Like salaries, partnerships normally deduct guaranteed payments. However, unlike salaries, guaranteed payments are not subject to withholding or payroll taxes.[52] Instead, a partner's compensation is treated as self-employment income.

### Example 18

H and W own their own company. This year the company made net income of $60,000 before consideration of any payments to H and W. Assume that H and W each receive a salary of $10,000 for total salary payments of $20,000. If the business is an S or C corporation, the salary is subject to withholding taxes and the corporation must pay FICA and unemployment taxes on it. If, however, the business is a partnership, there are no payroll taxes for owner compensation and partnership net income is $40,000 ($60,000 – $20,000), which is usually self-employment income and is subject to self-employment tax at the partner level. In addition, the salaries of $20,000 (i.e., guaranteed payments in the context of a partnership) would be subject to self-employment taxes.

The comparison of the two business forms for 2011 necessitates understanding of some temporary provisions enacted by the Tax Relief, Unemployment Insurance Reauthorization, and Job Creation Act of 2010. For 2011 only, the retirement portion of the social security withholding tax is 4.2%, a two percentage point reduction from its permanent rate of 6.2%. The employer's portion of the social security tax remains at 6.2%. Medicare tax remains at 1.45% for both the withholding and employer portions. [2010 Tax Relief Act §601(a)(2)].

There is a corresponding temporary reduction in the self-employment tax. For 2011 only, the retirement portion is 10.4%, down from its permanent 12.4% rate. The Medicare portion of this tax remains at 2.9%. For levels below 106,800, the base is 92.35% of the self-employment income, unchanged from its permanent level. The income tax deduction for self-employment tax for 2011 is set at 59.6% of the retirement portion and 50% of the Medicare portion. [2010 Tax Relief Act §601(b)] Thus the comparison of the two business forms yields the following for 2011.

| | *Partnership* | *S Corporation* |
|---|---|---|
| Net income before compensation | $60,000 | $60,000 |
| Guaranteed payment or salary | (20,000) | (20,000) |
| Employer FICA tax (6.2% × $20,000) | | (1,240) |
| Employer Medicare tax (1.45% × $20,000) | | (290) |
| Federal unemployment tax (6.2%) | | (868) |
| Flow-through income | $40,000 | $37,602 |
| Add guaranteed payment or salary | 20,000 | 20,000 |
| Employee FICA tax (4.2% × $20,000) | | (840) |
| Employee Medicare tax (1.45% × $20,000) | | (290) |
| Self-employment tax (10.4% * $60,000*.9235) | (5,763) | – |
| Self-employment Medicare tax (2.9% * $60,000*.9235) | (1,607) | |
| Deduction for Self employment tax (59.6%) | (3,435) | |
| Deduction for Self employment Medicare tax (50%) | (803) | |
| Net income after taxes | $48,392 | $56,472 |
| Income tax, assuming 15% rate | (7,259) | (8,471) |
| Cash flow after tax | $41,133 | $48,001 |

[52] Reg. § 1.707-1(c), Rev. Rul. 56-675, 1956-2 CB 459 and Rev. Rul. 69-180, 1969-1 CB 256.

> As this example demonstrates, the S corporation is preferred to the partnership if capital is to be retained in the business. This derives from the fact that the partners are subject to self-employment tax on their portions of partnership income, whether or not it is distributed. The S corporation and its shareholders, by contrast, are only subject to the FICA tax on money actually distributed to the shareholders as compensation.

### Employment Taxes and Undercompensation

It is important to note that, unlike partnerships, no self-employment income passes from an S corporation to its shareholders. In the S corporation setting, the only amounts subject to employment taxes are the salaries paid. In light of this treatment, owners of S corporations are tempted to undercompensate themselves in order to avoid social security and other payroll taxes. To illustrate, consider the example above. In this situation, the owners took only $20,000 in salary, paying employment taxes of $3,528 ($1240 + 290 + 868 + 840 + 290). This is far less than the $7,370 in self-employment tax that the owners would pay if they were partners in a partnership even though the amounts paid in both cases were identical ($20,000). The difference is due to the fact that the net income of the S corporation, $37,602, is not subject to employment taxes. However, there is another mitigating factor that reduces this difference. Each partner is allowed a deduction for A.G.I. for one-half of the self-employment tax paid on partnership income. Indeed, it would appear that the owners could avoid all employment taxes using an S corporation by not paying themselves any salary but simply distributing the profits. As might be expected, the IRS, with the support of the courts, frowns on this technique. In situations when this occurs, that is, when shareholders are undercompensated for their services, the Service generally recharacterizes all or a part of any distributions as compensation thereby securing the applicable payroll taxes.[53]

### Social Security Benefit Cutback

With the graying of America, the treatment of payments to S corporation owners is also becoming an increasingly important issue for social security purposes. An individual who retires before "normal" retirement age, must reduce his or her social security benefits if he or she earns income above a certain level. In 2010, the *normal retirement* age is 66 years of age. A person who is at least 62 but has not reached normal retirement age by the end of 2010 will be required to reduce his or her social security benefit by $1 for each $2 of earned income in excess of $14,160. After normal retirement age, an individual may receive full social security benefits regardless of the amount of earned income. For this reason, some owners of S corporations are tempted to take distributions from an S corporation rather than salary for services rendered. In a number of cases involving such attempts, however, the courts have upheld the Social Security Administration's bid to reclassify the distributions as wages.[54]

### Employee Benefits

One of the most important differences concerning the taxation of C corporations, partnerships, and S corporations is the treatment of fringe benefits provided to the owners (e.g., health and accident insurance, group-term life insurance). The taxation of a number of these benefits depends on whether the individual is an "employee" of the business. If the individual is an employee, the employer normally is allowed to deduct the cost of the benefit and its value is never subject to income or employment taxes. On the other hand, if the individual is not an employee, the benefit is usually considered compensation deductible by the employer but is subject to income and employment taxes to the payees.

It is not always clear as to whether or not a self-employed person is considered an "employee" for fringe benefit purposes. In the case of C corporations, an owner who works for the business is considered an employee. Therefore, shareholder-employees of C corporations enjoy the best of all possible worlds: the corporation is allowed to deduct the cost of these benefits yet their value to the shareholder-employees is never subject to income or employment taxes. In contrast, a partner (much like a sole proprietor) is normally not

---

[53] See Rev. Rul. 74-44, 1974-1 C.B. 287, *Radtke v. U.S.*, 90-1 USTC ¶50,113 and *Spicer Accounting, Inc., v. U.S.*, 918 F.2d 90 (CA-9, 1990).

[54] *Ludeking v. Finch*, 421 F.2d 499 (CA-8, 1970).

considered an employee of the business. Consequently, several of the key fringe benefits provided by partnerships to their partners are considered compensation (i.e., guaranteed payments) that are deductible by the partnership but subject to income and self-employment taxes to the partners. Unfortunately, the treatment of these key fringe benefits by an S corporation for the most part mirrors that for partnerships rather than that for C corporations.[55]

In determining the treatment extended to S corporations, shareholder-employees are divided into two groups: those who own more than 2 percent of the stock and those who own 2 percent or less.[56] The treatment for the two groups is summarized below.

> *Shareholders Owning 2 Percent or Less.* For those S shareholders who own 2 percent or less, the treatment follows the C corporation rules: the benefits are deductible by the corporation and nontaxable (both income and employment) to the employee.
>
> *Shareholders Owning More than 2 Percent.* More-than-2 percent shareholders are treated much like partners.[57] The fringe benefits requiring employee status are considered compensation: the benefits are deductible by the corporation but are included in the shareholder's gross income.[58] Unlike a partnership where these benefits are subject to self-employment tax, the value of health insurance provided to an S corporation employee is not subject to FICA or FUTA.[59] Note also that while the more-than-2 percent shareholder is required to include the benefit in income, he or she is also entitled to treat such amount as if he or she paid for the benefit. For example, in the case of medical insurance premiums paid by the S corporation on behalf of a more-than-2-percent shareholder, the shareholder is entitled to deduct 100 percent of the premiums as a deduction for A.G.I.[60]

In determining whether an individual owns more than 2 percent of an S corporation's stock, the constructive ownership rules of § 318 are applied.[61] For example, § 318 provides that an individual is deemed to own the stock of his or her spouse, children, parents or grandchildren. This rule prevents an owner (e.g., a husband) from employing a family member that does not own stock (e.g., a wife) in order to provide tax-free fringe benefits from the corporation to the family unit.

There are currently six fringe benefits which are nontaxable to owners of C corporations but which are treated as compensation to partners and more-than-2 percent shareholders. They are:

- Group-term life insurance (§ 79)
- Amounts received under accident and health (medical reimbursement) plans (§ 105)
- Premiums on employer-paid accident and health insurance (§ 106)
- Meals and lodging provided by the employer (§ 119)
- Value of transit passes (but this qualifies as a de minimis fringe if not greater than $21 per month) [§ 132(f)(5)(E)]
- Parking provided by the employer (except that provided away from the business such as at a client's) [§ 132(f)(5)(E)]

The value of all of these is included in the shareholder-employee's Form W-2 as noncash compensation. Premiums on accident and health insurance are not subject to FICA tax.

The remaining fringe benefits are eligible for exclusion not only by shareholder-employees of C corporations but also to partners and, therefore, more-than-2 percent shareholders of S corporations. In effect, the statutes governing these particular benefits specifically explain that, for purpose of the given exclusion, partners are considered

[55] § 1372(a)(1) and (2).

[56] § 1372(a) and (b).

[57] § 1372(a)(2).

[58] Rev. Rul. 91-26, 1991-1 C.B. 184, § 162(a) (subject to the capitalization rules of § 263), and § 61(a), respectively.

[59] Announcement 92-16, 1992-5 I.R.B. 53.

[60] §§ 162(l) and 106, respectively.

[61] § 1372(b). See Chapter 20 for discussion of § 318.

employees, thereby enabling exclusion not only for partners but also all S corporation shareholders. These include:

- Child and dependent care assistance (§ 129)
- Educational assistance plans (§ 127)
- No additional cost services [§ 132(b)]
- Qualified employee discounts [§ 132(c)]
- Working condition fringe benefits [§ 132(d)]
- De minimis fringes [§ 132(e)]
- Company dining room [§132(e)]
- On-premise athletic facilities [§132(h)]
- Employee achievement awards [§74(c)]

## Subdivision of Real Estate

Under the "subdivide and conquer" rules of § 1237, *individual* taxpayers are ensured capital gain rather than ordinary income treatment when they subdivide and sell land if they meet a number of requirements. To qualify, the land must be held more than five years (unless inherited); there must be no substantial improvements to the property; and the parcel sold, or any part thereof must not have previously been held by the taxpayer primarily for resale. An S corporation (as well as a partnership) is treated in the same manner as an individual and is entitled to this special treatment.[62]

## Section 291 Recapture

In most cases, an S corporation is not subject to the special rules of § 291 that require the recapture as ordinary income 20 percent of any straight-line depreciation claimed on residential or nonresidential real estate (see Chapter 19 for an example). However, an S corporation that was a C corporation for any of the three immediately preceding taxable years is subject to the special depreciation recapture rules of § 291(a)(1).[63]

## Accounting Methods

Certain entities are prohibited from using the cash method of accounting, and consequently are required to use the accrual method. The cash method normally cannot be used by a C corporation unless its annual gross receipts average $5 million or less for the past three years, or it is a qualified personal service corporation. In contrast, an S corporation can use the cash method (unless it is required to maintain inventories to clearly reflect income).[64]

## Charitable Contributions

Charitable contributions made by an S corporation are treated as if they are made directly by the shareholder. Consequently, unlike C corporations, an S corporation that uses the accrual method of accounting is not entitled to deduct accrued contributions.[65] Like an individual, contributions made by an S corporation can be deducted by the shareholders only in the tax year in which the contribution is made. Similarly, the special rule allowing C corporations to deduct the adjusted basis plus one-half of the foregone gross profit of inventory contributed to a organization for the care of the needy, the ill, or infants is not available to S corporations. However taxpayers other than C corporations are permitted to take an enhanced deduction for certain food contributions, but only to the extent of 10% of the income from businesses making such contributions.[66] This rule is scheduled to sunset after 2011.

---

[62] § 1237(a).

[63] See § 1363(b)(4).

[64] § 448. However, see Rev. Proc. 2001-10, which allows any taxpayer with no more than $1 million gross receipts to use the cash method. Also see Rev. Proc. 2002-28, which allows certain taxpayers with up to $10 million gross receipts to use the cash method.

[65] See § 1363, which incorporates the rules of § 702 that disallow the deduction of charitable contributions to partnerships.

[66] § 170(e)(3)(C)(iv).

### Qualified Production Activities Income Deduction

The deduction for Qualified Production Activities Income (QPAI) is allowed to all tax entities. However, for the S corporation, this deduction is to be computed at the shareholder level.[67]

## Reporting S Corporation Income

Once an S corporation identifies and measures the relevant items of income, deduction and credit, such items must be passed through to the shareholders for reporting on their own returns. The approach used is similar to that used by partnerships. Consistent with the conduit concept, the items normally retain their character when they are allocated to the shareholders. For example, charitable contributions made by the S corporation flow through and are reported as charitable contributions by the shareholders subject to all the special tax rules that apply to individuals. The amounts allocated to the shareholders are based on their percentage of stock owned during the year. Unlike partnerships, Subchapter S contains no provision for special allocations among owners. This can be a disadvantage if special allocations are desirable.

To accomplish the pass-through, the S corporation must file an annual information return, Form 1120S. Indeed, the similarity between the taxation of S corporations and partnerships becomes readily apparent when Forms 1120S and 1065 are compared. (See Exhibit 23-1 for an illustration of Form 1120S.) There are some differences in computing the net ordinary income on page one of the two tax forms, however. Unlike Form 1065, Form 1120S has a section for computing any taxes due on excessive passive investment income and Schedule D built-in gains (both are discussed in a later section of this chapter).

All income, expenses, gains, losses, and credits that may be subject to special treatment by one or more of the shareholders are reported separately on Schedule K, which is filed with Form 1120S.[68] Schedule K-1 is then prepared for the shareholders' use. (See Exhibit 23-1 for an illustration. Also see Exhibit 23-2 for a summary of items.) Again, these schedules are quite similar to the schedules applicable to partnerships and partners. There are differences, including the following:

- There are no guaranteed payments on the S corporation schedule.
- There is no self-employment income on the S corporation schedule.
- There are no reconciliations of capital accounts on the S corporation schedule.
- There is no allocation of liabilities on the S corporation schedule.

Finally, the S corporation schedule includes a section for reporting distributions. These are divided into two categories: (1) distributions from earnings of the S corporation, and (2) if it has been operated as a C corporation in previous years, distributions from earnings of the C corporation. (Distributions are discussed in a later section of this chapter.)

### Filing Requirements

Form 1120S, with the attached Schedule K-1s, must be filed for the S corporation on or before the 15th day of the third month following the close of its taxable year. An automatic extension of six months may be obtained. Thus a calendar year S corporation's normal due date is March 15 but may be extended until September 15. In order to obtain the extension, the corporation must file Form 7004 on or before March 15 (or two months and 15 days after the close of the corporation's fiscal year). In contrast, partnership returns are due on the 15th day of the fourth month following the close of the taxable year (e.g., April 15 for a calendar year partnership). So even though an S corporation is treated much like a partnership, its return is due at the same time as a C corporation return.

In addition to attaching the Schedule K-1s to Form 1120S, the S corporation is required to provide shareholders with Schedule K-1 by the due date of the return. The shareholder need not attach the K-1 to his or her Form 1040.

---

[67] §199(d)(1).

[68] § 1366(a)(1)(A).

**EXHIBIT 23.1** Forms 1120S

Form **1120S** Department of the Treasury Internal Revenue Service

## U.S. Income Tax Return for an S Corporation

▶ Do not file this form unless the corporation has filed or is attaching Form 2553 to elect to be an S corporation.
▶ See separate instructions.

OMB No. 1545-0130 **2010**

For calendar year 2010 or tax year beginning , 2010, ending , 20

| | | | |
|---|---|---|---|
| A S election effective date 1-1-10 | Use IRS label. Otherwise, print or type. | Name T COMPANY | D Employer identification number 88 : 9138761 |
| B Business activity code number *(see instructions)* 448110 | | Number, street, and room or suite no. If a P.O. box, see instructions. 8122 SOUTH 8TH STREET | E Date incorporated 1-1-10 |
| C Check if Sch. M-3 attached ☐ | | City or town, state, and ZIP code NORFORLK, VA 23508 | F Total assets *(see instructions)* $ 322,000 |

G Is the corporation electing to be an S corporation beginning with this tax year? ☑ Yes ☐ No If "Yes," attach Form 2553 if not already filed

H Check if: (1) ☐ Final return (2) ☐ Name change (3) ☐ Address change (4) ☐ Amended return (5) ☐ S election termination or revocation

I Enter the number of shareholders who were shareholders during any part of the tax year ▶

Caution. *Include **only** trade or business income and expenses on lines 1a through 21. See the instructions for more information.*

|  |  |  |  |  |
|---|---|---|---|---|
| Income | 1a | Gross receipts or sales 470,000 b Less returns and allowances -0- c Bal ▶ | 1c | 470,000 |
| | 2 | Cost of goods sold (Schedule A, line 8) | 2 | 300,000 |
| | 3 | Gross profit. Subtract line 2 from line 1c | 3 | 170,000 |
| | 4 | Net gain (loss) from Form 4797, Part II, line 17 *(attach Form 4797)* | 4 | |
| | 5 | Other income (loss) *(see instructions—attach statement)* | 5 | |
| | 6 | Total income (loss). Add lines 3 through 5 ▶ | 6 | 170,000 |
| Deductions (see instructions for limitations) | 7 | Compensation of officers $ 24,000 + $ 700 EMPLOYEE BENEFITS | 7 | 24,700 |
| | 8 | Salaries and wages (less employment credits) | 8 | 48,000 |
| | 9 | Repairs and maintenance | 9 | 12,000 |
| | 10 | Bad debts | 10 | |
| | 11 | Rents | 11 | |
| | 12 | Taxes and licenses $ 3,000 PROPERTY TAXES + $ 6,000 PAYROLL TAXES | 12 | 9,000 |
| | 13 | Interest | 13 | 3,300 |
| | 14 | Depreciation not claimed on Schedule A or elsewhere on return (*attach Form 4562*) | 14 | 15,000 |
| | 15 | Depletion (Do not deduct oil and gas depletion.) | 15 | |
| | 16 | Advertising | 16 | |
| | 17 | Pension, profit-sharing, etc., plans | 17 | |
| | 18 | Employee benefit programs LIFE INSURANCE COVERAGE | 18 | 1,400 |
| | 19 | Other deductions (*attach statement*) $ 2,500 UTILITIES & PHONE + $ 1,100 OFFICE EXPENSE + $ 3,100 INSURANCE EXPENSE | 19 | 6,700 |
| | 20 | Total deductions. Add lines 7 through 19 ▶ | 20 | 120,100 |
| | 21 | Ordinary business income (loss). Subtract line 20 from line 6 | 21 | 49,900 |
| Tax and Payments | 22a | Excess net passive income or LIFO recapture tax (*see instructions*) 22a | | |
| | b | Tax from Schedule D (Form 1120S) 22b | | |
| | c | Add lines 22a and 22b (*see instructions for additional taxes*) | 22c | NONE |
| | 23a | 2009 estimated tax payments and 2008 overpayment credited to 2009 23a | | |
| | b | Tax deposited with Form 7004 23b | | |
| | c | Credit for federal tax paid on fuels (*attach Form 4136*) 23c | | |
| | d | Add lines 23a through 23c | 23d | NONE |
| | 24 | Estimated tax penalty (*see instructions*). Check if Form 2220 is attached ▶ ☐ | 24 | |
| | 25 | Amount owed. If line 23d is smaller than the total of lines 22c and 24, enter amount owed | 25 | NONE |
| | 26 | Overpayment. If line 23d is larger than the total of lines 22c and 24, enter amount overpaid | 26 | |
| | 27 | Enter amount from line 26 Credited to 2011 estimated tax ▶ Refunded ▶ | 27 | NONE |

**Sign Here** Under penalties of perjury, I declare that I have examined this return, including accompanying schedules and statements, and to the best of my knowledge and belief, it is true, correct, and complete. Declaration of preparer (other than taxpayer) is based on all information of which preparer has any knowledge.

▶ adolph Z.T | 3-10-11 ▶ PRESIDENT
Signature of officer | Date | Title

May the IRS discuss this return with the preparer shown below (see instructions)? ☐ Yes ☐ No

**Paid Preparer's Use Only** Preparer's signature ▶ Date | Check if self-employed ☐ | Preparer's SSN or PTIN
Firm's name (or yours if self-employed), address, and ZIP code ▶ | EIN | Phone no. ( )

For Privacy Act and Paperwork Reduction Act Notice, see separate instructions. Cat. No. 11510H Form 1120S (2010)

## EXHIBIT 23.1 Continued

Form 1120S (2010) Page **2**

**Schedule A** **Cost of Goods Sold** (see instructions)

| | | Line | Amount |
|---|---|---|---|
| 1 | Inventory at beginning of year | 1 | 12,000 |
| 2 | Purchases | 2 | 302,000 |
| 3 | Cost of labor | 3 | |
| 4 | Additional section 263A costs (*attach statement*) | 4 | |
| 5 | Other costs (*attach statement*) | 5 | |
| 6 | **Total.** Add lines 1 through 5 | 6 | 314,000 |
| 7 | Inventory at end of year | 7 | 14,000 |
| 8 | **Cost of goods sold.** Subtract line 7 from line 6. Enter here and on page 1, line 2 | 8 | |

9a Check all methods used for valuing closing inventory: (*i*) ☐ Cost as described in Regulations section 1.471-3

(*ii*) ☑ Lower of cost or market as described in Regulations section 1.471-4

(*iii*) ☐ Other (Specify method used and attach explanation.) ▶

b Check if there was a writedown of subnormal goods as described in Regulations section 1.471-2(c) ▶ ☐

c Check if the LIFO inventory method was adopted this tax year for any goods (if checked, attach Form 970) ▶ ☐

d If the LIFO inventory method was used for this tax year, enter percentage (or amounts) of closing inventory computed under LIFO | 9d |

e If property is produced or acquired for resale, do the rules of section 263A apply to the corporation? ☐ Yes ☑ No

f Was there any change in determining quantities, cost, or valuations between opening and closing inventory? ☐ Yes ☑ No

If "Yes," attach explanation.

**Schedule B** **Other Information** (see instructions)

| | | Yes | No |
|---|---|---|---|
| 1 | Check accounting method: **a** ☐ Cash **b** ☑ Accrual **c** ☐ Other (specify) ▶ | | |
| 2 | See the instructions and enter the: **a** Business activity ▶ RETAIL SALES **b** Product or service ▶ MEN'S CLOTHING | | |
| 3 | At the end of the tax year, did the corporation own, directly or indirectly, 50% or more of the voting stock of a domestic corporation? (For rules of attribution, see section 267(c).) If "Yes," attach a statement showing: **(a)** name and employer identification number (EIN), **(b)** percentage owned, and **(c)** if 100% owned, was a QSub election made? | | ✓ |
| 4 | Has this corporation filed, or is it required to file, a return under section 6111 to provide information on any reportable transaction? | | ✓ |
| 5 | Check this box if the corporation issued publicly offered debt instruments with original issue discount ▶ ☐<br>If checked, the corporation may have to file **Form 8281,** Information Return for Publicly Offered Original Issue Discount Instruments. | | |
| 6 | If the corporation: **(a)** was a C corporation before it elected to be an S corporation **or** the corporation acquired an asset with a basis determined by reference to its basis (or the basis of any other property) in the hands of a C corporation **and (b)** has net unrealized built-in gain (defined in section 1374(d)(1)) in excess of the net recognized built-in gain from prior years, enter the net unrealized built-in gain reduced by net recognized built-in gain from prior years ▶ $ | | |
| 7 | Enter the accumulated earnings and profits of the corporation at the end of the tax year. $ | | |
| 8 | Are the corporation's total receipts (*see instructions*) for the tax year **and** its total assets at the end of the tax year less than $250,000? If "Yes," the corporation is not required to complete Schedules L and M-1 | | ✓ |

**Schedule K** **Shareholders' Pro Rata Share Items**

| | | | | | Line | Total amount |
|---|---|---|---|---|---|---|
| Income (Loss) | 1 | Ordinary business income (loss) (page 1, line 21) | | | 1 | 49,900 |
| | 2 | Net rental real estate income (loss) (*attach Form 8825*) | | | 2 | |
| | 3a | Other gross rental income (loss) | 3a | | | |
| | b | Expenses from other rental activities (*attach statement*) | 3b | | | |
| | c | Other net rental income (loss). Subtract line 3b from line 3a | | | 3c | |
| | 4 | Interest income | | | 4 | |
| | 5 | Dividends: **a** Ordinary dividends | | | 5a | 2,000 |
| | | **b** Qualified dividends | 5b | 2,000 | | |
| | 6 | Royalties | | | 6 | |
| | 7 | Net short-term capital gain (loss) (*attach Schedule D (Form 1120S)*) | | | 7 | |
| | 8a | Net long-term capital gain (loss) (*attach Schedule D (Form 1120S)*) | | | 8a | 1,000 |
| | b | Collectibles (28%) gain (loss) | 8b | | | |
| | c | Unrecaptured section 1250 gain (*attach statement*) | 8c | | | |
| | 9 | Net section 1231 gain (loss) (*attach Form 4797*) | | | 9 | |
| | 10 | Other income (loss) (*see instructions*) Type ▶ | | | 10 | |

Form **1120S** (2010)

## EXHIBIT 23.1 Continued

Form 1120S (2010) Page 3

| Section | Line | Shareholders' Pro Rata Share Items (continued) | Line | Total amount |
|---|---|---|---|---|
| Deductions | 11 | Section 179 deduction (*attach Form 4562*) | 11 | 7,000 |
| | 12a | Contributions | 12a | |
| | b | Investment interest expense | 12b | |
| | c | Section 59(e)(2) expenditures (1) Type ▶ (2) Amount ▶ | 12c(2) | |
| | d | Other deductions (*see instructions*) Type ▶ | 12d | |
| Credits | 13a | Low-income housing credit (section 42(j)(5)) | 13a | |
| | b | Low-income housing credit (other) | 13b | |
| | c | Qualified rehabilitation expenditures (rental real estate) (*attach Form 3468*) | 13c | |
| | d | Other rental real estate credits (*see instructions*) Type ▶ | 13d | |
| | e | Other rental credits (*see instructions*) Type ▶ | 13e | |
| | f | Alcohol and cellulosic biofuel fuels credit (*attach Form 6478*) | 13f | |
| | g | Other credits (*see instructions*) Type ▶ REHABILITATION CRERDIT | 13g | 2,000 |
| Foreign Transactions | 14a | Name of country or U.S. possession ▶ | | |
| | b | Gross income from all sources | 14b | |
| | c | Gross income sourced at shareholder level | 14c | |
| | | *Foreign gross income sourced at corporate level* | | |
| | d | Passive category | 14d | |
| | e | General category | 14e | |
| | f | Other (*attach statement*) | 14f | |
| | | *Deductions allocated and apportioned at shareholder level* | | |
| | g | Interest expense | 14g | |
| | h | Other | 14h | |
| | | *Deductions allocated and apportioned at corporate level to foreign source income* | | |
| | i | Passive category | 14i | |
| | j | General category | 14j | |
| | k | Other (*attach statement*) | 14k | |
| | | *Other information* | | |
| | l | Total foreign taxes (check one): ▶ ☐ Paid ☐ Accrued | 14l | |
| | m | Reduction in taxes available for credit (*attach statement*) | 14m | |
| | n | Other foreign tax information (*attach statement*) | | |
| Alternative Minimum Tax (AMT) Items | 15a | Post-1986 depreciation adjustment | 15a | |
| | b | Adjusted gain or loss | 15b | |
| | c | Depletion (other than oil and gas) | 15c | |
| | d | Oil, gas, and geothermal properties—gross income | 15d | |
| | e | Oil, gas, and geothermal properties—deductions | 15e | |
| | f | Other AMT items (*attach statement*) | 15f | |
| Items Affecting Shareholder Basis | 16a | Tax-exempt interest income | 16a | |
| | b | Other tax-exempt income | 16b | |
| | c | Nondeductible expenses | 16c | |
| | d | Property distributions LAND: FMV = $10,000 + $12,000 CASH | 16d | 22,000 |
| | e | Repayment of loans from shareholders | 16e | |
| Other Information | 17a | Investment income DIVIDENDS | 17a | 2,000 |
| | b | Investment expenses | 17b | |
| | c | Dividend distributions paid from accumulated earnings and profits | 17c | |
| | d | Other items and amounts (*attach statement*) | | |
| Reconciliation | 18 | **Income/loss reconciliation.** Combine the amounts on lines 1 through 10 in the far right column. From the result, subtract the sum of the amounts on lines 11 through 12d and 14l | 18 | 45,900 |

Form **1120S** (2010)

**EXHIBIT 23.1** **Continued**

Form 1120S (2010) Page **4**

**Schedule L** **Balance Sheets per Books**

| Assets | Beginning of tax year (a) | (b) | End of tax year (c) | (d) |
|---|---|---|---|---|
| 1 Cash | | | | |
| 2a Trade notes and accounts receivable | | | | |
| b Less allowance for bad debts | ( ) | | ( ) | |
| 3 Inventories | | | | |
| 4 U.S. government obligations | | | | |
| 5 Tax-exempt securities (*see instructions*) | | | | |
| 6 Other current assets (*attach statement*) | | | | |
| 7 Loans to shareholders | | *FIRST* | | |
| 8 Mortgage and real estate loans | | *YEAR* | | |
| 9 Other investments (*attach statement*) | | *CORPORATION* | | |
| 10a Buildings and other depreciable assets | | | | |
| b Less accumulated depreciation | ( ) | | ( ) | |
| 11a Depletable assets | | | | |
| b Less accumulated depletion | ( ) | | ( ) | |
| 12 Land (net of any amortization) | | | | |
| 13a Intangible assets (amortizable only) | | | | |
| b Less accumulated amortization | ( ) | | ( ) | |
| 14 Other assets (*attach statement*) | | | | |
| 15 Total assets | | | | *322,000* |
| **Liabilities and Shareholders' Equity** | | | | |
| 16 Accounts payable | | | | |
| 17 Mortgages, notes, bonds payable in less than 1 year | | | | |
| 18 Other current liabilities (*attach statement*) | | | | |
| 19 Loans from shareholders | | | | |
| 20 Mortgages, notes, bonds payable in 1 year or more | | | | |
| 21 Other liabilities (*attach statement*) | | | | |
| 22 Capital stock | | | | |
| 23 Additional paid-in capital | | | | |
| 24 Retained earnings | | | | |
| 25 Adjustments to shareholders' equity (*attach statement*) | | | | |
| 26 Less cost of treasury stock | | ( ) | | ( ) |
| 27 Total liabilities and shareholders' equity | | | | *322,000* |

**Schedule M-1** **Reconciliation of Income (Loss) per Books With Income (Loss) per Return**

**Note:** Schedule M-3 required instead of Schedule M-1 if total assets are $10 million or more—see instructions

| | | | |
|---|---|---|---|
| 1 Net income (loss) per books | *45,900* | 5 Income recorded on books this year not included on Schedule K, lines 1 through 10 (itemize): a Tax-exempt interest $ | |
| 2 Income included on Schedule K, lines 1, 2, 3c, 4, 5a, 6, 7, 8a, 9, and 10, not recorded on books this year (itemize): | | | |
| 3 Expenses recorded on books this year not included on Schedule K, lines 1 through 12 and 14l (itemize): a Depreciation $ b Travel and entertainment $ | | 6 Deductions included on Schedule K, lines 1 through 12 and 14l, not charged against book income this year (itemize): a Depreciation $ | |
| | | 7 Add lines 5 and 6 | |
| 4 Add lines 1 through 3 | *45,900* | 8 Income (loss) (Schedule K, line 18). Line 4 less line 7 | *45,900* |

**Schedule M-2** **Analysis of Accumulated Adjustments Account, Other Adjustments Account, and Shareholders' Undistributed Taxable Income Previously Taxed** (see instructions)

| | (a) Accumulated adjustments account | (b) Other adjustments account | (c) Shareholders' undistributed taxable income previously taxed |
|---|---|---|---|
| 1 Balance at beginning of tax year | *0* | | |
| 2 Ordinary income from page 1, line 21 | *49,900* | | |
| 3 Other additions | *3,000* | | |
| 4 Loss from page 1, line 21 | ( ) | | |
| 5 Other reductions | ( *7,000 charitable* ) | ( ) | |
| 6 Combine lines 1 through 5 | *45,900* | | |
| 7 Distributions other than dividend distributions | *22,000* | | |
| 8 Balance at end of tax year. Subtract line 7 from line 6 | *23,900* | | |

Form **1120S** (2010)

**EXHIBIT 23.1** Continued

651108

☐ Final K-1 ☐ Amended K-1 OMB No. 1545-0130

**Schedule K-1 (Form 1120S)** **2010**
Department of the Treasury
Internal Revenue Service

For calendar year 2010, or tax year beginning ______, 2010 ending ______, 20___

**Shareholder's Share of Income, Deductions, Credits, etc.** ► See back of form and separate instructions.

**Part I Information About the Corporation**

A Corporation's employer identification number
88 9138761

B Corporation's name, address, city, state, and ZIP code
T COMPANY
8122 SOUTH 8TH STREET
NORFOLK, VA 23508

C IRS Center where corporation filed return
MEMPHIS, TN

**Part II Information About the Shareholder**

D Shareholder's identifying number
467–63–5052

E Shareholder's name, address, city, state, and ZIP code
ADOLF Z.T
1291 MAPLE STREET
NORFOLK, VA 23508

F Shareholder's percentage of stock ownership for tax year 100 %

For IRS Use Only

**Part III Shareholder's Share of Current Year Income, Deductions, Credits, and Other Items**

| Line | Item | Amount |
|---|---|---|
| 1 | Ordinary business income (loss) | 49,900 |
| 2 | Net rental real estate income (loss) | |
| 3 | Other net rental income (loss) | |
| 4 | Interest income | |
| 5a | Ordinary dividends | |
| 5b | Qualified dividends | 2,000 |
| 6 | Royalties | 2,000 |
| 7 | Net short-term capital gain (loss) | |
| 8a | Net long-term capital gain (loss) | 1,000 |
| 8b | Collectibles (28%) gain (loss) | |
| 8c | Unrecaptured section 1250 gain | |
| 9 | Net section 1231 gain (loss) | |
| 10 | Other income (loss) | |
| 11 | Section 179 deduction | |
| 12 | Other deductions | CHARITABLE CONTRIBUTIONS = 7,000 |
| 13 | Credits | Rehabilitation Credit = 2,000 |
| 14 | Foreign transactions | |
| 15 | Alternative minimum tax (AMT) items | |
| 16 | Items affecting shareholder basis | $ 22,000 property distributions |
| 17 | Other information | INVESTMENT INCOME = 2,000 |

* See attached statement for additional information.

For Paperwork Reduction Act Notice, see Instructions for Form 1120S. Cat. No. 11520D **Schedule K-1 (Form 1120S) 2010**

## EXHIBIT 23.2 Separately and Nonseparately Stated Items

For each of the following items of income, deduction, loss, and credit, and "X" in the appropriate column indicates whether the item is includible in an S corporation's combined ordinary income or loss (reported on Form 1120S, page 1; Schedule K, line 1; and Schedule K-1, line 1) or whether the item must be separately stated (reported on Schedules K and K-1, and lines 2 and following).

| | | *Combined Ordinary Income or (Loss) (Form 1120S, p.1)* | *Separately Stated Item (Schedule K)* | *Reason* |
|---|---|---|---|---|
| a. | Sales | X | | No special shareholder treatment |
| b. | Income or loss from rental activities | | X | Passive income for § 469 purposes |
| c. | Dividends | | X | Investment (portfolio) income and qualification for capital gains tax rate. |
| d. | Taxable interest | | X | Investment (portfolio) income |
| e. | Tax-exempt interest | | X | May affect shareholder interest deductions (§ 265), or tax on social security benefits |
| f. | Cost of sales | X | | No special shareholder treatment |
| g. | State and local taxes | X | | Generally, no special shareholder treatment |
| h. | Net long-term capital gain or loss | | X | Requires netting at shareholder level |
| i. | Net short-term capital gain or loss | | X | Requires netting at shareholder level |
| j. | Net gain from sales of collectibles | | X | Requires netting at shareholder level |
| k. | Net unrecaptured § 1250 gain | | X | Requires netting at shareholder level |
| l. | Gain from sales of qualified small business stock | | X | Requires netting at shareholder level |
| m. | Charitable contribution | | X | Subject to A.G.I. limitation of shareholder |
| n. | Foreign income | | X | Required for foreign tax credit computation at shareholder level |
| o. | Foreign taxes | | X | Subject to election to credit or deduct |
| p. | Medical expenses | | X | Includible by shareholder; deductible by shareholder subject to A.G.I. limitation; deductible by S corporation |
| q. | Investment interest | | X | Subject to investment interest limitation |
| r. | MACRS or ACRS on plant and equipment | X | X | Subject to AMT tax liability at shareholder level[a] |
| s. | Section 179 expensing | | X | Subject to § 179 shareholder limit |
| t. | Research and experimentation expenditures | | X | Subject to special election by shareholder |
| u. | Work opportunity credit | | X | Subject to tax liability limitation at shareholder level |
| v. | Recovery of a bad debt | | X | Subject to § 111 determination at shareholder level |
| w. | Advertising | X | | No special shareholder treatment |
| x. | Repairs and maintenance | X | | No special shareholder treatment |
| y. | Expenses for production of income (§ 212) | | X | Miscellaneous itemized deduction at shareholder level |
| z. | QPAI information | | X | Deductions claimed at shareholder level |

[a]Any preference or adjustment resulting from the use of accelerated depreciation must be separately reported, along with any § 179 expense.

## Allocations to Shareholders

All S corporation items (except distributions) are allocated among the shareholders based on their *ownership percentage* of the outstanding stock on each day of the year.[69] Thus, a shareholder owning 20 percent of the outstanding stock all year is deemed to have received 20 percent of *each item*. The allocation rate can be changed only by increasing or decreasing the percentage of stock ownership. This precludes shareholders from dividing net income or losses in any other manner. Of course, a certain amount of special allocation can be achieved through salaries and other business payments to owners. If there is no change in stock ownership during the year, each item to be allocated is multiplied by the percentage of stock owned by each shareholder. In contrast, actual distributions of assets are assigned to the shareholder who receives them.

### Example 19

M owns 100 of an S corporation's 1,000 shares of common stock outstanding. Neither the number of shares outstanding nor the number owned by M has changed during the year. The S corporation items for its calendar year are allocated to M, based on her 10% ownership interest, as follows:

| | *Totals on Schedule K* | *M's 10% on Schedule K-1* |
|---|---|---|
| Ordinary income (from Form 1120S, page 1) | $70,000 | $7,000 |
| Net capital gain | 2,000 | 200 |
| Charitable contributions | 4,000 | 400 |

If the ownership of stock changes during the year, there are two methods for determining the allocations for those shareholders whose interests have changed. These are (1) the *per day allocation method* and (2) the *interim closing of the books* method. Generally, the per day allocation method must be used. However, the S corporation may elect to use either method if:

1. A shareholder's ownership interest is *completely* terminated;
2. There is a disposition by one shareholder of *more than* 20 percent of the outstanding shares of the corporation within 30 days; or
3. The corporation issues shares to one or more new shareholders and the new shares are at least 25 percent of the number previously outstanding.

### Per Day Allocation

This method assigns an equal amount of the S items to each day of the year.[70] When a shareholder's interest changes, the shareholder *must* report a pro rata share of each item for each day that the stock was owned. For this purpose, the seller is deemed to own the stock on the day of the sale. This computation may be expressed as follows:

$$\text{Percentage of shares owned} \times \text{Percentage of year stock was owned} = \text{Portion of item to be reported}$$

### Example 20

Assume the same facts as in *Example 19*, except that M sold all of her shares on August 7 to T. Because the S corporation uses the calendar year, M has held 100 shares for 219 days, or 60% of the year (219 ÷ 365). (The day of sale is considered an ownership day for the seller, M.) Thus M is allocated 6% (60% × 10%) of each corporate item

[69] §§ 1366(a) and 1377(a).

[70] § 1377(a)(1).

while T is allocated 4% (40% × 10%). Based on the per day allocation method, M's and T's shares of the S corporation items are as follows:

| | Totals on Schedule K | 10 Percent to M & T | M's Portion (10% × 219/365) | T's Portion (10% × 146/365) |
|---|---|---|---|---|
| Ordinary income . . . . . . | $70,000 | $7,000 | $4,200 | $2,800 |
| Net capital gain . . . . . . . | 2,000 | 200 | 120 | 80 |
| Charitable contributions. . | 4,000 | 400 | 240 | 160 |

The per day allocation method also is applicable for a shareholder whose stock interest varies during the year; however, the computation is more complex.

## Example 21

Assume the same facts as in *Example 20*, except M only sold 20 shares on August 7 to T. Thus, she owned 10% of the business the first 219 days and 8% the remaining 146 days. Based on the per day allocation method. M's and T's shares of the S corporation items are as follows:

| | Totals Schedule K | 1/1–8/7 (10% × 219/365) | 8/8–12/31 (8% × 146/365) | M's Schedule K-1 | T's Schedule K-1 (2% × 146/365) |
|---|---|---|---|---|---|
| Ordinary income . . . . . . | $70,000 | $4,200 | $2,240 | $6,440 | $560 |
| Net capital gain . . . . . . . | 2,000 | 120 | 64 | 184 | 16 |
| Charitable contributions. . | 4,000 | 240 | 128 | 368 | 32 |

### Interim Closing of the Books

As noted above, the per day method must be used unless there is either (1) a complete termination of a shareholder's interest, (2) a disposition of more than 20 percent of the outstanding stock of the corporation by one shareholder within a 30-day period, or (3) issuance of shares to persons who were not previously shareholders equal to at least 25 percent of the number previously outstanding. In any of these situations, the corporation may elect to use the interim closing of books method instead of the per day allocation method.[71] If the corporation elects, the year is divided into two short taxable years for allocation purposes and all owners report the actual dollar amounts that were accumulated while they owned their shares. A valid election must be filed by the corporation with Form 1120S. All parties who are affected by the transaction must consent to the election by filing personal tax returns consistent with the election. This election does not require the corporation to file separate returns for each portion of the year.

## Example 22

Assume the same facts as in *Example 20*, except the interim closing of books method is elected. since M sells *all* of her shares on August 7 to T, the S corporation's year ends the day before on August 6. Corporate records show the following amounts for the first 219 days, for the last 146 days, and M's share for the first 219 days.

| | First 219 days | Last 146 days | M's 10% on Schedule K-1 | T's 10% on Schedule K-1 |
|---|---|---|---|---|
| Ordinary income (from Form 1102S, page 1) . . . . . | $15,000 | $55,000 | $1,500 | $5,500 |
| Net capital gain . . . . . . . . . . . . . . . | 1,000 | 1,000 | 100 | 100 |
| Charitable contributions. . . . . . . . . . | 0 | 4,000 | 0 | 400 |

[71] § 1377(a)(2).

The computations for M's share are the amounts for the first 219 days *multiplied* by her 10% ownership interest. T's share are the amounts for the last 146 days *multiplied* by his 10% ownership interest. The combined amounts for M and T equal the amount for M in *Example 19*.

It is also possible for an S corporation to have an ordinary loss for part of the year and ordinary income for the remaining period.

## LOSSES OF THE S CORPORATION

One of the most common reasons a corporation elects Subchapter S status is because of the tax treatment for corporate losses. Recall that the C corporation's benefits are limited to those available from carrying the losses to another year to offset its own income. Refunds may be obtained to the extent *prior* year income is offset while losses carried to future years reduce the taxes due in those years. Frequently, these carryover benefits provide little or no value to the corporation. For example, many businesses report losses in the first few years so the carryback privilege is useless. In addition, many new businesses are never successful. But, even those that are successful receive no tax benefit from their losses currently—generally when the need is the greatest.

The pass-through feature of S corporations can be a significant advantage when a corporation has a net loss. Based on the flow-through concept, shareholders include their distributive shares of the S corporation's losses in their taxable income currently. Thus, the deduction for losses is transferred to the shareholder and generally results in tax savings for the current year. Even if a shareholder is unable to use the loss currently, carryover provisions may provide the shareholder with tax benefits in the near future.

### Limitations

Each shareholder's deductible share of net losses may not exceed that shareholder's basis in the corporation's stock and the basis in any debt that the corporation owes to the shareholder. (Shareholder basis is discussed in more depth later in this chapter.) Any losses that exceed a shareholder's basis may be carried forward indefinitely to be used when the shareholder's basis is increased.[72] When basis is insufficient and there is more than one item that reduces basis, the flow-through of each item is determined in a pro rata manner.[73] In addition, any income items that increase basis flow through to the owner before any items that reduce basis, including distributions on stock.[74]

### Example 23

G owns 200 of an S corporation's 1,000 shares of common stock outstanding and has a basis of $10,000 at the beginning of the year. Neither the number of shares outstanding nor those owned by G has changed during the year. The S corporation items for its calendar year are allocated to G, based on his 20% ownership interest, as follows:

| | *Totals on Schedule K* | *G's 20% on Schedule K-1* |
|---|---|---|
| Ordinary loss (from Form 1120S, page 1) . . . . . . | ($70,000) | ($14,000) |
| Net capital loss . . . . . . . . . . . . . . . . . . . . . . . . . | (5,000) | (1,000) |
| Section 1231 gain . . . . . . . . . . . . . . . . . . . . . . | 10,000 | 2,000 |

[72] § 1366(d)(2). Losses may also be subject to limitation under § 465 at-risk rules and § 469 passive activity rules.

[73] Reg. § 1.1366-2(a)(4).

[74] §§ 1366(d)(1) and 1367(a). After positive adjustments, basis is reduced by distributions and nondeductible items, before separately stated deductions and losses. See discussion below.

G's share of the S corporation's losses is limited as follows:

| | Basis | Loss Carryover |
|---|---|---|
| G's beginning basis | $10,000 | |
| Section 1231 gain | 2,000 | |
| Limitation on losses | $12,000 | |
| Ordinary loss* | (11,200) | $2,800 |
| Net capital loss** | (800) | 200 |
| G's ending basis | $ 0 | |

*($14,000/$15,000 × $12,000)
**($1,000/$15,000 × $12,000)

Because G's basis is less than the $15,000 total loss, G may report ordinary loss of only $11,200 and net capital loss of $800. The remaining ordinary loss of $2,800 and net capital loss of $200 are carried forward to be used at the end of the first year that G's basis increases.

The above allocation of losses is applicable to all losses and separate deductions (e.g., investment interest and state income taxes) for owners of both the S corporation and the partnership.

### Carryovers from C Corporation Years

Generally, no carryovers from a C corporation may be used during the years it is taxed as an S corporation (or vice versa). For example, a C corporation with a net operating loss may not use it to offset income in an S year. There is one exception: C corporate NOL carryforwards may be used to offset the S corporation's built-in gains (discussed later in this chapter).[75] The S years are counted, however, when determining the expiration period of the carryover. Thus, a carryback of two years means two fiscal or calendar years regardless of whether the corporation was a C corporation or an S corporation.[76]

## Determining Shareholder Basis

A shareholder's basis in his or her stock as well as any debt owed to the shareholder is critical for three principal purposes. First, upon a sale of stock, shareholders must know the basis of the stock to compute gain or loss on the sale. Second, the treatment of distributions depends on the basis of a shareholder's stock. Third, shareholders must know their stock basis as well as their debt basis in loss years since losses are deductible only to the extent of the basis in their stock and debt.

### Basis in S Corporate Stock

**LO.4**
Determine the shareholders' basis in the S corporation stock and debt, and understand the significance for loss deductions and distributions.

Conceptually, the computation of a shareholder's stock basis is similar to that for a partner's interest in a partnership. Both calculations are designed to ensure that there is neither double taxation of income nor double deduction of expenses. Consider a typical situation where two individuals form a business. Assume both parties contribute $10,000 for a 50 percent interest in an S corporation which immediately takes the money and invests it in land that it subsequently sells for $22,000. In this case, the S corporation has income of $2,000 ($22,000 − $20,000) and each shareholder reports his $1,000 share. Note that the shareholders report their share of the S corporation's income even if they receive no distributions from the

[75] § 1374(b)(2).

[76] §§ 1371(b) and 1362(e)(6)(A).

S corporation. However, to ensure that an S corporation's income is not taxed again when it is distributed, each shareholder must keep track of his or her investment, that is, basis in the S corporation. In this case, each shareholder has an original basis equal to the amount contributed to the S corporation, $10,000. Upon the reporting of S corporation income, each shareholder adjusts basis in the S corporation interest for his or her share of income, increasing it from $10,000 to $11,000. When a shareholder actually receives the $1,000 share of the income, the distribution is treated as tax-free to the extent of basis. Each shareholder would then reduce basis by $1,000 back to the original basis of $10,000. The end result is that the shareholders have reported and received income that has been subject to only one tax. The same rationale can be applied to situations involving tax-exempt income, deductible losses and nondeductible expenses to ensure the proper result is reached.

The steps for calculating a shareholder's stock basis are shown and compared to that for a partner in Exhibit 23-3.[77] Generally, both computations begin with the owner's initial investment, increased by items of taxable and tax-exempt income then decreased by distributions, nondeductible expenditures,[78] deductible expenses and losses in that order. As may be apparent in Exhibit 23-3, the primary difference between the two calculations is that an S corporation shareholder does not include a proportionate share of corporate debt to other lenders. In addition, as illustrated later, the treatment of the distribution of noncash property differs from that of a partnership.

**EXHIBIT 23.3** **Adjustments to Ownership Basis**

| *Shareholder's Basis in S Corporation Stock* | *Partner's Basis in Partnership Interest* |
|---|---|
| **Original Basis** | **Original Basis** |
| Cost | Generally same as S unless received in exchange for property contributed to partnership where partner assumed or reduced liabilities |
| Substitute for property contributed in § 351 exchange Donor's basis | |
| Inherited basis (estate tax value from deceased shareholder) | |
| **Increased by** | **Increased by** |
| Taxable income (ordinary or separately stated) | Same |
| Tax-exempt income | Same |
| **Decreased (but not below zero) by** | **Decreased (but not below zero) by** |
| Distributions of cash | Same |
| Distributions of property at fair market value | Partnership basis of distributed property (in most cases) |
| Nondeductible expenses (unless election)[a] | Same |
| Losses (ordinary and separately stated) | Same |
| **No Effect** | **Additional Effect** |
| Increase in corporate liabilities | Increase partner's basis for share of liabilities |
| Decrease in corporate liabilities | Decrease partner's basis for share of liabilities |

[a]Nondeductible expenses must be used to offset basis before deductible items unless the shareholder files a special election to reverse the order. Reg. § 1.1367-1(g).

[77] § 1367.

[78] With respect to the order of nondeductible and deductible expenditures, there is no special rule for partnerships and in absence of sufficient basis, presumably a pro rata portion of each type of expenditure is deducted as shown in *Example 23*. In contrast, S corporation shareholders must use the order shown unless they make a special election to reverse the order and agree to carry forward any disallowed expenses which exceed basis to reduce basis in future years. See Reg. § 1.1367-1(g).

## Basis in S Corporation Debt

If a shareholder's portion of the corporation's losses exceeds his or her stock basis, the shareholder must next turn to debt basis to determine whether or not any loss passing through from the corporation may be deductible. Unlike a partnership, in which a partner increases basis for his or her portion of the organization's debt to outsiders, a shareholder in an S corporation must actually loan money to the corporation in order to receive debt basis. This issue has been frequently litigated by shareholders with little success. The loan must represent an actual economic outlay on the shareholder's part, rather than a mere paper shuffling of debt instruments.[79] The loan must be made directly by the shareholder, rather than indirectly through a related party.[80] A shareholder guarantee of the corporation's debt to the lender does not create shareholder basis.[81] Thus there must be a debt directly from the corporation to the shareholder, based on the shareholder's economic outlay. Quite logically, the shareholder's basis, before any adjustments, is the amount loaned by the shareholder.

A shareholder's basis in the loan is adjusted *only* (1) when the actual indebtedness itself changes due to additional loans or repayment of loans, (2) when corporate net losses exceed the shareholder's basis in S stock, and (3) to restore any basis reduction due to the prior flow-through of net losses. The application of these latter two rules is somewhat tricky. As a general rule, losses first reduce the shareholder's stock basis (but not below zero). (Note that nondeductible expenses reduce basis before deductible expenses and losses unless a special election is made.) If there is insufficient stock basis to absorb the loss, the loss is deducted to the extent of the shareholder's debt basis. If there is insufficient stock and debt basis, the loss is carried over and used once there is sufficient basis to absorb the loss.

### Example 24

An S corporation incurs a net operating loss of $30,000 in 2010. L, its sole shareholder, has a basis in the stock of $24,000 and a note due him from the corporation totals $10,000.

| | *Stock Basis* | *Debt Basis* |
|---|---|---|
| Balance 12/31/2009 | $24,000 | $ 10,000 |
| Loss to extent of stock basis | (24,000) | |
| Loss to extent of debt | | (6,000) |
| Balance 12/31/2010 | $ 0 | $ 4,000 |

The $30,000 loss flows through to L, first to the extent of his $24,000 stock basis and the remaining $6,000 because of the $10,000 note owed to him.

If the 2010 loss had been $36,000, only $34,000 would be deductible by L, reducing his basis in both stock and debt to zero. The remaining $2,000 loss would be carried forward indefinitely until a positive basis adjustment occurs in stock or debt.

As the corporation earns income, the shareholder restores stock and debt basis. Debt basis is increased only for income in excess of current year distributions and deductible and nondeductible expenses and losses.[82] Thus if there are no distributions or losses during the year, the basis of the debt is increased first. However, in years where there are distributions and/or losses, the effect is to first allocate income to the stock's basis equal to the amount of any current year losses and distributions with any excess to the debt. While these rules are obviously confusing, failure to properly understand their operation may cause the shareholder to inadvertently have gain on the repayment of any corporate debt.

[79] *Wilson*, T.C. Memo. 1991-544.

[80] *Hitchins*, 103 T.C. 40 (1994).

[81] *Raynor*, 50 T.C. 762 (1968).

[82] § 1367(b)(2).

## Example 25

Refer to *Example 24*. The S corporation has net income of $3,000 in 2011 and $8,000 in 2012. There were no losses or distributions in either of these years.

| | *Stock Basis* | *Debt Basis* |
|---|---|---|
| Balance 12/31/2010 | $ 0 | $ 4,000 |
| 2011 net income | 0 | 3,000 |
| 2012 net income | 5,000 | 3,000 |
| Balance 12/31/2012 | $5,000 | $10,000 |

In 2011, the excess of income over distributions and losses is $3,000 ($3,000 – $0 – $0) and, therefore, the basis of the note is increased by $3,000. In 2012, the excess of income over distributions and losses is $8,000 ($8,000 – $0 – $0). Consequently, the basis of the debt is increased first by $3,000 to its original $10,000 face amount ($7,000 + $3,000). The remaining income of $5,000 ($8,000 – $3,000) is used to increase the basis of the stock.

## Example 26

The records of X, an S corporation, reveal the information below for 2010 and 2011. In addition, at the beginning of 2010, X's sole shareholder had a basis of $10,000 in her stock and $12,000 in a loan she had made to the corporation during 2008.

| | *2010* | *2011* |
|---|---|---|
| Tax-exempt income | $ 5,000 | |
| Loss | (30,000) | |
| Income | | $21,000 |
| Distribution | | 14,000 |

In 2010, the shareholder first increases the basis in her stock by the tax-exempt income of $5,000, resulting in a stock basis of $15,000. The $30,000 loss is then applied: first to the extent of her stock basis, $15,000, and then to the extent of her debt basis, $12,000. The remainder of the loss, $3,000, is carried over to 2011. These calculations are shown below:

| | *Stock Basis* | *Debt Basis* |
|---|---|---|
| Begin 2010 | $10,000 | $12,000 |
| Tax-exempt income | 5,000 | |
| Loss $30,000 | (15,000) | (12,000) |
| End 2010 | $ 0 | $ 0 |
| Loss in excess of basis | | $ 3,000 |

In 2011, the corporation reports taxable income of $21,000 and distributes $14,000. The $21,000 income is applied in the following order:

| | | *Stock Basis* | *Debt Basis* |
|---|---|---|---|
| Begin 2011 | | $ 0 | $ 0 |
| 2011 income | $21,000 | | |
| 2011 distribution | (14,000) | | 7,000 |
| Loss from 2010 | | | (3,000) |
| End 2011 | | $ 0 | $ 4,000 |

The shareholder deducts $27,000 of the 2010 loss in 2010 and carries the remaining $3,000 forward. In 2011, the shareholder reports $21,000 of income and deducts the remaining $3,000 of the 2010 loss.

After a shareholder's basis in the indebtedness is reduced, repayments of the debt in excess of basis result in taxable income. If the debt is a note, bond, or other written debt instrument, the shareholder recognizes capital gain to the extent the payment exceeds basis.[83] If the debt is an *open* account, the shareholder recognizes ordinary income.[84] This ordinary income can be recharacterized as capital gain by converting the open account to a capital contribution; no gain is recognized for this conversion, even if the open account has been reduced by net losses (i.e., its basis is less than its face or market value).[85]

In accounting for repayments, the following rules must be followed:[86]

1. Only the bases of loans outstanding at the close of the year are reduced.
2. Only loans outstanding at the beginning of the year are restored.

The operation of these rules generally favors the taxpayer. Observe that the basis of any loan that is completely paid off during the year may be increased for income earned during the year but is not reduced for losses.

## Example 27

J owns all of the stock of H, an S corporation. At the beginning of 2010, J had a basis in his S stock of $13,000 and a loan outstanding to the corporation of $10,000. On July 1, the corporation paid J the $10,000 it owed to him on the loan. As of July 1, the corporation's books and records revealed a loss of $15,000. The loss for the entire year was $20,000. J recognizes no gain on repayment of the loan since his basis is $10,000. Even though the losses suffered by the corporation at the date of the repayment, $15,000, and at the close of the year, $20,000, exceeded J's stock basis, there is no reduction in the basis of the loan since only the basis of a loan outstanding at the close of the year is reduced. However, J can only deduct $13,000 of the loss, the amount equal to his stock basis.

## Example 28

Assume the same facts above except that the corporation repaid the loan on June 1 of the following year, 2011. In this case, J's basis in the loan at the beginning of 2011 would be $3,000 computed as follows:

| | *Stock Basis* | *Debt Basis* |
|---|---|---|
| Begin 2010 | $13,000 | $10,000 |
| Loss for year $20,000 | (13,000) | (7,000) |
| End 2010 | $ 0 | $ 3,000 |

If the corporation had no income for 2011, J would report a gain on the repayment of $7,000 ($10,000 – $3,000). On the other hand, if the corporation had income for the year of $6,000 *and* no distributions were made, the basis of the loan would be increased

[83] § 1232 and Rev. Rul. 64-162, 1964-1 C.B. 304.

[84] Rev. Rul. 68-537, 1968-2 C.B. 372 and *Cornelius v. U.S.*, 74-1 USTC ¶9446, 33 AFTR2d 74-1331, 494 F.2d 465 (CA-5, 1974).

[85] §§ 108(e)(6) and (d)(7)(C). The holding period of the capital asset (the note) begins with the creation of the note—not the date of the unwritten loan.

[86] Reg. § 1.1367-2(d).

by the income of $6,000 to $9,000 and the gain on the repayment would be $1,000 ($10,000 – $9,000). Notice that in this latter case the basis of the loan is increased by income for the entire year even though the loan is paid off during the year. This follows from the rule that calls for loans outstanding at the first of the year to be restored.

## Relationship between an S Corporation and Its Shareholders

The S corporation is a legal entity, distinctly separate from its owners. As a result, transactions between an S corporation and its shareholders are treated as though occurring between unrelated parties unless otherwise provided. Of course, these transactions must be conducted in an arm's-length manner, based on market values that would be used by unrelated parties.

### Transactions between S Corporations and Their Shareholders

**LO.5**
Recognize transactions between shareholders and their S corporations that are subject to special treatment.

Owners may engage in *taxable transactions* with their S corporations. For example, shareholders may lend money, rent property, or sell assets to their S corporations (or vice versa). With few exceptions, owners include the interest income, rent income, or gain or loss from these transactions on their tax returns. Meanwhile, the S corporation is allowed a deduction for the interest, rent, or depreciation expense on assets purchased (if applicable).

#### Example 29

During the year, K received the following amounts from an S corporation in which she owns 30% of the stock outstanding:

1. $2,750 interest on a $25,000 loan made to the corporation;
2. $3,600 rental income from a storage building rented to the corporation; and
3. $6,300 for special tools sold to the corporation; the tools were acquired for personal use two years ago for $5,800.

Assume that the S corporation's net ordinary income, excluding the above items, is $40,000, and the depreciation deduction for the tools is $900. K's income is computed as follows:

| | *S Corporation* | *Shareholder K* |
|---|---|---|
| Ordinary income (before items below) | $40,000 | |
| Gain on sale of tools ($6,300 – $5,800) | | $ 500 |
| Depreciation of tools | (900) | |
| Interest | (2,750) | 2,750 |
| Rent | (3,600) | 3,600 |
| Ordinary income: | | |
| Corporation | $32,750 | |
| K ($32,750 × 30%) | | 9,825 |

There is a restriction, however, on when an S corporation may deduct expenses owed but not paid to a shareholder, regardless of the amount of stock owned. An accrual basis business (whether an S corporation or partnership) may not deduct expenses owed to a cash basis owner until the amount is paid.[87] This timing rule applies to all actual or constructive owners of any percent of the S corporation's stock.

[87] §§ 267(a)(2) and 267(e). This same restriction applies to a C corporation only if a cash basis shareholder owns more than 50 percent of its stock. § 267(b)(10).

**Example 30**

Assume the same facts as in *Example 29*, except that $2,000 of the $2,750 interest is accrued but not paid at the end of the current year, the S corporation is on the accrual basis, and K is on the cash basis. The corporation paid K the accrued interest of $2,000 on January 15, of the next year. Because K is a shareholder the corporation cannot deduct the $2,000 of accrued interest in the current year but must wait until it pays the amount. Consequently, the corporation will deduct the interest when it is paid in the next year. K will report the payment when she receives it.

Two special rules governing related-party transactions affect all business forms. Both are discussed in Chapter 22. *First*, realized *losses* on sales between related parties are disallowed.[88] This is not a deferral; therefore, there is no carryover of basis or holding period. However, if this property is later sold at a gain, the gain is offset by the previously disallowed losses.[89] *Second*, recognized gains on sales between related parties of *property* that will be *depreciable* to the new owner are taxed as ordinary income.[90] A related party is defined as one who owns directly or indirectly more than 50 percent of the business when losses are disallowed or when depreciable property is involved. (See the discussion and examples in Chapter 22 regarding these transactions and the definitions of related parties.) A *third* restriction, affecting transactions between partners and their 50 percent owned partnerships, is *not* applicable to either S or C corporations. For these partners, recognized gains on sales of capital assets that will not be capital assets to the partnership are taxed as ordinary income.[91] In contrast, shareholders may sell capital assets to their more than 50 percent owned S or C corporations and the gain is capital, as long as the assets will not be depreciable property to the corporation. Note that this rule may favor the S corporation over the partnership or LLC for certain activities such as real estate development.

## Selecting a Taxable Year

**LO.6**
Determine the appropriate taxable year for an S corporation.

Shareholders report their shares of S corporation income, deductions, and credits in their tax years in which the corporation's year ends regardless of when distributions of assets are actually made.[92] This timing requirement makes the selection of a year-end for the owners and the business an important tax planning decision. Under current law, an S corporation normally must use the calendar year. Fiscal years are available but only if very strict conditions are met.

Currently an S corporation may have as its taxable year:

- A calendar year.
- A fiscal year if it is a natural business year.
- A fiscal year if its majority shareholders are on the same year.
- A fiscal year under the special election of § 444.

### Calendar Years

An S corporation is allowed to have a calendar year.[93] No permission is needed to adopt the calendar year. As will become evident, the severe requirements that must be met to obtain a fiscal year force the vast majority of S corporations to use the calendar year.

### Natural Business Year

Section 1378 permits an S corporation to adopt a fiscal year if it "establishes a business purpose to the satisfaction of the Secretary." In this regard, the IRS has indicated that it will allow a

---

[88] §§ 267 and 707(b)(1).

[89] § 267(d).

[90] § 1239.

[91] § 707(b)(2).

[92] § 1366(a); § 706 provides a similar rule for partnerships.

[93] § 1378.

fiscal year only in the case of a *natural business year*. An S corporation can qualify for use of a fiscal year end if it considered to have a "natural business year-end." There are two general categories of the natural business year end for S corporations: fiscal year-ends that meet a "25 percent gross receipts test" and fiscal year ends that meet an "annual business cycle" or "seasonal business" test. Year-ends qualifying under the gross receipts test can be adopted automatically by the S corporation. The other category requires permission of the IRS.

**Automatic Adoption** A corporation that is electing S status, or a corporation that already has an S election in effect may automatically retain, adopt or change to a natural business year-end if it meets the "25 percent" test for its gross receipts of the past four years. To determine if this test is met, the corporation selects its desired year end (for example June 30) and determines its receipts for the two months ended on June 30 (May and June), and for the twelve months ending on that date in its most recent history (e.g., July through June). If the gross receipts for the final two months (e.g., May and June) exceed 25 percent of its gross receipts for the twelve months ending on that date (e.g., July through June), the S corporation meets the test. The S corporation must meet the test for its past three years ending on that date. A corporation that qualifies under this test may claim its fiscal year without receiving permission for the IRS, although it must file Form 1128 if it is changing its year.[94]

**Annual Business Cycle or Seasonal Business Tests** An S corporation may also qualify to apply for a natural business year-end under the annual business cycle test, or the seasonal business test. The annual business cycle test is for a corporation that has a "peak" period of receipts. The seasonal business test exists when there is a period of inactivity due to the nature of the business. Thus a retailer with peak sales during December holiday periods may qualify for the business cycle test, and a ski resort may qualify for the seasonal business test. However, the S corporation may not automatically claim a year-end based on either of these tests, but must apply to the National Office of the IRS and pay a ruling request fee.[95]

### Example 31

An S corporation is organized November 1, 2010. Its net ordinary income for the first 14 months is as follows:

| | |
|---|---|
| November 1, 2010–December 31, 2010 | $ 20,000 |
| January 1, 2011–October 31, 2011 | 200,000 |
| November 1, 2011–December 31, 2011 | 40,000 |

All shareholders report on the calendar year. If the S corporation's year-end also is December 31, the owners have includible income of $20,000 in 2010 and $240,000 ($200,000 + $40,000) in 2011. If, however, the S corporation meets the natural business year requirements and receives permission for an October 31 year-end, the owners have no includible income in 2010 but have includible income of $220,000 ($20,000 + $200,000) in 2011. The $40,000 will be combined with the net income or loss for the first ten months in 2012 and reported in 2012.

## Majority Ownership Year

Consistent with its concern about deferral, the IRS permits an S corporation to adopt a tax year that is identical to that of owners holding a majority of the corporation's stock.[96] For example, if an individual who operated a farm used a March 31 year-end, his wholly owned S corporation could use the same year-end since it conformed to the year of its majority owner. However, as a practical matter, this option is seldom used since most shareholders are individuals and certain trusts and they rarely use a fiscal year (e.g., trusts must use a calendar year).

[94] See Rev. Proc. 2002-37, 2002-22 I.R.B. 1030, § 5.06, Rev. Proc. 2002-38, 2002-22 I.R.B. 1037, § 5.05 and Rev. Proc. 2002-39, 2002-22 I.R.B. 1046, § 5.03(3).

[95] See Rev. Proc. 2002-39, 2002-22 I.R.B. 1046 for details.

[96] Rev. Proc. 2002-37, § 5.05 and Rev. Proc. 2002-38, § 5.06.

### Section 444 Year

A partnership or an S corporation may elect to adopt or change its tax year to any fiscal year that does not result in a deferral period longer than three months—or, if less, the deferral period of the year currently in use.[97] This election requires the electing partnership or S corporation to make a single deposit on or before May 15 of each year computed on the deferred income at the highest tax rate imposed on individual taxpayers *plus* one percent (for 2009, 35% + 1% = 36%).[98] This deposit does *not* flow through to the shareholders. In essence, the partnership or S corporation must maintain a non-interest-bearing deposit of the income taxes that would have been deferred without this requirement. Since this option eliminates some tax benefits of income deferral and has burdensome compliance requirements, few S corporations make the election. The deposit is refunded if the S corporation's income declines in the future.

Since restrictions on C corporation year-end choices are much more lenient than those for S corporations, an election by a fiscal year C corporation to become an S corporation also may require a change in the corporate year-end. This new year is applicable to all future years, even if the Subchapter S election is cancelled and the business reverts to a C corporation.

## Family Ownership

**LO.7**
Explain the unique concepts relevant to family members concerning ownership attribution, compensation, benefits and income allocation.

Many of the benefits available to family businesses from *income splitting* are dependent on which organizational form is selected. Some income splitting, however, may be achieved by employing relatives in the business regardless of the organizational form. For example, owners may hire their children to work for them. All reasonable salaries are deductible business expenses and includible salary income to the children. In addition to the tax benefits, some owners believe this provides personal advantages, including encouraging the children to take an interest in the business at an early age.

In some instances, family businesses are formed primarily for tax reasons. The most common example includes both a parent and one or more otherwise dependent children as owners. The basic tax rate structure provides considerable incentive for this type of arrangement when the child is at least 20 years of age.[99]

Rules similar to those affecting the family partnership (discussed in Chapter 22) are applicable to family S corporations.[100] Thus, if reasonable compensation is not paid for services performed or for the use of capital contributed by a family member, the IRS may reallocate S corporation income or expenses.[101] Unlike the partnership, this rule extends to all family members, including those who are *not* owners and when there is no donee/donor relationship.

### Example 32

This year, Dr. F created LME Corporation, an S corporation whose business is leasing medical equipment. He gave all of the stock in LME to his son and daughter. For the year, LME has $20,000 of net rental income. If Dr. F performs services for LME and is not adequately compensated, the IRS may adjust the income of the parties to force Dr. F to include reasonable compensation in his income, and reduce LME's income accordingly. The IRS is not required to make this adjustment.

---

[97] § 444 and Temp. Reg. § 1.444-1T(b). Partnerships and S corporations in existence before 1987 are allowed to continue their fiscal years even if the deferral period exceeds three months (i.e., the fiscal year is "grandfathered").

[98] § 7519 and Temp. Reg § 1.7519-2T(a)(4)(ii).

[99] Recall that many of the income-splitting advantages involving passive income are not available with children under 19 years of age.

[100] § 1366(e) and Reg. § 1.1366-3(a).

[101] Family member, as defined by the Code, is the same for the partnership and the S corporation. §§ 704(e)(3) and 1366(e).

## Current Distributions of Corporate Assets

**LO.8**
Calculate gain or loss for the S corporation and its shareholders when asset distributions are made and the S corporation (1) has no AE&P or (2) has AE&P.

The treatment of distributions by an S corporation borrows from the rules applying to distributions from partnerships and C corporations. Normally, distributions from an S corporation, like those from a partnership, represent accumulated income that has been previously taxed to its owners. Accordingly, this income should not be taxed again when it is distributed. Consistent with this approach, most distributions by an S corporation are considered nontaxable to the extent of the shareholder's stock basis. Any distribution in excess of the shareholder's stock basis is treated as gain from the sale of the underlying stock, producing capital gain.

Problems arise if the retained earnings of an S corporation consist of any C corporation earnings and profits (i.e., AE&P as discussed in Chapter 20). As might be expected, when this occurs, clarification is required regarding how the S and C corporation rules interact. Consequently, one of the first questions that must be considered before the treatment of a distribution can be determined is whether an S corporation has AE&P. Beyond this first concern, however, still other considerations may be relevant. For example, special rules can operate if the S corporation distributes property (i.e., assets other than cash) or the distribution occurs shortly after the S corporation election terminates. Each of these issues and several others are examined below.

### The E&P Question

As noted above, the treatment of an S corporation distribution can depend on whether the corporation has any AE&P. Normally a corporation that has been an S corporation since its inception will not have AE&P since it never operated as a C corporation.[102] Nevertheless, AE&P could be found in the retained earnings of a lifelong S corporation if a C corporation was merged or liquidated into the S corporation. An election to treat a subsidiary corporation as a QSub is a deemed liquidation of the subsidiary, governed by Code §§ 332 and 337. Accordingly, any AE&P of the subsidiary becomes AE&P of the parent S corporation.

An S corporation is far more likely to have AE&P if it operated as a C corporation before it elected S status. This is not at all uncommon. For example, it is estimated that due to substantial changes made by the Tax Reform Act of 1986, about 500,000 C corporations made S elections. Many of these converted C corporations are alive and operating today. There are also many other C corporations that for one reason or another have opted for S status. In these cases, AE&P is likely to exist. In any event, whether the corporation has always been an S corporation or is a converted C corporation, it is crucial to ascertain whether the corporation has AE&P. This determination often requires a long detailed study.

### S Corporations with No AE&P

All cash distributions by S corporations that have no AE&P are nontaxable unless they exceed the shareholder's basis in the stock.[103] It should be emphasized that the shareholder's stock basis is the critical variable in measuring the taxability of the distribution. The basis of any debt is irrelevant in this regard.

In determining whether a distribution exceeds the shareholder's stock basis, all distributions are deemed to be made on the last day of the tax year. For this purpose, the basis in the stock is increased for all positive adjustments before accounting for distributions. Like partnerships, distributions reduce the owner's basis before consideration of losses.[104] If the shareholder owns stock on the last day of the taxable year, all of the basis adjustments are made on the last day of the corporation's taxable year (or on the last day of ownership for a shareholder whose interest

[102] Prior to 1983, it was possible for an S corporation to generate AE&P while it was an S corporation. Starting in 1997, an S corporation's C earnings and profits do not include any AE&P that was produced while it was an S corporation prior to 1983. See § 1311 of the Small Business Jobs Protection Act. (P.L. 104-88).

[103] § 1368(b).

[104] Prior to 1997, distributions of S corporations were the final item absorbed (i.e., distributions were after losses and separately stated items of deductible and nondeductible expenses).

completely terminates). The general approach used by S corporations in accounting for distributions is illustrated below.

| | |
|---|---|
| | Original basis (purchase, formation, inherited, gift, etc.) |
| + | Additional capital contributions |
| + | Separately stated income items (taxable and tax-exempt) |
| + | Nonseparately stated income items (taxable and tax-exempt) |
| − | Distributions |
| − | Nondeductible, non-capital, expenses |
| − | Separately and nonseparately stated deduction and loss items |
| = | Ending basis of stock |

## Example 33

D and F have been equal owners of an S corporation for five years. D has a basis in his stock of $40,000 while F's stock basis is $10,000. The corporation's records for the year revealed the following:

| | |
|---|---|
| Ordinary taxable income | $50,000 |
| Tax-exempt income | 10,000 |
| Nondeductible portion of meals and entertainment | 2,000 |
| Capital loss (not fully deductible by shareholder) | 30,000 |

During the year, the corporation distributed $100,000, $50,000 to D and $50,000 to F. Based on these facts, the distribution to D would be nontaxable while the distribution to F would result in a capital gain of $10,000 as determined below.

| | *D's Share* | | *F's Share* | |
|---|---|---|---|---|
| | *Taxable Income* | *Basis* | *Taxable Income* | *Basis* |
| Beginning basis | | $40,000 | | $ 10,000 |
| Positive adjustments: | | | | |
| Exempt income | | 5,000 | | 5,000 |
| Ordinary taxable income | $25,000 | 25,000 | $25,000 | 25,000 |
| Basis before $50,000 distribution to each | | $70,000 | | $40,000 |
| Nontaxable portion of distribution | | (50,000) | | (40,000) |
| Taxable portion of distribution (capital gain) | 0 | — | 10,000 | — |
| Basis before negative adjustments | | $20,000 | | $ 0 |
| Negative adjustments: | | | | |
| Nondeductible meals and entertainment | | (1,000) | | — |
| Capital loss | | (15,000) | | *— |
| Ending basis | | $ 4,000 | | $ 0 |

*The capital loss would be allowed to F in any future year if F's basis were to increase.

In determining the treatment of the distributions, the stock basis for each shareholder is first adjusted for all positive adjustments before accounting for the distribution. In this case, the positive adjustments boost D's basis to $70,000 so that his $50,000 distribution is completely tax-free. After accounting for the distribution, D reduces his basis for his share of the nondeductible expenses and then the capital loss. The reduction to basis for the capital loss is made even though D is not able to fully deduct the loss on his own return. Any portion of the capital loss that D cannot deduct is carried over to subsequent years until it is exhausted.

The distribution to F results in a capital gain of $10,000 since his basis after positive adjustments, $40,000, is insufficient to absorb the entire $50,000 distribution. Note also that F cannot deduct any of the capital loss since losses are deductible only to the extent of the shareholder's basis. However, the capital loss carries over until such time that F has sufficient basis to enable its flow-through. Contrast the treatment of the capital loss with that of the nondeductible portion of meals and entertainment. There is no requirement that F must carry over the nondeductible expenses and reduce his basis. When it is known that distributions will exceed a shareholder's basis, the recognition of capital gain can be avoided if the shareholder increases his or her stock basis before the year ends. This may be done by (1) contributing capital to the S corporation, or (2) having debt owed this shareholder converted to capital.

## S Corporations With AE&P

The distribution rules for S corporations that have AE&P—regardless of the amount—are far more complex than those for S corporations without AE&P. This derives from the fact that the distributions that are out of an S corporation's earnings that were accumulated while it was a C corporation (C AE&P) are treated much differently from those out of its earnings accumulated while it was an S corporation. Distributions out of the S corporation's AE&P are treated as dividends and are fully taxable as ordinary income to the shareholder. In contrast, distributions out of the S corporation's earnings accumulated while it was an S corporation are generally nontaxable to the extent of the shareholder's stock basis. As a result, the source of the distribution is extremely important. This distinction—and a special concern about a potential abuse—requires the corporation to break down its retained earnings into several components. It is important to remember that while each of these components have its own special characteristics, all of them are simply part of the S corporation's total earnings that have been accumulated and not distributed over the years. There are four corporate level equity accounts. They are referred to as (1) the accumulated adjustments account (AAA); (2) previously taxed income (PTI); (3) AE&P; and (4) the other adjustments account (OAA). The treatment of the distributions from such accounts, as discussed below, can be summarized as follows:

| *Order* | *Source* | *Description* | *Treatment* | *Effect on Basis* |
|---|---|---|---|---|
| 1. | AAA | All S corps to the extent of AAA | Nontaxable unless exceeds shareholder's stock basis | Reduces stock basis to the extent thereof |
| 2. | PTI | Distributions to shareholders who have personal pre-1983 PTI accumulations | Nontaxable unless exceeds shareholder's stock basis | Reduces stock basis to the extent thereof |
| 3. | AE&P | S corps that have C AE&P | Ordinary dividend income | No effect |
| 4. | OAA | All remaining distributions from S corp's tax-exempt income | Nontaxable unless exceeds shareholder's stock basis | Reduce basis to the extent thereof |
| 5. | Paid-in Capital | All remaining distributions | Nontaxable unless exceeds shareholder's stock basis | Reduce basis to the extent thereof |

### Accumulated Adjustments Account

The *accumulated adjustments account* (AAA) is the initial reference point for determining the source of a distribution and therefore its treatment. All distributions are assumed to first come out of AAA to the extent thereof. While neither the name of the account nor its acronym are descriptive, this account generally represents post-1982 income of the S corporation that has been taxed to shareholders but has not been distributed. Consequently, distributions from the account are a *nontaxable* return of the shareholder's basis in his or her stock. Distributions from the AAA that exceed the shareholder's stock basis are capital gain.[105]

The AAA is a corporate-level equity account that must be maintained if the S corporation has accumulated E&P from years when it was operated as a C corporation.[106] The AAA is the cumulative total of the S corporation's post-1982 income and gains (other than tax-exempt income) as reduced by all expenses and losses (both deductible and nondeductible other than those related to tax-exempt income) and any distributions deemed

[105] § 1368(b).

[106] § 1368(c).

to have been made from the account. The specific formula for computing the balance in the AAA is shown in Exhibit 23-4. Note that the adjustments to the AAA are similar to those made by shareholders to their basis in their stock with some exceptions:[107]

1. Tax-exempt income increases the shareholder's stock basis but has no effect on the AAA. These items are posted to the OAA discussed below.
2. Expenses and losses related to tax-exempt income decrease the shareholder's stock basis but have no effect on the AAA. [However, other nondeductible expenditures reduce the AAA as they do the shareholder's stock basis (e.g., the 50 percent of meal and entertainment expenses that is not deductible, fines, and penalties).]
3. The various adjustments to the AAA (other than distributions) can create either a positive or negative balance in the AAA account. In contrast, the shareholder's stock basis can never be negative.
4. The ordering rules for the AAA are somewhat different than for basis. The corporation adjusts for income, then subtracts deductions and losses (but *only* to the extent of income items) before it calculates the balance available for distributions. In a year in which the corporation has deductions and losses in excess of income items, it reduces the AAA for this excess (called the "net negative adjustment") *after* reduction for distributions.

**EXHIBIT 23.4 Accumulated Adjustments Account Computations**

Beginning Balance

Add income items:

Taxable income

Separately stated gains and income (not including tax-exempt income)

Less losses and deductions (not to exceed income items above)

Nondeductible losses and expenses (excluding expenses relating to tax-exempt income)

Ordinary loss

Less distributions (to extent of beginning balance plus income less losses and deductions)

Less losses and deductions, to the extent they exceed income items (the net negative adjustment)

Equals AAA end of the year

## Example 34

In 1985, T formed ABC Inc. and operated it as a calendar year C corporation until 1992, when it elected to be treated as an S corporation. T has owned 100% of the stock since the corporation's inception. T's basis in his stock at the beginning of 2010 was $10,000. Other information related to the S corporation for 2010 is shown below.

| | |
|---|---|
| Net ordinary income | $50,000 |
| Charitable contribution | 9,000 |
| Tax-exempt interest income | 10,000 |
| Expenses related to tax-exempt interest income | 1,000 |
| Disallowed portion of meal expenses | 2,000 |
| Cash distributions | 20,000 |
| Beginning accumulated adjustments account | 10,000 |

[107] § 1368(e)(1).

The first five items listed above flow through to T. Of these, T must include the $50,000 of ordinary taxable income on his 2010 tax return. In addition, T is allowed to report the $9,000 charitable contribution made by the corporation as an itemized deduction on his return.

T's basis and the balances in the AAA and OAA accounts at the end of the year are computed in the following manner:

| | *Basis* | *AAA* | *OAA* |
|---|---|---|---|
| Beginning balance | $10,000 | $10,000 | $ 0 |
| Positive adjustments: | | | |
| Taxable income | 50,000 | 50,000 | 0 |
| Tax-exempt income | 10,000 | 0 | $10,000 |
| Basis before distributions | $70,000 | — | — |
| Negative items to AAA: | | | |
| Disallowed meal expense | — | (2,000) | |
| Charitable contributions | | (9,000) | |
| AAA before distribution | | $49,000 | |
| Less distribution | (20,000) | (20,000) | |
| Basis and AAA after distribution | $50,000 | $29,000 | |
| Negative items to basis: | | | |
| Disallowed meal expense | (2,000) | | |
| Expenses related to tax-exempt income | (1,000) | | (1,000) |
| Charitable contribution | (9,000) | | |
| Final balances | $38,000 | $29,000 | $ 9,000 |

Note that for purposes of the determining the treatment of the distribution, the shareholder's stock basis is determined after the positive adjustments but before the negative adjustments. In contrast, the AAA balance available for distributions is determined after the nondeductible and deductible items (including losses) but only to the extent of the positive adjustments. Also observe that the $9,000 ($38,000 − $29,000) difference between the increase in T's basis in his stock and the corporation's AAA is attributable to the tax-exempt interest income of $10,000 less the $1,000 of expenses related to this income, neither of which affects the AAA. These items are reflected in the OAA account.

As noted above, distributions from the AAA are nontaxable to the shareholder unless they exceed the shareholder's stock basis. However, it is rare for shareholders to receive distributions from the AAA that exceed the basis in their stock. Most of the time, the aggregate basis of the shareholders will equal or exceed the AAA (e.g., *see Example 34* above). Note also that the AAA is a corporate-level account and is unaffected by either shareholder transactions or shareholder basis in the stock. Therefore, if a shareholder sells stock, new shareholders are entitled to distributions from the AAA, which will be reductions of basis. On rare occasions a distribution from the AAA will exceed a shareholder's stock basis. In such case, the excess is treated as a gain from the sale of stock.

## Previously Taxed Income

The second account from which a distribution may come consists of undistributed income that has been previously taxed for S years before 1983, commonly referred to as previously taxed income (PTI).[108] As a practical matter, this account may be viewed as the AAA for years prior to 1983. The balance in this account represents taxable income that was earned by the corporation while it was an S corporation prior to 1983 and which has not been distributed to shareholders. Distributions from this account, like those from the AAA, are considered to be a nontaxable return of the shareholder's basis in his or her stock. Unlike AAA, PTI is considered a personal account and is nontransferable. Therefore buyers of a shareholder's interest do not obtain any of that shareholder's PTI.

---

[108] § 1368(c).

### Accumulated E&P of C Years

The third account from which a distribution may come represents earnings and profits accumulated in years when the corporation was a C corporation. Distributions from AE&P are taxable as dividend income. There is no schedule or reconciliation of AE&P on Form 1120S.

### Other Adjustments Account

Schedule M-2 of Form 1120S creates a fourth classification, entitled *other adjustments account* (OAA). The OAA represents post-1982 tax-exempt income and expenses related to such income and other items that do not flow into the AAA. Thus, the OAA is used to show amounts that affect shareholder bases but not the AAA.

### Schedule M-2

Schedule M-2 on page 4 of Form 1120S is a reconciliation of the beginning and ending balances in these corporate accounts: the AAA, the OAA, and shareholders' undistributed taxable income previously taxed (i.e., PTI). Interestingly, the M-2 does not reflect the ordering rules (i.e., distributions before losses and other expenses); nor does the M-2 provide for any reconciliation of AE&P.

## Example 35

Same facts as in *Example 34* above. The corporation's Schedule M-2 for the year would appear as follows:

**Schedule M-2** **Analysis of Accumulated Adjustments Account, Other Adjustments Account, and Shareholders' Undistributed Taxable Income Previously Taxed** (see instructions)

| | **(a)** Accumulated adjustments account | **(b)** Other adjustments account | **(c)** Shareholders' undistributed taxable income previously taxed |
|---|---|---|---|
| 1 Balance at beginning of tax year | 10,000 | | |
| 2 Ordinary income from page 1, line 21 | 50,000 | | |
| 3 Other additions | | 10,000 | |
| 4 Loss from page 1, line 21 | ( ) | | |
| 5 Other reductions | (11,000) | (1,000) | |
| 6 Combine lines 1 through 5 | 49,000 | 9,000 | |
| 7 Distributions other than dividend distributions | 20,000 | | |
| 8 Balance at end of tax year. Subtract line 7 from line 6 | 29,000 | 9,000 | |

Form **1120S** (2010)

### Source of Distribution

As discussed above, the treatment of a distribution depends on its source. For this purpose, distributions are presumed to flow out of the various accounts in the following order with the treatment as described.[109]

1. *Accumulated Adjustments Account (AAA).* Distributions are first considered distributions out of the AAA and, therefore, are nontaxable to extent of the shareholder's stock basis. Any amount received out of the AAA that is in excess of the shareholder's basis is treated as a sale of the underlying stock, resulting in capital gain.
2. *Previously Taxed Income (PTI).* Distributions of PTI are nontaxable to the extent of the shareholder's stock basis with any excess treated as capital gain.
3. *Accumulated Earnings and Profits (AE&P).* Distributions of AE&P are treated as dividends income just as if distributed from a C corporation and, therefore, are fully taxable as dividend income to the shareholder.
4. *Other Adjustments Account (OAA).* Distributions out of the OAA are nontaxable to the extent of the shareholder's stock basis with any excess treated as capital gain.
5. *Remaining Distributions.* Distributions in excess of the amounts in the accounts described above (i.e., the other accounts are exhausted) are treated as returns of the shareholder's capital and are nontaxable to the extent of the shareholder's stock basis. Any excess is treated as capital gain.

---

[109] § 1368(c).

Note that all of the distributions above reduce the shareholder's stock basis except amounts out of the corporation's AE&P.

## Example 36

J and W have been equal owners of a calendar year S corporation for several years. It has been operated as a C and an S corporation in the past. Balances at the beginning of the year are shown below in the schedule. Operations for the year show $12,000 net ordinary income, $2,000 tax-exempt interest income, and $24,000 cash distributions. Based on the approach described above, the $24,000 cash distribution exhausts (1) all of the $18,000 AAA, (2) all of the $4,000 PTI, and (3) $2,000 ($24,000 – $18,000 – $4,000) of the AE&P. The balances at the end of the year are determined as follows:

| | *Corporate Accounts* | | | | *Stock Basis* | |
|---|---|---|---|---|---|---|
| | *AAA* | *PTI* | *AE&P* | *OAA* | *J* | *W* |
| Beginning balances | $ 6,000 | $4,000 | $3,000 | $ 0 | $10,000 | $6,000 |
| Net ordinary income | 12,000 | | | | 6,000 | 6,000 |
| Tax-exempt interest income | | | | 2,000 | 1,000 | 1,000 |
| Cash distributions: | | | | | | |
| AAA | (18,000) | | | | (9,000) | (9,000) |
| PTI | | (4,000) | | | (2,000) | (2,000) |
| AE&P | | | (2,000) | | 0 | 0 |
| Ending balances | $ 0 | $ 0 | $1,000 | $2,000 | $ 6,000 | $2,000 |

Both J and W have $6,000 net ordinary income (from S operations) and $1,000 dividend income (from AE&P). Note that J and W recognize dividend income because tax-exempt income does not increase AAA. Also note that there is no longer any need to maintain an account for PTI once the corporation has distributed its PTI.

## Example 37

Refer to *Example 36*. Operations for the following year show net ordinary income of $9,400 and cash distributions of $16,000. The balances at the end of this year are determined as follows:

| | *Corporate Accounts* | | | *Stock Basis* | | |
|---|---|---|---|---|---|---|
| | *AAA* | *AE&P* | *OAA* | | *J* | *W* |
| Beginning balances | $ 0 | $1,000 | $2,000 | | $6,000 | $2,000 |
| Net ordinary income | 9,400 | | | | 4,700 | 4,700 |
| Cash distributions: | | | | | | |
| AAA | (9,400) | | | | (4,700) | (4,700) |
| AE&P | | (1,000) | | | 0 | 0 |
| OAA | | | (2,000) | | (1,000) | (1,000) |
| Remaining (basis) | | | | (3,600) | (1,800) | (1,000) |
| Remaining gain to W | | | | (800) | | |
| Ending balances | $ 0 | $ 0 | $ 0 | | $3,200 | $ 0 |

Both J and W have $4,700 net ordinary income and $500 dividend income (from AE&P). In addition, W has $800 capital gain since the distributions that reduce basis exceed her basis in the stock by $800. Because this S corporation no longer has AE&P, any future distributions will be nontaxable unless they exceed a shareholder's basis in the stock. Note that in this case there is no PTI component because the S corporation has no PTI.

## Distributions of Property

Although most distributions consist solely of cash, an S corporation may distribute property. Rules governing property distributions of an S corporation are a unique blend of both the partnership and C corporation provisions.

Like C corporations, the amount of any property distributed by an S corporation is the fair market value of the property less any associated liabilities. Also like a C corporation, an S corporation must recognize gain—but not loss—on the distribution of property. Any gain recognized by the S corporation on the distribution passes through to be reported by the shareholders. In addition, this gain increases each shareholder's stock basis. Upon receipt of the distribution, the shareholder reduces his or her basis by the fair market value of the property received (but not below zero). Any amount in excess of the shareholder's basis is capital gain. The shareholder's basis in the property is its fair market value. The treatment of property distributions is identical to the approach described above for cash distributions.[110]

### Example 38

After using the following equipment for four years of its five-year MACRS life, an S corporation distributes it to H, its sole owner.

| *Asset* | *Cost* | *Accumulated Depreciation* | *Basis* | *Fair Market Value* |
|---|---|---|---|---|
| Equipment | $10,000 | $7,900 | $2,100 | $4,300 |

H's stock basis, after all adjustments except the equipment distribution, is $1,800.

| | *Includible Income* | *Stock Basis* |
|---|---|---|
| H's basis, before. . . . . . . . . . . . . . . . . . . . . . . . . . . . . . . . . . | | $1,800 |
| S gain recognized (§ 1245: $4,300 FMV − $2,100 basis). . . . . . | $2,200 | 2,200 |
| Balance . . . . . . . . . . . . . . . . . . . . . . . . . . . . . . . . . . . . . . . | | $4,000 |
| Tax-free distribution . . . . . . . . . . . . . . . . . . . . . . . . . . . . . . | | (4,000) |
| Taxable distribution. . . . . . . . . . . . . . . . . . . . . . . . . . . . . . . | $300 | |
| H's basis, after . . . . . . . . . . . . . . . . . . . . . . . . . . . . . . . . . . | | $ 0 |

H must also recognize a $300 capital gain since the $4,300 FMV of the equipment exceeds his $4,000 stock basis. His basis in the equipment becomes $4,300.

## Special Rules Relating to Source of Distributions

While the normal rules for the sourcing of distributions usually is favored by shareholders, this is not always the case. For example, recall that an S election is terminated if an S corporation has excess passive income and AE&P for three consecutive years. In this

[110] Under current IRS instructions to Form 1120S, both property and cash reduce PTI.

**EXHIBIT 23.5 Sources of Distributions**

| Distribution Order | Normal Treatment | AAA and PTI Bypass Elections | Post-Termination Transition Period |
|---|---|---|---|
| 1 | AAA | AE&P | AAA |
| 2 | PTI | AAA | CE&P |
| 3 | AE&P | PTI | AE&P |
| 4 | OAA | OAA | Unspecified return of capital |

situation and others, the corporation may want to purge itself of its AE&P to avoid losing its election. Note, however, that under the normal rules, the corporation must distribute all of its AAA before it can begin distributing its AE&P. Fortunately, the law provides possible relief and makes a special election available to the corporation to alter the source of the distribution. Section 1368(e)(3) allows the corporation to make the so-called *bypass election*. As shown in Exhibit 23-5, this election enables the corporation to bypass AAA and treat accumulated E&P as being distributed before AAA.[111] The corporation files the election by attaching an appropriate statement to a timely filed or extended return. The election applies only to the year covered by the return. Thus, if AE&P remain at the beginning of the next year, the balance will again be behind the corporation's AAA.

When an S corporation has PTI and needs to eliminate AE&P, the election under § 1368(e)(3) is not sufficient. The corporation must also exhaust PTI before it can start distributing AE&P. The Regulations make this possible by allowing the corporation to elect to bypass PTI when determining the treatment of its distributions.[112] If the corporation elects to bypass both AAA and PTI (as shown in Exhibit 23-5), AE&P is deemed to be the first item distributed by the S corporation.

In many cases, an S corporation identifies the need to distribute its AE&P after the close of the taxable year—normally a time when it would be too late to take action. However, the Regulations rescue the corporation in this situation with a very valuable tool: the deemed dividend election.[113] When every shareholder who receives a distribution during the year consents to this election, the corporation is treated as having made a distribution of its AE&P on the last day of its taxable year. The shareholders must first include the deemed dividend in their income and then are treated as having contributed the amount to the corporation as a contribution to capital increasing the basis in their stock. The bypass and deemed dividend elections require the consent of all "affected shareholders" (those who have received distributions or deemed distributions during the tax year).

## Post-Termination Transactions

### Distributions

When a corporation election terminates its S election, the entity is immediately treated as a C corporation. Without special rules, this transition could be particularly severe. Recall that distributions for a C corporation are dividends to the extent of E&P. This is true even though the C corporation may have undistributed nontaxable income from S years. This could create a special hardship on a person who had been a shareholder during the corporation's final S corporation year and who had received an allocation of income from the corporation attributable to that period. In such a situation, the shareholder would not be able to withdraw money from the corporation, even to the extent necessary to pay taxes on his or her portion of the S corporation's taxable income, without the possibility of dividend treatment. To address this problem, special rules allow a shareholder to treat distributions as being from the AAA during the post-termination transition period (PTTP).

[111] Reg. § 1.1368-1(f)(2).

[112] Reg. § 1.1368-1(f)(4).

[113] Reg. § 1.1368-1(f)(3).

The PTTP begins the day after the S corporation's final tax year and lasts at least one year and perhaps longer.[114] During the PTTP, cash—but not property—distributions are deemed to come from AAA to the extent thereof.[115] But this is where the normal pattern of distributions ends. Any PTTP distributions in excess of AAA are *not* considered as having come from PTI or OAA but rather current or accumulated E&P. As shown in Exhibit 23-5, any distributions during the PTTP in excess of AAA would be fully taxable as dividends to the extent of the corporation's E&P. Note that this special ordering rule for distributions during the PTTP is deemed to occur unless the corporation elects not to have it apply. Also observe that a distribution during the PTTP is only treated as coming from the AAA if it is received by a person who was a shareholder on the corporation's final day as an S corporation.[116]

### Losses

In some cases, a shareholder who had sustained losses prior to the termination of an S election may have lacked sufficient basis to deduct those losses. Without some relief, those losses would provide no tax benefit after the termination since the corporation is no longer an S corporation but a C corporation. However, the Code enables shareholders to secure those losses by allowing them to increase their stock basis during the PTTP.[117] Note that a loan during this period does not create basis for prior losses. Only increases in stock basis can secure losses. For example, shareholders could cancel any corporate debt owed to them and treat the cancellation as a contribution to capital with a corresponding increase in basis. Similarly, a shareholder could exchange the debt for additional stock. A shareholder could also increase the stock's basis by simply contributing additional cash or property to the capital of the corporation.

# Taxes Imposed on the S Corporation

S corporations, like partnerships, normally are considered nontaxable entities. Unlike partnerships, however, S corporations may be required to pay one of the following taxes:

1. Excessive passive investment income tax
2. Tax on built-in gains
3. LIFO recapture tax

## Tax on Excessive Passive Income

**LO.9**
Calculate the special taxes on excessive passive income and on built-in gains.

When Congress revised Subchapter S in 1982, it was concerned that C corporations with a potential accumulated earnings tax or personal holding company tax, particularly those that are mere holding companies (i.e., those whose principal assets are investment properties such as stocks, securities, and real estate projects), would attempt to escape these penalty taxes by electing to be treated as S corporations. Subchapter S can provide a refuge for these corporations since S corporations normally are exempt from both penalty taxes. To guard against this possibility, Congress enacted two provisions. First, as previously explained, when a corporation has AE&P *and* excessive passive income in three consecutive years, the corporation's S election is terminated.[118] Second, an S corporation must pay a special tax on its passive income if (1) it has AE&P at the close of its tax year, *and* (2) passive investment income exceeds 25 percent of its gross receipts that year.[119] Note that this tax, as well as the termination provision for excessive passive income (discussed early in this chapter), only applies to corporations that have AE&P from C corporation years at the end of the taxable year. Consequently, the tax is not imposed on corporations that have distributed all of their AE&P or that have never been C corporations, unless the corporation has acquired E&P in a tax-free reorganization, tax-free liquidation or QSub election.

[114] § 1377(b).
[115] § 1371(e).
[116] Reg. § 1.1377-2(b).
[117] § 1366(d)(3).
[118] § 1362(d)(3).
[119] § 1375(a).

The tax on excessive passive income is equal to the maximum corporate rate for the year (35 percent in 2010 and 2011) multiplied by *excess net passive income* (ENPI). ENPI is computed as follows:

$$\text{ENPI} = \text{Net passive income} \times \frac{\text{Passive investment income} - 25\% \text{ of gross receipts}}{\text{Passive investment income}}$$

In computing the tax, several rules must be observed.

1. For any taxable year, *ENPI* cannot exceed the corporation's taxable income, computed as though it were a C corporation but before reduction for the dividends-received deduction and net operating loss deduction.[120]
2. *Passive investment income* is defined the same as it is for the termination provisions of § 1362(d) discussed previously:[121] generally gross receipts from dividends, interest (including tax-exempt interest), rents, royalties, and annuities.
3. *Net passive income* is passive investment income reduced by any allowable deductions directly connected with the production of this income. These deductions include such expenses as property taxes and depreciation related to rental property but exclude any deductions that are not directly connected with the sources of passive investment income.[122]

The amount of any tax paid reduces the amount of each item of passive investment income that flows through to shareholders. The tax is allocated proportionately based on net passive investment income.[123]

## Example 39

PTC is owned equally by R and S. At the close of the year, PTC, an S corporation, reports gross receipts of $200,000 and a balance in its AE&P account of $24,000. Gross receipts include $25,000 interest and $50,000 of passive rent. Deductions directly attributable to rents were $30,000, including depreciation, maintenance, insurance, and property taxes. Using this information, PTC has excess net passive investment income of $15,000 determined as follows:

| | |
|---|---|
| Total gross receipts: | |
| Gross receipts: | |
| Interest | $ 25,000 |
| Rent (passive) | 50,000 |
| Total passive gross receipts | $ 75,000 |
| Active gross receipts | 125,000 |
| Total gross receipts | $200,000 |
| Permitted passive portion (25% × $200,000) | $ 50,000 |
| Excess passive gross receipts ($75,000 − $50,000) | $ 25,000 |
| Net Passive Income: | |
| Passive gross receipts | $ 75,000 |
| Deductions connected with rent | (30,000) |
| Net passive income | $ 45,000 |

[120] § 1375(b)(1)(B) and Reg. § 1.1375-1(b)(1)(ii).

[121] §§ 1375(b)(3) and 1362(d)(3).

[122] § 1375(b)(2).

[123] Reg. § 1.1366-4(c).

| | |
|---|---|
| Excess net passive income: | |
| Excess passive gross receipts | $ 25,000 |
| Divide by total passive gross receipts | 75,000 |
| Excess fraction ($25,000/$75,000) | $\frac{1}{3}$ |
| Times net passive income | 45,000 |
| Excess net passive income | 15,000 |

Since the corporation has passive investment income exceeding 25% of its gross receipts ($25,000) *and* it has AE&P at the end of the taxable year, the tax on excessive passive income is imposed.

PTC's excessive passive investment income tax is $5,250 (35% × $15,000). This amount is allocated as follows:

| | *Interest* | *Rent* | *Total* |
|---|---|---|---|
| Gross receipts | $25,000 | $ 50,000 | $ 75,000 |
| Expenses | 0 | (30,000) | (30,000) |
| | $25,000 | $ 20,000 | $ 45,000 |
| Tax allocation | (2,916) | (2,334) | (5,250) |
| | $22,084 | $17,666 | $ 39,750 |
| To each shareholder (50%) | $11,042 | $ 8,833 | $ 19,875 |

## Tax on Built-in Gains

Without special rules, C corporations planning sales or distributions of appreciated property (e.g., as a dividend or in liquidation) could avoid double taxation by electing S status before making the distributions.

### Example 40

R, a regular C corporation, owns land worth $50,000 (basis $10,000). If R Corporation distributes the land to its sole shareholder, D, as a dividend, the corporation recognizes a gain of $40,000 ($50,000 – $10,000) and D recognizes dividend income of $50,000. Therefore, two taxes are imposed. In contrast, compare the result that occurs if R Corporation has S status. R still recognizes a $40,000 gain. However, that gain is not taxed at the corporate level but flows through to D to be included on his tax return. In addition, D increases his basis in his stock by $40,000. On receipt of the property, D does not report any income but simply reduces the basis in his stock. As a result, there is only a *single tax* if R Corporation has S status.

To eliminate the tax-avoidance possibility of electing S status before the distribution (or a sale), Congress enacted § 1374. This section imposes a special corporate-level tax—the *built-in gains tax*—on gains recognized by an S corporation that accrued while it was a C corporation. The tax applies *only* to certain gains recognized during the 10-year period following the S election. In 2009 Congress reduced the ten year period to seven years, but that rule is only in effect for 2009 and 2010. Congress reduced the recognition period for corporation's tax years beginning in 2011. This temporary rule excludes gains recognized in the 2011 tax year if five years have lapsed between the effective date of the S election and the beginning of the tax year.

Under § 1374, it is presumed that *any* gain recognized on the sale or distribution of any property by a "converted" S corporation is subject to the built-in gains tax. However, the corporation may rebut this presumption and avoid the tax by proving either of the following: (1) the asset sold or distributed was not held on the date that the corporation elected S status; or (2) the gain had not accrued at the time of the election. As a practical matter, this approach requires every C corporation electing S status to have an independent appraisal of its assets on the date the S election becomes effective (i.e., the conversion date) in order to rebut the presumption. Note that for purposes of this tax, built-in gains are applicable to *all* assets, including inventory, unrealized receivables of a cash basis taxpayer, any gain on a long-term contract that has not been recognized (e.g., the taxpayer uses the completed contract method of accounting), and any goodwill.

As a general rule, the special tax applies only to S corporations having a *net unrealized built-in gain*. A net unrealized built-in gain is defined as the difference between the value and basis of all assets held on the conversion date. This difference represents the *maximum* amount that may be subject to the built-in gains tax.

## Example 41

On November 3, 2010 T Corporation made an S election. The election was effective for calendar year 2011. On January 1, 2011 its balance sheet revealed the following assets:

| | *Adjusted Basis* | *Fair Market Value* | *Built-in Gain (Loss)* |
|---|---|---|---|
| Equipment . . . . . . . . . . . . . . | \$ 50,000 | \$ 75,000 | \$25,000 |
| Land . . . . . . . . . . . . . . . . . . | 30,000 | 70,000 | 40,000 |
| Stock. . . . . . . . . . . . . . . . . . | 20,000 | 15,000 | (5,000) |
| | \$100,000 | \$160,000 | \$60,000 |

T Corporation's net unrealized built-in gain is \$60,000. Note that the built-in loss on the stock effectively limits the taxpayer's future exposure to the built-in gains tax.

Only the *net recognized built-in gain* (NRBIG) is subject to tax.[124] According to the regulations, NRBIG is the lesser of:

1. The *Pre-Limitation Amount* (PLA). The PLA is the S corporation's taxable income as if its *only* recognized items for the year were its recognized built-in gains and losses. The S corporation must observe the C corporation rules in making this computation. However, in using the C rules, the corporation is not permitted to claim any dividends-received deduction or any loss carryforward.
2. The *Taxable Income Limit* (TIL). The TIL is the S corporation's taxable income computed in the same manner as a C corporation, including *all* of its recognized gross income and deductions for the taxable year. Again, it is not allowed to claim the dividends-received deduction or any loss carryforward. Due to this rule, NRBIG cannot exceed the taxable income that the corporation would have had if it had been a C corporation.
3. The *Net Unrealized Built-in Gain Limit* (NUL). In its first S corporation year, the NUL is the same as the net *unrealized* built-in gain (i.e., the maximum net built-in gain that could be recognized). In subsequent years, the NUL is the original net unrealized built-in gain reduced by all net recognized built-in gains in prior years. In this manner, the net unrealized built-in gain acts as the limiting factor on the total net recognized built-in gains that could be reported during the ten year recognition period.

The corporation computes each of these amounts and the lowest is the NRBIG for the year. After the corporation computes this amount, it is then allowed to reduce it by any unused net operating loss carryforwards from years in which it was a C corporation. The corporation applies a flat rate of 35 percent to this amount, which in turn may be offset by certain credit carryforwards from prior years.

[124] § 1374(b).

## Example 42

Refer to the facts in *Example 41*. During 2011 T Corporation sold the equipment and the stock for $77,000 and $15,000, respectively. Although T recognizes a gain of $27,000 ($77,000 – $50,000) on the sale of the equipment, T's built-in gain recognized is limited to the amount accrued on the date of conversion from a C corporation to S status, $25,000. T's net recognized built-in gain that is potentially subject to tax is $20,000 (the built-in gain of $25,000 less the $5,000 built-in loss recognized.)

## Example 43

Refer to the facts in *Example 41 and 42*. Assume that during 2011, T Corporation's taxable income, including the equipment and stock sales, is $38,000. This figure is computed using the modified C corporation rules. At this point, the TIL is greater than the PLA of $20,000, so the PLA is treated as the taxable built-in gain. The corporation then computes its NUL. In its first S corporation year, the NUL is the same as the net unrealized built in gain, $60,000. As a result, the net recognized built-in-gain (NRBIG) for the year is $20,000 (the lesser of PLA of $20,000, TIL $38,000, and NUL $60,000).

If the corporation had sold the land at a gain of $40,000 instead of selling the stock, the total gain for the first S corporation year would have been $67,000 ($40,000 gain from land + $27,000 gain from equipment). However, only $60,000 of this gain would be potentially subject to the § 1374 tax because T's NUL is the maximum amount subject to the tax. Moreover, since its TIL is $38,000, the gain would be further limited to $38,000.

In subsequent years, the NUL is computed by subtracting all net recognized built-in gains to date from the original net unrealized built-in gain. In this manner, the net unrealized built in gain may act as the limiting factor on the total net recognized built-in gains during the ten year recognition period.

In determining the built-in gains tax, the net recognized built-in gain (after applying all limitations) is reduced by any NOL and capital loss carryforward from C corporate years. In addition, business tax credit carryforwards arising in a C year can be used to reduce the tax.[125] Any net recognized built-in gain not subject to tax because of the TIL is carried over to the following year and treated as if it occurred in that year. The calculation of the tax is summarized below.

| | | |
|---|---|---|
| | Net recognized built-in gain | $ x,xxx |
| – | NOL and NCL carryforward from C year | (xxx) |
| = | Tax base | $ x,xxx |
| × | Top corporate tax rate | × xx% |
| = | Potential tax | $ x,xxx |
| – | Business credit and AMT carryforward from C year | (xxx) |
| = | Tax | $ x,xxx |

## Example 44

Refer to the facts in *Example 42*. Assume that T sold the land for $70,000 in its first S corporation year, but did not sell the equipment or stock. T recognizes a $40,000 gain, which is also the total PLA for the year. The TIL is $38,000 and the NUL is $60,000.

[125] § 1374(b)(2) and (3).

Assume T also has a NOL carryforward of $3,000 from C corporation years. The corporation's built in gains tax is:

| | | |
|---|---|---|
| Least of: | | |
| PLA | $40,000 | |
| NUL | $60,000 | |
| TIL | $38,000 | $38,000 |
| Less NOL carryforward | | (3,000) |
| Taxable amount | | $35,000 |
| Tax rate | | × 35% |
| Built in gains tax | | $12,250 |

After the S corporation calculates its built-in gains tax for the year, it needs to make some additional computations:

1. If the TIL is the least of the three net recognized built-in gain measures, the corporation will need to determine its recognized built-in gain carryforward to the next year.
2. The corporation must apportion the tax as a reduction to the income items flowing through to the shareholders, as well as the year's increment to the AAA.
3. The corporation must compute its NUL for its next taxable year.

For the corporation in *Example 44* above, the calculations are shown below.

Adjustment to next year's PLA to reflect the gain carryforward arising from the TIL for the current year.

| | |
|---|---|
| Lesser of NUL ($60,000) or PLA ($40,000) | $ 40,000 |
| Subtract TIL, if less | (38,000) |
| Gain carryforward to add to next year's PLA | $ 2,000 |

Adjustment to next year's NUL:

| | |
|---|---|
| NUL at beginning of current year | $ 60,000 |
| Less net recognized built-in gain of current year | (38,000) |
| NUL for next year | $ 22,000 |

The corporation must then subtract its built-in gains tax from the income items that created the built-in gain in order to determine the pass-through of items to the shareholders. Assuming that the recognized built-in gain of $40,000 was a § 1231 gain, the corporation would reduce this gain by the tax of $12,250 and pass through $27,750 of § 1231 gain ($40,000 − $12,250) to its shareholders. Assuming that the corporation had a net ordinary loss of $2,000, to yield the TIL of $38,000, the corporation would pass the loss of $2,000 through to its shareholder's and the year's net addition to the AAA would be $25,750 computed as follows:

| | |
|---|---|
| § 1231 gain | $40,000 |
| Built in gains tax | (12,250) |
| Ordinary loss | (2,000) |
| Net increment to AAA | $25,750 |

## LIFO Recapture

A corporation using the LIFO method of accounting for inventories in its last taxable year before an S election becomes effective must include in taxable income for its last C corporation year an additional amount, called the LIFO recapture amount.

The LIFO recapture amount is the excess of the inventory's value under FIFO (lower of cost or market) over its actual LIFO basis as of the end of the corporation's last

C corporation taxable year.[126] The increase in tax liability is referred to as the LIFO recapture tax, although it is not a separate tax per se, and it is not imposed on the income after the corporation becomes an S corporation. This portion of the tax is payable in four equal installments, with the first installment due on the due date of the corporation's last C corporation return and the subsequent payments due on the due dates of the first three S corporation returns.[127] No interest is due if the required installments are paid on a timely basis, and there is no requirement that estimated tax payments be made with respect to any LIFO recapture tax due.[128] Finally, the inventory's basis is increased by the LIFO recapture amount. Any additional appreciation attributable to the inventory (i.e., excess of fair market value over its FIFO basis) will be subject to the built-in gains tax as the inventory is sold. However, if the corporation does not report a decrement from its initial S corporation LIFO layer during its recognition period, it will not recognize income as a built-in gain.

**Example 45**

H Corporation converts to S corporation status for 2011. H used the LIFO method of accounting for its inventory in 2010 and had an ending LIFO inventory basis of $90,000. At the end of 2010, the inventory's actual fair market value was $175,000 and its FIFO value was $150,000. H must add the $60,000 LIFO recapture amount (FIFO value of $150,000 – $90,000 LIFO value) to its 2010 taxable income. Assuming a 35 percent corporate tax rate, H Corporation's 2010 tax liability is increased by $21,000, the LIFO recapture tax. Thus, H must pay $5,250 (one-fourth) of the LIFO recapture tax with its 2010 corporate tax return and the remaining three installments of $5,250 each must be paid with H's next three tax returns. Note also that after adjusting the inventory's basis to $150,000, there is $25,000 of remaining unrealized appreciation that may be subject to the built-in gains tax as the inventory is sold. However, the future gains will be calculated by the LIFO method.

### Estimated Taxes

S corporations are required to pay estimated taxes for (1) excessive passive investment income taxes (§ 1375), and (2) taxes on built-in gains (§ 1374). The computations of estimated taxes generally follow the rules applicable to C corporations.[129] Shareholders should include their portions of S corporation income or loss when calculating their own estimated tax payments.[130]

## Disposition of Ownership Interest

**LO.10**
Understand how dispositions of S corporate stock differ from those of C corporate stock.

Based on the entity theory, sales of stock by shareholders of an S corporation result in capital gain or loss. This, of course, is identical to how stock sales of a C corporation are treated. However, the amount of the gain or loss will differ since an S shareholder's basis is adjusted for income, losses, and distributions whereas a C shareholder's basis is not. All other stock transfers also follow the rules of an exchange or gift of a capital asset. This is a significant advantage for the S (or C) corporate shareholder when compared with the complicated and often unfavorable rules of the partnership. Shareholders who sell or otherwise dispose of their stock must report their share of the S corporation's current-year items, based either on the per-day allocation method or the interim closing-of-the-books method.

[126] § 1363(d)(3).

[127] § 1363(d)(2)(B).

[128] § 6655(g)(4).

[129] See § 6655 for estimated taxes applicable to C corporations.

[130] The Code and Regulations do not expressly provide that but the language of §§ 1366 and 6654 is broad enough to require inclusion of S corporation items. See Ltr. Ruls. 8542034 and 8544011.

## Worthless Securities

S and C shareholders who hold worthless securities, including stock and debt, are subject to the same provisions with one exception. The S corporation's flow-through rules apply *before* the deduction for worthless stock or debt. The loss on worthless securities is treated as though it occurred on the last day of the *shareholder's* taxable year (not the S corporation's year) from the sale or exchange of a capital asset. Thus, it is possible for stock to become worthless before corporate activities are completed. In addition, if the S corporation's year ends *after* the stockholder's year ends, worthlessness could occur before the flow-through is available. This potential loss of deduction could be a serious disadvantage to shareholders.

The deduction for worthless stock is a capital loss unless the stock qualifies for ordinary loss treatment under § 1244.[131] Bad debts also are capital losses unless the shareholder can establish that they are business bad debts.[132] For example, the debts may have arisen as a result of a business transaction or the shareholder's employment status with the corporation. Business bad debts are ordinary losses. Nonbusiness bad debts are short-term capital losses.

## Corporate Liquidation

Generally, provisions governing liquidations and reorganizations for C corporations are applicable to S corporations (see Chapter 20).

# Tax Planning

## Choice of Entity: Comparing S Corporations, C Corporations, Partnerships, and LLCs

**LO.11**
Compare the four business organizations—proprietorships, partnerships, S corporations, and C corporations (see Exhibit 11-6).

No doubt one of the most common questions asked by a taxpayer who is anticipating starting a new business or has an existing business concerns the form of organization that should be used. That decision has probably never been as confusing as it is today. For years, nontax factors, specifically the desire to limit an individual's liability, often were the key determinant in the choice of entity decision. Professional advisors, wishing to minimize the owner's personal liability, usually encouraged the owner to incorporate and secure the liability protection that the corporate entity offered. Assuming the owner took the advice, the only decision left from a tax perspective was whether the corporation would elect to be treated under the rules of Subchapter S or operate as a regular corporation subject to the rules of Subchapter C.

The limited liability company (authorized in all 50 states) has made the choice of entity decision far more difficult. This new creature, which provides limited liability yet is taxed as a partnership, has added an important new dimension to the business organization question. Business owners who seek limited liability are no longer constrained to accept the corporate form and the C or S tax treatment that accompanies it. They may now opt for partnership tax treatment provided by limited liability companies and still obtain the protection that was formerly available only with a corporation. In short, the limited liability company has for the most part made the liability factor moot. Consequently, the decision now turns on other critical factors, which for small business owners include tax considerations.

A complete comparison of these entities and the advantages and disadvantages of operating each can fill volumes and is beyond the scope of this text. Nevertheless, Exhibit 23-6 identifies some of the key transactions in the life of a business and explains how each of the various entities would be treated.

---

[131] Compare §§ 165(g) and 1367(b)(3) with § 1244(a).

[132] Compare §§ 166(a) and (d).

## EXHIBIT 23.6 Comparative Analysis of Business Forms

| *Items for Comparison* | *Proprietorship / Proprietor* | *Partnership / Partner* | *S Corporation / Shareholder* | *C Corporation / Shareholder* |
|---|---|---|---|---|
| 1. What are the restrictions on the number of owners or who may be an owner? | One owner who must be an individual | None, except there must be at least two owners | No more than 100 shareholders who must be individuals, estates, certain trusts, charities, pensions and ESOPs | None. |
| 2. Are owners liable for business debts that they have not personally guaranteed? | Yes, except if single-member LLC | Yes, for general partners but no for limited partners or partners in an LLP, LLC members | No | No |
| 3. What are the appropriate tax forms and schedules and who files them? | Schedules C, SE, and all supporting schedules and forms | Form 1065 and Schedules K-1 are prepared by partnership; partners report on Schedules E, SE and other supporting schedules | Form 1120S and its Schedules K-1 are prepared by corporation; shareholders report on Schedule E and other supporting schedules | Form 1120 and all supporting schedules are filed for the C corporation; shareholders report dividend income on Schedule B |
| 4. Who is the taxpayer? | Proprietor | Partners | Shareholders except tax on built-in gains, excess passive investment income, and LIFO recapture | C corporation: its shareholders are also taxed on dividend income when corporate earnings are distributed |
| 5. Do owners have self-employment (SE) income from the business? | Yes, the net income from Schedule C | Yes, each *general* partner's share of net (SE) income plus guaranteed payments; for *limited* partners, only guaranteed payments from services | No | No |
| 6. Must the business's taxable year be the same as that of the majority owners? | Yes | Generally, but a different year may be used if the partnership has natural business year or pays a tax on deferred income | Same as partnership | No, any period may be used except for personal service corporation |
| 7. Are contributions of assets for an ownership interest taxable transactions? | No | No, same as proprietorship | No, *if* parties to the exchange own more than 80 percent of the corporation after the contribution, but otherwise, a taxable exchange with no carryover of tax attributes | Same as S corporation |

**EXHIBIT 23.6 Continued**

| *Items for Comparison* | *Proprietorship / Proprietor* | *Partnership / Partner* | *S Corporation / Shareholder* | *C Corporation / Shareholder* |
|---|---|---|---|---|
| 8. Are distributions of cash includible income to owners? | No | No, except a distribution in excess of the partner's basis in the partnership is treated as a partial sale of the ownership interest | No, unless distribution exceeds shareholder's basis or is from accumulated E&P | Yes, if from the C corporation's earnings and profits |
| 9. Do property distributions result in taxable income to the business or the owners? | No: basis is preserved in distributed property | No, with several exceptions | Yes, S corporation must recognize realized gain—but not loss—if a nonliquidating distribution; shareholders have dividend income if the FMV of the property exceeds AAA | Yes. Corporation recognizes gain, but not loss; shareholders have dividend income to extent of property's value or E&P |
| 10. May an owner enter into taxable transactions (sales, loans, etc.) with the business? | No | Yes, when acting in a nonpartner capacity, but subject to related-party restrictions | Yes, subject to related-party restrictions | Same as S corporation |
| 11. May an accrual basis business deduct accrued expenses to cash basis owners? | No, not applicable | No, deductible only when paid (except see 12 below) | Not deductible until shareholder includes in income. Applies to any shareholder | Not deductible until shareholder includes in income. Applies to >50% shareholder |
| 12. Are accrued expenses of the business includible income to cash basis owners? If yes, when? | No, not applicable | Yes, when received, except guaranteed salary and interest on capital are includible when accrued | Yes, when received | When accrued to minority shareholders, when received by majority shareholders |
| 13. Can owners be employees of the business and be paid salaries subject to employment taxes and withholding? | No | No | Yes | Yes |
| 14. Are fringe benefits for owner/ employees deductible expenses? | No | Yes, but partner must include in gross income | Yes, but a more than 2 percent shareholder must include in gross income | Yes |

## EXHIBIT 23.6 Continued

| Items for Comparison | Proprietorship / Proprietor | Partnership / Partner | S Corporation / Shareholder | C Corporation / Shareholder |
|---|---|---|---|---|
| 15. May the business use the cash method? | Yes, depending on income and type of business unless it qualifies as a tax shelter | Yes, depending on income and type of business unless it qualifies as a tax shelter or has a C corporation as a partner | Yes, depending on income and type of business unless it qualifies as a tax shelter | No, unless gross receipts do not exceed $5 million or it qualifies under "type of business" exception |
| 16. Is the business a conduit with the original character of the items flowing through to its owners as of the last day of the business's taxable year? | Yes | Yes | Yes | No, the business is an entity and the flow-through concept is not applicable |
| 17. How are capital gains and losses of the business treated? | As though received by the proprietor | Flow through to each partner | Same as partnership | Net capital gain includible in corporate taxable income and taxed at regular rates; net capital losses carried back 3, forward 5 years, with no deduction against ordinary income |
| 18. How is dividend income received by the business treated? | Includible income as though received by the proprietor (may be subject to reduced rate) | Flows through to each partner as dividend income (may be subject to reduced rate) | Same as partnership | Includible income with a dividend-received deduction |
| 19. How are charitable contributions treated? | An itemized deduction as though contributed by the proprietor | Flow through to each partner as an itemized deduction | Same as partnership | Deductions may not exceed 10 percent of taxable income before certain deductions |
| 20. Who pays state and local income taxes on the business net income and how are they treated? | Proprietor; an itemized deduction as though paid by the proprietor | Each partner; an itemized deduction | Same as partnership, except some state and local income taxes are assessed on the S corporation | Deductible expense |
| 21. How are tax credits treated? | Offsets proprietor's tax | Qualifying credits flow through to each partner subject to any limitations applicable at the partner level | Same as partnership | Computed at the corporate level and reduces corporate tax liability |
| 22. How is net ordinary income treated? | Includible with proprietor's A.G.I. | Flows through to each partner | Same as partnership | Included in corporate taxable income |
| 23. How is net ordinary loss treated? | Reduction of proprietor's A.G.I. | Flows through to each partner, potentially deductible up to that partner's basis in the partnership; any excess is carried forward | Same as partnership except that basis rules differ | Subject to carryover rules (back two years and forward 20 years or forward 20 years only) and deductible against net ordinary income |

**EXHIBIT 23.6** **Continued**

| *Items for Comparison* | *Proprietorship / Proprietor* | *Partnership / Partner* | *S Corporation / Shareholder* | *C Corporation / Shareholder* |
|---|---|---|---|---|
| 24. How are AMT adjustments and preferences treated? | Included on proprietor's return | Flow through to partners | Same as partnership | Included in corporation's AMTI; ACE adjustment required: small corporations exempt |
| 25. Is § 291(a)(1) applicable? | No | No | Yes, if C corporation for any of three prior tax years | Yes |
| 26. How are items allocated among the owners? | Not applicable | According to profit and loss ratio or may be specially allocated | According to stock ownership ratio; special rules for years of termination or dispositions | Not applicable |
| 27. Is the basis of business assets adjusted when an ownership interest is sold? | Not applicable | Yes, if partnership has elected the optional adjustment to basis | No, unless § 338(h)(10) election is in effect | No, unless § 338(h)(10) election is in effect |
| 28. Is basis affected by business liabilities? | Not applicable | Yes, a partner's basis includes his or her share of partnership liabilities | No, except for loans directly from shareholders | No |
| 29. Is basis affected by business income, gains, deductions, and losses? | Not applicable | Yes, all income and gains increase basis and all expenses and losses (that flow through) decrease basis | Yes, same as partnership | No |
| 30. What is the character of gains and losses on the sale of a business interest? | Each asset is treated as sold individually and the character of the gain or loss is dependent on that asset | Capital gain or loss except ordinary income to the extent of partner's share of unrealized receivables, depreciation recapture, or inventory. Some gain may be taxed at 25 percent or 28 percent | Capital gains and losses, except losses may qualify as § 1244 ordinary losses if the corporation meets certain requirements. Some gain may be taxed at 28 percent (but not at 25 percent). | Same as S corporation, except no 28 percent portion. Special rules apply if stock is § 1202 stock. |
| 31. Must a reasonable salary be allocated to family members performing services for the business? | No | Yes | Yes | No |

## Problem Materials

### DISCUSSION QUESTIONS

**23-1** *Eligibility Requirements.* May the following corporations elect Subchapter S? If not, explain why.

**a.** A corporation is 100 percent owned by another corporation.

**b.** A corporation has 101 shareholders, including Mr. and Mrs. V and Mr. and Mrs. Z.

**c.** A family corporation is owned by a father and his three children. Since the children are under age 18, their shares are held in a trust.

**d.** A corporation has 1,000 shares of common stock outstanding and 500 shares of authorized but unissued preferred stock.

**e.** A corporation has 70 unrelated shareholders and 35 shareholders who are all descendants of Mr. and Mrs. A.

**23-2** *Eligibility Requirements.* Y corporation's shareholders want to elect S status. Do any of the following facts about the corporation prevent the election? Why?

**a.** It has a wholly owned subsidiary.

**b.** It has 99 shareholders who own their shares solely in their own name and a married couple who own the stock jointly.

**c.** It has 10 shareholders, and one is the estate of a former shareholder. It is expected that the shares held by the estate will be distributed to three U.S. citizens and one Englishman who is a U.S. resident.

**d.** It has 73 shareholders plus L, who owns no shares but serves as custodian for shares owned by her two minor children.

**e.** What if L, in (d) above, is a nonresident alien, but the children are U.S. citizens?

**f.** It has 15 owners of common stock and no owners of its authorized preferred stock.

**g.** It has 10 owners of voting common stock and five owners of nonvoting common. Except for voting, all other rights of the two sets of common stock are identical.

**h.** A corporation was formed many years ago by X, Y and Z. Several generations later there are 210 shareholders, 150 of whom are descendants of X, Y and Z.

**23-3** *Eligibility Requirements and Termination.* Refer to *Problem 23-2* and assume Y corporation made its S election in 2003. Do the following facts about the corporation terminate the election? When? Why? Can the shareholders prevent the termination?

**a.** Refer to a above. It has $5 billion in sales with various customers in the United States and $10,000 sales that it places through its subsidiary.

**b.** Refer to b above. The married couple is divorced December 29, 2010, and each receives one-half the shares in Y that were owned jointly by them prior to that date.

**c.** Refer to c above. The Englishman decides it is time to return home and moves to London, England, on March 3, 2010. He continues to own five shares of Y and gives up his residency in the United States.

**d.** Refer to f above. M exchanges her 500 shares of Y common for 700 shares of Y preferred. Although the number of shares differs, the dollar value of M's holdings remains the same.

**e.** The corporation elects to revoke its S election. Holders of 70 percent of the stock consent to the revocation. The other shareholders do not consent.

**f.** On June 5, 2010 a 20 percent shareholder transfers her stock to a C corporation she owns.

**g.** Y has $15,000 accumulated earnings and profits (AE&P) from C corporate years, and 30 percent of its gross receipts in 2009, 2010 and 2011 are from dividends and interest on investments.

**23-4** *Stock Requirements.* A mother wishes to establish an S corporation with her two children. However, she is concerned about the one class of stock requirement. She does not want to provide her children with voting control but does wish to give them 60 percent of the stock. Can she achieve her wishes? Explain.

**23-5** *Election.* F, M, and T are shareholders of a calendar year corporation. On February 15, 2011 they are advised they should elect Subchapter S status. All agree to the election. However, they state that they purchased a 10 percent ownership interest from V on January 4, 2011. V sold his interest because he said he never wanted to have any contact with F, M, or T again. Can the corporation make an S election for 2011? Explain.

**23-6** *Election.* B, C, and D are shareholders, each owning 1,000 shares. On February 20, 2011 they are advised to elect S status for 2011. Can they make the election for all of 2011 under the following circumstances? Explain.

**a.** B purchased 10 shares from R on January 5, 2011. R is hitchhiking across Europe and cannot be located until April 1, 2011.

**b.** C sells 10 percent of her interest (after the election) July 7, 2011 to X. X refuses to agree to the S election and wants it terminated.

**23-7** *Elections.* This year, RJ, an individual, formed ABC Corporation. ABC commenced business on April 17, 2011. The corporation issued its first shares on March 2, 2011. RJ transferred property (fair market value $100,000, adjusted basis $20,000) to the corporation on March 28, 2011 in a nontaxable § 351 exchange. ABC intends to use the calendar year for tax purposes. For the years in question ABC does not have any attribute that would disqualify it from S status.

**a.** By what date must ABC make an election to be an S corporation if the election is to be in effect for the corporation's first taxable year, assuming the corporation does not utilize any relief provisions?

**b.** Assume that ABC discovers, on February 15, 2012 that it has not made a timely S election for its year ended December 31, 2011. Could the corporation make an election to take effect for its taxable year beginning January 1, 2012?

**c.** If the corporation made an S election for its taxable year beginning January 1, 2012, would it have any exposure to the built-in gains tax?

**d.** Assume that on February 15, 2012 ABC discovered that no S election had been made. What would be needed for the corporation to make an S election to take effect for its year 2011 tax year?

**e.** Assume the same facts in (b) above except that the corporation discovered that it had not made an S election as of April 15, 2013. What would be required for the corporation to make an S election for its 2011 taxable year?

**23-8** *Termination of the Election.* Compare the effects of an intentional revocation, an unintentional violation of the eligibility requirements, and a termination due to the receipt of excessive passive investment income.

**23-9** *Termination of the Election.* A calendar year S corporation unexpectedly receives a government contract on April 3, 2011. The profits from the contract in 2011 will be substantial. The three equal shareholders wish to revoke the election for 2011. Can they? Explain.

**23-10** *Passive Investment Income.* An S corporation with AE&P of $5,000 is expected to receive 30 percent of its gross income from rents but only 18 percent of its net income from these rents. Will the excess passive investment income test be violated? Assume the S corporation's taxable year does not end for seven months and all income is earned equally over the year.

**a.** Can any action be taken during the next seven months to ensure the test will not be violated?

**b.** Could the corporation take any corrective action if it does not determine the nature of its gross receipts until after the end of its tax year?

**23-11** *Employee-Owner.* Which of the three organizational forms—S corporation, C corporation, or partnership—treats owners who work for the business in the following manner?

**a.** The owner's compensation is a deductible business expense.

**b.** The owner's compensation is subject to FICA withholding.

**c.** The employee benefits are deductible expenses.

**d.** The employee benefits are excluded from the owner-employee's gross income.

**23-12** *Schedule K-1.* Why must each shareholder of an S corporation be provided with a Schedule K-1?

**23-13** *Business Income.* How is each of the following items treated by an S corporation?

**a.** Dividend income
**b.** Accrued rental expense to a shareholder
**c.** Net capital gain
**d.** Distribution of assets with a market value in excess of basis

**23-14** *Family Ownership.* A taxpayer operates a retail store as an S corporation. He has a 16-year-old daughter and an 11-year-old son.

**a.** Can he employ either or both of them in the business and deduct their salaries?
**b.** Can they be shareholders in the S corporation?
**c.** Can a trust be formed to hold the shares of stock owned by a minor child?

**23-15** *Family Ownership.* A mother wants to transfer a substantial portion of her ownership in an S corporation to a trust for her son and daughter. She wants to transfer value but retain voting control. She also wants to be able to exercise some control over how the assets of the trust are distributed. However, she is willing to use an independent trustee to manage the assets.

**a.** Can she transfer nonvoting stock to the children and retain voting shares without creating a second class of stock?
**b.** If she transfers stock to a trust, but retains the ability to remove the shares from the trust, will she disqualify the corporation from S status?
**c.** How could she create a QSST for each child? What restrictions would the trusts face? Who would pay the tax on the income of the corporation allocated to the trusts' shares?
**d.** What would be the advantages of using an ESBT? Who would pay the tax on the income of the corporation allocated to the trust's shares?

**23-16** *Stock and Debt Basis.* What is the significance of stock basis and debt basis to a shareholder? How does a shareholder adjust basis for the activity of an S corporation for a year? How does a shareholder obtain debt basis?

**23-17** *Property Distributions.* What effect do noncash distributions have on the S corporation and on the shareholder if the S corporation has no AE&P, and:

**a.** The property's market value exceeds its basis, or
**b.** The property's basis exceeds its market value?

**23-18** *Distributions.* When do cash distributions result in includible income to the S shareholder?

**23-19** *Post-Termination Transition Period.* What is a post-termination transition period? How is it useful?

**23-20** *Basic Comparison.* List the tax advantages and the tax disadvantages of an S corporation when compared with:

**a.** A partnership.
**b.** A C corporation.

## PROBLEMS

**23-21** *Termination of Election.* T, the sole shareholder and president of T, Inc., had operated a successful automobile dealership as a regular C corporation for many years. In 2006, the corporation elected S corporation status. After T's unexpected illness in 2010, the corporation sold most of its assets and retained only a small used car operation. In 2010 and 2011, T, Inc. had paid the tax on excessive passive income and had AE&P (from its C corporation years) at the end of both years. In 2011, the corporation paid no dividends and had the following income and expenses:

| | |
|---|---:|
| Interest income | $50,000 |
| Dividend income | 5,000 |
| Gain from prior installment sale | 30,000 |
| Used car sales | 40,000 |
| Cost of sales | 20,000 |

Is the S election terminated, and if so, when?

**23-22** *Consequences of Revocation of an S Election.* In July 2011 S Inc., a calendar year corporation, revoked its S election as of August 1, 2011. The corporation's taxable income for January through December is $432,000, and the shareholders do not elect to perform an interim closing of the corporate books.

**a.** What tax return(s) must S file for the year, and what are the due dates of the return(s)?

**b.** Compute S's corporate taxable income for the short year for the (1) S corporation and (2) C corporation.

**c.** Compute the C corporation's Federal income tax.

**23-23** *Net Income from Operations.* A and B are MDs in the AB partnership. Because of limited liability considerations, their attorney has advised them to incorporate. A typical year for the MDs (who are equal partners) is as follows:

| | |
|---|---|
| Revenues | $400,000 |
| Operating expenses | 190,000 |
| Charitable contributions. | 10,000 |
| Owner compensation | 200,000 |

**a.** Calculate AB's ordinary net income if it is taxed as (1) a partnership or (2) an S corporation.

**b.** Calculate the effect on A's ordinary income if AB is taxed as (1) a partnership; (2) and S corporation; or (3) a C corporation.

**c.** Ignoring limited liability considerations, should the partners incorporate? If so, should they elect S status?

**d.** If A and B desire partnership tax treatment, is there any business entity that would meet their needs?

**23-24** *Net Income.* A calendar year S corporation has the following information for the current taxable year:

| | |
|---|---|
| Sales | $180,000 |
| Cost of goods sold | (70,000) |
| Dividend income | 5,000 |
| Net capital loss | (4,000) |
| Salary to Z | 12,000 |
| Life insurance for Z | 500 |
| Other operating expenses | 40,000 |
| Cash distributions to owners | 20,000 |

Assume Z is single and her only other income is $30,000 salary from an unrelated employer. She is a 20 percent owner with a $10,000 basis in the S stock at the beginning of the year. Calculate the S corporation's net ordinary income and Z's adjusted gross income and ending basis in the S corporation stock.

**23-25** *Net Losses.* A calendar year S corporation has the following information for the current taxable year:

| | |
|---|---|
| Sales | $180,000 |
| Cost of goods sold | (130,000) |
| Net capital loss | (6,000) |
| Salary to Z | 18,000 |
| Charitable contributions | 1,000 |
| Other operating expenses | 65,000 |
| Dividend income | 4,000 |

Assume Z is single and her only other income is $30,000 salary from an unrelated employer. She is a 40 percent owner with a $10,000 basis in the S stock and no corporate debt owed to her. Calculate the S corporation's net ordinary loss, Z's adjusted gross income, and the character and amount of S corporate items that flow through to her.

**23-26** *Net Income/Loss and Basis.* For 2010, an S corporation reported an ordinary loss of $100,000, a net capital loss of $10,000, and a § 1231 gain of $20,000. M owns 10 percent of the stock and at the beginning of the year had a basis in her stock of $7,500. In addition, M loaned the corporation $5,000 during the year. She materially participates in the S corporation.

**a.** Compute her deductible loss.

**b.** The following year, the corporation reported ordinary income of $70,000 and made no distributions. How does this income affect M's basis in the stock and the debt?

**23-27** *Allocations.* V owns 500 shares of stock of an S corporation with 2,000 shares outstanding. The calendar year S corporation's records show the following information:

| | |
|---|---|
| Net ordinary income | $200,000 |
| Net capital loss | (10,000) |

Calculate V's share of the items if on March 15 he sells:

**a.** 200 of his shares of stock;

**b.** All 500 shares of his stock and the per-day allocation method is used; or

**c.** All 500 shares of his stock and the interim closing of the books method is used. The records reveal that through March 15, net ordinary income was $60,000 and net capital loss was $ 10,000.

**23-28** *Basis.* A calendar year business reports the following information as of the end of 2010 and 2011:

| | 2010 | 2011 |
|---|---|---|
| Accounts payable to suppliers | $10,000 | $11,000 |
| Note payable to City Bank | 40,000 | 37,000 |
| Note payable to H | 12,000 | 10,000 |
| Cash distributions to owners | | 20,000 |
| Net ordinary income | 15,000 | |

H, a 30 percent owner, had a basis in the business at the end of 2010 of $9,000. Calculate H's basis in his ownership interest at the end of 2011 assuming the business is:

**a.** A partnership

**b.** An S corporation

**23-29** *Deductibility of Losses by Shareholders.* B, Inc. was incorporated and its shareholders made a valid S election for B's first taxable year. At the beginning of the current year, Shareholder Z had a basis of $14,500 in his B stock and held a $10,000 note receivable from B with a $10,000 basis. For the current year Z was allocated a $32,000 ordinary loss and a $4,000 capital loss from the corporation. B did not make any distributions to its shareholders during the current year.

**a.** How much of each allocated loss may Z deduct in the current year?

**b.** What happens to any losses in excess of the limits in (a) above?

**c.** How much basis will Z have in his B stock and his note receivable at the end of the current year?

**23-30** *Basis Adjustments—Restoration.* Refer to the facts in *Problem 23-29* above. In the next year Z is allocated $7,000 of ordinary income and $5,500 of tax-exempt income from B. B did not make any distributions to its shareholders during the year. What effect will these income allocations have on Z's basis in his B stock and note receivable?

**23-31** *Losses and Basis.* J, Inc. is an S corporation that reported the following selected items as of December 31, 2011.

| | |
|---|---|
| Ordinary loss (from Form 1120S, page 1) | $(30,000) |
| Long-term capital gain | 500 |
| Tax-exempt interest income | 1,000 |
| Notes payable to banks | 30,000 |
| (1/1/11 balance = $20,000) | |
| Notes payable to LJ | 5,000 |
| (1/1/11 balance = $0) | |

The corporation is owned 60 percent by LJ and 40 percent by RS. At the beginning of the year, they had a basis in their *stock* of $12,000 and $10,000, respectively. How much income or loss will each of the shareholders report for 2011?

**23-32** *Basis.* M, a 40 percent owner, has a basis in the S corporate stock of $15,000 and in a note receivable from the S corporation of $8,000. Compute the basis of the stock and the note and the amount of the ordinary loss and income that flow through to M in 2011 and 2012.

**a.** The S corporation has a net operating loss of $45,000 in 2011.

**b.** The S corporation has a net operating income of $20,000 in 2012.

**23-33** *Basis.* A calendar year S corporation has the following information for the two years:

| | *2010* | *2011* |
|---|---|---|
| Net ordinary income (or loss) | $(50,000) | $10,000 |
| Dividend income | 5,000 | 2,000 |

X, an unmarried 60 percent shareholder, has a basis in the stock on January 1, 2010 of $18,000 and a note receivable from the corporation for $12,000. X's only other income is salary from an unrelated business.

**a.** Calculate X's basis in the stock and in the note after the above income and loss are recorded for 2010.

**b.** Calculate X's basis in the stock and in the note after the above income items are recorded for 2011.

**c.** Assume the corporation paid the $12,000 note on April 3, 2011. Calculate X's basis in the stock after the above income distributions are recorded for 2011, and calculate the effect on X's adjusted gross income for all 2011 items, including the payment of the note.

**23-34** *Inside and Outside Basis. XYZ* is an S corporation owned equally by three shareholders. X has often disagreed with the other shareholders over business matters and now believes he should withdraw from the corporation. X's basis in his stock is $50,000. The corporation's balance sheet appears as follows:

| | |
|---|---|
| Cash | $100,000 |
| Accounts receivable | 50,000 |
| Land | 30,000 |
| Equipment (net) | 10,000 |
| Accounts payable | 30,000 |
| Note payable to X | 10,000 |
| Shareholders' equity | 150,000 |

The equipment's market value is approximately the same as its net book value, but the land is now valued at $60,000. X sells all of his stock to W for $60,000.

How much gain must X recognize?

**23-35** *Family Ownership.* K operates a small retail store as a proprietorship. Annual net ordinary income is expected to be $60,000 next year. The estimated value of her services to the business is $25,000. K's 14-year-old son is interested in the business. She is considering giving him a 30 percent ownership interest in the business. If she does this, she will be paid a salary of $25,000. K files as head of household and does not itemize deductions. Neither she nor her son has any other includible income. Ignore all payroll and self-employment taxes in the following computations.

**a.** Determine next year's tax savings that will be achieved if K establishes an S corporation with her son at the beginning of the year compared with continuing the business as a proprietorship.

**b.** Will K or her son have any includible income if they exchange the appreciated proprietorship assets for the 70 and 30 percent ownership interests, respectively, in the S corporation?

**c.** What advice should you give K on establishing and operating the S corporation?

**23-36** *Property Distributions.* M receives the following equipment from an S corporation as a distribution of profits.

| Asset | Cost | Accumulated Depreciation | Basis | Fair Value Market |
|---|---|---|---|---|
| Equipment | $10,000 | $7,900 | $2,100 | $2,280 |

The equipment was used in the business for four years of its five-year MACRS life and will be a nonbusiness asset to M. M is a 60 percent owner and has a basis in the stock of $11,000 before the property distribution. Calculate the following amounts.

**a.** The S corporation's recognized gain
**b.** M's basis in the equipment
**c.** The effect on M's basis in the stock
**d.** The effect on M's adjusted gross income

**23-37** *Property Distributions.* Refer to *Problem 23-36*. Calculate the same amounts if M's basis in the S corporation, before the distribution, is $1,200 instead of the $11,000.

**23-38** *Property Distribution.* J purchases 20 percent of an S corporation's stock for $50,000 when its records show the following:

| | Fair Market Value | Basis |
|---|---|---|
| Cash | $ 40,000 | $ 40,000 |
| Inventory | 60,000 | 45,000 |
| Land—investment | 80,000 | 20,000 |
| Other operating assets | 100,000 | 80,000 |
| Liabilities | (30,000) | (30,000) |
| Net assets | $250,000 | $155,000 |

Six months later, all of the land is distributed in equal plats to the shareholders. What is the effect of this distribution on J?

**23-39** *Cash and Property Distributions—No AE&P.* An S corporation with no AE&P distributes $10,000 cash, land ($7,000 FMV and $4,000 basis), and desks ($3,000 FMV and $4,500 basis) to *each* of its three equal shareholders. (That is, $30,000 in cash, $21,000 in land, and $9,000 in desks was distributed in total.) One of the shareholders, T, has a basis in the stock before the distribution of $12,000 and a long-term note from the corporation of $5,000. The other two shareholders have a basis in the stock before the distribution of $40,000 and no debt from the corporation. Calculate the effect of the distribution on the A.G.I. of each of the shareholders.

**23-40** *Computation of AAA and Basis.* J formed R Corporation in 1986. The corporation operated as a C corporation from 1986 until 2003, when it elected to be taxed as an S corporation. At the beginning of the current year, J had a basis in his stock of $100,000. The corporation's balance in the AAA at the beginning of the current year was $143,000. R's records for the current year reveal the following information:

| | |
|---|---|
| Sales | $300,000 |
| Cost of goods sold | (120,000) |
| Miscellaneous operating expenses | 50,000 |
| Salary to J | 40,000 |
| Nondeductible portion of entertainment | 4,000 |
| Tax-exempt interest income | 13,000 |
| Expenses related to tax-exempt interest income | 3,000 |
| Capital gain | 7,000 |

| | |
|---|---|
| Capital loss | (2,000) |
| Charitable contribution | 5,000 |
| Cash distribution to J | 10,000 |

The corporation also had AE&P from C years of $4,000.

Compute J's basis in his stock and the corporation's balance in the AAA as of the end of the taxable year. Assume J is the sole shareholder.

**23-41** *Treatment of Distributions: Converted C Corporation.* Assume the same facts as in *Problem 23-40* above. Explain the tax treatment to J if he receives the following distributions during the year.

**a.** $100,000
**b.** $220,000
**c.** $260,000

**23-42** *Cash and Property Distributions—AE&P.* S, Inc. had previously been a regular C corporation, but elected to be taxed as an S corporation in 1982. It is owned equally by J and G, who have a basis in their stock of $100,000 each at the beginning of the current year. Also at the beginning of the current year, the corporation had the following balances:

| | |
|---|---|
| Accumulated adjustments account | $50,000 |
| Previously taxed income | 40,000 |
| Accumulated earnings and profits | 30,000 |
| Other adjustments account | 0 |

During the current year, the corporation had ordinary income of $35,000 and distributed IM stock worth $75,000 to J and cash of $75,000 to G. The stock was purchased four years ago for $50,000.

**a.** What are the tax effects of the distribution on the corporation?
**b.** What are the consequences to each of the shareholders?

**23-43** *Cash Distributions—AE&P.* A calendar year S corporation has the following balance on January 1, of the current year:

| | |
|---|---|
| Accumulated adjustments account | $13,000 |
| Previously taxed income | 2,000 |
| Accumulated earnings and profits | 6,000 |
| Other adjustments account | 0 |

This year the S corporation records show $12,000 net ordinary income, $4,000 tax-exempt income net of related expenses, and $55,000 cash distributions. Y owns 70 percent of the stock. Her basis in the stock on January 1, was $7,000, and she has a note receivable from the corporation of $5,000. Y is single, and her only other income is salary from an unrelated business.

**a.** Calculate the balances in the corporate accounts as of December 31.
**b.** Calculate the effect on Y's adjusted gross income for the year.
**c.** Calculate the basis in Y's stock and note as of December 31.

**23-44** *Property Distributions—AE&P.* Assume the same facts as in *Problem 23-43* except the distribution is stock held more than one year as an investment with a market value of $55,000 and a basis of $53,000.

**a.** Calculate the balances in the corporate accounts as of December 31.
**b.** Calculate the effect on Y's adjusted gross income.
**c.** Calculate the basis in Y's stock and note as of December 31.

**23-45** *Cash Distributions—AE&P.* D, Inc. was incorporated in 1999, and its shareholders made a valid S election for D's 2003 calendar year. At the end of the current year but before the distribution is considered, D had $19,000 of accumulated earnings and profits from 1999 through 2002, and an accumulated adjustments account of $11,000. D made only one cash distribution of $20,000 during the current year, $5,000 of which was paid to shareholder M, who owns 25 percent of D's stock. After all adjustments *except* any required for the distribution, M's basis in his stock was $18,000.

**a.** What are the tax consequences of the distribution to M, and what is M's basis in his D stock after the distribution?

**b.** What are the balances in D's accumulated earnings and profits account and accumulated adjustments account after the distribution?

**23-46** *Cash Distribution—AE&P.* M and J have been equal owners of an S corporation for several years. It was operated as a C corporation its first two years and as an S corporation since then. This year it has $12,000 ordinary income, $2,000 tax-exempt interest income, $24,000 cash distributions, and the following balances at the end of the prior year:

| | |
|---|---|
| Accumulated adjustments account | $8,000 |
| Previously taxed income ($1,000 to M, $1,000 to J) | 2,000 |
| AE&P from C years | 3,000 |

M's stock basis at the end of last year was $8,500 and J's was $13,000.

**a.** Calculate the balances in the corporate accounts as of December 31.

**b.** Calculate the effect on M's and J's adjusted gross income.

**c.** Calculate the basis in M's and J's stock as of December 31.

**23-47** *Property Distribution—AE&P.* Refer to *Problem 23-46*, but assume the $24,000 distribution is of land that has a $23,000 basis.

**23-48** *Excess Passive Investment Income.* A calendar year S corporation has AE&P of $15,000 from years when it was operated as a C corporation. Its records show the following:

| | |
|---|---|
| Sales | $100,000 |
| Cost of goods sold | (55,000) |
| Operating expenses | (15,000) |
| Dividend income | 20,000 |
| Rental income (passive) | 40,000 |
| Rental expenses | (25,000) |

The corporation is owned equally by three brothers. Determine the tax effect on the S corporation and on each brother.

**23-49** *Tax on Built-in Gains.* A corporation, organized in 1983, was operated as a C corporation until Subchapter S was elected as of January 1, 2006, when it had total assets of $240,000 FMV and $185,000 basis. Assets held on that date ($80,000 market value and $50,000 basis) are distributed in 2010 when the market value is $90,000. Calculate the tax on built-in gains if taxable income, based on computations for a C corporation, is:

**a.** $60,000

**b.** $20,000

**23-50** *Tax on Built-in Gains.* On February 5, 2011 L Corporation, a cash basis calendar year C corporation, elected S status effective for January 1, 2011. On January 1, L's balance sheet revealed the following assets:

| | Adjusted Basis | Fair Market Value |
|---|---|---|
| Inventory | $20,000 | $85,000 |
| Land | 30,000 | 70,000 |
| Equipment | 45,000 | 15,000 |

During the current year, L sold all of its inventory for $90,000. It also sold the equipment for $9,000 (L did not claim any more depreciation on the equipment this year, so its basis at the time of sale was $45,000). L's taxable income limitation is $100,000 for the current year. Compute L Corporation's built-in gains tax.

**23-51** *LIFO Recapture Tax.* T Corporation converts to S corporation status for 2011. T used the LIFO method of accounting for its inventory in 2009 and had an ending LIFO inventory basis of $540,000. The ending inventory's FIFO value was $650,000 and its fair market value was $800,000.

**a.** What is T Corporation's LIFO recapture amount?

**b.** Assuming its corporate tax rate is 35 percent, what is T Corporation's LIFO recapture tax?

**c.** How is the LIFO recapture tax required to be paid?

**23-52** *Worthless Securities.* A calendar year S corporation is bankrupt. E, a 60 percent owner for several years, will not receive any assets from the business. His basis in the stock as of January 1, 2011 was $70,000, and he has a note receivable of $25,000 from the corporation. Both are determined to be uncollectible July 1, 2011. The S corporation has a net ordinary loss during 2011 of $30,000; $20,000 before July 1 and $10,000 after July 1. E lent the corporation the $20,000 last year and $5,000 four months ago in an effort to protect his ownership interest in the business. Calculate E's adjusted gross income and capital loss carryovers if his adjusted gross income from other sources totals $120,000.

## TAX RETURN PROBLEMS

**23-53** *Tax Return Problem.* Individuals P and K formed P&K Corporation on March 1, 1994 to provide computer consulting services. The company has been an S corporation since its formation, and the stock ownership is divided as follows: 60 percent to P and 40 percent to K. The business code and employer identification numbers are 7389 and 24-3897625, respectively. The business office is located at 3010 East Apple Street, Atlanta, Georgia 30304. P and K live nearby at 1521 South Elm Street and 3315 East Apple Street, respectively. Their social security numbers are 403-16-5110 for P and 518-72-9147 for K.

The calendar year, cash basis corporation's December 31, 2009 balance sheet and December 31, 2010 trial balance contain the following information:

| | Balance Sheet 12/31/09 | | Trial Balance 12/31/10 | |
|---|---|---|---|---|
| | Debit | Credit | Debit | Credit |
| Cash | $ 12,000 | | $ 22,000 | |
| Note receivable(1) | 14,000 | | 14,000 | |
| Equipment(2,3) | 150,000 | | 190,000 | |
| Accumulated depreciation | | $ 38,000 | | $ 63,500 |
| Notes payable(3,4) | | 94,000 | | 17,200 |
| Capital stock | | 10,000 | | 10,000 |
| Accumulated adjustments account | | 34,000 | | 34,000 |
| Cash distributed to P | | | 25,440 | |
| Cash distributed to K | | | 16,960 | |
| Revenues | | | | 235,000 |
| Dividend income(1) | | | | 1,400 |
| § 1245 gain | | | | 3,500 |
| Salary expense(5) | | | 110,000 | |
| Rent expense | | | 12,000 | |
| Interest expense | | | 16,600 | |
| Tax expense (property and payroll) | | | 13,800 | |
| Repair expense | | | 5,800 | |
| Depreciation expense | | | 29,200 | |

| | Balance Sheet 12/31/09 | | Trial Balance 12/31/10 | |
|---|---|---|---|---|
| | Debit | Credit | Debit | Credit |
| Health insurance expense(6) | | | 1,600 | |
| Property insurance expense | | | 1,500 | |
| Office supplies expense | | | 3,000 | |
| Utility expense | | | 2,200 | |
| Charitable contributions | | | 500 | |
| Totals | $ 176,000 | $ 176,000 | $ 464,600 | $ 464,600 |

(1) From a U.S. corporation.
(2) Equipment was sold May 12, 2009 for $9,800. It was purchased new on May 1, 2009 for $10,000 and its basis when sold was $6,300.
(3) New equipment was purchased March 1, 2010 with $5,000 cash and a $45,000 three-year note payable. The first note payment is March 1, 2011.
(4) Notes payable are long-term except for $20,000 of the note to be paid next year.
(5) Salary expense is composed of salary of $30,000 each to P and to K and $50,000 to unrelated employees.
(6) Health insurance premiums paid were for the unrelated employees.

Prepare Form 1120S (including Schedules K, L, and M), and Schedule K-l for shareholder P. Complete all six pages, including responses to all questions. If any necessary information is missing in the problem, assume a logical answer and record it. Do not prepare Schedule K-l for shareholder K or other required supplemental forms at this time.

**23-54** *Tax Return Problem.* During 2010, Lisa Cutter and Jeff McMullen decided they would like to start their own gourmet hamburger business. Lisa and Jeff believed that the public would love the recipes used by Lisa's mom, Tina Woodbrook. They also thought that they had the necessary experience to enter this business, since Jeff currently owned a fast-food franchise business while Lisa had experience operating a small bakery. After doing their own market research, they established Slattery's Inc. and elected to be taxed as an S corporation. The company's address is 5432 Partridge Pl., Tulsa, Oklahoma 74105 and its employer identification number is 88-7654321.

The company started modestly. After refurbishing an old gas station that it had purchased, the company opened for business on February 25, 2010. Shortly after business began, however, business boomed. By the end of 2010, the company had established two other locations.

Slattery's has three shareholders who own stock as follows:

| Shareholder | Shares |
|---|---|
| Lisa Cutter | 500 |
| Jeff McMullen | 200 |
| Tina Woodbrook | 300 |
| Total outstanding | 1,000 |

Slattery's was formed on February 1, 2010. On that date, shareholders made contributions as follows:

- Lisa Cutter contributed $30,000 in cash and 200 shares of MND stock, a publicly held company, which had a fair market value of $20,000. Lisa had purchased the MND stock on October 3, 1999 for $8,000.
- Jeff McMullen contributed equipment worth $35,000 and with a basis of $29,000.
- Tina Woodbrook contributed $30,000 in cash.

Assume 2010 depreciation for tax purposes is $11,500, and omit the detailed computations for depreciations from Form 4562.

The company is on the accrual basis and has chosen to use the calendar year for tax purposes. Its adjusted trial balance for *financial accounting* purposes reveals the following information:

| | *Debit* | *Credit* |
|---|---|---|
| Cash | $270,700 | |
| Ending inventory | 16,000 | |
| Equipment | 35,000 | |
| Land | 10,000 | |
| Building | 15,000 | |
| Improvements to building | 55,000 | |
| Accumulated depreciation | | $ 9,000 |
| Notes payable | | 78,000 |
| Accounts payable | | 40,000 |
| Taxes payable | | 8,000 |
| Salaries payable | | 20,000 |
| Capital stock | | 115,000 |
| Sales | | 400,000 |
| Gain on sale of MND stock | | 18,000 |
| Dividend from MND Corporation | | 2,000 |
| Cost of goods sold | 84,000 | |
| Legal expenses | 6,000 | |
| Accounting expenses | 4,000 | |
| Miscellaneous expenses | 2,100 | |
| Premium on life insurance policy | 800 | |
| Advertising | 8,600 | |
| Utilities | 8,000 | |
| Payroll taxes | 12,500 | |
| Salary expenses | 120,000 | |
| Insurance | 9,000 | |
| Repairs | 6,500 | |
| Charitable contributions | 17,600 | |
| Depreciation per books | 9,000 | |
| Interest expense | 200 | |

The company has provided additional information below.

The company took a physical count of inventory at the end of the year and determined that ending inventory was $16,000. Ten percent of the notes payable are due each year for the next ten years.

The legal costs were for work done by Slattery's attorney in February for drafting the articles of incorporation and by-laws. Accounting fees were paid in May for setting up the books and the accounting system. Miscellaneous expenses included a one-time $100 fee paid in February to the State of Oklahoma to incorporate.

The MND stock was sold for $38,000 on April. Shortly before the sale, MND had declared and paid a dividend. Slattery's received $2,000 on April 1. MND was incorporated in Delaware.

Slattery's has elected not to use the limited expensing provisions of Code § 179 but has otherwise claimed the maximum depreciation with respect to all assets. Any other elections required to minimize the corporation's tax liability were made.

Lisa Cutter (Social Security No. 447-52-7943) is president of the corporation and spends 90 percent of her working time in the business. She received a salary of $60,000. No other officers received compensation. Social security numbers are 306-28-6192 for Jeff and 403-34-6771 for Tina. The life insurance policy covers Lisa's life, and she has the right to name the beneficiary.

Prepare Form 1120S and other appropriate forms and schedules for Slattery's. On separate schedule(s), show all calculations used to determine all reported amounts except those for which the source is obvious or which are shown on a formal schedule to be filed with the return. If information is missing to answer a question on the return, make up an answer and circle it.

## TAX RESEARCH PROBLEMS

**23-55** *Expanding an S Corporation.* L Inc., an S corporation, manufactures computers. Most of its computers are sold through individually owned retail computer stores. This year it decided it wanted to expand its operations into the retail market. To this end, it has decided to acquire Micros Unlimited, which operates a chain of computer retail stores nationwide.

If L Inc. acquires all of the stock of Micro, may it operate Micro as a C corporation? May it operate Micro as a QSub? What would be some major considerations with each form of business?

**23-56** *Basis and Losses.* J and K, individuals, are equal shareholders in JK, Inc., an S corporation. For the current year, the corporation anticipates a loss of approximately $200,000. Neither shareholder has any substantial stock basis. The corporation has a $200,000 loan from First National Bank. J and K have personally guaranteed the loan. They are concerned about their ability to deduct the loss in the current year. Please advise if they have debt basis due to the current arrangement. If they do not have basis, explain how they might create basis without any outlay of additional funds.

***Research aids:***

Raynor, 50 T.C. 762 (1968).
Rev. Rul. 75-144, 1975-1 C.B. 277.

**23-57** *Losses and Basis.*Q, an individual, is the sole shareholder of QR Corporation, an S corporation. In past years, Q's losses have exceeded her basis by $100,000. Now QR Corporation is insolvent and is $100,000 in debt. The lenders realize that they will have no possibility of collecting the full amount and are writing down the $100,000. After the debt reduction, QR will not be solvent. QR's tax advisors have told Q that the write-down of debt will not result in taxable income to QR due to the insolvency exception of § 108. Q understands that tax-exempt income flows through to shareholders in S corporations and increases stock basis. She asks you to find out if any income realized by QR due to the cancellation of debt will give her basis to deduct her prior suspended losses.

***Research aids:***

§ 108(d)(7).
Reg. § 1.1366-1(a)(2)(viii).

**23-58** *Distribution Problems.*Dr. A has operated his medical practice as a sole proprietor. He has heard that there is no self-employment income passing through from an S corporation to a shareholder. He has also heard that distributions from corporations are not subject to social security tax. Accordingly, he intends to incorporate his medical practice. He will take no salary or other compensation for his services. Instead, he will cause the corporation to declare dividends each quarter and withdraw the profits as distributions from the corporation. He believes he will not be subject to self-employment tax or social security tax. Do you see any problems with this scheme?

***Research aid:***

Rev. Rul. 74-44, 1974-1 C.B. 287.

# Family Tax Planning

PART 9

**CHAPTER 24** The Federal Transfer Taxes

**CHAPTER 25** Income Taxation of Estates and Trusts

**CHAPTER 26** Family Tax Planning

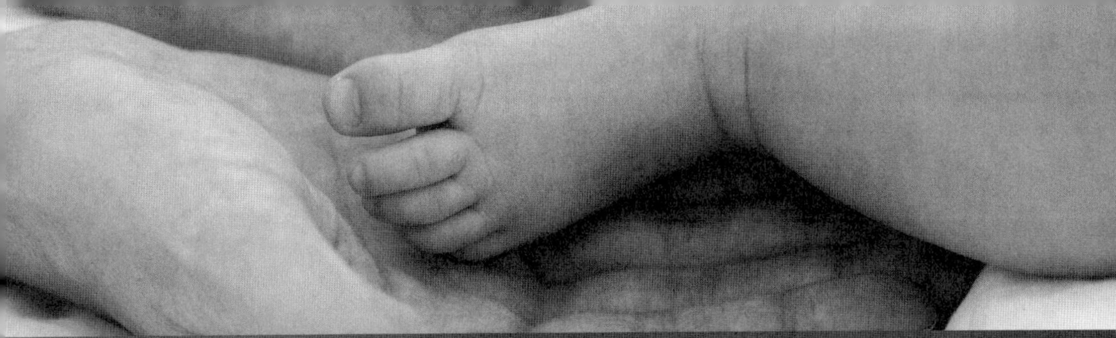

# 24

# The Federal Transfer Taxes

## Learning Objectives

Upon completion of this chapter you will be able to:

LO.1 Characterize the types of transfers that are subject to the Federal gift tax.

LO.2 Compute a donor's total taxable gifts for the current year, including:

- Determination of all available annual exclusions.
- Calculation of any available marital or charitable deduction.

LO.3 Explain the mechanics of the calculation of the gift tax, including the role of the unified credit.

LO.4 List the three basic steps involved in the computation of a decedent's taxable estate.

LO.5 Specify the various types of property interests that must be valued for inclusion in a decedent's gross estate.

LO.6 Describe any deductions from the gross estate.

LO.7 Explain the mechanics of the calculation of the estate tax, including the role of the unified credit.

LO.8 Discuss the purpose of the generation skipping transfer tax.

## Chapter Outline


Introduction 24-2
- History and Overview 24-2

Property Interests 24-3
- Forms of Co-Ownership 24-4
- Life Estates, Reversions, and Remainders 24-4

The Gift Tax 24-5
- Transfers Subject to Tax 24-6
- Valuation 24-7
- Basis 24-9
- The Gift Tax Exclusion 24-9
- Gift Splitting 24-10
- Gifts to Political and Charitable Organizations 24-10
- The Gift Tax Marital Deduction 24-10
- Computation and Filing 24-11
- The Overlap between the Gift and Estate Taxes 24-13

Transfers of Property at Death 24-14
- Role of a Will 24-14
- Intestacy 24-14
- Probate 24-14

The Taxable Estate 24-15

The Gross Estate Concept 24-16

Valuation of Gross Estate and Basis 24-16
Basis 24-18
Special Use Valuation: § 2032A 24-18
Gross Estate Inclusions 24-19
Insurance on the Life of the Decedent 24-19
Survivor Benefits 24-19
Joint Interests 24-20
General Powers of Appointment 24-20
Transfers Taking Effect at Death 24-22
Gifts in Contemplation of Death 24-24
Transfers for Insufficient Consideration 24-24
Deductions from the Gross Estate 24-25
Expenses, Indebtedness, and Taxes 24-25
Losses 24-26
State Death Taxes 24-27
Charitable Contributions 24-27
The Marital Deduction 24-28
Computation of the Estate Tax 24-29
Estate Tax Credits 24-30
A Comprehensive Example 24-31
Payment of the Estate Tax 24-32
The Generation-Skipping Transfer Tax 24-34
Tax Planning Considerations 24-34
Problem Materials 24-35


## Introduction

Since 1916 Congress has imposed taxes aimed solely at an individual's transfer of wealth: the estate tax (1916), the gift tax (1932), and the generation-skipping transfer tax (1976). As a practical matter, these taxes have produced relatively little revenue—about 1 percent of total revenues—and affected few individuals—also around 1 percent. Despite their limited impact, the taxes have survived. However, with the inauguration of President Bush in 2001, it appeared that the estate tax itself was about to die. Under the Economic Growth and Tax Relief Reconciliation Act of 2001, the estate tax—but not the gift tax—was scheduled for repeal in 2010. As a practical matter, most believed that repeal would never happen and ultimately Congress would reach some type of compromise that would extend the estate tax in some modified form. But, the unthinkable did occur and the estate tax was repealed—but only for one year, 2010. The Tax Relief, Unemployment Insurance Reauthorization, and Job Creation Act of 2010 resurrected the estate tax but only for 2011 and 2012, leaving everyone to wonder what will happen in 2013.[1]

### History and Overview

The estate tax became a permanent part of the tax system in 1916. In short, it is merely an excise tax on the transfer of the decedent's *net* wealth (fair market value of total assets less debts and expenses) that passes to his or her heirs at death. For example, if a taxpayer dies with a home worth $1,000,000 and a mortgage of $200,000, he or she is potentially taxed on the net amount of $800,000. Whether or not the taxpayer is actually taxed on such amount depends in part on a number of variables including who receives the property. For example, the law currently provides deductions for transfers to a spouse or qualifying charitable organizations.

Shortly after the enactment of the estate tax it became clear that without additional rules a taxpayer could easily avoid the estate tax simply by giving away property before he or she died. As might be expected, to prevent full scale avoidance of the estate tax Congress enacted a gift tax in 1924. A unique feature of the gift tax is the fact that unlike the income tax where the current year's tax is based on the current's year's income, the gift tax is computed on the cumulative amount of gifts made by an individual during his or her lifetime. Because of the progressive transfer tax rates, this approach makes every gift more expensive in terms of tax dollars than the last. Another important characteristic of the gift tax is the annual exclusion. To eliminate the vast administrative problems that would result if the gift tax were imposed on all gifts (e.g., birthday and Christmas presents) the gift tax is imposed only on those that exceed a certain threshold, currently $13,000 (2011) per donee per year.

Until 1976, the estate and gift tax were separate and distinct taxes. Although both taxes imposed a tax on transfers of wealth, one on lifetime transfers and one on transfers at death,

[1] Recent IRS statistics indicate the number of estate tax returns filed decreased from 130,000 in 2000 to 22,000 in 2006, but collections increased to $24 billion. Measured as a percent of deaths, taxable estates fell from 1.86% to .7% or seven for every thousand deaths. Net collections derived from the estate and gift taxes totaled $28 billion in 2006, representing 1.2% of total federal revenue.

they differed in several important ways. One important difference could be found in the rate structures. For many years, the gift tax rates were 25 percent less than estate tax rates, presumably to encourage taxpayers to transfer their assets during their lifetime rather than hoarding them until death. Another difference involved the amount of transfers exempted from tax. The gift tax had its own lifetime exemption of $30,000 while the estate tax exemption was $60,000. Any of the exemption for gifts that was not used during the taxpayer's lifetime could not be carried over and used at death but was lost. Another distinction concerned the tax computation. Transfers made during the taxpayer's lifetime (i.e., taxable gifts) did not enter into the calculation of the tax on the taxpayer's transfers at death (i.e., the taxable estate). However, these distinctions came to an end with the passage of the Tax Reform Act of 1976 when the two taxes were unified. Although current practice still refers to these transfer taxes as the estate tax and the gift tax, they are really part of what is a unified transfer tax system.

The unification of the estate and gift tax eliminated the differences between the two taxes, completely integrating the two systems into the one that exists today. The new law replaced the two separate rate schedules with a single, unified transfer tax rate schedule used to compute both the estate and the gift tax. Moreover, since 1976 a decedent's taxable estate is effectively treated as an individual's final taxable gift. This is accomplished by computing the estate tax on a base that includes not only the taxable estate but also any taxable gifts made during the decedent's life. The changes in 1976 also replaced the separate exemptions with a single unified credit. The credit is unified in the sense that whatever amount is used to offset the gift tax during life is unavailable to reduce the estate tax at death. For 2011, the exemption for both the estate tax and gift tax is $5,000,000.

Another change made in 1976 was the introduction of a third Federal transfer tax on generation-skipping transfers. This tax, designed to complement the gift and estate taxes, is quite complex and highly controversial. It is discussed later in this chapter.

The Economic Recovery Tax Act of 1981 (ERTA 1981) continued the restructuring of the transfer tax system begun in 1976. The most important feature of this legislation was the unlimited marital deduction. This deduction makes gifts between spouses completely nontaxable and allows the first spouse to die to leave the family wealth to the surviving spouse at no Federal transfer tax cost. Thus, after 1981, the taxable unit for the imposition of the gift or estate tax is no longer the individual but the marital unit.

As noted above, Congress allowed the estate tax to expire for one year in 2010. Under the Tax Relief, Unemployment Insurance Reauthorization, and Job Creation Act of 2010, estates for those dying in 2010 could elect *not* to pay the estate tax, in which case the heirs had to accept the modified carryover basis rules of § 1022. Estates that did not elect and did nothing were subject to the revised rules. These rules essentially exempted taxpayers with net wealth of $5,000,000 ($10,000,000 for married couples) from the estate tax. In addition, the basis of property passing to their heirs normally would be its fair market value at date of death.

## Property Interests

Since the estate and gift taxes concern transfers of property, understanding the two taxes requires an appreciation of the nature of property interests and the different forms of property ownership. In the United States, each of the 50 states has its own system of *property law*—statutory rules that govern an individual's right to own and convey both real and personal property during his or her lifetime. Unfortunately, the specific property laws of each state vary considerably and therefore generalizations about property laws can be dangerous. However, the various state legal systems can be divided into two basic categories: *common law systems* and *community property systems*. The common law system, derived from English laws of property ownership, focuses on individual ownership of assets, regardless of the marital status of the individual. This system has been adopted in 41 states. The community property system is a derivation of Spanish property law and is followed in nine states: Arizona, California, Idaho, Louisiana, Nevada, New Mexico, Texas, Washington, and Wisconsin. Under either system, an individual may own property alone or jointly with another. In addition, an individual may own only a partial interest in the property such as an income interest. The different forms of co-ownership and various types of partial interests are considered below.

## Forms of Co-Ownership

The consequences of holding property jointly with another can vary substantially, depending on the type of co-ownership. There are four forms of co-ownership: (1) tenancy in common, (2) joint tenancy, (3) tenancy by the entirety, and (4) community property ownership.

### Tenancy in Common

A tenancy in common exists when two or more persons hold title to property, each owning an undivided fractional interest in the whole. The percentage of the property owned by one tenant need not be the same as the other co-tenants but can differ as the co-tenants provide. The most important feature of this type of property interest is that it is treated in virtually all respects like property that is owned outright. Thus, the interest can be sold, gifted, willed, or, when there is no will, passed to the owner's heirs according to the laws of the state. Another important characteristic of a tenancy in common is the *right of partition*. This right permits co-owners who disagree over something concerning the property to go to court to secure a division of the property among the owners. In some cases, however, a physical division is impossible (e.g., 50 acres of land where each acre's value is dependent on the whole), and consequently, the property must be sold with the proceeds split between the owners.

### Joint Tenancy

Under a joint tenancy arrangement, two or more persons hold title to property, each owning the same fractional interest in the property. Joint tenancy normally implies the right of survivorship (joint tenancy with right of survivorship, or JTWROS). This means that upon the death of one joint tenant, the property automatically passes to the surviving joint tenants. Consequently, the disposition of the property is *not* controlled by the decedent's will. Like tenants in common, joint tenants have the right to sever their interest in the property. This is a particularly valuable right since the tenant may wish to disinherit the other joint tenants.

### Tenancy by the Entirety

A tenancy by the entirety is a JTWROS between husband and wife. The critical difference between a tenancy by the entirety and a JTWROS is that in most states a spouse cannot sever his or her interest without the consent of the other spouse. In addition, in some states the husband has full control over the property while alive and is entitled to all the income from it.

### Community Property

In a community property system, married individuals own an equal, undivided interest in all wealth acquired during the course of the marriage, regardless of which spouse made any individual contribution to the marital wealth. In addition to a half interest in such "community property," a spouse may also own property in an individual capacity as "separate property." Generally, assets acquired prior to marriage and assets received by gift or inheritance are separate property. However, in all nine community property states there exists a strong legal presumption that all property possessed during marriage is community, and that presumption can only be overcome by convincing proof of the property's separate nature.

### Marital Property

Before leaving the subject of joint ownership, the concept of marital property deserves attention. Except in community property states, it is a common mistake to assume that all property acquired during marriage is jointly held. State laws vary widely on this issue. In some states, only property specifically titled as JTWROS is treated as jointly held. In these and other states, it is not unusual that property acquired during marriage belongs to the husband regardless of whose earnings were used to acquire the property. In other states, each spouse is deemed to own that which can be traced to his or her own earnings. Because of the problems with marital property, transfers of such property should be evaluated carefully to ensure that the rights of either spouse are not violated.

## Life Estates, Reversions, and Remainders

Persons who own property outright have virtually unlimited rights with respect to their property. They can sell it, mortgage it, or transfer it as they wish. In addition, they can divide the ownership of the property in any number of ways. In this regard, it is not uncommon for property owners to transfer ownership in property to someone temporarily. During the period of temporary ownership, the beneficiary could have the right to use, possess, and benefit from the income of the property. Assuming that the beneficiary's interest is limited to the income from the property, he or she would be treated as having an *income interest*. The time to which the beneficiary is entitled to the income from the property could be specified in any terms, such as common measures of time: days, weeks, months, or years. Alternatively, the time period could be determined by reference to the occurrence of a specific event. For example, when an individual has an income interest for life, the interest is referred to as a life estate. In this case, the person entitled to the *life estate* is called the life tenant.

The owner of property has the right to provide for one or more temporary interests, subject only to the *rule against perpetuities*. This rule requires that the property pass outright to an individual within a certain time period after the transfer. Normally, ownership of the property must vest at a date no later than 21 years after the death of persons alive at the time the interest is created.

Interestingly, a few states have recently repealed the rule. For example, trusts in Alaska, Delaware, Washington D.C., Illinois, New Jersey, South Dakota, Virginia and Wisconsin can now be designed to last forever. Trusts in Utah and Wyoming can last for up to 1,000 years while those in Florida must end after 360 years.

After any temporary interests have been designated, the owner has the right to provide for the outright transfer of the property. If the owner specifies that the property should be returned to the owner or his or her estate, the interest following the temporary interest is referred to as a *reversionary interest*. If the property passes to someone other than the owner, the interest is called a *remainder interest*. The holder of the remainder interest is the *remainderman*.

Life estates, remainders, and reversions are property interests that can be transferred, sold, and willed (except for life estates) like other types of property. These interests can also be reached by creditors in satisfaction of their claims. However, a person can establish a trust with so-called *spendthrift* provisions, which prohibit the beneficiary from assigning or selling his or her interest (e.g., a life estate) or using the assets to satisfy creditors.

## The Gift Tax

The statutory provisions regarding the Federal gift tax are contained in §§ 2501 through 2524 of the Internal Revenue Code. These rules provide the basis for the gift tax formula found in Exhibit 24-1. The various elements of this formula are discussed below.

**EXHIBIT 24.1 Computation of Federal Gift Tax Liability**

| | | |
|---|---|---|
| Fair market value of all gifts made in the current year | | $xxx,xxx |
| Less the sum of | | |
| Annual exclusions ($13,000 per donee in 2011) | $xx,xxx | |
| Marital deduction | xx,xxx | |
| Charitable deduction | x,xxx | −xx,xxx |
| Taxable gifts for current year | | $xxx,xxx |
| Plus: All taxable gifts made in prior years | | +xx,xxx |
| Taxable transfers to date | | $xxx,xxx |
| Tentative tax on total transfers to date | | $ xx,xxx |
| Less the sum of | | |
| Gift taxes computed at current rates on prior years' taxable gifts | $ x,xxx | |
| Unified transfer tax credit | x,xxx | −xx,xxx |
| Gift tax due on current gifts | | $ xx,xxx |

## Transfers Subject to Tax

**LO.1**
Characterize the types of transfers that are subject to the Federal gift tax.

Section 2511 states that the gift tax shall apply to transfers in trust or otherwise, whether the gift is direct or indirect, real or personal, tangible or intangible. The gift tax is imposed only on transfers of property; gratuitous transfers of services are not subject to tax.[2] The types of property interests to which the gift tax applies are virtually unlimited. The tax applies to transfers of such common items as money, cars, stocks, bonds, jewelry, works of art, houses, and every other type of item normally considered property. It should be emphasized that no property is specifically excluded from the gift tax. For example, the transfer of municipal bonds is subject to the gift tax, even though the income from the bonds is tax free.

The gift tax reaches transfers of partial interests as well. One example is a transfer of property in trust where the income interest is given to someone—the income beneficiary—for his or her life, while the trust property or remainder interest is given to another person—the remainderman—upon the income beneficiary's death. In this case, the donor would be treated as having made two separate gifts, a gift of the income interest and a gift of the remainder interest.

The application of the gift tax to both direct and indirect gifts ensures that the tax reaches all transfers regardless of the method of transfer. Direct gifts encompass the common types of outright transfers (e.g., father transfers bonds to daughter, or grandmother gives cash to grandson). On the other hand, indirect gifts are represented primarily by transfers to trusts and other entities. When a transfer is made to a trust, it is considered a gift to the beneficiaries of the trust. Similarly, a transfer to a corporation or partnership is considered a gift to the shareholders or partners. However, if the donor owns an interest in a partnership or corporation, he or she is not treated as making a gift to the extent it would be a gift to himself or herself. An individual may also be treated as making a gift if he or she refuses to accept property and the property passes to another person on account of the refusal.

Most taxpayers understand that the gift tax is imposed on transfers of property motivated by affection and generosity. However, the tax may also be imposed on a transfer of property not intended as a gift within the commonly accepted definition of the word. The tax is intended to apply to any transfer of wealth by an individual that reduces his or her potential taxable estate. Therefore, § 2512 provides that any transfer of property, in return for which the transferor receives *less than adequate or full consideration* in money or money's worth, is a transfer subject to the gift tax.

### Adequate Consideration

Revenue Ruling 79-384 provides an excellent example of a transfer for insufficient consideration.[3] The taxpayer in the ruling was a father, who had made an oral promise to his son to pay him $10,000 upon the son's graduation from college. The son graduated but the father refused to pay him the promised amount. The son then successfully sued the father, who was forced to transfer the $10,000. The IRS ruled that the father had received no consideration in money or money's worth for the transfer and therefore had made a taxable gift to his son.

Revenue Ruling 79-384 illustrates two important concepts. First, *donative intent* on the part of a transferor of property is *not necessary* to classify the transfer as a taxable gift.[4] Second, anything received by the transferor in exchange for the property must be subject to valuation in monetary terms if it is to be consideration within the meaning of § 2512.[5] The father did receive the satisfaction resulting from his son's graduation, and this consideration was sufficient to create an enforceable oral contract between father and son. However, because the consideration could not be objectively valued in dollar terms it was irrelevant for tax purposes.

The question of sufficiency of consideration normally arises when transfers of assets are made between family members or related parties. When properties are transferred or exchanged in a bona fide business transaction, the Regulations specify that sufficiency of consideration will be presumed because of the arm's-length negotiation between the parties.[6]

Transfers of wealth to dependent family members that represent support are not taxable gifts. The distinction between support payments and gifts is far from clear, particularly when the transferor is not legally obligated to make the payments. Section 2503(e) specifies that

---

[2] Rev. Rul. 56-472, 1956-2 C.B. 21.

[3] 1979-2 C.B. 12.

[4] Reg. § 25.2511-1(g)(1).

[5] Reg. § 25.2512-8.

[6] *Ibid.*

amounts paid on behalf of any individual for tuition to an educational organization or for medical care shall not be considered taxable gifts to such individual. However, this rule only applies if the payments are made directly to the educational institution or the health care provider.

Payments that a divorced taxpayer is legally required to make for the *support* of his or her former spouse are not taxable gifts.[7] However, Regulation § 25.2512-8 specifies that payments made prior to or after marriage in return for the recipient's relinquishment of his or her *marital property rights* are transfers for insufficient consideration and subject to the gift tax. Section 2516 provides an exception to this rule. If a transfer of property is made under the terms of a written agreement between spouses and the transfer is (1) in settlement of the spouse's marital property rights, or (2) to provide a reasonable allowance for support of any minor children of the marriage, no taxable gift will occur. For the exception to apply, divorce must occur within the three-year period beginning on the date one year before such agreement is entered into.

### Retained Interest

The final criterion of a taxable transfer is that the transfer must be complete. A transfer is considered complete only if the donor has surrendered all control over the property. For this reason, when the donor alone retains the right to revoke the transfer, the transfer is incomplete and the gift tax does not apply. For example, creation of a joint bank account is not considered a completed gift since the depositor is free to withdraw the money deposited in the account. Similarly, the donor must not be able to redirect ownership of the property in the future; nonetheless, to have a completed gift it is not necessary that the donees have received the property or that the specific donees even be identified.[8]

#### Example 1

Donor D transfers $1 million into an irrevocable trust with an independent trustee. The trustee has the right to pay the income of the trust to beneficiaries A, B, or C *or* to accumulate the income. After 15 years, the trust will terminate and all accumulated income and principal will be divided among the surviving beneficiaries. Because D has parted with all control over the $1 million, it is a completed gift, even though neither A, B, or C has received or is guaranteed any specified portion of the money.

## Valuation

The value of a transfer subject to the Federal gift tax is measured by the fair market value of the property transferred less the value of any consideration received by the transferor. Determining fair market value can be the most difficult aspect of computing a gift tax due. Fair market value is defined in the Regulations as "the price at which such property would change hands between a willing buyer and a willing seller, neither being under any compulsion to buy or to sell, and both having reasonable knowledge of relevant facts."[9]

The determination of an asset's fair market value must be made on the basis of all relevant facts and circumstances. The Regulations under § 2512 are quite detailed and extremely useful in that they prescribe methods for valuation of a variety of assets.

#### Example 2

Donor S transfers 10 shares of the publicly traded common stock of XYZ Corporation on June 8, 2011. On that date, the highest quoted selling price of the stock was $53 per share. The lowest quoted selling price was $48 per share. Regulation § 25.2512-2(b)(1) specifies that the fair market value of the XYZ stock on June 8, 2011 shall be the mean between the highest and lowest quoted selling price [($53 + $48) ÷ 2], or $50.50 per share.

---

[7] Rev. Rul. 68-379, 1968-2 C.B. 414.

[8] Reg. § 25.2511-2(a).

[9] Reg. § 25.2512-1.

### Valuation of Income and Remainder Interests

In estate planning, it is quite common for individuals to make gifts of only a partial interest of property. These arrangements usually involve transfers to a trust such as the following:

- An individual transfers property to a trust, giving away an income interest to one beneficiary and a remainder interest to another beneficiary. In this case, the taxpayer has actually made two gifts—the income interest and the remainder interest—each of which must be valued for gift tax purposes.
- An individual transfers property to a trust, retaining the income interest and giving away the remainder interest. Here there is only a single gift of the remainder interest.
- An individual transfers property to a trust, giving the income interest to a beneficiary but providing that the remainder interest reverts or returns to the individual once the income interest has expired. In this case, the taxpayer has made a single gift of the income interest.

Gifts of income and remainder interests are valued using actuarial tables. These tables take into consideration current interest rates and, if necessary, current mortality rates. In valuing the various types of transfers, the tables assume that property transferred produces income at a certain rate, regardless of the actual amount of income that is produced.

For transfers after April 30, 1989, § 7520 requires valuations using the interest rate prevailing at the time of the transfer. Specifically, the rate to be used is 120 percent of the applicable Federal midterm rate in effect under § 1274(d)(1) for the month in which the transfer is made. These rates are published monthly. Using the appropriate rate, the values can be found in actuarial tables published by the IRS. The tables were first issued in 1989 in Notice 89-60.[10] Section 7520(c)(3) requires that the tables be revised at least once every 10 years thereafter to reflect the most recent mortality experience available. They were most recently revised in 2009 and can be found in IRS Publications 1457, 1458 or 1459.[11] These three massive volumes provide factors for interest rates of 2.2 percent to 26 percent and annuity factors for ages 0–110. The IRS issues monthly announcements indicating which of these tables applies for the month.[12] For example, the § 7520 rate for January, 2011 was 2.4 percent.[13] Table S shows the factors for determining the value of an annuity, a life estate, or a remainder interest based on a single life. Table B shows the factors for determining the value of an annuity, a life estate or a remainder interest for a term of years Selected portions of the tables can be found in Appendix A in this book.

In examining the tables, observe that if the value of the property is split between an income interest and a remainder interest, there are two factors and the sum of those two factors equals one. In a case where the remainder factor is known but the income factor is unknown or vice-versa, the income factor can be determined as follows:

$$\text{Income factor} = 1.000000 - \text{Remainder factor}$$

#### Example 3

In May, 20X9, H transferred $100,000 to a trust for his son, S, and his grandson, GS. According to the terms of the trust, S is to receive the income for life and upon his death, the remainder is to be paid to GS, if living, otherwise to GS's estate. S was 40 years old at the time the trust was created. H has made two gifts. The value of S's income interest is a function of three factors determined at the time of the gift:

[10] 1989-1 C.B. 700.

[11] IRS Publication 1457, Actuarial Values, Aleph Volume (2001), Version 3A (2009); IRS Publication 1458, Actuarial Values, Beth Volume (2001), Version 3B (2009); IRS Publication 1459, Actuarial Values, Gimel Volume (2001), Version 3A (2009). The rates can be found at the following IRS website: http://www.irs.gov/retirement/article/0,,id=206601,00.html.

[12] These rates are published monthly. For transfers after December 31, 1970 and before December 1, 1983 the interest rate used to compute the value of reversions and other interests was six percent. The factors can be found in the appropriate table contained in Reg § 20.2031-10(f). For transfers after November 30, 1983, and before May 1, 1989, the interest rate used to compute the value of reversions and other interests was 10 percent.

[13] Rev. Rul. 2011-2, 2011-2 IRB 12/22/2010.

(1) S's life expectancy, (2) the current interest rate, and (3) the value of the trust property. Assume the applicable rate for valuing the interest is five percent (120% of the May Federal mid-term rate). Using the table for valuing a remainder interest (Table S in Appendix A-1), the value of the remainder interest is \$18,619 (\$100,000 × .18619). The value of the income interest is \$81,381 [\$100,000 × (1 − .19516 = .81381)]. Note that thc sum of the remainder interest and the income interest equals the total value of the property.

### Example 4

In June, 20X2, M transferred \$100,000 to a trust for her daughter, D. Under the terms of the trust, D is to receive the income for 20 years at which time the trust will terminate and the property will revert to M. Assume the applicable rate for valuing the interest is 5.2% (120% of the June Federal mid-term rate). In this case, the factor for the income interest must be determined by subtracting the factor for the remainder interest from 1. Using the table for valuing a term certain remainder interest (Table B in Appendix A-2), the value of D's income interest for 20 years is \$63,719 (\$100,000 × .637185).

The valuation of a gift of a partial interest in property is subject to special rules when the donor retains an income interest. These rules are considered in Chapter 26 in conjunction with the discussion on special estate planning techniques [e.g., grantor retained income trusts, annuity trusts, and unitrusts (GRITS, GRATS, and GRUTS)].

## Basis

The basis of an asset in the hands of a donee is calculated under the rules of § 1015. Generally, the basis of property received as a gift is the basis of the asset in the hands of the donor, increased by the amount of any gift tax paid attributable to the excess of fair market value over the donor's basis at the date of gift. This general rule applies only if the asset is sold at a gain by the donee. If the carryover basis rule would result in a realized loss upon subsequent sale, the basis of the asset will be considered the *lesser* of the carryover basis (donor's basis) *or* the asset's fair market value at date of gift. If the asset is sold at a price greater than the fair market value at date of gift but less than its carryover basis, no gain or loss is recognized.

## The Gift Tax Exclusion

When the gift tax was enacted in 1932, Congress wanted to "eliminate the necessity of keeping an account of and reporting numerous small gifts." To this end, it created an annual exclusion designed to exempt gifts under a certain threshold from the gift tax.[14] The annual exclusion was initially set at \$3,000 until it was raised to \$10,000 in 1981 where it remained through 2001. Starting in 2002, the exclusion has been adjusted for inflation. For 2002–2005, the exclusion was \$11,000. For 2006 through 2008, the exclusion was \$12,000. For 2009 through 2011 the exclusion is \$13,000.

**LO.2**
Compute a donor's total taxable gifts for the current year, including:
- Determination of all available annual exclusions.
- Calculation of any available marital or charitable deduction.

A donor is entitled to exclude \$13,000 (2011) per year per donee. However, not all gifts are eligible for the annual exclusion. Congress was concerned about the problems that could arise in determining the number of exclusions when there was only a remote possibility that a donee would receive a gift (e.g., remote and contingent beneficiaries). For this reason, to qualify for the exclusion the gift must constitute a *present* interest. Regulation § 25.2503-3(b) defines a present interest as one that gives the donee "an unrestricted right to the immediate use, possession, or enjoyment of property or the income from property." Therefore, the annual exclusion is not available for a gift that can only be enjoyed by the donee at some future date, even if the donee receives a present ownership interest in the gift.

[14] § 2503(b).

### Example 5

Donor D gifts real estate worth \$20,000 to donees M and N. M is given a *life* estate (the right to the income from the property for as long as M lives) worth \$8,000. N receives *the remainder interest* (complete ownership of the property upon the death of M) worth \$12,000. Although both M and N have received legal property interests, D may claim only one exclusion for his gift to M. The gift to N is a gift of a future rather than a present interest. Thus D has made a taxable gift of \$12,000.

Securing the tax benefit of the annual exclusion can be difficult if the gift in question is made to a minor or an incapacitated donee. In such cases, the donor may be reluctant to give an unrestricted present interest in the donated property. Strategies for making gifts to minors or incapacitated donees is included in Chapter 26.

## Gift Splitting

A gift made by a married individual residing in a community property state may have two donors (husband and wife) because of state property law. Property laws in the 41 non-community property states do not produce this *two donor* result. To compensate for this difference, § 2513 provides a *gift splitting* election to a married donor.

If a donor makes the proper election on his or her current gift tax return, one-half of all gifts made during the year will be considered to have been made by the donor's spouse. Both spouses must consent to gift splitting for the election to be valid. Since evidence of the spouse's consent is necessary when gift splitting is used, a gift tax return must be filed.

### Example 6

In 2011, husband H gives \$100,000 to his son and \$100,000 to his daughter. His wife, W, makes a gift of \$5,000 to their daughter. H and W elect gift splitting on their current gift tax returns. As a result, H reports a gift to the daughter of \$52,500 (\$50,000 + \$2,500) and a gift to the son of \$50,000, and will claim two \$13,000 gift tax exclusions, resulting in total taxable gifts of \$76,500 (\$52,500 + \$50,000 – \$26,000). W will report exactly the same gifts and claim two \$13,000 exclusions, resulting in the same amount of taxable gifts as her husband H, \$76,000, for a total of \$152,000.

Without gift splitting, H would still be entitled to \$26,000 of exclusions, but W could only claim an exclusion of \$5,000 for her gift to the daughter. Without splitting, H and W would have total taxable gifts of \$174,000 compared to \$152,000 with splitting. By splitting, the couple is able to increase the exclusions by \$22,000 (\$13,000 for the gift to the son and \$9,000 for the gift to the daughter).

## Gifts to Political and Charitable Organizations

Code § 2501(a)(5) excludes gifts of money or other property to a political organization from the statutory definition of taxable transfers. If a gratuitous donation is made to a qualified charitable organization, § 2522 provides a deduction for such gift from the donor's taxable gifts for the calendar year. Thus, transfers made without sufficient consideration to qualifying political or charitable groups are not subject to the Federal gift tax.

## The Gift Tax Marital Deduction

Under § 2523, gifts to spouses are fully deductible by the donor. The marital deduction is permitted only if certain requirements are satisfied. A full discussion of these requirements is considered in conjunction with the discussion of the marital deduction for estate tax purposes.

The gift tax marital deduction allows an individual to make tax-free transfers of wealth to his or her spouse. This opportunity to equalize the wealth owned by husband and wife plays an essential role in family tax planning, a role that will be discussed in Chapter 26.

## Computation and Filing

Unlike the income tax, which is computed on annual taxable income, the Federal gift tax is computed on cumulative taxable gifts made during a donor's lifetime. This is done by adding taxable gifts for the current year to all taxable gifts made in prior years, calculating the gross tax on the sum of cumulative gifts, and subtracting the amount of gift tax calculated on prior years' gifts.[15] The transfer tax rate schedule currently in effect is reproduced in Exhibit 24-2. The maximum estate and gift tax rate has been gradually reduced as follows:

**LO.3**
Explain the mechanics of the calculation of the gift tax, including the role of the unified credit.

| *Year* | *Top Rate* |
|---|---|
| 2002 | 50% |
| 2003 | 49% |
| 2004 | 48% |
| 2005 | 47% |
| 2006 | 46% |
| 2007–09 | 45% |
| 2010–12 | 35% |

**EXHIBIT 24.2** **2010–2012 Estate and Gift Tax Rates**

| *If taxable transfer is* *Over* | *But not over* | *Tax liability* | *Of the amount over* |
|---|---|---|---|
| $ 0 | $ 10,000 | 18% | $ 0 |
| 10,000 | 20,000 | $ 1,800 + 20% | 10,000 |
| 20,000 | 40,000 | 3,800 + 22% | 20,000 |
| 40,000 | 60,000 | 8,200 + 24% | 40,000 |
| 60,000 | 80,000 | 13,000 + 26% | 60,000 |
| 80,000 | 100,000 | 18,200 + 28% | 80,000 |
| 100,000 | 150,000 | 23,800 + 30% | 100,000 |
| 150,000 | 250,000 | 38,800 + 32% | 150,000 |
| 250,000 | 500,000 | 70,800 + 34% | 250,000 |
| | over 500,000 | 155,800 + 35% | |

### Example 7

In 1995, X made his first taxable gift of $100,000 (after the exclusion). The tax (before credits) on this amount was $23,800. X made a second taxable gift of $85,000 in 2011. The tax (before credits) on the second gift is $26,200, computed as follows:

| | |
|---|---|
| 1995 taxable gift | $100,000 |
| 2011 taxable gift | +85,000 |
| Cumulative gifts | $185,000 |
| Tax on $185,000 | $ 50,000 |
| Less: Tax on 1995 taxable gift | −23,800 |
| Tax on 2011 gift | $ 26,200 |

This cumulative system of gift taxation and the progressive rate schedule cause a higher tax on the 2011 gift, even though the 2011 gift was $15,000 *less* than the 1995 gift.

[15] § 2502(a). The amount of gift tax calculated on prior years' gifts is based on current gift tax rates, regardless of the rates in effect when the gifts were actually made.

### Unified Credit

Both the estate and gift tax provisions have long contained exemptions to ensure that the taxes do not apply to modest transfers of wealth. As noted earlier, prior to their unification in 1976, each tax had its own separate exemption: the estate tax provided for an exemption of $60,000 while the gift tax allowed a lifetime exemption of $30,000 for otherwise taxable gifts (i.e., those not otherwise exempt by the annual exclusion). The unification in 1976 led to the creation of the unified credit. The unified credit is a lifetime credit available for offsetting the tax on all taxable transfers (i.e., the taxes imposed on taxable gifts or the taxable estate). In 2011, the credit is $1,730,800 for both the estate tax and gift tax. This gift tax credit of $1,730,800 completely offsets the tax on $5,000,000 of taxable transfers. For example, consider a taxpayer whose first *taxable* gift is $5,000,000. The tax on the $5,000,000 taxable transfer would be $1,730,800. However, the credit of $1,730,800 would completely eliminate the tax, effectively providing an exemption from tax for transfers of up to $5,000,000.

As can be seen in Exhibit 24-3, the amount of the credit has been increased over the years. In 1976, the credit was originally set so that when it was completely phased in by 1981 it would exempt from tax transfers of up to $175,625. However, by 1981, Congress and the Reagan administration viewed that amount as inadequate. Consequently, legislation was passed to gradually increase the credit so that it would reach $192,800 in 1987 where it would exempt $600,000 of transfers from tax. The credit remained at that level for more than 10 years until Congress acted again in the Taxpayer Relief Act of 1997. Beginning in 1998, the credit began to increase gradually. However, before the increase was complete, Congress changed course and moved toward ultimate repeal of the estate tax. From 2004 through 2010, the exemption amounts for the estate tax and the gift tax were no longer the same. The gift tax exemption was set at the $1,000,000 level. On the other hand, the exemption for the estate tax gradually increased to $3,500,000 in 2009. In 2010, Congress addressed the repeal of the

**EXHIBIT 24.3** **Credit and Exemption Equivalent**

| | Credit | | Exemption Equivalent | |
|---|---|---|---|---|
| Year | Estate Tax | Gift Tax | Estate Tax | Gift Tax |
| 1/1/77–6/30/77 | $ 6,000 | Same | $ 30,000 | Same |
| 7/1/77–12/31/77 | 30,000 | Same | 120,666 | Same |
| 1978 | 34,000 | Same | 134,000 | Same |
| 1979 | 38,000 | Same | 147,333 | Same |
| 1980 | 42,500 | Same | 161,563 | Same |
| 1981 | 47,000 | Same | 175,625 | Same |
| 1982 | 62,800 | Same | 225,000 | Same |
| 1983 | 79,300 | Same | 275,000 | Same |
| 1984 | 96,300 | Same | 325,000 | Same |
| 1985 | 121,800 | Same | 400,000 | Same |
| 1986 | 155,800 | Same | 500,000 | Same |
| 1987–97 | 192,800 | Same | 600,000 | Same |
| 1998 | 202,050 | Same | 625,000 | Same |
| 1999 | 211,300 | Same | 650,000 | Same |
| 2000–01 | 220,550 | Same | 675,000 | Same |
| 2002–03 | 345,800 | Same | 1,000,000 | Same |
| 2004–05 | 555,800 | $345,800 | 1,500,000 | $1,000,000 |
| 2006–08 | 780,800 | 345,800 | 2,000,000 | 1,000,000 |
| 2009 | 1,455,800 | 345,800 | 3,500,000 | 1,000,000 |
| 2010 | 1,730,800 | 345,800 | 5,000,000 | 1,000,000 |
| 2011–2012 | 1,730,800 | Same | 5,000,000 | Same |

estate tax. In so doing, it increased the exemption for the estate tax to $5,000,000 but the exemption for the gift tax for 2010 remained at $1,000,000. However, beginning in 2011, the exemptions for the estate and gift tax are united once again at $5,000,000.

The unified credit is the only credit available to offset the Federal gift tax. As noted above, the credit currently offsets the tax on $5,000,000 of taxable gifts. Thus, an individual may make substantial transfers of wealth before any tax liability is incurred. The unified credit must be used when available—a taxpayer may not decide to postpone use of the credit if he or she makes a taxable gift during the current year.[16]

## Example 8

In 1995, Y made her first taxable gift of $350,000. The tax calculated on this gift was $104,800, and Y used $104,800 of her available unified credit so that the actual gift tax due was reduced to zero. In 2011, Y made her second taxable gift of $6,000,000. The tax on this gift is $472,500, computed as follows:

| | | |
|---|---|---|
| Taxable gift for 2011 | | $ 6,000,000 |
| Plus: 1995 taxable gift | | +350,000 |
| Taxable transfers to date | | $ 6,350,000 |
| Tentative 2011 tax on total transfers to date (See Exhibit 24-2) ($155,800 + $2,047,500 [35%($6,350,000 – $500,000 = $5,850,000)] | | $ 2,203,300 |
| Less: Gift taxes calculated on 1995 gift | | –104,800 |
| Tentative tax on 2011 gift | | $ 2,098,500 |
| Less: Remaining unified transfer tax credit: | | |
| Total credit available for 2010 | $1,730,800 | |
| Less: Unified transfer tax credit used in 1995 | –104,800 | –1,626,000 |
| Gift tax due on 2011 gift | | $ 472,500 |

### Filing Requirements

The Federal gift tax return, Form 709, is filed annually on a calendar year basis. The due date of the return is the April 15th after the close of the taxable year. If a calendar year taxpayer obtains any extension to file his or her Federal income tax return, such extension automatically applies to any gift tax return due. If the donor dies during a taxable year for which a gift tax return is due, the gift tax return must be filed by the due date (nine months after death) plus any extensions of the donor's Federal estate tax return.[17]

## The Overlap between the Gift and Estate Taxes

A beginning student of the Federal transfer tax system might reasonably assume that an inter vivos (during life) transfer of property that is considered complete and therefore subject to the gift tax would also be considered complete for estate tax purposes, so that the transferred property would not be included in the decedent's taxable estate. This, however, is not the case. The gift tax and the estate tax are not mutually exclusive; property gifted away in earlier

[16] Rev. Rul. 79-398, 1979-2 C.B. 338.

[17] § 6075(b).

years can be included in the donor's taxable estate. The relationship between the two taxes is illustrated in the following diagram:

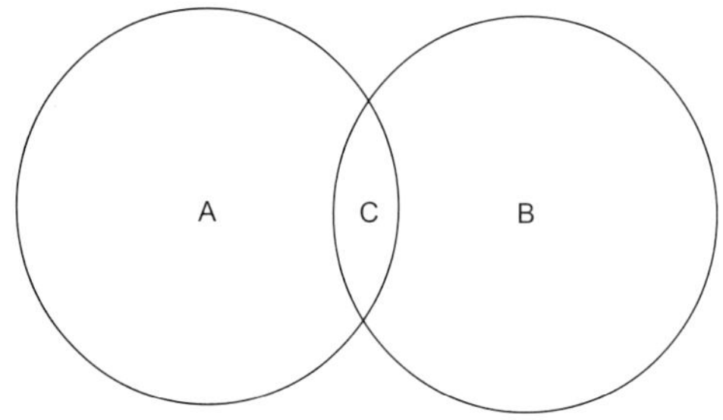


Circle A represents property transferred by the decedent during his or her lifetime and subject to the gift tax. Circle B represents the decedent's taxable estate. Overlap area C represents property already subject to a gift tax that is nevertheless included in the donor/decedent's taxable estate.

Examples of transfers that fall into the overlap area above will be presented later in the chapter. At this point, however, it is important to note that any gift tax paid on a transfer which is considered incomplete for estate tax purposes reduces the amount of estate tax payable.[18]

## Transfers of Property at Death

### Role of a Will

Each of the 50 states gives its citizens the right to transfer the ownership of their property at death by means of a valid will. State law provides various formal requirements for valid wills, and as a result great care must be taken that a will is drafted in strict accordance with such requirements. There are few restrictions on the right of an individual to dispose of property at death in any manner he or she chooses. The most common restriction is the right under state law of a surviving spouse to receive a specified statutory share of the deceased individual's wealth. The statutory share rules effectively prevent an individual from completely disinheriting a surviving spouse.[19]

### Intestacy

When a person dies with no will or an invalid will, the transfer of his or her wealth is determined under the intestacy laws of the deceased's state of residence. Again, the particulars of the intestacy laws of each state are different. As a general rule, property will pass in order in prescribed shares to a decedent's surviving spouse, children and lineal descendants, parents and lineal ancestors, collateral relatives, and finally, if no relatives of any degree can be located, to the state of residence itself. For example, in Indiana if the decedent is survived by his or her spouse, at least one parent and no children, ¾ of the property generally passes to the spouse and ¼ passes to the decedent's parents. If there were two children, the spouse normally would receive ½ while the children would receive ½ of the property.

### Probate

Probate is the legal process whereby a decedent's will is established as genuine and valid, and during which creditors of the decedent may submit their claims for payment from the estate. A decedent's probate estate consists of property interests owned at death that will pass under the terms of a decedent's will (or under the laws of intestacy if no valid will exists). It is extremely important for an individual engaged in estate planning to be aware of any property interests that he or she owns but which will *not* be included in the probate estate at death. A major example of such a property interest is a joint tenancy with right of survivorship

---

[18] § 2001(b)(2).

[19] Modern statutory share laws have their origins in the English common law property concepts of the "dower" rights of a widow and the "curtesy" rights of a widower.

(JTWROS). As previously explained, upon the death of one of the joint tenants, ownership of the asset automatically shifts to the surviving joint tenant or tenants. This is true *regardless* of the provisions of the deceased joint tenant's will. Similarly, survivor benefits, such as those from a life insurance policy or an annuity, or payments from pension and profit sharing plans, usually pass directly to the beneficiary and are not controlled by the will.

It should be apparent that those individuals who have amassed any amount of wealth and who wish to control the disposition of that wealth at death should have a validly executed will. However, there are compelling reasons why *every* responsible adult should have a will. When an individual dies intestate (without a valid will), the resulting legal and administrative complications can cause unnecessary hardship and confusion for the surviving family. Finally, one of the most critical functions of a will is to name a guardian for the decedent's minor children; failure to have a will can result in years of family discord and distress.

## The Taxable Estate

**LO.4**
List the three basic steps involved in the computation of a decedent's taxable estate.

Code §§ 2001 through 2056A contain the statutory rules providing for the imposition of a tax on the transfer of the taxable estate of every decedent who is a citizen or resident of the United States. Sections 2101 through 2108 provide for an estate tax on the value of assets located within the United States owned by a nonresident alien decedent. Discussion of this latter tax is beyond the scope of an introductory text.

Computation of a decedent's taxable estate involves three basic steps:

1. Identification and valuation of assets includible in the gross estate;
2. Identification of deductible claims against the gross estate and deductible expenses of estate administration; and
3. Identification of any deductible bequests out of the gross estate.

The formula for computing the estate tax is shown in Exhibit 24-4 below.

**EXHIBIT 24.4 Estate Tax Formula**

| | | |
|---|---|---|
| Gross estate (§§2031 through 2046) | | $x,xxx,xxx |
| Less the sum of | | |
| Expenses, indebtedness, and taxes (§ 2053) | $ xx,xxx | |
| Losses (§ 2054) | x,xxx | |
| State death taxes (§ 2058) | x,xxx | |
| Charitable bequests (§ 2055) | xx,xxx | |
| Marital deduction (§ 2056) | xxx,xxx | −xxx,xxx |
| Taxable estate (§ 2051) | | $ xxx,xxx |
| Plus: Taxable gifts made after December 31, 1976 [§ 2001(b)] | | + xx,xxx |
| Total taxable transfers | | $ xxx,xxx |
| Tentative tax on total transfers (§ 2001) | | $ xxx,xxx |
| Less the sum of | | |
| Gift taxes paid on post-1976 taxable gifts (§ 2001) | $ x,xxx | |
| Unified transfer tax credit (§ 2010) | xx,xxx | |
| Other tax credits (§§ 2012 through 2016) | x,xxx | −xx,xxx |
| Estate tax liability | | $ xx,xxx |

## The Gross Estate Concept

Section 2031 broadly states that "the value of the gross estate of the decedent shall be determined by including to the extent provided for in this part the value at the time of his death of all property, real or personal, tangible or intangible, wherever situated." The Regulations under this section make it clear that property located in a foreign country is included in this definition.[20]

Sections 2033 through 2044 identify the various types of property that are includible in a decedent's gross estate. Section 2033 is the most commonly applied of these Code sections. It requires the inclusion of any property interest owned by the decedent at date of death. The property interests specified in § 2033 correspond to the legal concept of a decedent's *probate estate*, property interests that will pass to the beneficiaries under the terms of the decedent's will.[21] If the decedent dies without a valid will, these interests will be distributed to the decedent's heirs under the state intestacy laws.

All individuals are, in a sense, on the accrual method of accounting for estate tax purposes. Any legal claim to or interest in an asset that exists at death is includible in the gross estate. For example, a cash basis taxpayer who performed substantial services and was to be paid $20,000 would not report the fee as income until collected. However, if death occurred before collection, the decedent is considered to have owned a $20,000 asset, the right to the fee which would be includible in his or her gross estate.

The concept of the gross estate is much broader than the legal probate estate. Exhibit 24-5 lists the various types of property interests and assets includible in the gross estate and the statutory authority for each inclusion. These various inclusions are discussed in more detail later in the chapter.

Although the estate tax reaches virtually all types of property interests, it does not extend to property in which the decedent owned a life estate created by another. Section 2033 does not require inclusion of such property since the decedent's only legal interest in the property terminated upon death.

**Example 9**

Upon W's death, she transferred stock worth $300,000 in trust, giving her son, S, a life estate and the remainder to her grandson. Several years later, S died when the property was worth $900,000. However, his estate does not include the stock, since his interest terminates at his death and he is not transferring the property to the grandson.

The above example illustrates why the life estate is one of the most important devices used in estate planning. Note that the son is entitled to use the property for his life, yet the property and all of the appreciation escapes taxation in his estate. In other words, the property was taxed in the first and third generations (i.e., in their estates) but not the second generation. Congress addressed this problem by enacting the generation-skipping transfer tax, discussed later in this chapter. This special tax, however, has not eliminated all of the benefits of using the life estate for family tax planning purposes.

### Valuation of Gross Estate and Basis

Once an asset is identified as part of the gross estate, its fair market value at date of death must be determined. Practically, valuation of assets is the most difficult and subjective problem in computing a decedent's gross estate. Many assets, such as stock in a closely held corporation, have no readily ascertainable fair market value. Fortunately, the estate tax Regulations, like their gift tax counterparts, provide detailed guidelines to the valuation of many types of assets.[22]

---

[20] Reg. § 20.2031-1(a).

[21] Reg. § 20.2031-1(a)(1).

[22] Reg. § 20.2031.

**EXHIBIT 24.5 Property Included in the Gross Estate**

| *Property* | *Statutory Authority* |
|---|---|
| Any property interest owned by the decedent at death | Section 2033 |
| Includes<br>cash<br>stocks, bonds, other investment securities<br>personal assets<br>personal residence<br>collectibles (antiques, etc.)<br>investment real estate<br>business interests (sole proprietorship, partnership interest) | |
| Certain gifts made within three years of death (limited application after 1981) | Section 2035 |
| Assets transferred during life in which the decedent retained an income interest or control over the enjoyment of the assets or the income therefrom | Section 2036 |
| Assets transferred during life in which the decedent retained more than a 5 percent reversionary interest and possession of which could only be obtained by surviving the decedent | Section 2037 |
| Assets transferred during life if, at death, the decedent possessed the right to alter, amend, revoke, or terminate the terms of the transfer | Section 2038 |
| Certain survivor benefits and annuities | Section 2039 |
| Joint tenancies with right of survivorship | Section 2040 |
| Assets over which the decedent held a *general* power of appointment | Section 2041 |
| Insurance proceeds on the decedent's life if<br>**1.** payable to the decedent's estate; *or*<br>**2.** the decedent possessed any incident of ownership in the policy at death. | Section 2042 |
| Assets in a QTIP trust in which the decedent had the income interest | Section 2044 |

In the 41 common law states, a surviving spouse may have a legally enforceable claim against assets owned by a decedent that cannot be defeated by the terms of the decedent's will. Section 2034 states that the value of property included in the decedent's gross estate is not diminished by such a claim. In the nine community property states, most property owned by a married individual is community property in which both spouses have equal interests. Only one-half the value of such community property is included in a decedent's gross estate.

Although the gross estate is normally valued as of the decedent's date of death, § 2032 allows the executor to elect an alternative valuation date of six months after death. If the election is made, the alternative valuation date must be used for every asset in the gross estate. If an asset is disposed of within six months of death, its value at date of disposition is used. This choice of two possible dates for valuation gives the executor some flexibility in minimizing the value of the gross estate and any estate tax liability.

## Basis

For income tax purposes, the basis of property in the hands of a person acquiring the property from a decedent is normally the property's fair market value at date of death or on the alternate valuation date under Code § 2032.[23] Under § 1223(11), assets acquired from a decedent are presumed to have a holding period in excess of one year. In the case of community property, the adjustment to fair market value is available for the *entire property* rather than just the one-half interest that is included in the gross estate of the decedent spouse.[24]

In situations in which the Federal estate tax to be imposed on a particular estate is minimal, an executor might actually elect the alternate valuation date in order to increase the valuation of assets included in the gross estate, thus achieving maximum step-up in the basis of the assets for income tax purposes. Section 2032(c) eliminates this particular tax planning option by providing that no § 2032 election may be made unless such election will decrease the value of the gross estate *and* the amount of the Federal estate tax imposed.

## Special Use Valuation: § 2032A

The requirement that property in a decedent's gross estate be valued at fair market value can create hardship if a principal estate asset is real property used in a family business. The value of such real property as it is used in the business may be considerably less than its potential selling price on the open market. As a result, an estate might be forced to sell the real estate and terminate the family business in order to pay the Federal estate tax.

Section 2032A provides that qualifying real estate used in a closely held business may be valued based on its business usage rather than market value. The requirements for qualification under this section are formidable, but can be summarized as follows:

- *Location.* The realty must be located in the United States.
- *Qualified Heir.* The realty must pass from the decedent to a "qualified heir" (generally a family member including the taxpayer's spouse, siblings, parents, grandparents and other ancestors, or children, grandchildren and other lineal descendants).
- *Qualified Farming or Business Use.* During the eight years prior to death (or disability or the time at which he begins to receive social security), there were at least 5 years when the realty was used for farming or in business and the decedent or a member of his family materially participated in the operation of the farm or business.
- *Realty and Personal Property Value (50 Percent Test).* The *adjusted value* of the real and personal property used in farming or business must be at least 50 percent of adjusted value of the gross estate. For purpose of this test and the test below, the adjusted value of the realty is the value of the property less any related debt while the adjusted value of the gross estate is the value of the gross estate less any debts related to property included in the estate.
- *Realty Value (25 Percent Test).* The adjusted value of the real property taken by itself is at least 25 percent of the adjusted value of the gross estate.

If these requirements are met, the maximum reduction from highest and best use value was originally $750,000, but is now adjusted for inflation. For 2011 the amount is $1,020,000. Note also that when special valuation is elected, the basis of the realty to the heirs is the reduced value.

### Example 10

F died in 2011. He owned a large farm south of a major urban center. As farming property, F's real estate was worth $4,000,000; however, developers wanting to acquire

[23] § 1014(a). Decedent's dying in 2010 have a choice to not pay the estate tax in which case the basis of the property to the heirs is what is referred to as a *modified carryover basis*. These rules are found in § 1022. These rules have limited application.

[24] § 1014(b)(6).

the real estate for future use as commercial and residential property had offered F $7,000,000 for the real estate. If all the qualifications of § 2032A can be met, F's real property would be valued at $5,980,000 ($7,000,000 – $1,020,000) in his gross estate, and would take an income tax basis of $5,980,000.

### Recapture of Tax Savings

The estate tax savings offered by the election of qualified-use valuation is conditional upon the continued use of the qualified real property in the family farm or other business. If the heirs of the decedent dispose of the real property or discontinue its qualified use within 10 years of the decedent's death, Code § 2032A(c) requires that the heirs repay the estate tax saved by the original use of the § 2032A election.

## Gross Estate Inclusions

The Federal estate tax is not a property tax levied on the value of property owned at death. Instead, it is a transfer tax levied on the value of any shift in a property interest that occurs because of a decedent's death. As a result, a decedent's gross estate may include assets not owned by a decedent at death, the transfer of which is not controlled by the terms of the decedent's will.

**LO.5**
Specify the various types of property interests that must be valued for inclusion in a decedent's gross estate.

### Insurance on the Life of the Decedent

The proceeds of an insurance policy on the life of a decedent do not come into existence until the death of the insured and are paid to the beneficiaries specified in the insurance contract, not the beneficiaries named in the decedent's will. However, § 2042 provides that such proceeds shall be included in the decedent's gross estate if either of the following is true:

1. The decedent's estate is the beneficiary, or
2. The decedent, at his or her death, possessed any incident of ownership in the life insurance policy, alone or in conjunction with any other person.

The term *incident of ownership* implies any economic interest in the policy and is broadly interpreted by the IRS. The Regulations under § 2042 list the power to change the policy's beneficiary, the right to cancel or assign the policy, and the right to borrow against the policy as incidents of ownership.[25]

**Example 11**

In 2005, T purchased a term insurance policy on his own life. Under the terms of the policy, beneficiary B would receive $150,000 upon T's death. In 2011 T died. Immediately before T's death the policy had no value since it was term insurance. Nevertheless, the $150,000 paid to B is includible in T's gross estate.

### Survivor Benefits

Section 2039 requires that the value of an annuity or any payment receivable by a beneficiary by reason of surviving a decedent be included in the decedent's gross estate. This rule only applies to the extent that the value of the annuity or payment is attributable to contributions made by the decedent or the decedent's employer. A second condition for applicability is that the payment or annuity be payable to the decedent or that the decedent possess the right to payment at death. For example, social security death benefits paid to a decedent's family are

[25] Reg. § 20.2042-1(c)(2).

not covered by § 2039 because the decedent had no right to the payments during his or her lifetime.

The value of an annuity includible under § 2039 is the replacement cost to the beneficiary of a comparable commercial annuity.[26]

### Example 12

H purchased a self and survivor annuity contract that was to pay him $1,500 a month for his life and, upon his death, $1,000 a month to his widow, W. At the date of H's death, W would have to pay $24,000 to purchase a $1,000 a month lifetime annuity for herself. Under § 2039, the value of the annuity received by W, $24,000, is includible in H's gross estate.

## JOINT INTERESTS

### Nonspousal Joint Tenancies

As discussed earlier in the chapter, a joint tenancy with right of survivorship is a form of equal co-ownership of an asset that causes full ownership of the asset to vest automatically in the survivor when the first joint tenant dies. The decedent's will cannot change this result; property owned in joint tenancy is not included in a decedent's probate estate. However, some portion of the value of this property may be includible in the decedent's gross estate. Under § 2040, it is necessary to determine the proportion of the decedent's original contribution toward the acquisition of the asset. This same proportion of the value of the asset at date of death must be included in the decedent's gross estate.

### Example 13

Brothers A and B decided to purchase a tract of real estate as equal joint tenants with right of survivorship. A contributed $40,000 and B contributed $10,000 toward the $50,000 purchase price. At A's death, the real estate was worth $150,000. A's gross estate must include $120,000, 80% [$40,000 ÷ ($40,000 + $10,000)] of the real estate's value. If B had died before A, only $30,000, 20% of the real estate's value, would be includible in B's gross estate.

Note in *Example 13* that in the year the real estate was acquired, A made a taxable gift to B of $15,000, the difference between half the value of the asset when purchased, $25,000, and B's $10,000 contribution. In spite of this completed gift, a portion of the property is taxed in A's gross estate under the authority of § 2040 if he dies before B.

### Spousal Joint Tenancies

If a husband and wife own property as joint tenants with right of survivorship, § 2040(b) contains a rule that requires 50 percent of the value of the property to be included in the gross estate of the first spouse to die, regardless of the original contribution of that spouse.

## GENERAL POWERS OF APPOINTMENT

A *power of appointment* is a right to dispose of property that the holder of the power does not legally own. It is normally created by the will of a decedent in conjunction with a transfer of property in trust. Typically, the decedent's will provides for the transfer of property in trust, giving an individual a life estate and a power to appoint the remainder interest during his or her life or at death through a will. By so doing, the decedent transfers the ability to control the

[26] Reg. § 20.2031-8(a).

property's disposition to the holder of the power, even though the holder does not own the property. In effect, a power of appointment gives a person the right to fill in the blanks of another person's will.

A power of appointment may be *specific*, meaning that the holder of the power may only give the property to members of a specified eligible group of recipients which does *not* include the holder. Alternatively, the power may be *general*, so that the holder may appoint the property to himself or herself, or his or her creditors, estate, or creditors of that estate. The terms of the power should specify to whom ownership of the property will go if the holder deliberately or inadvertently fails to exercise the power.

A *general power of appointment* over property is tantamount to actual ownership of the property. If the holder appoints the property to another person, the exercise is treated as a taxable gift per § 2514.[27] Section 2041 provides that if a decedent holds a general power over property at his or her death, the value of the property must be included in the gross estate.

**Example 14**

P has the right to appoint ownership of certain real estate to any of P's children or grandchildren. He may exercise the right during life or by will. Upon P's death, his will appoints the property to his daughter, D. Because P held only a *specific power*, the value of the appointed property is not included in P's gross estate.

**Example 15**

M has the right to appoint ownership of certain real estate to *himself* or any of his brothers and sisters. He may exercise the right during life or by will. However, M dies without exercising the power. The terms of the power provide that if the power is not exercised the property shall go to M's uncle. Because M possessed a *general power* of appointment, the date of death value of the property must be included in M's gross estate.

### Nontaxable Powers

As indicated above, a specific power of appointment over property will not result in inclusion of the property in the holder's gross estate. There are other situations where a power does not cause taxation. If the holder's power to appoint property for his or her benefit is limited to an *ascertainable standard*, it is not a general power of appointment and inclusion is not required. A power is considered limited to a standard if appointments of property may be made solely for the holder's health, education, maintenance, or support in his or her accustomed manner of living. The language used to describe the scope of the holder's power is extremely important. For example, a power is not considered limited if it permits appointments for the holder's comfort, happiness, or well-being.

**Example 16**

H's will provided for the transfer of $600,000 in trust, giving his wife a life estate and a power to appoint the property to herself for her support. Upon the wife's death, nothing is included in her gross estate since she does not have a general power of appointment. The power does not cause inclusion since it is limited to an ascertainable standard.

[27] If the holder of a general power releases the power or allows it to lapse, the transfer of ownership is still considered a taxable gift made by the holder. See §§ 2514(b) and (e).

Another nontaxable power which offers great planning flexibility is the so-called five and five power. Section 2041 generally does not require inclusion if the amount that the holder can appoint for his or her use in any one year does not exceed the greater of $5,000 or five percent of the value of the property. As long as the power is drawn within these limits, the power need not be restricted in any other manner to avoid taxation. However, in the year of the holder's death, the power is considered a general power to the extent of the greater of the two amounts and thus causes inclusion in the holder's estate to that extent.

**Example 17**

R created a $1,000,000 trust for his wife, giving her the income for life and the remainder to the children. R wanted to give his wife access to the corpus of the trust without causing it to be included in her estate. Therefore, he gave his wife the annual right to withdraw for her use any time during the year the greater of $5,000 or five percent of the aggregate value of the trust. As a result, assuming the value of the trust remained at $1,000,000, his wife could withdraw up to $50,000 (5% of $1,000,000) annually without having the entire corpus included in her estate. However, in the year of the wife's death, she must include $50,000 in her estate, the amount over which she might have exercised the power at death.

## Transfers Taking Effect at Death

Taxpayers who are reluctant to give away property during life but who also want to minimize the tax burden on their estate have designed a variety of inter vivos gifts with "strings attached." Such gifts are subject to a condition or restriction that enables the donor to continue to benefit from or enjoy the property until death. Such a transfer may be complete for gift tax purposes. Nevertheless, for estate tax purposes it may be classified as a transfer taking effect at death, with the result that the date of death value of the property is includible in the donor's gross estate.

Code §§ 2036, 2037, and 2038 govern transfers taking effect at death. Because these three sections were added to the Code at different times, there is a confusing amount of overlap in their coverage. The sections' requirements are very complex and difficult to apply. However, a brief description of each section can give the beginning tax student an idea of their general functions.

One important rule to remember is that all three sections can only require the inclusion in a decedent's gross estate of property that was originally owned by the decedent. A second rule is that the sections are inapplicable if the transfer of the property by the decedent was for sufficient consideration.

### Code § 2036

This section requires that the value of any property given away by the decedent, but to which the decedent retained the right to the property's income or the right to designate who may possess or enjoy the property, shall be included in the decedent's gross estate. Section 2036 also specifies that the retention of the voting rights of shares of stock in a controlled corporation represents a retention of enjoyment.[28]

**Example 18**

In 2003, F made a completed gift of rental property to his son, S, subject to the condition that F was to receive the net rent from the property for the rest of his life. Upon F's death in the current year, the date of death value of the rental property must be included in F's gross estate since he retained a right to income (i.e., rentals), even though S is the owner of the property.

---

[28] § 2036(b)(2) defines a controlled corporation as a corporation in which the decedent controlled (directly or indirectly) at least 20 percent of the voting power of all classes of stock.

> **Example 19**
>
> In the current year, M transferred assets into an irrevocable trust for the sole benefit of her grandchildren. Under the terms of the trust instrument, M reserved the right to designate which of the grandchildren should receive the annual income of the trust. Because M retained the right to designate the persons who shall possess the income from the trust assets, the value of the trust assets will be included in M's gross estate upon her death.

The IRS is very aggressive in applying § 2036. For example, in a situation in which a parent gifts a family residence to a child but continues to occupy the residence rent free, the parent is considered to have retained a beneficial interest in the residence, with the result that the value of the residence will be includible in the parent's gross estate.[29]

### Code § 2037

This statute requires inclusion in a decedent's gross estate of the value of previously transferred property if two conditions are met:

1. Possession or enjoyment of the property can only be obtained by surviving the decedent,
2. The decedent owns a reversionary interest in the property, the value of which exceeds 5 percent of the value of the property. The value of the reversion is computed as of the moment immediately before death, based on actuarial tables.[30]

Regulation § 20.2037-1(e) gives the following example of the application of Code § 2037.

> **Example 20**
>
> The decedent transferred property in trust, with the income payable to his wife for life and with the remainder payable to the decedent or, if he is not living at his wife's death, to his daughter or her estate. The daughter cannot obtain possession or enjoyment of the property without surviving the decedent. Therefore, if the decedent's reversionary interest immediately before death exceeded 5% of the value of the property, the value of the property less the value of the wife's outstanding life estate is includible in the decedent's gross estate.

Note in *Example 20* that the decedent's reversionary interest was extinguished at death and did not constitute an interest in property that would be transferred under the terms of the decedent's will. However, it is the event of the decedent's death that completes the transfer of the remainder interest in the trust to the daughter or her estate.

### Code § 2038

If, on the date of death, the decedent had the power to alter, amend, or revoke the enjoyment of any property previously given away by the decedent, § 2038 requires that the date of death value of the property be included in the decedent's gross estate. Obviously, a revocable transfer falls within § 2038. However, the scope of the section is broad enough to apply to much less obvious types of powers.

---

[29] Rev. Rul. 70-155, 1970-1 C.B. 189; and *Estate of Linderme*, 52 T.C. 305 (1966).

[30] Reg. § 20.2037-1(c)(3).

**Example 21**

Individual Z creates an irrevocable trust for the benefit of her children and names the trust department of a national bank as trustee. The only right retained by Z allows her to replace the trustee with a different trust department. Upon Z's death, Revenue Ruling 79-353[31] states that Code § 2038 applies and the value of the trust corpus must be included in Z's gross estate.

## Gifts in Contemplation of Death

For many years, Code § 2035 required that the date of death value of any gift made by the decedent during the three years prior to death, plus the amount of any gift tax paid on such gifts, be included in the decedent's gross estate. In 1981, Congress drastically altered this section so that it currently applies only to gifts of interests described in the sections governing transfers taking effect at death (§§ 2036, 2037, and 2038) and § 2042, relating to gifts of life insurance. In addition, § 2035 applies for determining the applicability of provisions such as § 2032A, concerning special use valuation (e.g., any property given away within three years of death is added back to the gross estate in applying the 50 and 25 percent tests). Notwithstanding the limited application of the general rule, § 2035(c) continues to require the inclusion in the gross estate of any gift tax paid within three years of death.

**Example 22**

Refer to the facts in *Example 18*. Assume that one year prior to his death, F made a gift of his retained income interest in the rental property to his granddaughter, D. Section 2035 applies to the transfer of the income interest, with the result that the date of death value of the rental property and any gift tax paid on the gift are included in F's gross estate.

## Transfers for Insufficient Consideration

A transfer for which the donor received consideration less than the value of the transferred property is vulnerable to the application of §§ 2035, 2036, 2037, or 2038 upon the donor's death. However, 2043 does allow the estate an offset for the consideration received.[32]

**Example 23**

A transferred her 100 shares of stock in Famco Corporation to her daughter, D, subject to the condition that A would retain the voting rights in the shares. At date of transfer, the fair market value of the stock was $500,000, and D paid A only $300,000 cash in exchange. The transfer constituted a taxable gift of $200,000. Upon A's death, the value of the stock, $1.2 million, is includible in A's gross estate under § 2036. However, A's estate may reduce this value by $300,000, the amount of the consideration received by A.

The § 2043 consideration offset equals the value of the consideration at date of receipt. Therefore, in *Example 23* only 40 percent ($200,000 ÷ $500,000) of the value of the property was transferred without consideration, but 75 percent [($1.2 million − $300,000) ÷ $1.2 million] of the date of death value of the property must be included in the gross estate.

[31] 1979-2 C.B. 325.

[32] See Reg. § 20.2043-1(a).

## Deductions from the Gross Estate

**LO.6**
Describe any deductions from the gross estate.

Not all of the value of a decedent's gross estate will be available for transfer to estate beneficiaries or other individuals. Some of the value must first be used to pay off debts of the decedent and other claims against the estate. The second step in computing an individual's taxable estate is to identify the debts and claims that are deductible against the gross estate.

### Expenses, Indebtedness, and Taxes

The estate tax is based on the *net* wealth that is actually transferred by the decedent. Consistent with this concept, the law permits deductions for expenses associated with death as well as costs of settling the estate and other claims against the property in the estate. As might be expected, the executor cannot spend and borrow willy-nilly and expect to deduct these items. Section 2053(a) generally allows deductions for funeral and administrative expenses, mortgages on property included in the gross estate and other personal debts owed by the decedent. Under § 2053(a), these items are deductible *only* if allowed by local law and *only* to the extent they are incurred in administering property subject to claims (i.e., creditors of the decedent can seek satisfaction of their claims from these assets). This normally encompasses those expenses relating to administering the probate estate. In addition, Section 2053(b) grants deductions for expenses incurred in administering property that is included in the gross estate but which is *not* subject to the claims of the estate's creditors. For example, expenses related to a revocable trust would be deductible even though creditors cannot seek satisfaction of their claims from the trust property. These deductions are allowed because the assets of the trust are included in the gross estate [§ 2053(b)].

#### Funeral Expenses

Deductible funeral expenses include costs for the funeral service, clergy, mortuary, hearse, limousines, casket, cremation, pianist, singers, flowers and the like. In addition, a deduction is allowed for costs of a tombstone, monument, mausoleum crypt, or for a burial lot, either for the decedent or his family. If the decedent had acquired the burial lots prior to death, no deduction is allowed but the lots are not included in the gross estate. Deductions are also allowed for a reasonable expenditure for the future care of the lot. Transportation costs of the person bringing the body to the burial site also are deductible as funeral expenses (e.g., a corpse is flown home). Traveling expenses for beneficiaries or others to attend the decedent's funeral are not deductible (e.g., costs of flying decedent's grandchildren to the funeral are not deductible).

#### Administrative Expenses

Section 2053 also permits deductions for administering and settling the decedent's estate. Deductions normally include all probate costs such as those incurred in collection and preservation of probate assets (bank charges), payment of debts and distribution of property (e.g., cost of wire transfer). Common administrative expenses are fees paid to the executor or administrator of the estate, accounting and legal expenses, court costs, and appraisal fees. In addition, expenses incurred in preserving the estate, including the costs of maintaining and storing property (e.g., utility bills on the decedent's home after death) are deductible.

It should be emphasized that deductions are limited for those expenses in the administration of the estate. Those that are not "essential" to the proper settlement of the estate, but are incurred for the benefit of the heirs or others, may not be claimed as deductions. In this regard, selling expenses are deductible administrative expenses, if the assets must be sold to pay debts, expenses or taxes. Regulation § 20.2053-3(d)(2) authorizes the deduction of the expenses of selling assets of the estate only if the sale is necessary (1) to pay debts, administrative expenses or tax; (2) to preserve the estate; or (3) to effect distribution.

**Example 24**

In *Estate of David Smith*, a famous sculptor died and left over 425 pieces of his work.[33] The executors of his estate paid commissions in excess of $1,000,000 to a gallery for

[33] 75-1 USTC ¶13,046, AFTR 2d 75-1594, 510 F.2d 479 (CA-2, 1975) aff'g 57 TC 650 (1972) cert. denied.

selling the decedent's work presumably to raise money to pay expenses of the estate. However, only $290,000 of those commissions were identified as attributable to sales needed to pay the decedent's debts, taxes, and other administration expenses. The Court held that only $290,000 of commissions were attributable to the estate's liquidity needs and denied a deduction for the remainder. Moreover, the court found no evidence that it was necessary to sell all of the works promptly. Presumably, such expenses could be claimed as selling expenses on the estate's income tax return. Note that *Smith* also stands for the proposition that assets cannot be valued in the gross estate at their value net of any expected selling expenses.

Adminstrative expenses incurred after death can be claimed as either a deduction on the estate tax return (Form 706) or on the estate's income tax return but not on both.[34]

The executor must be careful not to waste any deductions for administration expenses. This is a major concern when the estate owes no estate tax (e.g., due to the unlimited marital or charitable deductions or the unified credit) since the only potential benefit could be derived from deducting the expense for income tax purposes. Even if the executor properly waives the deduction for estate tax purposes, this does not ensure that an income tax benefit will be derived since the estate may have little or no income that could be reduced by the deduction. However, if the deduction exceeds income *in the year the estate terminates*, § 642(h) provides that all excess deductions pass through to the beneficiaries succeeding to the decedent's property who can then deduct them on their individual tax returns as itemized deductions. This is allowed only for the excess deductions that occur in the year of termination. If excess deductions occur in earlier years (e.g., because the estate chooses the wrong time to pay the expense) the deduction is generally lost.

### Claims against the Estate

Deductions are allowed for any debts that the decedent owed at the time of death. The deduction for these items reflects the fact that the estate must pay these amounts before the property is distributed thereby reducing the amount that is transferred to the heirs by the decedent. Debts of the estate typically include unpaid mortgages or liens on property included in the gross estate, unpaid income taxes on income received by the decedent before he or she died, property taxes accrued before death as well as personal obligations of the decedent. Examples of personal liabilities are balances due on credit card accounts, utility bills, interest on mortgages accrued before death, margin accounts, and other loans outstanding at the date of death. Interest accrued after the date of death is normally not deductible on the Form 706 even if the alternate valuation date is elected.[35]

Medical expenses of the decedent are deductible as a claim against the estate. However, if such expenses are paid within one year of death, they may be claimed as income tax deduction on the final return. The expenses cannot be claimed on both returns, however.

## Losses

Section 2054 allows deductions for casualty and theft losses occurring while the estate is being settled are deductible in computing the taxable estate. For example, the decedent's car may be stolen or his home destroyed by fire. The amount of the deductible loss is the value of the property reduced for any insurance proceeds received. If the alternate valuation date is elected, the property is valued at zero when determining the value of the gross estate. Therefore no loss deduction is allowed.

Although casualty and theft losses are also deductible for income tax purposes, there is no double deduction allowed.[36] The loss can be deducted on either the estate tax return or the estate's income tax return, but not both. In most cases, a greater benefit could be secured by deducting the expenses on the estate tax return since such expenses may be subject to limitations for income tax purposes.

---

[34] § 642(g).

[35] Reg. § 20.2053-7.

[36] *Supra* Footnote 34.

## STATE DEATH TAXES

In addition to the Federal estate tax, decedents must be concerned about state death taxes. Most states impose some type of death tax. These usually take the form of an inheritance tax, an estate tax or both. On the other hand very few states impose any type of gift tax. However, gifts made in contemplation of death (e.g., a deathbed transfer) are usually subject to the state's death tax.

### State Inheritance Taxes

Many states and some local jurisdictions impose an inheritance tax on the right to receive property at death. Unlike an estate tax, which is imposed on the estate according to the value of property transferred by the decedent at death, an inheritance tax is imposed on the recipient of property from an estate (although it is typically paid out of the estate). The amount of an inheritance tax payable usually is directly affected by the degree of kinship between the recipient and the decedent. The inheritance tax typically provides an exemption from the tax, which increases as the relationship between the recipient (e.g., the surviving spouse, children, grandchildren, etc.) and the decedent becomes closer. For example, under the Indiana inheritance tax rules, transfers to a surviving spouse are exempt while transfers to the decedent's children under 21 are entitled to an exemption of $100,000. The rate of tax also differs depending on the relationship. For example, the Indiana rates for transfers to children range from 1 to 10 percent while transfers to nonrelatives range from 10 to 20 percent. Observe that the small exemptions, at least in Indiana, make even modest estates subject to state inheritance taxes even though they may be exempt from the Federal estate tax.

### State Estate Taxes

These taxes are similar to the Federal estate tax and are based on the value of the property held by the decedent at the date of death.

### Deduction for State Death Taxes

Prior to 2005, the estate was allowed a credit for state death taxes. Beginning in 2005, however, the state death tax credit was eliminated and replaced by a deduction. Note that the deduction is for state death taxes. There is no deduction for Federal estate taxes.

Technically, § 2058 allows a deduction for the amount of any estate, inheritance, legacy, or succession taxes actually paid to any state or the District of Columbia, in respect of property included in the gross estate. The amount must be actually paid to the estate, not merely estimated or accrued. Observe that many states permit a discount for prompt payment. For example, Indiana allows a five percent discount if the tax is paid within 9 months of date of death. In such case, the amount paid, not the amount assessed, is the amount of the deductible state death tax.

## CHARITABLE CONTRIBUTIONS

An estate may deduct the value of any transfer of assets to a qualified charitable organization under § 2055. Qualifying organizations are specifically defined in the statute. If an individual is willing to leave his or her entire estate for public, charitable, or religious use, there will be no taxable estate.

For a charitable contribution to be deductible, it normally must consist of the decedent's entire interest in the underlying property. For example, if a decedent bequeaths a life interest in real estate to his son and the remainder interest in the property to charity, the value of the remainder interest is not deductible. Similarly, if the decedent bequeaths the interest in the real estate to a charity for a term of years (e.g., 20 years), and the remainder to his son, the value of the income interest is not deductible. However, this restriction does not apply if the transfer is in a specific statutory form: a *charitable lead trust*, where an income interest is given to the charity, or a *charitable remainder trust*, where a remainder interest is given to the charity.[37] A detailed description of such trusts is beyond the scope of this text, but they do allow a decedent to create both a charitable and a noncharitable interest in the same property and secure a deduction for the charitable interest. The restriction also is inapplicable to a

---

[37] § 2055(e)(2).

charitable contribution of a remainder interest in a personal residence or farm and to certain contributions for conservation purposes.[38]

If an individual taxpayer is considering making bequests to charity upon his or her death, his or her tax adviser should certainly explore the possibility of having the individual make such charitable contributions during his or her life. Such inter vivos contributions would serve a dual purpose: the donated assets would be removed from the individual's potential taxable estate, and the donation would create a deduction for income tax purposes.

## The Marital Deduction

Code § 2056 provides an unlimited deduction for the value of property passing to a surviving spouse. If a married taxpayer, no matter how wealthy, is willing to leave all his or her property to the surviving spouse, no transfer tax will be imposed on the estate.[39] Only upon the subsequent death of the spouse will the couple's wealth be subject to taxation. Planning for maximizing the benefit of the unlimited marital deduction is discussed in Chapter 26.

In certain instances, interests transferred to the surviving spouse are not deductible—so-called *nondeductible terminable interests*. If a decedent leaves an interest in property to his or her spouse that can or will terminate at a future date *and* if after termination another person receives an interest in the property from the decedent, the value of the interest passing to the spouse is ineligible for the marital deduction.[40] Absent this rule, the interest would escape taxation entirely, since it terminates prior to or with the death of the surviving spouse and thus is not included in his or her gross estate.

### Example 25

Decedent H leaves a life estate in real property to his surviving spouse, W, with the remainder after W's death left to their daughter. The interest passing to W is a terminable interest ineligible for the marital deduction. Note that without this rule barring a marital deduction, the value of the property would completely escape estate taxation since it would not be taxed in either H's estate (due to the marital deduction) or W's estate (since W's life estate terminates at her death).

The property need not pass directly to the surviving spouse to qualify for the marital deduction. Section 2056(b)(5) generally allows the deduction if the surviving spouse is entitled to annual payments of all of the income from the property for life and has a general power of appointment over the property exercisable during life or at death. In this case, the entire value of the property will be included in the estate of the surviving spouse because of his or her general power of appointment.

For many years, these two methods of leaving property to a spouse (outright or in trust with a general power of appointment to the surviving spouse) were essentially the only two techniques available if the decedent wanted to qualify the transfer for the marital deduction. This often left a married couple with a perplexing problem. Notice that in both situations, the decedent surrenders control of the property to the surviving spouse. When the surviving spouse is given a general power of appointment over the property, he or she has complete control over the ultimate disposition of the property—the same control that would have been obtained if he or she had received the property outright. Under either scenario, the surviving spouse is left with the choice of who will be the beneficiaries of the decedent's property. In other words, the decedent could not be assured that property that had been accumulated during marriage would reach the desired beneficiaries, typically the couple's children. For example, if the surviving spouse remarried, the decedent's property could end up being used for the benefit of the new spouse and new children, usually not the result desired by the decedent. Unfortunately, more suitable arrangements from a nontax point of view normally did not qualify for the marital deduction. Consequently, the tax law put taxpayers in an awkward position, requiring them to either give up control or face higher taxes.

---

[38] *Ibid.*

[39] No marital deduction is allowed for the value of property passing to a surviving spouse who is not a U.S. citizen unless the property is placed in a "qualified domestic trust."

[40] § 2056(b).

In 1981, Congress addressed this problem by sanctioning the marital deduction for a life estate for the surviving spouse. Observe that without this relief provision the life estate would be considered a nondeductible terminable interest. However, as explained below, the deduction is allowed only if the property (that would normally escape tax by virtue of the life estate rules) is included in the surviving spouse's estate upon his or her death. The special rules enabling this treatment are contained in § 2056(b)(7).

Under § 2056(b)(7), a marital deduction is allowed for the value of *qualifying terminable interest property* left to a surviving spouse. Qualifying terminable interest property is property from which the entire income must be paid to the spouse at least annually. During the spouse's lifetime, no one else must be able to receive any interest in the property. Upon the spouse's death, the property may pass to anyone. If the executor elects, the entire value of the property is deductible on the decedent's estate tax return. In most cases, these requirements are met by transferring property to a trust from which the spouse receives the income for life. Such arrangements are normally referred to as QTIPs, reflecting the fact that they are created to enable to the property to be considered Qualifying Terminable Interest Property.

Without further requirements, the interest described above is simply a life estate that would totally escape tax as described in *Example 25* above. However, § 2044 requires that when the surviving spouse dies, the entire value of the qualifying terminable interest property at that time must be included in the spouse's gross estate. If the surviving spouse gives away the income interest during life, § 2519 requires that the gift will consist of the entire value of the property.

### Example 26

H and W, husband and wife, have been married for ten years. They have three children, A, B, and C, ages 9, 7, and 4. H wants to ensure that their children receive the couple's assets after he dies. For this reason, he does not want to leave the property outright to his spouse nor does he want to leave the property in trust to her with a general power of appointment. To this end, his will provides that upon his death, all of his assets are transferred to a trust that gives W an income interest for life and the remainder interest to A, B and C upon W's death. Note that H has provided for W but has retained control over who ultimately receives the property. From a tax perspective, this normally would be considered a nondeductible terminable interest as described above and would not qualify for the marital deduction. However, if an election is made by the executor of H's estate, this otherwise nondeductible terminable interest becomes qualifying terminable interest property, that is, a QTIP, and qualifies for the marital deduction. When W dies, the value of the property at her death is automatically included in her gross estate. In this way, the property does not escape estate tax. Any estate tax that is attributable to inclusion of the property in the W's estate can be paid by her estate. However, if this is not suitable, the law requires that the tax will be paid from the property itself (e.g., the property could be sold to pay the estate tax and the property net of the estate tax would be passed to the children of H and W).

While the examples above provide some measure of the trade-offs that must be considered when planning with the marital deduction, these issues are just part of the story. Other factors that must be considered in order to effectively design marital bequests are discussed in Chapter 26.

## Computation of the Estate Tax

**LO.7**
Explain the mechanics of the calculation of the estate tax, including the role of the unified credit.

Once the value of the taxable estate has been determined, the first step in computing the estate tax liability is to add the taxable estate to the amount of the decedent's *adjusted taxable gifts*. Adjusted taxable gifts are defined in Code § 2001(b) as the total amount of taxable gifts (after any available exclusion or deduction) made after December 31, 1976 *other than* gifts includible in the gross estate of the decedent.

The transfer tax rates of § 2001(c) are then applied to the sum of the taxable estate plus adjusted taxable gifts. The tentative tax calculated is then reduced by any gift taxes paid or payable at current rates for gifts made after December 31, 1976. The result is the Federal estate tax liability *before* credits.

## Estate Tax Credits

There are several credits that can be used to reduce the estate tax. These are:

- Unified credit
- Foreign death tax credit
- Credit for taxes on prior transfers
- Credit for pre-1977 gift taxes

### Unified Credit

The major credit available to reduce the Federal estate tax is the unified credit of Code § 2010. As seen in Exhibit 24-3, the estate and gift tax credits have varied over the years. Currently, each is $1,780,300. The mechanics of the estate tax calculation ensure that the decedent's estate benefits from the credit only to the extent that it was not used to offset any gift tax during his or her lifetime. It is important to understand that the two credits combined will shelter a maximum of $5,000,000 (2011) of transfers from the imposition of transfers from the imposition of any Federal transfer tax.

### Portability of the Unused Unified Credit

The 2010 Tax Relief Act introduced the so-called portability rule. According to this rule, any credit that remains unused as of the death of a spouse who dies after 2010 (the "deceased spousal unused exclusion amount") is portable; that is, the unused amount is generally available for use by the surviving spouse as an addition to the surviving spouse's credit. Specifically, beginning in 2010 a surviving spouse may use the predeceased spousal carryover amount in addition to his or her own unified credit for taxable transfers made during life or at death.[41]

**Example 27**

H and W are husband and wife. H died in 2011 and used $3,000,000 of his $5,000,000 exemption to eliminate his estate from tax. As a result, $2,000,000 of his exemption is unused. In 2012, W dies. W's exemption amount is $7,000,000 (her $5,000,000 + the unused amount of her last deceased husband of $2,000,000). In effect, the couple is able to exempt up to $10 million from estate taxes ($3,000,000 when H died and $7,000,000 when W died).

If a surviving spouse is predeceased by more than one spouse, the amount of unused exclusion that is available for use by such surviving spouse is limited to the lesser of $5 million or the unused exclusion of the last such deceased spouse.

**Example 28**

H and W are married. H dies and his unused exclusion is $5,000,000. W remarried NH, a new husband. NH died and his unused exclusion is $2,000,000. By what amount can W increase her exemption? She can use only the unused amount of her last spouse, $2,000,000 (and not the $5,000,000 of her first spouse).

---

[41] § 2010(c).

The unused exclusion amount is available to a surviving spouse only if the executor of the estate of the deceased spouse files an estate tax return on which such amount is computed and makes an election on such return that such amount may be used. The election is irrevocable. The election cannot be made unless that estate tax return is filed on a timely basis as extended. Thus, even if a decedent normally is not required to file an estate tax return, it appears that a return is now necessary simply to preserve the unused exclusion amount.

### Foreign Death Tax Credit

Section 2014 allows the estate a credit for all or part of the death taxes that must be paid to a foreign country on account of property located in that country that is included in the gross estate. The amount of the credit is limited to the lesser of (1) the foreign death tax attributable to the foreign property, or (2) the Federal estate tax attributable to the foreign property.

### Credit for Tax on Prior Transfers

If two family members die within a short period of time, the same property may be included in both taxable estates and be subject to two rounds of estate taxation in rapid succession. Section 2013 provides a credit to the estate of the second decedent to mitigate this excessive taxation. The credit generally is computed as a percentage of the amount of tax attributable to the inclusion of property in the estate of the first decedent. The percentage is based on the number of years between the two deaths as follows:

| | |
|---|---|
| 0–2 years | 100% |
| 3–4 years | 80% |
| 5–6 years | 60% |
| 7–8 years | 40% |
| 9–10 years | 20% |

If the second decedent outlived the first by more than 10 years, no § 2013 credit is allowed.

#### Example 29

Individual A died in March 2008. Under the terms of his will, A left $1,000,000 in assets to his younger sister, B. B. died unexpectedly in May 2011 and the assets inherited from A were included in B's taxable estate. The amount of tax paid by A's estate that is attributable to the assets is calculated at $100,000. Since B died just over three years after A's death, 80% of the tax paid by A's estate is available to B's estate as a credit of $80,000 (80% × $100,000).

### Gift Taxes Paid on Pre-1977 Gifts

If a taxable gift was made prior to 1977 (i.e., prior to unification) and the gifted property is included in the transferor's gross estate (e.g., under the rules of §§ 2036, 2037, or 2038), § 2012 allows a credit for any gift tax paid. The amount of the credit is limited to the lesser of the gift tax paid or the estate tax attributable to inclusion of the gifted property in the taxpayer's gross estate.

## A Comprehensive Example

The following example illustrates the complete computation of the Federal estate tax. In 1997, taxpayer M makes his first taxable gift to his son S. The fair market value of the property transferred is $200,000. The gift tax is computed as follows:

| | |
|---|---|
| Value of gift | $ 200,000 |
| Less: Annual exclusion (1997) | −10,000 |
| Taxable gift | $ 190,000 |

| | |
|---|---|
| Gift tax before credits | $ 51,600 |
| Less: Unified credit | −51,600 |
| Gift tax liability for 1997 | $ 0 |

In 1998, M makes gifts to son S and daughter D. The value of each transfer is $250,000.

| | |
|---|---|
| Value of gifts | $ 500,000 |
| Less: Annual exclusions | −20,000 |
| Taxable gifts for 1998 | $ 480,000 |
| Plus: 1997 taxable gift | +190,000 |
| Taxable transfers to date | $ 670,000 |
| Tentative tax on total transfers to date | $ 218,700 |
| Less: Tax on 1997 gift | −51,600 |
| Less: 1998 unified credit ($202,050 − $51,600) | −150,450 |
| 1998 gift tax liability | $ 16,650 |

M dies in 2011, leaving a taxable estate valued at $8 million. The estate tax is computed as follows:

| | | |
|---|---|---|
| Taxable estate | | $8,000,000 |
| Plus: Taxable gifts made in prior years | | +670,000 |
| Total taxable transfers | | $8,670,000 |
| Tentative tax on total transfers ($155,800 + 35% (8,670,000 − 1,500,000 = $7,170,000) | | $2,665,300 |
| Less the sum of | | |
| Gift taxes paid on post-1976 taxable gifts (on 1998 gift) | $ 16,650 | |
| Unified credit (2011) | 1,730,800 | −1,747,450 |
| Estate tax liability | | $ 917,850 |

## PAYMENT OF THE ESTATE TAX

The Federal estate tax return, Form 706, is due nine months after the date of the decedent's death, and any tax liability shown is payable with the return. However, Congress appreciates the fact that the payment of the estate tax is often unforeseen, and has provided for a variety of relief measures for the estate with a substantial tax liability and insufficient liquidity to pay the tax nine months after death.

Section 6161 authorizes the Secretary of the Treasury to extend the time of payment of the estate tax for up to 10 years past the normal due date. To obtain an extension, the executor must show reasonable cause for the delay in payment. For example, the fact that the executor of an estate requires additional time to sell a particularly illiquid asset to generate the cash with which to pay the estate tax might be accepted as reasonable cause for an extension of the payment date for the estate tax.

Section 6166 allows an estate to pay a portion of its estate tax liability in installments if a substantial portion of the estate consists of the decedent's interest in a closely held business.[42] To be considered "closely-held" at least 20 percent of the total capital of the partnership or 20 percent of the total value of the corporation's voting stock must be included in the gross

[42] § 6166(b) provides specific definition of the phrase "interest in a closely held business."

estate or the decedent is a partner in the partnership or a shareholder in the corporation and such partnership or corporation has 45 or fewer partners or shareholders (as increased by the 2001 legislation). An estate is eligible if more than 35 percent of the *adjusted gross estate* (gross estate less §§ 2053 and 2054 deductions for debts of the decedent, funeral and administrative expenses, and losses) consists of the value of such an interest. The percentage of the estate tax liability that can be deferred is based on the ratio of the value of the closely held business to the value of the adjusted gross estate.

If a decedent owned an interest in more than one closely held business, the values of the interests can be combined to meet the 35 percent test *if* the decedent's interest represents 20 percent or more of the total value of the business.

## Example 30

The taxable estate of decedent X is composed of the following:

| | | Value |
|---|---|---|
| Sole proprietorship | | $ 600,000 |
| 40% interest in closely held corporation | | 3,000,000 |
| Other assets | | 5,000,000 |
| Gross estate | | $8,600,000 |
| Less sum of | | |
| Code §§ 2053 and 2054 deductions | $ 600,000 | |
| Code § 2055 charitable deduction | 1,000,000 | −1,600,000 |
| Taxable estate | | $7,000,000 |

The decedent owned 100% of the value of the sole proprietorship and 40% of the value of the closely held corporation. The combined values of these interests, $3,600,000, represents 45% of the adjusted gross estate of $8,000,000 ($8,600,000 – $600,000). Therefore, the executor may elect to defer payment on 45% of the estate tax liability.

The tax deferred under § 6166 is payable in 10 equal annual installments. The first installment is payable five years and nine months after death. The IRS does charge the estate interest on the unpaid balance for the entire 15-year period.[43] Historically the interest rate charged on the deferred tax has been substantially less than the current market rate. Legislation in 1997 cut the rate even more. Currently, the interest rate is only two-percent of the deferred tax on the so-called *two-percent portion*. The tax on the two-percent portion is limited to the tax on the sum of $1,360,000 (as adjusted for inflation in 2011) and the exemption equivalent for the year of death less the applicable unified credit. For example, in 2011, the maximum two percent portion would be $476,000 computed as follows:

| | |
|---|---|
| Base amount | $1,360,000 |
| Exemption equivalent (2011) | 5,000,000 |
| Two percent portion | $6,360,000 |

| | |
|---|---|
| Gross tax on two percent portion [$155,800 + (35% × ($6,360,000 – $500,000))] | $2,206,800 |
| Unified credit (2011) | (1,730,800) |
| Tax on two-percent portion | $ 476,000 |

In addition, the interest rate imposed on the amount of the deferred estate tax attributable to the taxable value of the business in excess of this amount ($1,360,000 + the exemption of $5,000,000 or $6,360,000 in 2011) is reduced to 45 percent of the rate applicable to underpayments of estimated taxes. No estate tax deduction is allowed for the interest paid. If the estate disposes of 50 percent or more of the value of the qualifying closely held interest, any outstanding amount of deferred estate tax must be paid immediately.

[43] See § 6601(j) for applicable interest rate.

## The Generation-Skipping Transfer Tax

**LO.8**
Discuss the purpose of the generation skipping transfer tax.

As part of the Tax Reform Act of 1976, Congress added a third type of transfer tax to the Internal Revenue Code. The *generation-skipping transfer tax* (GSTT) was designed to "plug a loophole" in the coverage of the gift and estate taxes. The original version of the GSTT was intimidatingly complex, and was criticized by tax practitioners from the moment of enactment.

The Tax Reform Act of 1986 retroactively repealed the 1976 version of the GSTT and replaced it with a new tax applicable to testamentary transfers occurring after the date of enactment and to inter vivos transfers made after September 25, 1985. Any tax actually paid under the 1976 GSTT is fully refundable.

A traditional generation-skipping transfer involves at least three generations of taxpayers. In its simplest form, a generation-skipping transfer occurs whenever there is a so-called *direct skip*, an outright transfer of wealth for the sole benefit of persons at least two generations younger than the transferor.[44]

### Example 31

This year Grandpa made a gift to his grandchild. Although a gift tax may be imposed on Grandpa, no gift or estate tax is imposed on the intervening generation, that is, the child's father. Therefore there is a direct skip of the estate and gift tax.

A more complicated yet equally important example involves a so-called *taxable termination* as illustrated below.

### Example 32

Several years ago, Mother, M, died. Her will created a trust with income to Daughter, D, for life, remainder to the grandchildren. In this case, M would pay an estate tax at the time of her death on the value of the property used to create the trust. More important, however, is the result when D dies and her interest terminates. Even though D is able to enjoy the income from the trust property for life, there is no estate tax imposed on her when she dies because her interest terminates at death. As a result, there is no estate or gift tax imposed on the second generation.

Generally, the value of property transferred in a taxable generation-skipping transaction is subject to a flat-rate tax of 35 percent (2011).[45] However, each transferor is allowed a lifetime exemption of $5,000,000 for 2011 for generation-skipping transfers of any type.[46] In addition, the tax is not imposed to the extent that the transfer is not subject to gift taxes (e.g., due to the annual exclusion or the exemption on transfers for medical or educational purposes). For example, small gifts from grandparents to grandchildren which fall within the annual exclusion would not be subject to the tax.

## Tax Planning Considerations

The statutory rules of Federal gift, estate, and generation-skipping taxes have been examined in this chapter. Any individual taxpayer who desires to maximize the accumulated wealth available to family members will want to minimize the burden of these three transfer taxes. Tax planning for transfer taxes would be incomplete, however, without consideration of any

[44] § 2612.

[45] § 2641.

[46] § 2631.

interrelated Federal income taxes. Many gifts are made by transfers to a trust, and the income taxation of the trust entity and its beneficiaries may have a significant impact upon the original tax minimization plan. For this reason, the Federal income taxation of trusts, estates, and beneficiaries is discussed in the next chapter (Chapter 25). The tax planning considerations for transfer taxes and any attendant income taxes are incorporated in Chapter 26, *Family Tax Planning*.

# Problem Materials

## DISCUSSION QUESTIONS

**24-1** *Interrelation of Federal Estate and Gift Taxes.* Discuss the various reasons why the Federal gift and estate taxes can be considered as a single, unified transfer tax.

**24-2** *Entity for Transfer Tax Purposes.* Why can the married couple rather than each individual spouse be considered the taxable entity for transfer tax purposes?

**24-3** *What Constitutes a Gift?* Businessperson B offers X $40,000 for an asset owned by X. Although X knows the asset is worth $60,000, he is in desperate need of cash and agrees to sell. Has X made a $20,000 taxable gift to B? Explain.

**24-4** *Adequate Consideration.* During the current year, K offered to pay $50,000 to his only son, S, if S would agree to live in the same town as K for the rest of K's life. K is very elderly and frail and desires to have a relative close at hand in case of emergency. Does the $50,000 payment constitute a taxable gift made by K?

**24-5** *When Is a Gift Complete?* Wealthy Grandmother G wants to provide financial support for her Grandson GS. She opens a joint checking account with $20,000 of cash. At any time, G or GS may withdraw funds from this account. Has G made a completed gift to GS by opening this account? At what point is the gift complete?

**24-6** *Cumulative Nature of Transfer Taxes.* The Federal income tax is computed on an annual basis. How does this contrast to the computation of the Federal gift tax?

**24-7** *Purpose of Unified Transfer Tax Rates.* A decedent's taxable estate can be considered the last taxable gift the decedent makes. Why?

**24-8** *Incomplete Transfers.* The Federal gift tax and estate tax are not mutually exclusive. Give examples of transfers that may be treated as taxable gifts but that do not remove the transferred assets from the donor's gross estate.

**24-9** *Computation of Taxable Estate.* What are the three steps involved in computing the taxable estate of a decedent?

**24-10** *Probate Estate vs. Gross Estate.* How can the value of a decedent's probate estate differ from the value of his or her gross estate for tax purposes?

**24-11** *Jointly Held Property.* Property held in joint tenancy with right of survivorship is often called a will substitute. In other words, if all property is held in joint tenancy, a will is unnecessary.

**a.** Does joint tenancy eliminate the need for a will?

**b.** Identify some of the problems that arise when property is titled in joint tenancy.

**24-12** *Special Use Valuation of § 2032A.* The gross estate of decedent F consists of a very successful farming operation located 80 miles east of an expanding metropolitan area. The estate includes 2,000 acres of real estate worth $400,000 as agricultural land. However, a real estate developer is willing to pay $1.5 million for the property because of its potential for suburban development. Discuss the utility of § 2032A to F's estate.

**24-13** *Powers of Appointment.* What are some *nontax* reasons for the creation of a power of appointment? What is the difference between a specific and a general power?

**24-14** *Gifts in Contemplation of Death.* Discuss the scope of § 2035 concerning gifts made within three years of death after the enactment of ERTA 1981.

**24-15** *Estate Tax Credits.* With the exception of the unified credit of § 2010, what is the basic purpose of the various estate tax credits?

**24-16** *Due Date of Estate Tax Return and Payment.* Why is the tax law particularly lenient in authorizing extensions for payment of the Federal estate tax?

**24-17** *Unified Transfer Tax Credit.* Section 2010 appears to allow a second $1,730,800 (2011) credit against the Federal estate tax (in addition to the credit allowed for gift tax purposes under § 2505). Is this the case?

**24-18** *Generation-Skipping Transfers.* Decedent T's will created a trust, the income from which is payable to T's invalid daughter D for her life. Upon D's death, the trust assets will be paid to T's two sons (D's brothers) in equal shares. Has T made a generation-skipping transfer? Explain.

## PROBLEMS

**24-19** *Gift Splitting.* During 2011, Mr. and Mrs. Z make the following cash gifts to their adult children:

| | |
|---|---|
| Mr. Z: | |
| to son M | $30,000 |
| to daughter N | 8,000 |
| Total | $38,000 |
| Mrs. Z: | |
| to son M | $ 2,000 |
| to daughter N | 12,000 |
| to daughter O | 18,000 |
| Total | $32,000 |

**a.** Assume Mr. and Mrs. Z do *not* elect to split their gifts per § 2513. Compute the total taxable gifts after exclusions for each.

**b.** How does the amount of taxable gifts change if Mr. and Mrs. Z *elect* to split their gifts?

**24-20** *Computing Gift Tax Liability.* B, a single individual, made a cash gift of $200,000 his niece C in 1996. In 2011, B gives C an additional $700,000 and nephew D $900,000. Compute B's gift tax liability for the current year.

**24-21** *Computing Taxable Gifts.* C, a single individual, makes the following transfers during current year:

| | *Fair Market Value* |
|---|---|
| Cash to sister D | $13,000 |
| Real estate: | |
| Life estate to brother B | 28,000 |
| Remainder to nephew N | 21,000 |
| Cash to First Baptist Church | 25,000 |

What is the total amount of taxable gifts C must report?

**24-22** *Amount of the Gift and the Annual Exclusion.* In 2011, Mr. C decided he wanted to set up trusts for his adult daughter and his grandson. To this end, he transferred $50,000 cash to a trust. The income of the trust was payable annually to his daughter, D, for 20 years with the remainder to D's son, R. For your computations, assume 120% of the applicable Federal midterm rate is 4.8 percent.

**a.** What is (are) the amount(s) of the taxable gift(s)?

**b.** Same as (a) except D is to receive the income for the rest of her life (she is age 40).

**24-23** *Computing Taxable Gifts.* During 2011, L, a widower, makes the following transfers:

| | *Fair Market Value* |
|---|---|
| Tuition payment to State College for nephew N, age 32 | $ 6,000 |
| New automobile to nephew N | 9,000 |
| Cash to a local qualified political committee | 15,000 |

What is the total amount of taxable gifts L must report?

**24-24** *Computing Taxable Gifts.* During 2011, Z, a widow, makes the following transfers:

| | *Fair Market Value* |
|---|---|
| Real estate located in France to son J | $500,000 |
| City of Philadelphia municipal bonds to daughter K | 120,000 |
| Payment to local hospital for medical expenses of brother-in-law M | 18,000 |

What is the total amount of taxable gifts Z must report?

**24-25** *Basis of Gifted Assets.* During the current year, L received a gift of land from his grandmother. The land had a basis to the grandmother of $100,000 and a fair market value of $250,000 on the date of the gift. A gift tax of $30,000 was paid on the transfer.

**a.** If L subsequently sells the land for $300,000, how much gain or loss will he recognize?

**b.** What would be the amount of L's recognized gain or loss on the sale if the land had a tax basis of $325,000 (rather than $100,000) to the grandmother?

**24-26** *Marital Deduction.* F died during the current year, leaving a gross estate valued at $5 million. F's will specifically provided that no amount of her wealth was to be left to her estranged husband, G. However, under applicable state law, G is legally entitled to $1 million of his deceased wife's assets. How does the payment of $1 million affect the value of:

**a.** F's *gross* estate,

**b.** F's *taxable* estate?

**24-27** *Gross Estate Inclusions.* Q was a cash basis taxpayer who died in the current year. On the date of Q's death, he owned corporate bonds, principal amount of $50,000, with accrued interest of $3,950. On the date of death, the bonds were selling on the open market for $54,000. Six months later the market price of the bonds had dropped to $51,500; there was $3,200 of accrued interest on the bonds as of this date. Neither market price includes any payment for accrued interest.

**a.** Assuming the executor of Q's estate does not elect the alternate valuation date, what amounts should be included in Q's gross estate because of his ownership of the bonds?

**b.** Assuming the executor does elect the alternate valuation date, what amounts should be included in Q's gross estate?

**24-28** *Interests in Trusts Included in Gross Estate.* M's mother left property in trust (Trust A), with the income payable to M for M's lifetime and the remainder to M's daughter. At M's death, Trust A was worth $6.5 million. M's grandfather created a trust (Trust B), with the income payable to M's father for his lifetime. Upon the father's death, the remainder in Trust B was payable to M or M's estate. At M's death, his 82-year-old father was still living and Trust B was worth $2.1 million. Assuming a 5.0 percent interest rate, what are the values of the inclusions in M's gross estate attributable to M's interests in Trust A and Trust B? (See Table S, contained in Appendix A-1.)

**24-29** *Computing Gross Estate.* Upon A's death, certain assets were valued as follows:

| | *Fair Market Value* |
|---|---|
| Probate estate | $ 750,000 |
| Insurance proceeds on a policy on A's life. The policy has always been owned by A's niece, the beneficiary | 150,000 |
| Corpus of Trust A. A possessed the right to give the ownership of the corpus to herself or any of her family. In her will she left the corpus to cousin K | 15,000,000 |

Based on these facts, what is the value of A's gross estate?

**24-30** *Computing Gross Estate.* Upon G's death, the following assets were valued:

| | *Fair Market Value* |
|---|---|
| Probate estate | $5,350,000 |
| Social security benefits payable to G's widow | 38,000 |
| Annuity payable to G's widow out of G's employer's pension plan | 20,000 |
| Corpus of revocable trust created by G for the benefit of his children 10 years prior to death. Upon G's death, the trust becomes irrevocable | 1,000,000 |

What is the value of G's gross estate?

**24-31** *Gifts Included in Gross Estate.* Donor D, age 66, makes a gift in trust for his grandchildren K and L. Under the terms of the trust instrument, D will receive the income from the trust for the rest of his life. Upon his death, the trust assets will be distributed equally between K and L. Upon the date of D's death, at age 77, the value of the trust assets is $2.5 million. What amount, if any, is included in D's gross estate?

**24-32** *Gifts in Contemplation of Death.* In 2009, S made a taxable gift of marketable securities to his nephew and paid a gift tax of $14,250. In 2010, S gave an income interest in trust property to the same nephew and paid a gift tax of $5,000. S originally created the trust in 1990, retaining the income interest for life (the same income interest that he later gave to S) and giving the remainder to another family member. S died in 2011, when the marketable securities were worth $300,000 and the trust property was worth $972,000. Based on these facts, what amounts, if any, are included in S's gross estate?

**24-33** *Gifts Included in Gross Estate.* In 1997, F transferred real estate into a trust, the income from which was payable to M during her lifetime. Upon M's death, the trust property will be distributed in equal portions among M's children. However, the trust instrument gives F the right to change the remainder beneficiaries at any time. F dies in the current year without ever having changed the original trust provisions. At date of death, the trust property is worth $3.9 million and M is 60 years old. Assuming a five percent interest rate, determine the amount, if any, to be included in F's gross estate. (See Table S, contained in Appendix A-1.)

**24-34** *Gifts Included in Gross Estate.* In 1993, P transferred $500,000 of assets into an irrevocable trust for the exclusive benefit of his children. Under the terms of the trust agreement, annual income must be distributed among the children according to P's direction. When the youngest child attains the age of 25 years, the trust corpus will be distributed equally among the living children. P dies in the current year while the trust is still in existence and the corpus has a fair market value of $3,200,000. How much, if any, of the corpus must be included in P's gross estate?

**24-35** *Powers of Appointment.* In 1999, donor D transferred $100,000 of assets into an irrevocable trust for the exclusive benefit of her minor grandchildren. Under the terms of the trust agreement, the grandchildren will receive the annual income from the trust, and when the youngest grandchild attains the age of 21, the trust corpus will be divided among the living grandchildren as S, D's only child, so directs. S dies in the current year while the trust is still in existence and the corpus has a fair market value of $400,000. S's valid will directs that the corpus of the trust will go entirely to grandchild Q. How much, if any, of the corpus must be included in S's gross estate?

**24-36** *Including Insurance in Gross Estate.* Decedent R left a probate estate of $3,000,000. Two years prior to his death, R gave all incidents of ownership in an insurance policy on his own life to his daughter S, the policy beneficiary. Because the policy had a substantial cash surrender value, R paid a gift tax of $77,000 on the transfer. Upon death, the insurance policy paid $5,000,000 to S. What is the value of R's gross estate?

**24-37** *Joint Tenancy.* In 2002, Q paid $500,000 for 100 acres of land and took title with his brother R as joint tenants with right of survivorship. R made no contribution toward the purchase price. This year Q died. At the time of his death, the land was worth $1.2 million. R became the sole owner of land upon Q's death.

**a.** What are the gift tax consequences of the creation of the joint tenancy?

**b.** How much of the date of death value of the land must be included in Q's gross estate?

**c.** How much would be included in the gross estate of R if R, rather than Q, died in the current year?

**24-38** *Computing Taxable Estate.* Decedent T left a gross estate for tax purposes of $8 million. T had personal debts of $60,000 and his estate incurred funeral expenses of $12,000 and legal and accounting fees of $35,000. T's will provided for $100,000 bequest to the American Cancer Society, with all other assets passing to his grandchildren. Compute T's taxable estate.

**24-39** *Sections 2053 and 2054 Expenses.* Decedent D died on July 1 of the current year. D owned a sailboat valued at $85,000 as of the date of death. However, on December 1 of the current year, the boat was destroyed in a storm, and the estate was unable to collect any insurance to compensate for the loss. In December, the executor of D's estate received a $2,200 bill from the company that had stored the sailboat from January 1 through December 1 of the current year.

**a.** If the executor does not elect the alternate valuation date, will the $85,000 value of the boat be included in D's gross estate? D's taxable estate?

**b.** May any portion of the $2,200 storage fee be deducted on D's Federal estate tax return? On the first income tax return filed by the estate?

**24-40** *Marital Deduction Assets.* J, who was employed by Gamma Inc. at the date of his death, had been an active participant in Gamma's qualified retirement plan. Under the terms of the plan, J's widow will receive an annuity of $1,500 per month for the next 20 years. The replacement value of the annuity is $145,000. In his will, J left his interest in a patent worth $50,000 to his widow; the patent will expire in eight years. To what extent will these transfers qualify for a marital deduction from J's gross estate?

**24-41** *Qualified Terminable Interest Trust.* Under the will of decedent H, all his assets (fair market value of $10 million) are to be put into trust. His widow, W, age 64, will be paid all the income from the trust every quarter for the rest of her life. Upon W's death, all the assets in the trust will be distributed to the couple's children and grandchildren. During W's life, no part of the trust corpus can be distributed to anyone but W.

**a.** What amount of marital deduction is available on H's estate tax return?

**b.** W dies eight years after H and under the terms of H's will the trust assets are distributed. What percentage, if any, of the value of these assets must be included in W's gross estate?

**24-42** *Deferring Estate Tax Payments.* Decedent X has the following taxable estate:

| | | |
|---|---|---|
| Sole proprietorship | | $ 8,800,000 |
| Ten percent interest in a closely held corporation | | 200,000 |
| Other assets | | 1,200,000 |
| Gross estate | | $10,200,000 |
| Less sum of | | |
| §§ 2053 and 2054 deductions | $800,000 | |
| § 2056 marital deduction | 400,000 | −1,200,000 |
| Taxable estate | | $ 9,000,000 |

Assume the estate tax liability on this estate is $3,000,000.

**a.** How much of the liability may be deferred under § 6166?

**b.** If X died in November 2011, when is the first installment payment of tax due?

**24-43** *Computing Estate Tax Liability.* Decedent Z died in 2011 and left a taxable estate of $10 million. During his life, Z made the following unrestricted gifts and did not elect gift splitting with his wife:

| | *Fair Market Value* |
|---|---|
| 1995: Gift of 2,000 shares of Acme stock to son S | $900,000 |
| 1997: Gift of cash to daughter D | 600,000 |
| 1999: Gift of cash to wife W | 700,000 |

Compute Z's estate tax liability after utilization of the available unified credit.

**24-44** *Unified Credit.* H and W are husband and wife. They own all of their property in joint tenancy with right of survivorship. This year H died. His estate included $4,000,000 (his ½ interest in all of the property). Will his unified credit be wasted?

## TAX RESEARCH PROBLEMS

**24-45** In 2000, JW gifted 30 percent of her stock in W Corporation to her favorite nephew, N. Although she retained a 50 percent interest in W Corporation and her husband owned the remaining 20 percent of the outstanding stock, JW was concerned that the family might eventually lose control of the firm. To reassure JW, the three stockholders agreed to restrict transferability of their stock by signing an agreement that any shareholder wishing to dispose of W Corporation stock must offer the stock to the corporation for a formula price based on the average net earnings per share for the three previous years. The corporation would then be obligated to purchase the stock at the formula price. At the time the buy-sell agreement was entered into, this formula resulted in a price very close to the stock's actual fair market value.

JW died in the current year at a time when the value of her W Corporation stock was substantially depreciated because of certain unfavorable local economic conditions. Several independent appraisals of the stock valued JW's 50 percent interest at $650,000. However, the formula under the 2000 buy-sell agreement resulted in a value of only $150,000 for the decedent's 50 percent interest. What is the correct value of the 50 percent interest in the corporation for estate tax purposes?

***Research aids*:**

Rev. Rul. 59-60, 1959-1 C.B. 237.
*Estate of Littick*, 31 T.C. 181 (1958), acq. 1959-2 C.B. 5.
Code § 2703.

**24-46** In 2003, Mr. and Mrs. B (residents of a common law state) created two trusts for the benefit of their children. Mr. B transferred $600,000 of his own property into trust, giving the income interest to his wife for her life, and the remainder interest to the children. Mrs. B transferred $640,000 of her own property into trust, giving the income interest to her husband for his life, and the remainder interest to the children. In the current year, Mrs. B dies. How much, if any, of the current value of the corpus of the 2003 trust created by Mrs. B will be included in her gross estate?

***Research aids*:**

*United States v. Estate of Grace*, 69-1 USTC ¶12,609.
23 AFTR 2d 69-1954, 395 U.S. 316 (USSC, 1969).

# 25

# Income Taxation of Estates and Trusts

## Learning Objectives

Upon completion of this chapter you will be able to:

LO.1 Compute fiduciary accounting income and determine the required allocation of such income among the various beneficiaries of the fiduciary.

LO.2 Identify the special rules that apply to the computation of fiduciary taxable income.

LO.3 Explain the concept of income and deductions in respect of a decedent.

LO.4 Compute both the taxable and nontaxable components of a fiduciary's distributable net income.

LO.5 Describe the defining characteristics of a simple and a complex trust, including:

- The computation of the deduction for distributions to beneficiaries for both types of trusts.
- The distinction between tier one and tier two distributions from a complex trust.

LO.6 Determine the tax consequences of fiduciary distributions to the recipient beneficiaries.

## Chapter Outline


Introduction 25-2
The Function of Estates and Trusts 25-2
- Estates 25-2
- Trusts 25-2
- Trust Beneficiaries 25-3
- Fiduciary Accounting Income 25-3

Income Taxation of Fiduciaries 25-5
Fiduciary Taxable Income 25-6
- Fiduciary Tax Rates 25-6
- Standard Deduction and Personal Exemption 25-6
- Limitations on Deductibility of Fiduciary Expenses 25-6
- Charitable Contributions 25-9
- Depreciation, Depletion, and Amortization 25-9
- Fiduciary Losses 25-10

Income and Deductions in Respect of a Decedent 25-11
- Estate Tax Treatment and the § 691(c) Deduction 25-11

The Distribution Deduction and the Taxation of Beneficiaries 25-13
- Computation of Distribution Deduction and DNI 25-14
- The Computation of DNI 25-15

Simple Trusts 25-16
Complex Trusts and Estates 25-16
Character of Beneficiary's Income 25-19
Reporting Requirements for Beneficiaries 25-21
The Separate Share Rule 25-21
A Comprehensive Example 25-22
The Sixty-Five Day Rule 25-24
Tax Planning Considerations 25-30
Problem Materials 25-30


## Introduction

Trusts and estates are taxable entities subject to a specialized set of tax rules contained in Subchapter J of the Internal Revenue Code (§§ 641 through 692). The income taxation of trusts and estates (commonly referred to as fiduciary taxpayers) and their beneficiaries is the subject of this chapter. Grantor trusts, a type of trust not recognized as a taxable entity and therefore not subject to the rules of Subchapter J, are discussed in Chapter 26.

## The Function of Estates and Trusts

### Estates

An estate as a legal entity comes into existence upon the death of an individual. During the period of time in which the decedent's legal affairs are being settled, assets owned by the decedent are managed by an executor or administrator of the estate. Once all legal requirements have been satisfied, the estate terminates and ownership of all estate assets passes to the decedent's beneficiaries or heirs.

During its existence, the decedent's estate is a taxable entity that files a tax return and pays Federal income taxes on any income earned.[1] Normally an estate is a transitional entity that bridges the brief gap in time between the death of an individual taxpayer and the distribution of that individual's wealth to other taxpayers. However, estates as taxpayers may continue in existence for many years if the correct distribution of a decedent's wealth is in question. If the administration of a decedent's estate is unreasonably prolonged, the IRS may treat the estate as terminated for tax purposes after a reasonable amount of time for settlement of the decedent's affairs has elapsed.[2]

### Trusts

A trust is a legal arrangement in which an individual, the *grantor*, transfers legal ownership of assets to one party, the *trustee*, and the legal right to enjoy and benefit from those assets to a second party, the *beneficiary* (or beneficiaries). Such an arrangement is usually designed for the protection of the beneficiary. Often trust beneficiaries are minor children or family members incapable of competently managing the assets themselves.

The terms of the trust, the duties of the trustee, and the rights of the various beneficiaries are specified in a legal document, the *trust instrument*. The assets put into trust are referred to as the trust *corpus*, or *principal*.

The role of the trustee is that of a fiduciary; he or she is required to act in the best interests of the trust beneficiaries rather than for his or her own interests. The position of trustee is usually filled by the professional trust department of a bank or a competent friend or family member. Professional trustees receive an annual fee to compensate them for services rendered.

The purpose of a trust is to protect and conserve trust assets for the sole benefit of the trust beneficiaries, not to operate a trade or business. A trust that becomes involved in an

[1] § 641(a)(3).

[2] Reg. § 1.641(b)-3(a).

active, profit-making business activity runs the risk of being classified as an *association* for Federal tax purposes, with the unfavorable result that it will be taxed as a corporation rather than under the rules of Subchapter J.[3]

## Trust Beneficiaries

An individual who desires to establish a trust has virtually unlimited discretion as to the identity of the trust beneficiaries and the nature of the interest in the trust given to each beneficiary. For example, assume grantor G creates a trust consisting of $1 million of assets. G could specify in the trust instrument that individual I is to receive all the income of the trust for I's life, and upon I's death the assets in the trust are to be distributed to individual R. In this example, both I and R are trust beneficiaries. I owns an *income interest* in the trust, while R owns a *remainder interest* (the right to the trust principal at some future date).

A grantor can give trust beneficiaries any mix of rights to trust income or principal (trust assets) that will best accomplish the goals of the trust. In the previous example, if grantor G decided that the trust income might be insufficient to provide for I, the trust document could specify that I also will receive a certain amount of trust principal every year. Alternatively, if G believed that I might not need all the trust income annually, the trust document could provide that the trustee could accumulate income to distribute to I at some later point. As may be apparent, a trust can be a very flexible arrangement for providing for the needs of specific beneficiaries.

## Fiduciary Accounting Income

**LO.1**
Compute fiduciary accounting income and determine the required allocation of such income among the various beneficiaries of the fiduciary.

There is no standard accounting system that applies to fiduciaries. The accounting income of an estate or trust is determined by reference to the decedent's valid will or the trust instrument. These documents can specify how fiduciary receipts, disbursements, and other transactions affect income, principal, or both. In other words, every fiduciary may have its own unique set of rules for the computation of accounting income, and the executor or trustee must refer exclusively to this income number in carrying out his or her duties. If a will or trust instrument is silent concerning the impact of a particular transaction on accounting income, such impact must be determined by reference to controlling state law. Most states have enacted a version of the Revised Uniform Principal and Income Act, a model set of fiduciary accounting rules proposed by the Uniform Commission on State Laws.

One common difference between fiduciary accounting income and taxable income is the classification of fiduciary capital gains. Typically, capital gains represent an increase in the value of the principal of the fiduciary and normally are not available for distribution to income beneficiaries. Of course, for Federal tax purposes capital gains represent taxable income. Similarly, stock dividends are often regarded as an increase in principal rather than trust income, even though the dividend may be taxable income under the Internal Revenue Code.

Trustee fees are generally deductible for tax purposes. However, for fiduciary accounting purposes such fees may be charged *either* to trust income or to trust principal.

Depreciation may or may not have an effect on fiduciary accounting income. If local law or the trust instrument requires the fiduciary to establish a reserve for depreciation, depreciation is computed in accordance with the local law or the trust instrument and subtracted in computing trust accounting income. In effect, the fiduciary transfers cash out of income (reducing the amount that can be distributed to the income beneficiary) and sets this amount aside for future replacement of the depreciable property. Note that the amount of depreciation computed for tax purposes can be quite different than the amount of depreciation for fiduciary accounting income purposes. For this reason, tax depreciation requires special treatment as described below.

Exhibit 25-1 identifies various items of income and expense and shows how they are normally allocated between income and corpus.

[3] See *Morrissey v. Comm.*, 36-1 USTC ¶9020, 16 AFTR 1274, 296 U.S. 344 (USSC, 1936), for this result.

**EXHIBIT 25.1** **Fiduciary Accounting Income**

***Typical income items***

- Interest
- Dividends
- Royalties
- Net rental income (income less expenses) from real or personal property
- Net profits from operation of a trade or business; losses are usually charged to corpus
- All or a portion of trustee commissions
- Depreciation to the extent of any required reserve

***Typical corpus items***

- Gain or loss on the sale or exchange of trust property (capital gains)
- Casualty losses
- Stock dividends
- All or a portion of trustee commissions

## Example 1

During the year, the records of a trust revealed the following information:

| | |
|---|---|
| *Receipts:* | |
| Dividends | $10,000 |
| Interest from municipal bonds | 12,000 |
| Long-term capital gain allocable to principal under state law | 6,500 |
| Stock dividend allocable to principal under the trust instrument | 4,000 |
| Total receipts | $32,500 |
| *Disbursements:* | |
| Trustee fee (half allocable to trust income; half allocable to principal under the trust instrument) | $ 3,000 |

Based on the above, the accounting income of the trust would be $20,500, computed as follows:

| | |
|---|---|
| Dividends | $10,000 |
| Interest from municipal bonds | 12,000 |
| | $22,000 |
| Less: One-half of the trustee fee ($3,000 ÷ 2) | (1,500) |
| Trust accounting income | $20,500 |

If the trustee of this particular trust was required to distribute the entire amount of trust income to a particular group of beneficiaries, the trustee would make a payment of $20,500. Note that this amount bears little relationship to the *taxable income* generated by the trust's activities.

## Income Taxation of Fiduciaries

For Federal tax purposes, fiduciaries are taxable entities.[4] Every estate that has annual gross income of $600 or more, and every trust that has either annual gross income of $600 or more *or* any taxable trust income, must file an income tax return. Furthermore, if a fiduciary has a beneficiary who is a nonresident alien, that fiduciary must file a return regardless of the amount of its gross or taxable income for the year.[5]

Form 1041, the U.S. Fiduciary Income Tax Return, must be filed by the 15th day of the fourth month following the close of the fiduciary's taxable year (see Appendix B for sample Form 1041). An estate may adopt a calendar or any fiscal taxable year. However, the taxable year of a trust must be a calendar year.[6] In the case of an estate, the first taxable year begins on the day following the date of death of the decedent.[7] In the case of a trust, the date of creation as specified in the controlling trust instrument marks the beginning of the first taxable year.

Fiduciaries generally must make quarterly estimated tax payments in the same manner as individuals. However, no estimated taxes must be paid by an estate or a grantor trust to which the residual of the grantor's estate is distributed for any taxable year ending within the two years following the decedent's death.[8] A trustee may *elect* to treat any portion of an excess estimated tax payment made by a trust as a payment of estimated tax made by a beneficiary. If the election is made, the payment is considered as having been distributed to the beneficiary on the last day of the trust's taxable year and then remitted to the government as estimated tax paid by the beneficiary on January 15th of the following year.[9]

### Example 2

On April 15, 2008, Trust T made an estimated tax payment of $14,000. However, later in the year, the trustee decided to distribute all 2008 trust income to beneficiary B. Because Trust T will have no 2008 tax liability, the trustee may elect to treat the $14,000 payment as a cash distribution made to beneficiary B on December 31, 2008. Beneficiary B will report the $14,000 as part of his 2008 estimated tax payment made on January 15, 2009.

Section 641 (b) provides that "the taxable income of an estate or trust shall be computed in the same manner as in the case of an individual, except as otherwise provided in this part." Thus, many of the rules governing the taxation of individuals apply to fiduciaries. Before examining the specific rules unique to fiduciary income taxation, it will be useful to look at the basic approach for computing fiduciary taxable income.

**Step One:** Compute fiduciary accounting income and identify any receipts and disbursements allocated to principal (under either the trust instrument or state law).

**Step Two:** Compute fiduciary taxable income *before* the deduction for distributions to beneficiaries authorized by Code §§ 651 and 661.

**Step Three:** Compute the deduction for distributions to beneficiaries. This step will require a computation of fiduciary "distributable net income" (DNI).

**Step Four:** Subtract the deduction for distributions to arrive at *fiduciary taxable income.*

Step One, the computation of fiduciary accounting income, was discussed earlier. Detailed discussions of Steps Two and Three constitute most of the remainder of this chapter.

---

[4] See §§ 7701(a)(6) and 641(a).

[5] § 6012(a)(3), (4), and (5).

[6] § 645. This requirement does not apply to tax-exempt and charitable trusts.

[7] See Reg. §§ 1.443-1(a)(2), and 1.461-1(b).

[8] § 6654(l).

[9] § 643(g).

## Fiduciary Taxable Income

**LO.2**
Identify the special rules that apply to the computation of fiduciary taxable income.

Unless otherwise modified, the fiduciary computes its taxable income in a manner identical to that of an individual taxpayer. The major difference is the deduction granted for distributions made to beneficiaries, explained later in this chapter. In addition, § 642 contains a number of special provisions that must be followed in computing fiduciary taxable income and the final tax. These unique aspects of estate and trust taxation are considered below.

### Fiduciary Tax Rates

The tax rates for estates and trusts for 2008 are shown in Exhibit 25-2. Note that the 10 percent rate that applies to individuals does not apply to trusts or estates. Also note that there is very little progressivity in the fiduciary rate schedule; taxable income in excess of $10,700 is taxed at the highest 35 percent rate. However, under § 1(j), any component of fiduciary taxable income consisting of net long-term capital gain or dividend income is taxed at a maximum 15 percent rate.

**EXHIBIT 25.2 Income Tax Rates for Estates and Trusts**

For Taxable Years Beginning in 2011

| *If taxable income is* | | | | | |
|---|---|---|---|---|---|
| **Over—** | **But not over—** | **The tax is** | | | **Of the amount over—** |
| $ 0 | $ 2,300 | $ 0 | | 15% | $ 0 |
| 2,300 | 5,450 | 345.00 | + | 25% | 2,300 |
| 5,450 | 8,300 | 1,132.50 | + | 28% | 5,450 |
| 8,300 | 11,350 | 1,930.50 | + | 33% | 8,300 |
| 11,350 | — | 2,937.00 | + | 35% | 11,350 |

In determining their final tax liability, fiduciaries are subject to the alternative minimum tax provisions.[10]

### Standard Deduction and Personal Exemption

Unlike individual taxpayers, fiduciaries are not entitled to a standard deduction.[11] However, a fiduciary, like an individual taxpayer, is entitled to a personal exemption. The amount of the exemption depends on the type of fiduciary. The personal exemption for an estate is $600. The exemption for a trust that is required by the trust instrument to distribute all trust income currently is $300. The exemption for any trust not subject to this requirement is $100.[12]

### Limitations on Deductibility of Fiduciary Expenses

Because fiduciaries generally do not engage in the conduct of a business, the gross income of a fiduciary usually consists of investment income items such as dividends, interest, rents, and royalties. Fiduciary expenses are normally deductible under the authority of § 212, which provides for the deduction of ordinary and necessary expenses paid for the management, conservation, or maintenance of property held for the production of income. However, there are several limitations on the deduction of expenses that apply to individuals that also apply to fiduciaries.

[10] See § 59(c). A special computation is used that is beyond the scope of this text.

[11] § 63(c)(6)(D).

[12] § 642(b).

### Limitations on Deductions Related to Tax-Exempt Income

As a general rule, § 265 denies the deduction for any expenses related to tax-exempt income. In contrast, any expense that is *directly related* to taxable fiduciary income is fully deductible. For example, rent expenses are directly related to rental income and would not be subject to this limitation. Expenses that are not directly related to a particular type of income—sometimes referred to as *indirect* expenses—must be allocated proportionately between taxable and tax-exempt income.[13] For example, consider a common expenditure of trusts such as trustee commissions. These fees are viewed as relating to both taxable and tax-exempt income and, therefore, an allocation is required. Assuming 20 percent of the trust's income is tax-exempt, then 20 percent of the trustee commission would be nondeductible. On the other hand, most practitioners take the position that tax preparation fees need not be allocated to tax-exempt income since they are only related to taxable income.

The portion of an indirect expense that is not deductible can be determined using the following formula:

$$\frac{\text{Tax exempt income}}{\text{Total trust income}} \times \begin{array}{c}\text{Expenses not directly related to}\\ \text{a particular type of income}\end{array} = \begin{array}{c}\text{Nondeductible}\\ \text{expenses}\end{array}$$

In computing the denominator of the above formula, trust accounting income does not include capital gains unless capital gains are actually included in trust accounting income.[14] In addition, the denominator is computed using gross receipts.

## Example 3

This year Trust T paid trustee fees of $7,000, $5,000 allocable to income and $2,000 allocable to corpus. Its records reveal the following additional information:

| | Amounts |
|---|---|
| Rental income | $70,000 |
| Rental expenses | (30,000) |
| Net rental income | $40,000 |
| | |
| Long-term capital gains allocable to corpus | $25,000 |
| Long-term capital losses allocable to corpus | (5,000) |
| Net capital gain | $20,000 |
| | |
| Sales | $20,000 |
| Costs of goods sold | (15,000) |
| Gross income | $ 5,000 |
| | |
| Interest on State of New York bonds | $10,000 |

To determine the amount of commissions that are not deductible, the denominator does not include the net capital gain allocable to corpus of $20,000. However, the denominator does include the gross amounts of income received and is not reduced by expenses. Thus the denominator includes the rent of $70,000, sales of $20,000, and tax-exempt interest of $10,000 for a total of $100,000. Therefore 10% ($10,000/$100,000) of the $7,000 of trustee's commissions or $700 is not deductible, and the remaining $6,300 is deductible. Note that in computing the amount of the deductible commissions, the fact that they are allocable to income or corpus for trust accounting purposes is irrelevant.

---

[13] Reg. § 1.642(g)-2.

[14] Rev. Rul. 77-365. Other approaches may be available. For example, see *Whittemore, Jr. v. U.S.* 20 AFTR 2d 5533, 67-2 USTC ¶9670 383 F.2d 824 (CA-8, 1967).

## Limitation on Double Deduction of Administrative Expenses

Section 642(g) provides a second major limitation on the deductibility of fiduciary expenses. If an administrative expense is claimed as a deduction on the estate tax return of a decedent, it may not also be claimed as a deduction on an income tax return of the decedent's estate or subsequent trust. However, Regulation § 1.642(g)-2 provides that administrative expenses that could be deducted for either estate tax or income tax purposes can be divided between the two returns in whatever portions achieve maximum tax benefit.

## Limitation on Miscellaneous Itemized Deductions

Section 67(a) limits certain miscellaneous itemized deductions, including the § 212 deduction for investment expenses. Such itemized deductions are allowed only to the extent they exceed 2 percent of adjusted gross income. Section 67(e) provides that the deduction for expenses paid or incurred in connection with the administration of a fiduciary that would have been avoided if the property were not held by the fiduciary shall be allowable in computing the adjusted gross income of the fiduciary. In other words, fiduciary expenses such as administration fees which are incurred only because of the trust or estate form are not considered itemized deductions subject to the 2 percent floor. Unfortunately, whether an expense is unique to a trust or an estate is not always clear. Most of the controversy has concerned investment management and advisory expenses. However, in 2008, the Supreme Court resolved the matter, holding that investment management and advisory fees were miscellaneous itemized deductions.[15] According to the Court, if an expense of a trust or estate is commonly incurred by an individual, it is not unique to a trust. Applying this theory to fees for investment management, the Court believed that it would not be uncommon or unusual for individuals to hire an investment adviser. Therefore, it held that such expenses are miscellaneous itemized deductions. In this regard, the proposed regulations would require that trustee fees be unbundled so that the proper amounts may be allocated properly between trust or estate administration and investment advice. After the *Knight* decision, it appears that such expenses as the costs of accounting, tax return preparation, division of income or corpus among beneficiaries, will or trust contests or construction, fiduciary bond premiums and communications with beneficiaries regarding trust or estate matters would not be miscellaneous itemized deductions.

The computation of the limitation on miscellaneous itemized deductions can be quite cumbersome. Since adjusted gross income of the trust depends on the amount of the distribution deduction and the distribution deduction in turn depends on taxable income after taking into account the deduction for miscellaneous itemized deductions (taxable DNI as explained below), the calculation of allowable miscellaneous itemized deductions may require the use of simultaneous algebraic equations.

## Deduction Cutback

Section 68 generally requires that the total of an individual's itemized deductions for the year be reduced by a percentage of the amount of adjusted gross income in excess of an inflation adjusted threshold. This requirement is expressly inapplicable to any estate or trust.[16]

## Medical Expenses

Medical expenses paid by an estate or trust require special consideration. Medical expenses paid for the care of a *decedent* prior to his death that are paid by an estate within one year after death can be deducted either on the income tax return of the decedent (final Form 1040) or the estate tax return (Form 706), but not both. Medical expenses paid after the one-year period are deductible only as liabilities on the estate tax return (Form 706) if such return is actually filed. Medical expenses of *beneficiaries* that are paid by the trust or estate are treated as distributions of income to the beneficiaries and are not deductible per se on the fiduciary income tax return.

---

[15] *Michael J. Knight, Trustee of the William L. Rudkin Testamentary Trust,*, 2008-1 USTC ¶50,132, 101 AFTR 2d 2008-544, 128 S. Ct. 782 (USSC, 2008).

[16] § 68(e).

## Charitable Contributions

Section 642(c) authorizes an unlimited charitable deduction for any amount of gross income paid by a fiduciary to a qualified charitable organization. Fiduciaries are given a great deal of flexibility as to the timing of charitable contributions; if a contribution is paid after the close of one taxable year but before the close of the next taxable year, the fiduciary may elect to deduct the payment in the earlier year.[17]

If a fiduciary receives tax-exempt income that is available for charitable distribution, its deduction for any charitable contribution made normally must be reduced by that portion of the contribution attributable to tax-exempt income.[18]

### Example 4

During the current year, Trust T receives $30,000 of tax-exempt interest, $25,000 of taxable interest, and $45,000 of taxable dividends. The trust makes a charitable contribution of $20,000 during the year. Because 30% of the trust's income available for distribution is nontaxable, 30% of the charitable distribution is nondeductible and the trust's deduction for charitable contributions is limited to $14,000.

## Depreciation, Depletion, and Amortization

The total allowable amount of depreciation, depletion, and amortization that may be deducted by the fiduciary (or passed through to the beneficiaries) is determined in the normal manner. A fiduciary is entitled to bonus depreciation but not allowed to expense any portion of the cost of eligible property under § 179.

Deductions for depreciation and depletion available to a fiduciary depend upon the terms of the controlling will or trust instrument. If the controlling instrument authorizes a reserve for depreciation or depletion, any *allowable* (deductible) tax depreciation or depletion will be deductible by the fiduciary to the extent of the specified reserve. If the allowable tax depreciation or depletion exceeds the reserve, the excess deduction is allocated between the fiduciary and beneficiaries based upon the amount of fiduciary income allocable to each.[19]

### Example 5

Trust R owns rental property with a basis of $300,000. The trust instrument authorizes the trustee to maintain an annual depreciation reserve of $15,000 (5% of the cost of the property). For tax purposes, however, the current year's depreciation deduction is $22,000. The trust instrument provides that one-half of annual trust income including rents will be distributed to the trust beneficiaries. For the current year, the trust is entitled to a depreciation deduction of $18,500 [5% of $300,000 + one-half the tax depreciation in excess of $15,000 (½ × $7,000 = $3,500)].

Note that if the controlling instrument is silent, depreciation and depletion deductions are simply allocated between fiduciary and beneficiaries on the basis of fiduciary income allocable to each. If a fiduciary is entitled to statutory amortization, the amortization deduction also will be apportioned among fiduciary and beneficiaries on the basis of income allocable to each.[20]

---

[17] § 642(c)(1). See Reg. § 1.642(c)-1(b) for the time and manner in which such an election is to be made.

[18] Reg. § 1.642(c)-3(b).

[19] Reg. § 1.167(h)-1; Reg. § 1.611-1(c)(4).

[20] Reg. § 1.642(f)-1.

## Fiduciary Losses

Because the function of a trust generally is to conserve and protect existing wealth rather than to engage in potentially risky business activities, it is unusual for a trust to incur a net operating loss. It is not unusual, however, for an estate or trust that owns a business interest (e.g., an interest in a partnership or an S corporation) to incur this type of loss. In any case, if a net operating loss does occur, a fiduciary may carry the loss back two years and forward for 20.[21] Capital losses incurred by a fiduciary are deductible against capital gains; a maximum of $3,000 of net capital loss may be deducted against other sources of income.[22] Nondeductible net capital losses are carried forward to subsequent taxable years of the fiduciary.[23]

Fiduciaries are also subject to the limitations imposed on passive activity losses and credits by § 469.[24] Therefore, a fiduciary may only deduct current losses from passive activities against current income from passive activities. Any nondeductible loss is suspended and carried forward to subsequent taxable years. If an interest in a passive activity is distributed by a fiduciary to a beneficiary, any suspended loss of the activity is added to the tax basis of the distributed interest.[25]

Section 469(i) normally provides for a $25,000 *de minimis* offset for losses attributable to rental real estate. However, this allowance is extended only to "natural persons" and, therefore, normally does not apply to trusts or estates. This rule prevents taxpayers from circumventing the $25,000 limitation by transferring multiple properties to multiple trusts with each claiming a $25,000 allowance. However, the provision is extended to estates for losses occurring for tax years ending less than two years after the decedent's date of death.

### NOLs, Capital Losses, and Excess Deductions

Unlike the net losses of a partnership or an S corporation, fiduciary losses do not flow through to beneficiaries. An exception to this rule applies for the year in which a trust or estate terminates. If the terminating fiduciary has net operating losses, capital loss carry-forwards, or current year deductions in excess of current gross income, § 642(h) provides that such unused losses and excess deductions become available to the beneficiaries succeeding to the property of the fiduciary.

#### Example 6

D died in 2011. In 2012, the year of termination, the estate had gross income of $5,000 and legal fees of $15,000. The excess deductions of $10,000 do not create an NOL (that would carryover to the beneficiaries) since legal fees are considered a nonbusiness expense and are not deductible in computing an NOL. However, because the excess deductions occur in the year of termination, they pass through to the beneficiary who can claim the $10,000 as an itemized deduction. It should be emphasized that had this not been the year of termination, the $10,000 excess would be wasted. Due to this treatment, the fiduciary should take steps to ensure that excess deductions occur only in the year of termination. For example, a cash basis estate could postpone paying the legal fees until the final year.

Casualty losses of a fiduciary are subject to the rules pertaining to individual taxpayers. For casualty losses, the limitation of the deduction to that amount in excess of 10 percent of adjusted gross income applies, although the concept of adjusted gross income is normally not associated with trusts or estates.[26] In addition, § 642(g) prohibits the deduction by a fiduciary of any loss that has already been claimed as a deduction on an estate tax return.

---

[21] §§ 172(b)(1) and 642(d).

[22] § 1211(b).

[23] § 1212(b).

[24] § 469(a)(2)(A).

[25] § 469(j)(12).

[26] See Form 4684 and its instructions for this computation.

# Income and Deductions in Respect of a Decedent

**LO.3**
Explain the concept of income and deductions in respect of a decedent.

The death of an individual taxpayer can create a peculiar timing problem involving the reporting of income items earned or deductible expenses incurred by the taxpayer prior to death. For example, if a cash basis individual had performed all the services required to earn a $5,000 consulting fee but had not collected the fee before death, by whom shall the $5,000 of *income in respect of a decedent* (IRD) be reported? The individual taxpayer who earned the income never received payment, but the recipient of the money, the individual's estate, is not the taxpayer who earned it. Section 691(a) gives a statutory solution to this puzzling question by providing that any income of an individual not properly includible in the taxable period prior to the individual's death will be included in the gross income of the recipient of the income, typically the estate of the decedent or a beneficiary of the estate. Common IRD items include unpaid salary or commissions, retirement income (e.g., IRA), rent income, or interest accrued but unpaid at death, and the amount of a § 453 installment obligation that would have been recognized as income if payment had been received by the decedent prior to death.

Certain expenses incurred by a decedent but not properly deductible on the decedent's final return because of nonpayment are afforded similar statutory treatment. Under § 691(b), these *deductions in respect of a decedent* (DRD) are deducted by the taxpayer who is legally required to make payment. Allowable DRD items include business and income-producing expenses, interest, taxes, and depletion.

## Estate Tax Treatment and the § 691(c) Deduction

Items of IRD and DRD represent assets and liabilities of the deceased taxpayer. As such, these items will be included on the decedent's estate tax return. Because IRD and DRD also have future income tax consequences, special provisions in the tax law apply to these items. First, even though the right to IRD is an asset acquired from a decedent, the basis of an IRD item does not become the item's fair market value at date of death. Instead, under § 1014(c), the basis of the item to the decedent carries over to the new owner. This special rule preserves the potential income that must be recognized when the IRD item is eventually collected. The character of IRD also is determined by reference to the decedent taxpayer.

Secondly, items of DRD that are deducted as administrative expenses on an estate tax return are *not* subject to the rule prohibiting a deduction on a subsequent income tax return.[27] Therefore, unlike administrative expenses of an estate that cannot be deducted on both the fiduciary income tax return (Form 1041) and the estate tax return (Form 706), DRD can be deducted on both.

Perhaps the most important reason for identifying items of IRD is the allowance of a special deduction for the recipient. To appreciate this deduction, consider the normal estate tax treatment given to a decedent's income. Such income is included *net* of any income tax that the decedent has paid. In contrast, items of IRD are included without reduction for the related income tax since the income tax on IRD is not a liability of the decedent but a liability of the recipient. Consequently, the amount of IRD income that is included in the gross estate is overstated and, therefore, the related estate tax is overstated. An heir who is the recipient of the income ends up with less than he would have had if the income had been taxed to the decedent and passed on to the heir net of the estate tax.

### Example 7

D died on March 7, 2011. For illustration purposes, assume he was in the 40% income tax bracket and the 50% estate tax bracket. At the time of his death, D's employer owed him $10,000 of income. The following analysis shows the tax consequences that result if D had collected the $10,000 before he died as compared to those which would occur if his son, his heir, collects the $10,000 (assuming he is in the 40% tax bracket).

[27] § 642(g).

| | *D Collects Before Death* | *Total Tax* | *Heir Collects After Death* | *Total Tax* |
|---|---|---|---|---|
| Income | $10,000 | | $10,000 | |
| Income tax to decedent | (4,000) | $4,000 | 0 | $ 0 |
| Aftertax income in estate | $ 6,000 | | $10,000 | |
| Estate tax at 50% | $ 3,000 | 3,000 | $ 5,000 | 5,000 |
| Income to heir | $ 0 | | $10,000 | |
| Income tax to heir | | | $ 4,000 | 4,000 |
| Total income and estate tax | | $7,000 | | $9,000 |

In this case, the total income and estate tax imposed on the $10,000 if D collected the $10,000 is $7,000. In contrast, if the heir collects the $10,000 from the employer the total income and estate tax is $9,000. The $2,000 difference is attributable to the fact that the entire $10,000 is subject to estate tax in the latter case while only $6,000 ($10,000 net of the income tax of $4,000) is subject to estate tax in the first case (50% × $4,000 = $2,000).

Perhaps the best way to treat this problem is to estimate the amount of income tax that the decedent would have paid had he or she received the income and give the estate a deduction for this amount. However, because this amount would presumably be difficult to estimate, the authors of § 691 opted for an alternative that produces about the same result. Section 691(c) allows the recipient of IRD a deduction for any estate tax attributable to the income.

The deduction is a percentage of the estate tax attributable to the total *net* IRD included in an estate based on the ratio of the recognized IRD item to all IRD items. Estate tax attributable to net IRD is the excess of the actual tax over the tax computed without including the IRD in the taxable estate.

The § 691(c) deduction can be computed using the following two steps:

1. Determine the estate tax attributable to net IRD:

   Estate tax actually incurred (including net IRD)
   − Estate tax without NIRD
   = Total estate tax attributable to IRD

2. Recipient's deduction is based on the proportionate amount of IRD (not net IRD) that is received.

$$\frac{\text{IRD received}}{\text{Total IRD}} \times \text{Total estate tax attributable to IRD} = \text{Section 691(c) deduction}$$

Note that if an estate or trust is the recipient of the IRD, it is not subject to the deduction cutback for itemized deductions. In contrast, if an individual taxpayer receives the IRD, the amount is considered an itemized deduction.

## Example 8

Taxpayer T's estate tax return included total IRD items valued at $145,000. DRD items totaled $20,000. If the *net* IRD of $125,000 had not been included in T's estate, the Federal estate tax liability would have decreased by $22,000. During the current year, the estate of T collected half ($72,500) of all IRD items and included this amount in estate gross income. T's estate is entitled to a § 691(c) deduction of $11,000.

## The Distribution Deduction and the Taxation of Beneficiaries

The central concept of Subchapter J is that income recognized by a fiduciary will be taxed *either* to the fiduciary itself or to the beneficiaries of the fiduciary. The determination of the amount of income taxable to each depends upon the amount of annual distributions from the fiduciary to the beneficiary. Conceptually, distributions to beneficiaries represent a flow-through of trust income that will be taxed to the beneficiary. Under §§ 651 and 661, the amount of the distribution will then be available as a *deduction* to the fiduciary, reducing the taxable income the fiduciary must report. Income that flows through the fiduciary to a beneficiary retains its original character; therefore, the fiduciary acts as a *conduit*, similar to a partnership in this respect.[28]

In computing the deduction for distributions, the law generally presumes that *every distribution consists of a pro rata portion of current taxable and nontaxable income that is in fact distributable*. Sections 651 and 661 refer to this quantity as *a distributable net income* (DNI) and allow the fiduciary a deduction for amounts distributed but limit the deduction to taxable DNI. It should be emphasized that whatever amount is deductible by the fiduciary is the same amount that is taxable to the beneficiaries. This follows from the fact that the deduction merely serves to allocate taxable income from the fiduciary to the beneficiary. Distributions exceeding DNI represent accumulated income of the fiduciary that has been previously taxed, or corpus. Such amounts are neither deductible by the fiduciary nor taxable to the beneficiary.

Before further examining the computation of the deduction concept and DNI, it is important to understand that a trust or estate can make distributions of either cash or property, both of which may or may not carry out DNI (i.e., taxable and nontaxable income). However, § 663(a)(1) provides that *specific* gifts or bequests properly distributed from a fiduciary to a beneficiary under the terms of the governing instrument are distributions of principal rather than of income. Correspondingly, the fiduciary does not recognize gain or loss upon the distribution of a specific property bequest.

### Example 9

During the current year, the Estate of Z recognized $30,000 of income, all of which is taxable. During the year, the executor of the estate distributed a pearl necklace to beneficiary B. The necklace had a fair market value of $6,000. If the will of decedent Z specifically provided for the distribution of the necklace to B, no estate income will be taxed to her. Alternatively, if there were no such specific bequest and B received the necklace as part of her general interest in estate assets, she will have received an income distribution.

The amount of income associated with a property distribution from a fiduciary depends upon the tax treatment of the distribution *elected* by the fiduciary. Section 643(e)(3) provides an election under which the fiduciary recognizes gain on the distribution of appreciated property as if the property had been sold at its fair market value. In this case, the amount of fiduciary income carried by the property distribution and the basis of the property in the hands of the beneficiary equals the property's fair market value. If the election is not made, the distribution of property produces no gain or loss to the fiduciary, and the amount of fiduciary income carried by the distribution is the lesser of the basis of such property in the hands of the fiduciary or the property's fair market value.[29] In the case where the election is not made, the basis of the property in the hands of the fiduciary will carry over as the basis of the property in the hands of the beneficiary.[30]

---

[28] §§ 652(b) and 662(b).

[29] § 643(e)(2).

[30] § 643(e)(1).

### Example 10

During the current year, Trust T distributes property to beneficiary B. The distribution is not a specific gift of property. On the date of distribution, the property has a basis to the trust of $10,000 and a fair market value of $17,000. If the trust so elects, it will recognize a $7,000 gain on the distribution, and B will be considered to have received a $17,000 income distribution and will have a $17,000 basis in the property. If the trustee does not make the election, it will not recognize any gain upon distribution of the property. B will be considered to have received only a $10,000 income distribution and will have only a $10,000 basis in the property.

When a beneficiary is entitled to a specific gift or bequest of a sum of money (a pecuniary gift or bequest), and the fiduciary distributes property in satisfaction of such gift or bequest, any appreciation or depreciation in the property is recognized as a gain or loss to the fiduciary.[31]

### Example 11

Under the terms of E's will, beneficiary M is to receive the sum of $60,000. E's executor distributes 600 shares of corporate stock to M to satisfy this pecuniary bequest. At the time of distribution, the stock has a fair market value of $100 a share and a basis to E's estate of $75 a share. Upon distribution, the estate must recognize a capital gain of $15,000 (600 shares × $25 per share appreciation). Note that because this distribution represents a specific bequest, it is not an income distribution to M and the § 643(e)(3) election is inapplicable. The basis of the stock to M will be its fair market value.

In any case in which the distribution of depreciated property by a trust or an estate to a beneficiary results in the recognition of loss, § 267 disallows any deduction of the loss by the trust.

## Computation of Distribution Deduction and DNI

To calculate the distribution deduction available to a fiduciary and the amount of fiduciary income taxable to beneficiaries, it is first necessary to calculate the *distributable net income* (DNI) of the fiduciary. DNI represents the net income of a fiduciary available for distribution to income beneficiaries.

DNI has several important characteristics. First, it does not include taxable income that is unavailable for distribution to income beneficiaries. For example, in most states capital gains realized upon the sale of fiduciary assets are considered to represent a part of *trust principal* and are not considered *fiduciary income*. Such capital gains, while taxable, are not included in DNI. Secondly, DNI may include nontaxable income that is available for distribution to income beneficiaries.

At this point, it would appear that the amount of DNI is the same amount as fiduciary accounting income. However, there is an important difference between the two concepts. All expenses that are deductible *for tax purposes* by the fiduciary enter into the DNI calculation, even if some of these expenses are chargeable to principal and not deducted in computing fiduciary accounting income.

A beneficiary who receives a distribution from a fiduciary with both taxable and nontaxable DNI is considered to have received a proportionate share of each.[32]

---

[31] Reg. § 1.661(a)-2(f)(1).

[32] Reg. § 1.662(b)-1.

### Example 12

Trust A has DNI of $80,000, $30,000 of which is nontaxable. During the year, beneficiary X receives a distribution of $16,000. This distribution consists of $10,000 of taxable DNI [$16,000 distribution × ($50,000 taxable DNI ÷ $80,000 total DNI)] and $6,000 of nontaxable DNI.

The amount of a fiduciary's *taxable* DNI represents *both* the maximum income that may be taxed to beneficiaries and the maximum deduction for distributions available to the fiduciary in computing its own taxable income.[33] Therefore, computing DNI is crucial to the correct computation of the taxable incomes of both beneficiary and fiduciary. Note that in *Example 12* Trust A is entitled to a deduction for distributions to beneficiaries of $10,000.

## The Computation of DNI

**LO.4**
Compute both the taxable and nontaxable components of a fiduciary's distributable net income.

Section 643 defines DNI as fiduciary taxable income before any deduction for distributions to beneficiaries, adjusted as follows:

1. No deduction for a personal exemption is allowed.
2. No deduction against ordinary income for net capital losses is allowed.
3. Taxable income allocable to principal and not available for distribution to income beneficiaries is excluded.
4. Tax-exempt interest reduced by expenses allocable thereto is included.

### Example 13

A trust that is not required to distribute all income currently has the following items of income and expense during the current year:

| | |
|---|---|
| Tax-exempt interest | $10,000 |
| Dividends | 5,000 |
| Rents | 20,000 |
| Long-term capital gains allocable to principal | 8,000 |
| Rent expense | 6,700 |
| Trustee fee allocable to income | 3,500 |

The trust's taxable income before any deduction for distributions to beneficiaries is $23,700, computed as follows:

| | | |
|---|---|---|
| Dividends | | $ 5,000 |
| Rents | | 20,000 |
| Capital gain | | 8,000 |
| | | $33,000 |
| Less: Rent expense | $6,700 | |
| Trust fee allocable to *taxable* trust income* | 2,500 | |
| Exemption | 100 | (9,300) |
| Taxable income before distribution deduction | | $23,700 |

[33] §§ 651(b) and 661(c).

$$*\$3,500 \text{ fee} \times \frac{\$25,000 \text{ taxable trust income}}{\$35,000 \text{ total trust income}}$$

The trust's DNI is $24,800, computed as follows:

| | |
|---|---|
| Trust taxable income before distribution deduction | $23,700 |
| Add back exemption | 100 |
| | $23,800 |
| Exclude: Nondistributable capital gain | (8,000) |
| Include: *Net* tax-exempt interest ($10,000 total − $1,000 allocable to trustee fee)** | 9,000 |
| Distributable net income (DNI) | $24,800 |

$$**\$3,500 \text{ fee} \times \frac{\$10,000 \text{ tax-exempt income}}{\$35,000 \text{ total trust income}}$$

## Simple Trusts

**LO.5**
Describe the defining characteristics of a simple and a complex trust, including:
- The computation of the deduction for distributions to beneficiaries for both types of trusts.
- The distinction between tier one and tier two distributions from a complex trust.

Section 651 defines a *simple trust* as one that satisfies these conditions:

1. Distributes all trust income currently
2. Does not take a deduction for a charitable contribution for the current year
3. Does not make any current distributions out of trust principal

Because of the requirement that a simple trust distribute all trust income to its beneficiaries, all taxable DNI of a simple trust is taxed to the beneficiaries, based upon the relative income distributable to each.

### Example 14

Trust S is required to distribute 40% of trust income to beneficiary A and 60% of trust income to B. The trust's DNI for the current year is $100,000, of which $20,000 is nontaxable. For the current year, beneficiary A must report $32,000 of trust income (40% of *taxable* DNI) and B must report $48,000 of trust income (60% of *taxable* DNI). Trust S's deduction for distributions to beneficiaries is $80,000 (i.e., taxable DNI).

In *Example 14*, the tax results would not change if the trustee had failed to make actual distributions to the beneficiaries. In the case of a simple trust, the taxability of income to beneficiaries is not dependent upon cash flow from the trust.[34]

## Complex Trusts and Estates

Any trust that does not meet all three requirements of a simple trust is categorized as a *complex trust*. The categorization of a trust may vary from year to year. For example, if a trustee is required to distribute all trust income currently but also has the discretion to make distributions out of trust principal, the trust will be *simple* in any year in which principal is not distributed, but *complex* in any year in which principal is distributed.

Computing the taxable income of complex trusts and estates generally is more difficult than computing the taxable income of a simple trust. Complex trusts and estates potentially may distribute amounts of cash and property that are less than or in excess of DNI.

[34] § 652(a).

If distributions to beneficiaries are less than or equal to DNI, each beneficiary is required to report the amount of the distribution representing *taxable* DNI in his or her gross income. Taxable DNI remaining in the fiduciary is taxed to the fiduciary.

### Example 15

In the current year, Trust C has DNI of $50,000, of which $20,000 or 40% is nontaxable. During the year, the trustee makes a $5,000 distribution to both beneficiary M and beneficiary N. M and N will each report $3,000 of income from Trust C [$5,000 distribution × ($30,000 taxable DNI ÷ $50,000 total DNI)]. Trust C is allowed a $6,000 deduction for distributions to beneficiaries.[35] As a result, $24,000 of taxable DNI will be reported by (and taxed to) Trust C.

### Example 16

Using the same facts as in *Example 13*, assume the trust distributes $10,000. The trust is generally entitled to a deduction for amounts distributed. However, this amount is further limited to the portion of taxable DNI contained in the distribution. In this case, the amount of the distribution deduction and the amount taxable to the beneficiaries is $6,371 computed as follows:

| | |
|---|---|
| Distributable net income | $24,800 |
| Net tax-exempt income ($10,000 – $1,000) | (9,000) |
| Taxable DNI | $15,800 |

$$\frac{\text{Taxable DNI}}{\text{Total DNI}} \times \text{Amount distributed} = \text{Distribution deduction}$$

$$\frac{\$15{,}800}{\$24{,}800} \times \$10{,}000 = \$6{,}371$$

In this case, the trust did not distribute all of its DNI, $24,800, but only a portion, $10,000. Consequently, the calculation effectively treats a portion of the amount distributed as taxable (63.71% or $6,371) and a portion as nontaxable (36.29% or $3,629). Taxable income of the trust would be $17,329 as computed below.

| | |
|---|---|
| Taxable income before distribution deduction | $23,700 |
| Deduction for distributions | (6,371) |
| Trust taxable income | $17,329 |

When distributions to beneficiaries exceed DNI, the entire taxable portion of DNI will be reported as income by the beneficiaries. Amounts distributed in excess of DNI are nontaxable, representing either accumulated income that has been previously taxed or corpus.

## Allocation of DNI

In those cases when distributions exceed DNI and there are multiple beneficiaries, DNI must be allocated among the beneficiaries. In determining the amount of DNI allocated to each beneficiary (and, therefore, the amount of taxable income and nontaxable income that is allocable to each), the distribution rules acknowledge that some beneficiaries' rights to income may be superior to those of others. For example, the trust agreement may provide

[35] § 661(c).

that distributions of income must be made to certain beneficiaries each year while other beneficiaries receive distributions solely at the discretion of the trustee. In recognition of this possibility, the Code establishes a so-called tier system to allocate DNI.[36]

Under the tier system, DNI (increased for charitable contributions) is first allocated proportionately to the distributions that are *required* to be made. These mandatory distributions are commonly referred to as *first-tier* or *tier-one* distributions. After allocating DNI to first-tier distributions, *any* DNI remaining (as reduced by first-tier distributions and charitable contributions) is allocated proportionately to *second tier* or *tier-two* distributions (i.e., discretionary distributions).

## Example 17

This year Trust T reported taxable DNI of $60,000. During the year, the trust made required distributions of $40,000 to beneficiary R. In addition, the trustee made discretionary distributions of $40,000 to R and $20,000 to S. DNI would be allocated as follows:

| | *Total* | *R* | *S* |
|---|---|---|---|
| Required distributions | $ 40,000 | $40,000 | — |
| Discretionary distributions | 60,000 | 40,000 | $20,000 |
| Total distributions received | $100,000 | $80,000 | $20,000 |

| | *Total* | *R* | *S* |
|---|---|---|---|
| DNI before contributions | $60,000 | | |
| First-tier distributions | (40,000) | $40,000 | — |
| DNI available for charity | 20,000 | | |
| Charitable distributions | ( 0) | | |
| DNI for second tier | $20,000 | | |
| Second-tier distributions | (20,000) | 13,333* | $ 6,667* |
| DNI received | | $53,333 | $ 6,667 |

*

$$\text{*DNI for second tier} \times \frac{\text{Beneficiary's second-tier distribution}}{\text{Total second-tier distribution}}$$

$20,000 × $40,000/$60,000 = $13,333 to R

$20,000 × $20,000/$60,000 = $ 6,667 to S

Observe that the first $40,000 of DNI must be allocated to R because this distribution was mandatory thus making it a first-tier distribution. The remaining $20,000 of DNI is allocated proportionally to the discretionary or second-tier distributions received by R and S. Note that all of the trust's DNI is allocated and taxed to the beneficiaries and none is taxed to the trust. In this case, R received $80,000 from the trust of which $53,333 is taxable while S received $20,000 of which $6,667 is taxable. The balance of each distribution represents either accumulated income or corpus. Although the trust distributed $100,000, its deduction for distributions is limited to its taxable DNI for the year, $60,000.

[36] §§ 662(a)(1) and (2).

In determining the treatment of a beneficiary's distributions, the treatment of charitable contributions can be a bit confusing. On the one hand, a contribution is treated as an expense that reduces the trust's taxable income (i.e., it is reported on Line 13 of Form 1041 and not on a Schedule K-1). On the other hand, the charity itself is treated like a beneficiary in the sense that it absorbs taxable and nontaxable DNI just like any other beneficiary. It should be emphasized that the charity is not considered a beneficiary when computing the deduction for distributions to beneficiaries. Instead, the distribution is accounted for as an expense.[37]

### Example 18

This year the F Trust reported $80,000 of dividend income. Pursuant to the trust instrument the trustee distributed $90,000 as follows: (1) a required distribution to beneficiary J of $50,000; (2) a charitable contribution of $30,000; and (3) a discretionary distribution to K of $10,000. Taxable DNI would be $50,000 ($80,000 – $30,000) all of which would be allocated to J as computed below.

| | |
|---|---|
| DNI before contributions ($50,000 + $ 30,000) | $80,000 |
| First-tier distribution to J | (50,000) |
| DNI available for charity | $30,000 |
| Charitable distribution | (30,000) |
| DNI for second tier | $ 0 |

Note that J would report $50,000 of DNI, all of which would be taxable. In contrast, K receives no taxable DNI since there is none available after taking into account the charitable contribution. Although the trust distributed $60,000 to J and K, its distribution deduction is limited to taxable DNI of $50,000. Trust taxable income would be $0 as calculated below.

| | |
|---|---|
| Dividends | $80,000 |
| Contribution | (30,000) |
| Distribution deduction (limited to taxable DNI) | (50,000) |
| Trust taxable income | $ 0 |

## Character of Beneficiary's Income

**LO.6**
Determine the tax consequences of fiduciary distributions to the recipient beneficiaries.

Not only must a beneficiary determine the amount of taxable income received from a trust or estate, but he or she must determine its character as well. As stated at the outset, estates and trusts generally serve as conduits to the extent they make distributions. Consequently, each distribution is deemed to contain a pro rata portion of each type of distributable income received by the trust or estate. For example, if a portion of a trust's income consisted of dividends, a portion of the distribution received by the beneficiary is considered dividend income.

To determine the composition of a distribution, the gross amount of each item of distributable income must be reduced by any deduction directly related to that item of income. Any other expenses may be allocated against whatever class of distributable income the fiduciary selects. However, charitable contributions are treated as consisting of a proportionate share of each type of distributable income.

---

[37] § 662(a)(2). For purposes of determining DNI available for first-tier distribution only, no charitable contribution deduction is allowed.

## Example 19

This year the records of the T Trust revealed the following information, resulting in DNI of $60,000:

| | *Income and Expenses* | *DNI* |
|---|---|---|
| Rental income | $70,000 | $70,000 |
| Dividends | 30,000 | 30,000 |
| Long-term capital gain | 50,000 | |
| Charitable contribution | 10,000 | (10,000) |
| Rent expense | 23,000 | (23,000) |
| Trustee commission allocable between income and corpus | 7,000 | (7,000) |
| DNI | | $60,000 |

During the year, the trust distributed $6,000 to its only beneficiary, X. The character of the distribution is determined below.

| *Elements of DNI* | *Rents* | *Dividends* | *Total* |
|---|---|---|---|
| Income | $70,000 | $30,000 | $100,000 |
| Expenses: | | | |
| Rental expenses | (23,000) | | (23,000) |
| Trustee fees | | (7,000) | (7,000) |
| Contribution | (7,000)* | (3,000)* | (10,000) |
| Total DNI | $40,000 | $20,000 | $ 60,000 |
| Percentage of DNI | 67% | 33% | 100% |

*$10,000 × $70,000/$100,000 = $7,000
$10,000 × $30,000/$100,000 = $3,000

Since X received 10% of the DNI ($6,000/$60,000) she is deemed to receive 10% of each item of DNI. Thus she will report rental income of $4,000 (10% × $40,000) and dividend income of $2,000 (10% × $20,000). In other words, of the $6,000 of DNI received, $4,000 or 67% is rents while $2,000 or 33% is dividends. Note how the expenses were allocated in determining the composition of DNI. The rental expenses are charged against the rental income since they are directly related. In contrast, the charitable contribution is charged proportionately against each type of distributable income. On the other hand, the trustee fees may be allocated however the trustee wishes. In this case, he elects to charge the trustee fees against the dividend income. In light of the 15% tax rate that applies to dividends, the trustee should consider allocating the fees to the rental income.

A special problem arises when the trust receives qualified dividends that are taxed at a maximum rate of 15 percent (5% if in the 15% tax bracket). A calculation must be made to determine the amount of qualified dividends *retained* by the trust to be taxed at the favorable rate. The amount deemed to be retained by the trust is equal to the proportion of distributable net income (DNI) retained by the trust.

## Example 20

Same facts as in *Example 19*. The total DNI was $60,000 and the trust distributed 10% of the DNI ($6,000/$60,000) to the beneficiary and retained 90% ($54,000/$60,000). Thus the qualified dividends retained by thc trust are $27,000 (90% × $30,000). Alternatively, the amount could be computed by using the amount of DNI allocated to the beneficiary as follows:

| | | |
|---|---|---|
| Qualified dividends. . . . . . . . . . . . . . . . . . . . . . . . . . . . . . | $30,000 | $30,000 |
| Allocation to beneficiary | | |
| DNI distributed to beneficiary $6,000 / Total DNI $60,000 | ×10% | (3,000) |
| Allocation to trust. . . . . . . . . . . . . . . . . . . . . . . . . . . . . . | | $27,000 |

Note that this method of allocating the amount of qualified dividends between the beneficiary and the trust is used solely for calculating the tax liability of the trust. The actual amount of qualified dividends to be reported on the Schedule K-1 which the beneficiary must report is not $3,000 but is $2,000 (10% × $20,000) as shown above.

## Reporting Requirements for Beneficiaries

A beneficiary who receives a distribution from a fiduciary will receive a summary of the tax consequences of the distribution in the form of a Schedule K-1 from the executor or trustee. The K-1 will tell the beneficiary the amounts and character of the various items of income that constitute the taxable portion of the distribution.

A beneficiary also may be entitled to depreciation or depletion deductions and various tax credits because of distributions of fiduciary income. Such items are also reflected on the Schedule K-1.

If the taxable year of a beneficiary is different from that of the fiduciary, the amount of fiduciary income taxable to the beneficiary is included in the beneficiary's tax year within which the fiduciary's year ends.[38]

## Example 21

Estate E is on a fiscal year ending January 31. During its fiscal year ending January 31, 2011, but prior to December 31, 2010, the estate made cash distributions to beneficiary Z, a calendar year taxpayer. Because of these distributions, Z must report income of $8,000. However, this income will be reported on Z's 2011 individual tax return.

## The Separate Share Rule

In certain circumstances, the rules governing the taxation of beneficiaries of a complex trust can lead to an inequitable result. Assume a grantor created a single trust with two beneficiaries, A and B. The grantor intended that each beneficiary have an equal interest in trust income and principal. The trustee has considerable discretion as to the timing of distributions of income and principal. Consider a year in which beneficiary A was in exceptional need of funds and, as a result, the trustee distributed $15,000 to A as A's half of trust income for the

[38] §§ 652(c) and 662(c).

year *plus* $10,000 out of A's half of trust principal. Because B had no need of current funds, the trustee distributed neither income nor principal to B.

If the trust's DNI was $30,000 for the year, the normal rules of Subchapter J would dictate that A would have to report and pay tax on $25,000 of trust income. However, the clear intent of the grantor is that A only be responsible for half of trust income and no more. To reflect such intent, § 663(c) provides the following rule: if a single trust contains substantially separate and independent shares for different beneficiaries, the trust shall be treated as separate trusts for purposes of determining DNI. Therefore, using this separate share rule, beneficiary A's *separate trust* would have DNI of only $15,000, the maximum amount taxable to A in the year of distribution. This rule is inapplicable to estates.

## A Comprehensive Example

The AB Trust is a calendar year taxpayer. In the current year, the trust books show the following:

| | |
|---|---|
| Gross rental income | $25,000 |
| Taxable interest income | 10,000 |
| Tax-exempt interest income | 15,000 |
| Long-term capital gain | 8,000 |
| Trustee fee | 6,000 |
| Rent expenses | 3,000 |
| Contribution to charity | 1,500 |
| Distributions to | |
| Beneficiary A | 20,000 |
| Beneficiary B | 20,000 |

Under the terms of the trust instrument the capital gain and one-third of the trustee fee are allocable to principal. The trustee is required to maintain a reserve for depreciation on the rental property equal to one-tenth of annual gross rental income. (For tax purposes, assume actual tax depreciation is $1,300.) The trustee is required to make an annual distribution to beneficiary A of $12,000 and has the discretion to make additional distributions to A or beneficiary B.

Based on these facts, the computation of the income taxable to the trust and the beneficiaries is as follows:

**Step One:** Compute fiduciary accounting income.

| | |
|---|---|
| Gross rental income | $25,000 |
| Taxable interest income | 10,000 |
| Tax-exempt interest income | 15,000 |
| | $50,000 |
| Trustee fee charged against income | (4,000) |
| Rent expenses | (3,000) |
| Depreciation (1/10 × $25,000) | (2,500) |
| Fiduciary accounting income | $40,500 |

**Step Two:** Compute fiduciary taxable income before the § 661 deduction for distributions to beneficiaries.

| | |
|---|---|
| Gross rental income | $ 25,000 |
| Taxable interest income | 10,000 |
| Long-term capital gain | 8,000 |
| | $ 43,000 |

| | |
|---|---|
| Deductible trustee fee | (4,200)* |
| Deductible rent expense | (3,000) |
| Deductible depreciation allocable to fiduciary | (1,300) |
| Deductible charitable contribution | (1,050)* |
| Exemption | (100) |
| Taxable income before § 661 deduction | $33,350 |

*$35,000 ÷ $50,000 of gross fiduciary accounting income is taxable; thus, only 70% of both the $6,000 trustee fee and $1,500 charitable contribution is deductible.

**Step Three:** Compute DNI and the § 661 deduction for distributions to beneficiaries.

| | |
|---|---|
| Taxable income from Step Two | $33,350 |
| Add back: | |
| Exemption | 100 |
| Net tax-exempt income | 12,750* |
| Subtract: | |
| Capital gain allocable to principal | (8,000) |
| Distributable net income (DNI) | $38,200 |

*$15,000 tax-exempt interest less 30% of the $6,000 trustee fee and $1,500 charitable contribution.

**Step Four:** Subtract the § 661 deduction for distributions to beneficiaries

| | |
|---|---|
| Taxable income before deduction | $33,350 |
| Section 661 deduction for distributions | (25,450)* |
| Trust taxable income | $ 7,900 |

Because distributions to beneficiaries exceeded DNI, the trust will deduct the entire amount of taxable DNI. $25,450 ($38,200 − $12,750).

## Tax Consequences to Beneficiaries

The $40,000 cash distribution to beneficiaries exceeds the total DNI of $38,200; thus, the entire amount of DNI must be allocated to the beneficiaries.

| | *Total* | *A* | *B* |
|---|---|---|---|
| DNI | $38,200 | | |
| Add-back charitable contribution | 1,500 | | |
| DNI before charitable contribution | $39,700 | | |
| First-tier distributions | (12,000) | $12,000 | — |
| DNI available for charity | $27,700 | | |
| Charitable distributions | (1,500) | | |
| DNI for second tier | $26,200 | | |
| Second-tier distributions | (26,200) | 7,483* | $18,717** |
| DNI received | (26,200) | $19,483 | $18,717 |
| Percentage of DNI received | | 51% | 49% |

$$*\text{DNI for second tier} \times \frac{\text{Beneficiary's second-tier distribution}}{\text{Total second-tier distributions}}$$

*$26,200 × $8,000/$28,000 = $7,483 to A
**$26,200 × $20,000/$28,000 = $18,717 to B

The composition of DNI is as follows:

| | *Rent* | *Taxable Interest* | *Tax-Exempt Interest* | *Total* |
|---|---|---|---|---|
| Gross receipts | $25,000 | $10,000 | $15,000 | $50,000 |
| Rent expense | (3,000) | | | (3,000) |
| Depreciation | (1,300) | | | (1,300) |
| Trustee fee* | | (4,200) | (1,800) | (6,000) |
| Charitable contribution** | (750) | (300) | (450) | (1,500) |
| Total | $19,950 | $ 5,500 | $12,750 | $38,200 |

*The trustee fee allocable to taxable income may be arbitrarily allocated to **any** item of taxable income. Reg. 1.652(b)-3(b).
**In the absence of a specific provision in the trust instrument, the charitable contribution is allocated proportionally to each class of income. Reg. § 1.642(c)-3(b)(2).

Each beneficiary should report the following:

| | *Rent* | *Taxable Interest* | *Tax-Exempt Interest* | *Total DNI Allocated* |
|---|---|---|---|---|
| Beneficiary A (51%) | $10,175* | $2,805 | $ 6,503 | $19,483 |
| Beneficiary B (49%) | 9,775 | 2,695 | 6,247 | 18,717 |
| Total | $ 19,950 | $5,500 | $12,750 | $38,200 |

*Beneficiary A's proportionate share of DNI 51% multiplied by $19,950 total rent income included in DNI equals beneficiary A's share of rent income. This same procedure is used to determine each beneficiary's share of all other items.

A completed Form 1041 for the AB Trust and Schedule K-1 for Beneficiary A are shown on the following pages.

## The Sixty-Five Day Rule

Fiduciaries may want to avoid accumulating income since such income may be taxed at very high rates. Because DNI is often not calculated until after the close of the trust's taxable year, the amount of current distributions necessary to avoid accumulation may be unknown. To alleviate this timing problem, § 663(b) provides that a trust or an estate *may elect* that any distribution made within the first 65 days of a taxable year will be considered paid to the beneficiary on the last day of the preceding taxable year.[39] This rule allows a trustee to make distributions after the close of a year to eliminate any accumulations of DNI for that year.

[39] See Reg. § 1.663(b)-2 for the manner and time for making such an election.

Form **1041** Department of the Treasury—Internal Revenue Service

**U.S. Income Tax Return for Estates and Trusts** **2010** OMB No. 1545-0092

For calendar year 2010 or fiscal year beginning , 2010, and ending , 20

**A** Type of entity (see instr.):
- ☐ Decedent's estate
- ☐ Simple trust
- ☐ Complex trust
- ☐ Qualified disability trust
- ☐ ESBT (S portion only)
- ☐ Grantor type trust
- ☐ Bankruptcy estate-Ch. 7
- ☐ Bankruptcy estate-Ch. 11
- ☐ Pooled income fund

Name of estate or trust (If a grantor type trust, see page 14 of the instructions.)

A B TRUST

Name and title of fiduciary

Number, street, and room or suite no. (If a P.O. box, see page 15 of the instructions.)

City or town, state, and ZIP code

**C** Employer identification number

**D** Date entity created

**E** Nonexempt charitable and split-interest trusts, check applicable boxes (see page 16 of the instr.):
- ☐ Described in section 4947(a)(1)
- ☐ Not a private foundation
- ☐ Described in section 4947(a)(2)

**B** Number of Schedules K-1 attached (see instructions) ▶

**F** Check applicable boxes: ☐ Initial return ☐ Final return ☐ Amended return ☐ Change in trust's name ☐ Change in fiduciary ☐ Change in fiduciary's name ☐ Change in fiduciary's address

**G** Check here if the estate or filing trust made a section 645 election . . . . . . ▶☐

**Income**

| | | Line | Amount |
|---|---|---|---|
| 1 | Interest income | 1 | 10,000 |
| 2a | Total ordinary dividends | 2a | |
| b | Qualified dividends allocable to: (1) Beneficiaries ______ (2) Estate or trust ______ | | |
| 3 | Business income or (loss). Attach Schedule C or C-EZ (Form 1040) | 3 | |
| 4 | Capital gain or (loss). Attach Schedule D (Form 1041) | 4 | 8,000 |
| 5 | Rents, royalties, partnerships, other estates and trusts, etc. Attach Schedule E (Form 1040) | 5 | 20,700 |
| 6 | Farm income or (loss). Attach Schedule F (Form 1040) | 6 | |
| 7 | Ordinary gain or (loss). Attach Form 4797 | 7 | |
| 8 | Other income. List type and amount ______ | 8 | |
| 9 | **Total income.** Combine lines 1, 2a, and 3 through 8 ▶ | 9 | |

**Deductions**

| | | Line | Amount |
|---|---|---|---|
| 10 | Interest. Check if Form 4952 is attached ▶ ☐ | 10 | |
| 11 | Taxes | 11 | |
| 12 | Fiduciary fees | 12 | 4,200 |
| 13 | Charitable deduction (from Schedule A, line 7) | 13 | 1,050 |
| 14 | Attorney, accountant, and return preparer fees | 14 | |
| 15a | Other deductions **not** subject to the 2% floor (attach schedule) | 15a | |
| b | Allowable miscellaneous itemized deductions subject to the 2% floor | 15b | |
| 16 | Add lines 10 through 15b ▶ | 16 | 5,250 |
| 17 | Adjusted total income or (loss). Subtract line 16 from line 9 . . . 17 | | 33,450 |
| 18 | Income distribution deduction (from Schedule B, line 15). Attach Schedules K-1 (Form 1041) | 18 | 22,450 |
| 19 | Estate tax deduction including certain generation-skipping taxes (attach computation) | 19 | |
| 20 | Exemption | 20 | 100 |
| 21 | Add lines 18 through 20 ▶ | 21 | 22,550 |

**Tax and Payments**

| | | Line | Amount |
|---|---|---|---|
| 22 | Taxable income. Subtract line 21 from line 17. If a loss, see page 23 of the instructions | 22 | 7,900 |
| 23 | **Total tax** (from Schedule G, line 7) | 23 | 840 |
| 24 | **Payments: a** 2009 estimated tax payments and amount applied from 2008 return | 24a | |
| b | Estimated tax payments allocated to beneficiaries (from Form 1041-T) | 24b | |
| c | Subtract line 24b from line 24a | 24c | |
| d | Tax paid with Form 7004 (see page 24 of the instructions) | 24d | |
| e | Federal income tax withheld. If any is from Form(s) 1099, check ▶ ☐ | 24e | |
| | Other payments: **f** Form 2439 ______ ; **g** Form 4136 ______ ; Total ▶ | 24h | |
| 25 | **Total payments.** Add lines 24c through 24e, and 24h ▶ | 25 | |
| 26 | Estimated tax penalty (see page 24 of the instructions) | 26 | |
| 27 | **Tax due.** If line 25 is smaller than the total of lines 23 and 26, enter amount owed | 27 | 840 |
| 28 | **Overpayment.** If line 25 is larger than the total of lines 23 and 26, enter amount overpaid | 28 | |
| 29 | Amount of line 28 to be: **a Credited to 2011 estimated tax** ▶ ; **b Refunded** ▶ | 29 | |

**Sign Here**

Under penalties of perjury, I declare that I have examined this return, including accompanying schedules and statements, and to the best of my knowledge and belief, it is true, correct, and complete. Declaration of preparer (other than taxpayer) is based on all information of which preparer has any knowledge.

▶ Signature of fiduciary or officer representing fiduciary | Date | ▶ EIN of fiduciary if a financial institution

May the IRS discuss this return with the preparer shown below (see instr.)? ☐ **Yes** ☐ **No**

**Paid Preparer's Use Only**

Preparer's signature | Date | Check if self-employed ☐ | Preparer's SSN or PTIN

Firm's name (or yours if self-employed), address, and ZIP code | EIN | Phone no.

**For Privacy Act and Paperwork Reduction Act Notice, see the separate instructions.** Cat. No. 11370H Form **1041** (2010)

Form 1041 (2010) Page 2

**Schedule A — Charitable Deduction.** Do not complete for a simple trust or a pooled income fund.

| | | | |
|---|---|---|---|
| 1 | Amounts paid or permanently set aside for charitable purposes from gross income (see page 25) | 1 | 1,500 |
| 2 | Tax-exempt income allocable to charitable contributions (see page 25 of the instructions) | 2 | 450 |
| 3 | Subtract line 2 from line 1 | 3 | 1,050 |
| 4 | Capital gains for the tax year allocated to corpus and paid or permanently set aside for charitable purposes | 4 | |
| 5 | Add lines 3 and 4 | 5 | 1,050 |
| 6 | Section 1202 exclusion allocable to capital gains paid or permanently set aside for charitable purposes (see page 25 of the instructions) | 6 | |
| 7 | **Charitable deduction.** Subtract line 6 from line 5. Enter here and on page 1, line 13 | 7 | 1,050 |

**Schedule B — Income Distribution Deduction**

| | | | |
|---|---|---|---|
| 1 | Adjusted total income (see page 26 of the instructions) | 1 | 33,450 |
| 2 | Adjusted tax-exempt interest | 2 | 12,750 |
| 3 | Total net gain from Schedule D (Form 1041), line 15, column (1) (see page 26 of the instructions) | 3 | |
| 4 | Enter amount from Schedule A, line 4 (minus any allocable section 1202 exclusion) | 4 | |
| 5 | Capital gains for the tax year included on Schedule A, line 1 (see page 26 of the instructions) | 5 | |
| 6 | Enter any gain from page 1, line 4, as a negative number. If page 1, line 4, is a loss, enter the loss as a positive number <GAIN> | 6 | <8000> |
| 7 | **Distributable net income.** Combine lines 1 through 6. If zero or less, enter -0- | 7 | 38,200 |
| 8 | If a complex trust, enter accounting income for the tax year as determined under the governing instrument and applicable local law — 8: 40,500 | | |
| 9 | Income required to be distributed currently | 9 | 12,000 |
| 10 | Other amounts paid, credited, or otherwise required to be distributed | 10 | 28,000 |
| 11 | Total distributions. Add lines 9 and 10. If greater than line 8, see page 27 of the instructions | 11 | 40,000 |
| 12 | Enter the amount of tax-exempt income included on line 11 | 12 | 12,750 |
| 13 | Tentative income distribution deduction. Subtract line 12 from line 11 | 13 | 27,250 |
| 14 | Tentative income distribution deduction. Subtract line 2 from line 7. If zero or less, enter -0- | 14 | 22,450 |
| 15 | **Income distribution deduction.** Enter the smaller of line 13 or line 14 here and on page 1, line 18 | 15 | 25,450 |

**Schedule G — Tax Computation** (see page 27 of the instructions)

| | | | | | |
|---|---|---|---|---|---|
| 1 | **Tax:** a Tax on taxable income (see page 27 of the instructions) | 1a | 840 | | |
| | b Tax on lump-sum distributions. Attach Form 4972 | 1b | | | |
| | c Alternative minimum tax (from Schedule I (Form 1041), line 56) | 1c | | | |
| | d **Total.** Add lines 1a through 1c ▶ | | | 1d | 840 |
| 2a | Foreign tax credit. Attach Form 1116 | 2a | | | |
| b | Other nonbusiness credits (attach schedule) | 2b | | | |
| c | General business credit. Attach Form 3800 | 2c | | | |
| d | Credit for prior year minimum tax. Attach Form 8801 | 2d | | | |
| 3 | **Total credits.** Add lines 2a through 2d ▶ | | | 3 | 0 |
| 4 | Subtract line 3 from line 1d. If zero or less, enter -0- | | | 4 | 840 |
| 5 | Recapture taxes. Check if from: ☐ Form 4255 ☐ Form 8611 | | | 5 | |
| 6 | Household employment taxes. Attach Schedule H (Form 1040) | | | 6 | |
| 7 | **Total tax.** Add lines 4 through 6. Enter here and on page 1, line 23 ▶ | | | 7 | 840 |

**Other Information**

| | | Yes | No |
|---|---|---|---|
| 1 | Did the estate or trust receive tax-exempt income? If "Yes," attach a computation of the allocation of expenses. Enter the amount of tax-exempt interest income and exempt-interest dividends ▶ $ 15,000 | ✓ | |
| 2 | Did the estate or trust receive all or any part of the earnings (salary, wages, and other compensation) of any individual by reason of a contract assignment or similar arrangement? | | ✓ |
| 3 | At any time during calendar year 2009, did the estate or trust have an interest in or a signature or other authority over a bank, securities, or other financial account in a foreign country? | | ✓ |
| | See page 30 of the instructions for exceptions and filing requirements for Form TD F 90-22.1. If "Yes," enter the name of the foreign country ▶ | | |
| 4 | During the tax year, did the estate or trust receive a distribution from, or was it the grantor of, or transferor to, a foreign trust? If "Yes," the estate or trust may have to file Form 3520. See page 30 of the instructions | | ✓ |
| 5 | Did the estate or trust receive, or pay, any qualified residence interest on seller-provided financing? If "Yes," see page 30 for required attachment | | ✓ |
| 6 | If this is an estate or a complex trust making the section 663(b) election, check here (see page 30) ▶ ☐ | | |
| 7 | To make a section 643(e)(3) election, attach Schedule D (Form 1041), and check here (see page 30) ▶ ☐ | | |
| 8 | If the decedent's estate has been open for more than 2 years, attach an explanation for the delay in closing the estate, and check here ▶ ☐ | | |
| 9 | Are any present or future trust beneficiaries skip persons? See page 30 of the instructions | | ✓ |

Form **1041** (2010)

**SCHEDULE D (Form 1041)**
Department of the Treasury Internal Revenue Service

# Capital Gains and Losses

▶ Attach to Form 1041, Form 5227, or Form 990-T. See the Instructions for Schedule D (Form 1041) (also for Form 5227 or Form 990-T, if applicable).

OMB No. 1545-0092

**2010**

Name of estate or trust: A B TRUST

Employer identification number:

**Note:** *Form 5227 filers need to complete **only** Parts I and II.*

## Part I Short-Term Capital Gains and Losses—Assets Held One Year or Less

| | (a) Description of property (Example: 100 shares 7% preferred of "Z" Co.) | (b) Date acquired (mo., day, yr.) | (c) Date sold (mo., day, yr.) | (d) Sales price | (e) Cost or other basis (see page 4 of the instructions) | (f) Gain or (loss) for the entire year Subtract (e) from (d) |
|---|---|---|---|---|---|---|
| 1a | | | | | | |
| | | | | | | |
| | | | | | | |
| | | | | | | |
| | | | | | | |

|  |  |  |  |
|---|---|---|---|
| b | Enter the short-term gain or (loss), if any, from Schedule D-1, line 1b . . . . . . . . . . . | 1b | |
| 2 | Short-term capital gain or (loss) from Forms 4684, 6252, 6781, and 8824 . . . . . . . . . . | 2 | |
| 3 | Net short-term gain or (loss) from partnerships, S corporations, and other estates or trusts . . . | 3 | |
| 4 | Short-term capital loss carryover. Enter the amount, if any, from line 9 of the 2008 Capital Loss Carryover Worksheet . . . . . . . . . . . . . . . . . . . . . . . . . . | 4 | ( ) |
| 5 | **Net short-term gain or (loss).** Combine lines 1a through 4 in column (f). Enter here and on line 13, column (3) on the back . . . . . . . . . . . . . . . . . . . . . . . ▶ | 5 | |

## Part II Long-Term Capital Gains and Losses—Assets Held More Than One Year

| | (a) Description of property (Example: 100 shares 7% preferred of "Z" Co.) | (b) Date acquired (mo., day, yr.) | (c) Date sold (mo., day, yr.) | (d) Sales price | (e) Cost or other basis (see page 4 of the instructions) | (f) Gain or (loss) for the entire year Subtract (e) from (d) |
|---|---|---|---|---|---|---|
| 6a | | | | | | 8,100 |
| | | | | | | |
| | | | | | | |
| | | | | | | |
| | | | | | | |

|  |  |  |  |
|---|---|---|---|
| b | Enter the long-term gain or (loss), if any, from Schedule D-1, line 6b . . . . . . . . . . . | 6b | |
| 7 | Long-term capital gain or (loss) from Forms 2439, 4684, 6252, 6781, and 8824 . . . . . . . . | 7 | |
| 8 | Net long-term gain or (loss) from partnerships, S corporations, and other estates or trusts . . . | 8 | |
| 9 | Capital gain distributions . . . . . . . . . . . . . . . . . . . . . . . . . . | 9 | |
| 10 | Gain from Form 4797, Part I . . . . . . . . . . . . . . . . . . . . . . . . . | 10 | |
| 11 | Long-term capital loss carryover. Enter the amount, if any, from line 14 of the 2008 Capital Loss Carryover Worksheet . . . . . . . . . . . . . . . . . . . . . . . . . | 11 | ( ) |
| 12 | **Net long-term gain or (loss).** Combine lines 6a through 11 in column (f). Enter here and on line 14a, column (3) on the back . . . . . . . . . . . . . . . . . . . . . . . ▶ | 12 | 8,100 |

**For Paperwork Reduction Act Notice, see the Instructions for Form 1041.** Cat. No. 11376V **Schedule D (Form 1041) 2010**

Schedule D (Form 1041) 2010 Page **2**

**Part III** **Summary of Parts I and II**

**Caution:** *Read the instructions* ***before*** *completing this part.*

| | | | (1) Beneficiaries' (see page 5) | (2) Estate's or trust's | (3) Total |
|---|---|---|---|---|---|
| 13 | **Net short-term gain or (loss)** | 13 | | | |
| 14 | **Net long-term gain or (loss):** | | | | |
| a | Total for year | 14a | | 8,000 | 8,000 |
| b | Unrecaptured section 1250 gain (see line 18 of the wrksht.) | 14b | | | |
| c | 28% rate gain | 14c | | | |
| 15 | **Total net gain or (loss).** Combine lines 13 and 14a ▶ | 15 | | 8,000 | 8,000 |

**Note:** *If line 15, column (3), is a net gain, enter the gain on Form 1041, line 4 (or Form 990-T, Part I, line 4a). If lines 14a and 15, column (2), are net gains, go to Part V, and* ***do not*** *complete Part IV. If line 15, column (3), is a net loss, complete Part IV and the* ***Capital Loss Carryover Worksheet,*** *as necessary.*

**Part IV** **Capital Loss Limitation**

16 Enter here and enter as a (loss) on Form 1041, line 4 (or Form 990-T, Part I, line 4c, if a trust), the **smaller** of:
a The loss on line 15, column (3) **or b** $3,000 . . . 16 ( )

**Note:** *If the loss on line 15, column (3), is more than $3,000,* ***or*** *if Form 1041, page 1, line 22 (or Form 990-T, line 34), is a loss, complete the* ***Capital Loss Carryover Worksheet*** *on page 7 of the instructions to figure your capital loss carryover.*

**Part V** **Tax Computation Using Maximum Capital Gains Rates**

**Form 1041 filers.** Complete this part **only** if both lines 14a and 15 in column (2) are gains, or an amount is entered in Part I or Part II and there is an entry on Form 1041, line 2b(2), **and** Form 1041, line 22, is more than zero.

**Caution:** *Skip this part and complete the worksheet on page 8 of the instructions if:*

- *Either line 14b, col. (2) or line 14c, col. (2) is more than zero, or*
- *Both Form 1041, line 2b(1), and Form 4952, line 4g are more than zero.*

**Form 990-T trusts.** Complete this part **only** if both lines 14a and 15 are gains, or qualified dividends are included in income in Part I of Form 990-T, **and** Form 990-T, line 34, is more than zero. Skip this part and complete the worksheet on page 8 of the instructions if either line 14b, col. (2) or line 14c, col. (2) is more than zero.

| | | | | | | | |
|---|---|---|---|---|---|---|---|
| 17 | Enter taxable income from Form 1041, line 22 (or Form 990-T, line 34) | | | 17 | 7,900 | | |
| 18 | Enter the **smaller** of line 14a or 15 in column (2) but not less than zero . LTCG | 18 | 8,000 | | | | |
| 19 | Enter the estate's or trust's qualified dividends from Form 1041, line 2b(2) (or enter the qualified dividends included in income in Part I of Form 990-T) | 19 | | | | | |
| 20 | Add lines 18 and 19 . LTCG | 20 | 8,000 | | | | |
| 21 | If the estate or trust is filing Form 4952, enter the amount from line 4g; otherwise, enter -0- ▶ | 21 | -0- | | | | |
| 22 | Subtract line 21 from line 20. If zero or less, enter -0- . LTCG | | | 22 | 8,000 | | |
| 23 | Subtract line 22 from line 17. If zero or less, enter -0- | | | 23 | 0 | | |
| 24 | Enter the **smaller** of the amount on line 17 or $2,300 | | | 24 | 2,300 | | |
| 25 | Is the amount on line 23 equal to or more than the amount on line 24?<br>☐ **Yes.** Skip lines 25 and 26; go to line 27 and check the "No" box.<br>☑ **No.** Enter the amount from line 23 | | | 25 | 0 | | |
| 26 | Subtract line 25 from line 24 | | | 26 | 2,300 | | |
| 27 | Are the amounts on lines 22 and 26 the same?<br>☐ **Yes.** Skip lines 27 thru 30; go to line 31. ☑ **No.** Enter the **smaller** of line 17 or line 22 | | | 27 | 7,900 | | |
| 28 | Enter the amount from line 26 (If line 26 is blank, enter -0-) | | | 28 | 2,300 | | |
| 29 | Subtract line 28 from line 27 | | | 29 | 5,600 | | |
| 30 | Multiply line 29 by 15% (.15) BALANCE OF LTCG AT 15% | | | | | 30 | 840 |
| 31 | Figure the tax on the amount on line 23. Use the 2009 Tax Rate Schedule for Estates and Trusts (see the Schedule G instructions in the instructions for Form 1041) | | | | | 31 | – |
| 32 | Add lines 30 and 31 | | | | | 32 | 840 |
| 33 | Figure the tax on the amount on line 17. Use the 2009 Tax Rate Schedule for Estates and Trusts (see the Schedule G instructions in the instructions for Form 1041) | | | | | 33 | 1,819 |
| 34 | **Tax on all taxable income.** Enter the **smaller** of line 32 or line 33 here and on Form 1041, Schedule G, line 1a (or Form 990-T, line 36) | | | | | 34 | 840 |

**Schedule D (Form 1041) 2010**

661108

Final K-1 | Amended K-1 | OMB No. 1545-0092

**Schedule K-1 (Form 1041)** **2010**

Department of the Treasury
Internal Revenue Service

For calendar year 2010, or tax year beginning, ________, 2010, and ending ________, 20 ____

## Beneficiary's Share of Income, Deductions, Credits, etc.

► See back of form and instructions.

### Part I Information About the Estate or Trust

A Estate's or trust's employer identification number

*A B TRUST*

B Estate's or trust's name

C Fiduciary's name, address, city, state, and ZIP code

*A B TRUST*

D ☐ Check if Form 1041-T was filed and enter the date it was filed

___/___/___

E ☐ Check if this is the final Form 1041 for the estate or trust

### Part II Information About the Beneficiary

F Beneficiary's identifying number

G Beneficiary's name, address, city, state, and ZIP code

*BENEFICIARY A*

H ☐ Domestic beneficiary ☐ Foreign beneficiary

### Part III Beneficiary's Share of Current Year Income, Deductions, Credits, and Other Items

|  |  |  |
|---|---|---|
| 1 | Interest income | *2,805* |
| 2a | Ordinary dividends | |
| 2b | Qualified dividends | |
| 3 | Net short-term capital gain | |
| 4a | Net long-term capital gain | |
| 4b | 28% rate gain | |
| 4c | Unrecaptured section 1250 gain | |
| 5 | Other portfolio and nonbusiness income | |
| 6 | Ordinary business income | *10,175* |
| 7 | Net rental real estate income | *12,980* |
| 8 | Other rental income | *12,980* |
| 9 | Directly apportioned deductions | |
| 10 | Estate tax deduction | |
| 11 | Final year deductions | |
| 12 | Alternative minimum tax adjustment | |
| 13 | Credits and credit recapture | |
| 14 | Other information | *6,503* |

*See attached statement for additional information.

**Note.** A statement must be attached showing the beneficiary's share of income and directly apportioned deductions from each business, rental real estate, and other rental activity.

For IRS Use Only

**For Paperwork Reduction Act Notice, see the Instructions for Form 1041.** Cat. No. 11380D **Schedule K-1 (Form 1041) 2010**

## Tax Planning Considerations

The tax planning considerations for the use of trusts are discussed in Chapter 26, *Family Tax Planning*.

## Problem Materials

### DISCUSSION QUESTIONS

**25-1** *Trusts and Estates as Conduits.* What does it mean to describe a fiduciary as *a conduit* of income? To what extent does a fiduciary operate as a conduit?

**25-2** *Purpose of Trusts.* Trusts are usually created for nonbusiness purposes. Give some examples of situations in which a trust could be useful.

**25-3** *Trust as a Separate Legal Entity.* A trust cannot exist if the only trustee is also sole beneficiary. Why not?

**25-4** *Trust Expenses Allocable to Principal.* For what reason might the grantor of a trust stipulate that some amount of trust expenses be paid out of trust principal rather than trust income?

**25-5** *Use of Fiduciaries to Defer Income Taxation.* Although a trust must adopt a calendar year for tax purposes, an estate may adopt any fiscal year, as well as a calendar year, for reporting taxable income. Why is Congress willing to allow an estate more flexibility in the choice of taxable year?

**25-6** *Trust Accounting Income vs. Taxable Income.* Even though a trustee may be required to distribute all trust income currently, the trust may still have to report taxable income. Explain.

**25-7** *Deductibility of Administrative Expenses.* Explain any options available to the executor of an estate with regard to the deductibility of administrative expenses incurred by the estate.

**25-8** *Capital Loss Deductions.* To what extent may a fiduciary deduct any excess of capital losses over capital gains for a taxable year?

**25-9** *Operating Losses of a Fiduciary.* How does the tax treatment of operating losses incurred by a fiduciary differ from the treatment of such losses by a partnership or an S corporation?

**25-10** *Purpose of DNI.* Discuss the function of DNI from the point of view of the fiduciary and the point of view of beneficiaries who receive distributions from the fiduciary.

**25-11** *Taxable vs. Nontaxable DNI.* Why is it important to correctly identify any nontaxable component of DNI?

**25-12** *Charitable Deductions.* Enumerate the differences in the charitable deduction allowable to a fiduciary and the charitable deduction allowable to an individual.

**25-13** *Timing Distributions from an Estate.* Why might a beneficiary of an estate prefer *not* to receive an early distribution of property from the estate?

**25-14** *Simple vs. Complex Trusts.* All trusts are complex in the year of termination. Why?

**25-15** *Trust Reserves for Depreciation.* Discuss the reason why a grantor of a trust would require the trustee to maintain a certain reserve for depreciation of trust assets.

**25-16** *Distributions Exceeding DNI.* How are distributions in excess of distributable net income treated?

**25-17** *Sixty-five Day Rule.* Explain the sixty-five day rule and what purpose it serves.

## PROBLEMS

**25-18** *Computation of Fiduciary Accounting Income.* Under the terms of the trust instrument, the annual fiduciary accounting income of Trust MNO must be distributed in equal amounts to individual beneficiaries M, N, and O. The trust instrument also provides that capital gains or losses realized on the sale of trust assets arc allocated to principal, and that 40 percent of the annual trustee fee is to be allocated to principal. For the current year, the records of the trust show the following:

| | |
|---|---|
| Dividend income | $38,000 |
| Tax-exempt interest income | 18,900 |
| Taxable interest income | 12,400 |
| Capital loss on sale of securities | (2,500) |
| Trustee fee | 5,000 |

Based on these facts, determine the required distribution to each of the three trust beneficiaries.

**25-19** *Tax Consequences of Property Distributions.* During the taxable year, beneficiary M receives 100 shares of Acme common stock from Trust T. The basis of the stock is $70 per share to the trust, and its fair market value at date of distribution is $110 per share. The trust's DNI for the year is $60,000, all of which is taxable. There were no other distributions made or required to be made by the trust.

**a.** Assume the stock distribution was in satisfaction of an $11,000 pecuniary bequest to M. What is the tax result to M? To Trust T? What basis will M have in the Acme shares?

**b.** Assume the distribution did not represent a specific bequest to M, and that Trust T did not make a § 643(e)(3) election. What is the tax result to M? To Trust T? What basis will M have in the Acme shares?

**c.** Assume now that Trust T did make a § 643(e)(3) election with regard to the distribution of the Acme shares. What is the tax result to M? To Trust T? What basis will M have in the Acme shares?

**25-20** *Trust's Depreciation Deduction.* Under the terms of the trust instrument, Trustee K is required to maintain a reserve for depreciation equal to $3,000 per year. All trust income, including rents from depreciable trust property, must be distributed currently to trust beneficiaries.

**a.** Assume allowable depreciation for tax purposes is $2,000. What is the amount of the depreciation deduction available to the trust? To the trust beneficiaries?

**b.** Assume allowable depreciation for tax purposes is $7,000. What is the amount of the depreciation deduction available to the trust? To the trust beneficiaries?

**25-21** *Trust Losses.* Complex Trust Z has the following receipts and disbursements for the current year:

| | |
|---|---|
| Receipts: | |
| Rents | $ 62,000 |
| Proceeds from sale of securities (basis of securities = $55,000) | 48,000 |
| Dividends | 12,000 |
| Total receipts | $122,000 |
| Disbursements: | |
| Rent expenses | $ 70,000 |
| Trustee fee (100% allocable to income) | 4,000 |
| Total disbursements | $ 74,000 |

The trustee made no distributions to any beneficiaries during the current year. Based on these facts, compute trust taxable income for the current year.

**25-22** *Deductibility of Funeral and Administrative Expenses.* Decedent L died on May 12 of the current year, and her executor elected a calendar taxable year for L's estate. Prior to December 31, L's estate paid $4,800 of funeral expenses, $19,900 of legal and accounting fees attributable to the administration of the estate, and a $6,100 executor's fee. Before consideration of any of these expenses, L's estate has taxable income of $60,000 for the period May 13 to December 31. Decedent L's taxable estate for Federal estate tax purposes is estimated at $1,700,000.

**a.** To what extent are the above expenses deductible on L's estate tax return (Form 706) or on the estate's income tax return (Form 1041) for the current year? On which return would the deductions yield the greater tax benefit?

**b.** Assume that L was married at the time of her death and that all the property included in her gross estate was left to her surviving spouse. Does this fact change your answer to (a)?

**25-23** *Amount of Distribution Taxable to Beneficiary.* During the current year, Trust H has DNI of $50,000, of which $30,000 is nontaxable. The trustee made a $10,000 cash distribution to beneficiary P during the year; no other distributions were made.

**a.** How much taxable income must P report?

**b.** What deduction for distributions to beneficiaries may Trust H claim?

**25-24** *Deductibility of Trust Expenses.* Trust A has the following receipts and disbursements for the current year:

| | |
|---|---|
| Receipts: | |
| Nontaxable interest | $ 40,000 |
| Taxable interest | 30,000 |
| Rents | 30,000 |
| Total receipts | $100,000 |
| Disbursements: | |
| Charitable donation | $ 10,000 |
| Rent expense | 6,500 |
| Trustee fee | 5,000 |
| Total disbursements | $ 21,500 |

**a.** What is Trust A's deduction for charitable contributions for the current year?

**b.** How much of the trustee fee is deductible?

**c.** How much of the rent expense is deductible?

**25-25** *Computation of DNI and Trust's Tax Liability.* Trust M has the following receipts disbursements for the current year:

| | |
|---|---|
| Receipts: | |
| Nontaxable interest | $ 4,000 |
| Taxable interest | 25,000 |
| Rents | 11,000 |
| Long-term capital gain allocable to principal | 9,000 |
| Total receipts | $49,000 |
| Disbursements: | |
| Rent expense | $ 2,400 |
| Trustee fee | 1,000 |
| Total disbursements | $ 3,400 |

The trustee is required to distribute all trust income to beneficiary N on a quarterly basis.

**a.** Compute Trust M's DNI for the current year.
**b.** Compute Trust M's taxable income for the current year.
**c.** Compute Trust M's tax liability for the current year.

**25-26** *Taxation of Trust and Beneficiaries.* Trust B has the following receipts and disbursements for the current year:

| | |
|---|---|
| Receipts: | |
| Nontaxable interest | $10,000 |
| Dividends | 10,000 |
| Rents | 30,000 |
| Long-term capital gain allocable to principal | 15,000 |
| Total receipts | $65,000 |
| Disbursements: | |
| Rent expense | $ 7,500 |
| Trustee fee | 5,000 |
| Total disbursements | $12,500 |

During the year, the trustee distributes $20,000 to beneficiary C and $10,000 to beneficiary D. None of these distributions is subject to the throwback rule. The trust and both beneficiaries are calendar year taxpayers.

**a.** Compute Trust B's DNI for the current year.
**b.** Compute Trust B's taxable income for the current year.
**c.** How much taxable income must each beneficiary report for the current year?

**25-27** *Distributions from Complex Trusts.* Under the terms of the trust instrument, the trustee of Trust EFG is required to make an annual distribution of 50 percent of trust accounting income to beneficiary E. The trustee can make additional discretionary distributions out of trust income or principal to beneficiaries E, F, or G. During the current year, the trust accounting income of $85,000 equaled taxable DNI.

**a.** Assume that the trustee made current distributions of $60,000 to E and $10,000 to G. How much taxable income must each beneficiary report for the current year? What is the amount of the trust's deduction for distributions to beneficiaries?
**b.** Assume that the trustee made current distributions of $80,000 to E and $40,000 to G. How much taxable income must each beneficiary report for the current year? What is the amount of the trust's deduction for distributions to beneficiaries?

**25-28** *First- and Second-Tier Distributions.* For the current year, Trust R has DNI of $100,000, of which $25,000 is nontaxable. The trustee is required to make an annual distribution of $60,000 to beneficiary S. Also during the year, the trustee made discretionary distributions of $40,000 to beneficiary T and $30,000 to beneficiary U. None of these distributions is subject to the throwback rules. How much taxable income must each beneficiary report?

**25-29** *Distribution Exceeding DNI.* In 2009 and 2010, complex Trust C had taxable DNI of $18,000 and $28,500, respectively. No distributions were made to beneficiaries in either year and the trust paid income taxes totaling $13,041 for the two years. In 2010, trust DNI was $33,000 and the trustee distributed $100,000 to beneficiary W. Explain how such distribution is taxed.

**25-30** *Income in Respect of a Decedent.* Individual K is a self-employed business consultant. In the current year, K performed services for a client and billed the client for $14,500. Unfortunately, K died on October 10 of the current year, before he received payment for his services. A check for $14,500 was received by K's executor on November 18. At the date of K's death, he owed a local attorney $1,600 for legal advice concerning a child custody suit in which K was involved. K's executor paid this bill on December 15.

**a.** Assuming that K was a cash basis taxpayer, describe the tax consequences of the $14,500 receipt and the $1,600 payment by K's executor.

**b.** How would your answer change if K had been an accrual basis taxpayer?

**25-31** *Income in Respect of a Decedent.* Early in 2010, Z (an unmarried cash basis taxpayer) sold investment land with a basis of $50,000 for $200,000. In payment, Z received an installment note for $200,000, payable over the next ten years. Z died on December 1, 2010. As of the date of death, Z had received no principal payments on the note. Accrued interest on the note as of December 1, 2010 was $18,000, although the first interest payment was not due until early in 2011.

**a.** Assuming that no election is made to avoid installment sale treatment, how much of the $150,000 gain realized by Z will be included on her final income tax return? How much of the accrued interest income will be included?

**b.** In 2011, the estate of Z collects the first annual interest payment on the note of $19,700, and the first principal payment of $20,000. What are the income tax consequences to the estate of these collections?

**c.** Assume that the amount of estate tax attributable to the inclusion of the IRD represented by the installment note and the accrued interest in Z's taxable estate is $10,000, and that there are no other IRD or DRD items on the estate tax return. Compute the § 691(c) deduction available on the estate's 2011 income tax return.

## TAX RETURN PROBLEMS

**25-32** The MKJ trust is a calendar year, cash basis taxpayer. The trust was created pursuant to the will of Murray Kyle Jacobs, who died on November 11, 2000. For 2011, the trust's book and records reflect these transactions:

| | | |
|---|---|---|
| Receipts: | | |
| Dividends (qualified) | | $30,000 |
| Gross rents | | 25,000 |
| Interest: | | |
| Bonds of the City of New York | | 25,000 |
| U.S. government bonds | | 20,000 |
| Capital gains: | | |
| General Motors stock received from estate of MKJ: | | |
| Sales price—December 2, 2011 | $48,000 | |
| Less: Basis (FMV on date of death) | (30,000) | 18,000 |
| Disbursements: | | |
| Trustee commissions (50% paid out of income, 50% paid out of principal) | | 5,300 |
| Legal fee | | 28,800 |
| Contribution—American Cancer Society (paid out of principal) | | 12,000 |
| Depreciation—rental property | | 2,000 |
| Real estate tax—rental property | | 4,000 |
| Repairs and maintenance—rental property | | 4,200 |
| Federal quarterly estimated tax payments | | 9,000 |

The legal fee was a legitimate trust expense and was incurred because of the choice of trust form. The fee was allocated by the trustee to the various income classes as follows:

| | |
|---|---|
| Dividends | $ 0 |
| Taxable interest | 16,000 |
| Tax-exempt interest | 6,000 |
| Rents | 6,800 |
| Total legal fee | $28,800 |

The propriety of this allocation is *not* in question. Under the terms of the trust instrument (i.e., Mr. Jacobs' will), the $2,000 depreciation reserve equals the available tax depreciation deduction for the year. The trust instrument also specifies that all capital gains are allocable to principal and that the trustee has discretion as to the amount of trust income distributed to Brenda Jacobs, the sole individual beneficiary, and several charities specified in Mr. Jacobs' will. During 2011, the trustee distributes $24,000 of income to Brenda and $12,000 of income to the American Cancer Society.

*Required:* Complete Form 1041 and Schedule D for the MKJ trust. If the 2011 forms are not available, use the 2010 forms. **Note**: If the student is required to complete a Schedule K-1 for Brenda Jacobs, he or she should refer to Reg. §§ 1.661(b)-1, 1.661(c)-2, and 1.661(c)-4, and the comprehensive example in this chapter in order to determine the character of any income distributed to the beneficiary.

## TAX RESEARCH PROBLEM

**25-33** In 2004, N transferred $600,000 of assets into an irrevocable trust for the benefit of her mother, M. The independent trustee, T, is required to distribute annually all income to M. The trust instrument also provides that any capital gains or losses realized upon the sale of trust assets are to be allocated to trust principal. In 2006, and 2008, the trustee sold trust assets and distributed an amount equal to the capital gain realized to M, in addition to the required distribution of trust income. During the current year, T sold certain trust securities and realized a net gain of $25,000. The trust also earned $10,000 of other income. During the year, $35,000 was distributed to M. Should the DNI of the trust for the current year include the $25,000 capital gain?

# 26 Family Tax Planning

## Learning Objectives

Upon completion of this chapter you will be able to:

LO.1 Explain the concept of income shifting and the judicial constraints on this tax planning technique.

LO.2 Describe the marriage penalty and the singles penalty and identify the taxpayer situations in which either might occur.

LO.3 Identify different planning techniques that achieve tax savings by the shifting of income among family members.

LO.4 Characterize a regular corporation, an S corporation, and a partnership in terms of their viability as intrafamily income-shifting devices.

LO.5 Explain how the "kiddie tax" is computed on the unearned income of a minor child.

LO.6 Understand the role of a trust as a vehicle for intrafamily income shifting.

LO.7 Distinguish between a grantor trust and a taxable trust.

LO.8 Specify the tax advantages of inter vivos gifts as compared to testamentary transfers of wealth.

## Chapter Outline


Introduction 26-2
Family Income Shifting 26-2
- Judicial Constraints on Income Shifting 26-3
- Joint Filing and the Singles Penalty 26-4
- The Marriage Penalty 26-4
- Income Shifting to Children and Other Family Members 26-5

Income-Shifting Techniques 26-6
- Family Members as Employees 26-6
- Family Employees of Partnerships and Corporations 26-6
- Family Members as Owners of the Family Business 26-7
- Family Partnerships 26-8
- Regular Corporations 26-9
- S Corporations 26-10
- Negative Aspects of Ownership Transfers 26-11
- Preservation of Control of the Business 26-11
- Shifts of Investment Income 26-12
- Taxation of Unearned Income of Minor Children 26-12

The Trust as a Tax Planning Vehicle 26-13
- Advantages of the Trust Form 26-13
- Tax Consequences of Transfers into Trust 26-14
- Gift-Leasebacks 26-14
- Gift Tax Considerations 26-14
- Section 2503(c) and Crummey Trusts 26-15

Grantor Trusts 26-15
Reversionary Trusts 26-16
Interest-Free Loans 26-16
Power to Control Beneficial Enjoyment 26-17
Other Grantor Trusts 26-18
Grantor Trusts and the Transfer Tax Rules 26-19
Transfer Tax Planning 26-19
Tax Planning with Intrafamily Gifts 26-20
"Freezing" the Value of Assets in the Gross Estate 26-21
Charitable Giving 26-30
Liquidity Planning 26-31
Source of Funds 26-32
Flower Bonds 26-32
Planning for Deferred Payment of the Estate Tax 26-32
Conclusion 26-33
Problem Materials 26-33

## Introduction

Under the United States system of taxation, individuals are viewed as the basic unit of taxation. However, most individuals who are members of a nuclear family tend to regard the family as the economic and financial unit. For example, the individual wage earner with a spouse and three children must budget his or her income according to the needs of five people rather than one individual. Similarly, the family that includes a teenager who has received a college scholarship may perceive the scholarship as a financial benefit to all its members.

The concept of family tax planning is a product of this family-oriented economic perspective. Such planning has as its goal the minimization of taxes paid by the family unit as opposed to the separate taxes paid by individual members. Minimization of the total annual income tax bill of a family results in greater consumable income to the family unit. Minimization of transfer taxes on shifts of wealth among family members increases the total wealth that can be enjoyed by the family as a whole.

Before beginning a study of family tax planning, it is important to remember that such planning is only one aspect of the larger issue of family financial planning. Nontax considerations may often be more important to a family than the tax consequences of a course of action. For example, a family that faces the possibility of large medical expenses might be more concerned with their short-term liquidity needs than minimization of their current tax bill. A competent tax adviser must always be sensitive to the family's nontax goals and desires before he or she can design a tax plan that is truly in the family's best interests.

## Family Income Shifting

A general premise in tax planning holds that, given a single amount of income, two taxpayers are always better than one. This premise results from the progressive structure of the United States income tax. As one taxpayer earns an increasing amount of income, the income is taxed at an increasing marginal rate. If the income can be diverted to a second taxpayer with less income of his or her own, the diverted amount will be taxed at a lower marginal rate. In 2011, the tax rates applicable to individuals range from 10 percent on the first dollar of taxable income to 35 percent on taxable income in excess of $373,650. This 25-percentage-point spread between the lowest and highest marginal rates is a powerful incentive for individuals to adopt tax plans that incorporate some type of income-shifting technique.

A family unit composed of several individuals theoretically represents a single economic unit, which nonetheless is composed of separate taxpayers. A shift of income from one of these taxpayers to another has no effect economically. However, if the shift moves the income from a high tax bracket to a low tax bracket, the family has enjoyed a tax savings. A simple example can illustrate this basic point.

## Example 1

Family F is composed of a father and his 15-year-old daughter. The father earns taxable income of $90,000 a year, an amount that represents total family income. During the summer, the daughter needs $10,000 for various personal expenses. To earn the money, she agrees to work for her father for a $10,000 salary, payment of which represents a deductible expense to him.

Based on this arrangement, the family saves $2,080 [$13,293 − ($10,793 + $420 = $11,213)] as computed below.

| | *Father Split* | *Daughter Split* | *Father No Split* |
|---|---|---|---|
| Gross income | $80,000 | $10,000 | $90,000 |
| Standard deduction | (8,500) | (5,800) | (8,500) |
| Exemptions | (7,400) | 0 | (7,400) |
| Taxable income | $64,100 | $ 4,200 | $74,100 |
| Tax (head of household rates) | $10,793 | | $13,293 |
| Tax (single rates) | | $ 420 | |

Note that the father's income tax, standard deduction and exemptions are based on the fact that he would be considered a head of household and can claim an exemption for his daughter. Observe also that the fact that the daughter is a taxpayer does not prevent the father from qualifying as a head of household for filing purposes. However, because the daughter is eligible to be claimed as a dependent on her father's return she is not entitled to a personal exemption.[1]

The tax savings in the above example is attributable to two factors. First, the daughter as a taxpayer with earned income is entitled to a $5,800 standard deduction, which shelters $5,700 of the income shifted to her from any taxation at all.[2] Second, the income taxable to the daughter is subject to a 10 percent tax rate; if this income had been taxed on the father's return, it would have been subject to a 25 percent tax rate.

## Judicial Constraints on Income Shifting

**LO.1**
Explain the concept of income shifting and the judicial constraints on this tax planning technique.

The Federal courts have consistently recognized that the United States system of taxation cannot tolerate arbitrary shifting of income from one family member to another. The decisions in a number of historic cases have established clear judicial doctrine that limits the assignment of income from one taxpayer to another.

The 1930 Supreme Court case of *Lucas v. Earl*[3] involved a husband and wife who entered into a contract providing that the earnings of either spouse should be considered as owned equally by each. The contract was signed in 1901, twelve years before the first Federal income tax law was written, and was legally binding upon the spouses under California law.

The taxpayers contended that because of the contract certain attorney fees earned by Mr. Earl should be taxed in equal portions to Mr. and Mrs. Earl. However, the Supreme Court agreed with the government's argument that the intent of the Federal income tax law was to tax income to the individual who earns it, an intent that cannot be avoided by anticipatory arrangements to assign the income to a different taxpayer. The decision of the Court ended with the memorable statement that the tax law must disregard arrangements "by which the fruits are attributed to a different tree from that on which they grew."[4]

The Supreme Court followed the same logic in its 1940 decision in *Helvering v. Horst*.[5] This case involved a father who owned corporate coupon bonds and who detached the

---

[1] § 151(d)(2).

[2] § 63(c)(5).

[3] 2 USTC ¶496, 8 AFTR 10287, 281 U.S. 111 (USSC, 1930).

[4] *Ibid.* 281 U.S. 115.

[5] 40-2 USTC ¶9787, 24 AFTR 1058, 311 U.S. 112 (USSC, 1940).

negotiable interest coupons from the bonds shortly before their due date. The father then gifted the coupons to his son, who collected the interest upon maturity and reported the income on his tax return for the year.

The Court's decision focused on the fact that ownership of the corporate bonds themselves created the right to the interest payments. Because the father owned the bonds, he alone had the right to and control over the interest income. In exercising his control by gifting the interest coupons to his child, the father realized the economic benefit of the income represented by the coupons and therefore was the individual taxable on the income.

These two cases illustrate the two basic premises of the *assignment of income doctrine*. Earned income must be taxed to the individual who performs the service for which the income is paid. Investment income must be taxed to the owner of the investment capital that generated the income. All legitimate efforts to shift income from one individual to another must take into account these judicial constraints.

## Joint Filing and the Singles Penalty

**LO.2**
Describe the marriage penalty and the singles penalty and identify the taxpayer situations in which either might occur.

The most obvious candidates for intrafamily income shifting are a husband and wife, one of whom has a much larger income than the other. However, since 1948 married couples have been allowed to file a joint income tax return, which reports the total income earned by the couple and taxes the income on the basis of one progressive rate schedule.[6]

Joint filing originally was intended as a benefit to married couples. Prior to 1969, the joint filing tax rates were designed to tax one-half of total marital income at the tax rates applicable to single individuals. The resultant tax was then doubled to produce the married couple's tax liability. This perfect split and the corresponding tax savings were perceived as inequitable by unmarried taxpayers, who felt they were paying an unjustifiable "singles penalty."

To illustrate, consider the situation of a single taxpayer with taxable income of $24,000. In 1965, this taxpayer owed $8,030 of income tax, with the last dollar of income taxed at a 50 percent marginal tax rate. A married couple with the same 1965 taxable income owed only $5,660 and faced a marginal tax rate of only 32 percent.

## The Marriage Penalty

In 1969, Congress attempted to alleviate the singles penalty by enacting a new (and lower) rate schedule for single taxpayers.[7] While this action did reduce (but not eliminate) the singles penalty, it also created a marriage penalty for certain individuals. In 2001, Congress addressed the marriage tax penalty by modifying the standard deduction and the tax rates. For 2010, the standard deduction for joint returns is exactly double that of single taxpayers. Similarly, the 10 percent and 15 percent rate brackets for joint filers are exactly twice the size of the corresponding bracket for an unmarried individual ($8,375 vs. $16,750 and $34,000 vs. $68,000). The brackets for the higher rates are *not* expanded to twice the corresponding single filer tax brackets. As a practical matter, these changes will eliminate the marriage tax penalty for most individuals. Nevertheless, a penalty may still result for higher income taxpayers as shown below.

### Example 2

J and S are thinking about getting married and starting a family. The calculations below demonstrate what may happen if (1) J and S do not marry and J earns $90,000; (2) J and S do marry and J earns $90,000; and (3) J and S marry and both earned $90,000.

[6] § 6013. Married individuals may choose to file separate returns, but they must use the rate schedule of § 1(d), which simply halves the tax brackets of the married filing jointly rate schedule of § 1(a). As a general rule, separate filing results in a greater tax than joint filing and such filing status is elected only for nontax reasons.

[7] Act. § 803(a), P.L. 91-172, Dec. 30, 1969.

| | J Single | J & S Married | J & S Married |
|---|---|---|---|
| Gross income of J | $90,000 | $90,000 | $ 90,000 |
| Gross income of S | – | – | 90,000 |
| Standard deduction | (5,800) | (11,600) | (11,600) |
| Exemption | (3,700) | (7,400) | (7,400) |
| Taxable income | $80,500 | $71,000 | $161,000 |
| Tax | $16,250 | $ 10,000 | $ 33,150 |
| Tax for two singles ($16,250 × 2) | | | (32,500) |
| Singles penalty ($16,250 – $10,000) | | $ 6,250 | |
| Marriage penalty | | | $ 650 |

Interpretations of these results differ depending on the point of view. If J is single, he may not like the fact that his married friends who make the same income pay $6,250 less tax than he does. Obviously, he needs to find a wife! If J and S are considering getting married and S does not work, they should marry immediately since they would save $6,250 or avoid the singles penalty that J currently pays. But what happens if both individuals earn income? If each had about the same income and the amounts did not exceed about $79,175, there would be no penalty. However, if they both earn $90,000, as seen above, getting married produces an additional tax of $650—some may say a small price for marital bliss. Most individuals contemplating marriage need not worry about the cost of marriage since the penalty normally occurs only at higher income levels.

Generally, a singles penalty may occur when *one* income can be taxed at married, rather than single, rates. A marriage penalty may occur when *two* incomes are combined and taxed at married, rather than single, rates. Today, two-income families have become the rule rather than the exception, and the marriage penalty has received considerable publicity. The recent changes by Congress will go a long way to putting an end to the controversy. Nevertheless there will be married couples who want to avoid the penalty. For these people who might entertain the notion of divorce, they should be wary. Because marital status is determined as of the last day of the taxable year,[8] couples have attempted to avoid the marriage penalty by obtaining a technically legal divorce shortly before year end. When a couple has immediately remarried and the only purpose of the divorce was to enable the husband and wife to file as single taxpayers, the IRS and the courts have had little trouble in concluding that the divorce was a sham transaction and therefore ineffective for tax purposes.[9]

Before leaving this topic, one last observation is worth noting. While the recent changes should eliminate most objections to the marriage tax penalty, this does not mean the system is neutral on marriage. Inequities between married and single taxpayers have not necessarily been resolved. No doubt singles who pay more taxes that their married counterparts who earn the same income will complain—much as their ancestors did in 1969. Only time will tell if Congress will once again provide relief and start the cycle once again.

## Income Shifting to Children and Other Family Members

Because a married couple is considered one rather than two taxpayers for Federal tax purposes, intrafamily income shifting usually involves a transfer of income from parents to children (or, less commonly, other family members) who are considered taxpayers in their own right.

The fact that children are taxpayers separate and distinct from their parents is recognized by § 73, which states "amounts received in respect of the services of a child shall be included in his gross income and not in the gross income of the parent, even though such amounts are not

[8] § 7703(a).

[9] Rev. Rul. 76-255, 1976-2 C.B. 40; and *Boyter v. Comm.*, 82-1 USTC ¶9117, 49 AFTR2d 451, 668 F.2d 1382 (CA-4, 1981).

received by the child." The regulations elaborate by stating that the statutory rule applies even if state law entitles the parent to the earnings of a minor child.[10]

Because children typically will have little or no income of their own, a shift of family income to such children can cause the income to be taxed at a lower marginal rate. The income shifted from parent to child also represents wealth that is owned by the child rather than the parent. Thus, the future taxable estate of the parent will not include the accumulated income that is already in the hands of younger-generation family members.

## Income-Shifting Techniques

**LO.3**
Identify different planning techniques that achieve tax savings by the shifting of income among family members.

The next section of this chapter explores a variety of techniques whereby income can be successfully shifted to family members in a lower marginal tax bracket. The circumstances of each particular family situation will dictate the specific technique to be used.

### Family Members as Employees

The first technique for intrafamily income shifting is for a low-bracket family member to become an employee of a family business. This technique does not involve the transfer of a capital interest in the business, so the family member who owns the business does not dilute his or her ownership by this technique.

In the simplest case in which the family business is a sole proprietorship, any family members who become employees must actually perform services the value of which equates to the amount of compensation received. This requirement implies that the employee is both capable and qualified for his or her job and devotes an appropriate amount of time to the performance of services.

**Example 3**

F owns a plumbing contracting business as a sole proprietorship. During the current year, F employs his son S as an apprentice plumber for an hourly wage of $10. The total amount paid to S for the year is $9,000.

If the father can prove to the satisfaction of the IRS that his son performed services worth $10 per hour and that the son actually worked 900 hours during the year, the father may deduct the $9,000 as wage expense on his tax return and the son will report $9,000 of compensation income on his own return.

If, on the other hand, the IRS concludes that the son was not a legitimate employee of his father's business, the transfer of $9,000 to the son would be recharacterized as a gift. As a result, the father would lose the business deduction, and no income shift from father to son would occur.

Obviously, the legitimacy of the employment relationship between father and son can only be determined by an examination of all relevant facts and circumstances. Facts to be considered would include the age of the son, his prior work experience and technical training, and his actual participation on contracted jobs requiring an apprentice plumber.

When a family member is an employee of a family business, any required payroll taxes on his or her compensation must be paid. However, compensation paid to an employer's children under the age of 18 is not subject to Federal payroll tax.[11]

### Family Employees of Partnerships and Corporations

If a family member wants to work as an employee of a family business operated in partnership or corporate form, the requirement that the value of his or her services equate to the amount of compensation received does not change. If the employment relationship is valid,

[10] Reg. § 1.73-1(a).

[11] §§ 3121(b)(3)(A) and 3306(c)(5).

the partnership or corporation may deduct the compensation paid to the family member. If the family member is not performing services that justify the salary he or she is drawing from the business, the IRS may recharacterize the payment.

In the case of a partnership, the payment may be recharacterized as a constructive cash withdrawal by one or more partners followed by a constructive gift of the cash to the pseudo employee.

### Example 4

Brothers X, Y, and Z are equal partners in Partnership XYZ. The partnership hires S, the sister of the partners, to act as secretary-treasurer for the business. S's salary is $20,000 per year. Assume that S has no business or clerical training and performs only minimal services for the business on a very sporadic basis. As a result, the IRS disallows a deduction to the partnership for all but $5,000 of the payment to the sister. The nondeductible $15,000 will be treated as a withdrawal by the partners that was transferred as a gift to the sister.

Constructive cash withdrawals from a partnership could have adverse tax consequences to the partners. If the withdrawal exceeds a partner's basis in his or her partnership interest, the excess constitutes capital gain to the partner.[12] Similarly, a constructive gift to a family member could result in an unexpected gift tax liability.

When the employer is a family corporation and a salary or wage paid to a nonshareholder family member is disallowed, the tax results can be extremely detrimental. Not only does the corporation lose a deduction, but the payment could be recharacterized as a constructive dividend to the family members who are shareholders, followed by a constructive gift to the family member who actually received the funds.[13] Thus, the corporate shareholders would have dividend income without any corresponding cash, and a potential gift tax liability.

The lesson to be learned from the preceding discussion should be clear. If an intrafamily income shift is to be accomplished by hiring a family member as an employee of a family business, the family member must perform as a legitimate employee. If the employment relationship has no substance, the unintended tax consequences to the family could be costly indeed.

## Family Members as Owners of the Family Business

**LO.4**
Characterize a regular corporation, an S corporation, and a partnership in terms of their viability as intrafamily income-shifting devices.

A second technique for intrafamily income shifting is to make a low-bracket family taxpayer a part owner of the family business. By virtue of his or her equity or capital interest, the family member is then entitled to a portion of the income generated by the business. This is a more extreme technique in that it involves an actual transfer of a valuable asset. Moreover, the disposition of a partial ownership interest may cause dilution of the original owner's control of the business. These and other negative aspects of this technique will be discussed in greater detail later in the chapter.

The gratuitous transfer of an equity interest in a business will constitute a taxable gift to the original owner.

### Example 5

M runs a very successful business as a sole proprietorship. She wants to bring her son S into the business as an equal general partner. Under the terms of a legally binding partnership agreement, she contributes her business, valued at $1 million, to the partnership. Although the son will have a 50% capital interest in the partnership, he contributes nothing. As a result, M has made a $500,000 taxable gift to S.

[12] § 731(a).

[13] *Duffey v. Lethert*, 63-1 USTC ¶9442, 11 AFTR2d 1317 (D.Ct. Minn., 1963).

Of course, if the transfer of the equity interest is accomplished by sale rather than gift, no initial gift tax liability will result. But in a typical family situation, the equity interest is being transferred to a family member without significant income or wealth, so that family member lacks the funds to purchase the interest. Also, the income tax consequences of a sale could be more expensive than gift tax consequences, depending upon the facts and circumstances. The prudent tax adviser should explore both possible methods of transfer when designing a particular plan.

## Family Partnerships

A family partnership can be used as a vehicle for the co-ownership of a single business by a number of family members. As a partner, each family member will report his or her allocable share of partnership income (or loss) on his or her individual tax return.[14] Therefore, through use of a partnership, business income can be shifted to family members with relatively low marginal tax brackets.

If the family partnership is primarily a service business, only a family member who performs services can receive an allocation of partnership income. In such service partnerships, the physical assets of the business (the capital of the partnership) are not a major factor of income production. Rather, it is the individual efforts and talents of the partners that produce partnership income. An attempt to allow a family member who cannot perform the appropriate services to participate in partnership income is an unwarranted assignment of earned income.

If the family partnership is one in which capital is a major income-producing factor, the mere ownership of a capital interest will entitle a family member to participate in partnership income. The determination of whether or not capital is a material income-producing factor is made by reference to the facts of each situation. However, capital is ordinarily a material income-producing factor if the operation of the business requires substantial inventories or investment in plant, machinery, or equipment.[15]

Section 704(e)(1) specifies that a family member will be recognized as a legitimate partner if he or she owns a capital interest in a partnership in which capital is a material income-producing factor. This is true even if the family member received his or her interest as a gift. However, § 704(e)(2) limits the amount of partnership income that can be shifted to such a donee partner. Under this statute, the income allocated to the partner cannot be proportionally greater than his or her interest in partnership capital.

### Example 6

Grandfather F is a 50% partner in Magnum Partnership. At the beginning of the current year, F gives his grandson G a 20% capital interest in Magnum (leaving F with a 30% interest). For the current year Magnum has taxable income of $120,000. The *maximum* amount allocable to G is $24,000 (20% × $120,000). If F wanted to increase the dollar amount of partnership income shifted to G, he must give G a greater equity interest in the partnership.

Section 704(e)(2) contains a second restriction on income allocation. A donor partner who *gifts* a capital interest must receive reasonable compensation for any services he or she renders to the partnership before any income can be allocated to the donee partner.

### Example 7

Refer to the facts in *Example 6*. During the current year, F performs services for Magnum worth $15,000 but for which he receives no compensation. Half of the $120,000 partnership income is still allocable to F and G with respect to their com-

[14] § 702(a).

[15] Reg. § 1.704-1(e)(1)(iv).

bined 50% capital interests; however, the maximum amount allocable to G decreases to $18,000 [($60,000 − $15,000 allocated to F as compensation for services) × 40%].

Note that in the above example, Grandfather F might be willing to forgo any compensation for the services performed for Magnum in order to increase the amount of partnership income shifted to his grandson. Unfortunately, § 704(e)(2) effectively curtails this type of indirect assignment of earned income.

Family members are not able to avoid the dual limitations of § 704(e) by arranging a transfer of a capital interest to a lower-bracket family member by sale rather than by gift. Under § 704(e)(3), a capital interest in a partnership purchased by one member of a family from another is considered to be created by gift from the seller. In this context the term *family* includes an individual's spouse, ancestors, lineal descendants, and certain family trusts.

## Regular Corporations

Family businesses are frequently owned as closely held corporations. There are a number of business reasons why the corporate form is popular. For example, shareholders in a corporation have limited liability so that creditors of the corporation cannot force the shareholders to pay the debts of the corporation out of the shareholders' personal assets. There are also tax benefits to the corporate form of business. The owners of the business can function as employees of the corporate entity. As employees, they may participate in a wide variety of tax-favored employee benefit plans, such as employer-sponsored medical reimbursement plans. If the family business were in sole proprietorship or partnership form, the owners of the business would be self-employed and ineligible to participate in such employee benefit plans.

The corporate form of business must be regarded as a mixed blessing from a tax point of view. The incorporation of a family business does result in the creation of a new taxable entity, separate and distinct from its owners. Business income has been shifted to the corporate taxpayer, and because corporate tax rates are progressive, a net tax savings to the business can be the result.[16]

### Example 8

Individual T, married, owns a sole proprietorship that produces $100,000 of net income before taxes. Ignoring the availability of any deductions or exemptions, T's 2011 tax on this income is $17,250 (married filing jointly rates). If T incorporates the business and draws a salary of $50,000, he will pay an individual tax of only $6,650. The corporation will also have income of $50,000 ($100,000 net income − $50,000 salary to T). The corporate tax on $50,000 is $7,500. Therefore, the *total* tax on the business income has decreased by $3,100 to $14,150 ($6,650 + $7,500).

The tax savings to T's business ($3,100) achieved by incorporation is certainly dramatic. However, the potential problem created by the incorporation of T's business is that the after-tax earnings of the business are now in the corporation rather than in T's pocket. If T needs or wants more than $43,350 ($50,000 salary − $6,650 tax liability) of after-tax personal income, he may certainly have his corporation pay out some of its after-tax earnings to him as a dividend. But any dividends paid must be included in T's gross income and taxed at the individual level.

This double taxation of corporate earnings paid to shareholders as dividends can quickly offset the tax savings resulting from using a corporation as a separate entity. Therefore, shareholders in closely held corporations usually become very adept in drawing business income out of their corporations as deductible business expenses rather than nondeductible dividends.

[16] Because of the 5 percent surtax on taxable income between $100,000 and $335,000, corporations with taxable income between $335,000 and $10 million face a flat 34 percent tax rate rather than a progressive rate. Qualified personal service corporations pay a flat 35 percent of their total taxable income. § 11(b)(2).

Shareholders who are also employees will usually try to maximize the amount of compensation they receive from the corporation. Section 162(a)(1) authorizes the corporation to deduct a *reasonable* allowance for salaries or other compensation paid. If the IRS determines that the compensation paid to an owner employee is unjustifiably high and therefore *unreasonable*, the excessive compensation can be reclassified as a dividend. As a result, the corporation loses the deduction for the excessive compensation, and to a corresponding extent, business earnings are taxed twice.

Other types of deductible payments from corporations to shareholders include rents paid for corporate use of shareholder assets and interest on loans made to the corporation by shareholders. The arrangements between corporation and shareholder that give rise to such rent or interest payments will be subject to careful scrutiny by the IRS. If an arrangement lacks substance and is deemed to be a device to camouflage the payments of dividends to shareholders, the corporate deduction for the payments will be disallowed.

Because it is a taxpayer in its own right, a regular corporation cannot be effectively used to shift business income to low-bracket family members. If such family members are made shareholders in the corporation and have no other relationship to the corporate business (employee, creditor, etc.), the only way to allocate business earnings to them is by paying dividends on their stock. As previously discussed, dividend payments are usually considered prohibitively costly from a tax standpoint.

Closely held regular corporations do have tremendous utility in other areas of tax planning. However, for purposes of intrafamily income shifting, the S corporation is a highly preferable alternative to a regular corporation.

## S Corporations

The complex set of statutory provisions that govern the tax treatment of S corporations is explained in Chapter 23. For family tax planning purposes, the most important characteristic of an S corporation is that the corporate income escapes taxation at the corporate level and is taxed to the corporation's shareholders. This characteristic makes an S corporation a very useful mechanism for intrafamily income shifting.

Section 1366(a) provides that the taxable income of an S corporation is allocated to the shareholders on a pro rata basis. Thus, any individual who is a shareholder will report a proportionate share of the corporate business income on his or her personal tax return for the year with or within which the S corporation's taxable year ends.

### Example 9

Individual M, married, owns a sole proprietorship with an annual net income before taxes of $200,000. Ignoring the availability of any itemized deductions or exemptions, M's personal tax on this income is $44,070 (joint return schedule). If at the beginning of 2011 M incorporates the business, gives each of his four unmarried children 20% of the stock, and has the shareholders elect S status for the corporation, the corporate income of $200,000 will be taxed in equal $40,000 amounts to the five shareholders. Ignoring other deductions or exemptions, the 2011 tax bill on the business income will be $29,650 [$5,150 on a joint return + (4 × $6,125 = $24,500 on a single return)]. By splitting the income, M saves $14,420 ($44,070 − $29,650).

A shareholder who is also an employee of a family-owned S corporation will not be able to divert corporate income to other shareholders by forgoing any compensation for services rendered to the corporation. Code § 1366(e) provides that if such a shareholder employee does not receive reasonable compensation from the S corporation, the IRS may reallocate corporate income to the shareholder employee so as to accurately reflect the value of his or her services.

Because shareholders of an S corporation are taxed on all the taxable income earned by the corporation, subsequent cash withdrawals of this income by shareholders are tax free.[17]

[17] § 1368(b).

However, the technical requirements for cash withdrawals from an S corporation are dangerously complicated. Because of the complexity of these requirements and many other tax aspects of S corporations, family tax plans involving their use should be carefully designed and monitored by the family tax adviser.

## Negative Aspects of Ownership Transfers

A high-bracket taxpayer who desires to shift income to low-bracket family members by making such members co-owners of the taxpayer's business must reconcile himself or herself to several facts. First, the transfer of the equity interest in the business must be complete and legally binding so that the recipient of the interest has "dominion and control" over his or her new asset. A *paper* transfer by which the transferor creates only the illusion that a family member has been given an equity interest in a business will be treated as a sham transaction, ineffective for income-shifting purposes.[18]

As a general rule, the recipient of an ownership interest in a family business is free to dispose of the interest, just as he or she is free to dispose of any asset he or she owns. If the recipient is a responsible individual and supportive of the family tax planning goals, his or her legal right to assign the interest may not be a problem. But if the recipient is a spendthrift in constant need of ready cash, he or she may sell the interest to a third party, thereby completely subverting the family tax plan.

One popular technique that can prevent an unexpected and undesired disposition of an interest in a family business is a buy-sell agreement. A taxpayer can transfer an equity interest to a low-bracket family member on the condition that should the family member desire to sell the interest he or she must first offer the interest to its original owner at an independently determined market value. Such an agreement is in no way economically detrimental to the family member, yet affords a measure of protection for both the original owner and the family tax plan.

A related aspect of the requirement that the taxpayer must legally surrender the ownership of the business interest transferred is that the transfer is irrevocable. Ownership of the interest cannot be regained if future events cause the original tax plan to become undesirable. For example, an estrangement between family members could convert a highly satisfactory intrafamily income-shifting plan into a bitterly resented trap. A father who has an ill-favored son as an employee can always fire him. It is another matter entirely if the son is a 40 percent shareholder in the father's corporation.

A change in economic circumstances could also cause a taxpayer to regret a transfer of a business interest. Consider a situation in which a formerly high-income taxpayer suffers a severe financial downturn. A tax plan that is shifting income *away* from such a taxpayer could suddenly become an economic disaster.

## Preservation of Control of the Business

A taxpayer who is contemplating transferring an ownership interest in a business to one or more family members should also consider any resultant dilution of his or her control of the business. The taxpayer may be willing to part with an equity interest in order to shift business income to low-bracket family members, but may be very reluctant to allow such family members to participate in the management of the business.

A limited partnership can be used to bring family members into a business without allowing them a voice in management. A family member who owns a capital interest as a limited partner in a partnership may be allocated a share of business income, subject to the family partnership rules, and yet be precluded from participating in management of the business.

If the family business is in corporate form, various classes of stock with differing characteristics can be issued. For example, nonvoting stock can be given to family members without any dilution of the original owner's voting power, and hence control, over the business. If the original owner does not want to draw any dividends out of the corporate business but is willing to have dividends paid to low-bracket family members, nonvoting preferred stock can be issued to such family members.

---

[18] For example, see Reg. § 1.704-1(e)(2).

Unfortunately, this flexibility in designing a corporate capital structure that maximizes income-shifting potential while minimizing loss of control is not available to S corporations. To qualify for S status a corporation may have only one class of stock outstanding.[19] Thus, all outstanding shares of stock in an S corporation must be identical with respect to the rights they convey in the profits and assets of the corporation. However, shares of stock in S corporations may have different *voting rights* without violating the single class of stock requirement.[20]

## Shifts of Investment Income

In many ways the shifting of investment income to family members is simpler than the shifting of business income. Questions of forms of co-ownership and control are not as difficult to resolve if the income-producing asset to be transferred is in the form of an investment security rather than a business interest.

The simplest means to shift investment income from one taxpayer to another is an outright gift of the investment asset. Even gifts to minors who are under legal disabilities with regard to property ownership can be accomplished under state Uniform Gifts to Minors Acts. By using a custodian to hold the property for the benefit of a minor, the donor has shifted the investment income to the minor's tax return.[21]

Although gifting of investment property is a relatively simple technique, the donor must be aware that the transfer must be complete. The asset (and the wealth it represents) is irrevocably out of the donor's hands. If the donor attempts to retain an interest in or control over the asset, the gift may be deemed incomplete and the attempted income shift ineffectual.

If a donee receives an unrestricted right to a valuable investment asset, there is always the worry that he or she will mismanage it, or worse, assign it to a third party against the wishes of the donor. Because of these negative aspects of outright gifts, the private trust has become a very popular vehicle for the transfer of investment assets, especially when minor children are involved. A subsequent section of the chapter explores the use of trusts in family tax planning.

## Taxation of Unearned Income of Minor Children

**LO.5**
Explain how the "kiddie tax" is computed on the unearned income of a minor child.

Tax law significantly limits the ability of parents to shift investment income to their children. Section 1(g) provides that any *net unearned income* of a minor child in excess of a $950 (2011) base is taxed at the marginal rate applicable to the income of the child's parents.[22] A minor child is one who by the close of the tax year has not obtained the age of 19 or is a full-time student less than the age of 24 who does not provide more than one-half of his or her support and who has at least one living parent on that date.

Net unearned income is generally defined as passive investment income such as interest and dividends, reduced by the $950 standard deduction available against unearned income of a dependent.[23] The amount of net unearned income for any taxable year may not exceed the child's taxable income for the year. The *source* of the unearned income is irrelevant for purposes of this so-called "kiddie tax."

### Example 10

Several years ago grandchild G, age 15, received a gift of corporate bonds from her grandparents. G's 2011 interest income from the securities totaled $8,000. G had no other income or deductions for the year. G's parents claimed G as a dependent and reported taxable income of $500,000 on their joint return. G's taxable income is $7,050

[19] § 1361(b)(1)(D).

[20] § 1361(c)(4).

[21] Rev. Rul. 56-484, 1956-2 C.B. 23. However, income earned by the custodian account used for the support of the minor will be taxed to the person legally responsible for such support (i.e., the parent).

[22] In the case of parents who are not married, the child's tax is computed with reference to the tax rate of the custodial parent. If the parents file separate tax returns, the tax rate of the parent with the *greater* taxable income is used. § 1(g)(5).

[23] § 63(c)(5).

($8,000 gross income – an $950 standard deduction) and her net unearned income to be taxed at her parents' rate is $6,100 ($8,000 – the $950 base – an $950 standard deduction). Thus $6,100 is taxed at her parents' rates and the balance, $950, is taxed at her rates, resulting in a tax liability of $2,230 computed as follows:

| | |
|---|---|
| Tax on unearned income at parents' rates: | |
| ($8,000 – $1,900 = $6,100 × 35%) | $2,135 |
| Tax on remaining taxable income at child's rates: | |
| ($950 × 10%) | 95 |
| Tax liability | $2,230 |

In this example, it is important to note that the income was interest and, therefore, subject to tax at the parents' highest tax rate. In contrast, dividend income or long-term capital gains that are shifted to a child are generally taxed at 15% (or 5%) but a special computation is required.

In certain cases parents may elect to include a dependent's unearned income on their return, rather than filing a separate return and making the "kiddie tax" calculation. As a general rule, this should not be done since the additional income increases the parents' adjusted gross income, which may reduce the amount of deductions that the parent may claim and have other unintended effects.

# The Trust as a Tax Planning Vehicle

As discussed in Chapter 25, a private trust is a legal arrangement whereby the ownership and control of property are vested in a trustee while the beneficial interest in the property is given to one or more beneficiaries. The trustee has a fiduciary responsibility to manage the property for the sole benefit of the beneficiaries.

## Advantages of the Trust Form

**LO.6**
Understand the role of a trust as a vehicle for intrafamily income shifting.

The use of a trust has many nontax advantages. If an individual desires to make a gift of property to a donee who is not capable of owning or managing the property, the gift can be made in trust so that a competent trustee can be selected to manage the property free from interference from the donee-beneficiary.

The trust form of property ownership is very convenient in that it allows the legal title to property to be held by a single person (the trustee) while allowing the beneficial enjoyment of the property to be shared by a number of beneficiaries. If legal ownership of the property were fragmented among the various beneficiaries, they would all have to jointly participate in management decisions regarding the property. This cumbersome and oftentimes impractical co-ownership situation is avoided when a trustee is given sole management authority over the property.

If a donor would like to give property to several donees so that the donees have sequential rather than concurrent rights in the property, the trust form for the gift is commonly the solution.

**Example 11**

Individual K owns a valuable tract of income-producing real estate. She would like ownership of the real estate to ultimately pass to her three minor grandchildren. She also would like to give her invalid brother an interest in the real estate so as to provide him with a future source of income. K can transfer the real estate into trust, giving her brother an income interest for a designated time period. Upon termination of the time period, ownership of the real estate will go to K's grandchildren.

## Tax Consequences of Transfers into Trust

The use of the trust form can have distinct income tax advantages to a family because both the trust itself and any beneficiaries who receive income from the trust are taxpayers in their own right.

> **Example 12**
>
> F, a high-bracket taxpayer, transfers income-producing assets into a trust of which his four grandchildren are discretionary income beneficiaries. In the current year, the trust assets generate $100,000 of income, of which the trustee distributes $24,000 to each child. The $100,000 of investment income will be taxed to five taxpayers, the four grandchildren and the trust itself.

In determining the benefit of splitting income in *Example 12*, it is important to remember that unearned income *distributed* from a trust to a beneficiary may be subject to the kiddie tax. The income will be taxed at the marginal rate applicable to the beneficiary's parents, even if the parents did not create the trust. However, if the beneficiary is not subject to the kiddie tax (e.g., a grandparent), substantial savings can be obtained.

## Gift-Leasebacks

A popular and controversial method for family income shifting through use of a trust involves a technique known as a gift-leaseback. Typically, a taxpayer who owns assets that he or she uses in a trade or business transfers the assets as a gift in trust for the benefit of the taxpayer's children (or other low-bracket family members). The independent trustee then leases the assets back to the taxpayer for their fair rental value. The rent paid by the taxpayer to the trust is deducted as a § 162 ordinary and necessary business expense and becomes income to the taxpayer's children because of their status as trust beneficiaries.

The IRS has refused to recognize the validity of gift-leaseback arrangements and has consistently disallowed the rent deduction to the transferor of the business assets under the theory that the entire transaction has no business purpose. However, if the trust owning the leased assets has an independent trustee and the leaseback arrangement is in written form and requires payment to the trust of a reasonable rent, the Tax Court and the Second, Third, Seventh, Eighth, and Ninth Circuits have allowed the transferor to deduct the rent paid.[24] To date, only the Fourth and Fifth Circuits have supported the government's position that gift-leaseback transactions are shams to be disregarded for tax purposes.[25]

## Gift Tax Considerations

The obvious income tax advantage of a family trust, such as the one described in *Example 12* above, can be offset if the original gift of property into the trust is subject to a substantial gift tax. Thus, the first step in designing a family trust is the minimization of any front-end gift tax. If the fair market value of the transferred property is less than the taxable amount sheltered by the unified credit of § 2505, no gift tax will be paid. However, the reader should bear in mind that the use of the credit against inter vivos gifts reduces the future shelter available on the donor's estate tax return.

An essential element in the minimization of any gift tax for transfers into trust is securing the $13,000 (2011) annual exclusion (§ 2503) for the amount transferred to each beneficiary-donee. This can be difficult when certain of the donees are given only a prospective or future interest in the trust property.

---

[24] See *May v. Comm.*, 76 T.C. 7(1981), *aff'd.* 84-1 USTC ¶9166, 53 AFTR2d 84-626 (CA-9. 1984).

[25] See *Mathews v. Comm.*, 75-2 USTC ¶9734, 36 AFTR2d 75-5965, 520 F.2d 323 (CA-5, 1975), cert. denied, 424 U.S. 967 (1976).

### Example 13

Donor Z transfers $100,000 into trust. The independent trustee has the discretion to distribute income currently among Z's five children, or she may accumulate it for future distribution. Upon trust termination, the trust assets will be divided equally among the children. Because the five donees have only future interests in the $100,000, Z may not claim any exclusions in computing the amount of the taxable gift.[26]

## SECTION 2503(C) AND CRUMMEY TRUSTS

One method of securing the exclusion for transfers into trust is to rely on the *safe harbor* rules of § 2503(c). Under this subsection a transfer into trust will not be considered a gift of a future interest if:

1. The property and income therefrom may be expended for the benefit of the donee-beneficiary before he or she reaches age 21; and
2. If any property or income is not so expended, it will pass to the donee-beneficiary at age 21 or be payable to his or her estate if he or she dies before that age.

One drawback to the "§ 2503(c) trust" is that the trust assets generally must go to the beneficiaries at age 21. Many parent-donors would prefer to postpone trust termination until their children-donees attain a more mature age. This goal can be accomplished through the use of a *Crummey trust*.[27]

A Crummey trust is one in which the beneficiaries are directly given only a future right to trust income or corpus. The term of the trust may extend well beyond the time when the beneficiaries reach age 21. However, the trust instrument contains a clause (the Crummey clause) that authorizes any beneficiary or his or her legal representative to make a current withdrawal of any current addition to the trust of up to $13,000 (2011). The withdrawal right is made noncumulative from year to year. As long as the beneficiary is given notification of this right within a reasonable period before it lapses for the year, the donor will be entitled to an exclusion for the current transfers into trust.[28] It should be noted that most donors anticipate that their donees will never exercise their withdrawal right; the Crummey clause is included in the trust instrument for the *sole purpose* of securing the $13,000 exclusion for gift tax purposes.

# Grantor Trusts

**LO.7**
Distinguish between a grantor trust and a taxable trust.

In certain cases a taxpayer may desire to transfer property into trust but does not want to surrender complete control over the property. Alternatively, the taxpayer may want to dispose of the property (and the right to income from the property) for only a limited period of time. Prior to the enactment of the 1954 Internal Revenue Code there was no statutory guidance as to when the retention of powers over a trust by the grantor (transferor) would prevent the trust from being recognized as a separate taxable entity. Nor was there statutory guidance as to the tax status of a reversionary trust, the corpus of which reverted to the grantor after a specified length of time.

The judicial attitude toward these *grantor* trusts was reflected in the Supreme Court decision of *Helvering v. Clifford*.[29] This case involved a taxpayer who transferred securities into trust for the exclusive benefit of his wife. The trust was to last for five years, during which time the taxpayer as trustee would manage the trust corpus as well as decide how much, if

[26] Reg. § 25.2503-3(c), Ex. 3.

[27] The amusing designation comes from the court case which established the validity of the technique—*Crummey v. Comm.*, 68-2 USTC ¶12,541, 22 AFTR2d 6023, 397 F.2d 82 (CA-9, 1968). The IRS *acquiesced* to this decision in Rev. Rul. 73-405, 1973-2 C.B. 321.

[28] Rev. Rul. 81-7, 1981-1 C.B. 27.

[29] 40-1 USTC ¶9265, 23 AFTR 1077, 309 U.S. 331 (1940).

any, of the trust income was to be paid to his wife. Upon trust termination, corpus was to return to the taxpayer while any accumulated income was to go to the wife.

In reaching its decision, the Court noted the lack of a precise standard or guide supplied by statute or regulations. As a result, the Court turned to a subjective evaluation of all the facts and circumstances of this particular short-term trust arrangement and held that "the short duration of the trust, the fact that the wife was the beneficiary, and the retention of control over the corpus by respondent all lead irresistibly to the conclusion that the respondent continued to be the owner."[30] As a result, the trust income was held to be taxable to the grantor rather than the trust or its beneficiary.

The authors of the 1954 Internal Revenue Code recognized that the uncertainty regarding the tax treatment of grantor trusts was undesirable and supplanted the subjective *Clifford* approach with a series of code sections (§§ 671 through 679) containing more objective rules as to the taxability of such trusts. The basic operative rule is contained in § 671. If §§ 673 through 679 specify that the grantor (or another person) shall be treated as the owner of any portion of a trust, the income, deductions, or credits attributable to that portion of the trust shall be reported on the grantor's (or other person's) tax return. If §§ 673 through 679 are inapplicable, the trust shall be treated as a separate taxable entity under the normal rules of Subchapter J (see Chapter 25).

## Reversionary Trusts

Section 673 provides that the grantor shall be treated as the owner of any portion of a trust in which he or she has a reversionary interest, if upon creation of the trust the value of the reversion exceeds 5 percent of the value of the assets subject to reversion.

**Example 14**

In the current year, grantor G transfers assets worth $500,000 into trust. Niece N, age 20, will receive the income from the trust for 15 years, after which the trust will terminate and the assets returned to G. On the date the trust is created, the reversion is properly valued at $121,000. Because the reversion is worth more than 5% of $500,000, the income will be taxed to G, even though it will be distributed to N.

**Example 15**

If in the previous example, N had been given the income from the trust for her life, the proper value of G's reversion would only be $13,000. Because this reversionary interest is worth only 2.6% of the value of the trust assets, the trust is not a grantor trust and the income will be taxed to N.

In the case of a trust in which a lineal descendant of the grantor (child, grandchild, etc.) is the income beneficiary, and the grantor owns a reversionary interest that takes effect only upon the death of the beneficiary prior to the age of 21, the trust *will not* be considered a grantor trust.[31]

## Interest-Free Loans

Through use of a reversionary trust, a taxpayer may divert income to low-bracket family members only if he or she is willing to part with control of the trust corpus for a significant period of time. For many years the use of an interest-free demand loan between family members provided an alternative to a reversionary trust. A taxpayer could loan a sum of money

[30] *Ibid.*, 309 U.S. 332.

[31] § 673(b).

to a family member on a demand basis and the money could be invested to earn income for that family member. Because the loan was interest-free, the creditor-taxpayer had no income from the temporary shift of wealth and could call the loan (demand payment) at any time.

The IRS was understandably hostile to such loans and argued that the creditor was making a gift of the use of the money to the borrower and that the amount of the gift equaled the interest that the creditor would have charged an unrelated borrower. In 1984, Congress codified the IRS position by enacting Code § 7872, concerning below- market-rate-interest and no-interest loans. The thrust of this provision is to impute interest income to the creditor donor and correspondingly allow an interest deduction for the borrower-donee. Therefore, the creditor-donor is effectively treated as having received interest income and then gifting such income to the borrower. The deemed transfer is subject to the gift tax to the extent the interest exceeds the annual exclusion. As a result, interest-free loans are no longer an effective device for shifting income.

### Example 16

On January 1 of the current year, father F loaned $175,000 to his daughter, S. The loan was interest free and F may demand repayment at any time. The current interest rate as determined by the IRS is 10% per annum. On December 31 of the current year, S is considered to have paid $17,500 of deductible interest to F, and F is considered to have received $17,500 of taxable interest income from S. On the same date, F is considered to have made a $17,500 gift to S which is eligible for the $13,000 (2011) annual gift tax exclusion.

## Power to Control Beneficial Enjoyment

Section 674(a) contains the general rule that a grantor shall be treated as the owner of any portion of a trust of which the grantor, a nonadverse party, or both, controls the beneficial enjoyment. However, if the exercise of such control requires the approval or consent of an *adverse party*, the general rule shall not apply. An adverse party is defined in § 672(a) as any person who has a substantial beneficial interest in the trust that would be adversely affected by the exercise of the control held by the grantor.

### Example 17

F transfers income-producing property into trust with City Bank as independent trustee. F's two children are named as trust beneficiaries. However, F retains the unrestricted right to designate which of the children is to receive annual distributions of trust income. This is a grantor trust with the result that all trust income is taxed to F.

### Example 18

Refer to the facts in *Example 17*. Assume that the trust instrument provides that the trust income will be paid out on an annual basis in equal portions to F's two children. However, F retains the right to adjust the amount of the income distributions at any time with the consent of the older child C. Because C is an adverse party with respect to the one-half of the income to which he is entitled, only the other half of the income is considered subject to F's control. As a result, only half the trust property is deemed owned by F and only half the trust income is taxable directly to him.[32]

[32] Reg. § 1.672(a)-1(b).

The general rule of § 674(a) is subject to numerous exceptions contained in §§ 674(b), (c), and (d). Any tax adviser attempting to avoid the grantor trust rules should be aware of these exceptions. For example, § 674(c) provides that the power to distribute income within a class of beneficiaries will not cause the grantor trust rules to apply if the power is solely exercisable by an *independent* trustee.

**Example 19**

M transfers income-producing property into trust and names Midtown Bank as independent trustee. The trustee has the right to *sprinkle* (distribute) the annual income of the trust among M's three children in any proportion the trustee deems appropriate. Even though the power to control the enjoyment of the income is held by a nonadverse party, such party is independent of the grantor and the trust is not a grantor trust.

## Other Grantor Trusts

Section 675 provides that the grantor shall be treated as the owner of any portion of a trust in respect of which he or she holds certain administrative or management powers.

**Example 20**

T transfers 60% of the common stock in his closely held corporation into trust with City National Bank as independent trustee. All income of the trust must be paid to T's only grandchild. However, T retains the right to vote the transferred shares. Because T has retained an administrative power specified in § 675(4), he will be taxed on the income generated by the corporate stock.

If a grantor, a nonadverse party, or both have the right to revest in the grantor the ownership of any portion of trust property, § 676 provides that such portion of the trust is considered to be owned by the grantor. Therefore, revocable trusts are grantor trusts for income tax purposes.

Under § 677, a grantor also is treated as owner of any portion of a trust the income of which *may be* distributed to the grantor or spouse without the approval of any adverse party. This rule also applies if trust income may be used to pay premiums for insurance on the life of the grantor and spouse. This provision is inapplicable if the beneficiary of the policy is a charitable organization.

**Example 21**

Individual J transfers income-producing assets into trust and designates Second National Bank as independent trustee. Under the terms of the trust instrument, the trustee may distribute trust income to either J's spouse or J's brother. In the current year the trustee distributes all trust income to J's brother. Because a nonadverse party (the trustee) could have distributed the trust income to J's spouse, this is a grantor trust and all income is taxed to J.

If trust income may be expended to discharge a legal obligation of the grantor, § 677 applies,[33] subject to two important exceptions. Section 682 creates an exception for *alimony trusts*. In certain divorce situations an individual who is required to pay alimony may fund a reversionary trust, the income from which will be paid to the grantor's former spouse in satisfaction of the alimony obligation. Under § 682, the recipient of the trust income rather

[33] Reg. § 1.677(a)-1(d).

than the grantor will be taxed on the income regardless of the applicability of any other of the grantor trust rules.

As a second exception, § 677(b) specifies that if trust income may be distributed for the support or maintenance of a beneficiary (other than the grantor's spouse) whom the grantor is legally obligated to support, such a provision by itself will not cause the trust to be a grantor trust. However, to the extent trust income is actually distributed for such purposes, it will be taxed to thc grantor.

The final type of trust that is not recognized as a separate taxable entity is described in § 678. Under this provision, a person *other than* the grantor may be treated as the owner of a portion of a trust if such person has an unrestricted right to vest trust corpus or income in himself or herself. Section 678 shall not apply to the situation in which a person, in the capacity of trustee, has the right to distribute trust income to a beneficiary whom the person is legally obligated to support. Only to the extent that trust income is actually so expended will the income be taxed to the person.

**Example 22**

Grantor G creates a trust with an independent corporate trustee and names his children and grandchildren as beneficiaries. The trust instrument also provides that G's sister S has the unrestricted right to withdraw up to one-third of trust corpus at anytime. S is considered the owner of one-third of the trust and will be taxed on one-third of the income, regardless of the fact that such income is not distributable to her.

### Grantor Trusts and the Transfer Tax Rules

As a general rule, a transfer of assets into trust that is incomplete for income tax purposes, so that the grantor is taxed on trust income, is also incomplete for gift and estate tax purposes.

**Example 23**

M transfers income-producing properties into a trust but retains the right to designate which of the specified trust beneficiaries will receive a distribution of trust income. The arrangement is a grantor trust per § 674. Under the gift tax Regulations, M has not made a completed gift of the income interest in the trust, and per § 2036 the value of the trust corpus will be included in M's gross estate upon his death.

However, it should be emphasized that the general rule does not always hold.

**Example 24**

Grantor G transfers assets into a reversionary trust that will last only eight years. During the existence of the trust, all income must be paid to G's cousin, C. For income tax purposes, this is a grantor trust and all trust income is taxable to G. However, for gift tax purposes G has made a completed gift of the income interest to C.

## Transfer Tax Planning

The first part of this chapter dealt with a variety of techniques to shift income within a family group and thereby minimize the family's income tax burden. The second part of the chapter focuses on family tax planning techniques designed to reduce any transfer tax liability on intrafamily shifts of wealth. At this point, the student should be cautioned against thinking of income tax planning and transfer tax planning as two separate areas; both types of planning should be considered as highly interrelated aspects of a single integrated family tax plan.

A second aspect of transfer tax planning of which any tax adviser should be aware is that a client's nontax estate planning goals may conflict with an optimal tax-oriented estate plan. From a client's point of view, an orderly disposition of wealth that benefits the heirs in the precise manner that the client desires may be the primary planning objective, regardless of the tax cost. A client planning for his or her own death may be most concerned with his or her own emotional and psychological needs as well as those of other family members. Minimization of the Federal estate tax levied on the estate simply may not be a central concern. A tax adviser who fails to appreciate the client's priorities and who designs an estate plan that fails to reflect the client's nontax needs is not acting in the best interest of that client.

## Tax Planning with Intrafamily Gifts

**LO.8**
Specify the tax advantages of inter vivos gifts as compared to testamentary transfers of wealth.

Before enactment of the Tax Reform Act of 1976, the Federal transfer tax savings associated with gifting assets to family members during the donor's life rather than transferring the assets at death were obvious. The gift tax rates were only 75 percent of the estate tax rates, and because of the progressive nature of both rate schedules, inter vivos gifts could shift an individual's wealth out of a high marginal estate tax bracket into a lower marginal gift tax bracket.

The Tax Reform Act of 1976 integrated the gift and estate taxes by providing a single rate schedule for both taxes and by including in the estate tax base the amount of post-1976 gifts made by a decedent.[34] Thus, any inter vivos gift made by a decedent after 1976 has the effect of boosting his or her taxable estate into a higher tax bracket.

### Example 25

In 2002, D made a taxable gift of $400,000, her only taxable inter vivos transfer. D dies in the current year, leaving a taxable estate of $5,000,000. The base for computing D's estate tax is $5.9 million, her taxable estate plus the $400,000 taxable gift.

Because of the integration of the gift and estate taxes, the tax benefit of inter vivos giving has been reduced but certainly not eliminated. The following advantages of making gifts have survived the integration process.

1. All appreciation in value of the transferred property that occurs after the date of gift escapes taxation in the donor's gross estate. Refer to *Example 25*. If the value of the gifted asset increased from $400,000 in 2002 to $700,000 in the current year, the $300,000 appreciation is not taxed in D's estate. It should be noted that inter vivos transfers of appreciating assets do have a potentially serious negative income tax consequence. The basis of such assets to the donee will be a carryover basis from the donor, increased by the amount of any gift tax paid attributable to the difference between the value of the gift and the donor's tax basis.[35] If the donor retained the property until death, the basis of the property would be stepped up to its fair market to value at date of death.[36] Thus, a transfer of the asset during life rather than at death preserves rather than eliminates pre-death appreciation in the value of the asset that will be subject to income taxation on subsequent sale.
2. Future income generated by property that the donor has transferred will be accumulated by younger generation family members rather than in the estate of the donor.
3. The availability of the annual $13,000 (2011) exclusion allows a donor to give away a substantial amount of wealth completely tax free.
4. All other factors being equal, it is cheaper to pay a gift tax rather than an estate tax. This is true because the dollars used to pay a gift tax are never themselves subject to a Federal transfer tax. However, dollars used to pay an estate tax have been included in the taxable estate and are subject to the estate tax.

[34] § 2001(b).

[35] § 1015.

[36] § 1014.

For this reason, the estate tax is said to be *tax inclusive* (since the estate tax is itself taxed) while the gift tax is sometimes said to be *tax exclusive* (the gift tax itself is not taxed).

### Example 26

D has $10,000,000 in assets and wants to transfer $6,500,000 to a beneficiary. Ignore the annual exclusion, the unified credit and assume a flat rate of 35%. If D dies with an estate of $10,000,000, the estate will pay a tax of $3,500,000 out of the estate's assets and $6,500,000 will be left to pass to the heirs. In contrast, if the individual had made a $6,500,000 gift before he died, he would have had to pay only a $2,275,000 tax for the privilege of transferring $6,500,000. In other words, it would cost $1,225,000 less ($3,500,000 – $2,275,000) to give $5,500,000 than to *will* such amount. In effect, if he gave $6,500,000 while he was living, he would have had $1,225,000 left to do with as he pleases. By making the gift and paying the gift tax, he is removing the gift tax amount ($2,275,000) from his estate, never to be taxed!

### Example 27

W has only $1,000,000 of assets. Assume a 35% rate and ignore the unified credit and annual exclusion. If W dies and leaves the $1,000,000 to her child, W pays a tax of $350,000 and the child receives $650,000. If W had used the same $1,000,000 to make a gift and pay the tax, she could have given her child $740,741, determined as follows:

$$x = \text{Amount of the gift}$$
$$.35x = \text{Gift tax}$$

$$x + .35x = \$1{,}000{,}000$$
$$1.35x = \$1{,}000{,}000$$
$$x = \$740{,}741$$
$$.35x = \$259{,}259$$

Thus if W makes a gift of $740,741, she will pay a gift tax of $259,259, exhausting the $1,000,000. Note that by giving, the child receives $740,741 rather than $650,000 or $90,741 more!

## "Freezing" the Value of Assets in the Gross Estate

A long-range plan of inter vivos giving from older generation to younger generation family members is a basic component of most family tax plans. However, elderly individuals can be very reluctant about making substantial gifts of their wealth, even when they fully understand the tax advantages in doing so. Psychologically it is difficult to part with wealth that is the result of a lifetime of endeavor. Elderly individuals often fear that gifts of property might leave them without sufficient income or capital to provide for their future comfort and security. They may even worry that their children and grandchildren might "desert" them if the offspring were given the family wealth too soon.

For these and many other reasons it may be difficult for the tax adviser to persuade an older client to transfer existing wealth during his or her lifetime. However, the same client may be much more amenable to simply "freezing" the value of his or her current estate, so that future accumulations of wealth are somehow transferred to younger members of the family and therefore not subject to estate tax upon the client's death.

### Gifts of Property

The simplest type of estate freeze is a gift. A gift of appreciating property is taxed at its current value for gift tax purposes and any future appreciation is forever removed from the estate tax base. Note, however, that this technique is not without problems. Taxpayers who want to maximize the amount of wealth that their heirs ultimately receive must balance the trade-offs between giving the property during their lifetime or willing the property at death.

If a taxpayer gives appreciating property during life, the gift removes any appreciation from the estate. However, the basis of the property to the donee will normally be the same as the donor's basis. In such case, the donee would be required to pay an income tax on a subsequent sale of the property. Note that this income tax would not have resulted had the property been retained till death due to the step-up in basis for inherited property. Moreover, if the taxpayer must pay gift tax on the transfer, the time value of any gift tax paid would be lost. In short, a gift of appreciating property normally saves transfer taxes at a rate up to 35 percent but results in an income tax of up to 15 percent (assuming the property is a capital asset) and loss of the time value of gift tax (net of estate tax). Conversely, retaining the property normally saves on income taxes but at the cost of an estate tax on the appreciation.

## Example 28

In 1991, T purchased 300 acres of land on the far west side of Dallas for $100,000. While the land was truly in a remote area, T expected that it would one day be prime property since it is near an interstate highway. By 2000, it was clear that an increase in the value of the property was imminent. Assume the property will triple in value to $300,000 by the time T dies in 10 years. Also assume that the transfer tax rate is 45%, the applicable income tax rate is 15%, and the aftertax interest rate is 8%. The following is a simple comparison (ignoring present values) of what happens if (1) T gives the property now, or (2) holds it until death.

| | | | |
|---|---|---|---|
| 1. | Give property now before it appreciates | | Tax cost |
| | Gift tax now ($100,000 × 45%) | | $ 45,000 |
| | Income tax to beneficiaries later due to carryover basis | | |
| | Gift: [($300,000 − $100,000 = $200,000) × 15%] | | 30,000 |
| | Value of gift tax paid today lost: | | |
| | Gift tax ($45,000 × 8% × 10 years) | $36,000 | |
| | Estate tax [$36,000 − (45% × $36,000)] | (19,800) | 16,200 |
| | Tax cost | | $ 91,200 |
| 2. | Retain property until death | | Tax cost |
| | Estate tax later ($300,000 × 45%) | | $135,000 |
| | No income tax later | | |
| | Bequest ($300,000 − $300,000 = $0 × 15%) | | 0 |
| | Tax cost | | $135,000 |

In this case, it would appear that giving the property away during T's life would produce a smaller overall tax cost than retaining it till death. However, this result is based on many assumptions and fails to consider many others. Nevertheless, the example illustrates some of the basic considerations that should be taken into account when doing estate planning.

### Interests in Closely Held Businesses

For individuals who have a stake in a business, such as stock in a family-held C or S corporation or an interest in a partnership or LLC, the interest in the company is not only their lifeblood but in most cases represents a substantial portion of their estate. Indeed, the business often represents the bulk of the assets that they wish to leave to their heirs. Unfortunately, without proper planning, the costs associated with transferring such business (e.g., illiquidity, the estate, gift and generation-skipping transfer taxes, probate) can decimate the business, leaving the heirs with little or no inheritance. Over the years, practitioners have addressed these problems in a number of ways. Most of these plans are directed at valuation of the assets and how that value can be reduced and frozen. In this regard, it should not be forgotten that for estate and gift tax purposes, the minimum marginal tax rate is 45 percent, meaning that every $1,000 of reduced valuation produces $450 of savings!

Closely held businesses normally present valuation problems of monumental proportions. The difficulty lies in the fact that, unlike their publicly traded cousins, there is no market where closely held businesses are actively traded.

For its part, the government's primary contribution concerning the valuation problem is contained in the often cited Revenue Ruling 59-60. In this ruling, the IRS has identified a list of factors to be considered in valuing such businesses. These are:

1. Book value and financial condition of the corporation.
2. Earning capacity of the company.
3. Dividend paying capacity.
4. Whether the enterprise has goodwill or other intangible value.
5. The economic outlook in general and the condition and outlook of the specific industry in particular.
6. The nature of the business and the history of the enterprise from its inception.
7. Sales of stock and the size of the block of stock to be valued.
8. The market price of stocks of corporations engaged in the same or a similar line of business that are actively traded in a free and open market.

Unfortunately, the ruling provides little guidance regarding how these factors are to be used. The ruling simply states that the weight to be accorded each factor depends upon the facts of each case. While experts in business valuation (a niche industry in and of itself) utilize these and other widely accepted methods, there is no certainty that the value obtained is objective and unbiased. As a practical matter, the estate is left to its own devices to determine the value of the company and convince the IRS and/or judge that its method and value are correct.

**Valuation: Premiums and Discounts.** In establishing the value of an interest in a closely held company, additional value is generally attributed to the interest if it represents control. A so-called *control premium* is warranted since it enables the holder to extract more value from the firm through his or her ability to dominate management. For example, an individual with control can elect the entire board of directors, remove a director, control the business and affairs of the company, elect and remove all of the officers, fix their salaries, and control the declaration of dividends. The major valuation issue when control is present is determining how much value, if any should be assigned to the control element. This has often been the source of a great deal of controversy.

### Example 29

The uncertainties of valuation are made abundantly clear in *Estate of Joseph E. Salsbury*.[37] In this case, the value of the company, particularly the amount of premium, was the primary issue. Salsbury died holding 51.8% of the stock of Salsbury Laboratories, a manufacturer of drug and health products for the poultry industry. At the time of his death, all of the stock of the corporation was owned by the decedent, members of his family, trusts for their benefit and a private charitable foundation. The IRS asserted an estate tax deficiency of $6,007,503 primarily attributable to the difference in values placed on the stock held by the decedent. The date of death values placed on the decedent's shares by the parties and the expert witnesses for the taxpayer and the IRS were worlds apart as shown below:

[37] T.C. Memo 1975-33.

| | |
|---|---|
| Value claimed on estate tax return | $ 372,152 |
| Value asserted by the IRS in deficiency notice | 11,655,000 |
| Expert witness for the taxpayer | 558,228 |
| Expert witness for the IRS | 8,748,152 |
| Expert witness for the IRS | 1,400,000 |

The sole issue of contention regarding the valuation was the amount that should be assigned to the control element held by the decedent. Note the difference in valuation even though these are valuation experts. Interestingly, the court ultimately held that the stock was worth $514,000.

**Discounts** In contrast to a control premium, a *discount* may be available. Over the years, taxpayers have identified a number of reasons why a discount should be allowed.

It is well accepted that a discount may be appropriate when valuing large blocks of stock. When a taxpayer owns such a large block of stock that the price at which the stock would be traded in the market would *not* be representative of the value, a *blockage discount* may be claimed. Blockage discounts are available if the executor can show that the block of stock to be valued is so large in relation to the actual sales on the existing market that the stock could not be liquidated in a reasonable time without depressing the market.

Discounts have also been granted for the tax consequences that could result upon a disposition of the business. For example, if a taxpayer owns stock in a C corporation, the ultimate value that the owner can extract from the company can be substantially reduced because of the double taxation problems that can occur on liquidation of the corporation.

By far the most important types of discount are those available if the taxpayer's ownership represents a minority interest or where there is lack of marketability or both. In reviewing the court decisions addressing this issue, it is not uncommon to see discounts of between 25 and 50 percent and sometimes more! With proper planning, taxpayers can successfully secure these discounts to obtain literally huge savings. For this reason, understanding the justification for these discounts and the techniques used to achieve them is extremely important.

*The lack of marketability discount* is based on the fact that an interest in a closely held business is generally less attractive because it is illiquid—hard to convert to cash—and more difficult to sell than an interest for which there is an active trading market. This is a particularly acute problem when the majority of interests are owned by family members. Stock that if publicly traded would be worth $1,000,000 would be worth far less because it would be unlikely to find an outside buyer to purchase the stock. Adding to the discount is the fact there would be substantial costs incurred such as underwriting expenses involved if a company were to go public.

The rationale for *minority interest discounts* is founded upon the owner's limited power to influence business decisions (e.g., control day-to-day or long-range managerial decisions, affect future earnings, control efforts for growth potential, establish executive compensation or dividend policy, or compel a sale of assets or a liquidation). As a practical matter, a discount is warranted due to the fact that an unrelated party interested in purchasing an interest in a family-owned business would not pay full value for such an interest.

## Example 30

D owns all of the stock of Close Corporation, which has a value of $9,000,000. If D were to die, the entire value of the stock would be included in his estate. D might be able to reduce the transfer cost substantially if he were to give one-third of the stock to his son, one-third to his daughter and die holding one-third. At first thought, it might appear that the value of the gifts would be one-third of the total or aggregate value or $3,000,000 each. However, by arguing that the each gift constitutes a minority interest, he may be able to claim a substantial discount when he makes the gifts or at death.

The IRS has not always accepted the minority discount theory, particularly when the person acquiring the interest is related. Historically, the government consistently argued that for purposes of valuing gifts and bequests of stock or partnership interests to family members, the ownership interests of the family members should be aggregated and valued as a whole.[38] Applying this approach to the example above, the IRS may take the position that no discount is allowed and the value of each gift is $3,000,000. In fact, when the IRS took this approach, using an aggregate value, it often included a control premium, and then used the increased value as the basis for assigning a value to the fraction of shares transferred.

After years of denying taxpayers minority discounts in the family setting, the IRS finally abandoned its position. In Revenue Ruling 93-12, the IRS stated that it would no longer challenge a discount solely because the transferred interest, when aggregated with interests held by family members, would be considered part of a controlling interest.[39] For example, when the taxpayer transferred all of his stock in equal gifts to each of his 11 children, the IRS ruled that the value of the gift to each is computed by considering each gift separately and not by aggregating all of the donor's holdings.[40]

Since the government's surrender in 1993, fractionalizing an owner's interest to obtain minority discounts has become virtually an indispensable part of estate planning. As explained below, corporate and partnership freezes, particularly the use of family limited partnerships, has become a staple of the estate planning industry.

## Freezing the Value of the Estate: C Corporations

To freeze the transfer tax value of an interest in a C corporation, the corporation engages in a type "E" reorganization referred to as a recapitalization. The following steps are taken:

1. The owner exchanges common stock for both new voting preferred and new non-voting common which together has a value equal to his original shares of common.
2. Pursuant to the reorganization provisions of § 368(a)(1)(E), this exchange of stock is nontaxable.
3. At the time of the exchange, the preferred stock is structured to represent the majority of the corporation's value, while the common stock has little value. The preferred stock typically carried a fixed-rate, non-cumulative dividend and preferential treatment for dividends and assets upon liquidation. Other rights and privileges may be attached.
4. The owner gives the nonvoting common stock to the heirs at little or no gift tax cost since all of the corporation's value is in the preferred stock which is held by the owner.
5. The result is that all of future appreciation of the corporation is attributable to the common stock and shifted to the donees since the preferred stock's value is locked in at time of exchange (i.e., its value is attributable to its preferred claim on assets in the event of liquidation and its yield). Also, the owner has retained income security.

### Example 31

F owns all of the voting common stock of C corporation with a value of $1,500,000 (basis $100,000). Approaching retirement, F wants to transfer the ownership of the business to his daughter and do so at the least possible tax cost. In addition, he wants to maintain control of the business and retain a steady stream of income for life. To this end, he exchanged his voting common stock for nonvoting common stock worth $1,000,000 and voting preferred stock with a par value set such that it is equal to $500,000. F has a non-cumulative "put" with the corporation that enables him to sell the preferred stock back to the corporation at its par value of $500,000. The preferred stock pays a non-cumulative dividend of 15 percent. The put and the dividend enable F to claim the stock is at least worth $500,000 since at any time the stock could be sold to

[38] See Revenue Ruling 81-253 1981-2 C.B. 187 which held that no minority interest discount would be allowed for intrafamily transfers of stock in a corporation controlled by the family absent discord among the family members.

[39] 1993-1 C.B. 202.

[40] TAM 9449001.

the corporation for $500,000. F realizes a gain of $1,400,000 ($500,000 + $1,000,000 – $100,000) but under the reorganization provisions this gain is not recognized. F subsequently gives the common worth $1,000,000 ($1,500,000 total value – $500,000 value of preferred) to his daughter and pays no gift tax due to the unified credit which shelters the $1,000,000 taxable gift. If the value of the preferred is respected, F has (1) retained control of the corporation since he owns all of the voting stock, (2) ensured a steady stream of income for retirement since he can vote himself a dividend at any time, (3) frozen the value of his estate at $500,000 and (4) shifted all of the appreciation to his daughter who holds the common stock. As might be expected, in these situations, the Service was reluctant to accept the value placed on the preferred since it was unlikely that F would ever exercise his put nor would he ever vote himself a dividend.

While this plan can be used successfully, there are certain restrictions that limit its value as discussed below.

### Freezing the Value of the Estate: Partnerships

Steps similar to that used in freezing the value of an interest in a family-held C corporation can be taken to freeze the value of an interest in a partnership (or LLC). In addition, a partnership could be used to freeze the value of appreciating property such as farms, ranches, timberland, and other unimproved or improved real estate. The partnership form provides an almost perfect vehicle to fractionalize interests in the property to create minority discounts. A partnership freeze normally involves recapitalizing an existing partnership or the formation of a new partnership. Family limited partnerships are the vehicle commonly used. The following steps are taken:

1. The owners of property (e.g., the senior members of the family such as parents or grandparents) normally transfer the property to a limited partnership in exchange for (1) a general partnership interest which represents growth interest and (2) a limited partnership interest which represents the frozen interest.
2. The exchange normally is nontaxable under § 721.
3. The transferors retain a small general partnership interest and transfer a large limited partnership interest.

#### Example 32

H and W transfer 1,000 acres of land worth $10,000,000 to a family limited partnership. In exchange H and W each receive one percent general partnership interests and 49% limited partnership interests. H and W then transfer the limited partnership interests to their children. Significant discounts are normally available for transfers of limited partnership interests. Normally there is a minority interest discount since limited partners have no control over the partnership (e.g., no voice in management and no right to force a liquidation) as well as a lack of marketability discount since such interests are usually illiquid.

### Valuation Issues in Corporate and Partnership Freezes

The approach normally used to value the interest transferred in a corporate or partnership freeze is a residual one. The entire business is valued and then the value of the retained interest is identified. Any residual value is the value of the transferred interest. This method is show in the formula below.

|   |   |
|---|---|
|   | FMV of business |
| – | FMV of retained interest |
| = | FMV of transferred interest and gift to heirs |

For many years, planners kept the value of the transferred interest (e.g., the common stock) low by assigning valuable rights to the retained interest (e.g., the preferred stock) in order to increase the value of the retained interest. For example, in a preferred stock freeze, these included an above market-rate cumulative (and often noncumulative) dividend, conversion rights, call rights, liquidation preferences and voting rights. Even if it was clear that it was unlikely that those rights would be exercised, the courts usually took them into account in valuing the preferred stock.[41]

Congress became concerned about assigning value to these "discretionary" rights given to the owner in that such rights probably would not be exercised. To address this problem, in 1987 Congress enacted the now infamous anti-freeze rules of §2036(c) that were so controversial that they were subsequently repealed in 1990. In their place, Congress substituted § 2701, which contains the rules currently in operation today. Section 2701 attempts to more accurately value the property that is transferred among family members when the transferor retains some interest in the business. The approach is to value certain retained discretionary rights (e.g., rights to dividends or distributions, liquidation rights, put, call, and conversion rights) at *zero* unless they meet tests that virtually guarantee their exercise. Note that if these retained rights are valued at zero, a transfer of the common stock or limited partnership interests would be treated as a gift of the full fair market value of the business.

Section 2701 generally operates only if the following conditions exist (note this is the normal pattern of a corporate or partnership freeze discussed above):

1. The taxpayer makes a transfer of an interest in a corporation or partnership.
2. The transferor controls the entity. Control is defined as ownership of at least 50 percent of the entity either directly or indirectly.
3. The transfer is made to a family member (i.e., spouse, lineal descendant of the transferor or spouse, or a spouse of such descendant).
4. The transferor retains an applicable retained right (distribution rights).

In general, the retained interests must provide for a periodic *qualified payment* (e.g., a dividend or distribution). If there is no provision for qualified payments, no value may be assigned to the retained interest, resulting in a gift of the full value of the business.

**Qualified Payments** A qualified payment depends on the type of entity. For corporations, a qualified payment is any dividend payable at a fixed rate on a periodic basis on cumulative preferred stock. For partnerships, a qualified payment is a comparable payment at a fixed rate made with respect to any partnership interest. The value of the retained interest must be determined by calculating the present value of the future cash flows from the retained interest or more precisely discounting the qualified payment. No value is assigned to any other rights (put, call, conversion) attached to the stock or partnership interest. Note that if a very low payout rate is selected, there will be a lower annual cash payout required but there will also be a lower value placed on the preferred stock or retained partnership interest. In contrast, if there is a high payout rate, the value of the retained interest is greater, yielding a smaller gift. However, selecting a high payout rate in order to increase the value of the retained interest and reduce the value of the gifted interest has the effect of returning more value (e.g., dividends) to the taxpayer's estate. In any event, a minimum value is placed on the common stock or partnership interest that is transferred. At least 10 percent of the value of the business must be assigned to the gifted stock or partnership interest. This ensures that there is a gift of at least 10 percent of the value of the corporation.

## Example 33

This year D decided to transfer her business, a C corporation, to her children. To this end, she exchanged all of her common stock in the corporation for nonvoting common and voting preferred in a transaction qualifying as a tax-free recapitalization. After the transfer, D owned 3,000 shares of $1,000 par value voting preferred stock, each share paying a cumulative annual dividend of seven percent. In addition, there are 10,000 shares of nonvoting common stock outstanding. D gave all of the common stock to her

[41] Rev. Rul. 83-120, 1983-2 C.B. 170.

daughter. Pursuant to an appraisal, the corporation's value was estimated to be \$3,100,000. The value of the preferred stock must be determined by discounting the future dividends. Here the annual dividends are \$210,000 (\$1,000 par value × 7% = \$70 per share × 3,000 shares). According to the regulations, the value is determined by assuming that the dividend is paid in perpetuity. Assuming the applicable federal rate is ten percent, the present value of a \$210,000 annuity discounted at ten percent is \$2,100,000 (1/.1 × \$210,000). Thus the value of the preferred is \$2,100,000 and the value of the common is \$1,000,000 (\$3,100,000 − \$2,100,000). Consequently, D is treated as making a \$1,000,000 gift. If D has not made any other taxable gifts during her lifetime, the entire transfer is tax-free. More important, if the corporation's value increases at a rate greater than the dividend rate of seven percent, all of the excess appreciation is attributable to the common and, therefore, out of her estate.

### Family Limited Partnerships

Although the corporate or partnership freeze can be useful, the qualified payment requirement can be a difficult hurdle when trying to accomplish the taxpayer's goals. For this reason, some plans do not meet or do not attempt to meet the qualified payment rule. In such case, the gift is the full value of the interest. However, to minimize this problem, a family limited partnership (FLP) is often formed to create minority and marketability discounts that reduce the value of the transferred interests.

#### Example 34

H and W, husband and wife, together own all of the stock of a corporation worth \$4,000,000. As part of a plan to transfer the stock to their children, they transfer all of the stock to a limited partnership in exchange for a one percent general partnership interest and a 99 percent limited partnership interest. The couple then transfers the limited partnership interest to their children, claiming minority and marketability discounts totaling 50 percent. As a result, the partnership interests transferred by each are about \$1,000,000 each and totally tax free because of the unified credit.

Due to the power of the FLP, they have become extremely popular and, at the same time, frequently abused. The most flagrant situations involve transfers of publicly traded securities to FLPs and taking substantial discounts. Although the IRS retreated in their challenge of such arrangements in Revenue Ruling 93-12, it is now pursuing these with some recent successes. Only time will tell the final outcome.[42]

### Sales of Property

Another technique for freezing the value of an asset in a taxpayer's estate is for the taxpayer to sell the asset to a younger generation family member.

#### Example 35

Grandfather G owns several acres of undeveloped real estate with a current value of \$1 million. The land is located near a rapidly growing metropolitan area and its value is expected to triple over the next decade. If G sells the real estate to his granddaughter D for \$1 million cash, the value of his current estate is unchanged. However, the future increase in the value of the land has been removed from G's estate and will belong to D. In addition, D's basis is at least equal to the value of the property at the time of the transfer rather than G's basis had it been gifted.

[42] For example, see *Estate of Charles Reichardt v. Comm.*, 114 T.C. 144 (2000).

An attractive variation of the selling technique illustrated in *Example 35* is an installment sale to the granddaughter. If D does not have $1 million of cash readily available (a most realistic assumption), G could simply accept his granddaughter's bona fide installment note as payment for the land. If the note is to be paid off over 20 years, G could use the installment sale method of reporting any taxable gain on the sale. If G had no need for cash during the term of the note, he could forgive his granddaughter's note payments and interest as they become due. Such forgiveness of indebtedness would not change the income tax consequences of the installment sale to G and would represent a gift to D eligible for the annual $13,000 (2011) exclusion.[43]

## GRITs, GRATs, and GRUTs

Another freezing technique that gained popularity over the years is the so-called *GRIT*, the acronym for *grantor retained income trust*. Under this arrangement, the grantor transfers property to a trust, retains the income for a period of years, and gifts the remainder. Under the right circumstances, substantial benefits can be obtained. If the grantor survives the term, nothing is pulled back into the grantor's estate under § 2036 since the grantor did not retain an interest until death. As a result, the taxpayer has transferred the property at the cost of a gift tax on the remainder which normally represents only a fraction of the value of the entire property. In addition, all of the appreciation in the property is out of the estate. Note, however, that if the grantor does not survive the term, the property is included in the estate at its date of death value and nothing has been accomplished.

### Example 36

R owns rapidly appreciating real estate. Its current value is $3,000,000. In 2011, he transferred the property to a trust, retaining the income from the property for 10 years and giving the remainder to his son. Assume the income interest is worth $2,000,000. As a result, the remainder interest is $1,000,000 and due to the unified credit there is no gift tax on the transfer. Eleven years after the transfer R died when the property was worth $9,000,000. Under prior law, nothing would be included in R's gross estate under § 2036 since he did not have an interest in the property at the time of his death. Moreover, if the property did not in reality produce any income, the $2,000,000 assigned to the retained interest is a fiction and is never subject to income or estate taxes. Thus, if R survives the transfer by more than 10 years, he was able to transfer property worth $9,000,000 and avoid all transfer tax.

### Example 37

Same facts as above except R died five years after the trust was created. In such case, all of the property is included in R's gross estate at its date of death value and nothing will have been accomplished.

Historically, the value of the retained income interest in a GRIT was determined using IRS tables that often placed a higher value on the retained income interest than was justified by the actual income generated on the property. The effect of this was to deflate the value of the gift of the remainder which could be sheltered by the donor's unified credit. As might be expected, the IRS attacked this technique primarily on the grounds that the retained income interest was undervalued. Consequently, legislation was enacted to ensure that the value of the income interest was indeed real.

Under § 2702, the value of the retained income interest is *zero* and the gifted value of the remainder is the entire value of the property unless the transfer is to a *grantor retained annuity*

[43] See Rev. Rul. 77-299, 1977-2 C.B. 343 for the IRS's negative reaction to this tax plan.

*trust (GRAT)* or a grantor retained unit trust (GRUT). When either of these is used, the value of the gift of the remainder is the value of the property less the value of the annuity or unitrust interest as shown below.

|   |   |
|---|---|
|   | Fair market value of property |
| − | Value of income interest |
| = | FMV of remainder and gift to heirs (no exclusion since future interest) |

When the transfer is made, the grantor specifies how much income will be retained [e.g., either a fixed dollar amount (i.e., an annuity trust) or a percentage of the annual asset value (i.e., a unitrust)] as well as the period for which the annuity will last. If the grantor retains an annuity interest, the arrangement is referred to as a GRAT. If the grantor retains a unitrust interest, the arrangement is called a GRUT. Note that in either case the income interest-retained annuity effectively replaces the transferred property. One of the biggest differences between a GRIT and GRATs and GRUTs is that annual payments under GRATs and GRUTs *must be made* even if the trust assets do not generate sufficient income to make the payments. Trust principal may have to be invaded to meet the distribution requirement (however, a debt obligation may suffice).

### Example 38

In 1997, R transferred land worth $1,000,000 to a GRAT. He wanted the amount of the gift of the remainder interest to be $600,000 in order to use his unified credit (exemption equivalent of $600,000 in 1997), but no more. R is 55 and he decides to use a term of 15 years to compute the required annuity. The present value of an annuity of $1 for 15 years using the IRS tables and a discount rate of 10% is $7.6061. Thus the present value of an annuity of $52,589 ($400,000/7.6061) at 10% for 15 years is $400,000. Therefore to achieve the desired result, the annuity rate is set at 5.26% and payments of $52,589 must be paid annually, even if the property does not generate sufficient income. This departs drastically from the GRIT where no payment was required if there was in fact no income. Note that if R lives the entire term, he will receive $788,835 ($52,589 × 15) which is the original $400,000 retained income interest plus the growth on the $400,000 at 10% for 15 years. Although R's estate may contain $788,835, he will have removed any appreciation from his estate. In short, if the property appreciates (or produces income at a rate exceeding the annuity rate) all of the excess appreciation or income is removed from his estate. In addition, R could remove part of this $788,835 by embarking on a gift-giving program.

## Charitable Giving

Another important tool that estate planners often use to reduce a family's tax burden is the charitable transfer. Obviously, an individual can reduce or even eliminate any estate taxes by simply leaving part or all of his or her property to a qualified charity. As explained in Chapter 24, bequests to qualified charitable organizations may be deducted from the gross estate without limitation. However, from a tax planning perspective it is usually preferable for the taxpayer to make a charitable donation during life rather than at death.

While many individuals would like to make large contributions of property to a charity during their lifetime, they often delay the contribution to their deaths believing they may need the income and the property before that time. Unfortunately, these kindhearted donors, while securing the contribution deduction for estate tax purposes, lose the income tax deduction. On the other hand, some individuals may be willing to give the property and its income to a charity temporarily but ultimately want to pass the property to their heirs. Long ago charitable organizations recognized these problems and designed a solution, the so-called split interest gift.

A split-interest gift is simply a transfer of property—typically to a trust—where part of the property is given to a charity and the other part is retained by the donor. There are two common types of charitable trusts: charitable remainder trusts, and charitable lead trusts.

### Charitable Remainder Trusts

With a charitable remainder trust, an individual transfers property to a trust, leaving the income from the property to a noncharitable beneficiary (e.g., a spouse or child) typically for life, and upon the beneficiary's death, the property passes to the charitable beneficiary. The beauty of a charitable remainder trust is that the donor retains the security of a steady income stream yet is entitled to an income tax deduction for the present value of the remainder interest—a deduction that would be lost had the gift been postponed until death. In order to secure the deduction for the remainder interest, a number of special requirements must be met to ensure that the charity in fact receives something once the income interest terminates.

### Charitable Lead Trusts

Charities also have an answer for individuals who wish to transfer property and its income to a charity for a period of years yet want the property returned after the term has run. The solution is referred to as a charitable lead trust. In this case, the donor receives both an income and gift-tax deduction for the present value of the income interest given to the charity. However, the income tax deduction is limited to 20 percent of A.G.I., since it is for the "use of the charity" rather than "to the" charity. No carryover is allowed.

For many years, the grantor of a charitable lead trust was not charged with the income of the trust but simply got a deduction for income given to the trust that he was never taxed on! In 1969, Congress believed that this was an "unwarranted tax advantage"—a duplication of benefits—and eliminated such favorable treatment. Currently, the trust must be a grantor trust to qualify. The effect in such case is to accelerate the deduction to the current year, yet defer the income to the year it is actually received.

Using a charitable lead trust is particularly beneficial when taxpayers want to bunch all of their charitable deductions in one year. Bunching or accelerating deductions to a particular year may be advantageous in situations when taxpayers have a particularly good year with high income and need the deduction or they simply expect to be in a lower bracket in the future. As with charitable remainder trusts, a number of requirements must be met in order to secure the deduction for the income interest.

#### Example 39

This year J sold his business, recognizing a large amount of income. To offset some of this income, J gave $100,000 to a charitable lead trust for his alma mater, the University of Nebraska. According to the terms of the gift, the university receives the income for the next five years after which the property is returned to J. Assuming the present value of the income over the next five years is $60,000, J receives a $60,000 deduction this year. Assume that next year, the trust earns $12,000. Because J has retained a reversionary interest that reverts too quickly, the trust is a grantor trust and J is taxed on the income of $12,000.

## Liquidity Planning

The Federal estate tax is literally a once-in-a-lifetime event. Because taxpayers do not have to pay the tax on a regular recurring basis, many individuals give little thought to the eventual need for cash to pay the tax.

When an individual dies leaving a large estate but little cash with which to pay death taxes and other expenses, serious problems can result. The family may be forced to sell assets at distress prices just to obtain cash. In a severe situation, a decedent's carefully designed dispositive plan may be shattered because of the failure to anticipate the liquidity needs of the estate.

One of the functions of a competent tax adviser is to foresee any liquidity problem of his or her client's potential estate and to suggest appropriate remedies. The remainder of this chapter covers some of the common solutions to the problem of a cash-poor estate.

## Source of Funds

An excellent source of funds with which to pay an estate tax is insurance on the life of the potential decedent. For a relatively small cash outlay, a taxpayer can purchase enough insurance coverage to meet all the liquidity needs of his or her estate. It is absolutely vital that the insured individual does not possess any incidents of ownership in the policies and that his or her estate is not the beneficiary of the policies. If these two rules are observed the policy proceeds will not be included in the insured's estate and needlessly subjected to the estate tax.[44]

A second source of funds is any family business in which the decedent owned an interest. Under the terms of a binding buy-sell agreement, the business could use its cash to liquidate the decedent's interest. If the business is in corporate form, a redemption of the decedent's interest under § 303 can be a highly beneficial method of securing funds. If the fairly straightforward requirements of § 303 are met, the corporation can purchase its own stock from the decedent's estate without danger of the payment being taxed as a dividend. Because the estate's basis in the stock has been stepped up to its fair market value at date of death, the estate normally will realize little or no taxable gain on sale. The amount of the corporate distribution protected by § 303 cannot exceed the amount of death taxes and funeral and administrative expenses payable by the estate.[45]

In order for a redemption of stock to qualify under § 303, the value of the stock must exceed 35 percent of the value of the gross estate less § 2053 and § 2054 expenses.[46] Careful pre-death planning may be necessary to meet this requirement.

### Example 40

C owns a 100% interest in F Corporation, a highly profitable business with substantial cash flow. However, the value of the F stock is only 29% of the value of C's projected estate. As C's tax adviser, you could recommend that C (1) gift away other assets to reduce the estate, or (2) transfer assets into F Corporation as a contribution to capital in order to increase the stock's value.

## Flower Bonds

Certain issues of Treasury bonds known as *flower bonds* may be used to pay the Federal estate tax at their par value plus accrued interest.[47] Because these bonds have very low interest rates, they are obtainable on the open market at a price well below their par value. Thus, an estate can satisfy its Federal tax liability with bonds that cost much less than the amount of that liability. The bonds must be included in the decedent's estate at their par, rather than market value.[48]

## Planning for Deferred Payment of the Estate Tax

Under § 6166, an estate may be entitled to pay its Federal estate tax liability on an installment basis over a 15-year period. This provision can be a blessing for an illiquid estate. However, only estates that meet the requirements of § 6166 may use the installment method of payment. As a result, pre-death planning should be undertaken to ensure qualification.

Basically, only an amount of estate tax attributable to a decedent's interest in a closely held business may be deferred.[49] In addition, the value of the closely held business must exceed 35 percent of the gross estate minus Code § 2053 and § 2054 deductions. If a deferral of estate tax is desirable in a specific situation, the tax adviser should make certain that such requirements are met on a prospective basis.

---

44 § 2042.

45 § 303(a).

46 § 303(b)(2)(A).

47 § 6312 provided the authorization for such usage. However, the section was repealed with respect to bonds issued after March 3, 1971. Bonds issued before this date and still outstanding continue to be eligible for payment of the estate tax.

48 Rev. Rul. 69-489, 1969-2 C.B. 172.

49 § 6166(a)(2).

## Conclusion

This chapter has introduced the reader to one of the most fascinating and satisfying areas of tax practice—family tax planning. Such planning involves arrangements whereby family income can be shifted to low-bracket members so as to reduce the income taxes paid by the family unit. The use of trusts also has been discussed, and grantor trusts whose income is taxed not to the trust or its beneficiaries but to the grantor have been described.

Transfer tax planning techniques for reducing the family transfer tax burden have been introduced. Such techniques include long-range programs of inter vivos giving, asset freezes, selective use of the marital deduction, and liquidity planning. The family tax planner should never lose sight of the basic premise of family tax planning: only a plan that meets the subjective nontax goals and desires of a family as well as the objective goal of tax minimization is a truly well-designed plan.

## Problem Materials

### DISCUSSION QUESTIONS

**26-1** *Assignment of Income Doctrine.* Explain the assignment of income doctrine as it relates to earned income. How does the doctrine apply to investment income?

**26-2** *Income Shifting.* Assignment of income from one taxpayer to another can result in a tax savings only in a tax system with a progressive rate structure. Discuss.

**26-3** *Family Employees.* List some of the factors the IRS might consider in determining whether a particular family member is a bona fide employee of a family business.

**26-4** *Shareholder/Employee.* Discuss the tax consequences if the IRS determines that a family member is receiving an amount of unreasonable compensation from a family-owned corporation if that family member is a shareholder. What if the family member is not a shareholder?

**26-5** *Gift of Business Interest.* An individual who transfers an equity interest in his or her business to a family member may be accomplishing an income shift to that family member. What are some nontax risks associated with such an equity transfer?

**26-6** *Buy-Sell Arrangements.* How may a buy-sell agreement be utilized when an intrafamily transfer of an equity interest in a business is contemplated?

**26-7** *Regular Corporation vs. S Corporation.* As a general rule, a regular corporation is an inappropriate vehicle by which to shift business income to low-bracket family members. Discuss.

**26-8** *Limitation on Using S Corporations.* An S corporation may have only a single class of common stock outstanding. How does this fact limit the utility of the S corporation in many family tax plans?

**26-9** *Use of Grantor Trusts.* Grantor trusts are ineffective as devices for shifting income to trust beneficiaries. However, such trusts may be very useful in achieving nontax family planning goals. Explain.

**26-10** *Crummey Trusts.* What is a Crummey trust and why might a grantor prefer a Crummey trust to a § 2503(c) trust?

**26-11** *Reversionary Trusts and Interest-Free Loans.* Can a trust in which the grantor has the right to receive his or her property back after a specified period of time be considered a valid trust for tax purposes so that the income is taxed to the beneficiaries rather than the grantor? Can an interest-free demand loan achieve an income shift from the lender to the debtor?

**26-12** *Inter Vivos Gifts.* Why are inter vivos gifts beneficial from a transfer tax planning viewpoint?

**26-13** *Limitations of Inter Vivos Gifts.* For what reasons might an elderly taxpayer be reluctant to make inter vivos gifts?

**26-14** *Estate Freezes.* Define an "asset freeze" as the term relates to estate planning.

**26-15** *Current vs. Testamentary Contributions.* Is it preferable to make a charitable contribution during a taxpayer's life or at his or her death under the terms of his or her will?

**26-16** *Marital Deduction.* Discuss the tax benefits associated with the unlimited marital deduction of § 2056.

**26-17** *Limiting Estate Taxes.* Why is it generally inadvisable for a taxpayer to plan to reduce his or her taxable estate to zero? What can be considered an "optimal" size for a decedent's taxable estate?

**26-18** *Qualifying Terminable Interests.* In what circumstances would a taxpayer desire to make a bequest to a surviving spouse in the form of qualifying terminable interest property? What are the tax consequences of such a bequest?

## PROBLEMS

**26-19** *Using Family Employees.* F runs a carpet installation and cleaning business as a sole proprietorship. In the current year, the business generates $83,000 of net income.

**a.** Assume F is married, has three children (all under the age of 19), does not have any other source of taxable income, and does not itemize deductions. What is his current year tax liability?

**b.** Assume F can use all three children in his business as legitimate part-time employees. He pays each child $6,000 per year, but continues to provide more than one-half of their support. Compute the family's total tax bill for the current year.

**26-20** *Sole Proprietorship vs. Corporation.* Single individual K owns a sole proprietorship that is K's only source of income. In the current year, the business has net income of $130,000.

**a.** If K does not itemize deductions, what is her current year tax liability?

**b.** If K incorporates the business on January 1 and pays herself a $40,000 salary (and no dividends), by how much will she have reduced the tax bill on her business income? (Assume the corporation will not be a personal service corporation.)

**26-21** *Sole Proprietorship vs. Corporation.* Mr. and Mrs. C own their own business, which they currently operate as a sole proprietorship. Annual income from the business averages $400,000. Mr. and Mrs. C are considering incorporating the business. They estimate that each of them could draw a reasonable annual salary of $75,000. In order to maintain their current standard of living, they would also have to draw an additional $50,000 cash out of the business annually in the form of dividends. Based on these facts, compute the income tax savings or cost that would result from the incorporation. In making your calculation, ignore any deductions or exemptions available on the C's joint return.

**26-22** *Singles Penalty.* Single taxpayer S has current year taxable income of $35,000 (after all available deductions and exemptions). His fiancé F has a taxable income of $6,000. Assuming they both itemize deductions, and that no deductions are affected by their combined adjusted gross income, should F and S marry before or after December 31? Support your conclusion with calculations.

**26-23** *Marriage Penalty.* Taxpayers H and W are married and file a joint return. Both are professionals and earn salaries of $150,000 and $120,000, respectively. Assuming H and W have no other income and do not itemize deductions, compute any *marriage penalty* they will pay.

**26-24** *Unearned Income of a Minor Child.* In the current year, taxpayer M receives $12,000 of interest income and earns a salary of $2,500 from a summer job. M has no other income or deductions. M is 13 years old and is claimed as a dependent on his parents' jointly filed tax return. His parents report taxable income of $200,000. Based on these facts, compute M's income tax liability.

**26-25** *Sheltering Unearned Income of a Minor Child.* Taxpayer P made a gift of investment securities to his 13-year-old dependent daughter, D, under the Uniform Gift to Minors Act. The securities generate annual dividend income of $4,000. P is considering a second gift to D that would generate an additional $3,000 of investment income annually. Calculate the amount of tax savings to the family if P could employ D in his business and pay her an annual salary of $3,000, rather than making the second gift. In making your calculation, assume P is in a 40 percent tax bracket.

**26-26** *Family Partnerships.* F owns a 70 percent interest in Mako Partnership, in which capital is a material income-producing factor. On January 1 of the current year, F gives his son S a 35 percent interest in Mako (leaving F with a 35% interest). For the current year, Mako has taxable income of $200,000.

**a.** Assume F does not perform any services for Mako. What is the maximum amount of partnership income allocable to S?

**b.** Assume F performs services for Mako for which he normally would receive $30,000. However, F has not charged the partnership for his services. Based on these facts, what is the maximum amount of partnership income allocable to S in the current year?

**26-27** *Gift of S Corporation Stock.* Grandfather G owns all 100 shares of the outstanding stock of Sigma, Inc., a calendar year S corporation. On January 1 of the current year, G gives 10 shares of Sigma stock to each of his four minor grandchildren under the Uniform Gift to Minors Act. For the current year, Sigma reports taxable income of $70,000. To whom is this income taxed?

**26-28** *Gift-Leaseback.* Taxpayer B owns land used in his sole proprietorship with a tax basis of $75,000 and a fair market value of $100,000. B gives this land to an irrevocable simple trust for the equal benefit of his three children (ages 19, 20, and 21) and leases back the land from the trust for a fair market rental of $9,000 per year.

**a.** Assuming that all three children are B's dependents and have no other source of income, calculate the tax savings to the family of this gift-leaseback arrangement. In making your calculation, assume B is in a 40 percent tax bracket.

**b.** What are the gift and estate tax consequences of this transaction to B and his family? Assume that B has made no prior taxable gifts and that he is married.

**26-29** *Use of Trusts.* Grandfather Z is in the habit of giving his 20-year-old grandchild, A, $10,000 annually as a gift. Z's taxable income is consistently over $500,000 per year, and A has no income. If Z creates a valid trust with investment assets just sufficient to yield $12,000 of income a year and specifies in the trust instrument that A is to receive the trust income annually, what will be the net tax savings to the family? (For purposes of this problem, assume that A is not a full-time student and *ignore* the fact that A may be claimed as a dependent on the return of another taxpayer.)

**26-30** *Reversionary Trusts.* Grantor G transfers $100,000 of assets into a trust that will last for 10 years, after which time the assets will revert to G or his estate. During the trust's existence all income must be paid to beneficiary M on a current basis. For the current year, ordinary trust income is $18,000. To whom is this income taxed?

**26-31** *Reversionary Trusts.* Refer to the facts in *Problem 26-30*. Assume that under the terms of the trust agreement the trust will last for M's lifetime. Upon M's death, the trust corpus will revert to G or his estate. On the date the trust is created, M is 18 years old. For the current year, ordinary trust income is $40,000. To whom is this income taxed?

**26-32** *Irrevocable Trusts.* F transfers assets into an irrevocable trust and designates First City Bank as independent trustee. F retains no control over the trust assets. The trustee may distribute income to either of F's two adult brothers or to S, F's minor son whom F is legally obligated to support. During the year, the trustee distributed all of the trust income to one of F's brothers. To whom will the income be taxed?

**26-33** *Irrevocable Trusts.* M transfers assets into an irrevocable trust and appoints National Bank independent trustee. M retains no control over trust assets. Under the terms of the trust agreement, M's sister N is given the right to determine which of M's three minor children will receive trust income for the year. N herself is not a trust beneficiary. During the year, N directs that trust income be divided equally among M's three children. To whom will the income be taxed?

**26-34** *Irrevocable Trusts.* Grantor B transfers assets into an irrevocable trust and designates Union State Bank independent trustee. B retains no control over trust assets. Under the terms of the trust instrument the trustee must use trust income to pay the annual insurance premium on a policy on B's life. Any remaining income must be distributed to B's grandson, GS. For the current year, trust income totals \$60,000, of which \$9,000 is used to pay the required insurance premium. To whom will the income be taxed?

**26-35** *Grantor Trusts.* Although T is not a beneficiary of the ABC Trust, T does have the right under the terms of the trust instrument to appoint up to 10 percent of the trust assets to himself or any member of his family. T has never exercised this right. For the current year, the trust income of \$80,000 is distributed to the income beneficiaries of the trust.

**a.** To whom will the income be taxed?

**b.** If T dies before exercising his right to appoint trust corpus, will the possession of the right have any estate tax consequences?

**26-36** *Gift Splitting.* Every year D gives each of her nine grandchildren \$15,000 in cash to be used toward their education.

**a.** If D is unmarried, what is the amount of her annual taxable gift?

**b.** If D is married and she and her husband elect to "gift split," what is the amount of her annual taxable gift?

**26-37** *Inter Vivos Gifts.* Decedent T died in 2011 and left the following taxable estate:

| | *Fair Market Value* |
|---|---|
| Investment real estate | \$6,000,000 |
| Cash and securities | 3,500,000 |
| Gross estate | \$9,500,000 |
| Less: § 2053 and § 2054 expenses | (500,000) |
| Taxable estate | \$9,000,000 |

After payment of all death taxes, the estate will be divided equally among T's five surviving married children.

**a.** If T has never made any inter vivos gifts, compute the estate's Federal estate tax liability (before credit for any state death tax paid).

**b.** How much tax could have been saved if T had made cash gifts equal to the maximum annual exclusion under § 2503 to each of his children and their spouses in each of the 10 years preceding his death?

**26-38** *Power of Giving.* W is thinking about the possibility of dying in the next ten years. She currently has an estate of \$10,000,000. Assuming W is in the 35% transfer tax bracket, how much more could she give to her child if she made a gift to her child rather than dying with the entire \$10,000,000? Ignore the annual exclusion and the unified credit.

**26-39** *Liquidity Planning.* Decedent D left the following taxable estate:

| | *Fair Market Value* |
|---|---|
| Life insurance proceeds from policy on D's life (D owned the policy at his death) | \$8,500,000 |
| Real estate | 1,300,000 |
| Stock in Acme Corporation (100% owned by D) | 650,000 |
| Gross estate | \$10,450,000 |
| Less: § 2053 and § 2054 expenses | (450,000) |
| Taxable estate | \$10,000,000 |

**a.** If D has never made any inter vivos gifts and dies in 2011, what is the estate's Federal estate tax liability (before credit for any state death tax paid)?

**b.** How much tax could have been avoided if D had not been the owner of the life insurance policy?

**c.** Can the Acme stock qualify for a § 303 redemption? What if the life insurance proceeds were not included in the gross estate?

## TAX RESEARCH PROBLEMS

**26-40** In 2001, P, a resident of St. Louis, Missouri, created an irrevocable trust for the benefit of his teenage son, S, and his brother, B. The independent trustee, T, has discretionary power to use the trust income for the "payment of tuition, books, and room and board at any institution of higher learning that S chooses to attend." After an 11-year period, the trust will terminate with any accumulated income payable to S and the trust corpus payable to B. In the current year, S received an income distribution of $7,000 from the trust, which he used to attend a state-supported school, the University of Missouri. To whom will the $7,000 of trust income be taxed?

***Research aids***:

§ 677 and accompanying regulations

*Morrill, Jr. v. United States*, 64-1 USTC ¶9463, 13 AFTR2d 1334, 228 F.Supp. 734 (D.Ct. Maine, 1964).

*Braun*, Jr., 48 TCM 210, T.C. Memo 1984-285.

**26-41** Decedent D died on January 19, 2006. Under the terms of D's will, D's sister S, age 57, is to receive $500,000 as a specific bequest. The remainder of D's estate will be distributed to D's various grandchildren. On June 8, 2008, S decides to join a religious community and take a vow of poverty. She makes written notification to the executor of D's estate that she will not accept her bequest from her late sister, and that the $500,000 should be added to the amount to be distributed to the grandchildren. What are the transfer tax consequences of S's action?

***Research aids***:

§ 2518

# Appendices

**APPENDIX A** Tax Rate Schedules and Tables

**APPENDIX B** Tax Forms

**APPENDIX C** Modified ACRS Tables

**APPENDIX D** Continuous Individual Tax Return Problems and Two Comprehensive Individual Tax Return Problems for 2010

**APPENDIX E** Glossary of Tax Terms

# A

# Tax Rate Schedules and Tables

## Appendix Outline


A-1 2010 Income Tax Rate Schedules A-2

A-2 2010 Income Tax Tables A-3

A-3 Unified Transfer Tax Rate Schedule A-15

A-4 Estate and Gift Tax Valuation Tables A-16

A-5 2010 Optional State Sales Tax Tables A-21

## A-1 2010 Income Tax Rate Schedules

# 2010 Tax Rate Schedules

**CAUTION**

*Do not use these Tax Rate Schedules to figure your 2009 taxes. Use only to figure your 2010 estimated taxes.*

**Schedule X**—Use if your **2010** filing status is **Single**

| If line 5 is: Over— | But not over— | The tax is: | of the amount over— |
|---|---|---|---|
| $0 | $8,375 | ---------- 10% | **$0** |
| 8,375 | 34,000 | **$837.50 + 15%** | **8,375** |
| 34,000 | 82,400 | **4,681.25 + 25%** | **34,000** |
| 82,400 | 171,850 | **16,781.25 + 28%** | **82,400** |
| 171,850 | 373,650 | **41,827.25 + 33%** | **171,850** |
| 373,650 | ------------ | **108,421.25 + 35%** | **373,650** |

**Schedule Z**—Use if your **2010** filing status is **Head of household**

| If line 5 is: Over— | But not over— | The tax is: | of the amount over— |
|---|---|---|---|
| $0 | $11,950 | ---------- 10% | **$0** |
| 11,950 | 45,550 | **$1,195.00 + 15%** | **11,950** |
| 45,550 | 117,650 | **6,235.00 + 25%** | **45,550** |
| 117,650 | 190,550 | **24,260.00 + 28%** | **117,650** |
| 190,550 | 373,650 | **44,672.00 + 33%** | **190,550** |
| 373,650 | ---------- | **105,095.00 + 35%** | **373,650** |

**Schedule Y-1**— Use if your **2010** filing status is **Married filing jointly or Qualifying widow(er)**

| If line 5 is: Over— | But not over— | The tax is: | of the amount over— |
|---|---|---|---|
| $0 | $16,750 | ---------- 10% | **$0** |
| 16,750 | 68,000 | **$1,675.00 + 15%** | **16,750** |
| 68,000 | 137,300 | **9,362.50 + 25%** | **68,000** |
| 137,300 | 209,250 | **26,687.50 + 28%** | **137,300** |
| 209,250 | 373,650 | **46,833.50 + 33%** | **209,250** |
| 373,650 | ---------- | **101,085.50 + 35%** | **373,650** |

**Schedule Y-2**— Use if your **2010** filing status is **Married filing separately**

| If line 5 is: Over— | But not over— | The tax is: | of the amount over— |
|---|---|---|---|
| $0 | $8,375 | ---------- 10% | **$0** |
| 8,375 | 34,000 | **$837.50 + 15%** | **8,375** |
| 34,000 | 68,650 | **4,681.25 + 25%** | **34,000** |
| 68,650 | 104,625 | **13,343.75 + 28%** | **68,650** |
| 104,625 | 186,825 | **23,416.75 + 33%** | **104,625** |
| 186,825 | ---------- | **50,542.75 + 35%** | **186,825** |

# A-2 2010 Income Tax Tables

## 2010 Tax Table

CAUTION *See the instructions for line 44 on page 35 to see if you must use the Tax Table below to figure your tax.*

**Example.** Mr. and Mrs. Brown are filing a joint return. Their taxable income on Form 1040, line 43, is $25,300. First, they find the $25,300–25,350 taxable income line. Next, they find the column for married filing jointly and read down the column. The amount shown where the taxable income line and filing status column meet is $2,961. This is the tax amount they should enter on Form 1040, line 44.

**Sample Table**

| At least | But less than | Single | Married filing jointly * | Married filing sepa-rately | Head of a house-hold |
|---|---|---|---|---|---|
| | | Your tax is— | | | |
| **25,200** | **25,250** | 3,365 | 2,946 | 3,365 | 3,186 |
| **25,250** | **25,300** | 3,373 | 2,954 | 3,373 | 3,194 |
| **25,300** | **25,350** | 3,380 | (2,961) | 3,380 | 3,201 |
| **25,350** | **25,400** | 3,388 | 2,969 | 3,388 | 3,209 |

| If line 43 (taxable income) is— | | And you are— | | | |
|---|---|---|---|---|---|
| At least | But less than | Single | Married filing jointly * | Married filing sepa-rately | Head of a house-hold |
| | | Your tax is— | | | |
| 0 | 5 | 0 | 0 | 0 | 0 |
| 5 | 15 | 1 | 1 | 1 | 1 |
| 15 | 25 | 2 | 2 | 2 | 2 |
| 25 | 50 | 4 | 4 | 4 | 4 |
| 50 | 75 | 6 | 6 | 6 | 6 |
| 75 | 100 | 9 | 9 | 9 | 9 |
| 100 | 125 | 11 | 11 | 11 | 11 |
| 125 | 150 | 14 | 14 | 14 | 14 |
| 150 | 175 | 16 | 16 | 16 | 16 |
| 175 | 200 | 19 | 19 | 19 | 19 |
| 200 | 225 | 21 | 21 | 21 | 21 |
| 225 | 250 | 24 | 24 | 24 | 24 |
| 250 | 275 | 26 | 26 | 26 | 26 |
| 275 | 300 | 29 | 29 | 29 | 29 |
| 300 | 325 | 31 | 31 | 31 | 31 |
| 325 | 350 | 34 | 34 | 34 | 34 |
| 350 | 375 | 36 | 36 | 36 | 36 |
| 375 | 400 | 39 | 39 | 39 | 39 |
| 400 | 425 | 41 | 41 | 41 | 41 |
| 425 | 450 | 44 | 44 | 44 | 44 |
| 450 | 475 | 46 | 46 | 46 | 46 |
| 475 | 500 | 49 | 49 | 49 | 49 |
| 500 | 525 | 51 | 51 | 51 | 51 |
| 525 | 550 | 54 | 54 | 54 | 54 |
| 550 | 575 | 56 | 56 | 56 | 56 |
| 575 | 600 | 59 | 59 | 59 | 59 |
| 600 | 625 | 61 | 61 | 61 | 61 |
| 625 | 650 | 64 | 64 | 64 | 64 |
| 650 | 675 | 66 | 66 | 66 | 66 |
| 675 | 700 | 69 | 69 | 69 | 69 |
| 700 | 725 | 71 | 71 | 71 | 71 |
| 725 | 750 | 74 | 74 | 74 | 74 |
| 750 | 775 | 76 | 76 | 76 | 76 |
| 775 | 800 | 79 | 79 | 79 | 79 |
| 800 | 825 | 81 | 81 | 81 | 81 |
| 825 | 850 | 84 | 84 | 84 | 84 |
| 850 | 875 | 86 | 86 | 86 | 86 |
| 875 | 900 | 89 | 89 | 89 | 89 |
| 900 | 925 | 91 | 91 | 91 | 91 |
| 925 | 950 | 94 | 94 | 94 | 94 |
| 950 | 975 | 96 | 96 | 96 | 96 |
| 975 | 1,000 | 99 | 99 | 99 | 99 |
| **1,000** | | | | | |
| 1,000 | 1,025 | 101 | 101 | 101 | 101 |
| 1,025 | 1,050 | 104 | 104 | 104 | 104 |
| 1,050 | 1,075 | 106 | 106 | 106 | 106 |
| 1,075 | 1,100 | 109 | 109 | 109 | 109 |
| 1,100 | 1,125 | 111 | 111 | 111 | 111 |
| 1,125 | 1,150 | 114 | 114 | 114 | 114 |
| 1,150 | 1,175 | 116 | 116 | 116 | 116 |
| 1,175 | 1,200 | 119 | 119 | 119 | 119 |
| 1,200 | 1,225 | 121 | 121 | 121 | 121 |
| 1,225 | 1,250 | 124 | 124 | 124 | 124 |
| 1,250 | 1,275 | 126 | 126 | 126 | 126 |
| 1,275 | 1,300 | 129 | 129 | 129 | 129 |
| 1,300 | 1,325 | 131 | 131 | 131 | 131 |
| 1,325 | 1,350 | 134 | 134 | 134 | 134 |
| 1,350 | 1,375 | 136 | 136 | 136 | 136 |
| 1,375 | 1,400 | 139 | 139 | 139 | 139 |
| 1,400 | 1,425 | 141 | 141 | 141 | 141 |
| 1,425 | 1,450 | 144 | 144 | 144 | 144 |
| 1,450 | 1,475 | 146 | 146 | 146 | 146 |
| 1,475 | 1,500 | 149 | 149 | 149 | 149 |
| 1,500 | 1,525 | 151 | 151 | 151 | 151 |
| 1,525 | 1,550 | 154 | 154 | 154 | 154 |
| 1,550 | 1,575 | 156 | 156 | 156 | 156 |
| 1,575 | 1,600 | 159 | 159 | 159 | 159 |
| 1,600 | 1,625 | 161 | 161 | 161 | 161 |
| 1,625 | 1,650 | 164 | 164 | 164 | 164 |
| 1,650 | 1,675 | 166 | 166 | 166 | 166 |
| 1,675 | 1,700 | 169 | 169 | 169 | 169 |
| 1,700 | 1,725 | 171 | 171 | 171 | 171 |
| 1,725 | 1,750 | 174 | 174 | 174 | 174 |
| 1,750 | 1,775 | 176 | 176 | 176 | 176 |
| 1,775 | 1,800 | 179 | 179 | 179 | 179 |
| 1,800 | 1,825 | 181 | 181 | 181 | 181 |
| 1,825 | 1,850 | 184 | 184 | 184 | 184 |
| 1,850 | 1,875 | 186 | 186 | 186 | 186 |
| 1,875 | 1,900 | 189 | 189 | 189 | 189 |
| 1,900 | 1,925 | 191 | 191 | 191 | 191 |
| 1,925 | 1,950 | 194 | 194 | 194 | 194 |
| 1,950 | 1,975 | 196 | 196 | 196 | 196 |
| 1,975 | 2,000 | 199 | 199 | 199 | 199 |
| **2,000** | | | | | |
| 2,000 | 2,025 | 201 | 201 | 201 | 201 |
| 2,025 | 2,050 | 204 | 204 | 204 | 204 |
| 2,050 | 2,075 | 206 | 206 | 206 | 206 |
| 2,075 | 2,100 | 209 | 209 | 209 | 209 |
| 2,100 | 2,125 | 211 | 211 | 211 | 211 |
| 2,125 | 2,150 | 214 | 214 | 214 | 214 |
| 2,150 | 2,175 | 216 | 216 | 216 | 216 |
| 2,175 | 2,200 | 219 | 219 | 219 | 219 |
| 2,200 | 2,225 | 221 | 221 | 221 | 221 |
| 2,225 | 2,250 | 224 | 224 | 224 | 224 |
| 2,250 | 2,275 | 226 | 226 | 226 | 226 |
| 2,275 | 2,300 | 229 | 229 | 229 | 229 |
| 2,300 | 2,325 | 231 | 231 | 231 | 231 |
| 2,325 | 2,350 | 234 | 234 | 234 | 234 |
| 2,350 | 2,375 | 236 | 236 | 236 | 236 |
| 2,375 | 2,400 | 239 | 239 | 239 | 239 |
| 2,400 | 2,425 | 241 | 241 | 241 | 241 |
| 2,425 | 2,450 | 244 | 244 | 244 | 244 |
| 2,450 | 2,475 | 246 | 246 | 246 | 246 |
| 2,475 | 2,500 | 249 | 249 | 249 | 249 |
| 2,500 | 2,525 | 251 | 251 | 251 | 251 |
| 2,525 | 2,550 | 254 | 254 | 254 | 254 |
| 2,550 | 2,575 | 256 | 256 | 256 | 256 |
| 2,575 | 2,600 | 259 | 259 | 259 | 259 |
| 2,600 | 2,625 | 261 | 261 | 261 | 261 |
| 2,625 | 2,650 | 264 | 264 | 264 | 264 |
| 2,650 | 2,675 | 266 | 266 | 266 | 266 |
| 2,675 | 2,700 | 269 | 269 | 269 | 269 |
| 2,700 | 2,725 | 271 | 271 | 271 | 271 |
| 2,725 | 2,750 | 274 | 274 | 274 | 274 |
| 2,750 | 2,775 | 276 | 276 | 276 | 276 |
| 2,775 | 2,800 | 279 | 279 | 279 | 279 |
| 2,800 | 2,825 | 281 | 281 | 281 | 281 |
| 2,825 | 2,850 | 284 | 284 | 284 | 284 |
| 2,850 | 2,875 | 286 | 286 | 286 | 286 |
| 2,875 | 2,900 | 289 | 289 | 289 | 289 |
| 2,900 | 2,925 | 291 | 291 | 291 | 291 |
| 2,925 | 2,950 | 294 | 294 | 294 | 294 |
| 2,950 | 2,975 | 296 | 296 | 296 | 296 |
| 2,975 | 3,000 | 299 | 299 | 299 | 299 |
| **3,000** | | | | | |
| 3,000 | 3,050 | 303 | 303 | 303 | 303 |
| 3,050 | 3,100 | 308 | 308 | 308 | 308 |
| 3,100 | 3,150 | 313 | 313 | 313 | 313 |
| 3,150 | 3,200 | 318 | 318 | 318 | 318 |
| 3,200 | 3,250 | 323 | 323 | 323 | 323 |
| 3,250 | 3,300 | 328 | 328 | 328 | 328 |
| 3,300 | 3,350 | 333 | 333 | 333 | 333 |
| 3,350 | 3,400 | 338 | 338 | 338 | 338 |
| 3,400 | 3,450 | 343 | 343 | 343 | 343 |
| 3,450 | 3,500 | 348 | 348 | 348 | 348 |
| 3,500 | 3,550 | 353 | 353 | 353 | 353 |
| 3,550 | 3,600 | 358 | 358 | 358 | 358 |
| 3,600 | 3,650 | 363 | 363 | 363 | 363 |
| 3,650 | 3,700 | 368 | 368 | 368 | 368 |
| 3,700 | 3,750 | 373 | 373 | 373 | 373 |
| 3,750 | 3,800 | 378 | 378 | 378 | 378 |
| 3,800 | 3,850 | 383 | 383 | 383 | 383 |
| 3,850 | 3,900 | 388 | 388 | 388 | 388 |
| 3,900 | 3,950 | 393 | 393 | 393 | 393 |
| 3,950 | 4,000 | 398 | 398 | 398 | 398 |
| **4,000** | | | | | |
| 4,000 | 4,050 | 403 | 403 | 403 | 403 |
| 4,050 | 4,100 | 408 | 408 | 408 | 408 |
| 4,100 | 4,150 | 413 | 413 | 413 | 413 |
| 4,150 | 4,200 | 418 | 418 | 418 | 418 |
| 4,200 | 4,250 | 423 | 423 | 423 | 423 |
| 4,250 | 4,300 | 428 | 428 | 428 | 428 |
| 4,300 | 4,350 | 433 | 433 | 433 | 433 |
| 4,350 | 4,400 | 438 | 438 | 438 | 438 |
| 4,400 | 4,450 | 443 | 443 | 443 | 443 |
| 4,450 | 4,500 | 448 | 448 | 448 | 448 |
| 4,500 | 4,550 | 453 | 453 | 453 | 453 |
| 4,550 | 4,600 | 458 | 458 | 458 | 458 |
| 4,600 | 4,650 | 463 | 463 | 463 | 463 |
| 4,650 | 4,700 | 468 | 468 | 468 | 468 |
| 4,700 | 4,750 | 473 | 473 | 473 | 473 |
| 4,750 | 4,800 | 478 | 478 | 478 | 478 |
| 4,800 | 4,850 | 483 | 483 | 483 | 483 |
| 4,850 | 4,900 | 488 | 488 | 488 | 488 |
| 4,900 | 4,950 | 493 | 493 | 493 | 493 |
| 4,950 | 5,000 | 498 | 498 | 498 | 498 |

* This column must also be used by a qualifying widow(er).

(Continued on next page)

**2010 Tax Table**–*Continued*

| If line 43 (taxable income) is— At least | But less than | And you are— Single | Married filing jointly * | Married filing separately | Head of a household |
|---|---|---|---|---|---|
| | | Your tax is— | | | |
| **5,000** | | | | | |
| 5,000 | 5,050 | 503 | 503 | 503 | 503 |
| 5,050 | 5,100 | 508 | 508 | 508 | 508 |
| 5,100 | 5,150 | 513 | 513 | 513 | 513 |
| 5,150 | 5,200 | 518 | 518 | 518 | 518 |
| 5,200 | 5,250 | 523 | 523 | 523 | 523 |
| 5,250 | 5,300 | 528 | 528 | 528 | 528 |
| 5,300 | 5,350 | 533 | 533 | 533 | 533 |
| 5,350 | 5,400 | 538 | 538 | 538 | 538 |
| 5,400 | 5,450 | 543 | 543 | 543 | 543 |
| 5,450 | 5,500 | 548 | 548 | 548 | 548 |
| 5,500 | 5,550 | 553 | 553 | 553 | 553 |
| 5,550 | 5,600 | 558 | 558 | 558 | 558 |
| 5,600 | 5,650 | 563 | 563 | 563 | 563 |
| 5,650 | 5,700 | 568 | 568 | 568 | 568 |
| 5,700 | 5,750 | 573 | 573 | 573 | 573 |
| 5,750 | 5,800 | 578 | 578 | 578 | 578 |
| 5,800 | 5,850 | 583 | 583 | 583 | 583 |
| 5,850 | 5,900 | 588 | 588 | 588 | 588 |
| 5,900 | 5,950 | 593 | 593 | 593 | 593 |
| 5,950 | 6,000 | 598 | 598 | 598 | 598 |
| **6,000** | | | | | |
| 6,000 | 6,050 | 603 | 603 | 603 | 603 |
| 6,050 | 6,100 | 608 | 608 | 608 | 608 |
| 6,100 | 6,150 | 613 | 613 | 613 | 613 |
| 6,150 | 6,200 | 618 | 618 | 618 | 618 |
| 6,200 | 6,250 | 623 | 623 | 623 | 623 |
| 6,250 | 6,300 | 628 | 628 | 628 | 628 |
| 6,300 | 6,350 | 633 | 633 | 633 | 633 |
| 6,350 | 6,400 | 638 | 638 | 638 | 638 |
| 6,400 | 6,450 | 643 | 643 | 643 | 643 |
| 6,450 | 6,500 | 648 | 648 | 648 | 648 |
| 6,500 | 6,550 | 653 | 653 | 653 | 653 |
| 6,550 | 6,600 | 658 | 658 | 658 | 658 |
| 6,600 | 6,650 | 663 | 663 | 663 | 663 |
| 6,650 | 6,700 | 668 | 668 | 668 | 668 |
| 6,700 | 6,750 | 673 | 673 | 673 | 673 |
| 6,750 | 6,800 | 678 | 678 | 678 | 678 |
| 6,800 | 6,850 | 683 | 683 | 683 | 683 |
| 6,850 | 6,900 | 688 | 688 | 688 | 688 |
| 6,900 | 6,950 | 693 | 693 | 693 | 693 |
| 6,950 | 7,000 | 698 | 698 | 698 | 698 |
| **7,000** | | | | | |
| 7,000 | 7,050 | 703 | 703 | 703 | 703 |
| 7,050 | 7,100 | 708 | 708 | 708 | 708 |
| 7,100 | 7,150 | 713 | 713 | 713 | 713 |
| 7,150 | 7,200 | 718 | 718 | 718 | 718 |
| 7,200 | 7,250 | 723 | 723 | 723 | 723 |
| 7,250 | 7,300 | 728 | 728 | 728 | 728 |
| 7,300 | 7,350 | 733 | 733 | 733 | 733 |
| 7,350 | 7,400 | 738 | 738 | 738 | 738 |
| 7,400 | 7,450 | 743 | 743 | 743 | 743 |
| 7,450 | 7,500 | 748 | 748 | 748 | 748 |
| 7,500 | 7,550 | 753 | 753 | 753 | 753 |
| 7,550 | 7,600 | 758 | 758 | 758 | 758 |
| 7,600 | 7,650 | 763 | 763 | 763 | 763 |
| 7,650 | 7,700 | 768 | 768 | 768 | 768 |
| 7,700 | 7,750 | 773 | 773 | 773 | 773 |
| 7,750 | 7,800 | 778 | 778 | 778 | 778 |
| 7,800 | 7,850 | 783 | 783 | 783 | 783 |
| 7,850 | 7,900 | 788 | 788 | 788 | 788 |
| 7,900 | 7,950 | 793 | 793 | 793 | 793 |
| 7,950 | 8,000 | 798 | 798 | 798 | 798 |

| If line 43 (taxable income) is— At least | But less than | And you are— Single | Married filing jointly * | Married filing separately | Head of a household |
|---|---|---|---|---|---|
| | | Your tax is— | | | |
| **8,000** | | | | | |
| 8,000 | 8,050 | 803 | 803 | 803 | 803 |
| 8,050 | 8,100 | 808 | 808 | 808 | 808 |
| 8,100 | 8,150 | 813 | 813 | 813 | 813 |
| 8,150 | 8,200 | 818 | 818 | 818 | 818 |
| 8,200 | 8,250 | 823 | 823 | 823 | 823 |
| 8,250 | 8,300 | 828 | 828 | 828 | 828 |
| 8,300 | 8,350 | 833 | 833 | 833 | 833 |
| 8,350 | 8,400 | 838 | 838 | 838 | 838 |
| 8,400 | 8,450 | 845 | 843 | 845 | 843 |
| 8,450 | 8,500 | 853 | 848 | 853 | 848 |
| 8,500 | 8,550 | 860 | 853 | 860 | 853 |
| 8,550 | 8,600 | 868 | 858 | 868 | 858 |
| 8,600 | 8,650 | 875 | 863 | 875 | 863 |
| 8,650 | 8,700 | 883 | 868 | 883 | 868 |
| 8,700 | 8,750 | 890 | 873 | 890 | 873 |
| 8,750 | 8,800 | 898 | 878 | 898 | 878 |
| 8,800 | 8,850 | 905 | 883 | 905 | 883 |
| 8,850 | 8,900 | 913 | 888 | 913 | 888 |
| 8,900 | 8,950 | 920 | 893 | 920 | 893 |
| 8,950 | 9,000 | 928 | 898 | 928 | 898 |
| **9,000** | | | | | |
| 9,000 | 9,050 | 935 | 903 | 935 | 903 |
| 9,050 | 9,100 | 943 | 908 | 943 | 908 |
| 9,100 | 9,150 | 950 | 913 | 950 | 913 |
| 9,150 | 9,200 | 958 | 918 | 958 | 918 |
| 9,200 | 9,250 | 965 | 923 | 965 | 923 |
| 9,250 | 9,300 | 973 | 928 | 973 | 928 |
| 9,300 | 9,350 | 980 | 933 | 980 | 933 |
| 9,350 | 9,400 | 988 | 938 | 988 | 938 |
| 9,400 | 9,450 | 995 | 943 | 995 | 943 |
| 9,450 | 9,500 | 1,003 | 948 | 1,003 | 948 |
| 9,500 | 9,550 | 1,010 | 953 | 1,010 | 953 |
| 9,550 | 9,600 | 1,018 | 958 | 1,018 | 958 |
| 9,600 | 9,650 | 1,025 | 963 | 1,025 | 963 |
| 9,650 | 9,700 | 1,033 | 968 | 1,033 | 968 |
| 9,700 | 9,750 | 1,040 | 973 | 1,040 | 973 |
| 9,750 | 9,800 | 1,048 | 978 | 1,048 | 978 |
| 9,800 | 9,850 | 1,055 | 983 | 1,055 | 983 |
| 9,850 | 9,900 | 1,063 | 988 | 1,063 | 988 |
| 9,900 | 9,950 | 1,070 | 993 | 1,070 | 993 |
| 9,950 | 10,000 | 1,078 | 998 | 1,078 | 998 |
| **10,000** | | | | | |
| 10,000 | 10,050 | 1,085 | 1,003 | 1,085 | 1,003 |
| 10,050 | 10,100 | 1,093 | 1,008 | 1,093 | 1,008 |
| 10,100 | 10,150 | 1,100 | 1,013 | 1,100 | 1,013 |
| 10,150 | 10,200 | 1,108 | 1,018 | 1,108 | 1,018 |
| 10,200 | 10,250 | 1,115 | 1,023 | 1,115 | 1,023 |
| 10,250 | 10,300 | 1,123 | 1,028 | 1,123 | 1,028 |
| 10,300 | 10,350 | 1,130 | 1,033 | 1,130 | 1,033 |
| 10,350 | 10,400 | 1,138 | 1,038 | 1,138 | 1,038 |
| 10,400 | 10,450 | 1,145 | 1,043 | 1,145 | 1,043 |
| 10,450 | 10,500 | 1,153 | 1,048 | 1,153 | 1,048 |
| 10,500 | 10,550 | 1,160 | 1,053 | 1,160 | 1,053 |
| 10,550 | 10,600 | 1,168 | 1,058 | 1,168 | 1,058 |
| 10,600 | 10,650 | 1,175 | 1,063 | 1,175 | 1,063 |
| 10,650 | 10,700 | 1,183 | 1,068 | 1,183 | 1,068 |
| 10,700 | 10,750 | 1,190 | 1,073 | 1,190 | 1,073 |
| 10,750 | 10,800 | 1,198 | 1,078 | 1,198 | 1,078 |
| 10,800 | 10,850 | 1,205 | 1,083 | 1,205 | 1,083 |
| 10,850 | 10,900 | 1,213 | 1,088 | 1,213 | 1,088 |
| 10,900 | 10,950 | 1,220 | 1,093 | 1,220 | 1,093 |
| 10,950 | 11,000 | 1,228 | 1,098 | 1,228 | 1,098 |

| If line 43 (taxable income) is— At least | But less than | And you are— Single | Married filing jointly * | Married filing separately | Head of a household |
|---|---|---|---|---|---|
| | | Your tax is— | | | |
| **11,000** | | | | | |
| 11,000 | 11,050 | 1,235 | 1,103 | 1,235 | 1,103 |
| 11,050 | 11,100 | 1,243 | 1,108 | 1,243 | 1,108 |
| 11,100 | 11,150 | 1,250 | 1,113 | 1,250 | 1,113 |
| 11,150 | 11,200 | 1,258 | 1,118 | 1,258 | 1,118 |
| 11,200 | 11,250 | 1,265 | 1,123 | 1,265 | 1,123 |
| 11,250 | 11,300 | 1,273 | 1,128 | 1,273 | 1,128 |
| 11,300 | 11,350 | 1,280 | 1,133 | 1,280 | 1,133 |
| 11,350 | 11,400 | 1,288 | 1,138 | 1,288 | 1,138 |
| 11,400 | 11,450 | 1,295 | 1,143 | 1,295 | 1,143 |
| 11,450 | 11,500 | 1,303 | 1,148 | 1,303 | 1,148 |
| 11,500 | 11,550 | 1,310 | 1,153 | 1,310 | 1,153 |
| 11,550 | 11,600 | 1,318 | 1,158 | 1,318 | 1,158 |
| 11,600 | 11,650 | 1,325 | 1,163 | 1,325 | 1,163 |
| 11,650 | 11,700 | 1,333 | 1,168 | 1,333 | 1,168 |
| 11,700 | 11,750 | 1,340 | 1,173 | 1,340 | 1,173 |
| 11,750 | 11,800 | 1,348 | 1,178 | 1,348 | 1,178 |
| 11,800 | 11,850 | 1,355 | 1,183 | 1,355 | 1,183 |
| 11,850 | 11,900 | 1,363 | 1,188 | 1,363 | 1,188 |
| 11,900 | 11,950 | 1,370 | 1,193 | 1,370 | 1,193 |
| 11,950 | 12,000 | 1,378 | 1,198 | 1,378 | 1,199 |
| **12,000** | | | | | |
| 12,000 | 12,050 | 1,385 | 1,203 | 1,385 | 1,206 |
| 12,050 | 12,100 | 1,393 | 1,208 | 1,393 | 1,214 |
| 12,100 | 12,150 | 1,400 | 1,213 | 1,400 | 1,221 |
| 12,150 | 12,200 | 1,408 | 1,218 | 1,408 | 1,229 |
| 12,200 | 12,250 | 1,415 | 1,223 | 1,415 | 1,236 |
| 12,250 | 12,300 | 1,423 | 1,228 | 1,423 | 1,244 |
| 12,300 | 12,350 | 1,430 | 1,233 | 1,430 | 1,251 |
| 12,350 | 12,400 | 1,438 | 1,238 | 1,438 | 1,259 |
| 12,400 | 12,450 | 1,445 | 1,243 | 1,445 | 1,266 |
| 12,450 | 12,500 | 1,453 | 1,248 | 1,453 | 1,274 |
| 12,500 | 12,550 | 1,460 | 1,253 | 1,460 | 1,281 |
| 12,550 | 12,600 | 1,468 | 1,258 | 1,468 | 1,289 |
| 12,600 | 12,650 | 1,475 | 1,263 | 1,475 | 1,296 |
| 12,650 | 12,700 | 1,483 | 1,268 | 1,483 | 1,304 |
| 12,700 | 12,750 | 1,490 | 1,273 | 1,490 | 1,311 |
| 12,750 | 12,800 | 1,498 | 1,278 | 1,498 | 1,319 |
| 12,800 | 12,850 | 1,505 | 1,283 | 1,505 | 1,326 |
| 12,850 | 12,900 | 1,513 | 1,288 | 1,513 | 1,334 |
| 12,900 | 12,950 | 1,520 | 1,293 | 1,520 | 1,341 |
| 12,950 | 13,000 | 1,528 | 1,298 | 1,528 | 1,349 |
| **13,000** | | | | | |
| 13,000 | 13,050 | 1,535 | 1,303 | 1,535 | 1,356 |
| 13,050 | 13,100 | 1,543 | 1,308 | 1,543 | 1,364 |
| 13,100 | 13,150 | 1,550 | 1,313 | 1,550 | 1,371 |
| 13,150 | 13,200 | 1,558 | 1,318 | 1,558 | 1,379 |
| 13,200 | 13,250 | 1,565 | 1,323 | 1,565 | 1,386 |
| 13,250 | 13,300 | 1,573 | 1,328 | 1,573 | 1,394 |
| 13,300 | 13,350 | 1,580 | 1,333 | 1,580 | 1,401 |
| 13,350 | 13,400 | 1,588 | 1,338 | 1,588 | 1,409 |
| 13,400 | 13,450 | 1,595 | 1,343 | 1,595 | 1,416 |
| 13,450 | 13,500 | 1,603 | 1,348 | 1,603 | 1,424 |
| 13,500 | 13,550 | 1,610 | 1,353 | 1,610 | 1,431 |
| 13,550 | 13,600 | 1,618 | 1,358 | 1,618 | 1,439 |
| 13,600 | 13,650 | 1,625 | 1,363 | 1,625 | 1,446 |
| 13,650 | 13,700 | 1,633 | 1,368 | 1,633 | 1,454 |
| 13,700 | 13,750 | 1,640 | 1,373 | 1,640 | 1,461 |
| 13,750 | 13,800 | 1,648 | 1,378 | 1,648 | 1,469 |
| 13,800 | 13,850 | 1,655 | 1,383 | 1,655 | 1,476 |
| 13,850 | 13,900 | 1,663 | 1,388 | 1,663 | 1,484 |
| 13,900 | 13,950 | 1,670 | 1,393 | 1,670 | 1,491 |
| 13,950 | 14,000 | 1,678 | 1,398 | 1,678 | 1,499 |

* This column must also be used by a qualifying widow(er).

*(Continued on next page)*

## 2010 Tax Table—*Continued*

| If line 43 (taxable income) is— At least | But less than | And you are— Single | Married filing jointly * | Married filing separately | Head of a household |
|---|---|---|---|---|---|
| | | Your tax is— | | | |
| **14,000** | | | | | |
| **14,000** | **14,050** | 1,685 | 1,403 | 1,685 | 1,506 |
| **14,050** | **14,100** | 1,693 | 1,408 | 1,693 | 1,514 |
| **14,100** | **14,150** | 1,700 | 1,413 | 1,700 | 1,521 |
| **14,150** | **14,200** | 1,708 | 1,418 | 1,708 | 1,529 |
| **14,200** | **14,250** | 1,715 | 1,423 | 1,715 | 1,536 |
| **14,250** | **14,300** | 1,723 | 1,428 | 1,723 | 1,544 |
| **14,300** | **14,350** | 1,730 | 1,433 | 1,730 | 1,551 |
| **14,350** | **14,400** | 1,738 | 1,438 | 1,738 | 1,559 |
| **14,400** | **14,450** | 1,745 | 1,443 | 1,745 | 1,566 |
| **14,450** | **14,500** | 1,753 | 1,448 | 1,753 | 1,574 |
| **14,500** | **14,550** | 1,760 | 1,453 | 1,760 | 1,581 |
| **14,550** | **14,600** | 1,768 | 1,458 | 1,768 | 1,589 |
| **14,600** | **14,650** | 1,775 | 1,463 | 1,775 | 1,596 |
| **14,650** | **14,700** | 1,783 | 1,468 | 1,783 | 1,604 |
| **14,700** | **14,750** | 1,790 | 1,473 | 1,790 | 1,611 |
| **14,750** | **14,800** | 1,798 | 1,478 | 1,798 | 1,619 |
| **14,800** | **14,850** | 1,805 | 1,483 | 1,805 | 1,626 |
| **14,850** | **14,900** | 1,813 | 1,488 | 1,813 | 1,634 |
| **14,900** | **14,950** | 1,820 | 1,493 | 1,820 | 1,641 |
| **14,950** | **15,000** | 1,828 | 1,498 | 1,828 | 1,649 |
| **15,000** | | | | | |
| **15,000** | **15,050** | 1,835 | 1,503 | 1,835 | 1,656 |
| **15,050** | **15,100** | 1,843 | 1,508 | 1,843 | 1,664 |
| **15,100** | **15,150** | 1,850 | 1,513 | 1,850 | 1,671 |
| **15,150** | **15,200** | 1,858 | 1,518 | 1,858 | 1,679 |
| **15,200** | **15,250** | 1,865 | 1,523 | 1,865 | 1,686 |
| **15,250** | **15,300** | 1,873 | 1,528 | 1,873 | 1,694 |
| **15,300** | **15,350** | 1,880 | 1,533 | 1,880 | 1,701 |
| **15,350** | **15,400** | 1,888 | 1,538 | 1,888 | 1,709 |
| **15,400** | **15,450** | 1,895 | 1,543 | 1,895 | 1,716 |
| **15,450** | **15,500** | 1,903 | 1,548 | 1,903 | 1,724 |
| **15,500** | **15,550** | 1,910 | 1,553 | 1,910 | 1,731 |
| **15,550** | **15,600** | 1,918 | 1,558 | 1,918 | 1,739 |
| **15,600** | **15,650** | 1,925 | 1,563 | 1,925 | 1,746 |
| **15,650** | **15,700** | 1,933 | 1,568 | 1,933 | 1,754 |
| **15,700** | **15,750** | 1,940 | 1,573 | 1,940 | 1,761 |
| **15,750** | **15,800** | 1,948 | 1,578 | 1,948 | 1,769 |
| **15,800** | **15,850** | 1,955 | 1,583 | 1,955 | 1,776 |
| **15,850** | **15,900** | 1,963 | 1,588 | 1,963 | 1,784 |
| **15,900** | **15,950** | 1,970 | 1,593 | 1,970 | 1,791 |
| **15,950** | **16,000** | 1,978 | 1,598 | 1,978 | 1,799 |
| **16,000** | | | | | |
| **16,000** | **16,050** | 1,985 | 1,603 | 1,985 | 1,806 |
| **16,050** | **16,100** | 1,993 | 1,608 | 1,993 | 1,814 |
| **16,100** | **16,150** | 2,000 | 1,613 | 2,000 | 1,821 |
| **16,150** | **16,200** | 2,008 | 1,618 | 2,008 | 1,829 |
| **16,200** | **16,250** | 2,015 | 1,623 | 2,015 | 1,836 |
| **16,250** | **16,300** | 2,023 | 1,628 | 2,023 | 1,844 |
| **16,300** | **16,350** | 2,030 | 1,633 | 2,030 | 1,851 |
| **16,350** | **16,400** | 2,038 | 1,638 | 2,038 | 1,859 |
| **16,400** | **16,450** | 2,045 | 1,643 | 2,045 | 1,866 |
| **16,450** | **16,500** | 2,053 | 1,648 | 2,053 | 1,874 |
| **16,500** | **16,550** | 2,060 | 1,653 | 2,060 | 1,881 |
| **16,550** | **16,600** | 2,068 | 1,658 | 2,068 | 1,889 |
| **16,600** | **16,650** | 2,075 | 1,663 | 2,075 | 1,896 |
| **16,650** | **16,700** | 2,083 | 1,668 | 2,083 | 1,904 |
| **16,700** | **16,750** | 2,090 | 1,673 | 2,090 | 1,911 |
| **16,750** | **16,800** | 2,098 | 1,679 | 2,098 | 1,919 |
| **16,800** | **16,850** | 2,105 | 1,686 | 2,105 | 1,926 |
| **16,850** | **16,900** | 2,113 | 1,694 | 2,113 | 1,934 |
| **16,900** | **16,950** | 2,120 | 1,701 | 2,120 | 1,941 |
| **16,950** | **17,000** | 2,128 | 1,709 | 2,128 | 1,949 |
| **17,000** | | | | | |
| **17,000** | **17,050** | 2,135 | 1,716 | 2,135 | 1,956 |
| **17,050** | **17,100** | 2,143 | 1,724 | 2,143 | 1,964 |
| **17,100** | **17,150** | 2,150 | 1,731 | 2,150 | 1,971 |
| **17,150** | **17,200** | 2,158 | 1,739 | 2,158 | 1,979 |
| **17,200** | **17,250** | 2,165 | 1,746 | 2,165 | 1,986 |
| **17,250** | **17,300** | 2,173 | 1,754 | 2,173 | 1,994 |
| **17,300** | **17,350** | 2,180 | 1,761 | 2,180 | 2,001 |
| **17,350** | **17,400** | 2,188 | 1,769 | 2,188 | 2,009 |
| **17,400** | **17,450** | 2,195 | 1,776 | 2,195 | 2,016 |
| **17,450** | **17,500** | 2,203 | 1,784 | 2,203 | 2,024 |
| **17,500** | **17,550** | 2,210 | 1,791 | 2,210 | 2,031 |
| **17,550** | **17,600** | 2,218 | 1,799 | 2,218 | 2,039 |
| **17,600** | **17,650** | 2,225 | 1,806 | 2,225 | 2,046 |
| **17,650** | **17,700** | 2,233 | 1,814 | 2,233 | 2,054 |
| **17,700** | **17,750** | 2,240 | 1,821 | 2,240 | 2,061 |
| **17,750** | **17,800** | 2,248 | 1,829 | 2,248 | 2,069 |
| **17,800** | **17,850** | 2,255 | 1,836 | 2,255 | 2,076 |
| **17,850** | **17,900** | 2,263 | 1,844 | 2,263 | 2,084 |
| **17,900** | **17,950** | 2,270 | 1,851 | 2,270 | 2,091 |
| **17,950** | **18,000** | 2,278 | 1,859 | 2,278 | 2,099 |
| **18,000** | | | | | |
| **18,000** | **18,050** | 2,285 | 1,866 | 2,285 | 2,106 |
| **18,050** | **18,100** | 2,293 | 1,874 | 2,293 | 2,114 |
| **18,100** | **18,150** | 2,300 | 1,881 | 2,300 | 2,121 |
| **18,150** | **18,200** | 2,308 | 1,889 | 2,308 | 2,129 |
| **18,200** | **18,250** | 2,315 | 1,896 | 2,315 | 2,136 |
| **18,250** | **18,300** | 2,323 | 1,904 | 2,323 | 2,144 |
| **18,300** | **18,350** | 2,330 | 1,911 | 2,330 | 2,151 |
| **18,350** | **18,400** | 2,338 | 1,919 | 2,338 | 2,159 |
| **18,400** | **18,450** | 2,345 | 1,926 | 2,345 | 2,166 |
| **18,450** | **18,500** | 2,353 | 1,934 | 2,353 | 2,174 |
| **18,500** | **18,550** | 2,360 | 1,941 | 2,360 | 2,181 |
| **18,550** | **18,600** | 2,368 | 1,949 | 2,368 | 2,189 |
| **18,600** | **18,650** | 2,375 | 1,956 | 2,375 | 2,196 |
| **18,650** | **18,700** | 2,383 | 1,964 | 2,383 | 2,204 |
| **18,700** | **18,750** | 2,390 | 1,971 | 2,390 | 2,211 |
| **18,750** | **18,800** | 2,398 | 1,979 | 2,398 | 2,219 |
| **18,800** | **18,850** | 2,405 | 1,986 | 2,405 | 2,226 |
| **18,850** | **18,900** | 2,413 | 1,994 | 2,413 | 2,234 |
| **18,900** | **18,950** | 2,420 | 2,001 | 2,420 | 2,241 |
| **18,950** | **19,000** | 2,428 | 2,009 | 2,428 | 2,249 |
| **19,000** | | | | | |
| **19,000** | **19,050** | 2,435 | 2,016 | 2,435 | 2,256 |
| **19,050** | **19,100** | 2,443 | 2,024 | 2,443 | 2,264 |
| **19,100** | **19,150** | 2,450 | 2,031 | 2,450 | 2,271 |
| **19,150** | **19,200** | 2,458 | 2,039 | 2,458 | 2,279 |
| **19,200** | **19,250** | 2,465 | 2,046 | 2,465 | 2,286 |
| **19,250** | **19,300** | 2,473 | 2,054 | 2,473 | 2,294 |
| **19,300** | **19,350** | 2,480 | 2,061 | 2,480 | 2,301 |
| **19,350** | **19,400** | 2,488 | 2,069 | 2,488 | 2,309 |
| **19,400** | **19,450** | 2,495 | 2,076 | 2,495 | 2,316 |
| **19,450** | **19,500** | 2,503 | 2,084 | 2,503 | 2,324 |
| **19,500** | **19,550** | 2,510 | 2,091 | 2,510 | 2,331 |
| **19,550** | **19,600** | 2,518 | 2,099 | 2,518 | 2,339 |
| **19,600** | **19,650** | 2,525 | 2,106 | 2,525 | 2,346 |
| **19,650** | **19,700** | 2,533 | 2,114 | 2,533 | 2,354 |
| **19,700** | **19,750** | 2,540 | 2,121 | 2,540 | 2,361 |
| **19,750** | **19,800** | 2,548 | 2,129 | 2,548 | 2,369 |
| **19,800** | **19,850** | 2,555 | 2,136 | 2,555 | 2,376 |
| **19,850** | **19,900** | 2,563 | 2,144 | 2,563 | 2,384 |
| **19,900** | **19,950** | 2,570 | 2,151 | 2,570 | 2,391 |
| **19,950** | **20,000** | 2,578 | 2,159 | 2,578 | 2,399 |
| **20,000** | | | | | |
| **20,000** | **20,050** | 2,585 | 2,166 | 2,585 | 2,406 |
| **20,050** | **20,100** | 2,593 | 2,174 | 2,593 | 2,414 |
| **20,100** | **20,150** | 2,600 | 2,181 | 2,600 | 2,421 |
| **20,150** | **20,200** | 2,608 | 2,189 | 2,608 | 2,429 |
| **20,200** | **20,250** | 2,615 | 2,196 | 2,615 | 2,436 |
| **20,250** | **20,300** | 2,623 | 2,204 | 2,623 | 2,444 |
| **20,300** | **20,350** | 2,630 | 2,211 | 2,630 | 2,451 |
| **20,350** | **20,400** | 2,638 | 2,219 | 2,638 | 2,459 |
| **20,400** | **20,450** | 2,645 | 2,226 | 2,645 | 2,466 |
| **20,450** | **20,500** | 2,653 | 2,234 | 2,653 | 2,474 |
| **20,500** | **20,550** | 2,660 | 2,241 | 2,660 | 2,481 |
| **20,550** | **20,600** | 2,668 | 2,249 | 2,668 | 2,489 |
| **20,600** | **20,650** | 2,675 | 2,256 | 2,675 | 2,496 |
| **20,650** | **20,700** | 2,683 | 2,264 | 2,683 | 2,504 |
| **20,700** | **20,750** | 2,690 | 2,271 | 2,690 | 2,511 |
| **20,750** | **20,800** | 2,698 | 2,279 | 2,698 | 2,519 |
| **20,800** | **20,850** | 2,705 | 2,286 | 2,705 | 2,526 |
| **20,850** | **20,900** | 2,713 | 2,294 | 2,713 | 2,534 |
| **20,900** | **20,950** | 2,720 | 2,301 | 2,720 | 2,541 |
| **20,950** | **21,000** | 2,728 | 2,309 | 2,728 | 2,549 |
| **21,000** | | | | | |
| **21,000** | **21,050** | 2,735 | 2,316 | 2,735 | 2,556 |
| **21,050** | **21,100** | 2,743 | 2,324 | 2,743 | 2,564 |
| **21,100** | **21,150** | 2,750 | 2,331 | 2,750 | 2,571 |
| **21,150** | **21,200** | 2,758 | 2,339 | 2,758 | 2,579 |
| **21,200** | **21,250** | 2,765 | 2,346 | 2,765 | 2,586 |
| **21,250** | **21,300** | 2,773 | 2,354 | 2,773 | 2,594 |
| **21,300** | **21,350** | 2,780 | 2,361 | 2,780 | 2,601 |
| **21,350** | **21,400** | 2,788 | 2,369 | 2,788 | 2,609 |
| **21,400** | **21,450** | 2,795 | 2,376 | 2,795 | 2,616 |
| **21,450** | **21,500** | 2,803 | 2,384 | 2,803 | 2,624 |
| **21,500** | **21,550** | 2,810 | 2,391 | 2,810 | 2,631 |
| **21,550** | **21,600** | 2,818 | 2,399 | 2,818 | 2,639 |
| **21,600** | **21,650** | 2,825 | 2,406 | 2,825 | 2,646 |
| **21,650** | **21,700** | 2,833 | 2,414 | 2,833 | 2,654 |
| **21,700** | **21,750** | 2,840 | 2,421 | 2,840 | 2,661 |
| **21,750** | **21,800** | 2,848 | 2,429 | 2,848 | 2,669 |
| **21,800** | **21,850** | 2,855 | 2,436 | 2,855 | 2,676 |
| **21,850** | **21,900** | 2,863 | 2,444 | 2,863 | 2,684 |
| **21,900** | **21,950** | 2,870 | 2,451 | 2,870 | 2,691 |
| **21,950** | **22,000** | 2,878 | 2,459 | 2,878 | 2,699 |
| **22,000** | | | | | |
| **22,000** | **22,050** | 2,885 | 2,466 | 2,885 | 2,706 |
| **22,050** | **22,100** | 2,893 | 2,474 | 2,893 | 2,714 |
| **22,100** | **22,150** | 2,900 | 2,481 | 2,900 | 2,721 |
| **22,150** | **22,200** | 2,908 | 2,489 | 2,908 | 2,729 |
| **22,200** | **22,250** | 2,915 | 2,496 | 2,915 | 2,736 |
| **22,250** | **22,300** | 2,923 | 2,504 | 2,923 | 2,744 |
| **22,300** | **22,350** | 2,930 | 2,511 | 2,930 | 2,751 |
| **22,350** | **22,400** | 2,938 | 2,519 | 2,938 | 2,759 |
| **22,400** | **22,450** | 2,945 | 2,526 | 2,945 | 2,766 |
| **22,450** | **22,500** | 2,953 | 2,534 | 2,953 | 2,774 |
| **22,500** | **22,550** | 2,960 | 2,541 | 2,960 | 2,781 |
| **22,550** | **22,600** | 2,968 | 2,549 | 2,968 | 2,789 |
| **22,600** | **22,650** | 2,975 | 2,556 | 2,975 | 2,796 |
| **22,650** | **22,700** | 2,983 | 2,564 | 2,983 | 2,804 |
| **22,700** | **22,750** | 2,990 | 2,571 | 2,990 | 2,811 |
| **22,750** | **22,800** | 2,998 | 2,579 | 2,998 | 2,819 |
| **22,800** | **22,850** | 3,005 | 2,586 | 3,005 | 2,826 |
| **22,850** | **22,900** | 3,013 | 2,594 | 3,013 | 2,834 |
| **22,900** | **22,950** | 3,020 | 2,601 | 3,020 | 2,841 |
| **22,950** | **23,000** | 3,028 | 2,609 | 3,028 | 2,849 |

* This column must also be used by a qualifying widow(er).

*(Continued on next page)*

**2010 Tax Table**—*Continued*

| If line 43 (taxable income) is— | | And you are— | | | |
|---|---|---|---|---|---|
| At least | But less than | Single | Married filing jointly * | Married filing sepa-rately | Head of a house-hold |
| | | Your tax is— | | | |
| **23,000** | | | | | |
| **23,000** | **23,050** | 3,035 | 2,616 | 3,035 | 2,856 |
| **23,050** | **23,100** | 3,043 | 2,624 | 3,043 | 2,864 |
| **23,100** | **23,150** | 3,050 | 2,631 | 3,050 | 2,871 |
| **23,150** | **23,200** | 3,058 | 2,639 | 3,058 | 2,879 |
| **23,200** | **23,250** | 3,065 | 2,646 | 3,065 | 2,886 |
| **23,250** | **23,300** | 3,073 | 2,654 | 3,073 | 2,894 |
| **23,300** | **23,350** | 3,080 | 2,661 | 3,080 | 2,901 |
| **23,350** | **23,400** | 3,088 | 2,669 | 3,088 | 2,909 |
| **23,400** | **23,450** | 3,095 | 2,676 | 3,095 | 2,916 |
| **23,450** | **23,500** | 3,103 | 2,684 | 3,103 | 2,924 |
| **23,500** | **23,550** | 3,110 | 2,691 | 3,110 | 2,931 |
| **23,550** | **23,600** | 3,118 | 2,699 | 3,118 | 2,939 |
| **23,600** | **23,650** | 3,125 | 2,706 | 3,125 | 2,946 |
| **23,650** | **23,700** | 3,133 | 2,714 | 3,133 | 2,954 |
| **23,700** | **23,750** | 3,140 | 2,721 | 3,140 | 2,961 |
| **23,750** | **23,800** | 3,148 | 2,729 | 3,148 | 2,969 |
| **23,800** | **23,850** | 3,155 | 2,736 | 3,155 | 2,976 |
| **23,850** | **23,900** | 3,163 | 2,744 | 3,163 | 2,984 |
| **23,900** | **23,950** | 3,170 | 2,751 | 3,170 | 2,991 |
| **23,950** | **24,000** | 3,178 | 2,759 | 3,178 | 2,999 |
| **24,000** | | | | | |
| **24,000** | **24,050** | 3,185 | 2,766 | 3,185 | 3,006 |
| **24,050** | **24,100** | 3,193 | 2,774 | 3,193 | 3,014 |
| **24,100** | **24,150** | 3,200 | 2,781 | 3,200 | 3,021 |
| **24,150** | **24,200** | 3,208 | 2,789 | 3,208 | 3,029 |
| **24,200** | **24,250** | 3,215 | 2,796 | 3,215 | 3,036 |
| **24,250** | **24,300** | 3,223 | 2,804 | 3,223 | 3,044 |
| **24,300** | **24,350** | 3,230 | 2,811 | 3,230 | 3,051 |
| **24,350** | **24,400** | 3,238 | 2,819 | 3,238 | 3,059 |
| **24,400** | **24,450** | 3,245 | 2,826 | 3,245 | 3,066 |
| **24,450** | **24,500** | 3,253 | 2,834 | 3,253 | 3,074 |
| **24,500** | **24,550** | 3,260 | 2,841 | 3,260 | 3,081 |
| **24,550** | **24,600** | 3,268 | 2,849 | 3,268 | 3,089 |
| **24,600** | **24,650** | 3,275 | 2,856 | 3,275 | 3,096 |
| **24,650** | **24,700** | 3,283 | 2,864 | 3,283 | 3,104 |
| **24,700** | **24,750** | 3,290 | 2,871 | 3,290 | 3,111 |
| **24,750** | **24,800** | 3,298 | 2,879 | 3,298 | 3,119 |
| **24,800** | **24,850** | 3,305 | 2,886 | 3,305 | 3,126 |
| **24,850** | **24,900** | 3,313 | 2,894 | 3,313 | 3,134 |
| **24,900** | **24,950** | 3,320 | 2,901 | 3,320 | 3,141 |
| **24,950** | **25,000** | 3,328 | 2,909 | 3,328 | 3,149 |
| **25,000** | | | | | |
| **25,000** | **25,050** | 3,335 | 2,916 | 3,335 | 3,156 |
| **25,050** | **25,100** | 3,343 | 2,924 | 3,343 | 3,164 |
| **25,100** | **25,150** | 3,350 | 2,931 | 3,350 | 3,171 |
| **25,150** | **25,200** | 3,358 | 2,939 | 3,358 | 3,179 |
| **25,200** | **25,250** | 3,365 | 2,946 | 3,365 | 3,186 |
| **25,250** | **25,300** | 3,373 | 2,954 | 3,373 | 3,194 |
| **25,300** | **25,350** | 3,380 | 2,961 | 3,380 | 3,201 |
| **25,350** | **25,400** | 3,388 | 2,969 | 3,388 | 3,209 |
| **25,400** | **25,450** | 3,395 | 2,976 | 3,395 | 3,216 |
| **25,450** | **25,500** | 3,403 | 2,984 | 3,403 | 3,224 |
| **25,500** | **25,550** | 3,410 | 2,991 | 3,410 | 3,231 |
| **25,550** | **25,600** | 3,418 | 2,999 | 3,418 | 3,239 |
| **25,600** | **25,650** | 3,425 | 3,006 | 3,425 | 3,246 |
| **25,650** | **25,700** | 3,433 | 3,014 | 3,433 | 3,254 |
| **25,700** | **25,750** | 3,440 | 3,021 | 3,440 | 3,261 |
| **25,750** | **25,800** | 3,448 | 3,029 | 3,448 | 3,269 |
| **25,800** | **25,850** | 3,455 | 3,036 | 3,455 | 3,276 |
| **25,850** | **25,900** | 3,463 | 3,044 | 3,463 | 3,284 |
| **25,900** | **25,950** | 3,470 | 3,051 | 3,470 | 3,291 |
| **25,950** | **26,000** | 3,478 | 3,059 | 3,478 | 3,299 |
| **26,000** | | | | | |
| **26,000** | **26,050** | 3,485 | 3,066 | 3,485 | 3,306 |
| **26,050** | **26,100** | 3,493 | 3,074 | 3,493 | 3,314 |
| **26,100** | **26,150** | 3,500 | 3,081 | 3,500 | 3,321 |
| **26,150** | **26,200** | 3,508 | 3,089 | 3,508 | 3,329 |
| **26,200** | **26,250** | 3,515 | 3,096 | 3,515 | 3,336 |
| **26,250** | **26,300** | 3,523 | 3,104 | 3,523 | 3,344 |
| **26,300** | **26,350** | 3,530 | 3,111 | 3,530 | 3,351 |
| **26,350** | **26,400** | 3,538 | 3,119 | 3,538 | 3,359 |
| **26,400** | **26,450** | 3,545 | 3,126 | 3,545 | 3,366 |
| **26,450** | **26,500** | 3,553 | 3,134 | 3,553 | 3,374 |
| **26,500** | **26,550** | 3,560 | 3,141 | 3,560 | 3,381 |
| **26,550** | **26,600** | 3,568 | 3,149 | 3,568 | 3,389 |
| **26,600** | **26,650** | 3,575 | 3,156 | 3,575 | 3,396 |
| **26,650** | **26,700** | 3,583 | 3,164 | 3,583 | 3,404 |
| **26,700** | **26,750** | 3,590 | 3,171 | 3,590 | 3,411 |
| **26,750** | **26,800** | 3,598 | 3,179 | 3,598 | 3,419 |
| **26,800** | **26,850** | 3,605 | 3,186 | 3,605 | 3,426 |
| **26,850** | **26,900** | 3,613 | 3,194 | 3,613 | 3,434 |
| **26,900** | **26,950** | 3,620 | 3,201 | 3,620 | 3,441 |
| **26,950** | **27,000** | 3,628 | 3,209 | 3,628 | 3,449 |
| **27,000** | | | | | |
| **27,000** | **27,050** | 3,635 | 3,216 | 3,635 | 3,456 |
| **27,050** | **27,100** | 3,643 | 3,224 | 3,643 | 3,464 |
| **27,100** | **27,150** | 3,650 | 3,231 | 3,650 | 3,471 |
| **27,150** | **27,200** | 3,658 | 3,239 | 3,658 | 3,479 |
| **27,200** | **27,250** | 3,665 | 3,246 | 3,665 | 3,486 |
| **27,250** | **27,300** | 3,673 | 3,254 | 3,673 | 3,494 |
| **27,300** | **27,350** | 3,680 | 3,261 | 3,680 | 3,501 |
| **27,350** | **27,400** | 3,688 | 3,269 | 3,688 | 3,509 |
| **27,400** | **27,450** | 3,695 | 3,276 | 3,695 | 3,516 |
| **27,450** | **27,500** | 3,703 | 3,284 | 3,703 | 3,524 |
| **27,500** | **27,550** | 3,710 | 3,291 | 3,710 | 3,531 |
| **27,550** | **27,600** | 3,718 | 3,299 | 3,718 | 3,539 |
| **27,600** | **27,650** | 3,725 | 3,306 | 3,725 | 3,546 |
| **27,650** | **27,700** | 3,733 | 3,314 | 3,733 | 3,554 |
| **27,700** | **27,750** | 3,740 | 3,321 | 3,740 | 3,561 |
| **27,750** | **27,800** | 3,748 | 3,329 | 3,748 | 3,569 |
| **27,800** | **27,850** | 3,755 | 3,336 | 3,755 | 3,576 |
| **27,850** | **27,900** | 3,763 | 3,344 | 3,763 | 3,584 |
| **27,900** | **27,950** | 3,770 | 3,351 | 3,770 | 3,591 |
| **27,950** | **28,000** | 3,778 | 3,359 | 3,778 | 3,599 |
| **28,000** | | | | | |
| **28,000** | **28,050** | 3,785 | 3,366 | 3,785 | 3,606 |
| **28,050** | **28,100** | 3,793 | 3,374 | 3,793 | 3,614 |
| **28,100** | **28,150** | 3,800 | 3,381 | 3,800 | 3,621 |
| **28,150** | **28,200** | 3,808 | 3,389 | 3,808 | 3,629 |
| **28,200** | **28,250** | 3,815 | 3,396 | 3,815 | 3,636 |
| **28,250** | **28,300** | 3,823 | 3,404 | 3,823 | 3,644 |
| **28,300** | **28,350** | 3,830 | 3,411 | 3,830 | 3,651 |
| **28,350** | **28,400** | 3,838 | 3,419 | 3,838 | 3,659 |
| **28,400** | **28,450** | 3,845 | 3,426 | 3,845 | 3,666 |
| **28,450** | **28,500** | 3,853 | 3,434 | 3,853 | 3,674 |
| **28,500** | **28,550** | 3,860 | 3,441 | 3,860 | 3,681 |
| **28,550** | **28,600** | 3,868 | 3,449 | 3,868 | 3,689 |
| **28,600** | **28,650** | 3,875 | 3,456 | 3,875 | 3,696 |
| **28,650** | **28,700** | 3,883 | 3,464 | 3,883 | 3,704 |
| **28,700** | **28,750** | 3,890 | 3,471 | 3,890 | 3,711 |
| **28,750** | **28,800** | 3,898 | 3,479 | 3,898 | 3,719 |
| **28,800** | **28,850** | 3,905 | 3,486 | 3,905 | 3,726 |
| **28,850** | **28,900** | 3,913 | 3,494 | 3,913 | 3,734 |
| **28,900** | **28,950** | 3,920 | 3,501 | 3,920 | 3,741 |
| **28,950** | **29,000** | 3,928 | 3,509 | 3,928 | 3,749 |
| **29,000** | | | | | |
| **29,000** | **29,050** | 3,935 | 3,516 | 3,935 | 3,756 |
| **29,050** | **29,100** | 3,943 | 3,524 | 3,943 | 3,764 |
| **29,100** | **29,150** | 3,950 | 3,531 | 3,950 | 3,771 |
| **29,150** | **29,200** | 3,958 | 3,539 | 3,958 | 3,779 |
| **29,200** | **29,250** | 3,965 | 3,546 | 3,965 | 3,786 |
| **29,250** | **29,300** | 3,973 | 3,554 | 3,973 | 3,794 |
| **29,300** | **29,350** | 3,980 | 3,561 | 3,980 | 3,801 |
| **29,350** | **29,400** | 3,988 | 3,569 | 3,988 | 3,809 |
| **29,400** | **29,450** | 3,995 | 3,576 | 3,995 | 3,816 |
| **29,450** | **29,500** | 4,003 | 3,584 | 4,003 | 3,824 |
| **29,500** | **29,550** | 4,010 | 3,591 | 4,010 | 3,831 |
| **29,550** | **29,600** | 4,018 | 3,599 | 4,018 | 3,839 |
| **29,600** | **29,650** | 4,025 | 3,606 | 4,025 | 3,846 |
| **29,650** | **29,700** | 4,033 | 3,614 | 4,033 | 3,854 |
| **29,700** | **29,750** | 4,040 | 3,621 | 4,040 | 3,861 |
| **29,750** | **29,800** | 4,048 | 3,629 | 4,048 | 3,869 |
| **29,800** | **29,850** | 4,055 | 3,636 | 4,055 | 3,876 |
| **29,850** | **29,900** | 4,063 | 3,644 | 4,063 | 3,884 |
| **29,900** | **29,950** | 4,070 | 3,651 | 4,070 | 3,891 |
| **29,950** | **30,000** | 4,078 | 3,659 | 4,078 | 3,899 |
| **30,000** | | | | | |
| **30,000** | **30,050** | 4,085 | 3,666 | 4,085 | 3,906 |
| **30,050** | **30,100** | 4,093 | 3,674 | 4,093 | 3,914 |
| **30,100** | **30,150** | 4,100 | 3,681 | 4,100 | 3,921 |
| **30,150** | **30,200** | 4,108 | 3,689 | 4,108 | 3,929 |
| **30,200** | **30,250** | 4,115 | 3,696 | 4,115 | 3,936 |
| **30,250** | **30,300** | 4,123 | 3,704 | 4,123 | 3,944 |
| **30,300** | **30,350** | 4,130 | 3,711 | 4,130 | 3,951 |
| **30,350** | **30,400** | 4,138 | 3,719 | 4,138 | 3,959 |
| **30,400** | **30,450** | 4,145 | 3,726 | 4,145 | 3,966 |
| **30,450** | **30,500** | 4,153 | 3,734 | 4,153 | 3,974 |
| **30,500** | **30,550** | 4,160 | 3,741 | 4,160 | 3,981 |
| **30,550** | **30,600** | 4,168 | 3,749 | 4,168 | 3,989 |
| **30,600** | **30,650** | 4,175 | 3,756 | 4,175 | 3,996 |
| **30,650** | **30,700** | 4,183 | 3,764 | 4,183 | 4,004 |
| **30,700** | **30,750** | 4,190 | 3,771 | 4,190 | 4,011 |
| **30,750** | **30,800** | 4,198 | 3,779 | 4,198 | 4,019 |
| **30,800** | **30,850** | 4,205 | 3,786 | 4,205 | 4,026 |
| **30,850** | **30,900** | 4,213 | 3,794 | 4,213 | 4,034 |
| **30,900** | **30,950** | 4,220 | 3,801 | 4,220 | 4,041 |
| **30,950** | **31,000** | 4,228 | 3,809 | 4,228 | 4,049 |
| **31,000** | | | | | |
| **31,000** | **31,050** | 4,235 | 3,816 | 4,235 | 4,056 |
| **31,050** | **31,100** | 4,243 | 3,824 | 4,243 | 4,064 |
| **31,100** | **31,150** | 4,250 | 3,831 | 4,250 | 4,071 |
| **31,150** | **31,200** | 4,258 | 3,839 | 4,258 | 4,079 |
| **31,200** | **31,250** | 4,265 | 3,846 | 4,265 | 4,086 |
| **31,250** | **31,300** | 4,273 | 3,854 | 4,273 | 4,094 |
| **31,300** | **31,350** | 4,280 | 3,861 | 4,280 | 4,101 |
| **31,350** | **31,400** | 4,288 | 3,869 | 4,288 | 4,109 |
| **31,400** | **31,450** | 4,295 | 3,876 | 4,295 | 4,116 |
| **31,450** | **31,500** | 4,303 | 3,884 | 4,303 | 4,124 |
| **31,500** | **31,550** | 4,310 | 3,891 | 4,310 | 4,131 |
| **31,550** | **31,600** | 4,318 | 3,899 | 4,318 | 4,139 |
| **31,600** | **31,650** | 4,325 | 3,906 | 4,325 | 4,146 |
| **31,650** | **31,700** | 4,333 | 3,914 | 4,333 | 4,154 |
| **31,700** | **31,750** | 4,340 | 3,921 | 4,340 | 4,161 |
| **31,750** | **31,800** | 4,348 | 3,929 | 4,348 | 4,169 |
| **31,800** | **31,850** | 4,355 | 3,936 | 4,355 | 4,176 |
| **31,850** | **31,900** | 4,363 | 3,944 | 4,363 | 4,184 |
| **31,900** | **31,950** | 4,370 | 3,951 | 4,370 | 4,191 |
| **31,950** | **32,000** | 4,378 | 3,959 | 4,378 | 4,199 |

* This column must also be used by a qualifying widow(er).

*(Continued on next page)*

## 2010 Tax Table–*Continued*

| If line 43 (taxable income) is— | | And you are— | | | |
|---|---|---|---|---|---|
| At least | But less than | Single | Married filing jointly * | Married filing sepa-rately | Head of a house-hold |
| | | Your tax is— | | | |
| **32,000** | | | | | |
| **32,000** | **32,050** | 4,385 | 3,966 | 4,385 | 4,206 |
| **32,050** | **32,100** | 4,393 | 3,974 | 4,393 | 4,214 |
| **32,100** | **32,150** | 4,400 | 3,981 | 4,400 | 4,221 |
| **32,150** | **32,200** | 4,408 | 3,989 | 4,408 | 4,229 |
| **32,200** | **32,250** | 4,415 | 3,996 | 4,415 | 4,236 |
| **32,250** | **32,300** | 4,423 | 4,004 | 4,423 | 4,244 |
| **32,300** | **32,350** | 4,430 | 4,011 | 4,430 | 4,251 |
| **32,350** | **32,400** | 4,438 | 4,019 | 4,438 | 4,259 |
| **32,400** | **32,450** | 4,445 | 4,026 | 4,445 | 4,266 |
| **32,450** | **32,500** | 4,453 | 4,034 | 4,453 | 4,274 |
| **32,500** | **32,550** | 4,460 | 4,041 | 4,460 | 4,281 |
| **32,550** | **32,600** | 4,468 | 4,049 | 4,468 | 4,289 |
| **32,600** | **32,650** | 4,475 | 4,056 | 4,475 | 4,296 |
| **32,650** | **32,700** | 4,483 | 4,064 | 4,483 | 4,304 |
| **32,700** | **32,750** | 4,490 | 4,071 | 4,490 | 4,311 |
| **32,750** | **32,800** | 4,498 | 4,079 | 4,498 | 4,319 |
| **32,800** | **32,850** | 4,505 | 4,086 | 4,505 | 4,326 |
| **32,850** | **32,900** | 4,513 | 4,094 | 4,513 | 4,334 |
| **32,900** | **32,950** | 4,520 | 4,101 | 4,520 | 4,341 |
| **32,950** | **33,000** | 4,528 | 4,109 | 4,528 | 4,349 |
| **33,000** | | | | | |
| **33,000** | **33,050** | 4,535 | 4,116 | 4,535 | 4,356 |
| **33,050** | **33,100** | 4,543 | 4,124 | 4,543 | 4,364 |
| **33,100** | **33,150** | 4,550 | 4,131 | 4,550 | 4,371 |
| **33,150** | **33,200** | 4,558 | 4,139 | 4,558 | 4,379 |
| **33,200** | **33,250** | 4,565 | 4,146 | 4,565 | 4,386 |
| **33,250** | **33,300** | 4,573 | 4,154 | 4,573 | 4,394 |
| **33,300** | **33,350** | 4,580 | 4,161 | 4,580 | 4,401 |
| **33,350** | **33,400** | 4,588 | 4,169 | 4,588 | 4,409 |
| **33,400** | **33,450** | 4,595 | 4,176 | 4,595 | 4,416 |
| **33,450** | **33,500** | 4,603 | 4,184 | 4,603 | 4,424 |
| **33,500** | **33,550** | 4,610 | 4,191 | 4,610 | 4,431 |
| **33,550** | **33,600** | 4,618 | 4,199 | 4,618 | 4,439 |
| **33,600** | **33,650** | 4,625 | 4,206 | 4,625 | 4,446 |
| **33,650** | **33,700** | 4,633 | 4,214 | 4,633 | 4,454 |
| **33,700** | **33,750** | 4,640 | 4,221 | 4,640 | 4,461 |
| **33,750** | **33,800** | 4,648 | 4,229 | 4,648 | 4,469 |
| **33,800** | **33,850** | 4,655 | 4,236 | 4,655 | 4,476 |
| **33,850** | **33,900** | 4,663 | 4,244 | 4,663 | 4,484 |
| **33,900** | **33,950** | 4,670 | 4,251 | 4,670 | 4,491 |
| **33,950** | **34,000** | 4,678 | 4,259 | 4,678 | 4,499 |
| **34,000** | | | | | |
| **34,000** | **34,050** | 4,688 | 4,266 | 4,688 | 4,506 |
| **34,050** | **34,100** | 4,700 | 4,274 | 4,700 | 4,514 |
| **34,100** | **34,150** | 4,713 | 4,281 | 4,713 | 4,521 |
| **34,150** | **34,200** | 4,725 | 4,289 | 4,725 | 4,529 |
| **34,200** | **34,250** | 4,738 | 4,296 | 4,738 | 4,536 |
| **34,250** | **34,300** | 4,750 | 4,304 | 4,750 | 4,544 |
| **34,300** | **34,350** | 4,763 | 4,311 | 4,763 | 4,551 |
| **34,350** | **34,400** | 4,775 | 4,319 | 4,775 | 4,559 |
| **34,400** | **34,450** | 4,788 | 4,326 | 4,788 | 4,566 |
| **34,450** | **34,500** | 4,800 | 4,334 | 4,800 | 4,574 |
| **34,500** | **34,550** | 4,813 | 4,341 | 4,813 | 4,581 |
| **34,550** | **34,600** | 4,825 | 4,349 | 4,825 | 4,589 |
| **34,600** | **34,650** | 4,838 | 4,356 | 4,838 | 4,596 |
| **34,650** | **34,700** | 4,850 | 4,364 | 4,850 | 4,604 |
| **34,700** | **34,750** | 4,863 | 4,371 | 4,863 | 4,611 |
| **34,750** | **34,800** | 4,875 | 4,379 | 4,875 | 4,619 |
| **34,800** | **34,850** | 4,888 | 4,386 | 4,888 | 4,626 |
| **34,850** | **34,900** | 4,900 | 4,394 | 4,900 | 4,634 |
| **34,900** | **34,950** | 4,913 | 4,401 | 4,913 | 4,641 |
| **34,950** | **35,000** | 4,925 | 4,409 | 4,925 | 4,649 |

| If line 43 (taxable income) is— | | And you are— | | | |
|---|---|---|---|---|---|
| At least | But less than | Single | Married filing jointly * | Married filing sepa-rately | Head of a house-hold |
| | | Your tax is— | | | |
| **35,000** | | | | | |
| **35,000** | **35,050** | 4,938 | 4,416 | 4,938 | 4,656 |
| **35,050** | **35,100** | 4,950 | 4,424 | 4,950 | 4,664 |
| **35,100** | **35,150** | 4,963 | 4,431 | 4,963 | 4,671 |
| **35,150** | **35,200** | 4,975 | 4,439 | 4,975 | 4,679 |
| **35,200** | **35,250** | 4,988 | 4,446 | 4,988 | 4,686 |
| **35,250** | **35,300** | 5,000 | 4,454 | 5,000 | 4,694 |
| **35,300** | **35,350** | 5,013 | 4,461 | 5,013 | 4,701 |
| **35,350** | **35,400** | 5,025 | 4,469 | 5,025 | 4,709 |
| **35,400** | **35,450** | 5,038 | 4,476 | 5,038 | 4,716 |
| **35,450** | **35,500** | 5,050 | 4,484 | 5,050 | 4,724 |
| **35,500** | **35,550** | 5,063 | 4,491 | 5,063 | 4,731 |
| **35,550** | **35,600** | 5,075 | 4,499 | 5,075 | 4,739 |
| **35,600** | **35,650** | 5,088 | 4,506 | 5,088 | 4,746 |
| **35,650** | **35,700** | 5,100 | 4,514 | 5,100 | 4,754 |
| **35,700** | **35,750** | 5,113 | 4,521 | 5,113 | 4,761 |
| **35,750** | **35,800** | 5,125 | 4,529 | 5,125 | 4,769 |
| **35,800** | **35,850** | 5,138 | 4,536 | 5,138 | 4,776 |
| **35,850** | **35,900** | 5,150 | 4,544 | 5,150 | 4,784 |
| **35,900** | **35,950** | 5,163 | 4,551 | 5,163 | 4,791 |
| **35,950** | **36,000** | 5,175 | 4,559 | 5,175 | 4,799 |
| **36,000** | | | | | |
| **36,000** | **36,050** | 5,188 | 4,566 | 5,188 | 4,806 |
| **36,050** | **36,100** | 5,200 | 4,574 | 5,200 | 4,814 |
| **36,100** | **36,150** | 5,213 | 4,581 | 5,213 | 4,821 |
| **36,150** | **36,200** | 5,225 | 4,589 | 5,225 | 4,829 |
| **36,200** | **36,250** | 5,238 | 4,596 | 5,238 | 4,836 |
| **36,250** | **36,300** | 5,250 | 4,604 | 5,250 | 4,844 |
| **36,300** | **36,350** | 5,263 | 4,611 | 5,263 | 4,851 |
| **36,350** | **36,400** | 5,275 | 4,619 | 5,275 | 4,859 |
| **36,400** | **36,450** | 5,288 | 4,626 | 5,288 | 4,866 |
| **36,450** | **36,500** | 5,300 | 4,634 | 5,300 | 4,874 |
| **36,500** | **36,550** | 5,313 | 4,641 | 5,313 | 4,881 |
| **36,550** | **36,600** | 5,325 | 4,649 | 5,325 | 4,889 |
| **36,600** | **36,650** | 5,338 | 4,656 | 5,338 | 4,896 |
| **36,650** | **36,700** | 5,350 | 4,664 | 5,350 | 4,904 |
| **36,700** | **36,750** | 5,363 | 4,671 | 5,363 | 4,911 |
| **36,750** | **36,800** | 5,375 | 4,679 | 5,375 | 4,919 |
| **36,800** | **36,850** | 5,388 | 4,686 | 5,388 | 4,926 |
| **36,850** | **36,900** | 5,400 | 4,694 | 5,400 | 4,934 |
| **36,900** | **36,950** | 5,413 | 4,701 | 5,413 | 4,941 |
| **36,950** | **37,000** | 5,425 | 4,709 | 5,425 | 4,949 |
| **37,000** | | | | | |
| **37,000** | **37,050** | 5,438 | 4,716 | 5,438 | 4,956 |
| **37,050** | **37,100** | 5,450 | 4,724 | 5,450 | 4,964 |
| **37,100** | **37,150** | 5,463 | 4,731 | 5,463 | 4,971 |
| **37,150** | **37,200** | 5,475 | 4,739 | 5,475 | 4,979 |
| **37,200** | **37,250** | 5,488 | 4,746 | 5,488 | 4,986 |
| **37,250** | **37,300** | 5,500 | 4,754 | 5,500 | 4,994 |
| **37,300** | **37,350** | 5,513 | 4,761 | 5,513 | 5,001 |
| **37,350** | **37,400** | 5,525 | 4,769 | 5,525 | 5,009 |
| **37,400** | **37,450** | 5,538 | 4,776 | 5,538 | 5,016 |
| **37,450** | **37,500** | 5,550 | 4,784 | 5,550 | 5,024 |
| **37,500** | **37,550** | 5,563 | 4,791 | 5,563 | 5,031 |
| **37,550** | **37,600** | 5,575 | 4,799 | 5,575 | 5,039 |
| **37,600** | **37,650** | 5,588 | 4,806 | 5,588 | 5,046 |
| **37,650** | **37,700** | 5,600 | 4,814 | 5,600 | 5,054 |
| **37,700** | **37,750** | 5,613 | 4,821 | 5,613 | 5,061 |
| **37,750** | **37,800** | 5,625 | 4,829 | 5,625 | 5,069 |
| **37,800** | **37,850** | 5,638 | 4,836 | 5,638 | 5,076 |
| **37,850** | **37,900** | 5,650 | 4,844 | 5,650 | 5,084 |
| **37,900** | **37,950** | 5,663 | 4,851 | 5,663 | 5,091 |
| **37,950** | **38,000** | 5,675 | 4,859 | 5,675 | 5,099 |

| If line 43 (taxable income) is— | | And you are— | | | |
|---|---|---|---|---|---|
| At least | But less than | Single | Married filing jointly * | Married filing sepa-rately | Head of a house-hold |
| | | Your tax is— | | | |
| **38,000** | | | | | |
| **38,000** | **38,050** | 5,688 | 4,866 | 5,688 | 5,106 |
| **38,050** | **38,100** | 5,700 | 4,874 | 5,700 | 5,114 |
| **38,100** | **38,150** | 5,713 | 4,881 | 5,713 | 5,121 |
| **38,150** | **38,200** | 5,725 | 4,889 | 5,725 | 5,129 |
| **38,200** | **38,250** | 5,738 | 4,896 | 5,738 | 5,136 |
| **38,250** | **38,300** | 5,750 | 4,904 | 5,750 | 5,144 |
| **38,300** | **38,350** | 5,763 | 4,911 | 5,763 | 5,151 |
| **38,350** | **38,400** | 5,775 | 4,919 | 5,775 | 5,159 |
| **38,400** | **38,450** | 5,788 | 4,926 | 5,788 | 5,166 |
| **38,450** | **38,500** | 5,800 | 4,934 | 5,800 | 5,174 |
| **38,500** | **38,550** | 5,813 | 4,941 | 5,813 | 5,181 |
| **38,550** | **38,600** | 5,825 | 4,949 | 5,825 | 5,189 |
| **38,600** | **38,650** | 5,838 | 4,956 | 5,838 | 5,196 |
| **38,650** | **38,700** | 5,850 | 4,964 | 5,850 | 5,204 |
| **38,700** | **38,750** | 5,863 | 4,971 | 5,863 | 5,211 |
| **38,750** | **38,800** | 5,875 | 4,979 | 5,875 | 5,219 |
| **38,800** | **38,850** | 5,888 | 4,986 | 5,888 | 5,226 |
| **38,850** | **38,900** | 5,900 | 4,994 | 5,900 | 5,234 |
| **38,900** | **38,950** | 5,913 | 5,001 | 5,913 | 5,241 |
| **38,950** | **39,000** | 5,925 | 5,009 | 5,925 | 5,249 |
| **39,000** | | | | | |
| **39,000** | **39,050** | 5,938 | 5,016 | 5,938 | 5,256 |
| **39,050** | **39,100** | 5,950 | 5,024 | 5,950 | 5,264 |
| **39,100** | **39,150** | 5,963 | 5,031 | 5,963 | 5,271 |
| **39,150** | **39,200** | 5,975 | 5,039 | 5,975 | 5,279 |
| **39,200** | **39,250** | 5,988 | 5,046 | 5,988 | 5,286 |
| **39,250** | **39,300** | 6,000 | 5,054 | 6,000 | 5,294 |
| **39,300** | **39,350** | 6,013 | 5,061 | 6,013 | 5,301 |
| **39,350** | **39,400** | 6,025 | 5,069 | 6,025 | 5,309 |
| **39,400** | **39,450** | 6,038 | 5,076 | 6,038 | 5,316 |
| **39,450** | **39,500** | 6,050 | 5,084 | 6,050 | 5,324 |
| **39,500** | **39,550** | 6,063 | 5,091 | 6,063 | 5,331 |
| **39,550** | **39,600** | 6,075 | 5,099 | 6,075 | 5,339 |
| **39,600** | **39,650** | 6,088 | 5,106 | 6,088 | 5,346 |
| **39,650** | **39,700** | 6,100 | 5,114 | 6,100 | 5,354 |
| **39,700** | **39,750** | 6,113 | 5,121 | 6,113 | 5,361 |
| **39,750** | **39,800** | 6,125 | 5,129 | 6,125 | 5,369 |
| **39,800** | **39,850** | 6,138 | 5,136 | 6,138 | 5,376 |
| **39,850** | **39,900** | 6,150 | 5,144 | 6,150 | 5,384 |
| **39,900** | **39,950** | 6,163 | 5,151 | 6,163 | 5,391 |
| **39,950** | **40,000** | 6,175 | 5,159 | 6,175 | 5,399 |
| **40,000** | | | | | |
| **40,000** | **40,050** | 6,188 | 5,166 | 6,188 | 5,406 |
| **40,050** | **40,100** | 6,200 | 5,174 | 6,200 | 5,414 |
| **40,100** | **40,150** | 6,213 | 5,181 | 6,213 | 5,421 |
| **40,150** | **40,200** | 6,225 | 5,189 | 6,225 | 5,429 |
| **40,200** | **40,250** | 6,238 | 5,196 | 6,238 | 5,436 |
| **40,250** | **40,300** | 6,250 | 5,204 | 6,250 | 5,444 |
| **40,300** | **40,350** | 6,263 | 5,211 | 6,263 | 5,451 |
| **40,350** | **40,400** | 6,275 | 5,219 | 6,275 | 5,459 |
| **40,400** | **40,450** | 6,288 | 5,226 | 6,288 | 5,466 |
| **40,450** | **40,500** | 6,300 | 5,234 | 6,300 | 5,474 |
| **40,500** | **40,550** | 6,313 | 5,241 | 6,313 | 5,481 |
| **40,550** | **40,600** | 6,325 | 5,249 | 6,325 | 5,489 |
| **40,600** | **40,650** | 6,338 | 5,256 | 6,338 | 5,496 |
| **40,650** | **40,700** | 6,350 | 5,264 | 6,350 | 5,504 |
| **40,700** | **40,750** | 6,363 | 5,271 | 6,363 | 5,511 |
| **40,750** | **40,800** | 6,375 | 5,279 | 6,375 | 5,519 |
| **40,800** | **40,850** | 6,388 | 5,286 | 6,388 | 5,526 |
| **40,850** | **40,900** | 6,400 | 5,294 | 6,400 | 5,534 |
| **40,900** | **40,950** | 6,413 | 5,301 | 6,413 | 5,541 |
| **40,950** | **41,000** | 6,425 | 5,309 | 6,425 | 5,549 |

* This column must also be used by a qualifying widow(er).

*(Continued on next page)*

**2010 Tax Table**–*Continued*

| If line 43 (taxable income) is— At least | But less than | And you are— Single | Married filing jointly * | Married filing separately | Head of a household |
|---|---|---|---|---|---|
| | | Your tax is— | | | |
| **41,000** | | | | | |
| **41,000** | **41,050** | 6,438 | 5,316 | 6,438 | 5,556 |
| **41,050** | **41,100** | 6,450 | 5,324 | 6,450 | 5,564 |
| **41,100** | **41,150** | 6,463 | 5,331 | 6,463 | 5,571 |
| **41,150** | **41,200** | 6,475 | 5,339 | 6,475 | 5,579 |
| **41,200** | **41,250** | 6,488 | 5,346 | 6,488 | 5,586 |
| **41,250** | **41,300** | 6,500 | 5,354 | 6,500 | 5,594 |
| **41,300** | **41,350** | 6,513 | 5,361 | 6,513 | 5,601 |
| **41,350** | **41,400** | 6,525 | 5,369 | 6,525 | 5,609 |
| **41,400** | **41,450** | 6,538 | 5,376 | 6,538 | 5,616 |
| **41,450** | **41,500** | 6,550 | 5,384 | 6,550 | 5,624 |
| **41,500** | **41,550** | 6,563 | 5,391 | 6,563 | 5,631 |
| **41,550** | **41,600** | 6,575 | 5,399 | 6,575 | 5,639 |
| **41,600** | **41,650** | 6,588 | 5,406 | 6,588 | 5,646 |
| **41,650** | **41,700** | 6,600 | 5,414 | 6,600 | 5,654 |
| **41,700** | **41,750** | 6,613 | 5,421 | 6,613 | 5,661 |
| **41,750** | **41,800** | 6,625 | 5,429 | 6,625 | 5,669 |
| **41,800** | **41,850** | 6,638 | 5,436 | 6,638 | 5,676 |
| **41,850** | **41,900** | 6,650 | 5,444 | 6,650 | 5,684 |
| **41,900** | **41,950** | 6,663 | 5,451 | 6,663 | 5,691 |
| **41,950** | **42,000** | 6,675 | 5,459 | 6,675 | 5,699 |
| **42,000** | | | | | |
| **42,000** | **42,050** | 6,688 | 5,466 | 6,688 | 5,706 |
| **42,050** | **42,100** | 6,700 | 5,474 | 6,700 | 5,714 |
| **42,100** | **42,150** | 6,713 | 5,481 | 6,713 | 5,721 |
| **42,150** | **42,200** | 6,725 | 5,489 | 6,725 | 5,729 |
| **42,200** | **42,250** | 6,738 | 5,496 | 6,738 | 5,736 |
| **42,250** | **42,300** | 6,750 | 5,504 | 6,750 | 5,744 |
| **42,300** | **42,350** | 6,763 | 5,511 | 6,763 | 5,751 |
| **42,350** | **42,400** | 6,775 | 5,519 | 6,775 | 5,759 |
| **42,400** | **42,450** | 6,788 | 5,526 | 6,788 | 5,766 |
| **42,450** | **42,500** | 6,800 | 5,534 | 6,800 | 5,774 |
| **42,500** | **42,550** | 6,813 | 5,541 | 6,813 | 5,781 |
| **42,550** | **42,600** | 6,825 | 5,549 | 6,825 | 5,789 |
| **42,600** | **42,650** | 6,838 | 5,556 | 6,838 | 5,796 |
| **42,650** | **42,700** | 6,850 | 5,564 | 6,850 | 5,804 |
| **42,700** | **42,750** | 6,863 | 5,571 | 6,863 | 5,811 |
| **42,750** | **42,800** | 6,875 | 5,579 | 6,875 | 5,819 |
| **42,800** | **42,850** | 6,888 | 5,586 | 6,888 | 5,826 |
| **42,850** | **42,900** | 6,900 | 5,594 | 6,900 | 5,834 |
| **42,900** | **42,950** | 6,913 | 5,601 | 6,913 | 5,841 |
| **42,950** | **43,000** | 6,925 | 5,609 | 6,925 | 5,849 |
| **43,000** | | | | | |
| **43,000** | **43,050** | 6,938 | 5,616 | 6,938 | 5,856 |
| **43,050** | **43,100** | 6,950 | 5,624 | 6,950 | 5,864 |
| **43,100** | **43,150** | 6,963 | 5,631 | 6,963 | 5,871 |
| **43,150** | **43,200** | 6,975 | 5,639 | 6,975 | 5,879 |
| **43,200** | **43,250** | 6,988 | 5,646 | 6,988 | 5,886 |
| **43,250** | **43,300** | 7,000 | 5,654 | 7,000 | 5,894 |
| **43,300** | **43,350** | 7,013 | 5,661 | 7,013 | 5,901 |
| **43,350** | **43,400** | 7,025 | 5,669 | 7,025 | 5,909 |
| **43,400** | **43,450** | 7,038 | 5,676 | 7,038 | 5,916 |
| **43,450** | **43,500** | 7,050 | 5,684 | 7,050 | 5,924 |
| **43,500** | **43,550** | 7,063 | 5,691 | 7,063 | 5,931 |
| **43,550** | **43,600** | 7,075 | 5,699 | 7,075 | 5,939 |
| **43,600** | **43,650** | 7,088 | 5,706 | 7,088 | 5,946 |
| **43,650** | **43,700** | 7,100 | 5,714 | 7,100 | 5,954 |
| **43,700** | **43,750** | 7,113 | 5,721 | 7,113 | 5,961 |
| **43,750** | **43,800** | 7,125 | 5,729 | 7,125 | 5,969 |
| **43,800** | **43,850** | 7,138 | 5,736 | 7,138 | 5,976 |
| **43,850** | **43,900** | 7,150 | 5,744 | 7,150 | 5,984 |
| **43,900** | **43,950** | 7,163 | 5,751 | 7,163 | 5,991 |
| **43,950** | **44,000** | 7,175 | 5,759 | 7,175 | 5,999 |
| **44,000** | | | | | |
| **44,000** | **44,050** | 7,188 | 5,766 | 7,188 | 6,006 |
| **44,050** | **44,100** | 7,200 | 5,774 | 7,200 | 6,014 |
| **44,100** | **44,150** | 7,213 | 5,781 | 7,213 | 6,021 |
| **44,150** | **44,200** | 7,225 | 5,789 | 7,225 | 6,029 |
| **44,200** | **44,250** | 7,238 | 5,796 | 7,238 | 6,036 |
| **44,250** | **44,300** | 7,250 | 5,804 | 7,250 | 6,044 |
| **44,300** | **44,350** | 7,263 | 5,811 | 7,263 | 6,051 |
| **44,350** | **44,400** | 7,275 | 5,819 | 7,275 | 6,059 |
| **44,400** | **44,450** | 7,288 | 5,826 | 7,288 | 6,066 |
| **44,450** | **44,500** | 7,300 | 5,834 | 7,300 | 6,074 |
| **44,500** | **44,550** | 7,313 | 5,841 | 7,313 | 6,081 |
| **44,550** | **44,600** | 7,325 | 5,849 | 7,325 | 6,089 |
| **44,600** | **44,650** | 7,338 | 5,856 | 7,338 | 6,096 |
| **44,650** | **44,700** | 7,350 | 5,864 | 7,350 | 6,104 |
| **44,700** | **44,750** | 7,363 | 5,871 | 7,363 | 6,111 |
| **44,750** | **44,800** | 7,375 | 5,879 | 7,375 | 6,119 |
| **44,800** | **44,850** | 7,388 | 5,886 | 7,388 | 6,126 |
| **44,850** | **44,900** | 7,400 | 5,894 | 7,400 | 6,134 |
| **44,900** | **44,950** | 7,413 | 5,901 | 7,413 | 6,141 |
| **44,950** | **45,000** | 7,425 | 5,909 | 7,425 | 6,149 |
| **45,000** | | | | | |
| **45,000** | **45,050** | 7,438 | 5,916 | 7,438 | 6,156 |
| **45,050** | **45,100** | 7,450 | 5,924 | 7,450 | 6,164 |
| **45,100** | **45,150** | 7,463 | 5,931 | 7,463 | 6,171 |
| **45,150** | **45,200** | 7,475 | 5,939 | 7,475 | 6,179 |
| **45,200** | **45,250** | 7,488 | 5,946 | 7,488 | 6,186 |
| **45,250** | **45,300** | 7,500 | 5,954 | 7,500 | 6,194 |
| **45,300** | **45,350** | 7,513 | 5,961 | 7,513 | 6,201 |
| **45,350** | **45,400** | 7,525 | 5,969 | 7,525 | 6,209 |
| **45,400** | **45,450** | 7,538 | 5,976 | 7,538 | 6,216 |
| **45,450** | **45,500** | 7,550 | 5,984 | 7,550 | 6,224 |
| **45,500** | **45,550** | 7,563 | 5,991 | 7,563 | 6,231 |
| **45,550** | **45,600** | 7,575 | 5,999 | 7,575 | 6,241 |
| **45,600** | **45,650** | 7,588 | 6,006 | 7,588 | 6,254 |
| **45,650** | **45,700** | 7,600 | 6,014 | 7,600 | 6,266 |
| **45,700** | **45,750** | 7,613 | 6,021 | 7,613 | 6,279 |
| **45,750** | **45,800** | 7,625 | 6,029 | 7,625 | 6,291 |
| **45,800** | **45,850** | 7,638 | 6,036 | 7,638 | 6,304 |
| **45,850** | **45,900** | 7,650 | 6,044 | 7,650 | 6,316 |
| **45,900** | **45,950** | 7,663 | 6,051 | 7,663 | 6,329 |
| **45,950** | **46,000** | 7,675 | 6,059 | 7,675 | 6,341 |
| **46,000** | | | | | |
| **46,000** | **46,050** | 7,688 | 6,066 | 7,688 | 6,354 |
| **46,050** | **46,100** | 7,700 | 6,074 | 7,700 | 6,366 |
| **46,100** | **46,150** | 7,713 | 6,081 | 7,713 | 6,379 |
| **46,150** | **46,200** | 7,725 | 6,089 | 7,725 | 6,391 |
| **46,200** | **46,250** | 7,738 | 6,096 | 7,738 | 6,404 |
| **46,250** | **46,300** | 7,750 | 6,104 | 7,750 | 6,416 |
| **46,300** | **46,350** | 7,763 | 6,111 | 7,763 | 6,429 |
| **46,350** | **46,400** | 7,775 | 6,119 | 7,775 | 6,441 |
| **46,400** | **46,450** | 7,788 | 6,126 | 7,788 | 6,454 |
| **46,450** | **46,500** | 7,800 | 6,134 | 7,800 | 6,466 |
| **46,500** | **46,550** | 7,813 | 6,141 | 7,813 | 6,479 |
| **46,550** | **46,600** | 7,825 | 6,149 | 7,825 | 6,491 |
| **46,600** | **46,650** | 7,838 | 6,156 | 7,838 | 6,504 |
| **46,650** | **46,700** | 7,850 | 6,164 | 7,850 | 6,516 |
| **46,700** | **46,750** | 7,863 | 6,171 | 7,863 | 6,529 |
| **46,750** | **46,800** | 7,875 | 6,179 | 7,875 | 6,541 |
| **46,800** | **46,850** | 7,888 | 6,186 | 7,888 | 6,554 |
| **46,850** | **46,900** | 7,900 | 6,194 | 7,900 | 6,566 |
| **46,900** | **46,950** | 7,913 | 6,201 | 7,913 | 6,579 |
| **46,950** | **47,000** | 7,925 | 6,209 | 7,925 | 6,591 |
| **47,000** | | | | | |
| **47,000** | **47,050** | 7,938 | 6,216 | 7,938 | 6,604 |
| **47,050** | **47,100** | 7,950 | 6,224 | 7,950 | 6,616 |
| **47,100** | **47,150** | 7,963 | 6,231 | 7,963 | 6,629 |
| **47,150** | **47,200** | 7,975 | 6,239 | 7,975 | 6,641 |
| **47,200** | **47,250** | 7,988 | 6,246 | 7,988 | 6,654 |
| **47,250** | **47,300** | 8,000 | 6,254 | 8,000 | 6,666 |
| **47,300** | **47,350** | 8,013 | 6,261 | 8,013 | 6,679 |
| **47,350** | **47,400** | 8,025 | 6,269 | 8,025 | 6,691 |
| **47,400** | **47,450** | 8,038 | 6,276 | 8,038 | 6,704 |
| **47,450** | **47,500** | 8,050 | 6,284 | 8,050 | 6,716 |
| **47,500** | **47,550** | 8,063 | 6,291 | 8,063 | 6,729 |
| **47,550** | **47,600** | 8,075 | 6,299 | 8,075 | 6,741 |
| **47,600** | **47,650** | 8,088 | 6,306 | 8,088 | 6,754 |
| **47,650** | **47,700** | 8,100 | 6,314 | 8,100 | 6,766 |
| **47,700** | **47,750** | 8,113 | 6,321 | 8,113 | 6,779 |
| **47,750** | **47,800** | 8,125 | 6,329 | 8,125 | 6,791 |
| **47,800** | **47,850** | 8,138 | 6,336 | 8,138 | 6,804 |
| **47,850** | **47,900** | 8,150 | 6,344 | 8,150 | 6,816 |
| **47,900** | **47,950** | 8,163 | 6,351 | 8,163 | 6,829 |
| **47,950** | **48,000** | 8,175 | 6,359 | 8,175 | 6,841 |
| **48,000** | | | | | |
| **48,000** | **48,050** | 8,188 | 6,366 | 8,188 | 6,854 |
| **48,050** | **48,100** | 8,200 | 6,374 | 8,200 | 6,866 |
| **48,100** | **48,150** | 8,213 | 6,381 | 8,213 | 6,879 |
| **48,150** | **48,200** | 8,225 | 6,389 | 8,225 | 6,891 |
| **48,200** | **48,250** | 8,238 | 6,396 | 8,238 | 6,904 |
| **48,250** | **48,300** | 8,250 | 6,404 | 8,250 | 6,916 |
| **48,300** | **48,350** | 8,263 | 6,411 | 8,263 | 6,929 |
| **48,350** | **48,400** | 8,275 | 6,419 | 8,275 | 6,941 |
| **48,400** | **48,450** | 8,288 | 6,426 | 8,288 | 6,954 |
| **48,450** | **48,500** | 8,300 | 6,434 | 8,300 | 6,966 |
| **48,500** | **48,550** | 8,313 | 6,441 | 8,313 | 6,979 |
| **48,550** | **48,600** | 8,325 | 6,449 | 8,325 | 6,991 |
| **48,600** | **48,650** | 8,338 | 6,456 | 8,338 | 7,004 |
| **48,650** | **48,700** | 8,350 | 6,464 | 8,350 | 7,016 |
| **48,700** | **48,750** | 8,363 | 6,471 | 8,363 | 7,029 |
| **48,750** | **48,800** | 8,375 | 6,479 | 8,375 | 7,041 |
| **48,800** | **48,850** | 8,388 | 6,486 | 8,388 | 7,054 |
| **48,850** | **48,900** | 8,400 | 6,494 | 8,400 | 7,066 |
| **48,900** | **48,950** | 8,413 | 6,501 | 8,413 | 7,079 |
| **48,950** | **49,000** | 8,425 | 6,509 | 8,425 | 7,091 |
| **49,000** | | | | | |
| **49,000** | **49,050** | 8,438 | 6,516 | 8,438 | 7,104 |
| **49,050** | **49,100** | 8,450 | 6,524 | 8,450 | 7,116 |
| **49,100** | **49,150** | 8,463 | 6,531 | 8,463 | 7,129 |
| **49,150** | **49,200** | 8,475 | 6,539 | 8,475 | 7,141 |
| **49,200** | **49,250** | 8,488 | 6,546 | 8,488 | 7,154 |
| **49,250** | **49,300** | 8,500 | 6,554 | 8,500 | 7,166 |
| **49,300** | **49,350** | 8,513 | 6,561 | 8,513 | 7,179 |
| **49,350** | **49,400** | 8,525 | 6,569 | 8,525 | 7,191 |
| **49,400** | **49,450** | 8,538 | 6,576 | 8,538 | 7,204 |
| **49,450** | **49,500** | 8,550 | 6,584 | 8,550 | 7,216 |
| **49,500** | **49,550** | 8,563 | 6,591 | 8,563 | 7,229 |
| **49,550** | **49,600** | 8,575 | 6,599 | 8,575 | 7,241 |
| **49,600** | **49,650** | 8,588 | 6,606 | 8,588 | 7,254 |
| **49,650** | **49,700** | 8,600 | 6,614 | 8,600 | 7,266 |
| **49,700** | **49,750** | 8,613 | 6,621 | 8,613 | 7,279 |
| **49,750** | **49,800** | 8,625 | 6,629 | 8,625 | 7,291 |
| **49,800** | **49,850** | 8,638 | 6,636 | 8,638 | 7,304 |
| **49,850** | **49,900** | 8,650 | 6,644 | 8,650 | 7,316 |
| **49,900** | **49,950** | 8,663 | 6,651 | 8,663 | 7,329 |
| **49,950** | **50,000** | 8,675 | 6,659 | 8,675 | 7,341 |

* This column must also be used by a qualifying widow(er).

*(Continued on next page)*

## 2010 Tax Table–*Continued*

| If line 43 (taxable income) is— | | And you are— | | | |
|---|---|---|---|---|---|
| At least | But less than | Single | Married filing jointly * | Married filing separately | Head of a household |
| | | Your tax is— | | | |
| **50,000** | | | | | |
| 50,000 | 50,050 | 8,688 | 6,666 | 8,688 | 7,354 |
| 50,050 | 50,100 | 8,700 | 6,674 | 8,700 | 7,366 |
| 50,100 | 50,150 | 8,713 | 6,681 | 8,713 | 7,379 |
| 50,150 | 50,200 | 8,725 | 6,689 | 8,725 | 7,391 |
| 50,200 | 50,250 | 8,738 | 6,696 | 8,738 | 7,404 |
| 50,250 | 50,300 | 8,750 | 6,704 | 8,750 | 7,416 |
| 50,300 | 50,350 | 8,763 | 6,711 | 8,763 | 7,429 |
| 50,350 | 50,400 | 8,775 | 6,719 | 8,775 | 7,441 |
| 50,400 | 50,450 | 8,788 | 6,726 | 8,788 | 7,454 |
| 50,450 | 50,500 | 8,800 | 6,734 | 8,800 | 7,466 |
| 50,500 | 50,550 | 8,813 | 6,741 | 8,813 | 7,479 |
| 50,550 | 50,600 | 8,825 | 6,749 | 8,825 | 7,491 |
| 50,600 | 50,650 | 8,838 | 6,756 | 8,838 | 7,504 |
| 50,650 | 50,700 | 8,850 | 6,764 | 8,850 | 7,516 |
| 50,700 | 50,750 | 8,863 | 6,771 | 8,863 | 7,529 |
| 50,750 | 50,800 | 8,875 | 6,779 | 8,875 | 7,541 |
| 50,800 | 50,850 | 8,888 | 6,786 | 8,888 | 7,554 |
| 50,850 | 50,900 | 8,900 | 6,794 | 8,900 | 7,566 |
| 50,900 | 50,950 | 8,913 | 6,801 | 8,913 | 7,579 |
| 50,950 | 51,000 | 8,925 | 6,809 | 8,925 | 7,591 |
| **51,000** | | | | | |
| 51,000 | 51,050 | 8,938 | 6,816 | 8,938 | 7,604 |
| 51,050 | 51,100 | 8,950 | 6,824 | 8,950 | 7,616 |
| 51,100 | 51,150 | 8,963 | 6,831 | 8,963 | 7,629 |
| 51,150 | 51,200 | 8,975 | 6,839 | 8,975 | 7,641 |
| 51,200 | 51,250 | 8,988 | 6,846 | 8,988 | 7,654 |
| 51,250 | 51,300 | 9,000 | 6,854 | 9,000 | 7,666 |
| 51,300 | 51,350 | 9,013 | 6,861 | 9,013 | 7,679 |
| 51,350 | 51,400 | 9,025 | 6,869 | 9,025 | 7,691 |
| 51,400 | 51,450 | 9,038 | 6,876 | 9,038 | 7,704 |
| 51,450 | 51,500 | 9,050 | 6,884 | 9,050 | 7,716 |
| 51,500 | 51,550 | 9,063 | 6,891 | 9,063 | 7,729 |
| 51,550 | 51,600 | 9,075 | 6,899 | 9,075 | 7,741 |
| 51,600 | 51,650 | 9,088 | 6,906 | 9,088 | 7,754 |
| 51,650 | 51,700 | 9,100 | 6,914 | 9,100 | 7,766 |
| 51,700 | 51,750 | 9,113 | 6,921 | 9,113 | 7,779 |
| 51,750 | 51,800 | 9,125 | 6,929 | 9,125 | 7,791 |
| 51,800 | 51,850 | 9,138 | 6,936 | 9,138 | 7,804 |
| 51,850 | 51,900 | 9,150 | 6,944 | 9,150 | 7,816 |
| 51,900 | 51,950 | 9,163 | 6,951 | 9,163 | 7,829 |
| 51,950 | 52,000 | 9,175 | 6,959 | 9,175 | 7,841 |
| **52,000** | | | | | |
| 52,000 | 52,050 | 9,188 | 6,966 | 9,188 | 7,854 |
| 52,050 | 52,100 | 9,200 | 6,974 | 9,200 | 7,866 |
| 52,100 | 52,150 | 9,213 | 6,981 | 9,213 | 7,879 |
| 52,150 | 52,200 | 9,225 | 6,989 | 9,225 | 7,891 |
| 52,200 | 52,250 | 9,238 | 6,996 | 9,238 | 7,904 |
| 52,250 | 52,300 | 9,250 | 7,004 | 9,250 | 7,916 |
| 52,300 | 52,350 | 9,263 | 7,011 | 9,263 | 7,929 |
| 52,350 | 52,400 | 9,275 | 7,019 | 9,275 | 7,941 |
| 52,400 | 52,450 | 9,288 | 7,026 | 9,288 | 7,954 |
| 52,450 | 52,500 | 9,300 | 7,034 | 9,300 | 7,966 |
| 52,500 | 52,550 | 9,313 | 7,041 | 9,313 | 7,979 |
| 52,550 | 52,600 | 9,325 | 7,049 | 9,325 | 7,991 |
| 52,600 | 52,650 | 9,338 | 7,056 | 9,338 | 8,004 |
| 52,650 | 52,700 | 9,350 | 7,064 | 9,350 | 8,016 |
| 52,700 | 52,750 | 9,363 | 7,071 | 9,363 | 8,029 |
| 52,750 | 52,800 | 9,375 | 7,079 | 9,375 | 8,041 |
| 52,800 | 52,850 | 9,388 | 7,086 | 9,388 | 8,054 |
| 52,850 | 52,900 | 9,400 | 7,094 | 9,400 | 8,066 |
| 52,900 | 52,950 | 9,413 | 7,101 | 9,413 | 8,079 |
| 52,950 | 53,000 | 9,425 | 7,109 | 9,425 | 8,091 |

| If line 43 (taxable income) is— | | And you are— | | | |
|---|---|---|---|---|---|
| At least | But less than | Single | Married filing jointly * | Married filing separately | Head of a household |
| | | Your tax is— | | | |
| **53,000** | | | | | |
| 53,000 | 53,050 | 9,438 | 7,116 | 9,438 | 8,104 |
| 53,050 | 53,100 | 9,450 | 7,124 | 9,450 | 8,116 |
| 53,100 | 53,150 | 9,463 | 7,131 | 9,463 | 8,129 |
| 53,150 | 53,200 | 9,475 | 7,139 | 9,475 | 8,141 |
| 53,200 | 53,250 | 9,488 | 7,146 | 9,488 | 8,154 |
| 53,250 | 53,300 | 9,500 | 7,154 | 9,500 | 8,166 |
| 53,300 | 53,350 | 9,513 | 7,161 | 9,513 | 8,179 |
| 53,350 | 53,400 | 9,525 | 7,169 | 9,525 | 8,191 |
| 53,400 | 53,450 | 9,538 | 7,176 | 9,538 | 8,204 |
| 53,450 | 53,500 | 9,550 | 7,184 | 9,550 | 8,216 |
| 53,500 | 53,550 | 9,563 | 7,191 | 9,563 | 8,229 |
| 53,550 | 53,600 | 9,575 | 7,199 | 9,575 | 8,241 |
| 53,600 | 53,650 | 9,588 | 7,206 | 9,588 | 8,254 |
| 53,650 | 53,700 | 9,600 | 7,214 | 9,600 | 8,266 |
| 53,700 | 53,750 | 9,613 | 7,221 | 9,613 | 8,279 |
| 53,750 | 53,800 | 9,625 | 7,229 | 9,625 | 8,291 |
| 53,800 | 53,850 | 9,638 | 7,236 | 9,638 | 8,304 |
| 53,850 | 53,900 | 9,650 | 7,244 | 9,650 | 8,316 |
| 53,900 | 53,950 | 9,663 | 7,251 | 9,663 | 8,329 |
| 53,950 | 54,000 | 9,675 | 7,259 | 9,675 | 8,341 |
| **54,000** | | | | | |
| 54,000 | 54,050 | 9,688 | 7,266 | 9,688 | 8,354 |
| 54,050 | 54,100 | 9,700 | 7,274 | 9,700 | 8,366 |
| 54,100 | 54,150 | 9,713 | 7,281 | 9,713 | 8,379 |
| 54,150 | 54,200 | 9,725 | 7,289 | 9,725 | 8,391 |
| 54,200 | 54,250 | 9,738 | 7,296 | 9,738 | 8,404 |
| 54,250 | 54,300 | 9,750 | 7,304 | 9,750 | 8,416 |
| 54,300 | 54,350 | 9,763 | 7,311 | 9,763 | 8,429 |
| 54,350 | 54,400 | 9,775 | 7,319 | 9,775 | 8,441 |
| 54,400 | 54,450 | 9,788 | 7,326 | 9,788 | 8,454 |
| 54,450 | 54,500 | 9,800 | 7,334 | 9,800 | 8,466 |
| 54,500 | 54,550 | 9,813 | 7,341 | 9,813 | 8,479 |
| 54,550 | 54,600 | 9,825 | 7,349 | 9,825 | 8,491 |
| 54,600 | 54,650 | 9,838 | 7,356 | 9,838 | 8,504 |
| 54,650 | 54,700 | 9,850 | 7,364 | 9,850 | 8,516 |
| 54,700 | 54,750 | 9,863 | 7,371 | 9,863 | 8,529 |
| 54,750 | 54,800 | 9,875 | 7,379 | 9,875 | 8,541 |
| 54,800 | 54,850 | 9,888 | 7,386 | 9,888 | 8,554 |
| 54,850 | 54,900 | 9,900 | 7,394 | 9,900 | 8,566 |
| 54,900 | 54,950 | 9,913 | 7,401 | 9,913 | 8,579 |
| 54,950 | 55,000 | 9,925 | 7,409 | 9,925 | 8,591 |
| **55,000** | | | | | |
| 55,000 | 55,050 | 9,938 | 7,416 | 9,938 | 8,604 |
| 55,050 | 55,100 | 9,950 | 7,424 | 9,950 | 8,616 |
| 55,100 | 55,150 | 9,963 | 7,431 | 9,963 | 8,629 |
| 55,150 | 55,200 | 9,975 | 7,439 | 9,975 | 8,641 |
| 55,200 | 55,250 | 9,988 | 7,446 | 9,988 | 8,654 |
| 55,250 | 55,300 | 10,000 | 7,454 | 10,000 | 8,666 |
| 55,300 | 55,350 | 10,013 | 7,461 | 10,013 | 8,679 |
| 55,350 | 55,400 | 10,025 | 7,469 | 10,025 | 8,691 |
| 55,400 | 55,450 | 10,038 | 7,476 | 10,038 | 8,704 |
| 55,450 | 55,500 | 10,050 | 7,484 | 10,050 | 8,716 |
| 55,500 | 55,550 | 10,063 | 7,491 | 10,063 | 8,729 |
| 55,550 | 55,600 | 10,075 | 7,499 | 10,075 | 8,741 |
| 55,600 | 55,650 | 10,088 | 7,506 | 10,088 | 8,754 |
| 55,650 | 55,700 | 10,100 | 7,514 | 10,100 | 8,766 |
| 55,700 | 55,750 | 10,113 | 7,521 | 10,113 | 8,779 |
| 55,750 | 55,800 | 10,125 | 7,529 | 10,125 | 8,791 |
| 55,800 | 55,850 | 10,138 | 7,536 | 10,138 | 8,804 |
| 55,850 | 55,900 | 10,150 | 7,544 | 10,150 | 8,816 |
| 55,900 | 55,950 | 10,163 | 7,551 | 10,163 | 8,829 |
| 55,950 | 56,000 | 10,175 | 7,559 | 10,175 | 8,841 |

| If line 43 (taxable income) is— | | And you are— | | | |
|---|---|---|---|---|---|
| At least | But less than | Single | Married filing jointly * | Married filing separately | Head of a household |
| | | Your tax is— | | | |
| **56,000** | | | | | |
| 56,000 | 56,050 | 10,188 | 7,566 | 10,188 | 8,854 |
| 56,050 | 56,100 | 10,200 | 7,574 | 10,200 | 8,866 |
| 56,100 | 56,150 | 10,213 | 7,581 | 10,213 | 8,879 |
| 56,150 | 56,200 | 10,225 | 7,589 | 10,225 | 8,891 |
| 56,200 | 56,250 | 10,238 | 7,596 | 10,238 | 8,904 |
| 56,250 | 56,300 | 10,250 | 7,604 | 10,250 | 8,916 |
| 56,300 | 56,350 | 10,263 | 7,611 | 10,263 | 8,929 |
| 56,350 | 56,400 | 10,275 | 7,619 | 10,275 | 8,941 |
| 56,400 | 56,450 | 10,288 | 7,626 | 10,288 | 8,954 |
| 56,450 | 56,500 | 10,300 | 7,634 | 10,300 | 8,966 |
| 56,500 | 56,550 | 10,313 | 7,641 | 10,313 | 8,979 |
| 56,550 | 56,600 | 10,325 | 7,649 | 10,325 | 8,991 |
| 56,600 | 56,650 | 10,338 | 7,656 | 10,338 | 9,004 |
| 56,650 | 56,700 | 10,350 | 7,664 | 10,350 | 9,016 |
| 56,700 | 56,750 | 10,363 | 7,671 | 10,363 | 9,029 |
| 56,750 | 56,800 | 10,375 | 7,679 | 10,375 | 9,041 |
| 56,800 | 56,850 | 10,388 | 7,686 | 10,388 | 9,054 |
| 56,850 | 56,900 | 10,400 | 7,694 | 10,400 | 9,066 |
| 56,900 | 56,950 | 10,413 | 7,701 | 10,413 | 9,079 |
| 56,950 | 57,000 | 10,425 | 7,709 | 10,425 | 9,091 |
| **57,000** | | | | | |
| 57,000 | 57,050 | 10,438 | 7,716 | 10,438 | 9,104 |
| 57,050 | 57,100 | 10,450 | 7,724 | 10,450 | 9,116 |
| 57,100 | 57,150 | 10,463 | 7,731 | 10,463 | 9,129 |
| 57,150 | 57,200 | 10,475 | 7,739 | 10,475 | 9,141 |
| 57,200 | 57,250 | 10,488 | 7,746 | 10,488 | 9,154 |
| 57,250 | 57,300 | 10,500 | 7,754 | 10,500 | 9,166 |
| 57,300 | 57,350 | 10,513 | 7,761 | 10,513 | 9,179 |
| 57,350 | 57,400 | 10,525 | 7,769 | 10,525 | 9,191 |
| 57,400 | 57,450 | 10,538 | 7,776 | 10,538 | 9,204 |
| 57,450 | 57,500 | 10,550 | 7,784 | 10,550 | 9,216 |
| 57,500 | 57,550 | 10,563 | 7,791 | 10,563 | 9,229 |
| 57,550 | 57,600 | 10,575 | 7,799 | 10,575 | 9,241 |
| 57,600 | 57,650 | 10,588 | 7,806 | 10,588 | 9,254 |
| 57,650 | 57,700 | 10,600 | 7,814 | 10,600 | 9,266 |
| 57,700 | 57,750 | 10,613 | 7,821 | 10,613 | 9,279 |
| 57,750 | 57,800 | 10,625 | 7,829 | 10,625 | 9,291 |
| 57,800 | 57,850 | 10,638 | 7,836 | 10,638 | 9,304 |
| 57,850 | 57,900 | 10,650 | 7,844 | 10,650 | 9,316 |
| 57,900 | 57,950 | 10,663 | 7,851 | 10,663 | 9,329 |
| 57,950 | 58,000 | 10,675 | 7,859 | 10,675 | 9,341 |
| **58,000** | | | | | |
| 58,000 | 58,050 | 10,688 | 7,866 | 10,688 | 9,354 |
| 58,050 | 58,100 | 10,700 | 7,874 | 10,700 | 9,366 |
| 58,100 | 58,150 | 10,713 | 7,881 | 10,713 | 9,379 |
| 58,150 | 58,200 | 10,725 | 7,889 | 10,725 | 9,391 |
| 58,200 | 58,250 | 10,738 | 7,896 | 10,738 | 9,404 |
| 58,250 | 58,300 | 10,750 | 7,904 | 10,750 | 9,416 |
| 58,300 | 58,350 | 10,763 | 7,911 | 10,763 | 9,429 |
| 58,350 | 58,400 | 10,775 | 7,919 | 10,775 | 9,441 |
| 58,400 | 58,450 | 10,788 | 7,926 | 10,788 | 9,454 |
| 58,450 | 58,500 | 10,800 | 7,934 | 10,800 | 9,466 |
| 58,500 | 58,550 | 10,813 | 7,941 | 10,813 | 9,479 |
| 58,550 | 58,600 | 10,825 | 7,949 | 10,825 | 9,491 |
| 58,600 | 58,650 | 10,838 | 7,956 | 10,838 | 9,504 |
| 58,650 | 58,700 | 10,850 | 7,964 | 10,850 | 9,516 |
| 58,700 | 58,750 | 10,863 | 7,971 | 10,863 | 9,529 |
| 58,750 | 58,800 | 10,875 | 7,979 | 10,875 | 9,541 |
| 58,800 | 58,850 | 10,888 | 7,986 | 10,888 | 9,554 |
| 58,850 | 58,900 | 10,900 | 7,994 | 10,900 | 9,566 |
| 58,900 | 58,950 | 10,913 | 8,001 | 10,913 | 9,579 |
| 58,950 | 59,000 | 10,925 | 8,009 | 10,925 | 9,591 |

* This column must also be used by a qualifying widow(er).

*(Continued on next page)*

**2010 Tax Table–*Continued***

| If line 43 (taxable income) is— | | And you are— | | | |
|---|---|---|---|---|---|
| At least | But less than | Single | Married filing jointly * | Married filing sepa-rately | Head of a house-hold |
| | | Your tax is— | | | |
| **59,000** | | | | | |
| 59,000 | 59,050 | 10,938 | 8,016 | 10,938 | 9,604 |
| 59,050 | 59,100 | 10,950 | 8,024 | 10,950 | 9,616 |
| 59,100 | 59,150 | 10,963 | 8,031 | 10,963 | 9,629 |
| 59,150 | 59,200 | 10,975 | 8,039 | 10,975 | 9,641 |
| 59,200 | 59,250 | 10,988 | 8,046 | 10,988 | 9,654 |
| 59,250 | 59,300 | 11,000 | 8,054 | 11,000 | 9,666 |
| 59,300 | 59,350 | 11,013 | 8,061 | 11,013 | 9,679 |
| 59,350 | 59,400 | 11,025 | 8,069 | 11,025 | 9,691 |
| 59,400 | 59,450 | 11,038 | 8,076 | 11,038 | 9,704 |
| 59,450 | 59,500 | 11,050 | 8,084 | 11,050 | 9,716 |
| 59,500 | 59,550 | 11,063 | 8,091 | 11,063 | 9,729 |
| 59,550 | 59,600 | 11,075 | 8,099 | 11,075 | 9,741 |
| 59,600 | 59,650 | 11,088 | 8,106 | 11,088 | 9,754 |
| 59,650 | 59,700 | 11,100 | 8,114 | 11,100 | 9,766 |
| 59,700 | 59,750 | 11,113 | 8,121 | 11,113 | 9,779 |
| 59,750 | 59,800 | 11,125 | 8,129 | 11,125 | 9,791 |
| 59,800 | 59,850 | 11,138 | 8,136 | 11,138 | 9,804 |
| 59,850 | 59,900 | 11,150 | 8,144 | 11,150 | 9,816 |
| 59,900 | 59,950 | 11,163 | 8,151 | 11,163 | 9,829 |
| 59,950 | 60,000 | 11,175 | 8,159 | 11,175 | 9,841 |
| **60,000** | | | | | |
| 60,000 | 60,050 | 11,188 | 8,166 | 11,188 | 9,854 |
| 60,050 | 60,100 | 11,200 | 8,174 | 11,200 | 9,866 |
| 60,100 | 60,150 | 11,213 | 8,181 | 11,213 | 9,879 |
| 60,150 | 60,200 | 11,225 | 8,189 | 11,225 | 9,891 |
| 60,200 | 60,250 | 11,238 | 8,196 | 11,238 | 9,904 |
| 60,250 | 60,300 | 11,250 | 8,204 | 11,250 | 9,916 |
| 60,300 | 60,350 | 11,263 | 8,211 | 11,263 | 9,929 |
| 60,350 | 60,400 | 11,275 | 8,219 | 11,275 | 9,941 |
| 60,400 | 60,450 | 11,288 | 8,226 | 11,288 | 9,954 |
| 60,450 | 60,500 | 11,300 | 8,234 | 11,300 | 9,966 |
| 60,500 | 60,550 | 11,313 | 8,241 | 11,313 | 9,979 |
| 60,550 | 60,600 | 11,325 | 8,249 | 11,325 | 9,991 |
| 60,600 | 60,650 | 11,338 | 8,256 | 11,338 | 10,004 |
| 60,650 | 60,700 | 11,350 | 8,264 | 11,350 | 10,016 |
| 60,700 | 60,750 | 11,363 | 8,271 | 11,363 | 10,029 |
| 60,750 | 60,800 | 11,375 | 8,279 | 11,375 | 10,041 |
| 60,800 | 60,850 | 11,388 | 8,286 | 11,388 | 10,054 |
| 60,850 | 60,900 | 11,400 | 8,294 | 11,400 | 10,066 |
| 60,900 | 60,950 | 11,413 | 8,301 | 11,413 | 10,079 |
| 60,950 | 61,000 | 11,425 | 8,309 | 11,425 | 10,091 |
| **61,000** | | | | | |
| 61,000 | 61,050 | 11,438 | 8,316 | 11,438 | 10,104 |
| 61,050 | 61,100 | 11,450 | 8,324 | 11,450 | 10,116 |
| 61,100 | 61,150 | 11,463 | 8,331 | 11,463 | 10,129 |
| 61,150 | 61,200 | 11,475 | 8,339 | 11,475 | 10,141 |
| 61,200 | 61,250 | 11,488 | 8,346 | 11,488 | 10,154 |
| 61,250 | 61,300 | 11,500 | 8,354 | 11,500 | 10,166 |
| 61,300 | 61,350 | 11,513 | 8,361 | 11,513 | 10,179 |
| 61,350 | 61,400 | 11,525 | 8,369 | 11,525 | 10,191 |
| 61,400 | 61,450 | 11,538 | 8,376 | 11,538 | 10,204 |
| 61,450 | 61,500 | 11,550 | 8,384 | 11,550 | 10,216 |
| 61,500 | 61,550 | 11,563 | 8,391 | 11,563 | 10,229 |
| 61,550 | 61,600 | 11,575 | 8,399 | 11,575 | 10,241 |
| 61,600 | 61,650 | 11,588 | 8,406 | 11,588 | 10,254 |
| 61,650 | 61,700 | 11,600 | 8,414 | 11,600 | 10,266 |
| 61,700 | 61,750 | 11,613 | 8,421 | 11,613 | 10,279 |
| 61,750 | 61,800 | 11,625 | 8,429 | 11,625 | 10,291 |
| 61,800 | 61,850 | 11,638 | 8,436 | 11,638 | 10,304 |
| 61,850 | 61,900 | 11,650 | 8,444 | 11,650 | 10,316 |
| 61,900 | 61,950 | 11,663 | 8,451 | 11,663 | 10,329 |
| 61,950 | 62,000 | 11,675 | 8,459 | 11,675 | 10,341 |
| **62,000** | | | | | |
| 62,000 | 62,050 | 11,688 | 8,466 | 11,688 | 10,354 |
| 62,050 | 62,100 | 11,700 | 8,474 | 11,700 | 10,366 |
| 62,100 | 62,150 | 11,713 | 8,481 | 11,713 | 10,379 |
| 62,150 | 62,200 | 11,725 | 8,489 | 11,725 | 10,391 |
| 62,200 | 62,250 | 11,738 | 8,496 | 11,738 | 10,404 |
| 62,250 | 62,300 | 11,750 | 8,504 | 11,750 | 10,416 |
| 62,300 | 62,350 | 11,763 | 8,511 | 11,763 | 10,429 |
| 62,350 | 62,400 | 11,775 | 8,519 | 11,775 | 10,441 |
| 62,400 | 62,450 | 11,788 | 8,526 | 11,788 | 10,454 |
| 62,450 | 62,500 | 11,800 | 8,534 | 11,800 | 10,466 |
| 62,500 | 62,550 | 11,813 | 8,541 | 11,813 | 10,479 |
| 62,550 | 62,600 | 11,825 | 8,549 | 11,825 | 10,491 |
| 62,600 | 62,650 | 11,838 | 8,556 | 11,838 | 10,504 |
| 62,650 | 62,700 | 11,850 | 8,564 | 11,850 | 10,516 |
| 62,700 | 62,750 | 11,863 | 8,571 | 11,863 | 10,529 |
| 62,750 | 62,800 | 11,875 | 8,579 | 11,875 | 10,541 |
| 62,800 | 62,850 | 11,888 | 8,586 | 11,888 | 10,554 |
| 62,850 | 62,900 | 11,900 | 8,594 | 11,900 | 10,566 |
| 62,900 | 62,950 | 11,913 | 8,601 | 11,913 | 10,579 |
| 62,950 | 63,000 | 11,925 | 8,609 | 11,925 | 10,591 |
| **63,000** | | | | | |
| 63,000 | 63,050 | 11,938 | 8,616 | 11,938 | 10,604 |
| 63,050 | 63,100 | 11,950 | 8,624 | 11,950 | 10,616 |
| 63,100 | 63,150 | 11,963 | 8,631 | 11,963 | 10,629 |
| 63,150 | 63,200 | 11,975 | 8,639 | 11,975 | 10,641 |
| 63,200 | 63,250 | 11,988 | 8,646 | 11,988 | 10,654 |
| 63,250 | 63,300 | 12,000 | 8,654 | 12,000 | 10,666 |
| 63,300 | 63,350 | 12,013 | 8,661 | 12,013 | 10,679 |
| 63,350 | 63,400 | 12,025 | 8,669 | 12,025 | 10,691 |
| 63,400 | 63,450 | 12,038 | 8,676 | 12,038 | 10,704 |
| 63,450 | 63,500 | 12,050 | 8,684 | 12,050 | 10,716 |
| 63,500 | 63,550 | 12,063 | 8,691 | 12,063 | 10,729 |
| 63,550 | 63,600 | 12,075 | 8,699 | 12,075 | 10,741 |
| 63,600 | 63,650 | 12,088 | 8,706 | 12,088 | 10,754 |
| 63,650 | 63,700 | 12,100 | 8,714 | 12,100 | 10,766 |
| 63,700 | 63,750 | 12,113 | 8,721 | 12,113 | 10,779 |
| 63,750 | 63,800 | 12,125 | 8,729 | 12,125 | 10,791 |
| 63,800 | 63,850 | 12,138 | 8,736 | 12,138 | 10,804 |
| 63,850 | 63,900 | 12,150 | 8,744 | 12,150 | 10,816 |
| 63,900 | 63,950 | 12,163 | 8,751 | 12,163 | 10,829 |
| 63,950 | 64,000 | 12,175 | 8,759 | 12,175 | 10,841 |
| **64,000** | | | | | |
| 64,000 | 64,050 | 12,188 | 8,766 | 12,188 | 10,854 |
| 64,050 | 64,100 | 12,200 | 8,774 | 12,200 | 10,866 |
| 64,100 | 64,150 | 12,213 | 8,781 | 12,213 | 10,879 |
| 64,150 | 64,200 | 12,225 | 8,789 | 12,225 | 10,891 |
| 64,200 | 64,250 | 12,238 | 8,796 | 12,238 | 10,904 |
| 64,250 | 64,300 | 12,250 | 8,804 | 12,250 | 10,916 |
| 64,300 | 64,350 | 12,263 | 8,811 | 12,263 | 10,929 |
| 64,350 | 64,400 | 12,275 | 8,819 | 12,275 | 10,941 |
| 64,400 | 64,450 | 12,288 | 8,826 | 12,288 | 10,954 |
| 64,450 | 64,500 | 12,300 | 8,834 | 12,300 | 10,966 |
| 64,500 | 64,550 | 12,313 | 8,841 | 12,313 | 10,979 |
| 64,550 | 64,600 | 12,325 | 8,849 | 12,325 | 10,991 |
| 64,600 | 64,650 | 12,338 | 8,856 | 12,338 | 11,004 |
| 64,650 | 64,700 | 12,350 | 8,864 | 12,350 | 11,016 |
| 64,700 | 64,750 | 12,363 | 8,871 | 12,363 | 11,029 |
| 64,750 | 64,800 | 12,375 | 8,879 | 12,375 | 11,041 |
| 64,800 | 64,850 | 12,388 | 8,886 | 12,388 | 11,054 |
| 64,850 | 64,900 | 12,400 | 8,894 | 12,400 | 11,066 |
| 64,900 | 64,950 | 12,413 | 8,901 | 12,413 | 11,079 |
| 64,950 | 65,000 | 12,425 | 8,909 | 12,425 | 11,091 |
| **65,000** | | | | | |
| 65,000 | 65,050 | 12,438 | 8,916 | 12,438 | 11,104 |
| 65,050 | 65,100 | 12,450 | 8,924 | 12,450 | 11,116 |
| 65,100 | 65,150 | 12,463 | 8,931 | 12,463 | 11,129 |
| 65,150 | 65,200 | 12,475 | 8,939 | 12,475 | 11,141 |
| 65,200 | 65,250 | 12,488 | 8,946 | 12,488 | 11,154 |
| 65,250 | 65,300 | 12,500 | 8,954 | 12,500 | 11,166 |
| 65,300 | 65,350 | 12,513 | 8,961 | 12,513 | 11,179 |
| 65,350 | 65,400 | 12,525 | 8,969 | 12,525 | 11,191 |
| 65,400 | 65,450 | 12,538 | 8,976 | 12,538 | 11,204 |
| 65,450 | 65,500 | 12,550 | 8,984 | 12,550 | 11,216 |
| 65,500 | 65,550 | 12,563 | 8,991 | 12,563 | 11,229 |
| 65,550 | 65,600 | 12,575 | 8,999 | 12,575 | 11,241 |
| 65,600 | 65,650 | 12,588 | 9,006 | 12,588 | 11,254 |
| 65,650 | 65,700 | 12,600 | 9,014 | 12,600 | 11,266 |
| 65,700 | 65,750 | 12,613 | 9,021 | 12,613 | 11,279 |
| 65,750 | 65,800 | 12,625 | 9,029 | 12,625 | 11,291 |
| 65,800 | 65,850 | 12,638 | 9,036 | 12,638 | 11,304 |
| 65,850 | 65,900 | 12,650 | 9,044 | 12,650 | 11,316 |
| 65,900 | 65,950 | 12,663 | 9,051 | 12,663 | 11,329 |
| 65,950 | 66,000 | 12,675 | 9,059 | 12,675 | 11,341 |
| **66,000** | | | | | |
| 66,000 | 66,050 | 12,688 | 9,066 | 12,688 | 11,354 |
| 66,050 | 66,100 | 12,700 | 9,074 | 12,700 | 11,366 |
| 66,100 | 66,150 | 12,713 | 9,081 | 12,713 | 11,379 |
| 66,150 | 66,200 | 12,725 | 9,089 | 12,725 | 11,391 |
| 66,200 | 66,250 | 12,738 | 9,096 | 12,738 | 11,404 |
| 66,250 | 66,300 | 12,750 | 9,104 | 12,750 | 11,416 |
| 66,300 | 66,350 | 12,763 | 9,111 | 12,763 | 11,429 |
| 66,350 | 66,400 | 12,775 | 9,119 | 12,775 | 11,441 |
| 66,400 | 66,450 | 12,788 | 9,126 | 12,788 | 11,454 |
| 66,450 | 66,500 | 12,800 | 9,134 | 12,800 | 11,466 |
| 66,500 | 66,550 | 12,813 | 9,141 | 12,813 | 11,479 |
| 66,550 | 66,600 | 12,825 | 9,149 | 12,825 | 11,491 |
| 66,600 | 66,650 | 12,838 | 9,156 | 12,838 | 11,504 |
| 66,650 | 66,700 | 12,850 | 9,164 | 12,850 | 11,516 |
| 66,700 | 66,750 | 12,863 | 9,171 | 12,863 | 11,529 |
| 66,750 | 66,800 | 12,875 | 9,179 | 12,875 | 11,541 |
| 66,800 | 66,850 | 12,888 | 9,186 | 12,888 | 11,554 |
| 66,850 | 66,900 | 12,900 | 9,194 | 12,900 | 11,566 |
| 66,900 | 66,950 | 12,913 | 9,201 | 12,913 | 11,579 |
| 66,950 | 67,000 | 12,925 | 9,209 | 12,925 | 11,591 |
| **67,000** | | | | | |
| 67,000 | 67,050 | 12,938 | 9,216 | 12,938 | 11,604 |
| 67,050 | 67,100 | 12,950 | 9,224 | 12,950 | 11,616 |
| 67,100 | 67,150 | 12,963 | 9,231 | 12,963 | 11,629 |
| 67,150 | 67,200 | 12,975 | 9,239 | 12,975 | 11,641 |
| 67,200 | 67,250 | 12,988 | 9,246 | 12,988 | 11,654 |
| 67,250 | 67,300 | 13,000 | 9,254 | 13,000 | 11,666 |
| 67,300 | 67,350 | 13,013 | 9,261 | 13,013 | 11,679 |
| 67,350 | 67,400 | 13,025 | 9,269 | 13,025 | 11,691 |
| 67,400 | 67,450 | 13,038 | 9,276 | 13,038 | 11,704 |
| 67,450 | 67,500 | 13,050 | 9,284 | 13,050 | 11,716 |
| 67,500 | 67,550 | 13,063 | 9,291 | 13,063 | 11,729 |
| 67,550 | 67,600 | 13,075 | 9,299 | 13,075 | 11,741 |
| 67,600 | 67,650 | 13,088 | 9,306 | 13,088 | 11,754 |
| 67,650 | 67,700 | 13,100 | 9,314 | 13,100 | 11,766 |
| 67,700 | 67,750 | 13,113 | 9,321 | 13,113 | 11,779 |
| 67,750 | 67,800 | 13,125 | 9,329 | 13,125 | 11,791 |
| 67,800 | 67,850 | 13,138 | 9,336 | 13,138 | 11,804 |
| 67,850 | 67,900 | 13,150 | 9,344 | 13,150 | 11,816 |
| 67,900 | 67,950 | 13,163 | 9,351 | 13,163 | 11,829 |
| 67,950 | 68,000 | 13,175 | 9,359 | 13,175 | 11,841 |

* This column must also be used by a qualifying widow(er).

*(Continued on next page)*

**2010 Tax Table**–*Continued*

| If line 43 (taxable income) is— | | And you are— | | | |
|---|---|---|---|---|---|
| At least | But less than | Single | Married filing jointly * | Married filing separately | Head of a household |
| | | Your tax is— | | | |
| **68,000** | | | | | |
| 68,000 | 68,050 | 13,188 | 9,369 | 13,188 | 11,854 |
| 68,050 | 68,100 | 13,200 | 9,381 | 13,200 | 11,866 |
| 68,100 | 68,150 | 13,213 | 9,394 | 13,213 | 11,879 |
| 68,150 | 68,200 | 13,225 | 9,406 | 13,225 | 11,891 |
| 68,200 | 68,250 | 13,238 | 9,419 | 13,238 | 11,904 |
| 68,250 | 68,300 | 13,250 | 9,431 | 13,250 | 11,916 |
| 68,300 | 68,350 | 13,263 | 9,444 | 13,263 | 11,929 |
| 68,350 | 68,400 | 13,275 | 9,456 | 13,275 | 11,941 |
| 68,400 | 68,450 | 13,288 | 9,469 | 13,288 | 11,954 |
| 68,450 | 68,500 | 13,300 | 9,481 | 13,300 | 11,966 |
| 68,500 | 68,550 | 13,313 | 9,494 | 13,313 | 11,979 |
| 68,550 | 68,600 | 13,325 | 9,506 | 13,325 | 11,991 |
| 68,600 | 68,650 | 13,338 | 9,519 | 13,338 | 12,004 |
| 68,650 | 68,700 | 13,350 | 9,531 | 13,351 | 12,016 |
| 68,700 | 68,750 | 13,363 | 9,544 | 13,365 | 12,029 |
| 68,750 | 68,800 | 13,375 | 9,556 | 13,379 | 12,041 |
| 68,800 | 68,850 | 13,388 | 9,569 | 13,393 | 12,054 |
| 68,850 | 68,900 | 13,400 | 9,581 | 13,407 | 12,066 |
| 68,900 | 68,950 | 13,413 | 9,594 | 13,421 | 12,079 |
| 68,950 | 69,000 | 13,425 | 9,606 | 13,435 | 12,091 |
| **69,000** | | | | | |
| 69,000 | 69,050 | 13,438 | 9,619 | 13,449 | 12,104 |
| 69,050 | 69,100 | 13,450 | 9,631 | 13,463 | 12,116 |
| 69,100 | 69,150 | 13,463 | 9,644 | 13,477 | 12,129 |
| 69,150 | 69,200 | 13,475 | 9,656 | 13,491 | 12,141 |
| 69,200 | 69,250 | 13,488 | 9,669 | 13,505 | 12,154 |
| 69,250 | 69,300 | 13,500 | 9,681 | 13,519 | 12,166 |
| 69,300 | 69,350 | 13,513 | 9,694 | 13,533 | 12,179 |
| 69,350 | 69,400 | 13,525 | 9,706 | 13,547 | 12,191 |
| 69,400 | 69,450 | 13,538 | 9,719 | 13,561 | 12,204 |
| 69,450 | 69,500 | 13,550 | 9,731 | 13,575 | 12,216 |
| 69,500 | 69,550 | 13,563 | 9,744 | 13,589 | 12,229 |
| 69,550 | 69,600 | 13,575 | 9,756 | 13,603 | 12,241 |
| 69,600 | 69,650 | 13,588 | 9,769 | 13,617 | 12,254 |
| 69,650 | 69,700 | 13,600 | 9,781 | 13,631 | 12,266 |
| 69,700 | 69,750 | 13,613 | 9,794 | 13,645 | 12,279 |
| 69,750 | 69,800 | 13,625 | 9,806 | 13,659 | 12,291 |
| 69,800 | 69,850 | 13,638 | 9,819 | 13,673 | 12,304 |
| 69,850 | 69,900 | 13,650 | 9,831 | 13,687 | 12,316 |
| 69,900 | 69,950 | 13,663 | 9,844 | 13,701 | 12,329 |
| 69,950 | 70,000 | 13,675 | 9,856 | 13,715 | 12,341 |
| **70,000** | | | | | |
| 70,000 | 70,050 | 13,688 | 9,869 | 13,729 | 12,354 |
| 70,050 | 70,100 | 13,700 | 9,881 | 13,743 | 12,366 |
| 70,100 | 70,150 | 13,713 | 9,894 | 13,757 | 12,379 |
| 70,150 | 70,200 | 13,725 | 9,906 | 13,771 | 12,391 |
| 70,200 | 70,250 | 13,738 | 9,919 | 13,785 | 12,404 |
| 70,250 | 70,300 | 13,750 | 9,931 | 13,799 | 12,416 |
| 70,300 | 70,350 | 13,763 | 9,944 | 13,813 | 12,429 |
| 70,350 | 70,400 | 13,775 | 9,956 | 13,827 | 12,441 |
| 70,400 | 70,450 | 13,788 | 9,969 | 13,841 | 12,454 |
| 70,450 | 70,500 | 13,800 | 9,981 | 13,855 | 12,466 |
| 70,500 | 70,550 | 13,813 | 9,994 | 13,869 | 12,479 |
| 70,550 | 70,600 | 13,825 | 10,006 | 13,883 | 12,491 |
| 70,600 | 70,650 | 13,838 | 10,019 | 13,897 | 12,504 |
| 70,650 | 70,700 | 13,850 | 10,031 | 13,911 | 12,516 |
| 70,700 | 70,750 | 13,863 | 10,044 | 13,925 | 12,529 |
| 70,750 | 70,800 | 13,875 | 10,056 | 13,939 | 12,541 |
| 70,800 | 70,850 | 13,888 | 10,069 | 13,953 | 12,554 |
| 70,850 | 70,900 | 13,900 | 10,081 | 13,967 | 12,566 |
| 70,900 | 70,950 | 13,913 | 10,094 | 13,981 | 12,579 |
| 70,950 | 71,000 | 13,925 | 10,106 | 13,995 | 12,591 |
| **71,000** | | | | | |
| 71,000 | 71,050 | 13,938 | 10,119 | 14,009 | 12,604 |
| 71,050 | 71,100 | 13,950 | 10,131 | 14,023 | 12,616 |
| 71,100 | 71,150 | 13,963 | 10,144 | 14,037 | 12,629 |
| 71,150 | 71,200 | 13,975 | 10,156 | 14,051 | 12,641 |
| 71,200 | 71,250 | 13,988 | 10,169 | 14,065 | 12,654 |
| 71,250 | 71,300 | 14,000 | 10,181 | 14,079 | 12,666 |
| 71,300 | 71,350 | 14,013 | 10,194 | 14,093 | 12,679 |
| 71,350 | 71,400 | 14,025 | 10,206 | 14,107 | 12,691 |
| 71,400 | 71,450 | 14,038 | 10,219 | 14,121 | 12,704 |
| 71,450 | 71,500 | 14,050 | 10,231 | 14,135 | 12,716 |
| 71,500 | 71,550 | 14,063 | 10,244 | 14,149 | 12,729 |
| 71,550 | 71,600 | 14,075 | 10,256 | 14,163 | 12,741 |
| 71,600 | 71,650 | 14,088 | 10,269 | 14,177 | 12,754 |
| 71,650 | 71,700 | 14,100 | 10,281 | 14,191 | 12,766 |
| 71,700 | 71,750 | 14,113 | 10,294 | 14,205 | 12,779 |
| 71,750 | 71,800 | 14,125 | 10,306 | 14,219 | 12,791 |
| 71,800 | 71,850 | 14,138 | 10,319 | 14,233 | 12,804 |
| 71,850 | 71,900 | 14,150 | 10,331 | 14,247 | 12,816 |
| 71,900 | 71,950 | 14,163 | 10,344 | 14,261 | 12,829 |
| 71,950 | 72,000 | 14,175 | 10,356 | 14,275 | 12,841 |
| **72,000** | | | | | |
| 72,000 | 72,050 | 14,188 | 10,369 | 14,289 | 12,854 |
| 72,050 | 72,100 | 14,200 | 10,381 | 14,303 | 12,866 |
| 72,100 | 72,150 | 14,213 | 10,394 | 14,317 | 12,879 |
| 72,150 | 72,200 | 14,225 | 10,406 | 14,331 | 12,891 |
| 72,200 | 72,250 | 14,238 | 10,419 | 14,345 | 12,904 |
| 72,250 | 72,300 | 14,250 | 10,431 | 14,359 | 12,916 |
| 72,300 | 72,350 | 14,263 | 10,444 | 14,373 | 12,929 |
| 72,350 | 72,400 | 14,275 | 10,456 | 14,387 | 12,941 |
| 72,400 | 72,450 | 14,288 | 10,469 | 14,401 | 12,954 |
| 72,450 | 72,500 | 14,300 | 10,481 | 14,415 | 12,966 |
| 72,500 | 72,550 | 14,313 | 10,494 | 14,429 | 12,979 |
| 72,550 | 72,600 | 14,325 | 10,506 | 14,443 | 12,991 |
| 72,600 | 72,650 | 14,338 | 10,519 | 14,457 | 13,004 |
| 72,650 | 72,700 | 14,350 | 10,531 | 14,471 | 13,016 |
| 72,700 | 72,750 | 14,363 | 10,544 | 14,485 | 13,029 |
| 72,750 | 72,800 | 14,375 | 10,556 | 14,499 | 13,041 |
| 72,800 | 72,850 | 14,388 | 10,569 | 14,513 | 13,054 |
| 72,850 | 72,900 | 14,400 | 10,581 | 14,527 | 13,066 |
| 72,900 | 72,950 | 14,413 | 10,594 | 14,541 | 13,079 |
| 72,950 | 73,000 | 14,425 | 10,606 | 14,555 | 13,091 |
| **73,000** | | | | | |
| 73,000 | 73,050 | 14,438 | 10,619 | 14,569 | 13,104 |
| 73,050 | 73,100 | 14,450 | 10,631 | 14,583 | 13,116 |
| 73,100 | 73,150 | 14,463 | 10,644 | 14,597 | 13,129 |
| 73,150 | 73,200 | 14,475 | 10,656 | 14,611 | 13,141 |
| 73,200 | 73,250 | 14,488 | 10,669 | 14,625 | 13,154 |
| 73,250 | 73,300 | 14,500 | 10,681 | 14,639 | 13,166 |
| 73,300 | 73,350 | 14,513 | 10,694 | 14,653 | 13,179 |
| 73,350 | 73,400 | 14,525 | 10,706 | 14,667 | 13,191 |
| 73,400 | 73,450 | 14,538 | 10,719 | 14,681 | 13,204 |
| 73,450 | 73,500 | 14,550 | 10,731 | 14,695 | 13,216 |
| 73,500 | 73,550 | 14,563 | 10,744 | 14,709 | 13,229 |
| 73,550 | 73,600 | 14,575 | 10,756 | 14,723 | 13,241 |
| 73,600 | 73,650 | 14,588 | 10,769 | 14,737 | 13,254 |
| 73,650 | 73,700 | 14,600 | 10,781 | 14,751 | 13,266 |
| 73,700 | 73,750 | 14,613 | 10,794 | 14,765 | 13,279 |
| 73,750 | 73,800 | 14,625 | 10,806 | 14,779 | 13,291 |
| 73,800 | 73,850 | 14,638 | 10,819 | 14,793 | 13,304 |
| 73,850 | 73,900 | 14,650 | 10,831 | 14,807 | 13,316 |
| 73,900 | 73,950 | 14,663 | 10,844 | 14,821 | 13,329 |
| 73,950 | 74,000 | 14,675 | 10,856 | 14,835 | 13,341 |
| **74,000** | | | | | |
| 74,000 | 74,050 | 14,688 | 10,869 | 14,849 | 13,354 |
| 74,050 | 74,100 | 14,700 | 10,881 | 14,863 | 13,366 |
| 74,100 | 74,150 | 14,713 | 10,894 | 14,877 | 13,379 |
| 74,150 | 74,200 | 14,725 | 10,906 | 14,891 | 13,391 |
| 74,200 | 74,250 | 14,738 | 10,919 | 14,905 | 13,404 |
| 74,250 | 74,300 | 14,750 | 10,931 | 14,919 | 13,416 |
| 74,300 | 74,350 | 14,763 | 10,944 | 14,933 | 13,429 |
| 74,350 | 74,400 | 14,775 | 10,956 | 14,947 | 13,441 |
| 74,400 | 74,450 | 14,788 | 10,969 | 14,961 | 13,454 |
| 74,450 | 74,500 | 14,800 | 10,981 | 14,975 | 13,466 |
| 74,500 | 74,550 | 14,813 | 10,994 | 14,989 | 13,479 |
| 74,550 | 74,600 | 14,825 | 11,006 | 15,003 | 13,491 |
| 74,600 | 74,650 | 14,838 | 11,019 | 15,017 | 13,504 |
| 74,650 | 74,700 | 14,850 | 11,031 | 15,031 | 13,516 |
| 74,700 | 74,750 | 14,863 | 11,044 | 15,045 | 13,529 |
| 74,750 | 74,800 | 14,875 | 11,056 | 15,059 | 13,541 |
| 74,800 | 74,850 | 14,888 | 11,069 | 15,073 | 13,554 |
| 74,850 | 74,900 | 14,900 | 11,081 | 15,087 | 13,566 |
| 74,900 | 74,950 | 14,913 | 11,094 | 15,101 | 13,579 |
| 74,950 | 75,000 | 14,925 | 11,106 | 15,115 | 13,591 |
| **75,000** | | | | | |
| 75,000 | 75,050 | 14,938 | 11,119 | 15,129 | 13,604 |
| 75,050 | 75,100 | 14,950 | 11,131 | 15,143 | 13,616 |
| 75,100 | 75,150 | 14,963 | 11,144 | 15,157 | 13,629 |
| 75,150 | 75,200 | 14,975 | 11,156 | 15,171 | 13,641 |
| 75,200 | 75,250 | 14,988 | 11,169 | 15,185 | 13,654 |
| 75,250 | 75,300 | 15,000 | 11,181 | 15,199 | 13,666 |
| 75,300 | 75,350 | 15,013 | 11,194 | 15,213 | 13,679 |
| 75,350 | 75,400 | 15,025 | 11,206 | 15,227 | 13,691 |
| 75,400 | 75,450 | 15,038 | 11,219 | 15,241 | 13,704 |
| 75,450 | 75,500 | 15,050 | 11,231 | 15,255 | 13,716 |
| 75,500 | 75,550 | 15,063 | 11,244 | 15,269 | 13,729 |
| 75,550 | 75,600 | 15,075 | 11,256 | 15,283 | 13,741 |
| 75,600 | 75,650 | 15,088 | 11,269 | 15,297 | 13,754 |
| 75,650 | 75,700 | 15,100 | 11,281 | 15,311 | 13,766 |
| 75,700 | 75,750 | 15,113 | 11,294 | 15,325 | 13,779 |
| 75,750 | 75,800 | 15,125 | 11,306 | 15,339 | 13,791 |
| 75,800 | 75,850 | 15,138 | 11,319 | 15,353 | 13,804 |
| 75,850 | 75,900 | 15,150 | 11,331 | 15,367 | 13,816 |
| 75,900 | 75,950 | 15,163 | 11,344 | 15,381 | 13,829 |
| 75,950 | 76,000 | 15,175 | 11,356 | 15,395 | 13,841 |
| **76,000** | | | | | |
| 76,000 | 76,050 | 15,188 | 11,369 | 15,409 | 13,854 |
| 76,050 | 76,100 | 15,200 | 11,381 | 15,423 | 13,866 |
| 76,100 | 76,150 | 15,213 | 11,394 | 15,437 | 13,879 |
| 76,150 | 76,200 | 15,225 | 11,406 | 15,451 | 13,891 |
| 76,200 | 76,250 | 15,238 | 11,419 | 15,465 | 13,904 |
| 76,250 | 76,300 | 15,250 | 11,431 | 15,479 | 13,916 |
| 76,300 | 76,350 | 15,263 | 11,444 | 15,493 | 13,929 |
| 76,350 | 76,400 | 15,275 | 11,456 | 15,507 | 13,941 |
| 76,400 | 76,450 | 15,288 | 11,469 | 15,521 | 13,954 |
| 76,450 | 76,500 | 15,300 | 11,481 | 15,535 | 13,966 |
| 76,500 | 76,550 | 15,313 | 11,494 | 15,549 | 13,979 |
| 76,550 | 76,600 | 15,325 | 11,506 | 15,563 | 13,991 |
| 76,600 | 76,650 | 15,338 | 11,519 | 15,577 | 14,004 |
| 76,650 | 76,700 | 15,350 | 11,531 | 15,591 | 14,016 |
| 76,700 | 76,750 | 15,363 | 11,544 | 15,605 | 14,029 |
| 76,750 | 76,800 | 15,375 | 11,556 | 15,619 | 14,041 |
| 76,800 | 76,850 | 15,388 | 11,569 | 15,633 | 14,054 |
| 76,850 | 76,900 | 15,400 | 11,581 | 15,647 | 14,066 |
| 76,900 | 76,950 | 15,413 | 11,594 | 15,661 | 14,079 |
| 76,950 | 77,000 | 15,425 | 11,606 | 15,675 | 14,091 |

* This column must also be used by a qualifying widow(er).

*(Continued on next page)*

## 2010 Tax Table–*Continued*

| If line 43 (taxable income) is— At least | But less than | And you are— Single | Married filing jointly * | Married filing separately | Head of a household |
|---|---|---|---|---|---|
| | | Your tax is— | | | |
| **77,000** | | | | | |
| 77,000 | 77,050 | 15,438 | 11,619 | 15,689 | 14,104 |
| 77,050 | 77,100 | 15,450 | 11,631 | 15,703 | 14,116 |
| 77,100 | 77,150 | 15,463 | 11,644 | 15,717 | 14,129 |
| 77,150 | 77,200 | 15,475 | 11,656 | 15,731 | 14,141 |
| 77,200 | 77,250 | 15,488 | 11,669 | 15,745 | 14,154 |
| 77,250 | 77,300 | 15,500 | 11,681 | 15,759 | 14,166 |
| 77,300 | 77,350 | 15,513 | 11,694 | 15,773 | 14,179 |
| 77,350 | 77,400 | 15,525 | 11,706 | 15,787 | 14,191 |
| 77,400 | 77,450 | 15,538 | 11,719 | 15,801 | 14,204 |
| 77,450 | 77,500 | 15,550 | 11,731 | 15,815 | 14,216 |
| 77,500 | 77,550 | 15,563 | 11,744 | 15,829 | 14,229 |
| 77,550 | 77,600 | 15,575 | 11,756 | 15,843 | 14,241 |
| 77,600 | 77,650 | 15,588 | 11,769 | 15,857 | 14,254 |
| 77,650 | 77,700 | 15,600 | 11,781 | 15,871 | 14,266 |
| 77,700 | 77,750 | 15,613 | 11,794 | 15,885 | 14,279 |
| 77,750 | 77,800 | 15,625 | 11,806 | 15,899 | 14,291 |
| 77,800 | 77,850 | 15,638 | 11,819 | 15,913 | 14,304 |
| 77,850 | 77,900 | 15,650 | 11,831 | 15,927 | 14,316 |
| 77,900 | 77,950 | 15,663 | 11,844 | 15,941 | 14,329 |
| 77,950 | 78,000 | 15,675 | 11,856 | 15,955 | 14,341 |
| **78,000** | | | | | |
| 78,000 | 78,050 | 15,688 | 11,869 | 15,969 | 14,354 |
| 78,050 | 78,100 | 15,700 | 11,881 | 15,983 | 14,366 |
| 78,100 | 78,150 | 15,713 | 11,894 | 15,997 | 14,379 |
| 78,150 | 78,200 | 15,725 | 11,906 | 16,011 | 14,391 |
| 78,200 | 78,250 | 15,738 | 11,919 | 16,025 | 14,404 |
| 78,250 | 78,300 | 15,750 | 11,931 | 16,039 | 14,416 |
| 78,300 | 78,350 | 15,763 | 11,944 | 16,053 | 14,429 |
| 78,350 | 78,400 | 15,775 | 11,956 | 16,067 | 14,441 |
| 78,400 | 78,450 | 15,788 | 11,969 | 16,081 | 14,454 |
| 78,450 | 78,500 | 15,800 | 11,981 | 16,095 | 14,466 |
| 78,500 | 78,550 | 15,813 | 11,994 | 16,109 | 14,479 |
| 78,550 | 78,600 | 15,825 | 12,006 | 16,123 | 14,491 |
| 78,600 | 78,650 | 15,838 | 12,019 | 16,137 | 14,504 |
| 78,650 | 78,700 | 15,850 | 12,031 | 16,151 | 14,516 |
| 78,700 | 78,750 | 15,863 | 12,044 | 16,165 | 14,529 |
| 78,750 | 78,800 | 15,875 | 12,056 | 16,179 | 14,541 |
| 78,800 | 78,850 | 15,888 | 12,069 | 16,193 | 14,554 |
| 78,850 | 78,900 | 15,900 | 12,081 | 16,207 | 14,566 |
| 78,900 | 78,950 | 15,913 | 12,094 | 16,221 | 14,579 |
| 78,950 | 79,000 | 15,925 | 12,106 | 16,235 | 14,591 |
| **79,000** | | | | | |
| 79,000 | 79,050 | 15,938 | 12,119 | 16,249 | 14,604 |
| 79,050 | 79,100 | 15,950 | 12,131 | 16,263 | 14,616 |
| 79,100 | 79,150 | 15,963 | 12,144 | 16,277 | 14,629 |
| 79,150 | 79,200 | 15,975 | 12,156 | 16,291 | 14,641 |
| 79,200 | 79,250 | 15,988 | 12,169 | 16,305 | 14,654 |
| 79,250 | 79,300 | 16,000 | 12,181 | 16,319 | 14,666 |
| 79,300 | 79,350 | 16,013 | 12,194 | 16,333 | 14,679 |
| 79,350 | 79,400 | 16,025 | 12,206 | 16,347 | 14,691 |
| 79,400 | 79,450 | 16,038 | 12,219 | 16,361 | 14,704 |
| 79,450 | 79,500 | 16,050 | 12,231 | 16,375 | 14,716 |
| 79,500 | 79,550 | 16,063 | 12,244 | 16,389 | 14,729 |
| 79,550 | 79,600 | 16,075 | 12,256 | 16,403 | 14,741 |
| 79,600 | 79,650 | 16,088 | 12,269 | 16,417 | 14,754 |
| 79,650 | 79,700 | 16,100 | 12,281 | 16,431 | 14,766 |
| 79,700 | 79,750 | 16,113 | 12,294 | 16,445 | 14,779 |
| 79,750 | 79,800 | 16,125 | 12,306 | 16,459 | 14,791 |
| 79,800 | 79,850 | 16,138 | 12,319 | 16,473 | 14,804 |
| 79,850 | 79,900 | 16,150 | 12,331 | 16,487 | 14,816 |
| 79,900 | 79,950 | 16,163 | 12,344 | 16,501 | 14,829 |
| 79,950 | 80,000 | 16,175 | 12,356 | 16,515 | 14,841 |
| **80,000** | | | | | |
| 80,000 | 80,050 | 16,188 | 12,369 | 16,529 | 14,854 |
| 80,050 | 80,100 | 16,200 | 12,381 | 16,543 | 14,866 |
| 80,100 | 80,150 | 16,213 | 12,394 | 16,557 | 14,879 |
| 80,150 | 80,200 | 16,225 | 12,406 | 16,571 | 14,891 |
| 80,200 | 80,250 | 16,238 | 12,419 | 16,585 | 14,904 |
| 80,250 | 80,300 | 16,250 | 12,431 | 16,599 | 14,916 |
| 80,300 | 80,350 | 16,263 | 12,444 | 16,613 | 14,929 |
| 80,350 | 80,400 | 16,275 | 12,456 | 16,627 | 14,941 |
| 80,400 | 80,450 | 16,288 | 12,469 | 16,641 | 14,954 |
| 80,450 | 80,500 | 16,300 | 12,481 | 16,655 | 14,966 |
| 80,500 | 80,550 | 16,313 | 12,494 | 16,669 | 14,979 |
| 80,550 | 80,600 | 16,325 | 12,506 | 16,683 | 14,991 |
| 80,600 | 80,650 | 16,338 | 12,519 | 16,697 | 15,004 |
| 80,650 | 80,700 | 16,350 | 12,531 | 16,711 | 15,016 |
| 80,700 | 80,750 | 16,363 | 12,544 | 16,725 | 15,029 |
| 80,750 | 80,800 | 16,375 | 12,556 | 16,739 | 15,041 |
| 80,800 | 80,850 | 16,388 | 12,569 | 16,753 | 15,054 |
| 80,850 | 80,900 | 16,400 | 12,581 | 16,767 | 15,066 |
| 80,900 | 80,950 | 16,413 | 12,594 | 16,781 | 15,079 |
| 80,950 | 81,000 | 16,425 | 12,606 | 16,795 | 15,091 |
| **81,000** | | | | | |
| 81,000 | 81,050 | 16,438 | 12,619 | 16,809 | 15,104 |
| 81,050 | 81,100 | 16,450 | 12,631 | 16,823 | 15,116 |
| 81,100 | 81,150 | 16,463 | 12,644 | 16,837 | 15,129 |
| 81,150 | 81,200 | 16,475 | 12,656 | 16,851 | 15,141 |
| 81,200 | 81,250 | 16,488 | 12,669 | 16,865 | 15,154 |
| 81,250 | 81,300 | 16,500 | 12,681 | 16,879 | 15,166 |
| 81,300 | 81,350 | 16,513 | 12,694 | 16,893 | 15,179 |
| 81,350 | 81,400 | 16,525 | 12,706 | 16,907 | 15,191 |
| 81,400 | 81,450 | 16,538 | 12,719 | 16,921 | 15,204 |
| 81,450 | 81,500 | 16,550 | 12,731 | 16,935 | 15,216 |
| 81,500 | 81,550 | 16,563 | 12,744 | 16,949 | 15,229 |
| 81,550 | 81,600 | 16,575 | 12,756 | 16,963 | 15,241 |
| 81,600 | 81,650 | 16,588 | 12,769 | 16,977 | 15,254 |
| 81,650 | 81,700 | 16,600 | 12,781 | 16,991 | 15,266 |
| 81,700 | 81,750 | 16,613 | 12,794 | 17,005 | 15,279 |
| 81,750 | 81,800 | 16,625 | 12,806 | 17,019 | 15,291 |
| 81,800 | 81,850 | 16,638 | 12,819 | 17,033 | 15,304 |
| 81,850 | 81,900 | 16,650 | 12,831 | 17,047 | 15,316 |
| 81,900 | 81,950 | 16,663 | 12,844 | 17,061 | 15,329 |
| 81,950 | 82,000 | 16,675 | 12,856 | 17,075 | 15,341 |
| **82,000** | | | | | |
| 82,000 | 82,050 | 16,688 | 12,869 | 17,089 | 15,354 |
| 82,050 | 82,100 | 16,700 | 12,881 | 17,103 | 15,366 |
| 82,100 | 82,150 | 16,713 | 12,894 | 17,117 | 15,379 |
| 82,150 | 82,200 | 16,725 | 12,906 | 17,131 | 15,391 |
| 82,200 | 82,250 | 16,738 | 12,919 | 17,145 | 15,404 |
| 82,250 | 82,300 | 16,750 | 12,931 | 17,159 | 15,416 |
| 82,300 | 82,350 | 16,763 | 12,944 | 17,173 | 15,429 |
| 82,350 | 82,400 | 16,775 | 12,956 | 17,187 | 15,441 |
| 82,400 | 82,450 | 16,788 | 12,969 | 17,201 | 15,454 |
| 82,450 | 82,500 | 16,802 | 12,981 | 17,215 | 15,466 |
| 82,500 | 82,550 | 16,816 | 12,994 | 17,229 | 15,479 |
| 82,550 | 82,600 | 16,830 | 13,006 | 17,243 | 15,491 |
| 82,600 | 82,650 | 16,844 | 13,019 | 17,257 | 15,504 |
| 82,650 | 82,700 | 16,858 | 13,031 | 17,271 | 15,516 |
| 82,700 | 82,750 | 16,872 | 13,044 | 17,285 | 15,529 |
| 82,750 | 82,800 | 16,886 | 13,056 | 17,299 | 15,541 |
| 82,800 | 82,850 | 16,900 | 13,069 | 17,313 | 15,554 |
| 82,850 | 82,900 | 16,914 | 13,081 | 17,327 | 15,566 |
| 82,900 | 82,950 | 16,928 | 13,094 | 17,341 | 15,579 |
| 82,950 | 83,000 | 16,942 | 13,106 | 17,355 | 15,591 |
| **83,000** | | | | | |
| 83,000 | 83,050 | 16,956 | 13,119 | 17,369 | 15,604 |
| 83,050 | 83,100 | 16,970 | 13,131 | 17,383 | 15,616 |
| 83,100 | 83,150 | 16,984 | 13,144 | 17,397 | 15,629 |
| 83,150 | 83,200 | 16,998 | 13,156 | 17,411 | 15,641 |
| 83,200 | 83,250 | 17,012 | 13,169 | 17,425 | 15,654 |
| 83,250 | 83,300 | 17,026 | 13,181 | 17,439 | 15,666 |
| 83,300 | 83,350 | 17,040 | 13,194 | 17,453 | 15,679 |
| 83,350 | 83,400 | 17,054 | 13,206 | 17,467 | 15,691 |
| 83,400 | 83,450 | 17,068 | 13,219 | 17,481 | 15,704 |
| 83,450 | 83,500 | 17,082 | 13,231 | 17,495 | 15,716 |
| 83,500 | 83,550 | 17,096 | 13,244 | 17,509 | 15,729 |
| 83,550 | 83,600 | 17,110 | 13,256 | 17,523 | 15,741 |
| 83,600 | 83,650 | 17,124 | 13,269 | 17,537 | 15,754 |
| 83,650 | 83,700 | 17,138 | 13,281 | 17,551 | 15,766 |
| 83,700 | 83,750 | 17,152 | 13,294 | 17,565 | 15,779 |
| 83,750 | 83,800 | 17,166 | 13,306 | 17,579 | 15,791 |
| 83,800 | 83,850 | 17,180 | 13,319 | 17,593 | 15,804 |
| 83,850 | 83,900 | 17,194 | 13,331 | 17,607 | 15,816 |
| 83,900 | 83,950 | 17,208 | 13,344 | 17,621 | 15,829 |
| 83,950 | 84,000 | 17,222 | 13,356 | 17,635 | 15,841 |
| **84,000** | | | | | |
| 84,000 | 84,050 | 17,236 | 13,369 | 17,649 | 15,854 |
| 84,050 | 84,100 | 17,250 | 13,381 | 17,663 | 15,866 |
| 84,100 | 84,150 | 17,264 | 13,394 | 17,677 | 15,879 |
| 84,150 | 84,200 | 17,278 | 13,406 | 17,691 | 15,891 |
| 84,200 | 84,250 | 17,292 | 13,419 | 17,705 | 15,904 |
| 84,250 | 84,300 | 17,306 | 13,431 | 17,719 | 15,916 |
| 84,300 | 84,350 | 17,320 | 13,444 | 17,733 | 15,929 |
| 84,350 | 84,400 | 17,334 | 13,456 | 17,747 | 15,941 |
| 84,400 | 84,450 | 17,348 | 13,469 | 17,761 | 15,954 |
| 84,450 | 84,500 | 17,362 | 13,481 | 17,775 | 15,966 |
| 84,500 | 84,550 | 17,376 | 13,494 | 17,789 | 15,979 |
| 84,550 | 84,600 | 17,390 | 13,506 | 17,803 | 15,991 |
| 84,600 | 84,650 | 17,404 | 13,519 | 17,817 | 16,004 |
| 84,650 | 84,700 | 17,418 | 13,531 | 17,831 | 16,016 |
| 84,700 | 84,750 | 17,432 | 13,544 | 17,845 | 16,029 |
| 84,750 | 84,800 | 17,446 | 13,556 | 17,859 | 16,041 |
| 84,800 | 84,850 | 17,460 | 13,569 | 17,873 | 16,054 |
| 84,850 | 84,900 | 17,474 | 13,581 | 17,887 | 16,066 |
| 84,900 | 84,950 | 17,488 | 13,594 | 17,901 | 16,079 |
| 84,950 | 85,000 | 17,502 | 13,606 | 17,915 | 16,091 |
| **85,000** | | | | | |
| 85,000 | 85,050 | 17,516 | 13,619 | 17,929 | 16,104 |
| 85,050 | 85,100 | 17,530 | 13,631 | 17,943 | 16,116 |
| 85,100 | 85,150 | 17,544 | 13,644 | 17,957 | 16,129 |
| 85,150 | 85,200 | 17,558 | 13,656 | 17,971 | 16,141 |
| 85,200 | 85,250 | 17,572 | 13,669 | 17,985 | 16,154 |
| 85,250 | 85,300 | 17,586 | 13,681 | 17,999 | 16,166 |
| 85,300 | 85,350 | 17,600 | 13,694 | 18,013 | 16,179 |
| 85,350 | 85,400 | 17,614 | 13,706 | 18,027 | 16,191 |
| 85,400 | 85,450 | 17,628 | 13,719 | 18,041 | 16,204 |
| 85,450 | 85,500 | 17,642 | 13,731 | 18,055 | 16,216 |
| 85,500 | 85,550 | 17,656 | 13,744 | 18,069 | 16,229 |
| 85,550 | 85,600 | 17,670 | 13,756 | 18,083 | 16,241 |
| 85,600 | 85,650 | 17,684 | 13,769 | 18,097 | 16,254 |
| 85,650 | 85,700 | 17,698 | 13,781 | 18,111 | 16,266 |
| 85,700 | 85,750 | 17,712 | 13,794 | 18,125 | 16,279 |
| 85,750 | 85,800 | 17,726 | 13,806 | 18,139 | 16,291 |
| 85,800 | 85,850 | 17,740 | 13,819 | 18,153 | 16,304 |
| 85,850 | 85,900 | 17,754 | 13,831 | 18,167 | 16,316 |
| 85,900 | 85,950 | 17,768 | 13,844 | 18,181 | 16,329 |
| 85,950 | 86,000 | 17,782 | 13,856 | 18,195 | 16,341 |

* This column must also be used by a qualifying widow(er).

*(Continued on next page)*

**2010 Tax Table**–*Continued*

| If line 43 (taxable income) is— | | And you are— | | | |
|---|---|---|---|---|---|
| At least | But less than | Single | Married filing jointly * | Married filing sepa-rately | Head of a house-hold |
| | | Your tax is— | | | |
| **86,000** | | | | | |
| **86,000** | **86,050** | 17,796 | 13,869 | 18,209 | 16,354 |
| **86,050** | **86,100** | 17,810 | 13,881 | 18,223 | 16,366 |
| **86,100** | **86,150** | 17,824 | 13,894 | 18,237 | 16,379 |
| **86,150** | **86,200** | 17,838 | 13,906 | 18,251 | 16,391 |
| **86,200** | **86,250** | 17,852 | 13,919 | 18,265 | 16,404 |
| **86,250** | **86,300** | 17,866 | 13,931 | 18,279 | 16,416 |
| **86,300** | **86,350** | 17,880 | 13,944 | 18,293 | 16,429 |
| **86,350** | **86,400** | 17,894 | 13,956 | 18,307 | 16,441 |
| **86,400** | **86,450** | 17,908 | 13,969 | 18,321 | 16,454 |
| **86,450** | **86,500** | 17,922 | 13,981 | 18,335 | 16,466 |
| **86,500** | **86,550** | 17,936 | 13,994 | 18,349 | 16,479 |
| **86,550** | **86,600** | 17,950 | 14,006 | 18,363 | 16,491 |
| **86,600** | **86,650** | 17,964 | 14,019 | 18,377 | 16,504 |
| **86,650** | **86,700** | 17,978 | 14,031 | 18,391 | 16,516 |
| **86,700** | **86,750** | 17,992 | 14,044 | 18,405 | 16,529 |
| **86,750** | **86,800** | 18,006 | 14,056 | 18,419 | 16,541 |
| **86,800** | **86,850** | 18,020 | 14,069 | 18,433 | 16,554 |
| **86,850** | **86,900** | 18,034 | 14,081 | 18,447 | 16,566 |
| **86,900** | **86,950** | 18,048 | 14,094 | 18,461 | 16,579 |
| **86,950** | **87,000** | 18,062 | 14,106 | 18,475 | 16,591 |
| **87,000** | | | | | |
| **87,000** | **87,050** | 18,076 | 14,119 | 18,489 | 16,604 |
| **87,050** | **87,100** | 18,090 | 14,131 | 18,503 | 16,616 |
| **87,100** | **87,150** | 18,104 | 14,144 | 18,517 | 16,629 |
| **87,150** | **87,200** | 18,118 | 14,156 | 18,531 | 16,641 |
| **87,200** | **87,250** | 18,132 | 14,169 | 18,545 | 16,654 |
| **87,250** | **87,300** | 18,146 | 14,181 | 18,559 | 16,666 |
| **87,300** | **87,350** | 18,160 | 14,194 | 18,573 | 16,679 |
| **87,350** | **87,400** | 18,174 | 14,206 | 18,587 | 16,691 |
| **87,400** | **87,450** | 18,188 | 14,219 | 18,601 | 16,704 |
| **87,450** | **87,500** | 18,202 | 14,231 | 18,615 | 16,716 |
| **87,500** | **87,550** | 18,216 | 14,244 | 18,629 | 16,729 |
| **87,550** | **87,600** | 18,230 | 14,256 | 18,643 | 16,741 |
| **87,600** | **87,650** | 18,244 | 14,269 | 18,657 | 16,754 |
| **87,650** | **87,700** | 18,258 | 14,281 | 18,671 | 16,766 |
| **87,700** | **87,750** | 18,272 | 14,294 | 18,685 | 16,779 |
| **87,750** | **87,800** | 18,286 | 14,306 | 18,699 | 16,791 |
| **87,800** | **87,850** | 18,300 | 14,319 | 18,713 | 16,804 |
| **87,850** | **87,900** | 18,314 | 14,331 | 18,727 | 16,816 |
| **87,900** | **87,950** | 18,328 | 14,344 | 18,741 | 16,829 |
| **87,950** | **88,000** | 18,342 | 14,356 | 18,755 | 16,841 |
| **88,000** | | | | | |
| **88,000** | **88,050** | 18,356 | 14,369 | 18,769 | 16,854 |
| **88,050** | **88,100** | 18,370 | 14,381 | 18,783 | 16,866 |
| **88,100** | **88,150** | 18,384 | 14,394 | 18,797 | 16,879 |
| **88,150** | **88,200** | 18,398 | 14,406 | 18,811 | 16,891 |
| **88,200** | **88,250** | 18,412 | 14,419 | 18,825 | 16,904 |
| **88,250** | **88,300** | 18,426 | 14,431 | 18,839 | 16,916 |
| **88,300** | **88,350** | 18,440 | 14,444 | 18,853 | 16,929 |
| **88,350** | **88,400** | 18,454 | 14,456 | 18,867 | 16,941 |
| **88,400** | **88,450** | 18,468 | 14,469 | 18,881 | 16,954 |
| **88,450** | **88,500** | 18,482 | 14,481 | 18,895 | 16,966 |
| **88,500** | **88,550** | 18,496 | 14,494 | 18,909 | 16,979 |
| **88,550** | **88,600** | 18,510 | 14,506 | 18,923 | 16,991 |
| **88,600** | **88,650** | 18,524 | 14,519 | 18,937 | 17,004 |
| **88,650** | **88,700** | 18,538 | 14,531 | 18,951 | 17,016 |
| **88,700** | **88,750** | 18,552 | 14,544 | 18,965 | 17,029 |
| **88,750** | **88,800** | 18,566 | 14,556 | 18,979 | 17,041 |
| **88,800** | **88,850** | 18,580 | 14,569 | 18,993 | 17,054 |
| **88,850** | **88,900** | 18,594 | 14,581 | 19,007 | 17,066 |
| **88,900** | **88,950** | 18,608 | 14,594 | 19,021 | 17,079 |
| **88,950** | **89,000** | 18,622 | 14,606 | 19,035 | 17,091 |

| If line 43 (taxable income) is— | | And you are— | | | |
|---|---|---|---|---|---|
| At least | But less than | Single | Married filing jointly * | Married filing sepa-rately | Head of a house-hold |
| | | Your tax is— | | | |
| **89,000** | | | | | |
| **89,000** | **89,050** | 18,636 | 14,619 | 19,049 | 17,104 |
| **89,050** | **89,100** | 18,650 | 14,631 | 19,063 | 17,116 |
| **89,100** | **89,150** | 18,664 | 14,644 | 19,077 | 17,129 |
| **89,150** | **89,200** | 18,678 | 14,656 | 19,091 | 17,141 |
| **89,200** | **89,250** | 18,692 | 14,669 | 19,105 | 17,154 |
| **89,250** | **89,300** | 18,706 | 14,681 | 19,119 | 17,166 |
| **89,300** | **89,350** | 18,720 | 14,694 | 19,133 | 17,179 |
| **89,350** | **89,400** | 18,734 | 14,706 | 19,147 | 17,191 |
| **89,400** | **89,450** | 18,748 | 14,719 | 19,161 | 17,204 |
| **89,450** | **89,500** | 18,762 | 14,731 | 19,175 | 17,216 |
| **89,500** | **89,550** | 18,776 | 14,744 | 19,189 | 17,229 |
| **89,550** | **89,600** | 18,790 | 14,756 | 19,203 | 17,241 |
| **89,600** | **89,650** | 18,804 | 14,769 | 19,217 | 17,254 |
| **89,650** | **89,700** | 18,818 | 14,781 | 19,231 | 17,266 |
| **89,700** | **89,750** | 18,832 | 14,794 | 19,245 | 17,279 |
| **89,750** | **89,800** | 18,846 | 14,806 | 19,259 | 17,291 |
| **89,800** | **89,850** | 18,860 | 14,819 | 19,273 | 17,304 |
| **89,850** | **89,900** | 18,874 | 14,831 | 19,287 | 17,316 |
| **89,900** | **89,950** | 18,888 | 14,844 | 19,301 | 17,329 |
| **89,950** | **90,000** | 18,902 | 14,856 | 19,315 | 17,341 |
| **90,000** | | | | | |
| **90,000** | **90,050** | 18,916 | 14,869 | 19,329 | 17,354 |
| **90,050** | **90,100** | 18,930 | 14,881 | 19,343 | 17,366 |
| **90,100** | **90,150** | 18,944 | 14,894 | 19,357 | 17,379 |
| **90,150** | **90,200** | 18,958 | 14,906 | 19,371 | 17,391 |
| **90,200** | **90,250** | 18,972 | 14,919 | 19,385 | 17,404 |
| **90,250** | **90,300** | 18,986 | 14,931 | 19,399 | 17,416 |
| **90,300** | **90,350** | 19,000 | 14,944 | 19,413 | 17,429 |
| **90,350** | **90,400** | 19,014 | 14,956 | 19,427 | 17,441 |
| **90,400** | **90,450** | 19,028 | 14,969 | 19,441 | 17,454 |
| **90,450** | **90,500** | 19,042 | 14,981 | 19,455 | 17,466 |
| **90,500** | **90,550** | 19,056 | 14,994 | 19,469 | 17,479 |
| **90,550** | **90,600** | 19,070 | 15,006 | 19,483 | 17,491 |
| **90,600** | **90,650** | 19,084 | 15,019 | 19,497 | 17,504 |
| **90,650** | **90,700** | 19,098 | 15,031 | 19,511 | 17,516 |
| **90,700** | **90,750** | 19,112 | 15,044 | 19,525 | 17,529 |
| **90,750** | **90,800** | 19,126 | 15,056 | 19,539 | 17,541 |
| **90,800** | **90,850** | 19,140 | 15,069 | 19,553 | 17,554 |
| **90,850** | **90,900** | 19,154 | 15,081 | 19,567 | 17,566 |
| **90,900** | **90,950** | 19,168 | 15,094 | 19,581 | 17,579 |
| **90,950** | **91,000** | 19,182 | 15,106 | 19,595 | 17,591 |
| **91,000** | | | | | |
| **91,000** | **91,050** | 19,196 | 15,119 | 19,609 | 17,604 |
| **91,050** | **91,100** | 19,210 | 15,131 | 19,623 | 17,616 |
| **91,100** | **91,150** | 19,224 | 15,144 | 19,637 | 17,629 |
| **91,150** | **91,200** | 19,238 | 15,156 | 19,651 | 17,641 |
| **91,200** | **91,250** | 19,252 | 15,169 | 19,665 | 17,654 |
| **91,250** | **91,300** | 19,266 | 15,181 | 19,679 | 17,666 |
| **91,300** | **91,350** | 19,280 | 15,194 | 19,693 | 17,679 |
| **91,350** | **91,400** | 19,294 | 15,206 | 19,707 | 17,691 |
| **91,400** | **91,450** | 19,308 | 15,219 | 19,721 | 17,704 |
| **91,450** | **91,500** | 19,322 | 15,231 | 19,735 | 17,716 |
| **91,500** | **91,550** | 19,336 | 15,244 | 19,749 | 17,729 |
| **91,550** | **91,600** | 19,350 | 15,256 | 19,763 | 17,741 |
| **91,600** | **91,650** | 19,364 | 15,269 | 19,777 | 17,754 |
| **91,650** | **91,700** | 19,378 | 15,281 | 19,791 | 17,766 |
| **91,700** | **91,750** | 19,392 | 15,294 | 19,805 | 17,779 |
| **91,750** | **91,800** | 19,406 | 15,306 | 19,819 | 17,791 |
| **91,800** | **91,850** | 19,420 | 15,319 | 19,833 | 17,804 |
| **91,850** | **91,900** | 19,434 | 15,331 | 19,847 | 17,816 |
| **91,900** | **91,950** | 19,448 | 15,344 | 19,861 | 17,829 |
| **91,950** | **92,000** | 19,462 | 15,356 | 19,875 | 17,841 |

| If line 43 (taxable income) is— | | And you are— | | | |
|---|---|---|---|---|---|
| At least | But less than | Single | Married filing jointly * | Married filing sepa-rately | Head of a house-hold |
| | | Your tax is— | | | |
| **92,000** | | | | | |
| **92,000** | **92,050** | 19,476 | 15,369 | 19,889 | 17,854 |
| **92,050** | **92,100** | 19,490 | 15,381 | 19,903 | 17,866 |
| **92,100** | **92,150** | 19,504 | 15,394 | 19,917 | 17,879 |
| **92,150** | **92,200** | 19,518 | 15,406 | 19,931 | 17,891 |
| **92,200** | **92,250** | 19,532 | 15,419 | 19,945 | 17,904 |
| **92,250** | **92,300** | 19,546 | 15,431 | 19,959 | 17,916 |
| **92,300** | **92,350** | 19,560 | 15,444 | 19,973 | 17,929 |
| **92,350** | **92,400** | 19,574 | 15,456 | 19,987 | 17,941 |
| **92,400** | **92,450** | 19,588 | 15,469 | 20,001 | 17,954 |
| **92,450** | **92,500** | 19,602 | 15,481 | 20,015 | 17,966 |
| **92,500** | **92,550** | 19,616 | 15,494 | 20,029 | 17,979 |
| **92,550** | **92,600** | 19,630 | 15,506 | 20,043 | 17,991 |
| **92,600** | **92,650** | 19,644 | 15,519 | 20,057 | 18,004 |
| **92,650** | **92,700** | 19,658 | 15,531 | 20,071 | 18,016 |
| **92,700** | **92,750** | 19,672 | 15,544 | 20,085 | 18,029 |
| **92,750** | **92,800** | 19,686 | 15,556 | 20,099 | 18,041 |
| **92,800** | **92,850** | 19,700 | 15,569 | 20,113 | 18,054 |
| **92,850** | **92,900** | 19,714 | 15,581 | 20,127 | 18,066 |
| **92,900** | **92,950** | 19,728 | 15,594 | 20,141 | 18,079 |
| **92,950** | **93,000** | 19,742 | 15,606 | 20,155 | 18,091 |
| **93,000** | | | | | |
| **93,000** | **93,050** | 19,756 | 15,619 | 20,169 | 18,104 |
| **93,050** | **93,100** | 19,770 | 15,631 | 20,183 | 18,116 |
| **93,100** | **93,150** | 19,784 | 15,644 | 20,197 | 18,129 |
| **93,150** | **93,200** | 19,798 | 15,656 | 20,211 | 18,141 |
| **93,200** | **93,250** | 19,812 | 15,669 | 20,225 | 18,154 |
| **93,250** | **93,300** | 19,826 | 15,681 | 20,239 | 18,166 |
| **93,300** | **93,350** | 19,840 | 15,694 | 20,253 | 18,179 |
| **93,350** | **93,400** | 19,854 | 15,706 | 20,267 | 18,191 |
| **93,400** | **93,450** | 19,868 | 15,719 | 20,281 | 18,204 |
| **93,450** | **93,500** | 19,882 | 15,731 | 20,295 | 18,216 |
| **93,500** | **93,550** | 19,896 | 15,744 | 20,309 | 18,229 |
| **93,550** | **93,600** | 19,910 | 15,756 | 20,323 | 18,241 |
| **93,600** | **93,650** | 19,924 | 15,769 | 20,337 | 18,254 |
| **93,650** | **93,700** | 19,938 | 15,781 | 20,351 | 18,266 |
| **93,700** | **93,750** | 19,952 | 15,794 | 20,365 | 18,279 |
| **93,750** | **93,800** | 19,966 | 15,806 | 20,379 | 18,291 |
| **93,800** | **93,850** | 19,980 | 15,819 | 20,393 | 18,304 |
| **93,850** | **93,900** | 19,994 | 15,831 | 20,407 | 18,316 |
| **93,900** | **93,950** | 20,008 | 15,844 | 20,421 | 18,329 |
| **93,950** | **94,000** | 20,022 | 15,856 | 20,435 | 18,341 |
| **94,000** | | | | | |
| **94,000** | **94,050** | 20,036 | 15,869 | 20,449 | 18,354 |
| **94,050** | **94,100** | 20,050 | 15,881 | 20,463 | 18,366 |
| **94,100** | **94,150** | 20,064 | 15,894 | 20,477 | 18,379 |
| **94,150** | **94,200** | 20,078 | 15,906 | 20,491 | 18,391 |
| **94,200** | **94,250** | 20,092 | 15,919 | 20,505 | 18,404 |
| **94,250** | **94,300** | 20,106 | 15,931 | 20,519 | 18,416 |
| **94,300** | **94,350** | 20,120 | 15,944 | 20,533 | 18,429 |
| **94,350** | **94,400** | 20,134 | 15,956 | 20,547 | 18,441 |
| **94,400** | **94,450** | 20,148 | 15,969 | 20,561 | 18,454 |
| **94,450** | **94,500** | 20,162 | 15,981 | 20,575 | 18,466 |
| **94,500** | **94,550** | 20,176 | 15,994 | 20,589 | 18,479 |
| **94,550** | **94,600** | 20,190 | 16,006 | 20,603 | 18,491 |
| **94,600** | **94,650** | 20,204 | 16,019 | 20,617 | 18,504 |
| **94,650** | **94,700** | 20,218 | 16,031 | 20,631 | 18,516 |
| **94,700** | **94,750** | 20,232 | 16,044 | 20,645 | 18,529 |
| **94,750** | **94,800** | 20,246 | 16,056 | 20,659 | 18,541 |
| **94,800** | **94,850** | 20,260 | 16,069 | 20,673 | 18,554 |
| **94,850** | **94,900** | 20,274 | 16,081 | 20,687 | 18,566 |
| **94,900** | **94,950** | 20,288 | 16,094 | 20,701 | 18,579 |
| **94,950** | **95,000** | 20,302 | 16,106 | 20,715 | 18,591 |

* This column must also be used by a qualifying widow(er).

*(Continued on next page)*

**2010 Tax Table**—*Continued*

| If line 43 (taxable income) is— | | And you are— | | | |
|---|---|---|---|---|---|
| At least | But less than | Single | Married filing jointly * | Married filing sepa-rately | Head of a house-hold |
| | | Your tax is— | | | |
| **95,000** | | | | | |
| **95,000** | **95,050** | 20,316 | 16,119 | 20,729 | 18,604 |
| **95,050** | **95,100** | 20,330 | 16,131 | 20,743 | 18,616 |
| **95,100** | **95,150** | 20,344 | 16,144 | 20,757 | 18,629 |
| **95,150** | **95,200** | 20,358 | 16,156 | 20,771 | 18,641 |
| **95,200** | **95,250** | 20,372 | 16,169 | 20,785 | 18,654 |
| **95,250** | **95,300** | 20,386 | 16,181 | 20,799 | 18,666 |
| **95,300** | **95,350** | 20,400 | 16,194 | 20,813 | 18,679 |
| **95,350** | **95,400** | 20,414 | 16,206 | 20,827 | 18,691 |
| **95,400** | **95,450** | 20,428 | 16,219 | 20,841 | 18,704 |
| **95,450** | **95,500** | 20,442 | 16,231 | 20,855 | 18,716 |
| **95,500** | **95,550** | 20,456 | 16,244 | 20,869 | 18,729 |
| **95,550** | **95,600** | 20,470 | 16,256 | 20,883 | 18,741 |
| **95,600** | **95,650** | 20,484 | 16,269 | 20,897 | 18,754 |
| **95,650** | **95,700** | 20,498 | 16,281 | 20,911 | 18,766 |
| **95,700** | **95,750** | 20,512 | 16,294 | 20,925 | 18,779 |
| **95,750** | **95,800** | 20,526 | 16,306 | 20,939 | 18,791 |
| **95,800** | **95,850** | 20,540 | 16,319 | 20,953 | 18,804 |
| **95,850** | **95,900** | 20,554 | 16,331 | 20,967 | 18,816 |
| **95,900** | **95,950** | 20,568 | 16,344 | 20,981 | 18,829 |
| **95,950** | **96,000** | 20,582 | 16,356 | 20,995 | 18,841 |
| **96,000** | | | | | |
| **96,000** | **96,050** | 20,596 | 16,369 | 21,009 | 18,854 |
| **96,050** | **96,100** | 20,610 | 16,381 | 21,023 | 18,866 |
| **96,100** | **96,150** | 20,624 | 16,394 | 21,037 | 18,879 |
| **96,150** | **96,200** | 20,638 | 16,406 | 21,051 | 18,891 |
| **96,200** | **96,250** | 20,652 | 16,419 | 21,065 | 18,904 |
| **96,250** | **96,300** | 20,666 | 16,431 | 21,079 | 18,916 |
| **96,300** | **96,350** | 20,680 | 16,444 | 21,093 | 18,929 |
| **96,350** | **96,400** | 20,694 | 16,456 | 21,107 | 18,941 |
| **96,400** | **96,450** | 20,708 | 16,469 | 21,121 | 18,954 |
| **96,450** | **96,500** | 20,722 | 16,481 | 21,135 | 18,966 |
| **96,500** | **96,550** | 20,736 | 16,494 | 21,149 | 18,979 |
| **96,550** | **96,600** | 20,750 | 16,506 | 21,163 | 18,991 |
| **96,600** | **96,650** | 20,764 | 16,519 | 21,177 | 19,004 |
| **96,650** | **96,700** | 20,778 | 16,531 | 21,191 | 19,016 |
| **96,700** | **96,750** | 20,792 | 16,544 | 21,205 | 19,029 |
| **96,750** | **96,800** | 20,806 | 16,556 | 21,219 | 19,041 |
| **96,800** | **96,850** | 20,820 | 16,569 | 21,233 | 19,054 |
| **96,850** | **96,900** | 20,834 | 16,581 | 21,247 | 19,066 |
| **96,900** | **96,950** | 20,848 | 16,594 | 21,261 | 19,079 |
| **96,950** | **97,000** | 20,862 | 16,606 | 21,275 | 19,091 |
| **97,000** | | | | | |
| **97,000** | **97,050** | 20,876 | 16,619 | 21,289 | 19,104 |
| **97,050** | **97,100** | 20,890 | 16,631 | 21,303 | 19,116 |
| **97,100** | **97,150** | 20,904 | 16,644 | 21,317 | 19,129 |
| **97,150** | **97,200** | 20,918 | 16,656 | 21,331 | 19,141 |
| **97,200** | **97,250** | 20,932 | 16,669 | 21,345 | 19,154 |
| **97,250** | **97,300** | 20,946 | 16,681 | 21,359 | 19,166 |
| **97,300** | **97,350** | 20,960 | 16,694 | 21,373 | 19,179 |
| **97,350** | **97,400** | 20,974 | 16,706 | 21,387 | 19,191 |
| **97,400** | **97,450** | 20,988 | 16,719 | 21,401 | 19,204 |
| **97,450** | **97,500** | 21,002 | 16,731 | 21,415 | 19,216 |
| **97,500** | **97,550** | 21,016 | 16,744 | 21,429 | 19,229 |
| **97,550** | **97,600** | 21,030 | 16,756 | 21,443 | 19,241 |
| **97,600** | **97,650** | 21,044 | 16,769 | 21,457 | 19,254 |
| **97,650** | **97,700** | 21,058 | 16,781 | 21,471 | 19,266 |
| **97,700** | **97,750** | 21,072 | 16,794 | 21,485 | 19,279 |
| **97,750** | **97,800** | 21,086 | 16,806 | 21,499 | 19,291 |
| **97,800** | **97,850** | 21,100 | 16,819 | 21,513 | 19,304 |
| **97,850** | **97,900** | 21,114 | 16,831 | 21,527 | 19,316 |
| **97,900** | **97,950** | 21,128 | 16,844 | 21,541 | 19,329 |
| **97,950** | **98,000** | 21,142 | 16,856 | 21,555 | 19,341 |
| **98,000** | | | | | |
| **98,000** | **98,050** | 21,156 | 16,869 | 21,569 | 19,354 |
| **98,050** | **98,100** | 21,170 | 16,881 | 21,583 | 19,366 |
| **98,100** | **98,150** | 21,184 | 16,894 | 21,597 | 19,379 |
| **98,150** | **98,200** | 21,198 | 16,906 | 21,611 | 19,391 |
| **98,200** | **98,250** | 21,212 | 16,919 | 21,625 | 19,404 |
| **98,250** | **98,300** | 21,226 | 16,931 | 21,639 | 19,416 |
| **98,300** | **98,350** | 21,240 | 16,944 | 21,653 | 19,429 |
| **98,350** | **98,400** | 21,254 | 16,956 | 21,667 | 19,441 |
| **98,400** | **98,450** | 21,268 | 16,969 | 21,681 | 19,454 |
| **98,450** | **98,500** | 21,282 | 16,981 | 21,695 | 19,466 |
| **98,500** | **98,550** | 21,296 | 16,994 | 21,709 | 19,479 |
| **98,550** | **98,600** | 21,310 | 17,006 | 21,723 | 19,491 |
| **98,600** | **98,650** | 21,324 | 17,019 | 21,737 | 19,504 |
| **98,650** | **98,700** | 21,338 | 17,031 | 21,751 | 19,516 |
| **98,700** | **98,750** | 21,352 | 17,044 | 21,765 | 19,529 |
| **98,750** | **98,800** | 21,366 | 17,056 | 21,779 | 19,541 |
| **98,800** | **98,850** | 21,380 | 17,069 | 21,793 | 19,554 |
| **98,850** | **98,900** | 21,394 | 17,081 | 21,807 | 19,566 |
| **98,900** | **98,950** | 21,408 | 17,094 | 21,821 | 19,579 |
| **98,950** | **99,000** | 21,422 | 17,106 | 21,835 | 19,591 |
| **99,000** | | | | | |
| **99,000** | **99,050** | 21,436 | 17,119 | 21,849 | 19,604 |
| **99,050** | **99,100** | 21,450 | 17,131 | 21,863 | 19,616 |
| **99,100** | **99,150** | 21,464 | 17,144 | 21,877 | 19,629 |
| **99,150** | **99,200** | 21,478 | 17,156 | 21,891 | 19,641 |
| **99,200** | **99,250** | 21,492 | 17,169 | 21,905 | 19,654 |
| **99,250** | **99,300** | 21,506 | 17,181 | 21,919 | 19,666 |
| **99,300** | **99,350** | 21,520 | 17,194 | 21,933 | 19,679 |
| **99,350** | **99,400** | 21,534 | 17,206 | 21,947 | 19,691 |
| **99,400** | **99,450** | 21,548 | 17,219 | 21,961 | 19,704 |
| **99,450** | **99,500** | 21,562 | 17,231 | 21,975 | 19,716 |
| **99,500** | **99,550** | 21,576 | 17,244 | 21,989 | 19,729 |
| **99,550** | **99,600** | 21,590 | 17,256 | 22,003 | 19,741 |
| **99,600** | **99,650** | 21,604 | 17,269 | 22,017 | 19,754 |
| **99,650** | **99,700** | 21,618 | 17,281 | 22,031 | 19,766 |
| **99,700** | **99,750** | 21,632 | 17,294 | 22,045 | 19,779 |
| **99,750** | **99,800** | 21,646 | 17,306 | 22,059 | 19,791 |
| **99,800** | **99,850** | 21,660 | 17,319 | 22,073 | 19,804 |
| **99,850** | **99,900** | 21,674 | 17,331 | 22,087 | 19,816 |
| **99,900** | **99,950** | 21,688 | 17,344 | 22,101 | 19,829 |
| **99,950** | **100,000** | 21,702 | 17,356 | 22,115 | 19,841 |

**$100,000 or over —** use the Tax Computation Worksheet on page 86

* This column must also be used by a qualifying widow(er)

## A-3 Unified Transfer Tax Rate Schedule

### 2010 Estate and Gift Tax Rates

| *If Taxable Transfer is* Over | But Not Over | Tax Liability | Of the Amount Over |
|---|---|---|---|
| $ 0 | $ 10,000 | 18% | $ 0 |
| 10,000 | 20,000 | $ 1,800 + 20% | 10,000 |
| 20,000 | 40,000 | 3,800 + 22% | 20,000 |
| 40,000 | 60,000 | 8,200 + 24% | 40,000 |
| 60,000 | 80,000 | 13,000 + 26% | 60,000 |
| 80,000 | 100,000 | 18,200 + 28% | 80,000 |
| 100,000 | 150,000 | 23,800 + 30% | 100,000 |
| 150,000 | 250,000 | 38,800 + 32% | 150,000 |
| 250,000 | 500,000 | 70,800 + 34% | 250,000 |
| 500,000 | 750,000 | 155,800 + 35% | 500,000 |

## A-4 Estate and Gift Tax Valuation Tables

**Section 1**

**Table S (4.4)**
**Single Life Factors Based on Life Table 2000CM**
**Interest at 4.4 Percent**

| Age | Annuity | Life Estate | Remainder | Age | Annuity | Life Estate | Remainder |
|---|---|---|---|---|---|---|---|
| 0 | 21.4812 | 0.94517 | 0.05483 | 55 | 14.3029 | 0.62933 | 0.37067 |
| 1 | 21.5798 | 0.94951 | 0.05049 | 56 | 14.0285 | 0.61725 | 0.38275 |
| 2 | 21.5405 | 0.94778 | 0.05222 | 57 | 13.7495 | 0.60498 | 0.39502 |
| 3 | 21.4955 | 0.94580 | 0.05420 | 58 | 13.4666 | 0.59253 | 0.40747 |
| 4 | 21.4469 | 0.94366 | 0.05634 | 59 | 13.1793 | 0.57989 | 0.42011 |
| 5 | 21.3952 | 0.94139 | 0.05861 | 60 | 12.8873 | 0.56704 | 0.43296 |
| 6 | 21.3405 | 0.93898 | 0.06102 | 61 | 12.5909 | 0.55400 | 0.44600 |
| 7 | 21.2835 | 0.93647 | 0.06353 | 62 | 12.2910 | 0.54080 | 0.45920 |
| 8 | 21.2234 | 0.93383 | 0.06617 | 63 | 11.9879 | 0.52747 | 0.47253 |
| 9 | 21.1603 | 0.93105 | 0.06895 | 64 | 11.6816 | 0.51399 | 0.48601 |
| 10 | 21.0942 | 0.92815 | 0.07185 | 65 | 11.3721 | 0.50037 | 0.49963 |
| 11 | 21.0250 | 0.92510 | 0.07490 | 66 | 11.0563 | 0.48648 | 0.51352 |
| 12 | 20.9527 | 0.92192 | 0.07808 | 67 | 10.7352 | 0.47235 | 0.52765 |
| 13 | 20.8780 | 0.91863 | 0.08137 | 68 | 10.4101 | 0.45804 | 0.54196 |
| 14 | 20.8018 | 0.91528 | 0.08472 | 69 | 10.0818 | 0.44360 | 0.55640 |
| 15 | 20.7246 | 0.91188 | 0.08812 | 70 | 9.7511 | 0.42905 | 0.57095 |
| 16 | 20.6468 | 0.90846 | 0.09154 | 71 | 9.4179 | 0.41439 | 0.58561 |
| 17 | 20.5678 | 0.90498 | 0.09502 | 72 | 9.0829 | 0.39965 | 0.60035 |
| 18 | 20.4874 | 0.90145 | 0.09855 | 73 | 8.7474 | 0.38488 | 0.61512 |
| 19 | 20.4051 | 0.89783 | 0.10217 | 74 | 8.4129 | 0.37017 | 0.62983 |
| 20 | 20.3200 | 0.89408 | 0.10592 | 75 | 8.0808 | 0.35556 | 0.64444 |
| 21 | 20.2324 | 0.89023 | 0.10977 | 76 | 7.7521 | 0.34109 | 0.65891 |
| 22 | 20.1419 | 0.88624 | 0.11376 | 77 | 7.4270 | 0.32679 | 0.67321 |
| 23 | 20.0480 | 0.88211 | 0.11789 | 78 | 7.1061 | 0.31267 | 0.68733 |
| 24 | 19.9498 | 0.87779 | 0.12221 | 79 | 6.7900 | 0.29876 | 0.70124 |
| 25 | 19.8469 | 0.87326 | 0.12674 | 80 | 6.4795 | 0.28510 | 0.71490 |
| 26 | 19.7389 | 0.86851 | 0.13149 | 81 | 6.1751 | 0.27170 | 0.72830 |
| 27 | 19.6256 | 0.86353 | 0.13647 | 82 | 5.8772 | 0.25860 | 0.74140 |
| 28 | 19.5071 | 0.85831 | 0.14169 | 83 | 5.5866 | 0.24581 | 0.75419 |
| 29 | 19.3837 | 0.85288 | 0.14712 | 84 | 5.3036 | 0.23336 | 0.76664 |
| 30 | 19.2556 | 0.84725 | 0.15275 | 85 | 5.0288 | 0.22127 | 0.77873 |
| 31 | 19.1225 | 0.84139 | 0.15861 | 86 | 4.7626 | 0.20956 | 0.79044 |
| 32 | 18.9844 | 0.83532 | 0.16468 | 87 | 4.5055 | 0.19824 | 0.80176 |
| 33 | 18.8412 | 0.82901 | 0.17099 | 88 | 4.2573 | 0.18732 | 0.81268 |
| 34 | 18.6932 | 0.82250 | 0.17750 | 89 | 4.0188 | 0.17683 | 0.82317 |
| 35 | 18.5402 | 0.81577 | 0.18423 | 90 | 3.7900 | 0.16676 | 0.83324 |
| 36 | 18.3820 | 0.80881 | 0.19119 | 91 | 3.5710 | 0.15712 | 0.84288 |
| 37 | 18.2186 | 0.80162 | 0.19838 | 92 | 3.3619 | 0.14792 | 0.85208 |
| 38 | 18.0496 | 0.79418 | 0.20582 | 93 | 3.1630 | 0.13917 | 0.86083 |
| 39 | 17.8755 | 0.78652 | 0.21348 | 94 | 2.9739 | 0.13085 | 0.86915 |
| 40 | 17.6962 | 0.77863 | 0.22137 | 95 | 2.7943 | 0.12295 | 0.87705 |
| 41 | 17.5114 | 0.77050 | 0.22950 | 96 | 2.6249 | 0.11549 | 0.88451 |
| 42 | 17.3214 | 0.76214 | 0.23786 | 97 | 2.4650 | 0.10846 | 0.89154 |
| 43 | 17.1253 | 0.75352 | 0.24648 | 98 | 2.3142 | 0.10182 | 0.89818 |
| 44 | 16.9238 | 0.74465 | 0.25535 | 99 | 2.1717 | 0.09556 | 0.90444 |
| 45 | 16.7166 | 0.73553 | 0.26447 | 100 | 2.0391 | 0.08972 | 0.91028 |
| 46 | 16.5033 | 0.72615 | 0.27385 | 101 | 1.9130 | 0.08417 | 0.91583 |
| 47 | 16.2844 | 0.71651 | 0.28349 | 102 | 1.7964 | 0.07904 | 0.92096 |
| 48 | 16.0595 | 0.70662 | 0.29338 | 103 | 1.6806 | 0.07395 | 0.92605 |
| 49 | 15.8285 | 0.69645 | 0.30355 | 104 | 1.5740 | 0.06926 | 0.93074 |
| 50 | 15.5907 | 0.68599 | 0.31401 | 105 | 1.4689 | 0.06463 | 0.93537 |
| 51 | 15.3462 | 0.67523 | 0.32477 | 106 | 1.3375 | 0.05885 | 0.94115 |
| 52 | 15.0949 | 0.66418 | 0.33582 | 107 | 1.1884 | 0.05229 | 0.94771 |
| 53 | 14.8370 | 0.65283 | 0.34717 | 108 | 0.9478 | 0.04170 | 0.95830 |
| 54 | 14.5728 | 0.64120 | 0.35880 | 109 | 0.4789 | 0.02107 | 0.97893 |

Section 1

## Table S (4.6)
## Single Life Factors Based on Life Table 2000CM
## Interest at 4.6 Percent

| Age | Annuity | Life Estate | Remainder | Age | Annuity | Life Estate | Remainder |
|---|---|---|---|---|---|---|---|
| 0 | 20.6611 | 0.95041 | 0.04959 | 55 | 13.9887 | 0.64348 | 0.35652 |
| 1 | 20.7593 | 0.95493 | 0.04507 | 56 | 13.7264 | 0.63141 | 0.36859 |
| 2 | 20.7249 | 0.95335 | 0.04665 | 57 | 13.4595 | 0.61914 | 0.38086 |
| 3 | 20.6853 | 0.95152 | 0.04848 | 58 | 13.1885 | 0.60667 | 0.39333 |
| 4 | 20.6421 | 0.94954 | 0.05046 | 59 | 12.9130 | 0.59400 | 0.40600 |
| 5 | 20.5961 | 0.94742 | 0.05258 | 60 | 12.6327 | 0.58110 | 0.41890 |
| 6 | 20.5474 | 0.94518 | 0.05482 | 61 | 12.3478 | 0.56800 | 0.43200 |
| 7 | 20.4964 | 0.94283 | 0.05717 | 62 | 12.0593 | 0.55473 | 0.44527 |
| 8 | 20.4426 | 0.94036 | 0.05964 | 63 | 11.7673 | 0.54130 | 0.45870 |
| 9 | 20.3859 | 0.93775 | 0.06225 | 64 | 11.4720 | 0.52771 | 0.47229 |
| 10 | 20.3264 | 0.93501 | 0.06499 | 65 | 11.1733 | 0.51397 | 0.48603 |
| 11 | 20.2639 | 0.93214 | 0.06786 | 66 | 10.8681 | 0.49993 | 0.50007 |
| 12 | 20.1986 | 0.92913 | 0.07087 | 67 | 10.5574 | 0.48564 | 0.51436 |
| 13 | 20.1310 | 0.92603 | 0.07397 | 68 | 10.2425 | 0.47115 | 0.52885 |
| 14 | 20.0620 | 0.92285 | 0.07715 | 69 | 9.9241 | 0.45651 | 0.54349 |
| 15 | 19.9921 | 0.91964 | 0.08036 | 70 | 9.6030 | 0.44174 | 0.55826 |
| 16 | 19.9217 | 0.91640 | 0.08360 | 71 | 9.2792 | 0.42684 | 0.57316 |
| 17 | 19.8502 | 0.91311 | 0.08689 | 72 | 8.9533 | 0.41185 | 0.58815 |
| 18 | 19.7775 | 0.90976 | 0.09024 | 73 | 8.6265 | 0.39682 | 0.60318 |
| 19 | 19.7030 | 0.90634 | 0.09366 | 74 | 8.3004 | 0.38182 | 0.61818 |
| 20 | 19.6258 | 0.90279 | 0.09721 | 75 | 7.9763 | 0.36691 | 0.63309 |
| 21 | 19.5463 | 0.89913 | 0.10087 | 76 | 7.6553 | 0.35214 | 0.64786 |
| 22 | 19.4640 | 0.89535 | 0.10465 | 77 | 7.3375 | 0.33752 | 0.66248 |
| 23 | 19.3786 | 0.89141 | 0.10859 | 78 | 7.0235 | 0.32308 | 0.67692 |
| 24 | 19.2891 | 0.88730 | 0.11270 | 79 | 6.7139 | 0.30884 | 0.69116 |
| 25 | 19.1950 | 0.88297 | 0.11703 | 80 | 6.4096 | 0.29484 | 0.70516 |
| 26 | 19.0961 | 0.87842 | 0.12158 | 81 | 6.1109 | 0.28110 | 0.71890 |
| 27 | 18.9922 | 0.87364 | 0.12636 | 82 | 5.8185 | 0.26765 | 0.73235 |
| 28 | 18.8833 | 0.86863 | 0.13137 | 83 | 5.5330 | 0.25452 | 0.74548 |
| 29 | 18.7696 | 0.86340 | 0.13660 | 84 | 5.2548 | 0.24172 | 0.75828 |
| 30 | 18.6514 | 0.85797 | 0.14203 | 85 | 4.9844 | 0.22928 | 0.77072 |
| 31 | 18.5285 | 0.85231 | 0.14769 | 86 | 4.7223 | 0.21722 | 0.78278 |
| 32 | 18.4007 | 0.84643 | 0.15357 | 87 | 4.4689 | 0.20557 | 0.79443 |
| 33 | 18.2679 | 0.84032 | 0.15968 | 88 | 4.2242 | 0.19431 | 0.80569 |
| 34 | 18.1306 | 0.83401 | 0.16599 | 89 | 3.9889 | 0.18349 | 0.81651 |
| 35 | 17.9884 | 0.82747 | 0.17253 | 90 | 3.7630 | 0.17310 | 0.82690 |
| 36 | 17.8411 | 0.82069 | 0.17931 | 91 | 3.5467 | 0.16315 | 0.83685 |
| 37 | 17.6888 | 0.81369 | 0.18631 | 92 | 3.3400 | 0.15364 | 0.84636 |
| 38 | 17.5311 | 0.80643 | 0.19357 | 93 | 3.1433 | 0.14459 | 0.85541 |
| 39 | 17.3684 | 0.79895 | 0.20105 | 94 | 2.9562 | 0.13598 | 0.86402 |
| 40 | 17.2005 | 0.79122 | 0.20878 | 95 | 2.7784 | 0.12781 | 0.87219 |
| 41 | 17.0274 | 0.78326 | 0.21674 | 96 | 2.6106 | 0.12009 | 0.87991 |
| 42 | 16.8490 | 0.77506 | 0.22494 | 97 | 2.4522 | 0.11280 | 0.88720 |
| 43 | 16.6649 | 0.76658 | 0.23342 | 98 | 2.3027 | 0.10592 | 0.89408 |
| 44 | 16.4752 | 0.75786 | 0.24214 | 99 | 2.1614 | 0.09943 | 0.90057 |
| 45 | 16.2800 | 0.74888 | 0.25112 | 100 | 2.0298 | 0.09337 | 0.90663 |
| 46 | 16.0788 | 0.73962 | 0.26038 | 101 | 1.9047 | 0.08762 | 0.91238 |
| 47 | 15.8720 | 0.73011 | 0.26989 | 102 | 1.7890 | 0.08229 | 0.91771 |
| 48 | 15.6593 | 0.72033 | 0.27967 | 103 | 1.6740 | 0.07700 | 0.92300 |
| 49 | 15.4405 | 0.71026 | 0.28974 | 104 | 1.5682 | 0.07214 | 0.92786 |
| 50 | 15.2150 | 0.69989 | 0.30011 | 105 | 1.4638 | 0.06734 | 0.93266 |
| 51 | 14.9828 | 0.68921 | 0.31079 | 106 | 1.3332 | 0.06133 | 0.93867 |
| 52 | 14.7439 | 0.67822 | 0.32178 | 107 | 1.1851 | 0.05451 | 0.94549 |
| 53 | 14.4983 | 0.66692 | 0.33308 | 108 | 0.9455 | 0.04349 | 0.95651 |
| 54 | 14.2464 | 0.65533 | 0.34467 | 109 | 0.4780 | 0.02199 | 0.97801 |

**Section 1**

**Table S (4.8)**
**Single Life Factors Based on Life Table 2000CM**
**Interest at 4.8 Percent**

| Age | Annuity | Life Estate | Remainder | Age | Annuity | Life Estate | Remainder |
|---|---|---|---|---|---|---|---|
| **0** | 19.8956 | 0.95499 | 0.04501 | **55** | 13.6857 | 0.65692 | 0.34308 |
| **1** | 19.9930 | 0.95966 | 0.04034 | **56** | 13.4349 | 0.64488 | 0.35512 |
| **2** | 19.9630 | 0.95822 | 0.04178 | **57** | 13.1795 | 0.63261 | 0.36739 |
| **3** | 19.9280 | 0.95654 | 0.04346 | **58** | 12.9198 | 0.62015 | 0.37985 |
| **4** | 19.8897 | 0.95470 | 0.04530 | **59** | 12.6555 | 0.60747 | 0.39253 |
| **5** | 19.8487 | 0.95274 | 0.04726 | **60** | 12.3863 | 0.59454 | 0.40546 |
| **6** | 19.8051 | 0.95065 | 0.04935 | **61** | 12.1124 | 0.58140 | 0.41860 |
| **7** | 19.7594 | 0.94845 | 0.05155 | **62** | 11.8347 | 0.56806 | 0.43194 |
| **8** | 19.7112 | 0.94614 | 0.05386 | **63** | 11.5534 | 0.55456 | 0.44544 |
| **9** | 19.6601 | 0.94369 | 0.05631 | **64** | 11.2686 | 0.54089 | 0.45911 |
| **10** | 19.6065 | 0.94111 | 0.05889 | **65** | 10.9802 | 0.52705 | 0.47295 |
| **11** | 19.5500 | 0.93840 | 0.06160 | **66** | 10.6852 | 0.51289 | 0.48711 |
| **12** | 19.4908 | 0.93556 | 0.06444 | **67** | 10.3845 | 0.49846 | 0.50154 |
| **13** | 19.4296 | 0.93262 | 0.06738 | **68** | 10.0793 | 0.48381 | 0.51619 |
| **14** | 19.3670 | 0.92962 | 0.07038 | **69** | 9.7705 | 0.46898 | 0.53102 |
| **15** | 19.3037 | 0.92658 | 0.07342 | **70** | 9.4587 | 0.45402 | 0.54598 |
| **16** | 19.2398 | 0.92351 | 0.07649 | **71** | 9.1439 | 0.43891 | 0.56109 |
| **17** | 19.1750 | 0.92040 | 0.07960 | **72** | 8.8267 | 0.42368 | 0.57632 |
| **18** | 19.1091 | 0.91724 | 0.08276 | **73** | 8.5084 | 0.40840 | 0.59160 |
| **19** | 19.0416 | 0.91400 | 0.08600 | **74** | 8.1904 | 0.39314 | 0.60686 |
| **20** | 18.9716 | 0.91063 | 0.08937 | **75** | 7.8741 | 0.37796 | 0.62204 |
| **21** | 18.8993 | 0.90717 | 0.09283 | **76** | 7.5605 | 0.36290 | 0.63710 |
| **22** | 18.8245 | 0.90358 | 0.09642 | **77** | 7.2498 | 0.34799 | 0.65201 |
| **23** | 18.7466 | 0.89984 | 0.10016 | **78** | 6.9425 | 0.33324 | 0.66676 |
| **24** | 18.6650 | 0.89592 | 0.10408 | **79** | 6.6393 | 0.31868 | 0.68132 |
| **25** | 18.5790 | 0.89179 | 0.10821 | **80** | 6.3409 | 0.30437 | 0.69563 |
| **26** | 18.4883 | 0.88744 | 0.11256 | **81** | 6.0480 | 0.29030 | 0.70970 |
| **27** | 18.3929 | 0.88286 | 0.11714 | **82** | 5.7608 | 0.27652 | 0.72348 |
| **28** | 18.2927 | 0.87805 | 0.12195 | **83** | 5.4803 | 0.26305 | 0.73695 |
| **29** | 18.1879 | 0.87302 | 0.12698 | **84** | 5.2067 | 0.24992 | 0.75008 |
| **30** | 18.0787 | 0.86778 | 0.13222 | **85** | 4.9407 | 0.23715 | 0.76285 |
| **31** | 17.9650 | 0.86232 | 0.13768 | **86** | 4.6825 | 0.22476 | 0.77524 |
| **32** | 17.8467 | 0.85664 | 0.14336 | **87** | 4.4328 | 0.21278 | 0.78722 |
| **33** | 17.7235 | 0.85073 | 0.14927 | **88** | 4.1916 | 0.20120 | 0.79880 |
| **34** | 17.5960 | 0.84461 | 0.15539 | **89** | 3.9594 | 0.19005 | 0.80995 |
| **35** | 17.4637 | 0.83826 | 0.16174 | **90** | 3.7364 | 0.17935 | 0.82065 |
| **36** | 17.3265 | 0.83167 | 0.16833 | **91** | 3.5226 | 0.16909 | 0.83091 |
| **37** | 17.1844 | 0.82485 | 0.17515 | **92** | 3.3183 | 0.15928 | 0.84072 |
| **38** | 17.0371 | 0.81778 | 0.18222 | **93** | 3.1238 | 0.14994 | 0.85006 |
| **39** | 16.8849 | 0.81048 | 0.18952 | **94** | 2.9387 | 0.14106 | 0.85894 |
| **40** | 16.7277 | 0.80293 | 0.19707 | **95** | 2.7626 | 0.13261 | 0.86739 |
| **41** | 16.5653 | 0.79513 | 0.20487 | **96** | 2.5965 | 0.12463 | 0.87537 |
| **42** | 16.3978 | 0.78710 | 0.21290 | **97** | 2.4395 | 0.11710 | 0.88290 |
| **43** | 16.2246 | 0.77878 | 0.22122 | **98** | 2.2913 | 0.10998 | 0.89002 |
| **44** | 16.0461 | 0.77021 | 0.22979 | **99** | 2.1512 | 0.10326 | 0.89674 |
| **45** | 15.8620 | 0.76138 | 0.23862 | **100** | 2.0207 | 0.09699 | 0.90301 |
| **46** | 15.6721 | 0.75226 | 0.24774 | **101** | 1.8965 | 0.09103 | 0.90897 |
| **47** | 15.4767 | 0.74288 | 0.25712 | **102** | 1.7816 | 0.08552 | 0.91448 |
| **48** | 15.2754 | 0.73322 | 0.26678 | **103** | 1.6674 | 0.08004 | 0.91996 |
| **49** | 15.0680 | 0.72326 | 0.27674 | **104** | 1.5624 | 0.07499 | 0.92501 |
| **50** | 14.8540 | 0.71299 | 0.28701 | **105** | 1.4588 | 0.07002 | 0.92998 |
| **51** | 14.6335 | 0.70241 | 0.29759 | **106** | 1.3290 | 0.06379 | 0.93621 |
| **52** | 14.4061 | 0.69149 | 0.30851 | **107** | 1.1817 | 0.05672 | 0.94328 |
| **53** | 14.1721 | 0.68026 | 0.31974 | **108** | 0.9433 | 0.04528 | 0.95472 |
| **54** | 13.9318 | 0.66873 | 0.33127 | **109** | 0.4771 | 0.02290 | 0.97710 |

## Table S (5.0) Section 1

### Single Life Factors Based on Life Table 2000CM
### Interest at 5.0 Percent

| Age | Annuity | Life Estate | Remainder | Age | Annuity | Life Estate | Remainder |
|---|---|---|---|---|---|---|---|
| 0 | 19.1799 | 0.95899 | 0.04101 | 55 | 13.3935 | 0.66968 | 0.33032 |
| 1 | 19.2763 | 0.96382 | 0.03618 | 56 | 13.1536 | 0.65768 | 0.34232 |
| 2 | 19.2501 | 0.96250 | 0.03750 | 57 | 12.9089 | 0.64545 | 0.35455 |
| 3 | 19.2192 | 0.96096 | 0.03904 | 58 | 12.6600 | 0.63300 | 0.36700 |
| 4 | 19.1851 | 0.95925 | 0.04075 | 59 | 12.4064 | 0.62032 | 0.37968 |
| 5 | 19.1485 | 0.95742 | 0.04258 | 60 | 12.1477 | 0.60739 | 0.39261 |
| 6 | 19.1095 | 0.95547 | 0.04453 | 61 | 11.8844 | 0.59422 | 0.40578 |
| 7 | 19.0685 | 0.95342 | 0.04658 | 62 | 11.6170 | 0.58085 | 0.41915 |
| 8 | 19.0251 | 0.95125 | 0.04875 | 63 | 11.3459 | 0.56729 | 0.43271 |
| 9 | 18.9791 | 0.94895 | 0.05105 | 64 | 11.0711 | 0.55355 | 0.44645 |
| 10 | 18.9306 | 0.94653 | 0.05347 | 65 | 10.7925 | 0.53963 | 0.46037 |
| 11 | 18.8795 | 0.94397 | 0.05603 | 66 | 10.5073 | 0.52536 | 0.47464 |
| 12 | 18.8258 | 0.94129 | 0.05871 | 67 | 10.2162 | 0.51081 | 0.48919 |
| 13 | 18.7702 | 0.93851 | 0.06149 | 68 | 9.9204 | 0.49602 | 0.50398 |
| 14 | 18.7133 | 0.93567 | 0.06433 | 69 | 9.6208 | 0.48104 | 0.51896 |
| 15 | 18.6558 | 0.93279 | 0.06721 | 70 | 9.3180 | 0.46590 | 0.53410 |
| 16 | 18.5978 | 0.92989 | 0.07011 | 71 | 9.0119 | 0.45060 | 0.54940 |
| 17 | 18.5391 | 0.92695 | 0.07305 | 72 | 8.7032 | 0.43516 | 0.56484 |
| 18 | 18.4793 | 0.92396 | 0.07604 | 73 | 8.3930 | 0.41965 | 0.58035 |
| 19 | 18.4180 | 0.92090 | 0.07910 | 74 | 8.0829 | 0.40414 | 0.59586 |
| 20 | 18.3543 | 0.91772 | 0.08228 | 75 | 7.7742 | 0.38871 | 0.61129 |
| 21 | 18.2886 | 0.91443 | 0.08557 | 76 | 7.4677 | 0.37339 | 0.62661 |
| 22 | 18.2205 | 0.91103 | 0.08897 | 77 | 7.1639 | 0.35819 | 0.64181 |
| 23 | 18.1495 | 0.90748 | 0.09252 | 78 | 6.8631 | 0.34316 | 0.65684 |
| 24 | 18.0749 | 0.90375 | 0.09625 | 79 | 6.5660 | 0.32830 | 0.67170 |
| 25 | 17.9962 | 0.89981 | 0.10019 | 80 | 6.2736 | 0.31368 | 0.68632 |
| 26 | 17.9131 | 0.89565 | 0.10435 | 81 | 5.9861 | 0.29931 | 0.70069 |
| 27 | 17.8253 | 0.89127 | 0.10873 | 82 | 5.7042 | 0.28521 | 0.71479 |
| 28 | 17.7330 | 0.88665 | 0.11335 | 83 | 5.4285 | 0.27142 | 0.72858 |
| 29 | 17.6363 | 0.88181 | 0.11819 | 84 | 5.1594 | 0.25797 | 0.74203 |
| 30 | 17.5354 | 0.87677 | 0.12323 | 85 | 4.8976 | 0.24488 | 0.75512 |
| 31 | 17.4302 | 0.87151 | 0.12849 | 86 | 4.6433 | 0.23217 | 0.76783 |
| 32 | 17.3205 | 0.86602 | 0.13398 | 87 | 4.3973 | 0.21986 | 0.78014 |
| 33 | 17.2061 | 0.86030 | 0.13970 | 88 | 4.1594 | 0.20797 | 0.79203 |
| 34 | 17.0875 | 0.85438 | 0.14562 | 89 | 3.9302 | 0.19651 | 0.80349 |
| 35 | 16.9643 | 0.84822 | 0.15178 | 90 | 3.7101 | 0.18550 | 0.81450 |
| 36 | 16.8364 | 0.84182 | 0.15818 | 91 | 3.4989 | 0.17495 | 0.82505 |
| 37 | 16.7038 | 0.83519 | 0.16481 | 92 | 3.2969 | 0.16485 | 0.83515 |
| 38 | 16.5661 | 0.82830 | 0.17170 | 93 | 3.1046 | 0.15523 | 0.84477 |
| 39 | 16.4236 | 0.82118 | 0.17882 | 94 | 2.9213 | 0.14607 | 0.85393 |
| 40 | 16.2762 | 0.81381 | 0.18619 | 95 | 2.7471 | 0.13735 | 0.86265 |
| 41 | 16.1238 | 0.80619 | 0.19381 | 96 | 2.5825 | 0.12912 | 0.87088 |
| 42 | 15.9665 | 0.79832 | 0.20168 | 97 | 2.4270 | 0.12135 | 0.87865 |
| 43 | 15.8035 | 0.79018 | 0.20982 | 98 | 2.2800 | 0.11400 | 0.88600 |
| 44 | 15.6353 | 0.78176 | 0.21824 | 99 | 2.1411 | 0.10706 | 0.89294 |
| 45 | 15.4617 | 0.77308 | 0.22692 | 100 | 2.0116 | 0.10058 | 0.89942 |
| 46 | 15.2823 | 0.76411 | 0.23589 | 101 | 1.8884 | 0.09442 | 0.90558 |
| 47 | 15.0975 | 0.75487 | 0.24513 | 102 | 1.7743 | 0.08872 | 0.91128 |
| 48 | 14.9069 | 0.74534 | 0.25466 | 103 | 1.6609 | 0.08305 | 0.91695 |
| 49 | 14.7103 | 0.73551 | 0.26449 | 104 | 1.5566 | 0.07783 | 0.92217 |
| 50 | 14.5071 | 0.72535 | 0.27465 | 105 | 1.4537 | 0.07269 | 0.92731 |
| 51 | 14.2974 | 0.71487 | 0.28513 | 106 | 1.3247 | 0.06624 | 0.93376 |
| 52 | 14.0810 | 0.70405 | 0.29595 | 107 | 1.1784 | 0.05892 | 0.94108 |
| 53 | 13.8580 | 0.69290 | 0.30710 | 108 | 0.9410 | 0.04705 | 0.95295 |
| 54 | 13.6286 | 0.68143 | 0.31857 | 109 | 0.4762 | 0.02381 | 0.97619 |

**Section 3**

## Table B
## Annuity, Income, and Remainder Interests For a Term Certain

| Interest Rates | 5.0% | | | | 5.2% | | |
|---|---|---|---|---|---|---|---|
| Years | Annuity | Income Interest | Remainder | Years | Annuity | Income Interest | Remainder |
| 1 | 0.9524 | .047619 | .952381 | 1 | 0.9506 | .045430 | .950570 |
| 2 | 1.8594 | .092971 | .907029 | 2 | 1.8542 | .096416 | .903584 |
| 3 | 2.7232 | .136162 | .863838 | 3 | 2.7131 | .141080 | .858920 |
| 4 | 3.5460 | .177298 | .822702 | 4 | 3.5295 | .183536 | .816464 |
| 5 | 4.3295 | .216474 | .783526 | 5 | 4.3056 | .223894 | .776106 |
| 6 | 5.0757 | .253785 | .746215 | 6 | 5.0434 | .262256 | .737744 |
| 7 | 5.7864 | .289319 | .710681 | 7 | 5.7447 | .298723 | .701277 |
| 8 | 6.4632 | .323161 | .676839 | 8 | 6.4113 | .333387 | .666613 |
| 9 | 7.1078 | .355391 | .644609 | 9 | 7.0449 | .366337 | .633663 |
| 10 | 7.7217 | .386087 | .613913 | 10 | 7.6473 | .397659 | .602341 |
| 11 | 8.3064 | .415321 | .584679 | 11 | 8.2199 | .427432 | .572568 |
| 12 | 8.8633 | .443163 | .556837 | 12 | 8.7641 | .455734 | .544266 |
| 13 | 9.3936 | .469679 | .530321 | 13 | 9.2815 | .482637 | .517363 |
| 14 | 9.8986 | .494932 | .505068 | 14 | 9.7733 | .508210 | .491790 |
| 15 | 10.3797 | .518983 | .481017 | 15 | 10.2408 | .532519 | .467481 |
| 16 | 10.8378 | .541888 | .458112 | 16 | 10.6851 | .555628 | .444374 |
| 17 | 11.2741 | .563703 | .436297 | 17 | 11.1075 | .577592 | .422408 |
| 18 | 11.6896 | .584479 | .415521 | 18 | 11.5091 | .598471 | .401529 |
| 19 | 12.0853 | .604266 | .395734 | 19 | 11.8907 | .618319 | .381681 |
| 20 | 12.4622 | .623111 | .376889 | 20 | 12.2536 | .637185 | .362815 |
| 21 | 12.8212 | .641058 | .358942 | 21 | 12.5984 | .655119 | .344881 |
| 22 | 13.1630 | .658150 | .341850 | 22 | 12.9263 | .672166 | .327834 |
| 23 | 13.4886 | .674429 | .325571 | 23 | 13.2379 | .688371 | .311629 |
| 24 | 13.7986 | .689932 | .310068 | 24 | 13.5341 | .703775 | .296225 |
| 25 | 14.0939 | .704697 | .295303 | 25 | 13.8157 | .718417 | .281583 |
| 26 | 14.3752 | .716759 | .281241 | 26 | 14.0834 | .732336 | .267664 |
| 27 | 14.6430 | .732152 | .267848 | 27 | 14.3378 | .745566 | .254434 |
| 28 | 14.8981 | .744906 | .255094 | 28 | 14.5797 | .758143 | .241357 |
| 29 | 15.1411 | .757054 | .242946 | 29 | 14.8096 | .770098 | .229902 |
| 30 | 15.3725 | .768623 | .231377 | 30 | 15.0281 | .781462 | .218538 |
| 31 | 15.5928 | .779641 | .220359 | 31 | 15.2358 | .792264 | .207736 |
| 32 | 15.8027 | .790134 | .209666 | 32 | 15.4333 | .802532 | .197468 |
| 33 | 16.0025 | .800127 | .199873 | 33 | 15.6210 | .812293 | .187707 |
| 34 | 16.1929 | .809645 | .190355 | 34 | 15.7994 | .821571 | .178429 |
| 35 | 16.3742 | .818710 | .181290 | 35 | 15.9691 | .830391 | .169609 |
| 36 | 16.5469 | .827343 | .172657 | 36 | 16.1303 | .838775 | .161225 |
| 37 | 16.7113 | .835564 | .164436 | 37 | 16.2835 | .846744 | .153256 |
| 38 | 16.8679 | .843395 | .156605 | 38 | 16.4292 | .854319 | .145681 |
| 39 | 17.0170 | .850852 | .149148 | 39 | 16.5677 | .861520 | .138480 |
| 40 | 17.1591 | .857954 | .142046 | 40 | 16.6993 | .868365 | .131635 |
| 41 | 17.2944 | .864718 | .135282 | 41 | 16.6245 | .874872 | .125128 |
| 42 | 17.4232 | .871160 | .128840 | 42 | 16.9434 | .881057 | .118943 |
| 43 | 17.5459 | .877296 | .122704 | 43 | 17.0565 | .886936 | .113064 |
| 44 | 17.6628 | .883139 | .116861 | 44 | 17.1639 | .892525 | .107475 |
| 45 | 17.7741 | .888703 | .111297 | 45 | 17.2661 | .897837 | .102163 |
| 46 | 17.8801 | .894003 | .105997 | 46 | 17.3632 | .902887 | .097113 |
| 47 | 17.9810 | .899051 | .100949 | 47 | 17.4555 | .907688 | .092312 |
| 48 | 18.0772 | .903858 | .096142 | 48 | 17.5433 | .912251 | .087749 |
| 49 | 18.1687 | .908436 | .091564 | 49 | 17.6267 | .916588 | .083412 |
| 50 | 18.2559 | .912796 | .087204 | 50 | 17.7060 | .920711 | .079289 |
| 51 | 18.3390 | .916949 | .083051 | 51 | 17.7814 | .924630 | .075370 |
| 52 | 18.4181 | .920904 | .079096 | 52 | 17.8530 | .928356 | .071644 |
| 53 | 18.4934 | .924670 | .075330 | 53 | 17.9211 | .931897 | .068103 |
| 54 | 18.5651 | .928257 | .071743 | 54 | 17.9858 | .935263 | .064737 |
| 55 | 18.6335 | .931674 | .068326 | 55 | 18.0474 | .938463 | .061537 |
| 56 | 18.6985 | .934927 | .065073 | 56 | 18.1059 | .941505 | .058495 |
| 57 | 18.7605 | .938026 | .061974 | 57 | 18.1615 | .944396 | .055604 |
| 58 | 18.8195 | .940977 | .059023 | 58 | 18.2143 | .947145 | .052855 |
| 59 | 18.8758 | .943788 | .056212 | 59 | 18.2646 | .949757 | .050243 |
| 60 | 18.9293 | .946464 | .053536 | 60 | 18.3123 | .952241 | .047759 |

# A-5 2010 Optional State Sales Tax Tables

## 2010 Optional State and Certain Local Sales Tax Tables

| Income: At least | Income: But less than | Alabama 4.0000% Exemptions 1 | 2 | 3 | 4 | 5 | Over 5 | Arizona[1] 6.1863% Exemptions 1 | 2 | 3 | 4 | 5 | Over 5 | Arkansas 6.0000% Exemptions 1 | 2 | 3 | 4 | 5 | Over 5 | California[2] 8.2500% Exemptions 1 | 2 | 3 | 4 | 5 | Over 5 | Colorado 2.9000% Exemptions 1 | 2 | 3 | 4 | 5 | Over 5 |
|---|---|---|---|---|---|---|---|---|---|---|---|---|---|---|---|---|---|---|---|---|---|---|---|---|---|---|---|---|---|---|---|
| $0 | $20,000 | 235 | 287 | 324 | 353 | 378 | 413 | 253 | 297 | 326 | 349 | 368 | 395 | 302 | 359 | 397 | 427 | 452 | 487 | 326 | 379 | 414 | 441 | 464 | 495 | 122 | 141 | 154 | 164 | 172 | 184 |
| 20,000 | 30,000 | 336 | 409 | 460 | 501 | 535 | 583 | 408 | 476 | 522 | 558 | 588 | 630 | 472 | 559 | 618 | 664 | 702 | 756 | 523 | 605 | 660 | 702 | 737 | 786 | 185 | 213 | 232 | 247 | 259 | 276 |
| 30,000 | 40,000 | 385 | 468 | 525 | 570 | 609 | 663 | 487 | 567 | 622 | 664 | 700 | 749 | 558 | 659 | 728 | 782 | 827 | 890 | 624 | 721 | 785 | 835 | 876 | 934 | 216 | 249 | 271 | 288 | 302 | 321 |
| 40,000 | 50,000 | 426 | 516 | 579 | 629 | 670 | 730 | 555 | 646 | 708 | 756 | 795 | 851 | 630 | 745 | 822 | 883 | 933 | 1004 | 710 | 820 | 892 | 949 | 995 | 1061 | 243 | 279 | 304 | 322 | 338 | 360 |
| 50,000 | 60,000 | 463 | 559 | 626 | 680 | 724 | 788 | 616 | 717 | 785 | 837 | 881 | 943 | 695 | 821 | 906 | 972 | 1027 | 1105 | 788 | 908 | 989 | 1051 | 1102 | 1174 | 267 | 306 | 333 | 353 | 370 | 393 |
| 60,000 | 70,000 | 495 | 597 | 669 | 725 | 773 | 840 | 671 | 781 | 855 | 912 | 960 | 1026 | 754 | 890 | 982 | 1053 | 1113 | 1197 | 859 | 989 | 1076 | 1144 | 1199 | 1277 | 288 | 331 | 359 | 381 | 399 | 424 |
| 70,000 | 80,000 | 525 | 633 | 708 | 767 | 817 | 889 | 724 | 842 | 921 | 982 | 1033 | 1105 | 809 | 954 | 1053 | 1129 | 1193 | 1283 | 926 | 1066 | 1159 | 1231 | 1291 | 1374 | 309 | 354 | 384 | 407 | 426 | 453 |
| 80,000 | 90,000 | 553 | 666 | 744 | 806 | 858 | 933 | 773 | 898 | 982 | 1048 | 1102 | 1178 | 860 | 1014 | 1118 | 1199 | 1267 | 1362 | 988 | 1136 | 1236 | 1312 | 1376 | 1464 | 327 | 375 | 406 | 431 | 451 | 479 |
| 90,000 | 100,000 | 579 | 696 | 778 | 842 | 897 | 974 | 819 | 951 | 1040 | 1109 | 1167 | 1247 | 908 | 1070 | 1180 | 1266 | 1337 | 1437 | 1047 | 1204 | 1308 | 1389 | 1456 | 1549 | 345 | 395 | 428 | 453 | 474 | 504 |
| 100,000 | 120,000 | 613 | 736 | 821 | 889 | 946 | 1028 | 881 | 1022 | 1117 | 1191 | 1252 | 1338 | 971 | 1144 | 1261 | 1353 | 1428 | 1535 | 1125 | 1292 | 1404 | 1490 | 1562 | 1662 | 368 | 421 | 456 | 483 | 505 | 536 |
| 120,000 | 140,000 | 659 | 790 | 881 | 953 | 1014 | 1100 | 965 | 1118 | 1222 | 1302 | 1369 | 1462 | 1058 | 1245 | 1372 | 1471 | 1553 | 1669 | 1231 | 1413 | 1535 | 1629 | 1706 | 1815 | 400 | 456 | 494 | 523 | 547 | 581 |
| 140,000 | 160,000 | 699 | 836 | 932 | 1008 | 1071 | 1162 | 1038 | 1202 | 1313 | 1399 | 1471 | 1571 | 1133 | 1333 | 1468 | 1574 | 1661 | 1785 | 1324 | 1519 | 1649 | 1750 | 1833 | 1949 | 427 | 487 | 527 | 558 | 583 | 619 |
| 160,000 | 180,000 | 739 | 882 | 982 | 1062 | 1128 | 1223 | 1111 | 1287 | 1405 | 1496 | 1572 | 1679 | 1207 | 1420 | 1564 | 1676 | 1769 | 1900 | 1417 | 1625 | 1763 | 1870 | 1959 | 2082 | 454 | 518 | 560 | 593 | 619 | 657 |
| 180,000 | 200,000 | 774 | 923 | 1027 | 1110 | 1179 | 1278 | 1178 | 1362 | 1487 | 1584 | 1664 | 1777 | 1274 | 1498 | 1649 | 1767 | 1865 | 2003 | 1501 | 1720 | 1866 | 1979 | 2072 | 2203 | 479 | 545 | 590 | 624 | 652 | 691 |
| 200,000 or more | | 947 | 1123 | 1246 | 1344 | 1425 | 1542 | 1508 | 1741 | 1898 | 2020 | 2121 | 2262 | 1605 | 1883 | 2072 | 2219 | 2341 | 2512 | 1921 | 2195 | 2378 | 2520 | 2637 | 2800 | 601 | 682 | 735 | 777 | 811 | 858 |

| Income: At least | Income: But less than | Connecticut 6.0000% Exemptions 1 | 2 | 3 | 4 | 5 | Over 5 | District of Columbia 6.0000% Exemptions 1 | 2 | 3 | 4 | 5 | Over 5 | Florida 6.0000% Exemptions 1 | 2 | 3 | 4 | 5 | Over 5 | Georgia 4.0000% Exemptions 1 | 2 | 3 | 4 | 5 | Over 5 | Hawaii[5] 4.0000% Exemptions 1 | 2 | 3 | 4 | 5 | Over 5 |
|---|---|---|---|---|---|---|---|---|---|---|---|---|---|---|---|---|---|---|---|---|---|---|---|---|---|---|---|---|---|---|---|
| $0 | $20,000 | 235 | 270 | 293 | 310 | 325 | 345 | 186 | 216 | 236 | 252 | 265 | 283 | 262 | 306 | 336 | 359 | 378 | 404 | 169 | 195 | 213 | 226 | 237 | 253 | 262 | 318 | 356 | 386 | 411 | 447 |
| 20,000 | 30,000 | 377 | 431 | 468 | 495 | 518 | 550 | 305 | 353 | 385 | 410 | 431 | 461 | 420 | 488 | 535 | 570 | 600 | 642 | 257 | 295 | 321 | 341 | 357 | 380 | 395 | 477 | 533 | 577 | 614 | 667 |
| 30,000 | 40,000 | 449 | 513 | 556 | 589 | 617 | 654 | 366 | 423 | 462 | 492 | 517 | 552 | 500 | 581 | 635 | 678 | 713 | 762 | 301 | 345 | 375 | 397 | 416 | 442 | 460 | 554 | 619 | 670 | 713 | 774 |
| 40,000 | 50,000 | 510 | 584 | 632 | 670 | 701 | 743 | 419 | 484 | 528 | 563 | 591 | 631 | 568 | 660 | 722 | 769 | 809 | 864 | 338 | 387 | 420 | 445 | 466 | 495 | 515 | 620 | 692 | 749 | 796 | 864 |
| 50,000 | 60,000 | 566 | 647 | 701 | 742 | 776 | 823 | 467 | 539 | 588 | 626 | 657 | 702 | 630 | 731 | 799 | 851 | 895 | 956 | 371 | 425 | 460 | 488 | 511 | 542 | 563 | 678 | 756 | 818 | 870 | 943 |
| 60,000 | 70,000 | 616 | 704 | 763 | 807 | 844 | 896 | 511 | 590 | 643 | 684 | 718 | 766 | 686 | 795 | 869 | 926 | 973 | 1040 | 401 | 458 | 497 | 526 | 551 | 584 | 607 | 730 | 814 | 880 | 936 | 1014 |
| 70,000 | 80,000 | 664 | 758 | 821 | 869 | 909 | 964 | 553 | 637 | 694 | 739 | 776 | 827 | 739 | 856 | 935 | 997 | 1047 | 1118 | 429 | 490 | 531 | 562 | 588 | 624 | 648 | 778 | 868 | 938 | 997 | 1081 |
| 80,000 | 90,000 | 708 | 808 | 875 | 926 | 968 | 1027 | 592 | 682 | 742 | 790 | 829 | 884 | 788 | 913 | 997 | 1062 | 1116 | 1191 | 455 | 519 | 562 | 595 | 623 | 660 | 685 | 823 | 917 | 992 | 1054 | 1142 |
| 90,000 | 100,000 | 749 | 856 | 926 | 980 | 1025 | 1087 | 628 | 724 | 788 | 838 | 880 | 938 | 834 | 966 | 1055 | 1123 | 1180 | 1260 | 480 | 547 | 592 | 627 | 655 | 695 | 721 | 865 | 964 | 1042 | 1107 | 1199 |
| 100,000 | 120,000 | 804 | 918 | 993 | 1051 | 1099 | 1165 | 677 | 779 | 848 | 902 | 946 | 1009 | 895 | 1036 | 1131 | 1204 | 1265 | 1350 | 512 | 583 | 631 | 668 | 698 | 740 | 767 | 920 | 1025 | 1107 | 1176 | 1274 |
| 120,000 | 140,000 | 879 | 1003 | 1085 | 1149 | 1200 | 1273 | 744 | 855 | 931 | 989 | 1038 | 1106 | 979 | 1133 | 1236 | 1315 | 1381 | 1474 | 556 | 633 | 684 | 723 | 756 | 801 | 829 | 994 | 1107 | 1196 | 1270 | 1375 |
| 140,000 | 160,000 | 944 | 1077 | 1166 | 1233 | 1289 | 1366 | 802 | 922 | 1003 | 1066 | 1118 | 1192 | 1052 | 1217 | 1327 | 1412 | 1483 | 1582 | 594 | 676 | 730 | 772 | 806 | 854 | 883 | 1058 | 1178 | 1272 | 1351 | 1463 |
| 160,000 | 180,000 | 1009 | 1151 | 1245 | 1318 | 1377 | 1459 | 861 | 989 | 1076 | 1143 | 1199 | 1277 | 1125 | 1300 | 1418 | 1508 | 1584 | 1689 | 632 | 718 | 776 | 820 | 856 | 907 | 937 | 1121 | 1248 | 1348 | 1431 | 1549 |
| 180,000 | 200,000 | 1068 | 1218 | 1317 | 1393 | 1456 | 1543 | 913 | 1049 | 1141 | 1212 | 1271 | 1354 | 1191 | 1375 | 1499 | 1595 | 1675 | 1786 | 666 | 757 | 817 | 863 | 901 | 954 | 985 | 1178 | 1311 | 1415 | 1503 | 1626 |
| 200,000 or more | | 1359 | 1549 | 1674 | 1770 | 1849 | 1959 | 1179 | 1351 | 1468 | 1558 | 1633 | 1738 | 1518 | 1750 | 1906 | 2026 | 2126 | 2265 | 836 | 946 | 1019 | 1075 | 1121 | 1186 | 1219 | 1456 | 1618 | 1745 | 1851 | 2002 |

| Income: At least | Income: But less than | Idaho 6.0000% Exemptions 1 | 2 | 3 | 4 | 5 | Over 5 | Illinois 6.2500% Exemptions 1 | 2 | 3 | 4 | 5 | Over 5 | Indiana 7.0000% Exemptions 1 | 2 | 3 | 4 | 5 | Over 5 | Iowa 6.0000% Exemptions 1 | 2 | 3 | 4 | 5 | Over 5 | Kansas[1] 5.8041% Exemptions 1 | 2 | 3 | 4 | 5 | Over 5 |
|---|---|---|---|---|---|---|---|---|---|---|---|---|---|---|---|---|---|---|---|---|---|---|---|---|---|---|---|---|---|---|---|
| $0 | $20,000 | 270 | 320 | 353 | 379 | 401 | 431 | 365 | 447 | 505 | 550 | 589 | 644 | 302 | 354 | 389 | 417 | 439 | 472 | 268 | 312 | 342 | 365 | 383 | 410 | 338 | 417 | 473 | 517 | 554 | 608 |
| 20,000 | 30,000 | 432 | 509 | 562 | 602 | 636 | 684 | 529 | 645 | 725 | 789 | 844 | 921 | 456 | 531 | 581 | 621 | 654 | 700 | 404 | 469 | 512 | 546 | 574 | 613 | 510 | 627 | 709 | 774 | 829 | 908 |
| 30,000 | 40,000 | 513 | 605 | 667 | 715 | 756 | 812 | 608 | 740 | 831 | 904 | 965 | 1052 | 532 | 618 | 676 | 721 | 759 | 812 | 471 | 546 | 596 | 635 | 667 | 711 | 595 | 730 | 824 | 900 | 963 | 1054 |
| 40,000 | 50,000 | 583 | 687 | 757 | 812 | 857 | 921 | 675 | 819 | 919 | 999 | 1066 | 1162 | 597 | 692 | 756 | 806 | 848 | 906 | 527 | 611 | 667 | 710 | 745 | 795 | 666 | 816 | 921 | 1005 | 1076 | 1177 |
| 50,000 | 60,000 | 646 | 760 | 838 | 898 | 948 | 1019 | 734 | 889 | 997 | 1083 | 1155 | 1258 | 655 | 757 | 827 | 881 | 926 | 990 | 578 | 669 | 729 | 776 | 815 | 868 | 730 | 893 | 1007 | 1098 | 1175 | 1285 |
| 60,000 | 70,000 | 703 | 827 | 911 | 977 | 1031 | 1108 | 787 | 952 | 1067 | 1158 | 1234 | 1344 | 707 | 816 | 891 | 949 | 997 | 1065 | 623 | 721 | 786 | 836 | 877 | 935 | 787 | 962 | 1085 | 1182 | 1265 | 1383 |
| 70,000 | 80,000 | 757 | 890 | 980 | 1050 | 1109 | 1191 | 836 | 1010 | 1131 | 1227 | 1308 | 1424 | 757 | 872 | 951 | 1012 | 1063 | 1135 | 665 | 769 | 838 | 891 | 935 | 997 | 840 | 1026 | 1157 | 1260 | 1348 | 1474 |
| 80,000 | 90,000 | 807 | 948 | 1044 | 1119 | 1181 | 1268 | 882 | 1064 | 1190 | 1291 | 1376 | 1497 | 802 | 923 | 1006 | 1070 | 1124 | 1199 | 705 | 814 | 887 | 943 | 989 | 1054 | 889 | 1085 | 1223 | 1332 | 1425 | 1557 |
| 90,000 | 100,000 | 854 | 1003 | 1105 | 1183 | 1249 | 1341 | 924 | 1114 | 1246 | 1351 | 1439 | 1565 | 845 | 972 | 1058 | 1125 | 1181 | 1260 | 741 | 856 | 932 | 991 | 1040 | 1107 | 935 | 1141 | 1285 | 1400 | 1497 | 1635 |
| 100,000 | 120,000 | 916 | 1076 | 1184 | 1268 | 1338 | 1437 | 980 | 1179 | 1318 | 1429 | 1521 | 1654 | 901 | 1035 | 1126 | 1197 | 1256 | 1339 | 790 | 911 | 992 | 1054 | 1105 | 1177 | 995 | 1214 | 1366 | 1488 | 1591 | 1737 |
| 120,000 | 140,000 | 1000 | 1175 | 1293 | 1384 | 1461 | 1568 | 1056 | 1268 | 1416 | 1534 | 1633 | 1774 | 978 | 1121 | 1219 | 1295 | 1358 | 1447 | 855 | 986 | 1073 | 1140 | 1195 | 1272 | 1077 | 1312 | 1477 | 1608 | 1718 | 1876 |
| 140,000 | 160,000 | 1074 | 1261 | 1387 | 1486 | 1567 | 1682 | 1121 | 1345 | 1501 | 1625 | 1729 | 1877 | 1045 | 1196 | 1299 | 1380 | 1446 | 1541 | 912 | 1051 | 1143 | 1214 | 1273 | 1354 | 1148 | 1398 | 1572 | 1711 | 1828 | 1995 |
| 160,000 | 180,000 | 1148 | 1347 | 1481 | 1586 | 1673 | 1796 | 1186 | 1421 | 1584 | 1714 | 1823 | 1979 | 1111 | 1271 | 1379 | 1464 | 1534 | 1633 | 968 | 1115 | 1212 | 1287 | 1349 | 1435 | 1219 | 1482 | 1666 | 1813 | 1937 | 2113 |
| 180,000 | 200,000 | 1214 | 1424 | 1566 | 1677 | 1769 | 1898 | 1244 | 1488 | 1659 | 1794 | 1907 | 2070 | 1171 | 1337 | 1451 | 1539 | 1612 | 1716 | 1019 | 1172 | 1274 | 1353 | 1418 | 1508 | 1281 | 1557 | 1751 | 1904 | 2034 | 2219 |
| 200,000 or more | | 1543 | 1807 | 1986 | 2125 | 2241 | 2403 | 1528 | 1819 | 2021 | 2182 | 2317 | 2510 | 1468 | 1668 | 1804 | 1910 | 1998 | 2123 | 1267 | 1455 | 1579 | 1675 | 1754 | 1864 | 1590 | 1927 | 2162 | 2350 | 2508 | 2733 |

| Income: At least | Income: But less than | Kentucky 6.0000% Exemptions 1 | 2 | 3 | 4 | 5 | Over 5 | Louisiana 4.0000% Exemptions 1 | 2 | 3 | 4 | 5 | Over 5 | Maine 5.0000% Exemptions 1 | 2 | 3 | 4 | 5 | Over 5 | Maryland 6.0000% Exemptions 1 | 2 | 3 | 4 | 5 | Over 5 | Massachusetts 6.2500% Exemptions 1 | 2 | 3 | 4 | 5 | Over 5 |
|---|---|---|---|---|---|---|---|---|---|---|---|---|---|---|---|---|---|---|---|---|---|---|---|---|---|---|---|---|---|---|---|
| $0 | $20,000 | 258 | 301 | 330 | 352 | 370 | 396 | 176 | 205 | 224 | 239 | 251 | 268 | 160 | 186 | 203 | 217 | 228 | 244 | 246 | 286 | 312 | 333 | 350 | 373 | 230 | 260 | 279 | 293 | 305 | 322 |
| 20,000 | 30,000 | 394 | 457 | 499 | 532 | 558 | 596 | 282 | 327 | 357 | 380 | 399 | 426 | 261 | 301 | 329 | 350 | 367 | 392 | 377 | 434 | 473 | 503 | 527 | 562 | 351 | 393 | 421 | 443 | 460 | 484 |
| 30,000 | 40,000 | 462 | 534 | 583 | 620 | 651 | 695 | 336 | 389 | 424 | 452 | 475 | 506 | 312 | 360 | 393 | 418 | 439 | 468 | 442 | 508 | 552 | 587 | 615 | 655 | 410 | 460 | 492 | 516 | 536 | 564 |
| 40,000 | 50,000 | 519 | 600 | 654 | 695 | 730 | 778 | 382 | 442 | 482 | 513 | 539 | 575 | 357 | 411 | 448 | 476 | 500 | 533 | 497 | 570 | 620 | 658 | 689 | 734 | 461 | 516 | 552 | 579 | 601 | 631 |
| 50,000 | 60,000 | 570 | 658 | 716 | 762 | 799 | 852 | 423 | 490 | 534 | 568 | 596 | 636 | 397 | 457 | 498 | 529 | 555 | 592 | 546 | 626 | 679 | 721 | 755 | 804 | 507 | 566 | 605 | 634 | 658 | 691 |
| 60,000 | 70,000 | 616 | 710 | 773 | 822 | 862 | 919 | 461 | 533 | 581 | 618 | 649 | 692 | 434 | 499 | 543 | 577 | 605 | 645 | 591 | 676 | 734 | 778 | 815 | 867 | 548 | 611 | 652 | 684 | 710 | 745 |
| 70,000 | 80,000 | 660 | 760 | 827 | 879 | 921 | 981 | 497 | 574 | 625 | 665 | 698 | 744 | 469 | 539 | 586 | 623 | 653 | 695 | 633 | 724 | 785 | 832 | 871 | 925 | 586 | 653 | 697 | 731 | 758 | 796 |
| 80,000 | 90,000 | 700 | 805 | 876 | 931 | 976 | 1039 | 530 | 612 | 666 | 709 | 744 | 792 | 501 | 576 | 626 | 665 | 697 | 742 | 672 | 767 | 831 | 881 | 922 | 980 | 622 | 692 | 739 | 774 | 803 | 843 |
| 90,000 | 100,000 | 738 | 848 | 922 | 980 | 1027 | 1093 | 561 | 647 | 705 | 750 | 787 | 838 | 532 | 611 | 664 | 705 | 739 | 787 | 709 | 809 | 876 | 928 | 971 | 1031 | 655 | 729 | 778 | 815 | 845 | 887 |
| 100,000 | 120,000 | 788 | 905 | 983 | 1044 | 1094 | 1164 | 602 | 694 | 756 | 804 | 844 | 899 | 573 | 657 | 714 | 758 | 794 | 845 | 757 | 863 | 934 | 989 | 1034 | 1098 | 699 | 778 | 829 | 868 | 900 | 944 |
| 120,000 | 140,000 | 856 | 982 | 1066 | 1131 | 1185 | 1260 | 658 | 759 | 826 | 878 | 921 | 981 | 629 | 721 | 782 | 830 | 870 | 925 | 824 | 937 | 1013 | 1072 | 1121 | 1189 | 759 | 844 | 899 | 941 | 975 | 1022 |
| 140,000 | 160,000 | 915 | 1049 | 1138 | 1207 | 1264 | 1344 | 708 | 815 | 887 | 943 | 989 | 1053 | 678 | 776 | 842 | 894 | 936 | 996 | 881 | 1001 | 1082 | 1144 | 1196 | 1268 | 811 | 901 | 959 | 1004 | 1040 | 1090 |
| 160,000 | 180,000 | 974 | 1115 | 1209 | 1282 | 1343 | 1427 | 757 | 871 | 948 | 1007 | 1056 | 1125 | 727 | 832 | 902 | 957 | 1002 | 1066 | 939 | 1065 | 1150 | 1216 | 1270 | 1347 | 863 | 958 | 1019 | 1066 | 1105 | 1158 |
| 180,000 | 200,000 | 1027 | 1174 | 1273 | 1350 | 1413 | 1501 | 801 | 922 | 1003 | 1065 | 1117 | 1189 | 771 | 882 | 956 | 1014 | 1062 | 1129 | 990 | 1122 | 1211 | 1280 | 1337 | 1417 | 910 | 1009 | 1073 | 1122 | 1163 | 1218 |
| 200,000 or more | | 1288 | 1469 | 1590 | 1683 | 1760 | 1867 | 1021 | 1173 | 1275 | 1354 | 1419 | 1509 | 994 | 1133 | 1227 | 1300 | 1360 | 1444 | 1247 | 1407 | 1514 | 1598 | 1667 | 1764 | 1141 | 1261 | 1340 | 1399 | 1448 | 1515 |

| Income: At least | Income: But less than | Michigan 6.0000% Exemptions 1 | 2 | 3 | 4 | 5 | Over 5 | Minnesota 6.8750% Exemptions 1 | 2 | 3 | 4 | 5 | Over 5 | Mississippi 7.0000% Exemptions 1 | 2 | 3 | 4 | 5 | Over 5 | Missouri 4.2250% Exemptions 1 | 2 | 3 | 4 | 5 | Over 5 | Nebraska 5.5000% Exemptions 1 | 2 | 3 | 4 | 5 | Over 5 |
|---|---|---|---|---|---|---|---|---|---|---|---|---|---|---|---|---|---|---|---|---|---|---|---|---|---|---|---|---|---|---|---|
| $0 | $20,000 | 248 | 287 | 313 | 333 | 349 | 372 | 256 | 296 | 322 | 343 | 360 | 384 | 426 | 520 | 585 | 637 | 680 | 742 | 187 | 223 | 247 | 267 | 283 | 305 | 247 | 289 | 317 | 339 | 357 | 382 |
| 20,000 | 30,000 | 379 | 436 | 474 | 504 | 528 | 561 | 413 | 476 | 518 | 551 | 578 | 616 | 644 | 783 | 879 | 956 | 1020 | 1111 | 285 | 338 | 374 | 402 | 426 | 459 | 395 | 461 | 505 | 540 | 569 | 609 |
| 30,000 | 40,000 | 444 | 510 | 554 | 588 | 616 | 655 | 493 | 568 | 618 | 657 | 689 | 734 | 751 | 912 | 1023 | 1112 | 1186 | 1291 | 334 | 395 | 436 | 469 | 496 | 535 | 470 | 548 | 601 | 642 | 676 | 723 |
| 40,000 | 50,000 | 500 | 573 | 622 | 659 | 690 | 733 | 561 | 646 | 703 | 748 | 784 | 835 | 841 | 1020 | 1144 | 1243 | 1325 | 1443 | 375 | 443 | 489 | 525 | 556 | 599 | 534 | 623 | 683 | 729 | 767 | 821 |
| 50,000 | 60,000 | 549 | 629 | 682 | 723 | 756 | 803 | 623 | 717 | 780 | 829 | 869 | 925 | 921 | 1116 | 1251 | 1358 | 1448 | 1576 | 412 | 486 | 536 | 576 | 609 | 655 | 592 | 690 | 756 | 807 | 849 | 908 |
| 60,000 | 70,000 | 594 | 679 | 736 | 780 | 816 | 866 | 679 | 782 | 850 | 903 | 947 | 1008 | 993 | 1203 | 1348 | 1462 | 1559 | 1696 | 446 | 524 | 578 | 621 | 656 | 706 | 644 | 751 | 823 | 878 | 924 | 988 |
| 70,000 | 80,000 | 636 | 727 | 787 | 834 | 872 | 925 | 732 | 842 | 916 | 973 | 1020 | 1086 | 1061 | 1283 | 1438 | 1560 | 1662 | 1808 | 477 | 561 | 618 | 663 | 701 | 754 | 694 | 808 | 885 | 945 | 994 | 1063 |
| 80,000 | 90,000 | 675 | 770 | 834 | 883 | 923 | 980 | 781 | 899 | 977 | 1037 | 1088 | 1157 | 1123 | 1358 | 1520 | 1649 | 1757 | 1911 | 506 | 594 | 655 | 702 | 742 | 798 | 740 | 862 | 943 | 1007 | 1059 | 1132 |
| 90,000 | 100,000 | 711 | 812 | 878 | 930 | 972 | 1031 | 828 | 952 | 1035 | 1099 | 1152 | 1226 | 1181 | 1427 | 1598 | 1733 | 1846 | 2008 | 533 | 626 | 689 | 739 | 780 | 839 | 783 | 912 | 998 | 1065 | 1120 | 1198 |
| 100,000 | 120,000 | 760 | 866 | 937 | 991 | 1036 | 1098 | 889 | 1022 | 1111 | 1179 | 1236 | 1315 | 1257 | 1518 | 1700 | 1843 | 1963 | 2134 | 569 | 667 | 735 | 787 | 831 | 893 | 840 | 978 | 1070 | 1142 | 1201 | 1284 |
| 120,000 | 140,000 | 825 | 940 | 1016 | 1074 | 1123 | 1190 | 973 | 1118 | 1215 | 1290 | 1351 | 1438 | 1361 | 1642 | 1837 | 1991 | 2121 | 2305 | 618 | 724 | 796 | 853 | 900 | 967 | 918 | 1068 | 1169 | 1247 | 1312 | 1402 |
| 140,000 | 160,000 | 883 | 1004 | 1085 | 1147 | 1198 | 1269 | 1047 | 1202 | 1306 | 1386 | 1452 | 1545 | 1451 | 1749 | 1956 | 2120 | 2257 | 2452 | 661 | 773 | 850 | 910 | 960 | 1030 | 986 | 1147 | 1255 | 1339 | 1408 | 1505 |
| 160,000 | 180,000 | 940 | 1068 | 1153 | 1218 | 1272 | 1348 | 1120 | 1286 | 1396 | 1482 | 1553 | 1651 | 1539 | 1855 | 2074 | 2247 | 2392 | 2598 | 703 | 822 | 903 | 966 | 1019 | 1093 | 1054 | 1226 | 1341 | 1430 | 1504 | 1607 |
| 180,000 | 200,000 | 991 | 1125 | 1214 | 1283 | 1339 | 1418 | 1186 | 1361 | 1478 | 1568 | 1643 | 1747 | 1619 | 1950 | 2179 | 2360 | 2512 | 2728 | 741 | 865 | 950 | 1017 | 1072 | 1150 | 1115 | 1297 | 1418 | 1512 | 1590 | 1699 |
| 200,000 or more | | 1245 | 1408 | 1517 | 1601 | 1670 | 1766 | 1514 | 1735 | 1883 | 1998 | 2092 | 2224 | 2008 | 2413 | 2693 | 2915 | 3100 | 3364 | 930 | 1081 | 1185 | 1266 | 1333 | 1428 | 1419 | 1648 | 1801 | 1920 | 2018 | 2155 |

(Continued on next page)

## 2010 Optional State and Certain Local Sales Tax Tables *(Continued)*

| Income: At least | But less than | Nevada[3] 6.8500%: 1 | 2 | 3 | 4 | 5 | Over 5 |
|---|---|---|---|---|---|---|---|
| $0 | $20,000 | 288 | 332 | 361 | 384 | 402 | 428 |
| 20,000 | 30,000 | 435 | 499 | 542 | 574 | 602 | 639 |
| 30,000 | 40,000 | 508 | 581 | 630 | 668 | 699 | 743 |
| 40,000 | 50,000 | 569 | 651 | 706 | 747 | 782 | 830 |
| 50,000 | 60,000 | 624 | 713 | 772 | 818 | 855 | 907 |
| 60,000 | 70,000 | 674 | 769 | 832 | 881 | 921 | 977 |
| 70,000 | 80,000 | 721 | 822 | 889 | 940 | 983 | 1042 |
| 80,000 | 90,000 | 764 | 870 | 941 | 995 | 1040 | 1102 |
| 90,000 | 100,000 | 805 | 916 | 990 | 1047 | 1093 | 1158 |
| 100,000 | 120,000 | 858 | 976 | 1054 | 1114 | 1163 | 1232 |
| 120,000 | 140,000 | 931 | 1058 | 1141 | 1206 | 1259 | 1333 |
| 140,000 | 160,000 | 995 | 1129 | 1217 | 1286 | 1342 | 1420 |
| 160,000 | 180,000 | 1058 | 1199 | 1293 | 1364 | 1424 | 1506 |
| 180,000 | 200,000 | 1115 | 1262 | 1360 | 1435 | 1497 | 1583 |
| 200,000 or more | | 1395 | 1575 | 1693 | 1784 | 1859 | 1964 |

| Income: At least | But less than | New Jersey[4] 7.0000%: 1 | 2 | 3 | 4 | 5 | Over 5 |
|---|---|---|---|---|---|---|---|
| $0 | $20,000 | 274 | 315 | 343 | 364 | 381 | 406 |
| 20,000 | 30,000 | 440 | 504 | 547 | 580 | 607 | 645 |
| 30,000 | 40,000 | 524 | 600 | 651 | 690 | 722 | 767 |
| 40,000 | 50,000 | 596 | 682 | 739 | 784 | 820 | 871 |
| 50,000 | 60,000 | 661 | 756 | 819 | 868 | 908 | 964 |
| 60,000 | 70,000 | 720 | 823 | 891 | 944 | 988 | 1048 |
| 70,000 | 80,000 | 776 | 886 | 959 | 1016 | 1063 | 1128 |
| 80,000 | 90,000 | 827 | 944 | 1023 | 1083 | 1133 | 1202 |
| 90,000 | 100,000 | 876 | 1000 | 1082 | 1146 | 1198 | 1272 |
| 100,000 | 120,000 | 940 | 1073 | 1161 | 1229 | 1285 | 1363 |
| 120,000 | 140,000 | 1029 | 1173 | 1269 | 1343 | 1404 | 1489 |
| 140,000 | 160,000 | 1106 | 1260 | 1362 | 1442 | 1507 | 1598 |
| 160,000 | 180,000 | 1182 | 1346 | 1456 | 1540 | 1610 | 1707 |
| 180,000 | 200,000 | 1251 | 1425 | 1540 | 1629 | 1702 | 1805 |
| 200,000 or more | | 1595 | 1813 | 1958 | 2070 | 2162 | 2291 |

| Income: At least | But less than | New Mexico[1] 5.0630%: 1 | 2 | 3 | 4 | 5 | Over 5 |
|---|---|---|---|---|---|---|---|
| $0 | $20,000 | 211 | 248 | 273 | 292 | 308 | 331 |
| 20,000 | 30,000 | 337 | 395 | 434 | 464 | 489 | 525 |
| 30,000 | 40,000 | 400 | 469 | 515 | 551 | 581 | 622 |
| 40,000 | 50,000 | 455 | 533 | 585 | 626 | 659 | 706 |
| 50,000 | 60,000 | 504 | 590 | 647 | 692 | 729 | 781 |
| 60,000 | 70,000 | 548 | 641 | 704 | 752 | 793 | 849 |
| 70,000 | 80,000 | 590 | 690 | 757 | 809 | 852 | 913 |
| 80,000 | 90,000 | 629 | 735 | 807 | 862 | 908 | 972 |
| 90,000 | 100,000 | 665 | 778 | 853 | 912 | 960 | 1028 |
| 100,000 | 120,000 | 713 | 834 | 915 | 977 | 1029 | 1101 |
| 120,000 | 140,000 | 779 | 911 | 999 | 1067 | 1123 | 1202 |
| 140,000 | 160,000 | 837 | 978 | 1072 | 1145 | 1205 | 1289 |
| 160,000 | 180,000 | 894 | 1044 | 1145 | 1222 | 1287 | 1376 |
| 180,000 | 200,000 | 946 | 1104 | 1210 | 1292 | 1360 | 1455 |
| 200,000 or more | | 1203 | 1402 | 1535 | 1638 | 1724 | 1843 |

| Income: At least | But less than | New York 4.0000%: 1 | 2 | 3 | 4 | 5 | Over 5 |
|---|---|---|---|---|---|---|---|
| $0 | $20,000 | 161 | 187 | 204 | 217 | 228 | 243 |
| 20,000 | 30,000 | 258 | 298 | 324 | 345 | 362 | 386 |
| 30,000 | 40,000 | 307 | 354 | 385 | 410 | 430 | 458 |
| 40,000 | 50,000 | 350 | 402 | 438 | 465 | 488 | 520 |
| 50,000 | 60,000 | 387 | 446 | 485 | 515 | 540 | 575 |
| 60,000 | 70,000 | 422 | 485 | 527 | 560 | 587 | 625 |
| 70,000 | 80,000 | 455 | 522 | 567 | 603 | 632 | 672 |
| 80,000 | 90,000 | 485 | 557 | 605 | 642 | 673 | 716 |
| 90,000 | 100,000 | 513 | 589 | 640 | 679 | 712 | 757 |
| 100,000 | 120,000 | 551 | 632 | 686 | 728 | 763 | 812 |
| 120,000 | 140,000 | 603 | 691 | 750 | 795 | 833 | 886 |
| 140,000 | 160,000 | 648 | 742 | 805 | 854 | 894 | 951 |
| 160,000 | 180,000 | 693 | 793 | 860 | 912 | 955 | 1015 |
| 180,000 | 200,000 | 733 | 839 | 910 | 965 | 1010 | 1073 |
| 200,000 or more | | 935 | 1067 | 1156 | 1225 | 1282 | 1361 |

| Income: At least | But less than | North Carolina 5.7500%: 1 | 2 | 3 | 4 | 5 | Over 5 |
|---|---|---|---|---|---|---|---|
| $0 | $20,000 | 281 | 336 | 374 | 404 | 428 | 463 |
| 20,000 | 30,000 | 436 | 519 | 576 | 621 | 658 | 711 |
| 30,000 | 40,000 | 513 | 610 | 677 | 729 | 773 | 834 |
| 40,000 | 50,000 | 578 | 687 | 762 | 821 | 870 | 930 |
| 50,000 | 60,000 | 636 | 756 | 838 | 902 | 956 | 1031 |
| 60,000 | 70,000 | 689 | 818 | 907 | 976 | 1033 | 1115 |
| 70,000 | 80,000 | 739 | 877 | 971 | 1045 | 1106 | 1193 |
| 80,000 | 90,000 | 784 | 930 | 1030 | 1108 | 1173 | 1265 |
| 90,000 | 100,000 | 827 | 981 | 1086 | 1168 | 1237 | 1333 |
| 100,000 | 120,000 | 884 | 1048 | 1159 | 1247 | 1319 | 1422 |
| 120,000 | 140,000 | 961 | 1138 | 1259 | 1353 | 1432 | 1543 |
| 140,000 | 160,000 | 1028 | 1217 | 1346 | 1446 | 1530 | 1649 |
| 160,000 | 180,000 | 1095 | 1295 | 1431 | 1538 | 1627 | 1753 |
| 180,000 | 200,000 | 1154 | 1365 | 1508 | 1620 | 1714 | 1846 |
| 200,000 or more | | 1449 | 1710 | 1887 | 2026 | 2142 | 2305 |

| Income: At least | But less than | North Dakota 5.0000%: 1 | 2 | 3 | 4 | 5 | Over 5 |
|---|---|---|---|---|---|---|---|
| $0 | $20,000 | 200 | 236 | 261 | 280 | 296 | 319 |
| 20,000 | 30,000 | 305 | 358 | 394 | 423 | 446 | 480 |
| 30,000 | 40,000 | 358 | 419 | 460 | 493 | 520 | 559 |
| 40,000 | 50,000 | 403 | 470 | 516 | 553 | 583 | 626 |
| 50,000 | 60,000 | 443 | 516 | 566 | 606 | 638 | 685 |
| 60,000 | 70,000 | 480 | 558 | 611 | 653 | 688 | 738 |
| 70,000 | 80,000 | 514 | 597 | 654 | 698 | 735 | 788 |
| 80,000 | 90,000 | 545 | 633 | 693 | 739 | 779 | 834 |
| 90,000 | 100,000 | 575 | 667 | 729 | 778 | 819 | 877 |
| 100,000 | 120,000 | 615 | 711 | 778 | 829 | 873 | 934 |
| 120,000 | 140,000 | 668 | 772 | 843 | 899 | 946 | 1011 |
| 140,000 | 160,000 | 715 | 825 | 900 | 959 | 1009 | 1078 |
| 160,000 | 180,000 | 762 | 878 | 957 | 1019 | 1071 | 1145 |
| 180,000 | 200,000 | 804 | 925 | 1008 | 1073 | 1127 | 1204 |
| 200,000 or more | | 1013 | 1159 | 1260 | 1339 | 1404 | 1498 |

| Income: At least | But less than | Ohio 5.5000%: 1 | 2 | 3 | 4 | 5 | Over 5 |
|---|---|---|---|---|---|---|---|
| $0 | $20,000 | 242 | 281 | 307 | 327 | 343 | 366 |
| 20,000 | 30,000 | 385 | 445 | 485 | 517 | 542 | 578 |
| 30,000 | 40,000 | 457 | 528 | 576 | 613 | 643 | 685 |
| 40,000 | 50,000 | 520 | 600 | 653 | 695 | 729 | 776 |
| 50,000 | 60,000 | 575 | 664 | 723 | 768 | 806 | 858 |
| 60,000 | 70,000 | 626 | 722 | 785 | 835 | 875 | 932 |
| 70,000 | 80,000 | 674 | 776 | 845 | 897 | 941 | 1002 |
| 80,000 | 90,000 | 718 | 827 | 900 | 956 | 1002 | 1066 |
| 90,000 | 100,000 | 760 | 875 | 951 | 1011 | 1059 | 1127 |
| 100,000 | 120,000 | 815 | 938 | 1020 | 1083 | 1135 | 1208 |
| 120,000 | 140,000 | 891 | 1024 | 1113 | 1182 | 1238 | 1317 |
| 140,000 | 160,000 | 957 | 1099 | 1194 | 1268 | 1328 | 1413 |
| 160,000 | 180,000 | 1022 | 1174 | 1275 | 1353 | 1418 | 1508 |
| 180,000 | 200,000 | 1081 | 1241 | 1348 | 1430 | 1498 | 1593 |
| 200,000 or more | | 1376 | 1576 | 1710 | 1813 | 1898 | 2017 |

| Income: At least | But less than | Oklahoma 4.5000%: 1 | 2 | 3 | 4 | 5 | Over 5 |
|---|---|---|---|---|---|---|---|
| $0 | $20,000 | 249 | 304 | 343 | 374 | 400 | 438 |
| 20,000 | 30,000 | 380 | 462 | 519 | 565 | 604 | 659 |
| 30,000 | 40,000 | 445 | 540 | 606 | 659 | 704 | 768 |
| 40,000 | 50,000 | 500 | 606 | 680 | 739 | 788 | 859 |
| 50,000 | 60,000 | 549 | 664 | 745 | 809 | 863 | 940 |
| 60,000 | 70,000 | 594 | 717 | 803 | 872 | 930 | 1013 |
| 70,000 | 80,000 | 635 | 767 | 859 | 932 | 993 | 1082 |
| 80,000 | 90,000 | 674 | 812 | 909 | 986 | 1051 | 1144 |
| 90,000 | 100,000 | 710 | 855 | 957 | 1038 | 1106 | 1204 |
| 100,000 | 120,000 | 758 | 912 | 1019 | 1105 | 1177 | 1281 |
| 120,000 | 140,000 | 823 | 988 | 1104 | 1197 | 1274 | 1386 |
| 140,000 | 160,000 | 879 | 1055 | 1178 | 1276 | 1358 | 1477 |
| 160,000 | 180,000 | 936 | 1121 | 1251 | 1354 | 1442 | 1566 |
| 180,000 | 200,000 | 986 | 1180 | 1316 | 1425 | 1516 | 1647 |
| 200,000 or more | | 1236 | 1472 | 1638 | 1770 | 1882 | 2041 |

| Income: At least | But less than | Pennsylvania 6.0000%: 1 | 2 | 3 | 4 | 5 | Over 5 |
|---|---|---|---|---|---|---|---|
| $0 | $20,000 | 223 | 256 | 279 | 296 | 310 | 329 |
| 20,000 | 30,000 | 355 | 407 | 441 | 468 | 490 | 520 |
| 30,000 | 40,000 | 422 | 483 | 524 | 555 | 581 | 617 |
| 40,000 | 50,000 | 480 | 548 | 594 | 629 | 658 | 699 |
| 50,000 | 60,000 | 531 | 607 | 657 | 696 | 728 | 773 |
| 60,000 | 70,000 | 578 | 660 | 714 | 756 | 791 | 839 |
| 70,000 | 80,000 | 622 | 710 | 768 | 813 | 850 | 902 |
| 80,000 | 90,000 | 663 | 756 | 818 | 866 | 905 | 960 |
| 90,000 | 100,000 | 702 | 800 | 865 | 916 | 957 | 1015 |
| 100,000 | 120,000 | 753 | 858 | 927 | 981 | 1026 | 1087 |
| 120,000 | 140,000 | 823 | 937 | 1012 | 1071 | 1119 | 1186 |
| 140,000 | 160,000 | 884 | 1005 | 1086 | 1149 | 1200 | 1272 |
| 160,000 | 180,000 | 944 | 1074 | 1160 | 1226 | 1281 | 1357 |
| 180,000 | 200,000 | 999 | 1135 | 1226 | 1296 | 1354 | 1434 |
| 200,000 or more | | 1270 | 1441 | 1555 | 1642 | 1714 | 1815 |

| Income: At least | But less than | Rhode Island 7.0000%: 1 | 2 | 3 | 4 | 5 | Over 5 |
|---|---|---|---|---|---|---|---|
| $0 | $20,000 | 271 | 311 | 337 | 357 | 373 | 396 |
| 20,000 | 30,000 | 408 | 465 | 503 | 532 | 556 | 589 |
| 30,000 | 40,000 | 476 | 541 | 585 | 618 | 645 | 683 |
| 40,000 | 50,000 | 533 | 605 | 653 | 690 | 720 | 763 |
| 50,000 | 60,000 | 583 | 662 | 714 | 754 | 787 | 833 |
| 60,000 | 70,000 | 629 | 713 | 769 | 812 | 847 | 896 |
| 70,000 | 80,000 | 671 | 761 | 820 | 865 | 903 | 954 |
| 80,000 | 90,000 | 711 | 805 | 867 | 915 | 954 | 1008 |
| 90,000 | 100,000 | 747 | 846 | 911 | 961 | 1002 | 1059 |
| 100,000 | 120,000 | 796 | 900 | 969 | 1022 | 1065 | 1125 |
| 120,000 | 140,000 | 861 | 973 | 1047 | 1104 | 1151 | 1215 |
| 140,000 | 160,000 | 918 | 1037 | 1115 | 1175 | 1225 | 1293 |
| 160,000 | 180,000 | 975 | 1100 | 1182 | 1246 | 1298 | 1370 |
| 180,000 | 200,000 | 1025 | 1156 | 1243 | 1309 | 1363 | 1439 |
| 200,000 or more | | 1273 | 1432 | 1537 | 1617 | 1683 | 1774 |

| Income: At least | But less than | South Carolina 6.0000%: 1 | 2 | 3 | 4 | 5 | Over 5 |
|---|---|---|---|---|---|---|---|
| $0 | $20,000 | 259 | 301 | 329 | 351 | 369 | 394 |
| 20,000 | 30,000 | 411 | 477 | 521 | 555 | 583 | 622 |
| 30,000 | 40,000 | 487 | 565 | 617 | 658 | 691 | 737 |
| 40,000 | 50,000 | 553 | 641 | 700 | 745 | 783 | 835 |
| 50,000 | 60,000 | 612 | 709 | 774 | 824 | 865 | 922 |
| 60,000 | 70,000 | 665 | 771 | 841 | 895 | 939 | 1002 |
| 70,000 | 80,000 | 716 | 829 | 904 | 962 | 1010 | 1076 |
| 80,000 | 90,000 | 762 | 882 | 962 | 1024 | 1074 | 1145 |
| 90,000 | 100,000 | 807 | 933 | 1017 | 1082 | 1136 | 1211 |
| 100,000 | 120,000 | 865 | 1000 | 1090 | 1159 | 1216 | 1296 |
| 120,000 | 140,000 | 944 | 1091 | 1189 | 1264 | 1327 | 1413 |
| 140,000 | 160,000 | 1013 | 1170 | 1275 | 1356 | 1422 | 1515 |
| 160,000 | 180,000 | 1082 | 1249 | 1361 | 1447 | 1518 | 1617 |
| 180,000 | 200,000 | 1144 | 1320 | 1438 | 1529 | 1603 | 1708 |
| 200,000 or more | | 1451 | 1673 | 1821 | 1934 | 2028 | 2159 |

| Income: At least | But less than | South Dakota 4.0000%: 1 | 2 | 3 | 4 | 5 | Over 5 |
|---|---|---|---|---|---|---|---|
| $0 | $20,000 | 242 | 297 | 335 | 366 | 391 | 428 |
| 20,000 | 30,000 | 368 | 449 | 506 | 551 | 589 | 644 |
| 30,000 | 40,000 | 429 | 524 | 590 | 642 | 686 | 749 |
| 40,000 | 50,000 | 482 | 587 | 661 | 719 | 768 | 838 |
| 50,000 | 60,000 | 528 | 643 | 723 | 786 | 840 | 916 |
| 60,000 | 70,000 | 570 | 693 | 779 | 847 | 905 | 987 |
| 70,000 | 80,000 | 609 | 740 | 832 | 904 | 965 | 1053 |
| 80,000 | 90,000 | 645 | 783 | 880 | 957 | 1021 | 1113 |
| 90,000 | 100,000 | 678 | 824 | 925 | 1006 | 1073 | 1170 |
| 100,000 | 120,000 | 723 | 877 | 985 | 1070 | 1142 | 1244 |
| 120,000 | 140,000 | 783 | 949 | 1065 | 1157 | 1235 | 1345 |
| 140,000 | 160,000 | 835 | 1012 | 1135 | 1233 | 1315 | 1432 |
| 160,000 | 180,000 | 887 | 1074 | 1204 | 1307 | 1394 | 1518 |
| 180,000 | 200,000 | 933 | 1129 | 1266 | 1374 | 1465 | 1595 |
| 200,000 or more | | 1159 | 1400 | 1567 | 1700 | 1811 | 1970 |

| Income: At least | But less than | Tennessee 7.0000%: 1 | 2 | 3 | 4 | 5 | Over 5 |
|---|---|---|---|---|---|---|---|
| $0 | $20,000 | 398 | 483 | 541 | 587 | 626 | 681 |
| 20,000 | 30,000 | 583 | 703 | 785 | 850 | 905 | 983 |
| 30,000 | 40,000 | 673 | 809 | 903 | 977 | 1039 | 1127 |
| 40,000 | 50,000 | 748 | 898 | 1001 | 1082 | 1151 | 1248 |
| 50,000 | 60,000 | 815 | 976 | 1087 | 1175 | 1249 | 1354 |
| 60,000 | 70,000 | 875 | 1046 | 1165 | 1259 | 1337 | 1449 |
| 70,000 | 80,000 | 930 | 1112 | 1237 | 1336 | 1419 | 1537 |
| 80,000 | 90,000 | 982 | 1172 | 1303 | 1407 | 1494 | 1617 |
| 90,000 | 100,000 | 1030 | 1228 | 1366 | 1474 | 1564 | 1693 |
| 100,000 | 120,000 | 1093 | 1302 | 1447 | 1560 | 1656 | 1791 |
| 120,000 | 140,000 | 1178 | 1402 | 1556 | 1678 | 1780 | 1925 |
| 140,000 | 160,000 | 1252 | 1488 | 1651 | 1779 | 1887 | 2039 |
| 160,000 | 180,000 | 1325 | 1573 | 1744 | 1879 | 1992 | 2152 |
| 180,000 | 200,000 | 1391 | 1649 | 1827 | 1968 | 2085 | 2253 |
| 200,000 or more | | 1711 | 2020 | 2234 | 2401 | 2542 | 2742 |

| Income: At least | But less than | Texas 6.2500%: 1 | 2 | 3 | 4 | 5 | Over 5 |
|---|---|---|---|---|---|---|---|
| $0 | $20,000 | 276 | 326 | 359 | 386 | 408 | 438 |
| 20,000 | 30,000 | 439 | 517 | 570 | 611 | 646 | 694 |
| 30,000 | 40,000 | 522 | 614 | 677 | 726 | 766 | 823 |
| 40,000 | 50,000 | 593 | 697 | 768 | 823 | 869 | 933 |
| 50,000 | 60,000 | 656 | 772 | 849 | 910 | 960 | 1031 |
| 60,000 | 70,000 | 714 | 839 | 924 | 989 | 1044 | 1121 |
| 70,000 | 80,000 | 769 | 903 | 993 | 1064 | 1122 | 1205 |
| 80,000 | 90,000 | 819 | 961 | 1058 | 1133 | 1195 | 1283 |
| 90,000 | 100,000 | 867 | 1017 | 1119 | 1198 | 1264 | 1356 |
| 100,000 | 120,000 | 929 | 1090 | 1199 | 1283 | 1354 | 1453 |
| 120,000 | 140,000 | 1015 | 1190 | 1308 | 1401 | 1477 | 1585 |
| 140,000 | 160,000 | 1090 | 1277 | 1404 | 1503 | 1584 | 1699 |
| 160,000 | 180,000 | 1164 | 1364 | 1499 | 1604 | 1691 | 1814 |
| 180,000 | 200,000 | 1231 | 1442 | 1584 | 1695 | 1787 | 1916 |
| 200,000 or more | | 1564 | 1829 | 2008 | 2147 | 2263 | 2425 |

| Income: At least | But less than | Utah 4.7000%: 1 | 2 | 3 | 4 | 5 | Over 5 |
|---|---|---|---|---|---|---|---|
| $0 | $20,000 | 249 | 300 | 335 | 363 | 386 | 419 |
| 20,000 | 30,000 | 384 | 461 | 514 | 556 | 591 | 640 |
| 30,000 | 40,000 | 451 | 541 | 603 | 651 | 692 | 750 |
| 40,000 | 50,000 | 509 | 609 | 678 | 732 | 778 | 842 |
| 50,000 | 60,000 | 560 | 669 | 745 | 804 | 854 | 925 |
| 60,000 | 70,000 | 606 | 724 | 805 | 869 | 923 | 999 |
| 70,000 | 80,000 | 649 | 775 | 862 | 930 | 987 | 1068 |
| 80,000 | 90,000 | 690 | 822 | 914 | 986 | 1047 | 1132 |
| 90,000 | 100,000 | 727 | 867 | 963 | 1039 | 1103 | 1193 |
| 100,000 | 120,000 | 777 | 926 | 1028 | 1108 | 1176 | 1272 |
| 120,000 | 140,000 | 845 | 1005 | 1116 | 1203 | 1276 | 1379 |
| 140,000 | 160,000 | 904 | 1074 | 1192 | 1285 | 1362 | 1472 |
| 160,000 | 180,000 | 962 | 1143 | 1268 | 1366 | 1448 | 1564 |
| 180,000 | 200,000 | 1014 | 1205 | 1335 | 1438 | 1525 | 1647 |
| 200,000 or more | | 1274 | 1508 | 1669 | 1796 | 1903 | 2053 |

| Income: At least | But less than | Vermont 6.0000%: 1 | 2 | 3 | 4 | 5 | Over 5 |
|---|---|---|---|---|---|---|---|
| $0 | $20,000 | 182 | 202 | 216 | 226 | 234 | 245 |
| 20,000 | 30,000 | 273 | 302 | 321 | 336 | 347 | 363 |
| 30,000 | 40,000 | 318 | 352 | 373 | 390 | 403 | 421 |
| 40,000 | 50,000 | 356 | 393 | 417 | 435 | 450 | 470 |
| 50,000 | 60,000 | 390 | 430 | 456 | 475 | 491 | 513 |
| 60,000 | 70,000 | 420 | 463 | 491 | 512 | 529 | 552 |
| 70,000 | 80,000 | 449 | 494 | 524 | 546 | 564 | 588 |
| 80,000 | 90,000 | 475 | 523 | 554 | 577 | 596 | 622 |
| 90,000 | 100,000 | 500 | 550 | 582 | 606 | 626 | 653 |
| 100,000 | 120,000 | 533 | 585 | 619 | 645 | 666 | 694 |
| 120,000 | 140,000 | 577 | 634 | 670 | 697 | 720 | 750 |
| 140,000 | 160,000 | 616 | 675 | 714 | 743 | 766 | 799 |
| 160,000 | 180,000 | 654 | 717 | 757 | 788 | 813 | 847 |
| 180,000 | 200,000 | 688 | 754 | 796 | 828 | 854 | 889 |
| 200,000 or more | | 857 | 936 | 988 | 1026 | 1057 | 1100 |

| Income: At least | But less than | Virginia 4.0000%: 1 | 2 | 3 | 4 | 5 | Over 5 |
|---|---|---|---|---|---|---|---|
| $0 | $20,000 | 185 | 220 | 244 | 263 | 279 | 301 |
| 20,000 | 30,000 | 276 | 327 | 361 | 389 | 411 | 443 |
| 30,000 | 40,000 | 321 | 379 | 419 | 450 | 476 | 512 |
| 40,000 | 50,000 | 359 | 423 | 467 | 501 | 530 | 570 |
| 50,000 | 60,000 | 393 | 462 | 510 | 547 | 578 | 621 |
| 60,000 | 70,000 | 423 | 498 | 548 | 588 | 621 | 667 |
| 70,000 | 80,000 | 452 | 531 | 584 | 626 | 661 | 710 |
| 80,000 | 90,000 | 478 | 561 | 617 | 661 | 698 | 750 |
| 90,000 | 100,000 | 503 | 590 | 648 | 694 | 733 | 787 |
| 100,000 | 120,000 | 536 | 627 | 689 | 738 | 778 | 835 |
| 120,000 | 140,000 | 580 | 678 | 744 | 797 | 840 | 901 |
| 140,000 | 160,000 | 619 | 722 | 792 | 847 | 893 | 958 |
| 160,000 | 180,000 | 657 | 766 | 840 | 898 | 946 | 1014 |
| 180,000 | 200,000 | 691 | 805 | 882 | 943 | 993 | 1065 |
| 200,000 or more | | 861 | 998 | 1091 | 1164 | 1225 | 1311 |

| Income: At least | But less than | Washington 6.5000%: 1 | 2 | 3 | 4 | 5 | Over 5 |
|---|---|---|---|---|---|---|---|
| $0 | $20,000 | 280 | 330 | 364 | 391 | 414 | 445 |
| 20,000 | 30,000 | 449 | 529 | 583 | 625 | 660 | 709 |
| 30,000 | 40,000 | 536 | 630 | 694 | 744 | 785 | 844 |
| 40,000 | 50,000 | 610 | 717 | 789 | 845 | 892 | 958 |
| 50,000 | 60,000 | 677 | 795 | 874 | 936 | 988 | 1061 |
| 60,000 | 70,000 | 738 | 865 | 952 | 1019 | 1076 | 1155 |
| 70,000 | 80,000 | 796 | 932 | 1025 | 1098 | 1158 | 1243 |
| 80,000 | 90,000 | 849 | 994 | 1093 | 1170 | 1234 | 1325 |
| 90,000 | 100,000 | 899 | 1053 | 1157 | 1239 | 1306 | 1402 |
| 100,000 | 120,000 | 966 | 1130 | 1242 | 1329 | 1401 | 1503 |
| 120,000 | 140,000 | 1057 | 1236 | 1358 | 1453 | 1531 | 1643 |
| 140,000 | 160,000 | 1137 | 1329 | 1459 | 1560 | 1645 | 1764 |
| 160,000 | 180,000 | 1216 | 1421 | 1560 | 1668 | 1758 | 1885 |
| 180,000 | 200,000 | 1288 | 1504 | 1650 | 1765 | 1860 | 1993 |
| 200,000 or more | | 1645 | 1917 | 2102 | 2246 | 2365 | 2534 |

| Income: At least | But less than | West Virginia 6.0000%: 1 | 2 | 3 | 4 | 5 | Over 5 |
|---|---|---|---|---|---|---|---|
| $0 | $20,000 | 306 | 368 | 411 | 445 | 474 | 514 |
| 20,000 | 30,000 | 478 | 573 | 638 | 690 | 733 | 795 |
| 30,000 | 40,000 | 564 | 675 | 752 | 812 | 863 | 934 |
| 40,000 | 50,000 | 637 | 762 | 848 | 916 | 972 | 1053 |
| 50,000 | 60,000 | 703 | 839 | 934 | 1008 | 1070 | 1158 |
| 60,000 | 70,000 | 762 | 910 | 1011 | 1091 | 1159 | 1254 |
| 70,000 | 80,000 | 818 | 976 | 1084 | 1170 | 1242 | 1343 |
| 80,000 | 90,000 | 870 | 1037 | 1152 | 1242 | 1318 | 1426 |
| 90,000 | 100,000 | 918 | 1094 | 1215 | 1310 | 1390 | 1503 |
| 100,000 | 120,000 | 982 | 1170 | 1298 | 1400 | 1485 | 1605 |
| 120,000 | 140,000 | 1070 | 1273 | 1412 | 1522 | 1614 | 1744 |
| 140,000 | 160,000 | 1146 | 1362 | 1511 | 1628 | 1726 | 1865 |
| 160,000 | 180,000 | 1222 | 1451 | 1609 | 1733 | 1837 | 1985 |
| 180,000 | 200,000 | 1290 | 1531 | 1697 | 1828 | 1937 | 2092 |
| 200,000 or more | | 1626 | 1926 | 2131 | 2293 | 2429 | 2621 |

| Income: At least | But less than | Wisconsin 5.0000%: 1 | 2 | 3 | 4 | 5 | Over 5 |
|---|---|---|---|---|---|---|---|
| $0 | $20,000 | 228 | 267 | 294 | 314 | 331 | 355 |
| 20,000 | 30,000 | 362 | 424 | 465 | 497 | 524 | 561 |
| 30,000 | 40,000 | 430 | 503 | 552 | 590 | 621 | 665 |
| 40,000 | 50,000 | 488 | 570 | 626 | 668 | 704 | 754 |
| 50,000 | 60,000 | 540 | 631 | 692 | 739 | 778 | 833 |
| 60,000 | 70,000 | 588 | 686 | 752 | 803 | 845 | 905 |
| 70,000 | 80,000 | 632 | 737 | 808 | 863 | 909 | 972 |
| 80,000 | 90,000 | 673 | 785 | 861 | 919 | 967 | 1035 |
| 90,000 | 100,000 | 712 | 830 | 910 | 971 | 1022 | 1094 |
| 100,000 | 120,000 | 763 | 890 | 975 | 1041 | 1095 | 1171 |
| 120,000 | 140,000 | 834 | 971 | 1063 | 1135 | 1194 | 1277 |
| 140,000 | 160,000 | 895 | 1042 | 1141 | 1217 | 1281 | 1369 |
| 160,000 | 180,000 | 955 | 1112 | 1218 | 1299 | 1367 | 1461 |
| 180,000 | 200,000 | 1010 | 1176 | 1287 | 1373 | 1444 | 1543 |
| 200,000 or more | | 1281 | 1489 | 1629 | 1737 | 1826 | 1951 |

| Income: At least | But less than | Wyoming 4.0000%: 1 | 2 | 3 | 4 | 5 | Over 5 |
|---|---|---|---|---|---|---|---|
| $0 | $20,000 | 171 | 200 | 219 | 234 | 246 | 264 |
| 20,000 | 30,000 | 274 | 319 | 349 | 373 | 392 | 419 |
| 30,000 | 40,000 | 327 | 380 | 415 | 443 | 466 | 498 |
| 40,000 | 50,000 | 372 | 432 | 472 | 503 | 529 | 565 |
| 50,000 | 60,000 | 412 | 478 | 523 | 557 | 586 | 626 |
| 60,000 | 70,000 | 449 | 521 | 569 | 606 | 637 | 681 |
| 70,000 | 80,000 | 484 | 561 | 613 | 653 | 686 | 732 |
| 80,000 | 90,000 | 516 | 598 | 653 | 696 | 731 | 780 |
| 90,000 | 100,000 | 547 | 633 | 691 | 736 | 773 | 826 |
| 100,000 | 120,000 | 587 | 679 | 741 | 790 | 829 | 885 |
| 120,000 | 140,000 | 642 | 743 | 810 | 863 | 906 | 967 |
| 140,000 | 160,000 | 690 | 798 | 870 | 926 | 973 | 1038 |
| 160,000 | 180,000 | 738 | 853 | 930 | 990 | 1039 | 1109 |
| 180,000 | 200,000 | 781 | 903 | 984 | 1047 | 1099 | 1172 |
| 200,000 or more | | 997 | 1150 | 1252 | 1331 | 1397 | 1489 |

**Note. Alaska** does not have a state sales tax. Alaska residents should follow the instructions on the next page to determine their local sales tax amount.

1 The rates for Arizona, Kansas, and New Mexico increased during 2010, so the rates given are averaged over the year.

2 The California table includes the 1% uniform local sales tax rate in addition to the 7.2500% state sales tax rate.

3 The Nevada table includes the 2.25% uniform local sales tax rate in addition to the 4.6000% state sales tax rate.

4 Residents of Salem County should deduct only half of the amount in the state table.

5 The 4.0% rate for Hawaii is actually an excise tax but is treated as a sales tax for purpose of this deduction.

## Which Optional Local Sales Tax Table Should I Use?

| IF you live in the state of... | AND you live in... | THEN use Local Table... |
|---|---|---|
| Alaska | Any locality | C |
| Arizona | Mesa or Tucson | A |
| | Chandler, Gilbert, Glendale, Peoria, Phoenix, Scottsdale, Tempe, Yuma, or any other locality | B |
| Arkansas | Any locality | C |
| California | Los Angeles County | A |
| Colorado | Adams County, Arapahoe County, Boulder County, Centennial, Colorado Springs, Denver City/Denver County, El Paso County, Greeley, Jefferson County, Larimer County, Pueblo County, or any other locality | A |
| | Arvada, Aurora, City of Boulder, Fort Collins, Lakewood, Longmont, City of Pueblo, Thornton, or Westminster | B |
| Georgia | Any locality | B |
| Illinois | Any locality | A |
| Louisiana | East Baton Rouge Parish | B |
| | Any other locality | C |
| Missouri | Any locality | B |
| New York | New York City | A |
| | One of the following counties: Albany, Allegany, Cattaraugus, Cayuga, Chemung, Clinton, Cortland, Dutchess, Erie, Essex, Franklin, Fulton, Genesee, Herkimer, Jefferson, Lewis, Livingston, Monroe, Montgomery, Nassau, Niagara, Oneida, Onondaga, Ontario, Orange, Orleans, Oswego, Otsego, Putnam, Rensselaer, Rockland, St. Lawrence, Saratoga, Schenectady, Schoharie, Seneca, Steuben, Suffolk, Sullivan, Tompkins, Ulster, Warren, Washington, Westchester, Wyoming, or Yates<br><br>Or the City of Oneida | B |
| | Any other locality | D |
| North Carolina | Any locality | B |
| South Carolina | Cherokee County, Chesterfield County, Darlington County, Dillon County, Horry County, Jasper County, Lee County, Lexington County, or Myrtle Beach | B |
| | Any other locality | C |
| Tennessee | Any locality | B |
| Utah | Any locality | B |
| Virginia | Any locality | B |

## 2010 Optional Local Sales Tax Tables for Certain Local Jurisdictions

**(Based on a local sales tax rate of 1 percent)***

| Income | | Local Table A | | | | | | Local Table B | | | | | | Local Table C | | | | | | Local Table D | | | | | |
|---|---|---|---|---|---|---|---|---|---|---|---|---|---|---|---|---|---|---|---|---|---|---|---|---|---|
| | | Exemptions | | | | | | Exemptions | | | | | | Exemptions | | | | | | Exemptions | | | | | |
| At least | But less than | 1 | 2 | 3 | 4 | 5 | Over 5 | 1 | 2 | 3 | 4 | 5 | Over 5 | 1 | 2 | 3 | 4 | 5 | Over 5 | 1 | 2 | 3 | 4 | 5 | Over 5 |
| $0 | $20,000 | 43 | 50 | 55 | 59 | 62 | 66 | 50 | 60 | 66 | 72 | 76 | 83 | 61 | 75 | 84 | 91 | 97 | 106 | 40 | 47 | 51 | 54 | 57 | 61 |
| 20,000 | 30,000 | 65 | 76 | 83 | 89 | 93 | 100 | 76 | 91 | 101 | 109 | 115 | 125 | 93 | 112 | 125 | 136 | 145 | 158 | 65 | 75 | 81 | 86 | 91 | 97 |
| 30,000 | 40,000 | 76 | 89 | 97 | 103 | 109 | 116 | 89 | 106 | 118 | 127 | 135 | 146 | 108 | 130 | 146 | 158 | 168 | 183 | 77 | 89 | 96 | 103 | 108 | 115 |
| 40,000 | 50,000 | 86 | 99 | 109 | 116 | 122 | 130 | 100 | 119 | 132 | 142 | 151 | 163 | 121 | 146 | 163 | 177 | 188 | 204 | 88 | 101 | 110 | 116 | 122 | 130 |
| 50,000 | 60,000 | 94 | 109 | 119 | 127 | 133 | 142 | 110 | 130 | 145 | 156 | 165 | 179 | 132 | 159 | 178 | 193 | 205 | 223 | 97 | 112 | 121 | 129 | 135 | 144 |
| 60,000 | 70,000 | 102 | 118 | 128 | 137 | 143 | 153 | 119 | 141 | 156 | 168 | 178 | 193 | 143 | 172 | 192 | 208 | 221 | 240 | 106 | 121 | 132 | 140 | 147 | 156 |
| 70,000 | 80,000 | 109 | 126 | 137 | 146 | 153 | 163 | 127 | 151 | 167 | 180 | 190 | 206 | 152 | 183 | 205 | 222 | 236 | 256 | 114 | 131 | 142 | 151 | 158 | 168 |
| 80,000 | 90,000 | 116 | 133 | 145 | 154 | 162 | 173 | 135 | 160 | 177 | 190 | 202 | 218 | 161 | 194 | 216 | 234 | 249 | 270 | 121 | 139 | 151 | 161 | 168 | 179 |
| 90,000 | 100,000 | 122 | 140 | 153 | 163 | 171 | 182 | 142 | 168 | 186 | 200 | 212 | 229 | 170 | 204 | 227 | 246 | 262 | 284 | 128 | 147 | 160 | 170 | 178 | 189 |
| 100,000 | 120,000 | 130 | 150 | 163 | 173 | 182 | 194 | 151 | 179 | 198 | 213 | 226 | 244 | 181 | 217 | 242 | 262 | 278 | 302 | 138 | 158 | 172 | 182 | 191 | 203 |
| 120,000 | 140,000 | 141 | 162 | 176 | 187 | 197 | 209 | 164 | 194 | 215 | 231 | 245 | 264 | 195 | 234 | 261 | 283 | 300 | 326 | 151 | 173 | 188 | 199 | 208 | 222 |
| 140,000 | 160,000 | 151 | 173 | 188 | 200 | 210 | 223 | 175 | 207 | 229 | 247 | 261 | 281 | 208 | 250 | 278 | 301 | 320 | 346 | 162 | 186 | 201 | 214 | 224 | 238 |
| 160,000 | 180,000 | 161 | 184 | 200 | 212 | 223 | 237 | 187 | 220 | 244 | 262 | 277 | 299 | 221 | 265 | 295 | 319 | 339 | 367 | 173 | 198 | 215 | 228 | 239 | 254 |
| 180,000 | 200,000 | 169 | 194 | 211 | 223 | 234 | 249 | 197 | 232 | 257 | 276 | 292 | 314 | 233 | 278 | 310 | 335 | 356 | 385 | 183 | 210 | 228 | 241 | 253 | 268 |
| 200,000 or more | | 213 | 242 | 263 | 278 | 291 | 309 | 246 | 290 | 319 | 343 | 362 | 390 | 289 | 344 | 383 | 413 | 439 | 475 | 234 | 267 | 289 | 306 | 321 | 340 |

*If your local rate is more than 1 percent, the local portion of your deduction for sales tax will be increased. See the instructions for line 3 of the *State and Local General Sales Tax Deduction Worksheet*.

# B

# Tax Forms

## Appendix Outline


| | | |
|---|---|---|
| **B-1** | Form 1040A U.S. Individual Income Tax Return | B-3 |
| **B-2** | Form 1040EZ Income Tax Return for Single and Joint Filers with No Dependents | B-5 |
| **B-3** | Form 1040 U.S. Individual Income Tax Return and Schedules | B-7 |
| | Schedules A&B Itemized Deductions and Interest and Dividend Income | B-9 |
| | Schedule C Profit or Loss from Business | B-11 |
| | Schedule D Capital Gains and Losses | B-13 |
| | Schedule E Supplemental Income and Loss | B-15 |
| | Schedule F Profit or Loss from Farming | B-17 |
| | Schedule R Credit for the Elderly or the Disabled | B-19 |
| | Schedule SE Self-Employment Tax | B-21 |
| | Schedule EIC Earned Income Credit | B-23 |
| **B-4** | Form 1041 U.S. Income Tax Return for Estates and Trusts | B-25 |
| | Schedule K-1 Beneficiary's Share of Income, Deductions, Credits, etc. | B-27 |
| | Schedule J Accumulation Distribution for a Complex Trust | B-29 |
| **B-5** | Form 1065 U.S. Partnership Return of Income | B-31 |
| | Schedule K-1 Partner's Share of Income, Credits, Deductions, etc. | B-36 |
| **B-6** | Form 1120 U.S. Corporation Income Tax Return | B-38 |
| **B-7** | Form 1120S U.S. Income Tax Return for an S Corporation | B-43 |
| | Schedule K-1 Shareholder's Share of Income, Credits, Deductions, etc. | B-47 |

**B-8** Amended Tax Return Forms

Form 1040X Amended U.S. Individual Income Tax Return B-49

Form 1120X Amended U.S. Corporation Income Tax Return B-51

**B-9** Application for Extension of Time to File Income Tax Returns

Form 4868 Application for Automatic Extension of Time to File U.S. Individual Income Tax Return B-53

Form 7004 Application for Automatic Extension of Time to File Corporation Income Tax Return B-54

**B-10** Underpayment of Estimated Tax

Form 2210 Underpayment of Estimated Tax by Individuals, Estates, and Trusts B-55

Form 2220 Underpayment of Estimated Tax by Corporations B-58

**B-11** Forms for Computation of Minimum Tax

Form 4626 Alternative Minimum Tax—Corporations B-60

Form 6251 Alternative Minimum Tax—Individuals B-61

**B-12** Forms for Tax Credits

Form 1116 Foreign Tax Credit B-63

Form 2441 Child and Dependent Care Expenses B-65

Form 3468 Investment Credit B-67

Form 3800 General Business Credit B-68

**B-13** Other Tax Forms

Form 2106 Employee Business Expenses B-70

Form 2120 Multiple Support Declaration B-72

Form 3903 Moving Expenses B-73

Form 4562 Depreciation and Amortization B-74

Form 4684 Casualties and Thefts B-76

Form 4797 Sales of Business Property B-78

Form 4952 Investment Interest Expense Deduction B-80

Form 6252 Installment Sale Income B-81

Form 8283 Noncash Charitable Contributions B-82

Form 8582 Passive Activity Loss Limitations B-84

Form 8615 Tax for Certain Children Who Have Investment Income of More than $1,900 B-87

Form 8814 Parents' Election to Report Child's Interest and Dividends B-88

Form 8829 Expenses for Business Use of Your Home B-89

Form 8863 Education Credits B-90

Form 8917 Tuition and Fees Deduction B-91

# B-1 Form 1040A U.S. Individual Income Tax Return

Form **1040A** | Department of the Treasury—Internal Revenue Service | **U.S. Individual Income Tax Return** (99) | **2010** | IRS Use Only—Do not write or staple in this space.

OMB No. 1545-0074

**Name, Address, and SSN**

See separate instructions.

PRINT CLEARLY

| Your first name and initial | Last name | **Your social security number** |
|---|---|---|
| If a joint return, spouse's first name and initial | Last name | **Spouse's social security number** |
| Home address (number and street). If you have a P.O. box, see instructions. | Apt. no. | ▲ Make sure the SSN(s) above and on line 6c are correct. |
| City, town or post office, state, and ZIP code. If you have a foreign address, see instructions. | | Checking a box below will not change your tax or refund. |

**Presidential Election Campaign** ▶ Check here if you, or your spouse if filing jointly, want $3 to go to this fund . . . . . . ▶ ☐ **You** ☐ **Spouse**

**Filing status**
Check only one box.

1 ☐ Single
2 ☐ Married filing jointly (even if only one had income)
3 ☐ Married filing separately. Enter spouse's SSN above and full name here. ▶
4 ☐ Head of household (with qualifying person). (See instructions.) If the qualifying person is a child but not your dependent, enter this child's name here. ▶
5 ☐ Qualifying widow(er) with dependent child (see instructions)

**Exemptions**

6a ☐ **Yourself.** If someone can claim you as a dependent, **do not** check box 6a.
b ☐ **Spouse**

Boxes checked on 6a and 6b

c **Dependents:**

If more than six dependents, see instructions.

| (1) First name Last name | (2) Dependent's social security number | (3) Dependent's relationship to you | (4) ✓ if child under age 17 qualifying for child tax credit (see page 16) |
|---|---|---|---|
| | | | ☐ |
| | | | ☐ |
| | | | ☐ |
| | | | ☐ |
| | | | ☐ |
| | | | ☐ |

No. of children on 6c who:
• lived with you
• did not live with you due to divorce or separation (see instructions)

Dependents on 6c not entered above

d Total number of exemptions claimed.

Add numbers on lines above ▶

**Income**

**Attach Form(s) W-2 here. Also attach Form(s) 1099-R if tax was withheld.**

If you did not get a W-2, see page 20.

Enclose, but do not attach, any payment. Also, please use **Form 1040-V.**

|  |  | | |  | |
|---|---|---|---|---|---|
| 7 | Wages, salaries, tips, etc. Attach Form(s) W-2. | | | 7 | |
| 8a | **Taxable** interest. Attach Schedule B if required. | | | 8a | |
| b | **Tax-exempt** interest. **Do not** include on line 8a. | 8b | | | |
| 9a | Ordinary dividends. Attach Schedule B if required. | | | 9a | |
| b | Qualified dividends (see instructions). | 9b | | | |
| 10 | Capital gain distributions (see instructions). | | | 10 | |
| 11a | IRA distributions. | 11a | **11b** Taxable amount (see instructions). | 11b | |
| 12a | Pensions and annuities. | 12a | **12b** Taxable amount (see instructions). | 12b | |
| 13 | Unemployment compensation and Alaska Permanent Fund dividends. | | | 13 | |
| 14a | Social security benefits. | 14a | **14b** Taxable amount (see instructions). | 14b | |
| 15 | Add lines 7 through 14b (far right column). This is your **total income.** ▶ | | | 15 | |

**Adjusted gross income**

|  |  | | |  | |
|---|---|---|---|---|---|
| 16 | Educator expenses (see instructions). | 16 | | | |
| 17 | IRA deduction (see instructions). | 17 | | | |
| 18 | Student loan interest deduction (see instructions). | 18 | | | |
| 19 | Tuition and fees. Attach Form 8917. | 19 | | | |
| 20 | Add lines 16 through 19. These are your **total adjustments.** | | | 20 | |
| 21 | Subtract line 20 from line 15. This is your **adjusted gross income.** ▶ | | | 21 | |

**For Disclosure, Privacy Act, and Paperwork Reduction Act Notice, see separate instructions.** Cat. No. 11327A Form **1040A** (2010)

Form 1040A (2010) Page **2**

**Tax, credits, and payments**

|  |  | | |
|---|---|---|---|
| 22 | Enter the amount from line 21 (adjusted gross income). | | 22 |
| 23a | Check if: { ☐ **You** were born before January 2, 1946, ☐ Blind / ☐ **Spouse** was born before January 2, 1946, ☐ Blind } **Total boxes checked** ▶ 23a ☐ | | |
| b | If you are married filing separately and your spouse itemizes deductions, see page 30 and check here ▶ 23b ☐ | | |
| 24 | Enter your **standard deduction** (see instructions). | | 24 |
| 25 | Subtract line 24 from line 22. If line 24 is more than line 22, enter -0-. | | 25 |
| 26 | **Exemptions.** Multiply $3,650 by the number on line 6d. | | 26 |
| 27 | Subtract line 26 from line 25. If line 26 is more than line 25, enter -0-. This is your **taxable income.** ▶ | | 27 |
| 28 | **Tax,** including any alternative minimum tax (see instructions). | | 28 |
| 29 | Credit for child and dependent care expenses. Attach Form 2441. | 29 | |
| 30 | Credit for the elderly or the disabled. Attach Schedule R. | 30 | |
| 31 | Education credits from Form 8863, line 23. | 31 | |
| 32 | Retirement savings contributions credit. Attach Form 8880. | 32 | |
| 33 | Child tax credit (see instructions). | 33 | |
| 34 | Add lines 29 through 33. These are your **total credits.** | | 34 |
| 35 | Subtract line 34 from line 28. If line 34 is more than line 28, enter -0-. | | 35 |
| 36 | Advance earned income credit payments from Form(s) W-2, box 9. | | 36 |
| 37 | Add lines 35 and 36. This is your **total tax.** ▶ | | 37 |
| 38 | Federal income tax withheld from Forms W-2 and 1099. | 38 | |
| 39 | 2010 estimated tax payments and amount applied from 2009 return. | 39 | |
| 40 | Making work pay credit. Attach Schedule M. | 40 | |
| 41a | **Earned income credit (EIC).** | 41a | |
| b | Nontaxable combat pay election. 41b | | |
| 42 | Additional child tax credit. Attach Form 8812. | 42 | |
| 43 | American opportunity credit from Form 8863, line 14. | 43 | |
| 44 | Add lines 38, 39, 40, 41a, 42, and 43. These are your **total payments.** ▶ | | 44 |

If you have a qualifying child, attach Schedule EIC.

**Refund**

|  |  | | |
|---|---|---|---|
| 45 | If line 44 is more than line 37, subtract line 37 from line 44. This is the amount you **overpaid.** | | 45 |
| 46a | Amount of line 45 you want **refunded to you.** If Form 8888 is attached, check here ▶ ☐ | | 46a |
| ▶ b | Routing number ☐☐☐☐☐☐☐☐☐ ▶ **c** Type: ☐ Checking ☐ Savings | | |
| ▶ d | Account number ☐☐☐☐☐☐☐☐☐☐☐☐☐☐☐☐☐ | | |
| 47 | Amount of line 45 you want **applied to your 2011 estimated tax.** | 47 | |

Direct deposit? See instructions and fill in 46b, 46c, and 46d or Form 8888.

**Amount you owe**

|  |  | | |
|---|---|---|---|
| 48 | **Amount you owe.** Subtract line 44 from line 37. For details on how to pay, see instructions. ▶ | | 48 |
| 49 | Estimated tax penalty (see instructions). | 49 | |

**Third party designee**

Do you want to allow another person to discuss this return with the IRS (see instructions)? ☐ **Yes.** Complete the following. ☐ **No**

Designee's name ▶ Phone no. ▶ Personal identification number (PIN) ▶ ☐☐☐☐☐

**Sign here**

Under penalties of perjury, I declare that I have examined this return and accompanying schedules and statements, and to the best of my knowledge and belief, they are true, correct, and accurately list all amounts and sources of income I received during the tax year. Declaration of preparer (other than the taxpayer) is based on all information of which the preparer has any knowledge.

Joint return? See page 13.

Keep a copy for your records.

| Your signature | Date | Your occupation | Daytime phone number |
|---|---|---|---|
| Spouse's signature. If a joint return, **both** must sign. | Date | Spouse's occupation | |

**Paid preparer use only**

| Print/type preparer's name | Preparer's signature | Date | Check ▶ ☐ if self-employed | PTIN |
|---|---|---|---|---|
| Firm's name ▶ | | | Firm's EIN ▶ | |
| Firm's address ▶ | | | Phone no. | |

Form **1040A** (2010)

# B-2 Form 1040EZ Income Tax Return for Single and Joint Filers with No Dependents

Department of the Treasury—Internal Revenue Service

Form **1040EZ** **Income Tax Return for Single and Joint Filers With No Dependents** (99) **2010** OMB No. 1545-0074

**Name, Address, and SSN**

See separate instructions.

PRINT CLEARLY

| Your first name and initial | Last name | Your social security number |
|---|---|---|
| If a joint return, spouse's first name and initial | Last name | Spouse's social security number |
| Home address (number and street). If you have a P.O. box, see instructions. | Apt. no. | ▲ Make sure the SSN(s) above are correct. ▲ |
| City, town or post office, state, and ZIP code. If you have a foreign address, see instructions. | | Checking a box below will not change your tax or refund. |

**Presidential Election Campaign** (see page 9) ▶ Check here if you, or your spouse if a joint return, want $3 to go to this fund . . ▶ ☐ **You** ☐ **Spouse**

**Income**

**Attach Form(s) W-2 here.**

Enclose, but do not attach, any payment.

You may be entitled to a larger deduction if you file Form 1040A or 1040. See *Before You Begin* on page 4.

| | | | |
|---|---|---|---|
| 1 | Wages, salaries, and tips. This should be shown in box 1 of your Form(s) W-2. Attach your Form(s) W-2. | 1 | |
| 2 | Taxable interest. If the total is over $1,500, you cannot use Form 1040EZ. | 2 | |
| 3 | Unemployment compensation and Alaska Permanent Fund dividends (see page 11). | 3 | |
| 4 | Add lines 1, 2, and 3. This is your **adjusted gross income.** | 4 | |
| 5 | If someone can claim you (or your spouse if a joint return) as a dependent, check the applicable box(es) below and enter the amount from the worksheet on back. ☐ **You** ☐ **Spouse** If no one can claim you (or your spouse if a joint return), enter $9,350 if **single;** $18,700 if **married filing jointly.** See back for explanation. | 5 | |
| 6 | Subtract line 5 from line 4. If line 5 is larger than line 4, enter -0-. This is your **taxable income.** ▶ | 6 | |

**Payments, Credits, and Tax**

| | | | |
|---|---|---|---|
| 7 | Federal income tax withheld from Form(s) W-2 and 1099. | 7 | |
| 8 | Making work pay credit (see worksheet on back). | 8 | |
| 9a | **Earned income credit (EIC)** (see page 13). | 9a | |
| b | Nontaxable combat pay election. 9b | | |
| 10 | Add lines 7, 8, and 9a. These are your **total payments and credits.** ▶ | 10 | |
| 11 | **Tax.** Use the amount on **line 6 above** to find your tax in the tax table on pages 27 through 35 of the instructions. Then, enter the tax from the table on this line. | 11 | |

**Refund**

Have it directly deposited! See page 18 and fill in 12b, 12c, and 12d or Form 8888.

| | | | |
|---|---|---|---|
| 12a | If line 10 is larger than line 11, subtract line 11 from line 10. This is your **refund.** If Form 8888 is attached, check here ▶ ☐ | 12a | |
| ▶ b | Routing number ☐☐☐☐☐☐☐☐☐ ▶ c Type: ☐ Checking ☐ Savings | | |
| ▶ d | Account number | | |

**Amount You Owe**

| | | | |
|---|---|---|---|
| 13 | If line 11 is larger than line 10, subtract line 10 from line 11. This is the **amount you owe.** For details on how to pay, see page 19. ▶ | 13 | |

**Third Party Designee**

Do you want to allow another person to discuss this return with the IRS (see page 20)? ☐ **Yes.** Complete the following. ☐ **No**

Designee's name ▶ Phone no. ▶ Personal identification number (PIN) ▶ ☐☐☐☐☐

**Sign Here**

Joint return? See page 6.

Keep a copy for your records.

Under penalties of perjury, I declare that I have examined this return, and to the best of my knowledge and belief, it is true, correct, and accurately lists all amounts and sources of income I received during the tax year. Declaration of preparer (other than the taxpayer) is based on all information of which the preparer has any knowledge.

| Your signature | Date | Your occupation | Daytime phone number |
|---|---|---|---|
| Spouse's signature. If a joint return, **both** must sign. | Date | Spouse's occupation | |

**Paid Preparer Use Only**

| Print/Type preparer's name | Preparer's signature | Date | Check ☐ if self-employed | PTIN |
|---|---|---|---|---|
| Firm's name ▶ | | | Firm's EIN ▶ | |
| Firm's address ▶ | | | Phone no. | |

**For Disclosure, Privacy Act, and Paperwork Reduction Act Notice, see page 36.** Cat. No. 11329W Form **1040EZ** (2010)

Form 1040EZ (2010) Page **2**

## Worksheet for Line 5 — Dependents Who Checked One or Both Boxes

Use this worksheet to figure the amount to enter on line 5 if someone can claim you (or your spouse if married filing jointly) as a dependent, even if that person chooses not to do so. To find out if someone can claim you as a dependent, see Pub. 501.

**A.** Amount, if any, from line 1 on front . . . . . . ______
+ 300.00 Enter total ▶ **A.** ______

**B.** Minimum standard deduction . . . . . . . . . . . . . . . . . . . . . . . . **B.** 950.00

**C.** Enter the **larger** of line A or line B here . . . . . . . . . . . . . . . . . . . . **C.** ______

**D.** Maximum standard deduction. If **single,** enter $5,700; if **married filing jointly,** enter $11,400 . **D.** ______

**E.** Enter the **smaller** of line C or line D here. This is your standard deduction . . . . . . . . **E.** ______

**F.** Exemption amount.
- If single, enter -0-.
- If married filing jointly and —
  - —both you and your spouse can be claimed as dependents, enter -0-.
  - —only one of you can be claimed as a dependent, enter $3,650.

**F.** ______

**G.** Add lines E and F. Enter the total here and on line 5 on the front . . . . . . . . . . **G.** ______

(keep a copy for your records)

**If you did not check any boxes on line 5,** enter on line 5 the amount shown below that applies to you.
- Single, enter $9,350. This is the total of your standard deduction ($5,700) and your exemption ($3,650).
- Married filing jointly, enter $18,700. This is the total of your standard deduction ($11,400), your exemption ($3,650), and your spouse's exemption ($3,650).

## Worksheet for Line 8 — Making Work Pay Credit

*Before you begin:* ✓ If you can be claimed as a dependent on someone else's return, you **do not** qualify for this credit.
✓ If married filing jointly, include your spouse's amounts with yours when completing this worksheet.

Use this worksheet to figure the amount to enter on line 8 if you **cannot** be claimed as a dependent on another person's return.

(keep a copy for your records)

**1a.** **Important.** See the instructions on page 12 if **(a)** you received a taxable scholarship or fellowship grant not reported on a Form W-2, **(b)** your wages include pay for work performed while an inmate in a penal institution, or **(c)** you received a pension or annuity from a nonqualified deferred compensation plan or a nongovernmental section 457 plan.
Do you (and your spouse if filing jointly) have 2010 wages of more than $6,451 ($12,903 if married filing jointly)?
☐ **Yes.** Skip lines 1a through 3. Enter $400 ($800 if married filing jointly) on line 4 and go to line 5.
☐ **No.** Enter your earned income (see instructions) . . . . . **1a.** ______

**b.** Nontaxable combat pay included on line 1a (see instructions) . . . . . . . . . . . **1b.** ______

**2.** Multiply line 1a by 6.2% (.062) . . . . . . . . . . . . . **2.** ______

**3.** Enter $400 ($800 if married filing jointly) . . . . . . . . . . **3.** ______

**4.** Enter the **smaller** of line 2 or line 3 (unless you checked "Yes" on line 1a) . . . . . . . **4.** ______

**5.** Enter amount from Form 1040EZ, line 4 (on front) . . . . . . **5.** ______

**6.** Enter $75,000 ($150,000 if married filing jointly) . . . . . . **6.** ______

**7.** Is the amount on line 5 more than the amount on line 6?
☐ **No.** Skip line 8. Enter the amount from line 4 on line 9 below.
☐ **Yes.** Subtract line 6 from line 5. . . . . . . . . . . . **7.** ______

**8.** Multiply line 7 by 2% (.02) . . . . . . . . . . . . . . . . . . . . . . . **8.** ______

**9.** Subtract line 8 from line 4. If zero or less, enter -0- . . . . . . . . . . . . . . . **9.** ______

**10.** Did you (or your spouse, if filing jointly) receive an economic recovery payment in **2010**? You may have received this payment in 2010 if you did not receive an economic recovery payment in 2009 but you received social security benefits, supplemental security income, railroad retirement benefits, or veterans disability compensation or pension benefits in November 2008, December 2008, or January 2009 (see instructions).
☐ **No.** Enter -0- on line 10 and go to line 11.
☐ **Yes.** Enter the total of the payments you (and your spouse, if filing jointly) received in **2010**. Do not enter more than $250 ($500 if married filing jointly). **10.** ______

**11.** **Making work pay credit.** Subtract line 10 from line 9. If zero or less, enter -0-. Enter the result here and on Form 1040EZ, line 8. . . . . . . . . . . . . . . . . . . . . . **11.** ______

## Mailing Return

Mail your return by **April 18, 2011.** Mail it to the address shown on the last page of the instructions.

Form **1040EZ** (2010)

# B-3 Form 1040 U.S. Individual Income Tax Return and Schedules

Form **1040** Department of the Treasury—Internal Revenue Service
**U.S. Individual Income Tax Return** **2010** (99) IRS Use Only—Do not write or staple in this space.

For the year Jan. 1–Dec. 31, 2010, or other tax year beginning , 2010, ending , 20 OMB No. 1545-0074

**Name, Address, and SSN**

See separate instructions.

PRINT CLEARLY

| | | | |
|---|---|---|---|
| Your first name and initial | Last name | | **Your social security number** |
| If a joint return, spouse's first name and initial | Last name | | **Spouse's social security number** |
| Home address (number and street). If you have a P.O. box, see instructions. | | Apt. no. | ▲ Make sure the SSN(s) above and on line 6c are correct. |
| City, town or post office, state, and ZIP code. If you have a foreign address, see instructions. | | | Checking a box below will not change your tax or refund. |

**Presidential Election Campaign** ▶ Check here if you, or your spouse if filing jointly, want $3 to go to this fund . . . . . ▶ ☐ **You** ☐ **Spouse**

**Filing Status**

Check only one box.

1 ☐ Single
2 ☐ Married filing jointly (even if only one had income)
3 ☐ Married filing separately. Enter spouse's SSN above and full name here. ▶
4 ☐ Head of household (with qualifying person). (See instructions.) If the qualifying person is a child but not your dependent, enter this child's name here. ▶
5 ☐ Qualifying widow(er) with dependent child

**Exemptions**

6a ☐ **Yourself.** If someone can claim you as a dependent, **do not** check box 6a . . . . .
b ☐ **Spouse** . . . . .

**Boxes checked on 6a and 6b**

c **Dependents:**

| (1) First name Last name | (2) Dependent's social security number | (3) Dependent's relationship to you | (4) ✓ if child under age 17 qualifying for child tax credit (see page 15) |
|---|---|---|---|
| | | | ☐ |
| | | | ☐ |
| | | | ☐ |
| | | | ☐ |

If more than four dependents, see instructions and check here ▶ ☐

**No. of children on 6c who:**
**• lived with you**
**• did not live with you due to divorce or separation (see instructions)**
**Dependents on 6c not entered above**

d Total number of exemptions claimed . . . . . **Add numbers on lines above** ▶

**Income**

**Attach Form(s) W-2 here. Also attach Forms W-2G and 1099-R if tax was withheld.**

If you did not get a W-2, see page 20.

Enclose, but do not attach, any payment. Also, please use **Form 1040-V.**

|  |  | | |
|---|---|---|---|
| 7 | Wages, salaries, tips, etc. Attach Form(s) W-2 . . . | | 7 |
| 8a | **Taxable** interest. Attach Schedule B if required . . . | | 8a |
| b | **Tax-exempt** interest. **Do not** include on line 8a . . . | 8b | |
| 9a | Ordinary dividends. Attach Schedule B if required . . . | | 9a |
| b | Qualified dividends . . . | 9b | |
| 10 | Taxable refunds, credits, or offsets of state and local income taxes . . . | | 10 |
| 11 | Alimony received . . . | | 11 |
| 12 | Business income or (loss). Attach Schedule C or C-EZ . . . | | 12 |
| 13 | Capital gain or (loss). Attach Schedule D if required. If not required, check here ▶ ☐ | | 13 |
| 14 | Other gains or (losses). Attach Form 4797 . . . | | 14 |
| 15a | IRA distributions . 15a | b Taxable amount . . . | 15b |
| 16a | Pensions and annuities 16a | b Taxable amount . . . | 16b |
| 17 | Rental real estate, royalties, partnerships, S corporations, trusts, etc. Attach Schedule E | | 17 |
| 18 | Farm income or (loss). Attach Schedule F . . . | | 18 |
| 19 | Unemployment compensation . . . | | 19 |
| 20a | Social security benefits 20a | b Taxable amount . . . | 20b |
| 21 | Other income. List type and amount | | 21 |
| 22 | Combine the amounts in the far right column for lines 7 through 21. This is your **total income** ▶ | | 22 |

**Adjusted Gross Income**

|  |  | | |
|---|---|---|---|
| 23 | Educator expenses . . . | 23 | |
| 24 | Certain business expenses of reservists, performing artists, and fee-basis government officials. Attach Form 2106 or 2106-EZ | 24 | |
| 25 | Health savings account deduction. Attach Form 8889 . | 25 | |
| 26 | Moving expenses. Attach Form 3903 . . . | 26 | |
| 27 | One-half of self-employment tax. Attach Schedule SE . | 27 | |
| 28 | Self-employed SEP, SIMPLE, and qualified plans . . | 28 | |
| 29 | Self-employed health insurance deduction . . . | 29 | |
| 30 | Penalty on early withdrawal of savings . . . | 30 | |
| 31a | Alimony paid **b** Recipient's SSN ▶ | 31a | |
| 32 | IRA deduction . . . | 32 | |
| 33 | Student loan interest deduction . . . | 33 | |
| 34 | Tuition and fees. Attach Form 8917 . . . | 34 | |
| 35 | Domestic production activities deduction. Attach Form 8903 | 35 | |
| 36 | Add lines 23 through 31a and 32 through 35 . . . | | 36 |
| 37 | Subtract line 36 from line 22. This is your **adjusted gross income** . . . ▶ | | 37 |

**For Disclosure, Privacy Act, and Paperwork Reduction Act Notice, see separate instructions.** Cat. No. 11320B Form **1040** (2010)

Form 1040 (2010) Page **2**

|  |  |  |  |  |
|---|---|---|---|---|
| **Tax and Credits** | 38 | Amount from line 37 (adjusted gross income) | 38 | |
| | 39a | Check if: ☐ **You** were born before January 2, 1946, ☐ Blind. ☐ **Spouse** was born before January 2, 1946, ☐ Blind. } **Total boxes checked ▶ 39a** ☐ | | |
| | b | If your spouse itemizes on a separate return or you were a dual-status alien, check here ▶ **39b** ☐ | | |
| | 40 | **Itemized deductions** (from Schedule A) **or** your **standard deduction** (see instructions) | 40 | |
| | 41 | Subtract line 40 from line 38 | 41 | |
| | 42 | **Exemptions.** Multiply $3,650 by the number on line 6d | 42 | |
| | 43 | **Taxable income.** Subtract line 42 from line 41. If line 42 is more than line 41, enter -0- | 43 | |
| | 44 | **Tax** (see instructions). Check if any tax is from: **a** ☐ Form(s) 8814 **b** ☐ Form 4972 | 44 | |
| | 45 | **Alternative minimum tax** (see instructions). Attach Form 6251 | 45 | |
| | 46 | Add lines 44 and 45 ▶ | 46 | |
| | 47 | Foreign tax credit. Attach Form 1116 if required | 47 | |
| | 48 | Credit for child and dependent care expenses. Attach Form 2441 | 48 | |
| | 49 | Education credits from Form 8863, line 23 | 49 | |
| | 50 | Retirement savings contributions credit. Attach Form 8880 | 50 | |
| | 51 | Child tax credit (see instructions) | 51 | |
| | 52 | Residential energy credits. Attach Form 5695 | 52 | |
| | 53 | Other credits from Form: **a** ☐ 3800 **b** ☐ 8801 **c** ☐ ______ | 53 | |
| | 54 | Add lines 47 through 53. These are your **total credits** | 54 | |
| | 55 | Subtract line 54 from line 46. If line 54 is more than line 46, enter -0- ▶ | 55 | |
| **Other Taxes** | 56 | Self-employment tax. Attach Schedule SE | 56 | |
| | 57 | Unreported social security and Medicare tax from Form: **a** ☐ 4137 **b** ☐ 8919 | 57 | |
| | 58 | Additional tax on IRAs, other qualified retirement plans, etc. Attach Form 5329 if required | 58 | |
| | 59 | **a** ☐ Form(s) W-2, box 9 **b** ☐ Schedule H **c** ☐ Form 5405, line 16 | 59 | |
| | 60 | Add lines 55 through 59. This is your **total tax** ▶ | 60 | |
| **Payments** | 61 | Federal income tax withheld from Forms W-2 and 1099 | 61 | |
| | 62 | 2010 estimated tax payments and amount applied from 2009 return | 62 | |
| If you have a qualifying child, attach Schedule EIC. | 63 | Making work pay credit. Attach Schedule M | 63 | |
| | 64a | **Earned income credit (EIC)** | 64a | |
| | b | Nontaxable combat pay election **64b** | | |
| | 65 | Additional child tax credit. Attach Form 8812 | 65 | |
| | 66 | American opportunity credit from Form 8863, line 14 | 66 | |
| | 67 | First-time homebuyer credit from Form 5405, line 10 | 67 | |
| | 68 | Amount paid with request for extension to file | 68 | |
| | 69 | Excess social security and tier 1 RRTA tax withheld | 69 | |
| | 70 | Credit for federal tax on fuels. Attach Form 4136 | 70 | |
| | 71 | Credits from Form: **a** ☐ 2439 **b** ☐ 8839 **c** ☐ 8801 **d** ☐ 8885 | 71 | |
| | 72 | Add lines 61, 62, 63, 64a, and 65 through 71. These are your **total payments** ▶ | 72 | |
| **Refund** | 73 | If line 72 is more than line 60, subtract line 60 from line 72. This is the amount you **overpaid** | 73 | |
| | 74a | Amount of line 73 you want **refunded to you.** If Form 8888 is attached, check here ▶ ☐ | 74a | |
| Direct deposit? See instructions. | ▶ b | Routing number ▶ **c** Type: ☐ Checking ☐ Savings | | |
| | ▶ d | Account number | | |
| | 75 | Amount of line 73 you want **applied to your 2011 estimated tax** ▶ **75** | | |
| **Amount You Owe** | 76 | **Amount you owe.** Subtract line 72 from line 60. For details on how to pay, see instructions ▶ | 76 | |
| | 77 | Estimated tax penalty (see instructions) **77** | | |

**Third Party Designee**

Do you want to allow another person to discuss this return with the IRS (see instructions)? ☐ **Yes.** Complete below. ☐ **No**

Designee's name ▶ Phone no. ▶ Personal identification number (PIN) ▶

**Sign Here**

Joint return? See page 12. Keep a copy for your records.

Under penalties of perjury, I declare that I have examined this return and accompanying schedules and statements, and to the best of my knowledge and belief, they are true, correct, and complete. Declaration of preparer (other than taxpayer) is based on all information of which preparer has any knowledge.

| Your signature | Date | Your occupation | Daytime phone number |
|---|---|---|---|
| Spouse's signature. If a joint return, **both** must sign. | Date | Spouse's occupation | |

**Paid Preparer Use Only**

| Print/Type preparer's name | Preparer's signature | Date | Check ☐ if self-employed | PTIN |
|---|---|---|---|---|
| Firm's name ▶ | | | Firm's EIN ▶ | |
| Firm's address ▶ | | | Phone no. | |

Form **1040** (2010)

**SCHEDULE A (Form 1040)**

Department of the Treasury
Internal Revenue Service (99)

# Itemized Deductions

▶ Attach to Form 1040. ▶ See Instructions for Schedule A (Form 1040).

OMB No. 1545-0074

**2010**

Attachment Sequence No. 07

Name(s) shown on Form 1040 | Your social security number

| Section | Line | Description | Box | Amount |
|---|---|---|---|---|
| **Medical and Dental Expenses** | | **Caution.** Do not include expenses reimbursed or paid by others. | | |
| | 1 | Medical and dental expenses (see instructions) | 1 | |
| | 2 | Enter amount from Form 1040, line 38 [2] | | |
| | 3 | Multiply line 2 by 7.5% (.075) | 3 | |
| | 4 | Subtract line 3 from line 1. If line 3 is more than line 1, enter -0- | | 4 |
| **Taxes You Paid** | 5 | State and local **(check only one box):** | | |
| | | a ☐ Income taxes, **or** / b ☐ General sales taxes | 5 | |
| | 6 | Real estate taxes (see instructions) | 6 | |
| | 7 | New motor vehicle taxes from line 11 of the worksheet on back (for certain vehicles purchased in 2009). Skip this line if you checked box 5b | 7 | |
| | 8 | Other taxes. List type and amount ▶ | 8 | |
| | 9 | Add lines 5 through 8 | | 9 |
| **Interest You Paid** | 10 | Home mortgage interest and points reported to you on Form 1098 | 10 | |
| **Note.** Your mortgage interest deduction may be limited (see instructions). | 11 | Home mortgage interest not reported to you on Form 1098. If paid to the person from whom you bought the home, see instructions and show that person's name, identifying no., and address ▶ | 11 | |
| | 12 | Points not reported to you on Form 1098. See instructions for special rules | 12 | |
| | 13 | Mortgage insurance premiums (see instructions) | 13 | |
| | 14 | Investment interest. Attach Form 4952 if required. (See instructions.) | 14 | |
| | 15 | Add lines 10 through 14 | | 15 |
| **Gifts to Charity** | 16 | Gifts by cash or check. If you made any gift of $250 or more, see instructions | 16 | |
| If you made a gift and got a benefit for it, see instructions. | 17 | Other than by cash or check. If any gift of $250 or more, see instructions. You **must** attach Form 8283 if over $500 | 17 | |
| | 18 | Carryover from prior year | 18 | |
| | 19 | Add lines 16 through 18 | | 19 |
| **Casualty and Theft Losses** | 20 | Casualty or theft loss(es). Attach Form 4684. (See instructions.) | | 20 |
| **Job Expenses and Certain Miscellaneous Deductions** | 21 | Unreimbursed employee expenses—job travel, union dues, job education, etc. Attach Form 2106 or 2106-EZ if required. (See instructions.) ▶ | 21 | |
| | 22 | Tax preparation fees | 22 | |
| | 23 | Other expenses—investment, safe deposit box, etc. List type and amount ▶ | 23 | |
| | 24 | Add lines 21 through 23 | 24 | |
| | 25 | Enter amount from Form 1040, line 38 [25] | | |
| | 26 | Multiply line 25 by 2% (.02) | 26 | |
| | 27 | Subtract line 26 from line 24. If line 26 is more than line 24, enter -0- | | 27 |
| **Other Miscellaneous Deductions** | 28 | Other—from list in instructions. List type and amount ▶ | | 28 |
| **Total Itemized Deductions** | 29 | Add the amounts in the far right column for lines 4 through 28. Also, enter this amount on Form 1040, line 40 | | 29 |
| | 30 | If you elect to itemize deductions even though they are less than your standard deduction, check here ▶ ☐ | | |

**For Paperwork Reduction Act Notice, see Form 1040 instructions.** Cat. No. 17145C **Schedule A (Form 1040) 2010**

**SCHEDULE B**
**(Form 1040A or 1040)**

Department of the Treasury
Internal Revenue Service (99)

# Interest and Ordinary Dividends

▶ **Attach to Form 1040A or 1040.** ▶ **See instructions on back.**

OMB No. 1545-0074

**2010**

Attachment Sequence No. **08**

Name(s) shown on return

**Your social security number**

## Part I Interest

(See instructions on back and the instructions for Form 1040A, or Form 1040, line 8a.)

**Note.** If you received a Form 1099-INT, Form 1099-OID, or substitute statement from a brokerage firm, list the firm's name as the payer and enter the total interest shown on that form.

| | | | **Amount** |
|---|---|---|---|
| 1 | List name of payer. If any interest is from a seller-financed mortgage and the buyer used the property as a personal residence, see instructions on back and list this interest first. Also, show that buyer's social security number and address ▶ | 1 | |
| 2 | Add the amounts on line 1 . . . . . . . . . . . . . . . . . . . . . | 2 | |
| 3 | Excludable interest on series EE and I U.S. savings bonds issued after 1989. Attach Form 8815 . . . . . . . . . . . . . . . . . . . . . | 3 | |
| 4 | Subtract line 3 from line 2. Enter the result here and on Form 1040A, or Form 1040, line 8a . . . . . . . . . . . . . . . . . . . . . ▶ | 4 | |

**Note.** If line 4 is over $1,500, you must complete Part III.

## Part II Ordinary Dividends

(See instructions on back and the instructions for Form 1040A, or Form 1040, line 9a.)

**Note.** If you received a Form 1099-DIV or substitute statement from a brokerage firm, list the firm's name as the payer and enter the ordinary dividends shown on that form.

| | | | **Amount** |
|---|---|---|---|
| 5 | List name of payer ▶ | 5 | |
| 6 | Add the amounts on line 5. Enter the total here and on Form 1040A, or Form 1040, line 9a . . . . . . . . . . . . . . . . . . . . . ▶ | 6 | |

**Note.** If line 6 is over $1,500, you must complete Part III.

## Part III Foreign Accounts and Trusts

(See instructions on back.)

| | You must complete this part if you **(a)** had over $1,500 of taxable interest or ordinary dividends; **(b)** had a foreign account; or **(c)** received a distribution from, or were a grantor of, or a transferor to, a foreign trust. | **Yes** | **No** |
|---|---|---|---|
| 7a | At any time during 2010, did you have an interest in or a signature or other authority over a financial account in a foreign country, such as a bank account, securities account, or other financial account? See instructions on back for exceptions and filing requirements for Form TD F 90-22.1 . . . . . . | | |
| b | If "Yes," enter the name of the foreign country ▶ | | |
| 8 | During 2010, did you receive a distribution from, or were you the grantor of, or transferor to, a foreign trust? If "Yes," you may have to file Form 3520. See instructions on back . . . . . . | | |

**For Paperwork Reduction Act Notice, see your tax return instructions.** Cat. No. 17146N **Schedule B (Form 1040A or 1040) 2010**

**SCHEDULE C (Form 1040)**

Department of the Treasury Internal Revenue Service (99)

# Profit or Loss From Business

(Sole Proprietorship)

▶ Partnerships, joint ventures, etc., generally must file Form 1065 or 1065-B.
▶ Attach to Form 1040, 1040NR, or 1041. ▶ See Instructions for Schedule C (Form 1040).

OMB No. 1545-0074
**2010**
Attachment Sequence No. 09

Name of proprietor | **Social security number (SSN)**

A Principal business or profession, including product or service (see instructions) | **B Enter code from pages C-9, 10, & 11** ▶

C Business name. If no separate business name, leave blank. | **D Employer ID number (EIN), if any**

E Business address (including suite or room no.) ▶
City, town or post office, state, and ZIP code

F Accounting method: **(1)** ☐ Cash **(2)** ☐ Accrual **(3)** ☐ Other (specify) ▶

G Did you "materially participate" in the operation of this business during 2010? If "No," see instructions for limit on losses ☐ **Yes** ☐ **No**

H If you started or acquired this business during 2010, check here . . . ▶ ☐

## Part I Income

1 Gross receipts or sales. **Caution.** See instructions and check the box if:
- This income was reported to you on Form W-2 and the "Statutory employee" box on that form was checked, or
- You are a member of a qualified joint venture reporting only rental real estate income not subject to self-employment tax. Also see instructions for limit on losses.

. . ▶ ☐ | 1

| | | |
|---|---|---|
| 2 | Returns and allowances | 2 |
| 3 | Subtract line 2 from line 1 | 3 |
| 4 | Cost of goods sold (from line 42 on page 2) | 4 |
| 5 | **Gross profit.** Subtract line 4 from line 3 | 5 |
| 6 | Other income, including federal and state gasoline or fuel tax credit or refund (see instructions) | 6 |
| 7 | **Gross income.** Add lines 5 and 6 ▶ | 7 |

## Part II Expenses. Enter expenses for business use of your home **only** on line 30.

| | | | | | | |
|---|---|---|---|---|---|---|
| 8 | Advertising | 8 | | 18 | Office expense | 18 |
| 9 | Car and truck expenses (see instructions) | 9 | | 19 | Pension and profit-sharing plans | 19 |
| 10 | Commissions and fees | 10 | | 20 | Rent or lease (see instructions): | |
| 11 | Contract labor (see instructions) | 11 | | a | Vehicles, machinery, and equipment | 20a |
| 12 | Depletion | 12 | | b | Other business property | 20b |
| 13 | Depreciation and section 179 expense deduction (not included in Part III) (see instructions) | 13 | | 21 | Repairs and maintenance | 21 |
| | | | | 22 | Supplies (not included in Part III) | 22 |
| | | | | 23 | Taxes and licenses | 23 |
| | | | | 24 | Travel, meals, and entertainment: | |
| | | | | a | Travel | 24a |
| 14 | Employee benefit programs (other than on line 19) | 14 | | b | Deductible meals and entertainment (see instructions) | 24b |
| 15 | Insurance (other than health) | 15 | | 25 | Utilities | 25 |
| 16 | Interest: | | | 26 | Wages (less employment credits) | 26 |
| a | Mortgage (paid to banks, etc.) | 16a | | 27 | Other expenses (from line 48 on page 2) | 27 |
| b | Other | 16b | | | | |
| 17 | Legal and professional services | 17 | | | | |

| | | |
|---|---|---|
| 28 | **Total expenses** before expenses for business use of home. Add lines 8 through 27 ▶ | 28 |
| 29 | Tentative profit or (loss). Subtract line 28 from line 7 | 29 |
| 30 | Expenses for business use of your home. Attach **Form 8829** | 30 |
| 31 | **Net profit or (loss).** Subtract line 30 from line 29. • If a profit, enter on both **Form 1040, line 12,** and **Schedule SE, line 2,** or on **Form 1040NR, line 13** (if you checked the box on line 1, see instructions). Estates and trusts, enter on **Form 1041, line 3.** • If a loss, you **must** go to line 32. | 31 |

32 If you have a loss, check the box that describes your investment in this activity (see instructions).
- If you checked 32a, enter the loss on both **Form 1040, line 12,** and **Schedule SE, line 2,** or on **Form 1040NR, line 13** (if you checked the box on line 1, see the line 31 instructions). Estates and trusts, enter on **Form 1041, line 3.**
- If you checked 32b, you **must** attach **Form 6198.** Your loss may be limited.

**32a** ☐ All investment is at risk.
**32b** ☐ Some investment is not at risk.

**For Paperwork Reduction Act Notice, see your tax return instructions.** Cat. No. 11334P **Schedule C (Form 1040) 2010**

Schedule C (Form 1040) 2010 Page **2**

**Part III** **Cost of Goods Sold** (see instructions)

33 Method(s) used to value closing inventory: **a** ☐ Cost **b** ☐ Lower of cost or market **c** ☐ Other (attach explanation)

34 Was there any change in determining quantities, costs, or valuations between opening and closing inventory? If "Yes," attach explanation . . . ☐ **Yes** ☐ **No**

| | | | |
|---|---|---|---|
| 35 | Inventory at beginning of year. If different from last year's closing inventory, attach explanation | **35** | |
| 36 | Purchases less cost of items withdrawn for personal use | **36** | |
| 37 | Cost of labor. Do not include any amounts paid to yourself | **37** | |
| 38 | Materials and supplies | **38** | |
| 39 | Other costs | **39** | |
| 40 | Add lines 35 through 39 | **40** | |
| 41 | Inventory at end of year | **41** | |
| 42 | **Cost of goods sold.** Subtract line 41 from line 40. Enter the result here and on page 1, line 4 | **42** | |

**Part IV** **Information on Your Vehicle.** Complete this part **only** if you are claiming car or truck expenses on line 9 and are not required to file Form 4562 for this business. See the instructions for line 13 to find out if you must file Form 4562.

43 When did you place your vehicle in service for business purposes? (month, day, year) ▶ ___ / ___ / ___

44 Of the total number of miles you drove your vehicle during 2010, enter the number of miles you used your vehicle for:

a Business ________ **b** Commuting (see instructions) ________ **c** Other ________

45 Was your vehicle available for personal use during off-duty hours? . . . ☐ **Yes** ☐ **No**

46 Do you (or your spouse) have another vehicle available for personal use?. . . ☐ **Yes** ☐ **No**

47a Do you have evidence to support your deduction? . . . ☐ **Yes** ☐ **No**

b If "Yes," is the evidence written? . . . ☐ **Yes** ☐ **No**

**Part V** **Other Expenses.** List below business expenses not included on lines 8–26 or line 30.

| | | |
|---|---|---|
| | | |
| | | |
| | | |
| | | |
| | | |
| | | |
| | | |
| | | |
| 48 **Total other expenses.** Enter here and on page 1, line 27 | **48** | |

**Schedule C (Form 1040) 2010**

**SCHEDULE D (Form 1040)**

Department of the Treasury Internal Revenue Service (99)

# Capital Gains and Losses

▶ Attach to Form 1040 or Form 1040NR. ▶ See Instructions for Schedule D (Form 1040).
▶ Use Schedule D-1 to list additional transactions for lines 1 and 8.

OMB No. 1545-0074

**2010**

Attachment Sequence No. **12**

Name(s) shown on return | **Your social security number**

**Part I** **Short-Term Capital Gains and Losses—Assets Held One Year or Less**

| **(a)** Description of property (Example: 100 sh. XYZ Co.) | **(b)** Date acquired (Mo., day, yr.) | **(c)** Date sold (Mo., day, yr.) | **(d)** Sales price (see page D-7 of the instructions) | **(e)** Cost or other basis (see page D-7 of the instructions) | **(f) Gain or (loss)** Subtract (e) from (d) |
|---|---|---|---|---|---|
| 1 | | | | | |
| | | | | | |
| | | | | | |
| | | | | | |
| | | | | | |

| | | |
|---|---|---|
| **2** Enter your short-term totals, if any, from Schedule D-1, line 2 | 2 | |
| **3** **Total short-term sales price amounts.** Add lines 1 and 2 in column (d) | 3 | |
| **4** Short-term gain from Form 6252 and short-term gain or (loss) from Forms 4684, 6781, and 8824 | 4 | |
| **5** Net short-term gain or (loss) from partnerships, S corporations, estates, and trusts from Schedule(s) K-1 | 5 | |
| **6** Short-term capital loss carryover. Enter the amount, if any, from line 10 of your **Capital Loss Carryover Worksheet** on page D-7 of the instructions | 6 | ( ) |
| **7** **Net short-term capital gain or (loss).** Combine lines 1 through 6 in column (f) | 7 | |

**Part II** **Long-Term Capital Gains and Losses—Assets Held More Than One Year**

| **(a)** Description of property (Example: 100 sh. XYZ Co.) | **(b)** Date acquired (Mo., day, yr.) | **(c)** Date sold (Mo., day, yr.) | **(d)** Sales price (see page D-7 of the instructions) | **(e)** Cost or other basis (see page D-7 of the instructions) | **(f) Gain or (loss)** Subtract (e) from (d) |
|---|---|---|---|---|---|
| 8 | | | | | |
| | | | | | |
| | | | | | |
| | | | | | |
| | | | | | |

| | | |
|---|---|---|
| **9** Enter your long-term totals, if any, from Schedule D-1, line 9 | 9 | |
| **10** **Total long-term sales price amounts.** Add lines 8 and 9 in column (d) | 10 | |
| **11** Gain from Form 4797, Part I; long-term gain from Forms 2439 and 6252; and long-term gain or (loss) from Forms 4684, 6781, and 8824 | 11 | |
| **12** Net long-term gain or (loss) from partnerships, S corporations, estates, and trusts from Schedule(s) K-1 | 12 | |
| **13** Capital gain distributions. See page D-2 of the instructions | 13 | |
| **14** Long-term capital loss carryover. Enter the amount, if any, from line 15 of your **Capital Loss Carryover Worksheet** on page D-7 of the instructions | 14 | ( ) |
| **15** **Net long-term capital gain or (loss).** Combine lines 8 through 14 in column (f). Then go to Part III on the back | 15 | |

**For Paperwork Reduction Act Notice, see your tax return instructions.** Cat. No. 11338H **Schedule D (Form 1040) 2010**

Schedule D (Form 1040) 2010 Page **2**

**Part III** **Summary**

**16** Combine lines 7 and 15 and enter the result . . . . . . . . . . . . . . . . . . . . . . **16**

- If line 16 is a **gain**, enter the amount from line 16 on Form 1040, line 13, or Form 1040NR, line 14. Then go to line 17 below.
- If line 16 is a **loss**, skip lines 17 through 20 below. Then go to line 21. Also be sure to complete line 22.
- If line 16 is **zero**, skip lines 17 through 21 below and enter -0- on Form 1040, line 13, or Form 1040NR, line 14. Then go to line 22.

**17** Are lines 15 and 16 **both** gains?

☐ **Yes.** Go to line 18.

☐ **No.** Skip lines 18 through 21, and go to line 22.

**18** Enter the amount, if any, from line 7 of the **28% Rate Gain Worksheet** on page D-8 of the instructions . . . . . . . . . . . . . . . . . . . . . . . . . . . . . ▶ **18**

**19** Enter the amount, if any, from line 18 of the **Unrecaptured Section 1250 Gain Worksheet** on page D-9 of the instructions . . . . . . . . . . . . . . . . . . . . . . . . . . . ▶ **19**

**20** Are lines 18 and 19 **both** zero or blank?

☐ **Yes.** Complete Form 1040 through line 43, or Form 1040NR through line 41. Then complete the **Qualified Dividends and Capital Gain Tax Worksheet** in the Instructions for Form 1040, line 44 (or in the Instructions for Form 1040NR, line 42). **Do not** complete lines 21 and 22 below.

☐ **No.** Complete Form 1040 through line 43, or Form 1040NR through line 41. Then complete the **Schedule D Tax Worksheet** on page D-10 of the instructions. **Do not** complete lines 21 and 22 below.

**21** If line 16 is a loss, enter here and on Form 1040, line 13, or Form 1040NR, line 14, the **smaller** of:

- The loss on line 16 or
- ($3,000), or if married filing separately, ($1,500)

. . . . . . . . . . . . . . . **21** ( )

**Note.** When figuring which amount is smaller, treat both amounts as positive numbers.

**22** Do you have qualified dividends on Form 1040, line 9b, or Form 1040NR, line 10b?

☐ **Yes.** Complete Form 1040 through line 43, or Form 1040NR through line 41. Then complete the **Qualified Dividends and Capital Gain Tax Worksheet** in the Instructions for Form 1040, line 44 (or in the Instructions for Form 1040NR, line 42).

☐ **No.** Complete the rest of Form 1040 or Form 1040NR.

**Schedule D (Form 1040) 2010**

**SCHEDULE E (Form 1040)**

Department of the Treasury Internal Revenue Service (99)

# Supplemental Income and Loss

**(From rental real estate, royalties, partnerships, S corporations, estates, trusts, REMICs, etc.)**

▶ **Attach to Form 1040, 1040NR, or Form 1041.** ▶ **See Instructions for Schedule E (Form 1040).**

OMB No. 1545-0074

**2010**

Attachment Sequence No. **13**

Name(s) shown on return | **Your social security number**

**Part I** **Income or Loss From Rental Real Estate and Royalties** **Note.** If you are in the business of renting personal property, use **Schedule C** or **C-EZ** (see page E-3). If you are an individual, report farm rental income or loss from **Form 4835** on page 2, line 40.

| 1 | List the type and address of each **rental real estate property:** | 2 For each rental real estate property listed on line 1, did you or your family use it during the tax year for personal purposes for more than the greater of: • 14 days **or** • 10% of the total days rented at fair rental value? (See page E-4) | | Yes | No |
|---|---|---|---|---|---|
| A | | | A | | |
| B | | | B | | |
| C | | | C | | |

| **Income:** | | Properties A | Properties B | Properties C | | **Totals** (Add columns A, B, and C.) |
|---|---|---|---|---|---|---|
| 3 Rents received | 3 | | | | 3 | |
| 4 Royalties received | 4 | | | | 4 | |
| **Expenses:** | | | | | | |
| 5 Advertising | 5 | | | | | |
| 6 Auto and travel (see page E-5) | 6 | | | | | |
| 7 Cleaning and maintenance | 7 | | | | | |
| 8 Commissions | 8 | | | | | |
| 9 Insurance | 9 | | | | | |
| 10 Legal and other professional fees | 10 | | | | | |
| 11 Management fees | 11 | | | | | |
| 12 Mortgage interest paid to banks, etc. (see page E-5) | 12 | | | | 12 | |
| 13 Other interest | 13 | | | | | |
| 14 Repairs | 14 | | | | | |
| 15 Supplies | 15 | | | | | |
| 16 Taxes | 16 | | | | | |
| 17 Utilities | 17 | | | | | |
| 18 Other (list) ▶ | 18 | | | | | |
| 19 Add lines 5 through 18 | 19 | | | | 19 | |
| 20 Depreciation expense or depletion (see page E-5) | 20 | | | | 20 | |
| 21 Total expenses. Add lines 19 and 20 | 21 | | | | | |
| 22 Income or (loss) from rental real estate or royalty properties. Subtract line 21 from line 3 (rents) or line 4 (royalties). If the result is a (loss), see page E-6 to find out if you must file **Form 6198** | 22 | | | | | |
| 23 Deductible rental real estate loss. **Caution.** Your rental real estate loss on line 22 may be limited. See page E-6 to find out if you must file **Form 8582.** Real estate professionals **must** complete line 43 on page 2 | 23 | ( ) | ( ) | ( ) | | |

| | | |
|---|---|---|
| 24 | **Income.** Add positive amounts shown on line 22. **Do not** include any losses | 24 |
| 25 | **Losses.** Add royalty losses from line 22 and rental real estate losses from line 23. Enter total losses here | 25 ( ) |
| 26 | **Total rental real estate and royalty income or (loss).** Combine lines 24 and 25. Enter the result here. If Parts II, III, IV, and line 40 on page 2 do not apply to you, also enter this amount on Form 1040, line 17, or Form 1040NR, line 18. Otherwise, include this amount in the total on line 41 on page 2 | 26 |

**For Paperwork Reduction Act Notice, see your tax return instructions.** Cat. No. 11344L **Schedule E (Form 1040) 2010**

Schedule E (Form 1040) 2010 Attachment Sequence No. **13** Page **2**

Name(s) shown on return. Do not enter name and social security number if shown on other side. | **Your social security number**

**Caution.** The IRS compares amounts reported on your tax return with amounts shown on Schedule(s) K-1.

## Part II Income or Loss From Partnerships and S Corporations

**Note.** If you report a loss from an at-risk activity for which **any** amount is **not** at risk, you **must** check the box in column **(e)** on line 28 and attach **Form 6198.** See page E-2.

27 Are you reporting any loss not allowed in a prior year due to the at-risk or basis limitations, a prior year unallowed loss from a passive activity (if that loss was not reported on Form 8582), or unreimbursed partnership expenses? If you answered "Yes," see page E-7 before completing this section. ☐ Yes ☐ No

| 28 | **(a)** Name | **(b)** Enter **P** for partnership; **S** for S corporation | **(c)** Check if foreign partnership | **(d)** Employer identification number | **(e)** Check if any amount is not at risk |
|---|---|---|---|---|---|
| A | | | ☐ | | ☐ |
| B | | | ☐ | | ☐ |
| C | | | ☐ | | ☐ |
| D | | | ☐ | | ☐ |

| | Passive Income and Loss | | Nonpassive Income and Loss | | |
|---|---|---|---|---|---|
| | **(f)** Passive loss allowed (attach **Form 8582** if required) | **(g)** Passive income from **Schedule K–1** | **(h)** Nonpassive loss from **Schedule K–1** | **(i)** Section 179 expense deduction from **Form 4562** | **(j)** Nonpassive income from **Schedule K–1** |
| A | | | | | |
| B | | | | | |
| C | | | | | |
| D | | | | | |
| 29a Totals | | | | | |
| b Totals | | | | | |

30 Add columns (g) and (j) of line 29a . . . . . 30

31 Add columns (f), (h), and (i) of line 29b . . . . . 31 ( )

32 **Total partnership and S corporation income or (loss).** Combine lines 30 and 31. Enter the result here and include in the total on line 41 below . . . . . 32

## Part III Income or Loss From Estates and Trusts

| 33 | **(a)** Name | **(b)** Employer identification number |
|---|---|---|
| A | | |
| B | | |

| | Passive Income and Loss | | Nonpassive Income and Loss | |
|---|---|---|---|---|
| | **(c)** Passive deduction or loss allowed (attach **Form 8582** if required) | **(d)** Passive income from **Schedule K–1** | **(e)** Deduction or loss from **Schedule K–1** | **(f)** Other income from **Schedule K–1** |
| A | | | | |
| B | | | | |
| 34a Totals | | | | |
| b Totals | | | | |

35 Add columns (d) and (f) of line 34a . . . . . 35

36 Add columns (c) and (e) of line 34b . . . . . 36 ( )

37 **Total estate and trust income or (loss).** Combine lines 35 and 36. Enter the result here and include in the total on line 41 below . . . . . 37

## Part IV Income or Loss From Real Estate Mortgage Investment Conduits (REMICs)—Residual Holder

| 38 **(a)** Name | **(b)** Employer identification number | **(c)** Excess inclusion from **Schedules Q,** line 2c (see page E-8) | **(d)** Taxable income (net loss) from **Schedules Q,** line 1b | (e) Income from **Schedules Q,** line 3b |
|---|---|---|---|---|
| | | | | |

39 Combine columns (d) and (e) only. Enter the result here and include in the total on line 41 below 39

## Part V Summary

40 Net farm rental income or (loss) from **Form 4835**. Also, complete line 42 below . . . . . 40

41 **Total income or (loss).** Combine lines 26, 32, 37, 39, and 40. Enter the result here and on Form 1040, line 17, or Form 1040NR, line 18 ▶ 41

42 **Reconciliation of farming and fishing income.** Enter your **gross** farming and fishing income reported on Form 4835, line 7; Schedule K-1 (Form 1065), box 14, code B; Schedule K-1 (Form 1120S), box 17, code U; and Schedule K-1 (Form 1041), line 14, code F (see page E-8) 42

43 **Reconciliation for real estate professionals.** If you were a real estate professional (see page E-2), enter the net income or (loss) you reported anywhere on Form 1040 or Form 1040NR from all rental real estate activities in which you materially participated under the passive activity loss rules . . 43

Schedule E (Form 1040) 2010

**SCHEDULE F (Form 1040)**

Department of the Treasury Internal Revenue Service (99)

# Profit or Loss From Farming

▶ Attach to Form 1040, Form 1040NR, Form 1041, Form 1065, or Form 1065-B.

▶ See Instructions for Schedule F (Form 1040).

OMB No. 1545-0074

**2010**

Attachment Sequence No. **14**

Name of proprietor | **Social security number (SSN)**

**A** Principal product. Describe in one or two words your principal crop or activity for the current tax year.

**B Enter code from Part IV** ▶

**D Employer ID number (EIN), if any**

**C** Accounting method: **(1)** ☐ Cash **(2)** ☐ Accrual

**E** Did you "materially participate" in the operation of this business during 2010? If "No," see instructions for limit on passive losses. ☐ Yes ☐ No

**Part I** **Farm Income—Cash Method.** Complete Parts I and II (Accrual method. Complete Parts II and III, and Part I, line 11.) Do not include sales of livestock held for draft, breeding, sport, or dairy purposes. Report these sales on Form 4797.

| | | | | | |
|---|---|---|---|---|---|
| 1 | Sales of livestock and other items you bought for resale | 1 | | | |
| 2 | Cost or other basis of livestock and other items reported on line 1 | 2 | | | |
| 3 | Subtract line 2 from line 1 | | | 3 | |
| 4 | Sales of livestock, produce, grains, and other products you raised | | | 4 | |
| 5a | Cooperative distributions (Form(s) 1099-PATR) | 5a | **5b** Taxable amount | 5b | |
| 6a | Agricultural program payments (see instructions) | 6a | **6b** Taxable amount | 6b | |
| 7 | Commodity Credit Corporation (CCC) loans (see instructions): | | | | |
| a | CCC loans reported under election | | | 7a | |
| b | CCC loans forfeited | 7b | **7c** Taxable amount | 7c | |
| 8 | Crop insurance proceeds and federal crop disaster payments (see instructions): | | | | |
| a | Amount received in 2010 | 8a | **8b** Taxable amount | 8b | |
| c | If election to defer to 2011 is attached, check here ▶ ☐ | | **8d** Amount deferred from 2009 | 8d | |
| 9 | Custom hire (machine work) income | | | 9 | |
| 10 | Other income, including federal and state gasoline or fuel tax credit or refund (see instructions) | | | 10 | |
| 11 | **Gross income.** Add amounts in the right column for lines 3 through 10. If you use the accrual method to figure your income, enter the amount from Part III, line 51 ▶ | | | 11 | |

**Part II** **Farm Expenses—Cash and Accrual Method.** Do not include personal or living expenses such as taxes, insurance, or repairs on your home.

| | | | | | | | |
|---|---|---|---|---|---|---|---|
| 12 | Car and truck expenses (see instructions). Also attach **Form 4562** | 12 | | 25 | Pension and profit-sharing plans | 25 | |
| 13 | Chemicals | 13 | | 26 | Rent or lease (see instructions): | | |
| 14 | Conservation expenses (see instructions) | 14 | | a | Vehicles, machinery, and equipment | 26a | |
| 15 | Custom hire (machine work) | 15 | | b | Other (land, animals, etc.) | 26b | |
| 16 | Depreciation and section 179 expense deduction not claimed elsewhere (see instructions) | 16 | | 27 | Repairs and maintenance | 27 | |
| | | | | 28 | Seeds and plants | 28 | |
| | | | | 29 | Storage and warehousing | 29 | |
| 17 | Employee benefit programs other than on line 25 | 17 | | 30 | Supplies | 30 | |
| | | | | 31 | Taxes | 31 | |
| 18 | Feed | 18 | | 32 | Utilities | 32 | |
| 19 | Fertilizers and lime | 19 | | 33 | Veterinary, breeding, and medicine | 33 | |
| 20 | Freight and trucking | 20 | | 34 | Other expenses (specify): | | |
| 21 | Gasoline, fuel, and oil | 21 | | a | | 34a | |
| 22 | Insurance (other than health) | 22 | | b | | 34b | |
| 23 | Interest: | | | c | | 34c | |
| a | Mortgage (paid to banks, etc.) | 23a | | d | | 34d | |
| b | Other | 23b | | e | | 34e | |
| 24 | Labor hired (less employment credits) | 24 | | f | | 34f | |

| | | | |
|---|---|---|---|
| 35 | **Total expenses.** Add lines 12 through 34f. If line 34f is negative, see instructions ▶ | 35 | |
| 36 | **Net farm profit or (loss).** Subtract line 35 from line 11. Partnerships, see instructions.<br>• If a profit, enter the profit on both **Form 1040, line 18,** and **Schedule SE, line 1a;** on **Form 1040NR, line 19;** or on **Form 1041, line 6.**<br>• If a loss, you **must** go to line 37. | 36 | |
| 37 | If you have a loss, you **must** check the box that describes your investment in this activity and whether you received any applicable subsidy (see instructions).<br>• If you checked 37a, enter the loss on both **Form 1040, line 18,** and **Schedule SE, line 1a;** on **Form 1040NR, line 19;** or on **Form 1041, line 6.**<br>• If you checked 37b, your loss may be limited. See instructions. | **37a** ☐ All investment is at risk and you did not receive a subsidy.<br>**37b** ☐ Some investment is not at risk or you received a subsidy. | |

**For Paperwork Reduction Act Notice, see your tax return instructions.** Cat. No. 11346H **Schedule F (Form 1040) 2010**

Schedule F (Form 1040) 2010 Page **2**

**Part III** **Farm Income—Accrual Method** (see instructions).
Do not include sales of livestock held for draft, breeding, sport, or dairy purposes. Report these sales on Form 4797 and do not include this livestock on line 46 below.

| | | | | |
|---|---|---|---|---|
| 38 | Sales of livestock, produce, grains, and other products | | **38** | |
| 39a | Cooperative distributions (Form(s) 1099-PATR) **39a** | **39b** Taxable amount | **39b** | |
| 40a | Agricultural program payments **40a** | **40b** Taxable amount | **40b** | |
| 41 | Commodity Credit Corporation (CCC) loans: | | | |
| a | CCC loans reported under election | | **41a** | |
| b | CCC loans forfeited **41b** | **41c** Taxable amount | **41c** | |
| 42 | Crop insurance proceeds | | **42** | |
| 43 | Custom hire (machine work) income | | **43** | |
| 44 | Other income, including federal and state gasoline or fuel tax credit or refund | | **44** | |
| 45 | Add amounts in the right column for lines 38 through 44 | | **45** | |
| 46 | Inventory of livestock, produce, grains, and other products at beginning of the year | **46** | | |
| 47 | Cost of livestock, produce, grains, and other products purchased during the year | **47** | | |
| 48 | Add lines 46 and 47 | **48** | | |
| 49 | Inventory of livestock, produce, grains, and other products at end of year | **49** | | |
| 50 | Cost of livestock, produce, grains, and other products sold. Subtract line 49 from line 48* | | **50** | |
| 51 | **Gross income.** Subtract line 50 from line 45. Enter the result here and on Part I, line 11 ▶ | | **51** | |

*If you use the unit-livestock-price method or the farm-price method of valuing inventory and the amount on line 49 is larger than the amount on line 48, subtract line 48 from line 49. Enter the result on line 50. Add lines 45 and 50. Enter the total on line 51 and on Part I, line 11.

**Part IV** **Principal Agricultural Activity Codes**

**CAUTION** *File Schedule C (Form 1040) or Schedule C-EZ (Form 1040) instead of Schedule F if* ***(a)*** *your principal source of income is from providing agricultural services such as soil preparation, veterinary, farm labor, horticultural, or management for a fee or on a contract basis, or* ***(b)*** *you are engaged in the business of breeding, raising, and caring for dogs, cats, or other pet animals.*

These codes for the Principal Agricultural Activity classify farms by their primary activity to facilitate the administration of the Internal Revenue Code. These six-digit codes are based on the North American Industry Classification System (NAICS).

Select the code that best identifies your primary farming activity and enter the six digit number on page 1, line B.

**Crop Production**

111100 Oilseed and grain farming
111210 Vegetable and melon farming
111300 Fruit and tree nut farming
111400 Greenhouse, nursery, and floriculture production
111900 Other crop farming

**Animal Production**

112111 Beef cattle ranching and farming
112112 Cattle feedlots
112120 Dairy cattle and milk production
112210 Hog and pig farming
112300 Poultry and egg production
112400 Sheep and goat farming
112510 Aquaculture
112900 Other animal production

**Forestry and Logging**

113000 Forestry and logging (including forest nurseries and timber tracts)

**Schedule F (Form 1040) 2010**

**Schedule R (Form 1040A or 1040)**

Department of the Treasury
Internal Revenue Service (99)

# Credit for the Elderly or the Disabled

*Complete and attach to Form 1040A or 1040.*

1040A / 1040 / R

OMB No. 1545-0074

**2010**

Attachment Sequence No. **16**

Name(s) shown on Form 1040A or 1040 | **Your social security number**

You may be able to take this credit and reduce your tax if by the end of 2010:

- You were age 65 or older **or** • You were under age 65, you retired on **permanent and total** disability, and you received taxable disability income.

But you must also meet other tests. See page R-1 of the instructions.

TIP In most cases, the IRS can figure the credit for you. See page R-1 of the instructions.

## Part I Check the Box for Your Filing Status and Age

| If your filing status is: | And by the end of 2010: | | Check only one box: |
|---|---|---|---|
| Single, Head of household, or Qualifying widow(er) | 1 You were 65 or older | 1 | ☐ |
| | 2 You were under 65 and you retired on permanent and total disability | 2 | ☐ |
| Married filing jointly | 3 Both spouses were 65 or older | 3 | ☐ |
| | 4 Both spouses were under 65, but only one spouse retired on permanent and total disability | 4 | ☐ |
| | 5 Both spouses were under 65, and both retired on permanent and total disability | 5 | ☐ |
| | 6 One spouse was 65 or older, and the other spouse was under 65 and retired on permanent and total disability | 6 | ☐ |
| | 7 One spouse was 65 or older, and the other spouse was under 65 and **not** retired on permanent and total disability | 7 | ☐ |
| Married filing separately | 8 You were 65 or older and you lived apart from your spouse for all of 2010 | 8 | ☐ |
| | 9 You were under 65, you retired on permanent and total disability, and you lived apart from your spouse for all of 2010 | 9 | ☐ |

**Did you check box 1, 3, 7, or 8?**
- **Yes** ▶ Skip Part II and complete Part III on the back.
- **No** ▶ Complete Parts II and III.

## Part II Statement of Permanent and Total Disability (Complete **only** if you checked box 2, 4, 5, 6, or 9 above.)

**If:** 1 You filed a physician's statement for this disability for 1983 or an earlier year, or you filed or got a statement for tax years after 1983 and your physician signed line B on the statement, **and**

2 Due to your continued disabled condition, you were unable to engage in any substantial gainful activity in 2010, check this box ▶ ☐

- If you checked this box, you do not have to get another statement for 2010.
- If you **did not** check this box, have your physician complete the statement on page R-4 of the instructions. You **must** keep the statement for your records.

**For Paperwork Reduction Act Notice, see your tax return instructions.** Cat. No. 11359K **Schedule R (Form 1040A or 1040) 2010**

Schedule R (Form 1040A or 1040) 2010 Page **2**

**Part III** **Figure Your Credit**

10 **If you checked (in Part I):** **Enter:**
Box 1, 2, 4, or 7 . . . . . . . . . . . . . $5,000
Box 3, 5, or 6 . . . . . . . . . . . . . $7,500
Box 8 or 9 . . . . . . . . . . . . . . $3,750 } . . . . . . . . . . . **10**

**Did you check box 2, 4, 5, 6, or 9 in Part I?**
- **Yes** ▶ You **must** complete line 11.
- **No** ▶ Enter the amount from line 10 on line 12 and go to line 13.

11 **If you checked (in Part I):**
- Box 6, add $5,000 to the taxable disability income of the spouse who was under age 65. Enter the total.
- Box 2, 4, or 9, enter your taxable disability income.
- Box 5, add your taxable disability income to your spouse's taxable disability income. Enter the total.

} . . . . . . . . **11**

TIP For more details on what to include on line 11, see page R-2.

12 If you completed line 11, enter the **smaller** of line 10 or line 11. **All others,** enter the amount from line 10 . . . . . . . . . . . . . . . . . . . . . . . . **12**

13 Enter the following pensions, annuities, or disability income that you (and your spouse if filing jointly) received in 2010.

a Nontaxable part of social security benefits and nontaxable part of railroad retirement benefits treated as social security (see page R-3 of the instructions). . . . . . . . . . . . . . **13a**

b Nontaxable veterans' pensions and any other pension, annuity, or disability benefit that is excluded from income under any other provision of law (see page R-3 of the instructions) . . . **13b**

c Add lines 13a and 13b. (Even though these income items are not taxable, they **must** be included here to figure your credit.) If you did not receive any of the types of nontaxable income listed on line 13a or 13b, enter -0- on line 13c . . . . . . . . . **13c**

14 Enter the amount from Form 1040A, line 22, or Form 1040, line 38 . . . . . **14**

15 **If you checked (in Part I):** **Enter:**
Box 1 or 2 . . . . . . $7,500
Box 3, 4, 5, 6, or 7 . . . $10,000
Box 8 or 9 . . . . . . $5,000 } **15**

16 Subtract line 15 from line 14. If zero or less, enter -0- . . . . . . . . . **16**

17 Enter one-half of line 16 . . . . . . . . . . . . . . . **17**

18 Add lines 13c and 17 . . . . . . . . . . . . . . . . . . . . . . . . . **18**

19 Subtract line 18 from line 12. If zero or less, **stop;** you **cannot** take the credit. Otherwise, go to line 20 . . . . . . . . . . . . . . . . . . . . . . . . **19**

20 Multiply line 19 by 15% (.15). . . . . . . . . . . . . . . . . . . . . . **20**

21 Tax liability limit. Enter the amount from the Credit Limit Worksheet on page R-3 of the instructions . . . . . . . . . . . . . . . . . . . . . . . . . . **21**

22 **Credit for the elderly or the disabled.** Enter the **smaller** of line 20 or line 21. Also enter this amount on Form 1040A, line 30, or include on Form 1040, line 53 (check box **c** and enter "Sch R" on the line next to that box) . . . . . . . . . . . . . . . . . . **22**

**Schedule R (Form 1040A or 1040) 2010**

| **SCHEDULE SE (Form 1040)** Department of the Treasury Internal Revenue Service (99) | **Self-Employment Tax** ▶ **Attach to Form 1040 or Form 1040NR.** ▶ **See Instructions for Schedule SE (Form 1040).** | OMB No. 1545-0074 **2010** Attachment Sequence No. **17** |
|---|---|---|
| Name of person with **self-employment** income (as shown on Form 1040) | Social security number of person with **self-employment** income ▶ | |

***Before you begin:*** To determine if you must file Schedule SE, see the instructions on page SE-1.

## May I Use Short Schedule SE or Must I Use Long Schedule SE?

**Note.** Use this flowchart **only if** you must file Schedule SE. If unsure, see *Who Must File Schedule SE* on page SE-1.

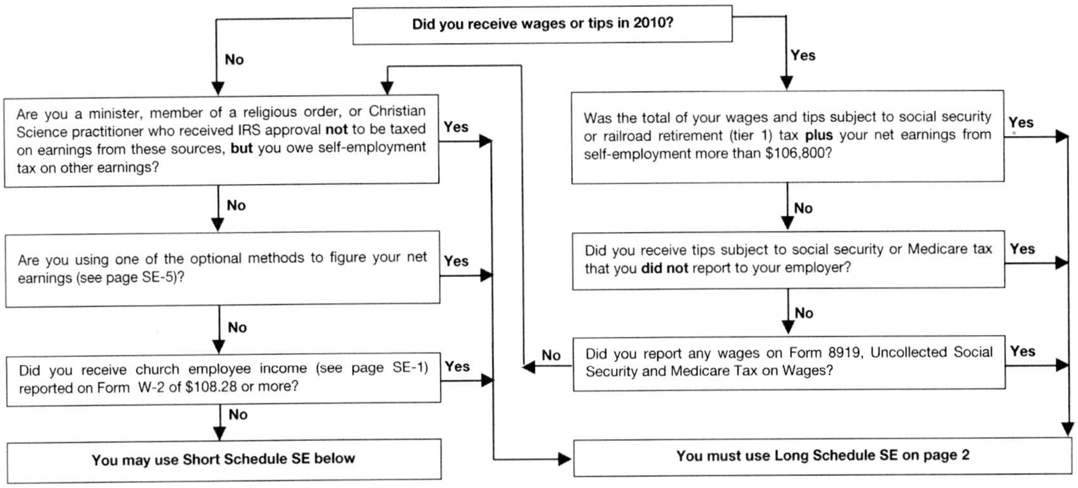


**Section A—Short Schedule SE. Caution.** Read above to see if you can use Short Schedule SE.

| | | | |
|---|---|---|---|
| **1a** | Net farm profit or (loss) from Schedule F, line 36, and farm partnerships, Schedule K-1 (Form 1065), box 14, code A . . . . . | **1a** | |
| **b** | If you received social security retirement or disability benefits, enter the amount of Conservation Reserve Program payments included on Schedule F, line 6b, or listed on Schedule K-1 (Form 1065), box 20, code Y | **1b** | ( ) |
| **2** | Net profit or (loss) from Schedule C, line 31; Schedule C-EZ, line 3; Schedule K-1 (Form 1065), box 14, code A (other than farming); and Schedule K-1 (Form 1065-B), box 9, code J1. Ministers and members of religious orders, see page SE-1 for types of income to report on this line. See page SE-3 for other income to report . . . . . | **2** | |
| **3** | Combine lines 1a, 1b, and 2. Subtract from that total the amount on Form 1040, line 29, or Form 1040NR, line 29, and enter the result (see page SE-3) . . . . . | **3** | |
| **4** | Multiply line 3 by 92.35% (.9235). If less than $400, you do not owe self-employment tax; **do not** file this schedule unless you have an amount on line 1b . . . . . ▶ | **4** | |
| | **Note.** If line 4 is less than $400 due to Conservation Reserve Program payments on line 1b, see page SE-3. | | |
| **5** | **Self-employment tax.** If the amount on line 4 is:<br>• $106,800 or less, multiply line 4 by 15.3% (.153). Enter the result here and on **Form 1040, line 56,** or **Form 1040NR, line 54**<br>• More than $106,800, multiply line 4 by 2.9% (.029). Then, add $13,243.20 to the result.<br>Enter the total here and on **Form 1040, line 56,** or **Form 1040NR, line 54** . . . . . | **5** | |
| **6** | **Deduction for one-half of self-employment tax.** Multiply line 5 by 50% (.50). Enter the result here and on **Form 1040, line 27,** or **Form 1040NR, line 27** . . . . . **6** | | |

**For Paperwork Reduction Act Notice, see your tax return instructions.** Cat. No. 11358Z **Schedule SE (Form 1040) 2010**

Schedule SE (Form 1040) 2010 | Attachment Sequence No. **17** | Page **2**

| Name of person with **self-employment** income (as shown on Form 1040) | Social security number of person with **self-employment** income ▶ | |
|---|---|---|

**Section B—Long Schedule SE**

**Part I Self-Employment Tax**

**Note.** If your only income subject to self-employment tax is **church employee income,** see page SE-3 for specific instructions. Also see page SE-1 for the definition of church employee income.

| Line | Description | Box | Amount | Cents |
|---|---|---|---|---|
| A | If you are a minister, member of a religious order, or Christian Science practitioner **and** you filed Form 4361, but you had $400 or more of **other** net earnings from self-employment, check here and continue with Part I ▶ ☐ | | | |
| 1a | Net farm profit or (loss) from Schedule F, line 36, and farm partnerships, Schedule K-1 (Form 1065), box 14, code A. **Note.** Skip lines 1a and 1b if you use the farm optional method (see page SE-5) | 1a | | |
| b | If you received social security retirement or disability benefits, enter the amount of Conservation Reserve Program payments included on Schedule F, line 6b, or listed on Schedule K-1 (Form 1065), box 20, code Y | 1b | ( | ) |
| 2 | Net profit or (loss) from Schedule C, line 31; Schedule C-EZ, line 3; Schedule K-1 (Form 1065), box 14, code A (other than farming); and Schedule K-1 (Form 1065-B), box 9, code J1. Ministers and members of religious orders, see page SE-1 for types of income to report on this line. See page SE-4 for other income to report. **Note.** Skip this line if you use the nonfarm optional method (see page SE-5) | 2 | | |
| 3 | Combine lines 1a, 1b, and 2. Subtract from that total the amount on Form 1040, line 29, or Form 1040NR, line 29, and enter the result (see page SE-3) | 3 | | |
| 4a | If line 3 is more than zero, multiply line 3 by 92.35% (.9235). Otherwise, enter amount from line 3 **Note.** If line 4a is less than $400 due to Conservation Reserve Program payments on line 1b, see page SE-3. | 4a | | |
| b | If you elect one or both of the optional methods, enter the total of lines 15 and 17 here | 4b | | |
| c | Combine lines 4a and 4b. If less than $400, **stop**; you do not owe self-employment tax. **Exception.** If less than $400 and you had **church employee income,** enter -0- and continue ▶ | 4c | | |
| 5a | Enter your **church employee income** from Form W-2. See page SE-1 for definition of church employee income. **5a** | | | |
| b | Multiply line 5a by 92.35% (.9235). If less than $100, enter -0- | 5b | | |
| 6 | Add lines 4c and 5b | 6 | | |
| 7 | Maximum amount of combined wages and self-employment earnings subject to social security tax or the 6.2% portion of the 7.65% railroad retirement (tier 1) tax for 2010 | 7 | 106,800 | 00 |
| 8a | Total social security wages and tips (total of boxes 3 and 7 on Form(s) W-2) and railroad retirement (tier 1) compensation. If $106,800 or more, skip lines 8b through 10, and go to line 11 **8a** | | | |
| b | Unreported tips subject to social security tax (from Form 4137, line 10) **8b** | | | |
| c | Wages subject to social security tax (from Form 8919, line 10) **8c** | | | |
| d | Add lines 8a, 8b, and 8c | 8d | | |
| 9 | Subtract line 8d from line 7. If zero or less, enter -0- here and on line 10 and go to line 11 ▶ | 9 | | |
| 10 | Multiply the **smaller** of line 6 or line 9 by 12.4% (.124) | 10 | | |
| 11 | Multiply line 6 by 2.9% (.029) | 11 | | |
| 12 | **Self-employment tax.** Add lines 10 and 11. Enter here and on **Form 1040, line 56,** or **Form 1040NR, line 54** | 12 | | |
| 13 | **Deduction for one-half of self-employment tax.** Multiply line 12 by 50% (.50). Enter the result here and on **Form 1040, line 27, or Form 1040NR, line 27** **13** | | | |

**Part II Optional Methods To Figure Net Earnings** (see page SE-4)

**Farm Optional Method.** You may use this method **only** if **(a)** your gross farm income[1] was not more than $6,720, **or (b)** your net farm profits[2] were less than $4,851.

| Line | Description | Box | Amount | Cents |
|---|---|---|---|---|
| 14 | Maximum income for optional methods | 14 | 4,480 | 00 |
| 15 | Enter the **smaller** of: two-thirds (2/3) of gross farm income[1] (not less than zero) **or** $4,480. Also include this amount on line 4b above | 15 | | |

**Nonfarm Optional Method.** You may use this method **only** if **(a)** your net nonfarm profits[3] were less than $4,851 and also less than 72.189% of your gross nonfarm income,[4] **and (b)** you had net earnings from self-employment of at least $400 in 2 of the prior 3 years. **Caution.** You may use this method no more than five times.

| Line | Description | Box | Amount | Cents |
|---|---|---|---|---|
| 16 | Subtract line 15 from line 14 | 16 | | |
| 17 | Enter the **smaller** of: two-thirds (2/3) of gross nonfarm income[4] (not less than zero) **or** the amount on line 16. Also include this amount on line 4b above | 17 | | |

[1] From Sch. F, line 11, and Sch. K-1 (Form 1065), box 14, code B.

[2] From Sch. F, line 36, and Sch. K-1 (Form 1065), box 14, code A—minus the amount you would have entered on line 1b had you not used the optional method.

[3] From Sch. C, line 31; Sch. C-EZ, line 3; Sch. K-1 (Form 1065), box 14, code A; and Sch. K-1 (Form 1065-B), box 9, code J1.

[4] From Sch. C, line 7; Sch. C-EZ, line 1; Sch. K-1 (Form 1065), box 14, code C; and Sch. K-1 (Form 1065-B), box 9, code J2.

**Schedule SE (Form 1040) 2010**

**SCHEDULE EIC**
**(Form 1040A or 1040)**

Department of the Treasury
Internal Revenue Service (99)

# Earned Income Credit

Qualifying Child Information

*Complete and attach to Form 1040A or 1040 only if you have a qualifying child.*

1040A
1040
EIC

OMB No. 1545-0074

**2010**

Attachment Sequence No. **43**

Name(s) shown on return

**Your social security number**

## *Before you begin:*

- See the instructions for Form 1040A, lines 41a and 41b, or Form 1040, lines 64a and 64b, to make sure that **(a)** you can take the EIC, and **(b)** you have a qualifying child.
- Be sure the child's name on line 1 and social security number (SSN) on line 2 agree with the child's social security card. Otherwise, at the time we process your return, we may reduce or disallow your EIC. If the name or SSN on the child's social security card is not correct, call the Social Security Administration at 1-800-772-1213.

**CAUTION**

- If you take the EIC even though you are not eligible, you may not be allowed to take the credit for up to 10 years. See page 2 of schedule for details.
- It will take us longer to process your return and issue your refund if you do not fill in all lines that apply for each qualifying child.

## Qualifying Child Information

| Qualifying Child Information | Child 1 | Child 2 | Child 3 |
|---|---|---|---|
| **1 Child's name**<br>If you have more than three qualifying children, you only have to list three to get the maximum credit. | First name / Last name | First name / Last name | First name / Last name |
| **2 Child's SSN**<br>The child must have an SSN as defined in the instructions for Form 1040A, lines 41a and 41b, or Form 1040, lines 64a and 64b, unless the child was born and died in 2010. If your child was born and died in 2010 and did not have an SSN, enter "Died" on this line and attach a copy of the child's birth certificate, death certificate, or hospital medical records. | | | |
| **3 Child's year of birth** | Year ___ ___ ___ ___<br>*If born after 1991 **and** the child was younger than you (or your spouse, if filing jointly), skip lines 4a and 4b; go to line 5.* | Year ___ ___ ___ ___<br>*If born after 1991 **and** the child was younger than you (or your spouse, if filing jointly), skip lines 4a and 4b; go to line 5.* | Year ___ ___ ___ ___<br>*If born after 1991 **and** the child was younger than you (or your spouse, if filing jointly), skip lines 4a and 4b; go to line 5.* |
| **4 a** Was the child under age 24 at the end of 2010, a student, and younger than you (or your spouse, if filing jointly)? | ☐ **Yes.** *Go to line 5.* ☐ **No.** *Continue.* | ☐ **Yes.** *Go to line 5.* ☐ **No.** *Continue.* | ☐ **Yes.** *Go to line 5.* ☐ **No.** *Continue.* |
| **b** Was the child permanently and totally disabled during any part of 2010? | ☐ **Yes.** *Continue.* ☐ **No.** The child is not a qualifying child. | ☐ **Yes.** *Continue.* ☐ **No.** The child is not a qualifying child. | ☐ **Yes.** *Continue.* ☐ **No.** The child is not a qualifying child. |
| **5 Child's relationship to you**<br>(for example, son, daughter, grandchild, niece, nephew, foster child, etc.) | | | |
| **6 Number of months child lived with you in the United States during 2010**<br>• If the child lived with you for more than half of 2010 but less than 7 months, enter "7."<br>• If the child was born or died in 2010 and your home was the child's home for the entire time he or she was alive during 2010, enter "12." | _______ months<br>*Do not enter more than 12 months.* | _______ months<br>*Do not enter more than 12 months.* | _______ months<br>*Do not enter more than 12 months.* |

**For Paperwork Reduction Act Notice, see your tax return instructions.** Cat. No. 13339M **Schedule EIC (Form 1040A or 1040) 2010**

# Purpose of Schedule

After you have figured your earned income credit (EIC), use Schedule EIC to give the IRS information about your qualifying child(ren).

To figure the amount of your credit or to have the IRS figure it for you, see the instructions for Form 1040A, lines 41a and 41b, or Form 1040, lines 64a and 64b.

**Taking the EIC when not eligible.** If you take the EIC even though you are not eligible and it is determined that your error is due to reckless or intentional disregard of the EIC rules, you will not be allowed to take the credit for 2 years even if you are otherwise eligible to do so. If you fraudulently take the EIC, you will not be allowed to take the credit for 10 years. You may also have to pay penalties.

**TIP** You may also be able to take the additional child tax credit if your child was your dependent and under age 17 at the end of 2010. For more details, see the instructions for line 42 of Form 1040A or line 65 of Form 1040.

## Qualifying Child

**A qualifying child for the EIC is a child who is your . . .**

Son, daughter, stepchild, foster child, brother, sister, stepbrother, stepsister, half brother, half sister, or a descendant of any of them (for example, your grandchild, niece, or nephew)

**AND**

**was . . .**

Under age 19 at the end of 2010 and younger than you (or your spouse, if filing jointly)
or
Under age 24 at the end of 2010, a student, and younger than you (or your spouse, if filing jointly)
or
Any age and permanently and totally disabled

**AND**

Who is not filing a joint return for 2010 or is filing a joint return for 2010 only as a claim for refund (as defined in the instructions for Form 1040A, lines 41a and 41b, or Form 1040, lines 64a and 64b)

**AND**

Who lived with you in the United States for more than half of 2010. If the child did not live with you for the required time, see *Exception to time lived with you* in the instructions for Form 1040A, lines 41a and 41b, or Form 1040, lines 64a and 64b.

**CAUTION** *If the child was married or meets the conditions to be a qualifying child of another person (other than your spouse if filing a joint return), special rules apply. For details, see* Married child *or* Qualifying child of more than one person *in the instructions for Form 1040A, lines 41a and 41b, or Form 1040, lines 64a and 64b.*

# B-4 U.S. Income Tax Return for Estates and Trusts

Form **1041** Department of the Treasury—Internal Revenue Service
**U.S. Income Tax Return for Estates and Trusts** **2010** OMB No. 1545-0092

**A** Type of entity (see instr.):
- ☐ Decedent's estate
- ☐ Simple trust
- ☐ Complex trust
- ☐ Qualified disability trust
- ☐ ESBT (S portion only)
- ☐ Grantor type trust
- ☐ Bankruptcy estate-Ch. 7
- ☐ Bankruptcy estate-Ch. 11
- ☐ Pooled income fund

**B** Number of Schedules K-1 attached (see instructions) ▶

For calendar year 2010 or fiscal year beginning , 2010, and ending , 20

Name of estate or trust (If a grantor type trust, see page 15 of the instructions.)

Name and title of fiduciary

Number, street, and room or suite no. (If a P.O. box, see page 15 of the instructions.)

City or town, state, and ZIP code

**C** Employer identification number

**D** Date entity created

**E** Nonexempt charitable and split-interest trusts, check applicable boxes (see page 16 of the instr.):
- ☐ Described in section 4947(a)(1)
- ☐ Not a private foundation
- ☐ Described in section 4947(a)(2)

**F** Check applicable boxes: ☐ Initial return ☐ Final return ☐ Amended return ☐ Change in trust's name ☐ Change in fiduciary ☐ Change in fiduciary's name ☐ Change in fiduciary's address

**G** Check here if the estate or filing trust made a section 645 election . . . . . . ▶☐

|  |  |  |  |  |
|---|---|---|---|---|
| Income | 1 | Interest income | 1 | |
| | 2a | Total ordinary dividends | 2a | |
| | b | Qualified dividends allocable to: **(1)** Beneficiaries ______ **(2)** Estate or trust ______ | | |
| | 3 | Business income or (loss). Attach Schedule C or C-EZ (Form 1040) | 3 | |
| | 4 | Capital gain or (loss). Attach Schedule D (Form 1041) | 4 | |
| | 5 | Rents, royalties, partnerships, other estates and trusts, etc. Attach Schedule E (Form 1040) | 5 | |
| | 6 | Farm income or (loss). Attach Schedule F (Form 1040) | 6 | |
| | 7 | Ordinary gain or (loss). Attach Form 4797 | 7 | |
| | 8 | Other income. List type and amount ______ | 8 | |
| | 9 | **Total income.** Combine lines 1, 2a, and 3 through 8 ▶ | 9 | |
| Deductions | 10 | Interest. Check if Form 4952 is attached ▶ ☐ | 10 | |
| | 11 | Taxes | 11 | |
| | 12 | Fiduciary fees | 12 | |
| | 13 | Charitable deduction (from Schedule A, line 7) | 13 | |
| | 14 | Attorney, accountant, and return preparer fees | 14 | |
| | 15a | Other deductions **not** subject to the 2% floor (attach schedule) | 15a | |
| | b | Allowable miscellaneous itemized deductions subject to the 2% floor | 15b | |
| | 16 | Add lines 10 through 15b ▶ | 16 | |
| | 17 | Adjusted total income or (loss). Subtract line 16 from line 9 . . . 17 | | |
| | 18 | Income distribution deduction (from Schedule B, line 15). Attach Schedules K-1 (Form 1041) | 18 | |
| | 19 | Estate tax deduction including certain generation-skipping taxes (attach computation) | 19 | |
| | 20 | Exemption | 20 | |
| | 21 | Add lines 18 through 20 ▶ | 21 | |
| Tax and Payments | 22 | Taxable income. Subtract line 21 from line 17. If a loss, see page 23 of the instructions | 22 | |
| | 23 | **Total tax** (from Schedule G, line 7) | 23 | |
| | 24 | **Payments: a** 2010 estimated tax payments and amount applied from 2009 return | 24a | |
| | b | Estimated tax payments allocated to beneficiaries (from Form 1041-T) | 24b | |
| | c | Subtract line 24b from line 24a | 24c | |
| | d | Tax paid with Form 7004 (see page 24 of the instructions) | 24d | |
| | e | Federal income tax withheld. If any is from Form(s) 1099, check ▶ ☐ | 24e | |
| | | Other payments: **f** Form 2439 ______ ; **g** Form 4136 ______ ; Total ▶ | 24h | |
| | 25 | **Total payments.** Add lines 24c through 24e, and 24h ▶ | 25 | |
| | 26 | Estimated tax penalty (see page 24 of the instructions) | 26 | |
| | 27 | **Tax due.** If line 25 is smaller than the total of lines 23 and 26, enter amount owed | 27 | |
| | 28 | **Overpayment.** If line 25 is larger than the total of lines 23 and 26, enter amount overpaid | 28 | |
| | 29 | Amount of line 28 to be: **a Credited to 2011 estimated tax** ▶ ; **b Refunded** ▶ | 29 | |

**Sign Here**

Under penalties of perjury, I declare that I have examined this return, including accompanying schedules and statements, and to the best of my knowledge and belief, it is true, correct, and complete. Declaration of preparer (other than taxpayer) is based on all information of which preparer has any knowledge.

Signature of fiduciary or officer representing fiduciary | Date | ▶ EIN of fiduciary if a financial institution

May the IRS discuss this return with the preparer shown below (see instr.)? ☐Yes ☐No

**Paid Preparer Use Only**

| Print/Type preparer's name | Preparer's signature | Date | Check ☐ if self-employed | PTIN |
|---|---|---|---|---|
| Firm's name ▶ | | | Firm's EIN ▶ | |
| Firm's address ▶ | | | Phone no. | |

**For Paperwork Reduction Act Notice, see the separate instructions.** Cat. No. 11370H Form **1041** (2010)

Form 1041 (2010) Page 2

## Schedule A Charitable Deduction. Do not complete for a simple trust or a pooled income fund.

| | | | |
|---|---|---|---|
| 1 | Amounts paid or permanently set aside for charitable purposes from gross income (see page 25) | 1 | |
| 2 | Tax-exempt income allocable to charitable contributions (see page 25 of the instructions) | 2 | |
| 3 | Subtract line 2 from line 1 | 3 | |
| 4 | Capital gains for the tax year allocated to corpus and paid or permanently set aside for charitable purposes | 4 | |
| 5 | Add lines 3 and 4 | 5 | |
| 6 | Section 1202 exclusion allocable to capital gains paid or permanently set aside for charitable purposes (see page 25 of the instructions) | 6 | |
| 7 | **Charitable deduction.** Subtract line 6 from line 5. Enter here and on page 1, line 13 | 7 | |

## Schedule B Income Distribution Deduction

| | | | |
|---|---|---|---|
| 1 | Adjusted total income (see page 25 of the instructions) | 1 | |
| 2 | Adjusted tax-exempt interest | 2 | |
| 3 | Total net gain from Schedule D (Form 1041), line 15, column (1) (see page 26 of the instructions) | 3 | |
| 4 | Enter amount from Schedule A, line 4 (minus any allocable section 1202 exclusion) | 4 | |
| 5 | Capital gains for the tax year included on Schedule A, line 1 (see page 26 of the instructions) | 5 | |
| 6 | Enter any gain from page 1, line 4, as a negative number. If page 1, line 4, is a loss, enter the loss as a positive number | 6 | |
| 7 | **Distributable net income.** Combine lines 1 through 6. If zero or less, enter -0- | 7 | |
| 8 | If a complex trust, enter accounting income for the tax year as determined under the governing instrument and applicable local law — 8 | | |
| 9 | Income required to be distributed currently | 9 | |
| 10 | Other amounts paid, credited, or otherwise required to be distributed | 10 | |
| 11 | Total distributions. Add lines 9 and 10. If greater than line 8, see page 26 of the instructions | 11 | |
| 12 | Enter the amount of tax-exempt income included on line 11 | 12 | |
| 13 | Tentative income distribution deduction. Subtract line 12 from line 11 | 13 | |
| 14 | Tentative income distribution deduction. Subtract line 2 from line 7. If zero or less, enter -0- | 14 | |
| 15 | **Income distribution deduction.** Enter the smaller of line 13 or line 14 here and on page 1, line 18 | 15 | |

## Schedule G Tax Computation (see page 27 of the instructions)

| | | | | | |
|---|---|---|---|---|---|
| 1 | **Tax:** a Tax on taxable income (see page 27 of the instructions) | 1a | | | |
| | b Tax on lump-sum distributions. Attach Form 4972 | 1b | | | |
| | c Alternative minimum tax (from Schedule I (Form 1041), line 56) | 1c | | | |
| | d **Total.** Add lines 1a through 1c ▶ | | | 1d | |
| 2a | Foreign tax credit. Attach Form 1116 | 2a | | | |
| b | General business credit. Attach Form 3800 | 2b | | | |
| c | Credit for prior year minimum tax. Attach Form 8801 | 2c | | | |
| d | Bond credits. Attach Form 8912 | 2d | | | |
| 3 | **Total credits.** Add lines 2a through 2d ▶ | | | 3 | |
| 4 | Subtract line 3 from line 1d. If zero or less, enter -0- | | | 4 | |
| 5 | Recapture taxes. Check if from: ☐ Form 4255 ☐ Form 8611 | | | 5 | |
| 6 | Household employment taxes. Attach Schedule H (Form 1040) | | | 6 | |
| 7 | **Total tax.** Add lines 4 through 6. Enter here and on page 1, line 23 ▶ | | | 7 | |

## Other Information

| | | Yes | No |
|---|---|---|---|
| 1 | Did the estate or trust receive tax-exempt income? If "Yes," attach a computation of the allocation of expenses<br>Enter the amount of tax-exempt interest income and exempt-interest dividends ▶ $ | | |
| 2 | Did the estate or trust receive all or any part of the earnings (salary, wages, and other compensation) of any individual by reason of a contract assignment or similar arrangement? | | |
| 3 | At any time during calendar year 2010, did the estate or trust have an interest in or a signature or other authority over a bank, securities, or other financial account in a foreign country?<br>See page 29 of the instructions for exceptions and filing requirements for Form TD F 90-22.1. If "Yes," enter the name of the foreign country ▶ | | |
| 4 | During the tax year, did the estate or trust receive a distribution from, or was it the grantor of, or transferor to, a foreign trust? If "Yes," the estate or trust may have to file Form 3520. See page 29 of the instructions | | |
| 5 | Did the estate or trust receive, or pay, any qualified residence interest on seller-provided financing? If "Yes," see page 29 for required attachment | | |
| 6 | If this is an estate or a complex trust making the section 663(b) election, check here (see page 29) ▶ ☐ | | |
| 7 | To make a section 643(e)(3) election, attach Schedule D (Form 1041), and check here (see page 29) ▶ ☐ | | |
| 8 | If the decedent's estate has been open for more than 2 years, attach an explanation for the delay in closing the estate, and check here ▶ ☐ | | |
| 9 | Are any present or future trust beneficiaries skip persons? See page 29 of the instructions | | |

Form **1041** (2010)

661110

☐ Final K-1 ☐ Amended K-1 OMB No. 1545-0092

**Schedule K-1**
**(Form 1041)**
Department of the Treasury
Internal Revenue Service

**2010**

For calendar year 2010,
or tax year beginning ____________, 2010,
and ending ____________, 20 ____

# Beneficiary's Share of Income, Deductions, Credits, etc.

▶ **See back of form and instructions.**

## Part I Information About the Estate or Trust

A Estate's or trust's employer identification number

B Estate's or trust's name

C Fiduciary's name, address, city, state, and ZIP code

D ☐ Check if Form 1041-T was filed and enter the date it was filed ____________

E ☐ Check if this is the final Form 1041 for the estate or trust

## Part II Information About the Beneficiary

F Beneficiary's identifying number

G Beneficiary's name, address, city, state, and ZIP code

H ☐ Domestic beneficiary ☐ Foreign beneficiary

## Part III Beneficiary's Share of Current Year Income, Deductions, Credits, and Other Items

| | | | |
|---|---|---|---|
| 1 | Interest income | 11 | Final year deductions |
| 2a | Ordinary dividends | | |
| 2b | Qualified dividends | | |
| 3 | Net short-term capital gain | | |
| 4a | Net long-term capital gain | | |
| 4b | 28% rate gain | 12 | Alternative minimum tax adjustment |
| 4c | Unrecaptured section 1250 gain | | |
| 5 | Other portfolio and nonbusiness income | | |
| 6 | Ordinary business income | | |
| 7 | Net rental real estate income | 13 | Credits and credit recapture |
| 8 | Other rental income | | |
| 9 | Directly apportioned deductions | | |
| | | 14 | Other information |
| 10 | Estate tax deduction | | |

*See attached statement for additional information.

**Note.** A statement must be attached showing the beneficiary's share of income and directly apportioned deductions from each business, rental real estate, and other rental activity.

For IRS Use Only

**For Paperwork Reduction Act Notice, see the Instructions for Form 1041.** Cat. No. 11380D **Schedule K-1 (Form 1041) 2010**

Schedule K-1 (Form 1041) 2010 Page **2**

**This list identifies the codes used on Schedule K-1 for beneficiaries and provides summarized reporting information for beneficiaries who file Form 1040. For detailed reporting and filing information, see the Instructions for Beneficiary Filing Form 1040 and the instructions for your income tax return.**

| | *Report on* |
|---|---|
| **1. Interest income** | Form 1040, line 8a |
| **2a. Ordinary dividends** | Form 1040, line 9a |
| **2b. Qualified dividends** | Form 1040, line 9b |
| **3. Net short-term capital gain** | Schedule D, line 5 |
| **4a. Net long-term capital gain** | Schedule D, line 12 |
| **4b. 28% rate gain** | Line 4 of the worksheet for Schedule D, line 18 |
| **4c. Unrecaptured section 1250 gain** | Line 11 of the worksheet for Schedule D, line 19 |
| **5. Other portfolio and nonbusiness income** | Schedule E, line 33, column (f) |
| **6. Ordinary business income** | Schedule E, line 33, column (d) or (f) |
| **7. Net rental real estate income** | Schedule E, line 33, column (d) or (f) |
| **8. Other rental income** | Schedule E, line 33, column (d) or (f) |
| **9. Directly apportioned deductions** | |
| *Code* | |
| **A** Depreciation | Form 8582 or Schedule E, line 33, column (c) or (e) |
| **B** Depletion | Form 8582 or Schedule E, line 33, column (c) or (e) |
| **C** Amortization | Form 8582 or Schedule E, line 33, column (c) or (e) |
| **10. Estate tax deduction** | Schedule A, line 28 |
| **11. Final year deductions** | |
| **A** Excess deductions | Schedule A, line 23 |
| **B** Short-term capital loss carryover | Schedule D, line 5 |
| **C** Long-term capital loss carryover | Schedule D, line 12; line 5 of the wksht. for Sch. D, line 18; and line 16 of the wksht. for Sch. D, line 19 |
| **D** Net operating loss carryover — regular tax | Form 1040, line 21 |
| **E** Net operating loss carryover — minimum tax | Form 6251, line 11 |

| **12. Alternative minimum tax (AMT) items** | |
|---|---|
| *Code* | *Report on* |
| **A** Adjustment for minimum tax purposes | Form 6251, line 15 |
| **B** AMT adjustment attributable to qualified dividends | See the beneficiary's instructions and the Instructions for Form 6251 |
| **C** AMT adjustment attributable to net short-term capital gain | (see B) |
| **D** AMT adjustment attributable to net long-term capital gain | (see B) |
| **E** AMT adjustment attributable to unrecaptured section 1250 gain | (see B) |
| **F** AMT adjustment attributable to 28% rate gain | (see B) |
| **G** Accelerated depreciation | (see B) |
| **H** Depletion | (see B) |
| **I** Amortization | |
| **J** Exclusion items | 2011 Form 8801 |
| **13. Credits and credit recapture** | |
| **A** Credit for estimated taxes | Form 1040, line 62 |
| **B** Credit for backup withholding | Form 1040, line 61 |
| **C** Low-income housing credit | Form 8586 (also see the beneficiary's instructions) |
| **D** Rehabilitation credit and energy credit | See the beneficiary's instructions |
| **E** Other qualifying investment credit | See the beneficiary's instructions |
| **F** Work opportunity credit | Form 5884, line 3 |
| **G** Credit for small employer health insurance premiums | Form 8941, line 15 |
| **H** Alcohol and cellulosic biofuel fuels credit | Form 6478, line 8 (also see the beneficiary's instructions) |
| **I** Credit for increasing research activities | Form 3800, line 1c |
| **J** Renewable electricity, refined coal, and Indian coal production credit | See the beneficiary's instructions |
| **K** Empowerment zone and renewal community employment credit | Form 8844, line 3 |
| **L** Indian employment credit | Form 3800, line 1g |
| **M** Orphan drug credit | Form 3800, line 1h |
| **N** Credit for employer-provided child care and facilities | Form 3800, line 1k |
| **O** Biodiesel and renewable diesel fuels credit | Form 8864, line 9 (also see the beneficiary's instructions) |
| **P** Nonconventional source fuel credit | Form 3800, line 1o |
| **Q** Credit to holders of tax credit bonds | Form 8912, line 8 |
| **R** Agricultural chemicals security credit | Form 3800, line 1v |
| **S** Energy efficient appliance credit | Form 3800, line 1q |
| **T** Credit for employer differential wage payments | Form 3800, line 1w |
| **U** Recapture of credits | See the beneficiary's instructions |
| **14. Other information** | |
| **A** Tax-exempt interest | Form 1040, line 8b |
| **B** Foreign taxes | Form 1040, line 47 or Sch. A, line 8 |
| **C** Qualified production activities income | Form 8903, line 7, col. (b) (also see the beneficiary's instructions) |
| **D** Form W-2 wages | Form 8903, line 17 |
| **E** Net investment income | Form 4952, line 4a |
| **F** Gross farm and fishing income | Schedule E, line 42 |
| **G** Foreign trading gross receipts (IRC 942(a)) | See the Instructions for Form 8873 |
| **H** Other information | See the beneficiary's instructions |

**Note.** If you are a beneficiary who does not file a Form 1040, see instructions for the type of income tax return you are filing.

**SCHEDULE J (Form 1041)**

Department of the Treasury
Internal Revenue Service

# Accumulation Distribution for Certain Complex Trusts

▶ Attach to Form 1041.

▶ See the Instructions for Form 1041.

OMB No. 1545-0092

2010

| Name of trust | Employer identification number |
|---|---|
| | |

**Part I** **Accumulation Distribution in 2010**

**Note:** *See the Form 4970 instructions for certain income that minors may exclude and special rules for multiple trusts.*

| | | | | | |
|---|---|---|---|---|---|
| 1 | Other amounts paid, credited, or otherwise required to be distributed for 2010 (from Form 1041, Schedule B, line 10) . . . . . . . . . . . . . . . . . . . . . . . . . . . . . | | | 1 | |
| 2 | Distributable net income for 2010 (from Form 1041, Schedule B, line 7) . . . . | 2 | | | |
| 3 | Income required to be distributed currently for 2010 (from Form 1041, Schedule B, line 9) . . . . . . . . . . . . . . . . . . . . . . . . . . . . . | 3 | | | |
| 4 | Subtract line 3 from line 2. If zero or less, enter -0- . . . . . . . . . . . . . . . . . . . . | | | 4 | |
| 5 | Accumulation distribution for 2010. Subtract line 4 from line 1 . . . . . . . . . . . . . . | | | 5 | |

**Part II** **Ordinary Income Accumulation Distribution** (Enter the applicable throwback years below.)

| **Note:** *If the distribution is thrown back to more than 5 years (starting with the earliest applicable tax year beginning after 1968), attach additional schedules. (If the trust was a simple trust, see Regulations section 1.665(e)-1A(b).)* | | **Throwback year ending** ---------- | **Throwback year ending** ---------- | **Throwback year ending** ---------- | **Throwback year ending** ---------- | **Throwback year ending** ---------- |
|---|---|---|---|---|---|---|
| 6 Distributable net income (see page 30 of the instructions) . | 6 | | | | | |
| 7 Distributions (see page 30 of the instructions) . . . . . | 7 | | | | | |
| 8 Subtract line 7 from line 6 . | 8 | | | | | |
| 9 Enter amount from page 2, line 25 or line 31, as applicable . . . . . . | 9 | | | | | |
| 10 Undistributed net income Subtract line 9 from line 8 . | 10 | | | | | |
| 11 Enter amount of prior accumulation distributions thrown back to any of these years . . . . . . . . | 11 | | | | | |
| 12 Subtract line 11 from line 10 | 12 | | | | | |
| 13 Allocate the amount on line 5 to the earliest applicable year first. Do not allocate an amount greater than line 12 for the same year (see page 30 of the instructions) . . . | 13 | | | | | |
| 14 Divide line 13 by line 10 and multiply result by amount on line 9 . . . . . . . . | 14 | | | | | |
| 15 Add lines 13 and 14 . . . | 15 | | | | | |
| 16 Tax-exempt interest included on line 13 (see page 30 of the instructions) . . . . . . | 16 | | | | | |
| 17 Subtract line 16 from line 15 | 17 | | | | | |

Schedule J (Form 1041) 2010 Page 2

**Part III** **Taxes Imposed on Undistributed Net Income** (Enter the applicable throwback years below.) (See page 30 of the instructions.)

**Note:** *If more than 5 throwback years are involved, attach additional schedules. If the trust received an accumulation distribution from another trust, see Regulations section 1.665(d)-1A.*

| If the trust elected the alternative tax on capital gains (repealed for tax years beginning after 1978), **skip** lines 18 through 25 and **complete** lines 26 through 31. | | **Throwback year ending** ______ | **Throwback year ending** ______ | **Throwback year ending** ______ | **Throwback year ending** ______ | **Throwback year ending** ______ |
|---|---|---|---|---|---|---|
| 18 Regular tax | 18 | | | | | |
| 19 Trust's share of net short-term gain | 19 | | | | | |
| 20 Trust's share of net long-term gain | 20 | | | | | |
| 21 Add lines 19 and 20 | 21 | | | | | |
| 22 Taxable income | 22 | | | | | |
| 23 Enter percent. Divide line 21 by line 22, but do not enter more than 100% | 23 | % | % | % | % | % |
| 24 Multiply line 18 by the percentage on line 23 | 24 | | | | | |
| 25 Tax on undistributed net income. Subtract line 24 from line 18. Enter here and on page 1, line 9 | 25 | | | | | |
| Do not complete lines 26 through 31 unless the trust elected the alternative tax on long-term capital gain. | | | | | | |
| 26 Tax on income other than long-term capital gain | 26 | | | | | |
| 27 Trust's share of net short-term gain | 27 | | | | | |
| 28 Trust's share of taxable income less section 1202 deduction | 28 | | | | | |
| 29 Enter percent. Divide line 27 by line 28, but do not enter more than 100% | 29 | % | % | % | % | % |
| 30 Multiply line 26 by the percentage on line 29 | 30 | | | | | |
| 31 Tax on undistributed net income. Subtract line 30 from line 26. Enter here and on page 1, line 9 | 31 | | | | | |

**Part IV** **Allocation to Beneficiary**

**Note:** *Be sure to complete* ***Form 4970,*** *Tax on Accumulation Distribution of Trusts.*

| Beneficiary's name | | | Identifying number | |
|---|---|---|---|---|
| Beneficiary's address (number and street including apartment number or P.O. box)<br>City, state, and ZIP code | | **(a)** This beneficiary's share of line 13 | **(b)** This beneficiary's share of line 14 | **(c)** This beneficiary's share of line 16 |
| 32 Throwback year ______ | 32 | | | |
| 33 Throwback year ______ | 33 | | | |
| 34 Throwback year ______ | 34 | | | |
| 35 Throwback year ______ | 35 | | | |
| 36 Throwback year ______ | 36 | | | |
| 37 Total. Add lines 32 through 36. Enter here and on the appropriate lines of Form 4970 | 37 | | | |

**Schedule J (Form 1041) 2010**

# B-5 U.S. Partnership Return of Income

Form **1065** | **U.S. Return of Partnership Income** | OMB No. 1545-0099

Department of the Treasury
Internal Revenue Service

For calendar year 2010, or tax year beginning ______, 2010, ending ______, 20____.

▶ See separate instructions.

**2010**

| | Print or type. | |
|---|---|---|
| A Principal business activity | Name of partnership | D Employer identification number |
| B Principal product or service | Number, street, and room or suite no. If a P.O. box, see the instructions. | E Date business started |
| C Business code number | City or town, state, and ZIP code | F Total assets (see the instructions) $ |

G Check applicable boxes: (1) ☐ Initial return (2) ☐ Final return (3) ☐ Name change (4) ☐ Address change (5) ☐ Amended return
(6) ☐ Technical termination - also check (1) or (2)

H Check accounting method: (1) ☐ Cash (2) ☐ Accrual (3) ☐ Other (specify) ▶

I Number of Schedules K-1. Attach one for each person who was a partner at any time during the tax year ▶

J Check if Schedules C and M-3 are attached . . . ☐

**Caution.** *Include **only** trade or business income and expenses on lines 1a through 22 below. See the instructions for more information.*

| | | | | | |
|---|---|---|---|---|---|
| Income | 1a | Gross receipts or sales | 1a | | |
| | b | Less returns and allowances | 1b | 1c | |
| | 2 | Cost of goods sold (Schedule A, line 8) | | 2 | |
| | 3 | Gross profit. Subtract line 2 from line 1c | | 3 | |
| | 4 | Ordinary income (loss) from other partnerships, estates, and trusts *(attach statement)* | | 4 | |
| | 5 | Net farm profit (loss) *(attach Schedule F (Form 1040))* | | 5 | |
| | 6 | Net gain (loss) from Form 4797, Part II, line 17 *(attach Form 4797)* | | 6 | |
| | 7 | Other income (loss) *(attach statement)* | | 7 | |
| | 8 | **Total income (loss).** Combine lines 3 through 7 | | 8 | |
| Deductions (see the instructions for limitations) | 9 | Salaries and wages (other than to partners) (less employment credits) | | 9 | |
| | 10 | Guaranteed payments to partners | | 10 | |
| | 11 | Repairs and maintenance | | 11 | |
| | 12 | Bad debts | | 12 | |
| | 13 | Rent | | 13 | |
| | 14 | Taxes and licenses | | 14 | |
| | 15 | Interest | | 15 | |
| | 16a | Depreciation (*if required, attach Form 4562*) | 16a | | |
| | b | Less depreciation reported on Schedule A and elsewhere on return | 16b | 16c | |
| | 17 | Depletion **(Do not deduct oil and gas depletion.)** | | 17 | |
| | 18 | Retirement plans, etc. | | 18 | |
| | 19 | Employee benefit programs | | 19 | |
| | 20 | Other deductions (*attach statement*) | | 20 | |
| | 21 | **Total deductions.** Add the amounts shown in the far right column for lines 9 through 20 | | 21 | |
| | 22 | **Ordinary business income (loss).** Subtract line 21 from line 8 | | 22 | |

**Sign Here**

Under penalties of perjury, I declare that I have examined this return, including accompanying schedules and statements, and to the best of my knowledge and belief, it is true, correct, and complete. Declaration of preparer (other than general partner or limited liability company member manager) is based on all information of which preparer has any knowledge.

May the IRS discuss this return with the preparer shown below (see instructions)? ☐ Yes ☐ No

▶ Signature of general partner or limited liability company member manager ▶ Date

| **Paid Preparer Use Only** | Print/Type preparer's name | Preparer's signature | Date | Check ☐ if self- employed | PTIN |
|---|---|---|---|---|---|
| | Firm's name ▶ | | | Firm's EIN ▶ | |
| | Firm's address ▶ | | | Phone no. | |

**For Paperwork Reduction Act Notice, see separate instructions.** Cat. No. 11390Z Form **1065** (2010)

Form 1065 (2010) Page 2

**Schedule A** **Cost of Goods Sold** (see the instructions)

| | | | |
|---|---|---|---|
| 1 | Inventory at beginning of year | 1 | |
| 2 | Purchases less cost of items withdrawn for personal use | 2 | |
| 3 | Cost of labor | 3 | |
| 4 | Additional section 263A costs (*attach statement*) | 4 | |
| 5 | Other costs (*attach statement*) | 5 | |
| 6 | **Total.** Add lines 1 through 5 | 6 | |
| 7 | Inventory at end of year | 7 | |
| 8 | **Cost of goods sold.** Subtract line 7 from line 6. Enter here and on page 1, line 2 | 8 | |

9a Check all methods used for valuing closing inventory:

**(i)** ☐ Cost as described in Regulations section 1.471-3

**(ii)** ☐ Lower of cost or market as described in Regulations section 1.471-4

**(iii)** ☐ Other (specify method used and attach explanation) ▶

b Check this box if there was a writedown of "subnormal" goods as described in Regulations section 1.471-2(c) ▶ ☐

c Check this box if the LIFO inventory method was adopted this tax year for any goods (*if checked, attach Form 970*) ▶ ☐

d Do the rules of section 263A (for property produced or acquired for resale) apply to the partnership? ☐ **Yes** ☐ **No**

e Was there any change in determining quantities, cost, or valuations between opening and closing inventory? ☐ **Yes** ☐ **No**
If "Yes," attach explanation.

**Schedule B** **Other Information**

| | | Yes | No |
|---|---|---|---|
| 1 | What type of entity is filing this return? Check the applicable box:<br>a ☐ Domestic general partnership b ☐ Domestic limited partnership<br>c ☐ Domestic limited liability company d ☐ Domestic limited liability partnership<br>e ☐ Foreign partnership f ☐ Other ▶ | | |
| 2 | At any time during the tax year, was any partner in the partnership a disregarded entity, a partnership (including an entity treated as a partnership), a trust, an S corporation, an estate (other than an estate of a deceased partner), or a nominee or similar person? | | |
| 3 | At the end of the tax year: | | |
| a | Did any foreign or domestic corporation, partnership (including any entity treated as a partnership), trust, or tax-exempt organization own, directly or indirectly, an interest of 50% or more in the profit, loss, or capital of the partnership? For rules of constructive ownership, see instructions. If "Yes," attach Schedule B-1, Information on Partners Owning 50% or More of the Partnership | | |
| b | Did any individual or estate own, directly or indirectly, an interest of 50% or more in the profit, loss, or capital of the partnership? For rules of constructive ownership, see instructions. If "Yes," attach Schedule B-1, Information on Partners Owning 50% or More of the Partnership | | |
| 4 | At the end of the tax year, did the partnership: | | |
| a | Own directly 20% or more, or own, directly or indirectly, 50% or more of the total voting power of all classes of stock entitled to vote of any foreign or domestic corporation? For rules of constructive ownership, see instructions. If "Yes," complete (i) through (iv) below | | |

| **(i)** Name of Corporation | **(ii)** Employer Identification Number (if any) | **(iii)** Country of Incorporation | **(iv)** Percentage Owned in Voting Stock |
|---|---|---|---|
| | | | |
| | | | |
| | | | |
| | | | |
| | | | |

| | | Yes | No |
|---|---|---|---|
| b | Own directly an interest of 20% or more, or own, directly or indirectly, an interest of 50% or more in the profit, loss, or capital in any foreign or domestic partnership (including an entity treated as a partnership) or in the beneficial interest of a trust? For rules of constructive ownership, see instructions. If "Yes," complete (i) through (v) below | | |

| **(i)** Name of Entity | **(ii)** Employer Identification Number (if any) | **(iii)** Type of Entity | **(iv)** Country of Organization | **(v)** Maximum Percentage Owned in Profit, Loss, or Capital |
|---|---|---|---|---|
| | | | | |
| | | | | |
| | | | | |
| | | | | |
| | | | | |

Form **1065** (2010)

Form 1065 (2010) Page **3**

| | | Yes | No |
|---|---|---|---|
| **5** | Did the partnership file Form 8893, Election of Partnership Level Tax Treatment, or an election statement under section 6231(a)(1)(B)(ii) for partnership-level tax treatment, that is in effect for this tax year? See Form 8893 for more details . . . . . | | |
| **6** | Does the partnership satisfy **all four** of the following conditions? | | |
| **a** | The partnership's total receipts for the tax year were less than $250,000. | | |
| **b** | The partnership's total assets at the end of the tax year were less than $1 million. | | |
| **c** | Schedules K-1 are filed with the return and furnished to the partners on or before the due date (including extensions) for the partnership return. | | |
| **d** | The partnership is not filing and is not required to file Schedule M-3 . . . . . | | |
| | If "Yes," the partnership is not required to complete Schedules L, M-1, and M-2; Item F on page 1 of Form 1065; or Item L on Schedule K-1. | | |
| **7** | Is this partnership a publicly traded partnership as defined in section 469(k)(2)? . . . . . | | |
| **8** | During the tax year, did the partnership have any debt that was cancelled, was forgiven, or had the terms modified so as to reduce the principal amount of the debt? . . . . . | | |
| **9** | Has this partnership filed, or is it required to file, Form 8918, Material Advisor Disclosure Statement, to provide information on any reportable transaction? . . . . . | | |
| **10** | At any time during calendar year 2010, did the partnership have an interest in or a signature or other authority over a financial account in a foreign country (such as a bank account, securities account, or other financial account)? See the instructions for exceptions and filing requirements for Form TD F 90-22.1, Report of Foreign Bank and Financial Accounts. If "Yes," enter the name of the foreign country. ▶ | | |
| **11** | At any time during the tax year, did the partnership receive a distribution from, or was it the grantor of, or transferor to, a foreign trust? If "Yes," the partnership may have to file Form 3520, Annual Return To Report Transactions With Foreign Trusts and Receipt of Certain Foreign Gifts. See instructions . . . . . | | |
| **12a** | Is the partnership making, or had it previously made (and not revoked), a section 754 election? . . . . . | | |
| | See instructions for details regarding a section 754 election. | | |
| **b** | Did the partnership make for this tax year an optional basis adjustment under section 743(b) or 734(b)? If "Yes," attach a statement showing the computation and allocation of the basis adjustment. See instructions . . . . | | |
| **c** | Is the partnership required to adjust the basis of partnership assets under section 743(b) or 734(b) because of a substantial built-in loss (as defined under section 743(d)) or substantial basis reduction (as defined under section 734(d))? If "Yes," attach a statement showing the computation and allocation of the basis adjustment. See instructions. | | |
| **13** | Check this box if, during the current or prior tax year, the partnership distributed any property received in a like-kind exchange or contributed such property to another entity (other than entities wholly-owned by the partnership throughout the tax year) . . . . . ▶ ☐ | | |
| **14** | At any time during the tax year, did the partnership distribute to any partner a tenancy-in-common or other undivided interest in partnership property? . . . . . | | |
| **15** | If the partnership is required to file Form 8858, Information Return of U.S. Persons With Respect To Foreign Disregarded Entities, enter the number of Forms 8858 attached. See instructions ▶ | | |
| **16** | Does the partnership have any foreign partners? If "Yes," enter the number of Forms 8805, Foreign Partner's Information Statement of Section 1446 Withholding Tax, filed for this partnership. ▶ | | |
| **17** | Enter the number of Forms 8865, Return of U.S. Persons With Respect to Certain Foreign Partnerships, attached to this return. ▶ | | |

**Designation of Tax Matters Partner** (see instructions)
Enter below the general partner designated as the tax matters partner (TMP) for the tax year of this return:

| | | | |
|---|---|---|---|
| Name of designated TMP ▶ | | Identifying number of TMP ▶ | |
| If the TMP is an entity, name of TMP representative ▶ | | Phone number of TMP ▶ | |
| Address of designated TMP ▶ | | | |

Form **1065** (2010)

Form 1065 (2010) Page **4**

**Schedule K — Partners' Distributive Share Items**

| Section | Line | Item | | Line | Total amount |
|---|---|---|---|---|---|
| Income (Loss) | 1 | Ordinary business income (loss) (page 1, line 22) | | 1 | |
| | 2 | Net rental real estate income (loss) (*attach Form 8825*) | | 2 | |
| | 3a | Other gross rental income (loss) | 3a | | |
| | b | Expenses from other rental activities (*attach statement*) | 3b | | |
| | c | Other net rental income (loss). Subtract line 3b from line 3a | | 3c | |
| | 4 | Guaranteed payments | | 4 | |
| | 5 | Interest income | | 5 | |
| | 6 | Dividends: a Ordinary dividends | | 6a | |
| | | b Qualified dividends | 6b | | |
| | 7 | Royalties | | 7 | |
| | 8 | Net short-term capital gain (loss) (*attach Schedule D (Form 1065)*) | | 8 | |
| | 9a | Net long-term capital gain (loss) (*attach Schedule D (Form 1065)*) | | 9a | |
| | b | Collectibles (28%) gain (loss) | 9b | | |
| | c | Unrecaptured section 1250 gain (*attach statement*) | 9c | | |
| | 10 | Net section 1231 gain (loss) (*attach Form 4797*) | | 10 | |
| | 11 | Other income (loss) (*see instructions*) Type ▶ | | 11 | |
| Deductions | 12 | Section 179 deduction (*attach Form 4562*) | | 12 | |
| | 13a | Contributions | | 13a | |
| | b | Investment interest expense | | 13b | |
| | c | Section 59(e)(2) expenditures: **(1)** Type ▶ ________ **(2)** Amount ▶ | | 13c(2) | |
| | d | Other deductions (*see instructions*) Type ▶ | | 13d | |
| Self-Employment | 14a | Net earnings (loss) from self-employment | | 14a | |
| | b | Gross farming or fishing income | | 14b | |
| | c | Gross nonfarm income | | 14c | |
| Credits | 15a | Low-income housing credit (section 42(j)(5)) | | 15a | |
| | b | Low-income housing credit (other) | | 15b | |
| | c | Qualified rehabilitation expenditures (rental real estate) (*attach Form 3468*) | | 15c | |
| | d | Other rental real estate credits (*see instructions*) Type ▶ | | 15d | |
| | e | Other rental credits (*see instructions*) Type ▶ | | 15e | |
| | f | Other credits (*see instructions*) Type ▶ | | 15f | |
| Foreign Transactions | 16a | Name of country or U.S. possession ▶ | | | |
| | b | Gross income from all sources | | 16b | |
| | c | Gross income sourced at partner level | | 16c | |
| | | *Foreign gross income sourced at partnership level* | | | |
| | d | Passive category ▶ ____ **e** General category ▶ ____ **f** Other ▶ | | 16f | |
| | | *Deductions allocated and apportioned at partner level* | | | |
| | g | Interest expense ▶ ____ **h** Other ▶ | | 16h | |
| | | *Deductions allocated and apportioned at partnership level to foreign source income* | | | |
| | i | Passive category ▶ ____ **j** General category ▶ ____ **k** Other ▶ | | 16k | |
| | l | Total foreign taxes (check one): ▶ Paid ☐ Accrued ☐ | | 16l | |
| | m | Reduction in taxes available for credit (*attach statement*) | | 16m | |
| | n | Other foreign tax information (*attach statement*) | | | |
| Alternative Minimum Tax (AMT) Items | 17a | Post-1986 depreciation adjustment | | 17a | |
| | b | Adjusted gain or loss | | 17b | |
| | c | Depletion (other than oil and gas) | | 17c | |
| | d | Oil, gas, and geothermal properties—gross income | | 17d | |
| | e | Oil, gas, and geothermal properties—deductions | | 17e | |
| | f | Other AMT items (*attach statement*) | | 17f | |
| Other Information | 18a | Tax-exempt interest income | | 18a | |
| | b | Other tax-exempt income | | 18b | |
| | c | Nondeductible expenses | | 18c | |
| | 19a | Distributions of cash and marketable securities | | 19a | |
| | b | Distributions of other property | | 19b | |
| | 20a | Investment income | | 20a | |
| | b | Investment expenses | | 20b | |
| | c | Other items and amounts (*attach statement*) | | | |

Form **1065** (2010)

Form 1065 (2010) Page 5

**Analysis of Net Income (Loss)**

1 Net income (loss). Combine Schedule K, lines 1 through 11. From the result, subtract the sum of Schedule K, lines 12 through 13d, and 16l . . . . . . 1

| 2 Analysis by partner type: | (i) Corporate | (ii) Individual (active) | (iii) Individual (passive) | (iv) Partnership | (v) Exempt organization | (vi) Nominee/Other |
|---|---|---|---|---|---|---|
| a General partners | | | | | | |
| b Limited partners | | | | | | |

**Schedule L Balance Sheets per Books**

| | Beginning of tax year | | End of tax year | |
|---|---|---|---|---|
| **Assets** | (a) | (b) | (c) | (d) |
| 1 Cash | | | | |
| 2a Trade notes and accounts receivable | | | | |
| b Less allowance for bad debts | | | | |
| 3 Inventories | | | | |
| 4 U.S. government obligations | | | | |
| 5 Tax-exempt securities | | | | |
| 6 Other current assets (*attach statement*) | | | | |
| 7 Mortgage and real estate loans | | | | |
| 8 Other investments (*attach statement*) | | | | |
| 9a Buildings and other depreciable assets | | | | |
| b Less accumulated depreciation | | | | |
| 10a Depletable assets | | | | |
| b Less accumulated depletion | | | | |
| 11 Land (net of any amortization) | | | | |
| 12a Intangible assets (amortizable only) | | | | |
| b Less accumulated amortization | | | | |
| 13 Other assets (*attach statement*) | | | | |
| 14 Total assets | | | | |
| **Liabilities and Capital** | | | | |
| 15 Accounts payable | | | | |
| 16 Mortgages, notes, bonds payable in less than 1 year | | | | |
| 17 Other current liabilities (*attach statement*) | | | | |
| 18 All nonrecourse loans | | | | |
| 19 Mortgages, notes, bonds payable in 1 year or more | | | | |
| 20 Other liabilities (*attach statement*) | | | | |
| 21 Partners' capital accounts | | | | |
| 22 Total liabilities and capital | | | | |

**Schedule M-1 Reconciliation of Income (Loss) per Books With Income (Loss) per Return**

**Note.** Schedule M-3 may be required instead of Schedule M-1 (see instructions).

| | | | |
|---|---|---|---|
| 1 Net income (loss) per books | | 6 Income recorded on books this year not included on Schedule K, lines 1 through 11 (itemize): a Tax-exempt interest $ | |
| 2 Income included on Schedule K, lines 1, 2, 3c, 5, 6a, 7, 8, 9a, 10, and 11, not recorded on books this year (itemize): | | | |
| 3 Guaranteed payments (other than health insurance) | | 7 Deductions included on Schedule K, lines 1 through 13d, and 16l, not charged against book income this year (itemize): a Depreciation $ | |
| 4 Expenses recorded on books this year not included on Schedule K, lines 1 through 13d, and 16l (itemize): a Depreciation $ b Travel and entertainment $ | | 8 Add lines 6 and 7 | |
| | | 9 Income (loss) (Analysis of Net Income (Loss), line 1). Subtract line 8 from line 5 | |
| 5 Add lines 1 through 4 | | | |

**Schedule M-2 Analysis of Partners' Capital Accounts**

| | | | |
|---|---|---|---|
| 1 Balance at beginning of year | | 6 Distributions: a Cash | |
| 2 Capital contributed: a Cash | | b Property | |
| b Property | | 7 Other decreases (itemize): | |
| 3 Net income (loss) per books | | | |
| 4 Other increases (itemize): | | | |
| | | 8 Add lines 6 and 7 | |
| 5 Add lines 1 through 4 | | 9 Balance at end of year. Subtract line 8 from line 5 | |

Form **1065** (2010)

651110

☐ Final K-1 ☐ Amended K-1 OMB No. 1545-0099

**Schedule K-1 (Form 1065)** **2010**

Department of the Treasury
Internal Revenue Service

For calendar year 2010, or tax year beginning ____________, 2010 ending ____________, 20____

## Partner's Share of Income, Deductions, Credits, etc.

► See back of form and separate instructions.

### Part I Information About the Partnership

A Partnership's employer identification number

B Partnership's name, address, city, state, and ZIP code

C IRS Center where partnership filed return

D ☐ Check if this is a publicly traded partnership (PTP)

### Part II Information About the Partner

E Partner's identifying number

F Partner's name, address, city, state, and ZIP code

G ☐ General partner or LLC member-manager ☐ Limited partner or other LLC member

H ☐ Domestic partner ☐ Foreign partner

I What type of entity is this partner? ____________

J Partner's share of profit, loss, and capital (see instructions):

| | Beginning | Ending |
|---|---|---|
| Profit | % | % |
| Loss | % | % |
| Capital | % | % |

K Partner's share of liabilities at year end:

Nonrecourse . . . . . . . $ ____________

Qualified nonrecourse financing . $ ____________

Recourse . . . . . . . . $ ____________

L Partner's capital account analysis:

Beginning capital account . . . $ ____________

Capital contributed during the year $ ____________

Current year increase (decrease) . $ ____________

Withdrawals & distributions . . $ ( ____________ )

Ending capital account . . . . $ ____________

☐ Tax basis ☐ GAAP ☐ Section 704(b) book
☐ Other (explain)

M Did the partner contribute property with a built-in gain or loss?
☐ Yes ☐ No
If "Yes", attach statement (see instructions)

### Part III Partner's Share of Current Year Income, Deductions, Credits, and Other Items

| | | | |
|---|---|---|---|
| 1 | Ordinary business income (loss) | 15 | Credits |
| 2 | Net rental real estate income (loss) | | |
| 3 | Other net rental income (loss) | 16 | Foreign transactions |
| 4 | Guaranteed payments | | |
| 5 | Interest income | | |
| 6a | Ordinary dividends | | |
| 6b | Qualified dividends | | |
| 7 | Royalties | | |
| 8 | Net short-term capital gain (loss) | | |
| 9a | Net long-term capital gain (loss) | 17 | Alternative minimum tax (AMT) items |
| 9b | Collectibles (28%) gain (loss) | | |
| 9c | Unrecaptured section 1250 gain | | |
| 10 | Net section 1231 gain (loss) | 18 | Tax-exempt income and nondeductible expenses |
| 11 | Other income (loss) | | |
| | | | |
| | | | |
| | | 19 | Distributions |
| 12 | Section 179 deduction | | |
| 13 | Other deductions | 20 | Other information |
| | | | |
| | | | |
| 14 | Self-employment earnings (loss) | | |

*See attached statement for additional information.

For IRS Use Only

For Paperwork Reduction Act Notice, see Instructions for Form 1065. Cat. No. 11394R **Schedule K-1 (Form 1065) 2010**

Schedule K-1 (Form 1065) 2010 Page **2**

**This list identifies the codes used on Schedule K-1 for all partners and provides summarized reporting information for partners who file Form 1040. For detailed reporting and filing information, see the separate Partner's Instructions for Schedule K-1 and the instructions for your income tax return.**

**1. Ordinary business income (loss).** Determine whether the income (loss) is passive or nonpassive and enter on your return as follows.

| | *Report on* |
|---|---|
| Passive loss | See the Partner's Instructions |
| Passive income | Schedule E, line 28, column (g) |
| Nonpassive loss | Schedule E, line 28, column (h) |
| Nonpassive income | Schedule E, line 28, column (j) |
| **2. Net rental real estate income (loss)** | See the Partner's Instructions |
| **3. Other net rental income (loss)** | |
| Net income | Schedule E, line 28, column (g) |
| Net loss | See the Partner's Instructions |
| **4. Guaranteed payments** | Schedule E, line 28, column (j) |
| **5. Interest income** | Form 1040, line 8a |
| **6a. Ordinary dividends** | Form 1040, line 9a |
| **6b. Qualified dividends** | Form 1040, line 9b |
| **7. Royalties** | Schedule E, line 4 |
| **8. Net short-term capital gain (loss)** | Schedule D, line 5, column (f) |
| **9a. Net long-term capital gain (loss)** | Schedule D, line 12, column (f) |
| **9b. Collectibles (28%) gain (loss)** | 28% Rate Gain Worksheet, line 4 (Schedule D instructions) |
| **9c. Unrecaptured section 1250 gain** | See the Partner's Instructions |
| **10. Net section 1231 gain (loss)** | See the Partner's Instructions |
| **11. Other income (loss)** | |
| *Code* | |
| A Other portfolio income (loss) | See the Partner's Instructions |
| B Involuntary conversions | See the Partner's Instructions |
| C Sec. 1256 contracts & straddles | Form 6781, line 1 |
| D Mining exploration costs recapture | See Pub. 535 |
| E Cancellation of debt | Form 1040, line 21 or Form 982 |
| F Other income (loss) | See the Partner's Instructions |
| **12. Section 179 deduction** | See the Partner's Instructions |
| **13. Other deductions** | |
| A Cash contributions (50%) | See the Partner's Instructions (A–F) |
| B Cash contributions (30%) | |
| C Noncash contributions (50%) | |
| D Noncash contributions (30%) | |
| E Capital gain property to a 50% organization (30%) | |
| F Capital gain property (20%) | |
| G Contributions (100%) | |
| H Investment interest expense | Form 4952, line 1 |
| I Deductions—royalty income | Schedule E, line 18 |
| J Section 59(e)(2) expenditures | See the Partner's Instructions |
| K Deductions—portfolio (2% floor) | Schedule A, line 23 |
| L Deductions—portfolio (other) | Schedule A, line 28 |
| M Amounts paid for medical insurance | Schedule A, line 1 or Form 1040, line 29 |
| N Educational assistance benefits | See the Partner's Instructions |
| O Dependent care benefits | Form 2441, line 12 |
| P Preproductive period expenses | See the Partner's Instructions |
| Q Commercial revitalization deduction from rental real estate activities | See Form 8582 instructions |
| R Pensions and IRAs | See the Partner's Instructions |
| S Reforestation expense deduction | See the Partner's Instructions |
| T Domestic production activities information | See Form 8903 instructions |
| U Qualified production activities income | Form 8903, line 7b |
| V Employer's Form W-2 wages | Form 8903, line 17 |
| W Other deductions | See the Partner's Instructions |
| **14. Self-employment earnings (loss)** | |

**Note.** *If you have a section 179 deduction or any partner-level deductions, see the Partner's Instructions before completing Schedule SE.*

| | |
|---|---|
| A Net earnings (loss) from self-employment | Schedule SE, Section A or B |
| B Gross farming or fishing income | See the Partner's Instructions |
| C Gross non-farm income | See the Partner's Instructions |
| **15. Credits** | |
| A Low-income housing credit (section 42(j)(5)) from pre-2008 buildings | See the Partner's Instructions |
| B Low-income housing credit (other) from pre-2008 buildings | See the Partner's Instructions |
| C Low-income housing credit (section 42(j)(5)) from post-2007 buildings | Form 8586, line 11 |
| D Low-income housing credit (other) from post-2007 buildings | Form 8586, line 11 |
| E Qualified rehabilitation expenditures (rental real estate) | See the Partner's Instructions (E–F) |
| F Other rental real estate credits | |
| G Other rental credits | |
| H Undistributed capital gains credit | Form 1040, line 71; check box a |
| I Alcohol and cellulosic biofuel fuels credit | Form 6478, line 8 |
| J Work opportunity credit | Form 5884, line 3 |

| *Code* | *Report on* |
|---|---|
| K Disabled access credit | See the Partner's Instructions |
| L Empowerment zone and renewal community employment credit | Form 8844, line 3 |
| M Credit for increasing research activities | See the Partner's Instructions |
| N Credit for employer social security and Medicare taxes | Form 8846, line 5 |
| O Backup withholding | Form 1040, line 61 |
| P Other credits | See the Partner's Instructions |
| **16. Foreign transactions** | |
| A Name of country or U.S. possession | Form 1116, Part I (A–C) |
| B Gross income from all sources | |
| C Gross income sourced at partner level | |
| *Foreign gross income sourced at partnership level* | |
| D Passive category | Form 1116, Part I (D–F) |
| E General category | |
| F Other | |
| *Deductions allocated and apportioned at partner level* | |
| G Interest expense | Form 1116, Part I |
| H Other | Form 1116, Part I |
| *Deductions allocated and apportioned at partnership level to foreign source income* | |
| I Passive category | Form 1116, Part I (I–K) |
| J General category | |
| K Other | |
| *Other information* | |
| L Total foreign taxes paid | Form 1116, Part II |
| M Total foreign taxes accrued | Form 1116, Part II |
| N Reduction in taxes available for credit | Form 1116, line 12 |
| O Foreign trading gross receipts | Form 8873 |
| P Extraterritorial income exclusion | Form 8873 |
| Q Other foreign transactions | See the Partner's Instructions |
| **17. Alternative minimum tax (AMT) items** | |
| A Post-1986 depreciation adjustment | See the Partner's Instructions and the Instructions for Form 6251 (A–E) |
| B Adjusted gain or loss | |
| C Depletion (other than oil & gas) | |
| D Oil, gas, & geothermal—gross income | |
| E Oil, gas, & geothermal—deductions | |
| F Other AMT items | |
| **18. Tax-exempt income and nondeductible expenses** | |
| A Tax-exempt interest income | Form 1040, line 8b |
| B Other tax-exempt income | See the Partner's Instructions |
| C Nondeductible expenses | See the Partner's Instructions |
| **19. Distributions** | |
| A Cash and marketable securities | See the Partner's Instructions (A–C) |
| B Distribution subject to section 737 | |
| C Other property | |
| **20. Other information** | |
| A Investment income | Form 4952, line 4a |
| B Investment expenses | Form 4952, line 5 |
| C Fuel tax credit information | Form 4136 |
| D Qualified rehabilitation expenditures (other than rental real estate) | See the Partner's Instructions |
| E Basis of energy property | See the Partner's Instructions |
| F Recapture of low-income housing credit (section 42(j)(5)) | Form 8611, line 8 |
| G Recapture of low-income housing credit (other) | Form 8611, line 8 |
| H Recapture of investment credit | See Form 4255 |
| I Recapture of other credits | See the Partner's Instructions |
| J Look-back interest—completed long-term contracts | See Form 8697 |
| K Look-back interest—income forecast method | See Form 8866 |
| L Dispositions of property with section 179 deductions | See the Partner's Instructions (L–W) |
| M Recapture of section 179 deduction | |
| N Interest expense for corporate partners | |
| O Section 453(l)(3) information | |
| P Section 453A(c) information | |
| Q Section 1260(b) information | |
| R Interest allocable to production expenditures | |
| S CCF nonqualified withdrawals | |
| T Depletion information—oil and gas | |
| U Amortization of reforestation costs | |
| V Unrelated business taxable income | |
| W Precontribution gain (loss) | |
| X Section 108(i) information | |
| Y Other information | |

# B-6 U.S. Corporation Income Tax Return

Form **1120** — Department of the Treasury, Internal Revenue Service

## U.S. Corporation Income Tax Return

For calendar year 2010 or tax year beginning ______________, 2010, ending ______________, 20 ___

▶ See separate instructions.

OMB No. 1545-0123 — **2010**

**A Check if:**
1a Consolidated return (attach Form 851) ☐
b Life/nonlife consolidated return ☐
2 Personal holding co. (attach Sch. PH) ☐
3 Personal service corp. (see instructions) ☐
4 Schedule M-3 attached ☐

Print or type: Name; Number, street, and room or suite no. If a P.O. box, see instructions.; City or town, state, and ZIP code

**B** Employer identification number
**C** Date incorporated
**D** Total assets (see instructions) $

**E** Check if: (1) ☐ Initial return (2) ☐ Final return (3) ☐ Name change (4) ☐ Address change

**Income**

| Line | Description | Box |
|---|---|---|
| 1a | Gross receipts or sales ____ **b** Less returns and allowances ____ **c** Bal ▶ | 1c |
| 2 | Cost of goods sold (Schedule A, line 8) | 2 |
| 3 | Gross profit. Subtract line 2 from line 1c | 3 |
| 4 | Dividends (Schedule C, line 19) | 4 |
| 5 | Interest | 5 |
| 6 | Gross rents | 6 |
| 7 | Gross royalties | 7 |
| 8 | Capital gain net income (attach Schedule D (Form 1120)) | 8 |
| 9 | Net gain or (loss) from Form 4797, Part II, line 17 (attach Form 4797) | 9 |
| 10 | Other income (see instructions—attach schedule) | 10 |
| 11 | **Total income.** Add lines 3 through 10 ▶ | 11 |

**Deductions (See instructions for limitations on deductions.)**

| Line | Description | Box |
|---|---|---|
| 12 | Compensation of officers (Schedule E, line 4) ▶ | 12 |
| 13 | Salaries and wages (less employment credits) | 13 |
| 14 | Repairs and maintenance | 14 |
| 15 | Bad debts | 15 |
| 16 | Rents | 16 |
| 17 | Taxes and licenses | 17 |
| 18 | Interest | 18 |
| 19 | Charitable contributions | 19 |
| 20 | Depreciation from Form 4562 not claimed on Schedule A or elsewhere on return (attach Form 4562) | 20 |
| 21 | Depletion | 21 |
| 22 | Advertising | 22 |
| 23 | Pension, profit-sharing, etc., plans | 23 |
| 24 | Employee benefit programs | 24 |
| 25 | Domestic production activities deduction (attach Form 8903) | 25 |
| 26 | Other deductions (attach schedule) | 26 |
| 27 | **Total deductions.** Add lines 12 through 26 ▶ | 27 |
| 28 | Taxable income before net operating loss deduction and special deductions. Subtract line 27 from line 11. | 28 |
| 29 | **Less: a** Net operating loss deduction (see instructions) — 29a | |
| | **b** Special deductions (Schedule C, line 20) — 29b | 29c |

**Tax, Refundable Credits, and Payments**

| Line | Description | Box |
|---|---|---|
| 30 | **Taxable income.** Subtract line 29c from line 28 (see instructions) | 30 |
| 31 | **Total tax** (Schedule J, line 10) | 31 |
| 32a | 2009 overpayment credited to 2010 — 32a | |
| b | 2010 estimated tax payments — 32b | |
| c | 2010 refund applied for on Form 4466 — 32c ( ) d Bal ▶ 32d | |
| e | Tax deposited with Form 7004 — 32e | |
| f | Credits: (1) Form 2439 ____ (2) Form 4136 ____ — 32f | |
| g | Refundable credits from Form 3800, line 19c, and Form 8827, line 8c — 32g | 32h |
| 33 | Estimated tax penalty (see instructions). Check if Form 2220 is attached ▶ ☐ | 33 |
| 34 | **Amount owed.** If line 32h is smaller than the total of lines 31 and 33, enter amount owed | 34 |
| 35 | **Overpayment.** If line 32h is larger than the total of lines 31 and 33, enter amount overpaid | 35 |
| 36 | Enter amount from line 35 you want: **Credited to 2011 estimated tax ▶** ____ **Refunded ▶** | 36 |

**Sign Here**

Under penalties of perjury, I declare that I have examined this return, including accompanying schedules and statements, and to the best of my knowledge and belief, it is true, correct, and complete. Declaration of preparer (other than taxpayer) is based on all information of which preparer has any knowledge.

▶ Signature of officer — Date — ▶ Title

May the IRS discuss this return with the preparer shown below (see instructions)? ☐ Yes ☐ No

**Paid Preparer Use Only**

| Print/Type preparer's name | Preparer's signature | Date | Check ☐ if self-employed | PTIN |
|---|---|---|---|---|
| Firm's name ▶ | | | Firm's EIN ▶ | |
| Firm's address ▶ | | | Phone no. | |

**For Paperwork Reduction Act Notice, see separate instructions.** Cat. No. 11450Q Form **1120** (2010)

Form 1120 (2010) Page 2

## Schedule A Cost of Goods Sold (see instructions)

| | | | |
|---|---|---|---|
| 1 | Inventory at beginning of year | 1 | |
| 2 | Purchases | 2 | |
| 3 | Cost of labor | 3 | |
| 4 | Additional section 263A costs (attach schedule) | 4 | |
| 5 | Other costs (attach schedule) | 5 | |
| 6 | **Total.** Add lines 1 through 5 | 6 | |
| 7 | Inventory at end of year | 7 | |
| 8 | **Cost of goods sold.** Subtract line 7 from line 6. Enter here and on page 1, line 2 | 8 | |

9a Check all methods used for valuing closing inventory:

(i) ☐ Cost

(ii) ☐ Lower of cost or market

(iii) ☐ Other (Specify method used and attach explanation.) ▶ ________

b Check if there was a writedown of subnormal goods ▶ ☐

c Check if the LIFO inventory method was adopted this tax year for any goods (if checked, attach Form 970) ▶ ☐

d If the LIFO inventory method was used for this tax year, enter percentage (or amounts) of closing inventory computed under LIFO | 9d |

e If property is produced or acquired for resale, do the rules of section 263A apply to the corporation? ☐ Yes ☐ No

f Was there any change in determining quantities, cost, or valuations between opening and closing inventory? If "Yes," attach explanation ☐ Yes ☐ No

## Schedule C Dividends and Special Deductions (see instructions)

| | | (a) Dividends received | (b) % | (c) Special deductions (a) × (b) |
|---|---|---|---|---|
| 1 | Dividends from less-than-20%-owned domestic corporations (other than debt-financed stock) | | 70 | |
| 2 | Dividends from 20%-or-more-owned domestic corporations (other than debt-financed stock) | | 80 | |
| 3 | Dividends on debt-financed stock of domestic and foreign corporations | | see instructions | |
| 4 | Dividends on certain preferred stock of less-than-20%-owned public utilities | | 42 | |
| 5 | Dividends on certain preferred stock of 20%-or-more-owned public utilities | | 48 | |
| 6 | Dividends from less-than-20%-owned foreign corporations and certain FSCs | | 70 | |
| 7 | Dividends from 20%-or-more-owned foreign corporations and certain FSCs | | 80 | |
| 8 | Dividends from wholly owned foreign subsidiaries | | 100 | |
| 9 | **Total.** Add lines 1 through 8. See instructions for limitation | | | |
| 10 | Dividends from domestic corporations received by a small business investment company operating under the Small Business Investment Act of 1958 | | 100 | |
| 11 | Dividends from affiliated group members | | 100 | |
| 12 | Dividends from certain FSCs | | 100 | |
| 13 | Dividends from foreign corporations not included on lines 3, 6, 7, 8, 11, or 12 | | | |
| 14 | Income from controlled foreign corporations under subpart F (attach Form(s) 5471) | | | |
| 15 | Foreign dividend gross-up | | | |
| 16 | IC-DISC and former DISC dividends not included on lines 1, 2, or 3 | | | |
| 17 | Other dividends | | | |
| 18 | Deduction for dividends paid on certain preferred stock of public utilities | | | |
| 19 | **Total dividends.** Add lines 1 through 17. Enter here and on page 1, line 4 ▶ | | | |
| 20 | **Total special deductions.** Add lines 9, 10, 11, 12, and 18. Enter here and on page 1, line 29b ▶ | | | |

## Schedule E Compensation of Officers (see instructions for page 1, line 12)

**Note:** *Complete Schedule E only if total receipts (line 1a plus lines 4 through 10 on page 1) are $500,000 or more.*

| | (a) Name of officer | (b) Social security number | (c) Percent of time devoted to business | Percent of corporation stock owned | | (f) Amount of compensation |
|---|---|---|---|---|---|---|
| | | | | (d) Common | (e) Preferred | |
| 1 | | | % | % | % | |
| | | | % | % | % | |
| | | | % | % | % | |
| | | | % | % | % | |
| | | | % | % | % | |

| | | |
|---|---|---|
| 2 | Total compensation of officers | |
| 3 | Compensation of officers claimed on Schedule A and elsewhere on return | |
| 4 | Subtract line 3 from line 2. Enter the result here and on page 1, line 12 | |

Form **1120** (2010)

Form 1120 (2010) Page **3**

## Schedule J Tax Computation (see instructions)

| | | | |
|---|---|---|---|
| 1 | Check if the corporation is a member of a controlled group (attach Schedule O (Form 1120)) . . . . ▶ ☐ | | |
| 2 | Income tax. Check if a qualified personal service corporation (see instructions) . . . . . . . . . ▶ ☐ | 2 | |
| 3 | Alternative minimum tax (attach Form 4626) . . . . . . . . . . . . . . . . . . . . . . . | 3 | |
| 4 | Add lines 2 and 3 . . . . . . . . . . . . . . . . . . . . . . . . . . . . . . . | 4 | |
| 5a | Foreign tax credit (attach Form 1118) . . . . . . . . . . . . . . . 5a | | |
| b | Credit from Form 8834, line 29 . . . . . . . . . . . . . . . . . 5b | | |
| c | General business credit (attach Form 3800) . . . . . . . . . . . . . 5c | | |
| d | Credit for prior year minimum tax (attach Form 8827) . . . . . . . . . 5d | | |
| e | Bond credits from Form 8912 . . . . . . . . . . . . . . . . . . 5e | | |
| 6 | **Total credits.** Add lines 5a through 5e . . . . . . . . . . . . . . . . . . . . . | 6 | |
| 7 | Subtract line 6 from line 4 . . . . . . . . . . . . . . . . . . . . . . . . . . | 7 | |
| 8 | Personal holding company tax (attach Schedule PH (Form 1120)) . . . . . . . . . . . . . . | 8 | |
| 9 | Other taxes. Check if from: ☐ Form 4255 ☐ Form 8611 ☐ Form 8697<br>☐ Form 8866 ☐ Form 8902 ☐ Other (attach schedule) . . . | 9 | |
| 10 | **Total tax.** Add lines 7 through 9. Enter here and on page 1, line 31 . . . . . . . . . . . . . | 10 | |

## Schedule K Other Information (see instructions)

| | | Yes | No |
|---|---|---|---|
| 1 | Check accounting method: **a** ☐ Cash **b** ☐ Accrual **c** ☐ Other (specify) ▶ ____________ | | |
| 2 | See the instructions and enter the: | | |
| a | Business activity code no. ▶ ____________ | | |
| b | Business activity ▶ ____________ | | |
| c | Product or service ▶ ____________ | | |
| 3 | Is the corporation a subsidiary in an affiliated group or a parent-subsidiary controlled group? . . . . . . . . . .<br>If "Yes," enter name and EIN of the parent corporation ▶ ____________ | | |
| 4 | At the end of the tax year: | | |
| a | Did any foreign or domestic corporation, partnership (including any entity treated as a partnership), trust, or tax-exempt organization own directly 20% or more, or own, directly or indirectly, 50% or more of the total voting power of all classes of the corporation's stock entitled to vote? If "Yes," complete Part I of Schedule G (Form 1120) (attach Schedule G) . . . . . . . | | |
| b | Did any individual or estate own directly 20% or more, or own, directly or indirectly, 50% or more of the total voting power of all classes of the corporation's stock entitled to vote? If "Yes," complete Part II of Schedule G (Form 1120) (attach Schedule G) . | | |
| 5 | At the end of the tax year, did the corporation: | | |
| a | Own directly 20% or more, or own, directly or indirectly, 50% or more of the total voting power of all classes of stock entitled to vote of any foreign or domestic corporation not included on **Form 851,** Affiliations Schedule? For rules of constructive ownership, see instructions<br>If "Yes," complete (i) through (iv). | | |

| **(i)** Name of Corporation | **(ii)** Employer Identification Number (if any) | **(iii)** Country of Incorporation | **(iv)** Percentage Owned in Voting Stock |
|---|---|---|---|
| | | | |
| | | | |
| | | | |
| | | | |
| | | | |
| | | | |

Form **1120** (2010)

Form 1120 (2010) Page **4**

**Schedule K** *Continued*

| | Yes | No |
|---|---|---|
| **b** Own directly an interest of 20% or more, or own, directly or indirectly, an interest of 50% or more in any foreign or domestic partnership (including an entity treated as a partnership) or in the beneficial interest of a trust? For rules of constructive ownership, see instructions. If "Yes," complete (i) through (iv). | | |

| **(i)** Name of Entity | **(ii)** Employer Identification Number (if any) | **(iii)** Country of Organization | **(iv)** Maximum Percentage Owned in Profit, Loss, or Capital |
|---|---|---|---|
| | | | |
| | | | |
| | | | |
| | | | |
| | | | |
| | | | |

| | | Yes | No |
|---|---|---|---|
| 6 | During this tax year, did the corporation pay dividends (other than stock dividends and distributions in exchange for stock) in excess of the corporation's current and accumulated earnings and profits? (See sections 301 and 316.) | | |
| | If "Yes," file **Form 5452,** Corporate Report of Nondividend Distributions. | | |
| | If this is a consolidated return, answer here for the parent corporation and on Form 851 for each subsidiary. | | |
| 7 | At any time during the tax year, did one foreign person own, directly or indirectly, at least 25% of **(a)** the total voting power of all classes of the corporation's stock entitled to vote or **(b)** the total value of all classes of the corporation's stock? | | |
| | For rules of attribution, see section 318. If "Yes," enter: | | |
| | **(i)** Percentage owned ▶ ______ and **(ii)** Owner's country ▶ ______ | | |
| | **(c)** The corporation may have to file **Form 5472,** Information Return of a 25% Foreign-Owned U.S. Corporation or a Foreign Corporation Engaged in a U.S. Trade or Business. Enter the number of Forms 5472 attached ▶ ______ | | |
| 8 | Check this box if the corporation issued publicly offered debt instruments with original issue discount ▶ ☐ | | |
| | If checked, the corporation may have to file **Form 8281,** Information Return for Publicly Offered Original Issue Discount Instruments. | | |
| 9 | Enter the amount of tax-exempt interest received or accrued during the tax year ▶ $ ______ | | |
| 10 | Enter the number of shareholders at the end of the tax year (if 100 or fewer) ▶ ______ | | |
| 11 | If the corporation has an NOL for the tax year and is electing to forego the carryback period, check here ▶ ☐ | | |
| | If the corporation is filing a consolidated return, the statement required by Regulations section 1.1502-21(b)(3) must be attached or the election will not be valid. | | |
| 12 | Enter the available NOL carryover from prior tax years (do not reduce it by any deduction on line 29a.) ▶ $ ______ | | |
| 13 | Are the corporation's total receipts (line 1a plus lines 4 through 10 on page 1) for the tax year **and** its total assets at the end of the tax year less than $250,000? | | |
| | If "Yes," the corporation is not required to complete Schedules L, M-1, and M-2 on page 5. Instead, enter the total amount of cash distributions and the book value of property distributions (other than cash) made during the tax year. ▶ $ ______ | | |
| 14 | Is the corporation required to file Schedule UTP (Form 1120), Uncertain Tax Position Statement (see instructions)? | | |
| | If "Yes," complete and attach Schedule UTP. | | |

Form **1120** (2010)

Form 1120 (2010) Page **5**

**Schedule L Balance Sheets per Books**

| Assets | Beginning of tax year (a) | (b) | End of tax year (c) | (d) |
|---|---|---|---|---|
| 1 Cash | | | | |
| 2a Trade notes and accounts receivable | | | | |
| b Less allowance for bad debts | ( ) | | ( ) | |
| 3 Inventories | | | | |
| 4 U.S. government obligations | | | | |
| 5 Tax-exempt securities (see instructions) | | | | |
| 6 Other current assets (attach schedule) | | | | |
| 7 Loans to shareholders | | | | |
| 8 Mortgage and real estate loans | | | | |
| 9 Other investments (attach schedule) | | | | |
| 10a Buildings and other depreciable assets | | | | |
| b Less accumulated depreciation | ( ) | | ( ) | |
| 11a Depletable assets | | | | |
| b Less accumulated depletion | ( ) | | ( ) | |
| 12 Land (net of any amortization) | | | | |
| 13a Intangible assets (amortizable only) | | | | |
| b Less accumulated amortization | ( ) | | ( ) | |
| 14 Other assets (attach schedule) | | | | |
| 15 Total assets | | | | |
| **Liabilities and Shareholders' Equity** | | | | |
| 16 Accounts payable | | | | |
| 17 Mortgages, notes, bonds payable in less than 1 year | | | | |
| 18 Other current liabilities (attach schedule) | | | | |
| 19 Loans from shareholders | | | | |
| 20 Mortgages, notes, bonds payable in 1 year or more | | | | |
| 21 Other liabilities (attach schedule) | | | | |
| 22 Capital stock: **a** Preferred stock | | | | |
| **b** Common stock | | | | |
| 23 Additional paid-in capital | | | | |
| 24 Retained earnings—Appropriated (attach schedule) | | | | |
| 25 Retained earnings—Unappropriated | | | | |
| 26 Adjustments to shareholders' equity (attach schedule) | | | | |
| 27 Less cost of treasury stock | | ( ) | | ( ) |
| 28 Total liabilities and shareholders' equity | | | | |

**Schedule M-1 Reconciliation of Income (Loss) per Books With Income per Return**

**Note:** Schedule M-3 required instead of Schedule M-1 if total assets are $10 million or more—see instructions

| | | | |
|---|---|---|---|
| 1 Net income (loss) per books | | 7 Income recorded on books this year not included on this return (itemize): Tax-exempt interest $ ______ | |
| 2 Federal income tax per books | | | |
| 3 Excess of capital losses over capital gains | | | |
| 4 Income subject to tax not recorded on books this year (itemize): ______ | | 8 Deductions on this return not charged against book income this year (itemize): | |
| 5 Expenses recorded on books this year not deducted on this return (itemize): | | a Depreciation $ ______ | |
| a Depreciation $ ______ | | b Charitable contributions $ ______ | |
| b Charitable contributions $ ______ | | | |
| c Travel and entertainment $ ______ | | 9 Add lines 7 and 8 | |
| 6 Add lines 1 through 5 | | 10 Income (page 1, line 28)—line 6 less line 9 | |

**Schedule M-2 Analysis of Unappropriated Retained Earnings per Books (Line 25, Schedule L)**

| | | | |
|---|---|---|---|
| 1 Balance at beginning of year | | 5 Distributions: **a** Cash | |
| 2 Net income (loss) per books | | **b** Stock | |
| 3 Other increases (itemize): ______ | | **c** Property | |
| | | 6 Other decreases (itemize): ______ | |
| | | 7 Add lines 5 and 6 | |
| 4 Add lines 1, 2, and 3 | | 8 Balance at end of year (line 4 less line 7) | |

Form **1120** (2010)

# B-7 U.S. Income Tax Return for an S Corporation

Form **1120S** | **U.S. Income Tax Return for an S Corporation** | OMB No. 1545-0130
Department of the Treasury
Internal Revenue Service

▶ Do not file this form unless the corporation has filed or is attaching Form 2553 to elect to be an S corporation.
▶ See separate instructions.

**2010**

For calendar year 2010 or tax year beginning , 2010, ending , 20

| | TYPE OR PRINT | |
|---|---|---|
| A S election effective date | Name | D Employer identification number |
| B Business activity code number *(see instructions)* | Number, street, and room or suite no. If a P.O. box, see instructions. | E Date incorporated |
| C Check if Sch. M-3 attached ☐ | City or town, state, and ZIP code | F Total assets *(see instructions)* $ |

G Is the corporation electing to be an S corporation beginning with this tax year? ☐ Yes ☐ No If "Yes," attach Form 2553 if not already filed

H Check if: (1) ☐ Final return (2) ☐ Name change (3) ☐ Address change
(4) ☐ Amended return (5) ☐ S election termination or revocation

I Enter the number of shareholders who were shareholders during any part of the tax year . . . . . . . . . . ▶

**Caution.** *Include **only** trade or business income and expenses on lines 1a through 21. See the instructions for more information.*

|  |  |  |  |  |
|---|---|---|---|---|
| Income | 1a | Gross receipts or sales ___ b Less returns and allowances ___ c Bal ▶ | 1c | |
| | 2 | Cost of goods sold (Schedule A, line 8) | 2 | |
| | 3 | Gross profit. Subtract line 2 from line 1c | 3 | |
| | 4 | Net gain (loss) from Form 4797, Part II, line 17 *(attach Form 4797)* | 4 | |
| | 5 | Other income (loss) *(see instructions—attach statement)* | 5 | |
| | 6 | **Total income (loss).** Add lines 3 through 5 ▶ | 6 | |
| Deductions (see instructions for limitations) | 7 | Compensation of officers | 7 | |
| | 8 | Salaries and wages (less employment credits) | 8 | |
| | 9 | Repairs and maintenance | 9 | |
| | 10 | Bad debts | 10 | |
| | 11 | Rents | 11 | |
| | 12 | Taxes and licenses | 12 | |
| | 13 | Interest | 13 | |
| | 14 | Depreciation not claimed on Schedule A or elsewhere on return *(attach Form 4562)* | 14 | |
| | 15 | Depletion **(Do not deduct oil and gas depletion.)** | 15 | |
| | 16 | Advertising | 16 | |
| | 17 | Pension, profit-sharing, etc., plans | 17 | |
| | 18 | Employee benefit programs | 18 | |
| | 19 | Other deductions *(attach statement)* | 19 | |
| | 20 | **Total deductions.** Add lines 7 through 19 ▶ | 20 | |
| | 21 | **Ordinary business income (loss).** Subtract line 20 from line 6 | 21 | |
| Tax and Payments | 22a | Excess net passive income or LIFO recapture tax *(see instructions)* — 22a | | |
| | b | Tax from Schedule D (Form 1120S) — 22b | | |
| | c | Add lines 22a and 22b *(see instructions for additional taxes)* | 22c | |
| | 23a | 2010 estimated tax payments and 2009 overpayment credited to 2010 — 23a | | |
| | b | Tax deposited with Form 7004 — 23b | | |
| | c | Credit for federal tax paid on fuels *(attach Form 4136)* — 23c | | |
| | d | Add lines 23a through 23c | 23d | |
| | 24 | Estimated tax penalty *(see instructions)*. Check if Form 2220 is attached ▶ ☐ | 24 | |
| | 25 | **Amount owed.** If line 23d is smaller than the total of lines 22c and 24, enter amount owed | 25 | |
| | 26 | **Overpayment.** If line 23d is larger than the total of lines 22c and 24, enter amount overpaid | 26 | |
| | 27 | Enter amount from line 26 **Credited to 2011 estimated tax ▶** ___ **Refunded ▶** | 27 | |

**Sign Here**

Under penalties of perjury, I declare that I have examined this return, including accompanying schedules and statements, and to the best of my knowledge and belief, it is true, correct, and complete. Declaration of preparer (other than taxpayer) is based on all information of which preparer has any knowledge.

▶ Signature of officer | Date | ▶ Title

May the IRS discuss this return with the preparer shown below (see instructions)? ☐ Yes ☐ No

**Paid Preparer Use Only**

| Print/Type preparer's name | Preparer's signature | Date | Check ☐ if self-employed | PTIN |
|---|---|---|---|---|
| Firm's name ▶ | | | Firm's EIN ▶ | |
| Firm's address ▶ | | | Phone no. | |

**For Paperwork Reduction Act Notice, see separate instructions.** Cat. No. 11510H Form **1120S** (2010)

Form 1120S (2010) Page **2**

**Schedule A** **Cost of Goods Sold** (see instructions)

| | | | |
|---|---|---|---|
| 1 | Inventory at beginning of year | 1 | |
| 2 | Purchases | 2 | |
| 3 | Cost of labor | 3 | |
| 4 | Additional section 263A costs (*attach statement*) | 4 | |
| 5 | Other costs (*attach statement*) | 5 | |
| 6 | **Total.** Add lines 1 through 5 | 6 | |
| 7 | Inventory at end of year | 7 | |
| 8 | **Cost of goods sold.** Subtract line 7 from line 6. Enter here and on page 1, line 2 | 8 | |

9a Check all methods used for valuing closing inventory: *(i)* ☐ Cost as described in Regulations section 1.471-3
*(ii)* ☐ Lower of cost or market as described in Regulations section 1.471-4
*(iii)* ☐ Other (Specify method used and attach explanation.) ▶

b Check if there was a writedown of subnormal goods as described in Regulations section 1.471-2(c) ▶ ☐

c Check if the LIFO inventory method was adopted this tax year for any goods (if checked, attach Form 970) ▶ ☐

d If the LIFO inventory method was used for this tax year, enter percentage (or amounts) of closing inventory computed under LIFO | 9d |

e If property is produced or acquired for resale, do the rules of section 263A apply to the corporation? ☐ Yes ☐ No

f Was there any change in determining quantities, cost, or valuations between opening and closing inventory? ☐ Yes ☐ No
If "Yes," attach explanation.

**Schedule B** **Other Information** (see instructions)

| | | Yes | No |
|---|---|---|---|
| 1 | Check accounting method: **a** ☐ Cash **b** ☐ Accrual **c** ☐ Other (specify) ▶ | | |
| 2 | See the instructions and enter the: **a** Business activity ▶ **b** Product or service ▶ | | |
| 3 | At the end of the tax year, did the corporation own, directly or indirectly, 50% or more of the voting stock of a domestic corporation? (For rules of attribution, see section 267(c).) If "Yes," attach a statement showing: **(a)** name and employer identification number (EIN), **(b)** percentage owned, and **(c)** if 100% owned, was a qualified subchapter S subsidiary election made? | | |
| 4 | Has this corporation filed, or is it required to file, **Form 8918,** Material Advisor Disclosure Statement, to provide information on any reportable transaction? | | |
| 5 | Check this box if the corporation issued publicly offered debt instruments with original issue discount ▶ ☐ If checked, the corporation may have to file **Form 8281,** Information Return for Publicly Offered Original Issue Discount Instruments. | | |
| 6 | If the corporation: **(a)** was a C corporation before it elected to be an S corporation **or** the corporation acquired an asset with a basis determined by reference to the basis of the asset (or the basis of any other property) in the hands of a C corporation **and (b)** has net unrealized built-in gain in excess of the net recognized built-in gain from prior years, enter the net unrealized built-in gain reduced by net recognized built-in gain from prior years *(see instructions)* ▶ $ | | |
| 7 | Enter the accumulated earnings and profits of the corporation at the end of the tax year. $ | | |
| 8 | Are the corporation's total receipts (*see instructions*) for the tax year **and** its total assets at the end of the tax year less than $250,000? If "Yes," the corporation is not required to complete Schedules L and M-1 | | |
| 9 | During the tax year, was a qualified subchapter S subsidiary election terminated or revoked? If "Yes," see instructions | | |

**Schedule K** **Shareholders' Pro Rata Share Items**

Income (Loss)

| | | | | | Total amount |
|---|---|---|---|---|---|
| 1 | Ordinary business income (loss) (page 1, line 21) | | | 1 | |
| 2 | Net rental real estate income (loss) (*attach Form 8825*) | | | 2 | |
| 3a | Other gross rental income (loss) | 3a | | | |
| b | Expenses from other rental activities (*attach statement*) | 3b | | | |
| c | Other net rental income (loss). Subtract line 3b from line 3a | | | 3c | |
| 4 | Interest income | | | 4 | |
| 5 | Dividends: **a** Ordinary dividends | | | 5a | |
| | **b** Qualified dividends | 5b | | | |
| 6 | Royalties | | | 6 | |
| 7 | Net short-term capital gain (loss) (*attach Schedule D (Form 1120S)*) | | | 7 | |
| 8a | Net long-term capital gain (loss) (*attach Schedule D (Form 1120S)*) | | | 8a | |
| b | Collectibles (28%) gain (loss) | 8b | | | |
| c | Unrecaptured section 1250 gain (*attach statement*) | 8c | | | |
| 9 | Net section 1231 gain (loss) (*attach Form 4797*) | | | 9 | |
| 10 | Other income (loss) (*see instructions*) Type ▶ | | | 10 | |

Form **1120S** (2010)

Form 1120S (2010) Page **3**

| Section | Line | Shareholders' Pro Rata Share Items (continued) | | Total amount |
|---|---|---|---|---|
| Deductions | 11 | Section 179 deduction (*attach Form 4562*) | 11 | |
| | 12a | Contributions | 12a | |
| | b | Investment interest expense | 12b | |
| | c | Section 59(e)(2) expenditures **(1)** Type ▶ ______ **(2)** Amount ▶ | 12c(2) | |
| | d | Other deductions *(see instructions)* Type ▶ | 12d | |
| Credits | 13a | Low-income housing credit (section 42(j)(5)) | 13a | |
| | b | Low-income housing credit (other) | 13b | |
| | c | Qualified rehabilitation expenditures (rental real estate) (*attach Form 3468*) | 13c | |
| | d | Other rental real estate credits (*see instructions*) Type ▶ ______ | 13d | |
| | e | Other rental credits (*see instructions*) Type ▶ ______ | 13e | |
| | f | Alcohol and cellulosic biofuel fuels credit (*attach Form 6478*) | 13f | |
| | g | Other credits (*see instructions*) Type ▶ | 13g | |
| Foreign Transactions | 14a | Name of country or U.S. possession ▶ ______ | | |
| | b | Gross income from all sources | 14b | |
| | c | Gross income sourced at shareholder level | 14c | |
| | | *Foreign gross income sourced at corporate level* | | |
| | d | Passive category | 14d | |
| | e | General category | 14e | |
| | f | Other (*attach statement*) | 14f | |
| | | *Deductions allocated and apportioned at shareholder level* | | |
| | g | Interest expense | 14g | |
| | h | Other | 14h | |
| | | *Deductions allocated and apportioned at corporate level to foreign source income* | | |
| | i | Passive category | 14i | |
| | j | General category | 14j | |
| | k | Other (*attach statement*) | 14k | |
| | | *Other information* | | |
| | l | Total foreign taxes (check one): ▶ ☐ Paid ☐ Accrued | 14l | |
| | m | Reduction in taxes available for credit (*attach statement*) | 14m | |
| | n | Other foreign tax information (*attach statement*) | | |
| Alternative Minimum Tax (AMT) Items | 15a | Post-1986 depreciation adjustment | 15a | |
| | b | Adjusted gain or loss | 15b | |
| | c | Depletion (other than oil and gas) | 15c | |
| | d | Oil, gas, and geothermal properties—gross income | 15d | |
| | e | Oil, gas, and geothermal properties—deductions | 15e | |
| | f | Other AMT items (*attach statement*) | 15f | |
| Items Affecting Shareholder Basis | 16a | Tax-exempt interest income | 16a | |
| | b | Other tax-exempt income | 16b | |
| | c | Nondeductible expenses | 16c | |
| | d | Distributions *(attach statement if required) (see instructions)* | 16d | |
| | e | Repayment of loans from shareholders | 16e | |
| Other Information | 17a | Investment income | 17a | |
| | b | Investment expenses | 17b | |
| | c | Dividend distributions paid from accumulated earnings and profits | 17c | |
| | d | Other items and amounts (*attach statement*) | | |
| Recon-ciliation | 18 | **Income/loss reconciliation.** Combine the amounts on lines 1 through 10 in the far right column. From the result, subtract the sum of the amounts on lines 11 through 12d and 14l | 18 | |

Form **1120S** (2010)

Form 1120S (2010) Page **4**

**Schedule L — Balance Sheets per Books**

| Assets | Beginning of tax year (a) | (b) | End of tax year (c) | (d) |
|---|---|---|---|---|
| 1 Cash | | | | |
| 2a Trade notes and accounts receivable | | | | |
| b Less allowance for bad debts | ( ) | | ( ) | |
| 3 Inventories | | | | |
| 4 U.S. government obligations | | | | |
| 5 Tax-exempt securities (*see instructions*) | | | | |
| 6 Other current assets (*attach statement*) | | | | |
| 7 Loans to shareholders | | | | |
| 8 Mortgage and real estate loans | | | | |
| 9 Other investments (*attach statement*) | | | | |
| 10a Buildings and other depreciable assets | | | | |
| b Less accumulated depreciation | ( ) | | ( ) | |
| 11a Depletable assets | | | | |
| b Less accumulated depletion | ( ) | | ( ) | |
| 12 Land (net of any amortization) | | | | |
| 13a Intangible assets (amortizable only) | | | | |
| b Less accumulated amortization | ( ) | | ( ) | |
| 14 Other assets (*attach statement*) | | | | |
| 15 Total assets | | | | |
| **Liabilities and Shareholders' Equity** | | | | |
| 16 Accounts payable | | | | |
| 17 Mortgages, notes, bonds payable in less than 1 year | | | | |
| 18 Other current liabilities (*attach statement*) | | | | |
| 19 Loans from shareholders | | | | |
| 20 Mortgages, notes, bonds payable in 1 year or more | | | | |
| 21 Other liabilities (*attach statement*) | | | | |
| 22 Capital stock | | | | |
| 23 Additional paid-in capital | | | | |
| 24 Retained earnings | | | | |
| 25 Adjustments to shareholders' equity (*attach statement*) | | | | |
| 26 Less cost of treasury stock | | ( ) | | ( ) |
| 27 Total liabilities and shareholders' equity | | | | |

**Schedule M-1 — Reconciliation of Income (Loss) per Books With Income (Loss) per Return**

**Note:** Schedule M-3 required instead of Schedule M-1 if total assets are $10 million or more—see instructions

| | | | |
|---|---|---|---|
| 1 Net income (loss) per books | | 5 Income recorded on books this year not included on Schedule K, lines 1 through 10 (itemize): a Tax-exempt interest $ ________ | |
| 2 Income included on Schedule K, lines 1, 2, 3c, 4, 5a, 6, 7, 8a, 9, and 10, not recorded on books this year (itemize): ________ | | | |
| 3 Expenses recorded on books this year not included on Schedule K, lines 1 through 12 and 14l (itemize): a Depreciation $ ________ b Travel and entertainment $ ________ | | 6 Deductions included on Schedule K, lines 1 through 12 and 14l, not charged against book income this year (itemize): a Depreciation $ ________ | |
| | | 7 Add lines 5 and 6 | |
| 4 Add lines 1 through 3 | | 8 Income (loss) (Schedule K, line 18). Line 4 less line 7 | |

**Schedule M-2 — Analysis of Accumulated Adjustments Account, Other Adjustments Account, and Shareholders' Undistributed Taxable Income Previously Taxed** (see instructions)

| | (a) Accumulated adjustments account | (b) Other adjustments account | (c) Shareholders' undistributed taxable income previously taxed |
|---|---|---|---|
| 1 Balance at beginning of tax year | | | |
| 2 Ordinary income from page 1, line 21 | | | |
| 3 Other additions | | | |
| 4 Loss from page 1, line 21 | ( ) | | |
| 5 Other reductions | ( ) | ( ) | |
| 6 Combine lines 1 through 5 | | | |
| 7 Distributions other than dividend distributions | | | |
| 8 Balance at end of tax year. Subtract line 7 from line 6 | | | |

Form **1120S** (2010)

671110

☐ Final K-1 ☐ Amended K-1 OMB No. 1545-0130

**Schedule K-1 (Form 1120S)** **2010**
Department of the Treasury
Internal Revenue Service

For calendar year 2010, or tax year beginning ____________, 2010
ending ____________, 20____

## Shareholder's Share of Income, Deductions, Credits, etc.

▶ See back of form and separate instructions.

**Part I Information About the Corporation**

A Corporation's employer identification number

B Corporation's name, address, city, state, and ZIP code

C IRS Center where corporation filed return

**Part II Information About the Shareholder**

D Shareholder's identifying number

E Shareholder's name, address, city, state, and ZIP code

F Shareholder's percentage of stock ownership for tax year . . . . . . . ________ %

For IRS Use Only

**Part III Shareholder's Share of Current Year Income, Deductions, Credits, and Other Items**

| | | | |
|---|---|---|---|
| 1 | Ordinary business income (loss) | 13 | Credits |
| 2 | Net rental real estate income (loss) | | |
| 3 | Other net rental income (loss) | | |
| 4 | Interest income | | |
| 5a | Ordinary dividends | | |
| 5b | Qualified dividends | 14 | Foreign transactions |
| 6 | Royalties | | |
| 7 | Net short-term capital gain (loss) | | |
| 8a | Net long-term capital gain (loss) | | |
| 8b | Collectibles (28%) gain (loss) | | |
| 8c | Unrecaptured section 1250 gain | | |
| 9 | Net section 1231 gain (loss) | | |
| 10 | Other income (loss) | 15 | Alternative minimum tax (AMT) items |
| 11 | Section 179 deduction | 16 | Items affecting shareholder basis |
| 12 | Other deductions | | |
| | | 17 | Other information |

* See attached statement for additional information.

For Paperwork Reduction Act Notice, see Instructions for Form 1120S. Cat. No. 11520D **Schedule K-1 (Form 1120S) 2010**

Schedule K-1 (Form 1120S) 2010 Page **2**

**This list identifies the codes used on Schedule K-1 for all shareholders and provides summarized reporting information for shareholders who file Form 1040. For detailed reporting and filing information, see the separate Shareholder's Instructions for Schedule K-1 and the instructions for your income tax return.**

**1. Ordinary business income (loss).** Determine whether the income (loss) is passive or nonpassive and enter on your return as follows:

| | *Report on* |
|---|---|
| Passive loss | See the Shareholder's Instructions |
| Passive income | Schedule E, line 28, column (g) |
| Nonpassive loss | Schedule E, line 28, column (h) |
| Nonpassive income | Schedule E, line 28, column (j) |
| **2. Net rental real estate income (loss)** | See the Shareholder's Instructions |
| **3. Other net rental income (loss)** | |
| Net income | Schedule E, line 28, column (g) |
| Net loss | See the Shareholder's Instructions |
| **4. Interest income** | Form 1040, line 8a |
| **5a. Ordinary dividends** | Form 1040, line 9a |
| **5b. Qualified dividends** | Form 1040, line 9b |
| **6. Royalties** | Schedule E, line 4 |
| **7. Net short-term capital gain (loss)** | Schedule D, line 5, column (f) |
| **8a. Net long-term capital gain (loss)** | Schedule D, line 12, column (f) |
| **8b. Collectibles (28%) gain (loss)** | 28% Rate Gain Worksheet, line 4 (Schedule D instructions) |
| **8c. Unrecaptured section 1250 gain** | See the Shareholder's Instructions |
| **9. Net section 1231 gain (loss)** | See the Shareholder's Instructions |
| **10. Other income (loss)** | |
| *Code* | |
| A Other portfolio income (loss) | See the Shareholder's Instructions |
| B Involuntary conversions | See the Shareholder's Instructions |
| C Sec. 1256 contracts & straddles | Form 6781, line 1 |
| D Mining exploration costs recapture | See Pub. 535 |
| E Other income (loss) | See the Shareholder's Instructions |
| **11. Section 179 deduction** | See the Shareholder's Instructions |
| **12. Other deductions** | |
| A Cash contributions (50%) | See the Shareholder's Instructions (A–F) |
| B Cash contributions (30%) | |
| C Noncash contributions (50%) | |
| D Noncash contributions (30%) | |
| E Capital gain property to a 50% organization (30%) | |
| F Capital gain property (20%) | |
| G Contributions (100%) | |
| H Investment interest expense | Form 4952, line 1 |
| I Deductions—royalty income | Schedule E, line 18 |
| J Section 59(e)(2) expenditures | See the Shareholder's Instructions |
| K Deductions—portfolio (2% floor) | Schedule A, line 23 |
| L Deductions—portfolio (other) | Schedule A, line 28 |
| M Preproductive period expenses | See the Shareholder's Instructions |
| N Commercial revitalization deduction from rental real estate activities | See Form 8582 instructions |
| O Reforestation expense deduction | See the Shareholder's Instructions |
| P Domestic production activities information | See Form 8903 instructions |
| Q Qualified production activities income | Form 8903, line 7b |
| R Employer's Form W-2 wages | Form 8903, line 17 |
| S Other deductions | See the Shareholder's Instructions |
| **13. Credits** | |
| A Low-income housing credit (section 42(j)(5)) from pre-2008 buildings | See the Shareholder's Instructions |
| B Low-income housing credit (other) from pre-2008 buildings | See the Shareholder's Instructions |
| C Low-income housing credit (section 42(j)(5)) from post-2007 buildings | Form 8586, line 11 |
| D Low-income housing credit (other) from post-2007 buildings | Form 8586, line 11 |
| E Qualified rehabilitation expenditures (rental real estate) | See the Shareholder's Instructions (E–F) |
| F Other rental real estate credits | |
| G Other rental credits | |
| H Undistributed capital gains credit | Form 1040, line 71, box a |
| I Alcohol and cellulosic biofuel fuels credit | Form 6478, line 8 |
| J Work opportunity credit | Form 5884, line 3 |
| K Disabled access credit | See the Shareholder's Instructions |
| L Empowerment zone and renewal communtiy employment credit | Form 8844, line 3 |

| *Code* | *Report on* |
|---|---|
| M Credit for increasing research activities | See the Shareholder's Instructions |
| N Credit for employer social security and Medicare taxes | Form 8846, line 5 |
| O Backup withholding | Form 1040, line 61 |
| P Other credits | See the Shareholder's Instructions |
| **14. Foreign transactions** | |
| A Name of country or U.S. possession | Form 1116, Part I (A–C) |
| B Gross income from all sources | |
| C Gross income sourced at shareholder level | |
| *Foreign gross income sourced at corporate level* | |
| D Passive category | Form 1116, Part I (D–F) |
| E General category | |
| F Other | |
| *Deductions allocated and apportioned at shareholder level* | |
| G Interest expense | Form 1116, Part I |
| H Other | Form 1116, Part I |
| *Deductions allocated and apportioned at corporate level to foreign source income* | |
| I Passive category | Form 1116, Part I (I–K) |
| J General category | |
| K Other | |
| *Other information* | |
| L Total foreign taxes paid | Form 1116, Part II |
| M Total foreign taxes accrued | Form 1116, Part II |
| N Reduction in taxes available for credit | Form 1116, line 12 |
| O Foreign trading gross receipts | Form 8873 |
| P Extraterritorial income exclusion | Form 8873 |
| Q Other foreign transactions | See the Shareholder's Instructions |
| **15. Alternative minimum tax (AMT) items** | |
| A Post-1986 depreciation adjustment | See the Shareholder's Instructions and the Instructions for Form 6251 (A–F) |
| B Adjusted gain or loss | |
| C Depletion (other than oil & gas) | |
| D Oil, gas, & geothermal—gross income | |
| E Oil, gas, & geothermal—deductions | |
| F Other AMT items | |
| **16. Items affecting shareholder basis** | |
| A Tax-exempt interest income | Form 1040, line 8b |
| B Other tax-exempt income | See the Shareholder's Instructions (B–E) |
| C Nondeductible expenses | |
| D Distributions | |
| E Repayment of loans from shareholders | |
| **17. Other information** | |
| A Investment income | Form 4952, line 4a |
| B Investment expenses | Form 4952, line 5 |
| C Qualified rehabilitation expenditures (other than rental real estate) | See the Shareholder's Instructions |
| D Basis of energy property | See the Shareholder's Instructions |
| E Recapture of low-income housing credit (section 42(j)(5)) | Form 8611, line 8 |
| F Recapture of low-income housing credit (other) | Form 8611, line 8 |
| G Recapture of investment credit | See Form 4255 |
| H Recapture of other credits | See the Shareholder's Instructions |
| I Look-back interest—completed long-term contracts | See Form 8697 |
| J Look-back interest—income forecast method | See Form 8866 |
| K Dispositions of property with section 179 deductions | See the Shareholder's Instructions (K–T) |
| L Recapture of section 179 deduction | |
| M Section 453(l)(3) information | |
| N Section 453A(c) information | |
| O Section 1260(b) information | |
| P Interest allocable to production expenditures | |
| Q CCF nonqualified withdrawals | |
| R Depletion information—oil and gas | |
| S Amortization of reforestation costs | |
| T Section 108(i) information | |
| U Other information | |

# B-8 Amended Tax Return Forms

Form **1040X** (Rev. December 2010)

Department of the Treasury—Internal Revenue Service

## Amended U.S. Individual Income Tax Return

▶ **See separate instructions.**

OMB No. 1545-0074

**This return is for calendar year** ☐ 2010 ☐ 2009 ☐ 2008 ☐ 2007

**Other year.** Enter one: calendar year **or** fiscal year (month and year ended):

| Your first name and middle initial | Your last name | **Your social security number** |
|---|---|---|
| If a joint return, your spouse's first name and middle initial | Your spouse's last name | **Your spouse's social security number** |
| Your current home address (number and street). If you have a P.O. box, see page 5 of instructions. | Apt. no. | Your phone number |
| Your city, town or post office, state, and ZIP code. If you have a foreign address, see page 5 of instructions. | | |

**Amended return filing status.** You **must** check one box even if you are not changing your filing status.
***Caution.*** *You cannot change your filing status from joint to separate returns after the due date.*

☐ Single ☐ Married filing jointly ☐ Married filing separately
☐ Qualifying widow(er) ☐ Head of household (If the qualifying person is a child but not your dependent, see page 5 of instructions.)

| Use Part III on the back to explain any changes | | **A. Original amount** or as previously adjusted (see page 6) | **B. Net change—** amount of increase or (decrease)—explain in Part III | **C. Correct amount** |
|---|---|---|---|---|
| **Income and Deductions** | | | | |
| 1 Adjusted gross income (see page 6 of instructions). If net operating loss (NOL) carryback is included, check here . . . . . . . . . ▶ ☐ | 1 | | | |
| 2 Itemized deductions or standard deduction (see page 7 of instructions) | 2 | | | |
| 3 Subtract line 2 from line 1 . . . . . . . . . . . . . . . . | 3 | | | |
| 4 Exemptions. **If changing, complete Part I on the back and enter the amount from line 30** (see page 7 of instructions) . . . . . . . | 4 | | | |
| 5 Taxable income. Subtract line 4 from line 3 . . . . . . . . . . | 5 | | | |
| **Tax Liability** | | | | |
| 6 Tax (see page 8 of instructions). Enter method used to figure tax: | 6 | | | |
| 7 Credits (see page 8 of instructions). If general business credit carryback is included, check here . . . . . . . . . . . . . . ▶ ☐ | 7 | | | |
| 8 Subtract line 7 from line 6. If the result is zero or less, enter -0- . . . | 8 | | | |
| 9 Other taxes (see page 8 of instructions) . . . . . . . . . . . | 9 | | | |
| 10 Total tax. Add lines 8 and 9 . . . . . . . . . . . . . . . | 10 | | | |
| **Payments** | | | | |
| 11 Federal income tax withheld and excess social security and tier 1 RRTA tax withheld (**if changing**, see page 8 of instructions) . . . . . . | 11 | | | |
| 12 Estimated tax payments, including amount applied from prior year's return (see page 9 of instructions) . . . . . . . . . . . . . | 12 | | | |
| 13 Earned income credit (EIC) (see page 9 of instructions) . . . . . . | 13 | | | |
| 14 Refundable credits from ☐ Schedule M or Form(s) ☐ 2439 ☐ 4136 ☐ 5405 ☐ 8801 ☐ 8812 ☐ 8839 ☐ 8863 ☐ 8885 or ☐ other (specify): | 14 | | | |
| 15 Total amount paid with request for extension of time to file, tax paid with original return, and additional tax paid after return was filed (see page 10 of instructions) . . . . . . . . . . . . . . | | | 15 | |
| 16 Total payments. Add lines 11 through 15 . . . . . . . . . . . . . . . . . . . . . | | | 16 | |
| **Refund or Amount You Owe** ***(Note. Allow 8–12 weeks to process Form 1040X.)*** | | | | |
| 17 Overpayment, if any, as shown on original return or as previously adjusted by the IRS (see page 10 of instructions) . . . . . . . . . . . . . . . . . . . . . . . . . . . | | | 17 | |
| 18 Subtract line 17 from line 16 (If less than zero, see page 10 of instructions) . . . . . . . . . . | | | 18 | |
| 19 **Amount you owe.** If line 10, column C, is more than line 18, enter the difference (see page 10 of instructions) | | | 19 | |
| 20 If line 10, column C, is less than line 18, enter the difference. This is the amount **overpaid** on this return | | | 20 | |
| 21 Amount of line 20 you want **refunded to you** . . . . . . . . . . . . . . . . . . . . . | | | 21 | |
| 22 Amount of line 20 you want **applied to your (enter year):** **estimated tax** | | 22 | | |

**Complete and sign this form on Page 2.**

**For Paperwork Reduction Act Notice, see page 11 of instructions.** Cat. No. 11360L Form **1040X** (Rev. 12-2010)

Form 1040X (Rev. 12-2010) Page **2**

**Part I** **Exemptions**

Complete this part **only** if you are:

- Increasing or decreasing the number of exemptions (personal and dependents) claimed on line 6d of the return you are amending, or
- Increasing or decreasing the exemption amount for housing individuals displaced by a Midwestern disaster in 2008 or 2009.

| See *Form 1040 or Form 1040A instructions and page 11 of Form 1040X instructions.* | | **A. Original number** of exemptions or amount reported or as previously adjusted | **B. Net change** | **C. Correct number or amount** |
|---|---|---|---|---|
| 23 Yourself and spouse. ***Caution.*** *If someone can claim you as a dependent, you cannot claim an exemption for yourself* . . . . . . | 23 | | | |
| 24 Your dependent children who lived with you . . . . . . . . . . | 24 | | | |
| 25 Your dependent children who did not live with you due to divorce or separation | 25 | | | |
| 26 Other dependents . . . . . . . . . . . . . . . . . . . . | 26 | | | |
| 27 Total number of exemptions. Add lines 23 through 26 . . . . . . . | 27 | | | |
| 28 Multiply the number of exemptions claimed on line 27 by the exemption amount shown in the instructions for line 28 for the year you are amending (see page 11 of instructions) . . . . . . . . . . . . | 28 | | | |
| 29 If you are claiming an exemption amount for housing individuals displaced by a Midwestern disaster, enter the amount from Form 8914, line 2 for 2008, or line 6 for 2009 . . . . . . . . . . . . . . . | 29 | | | |
| 30 Add lines 28 and 29. Enter the result here and on line 4 on page 1 of this form | 30 | | | |

31 List **ALL** dependents (children and others) claimed on this amended return. If more than 4 dependents, see page 11 of instructions.

| **(a)** First name | Last name | **(b)** Dependent's social security number | **(c)** Dependent's relationship to you | **(d)** Check box if qualifying child for child tax credit (see page 11 of instructions) |
|---|---|---|---|---|
| | | | | ☐ |
| | | | | ☐ |
| | | | | ☐ |
| | | | | ☐ |

**Part II** **Presidential Election Campaign Fund**

Checking below will not increase your tax or reduce your refund.

☐ Check here if you did not previously want $3 to go to the fund, but now do.

☐ Check here if this is a joint return and your spouse did not previously want $3 to go to the fund, but now does.

**Part III** **Explanation of changes.** In the space provided below, tell us why you are filing Form 1040X.

▶ Attach any supporting documents and new or changed forms and schedules.

## Sign Here

**Remember to keep a copy of this form for your records.**

Under penalties of perjury, I declare that I have filed an original return and that I have examined this amended return, including accompanying schedules and statements, and to the best of my knowledge and belief, this amended return is true, correct, and complete. Declaration of preparer (other than taxpayer) is based on all information about which the preparer has any knowledge.

▶ Your signature | Date | ▶ Spouse's signature. If a joint return, **both** must sign. | Date

**Paid Preparer Use Only**

▶ Preparer's signature | Date | Firm's name (or yours if self-employed)

Print/type preparer's name | Firm's address and ZIP code

PTIN | ☐ Check if self-employed | Phone number | EIN

For forms and publications, visit IRS.gov. Form **1040X** (Rev. 12-2010)

Form **1120X**
(Rev. January 2011)
Department of the Treasury
Internal Revenue Service

# Amended U.S. Corporation Income Tax Return

OMB No. 1545-0132
**For tax year ending** ▶
**(Enter month and year.)**

| Please Type or Print | Name | Employer identification number |
|---|---|---|
| | Number, street, and room or suite no. (If a P.O. box, see instructions.) | |
| | City or town, state, and ZIP code | Telephone number (optional) |

Enter name and address used on original return (If same as above, write "Same.")

Internal Revenue Service Center where original return was filed ▶

**Fill in applicable items and use Part II on the back to explain any changes**

| **Part I** **Income and Deductions** (see instructions) | | **(a)** As originally reported or as previously adjusted | **(b)** Net change — increase or (decrease) — explain in Part II | **(c)** Correct amount |
|---|---|---|---|---|
| 1 Total income | 1 | | | |
| 2 Total deductions | 2 | | | |
| 3 Taxable income. Subtract line 2 from line 1 | 3 | | | |
| 4 Total tax | 4 | | | |
| **Payments and Credits** (see instructions) | | | | |
| 5a Overpayment in prior year allowed as a credit | 5a | | | |
| b Estimated tax payments | 5b | | | |
| c Refund applied for on Form 4466 | 5c | | | |
| d Subtract line 5c from the sum of lines 5a and 5b | 5d | | | |
| e Tax deposited with Form 7004 | 5e | | | |
| f Credit from Form 2439 | 5f | | | |
| g Credit for federal tax on fuels and other refundable credits | 5g | | | |
| 6 Tax deposited or paid with (or after) the filing of the original return | 6 | | | |
| 7 Add lines 5d through 6, column (c) | 7 | | | |
| 8 Overpayment, if any, as shown on original return or as later adjusted | 8 | | | |
| 9 Subtract line 8 from line 7 | 9 | | | |
| **Tax Due or Overpayment** (see instructions) | | | | |
| 10 **Tax due.** Subtract line 9 from line 4, column (c). If paying by check, make it payable to the **"United States Treasury"** ▶ | 10 | | | |
| 11 **Overpayment.** Subtract line 4, column (c), from line 9 ▶ | 11 | | | |
| 12 Enter the amount of line 11 you want: **Credited to 20 Estimated tax** ▶ **Refunded** ▶ | 12 | | | |

**Sign Here**

Under penalties of perjury, I declare that I have filed an original return and that I have examined this amended return, including accompanying schedules and statements, and to the best of my knowledge and belief, this amended return is true, correct, and complete. Declaration of preparer (other than taxpayer) is based on all information of which preparer has any knowledge.

▶ Signature of officer | Date | ▶ Title

| **Paid Preparer Use Only** | Print/Type preparer's name | Preparer's signature | Date | Check ☐ if self-employed | PTIN |
|---|---|---|---|---|---|
| | Firm's name ▶ | | | Firm's EIN ▶ | |
| | Firm's address ▶ | | | Phone no. | |

**For Paperwork Reduction Act Notice, see instructions.** Cat. No. 11530Z Form **1120X** (Rev. 1-2011)

Form 1120X (Rev. 1-2011) Page **2**

**Part II** **Explanation of Changes to Items in Part I** (Enter the line number from page 1 for the items you are changing, and give the reason for each change. Show any computation in detail. Also, see **What To Attach** in the instructions.)

If the change is due to a net operating loss carryback, a capital loss carryback, or a general business credit carryback, see **Carryback Claims** in the instructions, and check here . . . . . . . . . . . . . . . . . . . . . . . . ▶ ☐

Form **1120X** (Rev. 1-2011)

# B-9 Application for Extension of Time to File Income Tax Returns

Form **4868**

Department of the Treasury
Internal Revenue Service (99)

## Application for Automatic Extension of Time To File U.S. Individual Income Tax Return

OMB No. 1545-0074

**2010**

There are three ways to request an automatic extension of time to file a U.S. individual income tax return.

1. You can file Form 4868 electronically by accessing IRS *e-file* using your home computer or by using a tax professional who uses *e-file.*
2. You can pay all or part of your estimate of income tax due using a credit or debit card.
3. You can file a paper Form 4868.

IRS e-file **It's Convenient, Safe, and Secure**

IRS *e-file* is the IRS's electronic filing program. You can get an automatic extension of time to file your tax return by filing Form 4868 electronically. You will receive an electronic acknowledgment once you complete the transaction. Keep it with your records. Do not send in Form 4868 if you file electronically, unless you are making a payment with a check or money order (see page 3).

Complete Form 4868 to use as a worksheet. If you think you may owe tax when you file your return, you will need to estimate your total tax liability and subtract how much you have already paid (lines 4, 5, and 6 below).

Several companies offer free e-filing of Form 4868 through the Free File program. For more details, go to IRS.gov and click on *freefile.*

**_E-file_ Using Your Personal Computer or Through a Tax Professional**

Refer to your tax software package or tax preparer for ways to file electronically. Be sure to have a copy of your 2009 tax return—you will be asked to provide information from the return for taxpayer verification. If you wish to make a payment, you can pay by electronic funds withdrawal or send your check or money order to the address shown in the middle column under *Where To File a Paper Form 4868* (see page 4).

**Pay by Credit or Debit Card**

You can get an extension if you pay part or all of your estimate of income tax due by using a credit or debit card. Your payment must be at least $1. You can pay by phone or over the Internet (see page 3).

**File a Paper Form 4868**

If you wish to file on paper instead of electronically, fill in the Form 4868 below and mail it to the address shown on page 4.

For information on using a private delivery service, see page 4.

**Note.** If you are a fiscal year taxpayer, you must file a paper Form 4868.

## General Instructions

### Purpose of Form

Use Form 4868 to apply for 6 more months (4 if "out of the country" (defined on page 2) and a U.S. citizen or resident) to file Form 1040, 1040A, 1040EZ, 1040NR, 1040NR-EZ, 1040-PR, or 1040-SS.

**Gift tax return (Form 709).** An extension of time to file your 2010 calendar year income tax return also extends the time to file Form 709 for 2010. However, it does not extend the time to pay any gift tax you may owe for 2010. To make a payment of gift tax, see Form 8892. If you do not pay the amount due by the regular due date for Form 709, you will owe interest and may also be charged penalties. If the donor died during 2010, see the instructions for Forms 709 and 8892.

### Qualifying for the Extension

To get the extra time you must:

1. Properly estimate your 2010 tax liability using the information available to you,
2. Enter your total tax liability on line 4 of Form 4868, and
3. File Form 4868 by the regular due date of your return.

CAUTION *Although you are not required to make a payment of the tax you estimate as due, Form 4868 does not extend the time to pay taxes. If you do not pay the amount due by the regular due date, you will owe interest. You may also be charged penalties. For more details, see* Interest *and* Late Payment Penalty *on page 2. Any remittance you make with your application for extension will be treated as a payment of tax.*

You do not have to explain why you are asking for the extension. We will contact you only if your request is denied.

Do not file Form 4868 if you want the IRS to figure your tax or you are under a court order to file your return by the regular due date.

▼ DETACH HERE ▼

Form **4868**

Department of the Treasury
Internal Revenue Service (99)

## Application for Automatic Extension of Time To File U.S. Individual Income Tax Return

OMB No. 1545-0074

**2010**

**For calendar year 2010, or other tax year beginning , 2010, ending , 20 .**

**Part I Identification**

1 Your name(s) (see instructions)

Address (see instructions)

City, town, or post office | State | ZIP Code

2 Your social security number | 3 Spouse's social security number

**Part II Individual Income Tax**

4 Estimate of total tax liability for 2010 . . $

5 Total 2010 payments . . . . . .

6 **Balance due.** Subtract line 5 from line 4 (see instructions) . . . . . . .

7 Amount you are paying (see instructions) ▶

8 Check here if you are "out of the country" and a U.S. citizen or resident (see instructions) . . . . . . ▶ ☐

9 Check here if you file Form 1040NR or 1040NR-EZ and did not receive wages as an employee subject to U.S. income tax withholding . . . . . . . . . . ▶ ☐

**For Privacy Act and Paperwork Reduction Act Notice, see page 4.** Cat. No. 13141W Form **4868** (2010)

Form **7004** (Rev. December 2008) Department of the Treasury Internal Revenue Service

# Application for Automatic Extension of Time To File Certain Business Income Tax, Information, and Other Returns

▶ File a separate application for each return.
▶ See separate instructions.

OMB No. 1545-0233

**Type or Print**

File by the due date for the return for which an extension is requested. See instructions.

Name | **Identifying number**

Number, street, and room or suite no. (If P.O. box, see instructions.)

City, town, state, and ZIP code (If a foreign address, enter city, province or state, and country (follow the country's practice for entering postal code)).

**Note. See instructions before completing this form.**

**Part I** **Automatic 5-Month Extension** Complete if Filing Form 1065, 1041, or 8804

**1a** Enter the form code for the return that this application is for (see below) . . . . . . . . . . . . . ☐☐

| Application Is For: | Form Code | Application Is For: | Form Code |
|---|---|---|---|
| Form 1065 | 09 | Form 1041 (estate) | 04 |
| Form 8804 | 31 | Form 1041 (trust) | 05 |

**Part II** **Automatic 6-Month Extension** Complete if Filing Other Forms

**b** Enter the form code for the return that this application is for (see below) . . . . . . . . . . . . . ☐☐

| Application Is For: | Form Code | Application Is For: | Form Code |
|---|---|---|---|
| Form 706-GS(D) | 01 | Form 1120-PC | 21 |
| Form 706-GS(T) | 02 | Form 1120-POL | 22 |
| Form 1041-N | 06 | Form 1120-REIT | 23 |
| Form 1041-QFT | 07 | Form 1120-RIC | 24 |
| Form 1042 | 08 | Form 1120S | 25 |
| Form 1065-B | 10 | Form 1120-SF | 26 |
| Form 1066 | 11 | Form 3520-A | 27 |
| Form 1120 | 12 | Form 8612 | 28 |
| Form 1120-C | 34 | Form 8613 | 29 |
| Form 1120-F | 15 | Form 8725 | 30 |
| Form 1120-FSC | 16 | Form 8831 | 32 |
| Form 1120-H | 17 | Form 8876 | 33 |
| Form 1120-L | 18 | Form 8924 | 35 |
| Form 1120-ND | 19 | Form 8928 | 36 |
| Form 1120-ND (section 4951 taxes) | 20 | | |

**2** If the organization is a foreign corporation that does not have an office or place of business in the United States, check here . . . . . . . . . . . . . . . . . . . . . . . . . . . . . ▶ ☐

**3** If the organization is a corporation and is the common parent of a group that intends to file a consolidated return, check here . . . . . . . . . . . . . . . . . . . . . . . . . . . . . ▶ ☐

If checked, attach a schedule, listing the name, address, and Employer Identification Number (EIN) for each member covered by this application.

**Part III** **All Filers Must Complete This Part**

**4** If the organization is a corporation or partnership that qualifies under Regulations section 1.6081-5, check here . ▶ ☐

**5a** The application is for calendar year 20 ____, or tax year beginning ____________, 20 ____, and ending ____________, 20 ____

**b** **Short tax year.** If this tax year is less than 12 months, check the reason:
☐ Initial return ☐ Final return ☐ Change in accounting period ☐ Consolidated return to be filed

| | | | |
|---|---|---|---|
| **6** | Tentative total tax . . . . . . . . . . . . . . . . . . . . . . . | 6 | |
| **7** | **Total** payments and credits (see instructions) . . . . . . . . . . . . . | 7 | |
| **8** | **Balance due.** Subtract line 7 from line 6. **Generally, you must deposit this amount using the Electronic Federal Tax Payment System (EFTPS), a Federal Tax Deposit (FTD) Coupon, or Electronic Funds Withdrawal (EFW)** (see instructions for exceptions) . . . . . . . | 8 | |

**For Privacy Act and Paperwork Reduction Act Notice, see separate Instructions.** Cat. No. 13804A Form **7004** (Rev. 12-2008)

# B-10 Underpayment of Estimated Tax

Form **2210**

Department of the Treasury
Internal Revenue Service

## Underpayment of Estimated Tax by Individuals, Estates, and Trusts

▶ See separate instructions.

▶ Attach to Form 1040, 1040A, 1040NR, 1040NR-EZ, or 1041.

OMB No. 1545-0140

**2010**

Attachment Sequence No. **06**

Name(s) shown on tax return | **Identifying number**

## Do You Have To File Form 2210?

Complete lines 1 through 7 below. Is line 7 less than $1,000? — **Yes** → **Do not file Form 2210.** You do not owe a penalty.

↓ **No**

Complete lines 8 and 9 below. Is line 6 equal to or more than line 9? — **Yes** → You do not owe a penalty. **Do not file Form 2210** (but if box **E** in Part II applies, you must file page 1 of Form 2210).

↓ **No**

You may owe a penalty. Does any box in Part II below apply? — **Yes** → You **must** file Form 2210. Does box **B, C,** or **D** in Part II apply?

- **Yes** → You must figure your penalty.
- **No** → You are **not** required to figure your penalty because the IRS will figure it and send you a bill for any unpaid amount. If you want to figure it, you may use Part III or Part IV as a worksheet and enter your penalty amount on your tax return, but **file only page 1 of Form 2210.**

↓ **No**

**Do not file Form 2210.** You are not required to figure your penalty because the IRS will figure it and send you a bill for any unpaid amount. If you want to figure it, you may use Part III or Part IV as a worksheet and enter your penalty amount on your tax return, but **do not file Form 2210.**

### Part I Required Annual Payment

| | |  |  |
|---|---|---|---|
| 1 | Enter your 2010 tax after credits from Form 1040, line 55 (see instructions if not filing Form 1040) | 1 | |
| 2 | Other taxes, including self-employment tax (see page 2 of the instructions) . . . . . . . . | 2 | |
| 3 | Refundable credits. Enter the total of your making work pay credit, earned income credit, additional child tax credit, American opportunity credit (Form 8863, line 14), first-time homebuyer credit (Form 5405, line 10), credit for federal tax paid on fuels, adoption credit, refundable credit for prior year minimum tax (Form 8801, line 27), and health coverage tax credit . . . . . | 3 | ( ) |
| 4 | Current year tax. Combine lines 1, 2, and 3. If less than $1,000, **stop;** you do not owe a penalty. **Do not** file Form 2210 . . . . . . . . . . . . . . . . . . . . . . | 4 | |
| 5 | Multiply line 4 by 90% (.90) . . . . . . . . . . . . . . 5 | | |
| 6 | Withholding taxes. **Do not** include estimated tax payments (see page 3 of the instructions) . . | 6 | |
| 7 | Subtract line 6 from line 4. If less than $1,000, **stop**; you do not owe a penalty. **Do not** file Form 2210 | 7 | |
| 8 | Maximum required annual payment based on prior year's tax (see page 3 of the instructions) . . | 8 | |
| 9 | **Required annual payment.** Enter the **smaller** of line 5 or line 8 . . . . . . . . . . . | 9 | |

**Next:** Is line 9 more than line 6?

☐ **No.** You **do not** owe a penalty. **Do not** file Form 2210 unless box **E** below applies.

☐ **Yes.** You may owe a penalty, but **do not** file Form 2210 unless one or more boxes in Part II below applies.

- If box **B, C,** or **D** applies, you must figure your penalty and file Form 2210.
- If box **A** or **E** applies (but not **B, C,** or **D**) file only page 1 of Form 2210. You are **not** required to figure your penalty; the IRS will figure it and send you a bill for any unpaid amount. If you want to figure your penalty, you may use Part III or IV as a worksheet and enter your penalty on your tax return, but **file only page 1 of Form 2210.**

### Part II Reasons for Filing. Check applicable boxes. If none apply, do not file Form 2210.

**A** ☐ You request a **waiver** (see page 2 of the instructions) of your entire penalty. You must check this box and file page 1 of Form 2210, but you are not required to figure your penalty.

**B** ☐ You request a **waiver** (see page 2 of the instructions) of part of your penalty. You must figure your penalty and waiver amount and file Form 2210.

**C** ☐ Your income varied during the year and your penalty is reduced or eliminated when figured using the **annualized income installment method.** You must figure the penalty using Schedule AI and file Form 2210.

**D** ☐ Your penalty is lower when figured by treating the federal income tax withheld from your income as paid on the dates it was actually withheld, instead of in equal amounts on the payment due dates. You must figure your penalty and file Form 2210.

**E** ☐ You filed or are filing a joint return for either 2009 or 2010, but not for both years, and line 8 above is smaller than line 5 above. You must file page 1 of Form 2210, but you are **not** required to figure your penalty (unless box **B, C,** or **D** applies).

**For Paperwork Reduction Act Notice, see page 6 of separate instructions.** Cat. No. 11744P Form **2210** (2010)

Form 2210 (2010) Page 2

## Part III Short Method

| | |
|---|---|
| ***Can You Use the Short Method?*** | You may use the short method if:<br>• You made no estimated tax payments (or your only payments were withheld federal income tax), **or**<br>• You paid the same amount of estimated tax on each of the four payment due dates. |
| ***Must You Use the Regular Method?*** | You must use the regular method (Part IV) instead of the short method if:<br>• You made any estimated tax payments late,<br>• You checked box **C** or **D** in Part II, **or**<br>• You are filing Form 1040NR or 1040NR-EZ and you did not receive wages as an employee subject to U.S. income tax withholding. |

**Note:** *If any payment was made earlier than the due date, you may use the short method, but using it may cause you to pay a larger penalty than the regular method. If the payment was only a few days early, the difference is likely to be small.*

| | | | | |
|---|---|---|---|---|
| **10** Enter the amount from Form 2210, line 9 | | | 10 | |
| **11** Enter the amount, if any, from Form 2210, line 6 | 11 | | | |
| **12** Enter the total amount, if any, of estimated tax payments you made (see page 3 of the instructions) | 12 | | | |
| **13** Add lines 11 and 12 | | | 13 | |
| **14** **Total underpayment for year.** Subtract line 13 from line 10. If zero or less, **stop**; you do not owe a penalty. **Do not file Form 2210 unless you checked box E in Part II** | | | 14 | |
| **15** Multiply line 14 by .02383 | | | 15 | |
| **16** • If the amount on line 14 was paid **on or after** 4/15/11, enter -0-.<br>• If the amount on line 14 was paid **before** 4/15/11, make the following computation to find the amount to enter on line 16.<br>Amount on line 14 × Number of days paid before 4/15/11 × .00008 | | | 16 | |
| **17** **Penalty.** Subtract line 16 from line 15. Enter the result here and on Form 1040, line 77; Form 1040A, line 49; Form 1040NR, line 73; Form 1040NR-EZ, line 26; or Form 1041, line 26. **Do not file Form 2210 unless you checked a box in Part II** ▶ | | | 17 | |

Form **2210** (2010)

Form 2210 (2010) Page 3

**Part IV** **Regular Method** (See page 3 of the instructions if you are filing Form 1040NR or 1040NR-EZ.)

| Section A—Figure Your Underpayment | | Payment Due Dates (a) 4/15/10 | (b) 6/15/10 | (c) 9/15/10 | (d) 1/15/11 |
|---|---|---|---|---|---|
| 18 **Required installments.** If box C in Part II applies, enter the amounts from Schedule AI, line 25. Otherwise, enter 25% (.25) of line 9, Form 2210, in each column | 18 | | | | |
| 19 Estimated tax paid and tax withheld (see page 3 of the instructions). For column (a) only, also enter the amount from line 19 on line 23. If line 19 is equal to or more than line 18 for all payment periods, stop here; you do not owe a penalty. **Do not file Form 2210 unless you checked a box in Part II** | 19 | | | | |
| ***Complete lines 20 through 26 of one column before going to line 20 of the next column.*** 20 Enter the amount, if any, from line 26 in the previous column | 20 | | | | |
| 21 Add lines 19 and 20 | 21 | | | | |
| 22 Add the amounts on lines 24 and 25 in the previous column | 22 | | | | |
| 23 Subtract line 22 from line 21. If zero or less, enter -0-. For column (a) only, enter the amount from line 19 | 23 | | | | |
| 24 If line 23 is zero, subtract line 21 from line 22. Otherwise, enter -0- | 24 | | | | |
| 25 **Underpayment.** If line 18 is equal to or more than line 23, subtract line 23 from line 18. Then go to line 20 of the next column. Otherwise, go to line 26 ▶ | 25 | | | | |
| 26 Overpayment. If line 23 is more than line 18, subtract line 18 from line 23. Then go to line 20 of the next column | 26 | | | | |

**Section B—Figure the Penalty** (Use the Worksheet for Form 2210, Part IV, Section B—Figure the Penalty on page 4 of the instructions to figure your penalty.)

| | | |
|---|---|---|
| 27 **Penalty.** Enter the total penalty from line 8 of the Worksheet for Form 2210, Part IV, Section B—Figure the Penalty. Also include this amount on Form 1040, line 77; Form 1040A, line 49; Form 1040NR, line 73; Form 1040NR-EZ, line 26; or Form 1041, line 26. **Do not file Form 2210 unless you checked a box in Part II** ▶ | 27 | |

Form **2210** (2010)

Form **2220**

Department of the Treasury
Internal Revenue Service

# Underpayment of Estimated Tax by Corporations

► See separate instructions.
► Attach to the corporation's tax return.

OMB No. 1545-0142

**2010**

Name | Employer identification number

**Note:** *Generally, the corporation is not required to file Form 2220 (see Part II below for exceptions) because the IRS will figure any penalty owed and bill the corporation. However, the corporation may still use Form 2220 to figure the penalty. If so, enter the amount from page 2, line 38 on the estimated tax penalty line of the corporation's income tax return, but* ***do not*** *attach Form 2220.*

## Part I Required Annual Payment

| | | | | | |
|---|---|---|---|---|---|
| 1 | Total tax (see instructions) | | | 1 | |
| 2a | Personal holding company tax (Schedule PH (Form 1120), line 26) included on line 1 | 2a | | | |
| b | Look-back interest included on line 1 under section 460(b)(2) for completed long-term contracts or section 167(g) for depreciation under the income forecast method | 2b | | | |
| c | Credit for federal tax paid on fuels (see instructions) | 2c | | | |
| d | **Total.** Add lines 2a through 2c | | | 2d | |
| 3 | Subtract line 2d from line 1. If the result is less than $500, **do not** complete or file this form. The corporation does not owe the penalty | | | 3 | |
| 4 | Enter the tax shown on the corporation's 2008 income tax return (see instructions). **Caution:** ***If the tax is zero or the tax year was for less than 12 months, skip this line and enter the amount from line 3 on line 5*** | | | 4 | |
| 5 | **Required annual payment.** Enter the **smaller** of line 3 or line 4. If the corporation is required to skip line 4, enter the amount from line 3 | | | 5 | |

## Part II Reasons for Filing— Check the boxes below that apply. If any boxes are checked, the corporation **must** file Form 2220 even if it does not owe a penalty (see instructions).

6 ☐ The corporation is using the adjusted seasonal installment method.

7 ☐ The corporation is using the annualized income installment method.

8 ☐ The corporation is a "large corporation" figuring its first required installment based on the prior year's tax.

## Part III Figuring the Underpayment

| | | | (a) | (b) | (c) | (d) |
|---|---|---|---|---|---|---|
| 9 | **Installment due dates.** Enter in columns (a) through (d) the 15th day of the 4th (*Form 990-PF filers:* Use 5th month), 6th, 9th, and 12th months of the corporation's tax year | 9 | | | | |
| 10 | **Required installments.** If the box on line 6 and/or line 7 above is checked, enter the amounts from Schedule A, line 38. If the box on line 8 (but not 6 or 7) is checked, see instructions for the amounts to enter. If none of these boxes are checked, enter 25% of line 5 above in each column | 10 | | | | |
| 11 | Estimated tax paid or credited for each period (see instructions). For column (a) only, enter the amount from line 11 on line 15 | 11 | | | | |
| | ***Complete lines 12 through 18 of one column before going to the next column.*** | | | | | |
| 12 | Enter amount, if any, from line 18 of the preceding column | 12 | | | | |
| 13 | Add lines 11 and 12 | 13 | | | | |
| 14 | Add amounts on lines 16 and 17 of the preceding column | 14 | | | | |
| 15 | Subtract line 14 from line 13. If zero or less, enter -0- | 15 | | | | |
| 16 | If the amount on line 15 is zero, subtract line 13 from line 14. Otherwise, enter -0- | 16 | | | | |
| 17 | **Underpayment.** If line 15 is less than or equal to line 10, subtract line 15 from line 10. Then go to line 12 of the next column. Otherwise, go to line 18 | 17 | | | | |
| 18 | **Overpayment.** If line 10 is less than line 15, subtract line 10 from line 15. Then go to line 12 of the next column | 18 | | | | |

***Go to Part IV on page 2 to figure the penalty. Do not go to Part IV if there are no entries on line 17—no penalty is owed.***

**For Paperwork Reduction Act Notice, see separate instructions.** Cat. No. 11746L Form **2220** (2010)

Form 2220 (2010) Page **2**

## Part IV Figuring the Penalty

| | | | (a) | (b) | (c) | (d) |
|---|---|---|---|---|---|---|
| 19 | Enter the date of payment or the 15th day of the 3rd month after the close of the tax year, whichever is earlier (see instructions). ***(Form 990-PF and Form 990-T filers:*** Use 5th month instead of 3rd month.) | 19 | | | | |
| 20 | Number of days from due date of installment on line 9 to the date shown on line 19 | 20 | | | | |
| 21 | Number of days on line 20 after 4/15/2009 and before 7/1/2009 | 21 | | | | |
| 22 | Underpayment on line 17 × $\frac{\text{Number of days on line 21}}{365}$ × 4% | 22 | $ | $ | $ | $ |
| 23 | Number of days on line 20 after 6/30/2009 and before 10/1/2009 | 23 | | | | |
| 24 | Underpayment on line 17 × $\frac{\text{Number of days on line 23}}{365}$ × 4% | 24 | $ | $ | $ | $ |
| 25 | Number of days on line 20 after 9/30/2009 and before 1/1/2010 | 25 | | | | |
| 26 | Underpayment on line 17 × $\frac{\text{Number of days on line 25}}{365}$ × 4% | 26 | $ | $ | $ | $ |
| 27 | Number of days on line 20 after 12/31/2009 and before 4/1/2010 | 27 | | | | |
| 28 | Underpayment on line 17 × $\frac{\text{Number of days on line 27}}{365}$ × 4% | 28 | $ | $ | $ | $ |
| 29 | Number of days on line 20 after 3/31/2010 and before 7/1/2010 | 29 | | | | |
| 30 | Underpayment on line 17 × $\frac{\text{Number of days on line 29}}{365}$ × *% | 30 | $ | $ | $ | $ |
| 31 | Number of days on line 20 after 6/30/2010 and before 10/1/2010 | 31 | | | | |
| 32 | Underpayment on line 17 × $\frac{\text{Number of days on line 31}}{365}$ × *% | 32 | $ | $ | $ | $ |
| 33 | Number of days on line 20 after 9/30/2010 and before 1/1/2011 | 33 | | | | |
| 34 | Underpayment on line 17 × $\frac{\text{Number of days on line 33}}{365}$ × *% | 34 | $ | $ | $ | $ |
| 35 | Number of days on line 20 after 12/31/2010 and before 2/16/2011 | 35 | | | | |
| 36 | Underpayment on line 17 × $\frac{\text{Number of days on line 35}}{365}$ × *% | 36 | $ | $ | $ | $ |
| 37 | Add lines 22, 24, 26, 28, 30, 32, 34, and 36 | 37 | $ | $ | $ | $ |
| 38 | **Penalty.** Add columns (a) through (d) of line 37. Enter the total here and on Form 1120, line 33; or the comparable line for other income tax returns | | | | 38 | $ |

*Use the penalty interest rate for each calendar quarter, which the IRS will determine during the first month in the preceding quarter. These rates are published quarterly in an IRS News Release and in a revenue ruling in the Internal Revenue Bulletin. To obtain this information on the Internet, access the IRS website at **www.irs.gov.** You can also call 1-800-829-4933 to get interest rate information.

Form **2220** (2010)

# B–11 Forms for Computation of Minimum Tax

Form **4626** — Department of the Treasury, Internal Revenue Service

## Alternative Minimum Tax—Corporations

▶ See separate instructions.
▶ Attach to the corporation's tax return.

OMB No. 1545-0175 — **2010**

Name | Employer identification number

**Note:** *See the instructions to find out if the corporation is a small corporation exempt from the alternative minimum tax (AMT) under section 55(e).*

| | | | |
|---|---|---|---|
| 1 | Taxable income or (loss) before net operating loss deduction | 1 | |
| 2 | **Adjustments and preferences:** | | |
| a | Depreciation of post-1986 property | 2a | |
| b | Amortization of certified pollution control facilities | 2b | |
| c | Amortization of mining exploration and development costs | 2c | |
| d | Amortization of circulation expenditures (personal holding companies only) | 2d | |
| e | Adjusted gain or loss | 2e | |
| f | Long-term contracts | 2f | |
| g | Merchant marine capital construction funds | 2g | |
| h | Section 833(b) deduction (Blue Cross, Blue Shield, and similar type organizations only) | 2h | |
| i | Tax shelter farm activities (personal service corporations only) | 2i | |
| j | Passive activities (closely held corporations and personal service corporations only) | 2j | |
| k | Loss limitations | 2k | |
| l | Depletion | 2l | |
| m | Tax-exempt interest income from specified private activity bonds | 2m | |
| n | Intangible drilling costs | 2n | |
| o | Other adjustments and preferences | 2o | |
| 3 | Pre-adjustment alternative minimum taxable income (AMTI). Combine lines 1 through 2o | 3 | |
| 4 | **Adjusted current earnings (ACE) adjustment:** | | |
| a | ACE from line 10 of the ACE worksheet in the instructions — 4a | | |
| b | Subtract line 3 from line 4a. If line 3 exceeds line 4a, enter the difference as a negative amount (see instructions) — 4b | | |
| c | Multiply line 4b by 75% (.75). Enter the result as a positive amount — 4c | | |
| d | Enter the excess, if any, of the corporation's total increases in AMTI from prior year ACE adjustments over its total reductions in AMTI from prior year ACE adjustments (see instructions). **Note:** *You **must** enter an amount on line 4d (even if line 4b is positive)* — 4d | | |
| e | ACE adjustment.<br>• If line 4b is zero or more, enter the amount from line 4c<br>• If line 4b is less than zero, enter the **smaller** of line 4c or line 4d as a negative amount | 4e | |
| 5 | Combine lines 3 and 4e. If zero or less, stop here; the corporation does not owe any AMT | 5 | |
| 6 | Alternative tax net operating loss deduction (see instructions) | 6 | |
| 7 | **Alternative minimum taxable income.** Subtract line 6 from line 5. If the corporation held a residual interest in a REMIC, see instructions | 7 | |
| 8 | **Exemption phase-out** (if line 7 is $310,000 or more, skip lines 8a and 8b and enter -0- on line 8c): | | |
| a | Subtract $150,000 from line 7 (if completing this line for a member of a controlled group, see instructions). If zero or less, enter -0- — 8a | | |
| b | Multiply line 8a by 25% (.25) — 8b | | |
| c | Exemption. Subtract line 8b from $40,000 (if completing this line for a member of a controlled group, see instructions). If zero or less, enter -0- | 8c | |
| 9 | Subtract line 8c from line 7. If zero or less, enter -0- | 9 | |
| 10 | Multiply line 9 by 20% (.20) | 10 | |
| 11 | Alternative minimum tax foreign tax credit (AMTFTC) (see instructions) | 11 | |
| 12 | Tentative minimum tax. Subtract line 11 from line 10 | 12 | |
| 13 | Regular tax liability before applying all credits except the foreign tax credit | 13 | |
| 14 | **Alternative minimum tax.** Subtract line 13 from line 12. If zero or less, enter -0-. Enter here and on Form 1120, Schedule J, line 3, or the appropriate line of the corporation's income tax return | 14 | |

**For Paperwork Reduction Act Notice, see the instructions.** Cat. No. 12955I Form **4626** (2010)

Form **6251**

Department of the Treasury
Internal Revenue Service (99)

# Alternative Minimum Tax—Individuals

▶ See separate instructions.

▶ Attach to Form 1040 or Form 1040NR.

OMB No. 1545-0074

**2010**

Attachment Sequence No. **32**

Name(s) shown on Form 1040 or Form 1040NR | Your social security number

## Part I Alternative Minimum Taxable Income (See instructions for how to complete each line.)

| | | | |
|---|---|---|---|
| 1 | If filing Schedule A (Form 1040), enter the amount from Form 1040, line 41, and go to line 2. Otherwise, enter the amount from Form 1040, line 38, and go to line 6. (If less than zero, enter as a negative amount.) | 1 | |
| 2 | Medical and dental. Enter the **smaller** of Schedule A (Form 1040), line 4, **or** 2.5% (.025) of Form 1040, line 38. If zero or less, enter -0- | 2 | |
| 3 | Taxes from Schedule A (Form 1040), lines 5, 6, and 8 | 3 | |
| 4 | Enter the home mortgage interest adjustment, if any, from line 6 of the worksheet on page 2 of the instructions | 4 | |
| 5 | Miscellaneous deductions from Schedule A (Form 1040), line 27 | 5 | |
| 6 | If filing Schedule L (Form 1040A or 1040), enter as a negative amount the sum of lines 6 and 17 from that schedule | 6 | ( ) |
| 7 | Tax refund from Form 1040, line 10 or line 21 | 7 | ( ) |
| 8 | Investment interest expense (difference between regular tax and AMT) | 8 | |
| 9 | Depletion (difference between regular tax and AMT) | 9 | |
| 10 | Net operating loss deduction from Form 1040, line 21. Enter as a positive amount | 10 | |
| 11 | Alternative tax net operating loss deduction | 11 | ( ) |
| 12 | Interest from specified private activity bonds exempt from the regular tax | 12 | |
| 13 | Qualified small business stock (7% of gain excluded under section 1202) | 13 | |
| 14 | Exercise of incentive stock options (excess of AMT income over regular tax income) | 14 | |
| 15 | Estates and trusts (amount from Schedule K-1 (Form 1041), box 12, code A) | 15 | |
| 16 | Electing large partnerships (amount from Schedule K-1 (Form 1065-B), box 6) | 16 | |
| 17 | Disposition of property (difference between AMT and regular tax gain or loss) | 17 | |
| 18 | Depreciation on assets placed in service after 1986 (difference between regular tax and AMT) | 18 | |
| 19 | Passive activities (difference between AMT and regular tax income or loss) | 19 | |
| 20 | Loss limitations (difference between AMT and regular tax income or loss) | 20 | |
| 21 | Circulation costs (difference between regular tax and AMT) | 21 | |
| 22 | Long-term contracts (difference between AMT and regular tax income) | 22 | |
| 23 | Mining costs (difference between regular tax and AMT) | 23 | |
| 24 | Research and experimental costs (difference between regular tax and AMT) | 24 | |
| 25 | Income from certain installment sales before January 1, 1987 | 25 | ( ) |
| 26 | Intangible drilling costs preference | 26 | |
| 27 | Other adjustments, including income-based related adjustments | 27 | |
| 28 | **Alternative minimum taxable income.** Combine lines 1 through 27. (If married filing separately and line 28 is more than $219,900, see page 8 of the instructions.) | 28 | |

## Part II Alternative Minimum Tax (AMT)

29 Exemption. (If you were under age 24 at the end of 2010, see page 8 of the instructions.)

| IF your filing status is . . . | AND line 28 is not over . . . | THEN enter on line 29 . . . |
|---|---|---|
| Single or head of household | $112,500 | $47,450 |
| Married filing jointly or qualifying widow(er) | 150,000 | 72,450 |
| Married filing separately | 75,000 | 36,225 |

If line 28 is **over** the amount shown above for your filing status, see page 8 of the instructions. — **29**

30 Subtract line 29 from line 28. If more than zero, go to line 31. If zero or less, enter -0- here and on lines 33 and 35 and skip the rest of Part II — **30**

31
- If you are filing Form 2555 or 2555-EZ, see page 9 of the instructions for the amount to enter.
- If you reported capital gain distributions directly on Form 1040, line 13; you reported qualified dividends on Form 1040, line 9b; **or** you had a gain on both lines 15 and 16 of Schedule D (Form 1040) (as refigured for the AMT, if necessary), complete Part III on the back and enter the amount from line 54 here. — **31**
- **All others:** If line 30 is $175,000 or less ($87,500 or less if married filing separately), multiply line 30 by 26% (.26). Otherwise, multiply line 30 by 28% (.28) and subtract $3,500 ($1,750 if married filing separately) from the result.

| | | | |
|---|---|---|---|
| 32 | Alternative minimum tax foreign tax credit (see page 9 of the instructions) | 32 | |
| 33 | Tentative minimum tax. Subtract line 32 from line 31 | 33 | |
| 34 | Tax from Form 1040, line 44 (minus any tax from Form 4972 and any foreign tax credit from Form 1040, line 47). If you used Schedule J to figure your tax, the amount from line 44 of Form 1040 must be refigured without using Schedule J (see page 11 of the instructions) | 34 | |
| 35 | **AMT.** Subtract line 34 from line 33. If zero or less, enter -0-. Enter here and on Form 1040, line 45 | 35 | |

**For Paperwork Reduction Act Notice, see your tax return instructions.** Cat. No. 13600G Form **6251** (2010)

Form 6251 (2010) Page **2**

## Part III Tax Computation Using Maximum Capital Gains Rates

|  |  | | |
|---|---|---|---|
| 36 | Enter the amount from Form 6251, line 30. If you are filing Form 2555 or 2555-EZ, enter the amount from line 3 of the worksheet on page 9 of the instructions | | 36 |
| 37 | Enter the amount from line 6 of the Qualified Dividends and Capital Gain Tax Worksheet in the instructions for Form 1040, line 44, or the amount from line 13 of the Schedule D Tax Worksheet in the instructions for Schedule D (Form 1040), whichever applies (as refigured for the AMT, if necessary) (see page 11 of the instructions). If you are filing Form 2555 or 2555-EZ, see page 11 of the instructions for the amount to enter | 37 | |
| 38 | Enter the amount from Schedule D (Form 1040), line 19 (as refigured for the AMT, if necessary) (see page 11 of the instructions). If you are filing Form 2555 or 2555-EZ, see page 11 of the instructions for the amount to enter | 38 | |
| 39 | If you did not complete a Schedule D Tax Worksheet for the regular tax or the AMT, enter the amount from line 37. Otherwise, add lines 37 and 38, and enter the **smaller** of that result or the amount from line 10 of the Schedule D Tax Worksheet (as refigured for the AMT, if necessary). If you are filing Form 2555 or 2555-EZ, see page 11 of the instructions for the amount to enter | 39 | |
| 40 | Enter the **smaller** of line 36 or line 39 | | 40 |
| 41 | Subtract line 40 from line 36 | | 41 |
| 42 | If line 41 is $175,000 or less ($87,500 or less if married filing separately), multiply line 41 by 26% (.26). Otherwise, multiply line 41 by 28% (.28) and subtract $3,500 ($1,750 if married filing separately) from the result ▶ | | 42 |
| 43 | Enter: • $68,000 if married filing jointly or qualifying widow(er), • $34,000 if single or married filing separately, or • $45,550 if head of household. | 43 | |
| 44 | Enter the amount from line 7 of the Qualified Dividends and Capital Gain Tax Worksheet in the instructions for Form 1040, line 44, or the amount from line 14 of the Schedule D Tax Worksheet in the instructions for Schedule D (Form 1040), whichever applies (as figured for the regular tax). If you did not complete either worksheet for the regular tax, enter -0- | 44 | |
| 45 | Subtract line 44 from line 43. If zero or less, enter -0- | 45 | |
| 46 | Enter the **smaller** of line 36 or line 37 | 46 | |
| 47 | Enter the **smaller** of line 45 or line 46 | 47 | |
| 48 | Subtract line 47 from line 46 | 48 | |
| 49 | Multiply line 48 by 15% (.15) ▶ | | 49 |
| | **If line 38 is zero or blank, skip lines 50 and 51 and go to line 52. Otherwise, go to line 50.** | | |
| 50 | Subtract line 46 from line 40 | 50 | |
| 51 | Multiply line 50 by 25% (.25) ▶ | | 51 |
| 52 | Add lines 42, 49, and 51 | | 52 |
| 53 | If line 36 is $175,000 or less ($87,500 or less if married filing separately), multiply line 36 by 26% (.26). Otherwise, multiply line 36 by 28% (.28) and subtract $3,500 ($1,750 if married filing separately) from the result | | 53 |
| 54 | Enter the **smaller** of line 52 or line 53 here and on line 31. If you are filing Form 2555 or 2555-EZ, do not enter this amount on line 31. Instead, enter it on line 4 of the worksheet on page 9 of the instructions | | 54 |

Form **6251** (2010)

# B-12 Forms for Tax Credits

Form **1116**

Department of the Treasury
Internal Revenue Service (99)

## Foreign Tax Credit

**(Individual, Estate, or Trust)**
▶ Attach to Form 1040, 1040NR, 1041, or 990-T.
▶ See separate instructions.

OMB No. 1545-0121
2010
Attachment Sequence No. 19

Name | **Identifying number** as shown on page 1 of your tax return

Use a separate Form 1116 for each category of income listed below. See **Categories of Income** in the instructions. Check only one box on each Form 1116. Report all amounts in U.S. dollars except where specified in Part II below.

a ☐ Passive category income
b ☐ General category income
c ☐ Section 901(j) income
d ☐ Certain income re-sourced by treaty
e ☐ Lump-sum distributions

f Resident of (name of country) ▶

**Note:** *If you paid taxes to only one foreign country or U.S. possession, use column A in Part I and line A in Part II. If you paid taxes to **more than one** foreign country or U.S. possession, use a separate column and line for each country or possession.*

**Part I Taxable Income or Loss From Sources Outside the United States (for Category Checked Above)**

| | | Foreign Country or U.S. Possession | | | Total |
|---|---|---|---|---|---|
| | | A | B | C | (Add cols. A, B, and C.) |
| g | **Enter the name of the foreign country or U.S. possession** ▶ | | | | |
| 1a | Gross income from sources within country shown above and of the type checked above (see instructions): | | | | 1a |
| b | Check if line 1a is compensation for personal services as an employee, your total compensation from all sources is $250,000 or more, and you used an alternative basis to determine its source (see instructions) ▶ ☐ | | | | |
| | **Deductions and losses** (***Caution:*** *See instructions*): | | | | |
| 2 | Expenses **definitely related** to the income on line 1a (attach statement) | | | | |
| 3 | Pro rata share of other deductions **not definitely related:** | | | | |
| a | Certain itemized deductions or standard deduction (see instructions) | | | | |
| b | Other deductions (attach statement) | | | | |
| c | Add lines 3a and 3b | | | | |
| d | Gross foreign source income (see instructions) | | | | |
| e | Gross income from all sources (see instructions) | | | | |
| f | Divide line 3d by line 3e (see instructions) | | | | |
| g | Multiply line 3c by line 3f | | | | |
| 4 | Pro rata share of interest expense (see instructions): | | | | |
| a | Home mortgage interest (use worksheet on page 14 of the instructions) | | | | |
| b | Other interest expense | | | | |
| 5 | Losses from foreign sources | | | | |
| 6 | Add lines 2, 3g, 4a, 4b, and 5 | | | | 6 |
| 7 | Subtract line 6 from line 1a. Enter the result here and on line 14, page 2 ▶ | | | | 7 |

**Part II Foreign Taxes Paid or Accrued** (see instructions)

| Country | Credit is claimed for taxes (you must check one) (h) ☐ Paid (i) ☐ Accrued | Foreign taxes paid or accrued | | | | | | | | |
|---|---|---|---|---|---|---|---|---|---|---|
| | | In foreign currency | | | | In U.S. dollars | | | | |
| | | Taxes withheld at source on: | | | | Taxes withheld at source on: | | | | |
| | (j) Date paid or accrued | (k) Dividends | (l) Rents and royalties | (m) Interest | (n) Other foreign taxes paid or accrued | (o) Dividends | (p) Rents and royalties | (q) Interest | (r) Other foreign taxes paid or accrued | (s) Total foreign taxes paid or accrued (add cols. (o) through (r)) |
| A | | | | | | | | | | |
| B | | | | | | | | | | |
| C | | | | | | | | | | |

8 **Add lines A through C, column (s). Enter the total here and on line 9, page 2** ▶ 8

**For Paperwork Reduction Act Notice, see instructions.** Cat. No. 11440U Form **1116** (2010)

Form 1116 (2010) Page **2**

## Part III Figuring the Credit

| Line | Description | Box | Amount |
|---|---|---|---|
| 9 | Enter the amount from line 8. These are your total foreign taxes paid or accrued for the category of income checked above Part I | 9 | |
| 10 | Carryback or carryover (attach detailed computation) | 10 | |
| 11 | Add lines 9 and 10 | 11 | |
| 12 | Reduction in foreign taxes (see instructions) | 12 | |
| 13 | Subtract line 12 from line 11. This is the total amount of foreign taxes available for credit (see instructions) | 13 | |
| 14 | Enter the amount from line 7. This is your taxable income or (loss) from sources outside the United States (before adjustments) for the category of income checked above Part I (see instructions) | 14 | |
| 15 | Adjustments to line 14 (see instructions) | 15 | |
| 16 | Combine the amounts on lines 14 and 15. This is your net foreign source taxable income. (If the result is zero or less, you have no foreign tax credit for the category of income you checked above Part I. Skip lines 17 through 21. However, if you are filing more than one Form 1116, you must complete line 19.) | 16 | |
| 17 | **Individuals:** Enter the amount from Form 1040, line 41, or Form 1040NR, line 39. **Estates and trusts:** Enter your taxable income without the deduction for your exemption | 17 | |
| | **Caution:** *If you figured your tax using the lower rates on qualified dividends or capital gains, see instructions.* | | |
| 18 | Divide line 16 by line 17. If line 16 is more than line 17, enter "1" | 18 | |
| 19 | **Individuals:** Enter the amount from Form 1040, line 44. If you are a nonresident alien, enter the amount from Form 1040NR, line 42. **Estates and trusts:** Enter the amount from Form 1041, Schedule G, line 1a, or the total of Form 990-T, lines 36 and 37 | 19 | |
| | **Caution:** *If you are completing line 19 for separate category* **e** *(lump-sum distributions), see instructions.* | | |
| 20 | Multiply line 19 by line 18 (maximum amount of credit) | 20 | |
| 21 | Enter the **smaller** of line 13 or line 20. If this is the only Form 1116 you are filing, skip lines 22 through 26 and enter this amount on line 27. Otherwise, complete the appropriate line in Part IV (see instructions) ▶ | 21 | |

## Part IV Summary of Credits From Separate Parts III (see instructions)

| Line | Description | Box | Amount |
|---|---|---|---|
| 22 | Credit for taxes on passive category income | 22 | |
| 23 | Credit for taxes on general category income | 23 | |
| 24 | Credit for taxes on certain income re-sourced by treaty | 24 | |
| 25 | Credit for taxes on lump-sum distributions | 25 | |
| 26 | Add lines 22 through 25 | 26 | |
| 27 | Enter the **smaller** of line 19 or line 26 | 27 | |
| 28 | Reduction of credit for international boycott operations. See instructions for line 12 | 28 | |
| 29 | Subtract line 28 from line 27. This is your **foreign tax credit.** Enter here and on Form 1040, line 47; Form 1040NR, line 45; Form 1041, Schedule G, line 2a; or Form 990-T, line 40a ▶ | 29 | |

Form **1116** (2010)

Form **2441** Department of the Treasury Internal Revenue Service (99)

# Child and Dependent Care Expenses

▶ Attach to Form 1040, Form 1040A, or Form 1040NR.
▶ See separate instructions.

1040 1040A 1040NR 2441

OMB No. 1545-0074
**2010**
Attachment Sequence No. **21**

Name(s) shown on return | **Your social security number**

**Part I** **Persons or Organizations Who Provided the Care—**You **must** complete this part.
(If you have more than two care providers, see the instructions.)

| 1 **(a)** Care provider's name | **(b)** Address (number, street, apt. no., city, state, and ZIP code) | **(c)** Identifying number (SSN or EIN) | **(d)** Amount paid (see instructions) |
|---|---|---|---|
| | | | |
| | | | |

Did you receive **dependent care benefits?** — **No** ⟶ Complete only Part II below.
— **Yes** ⟶ Complete Part III on the back next.

**Caution.** If the care was provided in your home, you may owe employment taxes. If you do, you cannot file Form 1040A. For details, see the instructions for Form 1040, line 59, or Form 1040NR, line 58.

**Part II** **Credit for Child and Dependent Care Expenses**

2 Information about your **qualifying person(s)**. If you have more than two qualifying persons, see the instructions.

| **(a)** Qualifying person's name First | Last | **(b)** Qualifying person's social security number | **(c) Qualified expenses** you incurred and paid in 2010 for the person listed in column (a) |
|---|---|---|---|
| | | | |
| | | | |

3 Add the amounts in column (c) of line 2. **Do not** enter more than $3,000 for one qualifying person or $6,000 for two or more persons. If you completed Part III, enter the amount from line 31 . . . . . **3**

4 Enter your **earned income**. See instructions . . . . . **4**

5 If married filing jointly, enter your spouse's earned income (if your spouse was a student or was disabled, see the instructions); **all others**, enter the amount from line 4 . . . . **5**

6 Enter the **smallest** of line 3, 4, or 5 . . . . . **6**

7 Enter the amount from Form 1040, line 38; Form 1040A, line 22; or Form 1040NR, line 37. . . . . **7**

8 Enter on line 8 the decimal amount shown below that applies to the amount on line 7

**If line 7 is:**

| Over | But not over | Decimal amount is |
|---|---|---|
| $0 | 15,000 | .35 |
| 15,000 | 17,000 | .34 |
| 17,000 | 19,000 | .33 |
| 19,000 | 21,000 | .32 |
| 21,000 | 23,000 | .31 |
| 23,000 | 25,000 | .30 |
| 25,000 | 27,000 | .29 |
| 27,000 | 29,000 | .28 |

**If line 7 is:**

| Over | But not over | Decimal amount is |
|---|---|---|
| $29,000 | 31,000 | .27 |
| 31,000 | 33,000 | .26 |
| 33,000 | 35,000 | .25 |
| 35,000 | 37,000 | .24 |
| 37,000 | 39,000 | .23 |
| 39,000 | 41,000 | .22 |
| 41,000 | 43,000 | .21 |
| 43,000 | No limit | .20 |

**8** X .

9 Multiply line 6 by the decimal amount on line 8. If you paid 2009 expenses in 2010, see the instructions . . . . . **9**

10 Tax liability limit. Enter the amount from the Credit Limit Worksheet in the instructions. . . . . . . **10**

11 **Credit for child and dependent care expenses.** Enter the **smaller** of line 9 or line 10 here and on Form 1040, line 48; Form 1040A, line 29; or Form 1040NR, line 46 . . . . **11**

**For Paperwork Reduction Act Notice, see your tax return instructions.** Cat. No. 11862M Form **2441** (2010)

Form 2441 (2010) Page **2**

## Part III Dependent Care Benefits

| | | | |
|---|---|---|---|
| **12** Enter the total amount of **dependent care benefits** you received in 2010. Amounts you received as an employee should be shown in box 10 of your Form(s) W-2. **Do not** include amounts reported as wages in box 1 of Form(s) W-2. If you were self-employed or a partner, include amounts you received under a dependent care assistance program from your sole proprietorship or partnership | | **12** | |
| **13** Enter the amount, if any, you carried over from 2009 and used in 2010 during the grace period. See instructions | | **13** | |
| **14** Enter the amount, if any, you forfeited or carried forward to 2011. See instructions | | **14** | ( ) |
| **15** Combine lines 12 through 14. See instructions | | **15** | |
| **16** Enter the total amount of **qualified expenses** incurred in 2010 for the care of the **qualifying person(s)** | **16** | | |
| **17** Enter the **smaller** of line 15 or 16 | **17** | | |
| **18** Enter your **earned income.** See instructions | **18** | | |
| **19** Enter the amount shown below that applies to you.<br>• If married filing jointly, enter your spouse's earned income (if your spouse was a student or was disabled, see the instructions for line 5).<br>• If married filing separately, see instructions.<br>• All others, enter the amount from line 18. | **19** | | |
| **20** Enter the **smallest** of line 17, 18, or 19 | **20** | | |
| **21** Enter $5,000 ($2,500 if married filing separately **and** you were required to enter your spouse's earned income on line 19) | **21** | | |
| **22** Is any amount on line 12 from your sole proprietorship or partnership? (Form 1040A filers go to line 25.)<br>☐ **No.** Enter -0-.<br>☐ **Yes.** Enter the amount here | | **22** | |
| **23** Subtract line 22 from line 15 | **23** | | |
| **24** **Deductible benefits.** Enter the **smallest** of line 20, 21, or 22. Also, include this amount on the appropriate line(s) of your return. See instructions | | **24** | |
| **25** **Excluded benefits. Form 1040 and 1040NR filers:** If you checked "No" on line 22, enter the smaller of line 20 or 21. Otherwise, subtract line 24 from the smaller of line 20 or line 21. If zero or less, enter -0-. **Form 1040A filers:** Enter the **smaller** of line 20 or line 21 | | **25** | |
| **26** **Taxable benefits. Form 1040 and 1040NR filers:** Subtract line 25 from line 23. If zero or less, enter -0-. Also, include this amount on Form 1040, line 7; or Form 1040NR, line 8. On the dotted line next to Form 1040, line 7; or Form 1040NR, line 8, enter "DCB." **Form 1040A filers:** Subtract line 25 from line 15. Also, include this amount on Form 1040A, line 7. In the space to the left of line 7, enter "DCB" | | **26** | |

To claim the child and dependent care credit, complete lines 27 through 31 below.

| | | |
|---|---|---|
| **27** Enter $3,000 ($6,000 if two or more qualifying persons) | **27** | |
| **28** **Form 1040 and 1040NR filers:** Add lines 24 and 25. **Form 1040A filers:** Enter the amount from line 25 | **28** | |
| **29** Subtract line 28 from line 27. If zero or less, **stop.** You cannot take the credit. **Exception.** If you paid 2009 expenses in 2010, see the instructions for line 9 | **29** | |
| **30** Complete line 2 on the front of this form. **Do not** include in column (c) any benefits shown on line 28 above. Then, add the amounts in column (c) and enter the total here | **30** | |
| **31** Enter the **smaller** of line 29 or 30. Also, enter this amount on line 3 on the front of this form and complete lines 4 through 11 | **31** | |

Form **2441** (2010)

Form **3468**

Department of the Treasury
Internal Revenue Service (99)

# Investment Credit

▶ Attach to your tax return. See instructions.

OMB No. 1545-0155
2010
Attachment Sequence No. 174

Name(s) shown on return | Identifying number

**Part I Information Regarding the Election To Treat the Lessee as the Purchaser of Investment Credit Property**

If you are claiming the investment credit as a lessee based on a section 48(d) (as in effect on November 4, 1990) election, provide the following information. If you acquired more than one property as a lessee, attach a statement showing the information below.

1 Name of lessor

2 Address of lessor

3 Description of property

4 Amount for which you were treated as having acquired the property . . . . . . . . . . . ▶ $

**Part II Qualifying Advanced Coal Project Credit, Qualifying Gasification Project Credit, Qualifying Advanced Energy Project Credit, and Qualifying Therapeutic Discovery Project Credit**

5 Qualifying advanced coal project credit (see instructions):

a Qualified investment in integrated gasification combined cycle property placed in service during the tax year for projects described in section 48A(d)(3)(B)(i) . . . . . . . $ ________ × 20% (.20) **5a**

b Qualified investment in advanced coal-based generation technology property placed in service during the tax year for projects described in section 48A(d)(3)(B)(ii) . . . . . $ ________ × 15% (.15) **5b**

c Qualified investment in advanced coal-based generation technology property placed in service during the tax year for projects described in section 48A(d)(3)(B)(iii) . . . . . $ ________ × 30% (.30) **5c**

d Total. Add lines 5a, 5b, and 5c . . . . . . . . . . . . . . . . . . . . . . . **5d**

6 Qualifying gasification project credit (see instructions):

a Qualified investment in qualified gasification property placed in service during the tax year for which credits were allocated or reallocated after October 3, 2008, and that includes equipment that separates and sequesters at least 75% of the project's carbon dioxide emissions . . . . . . . . . $ ________ × 30% (.30) **6a**

b Qualified investment in property other than in **a** above placed in service during the tax year . . . . . . $ ________ × 20% (.20) **6b**

c Total. Add lines 6a and 6b . . . . . . . . . . . . . . . . . . . . . . . . **6c**

7 Qualifying advanced energy project credit (see instructions):
Qualified investment in advanced energy project property placed in service during the tax year . . . . . . . . . . . . . $ ________ × 30% (.30) **7**

8 Qualifying therapeutic discovery project credit (see instructions):
Qualified investment in a qualifying therapeutic discovery project $ ________ × 50% (.50) **8**

9 Enter the applicable unused investment credit from cooperatives (see instructions) . . . . . . **9**

10 Add lines 5d, 6c, 7, 8, and 9. Report this amount on Form 3800, line 1a . . . . . . . . . . **10**

**Part III Rehabilitation Credit and Energy Credit**

11 Rehabilitation credit (see instructions for requirements that must be met):

a Check this box if you are electing under section 47(d)(5) to take your qualified rehabilitation expenditures into account for the tax year in which paid (or, for self-rehabilitated property, when capitalized). See instructions. **Note.** This election applies to the current tax year and to all later tax years. You may not revoke this election without IRS consent . . . . . . . . . . . . ▶ ☐

b Enter the dates on which the 24- or 60-month measuring period begins ________ and ends ________

c Enter the adjusted basis of the building as of the beginning date above (or the first day of your holding period, if later) . . . . . . . . . $ ________

d Enter the amount of the qualified rehabilitation expenditures incurred, or treated as incurred, during the period on line 11b above . . . . . $ ________

Enter the amount of qualified rehabilitation expenditures and multiply by the percentage shown:

e Pre-1936 buildings located in the Gulf Opportunity Zone . $ ________ × 13% (.13) **11e**

f Pre-1936 buildings affected by a Midwestern disaster . . $ ________ × 13% (.13) **11f**

g Other pre-1936 buildings . . . . . . . . . . . . $ ________ × 10% (.10) **11g**

h Certified historic structures located in the Gulf Opportunity Zone $ ________ × 26% (.26) **11h**

**For Paperwork Reduction Act Notice, see instructions.** Cat. No. 12276E Form **3468** (2010)

Form **3800**

Department of the Treasury
Internal Revenue Service (99)

# General Business Credit

▶ **See separate instructions.**
▶ **Attach to your tax return.**

OMB No. 1545-0895

**2010**

Attachment Sequence No. **22**

Name(s) shown on return

**Identifying number**

**Part I** **Current Year Credit**

**Important:** You may not be required to complete and file a separate credit form (shown in parentheses below) to claim the credit. For details, see the instructions.

| | | | |
|---|---|---|---|
| 1a | Investment credit (Form 3468, Part II only) (attach Form 3468) | 1a | |
| b | Reserved for future use | 1b | |
| c | Credit for increasing research activities | 1c | |
| d | Low-income housing credit (Form 8586, Part I only) (enter EIN if claiming this credit from a pass-through entity: ____________ ) | 1d | |
| e | Disabled access credit (Form 8826) (do not enter more than $5,000) | 1e | |
| f | Renewable electricity production credit (Form 8835) (see instructions) | 1f | |
| g | Indian employment credit | 1g | |
| h | Orphan drug credit (Form 8820) | 1h | |
| i | New markets credit (Form 8874) (enter EIN if claiming this credit from a pass-through entity: ____________ ) | 1i | |
| j | Credit for small employer pension plan startup costs (Form 8881) (do not enter more than $500) | 1j | |
| k | Credit for employer-provided child care facilities and services (Form 8882) (enter EIN if claiming this credit from a pass-through entity: ____________ ) | 1k | |
| l | Biodiesel and renewable diesel fuels credit (attach Form 8864) | 1l | |
| m | Low sulfur diesel fuel production credit (Form 8896) | 1m | |
| n | Distilled spirits credit (Form 8906) | 1n | |
| o | Nonconventional source fuel credit (Form 8907) | 1o | |
| p | Energy efficient home credit | 1p | |
| q | Energy efficient appliance credit (Form 8909) | 1q | |
| r | Alternative motor vehicle credit (Form 8910) (enter EIN if claiming this credit from a pass-through entity: ____________ ) | 1r | |
| s | Alternative fuel vehicle refueling property credit (Form 8911) | 1s | |
| t | Employer housing credit | 1t | |
| u | Mine rescue team training credit | 1u | |
| v | Agricultural chemicals security credit (Form 8931) (do not enter more than $2 million) | 1v | |
| w | Credit for employer differential wage payments | 1w | |
| x | Carbon dioxide sequestration credit (Form 8933) | 1x | |
| y | Qualified plug-in electric drive motor vehicle credit (Form 8936) | 1y | |
| z | Qualified plug-in electric vehicle credit (Form 8834, Part I only) | 1z | |
| aa | New hire retention credit (Form 5884-B) | 1aa | |
| bb | General credits from an electing large partnership (Schedule K-1 (Form 1065-B)) | 1bb | |
| 2 | Add lines 1a through 1bb | 2 | |
| 3 | Passive activity credits included on line 2 (see instructions) | 3 | |
| 4 | Subtract line 3 from line 2 | 4 | |
| 5 | Passive activity credits allowed for 2010 (see instructions) | 5 | |
| 6 | Carryforward of general business credit to 2010. See instructions for the schedule to attach | 6 | |
| 7 | Carryback of general business credit from 2011 (see instructions) | 7 | |
| 8 | Add lines 4 through 7. Subtract from that sum any eligible small business credits and enter the result (see instructions) | 8 | |

**For Paperwork Reduction Act Notice, see separate instructions.** Cat. No. 12392F Form **3800** (2010)

**Part II** **Allowable Credit**

| | | | |
|---|---|---|---|
| 9 | Regular tax before credits:<br>• Individuals. Enter the amount from Form 1040, line 44 or Form 1040NR, line 42<br>• Corporations. Enter the amount from Form 1120, Schedule J, line 2; or the applicable line of your return<br>• Estates and trusts. Enter the sum of the amounts from Form 1041, Schedule G, lines 1a and 1b, or the amount from the applicable line of your return | 9 | |
| 10 | Alternative minimum tax:<br>• Individuals. Enter the amount from Form 6251, line 35<br>• Corporations. Enter the amount from Form 4626, line 14<br>• Estates and trusts. Enter the amount from Schedule I (Form 1041), line 56 | 10 | |
| 11 | Add lines 9 and 10 | 11 | |
| 12a | Foreign tax credit ... 12a | | |
| b | Personal credits from Form 1040 or 1040NR (see instructions) ... 12b | | |
| c | Add lines 12a and 12b | 12c | |
| 13 | **Net income tax.** Subtract line 12c from line 11. If zero, skip lines 14 through 17 and enter -0- on line 18a | 13 | |
| 14 | **Net regular tax.** Subtract line 12c from line 9. If zero or less, enter -0- ... 14 | | |
| 15 | Enter 25% (.25) of the excess, if any, of line 14 over $25,000 (see instructions) ... 15 | | |
| 16 | Tentative minimum tax. If line 8 is zero and line 24 would be zero, skip lines 16 through 25 and go to line 26. Otherwise, see instructions ... 16 | | |
| 17 | Enter the greater of line 15 or line 16 | 17 | |
| 18a | Subtract line 17 from line 13. If zero or less, enter -0- | 18a | |
| b | For a corporation electing to accelerate the research credit, enter the bonus depreciation amount attributable to the research credit. (see instructions) | 18b | |
| c | Add lines 18a and 18b | 18c | |
| 19a | Enter the **smaller** of line 8 or line 18c<br>**C corporations:** See the line 19a instructions if there has been an ownership change, acquisition, or reorganization. | 19a | |
| b | Enter the smaller of line 8 or line 18a. If you made an entry on line 18b, go to line 19c; otherwise, skip line 19c (see instructions) | 19b | |
| c | Subtract line 19b from line 19a. This is the refundable amount for a corporation electing to accelerate the research credit. Include this amount on line 32g of Form 1120 (or the applicable line of your return) | 19c | |

# B-13 Other Tax Forms

Form **2106**

Department of the Treasury
Internal Revenue Service (99)

## Employee Business Expenses

▶ See separate instructions.

▶ Attach to Form 1040 or Form 1040NR.

OMB No. 1545-0074

2010

Attachment Sequence No. 129

| Your name | Occupation in which you incurred expenses | Social security number |
|---|---|---|
| | | |

**Part I** **Employee Business Expenses and Reimbursements**

| **Step 1 Enter Your Expenses** | | **Column A** Other Than Meals and Entertainment | **Column B** Meals and Entertainment |
|---|---|---|---|
| 1 Vehicle expense from line 22 or line 29. (Rural mail carriers: See instructions.) . . . . . . . . . . . . . . . . . . . . . | 1 | | |
| 2 Parking fees, tolls, and transportation, including train, bus, etc., that **did not** involve overnight travel or commuting to and from work . | 2 | | |
| 3 Travel expense while away from home overnight, including lodging, airplane, car rental, etc. **Do not** include meals and entertainment . | 3 | | |
| 4 Business expenses not included on lines 1 through 3. **Do not** include meals and entertainment . . . . . . . . . . . . . . . | 4 | | |
| 5 Meals and entertainment expenses (see instructions) . . . . . . | 5 | | |
| 6 **Total expenses.** In Column A, add lines 1 through 4 and enter the result. In Column B, enter the amount from line 5 . . . . . . . | 6 | | |

**Note:** *If you were not reimbursed for any expenses in Step 1, skip line 7 and enter the amount from line 6 on line 8.*

| **Step 2 Enter Reimbursements Received From Your Employer for Expenses Listed in Step 1** | | | |
|---|---|---|---|
| 7 Enter reimbursements received from your employer that were **not** reported to you in box 1 of Form W-2. Include any reimbursements reported under code "L" in box 12 of your Form W-2 (see instructions) . . . . . . . . . . . . . . . . . . . . . | 7 | | |

| **Step 3 Figure Expenses To Deduct on Schedule A (Form 1040 or Form 1040NR)** | | | |
|---|---|---|---|
| 8 Subtract line 7 from line 6. If zero or less, enter -0-. However, if line 7 is greater than line 6 in Column A, report the excess as income on Form 1040, line 7 (or on Form 1040NR, line 8) . . . . . . . . | 8 | | |
| **Note:** *If **both columns** of line 8 are zero, you cannot deduct employee business expenses. Stop here and attach Form 2106 to your return.* | | | |
| 9 In Column A, enter the amount from line 8. In Column B, multiply line 8 by 50% (.50). (Employees subject to Department of Transportation (DOT) hours of service limits: Multiply meal expenses incurred while away from home on business by 80% (.80) instead of 50%. For details, see instructions.) . . . . . . . . . . . . . . | 9 | | |

| | | |
|---|---|---|
| 10 Add the amounts on line 9 of both columns and enter the total here. **Also, enter the total on Schedule A (Form 1040), line 21** (or on **Schedule A (Form 1040NR), line 9**). (Armed Forces reservists, qualified performing artists, fee-basis state or local government officials, and individuals with disabilities: See the instructions for special rules on where to enter the total.) . . . . . ▶ | 10 | |

**For Paperwork Reduction Act Notice, see your tax return instructions.** Cat. No. 11700N Form **2106** (2010)

Form 2106 (2010) Page **2**

## Part II Vehicle Expenses

| **Section A—General Information** (You must complete this section if you are claiming vehicle expenses.) | | **(a)** Vehicle 1 | **(b)** Vehicle 2 |
|---|---|---|---|
| 11 Enter the date the vehicle was placed in service | 11 | / / | / / |
| 12 Total miles the vehicle was driven during 2010 | 12 | miles | miles |
| 13 Business miles included on line 12 | 13 | miles | miles |
| 14 Percent of business use. Divide line 13 by line 12 | 14 | % | % |
| 15 Average daily roundtrip commuting distance | 15 | miles | miles |
| 16 Commuting miles included on line 12 | 16 | miles | miles |
| 17 Other miles. Add lines 13 and 16 and subtract the total from line 12 | 17 | miles | miles |

| | | |
|---|---|---|
| 18 Was your vehicle available for personal use during off-duty hours? | ☐ Yes | ☐ No |
| 19 Do you (or your spouse) have another vehicle available for personal use? | ☐ Yes | ☐ No |
| 20 Do you have evidence to support your deduction? | ☐ Yes | ☐ No |
| 21 If "Yes," is the evidence written? | ☐ Yes | ☐ No |

**Section B—Standard Mileage Rate** (See the instructions for Part II to find out whether to complete this section or Section C.)

| | | |
|---|---|---|
| 22 Multiply line 13 by 50¢ (.50). Enter the result here and on line 1 | 22 | |

| **Section C—Actual Expenses** | | **(a)** Vehicle 1 | | **(b)** Vehicle 2 | |
|---|---|---|---|---|---|
| 23 Gasoline, oil, repairs, vehicle insurance, etc. | 23 | | | | |
| 24a Vehicle rentals | 24a | | | | |
| b Inclusion amount (see instructions) | 24b | | | | |
| c Subtract line 24b from line 24a | 24c | | | | |
| 25 Value of employer-provided vehicle (applies only if 100% of annual lease value was included on Form W-2—see instructions) | 25 | | | | |
| 26 Add lines 23, 24c, and 25 | 26 | | | | |
| 27 Multiply line 26 by the percentage on line 14 | 27 | | | | |
| 28 Depreciation (see instructions) | 28 | | | | |
| 29 Add lines 27 and 28. Enter total here and on line 1 | 29 | | | | |

**Section D—Depreciation of Vehicles** (Use this section only if you owned the vehicle and are completing Section C for the vehicle.)

| | | **(a)** Vehicle 1 | | **(b)** Vehicle 2 | |
|---|---|---|---|---|---|
| 30 Enter cost or other basis (see instructions) | 30 | | | | |
| 31 Enter section 179 deduction and special allowance (see instructions) | 31 | | | | |
| 32 Multiply line 30 by line 14 (see instructions if you claimed the section 179 deduction or special allowance) | 32 | | | | |
| 33 Enter depreciation method and percentage (see instructions) | 33 | | | | |
| 34 Multiply line 32 by the percentage on line 33 (see instructions) | 34 | | | | |
| 35 Add lines 31 and 34 | 35 | | | | |
| 36 Enter the applicable limit explained in the line 36 instructions | 36 | | | | |
| 37 Multiply line 36 by the percentage on line 14 | 37 | | | | |
| 38 Enter the **smaller** of line 35 or line 37. If you skipped lines 36 and 37, enter the amount from line 35. Also enter this amount on line 28 above | 38 | | | | |

Form **2106** (2010)

Form **2120**
(Rev. October 2005)
Department of the Treasury
Internal Revenue Service

# Multiple Support Declaration

▶ **Attach to Form 1040 or Form 1040A.**

OMB No. 1545-0074

Attachment
Sequence No. **114**

Name(s) shown on return | **Your social security number**

During the calendar year ................................ , the eligible persons listed below each paid over 10% of the support of:

..........................................................................................
Name of your qualifying relative

I have a signed statement from each eligible person waiving his or her right to claim this person as a dependent for any tax year that began in the above calendar year.

.......................................................................... ..............................
Eligible person's name | Social security number

..........................................................................................
Address (number, street, apt. no., city, state, and ZIP code)

.......................................................................... ..............................
Eligible person's name | Social security number

..........................................................................................
Address (number, street, apt. no., city, state, and ZIP code)

.......................................................................... ..............................
Eligible person's name | Social security number

..........................................................................................
Address (number, street, apt. no., city, state, and ZIP code)

.......................................................................... ..............................
Eligible person's name | Social security number

..........................................................................................
Address (number, street, apt. no., city, state, and ZIP code)

## Instructions

### What's New

The rules for multiple support agreements still apply to claiming an exemption for a qualifying relative, but they no longer apply to claiming an exemption for a qualifying child. For the definitions of "qualifying relative" and "qualifying child," see your tax return instruction booklet.

### Purpose of Form

Use Form 2120 to:

- Identify each other eligible person (see below) who paid over 10% of the support of your qualifying relative whom you are claiming as a dependent, and
- Indicate that you have a signed statement from each other eligible person waiving his or her right to claim that person as a dependent.

An eligible person is someone who could have claimed a person as a dependent except that he or she did not pay over half of that person's support.

If there are more than four other eligible persons, attach a statement to your return with the required information.

### Claiming a Qualifying Relative

Generally, to claim a person as a qualifying relative, you must pay over half of that person's support. However, even if you did not meet this support test, you may be able to claim him or her as a dependent if all five of the following apply.

**1.** You and one or more other eligible person(s) (see above) together paid over half of that person's support.

**2.** You paid over 10% of the support.

**3.** No one alone paid over half of that person's support.

**4.** The other dependency tests are met. See *Step 4, Is Your Qualifying Relative Your Dependent?* in the Form 1040 or Form 1040A instructions.

**5.** Each other eligible person who paid over 10% of the support agrees not to claim that person as a dependent by giving you a signed statement. See *Signed Statement* on this page.

**Note.** To find out what is included in support, see Pub. 501, Exemptions, Standard Deduction, and Filing Information.

### Signed Statement

You must have received, from each other eligible person listed above, a signed statement waiving his or her right to claim the person as a dependent for the calendar year indicated on this form. The statement must include:

- The calendar year the waiver applies to,
- The name of your qualifying relative the eligible person helped to support, and
- The eligible person's name, address, and social security number.

Do not file the signed statement with your return. But you must keep it for your records and be prepared to furnish it and any other information necessary to show that you qualify to claim the person as your dependent.

### Additional Information

See Pub. 501 for details.

**Paperwork Reduction Act Notice.** We ask for the information on this form to carry out the Internal Revenue laws of the United States. You are required to give us the information. We need it to ensure that you are complying with these laws and to allow us to figure and collect the right amount of tax.

You are not required to provide the information requested on a form that is subject to the Paperwork Reduction Act unless the form displays a valid OMB control number. Books or records relating to a form or its instructions must be retained as long as their contents may become material in the administration of any Internal Revenue law. Generally, tax returns and return information are confidential, as required by Internal Revenue Code section 6103.

The average time and expenses required to complete and file this form will vary depending on individual circumstances. For the estimated averages, see the instructions for your income tax return.

If you have suggestions for making this form simpler, we would be happy to hear from you. See the instructions for your income tax return.

Cat. No. 11712F    Form **2120** (Rev. 10-2005)

Form **3903**

Department of the Treasury
Internal Revenue Service (99)

## Moving Expenses

▶ **Attach to Form 1040 or Form 1040NR.**

OMB No. 1545-0074

**2010**

Attachment
Sequence No. **62**

| Name(s) shown on return | Your social security number |
| --- | --- |
| | |

***Before you begin:***

✓ See the **Distance Test** and **Time Test** in the instructions to find out if you can deduct your moving expenses.

✓ See **Members of the Armed Forces** in the instructions, if applicable.

| | | | |
| --- | --- | --- | --- |
| **1** | Transportation and storage of household goods and personal effects (see instructions) . . . | 1 | |
| **2** | Travel (including lodging) from your old home to your new home (see instructions). **Do not** include the cost of meals . . . . . . . . . . . . . . . . . . . . . . . . . | 2 | |
| **3** | Add lines 1 and 2 . . . . . . . . . . . . . . . . . . . . . . . . . . . . | 3 | |
| **4** | Enter the total amount your employer paid you for the expenses listed on lines 1 and 2 that is **not** included in box 1 of your Form W-2 (wages). This amount should be shown in box 12 of your Form W-2 with code **P** . . . . . . . . . . . . . . . . . . . . . . . . . | 4 | |
| **5** | Is line 3 **more than** line 4? | | |
| | ☐ **No.** You **cannot** deduct your moving expenses. If line 3 is less than line 4, subtract line 3 from line 4 and include the result on Form 1040, line 7, or Form 1040NR, line 8. | | |
| | ☐ **Yes.** Subtract line 4 from line 3. Enter the result here and on Form 1040, line 26, or Form 1040NR, line 26. This is your **moving expense deduction** . . . . . . . . . . | 5 | |

**For Paperwork Reduction Act Notice, see your tax return instructions.** Cat. No. 12490K Form **3903** (2010)

Form **4562**

Department of the Treasury Internal Revenue Service (99)

# Depreciation and Amortization
## (Including Information on Listed Property)

▶ See separate instructions. ▶ Attach to your tax return.

OMB No. 1545-0172

2010

Attachment Sequence No. 67

| Name(s) shown on return | Business or activity to which this form relates | Identifying number |
|---|---|---|
| | | |

**Part I** **Election To Expense Certain Property Under Section 179**
**Note:** *If you have any listed property, complete Part V before you complete Part I.*

| | | | |
|---|---|---|---|
| 1 | Maximum amount (see instructions) | 1 | |
| 2 | Total cost of section 179 property placed in service (see instructions) | 2 | |
| 3 | Threshold cost of section 179 property before reduction in limitation (see instructions) | 3 | |
| 4 | Reduction in limitation. Subtract line 3 from line 2. If zero or less, enter -0- | 4 | |
| 5 | Dollar limitation for tax year. Subtract line 4 from line 1. If zero or less, enter -0-. If married filing separately, see instructions | 5 | |

| 6 | (a) Description of property | (b) Cost (business use only) | (c) Elected cost |
|---|---|---|---|
| | | | |
| | | | |

| | | | |
|---|---|---|---|
| 7 | Listed property. Enter the amount from line 29 | 7 | |
| 8 | Total elected cost of section 179 property. Add amounts in column (c), lines 6 and 7 | 8 | |
| 9 | Tentative deduction. Enter the **smaller** of line 5 or line 8 | 9 | |
| 10 | Carryover of disallowed deduction from line 13 of your 2009 Form 4562 | 10 | |
| 11 | Business income limitation. Enter the smaller of business income (not less than zero) or line 5 (see instructions) | 11 | |
| 12 | Section 179 expense deduction. Add lines 9 and 10, but do not enter more than line 11 | 12 | |
| 13 | Carryover of disallowed deduction to 2011. Add lines 9 and 10, less line 12 ▶ | 13 | |

**Note:** *Do not use Part II or Part III below for listed property. Instead, use Part V.*

**Part II** **Special Depreciation Allowance and Other Depreciation (Do not** include listed property.**)** (See instructions.)

| | | | |
|---|---|---|---|
| 14 | Special depreciation allowance for qualified property (other than listed property) placed in service during the tax year (see instructions) | 14 | |
| 15 | Property subject to section 168(f)(1) election | 15 | |
| 16 | Other depreciation (including ACRS) | 16 | |

**Part III** **MACRS Depreciation (Do not** include listed property.**)** (See instructions.)

**Section A**

| | | | |
|---|---|---|---|
| 17 | MACRS deductions for assets placed in service in tax years beginning before 2010 | 17 | |
| 18 | If you are electing to group any assets placed in service during the tax year into one or more general asset accounts, check here ▶ ☐ | | |

**Section B—Assets Placed in Service During 2010 Tax Year Using the General Depreciation System**

| (a) Classification of property | (b) Month and year placed in service | (c) Basis for depreciation (business/investment use only—see instructions) | (d) Recovery period | (e) Convention | (f) Method | (g) Depreciation deduction |
|---|---|---|---|---|---|---|
| 19a 3-year property | | | | | | |
| b 5-year property | | | | | | |
| c 7-year property | | | | | | |
| d 10-year property | | | | | | |
| e 15-year property | | | | | | |
| f 20-year property | | | | | | |
| g 25-year property | | | 25 yrs. | | S/L | |
| h Residential rental property | | | 27.5 yrs. | MM | S/L | |
| | | | 27.5 yrs. | MM | S/L | |
| i Nonresidential real property | | | 39 yrs. | MM | S/L | |
| | | | | MM | S/L | |

**Section C—Assets Placed in Service During 2010 Tax Year Using the Alternative Depreciation System**

| | | | | | | |
|---|---|---|---|---|---|---|
| 20a Class life | | | | | S/L | |
| b 12-year | | | 12 yrs. | | S/L | |
| c 40-year | | | 40 yrs. | MM | S/L | |

**Part IV** **Summary** (See instructions.)

| | | | |
|---|---|---|---|
| 21 | Listed property. Enter amount from line 28 | 21 | |
| 22 | **Total.** Add amounts from line 12, lines 14 through 17, lines 19 and 20 in column (g), and line 21. Enter here and on the appropriate lines of your return. Partnerships and S corporations—see instructions | 22 | |
| 23 | For assets shown above and placed in service during the current year, enter the portion of the basis attributable to section 263A costs | 23 | |

**For Paperwork Reduction Act Notice, see separate instructions.** Cat. No. 12906N Form **4562** (2010)

Form 4562 (2010) Page 2

**Part V** **Listed Property** (Include automobiles, certain other vehicles, certain computers, and property used for entertainment, recreation, or amusement.)

**Note:** *For any vehicle for which you are using the standard mileage rate or deducting lease expense, complete **only** 24a, 24b, columns (a) through (c) of Section A, all of Section B, and Section C if applicable.*

**Section A—Depreciation and Other Information (Caution:** *See the instructions for limits for passenger automobiles.***)**

**24a** Do you have evidence to support the business/investment use claimed? ☐ **Yes** ☐ **No** **24b** If "Yes," is the evidence written? ☐ **Yes** ☐ **No**

| (a) Type of property (list vehicles first) | (b) Date placed in service | (c) Business/ investment use percentage | (d) Cost or other basis | (e) Basis for depreciation (business/investment use only) | (f) Recovery period | (g) Method/ Convention | (h) Depreciation deduction | (i) Elected section 179 cost |
|---|---|---|---|---|---|---|---|---|
| **25** Special depreciation allowance for qualified listed property placed in service during the tax year and used more than 50% in a qualified business use (see instructions) . | | | | | | **25** | | |
| **26** Property used more than 50% in a qualified business use: | | | | | | | | |
| | | % | | | | | | |
| | | % | | | | | | |
| | | % | | | | | | |
| **27** Property used 50% or less in a qualified business use: | | | | | | | | |
| | | % | | | | S/L – | | |
| | | % | | | | S/L – | | |
| | | % | | | | S/L – | | |
| **28** Add amounts in column (h), lines 25 through 27. Enter here and on line 21, page 1 . | | | | | | **28** | | |
| **29** Add amounts in column (i), line 26. Enter here and on line 7, page 1 . . . . . . . . . . . . . | | | | | | | **29** | |

**Section B—Information on Use of Vehicles**

Complete this section for vehicles used by a sole proprietor, partner, or other "more than 5% owner," or related person. If you provided vehicles to your employees, first answer the questions in Section C to see if you meet an exception to completing this section for those vehicles.

| | (a) Vehicle 1 | | (b) Vehicle 2 | | (c) Vehicle 3 | | (d) Vehicle 4 | | (e) Vehicle 5 | | (f) Vehicle 6 | |
|---|---|---|---|---|---|---|---|---|---|---|---|---|
| **30** Total business/investment miles driven during the year (**do not** include commuting miles) . | | | | | | | | | | | | |
| **31** Total commuting miles driven during the year | | | | | | | | | | | | |
| **32** Total other personal (noncommuting) miles driven . . . . . . . . . . . . | | | | | | | | | | | | |
| **33** Total miles driven during the year. Add lines 30 through 32 . . . . . . . . . | | | | | | | | | | | | |
| | **Yes** | **No** | **Yes** | **No** | **Yes** | **No** | **Yes** | **No** | **Yes** | **No** | **Yes** | **No** |
| **34** Was the vehicle available for personal use during off-duty hours? . . . . . . . | | | | | | | | | | | | |
| **35** Was the vehicle used primarily by a more than 5% owner or related person? . . . | | | | | | | | | | | | |
| **36** Is another vehicle available for personal use? | | | | | | | | | | | | |

**Section C—Questions for Employers Who Provide Vehicles for Use by Their Employees**

Answer these questions to determine if you meet an exception to completing Section B for vehicles used by employees who **are not** more than 5% owners or related persons (see instructions).

| | **Yes** | **No** |
|---|---|---|
| **37** Do you maintain a written policy statement that prohibits all personal use of vehicles, including commuting, by your employees? . . . . . . . . . . . . . . . . . . . . . . . . . . . . . | | |
| **38** Do you maintain a written policy statement that prohibits personal use of vehicles, except commuting, by your employees? See the instructions for vehicles used by corporate officers, directors, or 1% or more owners . . . . | | |
| **39** Do you treat all use of vehicles by employees as personal use? . . . . . . . . . . . . . . . . . . | | |
| **40** Do you provide more than five vehicles to your employees, obtain information from your employees about the use of the vehicles, and retain the information received? . . . . . . . . . . . . . . . . . . . . . | | |
| **41** Do you meet the requirements concerning qualified automobile demonstration use? (See instructions.) . . . | | |

**Note:** *If your answer to 37, 38, 39, 40, or 41 is "Yes," do not complete Section B for the covered vehicles.*

**Part VI** **Amortization**

| (a) Description of costs | (b) Date amortization begins | (c) Amortizable amount | (d) Code section | (e) Amortization period or percentage | (f) Amortization for this year |
|---|---|---|---|---|---|
| **42** Amortization of costs that begins during your 2010 tax year (see instructions): | | | | | |
| | | | | | |
| | | | | | |
| **43** Amortization of costs that began before your 2010 tax year . . . . . . . . . . . . . . . | | | | **43** | |
| **44** **Total.** Add amounts in column (f). See the instructions for where to report . . . . . . . . . | | | | **44** | |

Form **4562** (2010)

Form **4684**

Department of the Treasury
Internal Revenue Service

# Casualties and Thefts

▶ See separate instructions.
▶ Attach to your tax return.
▶ Use a separate Form 4684 for each casualty or theft.

OMB No. 1545-0177

**2010**

Attachment Sequence No. **26**

**Name(s) shown on tax return** | **Identifying number**

**SECTION A—Personal Use Property** (Use this section to report casualties and thefts of property **not** used in a trade or business or for income-producing purposes.)

**1** Description of properties (show type, location, and date acquired for each property). Use a separate line for each property lost or damaged from the same casualty or theft.

Property **A** ______

Property **B** ______

Property **C** ______

Property **D** ______

| | | Properties | | | |
|---|---|---|---|---|---|
| | | **A** | **B** | **C** | **D** |
| **2** Cost or other basis of each property | 2 | | | | |
| **3** Insurance or other reimbursement (whether or not you filed a claim) (see instructions) | 3 | | | | |
| **Note:** *If line 2 is **more** than line 3, skip line 4.* | | | | | |
| **4** Gain from casualty or theft. If line 3 is **more** than line 2, enter the difference here and skip lines 5 through 9 for that column. See instructions if line 3 includes insurance or other reimbursement you did not claim, or you received payment for your loss in a later tax year | 4 | | | | |
| **5** Fair market value **before** casualty or theft | 5 | | | | |
| **6** Fair market value **after** casualty or theft | 6 | | | | |
| **7** Subtract line 6 from line 5 | 7 | | | | |
| **8** Enter the **smaller** of line 2 or line 7 | 8 | | | | |
| **9** Subtract line 3 from line 8. If zero or less, enter -0- | 9 | | | | |

| | | |
|---|---|---|
| **10** Casualty or theft loss. Add the amounts on line 9 in columns A through D | 10 | |
| **11** Enter the **smaller** of line 10 or $100 | 11 | |
| **12** Subtract line 11 from line 10 | 12 | |
| **Caution:** *Use only one Form 4684 for lines 13 through 21.* | | |
| **13** Add the amounts on line 12 of all Forms 4684 | 13 | |
| **14** Add the amounts on line 4 of all Forms 4684. | 14 | |
| **15** • If line 14 is **more** than line 13, enter the difference here and on Schedule D. **Do not** complete the rest of this section (see instructions). • If line 14 is **less** than line 13, enter -0- here and go to line 16. • If line 14 is **equal** to line 13, enter -0- here. **Do not** complete the rest of this section. | 15 | |
| **16** If line 14 is **less** than line 13, enter the difference | 16 | |
| **17** Does the amount on line 12 include a loss from a disaster declared a federal disaster in tax years beginning after 2007 that occurred before 2010? ☐ **Yes.** Enter the amount from line 3 of the Worksheet for Line 17, in the instructions. If you are filing Schedule A (Form 1040), go to line 18. Otherwise, enter this amount on Schedule L (Form 1040A or 1040). Do not complete the rest of Section A. Form 1040NR filers, see instructions. ☐ **No.** Enter -0- and go to line 18 | 17 | |
| **18** Subtract line 17 from line 16 | 18 | |
| **19** Enter 10% of your adjusted gross income from Form 1040, line 38, or Form 1040NR, line 36. Estates and trusts, see instructions | 19 | |
| **20** Subtract line 19 from line 18. If zero or less, enter -0- | 20 | |
| **21** Add lines 17 and 20. Also enter the result on Schedule A (Form 1040), line 20, or Form 1040NR, Schedule A, line 8. Estates and trusts, enter the result on the "Other deductions" line of your tax return | 21 | |

**For Paperwork Reduction Act Notice, see page 5 of the instructions.** Cat. No. 12997O Form **4684** (2010)

Form 4684 (2010) Attachment Sequence No. **26** Page **2**

Name(s) shown on tax return. Do not enter name and identifying number if shown on other side. | **Identifying number**

## SECTION B—Business and Income-Producing Property

### Part I Casualty or Theft Gain or Loss (Use a separate Part I for each casualty or theft.)

22 Description of properties (show type, location, and date acquired for each property). Use a separate line for each property lost or damaged from the same casualty or theft.

Property **A** __________

Property **B** __________

Property **C** __________

Property **D** __________

| | | Properties | | | |
|---|---|---|---|---|---|
| | | A | B | C | D |
| 23 Cost or adjusted basis of each property | 23 | | | | |
| 24 Insurance or other reimbursement (whether or not you filed a claim). See the instructions for line 3 | 24 | | | | |
| **Note:** *If line 23 is **more** than line 24, skip line 25.* | | | | | |
| 25 Gain from casualty or theft. If line 24 is **more** than line 23, enter the difference here and on line 32 or line 37, column (c), except as provided in the instructions for line 36. Also, skip lines 26 through 30 for that column. See the instructions for line 4 if line 24 includes insurance or other reimbursement you did not claim, or you received payment for your loss in a later tax year | 25 | | | | |
| 26 Fair market value **before** casualty or theft | 26 | | | | |
| 27 Fair market value **after** casualty or theft | 27 | | | | |
| 28 Subtract line 27 from line 26 | 28 | | | | |
| 29 Enter the **smaller** of line 23 or line 28 | 29 | | | | |
| **Note:** *If the property was totally destroyed by casualty or lost from theft, enter on line 29 the amount from line 23.* | | | | | |
| 30 Subtract line 24 from line 29. If zero or less, enter -0- | 30 | | | | |

31 Casualty or theft loss. Add the amounts on line 30. Enter the total here and on line 32 **or** line 37 (see instructions) . . | 31 |

### Part II Summary of Gains and Losses (from separate Parts I)

| (a) Identify casualty or theft | | (b) Losses from casualties or thefts: (i) Trade, business, rental or royalty property | (ii) Income-producing and employee property | (c) Gains from casualties or thefts includible in income |
|---|---|---|---|---|
| **Casualty or Theft of Property Held One Year or Less** | | | | |
| 32 | | ( ) | ( ) | |
| | | ( ) | ( ) | |
| 33 Totals. Add the amounts on line 32 | 33 | ( ) | ( ) | |
| 34 Combine line 33, columns (b)(i) and (c). Enter the net gain or (loss) here and on Form 4797, line 14. If Form 4797 is not otherwise required, see instructions | | | 34 | |
| 35 Enter the amount from line 33, column (b)(ii) here. Individuals, enter the amount from income-producing property on Schedule A (Form 1040), line 28, or Form 1040NR, Schedule A, line 16, and enter the amount from property used as an employee on Schedule A (Form 1040), line 23, or Form 1040NR, Schedule A, line 11. Estates and trusts, partnerships, and S corporations, see instructions | | | 35 | |
| **Casualty or Theft of Property Held More Than One Year** | | | | |
| 36 Casualty or theft gains from Form 4797, line 32 | | | 36 | |
| 37 | | ( ) | ( ) | |
| | | ( ) | ( ) | |
| 38 Total losses. Add amounts on line 37, columns (b)(i) and (b)(ii) | 38 | ( ) | ( ) | |
| 39 Total gains. Add lines 36 and 37, column (c) | | | 39 | |
| 40 Add amounts on line 38, columns (b)(i) and (b)(ii) | | | 40 | |
| 41 If the loss on line 40 is **more** than the gain on line 39: | | | | |
| a Combine line 38, column (b)(i) and line 39, and enter the net gain or (loss) here. Partnerships (except electing large partnerships) and S corporations, see the note below. All others, enter this amount on Form 4797, line 14. If Form 4797 is not otherwise required, see instructions | | | 41a | |
| b Enter the amount from line 38, column (b)(ii) here. Individuals, enter the amount from income-producing property on Schedule A (Form 1040), line 28, or Form 1040NR, Schedule A, line 16, and enter the amount from property used as an employee on Schedule A (Form 1040), line 23, or Form 1040NR, Schedule A, line 11. Estates and trusts, enter on the "Other deductions" line of your tax return. Partnerships (except electing large partnerships) and S corporations, see the note below. Electing large partnerships, enter on Form 1065-B, Part II, line 11 | | | 41b | |
| 42 If the loss on line 40 is **less** than or **equal** to the gain on line 39, combine lines 39 and 40 and enter here. Partnerships (except electing large partnerships), see the note below. All others, enter this amount on Form 4797, line 3 | | | 42 | |

**Note:** *Partnerships, enter the amount from line 41a, 41b, or line 42 on Form 1065, Schedule K, line 11. S corporations, enter the amount from line 41a or 41b on Form 1120S, Schedule K, line 10.*

Form **4684** (2010)

Form **4797**

Department of the Treasury Internal Revenue Service (99)

# Sales of Business Property

**(Also Involuntary Conversions and Recapture Amounts Under Sections 179 and 280F(b)(2))**

**▶ Attach to your tax return. ▶ See separate instructions.**

OMB No. 1545-0184

**2010**

Attachment Sequence No. **27**

Name(s) shown on return | **Identifying number**

1 Enter the gross proceeds from sales or exchanges reported to you for 2010 on Form(s) 1099-B or 1099-S (or substitute statement) that you are including on line 2, 10, or 20 (see instructions) . . . . . . . . . | **1** |

**Part I Sales or Exchanges of Property Used in a Trade or Business and Involuntary Conversions From Other Than Casualty or Theft—Most Property Held More Than 1 Year** (see instructions)

| 2 (a) Description of property | (b) Date acquired (mo., day, yr.) | (c) Date sold (mo., day, yr.) | (d) Gross sales price | (e) Depreciation allowed or allowable since acquisition | (f) Cost or other basis, plus improvements and expense of sale | (g) Gain or (loss) Subtract (f) from the sum of (d) and (e) |
|---|---|---|---|---|---|---|
| | | | | | | |
| | | | | | | |
| | | | | | | |
| | | | | | | |

| | | | |
|---|---|---|---|
| 3 | Gain, if any, from Form 4684, line 42 . . . . . . . . . . . . . . . . . . . . . . . . . | **3** | |
| 4 | Section 1231 gain from installment sales from Form 6252, line 26 or 37 . . . . . . . . . . . . . . | **4** | |
| 5 | Section 1231 gain or (loss) from like-kind exchanges from Form 8824 . . . . . . . . . . . . . . . | **5** | |
| 6 | Gain, if any, from line 32, from other than casualty or theft. . . . . . . . . . . . . . . . . . . | **6** | |
| 7 | Combine lines 2 through 6. Enter the gain or (loss) here and on the appropriate line as follows: . . . . . . . . | **7** | |
| | **Partnerships (except electing large partnerships) and S corporations.** Report the gain or (loss) following the instructions for Form 1065, Schedule K, line 10, or Form 1120S, Schedule K, line 9. Skip lines 8, 9, 11, and 12 below. **Individuals, partners, S corporation shareholders, and all others.** If line 7 is zero or a loss, enter the amount from line 7 on line 11 below and skip lines 8 and 9. If line 7 is a gain and you did not have any prior year section 1231 losses, or they were recaptured in an earlier year, enter the gain from line 7 as a long-term capital gain on the Schedule D filed with your return and skip lines 8, 9, 11, and 12 below. | | |
| 8 | Nonrecaptured net section 1231 losses from prior years (see instructions) . . . . . . . . . . . . . . | **8** | |
| 9 | Subtract line 8 from line 7. If zero or less, enter -0-. If line 9 is zero, enter the gain from line 7 on line 12 below. If line 9 is more than zero, enter the amount from line 8 on line 12 below and enter the gain from line 9 as a long-term capital gain on the Schedule D filed with your return (see instructions) . . . . . . . . . . . . . . . | **9** | |

**Part II Ordinary Gains and Losses** (see instructions)

10 Ordinary gains and losses not included on lines 11 through 16 (include property held 1 year or less):

| | | | | | | |
|---|---|---|---|---|---|---|
| | | | | | | |
| | | | | | | |
| | | | | | | |
| | | | | | | |

| | | | |
|---|---|---|---|
| 11 | Loss, if any, from line 7 . . . . . . . . . . . . . . . . . . . . . . . . . . . | **11** | ( ) |
| 12 | Gain, if any, from line 7 or amount from line 8, if applicable . . . . . . . . . . . . . . . . . . | **12** | |
| 13 | Gain, if any, from line 31 . . . . . . . . . . . . . . . . . . . . . . . . . . | **13** | |
| 14 | Net gain or (loss) from Form 4684, lines 34 and 41a . . . . . . . . . . . . . . . . . . . . | **14** | |
| 15 | Ordinary gain from installment sales from Form 6252, line 25 or 36 . . . . . . . . . . . . . . . | **15** | |
| 16 | Ordinary gain or (loss) from like-kind exchanges from Form 8824. . . . . . . . . . . . . . . . | **16** | |
| 17 | Combine lines 10 through 16 . . . . . . . . . . . . . . . . . . . . . . . . . | **17** | |
| 18 | For all except individual returns, enter the amount from line 17 on the appropriate line of your return and skip lines a and b below. For individual returns, complete lines a and b below: | | |
| a | If the loss on line 11 includes a loss from Form 4684, line 38, column (b)(ii), enter that part of the loss here. Enter the part of the loss from income-producing property on Schedule A (Form 1040), line 28, and the part of the loss from property used as an employee on Schedule A (Form 1040), line 23. Identify as from "Form 4797, line 18a." See instructions . . | **18a** | |
| b | Redetermine the gain or (loss) on line 17 excluding the loss, if any, on line 18a. Enter here and on Form 1040, line 14 | **18b** | |

**For Paperwork Reduction Act Notice, see separate instructions.** Cat. No. 13086I Form **4797** (2010)

Form 4797 (2010) Page 2

## Part III Gain From Disposition of Property Under Sections 1245, 1250, 1252, 1254, and 1255 (see instructions)

| 19 (a) Description of section 1245, 1250, 1252, 1254, or 1255 property: | (b) Date acquired (mo., day, yr.) | (c) Date sold (mo., day, yr.) |
|---|---|---|
| A | | |
| B | | |
| C | | |
| D | | |

| These columns relate to the properties on lines 19A through 19D. ▶ | | Property A | Property B | Property C | Property D |
|---|---|---|---|---|---|
| 20 Gross sales price (**Note:** *See line 1 before completing.*) | 20 | | | | |
| 21 Cost or other basis plus expense of sale | 21 | | | | |
| 22 Depreciation (or depletion) allowed or allowable | 22 | | | | |
| 23 Adjusted basis. Subtract line 22 from line 21 | 23 | | | | |
| 24 Total gain. Subtract line 23 from line 20 | 24 | | | | |
| 25 **If section 1245 property:** | | | | | |
| a Depreciation allowed or allowable from line 22 | 25a | | | | |
| b Enter the **smaller** of line 24 or 25a | 25b | | | | |
| 26 **If section 1250 property:** If straight line depreciation was used, enter -0- on line 26g, except for a corporation subject to section 291. | | | | | |
| a Additional depreciation after 1975 (see instructions) | 26a | | | | |
| b Applicable percentage multiplied by the **smaller** of line 24 or line 26a (see instructions) | 26b | | | | |
| c Subtract line 26a from line 24. If residential rental property **or** line 24 is not more than line 26a, skip lines 26d and 26e | 26c | | | | |
| d Additional depreciation after 1969 and before 1976 | 26d | | | | |
| e Enter the **smaller** of line 26c or 26d | 26e | | | | |
| f Section 291 amount (corporations only) | 26f | | | | |
| g Add lines 26b, 26e, and 26f | 26g | | | | |
| 27 **If section 1252 property:** Skip this section if you did not dispose of farmland or if this form is being completed for a partnership (other than an electing large partnership). | | | | | |
| a Soil, water, and land clearing expenses | 27a | | | | |
| b Line 27a multiplied by applicable percentage (see instructions) | 27b | | | | |
| c Enter the **smaller** of line 24 or 27b | 27c | | | | |
| 28 **If section 1254 property:** | | | | | |
| a Intangible drilling and development costs, expenditures for development of mines and other natural deposits, mining exploration costs, and depletion (see instructions) | 28a | | | | |
| b Enter the **smaller** of line 24 or 28a | 28b | | | | |
| 29 **If section 1255 property:** | | | | | |
| a Applicable percentage of payments excluded from income under section 126 (see instructions) | 29a | | | | |
| b Enter the **smaller** of line 24 or 29a (see instructions) | 29b | | | | |

**Summary of Part III Gains.** Complete property columns A through D through line 29b before going to line 30.

| | | |
|---|---|---|
| 30 Total gains for all properties. Add property columns A through D, line 24 | 30 | |
| 31 Add property columns A through D, lines 25b, 26g, 27c, 28b, and 29b. Enter here and on line 13 | 31 | |
| 32 Subtract line 31 from line 30. Enter the portion from casualty or theft on Form 4684, line 36. Enter the portion from other than casualty or theft on Form 4797, line 6 | 32 | |

## Part IV Recapture Amounts Under Sections 179 and 280F(b)(2) When Business Use Drops to 50% or Less (see instructions)

| | | (a) Section 179 | (b) Section 280F(b)(2) |
|---|---|---|---|
| 33 Section 179 expense deduction or depreciation allowable in prior years | 33 | | |
| 34 Recomputed depreciation (see instructions) | 34 | | |
| 35 Recapture amount. Subtract line 34 from line 33. See the instructions for where to report | 35 | | |

Form 4797 (2010)

Form **4952** Department of the Treasury Internal Revenue Service (99)

# Investment Interest Expense Deduction

▶ Attach to your tax return.

OMB No. 1545-0191 **2010** Attachment Sequence No. **51**

Name(s) shown on return | Identifying number

**Part I Total Investment Interest Expense**

| | | | |
|---|---|---|---|
| 1 | Investment interest expense paid or accrued in 2010 (see instructions) | 1 | |
| 2 | Disallowed investment interest expense from 2009 Form 4952, line 7 | 2 | |
| 3 | **Total investment interest expense.** Add lines 1 and 2 | 3 | |

**Part II Net Investment Income**

| | | | | | |
|---|---|---|---|---|---|
| 4a | Gross income from property held for investment (excluding any net gain from the disposition of property held for investment) | 4a | | | |
| b | Qualified dividends included on line 4a | 4b | | | |
| c | Subtract line 4b from line 4a | | | 4c | |
| d | Net gain from the disposition of property held for investment | 4d | | | |
| e | Enter the **smaller** of line 4d or your net capital gain from the disposition of property held for investment (see instructions) | 4e | | | |
| f | Subtract line 4e from line 4d | | | 4f | |
| g | Enter the amount from lines 4b and 4e that you elect to include in investment income (see instructions) | | | 4g | |
| h | Investment income. Add lines 4c, 4f, and 4g | | | 4h | |
| 5 | Investment expenses (see instructions) | | | 5 | |
| 6 | **Net investment income.** Subtract line 5 from line 4h. If zero or less, enter -0- | | | 6 | |

**Part III Investment Interest Expense Deduction**

| | | | |
|---|---|---|---|
| 7 | Disallowed investment interest expense to be carried forward to 2011. Subtract line 6 from line 3. If zero or less, enter -0- | 7 | |
| 8 | **Investment interest expense deduction.** Enter the **smaller** of line 3 or 6. See instructions | 8 | |

Section references are to the Internal Revenue Code unless otherwise noted.

## General Instructions

### Purpose of Form

Use Form 4952 to figure the amount of investment interest expense you can deduct for 2010 and the amount you can carry forward to future years. Your investment interest expense deduction is limited to your net investment income.

For more information, see Pub. 550, Investment Income and Expenses.

### Who Must File

If you are an individual, estate, or a trust, you must file Form 4952 to claim a deduction for your investment interest expense.

**Exception.** You do not have to file Form 4952 if all of the following apply.

- Your investment income from interest and ordinary dividends minus any qualified dividends is more than your investment interest expense.
- You do not have any other deductible investment expenses.
- You do not have any carryover of disallowed investment interest expense from 2009.

### Allocation of Interest Expense

If you paid or accrued interest on a loan and used the loan proceeds for more than one purpose, you may have to allocate the interest. This is necessary because different rules apply to investment interest, personal interest, trade or business interest, home mortgage interest, and passive activity interest. See Pub. 535, Business Expenses.

## Specific Instructions

### Part I—Total Investment Interest Expense

#### Line 1

Enter the investment interest expense paid or accrued during the tax year, regardless of when you incurred the indebtedness. Investment interest expense is interest paid or accrued on a loan or part of a loan that is allocable to property held for investment (as defined on this page).

Include investment interest expense reported to you on Schedule K-1 from a partnership or an S corporation. Include amortization of bond premium on taxable bonds purchased after October 22, 1986, but before January 1, 1988, unless you elected to offset amortizable bond premium against the interest payments on the bond. A taxable bond is a bond on which the interest is includible in gross income.

Investment interest expense does not include any of the following:

- Home mortgage interest.
- Interest expense that is properly allocable to a passive activity. Generally, a passive activity is any trade or business activity in which you do not materially participate and any rental activity. See the Instructions for Form 8582, Passive Activity Loss Limitations, for details.
- Any interest expense that is capitalized, such as construction interest subject to section 263A.
- Interest expense related to tax-exempt interest income under section 265.
- Interest expense, disallowed under section 264, on indebtedness with respect to life insurance, endowment, or annuity contracts issued after June 8, 1997, even if the proceeds were used to purchase any property held for investment.

**Property held for investment.** Property held for investment includes property that produces income, not derived in the ordinary course of a trade or business, from interest, dividends, annuities, or royalties. It also includes property that produces gain or loss, not derived in the ordinary course of a trade or business, from the disposition of property that produces these types of income or is held for investment. However, it does not include an interest in a passive activity.

***Exception.*** A working interest in an oil or gas property that you held directly or through an entity that did not limit your liability is property held for investment, but only if you did not materially participate in the activity.

### Part II—Net Investment Income

#### Line 4a

Gross income from property held for investment includes income, unless derived in the ordinary course of a trade or business, from interest, ordinary dividends (except Alaska Permanent Fund dividends), annuities, and royalties. Include investment income

Form **6252**

Department of the Treasury
Internal Revenue Service

# Installment Sale Income

▶ Attach to your tax return.
▶ Use a separate form for each sale or other disposition of property on the installment method.

OMB No. 1545-0228

2010

Attachment Sequence No. 79

Name(s) shown on return | **Identifying number**

1 Description of property ▶

2a Date acquired (mm/dd/yyyy) ▶ ______ **b** Date sold (mm/dd/yyyy) ▶ ______

3 Was the property sold to a related party (see instructions) after May 14, 1980? If "No," skip line 4 . . . . ☐ Yes ☐ No

4 Was the property you sold to a related party a marketable security? If "Yes," complete Part III. If "No," complete Part III for the year of sale and the 2 years after the year of sale . . . . ☐ Yes ☐ No

**Part I Gross Profit and Contract Price.** Complete this part for the year of sale only.

| | | | | | |
|---|---|---|---|---|---|
| 5 | Selling price including mortgages and other debts. **Do not** include interest, whether stated or unstated | | | 5 | |
| 6 | Mortgages, debts, and other liabilities the buyer assumed or took the property subject to (see instructions) | 6 | | | |
| 7 | Subtract line 6 from line 5 | 7 | | | |
| 8 | Cost or other basis of property sold | 8 | | | |
| 9 | Depreciation allowed or allowable | 9 | | | |
| 10 | Adjusted basis. Subtract line 9 from line 8 | 10 | | | |
| 11 | Commissions and other expenses of sale | 11 | | | |
| 12 | Income recapture from Form 4797, Part III (see instructions) | 12 | | | |
| 13 | Add lines 10, 11, and 12 | | | 13 | |
| 14 | Subtract line 13 from line 5. If zero or less, **do not** complete the rest of this form (see instructions) | | | 14 | |
| 15 | If the property described on line 1 above was your main home, enter the amount of your excluded gain (see instructions). Otherwise, enter -0- | | | 15 | |
| 16 | **Gross profit.** Subtract line 15 from line 14 | | | 16 | |
| 17 | Subtract line 13 from line 6. If zero or less, enter -0- | | | 17 | |
| 18 | **Contract price.** Add line 7 and line 17 | | | 18 | |

**Part II Installment Sale Income.** Complete this part for the year of sale **and** any year you receive a payment or have certain debts you must treat as a payment on installment obligations.

| | | | | | |
|---|---|---|---|---|---|
| 19 | Gross profit percentage (expressed as a decimal amount). Divide line 16 by line 18. For years after the year of sale, see instructions | | | 19 | |
| 20 | If this is the year of sale, enter the amount from line 17. Otherwise, enter -0- | | | 20 | |
| 21 | Payments received during year (see instructions). **Do not** include interest, whether stated or unstated | | | 21 | |
| 22 | Add lines 20 and 21 | | | 22 | |
| 23 | Payments received in prior years (see instructions). **Do not** include interest, whether stated or unstated | 23 | | | |
| 24 | **Installment sale income.** Multiply line 22 by line 19 | | | 24 | |
| 25 | Enter the part of line 24 that is ordinary income under the recapture rules (see instructions) | | | 25 | |
| 26 | Subtract line 25 from line 24. Enter here and on Schedule D or Form 4797 (see instructions) | | | 26 | |

**Part III Related Party Installment Sale Income. Do not** complete if you received the final payment this tax year.

27 Name, address, and taxpayer identifying number of related party

28 Did the related party resell or dispose of the property ("second disposition") during this tax year? . . . . . ☐ Yes ☐ No

29 **If the answer to question 28 is "Yes," complete lines 30 through 37 below unless one of the following conditions is met. Check the box that applies.**

a ☐ The second disposition was more than 2 years after the first disposition (other than dispositions of marketable securities). If this box is checked, enter the date of disposition (mm/dd/yyyy) . . . . . ▶ ______

b ☐ The first disposition was a sale or exchange of stock to the issuing corporation.

c ☐ The second disposition was an involuntary conversion and the threat of conversion occurred after the first disposition.

d ☐ The second disposition occurred after the death of the original seller or buyer.

e ☐ It can be established to the satisfaction of the Internal Revenue Service that tax avoidance was not a principal purpose for either of the dispositions. If this box is checked, attach an explanation (see instructions).

| | | | |
|---|---|---|---|
| 30 | Selling price of property sold by related party (see instructions) | 30 | |
| 31 | Enter contract price from line 18 for year of first sale | 31 | |
| 32 | Enter the **smaller** of line 30 or line 31 | 32 | |
| 33 | Total payments received by the end of your 2010 tax year (see instructions) | 33 | |
| 34 | Subtract line 33 from line 32. If zero or less, enter -0- | 34 | |
| 35 | Multiply line 34 by the gross profit percentage on line 19 for year of first sale | 35 | |
| 36 | Enter the part of line 35 that is ordinary income under the recapture rules (see instructions) | 36 | |
| 37 | Subtract line 36 from line 35. Enter here and on Schedule D or Form 4797 (see instructions) | 37 | |

**For Paperwork Reduction Act Notice, see page 4.** Cat. No. 13601R Form **6252** (2010)

Form **8283**

(Rev. December 2006)

Department of the Treasury
Internal Revenue Service

# Noncash Charitable Contributions

▶ **Attach to your tax return if you claimed a total deduction of over $500 for all contributed property.**

▶ **See separate instructions.**

OMB No. 1545-0908

Attachment Sequence No. **155**

Name(s) shown on your income tax return

**Identifying number**

**Note.** Figure the amount of your contribution deduction before completing this form. See your tax return instructions.

**Section A. Donated Property of $5,000 or Less and Certain Publicly Traded Securities**—List in this section **only** items (or groups of similar items) for which you claimed a deduction of $5,000 or less. Also, list certain publicly traded securities even if the deduction is more than $5,000 (see instructions).

**Part I Information on Donated Property**—If you need more space, attach a statement.

| 1 | **(a)** Name and address of the donee organization | **(b)** Description of donated property (For a donated vehicle, enter the year, make, model, condition, and mileage, and attach Form 1098-C if required.) |
|---|---|---|
| A | | |
| B | | |
| C | | |
| D | | |
| E | | |

**Note.** If the amount you claimed as a deduction for an item is $500 or less, you do not have to complete columns (d), (e), and (f).

| | **(c)** Date of the contribution | **(d)** Date acquired by donor (mo., yr.) | **(e)** How acquired by donor | **(f)** Donor's cost or adjusted basis | **(g)** Fair market value (see instructions) | **(h)** Method used to determine the fair market value |
|---|---|---|---|---|---|---|
| A | | | | | | |
| B | | | | | | |
| C | | | | | | |
| D | | | | | | |
| E | | | | | | |

**Part II Partial Interests and Restricted Use Property**—Complete lines 2a through 2e if you gave less than an entire interest in a property listed in Part I. Complete lines 3a through 3c if conditions were placed on a contribution listed in Part I; also attach the required statement (see instructions).

**2a** Enter the letter from Part I that identifies the property for which you gave less than an entire interest ▶ ________ .
If Part II applies to more than one property, attach a separate statement.

**b** Total amount claimed as a deduction for the property listed in Part I: **(1)** For this tax year ▶ ________ .
**(2)** For any prior tax years ▶ ________ .

**c** Name and address of each organization to which any such contribution was made in a prior year (complete only if different from the donee organization above):

Name of charitable organization (donee)

Address (number, street, and room or suite no.)

City or town, state, and ZIP code

**d** For tangible property, enter the place where the property is located or kept ▶ ________

**e** Name of any person, other than the donee organization, having actual possession of the property ▶ ________

| | | Yes | No |
|---|---|---|---|
| **3a** | Is there a restriction, either temporary or permanent, on the donee's right to use or dispose of the donated property? . . . . . . . . . . . . . . . . . . . . . . . . . . . . . . . . . . | | |
| **b** | Did you give to anyone (other than the donee organization or another organization participating with the donee organization in cooperative fundraising) the right to the income from the donated property or to the possession of the property, including the right to vote donated securities, to acquire the property by purchase or otherwise, or to designate the person having such income, possession, or right to acquire? . . . . . . . . . . . . . | | |
| **c** | Is there a restriction limiting the donated property for a particular use? . . . . . . . . . . . . . . | | |

**For Paperwork Reduction Act Notice, see separate instructions.** Cat. No. 62299J Form **8283** (Rev. 12-2006)

Form 8283 (Rev. 12-2006) Page **2**

| Name(s) shown on your income tax return | **Identifying number** |
|---|---|
| | |

**Section B. Donated Property Over $5,000 (Except Certain Publicly Traded Securities)**—List in this section only items (or groups of similar items) for which you claimed a deduction of more than $5,000 per item or group (except contributions of certain publicly traded securities reported in Section A). An appraisal is generally required for property listed in Section B (see instructions).

**Part I** **Information on Donated Property**—To be completed by the taxpayer and/or the appraiser.

**4** Check the box that describes the type of property donated:

☐ Art* (contribution of $20,000 or more) ☐ Qualified Conservation Contribution ☐ Equipment
☐ Art* (contribution of less than $20,000) ☐ Other Real Estate ☐ Securities
☐ Collectibles** ☐ Intellectual Property ☐ Other

*Art includes paintings, sculptures, watercolors, prints, drawings, ceramics, antiques, decorative arts, textiles, carpets, silver, rare manuscripts, historical memorabilia, and other similar objects.

**Collectibles include coins, stamps, books, gems, jewelry, sports memorabilia, dolls, etc., but not art as defined above.

**Note.** In certain cases, you must attach a qualified appraisal of the property. See instructions.

| 5 | **(a)** Description of donated property (if you need more space, attach a separate statement) | **(b)** If tangible property was donated, give a brief summary of the overall physical condition of the property at the time of the gift | **(c)** Appraised fair market value |
|---|---|---|---|
| A | | | |
| B | | | |
| C | | | |
| D | | | |

| | **(d)** Date acquired by donor (mo., yr.) | **(e)** How acquired by donor | **(f)** Donor's cost or adjusted basis | **(g)** For bargain sales, enter amount received | See instructions: **(h)** Amount claimed as a deduction | See instructions: **(i)** Average trading price of securities |
|---|---|---|---|---|---|---|
| A | | | | | | |
| B | | | | | | |
| C | | | | | | |
| D | | | | | | |

**Part II** **Taxpayer (Donor) Statement**—List each item included in Part I above that the appraisal identifies as having a value of $500 or less. See instructions.

I declare that the following item(s) included in Part I above has to the best of my knowledge and belief an appraised value of not more than $500 (per item). Enter identifying letter from Part I and describe the specific item. See instructions. ▶ ____________

Signature of taxpayer (donor) ▶ Date ▶

**Part III** **Declaration of Appraiser**

I declare that I am not the donor, the donee, a party to the transaction in which the donor acquired the property, employed by, or related to any of the foregoing persons, or married to any person who is related to any of the foregoing persons. And, if regularly used by the donor, donee, or party to the transaction, I performed the majority of my appraisals during my tax year for other persons.

Also, I declare that I hold myself out to the public as an appraiser or perform appraisals on a regular basis; and that because of my qualifications as described in the appraisal, I am qualified to make appraisals of the type of property being valued. I certify that the appraisal fees were not based on a percentage of the appraised property value. Furthermore, I understand that a false or fraudulent overstatement of the property value as described in the qualified appraisal or this Form 8283 may subject me to the penalty under section 6701(a) (aiding and abetting the understatement of tax liability). In addition, I understand that a substantial or gross valuation misstatement resulting from the appraisal of the value of the property that I know, or reasonably should know, would be used in connection with a return or claim for refund, may subject me to the penalty under section 6695A. I affirm that I have not been barred from presenting evidence or testimony by the Office of Professional Responsibility.

**Sign Here** Signature ▶ Title ▶ Date ▶

| Business address (including room or suite no.) | **Identifying number** |
|---|---|
| City or town, state, and ZIP code | |

**Part IV** **Donee Acknowledgment**—To be completed by the charitable organization.

This charitable organization acknowledges that it is a qualified organization under section 170(c) and that it received the donated property as described in Section B, Part I, above on the following date ▶ ____________

Furthermore, this organization affirms that in the event it sells, exchanges, or otherwise disposes of the property described in Section B, Part I (or any portion thereof) within 3 years after the date of receipt, it will file **Form 8282,** Donee Information Return, with the IRS and give the donor a copy of that form. This acknowledgment does not represent agreement with the claimed fair market value.

Does the organization intend to use the property for an unrelated use? . . . . . . . . . . . . . . . . ▶ ☐ Yes ☐ No

| Name of charitable organization (donee) | **Employer identification number** | |
|---|---|---|
| Address (number, street, and room or suite no.) | City or town, state, and ZIP code | |
| Authorized signature | Title | Date |

*Printed on Recycled Paper* Form **8283** (Rev. 12-2006)

Form **8582**

Department of the Treasury
Internal Revenue Service (99)

# Passive Activity Loss Limitations

▶ See separate instructions.
▶ Attach to Form 1040 or Form 1041.

OMB No. 1545-1008

**2010**

Attachment Sequence No. **88**

Name(s) shown on return | **Identifying number**

**Part I** **2010 Passive Activity Loss**

**Caution:** *Complete Worksheets 1, 2, and 3 on page 2 before completing Part I.*

**Rental Real Estate Activities With Active Participation** (For the definition of active participation, see **Special Allowance for Rental Real Estate Activities** on page 3 of the instructions.)

| | | | | | |
|---|---|---|---|---|---|
| 1a | Activities with net income (enter the amount from Worksheet 1, column (a)) | 1a | | | |
| b | Activities with net loss (enter the amount from Worksheet 1, column (b)) | 1b | ( ) | | |
| c | Prior years unallowed losses (enter the amount from Worksheet 1, column (c)) | 1c | ( ) | | |
| d | Combine lines 1a, 1b, and 1c | | | 1d | |

**Commercial Revitalization Deductions From Rental Real Estate Activities**

| | | | | | |
|---|---|---|---|---|---|
| 2a | Commercial revitalization deductions from Worksheet 2, column (a) | 2a | ( ) | | |
| b | Prior year unallowed commercial revitalization deductions from Worksheet 2, column (b) | 2b | ( ) | | |
| c | Add lines 2a and 2b | | | 2c | ( ) |

**All Other Passive Activities**

| | | | | | |
|---|---|---|---|---|---|
| 3a | Activities with net income (enter the amount from Worksheet 3, column (a)) | 3a | | | |
| b | Activities with net loss (enter the amount from Worksheet 3, column (b)) | 3b | ( ) | | |
| c | Prior years unallowed losses (enter the amount from Worksheet 3, column (c)) | 3c | ( ) | | |
| d | Combine lines 3a, 3b, and 3c | | | 3d | |
| 4 | Combine lines 1d, 2c, and 3d. If the result is net income or zero, all losses are allowed, including any prior year unallowed losses entered on line 1c, 2b, or 3c. **Do not** complete Form 8582. Report the losses on the forms and schedules normally used | | | 4 | |

If line 4 is a loss and:
- Line 1d is a loss, go to Part II.
- Line 2c is a loss (and line 1d is zero or more), skip Part II and go to Part III.
- Line 3d is a loss (and lines 1d and 2c are zero or more), skip Parts II and III and go to line 15.

**Caution:** *If your filing status is married filing separately and you lived with your spouse at any time during the year,* **do not** *complete Part II or Part III. Instead, go to line 15.*

**Part II** **Special Allowance for Rental Real Estate Activities With Active Participation**

**Note:** *Enter all numbers in Part II as positive amounts. See page 9 of the instructions for an example.*

| | | | | | |
|---|---|---|---|---|---|
| 5 | Enter the **smaller** of the loss on line 1d or the loss on line 4 | | | 5 | |
| 6 | Enter $150,000. If married filing separately, see page 9 | 6 | | | |
| 7 | Enter modified adjusted gross income, but not less than zero (see page 9) | 7 | | | |
| | **Note:** *If line 7 is greater than or equal to line 6, skip lines 8 and 9, enter -0- on line 10. Otherwise, go to line 8.* | | | | |
| 8 | Subtract line 7 from line 6 | 8 | | | |
| 9 | Multiply line 8 by 50% (.5). **Do not** enter more than $25,000. If married filing separately, see page 9 | | | 9 | |
| 10 | Enter the **smaller** of line 5 or line 9 | | | 10 | |

If line 2c is a loss, go to Part III. Otherwise, go to line 15.

**Part III** **Special Allowance for Commercial Revitalization Deductions From Rental Real Estate Activities**

**Note:** *Enter all numbers in Part III as positive amounts. See the example for Part II on page 9 of the instructions.*

| | | | |
|---|---|---|---|
| 11 | Enter $25,000 reduced by the amount, if any, on line 10. If married filing separately, see instructions | 11 | |
| 12 | Enter the loss from line 4 | 12 | |
| 13 | Reduce line 12 by the amount on line 10 | 13 | |
| 14 | Enter the **smallest** of line 2c (treated as a positive amount), line 11, or line 13 | 14 | |

**Part IV** **Total Losses Allowed**

| | | | |
|---|---|---|---|
| 15 | Add the income, if any, on lines 1a and 3a and enter the total | 15 | |
| 16 | **Total losses allowed from all passive activities for 2010.** Add lines 10, 14, and 15. See page 11 of the instructions to find out how to report the losses on your tax return | 16 | |

**For Paperwork Reduction Act Notice, see page 13 of the instructions.** Cat. No. 63704F Form **8582** (2010)

Form 8582 (2010) Page **2**

**Caution:** *The worksheets must be filed with your tax return. Keep a copy for your records.*

**Worksheet 1—For Form 8582, Lines 1a, 1b, and 1c** (See page 8 of the instructions.)

| Name of activity | Current year | | Prior years | Overall gain or loss | |
|---|---|---|---|---|---|
| | (a) Net income (line 1a) | (b) Net loss (line 1b) | (c) Unallowed loss (line 1c) | (d) Gain | (e) Loss |
| | | | | | |
| | | | | | |
| | | | | | |
| | | | | | |
| | | | | | |
| Total. Enter on Form 8582, lines 1a, 1b, and 1c . . . . . . . . . . . . ▶ | | | | | |

**Worksheet 2—For Form 8582, Lines 2a and 2b** (See page 8 of the instructions.)

| Name of activity | (a) Current year deductions (line 2a) | (b) Prior year unallowed deductions (line 2b) | (c) Overall loss |
|---|---|---|---|
| | | | |
| | | | |
| | | | |
| | | | |
| Total. Enter on Form 8582, lines 2a and 2b . . . . . . . . . . . . . ▶ | | | |

**Worksheet 3—For Form 8582, Lines 3a, 3b, and 3c** (See page 8 of the instructions.)

| Name of activity | Current year | | Prior years | Overall gain or loss | |
|---|---|---|---|---|---|
| | (a) Net income (line 3a) | (b) Net loss (line 3b) | (c) Unallowed loss (line 3c) | (d) Gain | (e) Loss |
| | | | | | |
| | | | | | |
| | | | | | |
| | | | | | |
| | | | | | |
| Total. Enter on Form 8582, lines 3a, 3b, and 3c . . . . . . . . . . . . ▶ | | | | | |

**Worksheet 4—Use this worksheet if an amount is shown on Form 8582, line 10 or 14** (See page 9 of the instructions.)

| Name of activity | Form or schedule and line number to be reported on (see instructions) | (a) Loss | (b) Ratio | (c) Special allowance | (d) Subtract column (c) from column (a) |
|---|---|---|---|---|---|
| | | | | | |
| | | | | | |
| | | | | | |
| | | | | | |
| | | | | | |
| Total . . . . . . . . . . . . . . . . . . . . . ▶ | | | 1.00 | | |

**Worksheet 5—Allocation of Unallowed Losses** (See page 10 of the instructions.)

| Name of activity | Form or schedule and line number to be reported on (see instructions) | (a) Loss | (b) Ratio | (c) Unallowed loss |
|---|---|---|---|---|
| | | | | |
| | | | | |
| | | | | |
| | | | | |
| | | | | |
| Total . . . . . . . . . . . . . . . . . . . . . . . ▶ | | | 1.00 | |

Form **8582** (2010)

Form 8582 (2010) Page 3

**Worksheet 6—Allowed Losses** (See page 10 of the instructions.)

| Name of activity | Form or schedule and line number to be reported on (see instructions) | (a) Loss | (b) Unallowed loss | (c) Allowed loss |
|---|---|---|---|---|
| | | | | |
| | | | | |
| | | | | |
| | | | | |
| | | | | |
| Total . . . . . . . . . . . . . . . . . . . . . . . . ▶ | | | | |

**Worksheet 7—Activities With Losses Reported on Two or More Forms or Schedules** (See page 10 of the instructions.)

| Name of activity: | (a) | (b) | (c) Ratio | (d) Unallowed loss | (e) Allowed loss |
|---|---|---|---|---|---|
| Form or schedule and line number to be reported on (see instructions): | | | | | |
| 1a Net loss plus prior year unallowed loss from form or schedule . ▶ | | | | | |
| b Net income from form or schedule . . . . . . . ▶ | | | | | |
| c Subtract line 1b from line 1a. If zero or less, enter -0- ▶ | | | | | |
| Form or schedule and line number to be reported on (see instructions): | | | | | |
| 1a Net loss plus prior year unallowed loss from form or schedule . ▶ | | | | | |
| b Net income from form or schedule . . . . . . . ▶ | | | | | |
| c Subtract line 1b from line 1a. If zero or less, enter -0- ▶ | | | | | |
| Form or schedule and line number to be reported on (see instructions): | | | | | |
| 1a Net loss plus prior year unallowed loss from form or schedule . ▶ | | | | | |
| b Net income from form or schedule . . . . . . . ▶ | | | | | |
| c Subtract line 1b from line 1a. If zero or less, enter -0- ▶ | | | | | |
| Total . . . . . . . . . . . . . . . . . . . . . ▶ | | | 1.00 | | |

Form **8582** (2010)

Form **8615**

Department of the Treasury
Internal Revenue Service (99)

# Tax for Certain Children Who Have Investment Income of More Than $1,900

▶ Attach only to the child's Form 1040, Form 1040A, or Form 1040NR.
▶ See separate instructions.

OMB No. 1545-0074
2010
Attachment Sequence No. 33

Child's name shown on return | Child's social security number

***Before you begin:*** If the child, the parent, or any of the parent's other children for whom Form 8615 must be filed must use the Schedule D Tax Worksheet or has income from farming or fishing, see **Pub. 929,** Tax Rules for Children and Dependents. It explains how to figure the child's tax using the **Schedule D Tax Worksheet** or **Schedule J** (Form 1040).

**A** Parent's name (first, initial, and last). **Caution:** *See instructions before completing.* | **B** Parent's social security number

**C** Parent's filing status (check one):
☐ Single ☐ Married filing jointly ☐ Married filing separately ☐ Head of household ☐ Qualifying widow(er)

## Part I Child's Net Investment Income

| | | | |
|---|---|---|---|
| 1 | Enter the child's investment income (see instructions) | 1 | |
| 2 | If the child **did not** itemize deductions on **Schedule A** (Form 1040 or Form 1040NR), enter $1,900. Otherwise, see instructions | 2 | |
| 3 | Subtract line 2 from line 1. If zero or less, **stop;** do not complete the rest of this form but **do** attach it to the child's return | 3 | |
| 4 | Enter the child's **taxable income** from Form 1040, line 43; Form 1040A, line 27; or Form 1040NR, line 41. If the child files Form 2555 or 2555-EZ, see the instructions | 4 | |
| 5 | Enter the **smaller** of line 3 or line 4. If zero, **stop;** do not complete the rest of this form but **do** attach it to the child's return | 5 | |

## Part II Tentative Tax Based on the Tax Rate of the Parent

| | | | |
|---|---|---|---|
| 6 | Enter the parent's **taxable income** from Form 1040, line 43; Form 1040A, line 27; Form 1040EZ, line 6; Form 1040NR, line 41; or Form 1040NR-EZ, line 14. If zero or less, enter -0-. If the parent files Form 2555 or 2555-EZ, see the instructions | 6 | |
| 7 | Enter the total, if any, from Forms 8615, line 5, of **all other** children of the parent named above. **Do not** include the amount from line 5 above | 7 | |
| 8 | Add lines 5, 6, and 7 (see instructions) | 8 | |
| 9 | Enter the tax on the amount on line 8 based on the **parent's** filing status above (see instructions). If the Qualified Dividends and Capital Gain Tax Worksheet, Schedule D Tax Worksheet, or Schedule J (Form 1040) is used to figure the tax, check here ▶ ☐ | 9 | |
| 10 | Enter the parent's tax from Form 1040, line 44; Form 1040A, line 28, minus any alternative minimum tax; Form 1040EZ, line 11; Form 1040NR, line 42; or Form 1040NR-EZ, line 15. **Do not** include any tax from **Form 4972** or **8814** or any tax from recapture of an education credit. If the parent files Form 2555 or 2555-EZ, see the instructions. If the Qualified Dividends and Capital Gain Tax Worksheet, Schedule D Tax Worksheet, or Schedule J (Form 1040) was used to figure the tax, check here ▶ ☐ | 10 | |
| 11 | Subtract line 10 from line 9 and enter the result. If line 7 is blank, also enter this amount on line 13 and go to **Part III** | 11 | |
| 12a | Add lines 5 and 7 (12a) | | |
| b | Divide line 5 by line 12a. Enter the result as a decimal (rounded to at least three places) | 12b | × . |
| 13 | Multiply line 11 by line 12b | 13 | |

## Part III Child's Tax—If lines 4 and 5 above are the same, enter -0- on line 15 and go to line 16.

| | | | |
|---|---|---|---|
| 14 | Subtract line 5 from line 4 (14) | | |
| 15 | Enter the tax on the amount on line 14 based on the **child's** filing status (see instructions). If the Qualified Dividends and Capital Gain Tax Worksheet, Schedule D Tax Worksheet, or Schedule J (Form 1040) is used to figure the tax, check here ▶ ☐ | 15 | |
| 16 | Add lines 13 and 15 | 16 | |
| 17 | Enter the tax on the amount on line 4 based on the **child's** filing status (see instructions). If the Qualified Dividends and Capital Gain Tax Worksheet, Schedule D Tax Worksheet, or Schedule J (Form 1040) is used to figure the tax, check here ▶ ☐ | 17 | |
| 18 | Enter the **larger** of line 16 or line 17 here and on the **child's** Form 1040, line 44; Form 1040A, line 28; or Form 1040NR, line 42. If the child files Form 2555 or 2555-EZ, see the instructions | 18 | |

**For Paperwork Reduction Act Notice, see your tax return instructions.** Cat. No. 64113U Form **8615** (2010)

Form **8814**

Department of the Treasury
Internal Revenue Service (99)

# Parents' Election To Report Child's Interest and Dividends

▶ See instructions.
▶ Attach to parents' Form 1040 or Form 1040NR.

OMB No. 1545-0074

**2010**

Attachment Sequence No. **40**

| Name(s) shown on your return | **Your social security number** |
|---|---|
| | |

**Caution.** The federal income tax on your child's income, including qualified dividends and capital gain distributions, may be less if you file a separate tax return for the child instead of making this election. This is because you cannot take certain tax benefits that your child could take on his or her own return. For details, see **Tax benefits you cannot take** on page 3.

| **A** Child's name (first, initial, and last) | **B Child's social security number** |
|---|---|
| | |

**C** If more than one Form 8814 is attached, check here . . . . . . . . . . . . . . . . . . . . . . . . ▶ ☐

## Part I Child's Interest and Dividends To Report on Your Return

| | | | | | |
|---|---|---|---|---|---|
| **1a** | Enter your child's **taxable** interest. If this amount is different from the amounts shown on the child's Forms 1099-INT and 1099-OID, see the instructions . . . . . . . . . . . . . | | | 1a | |
| **b** | Enter your child's **tax-exempt** interest. **Do not** include this amount on line 1a . . . . . . . . . . . . . . . . . . . . . | 1b | | | |
| **2a** | Enter your child's ordinary dividends, including any Alaska Permanent Fund dividends. If your child received any ordinary dividends as a nominee, see the instructions . . . . . . . . . | | | 2a | |
| **b** | Enter your child's qualified dividends included on line 2a. See the instructions . . . . . . . . . . . . . . . . . . . . | 2b | | | |
| **3** | Enter your child's capital gain distributions. If your child received any capital gain distributions as a nominee, see the instructions . . . . . . . . . . . . . . . . . . . . . . | | | 3 | |
| **4** | Add lines 1a, 2a, and 3. If the total is $1,900 or less, skip lines 5 through 12 and go to line 13. If the total is $9,500 or more, **do not** file this form. Your child **must** file his or her own return to report the income . . . . . . . . . . . . . . . . . . . . . . . . . | | | 4 | |
| **5** | Base amount . . . . . . . . . . . . . . . . . . . . . . . . . . . | | | 5 | 1,900 00 |
| **6** | Subtract line 5 from line 4 . . . . . . . . . . . . . . . . . . . . . . . | | | 6 | |
| | **If both lines 2b and 3 are zero or blank, skip lines 7 through 10, enter -0- on line 11, and go to line 12. Otherwise, go to line 7.** | | | | |
| **7** | Divide line 2b by line 4. Enter the result as a decimal (rounded to at least three places) . . . . . . . . . . . . . . . . . . | 7 | . | | |
| **8** | Divide line 3 by line 4. Enter the result as a decimal (rounded to at least three places) . . . . . . . . . . . . . . . . . . | 8 | . | | |
| **9** | Multiply line 6 by line 7. Enter the result here. See the instructions for where to report this amount on your return . . . . . . . | 9 | | | |
| **10** | Multiply line 6 by line 8. Enter the result here. See the instructions for where to report this amount on your return . . . . . . . | 10 | | | |
| **11** | Add lines 9 and 10 . . . . . . . . . . . . . . . . . . . . . . . . . . . | | | 11 | |
| **12** | Subtract line 11 from line 6. Include this amount in the total on Form 1040, line 21, or Form 1040NR, line 21. In the space next to line 21, enter "Form 8814" and show the amount. If you checked the box on line C above, see the instructions. Go to line 13 below . . . . . . . | | | 12 | |

## Part II Tax on the First $1,900 of Child's Interest and Dividends

| | | | |
|---|---|---|---|
| **13** | Amount not taxed . . . . . . . . . . . . . . . . . . . . . . . . . . | 13 | 950 00 |
| **14** | Subtract line 13 from line 4. If the result is zero or less, enter -0- . . . . . . . . . . . . | 14 | |
| **15** | **Tax.** Is the amount on line 14 less than $950?<br>☐ **No.** Enter $95 here and see the **Note** below.<br>☐ **Yes.** Multiply line 14 by 10% (.10). Enter the result here and see the **Note** below. . . . | 15 | |

**Note.** If you checked the box on line C above, see the instructions. Otherwise, include the amount from line 15 in the tax you enter on Form 1040, line 44, or Form 1040NR, line 42. Be sure to check box **a** on Form 1040, line 44, or Form 1040NR, line 42.

**For Paperwork Reduction Act Notice, see your tax return instructions.** Cat. No. 10750J Form **8814** (2010)

Form **8829**

Department of the Treasury
Internal Revenue Service (99)

# Expenses for Business Use of Your Home

▶ **File only with Schedule C (Form 1040). Use a separate Form 8829 for each home you used for business during the year.**

▶ **See separate instructions.**

OMB No. 1545-0074

**2010**

Attachment Sequence No. **176**

| Name(s) of proprietor(s) | Your social security number |
|---|---|
| | |

## Part I Part of Your Home Used for Business

| | | | |
|---|---|---|---|
| 1 | Area used regularly and exclusively for business, regularly for daycare, or for storage of inventory or product samples (see instructions) | 1 | |
| 2 | Total area of home | 2 | |
| 3 | Divide line 1 by line 2. Enter the result as a percentage | 3 | % |
| | **For daycare facilities not used exclusively for business, go to line 4. All others go to line 7.** | | |
| 4 | Multiply days used for daycare during year by hours used per day — 4: hr. | | |
| 5 | Total hours available for use during the year (365 days x 24 hours) (see instructions) — 5: 8,760 hr. | | |
| 6 | Divide line 4 by line 5. Enter the result as a decimal amount — 6: . | | |
| 7 | Business percentage. For daycare facilities not used exclusively for business, multiply line 6 by line 3 (enter the result as a percentage). All others, enter the amount from line 3 ▶ | 7 | % |

## Part II Figure Your Allowable Deduction

| | | | (a) Direct expenses | (b) Indirect expenses | | |
|---|---|---|---|---|---|---|
| 8 | Enter the amount from Schedule C, line 29, **plus** any net gain or (loss) derived from the business use of your home and shown on Schedule D or Form 4797. If more than one place of business, see instructions | | | | 8 | |
| | **See instructions for columns (a) and (b) before completing lines 9–21.** | | | | | |
| 9 | Casualty losses (see instructions) | 9 | | | | |
| 10 | Deductible mortgage interest (see instructions) | 10 | | | | |
| 11 | Real estate taxes (see instructions) | 11 | | | | |
| 12 | Add lines 9, 10, and 11 | 12 | | | | |
| 13 | Multiply line 12, column (b) by line 7 | | 13 | | | |
| 14 | Add line 12, column (a) and line 13 | | | | 14 | |
| 15 | Subtract line 14 from line 8. If zero or less, enter -0- | | | | 15 | |
| 16 | Excess mortgage interest (see instructions) | 16 | | | | |
| 17 | Insurance | 17 | | | | |
| 18 | Rent | 18 | | | | |
| 19 | Repairs and maintenance | 19 | | | | |
| 20 | Utilities | 20 | | | | |
| 21 | Other expenses (see instructions) | 21 | | | | |
| 22 | Add lines 16 through 21 | 22 | | | | |
| 23 | Multiply line 22, column (b) by line 7 | | 23 | | | |
| 24 | Carryover of operating expenses from 2009 Form 8829, line 42 | | 24 | | | |
| 25 | Add line 22 column (a), line 23, and line 24 | | | | 25 | |
| 26 | Allowable operating expenses. Enter the **smaller** of line 15 or line 25 | | | | 26 | |
| 27 | Limit on excess casualty losses and depreciation. Subtract line 26 from line 15 | | | | 27 | |
| 28 | Excess casualty losses (see instructions) | | 28 | | | |
| 29 | Depreciation of your home from line 41 below | | 29 | | | |
| 30 | Carryover of excess casualty losses and depreciation from 2009 Form 8829, line 43 | | 30 | | | |
| 31 | Add lines 28 through 30 | | | | 31 | |
| 32 | Allowable excess casualty losses and depreciation. Enter the **smaller** of line 27 or line 31 | | | | 32 | |
| 33 | Add lines 14, 26, and 32 | | | | 33 | |
| 34 | Casualty loss portion, if any, from lines 14 and 32. Carry amount to **Form 4684** (see instructions) | | | | 34 | |
| 35 | **Allowable expenses for business use of your home.** Subtract line 34 from line 33. Enter here and on Schedule C, line 30. If your home was used for more than one business, see instructions ▶ | | | | 35 | |

## Part III Depreciation of Your Home

| | | | |
|---|---|---|---|
| 36 | Enter the **smaller** of your home's adjusted basis or its fair market value (see instructions) | 36 | |
| 37 | Value of land included on line 36 | 37 | |
| 38 | Basis of building. Subtract line 37 from line 36 | 38 | |
| 39 | Business basis of building. Multiply line 38 by line 7 | 39 | |
| 40 | Depreciation percentage (see instructions) | 40 | % |
| 41 | Depreciation allowable (see instructions). Multiply line 39 by line 40. Enter here and on line 29 above | 41 | |

## Part IV Carryover of Unallowed Expenses to 2011

| | | | |
|---|---|---|---|
| 42 | Operating expenses. Subtract line 26 from line 25. If less than zero, enter -0- | 42 | |
| 43 | Excess casualty losses and depreciation. Subtract line 32 from line 31. If less than zero, enter -0- | 43 | |

**For Paperwork Reduction Act Notice, see your tax return instructions.** Cat. No. 13232M Form **8829** (2010)

Form **8863**

Department of the Treasury Internal Revenue Service (99)

# Education Credits (American Opportunity and Lifetime Learning Credits)

**▶ See separate instructions to find out if you are eligible to take the credits.**
**▶ Attach to Form 1040 or Form 1040A.**

OMB No. 1545-0074

**2010**

Attachment Sequence No. **50**

Name(s) shown on return | **Your social security number**

CAUTION

***You cannot*** *take both an education credit and the tuition and fees deduction (see Form 8917) for the* ***same student*** *for the same year.*

## Part I American Opportunity Credit

**Caution:** *You* ***cannot*** *take the American opportunity credit for more than* ***4*** *tax years for the* ***same student.***

| 1 | **(a)** Student's name (as shown on page 1 of your tax return) First name / Last name | **(b)** Student's social security number (as shown on page 1 of your tax return) | **(c)** Qualified expenses (see instructions). **Do not** enter more than $4,000 for each student. | **(d)** Subtract $2,000 from the amount in column (c). If zero or less, enter -0-. | **(e)** Multiply the amount in column (d) by 25% (.25) | **(f)** If column (d) is zero, enter the amount from column (c). Otherwise, add $2,000 to the amount in column (e). |
|---|---|---|---|---|---|---|
| | | | | | | |
| | | | | | | |
| | | | | | | |

2 **Tentative American opportunity credit.** Add the amounts on line 1, column (f). If you are taking the lifetime learning credit for a different student, go to Part II; otherwise, go to Part III . . . . . . ▶ | 2 |

## Part II Lifetime Learning Credit

**Caution:** *You* ***cannot*** *take the American opportunity credit and the lifetime learning credit for the* ***same student*** *in the same year.*

| 3 | **(a)** Student's name (as shown on page 1 of your tax return) First name | Last name | **(b)** Student's social security number (as shown on page 1 of your tax return) | **(c)** Qualified expenses (see instructions) |
|---|---|---|---|---|
| | | | | |
| | | | | |
| | | | | |

| | | | |
|---|---|---|---|
| 4 | Add the amounts on line 3, column (c), and enter the total . . . . . . . . . . . . . . . . . . . | 4 | |
| 5 | Enter the **smaller** of line 4 or $10,000 . . . . . . . . . . . . . . . . . . . . . . | 5 | |
| 6 | **Tentative lifetime learning credit.** Multiply line 5 by 20% (.20). If you have an entry on line 2, go to Part III; otherwise go to Part IV . . . . . . . . . . . . . . . . . . . . . . . . | 6 | |

**For Paperwork Reduction Act Notice, see your tax return instructions.** Cat. No. 25379M Form **8863** (2010)

Form **8917**

Department of the Treasury
Internal Revenue Service

# Tuition and Fees Deduction

**See Instructions.**
**Attach to Form 1040 or Form 1040A.**

OMB No. 1545-0074
**2010**
Attachment Sequence No. **60**

Name(s) shown on return | **Your social security number**

CAUTION: *You **cannot** take both an education credit from Form 8863 and the tuition and fees deduction from this form for the **same student** for the same tax year.*

***Before you begin:***
- ✔ To see if you qualify for this deduction, see *Who Can Take the Deduction* in the instructions below.
- ✔ If you file Form 1040, figure any write-in adjustments to be entered on the dotted line next to Form 1040, line 36. See the 2010 Form 1040 instructions for line 36.

| 1 | **(a)** Student's name (as shown on page 1 of your tax return) First name | Last name | **(b)** Student's social security number (as shown on page 1 of your tax return) | **(c)** Qualified expenses (see instructions) |
|---|---|---|---|---|
| | | | | |
| | | | | |
| | | | | |

| | | | | | |
|---|---|---|---|---|---|
| 2 | Add the amounts on line 1, column (c), and enter the total . . . . . . . . . . . . . . | | | 2 | |
| 3 | Enter the amount from Form 1040, line 22, or Form 1040A, line 15 | 3 | | | |
| 4 | Enter the total from either:<br>• Form 1040, lines 23 through 33, plus any write-in adjustments entered on the dotted line next to Form 1040, line 36, **or**<br>• Form 1040A, lines 16 through 18 . . . . . . . . . . . | 4 | | | |
| 5 | Subtract line 4 from line 3.* If the result is more than $80,000 ($160,000 if married filing jointly), **stop**; you cannot take the deduction for tuition and fees . . . . . . . . . . . . . . .<br>*If you are filing Form 2555, 2555-EZ, or 4563, or you are excluding income from Puerto Rico, see *Effect of the Amount of Your Income on the Amount of Your Deduction* in Pub. 970, chapter 6, to figure the amount to enter on line 5. | | | 5 | |
| 6 | **Tuition and fees deduction.** Is the amount on line 5 more than $65,000 ($130,000 if married filing jointly)?<br>☐ **Yes.** Enter the smaller of line 2, or $2,000.<br>☐ **No.** Enter the smaller of line 2, or $4,000. . . . . . . . . . . . . . . . . . .<br>**Also enter** this amount on Form 1040, line 34, or Form 1040A, line 19. | | | 6 | |

Section references are to the Internal Revenue Code unless otherwise noted.

## General Instructions

### Purpose of Form

Use Form 8917 to figure and take the deduction for tuition and fees expenses **paid in 2010.**

This deduction is based on qualified education expenses paid to an eligible postsecondary educational institution. See *What Expenses Qualify,* on page 2, for more information.

TIP: *You may be able to take the American opportunity credit or lifetime learning credit for your education expenses instead of the tuition and fees deduction. Figure your tax both ways and choose the one that gives you the lower tax. See Form 8863, Education Credits, and Pub. 970, Tax Benefits for Education, for more information about these credits.*

### Who Can Take the Deduction

You may be able to take the deduction if you, your spouse, or a dependent you claim on your tax return was a student enrolled at or attending an eligible educational institution. The deduction is based on the amount of qualified education expenses you paid for the student in 2010 for academic periods beginning in 2010 and the first 3 months of 2011.

CAUTION: *Qualified education expenses must be reduced by any expenses paid directly or indirectly using tax-free educational assistance. See* Tax-free educational assistance and refunds of qualified education expenses *on page 2.*

Generally, in order to claim the deduction for qualified education expenses for a dependent, you must have paid the expenses in 2010 and must claim an exemption for the student as a dependent on your 2010 tax return (line 6c of Form 1040 or 1040A). For additional information, see chapter 6 of Pub. 970.

You **cannot** claim the tuition and fees deduction if any of the following apply.

- Your filing status is married filing separately.
- Another person can claim an exemption for you as a dependent on his or her tax return. You cannot take the deduction even if the other person does not actually claim that exemption.
- Your modified adjusted gross income (MAGI), as figured on line 5, is more than $80,000 ($160,000 if filing a joint return).
- You were a nonresident alien for any part of the year and did not elect to be treated as a resident alien for tax purposes. More information on nonresident aliens can be found in Pub. 519, U.S. Tax Guide for Aliens.

# C

# Modified ACRS Tables

## Appendix Outline


Accelerated Depreciation Percentages Using the Half-Year Convention for 3-, 5-, 7-, 10-, 15-, and 20-Year Property C-2

Depreciation Percentages Residential Rental Property (Placed in Service after December 31, 1986) C-3

Depreciation Percentages Nonresidential Real Property (Placed in Service after December 31, 1986 and before May 13, 1993) C-5

Depreciation Percentages for Nonresidential Real Property (Placed in Service after May 13, 1993) C-7

Accelerated Depreciation Percentages Using the Mid-Quarter Convention for 3-, 5-, 7-, 10-, 15-, and 20-Year Property C-8

Alternative Depreciation System Recovery Periods C-10

ACRS and ADS Straight-Line Depreciation Percentages Using the Half-Year Convention for Property with Certain Recovery Periods C-11

ADS Straight-Line Depreciation Percentages Real Property Using the Mid-Month Convention C-12

### Modified ACRS Accelerated Depreciation Percentages Using the Half Year Convention for 3-, 5-, 7-, 10-, 15-, and 20-Year Property Placed in Service after December 31, 1986

| Recovery Year | Property Class | | | | | |
|---|---|---|---|---|---|---|
| | 3-Year | 5-Year | 7-Year | 10-Year | 15-Year | 20-Year |
| 1 | 33.33 | 20.00 | 14.29 | 10.00 | 5.00 | 3.750 |
| 2 | 44.45 | 32.00 | 24.49 | 18.00 | 9.50 | 7.219 |
| 3 | 14.81 | 19.20 | 17.49 | 14.40 | 8.55 | 6.677 |
| 4 | 7.41 | 11.52 | 12.49 | 11.52 | 7.70 | 6.177 |
| 5 | | 11.52 | 8.93 | 9.22 | 6.93 | 5.713 |
| 6 | | 5.76 | 8.92 | 7.37 | 6.23 | 5.285 |
| 7 | | | 8.93 | 6.55 | 5.90 | 4.888 |
| 8 | | | 4.46 | 6.55 | 5.90 | 4.522 |
| 9 | | | | 6.56 | 5.91 | 4.462 |
| 10 | | | | 6.55 | 5.90 | 4.461 |
| 11 | | | | 3.28 | 5.91 | 4.462 |
| 12 | | | | | 5.90 | 4.461 |
| 13 | | | | | 5.91 | 4.462 |
| 14 | | | | | 5.90 | 4.461 |
| 15 | | | | | 5.91 | 4.462 |
| 16 | | | | | 2.95 | 4.461 |
| 17 | | | | | | 4.462 |
| 18 | | | | | | 4.461 |
| 19 | | | | | | 4.462 |
| 20 | | | | | | 4.461 |
| 21 | | | | | | 2.231 |

### Modified ACRS Depreciation Rates for Residential Rental Property Placed in Service after December 31, 1986

| Recovery Year | Month Placed in Service 1 | 2 | 3 | 4 | 5 | 6 |
|---|---|---|---|---|---|---|
| 1 | 3.485 | 3.182 | 2.879 | 2.576 | 2.273 | 1.970 |
| 2 | 3.636 | 3.636 | 3.636 | 3.636 | 3.636 | 3.636 |
| 3 | 3.636 | 3.636 | 3.636 | 3.636 | 3.636 | 3.636 |
| 4 | 3.636 | 3.636 | 3.636 | 3.636 | 3.636 | 3.636 |
| 5 | 3.636 | 3.636 | 3.636 | 3.636 | 3.636 | 3.636 |
| 6 | 3.636 | 3.636 | 3.636 | 3.636 | 3.636 | 3.636 |
| 7 | 3.636 | 3.636 | 3.636 | 3.636 | 3.636 | 3.636 |
| 8 | 3.636 | 3.636 | 3.636 | 3.636 | 3.636 | 3.636 |
| 9 | 3.636 | 3.636 | 3.636 | 3.636 | 3.636 | 3.636 |
| 10 | 3.637 | 3.637 | 3.637 | 3.637 | 3.637 | 3.637 |
| 11 | 3.636 | 3.636 | 3.636 | 3.636 | 3.636 | 3.636 |
| 12 | 3.637 | 3.637 | 3.637 | 3.637 | 3.637 | 3.637 |
| 13 | 3.636 | 3.636 | 3.636 | 3.636 | 3.636 | 3.636 |
| 14 | 3.637 | 3.637 | 3.637 | 3.637 | 3.637 | 3.637 |
| 15 | 3.636 | 3.636 | 3.636 | 3.636 | 3.636 | 3.636 |
| 16 | 3.637 | 3.637 | 3.637 | 3.637 | 3.637 | 3.637 |
| 17 | 3.636 | 3.636 | 3.636 | 3.636 | 3.636 | 3.636 |
| 18 | 3.637 | 3.637 | 3.637 | 3.637 | 3.637 | 3.637 |
| 19 | 3.636 | 3.636 | 3.636 | 3.636 | 3.636 | 3.636 |
| 20 | 3.637 | 3.637 | 3.637 | 3.637 | 3.637 | 3.636 |
| 21 | 3.636 | 3.636 | 3.636 | 3.636 | 3.636 | 3.636 |
| 22 | 3.637 | 3.637 | 3.637 | 3.637 | 3.637 | 3.637 |
| 23 | 3.636 | 3.636 | 3.636 | 3.636 | 3.636 | 3.636 |
| 24 | 3.637 | 3.637 | 3.637 | 3.637 | 3.637 | 3.637 |
| 25 | 3.636 | 3.636 | 3.636 | 3.636 | 3.636 | 3.636 |
| 26 | 3.637 | 3.637 | 3.637 | 3.637 | 3.637 | 3.637 |
| 27 | 3.636 | 3.636 | 3.636 | 3.636 | 3.636 | 3.636 |
| 28 | 1.970 | 2.273 | 2.576 | 2.879 | 3.182 | 3.485 |
| 29 | 0.000 | 0.000 | 0.000 | 0.000 | 0.000 | 0.000 |

## Modified ACRS Depreciation Rates for Residential Rental Property Placed in Service after December 31, 1986 (continued)

| Recovery Year | Month Placed in Service | | | | | |
|---|---|---|---|---|---|---|
| | 7 | 8 | 9 | 10 | 11 | 12 |
| 1 | 1.667 | 1.364 | 1.061 | 0.758 | 0.455 | 0.152 |
| 2 | 3.636 | 3.636 | 3.636 | 3.636 | 3.636 | 3.636 |
| 3 | 3.636 | 3.636 | 3.636 | 3.636 | 3.636 | 3.636 |
| 4 | 3.636 | 3.636 | 3.636 | 3.636 | 3.636 | 3.636 |
| 5 | 3.636 | 3.636 | 3.636 | 3.636 | 3.636 | 3.636 |
| 6 | 3.636 | 3.636 | 3.636 | 3.636 | 3.636 | 3.636 |
| 7 | 3.636 | 3.636 | 3.636 | 3.636 | 3.636 | 3.636 |
| 8 | 3.636 | 3.636 | 3.636 | 3.636 | 3.636 | 3.636 |
| 9 | 3.636 | 3.636 | 3.636 | 3.636 | 3.636 | 3.636 |
| 10 | 3.636 | 3.636 | 3.636 | 3.636 | 3.636 | 3.636 |
| 11 | 3.637 | 3.637 | 3.637 | 3.637 | 3.637 | 3.637 |
| 12 | 3.636 | 3.636 | 3.636 | 3.636 | 3.636 | 3.636 |
| 13 | 3.637 | 3.637 | 3.637 | 3.637 | 3.637 | 3.637 |
| 14 | 3.636 | 3.636 | 3.636 | 3.636 | 3.636 | 3.636 |
| 15 | 3.637 | 3.637 | 3.637 | 3.637 | 3.637 | 3.637 |
| 16 | 3.636 | 3.636 | 3.636 | 3.636 | 3.636 | 3.636 |
| 17 | 3.637 | 3.637 | 3.637 | 3.637 | 3.637 | 3.637 |
| 18 | 3.636 | 3.636 | 3.636 | 3.636 | 3.636 | 3.636 |
| 19 | 3.637 | 3.637 | 3.637 | 3.637 | 3.637 | 3.637 |
| 20 | 3.636 | 3.636 | 3.636 | 3.636 | 3.636 | 3.636 |
| 21 | 3.637 | 3.637 | 3.637 | 3.637 | 3.637 | 3.637 |
| 22 | 3.636 | 3.636 | 3.636 | 3.636 | 3.636 | 3.636 |
| 23 | 3.637 | 3.637 | 3.637 | 3.637 | 3.637 | 3.637 |
| 24 | 3.636 | 3.636 | 3.636 | 3.636 | 3.636 | 3.636 |
| 25 | 3.637 | 3.637 | 3.637 | 3.637 | 3.637 | 3.637 |
| 26 | 3.636 | 3.636 | 3.636 | 3.636 | 3.636 | 3.636 |
| 27 | 3.637 | 3.637 | 3.637 | 3.637 | 3.637 | 3.637 |
| 28 | 3.636 | 3.636 | 3.636 | 3.636 | 3.636 | 3.636 |
| 29 | 0.152 | 0.455 | 0.758 | 1.061 | 1.364 | 1.667 |

## Modified ACRS Depreciation Percentages for Nonresidential Real Property Placed in Service after December 31, 1986 and before May 13, 1993

| Recovery Year | Month Placed in Service 1 | 2 | 3 | 4 | 5 | 6 |
|---|---|---|---|---|---|---|
| 1 | 3.042 | 2.778 | 2.513 | 2.249 | 1.984 | 1.720 |
| 2 | 3.175 | 3.175 | 3.175 | 3.175 | 3.175 | 3.175 |
| 3 | 3.175 | 3.175 | 3.175 | 3.175 | 3.175 | 3.175 |
| 4 | 3.175 | 3.175 | 3.175 | 3.175 | 3.175 | 3.175 |
| 5 | 3.175 | 3.175 | 3.175 | 3.175 | 3.175 | 3.175 |
| 6 | 3.175 | 3.175 | 3.175 | 3.175 | 3.175 | 3.175 |
| 7 | 3.175 | 3.175 | 3.175 | 3.175 | 3.175 | 3.175 |
| 8 | 3.175 | 3.174 | 3.175 | 3.174 | 3.175 | 3.174 |
| 9 | 3.174 | 3.175 | 3.174 | 3.175 | 3.174 | 3.175 |
| 10 | 3.175 | 3.174 | 3.175 | 3.174 | 3.175 | 3.174 |
| 11 | 3.174 | 3.175 | 3.174 | 3.175 | 3.174 | 3.175 |
| 12 | 3.175 | 3.174 | 3.175 | 3.174 | 3.175 | 3.174 |
| 13 | 3.174 | 3.175 | 3.174 | 3.175 | 3.174 | 3.175 |
| 14 | 3.175 | 3.174 | 3.175 | 3.174 | 3.175 | 3.174 |
| 15 | 3.174 | 3.175 | 3.174 | 3.175 | 3.174 | 3.175 |
| 16 | 3.175 | 3.174 | 3.175 | 3.174 | 3.175 | 3.174 |
| 17 | 3.174 | 3.175 | 3.174 | 3.175 | 3.174 | 3.175 |
| 18 | 3.175 | 3.174 | 3.175 | 3.174 | 3.175 | 3.174 |
| 19 | 3.174 | 3.175 | 3.174 | 3.175 | 3.174 | 3.175 |
| 20 | 3.175 | 3.174 | 3.175 | 3.174 | 3.175 | 3.174 |
| 21 | 3.174 | 3.175 | 3.174 | 3.175 | 3.174 | 3.175 |
| 22 | 3.175 | 3.174 | 3.175 | 3.174 | 3.175 | 3.174 |
| 23 | 3.174 | 3.175 | 3.174 | 3.175 | 3.174 | 3.175 |
| 24 | 3.175 | 3.174 | 3.175 | 3.174 | 3.175 | 3.174 |
| 25 | 3.174 | 3.175 | 3.174 | 3.175 | 3.174 | 3.175 |
| 26 | 3.175 | 3.174 | 3.175 | 3.174 | 3.175 | 3.174 |
| 27 | 3.174 | 3.175 | 3.174 | 3.175 | 3.174 | 3.175 |
| 28 | 3.175 | 3.174 | 3.175 | 3.174 | 3.175 | 3.174 |
| 29 | 3.174 | 3.175 | 3.174 | 3.175 | 3.174 | 3.175 |
| 30 | 3.175 | 3.174 | 3.175 | 3.174 | 3.175 | 3.174 |
| 31 | 3.174 | 3.175 | 3.174 | 3.175 | 3.174 | 3.175 |
| 32 | 1.720 | 1.984 | 2.249 | 2.513 | 2.778 | 3.042 |
| 33 | 0.000 | 0.000 | 0.000 | 0.000 | 0.000 | 0.000 |

### Modified ACRS Depreciation Percentages for Nonresidential Real Property Placed in Service after December 31, 1986 and before May 13, 1993 (continued)

| Recovery Year | Month Placed in Service | | | | | |
|---|---|---|---|---|---|---|
| | 7 | 8 | 9 | 10 | 11 | 12 |
| 1 | 1.455 | 1.190 | 0.926 | 0.661 | 0.397 | 0.132 |
| 2 | 3.175 | 3.175 | 3.175 | 3.175 | 3.175 | 3.175 |
| 3 | 3.175 | 3.175 | 3.175 | 3.175 | 3.175 | 3.175 |
| 4 | 3.175 | 3.175 | 3.175 | 3.175 | 3.175 | 3.175 |
| 5 | 3.175 | 3.175 | 3.175 | 3.175 | 3.175 | 3.175 |
| 6 | 3.175 | 3.175 | 3.175 | 3.175 | 3.175 | 3.175 |
| 7 | 3.175 | 3.175 | 3.175 | 3.175 | 3.175 | 3.175 |
| 8 | 3.175 | 3.175 | 3.175 | 3.175 | 3.175 | 3.175 |
| 9 | 3.174 | 3.175 | 3.175 | 3.175 | 3.174 | 3.175 |
| 10 | 3.175 | 3.174 | 3.175 | 3.174 | 3.175 | 3.174 |
| 11 | 3.174 | 3.175 | 3.174 | 3.175 | 3.174 | 3.175 |
| 12 | 3.175 | 3.174 | 3.175 | 3.174 | 3.175 | 3.174 |
| 13 | 3.174 | 3.175 | 3.174 | 3.175 | 3.174 | 3.175 |
| 14 | 3.175 | 3.174 | 3.175 | 3.174 | 3.175 | 3.174 |
| 15 | 3.174 | 3.175 | 3.174 | 3.175 | 3.174 | 3.175 |
| 16 | 3.175 | 3.174 | 3.175 | 3.174 | 3.175 | 3.174 |
| 17 | 3.174 | 3.175 | 3.174 | 3.175 | 3.174 | 3.175 |
| 18 | 3.175 | 3.174 | 3.175 | 3.174 | 3.175 | 3.174 |
| 19 | 3.174 | 3.175 | 3.174 | 3.175 | 3.174 | 3.175 |
| 20 | 3.175 | 3.174 | 3.175 | 3.174 | 3.175 | 3.174 |
| 21 | 3.174 | 3.175 | 3.174 | 3.175 | 3.174 | 3.175 |
| 22 | 3.175 | 3.174 | 3.175 | 3.174 | 3.175 | 3.174 |
| 23 | 3.174 | 3.175 | 3.174 | 3.175 | 3.174 | 3.175 |
| 24 | 3.175 | 3.174 | 3.175 | 3.174 | 3.175 | 3.174 |
| 25 | 3.174 | 3.175 | 3.174 | 3.175 | 3.174 | 3.175 |
| 26 | 3.175 | 3.174 | 3.175 | 3.174 | 3.175 | 3.174 |
| 27 | 3.174 | 3.175 | 3.174 | 3.175 | 3.174 | 3.175 |
| 28 | 3.175 | 3.174 | 3.175 | 3.174 | 3.175 | 3.174 |
| 29 | 3.174 | 3.175 | 3.174 | 3.175 | 3.174 | 3.175 |
| 30 | 3.175 | 3.174 | 3.175 | 3.174 | 3.175 | 3.174 |
| 31 | 3.174 | 3.175 | 3.174 | 3.175 | 3.174 | 3.175 |
| 32 | 3.175 | 3.174 | 3.175 | 3.174 | 3.175 | 3.174 |
| 33 | 0.132 | 0.397 | 0.661 | 0.926 | 1.190 | 1.455 |

## Modified ACRS Depreciation Percentages for Nonresidential Real Property Placed in Service after May 12, 1993

| Month Placed in Service | Recovery Year 1 | 2 | ... | 39 | 40 |
|---|---|---|---|---|---|
| 1 | 2.461% | 2.564% | | 2.564% | 0.107% |
| 2 | 2.247 | 2.564 | | 2.564 | 0.321 |
| 3 | 2.033 | 2.564 | | 2.564 | 0.535 |
| 4 | 1.819 | 2.564 | | 2.564 | 0.749 |
| 5 | 1.605 | 2.564 | | 2.564 | 0.963 |
| 6 | 1.391 | 2.564 | | 2.564 | 1.177 |
| 7 | 1.177 | 2.564 | | 2.564 | 1.391 |
| 8 | 0.963 | 2.564 | | 2.564 | 1.605 |
| 9 | 0.749 | 2.564 | | 2.564 | 1.819 |
| 10 | 0.535 | 2.564 | | 2.564 | 2.033 |
| 11 | 0.321 | 2.564 | | 2.564 | 2.247 |
| 12 | 0.107 | 2.564 | | 2.564 | 2.461 |

### Modified ACRS Accelerated Depreciation Percentages Using the Mid-Quarter Convention for 3-, 5-, 7-, 10-, 15-, and 20-Year Property Placed in Service after December 31, 1986

| *Recovery Year* | *Quarter Placed in Service* | | | |
|---|---|---|---|---|
| | *1* | *2* | *3* | *4* |
| **3-Year Property:** | | | | |
| 1 | 58.33 | 41.67 | 25.00 | 8.33 |
| 2 | 27.78 | 38.89 | 50.00 | 61.11 |
| 3 | 12.35 | 14.14 | 16.67 | 20.37 |
| 4 | 1.54 | 5.30 | 8.33 | 10.19 |
| **5-Year Property:** | | | | |
| 1 | 35.00 | 25.00 | 15.00 | 5.00 |
| 2 | 26.00 | 30.00 | 34.00 | 38.00 |
| 3 | 15.60 | 18.00 | 20.40 | 22.80 |
| 4 | 11.01 | 11.37 | 12.24 | 13.68 |
| 5 | 11.01 | 11.37 | 11.30 | 10.94 |
| 6 | 1.38 | 4.26 | 7.06 | 9.58 |
| **7-Year Property:** | | | | |
| 1 | 25.00 | 17.85 | 10.71 | 3.57 |
| 2 | 21.43 | 23.47 | 25.51 | 27.55 |
| 3 | 15.31 | 16.76 | 18.22 | 19.68 |
| 4 | 10.93 | 11.37 | 13.02 | 14.06 |
| 5 | 8.75 | 8.87 | 9.30 | 10.04 |
| 6 | 8.74 | 8.87 | 8.85 | 8.73 |
| 7 | 8.75 | 8.87 | 8.86 | 8.73 |
| 8 | 1.09 | 3.33 | 5.53 | 7.64 |
| **10-Year Property:** | | | | |
| 1 | 17.50 | 12.50 | 7.50 | 2.50 |
| 2 | 16.50 | 17.50 | 18.50 | 19.50 |
| 3 | 13.20 | 14.00 | 14.80 | 15.60 |
| 4 | 10.56 | 11.20 | 11.84 | 12.48 |
| 5 | 8.45 | 8.96 | 9.47 | 9.98 |
| 6 | 6.76 | 7.17 | 7.58 | 7.99 |
| 7 | 6.55 | 6.55 | 6.55 | 6.55 |
| 8 | 6.55 | 6.55 | 6.55 | 6.55 |
| 9 | 6.56 | 6.56 | 6.56 | 6.56 |
| 10 | 0.82 | 6.55 | 6.55 | 6.55 |
| 11 | | 2.46 | 4.10 | 5.74 |

**Modified ACRS Accelerated Depreciation Percentages Using the Mid-Quarter Convention for 3-, 5-, 7-, 10-, 15-, and 20-Year Property Placed in Service after December 31, 1986 (continued)**

| Recovery Year | Quarter Placed in Service 1 | 2 | 3 | 4 |
|---|---|---|---|---|
| **15-Year Property:** | | | | |
| 1 | 8.75 | 6.25 | 3.75 | 1.25 |
| 2 | 9.13 | 9.38 | 9.63 | 9.88 |
| 3 | 8.21 | 8.44 | 8.66 | 8.89 |
| 4 | 7.39 | 7.59 | 7.80 | 8.00 |
| 5 | 6.65 | 6.83 | 7.02 | 7.20 |
| 6 | 5.99 | 6.15 | 6.31 | 6.48 |
| 7 | 5.90 | 5.91 | 5.90 | 5.90 |
| 8 | 5.91 | 5.90 | 5.90 | 5.90 |
| 9 | 5.90 | 5.91 | 5.91 | 5.90 |
| 10 | 5.91 | 5.90 | 5.90 | 5.91 |
| 11 | 5.90 | 5.91 | 5.91 | 5.90 |
| 12 | 5.91 | 5.90 | 5.90 | 5.91 |
| 13 | 5.90 | 5.91 | 5.91 | 5.90 |
| 14 | 5.91 | 5.90 | 5.90 | 5.91 |
| 15 | 5.90 | 5.91 | 5.91 | 5.90 |
| 16 | 0.74 | 2.21 | 3.69 | 5.17 |
| **20-Year Property:** | | | | |
| 1 | 6.563 | 4.688 | 2.813 | 0.938 |
| 2 | 7.000 | 7.148 | 7.289 | 7.430 |
| 3 | 6.482 | 6.612 | 6.742 | 6.872 |
| 4 | 5.996 | 6.116 | 6.237 | 6.357 |
| 5 | 5.546 | 5.658 | 5.769 | 5.880 |
| 6 | 5.130 | 5.233 | 5.336 | 5.439 |
| 7 | 4.746 | 4.841 | 4.936 | 5.031 |
| 8 | 4.459 | 4.478 | 4.566 | 4.654 |
| 9 | 4.459 | 4.463 | 4.460 | 4.458 |
| 10 | 4.459 | 4.463 | 4.460 | 4.458 |
| 11 | 4.459 | 4.463 | 4.460 | 4.458 |
| 12 | 4.460 | 4.463 | 4.460 | 4.458 |
| 13 | 4.459 | 4.463 | 4.461 | 4.458 |
| 14 | 4.460 | 4.463 | 4.460 | 4.458 |
| 15 | 4.459 | 4.462 | 4.461 | 4.458 |
| 16 | 4.460 | 4.463 | 4.460 | 4.458 |
| 17 | 4.459 | 4.462 | 4.461 | 4.458 |
| 18 | 4.460 | 4.463 | 4.460 | 4.459 |
| 19 | 4.459 | 4.462 | 4.461 | 4.458 |
| 20 | 4.460 | 4.463 | 4.460 | 4.459 |
| 21 | 0.557 | 1.673 | 2.788 | 3.901 |

## *Alternative Depreciation System Recovery Periods*

**General Rule: Recovery period is the property's class life unless:**
**1. There is no class life (see below), or**
**2. A special class life has been designated (see below).**

| *Type of Property* | *Recovery Period* |
|---|---|
| Personal property with no class life | 12 years |
| Nonresidential real property with no class life | 40 years |
| Residential rental property with no class life | 40 years |
| Cars, light general purpose trucks, certain technological equipment, and semiconductor manufacturing equipment | 5 years |
| Computer-based telephone central office switching equipment | 9.5 years |
| Railroad track | 10 years |
| Single purpose agricultural or horticultural structures | 15 years |
| Municipal waste water treatment plants, telephone distribution plants | 24 years |
| Low-income housing financed by tax-exempt bonds | 27.5 years |
| Municipal sewers | 50 years |

### *Modified ACRS and ADS Straight-Line Depreciation Percentages Using the Half-Year Convention for 3-, 5-, 7-, 10-, 15-, and 20-Year Property Placed in Service after December 31, 1986*

| | *Property Class* | | | | | |
|---|---|---|---|---|---|---|
| *Recovery Year* | *3-Year* | *5-Year* | *7-Year* | *10-Year* | *15-Year* | *20-Year* |
| 1 | 16.67 | 10.00 | 7.14 | 5.00 | 3.33 | 2.50 |
| 2 | 33.33 | 20.00 | 14.29 | 10.00 | 6.67 | 5.00 |
| 3 | 33.33 | 20.00 | 14.29 | 10.00 | 6.67 | 5.00 |
| 4 | 16.67 | 20.00 | 14.28 | 10.00 | 6.67 | 5.00 |
| 5 | | 20.00 | 14.29 | 10.00 | 6.67 | 5.00 |
| 6 | | 10.00 | 14.28 | 10.00 | 6.67 | 5.00 |
| 7 | | | 14.29 | 10.00 | 6.67 | 5.00 |
| 8 | | | 7.14 | 10.00 | 6.66 | 5.00 |
| 9 | | | | 10.00 | 6.67 | 5.00 |
| 10 | | | | 10.00 | 6.66 | 5.00 |
| 11 | | | | 5.00 | 6.67 | 5.00 |
| 12 | | | | | 6.66 | 5.00 |
| 13 | | | | | 6.67 | 5.00 |
| 14 | | | | | 6.66 | 5.00 |
| 15 | | | | | 6.67 | 5.00 |
| 16 | | | | | 3.33 | 5.00 |
| 17 | | | | | | 5.00 |
| 18 | | | | | | 5.00 |
| 19 | | | | | | 5.00 |
| 20 | | | | | | 5.00 |
| 21 | | | | | | 2.50 |

## ADS Straight-Line Depreciation Percentages Real Property Using the Mid-Month Convention for Property Placed in Service After December 31, 1986

| Month Placed In Service | Recovery Year 1 | 2–40 | 41 |
|---|---|---|---|
| 1 | 2.396 | 2.500 | 0.104 |
| 2 | 2.188 | 2.500 | 0.312 |
| 3 | 1.979 | 2.500 | 0.521 |
| 4 | 1.771 | 2.500 | 0.729 |
| 5 | 1.563 | 2.500 | 0.937 |
| 6 | 1.354 | 2.500 | 1.146 |
| 7 | 1.146 | 2.500 | 1.354 |
| 8 | 0.938 | 2.500 | 1.562 |
| 9 | 0.729 | 2.500 | 1.771 |
| 10 | 0.521 | 2.500 | 1.979 |
| 11 | 0.313 | 2.500 | 2.187 |
| 12 | 0.104 | 2.500 | 2.396 |

D

# Continuous Individual Tax Return Problems and Two Comprehensive Individual Tax Return Problems for 2010

## Continuous Tax Return Problems

**General Instructions.** Information is provided below for a continuous tax return problem. The tax return begins by providing a basic fact pattern, covering the topics found in Chapter 3. Additional facts are added to the facts for Chapter 3 in order to cover the topics discussed in Chapters 4, 5, 6, 7 and 8. In addition to the tax returns that must be prepared, questions relating to such returns are included.

### Chapter 3: Continuous Tax Return Problem

**3-1** **Problem Facts**. Larry K. and Cathy L. Zepp have been married 19 years. Larry is 62 years old (Social Security number 123-45-6789) while Cathy is 57 years old (Social Security number 123-45-6788). They live at 1234 Elm Dr. in Indianapolis, Indiana 46202. The couple uses the cash method of accounting and files their return on a calendar-year basis. They are tired of politics and do not want to contribute to the presidential election campaign.

**a.** Larry is a salesman employed by DSK Industries. This year he earned $110,000. Federal and state income taxes withheld were $17,000 and $6,000 respectively.

**b.** Cathy recently completed a graduate degree in computer technology. She freelances as an independent contractor in computer graphics. She uses her own name as the name of her business. Her earnings received from various engagements were $12,000. Her only expenses paid during the year were for miscellaneous office supplies of $3,000. She paid estimated federal taxes during the year of $1,000 ($250 on each due date). Her business uses the cash method of accounting.

**c.** Other income earned by the couple included interest income of $3,000 from a certificate of deposit issued by Highland National Bank and $975 of interest from tax-exempt bonds issued by the State of Indiana.

**d.** The couple paid moving expenses of $2,000 that are fully deductible.

**e.** The couple owns a duplex that it rents out. It is located at 111 Nowhere Ave., Indianapolis, Indiana. Their rental records reveal the following information for the year.

| | |
|---|---|
| Rental income | $12,000 |
| Rental expenses | |
| Insurance | 400 |
| Mortgage interest | 7,000 |
| Repairs | 1,000 |
| Real property taxes | 600 |

f. Other expenses paid during the year included:

| | |
|---|---|
| Unreimbursed medical expenses | $ 9,000 |
| Interest on home mortgage | 12,000 |
| Real property taxes on home | 1,900 |
| State income taxes withheld (see above) | 6,000 |
| Charitable contributions | 1,000 |
| Rental of safety deposit box to hold gold coins held for investment | 100 |
| Unreimbursed employee business expenses of Larry | 3,000 |

Prepare the 2010 individual income tax return for the Zepps. Complete Form 1040 and Schedules A, B, C, E and SE. Assume that all of the expenses except their business expenses are incurred jointly. Also assume that the "making work pay" credit is zero.

**3-2 Continuous Tax Return: Additional Questions.** Answer the following questions relating to the continuous tax return problem for Chapter 3 above:

**a.** What is the Zepp's marginal tax rate? Average tax rate?

**b.** The Zepps recently heard that making a contribution to an individual retirement account (IRA) may be a wise tax move. It is their understanding that contributions to a traditional or conventional IRA are deductible and the earnings on the accounts are not taxable until withdrawn (see Chapter 18 for more information). Assuming both Larry and Cathy make a deductible contribution of $4,000 each for a total of $8,000, compute the exact amount of tax the couple will save. Show computations illustrating how the savings are derived.

**c.** This question relates to the income tax of your state and may or may not be applicable. Check with your instructor for further instructions.

Larry incurred $3,000 of expenses related to his employment while Cathy incurred $3,000 related to her freelancing activity (i.e., self-employment). Which of the following statements is (are) true regarding the treatment of the expenses for state income tax purposes?

1. Both expenses were deductible in full.
2. Neither of the expenses was deductible.
3. The employment related expenses were deductible but the expenses related to self-employment were not deductible.
4. The expenses related to self-employment were deductible but the employment related expenses were not deductible.

**d.** Assume that Larry (instead of Cathy) had the self-employment income of $9,000. Which of the following statements is true?

1. Larry paid 15.3% self-employment tax on self-employment income of $9,000.
2. Larry paid 15.3% self-employment tax on self-employment income of $8,312.
3. Larry paid the same amount of self-employment tax that Cathy would have paid had she earned the income.
4. Larry pays less than the amount of self-employment tax that Cathy would have paid had she earned the income.

# Chapter 4: Continuous Tax Return Problem

**4-1 Problem Facts.** This is a continuation of the tax return problem beginning in Chapter 3. See previous facts above.

*New Facts:* Larry and Cathy Zepp just called and after a quick discussion the following additional information was obtained:

**a.** Larry received a corrected W-2 in the mail. The corrected W-2 (see below) reveals that federal income taxes withheld were $7,000 (rather than $17,000).

**b.** Last year's federal tax liability before prepayments was $10,000.

**c.** They forgot to note on their tax organizer that they had two children, a son and a daughter: Zachary W. Zepp (111-33-4444, date of birth 12/1/1999) and Jennifer A. Zepp (111-33-4445, 1/4/2001). Both children live with them the entire year. Zachary is a full-time student. Jennifer is considered legally blind.

**d.** Larry explained that he was formerly married to Sue Gottaway (443-44-1234) who currently has custody of their son Sam (447-93-9444, 4/14/1989). Sue has agreed to surrender the exemption for Sam to Larry and has provided Larry the necessary form. Sue provides all of Sam's support. Sam is time student at the University of Texas.

Prepare the 2010 individual income tax return for the Zepps. Complete Forms 1040, 2210, Schedules A, B, C, E, SE and any other forms required. Assume that all of the expenses except their business expenses are incurred jointly. Also assume that the "making work pay" credit is zero.

| 22222 | a Employee's social security number: 123-45-6789 | OMB No. 1545-0008 | |
|---|---|---|---|
| b Employer identification number (EIN): 25-2222345 | | 1 Wages, tips, other compensation: 110,000.00 | 2 Federal income tax withheld: 7,000.00 |
| c Employer's name, address, and ZIP code: DSK Industries, 1635 Longest Drive, Indianapolis, Indiana 46202 | | 3 Social security wages: $106,800 | 4 Social security tax withheld: $6,622 |
| | | 5 Medicare wages and tips: $110,000 | 6 Medicare tax withheld: $1,595 |
| | | 7 Social security tips | 8 Allocated tips |
| d Control number: 0068251111 | | 9 Advance EIC payment | 10 Dependent care benefits |
| e Employee's first name and initial / Last name / Suff.: Larry K. Zepp, 1234 Elm Dr., Indianapolis, Indiana 46202 | | 11 Nonqualified plans | 12a Code |
| | | 13 Statutory employee ☐ Retirement plan ☐ Third-party sick pay ☐ | 12b Code |
| | | 14 Other | 12c Code |
| f Employee's address and ZIP code | | | 12d Code |

| 15 State / Employer's state ID number | 16 State wages, tips, etc. | 17 State income tax | 18 Local wages, tips, etc. | 19 Local income tax | 20 Locality name |
|---|---|---|---|---|---|
| IN | | $6,000 | | | |
| | | | | | |

Form **W-2** Wage and Tax Statement **2010**  Department of the Treasury—Internal Revenue Service

**Copy 1—For State, City, or Local Tax Department**

**4-2 Continuous Tax Return: Additional Questions.** Refer to the facts for the continuous tax return problem (Chapters 3 and 4 above). The Zepp's tax organizer indicated that their daughter, Jennifer Zepp, received $3,000 of interest income from a savings account at Chase National Bank. Using this additional information and the facts above, prepare a separate Form 1040 for Jennifer Zepp. Do not include Jennifer's income on her parents' return.

**4-3 Continuous Tax Return: Additional Questions.** Answer the following questions relating to the continuous tax return problem above:

**a.** The Zepps generally could have avoided the estimated tax penalty by paying estimated taxes or by relying on their prior year's tax liability. Ignoring their prior year liability, how much should the couple have paid on each installment date to avoid the penalty? Alternatively, what would the amount of last year's tax liability have to be to avoid the penalty?

**b.** If Cathy had hired Jennifer as an employee and paid her $4,000 to help her on certain business-related projects, what effect would it have on the family's tax liability? Provide an explanation that shows precisely why the family's total tax liability increased or decreased. For simplicity, assume that Jennifer had no other income.

For purpose of the questions below, assume Cathy was also an employee and received wages of $50,000 in addition to her self-employment income. Also ignore (a) and (b) above.

**c.** Does the couple's taxable income increase by $50,000, more than $50,000 or less than $50,000? Explain specifically what accounts for the change in taxable income and tax liability, if any.

**d.** What would the Zepp's marginal tax rate be on the next $1,000 of income? For this question, use the actual change in tax to determine the marginal rate and compare it to the marginal rate in the tax rate schedule.

## Chapter 5: Continuous Tax Return Problem

**5-1 Problem Facts.** This is a continuation of the tax return problem covering Chapters 3 and 4. See previous facts above.

*New Facts:* This morning's mail contained a note from Larry Zepp, including the following information:

**a.** Cathy forgot to explain several things about her consulting income. First, $2,400 of the $12,000 she received was for services to be performed in 2011. Second, she performed consulting services in December but was not paid until January when she received $475. She had sent the client a bill for $475 in December and the amount was included in the $12,000 she reported earlier.

**b.** Larry paid federal estimated income taxes of $12,000 ($3,000 on each of the due dates). He made no state estimated tax payments.

**c.** A Schedule K-1 from a calendar-year partnership in which Larry is a small investor was included. The relevant portions of the Schedule K-1 are shown below. In addition, Larry received a $775 distribution from the partnership during the year.

Prepare the 2010 individual income tax return for the Zepps. Complete Forms 1040, 2210, Schedules A, B, C, E and SE. Assume that all of the expenses except their business expenses are incurred jointly. Also assume that the "making work pay" credit is zero.

651110

☐ Final K-1 ☐ Amended K-1 OMB No. 1545-0099

**Schedule K-1 (Form 1065)** **2010**

Department of the Treasury
Internal Revenue Service

For calendar year 2010, or tax year beginning ________, 2010 ending ________, 20____

## Partner's Share of Income, Deductions, Credits, etc.

► See back of form and separate instructions.

### Part I Information About the Partnership

**A** Partnership's employer identification number
*75-1234567*

**B** Partnership's name, address, city, state, and ZIP code
*KLM Associates*
*3214 Memorial*
*Houston, TX 77452*

**C** IRS Center where partnership filed return

**D** ☐ Check if this is a publicly traded partnership (PTP)

### Part II Information About the Partner

**E** Partner's identifying number
*123-45-6789*

**F** Partner's name, address, city, state, and ZIP code
*Larry L. Zepp*
*1234 Elm Drive*
*Indianapolis, IN 46202*

**G** ☐ General partner or LLC member-manager ☑ Limited partner or other LLC member

**H** ☐ Domestic partner ☐ Foreign partner

**I** What type of entity is this partner? ________

**J** Partner's share of profit, loss, and capital (see instructions):

| | Beginning | Ending |
|---|---|---|
| Profit | % | % |
| Loss | % | % |
| Capital | % | % |

**K** Partner's share of liabilities at year end:
Nonrecourse . . . . . . . $ ________
Qualified nonrecourse financing . $ ________
Recourse . . . . . . . . $ ________

**L** Partner's capital account analysis:
Beginning capital account . . . $ ________
Capital contributed during the year $ ________
Current year increase (decrease) . $ ________
Withdrawals & distributions . . $ ( ________ )
Ending capital account . . . . $ ________

☐ Tax basis ☐ GAAP ☐ Section 704(b) book
☐ Other (explain)

**M** Did the partner contribute property with a built-in gain or loss?
☐ Yes ☐ No
If "Yes", attach statement (see instructions)

### Part III Partner's Share of Current Year Income, Deductions, Credits, and Other Items

|  |  |  |
|---|---|---|
| 1 | Ordinary business income (loss) | *200* |
| 2 | Net rental real estate income (loss) | |
| 3 | Other net rental income (loss) | |
| 4 | Guaranteed payments | |
| 5 | Interest income | *150* |
| 6a | Ordinary dividends | |
| 6b | Qualified dividends | |
| 7 | Royalties | |
| 8 | Net short-term capital gain (loss) | |
| 9a | Net long-term capital gain (loss) | |
| 9b | Collectibles (28%) gain (loss) | |
| 9c | Unrecaptured section 1250 gain | |
| 10 | Net section 1231 gain (loss) | |
| 11 | Other income (loss) | |
| 12 | Section 179 deduction | |
| 13 | Other deductions | |
| 14 | Self-employment earnings (loss) | |
| 15 | Credits | |
| 16 | Foreign transactions | |
| 17 | Alternative minimum tax (AMT) items | |
| 18 | Tax-exempt income and nondeductible expenses | |
| 19 | Distributions | *775* |
| 20 | Other information | |

*See attached statement for additional information.

For IRS Use Only

For Paperwork Reduction Act Notice, see Instructions for Form 1065. Cat. No. 11394R **Schedule K-1 (Form 1065) 2010**

**5-2 Continuous Tax Return Problem. Additional Questions.** Refer to the facts for the continuous tax return problem (Chapters 3, 4 and 5 above).

**a.** According to the Schedule K-1, Larry Zepp received $775 of distributions from the partnership. How do the distributions impact the couple's individual income tax return? Explain.

**b.** Is the partnership income considered self-employment income of Larry Zepp for purposes of computing any self-employment tax he might owe? Explain.

**c.** Assume Cathy reached an agreement with a local fitness center to prepare various flyers, advertisements and do some work on the company's website. In exchange, she received an annual membership to the center worth $500. Explain the tax consequences to Cathy.

## Chapter 6: Continuous Tax Return Problem

**6-1 Problem Facts.** This is a continuation of the tax return problem covering Chapters 3, 4 and 5. See previous facts above.

*New Facts:*

**a.** This year Larry began receiving Social Security benefits. For the year, he received $12,000.

**b.** The couple received a Form 1099 from National Funds (see below) regarding an investment in a mutual fund.

**c.** Cathy was unemployed for a short period and received unemployment compensation of $800 reported on the Form 1099-G (see below).

**d.** Cathy received $2,000 of alimony from her first husband.

**e.** Cathy inherited $100,000 from her rich uncle.

**f.** The Zepps overpaid their income taxes for the prior year and received both a federal and state refund. The federal refund was $1700. They received a Form 1099-G from the state of Indiana reporting the state refund of $925. Last year, the Zepps' total itemized deductions were $19,000, including a deduction for state income taxes of $2,598.

**g.** Larry's father died this year and Larry was the beneficiary of his father's life insurance policy. Larry received life insurance proceeds of $25,000.

**h.** In June, DSK honored Larry for his 25 years of service. He received a plaque and a gift certificate for $400 at The Golf Shop, which he intends to use to buy a new driver.

**i.** Cathy's father had loaned her $5,000 to help her complete school and start her business. This year he told her that she did not have to repay him.

Prepare the 2010 individual income tax return for the Zepps. Complete Forms 1040, 2210, Schedules A, B, C, E and SE. Assume that all of the expenses except their business expenses are incurred jointly. Also assume that the "making work pay" credit is zero.

☐ CORRECTED (if checked)

**Dividends and Distributions** — OMB No. 1545-0110 — **2010** — Form **1099-DIV**

| PAYER'S name, street address, city, state, ZIP code, and telephone no. | | Field | Amount |
|---|---|---|---|
| National Funds<br>888 Toobad Drive<br>Boston, MA 02104 | | 1a Total ordinary dividends | $ 3,000 |
| | | 1b Qualified dividends | $ 3,000 |
| | | 2a Total capital gain distr. | $ 1,400 |
| | | 2b Unrecap. Sec. 1250 gain | $ |
| PAYER'S federal identification number | RECIPIENT'S identification number | 2c Section 1202 gain | $ |
| | | 2d Collectibles (28%) gain | $ |
| RECIPIENT'S name: Larry L. Zepp | | 3 Nondividend distributions | $ |
| | | 4 Federal income tax withheld | $ |
| | | 5 Investment expenses | $ |
| Street address (including apt. no.): 1234 Elm Drive | | 6 Foreign tax paid | $ 70 |
| | | 7 Foreign country or U.S. possession | |
| City, state, and ZIP code: Indianapolis, IN 46202 | | 8 Cash liquidation distributions | $ |
| | | 9 Noncash liquidation distributions | $ |
| Account number (see instructions) | | | |

**Copy B**
**For Recipient**

This is important tax information and is being furnished to the Internal Revenue Service. If you are required to file a return, a negligence penalty or other sanction may be imposed on you if this income is taxable and the IRS determines that it has not been reported.

Form **1099-DIV** (keep for your records) Department of the Treasury - Internal Revenue Service

☐ CORRECTED (if checked)

**Certain Government Payments** — OMB No. 1545-0120 — **2010** — Form **1099-G**

| PAYER'S name, street address, city, state, ZIP code, and telephone no. | | Field | Amount |
|---|---|---|---|
| Indiana Department of Revenue<br>100 N. Senate Ave.<br>Indianapolis, IN 46204-2253 | | 1 Unemployment compensation | $ 800 |
| | | 2 State or local income tax refunds, credits, or offsets | $ 925 |
| PAYER'S federal identification number | RECIPIENT'S identification number | 3 Box 2 amount is for tax year | |
| | | 4 Federal income tax withheld | $ |
| RECIPIENT'S name: Larry L. Zepp | | 5 ATAA payments | $ |
| | | 6 Taxable energy grants | $ |
| Street address (including apt. no.): 1234 Elm Dr. | | 7 Agriculture payments | $ |
| | | 8 Check if box 2 is trade or business income ▶ ☐ | |
| City, state, and ZIP code: Indianapolis, Indiana 46202 | | 9 Market gain | $ |
| Account number (see instructions) | | 10a State / 10b State identification no. / 11 State income tax withheld | |

**Copy B**
**For Recipient**

This is important tax information and is being furnished to the Internal Revenue Service. If you are required to file a return, a negligence penalty or other sanction may be imposed on you if this income is taxable and the IRS determines that it has not been reported.

Form **1099-G** (keep for your records) Department of the Treasury - Internal Revenue Service

**6-2 Continuous Tax Return Problem. Additional Questions.** Refer to the facts for the continuous tax return problem (Chapters 3, 4, 5 and 6 above).

**a.** What is the Zepp's marginal tax rate?

**b.** At what rate were the dividends taxed?

**c.** Which of the following statements is true regarding the tax treatment of Larry's social security benefits?

1. None of the social security payments was taxable.
2. 50% of the social security payments was taxable.
3. 85% of the social security payment was taxable.
4. None of the above.

**6-3 Continuous Tax Return Problem. Additional Questions.** Refer to the facts for the continuous tax return problem (Chapters 3, 4, 5 and 6 above). Note that the calculations required to complete the following questions are not explained in the text.

**a.** Assume that Jennifer received interest income of $3,000 and qualified dividend income of $1,000. Prepare Form 1040 for Jennifer. For simplicity purposes, assume that the taxable income of her parents was $200,000 and their return revealed qualified dividend income of $3,000.

**b.** At what rates were Jennifer's interest and dividend income taxed?

## Chapter 7: Continuous Tax Return Problem

**7-1 Problem Facts.** This is a continuation of the tax return problem covering Chapters 3, 4, 5 and 6. See previous facts above.

*New Facts:*

**a.** The $400 paid in 2010 for the insurance coverage related to the rental property was for a one-year term that begins on February 1, 2011.

**b.** On September 1, the couple refinanced the mortgage on the rental property to get a lower interest rate. They paid points of $1,800. The term of the new loan was 15 years.

**c.** Cathy paid medical insurance premiums of $4,000.

**d.** In early January, Cathy billed a customer $627 for setting up a website. The customer left town and Cathy indicates that the receivable is now worthless.

**e.** During the year, Larry explored the possibility of selling for a new employer. However, after some interviewing, he decided to stay with DSK. He paid $30 to have new resumes printed and another $20 to register his name on an employment website.

**f.** Larry paid several parking tickets during the year while calling on customers. Total cost was $48.

**g.** Larry contributed $250 to the Democratic National Party and Cathy contributed $250 to the Republican National Party.

**h.** The couple paid $3,000 premium for a $1,000,000 life insurance policy on Larry's life. Cathy was the beneficiary.

**i.** Cathy continued her hobby of breeding and selling terriers. This year she sold 10 puppies for $6,000. Her expenses for raising the dogs (food, shots, etc.) were $2,000.

Prepare the 2010 individual income tax return for the Zepps. Complete Forms 1040, 2210, Schedules A, B, C, E and SE. Assume that all of the expenses except their business expenses are incurred jointly. Also assume that the "making work pay" credit is zero.

**7-2 Continuous Tax Return: Additional Questions.** Refer to the facts for the continuous tax return problem (Chapters 3, 4, 5 and 6 above).

**a.** Larry incurred $3,000 of expenses related to his employment while Cathy incurred $3,000 related to her freelancing activity (i.e., self-employment). Which of the

following statements is true regarding the treatment of the expenses for federal income tax purposes?
1. The expenses of both Larry and Cathy were subject to the 2% limitation.
2. The expenses of both Larry and Cathy were fully deductible as deductions for A.G.I. (i.e., deductible in arriving at adjusted gross income).
3. The expenses of both Larry and Cathy were considered itemized deductions but only the employment expenses were subject to the 2% limitation.
4. The expenses of Cathy affected the amount of Larry's expenses that are deductible.
5. None of the above is correct.

**b.** Assume Larry is considered a statutory employee (see Box 13 of his W-2 in an earlier chapter). Indicate the amount, if any, by which the couple's taxable income increases or decreases.

**c.** Did Cathy's payment for medical insurance affect her self-employment tax?

**d.** The couple paid $1,000 for tax preparation of last year's return. Before last year, Larry did the return but since last year's return involved filing a Schedule C for Cathy he decided to get professional tax help. The accountant's fee was $400. Explain the treatment of the tax preparation fee.

## Chapter 8: Continuous Tax Return Problem

**8-1 Problem Facts.** This is a continuation of the tax return problem covering Chapters 3, 4, 5, 6 and 7. See previous facts above.

*New Facts:*

**a.** Cathy paid $1,000 of tuition for a course that she took at the local university. The course related to her to computer graphics business.

**b.** Cathy worked out of her home. According to her records, she drove 8,000 miles from her home to her clients and back during the year. She does not have a qualifying home office. She has records of her mileage but nothing for gas, oil or related expenses.

**c.** Cathy took a client to lunch and they discussed some of the work she was doing for the client. Cathy paid for her meal, $16, and the client's meal, $20. She kept the receipts.

**d.** The couple provided additional information regarding their moving expenses. On May 1, the couple moved downtown to try downtown living and reduce Larry's commute. Before the move, Larry's roundtrip commute from home was 60 miles and after the move the commute was only 5 miles. The cost of the move was $2,000 as previously reported.

Prepare the 2010 individual income tax return for the Zepps. Complete Forms 1040, 2210, Schedules A, B, C, E and SE. Assume that all of the expenses except their business expenses are incurred jointly. Also assume that the "making work pay" credit is zero.

**8-2 Continuous Tax Return: Additional Questions.** Refer to the facts for the continuous tax return problem (Chapters 3, 4, 5, 6 and 7 above).

**a.** Cathy had several options regarding the treatment of her educational expenses related to her job. Explain these options and demonstrate with calculations why one is better than another.

**b.** Were the moving expenses deductible? Why or why not? Explain.

## Comprehensive Tax Return Problems

### COMPREHENSIVE TAX RETURN PROBLEM I

**1. David R. and Susan L. Holman**

**a.** David and Susan Holman are married and file a joint return. David is 38 years of age and Susan is 36. David is a self-employed certified real estate appraiser (C.R. E.), and Susan is employed by Wells Fargo Bank as a trust officer. They have two children: Richard Lawrence, age 7, and Karen Ann, age 4. The Holmans currently live at 5901 W. 75th Street, Los Angeles, California 90034, in a home they purchased and occupied on September 6, 2010.

Until August 12, 2010 the Holman family lived at 3085 Windmill Lane in Dallas, Texas, where David was employed by Vestpar Company, a real estate appraisal company and Susan was a bank officer for First National Bank. They sold their home in Dallas and moved to Los Angeles so that Susan could assume her new job as a trust officer and David could become self-employed.

**b.** David and Susan sold their home in Dallas for $315,000 and incurred the following expenses:

| | |
|---|---|
| Sales commission | $18,900 |
| Attorney's fee | 1,800 |
| Title insurance | 2,650 |
| Document preparation fee | 90 |
| Recording fee | 30 |
| Pest inspection fee | 190 |
| Prepayment penalty for early retirement of home mortgage (3 points) | 1,500 |

The Holmans had purchased the Dallas home on August 4, 2002 and never held it for rent or used it for business purposes. The home originally cost $177,500, and they had paid $6,200 for a cedar fence and $7,900 for landscaping. Within seven weeks of receiving a contract of sale on their house, the Holmans paid $8,500 for interior and exterior painting and $600 for steam-cleaning of the carpets. The sale was closed on August 1, 2010 and the Holmans were required to move out of the home by August 15, 2010.

**c.** In moving from Dallas to Los Angeles, the Holmans incurred the following expenses, none of which were reimbursed:

| | |
|---|---|
| Cost of moving household goods | $9,250 |
| Meals | 295 |
| Lodging | 350 |
| House-hunting expenses (including $150 for meals) | 1,000 |
| Temporary living expenses (20 days; including meals costing $400) | 1,700 |

Not included in any of the above expenses are the costs for driving two automobiles from Dallas to Los Angeles. David and Susan each drove a car, taking turns driving with the children. Although neither one of them kept receipts, Susan noted that her auto mileage was 1,500 miles. In addition, David noted that the number of miles from their old home to their old workplace was 24 miles, and the number of miles from their old home to their new workplace is 1,514 miles.

**d.** The Holmans purchased their new home for $525,000 by making a $125,000 down payment and financing the remaining balance with a 30-year, 6% conventional mortgage loan from California Federal Savings and Loan. They were required to prepay 2 points ($8,000) in return for the favorable mortgage terms. New furniture and drapes cost an additional $27,500.

**e.** The Holmans received the following Forms W-2, reporting their salaries for 2010:

**1.** David R. Holman, Social Security No. 452-64-5837:

| | |
|---|---|
| Gross salary | $75,000 |
| Federal income taxes withheld | 9,050 |
| F.I.C.A. taxes withheld: | |
| Social security | 4,650 |
| Medicare | 1088 |

**2.** Susan L. Holman, Social Security No. 467-32-5452:

| | *First Nat'l Bank* | *Wells Fargo Bank* | *Total* |
|---|---|---|---|
| Gross salary | $17,500 | $34,000 | $51,500 |
| Federal income taxes withheld | 1,100 | 4,150 | 5,250 |
| F.I.C.A. taxes withheld: | | | |
| Social security | 1,085 | 2,108 | 3,193 |
| Medicare | 254 | 493 | 747 |
| California income taxes withheld | — | 2,950 | 2,950 |

**f.** On October 1, 2010 David rented office space at 5510 Wacker Drive, Los Angeles, California 90025. The terms of the one-year lease agreement called for a monthly rent of $800, with the first and last month's rent paid in advance.

David decided to operate his business in the name of "David R. Holman, Certified Real Estate Appraiser," and he elected to use the cash method of accounting for his revenues and expenses. The following items relate to his business for 2010:

| | |
|---|---|
| Gross receipts | $85,000 |
| Expenses: | |
| Advertising | 250 |
| Bank service charges | 50 |
| Dues and publications | 450 |
| Insurance | 600* |
| Interest | 275 |
| Professional services | 525 |
| Office rent | 3,200** |
| Office supplies | 700 |
| Meals and entertainment | 500 |
| Miscellaneous expenses | 75 |

*Three months of coverage
**Includes prepayment of rent for September, 2010

David drove his personal automobile, a 2007 Buick LeSabre, 5,000 miles for business pur poses from October 1 through December 31. Rather than keeping receipts, he elected to use the automatic mileage method for determining his auto expenses. David's total auto mileage for the year was 20,000 miles.

On October 3, 2010 David purchased the following furniture and equipment for use in his business:

| | |
|---|---|
| Office furniture | $17,000 |
| Copying machine | 5,800 |
| Computers | 6,500 |
| Laser printers | 2,500 |
| Telephone system | 3,100 |

David elects to expense the maximum amount allowed under the optional expensing rules of § 179. He also elects to compute the maximum depreciation allowance using the appropriate MACRS percentages.

**g.** The Holmans received interest income during 2010 from the following:

| | |
|---|---|
| U.S. Treasury bills | $1,475 |
| First National Bank, Dallas | 625 |
| Wells Fargo Bank | 400 |
| Tarrant County municipal bonds | 800 |

**h.** David and Susan received the following dividends during 2010:

| | |
|---|---|
| Ford Motor Company | $300 |
| Eastman Kodak Company | 575 |
| IBM Corporation | 125 |
| Apple stock dividend (20 new shares of stock valued at $60 per share, received March 9, 2010) | 1,200 |

**i.** The Holmans have never maintained foreign bank accounts or created foreign trusts.

**j.** The Holmans report the following stock transactions for 2010:

1. Sold 100 shares of IBM stock for $120 per share on August 1, 2010. David had inherited 500 shares of IBM stock from his uncle on July 18, 2006, and the stock was valued at $170 per share on the date of his uncle's death.
2. Sold 400 shares of Apple stock for $78 per share on July 20, 2010. Susan had received 1,000 shares of Apple stock as a wedding present from her grandfather on June 3, 1998. Her grandfather had purchased the stock for $35 per share on May 7, 1995, and the stock was valued at $60 per share on the date of the gift. Susan's grandfather paid gift taxes of $10,000 as a result of the gift. Note: the amount of the annual exclusion taken into account in determining the taxable gift was $10,000.
3. Sold 300 shares of Intel stock for $40 per share on December 28, 2010, but did not receive the sales proceeds until January 3, 2011. The Holmans had paid $25 per share for the stock on May 21, 2007.

**k.** Susan has summarized the following cash expenditures for 2010 from canceled checks, mortgage company statements, and other documents:

| | |
|---|---|
| Prescription medicines and drugs | $ 982 |
| Medical insurance premiums (paid by Susan) | 2,830 |
| Doctors' and hospital bills (net of reimbursements) | 1,535 |
| Contact lenses for David | 218 |
| Real estate taxes paid on | |
| Dallas residence | 3,400 |
| Los Angeles residence | 5,600 |
| Sales taxes paid on Susan's new auto | 1,485 |
| Ad valorem taxes paid on both autos | 350 |
| Interest paid for | |
| Dallas home mortgage | 5,250* |
| Los Angeles home mortgage | 10,200** |
| Credit card interest | 480 |
| Personal car loan | 1,720 |
| Cash contributions to | |
| United Methodist Church | 5,200 |
| Salvation Army | 1,500 |
| Barack Obama Campaign Fund | 250 |
| Susan's unreimbursed employee expenses | 470*** |
| David's unreimbursed employee expenses | 360 |
| Tax return preparation fee | 375 |

*Does not include the mortgage prepayment penalty identified in item (b) above.
**Does not include the interest points charged for the new mortgage identified in item (d) above.
***Does not include any costs for meals or entertainment.

Susan also noted that she and David had driven their personal automobiles 500 miles to receive medical treatment for themselves and their children. She also has a receipt for 100 shares of Apple stock that she gave to her alma mater, Southern Methodist University, on November 12, 2010. The stock was valued at $70 per share on the date of the gift and was from the block of Apple stock Susan had received as a wedding present from her grandfather [see item (j)(2) above for details].

**l.** The Holmans paid the following child care expenses during 2010:

1. Kindergarten Day Care School . . . . . . . . . . . . . . . . . . . . . . . . . . . . $2,800
   1177 Valley View
   Dallas, Texas 75210
   EIN: 74-0186254

2. Happy Trails Day Center . . . . . . . . . . . . . . . . . . . . . . . . . . . . . . . . 2,200
   3692 Airport Blvd.
   Los Angeles, California 90034
   EIN: 78-0593676

Of the $5,000 total child care expenses, $3,000 was for Karen, and the remaining $2,000 was for Richard.

**m.** Social security numbers for the Holman children are provided below:

Richard L. Holman, Social Security No. 582-60-4732
Karen A. Holman, Social Security No. 582-60-5840

**n.** David and Susan made estimated Federal income tax payments of $1,750 each quarter, on 4/15/10, 6/15/10, 9/15/10, and 1/15/11.

**o.** The Holmans have always directed that $6 go to the Presidential Election Campaign by checking the "yes" boxes on their Form 1040.

*Required:*
Complete the Holmans' Federal income tax return for 2010. If they have a refund due, they would prefer having it credited against their 2011 taxes.

## Comprehensive Tax Return Problem 2

**2. Richard M. and Anna K. Wilson**

**a.** Richard and Anna Wilson are married and file a joint return. Richard is 47 years of age and Anna is 46. Richard is employed by Telstar Corporation as its controller and Anna is self-employed as a travel agent. They have three children: Michael, age 22; Lisa, age 17; and Laura, age 14. Michael is a full-time student at Rutgers University. Lisa and Laura both live at home and attend school full-time. The Wilsons currently live at 3721 Chestnut Ridge Road, Montvale, New Jersey 07645, in a home they have owned since July 1989.

Richard and Anna provided over half of the support of Anna's mother, who currently lives in a nursing home in Mahwah, New Jersey. They also provided over half of the support of their son, Michael, who earned $4,750 during the summer as an accounting student intern for a national accounting firm.

**b.** Richard received a Form W-2 from his employer reporting the following information for 2010:

Richard M. Wilson, Social Security No. 294-38-6249:

| | |
|---|---|
| Gross wages and taxable benefits | $63,000 |
| Federal income taxes withheld | 11,400 |
| F.I.C.A. taxes withheld: | |
| Social security | 3,906 |
| Medicare | 914 |
| State income taxes withheld | 1,850 |

The taxable benefits reported on his W-2 Form include $2,700 (based on the currently deductible standard auto mileage rate) for Richard's personal use of the company car provided by his employer.

**c.** Anna operates her business under the name "Wilson's Travel Agency," located at 7200 Treeline Drive, Montvale, NJ 07645. Anna has one full-time employee, and her Federal employer identification number is 74-2638596.

Anna uses the cash method of accounting for her business, and her records for 2010 show the following:

| | |
|---|---|
| Fees and commissions | $134,000 |
| Expenses: | |
| Advertising | 1,425 |
| Bank service charges | 75 |
| Dues and subscriptions | 560 |
| Insurance | 1,100 |
| Interest on furniture loan | 960 |
| Professional services | 700 |
| Office rent | 6,000 |
| Office supplies | 470 |
| Meals and entertainment | 1,000 |
| Payroll taxes | 2,170 |
| Utilities and telephone | 3,480 |
| Wages paid to full-time employee | 22,800 |
| Miscellaneous expenses | 20 |

Automobile expenses and amounts paid to her children are not included in the above expenses. Anna paid her daughters Lisa and Laura $750 and $450, respectively, for working part-time during the summer. Since she did not withhold or pay any Federal income or employment taxes on these amounts, Anna is not certain that she is allowed a deduction. She does feel that the amounts paid to her children were reasonable, however.

Anna purchased a new 2009 Honda Accord on November 20 of last year, and her tax accountant used the actual cost method in determining the deductible business expenses for her 2009 Federal tax return. Because the deductible amount seemed so small, she is not certain whether she should claim actual expenses (including depreciation), or simply use the automatic mileage method. She has the following records relating to the business auto:

| | |
|---|---|
| Original cost | $26,000 |
| Depreciation claimed in 2009 ($26,000 × 5% = $1,300 × 80% business use) | 1,040 |
| Gas, oil, and repairs in 2010 | 1,790 |
| Parking and tolls paid in 2010 | 410 |
| Insurance for 2010 | 650 |
| Interest on car loan for 2010 | 750 |

Anna drove the auto 20,000 miles for business purposes and 5,000 miles for personal purposes during the year. The above expenses for 2010 have not been reduced to reflect her personal use of the vehicle.

On January 7, 2010 Anna purchased the following items for use in her business:

| | |
|---|---|
| Office furniture | $8,900 |
| Copying machine | 5,700 |
| Dell notebook computer | 1,500 |
| Printer | 1,600 |
| Fax machine | 300 |

Anna wishes to claim the maximum amount of depreciation deductions or other cost recovery allowed on the office furniture and equipment.

**d.** Richard attended an accounting convention in Washington, D.C. for three days in October. He incurred the following unreimbursed expenses related to the trip:

| | |
|---|---|
| Air fare (round-trip) | $470 |
| Registration fee for meeting | 225 |
| Hotel cost | 375 |
| Meals | 130 |
| Taxis | 20 |
| Airport parking | 18 |
| Road tolls | 2 |

**e.** Richard and Anna received Forms 1099-INT reporting interest income earned during 2010 from the following:

| | |
|---|---|
| Citibank of Mahwah | $845 |
| Montvale National Bank | 900 |
| Telstar Employees' Credit Union | 755 |

**f.** The Wilsons received the following dividends during 2010:

| | |
|---|---|
| Telstar Corporation | $300 |
| Chevron Corporation | 200 |

These dividends were labeled as "qualified dividends" on the respective Forms 1099- DIV.

**g.** The Wilsons have never had a foreign bank account or created a foreign trust.

**h.** The Wilsons had the following property transactions for 2010:

1. Anna sold 300 shares of Chevron Corporation stock on September 9, 2010 in order to pay for Michael's fall semester of college. She received a check in the amount of $14,950 from Shearson Lehman on September 16, 2010. The stock was from a block of 1,000 shares that Richard and Anna had purchased for $35 per share on February 1, 1987.
2. They gave each of the children 100 shares of Chevron stock on December 30, 2010, when the stock was valued at $62.50 per share. The stock was from the same block of stock purchased for $35 per share in February, 1987. No gift taxes were paid on these gifts.

3. They gave 100 shares of Chevron stock to Richard's alma mater, Rider University, on December 29, 2010. The average trading price of Chevron stock on that day was $61.25. This stock was also from the original block of 1,000 shares the Wilsons had purchased for $35 per share in 1987. The address of Rider University is 2083 Lawrenceville Road, Lawrenceville, New Jersey 08648
4. On May 17, 2010, Richard and Anna were notified by the bankruptcy judge handling the affairs of Bubbling Crude Oil Company in Houston, Texas that the company's shareholders would not receive anything for their stock ownership because all of the assets were used to satisfy claims of creditors. Richard had purchased 2,000 shares of the stock for $6 per share on April 1, 1993. Unfortunately, the stock did not meet the requirements of § 1244.

**i.** Richard and Anna own a rental condominium located at 7777 Boardwalk in Atlantic City, New Jersey. The unit was purchased on July 29, 2009 for $25,000 cash and a $175,000 mortgage. Of the purchase price, $50,000 was allocated to the land. The following items relate to the rental unit for 2010:

| | |
|---|---|
| Gross rents | $16,400 |
| Expenses: | |
| Management fee | 2,460 |
| Cleaning and maintenance | 1,200 |
| Insurance | 840 |
| Property taxes | 2,750 |
| Interest paid on mortgage | 13,675 |
| Utilities | 850 |

Although the unfurnished unit was vacant for 11 weeks during the year, the Wilsons never used the property for personal purposes. When the property is rented, the tenant is required to pay for all utilities, and the Wilsons are charged a management fee equal to 15 percent of the rents collected.

**j.** The Wilsons have prepared the following summary of their other expenditures for 2010:

| | |
|---|---|
| Prescription medicines and drugs | $ 425 |
| Medical insurance premiums (paid by Richard) | 1,595 |
| Doctors' and hospital bills (net of reimbursements) | 805(1) |
| Dentist | 2,750(2) |
| Real estate taxes paid on home | 1,625 |
| State income taxes paid during 2010 | 2,100(3) |
| Interest paid for | |
| Original home mortgage | 8,690 |
| Home equity loan (secured by home) | 410(4) |
| Credit card interest | 275 |
| Personal car loan | 725 |
| Cash contributions to First Presbyterian Church | 1,200 |
| Fee for preparation of 2009 tax return | 650(5) |

(1) Does not include $11,485 of doctor bills paid by Richard and Anna for medical treatment provided to Anna's mother at the nursing home. Also not included is $115 that Anna paid for a new pair of eyeglasses for her mother.

(2) $2,350 of this amount represents a prepayment of Laura's braces. The dentist required the prepayment before he would begin the two-year dental program involved.

(3) Does not include amounts withheld from Richard's wages.

(4) Represents interest paid on a $25,000 home equity loan obtained by the Wilsons in 2010 to obtain a new boat.

(5) $200 is related to preparation of Schedule C

**k.** Anna made an $11,500 deductible contribution to her Keogh plan on December 15, 2010.

**l.** Richard paid the following unreimbursed employee business expenses:

| | |
|---|---|
| Professional dues | $450 |
| Professional journals | 385 |
| Office gifts to subordinates (none over $25) | 115 |

**m.** During the year, the Wilsons paid tuition of $9,350 and spent $1,875 on books and supplies for Michael's senior year of college.

**n.** The Wilsons received a state income tax refund of $130 in 2009. They had $18,750 of itemized deductions for 2009, and their 2009 taxable income was $52,825.

**o.** Richard and Anna made timely estimated Federal income tax payments of $2,250 each quarter on 4/15/10, 6/15/10, 9/15/10, and 1/15/11.

**p.** Social security numbers for Anna, the children, and Anna's mother are provided below:

| | Number |
|---|---|
| Anna K. Wilson | 296-48-2385 |
| Michael D. Wilson | 256-83-4421 |
| Lisa M. Wilson | 257-64-7573 |
| Laura D. Wilson | 258-34-2894 |
| Ruth Knapp | 451-38-3790 |

**q.** The Wilsons have always checked the "no" boxes on their Form 1040 regarding the Presidential Election Campaign fund contribution.

*Required:*

Complete the Wilsons' Federal income tax return for 2010. If they have a refund due, they would prefer having it credited against their 2011 taxes.

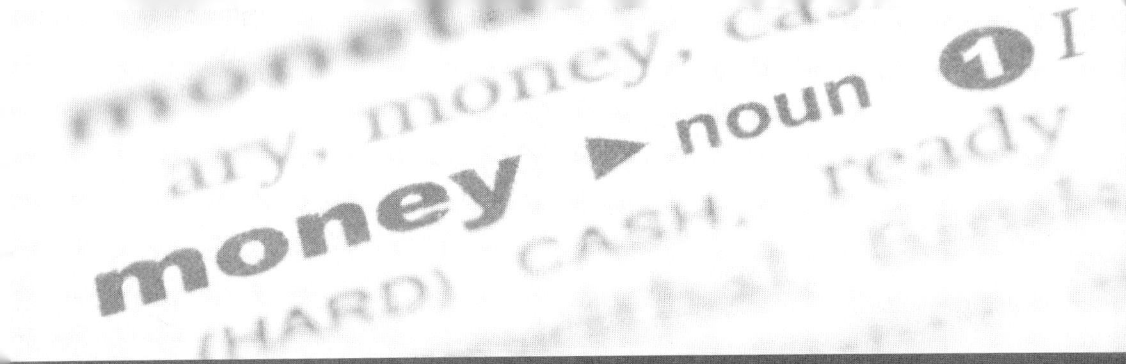

# E

# Glossary of Tax Terms

—A—

***A.*** (*see* Acquiescence).

***Accelerated Cost Recovery System (ACRS).*** An alternate form of depreciation enacted by the Economic Recovery Tax Act of 1981 and significantly modified by the Tax Reform Act of 1986. The modified cost recovery system applies to assets placed into service after 1986 and is referred to as MACRS. Under both systems, the cost of a qualifying asset is recovered over a set period of time. Salvage value is ignored. § 168.

***Accelerated Depreciation.*** Various depreciation methods that produce larger depreciation deductions in the earlier years of an asset's life than straight-line depreciation. Examples: double-declining balance method (200% declining balance) and sum-of-the-years'-digits method. § 167 (*see* Depreciation).

***Accounting Method.*** A method by which an entity's income and expenses are determined. The primary accounting methods used are the accrual method and the cash method. Other accounting methods include the installment method, the percentage-of-completion method (for construction), and various methods for valuing inventories, such as FIFO and LIFO. §§ 446 and 447 (*see also specific accounting methods*).

***Accounting Period.*** A period of time used by a taxpayer in determining his or her income, expenses, and tax liability. An accounting period is generally a year for tax purposes, either a calendar year, a fiscal year, or a 52-53 week year. §§ 441 and 443.

***Accrual Method of Accounting.*** The method of accounting that reflects the income earned and the expenses incurred during a given tax period. However, unearned income of an accrual basis taxpayer must generally be included in an entity's income in the year in which it is received, even if it is not actually earned by the entity until a later tax Period. § 446.

***Accumulated Adjustment Account (AAA).*** A summary of all includible income and gains, expenses, and losses of an S Corporation for taxable years after 1982, except those that relate to excludable income, distributions, and redemptions of an S Corporation. Distributions from the AAA are not taxable to the shareholders. §§ 1368(c)(1) and (3)(1).

***Accumulated Earnings Credit.*** A reduction in arriving at a corporation's accumulated taxable income (in computing the Accumulated Earnings Tax). Its purpose is to avoid penalizing a corporation for retaining sufficient earnings and profits to meet the reasonable needs of the business. § 535(c).

***Accumulated Earnings Tax.*** A penalty tax on the unreasonable accumulation of earnings and profits by a corporation. It is intended to encourage the distribution of earnings and profits of a corporation to its shareholders. §§ 531-537.

***Accumulated Taxable Income.*** The amount on which the accumulated earnings tax is imposed. §§ 531 and 535.

***Accuracy-Related Penalty.*** Any of the group of penalties that includes negligence or disregard of rules or regulations, substantial understatement of income tax, substantial valuation misstatement for income tax purposes, substantial overstatement of pension liabilities, and substantial estate or gift valuation understatement. § 6662.

***Acquiescence.*** The public endorsement of a regular Tax Court decision by the Commissioner of the Internal Revenue Service. When the Commissioner acquiesces to a regular Tax Court decision, the IRS generally will not dispute the result in cases involving substantially similar facts (*see* Nonacquiescence).

***Ad Valorem Tax.*** A tax based on the value of property.

***Adjusted Basis.*** The basis (i.e., cost or other basis) of property plus capital improvements minus depreciation allowed or allowable. See § 1016 for other adjustments to basis. § 1016 (*see* Basis).

***Adjusted Gross Income.*** A term used with reference to individual taxpayers. Adjusted gross income consists of an individual's gross income less certain deductions and business expenses. § 62.

***Adjusted Ordinary Gross Income (AOGI).*** A term used in relation to personal holding companies. Adjusted ordinary gross income is determined by subtracting certain expenses related to rents and mineral, oil, and gas royalties, and certain interest expense from ordinary gross income § 543(b)(2).

***Administrator.*** A person appointed by the court to administrate the estate of a deceased person. If named to perform these duties by the decedent's will, this person is called an executor (executrix).

***AFTR (American Federal Tax Reports).*** These volumes contain the Federal tax decisions issued by the U.S. District Courts, U.S. Court of Federal Claims, U.S. Circuit Courts of Appeals, and the U.S. Supreme Court (*see* AFTR2d).

***AFTR2d (American Federal Tax Reports, Second Series).*** The second series of the American Federal Tax Reports. These volumes contain the Federal tax decisions issued by the U.S. District Courts, U.S. Court of Federal Claims. U.S. Circuit Courts of Appeals, and the U.S. Supreme Court (*see* AFTR).

***Alternate Valuation Date.*** The property contained in a decedent's gross estate must be valued at either the decedent's date of death or the alternate valuation date. The alternate valuation date is six months after the decedent's date of death, or, if the property is disposed of prior to that date; the particular property disposed of is valued as of the date of its disposition. § 2032.

***Alternative Minimum Tax.*** A tax imposed on taxpayers only if it exceeds the "regular" tax of the taxpayer. Regular taxable income is adjusted by certain timing differences, then increased by tax preferences to arrive at alternative minimum taxable income.

***Amortization.*** The systematic write-off (deduction) of the cost or other basis of an intangible asset over its estimated useful life. The concept is similar to depreciation (used for tangible assets) and depletion (used for natural resources) (*see* Goodwill; Intangible Asset).

***Amount Realized.*** Any money received, plus the fair market value of any other property or services received, plus any liabilities discharged on the sale or other disposition of property. The determination of the amount realized is the first step in determining realized gain or loss. § 1001(b).

***Annual Exclusion.*** The amount each year that a donor may exclude from Federal gift tax for each donee. Currently, the annual exclusion is $13,000 per donee. The annual exclusion does not generally apply to gifts of future interests. § 2503(b).

***Annuity.*** A fixed amount of money payable to a person at specific intervals for either a specific period of time or for life.

***Appellate Court.*** A court to which other court decisions are appealed. The appellate courts for Federal tax purposes include the Courts of Appeals and the Supreme Court.

***Arm's-Length Transaction.*** A transaction entered into by unrelated parties, all acting in their own best interests. It is presumed that in an arm's length transaction the prices used are the fair market values of the properties or services being transferred in the transaction.

***Articles of Incorporation.*** The basic instrument filed with the appropriate state agency when a business is incorporated.

***Assessment of Tax.*** The imposition of an additional tax liability by the Internal Revenue Service (i.e., as the result of an audit).

***Assignment of Income.*** A situation in which a taxpayer assigns income or income-producing property to another person or entity in an attempt to avoid paying taxes on that income. An assignment of income or income-producing property is generally not recognized for tax purposes, and the income is taxable to the assignor.

***Association.*** An entity that possesses a majority of the following characteristics: associates; profit motive; continuity of life; centralized management; limited liability; free transferability of interests. Associations are taxed as corporations. §§ 7701(a)(3). Reg. § 301.7701-2.

***At-Risk Limitation.*** A provision that limits a deduction for losses to the amounts "at risk." A taxpayer is generally not "at risk" in situations where nonrecourse debt is used. § 465.

***Attribution.*** (*see* Constructive Ownership).

***Audit.*** The examination of a taxpayer's return or other taxable transactions by the Internal Revenue Service in order to determine the correct tax liability. Types of audits include correspondence audits, office audits, and field audits (*see also* Correspondence Audit; Office Audit; Field Audit).

—B—

***Bad Debt.*** An uncollectible debt. A bad debt may be classified either as a business bad debt or a nonbusiness bad debt. A business bad debt is one that has arisen in the course of the taxpayer's business (with a business purpose). Nonbusiness bad debts are treated as short-term capital losses rather than as ordinary losses. § 166.

***Bargain Sale, Rental, or Purchase.*** A sale, rental, or purchase of property for less than its fair market value. The difference between the sale, rental, or purchase price and the property's fair market value may have its own tax consequences, such as consideration as a constructive dividend or a gift.

***Bartering.*** The exchange of goods and services without using money.

***Basis.*** The starting point in determining the gain or loss from the sale or other disposition of an asset, or the depreciation (or depletion or amortization) on an asset. For example, if an asset is purchased for cash, the basis of that as set is the cash paid. §§ 1012, 1014, 1015, 334, 359, 362.

***Beneficiary.*** Someone who will benefit from an act of another, such as the beneficiary of a life insurance contract, the beneficiary of a trust (i.e., income beneficiary), or the beneficiary of an estate.

***Bequest.*** A testamentary transfer (by will) of personal property (personalty).

***Board of Tax Appeals (B.T.A.).*** The predecessor of the United States Tax Court, in existence from 1924 to 1942.

***Bona Fide.*** Real; in good faith.

***Boot.*** Cash or property that is not included in the definition of a particular type of nontaxable exchange [*see* §§ 351(b) and 1031(b)]. In these nontaxable exchanges, a taxpayer who receives boot must recognize gain to the extent of the boot received or the realized gain, whichever is less.

***Brother-Sister Corporations.*** A controlled group of two or more corporations owned (in certain amounts) by five or fewer individuals, estates, or trusts. § 1563(a)(2).

***Burden of Proof.*** The weight of evidence in a legal case or in a tax proceeding. Generally, the burden of proof is on the taxpayer in a tax case. However, the burden of proof is on the government in fraud cases. § 7454.

***Business Purpose.*** An actual business reason for following a course of action. Tax avoidance alone is not considered to be a business purpose. In areas such as corporate formation and corporate reorganizations, business purpose is especially important.

—C—

***Capital Asset.*** All proper by held by a taxpayer (e.g., house, car, clothing) except for certain assets that are specifically excluded from the definition of a capital asset, such as inventory and depreciable and real property used in a trade or business.

***Capital Contribution.*** Cash, services, or property contributed by a partner to a partnership or by a shareholder to a corporation. Capital contributions are not income to the recipient partnership or corporation. §§ 721 and 118.

***Capital Expenditure.*** Any amount paid for new buildings or for permanent improvements; any expenditures that add to the value or prolong the life of property or adapt the property to a new or different use. Capital expenditures should be added to the basis of the property improved. § 263.

***Capital Gain.*** A gain from the sale or other disposition of a capital asset. § 1222.

***Capital Loss.*** A loss from the sale or other disposition of a capital asset. § 1222.

***Cash Method of Accounting.*** The method of accounting that reflects the income received (or constructively received) and the expenses paid during a given period. However, prepaid expenses of a cash basis taxpayer that benefit more than one year may be required to be deducted only in the periods benefited (e.g., a premium for a three-year insurance policy may have to be spread over three years).

***CCH.*** (*see* Commerce Clearing House).

***C Corporation.*** A so-called regular corporation that is a separate tax-paying entity and is subject to the tax rules contained in Subchapter C of the Internal Revenue Code (as opposed to an S corporation, which is subject to the tax rules of Subchapter S of the Code).

***Certiorari.*** A Writ of Certiorari is the form used to appeal a lower court (U.S. Court of Appeals) decision to the Supreme Court. The Supreme Court then decides, by reviewing the Writ of Certiorari, whether it will accept the appeal or not. The Supreme Court generally does not accept the appeal unless a constitutional issue is involved or the lower courts are in conflict. If the Supreme Court refuses to accept the appeal, then the certiorari is denied (cert. den.).

***Claim of Right Doctrine.*** If a taxpayer has an unrestricted claim to income, the income is included in that taxpayer's income when it is received or constructively received, even if there is a possibility that all or part of the income may have to be returned to another party.

***Closely Held Corporation.*** A corporation whose voting stock is owned by one or a few shareholders and is operated by this person or closely knit group.

***Collapsible Corporation.*** A corporation that liquidates before it has realized a substantial portion of its income. Shareholders treat the gain on these liquidating distributions as ordinary income (rather than dividend income or capital gains). § 341.

***Commerce Clearing House.*** A publisher of tax materials, including a multivolume tax service, volumes that contain the Federal courts' decisions on tax matters (USTC) and the Tax Court regular (T.C.) and memorandum (TCM) decisions.

***Community Property.*** Property that is owned together by husband and wife, where each has an undivided one-half interest in the property due to their marital status. The ten community property states are Alaska, Arizona, California, Idaho, Louisiana, Nevada, New Mexico, Texas, Washington, and Wisconsin.

***Complex Trust.*** Any trust that does not meet the requirements of a simple trust. For example, a trust will be considered to be a complex trust if it does not distribute the trust income currently, if it takes a deduction for a charitable contribution for the current year, or if it distributes any of the trust corpus currently. § 661.

***Condemnation.*** The taking of private property for a public use by a public authority, an exercise of the power of eminent domain. The public authority compensates the owner of the property taken in a condemnation (*see also* Involuntary Conversion).

***Conduit Principle.*** The provisions in the tax law that allow specific tax characteristics to be passed through certain entities to the owners of the entity without losing their identity. For example, the short-term capital gains of a partnership would be passed through to the partners and retain their character as short-term capital gains on the tax returns of the partners. This principle applies in varying degrees to partnerships, S corporations, estates, and trusts

***Consent Dividend.*** A term used in relation to the accumulated earnings tax and the personal holding company tax. A consent dividend occurs when the shareholders consent to treat a certain amount as a taxable dividend on their tax returns even though there is no distribution of cash or property. The purpose of this is to obtain a dividends-paid deduction. § 565.

***Consolidated Return.*** A method used to determine the tax liability of a group of affiliated corporations. The aggregate income (with certain adjustments) of a group is viewed as the income of a single enterprise. § 1501.

***Consolidation.*** The statutory combination of two or more corporations in a new corporation. § 368(a)(1)(A).

***Constructive Dividends.*** The constructive receipt of a dividend. Even though a taxable benefit was not designated as a dividend by the distributing corporation, a shareholder may be designated by the IRS as having received a dividend if the benefit has the appearance of a dividend. For example, if a shareholder uses corporate property for personal purposes rent-free, he or she will have a constructive dividend equal to the fair rental value of the corporate property.

***Constructive Ownership.*** In certain situations the tax law attributes the ownership of stock to persons "related" to the person or entity that actually owns the stock. The related party is said to constructively own the stock of that person. For example, under § 267(c) a father is considered to constructively own all stock actually owned by his son. §§ 267, 318, and 544(a).

***Constructive Receipt.*** When income is available to a taxpayer, even though it is not actually received by the taxpayer, the amount is considered to be constructively received by the taxpayer and should be included in income (e.g., accrued interest on a savings account). However, if there are restrictions on the availability of the income, it is generally not considered to be constructively received until the restrictions are removed (e.g., interest on a 6-month certificate of deposit is not constructively received until the end of the 6-month period if early withdrawal would result in loss of interest or principal).

***Contributions to the Capital of a Corporation.*** (*see* Capital Contributions).

***Corpus.*** The principal of a trust, as opposed to the income of the trust. Also called the *res* of the trust.

***Correspondence Audit.*** An IRS audit conducted through the mail. Generally, verification or substantiation for specified items is requested by the IRS, and the taxpayer mails the requested information to the IRS (*see* Field Audit; Office Audit).

***Cost Depletion.*** (*see* Depletion).

***Court of Appeals.*** The U.S. Federal court system has 13 circuit Courts of Appeals, which consider cases appealed from the U.S. Court of Federal Claims, the U.S. Tax Court, and the U.S. District Courts. A writ of certiorari is used to appeal a case from a Court of Appeals to the U.S. Supreme Court (*see* Appellate Court).

***Creditor.*** A person or entity to whom money is owed. The person or entity who owes the money is called the debtor.

—D—

***Death Tax.*** A tax imposed on property upon the death of the owner, such as an estate tax or inheritance tax.

***Debtor.*** A person or entity who owes money to another. The person or entity to whom the money is owed is called the creditor.

***Decedent.*** A deceased person.

***Deductions in Respect of a Decedent (DRD).*** Certain expenses that are incurred by a decedent but are not properly deductible on the decedent's first return because of nonpayment. Deductions in respect of a decedent are deducted by the taxpayer who is legally required to make payment. § 691(b).

***Deficiency.*** An additional tax liability owed to the IRS by a taxpayer. A deficiency is generally proposed by the IRS through the use of a Revenue Agent's Report.

***Deficit.*** A negative balance in retained earnings or in earnings and profits.

***Dependent.*** A person who derives his or her primary support from another. In order for a taxpayer to claim a dependency exemption for a person, there are five tests that must be met: support test, gross income test, citizenship or residency test, relationship or member of household test, and joint return test. § 152.

***Depletion.*** As natural resources are extracted and sold, the cost or other basis of the resource is recovered by the use of depletion. Depletion may be either cost or percentage (statutory) depletion. Cost depletion has to do with the recovery of the cost of natural resources based on the units of the resource sold. Percentage depletion uses percentages given in the Internal Revenue Code multiplied by the gross income from the interest. subject to limitations. §§ 613 and 613A.

***Depreciation.*** The systematic write-off of the basis of a tangible asset over the asset's estimated useful life. Depreciation is intended to reflect the wear, tear, and obsolescence of the asset (*see* Amortization; Depletion).

***Depreciation Recapture.*** The situation in which all or part of the realized gain from the sale or other disposition of depreciable business property could be treated as ordinary income. See text for discussion of §§ 291, 1245, and 1250.

***Determination Letter.*** A written statement regarding the tax consequences of a transaction issued by an IRS District Director in response to a written inquiry by a taxpayer that applies to a particular set of facts. Determination letters are frequently used to state whether a pension or profit-sharing plan is qualified or not, to determine the tax-exempt status of nonprofit organizations, and to clarify employee status.

***Discretionary Trust.*** A trust in which the trustee or another party has the right to determine whether to accumulate or distribute the trust income currently, and/or which beneficiary is to receive the trust income.

***Discriminant Function System (DIF).*** The computerized system used by the Internal Revenue Service in identifying and selecting returns for examination. This system uses secret mathematical formulas to select those returns that have a probability of tax errors.

***Dissent.*** A disagreement with the majority opinion. The term is generally used to mean the explicit disagreement of one or more judges in a court with the majority decision on a particular case.

***Distributable Net Income (DNI).*** The net income of a fiduciary that is available for distribution to income beneficiaries. DNI is computed by adjusting an estate's or trust's taxable income by certain modifications. § 643(a).

***Distribution in Kind.*** A distribution of property as it is. For example, rather than selling property and distributing the proceeds to the shareholders, the property itself is distributed to the shareholders.

***District Court.*** A trial court in which Federal tax matters can be litigated; the only trial court in which a jury trial can be obtained.

***Dividend.*** A payment by a corporation to its shareholders authorized by the corporation's board of directors to be distributed pro rata among the outstanding shares. However, a constructive dividend does not need to be authorized by the shareholders (*see also* Constructive Dividend).

***Dividends-Paid Deduction.*** A deduction allowed in determining the amount that is subject to the accumulated earnings tax and the personal holding company tax. §§ 561-565.

***Dividends-Received Deduction.*** A deduction available to corporations on dividends received from a domestic corporation. The dividends-received deduction is generally 70 percent of the dividends received. If the recipient corporation owns 20 percent or more of the stock of the paying corporation, an 80 percent deduction is allowed. The dividends-received deduction is 100 percent of the dividends received from another member of an affiliated group, if an election is made §§ 243-246.

***Domestic Corporation.*** A corporation which is created or organized in the United States or under the law of the United States or of any state. § 7701(a)(4).

***Donee.*** The person or entity to whom a gift is made.

***Donor.*** The person or entity who makes a gift.

***Double Taxation.*** A situation in which income is taxed twice. For example, a regular corporation pays tax on its taxable income, and when this income is distributed to the corporation's shareholders, the shareholders are taxed on the dividend income.

—E—

***Earned Income.*** Income from personal services. § 911(d)(2).

***Earnings and Profits (E&P).*** The measure of a corporation's ability to pay dividends to its shareholders. Distributions made by a corporation to its shareholders are dividends to the extent of the corporation's earnings and profits. §§ 312 and 316.

***Eminent Domain.*** (*see* Condemnation).

***Employee.*** A person in the service of another, where the employer has the power to specify how the work is to be performed (*see* Independent Contractor).

***Employee Achievement Award.*** An award of tangible personalty that is made for length of service achievement or safety achievement. § 274(j).

***Encumbrance.*** A liability.

***Entity.*** For tax purposes, an organization that is considered to have a separate existence, such as a partnership, corporation, estate, or trust.

***Escrow.*** Cash or other property that is held by a third party as security for an obligation.

***Estate.*** All of the property owned by a decedent at the time of his or her death

***Estate Tax.*** A tax imposed on the transfer of a decedent's taxable estate. The estate, not the heirs, is liable for the estate tax. §§ 2001-2209 (*see* Inheritance Tax).

***Estoppel.*** A bar or impediment preventing a party from asserting a fact or a claim in court that is inconsistent with a position he or she had previously taken.

***Excise Tax.*** A tax imposed on the sale, manufacture, or use of a commodity or on the conduct of an occupation or activity; considered to include every Internal Revenue Tax except the income tax.

***Executor.*** A person appointed in a will to carry out the provisions in the will and to administer the estate of the decedent. (Feminine of *executor* is *executrix*.)

***Exempt Organization.*** An organization (such as a charitable organization) that is exempt from Federal income taxes. §§ 501-528.

***Exemption.*** A deduction allowed in computing taxable income. Personal exemptions are available for the taxpayer and his or her spouse. Dependency exemptions are available for the taxpayer's dependents. §§ 151-154 (*see* Dependent).

***Expatriate (U.S.).*** U.S. citizen working in a foreign country.

—F—

***F.2d (Federal Reporter, Second Series).*** Volumes in which the decisions of the U.S. Court of Federal Claims and the U.S. Courts of Appeals are published.

***F. Supp. (Federal Supplement).*** Volumes in which the decisions of the U.S. District Courts are published.

***Fair Market Value.*** The amount that a willing buyer would pay a willing seller in an arm's-length transaction.

***Fed. (Federal Reporter).*** Volumes in which the decisions of the U.S. Court of Federal Claims and the U.S. Courts of Appeals are published.

***FICA (Federal Insurance Contributions Act).*** The law dealing with social security taxes and benefits. §§ 3101-3126.

***Fiduciary.*** A person or institution who holds and manages property for another, such as a guardian, trustee, executor, or administrator. § 7701 (a)(6).

***Field Audit.*** An audit conducted by the IRS at the taxpayer's place of business or at the place of business of the taxpayer's representative. Field audits are generally conducted by Revenue Agents (*see* Correspondence Audit: Office Audit).

***FIFO (First-in, First-out).*** A method of determining the cost of an inventory. The first inventory units acquired are considered to be the first sold. Therefore, the cost of the inventory would consist of the most recently acquired inventory.

***Filing Status.*** The filing status of an individual taxpayer determines the tax rates that are applicable to that taxpayer. The filing statuses include Single, Head of Household, Married Filing Jointly, Married Filing Separately, and Surviving Spouse (Qualifying Widow or Widower).

***Fiscal Year.*** A period of 12 consecutive months, other than a calendar year, used as the accounting period of a business. § 7701(a)(24).

***Foreign Corporation.*** A corporation that is not organized under U.S. laws. other than a domestic corporation. § 7701(a)(5).

***Foreign Tax Credit.*** A credit available against taxes for foreign income taxes paid or deemed paid. A deduction may be taken for these foreign taxes as an alternative to the foreign tax credit. §§ 27 and 901-905.

***Fraud.*** A willful intent to evade tax. For tax purposes, fraud is divided into civil fraud and criminal fraud. The IRS has the burden of proof of proving fraud. Civil fraud has a penalty of 75 percent of the underpayment [§ 6653(b)]. Criminal fraud requires a greater degree of willful intent to evade tax (§§ 7201-7207).

***Freedom of Information Act.*** The means by which the public may obtain information held by Federal agencies.

***Fringe Benefits.*** Benefits received by an employee in addition to his or her salary or wages, such as insurance and recreational facilities.

***FUTA (Federal Unemployment Tax Act).*** A tax imposed on the employer on the wages of the employees. A credit is generally given for amounts contributed to state unemployment tax funds. §§ 3301-3311.

***Future Interest.*** An interest, the possession or enjoyment of which will come into being at some point in the future. The annual exclusion for gifts applies only to gifts of present interests, as opposed to future interests.

—G—

***General Partner.*** A partner who is jointly and severally liable for the debts of the partnership. A general partner has no limited liability (*see* Limited Partner).

***Generation-Skipping Tax.*** A transfer tax imposed on a certain type of transfer involving a trust and at least three generations of taxpayers. The transfer generally skips a generation younger than the original transferor. The transfer therefore results in the avoidance of one generation's estate tax on the transferred property. §§ 2601-2622.

***Gift.*** A transfer of property or money given for less than adequate consideration in money or money's worth.

***Gift-Splitting.*** A tax provision that allows a married person who makes a gift of his or her property to elect, with the consent of his or her spouse, to treat the gift as being made one-half by each the taxpayer and his or her spouse. The effect of gift-splitting is to take advantage of the annual gift tax exclusions for both the taxpayer and his or her spouse. § 2513.

***Gift Tax.*** A tax imposed on the donor of a gift. The tax applies to transfers in trust or otherwise, whether the gift is direct or indirect, real or personal, tangible or intangible. §§ 2501-2524.

***Goodwill.*** An intangible that has an indefinite useful life, arising from the difference between the purchase price and the value of the assets of an acquired business. Goodwill is amortizable over a 15-year period. § 263(b).

***Grantor.*** The person who creates a trust.

***Gross Estate.*** The value of all property, real or personal, tangible or intangible, owned by a decedent at the time of his or her death. §§ 2031-2046.

***Gross Income.*** Income that is subject to Federal income tax. All income from whatever source derived, unless it is specifically excluded from income (e.g., interest on state and local bonds). § 61.

***Guaranteed Payment.*** A payment made by a partnership to a partner for services or the use of capital, without regard to the income of the partnership. The payment generally is deductible by the partnership and taxable to the partner. § 707(c).

—H—

***Half-Year Convention.*** When using ACRS or MACRS, personalty placed in service at any time during the year is treated as placed in service in the middle of the year, and personalty disposed of or retired at any time during the year is treated as disposed of in the middle of the year. However, if more than 40 percent of all personalty placed in service during the year is placed in service during the last three months of the year, the mid-quarter convention applies. § 168(d)(4)(A).

***Heir.*** One who inherits property from a decedent.

***Hobby.*** An activity not engaged in for profit. § 183.

***Holding Period.*** The period of time that property is held. Holding period is used to determine whether a gain or loss is short-term or long-term. §§ 1222 and 1223.

***H.R. 10 Plans.*** (*see* Keogh Plans).

—I—

***Incident of Ownership.*** Any economic interest in a life insurance policy, such as the power to change the policy's beneficiary, the right to cancel or assign the policy, and the right to borrow against the policy. § 2042(2).

***Income Beneficiary.*** The person or entity entitled to receive the income from property. Generally used in reference to trusts.

***Income in Respect of a Decedent (IRD).*** Income that had been earned by a decedent at the time of his or her death, but is not included on the final tax return because of the decedent's method of accounting. Income in respect of a decedent is included in the decedent's gross estate and also on the tax return of the person who receives the income. § 691.

***Independent Contractor.*** One who contracts to do a job according to his or her own methods and skills. The employer has control over the independent contractor only as to the final result of his or her work (*see* Employee).

***Indirect Method.*** A method used by the IRS in order to determine whether a taxpayer's income is correctly reported when adequate records do not exist. Indirect methods include the Source and Applications of Funds Method and the Net Worth Method.

***Information Return.*** A return that must be filed with the Internal Revenue Service even though no tax is imposed, such as a partnership return (Form 1065), Form W-2, and Form 1099.

***Inheritance Tax.*** A tax imposed on the privilege of receiving property of a decedent. The tax is imposed on the heir.

***Installment Method.*** A method of accounting under which a taxpayer spreads the recognition of his or her gain ratably over time as the payments are received. §§ 453, 453A, and 453B.

***Intangible Asset.*** A nonphysical asset, such as goodwill, copyrights, franchises, or trademarks.

***Inter Vivos Transfer.*** A property transfer during the life of the owner.

***Intercompany Transaction.*** A transaction that occurs during a consolidated return year between two or more members of the same affiliated group.

***Internal Revenue Service.*** Part of the Treasury Department, it is responsible for administering and enforcing the Federal tax laws.

***Intestate.*** No will existing at the time of death.

***Investment Tax Credit.*** A credit against tax that was allowed for investing in depreciable tangible personalty before 1986. The credit was equal to 10 percent of the qualified investment. §§ 38 and 46-48.

***Investment Credit Recapture.*** When property on which an investment credit has been taken is disposed of prior to the full time period required under the law to earn the credit, then the amount of unearned credit must be added back to the taxpayer's tax liability-this is called recapture of the investment credit. § 47.

***Involuntary Conversion.*** The complete or partial destruction, theft, seizure, requisition, or condemnation of property. § 1033.

***Itemized Deductions.*** Certain expenditures of a personal nature that are specifically allowed to be deductible from an individual taxpayer's adjusted gross income. Itemized deductions (e.g., medical expenses, charitable contributions, interest, taxes, and miscellaneous itemized deductions) are deductible if they exceed the taxpayer's standard deduction.

—J—

***Jeopardy Assessment.*** If the IRS has reason to believe that the collection or assessment of a tax would be jeopardized by delay, the IRS may assess and collect the tax immediately. §§ 6861-6864.

***Joint and Several Liability.*** The creditor has the ability to sue one or more of the parties who have a liability, or all of the liable persons together. General partners are jointly and severally liable for the debts of the partnership. Also, if a husband and wife file a joint return, they are jointly and severally liable to the IRS for the taxes due.

***Joint Tenancy.*** Property held by two or more owners, where each has an undivided interest in the property. Joint tenancy includes the right of survivorship, which means that upon the death of an owner, his or her share passes to the surviving owner(s).

***Joint Venture.*** A joining together of two or more persons in order to undertake a specific business project. A joint venture is not a continuing relationship like a partnership, but may be treated as a partnership for Federal income tax purposes. § 761(a).

—K—

***Keogh Plans.*** A retirement plan available for self-employed taxpayers. § 401.

***Kiddie Tax.*** Unearned income of a child under age 19 is taxed at the child's parents' marginal tax rate. § 1(i).

—L—

***Leaseback.*** A transaction in which a taxpayer sells property and then leases back the property.

***Lessee.*** A person or entity who rents or leases property from another.

***Lessor.*** A person or entity who rents or leases property to another. Life Insurance. A form of insurance that will pay the beneficiary of the policy a fixed amount upon the death of the insured person.

***Life Estate.*** A trust or legal arrangement by which a certain person (life tenant) is entitled to receive the income from designated property for his or her life.

***Life Insurance.*** A form of insurance that will pay the beneficiary of the policy a fixed amount upon the death of the insured person.

***LIFO (Last-in, First-out).*** A method of determining the cost of an inventory. The last inventory units acquired are considered to be the first sold. Therefore, the cost of the inventory would consist of the earliest acquired inventory.

***Like-Kind Exchange.*** The exchange of property held for productive use in a trade or business or for investment (but not inventory, stock, bonds, or notes) for property that is also held for productive use or for investment (i.e., realty for realty; personalty for personalty). No gain or loss is generally recognized by either party unless boot (other than qualifying property) is involved in the transaction. § 1031.

***Limited Liability.*** The situation in which the liability of an owner of an organization for the organization's debts is limited to the owner's investment in the organization. Examples of taxpayers with limited liability are corporate shareholders and the limited partners in a limited partnership.

***Limited Liability Company (LLC).*** A form of business entity permitted by all states in the U.S. under which the owners are treated as partners and the company is subject to the rules of partnership taxation for Federal tax purposes.

***Limited Partner.*** A partner whose liability for partnership debts is limited to his or her investment in the partnership. A limited partner may take no active part in the management of the partnership according to the Uniform Limited Partnership Act (*see* General Partner).

***Limited Partnership.*** A partnership with *one* or more general partners *and* one or more limited partners. The limited partners are liable only up to the amount of their contribution plus any personally guaranteed debt. Limited partners cannot participate in the management or control of the partnership.

***Liquidation.*** The cessation of all or part of a corporation's operations or the corporate form of business and the distribution of the corporate assets to the shareholders. §§ 331-337.

***Lump Sum Distribution.*** Payment at one time of an entire amount due, or the entire proceeds of a pension or profit-sharing plan, rather than installment payments.

## —M—

***Majority.*** Of legal age (*see* Minor).

***Marital Deduction.*** Upon the transfer of property from one spouse to another, either by gift or at death. the Internal Revenue Code allows a transfer tax deduction for the amount transferred.

***Market Value.*** (*see* Fair Market Value).

***Material Participation.*** Occurs when a taxpayer is involved in the operations of an activity on a regular, continuous, and substantial basis. § 469(h).

***Merger.*** The absorption of one corporation (target corporation) by another corporation (acquiring corporation). The target corporation transfers its assets to the acquiring corporation in return for stock or securities of the acquiring corporation. Then the target corporation dissolves by exchanging the acquiring corporation's stock for its own stock held by its shareholders.

***Mid-Month Convention.*** When a taxpayer is using ACRS or MACRS, realty placed in service at any time during a month is treated as placed in service in the middle of the month, and realty disposed of or retired at any time during a month is treated as disposed of in the middle of the month. § 168(d)(4)(B).

***Mid-Quarter Convention.*** Used for all personalty placed in service during the year if more than 40 percent of all personalty placed in service during the year is placed in service during the last three months of the year. § 168(d)(4)(C).

***Minimum Tax.*** (*see* Alternative Minimum Tax).

***Minor.*** A person who has not yet reached the age of legal majority. In most states, a minor is a person under 18 years of age.

***Mortgagee.*** The person or entity that holds the mortgage; the lender; the creditor.

***Mortgagor.*** The person or entity that is mortgaging the property; the debtor.

## —N—

***NA.*** (*see* Nonacquiescence).

***Negligence Penalty.*** A penalty imposed by the IRS on taxpayers who are negligent or intentionally disregard the rules or regulations (but are not fraudulent), in the determination of their tax liability. § 6662.

***Net Operating Loss (NOL).*** The amount by which deductions exceed a taxpayer's gross income. § 172.

***Net Worth Method.*** An indirect method of determining a taxpayer's income used by the IRS when adequate records do not exist. The net worth of the taxpayer is determined for the end of each year in question, and adjustments are made to the increase in net worth from year to year for nontaxable sources of income and nondeductible expenditures. This method is often used when a possibility of fraud exists.

***Ninety-Day Letter.*** (*see* Statutory Notice of Deficiency).

***Nonacquiescence.*** The public announcement that the Commissioner of the Internal Revenue Service disagrees with a regular Tax Court decision. When the Commissioner non-acquiesces to a regular Tax Court decision, the IRS generally will litigate cases involving similar facts (*see* Acquiescence).

***Nonresident Alien.*** A person who is not a resident or citizen of the United States.

—O—

***Office Audit.*** An audit conducted by the Internal Revenue Service on IRS premises. The person conducting the audit is generally referred to as an Office Auditor (*see* Correspondence Audit; Field Audit).

***Office Auditor.*** An IRS employee who conducts primarily office audits, as opposed to a Revenue Agent, who conducts primarily field audits (*see also* Revenue Agent).

***Ordinary Gross Income.*** A term used in relation to personal holding companies. Ordinary gross income is determined by subtracting capital gains and § 1231 gains from gross income. § 1231 gains from gross income. § 543(b)(1).

—P—

***Partial Liquidation.*** A distribution that is not essentially equivalent to a dividend, or a distribution that is attributable to the termination one of two or more businesses (that have been active businesses for at least five years). § 302(e).

***Partner.*** (*see* General Partner; Limited Partner).

***Partnership.*** A syndicate, group, pool, joint venture, or other unincorporated organization, through or by means of which any business, financial operation, or venture is carried on, and which is not a trust, estate, or corporation. §§ 761(a) and 7701(a)(2).

***Passive Activity.*** Any activity that involves the conduct of any trade or business in which the taxpayer does not materially participate. Losses from passive activities generally are deductible only to the extent of passive activity income. § 469.

***Passive Investment Income.*** A term used in relation to S corporations. Passive investment income is generally defined as gross receipts derived from royalties, rents, dividends, interest, annuities, and gains on sales or exchanges of stock or securities. § 1362(d)(3)(D).

***Pecuniary Bequest.*** Monetary bequest (*see* Bequest).

***Percentage Depletion.*** (*see* Depletion).

***Percentage of Completion Method of Accounting.*** A method of accounting that may be used on certain long-term contracts in which the income is reported as the contract reaches various stages of completion.

***Percentage of Completion Method of Accounting.*** A method of accounting that may be used on certain long-term contracts in which the income is reported as the contract reaches various stages of completion.

***Personal Holding Company.*** A corporation in which five or fewer individuals owned more than 50 percent of the value of its stock at any a time during the last half of the taxable year and at least 60 percent of the corporation's adjusted ordinary gross income consists of personal holding company income. § 542.

***Personal Property.*** All property that is not realty; personalty. This term is also often used to mean personal use property (*see* Personal Use Property; Personalty).

***Personal Use Property.*** Any property used for personal, rather than business, purposes. Distinguished from "personal property."

***Personalty.*** All property that is not realty (e.g., automobiles, trucks, machinery, and equipment).

***Portfolio Income.*** Interest and dividends. Portfolio income, annuities, and royalties are not considered to be income from a passive activity for purposes of the passive activity loss limitations. § 469(e).

***Power of Appointment.*** A right to dispose of property that the holder of the power does not legally own.

***Preferred Stock Bailout.*** A scheme by which shareholders receive a nontaxable preferred stock dividend, sell this preferred stock to a third party, and report the gain as a long-term capital gain. This scheme, therefore, converts what would be ordinary dividend income to capital gain. Section 306 was created to prohibit use of this scheme.

***Present Interest.*** An interest in which the donee has the present right to use, possess, or enjoy the donated property. The annual exclusion is available for gifts of present interests, but not for gifts of future interests (*see* Future Interest).

***Previously Taxed Income (PTI).*** A term used to refer to the accumulated earnings and profits for the period that a Subchapter S election was in effect prior to 1983. Distributions from PTI are not taxable to the shareholders.

***Private Letter Ruling.*** A written statement from the IRS to a taxpayer in response to a request by the taxpayer for the tax consequences of a specific set of facts. The taxpayer who receives the Private Letter Ruling is the only taxpayer that may rely on that specific ruling in case of litigation.

***Probate.*** The court-directed administration of a decedent's estate.

***Prop. Reg. (Proposed Regulation).*** Treasury (IRS) Regulations are generally issued first in a proposed form in order to obtain input from various sources before the regulations are changed (if necessary) and issued in final form.

***Pro Rata.*** Proportionately.

—Q—

***Qualified Pension or Profit-Sharing Plan.*** A pension or profit-sharing plan sponsored by an employer that meets the requirements set forth by Congress in § 401. §§ 401-404.

***Qualified Residence Interest.*** Interest on indebtedness that is secured by the principal residence or one other residence of a taxpayer. §§ 162(h)(3) and (5)(A).

***Qualified Terminable Interest Property (QTIP).*** Property that passes from the decedent in which the surviving spouse has a qualifying income interest for life. An election to treat the property as qualified terminable interest property has been made. § 2056(b).

—R—

***RAR.*** (*see* Revenue Agent's Report).

***Real Property.*** (*see* Realty).

***Realized Gain or Loss.*** The difference between the amount realized from the sale or other disposition of an asset and the adjusted basis of the asset. § 1001.

***Realty.*** Real estate; land, including any objects attached thereto that are not readily movable (e.g., buildings, sidewalks, trees, and fences).

***Reasonable Needs of the Business.*** In relation to the accumulated earnings tax, a corporation may accumulate sufficient earnings and profits to meet its reasonable business needs. Examples of reasonable needs of the business include working capital needs, amounts needed for bona fide business expansion, and amounts needed for redemptions for death taxes § 537.

***Recapture.*** The recovery of the tax benefit from a previously taken deduction or credit. The recapture of a deduction results in its inclusion in income, and the recapture of a credit results in its inclusion in tax (*see* Depreciation Recapture; Investment Credit Recapture).

***Recognized Gain or Loss.*** The amount of the realized gain or loss that is subject to income tax. § 1001.

***Redemption.*** The acquisition by a corporation of its own stock from a shareholder in exchange for property. § 317(b).

***Reg.*** (*see* Regulations).

***Regulations (Treasury Department Regulations).*** Interpretations of the Internal Revenue Code by the Internal Revenue Service.

***Related Party.*** A person or entity that is related to another under the various code provisions for constructive ownership. §§ 267, 318, and 544(a).

***Remainder Interest.*** Property that passes to a remainderman after the life estate or other income interest expires on the property.

***Remainderman.*** The person entitled to the remainder interest.

***Remand.*** The sending back of a case by an appellate court to a lower court for further action by the lower court. The abbreviation for "remanding" is "rem'g."

***Reorganization.*** The combination, division, or restructuring of a corporation or corporations.

***Research Institute of America (RIA).*** A publisher of tax materials, including a multi-volume tax service and volumes that contain the Federal courts' decisions on tax matters (AFTR, AFTR2d).

***Resident Alien.*** A person who is not a citizen of the United States, and who is a resident of the United States or meets the substantial presence test. § 7701(b).

***Revenue Agent.*** An employee of the Internal Revenue Service who performs primarily field audits.

***Revenue Agent's Report (RAR).*** The report issued by a Revenue Agent in which adjustments to a taxpayer's tax liability are proposed. (IRS Form 4549; Form 1902 is used for office audits.)

***Revenue Officer.*** An employee of the Internal Revenue Service whose primary duty is the collection of tax. (As opposed to a Revenue Agent, who audits returns.)

***Revenue Procedure.*** A procedure published by the Internal Revenue Service outlining various processes and methods of handling various matters of tax practice and administration. Revenue Procedures are published first in the Internal Revenue Bulletin and then compiled annually in the Cumulative Bulletin.

***Revenue Ruling.*** A published interpretation by the Internal Revenue Service of the tax law as applied to specific situations. Revenue Rulings are published first in the Internal Revenue Bulletin and then compiled annually in the Cumulative Bulletin.

***Reversed (Rev'd).*** The reverse of a lower court's decision by a higher court.

***Reversing (Rev'g).*** The reversing of a lower court's decision by a higher court. Rev. Proc. (*see* Revenue Procedure).

***Revocable Transfer.*** A transfer that may be revoked by the transferor. In other words, the transferor keeps the right to recover the transferred property.

***Rev. Proc.*** (*see* Revenue Procedure).

***Rev. Rul.*** (*see* Revenue Ruling).

***Right of Survivorship.*** (*see* Joint Tenancy).

***Royalty.*** Compensation for the use of property, such as natural resources or copyrighted material.

—S—

***S Corporation.*** A corporation that qualifies as a small business corporation and elects to have §§ 1361-1379 apply. Once a Subchapter S election is made, the corporation is treated similarly to a partnership for tax purposes. An S corporation uses Form 1120S to report its income and expenses. (*see* C Corporation).

***Section 751 Assets.*** Unrealized receivables and appreciated inventory items of a partnership. A disproportionate distribution of § 751 assets generally results in taxable income to the partners.

***Section 1231 Property.*** Depreciable property and real estate used in a trade or business held for more than one year. Section 1231 property may also include timber, coal, domestic iron ore, livestock, and unharvested crops.

***Section 1244 Stock.*** Stock of a small business corporation issued pursuant to § 1244. A loss on § 1244 stock is treated as an ordinary loss (rather than a capital loss) within limitations. § 1244.

***Section 1245 Property.*** Property that is subject to depreciation recapture under § 1245.

***Section 1250 Property.*** Property that is subject to depreciation recapture under § 1250.

***Securities.*** Evidences of debt or of property, such as stock, bonds, and notes.

***Separate Property.*** Property that belongs separately to only one spouse (as contrasted with community property in a community property state). In a community property state, a spouse's separate property generally includes property acquired by the spouse prior to marriage, or property acquired after marriage by gift or inheritance.

***Severance Tax.*** At the time they are severed or removed from the earth. a tax on minerals or timber.

***Sham Transaction.*** A transaction with no substance or bona fide business purpose that may be ignored for tax purposes.

***Simple Trust.*** A trust that is required to distribute all of its income currently and does not pay, set aside, or use any funds for charitable purposes. § 651 (a).

***Small Business Corporation.*** There are two separate definitions of a small business corporation, one relating to S corporations and one relating to § 1244. If small business corporation status is met under § 1361(b), a corporation may elect Subchapter S. If small business corporation status is met under § 1244(c)(3), losses on § 1244 stock may be deducted as ordinary (rather than capital) losses, within limitations.

***Special Use Valuation.*** A special method of valuing real estate for estate tax purposes. The special use valuation allows that qualifying real estate used in a closely held business may be valued based on its business usage rather than market value. § 2032A.

***Specific Bequest.*** A bequest made by a testator in his or her will giving an heir a particular piece of property or money.

***Spin-off.*** A type of divisive corporate reorganization in which the original corporation transfers some of its assets to a newly formed subsidiary in exchange for all of the subsidiary's stock which it then distributes to its shareholders. The shareholders of the original corporation do not surrender any of their ownership in the original corporation for the subsidiary's stock.

***Split-off.*** A type of divisive corporate reorganization in which the original corporation transfers some of its assets to a newly formed subsidiary in exchange for all of the subsidiary's stock which it then distributes to some or all of its shareholders in exchange for some portion of their stock.

***Split-up.*** A type of divisive corporate reorganization in which the original corporation transfers some of its assets to one newly created subsidiary and the remainder of the assets to another newly created subsidiary. The original corporation then liquidates, distributing the stock of both subsidiaries in exchange for its own stock.

***Standard Deduction.*** A deduction that is available to most individual taxpayers. The standard deduction or total itemized deductions, whichever is larger, is subtracted in computing taxable income. §§ 63(c) and (f).

***Statute of Limitations.*** Law provisions that limit the period of time in which action may be taken after an event occurs. The limitations on the IRS for assessments and collections are included in §§ 6501-6504, and the limitations on taxpayers for credits or refunds are included in §§ 6511-6515.

***Statutory Depletion.*** (*see* Depletion).

***Stock Option.*** A right to purchase a specified amount of stock for a specified price at a given time or times.

***Subchapter S.*** Sections 1361-1379 of the Internal Revenue Code (*see also* S Corporation).

***Substance vs. Form.*** The essence of a transaction as opposed to the structure or form that the transaction takes. For example, a transaction may formally meet the requirements for a specific type of tax treatment, but if what the transaction is actually accomplishing is different from the form of the transaction, the form may be ignored.

***Surtax.*** An additional tax imposed on corporations with taxable income in excess of $100,000. The surtax is 5 percent of the corporation's taxable income in excess of $100,000 up to a maximum surtax of $11,750. § 11(b).

—T—

***Tangible Property.*** Property that can be touched (e.g., machinery, automobile, desk) as opposed to intangibles, which cannot (e.g., goodwill, copyrights, patents).

***Tax Avoidance.*** Using the tax laws to avoid paying taxes or to reduce one's tax liability (*see* Tax Evasion).

***Tax Benefit Rule.*** The doctrine by which the amount of income that a taxpayer must include in income when the taxpayer has recovered an amount previously deducted is limited to the amount of the previous deduction that produced a tax benefit.

***Tax Court (United States Tax Court).*** One of the three trial courts that hears cases dealing with Federal tax matters. A taxpayer need not pay his or her tax deficiency in advance if he or she decides to litigate the case in Tax Court (as opposed to the District Court or Claims Court).

***Tax Credits.*** An amount that is deducted directly from a taxpayer's tax liability, as opposed to a deduction, which reduces taxable income.

***Tax Evasion.*** The illegal evasion of the tax laws. § 7201 (*see* Tax Avoidance).

***Tax Preference Items.*** Those items specifically designated in § 57 that may be subject to a special tax (*see also* Alternative Minimum Tax).

***Tax Shelter.*** A device or scheme used by taxpayers either to reduce taxes or defer the payment of taxes.

***Taxable Estate.*** Gross estate reduced by the expenses, indebtedness, taxes, losses, and charitable contributions of the estate, and by the marital deduction. § 2051.

***Taxable Gifts.*** The total amount of gifts made during the calendar year, reduced by charitable gifts and the marital deduction. § 2503.

***T.C. (Tax Court: United States Tax Court).*** This abbreviation is also used to cite the Tax Court's Regular Decisions (*see also* Tax Court; T.C. Memo).

***T.C. Memo.*** The term used to cite the Tax Court's Memorandum Decisions (*see also* Tax Court; T.C.).

***Tenancy by the Entirety.*** A form of ownership between a husband and wife wherein each has an undivided interest in the property, with the right of survivorship.

***Tenancy in Common.*** A form of joint ownership wherein each owner has an undivided interest in the property, with no right of survivorship.

***Testator.*** A person who makes or has made a will; one who dies and has left a will.

***Thin Corporation.*** A corporation in which the amount of debt owed by the corporation is high in relationship to the amount of equity in the corporation. § 385.

***Treasury Regulations.*** (*see* Regulations).

***Trial Court.*** The first court to consider a case, as opposed to an appellate court.

***Trust.*** A right in property that is held by one person or entity for the benefit of another. §§ 641-683.

—U—

***Unearned Income.*** Income that is not earned or is not yet earned. The term is used to refer to both prepaid (not vet earned) income and to passive (not earned) income.

***Unearned Income of a Minor Child.*** (*see* "Kiddie" tax).

***Uniform Gift to Minors Act.*** An Act that provides a way to transfer property to minors. A custodian manages the property on behalf of the minor, and the custodianship terminates when the minor achieves majority.

***USSC (U.S. Supreme Court).*** This abbreviation is used to cite U.S. Supreme Court cases.

***U.S. Tax Court.*** (*see* Tax Court).

***USTC (U.S. Tax Cases).*** Published by Commerce Clearing House. These volumes contain all the Federal tax-related decisions of the U.S. District Courts, the U.S. Court of Federal Claims, the U.S. Courts of Appeals, and the U.S. Supreme Court.

—V—

***Valuation.*** (*see* Fair Market Value).

***Vested.*** Fixed or settled; having the right to absolute ownership, even if ownership will not come into being until sometime in the future.

# Index

## A


Abandoned spouse, *see* Filing Status
Abandonment losses, 14-15, 16-9
Accelerated Cost Recovery System (ACRS), *see* Modified Accelerated Cost Recovery System (MACRS)
Accelerated depreciation, *see* Depreciation and amortization
Accident and health benefits, *see* Insurance premiums; Insurance proceeds
Accounting methods, 5-14 to 5-15
  accrual basis (*see* Accrual method of accounting)
  advanced payments for goods, 5-27
  cash basis (*see* Cash method of accounting)
  cash receipts and disbursements method (*see* Cash method of accounting)
  changes in method, 5-21 to 5-24
    accounting for the adjustment, 5-22 to 5-23
  claim of right doctrine, 5-24 to 5-26
  constructive receipt doctrine, 5-16 to 5-17
  deferral of advance payments, 5-26 to 5-27. (*see also* Advance payments)
  financial, 7-17 to 7-18
  installment method (*see* Installment sale method of accounting)
  interest income, *see also* Interest income
    discount, 5-30 to 5-31
      other, 5-32
    general rules, 5-29
    non-interest bearing obligations issues at discount, 5-31 to 5-32
  inventories (*see* Inventories)
  long-term contracts, 5-28 to 5-29, 13-10
  prepaid dues and subscriptions, 5-29
  prepaid income, 5-26 to 5-29
  prepaid insurance, 7-12
  prepaid interest, 5-26
  prepaid rent, 5-26
  prepaid royalties, 5-26
  prepaid service income, 5-26 to 5-27
  Tax methods vs. Financial accounting methods, 5-15
Accounting periods, 5-12 to 5-14
  annual accounting period, 5-13 to 5-14
  income from partnerships, S corporations, fiduciaries, 5- 12to 5-13
  limitation on fiscal year, 5-13
Accrual method of accounting, 5-20 to 5-21, 7-13 to 7-17
  all events test, 7-13
  economic performance and recurring item exception, 7- 16
  economic performance test, 7-13 to 7-16
Accumulated Adjustments Account (AAA), *see* S corporations
Accumulated earnings and profits, *see* Earnings and profits
Accumulated earnings tax, 21-3 to 21-15, 21-28 to 21-29
  accumulated earnings credit, 21-12 to 21-14
  computation, 21-10 to 21-12
  dividends paid deduction, 21-14 to 21-15
    consent dividends, 21-15
    liquidating distributions, 21-15
    throwback dividends, 21-15
  intent, 21-4 to 21-5
  overview, 21-2 to 21-4
  reasonable needs of the business, 21-5 to 21-10
    acquisition of a business, 21-6
    business expansion or plant replacement, 21-5
    contingencies, 21-6
    investments, suppliers, customers, 21-6
    loans, suppliers, customers, 21-6
    product liability loss reserves, 21-5
    retirement of indebtedness, 21-6
    stock redemptions, 21-6 to 21-7
    stock redemptions from an estate, 21-5
    working capital, 21-7 to 21-10
  tax planning, 21-28 to 21-33
Accumulated earnings tax, tax planning, 2-3, 5-41 to 5-43
Accumulated taxable income, 2-3, 5-41 to 5-43
Accumulated taxable income (table), 21-10
Accumulation of earnings, *see* Accumulated earnings tax; Personal holding company
ACRS, *see* Modified Accelerated Cost Recovery System
Activity, *see* Passive-activity loss limitations
Activity not engaged in for profit, *see* Hobby losses
Additional Types of Taxes, 1-24 to 1-25
Additions to tax, *see* Penalties
Adjusted basis, *see* Basis
Adjusted gross income, 3-18 to 319
Adjusted sale price, *see* Sale of principal residence
Administrative concerns, 1-29
Administrative interpretations, *see* Tax law
Adoption expenses, 6-28, 13-52 to 13-53
  assistance program, 6-28
  credit for, 13-52 to 13-53
  foster care payments, 6-28
  interaction, with exclusion for qualified adoption expenses, 13-53
ADR (Asset depreciation range), *see* Depreciation and amortization
ADS (Alternative Depreciation System), *see* Depreciation and amortization
Advance payments, 5-27
Age, 3-3 to 3-4
Agreement not to compete, 6-48
Alcohol fuel credit, *see* Tax Credits
Aliens, 3-3. *see also* Foreign taxpayers
Alimony, *see also* Child support payments; Divorce, 6-36to 6-39
  limitations on front loading, 6-37 to 6-39
Allowance for bad debts, *see* Bad debts
Alternate valuation, 1-13
Alternative Depreciation System, *see* Depreciation and amortization
Alternative minimum tax (AMT), 3-24 to 3-26, 13-3 to 13-25, 19-28
  adjustments, 13-7 to 13-15
    applicable only to individuals, 13-10 to 13-13
      circulation and research expenditures, 13-12
      gains from incentive stock options, 13-12
      itemized deductions, 13-11 to 13-12
      personal exemptions, 13-13
      standard deduction, 13-13
      tax refunds, 13-13
    applicable to all taxpayers, 13-7 to 13-10
      Alternative Tax Net Operating Loss (ATNOL) deduction, 13-10
      depreciation, 13-7 to 13-9
      long-term contracts, 13-10
      mining Exploration and development costs, 13- 10
      pollution control facilities, 13-10
      Section 179 limited expensing, 13-10

Alternative minimum tax (AMT) (*Continued*)
applicable to corporations, 13-13 to 13-14
tax shelter adjustments, 13-14 to 13-15
farm losses, 13-14
passive-activity losses, 13-14 to 13-15
computations, 13-17 to 13-19
corporations, 19-28
exemptions, 13-5 to 13-6
minimum tax credit, 13-19 to 13-22
objectives, 13-3
overview, 13-3 to 13-5
preferences, 13-7, 13-15 to 13-16
excess depletion, 13-16
gain on sale of Qualified Small Business stock, 13- 16
intangible drilling costs, 13-16
private activity bond interest, 13-16
refundable tax credit, 13-23 to 13-24
Section 179, 13-10
tax rates, 13-5
Amortization, *see also* Depreciation and amortization, 7-32 to 7-33, 9-37 to 9-39
business investigation and start-up costs, 7-32 to 7-33
covenants not to compete, 9-38 to 9-39
five-year elective amortization, 9-39
goodwill, 9-38 to 9-39
leasehold improvements, 9-39
research and experimental expenditures, 9-42 to 9-44
Amount realized, *see* Gains and losses
Annual exclusion, *see* Gifts
Annuities, 6-10 to 6-14
simplified treatment, 6-13 to 6-14
taxation of, 6-11 to 6-13
Anti-churning rules, 9-36 to 9-37
Anti-discrimination rules, *see* Retirement plans
Appellate Courts, 2-19 to 2-21
Artists, expenses of, 7-23
Assessments for local benefits, *see* Taxes
Asset discovery, 6-51
Assets, *see* Property
Associations, 19-2 to 19-3
Assumption of liabilities, 15-29-11 to 15-30. *see also* Liabilities assumed
At-risk rules, 12-6 to 12-9
computation, 12-7 to 12-9
Authoritative sources of tax law, *see* tax law
Automobile expenses, *see* Depreciation and amortization; Transportation expenses
Automobile leases, 9-28
Average tax rates, 1-8
Awards, 6-42 to 6-43. *see also* Prizes and awards
Away-from-Home Test, 8-27 to 8-28

## B

Bad debts, 10-2 to 10-7, 10-38 16-34
basis, 10-5
bona fide debt, 10-4 to 10-5
business bad debts, 10-3
business vs. nonbusiness, 10-3 to 10-4
deduction methods, 10-5 to 10-7
experience method for service businesses, 10-6
loans between related parties (*see* Related-party transactions)
nonbusiness bad debts, 10-3 to 10-4
requirements, 10-4 to 10-5
tax planning, 10-37
worthlessness, 10-5
Bankruptcy Court, 2-18
Bankruptcy or insolvency, 6-44 to 6-45
Basis, 9-13, 10-5, 14-6 to 14-12
acquired by purchase, 14-6 to 14-7
acquisition costs, 7-29
adjusted basis defined, 3-29, 14-14
adjustments to basis, 14-12
allocation of basis, 14-18 to 14-19
bad debt (*see* Bad debts)
capital expenditures, 7-28 to 7-29
vs. repairs, 7-29
conversion from business use to personal, 14-11
conversion to business or income-producing use, 9-28
conversion to business use from personal, 14-11
conversion to personal use, 14-29
cost basis, 14-6
decedent, property acquired from a, 14-9 to 14-10
demolition, 14-15
depreciation, *see also* Depreciation and amortization, 9-2 to 9-4
determination, rules for, 14-6 to 14-12
election to capitalize or deduct, 7-31
environmental remediation costs, 7-30 to 7-31
gift, property acquired by, 14-7 to 14-9, 14-29 to 14-30
loss limitation rule, 14-8 to 14-9
goodwill, 7-28
identification problems, 14-7
inventories (*see* Inventories)
involuntary conversion (*see* Involuntary conversions)
liabilities, effect of, 14-13
like-kind exchanges, 15-24 to 15-38
long-term benefit theory, 7-29 to 7-30
nontaxable exchange, property acquired in, 14-10
nontaxable transactions, *see also* specific items, 15-38
options, 16-35 to 16-37
personal residence (*see* Sale of principal residence)
spousal transfers, 14-16
wash sales, 14-27 to 14-28
Below market loans, 5-35 to 5-36
Beneficiaries
character of income, 25-19 to 25-21
distributable net income (*see* Fiduciary)
filing requirements, 25-21
separate share rule, 25-21 to 25-22
tax treatment example, 25-22 to 25-24
taxable distributions from complex trusts and estates, 25-16 to 25-19
Beneficiaries, *see also* Trusts, 25-3, 25-13 to 25-29
Benefits, *see* Death benefits; Employee compensation and other benefits; Insurance proceeds
Bequests of property, 14-16 to 14-17, 14-29
Blindness, additional standard deduction, 3-20 to 3-21
Bonds, *see* Capital gains and losses; Interest income
Bonus depreciation, 9-23 to 9-25
Books and records, *see* Accounting methods
Bribes and illegal payments, 7-35
Business, sale of, 14-18 to 14-19, 16-6 to 16-7
Business assets, *see* Section 1231 property
Business bad debts, *see* Bad debts
Business expenses and losses
activity, 7-4 to 7-5
amortization (*see* Amortization)
automobile expenses (*see* Transportation expenses)
bad debts (*see* Bad debts)
bribes, kickbacks and other payments, 7-35
depreciation (*see* Depreciation; Modified Accelerated Cost Recovery System (MACRS))
distinguishing between 162 and 212, 7-6
election to capitalize, 7-31, 9-48
employee (*see* Employee business expenses; Employee compensation and other benefits)
entertainment (*see* Entertainment expenses)
environmental remediation costs, 7-30 to 7-31
fines and penalties, (*see* penalties)
general rules for deductibility, 7-43
gifts, 6-16 to 6-17, , 6-19, 8-40 to 8-41
goodwill, 6-50 to 6-51, , 9-38 to 9-39
home office expenses (*see* Home Office)
illegal business, 7-36
insurance (*see* Insurance premiums; Insurance Proceeds; specific types)
interest (*see* Interest expense)
investigation expenses, 7-31 to 7-34
job-*see* king expenses, 7-33 to 7-34
lobbying, 7-36
losses, 7-40

moving expense (*see* Moving expenses)
net operating losses (*see* Net Operating loss)
ordinary and necessary, 7-7
paid or incurred, 7-8 to 7-9
political contributions, 7-37
public policy restrictions, 7-34 to 7-36
reasonable, 7-8
related party transactions (*see* Related-party transactions)
relationship, 7-6
reporting, 8-44 to 8-49
self-employed versus employee, 7-21 to 7-24
start-up expenses, 7-31 to 7-34
amortization, 7-32 to 7-33
substantiation, 7-42
transportation (*see* Transportation expenses)
travel (*see* Travel expenses)
Business forms
C corporation (*see* Corporations)
choice, 3-36 to 3-37
limited liability company (*see* Limited liability company)
partnership (*see* Partnerships)
S corporation (*see* S corporations)
Sole proprietorship, 3-8 to 3-9 (*see also* Sole proprietorship)
Business income, 6-48 to 6-48
agreement not to compete and goodwill, 6-48
business interruption insurance proceeds, 6-48 to 6-49
contributions to capital, 6-51
damages, 6-49
lease cancellation payments, 6-49 to 6-50
leasehold improvements, 6-50
Business interruption insurance proceeds, 6-51
Business investigation costs, *see* Expenses
Business meals, *see* Entertainment expenses


## C


C corporations, *see* Corporations
Calendar year, *see* Accounting periods
Cancellation of debt, *see* Discharge of indebtedness
Capital additions, *see* Basis
Capital assets, 16-4 to 16-7
copyrights, artistic works, 16-5 to 16-6
defined, 16-4 to 16-5
inventory, 16-5
Capital assets, *see* Basis; Capital gains and losses
Capital budgeting, 15-39
Capital contributions, *see* Corporations; Partnerships
Capital expenditures, *see* Basis
Capital gain property, *see* Basis; Capital gains and losses; Charitable contributions
Capital gains and losses
abandoned property, 16-9
background, 2-7
bad debts, 7-18, 10-2 to 10-8, 10-39 to 10-49
basis (*see* Basis)
bonds, corporate, 16-37 to 16-42
conversion transactions, 16-41, 16-42
market discount, 16-41
original issue discount, 16-38 to 16-40
premium, 16-42
bonds, tax exempt, 6-8
business, disposition of, 16-6 to 16-7
calculating the tax, 16-20 to 16-24
capital assets, *see also* Basis, 16-4 to 16-7
capital loss deduction, 16-43
casualty and theft, 16-9 to 16-10
casualty and theft gains, 17-3, 17-36
computation of basis of residence, 15-4
constructive sale of appreciated financial positions, 16- 35
corporate taxpayers, and, 16-19 to 16-20
corporations, 6-4 to 6-5
dealers in securities, 16-31
decedent, 16-12
federal publications, 16-6
franchises, 9-43
holding period, 3-34 to 3-35
other rules, 7-16
special rules and exceptions, 16-11
property acquired by gift, 14-7, 16-12
property acquired from a decedent, 16-12
property acquired in a tax deferred transaction, 16-11
stock exchange transactions, 16-11
installment sales (*see* Installment sale method of accounting)
introduction, 17-2
inventory, 16-5
involuntary conversions (*see* Involuntary conversions)
lease cancellation payments, 6-49 to 6-50, 16-26
market discount, 16-41
net capital gains and losses, 16-15 to 16-17
netting process, 16-14 to 16-18
between groups, 16-14 to 16-16
within groups, 16-14
options, 16-35 to 16-37
buyer, 16-36
calls, 16-36 to 16-37
puts, 16-37
seller, 16-36 to 16-37
other transactions, 16-10
patents, 16-25 to 16-26
process, in general, 16-13 to 16-14
qualified small business stock, 16-27 to 16-30
rollover provision, 16-28 to 16-29
real estate, 16-32 to 16-33
related-party transactions (*see* Related-party transactions)
reporting procedures, 16-24
requirements for Capital Gain, 16-3
rollover of gain on certain publicly traded securities, 16- 30
sale or exchange, 16-7 to 16-10
Section 1202, 16-27 to 16-30
Section 1231 (*see* Section 1231 property)
Section 1244, Loss on small business stock, 16-26 to 16- 27
securities, rollover, 16-30
short sales, 16-34 to 16-35
stock, 16-43
tax planning, 16-42 to 16-43
tax rates, 13-5
treatment, 15-35 , 16-13 to 16-26
worthless securities, 16-8 to 16-9
Capital gains and losses, *see also* Basis; Gains and losses, 3- 34, 16-1 to 16-43
Capital losses, *see* Capital gains and losses
Capital recoveries, *see* Amortization; Depreciation and amortization
Capital stock, 16-31
Car pools, 6-51
Cash basis, *see* Cash method of accounting
Cash method of accounting, 5-15 to 5-20, 7-9 to 7-12
accounting for inventories, 10-22
constructive receipt, 18-31 to 18-32
general rule, § 83, 18-4 to 18-5
limitations on use of cash method, 5-17 to 5-19
other prepayments, 7-12
prepaid insurance, 7-11
prepaid interest, 7-12
prepaid rent, 7-11
restrictions on use of, 7-10
time of payment, 7-9 to 7-10
Cash or deferred arrangements (CODAs), *see* Retirement Plans
Casualty and theft, 16-9 to 16-10
Casualty and theft losses, 10-7 to 10-13, 11-13
defined, 10-8
gains and losses, 10-10
general rules, 10-7
loss computation, 10-8 to 10-9
reporting, 11-13
tax planning, 10-36
theft losses, 10-9
when to deduct, 10-11, 11-13

Change in accounting method, *see* Accounting methods
Change in accounting period, *see* Accounting Periods
Change in form of doing business, 15-38. *see also* Business forms
  choice, 3-36 to 3-37
Charge cards, *see* Interest expense
Charitable contributions, 11-35 to 11-45, 24-29 to 24-30, 25-9
  capital gain property, 11-40 to 11-41
  carryovers, 11-45 to 11-46
  corporations, 11-35
  deduction, 11-35 to 11-36
  disallowance, 11-36 to 11-37
  fair market value, 11-38
  gift tax, 24-10
  limitations, 11-37 to 11-45
  ordinary income property, 11-38 to 11-40
  other than money or property, 11-37 to 11-38
  percentage limitations, 11-39 to 11-46
    Fifty percent limitation, 11-41 to 11-42
    Thirty percent limitation, 11-42 to 11-44
    Twenty percent limitation, 11-44 to 11-45
  qualified donees, 11-37 to 11-38
  tax planning, 11-51
Child and dependent care assistance, 6-28
Child and dependent care credit, 13-44 to 13-48
  computation, 13-45
  dependents qualifying, 13-44 to 13-45
  earned income limitation, 13-47
  employment related expenses, 13-45
  Filing requirements, 13-48
  limitation, 13-46
  relationship to dependent care assistance programs, 13- 48
  relationship to other credits, 13-48
Child support payments, 6-40
Child tax credit, 4-12 to 4-14, 13-43 to 13-44, 13-59 to 13-61
  phase-out, 3-47, 4-12 to 4-13
  refundable child tax credits, 4-13, 13-59to 13-61
Children
  care (*see* Child and dependent care credit; Child tax credit)
  divorced or separated parents (*see* Personal and dependency exemptions)
  election to report child's income on parents' return, 4-31
  kiddie tax (*see* Kiddie tax)
Circulation expenditures, 13-12
Citizens and residents of the United States, 3-3
Citizenship or residency requirements test, *see* Personal and dependency exemptions
CLADR (Class Life Asset Depreciation Range, *see* Depreciation and amortization
Claim of right doctrine, 5-24 to 5-26
Classifying deductions, *see* Deductions
Classifying expenses, *see* Expenses
Cliff vesting, *see* Retirement plans
Club dues, *see* Entertainment expenses
Coal and iron ore, 17-5
CODA, *see* Retirement plans
Community property, 5-38 to 5-40
Commuting expenses, *see* Transportation
Comparison of business forms. *see also* Business forms
  choice, 3-36 to 3-37
Compensation damages, *see* Damages
Compete, agreement not to, *see* Amortization
Computation of tax. *see* Tax formula
Computers, *see* Depreciation and amortization; listed property
Condemnation, *see* Involuntary conversions
Construction contracts, 5-28, 13-10
Constructive ownership, *see* Related-party transactions
Constructive receipt doctrine, 5-16
Contributions, charitable, *see* Charitable contributions
Contributions to the capital of a corporation, *see* Corporations
Controlled corporations, *see* Corporations
Conventions and seminars, *see* Travel
Conversion, tax shelters, and, 12-4 to 12-5
Conversions, *see* Involuntary conversions
Copyrights, artistic works, 16-5 to 16-6
Corporate dividends, *see* Dividends
Corporate taxpayers, *see* Corporations
Corporations, 19-13 to 19-28, 19-33
  § 351, and, 19-29, 19-30, 19-31, 19-33, 19-34 to 19-35
  accounting periods and methods, 19-20 to 19-21
  alternative minimum tax, 13-3 to 13-25, 19-20
  associations, 19-2 to 19-3
  assumption of liabilities, 19-31 to 19-32
  boot, and, 19-30 to 19-31
  business form, 23-57 to 23-60
  capital contributions, 19-36 to 19-37
    made by shareholders, 19-37
  capital gains, 3-34, 16-13 to 16-25, 19-15 to 19-16
  capital losses, limitation, 19-25 to 19-26
  charitable contributions *see also* Charitable contributions, 19-12 to 19-14
    limitations, 19-14
  computing income tax, 19-18 to 19-21
  control, 19-30
  credits, *see also* Tax credits, 19-20
  deductions, 19-5 to 19-6
  defined, 19-2 to 19-4
  depreciation recapture (*see* depreciation; Recapture)
  estimated tax payments, 19-22 (*see also* Estimated tax)
  filing requirements, 19-22
  Form 1120, 19-24 to 19-28
  formation of, 19-29 to 19-36
    basis to shareholders, 19-33
    by one or more persons, 19-29 to 19-30
    solely for stock, 19-30
    transfer of property, 19-29
  limited liability corporations (LLCs), 19-3
  net operating loss (NOL), 19-11
  personal service, 19-20
  recapture, (*see* depreciation; Recapture)
  sales of depreciable property, 19-16 to 19-17
  sham, 19-3 to 19-4
  stock, 16-31 (*see also* Securities)
  subchapter S corporations (*see* S corporations)
  tax formula, 13-4, 19-4
  taxation, compared to individual, 19-4 to 19-5
Cost depletion, *see* Depletion
Court of Appeals, 2-19 to 2-21
Court of Federal Claims, 2-18
Court system, federal, 2-17 to 2-18
Covenants not to compete, 6-48, 9-38 to 9-39
Credit cards, *see* Interest expense
Credits, *see* Tax credits
Crops, unharvested, 17-5
Cruise Ships, *see* Travel expenses
Customs duties, 1-3


# D


Damages, 5-8 to 5-9, 6-49, 6-52 to 6-53
  compensatory, 6-52 to 6-53
  punitive, 6-53
Dealers and developers, *see* Capital gains and losses
Death benefits employee, 6-42
Death tax (Federal), 1-13, 1-18
Debts, *see* Bad debts; Discharge of indebtedness
Decedent, 1-13
Deduction and losses
  deduction for qualifies tuition, 8-6 to 8-7
  education, types and classifications for, 8-5 to 8-6
  for primary and secondary teachers' expenses, 8-8
Deductions and losses. *see* adjusted gross income; Itemized deductions
  accounting methods (*see* Accounting methods; Adjusted gross income)
  alternative minimum tax (*see* Alternative minimum tax)
  amortization (*see* Amortization)
  bad debts (*see* Bad debts)
  business expenses (*see* Business expenses and losses)
  capital losses (*see* Capital gains and losses)
  casualty and theft losses (*see* Casualty and theft losses)
  charitable contributions (*see* Charitable contributions)

depreciation (*see* Depreciation and amortization)
Education (*see* Education)
employee business expenses (*see* Employee business expenses)
goodwill (*see* Goodwill)
hobby expenses and losses (*see* Hobby losses)
medical (*see* Medical and dental expenses)
net operating losses (*see* Home office)
when to deduct (*see* Accounting methods)
Deductions and losses, *see also* Business expenses and losses, 1-6, 3-17 to 3-18, 7-1 to 7-44
Deductions and losses, *see also* Itemized deductions, adjusted gross incomeacquisition costs, 7-29
activity, 7-4 to 7-5
adjusted gross income, for *see also* Employee business expenses, 3-18, 7-19 to 7-20
A.G.I, and, 7-20
artist, performing, 7-23
carrying on a business or income-producing activity, 7-4 to 7-6
classification, 3-18 , 7-19 to 7-24
defined, 7-2
distinguishing between 162 and 212, 7-5
general rules for deductibility, 7-3 to 7-9
illegal business, 7-35, 7-36
INDOPCO and the long-term benefit theory, 7-29 to 7- 30
itemized, 3-21, 7-20 to 7-21, 11-1 to 11-49
limitations, 3-21, 7-24 to 7-42, 11-4 to 11-5, 11-20, 11-37
two-percent cutback rule, 11-27
losses, 7-18 to 7-19
medical (*see* Medical and dental expense)
miscellaneous deduction, 3-22, 11-46 to 11-47
ordinary and necessary expenses, 7-7
other, 11-47
payment, 7-9 to 7-42
payment of another's obligation, 7-41 to 7-42
personal living expenses, 7-26 to 7-28
contingent attorney fees, 7-27 to 7-28
legal, 7-27
real property tax, 7-16 to 7-17
reasonable expenses, 7-8
reimbursed expenses, 7-22
related to tax-exempt income, 7-37 to 7-38, 7-43
relationship, 7-6
self-employed versus employee, 7-21 to 7-24
standard, 3-20, 4-26
substantiation, 7-42
tax formula, 3-15 to 3-28
tax planning, 7-42 to 7-44
transportation, 8-19 to 8-26
Deferral, of tax, 12-3 to 12-4
Deferral of advance payments, 5-26 to 5-27
Deferred compensation, 18-3 to 18-4, 18-31 to 18-34
Demolition, 14-15
Dental expenses, *see* Medical and dental expenses
Dependency exemptions, *see* Personal and dependency exemptions
Dependent, special rules for person claimed as a dependent, *see also* Kiddie tax, 4-26 to 4-27
Depletion, 9-39 to 9-41, 13-16
alternative Minimum Tax, 13-2, 13-16
computation, 9-39 to 9-41
cost depletion, 9-40
percentage depletion, 9-40 to 9-41
Depreciation, 20-3 *see* Modified Accelerated Cost Recovery System (MACRS)
Depreciation and amortization, 9-2 to 9-4
ACRS (Accelerated Cost Recovery System) (*see* Modified Accelerated Cost Recovery System)
additional first year depreciation, 8-26
Alternative Depreciation System (ADS), 9-18 to 9-19
Alternative Minimum Due, 13-7
amortization (*see* Amortization)
automobiles (*see* Modified Accelerated Cost Recovery System; Transportation expenses)
basis (*see* Basis)
business and income producing property, 9-3
calculating under MACRS, 9-9 to 9-16
commencement, 9-4
computers (*see* Modified Accelerated Cost Recovery System, listed property)
exhaustion, wear and tear, and obsolescence, 9-3
general rules, 9-2 to 9-3
historical perspective, 9-4
listed property (*see* Modified Accelerated Cost Recovery System (MACRS))
modified accelerated cost recovery system (MACRS) (*see* Modified Accelerated Cost Recovery System (MACRS))
recapture (*see* Recapture depreciation)
straight-line, 9-17 to 9-18
tax planning, 9-45 to 9-47, 17-38 to 17-40
Determination Letter, 2-16
Determination of tax due or refund, 4-31
Development of U.S. Taxation, *see also* Tax law, 1-3 to 1-10
excise and customs duties, 1-3
federal income tax, 1-3 to 1-4
federal taxes as source of revenue, 1-4
federal wealth transfer taxes, 1-4
key tax terms, and *see also* Key tax terms, 1-4 to 1-10
Disabled access credit, 13-38 to 13-39
Disabled dependent care credit, *see* Child and dependent care credit
Disallowance of expenses and losses, *see also* Business expenses and losses, 14-27 to 14-28
Discharge of indebtedness,
bankruptcy or insolvency, 6-44 to 6-45
cancellation of student loans, 6-46 to 6-47
qualified real property business indebtedness, 6-45
seller reduction of purchases debt, 6-46
Discount, 5-30 to 5-32
Distributable net income, *see* Fiduciary
District Court, 2-17 to 2-18
Dividend distributions
liquidations
stock dividends (*see* Stock dividends)
stock rights (*see* Stock, rights)
Dividend distributions carryover *see also* Personal holding company tax, 3-12
dividends-paid deduction (*see* Dividends-paid deduction)
earnings and profits (*see* Earnings and profits)
liquidations (*see* Liquidations, complete; Redemptions)
Dividends, 6-3 to 6-6
adjustments, 20-5
Code § 179 expense, 20-3
constructive, 20-9
corporate dividends, 6-4 to 6-5
mutual fund dividends, 6-5
nondeductibility, 20-13
nonequivalance to redemptions, 20-14 to 20-15
other dividends, 6-5 to 6-6
stock, 20-9 to 20-13
rights, 20-11 to 20-13
stock, nontaxable, 20-10 to 20-11
stock, taxable, 20-11
stock "dividends," 6-6, 20-9 to 20-11
taxed at capital gain rate, 16-19 to 16-20
Dividends-paid deduction, 2-3, 5-41 to 5-43. *see also* Accumulated earnings tax; Personal holding company tax
Dividends-received deduction, 19-6 to 19-10
general rule, 19-6
other restrictions, 19-9 to 19-10
taxable income limitation, 19-6 to 19-9
Divorce, *see also* Alimony; Child support payments; Personal and dependency exemptions, 4-11 to 4-12, 6-56, 14-16
Doing-business penalty, 1-25
Domestic Travel, *see* Travel Expenses
Donations, *see* Charitable contributions
Drilling, 13-16
Due dates for filing returns, *see* Filing requirements

# E

E and EE bonds, 5-32
Earned income credit, 13-55 to 13-58

Earnings and profits
accumulated earnings and profits, 20-2 to 20-3
current earnings and profits, 20-4 to 20-5
depreciation, 20-3
distributions of, 20-5 to 20-7
property, distributions of, 20-8
basis, 20-8
gain or loss by corporation, 20-23 to 20-25
S corporations (*see* S corporations)
stock dividends, 6-6 (*see also* Stock Dividends)
stock redemptions and, 20-21 to 20-22
unreasonable accumulations, 2-3, 5-41 to 5-43 (*see also* Accumulated earnings tax)
Economic income, 5-41
Economic objectives of taxation, 1-26 to 1-27
Economic performance test, 7-13 to 7-15
Education, 6-9 to 6-10, 6-28, 8-2 to 8-9
credits (*see* Tax Credits)
529 saving plans, 6-15 to 6-16
gift and estate tax considerations, 6-16 to 6-17
interaction with HOPE and lifetime learning credits, 6-17
versus prepaid tuition plans, 6-16
maintain skills, 8-3
minimum education, 8-4
new trade or business, 8-3 to 8-4
prepaid tuition plans, 6-15
relationship to education credits and prepaid tuition, 8-6 to 8-7
required by employer or law, 8-3
requirements for deduction, 8-3 to 8-4
travel as a form of education, 8-4
types and classification, 8-4 to 8-5
Educational assistance plans, 6-28
Educational savings bonds, 6-9 to 6-10
Effective Tax Rates, 1-8 to 1-9
Elderly or blind taxpayers, 3-20 to 3-21
Elderly tax credit, 13-53 to 13-54
Election to report child's income on parent's return, 4-31
Electric vehicles, 9-28, 13-41
Electricity production credit, renewable, 13-40
Employee business expenses, 7-9, 8-1 to 8-52
automobile expenses (*see* Transportation expenses)
education expenses (*see* Education)
entertainment (*see* Entertainment)
home office expenses (*see* Home office)
job *see* king expenses, 7-33 to 7-34
moving expenses (*see* Moving expenses)
reporting, 8-44 to 8-49
accountable and nonaccountable plans, 8-46 to 8-47
substantiation, 8-47 to 8-49
tax planning, 3-37 to 3-38, 8-50 to 8-52
transportation expenses (*see* Transportation expenses)
travel expenses (*see* Travel expenses)
Employee compensation and benefits
annuities (*see* Annuities)
educational expenses (*see* Educational assistance plans)
entertainment expenses (*see* Entertainment)
retirement plans (*see* Retirement plans)
Employee compensation and other benefits, 6-17 to 6-34
achievement awards, 6-19 to 6-20, 8-40 to 8-41
adoption assistance programs, 6-28
annuities (*see* Annuities)
athletic facilities, 6-33
awards, 6-19 to 6-20, 6-42 to 6-43
child and dependent care assistance, 6-28
current compensation, 18-2 to 18-3
de minimis fringe benefits, 6-32
death benefits, 6-42
deferred compensation, 18-3 to 18-4
discounts, 6-31
educational expenses, 6-28
entertainment expenses (*see* Entertainment)
fringe benefits (§ 132), 6-29 to 6-33, 18-2 to 18-3
gifts to, 6-19
insurance, *see also* Insurance premiums; Insurance proceeds, 6-22 to 6-26
meals and lodging, 6-26 to 6-27
military personnel, 6-34
moving expenses, 6-33
no-additional cost services, 6-31
qualified employee discounts, 6-31
qualified long-term care benefits, 6-25
receipt of property for services, 18-4 to 18-6
general rule § 83, 18-4 to 18-5
Sec § 83(b) election, 18-5 to 18-6
reimbursed expenses, 6-19, 7-22
retirement plans (*see* Retirement plans)
Social Security benefits, 6-20 to 6-22
transportation benefits, 6-32
unemployment benefits, 6-22
working condition fringe benefits, 6-29 to 6-31
Employee fringe benefits, *see* Employee compensation and other benefits
Employer awards, 6-19 to 6-20
Employer social security credit, 13-40
Employer-provided child-care, 13-39 to 13-40
Employment taxes, 1-18 to 1-24
employee and employers, 1-19 to 1-20
FICA, 1-18 to 1-19
employee and employers, 1-19 to 1-20
self-employed taxpayers, 1-20
self-employment income, 1-20 to 1-21
calculation of, 1-21 to 1-23
Employment-related expenses, *see* Child and dependent care credit; Employee business expenses
Empowerment zone employment credit, 13-39
Energy tax credits, 13-26
Enhanced Oil Recovery Credit, 13-40
Entertainment expenses, 8-33 to 8-41, 8-50 to 8-52
business gifts, 8-40 to 8-41
business meals, 8-36
club dues, 8-37
deduction requirements, 8-33 to 8-36
associated-with expenses, 8-35 to 8-36
directly-related-to expenses, 8-34
actively engage in business, 8-35
business benefit, 8-34
principal character is business, 8-35
exceptions, 8-37
entertainment facilities, 8-37
exceptions, 8-37
excludable fringe benefits, 8-39
fifty percent limitation on entertainment and meals, 8-38 to 8-39
recordkeeping requirements, 8-41
reimbursed expenses, 8-39
Section 274(e) exceptions, 8-39
sporting events, charitable, 8-39
tax planning, 8-50 to 8-52
tickets, limitation on deduction, 8-39 to 8-40
Entertainment facilities, 8-37 to 8-38
Entities, taxable, 3-3 to 3-8
corporate, 3-5 to 3-7
fiduciaries, 3-7 to 3-8
individuals, 3-3 to 3-5
age, 3-3 to 3-4
citizens and residents of the U.S., 3-3
foreign taxpayers, 3-3
state income taxes, 3-4 to 3-5
worldwide income, 3-4
introduction, 3-2
limited liability companies, 3-11 to 3-12
partnerships, 3-9 to 3-10
S corporations, 3-11, 19-13 to 19-18
Environmental remediation costs, 7-30 to 7-31
Equity, 1-28 to 1-29
Estate tax
Code §§2053 and 2054, 24-33
comprehensive example, 24-31 to 24-32
computation, 24-29 to 24-33
credits, 24-30 to 24-32
credit for tax on prior transfers, 24-31

foreign death tax credit, 24-31
gift taxes paid on pre-1977 gifts, 24-31
state death tax credit, 24-27
computation of state death tax credit, 24-30 to 24-31
state estate taxes, 24-27
state inheritance taxes, 24-27
deductions from, 24-27
charitable contributions, 24-27 to 24-28
marital deduction, 24-28 to 24-29
family tax planning, 26-1 to 26-32
freeze, 26-21 to 26-30
generation-skipping transfer tax, 24-34
gross estate (*see* Gross Estate)
history and overview, 24-2 to 24-3
marital deduction, 24-28 to 24-29
overlap with gift tax, 24-13 to 24-14
property interests (*see* Property)
tax, payment of, 24-32 to 24-33
tax planning, 24-34 to 24-35
taxable estate, 24-15
transfers of property at death (*see* Property)
trusts (*see* Trusts)
Estate tax *see also* Beneficiaries, 24-2 to 24-3, 24-16 to 24-35, 26-21 to 26-29
Estate tax, *see also* Gifts, 1-13
Estates
function, of, 25-2
Estates and trusts
income taxation of
distribution deduction, taxation of beneficiaries, and, 25-13 to 25-29
Estimated tax, 4-37 to 4-39
annualized income installment, 4-39 to 4-40
Estimated tax payments, 19-22
Excess itemized deductions, *see* Itemized deductions
Exchanges of property, *see* Capital gains and losses; Like- kind exchanges; Property transactions; Recapture
Excise taxes, 1-3, 1-24
facilities and service, 1-24
manufacturers', 1-24
occupational, 1-24
state, 1-24
Exclusions from gross income, *see also* Employee compensation and other benefits, 3-16
Exempted loans, 5-37
Exemptions, *see* Personal and dependency exemptions
Expenses
business (*see* Business expenses and losses)
business investigation, 7-31 to 7-34
capital expenditures vs. repairs, 7-29
child care (*see* Child and dependent care credit)
classification, 7-19 to 7-24
deduction of (*see* Deductions and losses)
employee (*see* Employee business expenses)
farms and ranches (*see* Farmers and Ranchers)
interest (*see* Interest expense)
medical expense (*see* Medical and dental expenses)
obligations of another taxpayer, payment of, 7-41 to 7-42
related to tax-exempt income, 7-43
start-up costs, 7-31 to 7-34
Extension of time, *see* Filing requirements


# F


Facilities and services taxes, 1-24
Family, *see* Related-party transactions
Family members as employees, 26-6
Family ownership of business, *see* Tax planning
Family partnerships, *see* Tax planning
Family tax planning, 26-1 to 26-32
Farmers and ranchers, 9-44 to 9-45
development expenses, 9-45
expenses related to livestock, 9-44
livestock, 17-6
soil and water conservation, fertilizer, land clearing, 9-44
tax shelter losses, 13-14
unharvested crops, 17-5
Federal estate tax, 1-13 to 1-14
Federal gift tax, *see* Gifts
Federal income tax, 1-3 to 1-4
indexation, and, 4-43
source of revenue, 1-4
Federal Insurance Contributions Act (FICA), *see* FICA taxes
Federal Unemployment Tax Act (FUTA), 1-23 to 1-24
Federal Wealth Transfer Taxes, 1-4
Fees, 6-51
Fellowships, 6-43 to 6-44
Fertilizer, 9-44
FICA taxes, 1-18 to 1-19
employees and employers, 1-19 to 1-20
FUTA, 1-23 to 1-24
self-employed taxpayers, 1-20
Fiduciary, 25-3 to 25-10, 25-13 to 25-29
accounting income, 25-3 to 25-4
distribution deduction, 25-13 to 25-29
distributable net income, 25-15 to 25-16
allocation of, 25-17 to 25-19
computation, 25-14 to 25-16
expenses
charitable contributions, 25-9
limitation on deductibility
three percent cutback, 25-8
medical expenses, 25-8
income taxation, 25-5
tax rates, 25-6
taxable income, 25-6 to 25-10
depreciation, depletion, and amortization, 25-9
limitation on deductibility, 25-6 to 25-8
administrative expenses, 25-8
deduction cutback, 25-8
deductions related to tax exempt income, 25-7
medical cutback, 25-8
miscellaneous itemized deductions, 25-8
losses, 25-10
NOLs, capital losses, and excess deductions, 25-10
standard deduction and personal exemption, 25-6
trusts (*see* trusts)
FIFO, *see also* Inventories, 10-25
Filing requirements, 4-32 to 4-45
claim for refund, 4-40 to 4-41
due dates for filing returns, 4-35
estimated tax (*see* Estimated tax)
extensions of time to file, 4-37
Form 1040, 4-32 to 4-34
interest and penalties, 4-36to 4-40
partnership (*see* Partnerships)
S corporation (*see* S corporations)
statute of limitations, 4-41 to 4-43
Filing status, 4-14 to 4-22
abandoned spouse provision, 4-19
cost of maintaining a home, 4-18 to 4-19
determination (chart), 4-21
head-of-household, 4-15, 4-17 to 4-21
married, 4-14 to 4-15, 4-16 to 4-17
married filing jointly, 4-16
married filing separately, 4-17
single, 4-15, 4-19
summary, 4-15 to 4-16
surviving spouse, 4-16
Fines, *see* Penalties
First time homebuyer credit, 13-54 to 13-55
Fiscal year, *see* Accounting periods
529 plans, 6-15 to 6-16
Flow-through entities, 3-8 to 3-13
partnerships, 3-9 to 3-10
sole proprietorships, 3-8 to 3-9
tax-exempt organizations, 3-12 to 3-13

Foreign conventions, *see* Travel expenses
Foreign tax credit, 13-42 to 13-43
Foreign taxpayers, 3-3
Foreign travel, *see* Travel expenses
Form 1040, *see* Filing requirements
Formation of a business
  choice, 3-36 to 3-37
Forms, Tax
  corporate return example, 19-24 to 19-28
Forms, tax
  1040, 4-50 to 4-53
  1040, Schedule D, 17-30 to 17-31
  1040 Schedule C, 8-45
  1040A, 4-47 to 4-48
  1040EZ, 4-46
  1065, 22-13, 22-15
  1120, 19-21, 19-24 to 19-28
  1120S, 23-22 to 23-26
  2106, 8-51 to 8-52
  4797, 17-28 to 17-29
  6251, 13-20
Franchise agreements, 16-33 to 16-34
Franchise tax, 1-25
Fraud, 2-38 to 2-39
Fringe benefits, *see* Employee compensation and other benefits
FUTA (Federal Unemployment Tax Act), 1-23 to 1-24

## G

Gains and losses, *see also* Capital gains and losses
  adjusted basis, 3-29
  basis (*see* Basis)
  character of, 3-31 to 3-34
    capital gains, 3-31
      applicable rates, 3-32
      dividends, and, 3-33
      treatment of, 3-31 to 3-32
    treatment of losses, 3-34
  computation of, 3-29
  computing, 14-4 to 14-6
  dealers in securities, 16-31 to 16-32
  determining, 14-2 to 14-6
  disallowed losses, 14-27 to 14-28
    related parties (*see* Related-party transactions)
    wash sales, 14-27 to 14-28
  general rule of recognition, 14-3 to 14-4
  installment sale (*see* Installment sale)
  property transactions, 3-28 to 3-26, 14-1 to 14-30, 16-1 to 16-43
    adjusted basis, 3-29
    amount realized, 3-29
    gain or loss recognized, 3-30 to 3-31
  real estate subdivided, 16-32 to 16-33
  realized, 3-28 to 3-29
  recognized, 3-30 to 3-31
  rollover of gain on certain publicly traded securities, 16-30
  sale or other disposition, 14-13 to 14-18
    abandonment, 14-15
    bequest, (*see* Bequests)
    business, 14-18 to 14-19
    certain securities, 14-14
    demolition, 14-15
    gift (*see* Gifts)
    installment sale (*see* Installment sale)
    spousal transfers, 14-16
    tax-exempt bonds, 6-9
    transfers related to taxpayer's debt, 14-14
    transfers to charities, 14-17 to 14-18
  tax planning, 14-29 to 14-30
Gains and losses, *see also* Section 1231 property; Basis, 3-32
General Asset Account, *see* Modified Accelerated Cost Recovery System
General business credit, *see* Tax credits
General sales tax, 11-16 to 11-17
Generation-skipping tax, 24-34
Gift tax
  federal, *see also* Gifts, 24-5 to 24-14
    basis, 24-9
    charitable contributions (*see* Charitable contributions)
    computation, 24-11 to 24-13
    estate tax relation to, 24-13 to 24-14
    exclusions, 24-9 to 24-10
    filing requirements, 24-13
    gift property (*see* Property)
    gift splitting, 24-10
    marital deduction, 24-10
    overlap with estate tax, 24-13 to 24-14
    payment, deferred, 26-37
    political contributions, 24-10
    rates of tax, 24-11
    tax planning, 26-1 to 26-32
    transfers subject to tax, 24-6 to 24-7
      adequate consideration, 24-6 to 24-7
      retained interest, 24-7
      valuation
        income and remainder interests, 24-8 to 24-9
    unified credit, 24-12 to 24-13
    valuation, 24-7 to 24-9
      income and remainder interests, 24-8 to 24-9
Gift tax-Federal, *see also* Gifts, 1-15 to 1-17
Gift tax-State, 1-15 to 1-17
Gifts, *see also* Gift tax—Federal, 24-9 to 24-10
  basis of, 24-9
  charitable (*see* Charitable contributions)
  partnership interest (*see* Partnerships)
  property (*see* Property)
  to political and charitable organizations, 24-10
Gifts, *see also* Gift tax-Federal, 6-35, 14-7 to 14-9
  basis of, 14-7 to 14-9
  business, 8-40 to 8-41
  charitable (*see* Charitable contributions)
  exclusion from gross income, 1-5
  tax planning, 14-29
Goals of taxation, *see* Tax goals
"Good" tax, 1-28
Goodwill, 6-48, 7-28, 9-38 to 9-39
Government bonds issued at a discount, 5-31 to 5-32
Government transfer payments, 6-47
Graded vesting, *see* retirement plans
Grantor trust, 26-15 to 26-19
Grantor trusts, *see* Trusts
Gross estate, *see also* Estate tax
  deductions from (*see* Estate tax)
  "freezing" value, 26-21 to 26-29
  property, 26-22
    gifts, 26-22
    sales, 26-28 to 26-29
  property interests (*see* property interests)
  transfer taking effect at death, 24-14 to 24-15
  valuation, 24-7 to 24-9
Gross income, *see also* specific items; Business income, 5-1 to 5-42
  accounting concept, 5-5
  defined, 5-2 to 5-6
  economic concept, 5-3 to 5-5
  judicial concept, 5-5 to 5-6
  refinements in definition
    form-of-benefit principle, 5-7
    Indirect economic benefits, 5-10
    return of capital doctrine, 5-8 to 5-10
      damages, 5-8 to 5-9
      other considerations, 5-9 to 5-10
      sales or disposition, 5-8
  reporting, tax accounting, 5-12 to 5-24
    accounting methods, 5-14 to 5-15
      tax versus financial accounting, 5-15
    accounting periods, 5-12 to 5-14
      partnerships, S Corporations, Fiduciaries, 5-13
    accrual method, 5-20 to 5-21

cash method
accounting for inventory, 5-19 to 5-20
constructive receipt doctrine, 5-16
general rule, 5-15 to 5-16
limitations, 5-17 to 5-19
changes in, 5-21 to 5-23
accounting for changes, 5-22 to 5-23
Gross income test, *see* Personal and dependency exemptions
Group-term life insurance, *see* Insurance premiums; Insurance proceeds
Guidelines for CPA's, 2-42 to 2-43

# H

Half-year Convention, *see* Modified Accelerated Cost Recovery System
Head of household, *see* Filing status
Health and accident insurance plans, *see* Insurance premiums; Insurance proceeds
Health savings accounts, *see* Medical Savings Accounts
Heirs, *see* Beneficiaries
Hobby losses, 7-24 to 7-26
burden of proof, presumptive rule, 7-25
deduction limitation, 7-25 to 7-26
presumptive rule, 7-25
profit motive, 7-24 to 7-25
tax planning, 7-44
Holding period, *see* Capital Gains and Losses
Home equity indebtedness, *see* Interest expense
Home office, 8-13 to 8-19
amount deductible, 8-16 to 8-17
daycare use, 8-17
requirements for deductibility, 8-13 to 8-16
convenience of the employer, 8-14
exclusive use, 8-13 to 8-14
meeting place, 8-16
principal place of any business, 8-14 to 8-16
regular use, 8-14
separate structure, 8-16
trade or business, 8-16
residential phone service, 8-18
storage use, 8-17
HOPE Scholarship Credit, 6-17, 13-49 to 13-50
H.R. (Keogh) Plans, *see* Retirement plans

# I

Identification of taxpayer, *see* Taxpayer
Illegal business, 7-36
Immediate-expensing election, *see* Modified Accelerated Cost Recovery System
Incentive stock options, 13-12 to 13-13, 18-35 to 18-39
gains, 13-12 to 13-13
holding period requirements, 18-36
nonqualified stock options, 18-38
no readily ascertainable fair market value, 18-38
readily ascertainable fair market value, 18-38
qualification requirements, 18-37
stock appreciation rights, 18-38 to 13-39
Income, 1-6. *see also* Gross income
employee compensation and other benefits, 6-17 to 6-34
Income, investment, *see* Dividends
Income, tax exempt, 7-37 to 7-38, 7-43
Income from community property, 5-38 to 5-39
where spouses live apart, 5-38 to 5-39
Income from personal services, 5-34
Income from property, 5-34
Income in respect of a decedent, 25-11 to 25-12
estate tax treatment, 25-11 to 25-12
Section 691(c) deduction, 25-11 to 25-12
Income shifting, *see* Tax Planning
Income splitting, 5-40 to 5-41
Income tax (federal), 1-3 to 1-4
penalties (*see* Penalties)
Income tax credits, *see* Tax credits
Income taxation of estates, trusts, and beneficiaries, *see* Estate tax
Income taxes, *see* Taxes
Indebtedness, discharge of, *see* Discharge of indebtedness
Indexation, 4-43
Indian employment credit, 13-40
Individual retirement accounts (IRAs), *see* Retirement plans
Individual taxpayers, *see* Taxpayers
Inheritance taxes, *see* Estate tax
Inheritances, 6-35, 14-9 to 14-10
Insolvency, *see* Bankruptcy
Installment sale method of accounting, 14-19 to 14-26
contract price, 14-21
disposition of, 14-25 to 14-26
election out of, 14-20
exchange of, 15-25
gain reported in following years, 14-22
gain reported under, 14-21 to 14-22
general rules, 14-19 to 14-20
gross profit, 14-21
gross profit percentage, 14-22
imputed interest rules, 14-23 to 14-24
interest payments on deferred taxes, 14-26
limitations on, 14-23 to 14-26
mandatory reporting, 14-20
related-party sales, 14-24 to 14-25
reporting, 14-26
tax planning, 14-30, 17-37
total contract price, 14-21
Insurance premiums
accident and disability insurance, 6-25 to 6-26
group-term life insurance, 6-23
health insurance, 6-24 to 6-25, 11-12 to 11-13
life insurance, 6-23, 7-38
qualified long-term care, 6-25
Insurance proceeds
accident and disability insurance, 6-25 to 6-26
group-term life insurance, 6-23
health and accident insurance, 6-24
interruption of business, 6-48 to 6-49
life insurance, 6-40 to 6-42, 7-38
qualified long-term care, 6-25
reimbursements, 11-8 to 11-9
temporary living costs, 6-52
Intangible assets, *see* Amortization; Depreciation and amortization; specific items
Intangible drilling costs, *see* Alternative minimum tax
Interest expense, 7-37 to 7-38, 11-20 to 11-35
business, 11-25
classification of, 11-29 to 11-33
commingled funds, 11-30
computation and allocation, 11-32 to 11-33
debt repayments, refinancings, and reallocations, 11-32
graduated payment mortgages, 11-34
installment purchases, 11-34
investment, 11-25 to 11-26
net, 11-26
limitations, 11-20 to 11-29
loan proceeds received in cash, 11-31
loan proceeds received indirectly, 11-31
mortgage, 7-43 to 7-44
mortgage insurance, 11-24 to 11-25
note-discount interest, 11-34
paid in advance, 11-33 to 11-34
passive-activity, 11-27
personal, 11-20 to 11-21
points, 7-43 to 7-44
prepaid, 5-27, 7-10 to 7-11
proceeds deposited in borrower's account, 11-29
qualified residence, 11-21 to 11-24
limitations on deductible amounts, 11-23
qualifying indebtedness, 11-22
related-party transactions (*see* Related-party transactions)
student loans, 11-28 to 11-29

Interest expense (*Continued*)
tax-exempt securities, related to, 7-37 to 7-38
thirty-day rule, 11-31
trade or business, 11-25
when deductible, 11-3 to 11-4, 11-33 to 11-34
where reported, 11-34 to 11-35
Interest income, 5-29 to 5-32, 6-6 to 6-10
cap, 5-37
discount, 5-30 to 5-31
other, 5-31 to 5-32
education savings bonds, 6-9 to 6-10
general rules, 5-29 to 5-30
government obligations, 5-32
non-interest bearing obligations, 5-31 to 5-32
original issue discount, 5-32, 16-38 to 16-40
Series E and EE bonds, 5-31 to 5-32
state and local government obligations, 6-7 to 6-8
tax-exempt securities, 6-8 to 6-10
Treasury inflation-protection bonds, 5-32
Interest-free loans, 5-35
Internal Revenue Code, 2-6, 2-9 to 2-12
Internal Revenue Service (IRS), 2-6
Inventories, 7-10, 10-19 to 10-36
allocating inventoriable costs, 10-25 to 10-26
costs to be inventoried, 10-22 to 10-24
dollar value LIFO, 10-26 to 10-28
exceptions to requirement, 10-20 to 10-21
last in, first out (LIFO) election, 10-29
lower of cost or market, 10-29 to 10-30
qualified production activities deduction, 10-30 to 10-36
Investigation of new business, 7-31 to 7-34
Investment credit, 13-29 to 13-33
basis reduction, 13-31
carrybacks and carryovers, 13-32 to 13-33
energy investment credit, 13-30
recapture, 13-31 to 13-32
rehabilitation expenditure credit, 13-29 to 13-30
Investment income, *see* Interest expense
Investment income, *see also* Passive-activity loss limitations, 6-2 to 6-17
Investments, 6-53 to 6-56
employee benefits, 6-54 to 6-55
Involuntary conversions, 15-15 to 15-24
amount of gain realized, 15-21 to 15-23
condemned real estate, 15-18 to 15-19
control of corporation, 15-18
conversion of personal residence, 15-22
defined, 15-16 to 15-17
election, 15-20 to 15-21
interaction of § 121 and 1033, 15-23
livestock, 15-19
personal residence, 15-23
related party, 15-19
replacement period, 15-19 to 15-20
replacement property, 15-18 to 15-19
seizure, requisition, condemnation, 15-16 to 15-17
statute of limitations, 15-21
stock, control of corporation, 15-18
threat of imminence of condemnation, 15-17
IRA. *see also* Retirement plans
conversion, 18-28
education, 18-29 to 18-31
ROTH, 18-27 to 18-28
traditional, 18-22 to 18-26
IRS, 2-4, 2-5, 2-6
Itemized deductions, *see also* Deductions and losses; specific items, 3-19 to 3-20, 7-20 to 7-21, 11-1 to 11-49
alternative minimum tax (*see* Alternative minimum tax)
casualty and theft losses (*see* Casualty and theft losses)
charitable contributions (*see* Charitable contributions)
classification of expenses, 7-19 to 7-24
educational expenses (*see* Educational expenses)
employee business expenses (*see* Employee business expenses)
entertainment expenses (*see* Entertainment expenses)
interest (*see* Interest expense)
medical expenses (*see* Medical and dental expenses)
miscellaneous, 6-53 to 6-53, 11-49, *see also* Employee business expenses
other, 11-47
standard deduction, 3-19 to 3-20, 3-21 to 3-22, 3-37
tax planning, 1-29 to 1-30, 3-37, 11-48 to 11-49
taxes (*see* Taxes)
two-percent cutback rule, 11-26, 11-27

## J

Job-seeking expenses, 7-33 to 7-34
Joint ownership, 5-39 to 5-40
Joint return test, *see* Personal and dependency exemptions
Joint tenancies, 5-39 to 5-40
Judicial process, *see* Tax law
Judicial sources of tax law, *see* Tax law

## K

Keogh plans, *see* Retirement plans
Key tax terms, *see also* specific items, 1-4 to 1-10
Kickbacks, 7-35
Kiddie tax, 4-27 to 4-31, 5-34, 5-41
election to report child's income on parent's return, 4-31

## L

Land, *see* Property; Real estate
Land clearing, 9-44
Last in, first out (LIFO), *see* Inventories
Leasehold improvements, 6-50, 9-39
Leases, 6-8, 9-37
cancellation payments, 6-49 to 6-50, 16-26
improvements by lessee , 6-50
tax-exempt entities, 9-37
Legal expenses, 7-27
Legislative process, 2-6 to 2-7, 2-26 to 2-27
Letter Rulings, 2-15 to 2-16
Leverage, tax shelters, and, 12-5 to 12-6
Liabilities assumed amount realized, effect on, 14-13
Liability
assumption of corporate, 19-31 to 19-32
Life insurance, *see* Insurance premiums; Insurance proceeds
Lifetime learning credit, 6-17, 13-51, 13-52
LIFO (last in, first out), *see* Inventories
LIFO, *see also* Inventories, 10-25 to 10-29
Like-kind exchanges, 15-24 to 15-38
basis of property received, 15-30 to 15-33
boot, effect of, 15-28 to 15-30
delayed, 15-34 to 15-35
exchange requirement, 15-26, 15-33 to 15-35
holding period, 15-36
introduction, 15-2 to 15-3
liabilities, effect of, 15-24 to 15-25
like-kind property, 15-25 to 15-28
intangibles, 15-27
multiple property exchanges, 15-27 to 15-28
personal property, 15-26 to 15-27
real estate, 15-25
unqualified property outside the United States, 15- 28
mandatory treatment, 15-35 to 15-36
qualified property, 15-24 to 15-25
related-party exchanges, 15-35
three-corner exchanges, 15-33 to 15-34
types, 15-3
Limitation period, 4-44
Limited Expensing Election, 9-21 to 9-37
Limited liability company (LLC), 3-11 to 3-12, 19-3 *see also* Partnerships
Limited partners, *see* Partnerships
Limited partnership, *see* Partnerships

Liquidations
complete, 20-22 to 20-30
allocation of deemed purchase price, 20-28 to 20-30
defined, 20-22
purchase of assets, 20-27 to 20-28
subsidiaries, of, 20-25 to 20-30
Liquidations, partial, *see* Stock Redemptions
Liquidity planning, *see* Tax Planning
Listed property, 9-30 to 9-32, 9-34 to 9-35
Livestock, 9-44, 15-19, 17-6
Living expenses, 7-26 to 7-28
Loans, interest-free and below-market, 5-34 to 5-38
exempted loans, 5-37
interest income cap, 5-37
treatment, 5-35 to 5-36
Loans between related parties, *see* Related-party transactions
Lobbying expenditures, 7-36
Local Transfer Taxes, 1-17 to 1-18
Lodging, 6-26 to 6-27
Long-term Benefit Theory, 7-29 to 7-30
Long-term capital gains and losses, *see* Capital gains and losses
Long-term care, *see* Medical and dental expenses
Long-term care costs, 11-7
Long-term contracts, 5-28 to 5-29, 13-10
Look-back rule, 17-10
Losses, *see* Capital gains and losses; Casualty and theft losses; Deductions and losses; Gains and losses; Net operating loss; specific items
Losses between related parties, *see* Related-party transactions
Low-income housing credit, 13-38
Lump sum distributions, *see* Retirement plans

## M

MACRS, *see* Modified Accelerated Cost Recovery System
Major types of taxes, 1-10 to 1-25
Manufacturers taxes, 1-24
Marginal tax rate, 1-7 to 1-8
Marital deduction, 1-14
Marital property settlement, 5-39 to 5-40
Marriage effects, *see* Sale of principal residence
Marriage tax penalty, *see* Penalties
Meals, *see* Entertainment expenses
Meals and lodging employer provided, 6-26 to 6-27
Medical and dental expenses, 11-2 to 11-13, 11-48
accident and health insurance premiums (*see* Insurance premiums)
deductible limitations, 11-4 to 11-5
general rules, 11-2 to 11-3
insurance (*see* Insurance premiums; Insurance proceeds)
long-term care costs, 11-7
medical savings account (*see* Medical savings accounts)
reimbursement of, 11-8 to 11-9
self-employed taxpayers, 11-12 to 11-13
special care facilities, 11-6 to 11-7
special items and equipment, 11-5 to 11-6
tax planning, 11-48
travel and transportation expenses, 11-7 to 11-8
when deductible, 11-3 to 11-4
Medical Savings Accounts (MSAs), 11-9 to 11-12
contribution limitations, 11-11
eligible individuals, 11-11
penalty for distributions not used for medical expenses, 11-11
recordkeeping and filing requirements, 11-12
treatment of MSAs at death, 11-12
Medicine and drugs, *see* Medical and dental expenses
Members of Household Test, *see* personal and dependency exemptions
Method of accounting, *see* Accounting methods
Mid-month convention, *see* Modified Accelerated Cost Recovery System
Mid-quarter convention, *see* Modified Accelerated Cost Recovery System
Military personnel, 6-34
Minimum tax, *see* Alternative minimum tax
Mining costs, *see* Alternative minimum tax
Mining exploration and development costs, 13-10
Minor children, unearned income of, *see* Kiddie tax
Miscellaneous itemized deductions, *see also* Employee business expenses, 3-22, 11-46 to 11-47
Modified Accelerated Cost Recovery System (MACRS), 9-5 to 9-37
anti-churning rules, 9-36 to 9-37
automobiles, 6-29, 9-25 to 9-30
employer provided, 9-33 to 9-35
leased automobiles, 9-28 to 9-29
trucks, and vans, 9-27
bonus depreciation, 9-23 to 9-25
compared to Section 179, 925
changes in, 9-19 to 9-20
classes of property, 9-6 to 9-8
computation of depreciation, 9-9 to 9-16
conventions, 9-9 to 9-16
accounting, 9-9
half-year convention, 9-9 to 9-13
mid-month convention, 9-14
mid-quarter convention, 9-15 to 9-16
election to expense (Code § 179), 9-21 to 9-23, 13-10
eligible property, 9-22 to 9-23
recapture, 9-23
listed property, 9-30 to 9-35
employer provided cars, 9-33 to 9-35
limitations for personal use, 9-30 to 9-37
qualified business use, 9-32 to 9-33
recapture, 9-35
recordkeeping requirements, 9-35
nonresidential, 9-9, 9-12
other methods, 9-16 to 9-19
overview, 9-5
property leased to tax-exempt entities, 9-37
property subject to MACRS, 9-5
qualified film and television productions, 9-37
recovery periods, 9-9
straight-line, 9-17 to 9-18
SUVs, 9-29 to 9-30
tax planning, 9-45 to 9-47, 17-38 to 17-40
Money purchase plans, *see* Retirement plans
Mortgage, 7-43 to 3-44
Mortgage credit certificates, 13-54
Mortgage insurance, 11-24 to 11-25
Moving expenses, 8-9 to 8-13
classifying and reporting, 8-12
costs of moving household goods and personal belongings, 8-11
costs of traveling, 8-11
deductible amounts, 8-10 to 8-11
distance requirement, 8-9 to 8-10
nondeductible expenses, 8-11
tax planning, 8-50
time test, 8-10
Multiple support agreement, *see* Personal and dependency exemptions
Mutual fund dividends, 6-5

## N

Nature of a tax, 1-2
Negative income tax, 13-60 to 13-66
Negligence penalty, 2-33 to 2-34
Net capital gains and losses, *see* Capital gains and losses
Net earnings from self-employment, *see* Self-employment tax
Net operating loss (NOL), 10-13 to 10-19, 10-37, 19-27 to 19- 28
carrybacks and carryovers, 10-14
computation of, 10-15 to 10-19
corporations, 19-27
recomputing taxable income for year to which NOL is carried, 10-18 to 10-19
tax planning, 10-37
NOL, *see* Net operating loss
Nonbusiness bad debts, *see* Bad debts
Nonbusinesss tax credits, *see* Tax credits
Noncompete agreements, *see* Amortization; Business Income
Nonqualified stock option (NQSO), 18-38 to 18-39
Nonresident aliens, 3-3
Nontaxable exchanges, 15-1 to 15-35

Nontaxable transactions, 15-38
involuntary conversions (*see* Involuntary conversions)
like-kind exchanges (*see* Like-kind exchanges)
other nontaxable transactions, 15-38
changes in form of doing business, 15-38
exchanges of insurance policies, 15-38
exchanges of stock, 15-38
exchanges of stock in same corporation, 15-38
exchanges of U.S. obligations, 15-38
repossession of real property, 15-38
sale of a personal residence (*see* Sale of principal residence (§ 121))
tax planning, 15-39
capital budgeting, 15-39
current gain resulting in future reductions, 15-39
Section 121 considerations, 15-39

## O

Objectives of Taxation, *see* Tax Goals
Occupational taxes, 1-24
Office in the home, *see* Home office
Oil recovery credit, enhanced, 13-40
One percent cutback rule, 3-24
Options, *see also* Stock options; Capital Gains and Losses, 16-35 to 16-37
Ordinary and necessary expenses, *see* Deductions and losses
Ordinary gross income (OGI), *see* Personal holding company tax
Organizational expenditures, 19-10 to 19-11
Original issue discount, 5-33, 16-38 to 16-40
Orphan drug credit, 13-40 to 13-41

## P

Partnerships, 3-9 to 3-10, 22-1 to 22-48, 23-56, 26-8 to 26-9
aggregate theory, 22-4
basis adjustment to partnership property, 22-35 to 22-37
Section 754 election, 22-37
substantial basis reduction, 22-37
defined, 22-2 to 22-3
disposition of distributed property, 22-34
distributions, 22-24 to 22-37
current, 22-24 to 22-27
cash, 22-24 to 22-25
contributed property, 22-19 to 22-20
property, 22-25 to 22-27
disproportionate, 22-24
aggregate theory, 22-24
hot assets, 22-38 to 22-40
unrealized receivables, 22-38 to 22-40
mechanics of §751(a)
summary of tax consequences, 22-38
mechanics of §751(b), 22-24
consequences to distributing partnership, 22-24
consequences to recipient partner, 22-38
liquidating, 22-27 to 22-32
cash, 22-27 to 29-32
closing of partnership year, 22-32
property, 22-27 to 22-32
Section 736 payments, 22-32 to 22-34
payments for unrealized receivables and unspecified goodwill, 22-33 to 22-34
electing out of Subchapter K, 22-3
entity and aggregate theory, 22-4
family partnerships, 26-9 to 26-10
formation, 22-4 to 22-12
contribution of property, 22-5 to 22-6
contribution of services, 22-11 to 22-12
proposed regulations change rules for services, 22-12
receipt of capital interest, 22-11
receipt of profits interest, 22-12
effect of liabilities on basis, 22-6 to 22-11
liabilities transferred to the partnership, 22-10 to 22-11
partner's share of partnership liabilities, 22-7 to 22-9
general and limited partnerships, 22-3 to 22-4
operating, 22-12 to 22-17
adjustment to partner's basis, 22-16 to 22-17
computation of taxable income, 22-15
organizational expenditures, 22-14
reporting by partners, 22-16
syndication fees, 22-14
taxable year, 22-13 to 22-14
other dispositions of partnership interests
death of a partner, 22-46
exchanges, 22-47 to 22-48
gift of partnership interest, 22-45 to 22-46
partner's distributive shares, 22-17 to 22-21
allocations with respect to contributed property, 22-19 to 22-20
losses, limitations on, 22-21
basis limitations, 22-21
retroactive allocations, 22-20
substantial economic effect, 22-18 to 22-19
of partnership interest, 22-10 to 22-11
sales of partnership interests
effect of adjustment, 22-43 to 22-44
special basis adjustment, 22-42 to 22-43
special rule for built-in losses, 22-44 to 22-45
substantial built-in loss, 22-44
tax consequences to purchaser, 22-41 to 22-42
tax consequences to seller, 22-38
tax planning, 26-8
taxable income, 22-15
taxable year, 22-32
termination of, 22-47 to 22-48
effect of, 22-48
technical termination, 22-47 to 22-48
transactions between partners and partnerships, 22-22 to 22-23
sales between partners and controlled partnerships, 22-23
Passive-activity interest, 12-25
Passive-activity loss limitations, 12-9 to 12-25
general rule, 12-9 to 12-13
material participation, 12-21 to 12-25
passive activity, 12-14
appropriate economic unit, 12-15 to 12-16
conduit, activities conducted through, 12-16
consistency requirement, 12-16
definition, 12-14 to 12-15
grouping of rental and non-rental activities, 12-16 to 12-17
interest expense, 11-20 to 11-35, 12-25
passive income, recharacterized, 12-24 to 12-25
real estate developer exception, 12-23 to 12-24
rental real estate exception, 12-22 to 12-23
rental versus nonrental activities, 12-18 to 12-20
tax shelter adjustments, 13-14 to 13-15
Taxpayers affected, 12-13
Patents, 16-25 to 16-26
Payment of tax
estimated taxes (*see* Estimated tax)
Penalties
accuracy-related, 2- to 2-35
fines, 7-34 to 7-35
fraud, 2-38 to 2-39
marriage tax, 4-19 to 4-20
tax reform, and, 4-21
negligence, 2-33 to 2-34
substantial understatement, 2-34 to 2-35
substantial valuation misstatement, 2-35
summary, 2-35
tax preparer, 2-39 to 2-42
taxpayer, 2-32 to 2-33
Penalties, *see also* Filing requirements, 4-36 to 4-40, 7-34 to 7-35
Pension plans, *see* Retirement plans
Percentage depletion, *see* Depletion
Percentage of completion method, 5-28 to 5-29, 13-10

Performing artist, 7-23
Perks, *see* Employee compensation and other benefits
Personal and dependency exemptions, 4-2 to 4-14
  children of divorced or separated parents, 4-11 to 4-12
  citizenship or residency test, 4-9, 4-11
  dependency exemption tests, 4-3
  disallowance, 4-2
  gross income test, 4-8
  joint return test, 4-9
  multiple support agreements, 4-7
  personal exemptions, 4-2 to 4-3
    tie breaker rules, 4-4
  phase-out, 4-12
  provisions common to all, 4-9 to 4-11
  qualifying relative, 4-4 to 4-9
  relationship or member of household test, 4-8 to 4-9
  return filed by a dependent, 4-27
  support test, 4-5 to 4-7
Personal casualty & theft losses, *see* Casualty and theft losses
Personal holding company tax, 21-29 to 21-33
  adjusted ordinary gross income (AOGI), 21-18 to 21-20
    adjustments to ordinary gross income (OGI), 21-19 to 21-20
    from mineral, oil, and gas royalites, (table), 21-20
    from rents, (table), 21-20
    gross income, 21-18
    ordinary gross income (OGI), 21-18 to 21-19
  avoiding, 21-30
  candidates, 21-30
  computation of, 21-10 to 21-12, 21-25 to 21-27
  consent dividends, 21-26
  deficiency dividends, 21-26 to 21-27
  definition of personal holding company, 21-29 to 21-33
  dividend carryover, 21-26
  dividends-paid deduction, 21-25 to 21-27
  income test, 21-17 to 21-18
    reducing personal holding income, 21-31 to 21-32
  ownership test, 21-30 to 21-31
  passive income test, 21-31
    increasing operating income, 21-31
  personal holding company, defined, 21-16 to 21-17
    ownership test, 21-17
    passive income test, 21-31
  personal holding company income (PHCI), 21-20 to 21-25
    computation of (table), 21-24
    dividends, interest, royalties, annuities, 21-21 to 21-22
    personal service contracts, 21-24 to 21-25
    rental income, 21-22 to 21-24
  PHC ownership test, 21-19
  planned, 21-33
  reducing, 21-31 to 21-32
  removing the PHC taint, 21-32
  tax planning, 21-28 to 21-33
  Throwback dividends, 21-26
Personal interest, *see* Interest expense
Personal living expenses, 7-26 to 7-28
Personal property tax, 1-25
Personal residence, *see* Involuntary conversions; Sale of principal residence (§ 121)
Personal service corporations, 19-20
Personal services, 5-34
Personal transfers between individuals, 6-34 to 6-40
Points, 7-43 to 7-44
Political contributions, 7-37
Pollution Control Facilities, 13-10
Preference items, *see* Alternative minimum tax
Prelude to tax planning, *see* Tax planning
Prepaid, other, 7-12
Prepaid dues and subscriptions, 5-29
Prepaid income, 5-26 to 5-29
Prepaid insurance, 7-11
Prepaid interest, 5-26, 7-12
Prepaid rent, 5-26, 7-11
Prepaid royalties, 5-26
Prepaid service income, 5-26 to 5-27
Prepaid tuition plan, 6-15
  Estate and gift tax treatment, 6-16 to 6-17
  Interaction with Hope and Lifetime Learning Credit, 6- 17
Prepayment of tax, 3-24. *see also* Estimated tax
Principal residence, *see* Sale of principal residence (§ 121)
Private letter rulings, 2-15 to 2-16
Prizes and awards, 6-42 to 6-43
Property. *see also* Section 1231 property
  adjusted basis (*see* Basis)
  basis (*see* Basis)
  capital assets (*see* Capital assets)
  capital gains and losses (*see* Capital gains and losses)
  charitable contributions (*see* Charitable contributions)
  community property, 5-38 to 5-39
  condemned (*see* Involuntary conversions)
  conversion (*see* Involuntary conversions)
  depreciation (*see* Depreciation and amortization)
  depreciation recapture (*see* Recapture depreciation)
  gains and losses (*see* Gains and losses)
  gross estate, deductions from, 24-25 to 24-29
    charitable contributions, 24-27 to 24-28
    expense, indebtedness, and taxes
      administrative expenses, 24-25 to 24-26
      cliams against the estate, 24-26
      funeral expenses, 24-25
    losses, 24-26
    marital deduction, 24-28 to 24-29
    state death taxes, 24-27
      deduction for state death taxes, 24-27
      state estate taxes, 24-27
      state inheritance taxes, 24-27
  gross estate inclusions, 24-19 to 24-24
    inclusion
      code § 2036, 24-22 to 24-23
      code § 2037, 24-23
      code § 2038, 24-23
      gifts in contemplation of death, 24-24
    insurance on the life of the decendent, 24-19
    joint interests, 24-20
      nonspousal joint tenancies, 24-20
      spousal joint tenancies, 24-20
    powers of appointment, 24-20 to 24-22
      general powers, 24-20 to 24-22
      nontaxable powers, 24-21 to 24-22
    survivor benefits, 24-19 to 24-20
    transfer for insufficient consideration, 24-24
    transfer taking effect at death, 24-22 to 24-23
  gross estate, *see also* Estate tax, 24-16 to 24-19
    basis, 24-18
    survivor benefits, 24-19 to 24-20
    valuation, 24-16 to 24-17
      Special use valuation, (Section 2032A), 24-18 to 24-19
  income from, 5-35
  interests, forms of ownership, 24-3 to 24-5
    community property, 24-4
    joint tenancy, 24-4
    marital property, 24-4
    tenancy by the entirety, 24-4
    tenancy in common, 24-4
  introduction, 3-31
  inventory (*see* Inventories)
  leases (*see* Leases)
  life estates, reversions, remainders, 24-4 to 24-5
  qualifying terminal interest, 26-34
  trade or business, 3-33
  transfers at death, 24-14 to 24-15
    intestacy, 24-14
    probate, 24-14 to 24-15
    role of a will, 24-14
Property taxes, *see* Taxes
Property transactions, *see also* Involuntary conversions, 15-1 to 15-30
Property transactions, *see also* Involuntary conversions; Like-kind exchanges, 3-28 to 3-36, 14-1 to 14-30, 17-1 to 17-38

Property transfers to creditors, 14-14
Proprietorship, 3-8 to 3-9
Public assistance payments, 6-47
Public policy restriction, 7-34 to 7-36
Punitive damages, *see* Damages

## Q

QSub, 23-4
Qualified family owned business, 24-21 to 24-23
Qualified investment, *see* Investment credit
Qualified pension and profit sharing plans, *see* Retirement plans
Qualified Production Activities Income (QPAI), 10-32 to 10-33
Qualified real property business indebtedness, 6-45
Qualified residence interest, *see* Interest expense
Qualified retirement plans, *see* Retirement plans
Qualified small business stock, 13-16, 16-27 to 16-30
  alternative minimum tax, 13-17 to 13-19
  requirements, 16-29 to 16-30
  rollover provision, 16-30

## R

Rabbi trusts, 18-34
Ranching expenses, 9-44 to 9-45
Rates of tax, *see* Tax rates
Real estate, rental, *see* Passive-activity loss limitations
Real estate, rental vs. nonrental, 12-18 to 12-20
Real estate, subdivided, 16-32 to 16-33
Real estate developer, 12-23 to 12-24
Real property business indebtedness, 6-45
Realized amount, *see* Gains and losses
Realized gain or loss, *see* Gains and losses
Reasonable expenses, *see* Deductions and losses
Recapture depreciation, 17-13 to 17-34, 19-26
  applicability, 17-14
  corporations, 17-27 to 17-33
  Form 4797, 17-28 to 17-29
  historical perspective, 17-13 to 17-14
  installment sales, 17-35
  other provisions, 17-33
  summary, 17-25
  tax planning, 17-36 to 17-38
  types, 17-14 to 17-15
    Section 291, 17-15, 17-27
    Section 1245 (full), 17-15 to 17-17
      definition, 17-15
      exceptions, 17-17
      operation, 17-16
    Section 1250 (partial), 17-17 to 17-27
      combined results, 17-21 to 17-23
      definition, 17-20
      depreciation, 17-18 to 17-19
      exceptions, 17-23 to 17-27
      history, 17-23
      operation, 17-20
      real property, 17-18 to 17-19
      unrecaptured § 1250 gain, 17-20
Recognition of gain or loss, *see* Gains and losses
Recoveries
  bad debts (*see* Bad debts)
Redemptions of stock, *see* Stock redemptions
Refundable credits, *see* Tax credits
Refunds of tax, 6-51
Regulations, 2-12 to 2-14
Reimbursed expenses, 7-22, 8-39
Related-party transactions, 14-23 to 14-26, 14-27 to 14-28
  installment sales, 14-23 to 14-26, 14-30
  interest expense, 11-20 to 11-35
  like kind exchanges, 15-24 to 15-38
  losses, 7-40, 14-27 to 14-28
  payment of another taxpayers obligation, 7-41 to 7-42
  related taxpayers, 7-38 to 7-41
  sale of depreciable property, 14-19
  tax planning, 14-30
  unpaid expenses, 7-40 to 7-41
Relationship or member of household test, *see* Personal and dependency exemptions
Renewable electricity production credit, 13-40
Rental activities, 12-18 to 12-20
  real estate exception, 12-22 to 12-23
  rental of residence, 12-28 to 12-34
Rental of Residence, *see* Vacation Home Rentals
Rental real estate, *see* Passive-activity loss limitations
Rents, 21-22 to 21-24
Repairs vs. capital expenditures, 7-29
Replacement property, *see* Involuntary conversions
Replacement purchase price, *see* Sale of principal residence
Reporting business expenses and losses, 8-44 to 8-49
  statutory employees, 8-44 to 8-46
Reporting income, *see* Accounting methods
Repossessions, 15-38
Research, *see* Tax research
Research and experimental expenditures, 9-42 to 9-44, 13-12
  alternative incremental credit, 13-37
    limitations, 13-37 to 13-38
  alternative tax treatments, 9-42 to 9-43
  amount of credit, 13-35 to 13-36
  basic research expenditures, 13-37
  credit, 13-34 to 13-38
  defined, 9-42
  elections
    capitalize, 9-43
    deferral, 9-43
    expense, 9-42 to 9-43
  qualified expenditures, 13-37
  related provisions, 9-44
    amount, 13-35 to 13-36
    impact on current deductions, 13-35
    limitations, 13-37 to 13-38
Reserve for bad debts, *see* Bad debts
Residence, *see* Sale of principal residence (§ 121)
Residence requirements, *see* Personal and dependency exemptions
Retail sales of products and commodities tax, 1-24
Retirement plans, 18-6 to 18-13
  comparison, 18-41
  deductibility of contribution by employer, 18-17
  determination letters, 18-17
  funding, 18-15 to 18-17
    defined benefit plans, 18-16 to 18-17
    defined contribution plans, 18-16
  loans, 18-9 to 18-10
  low income individuals, 18-28 to 18-29
    tax credit for contributions, 18-28 to 18-29
  lump sum distributions, 18-7 to 18-8
  nonqualified deferred compensation plans, 18-31 to 18- 34
    constructive receipt, 18-31 to 18-32
    funded plans, 18-34
    Rabbi trusts, 18-34
    secular trusts, 18-34
    unfunded plans, 18-33
  premature distributions, 18-9
  qualifications requirements, 18-13 to 18-17
    50/40 rule, 18-15
    anti-discrimination rules, 18-13 to 18-14
    coverage and participation, 18-14 to 18-15
    qualified trust, existence of, 18-13
    top heavy plans, 18-17
    vesting, 18-15
      cliff vesting, 18-15
      grade vesting, 18-15
  qualified plans, 18-10 to 18-13
    deductibility, 18-17
    determination letters, 18-17
    employees

cash on deferred arrangements
catch-up adjustments, 18-21
[CODAs (401k) plans], 18-19 to 18-21
contribution limit, 18-29
deductible contributions, 18-22 to 18-23
deductible phase out, 18-23 to 18-24
distribution requirements, 18-26
distributions, 18-30
educational IRAs, 18-29 to 18-31
employer contributions, 18-20
excess contributions, 18-25
gift and estate tax treatment, 18-30 to 18-31
individual retirement accounts, 18-22
multiple education IRAs for a single beneficiary, 18-30
nondeductable contributions, 18-40
nondeductable IRA contributions, 18-25
plan requirements, 18-21
rollover contributions, 18-25 to 18-26
rollovers, 18-30
Roth IRAs, 18-27 to 18-28
spousal IRAs, 18-40
traditional IRA, 18-22 to 18-26
withdrawals, 18-26
married couples, and, 18-24
rollover contributions, 18-8 to 18-9, 18-25 to 18-26
self-employed individuals (Keogh plans; HR-10), 18-17 to 18-19
contribution limitations, 18-18 to 18-19
simplified employee pensions, 18-31
stock options, 18-34 to 18-35
summary, 18-42
tax benefits, 18-6 to 18-7
tax planning, 18-39 to 18-42
top heavy plans, 18-18
types, 18-10 to 18-13
employee stock ownership plans, 18-11 to 18-12
money purchase plans, 18-10 to 18-11
SIMPLE plans, 18-12
stock bonus plans, 18-11
Return of capital doctrine, *see* Gross income
Revenue Procedure (Rev. Proc.), 2-15
Revenue Ruling (Rev. Rul.), 2-14 to 2-15
Rollovers, *see* Retirement plans
Royalties, 5-26
Rules of tax practice: Responsibilities and ethics, 2-31 to 2-45
Rulings, 2-14 to 2-15


## S


S corporations, 1-3 to 1-4, 21-29, 23-1 to 23-60, *see* Tax planning: form of business
accounting elections, 23-16
basis, determining shareholder, 23-31 to 23-36
in debt, 23-33 to 23-36
in stock, 23-31 to 23-32
current distributions of assets
with AE&P, 23-42 to 23-47
accumulated adjustment account, 23-42 to 23-44
accumulated E&P of C Years, 23-45
Other Adjustments Account, 23-45
previously taxed income, 23-44
Schedule M-2, 23-45
earnings and profits, 23-40, 23-42 to 23-47
with no AE&P, 23-40 to 23-42
no earnings and profits, 23-40 to 23-42
sources of distributions
Accumulated Adjustment Account (AAA), 23-42 to 23-44
earnings and profits, accumulated (AEP), 23-42 to 23-47
Other Adjustment Account (OAA), 23-45
Post termination transactions, 23-48 to 23-49
distributions, 23-48 to 23-49
Previously Taxed Income (PTI), 23-44
special rules, 23-47 to 23-49
distributions, 23-48 to 23-49
losses, 23-49
election, 23-8 to 23-16
after termination, 23-16
making the election, 23-8 to 23-11
election effective for subsequent years, 23-11
shareholder consent, 11-10
time of the election, 23-9 to 23-10
termination of, 23-11 to 23-15
excessive passive income, 23-14 to 23-15
failure to meet requirements, 23-12 to 23-14
revocation, 23-11 to 23-12
eligibility requirements, 23-3 to 23-8
eligible corporations, 23-3 to 23-4
one class of stock, 23-7 to 23-8
debt as a second class of stock, 23-7 to 23-8
qualified Subchapter S subsidiary (Qsub), 23-4
taxes, excessive passive income tax
LIFO recapture tax, 23-54 to 23-55
eligible shareholders, 23-4 to 23-7
eligible trusts, 23-4 to 23-6
number, 23-6 to 23-7
type, 23-4
excess net passive income, 23-14 to 23-15
family ownership, 23-39
introduction, 23-2 to 23-3
net income, 23-16 to 23-21
number of shareholders [*see* eligibility requirements (above)]
one class of stock requirement [*see* eligibility requirements (above)]
operation, 23-16 to 23-32
determining net income, 23-16 to 23-21
accounting methods, 23-20
accumulated adjustments account (AAA), 23-42 to 23-44
charitable contributions, 23-20
depreciation recapture, 23-20
distributions, *see also* current distributions [above], 23-40 to 23-49
property, 23-49
Sources of distributions, 23-47 to 23-49
elections, 23-16
eligibility requirements
disposition of ownership interest, 23-55 to 23-56
estimated taxes, 23-55
LIFO recapture tax, 23-54 to 23-55
liquidations, 23-56
post-termination periods transaction, 23-48 to 23-49
tax planning, 23-56 to 23-60
taxes, 23-49 to 23-55
worthless securities, 23-56
employee benefits, 23-18 to 23-20
employment taxes, 23-18
Other Adjustments Account, 23-45
payments to a shareholder-employee, 23-17 to 23-18
previously taxed income (PTI), 23-44
qualified production activities deductions, 23-21
social security benefit cutback, 23-18
subdivision of real estate, 23-20
disposition of owner interest, 23-55 to 23-56
corporate liquidation, 23-56
worthless securities, 23-56
losses, 23-30 to 23-31
limitations, 23-30 to 23-31
reporting S corporation income, 23-21 to 23-30
allocations to shareholder, 23-28 to 23-30
interim closing of books, 23-29 to 23-30
per day allocation, 23-28 to 23-29
filing requirements, 23-21
taxes imposed, 23-49 to 23-55
estimated taxes, 23-55
LIFO recapture, 23-54 to 23-55
on excessive passive income, 23-49 to 23-51
passive investment income, 23-14 to 23-15
payments to shareholder-employees, 23-17
post-termination distributions [*see* distributions (above)]

S corporations (*Continued*)
  relations with shareholders
    distributions of property, sources of distributions
      special rules, 23-48 to 23-49
    eligibility requirements, taxes
      built-in gains, 23-51 to 23-54
      estimated, 23-55
      excessive passive income tax, 23-49 to 23-51
    transactions with shareholders, 23-36 to 23-37
    year, selecting taxable, 23-37 to 23-39
      calendar year, 23-37
      majority ownership year, 23-38
      natural business year, 23-37 to 23-38
      Section 444 year, 23-39
  revocation of election [*see* election (above)]
  shareholder requirements [*see* eligibility requirements (above)]
  subsidiary, 23-4
  types of shareholders [*see* eligibility requirements (above)]
Sale of business, 14-18
Sale of principal residence (§ 121), 15-3 to 15-15
  computations, 15-3 to 15-4
  gain or loss realized, 15-4
  gain or loss recognized, 15-4
    depreciation recapture, 15-10 to 15-11
    electing out, 15-14
    exceptions, frequency tests
      computation of reduced exclusion, 15-8
      depreciation recapture, 15-10 to 15-11
      incapacitated taxpayers, 15-10
      involuntary conversions, 15-10
      marriage, and, 15-9 to 15-10
      unsee n circumstances, 15-8 to 15-9
    incapacitated taxpayers, 15-10
    interaction with section 1031, 15-14
    involuntary conversions, 15-10
    marriage, effects of, 15-9 to 15-10
    maximum exclusion, 15-6
    one sale every two years, 15-7
    ownership and occupancy tests, 15-5
    rental and other nonqualified use, 15-12 to 15-13
    sale after like-kind exchange, 15-13
  principle residence, defined, 15-4 to 15-5
Sales tax, 1-25
Savings bonds, *see* Government bonds
Scholarships and fellowships, 6-43 to 6-44
School teachers, deductions for expenses, 8-8
Section 121, *see* Sale of principal residence (§ 121)
Section 179, 13-10, 17-37
Section 179 depreciation, 9-25
Section 1231 property, real and depreciable business property, 17-3 to 17-4
  applicability of lower rates, 17-11
  defined, 17-3 to 17-6
    coal and iron ore, 17-5
    crops, unharvested, 17-5
    livestock, 17-6
    timber, 17-4 to 17-5
  depreciation (*see* Depreciation and amortization)
  historical perspective, 17-13 to 17-14
  introduction, 17-2
  look-back rule, 17-10
  netting process, 17-6 to 17-10
  summary, 17-25
  tax planning, 17-36 to 17-38
Section 1245 property, *see* Recapture depreciation
Section 1250 property, *see* Recapture depreciation
Section 83, *see also* Employee Compensation and Other Benefits, 18-4 to 18-5
Section 1244 stock, 16-43
Section 83(b), 18-5 to 18-6
Secular trusts, 18-34
Securities, *see* Capital gains and losses
Securities, rollover, 16-30
Security dealers, 16-31
Self-employed business expenses, *see* Business expenses and losses
Self-employed reporting, 8-44
Self-employed vs. employee status, 6-55 to 6-56, 7-23 to 7-24
Self-employment tax, 1-18 to 1-23
Seller reduction of purchaser's debt, 6-46
Separate maintenance payments, *see also* Alimony, 6-35 to 6- 40
Separated parents, *see* Personal and dependency exemptions
Series E and EE savings bonds, 5-31 to 5-32
Services, receipt of property for, 18-4 to 18-6
Sham corporations, 19-3 to 19-4
Shareholder
  termination of interest, 20-17
Short sales, 16-34 to 16-35
Short-term capital gains and losses, *see* Capital gains and losses
Single filing status, *see* Filing status
Small business corporations
  qualified small business stock, 16-27 to 16-30
  Section 1202 stock, 16-27 to 16-30
  Section 1244 stock, 16-43
Small claims division, *see also* Tax court, 2-23
Small Tax Division *see also* Tax Court, 11-60 to 11-64, *see* Tax Law
Social Security number, 4-11
Social objectives of taxation, 1-27
Social security benefits, 6-20 to 6-22
Soil and water conservation, 9-44
Sole proprietorship, 3-8 to 3-9, 19-2 to 19-5, 19-29
Sources and applications of tax law, 2-5
Specific charge-off method, *see* Bad debts
Spouse Transfers, 14-16
Standard deduction, 3-20 to 3-22, 3-37, 4-26
Standard mileage deduction, *see* Transportation
Start-up expenditures, 7-31
State and local government obligations, 6-7 to 6-8
State and local taxes, *see* Taxes
State and local transfer taxes, 1-17 to 1-18
State excise taxes, 1-24
Statute of limitations, 4-41 to 4-43
Statutory employees, 8-44 to 8-46
Stock, 16-30
  constructive ownership, 20-18 to 20-20
  dividends, 20-9 to 20-13
  redemptions, 20-13 to 20-22
    to pay death taxes, 20-17 to 20-18
    substantially disproportionate, 20-15 to 20-17
    through related corporations, 20-20 to 20-21
  rights, 20-11 to 20-13
Stock bonus plans, 18-11
Stock dividends, 6-6
Stock options, *see also* Incentive stock options, 18-34 to 18-35
Straight-line depreciation, *see* Depreciation and amortization
Student loans, 6-47, 11-28 to 11-29
Subchapter S corporations, *see* S corporations
Subdivided real estate, 16-32 to 16-33
Substantial understatement penalty, 2-34 to 2-35
Substantial valuation misstatement, 2-35
Substantiation, 7-42, 8-47 to 8-49
Summary of penalties for inaccurate returns, 2-35
Support, 6-35, 6-39 to 6-40
Surtax
  corporate, 19-18 to 19-19
Surviving spouse, *see* Filing status
SUVs, 9-27, 9-29 to 9-30


## T


Tax
  compliance, 2-2
  computation for individuals, 4-22 to 4-32
  computing corporate, 19-18 to 19-21
  death, 20-17 to 20-18
  litigation, 2-3 to 2-4
  planning, 2-3
  preparation, 2-2 to 2-3

research, 2-4
schedules, 4-25 to 4-26
tables, 4-22 to 4-23
Tax accounting, *see* Accounting
Tax Accounting Methods, *see* Accounting Methods
Tax base, 1-4
Tax career, 2-4 to 2-5
Tax computation. *see* Tax formula
Tax Court, 2-17
Tax credits, 1-9, 13-4
adoption expenses, 13-52 to 13-53
alcohol fuel credit, 13-34
child and dependent care credit (*see* Child and dependent care credit)
child tax credit (*see* child tax credit)
credit for employer-provided child-care, 13-39 to 13-40
disabled access credit, 13-38 to 13-39
earned income credit, 13-55 to 13-58
computation, 13-56 to 13-57
eligibility requirements, 13-58
taxpayers with children, 13-58
taxpayers without children, 13-58
education credits, 13-49 to 13-52
eligible institutions, 13-51
eligible student, 13-50
Hope Scholarship credit, 13-49 to 13-50
Interaction, 13-52
phase-out for high income taxpayers, 13-51
qualified tuition and expenses, 13-50
elderly, credit for the, 13-53 to 13-54
electric vehicles, 13-41
Empowerment Zone Employment Credits, 13-39
energy credits, 13-30
first time homebuyer, 13-54 to 13-55
foreign tax credit, 13-42 to 13-43
general business credit, 13-28 to 13-29
carryover rules, 13-41 to 13-42
employer social security credit, 13-40
enhanced oil recovery credit, 13-40
Indian employment credit, 13-40
investment credit (*see* Investment credit)
low-income housing credit, 13-38
orphan drug credit, 13-40 to 13-41
rehabilitation investment credit, 13-29 to 13-30
renewable electricity production, 13-40
home mortgages, 13-54 to 13-55
income, 13-25 to 13-43
interaction of Hope credit, Lifetime Earning credit, education IRAs, series EE Savings Bonds, 13-52
Lifetime Learning credit, 13-52
Investments (*see* Investment credit)
limitation, 13-37 to 13-38, 13-46
limitation on nonrefundable credits, 13-26 to 13-28
low-income housing credit, 13-38
making work pay, 13-66 to 13-67
minimum tax credit, 13-19 to 13-21
mortgage credit certificates, 13-54 to 13-55
nonbusiness credits, 13-43 to 13-55
overview, 13-26
refundable, 13-28
refundable credits, 13-55 to 13-61
earned income credit, 13-55 to 13-58
other, 13-61
research credit (*see* Research and experimental expenditures)
welfare to work credit, 13-34
work opportunity credit, 13-33 to 13-34
amount, 13-33
rules for long term family assistance receipt, 13-34
summer youth employees, 13-33
Tax formula, 1-11, 3-15 to 3-28
adjusted gross income, 3-18
alternative minimum tax, 3-24 to 3-26, 13-3 to 13-25
credits, 3-23 to 3-24
deductions, 3-17
for adjusted gross income, 3-18 to 3-19
blind, 3-20 to 3-21
classifying, 3-18
elderly, 3-20 to 3-21
Itemized deductions, 3-19 to 3-20, 3-21
miscellaneous itemized deductions, 3-22
standard deductions limitations, 3-21
exclusions, 3-16
exemptions, 3-22
gross income, 3-16
income, 3-15
other taxes, 3-24 to 3-26
prepayments, 3-24
rates, 3-23
self employment tax, 3-24
special rules, 4-26 to 4-30
dependents, 4-26
election to report child's income on parents return, 4-31
kiddie tax, 4-27 to 4-30
standard deduction, 3-20
Tax goals, 1-25 to 1-29
economic objectives, 1-26 to 1-27
other objectives, 1-28 to 1-29
administrative, 1-29
equity, 1-28 to 1-29
social objectives, 1-27
tax indexation, 4-43
Tax law, 2-5 to 2-12
administrative interpretations, 2-12 to 2-16
letter rulings, 2-15 to 2-16
determination letter, 2-16
private letter ruling, 2-15 to 2-16
technical advice memorandum, 2-16
regulations, 2-12 to 2-14
citation, 2-14
interpretive, 2-13
legislative, 2-13
procedural, 2-13
temporary, 2-13
revenue procedures, 2-15
revenue rulings, 2-14 to 2-15
Administrative interpretations, Letter rulings, Citation, 2-17
Appellate Courts, 2-19 to 2-21
U.S. Courts of Appeals, 2-19 to 2-21
U.S. Supreme Court, 2-21
case citations, 2-21 to 2-25
tax court decisions, 2-21 to 2-23
judicial interpretations, 2-16 to 2-25
secondary sources, 2-25 to 2-26
tax periodicals, 2-26
tax services, 2-25 to 2-26
sources, 2-5
statutory, 2-6 to 2-12
committee reports, 2-7 to 2-8
making of a tax law, 2-6 to 2-7
organization of the code, 2-9 to 2-12
Tax research (*see* Tax Research Steps)
tax treaties, 2-12
Trial Courts, 2-17 to 2-18
Bankruptcy Court, 2-18
Small Claims Cases, 2-18
U.S. Court of Federal Claims, 2-18
U.S. District Courts, 2-17 to 2-18
U.S. Tax Courts, 2-17
citations, 2-23 to 2-25
Tax penalties, *see also* Penalties, 2-32 to 2-33
Tax periodicals, 2-26
Tax planning
Accelerated Depreciation with Cost Segregation, 9-46 to 9-47
accumulated earnings tax, 21-28 to 21-29
liquid assets and working capital, 21-28
reasonable needs, 21-28 to 21-29
S Corporation election, 21-29
after-tax cash flow, 9-45 to 9-46
bad debts, 10-37

Tax planning (*Continued*)
- bequests, 14-29
- business form, 3-36 to 3-37
- capital asset transitions timing, 16-42 to 16-43
- capital budgeting, 15-39
- casualty and theft losses, 10-36
- charitable contributions, 11-49
- current gain, 15-39
- current recognition versus deferral, 15-39
- deductions and losses, 7-42 to 7-43
- depreciation and amortization, 9-45 to 9-47, 17-36 to 17-37
  - accelerating depreciation with cost segregation, 9-46 to 9-47
  - recapture, 17-37
  - Section 179, 17-37
- divorce, 6-56
- employee business expenses, 3-37 to 3-38, 7-9
- employee compensation and retirement plans, 18-39 to 18-42
- employee fringe benefits, 3-11, 3-16
- employee vs self employed, 6-55 to 6-56
- excluded economic income, 5-41
- expenses related tax-exempt income, 7-43
- family
  - income shifting, 26-2 to 26-6
  - joint filing and the singles penalty, 26-4
  - judicial constraints, 26-3 to 26-4
  - marriage penalty, 26-4 to 26-5
  - members as owners of the family business, 26-7 to 26-8
  - negative aspects of ownership transfers, 26-11
  - partnerships, 26-6 to 26-7, 26-8 to 26-9
  - preservation of control of the business, 26-11 to 26-12
  - regular corporations, 26-10 to 26-11
  - S Corporations, 26-11 to 26-12
  - shifts of investment income, 26-12
  - techniques, 26-6 to 26-13
    - family members as employees, 26-6
      - of partnerships and corporations, 26-6 to 26-7
  - unearned income of minor children, 26-12 to 26-13
- form of business, 3-36 to 3-37
- forms of business, 11-56 to 11-60
  - choice of entity comparisons, 11-56 to 11-60
- gifts, 14-29
- goodwill, 9-47
- gross income, 5-40 to 5-41
- income splitting, 5-40 to 5-41
- installment sales, 14-30, 17-37
- investments, 6-53 to 6-54
- IRAs, 18-40 to 18-42
- itemized deductions vs. standard deductions, 3-40
- liquidity, 26-31 to 26-32
  - deferred payment of estate tax, 26-32
  - flower bonds, 26-32
  - source of funds, 26-32
- maximizing deductions, 7-42 to 7-43
- medical expenses, 11-48
- miscellaneous deductions, 11-49
- moving expenses, 8-50
- net operating losses, 10-37
- personal deductions, 11-48
- points on mortgages, 7-43 to 7-44
- preservation of control of the business, 26-11 to 26-12
- property, changes in use, 14-29
- qualifying terminal interest property, 26-34
- related parties, 14-30
- residence, sale of, 15-39
- retirement income, 18-39
- sale of property, 26-28 to 26-29
- Section 121, 15-37
- Section 179, 17-37
- Section 1231 assets, 17-37
- Section 1244 stock, 16-43
- self-employed vs. employee, 6-58 to 6-59
- tax-exempt income expenses, 7-43
- techniques
  - family members as owners of the family business, 26-7 to 26-8
  - family partnerships, 26-8 to 26-9
  - negative aspects of ownership transfers, 26-11
  - preservation of control of the business, 26-11 to 26- 12
  - regular corporations, 26-9 to 26-10
  - S Corporations, 26-10 to 26-11
  - shifts of investment income, 26-12
  - unearned income of minor children, 26-12 to 26-13
- timing income recognition, 5-40
- timing of capital asset transactions, 16-42 to 16-43
- timing of deductions, 7-43
- timing sales and dispositions, 17-36
- transfer tax, 24-34
  - charitable giving, 26-30 to 26-31
  - "freezing" value of assets, 26-21 to 26-32
    - C Corporations, and, 26-25 to 26-26
    - family limited partnerships, 26-28
    - gifts of property, 26-22
    - GRITs, GRATs, and GRUTs, 26-29 to 26-30
    - interests in closely held businesses, 26-22 to 26-25
    - partnerships, 26-26
    - sales of property, 26-28 to 26-29
    - valuation issues, 26-26 to 26-28
  - intrafamily gifts, and, 26-20 to 26-21
  - marital deduction planning, 16-32 to 16-33
  - qualifying terminal interest property, 16-34
- travel and entertainment, 8-50 to 8-52
- trusts, 26-15 to 26-20

Tax planning, *see also* below, 1-31 to 1-32

Tax practice, 2-2 to 2-4

Tax preference items, *see* Alternative minimum tax

Tax preparation
- circular 230 changes, 2-43
- guidelines for CPAs, 2-42 to 2-43
- penalties related to, 2-39 to 2-45
- positions, 2-40 to 2-42

Tax rate schedules, 4-27 to 4-28

Tax rates, 1-6 to 1-7, 4-26, 13-5 to 13-6, 19-20 to 19-21
- average, 1-8
- effective, 1-8 to 1-9
- marginal, 1-7 to 1-8

Tax reform, 4-20, 4-26

Tax refunds, 6-51

Tax research steps, 2-26 to 2-31
- communicate the findings, 2-31
- derive the solution, 2-31
- diagnose the issue, 2-27 to 2-28
- evaluate the authority, 2-28 to 2-31
  - code, 2-28 to 2-29
  - judicial authority, 2-29
  - rulings, 2-30 to 2-31
  - treasury regulations, 2-29
- locate the authorities, 2-28
- obtain the facts, 2-27

Tax return illustrations, 4-45

Tax return positions, 2-40 to 2-42

Tax services, 2-25 to 2-26

Tax shelters
- at-risk rules, and, 12-6 to 12-9
  - computation, 12-7 to 12-9
- elements of, 12-3 to 12-6
  - conversion, 12-4 to 12-5
  - deferral, 12-3 to 12-4
  - leverage, 12-5 to 12-6
- introduction to, 12-2 to 12-3

Tax treaties, 2-12

Taxable entities, *see* Entities

Taxable estate, 1-13 to 1-14

Taxable income, 3-23

Taxation
- corporate versus individual, 19-4 to 19-5

Taxation, career, 2-4 to 2-5

Taxation of business forms, 19-1 to 19-38

Taxes, deductibility of, 7-13 11-13 to 11-19
employment taxes (*see* Employment taxes)
estate taxes, 1-13 to 1-14
excise taxes, (*see* excise taxes)
general requirements for deductibility, 11-14 to 11-15
general sales tax, 11-16 to 11-17
income taxes, 11-15 to 11-16
property taxes, 11-17 to 11-19
reporting, 11-19
standard deduction increase for real property taxes, 11-18
types (*see* Types of taxes)
when deductible, 11-33 to 11-34
Tax-exempt securities, 6-8
Taxpayer, identification of, 5-33 to 5-40
Taxpayer identification
income from community property, 5-38 to 5-39
where spouses live apart, 5-38 to 5-39
income from personal services, 5-34
income from property, 5-34
interest-free and below market loans, 5-34 to 5-38
exempt loans, 5-37
loans to qualified continuing care facility, 5-37 to 5-38
treatment, 5-35 to 5-36
unearned income of children, 5-34
Taxpayers, 3-3 to 3-8
corporate, 3-5 to 3-7
fiduciary, 3-7 to 3-8
individual, 3-3 to 3-5
Technical advice memorandum, 2-16
Temporary living costs, 6-52
Tenancy in common, 5-39 to 5-40
Theft losses, *see* Casualty and theft losses
Tickets, *see* Entertainment Expenses
Timber, 17-4 to 17-5
Trade business property, *see* Property
Trade or business expenses, *see* Business expenses and losses
Trademarks, *see* Franchise agreements
Transfer payment, 6-47
Transfer tax, 26-19 to 26-31
Transfers, unrelated parties, 6-40 to 6-47
Transfers between individuals, personal, 6-34 to 6-40
Transportation expenses, 8-19 to 8-26, deductible transportation versus nondeductible
automobile expenses
actual expenses, 8-24
car pool receipts, 6-51
depreciation, 9-26
standard mileage rate, 8-25 to 8-26
classification of transportation and travel expenses, 8-26
commuting, 8-19 to 8-24
commuting between two jobs, 8-21
commuting to a temporary assignment, 8-22 to 8-23
commuting with tools and similar items, 8-20
temporary work location, 8-22
transportation between job sites, 8-23 to 8-24
deductible transportation versus nondeductible, commuting, 8-19 to 8-24
substantiation, 8-47 to 8-49
Travel, for Education, *see* Education
Travel expenses, 8-26 to 8-33
away from home test, 8-27 to 8-28
classification, 8-26
combined business and pleasure travel, 8-28 to 8-31
cruise ships, 8-32
domestic travel, 8-29
expense of spouse and dependents, 8-30
foreign conventions, 8-32
foreign travel, 8-30 to 8-31
luxury water travel, 8-31
substantiation, 8-47 to 8-49
tax planning, 8-50
Travel medical, *see* Medical and dental expenses
Travel recordkeeping, 8-41 to 8-42
Travel status, *see* Transportation expenses
Treasury department regulations, 2-12
Trial courts, 2-17 to 2-18
Trusts
beneficiary controlled, 23-5
electing small business (ESTB), 23-5 to 23-6
function of, 25-3
grantor, 23-5
qualified subchapter S (QSST), 23-5
testamentary, 23-6
voting, 23-6
Trusts, *see also* Beneficiaries, Fiduciaries, 25-2 to 25-30
accounting income (*see* Fiduciary)
as tax planning vehicle
advantages, 26-13
gift-leasebacks, 26-14
gifts to, tax considerations, 26-14
section 2503(C) and Crummey trusts, 26-15
transfers into trust, 26-14
beneficiaries (*see* Beneficiaries)
charitable lead trusts, 26-31
charitable remainder trusts, 26-31
complex trusts, 25-16 to 25-19
distributable net income (DNI), (*see* Fiduciary)
example, 25-22 to 25-29
grantor, 26-15 to 26-19
beneficial enjoyment, power to control, 26-17 to 26-18
loans, interest-free, 26-16 to 26-17
other grantor trusts, 26-18 to 26-19
reversionary, 26-16
transfer tax rules, 26-19
GRITs, GRATs, and GRUTs, 26-29 to 26-30
income in respect of a decedent, 25-11 to 25-12
losses (*see* Fiduciary) Trusts *see also* Beneficiaries; Fiduciaries
losses (*see* Fiduciary)
net operating loss (*see* Fiduciary)
simple trust, 25-16
sixty five day rule, 25-24
as tax planning vehicle
advantages, 26-13
gift-leasebacks, 26-14
gifts to, tax considerations, 26-14
section 2503(C) and Crummey trusts, 26-15
transfers into trust, 26-14
tax rates (*see* Fiduciary)
taxable income, (*see* Fiduciary)
Trusts *see also* Fiduciaries, 25-2 to 25-30
Tuition programs, *see* Education
Two percent limit, 11-47
Types of taxes, 1-10 to 1-25
doing-business penalty, 1-25
employment, 1-19 to 1-24
excise, 1-24
federal estate, 1-13 to 1-14
federal gift, 1-15 to 1-17
franchise, 1-25
income, 1-10 to 1-12
intangible property, 1-25
real property, 1-25
sales, 1-25
state and local transfer, 1-17 to 1-18
tangible property, 1-25
use, 1-25
wealth transfer, 1-12 to 1-13

# U

Understatement penalty, *see* Penalties
Unearned income of dependent child, *see* Kiddie tax
Unemployment benefits, 6-22
Unemployment tax, federal, *see* Employment taxes
Unharvested crops, 17-6
Uniform capitalization rules, *see* Inventories
U.S. Court of Federal Claims, 2-18
U.S. Courts of Appeals, 2-19 to 2-21

U.S. District Courts, 2-17 to 2-18
U.S. Supreme Court Report (USSC), 2-24
U.S. Tax Court, 2-17
Use tax, 1-25

## V

Vacation home rentals, 12-28 to 12-34
  allocation of expenses, 12-31 to 12-33
  basic rules, 12-28 to 12-30
Vacation pay, 7-18
Valuation misstatement penalty, 2-35
Vesting, *see* Retirement plans

## W

Wash sales, 14-27 to 14-28
Wealth transfer taxes, 1-12 to 1-18
Welfare payments, 6-47
Welfare to work credit, *see* Tax credits
Work opportunity credit, *see* Tax credits
Worldwide income, 3-4
Worthless securities, 16-7 to 16-8

## Y

Year taxable, *see* Accounting periods

## Corporate Tax Rate Schedule

| If taxable income is: *Over—* | *But not over—* | The tax is: | *of the amount over—* |
|---|---|---|---|
| $0 | $50,000 | ..... **15%** | $0 |
| 50,000 | 75,000 | **$7,500 + 25%** | 50,000 |
| 75,000 | 100,000 | **13,750 + 34%** | 75,000 |
| 100,000 | 335,000 | **22,250 + 39%** | 100,000 |
| 335,000 | 10,000,000 | **113,900 + 34%** | 335,000 |
| 10,000,000 | 15,000,000 | **3,400,000 + 35%** | 10,000,000 |
| 15,000,000 | 18,333,333 | **5,150,000 + 38%** | 15,000,000 |
| 18,333,333 | ..... | **6,416,666 + 35%** | 18,333,333 |

## Income Tax Rates for Estates and Trusts for Taxable Years Beginning in 2011

| If taxable income is: *Over—* | *But not over—* | The tax is: | *of the amount over—* |
|---|---|---|---|
| $0 | $2,300 | **$0 + 15%** | $0 |
| 2,300 | 5,450 | **345.00 + 25%** | 2,300 |
| 5,450 | 8,300 | **1,132.50 + 28%** | 5,450 |
| 8,300 | 11,350 | **1,930.50 + 33%** | 8,300 |
| 11,350 | ..... | **2,937.00 + 35%** | 11,350 |